## DATE DUE

| | | | |
|---|---|---|---|
| | | | |
| | | | |
| | | | |
| | | | |
| | | | |
| | | | |
| | | | |
| | | | |
| | | | |
| | | | |
| | | | |
| | | | |
| | | | |
| | | | |
| | | | |
| | | | |
| | | | |

DEMCO 38-296

# JANUARY — DECEMBER 1991

The right to make direct use of material contained in The CQ Researcher is strictly reserved
to newspaper, magazine, radio and television clients of the service. Others wishing to quote
from the reports for other than academic purposes must first obtain written permission.

Copyright 1991 by Congressional Quarterly Inc.
Published by Congressional Quarterly Inc.,
in conjunction with EBSCO Publishing
1414 22nd St., N.W. , Washington, D.C. 20037

ISBN 0-87187-695-7
ISSN 1056-2036

# Elements of The CQ Researcher

*(formerly Editorial Research Reports)*

The name of this publication changed effective May 10, 1991. This volume includes reports published under the name *Editorial Research Reports,* January 4 — April 26, 1991, and reports published under the name *The CQ Researcher,* May 10 — December 27, 1991.

Each report provides background on a current topic of widespread interest. Designed as a starting place for research, the reports define the issues and include a chronology and extensive bibliographies. A feature called "At Issue," which quotes opposing viewpoints from two experts, also is a part of each report.

The publication is available in various formats.

## THE REPORT

The report, about 12,000 words in length, is issued on Friday four times a month. Each report treats a subject that is in the news or likely to be in the news in the near future.

## BOUND REPORTS

The weekly reports are bound into quarterly paperback editions and an annual hardbound cumulation.

## INDEX

A subject index to the reports is published each quarter and cumulated annually. The latest index may be found (in the blue pages) at the back of this volume.

For more information call Congressional Quarterly, 800-432-2250 or 202-822-1438.

## CITATION

Recommended format for citing these reports in a bibliography, based on The Modern Language Association of America's *Handbook for Writers of Research Papers,* 3rd edition, follows.

Clark, Charles S. "The Obscenity Debate." *The CQ Researcher* 20 Dec. 1991: 969-992.

# THE CQ *Researcher*

*formerly Editorial Research Reports*

## CONTENTS                    1991

ERR

JANUARY 4, 1991

CONGRESSIONAL QUARTERLY'S
EDITORIAL RESEARCH REPORTS
FOUNDED 1923

# THE GROWING INFLUENCE OF BOYCOTTS

1991 No. 1

**EDITORIAL RESEARCH REPORTS**

EDITOR
**MARCUS D. ROSENBAUM**

MANAGING EDITOR
**SANDRA STENCEL**

ASSOCIATE EDITOR
**RICHARD L. WORSNOP**

STAFF WRITERS
**MARY H. COOPER**
**ROBERT K. LANDERS**
**PATRICK G. MARSHALL**

PRODUCTION EDITOR
**LAURIE DE MARIS**

EDITORIAL ASSISTANT
**AMY GORTON**

RICHARD M. BOECKEL (1892-1975)
FOUNDER

PUBLISHED BY
**CONGRESSIONAL QUARTERLY INC.**

CHAIRMAN
**ANDREW BARNES**

PRESIDENT
**RICHARD R. EDMONDS**

EDITOR AND PUBLISHER
**NEIL SKENE**

EXECUTIVE EDITOR
**ROBERT W. MERRY**

EDITORIAL RESEARCH REPORTS (LIBRARY OF CONGRESS CATALOGUE NO. 39-924; ISSN 0013-0958). Published weekly (48 times per year, excluding March 1, May 3, August 2 and November 1, 1991) by Congressional Quarterly Inc., 1414 22nd Street NW, Washington, D.C. 20037. Rates are furnished upon request. Application to mail at second-class postage rates is pending at Washington, D.C. POSTMASTER: Send address changes to EDITORIAL RESEARCH REPORTS, 1414 22nd Street NW, Washington, D.C. 20037.

# THE GROWING INFLUENCE OF BOYCOTTS

*by Mark Stencel*

Consumers, political activists and labor unions have adopted a new goal for an old strategy: They are boycotting companies with an eye toward the corporations' image, and not just their bottom line. Because effectively mounted boycotts can derail marketing strategies and drain employee morale, as well as damage that fragile corporate image, corporate executives now seem anxious to resolve disputes with boycotters. But as companies capitulate, they may be encouraging even more groups to engage in this form of protest.

Corporate executives once tried to ignore the threats posed to their business by consumer boycotts, but they are finding it a lot harder to do so now. "In the past," says Todd Putnam, the editor of the independent *National Boycott News*, "it seemed like it would take years for a company to acknowledge or even recognize that it was being boycotted. Now it seems like you even say the word 'boycott' and people in the board room jump."

There has been a lot of jumping in recent months. In November, for instance, McDonald's Corp. gave in to the growing environmental sensitivities of its customers and announced that it would scrap its hard-to-recycle plastic-foam food containers. Not long before that, when angry sports-bar owners threatened to boy-

---

*Mark Stencel is a free-lance writer who lives near Washington, D.C.*

cott the products of several leading network television advertisers, NBC and CBS shelved their plans to scramble satellite transmissions of professional football games. In April, three tuna companies, fighting an extended boycott, announced they would stop buying tuna caught in nets that also snared dolphins.

These and other recent corporate capitulations to consumer interest groups show how willing business leaders have been to respond to consumer boycotts — especially when such protests threaten their corporation's public image and marketing strategies. "A company's reputation is a critical ingredient in any product it makes," says D. Edward I. Smyth, vice president for corporate affairs at the H. J. Heinz Co., the parent corporation of StarKist. StarKist was the first seafood company to announce that it would make its tuna "dolphin-safe." *

StarKist had been the subject of a two-year consumer boycott over the dolphin issue, and Smyth says the company's decision to give in to its boycotters shows how large a role the desire to preserve consumer goodwill plays "in motivating the actions of global corporations." StarKist's announcement followed the publication of news stories about pupil-sponsored initiatives to ban tuna in school cafeterias. "The last thing Charlie the Tuna needed was a negative image with schoolchildren," Smyth says.[1]

This new corporate willingness to respond to consumer activists may be inspiring a growing number of interest groups to use boycotts as a tool for promoting social change. Putnam estimates that more than 150 groups around the country are currently engaged in 200 to 250 national consumer boycotts. This is about twice the number of boycotts Putnam's newsletter was tracking a year ago.

The number of boycotts had been increasing steadily over the past few years, Putnam says. "But in recent months it's been almost crazy. . . . I don't know if there have been this many boycotts . . . since the 1920s and 1930s, when [union] organizing efforts were still going on."

And the variety of interest groups that sponsor boycotts is staggering. The tactic is now being used by both anti-abortion and abortion-rights organizations, sometimes against the same companies but for different reasons (*see story, p. 6*). Animal rights activists used boycotts to convince many major cosmetic manufacturers to stop testing the safety of their products on laboratory animals. And a number of human rights organizations have boycotted firms that do business in countries with dubious rights records, including South Africa and El Salvador.

But most of the recent boycott boom can be

attributed to environmental groups, like Earth First! and the Rain Forest Action Network, which have used boycotts to pressure Burger King Corp. and other companies to stop buying beef from Latin American ranchers whose cattle graze on cleared land that was once tropical forest.

Boycotting — particularly environmental boycotting — caught on with the boycotts of Exxon Corp. in 1989. That April a number of organizations around the country called on customers to stop buying their gas from Exxon after one of the company's tankers dumped more than 10 million gallons of oil into Alaska's pristine Prince William Sound the month before. Within five months, nearly 40,000 of the company's 7 million credit card holders had returned their cards to Exxon in protest.[2]

"The reality is that, in ever greater numbers, consumers want environmentally safe products, packaging and processing," Smyth says. "The polls tell us that . . . nearly 30 percent of consumers claim to have boycotted a company's products because of its environmental policies." [3]

By renewing the public's awareness of this sort of consumer protest, environmentalists may also be helping traditional interest groups like labor unions, who frequently use boycotts — and sometimes just the threat of boycotts — as bargaining chips in their dealings with employers. Striking workers at the *New York Daily News*, for example, have been encouraging the newspaper's readers to support the unions by canceling subscriptions and refusing to buy the paper on the street. And circulation is way down, although the threat of violence against newsstands and other factors have undoubtedly played a part. Nevertheless, a drop in advertising followed the drop in circulation, and the *Daily News* is feeling a serious financial squeeze.

Boycotts are "one of the more powerful tools that labor has other than to strike," says Richard J. Perry, the secretary-treasurer of the AFL-CIO's Union Label and Service Trades Department, which sanctioned boycotts of nearly 30 corporations last fall. Among the 27 that were on the union's "Don't Buy" list for September and October were The Shell Oil Co., Eastern Airlines, Holly Farms Corp. and R. J. Reynolds Tobacco Co.

Putnam attributes the growing number of boycotts in part to Americans' lack of faith in the legislative process. "Boycotts are really a form of grass-roots democracy," he says. They offer "a way to bypass the legislative process when you think that your elected representatives aren't going to represent you on this issue or that issue."

But boycotts are not always successful. Sometimes companies fight back. That's what Nike Inc. did last summer when it became the boycott target of a civil rights organization. The Nike boycott was called by Operation PUSH, a Chicago-based group that has successfully used consumer protests to pressure the Ford Motor Co. and other large corporations into

___

*Activists continue to boycott some tuna companies, which they say have refused to submit their tuna procurement practices to the same verification standards Heinz has. Last month, the Earth Island Institute took out full-page ads in major newspapers accusing Bumble Bee Seafoods Inc. of violating its "dolphin-safe" pledge. Bumble Bee responded with its own ads denying the environmentalists' allegations.

investing more of their earnings in the black community. PUSH leaders say Nike targets black consumers with advertising campaigns that feature prominent African-Americans, like filmmaker Spike Lee and football/baseball player Bo Jackson, but at the same time fails to provide enough executive opportunities for its black employees. PUSH leaders also say the company has not invested enough of its revenue in black-owned businesses.

Unlike other PUSH targets, Nike officials responded to the group's boycott announcement with an unexpected public relations counteroffensive, accusing the boycott organizers of accepting contributions from Reebok International Ltd., a rival sportswear and athletic shoe manufacturer. Nike officials also suggested that the boycott was simply a publicity vehicle for the Rev. Tyrone Crider, who recently replaced Jesse Jackson as director of the 20-year-old group.

Nike did announce that it would adopt a two-year program to promote more minority employees into executive and senior management positions, including the company's first minority vice president and its first minority board member. But officials emphasized that "minority" did not necessarily mean "black." Meanwhile, local civil rights leaders in Nike's hometown of Portland, Ore., defended the company by arguing that it maintained a plant and outlet stores in predominantly black Portland neighborhoods while other companies were leaving the area.

The way in which a company like Nike responds to a boycott depends in large part on how sympathetic a company thinks its customers will be to the boycotters' message (*see p. 7*). But boycotts are generally getting harder to ignore, a fact Putnam attributes to the increasing sophistication of the consumer campaigns. Today's boycotters, he says, make a company's image as much of a target, or even more of a target, than a company's bottom line. "[C]orporations spend millions of dollars every year trying to present a certain type of image and if you can somehow damage that image you are going to indirectly cost the company a lot of money," he says.

Boycotters who can do that will be taken seriously by a target corporation, says Jerry Johnson, the research director at Powell, Adams & Rinehart, a Washington-based group that is part of the Ogilvy & Mather public relations group. "There is an intrinsic desire on the part of a firm to be perceived as doing the right thing," Johnson says. "It's good business."

## Boycott issues include labor, civil rights, environment

Boycotting got its name from Capt. Charles Boycott (1832-1897), a British land agent for Lord Erne's estates in County Mayo, Ireland, during the disputes

between Irish peasants and their mostly British landlords in 1880. Boycott's peasant tenants refused to work for him, sell his family food or deal with him in any way after the retired British army officer said he would not give in to nationalist demands that landowners lower their rents by 25 percent. Boycott was forced to hire expensive workers from Ulster to harvest his crops and seven regiments to protect these workers from his angry tenants. After the incident, the nationalists started talking about "boycotting" the landowners to assure that their demands were met.

That was just the first use of the term, however. Boycotts were used by disenfranchised people as a way of calling attention to their plights long before Capt. Boycott was around.[4] In 1765, for instance, groups of annoyed American colonists, including the Daughters of Liberty and the Sons of Liberty, organized boycotts of British goods to protest Parliament's Stamp Act. The Stamp Act was enacted that year as a way for the British government to recover the "expenses of defending, protecting and securing the British Colonies and plantations in America." Under this act, colonists were required to buy stamps ranging in cost from a few pence to several pounds for most legal documents, including law licenses, college diplomas, liquor licenses, mortgages and deeds. Parliament repealed the Stamp Act a year later after intense lobbying by merchants whose businesses were being hurt by the colonial boycott.

American colonists turned to boycotts again in 1774, when a resolution of the First Continental Congress stopped the importation of British goods until the king's government adequately redressed Colonial grievances. In violation of British law, this resolution also established local "committees of safety and inspection" to help enforce the boycott. The colonies and England were at war before the effectiveness of this effort could be gauged. But more than 150 years later and half a world away, Mohandas K. Gandhi's boycotts of British linen and salt proved instrumental in gaining India its independence from Britain.

American trade union organizers used boycotts throughout this century as a way to force employers into contract agreements with their workers. They have promoted these boycotts by circulating "fair" and "unfair" lists that named companies whose employees worked under union-approved conditions and wages. Union labels and stamps on products produced by the employees of unionized plants and factories also helped labor sympathizers decide which products to buy and which to shun. Employers frequently accused unions of violating antitrust laws with their boycotting activities and the legality of this form of protest has been challenged many times in U.S. courts, but the legality of primary boycotts — that is, boycotts against the "unfair" company itself — has routinely been upheld. Only secondary boycotts — boycotts, for example, against a store for carrying a boycotted product

*Continued on p. 6*

# The Boycotts of 1990

**Activists and interest groups sponsored more than 200 consumer boycotts in 1990. The following list includes some of those involving major corporations.**

**CATEGORY KEY:**

| | | |
|---|---|---|
| **A - animal rights** | **F - fairness** | **M - morality** |
| **C - civil rights and civil liberties, discrimination** | **H - human rights** | **P - peace** |
| **E - environment** | **L - labor** | **Q - quality or affordability** |

| Target | Sponsor | Category | Dates |
|---|---|---|---|
| Coors beer | Gay consumers | C | 1979† |
| Coors beer | National Organization for Women | C | 1979† |
| Coors beer | Earth First! and other ecology groups | E | 1980† |
| Banks dealing with South Africa | UN Centre Against Apartheid | H | Dec. 1981† |
| Products of the rabbit industry | Trans-Species Unlimited | A | 1983† |
| McDonald's Corp. | Boycott McDonald's Coalition | A | April 1983† |
| Military toys | Alliance for Non-Violent Action | P | 1984† |
| Chiquita bananas | United Farm Workers | L | Jan. 1984† |
| Tobacco subsidiaries | Georgians Against Smoking Pollution | H | 1984† |
| Cosmetic and toiletry companies | People for the Ethical Treatment of Animals | A | 1984?† |
| Milk-fed veal | Humane Society of the United States | A | 1985?† |
| Companies that use rainforest beef | Earth First! | E | Nov. 1985† |
| Hormel | United Food & Commercial Workers, P-9 | L | Jan. 1986† |
| Shell Oil Company | United Mine Workers of America, AFL-CIO | H, L | Jan. 1986† |
| Trans World Airlines | Independent Federation of Flight Attendants | L | March 1986† |
| Morton Salt | Nuclear Free America | P | April 1986-July 1990 |
| General Electric | INFACT | P | June 1986† |
| Coca-Cola Company | Coke Divestment Campaign | H | Fall 1986† |
| Gillette Company | ARK II, PETA | A | Sept. 1986† |
| Ford Motor Company | Irish National Caucus | C | Oct. 1986† |
| Redwood products, MAXXAM Corp. | Earth First! | E | Oct. 1986† |
| British Columbia Farm-raised Salmon | Ocean Resource Conservation Alliance | E | Jan. 1987† |
| United States Playing Card Company | Retail, Wholesale, Department Store Union | L | May 1987† |
| AT&T | Nuclear Free America | P | 1987?† |
| Colt Firearms Company | United Automobile Workers | L | Spring 1987-April 1990 |
| Styrofoam (polystyrene) products | Vermonters Organized for Clean Up | E | Aug. 1987† |
| Kellogg's | Educators Against Apartheid | H | 1988?† |
| Fur | Humane Society of the United States | A | 1988?† |
| Guess Jeans | Media Watch | H | Summer 1988-Summer 1990 |
| Advertisers in Sport Illustrated's swimsuit issue | Media Watch | H | 1988† |
| Burger King Corporation | Int'l Animal Right Alliance | A | Oct. 1988? |
| H.J. Heinz, StarKist | Earth Island Institute | A | Winter 1988-April 1990 |
| Domino's Pizza | National Organization for Women | C | Jan. 1989† |
| Eastern Airlines, Continental Airlines | Int'l Association of Machinists, ALPA | L | April 1989† |
| Mary Kay Cosmetics | Rocky Mountain Humane Society | A | May 1989-1990 |
| Exxon | Essential Info, Citizens for Environmental Responsibility | E | May 1989† |
| L'Oreal | People for the Ethical Treatment of Animals | A | July 1989† |
| Clorox | American Family Association, CLeaR-TV | M | July 1989-April 1990 |
| AeroMexico | Int'l Association of Machinists | L | Oct. 1989† |
| Weyerhauser | Rainforest Action Network | E | 1989† |
| Holly Farms | Int'l Brotherhood of Teamsters | L | Nov. 1989† |
| McDonald's | Kids Against Pollution, Environmental Club | E | 1990?-Nov. 1990 |
| AT&T†† | Christian Action Council, National Right to Life Committee | H | Jan. 1990?-March 1990 |
| Procter & Gamble | American Family Association, CLeaR-TV | M | Jan. 1990-April 1990? |
| Folger's coffee | Neighbor to Neighbor | H, P | Feb. 1990† |
| Greyhound Bus Lines | Amalgamated Transit Union | L | March 1990† |
| Chrysler, Cadillac, Honda, Oldsmobile | Waste Oil Action | E | March 1990† |
| Idaho Potatoes†† | National Organization for Women, NARAL | C | March 1990-April 1990 |
| Marlboro cigarettes and Miller beer | AIDS Coalition To Unleash Power (ACT-UP) | H | April 1990† |
| Dayton-Hudson Corp. | Minneapolis abortion rights activists | C | Spring 1990-Spring 1990 |
| Dayton-Hudson Corp. | anti-abortion activists | H | 1990? |
| Burger King | WISE, northwest loggers | F | June 1990† |
| Nike | Operation PUSH | F | Aug. 1990? |
| Burger King | American Family Association | M | Sept. 1990-Oct. 1990 |
| CBS, NBC network football sponsors | sports-bar owners | F | Sept. 1990-Sept. 1990 |
| Revlon | Media Watch | C, F | Fall 1990† |
| Advertisers in New York Daily News | striking workers | L | Oct. 1990? |
| Mitsubishi | Rainforest Action Network | E | 1990† |
| Bovine Growth Hormone Milk | Boycott BGH | Q, E, F | 1990† |

† *Indicates that the boycott is still underway*
†† *Boycott only threatened*
? *Indicates that the status or outcome of a boycott is not known*

*Source: Compiled by the Institute for Consumer Responsibility in November 1990.*

# *Abortion Issue: Boycotts on Both Sides*

Last spring, when Democratic Gov. Cecil D. Andrus of Idaho was presented with legislation restricting a woman's right to have an abortion, anti-abortion groups mounted an unusual lobbying campaign: They threatened to boycott Idaho potatoes if Andrus signed the abortion restrictions into law.

The boycott threat did not go unnoticed in the governor's mansion. "[A]nytime someone threatens one of our major cash crops, it becomes significant," Andrus said at the time.

Meanwhile, anti-abortion activists tried to counter the boycott threat by promising to increase their potato consumption. "[P]eople in the pro-life movement have more kids, and we'll go eat french fries at McDonald's," National Right to Life Committee spokeswoman Nancy Myers told *The Wall Street Journal*. In the end, the self-described "pro-life" governor vetoed the anti-abortion legislation.†

Boycotts sponsored by activists on both sides of the abortion issue make up only a small percentage of the more than 200 boycotts currently being mounted around the country. However, the volatile nature of the issue raises the stakes for any company that finds itself dragged into this emotional debate — a fact that some activist groups have used to solicit quick corporate capitulations.

Last spring, for example, the American Telephone and Telegraph Co. withdrew its financial contributions to the Planned Parenthood Federation of America, which advocates abortion

rights, after the anti-abortion Christian Action Council (CAC) threatened to boycott the telecommunications giant.

AT&T's contributions were specifically earmarked for one of Planned Parenthood's teenage pregnancy programs. But AT&T executives said they gave in to the CAC's demands because they didn't want the company's contributions to be perceived as a corporate endorsement of Planned Parenthood's pro-abortion rights views and abortion-related programs.

Planned Parenthood supporters responded to AT&T's announcement with a massive letter writing campaign and by taking out ads in newspapers in which they called on consumers to "voice their opposition to this act of corporate cowardice."

Meanwhile, the CAC launched boycotts against 43 other corporate contributors to Planned Parenthood, including Bristol-Myers Squibb Co., Pillsbury Co., H. J. Heinz Co., BP America Inc. and General Mills Inc. The CAC also sent letters to Planned Parenthood donors offering "to quietly remove your corporation from our list without any public statement should you decide to end your support for Planned Parenthood." CAC's public policy director, Doug Scott, says 15 corporations have accepted this offer, but he declines to name them. "We've agreed to not release that information," he says.

There have been other abortion-related boycotts as well. In May 1989, anti-abortion groups called for a boycott

of Maxwell House coffee after it sponsored the NBC made-for-television movie "Roe vs. Wade," which dramatized the story of the 1973 Supreme Court decision that legalized abortion. Abortion rights activists have called on consumers to boycott Domino's Pizza to protest personal contributions by Thomas Monaghan, the company's founder and its chief executive officer, to an anti-abortion group. And given the passions on both sides, both anti-abortion and abortion rights groups are likely to sponsor even more abortion-related consumer boycotts in the future.

Last summer, the National Organization for Women (NOW) suggested that it might boycott Hoechst AG, the German chemical company whose Paris-based Groupe Roussel Uclaf subsidiary manufactures the new abortion pill, RU-486. The pill currently is available only in France. NOW has been lobbying the chemical company to seek Food and Drug Administration approval for the drug in the United States, but the company has been slow to do so, in part because officials are concerned about the potential reaction of anti-abortion activists to such a move.

"It has been suggested that if in the end we are not successful, maybe we should consider a boycott," NOW President Molly Yard says. "I don't think it's outside the realm of possibility, but we aren't there yet."

† *See* The Wall Street Journal, *March 29, 1990, p. A14.*

---

*Continued from p. 4*
— have run into legal trouble. (*See story, p. 9.*)

Civil rights groups in the 1950s and '60s were also frequent boycotters, especially after the success of the Montgomery, Ala., bus boycott in 1955 and 1956. This effort — organized by the Montgomery Improvement Association (MIA) and its 27-year-old president, the Rev. Dr. Martin Luther King Jr. — began in December 1955, when a woman named Rosa Parks was arrested for refusing to comply with a bus driver's order to give up her seat for a white passenger. At first the boycotters' goal was simply to convince the bus company to adopt a modified but still segregated seating system in which riders were seated on a first-

come, first-served basis — blacks back-to-front and whites front-to-back. The boycotters did not adopt desegregation as their goal until after the city and the bus company rejected the MIA's proposed changes.

In February 1956, with a vast majority of Montgomery's black population walking to work and around town instead of riding the bus as they had before, the MIA challenged the city's bus segregation laws in federal court. Nine months later, the Supreme Court upheld an earlier district court ruling that sided with the boycotters, and in December, the MIA called off its boycott.[5]

Citing Gandhi's use of boycotts, King and other civil rights leaders continued to support this tactic as a form of "non-violent" protest throughout the 1950s and '60s. "[W]e must ... invest our finances in the cause of freedom," King wrote in 1957. "Freedom has always been an expensive thing. History is fit testimony to the fact that freedom is rarely gained without sacrifice and self-denial." But King also urged his followers to remember "that a boycott is not an end within itself; it is merely a means to awaken a sense of shame within the oppressor and challenge his false sense of superiority." [6]

"In the 1960s, we discovered ourselves as an interest group economically," says George Riddick, a senior vice president with Operation PUSH, which has used boycotts to pursue its goals for 20 years. "We [discovered] that our dollars had some real value in terms of the larger market economy. ... We are very brand-conscious and very brand-loyal [and] tend to represent the margin of profit for most consumer industries because of our consistent expenditures."

As a result, Riddick says, civil rights groups like PUSH have been able to use boycotts as tools for social and economic change. "The idea was that we should get a return for our investment ... in terms of jobs and in terms of opportunity for our businesses," he says. "We [have been] using our boycotts as leverage to increase economic benefits to our people."

Other groups were inspired by the labor and civil rights movements' boycott successes and also turned to this form of protest as a way of airing their grievances. In the mid-1960s and early '70s, Western farm workers led by Cesar Chavez of the United Farm Workers of America (UFW) organized national boycotts of table grapes and iceberg lettuce to pressure California growers into granting them union contracts.

These boycotts were extremely effective in mobilizing public support. By the end of 1968, retail grape sales were down by more than 10 percent nationally and 50 percent in major cities like New York. The boycotts also turned UFW President Chavez into a celebrity. Chavez's 25-day fast in February 1968 attracted national media attention, especially when the weakened labor leader was called into court for defying a picketing injunction. That March, Sen. Robert F. Kennedy, D-N.Y., a soon-to-be candidate for the Democratic presidential nomination, attended the Delano, Calif., mass at which Chavez ended his fast.[7] With Kennedy's accompanying throng of national television and print journalists making the most of the scene, boycotting — a form of protest used by disfranchised people for hundreds of years — entered the media age.

### Attacking image instead of economics

Earlier this year, a Massachusetts-based group called Stop Teenage Addiction to Tobacco (STAT)

decided to boycott all products made by Nabisco Brands Inc., Kraft Inc. and General Foods Corp. to protest the marketing strategies employed by parent companies R. J. Reynolds (Nabisco) and Philip Morris (Kraft/General Foods). But STAT President Joe Tye says he had no delusions about his group's ability to affect either of the tobacco companies' enormous profits. "We're not going to hurt them economically and we know that," Tye says. "Philip Morris could withstand anything we could do to them."

Instead, Tye says, STAT wants to damage both companies' corporate image — by associating the sales of Nabisco's Oreo, Chips Ahoy and Fig Newton cookies, for example, with the efforts of RJR Nabisco's tobacco units to promote smoking among teenagers. "We think the disruption of their public relations machine would be much more important than the actual economic loss."

This sort of thinking is a new development in the world of boycotts, says *National Boycott News* Editor Todd Putnam. "Boycotters used to play a numbers game by trying to enlist [other] boycotters ... and becoming a credible threat [to a company] that way." But economic impact has always been difficult to measure and isolate because so many different variables affect a company's sales. As a result, Putnam says, boycotters are targeting corporate image instead. This strategy is designed to change consumer attitudes by publicly associating a company's products — or even a subsidiary company's products — with an unpopular cause or practice. "That way they can get people to support a boycott without their even knowing that they're supporting a boycott," Putnam says.

One image-conscious interest group is San Francisco-based Neighbor to Neighbor, which is boycotting Folger's coffee because about 2 percent of the beans used in that company's blend come from El Salvador. Activists say the sale of Salvadoran coffee helps support the decade-long civil war in that country. To promote its campaign, Neighbor to Neighbor produced a 30-second television advertisement in which blood is shown oozing from an overturned coffee cup while a voice-over narration by actor Ed Asner accuses Folger's of "brew[ing] misery, destruction and death."

"I don't know that [Neighbor to Neighbor] really expected people to look at that ad and say, 'Wow, I really want to support this boycott,'" Putnam says. "I think they're more likely to turn people off ... to the product, thereby getting people to subconsciously not buy Folger's coffee because of this association with blood."

Folger's parent company, Procter & Gamble Co., the nation's second-largest advertiser,* recognized the threat. Calling the Neighbor to Neighbor ad "inaccurate, grossly misleading and offensive," the company

---

*The advertiser ranking is reported by *Advertising Age*, which says that the nation's leading advertiser in fiscal 1989 was Philip Morris.

yanked its entire $1 million a year account from Boston CBS affiliate WHDH-TV for running the ad and said it would cancel advertising agreements with any other station that ran it. Only one did — a UHF outlet in Massachusetts.[8]

From the boycotters' perspective, the advantage of an image-oriented strategy is that a company can see and measure a boycott's effectiveness simply by examining its own polling data. "You can actually measure whether companies are sticking in people's minds [and] whether they have a positive image or a negative image," Putnam says.

And companies take such findings very seriously. "Most companies want to be perceived by their immediate customers and their potential customers as being responsive and understanding and good corporate citizens," says Jerry Johnson of Powell, Adams & Rinehart. With positive image, "Your customers feel better about doing business with you, whether you deal directly with the public or your sales are mainly business-to-business."

As a result, a successful image-focused boycott can hurt a company's long-term sales by smothering its ability to move into new markets and by derailing expensive public relations and promotion strategies. Even after a boycott has been called off, says Richard Perry of the AFL-CIO's Union Label Department, the effects can linger. "The public becomes accustomed to patronizing someone else. ... Even though the all-clear has been signaled, the customer has become attuned to buying at another shop or to substituting that product with another product and becomes satisfied with it."

Credible boycotts can also affect a company's relations with its employees and potential employees, Johnson says. "You want to be able to hire and retain the highest-quality personnel available, [and] if those individuals ... don't think you're doing the right thing, that has an impact as well."

The Dow Chemical Co. discovered how long-lasting image problems can be in the mid-1980s. At that time the company found that many consumers were uncomfortable buying products from a company that had developed a reputation for resisting environmental regulation and that, 10 or 20 years earlier, had been widely associated with the manufacture of napalm bombs used in the Vietnam War. Some Dow employees were not happy with this reputation, either, so the company launched a multimillion-dollar advertising campaign that highlighted its charitable activities and the involvement of its scientists in environmental research. The company also changed its slogan from "Common sense — uncommon chemistry" to "Dow lets you do great things."

"I think we have a fair amount of work to do in terms of the way we are viewed," Dow's Frank Popoff told The New York Times a short time before he became the company's chief executive in 1987. "We know we'll never change Ralph Nader's mind. But

Dow is at peace with itself, and we want our people to feel good about the company, too." [9]

If it is difficult for a company to undo a negative public image, it also is difficult for boycotters to create that negative public image. Central to their fight is the fact that they generally must rely on the media to spread their message for them, either by providing news coverage of their boycotts, or by accepting the activists' advertising.

STAT, the anti-smoking group boycotting Nabisco, Kraft and General Foods, got some media attention recently when Ben & Jerry's Homemade Inc., the popular New England ice cream company, disclosed that it was looking for a substitute cookie to replace the Oreos it has been using in one of its flavors. Oreos are made by Nabisco. Lee Holden, the public relations coordinator for Ben & Jerry's, which has a reputation for using its products to promote social causes, says his company's announcement was not related to STAT's Nabisco boycott, and was a change the company had been considering for the past two years. Nevertheless, STAT has been using Ben & Jerry's announcement to help promote its cause with the press.

However, many media organizations do not want to jeopardize their own earnings by giving publicity to the wrong boycott and upsetting an advertiser, as Neighbor to Neighbor discovered with its anti-Folger's ad. "It is very, very difficult to get the media very much concerned [about a boycott, because] the people we are boycotting are huge advertisers," says Donovan McClure, a senior vice president with the Washington-based Kamber Group, a public relations firm that frequently works with labor unions. "When you announce the boycott you may get a one-day story. When the boycott's over, you get your second story. You don't get anything in between."

INFACT,* a peace group that has been boycotting General Electric Co. (GE) products to protest that company's involvement in the nuclear weapons industry, has had an especially tough time getting media attention, particularly on NBC. GE acquired the network in 1986 when it bought RCA, NBC's parent company. Fairness and Accuracy in Reporting (FAIR), a New York-based group that monitors the news media, recently criticized NBC's "Today" show for not discussing INFACT's efforts during a Nov. 26 segment on consumer boycotts.

In a letter responding to an advertisement FAIR placed in The New York Times on Dec. 11, NBC News Information Director Peggy Hubble defended the network's coverage of issues involving GE. "We attempt

*Continued on p. 10*

*INFACT was once an acronym for the Infant Formula Action Coalition, which mounted a successful seven-year boycott of Nestlé that ended in 1984. A spinoff organization, Action for Corporate Accountability, renewed the Nestlé boycott four years later (see p. 12). Meanwhile, INFACT retained the original acronym for its anti-nuclear campaign, even though it no longer calls itself the Infant Formula Action Coalition.

# The Complexities of Secondary Boycotts

In determining the legality of labor boycotts, U.S. courts have made a distinction between primary and secondary boycotts. In a primary boycott, employees call on consumers to shun the products or services of the company directly involved in the labor dispute. The courts have said that this form of protest is legal, as long as violence and intimidation are not used to keep people from doing business with the boycotted firm.

Secondary boycotts, on the other hand, have run into legal problems. This type of boycott is directed at businesses not directly involved in a labor dispute, such as firms that sell or distribute boycotted products. This type of boycott is generally illegal.

However, the distinction between what type of boycott is legal and what type is illegal is often easier to make in theory than it is in practice. As a result, labor-related boycotts have a long history of confusing litigation and legislation.

In the Danbury Hatters' case of 1908 (*Loewe v. Lawlor*), the U.S. Supreme Court upheld a lower court ruling that secondary boycotts constituted an illegal restraint of trade punishable under the provisions of the Sherman Antitrust Act of 1890. In this case, a union attempting to organize workers at a hat factory in Danbury, Conn., was supported by the American Federation of Labor, which set up boycotts of stores selling the hats in several states.

Speaking for the court, Chief Justice Melville W. Fuller asserted that because the antitrust act covered "any combination whatever" in restraint of trade, it extended to labor unions. The court therefore ruled that under the terms of the Sherman Act, the manufacturer could be awarded treble damages for business lost in the boycott.

In response to the Danbury decision, Congress added provisions to the Clayton Act of 1914 that specifically exempted labor unions from antitrust actions. Seven years later, however, the Supreme Court ruled in *Duplex Printing Press Co. v. Deering* that the Clayton Act exemptions pertained only to legal and normal operations of labor unions. There was nothing in the act, the court said, to protect unions that

engaged "in an actual combination or conspiracy in restraint of trade." The secondary boycott was such a restraint, the justices held.

The Supreme Court continued to use the antitrust laws against unions throughout the 1920s. Congress attempted to restrict the court's ability to interfere in labor disputes when it passed the Norris-LaGuardia Act of 1932, which prohibited the issuance of injunctions by federal courts in labor disputes except where unlawful acts were threatened or committed.

In 1938, in *Lauf v. E. G. Shinner & Co.*, the Supreme Court upheld the Norris-LaGuardia Act on the ground that Congress had the power to determine the jurisdiction of the federal courts. The ruling signaled a shift in attitude regarding union activities by the high court. In 1941, the court, in *U.S. v. Hutcheson*, sustained a provision of the Clayton Act that stated that certain acts such as strikes and secondary boycotts would not be considered violations of any federal law. In *Allen Bradley Co. v. International Brotherhood of Electrical Workers* (1945), the court ruled that a union was protected in conducting a secondary boycott as long as the union was not conducting its boycott in coordination with business groups.†

However, Congress reversed this trend with the passage of the Taft-Hartley Act of 1947. Passed over President Harry S Truman's veto and the opposition of organized labor, the act contained provisions barring certain labor union activities — including secondary boycotts — as "unfair labor practices." The prohibitions against secondary boycotts were strengthened by the Landrum-Griffin Act of 1959, which restricts union activities intended to "coerce" a person or business to stop doing business with another person or business.††

The current legal status of secondary boycotts is unclear, however, because of a 1988 Supreme Court ruling. In *Edward J. DeBartolo Corp. v. Florida Gulf Coast Building and Construction Trades Council*, the court ruled unanimously that federal law did not bar unions from distributing handbills urging customers to boycott a shopping mall because of a labor dispute with a

contractor working there. Attorneys for the mall owner claimed the handbill distribution was a coercive action that constituted an illegal secondary boycott. The National Labor Relations Board agreed, but an appeals court ruled in favor of the union.

The appeals court ruling in the *DeBartolo* case was upheld by the Supreme Court on April 20, 1988. The court said that while federal law outlaws "coercive" secondary boycotts, the union in this case was only trying "to persuade customers not to shop in the mall." There was no coercion, the justices said, because there was "no violence, picketing or patrolling."

According to Lawrence M. Cohen, an attorney for the Edward J. DeBartolo Corp., the 1988 ruling "broadened the area of industrial controversy until there's no limitation on the number of parties in a labor dispute." *Business Week* magazine said the *DeBartolo* ruling "significantly expands a union's right to conduct secondary boycotts. The decision gives a potentially powerful new weapon to the weakened labor movement, which has been searching for alternatives in recent years as its ability to mount strikes has diminished." ‡

But labor's right to mount secondary boycotts depends heavily on the specifics of each case. For example, it probably is legal for a labor union with a dispute against a widget manufacturer to hand out pamphlets in front of a store that carries the widgets, asking consumers not to buy them. It also is probably legal for the labor union to ask the store not to carry the widgets. But if the union did *both* activities, it would be on shaky legal ground.

Because the legality of such situations is so cloudy, many labor lawyers believe that secondary boycotts are likely to remain the subject of litigation and legal debate for the foreseeable future.

† *For more details on the Supreme Court rulings, see Elder Witt, ed.,* Congressional Quarterly's Guide to the U.S. Supreme Court, *2nd edition (1990), pp. 94, 96, 675.*

†† *For details, see Congressional Quarterly,* Congress and the Nation, 1945-1964 *(1965), pp. 566-568.*

‡ *"The Secondary Boycott Gets A Second Wind,"* Business Week, *June 27, 1988, p. 82. Cohen was quoted in the* Business Week *story.*

*Continued from p. 8*

to treat GE as we do any other entity — in a straightforward and aggressive manner — and we're confident that we achieve that goal." Hubble said GE was not mentioned in the "Today" show's boycott story because the segment's producer "made an independent news judgment about what products to include based on a specific type of story he was doing. He did so without conferring or receiving advice from any senior producer or news executive. Had he been taking a broader look at the boycott issue, he could and perhaps would have included GE." In the segment, Deborah Norville discussed a number of major consumer boycotts with Todd Putnam, including boycotts of Burger King, Nike, California table grapes, tuna, Marlboro, Miller beer and Philip Morris. But they did not discuss the GE boycott, even though Putnam says it is one of the largest under way in the country.

Meanwhile, activists have found other ways to call public attention to their boycotts. Members of the AIDS Coalition to Unleash Power (ACT-UP) have picketed and heckled speakers during Philip Morris' touted Bill of Rights tour to promote their boycott of Marlboro cigarettes and the Philip Morris-owned Miller Brewing Co. ACT-UP launched its boycott last spring to protest Philip Morris' political contributions to Sen. Jesse Helms, R-N.C., who has been an outspoken opponent of gay rights. "We've primarily tried to give [Philip Morris] a bad corporate image for supporting the most anti-gay senator there is, . . . [and] we thought it would be a good idea to boycott high-profile products of that company," says Michael Petrelis, a boycott organizer with ACT-UP's Washington chapter, which spearheaded the Philip Morris boycott in April.

Many leaders in the nation's arts community have called on their colleagues to support ACT-UP's boycott to protest Helms' efforts to restrict funding for the National Endowment for the Arts (NEA).* However, ACT-UP members have focused most of their efforts on gaining support for the boycott within the gay community. The boycott has received a great deal of coverage in gay newspapers, and its sponsors have convinced a number of gay bars to stop selling Miller products.

Putnam says the refocusing of boycott efforts on corporate image is one of the reasons companies seem

---

*In September, controversial performance artist Karen Finley, who had been denied an NEA grant, announced that she would not host an annual awards ceremony in New York that honors outstanding experimental performers, composers, designers and choreographers because Philip Morris provided funds for the event. Actor Ron Silver, the president of an organization of art professionals called Creative Coalition, has encouraged other artists to follow Finley's lead. "People in the arts community say, 'Please don't go after Philip Morris, because we get a lot of money from them,'" he recently told *The New York Times*. "But I feel there are enormous contradictions bordering on hypocrisy in accepting money from an organization that helps keep people like Jesse Helms afloat." See *The New York Times*, Dec. 18, 1990, pp. C15, 20. For background, see "Tying Down Federal Funds for the Arts," *E.R.R.*, May 25, 1990 (Vol. I, No. 20).

more willing to respond to these consumer protests. "The longer the boycott goes on, the more deeply entrenched this negative image is going to be with the consumer," he says.

But most companies still hold out in boycott situations, arguing that these protests amount to nothing more than "blackmail," or "economic extortion." As a result, the average amount of time it takes for a boycott to succeed remains between five and 10 years. Corporations "are playing the image game, too," Putnam says. "They think that if they can make boycotts look bad, or if they can make boycotts look unfair or unjust, they can . . . defeat a boycott — not individually by arguing their case, but simply by arguing against all boycotts in general."

## Companies' different ways of dealing with boycotts

If in business "the customer is always right," the way in which a company responds to a boycott depends in large part on how sympathetic its consumers — and potential consumers — will be to the boycotters' motives. But first, Putnam says, "the corporation has to decide . . . who their customers are."

Officials at McDonald's, for example, gave in to environmentalist boycotters who wanted the chain to stop using polystyrene, the lightweight plastic-foam material that keeps "the hot side hot and the cold side cold." On the other hand, these same officials do not seem worried about the possibility that Big Mac eaters will boycott the restaurants to support a vegetarian coalition's demand that McDonald's offer a less carnivorous menu.

Once it has determined that a boycott is "credible" with its customers, a company must answer other questions, says Jerry Johnson of Powell, Adams & Rinehart. "If it is credible, what type of economic impact does it have — not only directly, but indirectly in terms of company image and the future growth plans of the firm? What markets are they looking at? What things would they like to do in the next five to 10 years, and how would this boycott or threat of a boycott affect those things?"

Dave Fogelson, a spokesman for Miller Brewing Co., says his company responds to boycott threats on an individual basis, "based upon the issue that is being raised and how that may or may not relate to our role as an advertiser, as a sponsor and as a member of the community." Fogelson also says that his company's response to an interest group's call for a boycott "is not going to be predicated on what the sales or business situation is at any given time."

But when two coalitions of sports-bar owners threatened to boycott Miller and other prominent sponsors of television sports broadcasts last fall, the brewer arranged for the head of one of these groups to fly to New York and meet with NBC and CBS officials. Norman Lebovitz, who owns four sports bars in the San Diego area and is president of the Association for Sports Fans Rights, discussed his group's concerns about the networks' plans to comply with a National Football League edict and scramble their satellite transmissions of professional football games starting in September. Lebovitz said the scrambling would have destroyed the business of many sports bars, which rely on their presentation of out-of-market sporting events to attract customers. Within days, the networks announced that they were suspending their scrambling plans this season for technical reasons, and the Miller boycott was called off.

Lebovitz says he never expected Miller or the networks to respond to his group's demands as fast as they did. "I was real surprised. We were digging in for a lengthy fight." However, Lebovitz also says he knows why the companies responded the way they did: "All we are are sports fans, but we're also the guys who pay the bills."

Fogelson says it was appropriate for his company to respond the way it did because the satellite scrambling would have "affected a very important part of our market: number one, sports fans in general, and number two, sports-bar owners in particular. . . . [W]e realized that this was an issue that affected Miller Brewing Co. [because] it affected our customers." Fogelson denies that Miller "responded to the situation because of the threat of a boycott," but he concedes that the threat "might have hastened our response. It might have put things in motion a lot quicker than they normally would have. . . . Obviously [the beer market] is a very competitive market, and even minor ups and downs in sales can have affect."

Burger King recently negotiated its way out of a consumer protest sponsored by Christian Leaders for Responsible Television (CLeaR-TV), who called on their supporters to boycott the company for advertising during several TV programs they said exploited sex, violence and "anti-Christian stereotyping." One of CLeaR-TV's founders is American Family Association Executive Director Donald Wildmon, a minister whose organization used the threat of a consumer boycott against PepsiCo Inc. to pressure the soft-drink maker into dropping a television advertisement that featured pop star Madonna in April 1989.[10]

As Pepsi did more than a year before, Burger King officials responded to CLeaR-TV's boycott campaign quickly, meeting with members of the group to explain the company's existing advertising guidelines. Once CLeaR-TV leaders were convinced that Burger King would advertise the way they wanted them to, they called off the two-month-old boycott. Meanwhile, Burger King published half-page advertisements in hundreds of newspapers around the country in which the company pledged to use its advertising dollars to support "traditional American values on tele-

vision, especially the importance of the family."

Burger King officials say the publication of this advertisement was their idea and was not one of CLeaR-TV's conditions for ending the boycott. Instead, they say, it was a reflection of Burger King's concern about potential damage to its corporate image caused by CLeaR-TV's direct-mail campaign against the company. "We saw a possibility for a lot of confusion among our Christian consumers," says company spokesman Michael Evans.

Some corporations enjoy such high customer loyalty that they have not had to worry much about the threats posed to their businesses by consumer boycotts. This has been particularly true in the tobacco industry. "A person who smokes Marlboro probably has a high involvement with the brand," says Dr. Bernd Schmitt, a professor at Columbia University's graduate school of business who specializes in consumer behavior. "In most cases, when confronted with negative information about Marlboro, he'll engage in what we call biased information processing. He'll either disregard the information or rationalize it."[11]

But Philip Wilbur, director of the Advocacy Institute's Health Advocacy Resource Center, in Washington, D.C., believes smokers may not be as brand-loyal as tobacco companies might think. Wilbur works with a number of public interest organizations that publicize the health hazards associated with tobacco and alcohol use. These groups generally "don't talk about boycotting tobacco," because "the people who use the product are addicted to it," Wilbur says.

But one group Wilbur worked with, ACT-UP, found a solution to this problem by asking consumers to support their boycott of the Philip Morris-owned Miller Brewing Co. and Marlboro cigarettes by switching brands. STAT, on the other hand, has targeted the tobacco marketing efforts of Philip Morris and RJR Nabisco by boycotting their Kraft/General Foods and Nabisco subsidiaries. In both of these cases, Wilbur says, the groups "weren't asking for a boycott of tobacco products, so if you were addicted to tobacco, you didn't have to give it up to participate in the boycott."

The companies that are the targets of STAT's boycott have responded by trying to disassociate themselves with their parent corporations' tobacco units. "We believe their boycott is misguided . . . because Nabisco Brands is devoted solely to foods," says Nabisco spokesman Mark Gutsche. "We're a food company here. We deal with food. We make cookies and crackers."

But the independence of subsidiaries is not always so clear. Two years ago, RJR Nabisco canceled an 18-year-old, $84 million advertising contract for Nabisco and Life Savers with the New York-based advertising firm Saatchi and Saatchi after the firm produced a spot for Northwest Airlines that promoted the carrier's decision to ban smoking on all its domestic fights.[12] STAT President Tye says this incident exposed the company's "non-tobacco subsidiaries to our efforts to make people aware of how they use those non-tobacco subsidiaries to promote smoking."

Although a growing number of companies have decided to deal directly with consumer activists one way or the other, however, most companies still prefer to ignore boycotts if they can, as General Electric has tried to do with the four-year-old nuclear weapons-related boycott of its products. "We have not been awfully pro-active" in responding, says Ford Slater, GE's issues, planning and communications manager. Slater says he occasionally calls protesters who use the company's toll-free answer center to complain about GE's involvement in the production of certain weapons systems. "We reply when people are interested in knowing what our position is," he says.

After nine hospitals pledged to support the boycott last summer by not buying their equipment from GE, which is one of the nation's leading manufacturers of diagnostic technology, company marketing managers began accompanying sales representatives to meetings with officials from hospitals that expressed concern about the nuclear weapons issue. "The sales people aren't the best qualified to present our position in this matter," Slater told *The Wall Street Journal* in July.[13] But the company continues to approach the boycott in a low-key way.

One reason companies hesitate to respond too quickly to boycotts or threats of boycotts, says *Boycott News* Editor Todd Putnam, is that they believe they will become easy marks if they do. If that is the case, one company with such a problem may be Burger King. "They distinguish themselves as a company that is giving in to boycotts and [developing that image] is probably not a healthy thing to do," Putnam says. Putnam cites as examples the fast-food chain's recent appeasement of CLeaR-TV, its 1987 announcement that it would stop buying "rain forest beef" and two different decisions to remove veal items from its menus in the early 1980s.[14]

Burger King spokesman Evans says he doesn't think his company's products and services are "any more susceptible to boycotts than any other consumer product. . . . [A]ny company that is as visible as Burger King is subject to special interest group pressures, so I don't think we're being singled out one way or the other." Putnam isn't so sure. "There has got to be some degree of awareness on the part of the organizations that are calling the boycotts that the company has given in the past," he says.

There is another side to the story, however: Sometimes companies can gain more than just the end of a boycott by acquiescing. Heinz Vice President Edward Smyth says giving in to the StarKist tuna boycotters over the dolphin-killing issue presented his company with an "excellent opportunity to build credibility," given its customers' developing interest in environmental issues. "It was only a matter of time before someone else in the industry would capitalize on this

advancing consumer awareness if StarKist did not," he says. "[B]eing the first to seize the environmental initiative would affirm the company's leadership in the tuna industry [and] boost even further the loyalty of millions of consumers."[15]

Heinz has even used its capitulation in television advertisements promoting StarKist's new "dolphin-safe" tuna. "We used considerable internal and external public relations resources to get the greatest possible impact from our new policy," Smyth says. But some of the best PR for Heinz came in the form of endorsements for its products from former boycotters. As Smyth puts it, "Such a strong, high-profile activist network could be just as powerful an ally as an adversary."[16]

Putnam says more companies should consider responding to consumer protests the way Heinz and StarKist did. "I wish the corporations would just realize that it is in their long-term best interest not to alienate the public to their products and to damage their image over a five- to 10-year boycott."

And perhaps, if the boycott boom continues, a new corporate consensus will develop.

## *Are too many boycotts making them less effective?*

The increasing willingness on the part of corporations to respond to consumer boycotts has inspired even more groups to adopt this form of protest as a tool for social change. In fact, it has even inspired some former boycotters to jump-start their efforts and renew previously resolved boycotts.

In 1988, for example, Action for Corporate Accountability (ACA) — a Minneapolis-based coalition of churches and consumer groups — renewed its boycott of Nestlé S.A., accusing the Swiss-based firm of violating a four-year-old agreement that restricted the company's efforts to promote its baby formula in the Third World. According to the ACA, misuse of the formula contributes to malnutrition and high infant mortality rates in developing nations. ACA's original seven-year Nestlé boycott ended in 1984, when the company said that it would abide by World Health Organization guidelines on the marketing of infant formula in those countries. Nestlé has denied ACA's new claims.[17]

Meanwhile, the United Farm Workers union has renewed its California table grape boycott to call attention to the health threats posed to farm workers and consumers by the growers' use of certain pesticides. In 1988, UFW President Cesar Chavez even tried to recapture some of the widespread public support his union's original boycott efforts enjoyed by staging a 36-day fast, which ended at a mass attended by Jesse

*Continued on p. 14*

# AT ISSUE
*Does the current United Farm Workers union boycott unfairly target California grape growers?*

## YES
*says* **THE GRAPE WORKERS & FARMERS COALITION**, *a group established in 1985 that seeks to maintain "a steady, uninterrupted production and marketing cycle for the table grape industry."*

The Grape Workers & Farmers Coalition believes that grape growers have unfairly been singled out for their use of pesticides which are used throughout the agriculture industry. . . .

The four pesticides that the UFW [United Farm Workers] wants banned from table grapes — methyl bromide, Captan, Phosdrin, and Parathion [a fifth pesticide, Dinoseb has already been banned] — have been registered for use on hundreds of American-grown crops. The UFW itself permits the use of these four targeted pesticides in crops such as lettuce, cauliflower, citrus crops . . . , wine and raisin grapes, and broccoli. The UFW has contracts with many growers of these crops and represents the farm workers which harvest them. . . .

In addition, only the growers in California have been targeted, although the same chemicals are used in most other states.

Although the UFW is asking consumers to boycott all California-grown table grapes, statistics show that many California-grown grapes are free from the targeted pesticides. The Agricultural Commissioner of Riverside County, where approximately 15 percent of California's table grapes are grown, recently reported that the targeted pesticides methyl bromide, Parathion and Phosdrin were not used on table grapes in 1986 and 1987. Only 45 pounds of Captan was used in 1986, and none in 1987.

The UFW alleges that California table grape farmers are the worst violators of pesticide laws. . . . Yet not a single incident has been reported to the California Department of Food and Agriculture's Pesticide and Worker Safety Division involving negligent use of pesticides in the table grape industry. . . . California law requires that such cases be reported by physicians treating pesticide related illnesses.

While the UFW appears to blame the California table grape industry for incidents of cancer and birth defects, the Coalition maintains that these tragic incidents have nothing to do with grapes.

All government agencies that test for chemical residues in food have found California table grapes to be in solid compliance with all food safety standards. . . . Furthermore, California is the only state that has an independent and comprehensive pesticide registration and monitoring program that exceeds EPA and FDA standards. . . .

The Coalition also maintains that the UFW exploits the families of cancer victims by inviting parents of affected children to tell their story by promising medical and financial support that the parents need. Some parents . . . claim that the UFW misrepresents them and has not helped them to deal with their crises. [One parent] said that instead of assistance the parents "got a sophisticated boycott machine."

*From "The Grape Boycott: A Misguided Effort," National Boycott News, spring/summer 1989.*

## NO
*says* **THE UNITED FARM WORKERS** *union.*

During the previous grape boycott, the growers used much more open and explicit violence against farm workers and organizers. These widespread beatings did a lot to attract sympathy to the cause. Today, the growers are much more sophisticated and use other tactics in addition to violence and threats. During 1987, the Table Grape Commission's ad budget went up $2 million. Because of this and the more conservative mood of the country, the union decided that it must try a new approach. Right now, organizing is difficult, potentially dangerous, and not very fruitful. A successful boycott will enable the union to win important contracts and get back on the road toward organizing. . . .

Because the union hasn't the number of volunteers now that it had during the previous boycott, it *has* opted for a different approach. Without enough staff to do door-to-door and store-to-store, the union has had to make greater use of mass mailings and telephone canvassing to get the word out and to gather support. But [UFW President Cesar] Chavez has also taken the boycott on the road across the country and continues to build as much grass-roots support as is possible. . . .

The only reason that grape workers are not on strike as they were during the previous grape boycott, is that the UFW would not be able to afford to take care of them during such a strike. Also, many workers are scared and continue to receive threats from growers. . . .

[G]rapes are still the largest fresh fruit crop in California and the union has the most pesticide-related grievances with the grape industry. . . . The safety levels and regulations set by the federal and state agencies do not protect farm workers. A grower may endanger workers without necessarily violating current regulations. Furthermore, because cancers and other pesticide-related health effects may not show up for many months, or even years, there is no way to show the effects are tied to one specific incident.

Pesticides are a real concern to farm workers and to the UFW, and so is unionization. But the two issues are not separate. When workers are without a contract they have no say over what pesticides are used. The UFW uses contracts as opportunities to address the pesticide issue. . . . When a contract expires and it's time to renegotiate with a grower, the UFW gets a list of all pesticides used by the grower and asks experts which pesticide the union should target in contract talks. Sometimes the union succeeds in the outright banning of a chemical from use by the grower; other times the contract will include a gradual phase-out of specified chemicals. Such negotiations are part of the advantage of having a union.

*From "The UFW Replies," National Boycott News, spring/summer 1989.*

*Continued from p. 12*

Jackson and other celebrities.[18]

Putnam says the recent flurry of boycott activity — old and new — is a reflection of the American public's lack of faith in the political process, and that interest in this form of protest will continue to grow along with public cynicism. "As boycotts gain visibility they gain more public acceptance and they gain more clout," he says. "In the past you rarely ever heard of boycotts. The majority of Americans probably couldn't even name one boycott. Now I think most people could name two or three."

But the proliferating boycott movement also poses problems for the boycotters, who say they already have a hard time getting their message out in the battle for consumer attention. "Sometimes the public can get overburdened with all these special interest groups," says Richard Perry of the AFL-CIO. "The public can only assimilate so many of these things before they throw up their hands and say, 'The hell with all of them!'"

George Riddick of Operation PUSH says his group has also noticed the growth in the number of organizations sponsoring boycotts, and is concerned about how that growth might interfere with PUSH's efforts. "To date we have not been especially impeded by that, but it is certainly a factor that you have to take into account."

But Riddick and Perry also say this growth presents interest groups with opportunities to pool scarce resources and network, as some civil rights activists, religious groups and labor organizations have done by joining together to boycott the Shell Oil Co. over its operations in South Africa. "You have to form coalitions with religious groups and community groups to localize [a boycott] to the point where you know you can have an effect on a company's bottom line," Riddick says.

"You want to expand [the boycott] so that it has a larger focus of persons who have a direct interest in it," Riddick adds. "You have the assistance of these other persons and you incorporate their interests in the total focus of what you're negotiating for. ... That, of course, is the positive side of it."

The negative side is that when different interest groups boycott the same company they usually do so for different reasons, which can make it difficult to hold a coalition together when the company decides to appease one group and fight another. This happened after the Adolph Coors Co. came to an agreement with the AFL-CIO in August 1987, ending a bitter 10-year boycott of that company's products that hampered the brewer's efforts to expand into new markets.[19] Other groups had joined forces with the AFL-CIO to mount the Coors boycott, including human rights organizations, gay rights activists, Latino groups, feminist groups, environmentalists and civil rights organizations. But when the AFL-CIO ended its boycott, the other groups vowed to keep it going and expressed

disappointment with the union leaders for not consulting with them.[20] Nevertheless, coalition boycotting does help consumers in what is already a confusing field of boycotters and boycottees.

Todd Putnam of *Boycott News* says the proliferation of consumer boycotts has not yet reached the point where the interest groups need to be overly worried about overwhelming consumers. "As long as the average person on the street is only aware of two or three boycotts, I don't think there's any problem with any kind of backlash. If the American public becomes inundated with 10 or 15 boycotts, then there'd be some problem. Then they'd start to feel hopeless. But I'll only worry about that when there are maybe a thousand boycotts going on [and] I don't think that will happen. I think it will start dying down."

# NOTES

[1] Remarks by D. Edward I. Smyth before the Pittsburgh chapter of the Public Relations Society of America, Nov. 7, 1990.

[2] Exxon spokesman quoted by United Press International, Aug. 26 1989. The spill occurred on March 24.

[3] Smyth, *op. cit.*

[4] See Harry W. Laider, *Boycotts and the Labor Struggle* (1913), pp. 23-25.

[5] See David J. Garrow, ed., *The Walking City: The Montgomery Bus Boycott, 1955-1956* (1989), pp. 3-58.

[6] Quoted in Garrow, *ibid.*, pp. 157-159.

[7] See J. Craig Jenkins, *The Politics of Insurgency: The Farm Workers Movement in the 1960s* (1985), pp. 162-172, 193-197.

[8] See *Business Week*, June 4, 1990, and *The Washington Post*, May 12, 1990, p. A9.

[9] See *The New York Times*, Nov. 22, 1987, p. F6.

[10] See *The Wall Street Journal*, April 5, 1989, p. B11, and April 7, 1989 p. A1.

[11] Quoted by Richard Morgan in *Ad Week*, Aug. 20, 1990, p. 2.

[12] See *The Wall Street Journal*, April 6, 1988, p. A3.

[13] See *The Wall Street Journal*, July 16, 1990, p. B1.

[14] For details, see *Forbes*, Jan. 3, 1983, p. 14, and Jan. 2, 1984, p. 16; *Newsweek*, Sept. 14, 1987; *National Boycott News*, spring/summer 1989, pp. 1, 176-178; and *The New York Times*, Nov. 7, 1990, pp. D1, 9.

[15] Smyth, *op. cit.*

[16] *Ibid.*

[17] See *Los Angeles Times*, Oct. 5, 1988, sect. IV, p. 1.

[18] See *National Boycott News*, spring/summer 1989, p. 166.

[19] See *Business Week*, Sept. 7, 1987, p. 29.

[20] See *National Boycott News*, spring/summer 1989, pp. 157-165.

*Graphics: Cover, Margaret Scott.*

## RECOMMENDED READING

### BOOKS

Garrow, David J., editor, *The Walking City: The Montgomery Bus Boycott, 1955-1956*, Carlson Publishing Company, 1989.
Garrow has assembled a collection of essays and scholarly analyses of various aspects of the Montgomery bus boycott, which was the first of many significant boycotts of the civil rights movement. The book also includes the memoirs of several boycott leaders, including Ralph Abernathy, and a detailed chronology of boycott events.

Jenkins, J. Craig, *The Politics of Insurgency: The Farm Worker Movement in the 1960s*, Columbia University Press, 1985.
The author examines the farm workers movement of the 1960s — particularly the activities of the United Farm Workers of America and UFW President Cesar Chavez — in the context of the social movements and the political turmoil that was characteristic of that decade. Chapters six and seven include detailed descriptions of the tactics used by the UFW to mount national consumer boycotts against California growers. The successes of some of these boycotts inspired other activists to adopt this form of protest beginning in the early 1970s.

### ARTICLES

Atchison, S.D., "Will Labor's Joe Sixpack Come Back to Coors?" *Business Week*, Sept. 7, 1987.
The article discusses the AFL-CIO's decision to call off a 10-year boycott against the Adolph Coors Co., which effectively contained the brewer's ability to expand into new markets. The article analyzes the reasons behind the boycott's success and Coors' plans to overcome the boycott and become the nation's third largest brewer.

"Boycotting Corporate America," *The Economist*, May 26, 1990.
Noting the current boycott "epidemic," this article outlines various tactics adopted by consumer boycotters and lists examples. The article says that boycotts are effective tools for changing corporate policy simply because they work. The article includes a sidebar on Procter & Gamble Co.'s threat to cancel its advertising contracts with any television station that airs a spot produced by Neighbor to Neighbor, a San Francisco-based group that is calling on consumers to boycott P&G's Folger's coffee.

"Corporate Cointelpro," *Harper's Magazine*, July 1989.
Harper's reprinted "Pro-active Neutralization: Nestle Recommendations Regarding the Infant Formula Boycott," a confidential report prepared by the Ogilvy & Mather Public Relations unit for Nestle S.A. after Action for Corporate Accountability renewed its boycott of the company's products in the fall of 1988. The report outlines various image-related and public relations strategies Nestle could adopt to counter the boycott. Among its recommendations, Ogilvy & Mather suggested that Nestle infiltrate the sponsor organization to monitor the activists' plans. According to *The Wall Street Journal*, Nestle rejected this plan. Nevertheless, the report shows how seriously corporations consider the threats posed to their businesses by boycotts, and how public relations firms try to capitalize on these concerns.

Michael Kinsley, "Sour Grapes," *The New Republic*, Dec. 10, 1990.
The author proposes six rules for activists to help control the growing number of consumer boycotts, which he says "may be getting out of hand." Among other things, Kinsley suggests that consumer activists join unions in restricting their use of "secondary boycotts," which have run into legal trouble.

Savan, Leslie, "Activism in the Checkout Line: The Rising Tide of Boycotts," *Utne Reader*, September/October 1989.
The article, reprinted from *The Village Voice*, discusses the proliferation of boycotts and other forms of consumer protest sponsored by groups from both ends of the political spectrum, and lists a number of prominent examples.

Morgan, Richard, "It's High Time for Madison Avenue To Start Taking Boycotts Seriously," *Ad Week*, Aug. 20, 1990.
Morgan argues that boycotts are effective if the issue that led to the boycott is one that matters to the target company's customers. The article includes discussions with consumer behavior and public relations experts on how and when a company should respond to these protests.

Schiller, Zachary, and Landler, Mark, "P & G Can Get Mad, Sure, But Does It Have To Get Even?" *Business Week*, June 4, 1990.
Procter & Gamble Co. pulled its advertising from a Boston television station after it aired a spot produced by a group calling on consumers to boycott P&G's Folger's coffee. The powerful advertiser threatened to do the same to any other station that aired the anti-Folger's ad. According to the authors, this and similar moves by other large corporations "only fuel the public perception of corporate behemoths stomping on those who would dare oppose them." The authors suggest that corporations produce counter-ads or simply ignore such attacks.

### REPORTS AND STUDIES

*National Boycott News*, Institute for Consumer Responsibility, published irregularly.
*National Boycott News* is a 6-year-old newsletter-turned-magazine that monitors consumer boycotts around the nation. *NBN* is published by a mostly volunteer staff at the Institute for Consumer Responsibility in Seattle. Each issue includes lists of boycotts, addresses of sponsors and target companies, and in-depth unbiased articles on boycott developments, corporate reactions, the issues behind specific boycott efforts and activist tactics. Between main issues, *NBN* publishes update issues with stories on new boycotts and recent developments.

EDITORIAL RESEARCH REPORTS

MARCH 1990
Asbestos: Are the Risks Acceptable?
Public Health Campaigns
U.S. Role in South Africa's Future
Homeless Need More Than Shelter

APRIL 1990
How Fair is the Tax Burden?
Reforming Workers' Compensation
U.S. Pacific Forces
Curbing Auto-Insurance Premiums

MAY 1990
Should Teaching Be a Profession?
Will Canada Fall Apart?
Is the U.S. Patent System Outdated?
Federal Funding for the Arts

AUGUST 1989
Can Prisons Rehabilitate Criminals?
Transportation Crisis
Libel Law
Role of Ambassadors

SEPTEMBER 1989
Environmental Protection
Civil Servants' Discontent
Cambodia's Civil War
Defense Contractors

OCTOBER 1989
Good News and Bad About AIDS
Women and Combat
Crime's Link to Punishment
Politics of Refugee Policy

NOVEMBER 1989
Balkanization of Eastern Europe
Dealing With the Underclass
America Turns to Recycling
U.S. Role in New World Economy

DECEMBER 1989
North America Trade Pact
Influence Peddling
A Primer on German Reunification
Coping With Learning Disabilities

JANUARY 1990
Higher Education Curriculum
Photonics
Age of 'Infotainment'
Abortion: Politicians' Nightmare

FEBRUARY 1990
Free Politics and Economic Growth
Free Agency: Pro Sports' Challenge
Repetitive Motion: New Job Ailment
War on Drugs

JUNE 1990
Downsizing America's Armed Forces
Progress In Weather Forecasting
S & L Bailout
Bio-Chemical Disarmament

JULY 1990
Do Americans Still Love Marriage?
Death Penalty Debate
Decline of Rural America
United Nations in the 1990s

AUGUST 1990
Democracy in the Philippines
Initiatives: True Democracy?
Hard Times at Newspapers
Teens Balance School & Jobs

SEPTEMBER 1990
Dangers of Alcohol
Western Alliance After the Cold War
Tobacco Industry
Right to Die

OCTOBER 1990
Organ Transplants
Energy Policy Options
Search for Arab Unity
Child Support

NOVEMBER 1990
Lotteries and Gambling
Post Cold-War Choices
Setting Limits on Medical Care
Multicultural Education

DECEMBER 1990
Cable TV Regulation
Americans' Search For Their Roots
Is Insurance Going the Way of S&Ls?
Why Schools Still Have Tracking

*Coming soon*

- The Draft
- Archaeology
- Peace Corps at 30

Published weekly by Congressional Quarterly Inc., Editorial Research Reports analyze emerging issues of national interest across a broad range of social, scientific, political and economic fields. Reports are bound and indexed for permanent reference. Subscription information is available through Congressional Quarterly's Publications Sales Department by telephone (202) 887-8665. Copies of past issues are available through Customer Service, (202) 887-8621.

ERR

JANUARY 11, 1991

CONGRESSIONAL QUARTERLY'S

EDITORIAL RESEARCH REPORTS

FOUNDED 1923

# SHOULD THE U.S. REINSTATE THE DRAFT?

# SHOULD THE U.S. REINSTATE THE DRAFT?

## *by Patrick G. Marshall*

EDITOR
**MARCUS D. ROSENBAUM**

MANAGING EDITOR
**SANDRA STENCEL**

ASSOCIATE EDITOR
**RICHARD L. WORSNOP**

STAFF WRITERS
**MARY H. COOPER**
**ROBERT K. LANDERS**
**PATRICK G. MARSHALL**

PRODUCTION EDITOR
**LAURIE DE MARIS**

EDITORIAL ASSISTANT
**AMY GORTON**

RICHARD M. BOECKEL (1892-1975)
FOUNDER

PUBLISHED BY
**CONGRESSIONAL QUARTERLY INC.**

CHAIRMAN
**ANDREW BARNES**

PRESIDENT
**RICHARD R. EDMONDS**

EDITOR AND PUBLISHER
**NEIL SKENE**

EXECUTIVE EDITOR
**ROBERT W. MERRY**

EDITORIAL RESEARCH REPORTS (LIBRARY OF CONGRESS
CATALOGUE NO. 39-924; ISSN 0013-0958). Published weekly
(48 times per year, excluding March 1, May 3, August 2 and
November 1, 1991) by Congressional Quarterly Inc., 1414 22nd
Street NW, Washington, D.C. 20037. Rates are furnished
upon request. Application to mail at second-class postage
rates is pending at Washington, D.C. POSTMASTER: Send
address changes to EDITORIAL RESEARCH REPORTS, 1414
22nd Street NW, Washington, D.C. 20037.

Since 1973, when the United States abandoned military conscription in favor of an all-volunteer force, many people have come to regard military service as more of a job opportunity than a patriotic duty. But the threat of war in the Persian Gulf has changed things dramatically. With lives on the line, critics have charged that the all-volunteer forces put minorities and the poor disproportionately at risk. They say the United States should return to the draft to ensure that the sacrifices of war are more evenly shared.

The crisis in the Persian Gulf has revived an old debate: When America goes to war, who should do the fighting?

With its historical distrust of large standing armies, the United States traditionally has kept its active-duty forces relatively small, preferring to rely on a core group of volunteers whose numbers could be supplemented by a draft in the event of a national emergency. As a result, the question of when and if to draft civilians has had to be addressed each time a crisis arose.

The issue seemed to be settled once and for all in 1973, when President Richard M. Nixon abolished the draft and instituted the all-volunteer armed forces. But just seven years later, President Jimmy Carter reinstated mandatory draft registration in response to the 1980 Soviet invasion of Afghanistan. Since then, all men between the ages of 18 and 26 have been required to register for the draft. During the 1980s,

## Educational Levels of Recruits is Up

**Better pay and better benefits have attracted better people to the military. As the graph below indicates, the proportion of recruits with high school diplomas or higher levels of education has been above 90 percent since the early 1980s.**

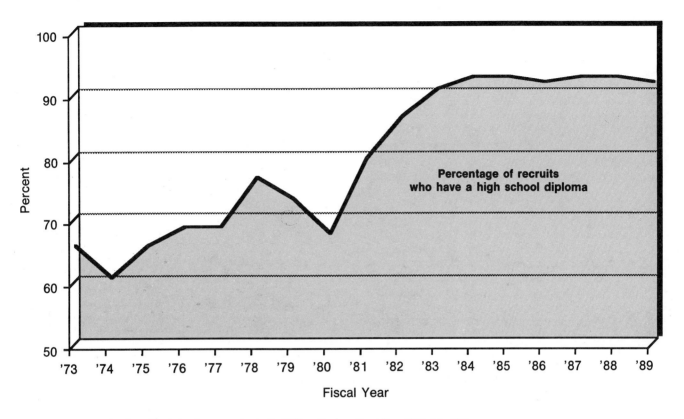

*Source: **Department of Defense**,* Population Representation in the Military Services, Fiscal Year 1989, *July 1990.*

however, U.S.-Soviet relations improved dramatically, so there was little reason to consider activating the draft.

That changed on Aug. 2, 1990, when Iraq invaded Kuwait. Over the past five months, the United States has sent nearly 400,000 troops to the Persian Gulf, enough to launch offensive action against Iraq.

As the possibility of armed conflict in the gulf has increased, so have calls for reviving conscription. "If the president is serious about going on the offensive, he should call for an immediate resumption of the draft," former Navy Secretary James Webb told the Senate Armed Services Committee Nov. 29. According to Webb, the 2 million-strong all-volunteer forces simply aren't large enough to sustain that many troops or replace casualties if combat breaks out.

Sen. Sam Nunn, D-Ga., chairman of the Armed Services Committee, agrees. Without a draft, Nunn said in a recent television interview, "we're not going to have the ability to sustain this level of forces, which is about half of our Army combat forces, about half of our Marines and about half of our Navy." Nunn made it clear that he was not calling for an immediate re-

sumption of the draft, but he intimated that the United States may have to consider this option if the gulf crisis drags on. "What happens if something else happens in the world that we don't expect?" he asked. "Do we have the military power to [deal with] it or are we inviting somebody else in the world to take aggressive steps now because America has gotten so committed in this part of the world?" [1]

Members of Congress are not the only ones questioning whether the United States should bring back the draft. In fact, according to a recent *Wall Street Journal* poll, 58 percent of voters already believe the draft should be reinstated if the United States goes to war against Iraq.[2]

Despite such sentiments, the Bush administration has made it clear that it is not considering activating the draft. Indeed, most defense experts agree that it is already too late for a draft to have any impact on the gulf crisis. "If you started the draft today, it would be six or eight months before you'd have these raw recruits out there," says Martin Binkin, a military manpower expert at the Brookings Institution in Washington. "Nobody expects the current crisis to last [that] long.

... And you wouldn't want to use that option anyway, because you still have probably 900,000 guys in the Army Reserve and National Guard ... who at least have had basic military training. ... [E]ven under a worst-case situation, you'd turn to them [first]."

Be that as it may, the Persian Gulf crisis clearly has brought the issue of the draft to the surface once again. And the debate, as it plays out, is a wide-ranging one. It concerns what kind of military is the most effective one, what kind brings the most benefits for the least cost, and — central to the issue — what kind of system spreads the burden of military service in the fairest way. The fact that it is too late to institute a draft for the Persian Gulf crisis does not mean that those questions will go away any time soon.

### Is military service just for the have-nots?

Since the early 1970s, the United States has relied on the rapid deployment of reserve forces as a basic tenet of its military policy. Some military analysts contend that making U.S. military effectiveness so dependent on part-time soldiers is a questionable gamble with national security.* The reserves may be better prepared for combat than untrained civilians, they argue, but reserve forces are not capable of replacing regular Army troops. "The basic problem with the reserves is that the line units, other than a few exceptions in the South, are a disaster," says Stephen Canby, a Washington-based defense consultant. "If you only train part of the time, as the reserves do, and you've got high turnover of personnel, of course your people aren't [as effective as active-duty forces]."

The alternative to relying on the reserves is to have a larger full-time military. But that would be particularly hard to do with an all-volunteer system. Nearly everyone agrees it would be extremely difficult to attract a sufficient number of volunteers for such a large military, especially in wartime. Moreover, even if the nation could attract that many volunteers, it would be prohibitively expensive. So the only way the United States could hope to afford a larger standing army is to reinstate the draft; draftees don't have to be paid as well or offered as many cash and educational incentives as volunteers. And some experts believe even a conscripted military would be too expensive.

For many people who support the draft, however, cost is not the issue. Nor is military preparedness. In their view, the chief issue is one of social equity. A draft, they say, would make the military more racially and economically balanced. Blacks, for example, ac-

count for 23 percent of all enlisted personnel and about 30 percent of the forces in the Persian Gulf, though blacks account for only about 13 percent of Americans between the ages of 18 and 24. Blacks make up a particularly high percentage of Army personnel, accounting for 32 percent of the troops.[3]

"Some people say it's simply unethical sending off the poor, black kids to die," says Martin Binkin. "Others say it's important that we have a representative military, not just for that reason, but to bring more sobriety to the decision-making process. The idea is that if we had congressmen's sons, CEOs' sons and journalists' sons [in the armed forces], then maybe we would have better checks and balances in the decision-making process."

Binkin says such sentiments have increased as tensions in the Persian Gulf have risen. "About four months ago, some black leaders were in the Pentagon concerned that the military was going to squeeze out blacks as it cut back on its force," he notes. "Now there are black leaders complaining that these young blacks are going to die disproportionately."

Gen. Colin L. Powell Jr., the first black chairman of the Joint Chiefs of Staff, insists that blacks are in the military because they want to be. "If it were unfair — and I don't accept that — the only way to correct that unfairness would be for somebody to instruct me to set a limit ... on the number of blacks allowed to enlist. The armed forces have always provided opportunities for blacks which blacks have found attractive and have gone after, and I see no reason to change that now." [4]

Though blacks and other minorities are disproportionately represented in the all-volunteer forces, there is conflicting evidence concerning whether a disproportionate number of those in the military come from lower-income families. According to a recent Defense Department study, the average recruit's socioeconomic status is only slightly below that of the average 18-to 24-year-old civilian.*

"The contention that the enlisted force is recruited primarily from the lower socioeconomic strata of society is not supported by the evidence," the report concludes. "In the last half of [fiscal year] 1989, the period for which data are available, the great majority of the parents of recruits had a high school education or better, were married, and owned their own homes. The overwhelming majority of those in the labor force were employed." [5]

Even critics of the all-volunteer forces concede that the military has not had to take the "dregs" of society to fill its forces. But they say it's also clear that the military has not been able to attract many recruits from

---

*For more details on the debate over the reserves, see "Downsizing America's Armed Forces," *E.R.R.*, June 8, 1990 (No. 21).

*Using an index that considered several factors about recruits' families — including parents' occupations, employment status, education and home ownership — the study found that recruits scored 36.0 as compared with 40.1 for the general population. The Defense Department study did not ask recruits about family income because the researchers found that recruits' estimates of family income were frequently in error.

# Potential Impact of the Draft

**The dotted line in the graph below shows the number of years of service for given numbers of enlisted personnel in the all-volunteer forces. The solid line shows the General Accounting Office's estimate of how many enlisted personnel would have specified years of service if the draft were implemented. Both volunteer and drafted forces would have about the same number of troops with 20 years of experience. But the GAO estimates that because of shorter enlistments and lower retention rates, there would be fewer experienced troops in a drafted force than in the all-volunteer forces.**

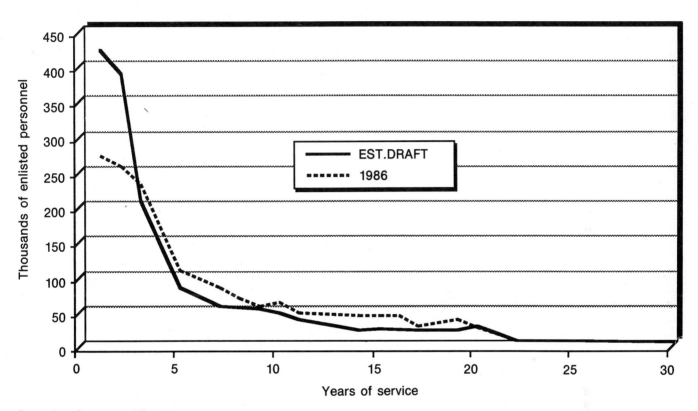

*Source: General Accounting Office,* Military Draft: Potential Impacts and Other Issues, *March 1988.*

higher socioeconomic levels. For example, a recent study by the RAND Corp. in Santa Monica, Calif., found that high school seniors from lower-income families were more likely to enlist than seniors from families with higher than average incomes. The study also found that high school seniors who wanted to attend college were less likely to enlist than those who weren't planning to go to college and that "applicants with relatively good civilian job opportunities were less likely to enlist than those with poorer civilian opportunities." [6]

Although the exact socioeconomic status of the volunteer forces is unclear, there is no question that better pay and educational benefits have been among the chief attractions of military service in recent years. "The pay and educational benefits we have provided over the past 10 years have helped the armed forces draw more motivated, middle-class Americans into the services," says Rep. G. V. "Sonny" Montgomery, D-Miss., chairman of the House Veterans' Affairs Committee. "... The bottom line is that we have a more representative sample of middle America in the vol-

unteer force ... than can be achieved in any draft, and we don't have the morale and discipline problems that accompany conscripts through their two-year hitches." [7]

Montgomery also argues that minorities and people from lower income levels have fared better in the all-volunteer forces than they did before the draft was abolished in 1973. "The draft tended to funnel minorities and lower-income recruits to the lesser technical skill areas, such as combat arms on the front lines," he says. "By contrast, the volunteer system offers more opportunities for its minority recruits to advance and to compete across the board for all skill positions."

But the opportunities offered by the military in peacetime obviously are far different from those offered during wartime — a reality underscored by the Persian Gulf crisis. "I think people got a wake-up call, that the military is not just a peacetime venture," Binkin says. Operation Desert Shield, as the deployment to the gulf is called, "has shown some of the warts of the volunteer force concept. People are

# *A History of Conscription in America...*

The draft was not the primary means of raising armies in Colonial America, even though, at times, large armies were needed. During the French and Indian Wars in the mid-1750s, for example, Massachusetts annually sent an expeditionary force that included about a third of the colony's men between the ages of 16 and 29. "It was not through impressment that such a mobilization was achieved, ...." writes Rutgers University historian John W. Chambers. "Rather, 88 percent enlisted voluntarily, inspired by economic, religious and patriotic reasons, and sometimes by the sheer desire for adventure." †

By the time of the American Revolution, there were clear differences between the state militia and the Continental Army. Because service in the Continental Army usually involved a long-term commitment, it tended to attract members of the lower classes, for whom the relatively small enlistment bonuses were sufficient inducement. "Unlike the celebrated 'embattled farmers' of the militia," Chambers observes, "the rank and file of the Continental Army ... eventually became composed overwhelmingly of the young and the poor whites and blacks — the sons of marginal farmers, laborers, drifters, indentured servants — and recent immigrants without roots in America."

As for the militias, there were many ways for members of the middle and upper classes to avoid service. In New England, wealthier individuals often hired others to serve in their place. "When not enough citizen-soldiers volunteered, local militia officers drafted the more affluent citizens who, in turn,

hired men to serve as substitutes," Chambers writes. "This selective draft functioned mainly as a kind of tax for raising individual enlistment bounties."

In the South, the system was more blatant. Many legislatures simply exempted those with property from the draft and forced the poor and unemployed into service. The Continental Congress had passed a law in 1775 exempting conscientious objectors from military duty, but that did not apply to service in the state militias.

The military system underwent significant changes in the early 1800s, with most states abandoning compulsory militia training. "With the expansion of citizenship, and of membership in the militia, to include large numbers of poor and working-class men, and with the end of major threats to national security, increasing numbers of the urban middle and upper classes shunned attendance at the semi-annual militia-training days, by paying a fine instead," Chambers writes. "Declining interest and consequent financial neglect led to the spectacle, lampooned by the urban press, of 'rabble' or 'scarecrow militia,' engaged in a parody of military drill, many without weapons or uniforms."

The first nationwide draft by the federal government came in 1863, in the midst of the Civil War. The 1862 law that provided for the draft allowed exemptions only for those considered physically, mentally or morally incapable of serving, as well as a few categories of state and federal officials. But there were two other escape hatches provided for those who had the money to use them: Draftees could avoid service by paying a $300 fee or by hiring a substi-

tute for whatever fee could be agreed upon.

Historian James M. McPherson called the Union draft "a clumsy carrot and stick device to stimulate volunteering." †† Of the approximately 2 million who served in the Union Army, more than 92 percent were volunteers. "The first federal call for volunteers, which included the threat of a draft, ... did in fact obtain several hundred thousand volunteers," Chambers relates. "In contrast, of the 300,000 men summoned by draft authorities, 40,000 failed to report for examination, 165,000 were examined and then exempted because of physical or other disability or dependency, 52,000 escaped service by paying the commutation fee, 26,000 provided substitutes, and only 10,000 were held to personal service."

While the draft didn't actually produce many troops, it did result in bloody riots in many major Northern cities. Historians are divided, however, on the question of whether the riots were in fact responses to the draft or to the war itself. "Rioters were not influenced by pacifist principles," argues law Professor Stephen M. Kohn. "Rather, these riots were violent rebellions against the very goals of the Civil War and were led mainly by racist or pro-Southern whites." ‡

The Confederacy also instituted a draft in 1863. It had fewer loopholes than the Union draft, but also was not very effective.

When the United States went to war against Spain in 1898, the draft was forsaken entirely in favor of locally raised volunteer forces. But less than 20 years later, conscription was brought

---

saying that they joined the service to learn a skill and for educational benefits and that they were kind of surprised when they got involved in a wartime situation and the prospect of dying on a sand dune in Kuwait."

Indeed, there are signs that the Persian Gulf crisis is making it more difficult for the military to meet its recruitment targets. A recent article in *The New York Times*, for example, said November enlistments were off by more than 25 percent at some Army recruiting stations.[8]

But spokesmen for the military insist that the news media are exaggerating the recruiting shortfalls. They say November enlistments were below projections because the Army pushed up its recruiting goals to September and October. Overall enlistments are below last year, they say, primarily because of congressionally mandated reductions in the size of the military. "Any wartime scenario is going to have an impact on recruiting," says a senior Army recruiting officer. "But the articles that were published gave a picture that recruiting was crumbling around us and that the

# ...From the Colonial Era to Vietnam

back when the United States entered World War I. Nearly three-quarters (72 percent) of the 3.5 million soldiers who served during that war were draftees.

Just as the government depended more on the draft during World War I than during previous wars, it also treated those who objected to the draft more harshly than in the past. In April 1918, the War Department ordered all conscientious objectors who were "active in propaganda" or "sullen and defiant" to be court-martialed. According to Kohn, 450 conscientious objectors were found guilty. Of these, 17 received death sentences (later commuted), 142 were sentenced to life in prison, 73 received 20-year terms, and only 15 received jail terms of three years or less.

The World War I draft was, at least on the surface, more egalitarian than previous drafts. The rich could no longer "buy out" or hire substitutes. But classifications were based on registrants' "value" to the economy. Hence, those in more "important" jobs — generally those making the most money — were frequently exempted from service.

World War II was a much more "popular" war in the United States, and so the draft was much less of an issue. Of the 3.5 million men who registered, only about 72,000 — less than two-tenths of 1 percent — requested classification as conscientious objectors.

Though being a conscientious objector in first half of the 1940s was not socially popular, COs received much better treatment than they did during World War I. According to Kohn, about 25,000 men entered the army in non-combatant service, and nearly 12,000 were assigned to alternative civilian service. About

20,000 had their requests for CO status turned down. In then end, 6,086 conscientious objectors were sent to prison.

"Unlike resisters from the previous war, the World War II objectors were tried in civilian courts and were not subjected to military courts-martial," Kohn notes. "The Selective Service System attempted to moderate the excessive brutality that had occurred during World War I. . . . After sentencing, COs were confined in federal prisons, not military jails. The maximum sentence for violating the Selective Service Act was five years (the average resister served 35 months behind bars), not the ridiculously long sentences doled out at the World War I courts-martial."

On March 17, 1948, as the Cold War between the United States and the Soviet Union emerged from the ruins of World War II, President Harry S Truman called both houses of Congress together and asked for a resumption of the draft. Although the United States did not go to war against the Soviet Union, war did break out five years later on the Korean Peninsula. Once again, the great majority of those who served were draftees.

America's next war, in Vietnam, would prove to be the undoing of the draft. As opposition to the war mounted in late 1960s and early 1970s, the draft became a major focus of protesters. Between 1964 and 1965 draft-card burning came into vogue. Congress reacted sharply to the new type of protest, passing legislation in 1965 that made the destruction of draft cards illegal.‡‡

The elimination of student deferments — under which many of the children of the middle- and upper-classes

had avoided service — and the introduction of a draft lottery in 1970 added to the opposition to conscription. As the war became more unpopular, the courts seemed to adopt a new attitude toward draft resisters. "In 1967, nearly 90 percent of all those convicted of draft law crimes received jail terms; that proportion had been cut in half by 1970," Kohn notes. "By 1975, less than 9 percent of all convicted defendants went to prison. For those sentenced to prison, the average length of their sentences also dropped, from a high of a 37.3 months in 1968 to a low of a 14.5 months in 1974."

In December 1972, President Nixon tried to reduce domestic discontent by stopping draft inductions. The draft officially ended the next year. In 1980, however, President Jimmy Carter responded to the Soviet invasion of Afghanistan by calling for a reinstitution of draft registration. Ronald Reagan criticized Carter's decision during the 1980 presidential campaign, arguing that peacetime registration would reduce by only a few days the time needed to call up draftees in case of war. After he became president, however, Reagan reversed his position, and on Jan. 7, 1982, he ordered the continuation of mandatory draft registration for 18-year-old men.

† *John W. Chambers,* To Raise an Army: The Draft Comes to Modern America *(1987), p. 15.*

†† *James M. McPherson,* Battle Cry of Freedom *(1988), p. 605.*

‡ *Stephen M. Kohn,* Jailed for Peace: The History of American Draft Law Violators, 1658-1985 *(1986), p. 21.*

‡‡ *Ultimately, 46 people were prosecuted under the law and 33 were convicted.*

---

services were in deep trouble. That's not true." The official, who asked not to be identified, concedes that there is generally less traffic at recruiting stations now, but says that a higher proportion of those who come in are enlisting.

Nevertheless, if war breaks out, there will almost certainly be increased pressure for a return to the draft — if not from the military as it finds it increasingly difficult to replace losses with volunteers, then from others insisting that the burdens of military service should be shared more broadly.

## The all-volunteer forces: 17 years old and fit

As recently as 10 years ago, critics of the all-volunteer forces were predicting its demise because the military seemed unable to attract enough quality recruits. The critics had a good deal of evidence to support their claim.

In 1973, the first year of the all-volunteer force, the Army alone fell 23,000 enlistments short of its goal. By the mid-1970s, however, the services were able to meet their recruiting goals, thanks in part to the 1974-75 recession, which encouraged many who might otherwise have been unemployed to enter the military. But when the recession ended, the services again had problems finding qualified recruits. In 1980, the year President Carter reinstated draft registration, only 54 percent of recruits had high school diplomas and 44 percent ranked in the lowest eligible category of mental ability on Defense Department aptitude tests. Only 5 percent ranked this low in 1975.[9]

During the 1980s, however, the all-volunteer forces came into their own. By 1989, most recruits (96 percent) had high school diplomas and only 6 percent ranked in the lowest eligible category of mental ability. What accounts for the turnaround? The answer is simple: Better pay and better benefits attracted better people.

In 1972, in preparation for the switch to the all-volunteer force, pay for new enlistees was increased 61 percent. By 1981, the average annual compensation of a typical recruit was $16,620. Military pay continued to rise by about 3-4 percent a year throughout the 1980s. Though military pay scales still are somewhat below those for corresponding jobs in the private sector, personnel in the volunteer forces clearly are making more money than did their draft-era counterparts.

Money also has been important in a negative sense: The military has an easier time attracting and retaining qualified recruits during economic downturns. This was certainly the case during the recessions of 1974-75 and 1982-83. In fact, one group of researchers found that for every percentage point increase in the unemployment rate, the military's retention rate goes up by as much as 2 percentage points.[10]

Keeping retention rates high is one of the keys to ensuring high quality in the military. By that measure, the all-volunteer forces have shown significant improvement. In 1973, just before the draft was abolished, the average age of enlisted personnel was 25 years, and the mean length of time in the service was 70 months. By 1989, the average age was up to 26 years, and the mean length of time in the service had climbed to nearly 80 months.

One of the most dramatic changes in the military over the past two decades has been the huge increase in the number of women in the forces. Though women are still barred from combat,* their presence in the military has grown from only about 2 percent in 1973 to 11 percent in 1990. This "has had a dramatic impact on the military, which has always been kind of a macho organization," says Martin Binkin. "Some of the problems associated with that [increase] are starting to show up. Some are going to say maybe this idea about [having more women in the military] is a little different in wartime when they're starting to leave their

babies at home." Indeed, many television news programs aired stories on women in active and reserve units who had to leave their children behind when they were deployed for duty in the Persian Gulf.

The increase in the number of women is not the only change in military demographics. More junior personnel are married today than in the past and more live off-base instead of in barracks. Some military analysts worry about the impact of these and other lifestyle changes on the military's esprit de corps. "As pay has grown, as recruiting campaigns have emphasized the armed services' advantages for vocational training, the soldier's calling has become a job, much like any other," Harvard political scientist Eliot A. Cohen wrote in 1985. "This is a perilous condition, for in wartime the soldier has a far grimmer set of duties, a far more difficult environment in which to live and work, than the automotive mechanic or crane operator." [11]

Such concerns have more urgency today. "Some say the members of the volunteer forces are seeming to be 'softer' than many people would like to see as far as their attitudes toward combat," Binkin says. "I was recently in the gulf for a month and a half and people were saying, 'When are we getting rotated?' That's a far cry from World War II, when people were over in the desert for four years."

Though admittedly not an unbiased observer, President Bush bluntly rejects such concerns about troop morale and readiness. "You'll read about one or two that say, 'Well, I didn't sign up to do this. I signed up because I thought I could get a free education,'" Bush told reporters at a Dec. 18 news conference. "But that's the tiny fraction of these kids that are over there [in the Persian Gulf]. The morale is good and they're motivated and they're well educated and they're dedicated, and if you'll excuse an old-fashioned reference, they're patriotic."

## Would conscription make for a better military?

Even critics of the volunteer forces concede that the quality of active-duty troops is relatively high. "The mode of the volunteer force is probably a notch higher than it was during the draft of the Vietnam era," says Charles Moskos, a professor of sociology at Northwestern University who favors a return to the draft.

Indeed, it is the professional nature of the all-volunteer military that is, in the view of many supporters, one of its major strengths. "We as a society hire police officers to risk their lives fighting criminals. We hire firefighters to risk their lives fighting fires. And we hire soldiers to risk their lives in defense of American interests," Michael Robinson of Midlothian, Va.,

---

*See "Should Women Be Allowed into Combat?" *E.R.R.*, Oct. 13, 1989 (Vol. II, No. 14).

wrote in a letter to the editor of *The Washington Post.* "To suggest ... that when fire — or war — strikes we should show our solidarity by grabbing people at random off the street and sending them into the inferno, when professionals are readily available, is just bizarre." [12]

However, Moskos and others support the draft not because they think draftees would be better qualified than volunteers, but because they believe it would not be possible to attract enough volunteers — at least at affordable prices — should the United States suddenly need to expand its forces to handle a future military conflict. And even if the military does not need to expand in size, these advocates of the draft warn, the job of attracting qualified recruits will get harder in the future. That's because the pool of eligible men and women is shrinking. According to Census Bureau figures, the number of Americans between the ages of 18 and 21 will fall by about 12 percent between 1989 and 1995.

Addressing such concerns, the Defense Department argues that the readiness of the volunteer forces cannot be judged without taking the reserves into account. Under the military's "Total Force" policy, in effect since the early 1970s, the reserves are expected to supplement active-duty forces on short notice. There currently are more than 1 million troops in the services' reserve components.*

The reserves' traditional role had been to be, literally, a force held in reserve, one that naturally needed time to be trained in the event of mobilization. Under the Total Force policy, however, reserve units are an integral part of military planning. Today, many reserve units have no counterpart in the active-duty forces. These include "heavy" non-attack helicopter units, infantry scout groups and railroad units. And reserve units are not limited to support roles. The Army National Guard, for example, represents more than 40 percent of the Army's total combat manpower. [13]

The chief advantage of relying on the reserves is that such units cost only a fraction of active-duty forces. According to a report by Martin Binkin and William W. Kaufman, a lecturer at Harvard University's John F. Kennedy School of Government, "personnel-related costs for a reserve Army unit are four to five times less than those for an active unit of the same size and rank structure." [14]

In line with their new responsibilities, the reserves now receive better training and equipment than they did during the Vietnam War era. According to Lt. Col. David Super of the Pentagon's Reserve Affairs Department, "The vast majority of guardsmen and reservists, if they've been in for more than three years

... have probably already gone at least once with their unit to either an overseas location or to some kind of major exercise in the states with their active-duty counterparts."

But while the training given to the reserves has improved over the past 10 years, critics say many reserve units still are not up to the job. They are particularly concerned about Army Reserve brigades and battalions assigned to "round out" active combat divisions. These reserve units are expected to deploy along with their parent active divisions in the event of war or other emergency.

Binkin and Kaufmann cite a 1986 report by a high-ranking Army official questioning the early reliance on the reserves. "In a scathing appraisal of the reserves, noteworthy because critical views held by high-ranking Army insiders are rarely aired in public, the official contended that 'our Reserve Components are not combat ready, particularly National Guard combat units. Round-out is not working. These forces will not be prepared to go to war in synchronization with their affiliated active duty formations.' " [15]

"It's always been a charade," defense analyst Stephen Canby says of the Total Force policy. According to Canby, some senior Army commanders in the Persian Gulf don't want the round-out reserve forces that are attached to their divisions to be shipped over "because they ... know what shape they're in." Canby concedes that the Air National Guard and "certain technical units" in the Army National Guard are "very good." The technical groups are usually manned by people who perform the same sorts of duties in their regular jobs. Most Air National Guard pilots, for example, are commercial pilots, just as most reserve doctors are full-time physicians outside the reserve. But in the case of front-line combat troops, their sole training consists of the usual one weekend of drills a month and two weeks training during the summer.

Though the Pentagon still officially touts the readiness of the reserves, the actual call-ups during the current crisis could be interpreted differently. According to Lt. Col. Super, of the more than 300,000 troops now assigned to the gulf, only 67,000 are from the reserves and the great majority are from air and other technical units.

Some of the reservists who've been sent to the Persian Gulf have also expressed concern about their readiness. Members of one Army Reserve company, whose mission is to decontaminate troops and equipment in the event of chemical attack, complained to a *New York Times* reporter that they were not as well equipped as their regular Army counterparts. "They want us to put our lives on the line," said one reservist. "And I'm willing to put my life on the line, but our guys deserve the proper equipment." [16] That anecdote is even more unsettling considering that more than 70 percent of the Army's chemical warfare units are reserve troops.

Even if the reserves were better equipped and

---

*There are seven different branches of the reserves: Army Reserve, National Guard, Naval Reserve, Air Force Reserve, Air National Guard, Marine Corps Reserve and Coast Guard Reserve. The last, like the Coast Guard itself, is part of the Department of Transportation during peacetime.

# All-Volunteer Forces Are Older, Stay Longer

**Keeping retention rates high is one of the keys to ensuring high quality in the military. By that measure, the all-volunteer forces have shown significant improvement. In 1973, just before the draft was abolished, the mean length of service of enlisted personnel was 70 months; by 1989, that figure had climbed to nearly 80 months. Likewise, the all-volunteer forces are older. In 1973, the average age of enlisted personnel was 25; in 1989 it was 26.**

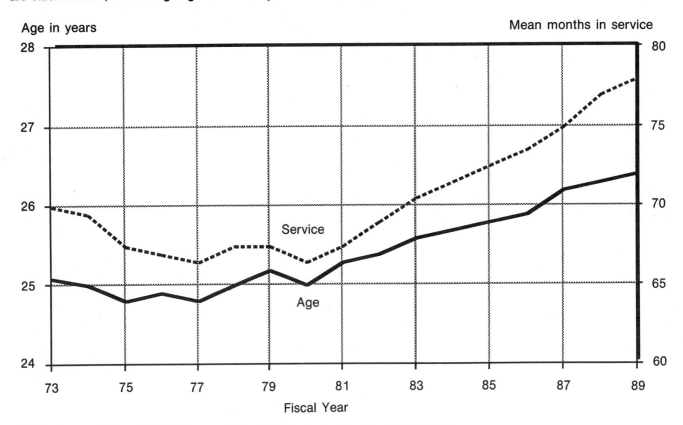

*Source: Department of Defense,* Population Representation in the Military Services, Fiscal Year 1989, *July 1990.*

prepared, advocates of the draft point out, there are certain areas where both the active-duty forces and the reserves are deficient, most notably medical personnel. *The New York Times* recently reported that the deployment of military medical staff to the Persian Gulf had left several Army base hospitals "critically short" in important specialties, such as diagnostic radiologists, surgeons and nurse anesthetists.[17] And that's without a shot being fired. "If you have a war, you've got to do something about filling in the spaces back here," says Canby. "I would assume that if push comes to shove, they'll have to contract out to civilian hospitals."

Some people think the only way to ensure that the military has an adequate number of physicians, pilots, computer programmers and other technical specialists is to activate the draft. In fact, in 1989 the Selective Service System announced it was preparing a plan to draft medical personnel in the event of a military crisis.

But doctors, pilots and other specialists aren't the only problem. In today's high-tech military, even the "grunts" need a level of technical ability that is often beyond today's recruits. "The electronics revolution in

the armed forces has not been matched by a comparable revolution in training in high schools and the recruiting pool," writes James W. Davis, a professor of political science at Washington University in St. Louis. "The increasing sophistication of weaponry will shrink the usable recruiting pool even further — and make the draft even more necessary." [18]

## Would conscription spread the burden of combat more evenly?

Many of the concerns regarding the all-volunteer forces stem from the fact that they are unrepresentative of the larger American society, both racially and socioeconomically. As noted above, the racial imbalance is particularly striking, with blacks accounting for 32 percent of enlisted personnel, though only 13 percent of youths between the ages of 18 and 24 are black. Most of those in the military come from families below the median economic levels of society, though the question of how far below the median is still hotly debated.

Supporters of the all-volunteer forces reject the notion that service in the military represents an unfair burden to the poor or minorities. "These arguments are simply wrong," says Assistant Secretary of Defense David J. Armor. "... Volunteers view service not as a burden, but as an opportunity." [19]

Joint Chiefs of Staff Chairman Powell says he is "proud of the fact that African Americans have seen fit to volunteer to join the armed forces" in such high numbers. "They come in for education. They come in for adventure. They come in to better themselves. They come in to serve a period of time and then get out and use the benefits we have provided them to go to college or get some kind of vocational training." [20]

Powell strongly opposes the idea of setting limits on the number of blacks allowed to enlist. "Is it unfair," he asks, "to allow Americans who wish to join the Army or the Navy, the Air Force or Marines Corps, because that's their choice?" Gary R. Nelson, a former deputy secretary of Defense, agrees with Powell: "Blacks and other groups would view any attempt to impose quotas as an act of discrimination," he writes.[21]

Critics of the all-volunteer forces argue that the military cannot be viewed simply as an educational and training program. Unlike a jobs program, military service is premised on the possibility of paying the ultimate sacrifice to defend the country. "Quite apart from the effect on minorities, there is a basic question of social fairness which the [all-volunteer force] simply assumes away," writes John G. Kester, an attorney and former deputy assistant secretary of the Army. "The issue is whether service in the armed forces (which no doubt is a positive experience for many people, but which also represents inconvenience and an enhanced risk of sudden death) should be distributed among citizens purely on economic incentives. In other words, should people be forced into the army by a lottery or because they need the money? How is the volunteer force different analytically from the Civil War draft's option of paying $300 to buy a substitute?" [22] (See story, p. 22.)

So far, the all-volunteer forces have yet to endure an all-out war. When and if a major conflict does erupt — in the Persian Gulf or elsewhere — "the first casualties, as well as combat replacements, would be disproportionately black because blacks comprise between 26 and 41 percent of the units likely to experience combat," according to the General Accounting Office, the investigative arm of Congress.[23]

"That will cause all kinds of furor," predicts Charles Moskos. There will undoubtedly be an increase in the voices that claim blacks and other minorities are being sacrificed for a war that the middle- and upper-class establishment — a predominately white establishment — have decided to wage. The social turmoil created by such a conflict could eventually affect the troops. "It'll be with the second wave that

goes over, and the reservists who follow, that the troubles will start," Moskos says. "The uproar at home would be going on, and the replacements would be coming out of a milieu that would be anti-war, and this will spill over for the troop morale."

Powell is not overly concerned about criticisms that blacks would take heavy causalities in a gulf war. "What would you have me do?" he asks. "Move the blacks from the positions they're in so that they will have a lower percentage of casualties? Every part of the force, whether its Hispanic Americans, Pacific Americans or lower-income white soldiers, will probably sustain casualties in relationship to the percentage that they represent in the overall force."

Some analysts question whether a conscripted military would be significantly more representative than the all-volunteer forces. During Vietnam, says Martin Binkin, "we had a pretty representative force as far as minorities are concerned. ... [A]bout 11 or 12 percent of the military was black, roughly the same proportion as society." Today, however, "It would be very difficult to alter the socioeconomic composition of the military unless you had a conscription system that denied volunteers the opportunity of serving. True, you'll draft a cross section, but only if you do away with deferments and other loopholes through which rich kids were able to get out of it earlier. Even then, you're still taking volunteers who do not represent the larger society."

And even if a system were adopted that eliminated the loopholes and drafted the affluent along with the poor, Binkin says, "there's no assurance that they would wind up in combat arms, unless you would set quotas or channel them there." People are usually assigned in the military on the basis of demonstrated aptitudes, and "a son of a steelworker from Gary, Ind., I would argue, is more likely to have aptitude for combat skills than a son of, say, Donald Trump. It's the middle class against the yuppies. Who do you want in a foxhole next to you?"

You might be better off if you picked the yuppie, says Stephen Canby. "Those are just the people you don't want to exempt from a draft," he says. Canby notes that the Germans and Israelis put their brightest troops into the light infantry. "They are the elite units that are assigned to do the most difficult tasks. They don't do assaults, per se. They're doing fancier things than that. They try to use deception, ambiguity and things of that ilk, but nevertheless they are the troops that are given the most demanding tasks. And potentially, if they screw up, get the most casualties."

But advocates of the draft respond that the all-volunteer army makes it easier for the government to go to war. Even some supporters of the all-volunteer force agree. "Military forces consisting entirely of volunteers give the nation greater flexibility in foreign policy. Public acceptance for military involvement in complex situations is much lower when the services are composed of draftees," Lawrence J. Korb wrote in

1986, when he was assistant secretary of Defense for manpower, installations and logistics.[24]

Critics of the all-volunteer force are quick to say that the reason public acceptance may be easier to gain with the volunteer forces is not so much that the soldiers are volunteers, but that they come from strata of society that have only limited political voice. As Canby observes, when the president's advisers and those in Congress do not have relatives serving in the gulf, the chances of war breaking out are probably greater. "My wife has become very political and anti-Bush, because we have a son who's in the Navy in the Persian Gulf," he says. "She doesn't like it one bit. She's become very bitter about the inside-the-Beltway politicians who don't have any relatives in the military." *Time* magazine recently reported that only two of the 535 members of Congress are known to have sons involved in Operation Desert Shield.[25]

Ironically, one of the goals of the Total Force policy from the military's point of view was to make sure that there *was* broad political support for any military action the United States became involved in. Military planners, wishing to avoid another political disaster like Vietnam, reasoned that early reliance on the reserves would cause great turmoil in the population, and that people would not put up with such turmoil unless they supported its goals.

In fact, the reserve call-up for the Persian Gulf has caused personal turmoil; the personal difficulties of reservists called to active duty have become the daily grist for the evening news. But as for the political consequences of the turmoil, that still is being played out — on the opinion pages of the nation's newspapers and in the halls of Congress.

## Without a war a draft is unlikely

The strongest argument against a peacetime draft is that it is politically unpopular. While a majority of Americans favor bringing back the draft if war breaks out, only about 25 percent support a peacetime draft.[26]

Given the low level of public support, "the administration is not going to propose conscription" in the near future, says Martin Binkin. "And Congress is not going to initiate it on their own. You can't even get those guys to take this conflict [in the Persian Gulf] by the horns. You're certainly not going to get them to vote for conscription." However, Binkin adds, public attitudes toward the draft could change if war breaks out in the Persian Gulf. "After it's all over, if we've taken casualties, I think . . . the American people may want to raise [the draft] issue once again. A lot will depend on how soon it's over, how many [women and minority] casualties there are. Once the dust settles, [advocates of the draft] will marshal their forces."

But in the end, Binkin doesn't think the draft will be reinstated. "I don't see a full-blown emotional debate about how we raise our military forces, especially since there seems to be few people who feel we're not going to be cutting our military forces when this crisis is over," he says.

Although he doesn't envision a return to the draft, Binkin thinks the Persian Gulf crisis is going to make military recruiting more difficult. "We're probably going to be seeing a negative impact on recruiting and retention because of this crisis. I think people will be leaving the reserve in large numbers after seeing what's happened." Moskos agrees. "What will probably happen in the post-gulf situation is that Army recruiting will suffer," he says. "I don't think it'll bounce back. I think this is a cold dash of water on people, that you can be put in harm's way."

For its part, the military seems confident that it will have no trouble filling its ranks, even in the event of a gulf war. "We're not sure what the impact [of] Desert Shield is going to be on the all-volunteer force, but I don't think it's going to be a scenario where we're going to have to get rid of the volunteer force and go back to the draft," says a Pentagon official who asked not to be identified. "The quality of the services right now is so high that we have a lot of flexibility in the quality level. We can fall back to lower quality and still meet the requirements."

Moskos is not so sure. "What you don't get in the present military is the bottom of the barrel," he says. "That's what [we] were getting in Vietnam, . . . which extended well into the early days of the volunteer force in the 1970s. With a harder time recruiting [after the gulf crisis] they'll have to go toward the bottom of the barrel again." The result, says Moskos, will be more pressure, even from within the military, for a return to the draft.

Budgetary pressures could also play a part in the debate over the draft. A 1988 report by the General Accounting Office concluded that if the government reinstated the draft "long-term budgetary savings would be $7.8 billion a year in 1987 dollars." The report assumed that draftees would serve for two years, that the military would stay the same size, and that pay for all first-term personnel would be cut by 50 percent for the first two years of service.[27]

But when the GAO tried to estimate the costs of switching to a conscript force of approximately the same "effectiveness" as the current all-volunteer forces, the picture changed dramatically. For one thing, a conscript military is certain to mean much higher turnover of personnel, and thus higher training costs. As a result, the GAO concluded, "the estimated budgetary cost savings associated with the draft diminish and eventually disappear. . . . Our analysis indicates that if force effectiveness is measured by the number of personnel with 12 months of service, the draft force results in net long-term budgetary savings of about $4

*Continued on p. 30*

# AT ISSUE    *Should the United States reinstate the draft?*

**YES** *says* **MARK SHIELDS**, *a* Washington Post *columnist.*

It hurts to admit that the critics of your adopted home town were right after all. But Washington turns out to be, as charged, an elitist place. And yes, the political and journalistic establishments of this city do live in a different country from those Americans whose lives are now at risk in the Persian Gulf....

A wise and just manpower policy is the foundation of our national defense. The all-volunteer American military, it was agreed, was to be a peacetime operation. Any major military engagement was to be a signal for a resumption of the draft. The reasoning was straightforward: If the goals of our nation are worth fighting for, then we ought not to hesitate to ask all Americans to share the obligation and the perils of that fighting....

In his landmark book on today's infantrymen, *The Mud Soldiers*, the [*Washington*] *Post*'s George Wilson quoted Col. Steve Siegfried, a combat veteran, on why the United States must have a draft in time of war: "Armies don't fight wars. Countries fight wars. I hope to hell we learned that in Vietnam.... A country fights a war. If it doesn't, then we shouldn't send an army."

Jim Webb knows that truth firsthand. Long before he was secretary of the Navy in the Reagan administration, he was a 1968 graduate of Annapolis. As a Marine platoon leader and company commander in Vietnam, Webb earned the Navy Cross, a Silver Star, two Bronze Stars, two Purple Hearts and, after several operations, a medical discharge.

With characteristic bluntness, Webb criticizes the "complete separation of people in power in Washington from the people at peril in the Persian Gulf." He continues, "If the U.S. military was truly representative of the country, you would have people going through the roof right now....

From the enlisted ranks of today's military, the sons of the powerful and the privileged, of the policy-makers and the politicians, are overwhelmingly missing from action.

If this war is worth Americans' fighting and dying for, then it must first be worth calling to service the sons of anchormen and of senators, of Cabinet members and college presidents, of columnists and CEOs. That would be a guaranteed antidote for Washington's current indifference.

*From a column that appeared in* The Washington Post *on Nov. 2, 1990.*

**NO** *says Rep.* **G. V. "SONNY" MONTGOMERY**, *D-Miss., chairman of the House Veterans' Affairs Committee.*

With the crisis in the Persian Gulf and the deployment of nearly half a million American service personnel has come a call by some people to reinstitute the draft. The idea is to avoid the situation we had during the Vietnam War, when a greater proportion of minorities and people from lower income levels ended up on the front lines. A draft, they say, would ensure that we have a more representative cross section of men and women in our military. I sympathize with that goal, but we don't need to go back to the draft to do it. The all-volunteer force is preferable for a number of reasons.

We have the best and brightest young men and women in the armed forces today that we have had at any time in the 35 years I have been associated with the military. The pay and educational benefits we have provided over the past 10 years have helped the armed forces draw more motivated, middle-class Americans into the services.

The cash bonuses, specific skills training, assignment-of-choice option and the new GI education bill have enabled the Pentagon to recruit from segments of the population that could not be tapped by a draft....

What has the volunteer system produced? It has filled the ranks with people who want to be there. They are better motivated and easier to train. They are career- and goal-oriented and present fewer discipline problems. All of the above characteristics would be lacking in a force assembled from conscription....

The bottom line is that we have a more representative sample of middle America in the volunteer force in 1990 than can be achieved in any draft, and we don't have the morale and discipline problems that accompany conscripts through their two-year hitches.

We have achieved this by providing education and cash incentives, which are where the focus should be in 1990. This has proved to be a successful formula, one we should expand on. We ought to be considering raising the GI Bill benefits from $300 a month to $400 a month for active-duty participants and from $140 to $200 a month for those in the National Guard and for reservists. That would help us maintain the high-quality personnel level we have today.

*From an article that appeared on the opinion page of* The Washington Post, *Dec. 4, 1990.*

*Continued from p. 28*
billion. But, if 24 months are required to become fully effective, the volunteer force is less expensive than the draft by about $2.6 billion." [28]

A 1988 study by a private consulting firm agreed with the GAO's conclusions. The study estimated that it would cost more than $1 billion a year more to return to conscription while maintaining the current quality of the armed forces.[29]

Estimates of military personnel costs are highly dependent on assumptions about the likelihood of war — and, therefore, the size of a standing military that is necessary — and also about the nature of the war that will be fought and the type of soldiers who will fight it. Do we need a small group of highly trained "technicians" to conduct surgical strikes, or do we need large numbers of foot soldiers to fight an extended war of attrition?

"A fully voluntary army is not desirable during a big and protracted war," University of Chicago economist Gary Becker argues, because "the high tax rates needed to finance a large voluntary army during such a war would greatly discourage long hours of work and high savings." By contrast, a draft tends to impose fewer direct budget costs per soldier, while imposing greater indirect societal costs in terms of lost income to draftees. "It is thus desirable in a major war to use the draft and impose more of the burden on young people," writes Becker. "But moderate-sized armed force prepared for limited conflict is better manned with volunteers than with draftees." [30]

Most defense strategists believe that the Third World is the likely source of military unrest in the coming years. "Regional conflict and crises — often erupting with very little warning — are the most likely future threats we will face," the members of a Defense Department task force said in a September 1990 report evaluating the effectiveness of the Total Force policy.[31]

But unlike most potential regional adversaries, Iraq is heavily armed with tanks and missiles and has a large, battle-hardened army. The question military planners must answer is whether the Persian Gulf situation is unique, or whether it represents the type of military engagement the United States can expect to face in the future.

# NOTES

[1] Nunn was interviewed on CBS-TV's *Face the Nation*, Nov. 11, 1990.

[2] Poll results published in *The Wall Street Journal*, Dec. 14, 1990.

[3] These figures are from the Defense Department and the General Accounting Office.

[4] Interview with *The Washington Post*, Nov. 28, 1990.

[5] Office of the Assistant Secretary of Defense for Force Management and Personnel, *Population Representation in the Military Services: Fiscal Year 1989*, Department of Defense, July 1990, p. 55.

[6] Bruce R. Orvis and Martin T. Gahart, *Enlistment Among Applicants for Military Service: Determinants and Incentives*, RAND Corp., January 1990, p. 17.

[7] Writing in *The Washington Post*, Dec. 4, 1990.

[8] *The New York Times*, Dec. 10, 1990. Also see *The Washington Post*, Nov. 28, 1990.

[9] Figures are from Defense Department and General Accounting Office statistics.

[10] C. Robert Roll Jr. and John T. Warner, "The Enlisted Career Manpower in the All-Volunteer Force," in *The All Volunteer Force After a Decade* (1986), edited by William Bowman, Roger Little and G. Thomas Sicilia, p. 61.

[11] Eliot A. Cohen, *Citizens and Soldiers: The Dilemmas of Military Service* (1985), p. 181.

[12] *The Washington Post*, Dec. 2, 1990.

[13] Martin Binkin and William W. Kaufmann, *U.S. Army Guard & Reserve: Rhetoric, Realities, Risks*, Brookings Institution, 1989, p. 12.

[14] *Ibid.*, p. 30.

[15] *Ibid.*, p. 96.

[16] *The New York Times*, Dec. 13, 1990.

[17] *The New York Times*, Dec. 19, 1990.

[18] James W. Davis, "Bring Back the Draft," *The New York Times*, Feb. 5, 1987.

[19] U.S. General Accounting Office, *Military Draft: Potential Impacts and Other Issues*, March 1988, p. 43.

[20] Interview with *The Washington Post*, Nov. 28, 1990.

[21] Gary R. Nelson, "The Supply and Quality of First-Term Enlistees Under the All-Volunteer Force," in Bowman, Little and Sicilia, *op. cit.*, p. 34.

[22] John G. Kester, "The Reasons to Draft," in Bowman, Little and Sicilia, *op. cit.*, p. 299.

[23] General Accounting Office, *op. cit.*, p. 14.

[24] Lawrence J. Korb, "Military Manpower Training Achievements and Challenges for the 1980s," in Bowman, Little and Sicilia, *op. cit.*, p. 7.

[25] "Why No Blue Blood Will Flow," *Time*, Nov. 26, 1990, p. 34.

[26] General Accounting Office, *op. cit.*, p. 18.

[27] General Accounting Office, *op. cit.*, p. 24.

[28] *Ibid.*, p. 34.

[29] The study assumed the draft would involve conscripting people for two years, instead of the standard four-year terms of the volunteer forces, and that drafted personnel would be paid less than the current volunteer forces are paid. The study was produced by Syllogistics, a consulting firm in Springfield, Va., for the Defense Department, and has not been publicly released.

[30] Gary S. Becker, "Why a Draft Would Only Damage the Army," *Business Week*, Feb. 8, 1988, p. 14.

[31] Total Force Policy Study Group, *Total Force Policy Interim Report to the Congress*, Department of Defense, September 1990, p. 5.

*Graphics: Cover, Margaret Scott; pp. 19, 21, 26, Jack Auldridge.*

# RECOMMENDED READING

## BOOKS

**Anderson, Martin, ed., *Registration and the Draft*, Hoover Institution Press, 1982.**

This book contains the proceedings — both presented papers and discussions — of a conference on the all-volunteer force held in 1979. Although sponsored by the conservative Hoover Institution, the conference brought together experts from a wide range of viewpoints and ideologies. At the time, critics of the all-volunteer force were predicting its demise because the military was finding it difficult to attract enough quality recruits. That attitude is reflected in much of the material in the book.

**Binkin, Martin, and Kaufmann, William W., *U.S. Army Guard & Reserve: Rhetoric, Realities, Risks*, Brookings Institution, 1989.**

In their concise but complete assessment of the military reserves, Binkin and Kaufmann conclude that while there has been great improvement in the quality of reserve units, many of them are far from combat ready.

**Bowman, William; Little, Roger; and Sicilia, G. Thomas, eds., *The All-Volunteer Force after a Decade*, Pergamon-Brassey's, 1986.**

An intriguing set of essays by some of the political and academic experts on military manpower. The articles all stem from a conference on the all-volunteer force that was held in late 1983. There are gung-ho contributions from former Defense Secretary Caspar Weinberger and former Deputy Defense Secretary Lawrence Korb, as well as critical articles from academia.

**Chambers, John Whiteclay II, *To Raise an Army: The Draft Comes to Modern America*, Free Press, 1987.**

Chambers offers a concise history of the draft in the United States, focusing primarily on the period immediately prior to the initiation of America's first major national draft during World War I.

**Cohen, Eliot A., *Citizens and Soldiers: The Dilemmas of Military Service*, Cornell University Press, 1985.**

This book looks at military conscription as a social and military phenomenon, tracing its development in Europe. Cohen examines conscription as a social institution that arises from the needs and demands of other social institutions.

**Kohn, Stephen M., *Jailed for Peace: The History of American Draft Law Violators, 1658-1985*, Greenwood Press, 1986.**

Kohn's interesting and very readable book traces draft laws and the fates of draft resisters through American history. This book is not argumentative; it is enjoyable and informative.

## REPORTS AND STUDIES

**Orvis, Bruce R., and Gahart, Martin T., *Enlistment among Applicants for Military Service: Determinants and Incentives*, RAND Corp., January 1990.**

This report presents the findings of a survey of applicants to the military taken during 1983. Those most likely to enlist, the study found, are young, black, either not interested in college or without the money to go to college, and without well-paying civilian jobs.

**U.S. Department of Defense, *Population Representation in the Military Services: Fiscal Year 1989*, Office of the Assistant Secretary of Defense, July 1990.**

This annual report provides statistics on the educational, racial and socioeconomic status of the military services.

**U.S. Department of Defense, *Total Force Policy Interim Report to the Congress*, Total Force Policy Study Group, September 1990.**

Though generally upbeat in tone, this report on the capability of the reserves to fulfill their role in the government's Total Force policy concedes that "most large reserve units — battalions, brigades, divisions — need additional training before employment in combat.

**U.S. General Accounting Office, *Military Draft: Potential Impacts and Other Issues*, March 1988.**

This short report summarizes the arguments for and against a reinstitution of the military draft, and provides its own cost estimates of making such a move.

EDITORIAL RESEARCH REPORTS

## Coming soon

- Archaeology
- Peace Corps at 30
- Recession

Published weekly by
Congressional Quarterly
Inc., Editorial Research
Reports analyze emerging
issues of national interest
across a broad range of
social, scientific, political
and economic fields.
Reports are bound and
indexed for permanent
reference. Subscription
information is available
through Congressional
Quarterly's Publications
Sales Department by
telephone (202) 887-8665.
Copies of past issues are
available through
Customer Service, (202)
887-8621.

ERR

JANUARY 18, 1991

CONGRESSIONAL QUARTERLY'S

EDITORIAL RESEARCH REPORTS®

# IS AMERICA ALLOWING ITS PAST TO BE STOLEN?

EDITORIAL RESEARCH REPORTS (LIBRARY OF CONGRESS
CATALOGUE NO. 39-924; ISSN 0013-0958). Published weekly
(48 times per year, excluding March 1, May 3, August 2 and
November 1, 1991) by Congressional Quarterly Inc., 1414 22nd
Street NW, Washington, D.C. 20037. Rates are furnished
upon request. Application to mail at second-class postage
rates is pending at Washington, D.C. POSTMASTER: Send
address changes to EDITORIAL RESEARCH REPORTS, 1414
22nd Street NW, Washington, D.C. 20037.

# IS AMERICA ALLOWING ITS PAST TO BE STOLEN?

*by Robert K. Landers*

In recent decades, the looting and mining of American Indian artifacts have become serious problems. Archaeologists fear that irreplaceable knowledge about America's historic and prehistoric past is being lost. The federal government has taken steps to try to deal with the problem on federal lands, but commercial looting continues — as does the legal mining of artifacts and destruction of valuable sites on private lands. The major underlying question is: Who owns the past?

When they entered the hidden cave in the Cherokee National Forest in Tennessee last March, Forest Archaeologist Quentin Bass and his co-workers had to crawl over a carpet of skulls and other human remains. They also found pottery and other artifacts that had been placed there by Cherokee Indians about 400 years ago. They soon realized that the remote cave and its contents represented an extremely unusual find, because the Cherokee usually buried their dead in or near their villages.

Unfortunately, Bass and his co-workers weren't the first modern-day persons to discover the cave: Grave robbers had been there first and had extensively damaged the site. But as it turns out, they didn't get away with it. After a stakeout, three men were caught inside the cave, and that led to the arrest of six others. All but one ultimately pleaded guilty to various charges — and that one person was convicted by a jury on Oct. 18 and sentenced on several charges to 22 years in prison. This was one of only two times that an individual had been tried and convicted on a felony charge under the Archaeological Resources Protection Act of 1979 (ARPA). But such convictions could become more common in the years ahead.[1]

"There's a network of these people around who deal in artifacts, and it's a real growing problem," Bass says. "It's not just Boy Scouts on the weekend, piddling around and doing haphazard vandalism. These people know what they're doing and they go after it. And there's a real market for [the artifacts]." Just this past year, Bass says, a Southwestern polychrome Indian pot was sold in Paris for a quarter of a million dollars, a Mississippi monolithic ax went in New Orleans for $150,000, and an arrowhead was sold for a record $20,000. "We're not talking inconsequential amounts," Bass observes.

The lure of such sums has helped turn the looting and mining of historic and prehistoric artifacts into a serious problem in the United States. Although the problem is often thought to be largely confined to the Southwest, where the most visually spectacular and easily appreciated archaeological sites are located, it's actually a nationwide problem, as the Cherokee National Forest case suggests.

"[W]hat's now the [entire] United States was occupied by prehistoric peoples from at least 12,000 years ago," says Francis P. McManamon, chief of the National Park Service's Archeological Assistance Division. "So there are archaeological sites from coast to coast . . . from the prehistoric period and also from the historic period."

Extensive looting of Indian artifacts has occurred even in New England. Metichawon, an area in New Milford, Conn., that was important to the Weantinock Indians for centuries, has been looted "on a scale that's really quite staggering," says Russell G. Handsman, director of research at the American Indian Archaeological Institute in Washington, Conn. Although the looters may not have found anything "real glamorous," they've taken away pieces of bowls, potsherds (pieces of broken pottery), whole pots, stone tools and other artifacts. "Lovers Leap [as the area is popularly known] is about as extensively and intensively looted a site as I think probably most people could find anywhere in the United States," Handsman says.

To archaeologists, such looting can mean the loss of irreplaceable knowledge. While collectors may value artifacts for their beauty or commercial worth, archaeologists value them primarily for the information they can provide about the past. If objects are thoughtlessly removed from a site, their archaeological value can sharply diminish. "[If] you just dig [an object] up and divorce it from where it came from, you lose any ability to really [tell] much of anything from it," says archaeologist Keith Kintigh of Arizona State University.

Persons bent on profit are not the only culprits responsible for the loss of that information. There are also so-called "casual looters" and mindless vandals.

The federal government in recent years has taken steps to crack down on commercial looting on federal lands and, by educating the public, to reduce casual looting and vandalism.

But the problem is not just a simple matter of good guys (archaeologists) vs. bad guys (looters). For one thing, the bad guys are not always so bad. Often they're just innocent hikers or campers who, as Utah State Archaeologist David B. Madsen has explained, "stumble upon a site and . . . scratch around, pick up a potsherd or a flake or two, and take it home as a souvenir."[2] For another thing, the good guys have not always been so good. In fact, for many decades Native Americans often regarded archaeologists and physical anthropologists (who study human remains and what they can reveal about human origins) as little better than looters. "Archaeologists and anthropologists have been looking at us [and our possessions] as their property . . . throughout the history of their professions," says Suzan Shown Harjo, president and executive director of the Morning Star Foundation and, from 1984-89, executive director of the National Congress of American Indians.

The public image of archaeologists is based in part on the popular "Indiana Jones" movies. Those movies, Kintigh says, "very graphically portrayed people's romantic image of what an archaeologist is. [But it] has nothing to do with what [modern] archaeologists actually do at all. And it in fact portrays exactly what the looters are doing: Basically, you're after some particular, wonderful object, and you go and you snatch it away, because of its inherent value."

Indiana Jones seldom pauses to study the context in which the object is found and never questions his right to snatch the object away. Yet if the movie archaeologist behaves more like a looter than a modern archaeologist, his cavalier attitude is not entirely untrue to that evidenced by many archaeologists in the past. Until recent decades, many archaeologists and physical anthropologists often failed to consult Indian tribes before digging up the burial sites of their ancestors. Even today, some archaeologists still fail to do that.

But Indians in recent years have become both more concerned about such excavations and more assertive about expressing their concern. And so attitudes have been changing. Archaeologists have been "finding that they need to be sensitive to the descendants of the people whom they are digging up," says Arizona Superior Court Judge Sherry Hutt, who handled many prosecutions under the Archaeological Resources Protection Act when she was an assistant U.S. attorney in Phoenix. And Indians, she says, have become more aware that archaeologists can help them to reclaim some of their own history.

Indians and archaeologists today share many of the same concerns, says Henry J. Sockbeson, an attorney with the Native American Rights Fund. "Indians don't want their ancestors dug up in any kind of uncontrolled fashion. Archaeologists don't want pot hunters going in and digging up Indian graveyards in the dead of night because it destroys archaeological information. So, from a preservation standpoint, clearly archaeologists and tribes have much the same interests. But where it gets touchy is when you talk about existing collections and returning existing collections [to tribes]."

A new law, the Native American Graves Protection and Repatriation Act, deals with that touchy subject. Signed by President Bush in November, it requires

---

*"Indians don't want their ancestors dug up in any kind of uncontrolled fashion. Archaeologists don't want pot hunters digging up Indian graveyards in the dead of night. So, from a preservation standpoint, clearly archaelogists and tribes have much the same interests," says Henry J. Sockbeson, an attorney with the Native American Rights Fund.*

---

museums and federal agencies to inventory their collections of Native American human remains and associated funerary objects, and then, where a close connection to living Indians or extant tribes can be shown, to return the items to them. Certain sacred and other important objects also will have to be turned over to tribes where a cultural affiliation with them can be shown. The law also states that Native American remains and funerary objects and certain other cultural objects newly excavated on federal or tribal lands belong to the tribes involved, and that archaeologists must "consult" the appropriate tribes before digging on federal lands. (They'd already been required to get the tribes' consent to dig on tribal lands.)

Native Americans regard the legislation as a big

step forward, and the final version of the bill had the backing of the Society for American Archaeology and the American Association of Museums. It "probably is the best compromise that we could have crafted," says archaeologist Lynne Goldstein of the University of Wisconsin-Milwaukee. It's "not the law that I would have written, it's not the law that most Indians, I think, would have written, but it's a law that all of us can live with."

The new legislation is complicated, and its implementing regulations have yet to be drawn up. While many archaeologists and museum officials are content with the legislation and hopeful that it will work tolerably well, others are not so sanguine. Clement Meighan, a professor of anthropology at the University of California in Los Angeles, for instance, says that "the aim [of the measure] is to kill off archaeology, to plow it under as a field. Fifty years from now, people — including the Indians — will look back and say, 'How could you be so stupid?'" [3]

James Reid, president of the Antique Tribal Art Dealers Association, which strongly opposed the legislation, says the new law fails to assume the legitimacy of museums' mission. "If the museums have no legitimate right to these pieces, then the next assumption might be that private persons have even less right." And, indeed, the private collecting of Indian artifacts has begun to come under fire. Many archaeologists and others, while supporting the mission of public museums, would like to see the private collecting of Indian artifacts become an activity that society regards with utter contempt. Until that happens, they say, the looting and mining of such artifacts are bound to continue — and with them, the theft of knowledge about America's past.

### Rising interest in Indian art prompts increased looting

The 1971 sale of a private collection at Parke-Bernet, a leading auction house in New York, signaled a sharp increase in interest in American Indian art and artifacts. The collection had been started by Col. George Green, a Civil War surgeon and businessman, and later expanded by his family. Before the sale, Parke-Bernet had estimated that the 310 items in the collection would fetch between $40,000 and $67,000. As it turned out, however, the proceeds came to more than $161,000.

A Navajo blanket that had sold at Parke-Bernet for $100 in 1963 brought $1,000. A tomahawk nearly three feet long brought $1,400. An Indian ceremonial hide shirt went for $4,500. Five baskets by Dat-so-la-Lee, the most famous basket maker of the Washo tribe of Nevada, were sold for prices ranging from $2,800 to $6,100, with three of the baskets going to private bidders and the other two going to the Museum of the American Indian, Heye Foundation, in New York. The headline in *The New York Times* the next day summed up the story: "For Indian Artifacts, Price Trend Is Up." [4] In the years since, strong interest in Indian artifacts has been manifested not only in the United States but in Japan, Germany and elsewhere.

The result of all this increased demand for Indian artifacts has been the increased mining of archaeological sites for profit. Among the pieces most in demand are beautiful Mimbres pottery, named for the valley in New Mexico in which it was first found. Almost all the major Mimbres sites, including those on federal or state-owned land, have been ravaged by pot hunters in recent decades. Most of the Mibres sites were on private lands, however, so as long as the mining was done by the landowner or with his consent, it was legal. "In the United States, which is not true of other countries, if you own a site, you can go out with dynamite and blow it to kingdom-come, you can go out there with a backhoe, you can do whatever you want, pretty much," archaeologist Keith Kintigh points out.

The looting of Indian artifacts on federal or tribal lands is a crime — and there's no question it's being committed. Some of the commercially looted items turn up on the open market. Among the items sold at one auction last summer, Kintigh says, were prehistoric Hopi pots of a sort found almost exclusively on federal or Indian lands. "It's virtually certain that that stuff was looted illegally," he says.

The reported incidents of looting on federal land rose steadily in the years for which statistics are available — from 430 incidents in fiscal 1985 to 627 the next year and 657 in fiscal 1987. The apparent increase may just reflect better reporting. But as the National Park Service's Archeological Assistance Division pointed out last year, the reported incidents "are only the tip of the iceberg. Many archaeological sites are in remote areas, many are unknown even to the federal agencies that are charged with managing them, and federal agencies have limited resources to systematically monitor the condition of sites that they do know exist." [5] The Bureau of Indian Affairs estimated that between 1980 and 1987, 560 archaeological sites on Indian lands in the Four Corners area* were vandalized or looted. On the Navajo Reservation alone, there was a 900 percent increase in the number of sites annually vandalized or looted — from 10 in 1980 to 100 in 1987. [6]

Although solid information on its true extent is very hard to obtain, many people believe that commercial looting has been on the increase. Profit-minded diggers have been reported active in the Southeast and the Pacific Northwest as well as in the Southwest. In the past few years, reports Francis McManamon of the Archeological Assistance Division, there may have been a reduction in commercial looting on federal lands — and increases in it elsewhere. The commercial looters, he says, "may have [been] pushed off onto private lands or onto state lands or other kinds of public lands, and we may be [having] an increase in those areas."

While "an awful lot of damage" has been done in the Southeast, notes Thomas F. King, an independent consulting archaeologist from Maryland who is conducting research into the general subject, the destructive digging of prehistoric sites is probably being done primarily in the West, where most of the federal lands are. The Four Corners states of Arizona, Colorado, New Mexico and Utah contain a wealth of archaeological resources — and of commercially valuable artifacts.

Since the late 19th century, Kintigh observes, the Southwest "has captured people's imagination" with such visually spectacular sights as the famous Cliff Palace in Mesa Verde. Nestled in the cliffs beneath the overhanging brow of a Colorado mesa, the elaborate stone structure, which once housed more than 400 people, was built by the Anasazi (a Navajo word meaning "Ancient Ones") some 900 years ago. [7] The ancestors of the modern Pueblo Indian culture — the Hopi, Zuni, and others — the Anasazi produced stunning pottery and woven baskets with intricate designs. The prehistoric Mogollon and Hohokam peoples also produced beautiful pottery. The finer and better-preserved pottery and baskets from these ancient cultures of the Southwest have high commercial value in the art market. Just a few years ago, an Anasazi basket fetched $152,000 at an auction at Sotheby's in London. [8]

"[M]any, many pieces of historic and prehistoric American Indian art have brought six figures in the past several years," says art dealer James Reid. But that, he adds, "doesn't make the one that your uncle brought back from the fair worth anything like that. It [has to be] something of extreme importance and a really exceptional piece within the context of the culture from which it came." An unbroken Anasazi mug or bowl that wasn't very well painted or very well made might bring $150-$200, Reid says. A bowl that was "pretty good" might be worth $500-$800, and one "that was really very finely made, beautifully painted, in excellent condition, might bring a couple of thousand [dollars] or more."

The sums obtained from unearthing Indian artifacts may often fail to match the dreams that inspire the digging, but they clearly are enough in many cases to keep the dreams alive. And the artifacts have an attraction all their own. "[P]eople have been interested in these things and collecting them for years and years, [even] before they really took off in terms of becoming identified as art," Reid observes.

---

*Arizona, Colorado, New Mexico, and Utah are called the Four Corners states because their boundaries meet at one point.

*Continued on p. 40*

# Controversy Over Indian Remains and Artifacts ...

In the spring of 1986, a group of Northern Cheyenne chiefs visited Washington, D.C. During their visit, they decided to examine the Smithsonian Institution's Cheyenne collection at the National Museum of Natural History. "As we were walking out," a Northern Cheyenne woman who worked on Capitol Hill later recalled, "we saw [the] huge ceilings in the room, with row upon row of drawers. Someone remarked that there must be a lot of Indian stuff in those drawers. Quite casually, a curator with us said, 'Oh, this is where we keep the skeletal remains,' and he told us how many — 18,500. Everyone was shocked." [1] The discovery helped lead to federal legislation that required museums and federal agencies to return some human remains and sacred artifacts to Native Americans.

Museums and federal agencies acquired the human remains of Native Americans in various ways, some of them quite unsavory to late 20th-century Americans. In the years after the Civil War, for instance, the Army Medical Museum eagerly sought out Indian remains, and an 1868 order by the U.S. surgeon general to all Army medical officers directed them to procure as many Indian crania as possible for the museum. These were collected from battlefields and from Indian graves and dispatched to the museum.

The reason given by the Army Medical Museum for wanting Indians' remains was so they could be used in a "comparative racial study." According to Robert E. Bieder of Indiana University's American Indian Studies Research Institute, the museum "sought to demonstrate racial characteristics. After his examination of 'osteological peculiarities,' Dr. George A. Otis of the Army Medical Museum announced in 1870 that data indicated that American Indians 'must be assigned a lower position in the human scale than has been believed heretofore.' " [2]

It was simple racism that was behind the collecting of Native American remains, according to Indian activists such as Suzan Shown Harjo, president and executive director of the Morning Star Foundation. "[T]here certainly was not a federally funded, federally directed, federally mandated white people's crania study. ... It was the *Indian* crania study," she notes.

Another Indian activist, Walter Echo-Hawk, who is an attorney with the Native American Rights Fund, told the Senate Select Committee on Indian Affairs last May that "The hundreds of thousands of dead Native Americans that have been dug up from their graves and now lie in the nation's museums, universities, government agencies, and tourist attractions provide mute testimony that the laws in all 50 states and the District of Columbia which so strongly protect the sanctity of the dead for other citizens and guarantee a decent burial for all citizens have never been extended to include Native Americans." [3]

In fact, however, it is not just Native Americans whose remains are in museum collections. In the case of the Smithsonian, for instance, Smithsonian Secretary Robert McCormick Adams testified in 1987 that the institution's collections included "something on the order of 15,000 skeletons that represent blacks and Orientals and Europeans and people from other parts of the world." [4] And of the more than 18,000 North American Indian skeletons, only 3,500 were from periods after Columbus first came to the New World — and of those, only about 800 came from the last 150 years.

Archaeologist Keith Kintigh rejects the Indian activists' contention "that this is an entirely racist enterprise. I think that that's really false. People in England ... go out and dig up prehistoric or 200- and 500- and 1,000-year-old, 10,000-year-old British cemeteries all the time, and those *are* in fact their ancestors. ... There is more interest in Native Americans in the United States simply because ... prior to 1540 there wasn't anybody else [here] and there's no historical records."

It's true, Kintigh says, that archaeologists and anthropologists too often failed to consult Indian tribes about excavations. On the other hand, he says, "I think Indian values on all of this have changed." He cites an instance from around 1920 in which an archaeologist was excavating many graves at a Zuni prehistoric and early historic site and had Zuni workmen helping him. "There's an interesting place in the field notes ... where it says that some of the workmen had excavated a particular grave, and the objects and so forth associated with the grave led them to conclude that this [was] the grave of ... a very important religious office, and they asked that that person be reburied, and [the archaeologist] said, yes, that was OK, and so they did that." Later, after four or five years of having done excavations, the archaeologist was forced to leave Zuni land as the result of a tribal dispute over his photographing a religious ceremony. "And so he got thrown out of town not for digging up the burials but for photographing the ceremonies. ... So I think Indian values about excavating prehistoric cemeteries have changed substantially. ... I think in the past, they objected less than in some cases people do today."

Harjo disagrees. She claims that "our people have been asking for [the] return [of the Indian remains and related objects] for as long as they've been held [by museums], as long as they've had knowledge that they were held. ... It's just that it has only been in recent times that any of us were in positions to be able to have someone pay attention to us, and to have assistance in that regard from non-Indian people, who also disdained the practices of their own past."

The human remains in museums' possession do have genuine scientific value, according to Adams and others. "Scholars arrive continually to study the documentation and collect data to pursue a wide range of problems ranging from the history of disease among American Indians to prehistoric culture ... ," Adams says. "Any hope of moving beyond oral history and ethnographic analogy in the reconstruction of the [prehistoric] past rests with archaeological approaches. ... Our ability to assess all biological factors and many biocultural aspects completely depends upon our recovery, curation, and analysis of well-documented human remains." [5]

Harjo, however, questions the scientific value of Indian remains that can't even be linked to particular tribes, and she contends that "human decency requires that they be reburied. ... That's the rule throughout the world. Everyone gets the right to be buried and stay buried. And the rules change when it comes to Indian country." Harjo, who is Cheyenne and Creek and a citizen of the Cheyenne and Arapaho tribes of Oklahoma, was asked whether she saw any difference between excavating the grave of someone

# ... Leads to New Law Requiring Repatriation

buried a year ago and excavating the grave of someone buried hundreds or thousands of years ago. "If they're Cheyenne, I don't. ... I see zero difference."

But that doesn't make archaeology impossible, she says. "If there are things that science wishes to learn and that can benefit the Indian people concerned ... then, if it's presented in a good way and discussed in a respectful way and if the consent of the affected Indians is obtained, I think that serves the interest of science. All sorts of terms can be worked out, and [this takes place] with great regularity."

Many archaeologists are sensitive to the Indians' concerns. "I don't know of a single archaeologist anywhere who would argue that, if you know that this is [someone's] uncle, that person should not have the right to decide what happens," says Lynne Goldstein, an archaeologist and an officer in the Society for American Archaeology. Furthermore, she adds, if "we can reasonably identify a set of human remains as belonging to a tribe ... then I think [the tribe] should be given the option to decide what happens to them."

Not all tribes, as it happens, want the remains back. For instance, Kintigh notes that the Zuni tribal council in New Mexico "has so far taken the position that while in retrospect [it] was inappropriate for the remains to [have been] excavated, they do not seek the repatriation, because you essentially can't undo the damage that's been done. ... Other [Indian] people feel that [repatriation is] appropriate, given that the excavations were done in the first place; that the best thing to do is to rebury them close to where they were found."

In the summer of 1989, the Smithsonian reached agreement with the Native American Rights Fund and the National Congress of American Indians about disposition of the remains in the institution's possession. The agreement was made part of the law creating the National Museum of the American Indian, which is to be located next to the National Air and Space Museum on the Mall in Washington. According to the law, the Smithsonian is to inventory the Indian remains and funerary objects it has and, "using the best available scientific and historical documentation," identify their origins. If the tribal origin is established, any affected Indian tribe is to be notified. "If any Indian human remains are identified by a preponderance of the evidence as those of a particular individual or as those of an individual culturally affiliated with a particular Indian tribe," then, at the request of the individual's descendants or of the tribe, the remains and any associated funerary objects are to be "expeditiously" returned to them.

The Smithsonian was exempted from the Native American Graves Protection and Repatriation Act signed into law last fall (the current Congress is expected to consider additional legislation that would cover the Smithsonian). In the controversy leading up to the enactment of that measure, Henry Sockbeson of the Native American Rights Fund says, "The remains weren't the major issue. All the controversy seemed to be driven by [concerns about] the sacred objects and the objects of cultural patrimony." The definitions of those terms were narrowed considerably in the final version that became law. Under the act, museums are obliged to turn over such objects to the tribes if they can demonstrate a "cultural affiliation" with them.

Such repatriation by museums actually has been going on for some time, even without the legislation. The idea behind repatriation, says Kintigh, who chairs the Society for American Archaeology's task force on reburial and repatriation, "is that there is a special claim that people who are in some way more closely tied to an object have over it." In the case of the new law, the claim that "a culturally affiliated Indian tribe would have over human remains, funerary objects, [or] sacred objects that were generated by their ancestors or by their culture ... essentially supersedes the public value that those things have, the value to science or to people who want to look at [the objects]."

In doing that, the law takes a middle position on repatriation, Kintigh says, and it should be viewed as "a line-drawing exercise. I don't think it's an absolute thing, where one could say, 'Yes, everything ought to be repatriated,' because at some point you have to ask the question of how far do you go."

The Antique Tribal Art Dealers Association thinks the new law goes too far. Although art dealers aren't directly affected by the law, they fought it vigorously. The value of objects in private collections to some extent derives from public collections, which generally are better researched, notes dealer James Reid. The new law, he says, embodies "an anti-institutional and an anti-scientific attitude that may seriously threaten collections" that are important to "the public's understanding, as well [as] that of Native Americans, of our collective past."

The legislation, Reid contends, failed to "assume the legitimacy of the museum structure, [or] that any of the sacred objects ever got there ... except by duplicity or theft. ... It's very easy to make a case for the wrongs that were done to the Indians, ... but it was more complex than our contemporary romantic view would have it. There was a great deal of trade and back and forth going on, and a lot of these objects were literally taken off the scrap heap of history and wouldn't exist except for somebody going out and collecting them."

The new law applies specifically to remains and artifacts of Native Americans. "This had to be done so as not to create a legal precedent that could then be applied to all museum collections," says Edward H. Able Jr., executive director of the American Association of Museums. As a result, the law contains a paragraph about the "unique relationship" between the federal government and the Indian tribes, and about how the law shouldn't be construed "to establish a precedent with respect to any other individual, organization or foreign government." Nevertheless, as Smithsonian Secretary Adams wrote recently, "[T]he issues that have now arisen with American Indians obviously have wider, international applications." [6]

Indeed, museums' concerns go far beyond their collections of Native American objects. "[W]hat about all the other culturally affiliated objects or religious affiliated objects in collections?" notes Able. "What are you going to do when the Catholic Church wants all of its artistic patrimony returned on the grounds that it could not be alienated from the church — whether you're talking about chalices or paintings or icons or whatever? What are you going to do about African cultures, or Asian cultures, who say, 'Well, these objects are the cultural patrimony of my culture and therefore they should be returned as well.' Where does it stop?"

*Continued from p. 37*

## *Efforts to protect archaeological resources*

Archaeologists have long been interested in preserving and protecting important archaeological sites. During the late 19th and early 20th centuries, a federal report has noted, "concern for American antiquities grew in both private and governmental sectors. Reports and warnings from individuals and professional organizations, such as the American Association for the Advancement of Science, the Anthropological Society of Washington, and the Archaeological Institute of America, increased public awareness of the destruction of archaeological sites." The result was the Antiquities Act of 1906, which made the federal government responsible for protecting archaeological sites on federal lands and prohibited looting and vandalism at them.[9]

Seventy-three years later, as a result of fresh concern about the increased threat to America's archaeological resources on federal and Indian lands, the Archaeological Resources Protection Act of 1979 was enacted.* It provided stiffer penalties for damaging or destroying those resources, and also prohibited trade in artifacts stolen from federal or Indian property. The maximum criminal penalty for repeated violations of the law was five years in prison and a $100,000 fine.

ARPA, however, proved to be a difficult weapon to use against individuals who looted or vandalized archaeological sites. Before the law was strengthened in 1988 (*see below*), there had been only one ARPA felony conviction by a jury. In that case, prosecuted by the U.S. attorney for Arizona in November 1987, the defendant was found guilty of attempting to sell the mummified remains of an Anasazi infant.[10]

One of the big difficulties with ARPA was that for a violation to be a felony instead of just a misdemeanor, the value of the stolen artifact or of the amount of damage to the site had to be more than $5,000. Attorney Kristine Olson Rogers, who had served for 10 years in the Portland, Ore., U.S. attorney's office, explained the problem to a congressional subcommittee in October 1987. Typically, she said, "A case is indicted accompanied by headlines touting massive damage estimates

*On tribal lands, if there are any tribal laws regulating the excavation or removal of archaeological resources, those laws, not ARPA, govern tribal members. The Bureau of Indian Affairs' jurisdiction in ARPA cases on lands with such tribal laws is limited to non-Indians. "What this means for the [Bureau of Indian Affairs]," Sidney L. Mills, director of the bureau's Albuquerque, N.M., area office, told a congressional subcommittee in 1987, "is that in many cases involving looting or destruction of sites by Indians, there are no enforcement actions that we can take. We can only help tribes to strengthen what laws they have governing archaeological resources and their means of enforcing them."

and then the jury convicts of a misdemeanor, utterly disregarding the experts' staggering damage totals. And any time there is a defense expert, the jury will opt for the lowest bidder's price."[11] Because it was so hard to get a felony conviction under ARPA, prosecutors often simply hung their cases against accused looters on other statutes, such as that prohibiting theft of government property, under which it was easier to get a conviction.

Another difficulty with ARPA was that it didn't prohibit the mere "attempt" to dig up artifacts from federal lands. As attorneys in Arizona told the U.S. General Accounting Office (GAO), this meant that law enforcement agents had to document that such attempts were successful before they could make any arrests. In short, the officers sometimes would find themselves "having to sit and watch looters damage a site before apprehending them. Then, when these cases have come to trial, the defense and jury have questioned whether the archaeological resources are really important and valuable, since agents were apparently willing to let them be destroyed."[12]

Enforcement of ARPA not only frequently failed to result in felony convictions, but sometimes backfired completely. The best-known example was what came to be called "The Great Pottery Raid of 1986." This operation, conducted by the U.S. attorney for Utah, with the assistance of the Forest Service and the Bureau of Land Management, was aimed at recovering Anasazi artifacts believed to have been stolen from federal lands. On the basis of information from a lone informant who himself had admitted to illegally digging up artifacts, federal agents searched 16 homes and businesses in the Four Corners area and seized more than 300 artifacts. Most were later returned, however, and the one man indicted and charged with aiding and abetting the sale and purchase of archaeological resources in violation of ARPA was acquitted by a jury.[13]

As Brent D. Ward, the U.S. attorney involved, later told a congressional subcommittee, the effort to enforce ARPA "does not seem to help in winning the hearts and minds of some people in southeastern Utah. By aggressively enforcing federal laws protecting archaeological resources we have aroused the antagonism of some citizens in San Juan and Grand counties. . . . This may stem in part from a tradition of pot-hunting spanning many years."[14]

Public attitudes have indeed been a major barrier to effective enforcement of ARPA. As the GAO reported, "[M]uch of the public in the Four Corners states condones the looting of archaeological sites on federal lands, both as a means of supplementing personal income and as a personal hobby." Two Arizona attorneys told the GAO "that before presenting the specific facts of a looting case they must often first convince the judge and jury that looting is indeed a crime and that the provisions of ARPA should be enforced." In a case of archaeological looting, the

# State Archaeological Protection Laws

**More than two-thirds of the states have laws protecting archaeological resources on state-owned property, according to a survey done by the State Historical Society of Iowa in 1989 for the National Conference of State Historic Preservation Officers. Many of the state laws are modeled after the federal Archaeological Resources Protection Act of 1979. Most states also have laws against the desecration of burial sites. Some states treat this offense as a misdemeanor, others as a felony.**

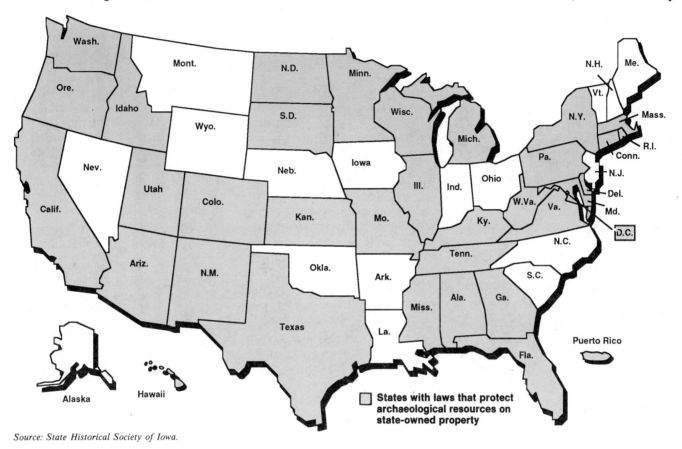

*Source: State Historical Society of Iowa.*

public often perceives it as having "no identifiable victim, and many do not believe it warrants strong (if any) punishment." [15]

Congress sought to bring about a change in such perceptions and to overcome some of the other obstacles in the way of effective archaeological protection, by amending ARPA in 1988. The amendments lowered the felony threshold from $5,000 to $500, and added a prohibition against any unauthorized *attempt* "to excavate, remove, damage, or otherwise alter or deface any archaeological resource located on public lands or Indian lands." And federal land managers were directed to set up programs "to increase public awareness of the significance of the archaeological resources located on public lands and Indian lands and the need to protect such resources."

"Many of the federal agencies are now taking very seriously their mandates to do public education," says archaeologist Kathleen Reinburg, who is the Society for American Archaeology's assistant Washington rep-

resentative. The Forest Service, for example, has a "Passport in Time" program in which the public is invited to visit archaeological sites that are being excavated or interpreted by archaeologists in national forests. Volunteers who want to participate in archaeological investigations and excavations are given training in basic field methods and allowed to take part. "The Passport in Time program has been going on for two years, and the response from the public has been overwhelming," Reinburg says. "There are thousands of people who have written the Forest Service wanting information and wanting to know where the sites are going to be open next year, can they come visit, can they participate."

Some states also have archaeological education programs. Arizona, for instance, has a Site Steward Program in which volunteers assist government agencies in monitoring the condition of selected archaeological sites. Boy Scouts or other groups, Reinburg explains, "go out and 'adopt' a site, and [then] whenever

# *Most Archaeological Resources Have Yet To Be Surveyed*

Nobody really knows the extent to which the nation's archaeological resources are being lost as a result of looting and vandalism. That's in large part because so little is known about the nature and extent of those resources. "There is such a small percentage of this country that has been inventoried, because we just don't have the time and staff to inventory all that, that we just don't really have any idea of what's being lost," says Ruthann Knudson, an archaeologist with the National Park Service's Archeological Assistance Division.

Federal agencies manage nearly 947 million acres of land — and more than 90 percent of these holdings haven't been surveyed.† In the Four Corners states alone (Arizona, Colorado, New Mexico, and Utah), officials estimate there may be almost 2 million archaeological sites — but only about 136,000 have been identified and recorded. Of these, a third or more are thought to have been looted.††

Most archaeological sites on federal lands have been identified

through surveys conducted mainly in response to proposed development projects. Some of the unrecorded sites may actually be of greater archaeological significance than the ones that have been identified and recorded.

A 1988 amendment to the Archaeological Resources Protection Act of 1979 directed the Secretaries of the Interior, Agriculture and Defense, as well as the chairman of the board of the Tennessee Valley Authority, "to develop plans for surveying the lands under their control to determine the nature and extent of archaeological resources on those lands."

But a comprehensive survey of all the archaeological resources on federal lands is not going to be completed any time soon, according to Francis P. McManamon, chief of the National Park Service's Archeological Assistance Division. It is technically possible "to get a comprehensive view of all of the resources and then to evaluate them and then to focus attention on protecting the ones that are most important," he

says. "But it's a very time-consuming and expensive undertaking, and it's certainly not funded at the level that it [would need to be] to accomplish that in the short term."

Most of the archaeological surveys that have been done, he says, have been in the Southwest, where "it's relatively easy to locate an archaeological site. Basically, you just have to walk around and you can see them on the ground. . . . [But in] other parts of the country . . . you can't just go out and walk around and find an archaeological site, for the most part, [because the sites are] buried underneath the soil and hidden beneath vegetation." While the federal government has put some money into uncovering the sites, he says, "it's at a very low level of effort. That idea of having a comprehensive view nationwide is something that's way out there in the future."

† *National Park Service, U.S. Department of the Interior,* Federal Archeology: The Current Program, *1989.*

†† *U.S. General Accounting Office,* Cultural Resources: Problems Protecting and Preserving Federal Archeological Resources, *December 1987.*

they're out hiking, they stop by and make sure the site hasn't been vandalized or looted. I think the more people you get out there on the ground, the better the sites will be protected."

## *Problems persist despite educational efforts and prosecutions*

The various educational efforts by federal, state, local and tribal agencies, as well as by the Society for American Archaeology and other groups, appear to be having some effect. Utah State Archaeologist David Madsen says that archaeologists working in the Four Corners area sense that the vandalism and casual looting of sites has substantially decreased. "I think that

the innocent kind of thing [done by] the 'boy scout' [type of] vandal has gone down," he says.

If so, that's a significant victory for those seeking to preserve archaeological resources. While campers, hikers and other casual visitors to an archaeological site do little damage individually, taken all together they can do a lot of damage. "If you get a hundred or a thousand people at a site each taking a potsherd, pretty soon the site is gone," Madsen has observed.[16] The damage that's done by all the repeated diggings by casual visitors and avocational collectors usually is just on the surface or the upper deposits of a site, while the lower deposits are left undisturbed. But that doesn't mean the damage is insignificant. Far from it. What's lost, Madsen says, is "the later part of the record. That's as important, if not more important, than the earlier part of the record." In seeking to understand the past, he explains, archaeologists must "relate modern groups — how they build houses, how they live — to prehistoric groups, and you sort of push that back through time. So if you miss that one major link between historically known people and the earlier people, it makes it almost impossible to describe what happened with the earlier record even if you have it. You need those connections all the way through."

But while the increased efforts at public education may already have had an effect on the casual looting and vandalism, it will take much longer for them to have any substantial impact on the commercial looting. Nevertheless, it's apparent that the amendments that beefed up ARPA have resulted in more vigorous enforcement of the law. "[I]t's made it a lot easier for the U.S. attorneys' offices to prosecute people who violate the statute by excavating illegally, or [who try] to traffic in artifacts across state borders, if they're obtained ... in violation of state law," says Francis McManamon. "Almost immediately after those amendments were passed ... there was an incident at Big South Fork National Recreation Area in the Southeastern part of the country. Some people were apprehended digging in a rock shelter on Park Service land and they were apprehended and successful prosecutions were made, because it was easier, based on the amendments, for the prosecuting attorney to demonstrate a violation of the statute. So that's been one immediate effect."

Judge Sherry Hutt says that in the past year there's been "a dramatic increase in the number of prosecutions" in the country. These have involved not only destruction at prehistoric sites but also destruction at historic ones, such as Civil War battlefields, which attract artifact-hunters armed with metal detectors. "[N]ot only is there an increasing use of the law," Hutt says, "but ... it spreads over a broader spectrum of the country. You can have an archaeological case being filed tomorrow in Florida or in Virginia or Washington as likely as you would in the Four Corners states."

Tougher law enforcement, however, sometimes has an unintended consequence: It drives up the prices of the artifacts that are available for sale and so increases the incentive for people to go out and loot more of them. That's what happened in the Cherokee National Forest case in Tennessee. "The net effect of all this," says Forest Archaeologist Quentin Bass, "is that it's inflated the price of artifacts around here now and put even more pressure on it, in a weird sort of way.... Just like cocaine on the streets. You make a big bust and street prices go up ... and propel them to do more." Still, Bass says, the enforcement certainly "scared the bunch we have got up there; we seem to have cooled them for a while."

The biggest obstacles to effective protection of archaeological resources on federal lands were not changed by the amendments to ARPA and will not be easily removed. The first is the vastness of the federal lands. In the Four Corners states alone, the

Bureau of Land Management, the Forest Service, and the National Park Service manage about 104 million acres of land. But according to a 1987 General Accounting Office report, the agencies have surveyed less than 6 million of those acres to identify archaeological sites and provide physical protection to only a small proportion of the known sites. (*See story, p. 42.*)

"The agencies are making efforts to protect their known archaeological resources," the GAO said, "but these efforts are limited by the vastness of their lands and archaeological resources, as well as funding and staffing constraints." [17] There's been some improvement since that GAO report, but the situation still remains essentially the same. "[W]hile there has been an increase in the funding for archaeological

*"The problem with looting is not here in the Four Corners area. It is in the drawing rooms of Washington, D.C., on the mantles of Boston fireplaces, and on the walls of Los Angeles condominiums," says Utah State Archaeologist David B. Madsen.*

resource protection at the field level — they have a better ability than they had a year or two ago to hire part-time staff, to buy electronic monitoring equipment — it still is not [all that the federal agencies] say they need," McManamon says.

The other hard-to-remove obstacle in the way of effective protection of archaeological resources on federal lands is the fact that mining artifacts continues to be legal on private lands. That means that once a looter makes it off federal property, he can simply claim that the artifacts in his possession came from private land. "Once an artifact is removed from the soil, it becomes very difficult, if not impossible, to prove whether it was removed from public or private lands," noted Stephen M. McNamee, then the U.S. attorney for the District of Arizona. "Without such proof, prosecution ... is not a viable option." [18]

Furthermore, the mining of artifacts on private

lands, even though legal, is a major problem in itself from an archaeological point of view. Indeed, McManamon says that it may even be "a bigger problem at this point than the situation on the federal land." At least with the federal lands, he says, "we are beginning to get that under control ... and federal agencies are beginning to take the steps that they need to take to prevent [looting] from happening and to prosecute those who continue to do it. . . . There is not a similar kind of protection on private land."

That was made dramatically evident in late 1987 when 10 pot hunters paid the new owner of a farm in western Kentucky $10,000 for the right to dig up the land, which overlooks the Ohio River. Archaeologists had long known that the site "was a large, relatively undisturbed Late Mississippian* settlement," archaeologist Brian Fagan recounts. "Judging from surface artifacts, the site dated to sometime between A.D. 1450 and 1650. The farm was of special importance, for it straddled the vital centuries of first European contact with the New World." Other sites along the river from the period had long since been ravaged by pot hunters. But the Slack family, which for many years owned the farm, had permitted no digging for artifacts, and so the property "had, remarkably, remained nearly intact, a unique archive of information about Late Mississippian lifeways." [19] But then, with the change in ownership, came the pot hunters.

"They rented a tractor and began bulldozing their way through the village midden [refuse heap] to reach graves," Fagan relates. "They pushed heaps of bones aside, and dug through dwellings and the potsherds, hearths and stone tools associated with them. Along the way, they left detritus of their own — empty pop-top beer and soda cans — scattered on the ground alongside Late Mississippian pottery fragments. Today, Slack Farm looks like a battlefield — a morass of crude shovel holes and gaping trenches. Broken human bones litter the ground, and fractured artifacts crunch under foot." [20] A *National Geographic* writer said the field "looked for all the world as if a low-flying squadron of bombers had just swooped over on a practice run. More than 450 small craters, each edged by a mound of raw earth, pocked the surface of the unplanted field." [21] In response to the destruction, the Kentucky legislature made the desecration of graves a felony. Other states also have adopted laws to protect burial sites, even on private lands. (*In addition, many states have adopted laws to protect archaeological resources on state lands. See map, p. 41.*)

But the problem with respect to private lands still, by and large, remains. "I think the United States should have a system as in Great Britain, that the past in all heritage sites belongs to the country, to the crown, and if it happens to be on your private land then you're responsible as a steward of the past," says Kathleen Reinburg. "You cannot go out and dig that site unless you have permission of the government." But while that system may work in Great Britain, it might well not work in the United States, where the Constitution's Fifth Amendment* protects people's right to do with their property pretty much as they will and where most people have no cultural or emotional link with America's prehistoric past.

"[M]ost Americans of non-Indian descent," Fagan observes, "tend to think of prehistoric Indian sites in impersonal, remote ways. Most would protest vigorously at the destruction of an important, privately owned, historic site from pioneer days, or shudder at the very thought of someone looting their neighbor's great-grandmother's grave. But a long-abandoned prehistoric Indian village and the graves of the people who once lived there are a different matter." [22]

Most of the Indian artifacts illegally looted from federal or tribal lands apparently wind up in the hands of private collectors. Museums are now extremely careful about buying American Indian artifacts purportedly unearthed on private lands. Most art dealers are, too, according to Reid. "As a businessperson, I have a responsibility to use due diligence in trying to ascertain that what I buy is legal," he says. However, the only way a dealer can be certain that he never handles any artifacts illegally taken from federal or tribal lands is not to deal in such artifacts at all. Some dealers are doing just that. Archaeologist Thomas King says he has been told that a lot of dealers are going out of the Indian artifacts business because of ARPA and laws limiting international traffic.

Even if that's so, however, it doesn't necessarily mean that the destruction of archaeological resources is decreasing, King says. He's been told that "a lot of the real big collectors, the folks with the major money in the game, don't work through dealers per se but work through private agents, or individuals who don't deal on the open market but simply have two or three major clients that keep them going." Legitimate dealers "may be withdrawing from the market because of the impact of the laws. But ... their place [may well be] being taken by the guys who, because they're not operating shops and not operating galleries ... are less threatened by the laws."

Private collecting is a legitimate activity in a capitalist society, Reid points out. "There's something really wonderful about being able to own a significant item and being able to handle it and show it to your friends and buy, sell and trade it," he says. "It's neat.

*Continued on p. 46*

---

*Mississippian culture, Fagan relates in *The Great Journey: The Peopling of Ancient America* (1987), began to emerge around 700 A.D. along the central Mississippi River and the major flood-plain corridors formed by its tributaries, into the Ohio, Tennessee, Arkansas, and Red rivers, and their branches. The Mississippian people grew maize, beans and squash, and also relied heavily on hunting and gathering.

---

*The Fifth Amendment, which also protects against self-incrimination, states that "No person . . . shall be deprived of life, liberty, or property, without due process of law; nor shall private property be taken for public use without just compensation."

# AT ISSUE
*Is the Native American Graves Protection and Repatriation Act needed?*

**YES** *says* **SUZAN SHOWN HARJO**, *president and executive director of the Morning Star Foundation, a nonprofit organization advocating Native Americans' traditional and cultural rights.*

[The] legislation is an honest, practical effort to do what can be done through modern legal mechanisms to bring the United States and its citizenry out of the shadows of a shameful past where good people let bad people commit atrocious actions against our people. Grave robbing, burial site desecration, sacrilege of our sacred sites and objects, theft of our items of native national patrimony, use of our dead relatives as commodities of trade and commerce, exhibition of our dead relatives' skulls and destruction of their remains in federal and private places of learning and education, classification of Native people as federal property, and other related practices are part of that shameful past and all continue today.

These heinous acts are burned into the hearts and minds of Native people and, together with the wholesale slaughters past and slower, more subtle methods of killing our people today, have left us in states of prolonged mourning as nations and as individuals. This legislation will not correct all our problems, but it is more than a beginning, and its implementation will go far toward educating by example and practice a U.S. population which still in great part views Native people in the past tense and allows official actions, which mirror many private and business actions, to dehumanize us today....

This legislation goes to the root cause of and incentive for the problem here — common greed — which must be stopped at the marketplace. Even though [federal law] already makes it illegal to be in possession of stolen Indian property, this has not solved the problem and has apparently not served as much of a deterrent. Only Congress can prevent the wholesale transportation of our property across state and international lines. The United States should seek accords with other countries toward this end, just as the governments of Peru [and] others have done and are doing. While the specified penalties and confinement terms [may not be adequate], given the meaning and injury related to the offense to Native people, and given the pricey nature of our property on the open market and in the black market, they are a starting point and could be reviewed after some experience is gained under the new law....

[R]equiring [museum] inventories and reports is essential, not only to the purpose of the legislation, but to good museum practice as well. All federal agencies, educational institutions and museums housing our property should have done this already and, if they have not done so, must now make up for their generations of neglect.

*From testimony given May 14, 1990, to the Senate Select Committee on Indian Affairs on the Senate version of the House bill that became the Native American Graves Protection and Repatriation Act (PL 101-601).*

**NO** *says* **JAMES REID**, *president of the Antique Tribal Art Dealers Association.*

The appeal of the antique and the exotic is a near universal phenomenon. Through objects ancient peoples speak across centuries of important lifestyles and aesthetics. The collection and conservation of important objects of antique art is a pursuit that channels man's natural sense of curiosity and acquisitiveness to a high purpose that refines his aesthetic awareness and enlarges his knowledge of history and science.

Objects of cultural significance may be treated with respect and admiration from divergent perspectives. The native artist creates a thing of beauty [and] usage that manifests the basic relationships of man in the context of nature and the individual to his clan and tribe. The scientist approaches the object through his discipline and relates the information gained to the larger body of human knowledge. The connoisseur sees the common thread of beauty that shines through art and that empowers history. There are few significant objects of tribal material culture that do not involve the concept of [the] sacred, but the truths these pieces address survive their creators and their religious interpretations....

That any group has a right to the quiet enjoyment of its religious practice and to communal or personal rights of ownership of objects associated with that practice is well established by law. That a group has a right to exclusive control of its own cultural history and the objects associated with that history that supersedes the rights of the general public and interested individuals is a concept foreign to the pursuit of knowledge and to commonly accepted rights of property....

Institutions have a clear mandate to acquire, study, and preserve items of cultural significance. Except for the efforts of early collectors there would be no record of many of the unique and diversified tribes of the American Indian. Tribal entities have a legitimate concern for the preservation of their cultural integrity and the right to protection of their religious practices, as do all Americans, and to protection of religious shrines and burials on Indian lands. It is much less clear that the state should seek to amend the rights of private or public ownership of items that have been in non-tribal hands for many years, [that] may have been given as gifts [or] sold or traded from institutions or tribes or by individuals apparently in good faith and where no cloud to their title is suggested....

Adequate laws exist for the protection of tribal, institutional and private interest[s] in most of the areas addressed by this [legislation]. ... Poorly conceived additional legislation that grandstands to special interest groups at the expense of other, equally legitimate interests and at the expense of basic individual rights is not in the public interest.

*From testimony given July 17, 1990, to the House Committee on Interior and Insular Affairs on the House bill that became the Native American Graves Protection and Repatriation Act.*

Continued from p. 44
[And it's] common all over the world, where any kind of wealth exists."

But many archaeologists and others dream of a day when private collecting of archaeological resources will be socially unacceptable. "The problem with looting is not here in the Four Corners area," Utah State Archaeologist Madsen told a congressional sub-committee. "It is in the drawing rooms of Washington, D.C., on the mantles of Boston fireplaces, and on the walls of Los Angeles condominiums. . . . Until the reaction to the private display of such artifacts is one of scorn rather than approval, those artifacts will continue to find a market." [23] So long as they do, it appears that the nation's finite and irreplaceable archaeological resources will continue to be lost.

# NOTES (Text)

[1] The defendant, Newall Charlton, 63, of Elizabethton, Tenn., was sentenced to two years in prison for the felony violation of the Archaeological Resources Protection Act, fined $499 and ordered to pay $2,500 in restitution. He also was given 10 years in prison for theft of federal government property, and 10 years for depredation of federal government property. The other defendants in the case received lesser sentences. For more details on the case, contact the U.S. Forest Service public affairs office at the Cherokee National Forest, 2800 Ocoee St., Cleveland, Tenn. 37312, (615) 476-9700.

[2] Testimony before the House Interior and Insular Affairs Committee's Subcommittee on General Oversight and Investigations at a hearing held in Cortez, Colo., Oct. 19, 1987.

[3] Quoted by Ann Gibbons in "New Law Requires Return of Indian Remains," *Science*, Nov. 9, 1990, p. 750.

[4] "For Indian Artifacts, Price Trend Is Up," *The New York Times*, Nov. 20, 1971; Karl E. Meyer, *The Plundered Past* (1973), pp. 8-10.

[5] *Archeological Looting, a Summary*, Archeological Assistance Division, National Park Service, U.S. Department of the Interior, briefing statement, Jan. 31, 1990.

[6] Subcommittee on General Oversight and Investigations, House Committee on Interior and Insular Affairs, *The Destruction of America's Archaeological Heritage: Looting and Vandalism of Indian Archaeological Sites in the Four Corners States of the Southwest*, February 1988, p. 9.

[7] Brian M. Fagan, *The Great Journey: The Peopling of Ancient America* (1987), p. 256.

[8] Jim Robbins, "Violating History," *National Parks*, July-August 1987, p. 29.

[9] National Park Service, U.S. Department of the Interior, *Federal Archeology: The Current Program*, 1989, p. 8.

[10] Subcommittee on General Oversight and Investigations, House Committee on Interior and Insular Affairs, *The Destruction of America's Archaeological Heritage*, op. cit., pp. 13-14.

[11] Subcommittee on General Oversight and Investigations, House Committee on Interior and Insular Affairs, *Theft of Indian Artifacts from Archaeological Sites*, Oct. 19, 1987, p. 149. The hearing was held in Cortez, Colo.

[12] U.S. General Accounting Office, *Cultural Resources: Problems Protecting and Preserving Federal Archeological Resources*, December 1987, p. 63.

[13] Subcommittee on General Oversight and Investigations, House Committee on Interior and Insular Affairs, *The Destruction of America's Archaeological Heritage*, op. cit., pp. 43-47.

[14] Subcommittee on General Oversight and Investigations, House Committee on Interior and Insular Affairs, *Theft of Indian Artifacts from Archeological Sites*, op. cit., pp. 122-123.

[15] U.S. General Accounting Office, *op. cit.*, p. 61.

[16] Subcommittee on General Oversight and Investigations, House Committee on Interior and Insular Affairs, *Theft of Indian Artifacts from Archeological Sites*, op. cit., p. 32. Madsen's other quoted comments are from an interview.

[17] U.S. General Accounting Office, *op. cit.*, pp. 37, 49.

[18] Subcommittee on General Oversight and Investigations, House Committee on Interior and Insular Affairs, *Theft of Indian Artifacts from Archeological Sites*, op. cit., p. 136.

[19] Brian Fagan, "Black Day at Slack Farm," *Archaeology*, July-August 1988, p. 15.

[20] Idem.

[21] Harvey Arden, "Who Owns Our Past?" *National Geographic*, March 1989, p. 378.

[22] Fagan, *op. cit.*, p. 16.

[23] Subcommittee on General Oversight and Investigations, House Committee on Interior and Insular Affairs, *Theft of Indian Artifacts from Archeological Sites*, op. cit., p. 34.

# NOTES (pp. 38-39)

[1] Quoted by Douglas J. Preston, who gives an account of the Northern Cheyenne chiefs' visit to Washington in "Skeletons in Our Museums' Closets," *Harper's*, February 1989, p. 68.

[2] Robert E. Bieder, "A Brief Historical Survey of the Expropriation of American Indian Remains," April 1990, in Senate Select Committee on Indian Affairs, *Native American Grave and Burial Protection Act (Repatriation); Native American Repatriation of Cultural Patrimony Act; and Heard Museum Report*, May 14, 1990, pp. 322-323.

[3] *Ibid.*, p. 51.

[4] Senate Select Committee on Indian Affairs, *Native American Cultural Preservation Act*, Feb. 20, 1987, pp. 65-66, 203-204.

[5] *Ibid.*, p. 189.

[6] Robert McCormick Adams, "Smithsonian Horizons," *Smithsonian*, October 1990, p. 10.

*Graphics: Cover, Margaret Scott; map, p. 41, Jack Auldridge.*

## RECOMMENDED READING

## BOOKS

**Fagan, Brian M., *Archaeology: A Brief Introduction*, 3rd ed., Scott, Foresman and Co., 1988.**

"Modern archaeology," writes the author of this excellent introduction to the subject, "is not treasure hunting, nor is it a fantasy search for lost worlds; *it is the systematic study of humanity in the past*. This general definition includes not only ancient technology and human behavior, but social organization, religious beliefs, and every aspect of human culture."

**Meyer, Karl E., *The Plundered Past*, Atheneum, 1973.**

This is an extremely well-written and researched book about the international illicit trade in antiquities. "In ancient Greece," journalist Meyer writes, "they were called *tymborychoi*, in modern Italy they are known as *tombaroli*, in India their name is 'idol-runners,' in Guatemala it is *esteleros*, and in Peru *huaqueros*, but in all times and places the terms signify the same thing: those who plunder tombs and temples. It is assuredly the second-oldest profession, practiced as widely if not always as profitably as the first. Like the courtesan, the tomb robber knows there is money in beauty, and rarely a shortage of customers. Laws, moral constraints, and bodily hazards have had roughly the same deterrent effect on the one calling as on the other."

## ARTICLES

**Arden, Harvey, "Who Owns Our Past?" *National Geographic*, March 1989, pp. 376-393.**

Superb color photographs accompanying this article show the destruction in late 1987 of an archaeologically important site on a farm in western Kentucky. The 10 men who, with the permission of the farm owner, dug into the field "disturbed more than bones and Indian relics," Arden writes. "They ripped out and crumpled an irreplaceable page of our common heritage — and raised in high relief the growing controversy over the looting, sale, and exhibition of Native American remains and grave goods."

**Cowley, Geoffrey *et al.*, "The Plunder of the Past," *Newsweek*, June 26, 1989, pp. 58-60.**

"Collecting Indian relics is a time-honored tradition in many parts of the country," notes *Newsweek*. "But what was once a rural hobby has lately blossomed into a multimillion-dollar industry. Spurred by the five-figure prices the most prized artifacts can fetch, small armies of treasure seekers are looting unmarked Indian graves from Arizona to North Carolina. Archaeologists express horror that the pot hunters are destroying an irreplaceable record of how the original Americans lived. Indian groups are horrified, too."

**Goodwin, Derek V., "Raiders of the Sacred Sites," *New York Times Magazine*, Dec. 7, 1986, pp. 64-66, 84-89.**

Archaeological looters are bringing to market artifacts from the Anasazi, Hopi, Hohokam, Caddo, Salado, Hopewell and Mimbres cultures, Goodwin reported. "Archaeologists and art historians link the present wave of desecration to the first major auction of American Indian art at New York's Parke-Bernet Galleries, in 1971. The record prices received then for domestic relics stunned the international art world, which had virtually ignored them, and caused raiders to turn their attention to treasures on American soil."

**Peerman, Dean, "Bare-Bones Imbroglio: Repatriating Indian Remains and Sacred Artifacts," *The Christian Century*, Oct. 17, 1990, pp. 935-937.**

Peerman, a senior editor at the magazine, provides a comprehensive look at the controversy over the repatriation of Indian remains and sacred artifacts. "As a matter of ethnic identity and pride, most Indians support the ongoing effort to recover and reconstitute their cultural heritage," he writes. "But they often differ on the details. Christianized Indians — and Mormonized Indians, of whom there are many — do not want returned to them items that they now regard as pagan. For a different reason, the Zunis do not want back their forebears' bones; they consider them to have become 'tainted' while in Anglo hands."

## REPORTS AND STUDIES

**National Park Service, U.S. Department of the Interior, *Federal Archeology: The Current Program*, 1989.**

Although there are numerous statutes designed to protect archaeological sites on federal lands, this report notes, widespread looting and vandalism have occurred. The reported incidents don't tell the whole story. "It is suspected that many incidents go unreported because the sites looted are in remote locations or the evidence of looting is not noticed."

**U.S. General Accounting Office, *Cultural Resources: Problems Protecting and Preserving Federal Archeological Resources*, December 1987. GAO/RCED-88-3.**

"Federal officials generally believe that enforcement efforts have deterred casual looting (looting to obtain artifacts for personal collections) but not commercial looting (looting to obtain artifacts for sale to others)," this important report said. "When an agency steps up its enforcement efforts, commercial looters shift their activities to other agencies' lands or other geographic areas."

# EDITORIAL RESEARCH REPORTS

## Coming soon

- Peace Corps at 30
- Recession
- Puerto Rico

Published weekly by Congressional Quarterly Inc., Editorial Research Reports analyze emerging issues of national interest across a broad range of social, scientific, political and economic fields. Reports are bound and indexed for permanent reference. Subscription information is available through Congressional Quarterly's Publications Sales Department by telephone (202) 887-8665. Copies of past issues are available through Customer Service, (202) 887-8621.

JANUARY 25, 1991

ERR

CONGRESSIONAL QUARTERLY'S

EDITORIAL RESEARCH REPORTS

FOUNDED 1923

# PEACE CORPS' CHALLENGES IN THE 1990s

# PEACE CORPS' CHALLENGES IN THE 1990s

*by Richard L. Worsnop*

March 1 marks the 30th anniversary of the Peace Corps, and by many measures, the agency is more popular today than it ever has been. Congress has encouraged it to expand to 10,000 volunteers, and Peace Corps programs are being established in more countries, including several in Eastern Europe. Nonetheless, the agency still faces problems of funding and recruiting as it enters its fourth decade.

No other federal agency is remotely like the Peace Corps. On the eve of its 30th anniversary, it still projects an image of vigor, youthfulness and altruism — a legacy from its close identification with the presidency of John F. Kennedy. Most people still think of the "typical" Peace Corps volunteer as being an idealist in his or her early 20s — a recent college graduate, in all likelihood — who willingly postpones career pursuits for two years of service in a remote village in some Third World country.

That image still mirrors reality in most cases. But increasingly, the Peace Corps is seeking out older volunteers, including retirees, who possess special skills needed by host countries. Moreover, some of the assignments today's volunteers receive amount to white-collar jobs, often performed in a big-city office building.

As before, the primary focus of Peace Corps assistance efforts is the Third World, notably sub-Saharan Africa. But the collapse of communism in Eastern Europe has given the agency an opportunity to establish programs in a region where it was not welcome before. Peace Corps volunteers already have been sent to Czechoslovakia, Hungary and Poland, and Romania is due to receive a contingent shortly. There is even speculation about setting up a program in the Soviet Union.

These changes, while not sweeping at this point, make some longtime supporters of the Peace Corps uneasy. They worry that the emphasis on special skills has left fewer openings for the young generalists who have long constituted the bulk of the volunteer force. The youngest volunteers may lack advanced professional training, the argument goes, but they often prove more adept at improvising than their elders.

Above all, critics of current Peace Corps policy are bothered by the move into Eastern Europe. Their concern found expression in a report submitted to Congress last fall by Peace Corps Inspector General Gerard A. Roy. When the agency sent volunteers into Eastern Europe, the report stated, "some of the existing Peace Corps programs in Africa, Asia and Latin America underwent actual budget cuts, while others received budget increases that, nevertheless, failed to keep pace with local inflation. . . . The agency must exercise great care in ensuring that the limited resources apportioned to existing countries are not redirected to support new country entries." [1]

Peace Corps Director Paul D. Coverdell views the Eastern European initiative in a positive light. "I don't see it as a change in direction at all," he says. "The ultimate mission of the Peace Corps is the pursuit of peace. In any of our capacities, if we can bring about a more peaceful world, that's what we ought to do."

Policy disputes are nothing new for the Peace Corps. For much of its existence, the agency has been a testing ground for sharply contrasting liberal and conservative theories on aiding the indigent. The Peace Corps came into being during the heady days of Kennedy's New Frontier, when Democratic liberalism held sway, but the Republican Party has controlled the executive branch for 19 of the agency's 30 years. As a result, the Peace Corps endured periods of decline and neglect after the ebullience of its formative period in the early and mid-1960s.

The Eastern Europe breakthrough could herald a new golden age for the agency. However, a number of nagging problems persist. One is funding. Annual appropriations for the Peace Corps have been climbing steadily since 1972, when expressed in current dollars, and now are at the highest level ever. In constant dollars, however, the agency today receives barely half the amount appropriated in 1966, its peak year.

A related problem concerns recruiting. From the beginning, the Peace Corps has fallen short of its goal of hiring enough volunteers from minority groups to form a rough facsimile of the U.S. racial and ethnic mosaic. Blacks, in particular, are said to view the Peace Corps as a preserve for middle-class whites. Thus, relatively few blacks have applied to become volunteers, thereby helping to perpetuate the stereotype.

In recruiting prospective volunteers of all kinds, the Peace Corps relies heavily on the efforts of returned volunteers who completed their full two years of

## Ugly Americans

*"This American is different from other white men. He knows how to work with his hands. He built this machine with his own fingers and his own brain. You people do not understand such things. But men that work with their hands and their muscles understand one another."*

— *The Ugly American*

One of the inspirations for the Peace Corps was a best-selling work of fiction published in 1958, *The Ugly American.* A loosely connected group of stories by William J. Lederer and Eugene Burdick, the book had a didactic purpose: to persuade Americans that U.S. foreign-aid programs in developing countries were misguided. The officials in charge of the programs, the authors charged, were largely unacquainted with local languages and customs and socialized mainly with their peers from other Western countries.

To illustrate their point, Lederer and Burdick invented a character named Homer Atkins. Nicknamed "the ugly American" because of his ungainly appearance, Atkins is an engineer (and self-made millionaire) who has little use for the bureaucrats and diplomatic personnel he encounters in the Southeast Asian country of Sarkhan.

Quite literally a hands-on type, Atkins teaches a group of rural villagers how to build a bicycle-powered pump for lifting water from one terraced field to another. He does this indirectly, letting the locals discover for themselves the correct way to design and build the pump.

In a subsequent chapter, Atkins' wife Emma uses the same approach to teach women in the area how to make long-handled brooms to replace the traditional short-handled ones that cause sore and stooped backs. The moral of the two episodes is that labor-saving devices are more appreciated if those benefiting from them do most of the work of "inventing" them — or at least think that they have.

Clearly, Homer Atkins is meant to be the hero of Lederer and Burdick's book. But the term "ugly American" has come to be associated instead with the insensitive bureaucrats that Atkins himself disdains.

In a "documentary epilogue" to the book, the authors pounded home their message in non-fictional terms: "We do not need the horde of 1,500,000 Americans — most amateurs — who are now working for the United States overseas," they wrote. "What we need is a small force of well-trained, well-chosen, hard-working, and dedicated professionals. They must be willing to risk their comforts and — in some lands — their health. They must go equipped to apply a positive policy promulgated by a clear-thinking government. They must speak the language of the land of their assignment, and they must be more expert in its problems than are the natives."

service. The returnees sometimes speak of their experience in near-reverent terms. Indeed, some of the most glowing appraisals come from volunteers who served in the most materially deprived areas. A common reaction is that the Peace Corps experience permanently alters one's outlook on life. (*See story, p. 53.*) To be sure, the Peace Corps is not and never has been for everyone; most young people are in a hurry to find a rewarding job and start a family, and understandably so. But three decades of experience strongly suggest that untold thousands of Americans still are willing to forgo financial security awhile and tackle what is, as a famous Peace Corps recruiting slogan put it, "the toughest job you'll ever love."

## Peace Corps' expansion into Eastern Europe

Several dozen of today's "toughest jobs" are in Eastern Europe, and many additional Peace Corps volunteers are due to go to host countries in that region this year. Poland eventually is to get 213 volunteers, which would give it one of the largest Peace Corps programs anywhere.*

The move into Eastern Europe was accomplished in short order. On Jan. 4, 1990, the Peace Corps announced that it would send its first volunteers to Poland and Hungary that June, and both contingents arrived on schedule. (Poland thus became the 100th country and Hungary the 101st to accept Peace Corps volunteers.) All 60 of the initial volunteers in Poland and all 65 in Hungary were assigned either to teach English or to train local teachers in English-language instruction techniques.

A Peace Corps task force that visited Hungary in 1989 found that people there had several reasons for wanting to become fluent in English. English is the working language of most international professions, the task force noted, so "Hungarian adults see English as the language of opportunity. Fluency in English prepares one for jobs in trade, commerce, business, interpreting and international travel. In addition, ambitious Hungarian professionals can increase their salary 8 percent by earning a state language proficiency certificate, while getting the advanced certificate can bring a 15 percent pay raise."

"Another factor in the popularity of English," the task force said, "is related to the rejection of compulsory Russian. ... The failure of most Hungarians to learn Russian is not attributed to the dissimilarity of the two languages, but rather to the resistance of being subordinate to a foreign power. English, on the other hand, represents to many Hungarians just the opposite: It provides a link to democracy and freedom." [2] The Peace Corps team also found that "High-school age students [in Hungary] are interested in English for a different

reason than their parents: They want to be part of the international pop culture."

The reasons cited by Polish adults and teenagers for wanting to learn English are substantially the same as those mentioned by the Hungarians. Catherine Peebles, a Peace Corps volunteer who teaches English at a high school in Bialystok, a city of 300,000 people about 100 miles northeast of Warsaw, reports that the Americans have been well received and are providing a vitally needed service.

"The Poles haven't had native speakers of English in their schools for 45 years," Peebles says. "The students who studied English before [the volunteers arrived] have very wonderful grammar. Grammar is something that can be taught from books only — and Polish teachers do that very well. But the students' English speech is really in need of help; it's heavily accented and very halting. If you know grammar and vocabulary well but you're not used to speaking, you can't use English in conversation. They're afraid to speak because oral work is not emphasized. One reason is that few Polish teachers of English have ever traveled to an English-speaking country. So the teachers aren't comfortable speaking English either."

Peebles adds that "English is a harder foreign language than Russian for most [Polish students]. It's much different from Polish. I guess English is just more exciting for them because it's something new and Western, and Western things are all the rage."

As more volunteers arrive in Eastern Europe and as more countries in the region establish Peace Corps programs, the scope of volunteer activities will expand beyond the teaching of English. "In Romania, [where Peace Corps volunteers are scheduled to arrive at the end of February] we will be helping institutionalized children," says Jon Keeton, the Peace Corps' director of international research and development. "We'll also be starting environmental efforts in Poland, Hungary and Czechoslovakia. Educational efforts, primarily."

The institutionalized Romanian children the Peace Corps intends to help are the orphans who have received so much attention in world news media since the downfall of the Communist dictatorship of Nicolae Ceaucescu in December 1989. Keeton says the agency plans to offer assistance "while retaining the goals and the motivation, the essence of Peace Corps — namely, that we are a development agency, not a humanitarian agency. Our volunteers will be looking for ways to educate the Romanians to link the institutions [housing the orphans] with nearby communities and to train the staff within those institutions."

Other Peace Corp opportunities beckon elsewhere in Eastern Europe. A program is just getting under way in Bulgaria, and Yugoslavia also has expressed interest. But the big question remains: Will the Peace Corps ever be invited to send volunteers to the Soviet Union? "We've had numerous inquiries from various parts of the Soviet Union and from citizens thereof

---

*As of January 1991, Honduras had the most volunteers (339), followed by Botswana (306), Guatemala (244), Thailand (219) and Zaire (210). No other country had more than 200 volunteers as of that date. For complete country-by-country totals worldwide, see map, p. 56-7.

# The Peace Corps Experience

**P**eople do not join the Peace Corps to make their fortune. While serving overseas, all volunteers receive a small living allowance in local currency. They also receive a lump-sum, $200-a-month readjustment allowance at the completion of their tour of duty. At that time they also may receive help in returning to college or finding a job.

Despite the modest monetary rewards, the vast majority of returned volunteers describe their experience as personally enriching in ways that cannot be measured in dollars. One such former volunteer is James V. Bullard, assistant director of promotion for *National Geographic* magazine, who taught English for the Peace Corps on the Caribbean island of St. Lucia from 1967 to 1969.

"Most of the people who joined Peace Corps came out of a very homogeneous and cloistered background," Bullard recalls. "They lived in suburbia, most of them, and they'd gone to decent colleges, worked hard. They had goals that were parent-defined. For most, Peace Corps represented their first exposure to the rest of the world — to different cultures, religions and races. That in itself was an eye-opener.

"Also, they were given unbelievable responsibility and freedom in which to operate. There was almost no hand-holding. Essentially, you were just cut loose. The support network you'd always had among family or in college — that was absolutely gone. To make matters even more frightening, you were looked up to by the people you were now living with. They expected you to know all the answers. And in many cases, you didn't know the answers.

"After you go through that, you're never quite the same person again. You become a lot more patient and tolerant, a lot more aware that there's more than one way to do things. Because it totally pulled you out of your environment, and forced you to adjust to another one, the Peace Corps put you in a unique position to evaluate the environment you came from and returned to. And to question it. [The Peace Corps experience] taught volunteers to question just about everything."

To be sure, Peace Corps service has its share of negative aspects. Two related problems encountered by most volunteers are "culture shock" and "culture fatigue." Culture shock, which volunteers usually feel soon after their arrival in the host country, is triggered by one or more of the following factors: homesickness, strange food, pervasive poverty and disease, harsh weather, and rigid class and caste distinctions. One volunteer stationed in the Far East acknowledged that when faced with "rotten teeth, foul breath, smells, sores, filth, rags, I couldn't take it. I was astonished to find that my reactions were so diametrically opposed to my ideals. . . . I simply and truthfully hated it and wanted to go home." †

Culture fatigue, which sets in about nine months after arrival, refers to the psychological and emotional letdown that accompanies volunteers' realization that their efforts will have little or no immediate impact. "We're in competition with Allah," remarked one volunteer while discussing his hosts' passive acceptance of their meager lot in life.††

Sometimes volunteers find themselves in life-threatening situations. Last June, for instance, the Peace Corps ordered its 261 volunteers out of the Philippines after intelligence reports indicated that they had become targets of Communist insurgents. The move came two weeks after volunteer Timothy Swanson was abducted on the central Philippine island of Negros by the Communist New People's Army. Swanson was released unharmed in early August. But the Peace Corps program in the Philippines, one of the agency's oldest and largest, remains suspended. Peace Corps officials hope, however, that volunteers will be able to return around October.

Over the years, there have been significant changes in the composition of the Peace Corps volunteer force. In the early 1960s, nearly 60 percent of all volunteers were young liberal-arts generalists holding only a bachelor's degree; today generalists account for only about 30 percent of volunteers. The difference has largely been made up by volunteers possessing professional skills in the fields of business, engineering, health and social work.

The increasing emphasis on skills has helped to raise the proportion of older volunteers. Throughout the 1960s, as many as 85 percent of volunteers were under 26 years old; today, that age bracket constitutes just over 50 percent of the total.

The Peace Corps also has done its part to topple gender-based job barriers. In 1963, only about one-third of volunteers were women; today's volunteer force is almost evenly divided between the sexes. Women also hold many executive jobs at the agency's Washington headquarters, including all three top deputy posts in Director Paul D. Coverdell's office.

† *Quoted by Lawrence H. Fuchs in* Those Peculiar Americans: The Peace Corps and the American National Character *(1967), p. 110.*
†† *Quoted by Kevin Lowther and C. Payne Lucas in* Keeping Kennedy's Promise: The Peace Corps, Unmet Hope of the New Frontier *(1978), p. 17.*

and from ethnic groups here in the United States supporting it," Keeton says. "There have been some semiofficial feelers also." But no official initiative from Moscow has been forthcoming thus far.

Some observers question whether the Soviets will ever take such a step. To do so would be tantamount to acknowledging that the country is, in many ways, at a Third World stage of economic development. This admission, by one superpower to another, might well be too humiliating to risk, notwithstanding the country's manifold needs.

In any case, the Peace Corps' Eastern Europe initiative has engendered some criticism, some of which was expressed while the Poland and Hungary programs were still being negotiated. Jeff Drumtra, editor of *WorldView Magazine*, the quarterly journal of the National Council of Returned Peace Corps Volunteers, said the agency's presence in Europe would raise "the philosophical question of what precisely is the role of Peace Corps in the world today — whether it should be confined to helping the less developed countries where the infant mortality rate is incredibly high, or [whether it should] ... be in European countries where the basic needs are not as great" [3]

Edward Patrick Healy, a former Peace Corps country director in Zaire, went further in a letter to *The Washington Post* last May. "The countries of Eastern Europe do not need expatriate teachers," he asserted. "Indeed, they are among the world's best-educated countries, with a literacy rate that is as high or higher than ours and universities that had world renown before there was a United States. Even those arguing from the short-term needs arising from Communist mismanagement must in fairness concede that those needs hardly equal those of countries where development, and the Peace Corps' contribution to it, may be the only alternative to death by starvation or disease." [4] (*For more of Healy's comments, see "At Issue," p. 61.*)

Peace Corps Director Coverdell dismisses such arguments. "Peace Corps should not turn down any legitimate request for assistance from any nation so long as the safety of our volunteers can be assured," he said in a statement released Jan. 4, 1990, the day the Hungary and Poland programs were announced. "There should be no political, economic or geographical boundaries placed on this people-to-people mission of peace." [5]

Many people involved in Peace Corps affairs or Third World development issues agree with Coverdell, though with qualifications. Drumtra, for instance, now says: "I think there's a role to be played [in Eastern Europe] as long as Peace Corps continues to focus the bulk of its resources on the poorest countries in the world, which are in Africa and Latin America."

John W. Sewell, president of the Overseas Development Council, a private research group that focuses on U.S. interests in developing countries, expresses similar views. He supports the decision to send Peace Corps volunteers to Eastern Europe, "as long as it's not at the expense of volunteers to the Third World. [Eastern Europe is] probably not a bad idea, but I don't think it should become a major focus of the Peace Corps at all."

Volunteer Catherine Peebles feels that such comments miss the point. "Teaching English to well-fed children in Czechoslovakia or Poland comes down to the same thing as teaching kids in West Africa how to build better stoves," she says. "It's all basically a matter of economic survival, and Poland isn't going to survive unless English is taught on a massive scale."

Robert J. Berg, president of the International Development Conference, a private organization concerned mainly with U.S.-Third World policies, approaches the question from a somewhat different angle. In his opinion, Peace Corps officials should insist that Eastern European countries underwrite at least some of the program's costs. He regards this as sound

policy for both the United States and the host countries. "Let us say that you normally pay 100 zlotys per whatever for [native Polish] English teachers. If you also had to pay the same 100 zlotys for the local support of a Peace Corps volunteer, you would have to decide whether you were getting better service out of the volunteer than you were from a Pole who was out of work but who could teach."

The recent debate on Peace Corps programs in Eastern Europe has tended to overshadow the agency's initiatives in other parts of the world. The Peace Corps is in more countries today than at any time in its history, and there are more countries seeking volunteers than at any time in the past 20 years. Congo, Mongolia, Mozambique and Uganda are among the countries due to start Peace Corps programs in 1991, and tentative overtures have been received from Bangladesh, Nicaragua and Turkey, among others. The agency estimates that 20 countries will set up programs in fiscal years 1991 and 1992 and that 40 more will do so between fiscal 1993 and 1996. [6]

## Origins of the Peace Corps; Kennedy's 'New Frontier'

Although the Peace Corps is closely identified with John F. Kennedy — indeed, it once was known as Kennedy's "special baby" — the idea for it did not originate with him. The concept was developed, both independently and jointly, by three of Kennedy's Democratic colleagues in Congress in the late 1950s — Sen. Hubert H. Humphrey of Minnesota, Sen. Richard L. Neuberger of Oregon and Rep. Henry S. Reuss of Wisconsin.

On June 15, 1960, seven months before Kennedy's inauguration, Humphrey introduced legislation to establish "a Peace Corps of American young men to assist the peoples of the underdeveloped areas of the world to learn the basic skills necessary to combat poverty, disease, illiteracy and hunger." In a floor speech explaining the rationale and objectives of his bill, Humphrey declared: "One of the most explosive situations today is that the rich nations are getting richer and the poor nations are getting poorer. ... In this type of a situation, communism can often look attractive. It is for this reason that we must offer them a suitable alternative."

Humphrey went on to stress that "the whole orientation of the corps and [its] director must be toward the people-to-people approach. The basic people-to-people orientation is sometimes missing in the way our foreign aid program is carried out."

The Humphrey Peace Corps bill, as well as similar legislation introduced earlier in the session by Neuberger and Reuss, went nowhere in 1960. Capitol Hill was preoccupied by that year's presidential election race. As it turned out, the Peace Corps figured as a pivotal campaign issue for Kennedy, a narrow winner over Republican nominee Richard M. Nixon.

Kennedy first mentioned the idea on Oct. 5, 1960, in a message directed at young voters. Acknowledging his debt to Humphrey and Reuss,* he said that he would, as president, "explore thoroughly the possibility of utilizing the services of the very best of our trained and qualified young people to give from three to five years of their lives to the cause of world peace by forming themselves into a Youth Peace Corps, going to the places that really need them and doing the sort of jobs that need to be done."

But the Peace Corps proposal did not really catch fire until Oct. 14. At 2 o'clock that morning, after an 18-hour day of campaigning, Kennedy delivered an impromptu speech from the steps of the University of Michigan student union in Ann Arbor. "How many of you," the candidate asked the assembled students, "are willing to spend 10 years in Africa or Latin America or Asia working for the United States and working for freedom? How many of you [who] are going to be doctors are willing to spend your days in Ghana? ... On your willingness ... to contribute part of your life to this country, I think, will depend the answer whether we as a free society can compete."

Reaction to Kennedy's speech, both at Ann Arbor and on other college campuses across the country, was wildly enthusiastic. The candidate's campaign strategists were quick to recognize that he had tapped a hidden reservoir of altruism among young people. As a result, the Peace Corps proposal was fleshed out and refined in the campaign's closing days.

Kennedy's most detailed presentation of his ideas on the subject came in a Nov. 2 speech at San Francisco's Cow Palace. Going beyond Humphrey, who had envisioned a Peace Corps of "American young men," Kennedy said volunteers "would be sought among talented young women as well — and from every race and walk of life." It was in this speech, too, that Kennedy developed at length a theme that he would return to again and again as the Peace Corps moved closer to reality. A major reason why such an overseas volunteer force was needed, he suggested, was to counteract the Communists' highly effective people-to-people programs in developing countries.

"[O]n the other side of the globe," Kennedy declared, "diplomats skilled in the languages and customs of the nation to whom [sic] they are credited — teachers, doctors, technicians and experts desperately needed in a dozen fields by underdeveloped nations — are pouring forth from Moscow to advance the cause of world communism. ... Already Asia has more of the Soviet than American technicians — and Africa may by this time. Russian diplomats are the first to arrive, the first to offer aid, the only ones represented

by key officials at diplomatic receptions. They know the country, they speak the language — and in Guinea, Ghana, Laos and all over the globe, they are working fast and effectively. Missiles and arms cannot stop them — neither can American dollars. They can only be countered by Americans equally skilled and equally dedicated — and if I am elected, I ask you to help me find those Americans."

Kennedy's words touched a nerve for at least two reasons. In 1960, Americans were still smarting from the Soviet feat of putting into orbit the first space satellite, Sputnik, in 1957. That achievement prompted nationwide soul-searching about the state of American education in general, especially in the sciences.

Then, in 1958, came the publication of *The Ugly American*, a collection of loosely related stories by William J. Lederer and Eugene Burdick. (*See story, p. 51.*) One of the book's main arguments was that U.S. government officials assigned to underdeveloped countries were ignorant of the local language and culture and rarely ventured from the capital into the countryside for anything but perfunctory inspection tours. Before long, "the ugly American" had become a popular shorthand term for all such U.S. officials serving overseas.

After Kennedy was elected, one of his first acts was to appoint a task force to study the Peace Corps idea. The panel submitted a report to the president-elect on Jan. 9, 1961, supporting the establishment of the Peace Corps on a "limited pilot basis," but saying it was "undesirable" that the agency be considered an alternative to the military draft, as Kennedy had proposed during the election campaign. The report said there was "abundant evidence that draft exemption is not required as a bait to induce an adequate number of applicants" for Peace Corps service.

On March 1, 1961, Kennedy — without waiting for congressional approval — signed an executive order establishing the Peace Corps on a temporary basis. He picked R. Sargent Shriver Jr., his brother-in-law, to head the new program. Shriver had served as president of the Chicago Board of Education from 1955-60 and as assistant general manager of the Merchandise Mart in Chicago. Shriver worked without compensation as head of the fledgling Peace Corps project. When the Peace Corps was approved by Congress on Sept. 21, 1961, Shriver was named its first director.

The enabling legislation reflected some of the Cold War concerns voiced by Kennedy in his Cow Palace address. It provided that volunteers' training "shall include instruction in the philosophy, strategy, tactics and menace of communism." It also required volunteers to take an oath of office and to swear that they did not advocate the overthrow of the U.S. government and did not knowingly belong to any organization that advocated the overthrow of the government.

These provisions failed to mollify the Peace Corps' critics, most of whom were political conservatives. Shriver later recalled that when the Peace Corps was

---

*Neuberger, not mentioned by Kennedy in the Oct. 5 message, had died on March 9, 1960.

# Peace Corps' Postings around the World

**The Peace Corps is in more countries today than at any time in its history. The numbers on the map below correspond to the alphabetized list below the map of the 83 countries that cur-** **rently have volunteers. The map is shaded to indicate which countries have the most and the fewest volunteers. The numbers in parentheses following the country names indicate the**

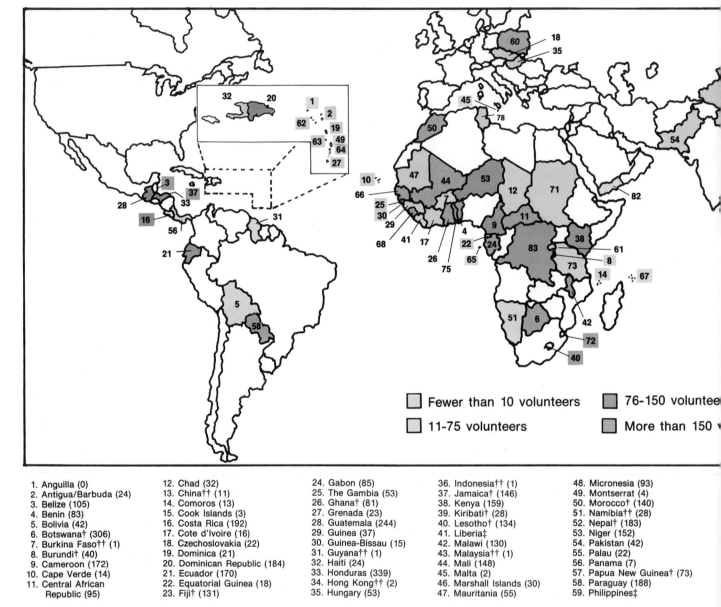

Fewer than 10 volunteers | 76-150 volunteer[s]
11-75 volunteers | More than 150 v[olunteers]

1. Anguilla (0)
2. Antigua/Barbuda (24)
3. Belize (105)
4. Benin (83)
5. Bolivia (42)
6. Botswana† (306)
7. Burkina Faso†† (1)
8. Burundi† (40)
9. Cameroon (172)
10. Cape Verde (14)
11. Central African Republic (95)
12. Chad (32)
13. China†† (11)
14. Comoros (13)
15. Cook Islands (3)
16. Costa Rica (192)
17. Cote d'Ivoire (16)
18. Czechoslovakia (22)
19. Dominica (21)
20. Dominican Republic (184)
21. Ecuador (170)
22. Equatorial Guinea (18)
23. Fiji† (131)
24. Gabon (85)
25. The Gambia (53)
26. Ghana† (81)
27. Grenada (23)
28. Guatemala (244)
29. Guinea (37)
30. Guinea-Bissau (15)
31. Guyana†† (1)
32. Haiti (24)
33. Honduras (339)
34. Hong Kong†† (2)
35. Hungary (53)
36. Indonesia†† (1)
37. Jamaica† (146)
38. Kenya (159)
39. Kiribati† (28)
40. Lesotho† (134)
41. Liberia‡
42. Malawi (130)
43. Malaysia†† (1)
44. Mali (148)
45. Malta (2)
46. Marshall Islands (30)
47. Mauritania (55)
48. Micronesia (93)
49. Montserrat (4)
50. Morocco† (140)
51. Namibia†† (28)
52. Nepal† (183)
53. Niger (152)
54. Pakistan (42)
55. Palau (22)
56. Panama (7)
57. Papua New Guinea† (73)
58. Paraguay (188)
59. Philippines‡

*† Includes United Nations volunteers.*   *†† United Nations volunteers only.*   *‡ Program temporarily suspended.*

Editorial Research Reports / January 25, 1991

proposed, "many . . . were frightened by the prospect of the United States loading contingents of beatniks with beards and guitars on jetliners, transporting them to trouble spots and turning them loose with vague admonitions to 'do good.'"[7]

The Peace Corps also was derided by Communist nations as a cover for American spy operations. Soviet and Chinese radio broadcasts beamed to Africa and Southeast Asia predicted that no country in those areas would accept volunteers. A Beijing broadcast to Asia

and Europe in August 1962 said the Peace Corps was a "fifth column of the Pentagon and the U.S. Central Intelligence Agency" and that its mission was "to export counterrevolution on behalf of U.S. imperialism." Humphrey commented on the Communist attacks in a Senate floor speech in September 1962. "I am happy to report," he said, "that the Communists are practically falling over themselves to malign, condemn and vilify the Peace Corps. . . . [This] tells me that the Peace Corps has done an outstanding job."

**actual number of volunteers in the countries as of January 1991. Honduras had the most volunteers (339), followed by Botswana (306), Guatemala (244), Thailand (219) and Zaire (210).**

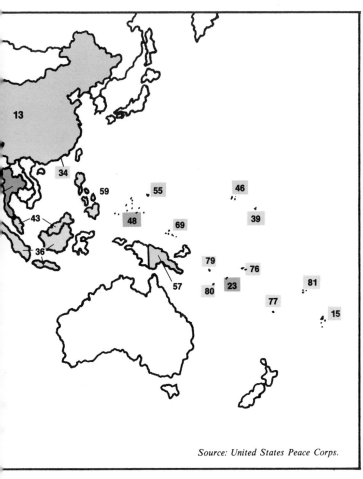

*Source: United States Peace Corps.*

60. Poland (84)
61. Rwanda (18)
62. St. Christopher-Nevis (17)
63. St. Lucia (20)
64. St. Vincent/Grenadines (18)
65. São Tomé (6)
66. Senegal (99)
67. Seychelles (13)
68. Sierra Leone† (107)
69. Solomon Islands (68)
70. Sri Lanka (33)
71. Sudan†† (13)

72. Swaziland (97)
73. Tanzania (45)
74. Thailand† (219)
75. Togo (91)
76. Tokelau†† (1)
77. Tonga (52)
78. Tunisia (72)
79. Tuvalu (3)
80. Vanuatu† (6)
81. Western Samoa (60)
82. Yemen‡
83. Zaire (210)

From the outset, the agency has had three distinct but interrelated goals. These are, in the words of the Peace Corps enabling law; (1) "to help the people of ... [host] countries and areas in meeting their needs for trained manpower, particularly in meeting the basic needs of those living in the poorest areas of such countries"; (2) "to help promote a better understanding of the American people on the part of the peoples served"; and (3) "a better understanding of other peoples on the part of the American people."

In addition, Peace Corps officials developed standards early on that still guide the selection of projects and countries: (1) A country must request Peace Corps aid. No volunteers are to be sent unless asked. (2) Agency officials should strive for balanced geographical distribution of host countries. (3) There must be a clear need for Peace Corps assistance. (4) Host countries must indicate that they intend to adopt measures for economic and social reform. (5) Peace Corps projects should never provide skills already sufficiently available in the country or fill a job that a skilled national of the country could fill. (6) The host country, so far as possible, should participate in the project and be able to carry on with it after the Peace Corps volunteers have left. (7) The project should have a significant impact on the host country in terms of psychological and educational effect and should stimulate related activities there.

Still another legacy of the Peace Corps' early days is Shriver's horror of bureaucratic stagnation. To guard against the chance that the agency would eventually be taken over by practitioners of the ways that things have always been done, Shriver devised the "five-year rule." This requirement limited all Peace Corps employees, up to and including the director, to no more than five consecutive years of service with the agency. The purpose was to assure a constant influx of new blood and fresh ideas.

James V. Bullard, a former Peace Corps volunteer who is now assistant director of promotion for *National Geographic* magazine, says the five-year rule was "one of the most powerful forces" within the Peace Corps organization. "The idea was, if tenure was limited to five years, only people who really wanted to work at Peace Corps would actually sign up," Bullard says. "And from the first day, they'd realize they had just five years to contribute. Whatever they wanted to accomplish, they'd know they had better get to work on it right away. The rule was brilliant. It made Peace Corps the most exciting, stimulating place to work."

The five-year limit still is in place, though with certain modifications. The rule has been amended to permit routine extensions of one year as well as an additional extension of 2½ years for up to 15 percent of the agency's U.S.-based staff. "Nevertheless, this employment limitation eliminates any possibility of a continuous long-term career in the Peace Corps," [8] the U.S. General Accounting Office observed in a report issued last spring.

### Peace Corps' ups and downs since agency was created

The Peace Corps grew steadily during the Kennedy and Lyndon B. Johnson administrations, reaching its all-time high total of 15,556 volunteers and trainees in fiscal year 1966. But the accession of Richard M. Nixon to the presidency in 1969 ushered in a long period of turmoil at the agency.

At first, rumors circulated that Nixon planned to abolish the Peace Corps, since he had been a longtime critic. Instead, he set about reshaping it. In the most significant change, the Nixon administration shifted recruiting away from the enthusiastic but inexperienced recent college graduates who had made up the bulk of volunteers until then. Under a program that new Peace Corps Director Joseph Blatchford called "New Directions," the agency sought older, more skilled volunteers who could offer greater technical competence.

In 1971, Nixon transferred the Peace Corps to ACTION, an agency he created by executive order to consolidate all federal volunteer programs.* Blatchford was appointed director of the new agency. Under ACTION, the Peace Corps became part of the federal bureaucracy. Volunteers, who had never felt they were federal employees, were directed by civil servants for the first time. The Peace Corps' administrative machinery was radically overhauled in the spring of 1972. Half of the country directors and 250 senior staff members in Washington were fired.

Blatchford was replaced as ACTION director early in 1973 by Michael P. Balzano, who had been a staff assistant at the White House. Balzano's "primary interests in the . . . Peace Corps seemed to be making it more cost-effective," former Peace Corps staffers Kevin Lowther and C. Payne Lucas wrote in 1978. "[T]his meant reducing staff and other support for volunteers — thus reducing both cost and effectiveness. . . . Under Balzano, the Peace Corps stagnated as it settled slowly into oblivion, a relic of the Soaring Sixties, forgotten at home and barely tolerated abroad." [9] Balzano, who served as director until January 1977, insisted that the smaller budgets stemmed not from an administration decision but from the fact that the Peace Corps was losing popularity both at home and overseas.

Democrat Jimmy Carter's election as president in 1976 brought no relief to the embattled Peace Corps. On the contrary, internal conflict became even more bitter under the ACTION director appointed by Carter — Sam Brown, a longtime New Left activist. Brown, wrote former Peace Corps volunteer T. Zane Reeves, "argued that volunteers should function as political organizers rather than as neutral observers. They should help organize oppressed peoples in developing countries rather than support petty right-wing dictators.

Supposedly peripheral Peace Corps projects such as recreation or teaching English as a second language were scrapped in favor of projects that addressed basic human needs in underdeveloped societies." [10]

Ironically, the Peace Corps began to recover its equilibrium during the conservative Republican administration of President Ronald Reagan. To head the Peace Corps, Reagan appointed Loret Miller Ruppe, who was to be a forceful advocate for the agency during her more than seven years as director. In another pivotal development, Congress in 1981 approved legislation formally separating the Peace Corps from ACTION.

During Senate debate on the issue, Sen. Alan Cranston, D-Calif., noted that ACTION Director Thomas Pauken had served with military intelligence units in Vietnam. Consequently, Cranston said, foreign countries might suspect that the Peace Corps had clandestine links to U.S. intelligence agencies. But in addition to dispelling these suspicions, Cranston said, separating the Peace Corps from ACTION would remove it from "unnecessary layers of bureaucracy — a bureaucracy that saps its strength and vitality."

The Peace Corps received still another boost in 1985, when Congress established an objective of 10,000 volunteers for the agency. At the time, only about half that many volunteers were active. The goal was written into the International Security and Development Cooperation Act of 1985, which declared it to be "the policy of the United States and a purpose of the Peace Corps to maintain, to the maximum extent appropriate and consistent with programmatic and fiscal considerations, a volunteer corps of at least 10,000 individuals." The legislation did not specify a deadline for reaching the 10,000 target. However, Ruppe and congressional leaders agreed in a subsequent exchange of letters to set a deadline of 1992. The deadline has since been moved back, to 1997.

## Agency's persistent problems in reaching recruiting goals

Even that may turn out to be wishful thinking. Despite the establishment of new programs in Eastern Europe and elsewhere in the past year, the number of active volunteers has changed little from the 6,264 employed in fiscal 1985. Lack of sufficient funding is one reason why the agency has been unable to expand more rapidly. Other contributing factors include difficulties in recruiting minorities and persons possessing skills wanted by Peace Corps host countries.

The minority-recruitment problem, such as it is, dates from the Peace Corps' earliest days. Numerous observers have asserted that blacks and other minorities of college age often view the Peace Corps as a club for middle-class whites. Furthermore, it is said that minorities feel more financial pressure to embark on

*The two main components of ACTION were the Peace Corps and Volunteers in Service to America (VISTA), sometimes called "the domestic Peace Corps." Founded in 1964, VISTA provides opportunities for volunteers to work on anti-poverty projects in the United States and its territories. Other ACTION programs included, at one time or another, the Foster Grandparent Program, the Retired Senior Volunteer Program (RSVP), the Senior Companion Program, the National Student Volunteer Program, the Urban Crime Prevention Program and the National Center for Service Learning.

their life's work immediately after college.

Edward J. Slevin, the Peace Corps' associate director for volunteer recruitment and selection, disputes the notion that minorities present unusual problems. He notes that more than 10 percent of all trainees who joined the Peace Corps in the current "program year" * were minorities — the first time, as far as he can determine, that this level of minority participation has been achieved.

Slevin also challenges the accuracy of statements that minorities regard the Peace Corps as a sanctuary for middle-class whites. "I don't think, from my experience in the field, that that's a general attitude minorities have," he says. Slevin makes the additional point that Peace Corps recruiters who visit college campuses "don't talk about anything any differently before minorities than they do [before] anybody else."

The Peace Corps' primary recruiting goal, Slevin says, is to "fill as close to 100 percent of the host country's requests for skills as we can. At the same time, we try to make the Peace Corps' presence more reflective of our society today; it isn't all 25-year-old single white males. We aim for a cross-section of ethnic groups and ages, marital status and so on. Our goal this year was 10 percent [minorities], and we met that. Next year, we're going to be shooting for 13 percent."

Slevin says the Peace Corps does not recruit generalist volunteers because it receives many more applications from generalists than it can accept. "What we want are the scarce skills," he says. "So our recruiters go to campuses where those skills are taught. They give classroom talks or try to persuade professors in fields like agriculture, math or the sciences to encourage some of their students to consider joining the Peace Corps."

Some countries request specific credentials as well as specific skills. "Countries that had a strong colonial background — ones that were ruled by France or Britain, let's say — tend to ask for volunteers with advanced degrees," Slevin says. "We've tried to steer them away from that and toward a competency-based system."

When Slevin was Peace Corps country director in the Philippines in the mid-1980s, he says he learned to appreciate the importance of prior experience on construction projects. "We found that the best volunteers, the most productive ones, were people who came out of the building trades," he says. "Or, perhaps, a person who went to college and spent his summers working as a carpenter. So we try to persuade the ministries [in host countries] not to get hung up over academic degrees. We ask them to identify the tasks needed to accomplish their goals and to let the Peace Corps worry about finding people with the skills to do the work."

Recruitment is only one of the Peace Corps' recur-

*The current program year includes spring and summer of fiscal 1990 plus fall and winter of fiscal 1991. The Peace Corps definition of minorities includes not only African Americans but also Hispanics, Asians, Pacific Americans and Native Americans.

rent personnel concerns. The agency also is constantly looking for ways to reduce the high rate of attrition among volunteers. According to the General Accounting Office, 33 percent of all volunteers fail to complete their scheduled two years of service, and 50 percent of older volunteers fail to do so. "Older volunteers often experience difficulties in training, especially with language; reduced ability to suffer difficult logistics; and a greater need for a correct fit between the assignment and the skills of the volunteer," the agency noted in a May 1990 report. "Our interviews with numerous volunteers indicate that early returns not only hurt the volunteers, who may feel a sense of failure at not being able to complete their tours, but also the host government, which may have been counting on a volunteer to perform a specific task, and the Peace Corps, which is seen as unreliable." [11]

In its Oct. 30 semiannual report to Congress, the Peace Corps Office of Inspector General cited the high cost of attrition. "Whenever a volunteer wishes to end service for any reason," the report said, "the agency pays all expenses in returning the volunteer home to the United States. The costs go beyond transportation, however, to the costs of recruiting and training replacement volunteers, and to the other costs associated with the disruption of the volunteer's in-country projects. ... We believe that the constant disruption of the continuity of ... the volunteer work force inhibits effective management and programming, and has become cost-prohibitive." [12]

Slevin says volunteers who are overqualified for their job assignments are more likely than others to drop out. He adds, however, that "going home early is usually due to a combination of factors. In some cases, reality fails to meet expectations. It could also be loneliness — or illness. In my experience, it takes two or three things to make a person decide to terminate Peace Corps service prematurely." Peace Corps Chief of Staff Jody Olsen reports that the agency recently began a study aimed at pinpointing the reasons for early termination and finding more effective ways of combating the problem. She says the survey is being conducted on a country-by-country basis because the mix of contributing factors may differ markedly from place to place.[13]

## Peace Corps' scramble for sufficient funding

The chief obstacle blocking achievement of the Peace Corps' 10,000-volunteer goal is lack of sufficient funding from Congress. "With a tightening U.S. budget and worsening economic conditions for our host countries," the Peace Corps Office of Inspector General warned last fall, "there is a very real danger that the agency may commit itself to a level of volunteers beyond the resources it has to properly support them.

Despite the fact that Congress continues to increase the agency's operating budget, the desperate requests for volunteers are outstripping the agency's resources." [14]

Although the Peace Corps' appropriations have risen steadily for nearly 20 years, as expressed in current dollars, the increases have failed to keep pace with inflation. Consequently, a different funding picture emerges when the agency's annual appropriations are converted into constant (that is, based on fiscal 1962 purchasing power) dollars. When this is done, the agency's $186 million budget for fiscal 1991 turns out to have less than half the purchasing power of the $114 million appropriation for fiscal 1966. On the other hand, the Peace Corps' fiscal 1991 budget increase of $17.4 million was its largest one-year gain in a quarter-century.

The additional money enabled the agency to expand into Eastern Europe without reducing its support of programs in the Third World, Peace Corps Chief of Staff Jody Olsen reports. In fact, she says, Peace Corps spending in Africa "increased over the last two years and is increasing again next year. The same is true of our programs in Asia, the Pacific and the inter-American region."

But further funding increases will be needed if the Peace Corps is to expand to 10,000 volunteers by 1997, the latest — but not necessarily the last — target date. Peace Corps Director Paul Coverdell has estimated that the agency will need $277.2 million (in 1990 dollars) to support 10,000 volunteers in 1997.

Meanwhile, Peace Corps officials have little choice but to scrimp and trim. The agency annually turns away an estimated 2,000 qualified applicants whom it is unable to place because of funding constraints. By the same token, the Peace Corps could meet many more host-country requests for experienced specialists if it had the money to support the families of married volunteers overseas. Another problem is that the agency's "public awareness" budget now amounts only to a fraction of the 1960s funding level. Increased spending in this area presumably would enhance recruitment and help promote "a better understanding of other peoples on the part of the American people" — one of the Peace Corps' three statutory goals (*see p. 57*).

Some such efforts are under way, however, including the agency's World Wise Schools Program. Participating U.S. schools are paired with a Peace Corps volunteer currently on assignment overseas. Through exchanges of letters and other materials, the American pupils gain a deeper understanding of a foreign culture than they could obtain through textbooks.

## Peace Corps in the 1990s: Old goals, shifting tactics

In Jody Olsen's opinion, the Peace Corps' adherence to the three objectives established at its formation have

helped keep the agency on a relatively steady course for 30 years. It hardly needs saying that much has changed in the world during that time. To stay afloat, the Peace Corps has sought to adapt to shifting conditions without compromising its fundamental principles.

Jeff Drumtra, the editor of *WorldView Magazine*, says the mere fact of the agency's survival for three decades speaks volumes about its determination to endure. "There were many people in the early '60s who thought Peace Corps would crumble along with its idealism," he says. "So there probably are quite a few people today who are surprised it has lasted. On the other hand, anyone who has served in Peace Corps *isn't* surprised — because it works, it's flexible, it can adapt itself to different countries and different situations. I think anything that adaptable can easily survive whatever is going on in Washington."

As Drumtra sees it, the collapse of communism in Europe will have little effect on the agency — except possibly to encourage more countries to apply for Peace Corps programs. From the early 1960s to the early '80s, he says, many countries "refrained from inviting Peace Corps because they did not want to appear to be taking sides with the United States against the Soviet Union. They viewed [Peace Corps] as a Cold War instrument. Now, with the Cold War melting away, a lot more countries have come out of the woodwork seeking volunteers. For 30 years, they ignored Peace Corps or railed against it as American imperialism. But now they're knocking on Peace Corps' door."

Communism's demise will have no effect on day-to-day Peace Corps operations abroad, Drumtra feels. "In the early '60s, Peace Corps sold itself as an instrument to fight communism. That was primarily for domestic consumption — to rally support for Peace Corps, to get Congress to appropriate money. But when the volunteers went overseas, communism or anticommunism was irrelevant to the lives of most of the people they were working with. Most people [in host countries] were wondering where their next meal was coming from, or how they could dig a well to get drinkable water — and that had nothing to do with whether they were Communists or not. And it had nothing to do with whether you, as a Peace Corps volunteer, were anti-Communist or not. It just didn't come up in conversation."

One ongoing change that Drumtra expects to have a lasting effect is urbanization. "The old scenario of the volunteer living in a mud hut in the middle of nowhere is becoming less and less true," he says. "More and more, you have the volunteer living in a barrio or a densely populated metropolis in Africa. That's where the people are moving. ... Even in the early to mid-1960s, there were quite a few volunteers who had white-collar jobs in national planning bureaus. There has always been a small cadre of white-collar volunteers: more of them now, maybe, because of the shift to

*Continued on p. 62*

# AT ISSUE

*Was it a good idea for the Peace Corps to send volunteers to Eastern Europe?*

## YES

*says* **PAUL D. COVERDELL**, *director of the Peace Corps.*

[S]ome people have asked me if serving in a European country such as Hungary is a radical departure from the traditional Peace Corps assignments in poor, developing nations. My answer is an emphatic "No, but what difference would it make if it were a departure from 'tradition'?"

The fact is that Hungary is not a wealthy country and it has tremendous needs. That includes the need for English teachers — the same need fulfilled in Ghana by the first Peace Corps volunteers in 1961.

As we enter the 1990s, I believe the Peace Corps must be on the leading edge of providing assistance to nations where great instability exists. Countries such as Hungary, Poland and other Eastern European nations are experiencing rapid . . . change. . . .

As its name has always symbolized, the primary mission of the Peace Corps is the promotion of peace. What better opportunity exists to promote peace than to play a positive role in bringing peaceful change to societies that have been turned literally upside down by events of revolutionary dimensions?

Having met more than 1,000 volunteers in 17 nations, I know these are extraordinary Americans who welcome the opportunity to serve under difficult conditions and who are capable of meeting the world's toughest challenges. I know they can make significant contributions in any nation that seeks assistance, whether it is teaching English in Hungary or nutrition in Haiti.

The Cold War has ended, and totalitarianism was clearly the loser. We are entering a new era in world history — an era that is both exciting and perilous. Democracy and free enterprise may eventually prove to be the dominant political and economic forces on the globe.

In the 1990s, . . . the Peace Corps will send volunteers to developing nations to help produce more food, to help educate the people and to help improve health care. But we must not stop there. Although some would argue that the Peace Corps should serve only in the poorest of nations, I reject that argument.

We must not place artificial barriers on the pursuit of peace. It is as important to teach Hungarians the international language of commerce as it is to teach Hondurans to grow crops on hillsides. It is as important to promote small-business development in Poland as it is to teach child nutrition in Paraguay.

*From* The Atlanta Journal-Constitution, *Dec. 25, 1989.*

## NO

*says* **EDWARD PATRICK HEALY**, *former Peace Corps director in Zaire.*

The Peace Corps . . . was ill served by two recent decisions of Director Paul Coverdell, both of which betrayed that he and the Bush administration do not understand much about the genesis of the Peace Corps' political strategy abroad.

In the biggest apparent change, it was announced that volunteers will soon go to Eastern Europe, thus joining the rush to redistribute even that small percentage of U.S. resources allocated to Third World countries to the more understandable, more personally felt problems of Europe.

But the Peace Corps was conceived as a way for the idealism and skills of U.S. citizens to help countries with severe development needs. As a former deputy Peace Corps director in Brazil . . . , I know that in the course of their service the volunteers and our country received as much as the recipient country from these encounters. . . .

The countries of Eastern Europe do not need expatriate teachers. Indeed, they are among the world's best-educated countries, with a literacy rate that is as high or higher than ours and universities that had world renown before there was a United States. Even those arguing from the short-term needs arising from Communist mismanagement must in fairness concede that those needs hardly equal those of countries where development, and the Peace Corps' contribution to it, may be the only alternative to death by starvation or disease.

Why are the volunteers being sent to Eastern Europe? I am forced to conclude that as an inexpensive and quickly marshaled development device, they are seen by the Bush administration as a means of muting some of the disappointment . . . of countries that are asking for money we no longer have.

The second change, renaming the Peace Corps as the United States Peace Corps, . . . is actually the biggest change of the two, because it represents a change in spirit which may be impossible to ever withdraw. It diminishes . . . the image of the Peace Corps in the countries it serves — the belief that . . . it is there because of the country's need, and not a response to U.S. geopolitical strategy, such as the decision to send volunteers to Eastern Europe. . . .

I find the changes disturbing. The Peace Corps can recover from a few years of ineffective programs in Eastern Europe, but if it becomes politicized, its clear call to the best in all of us could be . . . stilled.

*From* The Washington Post, *May 29, 1990.*

*Continued from p. 60*
urban areas, but I don't think that's necessarily bad. It's just a different image.

"You may not like the change, and I'm not sure I do. I was a volunteer, and my most precious memory is of being in a very rural setting, waking up at 5 a.m. to the sound of a rooster crowing, living outdoors and riding a horse. That experience is very important to me. But for a lot of [today's] volunteers, the experience will involve dodging traffic on the way to a high-rise office where they will help design water-filtration systems, or something. The need for volunteers still exists; it's just that the context is different."

Robert Berg of the International Development Conference believes that the Peace Corps should devote more of its efforts overseas to institution-building. "The Peace Corps is sporadic about that," he says. "It isn't a central [planning] feature. There are too many cases where the agency thinks the best thing it can do is provide technicians, and nothing else.

"Let's consider Czechoslovakia. If you look at statistics on the number of publishing houses and volunteer organizations that were in existence there in the late '40s and then were terminated when the Communists took over, you realize that pluralism was alive and functioning to a marvelous extent. That's what the Peace Corps ought to be helping [to resurrect] now. Providing only technical services would be unfortunate."

Berg also feels that the Peace Corps ought to enter into joint development projects with other countries. The agency, he says, "should be doing three-cornered deals where we and Brazil, say, team up with Mozambique or Angola. I have talked to the Brazilians about this. There are lots of things that could be done creatively in poorer countries or by giving status and responsibility to barely middle-class countries like Brazil."

Peace Corps Director Coverdell says he feels a "certain reticence" about adopting Berg's proposal. "The reticence is framed in strictly administrative terms," he says. "We already face difficulties in dealing with Congress, with volunteers, with determining what medical procedures and standards [for treating volunteers overseas] will be. Then I begin to imagine dealing also with the Brazilian Congress and president and wondering if their medical standards are the same as ours, and I see an organization that has become administratively unwieldy."

"One of the things that's impressive about Peace Corps," Coverdell adds, "is that we're reasonably fleet of foot. When an opportunity occurs, we can get there fast. The Central European thing is a classic example. We've gone there in a short time frame, while others are still thinking about it. I think it's useful to keep Peace Corps that way."

So no joint ventures of the sort envisioned by Berg are in the works at this time. All the same, Peace Corps officials are open to cooperative ventures with other agencies of the federal government. This represents a policy shift from the agency's early years, when it flaunted its newness and determination to be independent by holding itself aloof from the State Department and other mainstays of the executive branch.

Today, in contrast, the Peace Corps has helped arrange a number of joint programs with other governmental units, including the Department of Health and Human Services and the Agency for International Development. "For example, we have an agreement with the Environmental Protection Agency [EPA] under which they provide technical people to help us with our pre-service and on-site training of volunteers," Olsen says. "EPA does that free of charge. But they benefit from the arrangement, too, because it gives them a short-term opportunity to go to one of these [Peace Corps] countries to conduct the training."

Olsen says the Peace Corps is trying to set up similar joint programs with other federal agencies. "International development is a collaborative effort," she says. "No one agency can do it all alone." Coverdell is an enthusiastic supporter of interagency collaboration and would like to see much more of it. "I think Peace Corps, which has an environmental section now, will likely consort with EPA even more dramatically in Central Europe as these programs unfold," he says. "We'll find new and better avenues for putting the parts going together to produce a greater whole. We've only just scratched the surface."

# NOTES

[1] Peace Corps Office of Inspector General, *Semiannual Report to Congress,* Oct. 30, 1990, p. 4.
[2] Peace Corps/Hungary Program Design Team, *Findings and Recommendations,* October 1989, p. 10.
[3] Quoted by Susan Dillingham in "Peace Corps Broadens Its Horizons," *Insight,* Aug. 21, 1989, p. 22.
[4] *The Washington Post,* May 29, 1990.
[5] Peace Corps news release, Jan. 4, 1990.
[6] U.S. General Accounting Office, *Peace Corps: Meeting the Challenges of the 1990s,* May 1990, p. 18.
[7] Address to the National Press Club, Washington, D.C., Oct. 18, 1962.
[8] General Accounting Office, *op. cit.,* p. 12.
[9] Kevin Lowther and C. Payne Lucas, *Keeping Kennedy's Promise* (1978), p. 17. Lowther served as a Peace Corps training officer in Africa in the 1960s. Lucas served as deputy regional director of the African regional office and subsequently as regional director of that office in the 1960s.
[10] T. Zane Reeves, *The Politics of the Peace Corps and VISTA* (1988), p. 159.
[11] U.S. General Accounting Office, *op. cit.,* pp. 38-39.
[12] Peace Corps Office of Inspector General, *op. cit.,* p. 5.
[13] Remarks in a luncheon address before the Washington Chapter of the Society for International Development, Washington, D.C., Jan. 10, 1991.
[14] Peace Corps Office of Inspector General, *op. cit.,* p. 3.

*Graphics: Cover, Margaret Scott; pp. 56-7, Jack Auldridge.*

## RECOMMENDED READING

## BOOKS

**Hoopes, Roy,** *The Complete Peace Corps Guide*, **The Dial Press, 1961.**

This book, published the year the Peace Corps was established, obviously is not the source to turn to for a review of the agency's performance to date. But it contains as complete an account of the Peace Corps' origins as can be found in more recent works.

**Redmon, Coates,** *Come As You Are: The Peace Corps Story*, **Harcourt Brace Jovanovich, 1986.**

Redmon, a former feature editor of *Glamour* magazine and former senior writer for the Peace Corps, relates the story of the agency's formative years in anecdotal fashion.

**Reeves, T. Zane,** *The Politics of the Peace Corps and VISTA*, **The University of Alabama Press, 1988.**

Reeves, a former Peace Corps volunteer, focuses on the ideological infighting that has erupted periodically at his old agency and at VISTA (sometimes referred to as "the domestic Peace Corps"). "[A] particular ideological viewpoint is enforced within each party when it is in control of the presidency," he writes. "These ideologies differ markedly in the underlying assumptions regarding poverty, its causes and cures, and the proper role of agency volunteers."

**Rice, Gerard T.,** *The Bold Experiment: JFK's Peace Corps*, **University of Notre Dame Press, 1985.**

One of several histories of the Peace Corps published in the agency's 25th anniversary year, Rice's book is perhaps the most comprehensive of the lot. Besides reviewing all the maneuvering that preceded the Peace Corps' birth, Rice examines historical precedents for the volunteer-service concept, including philosopher William James' proposals in his famed 1911 essay, "The Moral Equivalent of War."

**Sadow, Sue,** *Into Africa With the Peace Corps*, **Beaumont Books, 1986.**

Sadow, the first senior citizen to become a Peace Corps volunteer, recounts her experiences as a teacher in Sierra Leone from 1961 to 1963.

**Viorst, Milton, ed.,** *Making a Difference: The Peace Corps at Twenty-Five*, **Weidenfeld & Nicolson, 1986.**

The essays in this anthology, published to coincide with the agency's silver anniversary, are grouped under the headings "The Ideal," "The People," "The Job" and "The Place." Many of the contributions consist of on-the-scene reports from volunteers.

## ARTICLES

**Marshall, Marilyn, "The Peace Corps: Alive and Well, and Looking for Blacks,"** *Ebony*, **October 1984.**

Marshall examines the Peace Corps' longstanding policy of encouraging minorities to become volunteers as well as the reasons why blacks have been reluctant to join the organization.

**Shute, Nancy, "After a Turbulent Youth, the Peace Corps Comes of Age,"** *Smithsonian*, **February 1986.**

Shute assesses the overall record of the Peace Corps while chronicling the activities of several Peace Corps volunteers in a remote area of Ecuador.

## REPORTS AND STUDIES

**American Enterprise Institute,** *The Peace Corps: Myths and Prospects*, **1978.**

The author of this "special analysis," Michael P. Balzano, served from 1973 to 1977 as the director of ACTION, the umbrella group of which the Peace Corps was part for a decade. Balzano generally is critical of the agency. The Peace Corps' presence, he writes, "is taken by some countries as an admission of poverty and dependence. Many nations that might need and want the technical assistance the Peace Corps could provide do not want to be saddled with the stigma it represents."

**U.S. General Accounting Office,** *Peace Corps: Meeting the Challenges of the 1990s*, **May 1990.**

Written in typical no-nonsense GAO style, this report lays particular stress on what it regards as the Peace Corps' subpar performance in minority recruitment — an area in which agency officials claim to have made substantial progress over the past year.

**U.S. General Accounting Office,** *Peace Corps: A Statistical Profile*, **July 1989.**

Consisting almost entirely of graphics, this brief report presents year-by-year data on Peace Corps funding, volunteer age groups, size of the volunteer force and other statistics in easy-to-grasp form.

**Peace Corps Office of Inspector General,** *Semiannual Report to Congress*, **Oct. 30, 1990.**

A balance sheet of the Peace Corps' strengths and weaknesses, this report sometimes seems to be straining hard to find negative things to say.

EDITORIAL RESEARCH REPORTS

*Coming soon*

■ Recession
■ Puerto Rico
■ Redistricting

Published weekly by
Congressional Quarterly
Inc., Editorial Research
Reports analyze emerging
issues of national interest
across a broad range of
social, scientific, political
and economic fields.
Reports are bound and
indexed for permanent
reference. Subscription
information is available
through Congressional
Quarterly's Publications
Sales Department by
telephone (202) 887-8665.
Copies of past issues are
available through
Customer Service, (202)
887-8621.

FEBRUARY 1, 1991    ERR

FOUNDED 1923

CONGRESSIONAL QUARTERLY'S
EDITORIAL RESEARCH REPORTS

# RECESSION'S REGIONAL IMPACT

# EDITORIAL RESEARCH REPORTS

**EDITOR**
**MARCUS D. ROSENBAUM**

**MANAGING EDITOR**
**SANDRA STENCEL**

**ASSOCIATE EDITOR**
**RICHARD L. WORSNOP**

**STAFF WRITERS**
**MARY H. COOPER**
**PATRICK G. MARSHALL**

**PRODUCTION EDITOR**
**LAURIE DE MARIS**

**EDITORIAL ASSISTANT**
**AMY GORTON**

**RICHARD M. BOECKEL (1892-1975)**
**FOUNDER**

**PUBLISHED BY**
**CONGRESSIONAL QUARTERLY INC.**

**CHAIRMAN**
**ANDREW BARNES**

**PRESIDENT**
**RICHARD R. EDMONDS**

**EDITOR AND PUBLISHER**
**NEIL SKENE**

**EXECUTIVE EDITOR**
**ROBERT W. MERRY**

EDITORIAL RESEARCH REPORTS (LIBRARY OF CONGRESS CATALOGUE NO. 39-924; ISSN 0013-0958). Published weekly (48 times per year, excluding March 1, May 3, August 2 and November 1, 1991) by Congressional Quarterly Inc., 1414 22nd Street NW, Washington, D.C. 20037. Rates are furnished upon request. Application to mail at second-class postage rates is pending at Washington, D.C. POSTMASTER: Send address changes to EDITORIAL RESEARCH REPORTS, 1414 22nd Street NW, Washington, D.C. 20037.

# RECESSION'S REGIONAL IMPACT

*by Mary H. Cooper*

The nation is in an economic recession, and while most states are feeling the pinch, some regions are faring better than others. New England has been hurt the hardest, and now the recession is deepening in other states along the Atlantic and Pacific Coasts. The Midwest and the South Central states are weathering the downturn better than they did in previous postwar recessions, but the nation's heartland may not be able to avoid the recession altogether. And how quickly any part of the country recovers depends to a great extent on what happens in the Persian Gulf.

The Bush administration has finally acknowledged what American consumers have known for months. "[I]t does appear that, after the longest economic expansion in the peacetime history of the United States, the economy probably has entered a recession," Michael J. Boskin, chairman of the president's Council of Economic Advisers, said in a recent television interview.[1]

Traditionally, economists pronounce the onset of a recession after the gross national product (GNP), the total value of the nation's output of goods and services, falls for two consecutive quarters. This time, however, economic forecasters moved up the official timetable. The National Bureau of Economic Research, a nonprofit think tank in Cambridge, Mass., that serves as the official timekeeper for the country's business cycles, announced Dec. 26 that the recession probably began sometime between June and September of 1990.*

The Commerce Department now says that GNP dropped 2.1 percent in the fourth quarter of 1990. This was the first quarterly drop in nearly five years and the largest drop since 1982, during the last recession. The Congressional Budget Office estimates that GNP will fall by an additional 1.7 percent in the first three months of this year.

Even before the year-end economic statistics were released, however, economists pointed to the data that were available as clear evidence that the recession had finally arrived. In November, for example, unemployment rose to a three-year high of 5.9 percent, construction spending fell to its lowest level in 11 months and the index of leading economic indicators** — the government's main forecasting tool — fell for the fifth month in a row. In December, industrial output fell for the third month in a row. In the last quarter of 1990 that important indicator of economic conditions fell by 8 percent, the sharpest drop in eight years.

But what stands out among all these national statistics is the current recession's unusual regional impact. "There is no question that there are regional differences," says Donald Ratajczak, director of economic forecasting at Georgia State University. "New England is getting smashed, California is starting to fade in the West, while the Midwest is holding up fairly satisfactorily because of export activity." The concentration of economic hardship on the East and West coasts contrasts sharply with the 1981-82 recession, when the industrial heartland suffered far more than the rest of the country.

It all began in the Northeastern states, where real estate values soared during the 1980s. "The Northeast, where the recession started in 1989, overbuilt, particularly in the commercial construction real estate market," says Clair Asklund, director of regional research at DRI/McGraw-Hill Inc., an economic research firm in Lexington, Mass. "The subsequent failure of financial institutions [in the region] added to consumer nervousness weakening industries throughout the trade and service sectors."

As real estate values peaked, homeowners found they could no longer sell their houses profitably and developers could no longer find tenants for commercial space. As mortgage loans went bad, banks saw profits plunge and began cutting back operations.

---

*The National Bureau of Economic Research's Business Cycle Dating Committee is expected to make its final determination about the onset of the recession within the next three months. The organization began tracking business cycles shortly after its founding in 1921. Since 1961, the U.S. Department of Commerce has published the bureau's findings in its official publication, now called the *Survey of Current Business*.

**Leading indicators are measures of economic activity, such as unemployment rates and corporations' plans to invest in new plants and equipment, that usually reach peaks and troughs before the rest of the economy.

For example, New York-based Citicorp, the biggest commercial bank in the country, recently announced it would lay off 8,000 employees, about 8.5 percent of its payroll.[2]

Unlike previous downturns, when consumers stopped buying only after manufacturers began closing factories, consumer behavior has played an important role in launching the current recession. "This particular recession is much more tied to consumer activity," Asklund says. "There is a tendency for it to be a national mood, although it's clearly worse in the Northeast at the moment."

Asklund attributes the falloff in consumer buying to the excesses of the 1980s. "It has to be put into the context of how the economy moved along through the mid- to late 1980s," he says. "We really did grow sharply, we were running at unemployment rates that were below balanced levels to keep inflation in check, and then people began to get a little nervous and started to pull back as they worried about their jobs. So the stimulus of that steady, strong spending has dropped off sharply."

What finally turned the economic downturn into a full-blown recession, many economists say, was the specter of war in the Middle East. The crisis began on Aug. 2, when Iraqi forces invaded Kuwait, and culminated in the outbreak of hostilities in mid-January. "Uncertainty in the Middle East, I would argue, [was] the major cause" of the recession, says Art Rolnick, senior vice president and director of research at the Federal Reserve Bank of Minneapolis. "That uncertainty [caused] a big drop in consumer confidence."

A big factor in this uncertainty was the fear that a war would further drive up oil prices. Prices rose sharply after the invasion, from $16 a barrel to a peak of $41 in early October. They then settled at $25-$30 a barrel after mid-November. So far, the fear of market disruption from war has proved unfounded. When hostilities finally broke out Jan. 16, the stock market rose and oil prices initially fell, returning within days to their prewar level of between $25 and $30 a barrel.

But many economists say it's a mistake to take these initial market reactions too seriously. "These are very volatile and highly sensitive markets, and I don't think they give you any reflection about the long-term prospects for the United States," says Jeff Faux, president of the Economic Policy Institute in Washington. "They are very misleading."

A protracted war in the Middle East could have "dire consequences" for the U.S. economy, Faux says. If the war causes a major cutoff of world oil supplies, for example, oil prices could soar. Analysts say a rise in oil prices to $50 a barrel would be enough to plunge the entire international economy into a severe depression.

"It will depend entirely on the direction of the war," says Philip K. Verleger Jr., an oil expert at the Institute for International Economics in Washington. "If [Iraqi President Saddam] Hussein has no success in

# The Recession's Impact on State and Local Governments

The recession is taking its toll on state and local governments, which are facing fiscal crises of unprecedented scope this year. Economic downturns always have the effect of reducing government revenues because as profits and incomes fall so, too, do tax payments by businesses and consumers. But this time there is another reason for the sudden depletion of government coffers.

Since the 1981-82 recession, the federal government has greatly reduced its payments to state and local governments. As long as the economy grew, as it did for the last eight years, state and local governments were able to absorb the greater financial burden fiscal federalism placed on them because prosperity meant higher tax revenues.

But as the economy began slowing in late 1989 and then contracted in the last quarter of 1990, many governments faced severe budget shortfalls. At the same time that tax revenues are shrinking, welfare and unemployment benefit rolls are growing. According to the National Governors' Association and the National Association of State Budget Officers, 28 state governments are now running budget deficits, for a total

shortfall of almost $10 billion.

Of course, budget deficits are nothing new to American government. But unlike the federal government, which has run a deficit every year since 1970, deficit spending is not an option for most state governments. All states except Vermont are required by law to balance their budgets.

Mirroring the recession's regional impact, the states' fiscal woes are most severe in the Northeast, California and Michigan, home of the ailing U.S. automakers. California alone faces a record deficit of $6 billion. But other states whose economies have been less severely damaged by the recession also are facing huge budget deficits. Virginia, for example, is expected to have a $2 billion shortfall this year.

Many of the country's biggest cities are suffering similar fiscal emergencies. Philadelphia barely managed to avoid bankruptcy in mid-January when it obtained a $150 million loan to tide the city over the winter. New York City Mayor David N. Dinkins has proposed eliminating almost 25,000 city jobs, mostly in the Board of Education, cutting social services and raising taxes and

user fees to overcome a projected $2.2 billion deficit. The recession pushed Washington, D.C.'s, projected deficit from $114 million in fiscal 1990 to $300 million for fiscal 1991.

Like the states, cities have lost federal funding over the past decade. The U.S. Conference of Mayors estimates that the federal contribution to city budgets has fallen from 18 percent of their budgets in 1980 to 6 percent a decade later.[†]

Governors and mayors alike are contemplating dire measures to meet their budget targets. Many will follow the lead of 26 states that raised taxes last year by a total of more than $10.3 million. Most are making severe cutbacks in spending for such essential services as education, fire stations and police forces.[††] More than half of the 50 cities surveyed by the Conference of Mayors raised taxes last year and 40 percent raised taxes on utilities, admission charges for zoos, parks and museums or user fees.

[†] *United States Conference of Mayors,* City Fiscal Conditions 1980-1990, *January 1991.*

[††] *National Governors' Association and National Association of State Budget Officers,* Fiscal Survey of the States, *September 1990.*

---

getting at the Saudi [oil] fields or interdicting Saudi supplies, I don't see much of an impact. If Hussein is able to get at Saudi oil, is able to disrupt refining capacity or shipping around the world, then it has an impact. To date he hasn't had any success."

## How the current downturn differs from last recession

All recessions have certain things in common. As business conditions worsen, employers cut back on production and lay off workers. With rising unemployment, fewer consumers are in a position to spend money. Even those who are still employed tend to reduce consumption out of fear of their own employment prospects. As consumers cut back, producers can sell fewer goods and services and they lay off more workers. The economy enters into a vicious cycle of layoffs, spending cutbacks and reduced production.

When inventories finally are used up, employers begin hiring workers once again. This boosts consumer confidence as well as incomes. Consumers begin making more purchases, increasing demand and completing the business cycle.

Rising inflation often is the first sign of an impending recession. In an effort to curtail increases in the cost of living, the Federal Reserve, the nation's central bank, raises interest rates, making it more expensive for consumers and businesses to borrow money. When consumers cut back on borrowing, they tend to put off buying unnecessary goods or ones they don't need immediately, especially big-ticket items such as automobiles and large appliances. Businesses also feel the pinch and delay investing in new plants and equipment.

This is what happened during the 1981-82 recession. As a result of the Federal Reserve's campaign to curb inflation, the prime rate, the interest banks charge their most creditworthy customers, stood at 20.5 percent in mid-1981. Factories that were already weakened by low productivity and growing competition from Japanese and European firms were unable to cope when consumers closed their pocketbooks. Massive layoffs and factory closings ensued, especially in the industrial heartland, producing the deepest recession since the Great Depression of the early 1930s.

Eight years later, the downturn looks different. Inflation, which stood at 6.1 percent in 1990, is far below the double-digit levels of the early 1980s. Likewise, interest rates have remained fairly constant at around 10 percent. Although this is high by historical standards, it is virtually unchanged from recent years when the economy was booming. In December, Federal Reserve Chairman Alan Greenspan lowered interest rates, prompting banks to lower their prime rate, the main benchmark rate to which consumer loans are pegged, from 10 percent to 9.5 percent.

So it wasn't high inflation or high interest rates that precipitated the current downturn; rather, many economists say, it was the situation in the Middle East. During the months following Iraq's invasion of Kuwait, businesses and consumers alike cut back on spending. But the possibility of war was not the only factor behind the drop in consumer confidence. Government economic policy did play a role.

Alarmed by the widespread failures of savings-and-loan institutions since the mid-1980s, federal regulators have tightened their grip over lending practices by both S&Ls and commercial banks, requiring them to keep more cash on hand to protect against defaults on mortgages and other loans. As a result, lending institutions in areas under close regulatory scrutiny, such as the Northeast, are unwilling to make loans to many consumers and small businesses, causing a "credit crunch" that is worsening the downturn.

Fortunately, the economic picture is not all bleak. One of the sharpest differences between today's recession and those of the past is the strength of some manufacturing industries, particularly those that export goods such as machine tools and heavy machinery. These are the very industries that took the worst beating in the early 1980s. Now, strong economic growth in Western Europe and East Asia has increased overseas demand for U.S. exports of capital goods, the components of factory assembly lines. At the same time, the dollar's value has fallen, making American products less expensive on world markets. As a result, some export-oriented industries have not yet felt the pinch of the recession.

Enhancing the favorable climate for American exports is the adjustment manufacturers made after the last recession to improve productivity. One of those adjustments was the adoption of "just-in-time" production methods, which Japanese manufacturers had long used to prevent backlogs of unsold inventory. By keeping on hand only enough supplies to keep assembly lines churning out what current demand warrants, American manufacturers have protected themselves from accumulating more inventory of finished products than consumers will buy.

This enables manufacturers to respond more quickly to changes in consumer demand by slowing production at the first signs of a fall in sales. In 1981-82, manufacturers closed hundreds of factories and laid off thousands of workers in an effort to avoid having to add to their already huge inventories of unsold goods. Today, the factory closings and layoffs have not been nearly as severe. "This time it's really not an inventory-driven downward adjustment, and we don't expect too much of it to be that as the recession proceeds," says Donald Ratajczak of Georgia State University.

## 'Bicoastal economy' of the 1980s gives way to a bicoastal recession

The unusual forces at work in the economy today have produced a recession that has markedly different regional impacts than past downturns. "At the onset of the slowdown, it was mainly something that was occurring on both the East and West coasts," says John Savacool, senior vice president of the WEFA Group, an economic forecasting firm in Bala Cynwyd, Pa. "The middle of the country was skating along and they thought they were going to escape it."

Now, as the recession deepens, most parts of the country are feeling the pinch, but to widely differing degrees. What follows is a look at the recession's impact in various regions:

**The Northeast.** No region is feeling economic hardship more acutely than the Northeast, which includes the Atlantic states from Maine to Maryland as well as the District of Columbia. Many of the region's difficulties can be traced to New England, where the recession began in 1989.

According to DRI/McGraw-Hill's fourth-quarter forecast, New England accounts for only 6 percent of the nation's jobs, but will suffer at least 20 percent of the nation's job losses during the recession.[3] Since the beginning of 1989, the region has lost 150,000 jobs, including 85,000 in manufacturing and 60,000 in construction.[4]

Ironically, the same ingredients that accounted for the so-called "Massachusetts miracle" of the 1980s have proved the undoing of the entire six-state New England region. The boom in consumer electronics along Boston's Route 128 corridor spurred the economy of all New England states — Connecticut, Maine, Massachusetts, New Hampshire, Rhode Island and Vermont — attracting suppliers and service businesses such as software firms, retail stores and restaurants. With the influx of new business, property values rose. The region's banks invested heavily in the thriving real estate market. When the bubble burst in 1989, consumers and developers were left with overvalued properties, and lenders were faced with spreading defaults on mortgage loans. According to the Mortgage Bankers Association of America, mortgage delinquencies — pay-

# Job Losses Reflect Recession's Regional Variations

**The effects of the recession have been spread unevenly across the nation. According to forecasts by DRI/McGraw-Hill Inc., an economic research firm in Lexington, Mass., New England will suffer about 20 percent of the nation's job losses during the recession. The Mid-Atlantic states will account for 25 percent of the job losses and the East North Central region for nearly 28 percent. Two regions — the Pacific Southwest and the West South Central states — will enjoy slight employment gains.**

| Region | Number of jobs 3rd quarter 1990 (thousands) | Number of jobs 2nd quarter 1991 (thousands) | Percent growth (annual rates) | Number of jobs lost/gained (thousands) | Share of nation's job loss (%) |
|---|---|---|---|---|---|
| New England (Conn., Maine, Mass., N.H., R.I., Vt.) | 6,410 | 6,306 | - 2.2 | - 104 | 20.3 |
| East South Central (Ala., Ky., Miss., Tenn.) | 6,181 | 6,132 | - 1.1 | - 49 | 9.6 |
| Middle Atlantic (N.J., N.Y., Penn.) | 17,072 | 16,944 | - 1.0 | - 128 | 25.0 |
| East North Central (Ill., Ind., Mich., Ohio, Wisc.) | 18,860 | 18,717 | - 1.0 | - 143 | 27.8 |
| West North Central (Iowa, Kan., Minn., Mo., Neb., N.D., S.D.) | 8,051 | 8,001 | - 0.8 | - 50 | 9.7 |
| Pacific Northwest (Alaska, Idaho, Mont., Ore., Wash., Wyo.) | 4,495 | 4,483 | - 0.4 | - 12 | 2.3 |
| South Atlantic (Del., D.C., Fla., Ga., Md., N.C., S.C., Va., W.Va.) | 19,906 | 19,868 | - 0.3 | - 38 | 7.4 |
| Pacific Southwest (Ariz., Calif., Colo., Hawaii, N.M., Nev., Utah) | 18,302 | 18,304 | 0.0 | + 2 | — |
| West South Central (Ark., La., Okla., Texas) | 10,584 | 10,594 | 0.1 | + 10 | — |
| U.S. Total | 109,861 | 109,348 | - 0.6 | - 513 | |

*Source: DRI/McGraw-Hill U.S. Markets Review, Regional Preview, fourth quarter 1990.*

ments that are at least 30 days late — and loan foreclosures rose in the third quarter of 1990 and are expected to "even drift up a bit more." [5]

Under pressure from federal regulators, the banking industry has cut back on lending, making it harder for businesses to invest and for consumers to buy on credit. After the collapse of Rhode Island's state insurance fund for credit unions, depositors in neighboring states withdrew their savings from federally insured institutions as well, prompting the Federal Deposit Insurance Corporation (FDIC) to intervene. The Jan. 6 rescue of the insolvent Bank of New England Corp., the holding company that owned three of the region's biggest commercial banks, was further evidence of the financial industry's plight.*

The rise in oil prices since last summer is further

undermining economic prospects in the region, where households and businesses depend more heavily on oil for heating and electricity than in other parts of the country. Local industry will continue to suffer as the spreading recession forces businesses throughout the country to cut their orders for New England's high-tech products and machines.

Cutbacks in defense spending are also hurting the region, especially among the shipbuilders in Maine and Connecticut that have depended heavily on Navy contracts. Some of the nation's biggest defense contractors, including United Technologies Corp.'s Pratt & Whitney unit and General Dynamics Corp., have laid off workers from their New England factories.

The war in the Middle East does not necessarily mean more defense jobs for the region. Raytheon Co., which manufactures the Patriot missiles that have proved so effective in destroying Iraqi Scud missiles over Israel and Saudi Arabia, may see an increase in Pentagon orders if the U.S. forces run out of existing

---

*The FDIC took control of the Bank of New England, Connecticut Bank and Trust Co. of Hartford and Maine National Bank of Portland. After pumping $750 million into the three institutions to cover their losses from bad real estate loans, the agency opened them for business the following day.

supplies. But so far inventories of the Patriot and other high-tech weapons built in the Northeast are sufficient to meet the expected demand for them. Although Raytheon and its subcontractors are working round-the-clock shifts to speed production of the Patriot missiles, the Pentagon has merely asked for early delivery of its existing order for about 4,000 Patriots by 1992. The Pentagon will not release information about its weapons stockpiles, but outside analysts say that even an extended air war would not exhaust existing supplies of high-tech weaponry, including aircraft and "smart" bombs and missiles.[6] Contractors that are more likely to see orders rise from Operation Desert Storm are suppliers of relatively low-tech items, such as rifles, uniforms and ammunition, most of which are located outside the region.

Cuts in defense spending also are hurting New England's neighbors in the Middle Atlantic states, especially New Jersey, New York and Pennsylvania, where such large employers as Grumman Corp. and General Electric Aerospace have laid off employees. The Mid-Atlantic states also depend heavily on the financial services industry, and problems in this sector have hurt their economies. The stock market crash of 1987 and the later demise of the junk bond market destroyed numerous securities firms on Wall Street, including Drexel Burnham Lambert Inc., that had prospered during the 1980s. At the same time, problem loans cut into commercial banks' profits, leading many to lay off workers.

In New York City alone, such banking giants as Citicorp, The Chase Manhattan Corp., Manufacturers Hanover Corp. and Chemical Banking Corp. announced layoffs last year totaling 15,500. Largely as a result of the crisis in finance, insurance and real estate, which represent major sources of local employment, the New York metropolitan area lost about 100,000 jobs in private industry in 1990.[7] This was the area's first significant drop in employment since 1982. Growing difficulties in the insurance business also are taking their toll in neighboring Connecticut, where some of the nation's biggest insurance companies are headquartered.*

Not all industries in the region are in a slump. Pharmaceuticals, chemicals, health care and some other service industries continue to thrive in New Jersey, Delaware and other Mid-Atlantic states. But throughout the Northeast, real estate and the financial industry that depends upon it are in a yearlong decline. As S&Ls and banks up and down the Northeast coast have cracked under the strain of overvalued property and consequent loan defaults, even healthy lending institutions have cut back on loans, preventing many small businesses from making the investments they need in order to expand.

**The Southeast.** The states south of the Ohio River and east of the Mississippi River are faring better than their neighbors to the north. As in the rest of the country, economic growth is hampered by the loss of consumer confidence sparked by the situation in the Middle East and the financial sectors' problems. But like most of the Sun Belt, which stretches from coast to coast across the southern half of the country, many parts of the Southeast have attracted businesses from the Midwest and the Northeast. Among the chief attractions are the lower cost of living and cheaper real estate.

This is not to say that the Southeast is without pockets of economic hardship. The Carolinas are suffering substantial job losses because of falling demand for locally produced furniture, textiles and clothing. As the disappointing retail sales during the Christmas season showed, these are among the first items American consumers have stopped buying. However, the region as a whole is expected to weather the recession in relatively good shape.

One strength the Southeast enjoys today is an improving agricultural economy. Following a period of widespread bankruptcies throughout the 1980s, Southern farmers, especially citrus growers, are showing profits once again. The region's harvests of corn, soybeans, peanuts and apples were all above normal in 1990.

The main catalyst for the Southeast's strength is Florida, which boasts one of the few recession-resistant economies in the country. Florida lacks a large manufacturing base, but one of its chief industries, tourism, is proving to be an especially valuable asset today. Some 40 million tourists went to Florida last year, many of them foreigners whose strong currencies are making travel to the United States the biggest bargain it has been in recent memory. Attracted by Florida's sunny climate and such entertainment centers as Walt Disney's Epcot Center in Orlando, foreign tourists are becoming a mainstay of the state's economy.

The crash in real estate values and the S&L crisis did not spare parts of Florida, especially the retirement communities of the Tampa Bay area. Though retirees from the North and Midwest continue to move into the state, the demand for housing has not been strong enough to prevent the fall in real estate values that followed the failure of local lending institutions. Despite this setback, the state as a whole continues to evade a steep downturn. The influx of retirees and tourists is spurring demand for local service and retail businesses. DRI/McGraw-Hill expects Florida to generate one out of every four new jobs in the country by the end of this year.[8]

**The Midwest.** For once, the industrial heartland is not bearing the brunt of the business cycle. The vast region, stretching west from Ohio to the Dakotas and Nebraska and south from the Canadian border to Kansas and Missouri, became known as the Rust Belt after four successive recessions left its manufacturers and other basic industries depleted.

*For background on the insurance industry's problems, see "Is Insurance Going the Way of the S&Ls?" *E.R.R.*, Dec. 21, 1990 (No. 47).

Some areas of the Midwest are suffering today as well, especially Detroit and other centers of auto production, including Cleveland, Chicago and St. Louis. Auto sales across the country are down, the result of the loss of consumer confidence and unwillingness to make big-ticket purchases. St. Louis has also suffered as a result of defense spending cuts, which have hurt McDonnell Douglas Corp. and other local contractors.

But outside these areas, the picture looks brighter for most of the region than it has in previous recessions. "There's no question that we're seeing a slowing here, but the situation clearly is better than in other areas of the country," says Art Rolnick of the Minneapolis Federal Reserve Bank. "Our employment numbers don't look quite as weak and retail sales don't look quite as weak." In addition, the region's banking system has fared relatively well, in large part because the real estate market did not undergo the boom and bust cycle experienced by other regions.

Farming in the Midwest presents a mixed picture. Wheat growers are suffering falling prices, Rolnick says, "but cattle and corn prices are very strong right now, and that money feeds back to the Twin Cities" of Minneapolis and St. Paul.

Many Midwestern cities are no longer as dependent on agriculture as they once were. Iowa's urban centers, for example, host numerous service industries and manufacturers such as Eastman Kodak Co., which is planning to build a biotechnology center in Cedar Rapids. Columbus, Ohio, has found its niche as a retail center; it serves as headquarters for The Limited Inc. fashion stores, Wendy's International Inc. fastfood restaurants and several other nationwide retail and franchise businesses.

The Midwest owes much of its relative economic strength today to the painful adjustment manufacturers undertook after the last recession. By adopting just-in-time production techniques, they have reduced inventories and thus the need to shut down assembly lines for long periods of time in anticipation of an upturn in demand for their products. Many workers who were displaced in the last recession have moved to the Sun Belt states of the South and West to find more available, if less well-paid, jobs in manufacturing and service industries.

But outside events have also helped the Midwest avoid another severe contraction this time. The weak dollar has made its products more competitive on world markets, boosting overseas demand just as domestic demand was falling. Some of the heavy manufacturing industries, which are concentrated in the Midwest, have profited from growing foreign demand for their products, especially manufacturers of farm equipment and machine tools, the capital goods needed to produce finished products and food.

Even the steel industry, which was decimated in the early 1980s by competition from Asian and European producers, has begun exporting again. After adopting the modern production methods introduced

by their overseas competitors, U.S. steelmakers became more efficient over the last decade. Helped by the weak dollar, American steel producers such as Chicago's Inland Steel Industries Inc., have resumed exporting their products to European manufacturers that are expanding production in preparation for the scheduled integration of the European Community in 1992. These exports have helped the industry weather the cutbacks in orders from ailing Detroit automakers.

As the recession moves across the country, however, the Midwest cannot expect to evade economic hard times for long. U.S. manufacturing employment fell by 200,000 jobs in November, the same month that industrial production saw its steepest decline since 1982. In December, some of the same steelmakers that were enjoying a revival in exports announced they would idle furnaces because of the drop in orders from the Big Three automakers.

"The Great Lakes area is starting to turn down," says John Savacool of the WEFA Group. "Some of the euphoria evident in the Midwest is starting to evaporate because it's pretty clear now that as we get a little bit farther into the recession they are not going to be able to escape it."

**The South Central states.** Site of a regional recession in the mid-1980s, Texas and its neighbors are now experiencing a recovery just as the rest of the nation sinks into recession. One of the region's advantages, of course, is its heavy reliance on energy markets, especially oil. The increase in oil prices that followed Iraq's invasion of Kuwait gave oil drillers a much greater incentive to drill new wells and renew extraction from marginal, hard-to-reach fields. This boosted employment in the industry and among support industries, especially those in Texas, Louisiana and Oklahoma.

While new jobs have declined throughout the country since mid-1990, the job market has held up better in the South Central states — Arkansas, Louisiana, Oklahoma and Texas — than anywhere else in the country, according to the Conference Board, a New York economic research organization that publishes a monthly survey of help-wanted advertising by region.[9] But economists stress that the region's economic health is less dependent on oil than in the past. "Oil is a great deal less important than it was in the early 1980s or even in the mid-'80s," says Bill Gruben, a regional economist at the Federal Reserve Bank in Dallas. In this region, Gruben says, "natural gas is also an important reason why people drill holes, and natural gas prices have not been substantively affected by the increase in oil prices."

Few analysts expect an oil boom similar to the one in the early 1980s that sent real estate prices soaring and, when oil prices fell later in the decade, crashing again. In the years since the region's severe downturn at mid-decade, a more diversified industrial base has slowly emerged, especially in Texas, creating the basis

# Economic Recovery Will Be Uneven

**Employment growth is an important indicator of the state of the economy. The maps below show employment-growth projections prepared by DRI/McGraw Hill, an economic research firm in Lexington, Mass. The map on the left shows projected employment growth from the third quarter of 1990 to the second quarter of 1991. The map on the right shows projected employment growth from the second quarter of 1991 to the fourth quarter of 1993. According to these projections, the Pacific Southwest and the South Atlantic regions will lose the fewest jobs in the early part of the recession and will bounce back the fastest.**

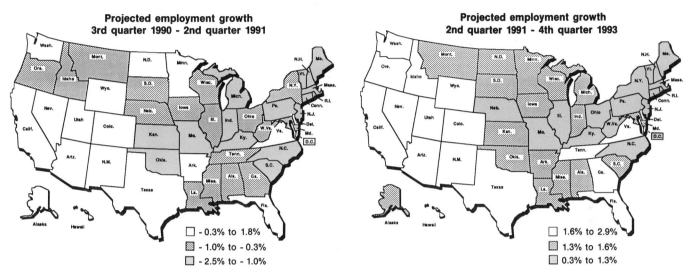

**Projected employment growth
3rd quarter 1990 - 2nd quarter 1991**

☐ - 0.3% to 1.8%
▥ - 1.0% to - 0.3%
▨ - 2.5% to - 1.0%

**Projected employment growth
2nd quarter 1991 - 4th quarter 1993**

☐ 1.6% to 2.9%
▥ 1.3% to 1.6%
▨ 0.3% to 1.3%

*Source: DRI/McGraw-Hill U.S. Markets Review*, Regional Preview, fourth quarter 1990.

for a healthier economy throughout the region.

Today, the South Central states offer an attractive environment for a wide array of businesses seeking a less expensive environment than the Northeast and Midwest. DRI/McGraw-Hill estimates that Texas has added almost two jobs for each one it lost during the 1986 oil recession.[10] Many of these new jobs have come with the relocation of corporate headquarters from the beleaguered Northeast. The 1989 transfer of J. C. Penney Co. from New York City and GTE Corp.'s telephone operations from Stamford, Conn., has boosted employment in the Dallas-Fort Worth area. The influx of new business to the area should help it weather the Pentagon's decision in January to cancel production of the Navy's A-12 Stealth carrier-based jet, which is expected to cost 8,000 jobs. Most of these would be in the Fort Worth area, where production of the new aircraft was centered.

The South Central region has lost relatively few manufacturing jobs thus far, a fact that Gruben attributes to diversification. "We've had some small declines in manufacturing employment over the last year, but it hasn't been anything like the rest of the United States has seen, maybe .005 percent or less." The reason for the South Central region's strength, Gruben says, is that most of the new industries that have set up headquarters here produce non-durable goods. "We have some durable goods that have had difficulties, such as electronics, but on the other hand the chemicals industry is very important in Texas and

Louisiana, and that industry has not suffered to the extent that the auto industry has." That, Gruben explains, is because "when you go into a recession, what people stop buying is things that don't wear out. And chemicals aren't that."

In sum, the South Central states seem well equipped to come out of the recession in relatively good condition. "Things are just kind of slow here," Gruben concludes, "but we're not as weak as they are on the East Coast."

**The Southwest.** Led by California, which accounts for 70 percent of the region's population and employment, the Southwestern region is suffering from losses in its manufacturing industries, especially defense contractors. According to the Conference Board's help-wanted index, the region is suffering the greatest loss of jobs of any area in the country, including the Northeast. New job listings fell by more than 10 percent in Los Angeles, Sacramento, San Diego and San Francisco between October and November alone. Southern California is likely to continue experiencing job losses as a result of falling orders from the Pentagon to such local contractors as Douglas Aircraft Co., a division of McDonnell Douglas Corp., and General Dynamics Corp., as well as the medium and small subcontractors that supply them.

At the same time, the region has undergone a crash in real estate values that mirrors the situation in the Northeast. Like banks and S&Ls on the Atlantic Coast, the Southwest's financial industry is suffering

# U.S. Industrial Outlook...

**S**ince the 1981-82 recession, many communities have diversified their economic base, and now host a wider variety of businesses than in the past. This is helping local economies weather the current recession. But economic diversification may be masking some very real differences in business conditions among the various sectors of American industry. What follows is a description of the strengths and weaknesses of some of the more important U.S. industries:

**Construction.** The bottom fell out of the home construction industry in the late 1980s, after one of the strongest housing booms in recent memory. Total construction of single-family homes and apartments peaked at 1.8 million in 1986 and fell to 1.2 million in 1990, the lowest level since the 1981-82 recession.

The Federal Reserve's recent moves to lower interest rates (*see p. 69*) pushed mortgage rates down to around 9.5 percent. This should help increase the demand for housing, especially in the glutted housing markets of the Northeast, Mid-Atlantic and Southwest. These conditions could place home ownership within the grasp of many Ameri-

cans who were priced out of the market when prices shot up in the 1980s.

However, the hesitancy of banks in many parts of the country to extend new loans to builders means that the construction industry will probably lag behind the rest of the economy in recovering from the recession. That will adversely affect businesses that supply the construction trade, including producers of glass, lumber, household furnishings and appliances.

**Automobiles.** Detroit's "Big Three" automakers — General Motors Corp., Ford Motor Co. and Chrysler Corp. — have suffered more than most manufacturers from the slack in public confidence over the past year, as many consumers put off purchasing such big-ticket items as automobiles. The stock market rally and the dip in oil prices that followed the outbreak of war in the Persian Gulf may restore some degree of consumer confidence. But with the recession still in force, it appears unlikely that the Big Three automakers will soon see a big boost in profitability. All three domestic automakers suffered a drop in earnings last year.

**Oil.** Domestic oil producers took

heart in the rise in oil prices that followed Iraq's invasion of Kuwait last August. Oil prices soared from $16 a barrel at the time of the invasion to a peak of around $41 a barrel before dropping back to $25-$30 a barrel. Philip K. Verleger Jr., an oil market analyst at the Institute for International Economics, believes the fluctua- tions in oil prices since August are more apparent than real. "It's a little like an earthquake," he says. "There's been a lot of noise, but we've returned back where we started from."

Verleger predicts that the current price of $25-$30 a barrel will remain in effect for some time unless Iraq destroys Saudi oil fields or in other ways disrupts the flow of Saudi oil. In any case, U.S. producers can expect a more profitable year than last year, when the price of oil was much lower.

**Defense.** Suppliers of the nation's military arsenal took a hard blow from the Pentagon's acknowledgement last year that the Cold War had ended. With little perceived need for massive troop deployments in Europe, the budget agreement between the White House and Congress last October called for a $9.8 billion cut in projected military

the consequences of the real estate collapse. The vacancy rate in commercial space in Los Angeles is among the highest in the nation, with little hope for a turnaround until mid-decade. Housing prices, which soared in the late 1980s, fell in 1990. As consumers see the value of their homes fall, they are reducing spending for goods and services, causing a contraction of business for retail stores, restaurants and other service providers.

But California's woes are good news for its neighbors. Because they did not experience a boom in real estate values to the extent California did, Arizona and Nevada now boast a lower cost of living. Both states are attracting businesses from California, and with them employees and service industries that support the growing population. As a result of this in-migration, Nevada has become the fastest-growing state in the country and continues to enjoy vigorous economic growth while California stagnates. Farther inland, Utah is enjoying something of an economic boom thanks to

the flourishing high-tech center around Provo and Orem, home to such software firms as WordPerfect.

**The Northwest.** The Pacific Northwest provided the main exception to this year's emerging bicoastal recession. The weakest component of the region's economy is the lumber industry, where demand has fallen sharply because of the nationwide drop in housing construction. Traditionally one of the Northwest's leading industries, the lumber and wood products business, centered in Oregon, saw a loss of almost 20 percent of its work force in 1990, a loss that accounts for much of the region's job losses to date.

The other traditional mainstay of the Northwest's economy, Seattle-based Boeing Co., has not suffered irreparable harm from the Pentagon's budget knife. Although defense contracts account for much of Boeing's business, the aerospace firm has enough civilian aircraft orders both in the United States and overseas to keep its operations healthy, and employment is expected to remain fairly steady at about

# ...*An Industry-by-Industry Survey*

spending during fiscal 1991.

Now, with the outbreak of war in the Middle East, the peace dividend expected from the end of the Cold War is not likely to materialize. But the prospects for military contractors are still unclear. Companies that manufacture ballistic missiles, nuclear submarines and long-range bombers may continue to be hurt by the Pentagon cuts, but other contractors seem likely to benefit from the war. These include Raytheon Corp., which manufactures the Patriot ground-to-air missiles that are being used so effectively to destroy Iraqi missiles.

Also likely to benefit from the war are the numerous companies that make uniforms, ammunition and chemical warfare equipment. In the longer term, however, military contractors as a group seem likely to lose business from the U.S. government.

**Steel.** Steelmakers have suffered from the loss of profits by one of their main customers, Detroit's automakers. But at the same time, they are exporting more of their products overseas, even to countries whose own steel industries have been their main competitors on the

world market. Steelmakers are profiting from the dollar's falling value, which makes their products less expensive than those made in Japan and Europe. Increased foreign demand for American steel is providing a vital cushion against the fall in domestic demand.

**Banks.** Hit by mortgage delinquencies and defaults on other loans in New England and other parts of the country, commercial banks are facing some of the same bleak prospects as the savings and loan industry.

After the Federal Deposit Insurance Corporation seized the Bank of New England in January, L. William Seidman, the agency's chairman, said no other big banks appeared to be on the verge of collapse. But he later qualified his prediction. Testifying before the Senate Banking Committee Jan. 9, Seidman said there would indeed be more big bank failures if the predictions of a "short and shallow" recession ending around the middle of the year proved to be wrong. Even under current conditions, he predicted that 180 banks would fail this year, at a cost to the government of around $5 billion.

**Retailers.** Worried about the country's economic prospects, con-

sumers held on to their wallets during the Christmas shopping season, capping an already meager year for the country's retailers. With few exceptions, stores were unable to boost sales during the last quarter of 1990 after a sluggish summer and fall. Many retailers count on last-quarter sales to produce as much as half of their earnings. One of the biggest losers, Sears, Roebuck & Co., announced in January that it would eliminate about 21,000 jobs across the country.

**Computers.** Although the United States continues to import more high-technology electronic equipment than it sells to the rest of the world, the industry is exporting more of its products than it has in recent years. One sector of this industry, the makers of computer chips such as Intel Corp. and Motorola Inc., reversed the steady decline in market share it had suffered during most of the 1980s. The U.S. Commerce Department predicts that high-tech industries in general, which make medical equipment and other electronic gear in addition to computers and semiconductors, will lead American manufacturers in sales this year.

100,000 this year.

But the Pacific Northwest has also developed other resources in recent years. Thanks to its location, the region has benefited from trade with East Asia through the ports of Seattle and Portland, which continues to grow despite some initial signs of slowdown.

Unlike California, whose real estate market is now in decline, the Northwestern states continue to enjoy a vigorous real estate market, bolstered by the arrival of workers and businesses from the southern Pacific Coast states and elsewhere attracted by the lower cost of living. As a result, the region's economy has diversified and now is home to transportation, communications and other service industries. According to a recent study conducted by the Northwest Policy Center at the University of Washington, four states in the region — Alaska, Idaho, Oregon and Washington — were among the top 10 states in the nation in employment growth in 1989.[11]

## *Prospects for recovery depend upon war's outcome*

The average duration of the eight recessions since the end of World War II has been just under a year. But there are signs that this recession may be shorter and less severe than usual. "The worst is behind us," Federal Reserve Chairman Alan Greenspan said Jan. 15. "Fortunately, for the moment the evidence seems to confirm [that this is] a recession of moderate dimensions and not one of extreme difficulty."[12] In testimony before the House Budget Committee Jan. 22, Greenspan predicted that the recession would end by the middle of this year.

The sources of strength in the economy that would allow for such a "soft landing" are the same ones that have enabled some areas of the country to weather the recession better than others. Manufacturers' success in keeping their inventories under control at the early stage of the recession will make it easier for them to boost production quickly when consumer demand picks up. The weak dollar continues to spur foreign demand for American exports, particularly manufactured goods that have been the most visible victims of past downturns. The plunge in real estate values that played such a big role in precipitating the downturn, appears to have hit bottom in most areas, giving rise to hopes that demand for new housing may materialize soon. This would boost the construction industry, as well as such related businesses as lumber, home furnishings and appliances.

Greenspan takes some credit for this improvement, citing the Fed's lowering of key interest rates at the end of 1990. "Our response has been in recent weeks to try to break the back of the credit crunch by increasing the profit margins of commercial banks," he says, "and we have done this by significantly lowering the cost of money to banks." [13] In his testimony before the House Banking Committee, Greenspan suggested that the Fed may soon cut interest rates further.

Lower interest rates should bring home ownership within the grasp of more Americans. Further, the lower cost of borrowing money should spur consumer purchases of goods and services. If Greenspan is correct in saying the credit crunch is easing, businesses also should find it easier to finance expansion of production facilities in order to meet the growing demand of consumers for their products. Employment would pick up, further boosting consumer demand.

Many economists are less optimistic about the prospects for job growth. "We expect something better than 40 states to end up with fewer jobs by mid-1991 than what they had going into the winter of 1990," says Clair Asklund of DRI/McGraw-Hill. "Most states will feel at least some pain in employment numbers." The firm predicts that total unemployment, which stood at 6.1 percent in December, will peak at 7.1 percent, and that inflation will fall from the 6.1 percent registered in December to around 3 percent by 1992.

However long the recession lasts, some of the regional differences that are evident now are likely to persist during the recovery. Donald Ratajczak of Georgia State University predicts that the Northeast, especially New England, will lag behind the rest of the nation in recovery because of the region's ailing financial institutions, which are vital ingredients in the revival of economic activity. "On the other hand, the recovery infrastructure looks pretty strong in the Midwest and reasonably strong in the South once you get south of Virginia," he says.

It remains to be seen, however, whether the bicoastal recession will turn into a bicoastal recovery. Ratajczak foresees faster improvement on the West Coast. "Even though both areas are feeling significant real estate pressures at the present time, the New England banking system is way over its head, whereas the banks out in California are experiencing just an earnings shock. This would indicate that California, as well as some states in the Southwest, would be in a better position to snap back than the Northeast."

But any scenario for recovery is strictly contingent upon the outcome of the war in the Middle East. If the U.S.-led forces score a speedy victory over Iraq and somehow manage to extricate themselves from the region, many experts believe the impact on the U.S. economy need not be severe, especially if the hostilities do not interrupt the bulk of oil supplies from the region. If, however, the forces dig in for a protracted conflict of attrition, the economic results could be disastrous.

"If we have war with significant damage to the oil flow, you've got worldwide recession," says Ratajczak. "If we have a war that doesn't damage the oil flow but only impacts our high costs and the costs of some of the [Allied] coalition members, you probably won't have worldwide recession. The duration of conflict would be a determining factor, but also its intensity. An important question is whether Iraq will use up all its missiles zapping out refineries. After all, they don't have an unlimited supply."

Any significant interruption of oil supplies from the Persian Gulf would have graver implications for other nations than for the United States. While this country depends on the Middle East for roughly half its energy needs, Western Europe relies on that source for the bulk of its energy requirements. While Japan has tried to diversify its energy sources to include Asian suppliers, it is even more dependent than Europe on the free flow of Persian Gulf oil.

What this means for the U.S. economy is a drastic fall in foreign demand for American goods and services if Persian Gulf oil supplies are interrupted for long. "With the exception of the United Kingdom and Canada, which are now in recession, too, our trading partners are still expanding," says John Savacool of the WEFA Group. "But the growth rates in Japan and many of the European countries are slowing down, and a slowdown in growth means that you're going to feel it in terms of sales abroad."

In that case, the whole country, including the Midwestern states, would feel the full brunt of recession. "If the world goes into recession, then of course the picture changes," says Ratajczak. "Our regional outlook then becomes who is early and who is late at going down, rather than who will and who will not go down. If this happens, the fact that the Midwest is export-oriented will no longer be positive."

A more ominous effect of a deep recession among the United States' main trading partners could be a sharp reduction in foreign investment here. Throughout the 1980s, as the federal budget deficit soared from $79 billion in fiscal 1981 to the $300 billion to $325 billion the administration has projected for the current fiscal year, Japanese and Western European investors have poured funds into U.S. Treasury bills and

*Continued on p. 78*

# AT ISSUE

*Is the United States likely to see sustained economic growth again in the near future?*

**YES** *says* **CHARLES R. MORRIS,** *author of* The Coming Global Boom.

On the eve of the fighting in the gulf, most analysts felt that, unless the conflict was prolonged, energy prices would stay under control. Even without production from Iraq and Kuwait, world oil supplies are bigger than they were a year ago. Once the gulf crisis is resolved, one way or the other, oil prices could fall quite sharply. . . .

If you are inclined toward pessimism, you see an economy that was unusually weak even before the technical recession got under way, which suggests that the recession will be unusually severe. If you are inclined toward optimism, you see an economy that had managed to handle more than a year of very bad news and still avoid a recession until the oil-price shock following Iraq's invasion of Kuwait last August, which suggests substantial underlying strengths. And the available data can easily be made to support either interpretation. . . .

There is no gainsaying the problems in commercial real estate, which, far more than junk bonds, are at the heart of the problems in the savings-and-loan and banking industries. But the picture in residential real estate — about three times as big as the commercial market — is more mixed. . . .

With the economy poised on a knife edge, much may turn on psychology. Consumers and businesses maintained remarkable stiff upper lips in the face of cascades of bad news through most of 1990, although confidence was clearly cracking by late fall. One reason for the cheeriness was that much of the country — the Midwest, and parts of the Southwest and West — chugged through the year at a respectable, if unspectacular rate. . . .

There is no way to know for sure how long the recession will last. It has been anticipated for so long, and so intently, that all the bad news may be out on the table. With the Federal Reserve easing up on interest rates and pushing banks back in to the lending business, a turnaround could come quite quickly — assuming, of course, that the crisis in the gulf is successfully resolved.

However long it takes, the restructuring of the financial-services industry is long overdue. Strikingly, [optimists and pessimists] . . . agree that the 1990s could be a period of very strong growth for the United States, as the average age of the work force rises and investment capital shifts away from real estate into factories and technology.

*From "Are Things as Bad as They Look?"* The New York Times Magazine, *Jan. 27, 1991, pp. 36-42.*

**NO** *says* **HOBART ROWAN,** *a columnist for* The Washington Post.

There are some positive elements in the economy that could lead to a turnaround. Business inventories are lean instead of fat, mortgage and other interest rates have come down (with the probability that the Federal Reserve can be expected to push them even lower) and a cheaper dollar helps make exports of American goods attractive. . . .

Yet it is difficult for anyone, including those who see only a moderate recession, to build a scenario that restores the economy quickly to a sustained period of vigorous economic growth. The federal budget deficit is huge, and a future tax increase to pay for the costs of Desert Shield and the S&L/bank bailouts looms on the not-so-distant horizon.

There is no blinking the reality of an overbuilt real estate market that helped precipitate the crisis among financial institutions. Even relative optimist [George] Perry [of the Brookings Institution in Washington] grants that commercial real estate is in its own depression: "It'll be a long time before anyone builds a commercial building again." Lenders are super-cautious in extending new credit for any purpose. And state and local governments are being forced to cut services and lay off workers.

What's more, although the rise in unemployment during the past year has primarily hit production workers, a severe crisis in the financial and business-services industries has had an early impact on white-collar jobs for the first time.

The showdown with Saddam Hussein further clouds the outlook. If there is no war — or, at worst, only a short one — most anticipate a revival of consumer and business confidence. If there is a protracted war, all bets are off.

But even a quick end to the Gulf crisis won't end the troubles of the economy. Lee Price of the Joint Economic Committee staff says, "We can't get back to 3 to 4 percent real growth until we write off some of the debt overload — junk bonds, real estate and so on. We can have a short, shallow recession, but we can stay at a sluggish level for a long time."

So how will the recession of 1990-91 wind up? Better not to ask. John Kenneth Galbraith, testifying Monday before a Senate Labor subcommittee, said that in forecasting recession, there are two kinds of economists: "There's the kind that doesn't know, and then there's the kind that doesn't know that it doesn't know."

*From* The Washington Post, *Jan. 11, 1991.*

*Continued from p. 76*

other instruments that have propped up the economy. They would have less money to invest abroad if their own economies suffered a severe downturn.

Already, there are signs of an investment pullback from overseas. Japanese banks are suffering from a collapse of the real estate market in Japan, while Germany, the main source of funds from Europe, is burdened by the high cost associated with German unification. If these big foreign investors reduce their U.S. holdings significantly, Americans will suddenly be left to foot the bill at a time when they are least able to do so.

The need for foreign investment is especially acute today, as the costs of waging war are pushing the federal budget deficit ever higher. The administration has not released information on the Persian Gulf War's cost to date, and estimates from other sources vary widely. Greenspan told the House Budget Committee that the United States was probably spending "several hundred million" dollars a day. But he was referring to expenditures for the early phase of the war, which to date has been largely confined to the air and involved relatively few losses to the U.S.-led forces.

Although the thousands of bombs and missiles the U.S. forces have launched against Iraq are costly, and the dozen or so aircraft that have been destroyed would cost tens of billions of dollars each to replace, further escalation of the war would undoubtedly raise war-related outlays considerably. The Congressional Budget Office estimates that a monthlong war would cost the U.S. government $17 billion, while the Center for Defense Information, a Washington research organization and frequent Pentagon critic, puts the figure as high as $80 billion if the conflict lasts six months.

Jeff Faux of the Economic Policy Institute says the war is jeopardizing the prospects of an early economic recovery. For one thing, he says, policy-makers are so preoccupied with the war that they are ignoring many important problems at home. "There are major policy decisions to be made and thought through regarding the U.S. economy, such as how to restructure the banking system, how long we can continue to absorb a recession without doing something about it and how to face the issues of education, training and other issues we've had with us for awhile and that continue to get worse every year."

Faux also believes the war will have a negative impact on U.S. competitiveness. "No matter what happens," he says, "our major competitors in the world — Europe, Japan and the newly industrialized countries of East Asia — will end up after this war stronger than we are." For one thing, he notes, the United States is likely to bear most of the financial burden of the war. America's allies are helping to defray some of the costs. Japan, for example, pledged Jan. 24 to contribute $9 billion to the military effort, in addition to the $4 billion it had previously commit-

ted. (The pledge is subject to approval by the Diet, Japan's parliament, where there has been some opposition.) But the cost to the United States will be huge. "Sooner or later you have to pay for that, and you pay for that by diverting resources that would have otherwise gone into productive investments. Secondly, while we have been turning our attention to the war, they are going on about their business."

House Speaker Thomas S. Foley, D-Wash., says Congress is not currently planning to raise taxes to pay for the war, but lawmakers may soon be forced to consider a tax increase. This is especially true if the recession spreads and deepens among America's major trading partners, causing them to reduce their purchases of American goods and services. A fall in foreign demand would further lower U.S. business earnings, deepen the recession here and thus reduce the government's tax revenues. "For the sake of everybody outside Iraq," Faux says, "this thing needs to be over fast."

# NOTES

[1] Boskin made his remarks Jan. 2, 1991, on NBC-TV's "Today" show.

[2] See "1991 Won't Be a Pretty Year," *Business Week*, Jan. 14, 1991, p. 62.

[3] See Beth Burnham Mace and Clair W. Asklund, "Winners Become Losers: The Regional Recessions," *Regional Preview, Fourth Quarter 1990*, DRI/McGraw-Hill.

[4] Estimate of the New England Economic Project, a nonprofit economic research organization, cited by Alan Deutschman in "A Map of Ups and Downs," *Fortune*, Jan. 14, 1991, pp. 73-74.

[5] Figures on mortgage delinquencies appear in the Mortgage Bankers Association of America's *National Delinquency Survey*, Dec. 17, 1990.

[6] See Benjamin Weiser, "No Shortage of Bombs, Missiles Foreseen for U.S.," *The Washington Post*, Jan. 25, 1991, p. A28.

[7] These figures were reported by the U.S. Department of Labor's Middle Atlantic Regional office. See Richard Levine, "New York Area Being Hit Hard by Loss of Jobs," *The New York Times*, Dec. 21, 1990, p. A1.

[8] Mace and Asklund, *op. cit.*, p. 6.

[9] The Conference Board released its latest help-wanted index Dec. 6, 1990.

[10] Mace and Asklund, *op. cit.*, p. 7.

[11] Northwest Policy Center, *Northwest Portrait 1991*, released Jan. 9, 1991.

[12] Greenspan spoke to Washington-area businessmen. See John M. Berry, "Fed Chairman Sees Signs Economy Is Stabilizing," *The Washington Post*, Jan. 16, 1991, p. A3.

[13] *Ibid.*

*Graphics: Cover, Margaret Scott; maps, p. 73, Jack Auldridge.*

# RECOMMENDED READING

## ARTICLES

Deutschman, Alan, "A Map of Ups and Downs," *Fortune*, Jan. 14, 1991, pp. 73-74.

The Northeast, birthplace of the current recession, will continue to suffer more than any other region of the country during 1991, the author predicts. The Pacific Northwest, on the other hand, stands to gain in economic activity despite the recession, as does, to a lesser extent, the Southeast. The rest of the country can expect little economic growth during the coming year.

Mace, Beth Burnham, and Asklund, Clair W., "Winners Become Losers: The Regional Recessions," *DRI/McGraw-Hill U.S. Markets Review*, Regional Preview, fourth quarter 1990.

DRI/McGraw-Hill, an economic forecasting firm in Lexington, Mass., publishes regional economic forecasts each quarter. This latest projection for the nine main regions in the country paints an uneven picture of economic conditions as the current recession spreads across the nation. New England is suffering the worst shock, and will account for one of every five non-agricultural job losses by June. A third of the job losses will occur in the larger East North Central region, the firm predicts. During the same period, Texas and other states in the South Central region stand to enjoy an increase in employment.

"Many That Are First Shall Be Last, and the Last First," *The Economist*, Dec. 22, 1990, pp. 25-26.

The last recession, which occurred in 1981-82, devastated the industrial Midwest but did far less damage to the East and West coasts, giving rise to the "bicoastal economy" dominated by the 1980s boom in financial services and real estate. But it was the collapse of those sectors on the two coasts that precipitated the latest downturn. As a result, the current recession is hitting the Atlantic and Pacific regions harder than the industrial heartland.

"1991 Industry Outlook," *Business Week*, Jan. 14, 1991, pp. 61-121.

As recession spreads across the country, few industries are likely to escape damage from the recession. Exports have grown with the falling value of the dollar on world markets, benefiting some manufacturers. But as unemployment rises, consumers at home are buying less, and the falling domestic demand is offsetting any gains made in exports for most industries. As a result, both industrial output and corporate profits are expected to fall this year.

## REPORTS AND STUDIES

Board of Governors of the Federal Reserve System, *Current Economic Conditions by Federal Reserve District*, January 1991.

The Federal Reserve releases its "beige book" each month to provide a regional snapshot of economic conditions. Compiled by economists at all 12 Federal Reserve banks, the report tracks consumer spending, manufacturing, construction and real estate, prices, banking and finance, state and local government finance and agriculture and natural-resource-related industries in each Federal Reserve district. This latest report finds that economic activity is declining in most parts of the country and the Persian Gulf situation is "a key determinant of both current and future economic activity."

Howard, Marcia A., *Fiscal Survey of the States*, National Governors' Association and National Association of State Budget Officers, September 1990.

Budget cuts and tax increases were the order of the day in 1990, as worsening economic conditions reduced tax revenues in most of the states. Unlike the federal government, all the state governments except Vermont are required to balance their budgets, so the states' budgets had to be changed to accommodate the fall in revenues. This semiannual report found the greatest drop in tax revenues to come from corporate taxes, reflecting the impact of recession on businesses. In 1990, 26 states raised taxes, primarily personal income taxes.

Northwest Policy Center, *Northwest Portrait 1991*, Jan. 9, 1991.

The Northwest Policy Center, a research organization at the University of Washington Graduate School of Public Affairs, predicts that most of the Northwest will manage to ward off the spreading recession and retain a healthy economy in 1991. The annual report covers Alaska, Washington, Oregon, Montana and Idaho, as well as the Canadian provinces of Alberta and British Columbia. With regard to the five U.S. described in the study, all but Montana were among the top 10 states in employment growth in 1989. Trade with Pacific Rim countries and abundant natural resources are among the region's assets.

United States Conference of Mayors, City Fiscal Conditions 1980-1990, January 1991.

This survey of 50 U.S. cities demonstrates the worsening fiscal condition of the nation's urban areas. The report blames "the shifting sands of federalism brought about by the Reagan Revolution" for their plight, as drastic cutbacks in federal funding to cities during the 1980s has left basic services underfunded. City governments have tried to bridge the funding gap with increases in taxes and user fees. But even these corrective measures are proving inadequate, as the drop in profits and income brought on by the recession means local taxes are bringing in less revenue to city coffers.

# EDITORIAL RESEARCH REPORTS

## Coming soon

- Puerto Rico
- Redistricting
- Pensions

Published weekly by
Congressional Quarterly
Inc., Editorial Research
Reports analyze emerging
issues of national interest
across a broad range of
social, scientific, political
and economic fields.
Reports are bound and
indexed for permanent
reference. Subscription
information is available
through Congressional
Quarterly's Publications
Sales Department by
telephone (202) 887-8665.
Copies of past issues are
available through
Customer Service, (202)
887-8621.

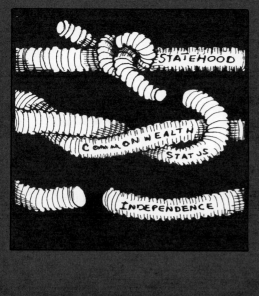

FEBRUARY 8, 1991

# PUERTO RICO: THE STRUGGLE OVER STATUS

EDITORIAL
RESEARCH
REPORTS

EDITOR
MARCUS D. ROSENBAUM

MANAGING EDITOR
SANDRA STENCEL

ASSOCIATE EDITOR
RICHARD L. WORSNOP

STAFF WRITERS
MARY H. COOPER
PATRICK G. MARSHALL

PRODUCTION EDITOR
LAURIE DE MARIS

EDITORIAL ASSISTANT
AMY GORTON

RICHARD M. BOECKEL (1892-1975)
FOUNDER

PUBLISHED BY
CONGRESSIONAL QUARTERLY INC.

CHAIRMAN
ANDREW BARNES

PRESIDENT
RICHARD R. EDMONDS

EDITOR AND PUBLISHER
NEIL SKENE

EXECUTIVE EDITOR
ROBERT W. MERRY

© 1991 BY CONGRESSIONAL QUARTERLY INC.

EDITORIAL RESEARCH REPORTS (LIBRARY OF CONGRESS
CATALOGUE NO. 39-924; ISSN 0013-0958). Published weekly
(48 times per year, excluding March 1, May 3, August 2 and
November 1, 1991) by Congressional Quarterly Inc., 1414 22nd
Street NW, Washington, D.C. 20037. Rates are furnished
upon request. Application to mail at second-class postage
rates is pending at Washington, D.C. POSTMASTER: Send
address changes to EDITORIAL RESEARCH REPORTS, 1414
22nd Street NW, Washington, D.C. 20037.

# DEBATE OVER PUERTO RICO'S POLITICAL STATUS

*by Patrick G. Marshall*

Puerto Rico's three political parties have united in calling for a vote on the island's future relationship with the United States. At the moment, islanders are closely divided over whether to continue the current commonwealth status or to opt for statehood, with only a small minority favoring complete independence. The U.S. Congress also is divided on the issue, however, and lawmakers may not give the islanders the chance to vote — a possibility many Puerto Ricans say would be intolerable.

After more than 92 years of living under U.S. domination, Puerto Rico may at last have a chance to decide whether it wants to become an independent country, enter the Union as the 51st state, or continue its current "commonwealth" status. The decision will not be an easy one for Puerto Ricans, for each status carries with it certain advantages and disadvantages.

Under commonwealth status, Puerto Ricans are U.S. citizens, but the island has no senators or voting representatives in Congress and islanders cannot vote in presidential elections. Puerto Rico also does not receive the same level or variety of social welfare programs as the states, although the federal government does give the island some money. On the other hand, commonwealth status carries benefits, too: Puerto Ricans are not required to pay federal income taxes, and companies establishing businesses on the island are given federal tax incentives that they could not receive in a state.

If Puerto Rico were to become a state, it would gain political power in Congress, and poor Puerto Ricans would qualify for many federal welfare benefits they cannot now receive. At the same time, however, they would have to pay income taxes, and the island would lose its corporate tax incentives, which could harm the economy.

Independence, the third option, would be emotionally gratifying to most Puerto Ricans, and it would give the island more flexibility in making trade arrangements with other countries. But it would mean the end of most of the subsidies currently provided by the United States — and an end to even the limited social welfare benefits that poor Puerto Ricans now receive.

Puerto Ricans are divided over which status would be best, but they are at one in their resentment over their continuing lack of power to decide the issue for themselves. Every president since Harry S Truman has conceded the right of Puerto Ricans to do so, but in spite of public plebiscites and diplomatic pleadings, legislation that would give Puerto Ricans control over their own destinies has yet to make it through Congress.

Legislators came close last year. The House passed a bill that would have provided funds for a referendum in Puerto Rico on the island's status and would have required Congress to take some action on the results of the referendum. In the Senate, however, a referendum bill was allowed to die in the commotion surrounding Congress' last-minute wrangling over a federal budget.

New bills were introduced in both houses early this year, and their respective sponsors have pledged to try to iron out the not inconsiderable differences between the two pieces of legislation so that an effective vote on Puerto Rico's status can finally be taken. Though many in Congress expect an uphill battle, an unexpected victory took place when the three Puerto Rican political parties issued a unified call for a referendum in November 1989. This agreement between Puerto Rican parties, says a staff member of a congressional committee that deals with the issue, has elevated the idea of a status referendum from a pipe dream to a potential reality. "That's always been tougher than the United States getting together on a process," says the staff member, who asked not to be identified.

The divisions within Puerto Rico over the island's relationship with the United States are clearly reflected in the political landscape. In fact, the three political parties are themselves largely defined by their respective positions on the status question. In recent years, the governorship has passed back and forth between the Popular Democratic Party, which currently occupies the governor's house and which favors commonwealth status, and the New Progressive Party, which favors statehood. The party that favors independence — appropriately named the Puerto Rican Independence Party — has been unable to gather more than about 5 percent of the vote in island elections.

But even though Puerto Ricans elected a pro-commonwealth governor — Rafael Hernández Colón — in 1988, that does not mean they would favor commonwealth status in a referendum today. Opinion polls

## Commonweath vs. Statehood

This table compares estimates of what the federal government would pay Puerto Rico (in billions of dollars) for certain entitlement programs under its current commonwealth status or under statehood. The increased costs under statehood are broken down by program.

| Programs | 1992 | 1993 | 1994 | 1995 |
|---|---|---|---|---|
| Outlays under commonwealth | 1.8 | 1.9 | 2.0 | 2.1 |
| Outlays under statehood | 3.5 | 3.7 | 4.6 | 5.1 |
| Increases under statehood | | | | |
| Food stamps | 0.7 | 0.7 | 0.7 | 0.7 |
| Medicaid | 0.9 | 1.0 | 1.1 | 1.2 |
| Medicare | 0.1 | 0.1 | 0.1 | 0.1 |
| Supplemental Security Income | 0 | 0 | 0.6 | 0.9 |
| Aid to Families with Dependent Children | - † | - † | 0.1 | 0.1 |
| Foster Care | - † | - † | - † | - † |
| Total increase | 1.7 | 1.8 | 2.6 | 3.0 |

† *Less than $50 million.*
*Source: Congressional Budget Office,* Potential Economic Impacts of Changes in Puerto Rico's Status Under S. 712, *April 1990.*

in January 1989 showed Puerto Ricans favoring commonwealth status by 52 percent to 41 percent, but a more recent poll in 1990 showed islanders favoring statehood 48 percent to 42 percent.[1]

On the surface, the most significant issues in the status debate seem to be economic. "Voters anywhere tend to vote their pocketbooks, and we're being shortchanged terribly in economic and social benefits," says Roland I. Perusse, a professor of U.S.-Puerto Rican relations at the Inter-American University of Puerto Rico.

Indeed, though Puerto Rico receives generous tax benefits and more than $6 billion a year from the U.S. government, the standard of living on the island, along with federal funds directed to the island, lags well behind states on the mainland. Federal expenditures in Puerto Rico amounted to only $1,893 per person in 1988, which put Puerto Rico at the bottom of the list. Of the 50 states, the lowest in terms of per capita expenditures was Michigan, which received an average of $2,543 per person in 1988.[2] Social welfare programs such as Aid to Families with Dependent Children (AFDC), food stamps and Medicare, are available in Puerto Rico, but expenditures are arbitrarily capped at levels far below those on the mainland.

"It's legal, geographical discrimination," complains Perusse, an advocate of statehood. And such disparity is all the harder to take, he says, when Puerto Ricans are expected to fight in America's wars. "There's a terrible feeling in Puerto Rico right now, especially in light of the Persian Gulf where we're expected to fight as equals with U.S. citizens, that we don't get equal benefits."

The reduced aid is certainly not a result of there being less need in Puerto Rico. While the island's standard of living is generally much higher than that found in nearby Caribbean countries, Puerto Ricans are

## Major Dates in Puerto Rican History

**1493** Columbus lands in Puerto Rico, an island inhabited by about 100,000 Indians.

**1508** Ponce de León arrives with Spanish settlers and becomes the island's first governor.

**1897** Spain grants autonomy to Puerto Rico.

**1898** On July 25, U.S. troops land in Puerto Rico. At the conclusion of the brief Spanish-American War, Spain cedes Puerto Rico to the United States. Puerto Rico becomes a U.S. colony.

**1917** President Woodrow Wilson signs the Jones Act, which grants U.S. citizenship to Puerto Ricans and sets up a bicameral legislature for the island.

**1947** Congress passes the Elective Governor Act, and Luis Muñoz Marín becomes the island's first elected governor.

**1948** Operation Bootstrap, a combination of federal and Puerto Rican tax incentives for industries setting up in Puerto Rico, is initiated.

**1952** With the adoption of a new constitution by Puerto Rico, and its ratification by the U.S. Congress, the island becomes a commonwealth of the United States.

**1953** The United Nations, taking note of Puerto Rico's popular vote in favor of becoming a U.S. commonwealth, removes the island from its list of non-self-governing territories.

**1978** The U.N. Decolonization Committee calls for the transfer of all political power to Puerto Rico.

far worse off than residents in the 50 U.S. states. According to a recent Congressional Research Service study, the incidence of poverty was six times greater in Puerto Rico in 1979, the most recent year for which figures were available, than in the United States as a whole.[3] Although more recent figures are not available, there does not seem to have been significant improvement over the past decade.

It is the promise of getting the additional benefits that would come with statehood, many analysts say, that has given new popularity to the idea of joining the Union. "If you're aged, blind and disabled in Puerto Rico, you get about one-eleventh what you'd get under Supplemental Security Income," says a congressional staff aide. "You could be a dedicated *independendista,* and if you knew your income was going to go up elevenfold, there'd be a lot of incentive to vote for statehood."

But the issue of Puerto Rico's future goes much deeper than just a question of economic benefits. "It's not simply a fill-your-belly situation like a lot of people would paint it," says Perusse. Rather, he says,

"it's civil rights that's probably the basic consideration right now."

Supporters of independence, who argue that Puerto Ricans are first of all Puerto Ricans and Latin Americans — with their own cultural and national identity — and only secondarily Americans, couldn't agree more. Manuel Rodríguez, electoral commissioner of the Puerto Rican Independence Party, warns that any attempt to absorb Puerto Rico into the United States through statehood would "create a problem for the United States by having a national minority — not an ethnic minority, but a national minority — with a thriving culture, language, literature and art that is distinctly different."

Indeed, it is these cultural and political issues that propel most Puerto Ricans' opinions about the island's ultimate status. "Probably 90 percent of Puerto Ricans will vote for one of those statuses" based on non-economic considerations, says a staff member of a Senate committee with jurisdiction over Puerto Rican issues. But ironically, because those who favor statehood and those who favor commonwealth are so close in numbers, it is the economic issues that will provide the swing vote and decide the issue. "Welfare payments are probably the single largest factor in making people switch their votes," the Senate staff member says. "We're really only talking about a 10 percent swing vote, and a fair percentage of those are poor people, and they'll vote for whatever gives them the most money."

Whether they have a chance to vote, however, depends on what happens in Congress, and the Popular Democratic Party has insisted that Congress reach some sort of consensus by Feb. 19. If no agreement is reached by that date, the party says it will withdraw its support. Even if consensus is reached by Feb. 19, many of those involved in the debate say final legislation would have to be enacted by early July for there to be enough time to prepare for a referendum next fall. If legislation is enacted any later, the referendum would probably be delayed until 1993 so that it wouldn't interfere with Puerto Rico's 1992 gubernatorial election.

## From colony to commonwealth

Ever since control over Puerto Rico was transferred to the United States at the end of the Spanish-American War in 1898, the island's relationship with the mainland has been an ambiguous one. Ruled as a colony after the war, Puerto Rico achieved a distinction unusual for colonies when, in 1917, the island's residents were given U.S. citizenship. Then in 1952 Puerto Rico, with the agreement of the U.S. Congress, adopted its own constitution. The colony thus became a commonwealth, an "autonomous body politic" in permanent union with the United States. In practical terms, the new agreement meant that the island had self-government for purely local matters, but all policies relating to defense and trade were set by the federal government in Washington.

As a commonwealth, Puerto Rico was "connected to" but not "part of" the United States. Citizens on the island could vote in presidential primaries, but not the final event. They could receive Medicare, food stamps and Social Security retirement benefits, but not at the same levels as mainlanders. Yet, if a Puerto Rican were to move to the mainland — and, as citizens, they have the right to do so — they could receive full welfare benefits and even vote for senators and presidents.

This political "limbo" has been matched by the development of a similar economic limbo. Historically, the primary economic feature of Puerto Rico's relationship with the mainland has been the island's transformation from a poor but largely self-sustaining economy into one somewhat richer but heavily dependent on the United States.

When the first U.S. governor arrived on the island in 1900, Puerto Rico's economy was almost exclusively agricultural. The country was, however, far from a pastoral paradise. Only 10 percent of the island consists of fertile flatlands that are well-suited to agriculture. An additional 25 percent of the island consists of uplands that are marginally arable. Thus, even before the turn of the century the island was not able to supply all of its own food directly, but had to rely on the export of specialty crops, mostly to Europe. Sugar, tobacco and coffee were the cash crops most suitable to the island's soil, and the best land was devoted to their cultivation. Production of domestic food crops — primarily by peasant landholders — took place on the marginal uplands.

The early period of the American occupation was relatively benign, with significant improvements in health care, sanitation and education. Apart from improvements in roads and other public infrastructure, however, the federal government did not get actively involved in restructuring the Puerto Rican economy. Nevertheless, increased access to the huge, and geographically close, American markets encouraged structural changes in the economy. A boom in exports of tobacco, coffee and, especially, sugar led to immense profits for the small elite that owned the rich agricultural land. Export crops came to predominate the island's economy, and as the sugar, tobacco and coffee farms grew in size and power, peasants were increasingly forced off their small farms.

The year 1947 marked a major turning point for Puerto Rico. That was the year that Operation Bootstrap — a program of industrial development based on tax incentives and tariff rebates — was inaugurated. Rewritten in 1976 as Section 936 of the Internal Revenue Code, the federal tax incentives introduced in the late 1940s featured rebates to mainland U.S. companies establishing facilities in Puerto Rico roughly in the amount of the taxes on earnings produced on the island.* At the same time, Puerto Rico itself also introduced nearly complete exemptions on local taxes for corporations moving to the island.

The incentives, combined with the low wages prevalent on the island, produced dramatic results. By 1952, about 70 new plants a year were opening in Puerto Rico. From being the site of only 82 industrial plants in 1952, Puerto Rico became the home for more than 1,000 such plants by 1970. "Rapid economic growth in the 1950s and 1960s became the hallmark of Operation Bootstrap," writes economist James L. Dietz. Between 1950 and 1960 Puerto Rico's gross national product (GNP), the total value of its annual output of goods and services, more than doubled, with the rate of annual growth averaging 8.3 percent. "From 1960 to 1970," Dietz writes, "GNP growth was even more spectacular, at an average rate of 10.8 percent per year, thus nearly tripling over the decade." [4]

At least at first, it was labor-intensive industries that were most attracted to the island. In 1949, for example, production of textiles and clothing accounted for 13.7 percent of all manufacturing companies. In 1954, the figure was 19.5 percent and by 1967 it was 19.9 percent. These manufacturers "were attracted to Puerto Rico not just by tax exemption," Dietz notes, "but also by the possibility of being able to pay wages substantially below mainland rates and by the absence of such risks as political instability that are often associated with foreign operations." [5]

## *Shaky economy, divided society*

Just behind Puerto Rico's observable economic success, however, there were some serious problems. While Operation Bootstrap accomplished a shift from an agriculture-dominated economy to a diversified one, it was an unbalanced development. To begin with, the fruits of Puerto Rico's boom were not evenly distributed. Even as a small middle class was developing, huge ghettos sprang up in the capital city of San Juan. Thousands of Puerto Ricans, unable to find enough work on the island, began emigrating to the mainland in search of opportunity. Perhaps the most distressing trend to government planners was that companies that came to Puerto Rico were not stimulating the kind of broad-based development that was hoped for.

Planners had hoped that Operation Bootstrap

---

*Section 936 of the Internal Revenue Code provides to qualifying companies a tax credit equal to the federal income taxes they would otherwise owe on income from their activities in Puerto Rico. To qualify, a company must be incorporated in the United States and must earn at least 80 percent of its income from activities in U.S. territory, including Puerto Rico.

## Lower Wages Helped Attract Industries

The graph below shows the hourly wages of manufacturing and apparel workers in Puerto Rico as a percentage of the wages of U.S. workers in those industries. Puerto Rican wages, while still significantly below wages on the mainland, rose dramatically in the 1960s and 1970s, but have leveled off in recent years. In the case of apparel workers, wages (as a percentage of wages on the mainland) have begun to decline.

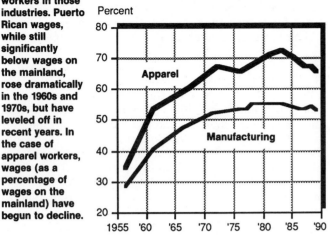

*Sources:* 1990 Statistical Abstract of the United States; *Office of the Resident Commissioner of Puerto Rico; Bureau of Labor Statistics.*

companies would stimulate the creation of new spinoff businesses created to supply raw materials and semi-finished goods, and to distribute the output of the manufacturing companies. "What actually happened was quite different," Dietz writes. "The firms that located on the island were integrated into sourcing and distribution networks with other firms in the United States or other countries. They made no attempt to forge linkages within the island economy, nor were they motivated to do so by the government or its incentive package." [6]

To make matters worse, even the partial success of Operation Bootstrap — as measured in employment gains and the number of companies attracted to the island — has waned in recent years. The reason is that there have been significant reductions both in the tax and tariff advantages of doing business in Puerto Rico and in the wage advantage of using Puerto Rican workers.

In 1951, the effective tax on corporate profits on the mainland was 54.2 percent. Since facilities of qualifying companies paid virtually no taxes on earnings in Puerto Rico, those companies enjoyed a tax advantage of 54.2 percent. But federal corporate tax rates fell significantly in the early 1980s. In 1981 alone, the Economic Recovery Tax Act at one stroke reduced the rate to below 30 percent. At the same time, Puerto Rico was itself increasing the amount it taxed companies on earnings leaving Puerto Rico. In 1976, a 10 percent withholding tax on such earnings was imposed. In 1978, a 4.5 percent tax on earnings was imposed, a rate that was to rise every five years until a total of 20.25 percent was imposed after 20 years. By 1982, according to Puerto Rican economist Bertram P. Finn, the tax advantage for a corporation locating in Puerto Rico had eroded to only 20.42 percent. [7]

At the same time, Puerto Rican wages, while still significantly below prevalent wages on the mainland, have risen dramatically. The average manufacturing wage in Puerto Rico climbed from below 30 percent of U.S. wages in the early 1950s to about 55 percent in the late '80s. (*See graph*) This has, of course, further reduced the advantages to mainland companies of doing business in Puerto Rico.

Another blow to Puerto Rico's economy was the reduction of U.S. tariffs. Negotiations during the 1960s reduced U.S. tariffs across the board, and further reductions were made specifically for Caribbean countries under the Caribbean Basin Initiative of the early '80s, a U.S. program aimed at aiding the development of economies in the Caribbean.* Lower tariffs for Puerto Rico's Caribbean competitors meant that the island's privilege of exporting goods to the United States on a tariff-free basis was less important.

The most noticeable result of these combined trends was a sharp reduction in economic growth rates. Where GNP growth exceeded 10 percent per year in the 1960s, in the late '70s and early '80s the economy grew at an annual rate of only 1.86 percent. [8] Since then, the growth rate has picked up slightly; it has grown at 3.6 percent since 1985. [9]

But the island's economy has changed structurally as well. Where the combination of tax incentives and low wages previously favored labor-intensive industry, beginning in the late 1970s it was capital-intensive industries — most notably, pharmaceuticals and electronics — that were attracted to Puerto Rico. "These capital-intensive endeavors required low levels of employment and did very little to solve chronic unemployment," writes Luis Neves Falcon, a Puerto Rican sociologist. "Ironically, many of the highly skilled positions opened by the new transnational subsidiaries could not be filled from local manpower and the employees had to be imported." [10] What's more, many of the labor-intensive industries that had come to Puerto Rico in earlier years began to flee. According to a recent report by the Congressional Budget Office (CBO), apparel and shoe manufacturers have been leaving the island in recent years for countries with lower wage rates. [11]

Today, after more than 90 years of association with the United States, Puerto Rico remains essentially a

### Economic Climate

Puerto Rico experienced strong economic growth in the 1950s and 1960s as a result of Operation Bootstrap, a combination of federal and Puerto Rican tax incentives begun in 1948. In the past two decades, however, the island's economy has grown more slowly and unemployment rates have risen.

| Decade | Average annual growth rate of real GNP per capita | Average annual unemployment rate |
|---|---|---|
| 1940s | 4.0 | N/A |
| 1950s | 4.7 | 14.3 |
| 1960s | 5.5 | 11.5 |
| 1970s | 1.6 | 15.5 |
| 1980s† | 1.5 | 19.5 |

† Data for the 1980s does not include 1990.
Source: Congressional Budget Office, Potential Economic Impacts of Changes in Puerto Rico's Status Under S. 712, *April 1990.*

*For background, see "Caribbean Basin Revisited," *E.R.R.*, Feb. 1, 1985 (Vol. I, No. 5).

Third World country, underdeveloped economically and with more than 60 percent of its people living under the U.S. federal poverty line. By comparison, in the United States as a whole, less than 10 percent of the population lives below the poverty line.[12]

"Unemployment hasn't been below 14 percent in over 15 years," complains Manuel Rodríguez, electoral commissioner of the Puerto Rican Independence Party. Even more telling, says Rodríguez, is the labor participation rate — the percentage of people who could be working who actually have jobs. According to the CBO, the U.S. rate in 1987 was 65.6 percent. In Puerto Rico the rate was only 44 percent.[13] "With those figures you can figure that unemployment is really closer to 25 or 30 percent," Rodríguez says.

One result of these trends is a very heavy reliance on federal welfare programs. For example, about 43 percent of the population receives some form of federal nutritional aid, compared with about 8 percent on the mainland.[14]

## Congress is deadlocked over procedures

Some analysts blame Puerto Rico's ambiguous political status for many of the island's economic problems. The relationship between Puerto Rico and the mainland has created an economy of dependency that has ill-served the island, argues Eric Negrón, an attorney and a tax adviser to the Puerto Rican Independence Party. "The main problem is that it's a structure almost exclusively reliant on just one single U.S. piece of legislation, Section 936 of the Internal Revenue Code," says Negrón. That reliance, he says, has resulted in an economy that is based on a handful of capital-intensive industries that actually employ few Puerto Ricans. At the same time, other U.S. laws tie the island's hands in dealing with other countries. "Japan, Canada, Germany have been interested in entering into tax agreements with Puerto Rico," says Negrón, "but have been prevented by the United States."

While each of the Puerto Rican parties has its own particular diagnosis for Puerto Rico's economic ills — and its own prescription for getting the patient back on its feet — it is the island's political relationship with the United States that is the focus of each party's analysis. And though each party bases its position on Puerto Rico's political status on cultural factors as well as economic factors, it is the economic issues that most clearly differentiate the parties.

And, as might be expected, support for each status option tends to be divided along socioeconomic class lines, though the fracture lines are far from rigid. Business people and members of the middle class are, analysts say, more likely than not to favor continuing commonwealth status. The poor and members of the

lower-middle class, attracted by the inevitable increase in social welfare benefits, are more likely to favor statehood. As for independence, while it is an emotionally attractive option to many, political support is largely confined to the universities.

If Puerto Ricans are divided on the status issue, so is Congress.

Many analysts thought that Congress might be finally on the verge of putting the island's status to a vote last year. But the House and Senate were not able to reach agreement on legislation before the 101st Congress finally adjourned in October.

At least on the surface, the disagreement in Congress is not over what status is best for Puerto Ricans, but how best to put the matter to a vote. The House passed legislation in 1990 — HR 4765 — that would have appropriated $13.5 million to conduct a status referendum in Puerto Rico. The House bill, sponsored by Democrat Ron de Lugo, the non-voting delegate from the Virgin Islands, offered voters four options: statehood, independence, a new commonwealth arrangement or no change. If any of the choices received a majority vote in the referendum, HR 4765 committed Congress to considering legislation implementing that status on an expedited basis.

Though the full House passed HR 4765 on a voice vote last October, and though the bill had the support of all three Puerto Rican parties, it was not good enough for Sen. J. Bennett Johnston, D-La., chairman of the Senate Committee on Energy and Natural Resources and a longtime champion of Puerto Rican status legislation. "What the House bill does is to provide for a referendum in Puerto Rico whereby the people of Puerto Rico would be able to make a choice between statehood, enhanced commonwealth, and independence. But that choice would be under a one-word definition or, in the case of, I think they call it improved commonwealth, a two-word definition," Johnston told his colleagues on Oct. 10, the day the House legislation passed.[15] Without specific definitions of the statuses — what benefits and obligations would go with each — the voters would not know what they were voting for, Johnston argued.

Johnston's own bill — S 712 — provided just such definitions. In its more than 3,500 lines of text, S 712 attempted to specify in detail the consequences of each status. In the event of statehood, for example, not only were the welfare benefits and tax obligations laid out, but the bill specified how U.S. military lands on the island would be handled, how electoral laws would apply to the election of Puerto Rico's new senators and congressmen, and even which courts would handle disputes arising from the electoral process.

The legislation also went beyond simply explaining in detail what would happen if Puerto Ricans voted for a given status. Johnston's bill included provisions that made it "self-executing." If a majority of Puerto Ricans voted for, say, statehood, no further vote would be required in Congress. Puerto Rico would become a state

*Editorial Research Reports / February 8, 1991*

under the conditions contained in S 712.

"The senator believes that unless you give the definitions first, you may get the wrong vote," explains a Senate committee staff member. "The way the process works down there is that each of the three parties makes wild claims about what statehood and commonwealth are. You could very likely have a vote for either statehood or commonwealth which would come back to Congress and Congress would just say it's ridiculous. In other words, the outcome of the vote would be different if Congress told people upfront what Congress was willing to implement in terms of statehood or commonwealth."

Indeed, even with the definitions of statehood spelled out in such detail in Johnston's bill, Senate staff members say that many misunderstandings remain. "Statehooders have the impression that they would still have some identity internationally even as a state, that they'd be able to be at the Olympics as their own team," says the committee staff member. "That's just not so. Also there's the impression that they'd still be able to set their quotas and tariffs on coffee. Obviously a state can't do that."

Though his Popular Democratic Party gave its support to the House bill, Gov. Rafael Hernández Colón agreed with much of Johnston's approach. "Congress has to express itself as to what each formula entails, and what transition schemes and measures are realistic and acceptable," Hernández said in a speech at Harvard University in April. "The people need to know what they are voting for, in order to make an intelligent choice. They need to know what to reasonably expect from each status option in terms of taxes, fiscal arrangements, trade, citizenship, language, social programs, Olympic representation, defense, transitional measures, and a wealth of related issues. For too long, myths and misconceptions have dominated the debate on political status in Puerto Rico, and it is about time that the people are told the truth, clearly and without reservations." [16]

Citing a referendum in 1967 in which Puerto Ricans voted for enhancing their commonwealth status only to have Congress take no action at all,* Hernández also endorsed the self-executing nature of S 712. "We cannot repeat the sad episode of the 1967 referendum, where the vote was overwhelmingly in favor of enhancing commonwealth status — more than 60 percent — yet Congress did not act."

In negotiations between the House and Senate last year, however, House members objected strongly to S 712's detailed definitions and its self-executing character. According to staff members, House leaders had two main problems with the detailed definitions in Johnston's bill. First, they felt it would be nearly impossible to get agreement on the definitions. Sec-

ondly, even if the legislature agreed on the definitions, they would be definitions that were created without the pressure of lobbyists, other than the Puerto Rican parties, and wouldn't likely stand up once those pressures came to bear.

"When you add the collective weight of all the companies — which now would rather see no bill or would rather see commonwealth prevail — if the decision is statehood and the companies know that it's going to be statehood, they might grandfather in for themselves all kinds of special deals, as every tax bill has, for companies that lose preferences," notes one House committee staff member. "Right now the Senate Finance Committee can make a very simple judgment about how Section 936 ought to be treated under statehood or independence. But that's in a situation where the committee is being told by the commonwealthers who control the government to shaft statehood, and where the companies are doing nothing to preserve their interest."

An additional problem with the definitions, some observers say, is that spelling out the consequences of each status tends to give undue weight to the short-term economic consequences of the choice. "It puts forward some goodies for the plebiscite," Del. de Lugo says of the Senate bill's treatment of the benefits that would go with statehood. As a result, voters would "not be looking at the overall long-term issue of what they're going to have to live with."

The only fair way to develop a political status, particularly with an area where the issue is as complicated as Puerto Rico, de Lugo says, "is where there's some process of bilateral negotiation between the people affected and the Congress." And that's something at least the House isn't willing to go through, he says, until the Puerto Rican people have decided which status they want to negotiate.

This year, de Lugo has stood his ground by reintroducing the very same bill the House passed last year. Sen. Johnston, on Jan. 23, introduced a revised version of his legislation — S 244. The major difference between S 244 and S 712 is that the new bill — though it contains the same lengthy, detailed explanations of each status option — is not self-executing. If S 244 were adopted, after Puerto Ricans selected a status, Congress would have to ratify the choice, and would have an opportunity to make changes in the implementing legislation. "The difference between the House and Senate bills has narrowed considerably," says a Senate staff member. "Structurally they're the same. The difference is in the length of definitions."

Key House members apparently disagree. "We argue that it's still self-executing," says a House staff analyst. "His bill is really a combination of three prospective implementing bills to the people of Puerto Rico. If you offer that in any seriousness to the people of Puerto Rico, then it's still self-executing, even if you don't say it's self-executing. Presumably, if

---

*One explanation for Congress' failure to respond to the referendum in Puerto Rico is that the Independence Party boycotted the vote, and the pro-statehood New Progressive Party also urged non-participation.

you're offering it to them with all these details, you've decided that it all makes sense." De Lugo agrees. "Detailed definitions are in fact binding on the Congress, and Congress is not ready to be bound at this time," he says.

Some legislators and staff members have argued — off the record — that there's more to the dispute between the House and Senate than simply a matter of procedure. Supporters of Johnston's bill have intimated that many House members — and possibly many senators — are against Puerto Rico becoming a state, though they'd rather not go on record saying so. Hence, there's a reluctance to make the legislation self-executing, and thereby putting the choice in Puerto Rico's hands.

Johnston says he would rather force the issue sooner rather than later. "If there's going to be a disappointment, it's a whole lot better to have it in advance of the vote," he says. "The worst thing we can do is to string these people along, have a congressionally mandated choice and then not deliver on their choice." But de Lugo contends that it's too early to force the issue. "I want to see the people of Puerto Rico given the opportunity to have this plebiscite," he says. Once the people have spoken, then Congress will respond. "And let's see how decisively they speak," de Lugo adds. "That goes into the equation, too, as to how Congress will respond."

## *Statehood, commonwealth or independence?*

Sen. Johnston's bills, with their detailed and lengthy definitions of each status, clearly demonstrate one thing: While some of the implications of the various status options for Puerto Rico are clear, a great many are not. In the process of writing S 712, many of the subtle but potentially explosive issues were brought to light.

Whether decisions on those issues are made before a status is selected, as Sen. Johnston would have it, or after, as Del. de Lugo would have it, the decisions will have to be faced. Even a clear choice by the Puerto Rican

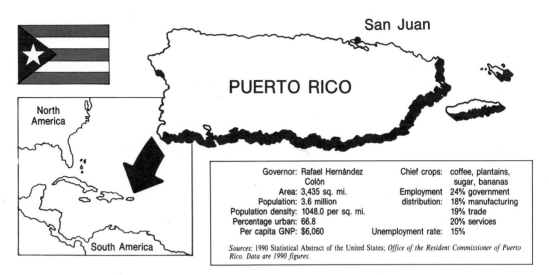

# *Puerto Rico*

San Juan

PUERTO RICO

North America

South America

| Governor: | Rafael Hernández Colón | Chief crops: | coffee, plantains, sugar, bananas |
| Area: | 3,435 sq. mi. | Employment | 24% government |
| Population: | 3.6 million | distribution: | 18% manufacturing |
| Population density: | 1048.0 per sq. mi. | | 19% trade |
| Percentage urban: | 66.8 | | 20% services |
| Per capita GNP: | $6,060 | Unemployment rate: | 15% |

*Sources:* 1990 Statistical Abstract of the United States; *Office of the Resident Commissioner of Puerto Rico. Data are 1990 figures.*

people in favor of continuing the current commonwealth status will probably not save legislators from having to deal with many of the intractable tradeoffs between sovereignty and dependency that represents the uncomfortable status quo for Puerto Ricans.

**Statehood.** If a vote were held today, the likely winner would be statehood. That is also the result that would entail the most dramatic and complex changes in the U.S.-Puerto Rican relationship.

Politically, statehood would mean a stronger political presence in Congress for Puerto Rico. Instead of merely having one non-voting representative (called the "resident commissioner") in the House, the island would send two senators and six or seven representatives to Congress. Political analysts seem to be in agreement that virtually all of those sent to Congress from Puerto Rico would be Democrats, which may explain what one Senate committee staff member describes as the "skittishness" of Senate Republicans toward the idea of Puerto Rican statehood.

Economically, one of the most dramatic effects of statehood would be huge increases in the amounts of social benefits islanders would receive. Currently, many of the welfare benefits Puerto Ricans receive are capped at levels significantly below those received by the states. Medicaid payments, for example, are only about one-tenth what they would be if Puerto Rico were a state. And islanders cannot participate in some programs — such as Supplemental Security Income (SSI) — at all.

While stressing that cost projections of entitlement programs like food stamps and unemployment involve a lot of guesswork — since they are so dependent on future economic conditions and on decisions by the Puerto Rican government — the Congressional Budget Office estimated in April 1990 that if Puerto Rico became a state, U.S. payments to the island would

*Editorial Research Reports / February 8, 1991*

increase by $1.7 billion in 1992, and as much as $3 billion in 1995.[17] The big-ticket items in the estimate were Supplemental Security Income ($900 million in 1995), Medicaid ($900 million over current payments in 1995) and food stamps ($700 million above current payments).

The benefit increases, as spelled out in detail last year in S 712, were so attractive that many critics, particularly advocates of commonwealth status, charged that Johnston's bill was "front-loaded" in favor of statehood. "This offer," said Gov. Rafael Hernández Colón in a speech last April, "has already had an impact on the Puerto Rican electorate. For the first time in history, statehood has come out ahead in the polls in Puerto Rico, having gained 15 points since the . . . bill was reported out." Commonwealthers argued that the same improvements in welfare benefits should be provided under the commonwealth option in order to "level the playing field."

Instead, in an attempt to keep both the statehood and commonwealth options "revenue neutral" — that is, incurring no net cost to the federal Treasury — Sen. Johnston in his new bill has reduced the benefits available to Puerto Ricans under statehood. Specifically, the legislation calls for SSI payments to Puerto Rico to be phased in gradually to a maximum of only about 75 percent of what islanders would otherwise qualify for by the time Puerto Rico actually became a state, five years after the referendum. Similarly, food-stamp benefits to Puerto Ricans would be capped at levels well below those available on the mainland.

Some observers, however, have described these measures as nothing more than a ruse to placate advocates of commonwealth and to maintain the illusion that statehood would not be a drain on the federal Treasury. To begin with, it's not at all clear that, once Puerto Rico became a state, islanders could be limited to lower benefits than citizens of other states — particularly in light of Article IV of the Constitution, which holds that "the citizens of each state shall be entitled to all privileges and immunities of citizens in the several states." Even a Senate analyst concedes that such discrimination is "probably unconstitutional," and would not stand up to a court challenge.

Another major change that would come with statehood is the repeal of the special tax benefits to U.S. corporations setting up businesses in Puerto Rico under Section 936 of the Internal Revenue Code. According to the Treasury Department, in 1989, tax benefits received by Section 936 companies amounted to about $1.9 billion.[18]

The effect of losing Section 936 on Puerto Rico is uncertain. Commonwealth advocates, citing the 160,000 employed directly by Section 936 companies, along with an additional estimated 150,000 jobs dependent on those companies, claim that removal of federal tax exemption would be disastrous. "About three-fourths of all manufacturing employment in Puerto Rico is in 936 companies," Jaime B. Fuster, Puerto Rico's non-voting representative to Congress, told the Senate Finance Committee in 1989. "Moreover, 936 deposits in Puerto Rican banks have allowed the financial sector to grow and thrive to unprecedented levels. Together manufacturing and banking and the indirect service jobs they create account for close to a third of the island's labor force. . . . The elimination of federal tax exemption will inevitably result in a sharp decline of the existing manufacturing and financial structure with the loss of thousands of jobs and the removal of hundreds of millions of dollars from the productive sector of the island's economy."

Statehood advocates, on the other hand, claim that commonwealthers' estimates are grossly inflated. "The industries that take advantage of 936 now aren't labor intensive. They're all mechanized," says political scientist Roland Perusse. "You'll pick up story after story by responsible reporters that talk about the 936 program being the economic cornerstone of Puerto Rico. It *was*, in the 1950s and '60s, no question it was." In the 1980s, however, this assertion "wasn't justified any more. And it's even less justified now in the 1990s."

The truth probably lies somewhere in between. The Congressional Budget Office has put the effects of losing Section 936 at about 1 or 2 percentage points of annual economic growth in Puerto Rico. "Increased federal transfers (less new taxes) would initially stimulate the economy," reads the CBO report. "Later, however, statehood could lead to slower economic growth than would be expected under commonwealth status because statehood could reduce the growth of investment, output and employment in the manufacturing sector." [19]

In claiming overall revenue neutrality for the statehood option, however, Johnston's new bill relies on the full $2 billion of new taxes from Section 936 companies to balance the increase in expenditures on entitlement programs. The crucial assumption is that repeal of Section 936 would not affect Puerto Rico's economy. Under the circumstances, most experts think that is unlikely.

At the same time as Puerto Rico would lose Section 936, individual Puerto Ricans would lose their exemption from federal income taxes. Though loss of the exemption could have a notable impact on Puerto Ricans' standard of living, and could add to those seeking federal entitlement benefits, given the low per capita incomes on the island, experts do not expect income taxes to add noticeably to federal revenue.

In the long run, statehooders argue that the tradeoffs of statehood would work in favor of Puerto Ricans by attracting more businesses and tourism. "Statehood will immediately make the island a more attractive place for investment," writes Hector Ricardo Ramos Díaz, a former secretary of consumer affairs in Puerto Rico. "In the business world potential profit is seen as a direct function of risk. The political security and stability offered by statehood will reduce the perceived risk of investing in Puerto

Rico. Statehood will reduce the current demand of corporations for a larger return on investments in Puerto Rico than on the mainland." [20]

Commonwealth advocates paint a dramatically different picture. "Puerto Rico would be the first state to come into the Union as a dependent of the federal Treasury," Gov. Hernández argued last year. "After our transition to statehood, our economy almost certainly would decline. The federal government would have to spend $2 billion to $3 billion annually in excess of revenue generated in federal taxes paid by Puerto Ricans to provide the safety net necessary to make up for a devastated economy." [21]

**Commonwealth.** If Puerto Ricans choose the commonwealth option, very little would change. In fact, it is possible that nothing at all would change, though both the House and Senate bills have proposed the inclusion of an "enhanced" commonwealth status among the options.

The House bill does not actually specify what a new commonwealth relationship would entail. The Senate bill goes into great detail as to what enhancing the commonwealth relationship would involve. The major features that would change would be the increase in nutritional aid for the poor to match that which the island would enjoy under statehood. The new commonwealth would also receive increased grants for the aged, blind and disabled, to a level equal to what would be available to the island under statehood with SSI. In both cases, the benefits would increase significantly over their current levels, but would still not match the levels of benefits received by the states.

The only other significant change of commonwealth status under Johnston's bill would be the creation of an "office of liaison" to the Senate. Unlike the island's non-voting representative to the House, however, the liaison to the Senate would not be allowed to serve and vote on committees.

As a commonwealth, Puerto Rico would still not receive the same level of benefits in other entitlement programs, such as AFDC and Medicaid, as it would as a state. On the other hand, commonwealth advocates argue that for the foreseeable future the island would retain the benefits of Section 936 tax exemptions. But there's no guarantee as to how long such exemptions would be kept in place. As statehood advocates point out, Section 936 benefits are totally at the discretion of Congress. And the Treasury Department has several times in recent years suggested scrapping the program as too costly.

Commonwealth advocates have also argued for a host of other changes, including Puerto Rican control over negotiating air routes, shipping rates, and other trade arrangements with foreign countries. In fact, Gov. Hernández has even argued that legislation "should make clear that the sovereignty of the commonwealth government would be unequivocal." [22] It is considered unlikely that Congress would grant many if any of these changes, and certainly not "unequivocal sover-

## Puerto Rican Extremists

The great majority of Puerto Ricans who favor independence have pursued that goal peacefully through the political process. But over the years extremists have resorted to terrorist acts.

The most dramatic incident occurred in 1950, when two Puerto Rican nationalists attempted to assassinate President Harry S Truman at Blair House in Washington, where the president was living while the White House underwent repairs. Truman was not harmed, but a Secret Service agent and one of the would-be assassins were killed in a gun battle during the attempt. The other assailant was captured.

Then in 1954, shortly after Puerto Rico became a commonwealth, four militant nationalists sprayed the floor of the House of Representatives with gunfire, wounding five members of Congress.

Over the next 25 years, terrorist activities were limited, with only an occasional pipe-bombing or sniping at U.S. military facilities on the island. In 1979, however, a series of incidents began that demonstrated greater organization on the part of extremists. The two most dangerous groups were the *Macheteros*, which operated primarily in Puerto Rico, and the Armed Forces for National Liberation (FALN), which operated mostly on the mainland.

The *Macheteros* claimed credit for a 1979 ambush on a U.S. Navy bus in Puerto Rico that left two sailors dead and eight wounded. In January 1981, the group followed up with an attack on Muñoz Marín Air Base in San Juan, destroying nine National Guard fighter planes. In November 1981, the *Macheteros* blew up two electric power stations on the island.

In September 1983, in an effort to get funds for future operations, members of the *Macheteros* pulled off a $7 million robbery of a Wells Fargo armored car in Hartford, Conn. One of the most recent actions by the *Macheteros* was a bazooka attack on a U.S. District Court building in San Juan in August 1985. Shortly after that attack, the FBI arrested a dozen *Macheteros*, effectively neutralizing the group at least for the time being.

In 1984, the FBI described the FALN as the most dangerous terrorist group in the United States. Though the FALN did not undertake the sort of high-profile actions executed by the *Macheteros*, the group was responsible for more than 150 attacks between 1973 and 1987, which involved six deaths and more than $3.5 million in property damage.†

There have been no significant terrorist actions related to Puerto Rico in the past few years.

† Roland I. Perusse, The United States and Puerto Rico: Decolonization Options and Prospects (1987), p. 30.

eignty." "The commonwealth people are *independendistas* in their hearts," says one congressional analyst. "But they can't have their cake and eat it too. Commonwealth status does not carry the same sovereignty as independence."

**Independence.** Virtually everyone, including most of those who favor independence, agree that this option doesn't have much chance of winning a plebiscite in the near future. The main appeal of independence to Puerto Ricans is emotional, not economic. And though many Puerto Ricans yearn for the dignity that would come with independence, the "stomach issues" for the time being dictate against such a choice.

Analysts are generally agreed that, over the short-term at least, independence would mean a serious dislocation for Puerto Rico's economy. The island would lose most of the federal entitlement benefits it has received, with the exception only of pension and Social Security benefits. And it is almost certain that Congress would also revoke the Section 936 tax exemptions.

What's more, the CBO notes that as an independent country, Puerto Rico would face interest rates on funds borrowed abroad "at least two percentage points higher than those it would pay under other status options." Some analysts, the report adds, "are concerned that, like other developing countries in Latin America and elsewhere, the island might suffer from a shortage of external capital." [23] Also, while those Puerto Ricans currently holding U.S. citizenship would likely be allowed to retain it, those born in Puerto Rico after independence would not be U.S. citizens. Accordingly, the "escape valve" of migration to the mainland United States would be abruptly shut off.

It is likely, however, that if and when Puerto Ricans opt for independence, the United States would provide some transition assistance. The Senate bill, in fact, provides for payment to an independent Puerto Rico of block grants equal in value to the social benefits currently provided, including Medicare, for a period of 10 years. Also, tax benefits, including Section 936, would not be ended abruptly, but would be phased out over a five-year period. Even if the United States were to decide to provide all the transition benefits listed in the Senate bill, however, the Congressional Budget Office projects that by 1995 the U.S. Treasury would be better off by about $1.6 billion than it would if Puerto Rico retained its current status. [24]

Despite the loss of U.S. funds, however, the Puerto Rican Independence Party argues that independence is the only long-term answer for Puerto Rico, economically as well as politically. "The relationship between Puerto Rico and the United States has created an inordinate amount of economic dependency," says Manuel Rodríguez, electoral commissioner of the Independence Party. "It's an economic dependency that, while it does help in some ways to at least raise the level of the standard of living, it doesn't solve the problem structurally. You might have someone who lives on food stamps for $800 a month, or someone living on food stamps for $1,500 a month. But they're still living on food stamps."

The key change that needs to be made in the Puerto Rican economy, says Eric Negrón, tax adviser to the Independence Party, is to diversify it. "Under independence, our aim is to diversify our sources of capital and our export markets," he says. "About 30

percent of our imports are from European countries. We have very few products going to those markets. That's partly due to the fact that we don't have the favorable access we could get if we were considered a developing nation in terms of not only market access to those otherwise sheltered markets, but also in terms of permitting companies from those areas to come into Puerto Rico without having to face taxes both here and at home." Until Puerto Rico is independent, he adds, the island cannot negotiate such arrangements with foreign countries.

Those who favor independence don't see the loss of Section 936 benefits as an insurmountable hurdle. The kinds of companies that have been attracted to Puerto Rico by Section 936 in recent years have been the kind "that do not engage in the research and development stages of production here," Negrón says. "Here they just do their assembly portions, which yields a lot of nominal value added. They strive to operate here without incurring expenses. They don't have incentive to employ many people, or to engage in labor-intensive activities whatsoever. So we have a system that is not conducive to very high employment." Unfortunately, high-employment industries are just what Puerto Rico needs.

Negrón believes that as an independent country Puerto Rico could continue to attract foreign investment, and it would at the same time be better able to direct what sorts of industries it brought to the island. CBO analysts agree that such a scenario is at least feasible. "As an independent nation, Puerto Rico might offset, wholly or in part, the loss of tax incentives for direct investment by U.S. corporations and, in addition, may be better able to attract direct investment from third countries than the island has in the past," the CBO report notes. [25]

Most analysts agree, however, that even if Puerto Rico were eventually to prosper under independence, there would likely be a lengthy period of painful adjustment to go through first.

## Is Puerto Rico fit to be a state?

It's not clear what action will be taken on Puerto Rico during this session of Congress. Congressional staff members rate the chances of legislation clearing both houses at about 50-50.

But most legislators and analysts involved with the issue seem to believe that it is not a question of "if" but "when" Congress will pass status legislation for Puerto Rico. "Ultimately, the arguments for doing it are so persuasive that I have confidence it'll get done," says a Senate committee staff member. "How can Congress deny after 90 years the people a simple

*Continued on p. 94*

# AT ISSUE
*Would statehood hurt Puerto Rico's economy?*

## YES

*says* **JAIME B. FUSTER**, *non-voting member of Congress from Puerto Rico.*

In 1966 the U.S.-Puerto Rico Status Commission, headed by Sen. Henry Jackson, D-Wash., said: "Unless an appropriate substitute for Puerto Rico's present economic arrangements can be provided, it is clear that statehood ... would have severe and probably disastrous consequences. ... It is not helpful to the people of Puerto Rico to claim that the economic question of statehood is not potentially a very serious one."

That assessment is still valid. No one favoring statehood has yet developed a cogent economic model explaining how to make statehood economically viable for Puerto Rico, an overpopulated island with limited natural resources where unemployment is very high and per capita income low. Statehood advocates in both Puerto Rico and on the mainland limit themselves to crude generalizations such as "no state has ever gone broke" or "political equality will translate into economic progress."

No one has explained what would take the place of the existing tax incentives program that accounts for one of every three jobs in Puerto Rico. No one has explained what would take the place of Puerto Rico's current fiscal autonomy, which has allowed centralized local government to employ hundreds of thousands and to provide extensive public services on a scale that no state government in the United States can afford.

The Bush administration has not addressed at all the potentially explosive language issue. When the United States took over Puerto Rico as war booty in 1898, policy makers in Washington, deeply distrustful of the capabilities of the Puerto Rican people, decided they had to be educated about American institutions before these institutions were transplanted to the island. For 50 years, Americanization meant imposing the English language and casting aside old values; the army, schools, judicial system and labor movement were important tools. This policy was deeply resented and strongly resisted by most Puerto Ricans, and it failed. Thus, after 91 years of intimate association, Puerto Rico remains a separate cultural nationality.

All parties in Puerto Rico want to preserve this distinct personality under any status option. Statehood advocates have adamantly declared that "language is non-negotiable."

Will the United States accept a new state where 60 percent of the people speak no English, and where most will resist efforts to meld? Should Puerto Ricans be encouraged to vote for statehood when the United States is debating the issue of bilingualism?

The last thing the United States needs to do is create grave instability in an island that plays a crucial role in the important Caribbean Basin. Policy makers must think through their position on Puerto Rico's political status and come to understand better what is in the best interests of both the United States and Puerto Rico.

*From a column in* The Washington Post, *July 31, 1989.*

## NO

*says* **ROLAND I. PERUSSE**, *professor of political science at the Inter American University of Puerto Rico.*

Jaime B. Fuster ... greatly underestimates the benefits that would accrue to both the United States and Puerto Rico if the island becomes a state of the union as a result of a plebiscite. ...

Statehood's fresh winds of equality and freedom would bring an economic boom to our island, as it did to Hawaii, and in much the same way. Liberation of the human spirit would stimulate the people to even greater achievement. Tourism would flourish as Americans on the mainland learned that another state of the Union exists with a near-perfect, year-round climate. For the same reason, retirement communities would multiply, property values would soar and additional dollars would enter the Puerto Rican economy.

For these and other reasons, business would boom as investors recognized the degree of security, stability and permanent prosperity that statehood brings. Our professional class would stay on the island and to continue to contribute to our economy instead of migrating to the United States in search of greater economic opportunity. ...

Puerto Rico's present economic model, commonwealth, is the greatest ideological oddity ever conceived by the mind of man. It is a corruption of capitalism, with fascist and socialist undertones. Its most serious flaw is that it doesn't work. It worked well in the '50s and '60s but sputtered in the '70s and [was] a wreck at the end of the '80s. After 37 years of commonwealth, our per capita income remains half that of the poorest U.S. state, and unemployment in [the '80s] has varied from 14 to 25 percent — three to five times that of the United States.

Fuster replays the broken record of an overpopulated island with limited natural resources. The fact is that our population rate is declining. ... We have always had enviable resources in the sea, sand, sun and soil around us, not to speak of the human resources of the island, but Fuster's model has failed to take advantage of these God-given bounties.

Commonwealth has relied instead on artificial arrangements that have generated dependency rather than prosperity at a considerable cost to the U.S. taxpayer. We have become a nation of beggars instead of standing tall and proud. ...

Unable to make an economic argument for commonwealth, Fuster raises cultural non-issues. He accuses the Bush administration of not addressing the "potentially explosive language issue."

If the language issue is "potentially explosive" in Puerto Rico, it is only because Fuster and others like him try to make it so. Both the Bush administration and the U.S. Congress have done the right thing by leaving well enough alone.

*From a column in* The Washington Post, *Aug. 15, 1989.*

*Continued from p. 92*

petition to be consulted on their future?" If legislation is not passed this session, the issue will be right back on the legislators' doorstep, just as soon as the 1992 elections are over in Puerto Rico.

But even if legislation is passed this year or next, there's no assurance that Congress would act favorably on Puerto Ricans' choice. In particular, if statehood is the island's choice — and that is the status that is currently leading in the polls — many doubt that Congress would in the end approve Puerto Rico's joining the Union. "Is there anyone that thinks the Congress is ready to vote favorably on statehood today?" Del. de Lugo asks rhetorically. "No." According to de Lugo, there is a lot of negotiating that will have to take place between Puerto Rico and the Congress before a majority vote for statehood could be hoped for.

Statehood is, indeed, the one option that causes the most uneasiness in the United States. Though legislators are reluctant to go on the record, some have reportedly expressed concerns about the potential costs to the U.S. Treasury, particularly in this era of high federal deficits. And some worry about whether Puerto Rico — with its predominance of Latino culture and with only 40 percent of its people able to speak English — really "fits" in the United States.

Concerns about whether Puerto Rico is "suited" to become a state often draw charges of racism, but Manuel Rodríguez of the Puerto Rican Independence Party says there are some good reasons to ask the question. "There comes a realization that U.S. citizenship is a label, and being Puerto Rican is what's inside the bottle," says Rodríguez. "Many Americans tend to feel uncomfortable with saying they don't feel Puerto Rico should become a state because they're afraid of being labeled racist or discriminatory. I think that it should be made clear to the American people that there is no shame in the United States saying, 'Wait a minute — it's one thing for immigrants to come here because they want to become Americans, to integrate, and another thing for those who want to receive the benefits of statehood without really becoming Americans.'"

Puerto Ricans are not just an ethnic group, argues the Independence Party, but a nationality. "Minorities and majorities come and go; but nationalities remain," Rubén Berríos Martínez, president of the party, wrote recently. "The United States is a unitary, not a multinational, country, and statehood was made for Americans, not for Puerto Ricans or other distinct nationalities." Berríos added that even under statehood, "We Puerto Rican *independendistas* will never give up our inalienable right to struggle for independence." [26]

Indeed, the possibilities for social unrest on the island has many observers concerned. Though the Puerto Rican Independence Party has publicly forsworn violence as a means of achieving independence, there are many fringe elements that have resorted to terrorist activities in the past. (*See story, p. 91.*) "If

statehood were to win and the Congress were to take the necessary steps, the U.S. would have on its hands a situation in which a permanent, hard-core group of people who favor independence for Puerto Rico would always be in favor of that," says a congressional aide. "There have been concerns expressed that if that scenario came into being that those people who favor independence would not just go down gracefully. You could make the case that there would be terrorism. Certainly, that's happened in the past."

Rodríguez agrees. Though he and his party have opted for a strictly non-violent struggle, Rodríguez says: "I can't answer for my children." A separatist movement would continue to exist, and would become a national security problem for the United States, he warns. "At some point in this process, the low level of violence practiced for years by small groups of fanatics could become more generalized."

Still, others feel that if the majority of Puerto Ricans want statehood, it is not something that can in good conscience be denied. "We want to become a state. We love America and want to become a part of it. We can't understand why America won't act," says Roland Perusse. "My God, how much longer are we going to take this in Puerto Rico?"

# NOTES

[1] See *Congressional Quarterly Weekly Report*, Dec. 8, 1990, p. 4078.
[2] U.S. Department of Commerce, *Statistical Abstract of the United States, 1990*, Bureau of the Census, p. 317.
[3] Congressional Research Service memorandum to Congress, July 6, 1989.
[4] James L. Dietz, *Economic History of Puerto Rico: Institutional Change and Capitalist Development* (1986), p. 243.
[5] *Ibid.*, p. 247.
[6] *Ibid.*, p. 254.
[7] Bertram P. Finn, "Puerto Rico's Economic Development: The Old Formula No Longer Works -A New Strategy is Needed," in *Puerto Rico: The Search for a National Policy* (1985), edited by Richard J. Bloomfield, p. 24.
[8] Finn, *op. cit.*, p. 29.
[9] Congressional Budget Office, *Potential Economic Impacts of Changes in Puerto Rico's Status Under S 712*, April 1990, p. 6.
[10] Luis Neves Falcon, "The Social Pathology of Dependence," in Bloomfield, *op. cit.*, p. 49.
[11] Congressional Budget Office, *op. cit.*, p. 7.
[12] In 1988, the official poverty line was $6,024 for an individual and $12,092 for a family of four. See *Statistical Abstract of the United States: 1990*, p. 423.
[13] *Idem.*
[14] Congressional Research Service memorandum to Congress, July 6, 1989.
[15] *Congressional Record*, Oct. 10, 1990.
[16] Hernández's April 19, 1990, speech was entered into the *Congressional Record* on April 24, 1990.
[17] Congressional Budget Office, *op. cit.*, p. 14.
[18] Testimony by Kenneth W. Gideon, assistant secretary for tax policy of the Treasury Department, before the Senate Energy and Natural Resources Committee on July 13, 1989.
[19] Congressional Budget Office, *op. cit.*, p. 1.
[20] Hector Ricardo Ramos Díaz, "The Path to Statehood: Puerto Rico is No Exception," in Bloomfield, *op. cit.*, p. 164.
[21] Writing in *The New York Times*, Feb. 26, 1990.
[22] *Ibid.*
[23] Congressional Budget Office, *op. cit.*, pp. 2, 3.
[24] This figure is contained in a Congressional Budget Office cost-estimate memorandum sent to the Senate Finance Committee, Sept. 14, 1990.
[25] Congressional Budget Office, *op. cit.*, p. 4.
[26] Writing in *The Washington Post*, May 23, 1990.

*Graphics: Cover, Margaret Scott; pp. 86, 89, Jack Auldridge.*

**RECOMMENDED READING**

## BOOKS

**Bloomfield, Richard J., ed., *Puerto Rico: The Search for a National Policy*, Westview Press, 1985.**

Though much of the economic data in this book is now dated, the assembled essays present well-written arguments over development strategies for Puerto Rico. The book concludes with policy statements from each of the three Puerto Rican political parties on what the United States should do for Puerto Rico.

**Dietz, James L., *Economic History of Puerto Rico: Institutional Change and Capitalist Development*, Princeton University Press, 1986.**

This is an excellent book on the economic history of Puerto Rico. Though unavoidably dense in places, it is filled with lots of useful data placed in context by insightful analysis.

**Falk, Pamela S., ed., *The Political Status of Puerto Rico*, Lexington Books, 1986.**

This book consists primarily of policy statements by political figures, from the mayor of San Juan, to a columnist at the *San Juan Star*, to a U.S. congressman. The brief essays — an average of only five pages each — are more rhetorical than analytical.

**García-Passalacqua, Juan M., *Puerto Rico: Equality and Freedom at Issue*, Praeger, 1984.**

As might be expected from the pen of a columnist for the *San Juan Star*, this book takes an approach more journalistic than academic to covering the history of Puerto Rico since the end of the Spanish-American War. Garcia-Passalacqua writes clearly and outlines the main issues at stake in the debate over the island's political status.

**Meléndez, Edgardo, *Puerto Rico's Statehood Movement*, Greenwood Press, 1988.**

Melendez offers a thorough and readable history of Puerto Rico's statehood movement from 1898 to the present.

**Perusse, Roland I., *The United States and Puerto Rico: Decolonization Options and Prospects*, University Press of America, 1987.**

Perusse, a professor of U.S.-Puerto Rican relations at the Inter American University of Puerto Rico, presents the positions of more than a dozen major politicians and analysts on the three status options for Puerto Rico. These analyses are sandwiched between Perusse's own broad ranging analysis of the challenges facing Puerto Rico.

## REPORTS AND STUDIES

**Congressional Budget Office, *CBO Papers: Potential Economic Impacts of Changes in Puerto Rico's Status under S. 712*, April 1990.**

This report analyzes the economic implications of S 712, the Puerto Rican referendum bill sponsored by Sen. J. Bennett Johnston, D-La. The report is obviously dated by the fact that S 712 died with the last Congress and has been superseded by Bennett's new bill, S 244. But very little that the CBO looks at has been changed from the previous bill to the current one, so careful readers will still find the bulk of the report relevant. The particulars of legislation aside, this report represents the most detailed analysis available of the effects of status changes on Puerto Rico. Readers of this report will want to also obtain the CBO's Sept. 14, 1990, memo to the Senate Committee on Finance, which provides additional details on the effects of repealing tax incentives and other matters.

**Puerto Rico Economic Development Administration, *Puerto Rico: A Brief Introduction*, March 1990.**

This annual report from a government-funded agency has something of the feel of a chamber of commerce publication, but it is nevertheless a valuable source of economic and social data.

EDITORIAL RESEARCH REPORTS

*Coming soon*

Redistricting

Pensions

Nuclear Power

Published weekly by
Congressional Quarterly
Inc., Editorial Research
Reports analyze emerging
issues of national interest
across a broad range of
social, scientific, political
and economic fields.
Reports are bound and
indexed for permanent
reference. Subscription
information is available
through Congressional
Quarterly's Publications
Sales Department by
telephone (202) 887-8665.
Copies of past issues are
available through
Customer Service, (202)
887-8621.

FEBRUARY 15, 1991

CONGRESSIONAL QUARTERLY'S

# EDITORIAL RESEARCH REPORTS

FOUNDED 1923

# REDISTRICTING: DRAWING POWER WITH A MAP

1991 No. 7

# EDITORIAL RESEARCH REPORTS

**EDITOR**
**MARCUS D. ROSENBAUM**

**MANAGING EDITOR**
**SANDRA STENCEL**

**ASSOCIATE EDITOR**
**RICHARD L. WORSNOP**

**STAFF WRITERS**
**MARY H. COOPER**
**PATRICK G. MARSHALL**

**PRODUCTION EDITOR**
**LAURIE DE MARIS**

**EDITORIAL ASSISTANT**
**AMY GORTON**

**RICHARD M. BOECKEL (1892-1975)**
**FOUNDER**

**PUBLISHED BY**
**CONGRESSIONAL QUARTERLY INC.**

**CHAIRMAN**
**ANDREW BARNES**

**PRESIDENT**
**RICHARD R. EDMONDS**

**EDITOR AND PUBLISHER**
**NEIL SKENE**

**EXECUTIVE EDITOR**
**ROBERT W. MERRY**

© 1991 BY CONGRESSIONAL QUARTERLY INC.

EDITORIAL RESEARCH REPORTS (LIBRARY OF CONGRESS
CATALOGUE NO. 39-924; ISSN 0013-0958). Published weekly
(48 times per year, excluding March 1, May 3, August 2 and
November 1, 1991) by Congressional Quarterly Inc., 1414 22nd
Street NW, Washington, D.C. 20037. Rates are furnished
upon request. Application to mail at second-class postage
rates is pending at Washington, D.C. POSTMASTER: Send
address changes to EDITORIAL RESEARCH REPORTS, 1414
22nd Street NW, Washington, D.C. 20037.

# REDISTRICTING: DRAWING POWER WITH A MAP

## *by Ronald D. Elving*

This year the states are undertaking their constitutional duty of "redistricting" — drawing new borders and creating new constituencies for politicians — because of the 1990 census. At the congressional level, some states gained seats and some lost them, but only the few states with a single representative will escape the need to draw new district lines to reflect shifting population patterns. Thus, redistricting could be a major impetus for changing the makeup of Congress and state legislatures. But because politicians put their own survival first, redistricting generally serves to preserve the status quo.

Long before talk of "permanent incumbents" and limits on lawmakers' terms, the authors of the Constitution had an idea that would keep Congress representative and responsive: The seats in the House of Representatives would be redistributed — "reapportioned" — among the states every 10 years to reflect population changes. Besides promoting equal representation, the idea had at least the potential to force turnover by trimming seats from some delegations and adding

*Ronald D. Elving is the deputy political editor of*
Congressional Quarterly Weekly Report.

them to others. The same idea was incorporated into state and local institutions, and, given a chance to work, it still provides transfusions of new blood in the House and in every other legislative body at each level of government.

For obvious reasons, when reapportionment expands or shrinks a state's delegation in Congress, the lines between that state's districts must be redrawn. More recently, however, federal courts have required that districts be as equal in population as possible. So even when reapportionment leaves the number of seats unchanged, the district lines must be adjusted to reflect population shifts within the state.

Reapportionment, then, begets redistricting. And their combined effect is the slow but sure enforcement of change. Incumbents may find themselves suddenly representing many thousands of new constituents, people who may have different interests and leanings. New constituents may not know the incumbent's record — or name, for that matter. New constituents are far less likely to have received the incumbent's frequent mailings, or to have enjoyed his help in finding a missing government check. That is why members of Congress returned to work in January preoccupied not only with the Persian Gulf and the recession but with the tricky mechanical problem of predicting who their constituents will be in 1992.

Some members may find their old district no longer recognizable, or their home located in someone else's district. Others will find the music has stopped and they are, quite literally, without a seat. Or they will find themselves thrown together in a single district with another incumbent — often from the same party. The scramble to prevent or minimize such political problems involves some of the most brutal combat in American politics, for the power to draw district lines is the power not only to end one politician's career but often to enfranchise or disenfranchise a neighborhood, a city, a party, a social or economic group or even a race by concentrating or diluting their votes within a given district.[1]

In each new decade, the upheaval of redistricting is triggered by the census. Once the national population has been established and the state figures are known, the 435 seats (a number fixed in 1912) can be apportioned.* Then the process generally falls into the hands of the state legislatures, where the two parties fight between themselves and within themselves over whose seat will be protected and whose rendered vulnerable. Most governors have veto power over the

maps drawn by legislators, which means a legislature of one party may have to allow a governor of the other party to take a hand as soon as the dealing begins.

Recently, this game has been radically rearranged by the arrival of a new player — the federal judiciary. Until just a generation ago, legislators often drew districts to preserve the rural tilt of the past despite large migration toward the cities. When the Supreme Court finally addressed the question with its landmark "one person, one vote" decision in the early 1960s (see p. 103), Louisiana had not redrawn its district lines since 1912 and Tennessee had not done so since 1901. States as diverse as South Carolina, Colorado and Wisconsin had not changed theirs since the 1930s.

Having decided each person's vote should be weighed equally, regardless of where he or she lived, the court soon found itself confronted with line-drawing intended to dilute the voting strength of a race or a party. For example, when the Voting Rights Act came to Mississippi in the mid-1960s and forced local registrars to enroll black voters, legislators promptly redrew the districts so as to divide black votes in the Delta counties among as many different white legislators and congressmen as feasible.

After outlawing such endeavors, the high court later indicated that minority voter strength had to be *maximized* in the states where it had once been diluted. And, while it has been far less decisive regarding maps drawn not with race but with politics in mind — to disadvantage a given party — it has hinted that these schemes may be illegal, too.[2]

Meanwhile, there is a new factor at play in the arcane business of redistricting: technology. In the past, redistricting required painstaking calculations and recalculations of volumes of census data. The process was time-consuming and difficult not only to do, but also to check for accuracy. Now, however, anyone with a personal computer and the right software can participate. As the politicians work on the new maps required by the 1990 census, every lobbyist and every citizens' group will be looking over their shoulders — and offering their own maps for consideration. (See story, p. 101.)

At the same time, the politicians themselves may be playing the game differently this year. In past years, members of Congress, although legally only observers of the redistricting process, have worked behind the scenes to get district lines to their liking; plans mutually agreed upon by the incumbents of both parties have often been acceptable to the state legislators (who have generally been more concerned about their own — and their colleagues' — futures, anyway). This year, the congressional incumbents are likely to attempt the same approach, but as term limits and anti-incumbent movements gain momentum, fewer legislators may be willing to accommodate them. On the contrary, with the clock running out on their own terms, some may want to design districts in which they themselves could successfully challenge those congressional incumbents.

---

*This has usually been an objective undertaking run by demographers and other disinterested technicians. But in recent years, even the basic head count has become controversial. The big cities and states of the Northeast have sued, alleging their poorest residents have been systematically undercounted. The pending litigation could cause the delay of apportionment and redistricting — into late 1991 or even 1992. That would leave thousands of congressional and legislative candidates uncertain of their constituencies. For background, see "1990 Census: Undercounting Minorities," *E.R.R.*, March 10, 1989 (Vol. I, No. 9).

However the game is played in the individual states, it is clear from the 1990 census that nationally power is continuing its shift away from the industrial North and toward the South and the West. When the new Congress convenes in 1993, 17 more seats will have moved from the Frost Belt to the Sun Belt. California will gain seven seats to reach an unprecedented total of 52. Florida, gaining four seats to a total of 23, will have a larger delegation than Pennsylvania, with 21, losing two.

Each congressional seat gained or lost also means a vote gained or lost in the Electoral College, the mechanism by which the president is actually elected after the popular vote has been tallied (each state is allotted electoral votes equal to its representation in both houses of Congress). The meaning here is not hard to discern. In 1948, New York still had 47 electoral votes and one of the two major parties usually nominated a New Yorker for president. Forty years later, California had 47 electoral votes, and a Californian had won four of the previous five presidential elections.

The population shift diminishes the pre-eminence of the old population centers with their traditional labor-liberal Democratic politics. The Southern states gain seats even as they become less monolithically Democratic. Moreover, within the states, the shift is from urban venues to suburban, from traditionally Democratic districts to traditionally Republican ones.

For that reason, redistricting has been a pillar of Republican hopes for regaining control of the House of Representatives for the first time since 1954. But to date, fulfillment of those hopes has remained elusive. Democratic control of state legislatures, which draw the lines for legislative and congressional districts, has shown remarkable resilience. And where districts have been drawn to favor Republicans, the GOP has often failed to produce candidates to exploit the opportunity.

Moreover, although the growth regions of the Sun Belt have been presumed to be more conservative, the new districts in the South and West often include substantial populations of blacks, Hispanics and other minorities. And while the GOP wants badly to make minority voters a positive factor in their electoral equation, much work remains to be done if that desire is to bear fruit.

Nonetheless, for both parties each census means a fresh map, an untouched field and an unspoiled day. As each decade dawns, the prospect of redistricting renews the political hunt.

In many ways the internecine aspect of these struggles obscures what is really at stake. Because redistricting is politics at its most elemental — survival and power are the issues of the day — the relevance of these backroom maneuverings may not be apparent. But policy is not made in a vacuum; it is made by individuals. So ultimately redistricting influences much more than the distribution of political office and money. In a real sense it determines the direction of the nation's history.

## From quill and scroll to custom computer software

The Constitution itself apportioned the first House's 65 seats among the 13 original states, with each seat representing approximately 30,000 people. After the 1790 census, new districts were to be added in response to state growth. But just how much growth would suffice to create a new seat was not clear. That was left up to Congress.

It wasn't an easy job. The first bill ever to attempt reapportionment, in 1792, displeased George Washington enough to occasion the first presidential veto. Thomas Jefferson devised an alternative by which the number of seats was fixed at 105 and the required number of residents for one representative was set at 33,000. With subsequent censuses, the size of the House was simply enlarged to reflect the larger number of residents. However, in 1840, with the House of Representatives having grown to 242 members, Congress put a halt to that system and set up one by which the size of the House was fixed prior to each apportionment, and the number of constituents for each representative was allowed to fluctuate. After another half century of growth, Congress permanently fixed the size of the House in 1912 at the present 435 seats.[3]

How those seats have been apportioned has followed the basic trends of the nation itself. In the early years, Virginia dominated the House as no state has since. Even California's gargantuan delegation in 1993 will not bulk as large in percentage terms as Virginia's once did. In the 1790s, Virginia's 19 seats represented about 18 percent of the House; in 1993, California's 52 will represent only about 12 percent.

The Eastern Seaboard overshadowed all other regions through 1900. But by 1912 the six Great Lakes states from Ohio west accounted for nearly a quarter of the House. And in the late 1920s the states of the Great Plains had more House members than they do today. But the Depression, the Dust Bowl, World War II and the rise of air conditioning all conspired to wrench destiny in a new direction — and reapportionment forced Congress to respond. The 10 states stretching along the nation's southern rim from California to South Carolina had just 80 seats among them at the end of the 1920s. Three decades later they had risen to just 103. But in the three decades since, they have come to claim (after the 1990 census) more than 150 seats, or more than one-third of the House. And in most of these states, growth is still accelerating.

Technically, the Census Bureau's task is merely to chronicle and calculate the pace of these historic changes. But in recent years, the bureau has seemed to lose some of its political innocence. One reason is that federal program formulas use census data to determine how many federal dollars a particular community may receive. But another is the growing awareness that uncounted residents weaken a state or municipal-

# *Costs and Benefits of High-Tech Cartography*

Redistricting in the 1990s may be a game any number can play, but would-be players will find the requisite computer hardware, software and data bases carry substantial price tags.

For generations, Census Bureau data have been "hard copy" phenomena so voluminous and complex that only states and major-party organizations had the staff to tackle the task of sorting through it. The mountain of material became truly daunting as court decisions on "one person, one vote" and other issues demanded that more and more information be generated.

After the early 1970s redistricting, Congress passed a law (PL 94-171) that required the Census Bureau to produce computer data files to facilitate future remapping. "Computer" meant big mainframes that could not only store information about population, demographics and voting history but rearrange it on command as programmers tried out various mapping alternatives.

The so-called PL 94 files have since grown and evolved. This year, the Census Bureau will supply 24 demographic breakdowns (there were seven in 1980) for every county, town, precinct and block in the 50 states. On paper, the data for Michigan alone will run to 11,000 pages.

Now, the bureau is also selling a new product called "Tiger" files (short for Topologically Integrated Geographic Encoding and Referencing). They are detailed electronic maps. By integrating Tigers with the latest census data, computerized remappers can rearrange districts not only by numbers of people but by race and other characteristics down to the street and block. Add in a data base for voting results (precinct by precinct), and you can reallocate votes with far greater accuracy and speed than ever before.

With all these tools, smaller organizations, individual legislators or other interested parties will be able to analyze proposed new maps on their own. They can even design their own and shop them around.

But before assuming redistricting will replace Nintendo, consider the costs. To do it right, you need some expertise. Some Tiger files may not match up perfectly with the formats of the voting data obtained from different sources, and adjusting them will not be simple. Much of the voting data will have to be entered into the data base by hand, as only some states have the data in "machine readable" form. All such data will need to be verified.

Moreover, when people talk about "doing it on a PC," they generally do not mean an inexpensive home model. If one is going first-class, a $25,000 investment in a "high-end hardware platform" and another $2,500 or so in operating software will be just the beginning, says Mark Acton, assistant director of redistricting for the National Republican Congressional Committee.

It is a matter of how big and how small. How much area and how many people do you need to cover? And how much detail, especially in voting results, do you want?

William H. McGee, vice president of Geographic Systems Integration Inc., says those interested in a small state might get away with spending only $15,000 to $20,000. But a quality system for a big state might total $70,000 and will need color graphics cards, sophisticated plotters and perhaps such extras as 3-foot diagonal high-resolution monitors and other means of making the process vivid and precise.

But with these tools, anyone interested in redistricting can plot districts through endless permutations, keyboarding instructions and watching the ramifications develop on-screen. And it will be possible to run through permutations quickly. "If you get handed a map at 6 o'clock and you're voting on it the next morning, you need speed," notes McGee.

---

ity's clout in either the state or the national capitol.

In each of the last three censuses, Democratic enclaves in the North have been counted as losing population — not just the population they acknowledged having lost but hundreds of additional thousands. In 1987, several Northeastern cities and states filed suit to force the Census Bureau to supplement traditional head-counting methods with population estimates derived from sampling techniques.

Responding to the lawsuits, the Commerce Department (parent agency to the Census Bureau) agreed in 1987 to consider adjusting its head count once the regular enumeration was completed. Its latest deadline for announcing a decision on adjustment is July 15. Few experts in the field expect the department to adjust the figures significantly, and a final decision against adjustment will almost certainly prompt court challenges.

"These are uncharted waters," says Marshall Turner, the acting chief of the Data User Services Division of the Census Bureau and a veteran of 26 years of redistricting battles at the agency. "We've had lawsuits before, but not of this kind with this potential for delay. Most of the states are proceeding with the caveat that there could be new numbers later this year. How they handle it if there is, is really a question for them."

The problem is particularly acute for the four states that hold legislative elections in 1991. Three of the four, in fact, have already begun the legislative session in which the new map is supposed to be drawn. If no final decision is available on census adjustment until July, the actual shape of electoral districts in these four states will not be available until well after campaigns have begun.

And the potential panic extends well beyond these states. If the Census Bureau refuses to adjust for an undercount, various federal judges around the country could begin issuing rulings later in 1991 or 1992. Those rulings will surely be challenged in the federal appellate courts and then in the Supreme Court itself. And the outcome of any high court decision could send everyone back to the drawing board to determine legislative and congressional maps for 1992 — possibly just a few months before the election is to take place.

Under more normal circumstances, the legislatures could be collecting their final numbers from the Census Bureau this spring and delegating to staff the task of redrawing districts as acceptable as possible to incumbents. The idea is to reach a critical mass of placated members — congressional and legislative — so that a plan can be passed and sent to the governor.

In 20 states, the governor will be of the same party that controls both houses of the legislature. (*See pp. 104-105.*) Absent some special pique, these governors will usually be involved in designing the map from the outset and will sign the legislators' product without fuss.

But in the rest of the states, at least one house of the legislature is of a different party and the threat of a veto comes into play. All but five states (Connecticut, Hawaii, Montana, North Carolina and Washington) allow the governor to veto the legislature's handiwork. Of the five, only Washington and North Carolina have a sizable number of seats to distribute.

In some cases, vetoes can be overridden by top-heavy majorities (not unknown in the South) or by coalitions between the two parties' legislators. In some cases, the desire to see a particular set of lines in place for individual political reasons can undermine a minority-party legislator's team spirit.

After witnessing the rancorous and time-consuming fights that often arise over redistricting, several states passed legislation attempting to rationalize and depoliticize the process. In Connecticut, the legislature has until Oct. 1 to pass a plan of its own; after that, the legislative leaders select eight members of a special committee that selects its own ninth member and must submit a legally binding compromise within 30 days. In Iowa, a nonpartisan agency of government submits a plan to the legislature. In Maine, Rhode Island and Washington, a commission devises a plan for legislators' approval. In New York, a task force submits a plan for legislators' approval. In Hawaii, another eight-pick-a-ninth panel does the job and sends its product straight into law. A similar plan handles the task for legislative districts in Montana, which will have only one seat in the House.

## Orders from the courts redefine the landscape

In the first years of the Republic, reapportionment did not automatically mean redistricting. In fact, many states obviated district lines altogether and simply filled their apportioned seats in the House by electing representatives statewide. This at-large approach allowed a powerful region or faction within a state to dominate its delegations. With the same powers probably running the state government as well, objections from the underrepresented were often in vain. The federal government was reluctant to discipline states over such a relatively technical matter, however, and such statewide schemes were common for half a century. In 1842, Congress passed a law that specifically forbade at-large delegations, but even so, such arrangements continued to crop up in response to (or under the color of) peculiar circumstances.

These "general ticket" elections of representatives, as they're called, usually occurred when states were first added to the Union or when they were unable or unwilling to arrive at a post-apportionment redistricting plan. Five multiple-member delegations were all "general ticket" for the 73rd Congress (1933-35), for instance. Each had seen its apportionment reduced after the census of 1930, an especially sharp shock because there had been no reapportionment after the census of 1920.

Another kind of at-large representative came from states that elected all but one or two members by districts. Here again, the practice primarily functioned as a pressure valve or safety device after a census and reapportionment. It was most common in the 43rd Congress (1873-75), when nine states did it. But this type of at-large member appeared as recently as the 89th Congress (1965-67), when Maryland, Ohio and Texas each had one such seat. The practice was finally outlawed in December 1967.[4]

Until 30 years ago, the courts were reluctant to interfere in the way states chose their congressional representatives. Even as the decade of the 1960s began, the venerable Supreme Court Justice Felix Frankfurter continued to dismiss the issue as "a political thicket" best shunned by jurists. But the activist court of that era, under Chief Justice Earl Warren, was not one to pass thorny problems by, and in 1962 it grasped one of the thorniest. The case was called *Baker v. Carr,* and in it a group of urban-dwellers from Tennessee asked whether a state could draw legislative (and, by extension, congressional) district maps subordinating population to other criteria. Justice William J. Brennan Jr., the trailblazer here as on other issues, led a 6-2 majority that, while it did not overturn the existing districts, did grant that the plaintiffs had a point.[5]

The question was far from academic. Practically since the Republic's founding, state legislatures had found it to their advantage to structure seats not by relative population but by political subdivisions such as counties. The abuse had become particularly acute after World War I and the upheavals of population it had produced. The 1920 census found such radical shifts from rural to urban areas that Congress could not manage to pass a bill of apportionment; legislators from rural venues blocked enactment of the census results throughout the decade. Thereafter, Congress adopted a more scientific method of distributing seats developed by a Harvard professor in 1921, which

# Reapportionment's Close Calls

**W**hen congressional and legislative seats are reapportioned, even slight shifts can make a difference. Of the 13 states that will lose some representation in the next Congress, *most* could have had another seat if their head count had been higher by 2 percent or less. Four states were losers by an eyelash, forfeiting a seat they could have kept with a count just 1 percent higher or even less. Massachusetts and New Jersey lost out by about one-half of one percentage point.

In raw numbers, the frustration trophy went to Kentucky, where just 3,981 more residents in the preliminary count would have kept the state's delegation intact. Montana could have kept both its districts with just 8,157 more residents. Among the luckier stories: Mississippi avoided losing a seat by a margin of just 2,747 people.

Each of these states improved slightly in the final figures released Dec. 26. But so did every other state — none was adjusted downward — so the prospective losers from reapportionment in August remained so at year's end.

The current method by which House seats are apportioned was not established until 1941. Previously, different methods were used to produce competing bills of apportionment that vied for congressional approval. Now, Congress merely rubber stamps the application of the "method of equal proportions" (devised by Edward V. Huntington of Harvard in 1921).

The system first assigns each of the 50 states one seat. Then the remaining 385 seats are apportioned by assigning states a priority value rank. The ranks are assigned using a mathematical formula that measures population against the number of seats remaining. Not surprisingly, this assigns the 51st seat to California, the most populous state, and the 52nd to New York, the second most populous.

Then it gets a bit trickier. The 53rd seat goes not to Texas, the third most populous state, but to California, which gets its third helping before any state but New York has qualified for a second. Texas then claims the 54th seat and Florida the 55th before California

shoulders to the front of the line again and receives the 56th. And so on until all 435 seats are allocated.

Judged against other mechanisms, Huntington's produces the smallest deviation between the most and the least populous districts. It also yields the smallest deviation from a population-per-district average nationwide. After the 1981 reapportionment, for example, the most populous district was South Dakota's single district (690,768). The least was either of Montana's two districts, both of which were slightly under 400,000. In the 1990s, however, having lost its second seat, Montana will have the one most populous district (803,655 by the Dec. 26 figures). The distinction of being least populous will move south across the state line into Wyoming, where one House member will represent just 455,975.

Among states with multiple districts, Rhode Island will have the smallest at about 503,000 each and New Mexico will be next at about 507,000 each. The mean population per district nationwide will be about 572,500.

obviated any direct congressional role.[6]

But if the rural interests could not forever resist the loss of seats through reapportionment, they could still control the redistricting of their remaining seats. And this they did with a vengeance. Several states simply stopped redrawing the district lines for Congress or the legislative seats. As late as 1960, for example, California allotted a state senator to three remote mountain counties with a total population of 15,000 and one state senator to Los Angeles County with a population of 6 million. Nevada's state Senate had one member with 223 times as many constituents as another, while in the Vermont House the maximum ratio of discrepancy was a staggering 1,480-to-1.[7]

Technically, the *Baker* case decided little other than the justiciable nature of the issue at hand — that is, that it would be fair game should the justices choose to deal with it later. But with the gate open, the flood was not long in pouring through. The next year, writing for the majority in *Gray v. Sanders,* Justice William O. Douglas penned the phrase that still resounds, stating that the "conception of political equality from the Declaration of Independence to Lincoln's Gettysburg Address to the 15th, 17th and 19th Amendments can mean only one thing — one

person, one vote." In the succession of cases that followed, the court established that legislative districts had to be "substantially equal" in size but that congressional districts had to be "as nearly equal in population as practicable" — a standard that, in the computer age, approximates a deviation of zero.[8]

The standard has been taken seriously. Of the 435 representatives elected in 1972, 385 were elected in districts that deviated from the average district population in their state by less than 1 percent. The *reductio ad absurdum* was reached in the early 1980s, when a court-imposed map in Michigan created 16 districts with the exact same population of 514,560 each and two more with 514,559. "Will we be faced with that kind of absurdity again this time? I don't know," says Kimball Brace, whose Election Data Services provides census analysis and other redistricting help for parties and candidates. But when rival groups, such as the two major parties, submit competing state redistricting plans to the courts for review, equality of district population will inevitably be a major criterion in the judging.

The language employed by Douglas back in 1963, however, implied a question of equality beyond that

*Continued on p. 106*

# *Remapping State by State*

This chart shows, for each state, the current number of House seats, how they are divided between the parties, the number of seats after 1992, the party in control of each house of the legislature and the governorship, and a brief description of the redistricting battle ahead. States that gain House seats are shaded blue; states that lose seats are shaded gray; states that remain the same are white. States in which both houses of the legislature and the governor are of the same party are in light type; states in which there is divided control are in boldface. The six current single-seat states are not listed. They are (with the party of their representative in parentheses) Alaska (R), Delaware (D), South Dakota (D), North Dakota (D), Vermont (I) and Wyoming (R). Each of them will continue to have one representative after 1992.

| State | Number of Seats Current (D/R) | After 1992 | Party in Power Legis. Lwr. | Uppr. | Gov. | Redistricting |
|-------|--------|------|------|------|------|---------------|
| Ala. | 7 (5/2) | 7 | D | D | D | The big question mark in Alabama is whether the Democrats can create a black-majority district in Birmingham without giving the GOP a shot at a third seat in the process. |
| **Ariz.** | **5 (1/4)** | **6** | **R** | **D** | **?** | **The governorship will be decided by a runoff Feb. 26. But the split legislature is likely to preserve the status quo by allowing Democrats a shot at two to three seats out of six.** |
| Ark. | 4 (3/1) | 4 | D | D | D | One of the more secure situations in the country if the Democrats draw the lines skillfully enough. Total control may allow them to keep three seats of four. |
| **Calif.** | **45 (26/19)** | **52** | **D** | **D** | **R** | **Historic opportunity to break through to the biggest payoff anywhere may come a cropper if new GOP Gov. Pete Wilson cannot enforce discipline in the legislature. GOP has a chance for something close to an even split. (For details, see story, p. 108.)** |
| **Colo.** | **6 (3/3)** | **6** | **R** | **R** | **D** | **Democrats must scramble to protect the district that includes Boulder from becoming any more Republican than it already is. Otherwise, the 3-3 tie looks solid.** |
| **Conn.** | **6 (3/3)** | **6** | **D** | **D** | **I** | **Legislature must pass a plan by Sept. 15 or cede the chance to a commission. Legislative leaders would pick eight commissioners who would then pick a ninth. The nine would have one month to write a plan directly into law. Party split likely to remain even.** |
| Fla. | 19 (9/10) | 23 | D | D | D | Fireworks here likely to happen in court, where GOP and minorities may challenge Democrats' map, which will try to regain the delegation majority. |
| Ga. | 10 (9/1) | 11 | D | D | D | Another case for the GOP to take to court after no-compromise redistricting by an untrammeled Democratic power structure; in the long run, two GOP seats look likely. |
| Hawaii | 2 (2/0) | 2 | D | D | D | Legislative leaders appoint an eight-member commission that chooses its own ninth member and has 150 days to draw a plan for publication into law. It's a sure pair of Democrats whatever the commission does. |
| **Idaho** | **2 (2/0)** | **2** | **R** | **R** | **D** | **By state law, legislature is not required to deal with redistricting until 1993. A simple majority overrides the governor, making him almost irrelevant. But then redistricting is not the GOP's answer anyway in a heavily Republican state that elects an all-Democratic House delegation.** |
| **Ill.** | **22 (15/7)** | **20** | **D** | **D** | **R** | **Even if the Democrats had all three legs of the Illinois tripod, they probably would have to give up one more Democratic enclave in Chicago. The new delegation should be 13-7 or 14-6 Democratic.** |
| **Ind.** | **10 (8/2)** | **10** | **D** | **R** | **D** | **Having fouled their own nest a decade ago, Hoosier Republicans can do no worse by Democratic remappers than they did by themselves. Delegation could well pick up a third or fourth Republican during the 1990s.** |
| **Iowa** | **6 (2/4)** | **5** | **D** | **D** | **R** | **The non-partisan Legislative Services Bureau has until April 1 to submit a plan. The legislature may reject one or two bureau plans but can only amend a third. In the case of a stalemate, the process goes to the state Supreme Court.** |
| **Kansas** | **5 (2/3)** | **4** | **D** | **R** | **D** | **With split-control in Topeka, dismemberment of the fifth district means GOP can count on only two seats.** |
| Ky. | 7 (4/3) | 6 | D | D | D | By state law, legislature not required to deal with redistricting until 1993, but needs to do something before 1992 because of the surprise loss of a seat. The loss increases pressure on 81-year-old Republican William H. Natcher to retire. |
| La. | 8 (4/4) | 7 | D | D | D | Heavily Democratic legislature will try to reverse GOP trend in delegation, but must invest many votes in preserving minority district in New Orleans. Republican Clyde C. Holloway's central 8th District is likely target. |
| **Maine** | **2 (1/1)** | **2** | **D** | **D** | **R** | **A 15-member commission, which is appointed by legislative leaders and party chairmen and includes three private citizens, submits a plan the legislature must approve by two-thirds vote. If it fails, the legislature needs a two-thirds vote to substitute a plan of its own. Process makes outcome unpredictable.** |
| Md. | 8 (5/3) | 8 | D | D | D | Total-control Democrats may seek to reclaim district lost in 1990, while two Democratic districts east of Washington, D.C., could be reconfigured to create another minority district under court order. |
| **Mass.** | **11 (10/1)** | **10** | **D** | **D** | **R** | **The death of 17-term Republican Rep. Silvio O. Conte Feb. 8 left the GOP without an incumbent. Years of gerrymander have left Republicans without a natural district. New GOP Gov. William F. Weld faces a deeply Democratic legislature and may need help from the courts to break the lock.** |
| **Mich.** | **18 (11/7)** | **16** | **D** | **R** | **R** | **Democrats chose a bad time to lose control of two-thirds of the tripod in Michigan. Not only is the state losing two seats, but the population loss is centered in urban southern Michigan. The logjam of senior Democrats sharing a voter base shows no sign of breaking, yet there seems no way to spike one GOP district, let alone two.** |
| **Minn.** | **8 (6/2)** | **8** | **D** | **D** | **R** | **Although the Republicans have reclaimed the governorship, it may not mean much. Still, the Democrats could have one seat more than they can comfortably defend.** |

| State | Number of Seats | | Party in Power | | | Redistricting |
|---|---|---|---|---|---|---|
| | Current (D/R) | After 1992 | Legis. Lwr. | Uppr. | Gov. | |
| Miss. | 5 (5/0) | 5 | D | D | D | Historically among the most sensitive redistricting cases, Mississippi may be quiet this time around: Democrats hold all the levers and one minority district is already in place. |
| Mo. | 9 (6/3) | 9 | D | D | R | **Three Missouri Democrats look safe, but three others are suddenly sharing the party's shrinking base of voters in metropolitan St. Louis. One, freshman Joan Kelly Horn, will not find life getting easier.** |
| Mont. | 2 (1/1) | 1 | D | D | R | **Montana will lose its second district and will no longer need to redistrict (its two incumbents look bound for a showdown). As for the legislators' remap, legislative leaders choose four members of a commission who then choose a fifth as chairman. None of the five can be public officials. The commission map is not subject to politicians' review and becomes law 90 days after final census figures are available.** |
| Neb. | 3 (1/2) | 3 | n/a | n/a | D | Nebraska has a non-partisan, unicameral legislature and a Democratic governor. None of the incumbents has too much to fear from redistricting. |
| Nev. | 2 (1/1) | 2 | D | D | D | Most two-seater states draw a map protecting both incumbents, but adding more of metropolitan Las Vegas to the state's GOP district could weaken five-term GOP Rep. Barbara F. Vucanovich. |
| N.H. | 2 (1/1) | 2 | R | R | R | Freshman Democrat Dick Swett has enough of a fight on his hands here without having to have the map redrawn just before his first re-election bid. |
| N.J. | 14 (8/6) | 13 | D | D | D | Democrats' total control of the redistricting process may not be enough to save some Democratic House incumbents in 1992 if voters remain as angry at the party as they were late in 1990. But it should be some help. |
| N.M. | 3 (1/2) | 3 | D | D | D | Taking over the governorship here may help the Democrats weaken one GOP House incumbent enough to make a difference in 1992. They must preserve the Hispanic character of the northernmost district, however. |
| N.Y. | 34 (21/13) | 31 | D | R | D | **A permanent legislature task force on redistricting consists of two legislators and four non-legislators. But its plan must be approved by the legislature. Democrats have done so well in so many swing districts that it will be hard to stick GOP with more than one of the seat losses.** |
| N.C. | 11 (7/4) | 12 | D | D | R | **On paper, the GOP has a role in North Carolina. But in practice, this one will pit the Democrats against minorities (and Republicans) in the courts. Extra seat could be a boon to rural Dixiecrats or to blacks and liberals in the Research Triangle. Given the latter scenario, Republicans could solidify claim on one or two swing districts.** |
| Ohio | 21 (11/10) | 19 | D | R | R | **If Democrats had a chance of sticking downstate Republicans with both the seat losses, it expired in November when the GOP won the governorship. A retirement or two could still ease the process.** |
| Okla. | 6 (4/2) | 6 | D | D | D | Republicans nearly invalidated the last redistricting map with a ballot initiative in 1982. But they continue to trail badly in the legislature and may have to take their case to court. |
| Ore. | 5 (4/1) | 5 | R | D | D | **Oregon Democrats cannot expect to do better than four seats and so will probably try to shore up what they have. A similar strategy worked well for them a decade ago.** |
| Pa. | 23 (11/12) | 21 | D | R | D | **Pennsylvania's partisan politics may be more evenly matched than those of any other state. Legislative redistricting is handled by a commission, but the House seat losses must be distributed by the legislature. Look for an even split between the parties and between the state's eastern and western halves.** |
| R.I. | 2 (1/1) | 2 | D | D | D | A commission will redraw the map — subject to approval by the legislature — but it is not likely to matter much. Right now, Rhode Island's more Democratic half has a Republican representative and vice versa. |
| S.C. | 6 (4/2) | 6 | D | D | R | **South Carolina is a solid GOP state in presidential elections and two of its top three statewide offices are held by Republicans. But Democrats so control the legislature that they keep a majority of the House seats. This could change if the state is compelled to create a minority district.** |
| Tenn. | 9 (6/3) | 9 | D | D | D | The governor's veto can be overridden by a mere majority, but the governor is not likely to veto his own party's plans. With senior Republican Jamie Quillen retiring, Democrats may try to dismember his district, but they will have trouble improving on their current 2-1 split. |
| Texas | 27 (19/8) | 30 | D | D | D | Republicans were itching to carve unpleasant lines for Democrats in Dallas, Houston and elsewhere after 1990 but lost a governor's race they expected to win. As a result, Texas Democrats may not lose any seats after all — and they could even add one or two. But watch for a major lawsuit if they do not increase the number of minority members. |
| Utah | 3 (2/1) | 3 | R | R | R | Republicans must despair when they consider the case of Utah. Despite controlling the state government top to bottom, they will have but one House seat. Efforts will be made to ease recapture of at least one in 1992, probably by dividing Salt Lake City voters between the two Democrats. |
| Va. | 10 (6/4) | 11 | D | D | D | Just a decade ago, Virginia was Exhibit A in the realignment of the South. Since then, Democrats have returned to dominating statewide offices, preserved their hold on the legislature and battled back to majority status in the House delegation. In redistricting they may create a minority district, risking two white Democrats' House seats. |
| Wash. | 8 (5/3) | 9 | D | R | D | **Legislative leaders appoint four members of a commission and the four then choose a fifth member to be chairman. The plan they submit can only be slightly amended by the legislature, which must approve it by two-thirds vote. If the commission fails or the legislature balks, the state Supreme Court takes over. Process makes outcome unpredictable.** |
| W.Va. | 4 (4/0) | 3 | D | D | D | Despite total control, the Democrats cannot help but lose in a state where they hold all the seats and one seat must go. |
| Wis. | 9 (4/5) | 9 | D | D | R | **Wisconsin was thought likely to lose a seat but did not. The defeat of 32-year veteran Robert W. Kastenmeier in 1990 further loosened the redistricting knot. An expected fight over the division of Milwaukee's votes between two Democrats may now be postponed for another decade.** |

*Continued from p. 103*

raised by any of the cases the court had taken until that time. Although the high court had begun handling civil rights cases of historic importance, including *Brown v. Board of Education*, which integrated public schools, it had yet to tackle the established practice of drawing district maps to dilute the voting strength of racial minorities. But even as "one person, one vote" was taking hold, Congress was opening a new front by enacting the Voting Rights Act of 1965. That act, extended in 1970, 1975 and 1982, outlawed district maps drawn to dilute minority voters' impact on elections.

The state of Mississippi, already a focus of the civil rights movement, became the testing ground for the 1965 law. The Legislature adopted a program of "massive resistance." It redrew its legislative and congressional maps so that, if other obstacles to voting by blacks were forcibly removed (as also required by the Voting Rights Act), black votes would be sufficiently dispersed to minimize their effect. At that time, according to the 1960 census, the state had 29 counties where blacks constituted the majority. All but a half dozen of these were packed tightly along the Mississippi River Delta, which had been a single congressional district. The Legislature proceeded to redraw the five congressional district lines east to west, slicing the black vote like a layer cake. When they discovered that this still left a small black majority in the northernmost district, they revised the map to correct that oversight. Districts for state legislators were redrawn along similar lines.[9]

The Supreme Court's new attitude toward redistricting at first did Mississippi blacks little good. Because the 1966 plan kept the five congressional districts about equal in size, the court at first did not see its way clear to rule on the racial aspects of the gerrymander.* The court did not overcome that reluctance until March 3, 1969, when, in *Allen v. State Board of Elections*, Warren himself wrote that the 1965 Voting Rights Act should be given "the broadest possible scope" and that it was "aimed to the subtle, as well as the obvious" efforts to dilute minority political power. Because of past practices, 16 states remain on a special list that requires them to submit their redistricting plans — for all or part of the state — for review by the Justice Department under Section 5 of the 1965 Act.**

Voter rights law took another significant turn in 1980, when the court narrowed the scope of the 1965 Act

---

*The term "gerrymander," now used as either a noun or a verb, describes the creation of oddly shaped districts that violate communities of interest (such as cities, towns or other areas of natural affinity) in pursuit of a political goal. The term comes from an 1812 example of the art that involved Massachusetts Gov. Elbridge Gerry and a legislative district with a shape resembling a salamander.

**They are Alabama, Alaska, Arizona, Georgia, Louisiana, Mississippi, South Carolina, Texas and Virginia (all statewide) and certain local jurisdictions of California, Florida, Michigan, New Hampshire, New York, North Carolina and South Dakota.

in *Mobile v. Bolden*. The court held that the mere absence of elected minorities in a given jurisdiction did not prove discrimination unless there was also evidence of intent to discriminate. Congress reacted to *Mobile* by passing the 1982 amendments to the 1965 Voting Rights Act, which included the explicit provision that results — the absence of minority elected officials — were sufficient evidence of discrimination. The Supreme Court adopted this test in *Thornburg v. Gingles* in 1986, when it ruled that six districts in North Carolina had produced so few minority legislators that they violated the 1982 act.[10]

The 1982 amendments were generally welcomed not only by the civil rights community but by its allies among congressional Democrats. In recent months, however, the Bush administration's Justice Department has seen a Republican opportunity in them, as well. Building on the *Thornburg* precedent, GOP lawyers have noted that, where minorities lack representatives of their own race, the beneficiaries of their votes are usually Democrats. In certain legislative and congressional situations, then, concentrating minority votes within a given district might increase the chances of a minority candidate being elected *and* siphon probable Democratic voters out of adjacent districts. The adjacent districts may then become more fertile ground for a Republican candidate, leading to an overall increase in the number of districts in which the GOP can compete. (*For a discussion of whether minority voter concentration helps or hurts minorities, see "At Issue," p. 109.*)

This is the context in which many political observers have placed the "Read my lips: No minority dilution" dictum from John R. Dunne, the 24-year veteran of the New York Senate who now heads up the Justice Department's Civil Rights Division.[11] The old ban on splitting black votes to *prevent* a black winner has now been reinterpreted. It now provides that legislatures must *create* minority districts wherever minority votes can be assembled in sufficient numbers. The Supreme Court has even specified the three conditions that must exist for legislatures to be required to act: sufficient concentration of numbers, an established pattern of racial voting and of white voting en bloc to defeat minority candidates.

Benjamin Ginsberg, chief counsel to the Republican National Committee, argues that lawsuits based on these criteria can be used to force Democratic legislators to increase the concentration of minority voters in a handful of districts. Experience shows minorities must constitute 60 percent to 65 percent of a district's voting-age population to guarantee a minority winner. But such districts could be created where they do not now exist in Maryland, Virginia, North Carolina, South Carolina, Georgia, Alabama, Texas and possibly California. Ginsberg says this could double the number of minority members in Congress (which now stands at 25 blacks, 10 Hispanics). While he has not said how many white Democrats would have to lose their seats for this to happen, neither he nor a panoply of state GOP officials attempt to conceal their interest in that corollary outcome.

For his part, Jeffrey Wice, counsel for the Democratic State Legislative Leaders Association, argues that Ginsberg's estimates are too high by half. He argues that while some new minority districts will doubtless be created, meeting the three tests set down by the court in *Thornburg* proves more difficult in practice than either party had hoped or feared.

## *Partisan gerrymanders: The golden rule reversed*

Even more basic to the redistricting ethos is another species of gerrymandering, the kind done to scatter, and thus to devalue, the votes likely to be cast for a rival or a rival party. To date, the courts have done no more than declare the issue justiciable (worthy of consideration). The court raised a similar warning flag in 1962 before the torrent of "one person, one vote" cases. But in this instance, the pace of judicial involvement has remained gradual. Still, as lower courts build up a backlog of rulings, the Supreme Court may eventually see fit to rule on one.

In the meantime, the two parties will pursue the fine and ancient art of political homicide by political cartography. The ethics are elemental. "We are going to adopt a very high standard of fairness," says the Democratic chairman of the Senate Reapportionment Committee in Florida. "We're going to treat the Republicans as fairly as they would have treated us." [12]

Offensive to some, this swashbuckling attitude persists in part because the public pays so little attention to the entire enterprise. Serious newspapers strive to educate readers on the subject, yet from era to era, reapportionment and redistricting remain unintelligible or uninteresting to the public. "The problem is that the average citizen does not believe that by moving the lines over a few blocks you decide in advance who wins the election," says California Rep. Bill Thomas, co-chairman of the GOP's ad hoc committee on redistricting in the U.S. House.

For this reason, parties in power have practiced partisan gerrymandering to the extent of their ability and with near total impunity. The only constraints have been the sheer difficulty of assessing alternative plans rapidly, of obtaining reliable and precise information about voters and their patterns and of predicting how voters will turn out or vote in a given circumstance. Nonetheless, those with the right combination of data and acumen have proved uncanny in their ability to structure and prefigure the results of elections.

Shortly after the 1980 census, Rep. Phillip Burton, leader of California's congressional Democrats, sat down with some of the relatively crude electronic data processing equipment then available (legend has it he did it all on a hand calculator) and drew a plan for the 45 California districts. Burton's plan (he called it his "contribution to modern art") included such personal touches as tough districts for people he disliked and a cream-puff Democratic district for his brother, John. But Burton's primary purpose was to isolate Republican votes in as few districts as possible while placing just enough Democrats in each of the remaining districts to win.

It may well rank as the most masterful gerrymandering in history, even after computers and block-by-block software enable others to emulate it. Burton carefully stretched districts from one Democratic enclave to another — sometimes joining them with nothing but a bridge, a stretch of harbor or a spit of land (courts have ruled that districts must be "contiguous") — avoiding Republicans block for block and household for household. In the end, he packed enough Republicans into a few safe havens and "cracked and stacked" enough away from swing districts and into safe Democratic venues that his party went from holding about half the state's seats to holding three out of five. The GOP spent millions of dollars and the rest of the decade challenging Burton's handiwork in court and in a series of voter referendums. But after Burton made a few refinements in 1982 (he died shortly thereafter), his map stood up through the rest of the decade against lawsuit and public referendum.

But gerrymanders on that order rarely work to such perfection. In the same way Burton drew his map, Indiana Republicans outraged Indiana Democrats with an aggressive reworking of their state's district lines. But their plan backfired. Whereas in California the number of incumbents defeated since 1982 can be counted on the fingers of one hand, in Indiana most of the state's seats have turned over, some more than once.

What happened? In 1981, Indiana had six Democrats and five Republicans in the House. Ordered to eliminate one district, Republicans, who controlled both houses of the legislature and the governorship, fashioned a map they thought would reduce the Democrats to three. But they cut the lines too close and then fielded candidates that many analysts have said were too weak. A decade later, the delegation stands at eight Democrats and two Republicans. No wonder Democrats in the state Capitol joke about letting the Republicans do the remapping all by themselves again. (The Indiana GOP will not have that option, of course, because it has lost control of the governorship and the Indiana House.)

While it is important for either party to maintain its hold on at least one leg of this tripod, the real benefits in redistricting accrue when one party holds all three — Indiana's experience notwithstanding. This has been the key to Democrats' success in holding a preponderance of state legislative seats over the decades and thus drawing congressional maps to similar

# *California Remapping: Carrots, Sticks and Politics*

**G**oing into the 1990 elections, national Republicans figured that if they wanted to gain ground on the Democrats in the House of Representatives, the California governor's race was the key. California was bound to gain seats from the 1990 census (it actually gained seven, bringing its total representation to an unprecedented 52 seats). And with Democrats continuing to control both houses of the state Legislature, winning the governorship was the only way to avoid being locked out of the redistricting process as they were in 1981 and 1982.

In the event, they were pleased. Sen. Pete Wilson won and is now in the governor's mansion. But his power in the remapping process remains in doubt. "Gov. Wilson may not have as big a role as some initially thought," warns Rep. Bill Thomas, R-Calif., chairman of the House GOP's ad hoc committee on redistricting. The problem for Republicans is that their own members in the Legislature may be more interested in facilitating their own futures than in serving their party's state or national agenda.

A decade ago, only a handful of power brokers in Sacramento had the means to tinker with redistricting plans. This time, things will be different. Personal computers now allow virtually any legislator to become as sophisticated about shaping his or her district as the party leaders. Far more detailed census data is available in computer-readable form than ever before. So using the storage capacity of read-only-memory compact discs (CD-ROM), individuals can even design their own statewide plans using customized software already commercially available, complete with graphics

(*see story, p. 101*).

If the means to participate in remapping have been augmented, the will to do so has been strengthened as well. Far more legislators are likely to take the congressional remapping for 1992 personally. An unusual number of House seats may be vacated in 1992. Not only does redistricting nudge older members into retirement, but the state will have two races for the U.S. Senate that year† and a half-dozen House members may run in one or the other.

Even more important than these elective carrots, however, is an unprecedented stick. In November, Californians approved a ballot measure limiting legislators' terms. The legislators who will draw the next congressional map, hearing the clock ticking on their own political careers, are more anxious than ever to fashion congressional districts hospitable to their own ambitions.

Taken together, these factors sharply reduce Wilson's power to hold his troops together. Democrats may be more than willing to play along. They could pick off an individual Republican's vote by tailoring a safe GOP congressional district perfectly to that one legislator's needs. Thomas paints the picture this way: "The Democrats are offering you a seat in Congress; Wilson's offering you good government."

All the majority needs to override a Wilson veto is a two-thirds vote, which requires just one Republican crossover in the Senate and five in the Assembly. And here the new technology may be pivotal. Because when an individual legislator is deciding which way to vote, he or she will be able to verify whatever blandishments the Democrats are offer-

ing. "You don't have to buy anything on faith," says Thomas. "You can see the hard goods. It's even easier to buck the governor if you can see a district you know is yours."

Some Republicans fear that another Democratic-tilted map is in the making, and only a breakthrough in the courts will save them from another decade of defeat in the Golden State sweepstakes. The judicial hope remains a slender one at this point, given that the Supreme Court refused to review the notorious map drawn a decade ago by then-Rep. Phillip Burton, D-Calif. (*See p. 107.*) Now led by Rep. Vic Fazio, D-Calif., California Democrats are unlikely to draw a map as aggressive as that again. Even Fazio calls the Burton map "a little overkill" and promises to be "more accommodating" of Republicans this time.

On the other hand, judicial attitudes are never easy to predict. Southern California was stunned by a federal court's ruling in June 1990 that the Los Angeles County Board of Supervisors had gerrymandered its five districts to deny the county's 3 million Hispanics a seat. The judge imposed a new map that not only enfranchises Latinos but may end the careers of two or three current supervisors. A federal appeals court has since upheld the ruling, and the U.S. Supreme Court has let the appeals court ruling stand.

The ramifications of that precedent add one more uncertain element to the mix as California's power structure undertakes redistricting this spring.

*† Wilson's appointed successor in the Senate, John Seymour, must go before the voters in 1992, while Democratic Sen. Alan Cranston, under treatment for prostate cancer, is retiring.*

specifications. This year the Democrats have total control in 17 states (with 145 seats) and control two legs of the tripod in an additional 20 states (with another 224 seats). The GOP, by contrast, holds all three legs in just three states — Utah, South Dakota and New Hampshire — with a total of just six congressional seats among them. (*See pp. 104-105.*)

After Ronald Reagan was first elected president in 1980, the GOP appeared poised to make a run at this long-term Democratic hegemony. But the Reagan years proved disappointing. "Despite a long, costly and

ambitious plan for developing more Republican muscle, the GOP is in a much weaker position today than it was 10 years ago," writes Karen Hansen, editor of the magazine *State Legislatures*.[13] As Reagan was inaugurated the first time, Republicans controlled 15 state legislatures. They are now back down to their post-Watergate low of five. Nationwide, they hold only about 40 percent of the legislative seats — which is about where they have been since Dwight D. Eisenhower left the White House 30 years ago.

*Continued on p. 110*

# AT ISSUE

*Should states be compelled to create congressional districts with black or Hispanic majorities wherever possible?*

## YES

*says* **BENJAMIN L. GINSBERG**, *chief counsel, Republican National Committee.*

The fact is that minorities remain grossly underrepresented in Congress, state legislatures and local boards and commissions. Racial minorities make up 20 percent of the population but hold only 10 percent of the seats in the House of Representatives. Blacks are 12 percent of the population but hold only 8 percent of elected positions nationwide. Latinos ... are 8 percent of the population but hold only 2 percent of elected positions.

The culprit is the gerrymander — the drawing of representational districts by a majority that ignores established communities so it can lock in the status quo (i.e., incumbents) — and lock out emerging groups. ... It has been done to Republicans (who now get about 48 percent of the congressional vote but hold only 40 percent of the seats) and to racial minority groups. ...

Full enforcement of the Voting Rights Act can change this. As passed by Congress and interpreted by the courts, the Voting Rights Act now requires the drawing of majority-minority districts wherever possible. This mandate will have a dramatic effect on the redistricting process because it means the first lines drawn must be for a required minority district, rather than for ... white incumbent Democrats. ... The bottom line is that if the minority community is not packed, cracked, stacked or fractured, minority representation should be dramatically increased. ...

Another major development in the drive to political empowerment is the sea change in technology. In the 1980s, only the majorities in the Legislatures had computers. In the 1990s, anyone with a PC will be able to draw plans... The Republican National Committee ... has made its state-of-the-art redistricting software package available to all those traditionally excluded from the process. Of course, the notion of Republicans aiding racial minorities cuts against political stereotypes. But it is a natural alliance born of the gerrymander. ...

[Some] elected black Democrats have suggested racial minorities are better off allowing their communities to be split among a series of districts, apparently on the theory that this will maximize their influence on a larger number of white representatives. ...

[A] numerical minority should be content ... only if its current representative can pass the rhetoric-versus-reality test. ... To take the test, tour the minority's neighborhoods and compare them with the majority's neighborhoods: Are the roads as good? The schools? Police protection? If the answers are yes, the current representational system is working for the minority groups. But if the answer is no, then that is why the Voting Rights Act was passed and why every community deserves ... elected officials whose only priority is being sure his or her community gets its fair share.

*From remarks before the Congressional Black Caucus Foundation, Sept. 28, 1990.*

## NO

*says* **JEFFREY M. WICE**, *counsel to Democratic State Legislative Leaders Association.*

The media has made much of the GOP effort to create "unholy alliances" with black and Hispanic groups in upcoming legislative redistricting by offering legal assistance and computer software programs (without necessarily providing the thousands of dollars of hardware necessary to run the programs). There has been scant discussion of lack of recent Republican support for strong voting rights enforcement. Similarly, there has been little, if any, discussion of the real political and legal factors that go into the creation of true majority-black or Hispanic voting districts.

Since its enactment 26 years ago, the Voting Rights Act has worked. While there were only about 500 black elected officials in the country when the law was enacted, today there are over 7,200. Black Democrats have been elected as governor of Virginia and as mayors in the cities of New York, Seattle and Hartford. Black and Hispanic Democratic state legislative leaders and redistricting committee chairs are in control of the redistricting process in a number of important states including New York, Colorado, Arizona, California, New Mexico, North Carolina and Georgia.

Republicans support the notion of creating more minority districts only when it serves their partisan interest. While the Democratic Party has consistently supported a strong Voting Rights Act, the Republican record pales in comparison. ...

Voting Rights Act compliance means that decisions must be made on a local case-by-case basis. Important factors involving racial polarization, population characteristics, geography and other political factors must all be weighed against the total picture. The simple "packing" of minorities into either small and compact districts or tortured geographical shapes ... contradict a number of realistic factors. Census data must be carefully analyzed to determine the necessary and realistic thresholds for minority-candidate electability. Political considerations will help decide whether black and Hispanic populations can be joined together to form single districts or whether a lack of racial cohesion prevents the creation of such districts.

Minority communities must decide whether it is in their best interest to be represented by single districts or whether their goals will best be achieved in the state capitols and Congress through a coalition with other racial groups through the creation of several districts where minority influence can be greater. Critical to the election of more minority candidates is the election of minority candidates in non-majority black or Hispanic districts. Many black members of Congress have been elected from majority-white congressional districts.

Similarly, non-minority candidates can just as effectively represent minority-group constituencies. The future electability of white representatives from districts with large minority-group constituencies will be determined, in a large part, by the ability of non-minority candidates to effectively represent minority interests.

*Continued from p. 108*

In November of 1990, national GOP spokesman Charles Black said the 1990 elections had improved his party's influence in state redistricting decisions. He said Republicans would have a seat at the table for the remapping of 50 percent more districts in the 1990s than it had in the 1980s. While true, that statement mostly denoted the sheer size of the mountain the GOP has to climb. In the early 1980s, Democrats had untrammeled control over the drawing of more than 200 districts and dominant influence over most of the rest. The Republicans' 65-seat improvement this time around is almost entirely due to holding the governorship in California, where 52 districts must be drawn. And even that prize, important as it is, may be tarnished if its winner, Pete Wilson, cannot tame the teeming impulses of his own party members in the Legislature. (*See story, p. 108.*)

## *By fits and starts to shape a new landscape*

And so 1991 began with states awaiting official word on their census counts, wondering whether even the "final" numbers might be changed by adjustment before (or after) July 15 and pondering what disruption might follow from court rulings thereafter. Yet even in this awkwardly uncertain atmosphere, legislators got to work redividing the voter base that is their source of authority. The struggle is intense and complicated in all but the six states that had a single seat after the 1980 census and will continue to have a single representative in the '90s — Alaska, Delaware, North Dakota, South Dakota, Vermont and Wyoming. But it is most visible, and most meaningful to the balance of power in national politics, in the 21 states that are either gaining or losing seats. The largest of these, and the most difficult to predict, is California. (*See story, p. 108.*)

California aside, the other 20 gaining-or-losing states divide into four categories of political circumstance. In eight states, Democrats control all three levers of redistricting power (the governorship and both chambers of the legislature): Florida, Georgia, Kentucky, Louisiana, New Jersey, Texas, Virginia and West Virginia. In seven states, the parties appear to share control but Democrats predominate *de facto*: Illinois, Iowa, Kansas, Massachusetts, New York, North Carolina and Pennsylvania. In three states, the parties share control but Republicans have an upper hand: Arizona, Michigan and Ohio. And in the two remaining states, redistricting may be conducted on a bipartisan basis: Montana and Washington. (*For a state-by-state breakdown, see pp. 104-105.*)

In none of the 21 pivotal states do Republicans control all three levers of power. This is indicative of the frustration the GOP is experiencing nationwide.

Having made large gains after the 1974 Watergate disaster, the GOP had hoped to build on Ronald Reagan's 1980 breakthrough and to become the nation's majority party. To be lagging 100 seats behind the Democrats a full decade later is discouraging. Yet the vagaries of voter behavior are such that even as the population moves toward the sun and the suburbs and becomes more nominally Republican, the candidates of the GOP do not proportionately benefit. Congress is renewed not by one or two elections but over an era. Redistricting, with its fits and starts and confusion, is very much a part of that.

Redistricting could do far more to freshen the air in legislative chambers than it does. The problem is the instinct of self-preservation so pervasive in politics. Each decade's remapping is controlled, state by state, by the party in power. Each state legislator reviews the new map with an eye toward protecting turf and the thought of expanding career horizons.

Thus, the party that dominates the legislatures tends naturally to dominate the Congress, and there is little that governors — and even less that presidents — can do about it.

With some exceptions, therefore, the status quo is generally respected. This kind of political buddy system might well be changed if the public ever took an interest and demanded it. But that has not happened to date, and as an engine for change redistricting remains a perennial underachiever.

Today the House of Representatives consists of 267 Democrats, 166 Republicans and one independent (one seat is vacant). Barring a Supreme Court ruling that outlaws partisan gerrymandering, the GOP's best-case scenario would give them only 20-30 more seats — still a long way from control of the House.

# NOTES

[1] See Chandler Davidson, *Minority Vote Dilution* (1984). Davidson has been a political scientist and activist in Texas for a generation.
[2] The court came tantalizingly close to tackling the issue in *Badham v. Eu* in January 1989. See Rhodes Cook, "Map-drawers Must Toe the Line in Upcoming Redistricting," *Congressional Quarterly Weekly Report*, Sept. 1, 1990, p. 2786.
[3] Robert Benenson, *Jigsaw Politics: Shaping the House After the 1990 Census* (1990), pp. 7-8. When Alaska and Hawaii entered the Union in 1959, each was given a single representative in the House, and the size of the House was increased temporarily to 437. In the apportionment that followed the 1960 census, the House returned to 435 members.
[4] See Kenneth C. Martis, *The Historical Atlas of United States Congressional Districts* (1982), pp. 2, 4-5, 166-167, 199.
[5] See National Conference of State Legislatures, *Reapportionment Law: The 1990s*, (1990), pp. 17-40.
[6] Benenson, *op. cit.*, p. 15.
[7] Cook, *op. cit.*, p. 2787.
[8] National Conference of State Legislatures, *op. cit.*, p. 39.
[9] Frank R. Parker, *Black Votes Count: Political Empowerment in Mississippi after 1965* (1990), pp. 34-77.
[10] See Armand Derfner, "Vote Dilution and the Voting Rights Act Amendments of 1982," *Minority Vote Dilution* (1984), pp. 145-163.
[11] Quote by Cook, *op. cit.*, p. 2792.
[12] Quoted in *The Wall Street Journal*, Jan. 22, 1991.
[13] Karen Hansen, *State Legislatures*, November-December 1990, p. 15.

*Graphics: Cover, Margaret Scott.*

# RECOMMENDED READING

## BOOKS

**Benenson, Robert,** *et al.*, *Jigsaw Politics: Shaping the House After the 1990 Census*, **Congressional Quarterly Inc., 1990.**

A compendium of several articles published during 1989 and 1990 in *Congressional Quarterly Weekly Report* regarding the approaching process of census, reapportionment and redistricting. Particularly valuable and interesting for the background and process sections, the book also deals with each of the 50 states. Much of the detail remains useful, although some has been overtaken by events since the release of the census figures.

**Davidson, Chandler, ed.,** *Minority Vote Dilution*, **Howard University Press, 1984.**

The volume includes an overview of the subject by Davidson, a Rice University sociologist who has been involved in many voting rights and other discrimination cases throughout the South. There are 11 other scholarly essays ranging from historical review to legal analysis and focusing on vote dilution's roots, current forms, possible remedies and eventual prospects. The final essay asks what benefits blacks have enjoyed to date from decades of seeking full political participation. It concludes that the benefits have been most tangible at the local level.

**Ehrenhalt, Alan, "Reapportionment and Redistricting," in Mann, Thomas E., and Ornstein, Norman J.,** *The American Elections of 1982*, **The American Enterprise Institute for Public Policy Research, 1983.**

Ehrenhalt, an experienced reporter of congressional politics, notes that the effort devoted to redistricting often yields disappointing results for party planners and political observers alike.

**Martis, Kenneth C.,** *The Historical Atlas of United States Congressional Districts*, **The Free Press, 1982.**

Martis' oversized maps of all the Congresses from 1789 forward offer a vivid sense of how geographical representation has shaped American democracy. The gathering of all the geographic data (provided in written descriptions as well as maps) was begun as a WPA project in the 1930s. Martis' introduction is also a valuable overview of the subject matter in historical context.

**Parker, Frank R.,** *Black Votes Count: Political Empowerment in Mississippi after 1965*, **The University of North Carolina Press, 1990.**

Parker is director of the Voting Rights Project of the Lawyers' Committee for Civil Rights Under Law. He was a civil rights lawyer in Mississippi from 1968 until 1981. Although his book focuses on just one state, it focuses on what was in many ways *the* state in the "massive resistance" years.

This account is particularly useful in meshing the various political fronts — judicial, electoral and social — within the voting rights movement.

## ARTICLES

**Atwater, Lee, "Altered States: Redistricting Law and Politics in the 1990s,"** *The Journal of Law and Politics*, **Vol. VI, No. 4, summer 1990, pp. 661-672.**

In an article produced shortly before he was stricken by a brain tumor, Atwater as chairman of the Republican National Committee and Atwater as political science doctoral candidate briefly share the limelight.

**Cook, Rhodes, "Map-Drawers Must Toe the Line in Upcoming Redistricting,"** *Congressional Quarterly Weekly Report*, **Sept. 1, 1990, pp. 2786-2793.**

Perhaps the most thorough layman's tour of the legal and political thickets surrounding redistricting in the post-1990 round, including a catalog of all districts with more than 30 percent racial-minority population.

**Hansen, Karen, "To the Democrats Go the Spoils,"** *State Legislatures*, **November/December 1990, pp. 15-18.**

A short-form summary of why the 1990 elections disappointed Republicans hoping to usher in an era of parity in the control of redistricting decisions.

**Schneider, Ed, "1990s Redistricting: High Stakes, High Tech,"** *State Legislatures*, **September 1990, pp. 20-22.**

A rundown on how hardware (and software) will figure in the hardball politics of redistricting, this time and hereafter.

**Shogan, Robert, "GOP Seeking Remap Gains by Wooing Blacks, Latinos,"** *Los Angeles Times*, **April 14, 1990, p. A1.**

One of the earliest, and most comprehensive, journalistic looks at the Republican strategy for maximizing minority representation and trimming the Democratic majority in the House.

## REPORTS AND STUDIES

**Reapportionment Task Force, National Conference of State Legislatures,** *Reapportionment Law: The 1990s*, **October 1989.**

An authoritative summary of reapportionment and redistricting from the constitutional origins to the late-1980s applications of the Voting Rights Act Amendments of 1982. This detailed product of the task force (an ad hoc committee of 56 state legislators and other officials from around the country) covers the laws and court rulings on the essential issues of partisan gerrymandering, equal representation by population and race and other matters affecting the states directly. Useful appendixes include deadlines state by state, a table of relevant court case citations and a bibliography.

**Reapportionment Task Force, National Conference of State Legislatures,** *Redistricting Provisions: 50 State Profiles*, **October 1989.**

A compendium of the system in all its permutations, state by state, as it stood at the end of a tempestuous decade of court challenge and compliance. Each state's entry includes the state constitutional and statutory references, the relevant numbers on partisan lineups, the relevant historical data, deadlines for legislative action following the census and a contact person for further information.

# EDITORIAL RESEARCH REPORTS

## Coming soon

- Nuclear Power
- Gun Control
- The Cost of War

Published weekly by Congressional Quarterly Inc., Editorial Research Reports analyze emerging issues of national interest across a broad range of social, scientific, political and economic fields. Reports are bound and indexed for permanent reference. Subscription information is available through Congressional Quarterly's Publications Sales Department by telephone (202) 887-8665. Copies of past issues are available through Customer Service, (202) 887-8621.

FEBRUARY 22, 1991

ERR

CONGRESSIONAL QUARTERLY'S

EDITORIAL RESEARCH REPORTS

FOUNDED 1923

# WILL NUCLEAR POWER GET ANOTHER CHANCE?

1991 No. 8

EDITOR
**MARCUS D. ROSENBAUM**

MANAGING EDITOR
**SANDRA STENCEL**

ASSOCIATE EDITOR
**RICHARD L. WORSNOP**

STAFF WRITERS
**MARY H. COOPER**
**PATRICK G. MARSHALL**

PRODUCTION EDITOR
**LAURIE DE MARIS**

EDITORIAL ASSISTANT
**AMY GORTON**

**RICHARD M. BOECKEL (1892-1975)**
FOUNDER

PUBLISHED BY
**CONGRESSIONAL QUARTERLY INC.**

CHAIRMAN
**ANDREW BARNES**

PRESIDENT
**RICHARD R. EDMONDS**

EDITOR AND PUBLISHER
**NEIL SKENE**

EXECUTIVE EDITOR
**ROBERT W. MERRY**

EDITORIAL RESEARCH REPORTS (LIBRARY OF CONGRESS CATALOGUE NO. 39-924; ISSN 0013-0958). Published weekly (48 times per year, excluding March 1, May 3, August 2 and November 1, 1991) by Congressional Quarterly Inc., 1414 22nd Street NW, Washington, D.C. 20037. Rates are furnished upon request. Application to mail at second-class postage rates is pending at Washington, D.C. POSTMASTER: Send address changes to EDITORIAL RESEARCH REPORTS, 1414 22nd Street NW, Washington, D.C. 20037.

# WILL NUCLEAR POWER GET ANOTHER CHANCE?

*by Richard L. Worsnop*

Five years after it happened, the calamitous nuclear reactor accident at Chernobyl in the Soviet Union continues to cloud the future of nuclear power worldwide. In the United States, it has reinforced anti-nuclear sentiment dating from the 1979 Three Mile Island power-plant mishap; no U.S. utility has ordered a new nuclear plant in more than a dozen years. Nonetheless, the development of safer reactors and rising concern over the global warming associated with the burning of fossil fuels could spark a revival of interest in commercial nuclear power before the end of the century.

Are Americans ready to give commercial nuclear power a second chance? The Bush administration intends to find out. As part of its long-awaited national energy strategy, the White House recently floated legislative proposals that could help break the de facto moratorium on construction of new nuclear-power plants.

One proposal would restrict the ability of states to block the location of nuclear-waste repositories within their borders. Another would speed up the review process for new nuclear plants by limiting public comment. Lack of storage sites for radioactive waste and protracted review proceedings are often cited as prime reasons for the power industry's reluctance to build more nuclear reactors.

Supporters of nuclear power insist it deserves another trial. In many ways, they say, it is an ideal source of electric power. Uranium ore, from which the fuel used in nuclear fission is obtained, is widely distributed throughout the world. Major deposits exist in the United States, enabling the American nuclear industry to boast that it provides "The Power of Independence."

Such energy-security considerations seem especially pertinent now. "Clearly, events in the Persian Gulf have reinforced the importance of all domestic sources of energy," says James E. McDonald Jr., vice president for governmental communications at the American Nuclear Energy Council, a pro-nuclear-power industry group. Although he notes that nuclear power is not an immediate replacement for foreign oil, he still believes it "must be maintained."

Most U.S. oil consumption goes for transportation, not the generation of electricity. Today, only about 5 percent of U.S. electricity is generated by oil, compared with 17-18 percent in 1973. "However, if the country uses more and more electricity," McDonald says, "it enables us to back out of foreign oil more efficiently — more effectively, quicker. And if that happens, then nuclear energy clearly plays a major role. It's not a short-term solution. It's a solution that needs to be pursued on a continuing basis."

What's more, its proponents argue, nuclear energy is an uncommonly clean source of power. Unlike oil or coal, which foul the air with sulfur oxides, nitrogen oxides and "greenhouse" gases like carbon dioxide, nuclear power emits little noxious matter. In this sense, at least, it poses little threat to the environment.

However, nuclear energy has one immense drawback that has prevented it from realizing its potential as a source of electricity: Both the fuel consumed by nuclear plants and the resulting waste are highly radioactive. A nuclear-plant accident can lead to the release of radioactivity into populated areas, threatening countless lives. In addition, all nuclear plants, including those with accident-free records, must dispose of wastes that will remain radioactive for hundreds — even thousands — of years.

Popular concern about these problems is well-founded. Though most commercial reactors have operated without incident since the "peaceful" nuclear-energy era began in the late 1950s, major mishaps have occurred. The worst of these took place five years ago this spring at Chernobyl, about 50 miles north of the Ukrainian city of Kiev in the Soviet Union.

Due to human error and faulty plant design, an explosion blew the roof off of one of the four Chernobyl reactors on April 26, 1986, spewing a huge cloud of radioactive gas and dust into the atmosphere. Over the next few days, the cloud spread over much of eastern and northern Europe, depositing radioactivity on the ground. The magnitude of the disaster, combined with the Soviet government's initial reluctance to furnish details of the event, stirred global outrage.

## Editor's Note

This issue of *Editorial Research Reports* concerns the nation's nuclear-powered electricity generating plants. It does not deal with their military counterpart — the 17 major plants, in 12 states, that produce components for nuclear weapons. The plants employ 80,000 people and cost about $10 billion a year to operate. Three of the better-known facilities are the Savannah River plant in South Carolina, the Rocky Flats plant in Colorado and the Hanford Reservation in Washington.

All three of these plants, as well the others, have been plagued by discoveries of radioactive contamination in recent years. A National Research Council committee asserted in December 1989 that the problem would take many years and more than $100 billion to correct. At Hanford and Rocky Flats, the panel said, plutonium was found in exhaust ducts. This kind of contamination has not been found around power plants. Because of the dangers, some of the military plants have been shut down, which could adversely affect the nation's nuclear-weapons program.

— *Marcus D. Rosenbaum*

Chernobyl also provided opponents of nuclear power with fresh ammunition. To many Americans, it proved that the 1979 accident at Three Mile Island (TMI) in Pennsylvania was no fluke. Even if nuclear power were not inherently unsafe, opponents argued, the risk of catastrophe was too great to allow the technology to continue developing without strict safeguards.

And for many opponents of nuclear energy, there is no conceivable safeguard that is strong enough. Diane D'Arrigo of the Nuclear Information and Resource Service, a group that promotes alternatives to nuclear power, says that the problem of nuclear waste illustrates that reasoning. Even low-level radioactive waste is life-threatening, she says, and genuinely safe disposal facilities are simply not available for the thousands of years it must be kept. "We're not advocating coal over nuclear, either," she adds. "We've got to phase out of both of those polluting technologies." In their place, she favors a mix of demonstrably clean and renewable energy sources, including solar and thermal.

The nuclear-power industry says that such alternatives are impractical, and it vigorously disputes charges that nuclear energy is unsafe. Nonetheless, "anti-nuke" forces have held the upper hand in the public-opinion battle that has raged for the past dozen years. In part because of this, no U.S. utility has ordered a nuclear plant since 1978.

Because the gestation period of nuclear plants is so long, however, new commercial reactors continue to come on-line. The Nuclear Regulatory Commission (NRC) reports that 114 plants are now in service, supplying about 20 percent of the nation's electricity. At the time of the TMI accident, there were 72 nuclear-

# Nuclear Power Plants

**All U.S. commercial nuclear plants are light-water reactors, and most of them have this pressurized-water design. When the control rods containing uranium are lowered into the core, a nuclear reaction begins. This heats the water in the pressure vessel. The hot water (which is under pressure so it does not become steam) is pumped into a second vessel containing water. The water in the second vessel boils, and the steam is used to drive a turbine and produce electricity. The pressurized water is cooled in the process and pumped back into the pressure vessel. The pressurized water is used not only to generate the steam, but also to keep the nuclear reaction in check. This is why it is called the "coolant." (About a third of U.S. reactors are boiling-water reactors, in which the coolant water itself is allowed to boil and drive the turbine.)**

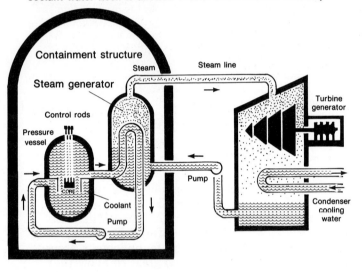

power plants, meeting 11.4 percent of the nation's electricity needs. Only nine more plants are still in the construction pipeline, according to the NRC, and not all of them are assured of completion. Unless orders for new plants are placed before the end of the decade, nuclear's share of U.S. electricity output is fated to decline as older plants reach the end of their useful life and are decommissioned.

Some proponents of nuclear power express confidence that a new age of commercial reactor-building already is at hand, thanks to various breakthroughs in nuclear-power technology. Advanced reactor designs, nuclear-power advocates say, are safer than existing models and can be built faster and for less money. All that remains to be done, as the advocates see it, is to convince a skeptical public that commercial nuclear power is more reliable than ever.

That is likely to require a world-class job of persuasion. To be sure, concern about the United States' mounting dependence on foreign oil and about environmental damage from the burning of coal could help erode resistance to nuclear power. At the same time, deep-seated fear of radioactive contamination may prove much harder to dislodge from people's minds. Although the Chernobyl disaster occurred five years ago, it has lost little of its power to inspire dread among ordinary people the world over.

## How nuclear reactors work; efforts to make them safer

Nuclear power, *Physics Today* reporter and editor William Sweet has written, "simply provides another way of boiling water." "In a nuclear plant, as in a coal-or oil-fired plant," he explained, "water is heated to generate steam, pressure from the steam causes turbines to turn, and the turbines generate electricity. The one big difference between a nuclear plant and a conventional plant is this: In a nuclear plant, controlled atomic reactions . . . heat the water, while in a conventional plant an ordinary fire generates the heat." [1]

The fuel used in all commercial reactors is uranium, either in its pure metallic state or in the form of uranium oxide. Usually, the fuel pellets (about the size of pencil erasers) are inserted in metal tubes, groups of which form the reactor core. When the tubes are placed in close proximity to each other, the core is "activated"; uranium atoms begin to collide, releasing energy and neutrons as they do so. The stray neutrons then are absorbed by other atoms, which release still more energy and neutrons. This self-sustaining chain reaction produces the heat that, converted to steam, drives the turbines that generate the plant's electricity.

All U.S. commercial nuclear plants are light-water reactors (LWRs), meaning that ordinary water is the substance that cools the fuel core, keeping the nuclear reaction in check. As the water is heated, it provides steam, directly or indirectly.

Not all LWRs are alike. About two-thirds of them are pressurized-water reactors, a type developed by Adm. Hyman G. Rickover. In such a reactor (*see illustration*), the coolant water is kept under pressure to prevent it from boiling. The coolant circulates by pipe between the vessel containing the fuel core and a second vessel, also containing water. As the piped water passes through the second vessel, it raises the temperature of the water in that vessel to the boiling point, producing steam that makes the turbine blades turn.

The second type of LWR, accounting for about one-third of those used in the United States, is the boiling-water reactor. As the name suggests, the coolant water itself is allowed to boil, and the radioactive steam that is generated drives the turbines directly. The boiling-water reactor might seem to be simpler and therefore cheaper to build than the pressurized-water variety. But for a number of reasons having to do with construction and refueling, the two reactors cost roughly the same to build and operate.

In all reactors, a sudden loss of coolant spells trouble. That is because a number of things — all of them bad — can happen if the temperature of the reactor core is allowed to reach the melting point. Within a minute, the core would begin to collapse to the bottom of the containment vessel. The molten radioactive material would eventually burn its way through the vessel and then through the slab of concrete beneath it — the dreaded phenomenon known as a "meltdown."

The ball of atomic fire would proceed to burn itself into the Earth in what has been called the "China syndrome" — that is, it would sink (figuratively) "all the way to China." A more scientific guess is that the molten material would eventually reach the water table, where it would turn ground water into highly radioactive steam, which would be vented to the atmosphere. Another possibility is that the material would congeal into a fiery blob that would burn uncontrollably in a radioactive mess for a decade or more.

Two advanced reactors now under development offer what their supporters claim are safer alternatives to the LWR. More disinterested observers say both types have drawbacks as well as advantages. In liquid-metal reactors (LMRs), the coolant is liquid sodium, which has a much higher boiling point than water and superior ability to absorb unexpected heat surges. The coolant in pressurized-water reactors must be maintained at high pressure — up to 150 times atmospheric pressure — to keep it from turning to steam. In contrast, liquid sodium needs no pressurization. If pumps circulating the metal broke down, the coolant itself, along with the natural circulation of air outside the reactor, would prevent fuel damage indefinitely.

On the other hand, liquid sodium reacts violently when exposed to air or water. Thus, an LMR reactor vessel would have to be double-walled, with nitrogen occupying the middle space, to keep the sodium isolated.

A major advantage of the gas-cooled reactor (GCR), which uses helium as the coolant, is that it is practically impossible for it to experience a core meltdown. Its fuel core would heat up very slowly during an accident, taking hours and possibly days to reach dangerously high temperatures. By contrast, at Three Mile Island, the light-water reactor's core partially melted in less than two minutes. According to nuclear engineer Lawrence M. Lidsky of the Massachusetts Institute of Technology, operators of a helium-cooled reactor "could go down the street and have a cup of coffee while they ponder what to do about any trouble." [2]

Unfortunately, gas-cooled plants have problems, too. The nuclear-power industries of Britain and France initially were based on versions of GCR technology. However, the high capital costs and low reliability of the early gas-cooled plants led both countries to abandon them in favor of LWRs.

But even for LWRs, the technology is improving. Many of the advanced reactors now under development contain "passive" safety devices that are activated by gravity or natural convection instead of pumps. Some manufacturers contend that such features make their reactors "inherently safe." In fact, General Electric has named its advanced LMR model PRISM — an acronym for Power Reactor Inherently Safe Module.

A report prepared last year for the Union of Concerned Scientists, a group that monitors the impact of technology on society, took a dim view of such

## Breeder Reactor's Demise

One of the chief victims of the nation's mounting disenchantment with nuclear power in the 1980s was the Clinch River (Tenn.) breeder reactor. First authorized by Congress in 1970, the Clinch River plant was intended to prove that breeder reactors, which run on plutonium and produce (that is, "breed") more plutonium as a byproduct than they consume, could generate electricity while also producing additional nuclear fuel. To its supporters, the project promised an almost inexhaustible source of electrical energy. "The breeder could extend the life of our natural uranium fuel supply from decades to centuries," President Richard M. Nixon told the nation in 1971.

Environmentalists opposed Clinch River from the outset, contending that breeder technology would increase the world's supply of plutonium, a key ingredient in nuclear weapons. Criticism spread throughout the 1970s as the plant's estimated cost soared from $700 million initially to more than $3.2 billion by 1981. In 1977, President Jimmy Carter renounced plans to use plutonium as nuclear-power-plant fuel in the United States and tried unsuccessfully to persuade Congress to abandon the Clinch River project.

By the early 1980s, however, congressional support was being eroded by construction delays, rising costs, flattening demand for electric power and concern about the safety of nuclear technology. Although the government had spent $1.5 billion on planning the project, construction never got under way.

Congress nearly pulled the plug on the project in 1981-82, despite strong support by President Ronald Reagan and Senate Majority Leader Howard H. Baker Jr., in whose state the plant was to be built. By 1983, most members had concluded that the potential energy yield no longer justified the project's escalating costs or the technology's risks.

Both the House and the Senate voted that year to scrap the project. In addition, Congress ignored the Reagan administration's plea to salvage the plant through a new plan for sharing its cost with private industry.

claims. "As a general proposition, there is nothing 'inherently' safe about a nuclear reactor," the report stated. "Regardless of attention to design, construction, operation, and management of nuclear reactors, there is always something that could be done (or not done) to render the reactor dangerous. The degree to which this is true varies from design to design, but we believe that our general conclusion is correct." [3]

The report went on to assert that "some of the advanced reactor designs appear to be quite vulnerable to sabotage." It specifically cited GE's PRISM and General Atomics' Modular High Temperature Gas-Cooled Reactor. In both models, the report declared, although the reactors themselves are below-ground, the passive heat removal systems that make the plants safer are located above-ground, where saboteurs could have relatively easy access. [4]

Another key feature of today's advanced reactor designs is modular construction. Rather than being custom-built at the site, as all U.S. commercial reactors now in service were, the next generation of nuclear-power plants may well be assembled from standardized components made in a factory and shipped to their destination by rail or barge. Plants of the future may also have only about half the generating capacity of today's 1,000-megawatt units. This would enable utilities to expand their electricity output in smaller increments. Modestly sized plants may lack the economies of scale that giant reactors possess, advocates say, but the savings gained from standardization could make up much of the difference.

However, some veteran nuclear engineers question whether scaled-down modularity is the wave of the future. Thomas H. Pigford, a professor of nuclear engineering at the University of California, Berkeley, and a member of the presidential commission that investigated the Three Mile Island accident, says that any facility with a generating capacity of under 600 megawatts would be "very speculative" economically. Pigford also is skeptical about the prospects for standardized plant design. "Nuclear plants will not be standardized like automobiles as long as we have so many different architect-engineers," he says. "Utilities like to work with different architect-engineers, and each has his own way of doing things."

Be that as it may, the obstacles facing the nuclear-power industry are not simply technological ones. As the U.S. Office of Technology Assessment put it as far back as 1984: "Problems such as large cost overruns and subsequent rate increases, inadequate quality control, uneven reliability, operating mishaps, and accidents, have been numerous enough that the confidence of the public, investors, rate and safety regulators, and the utilities themselves is too low to be restored easily. *Unless this trust is restored, nuclear power will not be a credible energy option for this country.*" [5] With Chernobyl, hopes of restoring that trust plummeted.

## Chernobyl accident's origin and its lingering aftermath

The Chernobyl accident began, ironically, with a safety test. The purpose of the exercise was to determine how long the steam-driven turbines at the plant would continue to generate electricity in the event of an electrical blackout. While the plant operators were in the process of shutting down reactor No. 4 at the start of the test, they simultaneously reduced the flow of water needed to control the temperature of the reactor's radioactive fuel. They also disconnected the backup systems on which the plant relied in case of a loss of cooling water.

This combination of events led to a runaway nuclear reaction, culminating in two explosions. Burning debris from the first blast started numerous fires inside the plant. Within the reactor core, graphite, which cannot be extinguished with water, also caught fire. This led to the second, more powerful explosion, which lifted the concrete roof above the fuel core into the air and spewed out radioactive debris in a high plume, dispersing radioactivity over much of Europe. The crippled reactor continued to emit radioactive matter for the next 10 days.

A distinctive feature of the Chernobyl reactor's design contributed to the severity of the accident. American reactors contain a safety device that automatically stops the nuclear reaction when the water used to cool the radioactive fuel rises or even boils away. The Chernobyl plant did not have such automatic controls, and when the water temperature rose, the nuclear reaction naturally speeded up.

The initial Soviet response to the Chernobyl accident was swift but also cautious — perhaps fatally so. People living within a six-mile danger zone were evacuated within 36 hours. One week later, everyone except emergency workers was ordered to leave a widened 18.6-mile danger zone.*

There remained the complex and highly hazardous task of damage control — putting out the fire and stopping the release of radioactivity from the reactor. To accomplish this, 5,000 tons of sand, limestone, clay and lead were dropped from helicopters onto the reactor between April 28 and May 2. The idea was to form a seal over the core, but radioactivity continued to seep through nonetheless. Furthermore, the seal trapped heat inside the reactor, increasing the danger of another core meltdown. As a precautionary measure, emergency workers drilled holes in the earth beneath the reactor and filled them with liquid nitrogen to freeze the ground.

Despite everything, emission of radioactivity persisted, though at a greatly reduced rate. Not until the reactor was entombed in a "sarcophagus" of reinforced concrete in October — six months after the accident — did the Chernobyl plant cease to be a major source of contamination.

It did not, of course, cease to be a major source of controversy. In the Soviet Union, wrote David Holloway, a political science professor at Stanford University, "Chernobyl has helped to inspire a distrust of political authority, which has rubbed off on scientists and experts more generally." [6] In the rest of the world, it has inspired distrust, too.

First there was outrage over Moscow's reluctance to acknowledge the magnitude of the disaster. Then chang-

---

*Soviet Prosecutor General Nikolai Trubin announced on Feb. 7, 1991, that some officials involved in the Chernobyl cleanup failed to evacuate people as quickly and safely as they should have done; ignored dangerous radiation readings; used faulty methods to bury contaminated waste; and built resettlement shelters in areas polluted with radioactivity.

# A Future for Fusion?

Scientists have long dreamed of harnessing nuclear fusion, the energy that makes stars shine and thermonuclear bombs explode. Unlike fission, which occurs when the nuclei of heavy atoms like uranium split, fusion takes place when two nuclei — usually of light elements such as hydrogen or helium — merge to form a new atom, releasing vast amounts of energy in the process.

The fusion reaction itself forms no radioactive waste. Its fuel, moreover, can be ordinary water — a virtually limitless resource. With fusion, says nuclear physicist Edson C. Brolin, "the top two inches of Lake Erie contain 1.6 times more energy than all the world's oil supplies."

The trouble is that no one has yet demonstrated a way to create a self-sustaining fusion reaction, in which more energy is produced than is required to confine and ignite the atoms that keep the reaction going. Over the past 30 years, most fusion research has concentrated on building a machine capable of heating the fuel to ignition temperature — estimated to be as high as hundreds of millions of degrees Celsius. So far, no one has been able to construct such a reactor.

Because their goal seemed so far out of reach, fusion researchers were elated when two chemists announced in March 1989 that they had produced heat from nuclear fusion at room temperature. B. Stanley Pons of the University of Utah and Martin Fleischmann of the University of Southampton, England, reported on a simple table-top experiment in which they ran an electric current through deuterium (an isotope of hydrogen that is also known as heavy water) with the aid of a metal rod made of palladium. Pons and Fleischmann claimed that their apparatus liberated heat from the fusion of heavy hydrogen atoms that the current forced into the palladium.

In an attempt to see if they, too, could generate "cold fusion," researchers the world over hastened to replicate the chemists' experiment. Nearly all the efforts failed to yield unambiguous evidence that a fusion reaction had occurred. As skepticism about cold fusion spread, media coverage tailed off. Pons and Fleischmann still insist that they will ultimately be vindicated, but the scientific community takes the position that the burden of proof rests with them — and so far they haven't provided it.

Proponents of fusion power often argue that the technology is an uncommonly "clean" source of energy. But now that claim has been called into question because of the fact that fusion involves the release of neutrons, which contaminate almost any material they come in contact with. In 1990, the congressional Office of Technology Assessment estimated that the walls of a fusion reactor would have to be replaced every five to 10 years — though they would be far less radioactive than a fission plant's waste.

Nuclear engineer Robert W. Deutsch described a gloomier fusion scenario in 1987. "The amount of radiation produced by the fusion process will contaminate the entire plant, which could be the size of the Houston Astrodome," he wrote, "and all maintenance will have to be performed remotely. Thus, a nuclear fusion power plant, just like any other alternative source of energy, has its own risks that could prove to be far worse than a nuclear fission power plant." [†]

[†] *Robert W. Deutsch,* Nuclear Power: A Rational Approach, *fourth edition, 1987, p. 87.*

ing estimates of Chernobyl's toll aroused suspicions at home and abroad of a deliberate coverup by Soviet officials. For instance, Kremlin authorities insisted for more than three years that only 31 people had died as a result of the accident, most of them from radiation sickness. In November 1989, however, a brief report in the weekly newspaper *Moscow News* said that at least 250 persons who were at Chernobyl during and after the disaster had perished. But the article provided no details on how and when the deaths occurred.

Estimates of Chernobyl's economic cost also have been revised upward over the past five years. In a study released last March, a leading Soviet nuclear-industry economist, Yuri Kuryakin, said Chernobyl could cost the country 170 billion to 215 billion rubles by the year 2000, mainly from lost electricity and farm production. Moscow's previous official estimate, which covered only immediate cleanup costs, was 10 billion rubles. (Although the Soviet currency is not freely convertible in world foreign-exchange markets, at the Moscow-fixed exchange rate prevailing when the study was released, the March 1990 estimates ranged between $283 billion and $358 billion.)

Soviet popular response to the 1986 accident has gone well past the grumbling stage. According to Holloway, Chernobyl "has given the environmental movement in the Soviet Union an enormous impetus and has led to the scaling back of plans for nuclear power." [7] The Chernobyl Atomic Energy Station itself has not escaped the backlash. Last March, the Ukrainian Supreme Soviet announced that the plant, which still has three functioning reactors, will be phased out of operation over the next five years and that no additional nuclear plants will be built in the republic, the second most populous in the Soviet Union.

Chernobyl-inspired agitation against nuclear power soon spread to Eastern Europe, which then was still firmly within the Soviet orbit. Bulgaria, Czechoslovakia and East Germany announced after the accident that they were installing new safety devices at their nuclear generating stations. Czechoslovakia canceled two of four planned reactors. Poland postponed indefinitely its first nuclear plant; the project previously had been on temporary hold. And Bulgaria closed two of the five

# Effects of Three Mile Island

**The 1979 accident at the Three Mile Island nuclear facility in Pennsylvania was a major setback from which the nuclear-power industry in the United States has never recovered. Not only did it shake public confidence in nuclear power, but it led to much tighter regulation — and skyrocketing construction costs (Graph 1). As a result, no U.S. utility has ordered a new nuclear facility in more than a dozen years. Nevertheless, because the lead-time to build a nuclear power plant is so long, new facilities have continued to go into operation (Graph 2), and the amount of electricity generated by nuclear power and the percentage of the nation's electricity that comes from it have continued to climb (Graph 3). Proponents of nuclear power fear these trends will not continue into the next century if new facilities are not ordered soon, but the accident at Chernobyl five years ago further eroded support for the industry.**

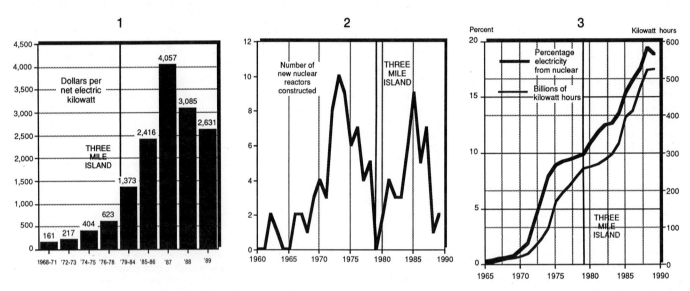

*Sources: U.S. Bureau of the Census, Statistical Abstract of the United States: 1990, 1990, and Edison Electric Institute, 1989 Statistical Yearbook of the Electric Utility Industry, 1990 (graphs 2 and 3); U.S. Department of Energy, Energy Information Administration, Nuclear Power Plant Construction Activity 1988 (graph 1).*

reactors at its only nuclear plant after a breakdown.

Anti-nuclear sentiment in Eastern Europe, especially in the former state of East Germany, has grown even stronger since the region's Communist governments collapsed in late 1989. East German nuclear reactors, all Soviet-built, were subjected to more stringent West German performance standards when the government of unified Germany took power last year.

West German inspectors found the East German reactors to be so deficient that all five were ordered permanently shut down. Four of the reactors were clustered at a plant near Greifswald, on the Baltic coast, and one was at Rheinsberg, 45 miles northwest of Berlin. The reactors' flaws included substandard materials, inadequate fire-protection safeguards, inferior cooling systems and slipshod maintenance procedures. On Jan. 22, 1990, East Germany disclosed for the first time that the Greifswald plant had suffered the country's "most serious and grave" nuclear accident — a near meltdown of the radioactive core of one of its reactors — in 1976, three years before the Three Mile Island accident in the United States caught the world's attention.

## Three Mile Island mishap: U.S. version of Chernobyl

Before Chernobyl, the world's most publicized nuclear power-plant accident was the one that occurred March 28, 1979, at Three Mile Island Nuclear Station, situated on a small island in the Susquehanna River near Harrisburg, Pa. Like the subsequent Soviet disaster, the TMI mishap resulted from a combination of equipment failure and human error.

It started when a valve stuck open, enabling water to drain from the core of TMI reactor No. 2. Not realizing what had happened, operators turned off the emergency cooling pumps that had come into operation automatically. As a result, the reactor soon became overheated. By the time operators realized something was wrong, materials in the core had started to melt. Later studies indicated that the reactor had come within a half hour to an hour of complete meltdown.

Media coverage focused national attention on the TMI plant as an emergency team from the Nuclear Regulatory Commission worked with utility engineers to bring the stricken reactor under control. "In news reports from the scene, it was clear that the experts were encountering problems they were not confident they could solve," wrote William Sweet, the *Physics Today* writer and editor. "It was apparent, in fact, that they were not even sure they understood what was happening in the reactor." [8]

The most serious problem was a buildup of hydrogen, which is highly flammable, in the reactor dome. A small hydrogen explosion apparently did take place, but it was not strong enough to rupture the containment vessel. All the same, tens of thousands of people were evacuated from the area because of concern that a hydrogen blast might rip the reactor apart, scattering radioactivity over a wide area. More than anything else, the evacuation brought home the seriousness of the TMI accident to the American public.

Subsequent cleanup operations showed that the damage at TMI was much greater than initial estimates had suggested. At least 70 percent of the reactor core was destroyed, and 40,000 pounds of core material had migrated to the bottom of the containment vessel as the core melted, although it did not break through the bottom.

To study the accident and recommend preventive measures, President Carter appointed a commission headed by Dartmouth College President John Kemeny. The panel's report, issued Oct. 30, 1979, called for sweeping reform of procedures then used for operating and regulating nuclear power plants in the United States.

"If the country wishes, for larger reasons, to confront the risks that are inherently associated with nuclear power, fundamental changes are necessary if those risks are to be kept within tolerable limits," the report asserted. Because of shortcomings it had found in utility operation and government regulation of nuclear power, the commission said, an accident like the one at Three Mile Island was "eventually inevitable." Even if changes were made, it added, a similar accident still could occur. [9]

In its most eye-catching recommendation, the Kemeny commission urged that the five-member, independent NRC be replaced by an executive branch agency headed by a single administrator appointed by the president. But Carter, after studying the report, declined to adopt the suggestion for abolishing the NRC. Instead, he reaffirmed the administration's support, and the nation's need, for nuclear power. He agreed with the commission that reforms were needed, but he urged that once they were instituted, the nation should move ahead to reduce U.S. dependence on foreign oil.

For its part, the NRC responded to the Kemeny commission's critique by issuing hundreds of new safety regulations. Among other things, it increased the number of nuclear-plant personnel and the training required of them and mandated extensive backfitting of equipment. "For those plants under construction, the utilities had no choice but to tear apart nearly completed plants or redesign plants just under way," nuclear engineer Robert W. Deutsch wrote in

*Nuclear Power: A Rational Approach.* "The NRC paid little attention to the cost effect of the regulations it imposed. The industry itself was on the ropes, and most companies were prepared to do whatever was asked of them, regardless of the cost." [10]

In this connection, William Sweet noted that "Regulatory changes were so great after the accident ... that specialists in nuclear economics now distinguish as a matter of course between pre-TMI and post-TMI generating costs." [11] (*See Graph 1 at left.*) A study released by Cambridge Energy Associates in November 1983 concluded that electricity from the most recent nuclear power plants could cost up to 20 times as much as electricity from the first plants. During the 1980s, the costs of new nuclear plants reached three to five times the amounts that had originally been projected. No longer did the nuclear-power industry boast, as it had in its early years, of electricity "too cheap to meter."

By tightening its safety rules, the NRC presumably hoped to bolster public confidence in the reliability of nuclear energy. Whether it succeeded in doing so is hard to gauge, but public support for nuclear power seems to have continued to fall, especially after Chernobyl. Similarly worded Gallup polls taken several years before TMI and several weeks after Chernobyl showed that the percentage of respondents who said it was "extremely important" or "somewhat important" for the United States "to have more nuclear power plants ... to meet the future power needs of the nation" fell from 71 percent to just 50 percent. [12]

## Many factors line up against nuclear power

After the TMI accident, new federal regulations and slumping public support combined to dry up orders for new plants and cast doubt on the fate of those already under construction. One of the chief casualties was the Long Island Lighting Co.'s (LILCO) facility at Shoreham, on Long Island's North Shore.

When LILCO applied in 1968 to the old Atomic Energy Commission (forerunner of the NRC) to build a 500-megawatt nuclear plant at Shoreham, it estimated the cost at about $70 million. That figure rose to $260 million as the plant's projected capacity was expanded to 900 megawatts. By the time the project was completed in 1983, Shoreham had cost $5.5 billion.

Worse was soon to befall LILCO, however. Galvanized by TMI, the utility's customers turned decisively against Shoreham. Anti-nuclear activists contended that evacuating even a portion of densely populated Long Island* would be impossible if a serious nuclear

*Long Island, including New York City's Kings and Queens counties, with 1,396 square miles and some 6.7 million residents, has a population density of about 4,800 per square mile.

# Changing Demand for Electricity

**Lower-than-projected demand for electricity after the 1973 cutoff of oil from the Middle East meant that many utilities were building plants that were not needed as soon as expected — or not at all. This graph shows electricity generation in billions of kilowatts since 1950. Before 1973, electricity usage increased steadily at about 7 percent per year. After 1973, the increase in usage was much more erratic, and even declined in some years.**

Billions of kilowatts

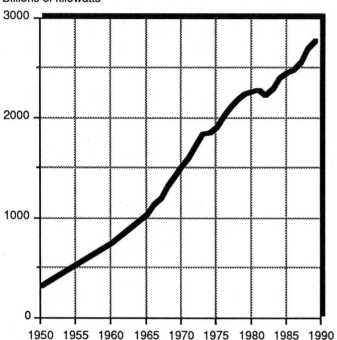

*Source: U.S. Bureau of the Census,* Statistical Abstract of the United States: 1990.

accident occurred. Accepting this argument, New York Gov. Mario M. Cuomo determined to prevent the Shoreham plant from opening on safety grounds. Gary R. Fryer, a spokesman for the governor, called the plant "a radioactive elephant." [13]

The impasse was finally broken in June 1989, when LILCO shareholders approved a settlement reached by utility executives and the New York state government. Under the accord, LILCO agreed to sell the plant to the state for $1. In return, the state pledged to allow LILCO to raise customers' electricity rates at least 5 percent annually for 10 years. The Shoreham facility, which has since been partially dismantled, thus became the nation's first nuclear power plant to be abandoned even before going into commercial operation.

For a time, the ill-starred Seabrook nuclear-power plant in New Hampshire seemed destined for a fate much like Shoreham's. It, too, was plagued by massive cost overruns prior to its completion in October 1986; the total bill came to $6.6 billion. Anti-nuclear activists charged that the Seabrook site, on the Atlantic coast barely 40 miles north of Boston, posed an unacceptable threat to one of the nation's largest metropolitan areas. To keep the plant from being commissioned,

Massachusetts Gov. Michael S. Dukakis refused to prepare an evacuation plan required by federal law.

The Seabrook controversy eventually depleted the financial reserves of the plant's principal owner, Public Service Co. of New Hampshire. In January 1988, the company was forced to file for bankruptcy protection, making it the first utility driven to such action since the Great Depression. Seabrook, however, has not ended up in mothballs. In May 1989, the NRC issued a license to Public Service Co. and Seabrook's other owners authorizing them to begin low-power testing of the reactor. The plant began regular, full-power operation last Aug. 19.

As anti-nuclear public sentiment and new regulations took their toll on the nuclear-power industry, other economic factors also began to stand in the way. In the last two decades especially, lower-than-projected demand for electricity meant that many utilities began to build plants only to discover midway through the construction process that the plants would not be needed as soon as expected — or not at all. From the end of World War II to the cutoff of oil from the Middle East in 1973, U.S. electricity use had increased by an average of about 7 percent annually. But over the next decade, annual electricity growth dropped to about 3-4 percent (*see graph*).

As a rule, state regulatory bodies do not allow utilities to add the costs of a new power plant to the rate base until the plant begins to generate electricity, so the decline in demand presented the utilities with a major financial crisis. And when some hard-pressed utilities sought permission to charge customers for work in progress, their requests became hot political issues. In New Hampshire, some election analysts attributed Gov. Meldrim P. Thomson Jr.'s defeat for re-election in 1978 to his veto of a bill that would have prevented utilities from charging customers for the cost of building a nuclear-power plant — a measure clearly inspired by the Seabrook controversy.

Another utility severely affected by the changing outlook for nuclear electricity in the 1980s was the Washington Public Power Supply System (WPPSS), a consortium of 88 utilities in Idaho, Montana, Oregon and Washington. WPPSS, or "Whoops," as it came to be called, set out to build five nuclear-power plants in the early 1970s. After large cost overruns and long construction delays, WPPSS was forced to cancel two plants, and in July 1983 it defaulted on $2.25 billion in bonds.

The WPPSS default, the largest tax-exempt bond default in U.S. history, left the system unable to borrow more funds from private lenders to complete its ambitious power-generation plans. To cushion the blow, Senate Energy and Natural Resources Committee Chairman James A. McClure, R-Idaho, introduced legislation to help WPPSS finish building as many as three of its five planned nuclear plants. McClure's measure would have allowed the consortium to establish a new lending authority under state law to finance completion of at least two of the plants that sponsors hoped to salvage. But on the Senate floor Howard M. Metzenbaum, D-Ohio, and William Proxmire, D-Wis., threatened to filibuster against the McClure amendment, calling the plan a bailout that would be borne by federal taxpayers. After a six-week standoff, McClure abandoned his effort.

### Closing down old plants and managing nuclear waste

Even as they have struggled to get nuclear-power plants built, utilities have had to prepare for the day when the plants reach the end of their useful life and must be dismantled. The presence of radioactive material makes this "decommissioning" process exceedingly complex and costly — more costly, perhaps, than the industry yet imagines. Because nuclear-power technology still is in an early stage of development, utilities have had only limited experience with decommissioning. As a result, the money they have set aside for closing down a plant and decontaminating its grounds may not turn out to be adequate.

The Shippingport (Pa.) Atomic Power Station, the nation's first nuclear-power plant, was also the first to be decommissioned. It was, in fact, the largest nuclear unit and first commercial reactor in the world to be taken out of service and dismantled. The five-year task, which began in September 1985, cost $98.3 million and was carried out as a demonstration project by the U.S. Department of Energy. The department estimates that 15 additional reactors will reach decommissioning age by the year 2000.

When a nuclear-power plant is decommissioned, NRC rules require the operators to decontaminate the site, which is defined as including land, ground water, buildings, equipment and supplies. Any residual radioactivity must be low enough to permit unrestricted use of the property. The trouble is that no federal standards for residual radioactivity yet exist. In 1970, Congress assigned the job of developing standards to the Environmental Protection Agency. EPA began work on the job only in 1984 and expects to complete it by 1992.

According to the U.S. General Accounting Office (GAO), the investigative arm of Congress, the decommissioning process has other shortcomings as well. Testifying before a congressional subcommittee in August 1989, GAO Associate Director Keith O. Fultz asserted that "Little actual data exist on decommissioning costs, and estimates range from the tens of millions [of dollars] to $3 billion, depending on the facility. We found that NRC's decommissioning cost estimates averaged 29 percent, or $45 million, lower than those prepared by a private consulting firm for 25 nuclear power plants and were between $6 million and $19 million lower than two ... owners' estimates

## Types of Radioactive Waste

Most radioactive waste falls into one of the following categories, listed in descending order of their hazard to human health:

**Spent fuel** — Used reactor fuel rods that are no longer capable of facilitating a nuclear chain reaction. Nonetheless, the rods are extremely hot in both the thermal and radioactive senses of the word. As a result, they require heavy shielding while in storage.

**High-level waste** — The residue that remains when spent fuel is reprocessed to retrieve plutonium and uranium. This form of waste is highly radioactive, generates some heat and requires heavy shielding.

**Transuranic waste** — Radioactive elements with atomic numbers higher than 92, the atomic number of uranium. It is produced during the refurbishing or decommissioning of nuclear-power plants.

**Low-level radioactive waste** — Includes all radioactive waste not classified as spent fuel, high-level waste or uranium mill tailings. About 97 percent of low-level waste requires no shielding to protect workers or the public.

**Uranium mill tailings** — The earthen residues that remain after uranium is extracted from its ore. Though large in volume, the tailings contain low levels of radioactivity.

**Byproduct material** — Objects that become contaminated during the production or use of radioactive material.

*Source: Weber, I. P., and Wiltshire, S. D., The Nuclear Waste Primer: A Handbook for Citizens, Nick Lyons Books, 1985.*

for their facilities." * [14]

One aspect of decommissioning posed only a minor problem for operators of the Shippingport plant — disposal of nuclear waste. Because the plant was owned by the federal government, it was able to dispatch its spent uranium fuel rods to a military dump in Idaho. Low-level waste from Shippingport was sent to the government-owned nuclear facility at Hanford, Wash., for burial.

Privately owned nuclear-power plants have only limited access to disposal sites for low-level radioactive waste — and none at all to sites capable of safely storing high-level waste. In the absence of permanent disposal arrangements, nuclear-plant operators store spent fuel rods in cooling ponds at plant sites. Nationwide, there are only three commercial low-level waste sites — at Beatty, Nev.; Barnwell, S.C.; and Hanford,

---

*In a preliminary funding certification filed with the NRC in July 1990, cost of cost of decommissioning the destroyed TMI-2 reactor was placed at $196.6 million. The figure is to be updated annually. Present plans call for decommissioning TMI-2 in the year 2014, when the still-functional TMI-1 is due for decommissioning.

Wash. Until more storage facilities become available, utilities may conclude that the radioactive waste-disposal problem alone makes nuclear power an unattractive option for the near future.

Progress toward solving the waste-storage problem has been painfully slow thus far. In passing the Low-Level Radioactive Waste Policy Act of 1980, Congress required every state to become responsible for disposing of the low-level waste generated within its borders. But the original deadline of Dec. 31, 1985, was not met, forcing Congress to move it back to Dec. 31, 1992. After that date, all existing facilities for storing low-level waste will be closed to out-of-region users.

Because of the high disposal costs and small volumes of low-level nuclear waste, states were encouraged to form regional compacts in which one state agrees to provide the site for a disposal facility available to all of its partners. Nine such accords have been negotiated so far. Seven states (Maine, Massachusetts, New Hampshire, New York, Rhode Island, Texas and Vermont), the District of Columbia and Puerto Rico have elected to go it alone — either because they are confident of their ability to handle their own waste or because they feel they do not generate enough of it to justify membership in a compact.

Finding a permanent storage site for high-level radioactive waste from commercial nuclear plants has been far more frustrating. The Nuclear Waste Policy Act of 1982 represented a step in that direction, but no more. The law directed the Energy Department to choose five potential sites and recommend three of them to the president by Jan. 1, 1985. By March 31, 1987, the president was to recommend to Congress the first repository site, which would begin receiving nuclear waste no later than Jan. 31, 1998.

In 1987, however, Congress amended the 1982 act by ordering the Energy Department to concentrate all its waste-disposal efforts on a site at Yucca Mountain, Nev., 100 miles northwest of Las Vegas. The department was instructed to build the storage facility there unless it found the area totally unsuitable.

Indeed, the Nevada site seemed ideal in several respects: Located in a remote desert region with little rainfall, no surface water and a low water table, it gave promise of providing a secure, moisture-free environment for spent reactor fuel and lethal waste from nuclear-weapons production. But some scientists challenged that assumption, noting that the Earth appears to be entering a period of significant climatic change. Consequently, these scientists argued, it is too early to say that the Yucca Mountain area will remain a desert indefinitely.

Diane D'Arrigo of the Nuclear Information and Resource Service points to two other drawbacks of Yucca Mountain. "That site is 12 miles from a potentially active volcano above a seismic risk zone, which could result in flooding of the repository while the waste is still in a hazardous state," she says. "Also, it's on Native American land, which has never been

signed over to the federal government."

But Bernard I. Spinrad, retired chairman of the Iowa State University department of nuclear engineering, argues that the hazards of nuclear-waste storage have been greatly overblown. "Waste disposal truly is no problem," he says. "Every item of technology that's involved is practiced all the time in deep mining. People burrow way, way down, they dig into rock, mine out rooms and pillars, the whole works."

Spinrad adds that he "could pick almost any acreage in the United States and be reasonably sure it would be safe [for storing radioactive waste]. I wouldn't pick a site on the San Andreas Fault, and I wouldn't put nuclear waste on top of Mount St. Helen's or in the Ogallala Aquifer. But there's a lot of real estate where I *could* put it, and where it would be much better guarded than the radioactive ores that exist in nature."

In any case, construction of a high-level nuclear-waste depository at Yucca Mountain or elsewhere appears a long way off. In November 1989, the Energy Department decided to move the target date for opening a storage facility at Yucca Mountain to the year 2010 at the earliest.

## Prospects for a revival of nuclear-plant building

Regardless of the ultimate fate of President Bush's national energy strategy, the United States will remain much less dependent on nuclear power than a number of other industrialized countries for many years to come. France, the world leader, derives more than 70 percent of its electricity from nuclear energy. Other countries that outperform the United States in this regard include Japan, Germany, Britain and South Korea.

However, these countries are by no means immune to the kind of anti-nuclear activism that emerged after Three Mile Island and Chernobyl. For example, Japanese public opinion was shaken by a Feb. 9 accident at the Mihama Nuclear Power Plant, not far from the old imperial capital of Kyoto. Described as the worst such accident in the country's history, the mishap led to emergency flooding of the reactor core to prevent a fuel meltdown.

Although it is too early to draw firm conclusions, popular reaction to the Mihama accident could set back the Japanese government's plans for additional nuclear-plant construction. According to the U.S. Council for Energy Awareness, the nuclear-power industry's main lobbying group, nuclear power provides a little more than 25 percent of Japan's electricity at present. With no significant domestic reserves of fossil fuels to draw upon, the Japanese government wants to increase nuclear's share to 36 percent by 1995.

*Continued on p. 126*

# AT ISSUE

*Should the United States turn increasingly to nuclear power to meet its future energy needs?*

## YES

*says* **BILL HARRIS**, *senior vice president of the U.S. Council for Energy Awareness.*

There are many important reasons [that nuclear power] must be a part of our energy mix. But none more important than this: It's in our national interest. The more electricity we make using nuclear energy, the less we must make with imported oil. Since the 1973 Arab oil embargo, nuclear energy has saved this country over 4 billion barrels of oil . . . enough to fuel every motor vehicle in America — cars, buses, trucks, you name it — for well over a year. And nuclear energy has kept $125 billion . . . from flowing into the pockets of foreign oil producers. That amounts to almost half of America's entire 1991 budget for national defense.

Those are just the savings in the United States. Throughout the world, 426 nuclear electric plants in 26 nations displace 6 million barrels of OPEC oil each day. So you can see that nuclear energy furthers not just U.S. energy independence, but that of our allies as well. . . .

Nuclear energy is one of the cleanest sources of electricity. It emits no sulfur oxides, no nitrogen oxides, no carbon dioxides or other greenhouse gases.

Take away the nation's . . . nuclear energy plants, and utility sulfur dioxide emissions would be 5 million tons a year higher. That's one-half the reduction mandated in the new Clean Air Act.

Take away our nuclear energy plants, and utility nitrogen oxide emissions would be 2 million tons a year higher. That's equal to the reduction required in the Senate version of the new law.

In France, where over 70 percent of electricity comes from nuclear energy — far more than in the U.S. — there have been even more dramatic environmental benefits. Back in 1979, when France was still heavily dependent on oil and coal-fired power, their plants emitted large amounts of nitrogen oxides and sulfur dioxide. By 1987, in less than 10 years, the use of nuclear energy had tripled — and those emissions had dropped dramatically. Total pollution from the French power system decreased by 80-90 percent. You don't hear many French environmentalists opposing nuclear energy. . . .

Let's learn from what is happening in the Persian Gulf.

*From an address before the American Legion national convention, Indianapolis, Aug. 25, 1990.*

## NO

*writes* **THE PROGRESSIVE** *magazine in an editorial.*

Long-suppressed tales of horror continue to surface about the reckless disregard for human health and safety in the government's nuclear-weapons production program. Investigations are under way about reckless releases or leaks of toxic radioactive substances at the Hanford Reservation in the state of Washington, at the Feed Materials Production Center near Fernald, Ohio, at the National Engineering Laboratory in Idaho, and at the Rocky Flats plant in Colorado. The total number of workers and nearby residents exposed to illness and premature death may never be established, but it is clear that the human toll has been high.

The costs of cleanup will be astronomic. The Department of Energy, which presides over the production of nuclear weapons, has estimated that repairing defective equipment and cleaning up . . . pollution could cost more than $150 billion. . . .

More has been at stake here than the normal bureaucratic impulse to conceal incompetence or the usual corporate drive for profit-maximization regardless of human consequences. A powerful motive for hiding the catastrophic risks in the weapons-production program is the determination to shield the civilian nuclear-power industry from close scrutiny. If Americans were to conclude — as they have every reason to conclude — that radioactive substances are inherently and unavoidably dangerous — nuclear power would finally receive the death sentence it so richly deserves.

But the industry clings stubbornly to life. Though no new reactors have been ordered in the past decade, though some five dozen scheduled projects have been canceled, nuclear-power advocates continue to insist they have the long-range answer to energy needs. . . .

The cost of constructing nuclear plants rose from $1,355 per kilowatt in 1980 to $4,590 in 1989. At the same time, the cost of such renewable energy sources as hydroelectric, solar, and wind power declined, and their generating capacity grew by 27 percent, producing more electricity than nuclear power plants.

The nuclear snake-oil salesmen are expected to begin another push for their quack medicine. The United States *will* be facing an energy crunch in the years ahead. It can meet that crisis first of all by practicing conservation, and second by resorting to forms of energy that are safer, cheaper, and less environmentally destructive than nuclear power.

*From* The Progressive, *February 1990.*

*Continued from p. 124*

Nuclear power's future in the United States will hinge at least partially on whether Congress goes along with the Bush administration's proposal to streamline the way nuclear plants are licensed. In April 1989, the NRC issued a regulation to permit the granting of "combined licenses." Previously, two separate NRC reviews were required — the first for a construction permit based on a preliminary design, and the second for an operating license based on a final design. The combined license was intended to allow both construction and operation to proceed on the basis of a final design. Now the administration has recommended, in effect, that the 1989 NRC regulation be codified into law, as the nuclear-power industry has urged.

James McDonald of the American Nuclear Energy Council believes that combined licensing is essential. "The problem the industry has had is with the second hearing after construction is finished. That has delayed completed plants from operating for years and has dramatically increased costs. So there needs to be a comprehensive, safe and yet fair system for licensing these plants. And it needs to be done prior to completion of construction."

Thomas Pigford of the University of California concurs. "Utilities want assurance that once they have gone through the major safety analysis for construction and the plant is built according to approved specifications, they will be allowed to operate it," he says.

Bernard Spinrad, the retired Iowa nuclear-engineering professor, foresees a new era of nuclear-power-plant construction getting under way in the United States, but not until the year 2010 at the earliest. One reason he does not expect utilities to act before then is that he feels they have been intimidated by environmentalists. "In my opinion, utilities ... don't think straight about these matters any more," he says. "They're no longer players in the environmental game. They would like to be, but they've been beaten over the head so many times that they've sort of quit the game."

The Nuclear Power Oversight Committee, which represents utilities and other groups involved in supplying nuclear-generated electricity to the American people, would not be likely to agree with that description. The organization has made the environment a major element of its pro-nuclear arguments. Unlike oil- and coal-fired power plants, the committee asserted in a November 1990 position paper, "Nuclear energy plants do not pollute the atmosphere with emissions of sulfur oxides, nitrogen oxides, particulate matter or 'greenhouse' gases like carbon dioxide. The waste byproducts of nuclear energy are small in volume and, given the special care with which they are (and always have been) managed, represent no threat to the environment." [15]

Environmental groups disagree, especially with the part about waste from nuclear-power plants. Nuclear waste classified as low-level "is not low-risk," says Diane D'Arrigo of the Nuclear Information and Resource Service. "You still have radioactive plutonium, strontium, cesium and iodine in the so-called low-level waste," she says. "Also, the metal piping in the plant that carries radioactive water becomes contaminated over the years. One of the radioactive substances that is formed in the pipes is nickel 59, which has a half-life of 80,000 years. That means it'll be hazardous for 800,000 to 1.6 million years.* But it is still considered, quote, low-level, unquote, waste."

Environmentalists insist that the alternative to nuclear energy is not greenhouse-gas-producing coal but renewable sources like wind and solar power. But nuclear-power advocates point out that large-scale windmill farms and solar-energy collectors can be built economically only in areas where the wind blows or the sun shines virtually year-round. Moreover, nuclear advocates say, long rows of windmills or solar-cell panels take up a lot of space and are unsightly besides.

Spinrad goes still further. "Windmills are fine. Solar power is fine. Do it! Just don't complain about the bill. ... The most compelling argument for nuclear power will ultimately be cost. Nuclear power still has the potential to be quite cheap. When that happens, it'll come in."

---

*Half-life is the time required for half the atoms of a given radioactive substance to disintegrate, losing their radioactivity in the process. A rule of thumb holds that it takes 10 half-lives for radioactivity to fall to the background level found in nature.

# NOTES

[1] William Sweet, *The Nuclear Age: Atomic Energy, Proliferation, and the Arms Race*, second edition, Congressional Quarterly Inc., 1988, p. 29.
[2] Lawrence M. Lidsky, "The Reactor of the Future?" *Technology Review*, February-March 1984, p. 54.
[3] MHB Technical Associates, *Advanced Reactor Study*, July 1990, p. 0-4. MHB Technical Associates, of San Jose, Calif., is a consulting firm specializing in energy and the environment.
[4] *Ibid.*, p. 0-7.
[5] U.S. Office of Technology Assessment, *Nuclear Power in an Age of Uncertainty*, February 1984, p. xi. (Emphasis included in original text.) OTA provides Congress with information and analyses on the political, physical, economic and social effects of technological applications.
[6] David Holloway, "The Catastrophe and After," *The New York Review of Books*, July 19, 1990, p. 6.
[7] Ibid., p. 6.
[8] Sweet, *op. cit.*, p. 93.
[9] Report of the President's Commission on the Accident at Three Mile Island, *The Need for Change: The Legacy of TMI*, Oct. 30, 1979.
[10] Robert W. Deutsch, *Nuclear Power: A Rational Approach*, fourth edition, 1987, p. 19.
[11] Sweet, *op. cit.*, p. 58.
[12] The earlier Gallup Poll was conducted June 6-11, 1976; the later one was conducted June 9-16, 1986, less than two months after Chernobyl.
[13] Quoted in *The New York Times*, Oct. 6, 1989.
[14] Testimony before Environment, Energy, and Natural Resources Subcommittee, House Committee on Government Operations, Aug. 3, 1989.
[15] Nuclear Power Oversight Committee, "A Perfect Match: Nuclear Energy and the National Energy Strategy," November 1990, p. 5.

*Graphics: Cover, Margaret Scott; pp. 116, 121, 122, Jack Auldridge.*

## RECOMMENDED READING

## BOOKS

**Deutsch, Robert W.,** *Nuclear Power: A Rational Approach,* **fourth edition, GP Courseware, 1987.**

The author, who has taught nuclear engineering and founded a company that provided training and support services to the nuclear-utility industry, is well-placed to evaluate the industry from an insider's perspective. His short but highly informative book covers the main issues in the nuclear-power debate in terms that a reader approaching the subject for the first time can easily grasp.

**Gale, Dr. Robert Peter, and Hauser, Thomas,** *Final Warning: The Legacy of Chernobyl,* **Warner Books, 1988.**

Dr. Gale, head of the Bone Marrow Transplant Unit at the UCLA Medical Center in Los Angeles, gained instant worldwide celebrity when he was summoned to the Soviet Union after Chernobyl to try and save the lives of people who had been exposed to dangerous doses of radiation. He describes his experiences with the help of Hauser, an attorney and author whose previous books include *Missing,* which was made into an Academy Award-winning film.

**Gould, Jay M., and Goldman, Benjamin A.,** *Deadly Deceit: Low-Level Radiation, High-Level Cover-Up,* **Four Walls Eight Windows, 1990.**

Gould and Goldman concentrate on the health problems caused by radiation released by nuclear technologies. In particular, they challenge the notion that low-level radiation causes little harm in small doses. "There is now reason to fear that low-level radiation from fallout and from nuclear reactors may have done far more damage to humans and other living things than previously thought," they write, "and that continued operation of civilian and military nuclear reactors may do irreversible harm to future generations as well."

**Haynes, Viktor, and Bojkun, Marko,** *The Chernobyl Disaster,* **The Hogarth Press, 1988.**

Haynes and Bojkun use the Chernobyl disaster as a springboard for a sweeping indictment of nuclear energy, whether used for weapons production or electricity

generation. "The aging and proliferation of such power plants will make [Chernobyl-like] accidents even more frequent," they charge, "and once again the bitter fruit of the nuclear age will be delivered to our doorstep. Unless we find another way to satisfy our energy needs, we must be prepared for what the people of Chernobyl have now tasted."

**Sweet, William,** *The Nuclear Age: Atomic Energy, Proliferation and the Arms Race,* **second edition, Congressional Quarterly Inc., 1988.**

An editor and writer for *Physics Today,* the journal of the American Institute of Physics, Sweet surveys the main areas of concern involving nuclear power. "The world as a whole is violently split by huge economic disparities between the North and South, complicated by the various Christian, Jewish, Hindu and Islamic heritages," he concludes. "Only as all these divisions are gradually transcended or reconciled will it be possible to come to terms, once and for all, with the nuclear menace."

## REPORTS AND STUDIES

**MHB Technical Associates,** *Advanced Reactor Study,* **July 1990.**

Prepared for the Union of Concerned Scientists, perhaps the most respected group of critics of the nuclear-power industry, this study examines the coming generation of reactors with a view to determining if they can live up to the claims made by their advocates. While acknowledging that many of the claims are indeed valid, the study points out that some advanced safety features create new problems of their own.

**Nuclear Power Oversight Committee,** *A Perfect Match: Nuclear Energy and the National Energy Strategy,* **November 1990.**

Anticipating the release of the Bush administration's national energy strategy, the Nuclear Power Oversight Committee sets forth its arguments in favor of giving nuclear energy a key role in U.S. electricity generation. "America's electric consumers — for economic and environmental reasons — need this opportunity," the committee asserts.

## ARTICLES

**Golay, Michael W., and Todreas, Neil E.,** "Advanced Light-Water Reactors," *Scientific American,* **April 1990.**

The authors, professors of nuclear engineering at the Massachusetts Institute of Technology, suggest that improved light-water reactors incorporating "passive" safety features can be both safe and profitable — provided utilities improve their management techniques. They also examine the two main rival nuclear-power technologies, liquid-metal-cooled and gas-cooled reactors.

## Coming soon

Gun Control
The Cost of War
Acid Rain

Published weekly by
Congressional Quarterly
Inc., Editorial Research
Reports analyze emerging
issues of national interest
across a broad range of
social, scientific, political
and economic fields.
Reports are bound and
indexed for permanent
reference. Subscription
information is available
through Congressional
Quarterly's Publications
Sales Department by
telephone (202) 887-8665.
Copies of past issues are
available through
Customer Service, (202)
887-8621.

ERR

MARCH 8, 1991

FOUNDED 1923

CONGRESSIONAL QUARTERLY'S
EDITORIAL RESEARCH REPORTS

# ACID RAIN: NEW APPROACH TO OLD PROBLEM

**1991 No. 9**

**EDITORIAL RESEARCH REPORTS**

EDITOR
**MARCUS D. ROSENBAUM**

MANAGING EDITOR
**SANDRA STENCEL**

ASSOCIATE EDITOR
**RICHARD L. WORSNOP**

STAFF WRITERS
**MARY H. COOPER**
**PATRICK G. MARSHALL**

PRODUCTION EDITOR
**LAURIE DE MARIS**

EDITORIAL ASSISTANT
**AMY GORTON**

**RICHARD M. BOECKEL (1892-1975)**
**FOUNDER**

PUBLISHED BY
**CONGRESSIONAL QUARTERLY INC.**

CHAIRMAN
**ANDREW BARNES**

PRESIDENT
**RICHARD R. EDMONDS**

EDITOR AND PUBLISHER
**NEIL SKENE**

EXECUTIVE EDITOR
**ROBERT W. MERRY**

© 1991 BY CONGRESSIONAL QUARTERLY INC.

EDITORIAL RESEARCH REPORTS (LIBRARY OF CONGRESS CATALOGUE NO. 39-924; ISSN 0013-0958). Published weekly (48 times per year, excluding March 1, May 3, August 2 and November 1, 1991) by Congressional Quarterly Inc., 1414 22nd Street NW, Washington, D.C. 20037. Rates are furnished upon request. Application to mail at second-class postage rates is pending at Washington, D.C. POSTMASTER: Send address changes to EDITORIAL RESEARCH REPORTS, 1414 22nd Street NW, Washington, D.C. 20037.

# ACID RAIN: NEW APPROACH TO OLD PROBLEM

## *by Thomas H. Moore*

As the United States sails toward the 21st century, it is setting a new course on acid rain — the deadly precipitation that results from airborne pollutants. Last November, President Bush signed into law a Clean Air Act that offers industries financial incentives to reduce the emissions that cause acid rain. Industry officials and environmentalists are closely watching to see how this market-based approach works, because it may be useful in attacking other environmental problems.

After years of frustration, those pushing for action on acid rain finally got it last year. The 1990 Clean Air Act Amendments officially recognized acid rain as a serious environmental problem for the first time and set into motion radical reforms that could transform the way that government controls air pollution. The legislation, passed in the final days of the 101st Congress and signed into law by President Bush on Nov. 15, sets up an ambitious program to reduce toxic emissions from industry, including pollutants that cause acid rain. It also includes provisions for cleaning up motor vehicles and fuels, reducing smog and phasing out chemicals that harm the Earth's protective ozone layer.[1]

Final passage of the clean air amendments, which took months of intense negotiations between the House and Senate, ended more than a decade of legislative gridlock over the nation's clean air laws. But nearly lost

---

*Thomas H. Moore is a free-lance writer who lives in Washington, D.C.*

in the excitement over passage of the clean air bill was the release of a 10-year, half-billion-dollar government study on the causes and effects of acid rain and on control strategy options.

The September 1990 report was prepared by the National Acid Precipitation Assessment Program (NAPAP), an interagency body created by Congress in 1980.[2] The document was an external review draft of NAPAP's final report, which will be released by May 1991. Some interpreted the report as raising questions about the severity of the acid rain problem — opening lawmakers up to charges that they were applying a billion-dollar solution to a million-dollar problem.

The NAPAP report actually challenged the views of extremists on both sides of the acid rain debate: It dismissed the arguments of those who say acid rain is no problem at all as well as those who portray acid rain as an impending environmental disaster. NAPAP Director James R. Mahoney summarized the report's findings this way: "The sky is not falling, but there is a problem that needs addressing."[3]

Acid rain is the popular term that describes a phenomenon more appropriately called acid deposition. It occurs when sulfur dioxide and nitrogen oxides emitted from coal-burning electric power plants, industrial furnaces, motor vehicles and other sources combine with moisture in the atmosphere and return to earth as acid compounds. Carried by the winds, these acidic compounds fall to earth in either wet or dry forms, building up in soils, rivers, streams and lakes.

While acid rain is not corrosive enough to burn people or melt leaves off trees, it increases the acidity of the land and water it touches, altering some environments to the point that they can no longer support life. Hundreds of lakes in the Northeastern United States, southeastern Canada and throughout Europe already have been "killed" by acid rain, and some forests in these areas are showing signs of stress. Over time, acid rain can eat away at monuments and buildings. Some experts believe it contributes to asthma, emphysema and other respiratory diseases, particularly in young children, and scientists are beginning to explore possible links between acid rain and other health problems.

Acid rain has been a recognized environmental danger for more than a decade, but there has been intense debate over the precise causes and severity of the problem and the best control strategies.* Prospects for a legislative compromise on acid rain and other air pollution problems dimmed during the eight years of the Reagan administration, when the federal government seemed more interested in spurring industrial growth than in protecting the environment.

George Bush, who during the 1988 campaign claimed he wanted to be "the environmental president," is given much of the credit for breaking the legislative logjam. The president introduced his own clean air proposal in June 1989, and according to *Congres-*

*For background, see "Acid Rain," *E.R.R.*, June 20, 1980 (Vol. I, No. 23).

## Acidity of Precipitation

**Because prevailing winds blow from west to east, much of the sulfur dioxide emitted by Midwestern power plants ends up in the northeastern states and in southeastern Canada. The map below shows the average level of acidity found in the two countries' precipitation as measured by the pH scale. *(See p. 135)* The lower the number, the more acidic the precipitation. Since the scale is logarithmic, a change of one point indicates a tenfold change in acidity. Thus the pH 4.5 precipitation that falls on much of the Northeast and southern Canada is 10 times as acidic as the 5.5 precipitation that falls on the Rocky Mountain states.**

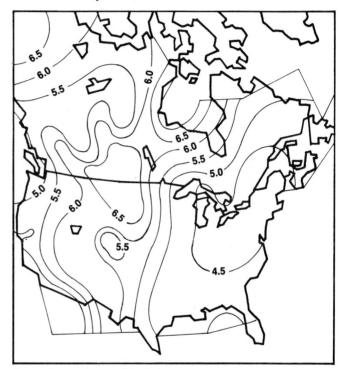

*Source: Ontario Ministry of the Environment.*

*sional Quarterly Weekly Report,* "Bush's move strengthened the hand of congressional proponents of clean air legislation, whose proposals had repeatedly been killed or stalled to death at the behest of industry."[4]

But from industry's perspective, Bush also created a monster he could not contain. Congress broke from the administration's leash early on, approving in many cases tougher and far more costly controls on industry than Bush had proposed.[5] The Clean Air Act Amendments built up so much momentum that the House and Senate ended up forging the bulk of them before the agency charged with providing Congress with reliable data on acid rain had finished its work. By the time the National Acid Precipitation Assessment Program released its external review report in September, the last details of the clean air legislation were already being banged out.

Lawmakers say the requirements of the clean air amendments are in line with the findings of the NAPAP report. "Even though the final report wasn't out"

# *History of Acid Rain Research*

**A**lthough it wasn't until the 1960s that acid rain was recognized as a serious environmental problem, scientists have been studying the phenomenon since at least the mid-1800s. One of the earliest researchers was Robert Angus Smith, Britain's first chief alkali inspector. Smith discovered a link between the sooty air in Manchester and the acidic precipitation the town suffered from, which he described in his 1872 book, *Air and Rain: The Beginnings of a Chemical Climatology*. It was in this book that Smith coined the term "acid rain."

Acid rain first gained wide public attention 80 years later, when about 4,000 people died in London in 1952 from a mix of particulates, sulfur dioxide and acidic fog. But while London's "killer fog" raised public awareness about the dangers of air pollution, it would be at least another decade before the public recognized acid rain as a unique kind of air pollution.

Some of the most important data on acid precipitation developed from the work of Swedish soil scientists in the late 1950s and early '60s. Their work, together with a series of papers published during this period by Canadian ecologist Eville Gorham, provided the basis for understanding how acid rain is generated and dispersed. Working in England and Canada, Gorham and his colleagues found that abnormally acidic precipitation could be attributed to combustion of fossil fuels and that changes in lake and soil chemistry could be traced to the precipitation.

But as a leading U.S. authority on acid rain, Ellis B. Cowling of North Carolina State University, put it, Gorham's research was "met by thundering silence from both the scientific community and the public at large."†

Wider appreciation of the acid rain problem came only after a young Swedish scientist, Svante Odén, published a comprehensive story on acid precipitation in a leading Swedish newspaper in 1967. According to Cowling, Odén's "analysis of air-mass trajectories clearly showed that acid precipitation was a large-scale regional phenomenon in much of Europe, that both precipitation and surface waters were becoming more acidic, and that long-distance . . . transport of both sulfur- and nitrogen-containing air pollutants was occurring among the various nations of Europe."

Because of southern Scandinavia's special vulnerability to acid rain from England and Western Europe, Odén's article attracted wide attention, and the Swedish government initiated an inquiry that led eventually to a presentation at the United Nations Conference on the Human Environment in 1972. Odén is now referred to as "the father of acid rain research."

† *Ellis B. Cowling*, From Research to Public Policy: Progress in Scientific and Public Understanding of Acid Precipitation and Its Biological Effects *(1980), p. 12.*

during the final negotiations on the clean air bill, "the testimony that outlined the conclusions was in the congressional milieu for over a year, so the final report was not a shocker or a surprise," explained a House committee staff member who asked not to be identified.

Some environmentalists had argued that the decade-long National Acid Precipitation Assessment Program was being used as an excuse to delay taking action on acid rain. "It became a very convenient excuse for the Reagan administration," says Deborah Sheiman, a resource specialist at the Natural Resources Defense Council in Washington. "It was the Reagan line: 'We've got to research acid rain, [so] we can't do anything to control it.'" And NAPAP's credibility suffered a tremendous blow in 1987 when the program's director, Lawrence Kulp, resigned after he reportedly wrote an introduction to a NAPAP interim report that reflected what he thought the Reagan administration wanted to hear — and not what the data in the report actually said.[6]

Environmentalists generally are satisfied with NAPAP's final results, although some say the report has added little to the existing body of scientific knowledge about acid rain. "It's a big report," says Sheiman. "But if you read it closely, I think it says more about what isn't known, in terms of some of the effects that they never really got around to studying." Sheiman also accuses industry groups of

"mischaracterizing" the report's conclusions in order to belittle the dangers of acid rain.

Industry's interpretation of the report leads to the conclusion that the government went after a relatively small problem with a mighty big stick. "We felt that the Congress paid precious little attention to the NAPAP study, and I wish that they had [paid more]," says Bill Fay, vice president for congressional affairs for the National Coal Association and former executive director of the Clean Air Working Group, a now-disbanded industry coalition that favored less regulation. "I think what NAPAP was saying was that this is a problem," but not a crisis, "and there were certainly ways to approach the problem that would have been much more affordable than the approach that [the clean air amendments] took."

Although the final version of the clean air amendments went further than the president wanted, the Bush administration has defended the law's acid rain provisions. The provisions represent "a measured response to a serious long-term environmental problem," states a report by the Environmental Protection Agency's Office of Air and Radiation. "The issue is not whether or not acid rain is an environmental catastrophe or crisis," the report said, "but if acid rain is a serious enough problem to warrant action. The answer is yes."[7]

Bill Roberts, legislative director of the Environmental Defense Fund, agrees. "Everyone, including the president, did seem to agree that we have a serious problem that justified an aggressive solution, and in fact, that's what we have," Roberts says.

This "aggressive solution" calls for annual sulfur dioxide emissions to be cut almost in half from 1980 levels — which would mean about a 10 million ton reduction by the year 2000. Annual nitrogen oxides emissions would have to be cut by 2 million tons by that year, roughly a 25 percent cut. Midwestern utility plants that are the source of most acid rain pollutants will have to clean up first; beginning in 1995, 111 of the dirtiest coal-fired plants in 21 states will have to reduce sulfur dioxide emissions. About 200 more will have to comply by 2000.[8]

The acid rain provisions of the clean air amendments reflect a dramatic shift in the philosophy of pollution control. Since the government began regulating pollution 20 years ago, it has relied on a "command and control" approach to limit emissions. The 1990 amendments mark the first time that a market-based "emissions cap" has been used to manage pollutants.

Under the "command and control" approach, individual power plants were regulated, but the total amount of emissions was unlimited. The "emissions cap" approach allows individual plants to pollute at different rates, but the total amount of pollutants emitted is limited; no matter how many new power plants are built in the future, the total amount of pollutants they emit must be under this cap. A market will be set up to enable utilities that can reduce emissions below what the law requires to sell those reductions to other utilities. This system is expected to provide great reductions in emissions at low costs.

Many in the environmental community are cautiously optimistic about the impact of the clean air amendments on the acid rain problem, but they are withholding final judgment until the EPA's implementing regulations emerge over the next year or so and the system is up and running. "We have to make sure it happens before we claim complete victory over this problem," says Bill Roberts.

## Effects of acid rain on lakes and streams

Excess acidity in precipitation arises primarily from the reaction of sulfur and nitrogen oxides with water.* Numerous factors such as the intensity of sunlight can influence the type of reaction that takes place and the speed with which sulfuric and nitric acids are formed. Atmospheric conditions also have a strong effect on the concentration and dispersal of pollutants.

The acidity of precipitation and of waters or soil contaminated by pollutants is measured by what scientists call a pH scale. Measurements range from 0, most acidic, to 14, which is alkaline and thus shows no acidity. A reading of 7 is neutral. For example, battery acid is pH 1.0, lemon juice is pH 2.0, and vinegar is pH 2.2. (*See pH scale, p. 135.*) Unpolluted rainfall is not neutral; it is somewhat acidic, generally having a pH level of 5.6, although there are naturally occurring regional and seasonal variations. Acid rain is any precipitation with a pH level lower — that is, more acidic — than 5.6.

Since the pH scale is logarithmic, a change in one point on the scale indicates a tenfold change in acidity. Thus, if the acidity of rainfall goes from 5.6 to 4.6, then it has become 10 times more acidic. A drop in pH to 3.6 would signify it had become 100 times more acidic.

Sulfur dioxide is roughly twice as acidic as nitrogen oxides, and is the chief target of the new emission controls. Electric utilities accounted for 70 percent of the 23 million tons of sulfur oxides emitted nationwide in 1985. Once in the atmosphere, these emissions may fall back to earth within a few miles, or be carried many hundreds of miles from their source.

The National Acid Precipitation Assessment Program reports that sulfur dioxide emissions from utilities have decreased by approximately 30 percent since 1975, primarily because of adoption of cleaner combustion technologies and use of low-sulfur coal. But utility power plants still emitted 16 million tons of sulfur oxides in 1985.[9] These emissions were concentrated in the Ohio River Valley. (*See map, p. 137.*)

(Motor vehicle exhaust is the main source of nitrogen oxide emissions in the United States, accounting for 45 percent of the 20.5 million tons emitted in 1985. For this reason, these emissions are more evenly dispersed around the country than are sulfur dioxide emissions.[10])

The ecosystems most likely to be affected by acid rain are lakes, streams, forests and croplands. The scientific evidence to date indicates that acid precipitation is particularly damaging to aquatic systems. "The whole water system changes" as a result of acidification, says Harold Harvey, a zoologist from the University of Toronto. "The clams go first, then the snails, then the crayfish; and many of the aquatic insects like the mayfly, damselfly, stonefly, and the dragonfly. Then you start dropping off things like amphibians. God only knows what happened to the reptiles, we haven't got a fix on them yet. Then out go the fish, and so on."[11]

Although acidification affects the full spectrum of life in aquatic systems, acidic lakes aren't really "dead" — they're just radically altered. Different organisms flourish; high acid levels promote the growth of sphag-

---

*There also are natural causes of acid precipitation. Lightning bolts form nitrogen oxides, volcanoes spew sulfur dioxide, and forest fires and bacterial decomposition release acid-forming gases.

# An International Problem

The problem of acid rain is not limited to North America. Europe and many parts of the developing world have suffered from its effects, and very few places are doing anything about it.

The problem has been particularly acute in Europe, China and India, all of which have large deposits of high-sulfur coal. In 1983, for instance, West Germany's media reported that a third of the country's forests were showing classic effects of acid rain: they were yellowing and dropping leaves and needles. A later study found that the damage was spreading: nearly half of Germany's 18 million forested acres — and two-thirds of the famed Black Forest — were measurably damaged. The Germans even coined a new word for acid rain: *Waldsterben* — "forest death," later amended to *neuartige Waldschäden* — "new type of forest damage."

In the mid-1980s, West Germany passed laws requiring all its power plants to be retrofitted with scrubbers as well as with devices to reduce nitrogen oxide emissions. Nearly all the plants in what used to be West Germany now have the systems in place. Other Western European countries also have taken steps to reduce emissions in recent years. But it has only been with German unification and the fall of communism in the region that Eastern Europe has begun to confront the problem of acid rain.

By contrast, more than 20 years ago Japan recognized that its dependence on coal could lead to problems. It instituted strict controls in 1968, reducing its sulfur dioxide emissions by 50 percent between 1968 and 1975. It has toughened its rules even more since then, encouraging the use of low-sulfur coal scrubbers; more than 1,200 scrubbers are now operating in the country.

num mosses and filamentous algae, which create "mats" that seal off oxygen from the lake floor; this makes the decomposition process less efficient. As a result, Harvey says, "the lakes look like they've got Astroturf on the bottom." [12]

The effects of acidification are usually difficult for the average person to detect. In fact, an acid lake may actually look better than one with a lower acid level. "It is a chilling and ironic twist that as a lake acidifies it becomes more attractive," states a Canadian report on acid rain, "for as the various life forms within it die off, the water clears and appears to be in radiant health — until you look beneath the surface." [13]

The sensitivity of freshwater systems to acid precipitation depends largely on their buffering capacity,

that is, their ability to neutralize acids. When the bedrock under lakes or streams consists largely of siliceous types such as granite and quartz, the water generally is highly sensitive to added acid. Siliceous bedrock is found in Scandinavia, New England, the Adirondacks and the Appalachians, precisely the areas where the most drastic changes in lake ecology have been detected.

A decade ago, when NAPAP was chartered, many scientists thought that hundreds of lakes throughout the United States would become acidic during the 1980s. But the findings of the NAPAP report dispute this prediction. According to the report, acid rain has adversely affected less than 5 percent of the nation's lakes and only 10 percent of the streams. "In most of the country," the report states, "there are sufficient materials in the soil, ground water, and surface water to neutralize acid effectively, and environmental quality is apparently unaffected by sulfate deposition. ... Instead of widespread acidity in U.S. lakes and streams, acidic surface waters are concentrated in specific regions." [14]

The highest percentage of acidic lakes is found in the Adirondack region of New York; up to 15 percent of the large lakes in this area (those greater than 10 acres in size) and up to 30 percent of the small lakes are chronically acidic. (Florida actually has a higher percentage of acidic lakes, but most are acidic because of natural processes.) Lakes and streams in the Mid-Atlantic region also have higher than average acidic levels. But while NAPAP did not find evidence of extreme acid rain damage in other parts of the country, its report warned that "in some regions, future acid inputs could place sensitive waters at greater risk. ... These waters exhibit low capacities to retain incoming sulfate and neutralize acidic inputs. The number of these sensitive surface waters is at least twice the present number of acidic lakes and streams." [15]

Dan Binkley, an associate professor of forest ecology at Colorado State University, thinks the NAPAP report greatly understated the extent of acid rain damage in North America because it did not pay enough attention to the situation in Canada. "[T]he characteristics of those lakes in the Adirondacks that allowed them to be acidified aren't real common in the Northeastern United States," he says, but they are common in Canada. Based on the NAPAP report, acid rain may not seem like that big a problem, Binkley adds, "but if you move northward and worry about Canada, [the situation is] not necessarily quite as reassuring."

Acid rain has been a major irritant in the relationship between the United States and Canada for more than a decade.* About half of the acid compounds that fall on Canada come from power plants and other sources within the United States. Canada's soils and aquatic systems tend to be less buffered than those in

*For background, see "Acid Rain: Canada's Push for U.S. Action," *E.R.R.*, March 7, 1986 (Vol. I, No. 9).

the United States and are therefore more vulnerable to acid precipitation.

Freshwater fish are particularly affected by acid rain. Female fish fail to reproduce after the pH hits a certain level. By the time the water's pH reaches 5.5, most species of fish are endangered, and by pH 4.5, all fish are gone. They are also an easy casualty to track, since their disappearance in a lake or stream is quickly noted by fishermen and sportsmen.

Increases in acidity hurt fish in a number of ways. As the acid levels increase, metals like aluminum that had settled into the sediment of lakes and streams are released back into the water in unnatural amounts. This process is known as "mobilization." In 1977, Dr. Carl Schofield of Cornell University demonstrated that young Adirondack fish, called fry, picked up the aluminum in their gills. In attempting to get rid of it, they pump out so much mucus that they strangle. In other studies, fish have actually been spotted sneezing to try to clear their gills of aluminum.

The acidity also hampers the ability of fish to absorb calcium and sodium. The lack of calcium makes them deformed, humpbacked or dwarfed; while their skeletons wither, their muscles stay strong, and they end up pulling themselves apart. Sodium deficiencies cause fish to twitch uncontrollably until they die.

Fish are also extremely vulnerable to a phenomenon known as "acid shock," or "episodic acidification." Acid collects with the snows of winter and reaches the streams and lakes during the spring runoff just when fish are spawning, an exceptionally sensitive stage in the aquatic life cycle.

Acid shock is a difficult phenomenon to track, because its effects quickly dissipate. Sheiman of the Natural Resources Defense Council estimates that compared with the number of lakes classified as chronically acidic, "You probably have three times the number of water bodies that are affected by acidification on a temporary basis." Acid shock is more of a problem in Canada than in the United States, Sheiman says, because that nation is more likely to be covered with snow all winter long.

## Impact on forests and human health

One of the most controversial conclusions of the NAPAP report is that there is currently no widespread forest damage in the United States or Canada that can be directly linked to acid rain. "In general ... the majority of North American forests are healthy," said NAPAP Director James Mahoney.[16]

The report linked most forest damage to ozone and "localized soil nutrient deficiencies." Studies conducted for NAPAP did find that acidic cloud water, "together with a complex combination of other factors (ozone, soil acidification climate)," can reduce the cold tolerance of one tree species, the red spruce, at high elevations in the Eastern United States. According to the report, "This can contribute to damage to trees above cloud level during winters with particularly low

# The pH Scale Measures Acidity

The acidity of precipitation and other substances is measured by what scientists call a pH scale. Measurements range from 0, most acidic, to 14, which is alkaline and thus shows no acidity. A reading of 7 is neutral. The pH level of various substances is indicated on the scale below. Acid rain is any precipitation with a pH level lower — that is, more acidic — than 5.6.

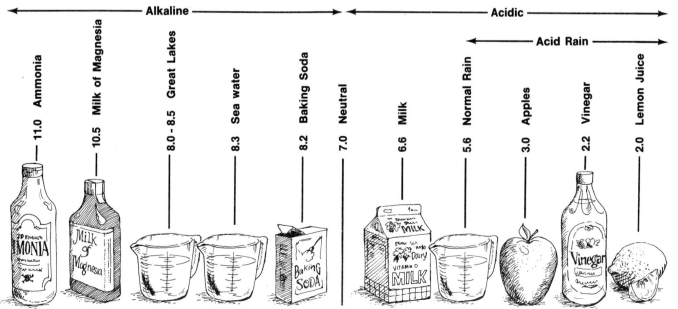

temperatures." The report also said that over the next several decades acid deposition could aggravate soil nutrient deficiencies in some regions and that this could adversely affect sugar maples in eastern Canada. "However," the report added, "there is no evidence to indicate that forest health in general is currently affected by nutrient deficiency or will be affected in the next half century." [17]

Acid rain actually boosts the growth of some trees, especially Scotch pines, but the beneficial effects are only temporary. Nitrogen and sulfur "emissions can be fertilizers, but only to a certain point," says Dan Binkley of Colorado State University. Eventually, the soil's buffering capacity is overwhelmed and acids can no longer be neutralized. According to Binkley, the accumulation of acid in the soil, along with the resulting buildup of metals and the retardation of decomposition, damage the trees.

Binkley and many other environmentalists disagree with NAPAP's conclusions about the impact of acid rain on forests. Sheiman of the Natural Resources Defense Council thinks NAPAP didn't conduct enough research in this area. "At most what they can say is that they don't understand what's going on in these forest systems," she says, ". . . [and that] there seem to be a variety of factors involved, some natural stresses, and some additional stresses from man-made air pollution." In Sheiman's view, the fact that there are different stress factors involved should not be used as an excuse to avoid tackling the acid rain problem. "It's hard to say that you're going to do something about the fact that you had a drought last year, but you can do something about the man-made air pollution."

Sheiman also thinks that NAPAP should have spent more time and money studying acid rain's impact on human health. Many scientists believe acid rain aggravates respiratory disorders such as chronic bronchitis, asthma and emphysema, especially in small children.

"Infants and children breathe more rapidly, and therefore move more pollutant through the lungs," says Dr. Richard M. Narkewicz of the American Academy of Pediatricians. "The repair process of children for damaged airways is less efficient than that of adults, and the immunologic immaturity of children contributes to more respiratory disease. The obvious risk is that children's exposure to pollution will be longer, because of their life span, which potentially exposes them to more long-term crippling events." [18]

Scientists also worry about the risks posed to people who eat large amounts of fish from acidic lakes or streams. Such fish often have extremely high levels of aluminum, mercury, lead, zinc, copper and other metals that can adversely affect human health. Some scientists believe that aluminum from fish tissue may be linked to the onset of Alzheimer's disease. Autopsies of those who die from Alzheimer's often reveal large plaques of aluminum — sufficient quantities to im-

pede neural function. This could cause the progressive dementia typical of the disease. [19]

Although some environmentalists think the NAPAP report understates the overall damage caused by acid rain, the report does confirm some long-held suspicions. For example, the report says that acid rain contributes to reduced visibility throughout the Eastern United States and in some large metropolitan areas of the West. It also says that acid rain contributes "to the corrosion of metals and deterioration of stone in buildings, statues and other cultural resources." [20]

The effect of acid rain on man-made structures is receiving increased attention as the deterioration accelerates. At risk are stone objects throughout the world, ranging in size from gravestones to the Lincoln Memorial. For example, acid rain has been blamed for the extensive deterioration of the Caryatids, six marble maidens carved by the Greek sculptor Phidias in the fifth century B.C. The statues supported the Erectheum porch of the Acropolis in Athens until 1977, when they had to be replaced by fiberglass replicas.

## Giving industry incentives to reduce air pollution

The damage acid rain has done to structures, forests, lakes, and people might have been even greater had the United States not taken steps to reduce air pollution over the past 30 years. Congress enacted the nation's first Clean Air Act in 1963, but it was the 1970 amendments to this act that were considered the first comprehensive air pollution law.

The 1970 legislation required states to regulate industrial emissions of air toxics within their own boundaries. Unfortunately, this requirement had an unintended effect: It encouraged utilities and industries to build tall smokestacks that wafted the gases beyond a state's lines. By 1981, the United States had 179 smokestacks higher than 500 feet and 20 that were 1,000 feet or more. [21]

The 1970 legislation also allowed states to set their own emissions limits. Some environmentalists felt this provision actually made the acid rain problem worse. "The [1970] Clean Air Act [was] one of the chief reasons for the increase in acid rain," Robert B. Flacke, commissioner of New York State's Department of Environmental Conservation, told a reporter in 1981. "Not only did its . . . policy bring about the long-range transport of air pollution via tall stacks, it also permit[ted] New York and other clean-plant states to be dirtied by states with looser air standards." [22]

Congress amended the Clean Air Act in 1977, and while the amendments did not address the problem of tall smokestacks, they did impose stringent emission limits on new power plants. Under the 1977 law, new power plants could emit only 15 pounds of sulfur

# Sulfur Emissions by State

Concentrations of sulfur dioxide emissions vary widely from state to state. The heights of the bars in the map below indicate the number of tons of sulfur dioxide that electric power utilities emitted in each state per square mile in 1988. The table lists the *total* number of tons of sulfur dioxide that the utilities emitted that year. Power plants in the Midwest tend to use high-sulfur coal mined from the Midwest and the northern Appalachians, while power plants in the Far West tend to burn low-sulfur coal mined from the West and the southern Appalachians. So while Illinois emitted fewer tons overall than Texas (1,166,000 vs. 1,341,000), concentrations of emissions were much higher in Illinois (20.9 tons/sq. mile vs. 5.1 tons/sq. mile).

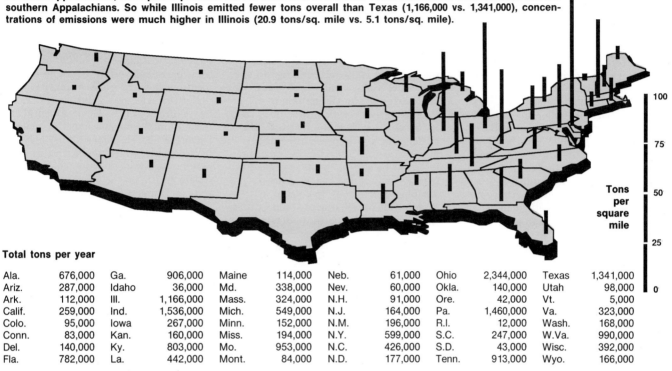

**Total tons per year**

| Ala. | 676,000 | Ga. | 906,000 | Maine | 114,000 | Neb. | 61,000 | Ohio | 2,344,000 | Texas | 1,341,000 |
|------|---------|-------|-----------|-------|---------|------|---------|------|-----------|-------|-----------|
| Ariz. | 287,000 | Idaho | 36,000 | Md. | 338,000 | Nev. | 60,000 | Okla. | 140,000 | Utah | 98,000 |
| Ark. | 112,000 | Ill. | 1,166,000 | Mass. | 324,000 | N.H. | 91,000 | Ore. | 42,000 | Vt. | 5,000 |
| Calif. | 259,000 | Ind. | 1,536,000 | Mich. | 549,000 | N.J. | 164,000 | Pa. | 1,460,000 | Va. | 323,000 |
| Colo. | 95,000 | Iowa | 267,000 | Minn. | 152,000 | N.M. | 196,000 | R.I. | 12,000 | Wash. | 168,000 |
| Conn. | 83,000 | Kan. | 160,000 | Miss. | 194,000 | N.Y. | 599,000 | S.C. | 247,000 | W.Va. | 990,000 |
| Del. | 140,000 | Ky. | 803,000 | Mo. | 953,000 | N.C. | 426,000 | S.D. | 43,000 | Wisc. | 392,000 |
| Fla. | 782,000 | La. | 442,000 | Mont. | 84,000 | N.D. | 177,000 | Tenn. | 913,000 | Wyo. | 166,000 |

*Source: U.S. Department of Energy.*

dioxide per ton of coal burned. By contrast, older plants had been allowed to pump out up to 200 pounds of sulfur dioxide per ton of coal burned.

The new emission-control requirements meant that most new power plants would have to be built with expensive pollution-control devices known as "scrubbers," which remove sulfur from flue gases. (*See story, p. 138.*) "The 1977 act itself did not mention the word 'scrubber,'" explains Jeff Smith, executive director of the Industrial Gas Cleaning Institute, the scrubber manufacturers' trade group. But this was the only technology available that could get emissions down to the levels required by law.

The 1977 amendments did not solve the nation's air pollution problems. For one thing, they only restricted the emissions of power plants built after 1977; operators of older plants did not have to comply with the new emissions standards. The older plants, many of which are still in use today, "are totally uncontrolled in terms of their sulfur air pollution," says Sheiman of the Natural Resources Defense Council. "It's a pretty shocking situation when you consider that here it is 1991, in this advanced industrialized society, and the power plants operate as if they were in Eastern Europe."

According to Sheiman, "The utilities have been extending the lifetime [of power plants] well beyond

what their initial projected life was. Most had a projected life of 30 years, but they've been fixing up the plants piece by piece, so now many of them have lifetimes that extend 50 or 60 years into the future." Because of this, "they don't [have to] build new power plants which would have to meet new [emissions] standards."

No progress was made in formulating new clean air legislation during the 1980s. The Reagan administration's lack of enthusiasm for new regulations strengthened the hand of key congressional opponents of air-pollution regulation. "Chief among them was auto industry ally John D. Dingell, D-Mich., who used his House Energy and Commerce Committee chairmanship to stall any bills that would impose tough new standards on Detroit automakers. In the Senate, then-Majority Leader Robert C. Byrd discouraged action because of fear that acid rain proposals would throw coal miners out of work by destroying the market for high-sulfur coal mined in his home state of West Virginia." [23]

Underlying their opposition were important regional concerns. The Midwestern states, for example, opposed acid rain bills year after year because of the heavy cost to utilities in their states, which burn high-sulfur coal. Lawmakers also had to address the concerns of states with utilities that burn less polluting,

# Scrubber Technology Reduces Emissions

Scrubbers are elaborate, and very expensive, devices that are used to take the sulfur out of electric power plant emissions. Scrubbers do their work after the coal has been burned in the plant's boiler, but before it goes up the smokestack.

Inside a scrubber, limestone mixes with the gases the boiler has produced and attaches itself to the sulfur dioxide. The resulting "sludge" can then be easily collected. Scrubbers can capture about 92 percent of the sulfur dioxide a plant would normally emit. But because of their high cost, the devices have never been popular with the utility industry.

Putting a scrubber in an existing power plant ("retrofitting" a scrubber) costs between $150,000-$160,000 per megawatt expended. A typical American electric power plant puts out 500 megawatts of power every year. A megawatt is 1 million watts, so the total cost of retrofitting a plant generally runs between $75 million and $80 million. If space is limited and ductwork has to be piped all over, it can bring the total cost up to $130 million. And that's for an average-sized plant. Some power plants produce up to 1,500 megawatts of power a year.

It's more expensive to retrofit an existing power plant than to put a scrubber in a new plant, but even these costs are substantial. Pennsylvania officials estimate that when the Bruce Mansfield power plant in Shippingport was built in 1980, one-third of the $1.4-billion price

tag went for scrubbers and for dams to hold the sulfuric sludge. The extra costs raised area utility bills 7 percent.[†]

And construction costs aren't the only expense related to scrubber use. Once the scrubber is up and running, up to 8 percent of a power plant's output has to be diverted to run the scrubber.

Jeff Smith, executive director of the Industrial Gas Cleaning Institute, the trade group that represents scrubber manufacturers, concedes that costs are high, but he says they "have come down substantially in the last 10 years. A scrubber costs about 30 percent less than it did in 1980 due to standardization of design and better understanding of chemistry and materials."

Costs aren't the only problem, however. "Some utilities don't have the space" for a scrubber, says Bill Fay, vice president for congressional affairs for the National Coal Association and former executive director of the Clean Air Working Group, a now-disbanded industry coalition that represented industry's views during the Clean Air Act negotiations. "They take up as much space as the generating unit itself."

Getting rid of the sulfuric sludge is also a problem. "We have a whole valley outside of Pittsburgh that's starting to fill up with this scrubber sludge," says Fay. "It's not a usable product. When it's hot, it turns into a liquid, when it's cold, it's very, very solid, but it never really congeals."

The system of pollution "allowances"

contained in the new clean air amendments are designed to reduce the need for utilities to install scrubbers. (*For a description of the allowance system, see p. 139.*) "Installing a scrubber may in some cases be overkill for purposes of meeting their compliance obligations under the act," says Bill Roberts, legislative director of the Environmental Defense Fund. "People way out of whack [with the new emissions limits] may put in a scrubber, while people who are close may buy allowances or switch fuels."

Jeff Smith, on the other hand, thinks the new law could encourage scrubber use. "Congress has chosen to provide rather breathtakingly significant incentives for scrubber use and I think that speaks well of the performance of the technology. The outright hatred of scrubber technology by utility executives and utility engineers has been replaced by a measured acceptance of the technology due to improvements in reliability."

Bill Fay agrees that industry in general prefers scrubbers to the even more expensive alternatives outlined in the Clean Air Act. Using scrubbers, he says, "We can burn high-sulfur coals cleanly. We can continue to use a resource that is the epitome of our energy independence. We have 400 years of energy in our coal reserves in this country, and we need to utilize both high- and low-sulfur coals."

[†] *See Anne LaBastille, "Acid Rain: How Great a Menace?" National Geographic, November 1981, p. 679.*

low-sulfur coal, or that had installed pollution-control devices. These states felt that the Midwest had been able to snatch industries from other areas by promising them a work climate that featured low utility rates and loose emissions rules. So these areas did not want to share the burden of paying for the Midwest's costly cleanup.

The political climate finally changed when President Bush presented his clean air bill on June 12, 1989. Bush's plan did not resolve regional conflicts, but it gave the clean air legislation a legitimacy it hadn't had throughout the Reagan years. One measure of this change was a newly active Environmental Protection Agency (EPA) headed by William K. Reilly. The EPA had been largely silenced during the Reagan years.

The climate in Congress changed, too; Byrd, a powerful foe of tougher acid rain legislation, stepped down as Senate majority leader as environmentalist George Mitchell of Maine stepped up in late 1988. In his new role, Mitchell was able to push a tough clean air bill through the Senate.

In the House, an unlikely alliance emerged when Bush was able to line up Energy Committee Chairman Dingell, usually a fierce opponent of clean air legislation. Dingell, realizing that a bill was inevitable, got on board so he could steer the bill, rather than watch it go by. While the final House bill was stronger than Bush's original plan, Dingell was able to keep it weaker than Mitchell's Senate bill, and the House bill was eventually the one that won out in conference committee negotiations.[24]

While the final bill included provisions that went far beyond Bush's proposal, it did include three key aspects of Bush's plan: a multimillion-ton reduction in sulfur dioxide emissions, an "emissions cap" that put a permanent lid on the country's total air emissions, and a market-based system of pollution "allowances" that offered industry financial incentives to clean up their own acts by charging them for polluting and rewarding them if they didn't.

The idea behind Bush's proposal was to give plants the flexibility to clean up in the most cost-effective manner. Because utilities could sell or trade their allowances,* they would be encouraged to clean up more than required and recover their costs by selling valuable credits. The buyers: utilities that want to expand but that would have little or no room to do so under the tough new emissions cap.

Bill Roberts of the Environmental Defense Fund says many environmentalists initially were skeptical about Bush's market-based approach, which his organization was instrumental in developing.** "There was some concern [among environmentalists] about the effectiveness of emissions trading, but what people really began to focus on after getting adjusted to the idea was that this proposal, unlike most proposals before it, imposed a cap on emissions. Limiting emissions to a fixed level into the future, despite all growth, is a process by which we don't allow for the erosion of the gains we make over the long haul in acid rain emissions reductions. Cutting the emissions in half — and keeping it there — was a real environmental home run."

Emissions trading had been used on a limited basis before, but according to Roberts, "It had had enforcement problems and a number of other problems, so it left people feeling dissatisfied with its ability to work." But the Environmental Defense Fund came to believe that in the case of acid rain, emissions trading "had unique applications ... because the goal is to reduce emissions over the whole [country]. So the fact that one facility might decrease while another one increases, all the while getting the cumulative reductions down, gets you to the goal."

Roberts estimates that the market-based system will save 30-50 percent of the costs of reducing sulfur dioxide emissions. What emissions trading does, Roberts says, "is accommodate the environmental objective ... in a way that reduces the cost as much as possible on the affected industry by allowing Utility A to effectively share the costs of reductions with Utility B and

with Utility C and so forth. So that if Utility A has the cheapest way to get those kinds of reductions, it can sell that advantage to the other utilities for something less than they might spend if they had to do it all on their own. So in other words, you get the same environmental result at a lot lower cost — which made it, frankly, a lot more politically palatable."

Bill Fay of the National Coal Association agrees that the new system should help keep compliance costs down, but he says industry is still concerned about the costs of the entire law. The Clean Air Working Group that Fay headed estimated that the annual costs of complying with just the acid rain provisions of the 1990 Clean Air Act will be about $6 billion.[25] Ten states in the Midwest will pick up most of the tab: Illinois, Indiana, Kentucky, Missouri, Michigan, Pennsylvania, Ohio, Tennessee, West Virginia, and Wisconsin will bear 80-90 percent of the costs of the 10-million-ton reduction in sulfur dioxide emissions. Most states in other regions already have taken steps to stem sulfur dioxide emissions and other sources of air pollution.

## Acid rain provisions of 1990 clean air law

The Clean Air Act breaks acid rain regulation into two phases, with the Midwest getting a bit of a break during the first phase. Phase I, beginning in 1995, will control the emissions of large units (100 megawatts of power per year or greater) that currently emit more than 2.5 pounds of sulfur dioxide for every million British thermal units (mmBtu) of energy produced.* The Phase I plants are the dirtiest in the nation and most of them are located in the Midwest. To ease that region's initial burden, 50,000 extra, free allowances will go to plants targeted for Phase I. Phase II, beginning in the year 2000, will cover all plants with outputs of more than 25 megawatts per year that emit 1.2 or more pounds of sulfur dioxide per mmBtu produced.

EPA will issue each plant allowances according to the following formula: 2.5 lbs. (or, in Phase II, 1.2 lbs.) per mmBtu multiplied by the "baseline," or average amount of fuel used by the utility per year from 1985-87.[26]

Under this formula, a plant that emitted 5 lbs. of sulfur for every mmBtu in 1985 — that's about average for an old coal-burning power plant — will, by 1995, only get enough allowances to emit 2.5 lbs. per mmBtu.** By 2000, the plant will only receive

*An allowance is a license to emit a single ton of sulfur dioxide (or nitrogen oxide) in a single calendar year.

**The market-based system was conceived by two economists at the Environmental Defense Fund, Daniel Dudek and Joseph Goffman. Goffman ended up joining the staff of the Senate Environment Committee, where he helped write the new clean air bill. For background on the market-based approach to environmental protection, see "Free Market Environmental Protection," *E.R.R.*, Sept. 8, 1989 (Vol. II, No. 9).

*A British thermal unit represents the quantity of heat required to raise the temperature of one pound of water one degree Fahrenheit.

**The 1990 law mainly affects plants built before 1977. Because of the 1977 Clean Air Act, the few plants built since then essentially meet the requirements for emissions under the new bill.

enough allowances to emit 1.2 lbs. of sulfur per mmBtu. This plant's emissions, then, will have been chopped by 76 percent over 10 years. The utility has only a few ways to get the emissions down that far: switch to low-sulfur coal, install a scrubber, buy allowances from other utilities, or shut the plant down.

Although the focus of the acid rain titles of the Clean Air Act is on sulfur dioxide emissions, nitrogen oxides will also be controlled beginning in 1995. Many plants' emissions will then be limited to only .45 lbs. of nitrogen oxides per mmBtu produced. In 1997, other types of boilers will fall under standards that the EPA still has to develop.

By the year 2000, utilities' overall sulfur dioxide emissions will be 10 million tons less than they were in 1980. Nitrogen oxide emissions will be 2 million tons less than in 1980. If a plant emits more sulfur dioxide or nitrogen oxides than it has allowances for, it will be fined $2,000 per ton over the limit and the plant will be required to reduce its emissions by an additional ton the next year.

If a utility wants to build a new power plant after 1999, it will first need to accumulate enough allowances to run it. There are four ways it can do this:

■ Shut down an old plant and transfer the allowances to the new plant.

■ Clean up existing units.

■ Implement conservation measures or build the new plant to use renewable sources such as solar or hydroelectric power.

■ Buy allowances on the open market (which are forecast to cost between $300 and $1,500 per ton per year).

Most new plants will be built in areas experiencing high growth, such as the Far West. "It's a complicated game," Roberts says, "but essentially we think there's enough flexibility in the system to permit growth to occur in the West."

To prime the allowance market, and to avoid restricting growth, the EPA will auction off 2.8 percent of all the allowances each year. From 1995-1999, 150,000 allowances will be auctioned off to the highest bidder, and from 2000 onward, 250,000 allowances per year will be auctioned off. Additionally, after 1999, 50,000 allowances will be sold at $1,500 per ton. These measures ensure that utilities building new plants will be able to purchase allowances to run them; there had been some fear that existing utilities would hoard their allowances and not sell.

Why wouldn't existing utilities want to sell their allowances? One way to look at this issue is through its effect on growth. Cheap and available electric power, for all practical purposes, equals growth. As an area adds industries, office buildings and residences, it needs more electric power, and eventually, more electric power plants. This also means more sulfur dioxide and nitrogen oxide emissions if the plants are coal-fired, as most in the United States are. Limiting the ability of a utility to emit pollutants — as the allowance system

does — can also limit the area's ability to grow.

Bill Roberts says that reluctance to sell allowances shouldn't be a big problem. "We believe that Midwestern utilities will find it economically in their interests to sell those allowances to anyone who may need them," he says. Also, Midwestern public utility commissions will be concerned about the huge utility rate hikes that may be needed to cover the costs of clean air compliance — and they will be looking for ways to keep those hikes as low as possible. "To the extent that a utility company is holding allowances that could, if sold, lower the costs to consumers in those states, there'll be every impetus on the part of these utility commissioners to try and encourage those kinds of sales or require them," Roberts says.

One of the additional benefits of the emissions trading system, says Roberts, is that it will defuse the pressure to raise the emissions cap in the future. If the law merely required lower emissions, he says, there would be a lot of pressure to move the cap up to maintain growth. But "by investing the existing utilities with these allowances, they become interested in maintaining that cap, because to the extent that more emissions are permitted, the value of what they're holding goes down."

## *Looking to the future: Implementation and assessment*

Industry and the environmental community agree that what happens in the next year or so will determine the path of progress against acid rain for the next decade. The Environmental Protection Agency is busy writing regulations — putting flesh on the bones of the Clean Air Act amendments. What the agency does will determine in large part how well the emissions trading system works.

"I think that the goals are realistic," says Jeff Smith of the Industrial Gas Cleaning Institute. "An awful lot depends on implementation. And that ... burden falls initially on EPA to come out with clear and timely regulations."

Bill Roberts of the Environmental Defense Fund agrees. "I think we have to make sure that this thing is implemented properly, and that it's given a chance to work," he says. It's important to "see if, in fact, we've found a mechanism to address an environmental problem that really does rely on the market as an ally rather than an opponent of environmental change."

Roberts says the new law contains a provision that may help avoid the delays that plagued enforcement of previous clean air laws. "In the acid rain title there is a specific requirement that whether the acid rain emissions trading program is up and running or not, you are required to meet the emission targets notwithstand-

*Continued on p. 142*

# AT ISSUE  *Is acid rain a serious environmental problem?*

**YES** *says an editorial in* **THE NEW YORK TIMES.**

The rain that falls over much of the northeastern United States is mildly acidic from pollutant gases. Like many weak poisons, its effects are subtle and hard to pinpoint. The preliminary results of a monumental 10-year Federal study [by the National Acid Precipitation Assessment Program] now establish how harmful this acid deluge is. They lend urgency to proposals that coal-burning utilities sharply cut their emissions of acid gases.

The $500 million study began in 1980 and seven years later produced a much criticized interim report. In accord with the Reagan Administration's belief that acid rain was not a serious problem, the interim study indicated that no more lakes were likely to become acidified and damage to trees was highly unlikely.

Drafts of the final report paint a darker picture. Acid rain is not about to cause the sudden ecological collapse predicted by some accounts in the early 1980s. Lakes are acidifying over decades, not seasons. But acid rain is indeed a serious threat to the ecology, especially in regions where the soil lacks a natural capacity for neutralizing acid.

In the southwestern Adirondacks, 11 percent of lakes are already acidified and 36 percent in danger of becoming so. In Appalachia, the Atlantic coastal plain, and parts of Michigan and Wisconsin, some 10 percent of lakes and streams have already been acidified past the point at which ecological damage is likely.

The draft report does not settle the longstanding issue of the widespread decline in some American forests. It finds no evidence to link forest decline in North America to acid rain, other than for high-altitude red spruce. With these trees, acid rain seems to worsen natural stresses. But acid rain may reduce the fertility of some forest soils over the long term.

Opponents of acid rain control have argued that all the lakes likely to go acid have already done so, and that reducing acid rain won't revive any of them. But James Mahoney, director of the study, told a Senate subcommittee last year that more streams could acidify at current levels of pollution.

Political solutions should follow, not precede, scientific conclusions, especially conclusions reached at the cost of $500 million. Fortunately, the National Acid Precipitation Assessment Program has already provided ample evidence for acting to curb acid rain.

*From "Acid Rain: Plenty Bad Enough," The New York Times, Jan. 29, 1990.*

**NO** *says syndicated economics columnist* **WARREN T. BROOKES**

At a hearing on Oct. 5, [1990,] members of the Senate Subcommittee on Environmental Protection discovered that the Bush administration acid rain program is expensively futile.

A preview of the 1990 final report by the National Acid Precipitation Assessment Project [*sic*] shows the Bush proposal to spend up to $4 billion to $6 billion per year to cut sulfur dioxide emissions will deacidify only 26 lakes in the Northeast after 20 years — and only 75 lakes after 50 years.

This means a 20-year cumulative cost of almost $5 billion per deacidified lake and after 50 years about $4 billion per lake. (By contrast, the 20-year cost of liming the average lake is less that $50,000.)

In his report to the Senate, James Mahoney, NAPAP director, admitted that even this scandalously small projection of benefits from the proposed Clean Air Program was iffy because: "There are significant uncertainties about the role that watershed mineral processes, organic acids and nitrates (in the soils) may play in the acidification and recovery process."

This is "science-ese" for admitting that, despite protestations, NAPAP knows there is very little correlation between acid-rain levels and acid lakes. For example, Mr. Mahoney acknowledged that the highest acid lake concentration in any U.S. state is in Florida. Yet Florida gets hardly any acid-rain depositions, and, as Mr. Mahoney noted, its acid lakes were the result of natural causes.

Mr. Mahoney granted that "the effects of constant, increased and decreased acid-rain deposition are not always statistically significant."

In fact, the EPA's own data shows that land use and soil composition are at least three times as statistically significant "causes" of acidic lakes as acid rain.

This is why NAPAP was forced to project that even if we do nothing, the number of acidic lakes in the Northeast will actually *decline* by one in the next 20 years, to a total of 161 and will only rise to 186 by the end of the next 50 years. Mr. Mahoney admitted, "What that really means, statistically, is no change at all."

In short, the NAPAP analysis shows now what it did in 1987: Acid rain is *not* a serious environmental problem . . . and the costs of $SO_2$ reduction are ludicrously out of line with the benefits.

It's a scandal waiting to be legislated.

*From "On Gold-Plated Ponds," The Washington Times, Oct. 26, 1989.*

*Continued from p. 140*

ing anything else. That is just a legal requirement that you are required to comply with."

Jeff Smith doesn't think industry will drag its feet on complying with the new law. "There are a lot of incentives under the acid rain title [that] provide a lot of benefits for industries that choose to comply by installing technologies such as scrubbers," he says. "So it certainly would behoove the utility industry to see that allowance program up and running as soon and as smoothly as possible."

By getting acid rain emissions reductions on track, other environmental problems such as ozone and global warming may also be affected positively. "The precursors to ozone are hydrocarbons and nitrogen oxides," says Deborah Sheiman. "The precursors to acid rain are nitrogen oxides and sulfur oxides. Ozone-depleting compounds like [chlorofluorocarbons] have global warming properties. All of these issues are interrelated."

Acid rain may not even be the most pressing of these problems. The NAPAP report notes that many of the environmental effects ascribed to acid rain are actually caused by ozone in the atmosphere. Some environmentalists agree. "In terms of harming plants, trees and agricultural crops, the ozone really is more threatening than acid rain," says Binkley of Colorado State University.

Bill Roberts thinks the market-based system being used to attack acid rain also could be used to tackle other air pollution problems. "We're seeking reductions in carbon dioxide and methane and a number of other pollutants where, once again, it doesn't really matter where those reductions occur," he says. "We're hopeful that it can offer a real solution to that problem by allowing costs for those kinds of reductions to be spread not just across industries, but potentially across countries."

For right now, at least, all eyes are on acid rain. The battle has shifted from the Capitol to EPA's headquarters, where the agency is bolstering its staff to manage the process. In fiscal 1992, EPA's acid rain staff will leap from 15 to 63 people; overall, more than 600 people at EPA will be working on the Clean Air Act Amendments.

NAPAP's final report is scheduled to be issued by May 1991. Its final conclusions may change slightly, based on the response NAPAP has received from scientists and others since its external review report was released in September. NAPAP's role in monitoring acid rain is up in the air. The program itself may be dissolved, but the compromise worked out in the clean air amendments called for the continuation of its research and provided funds for it. It is expected that NAPAP's work will continue in some form under the EPA and other agencies. Whatever takes its place will review the status of research activities conducted and report to Congress on gaps in research. It will also create a program to address current and future research priorities.

One of the benefits of all the money invested in NAPAP could be the mass of data accumulated on ozone, global warming and other environmental problems. "It's hoped that we'll get a lot of information back that will have a broader impact than just on acid rain," says a House committee staff member.

It seems that acid rain may actually be under control, but the committee staff member warns that the situation still will have to be monitored closely. "Given the fact that we've acted fairly quickly and we're addressing this issue, the impact hasn't been disastrous," she says. "But that doesn't mean that had we ignored it, it wouldn't have been. And it doesn't mean that you can just drop it, and move on."

# NOTES

[1] The amendments revise and extend the 1977 Clean Air Act. For a complete description of the provisions of the Clean Air Act Amendments, see *CQ Weekly Report*, Nov. 24, 1990, pp. 3934-3963.
[2] Agencies participating in the National Acid Precipitation Assessment Program are the Environmental Protection Agency, National Oceanic and Atmospheric Administration, Department of Agriculture, Department of Energy, Department of the Interior, Department of State, Tennessee Valley Authority, Executive Office of the President, Department of Commerce, Department of Health and Human Services, National Science Foundation, and the National Aeronautics and Space Administration.
[3] Quoted in *The New York Times*, Feb. 20, 1990.
[4] *CQ Weekly Report*, Nov. 3, 1990, p. 3692.
[5] See Alyson Pytte, "A Decade's Acrimony Lifted In the Glow of Clean Air," *CQ Weekly Report*, Oct. 27, 1990, p. 3587.
[6] See Margaret E. Kriz, "Dunning the Midwest," *National Journal*, April 14, 1990, p. 895.
[7] Environmental Protection Agency, Office of Air and Radiation, "Response to *60 Minutes* Story on Acid Rain," Jan. 10, 1991, pp. 1-2.
[8] See Pytte, *op. cit.*, p. 3592.
[9] National Acid Precipitation Assessment Program, *Assessment Highlights*, Sept. 5, 1990, pp. 1-2, 10.
[10] Electric utilities accounted for 30 percent of the nitrogen oxide emissions in 1985. *Ibid.*, p. 11.
[11] Quoted in *Downwind: The Acid Rain Story*, a booklet published in 1981 by Environment Canada, the Canadian equivalent of the Environmental Protection Agency.
[12] *Ibid.*
[13] *Ibid.*
[14] National Acid Precipitation Assessment Program, *op. cit.*, p. 5.
[15] *Ibid.*, pp. 5-6.
[16] Statement presented at the NAPAP final task force meeting at the National Academy of Sciences in Washington, Sept. 5, 1990.
[17] National Acid Precipitation Assessment Program, *op. cit.*, p. 7.
[18] Testimony before the Senate Committee on Environment and Public Works Subcommittee on Environmental Protection Feb. 3, 1987, as quoted in George J. Mitchell's *World on Fire: Saving an Endangered Earth* (1991), pp. 103-104.
[19] See Alan Wellburn, *Acid Rain and Air Pollution* (1988), p. 128.
[20] National Acid Precipitation Assessment Program, *op. cit.*, p. 7.
[21] See Anne LaBastille, "Acid Rain: How Great a Menace?" *National Geographic*, November 1981, p. 652.
[22] *Ibid.*, p. 652.
[23] Pytte, *op. cit.*, p. 3590.
[24] For more details, see *CQ Weekly Report*, Oct. 27, 1990, pp. 3934-3963.
[25] See Kriz, *op. cit.*, p. 897.
[26] The years 1985, 1986 and 1987 are used because those are the years for which the EPA has the best data. Plants that had prolonged outages during that time, and therefore used much less fuel than normal, will receive special permits.

*Graphics: Cover, Margaret Scott; pp. 131, 135, 137, Jack Auldridge.*

# RECOMMENDED READING

## BOOKS

**Mitchell, George, *World on Fire: Saving an Endangered Earth*, Charles Scribners' Sons, 1991.**

Mitchell, who is the Senate majority leader, maps out a scientific and political strategy for addressing what he calls "The Four Horsemen of the Apocalypse" — acid rain, global warming, ozone holes and wholesale rainforest destruction. Mitchell believes the United States must play a leading role in cleaning up the Earth. "We have a clear moral obligation to lead the world in undoing the damage we have done," says the Maine Democrat. Mitchell also provides an insider's perspective on the legislative maneuvers performed during negotiations over the 1990 Clean Air Act.

**Wellburn, Alan, *Air Pollution and Acid Rain: The Biological Impact*, Longman Scientific and Technical, 1988.**

This book tackles the acid rain question from the perspective of the affected organisms. The author, director of the biochemistry department at the University of Lancaster in Britain, examines the mechanisms by which acids kill fish, forests and people. "If one turns to books for information on the subject the problem is not the lack of it but the abundance," he says. But while there are many sources for information on the social, economic, and political effects of acid rain, there are few dealing exclusively with the science.

**MacKenzie, James J., and El-Ashry, Mohamed T., *Ill Winds: Airborne Pollution's Toll on Trees and Crops*, World Resources Institute, 1988.**

This book focuses on the combined effects of atmospheric ozone and acid deposition on forests and agricultural soils. The authors point to forest damage from Vermont to North Carolina that can be traced to air pollutants, and warn that the long-term threat to trees and crops is substantial. While ozone is the chief problem — annually costing the United States about $3 billion in losses of major crops alone — the combination of ozone and acid rain is even deadlier and cannot be ignored.

## ARTICLES

**"Clean Air Act Amendments," *Congressional Quarterly Weekly Report*, Nov. 24, 1990, p. 3934.**

CQ provides a complete list of all the provisions of the 1990 Clean Air Act Amendments.

**Kriz, Margaret E., "Dunning the Midwest," *National Journal*, April 14, 1990, p. 893.**

This article discusses the extent to which the Midwest got stuck with the bill for the 1990 Clean Air Act Amendments. After decades of putting up with the Midwest refusing to share the costs of acid rain controls, the rest of the country finally got fed up and handed the region most of the bill.

**Kurtz, Howard, "Is Acid Rain a Tempest in News Media Teapot?: Study Questioning Harm Gets Little Attention," *The Washington Post*, Jan. 14, 1991, p. A3.**

This article examines the controversy over whether the government and the news media ignored the work of the National Acid Precipitation Assessment Program. Kurtz interviews several science reporters, including the *Post's*, to see why they paid so little attention to the study.

**Pytte, Alyson, "A Decade's Acrimony Lifted in the Glow of Clean Air," *Congressional Quarterly Weekly Report*, Oct. 27, 1990, p. 3587.**

After a marathon negotiating session, Pytte writes, "The sky opened up on Oct. 22." The last of the major disagreements over the 1990 Clean Air Act Amendments were ironed out and the bill was on its way to the floors of the House and Senate. Pytte outlines the players and the compromises they made in hammering out the law.

**Steinzor, Rena I., and Straus, David R., "What Will the New Acid Rain Law Mean to You?" *Public Power*, January/February 1991, pp. 20-24.**

This summary of the 1990 Clean Air Act's acid rain provisions was written by two partners of a Washington, D.C., law firm. It analyzes the new provisions from the perspective of what they will mean to public power utilities. The new rules in place could so distort the energy markets, the authors suggest, that anyone who wants to work in the field must understand them inside and out. "Some predict, for example, that the law will inflate natural gas profits beyond producers' wildest dreams, notwithstanding their protestations to the contrary," they write. "Others claim it will accelerate demand-side programs and renewable energy while another industry faction believes it will resuscitate nuclear power."

**Weisskopf, Michael, "Best Intentions: The Unfulfilled Promise of the Clean Air Act," *The Washington Post*, June 5, 6, 7, 8, 1989 (four-part, front-page series).**

This series of articles is an intensive look at the failures of the 1970 Clean Air Act — both in the way it was originally written and in the way the federal government implemented it. Weisskopf, the *Post's* science reporter, winds up the series with a preview of the clean air debate to come in 1990.

## REPORTS AND STUDIES

**National Acid Precipitation Assessment Program, *Assessment Highlights*, Sept. 5, 1990; National Acid Precipitation Assessment Program, *NAPAP: Key Results*, Sept. 5, 1990.**

These are good summaries of the findings of the 10-year, $500 million NAPAP study and are invaluable as a starting point for research. NAPAP's final conclusions may change slightly in May 1991 when the final report is due to be published. *Key Results* is the text of a presentation made by NAPAP Director James R. Mahoney to the final NAPAP task force meeting.

**Office of Air and Radiation, the Environmental Protection Agency, "Response to 60 Minutes Story on Acid Rain," Jan. 10, 1991.**

This six-page memo is a response to a Dec. 30, 1990, edition of CBS' *60 Minutes*. The *60 Minutes* segment charged that the government had ignored the NAPAP's data in deciding the provisions of the Clean Air Act. The memo responds point by point to the accusations, and gives a good idea of how the government itself has interpreted the NAPAP report.

# EDITORIAL RESEARCH REPORTS

## Coming soon

- Gun Control
- The Cost of War
- Space Exploration

Published weekly by Congressional Quarterly Inc., Editorial Research Reports analyze emerging issues of national interest across a broad range of social, scientific, political and economic fields. Reports are bound and indexed for permanent reference. Subscription information is available through Congressional Quarterly's Publications Sales Department by telephone (202) 887-8665. Copies of past issues are available through Customer Service, (202) 887-8621.

ERR

MARCH 15, 1991

CONGRESSIONAL QUARTERLY'S

EDITORIAL RESEARCH REPORTS

FOUNDED 1923

# CALCULATING THE COSTS OF THE GULF WAR

EDITOR
**MARCUS D. ROSENBAUM**

MANAGING EDITOR
**SANDRA STENCEL**

ASSOCIATE EDITOR
**RICHARD L. WORSNOP**

STAFF WRITERS
**MARY H. COOPER**
**PATRICK G. MARSHALL**

PRODUCTION EDITOR
**LAURIE DE MARIS**

EDITORIAL ASSISTANT
**AMY GORTON**

RICHARD M. BOECKEL (1892-1975)
FOUNDER

PUBLISHED BY
**CONGRESSIONAL QUARTERLY INC.**

CHAIRMAN
**ANDREW BARNES**

PRESIDENT
**RICHARD R. EDMONDS**

EDITOR AND PUBLISHER
**NEIL SKENE**

EXECUTIVE EDITOR
**ROBERT W. MERRY**

EDITORIAL RESEARCH REPORTS (LIBRARY OF CONGRESS
CATALOGUE NO. 39-924; ISSN 0013-0958). Published weekly
(48 times per year, excluding March 1, May 3, August 2 and
November 1, 1991) by Congressional Quarterly Inc., 1414 22nd
Street NW, Washington, D.C. 20037. Rates are furnished
upon request. Application to mail at second-class postage
rates is pending at Washington, D.C. POSTMASTER: Send
address changes to EDITORIAL RESEARCH REPORTS, 1414
22nd Street NW, Washington, D.C. 20037.

# CALCULATING THE COSTS OF THE GULF WAR

*by Patrick G. Marshall*

By the Bush administration's accounting, the costs of the Persian Gulf War were remarkably low, both in dollars and American lives. Pledges of financial support from America's coalition allies could cover most of the $77 billion the administration estimates the war will cost. But some analysts think the actual cost of the war could run as much as three times that amount. And if the allies' contributions fall short, American taxpayers still could end up paying most of the war-related bills.

Live satellite broadcasts brought the war in the Persian Gulf home to Americans with an immediacy unknown in previous wars. Citizens could follow the war's progress not merely on a daily basis, but on an hourly and even a minute-by-minute basis. Still, for many Americans — particularly those who did not have a loved one in the gulf — the war hardly touched home. Citizens were not called upon to make the sort of economic sacrifices required in earlier conflicts. There were no film stars peddling war bonds, no gas coupons, rubber collection drives or victory gardens, as in World War II. There was not even much talk about a war tax, as was finally imposed toward the end of the Vietnam War.

Indeed, some experts say the United States could eventually close the books on the gulf war without incurring any direct costs at all. According to MIT Professor Emeritus William Kaufmann, a former adviser to several secretaries of Defense, the debits and credits of the war could come close to balancing if — and it's still a big if — America's coalition allies come through with the $53.5 billion they have pledged so far to help defray the costs of liberating Kuwait. (*See story, p. 149.*)

"I find it hard to run up the costs [of the war] beyond, say, $60 billion, and I regard those numbers as conservative," Kaufmann says. That figure would be even lower, he adds, if the United States decides not to replace all the equipment it has used in the gulf. "Since we're already planning to downsize the armed forces, there's a question as to how much of the war reserves stocks we really need to replace, and if the allies do come through with their pledges, then [the gulf war] essentially could be free."

No one, including the Defense Department, has yet provided an authoritative accounting of all of the direct costs of the war to the United States. Recent estimates by the Bush administration were slightly higher than Kaufmann's. Richard G. Darman, director of the Office of Management and Budget, told reporters Feb. 22 — two days before the ground phase of the war began — that the conflict could cost the United States up to $77 billion.

As it happened, the allied troops met with far less resistance from Iraqi forces than many had expected. A cease-fire took effect at midnight on Feb. 27, just 100 hours after the ground war began. The unanticipated brevity of the fighting should presumably lower the direct costs of the war.

The House on March 7 approved the creation of a $42.6 billion fund to pay for war costs for which the Defense Department has accounted so far. That fund is to be filled primarily by the contributions of coalition allies — some of whom, such as Saudi Arabia, fought alongside the United States, and some of whom, such as Japan, did not.* And since at last count $53.5 billion in foreign contributions had been pledged, it is possible that no U.S. funds will be required to cover the Defense Department's war-related expenses. But just in case foreign pledges are not fulfilled in time, the House voted to provide $15 billion to the fund as a sort of "bridge loan" until the foreign contributions are received.

One of the major causes of uncertainty about the actual costs of the war, as Kaufmann and others note, is the question of whether the military really needs to replace all of the equipment and munitions used during the war. Unlike previous wars, the gulf conflict was fought almost entirely out of existing inventories. During the Cold War, the United States built huge stockpiles of weapons and other military equipment and supplies — up to $120 billion worth, according to Kaufmann.

In recent years, as U.S.-Soviet relations improved, the rationale for maintaining all the weapons diminished. Congress started trimming the defense budget, calling for significant cuts in both active-duty personnel and in weapons systems.** The war in the gulf has revived the debate over downsizing America's military (*see p. 152*), but it still seems unlikely that defense spending will return to the levels of the Reagan years.

Much of the credit for the swiftness of the allies'

victory and for the relatively low number of allied casualties goes to the coalition's superior air power and to the effectiveness of America's high-tech weapons. But not all of the weapons used against Iraq were state-of-the-art. For example, many of the B-52 bombers — and their so-called "dumb" bombs, which cannot be guided once they are released — date from the 1960s, and will not be replaced. "There's an awful lot of stuff out there that's reasonably long in the tooth, so it may not be necessary to replace it all," says retired Rear Adm. Eugene Carroll, deputy director of the Center for Defense Information, a Washington research organization that is often critical of U.S. defense policy.

Some military analysts are even questioning whether the country needs to replace all the Patriot missiles used in the war. The Patriots, one of the stars of America's gulf arsenal, were used to shoot down Iraq's Scud missiles. "During the 1980s, we bought somewhere between 4,000 and 5,000 Patriots," says Brookings Institution scholar Lawrence J. Korb, an assistant secretary of Defense under President Reagan. "One of the reasons we were buying so many is we were going to be fighting the Soviets in Europe and we wanted these things to shoot down *their* planes and missiles. Let's say ... we [now] have 4,000 Patriots [left]. Is that enough?"

Some experts argue that as long as the Soviets are not a major threat, 4,000 Patriots is enough, but others disagree. "They'll probably be replaced in even larger numbers now that people see how valuable they are," says defense consultant Jacques Gansler.[1]

In fact, in its first supplemental budget request to cover war costs, the administration asked for $6.4 billion to replace missiles and ammunition, including $324 million to buy 500 Patriot missiles. But according to the Defense Budget Project, a Washington-based policy group, only about 200 Patriots actually were used in the war. Concerned that the Defense Department might be trying to pad its request, the House cut the administration's request for weapons replacement funds to $3.2 billion.

But even if Congress keeps a lid on appropriations for weapons replacement in this current supplemental request, that's not necessarily the end of the matter. "Probably what's going to happen is that later, under future supplemental requests, these figures are going to be raised," says Greg Bischak, an analyst at the National Commission for Economic Conversion Analysis, a Washington think tank. "I suspect the president is trying to manage the budgetary politics of this by stretching out the replacements."

Indeed, some critics of defense spending are concerned that, far from being a no-cost war fought with expendable munitions, the war could result in even greater expenditures on new high-tech weapons. "Already the drums are beating, saying, 'Hey, this stuff works; this proves it. Now we've got to keep spending money on it,'" says Jeff Faux, director of the Washington-based Economic Policy Institute. "Would you bet your house that the administration is not going to come in with more proposals for spending more money?"

And if the administration does ask, there are signs that Congress may be more disposed to the idea than before the war. "I think you'll find the members of Congress voicing much less criticism with respect to high-

---

* According to the *Defense Budget Project*, a Washington-based policy group, 28 allied countries had ground, air or naval forces deployed in the gulf; 16 of these countries had grounds troops deployed in the area.

**For background, see "Downsizing America's Armed Forces," *E.R.R.*, June 8, 1990 (No. 21), and "The Military Build-Down in the 1990s," *E.R.R.*, April 22, 1988 (Vol. I, No. 15).

tech weapons," Sen. John W. Warner of Virginia, ranking Republican on the Armed Services Committee, told reporters recently. "The investment in these weapons systems has paid off." [2]

In addition to the uncertainties over the direct costs of the gulf conflict, there are other factors that have to be taken into account in figuring the costs of the war. For example, will the United States help pay for the reconstruction of Kuwait and Iraq? How much aid will be given to help allies such as Israel* and Turkey that suffered economically from the conflict? Will it be necessary to maintain troops in the gulf region, and if so, for how long? How will the war affect oil prices in the long-term?

Faux says indirect costs will add at least $15 billion, and possibly much more, to the costs of the war. The nonprofit advocacy group Public Citizen, in a report released before the ground war began, estimated that if all the indirect costs were included, the actual cost of the war would come to between $164 billion and $268 billion, depending on the length and severity of the combat. On a per capita basis, that would mean between $656 and $1,072 for each American.[3] No one has done a comprehensive report on indirect costs since the cease-fire.

Faux and other critics of the war are particularly bothered by the fact that there has been no real debate yet on how the country will cover all the costs. "I think the military triumph has thrown sand in everybody's face on this," he says. "The Democrats are so shy now of talking about any question that has to do with the war. So there's no debate."

## Waging war on the layaway plan

By some estimates, the Vietnam War cost the United States about $570 billion in 1991 dollars.[4] The United States spent about $3.1 trillion in today's dollars fighting World War II. The money spent on the gulf war may seem small in comparison, even considering the much shorter duration of the conflict. But appearances can be deceiving.

All of these figures reflect *incremental* costs — direct costs that would not have been incurred except for the war. When World War II broke out, for example, the United States had a very small army and virtually no defense industry, so nearly all the war costs were incremental ones. During World War II, the United States also faced significant incremental costs for registering, inducting and training the large numbers of soldiers needed to do the fighting. With the latest conflict, however, most of the outlays by the United States are included in existing military expenditures, not in incremental costs that can be attributed to the war.

For each of the past 15 years, the United States has been spending the equivalent of more than $200 billion on

---

*The House on March 7 voted to give Israel $650 million in aid to help that country pay for additional defense costs related to the gulf conflict (*see p. 151*).

the military. Between 1984 and 1990, total annual defense expenditures exceeded $300 billion (in 1991 dollars). That money has supported a relatively large standing army and the stockpiling of billions of dollars of weapons.

For this reason, the gulf war did not require huge outlays of funds for conscripting and training soldiers or for retooling industry for war production. As Secretary of Defense Dick Cheney told Congress in early February, "America's past investment in defense is on display [in the gulf]." [5]

The transition from a pattern of raising defense spending only during wars to one of constantly high defense spending occurred suddenly, and with dramatic impact, in the years after World War II. "From 1900 to 1930, apart from the two years of World War I, less than 1 percent of the country's gross national product (GNP) [the total value of the nation's output of goods and services] was used on average for military purposes," writes Columbia University Professor Seymour Melman. "From 1931 to 1939, 1.3 percent of the country's gross national product was used for military purposes." [6] But with the advent of the nuclear age after World War II, and the perception of a more or less constant Soviet threat to U.S. security, the United States boosted peacetime defense spending nearly to wartime levels. In 1953, more than 12 percent of the GNP was devoted to national security. During the 1960s, between 7 percent and 10 percent of GNP was devoted to defense. America had inaugurated what Melman calls a "permanent war economy."

Defense spending did fall considerably as a proportion of GNP after the Vietnam War, reaching a post-World War II low of about 5 percent at the end of the 1970s. Then came the immense spending hikes during the Reagan era. Between 1980 and 1987, real defense outlays increased by 52 percent. During the same period, defense expenditures took an increasing share of the country's GNP, up from 5 percent in 1980 to 6.2 percent in 1987. The increase might have been even higher except that the U.S. economy was expanding nearly as fast as the defense budget.

The buildup of the 1980s was tailored specifically as a response to the Soviet threat. Accordingly, procurement and research and development were focused primarily on systems suited to dealing with the Soviets. Much of the emphasis of President Ronald Reagan's defense buildup was on strategic nuclear weaponry. The United States undertook a program to modernize each of the three components of the U.S. triad of strategic nuclear weapons — land (the MX intercontinental ballistic missile), air (the B-1 and stealth bombers), and sea (Trident II submarines).

Reagan also began a controversial program to build a space-based defense system to shield the United States from nuclear attack. The strategic defense initiative (SDI), popularly known as "star wars," called for the development of a high-technology defense system capable of destroying incoming ballistic missiles before they could reach their targets. More than $12 billion already has been spent on SDI research and development.

The Reagan buildup was not limited to weapons and equipment procurement. The administration also improved the quality of U.S. troops and raised troop

# Who Picks Up the Check

*By Pat Towell*
*Congressional Quarterly*

It will be months before Pentagon accountants can tote up the cost of liberating Kuwait, but if allies deliver on their promises, they will cover most of the United States' direct costs of waging the Persian Gulf War.

Pledges toward U.S. costs from the beginning of the gulf deployment last August through March 31 total $53.5 billion. Arab states bordering the gulf — Saudi Arabia, the United Arab Emirates and the government of Kuwait — have pledged $36 billion, about two-thirds of the total. Most of the remaining $17 billion has been promised by Japan, Germany and South Korea, all of which depend heavily on Persian Gulf oil.

For Pentagon costs through the end of December, foreign governments pledged $9.74 billion — 88 percent of the actual direct U.S. costs — leaving $1.35 billion to be covered by U.S. funds.

Of the $9.74 billion pledged for last year's costs, the U.S. Treasury collected $5.37 million as of Feb. 26. The Pentagon valued "in-kind" contributions — such as fuel, equipment and transportation services — as being worth an additional $1.98 billion.

According to the Bush administration, most of the unpaid balance ($2.93 billion) has been awaiting the Defense Department's preparation of detailed invoices. For example, the Saudi government has promised to pay for all food, fuel and building materials used by U.S. forces in the gulf region and for the cost of transporting U.S. troops deployed since mid-November.

The $9 billion Japan has promised to cover costs for the first three months of 1991 was recently approved by that country's parliament. To accommodate demands by opposition parties that the payment be squared with Japan's constitutional ban on war-making, Prime Minister Toshiki Kaifu has stipulated that the Japanese funds be used only for non-lethal purposes, such as payment of transportation costs. Such limitations will pose no difficulty, according to the Bush administration.

Congressional critics of allied burden-sharing have dismissed as self-serving some governments' in-kind contributions. Rep. Charles E. Schumer, D-N.Y., has complained that Germany's donations included decrepit equipment that had belonged to the disbanded army of East Germany and that Japan's included vehicles and electronic gear purchased in Japan.

But the Pentagon insists that the in-kind donations meet requirements set by the U.S. command in Saudi Arabia. And Pentagon official Henry S. Rowen assured the House Armed Services Committee on Feb. 27 that most equipment donated by Japan was purchased from U.S. companies.

*(Dollar amounts in millions)*

| | Promised | | | Delivered | | | To Come |
|---|---|---|---|---|---|---|---|
| | **1990** | **1991** | **Total** | **Cash** | **In-kind** | **Total** | |
| Saudi Arabia | $ 3,339 | $ 13,500 | $ 16,839 | $ 4,457 | $ 1,566 | $ 6,023 | $10,816 |
| Kuwait | 2,506 | 13,500 | 16,006 | 3,500 | 10 | 3,510 | 12,496 |
| United Arab Emirates | 1,000 | 2,000 † | 3,000 | 870 | 140 | 1,010 | 1,990 |
| Germany | 1,072 | 5,500 | 6,572 | 2,432 | 531 | 2,963 | 3,609 |
| Japan | 1,740 | 9,000 | 10,740 | 866 | 457 | 1,323 | 9,417 |
| South Korea | 80 | 305 | 385 | 50 | 21 | 71 | 314 |
| Others | 3 | 3 | 3 | 3 | — | — | — |
| **Total** | **$ 9,740** | **$ 43,805** | **$ 53,545** | **$ 12,175** | **$ 2,728** | **$ 14,903** | **$ 38,642** |

*† An additional pledge of at least $2 billion is under consideration.*
*Note: Numbers may not add due to rounding.*
*Source: Congressional Quarterly Weekly Report, March 2, 1991.*

levels. The percentage of high school graduates among the armed forces went from 68 percent in 1980 to 96 percent in 1989. The average level of expertise also improved, as more enlisted personnel remained in the service, attracted by better pay and benefits.

Critics of the Reagan buildup note that many of the weapons used during the gulf war were actually products of earlier administrations. "We should recognize that a great many of the weapons . . . came long before Ronald Reagan ever heaved into view," says Adm. Carroll of the Center for Defense Information. "The Patriot missile was a missile in 1972. The Tomahawk cruise missile that's been touted so highly was in the budget in 1977." And the F-117 stealth fighter was under development in 1979.

But many analysts — even some critical of Reagan's

defense policies — have credited the large expenditures of the Reagan era as finally paying off in the gulf war. "For the most part, this war is being fought with technologies that were being developed in the 1970s," says Alexis Cain, research director of the Defense Budget Project. "But the increases in the Reagan budgets allowed us to buy them in large numbers, and the Reagan buildup deserves credit for that."

Defense consultant Jacques Gansler agrees. "If it hadn't been for the buildup of the 1980s, we wouldn't have any of the expendable equipment that we have, neither platforms nor weapons," he says. "The things we bought in the 1980s — the smart bombs, the advanced fighters such as the F-117 [stealth fighter] — are really the big payoff items from this war."

On the other hand, says Carroll, the high spending of the Reagan era has also left the military burdened with a host of weapons systems the Reagan administration purchased to counter the Soviet Union, but which are of questionable utility in other situations. According to Carroll, as much as 25 percent of the Reagan defense budgets "went into preparations for nuclear war with the Soviet Union, which have no bearing on [the Persian Gulf War] or any comparable situation in the Third World. We've overdesigned the military forces to fight the Soviet Union with equipment that is far too expensive and difficult to maintain and unnecessarily complex for Third World scenarios."

Carroll is willing to concede one major debt to Reagan: not the quality of weapons, but the quality of troops. "The Reagan pay raises of 1981-82 were the most important step in creating a really high-quality all-volunteer force," he says. "He restored the pay scales of the military so they were competitive. We suddenly found ourselves for the first time with really high-quality volunteers in adequate numbers. That is the foundation of a top-notch personnel structure that is really the basis for our strong performance out there in the gulf. Weapons are just pieces of stuff, hardware. It's the people who either make them work or let them fall apart." *

Even with all the spending on defense during the 1980s, however, there were some serious gaps in procurement. "We've got a lot of everything except the bullets we need to shoot," Sen. Alan J. Dixon, D-Ill., chairman of the Senate Armed Services Readiness, Sustainability and Support Subcommittee, told a reporter before the ground war began. "The smart stuff is great, but when we get going on the ground with the grunts, we need the dumb stuff, and the military never bought enough of it." [7]

A recent article in *The Philadelphia Inquirer* cited potentially serious shortages of 25mm ammunition for the Bradley infantry fighting vehicle, 120mm ammo for the main gun of the M-1A1 tank, and rockets for the Apache and Cobra attack helicopters. The article quoted one government official familiar with inventories as saying, "For some munitions, less than a 10-day anticipated wartime supply is available in U.S. stocks. In other cases, once the preferred munitions run out, troops will be forced to use substitute rounds that are dramatically inferior." [8] As it turned out, of course, a 10-day supply was all that was needed, but the shortages could have been serious.

Kaufmann blames the situation on Reagan's emphasis on high-tech weapons programs, such as the strategic defense initiative. "If we had not done the SDI folly," he says, "we could have bought lots of things that are truly useful. I don't think people have looked adequately at what actually happened. One of the things they neglected was precisely building up war reserves stocks."

Whether or not the Reagan administration wasted defense dollars, it's clear that the true cost of the gulf war cannot be accounted for — and certainly cannot be compared with previous wars — without taking into consideration the high spending on the military that occurred during the 1970s and '80s. Exactly how many of the billions that have been spent in previous years actually contributed to the gulf war can only be guessed at. But the spending did establish such a large and generally well-equipped military that the war against Iraq could be fought largely out of the U.S. "hip pocket," with only small requests for new funding to support it.

Whether those small requests will turn into large ones in the months ahead will depend on how much of the equipment and weaponry used in the gulf war — some of it very expensive — will be replaced. And that decision has not been made.

## Hidden economic effects of the Persian Gulf War

In addition to the direct costs of the gulf conflict, there are other factors that have to be taken into account in figuring the total cost of the war. Again, accurate figures are hard to come by, either because the total will depend on political decisions yet to be made, or because the economic impacts are difficult to quantify. But in the long run, the financial impact of these decisions could be much greater than the expenses involved in fighting the war.

**Future military costs in the region.** American troops already have started leaving the gulf, and the Bush administration has said it would like to bring most of the troops home by July 4. But some experts envision a variety of scenarios that might require the presence of at least some U.S. troops for an extended period of time.

How long U.S. troops will have to stay in the region depends on a number of factors. If the war's end results in the relatively rapid removal of Iraqi President Saddam Hussein from power, there could be a period of turmoil as various factions struggle for control. If, on the other hand, Saddam remains in power, Iraq will likely continue to maintain a hostile attitude. In either event, the presence of coalition forces could be required in the gulf region for much longer than four months.

One alternative to an extended stay for U.S. forces in the gulf region would be the establishment of a U.N. peacekeeping force. Since the costs of such a force would be borne by member nations of the United Nations, the cost to the United States would probably be less than maintaining U.S. forces in the region, though it still would be considerable. For example, the United States picked up 31 percent of the tab for the five U.N. peacekeeping operations that were set up in 1988 and 1989 — Afghanistan-Pakistan, Iran-Iraq, Angola, Central America, and Namibia — and those operations were in areas where U.S. involvement had not been as direct as in the Persian Gulf.

The United Nations has been working on contingency plans for a peacekeeping force in the gulf since the Aug. 2 invasion of Kuwait. It will not discuss details, however, because, as one U.N. official, who asked not to be identified, put it, "the political process of creating peacekeep-

*For background on the all-volunteer forces, see "Should the U.S. Reinstate the Draft?" *E.R.R.,* Jan. 11, 1991 (No. 2).

ing operations is so sensitive." One unconfirmed report cited U.N. contingency plans as figuring on a force of 6,000, a number that seems very low to many analysts. By way of comparison, the U.N. Interim Force in Lebanon, which is comprised of slightly fewer than 6,000 troops, cost $142 million to maintain during 1990.

It's possible that the United States may establish a long-term military presence in the region. President Bush, in a speech before a joint session of Congress March 6, noted that "Our vital national interests depend on a stable and secure gulf." While disclaiming any need for permanently stationing U.S. ground forces on the Arabian Peninsula, Bush said that securing peace in the region "does mean American participation in joint exercises involving both air and ground forces" and "maintaining a capable U.S. naval presence in the region, just as we have for over 40 years."

**Loans forgiven and aid promised to allies.** In its effort to maintain the coalition against Iraq, the United States has spent billions of dollars, and forgiven billions more in funds owed to the United States.

Citing Turkey's cooperation in allowing the coalition to use air bases in Turkish territory for raids against Iraq, President Bush has recommended that Turkey receive an additional $82 million in military aid during 1991, and an additional $186 million in 1992. Last November, Bush also approved a 40 percent increase in Turkey's quota for exports to the United States of textiles and apparel, a move that some critics say could cost thousands of American jobs.

Bush, with congressional approval, rewarded Egypt for its participation in the effort against Iraq by forgiving $7 billion in outstanding debts, though that figure may be deceptive. "The real effect on us is that that means they don't repay about $700 million a year or so that they otherwise would have if they could have but they probably wouldn't have because they couldn't have," says William Quandt, a Middle East expert at the Brookings Institution. "It's a paper transaction of sorts. We almost certainly would have had to give them debt rescheduling if we hadn't given them debt forgiveness. So it's almost impossible to measure the real impact." Nevertheless, Quandt notes that Egypt has also requested an additional $1 billion in economic aid.

Israel, already the single largest recipient of U.S. foreign aid, originally asked for an additional $1 billion to pay for the damage caused by Iraqi Scud missiles and other costs associated with the war. After negotiations with administration officials,[9] Israel agreed to a compromise aid package that includes $650 million in cash. The aid is included in a supplemental funding bill approved by the House March 7.

It is not known what other concessions or aid may have been granted or may soon be granted to coalition allies, but some analysts feel there may be considerable amounts that have not been made public. For example, both the World Bank and the International Monetary Fund have indicated that they will provide assistance to countries affected by the gulf crisis. No figures have been made public, but since the United States provides large contributions to both organizations, it is likely that it will bear much of the burden of that additional assistance as well.

**Paying for the reconstruction of Kuwait and Iraq.** The most expensive part of the gulf crisis by far will be the reconstruction of Iraq and Kuwait. Some Kuwaiti officials have estimated that the cost of rebuilding Kuwait could run as high at $100 billion. That figure includes primarily the costs of rebuilding the public infrastructure and repairing major damage to oil fields. It does not include rebuilding and repairing individuals' residences, stores, or replacing looted or destroyed personal property.

Iraq has agreed in principle to an allied demand that it pay reparations to Kuwait. But at least in the short-term, Iraq is not likely to contribute much to Kuwait. "Iraq is not going to be in a position to bear the cost [of rebuilding Kuwait] entirely," says Harvard economist Robert Reich. "Kuwaiti families certainly have a lot of money, but how much are they going to be putting in? The United States is probably going to be involved in some of the rebuilding effort there" — and may foot some of the bill.

The costs of reconstructing Iraq are probably much greater, though no international agencies have been able to make any actual assessments of the damage. "We don't have a clue," says Norman Lauzon, director of the United Nations Development Project's Gulf Task Force. "As long as we are not in a position to send preliminary needs assessments missions, and as long as we do not have a clearer picture as to what damage has been done, which is still only known by the military, we're not in a position to hazard any figures." Based on what is known about the Iraqi infrastructure, however, Reich estimates that the job of rebuilding may take $300 billion to $400 billion.

President Bush has said that he doesn't want to see "a single dime" of U.S. money go to Iraq. Nevertheless, some analysts expect that the United States will eventually contribute to Iraq's reconstruction. The issue has not been debated yet, much less decided. But in past conflicts, when the United States has emerged victorious, it has generally felt obliged to aid in reconstruction. "Even if we're only talking about 10 percent of the total [as the U.S. share]," Reich says, "it's another $40 billion to $50 billion."

Reich believes the United States will contribute even more. Others, however, offer more conservative, but still significant, estimates. Based on per-capita levels of reconstruction aid to Germany and Japan after World War II, Public Citizen estimated that the United States would end up giving Iraq between $3.5 billion and $7 billion over the next five years.[10]

**Higher oil prices.** As many commentators have pointed out, although prices have now fallen, economies around the world sustained billions of dollars in losses through having to pay higher prices for oil in the months that followed Iraq's invasion of Kuwait.

Though most analysts have declined to attach spec[ ] figures to the cost increases caused by the crisis, [ ] Citizen has estimated that the "war premium" [ ] consumers — including the effects on oil p[ ] combat and economic sanctions — amou[ ] billion to $32 billion for 1990, and $10 bi[ ] for 1991. Public Citizen also noted that[ ] translate into reduced GNP. According to its figures, the lost output for 1990 and 1991 would amount to $55 billion, which would translate into a drop in federal revenue of some $15 billion for the period.[11]

Of course, there's a lot of guesswork in these estimates, if only because no one can know what would have happened to oil prices and other economic inputs if the coalition forces had not forced the issue in the gulf. Prices could have stayed low, or they could have gone up if oil producers had been able to enforce production quotas.

As for the future, some analysts have predicted that the gulf war could seriously damage the Organization of Petroleum Exporting Countries (OPEC) and result in much lower oil prices over the long-term. "Oil from Iraq and Kuwait has been embargoed since the Aug. 2 invasion of Kuwait by Iraq. But the other 11 members of OPEC are producing at least as much oil as all 13 did before the war, and when Kuwaiti and Iraqi oil returns to the market a glut is likely, depressing prices," *New York Times* reporter Matthew Wald wrote. "And to raise money for reconstruction, Iraq and Kuwait may well want to produce far more than the prewar quotas assigned to them by OPEC."[12] Oil prices already are down to about where they were before Iraq's invasion of Kuwait, and a market glut would likely bring them even lower.

There are, of course, a host of economic impacts that, while obvious, cannot be quantified with enough accuracy to provide meaningful figures. For example, many travel agencies, hotels, airlines and other businesses have suffered from lack of business that many ascribe to fears of terrorism. And many federal and state agencies, as well as private corporations, have incurred significant expenses providing additional security. Without explaining the basis of its estimate, Public Citizen pegged the costs of additional security measures at $1 billion for a short war.

There are also many costs that will be impossible to track down, such as the impact of environmental damage from the gulf oil spill or from the smoke produced by burning oil wells in Kuwait. Some experts have warned that the smoke from the approximately 600 oil wells that are on fire in Kuwait could cause disease and deaths in the region, primarily from particles in the lungs and carcinogens that may be inhaled or ingested from food and drinking water. And some scientists have speculated that the smoke could affect the world's climate patterns and could cause environmental damage potentially as far away as North America, although there is no consensus on that.

And there are many unpredicted costs likely to emerge from Congress — such as an increase in veterans' benefits. Senate leaders have named John Glenn, D-Ohio, and John McCain, R-Ariz., as co-chairman of an ad hoc task force on troop benefits legislation. The package they are drafting will incorporate language from dozens of bills that have been introduced in the last few months. Among the recommendations are proposals to exclude from income taxation all enlisted troops' pay and $2,000 per month of officers' pay for those who served in combat zones; increase servicemen's life insurance from $50,000 to $100,000; grant military personnel involuntarily leaving the service employment compensation equal to that received by civilians; defer student loan payments for activated person-

nel; and ensure that accrued leave benefits be paid to the survivors of personnel killed in action. The House is considering similar legislation.[13]

Public Citizen is the only organization that has attempted to include economic impacts in its estimate of the total cost of the war. The group estimated that the war would cost the United States between $164 billion and $268 billion.[14] The wide margin of error in the estimate reflected not only uncertainty about how the conflict would progress, and with what damage, but the inevitable uncertainties involved in attempting to quantify the impact of a complex political and economic event on systems that are also influenced by many other factors.

"The trouble with any of these projections is that they're going to be based on a whole battery of assumptions, any one of which could change," says Robert Reich. "I think the important thing is to at least get on the table the important categories of expenditures."

## Encouraging debate on the war's costs

Since so many of the costs of war are hard to pin down, they often don't enter into the national debate over what course to pursue, and over how to pay for the course eventually decided upon.

If the cost of the gulf war to American society were truly limited to the direct incremental costs of the military operation, the impact on an economy the size of the United States' would probably not be noticed, particularly if the allies do come through with the full $53.5 billion they have pledged to the effort. And if, as several analysts have recommended, the United States takes advantage of plans to downsize the military and decides not to replace all the weapons and munitions expended in the gulf, the nation may encounter no direct incremental costs at all. In that case, there might be no need for a decision about how to pay for the war.

But the Defense Department may have something else in mind. "They were very clever," Lawrence Korb says of the Defense Department's first supplemental request in February to cover war costs. "A lot of the stuff was in the baseline defense budget anyway." The two-year defense budget submitted last year, for example, called for the purchase of 440 Patriot missiles in 1992, but none in 1991. With the war, the government pushed the purchase into 1991 and now expects to pay for the missiles with a supplemental appropriation. "We're putting those things in the supplemental so that we can get the Japanese and the Germans to pay for them," Korb says. "But the fact of the matter is, do you count that as a war cost? I wouldn't. We were going to buy them anyway."

What's more, voices are already being heard saying that the gulf experience demonstrates that the country cannot afford to downsize the military. In a column published Feb. 28, the day after the gulf war ended, Anthony Cordesman, a Georgetown University national security expert, recommended restoring military spending

*Continued on p. 152*

# AT ISSUE
*Should the United States impose an income surtax to help pay for the Persian Gulf War?*

**YES** *says* **JEFF FAUX**, *president of the Economic Policy Institute.*

The conventional wisdom is that the cost of the war is crowding domestic problems from Washington's agenda. Not so. The problem is the willingness of George Bush and Congress to fight a war without raising the revenue to pay for it. The responsible way to finance the war is a war tax coupled, whatever the political discomfort, with a drastic cut in the still bloated military budget.

Estimates vary, but ... the cost may well be at least $45 billion. The total military costs, including the replacement of inventory, could double that figure. Add the price of aid and forgiving our allies' debt, the postwar cleanup and the burden of maintaining a military presence in the Middle East, and we are into big money. Even if promised aid from other nations comes through, the addition to the high U.S. debt will be substantial....

It is patently foolish to finance the war on credit and then use the higher deficit as grounds for not making the education, infrastructure and other investments needed to compete in the global economy.

Federal budget policy inverts the common-sense principle that current expenses should be paid for out of current income, with borrowing used for capital spending that produces income to pay off the new debt.

Since most troops in the gulf are young and in the working class, a war tax should be tilted toward the older and richer. A 38 percent bracket for the top-income group would bring in some $60 billion over the next three years — enough to pay the out-of-pocket expenses of a six-month war and some of its immediate aftermath.

The economy's primary problem is not a temporary recession but slow growth stemming from a lack of investment. Ending the need to finance the war with credit would free the government's borrowing capacity for an investment program, which would help counter a longer downturn and is needed, recession or not....

President Bush and most members of Congress are basking in the reflected glory of the young people sent to the gulf. The least they can do is finance the war properly so that those who return have a more secure place in whatever new world order they are risking their lives to create.

*From* The New York Times *Feb. 19, 1991.*

**NO** *says economics columnist* **ROBERT J. SAMUELSON.**

Let's talk about the economics of the war. We're told that it [was] frightfully expensive (perhaps $1 billion a day) and that perhaps we ought to pay for it with a surtax. Please, keep cool. Yes, the war may ultimately cost tens of billions of dollars, but as wars go, it will be relatively cheap. And this is not the right moment for new taxes.

The idea that American's economic base can't support this war is absurd. The worries partly reflect our obsession with budget deficits. But the deficit preoccupation obscures larger issues. The major economic effects of the crisis so far have involved psychology, not deficits. Anxiety and high oil prices have depressed consumer spending and business investment, worsening the recession....

The classic challenge of war economies is preventing spending booms and runaway inflation. Rather than raise taxes, governments sometimes pay for wars by printing more money. In part, this happened in the Vietnam War. By late 1965, Lyndon Johnson's economic advisers urged him to raise taxes. But Johnson didn't propose a surtax until 1967, and Congress didn't pass one until 1968. Between 1964 and 1969, inflation jumped from 1.3 percent to 5.5 percent.

The danger of rising inflation is muted now. In the 1960s, the extra defense spending fed an economy near "full employment." Today there's a recession and rising unemployment. Even when taxes are raised, they usually don't cover all war costs. In World War II, the national debt nearly quintupled. Taxes paid only 43 percent of costs. Rationing forced Americans to funnel idle funds into government bonds. The idea was to spread war costs over more years by repaying the debt later through budget surpluses.

The trouble today is that we already have huge deficits. The current deficit — $300 billion or more — seems to say that last fall's budget agreement achieved nothing. This is misleading. A big part of the deficit now reflects temporary costs; up to $110 billion for deposit insurance (mainly S&Ls); perhaps $25 billion or so for the recession (it lowers taxes and raises spending) and an unknown amount for the war. With time, these will disappear. Meanwhile, the budget agreement's tax increases and spending cuts will shrink the remaining deficit, which is probably about $160 billion.

*From* The Washington Post *Jan. 30, 1991.*

*Continued from p. 150*

to Reagan-era levels. If the nation proceeds with downsizing, Cordesman warned, "many of our technological assets will be gone — perhaps much of our readiness as well. If this goes on, we will be unable to refight our last war, much less the next one." [15]

At the very least, the gulf war has called into question the planned time line for reducing the military. "That's going to be a major issue that's going to have to be revisited," says Rep. Norm Dicks, D-Wash., a member of the House Defense Appropriations Subcommittee. "How do we get from where we are today, with a million people in the Army, down to the lower levels that are called for in the 1991 budget and beyond? I don't think people are going to be very comfortable with the 1991 targets, and we may have to grab some relief on that."

As for whether downsizing still seems to be a good idea at all, Dicks says "that's another discussion that's going on. Unfortunately, we've gotten ourselves caught on this budget agreement and it's very difficult for us to back away from that." Dicks also says that the role of the National Guard and reserves — which would be relied on even more under the downsizing plan — needs to be reassessed in light of the gulf experience. It's not clear, he says, "that we can really count on the Guard and reserve units for actual combat."

If, in fact, the debate over whether to downsize is to be revived, Congress and the public will need to understand the true costs of going to war — direct and indirect, prepaid and incremental. According to Jeff Faux of the Economic Policy Institute, even with all the uncertainties, the real costs of the war will surely exceed the figures given by the administration by at least $15 billion. Robert Reich puts the total at at least an additional $100 billion beyond the $77 billion estimated by the Bush administration. Public Citizen's estimate was as much as three times the administration's estimate.

One way or another the costs will have to be paid. And there are only two ways to do it: One is to borrow money, and the other is to tax.

"Historically, we went to war and we borrowed. And then we stopped borrowing and paid it back," says John Marlin, an analyst at the Council on Economic Priorities in New York City. But this war is different. "This time we've already been borrowing for five years. And now we have a war. So it's like the boy who cried wolf. We may discover that our friends aren't going to cover the money we need to borrow anymore, and that the credit window in Tokyo is shutting down, and that will not be good."

Borrowing money can be accomplished by selling war bonds, as during World War II, by selling bonds on the international market, or by any of a host of other financial vehicles. But with deficits already high, many analysts are concerned that further borrowing could be dangerous.

The alternative — imposing a war tax — is an option that has not even been hinted by the Bush administration. Some analysts have suggested that the White House is concerned that imposing a new tax now could worsen the current economic recession. Others have suggested that the administration has been loath to take any step that

could lessen public support for the war. (*See "At Issue," p. 153.*)

Still, Faux is convinced that a tax is both necessary and feasible. "The resistance to taxes on the part of the majority of Congress and the White House is, we're told, because 'the people' don't want any taxes," he says. "Well, here you have a situation where 85-90 percent of the people support this war. If ever there was an opportunity to say, 'OK, America, let's pay for what we've decided to do,' this is it."

Reich agrees, and specifically proposes a tax on people with incomes of over $100,000 or an income tax surcharge in the neighborhood of 2 or 3 percent on the highest marginal tax rate. "I think it's quite important to debate this," Reich says. "This is really a down payment on the new world order of George Bush. The decisions we make now in terms of how to keep the peace are setting precedents for how we maintain the peace. At one extreme, we're going to be the world's policeman. At the other extreme, this is going to be very much of a multilateral effort and we're going to do very little. I don't know what the answer is, but I do know that we do need to debate it, because the long-term financial implications are extraordinarily high."

# NOTES

[1] Gansler is senior vice president and director of the Analytic Sciences Corporation in Arlington, Va., and is the author of several books on the defense industry, including *Affording Defense* (1989).
[2] John Huey and Nancy J. Perry, "The Future of Arms," *Fortune*, Feb. 25, 1991, p. 34.
[3] James P. Love, *Costs of the U.S. War with Iraq*, Public Citizen, Feb. 5, 1991.
[4] See, for example, a column by Robert J. Samuelson in *The Washington Post*, Jan. 30, 1991.
[5] Cheney testified before the House Armed Services Committee on Feb. 7, 1991.
[6] Seymour Melman, *The Permanent War Economy* (1985), p. 137.
[7] Quoted in *The Philadelphia Inquirer*, Feb. 13, 1991.
[8] *Ibid.*
[9] For details on the negotiations, see story by Thomas L. Friedman in *The New York Times*, March 6, 1991.
[10] Public Citizen, *op. cit.*, p. 10.
[11] *Ibid.*, p. 30.
[12] *The New York Times*, Feb. 11, 1991.
[13] See *The Congressional Monitor*, Congressional Quarterly, March 8, 1991.
[14] Public Citizen, *op. cit.*, p. 1. The estimate includes such indirect expenditures as aid to allied governments and increased oil costs, but excludes the impact on the economy of sustaining the large military-industrial complex.
[15] The column appeared in *The New York Times*, Feb. 28, 1991.

*Graphics: Cover, Margaret Scott.*

# RECOMMENDED READING

## BOOKS

**Clem, Harold J.,** *Mobilization Preparedness*, **National Defense University Press, 1983.**

Clem offers a broad historical background on American mobilization efforts in times of war. The book deals with both manpower mobilization for the armed forces and with industrial mobilization of the economy to supply those forces.

**DeGrasse, Robert W.,** *Military Expansion, Economic Decline: The Impact of Military Spending on U.S. Economic Performance*, **Sharpe, 1983.**

DeGrasse, an economist at the Council on Economic Priorities in New York City, marshals an impressive amount of evidence to support his argument that defense spending acts as a drag on the civilian economy. Since DeGrasse supplies so many economic statistics, it's a pity that his book has not been updated since 1983.

**DiFilippo, Anthony,** *From Industry to Arms: The Political Economy of High Technology*, **Greenwood, 1990.**

This book addresses the relationship between defense research and development programs and the decline of U.S. competitiveness in civilian high-technology fields. DiFilippo's conclusion is that, as military and civilian applications of high technologies grow further apart, the contributions of military research dollars to the civilian economy are shrinking, and the dollars would be better spent — at least from the standpoint of economic competitiveness — on civilian programs.

**Gansler, Jacques S.,** *Affording Defense*, **MIT Press, 1989.**

Gansler is one of the best analysts on the nuts and bolts of the defense industry. He is highly critical of the way the Defense Department handles contracts with defense companies, and argues that the way business is done almost guarantees high-cost, low-quality products. Gansler argues that the defense industry needs to be more closely integrated with related civilian industries.

**Melman, Seymour,** *The Permanent War Economy: American Capitalism in Decline*, **Simon & Schuster, 1985.**

This book was originally published in 1974, and was brought out again in 1985 with modest updating of statistics. Though more thorough updating would have been welcome, the basics of Melman's argument are as strong today as they were more than 15 years ago. The thrust of the book is summarized nicely by its title; Melman holds that America's economic decline over the past 20 years is a direct result of the nation's maintenance of a permanent defense industry.

**Vawter, Roderick L.,** *Industrial Mobilization: The Relevant History*, **National Defense University Press, 1983.**

Vawter details post-World War II industrial mobilization planning and efforts. The majority of the book focuses on the many pieces of legislation enacted just prior to the Korean War.

## ARTICLES

**Huey, John, and Perry, Nancy J., "The Future of Arms,"** *Fortune*, **Feb. 25, 1991.**

This article offers some interesting histories of specific weapons systems' development and production. The focus is on those weapons most prominently featured in the gulf war: the Patriot missile, the M-1A1 tank, the Bradley fighting vehicle, the Apache attack helicopter.

## REPORTS AND STUDIES

**Congressional Budget Office,** *Costs of Operation Desert Shield*, **January 1991.**

Prepared before the war in the Persian Gulf broke out, this CBO study details its own estimates of the direct costs of both Operation Desert Shield and Desert Storm. The report also provides summaries of other experts' estimates. The report obviously does not benefit from knowledge about how the war actually progressed, but until the Defense Department releases more details it is still one of the best sources for estimating the costs of the conflict.

**Love, James P.,** *Costs of the U.S. War with Iraq*, **Public Citizen, Feb. 5, 1991.**

This report by Ralph Nader's Washington-based public interest group represents the first — and, at this date, only — attempt to specify and compile all the costs, direct and indirect, of the gulf war. As might be expected, the report is very detailed about its basis for estimating military costs, and much less so regarding its basis for estimating indirect impacts such as the effects on national GNP of higher oil prices. In addition, it should be pointed out that the report was written before the ground war commenced — or ended so quickly.

# EDITORIAL RESEARCH REPORTS

## Coming soon

- Gun Control
- Space Exploration
- California Drought

Published weekly by Congressional Quarterly Inc., Editorial Research Reports analyze emerging issues of national interest across a broad range of social, scientific, political and economic fields. Reports are bound and indexed for permanent reference. Subscription information is available through Congressional Quarterly's Publications Sales Department by telephone (202) 887-8665. Copies of past issues are available through Customer Service, (202) 887-8621.

MARCH 22, 1991

ERR

CONGRESSIONAL QUARTERLY'S

EDITORIAL RESEARCH REPORTS

FOUNDED 1923

# REASSESSING THE NATION'S GUN LAWS

1991 No. 11

# REASSESSING THE NATION'S GUN LAWS

*by Mary H. Cooper*

Gun-control advocates are trying once again to gain passage of a mandatory waiting period for handgun purchases. Although few observers suggest that the so-called Brady bill alone will prevent the rising tide of firearm violence, there are signs that support for it is building in Congress. The powerful National Rifle Association is gearing up in opposition, however, and new federal gun-control legislation is far from assured.

With the war then raging in the Persian Gulf, few Americans may have noticed when a bill was introduced in Congress that would make it harder for people to buy handguns. The legislation, supported by advocates of gun control, would require purchasers of these small, easily concealed firearms to wait seven days before they take possession of their new weapons. The one-week "cooling-off period" would make it less likely, supporters say, that handguns would be used in crimes of passion or suicide, acts of violence that often are committed on impulse. The delay also would allow law enforcement authorities to complete background checks on would-be handgun buyers and deny them access if they have criminal records or a history of mental illness.

"While our thoughts are on the crisis in the Persian Gulf, too many of us are blind to the crisis going on here on the nation's streets," said Sarah Brady, chairman of Handgun Control Inc., the country's largest gun-control group and a major backer of the measure. "No one wants to see body bags of American men and women coming home, but right now we're seeing 60 body bags each and every day here in this country." [1]

Sarah Brady became one of the most vocal supporters of gun control — the movement to restrict access to firearms — after her husband, James S. Brady, was shot during a 1981 assassination attempt on President Ronald Reagan. Brady was Reagan's press secretary, and the bullet that struck him in the head March 30, 1981, left him permanently disabled. The man who shot him, John W. Hinckley Jr., had a history of mental illness but had easily bought his handgun in Texas after lying on the registration form. It is this kind of criminal use of firearms that the proposed legislation — also known as the Brady bill — is designed to deter.

Attempted assassinations of government officials, of course, constitute only a small part of the picture of firearms violence in this country. If current estimates prove correct, 23,220 Americans were murdered last year, breaking the previous national record of 23,040 set in 1980. Most of these homicides were committed with firearms, principally handguns.[2] In many big cities, 1990 was merely the latest in a series of record-breaking years for firearms violence.

To explain the high rate of gun murders, crime experts point to the trade in illegal drugs, in which competition for market share often ends in murder. Drug dealers' preference for easily concealed and rapid-firing guns has fostered the spread of these more lethal weapons. "There is a fair amount of epidemiological evidence to tell us that what is of utmost concern are handguns and assault-type weapons," says Daniel Webster, director of violence research at the Washington Hospital Center in the nation's capital. "They are easily concealed, and in the case of assault-type weapons they can fire dozens of rounds in a matter of seconds. They pose an obvious threat and very little social gain."

All 50 states and the District of Columbia already have restrictions on public access to certain firearms, but critics of the system say gun control is doomed to failure without federal legislation. "One state's gun-control legislation is only as good as the weakest link in the national chain," says James Fox, a criminologist at Northeastern University in Boston, Mass. "What we need is more national policy so that we have consistency in coverage. That's why things like the Brady bill can only help."

This is not the first time that the Brady bill has gone before Congress. Last year a similar measure was approved by the House Judiciary Committee, but Speaker Thomas S. Foley, D-Wash., prevented it from coming to a vote by the full House.* Other federal gun-control legislation has fared no better. A proposal

*Foley later defended his action by saying that it was so late in the legislative year that there had not been enough time to get the Brady bill through the entire legislative process even if it had made it to the House floor and won approval. Speaking before the National Press Club Feb. 7, Foley said proposing the bill at the end of the session was "a mere exercise at a very difficult time in our congressional calendar of a contentious issue without purpose or result."

to ban assault weapons — military-style rifles and pistols — also died in Congress last year.

For his part, President Bush, like Reagan before him, supports a tougher stance against crime, including more extensive use of the death penalty, but he has opposed gun-control measures such as an overall ban on assault-type weapons. Reflecting the administration's focus on criminal behavior rather than the tools used to carry it out, a Justice Department summit on crime held March 3-5 included no specific panel discussions on the place of gun control in policy options to combat crime.

Given the high incidence of deaths and injuries from firearms, why has Congress not acted more forcefully to curb the availability of weapons that have no legitimate use for hunting purposes? The reason, many critics of gun policy say, is the National Rifle Association (NRA). With 2.8 million members, including life members Bush and Reagan, and a budget of $88 million in 1989,[3] the NRA is one of the most powerful lobbies in the capital. And, judging from congressional voting records on the issue, few lawmakers dare cross the gun lobby's legislative agenda. Says Fox: "If politicians come out strongly against guns, their political careers are in jeopardy."

The NRA opposes gun-control legislation because the organization says it violates the individual's right to own and bear arms. This right, the NRA contends, is enshrined in the Second Amendment. (Many constitutional lawyers dispute this reading of the Constitution, however, and courts have consistently failed to uphold it. *See "At Issue," p. 169.*) In the NRA's view, even waiting periods violate this "right to bear arms," as do initiatives to ban assault weapons and other non-sporting firearms.

There is evidence that the NRA does not represent the views of most Americans — even the estimated 45 percent who own guns. According to a recent Gallup Poll, 78 percent of the public favors stricter laws covering the sale of firearms, up from 60 percent in 1986.[4] An earlier Harris Poll found that 73 percent of gun owners — and 53 percent of NRA members — favored some federal law to control the sale of firearms.[5] To explain the apparent discrepancy between the views of the NRA membership and its leaders in Washington, a Justice Department official, who spoke on condition he not be identified, said, "The NRA is whoever happens to be in control of it at the time. Like any other organization it's run by its leaders, whether or not they represent the true views of the membership."

But as public opinion in favor of some steps to curtail gun violence grows, gun-control advocates are beginning to see chinks in the NRA's armor. Organizations of law enforcement officers, which once stood behind the NRA, now endorse the Brady bill and some other gun-control initiatives because their members are increasingly being victimized by criminals using the very weapons the NRA wants to have freely

*Continued on p. 161*

# Gun Control Laws in the States

**Most gun control in the United States is at the state level, and laws vary widely from state to state. In addition, many cities have their own gun-control laws. Gun-control proponents argue that only federal legislation will work because gun control is only as effective as its weakest link.**

| State | Waiting period | Permit to purchase | Registration of firearms | Licensing of owner | Permit to carry |
|---|---|---|---|---|---|
| Ala. | 48 hours[1] | no | no | no | only for handguns |
| Alaska | no | no | no | no | no concealed weapons |
| Ariz. | no | no | no | no | no concealed firearms |
| Ark. | no | no | no | no | no concealed weapons |
| Calif. | 15 days[2] | no | yes[3] | no | for concealed handguns |
| Col. | no | no | no | no | for all concealed guns |
| Conn. | 14 days[2] | no | no | no | only for handguns |
| Del. | †[4] | no | no | no | for concealed handguns only |
| D.C. | no | rifles and shotguns; no handgun sales | yes | yes | yes |
| Fla. | †[1] 3 days[2] | no | no | no | yes |
| Ga. | no[5] | no | no | no | yes |
| Hawaii | no | yes[2] | yes | no | only for handguns |
| Idaho | no | no | no | no | only for concealed firearm |
| Ill. | 72 hours[1] 24 hours[6] | 30 days[2] | no[7] | yes | yes; no concealed firearms |
| Ind. | 7 days[1] | no | no | no | only for handguns |
| Iowa | no | 3 days[1] | no | no | only for handguns |
| Kan. | no | no | no | no | no concealed firearms |
| Ky. | no | no | no | no | no concealed weapons |
| La. | no | no | no | no | for concealed weapons |
| Me. | no | no | no | no | for concealed firearms |
| Md. | 7 days[8] | no[9] | no[8] | no | only for handguns |
| Mass. | no | 90 days[2] | no | yes | yes |
| Mich. | no | yes[1] | yes[1] | no | only for handguns |
| Minn. | no | 7 days[1] | no | no | only for handguns |
| Miss. | no | no | no | no | restricted, only for hand guns |
| Mo. | no | 7 days[1] | no | no | no concealed firearms |
| Mon. | no | no | no | no | for concealed firearms |
| Neb. | no | no[10] | no | no | no concealed weapons |
| Nev. | no | no | no | no | for concealed firearms |
| N.C. | no | 30 days[1] | no[8] | no | no, but no concealed handguns |
| N.D. | no | no | no | no | only for concealed handguns |
| N.H. | no | no | no | no | only for handguns |
| N.J. | 7 days[1] | 3 month[1] 6 month[6] | no[11] | yes | yes |
| N.M. | no | no | no | no | no concealed weapons |
| N.Y. | no | yes[1] | yes[1] | yes[1] | for handguns only[12] |
| Ohio | no[13] | no[11] | no[11] | no[11] | no[11] |
| Okla. | no | no | no | no | no concealed weapons |
| Ore. | 15 days[1] | no | no | no | for concealed weapons |
| Pa. | 48 hours[1] | no | no | no | handguns and short rifles |
| R.I. | 7 days[2] | no | no | no | only for handguns |
| S.C. | no | no[14] | no | no | only for handguns |
| S.D. | 48 hours[1] | no | no | no | only for concealed hand guns |
| Tenn. | 15 days[1] | no | no | no | no, but handguns may not be carried "with intent to go armed" |
| Texas | no | no | no | no | restrictions on carrying handguns; no permit |
| Utah | no | no | no | no | for concealed weapons |
| Vt. | no | no | no | no | no |
| Va. | †[4] | no | no | no | for concealed handguns |
| Wash. | 5 days[1] | no[9] | no[9] | no | for handguns only |
| W.Va. | no | no | no | no | for handguns only |
| Wis. | 48 hours[1] | no | no | no | no concealed weapons |
| Wyo. | no | no | no | no | for concealed handguns |

† Instantaneous criminal records check at point of purchase

[1] Handguns only

[2] All firearms: handguns, rifles and shotguns

[3] Assault rifles and pistols only. Police record all gun purchases from dealers.

[4] Handguns and rifles only

[5] Atlanta has a 15-day waiting period and background check for handgun sales.

[6] Rifles and shotguns

[7] Chicago requires registration of all firearms

[8] Handguns and military-style firearms

[9] Police record handgun purchases from dealers

[10] Omaha requires permit to purchase.

[11] Police must record all handgun transfers

[12] New York City requires a 6-month permit to purchase, registration and owner licensing for all firearms

[13] Some municipalities control the possession, sale and transfer of firearms through waiting periods, registration, bans on small, cheap handguns and use of firearms by children.

[14] Only one handgun purchase permitted every 30 days

*Continued from p. 159*
available to the public. "What we believe in is a common-sense approach to curbing some of the problems that have come about from the free flow of weapons in this country," says Dewey R. Stokes, president of the Fraternal Order of Police and a police officer in Columbus, Ohio.

The Brady bill has also gained the endorsement of other groups, such as the American Medical Association, which views gun violence as a public-health hazard, and the National Congress of Parents and Teachers, which is alarmed at the high number of gun deaths among children. Even Rep. Les AuCoin (D-Ore.), who says he has a 100 percent rating from the NRA, has announced he will break ranks and vote for the Brady Bill.

However, it is too soon to write off the NRA's ability to block federal gun-control legislation. Supporters of the organization's hard-line approach to gun control won a major battle on Feb. 22 when J. Warren Cassidy, the NRA's executive vice president, stepped down. NRA hard-liners, one of whom calls gun-control advocates "eco-terrorists and militant carrot-killer vegetarians," [6] had long criticized Cassidy's leadership as excessively moderate. They hope to elect a board of directors in April that will concentrate the lobby's energies on what they see as the organization's primary mission, defense of the public's right to own and bear the arms of their choice.

But Handgun Control Inc. and the Brady bill's congressional sponsors hope to win passage of the measure this year. "We have never said that we believe that the Brady bill is going to totally solve the gun-violence problem in America," says Susan Whitmore, the organization's spokesman. "But we do know that it is the single most important piece of legislation that we can pass."

## High level of firearms violence spurs the push for new laws

A look at the statistics on deaths and injuries from firearms in the United States reveals why even supporters of the handgun waiting period required by the Brady bill predict that the measure would have a limited impact. "We have over 30,000 deaths and approaching 200,000 injuries per year from firearms, if you consider homicide, suicide and the non-fatal equivalent of those as well as accidents," says Dr. Garen J. Wintemute, assistant professor of family practice at the School of Medicine of the University of California at Davis.

Between 1979 and 1987, the Justice Department reports in a survey of victims of handgun crimes, offenders used their weapons to kill an average of 9,200 Americans each year and to wound 15,000.[7] Even more deaths caused by handguns were not murders. According to Handgun Control Inc., 1,200 people die each year from handgun accidents, and handguns were used by 12,701 Americans to take their own lives in 1987. Of the more than 30,000 total deaths from all kinds of firearms each year, the organization reports, more than 23,000 are caused by handguns, the weapons targeted by the Brady bill.

The Justice Department reports that an average of 639,000 people in this country faced an offender wielding a handgun each year between 1979 and 1987.[8] The typical handgun crime involved a single offender armed with no other weapon besides the handgun, confronting a stranger on the street. The vast majority of offenders — 87 percent — did not fire their weapons at all but used them to threaten their victims. Most victims of handgun crimes were assaulted. About a third were robbed. One in 50 was raped.[9]

Big-city residents are more than twice as likely to be victimized by guns as their suburban neighbors and more than three times as likely as people living in non-metropolitan areas. The risks are even greater for residents of cities where the illegal drug trade flourishes. Washington, D.C., and its immediate suburbs — which boast the highest per capita murder rate in the nation — lost 703 people to homicide last year, 75 percent of whom were killed with firearms. It was the capital's third-straight record year for homicides. New York City, another important hub of the East Coast's drug trade, also witnessed its third-straight record year in 1990, when more than 2,200 homicides were recorded. Los Angeles County, the West Coast's drug capital, broke its 1980 homicide record last November.

Firearm violence is now spreading to smaller cities as well. In 1990, homicide rates jumped to record levels in Richmond, Va., Milwaukee, Wis., Fresno, Calif., and many other smaller urban centers the recent wave of violence had previously passed by. In many cases, the spread has followed the dispersal of the urban drug markets to the surrounding areas. Thus, the rise in homicides seen in Milwaukee is seen as the natural consequence of the spread of Chicago-based drug gangs.[10]

And yet as important as the drug trade has been in increasing the use of firearms in criminal activities, police report a fall in drug-related homicides. In Washington, D.C., police say the percentage of killings that were directly linked to drugs fell from 60 percent in 1988 to 41 percent in 1990. They conclude that even as the drug trade has diminished in the past two years, it has left in its wake a pernicious "culture of guns" in which people are more willing to use firearms to settle disputes.[11]

Having witnessed members of drug gangs wield virtually absolute power in their neighborhoods, many residents in and around the nation's main drug markets are cynically turning to guns as a quick and sure way to settle their differences. These killings take a high toll among innocent bystanders; the number of people killed by stray bullets more than tripled over the last five years.[12] The Washington area, jaded in recent years by the scores of drive-by shootings in which innocent bystanders have been killed, was stunned last December when 20-year-old James Bias was shot while driving away in a car from the scene of an argument with an apparent stranger. Bias' older brother Len, a University of Maryland basketball star, had died of a cocaine overdose in 1986.

Handgun crime takes a disproportionate toll among Americans like Bias — young black male residents of large American cities. The Justice Department survey found that about one in 32 urban black males ages 16-24 is victimized each year by handgun-bearing criminals. That is about seven times the rate suffered by the population as a whole.

Further, the risk of being killed among young black males is growing faster than among any other group of Americans. The federal Centers for Disease Control reports that the rate of homicide among young black males rose by 50 percent between 1984 and 1987, with firearms accounting for almost all of the increase.[13] It was statistics such as these that prompted Louis W. Sullivan, secretary of Health and Human Services, to part company with the rest of the Bush Cabinet and advocate gun control because, he said, he was "very concerned about the high number of deaths from handguns in our society in general and certainly in the black community."[14]

The escalation of street violence is taking its toll among law enforcement officers as well. Dewey Stokes, president of the Fraternal Order of Police, says that 63 city, county, state and federal law enforcement officers were killed due to criminal action last year. The vast majority, 45 officers, were killed by handguns.

Even children have not been spared. In New York City, 39 children under 16 years of age were killed with guns last year. According to Handgun Control Inc., 10 children age 18 and under are killed every day by handguns. Every three hours, the group estimates, an American teenager commits suicide with a handgun. The Justice Department found that people 16-24 years old were confronted by offenders bearing handguns more that any other age group.

Ominously, children are the victimizers as well as

## Handgun Crime

**Handgun crime takes a disproportionate toll among young black males in large urban areas.**

| Place of residence and age of victim | Average annual rate[†] of crimes committed with handguns (per 1,000 persons) | |
| --- | --- | --- |
| | White | Black |
| *Central city* | | |
| 12-15 years | 3.5 | 7.0 |
| 16-19 | 9.8 | 23.1 |
| 20-24 | 9.4 | 20.1 |
| 25-34 | 5.8 | 13.9 |
| 35-49 | 3.4 | 7.2 |
| 50-64 | 2.3 | 6.1 |
| 65 or older | .6 | 2.6 |
| *Suburbs* | | |
| 12-15 years | .8 | — |
| 16-19 | 5.0 | 10.6 |
| 20-24 | 5.7 | 9.1 |
| 25-34 | 3.6 | 6.8 |
| 35-49 | 1.7 | 4.0 |
| 50-64 | 1.3 | — |
| 65 or older | .6 | — |
| *Nonmetropolitan area* | | |
| 12-15 years | .7 | — |
| 16-19 | 2.6 | 4.7 |
| 20-24 | 4.9 | 6.8 |
| 25-34 | 2.4 | 4.5 |
| 35-49 | 1.5 | — |
| 50-64 | .6 | — |
| 65 or older | — | — |

† *Average annual rate 1979-1987.*

*Source: Department of Justice, Bureau of Justice Statistics, Special Report: Handgun Crime Victims, July 1990.*

the victims in handgun violence. In Washington, D.C., last year, 68 juveniles — 17 of them younger than 15 years of age — were charged with homicide. And Fox of Northeastern University says such statistics will only get worse. In what he calls the "baby boomerang effect," Fox predicts more murders by teenagers as the children of the baby boomers reach their teens, just as a similar rise in homicide rates by that age group occurred among their parents when they were teenagers in the 1960s.

And yet demographics are only part of the picture, Fox says. "It's not just a matter of how many kids there are, but also how deadly the weapons are they have in their hands." Handguns, which are responsible for most firearms deaths and injuries, include not only the traditional revolvers, which must be reloaded after five or six bullets are fired, but also more powerful semiautomatic and even fully automatic pistols, such as the Tec-9 and Uzi pistol, which can fire as many shots as the ammunition clip can hold, often 30 or 32 rounds.

Slightly less easily concealed than pistols but still shorter than hunting rifles or shotguns are assault rifles such as the Russian-made AK-47. Semiautomatic versions fire one round and instantly reload the next round with each pull of the trigger, while fully automatic guns literally spray bullets for as long as the trigger is depressed and the 30-odd (or more) rounds of ammunition hold out. Further, newer handguns are often more powerful and thus more deadly than those produced 10 or 15 years ago. "At one time a gunshot wound victim might be saved," Fox says. "But now, firearms being as powerful as they are, that same gunshot-wound victim today may not be salvageable in our emergency rooms because rather than having an organ penetrated, it may be annihilated."

## The place of guns in American society

The level of gun violence in the United States becomes even more striking when U.S. crime statistics are compared with those of other countries. Violent crimes are far more common in this country than in Europe, for example. Murders, rapes and robberies occurred at rates four to nine times higher in the United States than in Europe in the early 1980s, according to a Justice Department study of crime in 41 countries, mostly in Europe and the Western Hemisphere.[15]

Although the differences in violent crime rates between the United States and other industrialized countries were narrowing as the decade drew to a close, this country's lead in violent crimes remained overwhelming. (*See chart, p. 163*) The difference becomes even more stunning when the choice of weapons for violent crimes is examined. From its review of the literature, Handgun Control Inc. found that in 1988 handguns were used to kill seven people in Great Britain, 19 in Sweden, 53 in Switzerland, 25 in Israel, 13 in Australia and eight in Canada. In the United States that year, 8,915 people died from handgun violence.

There are several theories to explain the disparity. One is historical: The barely 200-year story of the United States is steeped in violence. It was founded as a result of armed insurrection and expanded by violently wresting the land from Native Americans. Before the country's centennial, it had experienced a bloody civil war that claimed more victims than all subsequent wars the United States has participated in. A sizable minority of the country's inhabitants suffered the violence of enslavement, only to become victims of harassment and discrimination after their emancipation. The most recent chapter of American violence opened in the nation's city streets in the early 1980s, when the market for illegal drugs began its decade-long boom. The drug trade brought a new level of violence to American society.

Not surprisingly, firearms have figured prominently in this history of violence. "In American history the gun has been more than just present — it has been prominent," write historians Lee Kennett and James LaVerne Anderson. "An armed population was long held to be a necessary prop to the American way of life. No amount of historical evidence has ever shaken the popular notion that individual Americans and their guns preserved the nation from foreign dangers, whether they were the Minutemen at Lexington, Davy Crockett at the Alamo, or Sergeant York in the trenches of France." [16]

Today, the Bureau of Alcohol, Tobacco and Firearms (BATF), the federal agency in charge of firearms regulations, estimates that private citizens in the United States possess some 200 million firearms of all types, including 60-70 million handguns. Although the government does not keep records on assault weapons, the bureau estimates that between 1 million and 3 million semiautomatic assault-type weapons are in the hands of private citizens.

Paralleling the nation's history of violence is its reflection in films and television entertainment, another

## World Homicide Rates

This chart shows the number of homicides per 100,000 population in 1987.

| Country | Men | Women |
|---------|-----|-------|
| United States† | 13.9 | 4.1 |
| Australia† | 2.4 | 1.5 |
| Austria | 1.4 | 1.2 |
| Canada† | 2.7 | 1.4 |
| Chile† | 5.4 | 0.8 |
| Costa Rica† | 6.0 | 2.1 |
| Czechoslovakia† | 1.3 | 1.0 |
| Denmark† | 1.4 | 1.0 |
| Ecuador† | 17.6 | 2.1 |
| United Kingdom | 1.3 | 0.7 |
| France | 1.5 | 0.9 |
| Greece† | 1.2 | 0.7 |
| Hungary | 3.1 | 1.9 |
| Ireland† | 0.7 | 0.6 |
| Japan | 0.9 | 0.6 |
| Luxembourg | 2.2 | 1.0 |
| Netherlands† | 1.4 | 0.7 |
| New Zealand† | 2.8 | 1.6 |
| Norway† | 2.8 | 1.6 |
| Panama† | 9.3 | 1.6 |
| Portugal | 1.7 | 0.8 |
| Scotland | 2.8 | 1.3 |
| Spain | 1.3 | 0.3 |
| Sweden† | 1.9 | 0.9 |

† Data are for 1986.

*Source: World Health Organization, 1988 World Health Statistics Annual, 1988. Data are for 1987 unless otherwise indicated.*

important cause of the high rates of violent crime in this country in the view of some mental health professionals. Viewers, especially young ones, it is often said, take cues on how to commit a crime of violence from fictional depictions they see on screen.

There is only anecdotal evidence to support the notion that viewing violence makes people more violent, but some experts say that these depictions do have an impact on viewers' attitudes and behavior in more subtle ways. Dr. Thomas Radecki, a psychiatrist in Champaign, Ill., and chairman of the National Coalition on Television Violence, says television viewing tends to distort people's sense of reality. Radecki charges Hollywood with perpetrating the "myth of violence" by using "violent themes as a way of exciting us and bringing programs to rapid resolution."

He cites the case of "Miami Vice," a popular television series, in which the two hero cops killed 43 people in 18 episodes. In contrast, Radecki found that the real Miami police force killed only eight people in a year. "We calculated that the TV killer cops were 12,000 times more violent than real-life police officers and that if all police officers in America were like these TV cops, all the rest of us would be dead in six months."

Radecki conducted his own experiment to test his theory that viewing depictions of violence distorts people's perceptions of reality. When he asked people how often they thought a real-life police officer in nearby Chicago, Ill., fired his gun, his patients said once a week and other health-care professionals guessed once a month. According to Chicago police statistics, Radecki said, the actual figure is once every 27 years. "So even for a normal, college-educated adult in America, we overestimate the necessity of police violence by 400-fold, or 40,000 percent. That's how we perceive reality."

Researchers also have found that the more people watch violent programs on television, the more likely they are to overestimate the dangers of violent attack. "Obviously, we live in a very violent country," Radecki says. "But the people who don't watch television or who watch small amounts of television or who select away from violent television tend to make more accurate estimates of how dangerous it is in their own neighborhoods."

Radecki also cites studies that show a high correlation between the amount of television people watch and gun ownership. Their heightened sense of vulnerability, Radecki says, explains why. "And once people own a gun, the more likely they are to use a gun."

To some observers, the historical and cultural explanations of the extraordinarily high rate of firearm violence in the United States do not go far enough. They focus instead on the ready availability of guns in this country. Other countries impose sweeping restrictions on gun ownership and prohibit almost all gun owners from carrying their weapons outside. In Spain, for example, carrying a gun was until recently considered an act of military insurrection punishable by death. Even today, in Germany the only type of gun a civilian is allowed to carry is a hunting rifle, whose size makes it hard to conceal. And before gun owners receive a hunting license, which is required to carry rifles, they must first pass a government-conducted firearms safety test.

To test the hypothesis that it is gun availability rather than some other cause that accounts for the high level of firearm violence in the United States, researchers compared the crime rates of Seattle, Wash., and Vancouver, British Columbia, cities with very similar cultural, ethnic and economic characteristics but very different approaches to firearms. Canadian law requires handgun purchasers to obtain permits and to register their weapons. It does not recognize self-defense in the home or on the street as a legally acceptable reason to buy a handgun. Seattle residents, however, need not register their handguns and are free to buy them for self-defense in the home. They may also obtain a permit to carry a concealed gun for self-defense in the street. The researchers found that while the rates of most types of crimes were similar in both cities, there were seven times as many assaults with firearms in Seattle and that the risk of being murdered with a handgun was almost five times greater there than in Vancouver.[17]

"People feel like they need to protect themselves. It's a feeling of safety, a feeling of taking control of one's life instead of being a victim," says criminologist Fox of Northeastern University. "What they don't understand is that if they pull a gun on someone, they stand a good chance of having that gun taken away and used against them." Fox says gun ownership among private citizens helps raise the threshold of firearm violence. "If we try to arm ourselves with guns, criminals will arm themselves with bigger guns. It's often said the Americans have a love affair with violence. Actually it's more like a marriage, and if we're not careful, this marriage will become until death do us part."

## Court rulings and gun-control legislation

American gun owners' chief lobby, the NRA, attributes the high rate of gun violence in this country to lax treatment of criminals and says harsher punishment of felons using firearms to commit crimes is the best way to reduce that rate. "Guns don't kill people — people do," reads a popular NRA bumper sticker. The gun lobby stands firm in its defense of the individual's right to keep and bear arms, a right it says is protected by the Second Amendment to the Constitution. It reads: "A well regulated Militia, being necessary to the security of a free State, the right of the people to keep and bear Arms, shall not be infringed."

The clumsy syntax and ambiguous phrasing of this amendment have given rise to differences in its interpretation ever since (*see "At Issue," p. 169*). Most constitutional experts, including the American Bar Association, assert that the two clauses are inseparable, that the amendment was meant to protect the right of states to maintain organized militias — today called the National Guard. The NRA emphasizes only the second half of the sentence, which is etched in the stone that frames the doorway of its headquarters in downtown Washington. The organization believes the protected right is that of the population at large.

The Supreme Court has addressed the Second Amendment question on several occasions. Although it has never directly ruled which interpretation is correct, it has always ruled against gun-control opponents on the constitutional question. "The Supreme Court," explains Bruce Nicholson, a lobbyist for the American Bar Association who works on gun-control issues, "has never found language in the Second Amendment as a bar to reasonable regulation of firearms. More affirmatively, the Supreme Court has upheld laws from attack on these grounds, even though it hasn't squarely faced the issue and given a definitive answer."

# *Murders by Type of Weapon, 1974-1989*

**The vast majority of murders in the United States are committed by firearms, and the vast majority of firearms murders are committed by handguns. Note that the number of murders has remained relatively steady over the years, with only a slight peak in 1980. Nevertheless, many cities have reported record numbers of murders in recent years, and, although the final figures have not been released, there are indications that 1990 may have broken the 1980 record. (This chart shows only murders for which the weapon was known; several thousand additional murders each year are committed with an unknown weapon.)**

| | 1974 | 1975 | 1976 | 1977 | 1978 | 1979 | 1980 | 1981 | 1982 | 1983 | 1984 | 1985 | 1986 | 1987 | 1988 | 1989 |
|---|---|---|---|---|---|---|---|---|---|---|---|---|---|---|---|---|
| TOTAL MURDERS | 18,627 | 18,642 | 16,605 | 18,032 | 18,714 | 20,591 | 21,860 | 20,053 | 19,485 | 18,673 | 17,260 | 17,545 | 19,257 | 17,963 | 17,971 | 18,954 |
| Total firearms | 12,470 | 12,061 | 10,592 | 11,274 | 11,910 | 13,040 | 13,650 | 12,523 | 11,721 | 10,895 | 10,175 | 10,296 | 11,381 | 10,612 | 10,895 | 11,832 |
| Handgun | 9,334 | 8,767 | 7,649 | 8,076 | 8,495 | 9,459 | 10,012 | 9,193 | 8,474 | 8,193 | 7,557 | 7,548 | 8,460 | 7,847 | 8,147 | 9,013 |
| Rifle | 952 | 996 | 975 | 1,046 | 1,091 | 1,075 | 1,124 | 968 | 1,017 | 831 | 785 | 810 | 788 | 776 | 753 | 865 |
| Shotgun | 1,539 | 1,563 | 1,433 | 1,580 | 1,582 | 1,719 | 1,636 | 1,528 | 1,377 | 1,243 | 1,194 | 1,188 | 1,296 | 1,101 | 1,105 | 1,173 |
| Other guns | † | † | 23 | 24 | 7 | 40 | 53 | 82 | 38 | 19 | 19 | 24 | 22 | 16 | 15 | 34 |
| Firearm not stated | 645 | 735 | 512 | 548 | 735 | 747 | 825 | 752 | 815 | 609 | 620 | 726 | 815 | 872 | 875 | 747 |

† *Data not collected.*

*Source: Federal Bureau of Investigation, Uniform Crime Reporting.*

In its first ruling on the issue, in *United States v. Cruickshank*, the court determined in 1876 that the right to bear arms "is not a right granted by the Constitution" and that if such a right exists, it does so independently of the Second Amendment. The court also ruled that the amendment itself restricted the power of Congress, but not the state governments, to regulate firearms.

The Supreme Court further endorsed the states' right to regulate firearms in 1886, in *Presser v. Illinois*, by upholding a state statute banning the formation and parading of armed groups of men. In 1939, the court decided in *United States v. Miller* that Congress could regulate guns as long as the regulations do not impede the efficiency of the state militia. That case involved the arrest of a man who had carried a sawed-off shotgun across state lines in violation of a law passed several years before.

The law in question in the *Miller* case was the National Firearms Act, which Congress passed in 1934 under its power to raise revenue. That law, the first federal gun law, imposed a $200 excise tax on the sale of fully automatic weapons as well as short-barreled rifles and shotguns. Because the purchaser was identified upon payment of the tax, the law also indirectly imposed the requirement to register these weapons. Four years later, the Federal Firearms Act of 1938 placed some restrictions on the sale of all other firearms as well. It required any gun dealer selling firearms across state lines to obtain a federal license and to keep records identifying all gun buyers. The law prohibited dealers from selling any firearms to people who had been convicted of violent felonies.

Federal gun legislation remained unchanged until the late 1960s. Prompted by the assassinations of President John F. Kennedy, Sen. Robert F. Kennedy and the Rev. Dr. Martin Luther King Jr., Congress introduced several changes in federal firearms law with the Gun Control Act of 1968. This measure extended the licensing requirement to all firearms dealers, prohibited dealers from selling handguns to out-of-state residents, and prohibited individuals from buying handguns out of state. It also banned, for the first time, the mail-order sale of guns and expanded the list of people to whom dealers were prohibited from selling firearms to include almost all convicted felons (except those convicted for certain business-related felonies), people with certain mental illnesses and illegal-drug users. Finally, the Gun Control Act banned the importation of guns that are not "particularly suitable for or readily adaptable to sporting purposes."

Enforcement of the 1968 Gun Control Act, like its predecessors, fell under the authority of the Treasury Department, specifically an agency in the Internal Revenue Service responsible for pursuing illegal producers of alcohol. Renamed the Bureau of Alcohol, Tobacco and Firearms in 1972, this department has since devoted most of its energies to enforcing firearms laws.

Since 1968, Congress has made only slight changes to federal gun laws. A law passed in 1969 (PL 91-128) weakened the Gun Control Act by removing the recordkeeping requirements that the law imposed for some types of rifle and shotgun ammunition. But a year later, lawmakers tightened the statute by adding an amendment that made it a crime to carry a gun while committing a federal crime. The amendment, part of the 1970 Omnibus Crime Control Act (PL 91-644), also established minimum mandatory sentences for these offenders. The mandatory sentencing provision was strengthened under the 1984 Crime Control Act (contained in PL 98-473), which also set a minimum mandatory five-year prison sentence for anyone who carries or uses a handgun with armor-piercing bullets while committing a violent crime.

In 1986, Congress passed two gun-related measures whose effect on law enforcement prompted most police organizations for the first time to declare their support for gun control. One law, strongly backed by law enforcement groups, curbed the sale of armor-piercing bullets, called "cop-killers" because they are able to penetrate the bulletproof vests worn by police officers. Congress also passed an NRA-sponsored measure, the Firearms Owners Protection Act, which eliminated some of the recordkeeping requirements for gun dealers imposed by earlier legislation and allowed people once again to buy rifles out of state.

The bill also included an amendment, which was supported by law enforcement groups, that banned the manufacture or sale of fully automatic machine guns after May 19, 1986, and banned ownership of such weapons after that date. The amendment, introduced by Rep. William J. Hughes, D-N.J., exempted machine guns made "under the authority of the United States" or any state agency. The Bureau of Alcohol, Tobacco and Firearms (BATF) interpreted this clause to mean that only the U.S. military and police forces were authorized to possess machine guns, an interpretation the NRA challenged as too restrictive. When a Georgia gun manufacturer, J. D. Farmer, was denied a license by BATF to make a machine gun in 1987, he sued the bureau. The case, *Farmer v. Higgins*, made its way to the U.S. Supreme Court, which on Jan. 14, 1991, let stand the new machine-gun ban and declined to consider the NRA's arguments.

In 1988, Congress passed a law (PL 100-649) banning the sale of plastic handguns that cannot be readily spotted by metal detectors. Another law enacted that year, the Federal Energy Management Improvement Act (PL 100-615), prohibits the manufacturing and sale of toy or imitation firearms unless they have distinctive color markings that allow law enforcement agents to distinguish them from the real thing. The law was prompted by the rising number of assaults and robberies committed by criminals bearing imitation guns as well as shootings by police of people who appeared to be armed with lethal weapons.[18] In 1989, President Bush — who like most Republican lawmakers generally opposes gun control — banned the importation of 43 types of semiautomatic assault weapons, under authority granted by the 1968 Gun Control Act. But since almost three-quarters of all assault weapons are made in the United States, gun-control advocates have since pushed for passage of a ban on the domestic manufacture of these firearms, which include the AK-47 and Uzi rifles as well as the more easily concealed Tec-9 and Mac-11 pistols.

More recently, gun-control advocates have had little success on the federal level. Despite support from President Reagan, the Brady bill failed to win congressional support when it was first introduced in 1987. Though the bill finally was cleared by a wide margin in the House Judiciary Committee in July 1990, House Speaker Foley, an NRA member and longstanding opponent of gun-control laws, prevented the seven-day waiting period for handgun purchases from making it to the floor for a vote as part of the Omnibus Crime Bill. The ban on assault weapons also was dropped from the crime bill.

In sum, public access to firearms is more loosely regulated than in most other countries. The restrictions that do exist vary in severity according to weapon type. Long guns, which include rifles and shotguns, may be purchased across state lines, but handguns may be bought only in the purchaser's state of residence.

Purchasers of all types of firearms must answer several questions on a federal form supplied by the dealer, aimed at identifying convicted felons, drug or alcohol abusers and people who have been adjudicated mentally ill. But under federal law, this system works on the honor system, as there is no check on the validity of the answers. Anyone who denies falling into the categories of prohibited purchasers can buy rifles and handguns under federal law.

There is no federally mandated system for registering rifles or handguns under current law. The most stringent federal regulations apply to fully automatic machine guns. Since 1934, machine-gun owners have been required to register their weapons, submit to a background check and pay a tax. Since 1986, the production, importation and sale of new machine guns has been prohibited. However, people who already legally owned these firearms were allowed to keep or sell them.

## Most firearms regulations are enforced by the states

With the federal government taking such a limited role, most gun-related legislation has been introduced at the state level. But the conditions for gun ownership vary greatly from state to state, and in certain cases among local jurisdictions, producing a patchwork of gun restrictions across the country. In some states the

right to gun ownership is less ambiguous than in the country as a whole. Indeed, 40 state constitutions specifically guarantee the right to bear arms, and 22 of these define that right as pertaining to "personal defense." * (*See chart, p. 160.*)

But other states have acted to restrict gun availability. In 1981, the town of Morton Grove, Ill., passed an ordinance banning handguns for all but gun clubs, collectors and police and security personnel. Challenges to the ordinance went to the U.S. Supreme Court, which declined to hear the case on Second Amendment grounds and thus implicitly upheld the town's right to ban the guns under its police powers. Other local jurisdictions that have imposed unusually stiff restrictions on gun ownership include Washington, D.C., which in 1976 banned the sale of all handguns.

Several Southern states, as a result of their relatively lax controls on gun sales, have emerged as leading gun-running states by providing firearms to criminals who illegally transport them to jurisdictions such as Washington, D.C., and New York City, where gun ownership is strictly limited. "In the big cities like New York and Washington, most of the guns come from out of town," says James Fyfe, a professor of justice, law and society at American University in Washington, D.C., and a former New York City police lieutenant. "They historically come from the same states over and over again — Virginia, Georgia, the Carolinas and Florida."

Voters in some of these states are beginning to take steps to make it harder to obtain firearms. Last November, 84 percent of Florida voters chose to amend their state Constitution to add a three-day "cooling-off" period for all gun sales. The Florida Legislature had earlier passed a law requiring adults to keep loaded guns away from children and imposing fines and prison sentences on those who violated the law.

But gun-control advocates still face strong opposition in these states. The Virginia General Assembly, for example, recently killed a proposal for a three-day waiting period for handgun purchases, which supporters hoped would discourage the use of firearms for suicide and crimes of passion. Opponents of the measure, including the NRA, say the measure is a form of harassment. They support instead the state's existing system for checking the criminal records of gun buyers — a two-year-old computerized instantaneous background check similar to credit-card validation procedures in other retail stores.

As a compromise, both the NRA and Virginia lawmakers are backing a measure that would expand the existing background check to cover not only handguns and semiautomatic weapons but all firearms. The NRA would like to see the computerized system instituted nationwide as an alternative to waiting periods. The Justice Department, however, says that only

*State constitutions often define rights more broadly than the federal Constitution. See "Protecting Rights in State Courts," *E.R.R.*, May 27, 1988 (Vol. I, No. 20).

# The U.S. Firearms Industry

Considering the number of firearms in private hands in the United States, the industry that produces them is surprisingly small. According to the Census Bureau, the American small-arms industry, which makes rifles, shotguns and handguns for private sale as well as for law enforcement and the military, employed only 13,300 people in 1987, the last year for which statistics are available.†

There were 144 gun manufacturers in the United States, but only two — Remington Arms Co. Inc., a subsidiary of Du Pont, and Smith & Wesson, a division of Tomkins Corp. — accounted for almost half of the industry's $1.1 billion in sales. Handgun manufacture is similarly concentrated, as two companies — Smith & Wesson and Sturm, Ruger & Co. Inc., — produce almost two-thirds of the handguns manufactured in the United States. No company employed more than 2,000 people, and the vast majority of gunmakers counted fewer than 10 workers.

Although the Bureau of Alcohol, Tobacco and Firearms lists gun manufacturers in 42 states, the industry is concentrated, as it has been since the Revolutionary period, along the Connecticut River Valley from Springfield, Mass., home of Smith & Wesson, to the Atlantic Ocean and along the coast from New Haven, Conn., to New York City. Five of the six largest gunmakers are headquartered in this region, and many small firms are located there as well.

Despite their small size and lack of a separate lobbying arm in Washington to represent them before Congress, lawmakers have looked after the industry's interests through the years. The Gun Control Act of 1968, for example, was aimed in part at restricting public access to cheap handguns like the one used to assassinate Sen. Robert F. Kennedy. To that end it established certain performance standards for handguns.

But the bill, introduced by Thomas J. Dodd, a Democratic senator from Connecticut, a major gun-producing state, applied only to imported handguns, not to domestically produced weapons. As a result, says Dr. Garen J. Wintemute, a public health specialist who is an authority on gun violence, "we enacted a whole series of standards, some having to do with general design, some having to do with performance, that imports have to meet. But guns that are made in the United States do not have to meet those tests."

Twenty years later, Wintemute explains, similar discriminatory measures were taken to protect the domestic manufacturers of assault weapons. In 1989 and 1990, the Bureau of Alcohol, Tobacco and Firearms, under orders from President Bush, banned the importation of several assault-type weapons, including the Israeli-designed Uzi and the Soviet-designed AK-47, but not the domestic manufacture of these guns.

"As a result, companies were set up in the United States precisely to produce weapons which were banned from importation," Wintemute says. He cites the examples of the AK-47, now manufactured and sold in this country by a company in Arizona, and the Striker-12, an assault shotgun also known as the Street Sweeper, which can no longer be imported but is now produced in the United States.

Domestic gun manufacturers received another benefit last fall with an amendment to the Omnibus Crime Bill that would have banned the assembly of semiautomatic weapons identical to weapons banned from importation. That amendment, introduced by Rep. Jolene Unsoeld, D-Wash., allows these firearms to be assembled with U.S.-made parts.

Virtually the only constraints placed on the domestic small arms industry concerning the kinds of weapons it makes come from product-liability lawsuits brought against gun manufacturers for injuries caused by malfunctioning firearms. But lawyers have been less successful when they argue in injury cases that handguns are inherently defective because their small size allows them to be easily concealed. Wintemute says the only successful lawsuit of this kind was *Kelley et al. v. RG Industries Inc. et al.*, in which the maker of a handgun was held responsible for injuries it caused in Maryland. As a result of that case, the manufacturer went out of business. However, a 1988 state law banning cheap handguns known as Saturday night specials in Maryland legislatively repealed the use of the *Kelley* case as legal precedent in the state.

The District of Columbia almost became the first jurisdiction to make the manufacturers of assault weapons liable for damages and injuries caused by their products when the City Council passed the Assault Weapon Manufacturing Strict Liability Act last December. The council later repealed the bill, however, when it became apparent that Congress might otherwise withhold desperately needed federal aid to the District.

But in Wintemute's view, firearms manufacturers may soon face similar challenges from other cities that, like Washington, are victims of gun violence but do not depend on Congress for direct funding. "I would bet you that we will see attempts to enact such laws in places like New York City and Oakland, Calif.," he predicts.

† *Bureau of the Census, U.S. Department of Commerce, 1987 Census of Manufactures, Industry Series, Ordnance and Accessories, N.E.C., March 1990.*

10 states have fully automated their criminal records. "The main problem [with an instant computer check]," one Justice Department official told *The Washington Post*, "is you don't have the computer record system that makes it worthwhile."[19]

Many states that already imposed greater restrictions on gun sales than the traditional "gun-runner" states have recently tightened their firearm laws in response to the rising rate of firearm violence. Maryland legislators banned the manufacture and sale of cheap handguns known as Saturday night specials in 1988, a measure that the state's voters upheld in a referendum later that year despite a $6 million campaign financed by the NRA to repeal the ban.

In the aftermath of the January 1989 killing of five children in a Stockton, Calif., schoolyard in a hail of gunfire from an AK-47, some states enacted measures to restrict public access to military-style assault weapons. California and New Jersey banned assault-type weapons shortly after the killings. New Jersey's 1990 law, the most restrictive assault-weapon measure in the country, banned the sale and restricted the ownership of many semiautomatics. Owners of such guns purchased before May 31, 1990, are required either to surrender their weapons or to make them inoperable by May of this year. A drive to weaken the law is currently under consideration.[20]

The California law banned the sale of 56 types of semiautomatic weapons and required the registration of semiautomatic assault-type weapons by Dec. 31. But most of the state's gun owners have defied the law, and one group called a news conference to announce openly that its members would not register their semi-automatics. Of the estimated 200,000-300,000 assault-type weapons in the state, only about 13,000 were registered by the deadline. Despite the apparent setback in California, Maryland Gov. William Donald Schaefer has called for a ban on the AK-47 and 38 other guns in his state and a new requirement for the registration of the estimated 30,000 such weapons currently in the hands of Marylanders.

The District of Columbia, already home of the nation's strictest gun law, passed a landmark bill in 1990 that held manufacturers of assault weapons liable for deaths and injuries caused by these guns. The measure was later dropped when it became clear that Congress, which has the authority to repeal D.C. laws, opposed it and might hold up the transfer of $300 million in federal funds to the financially strapped city if the city government failed to drop the assault-weapons law on its own.

### New supply-side and demand-side proposals to limit access to guns

Both sides of the debate over gun control agree that none of the measures enacted to date provides an adequate solution to the scourge of firearms violence in this country. Gun-control advocates say that their agenda has not been given a chance, that the patch-work of state laws makes it impossible to prevent firearms from falling into the hands of criminals. "Right now in more than half the states in this country criminals are walking into gun stores, lying on the federal forms and walking out with the weapons of their choice," says Susan Whitmore of Handgun Control. "They are contributing to the so-called black market of weapons we see on the street corners of New York and the District of Columbia. We know that if we can have a minimum uniform standard law that can stop

the easy and quick, over-the-counter access of weapons to criminals that we're going to make a significant dent in the level of gun violence and crime."

The National Rifle Association agrees that current gun-control measures don't work, but the gun lobby says that is because gun control of any kind is inherently wrong. "Gun control bears no relation to criminality or crime control," says Paul Blackman, research coordinator for the NRA. The way to reduce firearms violence, the organization says, is to attack criminals, not the weapons they use. Blackman notes that the NRA's solution to firearms violence continues to be one the organization first proposed in 1958 — mandatory prison terms for people who use guns while committing drug-trafficking offenses or violent offenses.

While the two main spokesmen for the opposing views on gun control stand by their proposals, experts on firearms violence who work in various fields are offering novel approaches to the problem. Some suggest that current laws, while better than nothing, are flawed because they attempt to tackle the problem too late. One such critic is Dr. Garen Wintemute of the University of California at Davis, who views gun violence from his perspective in the field of public health.

Wintemute equates firearms violence with what health professionals call a point-source epidemic. Just as a contaminated well can be the source of a cholera epidemic, Wintemute explains, domestic gun manufacturers and gun distributors are the source of the vast majority of guns used to commit acts of violence in this country. In much the same way that a cholera epidemic in London was once curtailed by removing the handle used to pump water from a contaminated well, the epidemic of gun violence could be curtailed by stopping the production and importation of firearms.

Wintemute acknowledges that political obstacles to this ideal goal are too great to surmount. But other supply-side approaches to gun control are well within society's reach, in his view. One is the tighter regulation of the gun manufacturing industry (*see story, p. 167*). "We talk about how many regulations there are having to do with guns, but those all have to do with how guns are handled once they are manufactured and sold," Wintemute notes. "With very rare exceptions, there are almost no regulations on the manufacture of guns."

Wintemute proposes applying current standards for imports to domestically produced guns as well. These include a requirement that guns be easily adaptable to sporting purposes — to screen out assault weapons — and size and safety standards for handguns, to eliminate Saturday night specials. Wintemute also would support additional standards to improve the safety of firearms, such as requiring that all revolvers have safety mechanisms to prevent accidental firing.

If Wintemute's proposals for heavier regulation of the manufacture of firearms can be seen as a supply-side solution to gun violence, other experts say this approach is flawed and suggest novel demand-side

*Continued on p. 170*

# AT ISSUE

*Does the Second Amendment give individuals the right to have guns without restrictions?*

## YES

*says* **DAVID I. CAPLAN**, *a member of the board of directors of the National Rifle Association.*

Today grave dangers and assaults from many directions threaten all the individual rights of the people. The most fierce assault is the erosion of rights by legal process, a procedure most dangerous because it is so effective.

The realization that an erosion of the individual right to have arms under the Second Amendment spells dire peril for all our other constitutional rights has caused fear and alarm among those who own guns, as well as among those who don't.

Existing legal principles and historical precedents fully justify this fear and alarm.

One of the favorite arguments disparaging the Second Amendment is that "the right of the people to keep and bear arms" is merely a collective right referring only to the people collectively as a common body.

However, in the consideration of the proposal for inclusion of the Second Amendment in the Bill of Rights, the U.S. Senate in 1789 soundly rejected a motion on the floor to add the restrictive words "for the common defense" after the words "to keep and bear arms." (The British Parliament earlier had rejected an identical attempt to restrict the right to "have arms" in the English Bill of Rights of 1689.) . . .

On the other hand, it is important to remember also that the Congress not only is able to enact legislation encroaching on fundamental rights, but also is legally presumed by the courts to have acted in accordance with the Constitution. As a consequence, anyone who attempts to challenge in court any act of Congress on constitutional grounds has a correspondingly heavy burden of proof in the face of that strong legal presumption of constitutionality of all congressional acts.

Such a presumption becomes even stronger when legislators who vote for legislation eroding a constitutional right keep winning elections — courts follow the election returns. Accordingly, it is clear that the legislative process can erode and ultimately even abolish constitutional rights of all kinds. That is why it is important to realize that any restrictive or prohibitory "gun control" legislation threatens the Second Amendment and hence similarly threatens the rest of the Bill of Rights.

Therefore, those who cherish liberty under the Constitution must oppose any restrictive "gun control" legislation — whether past, present, or future — as well as any other legislation encroaching on constitutional rights. All free men should proudly support legislation repealing any and all restrictive aspects of previously enacted "gun control" legislation.

*From "Constitutional Rights in Jeopardy: The Push for 'Gun Control,'" a pamphlet published by the National Rifle Association, dated March 1990.*

## NO

*says* **WARREN E. BURGER**, *chief justice of the United States from 1969 to 1986.*

The Constitution of the United States, in its Second Amendment, guarantees a "right of the people to keep and bear arms." However, the meaning of this clause cannot be understood except by looking to the purpose, the setting and the objectives of the draftsmen. The first 10 amendments — the Bill of Rights — were not drafted at Philadelphia in 1787; that document came two years later than the Constitution. Most of the states already had bills of rights, but the Constitution might not have been ratified in 1788 if the states had not had assurances that a national Bill of Rights would soon be added. . . .

The victory at Yorktown — and the ratification of the Bill of Rights a decade later — did not change people's attitudes about a national army. They had lived for years under the notion that each state would maintain its own military establishment, and the seaboard states had their own navies as well. These people, and their fathers and grandfathers before them, remembered how monarchs had used standing armies to oppress their ancestors in Europe. Americans wanted no part of this. A state militia, like a rifle and powder horn, was as much a part of life as the automobile is today; pistols were largely for officers, aristocrats — and dueling.

Against this background, it was not surprising that the provision concerning firearms emerged in very simple terms with the significant predicate — basing the right on the *necessity* for a "well regulated militia," a state army.

In the two centuries since then — with two world wars and some lesser ones — it has become clear, sadly, that we have no choice but to maintain a standing national army while still maintaining a "militia" by way of the National Guard, which can be swiftly integrated into the national defense forces.

Americans also have a right to defend their homes, and we need not challenge that. Nor does anyone seriously question that the Constitution protects the rights of hunters to own and keep sporting guns for hunting game any more than anyone would challenge the right to own and keep fishing rods and other equipment for fishing — or to own automobiles. To "keep and bear arms" for hunting today is essentially a recreational activity and not an imperative of survival, as it was 200 years ago; "Saturday night specials" and machine guns are not recreational weapons and surely are as much in need of regulation as motor vehicles.

The Constitution does not mention automobiles or motorboats, but the right to keep and own an automobile is beyond question; equally beyond question is the power of the state to regulate the purchase or the transfer of such a vehicle and the right to license the vehicle and the driver with reasonable standards. In some places, even a bicycle must be registered, as must some household dogs.

*From "The Right to Bear Arms," Parade Magazine, Jan. 14, 1990.*

*Continued from p. 168*

solutions to the problem instead. Many come from professionals in the criminal-justice system. Fyfe, of American University, is hardly in the camp of the NRA. But he does acknowledge the validity of the gun lobby's criticism of measures like the Brady bill's waiting period — a "downstream" supply-side solution to gun violence — for punishing gun dealers because some of their customers commit crimes.

Fyfe proposes instead a demand-side solution to gun violence that he says has not as yet found support among lawmakers — a federal law that would make it a federal felony to commit a state crime while armed with a gun brought under any circumstances across state lines. The 1968 Gun Control Act provides the framework for such a law; under it, handguns may not be sold to out-of-state residents, and all firearms must bear serial numbers, which can be used to determine the place of original sale.

But Fyfe wants a new law with tough penalties and tough enforcement. "So if you stick up a store in the Bronx [in New York City] with a gun that was bought in Georgia, the fact that you were in possession of the gun that was illegally transported across state lines would mean the federal government, under its authority to control interstate commerce, could charge you with a felony and send you to Leavenworth or Atlanta, rather than Riker's Island [in New York City]." The prospect of serving time in a federal penitentiary rather than a local prison, Fyfe maintains, would act as a meaningful deterrent in the eyes of potential criminals.[21]

While experts in various fields debate the merits of alternative ways to curtail gun violence in the United States, the focus in Washington remains the "downstream" restriction of public access to handguns as reflected in the Brady bill. Although the measure failed to survive the legislative process long enough to be voted on by either chamber last year, it appears likely that Congress will consider the seven-day waiting period for handgun purchases this year. House Speaker Foley, who was criticized for obstructing the Brady bill's consideration by the full House in 1990, has assured the measure's supporters that he "would not in any way be a barrier to its consideration early in the first session of the 102nd Congress," which convened in January. If the Judiciary Committee reports the Brady bill, Foley promised, "you will be surprised to see how quickly it is scheduled" for a floor vote.[22] A companion measure to the House version of the Brady bill has been introduced in the Senate by Howard M. Metzenbaum, D-Ohio.

Judging from public opinion polls, the Brady bill should receive congressional passage by a wide margin. Recent surveys show growing support for some types of gun control, including a ban on semiautomatic weapons, registration of handguns and a requirement that anyone carrying a gun must have a license. Nearly everyone appears to favor the Brady bill. According to a Gallup Poll conducted last September, 95 percent of Americans support the seven-day waiting period before a handgun can be purchased, up from 91 percent in 1988.[23]

Given the degree of public support for this approach to gun regulation, it may seem surprising that Speaker Foley, a firm opponent of gun control in the past, predicts the Brady bill will face rough sailing in Congress. "I think the problems the Brady bill will face, if it faces any, is not that it won't be scheduled . . . but whether the people who support it have the support in the House to pass it."[24] Despite the recent turmoil in its leadership, the National Rifle Association may still live up to its reputation as the most powerful lobby in Washington.

# NOTES

[1] The measure, HR 7, was introduced Jan. 3 by Rep. Edward F. Feighan, D-Ohio. A companion bill, S 257, was introduced Jan. 23 by Sen. Howard M. Metzenbaum, D-Ohio.

[2] In 1989, the latest year for which figures are available, 62 percent of all murders were committed with firearms, and handguns were the weapons used in 48 percent of all murders. See U.S. Department of Justice, Federal Bureau of Investigation, *Crime in the United States*, Aug. 5, 1990, p. 11.

[3] The National Rifle Association of America, *1989 Annual Report*, 1989.

[4] The poll was conducted Sept. 10-11, 1990.

[5] The poll was conducted March 23-29, 1989.

[6] John D. Aquilino, a leading NRA dissident and editor of *The Insider Gun News*, made this reference in the September-October 1990 issue of the newsletter.

[7] U.S. Department of Justice, Bureau of Justice Statistics, *Handgun Crime Victims*, July 1990, p. 1.

[8] Bureau of Justice Statistics, *op. cit.*, p. 1.

[9] *Ibid.*

[10] See "Murder on Main Street," *Business Week*, Jan. 14, 1991, p. 42.

[11] See Gabriel Escobar, "Washington Area's 703 Homicides in 1990 Set a Record," *The Washington Post*, Jan. 2, 1991, p. A1.

[12] See Donatella Lorch, "Record Year for Killings Jolts Officials in New York," *The New York Times*, Dec. 31, 1990, p. B1.

[13] "Homicide among Young Black Males — United States, 1978-1987," *Morbidity and Mortality Weekly Report*, Centers for Disease Control, Dec. 7, 1990, pp. 869-888.

[14] Jack Nelson, "Activist Secretary of Health Sets His Sights on Weapons," *Los Angeles Times*, May 9, 1990.

[15] U.S. Department of Justice, Bureau of Justice Statistics, *International Crime Rates*, May 1988.

[16] Lee Kennett and James LaVerne Anderson, *The Gun in America: The Origins of a National Dilemma* (1975), pp. 249, 251.

[17] John Henry Sloan, *et al.*, "Handgun Regulations, Crime, Assaults, and Homicide: A Tale of Two Cities," *The New England Journal of Medicine*, Nov. 10, 1988, pp. 1256-1262.

[18] See Bureau of Justice Statistics and Police Executive Research Forum, *Toy Guns: Involvement in Crime & Encounters with Police*, June 1990.

[19] Michael Isakoff, "Computer Check of Gun Buyers Is Sought," *The Washington Post*, March 13, 1991, p. A4.

[20] See Peter Kerr, "Legislators Are Eager to Curb New Jersey's Weapons Law," *The New York Times*, Jan. 17, 1991, p. B1.

[21] Fyfe and several other criminologists also presented their views in an oped page dedicated to the issue of gun control. See "Guns, Guns Everywhere — Strategies for Arms Control." *The New York Times*, Jan. 4, 1991, p. A27.

[22] Feb. 7, 1991, address to the National Press Club.

[23] George Gallup Jr. and Frank Newport, "Support for Gun Control at All Time High," *The Gallup Poll News Service*, Sept. 26, 1990.

[24] Feb. 7, 1991, address to the National Press Club.

*Graphics: Cover, Margaret Scott.*

# RECOMMENDED READING

individual right to bear arms and not merely a state's right to maintain an armed militia. "I want to suggest," writes Levinson, who calls himself a "card-carrying member" of the American Civil Liberties Union, "that the Amendment may be profoundly embarrassing for many who both support such [gun-control] regulation and view themselves as committed to zealous adherence to the Bill of Rights."

**Witkin, Gordon, with Gest, Ted, and Friedman, Dorian, "Cops under Fire," *U.S. News & World Report*, Dec. 3, 1990, pp. 32-44.**

As violent crimes spread among the nation's cities in the 1980s, law enforcement officers are paying a heavy price. Offenders armed with semiautomatic pistols have an edge over policemen bearing revolvers, while drug dealers' penchant for violence has made the police beat an increasingly dangerous job. In 1989, 146 police officers were killed in the line of duty, twice the number killed in 1961.

**Zimring, Franklin E., "Gun Control," *Bulletin of the New York Academy of Medicine*, June 1986, pp. 615-621.**

A noted expert on gun control who teaches at the University of California School of Law at Berkeley, Zimring reviews the statistics on gun violence and the range of state laws designed to restrict public access to firearms. Because some 35 million handguns are currently in civilian hands, he points out, even the stiffest regulatory system would have a limited impact on gun violence well into the 21st century.

## BOOKS

**Kennett, Lee, and Anderson, James La Verne, *The Gun in America: The Origins of a National Dilemma*, Greenwood Press, 1975.**

The authors trace the role of firearms in American society and conclude that "in American history the gun has been more than just present — it has been prominent. The country is uniquely 'gun-minded.' " But as the country becomes increasingly urbanized, they write, the place for guns is rapidly dwindling.

## ARTICLES

**King, Wayne, "Sarah and James Brady, Target: The Gun Lobby," *The New York Times Magazine*, Dec. 9, 1990, pp. 42-45, 75-84.**

James S. Brady, President Ronald Reagan's press secretary, was seriously wounded in March 1981 by a bullet would-be assassin John W. Hinckley Jr. had aimed at the president. Since then, Brady's wife, Sarah, has become an outspoken advocate of gun control, joined in recent years by Brady himself. A bill currently before Congress, known as the Brady bill, would impose a national, seven-day waiting period on all handgun purchases. The bill's purpose would be to prevent people like Hinckley, with a history of mental illness, and convicted felons from buying handguns. The gun lobby, notably the National Rifle Association, has prevailed upon members of Congress to block passage of the bill in the past.

**Kleck, Gary, "Policy Lessons from Recent Gun Control Research," *Law and Contemporary Problems*, winter 1986, pp. 35-62.**

Kleck, an associate professor at Florida State University's School of Criminology, opposes gun control. He questions the relationship between guns and violent actions and challenges the effectiveness of gun-control laws because they inhibit gun ownership by law-abiding citizens while doing little to disrupt the illegal market in firearms which is the source of most gun purchases by criminals.

**Levinson, Sanford, "The Embarrassing Second Amendment," *The Yale Law Journal*, December 1989, pp. 637-659.**

In this well-written essay, the author, a professor at the University of Texas Law School, argues that there is legal merit to the belief that the Second Amendment grants an

## REPORTS AND STUDIES

**U.S. Department of Justice, Bureau of Justice Statistics, *Criminal Victimization 1989*, October 1990.**

This latest report by the National Crime Survey found 19.7 million incidents of violence, not counting homicide, and personal theft in 1989. Certain types of criminal activity, such as burglary, decreased, while there was a rise in household larcenies for the period. "Males, younger persons, blacks, Hispanics, residents of central cities, and the poor tended to have higher risks of victimization than persons who did not share these characteristics."

**\_\_\_\_, *Handgun Crime Victims*, July 1990.**

Every year an estimated 639,000 Americans face an offender with a handgun, the study found. These include 9,200 people murdered with handguns and 15,000 others wounded by these easily concealed weapons. An additional 76,000 victims are injured in other ways each year by offenders armed with handguns. Urban black males are the most frequent victims of handgun violence: one in 32 black males ages 16 through 25 years is a handgun victim in the nation's cities each year.

**U.S. Department of Justice, Federal Bureau of Investigation, *Crime in the United States: Uniform Crime Reports 1989*, Aug. 5, 1990.**

The Uniform Crime Reporting Program run by the FBI since 1930 issues annual reports that provide the most complete picture of crime in the United States. The report breaks down crime statistics by types of offenses, relationships of offenders to victims, types of weapons used, regional incidence and age of offender.

# EDITORIAL RESEARCH REPORTS

## Coming soon

Space Exploration

Social Security

Canada Update

Published weekly by
Congressional Quarterly
Inc., Editorial Research
Reports analyze emerging
issues of national interest
across a broad range of
social, scientific, political
and economic fields.
Reports are bound and
indexed for permanent
reference. Subscription
information is available
through Congressional
Quarterly's Publications
Sales Department by
telephone (202) 887-8665.
Copies of past issues are
available through
Customer Service, (202)
887-8621.

ERR

MARCH 29, 1991

FOUNDED 1923

CONGRESSIONAL QUARTERLY'S

EDITORIAL RESEARCH REPORTS

# UNCERTAIN FUTURE FOR MAN IN SPACE

# UNCERTAIN FUTURE FOR MAN IN SPACE

*by Richard L. Worsnop*

EDITOR
**MARCUS D. ROSENBAUM**

MANAGING EDITOR
**SANDRA STENCEL**

ASSOCIATE EDITOR
**RICHARD L. WORSNOP**

STAFF WRITERS
**MARY H. COOPER**
**PATRICK G. MARSHALL**

PRODUCTION EDITOR
**LAURIE DE MARIS**

EDITORIAL ASSISTANT
**AMY GORTON**

RICHARD M. BOECKEL (1892-1975)
FOUNDER

PUBLISHED BY
**CONGRESSIONAL QUARTERLY INC.**

CHAIRMAN
**ANDREW BARNES**

PRESIDENT
**RICHARD R. EDMONDS**

EDITOR AND PUBLISHER
**NEIL SKENE**

EXECUTIVE EDITOR
**ROBERT W. MERRY**

© 1991 BY CONGRESSIONAL QUARTERLY INC.

EDITORIAL RESEARCH REPORTS (LIBRARY OF CONGRESS
CATALOGUE NO. 39-924; ISSN 0013-0958). Published weekly
(48 times per year, excluding March 1, May 3, August 2 and
November 1, 1991) by Congressional Quarterly Inc., 1414 22nd
Street NW, Washington, D.C. 20037. Rates are furnished
upon request. Application to mail at second-class postage
rates is pending at Washington, D.C. POSTMASTER: Send
address changes to EDITORIAL RESEARCH REPORTS, 1414
22nd Street NW, Washington, D.C. 20037.

Thirty years after President John F. Kennedy proposed that the United States land a man on the moon within a decade, the Bush administration is pressing for several new manned space projects. Chief among them is a mission to Mars by the year 2019, the 50th anniversary of the first lunar landing. In contrast to the early 1960s, however, the new space proposals are meeting with considerable resistance. Not only do many experts question whether manned missions are worth their great cost, but memories of the 1986 explosion of the space shuttle *Challenger* still cast doubt on the safety of manned space flight in general.

During its brief history, the American manned space program has performed best when working toward a clear-cut, glamorous goal. In the 1960s, that goal was to land a man on the moon and return him to Earth before the end of the decade — a deadline that was met with five months to spare.

Since then, though, the manned space program has been limited to Earth-orbital flights, mostly on space shuttles. That program suffered a crippling blow in January 1986, when the shuttle *Challenger* exploded soon after liftoff, killing the entire seven-person crew. All shuttle flights were suspended for more than two years as scientists and government officials debated whether the benefits of sending astronauts into space outweighed the risks. Then, when flights resumed in 1988, confidence in the reusable space vehicle was further eroded as the shuttles were plagued by mechanical defects.

Now the White House is attempting to breathe new life into the manned space program. "The time has come to look beyond brief encounters," President Bush declared in a speech marking the 20th anniversary of the first manned landing on the moon. "We must commit ourselves anew to a sustained program of manned exploration of the solar system — and yes — the permanent settlement of space. We must commit ourselves to a future where Americans and citizens of all nations will live and work in space." [1]

To this end, he proposed three objectives: an Earth-orbiting space station, a permanent colony on the moon and, as the program's centerpiece, a manned mission to Mars. Paraphrasing astronaut Neil Armstrong's words when he became the first man to set foot on the moon in 1969, Bush added: "We cannot take the next giant leap for mankind tomorrow unless we take a single step today."

In a commencement address nearly a year later, the president suggested a rough timetable for the Mars mission. "Thirty years ago NASA was founded and the space race began," he said. "And 30 years from now I believe man will stand on another planet. ... I believe that before Apollo celebrates the 50th anniversary of its [first] landing on the moon, the American flag should be planted on Mars." [2] However, Bush made no mention of the lunar colony, a more near-term space objective. Nor did he say anything about the cost of the Mars program, which some space analysts have placed at between $400 billion and $500 billion.

Even at that early point, the president's space initiative was running into difficulty. One source of embarrassment was a 12-man investigative panel appointed by the National Aeronautics and Space Administration (NASA) to evaluate the space station, which is to be named *Freedom*. In a preliminary report, released in March 1990, the study team said the station would require more than 2,200 hours of maintenance a year by spacewalking astronauts — vastly more time than the 130 hours originally budgeted by NASA. Spacewalking is dangerous, and it seriously cuts into time for scientific experiments. So to Sen. Al Gore, D-Tenn., chairman of the Senate Subcommittee on Science, Technology and Space, even the preliminary report was "cause for great alarm." "Very simply," he said, "the space station *Freedom* is in jeopardy." [3]

The study group's final report, issued July 20, 1990, was even more disheartening to advocates of manned space flight. It estimated that astronauts would have to spend an average of 3,276 hours a year on extravehicular maintenance, which would amount to more than five two-person missions a week. Maintenance also would be a problem while the space station was being assembled in orbit, the panel declared. It said 6,267 hours of external maintenance would be needed to make the station habitable. This, in turn, would require several round-trip shuttle flights a week, an impossible task.

Criticism of the space station capped a summer of dismal developments for NASA. In June, a major flaw had been discovered in the $1.6 billion orbiting Hubble Space Telescope. The shuttle fleet was grounded the same month because of hydrogen leaks in two of the three vehicles. (*See below.*)

This cascade of bad news led to the appointment, in September, of another blue-ribbon investigative body. Headed by Norman R. Augustine, the chairman and chief executive officer of Martin Marietta Corp., the Advisory Committee on the Future of the U.S. Space Program was directed to review the entire range of civil space activities and recommend changes in program content and organizational structure to the administrator of NASA.

NASA came under additional pressure in October, when Congress ordered it to trim $6 billion from space station outlays through fiscal 1996. The agency also was told to redesign the platform as a set of interlocking modular components. This approach would enable some testing and assembly to be done on Earth, thus reducing the number of shuttle flights required to carry the modules into space.

The Augustine panel's report, issued Dec. 17, 1990, proposed what seemed to be far-reaching changes in the nation's space activities. NASA, it charged, "is currently over-committed in terms of program obligations relative to resources available — in short, it is trying to do too much, and allowing too little margin for the unexpected." The panel called for a new focus for the agency: Instead of devoting the bulk of its resources to manned space flight, the agency should devote the "highest priority for funding" to "the space science program" [4] — that is, non-manned missions.

On the other hand, the advisory committee did not write off the manned space program, asserting that the human element is indeed crucial. "There *is* a difference between [Edmund] Hillary reaching the top of Everest and merely using a rocket to loft an instrument package to the summit," the panel said by way of analogy. "There *is* a difference between the now largely forgotten Soviet robotic moon explorer that itself returned lunar samples, and the exploits of [*Apollo 11*] astronauts Neil Armstrong, Buzz Aldrin and Mike Collins." [5]

The panel expressed support for the space station as "the next logical and essential element" of the manned space program and for a "permanent (although not necessarily continually inhabited)" moon colony as the goal after that. It even endorsed the manned Mars mission, although it recommended that the mission proceed on a go-as-you-pay basis.

"[T]he committee believes that the progress of any program with the ultimate, long-term objective of human exploration of Mars should be tailored to the availability of funding — and not to some fixed date for accomplishment," the panel said. "This is not only because we cannot exactly predict costs, or the rate of progress of the revolutionary technology that will be required, but because we must ultimately limit the risk to pioneering astronauts. Clearly, their safety is of greater concern than meeting any challenging, but in truth arbitrary, schedule." [6]

Despite its somewhat contradictory recommendations on manned space flight, the advisory committee's report has received generally favorable reaction from opponents and supporters of manned missions. "The report is not brilliant; it's just great common sense," says Daniel S. Greenberg, editor and publisher of the newsletter *Science & Government Report*. "The panel members were saying to the space establishment, 'Come on, grow up! The circus days are over!'"

John E. Pike, head of space policy for the Federation of American Scientists, also is supportive. But he is skeptical that the Augustine panel's recommendation to give science top priority in the space program will ever amount to anything. "Everybody agrees with that, but nobody knows what it means," he says. "In the real world, science's relative priority amounts to 20 percent of the overall [NASA] budget. Sometimes it's 17 percent and sometimes it's 22 percent, but, basically, one-fifth of the budget goes to science." Pike expects it will remain about the same.

## Continuing difficulties with the space shuttle

The advisory committee's conclusion that "the civil space program is overly dependent on the space shuttle for access to space" met with universal approval. While acknowledging that the shuttle "provides the flexibility and capability attendant to human presence and ... permits the recovery of costly launch vehicle hardware which would otherwise be expended," the panel noted that the vehicle "tends to be complex, with relatively limited margins; it has not realized the promised cost savings; and should it fail catastrophically, it takes with it a substantial portion of the nation's future manned launch capability and, potentially, several human lives." [7]

The panel's unflattering appraisal appeared at a time when the three-vehicle space shuttle fleet* was experiencing repeated mechanical troubles and flight delays. In 1990, the problem was fuel leaks that led to grounding of the fleet for much of the summer and to the postponement of three scheduled missions until 1991.

*The shuttles currently in service are named *Atlantis, Columbia* and *Discovery*. A fourth shuttle, *Endeavour*, is under construction and due for completion in 1992.

The jinx hovering over the manned space program carried over into 1991 as NASA personnel found cracks in the hinges of the doors of two shuttles. In both cases, the hinges were on the two doors on the shuttle's underside that are supposed to close when the external fuel tank drops away minutes after liftoff. If the doors do not form a tight seal after closing, the vehicle could be destroyed when it re-enters the Earth's atmosphere at the end of the mission. The hinge problem has cast doubt on NASA's ability to carry out the seven shuttle missions planned for this year.

But the concerns raised by the fuel leaks and defective hinges extend well beyond the 1991 flight schedule. They have underscored the fact that the space shuttle, once regarded as being at the cutting edge of high technology, is becoming obsolete. That prospect has imparted fresh urgency to the quest for a new generation of vehicles to lift manned and unmanned capsules into space.

In a 1989 report, the congressional Office of Technology Assessment noted that shuttle obsolescence is a multifaceted problem. "After sufficiently many flights, an orbiter's airframe could be so weakened by [metal] fatigue as to be unsafe," the report said. "Replaceable parts may also wear out; when they do, replacement parts may no longer be available from manufacturers. The manufacturers that built them originally may have stopped making such parts, the tooling used to build them may have been destroyed, and the skilled workers who made them may have left or retired." [8]

Such considerations led the Augustine panel to propose that the shuttle gradually be retired from service. But since the transition period is likely to last many years, it said NASA "simply must take those steps needed to enhance the shuttle's reliability, minimize wear and tear, and enhance launch schedule predictability." At the same time, the panel urged the space agency to "proceed immediately to phase out some of the burden being carried by the space shuttle to a new unmanned ... launch vehicle." [9]

NASA, however, still is thinking primarily in terms of manned flight. Under its Advanced Manned Launch System program, the agency is evaluating five different vehicle designs, all of which would be at least partially reusable. Also under consideration is the National Aero-Space Plane, a fully reusable vehicle that would take off from a runway like a conventional airplane and climb all the way to Earth orbit, powered by a single propulsion stage. For the aero-space plane to become a reality, however, scientists will have to develop designs, structural materials and propulsion systems far more advanced than those available today.

While this research goes on, NASA also has embraced one of the Augustine panel's chief proposals for manned space flight — that the orbiting space station be substantially reduced in size. NASA's plan, submitted to Congress on March 21, shortens the length of the space station from 508 to 300 feet and

# Shuttle Launches: Planned vs. Actual

**NASA rarely has launched as many space shuttle missions as it planned. This was the case even before the *Challenger* explosion. In this graph, the gray bar represents the number of missions planned for each year during the previous year, the white bar represents the number of missions planned during the course of the year, and the black bar represents the number of actual launches. In 1988, for instance, the space agency planned to launch seven shuttle missions during 1989; in 1989, that number was cut back to six; and only five shuttles actually were launched.**

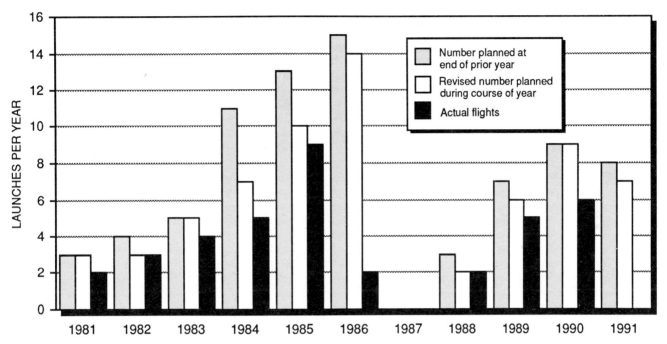

Legend:
- Number planned at end of prior year
- Revised number planned during course of year
- Actual flights

*Source: National Aeronautics and Space Administration.*

trims the number of resident astronauts from eight to four.

The range of experiments to be conducted aboard the space station will shrink as well. The main focus now is to be the effect of weightlessness on the human body and the manufacture of various materials. Before a manned flight to Mars can be attempted, more will have to be learned about how prolonged exposure to the zero-gravity environment of outer space alters an astronaut's physiological and psychological health. Also, the space station will serve as a laboratory for making exceptionally pure crystals, alloys and pharmaceuticals. By doing this, NASA would be fulfilling its mandate to encourage the commercial development of outer space. (*See story, p. 178.*)

The facility is now projected to cost $30 billion, and NASA says the new design will require substantially less spacewalking time than the one it replaced — 50 percent less time for assembly and 40 percent less for maintenance. The NASA plan calls for assembly to begin early in 1997, with completion in the year 2000.

The scaled-down space station has some critics wondering whether it will be worth the money to build it at all. For instance, the National Research Council's Space Studies Board asserted in a report that the new design "does not meet the basic research requirements" for its two chief scientific objectives. The report also said "The *monthly* cost of constructing the redesigned station would approach the *annual* total funding devoted to both NASA's life sciences and microgravity science" in the current fiscal year.[10] *

Despite such criticism, at a March 20 meeting, the National Space Council, headed by Vice President Dan Quayle,** decided to press ahead with the project. Sen. Phil Gramm, R-Texas, one of several key members of Congress who attended the meeting, said, "There's nothing in this [Space Studies Board] report that calls the design into question, in my mind."

But a spokeswoman for the Space Science Board, who asked not to be quoted directly, disagreed with Gramm's assessment. The Space Council did not rebut the Space Science Board's criticisms of the space station in detail, and the spokeswoman said the Space Council's decision may not be the last word on the

---

*Microgravity is a scientific term for weightlessness.

**In addition to the vice president, the National Space Council also includes the members of the Cabinet, the administrator of NASA, the director of central intelligence, the director of the Office of Management and Budget, the White House chief of staff and the president's science adviser.

# *Commercial Opportunities in Space*

In the early days of the U.S. civilian space program, the National Aeronautics and Space Administration had the field to itself. Today, though, the agency is under orders to help private enterprise investigate and exploit commercial applications of space.

The policy dates from the Reagan administration, which put great store by the privatization of government services. In his 1984 State of the Union address, President Ronald Reagan asserted that "space holds enormous potential for commerce today" and recommended that the federal government help private business realize that potential. Later in 1984, Congress expanded the scope of the National Aeronautics and Space Act of 1958 by directing NASA to "seek and encourage to the maximum extent possible the fullest commercial use of space."

Space commerce generally falls within one of four broad categories: satellite communications, Earth and ocean observations, materials research and processing, and space transportation and industrial services. Satellite communications, though established and mature, continues to develop through new applications and technological advances. This $3-billion-a-year industry did not even exist a quarter-century ago.

Today, the chief emphasis in space commerce is the manufacture of crystals, alloys and pharmaceuticals in the weightless environment of Earth orbit. This is one of the two principal missions of the proposed U.S. space station. The Soviet Union reportedly has produced some 2,000 pounds of crystals aboard its orbiting space stations, and similar programs are being developed by France, Germany and Japan.

Nonetheless, some U.S. experts question whether outer space is as ripe for commercial development as is often claimed. John E. Pike, head of space policy for the Federation of American Scientists, says he doesn't believe "there's enough scientific or commercial promise in microgravity materials research to warrant spending $25 billion on it. On the other hand, it's real popular with Congress, and NASA's thinking seems to be that that's what Congress wants."

Daniel S. Greenberg, editor and publisher of the newsletter *Science & Government Report*, is even more dismissive. "Manufacturing in space is one of the great hallucinations," he says. "When industry is told that there's an opportunity for manufacturing in space and asked to come on board and put down a few bucks to help pay for it, nobody shows up. Or practically nobody. Manufacturing in space requiring zero gravity or near-zero gravity is something that may have some validity, but there's certainly no great hurry to do it. For one thing, you can achieve some of that near-gravity effect on Earth. So the idea of putting up a $37 billion space station to fiddle around with a few crystals is absolutely crazy."

subject. Congress still must appropriate the funds.

Nevertheless, many scientists see the space station as crucial to the future of the manned space program. "We can and probably will go to the moon without heavy use of the station," says Dr. John M. Logsdon, director of the George Washington University Space Policy Institute. "But in order to do the life-science research required to design a Mars mission, we certainly need some form of a space station." The question, of course, is whether the scaled-down version will fill the bill.

## *Debate on whether astronauts are crucial to space program*

All the recent controversy over the space platform and mission to Mars has revived the longstanding debate over the merits of manned space flight vs. unmanned space flight. The controversy has raged since the earliest days of NASA, and it seems unlikely to be resolved any time soon to the satisfaction of all parties. Up till now, proponents of manned space flight clearly have had the best of it. Year after year, manned space programs claim about 70 percent of overall NASA spending.

Manned space flight advocates say the disproportionate allocation of resources is justified. John Logsdon offers this rationale: "The [manned] space program is a visible symbol of U.S. world leadership; its challenges and accomplishments motivate scientific and technical excellence among U.S. students; and it provides for a diverse American population a sense of common national accomplishment and shared pride in American achievement." [11] Space policy analysts H. Guyford Stever and David L. Bodde offer additional reasons: "The will to explore is fundamental to mankind," they said in a joint statement to a congressional committee, "and manned exploration lends meaning and popular support to much of the rest of the space program." [12]

Supporters of unmanned space flight find such arguments unpersuasive. "Man is extremely fragile in space — and to a large extent, kind of useless," says Daniel Greenberg. "Man can fix a stopped-up toilet on a space shuttle, but you wouldn't have to have a toilet there in the first place if a man weren't there." As for the need for public support, Greenberg is equally skeptical. "NASA has always adopted the attitude that it's on stage, that if it isn't putting on a three-ring circus with lots of jugglers and flashing lights, then its budget gets killed," he says. "The evidence for this is non-existent."

Indeed, opinion surveys taken over the past 30 years have consistently shown that popular support is less than wholehearted regardless of what the space program is doing. In a Gallup Poll conducted in May 1961, shortly before President John F. Kennedy unveiled his lunar flight proposal, only 33 percent of the respondents said they favored spending $40 billion to send a man to the moon; 58 percent were opposed.

Even at the time that Neil Armstrong became the first person to walk on the moon Americans were not supportive of going farther. According to a Gallup survey taken July 24-29, 1969 — just a few days after the *Apollo 11* mission — 53 percent of those polled said they were opposed to sending a man to Mars. Only 39 percent favored a Mars mission.

The most recent national poll on U.S. space programs, taken in July 1989 by Gallup, produced similarly inconclusive results. Forty-three percent of the respondents said the nation's space effort should focus on maintaining a "manned space program like the space shuttle," while 40 percent said it should concentrate on "unmanned missions like Voyager 2, which will send back information . . . from the planet Neptune." Asked about a possible manned mission to Mars, the respondents again were closely divided. Fifty-one percent said it was "very important" or "somewhat important" for an American to be the first to land on Mars. But 48 percent said this goal was "not very important" or "not important at all."

Commenting on the most recent findings, the Gallup Organization said: "Twenty years after America first put men on the moon, the public shows only a limited commitment to the U.S. space program. This lukewarm attitude about future space exploration is a consequence of increased awareness of domestic problems, coupled with decreased concern for the U.S.-Soviet rivalry that propelled the space race during the 1960s." [13]

Another point of disagreement is whether the tangible and intangible benefits of space exploration justify the amount of money poured into it. Defenders of the space program often point out that materials developed for space flight have found many applications in consumer products. The stick-proof plastic coating called Teflon and heat-resistant ceramic cookware are both spinoff products of space research. In addition, the miniature electronic components used in space vehicles have helped to reduce the bulk and prolong the life of such appliances as television sets, radios and tape recorders. Several producers of home and industrial paints have used space technology in their manufacturing processes to develop a longer-lasting, heat-resistant product.

In Greenberg's view, however, "it's hard to say" whether the space program yields returns commensurate with its costs. "Space clearly is very, very useful for communications, for earth-sensing, for military intelligence, for scientific exploration of the planets," he says. "For weather forecasting and weather studies,

it's immensely important. For the greenhouse studies now going on, it's absolutely indispensable. But how you work out the arithmetic of whether we're getting our money's worth out of it, I don't know."

As time goes on, the proposed mission to Mars is sure to be subjected to rigorous cost-benefit analysis. The Augustine panel dealt briefly with the issue in its report of last December. "It needs to be stated straightforwardly," the panel stated, "that such an undertaking probably must be justified largely on the basis of intangibles — the desire to explore, to learn about one's surroundings, to challenge the unknown and to find what is to be found." [14] Is that worth the enormous cost?

Thanks to previous unmanned missions to Mars, notably the successful soft landings of the Viking 1 and 2 spacecraft in 1976, scientists already have a fairly good idea of what astronauts are likely to find there. The Planetary Society, a group that promotes space exploration and the search for extraterrestrial life, drew on the data transmitted from the Viking probes in drawing up its Mars Declaration: "Mars is the world next door, the nearest planet on which human explorers could safely land. Although it is sometimes as warm as a New England October, Mars is a chilly place, so cold that some of its thin carbon dioxide atmosphere freezes out at the winter pole. There are pink skies, fields of boulders, sand dunes, vast extinct volcanoes that dwarf anything on Earth, a great canyon that would cross most of the United States, sandstorms that sometimes reach half the speed of sound, strange bright and dark markings on the surface, hundreds of ancient river valleys, mountains shaped like pyramids and many other mysteries." [15]

NASA scientists generally agree that a manned Mars mission should be preceded by several unmanned probes that would gather soil and rock samples from the planet's surface and return them to Earth. Analysis of the samples could establish whether there are toxic substances or hostile organisms on Mars that could be hazardous or lethal to human explorers. The samples should also help mission planners choose the safest and most scientifically productive site for a manned landing. High on the current priority list is an ancient Martian lake bed, where fossils of extinct life forms — if they ever existed — most likely would be found. A lake bed might also lie above subsurface permafrost, which the Mars astronauts could use as a water supply.

Obviously, a round trip to Mars would be vastly more difficult than journeying to the moon and back. A major problem is distance. While orbiting around Earth, the moon remains at a relatively fixed distance — between 221,000 and 252,000 miles — from the planet. But the distance between Mars and Earth varies greatly, principally because each planet moves in a different orbit around the sun. The closest approaches of Mars to Earth occur when the two planets are in opposition — that is, when they are so aligned that a straight line would pass from the sun through Earth and through Mars, in that order. Since Mars takes almost twice as long — 687 days — to orbit the sun as does Earth, the planets are in opposition only once every two years and seven weeks.

Moreover, because the eccentricity of the orbit of Mars is significantly greater than that of Earth's orbit, the distance between the two planets varies from one opposition to the next. The distance ranges from somewhat less than 35 million miles at the most favorable opposition to a little over 63 million miles at the least favorable. The straight-line distance between Mars and Earth at opposition gives little indication, however, of how far a space ship actually must travel from one planet to the other. Since Mars is a moving target, Mariner 6 logged 226 million miles and Mariner 7 logged 193 million miles before the two unmanned spacecraft passed by the red planet in the summer of 1969.

Before a manned spaceship is assembled in Earth orbit and sent on its way to Mars, much remains to be learned about the effects of prolonged weightlessness on the astronauts who will be aboard. To date, the longest time Americans have stayed in space is 84 days on Skylab 4 — and that was more than 17 years ago.* At present, the longevity record is held by Soviet cosmonauts Vladimir Titov and Musa Manarov, who returned to Earth on Dec. 21, 1988, after spending 366 days aboard the space station *Mir*. But a Mars mission would entail a much longer period in weightless or near-weightless conditions; the round trip plus time spent on the Martian surface could add up to as much as three years.

---

*Astronauts Gerald Carr, Edward Gibson and William Pogue stayed aboard Skylab 4 from Nov. 16, 1973, to Feb. 8, 1974.

According to Dr. Joseph Steffen, a University of Louisville biologist and an expert on weightlessness, space flight affects the human body in three important ways. "One is the effect on muscle, where we get muscle atrophy and a decrease in the [muscles'] work capacity, which is critical to things like building a space station. Then we have bone atrophy, also known as osteoporosis. Third, we have cardiovascular problems, often referred to as cardiovascular deconditioning."

All these changes occur as a result of the absence of gravity. Because strong bones aren't needed in zero-g conditions, they gradually start to lose calcium. At the same time, body height increases by about 2 inches as gravity compression is removed from the skeletal frame. Muscles, including the heart, lose strength without the demands made upon them by Earth's gravitational forces. Moreover, weightlessness causes hemoglobin in the blood — the substance that carries oxygen to the body's cells — to drop by as much as one-third. Fluids, meanwhile, migrate toward the upper body, placing stress on the heart and producing facial puffiness.

Regular exercise aboard the spacecraft can minimize deterioration of the body. Soviet cosmonaut Yuri Romanenko, who logged 326 days in space in 1987, reportedly spent two hours or more a day jogging on a treadmill, pumping a stationary bicycle and performing stretching and push-pull exercises. On returning to Earth, he told reporters that he felt better than he had after an earlier, 96-day mission. "When I returned in 1978, doctors flying with me in a helicopter suggested I try to stand up," he said. "My legs felt like lead. This time, I didn't have any trouble at all and managed to jog about a hundred yards the next day." [16]

However, exercise may be of little help in combating other adverse effects of weightlessness. Steffen

## *Manned Space Flights*

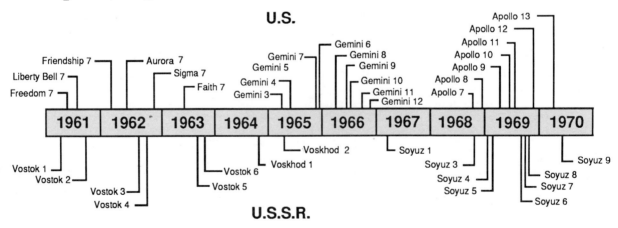

*Source: National Aeronautics and Space Administration.*

points to studies indicating that astronauts' bones do not recover all of their lost mass after return to Earth. Another problem concerns the impact of weightlessness on the body's immune system. "There have been studies on isolated immune cells that were flown on various shuttle missions, and tested in-flight for their ability to respond to a particular substance that would normally trigger an immune response," Steffen says. "And the cells were unable to do that. They didn't respond very well at all."

There could be psychological problems, too. Experience has shown that the cramped quarters and enforced companionship of manned space missions can produce emotional stresses that may impair the performance of essential tasks. Consequently, "Private personal space is a very important need for high human productivity on long-term space station missions," wrote Gordon R. Woodcock, an aerospace industry executive who has studied the problem. "Although the crew habitation areas on a space station are generous compared to early spacecraft, astronauts have reported a strong confinement effect, especially on long missions. One cannot even go outside to be alone; EVA [extravehicular activity] is always conducted using a buddy system and with continuous communications with other crew members."[17]

Astronauts on long missions also are vulnerable to boredom. To counteract the feeling, Woodcock wrote, astronauts have recommended that "some form of entertainment, e.g., TV, audio, or electronic text display for reading, be provided." Crew members on long-duration flights also have remarked on the desirability of windows, because "watching the Earth 'go by' out the window was one of their favorite forms of entertainment."[18]

## Assessing the likelihood of another space disaster

Although NASA officials are concerned about the health consequences of weightlessness, their overriding worry is the manned space program's worst-case scenario: another *Challenger*-type disaster. Because the shuttle fleet still is scheduled to make dozens of flights over the next decade or so, some experts have concluded that a major accident is virtually inevitable.

In their 1989 congressional testimony, space policy analysts Guyford Stever and David Bodde observed that existing shuttles are bound to "wear out, as each launch stresses the orbiter near its design limits." But the risk of major accident would remain high even if wear and tear were not a factor, they said. "Even if the probability of avoided accident for each flight were 99 percent, the cumulative likelihood of disabling an orbiter after six years at a flight rate of 12 per year would be over 50 percent. Thus, we must count on exceedingly good fortune, or plan to keep [shuttle] production lines openable over the next 15 to 20 years, or develop an alternate transportation system for use beyond the turn of the century."[19]

Stever and Bodde's remarks attracted little attention at the time. But a similar analysis issued later in 1989 by the Office of Technology Assessment (OTA) provoked extensive comment in the national news media. "Whatever the [shuttle] launch rate, the fleet will be subject to a growing cumulative risk of attrition," OTA reported. "...If [shuttle] reliability is and remains 98 percent, there would be a 50 percent chance of losing an orbiter on the next 34 flights, a 72 percent chance of losing an orbiter before the first space station assembly

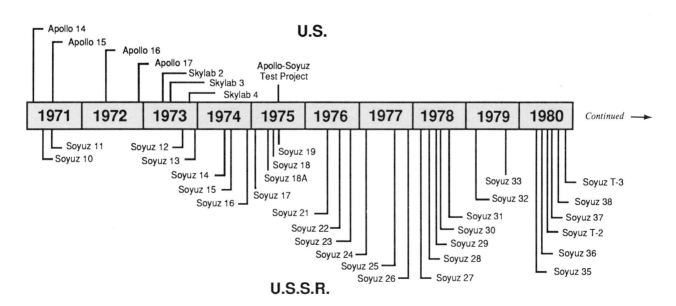

flight (if scheduled for flight 92), and an 88 percent chance of losing an orbiter before space station assembly is completed 42 flights later." [20]

Scaling down of the space station design will reduce the number of shuttle flights needed to carry structural components into orbit. Nonetheless, the basic thrust of OTA's message remains the same: "If the United States wishes to send people into space on a routine basis, the nation will have to come to grips with the risks of human space flight. In particular, it will have to accept the likelihood that loss of life will occur. If such risks are perceived to be too high, the nation may decide to reduce its emphasis on placing humans in space." [21]

The impact of a major shuttle mishap would be especially severe if it occurred during the period when the space station is being assembled in orbit. At the very least, resupply and servicing flights by the surviving shuttles would have to be rescheduled. But if a shuttle were lost while carrying a critical space station component in its cargo hold, the result could be long delays in completing the station — or even a decision to abandon it.

And after the space station is operational, the threat of accident would still linger, though the most likely sources of trouble would be different. Orbital debris from previous space activities conceivably could puncture one of the station's crew modules, necessitating the evacuation and return to Earth of everyone aboard. Or there could be a major medical emergency or equipment breakdown that would require evacuation. Or the station could run out of vital provisions because of the postponement or failure of shuttle resupply flights.

At present, NASA lacks the capability to deal with such a contingency. However, the agency is studying various designs for vehicles to be used on escape and rescue missions. One possibility is a simple capsule with a protective heat shield, much like the re-entry vehicles used in the Apollo moon program. Because the technology is familiar, development costs would be relatively low. In addition, the fact that capsules need little or no piloting would be a plus if an experienced pilot were not among the evacuees.

Another emergency return vehicle under consideration is a small, aerodynamically stable glider whose shape would provide lift. It would be able to land either by parachute or at low speed on a conventional runway. A glider could reach a broader range of landing sites than a capsule and also would provide a more comfortable ride. However, projected development costs are 20 to 50 percent greater than for a capsule.

## United States and Soviet Union: Space rivals, potential partners

Just as space technology has evolved over the years, so has the nature of the U.S.-Soviet "space race." At the dawn of the space age, signaled by the launching in October 1957 of the unmanned capsule *Sputnik*, outer space was seen as a vast new arena of Cold War conflict between the Soviet Union and the United States. Indeed, the immediate post-*Sputnik* period was a time of national chagrin for the United States as it

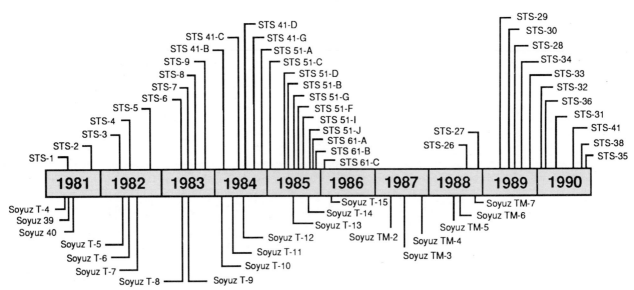

**U.S.**

**U.S.S.R.**

*Data for Soviet shuttle missions 1989-1990 not available.*

# *Europeans, Other Nations Send Satellites into Orbit*

For years, the United States and the Soviet Union were the world's only spacefaring nations. They still are the only nations operating manned space programs. But several other countries have established an independent presence in space over the past two decades, lured by the promise of scientific and commercial gain.

The European Space Agency (ESA), formed in 1973 by the member nations of the European Community, developed the *Ariane* family of vehicles as the centerpiece of its program. *Ariane IV*, the program's workhorse at present, has four different possible configurations and can lift a payload of from 2 to 4.5 tons into geostationary orbit roughly 22,300 miles above Earth at the equator — a height and latitude that make a satellite hover in a fixed position in the sky. *Ariane V*, due to become operational in 1995, will be able to place 6.8 tons into geostationary orbit or 21 tons into low Earth orbit. Arianespace, a commercial offshoot of ESA, already has

captured 50 percent of the global commercial launch market, and it intends to maintain or increase its market share in coming years.

ESA also is working on *Hermes*, a manned space vehicle. The first *Hermes* flight, to be launched on an *Ariane V*, is scheduled for 1998. *Hermes* is designed to carry a crew of three and a payload of up to 1.5 tons.

Japan, too, is well on the way to becoming a major player in space. Starting in the early 1970s, the Japanese developed a group of launchers by using U.S. technology obtained under license. As part of the licensing deal, the United States was able to restrict Japan's ability to launch satellites for third parties. Now, however, Japan is building a new launch vehicle, the *H-II*, with technology of domestic origin. Capable of placing 2 tons in geostationary orbit or 10 tons in low Earth orbit, *H-II* will provide Japan with unfettered access to space for the first time.

Although China has had launch ca-

pability since the early 1970s, it achieved the status of serious competitor in space only with the development in recent years of the *Long March* family of vehicles. China has been aggressively marketing its *Long March* launch services worldwide since 1985. Experience to date has shown the spacecraft to be reliable.

Several other nations are only bit players in space today, but they may strive for more prominent roles in the future. India has been launching small satellites since 1980, for instance, and is pressing ahead with a larger launch vehicle despite some setbacks. Israel launched its first test satellite in 1988, and Brazil and Pakistan also are developing launch vehicles. In addition, astronauts from 17 countries have flown on U.S.- or Soviet-manned space missions.†

† *The countries are Afghanistan, Bulgaria, Canada, Cuba, Czechoslovakia, France, Germany, Hungary, India, Mexico, Mongolia, the Netherlands, Poland, Romania, Saudi Arabia, Syria and Vietnam. Astronaut Mamoru Mark Mohri of Japan is scheduled to become his country's first space traveler on a U.S. shuttle flight late this year.*

scrambled to overcome the Soviets' early lead.

Progress was frustratingly slow at first, with each modest U.S. space achievement soon topped by a more impressive Soviet feat. But then, in a message to Congress on May 25, 1961, President Kennedy urged the United States to embark on "a great new American enterprise." He called on the nation to achieve nothing less than the goal, "before this decade is out, of landing a man on the moon and returning him safely to the Earth." Kennedy's message came at a time when public attention was riveted on outer space. Soviet Maj. Yuri Gagarin had become the first person in space, orbiting around the Earth on April 12, 1961; three weeks later, on May 5, Cmdr. Alan B. Shepard rode a Project Mercury capsule, *Freedom 7*, up 115 miles into space in a suborbital flight from Cape Canaveral, landing safely some 300 miles from the starting point.

Kennedy said that "no single space project [in the 1960s] will be more impressive to mankind, or more important for the long-range exploration of space" than getting to the moon, but he warned that "none will be so difficult or expensive to accomplish." He asked Congress and the American people to consider the matter carefully. In response, Congress approved almost in its entirety an administration request for

appropriation of $1.8 billion for NASA in fiscal 1962.[22] There was little opposition, even though the amount was nearly twice as large as the space agency's appropriation for fiscal 1961.

In a pattern that was to be repeated later, support for the manned space program began to erode as it lost its novelty. One of the most acerbic early critics was former President Dwight D. Eisenhower, who complained in a March 1963 letter to House Minority Leader Charles A. Halleck, R-Ind., that the entire space program was "downright spongy." Eisenhower said he had never believed that "a spectacular dash to the moon, vastly deepening our debt, is worth the added tax burden it will eventually impose."

Despite such complaints, the American manned space program went briskly forward, intent on meeting Kennedy's deadline for a moon landing. By 1963, when the two-astronaut Gemini missions began, the United States had achieved rough parity with the Soviet Union in manned space flight. Ten Gemini capsules were launched over the next two years to perfect the orbital rendezvous and docking techniques that would later be used to retrieve men from the moon and return them to Earth. During the same period, by contrast, the Soviet Union launched only two piloted spacecraft.

Both the U.S. and Soviet manned space programs suffered serious setbacks in 1967. On Jan. 27 of that year, three Apollo astronauts perished in a fire at Cape Kennedy during a pre-launch test of the first Apollo mission. Three months later, on April 24, the pilot of the first Soviet *Soyuz* capsule was killed when the spacecraft's parachute lines became entangled during descent, causing it to crash to Earth. The two countries reacted to their respective tragedies by closing down their manned space programs for a year and a half.

In the ensuing years the United States surged ahead. By July 20, 1969, the day of the *Apollo 11* moon landing, the United States had taken a commanding lead in manned space flight. Though additional Apollo flights were to take place, NASA officials began to cast about for a new goal to maintain the agency's momentum. They did not have to look far. In press interviews at Cape Kennedy when *Apollo 11* was launched, Vice President Spiro T. Agnew said it was his "individual feeling that we should articulate a simple, ambitious, optimistic goal of a manned flight to Mars by the end of this century." Two months later, a space task force headed by Agnew made the same recommendation.

President Richard M. Nixon had other ideas. "By no means should we allow our space program to stagnate," he said in a policy statement on March 7, 1970. "But with the entire future and the entire universe before us, we should not try to do everything at once. Our approach to space must continue to be bold — but it must also be balanced." Alluding to Agnew's proposal, the president said only that "we will eventually send men to explore the planet Mars."

There matters stood until Jan. 5, 1972, when Nixon declared that the United States "should proceed at once" with the development of a reusable space shuttle that would "take the astronomical costs out of astronautics." The shuttle and Skylab, an experimental space laboratory that had been authorized earlier, were thus left as the nation's only manned space programs for the post-Apollo era.

That gave the Soviet Union an opportunity to close the manned-flight gap with the United States, and it proceeded to do just that. *Salyut 1*, the first space station, was placed in orbit in 1971. *Salyut 6*, a second-generation model, followed in 1977. Because *Salyut 6* had two docking ports, the Soviets were able to resupply the station with fuel, food, water and air, permitting it to continue operating for six years. By 1980, the Soviets had logged more than twice as many hours of manned space flight as the United States.

Since then, the Soviet Union has continued to pad its lead. *Salyut 7*, launched in 1982, was essentially a clone of its predecessor. *Mir*, the third-generation Soviet space station where the current record for longest manned space flight was set, has been in orbit since 1986.

With the passage of years, the intense space rivalry between the superpowers has mellowed. There was an indication of change as far back as 1975. Then, in the Apollo-Soyuz Test Project, U.S. astronauts docked with Soviet cosmonauts for two days of joint experimentation in Earth orbit. The United States thereupon suspended all manned space activities until the first shuttle flight in 1981.

In recent years, with the warming of relations between the superpowers, there has been additional U.S.-Soviet cooperation in space. Joseph Steffen, the University of Louisville biologist, notes that the Soviets "are going to do some experiments on one of our next shuttle flights. They are also sharing a lot more of their human weightlessness data [from long-duration flights], which is something they wouldn't do before because of national security reasons. It's a much better atmosphere now."

Meanwhile, though, the Soviet space program has been plagued by funding and technological problems. In 1989, for example, *Mir* was evacuated for four months as an economy measure. The move came at a time of rising complaints about the cost and effectiveness of Soviet space exploration. One of the leading critics has been Boris N. Yeltsin, the president of the Russian Republic, who contends the money spent on space should go to production of consumer goods instead. "Mars, Venus, the stars will be there 10 years from [now], just as they are today," he said.[23]

The Soviet space program suffered a more serious setback when it lost *Phobos 1* and *Phobos 2*, twin spacecraft that were launched in 1988 for a rendezvous with the Martian moon of that name. Embarrassing enough in their own right, the Phobos failures were the latest in a long string of botched Soviet interplanetary probes. But Soviet space officials still insist that there has been no change in plans for an unmanned landing on Mars in 1994 and a project to be launched in 1998 to bring back samples of Martian soil.

As the two superpowers lay plans for their respective Mars missions, there is increasing speculation that they may ultimately decide to pool their efforts. With their greater experience in long-duration space flight, the Soviets presumably have gathered much of the data about the effects of weightlessness that the U.S. space station is meant to gather. For its part, the United States has accomplished much more in the way of planetary exploration than the Soviet Union has.

The superpowers already have begun to collaborate on a limited basis. Under a 1987 agreement, they established a joint working group in space biology and medicine. At the group's annual meetings, says Frank M. Sulzman, chief of NASA's life support branch, "the Soviets give us a presentation on the significant medical results of their long-duration flights that have occurred during the preceding year. We reciprocate with the significant medical events that we have encountered in the shuttle flights, which

*Continued on p. 186*

# AT ISSUE

*Should the United States support manned space exploration?*

**YES** *writes* **Rep. ROBERT A. ROE**, *D-N.J., former chairman of the House Committee on Science, Space and Technology.*

Exploration is a search for knowledge. There is a legitimate question whether men or machines should be used for exploration. Clearly in cases of our distant space science probes to Jupiter, Venus, Uranus and Neptune, we had no choice but to use unmanned mechanisms.

In the particular cases where either manned or unmanned vehicles could be utilized, we must base our decision on whether we are only searching for data or whether our objective is also to gain experience for an expanded mission.

If we had been searching only for samples of moon dust or had been interested only in photographs of the moon's geographical features, then an unmanned vehicle would have substituted well for the whole Apollo program. But our goals were political and developmental as well as exploratory.

We were not racing against the Russians to scoop moon rocks but rather to prove the supremacy of our science and technology over theirs. That supremacy was defined by solving the myriad scientific and technological challenges of keeping a human being alive and safe in going to the moon and back.

The inevitable tide of progress is moving contemporary civilization into space. All of the world's major industrial nations are headed there.

If America is lulled into believing that unmanned space exploration missions are a reasonable and budget-conscious substitute for a manned space station, a space transportation system and an eventual moon base, then we are effectively cutting ourselves off from the primary frontier of the 21st century.

Our space science program was not intended to replace our manned space program. It was designed to be a companion to manned space efforts. Together the two form the exploration and development balance needed for continuous space expansion.

With only unmanned missions, we will be space information gatherers in an age of space infrastructure builders. We will be space explorers in an age of space settlers.

After 30 years of spectacular space achievements, some of them surely in space science, we are poised at a crossroads. We can continue to lead and let others follow in our footsteps or we can step aside and watch them build along the path we have blazed.

*From* American Legion Magazine, *July 1990.*

**NO** *writes* **Rep. BILL GREEN**, *R-N.Y., ranking Republican member of the House Appropriations Subcommittee in charge of funding for the National Aeronautics and Space Administration (NASA).*

In August [1989], Voyager II skirted Neptune and transmitted to Earth a treasure of stunning pictures and scientific information. . . . [A]nother U.S. space probe . . . [later went] to Venus to learn why a body so near and similar in size to Earth suffers 900 degree temperatures and a veil of sulfur rain. No one [was] aboard either spacecraft; none [was] needed.

During the Apollo "moon shots" two decades ago, the idea of a man on the moon was exciting. Today such "go-man-go" gestures as placing men on the moon and Mars should be set aside for more valuable and less costly earth and planetary sciences.

We can't afford great manned missions; there is a huge federal budget deficit. NASA's planned manned space station will cost at least $30 billion. Manned missions to the moon and Mars would raise NASA's budget to more than that each year.

Further, when NASA pushes manned space operations, more valuable scientific work tends to take a back door. Apollo is recognized now as a costly jaunt. Subsequently, the shuttle ate up most of the agency budget. By contrast, since 1977, the cheap, unmanned *Voyager II* spacecraft has been teaching us about our solar system with flybys of Jupiter, Saturn, Uranus and Neptune.

Closer to home, most scientific work planned for the manned station could be done by a smaller, less expensive platform merely visited by man while experiments are measured or altered.

NASA has funding for small, specialized missions to study the complex chemistry of the stratosphere and mesosphere. The House Appropriations subcommittee on which I serve will propose a Tropical Rain Measuring Mission to study tropical zone precipitation, an important element in understanding weather systems and evaluating the greenhouse effect. A major earth science satellite is slated for launch in 1997.

Such missions depend on the support of Congress and the White House, and restraint on manned projects. Currently, Congress is split between science and "go-man-go." It is hoped that the number of man-in-space boosters can be restrained until needed earth and space science projects are secured.

*From* American Legion Magazine, *July 1990.*

*Continued from p. 184*

are more numerous and of shorter duration but are still very significant for a number of reasons — and are of interest to the Soviets."

But the sharing of experiences and data goes well beyond that. Sulzman notes that NASA flight surgeons and researchers are now allowed to take part in the medical exams of cosmonauts who have just returned from long-duration flights. "We have some medical diagnostic equipment in the Soviet Union at Star City, the training center for the cosmonauts, that we use," Sulzman says. "It's the same kind of gear that we use in the United States. So now we can do better at interpreting the results of their long-duration flights."

In Sulzman's opinion, "the experience that we're gaining with the Soviets will really save us time by pointing us in the direction of the most critical areas [of research on the effects of weightlessness] and perhaps indicate what would ameliorate these problems."

One area of research that remains relatively unexplored is the effect of weightlessness on women. "The longest a Soviet woman has ever flown is about 10 days," Sulzman says, "whereas we expect that U.S. space station crews will be of both sexes."

More extensive U.S.-Soviet collaboration in space should be forthcoming in the near future. At a meeting in Washington in November 1988, American and Soviet space scientists announced they had agreed to cooperate in a planned exploration of Mars. The Soviet scientists offered to carry American scientific instruments on future flights to Mars, while the U.S. side volunteered to provide mapping information to aid in the selection of a landing site for the Soviet Mars mission due to be launched in 1994.

John Pike of the Federation of American Scientists views a collaborative Mars venture as almost inevitable. "It's difficult for me to imagine how we're going to go to Mars without the Russians," he says. "Mars is going to be too expensive for us to pay for by ourselves." In this connection, he observes that "All the cheap and easy space projects have been done. Increasingly, we're dealing with space projects that are just too big for any one country."

John Logsdon of George Washington University also supports the idea of a collaborative Mars mission. But he feels that the United States must first demonstrate its reliability as a partner by honoring its commitment to the space station, which was conceived as a joint project with several other countries. "We've already got collaboration on the space station," he says. "That's a more difficult issue right now than going to Mars with the Soviet Union. We're not going anywhere with anybody unless we can salvage this."

# NOTES

[1] Remarks at Air and Space Museum, Washington, D.C., July 20, 1989.

[2] Speech at Texas A&I University, Kingsville, Texas, May 11, 1990.

[3] Remarks at hearing of Senate Subcommittee on Science, Technology and Space, March 28, 1990.

[4] Advisory Committee on the Future of the U.S. Space Program, *Report of the Advisory Committee on the Future of the U.S. Space Program*, December 1990, pp. 2, 5.

[5] *Ibid.*, p. 6.

[6] *Ibid.*, p. 24.

[7] *Ibid.*, pp. 2-3.

[8] Office of Technology Assessment, *Round Trip to Orbit: Human Spaceflight Alternatives*, August 1989, p. 40.

[9] Advisory Committee, *op. cit.*, p. 7.

[10] Space Science Board, National Research Council, *Space Science Board Position on Proposed Redesign of Space Station Freedom*, March 15, 1991.

[11] John M. Logsdon, "A Sustainable Rationale for Manned Space Flight," *Space Policy*, Vol. 5, 1989, pp. 3-6.

[12] Prepared statement before the Subcommittee on Space Science and Applications, House Committee on Science, Space and Technology, Feb. 8, 1989. Stever is chairman of the space policy committee of the National Academy of Sciences and National Academy of Engineering; Bodde is executive director of the National Research Council's commission on engineering and technical systems.

[13] George Gallup Jr., *The Gallup Poll: Public Opinion 1989*, 1990, p. 172.

[14] Advisory Committee, *op. cit.*, p. 6.

[15] Quoted by Bruce C. Murray, *Journey Into Space: Three Decades of Space Exploration*, 1989, p. 340. Murray was one of the declaration's co-authors.

[16] Quoted in *U.S. News & World Report*, May 16, 1988.

[17] Gordon R. Woodcock, *Space Stations and Platforms* (1986), p. 130.

[18] *Ibid.*, pp. 127, 131.

[19] Prepared statement before the Subcommittee on Space Science and Applications, House Committee on Science, Space and Technology, Feb. 8, 1989.

[20] Office of Technology Assessment, *op. cit.*, p. 25.

[21] *Ibid.*, p. 4.

[22] Both the Senate and the House authorized appropriation of the full amount on July 21, 1961, the day Capt. Virgil I. Grissom duplicated Shepard's feat.

[23] Quoted in the *Los Angeles Times*, April 12, 1989.

*Graphics: Cover, Margaret Scott; pp. 177, 180-182, Jack Auldridge.*

# RECOMMENDED READING

## BOOKS

**Bond, Peter R.,** *Heroes in Space — From Gagarin to Challenger,* **Basil Blackwell Ltd., 1987.**

A British free-lance writer, Bond gives the story of U.S. and Soviet space exploration a human-interest spin by focusing on the feelings as well as the exploits of individual astronauts and cosmonauts.

**Connors, Mary M., Harrison, Albert A., and Akins, Faren R.,** *Living Aloft: Human Requirements for Extended Spaceflight,* **National Aeronautics and Space Administration, 1985.**

The three authors provide an exhaustive and provocative summary of current knowledge about the effects of prolonged weightlessness on the human body. Among their more unexpected conclusions is that older persons may be better adapted to long-duration space flight than are the young, athletic astronauts who have been selected in the past.

**Murray, Bruce C.,** *Journey Into Space,* **W. W. Norton & Co., 1989.**

Murray, a planetary scientist at California Institute of Technology in Pasadena, Calif., caps this review of the first three decades of space exploration with a proposal that the United States and the Soviet Union pool their resources for a manned mission to Mars. "U.S. and Soviet energies must be fused into peaceful *cooperative* accomplishments," he writes. "The second golden age of planetary exploration would not repeat the American domination of the Apollo era. But there could be a magnificent new era of international discovery and adventure, fueled by enlightened U.S.-Soviet collaboration."

**Trento, Joseph J.,** *Prescription for Disaster,* **Crown Publishers Inc., 1987.**

With considerable bitterness, Trento recounts the events leading to the decision to build the space shuttle and to the *Challenger* disaster of 1986. He reserves some of his harshest comments for former NASA Administrator Thomas C. Fletcher. "He is the same man who made the decision to build the shuttle on the cheap, using solid rockets," writes Trento.

**Woodcock, Gordon R.,** *Space Stations and Platforms,* **Orbit Book Co., 1986.**

Although this book was published five years ago, the current controversy over the U.S. space station has made it timely again. Woodcock, an aerospace industry executive, covers such questions as space station design and operations, cost considerations and the effects of zero-gravity conditions on crew members.

## REPORTS AND STUDIES

**Advisory Committee on the Future of the U.S. Space Program,** *Report of the Advisory Committee on the Future of the U.S. Space Program,* **December 1990.**

On first reading, the committee's report seems to call for a bold reordering of U.S. space priorities. But on reflection or a second reading, its recommendations do not seem quite so sweeping as all that. Still, it is a thoughtful evaluation of the nation's space program and an especially impressive achievement, considering that it was published barely three months after the committee was appointed.

**U.S. Congress, Office of Technology Assessment,** *Round Trip to Orbit: Human Spaceflight Alternatives — Special Report,* **August 1989.**

The highlight of this report is its assessment of the high chances for another space shuttle accident like the one that destroyed *Challenger* and its crew in January 1986. Space transportation options in the post-shuttle era also are evaluated.

**U.S. House Subcommittee on Space Science and Applications, Committee on Science, Space and Technology,** *Review of Major Space Program Studies and Recommendations Made to Bush Transition Team* **(published proceedings of hearings held Feb. 8 and 9, 1989).**

Expert witnesses present their ideas about what the space priorities of the newly installed Bush administration should be.

**U.S. Senate Subcommittee on Science, Technology and Space, Committee on Commerce, Science and Transportation,** *Comparative Assessment of U.S. Space Program* **(published proceedings of hearing held July 19, 1989).**

Held on the eve of the 20th anniversary of the historic *Apollo 11* moon landing, this hearing provides a comprehensive look at the current state of U.S. space exploration as well as a survey of previous developments.

## ARTICLES

**"U.S. Planetary Launch Surge," a special section of *Aviation Week & Space Technology,* Oct. 9, 1989.**

In a special section comprising 12 articles by various authors, *Aviation Week* surveys U.S. plans to send a manned mission to Mars and unmanned missions to Venus, Mars, Jupiter and Saturn, as well as to the realm of outer space that lies beyond the solar system.

EDITORIAL RESEARCH REPORTS

## Coming soon

Published weekly by
Congressional Quarterly
Inc., Editorial Research
Reports analyze emerging
issues of national interest
across a broad range of
social, scientific, political
and economic fields.
Reports are bound and
indexed for permanent
reference. Subscription
information is available
through Congressional
Quarterly's Publications
Sales Department by
telephone (202) 887-8665.
Copies of past issues are
available through
Customer Service, (202)
887-8621.

CONGRESSIONAL QUARTERLY'S

EDITORIAL RESEARCH REPORTS ®

ERR

APRIL 5, 1991

# SOCIAL SECURITY: THE SEARCH FOR FAIRNESS

## EDITORIAL RESEARCH REPORTS

**EDITOR**
**MARCUS D. ROSENBAUM**

**MANAGING EDITOR**
**SANDRA STENCEL**

**ASSOCIATE EDITOR**
**RICHARD L. WORSNOP**

**STAFF WRITERS**
**MARY H. COOPER**
**PATRICK G. MARSHALL**

**PRODUCTION EDITOR**
**LAURIE DE MARIS**

**EDITORIAL ASSISTANT**
**AMY GORTON**

**RICHARD M. BOECKEL (1892-1975)**
**FOUNDER**

**PUBLISHED BY**
**CONGRESSIONAL QUARTERLY INC.**

**CHAIRMAN**
**ANDREW BARNES**

**PRESIDENT**
**RICHARD R. EDMONDS**

**EDITOR AND PUBLISHER**
**NEIL SKENE**

**EXECUTIVE EDITOR**
**ROBERT W. MERRY**

EDITORIAL RESEARCH REPORTS (LIBRARY OF CONGRESS CATALOGUE NO. 39-924; ISSN 0013-0958). Published weekly (48 times per year, excluding March 1, May 3, August 2 and November 1, 1991) by Congressional Quarterly Inc., 1414 22nd Street NW, Washington, D.C. 20037. Rates are furnished upon request. Application to mail at second-class postage rates is pending at Washington, D.C. POSTMASTER: Send address changes to EDITORIAL RESEARCH REPORTS, 1414 22nd Street NW, Washington, D.C. 20037.

© 1991 BY CONGRESSIONAL QUARTERLY INC.

# SOCIAL SECURITY: THE SEARCH FOR FAIRNESS

*by Pamela M. Terrell*

The aging of the American population and the piling up of huge federal deficits are putting new pressures on the Social Security system. Caught in the crunch, policy-makers are talking about various reform proposals. These include tinkering with the benefit formulas, shifting a greater portion of the tax burden to the rich and restructuring the system to allow workers to put their Social Security contributions into private retirement accounts. Although the approaches differ, the reform proposals have one thing in common: They are intended to redress perceived inequities in the Social Security system. But they also demonstrate how little confidence exists among policy-makers about the long-term financial and political stability of the program.

The myths about Social Security are as enduring as the realities. Americans justify their participation in the program with the fictional belief that they are underwriting their own retirements. Yet the reality is that

*Pamela M. Terrell is a free-lance writer who lives near Washington, D.C. David S. Cloud, a reporter for* Congressional Quarterly Weekly Report, *contributed to this story.*

benefits have become so costly — and recipients so unwilling to accept cuts — that Social Security's long-term solvency remains an ongoing concern to policy-makers.

The dichotomy between myth and reality is at the root of the controversies surrounding the Social Security system. Of course, everyone who wants to change the system — and even those who do not — uses the same word: fairness. What is the fairest way to collect revenues for the program? What level of reserves should the system have to ensure that obligations to current and future retirees are fairly met? What is the fairest way to distribute the benefits? But the answers to those questions — that is, what *fair* really means — depend to a great extent on one's point of view.

A decade ago, policy-makers had to rescue the system from the brink of insolvency. Now, with Social Security reserves soon to be counted in the trillions of dollars, a different problem is arising: The surplus is being spent as fast as it comes in. Funds that were supposed to be accumulating in trust funds to pay for baby boomers' retirements are being funneled into the federal government's general revenue pot and replaced with IOUs that come due in the next century. Some policy-makers say that is the wrong way to finance the government. They say fairness demands another overhaul of the system, even though it is on its strongest financial footing in decades. But any proposal to cut Social Security revenues raises concern about returning the system to insolvency.

In the broadest sense, the critique of Social Security financing comes from one of two directions. Some critics argue for a more direct relationship between paid-in contributions and benefits received. Others argue just as fervently for reforms that would lower the tax rates and distribute the benefits more on the basis of need, rather than on past contributions. Most policy-makers prefer the status quo. These various forces have wrestled before, and they will again in 1991, which is shaping up as another year of voluble debate over Social Security.

Confusing the issue is the complexity of the system. Social Security commonly refers to the old-age, survivors', and disability insurance programs, collectively known as OASDI. OASDI is financed through a 6.2 percent payroll tax on income up to a specified cutoff. An additional 1.45 percent payroll tax is levied to finance the hospital component of Medicare, the federal health insurance program for persons age 65 and older.* Employers must match worker contributions.

The programs are designed to be self-supporting and are funded through a year-to-year transfer of income between generations. Each is backed by a

*Medicare, which is now administered by the Health Care Financing Administration, is actually two programs in one. Part A, which is financed by payroll taxes, covers hospital stays. Part B, the optional portion of Medicare that helps cover doctor and other outpatient bills, is financed in part through monthly premiums deducted from the Social Security checks of beneficiaries. The rest is financed by general tax revenues.

## Payroll Tax Increases

**Congress raised Social Security taxes in 1973, 1977 and 1983. The increases affected not only tax rates but also the maximum amount of earnings subject to the tax.**

*(Historically and under current law)*

| | Maximum Taxable | Rate |
|---|---|---|
| 1937 | $ 3,000 | 1.0 |
| 1950 | 3,000 | 1.5 |
| 1955 | 4,200 | 2.0 |
| 1959 | 4,800 | 2.5 |
| 1966 | 6,600 | 4.2 |
| 1970 | 7,800 | 4.8 |
| 1974 | 13,200 | 5.85 |
| 1978 | 17,700 | 6.05 |
| 1979 | 22,900 | 6.13 |
| 1981 | 29,700 | 6.65 |
| 1982 | 32,400 | 6.70 |
| 1984 | 37,800 | 6.70 † |
| 1985 | 39,600 | 7.05 |
| 1986 | 42,000 | 7.15 |
| 1987 | 43,800 | 7.15 |
| 1988 | 45,000 | 7.51 |
| 1989 | 48,000 | 7.51 |
| 1990 | 51,300 | 7.65 |
| 1991 | 53,400 | 7.65 |

† *Effective rate.*

*Source: House Ways and Means Committee.*

reserve trust fund to cover deficits in fund-short years. Congress accelerated a series of automatic payroll tax increases in 1983 to build surpluses in the reserves that are intended to ensure the solvency of the system well into the retirement of the baby-boom generation in the 21st century. The 1983 overhaul was a watershed because it promised to transform Social Security gradually from a "pay-as-you-go" system to a partially pre-funded system.

Social Security is the largest federal program. More than 95 percent of the work force is subject to the Social Security and Medicare payroll taxes, and one of every seven people in the country — about 40 million Americans — receives a check from the Social Security Administration (SSA). Receipts from payroll taxes represent 33 percent of all federal revenues, and the programs' expenditures constitute 28 percent of all federal spending.

Given how immense and complex the system is, it is surprising that disputes about equitable treatment among Social Security's various constituencies do not arise more frequently. The program is extremely popular, drawing strength from the emotional, as well as financial, investment ordinary Americans have made in it. But that investment is also grist for critics. The

Social Security Administration estimated that in 1990 about 74 percent of the taxpayers would pay more in payroll taxes — if employers' contributions are included — than they pay in income taxes.

Critics say that payroll taxes are unfair to lower-income workers for two reasons. First, they apply at a fixed rate to all earned income up to a stipulated ceiling, at which point they are no longer levied, so the higher one's income, the smaller the percentage that is paid in Social Security taxes.* Second, Social Security taxes do not apply at all to unearned income such as interest, dividends and capital gains, which are received chiefly by wealthier taxpayers.

High earners, on the other hand, complain that they don't get a fair return on their contributions to the system because the benefit formulas favor lower-income wage earners. (*See story, p. 193.*) Working women complain that they are unfairly treated by benefit formulas that punish them for years spent at home taking care of children and elderly parents. Blacks say they don't get their fair share because, on average, they begin to work earlier, pay into the system longer, then die younger. And businesses blame increasing payroll taxes for raising the cost of labor.

The concerns of these groups are reflected in various legislative proposals recently introduced or currently being drafted on Capitol Hill. Sen. Daniel Patrick Moynihan, D-N.Y., has reintroduced his plan of a year ago to cut Social Security payroll taxes and increase the amount of income subject to the tax. One of Moynihan's goals is to highlight the fact that Congress and the administration have failed to eliminate the deficit and thus are forced to spend the surplus that resulted from the 1983 overhaul in order to pay the country's bills. He is concerned about the increasing reliance on regressive taxes, of which the payroll tax is a leading example, to finance general government expenses. And he would prefer to eliminate the surplus in Social Security rather than allow it to continue to be spent to finance the deficit. His bill has the residual benefit of providing tax relief for all workers and employers paying the payroll tax, but it would be particularly welcome to lower- and middle-income wage earners, he argues.

According to a draft report on the status of Social Security legislation prepared by the Senate Special Committee on Aging, Moynihan's proposal is likely to be "the most controversial and widely debated Social Security issue in 1991." "Although [Moynihan] was unable to forge a consensus around his proposal [last year], he succeeded in building a considerable coalition in its support," the report stated.[1]

Critics of Moynihan's plan fear that without a hefty surplus the Social Security system will be ill-equipped in the next century to take care of the tidal wave of baby boomers, those born between 1946 and

1964, who will start to retire around the year 2010. The fact that the baby boom was followed by the baby bust of the 1970s will increase the demographic strain on the Social Security system. The ratio of taxpayers to beneficiaries is expected to fall from about 3.4 taxpayers to each beneficiary in 1990 to only two taxpayers for each beneficiary in 2030.[2]

Free-market advocates believe that the best way to deal with the retirement needs of the baby boomers is to let individuals opt out of the Social Security system and contribute some or all of their payroll taxes to private retirement accounts. Advocates of this approach, including Rep. John Porter, R-Ill., say it would pay individuals higher returns on their investments. Porter says he intends to introduce legislation later this year that would set up a program to turn back surplus Social Security revenues to individual contributors. Under his plan this money would have to be invested in private retirement accounts. Porter and others who support the idea of "privatizing" Social Security, at least to some degree, say it would benefit both low- and high-income wage earners, but opponents say it could result in lower retirement incomes compared with benefits under current law (*see p. 198*).

Besides such sweeping proposals, Congress also may debate proposals for changing the way Social Security benefits are calculated for certain groups. Two such issues are perennials. One concerns the "earnings test," which limits the amount of income a retired person can earn before old-age benefits are reduced. Moves are afoot to either liberalize or eliminate the test.

The other issue concerns the grievances of the so-called "notch babies," who were born between 1917 and 1921. Because of a technical error in the benefit formula that was subsequently corrected, retirees born before 1917 receive higher benefits than those who retired after them. The notch babies feel wronged by the difference, but those who are against assuaging their grievances say the notches weren't unfairly treated. Rather, the retirees who preceded them lucked into a windfall before the formula was corrected.

The concerns of the elderly are taken seriously on Capitol Hill, but lawmakers are finding it more difficult to justify lavishing benefits on this group. That's because the elderly have greatly improved their economic well-being over the past two decades.* As Nancy M. Gordon, the Congressional Budget Office's assistant director for human resources and community development, told a House subcommittee in 1989, "The elderly as a group are doing well. Since 1970, their median income has grown faster than that of the non-elderly. Their poverty rate has fallen to an all-time low and is now less than that of the rest of the population."[3] Between 1974 and 1989, the percentage of elderly living below the poverty level fell from

*Continued on p. 194*

---

*The maximum taxable annual income is currently $53,400 for the OASDI program and $125,000 for Medicare.

---

*For background, see "The Elderly in An Aging America," *E.R.R.*, Aug. 19, 1988 (Vol. II, No. 7).

# Calculating Old-Age Benefits

**A** retiree's basic monthly Social Security benefit, also called primary insurance amount (PIA), is based on a complicated formula. The calculation starts with a review of his average monthly earnings from employment covered by the program. The PIA is the benefit for a single retired worker who starts receiving his monthly Social Security check at the normal retirement age.†

The benefit computations are based on earnings during the 35 years of highest covered earnings up to age 62 or the worker's age when he applies for benefits, whichever is later. The wages in each year of the earnings' record before age 60 are multiplied by an index factor to take into account the growth in national average earnings since that year. The result is called the average indexed monthly earnings (AIME). The earnings from age 60 on are not indexed.

Once the AIME has been determined, it is multiplied by percentages that are weighted in favor of low-income earners. As an example, which is illustrated in the chart at right, here is the benefit formula that applies to a worker who retired at the beginning of 1991 at age 65, having worked through 1990:

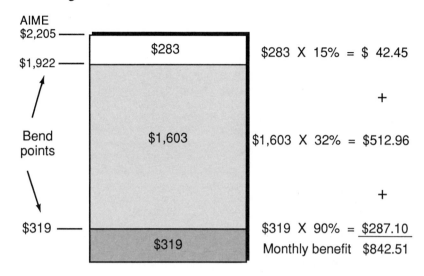

Here is how monthly Social Security benefits are calculated for someone who retired at the beginning of 1991 at age 65 with average indexed monthly earnings of $2,205.

*Source: Congressional Research Service.*

■ 90 percent of the first $319 of AIME, plus
■ 32 percent of the next $1,603 of AIME, plus
■ 15 percent of the rest of AIME, to a maximum of $2,531.

The dollar amounts where the percentages change are referred to as "bend points." They are adjusted each year in tandem with average wages.

Such a formula weights the benefits in favor of lower-income workers, as the chart at left shows. Although high earners receive higher benefits than low earners, low earners receive a higher proportion of their average pre-retirement wages than high earners. (High earners, of course, also have contributed more in Social Security taxes over the years than low earners.)

If a person chooses to retire between 62, the earliest eligible age to receive Social Security, and 65, the benefit is reduced by five-ninths of 1 percent for each month short of age 65 that benefits are received. The reduction will start getting larger after the year 2000 until the reduced benefit drops to 70 percent of PIA for people turning 62 in 2022 or later.

Conversely, if a worker who turns 65 in 1991 postpones retirement, he receives a delayed retirement credit of 3.5 percent of the PIA for each year he delays receiving old-age benefits. The credit is scheduled to increase until it reaches 8 percent per year in 2008.

† *Normal retirement age is now 65. It will rise to 66 in 2008 and to 67 in 2027.*

## Benefits by Income

These are benefits to workers retiring (at age 65) at the beginning of 1991.

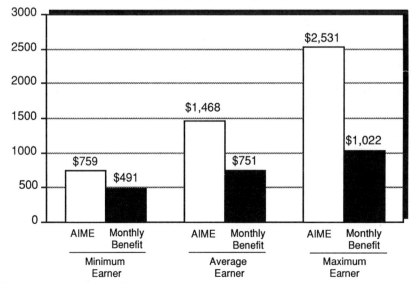

*Source: Congressional Research Service.*

*Continued from p. 192*
14.6 percent to 11.4 percent. During the same period, the percentage of children living in poverty rose from 15.4 percent to 19.6 percent.

Nevertheless, there is a hard core of elderly poor. Most of them are women and many of them live alone. The issue of benefits for the poorest elderly is being addressed by the Social Security Administration as part of its yearlong Supplemental Security Income (SSI) Modernization Project. SSA plans to issue a report later this year after completing hearings around the nation designed to solicit suggestions for improving SSI, a means-tested program for the aged poor, the blind and the permanently disabled.*

Whatever proposed changes to Social Security come before Congress in 1991, they will likely provoke careful consideration if not heated debate among lawmakers, because even though the elderly as a group may not be as poor as they once were, they, unlike children, *do* vote. And politicians have become reluctant over the years to provoke their ire by tinkering with benefits — or proposing to change the Social Security system in a way that could be portrayed as a threat to benefits. Members of Congress will be very careful, therefore, before changing the system. Many will take to heart the attitude expressed by House Ways and Means Committee Chairman Dan Rostenkowski, D-Ill.: "It ain't broke," he says, "so we shouldn't try to fix it." But that doesn't mean that others won't try.

## More generous benefits for greater numbers of workers

Born of the bitter poverty and widespread unemployment of the Great Depression, the Social Security Act was signed into law Aug. 14, 1935, by President Franklin D. Roosevelt. The original law's old-age provisions covered only retirees who had worked in commerce or industry, about 6 million people, or less than 15 percent of the work force at the time. Over the years, coverage gradually was extended to new groups of workers, including regularly employed agricultural and household workers; farmers, professionals and others who are self-employed; employees of nonprofit organizations; and federal, state and local government workers not covered by other benefit plans. Today, Social Security covers about 95 percent of the work force, or 132.8 million workers.

From the earliest days, retiring workers weren't the only ones covered by the Social Security system. In 1939, a year before the first monthly Social Security checks were mailed, Congress expanded coverage to include survivors and dependents of covered workers. During the 1950s coverage was extended to disabled persons below retirement age and to their dependents. By the early 1960s, Social Security had become the nation's single most important entitlement program, accounting in fiscal 1964 for 37 percent of all welfare expenditures compared with only 6 percent in fiscal 1950.[4]

Rising inflation in the late 1960s led Congress to raise OASDI benefits three times between 1969 and 1972: 15 percent in 1969, 10 percent in 1971 and 20 percent in 1972. Also in 1972, Congress decided to tie future increases in Social Security benefits to the Consumer Price Index by providing for annual cost-of-living adjustments, known as COLAs. The 1972 law also introduced a new formula for computing the initial benefit at retirement. The new formula contained the technical error that gave birth to the notch-baby complaints. A correction was made in 1977 amendments to the law, which also contained steep increases in both the payroll tax rate and the taxable earnings base.

The 1977 Social Security tax increase — one of the nation's largest peacetime tax increases — was designed to yield $227 billion over 10 years. The legislation raised payroll taxes, starting in 1979, to 6.13 percent and locked in increases that were supposed to bring the tax to 7.65 percent in 1990. The maximum tax payment an individual could make was to more than triple over the same period. Nevertheless, the 1977 bailout was not enough to carry the system through continuing periods of high inflation and soaring unemployment. Inflation drove up the cost of benefits, while high unemployment and slow growth in wages meant revenue from payroll taxes was less than expected. In addition to the short-term problems, there was growing fear that after baby boomers started to collect benefits in the 21st century, the strain on the work force and the Social Security system itself would become intolerable.

With the system nearing collapse, President Ronald Reagan in 1981 formed a bipartisan commission to find ways to put Social Security on solid ground again. The 15-member commission, which was chaired by Alan Greenspan, was made up of liberals, moderates and conservatives who inauspiciously started out by "circling and glowering at each other like gang members before a brawl," recounts Peter J. Ferrara, an attorney and an adjunct scholar of the Cato Institute, a libertarian think tank in Washington.[5] Nevertheless, the commission finally agreed on a number of recommendations that Congress used as a basis for the 1983 amendments to the Social Security Act.

The landmark amendments gradually increased the normal retirement age — the age when workers can retire and receive unreduced benefits — from 65 to 66 by the year 2009 and to 67 by the year 2027. Benefits for those who retire early were reduced gradually

---

*Some people believe SSI benefits for the elderly, now based on about 78 percent of the poverty level, should be raised to the regular poverty threshold, which in 1990 was $6,268 for a person living alone. The measuring stick for poverty is lower for the elderly because it is assumed that older people eat less, but the formula fails to account for extra medical expenses typically incurred by older people.

from 80 percent to 75 percent and then to 70 percent. It delayed retirees' annual cost-of-living adjustments six months, speed up previously approved increases in payroll taxes for both employees and employers, and brought new federal employees and workers in the nonprofit sector into the system.

Congress also agreed to a fundamental change in the program: For the first time, federal income taxes would be imposed on up to half of Social Security benefits for those with incomes over a specified level ($25,000 for an individual or $32,000 for a married couple). That tax revenue is turned back into the retirement trust fund.[6]

President Reagan signed the bill at a large White House ceremony April 20, 1983, noting that the legislation would " allow Social Security to age as gracefully as all of us hope to do ourselves, without becoming an overwhelming burden on generations to come." [7]

## Debate over Moynihan plan for cutting payroll taxes

One of the results of the 1983 bailout was to build up a surplus in the Social Security trust fund that would help ensure the system's solvency through the 21st century, when the baby boomers would retire.[8] Indeed, the success of the 1983 reforms has belied critics who said that the Greenspan commission had not ensured the system's long-term solvency because it had failed to restrain the skyrocketing growth of benefit payments. But the health of the system is due in no small measure to the economy, which, before this year, had enjoyed seven recession-free years with low inflation and low unemployment.

On the surface, the growth of the surplus may seem like good news for the baby boomers. The problem, however, is that the surplus is not being invested the way a normal retirement fund would be; it is being used to help finance the federal budget deficit. It's not that payroll tax revenues are being used to finance other government programs directly. Rather, the trust fund surplus, by law, must be invested in Treasury securities, which are a form of federal debt. Thus the accumulating surplus is not in the form of cash but IOUs from the government. These will have to be redeemed for cash when the boomers retire.

The fact that the Social Security surplus is being used to mask the true size of the budget deficit angers Sen. Moynihan, who was a member of the Greenspan commission. When Congress enacted the 1983 payroll tax increases, he says, it assumed the federal deficit would be eliminated before the system began running a surplus. According to Moynihan, the inclusion of the Social Security surplus disguised the actual size of the 1989 deficit by $52 billion.[9] Last year Congress removed the Social Security reve-

nue from the deficit calculation as part of the 1990 budget agreement.

Moynihan's opponents concede that it is technically true that there is no accumulating Social Security reserve segregated from the rest of the government revenue. But the fact that the surplus is invested in Treasury securities constitutes an ironclad assurance by the federal government that the funds, augmented by interest, will be pumped back into the Social Security system when they are needed to pay for benefits in the next century. Cutting the payroll tax now, critics argue, would require either tax increases later, or worse, adding the cost of the baby boomers' retirements to the federal deficit.

But Moynihan has a broader concern. He is bent upon reversing the trend toward financing general government activities using regressive taxes because they place a greater burden on middle- and low-level wage earners. The Social Security tax is one of the more regressive U.S. levies. As long as the country continues to run a deficit, the Social Security surplus will get spent as part of the general revenue pot, thus reducing the need to raise revenue through the more progressive income tax, he argues.*

To reduce the size of the surplus — and thus, presumably, force the administration to find other ways of dealing with the gap between federal revenues and outlays — Moynihan on Dec. 29, 1989, introduced a plan to cut Social Security payroll taxes. Although Moynihan's proposal stalled in the 101st Congress,[10] it got the attention of his colleagues and provoked a national debate.

Moynihan reintroduced his payroll tax plan on Jan. 14, 1991, arguing that it would "strengthen the financing of the Social Security program, stimulate the weakening economy, and provide a fair tax cut to 132 million workers and 6 million employers and self-employed individuals." Moynihan wants to cut the Social Security payroll tax from 6.2 percent to 5.7 percent in July 1991, to 5.5 percent on Jan. 1, 1994, and to 5.2 percent on Jan. 1, 1996. He also wants to increase the amount of income subject to the tax from $53,400 this year to $60,000 in 1992 and to $82,200 by 1996. "Workers with earnings at or above the proposed maximum wage levels would still, with the proposed tax rates, realize a tax cut," Moynihan says.

Moynihan stresses that his proposal would affect only the surplus in Social Security and says he still favors keeping a reserve equal to 18 months' worth of benefits. He also disputes the argument that the surplus is needed to accumulate reserves to finance the baby boomers' retirement. Under his plan, tax rates would start to rise again after the turn of the century, when the baby boomers start to retire. The rate would climb

---

*Social Security is considered a regressive tax because it decreases as a percentage of income as income rises. Federal personal income taxes, on the other hand, usually are considered progressive because rates go up as income increases.

back to 6.2 percent by 2015 and would reach 8.1 percent in 2050.

Moynihan's plan has been endorsed by a wide range of individuals and groups — from the AFL-CIO to the U.S. Chamber of Commerce to the Democratic National Committee. Some of the strongest support has come from conservatives. According to Daniel Mitchell, an expert in budget and tax issues at the conservative Heritage Foundation, "Lower Social Security taxes would spur economic growth by returning billions of dollars to workers. ... Further, since payroll taxes directly increase the cost of labor, lower Social Security taxes would create as many as 1 million new jobs — depending on how much the tax is reduced. In addition to creating new jobs, businesses would be able to purchase additional new plant and equipment and increase rewards for investors with savings from lower labor costs." [11]

Robert J. Myers, who was a member of the 1934 panel that created the Social Security system and who served as the Social Security Administration's chief actuary for 23 years until 1970, says he supports Moynihan's plan "110 percent." The buildup of a trust surplus is dangerous, he says, because it may tempt lawmakers to raise Social Security benefits, which would create new problems for the future financing of the system.*

Moynihan's plan also has notable critics, however, who argue that reducing Social Security taxes would damage the retirement program and hurt the economy. Among their specific criticisms:

■ **Cutting Social Security taxes would push up interest rates and reduce national savings.** Ralph C. Bryant, a senior fellow in economic studies at the Brookings Institution in Washington, predicts that the Federal Reserve would respond to the enactment of the Moynihan proposal by tightening monetary policy. This, he says, "would lead to dramatically higher nominal interest rates. ... The added interest costs of servicing the government's debt would lead to still more ballooning of the budget deficit [and] a sizable additional appreciation of the dollar in exchange markets. ..." As a result, Bryant writes, the proposal's effects on the economy "would be precisely the opposite of what the country needs to increase national saving and domestic investment." [12]

Charles L. Schultze, director of Economic Studies at Brookings and chairman of the Council of Economic Advisers under President Jimmy Carter, agrees. Sen. Moynihan's proposal, he writes, "would cost some $60 billion annually in lost payroll tax revenues. Because this initial increase in the budget deficit would result in higher interest rates and a higher federal debt, federal interest outlays would grow sharply. The combina-

tion of lower tax revenues and increased interest outlay would add $90-$100 billion a year to the budget deficit." As a result, Schultze says, "National savings in the United States — which is equal to private savings less the amount absorbed in financing the overall budget deficit — would fall still further below the abysmal level to which it has sunk in the past decade." [13]

■ **Cutting payroll taxes would bankrupt the Social Security system.** An analysis prepared by Social Security actuaries for the Senate Finance Committee says the tax cuts proposed by Sen. Moynihan could bankrupt the system by the year 2005 if the economy took a turn for the worse and pessimistic long-term economic projections proved correct. The study worries Senate Finance Committee Chairman Lloyd Bentsen, D-Texas. "We're in a recession with no certainties about when it will end," Bentsen told a reporter recently. "We're burdened with debt. I think we have to take [this new analysis] seriously. ... I want a big margin of safety. You bet I do." [14]

■ **Returning to pay-as-you-go financing would necessitate a big increase in payroll taxes in the 21st century to finance the baby boomers' retirement.** According to Alice M. Rivlin, a senior fellow at the Brookings Institution and the former director of the Congressional Budget Office, "The big payroll taxes that would be necessary when the baby boomers retire would likely lead to intergenerational conflict, benefit cuts, and perhaps conversion of Social Security to a means-tested program." [15] However, Moynihan's legislation calls for increasing the payroll tax for the next century as projected costs rise, consistent with pay-as-you-go financing.

■ **Reducing payroll taxes would exacerbate the budget deficit, even though technically Social Security is not counted in the deficit.** "To reduce the payroll tax rate at this time would be fiscally irresponsible and could seriously jeopardize the Social Security system," says Gwendolyn S. King, the commissioner of Social Security. "I can only repeat the president's own admonition: 'Don't mess with Social Security.'"

Similar sentiments have been expressed by Bush administration officials, including budget director Richard G. Darman, and Ways and Means Committee Chairman Rostenkowski, one of the most outspoken critics of Moynihan's plan. "People don't want their Social Security tampered with," he said recently. Changing the system "would be stepping in a field full of mines." [16]

## Moynihan's isn't the only plan for cutting payroll taxes

Sen. Moynihan is not the only one with designs on Social Security. Sens. Malcolm Wallop, R-Wyo., and Bob

---

*Myers also recommends another option for meeting the benefit burden of the next century — raising the retirement age, to at least 68 and perhaps to 70. This would raise revenues and reduce benefit costs at the same time, he says. Skeptics say a later retirement date is fine for white-collar workers but is not a realistic option for other kinds of workers.

Kasten, R-Wis., in February joined with Rep. Tom DeLay, R-Texas, in sponsoring a bill that would couple a payroll tax cut with a reduction in the capital gains rate. The Wallop-DeLay bill is a favorite among conservatives who want to piggyback on Moynihan to push Reagan-style tax cuts promoting savings and investment.

Senate Majority Leader George J. Mitchell, D-Maine., and other Democrats want to use the Moynihan proposal to revive their campaign for "tax fairness" — their campaign to raise taxes on the rich to pay for tax cuts for the middle class. Mitchell has expressed interest in coupling a payroll tax cut with a lifting of the cap on wages subject to the tax — a move that would result in a massive tax increase on employers and higher-paid workers.

The Progressive Policy Institute, a research organization connected with the Democratic Leadership Council,* has proposed a plan for reducing Social Security tax rates without reducing the Social Security trust fund balances. The institute says its proposal would raise the same revenues expected under the current tax schedule by applying a lower tax rate to a larger tax base.

This reform "would bring tax relief to 95 percent of all workers and finance it with a dose of tax equity in which highly paid people, like everyone else, would pay Social Security tax on all or at least on more of their wages," says Robert J. Shapiro, vice president and director of economic studies at the institute.

The institute proposes two options. One would subject all wage and salary income to the Social Security taxes while decreasing the OASDI tax rate from 6.2 percent to 5.55 percent and lowering the Medicare tax rate from 1.45 percent to 1.4 percent. A family earning $50,000 a year would get a $350 tax break in 1991, while a family earning the national median income of $37,000 would get a tax break of $260.

Option No. 2 would have Congress raise the cap on salaries subject to the OASDI tax to $125,000. According to the institute, this would expand the tax base enough to produce the same revenues with an OASDI tax rate of 5.7 percent instead of the current 6.2 percent. Under this option, a median-income family would have $185 extra in take-home pay by the end of the year, and a family earning $50,000 annually would get about $250 more.

Shapiro says the institute's proposals offer "a progressive alternative" to President Bush's argument that a capital gains tax cut could help turn the economy around. "Under the current system," Shapiro says, "ordinary Americans feel the full brunt of any payroll tax rate increase, while more highly paid people avoid most of the additional burden. The chief reason is that the cap on wages and salaries subject to payroll tax covers all of a middle-class family's income, but only a minor share of the income of families in the top 5 percent. In addition, the payroll tax

## Elderly Count on Social Security

**Social Security payments represent the largest share of an older person's income. The rest comes from savings and other assets, pensions and earnings.**

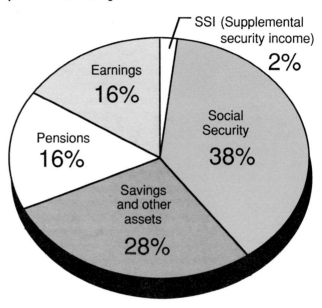

*Source: U.S. Bureau of the Census, 1989.*

covers only a person's wages or salary, which account for virtually all of an average worker's income, while wealthy people derive more than half of their income in other forms, such as dividends and capital gains."

The institute's proposals have been criticized both by former Social Security Commissioner Robert M. Ball,* who opposes Moynihan's plan, and Robert Myers, who supports it. In a joint statement issued last year from the National Academy of Social Insurance, a nonpartisan research and educational organization in Washington where they serve on the board of directors, Ball and Myers argue that the balance of the flat-rate payroll tax with the benefits formula is fair as it is: "Although everyone pays the same percentage of earnings, those with lower earnings get more in relation to what they pay. The benefits of the higher paid are higher, but they are a smaller percentage of past earnings."

### Would private retirement accounts offer a better rate of return?

While Sen. Moynihan and others propose changing Social Security tax rates, still others are interested in

---

*The Democratic Leadership Council is a coalition of Democratic governors, members of Congress, mayors and state legislators.

*Ball served as commissioner of Social Security from 1962 to 1973 and is a member of the 1991 Advisory Council on Social Security. He also served on the Greenspan commission.

changing Social Security benefits in one way or another. The proposals range from radical initiatives to divert Social Security contributions into private retirement accounts to those that would bend the established structure to even out benefit inequities, perceived or real.

Rep. Porter says his plan to privatize the old-age insurance portion of Social Security would not only result in better rates of return on contributions but would ensure that real dollars — not IOUs from the Treasury — would be there to pay for the baby boomers' retirement.

Porter's plan would take surplus Social Security funds, the amount of contributions that exceed benefit payments for the year, and return the money to individual workers. This money would have to be invested in Individual Social Security Retirement Accounts (ISSRAs) that would be administered by bonded trustees, such as banks or insurance companies. Porter estimates that in 1990 about $60 billion would have been returned to some 130 million workers, averaging out to approximately $430 per worker.

Under Porter's plan, the amount refunded to the individual, which would depend on the level of taxes paid by the worker, as well as the interest from the investments would not be subject to additional income tax. Early withdrawals would not be permitted. At retirement, each worker would purchase a lifetime annuity from which he would receive retirement income.

It is not known yet how the plan might make the annuity inflation-proof, as COLAs now do for Social Security benefits. The plan is "fluid" at this point, says Robert Gustafson, Porter's legislative director. Porter "doesn't have everything nailed down yet." In any event, a retiree's annuity income would be tacked on to his Social Security benefit.

The General Accounting Office (GAO), the investigative arm of Congress, issued a report in December 1990 analyzing Porter's proposal at his request. The GAO gave Porter's plan mixed reviews. "Given favorable financial market conditions [ISSRAs] could improve retirement incomes," the report stated, but ISSRAs "could also yield lower rates of return," resulting in lower retirement incomes compared with benefits under current law. The GAO noted that rates of return will depend on how retirees invest their ISSRAs. "If the ISSRA proposal precludes riskier investments to enhance the security of private retirement income, it also limits the gains individuals can expect from the program." [17]

According to GAO estimates, if ISSRAs were to pay on average a rate somewhat higher than bonds have paid historically, they would earn about 3 percent a year. A more optimistic assumption would be a 7 percent return, which would reflect the historical performance of Standard & Poor's 500 stocks. Social Security pays a rate of return of about 2 percent, adjusted for inflation, according to the GAO.

Because the likely variation in market returns could result in some retirees' being worse off under the ISSRA program than they would be under Social Security, the GAO cautioned that the government could be pressured to guarantee that every retiree be at least as well off under the ISSRA system as under Social Security. If the government agreed to provide such a guarantee, GAO warned, it might encourage ISSRA holders to make riskier investments. Many people might be tempted to aim for the highest returns possible knowing they had a safety net below. "While investment restrictions may mitigate this problem," the GAO said, "the possibility that losses may still occur could expose the government to significant costs."

Despite these cautions, as well as outright objection to the concept in other quarters, believers in privatization remain undaunted. Ferrara of the Cato Institute says he supports the privatization concept because it will increase returns on investment. As a tax-transfer system like Social Security matures, Ferrara says, returns on investment inevitably worsen. When the system was starting out, workers had not been paying into it for very long before they received benefits, so their return on contributions was high. But as the system matures, workers pay into it for a longer time and therefore receive lower rates of return.

"For those entering the work force today, even if they receive all the Social Security benefits they are currently promised, the program will still be a miserable deal, given the enormous tax burden to be imposed under current law over their working careers," Ferrara wrote in a 1985 book on the subject. [18]

Proposals for privatization began to crop up in the 1960s about the time payroll taxes started to shoot up, Ferrara said. In 1950, the tax rate was 1.5 percent on maximum taxable earnings of $3,000. The top contribution paid by an employee that year was $45. By 1960, the tax rate was up to 3 percent, the income cap was up to $4,800 and the maximum annual payroll tax was $144. Ten years later, the tax rate had reached 4.8 percent, the income cap was $7,800 and the maximum employee contribution was $374. In 1990, employee payments shot up to a maximum of $3,924, the result of the 7.65 percent tax on income up to $51,300. [19]

Ferrara predicts that Social Security taxes will continue to rise. Citing the SSA's predictions for the 21st century based on a pessimistic set of demographic and economic assumptions — which, in Ferrara's view, are realistic — he says paying all the benefits promised to those entering the work force today would require a payroll tax rate of 37.5 percent, divided between employers and employees. Even under remarkable economic conditions, Ferrara says, Social Security's rate of return for the next century's retirees would at most reach 4 percent, while a system of private investment accounts would give the retiree a return of 12 to 13 percent, based on historical returns on capital investment. [20]

Opponents of privatization say the lure of possible high returns does not give the peace of mind that Social Security has offered retirees for more than five decades. If the economic growth needed to support privatization fails to materialize, says Gary Burtless, an economist at the Brookings Institution, people will be left asking for handouts from the government. So instead of the relative dignity of Social Security, retirees would face the "stigma" of welfare.

John Rother, director of federal policy for the 33-million-member American Association of Retired Persons, calls the privatization proposal an "elitist idea" based on the notion that "everyone will be home with his personal computer" figuring out how to invest his money. "Not everyone is a wise investor," Rother says. "You would have a whole lot of losers out there," as well as an opportunity for fraud for those would prey upon them.

## Proposals to put equity in benefit allocation

Social Security payments represent the largest share of an older person's income (*see chart, p. 197*). The rest comes from savings and other assets, pensions and earnings. Some experts think the proportion of income coming from earnings, currently 16 percent, might be higher if it were not for the "earnings test," which limits the amount of income those under 70 can earn before old-age benefits are reduced. Moves are afoot either to liberalize or to eliminate the test.

The earnings test, which applies only to income from work (not from investments), was a feature of the original Social Security Act. It has been modified a number of times to liberalize the amount a retiree may earn before incurring a reduction in old-age benefits. In 1991, a retiree under age 65 may earn $7,080 before starting to lose $1 in benefits for every $2 earned above that amount. Retirees age 65-69 can earn up to $9,720 before losing $1 in benefits for every $3 earned above the income cap. There is no earnings' limit on retirees age 70 and older.

Senate Minority Leader Bob Dole, R-Kan., wants to phase out the earnings test; Rep. Dennis Hastert, R-Ill., wants to do away with it altogether. Hastert contends that no other demographic group in the country is so "blatantly discriminated against" in the effort to become financially self-reliant. His bill would eliminate the earnings cap for those age 65-69. Hastert's press secretary, Eron S. Shosteck, says the bill would help retirees who really need the break, as evidenced by the letters the congressman receives every day from the elderly who are trying to make ends meet.

Opponents of Hastert's bill, which has 219 cosponsors, say it would cost too much, taking about $5 billion

a year from the Social Security trust fund. Opponents also say eliminating the earnings test would allow six-figure-salary earners to pad their income with retirement benefits.

Among those who argue that dropping the test would mainly be a windfall for the highly paid is Marsha Simon, legislative director for Families USA, a Washington group that represents the interests of poor people. She says 40 percent of those who would be affected by the change have family incomes of more than $42,000 annually, while 5 percent earn below $15,000 and 1 percent earn less than $10,500. The money that would be spent on the cost of dropping the test could be used better elsewhere, she says.

Robert Ball says there would be a public relations problem in paying full benefits to someone who at the

> *"For those entering the work force today, even if they receive all the Social Security benefits they are currently promised, the program will still be a miserable deal, given the enormous tax burdens to be imposed under current law over their working careers," says Peter J. Ferrara of the Cato Institute.*

same time is making a good living. "Full-time executives of corporations would be paid benefits just because they reach 65," he says. "That's not going to look real good." Ball points out that people who want to continue to work after age 65 also have the option of postponing their benefits and earning delayed retirement credits. For every year benefits are postponed, the monthly benefit increases by 3.5 percent. The delayed retirement credit will gradually increase until it reaches 8 percent in 2008.

While Dole and Hastert are focusing their attention on the elderly who want to continue to work, others are looking to make the benefits for those who retire more equitable. Rep. William J. Hughes, D-N.J., for instance, is concerned about retirees, primarily women, who receive lower benefits because of the time they spend out of the work force to care for children and elderly parents. Lou Glasse, president of the Older Women's League, points out that the average monthly Social Security benefit is $627 for a man and $458 for a woman. "We believe this is due in part to pay inequities throughout the years," Glasse says, referring to the fact that many women who are now retired worked in fields such as teaching, nursing and social work that historically have paid lower wages.

The discrepancy between men's and women's benefits also stems from a difference in work patterns. A woman typically goes in and out of the work force as she straddles the responsibilities of earning a living and taking care of children and elderly parents. This in-and-out pattern deviates from the male work pattern upon which benefit formulas are based. Years of zero earnings for those years spent out of the work force are averaged into calculations for the retiree's monthly benefit. The bias in the formula potentially affects a large number of women. "Eighty-nine percent of all women over age 18 will be care givers either of children, parents, or both," Glasse says.

Hughes has proposed legislation that would address these inequities. Now, five years of low or zero earnings may be dropped from the calculations that determine a retiree's monthly benefit. Hughes' bill would allow a worker to drop up to another five years of zero or very low earnings from the calculations, provided those years were spent giving care to children or elderly parents. "While women often assume the majority of care-giving responsibilities . . . the Social Security program does not recognize those years" spent out of the work force, Hughes said in a Jan. 31 letter to congressional colleagues. "I strongly believe this bill takes an important first step towards addressing some of the inequities and inadequacies of the Social Security program."

## Does the public support Social Security reform?

The Social Security program enjoys such overwhelming popular support that lawmakers who want to change it may face an uphill battle. A survey conducted for the American Association of Retired Persons (AARP) in 1985 found that 96 percent of the respondents thought Social Security was an important government program and 92 percent deemed it a success.[21]

Even if the public accepted the concept of a particular change, it's not clear that they would be willing to spend the money to implement it. There are some indications that this may depend in part on the economic climate at the time. For example, a poll conducted by Louis Harris and Associates Inc. during the recession of the early 1980s found that only a slim majority, 51 percent, agreed that taxes should be raised if needed to provide adequate income for the elderly.

On the other hand, a survey conducted by AARP in the healthier economic climate of the mid-1980s showed the public was more amenable toward spending money for the needs of the elderly. The 1986 survey found that 64 percent of the population strongly agreed that the government was not doing enough for the elderly; the same percentage thought the government should spend more for Social Security payments.[22] It remains to be seen how open to change the public is this year, one that has so far been in an economic downturn.

Besides public opinion, which influences lawmakers, lobbyists will also have their say. Several groups have already made their views on the Moynihan plan known. Because of its perceived threat to the Social Security trust fund, the Older Women's League has come out against it. Glasse says the league views the proposal with "alarm." The AARP also opposes the Moynihan proposal. Business as well as labor groups have endorsed the plan, as has the National Committee to Preserve Social Security and Medicare, a group formed in 1982 when the trust fund was in trouble. The committee adds one proviso to its endorsement, however. To protect the contingency fund, the plan should include an automatic tax rate increase if the fund falls below a certain level, says Lloyd Duxbury, legislative representative for the committee.

Whatever proposed changes to Social Security come before Congress this year, they will face extra procedural hurdles because of "fire wall" protections to the program that were written into the 1990 Omnibus Budget Reconciliation Act. The procedures differ in the House and Senate, but the objective is the same: to make it more difficult to pass a tax cut or an increase in benefits.

Moynihan's plan already has a head start in the Senate. Last year it received a majority vote of 54, 42 Democrats and 12 Republicans. At that time, however, 60 votes were needed to pass the measure. This year, Moynihan will need only 51 votes in the Senate, because of a phrase inserted into last year's budget agreement by Budget Committee Chairman Jim Sasser, D-Tenn. The 60-vote requirement to reduce Social Security revenues only applies to a budget resolution "as reported" out of the Budget Committee. When the budget resolution gets to the Senate floor, the 60-vote requirement does not apply. Thus, when the Senate budget resolution goes to the floor, probably in April, Moynihan intends to offer an amendment reducing the assumed level of Social Security revenues. If that passes, it would pave the way for Senate consideration of the actual bill reducing the payroll tax later this year.

Opponents say Moynihan's maneuver would violate the spirit of the budget act. If he triumphs in the Senate, Moynihan will still have a fight in the House, which has its own set of procedures to guard against hasty reductions of Social Security revenues.

*Continued on p. 202*

# AT ISSUE
*Would private retirement accounts give today's workers a better deal at retirement than Social Security?*

**YES** says **PETER J. FERRARA,** editor of *Social Security: Prospects for Real Reform.*
The rate of return paid by Social Security on the tax funds paid into the system has been falling steadily. Today's retirees are still receiving a good deal from the program in return for past tax payments. But for those entering the work force today, *even if they receive all the Social Security benefits they are currently promised*, the program will still be a miserable deal, given the enormous tax burden to be imposed under current law over their working careers. . . .

If these workers could invest the same amounts as paid into Social Security in private IRA-type vehicles, they could receive much higher benefits. . . .

Fortunately, fundamental reform can be structured to address the problems of Social Security without benefit cuts for the elderly or tax increases for workers. Such reform would involve the creation of "Super IRAs," an expanded version of currently available Individual Retirement Accounts. Workers would have the freedom to choose to substitute Super IRAs for some, and eventually all, of their Social Security coverage through a carefully structured option designed at the same time to maintain, and indeed strengthen, essential Social Security financing. . . .

Through the proposed Super-IRA reform, baby boomers could be relying heavily on their own individual savings pools in retirement and less heavily on Social Security. They would be allowed to receive market returns on these funds through the Super IRAs, and much higher benefits, instead of the scandalous returns and inadequate benefits offered them by Social Security. . . .

The reform itself would directly eliminate some current waste. Shifting from Social Security to a private system would mean that the portion of Social Security benefits in effect constituting welfare assistance would instead be paid only through other, means-tested government programs, as the private system would not pay any such redistribution benefits. This would eliminate the current waste of welfare benefits paid through Social Security to many who are not poor, which occurs because the program has no means test.

. . . The supplemental security income (SSI) program would continue to provide means-tested, general revenue-financed welfare benefits to the elderly poor, ensuring that their retirement income would not in any event fall below a basic minimum. Moreover, SuperIRAs would allow for greater reliance on this program and for the reduction or elimination of the current waste resulting from the payment of welfare benefits through Social Security.

The proposed Super-IRA reform would also strengthen the economy. Based on the initial reform package alone, workers paying into Super IRAs could potentially increase national savings by tens of billions of dollars each year. This in turn would provide the capital necessary for technological innovation, the creation of new jobs and more rapid economic growth.

*From Social Security: Prospects for Real Reform, Cato Institute, 1985.*

**NO** say **HENRY J. AARON, BARRY P. BOSWORTH** and **GARY BURTLESS,** co-authors of *Can America Afford to Grow Old?*
Social insurance programs continue to enjoy enormous popularity. They possess unique advantages that set them apart from privately funded alternatives. Based on experience over the past half century, Social Security and Medicare seem much more secure than privately financed retirement benefits. Social Security is not affected by financial market fluctuations, and benefits under the program have never been in jeopardy because of competitive losses suffered by individual companies, industries, or regions. Nor have benefits been substantially eroded by inflation. . . .

The economic case for privatization rests on the arguments that privatization will increase national saving and that retirement saving will be invested more efficiently than it now is, thus reducing the burden of future retirement benefits. But privatization raises important political questions. Can private plans offer the secure, inflation-proof benefits now offered under Social Security and Medicare? Can alternative plans achieve the redistributional goals attained by these two programs?

Shifting to private savings accounts would eliminate or reduce the possibility of paying extra benefits to workers whose earnings have been low or to survivors and dependents in large families, and it would increase the number of applicants for welfare or other income-tested benefits. Such a course would pose an unattractive dilemma. Either it would necessitate a reduction or elimination of assistance to low-income households or it would require an increase in the number of elderly, survivors, and disabled who must apply for income- or means-tested payments.

In the short run, privatization cannot increase national saving, unless benefits to current retirees and workers on the verge of retirement are reduced or taxes on active workers are increased. Advocates of privatization typically do not favor either course. . . . Over the long run, privatizing OASDI would raise national saving only to the extent that it leads to the accumulation of increased pension reserves or to smaller deficits. . . .

In short, the move to privatize Social Security, like many other measures, might facilitate an increase in national saving; but so too would a change in fiscal policy that permits future Social Security surpluses to be reflected in smaller federal deficits or larger federal surpluses. Privatization would not change the physical assets in which national saving is invested. For that reason, the policy should be viewed primarily in political terms. It is a device that would eliminate the Social Security link between pension-type benefits and assistance to workers with lower-than-average earnings or larger-than-average families. It would thereby either increase the number of elderly and disabled persons who would require recourse to welfare or reduce the financial assistance provided to such workers.

*From Can America Afford to Grow Old? Paying for Social Security, Brookings Institution, 1989.*

*Continued from p. 200*

Robert Shapiro of the Progressive Policy Institute maintains that his organization's proposal to eliminate the cap on wages that are subject to payroll taxes has popular support. He cites a recent poll by Penn+Schoen Associates Inc., a political consulting and polling firm in New York City, that found 73 percent of Americans favor eliminating the cap, with support rising to 83 percent when the additional funds are used to lower the tax rate.

Shapiro says such evidence outweighs critics' concern that an increase in the burden on high-salary earners would undermine their backing for Social Security, "with ruinous long-term effects for the whole program." To the contrary, he says, "over the long run, support for Social Security will rest most truly on the judgment by the vast middle class that the tax is fair, the system is secure and their burden is reasonable."

Although the proponents of privatization are not claiming a groundswell of support for their cause at this stage, they believe their time is nearing. As people become more cognizant of the financing problems Social Security will face in the next century, "the status quo will be politically untenable," Ferrara maintains. He says there are signs that the younger generation is already receptive to privatization, citing a poll by Market Opinion Research in which 87 percent of workers age 18-25 said they liked the idea of the Porter plan. The plan received an overall 68 percent favorable response.

In recent years, Social Security has become known as a 'third rail" of American politics: To touch it, politicians say, means instant death. Most of the proposals to change the system do not touch Social Security in the conventional sense; they do not directly reduce benefits. Nonetheless, they cannot escape the myths that politicians have nurtured over the years and that sustain the program, frustrating efforts to overhaul it. Most policy-makers automatically hold any proposal to change Social Security at arms-length, out of fear that — justifiably or not — it will be portrayed as a threat to benefits. And once that happens, the powerful elderly lobby will swing into action.

Two competing forces are at work. One pulls to adapt Social Security to changing demographic and economic realities. The other pushes toward the status quo because of the program's enormous popularity. Unless Social Security falls into a crisis, as it did in 1983, the status quo will probably prevail.

# NOTES

[1] The final report, *Developments in Aging: 1990*, is scheduled to be published by the committee in early April. It is an annual report the committee is required to publish each year under law.

[2] *1990 Annual Report of the Federal Old-Age and Survivors Insurance and Disability Insurance Trust Funds*, p. 76.

[3] Testifying before the House Ways and Means Subcommittee on Social Security, May 23, 1989.

[4] *Aging in America: The Federal Government's Role*, Congressional Quarterly Inc., 1989, p. 18.

[5] Peter J. Ferrara, ed., *Social Security: Prospects for Real Reform* (1985), p. 36.

[6] It is the employer's half of the payroll contributions that is taxed, because a retiree has already paid income tax on his portion while in the work force. See David Koitz, *Social Security: Brief Facts and Statistics*, Congressional Research Service Report for Congress, Nov. 1, 1990, p. 10.

[7] "Social Security Rescue Plan Swiftly Approved," *1983 CQ Almanac*, p. 219.

[8] By the end of 1991, the trust fund is expected to reach $297 billion, according to "intermediate" forecasts, those lying somewhere between outlooks based on optimistic and pessimistic demographic and economic assumptions. By the end of 1994, the fund will reach $562 billion, and by 2027, about $9.4 trillion. See Koitz, *op. cit.*, p. 12.

[9] At a Dec. 29, 1989, press conference, Moynihan said the 1989 deficit was not the officially announced figure of $152 billion but $204 billion.

[10] The bill was effectively killed when Sen. Ted Stevens, R-Alaska, asked to have it ruled out of order because it would violate the statutory requirement that bills may not be considered if they would increase the federal deficit above the Gramm-Rudman target. Moynihan's motion to waive the Gramm-Rudman requirement got only 54 of the 60 votes needed to pass. The House did not consider the measure in 1990. See *Congressional Quarterly Weekly Report*, Oct. 13, 1990, p. 3399.

[11] Daniel J. Mitchell, "The Facts About Cutting Social Security Taxes," The Heritage Foundation, March 15, 1991, p. 1.

[12] Ralph C. Bryant, "Four Reasons Not to Cut Social Security Taxes: Effects on the Economy" *The Brookings Review*, spring 1990, p. 5.

[13] Charles L. Schultze, "Four Reasons Not to Cut Social Security Taxes: Effects on National Savings," *The Brookings Review*, spring 1990, p. 5.

[14] Quoted by Spencer Rich in *The Washington Post*, Feb. 22, 1991, p. C2.

[15] Alice M. Rivlin, "Four Reasons Not to Cut Social Security Taxes: What Kind of Social Security System?" *The Brookings Review*, spring 1990, p. 4.

[16] Quoted by Paul Clancy in *USA Today*, March 21, 1991.

[17] General Accounting Office, *Social Security: Analysis of a Proposal to Privatize Trust Fund Reserves*, December 1990.

[18] Peter J. Ferrara, ed., *Social Security: Prospects for Real Reform*, Cato Institute, 1985, p. 2.

[19] Koitz, *op. cit.*, p. 5.

[20] See Peter J. Ferrara and John R. Lott, Jr., "Rates of Return Promised by Social Security to Today's Young Workers," in *Social Security: Prospects for Real Reform, op. cit.*, pp. 16-18.

[21] The survey was conducted by Yankelovich, Skelly, and White Inc. It included a national sample of people age 25 and older. See Sally R. Sherman, "Public Attitudes Toward Social Security," *Social Security Bulletin*, December 1989/Vol. 52, No. 12, p. 13.

[22] *Ibid.*, pp. 10, 14.

*Graphics: Cover, Margaret Scott; pp. 192, 196, Jack Auldridge.*

# RECOMMENDED READING

## BOOKS

**Aaron, Henry J.; Bosworth, Barry P.; and Burtless, Gary,** *Can America Afford to Grow Old? Paying for Social Security,* **Brookings Institution, 1989.**

As the title suggests, this book delves into the challenges of financing the Social Security system as the baby boomers begin to retire. The authors, all three of whom are senior fellows in Brookings' Economic Studies program, conclude that future workers will have to bear a greater tax burden if promised benefits are to be fulfilled.

**Ball, Robert M.,** *Social Security: Today and Tomorrow,* **Columbia University Press, 1978.**

The author, a former commissioner of Social Security, draws on decades of expertise to clarify the provisions and issues in the vast and complex program of Social Security. The information in this volume, presented in a question-and-answer format, also puts Social Security in historical perspective and makes recommendations for its future.

**Ferrara, Peter J., ed.,** *Social Security: Prospects for Real Reform,* **Cato Institute, 1985.**

With this collection of 11 articles Ferrara advances his quest to privatize Social Security. The book discusses various options and degrees of privatization and suggests ways to make the transition.

## ARTICLES

**Schwartz, David, and Grundmann, Herman, "Social Insurance Programs,"** *Social Security Bulletin,* **July 1989.**

Staff members of the Social Security Administration provide a history of old-age, survivors' and disability insurance programs as well as a layman's guide to current provisions of the Social Security Act.

**Moynihan, Daniel Patrick, "Surplus Value,"** *The New Republic,* **June 4, 1990.**

The Democratic senator from New York tells how his proposal to cut payroll taxes, and return to a pay-as-you-go funding arrangement for Social Security, has picked up support. He argues that Democrats ought to be attracted to his proposal to raise take-home pay for the average worker, who has experienced stagnant wages. Rather than being regarded as insurance contributions, Moynihan says, the billions of dollars in surplus Social Security funds are wrongly seen as revenues to be used to pay for deficit spending.

**Rivlin, Alice M.; Bryant, Ralph C.; Schultze, Charles L.; White, Joseph; and Wildavsky, Aaron, "Four Reasons Not To Cut Social Security Taxes,"** *The Brookings Review,* **spring 1990.**

These authors slice up the proposal by Sen. Daniel Patrick Moynihan, D-N.Y., to cut payroll taxes and return to a pay-as-you-go financing arrangement. They contend the buildup of Social Security reserves is prudent in light of the aging of the American population and that Moynihan's plan would dash chances of increasing national saving and investment.

## REPORTS AND STUDIES

**Thompson, Lawrence H.,** *Social Security: Analysis of a Proposal to Privatize Trust Fund Reserves,* **U.S. General Accounting Office, December 1990.**

This study analyzes a proposal by Rep. John Porter, R-Ill., to return surplus Social Security funds to taxpayers for mandatory investment in private retirement accounts. It projects what the proposal's consequences would be under differing market conditions and various degrees of risk in investments. Potential losses raise concerns about benefit security, and implementation of the proposal poses numerous challenges, the study says.

**Koitz, David, and Kollmann, Geoffrey,** *Social Security: Surplus Receipts Trigger New Financing Debate,* **Congressional Research Service, Jan. 9, 1991.**

This report puts the Moynihan pay-as-you-go plan into historical and economic contexts, and sums up congressional action on various proposals to cut payroll taxes.

**Koitz, David,** *Social Security: Brief Facts and Statistics,* **Congressional Research Service, Nov. 1, 1990.**

Salient statistics on Social Security recipients, taxes and benefits are presented in an at-a-glance format in this report.

**House Ways and Means Committee,** *1990 Green Book: Overview of Entitlement Programs,* **June 5, 1990.**

This report, issued annually, includes a section on Social Security that gives the latest legislative changes and a detailed description of the law's major provisions.

**U.S. House Subcommittee on Retirement Income and Employment, Select Committee on Aging,** *Women in Retirement: Are They Losing Out?* **(published proceedings of hearing held May 22, 1990).**

This hearing includes testimony from women who contend the Social Security benefit formula has shortchanged them because of the years they left the work force to take care of children and elderly parents.

**U.S. House Subcommittee on Social Security, Committee on Ways and Means,** *The Oldest and Poorest Social Security Beneficiaries* **(published proceedings of hearing held May 23, 1989).**

The subcommittee transcript is replete with information on the financial status of the elderly in general and descriptions of the oldest and poorest of the age group, namely women who live alone. There is a broad range of recommendations on how to help these poor Social Security beneficiaries.

EDITORIAL
RESEARCH
REPORTS

## Coming soon

Canada Update

California Drought

Electromagnetic Radiation

Published weekly by
Congressional Quarterly
Inc., Editorial Research
Reports analyze emerging
issues of national interest
across a broad range of
social, scientific, political
and economic fields.
Reports are bound and
indexed for permanent
reference. Subscription
information is available
through Congressional
Quarterly's Publications
Sales Department by
telephone (202) 887-8665.
Copies of past issues are
available through
Customer Service, (202)
887-8621.

CANADA

ERR

APRIL 12, 1991

CONGRESSIONAL QUARTERLY'S

EDITORIAL RESEARCH REPORTS

FOUNDED 1923

# THE DEEPENING CANADIAN CRISIS OVER QUEBEC

# EDITORIAL RESEARCH REPORTS

**EDITOR**
**MARCUS D. ROSENBAUM**

**MANAGING EDITOR**
**SANDRA STENCEL**

**ASSOCIATE EDITOR**
**RICHARD L. WORSNOP**

**STAFF WRITERS**
**MARY H. COOPER**
**PATRICK G. MARSHALL**

**PRODUCTION EDITOR**
**LAURIE DE MARIS**

**EDITORIAL ASSISTANT**
**AMY GORTON**

**RICHARD M. BOECKEL (1892-1975)**
**FOUNDER**

**PUBLISHED BY**
**CONGRESSIONAL QUARTERLY INC.**

**CHAIRMAN**
**ANDREW BARNES**

**PRESIDENT**
**RICHARD R. EDMONDS**

**EDITOR AND PUBLISHER**
**NEIL SKENE**

**EXECUTIVE EDITOR**
**ROBERT W. MERRY**

EDITORIAL RESEARCH REPORTS (LIBRARY OF CONGRESS CATALOGUE NO. 39-924; ISSN 0013-0958). Published weekly (48 times per year, excluding March 1, May 3, August 2 and November 1, 1991) by Congressional Quarterly Inc., 1414 22nd Street NW, Washington, D.C. 20037. Rates are furnished upon request. Application to mail at second-class postage rates is pending at Washington, D.C. POSTMASTER: Send address changes to EDITORIAL RESEARCH REPORTS, 1414 22nd Street NW, Washington, D.C. 20037.

© 1991 BY CONGRESSIONAL QUARTERLY INC.

# THE DEEPENING CANADIAN CRISIS OVER QUEBEC

## by Mary H. Cooper

Less than a year after the failure of a plan to resolve Canada's longstanding constitutional crisis, Quebec has thrown down the gauntlet to the rest of Canada: Either give the French-speaking province greater autonomy, or Quebec will set its own course. Opinion polls now say that Quebeckers over-whelmingly favor some form of inde-pendence. At the same time, many English-speaking Canadians would rather see Quebec break away than give in to its demands. But others say there is still room for compromise.

"We have a rendezvous with the future of Quebec, and if we remain united, we shall succeed." With these words, Quebec Premier Robert Bourassa opened the pivotal convention of his Quebec Liberal Party* in Montreal. Before the convention was over, Quebec's governing party delivered an ultimatum to the rest of Canada: Either accept a radical decentralization of power that would allow the French-speaking province to develop according to its own linguistic and cultural priorities, or Quebec will hold a referendum to decide for itself whether to remain a part of Canada or to break away.

More than 2,700 party delegates rose to their feet and greeted the premier's words with a thunderous

---

*The Quebec Liberal Party is separate from the national Liberal Party, whose former leader, Pierre Elliott Trudeau, was prime minister for 16 years before he resigned in 1984. The government then passed into the hands of the Progressive Conservative Party under Brian Mulroney, the current prime minister.

ovation. "You have just witnessed a historic moment," said one enthusiastic delegate as the crowd dispersed into Montreal's cold night air. They would return over the weekend of March 8-10 to the immense Palais des Congrès to hammer out the details of Quebec's most recent plan to determine its place in the 10-province Canadian confederation.

This was not the first time that Quebec had proclaimed dissatisfaction with its role in English-dominated Canada. But the Quebec Liberal Party's challenge has a special meaning today. It comes less than a year after the failure of a long-awaited compromise solution to the country's chronic constitutional crisis. The compromise, called the Meech Lake Accord after a resort in northern Quebec where it was reached, satisfied Quebec's terms for accepting the Canadian Constitution, which it alone among the 10 provinces has not ratified. The failure of two English-speaking provinces to ratify Meech Lake by the June 23, 1990, deadline was seen by Bourassa's government and the majority of Quebeckers as a rejection of Quebec itself.*

The chief focus of Canada's constitutional crisis is the conflict between Quebec's majority Francophone, or French-speaking, population and the English-speakers who dominate the rest of Canada. But there is another, and almost as deeply rooted power struggle in Canadian politics that transcends the language barrier, and that is the struggle between the provinces and the central government.

Based in Ottawa, Ontario, the richest and most populated province, the central government is resented in the peripheral provinces of Eastern and especially Western Canada as being overly sensitive to local interests at the expense of their own. Because of its central location and broad representation in the Cabinet of Canadian Prime Minister Brian Mulroney, Quebec also is a target of the periphery's attacks on the center. "There is a perception out West that everything's done for Ontario and Quebec, particularly for Ontario," explains Desmond Morton, a history professor and the principal (president) of the University of Toronto's Erindale College.

These sentiments have complicated attempts to resolve the constitutional crisis. Many English-speaking Canadians resented the provisions in the Meech Lake Accord that would have recognized Quebec as a "distinct society" and granted the province special rights. At the same time, some English Canadians felt little obligation to accept the compromise simply because it was championed by the prime minister. Support for Mulroney (pronounced *Mul-ROO-ney*) was already waning because of a highly unpopular sales tax his government put into effect last December. Since then, Mulroney's standing in public opinion polls has plummeted still further. His government is blamed

for the high interest rates that have dragged down the already depressed Canadian economy. Today, Mulroney and his Progressive Conservative Party enjoy the support of less than 20 percent of the population, according to numerous opinion polls. (Under Canadian law, Mulroney does not have to call an election until November 1993.)

Since Meech Lake failed to gain all the provinces' approval last June, both the Quebec government and the central government have been groping for alternative solutions to the constitutional crisis. Myriad committees and commissions have been set up to study new proposals to bring Quebec into the constitution. In Quebec, this process has pitted the interests of federalists, who want to remain a part of Canada, against those calling themselves sovereigntists, who would rather break free.

This division was apparent as delegates to the Quebec Liberal Party convention debated the recommendations of a commission headed by Jean Allaire, a Montreal lawyer. The commission's report calls for a radical decentralization of Canada's current political system. It would make Quebec an autonomous political entity and have the federal government surrender most of its current powers over Quebec to the provincial government. The party eventually accepted most of the commission's recommendations.

In adopting the Allaire report, the Quebec Liberal Party gave the federal government less than two years to negotiate these changes. If negotiations between Quebec and Ottawa produce an agreement, Quebec's voters will be asked to approve it in a referendum to be held in the fall of 1992. If the negotiations fail to produce an agreement by that time, the referendum will be held anyway, but voters will instead choose whether to make Quebec a sovereign country.

If such a vote were held today, it would almost certainly be in favor of sovereignty for Quebec. Several polls taken since the failure of Meech Lake show a majority of Quebeckers in favor of greater autonomy for the province. "The trend now in Quebec is strongly in favor of sovereignty," says Daniel Bonin, research associate at the Institute of Intergovernmental Relations at Queen's University in Kingston, Ontario. He cites the most recent survey, conducted after Bourassa's party adopted the Allaire commission's recommendations, showing even heavier support for such an outcome. Asked whether they would like to see Quebec become a sovereign country, 63 percent of those polled said yes, while only 37 said they would not.[1]

Pro-sovereignty forces are in fact pushing Bourassa to make even stronger demands on federal Canada. Federalist forces, including English-speaking Quebeckers, suffered a resounding defeat at the Liberal Party congress when members refused to soften the Allaire report's language. When the congress refused, for example, to include the other provincial premiers in Quebec's negotiations with Ottawa, leaders of the party's federalist camp walked out of the meeting.

---

*For background information on the Meech Lake Accord, see "Will Canada Fall Apart?" *E.R.R.*, May 11, 1990 (No. 18).

Bourassa, known for his consensus-building skills, managed to smooth over the differences within his own party. While his own views on the issue of Quebec's sovereignty are unclear, he appears to favor what Quebec watchers call "renewed federalism," meaning broad autonomy stopping short of the true independence espoused by the Allaire report. A bigger test of Bourassa's abilities as a political broker will come from outside his party, where forces supporting an independent Quebec are pushing for even stronger demands on Ottawa. The Parti Québécois (PQ), the unequivocal champion of Quebec sovereignty and the leading opposition party in the Quebec National Assembly, is represented in another Quebec commission — this one appointed by the Bourassa government — which issued its recommendations on March 28.

Both the Quebec Liberal Party and the Parti Québécois are now eager to agree between themselves on Quebec's demands. "They are trying to reach a consensus because they don't want to give more arguments for English Canada to present Quebec as a divided province," Bonin says. Their goals remain divided, however, with the PQ sovereigntists pushing for a referendum on the sovereignty question alone. Bourassa, on the other hand, wants to wait and see if English Canada will negotiate a deal that Quebeckers could live with before posing that question. "Bourassa and his renewed federalist camp would like to get more maneuvering room in case they get an interesting response from English Canada," Bonin explains.

While political forces inside Quebec prepare to finalize their proposals for determining Quebec's status in Canada, the federal government is only just beginning to provide some ideas of its own. Although the Mulroney government has appointed four separate commissions to study the issue, none is expected to release its findings until this summer. As for Mulroney himself, the prime minister has spoken of the need for "reconfederation." That term awaits precise definition, however, and the prime minister's position on Quebec's future remains vague. In the view of Peter Russell, a constitutional expert and professor of political science at the University of Toronto, reconfederation would probably amount to "a reshuffling of the division of powers between the provinces and Ottawa, but with still considerable strength at the national level."

However Quebec and Ottawa position themselves for negotiations later this year, they cannot ignore the views of "the rest of Canada," an entity that has emerged as such a distinct player in the constitutional debate that it now is sometimes identified by its acronym, TROC. Reaction there to the Quebec Liberal Party's almost complete adoption of the Allaire report was almost unanimously negative. "Many people in Western Canada are saying let's let the buggers go and the sooner the better," says Morton. Although the reactions are less harsh in Ontario, Morton says that even there many people are eager to get over what they

see as the inevitable breakup of their country. In this view, Morton explains, "people are saying let's get out the divorce papers and finalize the deal and let's be tough as hell with them."

While editorial opinions across Canada reflect disappointment with the growing sovereigntist mood in Quebec, not everyone in English Canada views the developments with pessimism. In the West, where some of the most anti-Quebec sentiment can be heard, there are also voices of hope who see in the Allaire report not so much a declaration of independence as a demand for decentralization that may benefit the Western provinces as well as Quebec. "In the Allaire report they are insisting on decentralizing a number of economic powers, and that just happens to coincide with what the government here and the government of Alberta for their own economic reasons, have been saying," says Edward McWhinney, a professor of constitutional law at Simon Fraser University in Barnaby, British Columbia. While no one will predict at this stage that Quebec will be able to negotiate a new political framework based on a broad decentralization of powers to the provinces, McWhinney calls this aspect of the crisis "a sort of cross-current, but at best a new, unifying, cohesive factor in the federal system."

## Quebec's sporadic attempts to gain special status

Quebec's search for its rightful place in Canada is as old as the country itself. Although Francophone Canadians are present in small numbers in other provinces, Quebec is the home of the vast majority of French-speakers. It is also the main source of the French culture that was first introduced by fur traders in the 17th century and that still prevails there. Since the British claimed Canada as its own in 1760, however, Quebeckers have lived under the dominance of English Canadians, who hold the economic as well as political power in Quebec and the rest of Canada.

Although Quebeckers have made sporadic attempts to gain greater political autonomy ever since, it was not until the 1960s that separation from Canada was a seriously considered option for the province. The initial "Quiet Revolution" at the beginning of the decade gave way to a separatist movement that later took a violent turn, culminating in 1970 with the murder of a provincial Cabinet minister and the kidnapping of a British diplomat in Montreal. Under the martial law subsequently imposed in the province by Prime Minister Trudeau, the movement's terrorist phase came to an end.

Quebec separatism assumed a more respectable face with the 1976 election of René Lévesque and his Parti Québécois. English-speaking Quebeckers chafed under

*Continued on p. 210*

# *What Does Quebec Want?*

Canada's latest constitutional crisis began when two of the 10 provincial governments failed to ratify the Meech Lake Accord by June 23, 1990. The accord included a package of amendments to the Canadian Constitution that had been demanded by Quebec as conditions for its approval of the constitution.

After the failure of Meech Lake, the Quebec government decided to find out what the province's population wanted to do next. As part of this plan, Quebec Premier Robert Bourassa's ruling Quebec Liberal Party appointed a commission headed by Montreal lawyer Jean Allaire.

At its annual congress held March 8-10 in Montreal, the Quebec Liberal Party adopted the Allaire commission's recommendations on Quebec's future with only a few modifications. The main demands contained in the Allaire report, entitled "A Quebec Free To Choose," are listed below. They would make Quebec a semi-sovereign state without breaking away completely from the Canadian confederation.

Together with similar recommendations put forward by a Quebec government commission — the Bélanger-Campeau commission, which included members of the opposition Parti Québécois (*see p. 212*) — these demands will be placed on the negotiating table when talks with the rest of Canada commence later this year. Although no dates have yet been set, talks cannot begin before the federal government completes its own studies on Canada's future, probably around midsummer.

## Recommendations of the Allaire Commission

— The Canadian political system will undergo a drastic reorganization resulting in political autonomy for Quebec and a stronger Canadian economic union.

— The federal government will cede many powers to Quebec, including exclusive jurisdiction over 22 areas. These include the following 11 areas currently under Quebec jurisdiction:

- Social affairs
- Municipal affairs
- Culture
- Education
- Housing
- Recreation and sports
- Family policy
- Manpower and training
- Natural resources
- Health
- Tourism

They also include 11 more areas now administered jointly with Ottawa or under exclusive federal authority:

- Agriculture
- Unemployment insurance
- Communications
- Regional development
- Energy
- Environment
- Industry and commerce
- Language
- Research & development
- Public security
- Income security

— Power over the following nine areas will be jointly shared between the governments of Quebec and Canada:

- Native affairs
- Taxation and revenue
- Immigration
- Justice
- Fisheries
- Foreign policy
- Post office and telecommunications
- Transport
- Financial institutions

— That would leave the federal government in exclusive control over only four jurisdictions:

- Defense and territorial security
- Customs and tariffs
- Currency and common debt
- Equalization (apportioning federal transfer payments to the provinces based on need)

— The Quebec National Assembly will write a Constitution of Quebec, which will include the existing Quebec Charter of Human Rights and Freedoms.

— Under the Canadian economic union, there will be no obstacle to the free movement of people, goods and capital throughout Canada, and both Quebec and Canada will share a common currency and customs union.

— Canada will be required to rewrite its constitution in such a way as to guarantee all provinces' right to withdraw upon advance notice. Constitutional amendments must be approved by a majority of the provinces together representing at least half Canada's population, and must be approved in any case by Quebec. The Senate in its current form — appointed by the federal government — will be abolished. The Bank of Canada will continue to be an independent entity but will come under some control of regional representatives.

— The Quebec government will hold a provincial referendum before the end of the fall of 1992 to vote on these reforms. If no agreement is reached, the referendum will be held anyway, but the proposal will instead be to make Quebec a sovereign state. (The Bélanger-Campeau commission suggested that the referendum be held no later than Oct. 26, 1992, and that it propose simply that Quebec become independent. If Quebeckers agree, the province would become an independent country by 1993.)

*Continued from p. 208*
some of the Lévesque government's measures, such as a 1977 law banning English on commercial signs. Lévesque's call for "sovereignty-association" — political independence with strong economic ties to Canada — garnered widespread support among the French-speaking majority in Quebec. But it also prompted many English-speaking business leaders to migrate west to Ontario, taking their manufacturing plants and other considerable economic assets with them. The flight of capital from their province startled Quebeckers, who voted against Lévesque's call to separate from Canada in a referendum held May 20, 1980.*

The most recent chapter in Quebec's quest for self-determination began in 1982, when Canada acquired a constitution. Until that time, the country's basic charter had consisted of the 1867 British North America Act, a law passed by the British Parliament. That law established the Canadian confederation, which today consists of Quebec, the other nine provinces and two federal territories — the Northwest Territories and the Yukon. (*See map, p. 212.*) As part of his goal to strengthen the confederation under a strong central government, Prime Minister Trudeau petitioned the British government to "patriate" the basic charter to Canada. In 1982, Britain's Parliament did so by passing the Constitution Act, and Queen Elizabeth II appeared in Ottawa that summer to transmit the law to Canada.

The new constitution retained the basic political structure of the Canadian confederation established by the North America Act. The Canadian Parliament has power over jurisdictions that are not specifically reserved for the provinces, such as foreign trade, national defense and international relations. The provinces maintain the power to collect taxes, provide social services such as health care and education and to run provincial affairs. But the constitution also added some new elements. One is the Charter of Rights and Freedoms, which like the American Bill of Rights enumerates individual rights, such as freedom of speech. The Charter also establishes collective rights, including those of women and of Canada's minority aboriginal populations.

All the provinces except Quebec ratified the new constitution in 1982. Then, as now, the Quebec government protested that the constitution vested too much power in the central government and denied Quebec sufficient autonomy to preserve its unique culture within the confederation.

After winning the elections of December 1985, Quebec Premier Robert Bourassa presented the federal government with what he called Quebec's five minimal demands for accepting the constitution. These were the explicit recognition of Quebec as a "distinct society" and of its right to opt out of federal laws that

adversely affect the province; greater provincial control over immigration; stricter limits on the federal government's spending authority; and the right to nominate Supreme Court justices.

All five of Quebec's demands were incorporated into amendments contained in the Meech Lake Accord, which Prime Minister Mulroney and all 10 provincial premiers agreed to June 3, 1987. Under the terms of the agreement, the constitutional amendments were to take effect if they were ratified separately by the federal government and by all 10 provincial governments by June 23, 1990. The Canadian government and seven provinces quickly ratified Meech Lake. But Manitoba and New Brunswick refused to do so unless the distinct-society clause was deleted. Later, newly elected Newfoundland Premier Clyde Wells rescinded his predecessor's approval of Meech Lake. On June 15, 1990, the New Brunswick legislature finally approved the pact. But on June 22, the day before the deadline, the Manitoba and Newfoundland legislatures adjourned without ratifying Meech Lake.

## Events following the collapse of the Meech Lake Accord

Of all Quebec's demands in the Meech Lake Accord, the one that effectively torpedoed the agreement was recognition of Quebec as a distinct society. "By recognizing Quebec as a distinct society, which most Canadians do, and not recognizing other people as important and distinct, like the aboriginals, it really got people's egos involved," says Peter Russell of the University of Toronto. "It was like giving out lollipops to kids. Quebec was getting the big lollipop and others were not. People said, 'We think Quebec's distinct, sure, but aren't we important, too? Don't we deserve some sort of mention in the constitution?'"

Bourassa, who like Mulroney had given his full support to the Meech Lake constitutional amendments, interpreted the accord's failure as a rebuff by English Canada of Quebec. On June 23, just after the deadline for ratification passed, Bourassa declared that because the negotiating process had failed, Quebec was now "free to choose" its fate. He then appointed a commission of Quebec Liberal Party members to canvass the province to find out what Quebeckers wanted to do next.

The result was the Allaire report, entitled "A Quebec Free to Choose," whose recommendations were adopted almost in full at the recent party congress. The report recommended a vast political and constitutional reform that would make Quebec an autonomous state within a reorganized Canada. The reform would leave the federal government in Ottawa with exclusive control over only four jurisdictions: defense and territorial security; customs and tariffs; currency and the

---

*For background, see "Canada's Political Conflicts," *E.R.R.*, Dec. 24, 1981 (Vol. II, No. 24).

common debt; and equalization, payments that the federal government currently pays to poorer provinces.

The provincial and federal governments would share jurisdiction over nine areas, including several that are traditionally the domain of central authority, such as the postal system and telecommunications, justice and foreign policy. The reform would grant Quebec exclusive control over 22 areas now controlled either entirely or in part by the federal government. Quebec would have its own constitution and Supreme Court. Ottawa would be required to abolish the Senate in its present form, reorganize the Bank of Canada and rewrite the Canadian Constitution. Quebec would have veto power over amending that constitution and would be free to pull out.

Even Liberal Party members were surprised at the degree of support the Allaire report received. Largely as a result of the strong sovereigntist feeling among the party's youth organization, who made up about a third of the delegates, the party's federalist faction succeeded in making only two significant changes to the commission's report. One change specifically guaranteed English rights in Quebec and the other called for inclusion of the Canadian Charter of Rights and Freedoms in any new Canadian Constitution.

But the federalists went down to defeat in their effort to dilute one of the Allaire report's most controversial demands for negotiating constitutional changes with the rest of Canada. The Meech Lake Accord had been drawn up by the prime minister as well as all 10 provincial premiers. But because the agreement had been torpedoed by two provincial governments, the Allaire commission decided Quebec should now bypass the other provinces and negotiate exclusively with the federal government, which in the past has supported many of Quebec's demands. The federalists in the party feared that the other provinces would refuse to accept any agreement based on negotiations on constitutional questions that would affect them all but from which they had been excluded.

The federalists also were counting on the other provinces to use their bargaining clout to dilute the strong decentralizing theme of the Allaire report and retain greater federal control over the country and the province. When the party delegates voted against their proposal and kept the Allaire report's demand to negotiate exclusively with Ottawa, the federalists walked out of the meeting, prompting fears among supporters of a united Canada that the party — and the Quebec government — would be left in the hands of sovereigntists bent on leading Quebec into independence.

Eager to keep his party intact, Premier Bourassa was able to prevent a split in his ranks by declaring in his closing speech to the party congress March 10 that his first priority was to "develop Quebec inside Canada in a federal structure. That's the first choice of the Quebec Liberal Party. We have common values. We have two centuries of common history, and Canada, as we know, is one of the most envied countries in the world."

But Bourassa will find it much more difficult to placate the sovereigntist forces outside his party. For the Parti Québécois under its current leader, Jacques Parizeau, negotiations with the rest of Canada are a waste of time. Sovereignty is the party's sole agenda. Party officials outline a number of reasons why it is only as a sovereign state that Quebec can survive and prosper.[2] First, they say, sovereignty is necessary for Quebec to flourish as a Francophone nation. Quebec's low birth rate and the preference of most immigrants to live in English-speaking Canada threaten the survival of French language and culture in the province. Even the stringent language law passed in 1977 barring English on commercial signs, they point out, has been undermined by later Canadian Supreme Court decisions and by the federal law promoting bilingualism as Canada's official language policy. A related reason for Quebec's need to achieve sovereign status, the Parti Québécois says, is to make French-speakers a majority in their own nation. Francophones, who constituted half of Canada's population in 1840, now account for barely a quarter, and most of them live in Quebec.

Parti Québécois supporters also claim that sovereignty would end the waste produced by the current power-sharing arrangement between Ottawa and the provinces in certain sectors. Like most U.S. citizens, Canadians have to file two income tax returns. In addition, each province has separate federal and provincial departments of finance, health, agriculture and immigration, to name a few. Of course, grumbling about government waste and red tape is nothing new to Americans: Ronald Reagan's call to "get the government off our backs" helped catapult him and the Republican Party to power in the 1980s. But in Quebec, sentiment against Ottawa is strong enough for sovereigntists to cite government waste as one more reason to break away from the federal system altogether.

Quebec sovereigntists claim the federal government has acted against the province's economic interests and favored the English provinces, especially Ontario. The Parti Québécois cites as an example of Ottawa's bias against Quebec the 1965 auto pact with the United States, which has created 175,000 new jobs in Ontario, accounting for 90 percent of the auto industry's expansion in Canada that the pact was designed to accomplish. Quebec, by contrast, has garnered only 9 percent of the new auto industry jobs. Further, Quebec sovereigntists, like government critics in the Western provinces, say that by pushing up interest rates, the Bank of Canada has geared its monetary policy toward the needs of Ontario. While high interest rates may help cool Ontario's overheated economy, they are deepening the already severe recession in Quebec and other provinces.

In calling for autonomy, the Parti Québécois points to Quebec's healthy local economy as the basis for its future prosperity. Even after the flight of capital from Quebec that accompanied the exodus of English

| Province/Territory | Population (in thousands) |
|---|---|

**1991 population†**

| Province/Territory | Population (in thousands) |
|---|---|
| Newfoundland | 571.7 |
| Prince Edward Island | 129.9 |
| Nova Scotia | 897.5 |
| New Brunswick | 725.6 |
| Quebec | 6,811.8 |
| Ontario | 9,840.3 |
| Manitoba | 1,092.6 |
| Saskatchewan | 995.3 |
| Alberta | 2,501.4 |
| British Columbia | 3,185.9 |
| Yukon Territory | 26.5 |
| Northwest Territories | 54.0 |

† As of Jan. 1, 1991.

**Language spoken at home**

| Province/Territory | English | French | Other |
|---|---|---|---|
| Newfoundland | 99.2 % | 0.4 % | 0.4 % |
| Prince Edward Island | 96.8 | 2.8 | 0.4 |
| Nova Scotia | 96.0 | 2.9 | 1.1 |
| New Brunswick | 68.1 | 31.3 | 0.6 |
| Quebec | 12.3 | 82.8 | 4.9 |
| Ontario | 86.6 | 3.8 | 9.6 |
| Manitoba | 87.2 | 2.8 | 9.9 |
| Saskatchewan | 93.8 | 0.9 | 5.3 |
| Alberta | 92.0 | 1.1 | 6.9 |
| British Columbia | 91.4 | 0.6 | 8.0 |
| Yukon Territory | 97.0 | 1.2 | 1.8 |
| Northwest Territories | 66.2 | 1.5 | 32.4 |

★ Province/Territory capital
⊛ National capital

Source: Statistics Canada.

business interests in the 1970s, the province's economic base has continued to expand. In recent years it has grown faster than that of the country as a whole. Local manufacturing industries, such as Bombardier Inc.'s subway car production, have been joined by subsidiaries of foreign firms, such as South Korea's Hyundai and General Motors Corp. And the province's generation of hydroelectric power, which it exports to New England and New York, continues to be an important source of revenue. All this leads sovereigntists to predict that an independent Quebec could go it alone, even in an increasingly interdependent world.

"We Quebeckers have a problem to solve," Parti Québécois leader Jacques Parizeau told U.S. businessmen recently. "We are undoubtedly North Americans, of French roots and culture. We have developed an economy that is, in North America, rather peculiar: We do not do things quite in the same way.... We are ready to take our chances in the global village and according to its rules."[3]

Premier Bourassa appears, for now at least, to reject the Parti Québécois' agenda for full sovereignty. The recommendations of another Quebec study group, this one a 37-member commission appointed by Bourassa's provincial government and headed by businessmen Michel Bélanger and Jean Campeau, were far more solidly in the sovereigntist camp than the Allaire report. But even after the Bélanger-Campeau commission released its proposals in late March, the Quebec premier seemed to maintain control over the sovereigntist-federalist debate in his province.

## *How English Canada views the new constitutional talks*

English Canada expressed little appreciation of Bourassa's struggle to keep the lid on sovereigntist forces in Quebec. "People outside Quebec, with the exception of the Mulroney government, don't trust Bourassa because they think he has to answer to his sovereigntist camp," explains Daniel Bonin of Queen's University in Ontario.

The Quebec Liberal Party's insistence on conducting future negotiations solely with the federal government was roundly denounced by several provincial leaders. New Brunswick Premier Frank McKenna, whose government originally rejected the Meech Lake Accord, made it clear he was not prepared to delegate the job of changing the constitution to Ottawa. "We have a very real stake in those talks and we are not prepared to abandon the interests of the people of New Brunswick," McKenna said. Spokesmen for Western provinces, which have supported Quebec's goal of decentralizing Canada's federal government, also balked at Bourassa's proposal to cut them out of the process of constitutional change.

There was little encouragement from the opponents of Meech Lake for Quebec's emerging position on constitutional change. Premier Clyde Wells of Newfoundland, who withdrew his province's earlier support for the Meech Lake Accord, advanced a proposal of his own for getting constitutional talks started once again. In a speech delivered in Ottawa the same night the Quebec Liberal Party opened its debate on the Allaire report, Wells suggested that Quebec have a limited veto power over constitutional reforms concerning language, culture and civil law. Wells said such a veto power should be granted Quebec through its representatives in a future elected Senate.

Wells' proposal and Quebec's response to it provide little hope for resolution of the constitutional dilemma, however. Bourassa, who is often referred to as "the accountant" and is not given to colorful remarks, responded tersely to Wells' proposal, saying "it would have been a lot easier if he had ratified the Meech Lake Accord." Gil Rémillard, Bourassa's minister for intergovernmental affairs, was more outspoken. "Asking Clyde Wells to suggest constitutional reform to Quebec is like putting Dracula in charge of the blood bank," he quipped.[4]

For the federal government, the Quebec Liberal Party's ultimatum set the clock ticking toward a deadline in the fall of 1992. This meant Brian Mulroney would have little time to act on the findings of the three

commissions that are still at work on proposals of their own.* All are due to release their findings on the symbolic date of July 1, Canada Day.**

Assuming the three commissions meet their July 1 deadlines, the Mulroney government will have about 17 months to decide which proposals to put forward to Quebec and — assuming the other nine provinces continue to insist on participating in the subsequent negotiations — to the other players in the failed Meech Lake process as well. His ability to do so will become more apparent in mid-August, when his party, the Progressive Conservative Party, holds its national policy congress in Toronto. Like Bourassa, Mulroney must gain his party's blessing for any plan he takes before the nation to resolve the constitutional crisis.

So far, Mulroney's plans are obscure. He has referred vaguely to what he calls a "*project de pays,*" or national plan, that he said in a recent speech would "allow a rebuilt Canada to emerge." But he left no doubt that such a reconstituted Canada would include Quebec, and he condemned the notion of negotiating with sovereigntist "dream merchants" on a withdrawal of the province from the Canadian confederation. Speaking before the Chamber of Commerce in Quebec City Feb. 13, Mulroney said, "My responsibility as prime minister is not to treat with kid gloves those who are set on destroying or abandoning our country, but to represent those who want to preserve and improve it for their children and grandchildren. The real choice facing Quebeckers is between remaining citizens of Canada and becoming citizens of another country. You can't have a part-time country."

For the moment, Mulroney is taking an optimistic position on Quebec's constitutional proposals and emphasizes the Quebec premier's stated support for Quebec's continued role in the Canadian confederation. "Premier Bourassa said that the Liberal Party had, as its first choice, a stronger Quebec, within a united and strong Canada," Mulroney told the House of Commons the day after the Quebec Liberal Party congress ended.

For Mulroney, himself a Quebecker, new negotiations for a constitutional agreement could hardly come at a worse time. He and his Conservative Party are at the lowest point in the opinion polls since Mulroney became party leader in 1983, mostly for reasons having little to do with the constitutional impasse.

---

*One of these commissions, the 12-member Citizen's Forum on Canada's Future, has met with considerable controversy because its chairman, Keith Spicer, has already spent the group's entire budget. News of the scandal fanned the flames of antifederal sentiment throughout Canada, which has long focused on reports of government waste and fraud. Another commission, made up of deputy ministers of Mulroney's government, has been meeting regularly once a week and is said to favor a highly decentralized plan for the confederation. A third commission, chaired by Sen. Gerald Beaudoin and Jim Edwards, a member of Parliament from Alberta, is more narrowly focused on finding a constitutional amending formula that would satisfy all the provinces.

**Canada's national day, formerly known as Dominion Day, commemorates the confederation of Upper and Lower Canada and some of the Maritime Provinces into the Dominion of Canada on that day in 1867.

# Canada and the Free Trade Agreement

**W**hen Canada and the United States signed a free-trade agreement in 1988, which was designed to eliminate tariffs and other obstacles to the free trade of goods and services between the two countries, many Canadians feared their country would be hurt by the deal. The fear north of the border was that small Canadian businesses could not compete against bigger firms in the United States without protection. Protests against the pact were widespread, and the Progressive Conservative government of Prime Minister Brian Mulroney suffered in the opinion polls.

Two years later, Canadian opinion about the arrangement is still largely negative. Many small businesses have indeed folded as predicted, and many Canadians blame their country's 10.2 percent unemployment rate on free trade with the United States. Recent plant closings in Canada, including a General Motors Corp. plant near Montreal and several auto parts plants in Ontario, have heightened antagonism toward the pact.

"The downside of free trade up here is getting a lot more publicity than the upside," says Peter Russell, a professor

of political science at the University of Toronto. "It's small potatoes for the American economy, but it's big stuff here."

Similar fears are being expressed about current negotiations to extend the free-trade area to include Mexico.† Although Canada is among the seven leading industrial economies in the world and Mexico is far less developed than either of its potential partners, many Canadians fear that removing all protections from competition from Mexico will further undermine their well-being. Because of Mexico's lower labor costs, Canadian goods may not be able to compete with Mexican goods in the U.S. market. McGill University economist William G. Watson points out that "fully $59 billion worth of Canadian exports to the U.S. market, or 60 percent of the total, is in direct competition with Mexican goods." ††

The Mulroney government strongly supports Canada's participation in a North American Free Trade Area, as the enlarged liberalized trade area is to be called. "We are more dependent on trade than either Mexico or the United States

for our economic well-being," says Canadian Ambassador D. H. Burney. "We're looking for avenues of trade liberalization wherever we can find them."

Opposition to the government's plan to support a North American Free Trade Area is concentrated in English Canada. Despite the recent shutdown of GM's operations near Montreal, trade liberalization remains popular in Quebec as a means of enhancing the province's strong export industries if it should become a sovereign state.

But if Quebec leaves Canada, it will have to renegotiate its place in the free-trade area with Canada, the United States and Mexico. And there is no guarantee that it will enjoy the same benefits it does today. "Indeed," says Russell, "one of the things that may keep Quebec in Canada is their fear of being kicked out of the Free Trade Agreement."

† *For background, see "North American Trade Pact: A Good Idea?" E.R.R., Dec. 8, 1989 (Vol. II, No. 21).*

†† *William G. Watson, "Canada's Trade With and Against Mexico," an unpublished paper prepared while a visiting associate for Canadian affairs at the Americas Society in New York City.*

---

Mulroney is blamed for Canada's recession, which has been prolonged by high interest rates imposed by the Bank of Canada. He also came under fire for imposing the new General Sales Tax, which went into effect last December and raised the price of most goods sold in Canada. Mulroney also is blamed for what many Canadians see are the negative effects of the two-year-old Free Trade Agreement with the United States. (*See story, above.*)

As a result, Mulroney must negotiate on behalf of the rest of Canada at a time when his ability to do so is faltering, especially in the Western provinces, where antifederal and anti-Quebec sentiments often coincide. "I can think of no one less qualified than Brian Mulroney to speak for English Canada in the controversy over the place of Quebec in the Constitution...," a resident of British Columbia wrote to the editor of *Maclean's*, Canada's leading weekly newsmagazine. "Mulroney has amply demonstrated his devotion to the interests of Quebec ever since he came to office. The Liberals have played the game for many decades of buying votes in Quebec with gross conces-

sions from English Canada. ... We must stop the practice of letting Quebeckers in Ottawa make deals with Quebec." [5]

But Mulroney was not the lone English Canadian voice to express some hope after the Quebec Liberal Party congress. Federalists outside Quebec were heartened by the changes the party delegates did make to the Allaire report. One in particular called for abolition of Canada's Senate as it is currently constituted. Senators today are not elected, but rather appointed by the federal government. The Senate rarely exercises any power, though nominally it has the same powers as the elected House of Commons. Support for an elected Senate with an equal number of senators from each province has been especially strong in the Western provinces, which already feel underrepresented in Ottawa. The Allaire report had recommended the abolition of the Senate without further qualification, a measure that would have killed many Westerners' vehicle for greater representation. By asking instead that the *existing* Senate be abolished, Quebec has left open the door of Senate reform and won the potential support of many of its harshest critics.

But the overall theme of the Allaire report, both in its original form and as it was endorsed by the Quebec Liberal Party, has found support among some federal government critics in ways that cannot be good news to Mulroney and other supporters of Canada's strong federal system. Edward McWhinney of Simon Fraser University suggests that the Western provinces may overcome their traditional antipathy toward Quebec as an integral element of the hated "center" in the Canadian polity. "A good deal of the Allaire commission report coincides with thinking in British Columbia," he says. "If Quebec wants decentralization for nationalistic reasons, it may be that what it is asking for coincides with desires for decentralization in the provinces — other than Ontario — for economic reasons."

The push for decentralization, long a priority in the West, is spreading to other provinces because of growing resentment of the federal government's monetary policy. John Crow, the governor of the Bank of Canada and a Mulroney appointee, has come under fire throughout the country, except in Ontario, for raising interest rates and deepening the recession.

While the United States appears poised to enter into a recovery after only two months of recession, Canada sees no relief in sight. In February, the national unemployment rate hit 10.2 percent, its highest level since October 1985. In some cities — including St. John, Newfoundland; Montreal; Quebec; and Windsor, Ontario — the jobless rate exceeds 12 percent of the work force. While the Western provinces are not faring as badly, high interest rates are impeding the development programs of British Columbia, especially the province's plans to promote trade with Asia. The Allaire report's recommendation that regional representatives share some control over Bank of Canada policies has thus found sympathy in parts of English Canada, especially British Columbia and Alberta.

## Prospects for a negotiated settlement with Quebec

As the study commissions complete their recommendations for a federal response to Quebec's proposals, the rhetoric is likely to escalate on both sides of the issue. Peter Russell, who has been involved in the constitutional debate for many years, predicts that "there will be some tough bargaining in the year ahead, and I think it's going to start off pretty hard-nosed on each side." If he is right, Prime Minister Mulroney's earlier warning to the sovereigntist "dream merchants" of Quebec means they are likely to come under heavy fire this summer. English Canada is taking the position, Russell says, that "we're not going to tear this country apart to accommodate Quebec; we're not gong to weaken the center to the point of idiocy, where

we have a non-government in Ottawa, just in order to keep Quebec part of Canada. That would really be unity at any price, and the price would be too great."

Although Bourassa did not concede that his party's platform is negotiable, most observers say it is only the opening proposal in what is likely to be a protracted bargaining session. "It is well understood that neither the Allaire commission report nor the Bélanger-Campeau report is necessarily Mr. Bourassa's present position or his opinion," says Edward McWhinney. An adviser to Bourassa at an earlier point in his political career, McWhinney agrees with many analysts that the Quebec premier is above all pragmatic. "He's not an ideologue. He's almost value-neutral, and I don't think he has strong views on federalism or on non-federalism."

If McWhinney is correct, Bourassa may well place some of his province's more controversial demands on the table. Some of the powers Quebec wants to control exclusively, for example, could be up for discussion at the negotiating table. Even the insistence that Quebec no longer deal with the other provincial governments may well be dropped if it becomes clear that no agreement can be reached by negotiating with the central government alone. "You really can't avoid the provincial political leaders," McWhinney explains. "The key element in studying the Allaire report is to determine what amounts to throwaway points that were just put in there for the negotiations to drop at the appropriate moment as a concession to the other side, and what is really core thinking."

As for the majority of Quebeckers who today say they want sovereignty, McWhinney says that, too, may change. "People who want their own state are not necessarily a majority. The independence movement, like any political movement, is a coalition, and it includes some very disappointed federalists who might choose the federal option again if they were satisfied it was the better one."

The better option McWhinney describes might be the decentralized federal system desired by many Westerners. "Something like that would be supported by British Columbia and, I think, by the neighboring province of Alberta as well as by Quebec. So you've immediately got three votes, and it's not too difficult to get perhaps nine out of 10 provinces going along with that idea."

Such an outcome may be more than wishful thinking by frustrated Westerners who are eager to wrest greater powers from Ottawa. Some Francophone Quebeckers, although they may not support the move, agree that Bourassa may well prove willing to negotiate away some of his province's demands if that means he obtains an agreement with Ottawa. The reason, says Daniel Bonin, is that "Bourassa is not a real sovereigntist."

But while Bourassa himself may be willing to throw away some of his party's demands in the interests of keeping Canada whole, his freedom to maneuver will be limited by sovereigntists whose support has been essential to his political survival. Bonin says that of the 22 exclusive powers the Quebec Liberal Party claims, Bourassa can only afford to negotiate away a few without tearing up the fragile consensus he has built. "He has to claim at least 12 to 15 exclusive powers for Quebec, which is already too much for the rest of Canada. Even though Bourassa doesn't present those claims as just something for Quebec but rather as something the other provinces should ask for as well, it is not necessarily in their interests to do so." And although some of the Western provinces, especially British Columbia and Alberta, are interested in decentralizing the federal system, Bonin says, "Quebec is really the only province to be really interested in such broad decentralization."

Nevertheless, there may be another road toward compromise in the negotiations on Canada's future. Despite the seemingly stiff demands coming out of Quebec, Peter Russell sees hope in the fact that they do not include such symbolic and vague claims as the recognition of Quebec as a distinct society — the demand that was largely responsible for the demise last year of the Meech Lake Accord. "Constitutional politics are fundamentally about symbols, and people are much more concerned about the symbols of power," he says. The fact that Quebec's demands today include only a few such symbols may ease the process toward a constitutional agreement, in Russell's view. "This time they're really down to brass tacks, and they're not talking about flags and symbols but some real powers. That may be an easier agenda even though it's more brutal in real, functional terms." With the talks aimed at real, technical issues, Russell hopes, agreement can be found on technical grounds.

One technical key to agreement, Russell says, may be a concept that already exists in the Canadian Constitution that allows the provinces to have their way when federal laws conflict with their own. As in the United States, federal legislation in Canada ordinarily supersedes provincial, or state, legislation when conflicts between the two jurisdictions arise. But there is an exception to this rule in Canadian law. Section 94 of the constitution, which governs pension legislation, states that both the federal government and the provinces can pass laws relating to pensions. But under terms added to the constitution in the 1950s, Russell explains, provincial law will prevail if there is a conflict in pension laws. Called "concurrent power with provincial paramountcy," this legal concept has been invoked to date only by Quebec, which now has its own pension system while the other provinces remain covered by the federal pension system. Because all the provinces enjoy the same right as Quebec to override federal law in pension policy, Russell says, "everybody's been very happy and it's not an issue in Canada."

In Russell's view, "you could extend that concept [of provincial paramountcy] to social policy, cultural policy and communications and just put it in the

constitution for all provinces to have this opportunity and not single out Quebec. Then Quebec could exercise some real autonomy in some of these areas."

While Russell supports extending the concurrent-power notion to some of the areas Quebec wants to control exclusively, he emphasizes that the process of negotiating changes to the constitution could collapse at any time. While Bourassa concluded the recent party congress saying the ball is now in federal Canada's court, Russell urges caution to Quebeckers who want to stop short of leaving the confederation. To his friends in the Quebec government, Russell warns, "You may get committed to your own rhetoric, you may get on a sort of a political course that you can't reverse, once you've got all this out in public and made such a to-do out of it."

## Impact of Quebec sovereignty on the rest of Canada

Many close observers of past constitutional talks say that Quebec has already gone too far in its demands to find a compromise solution with the rest of Canada. If they prove right, there is considerable disagreement over the impact a breakup of the confederation would have on both Quebec and the rest of Canada.

In the view of Parti Québécois and other sovereigntists, Quebec stands to profit from independence. Fears that the Quebec economy could not survive separation from Canada drove Quebeckers to reject sovereignty in 1980. Today, however, many view the situation differently, says PQ leader Jacques Parizeau. "What studies have shown . . . is that after the divorce the Quebec household would be viable and could even have better growth prospects providing that quarreling and working at cross-purposes with Canada be put to rest," he says.

Quebec's economy has indeed grown since the early 1980s when many English-speaking business owners left the province. Today, the province boasts an economy the size of Austria's and a per capita income — a measure of standard of living — that ranks 16th in the world.[6] Quebec is headquarters to some of Canada's leading enterprises, such as Air Canada, the national airline that passed into private ownership under the Mulroney government's drive to privatize many of Canada's state-owned businesses in the late 1980s. Primary resources continue to bolster the local economy. Hydro Quebec, the electric utility, is owned by the provincial government, which is planning to expand its production from James Bay. Alcan Aluminium, a large aluminum producer, also is headquartered in Montreal.

Quebec — one of the few provinces where supporters of the free-trade agreement with the United States seem to outnumber its critics — would continue to

*Continued on p. 218*

# AT ISSUE
*Are negotiations to keep Quebec part of Canada doomed to fail?*

## YES
*says the* **PARTI QUEBECOIS**, *the main opposition party in Quebec and the leading advocate of sovereignty for the province for the past 30 years.*

To allow Quebec to reintegrate the Canadian Constitution with pride and enthusiasm, the Bourassa government imposed the five conditions enumerated in the Meech Lake Accord signed in 1987. These minimal conditions are the lowest ever presented by a Quebec government in the last 30 years, but it is now evident that it is still too much to ask of English Canada. The constitutional deadlock is a clear indication of Canada's incapacity to recognize any type of specific status within the federation.

Two very different and clearly incompatible visions of the federal system and of Quebec's place in it are clashing: While English Canada favors a strong central government placed above equal provinces, Quebec rather considers its Parliament as the legitimate advocate of its national interests and demands maximum autonomy within the federation. Two nations oppose one another: Quebec and Canada. *It is clear that we will never agree!*

Anglophone provinces show an unprecedented anti-francophone trend. Quebec is considered as the one who always asks for more and who is never satisfied. The Meech Lake Accord, however, does not give Quebec any real additional powers. There is no new distribution of powers such as it has historically been claimed by Quebec. And as for the famous recognition of Quebec as being a distinct society, it is now defined in the accord and no one can really describe its implications. It is now clearer than ever that Quebeckers will never obtain from Canada the powers essential to its full development. The debate over Meech served as revealing a situation and as a catalyst for history to renew itself.

In such a context, it is not surprising that sovereignty is seen by an increasingly large number of Quebeckers as the alternative to a centralizing federalism. The most recent surveys reveal that an unprecedented 60 percent of Quebeckers now favor sovereignty. In addition ... the business community is now openly confident in Quebec's capacity to confidently undertake the challenge of a new political status. Even major financial institutions, banks and brokerage firms are now reassuring the population about the economic future of a sovereign Quebec. *Sovereignty has never been closer.*

*From "Sovereignty: Why? How?" an undated paper by the Parti Québécois.*

## NO
*says* **CHARLES GORDON**, *a columnist with* The Ottawa Citizen.

Intelligent, tolerant and open-minded Canadians, people who fought hard to keep the country together through the flag debate, the early bilingualism wars, the October Crisis, the Parti Québécois election victory of 1976, the Quebec referendum, the constitutional debates of the early 1980s, Meech Lake — many such Canadians are uttering what may be the mantra of the 1990s: "It's over," they say, too tired from carrying the weight of doom to ponder any more steps.

What weighs them down, aside from at least two decades' worth of words, is a growing sense of inevitability. Each setback adds to the feeling that the whole thing was doomed from the start. What is easily forgotten, however, is how close we have been, in many occasions, to success. If, pardon the expression, the dice had come up a bit differently, we would not be in our current mess.

Everybody remembers the failure of Meech Lake; few remember how close the accord was to succeeding. ... The breaks of politics, not historical inevitability, destroyed Meech Lake. The lesson to be learned from that is not that we are doomed, but that the breaks of politics might work in our favor the next time....

The Bourassa government put forward a law saying that the English language could be used only on indoor commercial signs. Historical inevitability? No, the response of a nervous politician, desperate to hang on to nationalist votes. Yet, more than any other factor, Bill 178 created in English Canada the backlash that made the defeat of Meech Lake possible, even popular....

Without Bill 178, Meech Lake might have passed. Even with Bill 178, Meech might have had support in English Canada had different political forces been at work — one such being enthusiastic leadership by the prime minister....

The situation can change, will change. Time and inertia are on our side. For Quebec, leaving Canada is much more difficult to do than staying in. Divorce takes an effort of will and it takes considerable time, during which the political climate and the political cast of characters can change....

Change is all around us and there is no reason why change cannot be for the better, if we don't give up. Even doom is not forever.

*From "Changing the Words to Change the Mood,"* Maclean's, *Feb. 25, 1991, p. 11.*

*Continued from p. 216*

benefit from that pact, sovereigntists say. Although the sovereigntists are calling for an economic union with the rest of Canada, they are also looking to the United States, already a major source of export revenue, as a natural focus of economic expansion. But if Quebec separates from Canada, it would also leave the existing free-trade area. "They would have to work out some kind of terms of accession for Quebec to the agreement because it's an agreement between Ottawa and Washington," says William Watson, a professor of economics at McGill University in Montreal who is currently on leave to study the impact of free trade for the Americas Society in New York. "The international law is not even ambiguous on this matter. Quebec is not a party to it." If Quebec must negotiate a separate trade pact with the United States, it may end up with less favorable terms than it now enjoys. "People naturally ask what they can get out of people in negotiations, and if I were Washington I would do the same thing," Watson says. "That's not emphasized very much in the Quebec debate."

For Quebec, then, sovereignty is a risky affair, but one that many federalists now concede may not spell disaster for the province as many previously feared. As for the impact of Quebec's secession on the rest of Canada, opinions vary widely. Some critics have predicted dire consequences for the four small provinces that lie to the east of Quebec — New Brunswick, Newfoundland, Nova Scotia and Prince Edward Island — and that would be cut off physically from the rest of Canada. These Maritime Provinces, it has been said, would be "Pakistanized," or impoverished by their isolation from Ontario and the other centers of wealth much as Pakistan has fared following its break with India. Watson dismisses this fear, reminding critics that the Maritimes "do have telephones and fax machines and much of their overland travel is done via the United States." And in any case, he points out, Alaska has fared well despite its physical separation from the lower 48 states.[7]

There are proposals afloat for the rest of Canada to pursue Quebec's scheme for radical decentralization one step further and transform the remaining provinces into a loose association of five nations consisting of Canada East (the Maritimes), Canada West (present-day British Columbia, Alberta, Saskatchewan and Manitoba), Quebec, Ontario and the Territories (today the Yukon and Northwest Territories). The five Canadian nations could form a common market and share some political functions much as the European Economic Community is planning to do beginning in 1992.

But all these visions assume that Quebec and the rest of Canada will separate peaceably. Desmond Morton, one of the more pessimistic Canadian observers, says history provides little encouragement for such an optimistic outcome. "I've been pretty much denounced for my pains because it does lead you to make dangerous assertions about a violent future," he says.

Many analysts compare Quebec's quest for independence to that of the Baltic States that are now struggling for independence from the Soviet Union. That struggle has not been free of violence, and yet Quebec is a far more integral part of Canada than the Baltics are to the Soviet Union. Morton cautions against straining the analogy, but repeats his warning that Quebec's separation would not be easy. "There are integral problems of who splits the national debt and who splits the national assets, all of which can be resolved if you have time, patience and good will. But how often have we had divorces among our friends described in those terms? They always start that way, in my experience, saying they are going to be adult and different. But they aren't."

Watson is less worried than Morton that Quebec's eventual secession would cause severe economic or political problems there or in the rest of Canada. Once English Canada realizes Quebec really does want to go its own way, he says, "I think most English Canadians will take the view that we should do everything we can to make the break as painless as possible." But even English Canadians like Watson, who are pretty much resigned to the notion that Quebec will eventually secede from Canada, are saddened by the prospect. "The prospect of my country's breaking up is dismaying," Watson said recently. "I was in Ottawa last week. On the point of land behind the new national art gallery stands a statue of Samuel de Champlain, looking out at the Parliament buildings just upriver. The hardy souls and bold spirits who explored and settled Canada and, in the middle of last century, built a federal Parliament in a small, rude logging town would be dismayed at the prospect, too."[8]

# NOTES

[1] The poll was conducted among 1,000 Quebeckers on March 20, 1991, by the polling firm IQOP. The margin of error was reported to be 3 percent.

[2] The Parti Québécois' platform is described in an undated paper entitled "Sovereignty: Why? How?" obtained from Quebec Government House in New York.

[3] Parizeau addressed the New York Forum on International Business, Feb. 26, 1991.

[4] Quoted in Don MacDonald, "Les propos de Wells n'intéressent aucunement Rémillard," *La Presse*, March 10, 1991, p. A3.

[5] Writing in *Maclean's*, March 18, 1991, p. 6.

[6] Figures taken from "Québec," an undated document prepared by the Parti Québécois.

[7] Speaking before the Americas Society, Jan. 24, 1991.

[8] From Watson's Jan. 24 speech.

*Graphics: Cover, Margaret Scott; p. 212, Jack Auldridge.*

# BOOKS

**Cohen, Andrew, *A Deal Undone: The Making and Breaking of the Meech Lake Accord*, Douglas & McIntyre, 1990.**

The author, a journalist who has covered Canada's constitutional crisis for more than 10 years, presents a close look at the process that produced the Meech Lake Accord to obtain Quebec's acceptance of the constitution. Interviews with provincial premiers and other players in the negotiations reveal the fundamental disagreements among various parts of the country that torpedoed the pact last June.

**Milne, David, *The Canadian Constitution: From Patriation to Meech Lake*, James Lorimer & Company, 1989.**

Milne, a constitutional expert who teaches Canadian politics at the University of Prince Edward Island, describes the story of Canada's Constitution from 1980 through the Meech Lake Accord reached in 1987. He also analyzes the origins of the Charter of Rights and Freedoms, Canada's equivalent to the U.S. Bill of Rights.

# ARTICLES

**"The Choice Facing Canada," *Maclean's*, Feb, 18, 1991, pp. 16-23.**

The cover story of Canada's leading weekly news magazine is actually a series of articles that describe the choices Canadians must make as Quebec prepares to present its latest challenge over provincial rights. One story describes the federal government's formulation of counter-proposals to Quebec's demands, while another describes the growing debate across Canada about the benefits of keeping the country whole.

**Reitsma, Steven, "Canada-United States-Mexico: Trade Policy Options," *Canadian Business Review*, winter 1990, pp. 17-20.**

The author, a research associate at the Conference Board of Canada, analyzes the impact of free trade on the Canadian economy. His focus is on negotiations for extension of the bilateral U.S.-Canada Free Trade Area to include Mexico. He also examines two proposals for Canada's role in the trade negotiations.

# REPORTS AND STUDIES

**Conference Board of Canada, "Central Canada Hardest Hit by Recession but Recovery in Sight," *Provincial Outlook*, winter 1991.**

Canada is suffering from a much deeper recession than the United States. This report examines its impact on the country's 10 provinces. Poor harvests and low grain prices are contributing to the downturn in the Prairie provinces, while fishing and oil exploration are helping the chronically depressed Maritimes. Ontario, Canada's most industrialized province, has been hardest hit by this recession because of the severe downturn in the manufacturing sector. The business research organization predicts that recovery will begin in the spring.

**External Affairs and International Trade Canada, *North American Free Trade: Securing Canada's Growth through Trade*, undated.**

This Canadian government publication reports the benefits of entering into a North American free trade agreement with the United States and Mexico. Following Mexico's 1986 entrance into the General Agreement on Tariffs and Trade (GATT), the report states, trade between Mexico and Canada has grown dramatically and now exceeds $2 billion a year. Further, almost half the goods produced in Canada are exported, and Canada is more than twice as dependent on sales abroad as the United States. Any extension of the free trade area, therefore, is favorable to the Canadian economy, the report concludes.

**Parti Québécois, *Sovereignty: Why? How?* undated.**

The original Quebec separatist party, now the leading opposition party in the Quebec National Assembly, presents the reasons for its support of Quebec sovereignty. The report points to the erosion of Quebec's French language and culture since the province has been part of the Canadian federal system, especially since that system was strengthened under the government of former Prime Minister Pierre Elliott Trudeau. In the PQ's view, Quebec can survive only as a sovereign nation.

**Quebec Liberal Party, Constitutional Committee, *A Quebec Free to Choose*, Jan. 28, 1991.**

The famous Allaire report, named for the committee's chairman, Montreal lawyer Jean Allaire, is the ruling Quebec Liberal Party's official proposal to the rest of Canada for resolving the longstanding crisis surrounding the constitution, which Quebec refuses to ratify. The report calls for radical changes in the federal structure that would transfer many powers now held by the federal government in Ottawa to Quebec. It sets a deadline of the fall of 1992 for agreement on the plan, which would then be put before Quebeckers for approval in a referendum. If no agreement is reached, Quebeckers will be asked to approve secession from Canada.

**EDITORIAL RESEARCH REPORTS**

## Coming soon

Published weekly by
Congressional Quarterly
Inc., Editorial Research
Reports analyze emerging
issues of national interest
across a broad range of
social, scientific, political
and economic fields.
Reports are bound and
indexed for permanent
reference. Subscription
information is available
through Congressional
Quarterly's Publications
Sales Department by
telephone (202) 887-8665.
Copies of past issues are
available through
Customer Service, (202)
887-8621.

ERR

APRIL 19, 1991

CONGRESSIONAL QUARTERLY'S

EDITORIAL RESEARCH REPORTS

FOUNDED 1923

# CALIFORNIA: ENOUGH WATER FOR THE FUTURE?

# CALIFORNIA: ENOUGH WATER FOR THE FUTURE?

*by Patrick G. Marshall*

California is now in the fifth year of the worst drought in its history, and urban and environmental interests are calling for an end to farmers' guarantee of current supplies of cheap irrigation water from federal and state water projects. Unless there is some change in water policy, they say, California will be unable to sustain its phenomenal growth and its huge agricultural sector. Most experts agree that there are, indeed, serious problems with Western water policy, because low prices and arcane laws do nothing to encourage conservation in the arid climate. But there are practical, political, legal and economic obstacles to overcome.

During his sojourn in California in the 1860s, Mark Twain is reputed to have observed that in the West, "Whiskey is for drinking, water is for fighting." For once, at least as far as the water is concerned, Twain cannot be accused of exaggeration. For well over a hundred years, conflict over access to water in the fertile but arid state has pitted city dwellers against farmers, north against south, family farms against corporate farms, and the entire state against its neighbors.

During the past five years, such battles have intensified as California has struggled to deal with the worst drought in its history. Few Californians have escaped its effects, and most residents are still feeling them, even though heavy March rains brought some relief.

Farmers have been particularly hard hit. In February, the state shut the tap on irrigation water from its State Water Project — which carries water from the Sacramento River delta in the north to farms in the state's Central Valley and cities in Southern California. At the same time, the federal Central Valley Project — which carries water from rivers in the Sierra and Coastal Range mountains to farmers in the fertile San Joaquin Valley — cut deliveries by 75 percent.

The cutbacks have continued despite the March rains. Some farmers have been able to pump groundwater, at significantly higher cost, to replace federal and state water deliveries. Others, without groundwater supplies, have been forced to leave fields fallow. "We are looking at losses of billions of dollars in Kern County alone," Donald W. Marquez, an engineer with the county's water agency, told a reporter in February.[1] Kern County, larger than the entire state of Massachusetts, is in the San Joaquin Valley and comprises some of the state's most fertile farmland.

Urban areas have not been spared, either. When the State Water Project cut off water to the farmers in February, it also cut deliveries to Southern California cities to only about 10 percent of normal. In early March, the Metropolitan Water District, which supplies water to Los Angeles, announced that customers would have to reduce water use by 50 percent or face stiff fines. It could have been much worse, except that Los Angeles, unlike other metropolitan areas in the state, receives water not only from in-state sources but also from the Colorado River, which has not been affected by the drought.

Other major California cities, relying on reservoirs that then were only at about 15 percent of capacity, already had instituted draconian limits on water use during the previous year. For instance, Santa Barbara, with one of its main reservoirs completely dry and the other at only 20 percent of capacity, imposed cuts of 40 percent. "Water police" roamed the city's neighborhoods, handing out citations to people illegally watering lawns or washing cars with running hoses.

Even San Francisco, in the normally wet north, passed ordinances to enforce water-use cuts of 55 percent of normal use, making it illegal for residents to fill hot tubs and swimming pools. San Franciscans had already adjusted to cuts of 25 percent from the previous year.

Necessity being the mother of invention, the drought has given rise to a number of efforts to generate additional sources of water. For example, according to Bill Helms, a spokesman for the state Department of Water Resources, the state already has undertaken 13 cloud-seeding projects in 1991. The results have been mixed. "It's improving our yield from the storms a little bit," says Helms, "but of course you have to have moisture in the clouds to begin with for it to do any good."

At least one city — Santa Barbara — contracted to build a desalination plant to produce drinking water from seawater. (*See story, p. 224.*) And Goleta, right next door to Santa Barbara, planned to have fresh water from Canada delivered by supertankers.

As in previous droughts, there have also been some suggestions that, while of dubious practicality, earn high scores for imagination. Several letter writers to newspapers, for example, have proposed towing huge icebergs from the arctic. And last May a Los Angeles County supervisor suggested diverting water from the Columbia River in Washington state to Southern California. Perhaps not a bad idea, except for the price tag: $400 billion.[2]

Some relief — both from the drought and from outlandish ideas to counteract it — came with the heavy rains at the end of March. Farmers, particularly those with orchards and vineyards that were in danger of dying, were helped especially. Urban areas were, too. Goleta canceled its plan to fill supertankers with Canadian water, Santa Barbara has lifted some of its water restrictions (lawns can now be watered at night), and the state says it may be able to increase urban water deliveries to 20 percent and maybe even 35 percent of normal. The Metropolitan Water District relaxed mandatory conservation from 50 percent to 31 percent, and San Francisco and Monterey water officials will hold hearings next week to discuss whether to ease restrictions.

"Our snow pack statewide was 14 percent of average before the storms and now it's jumped up to 60 percent," Helms notes. In an average year, California receives about 19 million acre-feet of runoff. In its driest year of record, 1977, the state received only 5.1 million acre-feet. According to Helms, before the recent rains it seemed that runoff for 1991 would be below 5 million feet. Now, however, the state should receive about 8 million acre-feet for the year. Helms says the situation is no longer desperate, but it's still critical. "It's like the man thirsting in the desert getting a full glass of water instead of half a glass," he says.

So in spite of the recent rainfall, the State Water Project says farmers still will have to do without. The agency won't send any water to farmers until it can supply 50 percent of normal deliveries to urban users, and Doug Priest, manager of the State Drought Center, told reporters on March 26 that "chances of that happening this year range from zero to none."[3]

There is, however, a silver lining to the drought, say advocates of water policy reform: It has served as a clear signal of the need for changes in the system. The question, of course, is what can and should be done?

Most of the major interest groups in California appear to be in accord on two things: First, the state needs more water. And second, the outlook for major new water diversion projects like the State Water Project and the Central Valley Project is poor at best. Such projects are too expensive in light of current budget deficits, they generate too much opposition from environmental groups, and the political constituency isn't there to support them. Farm interests have pushed hard for new projects, but California voters have not approved a single major new water project since 1960. "There are no new sources in the state," Rep.

# *Water From the Ocean?*

The technology for turning saltwater into drinking water has been around for a long time, and it is widely used in the desert areas of the Middle East. In the United States, small desalination plants have been used in a limited way to purify brackish water, particularly in Florida. But the only seawater desalination plant in the nation was put into operation by the U.S. Navy last October on San Nicolas Island off the coast of California. A second plant, operated by Southern California Edison, is due to open on Santa Catalina Island sometime in the next several months.

Desalination has seen such limited use for one very compelling reason: cost. That's why the only saltwater plants currently under construction are on arid islands, where transportation costs for water are extremely high. According to Gene Reahl, regional director in California for the Massachusetts-based Ionics Inc., the cost of desalinated water can run between $1,000 and $2,500 per acre-foot, depending on the size and type of plant constructed. With water for urban areas in Southern California costing between $200 and $500 per acre-foot, opting for desalination is an expensive proposition.

But expensive water is a good sight better than no water at all, so many communities in California that have faced the prospect of running dry during the drought are considering investing in desalination.

In fact, Santa Barbara — one of the cities hardest hit by the drought — has contracted with Ionics to build a desalination plant that should be in production by February 1992. The city has not decided whether to build a 5,000 acre-feet plant or a 10,000 acre-feet plant. Reahl says the cost of water from a 5,000 acre-feet plant will be about $2,000 an acre-foot; for a 10,000 acre-feet plant, economies of scale should bring the cost down to about $1,866 an acre-foot.

Many other coastal communities that, like Santa Barbara, are not connected to state or federal water projects, have also been investigating the desalination option. "It's unbelievable," Reahl says of the number of calls he's received. "I want to take a week's vacation and then hire two more people." Morro Bay, San Luis Obispo, Monterey and Ventura are all looking into the possibility of building plants. And Los Angeles and Mexican officials jointly announced in March a $600,000 feasibility study of a 125,000 acre-foot plant.

There are actually two basic types of desalination plants: those that use a distillation process, and those that rely on reverse osmosis. In distillation plants, water is sent through a cycle of being boiled into steam and then condensed, leaving behind salt and other impurities. In reverse osmosis plants, water is pumped through a special membrane that filters out salt and impurities.

Each process has its advantages. Reverse osmosis requires less energy than distillation, since the water does not need to be boiled. But the membrane used in reverse osmosis has a limited life span and can only withstand a certain amount of water pressure. The result is less capacity than a similarly sized distillation plant.

Generally, experts prefer reverse osmosis for smaller plants, and distillation for larger ones, particularly if the steam used in the process can be harnessed to produce energy for other uses. Accordingly, all of the distillation plants being planned in California would use reverse osmosis, with the exception of the huge Los Angeles-Mexico plant, which would use distillation.

In addition to the high cost of a desalination plant itself, there are other limitations on the feasibility of desalination. First of all, the cost estimates don't include the expense of disposing of the brine that results from the process. "If you have a sewage outlet to the ocean, or accessible facilities for disposing of industrial waste, you're in good shape," says Reahl. "But where those do not exist, it is very expensive to put them in." Inland communities can't dispose of the brine in their sewage treatment plants, Reahl adds, because those sewage plants generally want to reclaim water for irrigation use, and brine would prevent that.

Another potential problem is that going the desalination route involves building large facilities, generally right on the coast. And that's bound to spur opposition from environmentalists and others.

In light of the cost and other problems, experts see desalination as an option limited to supplying a small, but critical, cushion for a certain type of community: primarily coastal communities that are particularly drought-prone. In addition to coastal cities, inland communities that have large supplies of brackish underground water might find it cost-effective to construct desalination plants. Disposal costs might be higher at inland sites, but brackish water can be processed for $300 to $800 an acre-foot, a rate much less than for seawater, because fewer impurities need to be removed.

"Each town has a different situation, and you have to look at it on a site-specific basis," says Reahl. In all, he estimates that desalination plants could end up adding between 5 and 7 percent to the total water supply. "It's significant, but it's not going to solve the problem. It tends to help localized communities more than the overall general population of California."

And desalination will be of virtually no help at all to most farmers. The costs are generally far too high to produce irrigation water.

George Miller, D-Calif., says bluntly.

That opinion isn't unanimous. "We believe that if the question of environmental protections and guarantees can be worked out to a mutually satisfactory answer, then there is ample room for certain kinds of additional diversions," says Lyle Hoge, director of California Urban Water Agencies. He specifically cites the possibility of eventually constructing the long-debated Peripheral Canal, which would take water from the upper reaches of the Sacramento River.

Nevertheless, in light of the difficulties of developing new sources of water, state water officials have directed most of their efforts at stretching current supplies. The goal of the Department of Water Resources, say officials, is not to build more diversion projects, but to create more storage facilities for saving water collected during wet years for use in dry years. At the same time, both water officials and environmental groups have called for new water conservation measures.

Even with more conservation and better storage facilities, however, it's not clear that the state will have enough water to support its extensive and expensive agricultural sector as well as to sustain its phenomenal metropolitan growth. Some experts argue that there will have to be a thorough reform of the current allocation system, probably involving higher water prices for farmers, more stringent mandates for conservation and quite possibly future limits on irrigation.

## Maximum water use, minimum conservation

California's arid climate is, of course, the most obvious cause of the state's continuing water problems. But blame also falls on the state's pattern of development. Much of California's history, in fact, can be described in terms of conflicts between various interest groups searching for more water for growth — growth of urban areas as well as agriculture. And as those interest groups have fought over water, they have pushed demand to the outer limits of, and frequently beyond, available water supplies.

Southern California, the world's largest urban area dependent upon imported water,[4] is a case in point. Its phenomenal growth could not have taken place without the securing — some would say theft — of water supplies from other areas. Los Angeles receives most of its water from three sources: the State Water Project, the Colorado River and the Los Angeles Aqueduct (also called the Owens Valley/Mono Lake aqueduct). Two of those three sources are regularly being challenged — sometimes successfully. As a result of a 1963 Supreme Court ruling,[5] for example, Los Angeles soon will lose almost half of its annual 650,000 acre-feet share of the Colorado River to Arizona, which has prior rights to the river's water. Residents of the Owens Valley, northeast of Los Angeles, meanwhile, have long maintained that the Metropolitan Water District stole their water in 1905, when district officials surreptitiously purchased water rights in the valley. Farmers there now complain — sometimes in court — that Los Angeles is pumping so much water that its underground aquifers are not replenishing, and environmentalists have charged that the withdrawal of too much water is damaging the ecosystem of Mono Lake.

In the 1970s and early '80s, in its search for new sources of water, the Metropolitan Water District pushed hard for passage of legislation to expand the California Water Project by building the Peripheral Canal in

Northern California. Northern voters turned down the measure, amid charges that Los Angelenos were trying to subsidize their own extravagant water use. Environmental groups also warned that extraction of more water from the Delta could result in dangerously high levels of salt water in San Francisco Bay.

With current supplies being cut and future water projects nowhere on the horizon, then, Southern California's future water supplies are in doubt. "In the simplest terms," journalist Marc Reisner has written, "the five-county Los Angeles area, which has gained almost 5 million people in the past 20 years and could easily gain 5 million more in the next 20 years, stands to lose water for 7 million people during that time. And the California Water Project, which was supposed to have compensated for that stupefying loss, has no chance of being expanded any time soon."[6]

As dependent as Los Angeles and other cities in Southern California are on imported water, however, it has been the state's farms that are real guzzlers. Ironically, a major reason that California's agricultural sector is so lucrative is that the climate is so dry, so crops are not so susceptible to damage from pests and plant diseases that plague farmers in the East. That, combined with the state's temperate climate, which allows crops to be grown virtually year-round, makes California in many ways ideal for agriculture. Farms in the state's Central Valley alone produce half of the entire nation's fruits, vegetables and nuts.

The key to California's agricultural success has been irrigation. Specifically, the state's farms have thrived on cheap, heavily subsidized water from federal and state water projects. Farmers use more than 80 percent of that water. Many city dwellers believe that's more than the farmers' fair share — and that they're getting it too cheaply, too.

Indeed, critics point to the fact that despite the state's dry climate, farmers' water is so cheap that California even produces water-intensive crops like alfalfa, rice and cotton. Many farmers receiving water from the federal Central Valley Project are charged less than $10 per acre-foot of water, while the average resident of Southern California is paying more than $200 per acre-foot, and some residents are paying nearly $500 per acre-foot.

Federal water projects were built on the understanding that the people who used the water would eventually pay capital costs for construction as well as all costs for operating and maintaining the system. Unlike non-agricultural water consumers, however, farmers are not charged interest on the money that was used to build the projects. In reality, therefore, farmers pay very little of the true capital costs. "If federal borrowing costs 4 percent annually, then repayment 40 years later interest-free returns to the United States only 20.8 percent of the true cost of the loan," according to Interior Department economist Richard Wahl. "At a borrowing cost of 7 percent, only 6.7 percent is returned."[7]

# California Water Projects

**California's huge agricultural industry is fueled by irrigation. The water is provided by canals from two giant systems — the State Water Project and the federally run Central Valley Project. The canals also provide water for some urban areas. Los Angeles gets water from the Los Angeles Aqueduct and the Colorado River, in addition to the State Water Project.**

**California**

Klamath River
Trinity River
Shasta Lake
● Redding
*Feather River*
Sacramento River
**LAKE OROVILLE**
Yuba River
American River
*TEHAMA COLUSA CANAL*
Folsom Lake
● Sacramento
*FOLSOM-SOUTH CANAL*
*CONTRA COSTA CANAL*
New Melones Reservoir
**MONO LAKE**
*Stanislaus River*
*DELTA MENDOTA CANAL*
San Francisco ●
San Joaquin R.
Owens River
**LAKE DEL VALLE**
*SANTA CLARA CANAL*
Millerton Lake
*FRIANT KERN CANAL*
Los Angeles Aqueduct
*HOLLISTER CONDUIT*
**SAN LUIS RES.**
*JOINT USE*
● Fresno
CALIFORNIA AQUEDUCT
*PLEASANT VALLEY CANAL*
San Luis Obispo ●
● Bakersfield
**LAKE HAVASU**
**PYRAMID LAKE**
**SILVERWOOD LAKE**
**CASTAIC LAKE**
Los Angeles ●
**LAKE PERRIS**
Los Angeles ●
Colorado River Aqueduct
San Diego ●
**SALTON SEA**

━━━━ **STATE WATER PROJECT AQUEDUCTS**
LAKES AND RESERVOIRS

••••••• *CENTRAL VALLEY PROJECT CANALS*
Lakes and Reservoirs

━ ∙ ━ ∙ **JOINT USE FACILITIES**

━━━━ L.A. Metropolitan Water District

In addition, farmers generally have long-term, fixed-rate contracts, which shield them from rising operating and maintenance costs. From the government's point of view, the fixed payments mean that all the money goes to operation and maintenance, with none left over for paying off the capital costs of building the project. "As of 1985, 37 years after project repayment began," Wahl writes of the Central Valley Project, "less than 4 percent of capital costs ($38 million out of $950 million) had been repaid." [8] In fact,

according to an Interior Department official, the department does not expect any actual repayments of farmers' share of capital costs until after 1995.

For farms smaller than 960 acres, there is even more: Rates for water delivery are based on the farmers' "ability to pay." The policy basically means that regardless of the size of their water bill, qualifying farmers never have to pay more than their net income for water — and often they are charged less, even if they cannot pay the entire bill. Thus, in bad years, when smaller farmers lose money, their water bills go unpaid.

In all, the subsidies for farmers are substantial. Wahl estimates that nationally, farmers pay only 18 percent of the total cost of providing the water they use from federal projects. California farmers may pay even less.

Water from the State Water Project also includes subsidies for farmers, though at a much lower level. For one thing, the state does not offer 40-year contracts with fixed prices. "Our contractors pay the full costs on capital cost repayments for building the projects, including interest," says Larry Gage, a water project spokesman. "They also pay minimum operations power and recovery costs, which vary according to how much we have to pay for electricity, replacement equipment, etc." According to Gage, prices for 1989 in the San Joaquin Valley ranged from just over $23 an acre-foot to more than $48 an acre-foot, still well below rates for metropolitan areas.

The original rationale for the high subsidization of irrigation water, say critics, has long since disappeared. The Reclamation Act of 1902, the legislation that set up the federal water projects in the West, was designed "to encourage the settlement of the arid West through the provision of water to lands that could be homesteaded," according to Wahl.[9] Now the state has, if anything, too many farmers rather than too few; requests for water from the Central Valley Project alone are running some 3 million acre-feet above capacity.

Thus, the subsidies have generated increasing opposition in recent years. "What possible justification is there that gives taxpayer dollars to rice growers in the amount of $7 for rice that costs $6 to grow and sells for $3?" State Assemblyman Richard Katz asked U.S. senators at a recent hearing in Los Angeles. "Who benefits from this type of arrangement? Those who grow rice, cotton and other water-intensive subsidized crops — corporations who farm their IRS forms." [10]

But the biggest problem with the federal and state subsidies isn't the drain on taxpayers' pocketbooks, say many environmentalists. The worst effect of the subsidies, says Hal Candee, senior attorney for the Natural Resources Defense Council, is that they undermine economic incentives to conserve the water. When adoption of conservation measures — such as installing more efficient drip irrigation systems — inevitably cost many times more than the federal price of the water saved, Candee says, "the economic signals are all skewed toward waste instead of efficiencies."

And there are other features of the agricultural water system that discourage conservation, too. For example, it has long been the policy of the Bureau of Reclamation, the Interior Department agency that runs federal water projects, that recipients could not resell federal water at a profit. Without the ability to make a profit, there is little reason for a farmer to conserve unused water. In December 1988, the Interior Department adopted a new policy of facilitating transfers of water and allowing profits to be made. According to an Interior Department analyst who asked not to be identified, however, "The Central Valley Project hasn't yet implemented that policy."

There is clearly increasing pressure in Congress for measures that would provide greater incentives for water conservation, and perhaps for reallocation of water resources between farm regions or from agricultural to urban uses. Currently three major bills have been introduced that would either mandate conservation and reallocation, or would provide incentives for the same by allowing project recipients to resell water at a profit.

The most prominent bill is S 484, sponsored by Senate Water and Power Subcommittee Chairman Bill Bradley, D-N.J. Known as the Central Valley Improvement Act, the bill would allow sale of project water at a profit by contracting recipients as long as either 25 percent of the net proceeds went to a fund for repairing environmental damage caused by the project, or 25 percent of the water transferred was dedicated to fish and wildlife restoration.

Farmers are particularly leery about other provisions of the bill that would offer 100,000 acre-feet of project water to the highest bidder, and that would add a surcharge to water rates to raise $30 million a year for fish and wildlife restoration. Farmers are also upset about a provision that would limit contract renewals to one year until plans for mitigation of environmental damage have been formed and implemented. (*See "At Issue," p. 233.*)

## *Recent conservation efforts have yielded mixed results*

The dramatic reductions in water use in Los Angeles, Santa Barbara and San Francisco demonstrate that,

in a pinch, urban use can be cut by as much as 35 percent without major changes in lifestyle. For short terms, it can be cut even more. So far, it has been the government that has been the driving force behind these reductions, through the threat of fines, building restrictions, shutting off service to consumers who don't meet reduction goals, and similar policies.

As early as January 1989, for example, Monterey adopted a wide variety of such measures, including a surcharge on residents who did not cut water usage sufficiently. Since then, other California cities have followed suit. Now the state is getting into the act, too. As of Jan. 1, 1992, toilets in new construction in California cannot use more than 1.6 gallons per flush (ordinary toilets now use about 3½ gallons per flush; many older toilets use more). And the state Legislature is now considering a bill that would require toilets to be replaced when houses are resold. Another measure under consideration would require industries to design their cooling systems to use water more than once before disposing of it.

Obviously, many of these drought-inspired measures are the sort that are likely to disappear as soon as the drought is over. Communities are unlikely to continue imposing fines for watering lawns or washing cars once the reservoirs·are once again full. Stiff surcharges for excess water usage will almost certainly be repealed and, once they are, consumers are unlikely to continue doing such things as watering their shrubs with bathwater.

But many of the measures being taken — such as requirements for low-flow toilets and more efficient cooling systems in industry — will result in continuing savings. In fact, Jonas Minton, a spokesman for the state Office of Water Conservation, estimates that as a result of conservation measures adopted during the drought, urban water consumption will be cut by some 10 to 15 percent even after the drought is over.

Many experts say much more could be done to encourage long-term conservation. They recommend greater use of pricing incentives in addition to government mandates. "Traditionally, water is priced in declining block quantities: the more water a household uses, the less it costs for each successive increment," note Mohamed T. El-Ashry and Diana C. Gibbons, researchers at the World Resources Institute in Washington, D.C. "The odd result is that the heaviest users pay the lowest average water price." Now, some cities are inverting the rate structure, so that each successive block of water costs more — "a sensible way to discourage profligate water use." [11]

But even better than inverting the traditional pricing structure, according to El-Ashry and Gibbons, would be pricing water at its "marginal cost" — the amount that would be required to replace current supplies of water. The authors offer Tucson, Ariz., as an example: "Tucson currently mines good quality groundwater costing approximately $45 per acre-foot." But the city is running out of groundwater, and it soon will have to get water from the Central Arizona Project. The new water will cost about $250 per acre-foot. If Tucsonans were made to pay the marginal $250 cost for the water now, the researchers argue, they would "base their consumption patterns on full knowledge of the cost of the next source of water" — and use much less.[12]

According to El-Ashry and Gibbons, a change to marginal pricing by Los Angeles' Metropolitan Water District would increase prices by 12.6 percent over the next 30 years, and people would therefore use about 10 percent less water per person.

"The most effective demand-curtailment program would contain elements of pricing, regulation and education," conclude the researchers. "The 'carrot and stick' approach to water management combines pricing water at its marginal cost to give consumers a clear idea of water scarcity with educating them on the need to reduce use and, perhaps, rewarding them for water saved." [13]

With long-term incentives for conservation — instead of just short-term penalties for overuse — consumers would be more likely to take the kinds of steps that result in long-term savings, such as installing automatic sprinkler controls and low-flow toilets. Another major opportunity for long-term savings, according to Bill Helms of the state Department of Water Resources, is the use of drought-tolerant plants in landscaping. "In an average household, half the water use is outside use, for lawns and shrubs," says Helms. "By planting drought-tolerant plants, you can have a yard that needs to be watered as infrequently as once a week, or maybe only three or four times a year."

In addition, if consumers are to be charged the marginal cost of new water, water districts are likely to look for creative ways to save water. The Metropolitan Water District took one such step in 1989. It agreed to pay more than $100 million to the Imperial Irrigation District — one of its main suppliers — to line more than 300 miles of canals with concrete. The project is expected to save an estimate 100,000 acre-feet of water each year, and under the deal, the water district gets that 100,000 acre-feet per year for the next 35 years.

## How to get farmers to conserve water

No matter how much urban areas save through conservation, if California continues to grow at the rapid pace it has in the past, the cities will need more water. And with no new water projects in the offing, the only way for cities to get more water is for agriculture to use less. With farms, however, the situation is bleak. It's not that there are no ways to save water. It's that current policies — particularly pricing policies — discourage conservation.

According to agriculture experts, there are four basic kinds of actions that can be taken to reduce agricultural water consumption:
■ Improve sprinkler or drip irrigation systems.
■ Reduce water applications below the crop's maximum need.
■ Change cropping patterns.
■ Cease irrigation of some cropland.

Some of these options, however, have the potential to backfire if not implemented carefully. As one group of researchers has noted, in areas that have problems with salt buildup, drip irrigation can greatly increase the salinity of the soil, making it unsuitable for some crops.[14] In other areas, where water drainage is good and unused irrigation water generally percolates to underground aquifers or drains easily to surface water flows, expensive new irrigation systems would simply reduce the recycling of water and have little or no actual benefit.

Of all the options, the greatest opportunities for saving water probably lie in changing crops to more water-efficient varieties and in ceasing irrigation of marginal lands. In general, that means a move away from water-intensive crops like cotton, rice, alfalfa, corn and soybeans, to drought-resistant crops such as jojoba, crambo, pearl millet and guar.

Another major source of savings, say state water experts, is greater use of reclaimed water.* Currently, about 1 percent of California's 35 million acre-feet of water use per year is from reclaimed water, according to the Department of Water Resources. With proper planning that takes into account the need to replenish aquifers, there's room for much more reclamation. But at least for now the costs of reclaiming water are generally too high. In 1982, the cost was estimated at $240-$350 per acre-foot in the immediate area of the treatment plant.[15] The farther the water had to be transported from there, the higher the costs. For those who can get federal and state water for $4 to $40 an acre-foot, reclaimed water does not look like such a good deal.

According to David Davidoff, chief of the agriculture section of California's Office of Water Conservation, "the industry as a whole is already fairly efficient [in its water use]." The major canals are already lined to prevent water loss, says Davidoff, though many of the smaller irrigation ditches aren't. And many growers are already using the newer, more efficient irrigation systems.

The drought has been a stimulus for further efforts. According to Davidoff, farmers have been streaming to his agency's training and workshops on irrigation techniques since the drought started, and more farmers have applied for loans from the state and their own water districts to install more efficient equipment.

Nevertheless, Davidoff concedes, "The price of

*Continued on p. 230*

---

*Reclaimed water is runoff from irrigation that has been captured and cleaned enough for reuse.

# *Elsewhere in the Nation*

This map of average annual precipitation shows clearly why water supplies are so critical in California, especially in the southern part of the state's Central Valley. But other parts of the West also are chronically dry.

Nevada, southeastern Oregon, southern Idaho and parts of Utah have been suffering from the same drought as California, although they have received less attention. Nevada is probably the worst off, according to the National Weather Service. "Hydrologically, they're a basket case," says Frank Richards, a Weather Service hydrologist.

Even though the inland regions from Southern California through Nevada to Idaho are generally dry and prone to drought, precipitation statistics don't tell the whole story. Many areas of the country, even some of those that receive heavy average annual rainfall, are susceptible to periodic drought. Lower New York state, for example, has experienced three significant droughts in the past 10 years: 1981, 1985 and 1989. There also was a serious drought in 1964.

The Farm Belt of the Midwest also faces periodic droughts. Most recently, in 1988, about 80 percent of the farmland between Pennsylvania and Montana suffered from drought, and corn production dropped 30 percent.

And, despite receiving on average nearly a hundred inches of rainfall during normal years, Florida is currently in the grip of its own drought. The Sunshine State's water shortage is not nearly as critical as California's, but it's bad enough that some counties are limiting outdoor water usage for such things as watering lawns and washing cars.

Why a water shortage in a state with so much rain? In large part, says Frank Richard, it's because Florida has not developed an extensive infrastructure for storing water runoff for use in dry periods. At the same time, Florida's population has been growing by leaps and bounds, putting stress on available supplies of water. "What's happening in Florida is that the infrastructure to increase water hasn't increased with its population," says Richards. "We are making demands on water that are pushing us right to the edge of capabilities." With those additional demands, a dry spell that could have been ridden out with ease became a water crisis.

In addition to considering more stringent conservation measures, the five hardest-hit counties — in central Florida — are on the verge of approving a new water project that includes drilling of additional well fields and more than 70 miles of distribution pipes. According to *St. Petersburg Times* reporter Sue Landry, the multi-county cooperation on the proposed Cypress Bridge Project is serving as a "template" for other areas. After years of fighting each other over water, says Landry, "at least two other water authorities are beginning to address water on a regional basis."

Another long-term measure taken by the 16-county water management district in the Tampa Bay region was to require utilities to reduce their water usage. According to Landry, it's part of a plan to cut annual per capita water consumption from 175 gallons to 130 gallons over the next 20 years.

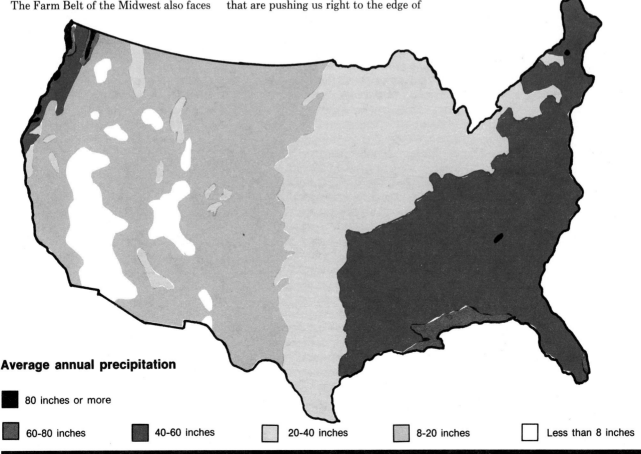

**Average annual precipitation**

- ■ 80 inches or more
- ■ 60-80 inches
- ■ 40-60 inches
- ▢ 20-40 inches
- ▢ 8-20 inches
- ▢ Less than 8 inches

*Continued from p. 228*

water is not an incentive to conserve water. In fact, in certain areas, if someone tries to conserve water, the cost of conservation may be significantly more than the savings." There's no doubt, he adds, that "if the price of water were higher, they'd use it more efficiently."

As for how much water could potentially be conserved, that depends on how expensive water is compared with the cost of the conservation measures. Unfortunately, state officials are decidedly in the dark on the matter. "There has been no real study to answer the question," says Davidoff.

Though he, too, is without any solid figures, Tom Graff, a senior attorney of the Environmental Defense Fund insists that "most sensible people will agree you can do an awful lot of conservation in the range between $30 an acre-foot and $150 an acre-foot." Unfortunately, those are prices well above what many farmers are currently paying for their water.

Just as inexpensive water has discouraged conservation, it has also discouraged research into new technologies and innovations that could result in less expensive means of conserving water. With enough research funds, "advances in science and technology can be a major factor in ameliorating the consequences of water shortages throughout the West," according to researchers Ann F. Scheuring, Ernest A. Engelbert and Robert M. Hagan.[16] They look for "improved irrigation technologies, better plant breeding for drought resistance [and] precise monitoring of water needs." But it's not likely that many dollars will be devoted to research in those areas as long as such heavily subsidized water is provided to agriculture.

If price is the primary incentive for conservation, a couple of recent actions may improve the situation. At least for the short-term purpose of dealing with the drought, the state has established a water bank that buys water from farmers who have excess water or who are willing to take acreage out of production. Farmers have been paid about $450 an acre to forgo their water supplies, which — figuring that about 3.5 acre-feet of water would be used to grow an acre of rice or alfalfa — amounts to about $125 per acre-foot of water. In turn, farmers who need additional water will be allowed to purchase water from the bank. But critics say that with the state setting the price for the water and determining who gets to buy it, the bank will do little for conservation. Besides, they say, it's only a temporary measure, anyway.

More encouraging, perhaps, is the fact that most of the 40-year federal contracts for Central Valley Project water are due to expire during the 1990s. Critics of subsidies have argued that those contracts should be renewed at significantly higher rates and for much shorter periods of time. But thus far the critics are not getting what they want. When recently expired contracts were renewed, the rates did go up — with the cheapest ones now about $16.50 an acre-foot instead of $3.50 under the old contracts. But that's not nearly

enough for some critics. And the farmers also got the long-term renewals they wanted.

Rep. George Miller believes that is a major problem. "This water was developed with public money. There's billions of dollars invested, and there's billions of dollars of debt in this system," he says. "And so I think we have a right to review the contract period, just like the bank does on home mortgages. The terms should be shortened, to a period of 10 years or something like that, so there is a continued flexibility for California to review its allocations of water."

That brings a chorus of objections from farmers. "If a person wants to be in the farming business, and he's going to make a multimillion-dollar improvement to his facilities, to laser-level his land or line all of his ditches, he has to have a length of time in which to recoup those investments," explains Frank Dimick of the Bureau of Reclamation. "If he goes down to the bank and says he's only got a contract to get water for the next six years, yet he wants a loan for the next 40 or 30 years to pay for the improvements, it might be very awkward. So the investment time is a very critical thing for these people."

As understandable as farmers' concerns may be, however, critics complain that accommodating those concerns has resulted in ever-increasing demands for more water. Indeed, according to John L. Winther, president of the Delta Wetlands association of farmers, "The CVP [Central Valley Project], with its present water supply, will be unable to supply even half of the water demands which will be placed upon it in the near future."[17] And most critics believe that charges of $16.50 per acre-foot are far too small to encourage farmers to undertake significant conservation efforts.

## Some say free markets in water are the answer

Increasingly, city officials and academic water experts — even some farmers — seem to be coming to the same conclusion. The best long-term answer to water scarcity, they say, is a free market in water. Such a free market would go well beyond district-by-district marginal pricing of water based on estimates of the costs of obtaining new supplies, and well beyond the state's current water bank as well. It would allow water districts and even individuals to buy and sell water largely without restriction. Under such circumstances, those who are willing to pay a higher price would be able to obtain greater amounts of water.

If the marketplace determines prices, free-market proponents say, water will naturally be put to uses that have the highest value. If rice can't be grown profitably when water costs $150 a gallon but a semiconductor plant is willing to pay that much and possibly even more, then rice paddies will lie fallow or be

# *The Byzantine World of Water Law*

Any major reform of water policy in California — whether it's water banking, free markets or various conservation measures — will run headlong into the state's web of arcane laws governing who owns rights to water. Historical circumstances have turned the relatively simple set of water rights laws inherited from England into a system that is, as one expert described it, "complex, inflexible, and fraught with uncertainties." †

California got its system of water rights in 1850, when the Legislature adopted the common law of England as the basis for the state's legal system. Under English common law, the owner of land abutting a river has a right to take water from the river. These "riparian" rights, as they are called, are held equally with other owners. That is, while there is no specific limit on the amount of water a landowner can use, one landowner cannot take so much water that it would affect the rights of other riparians.

But California is not England, and, as Professors Gerald D. Bowden, Stahrl W. Edmunds and Norris C. Hundley put it, "a water doctrine that had worked well in England and in the eastern United States . . . would prove ill suited to California's drier climes." ††

Unlike water laws on the East Coast, which was settled first by farmers, California's water laws were shaped largely by miners. The predominant form of mining in the region in the late 1840s required great amounts of water to process soil in search of gold. The miners solved the problem by diverting nearby streams to their diggings for use with sluice boxes and hydraulic equipment. In the sparsely populated territory, there were few downstream users to complain.

"Necessity, not the law, sanctioned such action, but the law soon fell into line," the three professors explain. "At first the miners relied on their own self-imposed regulations. Acting on the assumption that natural resources like gold and water were free for the taking, they concluded that the person with the best right to them was the person who first appropriated them to his use."

This principle was later endorsed by the state Supreme Court as the "right of prior appropriation": Other users could appropriate water from a stream, but the first person to do so had priority so long as he put the water to "beneficial use."

The obvious potential for conflict between riparian rights and prior appropriation rights to the same water was resolved by the California Supreme Court in 1886. In *Lux v. Haggin*, the court held that if the property with riparian rights was originally acquired before water was appropriated, the riparian rights had priority. If water was appropriated before riparian land was originally acquired, the appropriator had priority to the water.

One problem that was not resolved, and has since caused many difficulties, is that appropriation rights were not recorded until a 1914 law required them to be. Even today, about half of California's water demand is allotted under appropriative rights, and about one-fourth of those rights are unrecorded pre-1914 appropriations.

The third major type of water rights is groundwater rights. Groundwater rights generally parallel riparian rights. Landowners have rights to water lying under their property, and, since underground aquifers often stretch under the property of dozens if not hundreds of landowners, those rights have been considered correlative. Landowners, owners of

property along a river, have the right to as much water as they need. If they do not use the water, they do not lose the right to the water.

In 1903 the California Supreme Court ruled that if landowners did not need all the underground water, others could pump it on a "first-in-time, first-in-line" basis. Those who first put the excess water to beneficial use had prior rights to other appropriators. Courts limited some appropriative groundwater rights when aquifers were being overdrawn, but most groundwater supplies in California, even those being drawn down below their replenishment levels, have not been apportioned by the courts.

Each of these historically defined rights carries with it certain difficulties for water policy reform. Riparian rights are clear and easy to establish, but they do not clearly specify the quantity of water a landowner is entitled to.

Appropriative rights have always been sensitive to issues of quantity, too: They are based on how much how much water is put to "beneficial use." This raises two problems. First, it encourages a "use-it-or-lose-it" attitude. If a farmer with appropriative rights reduces his water usage through conservation, he may lose the legal right to that quantity of water.

Second, "beneficial use" is a vague term. Under a free market for water, would those with appropriative rights to water be putting their water to beneficial use if they chose to sell it?

† H. J. Vaux Jr., "Water Scarcity Gains from Trade in Kern County, California," in Scarce Water and Institutional Change, edited by Kenneth D. Frederick, Resources for the Future, 1986, p. 77.

†† Gerald D. Bowden, Stahrl W. Edmunds, and Norris C. Hundley, "Institutions: Customs, Laws and Organization," in Competition for California Water, edited by Ernest A. Engelbert, University of California Press, 1982, p. 166.

---

converted to other more water-efficient crops and the water will be used to make semiconductors.

Because of the drought, says Frederick Cannon, an agricultural economist at the Bank of America in San Francisco, "we had semiconductor firms in Silicon Valley saying that if they had to meet what had been proposed allocation schemes, they'd have to lay off tens of thousands of people. Now the idea that you would have an economy where a firm would be laying off thousands of people at the same time as anybody is

watering their lawn in the entire Santa Clara Valley means you have an allocation problem." If there were a market mechanism, says Cannon, "you know that these Silicon Valley firms could pay a hell of a lot for their water to keep their firm going."

What's more, say advocates of water markets, the higher prices would be a major incentive to all users to conserve water resources. "If you get a market going," says Tom Graff of the Environmental Defense Fund, "a lot of the sensible conservation measures would emerge."

What would be the economic effect of such a free-market system? Agricultural economists believe that as far as consumer prices are concerned, it would be very small. That's because the crops most sensitive to water prices — such as hay, corn, barley, wheat and cotton — are grown in large quantities elsewhere in the country. "California doesn't have a very big share of that market, says Richard Howitt of the University of California at Davis, "so the price impact won't be large."

In those crops where California accounts for a large share of the national production — that is, fruits and vegetables — the cost of water is much less a factor in the cost of producing the crop. "You can make about $40 out of an acre-foot of water growing hay, and perhaps you can make $300 out of it growing tomatoes," says Howitt. "So [if] that $40 jumps to $55 in the marketing scheme, it may affect your hay, wheat and cotton, but it won't affect tomatoes." Howitt figures that with larger profit margins, fruit and vegetable farmers will probably absorb most of the cost increases for water, and whatever is passed on to consumers will hardly be noticeable.

This does not mean that moving to such a system would be easy, however. In addition to vociferous objections from California's politically powerful agricultural interests, there also would be many practical obstacles to overcome. The first and most obvious problem is the fragmentation of the current water system, both physically and bureaucratically. To begin with, all major sectors of the water industry would have to participate in the water market. The federal water projects, for example, could not continue to sell water at subsidized prices to farmers while the state projects sold at market prices. Bringing the federal water system into a free market would almost certainly involve federal legislation, and could run into opposition from other states.

There's also the question of whether current contracts for federal water at subsidized rates could be broken. "Does the farmer getting water from the Central Valley Project have the right to the water at the price they've been charged, and can he then turn around and resell it at a huge profit?" asks Ron Schmidt, an analyst at the Federal Reserve Bank in San Francisco who has followed the water industry. Perhaps not, says Schmidt, adding that state courts have long held the view that water should go to the highest-valued use. "If you can show that breaking the contract is in the spirit of the public trust, then you could do that," he says. Lacking that, Schmidt suggests imposing windfall-profit taxes on those still receiving subsidized water.

Howitt thinks Schmidt is wrong. Not only does he doubt that water contracts could be easily broken, but he says that "there's nothing wrong with a windfall that encourages farmers to put the water to a higher value use by selling it. You have to let the farmers have their slice of the pie [because farmers] can stop the deal."

Another source of difficulties would be in clarifying water rights. Historically, rights to water have been determined in a variety of ways (*see story, p. 231*). "Riparian rights" to water, for example, mean that anyone who owns property abutting a river has the right to take water for "beneficial use" on that land. Similarly, "appropriative rights" allow the first person who diverts water from a source (without, that is, infringing on the rights of existing downstream rights holders), to take as much water as he can put to beneficial use. How much water could holders of such rights sell on the open market?

"The costs of defining and quantifying water rights may be high and the process may require considerable time," Howitt and colleagues Dean E. Mann and H. J. Vaux Jr. have written. "Some of these rights are recorded and defined and therefore meet the test of property rights that can be sold, purchased rented or leased. Other rights, such as most riparian and some appropriative rights, are not recorded and defined. For those rights to be made part of a transfer market they would have to be defined." [18]

Another set of rights that would have to be defined is groundwater rights. Groundwater collects in underground aquifers that generally stretch under the property of dozens or even hundreds of landowners. Currently, in most areas of the state, there are no limits on the amount of groundwater that can be pumped by landowners. And there is little need for such regulation in California, since the cost of pumping groundwater starts at about $45 per acre-foot, a price well above most other sources of irrigation water. But if surface water prices rose significantly, as would be expected under a free-market system, there would be incentive for farmers to turn increasingly to groundwater. The problem, says Helms of the Department of Water Resources, is that Californians are already using 2 million acre-feet more groundwater each year than is being replenished.

"We're continually drawing on the groundwater supply, and the water table keeps moving lower and lower," says Helms. "There's a long-range possibility of contamination as water is drawn in from more distant areas, where the water supply may not be as clean. Also, in some areas, where the soil becomes compacted after water is withdrawn, removing too much groundwater can make replenishment impossible."

Accordingly, rights to groundwater, as well as limits on pumping that will ensure replenishment, would have to be established for all areas of the state.

Finally, many question whether there is sufficient infrastructure to support the huge water transfers that could be expected with a free market. State officials have contended in the past that the current system is handling all the water it can, so establishing a free market might mean new canals and storage facilities, an expensive proposition.

And there's also the question of who would coordi-

*Continued on p. 234*

**YES** *says* **DAVID BOLLING**, *executive director of Friends of the River.*

Given this simple formula — 85 percent of the water goes to agriculture, less than 10 percent goes to people — it doesn't require a MENSA certificate to understand the bottom line. . . .

The fact is there's one set of water rules for agriculture, and another set of water rules for everyone else.

Agriculture doesn't pay very much for its water. People pay a lot. If you live in San Diego, which has the state's highest water rates, you get about 7.5 gallons for each penny you spend on water.

If you're a Central Valley farmer, you get from 250 to 900 gallons of water for each penny. The average cost of water for Central Valley farmers is about $6 per acre-foot. The cost for an acre-foot of water in San Francisco is more than $225 and in Los Angeles it's more than $300.

What we're talking about here is subsidy, frequently double subsidy, and in some cases, triple subsidy. Cotton farmers, for instance, get subsidized water to grow subsidized crops. Some of those cotton farmers use that subsidized water to grow subsidized crops on massive "farms" covering tens of thousands of acres. . . .

Lest you discover an errant chord of sympathy stirring in your breast for the plight of these struggling farmers, listen to these numbers from the Bank of America's recent "California Agricultural Outlook." Farm income, says the B of A, has been on a steady rise since 1986 and is expected to increase 7 percent in 1990, reaching a record level of $19.2 billion. Production expenses, meanwhile, will have climbed only 2.5 percent.

Given these illuminating facts, does it not make simple common sense to expect that irrigated agriculture should adopt water conservation and increased efficiency standards at least slightly as stringent as those imposed on residential water customers?

Get out your calculators, students, and let's do some simple math. . . . If all urban users cut their water use by 25 percent, that would be the equivalent of agriculture cutting its water use by 3 percent. Do you think agriculture can cut its water use by 3 percent? Do you think the Earth is round?

The simple truth is that improved efficiency in the use of agricultural water could produce enough new supplies to keep us, our swimming pools and our incongruously green lawns drenched for decades to come.

But that message does not mean music to the ears of the water lobby. The water lobby would like us to spend $2 billion on Auburn Dam; they'd like us to raise Shasta, plug the Yuba, drain the delta. . . .

None of this should be construed as suggesting that farmers are evil, that agriculture is bad. Except for the corporate giants, farming is a tough way to make a living.

But the painful truth is that . . . irrigated agriculture has developed an expensive addiction to cheap water and has never had adequate incentive to kick the habit.

*From Headwaters (bimonthly publication of the Friends of the River), July-August 1990.*

**NO** *says* **JASON PELTIER**, *manager, Central Valley Project Water Association.*

When President Roosevelt ordered the construction of the Central Valley Project (CVP) as a public works project during the Depression, the principle behind subsidized water was that an economically strong agricultural sector and rural communities that can grow with the farmers are in the best interest of America. Pasture and grain fields were converted to high-value fruit and vegetables. With this conversion came more and higher paying jobs — not only on the farm but in the surrounding communities as well. Water converted marginal land to prime land, and we are all enjoying the bounty.

What is the subsidy? It is just the interest payments on the federal expenditures to enhance California's water infrastructure. Farmers themselves will repay all of the capital and operating costs of the $1.3 billion spent for the irrigation features of the CVP, the largest irrigation project in the world.

The interest payment should be viewed as a federal investment. This investment has generated a $50 billion increase in primary economic activity over the last 30 years and upwards of $200 billion in broader economic contributions.

I challenge any other activity of our government to match that return on investment. And I am not talking merely in economic terms. The human and societal benefits are incalculable. Rural California has benefited. Consumers have benefited. The Federal Treasury has benefited. In fact, the initial federal expenditure is returned every three years, through increased tax revenues.

This is not a cash subsidy. For the most part, the value of the subsidy has been incorporated into the value of the land and was "captured" by the first person to sell the land after project water arrived. So while a farmer with subsidized water may pay a little less than his neighbor, he will most often have higher mortgage payments, reflecting the greater value of his land.

Some say, "Take the subsidy away. They can afford it." This short-sightedness comes from the same people who will tell you our agriculture is dominated by corporate farms.

Here are the facts: (1) They are small farmers (the average farm in California is considerably smaller than the national average). (2) They are struggling to stay in business — and who wouldn't when the return on investment runs at 4-5 percent? And (3) if you raise their water costs, you eliminate their ability to invest in capital improvements to increase on-farm efficiency.

So who advocates the elimination of water subsidies? Is it the cities, so they can continue to sprawl? Or is it other interests seeking to drive farmers out of business so their water can be redirected to environmental or aesthetic purposes? It does not really matter to the people working the land. They will suffer with the burden of higher production costs, as will their employees, and you, the consumer of their bounty.

*Continued from p. 232*

nate all the buying, selling and transferring of water. "Given the central role of the state of California in managing water, it is possible that the Department of Water Resources would perform the function of brokering water," Professors Howitt, Mann and Vaux propose. "Its capacity to deliver water over long distances, its ability to make exchanges that might avoid large transportation charges, and its concern for the protection of water quality would all tend to justify a central role for some state institution." [19]

How likely is it that all these hurdles could be cleared? Tom Graff of the Environmental Defense Fund believes that transition won't be easy, but it will eventually happen. "I'm hopeful that we've gotten enough of a scare from the drought, and that an active water market will emerge," says Graff. "The existing water institutions and their leaders are only slowly coming around to supporting a method of allocation of water that is significantly different than the one they grew up with. Institutional inertia is the major stumbling block."

Lyle Hoge, director of the California Urban Water Agencies organization, agrees that some type of free market for water is probably inevitable. "Conservation alone won't do the job," says Hoge. "Urban conservation, which may be able to achieve another 10, 15 or even 20 percent, certainly isn't going to provide for growth. It's going to take all sorts of tactics to provide a reliable supply into the next century: transfers, marketing, wet-weather banking and everything."

Some experts fear that free markets in water could create significant problems in the state. Calling a complete deregulation of the water market a "serious mistake," Judith Redmond, executive director of the California Action Network, a nonprofit citizens' group that deals with rural issues, warned visiting U.S. senators recently that "water transfers are sure to result in loss of jobs and loss of economic opportunity for rural residents." Others have noted that farmland that is currently highly valued in part because of its access to cheap water may lose much of its value, which would be an unfair burden on farmers.[20]

Advocates of free water markets, however, argue that such problems could be dealt with. "Lost value in real estate could be compensated," says Ron Schmidt, "and other schemes could be devised to protect those facing potential harm."

In any event, says Rep. George Miller, the impact on the agricultural sector is not likely to be nearly as severe as some have warned. "Over the next 25 years, I think we'll see a marginal change in agriculture in terms of volume, changing crop patterns — some crops just won't be as economical as they are today because of the subsidies. We'll see some rather bad land no longer being irrigated. You're really trimming agriculture around the margins, and that's about it."

Far more daunting than the consequences of re-allocating water, say some experts, are the consequences of failing to do so. The current system strongly favors agriculture, says Miller. "But the long-term economic future of California is not agriculture. That's not to diminish the importance of agriculture, but that's not where long-term growth is going to take place, simply because we're adding people faster than we're adding farms."

And it is the possibility of losing companies in the industrial sector that has many urban officials concerned, says Lyle Hoge. Industrial users currently account for about one-fourth of urban water use. "Many of the big water users like refiners and food processors have over the last several years taken steps to find alternative supplies or taken conservation measures to 'drought proof' themselves," says Hoge. "But the specter of what could have occurred with another year of drought was very stark to some companies. . . . The industrial folks have been able to do OK so far, but when they look in the planning direction, it's quite scary and they tend to look elsewhere."

Any fundamental changes in the current water system will, however, require an unprecedented degree of cooperation among the various interest groups in the state. "If we get enough cooperation among the interests, then there's enough water around to have a rational allocation scheme," says Graff. "If we end up fighting each other, then someone's going to get hurt. I'm not sure exactly who."

# NOTES

[1] *The New York Times*, Feb. 5, 1991.
[2] *Los Angeles Times*, June 21, 1990. The supervisor was Kenneth Hahn.
[3] *The Washington Post*, March 27, 1991.
[4] Mohamed T. El-Ashry and Diana C. Gibbons, *Troubled Waters: New Policies for Managing Water in the American West*, October 1986, p. 41.
[5] *California v. Arizona*, 1963.
[6] Marc Reisner, "The Big Thirst," *The New York Times Magazine*, Oct. 28, 1990, p. 57.
[7] Richard Wahl, *Markets for Federal Water: Subsidies, Property Rights and the Bureau of Reclamation*, Resources for the Future, 1989, p. 27.
[8] *Ibid.*, p. 57.
[9] *Ibid.*, p. 45.
[10] Katz testified before the Senate Water and Power Subcommittee on March 18, 1991.
[11] El-Ashry & Gibbons, *op. cit.*, p. 57.
[12] *Ibid.*, p. 56.
[13] *Idem.*
[14] Ernest A. Engelbert, ed., *Competition for California Water: Alternative Resolutions*, University of California Press, 1982, p. 25.
[15] *Ibid.*, p. 6.
[16] Ann F. Scheuring, Ernest A. Engelbert, and Robert M. Hagan, "No Simple Solutions," in *Water Scarcity*, edited by Ernest A. Engelbert, University of California Press, 1984, p. 6.
[17] John L. Winther testified before the Senate Water and Power Subcommittee on March 18, 1991.
[18] Richard E. Howitt, Dean E. Mann and H. J. Vaux Jr., "The Economics of Water Allocation," in *Competition for California Water: Alternative Resolutions*, edited by Ernest A. Engelbert, University of California Press, 1982, p. 146.
[19] *Idem.*
[20] Redmond testified before the Senate Water and Power Subcommittee on March 18, 1991, in Los Angeles.

*Graphics: Cover, Margaret Scott; pp. 226, 229, Jack Auldridge.*

## RECOMMENDED READING

## BOOKS

**Berk, Richard A., LaCivita, C. J., Sredl, Katherine, and Cooley, Thomas F.,** *Water Shortage: Lessons in Conservation from the Great California Drought, 1976-1977,* **Abt Books, 1981..**

The authors study the California drought of 1976-77, and community responses to it, in great detail and assess the effectiveness of various conservation measures. The book focuses almost entirely on residential consumption, rather than industrial and agricultural.

**El-Ashry, Mohamed T., and Gibbons, Diana C.,** *Troubled Waters: New Policies for Managing Water in the American West,* **World Resources Institute, October 1986.**

A concise (89 pages) and very readable book, *Troubled Waters* is probably the best quick primer available on the issues of Western water policies. There's not a lot of detail in the book, but it does offer a very good overview of the policy conflicts surrounding water issues.

**Engelbert, Ernest A., ed.,** *Competition for California Water: Alternative Solutions,* **University of California Press, 1982.**

This set of essays, which resulted from a conference held in California in 1981, examines the impact of water scarcity on all the major sectors: agriculture, industry, residential, energy and environment. The writing is dense in places, and some of the data are by now out of date. But since there have been no new major water projects in the past 10 years, most of the essays hold up well.

**Engelbert, Ernest A., ed.,** *Water Scarcity: Impacts on Western Agriculture,* **University of California Press, 1984.**

The articles in this book examine the effect of insufficient water — and strategies for dealing with it — on agriculture in the West. Included are case studies that cover regions from California to Montana.

**Frederick, Kenneth D., ed.,** *Scarce Water and Institutional Change,* **Resources for the Future, 1986.**

A bit on the technical side for many readers, this collection of essays explores the nuts and bolts of dealing with water scarcity in several regions. There are, for example, chapters on "Satisfying Southern California's Thirst for Water," "Water Scarcity and Gains from Trade in Kern County, California," and "Competition Between Irrigation and Hydropower in the Pacific Northwest."

**Gottlieb, Robert,** *A Life of its Own: The Politics and Power of Water,* **Harcourt Brace Jovanovich, 1988.**

Gottlieb's book is a well-written history of the development of water and water policy in the West. Gottlieb brings to his book the insight of a former dissident member of the board of Southern California's Metropolitan Water District.

**Reisner, Marc,** *Cadillac Desert: The American West and its Disappearing Water,* **Viking Penguin, 1986.**

Written by a longtime environmental journalist, *Cadillac Desert* is a good history of the emergence of Western water projects and policies. The book reads like a novel.

**Wahl, Richard W.,** *Markets for Federal Water: Subsidies, Property Rights and the Bureau of Reclamation,* **Resources for the Future, 1989.**

Wahl, an Interior Department economist, has produced a clearly written, definitive account of the way federal water projects subsidize agriculture. The book also explores in detail what would be involved in creating nearly free markets for water.

## ARTICLES

**Reisner, Marc, "The Big Thirst,"** *The New York Times Magazine,* **Oct. 28, 1990.**

Reisner, author of *Cadillac Desert,* offers a capsule history of water development in California, and carries the story up to the present to explain just why the current drought has hit the state so hard.

**Peterson, Cass, "Washed Out,"** *Mother Jones,* **May 1990.**

Peterson's article is a highly critical account of the Bush administration's decision to allow the Department of the Interior to renew federal water contracts with farmers for full 40-year periods despite strong lobbying by environmental groups and others.

# EDITORIAL RESEARCH REPORTS

## Coming soon

Electromagnetic Radiation

School Choice

Quotas

Published weekly by
Congressional Quarterly
Inc., Editorial Research
Reports analyze emerging
issues of national interest
across a broad range of
social, scientific, political
and economic fields.
Reports are bound and
indexed for permanent
reference. Subscription
information is available
through Congressional
Quarterly's Publications
Sales Department by
telephone (202) 887-8665.
Copies of past issues are
available through
Customer Service, (202)
887-8621.

ERR

APRIL 26, 1991

FOUNDED 1923

CONGRESSIONAL QUARTERLY'S

EDITORIAL RESEARCH REPORTS

# ELECTROMAGNETIC FIELDS: ARE THEY DANGEROUS?

1991 No. 16

# EDITORIAL RESEARCH REPORTS

**EDITOR**
**MARCUS D. ROSENBAUM**

**MANAGING EDITOR**
**SANDRA STENCEL**

**ASSOCIATE EDITOR**
**RICHARD L. WORSNOP**

**STAFF WRITERS**
**MARY H. COOPER**
**PATRICK G. MARSHALL**

**PRODUCTION EDITOR**
**LAURIE DE MARIS**

**EDITORIAL ASSISTANT**
**AMY GORTON**

**RICHARD M. BOECKEL (1892-1975)**
**FOUNDER**

**PUBLISHED BY**
**CONGRESSIONAL QUARTERLY INC.**

**CHAIRMAN**
**ANDREW BARNES**

**VICE CHAIRMAN**
**ANDREW P. CORTY**

**EDITOR AND PUBLISHER**
**NEIL SKENE**

**EXECUTIVE EDITOR**
**ROBERT W. MERRY**

© 1991 BY CONGRESSIONAL QUARTERLY INC.

# ELECTROMAGNETIC FIELDS: ARE THEY DANGEROUS?

*by Sarah Glazer*

Are electromagnetic fields given off by electricity dangerous? For the past decade, a debate over that question has raged among scientists and activists. Now a scientific consensus is developing — not that EMFs *are* dangerous, but that they may be and that they must be investigated further. Over the next few years, therefore, scientists will try to decide the issue conclusively. In the meantime, experts advise only "prudent avoidance" of EMFs. Although they say further action is not warranted, in many places fierce political and legal battles are being waged by a frightened public.

When epidemiologist Nancy Wertheimer, working with physicist Ed Leeper, published her findings in 1979,[1] nobody believed her. That Wertheimer had just returned to her scientific career after a break to raise children and was working on her own time and money didn't lend her much credibility, either. It was her hypothesis that seemed so bizarre. What she found was that Denver children living near certain power lines were more likely to develop cancer than children living in houses without such exposure — twice as likely, in fact, to develop leukemia, the most

*Sarah Glazer writes about health and science issues from Washington, D.C.*

common childhood cancer.* Thus, she reasoned, the magnetic field emanating from outdoor power lines could affect the risk of cancer.

At the time, that hypothesis drew only a few skeptical shakes of the head. "It was like a tree falling in the forest," recalls Leonard A. Sagan, who directs radiation studies at the Electric Power Research Institute (EPRI), a research organization funded by electric utilities in Palo Alto, Calif. "The possibility that [human] cells could detect these signals seemed, and still seems to many physicists, to be implausible."

There was a scientifically sound basis for the skepticism. The electric and magnetic fields that emanate from anything electric — whether overhead wires or indoor appliances — are extraordinarily weak sources of energy. Unlike ionizing radiation, which comes from nuclear energy, these fields don't break molecular bonds and don't cause mutations. And compared with other forms of non-ionizing radiation, such as microwaves from powerful military radar, energy from electric-power-generated electromagnetic fields, or EMFs, is among the weakest. Physicists have long believed that such weak EMFs could not possibly cause biological damage because unlike, say, microwaves, they do not produce significant heat.

Further, the strength of the fields produced by man-made electric gadgets pales next to the natural fields emitted by the Earth and by the human body. The magnetic field generated by a power line is normally only about 1 percent of the Earth's magnetic field. Even the electric field generated by a high-voltage power line will induce a corresponding field inside the body no bigger than the electric fields naturally generated by some cells.

Wertheimer's low-budget investigation had methodological flaws as well, in the view of most scientists. Wertheimer had begun her study by gathering the addresses of 344 Denver children who had died of cancer between 1950 and 1973 and comparing them with an approximately equal number of children born around the same time who did not get cancer. Having personally obtained the addresses from the Cancer Registry, a local data bank, Wertheimer already knew which houses were the sites of cancer deaths when she went to examine their relationship to outdoor electric wires. In epidemiologic parlance, she had thus failed to conduct a "blind" study, opening the possibility that her observations of wiring were subject to unconscious bias favoring her theory of cancer association.

Another major weakness was the lack of actual measurements of the EMF levels. As a proxy for measuring the fields, Wertheimer recorded the distance of the homes from the outdoor electric wires, the thickness of electric wires and the presence of other nearby power sources that might contribute to the amount of current. This method, which came to be known as the Wertheimer-Leeper "wiring code," was criticized as a possibly inaccurate way of measuring the children's exposure.

Although scientists paid little attention to Wertheimer's findings when they were published in 1979, citizens fighting various large-scale electric power projects earlier in the 1970s had cited previous scientific findings of EMFs' biological effects on animals. One of the most drawn-out of these battles, concerning several large transmission lines proposed by the Power Authority of New York, raised enough troubling questions that in 1978 New York's Public Service Commission called for a five-year research program on the biological effects of power-line radiation.

During the 1980s, as the data from that study and others began to come in, the scientific debate over the biological power of electromagnetic fields began in earnest. Numerous studies were designed either to disprove or to uphold the Wertheimer thesis, leading to conflicting findings on almost any EMF question that has been investigated. Often the debate has been clouded by the vested interests of warring camps, fighting over such issues as the siting of high-voltage power lines or of military radio antennae. Typically, in debates before public utility commissions, consumers have presented scientists who warn of potential health risks while electric utilities have paraded scientific skeptics to counter them.

There is a non-scientific element that has colored the debate as well, notes Karen Larsen, a senior analyst at the congressional Office of Technology Assessment (OTA).* "Lines are drawn," she says, "and there's a lot more personal animosity than I've seen on a lot of other topics. ... These [scientists] are carrying 10-15 years of vicious personal attacks on each other."

The most friction has been between scientists like Wertheimer, who have linked EMF to health risks, and researchers funded by EPRI. EPRI now conducts the world's largest program of research on the health effects of electric and magnetic fields, and EPRI-funded attacks on Wertheimer's methodology in the early 1980s have been portrayed as an electric utility industry campaign "to discredit Wertheimer" in *New Yorker* journalist Paul Brodeur's controversial book, *Currents of Death.*[2]

But such clear battle lines may soon be considered an anachronism. In a historically symbolic turn-around, preliminary findings released in February of a long-awaited EPRI-funded study supported the association between the Wertheimer-Leeper wiring code and the risk of childhood cancer.[3] The study, authored by John M. Peters of the University of Southern California School of Medicine in Los Angeles, found that children

*The normal rate of leukemia in children is 1 out of 20,000 per year. (*For a comparison with other health risks, see story and chart, p. 241.*)

*OTA conducted its own investigation of the subject, and in 1989, it produced a report that concluded: "Epidemiological evidence, while controversial and subject to a variety of criticisms, is beginning to provide a basis for concern about risks from chronic exposure." See Office of Technology Assessment, *Biological Effects of Power Frequency Electric and Magnetic Fields* (May 1989), p. 3.

who lived near clusterings of high-current wires were two and a half times as likely to have leukemia as other children. Although the study leaves unanswered many of the same questions about cause and effect raised by Wertheimer's study, its large size (464 children) and well-regarded design spared it from the criticisms traditionally leveled by EPRI researchers against the Wertheimer study. The EPRI-funded study is the third major report in the United States to support an association of childhood cancer with electric wiring patterns.

The scientific respect and interest focused on this new study are a dramatic illustration of how far the subject of EMF has shifted in scientific circles. What had been only the alarms expressed in occasional reports of a scientific fringe have developed into a mainstream consensus that there is indeed something strange about electric power sources that should be investigated. Experts caution that the epidemiologic rule of thumb still applies: Statistical association does not equal causation. Yet as growing numbers of population studies in a variety of countries find similar kinds of health effects, and as laboratory experiments start to suggest possible biological mechanisms, scientists are becoming intrigued by a variety of explanations for a phenomenon considered inexplicable.

OTA's Larsen sums up the current situation this way: "There's been a shift in the consensus taking place as to whether or not it's likely or possible that electromagnetic fields do have interaction with living things. Now the question is: Is it harmful and how do we measure it? How serious is the risk? How serious is it compared to other risks?" On those questions there are still wide differences of opinion.

## States introduce regulations in response to public concern

Although there is no scientific consensus on the answers to those questions, some states have already moved to regulate EMF exposure. Currently, seven states (Montana, Minnesota, New Jersey, New York, North Dakota, Oregon and Florida) limit the strength of the electric field at the edge of transmission line rights-of-way. Two of those states, New York and Florida, also limit the intensity of magnetic fields near transmission lines, reflecting the growing belief among researchers that magnetic fields are of greater concern than electric fields.

Most observers view these state regulations as a response to the public's fears rather than to scientific evidence. One indication of that is the fact that New York's and Florida's magnetic field limits are about 100 times higher than the magnetic field levels that appear to be hazardous from childhood cancer studies. "The standard is so high, it clearly is not being set on

the basis of any health effect," says David O. Carpenter, dean of the School of Public Health at the State University of New York at Albany. He says New York designed its limits to match levels that already exist near transmission lines; the purpose was to keep utilities from going any higher.

Carpenter headed the landmark $5 million, five-year New York State Powerlines Project, one of the largest research efforts ever undertaken to determine the connection between EMFs and health. The program funded 16 separate studies between 1982 and 1987. It was spawned by the bitter, lengthy public battle over the proposed construction of several 765-kilovolt power lines, but ironically, says Carpenter, the project found "that the problem is not high-voltage lines. The problem is [neighborhood] distribution lines, appliances and household wiring, because that's where people are and that's where they're exposed."

The report concluded that magnetic fields, which penetrate through common objects as thick as concrete walls without losing their strength, were of the greatest health concern. Little or no connection was found between health risks and electric fields, which can be shielded by materials like wood, aluminum or the covering around wires. Few people, Carpenter notes, live close enough to transmission lines to be affected by magnetic fields, but not so with regard to neighborhood distribution lines.

Exposure to magnetic fields from electric appliances at home and at work are probably of equal health importance, Carpenter adds. "Most electric blankets on sale in this country generate magnetic fields, for someone sleeping under them, about 10 times larger than fields shown to cause an increase in childhood cancer," he says. Carpenter believes warnings should be placed on electric blankets. That has not been done. But partly at the urging of the Food and Drug Administration (FDA), the three American manufacturers of electric blankets — Northern Electric Co. in Chicago, Casco-Belton Corp. in Grover, N.C., and Fieldcrest Cannon in Greensboro, N.C. — are redesigning their products to reduce the magnetic field to "virtually zero," according to F. Alan Anderson, director of FDA's Office of Science and Technology. The first two companies already have such products on the market, and the third has promised to do so this year.

The impetus for FDA action, according to Anderson, comes from the growing pattern of "well-done studies which suggest an association" between exposure and health effects. "We don't know if it's going to be demonstrated that there's a causal relationship. The jury's still out on that. But prudence would suggest if it's possible that you go ahead and take steps to reduce emissions."

FDA is also developing a voluntary EMF emissions standards for video-display terminals (VDTs) along the lines of a voluntary standard introduced by Sweden this year, according to Anderson. Although the Swedish standard is voluntary, the strength of European labor

# Risks Are Comparatively Low

Current studies suggest that if electromagnetic fields do turn out to be dangerous, the dangers are not very high when compared with other health hazards.

A recent study by John M. Peters of the University of Southern California, for example, found that children who live close to neighborhood power lines are about 2.5 times as likely to have leukemia as children who don't. That sounds like a lot. But since the overall frequency for childhood leukemia is about one case for each 20,000 children per year, the increased risk would raise the rate only to one case for each 8,000 youngsters — higher, to be sure, but still rare.

The risk of death suggested by such studies is generally no more than one out of many thousands. Traffic patterns in one's neighborhood are likely to pose a much greater risk to one's child than electromagnetic fields. The danger from EMFs, then, seems to be much lower than the risks American society now spends money to avert, notes M. Granger Morgan, head of the Department of Engineering and Public Policy at Carnegie Mellon University.

Generally, society chooses to spend large sums of money primarily on hazards for which the lifetime risk of death is well above 1 in 1,000 — the kinds of risks listed above the shaded band in the chart at right. For example, the chances that the average American will die from an auto accident are relatively high — about 1 in 40 — and the United States spends a few hundred thousand dollars per death avoided.

By that measure, says Morgan, it would be hard to justify spending more than a few thousand dollars for each person exposed to electromagnetic fields. Because the health of only a small

| Cause of death | Approximate number who die each year from this cause | Approximate odds, on average, that death was from this cause |
|---|---|---|
| Disease (all kinds) | 1,600,000 | 1 in 1.3 |
| Heart disease | 710,000 | 1 in 3 |
| Cancer (all kinds) | 410,000 | 1 in 5 |
| Accidents (all kinds) | 100,000 | 1 in 20 |
| Auto accidents | 50,000 | 1 in 42 |
| Diabetes | 32,000 | 1 in 66 |
| Suicide | 26,000 | 1 in 81 |
| Homicide | 25,000 | 1 in 84 |
| Drowning | 7,500 | 1 in 280 |
| Fire | 6,000 | 1 in 350 |
| Firearm accidents | 2,200 | 1 in 1,000 |
| Asthma | 2,000 | 1 in 1,000 |
| Electrocution | 1,000 | 1 in 2,100 |
| Car-train accidents | 1,000 | 1 in 2,100 |
| Appendicitis | 650 | 1 in 3,200 |
| Infectious hepatitis | 350 | 1 in 5,900 |
| Pregnancy and related | 250 | 1 in 4,200 |
| Floods | 140 | 1 in 15,000 |
| Lightning | 110 | 1 in 20,000 |
| Tornado | 92 | 1 in 25,000 |
| Botulism | 6 | 1 in 360,000 |
| Fireworks | 5 | 1 in 430,000 |

*Note: This chart applies only to the United States.*
*Source: M. Granger Morgan, "Electric and Magnetic Fields from 60 Hertz Electric Power: What do we know about possible health risks?" Carnegie Mellon University. Copyright 1989. Reprinted by permission.*

fraction of those exposed to electromagnetic fields is likely to be affected, an investment of $1,000 per exposure avoided could amount to an investment of millions of dollars or more per health danger avoided, he calculates.

"Much larger expenditures can almost certainly not be justified," Morgan argues. "If you think the risk, if any, for exposed people probably does not lie well above this shaded band, you should seriously consider selecting either the strategy of 'prudent avoidance' or 'no action.' " †

Morgan likens the strategy of prudent avoidance to that of changing one's diet to reduce cholesterol intake and increase fiber. Even though the various health associations have not been proven, many people have decided it does not cost much to change their eating habits to avoid a potential health problem. Similarly, he proposes low-cost, easy steps to avoid the unproven risks of electromagnetic fields. These would include getting rid of electric blankets and reducing one's exposures to appliances with motors, like hair dryers, which emanate strong magnetic fields when held close to the body.

Morgan and others have pointed out that there have not been dramatic increases in the numbers of deaths or illness in the decades since society has become electrified. If anything, there has been a dramatic decrease in death and disease since the onset of the industrial age. But those who are concerned about electromagnetic fields argue that increases in life-expectancy might have been even greater without EMF exposure.

† *M. Granger Morgan, Electric and Magnetic Fields from 60 Hertz Electric Power: What do We Know About the Risks? Department of Engineering and Public Policy, Carnegie Mellon University, 1989.*

---

unions is expected to make it a de facto standard in other European countries as well. Several major manufacturers of VDTs — including International Business Machines Co. and Sigma Designs Inc. — have announced they will offer low-emissions monitors on the U.S. market that would meet the Swedish standard. According to Tom Quinlan of *InfoWorld*, a Menlo Park, Calif., weekly that covers microcomputers for business users, low-emission monitors will not cost much more than current ones.

Computer industry spokesmen say they're not convinced that there are EMF health risks associated with VDTs but that the Swedish standard is "technically achievable" and reasonable in cost. "The industry does

not perceive it as a health issue," says Maryann Karinch, communications director for the Computer and Business Equipment Manufacturers Association, a Washington, D.C., trade association of large manufacturers. "But as long as the market does, that's the important thing."

## Complex and confusing scientific evidence

A major reason that scientists have been unable to determine unequivocally whether EMFs are dangerous is that the scientific evidence is so complex and confusing. If EMFs cause health problems, they do so in very strange ways.

This year's EPRI-funded study, for instance, found an association between leukemia and wiring near the homes of Los Angeles children. Curiously, however, the study found little relationship between the magnetic field strength *inside* a child's home — as measured by a specially developed dosimeter known as an EMDEX — and the child's likelihood of developing leukemia, except at the very highest levels.

This lack of systematic association between dose and risk also characterized an earlier study of Denver children conducted by David A. Savitz, an epidemiologist now at the University of North Carolina at Chapel Hill.[4] Savitz's study, an analysis of 356 childhood cancer cases between 1976 and 1983, was an attempt to see if the famous Wertheimer results could be replicated. He concluded that children with high exposure to power line EMFs, as measured by the Wertheimer-Leeper wiring code, were about one and a half times as likely to develop cancer as children with very low exposure. That conclusion, coming from a study seen as methodologically stronger than the Wertheimer study, surprised many scientists and changed some from skeptics into believers.

Yet Savitz's indoor spot measurements of magnetic field strength did not show a clear relationship with cancer rates. Savitz theorized that this might be because his one-time measurement did not capture a child's long-term exposure to magnetic fields, which would vary over the course of a day depending on what appliances were being used in the house, how close the child was to the appliances, and so on.

The EPRI-funded study by John Peters was expected to clarify this question because it kept 24-hour to 72-hour records of actual EMF exposures in the children's sleeping areas. Yet even those measurements failed to show a statistically significant relationship with cancer risk, according to preliminary findings released by EPRI. Some scientists, especially those who are convinced there is a health risk, theorize that a child's long-term exposure over many years may be better captured by the wiring code outside than by the indoor recorded exposure over a day or two. An alternative theory is that sudden increases in EMF exposure — by turning certain appliances on and off, for example, or walking under a power line on the way to school — may be more important than the chronic exposure at a child's bedside.

Another possible explanation, posed by EPRI's Leonard Sagan, is that the wiring code correlation now found by three childhood studies has nothing to do with magnetic fields. It may be that families who live closest to power lines share some other characteristic that makes them more prone to cancer, such as low socioeconomic status or cigarette smoking. The wires themselves might leach toxic materials or play some other role in promoting cancer. Or the wiring clusters

could simply be a false lead in the search for cancer causation.

Savitz's Denver study, for example, found childhood cancer associations with the neighborhood's traffic density, not just with wiring codes. Similarly, in the EPRI-funded study, Peters reports associations of childhood leukemia risk with a variety of other factors, including indoor pesticide use, the father's exposure to spray paints and children's exposure to hair dryers and black and white televisions. Children's use of hair dryers and TVs are a possible link to the theory that intermittent high-level spikes in electricity use are more important than chronic average exposure.

Many experts contend that despite these remaining questions, the case in favor of EMF health risks has become stronger since the Peters study. "Once again, you have something you have to put on the side of saying, 'This found an association like the Wertheimer and Savitz studies did,'" says OTA's Karen Larsen. Others share Sagan's view that "The mystery is building rather than clarifying."

## Mixed scientific results get mixed scientific reviews

To some scientists, none of the childhood cancer studies is persuasive evidence that EMFs are dangerous. One such skeptic, Yale School of Medicine epidemiologist Michael B. Bracken, notes that virtually all the published cancer studies of adults and children have been "retrospective," relying on interviews with subjects about past electric power use and exposure, sometimes as long as 20 years after the fact. Such studies are inherently subject to the vagaries of faulty memory and "recall bias" on the part of investigators or interviewees, who may employ the benefits of hindsight to put stress on certain past events and not others. "These studies have a problem which they can't do much about," says Bracken. "I think the [studies] in the literature are not at all convincing. My own feeling right now is the evidence does not lead to a conclusion that magnetic fields affect health status."

Methodological criticisms like Bracken's may be answered in the next few years by a six-state, four-year "prospective" study of childhood leukemia by the National Cancer Institute initiated in September 1989. The study will compare the EMF exposure of 1,000 children with leukemia to 1,000 other children through a combination of interviews with parents, dosimeters worn by selected children, and spot and 24-hour measurements of EMFs in most of the places children spend their time, including schools and day-care centers. Results of the study are expected in early 1995.

But that study may not be the final word. "Human epidemiologic studies of EMFs and cancer have been inconsistent and inconclusive," the institute has

# What Are Electromagnetic Fields?

**W**herever electricity is present, there are electromagnetic fields. The electric fields of power lines, wall wiring and appliances are produced by electric charges that are sent through the power system by electric power generating stations. **Electric fields** arise from the strength of that charge, and **magnetic fields** result from the motion of that charge. Taken together, these fields are referred to as **electromagnetic fields**, or **EMFs**.

The electric and magnetic fields created by power systems oscillate with the **current**, measured in **amperes** or **amps**, which is the rate of electric charge flowing in a power line or wire. The strength of the magnetic field, measured in a unit called **gauss** depends upon the amount of current; the stronger the current, the stronger the magnetic field. The strength of the electrict field, on the other hand, comes from **voltage** — how much energy an electron will gain going from one point to another. The strength of the electric field is measured in units of **volts per meter**.

(An analogy is helpful in understanding the difference between current and voltage. Think of someone rolling balls down a trough. The "current" would be the number of balls he rolls over a certain period of time. The "voltage" would be how much energy the ball would gain going from the top of the trough to the bottom. He could increase the "current" by rolling more balls per minute; he could increase the "voltage" by making the trough longer and higher.)

The electric power used in North America alternates back and forth at a **frequency** of 60 times each second. Scientists call this 60 **hertz** power (abbreviated **Hz**). Sixty Hz electric and magnetic fields are those associated with 60 Hz power. These **power-frequency** fields are only one type of the **non-ionizing** electric and magnetic fields that people regularly encounter. Electric and magnetic fields at higher frequencies are produced by video-display terminals (about 15 kilohertz, or 15,000 cycles per second), TV sets (about 20 kilohertz), AM radio transmitters (about 1 megahertz, or 1 million cycles per second) and microwave ovens (about 2 gigahertz, or 2 billion cycles per second). All of the possible frequencies of electromagnetic waves and fields can be put onto an **electromagnetic spectrum** (*see chart*). Frequencies of oscillation above visible light are considered to be **ionizing** and include X-rays. Ionizing radiation carries enough energy to break chemical and electrical bonds. Nonionizing radiation does not.

Recently, scientists have focused their attention on magnetic fields, because epidemiologic and laboratory studies that suggest a health risk tend to find correlations with magnetic rather than electric fields. Among the factors that scientists are examining for possible links to health are these:

■ **Strength of the field.** Appliances that heat, such as hair dryers, room heaters and electric stoves, have strong fields associated with them because they draw a lot of current.

■ **Distance from the source.** Magnetic fields fall off quickly with distance, though with some variations. For example, the strength of magnetic fields from appliances typically declines faster with distance than does the strength of fields from overhead power lines, because appliances are less extended in space than long power lines. On the other hand, some appliances, such as hair dryers, are used very close to the body.

■ **Length of exposure.** Electric blankets, which give off weaker magnetic fields than electric stoves, are probably a bigger contributor to a person's overall magnetic field exposure if used all night.

---

**The electromagnetic spectrum shows the frequencies of electromagnetic waves or fields, measured in hertz (Hz), of everything from electricity to radio to visible light to X-rays. Some of the more important areas of the spectrum are labeled on this graph. In the United States, electricity oscillates at 60 Hz; it may use slightly different frequencies in other countries.**

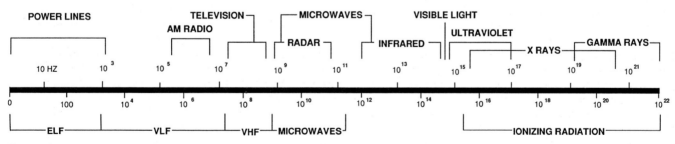

*Source: Electric Power Research Institute,* EPRI Journal, *October/November 1987.*

---

noted.[5] The cancer associations found in the Denver studies and in a Swedish study were not confirmed in similar studies from Rhode Island, Washington state and England.

Further clouding the cancer question are the generally negative results from studies of adults living near power lines. In a review of the literature last year, *Science* magazine noted that several studies conducted since a 1982 Wertheimer-Leeper study claiming increased cancer rates among Colorado adults with high EMF exposure found "little or nothing." [6] One possible explanation, *Science* noted, is that it may be more difficult to separate out EMFs from the multitude of potential cancer risks faced by adults than it is for children during their much shorter life span. Nevertheless, the lack of evidence from these residential adult studies feeds some scientists' overall skepticism of health hazards.

# EMF Exposure

**If there are any health effects at all from exposure to electromagnetic fields from electricity, they could depend on a variety of factors. This chart shows, for various sources of electromagnetic fields, some of these factors: the strength of the electric field (measured in kilovolts per meter), the strength of the magnetic field (measured in milligauss), the length of exposure and the fraction of the population exposed. It is clear that the answer to the question, "What produces the biggest exposure?" depends on which factor is being examined.**

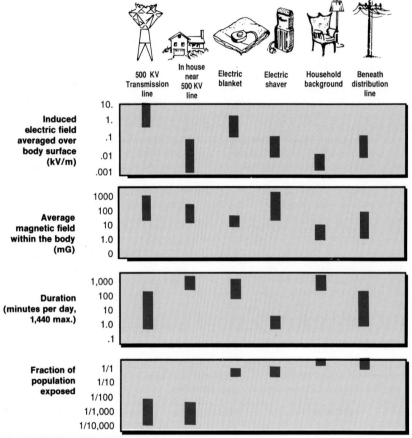

*Source: M. Granger Morgan, "Electric and Magnetic Fields from 60 Hertz Electric Power: What do we know about possible health risks?" Carnegie Mellon University. Copyright 1989. Reprinted by permission.*

fetal development among more than 2,000 pregnant New Haven, Conn., women, whose EMF exposure will be monitored throughout pregnancy, starting with their first prenatal visit.

For many members of the public, concerns about the effect of EMF emissions on pregnancy may have been laid to rest prematurely when the National Institute for Occupational Safety and Health (NIOSH) released a good-news study of computer monitors last month.[9] The study of 730 telephone operators found that those who used VDTs had no greater risk of suffering miscarriages than operators using an older type of work station equipped with neon tubes.

But some experts noted that the study was of limited significance for the larger question of whether EMFs generally are harmful because it only measured frequencies special to VDTs — called Very Low Frequency EMFs — and not the Extremely Low Frequencies that are emitted by all electric equipment. Extremely Low Frequencies have been the focus of most EMF epidemiologic studies to date. Another analysis of the NIOSH study data found that VDTs do not add significantly to ambient EMF levels in offices, probably because the electric wiring systems in a building are a greater influence on the overall environment.[10]

Mixed results also dog studies looking into effects of EMFs on pregnancies. Two studies by Nancy Wertheimer in the mid-1980s showed a seasonal pattern of miscarriages in families that used electric blankets or electrically heated water beds, or had electric heating cables installed in their bedroom ceilings, a practice common in some places during the 1960s and '70s.[7] A study by Savitz published in the May 1990 issue of the *American Journal of Epidemiology* indicated that children borne by women who used electric blankets when they were pregnant had two and a half times the expected incidence of brain tumors and a 70 percent greater likelihood of developing leukemia.[8]

Bracken, the skeptic, notes that Savitz asked women about their electric blanket use some 10 years earlier. "I think the potential for biased recall of use is very obvious in that kind of study," he says. For his part, Bracken is currently conducting an EPRI-funded prospective study of electric blankets' effects on

## Occupational studies raise serious concerns

Compared with the equivocal picture for pregnancies and residential adult exposure, occupational studies of workers in electrically associated occupations have consistently raised red flags for increased cancer risk. Numerous studies have found increased rates of various forms of brain tumors, leukemia and, most startlingly, male breast cancer, an extremely rare form of the disease. One recent study, for example, found that Los Angeles men who had worked for 10 years or more in a variety of electrical occupations had a 10 times greater chance of getting brain cancer than men in a control group.[11]

The reports of male breast cancer are particularly intriguing because they present one of the few diseases that could be explained by EMF-produced biological changes observed in laboratory experiments. One widely discussed study, conducted by epidemiologist Genevieve M. Matanoski of Johns Hopkins University in Baltimore, found that New York telephone company workers with line-related jobs suffered cancer at almost twice the rate of other telephone company employees. She discovered two cases of male breast cancer in a group of 9,500 central office technicians, where zero cases of this disease would normally be expected.[12] A nationwide study of Norwegian adult males published last December found that workers in electrical occupations suffered from breast cancer at twice the rate that would be expected for the general population.[13]

The two men in Matanoski's study with breast cancer worked in an office in which telephone switching equipment is frequently turned on and off, creating spikes of EMF exposure. In a letter to the British medical journal *Lancet* last month, Matanoski suggested that these cases might be explained by laboratory experiments with rats showing that EMF exposure can reduce melatonin, a hormone linked to suppression of breast cancer.[14]

This explanation would fit in nicely with a theory put forward by Richard G. Stevens, a cancer epidemiologist at Battelle Pacific Northwest Laboratories in Richland, Wash. He has suggested that the very high breast cancer rate among women in industrialized countries, as compared with women in underdeveloped countries, might be explained by their chronic exposure to EMFs from living around electrical equipment.

Stevens calls the recent studies finding breast cancer among male workers "tantalizing. It adds support to the idea that we ought to do more big studies of female breast cancer and electric power." To date, female breast cancer has not been a target of EMF epidemiologic research.

Because of its simplicity, the melatonin theory is probably the most attractive of various explanations that have been put forward to explain how EMFs could affect humans. But it does not explain the entire range of cancers found so far, Stevens concedes. For example, the melatonin theory does not explain the non-hormonal kinds of cancers found at elevated levels among electrical workers, such as leukemia, an association found in more than 20 occupation studies.

Other aspects of electrical work that have nothing to do with EMF could also account for the elevated breast cancer among electrical workers, Stevens points out. For example, the presence of light has been shown in rat experiments to reduce melatonin, and that syndrome might be taking place among the electrical workers if they work in artificial light during normal sleeping hours. It is also possible that chemicals present in electrical work environments are responsible for the increased cancers.

## 'Windows' theory: EMFs' unusual pattern

Further complicating attempts to establish a cause-effect relationship between EMFs and health problems is the fact that if EMFs do cause problems, they do not follow the usual pattern of known carcinogens. Typically, in studies of cancer-causing substances, researchers expect to find that as the dose of a substance increases, the risk will increase proportionally in a "dose-response relationship." Most epidemiologic studies have failed to find such a relationship in connection with EMF. One reason may be that it simply doesn't work that way.

For example, in laboratory experiments on the brains of baby chicks, one researcher found that he could produce an important biological effect — the leaching of calcium — only at specific "windows" of frequencies and intensities of electromagnetic fields. The researcher, biologist Carl F. Blackman of the Environmental Protection Agency's Health Effects Research Laboratory at Research Triangle Park, N.C., reports that as he increases or lowers the strength of the EMF fields, he loses the effect — until he gets to the next "window."

Blackman has published work showing six such "windows."[15] He is one of the few researchers who has observed biological effects at the low electric and magnetic field strengths typical of the background level inside a house. Because calcium is considered an important biological "messenger" for activity in the cell, Blackman suggests that the magnetic field is causing some important change either inside or on the surface of the cell. But he cautions: "We don't know if these changes are hazards. We don't know what the physiological significance is. It reflects a response we had no reason to predict and that we do not understand."

Epidemiologists, however, are intrigued by the windows research as a possible explanation for the links between cancer and short spurts of high-level EMF exposure from appliances like hair dryers, as suggested by John Peters' study of Los Angeles children.

Blackman's research also may help explain another mysterious aspect of EMF studies — the frequent inability of scientists to replicate the biological effects produced by their colleagues at other laboratories. Blackman and other scientists call it the "now-you-see-it-now-you-don't Cheshire Cat" phenomenon, and Blackman says the Earth's magnetic field can affect which frequencies produce change. For example, when Blackman artificially reduces the Earth's magnetic field by half in his laboratory, he no longer sees the biological results that had consistently come about at the 15 hertz frequency.

If the Earth's magnetic field is as important as Blackman thinks it is, it could explain why epidemiologic studies in different locations sometimes come up with conflicting results. The lesson for public health, however, would be extremely complicated. It would

# *Paul Brodeur's Crusade*

**S**cience magazine called it "sensationalistic." The *New York Times* branded it an "alarmist" tract. *Scientific American* called it "a disservice to the public interest." †

The target of all this outrage was journalist Paul Brodeur's three-part article tracing the scientific investigation into health hazards of electromagnetic radiation. The series first appeared in *The New Yorker* in 1989 and then later that year in book form under the title *Currents of Death*.

Brodeur, who first made a name for himself in exposing the dangers of asbestos, concluded that electromagnetic fields are, indeed, dangerous. "[T]he de facto policy that power lines, electric blankets, and video display terminals be considered innocent until proved guilty should be rejected out of hand by sensible people everywhere," he wrote. "To do otherwise is to accept a situation in which millions of human beings continue to be test animals in a long-term biological experiment whose consequences remain unknown."

That extreme view is not one that is shared by many. "This turns logic on its head," wrote *New York Times* science reporter William J. Broad in a review of Brodeur's book. "Alarming claims need large amounts of evidence." Broad likened Brodeur's claims to someone asserting the presence of space aliens on Earth.

Scientists who reviewed the book objected that it told only one side of the story. David A. Savitz of the University of North Carolina at Chapel Hill, one of the leading epidemiologists in the field, found the book "generally accurate in citing evidence of health harm but not giving equal consideration to opposing findings. . . . Personal or institutional bias is invoked as the only possible reason for failure to accept what the author but [few others] considers irrefutable evidence." ††

Brodeur glosses over inconsistencies with his belief that utility-funded studies have been designed purely to discredit scientists who find health harms, Savitz said, citing his own work. In a widely respected study funded by utilities, Savitz found elevated leukemia risks for children living near high-current wires.

M. Granger Morgan, professor of engineering at Carnegie Mellon University, expressed the worries of many scientists in his *Scientific American* review when he said that "Brodeur's book is already shaping the way many concerned technologically untrained citizens, including some decision makers, frame and think about these issues." Morgan charged that Brodeur "deliberately oversimplifies and misrepresents the complexity of the scientific process and the evidence it has produced."

But Brodeur himself continues to appear on TV talk shows, at conferences and at school board meetings in a personal crusade, pressing his charge that electric utility and media interests are covering up the health hazards of EMF. And people seem to be listening. When National Public Radio interviewed Cleveland, Ohio, business executives this month about their suit to block construction of a local transmission line, the executives cited *Currents of Death* as a prime authority for their health concerns.

Electric utilities and engineers are starting to strike back. The utility-funded Electric Power Research Institute, for example, has published a booklet refuting Brodeur's July 9, 1990, *New Yorker* article, "Calamity on Meadow Street," which claims that clusters of cancer cases have arisen in Guilford, Conn., and Dukeville, N.C., because of EMFs. And another critique of Brodeur is being circulated by the Institute of Electrical and Electronics Engineers, a national professional organization.‡

† *Robert Pool, "Is There an EMF-Cancer Connection?" Science, Sept. 7, 1990, pp. 1096-8; William J. Broad, "Science Books," New York Times Book Review, April 8, 1990, p. 21; M. Granger Morgan, "Exposé Treatment Confounds Understanding of a Serious Public Health Issue," Scientific American, April 1990, pp. 118-123.*
†† *David A. Savitz, "Electric Current and Health," JAMA, Aug. 1, 1990, pp. 636-7.*
‡ *See "Power Line Talk," Microwave News, March/April 1991, p. 2.*

---

mean that humans experience different effects from EMF depending on where they live, because geomagnetic fields vary by location. And because the strength of the Earth's magnetic field can also be affected by geological anomalies in a neighborhood and by construction materials, a person's biological reaction to EMFs could depend on the kind of building he lived in or even where in the building he spent the most time, Blackman says.

Laboratory studies have also found other effects of EMFs, including changes in neurotransmitters, the chemicals that send signals between nerves; changes in the rate at which the genetic material DNA is made and in the rate of errors when RNA is copied from it; and changes in the rate of growth and cell division of some cells. Some studies in which people have been exposed to magnetic fields that are turned on an off repeatedly report more pronounced effects, such as changes in heart rate and reaction time, than when people are exposed to the same continuous level of EMFs.

All of these experiments show that EMFs from everyday power sources, once considered too weak to affect humans, do have a biological impact. This should not be surprising. It has long been thought that other animals can sense magnetic fields, that this is one of the ways homing pigeons, for example, find their way home. But for humans whether the effects of EMFs translate into health dangers is far from clear. And no one has yet come up with a comprehensive theory that would explain exactly what biological mechanism, as seen in the laboratory, could cause the varied health effects found in epidemiologic studies.

## Despite some consensus, major divisions still exist

Although researching potential health risks of EMFs has become a respectable activity in the 1990s, wide divisions remain. A major concern often expressed is the objectivity of EPRI, the major funder of EMF research. EPRI's $7.5 million annual research budget is more than twice the size of the largest federal program, a $3 million effort by the Department of Energy (DOE). (The Environmental Protection Agency's (EPA) research program in the area was eliminated during the Reagan administration.) And EPRI's effort dwarfs that of any of the 17 countries researching the issue. The largest overseas program is run by Sweden at about $1.9 million per year.

"The problem of the moment is 90 percent of the research is done by two groups: EPRI and DOE. They have too much to lose," says Louis Slesin, editor of *Microwave News*, a New York City-based newsletter that pioneered reporting on the health risks of EMF. "We've learned over and over, whether it's asbestos or chemicals, you don't have the person who has the most to lose doing the work."

EPRI's Leonard Sagan retorts that unlike asbestos or toxic chemicals, "people are not going to stop using electricity. ... The problem is not that we're doing too much. The problem is others are doing too little." On that score, even EPRI critic David Carpenter agrees: "The federal government has not been a player here. That's just ludicrous."

Citing a similar concern that industry-funded studies "will never have full credibility with the public," Rep. Frank Pallone Jr., D-N.J., introduced legislation (HR 1483) in March to establish a coordinated federal EMF research program involving the Department of Energy, the Environmental Protection Agency and the National Institute of Environmental Health Sciences. The proposal, which also includes a public information program, would reach a $10 million annual funding level by 1995. Pallone introduced the bill after constituents from Middletown Township, N.J., fought the construction of a new power line by New Jersey Central Power and Light. (Last fall, the utility announced that it would not build the power line, but it cited economic, not health reasons.) Although no action was taken on a similar Pallone bill last session, the legislation has the support of the new House Science Committee chairman, George E. Brown Jr., D-Calif. Pallone's bill is scheduled to be considered, along with other research approaches, at a June 25 hearing of the House Science Subcommittee on the Environment.

Even within the federal government, views on EMF have been strikingly divided. An EPA report released last December, calling EMFs emitted from power lines and home sources a "possible" human carcinogen, became a political football when White House science adviser D. Allan Bromley objected to EPA's conclusions. EPA's report cited the accumulated childhood studies and adult occupational studies as showing "a consistent pattern of response which suggests a causal link" to cancer.[16] Bromley disagreed. He insisted that the agency attach a "Note to Reviewers" warning that there had been "disagreement among the reviewers from various agencies about the weight of evidence and the conclusions presented in the executive summary." In boldface type, the note cautioned, "There are insufficient data to determine whether or not a cause and effect relationship exists" between EMF and cancer. Bromley also insisted that the report be evaluated by another scientific panel, in addition to EPA's own group of outside advisers. In an interview with *Time* magazine, he made it clear he found EPA's finding of a positive association between EMF and childhood cancer "quite incorrect."[17]

Air Force scientists also weighed in with a blistering attack on the report, charging that the EPA authors presented "no evidence of causation between electromagnetic fields and cancer, but rather argue as if this hypothesis were accepted fact." Many scientists viewed the Air Force's position as the legacy of the longstanding military contention that EMF radiation is incapable of producing health effects because it does not induce heating.[18] In his book *Currents of Death*, reporter Paul Brodeur has portrayed the military's scientific position as the self-interested corollary of its campaigns to overcome public opposition to constructing military radio antennae and radar facilities in populated areas.

The Brodeur book drew strong criticism from researchers like David Savitz, who condemned as oversimplified Brodeur's division of scientists "into heroes working on behalf of the people and villains working for the military-industrial complex." At the same time, the issue of financial incentives for scientists hired as consultants to the military and to electric utilities to support their skepticism in the courts "deserves to be more carefully examined than it has been in the past," Savitz said. "Prominent scientists may indeed hold views supportive of their position, but the payment of tens of thousands of dollars to express those views may be corrupting."[19]

In contrast, scientific observers viewed last year's disagreement between the EPA and White House science adviser Bromley as a classic conflict between physicists like Bromley, who tend to be skeptical of EMF health effects, and biologists, who have led the recent research in this area. Anticipating White House criticism, for example, EPA last February added Harvard physicist Richard Wilson, widely viewed as a skeptic, to its advisory panel on the EMF report; until then, there had been no physicists on the panel. An EPA staffer explained at the time that physicists, unable to reconcile EMF-cancer correlations with traditional physical theories, "have trouble accepting what's going on in the field."[20]

Nevertheless, even though the skepticism continues, as do the divisions among scientists, today's scientific atmosphere on the subject of EMFs is a long way from the utter disbelief that greeted Nancy Wertheimer's first reports of childhood cancer in 1979.

## Protecting public health through 'prudent avoidance'

Federal officials charged with regulating public health hazards have shied away from siding with either extreme in the debate, but the mounting scientific evidence means the issue can no longer be ignored, they say.

"I have never seen an epidemiologically more compelling case [of a link to cancer] in the last 10 years," says Martin P. Halper, director of the Analysis and Support Division of EPA's Office of Radiation Programs. What makes it compelling, at least to Halper, is that "the results are very consistent. All the studies done by different people on different populations in different parts of the world are all correlating to the same group of cancers."

Nevertheless, Halper says, "We cannot say at this point that we're dealing with a significant public health risk. Even if we said there's a real problem, no one knows what to do with it." From existing studies, he points out, it's not clear what level of exposure is a risk, nor is it clear what proportion of the population is at risk. Huge gaps in current understanding of EMF must be closed before EPA could begin to regulate electromagnetic fields as a carcinogen, he says.

FDA's Alan Anderson takes a similar approach on the issue of whether electric blankets should carry warnings. "Given the current status of knowledge, it's not clear what you warn people. There's no sense of a cause and effect relationship that's been established or what level it would occur at if it existed."

Most experts agree that there will not be a clear idea of what levels of EMF exposure constitute a health hazard — if any — until there have been extensive animal studies. Several such studies are currently under way around the world. Researchers believe that if EMF is linked to cancer, it probably plays a role in promoting carcinogenesis in the later stages, affecting the growth or spread of cancer cells rather than initiating the disease. Animal experiments designed to observe this process are expected to take years before they produce results.

But the public may not be willing to wait for long-term animal studies to come to a conclusion, particularly at the current pace of government research efforts, warns Louis Slesin of *Microwave News*. If federal research agencies "don't start doing the work that will pinpoint where the problem really lies, you're going to have the public decide. And the public has

this nasty habit of overreacting," he says.

Citizen-led siting battles over the construction of new power lines are now taking place in practically every state, Slesin reports. Major transmission line projects in New York, Montana, Florida and several other states have encountered considerable opposition. And some of these battles have ended up in the courts. Few cases have been decided, but two of them stand out:

■ In *Houston Power and Lighting v. Klein*, the Houston utility initially was ordered to pay the Klein Independent School District $25 million in damages for building a 345 kilovolt transmission line close to a school. The Texas Court of Appeals reversed the damage award, but affirmed the lower court's finding that there are potential health effects from exposure to power-line fields. Because the utility was prevented from using the power line during the appeals process, it rerouted it at a cost of $8.6 million in 1987.[21]

■ The other case that gained wide notice in the industry was a personal injury lawsuit brought by Robert Strom, a former Boeing Co. employee, who alleged that he had contracted terminal leukemia after being exposed to dangerous EMF levels in his job as an electrician. In a settlement reached last year with Strom, who brought a class action suit on behalf of some 750 Boeing workers, the Seattle company paid him $500,000 in damages and agreed to fund free independent medical exams for all class members for up to 10 years.

"We expect that this case and the increasing scientific evidence being developed about the health effects of non-ionizing radiation will prompt the filing of additional lawsuits, both property damage and personal injury lawsuits," says Arthur H. Bryant, executive director of Trial Lawyers for Public Justice in Washington, D.C., a national public interest law firm that represented Strom.

Growing numbers of expensive lawsuits and battles over the siting of power lines could translate into huge costs for the electric power industry. Researchers for the utilities express concern that the technical solutions resulting from court cases and government action may not be scientifically justified. "I'm terribly worried that people are going to panic and we'll be made to do costly things," says EPRI's Leonard Sagan. "Dollars will be squandered."

For many utility managers, however, regulatory limits of some kind on EMF would be a welcome ceiling on the current uncertainty that now threatens the future of power line construction, according to a recent survey by *The Wall Street Journal*. Many utilities are putting together technical teams to make free EMF measurements in homes and offices for customers who request them, the Journal reported.[22]

In the absence of good scientific evidence, what steps should be taken to protect public health? M. Granger Morgan, head of the Engineering and Public Policy Department at Carnegie Mellon University in

*Continued on p. 250*

# AT ISSUE — Is "prudent avoidance" of electromagnetic fields a good strategy for people to follow?

**YES** *say* **INDIRA NAIR, M. GRANGER MORGAN** *and* **H. KEITH FLORIG**, *co-authors of a 1989 report for the congressional Office of Technology Assessment (OTA).*

Why not just use the standard techniques of probabilistic risk assessment and risk analysis to decide how serious the possible risks of human exposure to [electromagnetic] fields [from electrical sources] may be and develop appropriate regulatory recommendations from those studies? . . . The basic problem . . . is the inability to define dose. We do not yet know what attribute or combination of attributes, of the field produces public health effects. . . .

Better scientific understanding may in the future clearly demonstrate the existence of adverse public health effects from field exposure and may point the way to specific risk management regulations. But, for the moment we have to operate with what we have. Available policy options include . . . do nothing until the science becomes better, [or] adopt a "prudent avoidance" strategy. . . . By avoidance we mean taking steps to keep people out of fields, both by rerouting facilities and by redesigning electrical systems and appliances. By prudence we mean undertaking only those avoidance activities which carry modest costs. When, as individuals, we think a risk may exist but we are not sure, we exercise prudence. For example . . . dietary fiber may help reduce the risk of certain cancers. . . . As a matter of prudence many people have tried to increase . . . their fiber intake. . . . But reasonable people do not rent a helicopter to fly high-fiber bread in to them when they spend a week at a mountain ski resort which serves only regular bread. . . .

What would constitute prudence in the context of keeping people out of [electric power] fields? Here are a few possibilities: attempt to route new transmission lines so that they avoid people; widen transmission line rights of way; develop designs for distribution systems, including new grounding procedures, which minimize the associated fields; develop new approaches to house wiring that minimize associated fields; redesign appliances to minimize or eliminate fields. . . .

[C]learly it makes no sense to invest more per person-exposure avoided than we invest per *death* avoided for various *known* risks in our society. . . . [F]or example, while it might make sense to work to avoid exposing people in siting new lines, in most cases, with our current knowledge, it would not make sense to tear out and rebuild old lines. Similarly it might make sense to redesign new appliances to reduce fields exposure if this can be done for small increments in their costs. . . . But it probably would not make sense to throw out all old appliances before they wear out and replace them all immediately with new "field-free" ones.

*From* Biological Effects of Power Frequency Electric and Magnetic Fields, *prepared for the Office of Technology Assessment, May 1989.*

**NO** *says* **THE ELECTROMAGNETIC ENERGY POLICY ALLIANCE (EEPA)**, *a Washington, D.C.-based association of manufacturers and users of electronic and electrical systems.*

Despite the seductive phrase "prudent avoidance," and the representation of the concept as a pragmatic response for policy setting when the scientific basis is inadequate, an examination of the origins and implications of this proposal reveals that it actually involves a rejection of the modern concept of rational, scientifically based guidance of safety policy and a return to the alternative, emotional, medieval concept of acting to mitigate fear of the unknown. . . . EEPA perceives a great danger to society, as we know it, if "prudent avoidance" becomes accepted as a principle for setting public policy whenever there is scientifically unfounded public concern and/or fear. . . .

Taking the assessment of the OTA report at face value [that there are "increasingly suggestive findings" of health risks from electromagnetic fields, we ask:] . . . Is "suggestive science" a basis [upon which] to abandon scientific standard setting? The scientist has only one answer to the question, a resounding no! Politicians, however, may very well find [the "prudent avoidance"] option appealing since it also dispenses with their requirement to grapple with science. . . .

We do not agree . . . that the primary reason for the inadequate state of knowledge for scientific standard setting is complexity of the subject matter: Rather, EEPA views the confusion as primarily attributable to insufficient "good" science. . . . Many of these studies concern field strengths at cells and in cells which are many orders of magnitude below any established bioeffects and even appear to violate basic laws of physics, a non-trivial objection. . . .

The prospects of causing a major impact on the generation, transmission, distribution and end use of electricity are actually contrary to the OTA report authors' perceptions of prudence. Nevertheless, the intuitive appeal of the phrase "prudent avoidance" coupled with a "less is safer" mind set, could have that end result. More importantly, the precedent set for rejecting the scientific approach to dealing with hazards in favor of deferring to the political need to assuage media-induced public concern undermines the accepted role of scientific knowledge as the proper basis for determining appropriate action by legislators, regulators, judges and juries for all popularly perceived risks. . . .

In EEPA's opinion, a policy of "prudent avoidance" represents the triumph of fear of the unknown over reason. . . . The concern over possible health risks, if any, from exposure to ambient . . . electric and magnetic fields can and properly should be resolved by scientific research. Interim exposure guidelines should be adopted that are based upon scientific consensus and reviewed periodically by consensus groups. . . .

*From* 'Prudent Avoidance': The Abandonment of Science, *unpublished position paper from EEPA, April 1991.*

*Continued from p. 248*

Pittsburgh, argues that even if the risk of childhood cancer proves true, that does not mean that the nation should necessarily spend great amounts of money to do something about it. The risk to health would still be very low — still only one in many thousands. (*See story, p. 000.*)

However, other experts, such as David Carpenter, believe that the risks could turn out to be significantly higher with more study, and even if they don't, the current level is significant because it involves children, who have their entire lives ahead of them.

Nevertheless, Carpenter agrees with Morgan that it's too early to start setting health-based standards. And Morgan believes there are steps that can be taken short of setting standards — what he calls "prudent avoidance," or taking low-cost, relatively painless steps to reduce one's EMF exposure. He advises replacing an electric blanket with a comforter and moving electric clocks away from the bedside, because both devices produce strong magnetic fields for extended periods at night. And he says that someone buying a new home might want to consider the location of distribution and transmission lines. But selling one's home solely to move away from power lines would for the most part "go beyond prudence," in his view.

Carpenter offers some other advice along those lines. Position beds against walls that don't carry wiring, he says, because the strength of the magnetic field falls off sharply as a person moves away from an electricity source. He also recommends arranging offices so that workers are not seated near the rear of a neighbor's VDT terminal, because the back of a terminal emits a much stronger magnetic field than the screen side.

These kinds of steps are easy. But if electric current turns out to be as dangerous as some people think, the cost could be enormous. Many houses, for example, have their power grounded through underground water and sewer pipes, which can produce strong magnetic fields. EPRI has been experimenting with alternative grounding techniques that could reduce magnetic fields in houses considerably. "I'm relatively optimistic that utilities are going to be able to find ways to bring power to new homes with much reduced fields," says Carpenter of the EPRI efforts. "The problem, of course, is what do you do with all the existing homes?"

Morgan says it is not too early to start studying how the nation would re-engineer electric energy systems, appliances and house wiring. "If and when we get clear evidence from animal studies, then . . . regulatory and public pressures aren't going to let folks sit around for a few years trying to figure out what to do. If we haven't done our homework at that point, a lot of dumb and silly things could happen."

Unfortunately, such planning is difficult, if only because the scientific research seems to offer contradictory advice. If it's sudden spikes in exposure that are most hazardous, then chronic exposure to a bedside clock may be less important than turning on a hair dryer or walking under a power line, notes Sagan. And if only certain intensities or frequencies have an effect, the overall amount of exposure may be irrelevant.

In the long run, if a link between EMFs and health is firmly established, there will be many cost-benefit decisions that will have to be made. It's not as if electricity is an optional characteristic of the modern world. "We all want it. We all need it. We're going to keep it whether we've got a problem or not," says Morgan. "What we'll do is redesign it. If we do have a problem, there have to be collective ways of solving it short of suing everybody in sight."

# NOTES

[1] Nancy Wertheimer and Ed Leeper, "Electrical Wiring Configurations and Childhood Cancer," *American Journal of Epidemiology*, March 1979, pp. 273-284

[2] Paul Brodeur, *Currents of Death* (1989), p. 67.

[3] EPRI printed a summary of this not-yet-published study in a Feb. 7, 1991, press release.

[4] David A. Savitz, *et.al*, "Case Control Study of Childhood Cancer and Exposure to 60-Hertz Magnetic Fields," *American Journal of Epidemiology*, July 1988, pp. 21-28.

[5] In a March 1990 press release.

[6] Robert Pool, "Is There an EMF-Cancer Connection?" *Science*, Sept. 7, 1990, pp. 1096-1097.

[7] Nancy Wertheimer and Ed Leeper, "Possible Effects of Electric Blankets and Heated Waterbeds on Fetal Development," *Bioelectromagnetics*, 1986, Vol. 7, pp. 13-22. And Wertheimer and Leeper, "Fetal Loss Associated with Two Seasonal Sources of Electromagnetic Field Exposure," *American Journal of Epidemiology*, 1989, Vol. 120, pp. 220-224.

[8] Study by Savitz cited in Gary Stix, "Field Effects: A health worry for electric blanket makers," *Scientific American*, December 1990, pp. 122-3.

[9] Teresa M. Schnorr, "Video Display Terminals and the Risk of Spontaneous Abortion," *New England Journal of Medicine*, March 14, 1991, pp. 727-733.

[10] "NIOSH EMF Survey Most Comprehensive to Date," *Microwave News*, March/April 1991, p. 11.

[11] Study by Susan Preston-Martin and Wendy Mack of the University of Southern California, cited in Pool, *op. cit.*, p. 1097.

[12] Genevieve M. Matanoski *et al.*, "Electromagnetic field exposure and male breast cancer," *Lancet*, Mar. 23, 1991, p. 737. This letter is Matanoski's only published summary of her findings.

[13] Tore Tynes and Aage Andersen, "Electromagnetic fields and male breast cancer," *Lancet*, Dec. 22/29, 1990, p. 1596. This letter reports 12 male breast cancer cases in a population of 37,952 men, where only six cases would normally be expected.

[14] Matanoski, *op. cit.*

[15] Bary W. Wilson *et al.*, ed., *Extremely Low Frequency Electromagnetic Fields: The Question of Cancer* (1990), pp. 187-208.

[16] Environmental Protection Agency, *Evaluation of the Potential Carcinogenicity of Electromagnetic Fields*, October 1990, pp. 1-5.

[17] Philip Elmer-Dewitt, "Mystery — and Maybe Danger — in the Air," *Time*, Dec. 24, 1990, pp. 67-69.

[18] "U.S. Air Force Labels EPA Report Biased and Political," *Microwave News*, November/December 1990, p. 7.

[19] David A. Savitz, "Electric Current and Health," *JAMA*, Aug. 1, 1990, pp. 636-637.

[20] "EPA: Physicists Unwelcome on EMF Panel," *Science*, Feb. 22, 1991, p. 863.

[21] OTA, *op. cit.*, p. 73.

[22] Frederick Rose, "Utilities React to Electromagnetic Fields," *The Wall Street Journal*, April 11, 1991, pp. B1, B10.

*Graphics: Cover, Margaret Scott; pp. 243, 244, Jack Auldridge.*

# RECOMMENDED READING

## BOOKS

**Brodeur, Paul,** *Currents of Death*, **Simon & Schuster, 1989.**

Journalist Brodeur's book-length version of his three-part *New Yorker* series has been responsible for arousing much of the public concern over electromagnetic radiation. But most scientists who have reviewed the book consider it unfairly alarmist. Although they find Brodeur's account of the research pioneers generally accurate, they object that Brodeur gives short shrift to studies that find conflicting or ambiguous results. Brodeur tends to portray such studies, where he does discuss them, as industry-backed efforts to discredit the pioneers. The result is a rather one-sided account, but interesting reading.

**Robert O. Becker,** *Cross Currents*, **Jeremy P. Tarcher Inc., 1990.**

In the early 1970s, Becker, an orthopedic surgeon and research scientist, was among the first scientists to become convinced that electromagnetic fields from power lines could pose a serious threat to human health. Becker calls for citizen action to protest hazardous power lines and to redesign electrical appliances. The bulk of the book is devoted to a discussion of electromagnetic fields aimed at the layman. It contains some helpful scientific explanations and interesting history of early research in this field.

## ARTICLES

**Blumberg, Peter, "Paul Brodeur's War on Electromagnetic Fields,"** *Washington Journalism Review*, **January/February 1991, pp. 40-44.**

Blumberg investigates Brodeur's charges that newspapers downplay the EMF story because they fear advertising losses and because their employees are heavily exposed to video-display terminals. An interesting review of the media coverage.

**Morgan, M. Granger, "Exposé Treatment Confounds Understanding of a Serious Public-Health Issue,"** *Scientific American*, **April 1990, pp. 118-123.**

Carnegie Mellon University engineer Morgan provides a good summary of scientific thinking on EMF in this critical review of Paul Brodeur's book, which he charges with "simplifying a complex problem by sweeping all complexity under the rug of cover-up."

**Pool, Robert, "Is There an EMF-Cancer Connection?"** *Science*, **Sept. 7, 1990, pp. 1096-98; "Electromagnetic Fields: The Biological Evidence," Sept. 21, 1990, pp. 1378-81; "Flying Blind: The Making of EMF Policy," Oct. 5, 1990, pp. 23-25.**

This three-part series provides an excellent summary of EMF research, replete with all its contradictions. Pool portrays both epidemiologic and laboratory results as "maddeningly inconclusive." His final article explores the difficulties of setting policy in the face of scientific uncertainty.

## REPORTS AND STUDIES

**Environmental Protection Agency,** *Evaluation of the Potential Carcinogenicity of Electromagnetic Fields*, **October 1990.**

This EPA "review draft" released last December added to the growing public concern by calling EMFs "a possible, but not proven, cause of cancer in humans." The report attracted the displeasure of the White House science adviser, who insisted on the addition of a cover note cautioning that "a cause and effect relationship" cannot be established from existing data. The draft is currently under review by two panels of outside experts, one appointed by EPA and one by the president. The report is a comprehensive review of existing research on EMFs through 1990.

**Morgan, M. Granger,** *Electric and Magnetic Fields from 60 Hertz Electric Power: What Do We Know about Possible Health Risks?* **1989.**

An easy-to-understand primer on electromagnetic fields and the ongoing health risks debate, written for the layman. Available from the Department of Engineering and Public Policy, Carnegie Mellon University, Pittsburgh, Pa. 15213.

**Office of Technology Assessment,** *Biological Effects of Power Frequency Electric and Magnetic Fields*, **May 1989.**

This report by the congressional Office of Technology Assessment was the first widely circulated literature review to put the stamp of respectability on health concerns about EMF. "In our view, the emerging evidence no longer allows one to categorically assert that there are no risks," the report states. "But it does not provide a basis for asserting that there is significant risk."

EDITORIAL RESEARCH REPORTS

## Coming soon

- School Choice
- Quotas
- Animal Rights

Published weekly by Congressional Quarterly Inc., Editorial Research Reports analyze emerging issues of national interest across a broad range of social, scientific, political and economic fields. Reports are bound and indexed for permanent reference. Subscription information is available through Congressional Quarterly's Publications Sales Department by telephone (202) 887-8665. Copies of past issues are available through Customer Service, (202) 887-8621.

# NOTE

*Editorial Research Reports* became *The CQ Researcher* on May 10, 1991 effective with page 253.

PUBLISHED BY CONGRESSIONAL QUARTERLY INC., IN CONJUNCTION WITH EBSCO PUBLISHING

# School Choice

*Would it strengthen or weaken public education in America?*

A MONG EDUCATIONAL REFORMERS, "CHOICE" is the buzzword of the hour. Supporters say the entire educational system would benefit if parents could choose their children's schools. In this view, competition for students would force schools to improve. Better schools, in turn, would prod students to do better. And parents, having set the whole process in motion, would take a greater interest in the schools and in their children's academic progress. President Bush supports the concept, but many teachers and school administrators are deeply skeptical. They fear that choice plans will siphon money and interest from public schools, will create elite schools for the few and second-rate schools for the many, will lead to increased segregation of students by race and income, and will cost taxpayers more money.

## I N S I D E  THIS ISSUE

May 10, 1991 • Volume 1, No. 1 • 253-276

*Formerly Editorial Research Reports*

May 10, 1991
Volume 1, No. 1

**MANAGING EDITOR**
Sandra Stencel

**ASSOCIATE EDITOR**
Richard L. Worsnop

**STAFF WRITERS**
Charles S. Clark
Mary H. Cooper
Patrick G. Marshall

**PRODUCTION EDITOR**
Laurie De Maris

**EDITORIAL ASSISTANT**
Thomas H. Moore

**GRAPHICS**
Jack Auldridge

**PUBLISHED BY**
Congressional Quarterly Inc.

**CHAIRMAN**
Andrew Barnes

**VICE CHAIRMAN**
Andrew P. Corty

**EDITOR AND PUBLISHER**
Neil Skene

**EXECUTIVE EDITOR**
Robert W. Merry

**EDITOR, EBSCO PUBLISHING**
Melissa Kummerer

The CQ Researcher (ISSN 1056-2036). Formerly Editorial Research Reports. Published weekly (48 times yer year, excluding March 1, May 3, Aug. 2 and Nov. 1, 1991) by Congressional Quarterly Inc., 1414 22nd St., N.W., Washington, D.C. 20037. Rates are furnished upon request. Application to mail at second-class postage rates is pending at Washington, D.C. POSTMASTER: Send address changes to The CQ Researcher, 1414 22nd St., N.W., Washington, D.C. 20037.

COVER ART: BARBARA SASSA-DANIELS

# School Choice

BY RICHARD L. WORNSOP

## THE ISSUES

Few issues generate more emotion these days than the quality of public education in America. The widespread disenchantment with the state of the country's schools found eloquent expression in a report issued in April 1983 by a blue-ribbon federal panel.[1] Entitled *A Nation at Risk: The Imperative for Educational Reform*, the report warned that "the educational foundations of our society are presently being eroded by a rising tide of mediocrity that threatens our very future as a nation and a people." The report caused a stir at the time, and public opinion polls and political discourse indicate its conclusions are considered by many Americans to be as accurate and timely today as they were eight years ago.

Now some academics, politicians and public-policy experts have stepped forward with what they consider a solution to the woes of American public education. It goes by the name of "choice," and it aims to give parents a much broader range of options in deciding where to send their children to school. For parents, the idea is that this would mean greater "empowerment" in determining what kind of education their children will get. For schools, the idea is that it would mean a heightened awareness of parents' wishes and greater incentives for responding to them.

Proponents of choice say this concept of bringing free-market principles to the world of public education would greatly improve the quality of teaching. Parents would vote with their feet — or their car pools — in determining where to send their children.

Schools that respond to parents' wishes would thrive. Bad schools would wither and die. In the view of choice advocates, the winners would be parents, students and educators committed to excellence. They say the losers would be the country's entrenched education bureaucracy and educators who either failed or refused to respond to the call for excellence.

The choice concept has caught on in many quarters throughout the country. Minnesota has what is probably the most comprehensive statewide program, but more limited versions have sprung up in other states. (*For a description of selected state programs, see p. 269.*) And President Bush made choice a centerpiece of his recent comprehensive education plan, which also included calls for national standardized tests in five core curriculum subjects, merit pay for superior teachers and grants for "merit schools" that make progress toward specified education goals.

But while choice seems to be to-day's leading answer to the lingering problem of educational mediocrity, it raises a host of questions that many educators and academic experts find troubling. They say that choice plans will siphon money and interest from public schools, will create elite schools for the few and second-rate schools for the many, will lead to increased segregation of students by race and income, and will cost taxpayers more money. Teachers and school officials, moreover, are apprehensive about the changes that free-wheeling competition among schools might bring. Among the questions raised by this new concept:

### Does school choice lead to improved student achievement in the classroom?

The key contention of choice advocates is that their approach will enhance student performance. A major reason for poor academic performance, they say, is that students are not challenged to perform at the top of their academic potential. Courses often are dull or frivolous or ineptly taught, prompting even (or especially) the brightest students to lose interest.

Under a choice system, by contrast, schools would have to compete with each other for the best students. Accordingly, they would develop challenging courses and give faculty members free rein to use innovative teaching methods. At best, choice advocates say, all participating schools would improve; at worst, the schools that failed to show any improvement would be forced to shut down.

Either way, choice proponents argue, the more stimulating classroom environment would surely yield higher overall scores on standard achievement tests.

Choice advocates note that parental involvement in their children's education is an important indicator of student achievement, and they argue that the mere act of choosing a school can serve as a catalyst for increased parental involvement. "Freedom to choose may generate a sense of power that itself enhances [parents'] commitment," says Donald Erickson, professor of education at UCLA.[2]

But critics contend that many school choices will be made on the basis of factors that have nothing to do with academics. They foresee parents choosing schools because of their proximity to their homes or because they excel in a particular sport. Indeed, some critics suggest the choice system will foster intense programs of athletic recruiting run by coaches out to make names for themselves. "You can bet that there are going to be some schools that will be recruiting kids for their athletic teams," says Gary Marx, associate director of the American Association of School Administrators. "You may [even] have a draft of some kind." The implications of athletic recruiting work both ways, Marx adds. "You'll also find some kids who want to play college sports trying to work their way into another school just so that they can gain some prestige," he says.

Choice proponents argue that switching schools for the sake of convenience or a better sports program is not necessarily a bad thing. "People do better in schools they want to be in," says Chester E. Finn Jr., a close adviser to Education Secretary Lamar Alexander and a Vanderbilt University professor, "... so even if the initial motivation is [non-academic], they might learn more, too."[3]

Choice proponents often point to test-score statistics from schools in choice programs to bolster their contention that choice promotes academic improvement. Critics argue that these statistics are open to differing interpretations. Student test scores in one highly touted New York school district with a choice program rose significantly, for example, but so did those in many other traditional New York schools over the same time period (*see p. 263*). And critics note that if choice schools draw brighter and more motivated students, higher test scores could just as likely reflect that increased proportion of bright and motivated students than anything related to the curriculum.

### Will choice programs lead to the creation of segregated or elitist schools, with the best students being lured to the best schools and the less gifted left behind?

Choice critics warn that the best schools will lure most of the brightest students — a process sometimes called "skimming" or "creaming." Gary Marx of the American Association of School Administrators fears the choice concept will make some schools "absolutely wonderful" while others get left on the "ash heap." He adds: "That would create an even greater gap between the rich and the poor, between the motivated and the unmotivated, and would push this country even further toward a two-tier society."

Proponents argue that this doesn't have to happen. For one thing, most existing choice programs prohibit transfers that would undermine school desegregation plans. Proponents also say schools in choice networks won't necessarily tailor their academic programs merely to the brightest students. More likely, says education Professor Mary Anne Raywid of Hofstra University, they will construct curricular programs designed to draw a wide diversity of students — those who need special help, those interested in math, science, the arts, etc. "If . . . you put the programs together so that they appeal across ability and achievement levels, then [a two-tier system] is not an inescapable outcome at all," she says.

Secondly, some choice advocates argue, sometimes heatedly, that parents from all backgrounds will respond to the challenge and opportunity posed by choice. The skimming argument, says Chester Finn, "assumes that poor people and minority-group people are incapable of availing themselves of the same kind of system that rich people and middle-class people and white people can avail themselves of. It's the most racist, condescending argument imaginable." He adds that the key test of a choice system is whether it will yield improvement over the current situation, which "leaves behind the vast majority of American kids."

Some public opinion polls indicate that blacks and other minorities favor choice plans even more than whites. For example, a Gallup Poll released in August 1990 found that 72 percent of non-whites supported choice compared with 60 percent of whites.

This doesn't surprise State Sen. Polly Williams of Wisconsin, a Democrat from inner-city Milwaukee who was the main sponsor of that state's choice legislation (*see p. 266*). "Most African-Americans and low-income people feel very helpless when it comes to the education of their children," she says. "We don't have choice because we don't have the money."[4]

### Should secular and church-related private schools be included in a choice program designed primarily for public school students?

This is among the most sensitive issues surrounding the school-choice debate. The idea is that, through some kind of voucher system, parents could take moneys that normally would be applied to their children's public education and apply them to private-school enrollment instead. Many experts, including choice advocates as well as opponents, argue that including private and parochial schools in a choice system could destroy the public education system in America. They predict that great numbers of private schools would emerge to answer parental desires and avail themselves of funds previously reserved to the public education system. "There needs to continue to be a public education system," says Mary Anne Raywid of Hofstra, "and I think that public funds ought to be restricted to that system."

Others suggest that if parents would abandon the public schools to such an extent, it reflects just how bad they are — and how desperately parents want to see improvements. The way to really make choice work, say these proponents of choice, is to open it up to the broadest possible range of options — and that inevitably includes private schools. "We should quit the old-fashioned way of classifying schools into either public or private," says Chester Finn. "If they serve the public interest, if they are publicly accountable, then as far as I'm concerned they qualify as public schools."

This debate also touches on the question of whether inclusion of parochial schools in choice plans* would violate the U.S. Constitution's doctrine of separation of

church and state. A 1983 U.S. Supreme Court decision suggested that this would be permissible under certain conditions.

The case, *Mueller v. Allen*, challenged the constitutionality of a Minnesota law that allowed parents to deduct up to $700 a year from their state income taxes for tuition, school-related transportation fees and the cost of school supplies. The deduction was available regardless of whether the children attended public or private elementary and secondary schools — a fact that was central to the court's ruling. However, because few public school students have large educational expenses, the lion's share of the benefits accrued to parents with children in private non-sectarian and parochial schools.

Citing an earlier ruling on the issue (*see p. 260*), the court said such indirect aid to parochial schools was constitutional if it had a secular aim, neither promoted nor denigrated religion and did not foster "an excessive government entanglement with religion." Taking a broader view of the issue, the court went on to argue that "a state's decision to defray the cost of educational expenses incurred by parents, regardless of the types of schools their children attend, is both secular and understandable. . . . Minnesota, like other states, could conclude that there is a strong public interest in assuring the continued financial health of private schools, both sectarian and non-sectarian. By educating a substantial number of students, such schools relieve public schools of a correspondingly great burden, to the benefit of all taxpayers."

***Would choice undermine the current education establishment and transfer responsibility for choosing curricula, setting graduation standards and running the***

***schools? And, if so, is that a good idea?***

Two leading choice advocates — John E. Chubb and Terry M. Moe, authors of a recent Brookings Institution book on the subject — argue that the education establishment itself is the problem and needs to be dismantled. *(See story, p. 265.)* They would place nearly all accountability in the hands of individual schools, teachers and parents. Writing approvingly of a choice program in New York City's East Harlem district, they said, "[T]he schools control their own admissions — they set up their own criteria and make their own decisions about whom to accept and reject. More generally, the schools are largely (but not entirely) free to make their own decisions about programs, methods, structure, and virtually everything else pertaining to the kind of education they provide." [5]

They add that these schools have eliminated many of the old rules and requirements that emerged from the education bureaucracy and stifled creativity. In these schools, they write, "teachers, parents and students are all encouraged to think of themselves as their schools' 'owners' and to take the responsibilities — and the pride and involvement — that real ownership entails."

Others balk at this expansive free-market approach to education, arguing that any choice system should operate within a framework of at least some outside political control. Says Raywid, "I think that school choice that combines some kind of broad control or the setting of broad parameters by elected officials and then leaves individual schools free to operate within those parameters would be a good way to downscale bureaucracy and the damage it does." Similarly, Finn advocates a system in which states

---

*At its annual meeting last November, the National Conference of Catholic Bishops voted to establish a central office to help parents' groups pressure Congress and state legislatures to support school choice programs. The Catholic school system currently serves about 630,000 high school and 2 million elementary school students.

would set what he calls "essential outcome standards" — the body of knowledge required for graduation — and then leave the schools free to meet those standards in their own way. He also says states should institute systems of testing to ensure their broad standards are being met.

### Would choice programs increase educational expenditures?

Supporters and critics of school choice differ sharply on its budgetary impact. Critics say choice programs could end up adding to educational expenditures because a new layer of bureaucracy will be needed to supervise the programs. "A program of that nature doesn't just happen," says Gary Marx. "It needs to be managed . . . and the people who did it would have to be paid." Mary Anne Raywid, on the other hand, "can't see" why choice programs should mean more bureaucrats. Choice might entail setting up an Office of Information to help parents and students make their selections, she says, "but it also ought to result in the closing down of a lot of central office supervision."

One of the chief concerns about choice plans is their impact on school transportation costs. Even supporters of choice say such plans won't work unless school districts provide transportation or reimburse parents for transportation expenses. "Otherwise you're creating choice for affluent families," says Joe Nathan, who is director of the Center for School Change at the University of Minnesota's Hubert H. Humphrey Institute of Public Affairs.[6]

The issue of choice-related costs came to national attention last month when the Richmond Unified School District in Northern California filed for bankruptcy. Dr. Fred Stewart, named by the state last year to oversee the debt-ridden district,

announced in mid-April that he was closing all schools more than a month before the scheduled start of summer vacation on June 14. But on April 29, Judge Ellen S. James of the Contra Costa County Superior Court ordered the state to come up with the money to keep the district's schools open. Gov. Pete Wilson said the state would appeal the judge's ruling on the ground that it sets a "dangerous precedent" by requiring that the state come to the rescue of school districts that are in fiscal trouble because of their own mismanagement. But Wilson also indicated that the state would keep the school district running until the end of the school year. It's unclear what will happen next year.

Many blame Richmond's financial woes on an ambitious school reform program introduced in 1987 by former Superintendent Walter L. Marks. The program included a "system for choice" plan that attracted national attention. Most of the 47 campuses in the district became specialty schools, and parents were allowed to choose among them. The overall objective was to persuade middle-class, suburban families to enroll their children in inner-city schools.

Marks' mistake, audits conducted by Stewart suggested, was in trying to do too much too soon. "People should realize from [the Richmond experience] that choice is not cheap, it is expensive," says Maureen DiMarco, the California secretary for child development and education. "If schools go into something like this, they should go in with their eyes open and operate in a fiscally responsible manner. . . . I don't know if [Richmond's experience] will deter others from [trying a system of] choice, but it should certainly deter them from trying for a quick fix."[7]

But others point out that the Richmond school district was in precarious financial shape even before Marks launched the choice program. For one thing, the district had been outspending its general fund revenues since 1984. By the time Marks took office as superintendent three years later, the fund had a deficit of more than $2 million. The district's deficit is now over $20 million.

In Minnesota, most of the financial trauma associated with school choice has been at the local level, as school systems adjust to the loss or gain of state aid that results from student transfers across district lines. But according to Richard Anderson, executive director of the Minnesota School Boards Association, choice has had little financial impact on a statewide basis. Indeed, he notes, the Minnesota program was designed to be "revenue-neutral." ∎

# BACKGROUND

## Movement's Origins

There is little that is genuinely new about school-choice plans. Wealthy families, it is often noted, have always been able to send their children to the best schools — private ones, for the most part, or the

public school system of an affluent suburb. The most highly regarded suburban public schools are almost as exclusive as the top private schools, since admission usually is restricted to community residents.

Some cities offer bright students from families of limited means the chance to attend a college-prep high school, provided they pass a rigorous entrance exam. Examples of such schools include Boston

# Magnet Schools

Typically situated in a minority neighborhood, magnet schools try to attract white students from more affluent areas by offering additional resources, innovative teaching methods and a highly focused curriculum in such fields as the performing arts, classical studies, science and mathematics.

Magnet schools have been operating for a long time in many parts of the country. Several Northern school districts initiated magnet schools in the late 1960s and early '70s as part of a voluntary approach to school desegregation. Boston University political scientist Christine H. Rossell cites Tacoma, Wash., and Portland, Ore., as two of the earliest school districts to experiment with magnet schools. In the 1970s, magnet schools became increasingly popular as elements of court-ordered desegregation plans.

President Ronald Reagan, a longstanding opponent of forced busing to desegregate public schools, adopted the cause of magnet schools after taking office in 1981. The Justice Department moved away from taking school boards to court, as it had done during the Carter administration, and instead supported consent decrees. In these, school boards agreed to establish magnet schools or other forms of parental choice to achieve desegregation.

In their book *Politics, Markets and America's Schools*, John E. Chubb and Terry M. Moe conclude that magnet schools have gone far toward achieving the goal of racial balance. But they also say that magnet schools "have worked less well in promoting district-wide improvement in school effectiveness. . . . Magnets tend to attract the best, most innovative teachers away from regular schools of assignment, which then threaten to become dumping grounds for the district's mediocre teachers. . . . Magnets also tend to attract the best, most interested students and parents, making the job of regular schools still more diffi-

cult." †

Indeed, some students and educators associated with magnet schools openly revel in standing above the crowd. Consider the remarks of William Pasderin, a teacher at the Francisco Bravo Medical Magnet High School in East Los Angeles. "This is heaven — the best students, the latest equipment," Pasderin told his first computer class shortly after the school opened last September. "This is a private school in a public system, and this is where you go when you want to get into UCLA, Harvard, Cal-Berkeley, MIT." ††

In some areas, magnet schools may be fast approaching the limit of their effectiveness as a desegregation tool. Prince George's County, Md., adjacent to Washington, D.C., has operated magnet schools since 1985. "The magnet solution was a good vehicle for the problems of the mid '80s," county School Superintendent John A. Murphy said early last year. "But the problems of the '90s need different solutions, and I don't think that magnet schools alone are the best answer." ‡

Prince George's County now has a majority-black population, making it more difficult for the school system to comply with court-ordered desegregation guidelines, which state that county schools should be at least 10 percent black but no more than 80 percent black. As a result, county officials are weighing an alternative approach called "educational equity." This concept rests on the notion that a school system should make sure that all students have the educational tools they need, regardless of the racial composition of the school they attend.

---

† John E. Chubb and Terry M. Moe, *Politics, Markets and America's Schools* (1990), p. 209.

†† Quoted in the *Los Angeles Times*, Sept. 12, 1990.

‡ Quoted in *The Washington Post*, Jan. 5, 1990.

---

Latin School, one of the nation's oldest public schools, as well as New York's Bronx High School of Science, Chicago's Lane Technical High, Philadelphia's Central High and Cincinnati's Walnut Hills High.

These "exam schools" are not strictly comparable to the newer "magnet schools" now found throughout the country. Magnet schools offer specialized programs and generally are better funded and equipped than other schools in the district. In many cases, magnet schools are established in inner-city

neighborhoods as part of a desegregation plan. The idea is to attract white suburban students, thus achieving racial balance by voluntary means. (*For details on magnet-school programs, see story, above.*)

### Friedman's Voucher Proposal

Many students of school choice trace the movement's origins to a 1962 book by economist Milton Friedman, *Capitalism and Freedom*. In this work, Friedman expounded his proposal for government-funded vouchers that would

permit parents to send their children to a school — public or private — of their choice. Under Friedman's plan, the government would provide parents with vouchers financed from tax revenues earmarked for education. The vouchers would be redeemed for cash by whatever school enrolled the children. Friedman suggested that the face value of the voucher be equivalent to the cost of educating a child in public school.

Friedman argued that a voucher system would improve the quality of education in America by forcing schools to compete with one another for students. "If present public expenditures on schooling were made available to parents regardless of where they send their children," Friedman wrote, "a wide variety of schools would spring up to meet the demand. Parents could express their views about schools directly by withdrawing their children from one school and sending them to another, to a much greater extent than is now possible." [8]

A free market in education would operate much as it does in other areas of life, Friedman asserted. "The role of government would be limited to insuring that the schools met certain minimum standards," he wrote, "... much as it now inspects restaurants to insure that they maintain minimum sanitary standards." [9]

## Supreme Court Rulings

The tuition voucher idea and its companion concept, tuition tax credits, appealed to political conservatives because of their free-market connotations. Civil libertarians, on the other hand, opposed such plans on constitutional grounds. They argued that vouchers and tuition tax credits that could be used in church-related schools violated the First Amendment's ban on government "establishment" of religion.

Over the years, the Supreme Court has taken a dim view of educational aid programs that mainly benefit parochial school pupils. On the other hand, the court has upheld the constitutionality of laws extending education benefits to all children, regardless of the type of school they attend.

In its first "parochiaid" decision (*Cochran v. Louisiana Board of Education*), the court in 1930 upheld a Louisiana program that provided secular textbooks to all pupils in the state, including those in parochial schools. Seventeen years later, in *Everson v. Board of Education*, the court upheld a New Jersey law reimbursing parents for the cost of sending their children to school on public transportation. Although parents of parochial school students qualified for the reimbursement, the court ruled that the law did not aid religion but was instead public welfare legislation that benefited children rather than schools. In the 1968 case of *Board of Education of Central School District No. 1 v. Allen*, the court endorsed New York's program of lending publicly purchased textbooks to students attending public or private secondary schools.[10]

The court's rulings in all three cases rested in whole or in part on the theory that aid to parochial school students is permissible so long as public school students have equal access to the aid. In the 1947 New Jersey case, for instance, the court viewed state subsidies for bus transportation of parochial school children as a service to citizens, comparable to that provided by police and fire departments, without regard to the religion of those served.

In 1971, the court issued a ruling in the case of *Lemon v. Kurtzman* that set forth a three-part test for determining whether aid to parochial schools is constitutional. To avoid running afoul of the First Amendment, the court held, a state law benefiting parochial schools (1) must have a secular purpose, (2) must not have the primary effect of advancing or retarding religion and (3) must not foster the "excessive entanglement" of government in religious affairs.

A New York law flunked the second part of this test in a case that reached the Supreme Court in 1973. In *Committee for Public Education and Religious Liberty v. Nyquist*, the court invalidated a state program that authorized maintenance and repair grants to certain private and parochial schools, reimbursed low-income families for a portion of their private and parochial school expenses, and allowed tax credits to parents of non-public school students who did not qualify for the tuition reimbursement. The court struck down the law on the ground that parochial schools were its chief beneficiaries. However, the court raised no such objection to a Minnesota law that was challenged in the 1983 case of *Mueller v. Allen*. The key difference was that the Minnesota law offered parents a tax deduction for school expenses regardless of what kind of school their children attended — private or public. (*For details on the case, see p. 257.*)

## Action in Congress

In the last dozen years or so, Congress has considered a number of tuition tax credit proposals, but none have been enacted into law. In 1978, for example, the House passed a bill that would have granted parents who sent their children to private elementary and high schools, including parochial schools, a tax credit for tuition expenses. Under the plan, parents would have been able to reduce their federal income taxes by an amount equal to 25 percent of tuition expenses for each student in private school. The bill also provided federal income tax relief to help pay college tuition costs. The credit for higher education tuition would at first have been limited to $100 per student; for lower-school children, the initial

*Continued on p. 262*

# Chronology

## 1960s
*Economist Milton Friedman proposes publicly funded educational vouchers in his 1962 book* Capitalism and Freedom. *Under Friedman's plan, parents who choose to send their children to private school would be paid a sum equal to the estimated cost of educating a child in a public school.*

———— • ————

## 1970s
*The federal government funds an experimental school voucher program in the Alum Rock Unified School District near San Jose, Calif., and New York City's District 4 in East Harlem adopts a parental choice program for its schools.*

### June 28, 1971
Supreme Court invalidates state laws authorizing state reimbursement of nonpublic schools for costs of teachers' salaries, textbooks and instructional materials in secular subjects (*Lemon v. Kurtzman*). In its ruling, the court sets forth a three-part test for determining whether aid to parochial schools is constitutional.

### June 25, 1973
Supreme Court strikes down a New York law under which low-income families were reimbursed for a portion of their private and parochial school tuition expenses and higher-income parents received a comparable income tax credit (*Committee for Public Education and Religious Liberty v. Nyquist*).

## 1980s
*Support for school choice grows.*

### April 1983
*A Nation at Risk*, a report by a blue-ribbon federal panel, warns that the nation's schools are being eroded by "a rising tide of mediocrity."

### June 29, 1983
Supreme Court upholds the constitutionality of a Minnesota law permitting parents to deduct part of their childrens' private or parochial school expenses from the family's taxable income (*Mueller v. Allen*).

### Nov. 16, 1983
Senate defeats a Reagan administration proposal to extend federal tuition tax credits to parents of children attending secular or church-related private schools.

### Jan. 10, 1989
A White House Workshop on Choice in Education, held during the closing days of the Reagan administration, serves notice that choice will be a prime objective of the incoming Bush administration.

### 1989
Minnesota becomes the first state to institute open enrollment on a statewide basis for all school districts. The plan covers only public schools.

———— • ————

## 1990s
*Debate over school choice escalates.*

### 1990
The Brookings Institution publishes *Politics, Markets and American Schools.* Authors John E. Chubb and Terry M. Moe prescribe "truly fundamental reforms" and "new institutions of educational governance" for the nation's schools. The key to education reform, they say, is parental choice.

### Aug. 6, 1990
Judge Susan Steingass of the Dane County (Madison) Circuit Court upholds the constitutionality of a Wisconsin law allowing more than 900 low-income students from Milwaukee to use state funds to attend private, non-sectarian schools. The plaintiffs appeal the decision.

### Nov. 6, 1990
Oregon voters decisively reject the most far-reaching choice plan proposed to date — one that would have covered not only all public, private and parochial schools in the state but also children who are taught at home.

### Nov. 13, 1990
Wisconsin State Court of Appeals strikes down the Milwaukee school-choice program on the ground that the law authorizing it was enacted in a way that violates the state constitution. The program's supporters appeal to the Wisconsin Supreme Court, which agrees to review the case.

### Dec. 4, 1990
Center for Choice in Education is established within the U.S. Department of Education to assist parents and educators involved in school-choice programs.

### April 18, 1991
President Bush unveils his strategy for improving U.S. public schools. His plan includes financial incentives to encourage state and local governments to develop school-choice policies.

*Continued from p. 260*
tuition tax credit would have been limited to $50.

There was strong support in the Senate for college tuition tax credits and little organized opposition to the concept. But the elementary and secondary credits attracted the opposition of the powerful public education lobby, which worried that federal incentives for private school education would weaken public school systems. Civil rights leaders worried that private school credits would undermine integration efforts by subsidizing students in all-white private schools, which had sprung up throughout the South in the 1960s and early '70s.

Supporters pointed out that the bill would not allow credits for students in schools found by the Internal Revenue Service to be discriminatory. They also argued that the chief beneficiaries would be parochial schools, which had a long history of integration.

In the end, however, the Senate voted to delete credits for elementary and secondary school students from its bill. When the House refused to accept tax credits for college tuition only, the bill died.

### Reagan Backs Choice Plans

The tuition tax credit concept was one of the cornerstones of the Reagan administration's education policy. Although Reagan had supported tuition tax credits during his 1980 campaign, the administration did not submit its legislative proposal to Congress until June 1982. Reagan said tuition tax credits were needed because parents were hard pressed to pay both private school tuition and taxes to support public schools. "Our proposal is intended to relieve that dual financial burden

threatening to usurp the traditional right of parents to direct the education of the children," he said.[11]

Reagan stressed that his tuition credit proposal would be focused on the needs of low- and middle-income families. He proposed a relatively small credit — no more than $100 per student to begin with. That

**In the last dozen years or so, Congress has considered a number of tuition tax credit proposals. But in each case, the public education lobby succeeded in keeping the proposals from being enacted into law.**

would make it a more significant factor for parents of students in parochial schools, where tuitions were low, than for those attending exclusive prep schools with very high tuitions.

Under Reagan's proposal, parents would have received an income tax credit — to be subtracted from taxes owed — equal to 50 percent of tuition in a nonprofit, private elementary or secondary school. The limit on the credit for each child would have been $100 in 1983, $300 in 1984 and $500 in 1985. Parents with incomes over $50,000 a year would have received only partial credits. Those with incomes over $75,000 would have gotten no credits.

The Senate Finance Committee reported a compromise version of Reagan's proposal on Sept. 23,

1982, but there was no further congressional action on the issue, and the legislation died when Congress adjourned.

Reagan revived the issue the following year, arguing that greater competition would improve American education. The administration's proposal, introduced in the Senate by Bob Dole, R-Kan., called for a tax credit of 50 percent of the tuition paid to a qualified school that met standards prohibiting racial discrimination. During the first year, the maximum credit would have been $100 per student. The maximum would rise to $200 the second year and $300 in subsequent years. Parents with incomes over $40,000 would receive a smaller credit and those with incomes above $50,000 would receive none at all.

Opponents of the 1983 tuition tax credit bill said it would not appreciably help low- and middle-income parents who wished to send their children to private schools. "Even with the tax break," said Sen. Mack Mattingly, R-Ga., "lower middle-class and poor families still could not afford to pay the balance due on private school tuition. Additionally, how will a tax refund coming after the first of the year help a family whose private school tuition is due . . . in September, at the beginning of the school year?"

Opponents of the tuition tax credit proposal also said it failed to meet the requirements of the Supreme Court's ruling in *Mueller v. Allen* upholding a Minnesota state income tax deduction for public and private school tuition, textbooks and transportation. They argued that the legislation was not sufficiently similar to the Minnesota law to survive Supreme Court scrutiny. First and foremost, it benefited only parents of private and parochial school students. The Minnesota deduction was available regardless of whether the children attended public or private school.

The measure's opponents also objected that the administration was proposing an expensive new program at the same time it was invoking the need to reduce budget deficits as a reason not to increase federal aid to public schools. A tuition tax credit bill would be, in the words of Sen. David L. Boren, D-Okla., "another major step down the road of destruction of public education in the United States."

On Nov. 16, 1983, the Senate overwhelmingly rejected the White House-backed measure. A similar House measure remained bottled up in the Ways and Means Committee.

Undaunted, the Reagan administration in 1985 proposed transforming federal education aid for the disadvantaged into a school voucher program. The plan would have provided low-income parents with vouchers worth around $600 a year to be used to send their children to public or private schools. The vouchers would have functioned much as food stamps do — as a credit toward a purchase approved by the government.

In education, however, vouchers are a credit to be claimed by the school that enrolls a voucher-holder's child. The parents pick the school, and the school then applies for reimbursement in accordance with procedures prescribed by statute or regulation.

President Reagan submitted various versions of the voucher proposal over the next three years, but each time the public education lobby succeeded in keeping the proposal from being enacted into law.

## State and Local Plans

Choice programs have made considerably more headway at the local and state level than at the federal level. For instance, those who believe that school choice inspires students and teachers to do better often cite New York City's Community District 4, which encompasses largely black and Hispanic East Harlem. Before choice began there on a limited basis in 1973-74, the district ranked last academically among the 32 school districts in the city. District 4's ranking has since climbed to No. 16. In addition, more than 65 percent of East Harlem students in kindergarten through eighth grade now read at or above grade level, compared with only 15 percent in 1973-74. Hoping to share in the turnaround, parents in other parts of the city are enrolling their children in District 4 schools.

While acknowledging that East Harlem schools have improved, some policy analysts say the change has been less dramatic than choice enthusiasts say. For instance, District 4 recorded its largest increases in reading proficiency in 1975, when the choice program was in its infancy, and in 1986, when New York City changed its test for measuring reading skills. In both those years, schools in other parts of the city achieved gains in reading scores similar to District 4's. Another reason for the rise in District 4 test scores, these analysts say, could be the infusion of academic talent from other parts of the city. More than 10 percent of students enrolled in East Harlem schools live outside the district.

### Alum Rock Experiment
Another early experiment in school choice also yielded inconclusive results. From 1972 to 1976, the federal government spent about $7 million on a demonstration pro-

gram in California under which parents received publicly funded tuition vouchers to spend at public schools of their choice in the Alum Rock Unified School District near San Jose. The purpose of the experiment was to encourage community control of the schools, especially in poor and minority neighborhoods.

Participating Alum Rock students in kindergarten through sixth grade got vouchers worth $680; seventh- and eighth-graders got vouchers worth $970. Low-income students also received a bonus voucher worth $275, which gave schools an incentive to enroll them and cater to their special needs. All voucher students were bused to their schools for free. By 1976, the experiment's final year, 14 of Alum Rock's 24 elementary and middle schools were taking part in the voucher plan. These schools had subdivided themselves into 55 minischools, each with a highly focused curriculum.

The Alum Rock experiment seems to have had only a modest impact on established patterns of school attendance. Initially, the vast majority of parents chose schools near their homes. By the third year of the program, the proportion of parents choosing schools *outside* their neighborhood had doubled — rising from about 11 percent to about 22 percent. But as a recent report noted, "Even this increase in the number of parents who overtly exercised choice left the majority of parents sending their children to the neighborhood school either as a result of a conscious choice or without exercising their right to choose." [12]

The authors of the report found little evidence that the voucher program led to improvements in reading scores or innovations in teaching methods. But they also cautioned that it would not be fair to use the results of the Alum Rock experiment to judge the success or failure of choice plans. As they noted in their report, there initially was local political opposition to the program and "the ground rules of parent choice were changed several times. ... For these reasons, most choice advocates feel the Alum Rock experiment does not accurately portray what choice can do under more favorable circumstances."

But others who have studied the Alum Rock program are less equivocal. "What we learned from Alum Rock is that a system of vouchers and choice is not the solution to the educational problems of low-income students," says R. Gary Bridge, an associate professor of psychology and education at Columbia University's Teachers College. According to Bridge, middle-class and well-educated parents were much more informed about the various mini-school programs than lower-income parents. "It is assumed that poor parents can make informed educational choices for their children, and they can't, which is why these children aren't doing well in school to begin with," Bridge says.[13]

### Minnesota's Choice Plan

The Alum Rock and East Harlem choice programs each covered only a single school district. Minnesota, which operates the most comprehensive statewide program of school choice, may provide a more instructive model for the nation at large.

Introduced in stages over the past six years, the Minnesota plan has three main features. The Postsecondary Options Act enables juniors and seniors attending public high schools to take courses at state colleges and universities. Participating students may take the courses for either high school or college credit. If the student is taking the course for high school credit, the state picks up the tab for tuition, textbooks and other fees. (If the student wants postsecondary credit for the college courses, he or she must bear all the costs.)*

According to Joe Nathan of the University of Minnesota's Hubert H.

> In Minnesota, relatively few families have exercised the choice option so far. Only about 6,000 students — less than 1 percent of the state's school-age population — applied for a transfer to a different school district this year.

Humphrey Institute of Public Affairs, more than 25,000 Minnesota youngsters have participated in the postsecondary options program. In Nathan's view, the program has been a great success. He cites the case of a bored high school student who "was ready to drop out of school at 16 and become a drummer in a rock band. Instead ... she agreed to try a couple of courses at the University of Minnesota. Two

---

*Reimbursement for transportation expenses is available in some cases. Students who meet the financial-need requirements receive 25.5 cents a mile to cover transportation costs. The reimbursement covers up to 250 miles a week, unless the closest school offering the particular course the student wants to take is a greater distance from the student's home. In that case, the state will reimburse the student for actual mileage.

years ago, she graduated from high school. She had also earned 45 credits at the university, and she had a high B average. She had always had the ability to do well, but her mother says she never would have graduated from high school without this program."

The second part of the Minnesota choice plan is the High School Graduation Incentives Program, also known as the "second chance" program. Its aim is to persuade students aged 12 to 21 who have not succeeded in one school to enroll in another and remain there until they graduate. Many of the 12,000 to 15,000 participants in the second-chance program got into trouble because of drug abuse, pregnancy or chronic truancy. Nathan mentions a star student whose troubles began when she became pregnant. School officials expelled her from the Honor Society and the cheerleading squad, prompting her to drop out. After giving birth, she took advantage of the second-chance program and enrolled in a neighboring school that had a day-care center. Before long, she was again doing well academically. "There are thousands of stories like hers," Nathan says.

The newest segment of the Minnesota plan is open enrollment, introduced on a voluntary basis in 1987 and since made mandatory. Under this program, all school students from kindergarten through 12th grade are free to attend any public school in the state. The plan does not include private schools. State aid automatically accompanies students who transfer out of their school districts. Transportation to the border of the receiving district is arranged by the students' parents; from there, the receiving district provides transportation to the

# Brookings Book Sparks Debate Over Choice Plans

Much of the recent debate over school choice has focused on a book published last June by the Brookings Institution, a Washington-based think tank. The authors of the book are John E. Chubb, a senior fellow in Brookings' Governmental Studies Program, and Terry M. Moe, a professor of political science at Stanford University and a former Brookings fellow.

In their book *Politics, Markets and American Schools*, Chubb and Moe proposed a radical restructuring of American education. Under their plan, private schools — including religious schools — would compete for students with public schools in a free market. They based their recommendations on findings that private schools were able to function with more autonomy and less bureaucracy than public schools and were therefore more effective in raising student achievement levels.

In order to qualify for public funding under Chubb and Moe's plan, a private school would have to meet certain requirements set by the state. But Chubb and Moe emphasize that these requirements "should be minimal — roughly corresponding to the criteria many states now use in accrediting private schools." They go on to say that "any educational group or organization that applies to the state and meets these minimal criteria must then be chartered as a public school and granted the right to accept students and receive public money."

Chubb and Moe say that the choice plans now in existence in various states and localities don't go nearly far enough. The key to making choice work, they say, is to withdraw authority from existing educational institutions and vest it directly "in the schools, parents, and students."

Choice, they write, "has been embraced half-heartedly and in bits and pieces — for example, through magnet schools and limited open enrollment plans.... [B]y treating choice like other system-preserving reforms ... reformers completely miss what choice is all about.... The whole point of a thoroughgoing system of choice is to free the schools of ... disabling constraints by sweeping away the old institutions."

Opponents of Chubb and Moe's plan say the creation of state-financed "choice offices" and "parent information centers" in each district, as Chubb and Moe propose, would create a new level of bureaucracy. Some have also criticized the methodology they used to demonstrate that choice would bring about substantial gains in achievement.[†]

One of the most controversial aspects of Chubb and Moe's plan is that it would allow schools to restrict student entry, subject only to non-discrimination requirements. "Schools must be able to define their own missions ... and they cannot do that if their student population is thrust on them by outsiders," they write. "Schools must be free to admit as many or as few students as they want, based on whatever criteria they think relevant — intelligence, interest, motivation, special needs — and they must be free to exercise their own, informal judgments about individual applicants."

Bill Honig, the California superintendent of public instruction, says this would lead to the creation of "elite academies for the few and second-rate schools for the many." Honig also predicts that the deregulation of public education would lead to an educational version of the savings and loan debacle. "Nobody seriously proposes rescinding environmental safeguards," he says. "Why should our children not be similarly protected?" [††]

---

† See Robert Rothman, "Paper Launches Academic Attack on Chubb-Moe Book on Education," *Education Week*, Nov. 14, 1990, p. 1.

†† Bill Honig, "Why Privatizing Public Education Is a Bad Idea," *The Brookings Review*, winter 1990/91, pp. 15-16.

---

school and is reimbursed by the state. Families falling below certain income levels are reimbursed for their transportation costs.

Though it may be too early to pass judgment on Minnesota's open-enrollment program, commentators have been quick to note certain trends. As was the case in Alum Rock, relatively few families have exercised the choice option so far. Only about 6,000 students — less than 1 percent of the state's school-age population of about 700,000 — applied for transfer to a different school district this year. The small number of participating students, critics say, means there hasn't been enough competitive pressure to force dramatic changes in the schools.

Richard Anderson of the Minnesota School Boards Association characterizes the plan as "a lot of smoke and not much fire." Most children want to go to school with their friends, he says, so open enrollment hasn't had a "major impact" on the state's educational system. But while the program hasn't been the educational panacea many people said it would be, Anderson adds, it hasn't been entirely negative. "There are those who said that this would just destroy public education," he says. "But that hasn't happened either."

### Keeping Parents Informed

Joe Nathan takes the position that a choice plan must contain safeguards to assure that all eligible students have an equal chance of benefiting from it. In Minnesota, he observes, "We have had materials translated into various languages. Information is mailed to welfare recipients along with their checks, letting them know that there's an 800 number they can call from all over the state. We have worked with grocery store chains to print up a million bags displaying that toll-free number. There have also been workshops for probation officers and youth service workers; the idea is to make sure they know about these [school-choice programs] and can tell their clients about them."

Keeping students and families informed also is an integral part of the choice program in East Harlem's District 4. During sixth grade, each

student receives a booklet describing the choices available in the district's junior high schools, all of which are "open zoned." Some are traditional junior highs but many are specialized, concentrating on such areas as environmental science, the performing arts, health and biomedical studies, music, the humanities and computer science.

The director of each junior high explains what the school offers. Teachers consult with students to help them decide where they would like to go. The students and their parents then fill out an application listing their six top choices. About 60 percent of all students usually are accepted into their first-choice school, and 35 percent into their second or third choice. ■

# CURRENT SITUATION

## Recent State Action

At present, the only choice plan in the country that provides public vouchers for private schools is operating on a limited basis in Milwaukee. A law approved by the Wisconsin Legislature in March 1990 established a pilot program for up to 1 percent of Milwaukee's school population, or about 950 students in all. Only students from families whose income does not exceed 1.75 times the federal poverty level (net monthly income of $1,059 for a family of four) are eligible for consideration. The law commits the state to pay participating private, non-sectarian schools up to $2,500 per pupil, which equals the state contribution per pupil to the Milwaukee public school system. The total is

then deducted from the system's aid package.

State Sen. Polly Williams, a Democrat from inner-city Milwaukee, was the main sponsor of the Wisconsin choice legislation. "The Milwaukee schools constantly ask for more money each year, blame the students and say they can't learn," she complained. "But the problem is [that] the schools can't teach. These schools have to change." [14]

As expected, the Milwaukee choice program generated strong opposition, including a lawsuit brought by the Wisconsin Education Association Council, the state's largest teachers' union, and officials of the NAACP. In a ruling handed down last August, Judge Susan Steingass of the Dane County (Madison) Circuit Court held that the Milwaukee plan was legal because the Wisconsin Constitution "does not expressly require that public expenditures be made only for public purposes."

The plaintiffs fared better when

they carried their case to a higher court. In a Nov. 14 decision, the Wisconsin State Court of Appeals did not comment directly on the merits of the Milwaukee program. Nonetheless, it struck down the plan because the Legislature had violated a state constitutional provision barring bills benefiting specific communities from being attached to statewide legislation. The Milwaukee plan was enacted as an amendment to a statewide budget measure.

Supporters of the choice program have now taken the case to the Wisconsin Supreme Court, which has agreed to hear it but has not issued a decision. In the meantime, the program remains in force. Herbert Grover, the state superintendent of public instruction, decided it would be unfair to participating students to terminate the program before the end of the current school year, at the earliest.

Polly Williams says attacks on Milwaukee's choice program are attempts to hide the fact that the public schools in the city have done a poor job educating inner-city blacks. She says the private schools that have elected to participate in the plan "help instill pride in the African American heritage through history and other courses the public schools aren't interested in." [15]

But there are indications that the choice program isn't meeting students' needs either. Although the Legislature agreed to provide up to 1,000 disadvantaged children with vouchers to cover private school tuition, only 350 signed up. "We're now down to about 250-260 kids," says Pat Sweeney, a spokesman for the Wisconsin Department of Public Instruction. "A couple of schools have dropped out, too. So while the program still has a high visibility, its actual impact in [terms of] number of kids in school is relatively small."

*Continued on p. 268*

# At Issue:

## Will school-choice plans improve public education in America?

### *yes*

**JOE NATHAN**

*Senior fellow at the University of Minnesota's Hubert H. Humphrey Institute of Public Affairs.*
**FROM *THE CHRISTIAN SCIENCE MONITOR*, APRIL 5, 1989.**

*t*en years from now, people will be surprised that there ever was a vigorous debate about public school choice. It will be an accepted right, like voting, equal pay for equal work, and nondiscriminatory housing. . . .

The best public school choice plans, like the one in the East Harlem section of New York City, illustrate the possibilities. Ten years ago, the district ranked last among 32 community districts in student achievement. Only about 15 percent of its students could read and do math at grade level. Today, 65 percent of the students score at or above grade level, and the district has moved to 16th among the districts. East Harlem is one of the rare urban districts which have a waiting list of people who want to work there. What happened?

The district began allowing teachers to create distinctive schools from which families could select. Gradually, every junior high school became a magnet; there are no assigned schools. . . .

Minnesota . . . pioneered programs that allow public-school juniors and seniors to attend colleges and universities with tax funds following students and permit students to move across district lines so long as the movement does not have a negative impact on desegregation and receiving districts have room. . . . [M]ore than 90 percent of students and parents report satisfaction with the programs. . . .

[C]hoice programs can help stimulate widespread improvement and serve the needs of all students. However, not all programs are equally effective. While choice plans differ, the best specify goals and procedures all schools use; provide parent information and counseling; avoid "first-come, first-served" admissions procedures; prohibit admissions on the basis of past achievement or behavior; help most schools within a geographical area to become distinctive rather than developing a few "super magnet" schools; provide transportation within a reasonable area for all students; use racial balance procedures that promote integration; and continue oversight.

Permitting choice among public schools will not solve all of education's problems. But it complements other reform proposals by expanding opportunity, recognizing that there is no one best school for all students or educators, and changing the monopoly relationship schools have with many families. Choice is a powerful, progressive reform.

### *no*

**WILSON C. RILES**

*Former state superintendent of public instruction in California.*
**FROM THE *LOS ANGELES TIMES*, APRIL 5, 1989.**

*a*lthough at first blush the idea of parental choice seems reasonable, a careful study of the implications of . . . will reveal that it has serious flaws. . . .

Some advocates equate the freedom of parents to choose schools with supply-side economic theory and honestly believe that if large numbers of parents remove their children from schools considered to be inadequate, competition will force the inadequate schools to improve. And some politicians have been quick to discover that the word "choice," like "motherhood," has such a virtuous connotation that they have been anxious to endorse and advocate a sweeping expansion of the idea. . . .

A case can be made for some degree of flexibility in school attendance policies. But it would be extremely unfortunate if, in the name of school reform, parents were misled into believing that it is possible for the state to provide them with unlimited school choices. There is no evidence that such a policy would make schools better.

As a first order of business, school policy-makers should take a hard look at the realities underlying the choice issue. In the first place, classroom space is a limiting factor. Unless provisions are made to accommodate the students where parents choose to send them, the promise of unlimited choice will only lead to confusion, frustration and disappointment.

Second, unless the state is prepared to provide transportation, low-income parents would not have the means to exercise options even if they existed. Third, concepts of marketing that apply to business are totally inappropriate when applied to schools. And the notion that competition will force improvements at the schools from which children transfer is perhaps the greatest fallacy of all. Schools that are being abandoned will get worse since they will lose the support of their most vocal and influential parents. The children that are left behind will undoubtedly be the most disadvantaged and in the greatest need of an effective educational program. . . .

Admittedly, there is an imperative need for school improvement. But schools will not be improved by quick-fix, mechanical solutions based on myths and hunches rather than research and experience.

Policy-makers should not be diverted from the goal of making all schools capable of ensuring that each child achieves to the best of his or her ability. To the extent that goal is reached, "choice" will cease to be a major issue.

Continued from p. 266

### Regional Differences

The most far-reaching school choice plan yet proposed in the United States was put before Oregon voters last November in the form of a ballot initiative. Under the proposal, parents or others paying tuition at private non-sectarian or church-related schools, or bearing the cost of educating a child at home, would have received a tax credit of up to $2,500 a year for each child. Also, students would have been able to transfer between school districts under an open-enrollment program. The ballot measure was soundly defeated by a 2-1 margin.

Seven states did pass legislation last year permitting greater parental choice in varying degrees — Colorado, Idaho, Kentucky, Utah, Vermont, Washington and Wisconsin. They joined five other states — Arkansas, Iowa, Minnesota, Nebraska and Ohio — that, by the end of 1989, had enacted laws allowing parents to send their children to schools across district lines.

These laws all differ in some degree, reflecting regional or other differences. (*For details on the state programs, see p. 269.*) In Joe Nathan's opinion, that is as it should be. "There are a variety of carefully developed choice plans around the country," he says, "and I don't think there's one plan that's appropriate for every school district, or every town, or every city, or every community, or every state."

Last December, for example, the town of Epsom, N.H., became the first jurisdiction in the country to adopt a choice plan based on the local property tax. Under the Epsom Educational Tax Abatement Plan, property owners may receive abatements of up to $1,000 from town property taxes to send their children to private schools. The children of families who don't own property may be sponsored by other property owners, including businesses.*

The plan was approved by the town's Board of Selectmen, but the Epsom school district is challenging it, as are the American Civil Liberties Union and the National Education Association. Opponents claim that the New Hampshire Constitution prohibits the spending of state money on parochial schools, and that those receiving the abatement are not paying their fair share for the public schools as the constitution requires.

Nathan says further innovations may be forthcoming in Minnesota, which already has the nation's most comprehensive school choice program. "We're discussing this year the so-called charter school idea, which would allow groups of teachers and parents to come to the state board or to go to an intermediate unit and get permission to establish a new public school," he says. The state's education establishment opposes the idea. Richard Anderson of the Minnesota School Boards Association says charter schools have "a much greater capacity to destroy public education" than the state's current open-enrollment plan. "The danger is that there isn't going to be any accountability other than the marketplace," he says.

## Bush's Education Plan

Like Reagan before him, President Bush has embraced school choice as the centerpiece of his education policy. Indeed, Bush's attachment to the idea may be even stronger than Reagan's, for he announced during the 1988 election campaign that he intended to build a record as "the education president."

At a White House Workshop on Choice in Education held shortly before his inauguration, Bush hailed school choice as perhaps the single most promising new idea in American education. Choice programs would, he said, "give parents back their voices and their proper determining roles in the makeup of children's education, and they give schools a chance to distinguish themselves from one another."

Last December, the administration established a Center for Choice in Education in the Education Department to field questions from people calling a nationwide, toll-

Continued on p. 270

---

*Under this part of the plan, a family or business in Epsom receives a property tax abatement of up to $1,000 for sending a child from a non-property-owning family to private school. The sponsoring family or business must present proof that they have aided such a child — a receipt from the child's school, for example — in order to qualify for the abatement. Charles Bauer, the Epsom town counsel, says a number of local children have benefited from the program, but he has no precise numbers.

> Seven states passed legislation last year permitting greater parental choice in varying degrees. But the most far-reaching choice plan yet proposed in the United States was defeated by Oregon voters last November by a 2-1 margin.

# How Choice Plans Operate in the States

The list below provides a capsule look at how school-choice plans operate in selected states and school districts. Some programs allow parents to select schools only within a given school district. Interdistrict plans allow parents to select schools outside their home districts.

### Arkansas
Students aged 5 to 18 may attend schools outside their home districts provided the receiving district has room for them and the transfer does not disturb desegregation efforts.

### California (Cupertino)
The Cupertino Union School District near San Jose subsidizes home schooling. Parents who choose to educate their children at home can receive an annual $1,000 subsidy that can be used to purchase products or services available to public school students. The subsidy covers such educational expenses as textbooks, foreign-language tapes and computer software. The subsidy may not be used for private school tuition or religious curricula. The school district's purchasing department reviews the parents' receipts to determine whether they are reimbursable.

### Connecticut
The state finances a limited number of interdistrict choice plans to promote racial balance between cities and suburbs through the use of magnet schools.

### Idaho
The governor has signed a statewide school choice plan into law that permits a receiving district to reject a student only because the district is full, and not because of the student's academic record or other personal characteristics. Parents are responsible for the students' transportation. The plan is scheduled to go into effect next school year.

### Iowa
Under a 1989 open-enrollment law, pupils aged 5 to 18 may attend schools across district lines if the receiving district has room and the transfer does not disrupt desegregation plans. In addition, public school students may take college courses not available at their high school with the state paying up to $200 in tuition.

### Massachusetts (Cambridge)
The Cambridge School District has had a choice plan since 1981 that has served as a model for others in the state and around the nation. The district abolished school attendance zones, and parents may send their children to any of the district's 13 elementary schools. Assignments are made on a first-come, first-served basis, providing space is available and subject to desegregation constraints. According to the U.S. Department of Education, the proportion of students attending public schools in the district rose from 74 to 82 percent after the introduction of the choice plan.

### Minnesota
Students in all parts of the state may attend public schools outside their district if the receiving district has space available and racial balance is not adversely affected. Young people who have not succeeded in one high school may transfer to another school to complete their secondary education. High school juniors and seniors may take college courses for high school or college credit.

Parents may deduct from their taxable income up to $650 for elementary school students and up to $1,000 for secondary school expenses.

### Missouri
The state has financed a magnet school system linking St. Louis and adjacent suburban school districts to encourage voluntary desegregation. The state has also paid for magnet schools in Kansas City.

### Nebraska
Students from kindergarten through grade 12 may attend schools across district lines if the receiving district has room and the transfer does not upset desegregation plans.

### New Hampshire (Epsom)
The small town of Epsom has enacted a controversial choice plan that allows parents who educate their children outside the public school system to receive a $1,000 property tax abatement. The plan was approved by the town's Board of Selectmen, but the Epsom school district is challenging it, as are the American Civil Liberties Union and the National Education Association. Opponents claim that the New Hampshire Constitution prohibits the spending of state money on parochial schools, and that those receiving the abatement are not paying their fair share for the public schools as the constitution requires.

### Vermont
Since 1869, Vermont has had a plan that allows parents in areas without public high schools to have the school district pay to send their children to public or private secondary schools (excluding parochial schools) in or out of the state. The plan covers the full tuition to a public high school and provides a capped tuition payment equal to the average tuition of the state's high schools to private schools. The plan was modified in 1990 to allow parents in areas that do have public high schools to participate. The 1990 law also extended the plan to elementary school students.

### Washington
The Legislature passed a new choice law during the 1990 session. It expanded the current choice law, and widened the reasons a parent could give for requesting a transfer, such as proximity to day care or the parent's place of employment. It also provided that every school district have a policy on interdistrict transfers. Receiving districts must have a set policy for accepting or rejecting students. The state is considering a plan to pay the transportation costs for students who cross district lines.

### Wisconsin (Milwaukee)
The state "double-funds" the movement of students between Milwaukee and suburban school districts by providing financial support to both the receiving and sending districts. Moreover, a small number of Milwaukee students from low-income families may take part in a program enabling them to transfer to private schools at state expense. The program has been challenged in court. It was first upheld, then was overturned on narrow procedural grounds, and is now being appealed to the state Supreme Court.

Sources: U.S. Department of Education, Education Commission of the States.

*Continued from p. 268*
free telephone number.* The center also will recruit a band of experts to help parents and educators deal with choice-related issues and to staff workshops and seminars for school administrators, teachers, legislators and other interested parties.

### *"America 2000"*

School choice also received prominent play when Bush unveiled his "America 2000" program of education reform on April 18, 1991, before a White House audience of educators, business executives, governors and members of Congress. Bush did not propose financing school-choice programs directly. Instead, the federal government would provide about $200 million in financial incentives to state and local governments to develop school-choice policies. Secretary of Education Lamar Alexander also plans to ask Congress to change the Chapter 1 program of federal aid to schools with disadvantaged students* to allow federal dollars to follow a low-income student if he or she transfers to another school, even if the new school is a private or parochial one.

School choice was just one aspect of the educational reform package President Bush outlined April 18. The president also called for:

■ **National standards and tests.** Standards would be set in five core subjects — English, mathematics, science, history and geography. The president will ask governors to adopt voluntary tests for fourth-, eighth- and 12th-graders.

■ **Flexibility.** Schools could ignore federal rules governing their funding in order to cut through red tape and raise achievement levels. This idea needs congressional approval.

■ **Merit schools.** The federal gov-

*The number is 1-800-442-PICK.

ernment would award grants to schools that have made progress toward national goals. This would require congressional authorization.

■ **Merit pay.** School districts would be urged to boost pay for those who teach well, who teach core subjects, who teach in "dangerous" settings or who are mentors for new teachers.

■ **New Schools.** Bypassing Congress, the president plans to raise up to $200 million from the business community to fund research and development of non-traditional schools. Bush will then ask Congress for $550 million to create 535 "new American schools," one in each congressional district, by 1996.[16]

The estimated price tag for the president's proposals was a relatively low $690 million. "People who want Washington to solve our educational problems are missing the point," Bush said. "We can lend appropriate help . . . but what happens here in Washington won't matter half as much as what happens in each school, each local community and, yes, each home." ■

---

*Under the Chapter 1 program, a school receives money if a large proportion of its students qualify as needy either under the federal free-lunch program or the Aid to Families with Dependent Children program. The money must be spent on remedial classes and services for those children, unless a school's poverty rate exceeds 75 percent, in which case Chapter 1 funds can be spent on schoolwide programs.

---

# OUTLOOK

## Political Prospects

President Bush's legislative initiative makes it likely that Congress will be the main forum for debate on school choice this year and next. The congressional battle lines on school choice do not always coincide with party lines. Members who represent districts with large numbers of private schools are more likely to favor choice. By the same token, members from districts containing mostly public schools tend to oppose policies that would divert federal education aid from those schools.

The retirement last year of Rep. Augustus F. Hawkins, D-Calif., long-time chairman of the House Education and Labor Committee, removed one of the leading opponents of school choice from Congress. Hawkins took a consistently hostile view of the concept, asserting that

"there's not enough room for everybody in the 'good' schools. Choice will segregate on the basis of income, race and national origin."

Rep. William D. Ford, D-Mich., Hawkins' successor as chairman of the Education panel, says he plans to withhold comment on the administration plan until it is translated into legislative form. "The details are more than fuzzy," he says. Rep. Dale E. Kildee, D-Mich., chairman of the House Education Subcommittee on Elementary, Secondary and Vocational Education, is more outspoken. He worries that choice plans would leave some students behind in the poorer schools. "If students have this choice and go from school A to school B because they perceive that B is a better school," he asks, "what do we do for school A and for the students that remain in school A?"

Rep. Bill Goodling, R-Pa., the ranking Republican member of the House Education and Labor Committee, expresses similar sentiments. "If you have 500 students in a school and 250 of them . . . decide to go to a school of choice, that leaves 250 fallen angels behind," he says.

Goodling is a close friend and adviser to President Bush on educational issues, but he has reservations about the choice concept. The president "really believes [choice] will give low-income parents and children a greater opportunity for a better education," Goodling says. "I want to make sure that the opposite does not happen."

Given such bipartisan concerns, House members are likely to force the administration to modify its proposal significantly. The administration's education package may also receive rough handling by the Senate Labor and Human Resources Committee, which is headed by Edward M. Kennedy, D-Mass. Kennedy says he supports choice for public schools but not for private or parochial ones. Choice, in his opinion, "should not become a death sentence for public schools struggling to serve disadvantaged students."

Kennedy believes that including parochial schools in choice plans raises questions about the separation of church and state. "By offering public dollars to private schools, including religious schools, the administration is reopening the bitter and divisive policy and constitutional debates of the past about public aid to private schools," Kennedy told Education Secretary Lamar Alexander at a hearing before the Labor and Human Resources Committee April 23.[17]

But most experts on constitutional law now dismiss this question as moot. Says Laurence Tribe, a constitutional scholar at Harvard Law School, "I don't think there is any chance at all that the [Supreme Court] as currently composed would find a reasonably designed school-choice plan as a violation of church and state. If there are objections, they should be debated on policy grounds and not recast as constitutional arguments."[18]

Denis P. Doyle, a senior fellow at the Hudson Institute who has written extensively on education issues, supports the administration's proposal to convert the Chapter 1 program into a vouchers plan. If Congress goes along with the idea, Doyle says, "it would be simply a tour de force" for the White House. But, he adds, "The likelihood of Congress enacting this is not high, given the fact that Congress views education principally as a pork-barrel issue rather than a substantive issue. They tend to be quite happy with Chapter 1 the way it is."

As Congress prepares to grapple with the issue, state legislatures are dealing with the choice question on their own. According to the Center for Choice in Education, choice-related bills have been introduced in at least 30 states this year. The only one enacted so far has been in Massachusetts, where Gov. William F. Weld signed an open-enrollment bill into law in March. Under the plan, which will go into effect June 30, a child may attend a public school in a city or town where he does not reside, *providing* that school district has chosen to admit non-resident students. Districts that agree to accept non-resident students set a tuition rate that will be paid by the state. The tuition rate cannot exceed the average expense per student for such a school.

Doyle believes other states eventually will adopt choice plans. "Popular support for school choice is very high," he says. Whether that support will be mobilized in the short run "remains to be seen," he adds, but "there is every reason to believe it will be." ■

## Notes

[1] The 18-member National Commission on Excellence in Education, composed primarily of educators, was appointed by Education Secretary T. H. Bell on Aug. 26, 1981, to assess the quality of education at all levels in both public and private schools. The commission disbanded in August 1983.

[2] Quoted by Nancy Paulu in *Improving Schools and Empowering Parents,* October 1989, p. 20. The report was based on a White House Workshop on Choice in Education held Jan. 10, 1989.

[3] Finn was assistant secretary of Education during the Reagan administration and is currently a professor of education and public policy at Vanderbilt University's branch in Washington.

[4] Quoted in *USA Today,* Aug. 24, 1990.

[5] John E. Chubb and Terry M. Moe, *Politics, Markets and America's Schools* (1990), p. 213. Chubb is a senior fellow at Brookings and Moe is a political science professor at Stanford University.

[6] Quoted by Jill Zuckman in "School 'Choice' a Tough Choice for Members of Congress," *Congressional Quarterly Weekly Report,* April 27, 1991, p. 1062.

[7] Quoted in the *Los Angeles Times,* March 12, 1991.

[8] Milton Friedman, *Capitalism and Freedom* (1962), p. 91.

[9] *Ibid.,* p. 89.

[10] For details on these and other "parochiaid" cases, see Congressional Quarterly's *Guide to the U.S. Supreme Court* (1979), pp. 466-470.

[11] Quoted in the *1982 CQ Almanac,* p. 489.

[12] Association for Supervision and Curriculum Development, *Public Schools of Choice,* 1990, p. 10.

[13] Quoted in *The New York Times,* Aug. 22, 1990.

[14] Quoted in *The Wall Street Journal,* March 26, 1990.

[15] Quoted in "Hero of Choice," *The New Republic,* Oct. 22, 1990, p. 16.

[16] See *Congressional Quarterly Weekly Report,* April 20, 1991, pp. 983-986.

[17] Most of the members of Congress quoted in this section were interviewed by Congressional Quarterly reporter Jill Zuckman. See Zuckman, *op. cit.,* pp. 1061-1062.

[18] *Ibid.,* p. 1061.

# Bibliography

## Selected Sources Used

### Books

**Chubb, John E., and Moe, Terry M., *Politics, Markets, and America's Schools,* The Brookings Institution, 1990.**

With the publication of this book, Chubb and Moe succeeded in shaking up not only the education establishment, which was their intention, but also many supporters of school choice. Those who take issue with the book usually object to its argument that an open market with minimal regulation will lead to more effective schools and improved student performance.

**Friedman, Milton, *Capitalism and Freedom*, The University of Chicago Press, 1962.**

In this influential work, Friedman sets forth his proposal for tuition vouchers to give parents greater choice in deciding where to send their children to school. American thinking about education, he writes, is "still dominated by the small town which had but one school for the poor and rich residents alike. Under such circumstances, public schools may well have equalized opportunities. With the growth of urban and suburban areas, the situation has changed drastically. Our present school system, far from equalizing opportunity, very likely does the opposite. It makes it all the harder for the exceptional few — and it is they who are the hope of the future — to rise above the poverty of their initial state."

**Glenn, Charles L., *Choice of Schools in Six Nations*, U.S. Department of Education, 1989.**

Glenn, who has been involved in equity and urban education programs in the Massachusetts Department of Education for 20 years, examines the status of school choice in six industrial nations — Belgium, Britain, Canada, France, [West] Germany and the Netherlands. Among other things, he concludes, "The advance of universal education as a result of government efforts has resulted, in nation after nation, in a generation of educational consumers who are more sophisticated about what they want for their children."

**Lieberman, Myron, *Privatization and Educational Choice*, St. Martin's Press, 1989.**

Lieberman, a veteran education policy analyst, takes the position that "education for profit may be our best hope for educational improvement." He also lashes out at the mass media for failing to articulate "the important developments and issues in education."

### Articles

**Honig, Bill, "Why Privatizing Public Education Is a Bad Idea," *The Brookings Review*, winter 1990-91.**

Honig, who is California's superintendent of public instruction, is sharply critical of the free-market approach to school choice espoused by John E. Chubb and Terry M. Moe. "We *should* give public school parents more choice, either through magnet schools or through open-enrollment plans," he writes. "But limits are necessary to prevent skimming of the academic or athletically talented or furthering racial segregation."

### Reports and Studies

**Designs for Change, *The New Improved Sorting Machine*, February 1989.**

This study of high schools in Boston, Chicago, New York and Philadelphia concludes that "high school options have great potential for increasing educational inequality, creating a new form of segregation based on a combination of race, income level and previous success in school." Choice programs in the four cities, the report states, "frequently ended up bringing disproportionate benefits to white students and to selected middle-class students whose families have mastered the intricacies of the high school admissions process."

**Paulu, Nancy, *Improving Schools and Empowering Parents*, October 1989.**

Paulu's report consists largely of excerpts from the remarks of participants in the January 1989 White House workshop on school choice.

**U.S. House Subcommittee on Elementary, Secondary and Vocational Education, Committee on Education and Labor, *Oversight Hearing on Parental Choice* (published proceedings of field hearing in St. Paul, Minn., Feb. 16, 1989).**

Numerous witnesses testify about various aspects of the Minnesota school choice plan, which is the most comprehensive choice program in the nation today.

**U.S. Senate Committee on Labor and Human Resources, *Incentives in Education* (published proceedings of field hearing in Boston, Oct. 5, 1987).**

Although the focus of this hearing was school choice in Boston, a secondary aim was to determine whether programs in operation there could be successfully replicated in other parts of the country.

# The Next Step

## Additional Articles from Current Periodicals

### Addresses & essays

**"President Bush and school choice,"** *America*, Feb. 11, 1989, p. 99.

Editorial. Considers President Bush's support for a policy allowing parents to choose the public school that their children attend. Opponents say the plan needs to include private schools as well.

**Bamber, C., "Public school choice: Will we be ready?"** *Education Digest*, January 1990, p. 19.

Discusses public school choice and cites some of the misgivings voiced by the National Committee for Citizens in Education (NCCE). Restrictive transfer policies.

**Becker, G. S., "What our schools need is a healthy dose of competition,"** *Business Week*, Dec. 18, 1989, p. 28.

Opinion. Argues that if Americans want a better education system, they must give parents the right to choose their children's schools, and help poor students gain access to private schools.

**Caminiti, S., "A bigger role for parents,"** *Fortune (Special Issue: Saving Our Schools)*, spring 1990, p. 25.

Reports how giving mom and dad a choice of schools is only one of many new programs to pull parents into the educational process. Describes how the main beneficiaries of these programs are kids. Closing the parent-teacher gap; Profiles several communities, including Rochester, N.Y., and Chicago; The choice option; Critics of the plans.

**Cavazos, L. F., "Restructuring American education through choice,"** *Vital Speeches*, June 15, 1989, p. 514.

Presents a speech given by Lauro F. Cavazos, former U. S. secretary of Education, at the Education Press Association, dealing with the issue of improving the national commitment to excellence in education through the provision of choice at the elementary and secondary school levels.

**Clinchy, E., "Public school choice: Absolutely necessary but not wholly sufficient,"** *Phi Delta Kappan*, December 1989, p. 289.

Discusses some of the reasons the current trend toward public school choice may not be successful. Necessity of choice; Requirements of choice; Need for autonomy; Educational equity; Role of central administration;

New restructuring framework; Need for a different set of national priorities.

**Lieberman, M., "Education reform as a conservative fiasco,"** *Education Digest*, February 1990, p. 3.

Examines ways in which conservatives have failed to make a significant improvement in public education since the reform movement began in the 1980s. Understatement of the cost of public education; Misconceptions about merit pay; Public school choice.

### Book reviews

**"Choosing choice,"** *Commonweal*, Oct. 12, 1990, p. 588.

Reviews the book "Politics, Markets, & America's Schools," by John E. Chubb and Terry Moe. Analysis of what makes an effective school.

**"New materials,"** *Education Digest*, November 1990, p. 77.

Reviews the book 'Public School Choice: Current Issues/Future Prospects,' by Myron Lieberman.

### Case studies

**Buckley, W. F. Jr., "The Milwaukee plan,"** *National Review*, Aug. 6, 1990, p. 54.

Editorial. Discusses a recent bill passed in Milwaukee that was designed to offer educational choice to parents. Overview of the bill, proposed by state Rep. Polly Williams; Challenges faced in passing the bill; Current efforts to nullify the law.

**Leo, J., "School reform's best choice,"** *U. S. News & World Report*, Jan. 14, 1991, p. 17.

Considers the work of Polly Williams, a black Wisconsin state legislator, who pushed through a bill allowing up to 1,000 poor children to attend private, non-sectarian schools with the state paying $2,500 a year for each pupil. The coalition of organizations for school choice that will produce change and ferment from coast to coast; Excellence and empowerment more important than integration; Problems with the theory; No panacea.

**Nathan, J., "Helping all children, empowering all educators: Another view of school choice,"** *Phi Delta Kappan*, December 1989, p. 304.

Discusses the positive aspects of the public school choice plan implemented in Minnesota. Educational, parental, and political support; Implementation of Minnesota plan; Improvements in existing plan.

**Pearson, J., "Myths of choice: The governor's new clothes?" *Phi Delta Kappan*, June 1989, p. 821.**

Opinion. Argues against the Minnesota statewide open enrollment plan, which allows students to attend any school of their choice. The author claims that the plan will harm certain schools and districts while helping others, and will present increased problems in budgeting, staffing, and scheduling for school districts.

**Walberg, H. J., Bakalis, M. J., et al., "Reconstructing the nation's worst schools," *Phi Delta Kappan*, June 1989, p. 802.**

Summarizes a plan drawn up by a Chicago, Ill., coalition called Chicagoans United to Reform Education (CURE) to improve Chicago schools, which some consider the worst in the nation. Some of the plan's components include individual elected school governing councils and school-choice provisions, and education rebates, designed to increase competition between Chicago's private and public schools.

## Debates & issues

**Atkins, A., "C-H-O-I-C-E the hottest education issue of the '90s," *Better Homes & Gardens*, October 1989, p. 18.**

Reports on the issue of choice or open enrollment which offers students the freedom to attend any public school within a district or in some cases, within an entire state. How it has worked successfully in Montclair, N.J., for the past 10 years, and other areas which are attempting the system; How it works; Why parents like it; What critics say. INSETS: If choice comes to your district; How to pick a school; Debating choice: How to recognize a good choice plan.

**Bastian, A., "Thoughts on school choice," *Education Digest*, February 1990, p. 17.**

Examines potential negative impacts of school choice on equal opportunity, accountability, and democratic governance.

**Finn, C. E. Jr., "The choice backlash," *National Review*, Nov. 10, 1989, p. 30.**

Criticizes the National Education Association's opposition to school choice as a means of education reform. Three key premises behind the school-choice viewpoint; Four arguments against choice; Argues for giving choice a chance. INSET: Voice against choice.

**Glastris, P., Toch, T., et al., "The uncertain benefits of school choice," *U. S. News & World Report*, Nov. 6,**

1989, p. 79.

Examines the pros and cons of the new trend toward parental choice of public schools. Case study of an open-enrollment system in Minnesota; Opposing viewpoints on the concept. INSET: Choosing hockey.

**Leslie, C., "In search of excellence," *Newsweek*, Oct. 24, 1988, p. 81.**

Discusses the ways parents get their children into the public school of their choice, usually by lying or by paying hefty non-resident tuitions. Examples; School crackdown measures.

**Moore, D. R. and Davenport, S., "High school choice and students at risk," *Education Digest*, September 1989, p. 7.**

Describes a study that analyzes how students at risk are affected by open choice of high schools. Study details; Results; Conclusions; Recommendations.

**Pipho, C., "State and local control: rainbows and dark. . ." *Phi Delta Kappan*, September 1988, p. 7.**

Forecast of the upcoming educational year based on recent state actions and programs. Academic bankruptcy; Restructured schools; Parental choice of school districts.

**Rist, M. C., "Should parents choose their child's school?" *Education Digest*, September 1989, p. 3.**

Debates the issue of parental school choice and examines Minnesota's statewide enrollment-options plan. Comments by advocates and opponents.

**Rosenberg, P., "How do we balance public school choice?" *Education Digest*, November 1989, p. 7.**

Comments on different points of view concerning the question of public school choice. Lack of diversity between schools; School finance equalization; Magnet schools and intra- and inter-district choice.

**Tifft, S., "The fight over school choice," *Time*, March 13, 1989, p. 54.**

Report on President Bush's backing of giving parents the right to choose which public school their children will attend. Pros and cons; Who likes and dislikes the choice program for open enrollment; What states are doing. INSET: Report card.

## General

**"Teachers are talking about. . ." *Instructor*, October 1990, p. 12.**

Presents reports on class-size studies, the drawbacks of reward systems, and the growing trend of state-mandated school-choice programs. Also includes information about the JASON project and Landmark Edition's "Written &

Illustrated By. . ." contest.

**Chubb, J. E. and Moe, T. M., "America's public schools," *Current*, December 1990, p. 4.**

Reprints the article "America's Public Schools: Choice Is a Panacea," written by John E. Chubb and Terry M. Moe in the summer issue of "The Brookings Review." Proposes a new system of public education based on indirect control through markets and parental choice. Failure of those institutions which have traditionally governed America's schools; How a system based on choice would work.

**Fierman, J., "Giving parents a choice of schools," *Fortune*, Dec. 4, 1989, p. 147.**

Discusses public school choice, in which families choose the school the children will attend, which has been supported by President Bush, most governors, and over half of the Americans recently polled, but which also has many vocal critics who say it will further encourage racial and class divisions. Business support; Examples.

**Leslie, C., "Giving parents a choice," *Newsweek*, Sept. 19, 1988, p. 77.**

Report on a new reform in public education allowing parents to have a choice in the education their children receive, whether special needs or custom-tailored for gifted students. The open enrollment concept is working in some form in at least 15 states. Concept, goals, models, lessons learned, examples, logistics, and problems.

**Lomax, S. M., "Declaring independence," *Essence*, February 1991, p. 96.**

Presents guidelines for parents to help them choose an independent black elementary or secondary school. Afrocentric focus; Price.

**Shapiro, W., and Horowitz, J. M., "Pick a school, any school." *Time*, Sept. 3, 1990, p. 70.**

Reports that a conservative idea — vouchers that would give parents freedom to choose where their kids will be educated — is gaining liberal disciples. Milwaukee students with grants from the state of Wisconsin; November Oregon initiative for tuition tax credits for private schools; Inflated public-education costs.

**Theroux, P., "Pick a school (but not any school)," *Parents*, September 1988, p. 62.**

Discusses how to choose a school to suit each individual child, types of schools, meetings with teachers, and curricula.

## *Implementation*

**Glenn, C. L., "Putting school choice in place," *Phi Delta Kappan*, December 1989, p. 295.**

Gives advice on introducing and implementing a policy of public school choice, which incorporates fairness, clear communication, autonomy, and diversity. Context of expectations and requirements; Concrete implementation steps; Checklist.

**Uchitelle, S., "What it really takes to make school choice work," *Phi Delta Kappan*, December 1989, p. 301.**

Discusses some of the essential elements of public school choice plans, which were successfully implemented in a St. Louis school choice program. Equitable access; Transportation services; Funding.

## *Law & legislation*

**McHenry, S. P., "The 'Education President' meets with Catholic educators," *America*, Aug. 5, 1989, p. 52.**

Reports on a recent meeting of educational leaders from 11 Catholic dioceses with President George Bush. Urging Bush to support a tuition tax credit for parents who choose private schools.

**Pipho, C., "Watching the legislatures," *Phi Delta Kappan*, January 1990, p. 342.**

Reports on issues related to state budgets and finance, with education playing a prominent role, that are expected to come before the more than 40 state legislatures convening this year. State lotteries and education financing; Tax initiative results; Parental choice; Collaboration on early education and problems of youth at risk.

## *Public opinion*

**Elam, S. M. and Gallup, A. M., "The 21st annual Gallup poll of the public's attitudes toward the public schools," *Phi Delta Kappan*, September 1989, p. 41.**

Presents results of the 21st annual Gallup/Phi Delta Kappa poll of the public's attitude toward public schools. Results show the public favors letting students choose the school they attend, uniformity in public school programs, and higher quality schools in poor areas, among other issues. INSETS: Acknowledgements; Research procedure; Composition of the sample; Design of the sample; Sampling tolerances; How to order the poll.

# Back Issues

*Great Research on Current Issues Starts Right Here. . . Recent topics covered by The CQ Researcher are listed below. Issues dated before May 10, 1991, were published under the name of Editorial Research Reports.*

**NOVEMBER 1989**
Balkanization of Eastern Europe
Dealing With the Underclass
America Turns to Recycling
New World Economy

**DECEMBER 1989**
North America Trade Pact
Influence Peddling
German Reunification
Learning Disabilities

**JANUARY 1990**
Higher Education Curriculum
Photonics
Age of 'Infotainment'
Abortion: Politicians' Nightmare

**FEBRUARY 1990**
Politics and Economic Growth
Free Agency in Sports
Repetitive Motion
War on Drugs

**MARCH 1990**
Asbestos: Are Risks Acceptable?
Public Health Campaigns
South Africa's Future
Homeless Need More Than Shelter

**APRIL 1990**
How Fair is the Tax Burden?
Workers' Compensation
U.S. Pacific Forces
Curbing Insurance Premiums

**MAY 1990**
Should Teaching Be a Profession?
Will Canada Fall Apart?
Is U.S. Patent System Outdated?
Federal Funding for the Arts

**JUNE 1990**
Downsizing America's Armed Forces
Progress In Weather Forecasting
S & L Bailout
Bio-Chemical Disarmament

**JULY 1990**
Do Americans Still Love Marriage?
Death Penalty Debate
Decline of Rural America
United Nations in the 1990s

**AUGUST 1990**
Democracy in the Philippines
Initiatives: True Democracy?
Hard Times at Newspapers
Teens Balance School & Jobs

**SEPTEMBER 1990**
Dangers of Alcohol
Western Alliance After the Cold War
Tobacco Industry
Right to Die

**OCTOBER 1990**
Organ Transplants
Energy Policy Options
Search for Arab Unity
Child Support

**NOVEMBER 1990**
Lotteries and Gambling
Post Cold-War Choices
Setting Limits on Medical Care
Multicultural Education

**DECEMBER 1990**
Cable TV Regulation
Americans' Search For Their Roots
Is Insurance System a Failure?
Why Schools Still Have Tracking

**JANUARY 1991**
Growing Influence of Boycotts
Should the U.S. Reinstate the Draft?
America's Archaeological Past
Peace Corps' Challenges in '90s

**FEBRUARY 1991**
Regional Impact of Recession
Puerto Rico's Status
Redistricting: Mapping Power
Nuclear Power

**MARCH 1991**
Acid Rain
Cost of the Gulf War
Reassessing Gun Laws
Future for Man in Space

**APRIL 1991**
Social Security
Canadian Crisis Over Quebec
California Drought
Electromagnetic Radiation

Back issues are available for $4.00 (subscribers) or $7.00 (non-subscribers). Quantity discounts apply to orders over ten. To order, call Congressional Quarterly 1-800-432-2250.

# Future Topics

▶ *Quotas*

▶ *Animal Rights*

▶ *U.S.-Japan Relations*

# ERRATUM

Correction for "Racial Quotas," May 17, 1991, *CQR:*

Reference to *Firefighters Local Union No. 1794 v. Stoots*, p. 283:

The correct case name is *Firefighters Local Union No. 1794 v. Stotts*.

# Racial Quotas

*Can there be affirmative action without special preferences?*

T
HE CIVIL RIGHTS DEBATES OF THE 1990s are a far cry from those of the 1960s. Gone is the stirring rhetoric of Martin Luther King's "I Have a Dream" speech. In its place is a single word: quotas. The resentments generated by the quota issue can be seen in debates over college admissions policies and in controversies over hiring and promotion. But the main focus is in Congress, where supporters of affirmative action are pushing a new civil rights bill. President Bush vetoed a similar measure last year, saying it would force employers to adopt racial quotas. The bill's supporters say it would do no such thing, and they accuse the president of using the quota issue to scare white voters. Looming over the debate is the 1992 presidential and congressional elections, which could be powerfully affected by the quota issue.

CQ    May 17, 1991 • Volume 1, No. 2 • 277-300

*Formerly Editorial Research Reports*

COVER ART: BARBARA SASSA-DANIELS

# CQ Researcher

May 17, 1991
Volume 1, No. 2

**EDITOR**
Sandra Stencel

**ASSOCIATE EDITOR**
Richard L. Worsnop

**STAFF WRITERS**
Charles S. Clark
Mary H. Cooper
Patrick G. Marshall

**PRODUCTION EDITOR**
Laurie De Maris

**EDITORIAL ASSISTANT**
Thomas H. Moore

**GRAPHICS**
Jack Auldridge

**PUBLISHED BY**
Congressional Quarterly Inc.

**CHAIRMAN**
Andrew Barnes

**VICE CHAIRMAN**
Andrew P. Corty

**EDITOR AND PUBLISHER**
Neil Skene

**EXECUTIVE EDITOR**
Robert W. Merry

**EDITOR, EBSCO PUBLISHING**
Melissa Kummerer

The CQ Researcher (ISSN 1056-2036). Formerly Editorial Research Reports. Published weekly (48 times yer year, excluding March 1, May 3, Aug. 2 and Nov. 1, 1991) by Congressional Quarterly Inc., 1414 22nd St., N.W., Washington, D.C. 20037. Rates are furnished upon request. Application to mail at second-class postage rates is pending at Washington, D.C. POSTMASTER: Send address changes to The CQ Researcher, 1414 22nd St., N.W., Washington, D.C. 20037.

# Racial Quotas

BY MARY H. COOPER

## THE ISSUES

It has been a generation since the emotional confrontations in Southern restaurants, schools and streets led to the historic civil rights legislation of the 1960s. Today, Americans still express pride in the social and political revolution that placed on the lawbooks a national commitment to equal treatment for all citizens.

But that commitment has led also to a patchwork of policies and practices in the country aimed not only at preventing discrimination in the present or the future, but also at redressing the injustice of past discrimination. And these policies and practices have generated a new wave of political and cultural controversy that seems to be rapidly intensifying.

The buzzword for this controversy is "quotas." Opinion polls indicate that Americans overwhelmingly support laws that ensure fairness and prohibit discrimination in hiring, promotions and academic admissions. The vast majority believe that special efforts at education or encouragement or recruitment are warranted to increase the representation of minorities in the workplace, among managers and in colleges and universities. But at the same time, most Americans strongly oppose policies that result in numerical goals, or quotas, for minority hires or admissions.

The issue isn't new; it has reverberated in court cases, Congress and in political discourse since the 1970s. But recent developments suggest it has become lodged in the nation's political maw and is likely to inflame the domestic debate for some time to come.

One such development was President Bush's controversial veto of a civil rights bill cleared by Congress in the closing days of the 1990 session. The legislation's aim was to reverse several Supreme Court decisions that critics said narrowed the remedies open to minorities who believed they were victims of discrimination. Bush professed support for that aim, but argued Congress' approach had produced a "quota bill." Waving the quota argument, the bill's opponents sustained the veto amid suggestions their action helped foster ongoing racism in America.

Another development was the hard line adopted by North Carolina's Republican Sen. Jesse Helms in his successful 1990 effort to fight off a powerful challenge from Democrat Harvey Gantt, a black politician from Charlotte. Helms pummelled Gantt with commercials showing a pair of white hands crumpling a rejection letter and suggesting the person had lost the job to a less qualified minority worker.

The quota issue is cropping up in less dramatic form across the country in colleges, law schools, government agencies and private companies, and it is generating plenty of public debate and civic emotion. Through this debate and emotion, some fundamental questions have emerged:

### How widespread is the use of quotas today?

There is little definitive information on quota usage among employers and college officials. "It's very difficult to get data on how many individual employers do it," says Carl Hampe, a staffer for Sen. Alan K. Simpson, R-Wyo. In part, he says, this reflects a cross-fire faced by many employers and academic institutions in America. Though committed to "affirmative action" programs to help minorities and women, they also fear being accused of "reverse discrimination" by disgruntled whites.

The result is that evidence on the matter is largely anecdotal. But many industrial relations specialists say the practice in corporate hiring and promotions is widespread. James Sharf, special assistant to the chairman of the U.S. Equal Employment Opportunity Commission (EEOC), says industrial psychologists "will tell you strictly off the record, 'Of course we're doing that [hiring and promoting by quota].'" But he adds they can't acknowledge the practice publicly for fear of getting their clients into legal trouble for reverse discrimination. "So what you've got is everyone tacitly using race-conscious hiring — either formally or informally ... hiring by the numbers."

Organizations that formally adopt quota policies, or are revealed as having them in place, generally find themselves in the midst of controversy. When the *Philadelphia Inquirer* instituted a quota-based hiring policy earlier this year aimed at boosting the number of women and minorities in the newsroom, anger quickly welled up among some white males. Amid the subsequent controversy, Inquirer editors backed away from the "quota" label. And a fierce controversy erupted at the Washington, D.C., campus of Georgetown University in April when a white male law student accused the administration of admitting black students with academic credentials that were "dramatically unequal" to those of white students at the school. (*For more details, see Current Situation, p. 290.*)

Minority commentators quickly weighed in with the argument that preferential hiring and academic admissions have been going on in the country for centuries. The only difference was in who was preferred. "There is one group of people who were powerfully, thoroughly, completely and aggressively preferred, and those are white males," says Roger Wilkins, professor of history and American culture at George Mason University in Fairfax, Va. He adds that this preferential treatment didn't end with the civil rights and women's movements of the 1960s and '70s, but continued as a kind of "snobbish, elitist ... passing [of] the torch from generation to generation."

In this view, the quota issue is little more than a tool wielded by the white male establishment to make white workers fear they will lose their jobs to less qualified minorities or women. "And yet there is this enormous whine across the country from white men about these unqualified black people taking over," says Wilkins.

But others argue the hiring and promotion processes are being skewed in ways that damage the American idea of a meritocracy in

which people rise to their natural level based on their relative talents. This is happening, they say, largely as a result of employers' concerns about compliance with federal legislation.

Title VII of the landmark 1964 Civil Rights Act specifically prohibits discriminatory practices that would deprive any individual of employment opportunities because of race, color, religion, sex or national origin. Subsequent affirmative action measures went a step further by specifically encouraging active efforts to recruit workers from targeted minority groups.

Quota opponents say from such policies it was a short step to actual quotas. The progression reached its culmination, they argue, with the Supreme Court's 1971 decision in *Griggs v. Duke Power Co.*, affirming the constitutionality of so-called "disparate impact analysis," a statistical method for determining employers' compliance with Title VII. Essentially, the court said plaintiffs in discrimination suits could use the racial composition of the surrounding community as evidence of their compliance. The result, say quota opponents, is that more and more employers adopted quota policies to bring their work force into balance with the surrounding community and thus ensure Title VII compliance.

But Clint Bolick, director of the Landmark Legal Foundation Center for Civil Rights, a conservative group based in Washington, says large corporations and government agencies are more likely to pursue such policies than small businesses. Bolick, an EEOC official during the Reagan administration, says large organizations often opt for compliance even if it means a decline in productivity, while small businesses "simply cannot afford to do that."

Even small businesses may unknowingly apply a form of racial quota when they turn to state em-

ployment agencies in search of candidates for lower-level positions. Many of these agencies use a skills test called the GATB (for Generalized Aptitude Test Battery), which is approved by the U.S. Department of Labor as a reliable predictor of job performance.

But the test results are adjusted on the basis of race, with the raw scores of blacks and Hispanics scaled upward to account for the fact that they generally score lower than whites and Asian Americans. Under this process, known as "race-norming" (*see story, p. 289*), an employer may get a list of test scores indicating a minority applicant scored higher than a white applicant when in fact the reverse was true.

"Race-norming," R. Gaull Silberman, vice chairman of the EEOC, told the Equal Employment Advisory Council, "is the oil which greases the quota engine which drives much of employment policy today under the guise of government-required contract compliance." [1]

### Are quotas an inevitable result of affirmative action policies?

This may lie at the heart of the dispute. For example, when President Bush called last year's civil rights measure a quota bill, he was not referring to the text itself, which included explicit language denying it was intended to establish racial quotas. Bush, echoing the views of many critics, predicted that employers would be forced to adopt quota policies in order to protect themselves from the litigation he said the bill would encourage.

The question boils down to whether statistical analyses can be used for judging compliance with affirmative action statutes without encouraging quotas. Nathan Glazer, professor of education and sociology at Harvard University's School of Education, suggests statistical patterns can be "determinative" in some circumstances, but they shouldn't be applied too broadly. After all, he argues, employers must consider other factors in hiring and promotion, such as "achievement on tests or appearance or factors which suggest loyalty and teamwork." He adds: "At some point one has to declare a compromise to this war over the use of statistical factors to demonstrate discrimination."

But some experts, including some who oppose quotas, say statistical analyses don't necessarily have to lead to quotas. Herman Belz, professor of American constitutional history at the University of Maryland, advocates tracking an employer's progress by considering the number of applicants, acceptances and promotions, broken down by race, over five or 10 years. In this way, he says, "you can examine the outcome of his equal employment opportunity procedures. . . . If there is not a gross disparity, that implies a proper relationship [in hiring patterns]."

He cites the example of the Office of Federal Contract Compliance Programs (OFCCP), which uses a statistical rule of thumb to decide when to investigate federal contractors for possible discrimination in hiring. It investigates a company only if the job acceptance rate among black applicants falls below 80 percent of the rate for whites. "Disparate impact analysis doesn't have to result in gross class action quotas," says Belz, who is the author of a recently published history of affirmative action called *Equality Transformed*.

But others suggest that five- or 10-year averages aren't as important to employers as the here and now, and it is difficult to escape the reality that employers often feel vulnerable to lawsuits when numerical standards are applied in affirmative action cases. "If employers can be dragged into court because of the racial body count among their employees," writes Thomas Sowell, a conservative black critic of affirmative action, "then they are going to save themselves megabucks in legal bills by hiring through quotas. There is nothing mysterious about that." [2]

### Do quotas affect minorities adversely by leaving questions about their professional worth?

Critics suggest that quotas undermine black people's self-esteem by leaving them always unsure about whether they gained a particular position on merit. Some also suggest the use of quotas can generate suspicions among whites that individual minority-group members didn't earn their way up the ladder even when they actually did.

"The logic of affirmative action is to categorize people as unable to compete without some kind of tilt on their side," Belz says. "It makes blacks seem to be unqualified and unable to compete and therefore just not up to snuff."

Even some blacks raise concerns about this psychological effect. Shelby Steele, professor of English at San Jose State University in California, suggests that when blacks acknowledge their race on an application form with the view that it could be used to grant preferential treatment, they enter into a Faustian bargain. "One of the most troubling effects of racial preferences for blacks is a kind of demoralization or . . . an enlargement of self-doubt," he says. "Under affirmative action the quality that earns us preferential treatment is implied inferiority." [3]

Roger Wilkins dismisses such views as "ahistorical." He says it is centuries of racism, not preferential treatment, that has undermined the self-esteem of American blacks. "If you're black in this country, you pay a psychic tax," he says. "It is significant, and it wasn't invented with affirmative action." He adds black people will have to grapple with these psychological pressures whether or not they get into, say, Berkeley. "I would rather have a guy feel bad with a degree from Berkeley than feel bad walking the streets with a high school diploma."

### In a society committed to equal opportunity, are there alternatives to affirmative action?

For traditional civil rights activists, the problems facing minorities in America stem from such deeply rooted causes that only strong remedies could make a difference. Thus, they argue, relaxing preferential hiring and numbers-oriented guidelines would amount to turning back the clock.

"Racism and sexism are so deep in this society that when you give people freedom of choice they just go back to doing that old, easy thing," says Wilkins. "You cannot rely on the good faith of white males, who are used to being privileged." He points to freedom-of-choice plans in the South, which were designed to produce integration but which failed for lack of commitment from the white power structure. White males, he says, "have to be held to standards, they have to be made to be accountable." And that isn't possible, he adds, without numerical guideposts.

Wilkins doesn't insist that every workplace reflect the precise proportion of minorities in the surrounding community. But if blacks constitute 8 percent of an area's work force, then an 8 percent goal for employers in that area isn't unreasonable. "If the efforts are really commendable and they still were able to find only two people they could hire, by me that would be fine," he says, adding his position calls for merely "some kind of tangible target plus some kind of demonstrated effort to meet that target."

But those who dispute the wisdom of quotas argue there are ways to ensure minority progress without them. Steele calls for a two-pronged social policy: the educational and economic development of disadvantaged people; and the eradication from society, through close monitoring and severe sanctions, of racial, ethnic or gender discrimination. In this view, color-blind programs to help the poor of all races and elimination of private-sector roadblocks to minority progress would be sufficient.

Others suggest greater self-help efforts among minority groups themselves. Roy L. Brooks, a black professor of law at the University of Minnesota, accepts affirmative action as it has evolved over the past 30 years, but he questions whether minorities can rely on government to erase racism. He calls on black Americans who have made it economically to devote themselves to programs aimed at helping poor blacks.[4]

Still others emphasize private-sector programs aimed at increasing the number of "employable" people in the work force. Clint Bolick, in a study of private companies he conducted for the Labor Department,[5] found "literally hundreds of companies" pursuing such efforts. He cites day-care programs, basic skill training, literacy training, transportation of inner-city workers to suburban jobs and the opening of training centers by companies in the inner city. "To me that is what affirmative action was originally intended to be," he says. And such actions, he adds, also are "synonymous with increasing productivity."

Indeed, some experts say the economic costs of quota-oriented programs are too high at a time when American business faces serious competitive pressures from abroad. However well intentioned, racial policies that hamper productivity only harm workers of all races by preventing job growth, these critics argue. "American business is already so burdened by litigation and antitrust action . . . ," says Nathan Glazer, "that a nondiscrimination requirement should not be turned into a pattern which simply . . . pushes the employer to develop a representative labor force . . . to avoid further litigation." ∎

# BACKGROUND

## Civil Rights Movement

The civil rights movement of the 1950s and '60s was born of the frustration of blacks over their lack of economic, educational and social progress in America since the end of the Civil War. The 13th Amendment to the Constitution, ratified in 1865, prohibited slavery, but it did not specify what civil rights the freed slaves were to enjoy.

That issue was addressed the following year by the nation's first Civil Rights Act. It declared that all individuals born or naturalized in the United States are U.S. citizens, with the exception of untaxed Indians. The law guaranteed all citizens the right to buy and sell real estate and other property and to enter into contracts, but it did not prohibit citizens from discriminating against one another. Neither did the 14th Amendment, ratified in 1868, which prohibits states from violating the rights of citizens by denying them equal protection under the law.

It would be nearly 70 years before the nation passed its first anti-discrimination law. The National Labor Relations Act of 1935 prohibited private employers from discriminating against members of labor unions. That law set the stage for the country's first measure banning racial discrimination — Executive Order 8802, issued by President Franklin D. Roosevelt in 1941.* It prohibited defense contractors and the federal government from discriminating against anyone on the basis of race, color, religion or national origin. President Roosevelt also set up the first federal agency responsible for measuring compliance with anti-discrimination measures, the Fair Employment Practices Commission.

Presidents Harry S Truman, Dwight D. Eisenhower and John F. Kennedy all issued executive orders expanding the anti-discrimination provisions introduced by Roosevelt. Their actions were prompted in large part by the growing civil rights movement, which gained support following the Supreme Court's 1954 ruling in *Brown v. Board of Education*, which banned school segregation, and the 1955 Montgomery bus boycott led by the Rev. Dr. Martin Luther King Jr.

The Civil Rights Act, drawn up during the Kennedy administration and signed into law in 1964 by President Lyndon B. Johnson, was the first major piece of legislation dealing with civil rights since 1866. It remains the principal body of law regarding racial discrimination today. The core section of the act regarding discrimination in hiring is Title VII, which outlaws employment discrimination on the basis of race, color, religion, sex or national origin by private employers and

Continued on p. 284

---

*Although executive orders do not require congressional approval, they have the full weight of law. They can, however, be rescinded by later presidents.

# Chronology

**1950s** *Civil rights movement springs from blacks' frustration over continuing obstacles to equal rights.*

### May 17, 1954
Supreme Court declares school segregation unconstitutional (*Brown v. Board of Education*).

———•———

**1960s** *Major anti-discrimination laws are enacted.*

### July 2, 1964
Congress passes the Civil Rights Act of 1964, the most far-reaching civil rights law ever to go into effect. Title VII of the act specifically addresses equal employment opportunity, outlawing employment practices that discriminate against individuals on the basis of race, color, religion, sex, or national origin. To enforce these provisions, the law creates the Equal Employment Opportunity Commission.

———•———

**1970s** *Affirmative action plans to promote the hiring of minorities and women become an increasing part of employment policies, prompting white men denied employment or admission to colleges and universities to charge "reverse discrimination."*

### March 8, 1971
Supreme Court adopts "disparate impact" analysis as a means of determining discrimination (*Griggs v. Duke Power Co.*). The ruling requires employers to demonstrate that employment tests and other criteria for hiring that result in unintentional discrimination are justified by business necessity.

### June 28, 1978
Supreme Court rules in its first "reverse discrimination" case (*Regents of the University of California v. Bakke*) that an affirmative action program that uses quotas for medical school admissions violates the Civil Rights Act of 1964. But the court also declares that admissions programs that consider race as one of a complex of factors involved in admissions decisions are not unconstitutional in and of themselves.

———•———

**1980s** *Reagan and Bush administrations try to reverse the trend in affirmative action toward numbers-oriented hiring and admissions practices. Supreme Court overturns previous rulings and restricts affirmative action plans.*

### June 11, 1984
Supreme Court upholds the seniority rights of white workers who charged that a court-ordered affirmative action promotion plan was discriminatory (*Firefighters Local Union No. 1794 v. Stoots*).

### Jan. 23, 1989
Supreme Court strikes down a minority set-aside program reserving a percentage of local government contracts for minority-owned firms (*City of Richmond v. J. A. Croson Company*).

### June 5, 1989
Supreme Court makes it more difficult for workers to prove racial discrimination by citing statistics that show a particular group is underrepresented in a particular work force (*Wards Cove Packing Co. v. Atonio*). Court issues other rulings that narrow the reach of anti-bias laws (*Patterson v. McLean Credit Union, Martin v. Wilks, Lorance v. AT&T Technologies, Independent Flight Attendants v. Zipes and Price Waterhouse v. Hopkins*).

———•———

**1990s** *Congress tries to pass new civil rights legislation that would close loopholes in the law opened by the 1989 Supreme Court rulings.*

### Oct. 22, 1990
President Bush vetoes the Civil Rights Act of 1990, saying it would force employers to adopt racial quotas to avoid discrimination lawsuits.

### Nov. 6, 1990
North Carolina's Republican Sen. Jesse Helms defeats Democratic challenger Harvey Gantt, a black politician from Charlotte. In the final days of the campaign, Helms pummelled Gantt with commercials showing a pair of white hands crumpling a rejection letter and suggesting the person had lost the job to a less qualified minority worker.

### 1991
Democrats reintroduce the Civil Rights Act (HR 1) with few modifications. Bush administration says the new bill, like its predecessor, is a quota bill and introduces its own civil rights legislation.

Continued from p. 282
unions with 25 or more employees or members. The law also established the Equal Employment Opportunity Commission (EEOC) to investigate and resolve discrimination complaints by individuals.

## Affirmative Action

When Congress passed the Civil Rights Act of 1964, it was generally believed that discrimination took place primarily through conscious, overt actions against individuals. But it quickly became apparent that the processes of discrimination were much more subtle and complex than originally envisioned. It was discovered that normal, seemingly neutral policies such as seniority, aptitude and personnel tests, high school diploma requirements and college admission tests could perpetuate the effects of past discrimination. This led to the development of the affirmative action concept.

The need for affirmative action was spelled out by President Johnson in a commencement address at Howard University on June 4, 1965. "Freedom is not enough," Johnson said. "You do not wipe out scars of centuries by saying, 'now you're free to go where you want and do as you desire.'"

The following September, Johnson issued Executive Order 11246 requiring federal contractors "to take affirmative action to ensure that applicants are employed ... without regard to their race, creed, color or national origin." * Every major contractor — one having more than 50 employees and a contract of $50,000 or more with the federal government — was required

---

*Executive Order 11246 was amended in 1967 to apply to sexual discrimination.

to submit a written affirmative action compliance program to the federal government.

The term "affirmative action," as originally used by President Johnson, meant that federal contractors would take steps to recruit workers, without discrimination. "[It] meant that one should not only not discriminate, but inform people one did not discriminate; not only treat those who applied for jobs without discrimination, but seek out those who might not apply," notes sociologist Nathan Glazer.[6]

In subsequent years, however, affirmative action came to mean something quite different. As a result of interpretations made in federal regulations and court rulings, federal contractors and private employers began to be required to take race (and gender) into account in their hiring and promotions. If their work forces were found to be racially imbalanced, the employers had to establish numerical "goals" to correct that imbalance, along with "timetables" for reaching the goals — and then to make "good faith" efforts to do so.

Critics said all this amounted to illegal racial quotas, but advocates of affirmative action denied this and insisted that, as Supreme Court Justice Harry A. Blackmun once put it, "In order to get beyond racism we must first take race into account."[7]

### Disparate Impact

The passage from a simple ban against discrimination to numerical standards intended to enforce that ban received further impetus from a 1971 Supreme Court decision, *Griggs v. Duke Power Co.* Black workers charged that the North Carolina power company had discriminated against them when the company required a high school diploma or the passing of a standardized general intelligence test as a condition for employment or

promotion. There was no evidence that the company intended to discriminate. But the requirements disqualified blacks at a substantially higher rate than whites and, the workers contended, were irrelevant to successful job performance.

The Supreme Court agreed. In a unanimous decision, the justices found that the job requirements were discriminatory because they had a "disparate impact" on one of the groups protected by Title VII of the Civil Rights Act. If a hiring practice "substantially" excludes people belonging to one of those groups, the justices ruled, the employer must demonstrate that the requirement has "a manifest relationship to the employment in question." As a result, employers were required to prove that tests or other means of selecting employees that had a discriminatory impact were justified by business necessity.

## Reverse Discrimination

The nation's colleges and universities also were under pressure to increase the number of women and minority students, particularly in graduate and professional schools. To meet these demands, many schools adopted preferential admissions programs favoring women and minority group members. That practice came under increasing attack in the 1970s. White applicants charged that they were being denied admission to universities in favor of less qualified minority applicants, making them victims of "reverse discrimination."

Among the schools adopting a preferential admissions policy was the University of Washington. In 1971 its law school received 1,600 applications for 150 openings. Among the applicants rejected was Marco DeFunis, a white Phi Beta

# Asian-American Quotas

As quotas of preference were gaining attention as a hot issue on American campuses, a new controversy began brewing over quotas of exclusion.

This controversy centers on allegations that some major universities and professional schools restrict the number of Asian-Americans they will admit. The issue has been getting increasing attention in Congress, governmental agencies and the news media. Asian-Americans, a fast-growing segment of the population and an increasingly influential one, complain that these maximum quotas violate the 1964 Civil Rights Act's prohibition of discrimination on the basis of race, color or national origin.

Responding to complaints, the U.S. Education Department's Office of Civil Rights in 1988 undertook an investigation of the admissions policies at UCLA and Harvard. The department declared last October that UCLA had indeed violated the civil rights of Asian-Americans who had applied to the university's graduate program in mathematics. This marked the first time a federal agency had found illegal discrimination against Asian-Americans in higher education.

The Asian-Americans' complaint against Harvard focused on the university's policy of granting preferential treatment in admissions to the children of alumni, or "legacies," and to outstanding athletes — two groups that contain few Asian-Americans. Last October the Education Department ruled that the consideration Harvard gives to legacies and to athletes is shared by many institutions and does not constitute illegal discrimination. It accepted Harvard's contention that some preference for legacies is necessitated by alumni-fundraising considerations.

This controversy comes at a time when the presence of Asian-Americans on college campuses is growing dramatically. In 1976, according to Don T. Nakanishi, a professor at UCLA's Graduate School of Education, there were 150,000 Asian-American undergraduates throughout the country. By 1986 the number had nearly tripled to 448,000.[†]

And Asian-Americans as a group accumulate relatively high grade averages in high school and score well on college entrance exams. The result has been that, by quantitative measurements, Asian-Americans compete powerfully for enrollment at America's most prestigious universities. And yet statistics indicate they are admitted at rates significantly below those of other groups.

At the heart of the controversy, some experts and commentators argue, is affirmative action programs aimed at aiding other minorities, such as blacks and Hispanics, who as groups don't score as high in high school grades or college entrance exams. In order to ensure positions for members of these groups, according to this view, college officials effectively place limits on Asian-Americans.

"You cannot have the statistical representation of all groups in proportion to their percentage of the population if you use performance as a criterion," argues Thomas Sowell, a black economist and a senior fellow at Stanford University's Hoover Institution. Thus, he says, college administrators hold back Asian-Americans in order to protect what they consider to be "their prerogative to mix and match different groups to present a pretty public relations picture."[††]

Sowell and others suggest such policies are akin to the practice of Harvard and other prestigious universities before World War II of placing a quota limit on admissions for Jews. "Asians have, in effect, inherited the anti-Semitic quotas of the past," Sowell says.

But some liberal commentators criticize conservatives for using the Asian-American admissions controversy as a rhetorical weapon against affirmative action programs. Referring to an ongoing debate over the issue at the University of California at Berkeley, syndicated columnist Clarence Page says, "The Berkeley problem was not 'reverse discrimination.' It was plain, old-fashioned discrimination of a sort affirmative action programs were intended to remedy, not create. The big difference this time is that it penalizes a people who have a reputation for over-achieving." [‡]

---

† Don T. Nakanishi, "A Quota on Excellence: The Asian American Admissions Debate," *Change*, November/December 1989, p. 39.

†† Thomas Sowell, "Quotas Against Asians," *New Dimensions*, December 1990.

‡ Quoted by Nakanishi, *op. cit.*, p. 41.

---

Kappa graduate of the university's undergraduate program. Among those admitted were 36 minority-group students whose grades and law school admission test scores were lower than those of DeFunis. The law school acknowledged that minority applicants had been judged separately. DeFunis sued, charging that he had been deprived of his constitutional right to equal protection under the law.

A trial court in Seattle agreed and ordered the school to enroll him. The university complied but appealed and the state Supreme Court, in 1973, ruled in favor of the school. DeFunis then appealed to the U.S. Supreme Court, and Justice William O. Douglas granted a stay that permitted him to remain in school pending a Supreme Court decision. But the court, by a 5-4 vote on April 23, 1974, refused to decide the case on the ground that the question was moot because DeFunis was about to graduate.

The issue of reverse discrimination came before the Supreme Court again in 1978. That case involved Allan Bakke, a 38-year-old white engineer who had been twice denied admission to the medical school at the University of California at Davis. To ensure minority representation in the student body, the university had set aside 16 seats in each 100-member medical school class for minority applicants. Each year that Bakke's application had been rejected, minority applicants with qualifications inferior to his had been accepted.

The Supreme Court, by a 5-4 vote, ruled in *Regents of the University of California v. Bakke* that state universities may not set aside a fixed quota of seats in each class for minority-group members, denying white applicants the opportunity to compete for those places. Bakke was ordered admitted to the medical school. But at the same time, the court also ruled that the equal protection clause of the 14th Amendment did not bar colleges from considering race as a factor in their admissions decisions.

## Debate and Controversy

Although it was not the only factor in the enormous progress African-Americans have made in the past half century, affirmative action has had an effect. There's been a marked increase in the number of blacks employed by firms and industries covered by the EEOC and a significant increase in the number of blacks holding professional and managerial jobs in these firms. From 1950 to 1980, the percentage of black men employed in profes-

sional and managerial positions tripled.[8] There has also been an increase in the number of blacks employed by federal contractors.

But while affirmative action greatly increased minority access to jobs, especially in the decade immediately after the 1964 civil rights law went into effect, it seems to have had less impact on minority

**Many civil rights organizations take a dim view of the Reagan administration's positions on minority issues. Some of that animosity has spilled over to the Bush administration.**

earnings. A study conducted by the Rand Corporation found that affirmative action "had no significant ... impact" on the closing of the wage gap between black and white males.[9] The gradual closing of the gap between the average income of black and white males that began after World War II continued at roughly the same pace after the Civil Rights Act was passed, the Rand researchers found. They attributed most of the decline in the wage gap to improved educational opportunities for minorities and the migration of black farm workers from the rural South to better-paying jobs in the industrial centers of the Northeast and Midwest.

Experts have also found that the principal beneficiaries of affirmative action have been those minorities who have already achieved a

high level of education and training. To unskilled blacks trapped in the underclass, however, affirmative action has meant virtually nothing. Clint Bolick of the Landmark Legal Foundation Center for Civil Rights doesn't find this surprising. "If you have a numerical goal, you're most likely to hire the most qualified member of the favored group that you can find," he says.

The failure of affirmative action to reach the most disadvantaged minorities may help explain the growing disparity in income between higher- and lower-income minorities since the 1960s. Between 1969 and 1984, for example, there was a significant increase both in the proportion of black men ages 25 to 55 earning over $30,000 a year and those earning less than $10,000 a year.[10]

### Reagan's Record

Critics of affirmative action found a champion in Ronald Reagan. Elected president in 1980 and again in 1984, Reagan adopted a conservative social agenda whose main emphasis was to shift as much responsibility as possible from the federal government to the states and localities. Reagan's agenda also envisioned a shift from coercive policies, such as affirmative action hiring programs, to volunteer efforts.

Reagan criticized affirmative action programs for attempting to shift the aim of anti-discrimination policy from equality of opportunity to equality of result.[11] William Bradford Reynolds, then assistant attorney general for civil rights, expressed the administration's position in September 1981, when he told the House Education and Labor Subcommittee on Employment Opportunities that the Justice Department "no longer will insist upon or in any respect support the use of quotas or any other numerical or statistical formulae designed to provide to non-victims of discrimination preferential treatment based on race, sex, national origin or religion." In the Justice Department's view, remedies for discrimination should go only to specific victims of past discrimination.

Others in the Reagan administration had a more positive view of affirmative action programs, however. Clarence Thomas, a black conservative appointed by Reagan to head the EEOC in 1982, criticized the Justice Department's efforts to eliminate quotas.

Thomas supported the use of numerical data as a useful standard for assuring compliance with Title VII. But under his direction, the agency shifted its focus from class action enforcement, involving large numbers of racial groups in single discrimination suits, to discrimination complaints filed by individuals.

Clint Bolick, who worked at the EEOC from 1986-87, says Thomas actually improved the use of statistics in affirmative action programs in federal agencies. Under the old system, Bolick explains, "you couldn't really tell whether the recent black hires were secretarial or shunted into specific jobs as often happens under numbers-oriented affirmative action." Thomas required the agencies to report exactly what they were doing to increase opportunities for minorities. Agencies could no longer satisfy their affirmative action requirements by simply "showing the right numbers," Bolick recalls. "The whole idea was . . . to get into more structural changes to produce more meaningful changes."

Thomas was not the only administration official to support affirmative action. When Reynolds and Attorney General Edwin Meese III in 1985 began pushing a proposal that President Reagan rewrite the 1965 executive order to combat discrimination by federal contractors so as to relax the affirmative action requirements, they ran into opposition from Secretary of Labor William E. Brock II, who told an NAACP national convention that he believed "the country would have to have some form of affirmative action for the foreseeable future." The Justice Department officials ultimately lost the battle over the executive order. Reagan never had it rewritten.

### Willie Horton

Nevertheless, many civil rights leaders and organizations take a dim view of the Reagan administration's positions on minority issues. Some of that animosity has spilled over to the Bush administration. "Since 1980, we've had two kinds of white leadership in the White House," says Roger Wilkins. "One was just flat-out bigoted, and that was Ronald Reagan. The other is fundamentally corrupt, and that's George Bush."

To illustrate his point, Wilkins recalls the 1988 presidential election campaign, when candidate Bush exploited the racial fears of white voters to help defeat Democrat Michael S. Dukakis. Bush repeatedly accused Dukakis of being soft on crime, citing as evidence Dukakis' decision while he was governor of Massachusetts to furlough Willie Horton, a black man who was serving a sentence for murder. Horton escaped while out on furlough; he was caught after he raped a Maryland woman and stabbed her boyfriend.

But race was not the only factor that made the Willie Horton issue so powerful. "Republican strategists recognized that the furloughing of Willie Horton epitomized an evolution of the far-reaching rights movement," writes journalist Thomas Edsall, "an evolution resented and disapproved of by significant numbers of voters. These voters saw crime as one of a number of social and moral problems aggravated by liberalism. . . . 'Crime' became a shorthand signal . . . for broader issues of social disorder, evoking powerful ideas about authority, status, morality, self-control, and race." [12]

### Scholarship Policy

The Bush administration, like its predecessor, also has come under fire from civil rights groups for taking the position that civil rights measures should be "colorblind" and "race-neutral." This "has resulted in continuing hostility to any measures — either in legislative proposals or litigation — that incorporate race- or gender-conscious remedies or require affirmative relief," notes a recent report by the Citizens' Commission on Civil Rights, a bipartisan group of former officials who have served in the federal government in positions with responsibility for equal opportunity. [13]

Last December, an administration official attempted to apply the administration's colorblind theory to civil rights policy. Michael L. Williams, assistant secretary of Education for civil rights, declared that scholarships reserved for members of minority groups could not legally be offered by colleges and universities that receive federal aid. Race-based scholarships have long been used by many institutions to help diversify their student bodies. The policy announcement apparently caught the White House off guard. When civil rights organizations and many news organizations denounced the change, the administration said the targeted scholarships would be allowed if they were funded by private sources rather than from university funds.

## Supreme Court Rulings

The main setbacks to the civil rights movement's agenda in recent years have come arguably from the Supreme Court, not the White House. In 1989 alone, the court issued seven rulings that made it harder to prove job discrimination and easier to challenge affirmative action programs. Civil rights advocates refer to the rulings, which are described below, as the "civil rights massacre of 1989."

■ **City of Richmond v. J. A. Croson Company**. The court struck down a Richmond, Va., affirmative action plan that set aside 30 percent of the dollar amount of city construction contracts for minority-owned firms. Writing for the majority, Justice Sandra Day O'Connor said the city had failed to provide any evidence of any "identified discrimination" in the Richmond construction industry, and so had failed to demonstrate a "compelling interest" that would justify such a race-based remedy. "While there is no doubt that the sorry history of both private and public discrimination in this country has contributed to a lack of opportunities for black entrepreneurs," the court said, "this observation, standing alone, cannot justify a rigid racial quota in the awarding of public contracts in Richmond, Va."

■ **Wards Cove Packing Co v. Atonio**. The court ruled that it was up to the plaintiffs in Title VII cases to prove that an employer had no legitimate business reason for employment practices that had an adverse "disparate impact" on women and minorities. The decision involving Alaskan cannery workers effectively overturned the standard in effect since the 1971 *Griggs* ruling. In that decision, the court held that violations of Title VII could be established through statistical evidence showing that personnel prac-

tices had an adverse effect on minorities, even if there was no proof an employer intended to discriminate. In *Wards Cove*, the court not only shifted the burden of proof to the plaintiff, it also ruled that statistics showing even dramatic racial imbalances in job categories were not enough to prove discrimination. It said plaintiffs must prove, instance by instance, that particular employment practices had a discriminatory effect.*

■ **Martin v. Wilks**. The court held that white firefighters in Birmingham, Ala., could challenge a court-approved consent decree that black firefighters had negotiated with the city and a county personnel board. The consent decree included goals for hiring and promoting blacks. The defendants argued that the interests of the white firefighters had already been adequately considered before the consent decree went into effect, but the court ruled that because the white plaintiffs were not a party to the consent decree, they had the right to bring a discrimination suit on their own behalf.

■ **Patterson v. McLean Credit Union**. In this case, the court ruled that the Civil Rights Act of 1866, which protects the rights of U.S. citizens to enter into contracts, could be used as the basis for monetary-damage suits challenging a hiring agreement, but that it had no applicability once an individual was on the job. In those situations, a plaintiff has to use Title VII, which permits injunctive relief and back pay, but no monetary damages.

---

*The *Wards Cove* case involved complaints brought by minority workers at two salmon canneries in Alaska. Jobs at the plants were divided into those on the cannery line, which were low-paid and low-skilled positions, and "non-cannery jobs," which fell into a variety of skilled-job classifications and paid more than the cannery jobs. The cannery jobs were filled mainly by non-whites — Filipinos and Alaska Natives. The non-cannery jobs were filled predominantly by whites.

■ **Price Waterhouse v. Hopkins**. The court ruled once a worker proved sex discrimination played a part in an adverse employment decision, the employer had to prove the same decision would have been made in the absence of such bias.

■ **Lorance v. AT&T Technologies**. The court ruled that a seniority plan could not be challenged as "intentionally discriminatory" unless complaints were filed within 300 days of when the plan was adopted, even if workers were not sure by then whether they were adversely affected.

■ **Independent Federation of Flight Attendants v. Zipes**. This ruling made it more difficult for parties who prevail in job-discrimination suits to collect attorneys' fees.

The overall impact of these decisions was to restrict the ability of plaintiffs to bring job-discrimination complaints.

## 1990 Civil Rights Bill

The Civil Rights Act of 1990 was designed to counter the impact of the 1989 Supreme Court rulings. One of its key provisions would have returned to the employer the burden of proving that a practice with a disparate impact on minorities and women was necessary to the business. This provision, which was designed to counter the *Wards Cove* decision, would have allowed employee-plaintiffs to establish that a practice had a disparate impact without pinpointing the specific cause of the discrimination. The bill also would have allowed money damages for women who were victims of job bias, similar to remedies for racial minorities allowed under current law.

President Bush said he wanted to

*Continued on p. 290*

# "Race-Norming" Could Be Political Bombshell in 1992

I f Republican office-seekers were able to benefit last year from President Bush's denunciation of the Democratic Civil Rights Act as a "quota bill," they may well turn to an even more effective weapon in 1992. "Race-norming," the little-known practice of weighting test results on the basis of race and ethnic origin, promises to reap big dividends for Republicans on the lookout for swing votes among white and Asian-American workers.

Race-norming is currently used by state employment services that administer the General Aptitude Test Battery (GATB) to screen some 20 million job applicants each year before referring them to private employers. This standardized test, the most widely used employment test in the country, is used as a predictor of future job performance.

All applicants take the same test; it is the results of the test that are subjected to race-norming, which works like this. Imagine four job-seekers who apply for work at a state employment agency — a black, a Hispanic, a white and an Asian-American. All four score in the 50th percentile of the GATB. But an employer who wants to fill a new opening will receive from the agency a referral list with the following final scores: the black applicant, 84; the Hispanic, 66; the white and the Asian-American, 50. Because blacks and Hispanics historically have scored lower on the GATB and other standardized tests, their test results are subjected to "within-group scoring," by which they are compared with the results of other blacks or Hispanics rather than with the wider universe of all applicants.

Because the employer would, on the basis of the test alone, naturally hire the highest-scoring applicant, the practice of race-norming has been praised by affirmative action supporters for helping to integrate blacks and Hispanics into the work force. Critics say race-norming amounts to racial quotas and promotes reverse discrimination against whites and Asian-Americans.

Race-norming has its roots in the 1971 Supreme Court ruling in *Griggs v. Duke Power Co.*, which expanded the definition of discrimination to comprise the notion of "disparate impact." Under this definition, employers are held responsible for showing that hiring practices that result in disparate impact on minorities in the surrounding community are required by business necessity. To help employers meet the new requirements, the Labor Department's Employment Service began in 1981 to encourage state employment agencies to use the race-norming technique in determining final scores on the GATB, which the service developed in the late 1940s for vocational counseling and job referral in state employment agencies.

The GATB is not the only employment test whose results are race-normed. In 1976, the testing firm of E. F. Wonder-lic & Associates Inc., of Northfield, Ill., introduced a test for employers themselves to use for a wide array of job applicants, from unskilled laborers to engineers. Final scores are race-normed for a broader range of racial and ethnic categories than the GATB: Caucasian, Negro, Spanish Surnamed, Oriental and American Indian. In a letter to private employers dated May 1976, the firm promoted its Wonderlic Personnel Test citing its approval by the Labor Department's Office of Federal Contract Compliance and concluded in a P.S.: "Select to fill proper ratios and quotas. Select the best-suited individuals by ethnic class."

The Reagan administration, which disapproved of affirmative action programs resulting in quotas, took steps to discontinue the practice. In November 1986, the Justice Department ordered the Labor Department Employment Service to cease and desist from encouraging race-norming, saying the practice was in violation of the 1964 Civil Rights Act barring discrimination in employment. The service responded by promising not to expand its efforts to race-norm the GATB, pending a review of the practice's effects which was commissioned to the National Research Council, a branch of the National Academy of Sciences. The council completed its review in 1989, concluded that the test puts blacks and Hispanics at a disadvantage and recommended that race-norming of GATB scores for these two groups be continued.†

The Bush administration, in formulating its alternative to the Civil Rights Act of 1991 (HR 1), refrained from specifically prohibiting race-norming. It did, however, invite congressional Republicans to do so. Henry J. Hyde, R-Ill., offered an amendment to HR 1 banning the practice that the House Judiciary Committee rejected March 19. On Feb. 22, Sen. Alan K. Simpson, R-Wyo., introduced a separate bill, the Civil Rights Amendments of 1991 (S 478), that bans race-norming. That bill, reported to the Senate Labor and Human Resources Committee, has yet to be acted on.

Like racial hiring quotas, the race-norming issue promises to be a political football in the upcoming election campaigns. When race-norming was explained to them, 77 percent of the respondents to a poll conducted March 19-24 by Market Opinion Research, a Republican polling firm, said they oppose the practice. Only 16 percent said they approved. Republicans can expect to benefit from the public's disdain for the practice because they have been more outspoken in their opposition to numerical goals and timetables in affirmative action programs.

---

† John A. Hartigan and Alexandra K. Wigdor, eds., *Fairness in Employment Testing: Validity Generalization, Minority Issues, and the General Aptitude Test Battery* (1989).

Continued from p. 288

sign a civil rights bill — he even submitted his own proposal. But the president insisted he would veto any bill that led to hiring quotas. Bush, his allies on Capitol Hill, and the business community contended that if standards established by the Supreme Court for a defense of employment practices were reversed, companies would adopt hiring and promotion quotas for women and minorities in order to avoid discrimination lawsuits. Proponents of the measure insisted it had nothing to do with quotas and would not encourage them. They also were confident that President Bush would not risk the political cost of vetoing a civil rights measure in an election year.

After months of debate, the House and Senate approved the Democratic bill by strong majorities Oct. 16-17, but not the two-thirds needed to override Bush's anticipated veto. The veto came Oct. 22. "I deeply regret having to take this action . . . ," Bush said. "But when our efforts, however, well intentioned, result in quotas, equal opportunity is not advanced but thwarted." Two days later, the Senate failed by one vote to override the veto.

### 1990 Elections

President Bush was not the only politician to use the quota issue in 1990. David Duke, a former Ku Klux Klan leader, made quotas a central theme of his campaign to unseat Sen. J. Bennett Johnston, D.-La. Although Duke lost the election, he won about 60 percent of the white vote in the state's October primary. The quota issue also came up in the California governor's race between Dianne Feinstein, the former Democratic mayor of San Francisco, and Pete Wilson, then the state's Republican senator.

During the Democratic gubernatorial primary, Feinstein said she would be willing to appoint women and minorities to state jobs on the basis of their gender and race. Wilson used the issue against her in a series of ads in the fall campaign. Although the issue had faded by Election Day, political observers believe it contributed to her defensive posture through much of the campaign. Wilson won, 49-46 percent.[14]

The quota issue played a more significant role in North Carolina, where Republican Sen. Jesse Helms was elected to a fourth term by defeating black Democratic challenger Harvey Gantt. Gantt had maintained a narrow lead in the polls until November, but Helms won by 52 percent of the vote. Although many observers think Helms would have won anyway, they don't diminish the importance of the hard-hitting quota ad Helms put on the air in the final week of the campaign. In it, a pair of white hands crumple a rejection letter while the narrator says: "You needed that job, and you were the best qualified. But they had to give it to a minority because of a racial quota. Is that really fair?" The quota ad, writes Congressional Quarterly Deputy Political Editor Ronald D. Elving, "may have crystallized in seconds what Helms had been trying to do for months: depict Gantt as a threat to the average Carolinian's values." [15] ■

# CURRENT SITUATION

## Turning Point

Last year marked a turning point in race relations in the United States. President Bush's veto of the 1990 civil rights bill and national press coverage of the North Carolina Senate race helped bring to the surface racial tensions that had been brewing for many years. Bush's attacks on quotas and his call for "color-blind" civil rights policies gave vent to the resentments felt by many whites who opposed quotas as being unfair but who had restrained their open criticism for fear of being branded as racists. With the ideological imprimatur offered by the White House, these resentments — and those of minorities who came to feel their hard-won battle for equal opportunity was threatened — came more freely to the surface.

They are seen today across the country in the debates over preferential college admissions, in minority-group pressures to shift the focus of academic study away from traditional Western civilization courses and more toward "multiculturalism," and in controversies over hiring and promotions. But the main focus is in Congress, where supporters of affirmative action are pushing a new version of the bill vetoed by President Bush in 1990. Their aim is to protect the gains made by the civil rights movement from erosion by the 1989 Supreme Court rulings and by the growing white resentment over affirmative action. Looming over the entire struggle is the 1992 presidential and congressional elections, which could be powerfully affected by the debate over quotas.

## 1991 Civil Rights Bill

Following Bush's veto of the 1990 civil rights proposal, congressional Democrats made the law's passage their top domestic priority for 1991. They reintroduced the measure as the first proposal in the House to give it the symbolically important title of HR 1. The bill's sponsors strengthened language aimed at circumventing the Bush administration's "quota bill" rhetoric. Section 13 of HR 1 explicitly states that "nothing in the amendments made by this Act shall be construed to require or encourage an employer to adopt hiring or promotion quotas on the basis of race, color, religion, sex or national origin." Also, to maximize white support for the proposal, the bill's sponsors are emphasizing its importance for the advancement of equal opportunity for women.

Once again, the Bush administration has proposed a civil rights law of its own (HR 1375, S 611). It differs from the Democratic version in two main respects. The first concerns limits on punitive damages women can collect for intentional discrimination. The Democratic bill would place no limits, citing the lack of such limits for minorities under the 1866 Civil Rights Act. The more restrictive administration bill would place a $150,000 cap on damage awards.

The second major difference regards the old question of business necessity as defined by the Supreme Court in *Griggs* and then revised in *Wards Cove*. Once again, the Democratic proposal states that business practices that have unintentional discriminatory effects are permissible only if they "bear a significant relationship to successful performance of the job." And once again, the Republicans say that language will force employers to impose hiring quotas to ward off lawsuits.

The two versions differ in some less critical respects also. One involves the right to sue in discrimination cases, which the administration would limit in an effort to reduce litigation. Under the Republican proposal, plaintiffs would be allowed to bring suit only after they have made an unsuccessful attempt to resolve their disagreement through arbitration. Democrats respond that such binding arbitration effectively denies employees their right to sue. Finally, the Democratic proposal would ban discrimination in employment even when the employer's action was motivated by other concerns. The Republican bill would permit such unintentional discrimination if the employer can demonstrate that the discriminatory action was motivated by other reasons.

### Power Shift

The Bush administration and Republicans in Congress have the upper hand in the current legislative struggle over civil rights. Republicans' successful exploitation of Bush's "quota bill" label of last year's civil rights measure during last fall's election campaigns demonstrated a visible shift in public attitudes toward affirmative action. And that shift has come among a key segment of the population — blue-collar and lower-middle-class whites. Because Democrats have long depended upon these groups for their own political support, Republicans are discovering they can use the quota issue to drive a wedge into the Democratic Party, dividing the party's black voters from much of its white constituency. Swing votes by white Democrats lured away from their traditional party by the quota issue may provide many Republicans, including George Bush, a ticket to office.

As Republicans have run away with the quota issue, the Democrats themselves are left to defend the traditional approach toward civil rights. While they argue that there is nothing in HR 1 that would produce quotas, they also continue to defend the need for legislation that will level the playing field for minorities and right the wrongs they have suffered in the past.

The Democrats' principal ally in this campaign is the Leadership Conference on Civil Rights, a broad coalition of groups representing minorities, women, senior citizens, religious organizations and the disabled — in short, all the classes of citizens protected from discrimination by Title VII of the 1964 Civil Rights Act. The Leadership Conference comprises most of the organizations that make up the traditional civil rights movement. However, opinion surveys seem to confirm what key Republican victories last fall suggested, that these groups are losing support among key segments of white voters.

Celinda Lake, a pollster with Greenberg-Lake, a Washington-based firm that conducts opinion surveys for Democrats, says nationwide studies she has conducted over the past 10 years clearly show this trend. "There is broad-based support for norms of equality, equal opportunity and non-discrimination," Lake says. However, "voters are not always clear that the civil rights movement is advocating those broad norms. The key here for the civil rights movement is to demonstrate its broad-based support for non-discrimination." While they may not understand all the details involved in affirmative action programs, Lake says, voters are clear about where they draw the line. "They want measures that fight discrimination, they want measures that can include themselves when they are discriminated against, and they don't want quotas."

With the civil rights movement under fire and support for HR 1 in question among voters, congressional Democrats are in a quandary. On the one hand, they have made the Civil Rights Act of 1991 their top domestic priority. They have tried to steer clear of the quota label by emphasizing the bill's specific language denying it is intended to promote quota hiring. They have also tried to broaden the bill's appeal by stressing its expansion of equal opportunity for women, regardless of race. But there is evidence that the Democrats are not jumping into the fray with the same enthusiasm as they did last fall. In the Senate, for example, Democrats have yet to even offer companion legislation to HR 1.

Another sign of division in Democratic ranks came at a meeting of the Democratic Leadership Council (DLC) in Cleveland earlier this month. Black delegates were angry that the group, created in 1985 by moderate, mostly Southern Democrats, had not invited civil rights leader Jesse Jackson to speak. They also were unhappy about a resolution adopted by the DLC renouncing quotas.

### *Business Group Backs Out*

Another sign the 1991 civil rights bill may be in trouble came with the collapse of talks between big business and civil right groups that many had hoped would produce a compromise bill both sides could live with. Representatives of The Business Roundtable, a group representing the nation's largest corporations, and the Leadership Conference on Civil Rights reportedly were nearing agreement on some of the most controversial elements of the Democratic bill, including unlimited damage awards to women who are victims of intentional discrimination. But the Roundtable pulled out of the talks April 19 under pressure from the White House.

White House Chief of Staff John H. Sununu and counsel C. Boyden Gray had long pressed the business executives to support the administration's civil rights bill. "I don't

need . . . the grief I and my company are taking," AT&T Chairman Robert Allen said in announcing his withdrawal from the negotiations.

Representatives of small business also were opposed to a negotiated settlement that would have eased passage of HR 1. David K. Rehr, chief House lobbyist for the National Federation of Independent Business, says small businesses would find it more difficult than large corporations to handle the bill's complicated anti-discrimination rules. "If you pass HR 1," he says, "small-business owners . . . will make a rational, economic calculation to avoid being taken to court. And therefore they will hire by a quota."

## Campus Turmoil

While policy-makers in Washington continue the debate over racial quotas in employment, many college and university administrators are facing deepening racial tensions on their campuses. Some of the tensions can be traced to academic affirmative action programs. In much the same way employers seek to integrate their payrolls, colleges and universities actively recruit minority applicants, offer special scholarships to members of certain racial or ethnic groups and grant minorities preferential treatment by lowering standardized test requirements for these groups. Opponents of these practices say they unfairly discriminate against white students.

Resentment over quota-based affirmative action policies exploded into a heated debate at Georgetown University's Law Center in April, when a white student published an article in the campus newspaper decrying the admissions department's policy of admitting minority stu-

dents with lower test scores and grades than white students.[16] Georgetown, one of the most prestigious law schools in the country, has an 11 percent black enrollment, one of the highest in the country.

The campus's Black Law Student Association denounced the article for insinuating that minority students are less qualified than whites. "I think people have been internalizing . . . feelings of subtle racism for a long time," said association member Caroline Smith. "That is why the [article] had so much impact." [17]

### *Political Correctness*

The situation at Georgetown is not unique. Reports of intolerance, sexual harassment, as well as racist and anti-Semitic acts are on the increase at campuses throughout the United States. Some commentators say these events are partly the result of the diversity among student populations that affirmative action programs have sought to promote.

Dinesh D'Souza, an analyst at the conservative American Enterprise Institute for Public Policy Research, presents this argument in his controversial book, *Illiberal Education*.[18] D'Souza argues that lowering test requirements or otherwise offering preferential treatment to certain groups of applicants has produced a feeling of victimization among blacks, women and other beneficiaries of affirmative action in colleges and universities. This feeling makes them identify ever more closely with their group, he maintains, defying one of the main aims of affirmative action.

The outburst of racial resentments at Georgetown should also be viewed in the context of a spreading intellectual current on American campuses. Over the past decade, while the political mainstream in the Unites States was moving to the right, there was growing

*Continued on p. 294*

# At Issue:

## Is President Bush justified in calling the Democrat-sponsored civil rights bill a "quota bill?"

JOHN R. DUNNE

*U.S. Assistant Attorney General, Civil Rights Division.*
FROM TESTIMONY BEFORE THE JUDICIARY SUBCOMMIT-
TEE ON CIVIL AND CONSTITUTIONAL RIGHTS ON THE
CIVIL RIGHTS ACT OF 1991, FEB. 7, 1991.

*t*he Administration remains committed — as I know all of the members of this subcommittee do — to the elimination of barriers to equal employment opportunity grounded in race, color, religion, sex, and national origin, as well as disability and age. Disagreements with the last Congress were not over this goal, but how to achieve it. As it did last Congress, the Administration supports legislation that will provide adequate remedies for all forms of discrimination. It remains steadfast in its view, and this continues to be a high priority for our Nation. . . .

The President remains steadfast as well, however, in his opposition to the legislation he was compelled to veto last year. As the President said in his veto message, that legislation was returned to Congress because "[d]espite the use of the term 'civil rights' . . . the bill employs a maze of highly legalistic language to introduce the destructive force of quotas into our Nation's employment system. . . ."

Unfortunately, H.R. 1 is nearly identical to — and in at least one respect more troublesome than — that legislation. There are no provisions in H.R. 1 which respond to the President's objections; in fact, this bill is even more of an engine of litigation for lawyers at the expense of conciliation, settlement and harmony in the workplace than its predecessor. H.R. 1 is not legislation the Administration can support. . . .

Let me reiterate for the Administration . . .: we will not accept a bill that results in quotas or other unfair preferences. Such quotas are not only unfair; they are counterproductive. This Administration understands the crucial difference between inclusive affirmative action to cast the recruitment net as widely as possible, which helps overcome the effects of discrimination, and rote adherence to racial and ethnic quotas — a pernicious practice which provides at most a Pyrrhic victory even for those who temporarily benefit.

Quotas are not the antidote to racism and discrimination. At its core, quota hiring is decision making based upon one's status in a particular class, rather than upon one's individual ability. . . . Our goal ought to be an equal opportunity society, and that is not achieved when we predetermine the results. In the words of the President: "Our war against discrimination is impeded, not advanced, by a bill that encourages the adoption of quotas."

CITIZENS' COMMISSION ON CIVIL RIGHTS

*Bipartisan group of former government officials that monitors civil rights policies.*
FROM *LOST OPPORTUNITIES: THE CIVIL RIGHTS RECORD OF THE BUSH ADMINISTRA-TION MID-TERM*, 1991.

*t*he proposed Civil Rights Act of 1990 provided the first major test of the civil rights policies of the Bush Administration. The Act was designed to reverse the serious damage done to federal civil rights laws by a series of 1989 Supreme Court decisions and to strengthen civil rights remedies. Despite significant bipartisan backing and repeated efforts to obtain Administration support, however, the Act was opposed and ultimately vetoed by President Bush, making him only the third President in United States history — following Andrew Johnson and Ronald Reagan — to veto civil rights legislation. The Administration's rhetoric in opposing the bill, moreover, not only mischaracterized the legislation, but has also fanned the flames of racial intolerance and division. In short, the Bush Administration has failed its first critical test on civil rights. . . .

Despite the urging of key Republican legislators, a Cabinet member, the Chairman of the U.S. Commission on Civil Rights, and other high Administration officials, President Bush vetoed the Act in October, after it had been passed by significant bipartisan majorities. In vetoing the bill, the President relied on the same misleading label his Administration had used throughout the debate over the bill — that the bill would require employers to adopt hiring "quotas." The Senate failed by a single vote to override the veto.

Just as disturbing as the Administration's actions was its rhetoric. The Administration's primary argument has been the claim that the Act, particularly its sections remedying the effect of [the Supreme Court's ruling in] *Wards Cove,* would cause employers to adopt job quotas. This assertion is flatly contradicted by the language of the bill itself, by the many quota opponents who support the Act, and by the fact that the Act would simply restore the principles of [the Supreme Court's ruling in] *Griggs,* which was the law for 18 years and never produced such results. Despite its inaccuracy, however, the quota claim has sparked racial divisiveness. . . . It suggests a willingness by the Administration to exploit code words and racial division for purposes of political gain.

Continued from p. 292

support in the faculties of many colleges and universities for a radical movement to supplant the teaching of classics reflecting the accumulated wisdom of Western, or white, culture, with texts representing other cultures. Supporters of "multiculturalism," as this movement is known, promoted the creation of new disciplines, such as women's studies and African-American history, to achieve on the intellectual level what affirmative action was intended to achieve in employment — better integration of minorities into positions of power in American society. But D'Souza and other critics of multiculturalism say the movement has produced an intolerance of traditional Western values and polarized faculties and students between the "politically correct" supporters of multiculturalism and defenders of traditional curricula who often are branded as racists for their views.

### Newspaper Dispute

Colleges and universities aren't the only organizations feeling the heat for adopting quota-based affirmative action programs. A major controversy erupted at the *Philadelphia Inquirer* earlier this year when the daily newspaper announced it would adopt hiring quotas for its newsroom. Editor Maxwell King said the objective was to boost the newsroom's minority presence from 13 percent to 18 percent and the proportion of women from 33 percent to 49 percent.

Many black reporters were elated by the policy, but anger quickly welled up among some whites. One white male reporter said he was "angry about being stereotyped as a [member of] a group that some seem to feel is responsible for . . . all the evils of society." The reporter added, "What was supposed to be a plan to bring us together is instead pulling us apart." [19]

Amid the subsequent controversy, Inquirer editors backed away from the "quota" label and called the numerical goals "objectives." Said Managing Editor James M. Naughton, "It was never regarded as a quota that would be met come hell or high water." [20] ∎

# OUTLOOK

## Conservative Populism

The struggle over the 1991 civil rights bill marks a new phase in the civil rights movement. Until recently, few Republicans dared to stand in the way of anti-discrimination measures. To do so meant risking charges of racism from Democrats, the traditional champions of civil rights laws and affirmative action programs. But today it is the Democrats who are on the defensive. Many voters now see them as the party of special interests, not as the defender of the average working man and woman.

The Republican Party, on the other hand, is successfully portraying itself as the champion of a new color-blind fairness. Republican strategists, writes journalist Tom Edsall, are establishing a new and evolving ideology: "conservative egalitarianism, opposed to preferences whether for blacks, unions, or any other liberal interest. Liberal Democratic support for preferential hiring . . . has enabled a conservative Republican Party to lay claim to the cause of equal opportunity, once the rallying cry of the civil-rights movement." [21]

Both Republicans and Democrats are viewing the intensifying debate over civil rights and quotas through the prism of next year's elections. As the 1990 midterm contests showed, the quota issue evokes strong emotions. Some Democrats have accused the Bush administration of using the civil rights bill to scare white voters. The temptation to use the quotas issue as a campaign theme is likely to intensify if the recession continues. In hard economic times, competition for employment grows, creating an atmosphere in which the quota issue can more readily be exploited to capture white votes.

Even some Democratic supporters of HR 1 acknowledge that there is little popular support for their legislation, even among the people who stand to benefit from it — minorities and women. The reason, they say, is that the legislation is couched in legal terms that do not lend themselves to campaign rhetoric. "The Civil Rights Act actually has nothing to do with quotas," says Ralph G. Neas, executive director of the Leadership Conference on Civil Rights. "It has a lot to do with just about every working American family in this country. But the burden is on us to articulate our positive measures as well as underscore our opposition to quotas. Our side has got to do a much more aggressive job in articulating that."

### Legislative Prospects

It's still not clear whether the Democrats will be able to bring big business back into the negotiations over the civil rights bill. Some members of The Business Roundtable have expressed interest in resuming negotiations with civil rights advocates, but that is not expected to happen before the House votes on the bill. "The reason," says one participant in the failed negotiations who spoke on condition he not be identified, is that conservative Republicans in the House "do not want a bill enacted into law. They want a campaign issue." This source, who supports HR 1, expresses optimism that the House will overcome the opposition of conservative Republicans and pass the measure by the end of May. Once it passes the House, he predicts, Senate Democrats will submit a comparable proposal.

If the House does pass a civil rights bill, The Business Roundtable may then re-enter negotiations to reach compromise language for the measure. Because there is less pressure on the Senate side, even among conservative Republicans, to reject the bill out of hand, the ultimate prospects for the bill's enactment would likely improve during Senate deliberation of the measure.

"We were within days of making a joint recommendation to Congress and the president" before the talks broke down last month, the participant says. "We had made enormous progress on non-monetary damages issues and were about to agree on monetary issues." If the business community and civil rights organizations could agree on acceptable terms for legislation, the White House might be more reluctant to veto the measure.

If optimistic supporters are correct, the Senate will take up the measure in June or July and the Civil Rights Act, as amended to reflect corporate leaders' interests, could be approved by Congress by August. On the other hand, the Bush administration has demonstrated its ability and willingness to derail progress in these negotiations. Whether it will decide to do so again in an attempt to gain passage of its own civil rights measure or to use the failure of HR 1 as a way to pursue the quota issue into next year's election campaign, remains to be seen.

## Quotas and the Courts

Following its series of rulings on affirmative action in 1989, the Supreme Court may refrain from acting on cases involving employment discrimination or quotas until Congress and the White House agree on new legislation. "The court was extremely active for several years on this issue," says Clint Bolick of the conservative Landmark Legal Foundation Center for Civil Rights. "It thinks it has framed the applicable rules now and probably will not be active for the next several years in that area unless it appears there are more problems."

But in the longer run, Bolick predicts, the Supreme Court, now dominated by conservative justices appointed by Presidents Reagan and Bush, will likely strike down racial preference systems. "This court does not believe there are differences among types of discrimination cases, and so they would be as willing to strike down a preference in favor of minorities as they would discrimination against minorities," Bolick says. "The court is taking a very dim view of racial preferences generally, and that has improved the prospects for successful reverse discrimination lawsuits around the country."

While the Supreme Court is expected to step back from the issue of employment discrimination until new civil rights legislation takes effect, it is turning toward desegregation in education, an area it has not been active in for a decade. The court recently accepted a case involving desegregation decrees in higher education. At issue is whether colleges should maintain racial preference systems in student admissions once they have eliminated their prior discriminatory policies, or whether quotas are still needed to undo the damage caused by past discrimination. Desegrega-

tion cases such as these, Bolick predicts, represent the "next generation of civil rights cases." ■

## Notes

[1] Silberman spoke before the Equal Employment Advisory Council on Feb. 28, 1991.
[2] Thomas Sowell, "The Un-Quota," *The Richmond Times-Dispatch*, April 14, 1991.
[3] Shelby Steele, *The Content of Our Character* (1990), p. 116.
[4] See Roy L. Brooks, *Rethinking the American Race Problem* (1990).
[5] Clint Bolick, *Opportunity 2000: Creative Affirmative Action Strategies for a Changing Work Force*, 1987.
[6] Nathan Glazer, *Affirmative Discrimination* (1975), p. 58.
[7] Quoted in U.S. House Committee on Education and Labor, *A Report of the Study Group on Affirmative Action to the House Committee on Education and Labor*, August 1987, p. 33.
[8] See Frank Levy, *Dollars and Dreams: The Changing American Income Distribution* (1987), p. 134.
[9] James P. Smith and Finis R. Welch, *Closing the Gap: Forty Years of Economic Progress for Blacks*, The Rand Corporation, February 1986, p. xxi.
[10] Levy, *op. cit.*, p. 140.
[11] See John L. Palmer, ed., *Perspectives on the Reagan Years* (1986), pp. 12-13.
[12] Thomas Byrne Edsall and Mary D. Edsall, "Race," *The Atlantic*, May 1991, p. 77.
[13] Citizens' Commission on Civil Rights, *Lost Opportunities: The Civil Rights Record of the Bush Administration Mid-Term*, 1991, p. 3.
[14] *Congressional Quarterly Weekly Report*, Feb. 9, 1991, pp. 368-369.
[15] *Ibid.*, p. 369.
[16] Timothy Maguire, "Admissions Apartheid," *Law Weekly*, April 8, 1991.
[17] Quoted in *The Washington Post*, April 16, 1991.
[18] Dinesh D'Souza, *Illiberal Education: The Politics of Race and Sex on Campus* (1991).
[19] Quoted in *The Washington Post*, Feb. 26, 1991.
[20] Quoted in *The Washington Post*, April 14, 1991.
[21] Edsall, *op. cit.*, p. 54.

# Bibliography

## Selected Sources Used

## Books

**Belz, Herman, *Equality Transformed: A Quarter-Century of Affirmative Action*, Transaction Publishers, 1991.**

Belz, a professor of American constitutional history at the University of Maryland, examines the development of affirmative action after the Civil Rights Act of 1964. From a policy to prevent discrimination, he writes, affirmative action has evolved into a system of preferences, goals and timetables that undermine the policy's original purpose.

**Bolick, Clint, *Unfinished Business: A Civil Rights Strategy for America's Third Century*, Pacific Research Institute for Public Policy, 1990.**

Bolick, an official of the Equal Employment Opportunity Commission during the Reagan administration, is now director of the Landmark Legal Foundation Center for Civil Rights, a conservative group based in Washington, D.C. He argues that affirmative action has evolved in ways that hurt the people it was intended to help.

**Branch, Taylor, *Parting the Waters: America in the King Years 1954-63*, Touchstone, 1988.**

This Pulitzer Prize winner describes the birth of the civil rights movement as it developed from the 1950s until the eve of the passage of the 1964 Civil Rights Act. The book provides detailed information about the social setting of the South and the personalities involved in the movement's progress, especially its early leader, the Rev. Dr. Martin Luther King Jr.

**Brooks, Roy L., *Rethinking the American Race Problem*, University of California Press, 1990.**

Brooks, a professor of law at the University of Minnesota Law School, writes that civil rights laws have fallen far short of their intended purpose to provide equal opportunity for black Americans. He outlines a blueprint of black American self-help, in which middle-class blacks would work personally with poor blacks to help them find skills and employment.

**Steele, Shelby, *The Content of Our Character*, St. Martin's Press, 1990.**

To Steele, a black professor of English at San Jose State University in California, affirmative action has exacerbated the racial divisions in American society by continuing to focus on race instead of on achievement. While stressing the need for protections of equal opportunity, Steele advocates better education and economic development for disadvantaged minorities.

## Articles

**Edsall, Thomas Byrne, and Edsall, Mary D., "Race," *The Atlantic*, May 1991.**

American society has become increasingly polarized since the end of the 1970s, when the gradual convergence between the incomes of employed blacks and whites halted. "The failure of the trend toward wage equality to continue has encouraged the conflict between black and white world views," the Edsalls write, "in which black gains are seen as a cost to whites, and white advantages are seen as a manifestation of racism." This thoughtful article also has a lot to say about the politics of race. "Race is no longer a straightforward, morally unambiguous force in American politics; instead," the Edsalls write, "considerations of race are now deeply imbedded in the strategy and tactics of politics. . . ."

**Lerner, Barbara, "Good News About American Education," *Commentary*, March 1991.**

The author, who runs a consulting firm in Princeton, N.J., criticizes the practice of adjusting test scores on the basis of race. She believes this means of applying affirmative action is inherently racist, reflecting an "American prejudice that intelligence is a fixed and unchanging phenomenon." She views standardized tests as valuable tools and suggests that minority groups that do poorly on these tests should be helped to achieve a better education rather than granted preferential treatment.

## Reports and Studies

**Citizens' Commission on Civil Rights, *Lost Opportunities: The Civil Rights Record of the Bush Administration Mid-Term*, 1991.**

The commission, a bipartisan group of former officials who have served in the federal government in positions with responsibility for equal opportunity, was formed in 1982 to monitor and promote civil rights policies. The Bush administration's emphasis on "colorblindness" and "race neutrality," the study concludes, "has resulted in continuing hostility to any measures — either in legislative proposals or litigation — that incorporate race- or gender-conscious remedies or require affirmative relief."

**Smith, James P., and Welch, Finis R., *Closing the Gap: Forty Years of Economic Progress for Blacks*, The Rand Corporation, February 1986.**

The study, commissioned by the Labor Department, finds that affirmative action has "reshuffled" black jobs in the labor force more than it has provided advancement.

# The Next Step

## Additional Articles from Current Periodicals

### Actions & defenses

**Dwyer, P., "The blow to affirmative action may not hurt that much,"** *Business Week*, **July 3, 1989, p. 61.**

Opinion. Discusses how the Supreme Court has recently issued a series of rulings that erect new barriers for minorities and women trying to use the legal system to redress discrimination in the workplace. Suggests that the court rulings won't matter too much, now that business views affirmative action as a competitive necessity. Brief descriptions of five court rulings.

**Dyson, M. E., "Deaffirmation,"** *The Nation*, **July 3, 1989, p. 4.**

Editorial. Discusses the effects of the Supreme Court's majority ruling on court-approved affirmative action plans, which may now be challenged by white workers, and how this and other recent rulings threaten the foundation of equal employment opportunities for women and racial minorities. Affirmative action plans may be abandoned; Voluntarily adopted plans; White men have successfully called themselves victims.

**Eastland, T., "Toward a real restoration of civil rights,"** *Commentary*, **November 1989, p. 25.**

Surveys the implications of three recent Supreme Court decisions for civil rights. Affirmative action; Discrimination and quotas; Legislative responses; Redefinitions of civil rights.

**Hertzberg, H., "Wounds of race,"** *The New Republic*, **July 10, 1989, p. 4.**

Editorial. Critical analysis of a recent series of Supreme Court decisions curtailing equal employment provisions of the Civil Rights Act of 1964. Need for continued affirmative action programs despite their unpopularity; Lack of equality for blacks in America still a major issue in society today.

**Kaplan, D. A. and Cohn, B., "The court's Mr. Right,"** *Newsweek*, **Nov. 5, 1990, p. 62.**

Profiles Antonin Scalia, Supreme Court Justice. His political position; Most provocative justice after only four years on the bench; Ardent judicial supporter of a strong executive branch; Hostility to affirmative action; How the conservatives view him as opposed to the liberals; Comments by lawyers and other judges. INSET: Read his clips.

**Simpson, P., "Constitutional crisis,"** *Ms.*, **September 1989, p. 90.**

Examines recent U.S. Supreme Court civil rights and affirmative action decisions. The court's new conservatism; 1971 *Griggs v. Duke Power Company* decision; Title VII; Greater difficulty in proving discrimination; 1989 *Martin v. Wilks* decision; "Reverse discrimination"; Reaction of business community; Policies of Presidents Ronald Reagan and George Bush.

### Addresses & essays

**Blits, J. H. and Gottfredson, L. S., "Equality or lasting inequality?"** *Society*, **March/April 1990, p. 4.**

Examines the concept of race-norming, where job candidates' scores on employment tests are ranked relative only to those of the same race. Results of an analysis of the practice completed by the National Academy of Science (NAS); History of race-norming; Authors' arguments against race-norming.

**Bunzel, J. H., "Minority faculty hiring,"** *American Scholar*, **winter 1990, p. 39.**

Traces the history of affirmative action programs in the last 25 years. How useless many were; Detracted from quality of education; What must be done, including bettering public schools.

**Kelman, M., "The problem of false negatives,"** *Society*, **March/April 1990, p. 21.**

Comments on an article by Jan H. Blits and Linda S. Gottfredson that challenges the validity of race-norming in hiring. Private and social costs; Issue of false negatives; Balancing the elimination of test-based screening with meeting racial quotas.

**Steele, S., "Booker T. Washington was right,"** *New Perspectives Quarterly*, **fall 1990, p. 23.**

Asserts that blacks can have no real power in this country without taking responsibility for their own educational and economic development. Leaders are needed who champion the concept of personal responsibility; Negative effects of affirmative action. INSET: Attitude, not aptitude (details the "cities in schools" dropout program), by W. Milliken.

### Case studies

**Berger, J., "Pessimism in air as schools try affirmative action,"** *The New York Times*, **Feb. 27, 1990, p. B1.**

Says there is little confidence among officials and scholars that the New York City school system's first affirmative action plan in its history will significantly increase the numbers of minority teachers, and little evidence that it will improve student performance.

**Greenhouse, L., "Signal on job rights," *The New York Times*, Jan. 25, 1989, p. 1.**

Editorial. In declaring unconstitutional the effort by the city of Richmond, Va., to increase opportunities for blacks in the construction industry, the Supreme Court did not declare an end to government-sponsored affirmative action programs. Under the principle of "strict scrutiny," only those programs aimed at eliminating specific racial obstacles will meet with judicial approval. The court has decided to interpret the Constitution on a racially level playing field.

**Kilborn, P. T., "A company recasts itself to erase decades of bias," *The New York Times*, Oct. 4, 1990, p. A1.**

Presents a special report on affirmative action. Describes the ambitious experiment in cultural engineering at Corning, the giant family-controlled maker of Pyrex, Corning Ware and Steuben crystal. The company accommodates women and blacks in scores of ways, all ultimately intended to assure them of a good crack at the top jobs in the company. Eventually, the company wants to do the same for other minority members.

**Rockwell, P., "Fighting the fires of racism," *The Nation*, Dec. 11, 1989, p. 714.**

Describes the ways in which the International Association of Fire Fighters, an AFL-CIO union, is crusading against affirmative action, and particularly against African-Americans, in several U.S. cities.

**Thomas, R. R., "From affirmative action to affirming diversity," *Harvard Business Review*, March/April 1990, p. 107.**

Urges American business to re-evaluate the principles of affirmative action. How the work force and nature of business has changed; New problems; 10 new guidelines for managing diversity. INSETS: Out of the numbers game and into decision making (Avon); "It simply makes good business sense" (Corning); Turning social pressures into competitive advantage (Digital); Discovering complexing and value in P&G's diversity; The daily experience of genuine workplace diversity (Xerox).

## Civil Rights Act, 1990

**"Civil-rights bills are supposed to prevent quotas," *Nation's Business*, August 1990, p. 67.**

Editorial. Argues against passage of the Civil Rights Act of 1990. Explains why it could force many employers to establish quota systems in hiring.

**Smart, T., Garland, S. B., et al., "Why business is suddenly gunning for the 1990 Civil Rights Act," *Business Week*, May 14, 1990, p. 49.**

Reports on a measure, written by Sen. Edward M. Kennedy, D-Mass., and Rep. Augustus F. Hawkins, D-Calif., which was designed to overturn a series of 1989 Supreme Court decisions. The high court restricted individuals' ability to bring discrimination suits and expanded the right of white males to challenge longstanding affirmative action plans.

## Colleges & universities

**D'Souza, D., "Sins of admission," *The New Republic*, Feb. 18, 1991, p. 30.**

Analyzes the controversial issue of affirmative action in America's universities and colleges. Major flaws with its premise that diversity should be pursued through proportional representation; Resulting pressures on affirmative action students; How affirmative action has increased racial tensions on campuses. INSET: Mea culpa (a liberal who has become politically incorrect), by R. Blow.

**Gillespie, P., "Campus stories, or the cat beyond the canvas," *Vital Speeches*, Feb. 1, 1988, p. 235.**

All the hoopla over equal opportunity and affirmative action has created the illusion of a profound change in colleges and universities. But the change has not occurred. Schools have fewer black undergraduate and graduate students than a few years ago, and the number and proportion of black faculty members is declining. Women haven't fared much better. The blame is not to be put on the media but on the academies themselves. Examples.

**Williams, W. E. and Seligman, D.,"Race, scholarship, and affirmative action," *The National Review*, May 5, 1989, p. 36.**

Two articles dealing with how affirmative action programs have as victims white and Asian students, independent scholars, and the minority students who are their supposed beneficiaries. Campus racism; The case of Michael Levin.

## Debates & issues

**"Facing the moment of truth," *Black Enterprise*, June 1990, p. 97.**

Forecasts the future of the nation's black businesses over the next decade. Impact of a slowing economy; Changing public policy on affirmative action and minority set-aside programs; Key industries that will be deeply affected, such as auto dealerships and contractors; Businesses that have already gone bankrupt; Lessons on beating the competition.

**Johnson, C., "The hidden perils of racial conformity,"** *U.S. News & World Report*, Dec. 24, 1990, p. 42.

Outlines the silent commandment among black leaders: "Thou shalt refrain from second-guessing the civil-rights agenda, particularly the need for new government-aid programs in the inner city and affirmative action." Author Shelby Steele and his best-selling "The Content of Our Character," which has set off a firestorm of protest from black leaders; Polly Williams in Milwaukee vs. the NAACP; Intra-racial name-calling.

**Lewis, A. F., "Thanks, guys,"** *Ms.*, September 1989, p. 86.

Opinion. Refutes recent articles in several establishment newspapers and magazines which assert that affirmative action can be mentally and emotionally damaging to women and minorities.

**Manning, S., "What's fair?"** *Scholastic Update*, Jan. 11, 1991, p. 10.

Debates the pros and cons of affirmative action plans. Why they were originally established, as a means of fighting discrimination; Critics' charges that they actually promote reverse discrimination.

**Steele, S., "A negative vote on affirmative action,"** *The New York Times Magazine*, May 13, 1990, p. 46.

Discusses the negative implications of affirmative action. Reverse discrimination; Artificial diversity; Racial development needed, not racial representation; Demoralizing effects of racial preferences; Exploiting victimization; Impossibility of repaying suffering.

**Villarosa, L., "What have they done for us lately?"** *Essence*, May 1990, p. 66.

Discusses the dismantling of the two-decade legacy of affirmative action by the conservative Supreme Court, with several controversial decisions. Case of Brenda Patterson; Other cases; Affirmative action ideals; Backlash; Reagan administration and affirmative action; Tracy Juzang's affirmative action success story. INSET: Do you think affirmative action has been effective?

**Wilkins, R., "In ivory towers,"** *Mother Jones*, July/August 1990, p. 10.

Opinion. Talks about how affirmative action opens doors of opportunity often thought closed, and makes the country better and stronger. Problems and confusion; Desires for excellence; Racism remaining.

## Political aspects

**Barnes, F., "The race card,"** *The New Republic*, Dec. 17, 1990, p. 10.

Studies the controversial role of quotas in the recent elections and the defeat of the Kennedy-Hawkins Civil Rights Act. Successes of Republicans Jesse Helms and Pete Wilson in exploiting the quota issue; Bush's emphasis on quotas to win support for his veto of the civil rights bill; How Americans, black and white, appear to view quotas; Dangers of using the issue to promote racism.

**Cooper, M., Friedman, D., et al., "Hyping the 'quota' wars,"** *U.S. News & World Report*, Dec. 24, 1990, p. 40.

Comments that the charge of racial quotas is at the center of a political struggle, started when Republicans hurled "racial quota" at the Democrats, who threw "race baiting" back. Education Department decision to halt the awarding of scholarships based solely on race; Affirmative action mostly a done deal; Factors keeping the quota ward raging; David Duke. INSET: Affirmative action status report.

**Mathews, T., "Quotas,"** *Newsweek*, Dec. 31, 1990, p. 28.

Predicts that political talk about quotas will become the polite way to talk race and class. Asserts that the real issue behind quotas will be the future of affirmative action. INSETS: Predictions; Clarence Thomas (federal appeals court judge).

## Women

**"They haven't come far enough, baby,"** *Business Week*, Aug. 6, 1990, p. 90.

Editorial. Discusses how it is true that women have come a long way in American business, but they still have a long way to go. Changes made in the work force; Conflicting demands of work and family playing a part; Going beyond affirmative action.

**Eisenberg, S., "Women hard hats speak out,"** *The Nation*, Sept. 18, 1989, p. 272.

Describes female workers' experiences in the construction industry since the beginning of affirmative action for women in the construction unions. Informal support networks; Statistics of women in construction jobs; Minority women in construction jobs; Fight for equal access to hands-on-training.

**King, S. R., "At the crossroads,"** *Black Enterprise*, August 1988, p. 45.

Part of a special report: Black Women in Corporate America. Profiles several black women in the upper echelons of corporate life. Opportunities and barriers; Why so few make it to the top; Internationalism in the marketplace; Breaking into the corporate club. INSETS: The path to the executive suite; Detoured by deferred affirmative action.

# Back Issues

*Great Research on Current Issues Starts Right Here... Recent topics covered by The CQ Researcher are listed below. Issues dated before May 10, 1991, were published under the name of Editorial Research Reports.*

**NOVEMBER 1989**
Balkanization of Eastern Europe
Dealing With the Underclass
America Turns to Recycling
New World Economy

**DECEMBER 1989**
North America Trade Pact
Influence Peddling
German Reunification
Learning Disabilities

**JANUARY 1990**
Higher Education Curriculum
Photonics
Age of 'Infotainment'
Abortion: Politicians' Nightmare

**FEBRUARY 1990**
Politics and Economic Growth
Free Agency in Sports
Repetitive Motion
War on Drugs

**MARCH 1990**
Asbestos: Are Risks Acceptable?
Public Health Campaigns
South Africa's Future
Homeless Need More Than Shelter

**APRIL 1990**
How Fair is the Tax Burden?
Workers' Compensation
U.S. Pacific Forces
Curbing Insurance Premiums

**MAY 1990**
Should Teaching Be a Profession?
Will Canada Fall Apart?
Is U.S. Patent System Outdated?
Federal Funding for the Arts

**JUNE 1990**
Downsizing America's Armed Forces
Progress In Weather Forecasting
S & L Bailout
Bio-Chemical Disarmament

**JULY 1990**
Do Americans Still Love Marriage?
Death Penalty Debate
Decline of Rural America
United Nations in the 1990s

**AUGUST 1990**
Democracy in the Philippines
Initiatives: True Democracy?
Hard Times at Newspapers
Teens Balance School & Jobs

**SEPTEMBER 1990**
Dangers of Alcohol
Western Alliance After the Cold War
Tobacco Industry
Right to Die

**OCTOBER 1990**
Organ Transplants
Energy Policy Options
Search for Arab Unity
Child Support

**NOVEMBER 1990**
Lotteries and Gambling
Post Cold-War Choices
Setting Limits on Medical Care
Multicultural Education

**DECEMBER 1990**
Cable TV Regulation
Americans' Search For Their Roots
Is Insurance System a Failure?
Why Schools Still Have Tracking

**JANUARY 1991**
Growing Influence of Boycotts
Should the U.S. Reinstate the Draft?
America's Archaeological Past
Peace Corps' Challenges in '90s

**FEBRUARY 1991**
Regional Impact of Recession
Puerto Rico's Status
Redistricting: Mapping Power
Nuclear Power

**MARCH 1991**
Acid Rain
Cost of the Gulf War
Reassessing Gun Laws
Future for Man in Space

**APRIL 1991**
Social Security
Canadian Crisis Over Quebec
California Drought
Electromagnetic Radiation

**MAY 1991**
School Choice

Back issues are available for $4.00 (subscribers) or $7.00 (non-subscribers). Quantity discounts apply to orders over ten. To order, call Congressional Quarterly 1-800-432-2250.

# Future Topics

▶ *Animal Rights*

▶ *U.S.-Japan Relations*

▶ *Divorce and Children*

# THE CQ Researcher

PUBLISHED BY CONGRESSIONAL QUARTERLY INC., IN CONJUNCTION WITH EBSCO PUBLISHING

PUBLISHED BY CONGRESSIONAL QUARTERLY INC., IN CONJUNCTION WITH EBSCO PUBLISHING

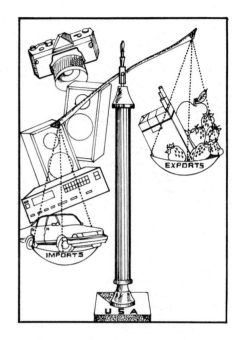

# The U.S. and Japan

*Trade and strategic issues create tensions in U.S.-Japan relations*

THE PERSIAN GULF WAR INCREASED TENSIONS between the United States and Japan. U.S. officials were unhappy with Japan's slow response to U.S. entreaties for financial support for Operation Desert Storm and its decision not to send any personnel. The dissatisfaction with Japan's role in the war is only the latest irritant in relations between the two nations. Underlying most of the tensions is Japan's huge trade surplus with the United States. Many Americans believe the trade imbalance is the result of unfair trade practices by the Japanese. U.S. critics also say Japan isn't carrying its fair share of the defense burden. Japanese officials, meanwhile, say U.S. companies aren't trying hard enough to sell in Japanese markets. And many Japanese are questioning how much Japan should be giving in to the United States.

 May 31, 1991 • Volume 1, No. 4 • 325-348

*Formerly Editorial Research Reports*

COVER ART: BARBARA SASSA-DANIELS

May 31, 1991
Volume 1, No. 4

**EDITOR**
Sandra Stencel

**ASSOCIATE EDITOR**
Richard L. Worsnop

**STAFF WRITERS**
Charles S. Clark
Mary H. Cooper
Patrick G. Marshall

**PRODUCTION EDITOR**
Laurie De Maris

**EDITORIAL ASSISTANT**
Thomas H. Moore

**GRAPHICS**
Jack Auldridge

**PUBLISHED BY**
Congressional Quarterly Inc.

**CHAIRMAN**
Andrew Barnes

**VICE CHAIRMAN**
Andrew P. Corty

**EDITOR AND PUBLISHER**
Neil Skene

**EXECUTIVE EDITOR**
Robert W. Merry

**PUBLICATIONS MARKETING/SALES**
Robert Smith

**EDITOR, EBSCO PUBLISHING**
Melissa Kummerer

The CQ Researcher (ISSN 1056-2036). Formerly Editorial Research Reports. Published weekly (48 times per year, excluding March 1, May 3, Aug. 2 and Nov. 1, 1991) by Congressional Quarterly Inc., 1414 22nd St., N.W., Washington, D.C. 20037. Rates are furnished upon request. Application to mail at second-class postage rates is pending at Washington, D.C. POSTMASTER: Send address changes to The CQ Researcher, 1414 22nd St., N.W., Washington, D.C. 20037.

# The U.S. and Japan

By Patrick G. Marshall

## THE ISSUES

Ever since World War II, when the United States defeated and subsequently occupied Japan,* the relationship between the two countries has been an uneasy one. No doubt the strains of occupation — and the paternalism that accompanied it — explain some of the uneasiness. But other factors have divided the two nations as well.

To begin with, the two countries have dramatically different political and cultural backgrounds. Historically, the United States has adapted its politics, as well as its cultural undertakings, toward Europe, while Japan has rarely emerged from self-imposed cultural and political isolation. The same distance applies to languages: English and Japanese are not closely related and are extremely difficult tongues for non-native speakers to learn.

The primary tie that has bound the two countries for the past 45 years has been opposition to Soviet expansion in the Pacific. But this threat, which resulted in the basing of U.S. military forces in Japan, has receded in recent years while other tensions between the United States and Japan have increased.

The most notable irritant in relations between the two countries in recent years has been Japan's large trade surplus with the United States. Many Americans believe the trade imbalance is the result of unfair trade practices by the Japanese. U.S. critics also say the Japanese have had an unfair economic advan-

*The American occupation of Japan lasted from the end of World War II in 1945 until April 1952.

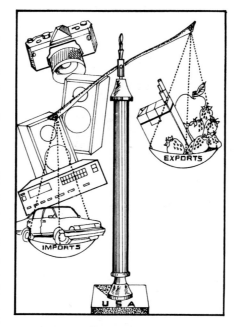

tage because the island nation has enjoyed the benefit of the American defense umbrella while only having to devote a fraction of its own national wealth to defense. This accusation has been heard even more vociferously since the war in the Persian Gulf.

Japan's slow response to U.S. entreaties for financial support for Operation Desert Storm — and its failure to send any personnel at all — didn't sit well with many Americans, who felt Japan, which is dependent on the Middle East for nearly 70 percent of its oil, was taking another free ride on America's back. A poll conducted in March for *USA Today* asked people if they would be less likely or more likely to buy Japanese products than before the war. Although 42 percent said the war had no impact on their buying decisions, 31 percent said they would be less likely to buy Japanese goods than before the war.[1]

It was Japan's bad luck that the gulf conflict came just as the United States was entering a recession.

With unemployment growing, profits falling, and Japan's trade surplus with the United States remaining uncomfortably high, complaints over Japan's trade practices have escalated. Congress has responded to the controversy with a rash of bills aimed at punishing Japan. And President Bush recently started the ball rolling on what would be the first trade retaliation against Japan since 1987. On April 27, the administration announced that because of insufficient progress in talks aimed at opening the Japanese construction market to U.S. firms, it was taking steps to ban Japanese companies from U.S. government contracting.

Just how the U.S.-Japan economic and strategic relationship will emerge from the current tensions is uncertain. "One's reputation is rather like a crystal goblet — when it's dropped, it's hard to put back together again," U.S. Trade Representative Carla A. Hills said in response to a question about Japan's image in the United States since the gulf war.[2] Full payment of the $9 billion promised by Japan for the war effort would go a long way toward repairing the damage, Hills said. But there are deeper questions about trade and security issues that will be harder to resolve.

### Is Japan a fair trader?

Underlying most of the tensions between the United States and Japan is the conviction on the part of many Americans that Japan's huge trade surpluses with the United States — $41.71 billion in 1990 — are the result of unfair trade practices on the part of the Japanese. Last March, for example, many U.S. newspapers ran front-page stories about Japanese threats to arrest U.S. farmers who were displaying Ameri-

May 31, 1991    327

can rice at an international trade show in Tokyo. Japanese rice growers claimed the display was a violation of Japan's law prohibiting rice imports.

"Showrooms all over America display Hondas, Toyotas, and Nissans, but in Japan you cannot display a 10-pound bag of American rice," complained Rep. William S. Broomfield, R-Mich., expressing the view of many Americans. "I cannot think of a country that has benefited more from our open markets than Japan. And I cannot think of any country that has done less to deserve it." [3]

As Japanese officials are quick to point out, however, their ban on rice imports is only different in degree from the strict quotas the United States places on imports of sugar and textiles. In fact, Japanese officials continually note that official trade barriers — tariffs, quotas and outright exclusion of products — are lower in Japan than in many industrial countries. Indeed, Japan's average tariffs of 2 percent are among the lowest in the world.

Japanese officials say U.S. companies are not trying hard enough to sell in what they admit is a tough, quality-conscious market. They cite recent statistics showing a doubling of Japan's manufactured imports between 1985 and 1988 — from $40 billion to $92 billion — most of which was accounted for by Asian and Western European exporters. Over the same period, American goods dropped from 35 percent of Japan's manufactured imports to only 25 percent.[4] These figures, Japanese officials say, are evidence their markets can be cracked, if only American companies would try harder.

But the most serious obstacles facing U.S. exporters, Japanese officials have repeatedly stressed, are the high U.S. budget deficits, which make borrowing money more expensive for U.S. companies. This

combined with a low national savings rate, which means less money available for investment, and a financial system that favors short-term profits over long-term investment hurts the competitiveness of U.S. companies, Japanese officials say.

While not denying the importance to U.S. trade of bringing down federal deficits, U.S. officials have alleged that Japan is, indeed, an unfair trader. Despite Japan's relatively low official trade barriers, Japan's entry in the U.S. trade representative's annual report on foreign trade barriers is (at 18 pages) the longest in the book. That, according to American trade experts, is in large part because the remaining Japanese tariffs and quotas are concentrated in product areas where the United States is most competitive. The chief problem areas cited in the report are supercomputers, telecommunications equipment, semiconductors, intellectual property matters, paper products and a variety of agricultural products.

U.S. and European trade experts have long complained that non-traditional barriers to trade are systemically entrenched in Japan's manufacturing and distribution sectors. Japan's informal trade barriers include:

■ Product standards and testing procedures intentionally designed to exclude foreign products.

■ Inadequate intellectual property rights, including a patent system critics say makes it easy for Japanese companies to steal foreign inventions.

■ Collusive behavior by Japanese firms.

■ Government procurement practices aimed at favoring non-competitive domestic industries over foreign companies.

Critics of Japan cite an array of anecdotal evidence of such barriers. Economist Edward J. Lincoln of the Brookings Institution tells of a building supply firm in Japan that

created a local uproar in 1987 when it tried to import South Korean cement. Japanese cement companies and their distributors complained that the errant supplier was "upsetting order" in the domestic cement industry.[5]

The best-known example of Japan's informal trade barriers is the way Japanese companies are combined in closely knit groups called *keiretsu*, which finance each other's projects, use each other as suppliers and so forth. Japanese officials have long maintained that *keiretsu* only work to maximize efficiency and do not unfairly exclude foreign products. And Western economists have not had access to the kind of data needed to prove that *keiretsu* are a trade barrier.

One recent study, however, found that at least some *keiretsu* clearly act to impede imports, largely by doing business with each other instead of negotiating with other Japanese firms and foreign companies for lower prices. The author of the study — Robert Z. Lawrence, an economist at the Brookings Institution — also noted that many Japanese distributors "apply unusually high mark-ups to foreign products sold in Japan." [6]

Other critics have noted that the Japanese government, intentionally or not, favors collusive behavior by having lax antitrust laws. Not only are antitrust actions rarely filed in Japan, U.S. officials complain, but when they are, resulting fines only amount to 2 percent of the sales affected. In the United States, fines amount to 50 percent of affected sales.[7]

Bill Krist, vice president for international affairs of the American Electronics Association, says the barriers to foreign goods aren't just at Japan's shores — they follow Japanese companies abroad. "Japanese electronics companies in the United States purchase only 23 percent locally and import 74 percent from Japan, preferring instead to source from their own *keiretsu*," Krist said at a recent congressional hearing.[8]

As for why Asian and European countries have managed to significantly increase their exports to Japan in recent years, while U.S. companies have not, some American experts argue that there are explanations besides lack of U.S. competitiveness. In the case of Asia, the increase in imports is due in large part to imports from Japanese companies that have responded to rising wages in Japan by siting in nearby Asian countries such as Malaysia and Thailand. The rise in imports from Europe is accounted for mostly by luxury items, such as Gucci leather goods and high-priced German cars — product sectors in which Japan has not yet attempted to compete.

As one critic has noted, Japan's behavior is unfair in that "Japanese business does to other countries what Japan will not permit to be done to itself." [9] Many trade experts in the United States and Europe argue that Japan is engaging in trade practices that are unfair at least in the sense that if the rest of the world adopted them, world trade would suffer.

The problem, as many see it, is that many trade barriers at issue are either an entrenched part of the Japanese "way of life" — such as the cooperation between companies within *keiretsu*, and between *keiretsu* and the government — or are so hidden as to allow the Japanese government "plausible deniability." "The failure of most mainstream Japanese economists and government officials to acknowledge a market-access problem is both discouraging and a measure of how far they are from comprehending the nature of their own protectionism," Lincoln concludes.

## Should the United States take a harder line with Japan?

Most Western analysts — whether from government or academia — seem to agree that outside pressure is required to open up Japanese markets. But disagreement comes over how much and what type of pressure is needed.

For the past couple of years, the Bush administration has argued against taking drastic steps against Japan. Despite the great number of outstanding trade complaints, U.S. Trade Representative Carla A. Hills announced in April 1990 that the administration had decided against naming Japan as an unfair trader.* She said cooperation, not confrontation, was what was needed to bring about change.

Over recent months, the U.S. trade representative's office has said that it sees great progress in negotiations with Japan. "When the administration took over, there were about 12 outstanding issues between the U.S. and Japan," says a trade official who spoke on the condition he not be identified. "In the last couple of years, we have resolved those specifics and entered into agreements. In some of them — for example, in telecommunications — there has been a substantial increase in our exports, or in market penetration."

But where the administration tends to measure progress by agreements reached, business interests tend to look to the bottom line. And the bottom line hasn't changed much. "If you're a chef you may say that dinner's coming along fine, but if you're the person who's waiting for the meal it's too early to say that," says Judge Morris, director of the international trade division of the National Association of Manufacturers (NAM).

---

*Japan had been included in the list of unfair traders in 1989 (*see p. 342*).

That view is echoed by Bill Krist of the American Electronics Association. "You can't say there's progress because Japan has made yet another promise in the trade area," Krist says. He notes that between 1979 and 1989 there were a total of 15 agreements related to market access in electronics, yet the Japanese trade surplus with the United States in electronics continues to run at about $20 billion a year. "Clearly, individual agreements without a comprehensive strategy for monitoring and implementation will not be successful," Krist says.

Over the past couple of years, there have been increasing calls for harsher measures against Japan. Former Secretaries of State Henry A. Kissinger and Cyrus R. Vance in 1989 suggested that the United States abandon the idea of negotiating away barriers with Japan and simply set an appropriate trade balance and let Japan meet the goal however it chose. A variant of that idea, suggested by economics Professor Rudiger Dornbusch of the Massachusetts Institute of Technology, is imposing a tariff tied to Japan's performance: Any year in which the United States doesn't increase its exports to Japan by, say, 15 percent, the United States would automatically impose a tariff on Japanese products.[10]

Finally, some analysts have proposed that the United States emulate at least parts of Japan's strategy by encouraging closer cooperation between U.S. companies, and between those companies and the government. One proposal that keeps cropping up in Congress is for suspension of U.S. antitrust laws to allow high-tech companies to cooperate not only on the research and design of products, but on production and marketing as well.

Many economists warn, however, that putting the government in the position of "picking winners and losers" is not a strategy that will work over the long haul. "Few subsidized industries have earned high or even normal rates of return," writes economist Pietro S. Nivola. "Much public financing has been squandered on antiquated, high-cost industries." [11]

### Is the United States too dependent on Japanese capital?

The extent of Japanese investments in the United States has long been a source of concern. Whenever a major department store chain or a landmark building is sold to Japanese investors, it seems to automatically attract the attention of the national media.

The most visible instance of U.S. sensitivity to Japanese investment in recent years occurred when the Matsushita Electric Industrial Co. acquired the U.S. company MCA Inc. in January 1991, and thereby gained control of concessions at Yosemite National Park. The idea that profits from Yosemite — one of this country's greatest natural treasures — would flow to a Japanese company upset many, including Interior Secretary Manuel Lujan Jr., who tried to pull the concessions back. In the end, Matsushita sold the concessions to the Interior Department at a cut-rate price.

American worries over Japanese investment appear to be grounded on two fears. First, there is a concern that somehow America's identity is being purchased by foreigners, that a Rockefeller Center owned by Japanese investors is no longer "American." Secondly, and more serious, is the fear that Japan might gain political leverage over the United States as a result of its huge capital investments and U.S. dependence on the Japanese for purchases of Treasury bills.

So far, Japan has not used its financial leverage against the United States, though one senator recently accused Japan of threatening to do so. In February, Japan's vice minister of finance for international affairs, Makoto Utsumi, warned that if the United States passed legislation aimed at curbing Japanese banks' activities in the United States* the relationship between the United States and financial institutions "could be endangered." Sen. John Heinz, R-Pa., angrily characterized Utsumi's statement as "financial blackmail." [12]

Economists warn that there are, in fact, legitimate reasons to worry about how much of U.S. assets are held by foreigners generally. After all, when Treasury bills come due, the money that is paid may well leave the country. "In 1988 these payments exceeded $100 billion, almost equaling receipts from accumulated U.S. investments abroad," writes economist Philip Trezise. "Clearly enough, the nation would be better off if these payments were made to other Americans rather than to foreigners." [13]

But if the overall amount of assets held by foreigners can be a problem, most experts agree there is little reason to fear how much of those assets are held by a specific country.

In 1989, foreigners owned about $1.3 trillion, or 8.7 percent of the estimated $15 trillion in total U.S. assets.** "Japanese direct investments totaled $53 billion, or slightly more than three-tenths of a

percent of our national wealth," writes Trezise. "These are not numbers that would imply the imminent domination of American economic or political life by Japan or by foreigners generally." [14]

According to economist Paul Samuelson, the question of Japanese investments in the United States "is a non-issue. There may be some industries where we want to limit foreign ownership. But otherwise, foreign investment — including Japanese investment — doesn't hurt the U.S. economy." [15]

Even so staunch a critic of Japan as Clyde V. Prestowitz Jr. does not find Japanese investment a threat. Prestowitz, a former U.S. trade negotiator and currently president of the Economic Strategy Institute in Washington, says "Japanese threats to withdraw financing or technology would have limited credibility because such actions would involve many private actors, such as insurance companies, banks and individual investors, who are not easy to control and are subject to U.S. as well as foreign administrative authority." [16]

The one sector in which analysts agree too much foreign ownership could be a legitimate problem is the defense industry. With that in mind, Congress in 1988 passed legislation setting up procedures for reviewing foreign takeovers of U.S. businesses. It gave the president authority to block a sale if he felt it could harm national security. The authority — which was used only once, to block the sale of an aircraft-parts manufacturer to China — has recently lapsed, but many in Congress expect it to be renewed soon.

### Is Japan holding up its end of the U.S.-Japan strategic relationship?

The gulf war revived allegations, particularly on Capitol Hill, that Japan isn't carrying its fair share of the allies' defense burden. It was only after many weeks, and a close vote

---

*The bill in question is S1019, the Foreign Bank Supervision Enhancement Act of 1991, sponsored by Donald W. Riegle Jr., D-Mich., chairman of the Senate Banking Committee. The legislation would empower federal bank regulators to deny foreign banks approval to open U.S. branches if equivalent opportunities are not available for U.S. banks in the foreign bank's home market.

**Foreign investment in the United States appears to be declining. In 1990, according to the Securities Industries Association, new investments amounted to $49 billion, down from $170 billion in 1989.

in the Diet, or Japanese legislature, that Japan pledged $9 million toward allied costs. Some U.S. officials also were upset that Japan would not consider sending troops to the gulf. When Japan promised in late August to transport food, water and medical supplies to the gulf, one American official commented: "There's a limited amount of Girl Scout cookies that can be used there." [17]

The dissatisfaction with Japan's role in the gulf war is only the latest episode in a security relationship that has been growing increasingly frustrating for the United States. Many Americans have questioned whether the United States should continue to include Japan under the very expensive U.S. defense umbrella, particularly while Japan is running such large trade surpluses with the United States.

Throughout the 1980s, the Reagan administration pressed Japan to increase its defense budgets and to assume more responsibility for its own defense. Japan's defense budgets have, in fact, grown in recent years. By the late 1980s, Japan was the world's third-biggest spender on defense, behind the United States and the Soviet Union. Still, Japan spends only about 1 percent of its gross national product (GNP) on defense, compared with about 5-6 percent for the United States. For many Americans, especially members of Congress, that's not enough. Legislation repeatedly has been introduced that would require Japan to pay the full price of stationing U.S. forces there. (Japan just recently agreed to increase its share of the costs from 40 percent to 50 percent.)

Since the gulf war, new legislation has been introduced aimed at getting Japan to contribute more to the strategic relationship. A bill introduced by Rep. Stephen L. Neal, D-N.C., would require the president to negotiate a deal with Japan whereby Japan would pay an annual "security fee" equal to 3 percent of its GNP, less the amount spent by the Japanese government for defense during that year. That way, Neal said, either Japan would increase its defense spending, or pay the United States a more appropriate amount to provide the service.

Others, however, would prefer not to see a larger role for Japanese forces in the North Pacific. In fact, the U.S. Marine commander in Japan, Maj. Gen. Henry Stackpole III, has described U.S. forces in Japan as a "cap in the bottle" to prevent resurgence of Japanese militarism.[18] That's a sentiment shared by many of Japan's Asian neighbors, who experienced Japanese military aggression in World War II. Some analysts have warned that a larger Japanese military presence could trigger a regional arms race.

Vice Adm. Henry H. Mauz Jr., commander of the U.S. 7th Fleet, made headlines in February 1990 when he warned the Bush administration against pushing Japan to assume more of the U.S. costs in the region. To raise the figures, Mauz said, "may in the long run have some impact on our flexibility. . . . If Japan pays essentially a very large share of those costs, and Japan doesn't agree with our course of action elsewhere in the world, which is not inconceivable, there may be some inclination to suggest that the force that Japan is paying for ought to stay closer to Japan." [19]

"The United States clearly has very ambivalent feelings about what it is we want the Japanese to do," observes Paul Kreisberg, a foreign policy analyst at the Carnegie Endowment for International Peace in Washington. "You get different views on [Capitol] Hill and in the Defense Department and in the State Department." ∎

# BACKGROUND

## Roots of the Problem

The roots of today's ambiguous U.S.-Japan relationship can be traced to actions taken by the United States during the occupation of Japan at the end of World War II. In fact, historians point to three decisions in particular as being largely responsible for the current tensions between the United States and Japan.

The first was the clause in the 1947 Japanese Constitution, imposed by the United States, that forbids the use of military force by Japan except in defense of the Japanese islands. The result was that the United States assumed responsibility for Japan's defense and for maintaining peace in the Pacific generally.

The second decision was to leave Japan's government-industrial bureaucracy largely intact. Actually, the occupation authorities did break up the huge *zaibatsu* — large groups of companies owned by a small number of families — that were blamed in part for Japan's role in the war. But with the same industrial leaders and government bureaucrats left in place, the breakup was not thorough enough to prevent the reassembling of the *zaibatsu* in a new form even before the occupation officially ended in 1952.

The third decision was to allow Japan, as well as other selected Asian countries, to have virtually free access to U.S. markets without demanding the same in return. The motive behind the decision was similar to what guided the Marshall Plan aid to

## U.S. Trade Deficits

*Throughout the 1980s, U.S. trade deficits with Japan far exceeded those with other countries. Total U.S. trade deficits peaked in 1987. American consumers bought $152 billion more in imported goods that year than U.S. companies sold abroad. From 1987 to 1990, the U.S. trade deficit shrunk by nearly a third, but the trade deficit with Japan is still more than $40 billion.*

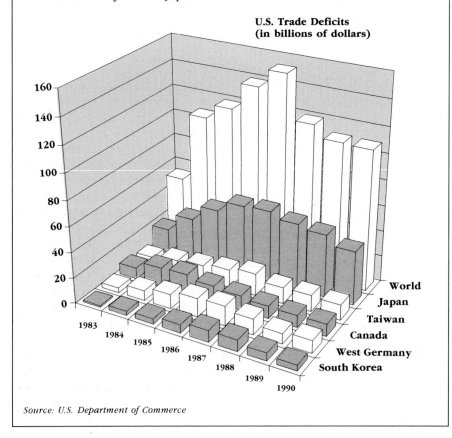

**U.S. Trade Deficits
(in billions of dollars)**

World
Japan
Taiwan
Canada
West Germany
South Korea

1983 1984 1985 1986 1987 1988 1989 1990

*Source: U.S. Department of Commerce*

Europe — to shore up the economies of a war-shattered area. But providing aid in the form of relatively unrestricted market access while allowing virtually closed markets in Japan encouraged an unusually strong export orientation in Japan.

It didn't take Japan long to take advantage of the situation. Before 1950, Japan erected strong tariff and quota barriers — even as the world's industrial countries were negotiating to dismantle tariffs and quotas under the fledgling General Agreement on Tariffs and Trade (GATT). In 1949, Japan's Diet passed a Foreign Exchange and Foreign Trade Control Law that re-

quired licenses from the government for all imports.

At first, such measures met with relatively few foreign complaints, since the country's economy was in such bad shape. If there was a role for tariffs and quotas in the new economic order of things, it was precisely for countries like Japan that needed to protect "infant" industries from foreign competition. As Japan's economy stabilized at the end of the 1950s, however, the country came under increasing pressure to reduce its trade barriers. Most quotas were eliminated in the early 1960s, but as economist Edward Lincoln notes, "in many cases

liberalization of quotas on products was offset by the imposition of high tariffs on those same products." [20]

Lincoln points out that Japan's decision to liberalize trade barriers was motivated by foreign pressure, not any free-trade sentiments. "The predominant domestic intellectual rationale for liberalization from the early 1960s to the mid-'80s has been the need to meet international obligations, with an implicit belief that liberalization held no direct benefit for the Japanese economy," he says.

## Friction Grew in 1980s

As long as the United States was running overall trade surpluses, U.S. officials seemed willing to overlook Japanese trade surpluses in the interest of not upsetting its security arrangements with Japan. But when the United States started to show overall trade deficits in the mid-1970s, concern began to grow. And by the 1980s, as the U.S. trade deficit mushroomed,* Congress and the White House concluded that some sort of action was necessary.

"It seemed that the Japanese economy suddenly was challenging or outstripping the United States in many fields — from the ubiquitous presence of Japanese consumer electronics products and automobiles in the American market, to computer chips and petrochemical plants worldwide," notes Richard Fairbanks, president of the U.S. National Committee for Pacific Economic Cooperation.[21]

It took a while, Fairbanks says, but "slowly, Americans realized that ... the energies of this remarkably

---

*The U.S. trade deficit rose from a little over $35 billion in 1980 to $152 billion in 1987. Japan alone accounted for about $50 billion of that increase.

cohesive and determined society were able to be directed toward product and market development by a combination of dynamic private businesses reinforced by government policies." Japan was limiting competition at home and often excluding it from abroad while also marshaling business-expansion capital at the expense of consumers and social imperatives. In other words, Japan wasn't playing fair. It was shutting out U.S. and other foreign products, partly through trade barriers and partly by holding down consumption at home.

At the same time, the United States in the early 1980s entered upon a binge of deficit spending, much of it devoted to an immense and expensive military buildup. Between 1981 and 1983, the federal deficit tripled in size, rising from 2 percent of gross national product to 6 percent. To attract enough money to fund that deficit, the government had to offer high interest rates when it sold U.S. Treasury notes. As more dollars were put into Treasury notes, dollars became scarcer, and therefore more valuable. The high dollar made imports cheaper for Americans, but it also made U.S. exports less competitive overseas.

Many countries benefited from the high dollar, but none more than Japan, which moved from a global trade deficit of more than $10 billion in 1980 to a surplus of more than $80 billion by 1987. The United States tried to stem the tide in 1985 by engineering a 60 percent drop in the value of the dollar over three years. But the move failed to reduce U.S. trade deficits significantly. In fact, it seemed to improve Japan's economic standing. "The high yen drove Japan to hyperefficiency," says Chalmers Johnson, professor of Asian studies at the University of California at San Diego. "Simultaneously, the low dollar seriously lowered the price

of American assets, and they became bargain-sale items." The result was a wave of Japanese acquisitions in the United States.

One reason the devaluation of the dollar didn't have as great an impact on the trade balance as economists had estimated was that the American consumption spree gave birth to overseas producers who did whatever they had to do — cut wages, cut costs, cut profit margins — to hold onto market share.

As charges of unfair trade practices increased, the United States initiated a series of bilateral trade negotiations with Japan.

### Decade of Trade Talks

When Reagan administration trade negotiators sat down to talk to Japanese negotiators in the early 1980s, Edward Lincoln suggests, they "brought a bedrock ideological commitment to the concept of free trade" that "became a stumbling block in the tactical approach to Japan." He argues that administration officials assumed that Japan (as another market-oriented capitalist country) behaved according to the same principles and thus opposed any action that could be construed as protectionist.[22]

The Reagan administration soon fell into a pattern of negotiating for greater market access in specified narrow sectors, or even specified products — a "laundry-list strategy," in Lincoln's words[23] — rather than trying to deal with Japan's economic structure and its systemwide impediments to imports. One of the few successes of this approach was in tobacco products. The U.S. share of the Japanese market increased from 2 percent in 1985 to more than 10 percent by late 1987. The Reagan administration also was successful in negotiating voluntary restrictions on Japanese automobile imports. (*See story, p. 342.*)

In 1984, the Reagan administra-

tion adopted a different tactic. Instead of focusing efforts on narrow products areas, the United States decided to choose four broad product categories for intensive discussion in the so-called Market-Oriented Sector Selective (MOSS) negotiations. They were forest products, medical and pharmaceutical products, electronics and telecommunications.

The results of the MOSS talks were spotty. Some products did find more open markets in Japan, but most U.S. companies were dissatisfied with the results. Despite the MOSS emphasis on telecommunications, for example, Japanese restrictions on international telecommunications services resulted in new talks in 1987, and restrictions on cellular telephones had to be dealt with in 1989.

Another major sore point was semiconductors. In the mid-1980s, U.S. chipmakers began complaining that the Japanese were selling chips in the U.S. market at below-cost prices in order to run U.S. chipmakers out of business. Reagan administration trade negotiators reached an agreement with Japan in 1986 that Japanese chipmakers would boost their prices. There also was a semi-secret attachment to the agreement: In it the Japanese agreed to try to expand foreigners' share of the Japanese chip market to 20 percent by 1991.

Unfortunately, the pact backfired on the United States, primarily because by the time it was instituted U.S. manufacturers had already nearly abandoned the market. "Though government-sanctioned production cutbacks in Japan did help boost [chip] prices . . .," observes economist Kenneth Flamm of the Brookings Institution, "only a small share of the resulting profits dribbled back to American . . . vendors, while U.S. chip consumers paid billions in increased prices."[24]

One part of the agreement has been modestly successful: Chip imports to Japan have increased from below 10 percent in 1986 to slightly more than 13 percent today — a clear improvement, though still well below the target of 20 percent.

Aside from narrow concessions where it could not avoid them, Japan responded to the increasing pressure from the United States with a series of reports — the Okita report in 1985 and the Maekawa report a year later. Both called for significant structural changes in Japan and an all-out effort to increase imports.

"Nakasone's government released the Maekawa report and indicated that it represented a step almost as dramatic as the Marshall Plan," writes James Fallows. "No longer would salarymen be admired for toiling 18 hours a day in order to expand Japan's market share. No longer would Japan's standard of living be so far out of whack with its paper wealth, and no longer would Japan view its trade surplus as an indication of its superiority over the West." [25]

Though the U.S. media generally trumpeted the reports as signifying a major change in Japanese attitudes, there actually was little change. "There have been a few symbolic changes — banks and some government offices are closed on Saturday mornings — but compared with the claims that were made when it was presented, the report has been a major disappointment," Fallows observes.

The disappointment in the United States was great enough that on March 27, 1987, the Reagan administration announced it was taking retaliatory measures against Japan. The decision was made in response to Japan's alleged failure to live up to the 1986 agreement barring Japanese companies from selling semiconductor chips in the United States for less than a "fair market value." In retaliation, the

administration imposed punitive tariffs on a wide range of Japanese electronics products, including certain color televisions, computers and power tools.* The White House lifted most of the tariffs by the end of the year, however, saying the Japanese appeared to have stopped dumping computer chips in the United States.

Congress, too, showed its impatience with Japan when it passed the Fair Trade and Competitiveness Act of 1988. The legislation — which applies to any country exporting to the United States, but which was designed with Japan in mind — contained a set of deadlines for identifying and resolving trade disputes. The legislation required the U.S. trade representative to submit a report to Congress on other countries' trade practices by April 30 of each year. Within a month, the trade representative was required to target specific countries' practices and begin negotiations to resolve the problems. If those negotiations failed, the act called for retaliation, though ultimately the president had the authority to suspend any such steps.

For its part, Japan's Diet in December 1988 responded to persistent American complaints with a sweeping tax reform bill that many economists predicted would spur consumer spending and, hence, increase Japanese imports. Under the legislation, the highest individual tax rate fell from 60 percent to 50 percent. The corporate tax rate dropped from 42 percent to 37.5 percent, and taxes on luxury items such as autos, liquor, electrical appliances and sports equipment,

were cut from 20 percent to 3 percent.

### Bush Tries New Approach

Despite all these efforts, the United States was still running an annual trade deficit with Japan of nearly $52 billion when George Bush assumed the presidency in 1989. This was down only about $4 billion from the high point of 1987. Bush trade officials decided to try a new tactic: the Structural Impediments Initiative (SII). In July 1989, just two months after having branded Japan an unfair trade partner under the 1988 trade law, the Bush administration coerced Japan into a series of negotiations not on specific products, but on the "structural impediments" to bilateral trade — such things as government regulations, business practices, lax antitrust laws and so forth.

In a report issued by the joint working group on SII in June 1990, the Japanese government committed itself to take action in six broad areas: reforming savings and investment patterns, land policy, the distribution system, exclusionary business practices, *keiretsu* relationships and pricing. In return, the United States committed itself to one major task: bringing down the federal deficits, which the Japanese had argued were the main problem for U.S. exporters all along.

At the same time, Bush administration negotiators continued to pursue sector-specific and product-specific negotiations, and with some apparent success. In April 1990, U.S. Trade Representative Carla A. Hills told Congress that Japan had moved "further this year than any other country" in opening its markets and shouldn't be cited as an unfair trader. [26]

Indeed, throughout 1990 the U.S. trade representative's office announced a series of agreements on trade disputes. On April 3 of last

*Continued on p. 336*

---

*The White House chose not to retaliate directly by imposing tariffs on Japanese semiconductors because such a move would have angered U.S. computer makers, who needed to buy chips cheaply to keep their products competitive.

# Chronology

**1940s** *U.S. occupies Japan after World War II. Japan struggles to rebuild its war-torn economy.*

### May 3, 1947
New Japanese Constitution takes effect.

———•———

**1950s** *Japan's economy stabilizes.*

———•———

**1960s** *Japan eliminates most quotas on imports, but replaces them with higher tariffs and non-formal trade barriers.*

———•———

**1970s** *The United States begins to show chronic and increasing trade deficits.*

———•———

**1980s** *Trade friction grows despite a series of negotiations aimed at settling disputes.*

### 1984
Reagan administration initiates talks aimed at lowering Japanese trade barriers in forest products, medical and pharmaceutical products, electronics and telecommunications.

### April 7, 1986
Japanese government issues Maekawa report calling for "historic shift" away from dependence on growth through exports.

### July 31, 1986
U.S. and Japanese negotiators sign an accord to end a microchip dispute. Japan agrees to raise prices of its semiconductors and to let foreign chip manufacturers increase their share of the Japanese market.

### Sept. 18, 1986
For the first time since World War II, Japan spends more than 1 percent of its GNP on defense.

### March 27, 1987
Reagan administration accuses Japan of violating 1986 microchip agreement and places a 100 percent tariff on selected Japanese electronics products.

### Aug. 23, 1988
The Fair Trade and Competitiveness Act is signed into law. It requires the U.S. trade representative to submit reports annually listing countries that engage in unfair trade practices and requires sanctions against those that refuse to change.

### Dec. 24, 1988
Japan's Diet (legislature) passes sweeping tax reform measure aimed at increasing the country's consumption of imports.

### May 25, 1989
Bush administration brands Japan as an unfair trade partner.

### July 1989
Beginning of the Structural Impediments Initiative talks, aimed at reducing impediments to trade in the U.S. and Japan.

**1990s** *Some progress in trade negotiations, but U.S. recession and Persian Gulf War increase tensions between the U.S. and Japan.*

### April 27, 1990
Bush administration says Japan has made progress in opening its markets and announces it will not name Japan as an unfair trader.

### June 1990
Japan and U.S. release year-end report of the Structural Impediments Initiative. U.S. promises to work to reduce federal budget deficits and increase national savings. Japan promises to reform savings and investment patterns and exclusionary business practices.

### December 1990
Japan agrees to increase payments for maintaining U.S. forces in Japan from 40 percent of costs to 50 percent.

### Dec. 12, 1990
U.S. Commerce Department issues preliminary finding that Japan is skirting an anti-dumping order by shipping television tubes to Mexico for assembly and export to the U.S.

### April 24, 1991
Japan announces it is sending a flotilla of minesweepers to the Persian Gulf.

### April 26, 1991
Bush administration announces it is initiating procedures to ban Japanese construction companies from contracts with the U.S. government.

*Continued from p. 334*

year, Japan agreed to open some bidding on satellites for purchase by Japan. On April 25, negotiators agreed on measures to open the Japanese market to more U.S. wood products. On June 15 an agreement was concluded that would require publicly funded organizations in Japan to select supercomputers not on the basis of cost alone, but on cost and performance, a change thought to favor U.S. supercomputers. On June 28, Japan agreed to open access to its mobile telephone market. On Aug. 1, Japan agreed to measures aimed at liberalizing its telecommunications markets.

But these agreements did not end the U.S.-Japan trade disputes. In August 1990, for example, a coalition of television manufacturers — the Committee to Preserve American Color Television — accused Japan of getting around anti-dumping laws by shipping picture tubes to Mexico for assembly and export to the United States. On Dec. 12, 1990, the Commerce Department issued a preliminary ruling finding circumstantial evidence that Japan was guilty of skirting the anti-dumping order.

## Eroding Security Alliance

The U.S.-Japan security relationship, though not as public an issue, has been nearly as turbulent as the trade relationship. For both countries, the postwar relationship has been one that traded off economic and strategic concerns.

In the early years, the United States was willing to make economic concessions in favor of larger strategic interests. The larger strategic interest at stake was that of containing the Soviet Union and maintaining a dominating presence in the Pacific. Japan's part of the bar-

gain was to tolerate the presence of American forces in exchange for protection from the Soviets.

For the next 20 years or so, the deal was considered a good one for the United States, which was able to contain the Soviet fleet and also eliminate any need for the Japanese to rebuild its own armed forces. This latter factor, though generally not discussed publicly, had great importance both to U.S. planners and to countries in the Pacific — including South Korea, Singapore and the Philippines — that had suffered under Japanese occupation during World War II.

It wasn't until the late 1970s and early '80s that many in the United States began to question the arrangement. The reasons were simple: The U.S. budget was moving into heavy deficits even as Japan's trade surpluses, especially those with the United States, were climbing higher and higher. Frustration with the deficits caused many in Congress to point the finger at Japan, alleging that it was beating the United States in the market place in part because it didn't have to spend the billions Americans did on defense.

A slew of legislation calling for greater "burden-sharing" began to appear in Congress. Although none of the proposals was ever enacted, they reflected Americans' growing frustration with Japan. ∎

# CURRENT SITUATION

## Japanese Resentment

The most important single event in the recent history of the U.S.-Japan relationship is without question the end of the Cold War with the Soviet Union. Without the Soviet threat, the U.S.-Japanese relationship has changed in subtle but very important ways. For Japan, there seems to be a new sense of self-confidence and more questioning of how much Japan should be giving in to the United States.

Evidence of this new self-confidence abounds. A particular stir was raised with the publication of the 1989 book *The Japan that Can Say No*, in which former Japanese legislator Shintaro Ishihara warns the United States that Japan could easily alter the global balance of power by selling microchip technologies to the Soviets. "The more technol-

ogy advances, the more the U.S. and Soviet Union will become dependent upon the initiative of the Japanese people," Ishihara wrote.

Though extreme, Ishihara's views appear to reflect a trend. A recent study of U.S.-Japan relations commissioned by the Japanese Foreign Ministry observed that Japan's economic strength was reawakening Japanese nationalism. According to the report, "There is a growing feeling that further [trade] concessions to the U.S. are unnecessary." [29]

Karel van Wolferen, a Dutch journalist who has lived and worked in Japan for quite some time, says Japanese resentment over complaints about its trade practices is growing. "The Japanese people take it almost for granted that the rest of the world begrudges them the fruit of their hard work," he writes, adding that many Japanese believe Washington's pressure tactics are "based on anti-Japanese, even racist, sentiment." [30]

Even as Western observers are noting a more independent attitude on Japan's part, Japanese investors have focused increasingly on markets in Asia and, accordingly, putting less emphasis on U.S. markets. Between 1985 and 1989, Japan's direct investment in Asia quadrupled, to a total of about $5.6 billion. Japan's trade with Asian countries has also grown dramatically. In 1989, Japan for the first time imported more from Asian countries — $49 billion worth of goods — than it did from the United States.

## Ongoing Negotiations

With security issues in the Pacific no longer carrying the same degree of overriding importance, the United States is less inclined to overlook trade issues. "Whatever the ultimate verdict of history," write Clyde Prestowitz and Selig Harrison, "Soviet President Mikhail [S.] Gorbachev has now made it possible for Washington to put economic priorities first and to strengthen its leverage with the East Asian capitals hitherto regarded as indispensable pillars of U.S. security." [31]

And there are currently plenty of issues in dispute between the two countries. To begin with, Japan's trade surplus with the United States remains unacceptably high, totalling more than $41 billion for 1990. The Foreign Trade Barriers report of the U.S. trade representative's office, released in April, contains a litany of complaints against Japan, including:

■ High tariff rates and quantity restrictions on agricultural products.

■ Quotas on leather goods.

■ Government subsidies for Japanese lumber companies.

■ Prohibition on rice imports.

But these formal barriers are only the beginning. The trade representative's report also complains of a host of "invisible" barriers, from

government procurement practices to lax enforcement of antitrust laws. For example, the report complains that "foreign computer suppliers have been selected for only about 10 percent of the Japanese government's computer purchases. By con-

**Without the Soviet threat, the U.S.-Japanese relationship has changed in subtle but very important ways. For Japan, there seems to be a new sense of self-confidence and more questioning of how much Japan should be giving in to the United States.**

trast, foreign companies supplied 36.8 percent of the Japanese private-sector computer market in 1989." And, though legal restrictions on foreign direct investment have been eased in Japan, the report says that "the Japanese government continues to regulate foreign investment in certain specified sectors: aircraft, space development, agriculture, fishing and forestry, oil and gas, mining, and leather and leather product manufacturing."

The two most contentious issues currently are construction and semiconductors. On April 26, the Bush administration announced it was going to ban Japanese construction companies from contracts with the U.S. government because talks on access of U.S. construction firms to Japanese projects were going nowhere. While Japanese firms received $2.8 billion in new contracts from the United States in 1989, U.S. firms have been able to secure only

$310 million in Japanese contracts since May 1988.

If the Bush administration actually carries through on the sanctions at the end of May — under U.S. law, the government must give 30 days' notice — it would be the first retaliation ordered by the White House since 1987, when the Reagan administration imposed punitive tariffs on certain Japanese electronics goods in response to alleged dumping of computer chips (see p. 334).

Japan's economics minister, Hiroshi Hirabayashi, has already warned that if the United States resorts to sanctions, Japan would revoke contracts already granted to U.S. construction firms.

As for semiconductors, the chip pact negotiated in 1986 expires in July 1991, and U.S. firms are pushing to have a new agreement in place before then. The old agreement "certainly didn't meet the expectations of U.S. semiconductor producers," says Judge Morris of the National Association of Manufacturers. "The agreement needs to be continued for another five years or so, so that we can solidify the gains and improve upon them."

For its part, Japan is demanding that the United States lift the remaining tariffs on Japanese electronic goods. Japan is also likely to argue against setting a firm market share for foreign chips.

U.S. and Japanese negotiators also are currently engaged in a continuation of the Structural Impediments Initiative talks begun by the Bush administration in 1989. American negotiators are generally upbeat about the course of the negotiations. A trade official who asked not to be identified said the Japanese seem to have done all the things they promised.

## Trade in Manufactured Goods

*In the 1980s, exports of U.S. manufactured goods to Japan actually grew at a more rapid pace than Japan's exports of manufactured goods to the U.S. But Japan still exports significantly more to the U.S. than the U.S. does to Japan.*

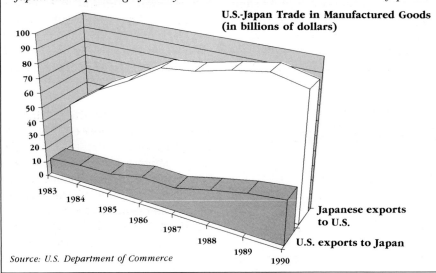

**U.S.-Japan Trade in Manufactured Goods (in billions of dollars)**

Japanese exports to U.S.

U.S. exports to Japan

*Source: U.S. Department of Commerce*

Other analysts are taking a wait-and-see attitude. Judge Morris, for example, says it will take years to judge the success or failure of SII. "We hope SII can be kept going," he says, "but we also think there are clear limits to it, and that other avenues are necessary." Bill Krist of the American Electronics Association echoes that judgment. "We support the SII activity.... But SII is basically a blueprint for future action," he says. "The things that are set out in SII, many of them Japan has been talking about doing for decades. There's no progress until they're done and done in a way that leads to results in the marketplace."

### Signs of change in Japan

Despite the pessimism that has been engendered among many American analysts by past Japanese actions, some believe Japan is finally turning a corner. In part, the change they see is the result of a maturing economy. In part, the change is one of attitude.

To begin with, recent events,

most notably the crash of the Japanese stock market in 1990, have changed the financial outlook for Japanese businesses. The decline of nearly 40 percent of stock values in the first nine months of 1990 cut deeply into the assets and borrowing power of Japanese companies. Japanese banks, which rely on stock holdings for about half of their lending capital, were hurt by the crash. "As a result," writes banker Roy C. Smith, "the huge Japanese comparative advantages in banking and finance have disappeared. ... The result may be less money to finance the U.S. budget deficits, but far less pressure on the U.S. and European companies that compete with the Japanese." [32]

Many analysts also see fundamental structural changes taking place within Japan. The people who have benefited most from the old protectionist system are distributors, small retailers and farmers. "It's a political artifact," says Frances Rosenbluth, a professor at the Center for International Relations and

Pacific Studies at the University of California at San Diego. "It's not there for the sake of economic efficiency [or] to maximize consumer welfare. It's there because small retailers are politically powerful."

Now, Rosenbluth says, large businesses are growing "increasingly weary of carrying along the less efficient sectors of the economy that are always flagged by the U.S." But it's not just big business that wants to scrap the old protectionist system, Rosenbluth adds. "Over time the [ruling party's] demographic base has been shifting. There are more urban voters who are harder to woo in the usual way, with the usual protectionist favors."

The Structural Impediments Initiative has helped this process along, U.S. trade officials say. "The SII process engendered a very broad debate within Japanese society about the goals and objectives of the process," says one U.S. negotiator. He adds that approval ratings in the polls for SII have been extremely high. "It's not just a case of foreign pressure and Japanese concessions ..., [but also] of intentions and undertakings between the Japanese people and the Japanese government."

At the same time, he says, "the existence of foreign pressure to make changes does seem to be a permanent part of the landscape. I think we must expect that we will have to live with a certain amount of friction in our relationship. It will be with us indefinitely."

## Strategic Realignments

Beyond the trade issues, it is clear that the entire U.S.-Japanese relationship is undergoing change. For the United States, the change requires an adjustment to the fact that America no longer controls the helm of the world economy by itself. Though Japan's GNP is still behind that of the United States, Japan is now such an economic power that it must be reckoned with in most international undertakings.

For the Japanese, the adjustments are even more challenging. As the behavior of Japan during the gulf war demonstrates, the country is undergoing something of an identity crisis. One part of Japan very clearly wants to assume a larger role on the world stage, while another part wants to remain isolated.

As early as Oct. 16, 1990, for example, the Japanese Cabinet approved a plan to send troops to the Persian Gulf to perform behind-the-lines support tasks, but the plan was quickly shot down by opposition at home. And though the Takeshita government subsequently pushed hard for Japan to do more for the allied effort, an opinion poll conducted in early February revealed that the majority of Japanese opposed even the $9 billion of financial aid the government said it would contribute to the gulf war effort.[33] "It was an agonizing period for the government," says a U.S. trade official. "It showed that Japan has not come to terms with its own history."

But while Japan was unable to bring itself to take an active role in the gulf war, many Japanese are increasingly chafing at being militarily dependent on the United States. "The American policy of keeping Japan militarily weak while pressuring Japan to pay more and more has built up suppressed anger and resentment among many Japanese politicians and bureaucrats," writes Kan Ito, a Japanese journalist. "They feel that the United States is demanding burden sharing without offering power sharing and leadership sharing in return. They feel treated as inferiors; they feel distrusted. They feel, in fact, more than a little insulted."[34]

Ito warns that "the current U.S.

policy of pressuring Japan to spend more while keeping it weak cannot last; it will eventually invite an unhealthy nationalistic backlash." According to Ito, "the only fair and acceptable solution to this burden-sharing problem is to create a new integrated defense system to share missions and leadership in the Asia-Pacific region."

Yet many Japanese — particularly those who lived through World War II — are themselves very distrustful of a resurgent Japanese military. That is one reason there was so much opposition to Japan providing any sort of military support to the allied effort in the Persian Gulf War.  ■

# OUTLOOK

## Ties That Bind?

Are the ties that bind the United States and Japan together stronger than the forces that pull the two countries apart? Most analysts believe they are. "Fundamentally, I believe the leadership in Japan feels that our bilateral relationship is their most important relationship," says the U.S. trade official. Judge Morris of the NAM also believes the relationship will survive the current strains. "There are going to be clashes. And they're going to be slightly more serious than the usual trade frictions over 'you blocked my widget,'" Morris says. "That doesn't mean we aren't also going to forge a successful relationship."

Ito is not so sure. "Many Americans would like to believe . . . they are innocent victims of Japan's trade and investment activities, which are variously described as unbalanced, unfair, aggressive, one-sided and predatory," he writes. "Many Japanese would like to believe that they are innocent victims of what they call America's envy, economic mismanagement, hypocrisy and racism. Both sides, in fact, have legitimate complaints and grievances; but both sides are also myopic, self-centered and self-righteous."[35]

A book published this year in the

United States actually predicts a shooting war between the two countries within the next two decades. "Just as Iraq, after its war with Iran, presented its bill to Kuwait and the rest of the Persian Gulf, so, too, the United States, after the Cold War, is adding up the bill for its allies, and in particular Japan," George Friedman, a national security expert at the Heritage Foundation, a conservative think tank in Washington, writes in *The Coming War with Japan*. "The price, permanent subordination to the United States and a willingness to suffer economic damage on American demand, is too high a price for Japan — or any sovereign state — to pay. On the other hand, for the United States to continue protecting Japan's global interests free of charge after the Soviets have collapsed is too high a price for Americans to pay."[36]

### Trade Issues

Whether the United States and Japan can find their way to a new equilibrium will depend on many factors. The primary one, of course, is whether the imbalance in the trade relationship can be corrected.

Ultimately, economists say that balancing trade between Japan and the United States depends more on actions by the United States than Japan. Huge federal budget deficits will have to be cut down, and the low U.S. savings rate will have to be raised. Most experts are not willing to predict how soon those goals might be achieved.

Precisely because it may take some time to address the problems of the U.S. deficit and low savings rates, some analysts argue that it is essential that Japan do its part — for political reasons, if not domestic economic ones — to ease the trade relationship by opening its markets.

The camp of analysts that believes Japan is already changing in the direction of trade liberalization argues that the best course for the United States is to encourage that trend through continuing trade negotiations. "I think over 20 years the Japanese will be consuming more, saving less, and their trade surplus will be shrinking," says Frances Rosenbluth. "But that's way down the road, and I don't think politically in the U.S. that's going to fly. Japan will have to make its incremental concessions right along the way." So long as the United States doesn't make an emotional issue of it, Japan will make those concessions, Rosenbluth says, because they really can't afford not to. "There are noises in Japan about, 'How much do we have to put up with?' But from the standpoint of big corporations I don't think there's really much of a choice. They don't have an alternative. The U.S. market is far and away the most attractive. They're not about to give that up."

Economist Edward Lincoln agrees that Japan is changing, albeit slowly, in the right direction. But he says that further pressures, while necessary "to strengthen the hand of those in Japan desiring change," should come in the forum of multilateral negotiations under the General Agreement on Tariffs and Trade, and not through bilateral trade deals. Not only does the mul-

tilateral approach encourage freer trade, Lincoln says, GATT decisions tend to have greater impact in Japan than bilateral deals. "To lose a decision represents an international humiliation for the Japanese, especially given the importance of

**Whether the United States and Japan can find their way to a new equilibrium will depend on many factors. The primary one, of course, is whether the imbalance in the trade relationship can be corrected.**

international economic and trade issues in Japan," he writes.[37]

Many other analysts, however, believe the Japanese will rigidly resist any real change in their system, and that stronger actions by the United States are called for. "The common suggestion that the Japanese public will at some point grow tired of subsidizing exports (by paying the world's highest prices for consumer products), and thus help bring about major structural changes, shows how little is understood in the West about the informal political arrangements that serve to prevent such a development," writes Karel van Wolferen. "Any of the structural changes desired by Washington would, in the eyes of Japanese powerholders, introduce an intolerable degree of disorder and threaten their world."[38]

That being the case, van Wolferen argues, "Whatever formal Japanese concessions emerge from negotia-

tions, informal arrangements will spring up to preserve the status quo in every case." This, he says, could lead to a kind of vicious cycle of growing frustration and anger in both countries.

Instead of "haranguing and negotiating with Japan," James Fallows suggests, the United States should "act politely but firmly to defend the industries and technologies that are important to us." In Fallows' view, such action would likely include not only efforts to reduce the federal deficits, but also government involvement in subsidizing strategic industries, and some types of market-sharing agreements.

While most U.S. economists favor free trade, many, including Edward Lincoln, believe that managed trade in a few products may be unavoidable. Still, they warn that relying on bilateral managed-trade agreements to share markets, and increased protectionism at home through subsidizing industries, could lead to an erosion of the current trading system.

The big fear of free-market economists is that the U.S.-Japan trade conflict could encourage the evolution of regional trade blocs to replace a crumbling international system. There are, in fact, already some signs that Japan — always concerned about being shut out of coordinated North American and European trading blocs — may be preparing for a regional Asian trade bloc. For example, a 1988 study prepared for the Japanese Economic Planning Agency carried the title "Promoting Comprehensive Economic Cooperation in an International Economic Environment Undergoing Upheaval: Towards the Construction of an Asian Network." And many economists have sug-

*Continued on p. 342*

# At Issue:

## Are lobbyists for Japan a threat to American interests?

**PAT CHOATE**

*Economist, author of* Agents of Influence
FROM *HARVARD BUSINESS REVIEW*, SEPTEMBER/
OCTOBER 1990.

*yes*

*i*magine [a nation] spending more than $100 million each year to hire 1,000 Washington, D.C., lobbyists, superlawyers, former high-ranking public officials, public relations specialists, political advisers — even former presidents. Imagine it spending another $300 million each year to build a nationwide grass roots political network to influence public opinion. Imagine that its $400 million per year political campaign sought to advance its economic interests, influence U.S. trade policy and win market share in the United States for its target industries.

None of this is imaginary; none of it is illegal. The country that is actually undertaking this political campaign is Japan. Today Japan controls the most sophisticated and successful political-economic machine in the United States. . . .

In politics, as in manufactured products, Japanese strategy follows a simple and predictable pattern: protect your own domestic market from foreign penetration, capture as much of your competitor's market share as possible. . . . Japan is gaining political market share in the United States, spending hundreds of millions of dollars for competitive advantage. To the Japanese, politics is another legitimate business expense. . . .

Japan's political machine in the United States is designed to serve six national and corporate goals:

1. To keep the U.S. market open for exports from Japan.

2. To smooth the way for additional purchases of key assets in the United States.

3. To blunt criticism of Japan's adversarial trade practices.

4. To neutralize or, even better, to capture the political influence of the U.S. companies that compete with Japan.

5. To influence U.S. trade policies toward Japan, Europe and all other markets where Japan has significant economic interest.

6. To create an integrated U.S.-Japan economy that prevents the United States from confronting Japan economically and politically. . . .

In one critical industry after another, U.S. companies originally challenged by Japanese manufacturing prowess, now run the added risk of losing out to the Japanese competition because of Japan's well-managed political strategy. American companies, pressed in the market for the consumer's favor, may now face the defection of their own government as an ally in global competition. For the American public, the issue is even more stark. With so much Japanese money influencing so many officials in government, the question for the American people is "Who do you trust?"

**TOMOHITO SHINODA**

*Washington representative for Taro Kimura Inc. and author of* Lobbying U.S. Congress: U.S.-Japan Relations Within Washington *(1989)*
FROM *HARVARD BUSINESS REVIEW*, NOVEMBER/DECEMBER 1990.

*no*

*l*ike many critics of Japan, Pat Choate has a monolithic view of Japanese corporate activities that is inaccurate. When the U.S. media write about Japanese investments in the United States, reporters say, "Japan bought Rockefeller Center," or "Japan bought Columbia Pictures," rather than say Americans sold them to the individual Japanese corporations, Mitsubishi and Sony. Such reports give the impression that the Japanese business community has teamed up to buy America. In the same way, Mr. Choate argues, "Japan's political machine in the United States is designed to serve six national and corporate goals," including "to keep the U.S. market open for Japanese exports."

My research suggests that the only example of concerted multisector effort to influence U.S. government policy by Japanese corporations was against the unitary tax, a state tax that would impose double taxation on foreign corporations in the United States. This lobbying effort was organized only because the participants had common commercial interests in that specific matter.

Japanese corporations and industry organizations, independent of one another, do spend outstanding amounts of money on their lobbying activities. Each individual corporation, however, like its U.S. counterpart, seeks its own commercial interest, not "national" interests. . . .

Undoubtedly, Japanese companies do spend large sums on lobbying. . . . But this fact is often exaggerated. Choate compares Japan's "1,000-person lobby" with domestic groups — a rather misleading comparison. Large U.S. institutions, including the National Association of Manufacturers, have at least a dozen full-time lobbyists, besides hundreds of consultants and public relations personnel within their own organizations, so they do not have to be as dependent on outside lobbyists as do Japanese interests in Washington. . . .

My research shows that Japanese lobbying is rarely arm-twisting. Japan's presence in Washington is, in effect, a kind of insurance policy, which is usually defensive rather than offensive and usually not as effective as domestic groups. When rational arguments are used and reasonable requests are made, Japanese lobbying can be effective. . . .

The issue involved is not whether or not foreign influence is good but whether or not the consequent policy outcomes are in the best interest of U.S. society.

# Japanese Auto Imports

Fifteen years ago, as gasoline prices soared, American consumers abandoned their gas-guzzling American automobiles and snapped up the no-nonsense, subcompact "econoboxes" manufactured by Honda Motor Co., Toyota Motor Corp., Nissan Motor Co. and other Japanese companies. Americans soon learned they were getting more for their money than they had bargained for. Not only were the Japanese cars cheap to buy and fuel, they were cheap to run because of the high quality of the workmanship that went into both engines and auto bodies.

The number of Japanese imports sold in the United States doubled from 1976 to 1980 to more than 1.9 million vehicles. By 1982, Japan had captured 22.6 percent of the U.S. market.

As sales of Japanese cars soared, American automakers began pressuring Congress and the White House to impose quotas on the Japanese. The Reagan administration was committed to the concept of free trade, but in May 1981 it negotiated a "voluntary" export-restraint agreement with the Japanese government. The Japanese agreed to a quota of fewer than 2 million exports of cars, vans and station wagons for the year beginning Aug. 1, 1981, amounting to an 8 percent cut from the previous year.

With only a limited number of cars to export, Japan began shipping to America more of their upscale models, loaded with expensive options. The Japanese soon were making more money selling fewer cars. And with prices rising for Japanese imports, American automakers were able to raise prices on their models as well.

The quotas were not all good news for Detroit, however. Beginning in December 1982, when Honda opened an auto-assembly plant in Marysville, Ohio, Japanese automakers increasingly have transferred some of their assembly operations to the United States. U.S. automakers now must compete with some of their biggest Japanese rivals on their home turf. This has not only allowed the Japanese to circumvent the export-quota agreement, but also to save production costs. By assembling cars close to their principal wholesale market, the Japanese cut down on the cost of shipping finished vehicles across the Pacific.

After nearly a decade of voluntary export quotas, American automakers still are having trouble competing with the Japanese. Sales of American-built cars have slumped badly during the current recession. General Motors Corp.'s sales in March were down 12.3 percent from a year earlier. Ford Motor Co.'s sales were down 14.8 percent for the month and Chrysler Corp.'s sales were off 18.3 percent.

Japanese automakers have fared better. Led by Honda, Japanese automakers boosted their combined share of the U.S. car market to 31 percent in March from 29 percent a year earlier. Honda's sales were up 9.5 percent from March 1990. Mazda's sales were up 5.5 percent. But Toyota's sales were down 5 percent in March and Nissan's sales were down 24 percent.

The strong showing by Japanese automakers led Chrysler Chairman Lee A. Iacocca to ask President Bush for more protection from Japanese imports. While Iacocca's March 6 letter reportedly got a cool reception at the White House, Japanese auto executives are said to be increasingly anxious about the threat of trade retaliation.†

---

† See *The Wall Street Journal*, April 5, 1991.

---

*Continued from p. 340*

gested that Japan's recent surge in investments in Asian countries could, in Lincoln's words, "foreshadow a regionalism that seeks to exclude the United States." [39]

### Strategic Issues

Increased trade tensions between the United States and Japan could, of course, erode the relationship in other realms. Harsher demands by the United States on Japan could lead to increased nationalism in that country. "Officials in Tokyo have privately warned Washington that perennial demands in the context of the bilateral trade conflict abet the proliferation of nationalistic sentiment in Japan, and that this sentiment could get out of hand," writes van Wolferen. "While the U.S. administration must contend with a Congress that is increasingly restive on the subject of Japan, Japanese bureaucrats today must take into account a newly emerging and intimidating right-wing force." [40]

Under such circumstances the possibility of Japan actively rearming and assuming a military role in the region would increase dramatically. And if, indeed, the international trading regime broke into three major trading blocs — North America, Europe, and Asia — the result would almost certainly be a heightening of political tensions and an increase in Japanese militarism.

If the American-Japanese strategic alliance were ended, "the strategic architecture of the region would be unhinged," write former Defense Department official Fred C. Ikle and Terumasa Nakanishi, professor of international relations at the University of Shizuoka. [41] Among the immediate results would probably be a regional arms race, with Asian nations still nervous about past Japanese aggressions seeking to protect themselves.

"So much depends upon what happens in the short run," says foreign policy analyst Paul Kreisberg. "One extreme view is that the Japanese will come to the conclusion that they must assert a stronger political and military role if they want to be respected in the world. The other view is that so long as threats stay away from Asia the Japanese are unlikely to change the policy they've been following."

Kreisberg thinks the latter course is more likely. "But there are big changes in attitudes going on in both countries," he adds. "A lot depends on how long our recession lasts, how hard we beat up on the Japanese, what happens politically inside Japan. I think we're moving into a decade where looking into the future is a lot harder than it was 10 or 15 years ago." ■

## Notes

[1] *USA Today,* March 6, 1991.

[2] Quoted in *National Journal,* March 9, 1991, p. 586.

[3] *Congressional Record,* March 19, 1991.

[4] Figures cited by Kan Ito in "Trans-Pacific Anger," *Foreign Policy,* spring 1990, p. 138.

[5] Edward J. Lincoln, *Japan's Unequal Trade,* Brookings Institution, 1990, p. 132. The Brookings Institution is a think tank in Washington, D.C.

[6] Robert Z. Lawrence, *Efficient or Exclusionist: The Import Behavior of Japanese Corporate Groups,* draft of paper delivered at the Brookings Institution on April 4, 1991.

[7] See *The New York Times,* Jan. 7, 1991.

[8] Krist testified before the Senate Finance Subcommittee on International Trade on April 15, 1991.

[9] James Fallows, "Containing Japan," *The Atlantic,* May 1989, p. 41.

[10] Cited by James Fallows in "Getting Along with Japan," *The Atlantic,* December 1989, p. 64.

[11] Pietro S. Nivola, "More Like Them? The Political Feasibility of Strategic Trade Policy," *The Brookings Review,* spring 1991, p. 16.

[12] *Congressional Record,* Feb. 20, 1991. Sen. Heinz died in a plane crash April 4, 1991.

[13] Philip Trezise, "Japan, the Enemy?" *The Brookings Review,* winter 1989/90, p. 8.

[14] *Idem.* By 1990, total Japanese investment in the United States was valued at $75.8 billion, a total significantly less than Great Britain's $121.6 billion. See *The New York Times,* Jan. 7, 1991.

[15] Writing in *The Washington Post,* April 10, 1991.

[16] Clyde V. Prestowitz Jr. and Selig S. Harrison, "Pacific Agenda: Defense or Economics," *Foreign Policy,* summer 1990, p. 76.

[17] The official, who was not identified, was quoted in *The New York Times,* Aug. 30, 1990.

[18] Quoted in Prestowitz and Harrison, *op. cit.,* p. 62.

[19] Quoted in *The Washington Post,* Feb. 8, 1990.

[20] According to Japanese figures cited by Lincoln, the percentage of Japan's imports that were under quotas went from 59 percent in 1960 to 12 percent in 1963. See Lincoln, *op. cit.,* p. 13.

[21] Speech delivered at the Japan-Western U.S. Association in Washington, Sept. 13, 1990.

[22] Lincoln, *op. cit.,* p. 143.

[23] *Ibid.,* p. 147.

[24] Kenneth Flamm, "Making New Rules: High-Tech Trade Friction and the Semiconductor Industry," *The Brookings Review,* spring 1991, p. 23.

[25] Fallows, "Containing Japan," *op. cit.,* p. 45.

[26] Quoted in *The New York Times,* April 26, 1990.

[27] James E. Auer, "Japan's Defense Policy," *Current History,* April 1988, p. 147.

[28] Quoted in the *Los Angeles Times,* May 3, 1989.

[29] Quoted by Carla Rapoport in "The Big Split," *Fortune,* May 6, 1991.

[30] Karel van Wolferen, "The Japan Problem Revisited," *Foreign Affairs,* fall 1990, p. 44.

[31] Prestowitz and Harrison, *op. cit.,* p. 57.

[32] Op-ed column in *The New York Times,* Oct. 24, 1990.

[33] Forty-four percent of those polled were against the aid, while 39 percent were in favor of it. See Economist Intelligence Unit, *Country Report: Japan,* March 8, 1991, p. 11.

[34] Ito, *op. cit.,* p. 149.

[35] *Ibid.,* p. 135.

[36] George Friedman and Meredith LeBard, *The Coming War with Japan* (1991), p. 256.

[37] Lincoln, *op. cit.,* p. 102.

[38] Van Wolferen, *op. cit.,* p. 45.

[39] Lincoln, *op. cit.,* p. 139.

[40] Van Wolferen, *op. cit.,* p. 51.

[41] Fred C. Ikle and Terumasa Nakanishi, "Japan's Grand Strategy," *Foreign Affairs,* summer 1990, p. 85.

# Bibliography

## Selected Sources Used

### Books

**El-Agraa, Ali M., _Japan's Trade Friction, Realities or Misconceptions?_, St. Martin's Press, 1988.**
His data is a bit dated, but El-Agraa offers valuable historical details on the development of Japan's trade policies.

**Johnson, Chalmers; Tyson, Laura D'Andrea; and Zysman, John, eds., _Politics and Productivity: How Japan's Development Strategy Works_, Ballinger, 1989.**
This book offers sophisticated analyses of Japan's industrial policy and what it implies for the United States.

**Kotkin, Joel, and Kishimoto, Yoriko, _The Third Century: America's Resurgence in the Asian Era_, Crown, 1988.**
Not everyone thinks the United States is losing the battle with Japan. Kotkin and Kishimoto argue that Japan's industrial policy discourages innovation. They believe the Japanese economy is already losing steam and say the United States should not change its economy to compete with Japan.

**Lincoln, Edward J., _Japan's Unequal Trade_, Brookings, 1990.**
The economists have finally begun to move beyond the anecdotal in discussing Japan's trade practices, since an increasing amount of data is becoming available. Lincoln reviews the arguments on both sides and comes to the conclusion that Japan's trade practices are, indeed, unfair. But he also believes the United States should not abandon its commitment to free trade in order to counter Japan.

**Olsen, Edward A., _U.S.-Japan Strategic Reciprocity_, Hoover Press, 1985.**
This book is obviously dated, but it provides an excellent history of a crucial period in U.S.-Japan strategic relations. It was during the early 1980s that the United States began to make a concerted effort to get Japan to increase its military preparedness.

**Prestowitz, Clyde V., _Trading Places: How We Allowed Japan to Take the Lead_, Basic Books, 1988.**
When it first appeared, Prestowitz's book attracted a lot of attention because it was the most convincing argument to date that the Japanese systematically practiced unfair trading practices. Today, most of Prestowitz's arguments are almost taken for granted.

### Articles

**Fallows, James, "Containing Japan," _The Atlantic_, May 1989.**
Fallows, a well-known critic of Japanese trade policies, makes a strong case for why the United States has to find a way to force Japan to open its markets and stop unfair trade practices.

**Fallows, James, "Getting Along with Japan," _The Atlantic_, December 1989.**
In this article, Fallows follows up his article on the need to contain Japan with a discussion of the best ways of doing so. The first thing the United States needs to do, Fallows argues, "is to stop haranguing and negotiating with Japan, and instead act politely but firmly to defend the industries and technologies that are important to us."

**Harrison, Selig S. and Prestowitz, Clyde V., "Pacific Agenda: Defense or Economics?, _Foreign Policy_, summer 1990.**
The authors write that the end of the Cold War with the Soviet Union has now made it possible for the United States to focus on economic issues, particularly in the Pacific Rim.

**Ito, Kan, "Trans-Pacific Anger," _Foreign Policy_, spring 1990.**
Ito, a Japanese journalist, says U.S. policy-makers had better wake up to the fact that Japan can no longer be treated as a dependent vassal state. The only way the U.S.-Japan relationship can be maintained, Ito argues, is if the United States willingly gives Japan a larger strategic role.

**Van Wolferen, Karel, "The Japan Problem Revisited," _Foreign Affairs_, fall 1990.**
Wolferen is convinced that Japanese policy-makers "are simply not ready to discuss with the outside world how their economy and informal power system interact." Accordingly, the United States will have to apply more pressure than it has in the past to achieve change in Japan. If both countries don't deal with the situation maturely, Wolferen says, it could mean the end of the international trading system.

**"The Yen Block: A New Balance in Asia," _The Economist_, July 15, 1989.**
This excellent essay documents Japan's growing involvement in the economies of other nations throughout Asia. The article explores factors that might lead to a regional trading bloc centered on Tokyo, as well as factors that will impede such a development.

# The Next Step

## Additional Articles from Current Periodicals

### Diplomatic relations

**Baker, J. A. III, "A new Pacific partnership: Framework for the future," *Department of State Bulletin*, August 1989, p. 64.**

Presents Secretary of State James A. Baker III's address prepared for delivery before the Asia Society in New York City on June 26, dealing with the establishment of a framework for a new Pacific partnership. U.S.-Japan global partnership; Economic cooperation; Constructive relations with China; Conflict.

**Denoon, D. B. H., "Japan and the U.S. — the security agenda," *Current History*, January 1989, p. 37.**

Discusses U.S.-Japanese relations since 1978. Japanese security and defense policies; Carter and Reagan administration policies; U.S.-Japanese military security relationship; U.S.-Japan economic competition as a source of tension; Strong U.S.-Japan political relationship; U.S.-Japanese Mutual Security Treaty.

**Fallows, J., "The Japan-handlers," *The Atlantic*, August 1989, p. 14.**

Discusses U.S. policy toward Japan and the specialists who shape it. Who are the specialists; Division among the experts; Influence on public perception of Japan.

**Mansfield, M., "The U.S. and Japan: Sharing our destinies," *Foreign Affairs*, spring 1989, p. 3.**

Argues that the most important bilateral relationship in the world today is that between the U.S. and Japan. Examines the substance of this partnership and why the relationship is of immense benefit to the peoples of both nations.

**Nacht, M., "United States-Japanese relations," *Current History*, April 1988, p. 149.**

Examines U.S.-Japanese political and economic relations. Discusses ways in which the Japanese and U.S. governments can manage their economic differences effectively while promoting an international political order in the best interests of the global democracies. Economic, domestic, and strategic considerations; Conclusions.

**Palmer, N. D., "United States policy in East Asia," *Current History*, April 1989, p. 161.**

Summarizes current U.S. policy in East Asia. Recent Soviet policy in East Asia; "Core relationship" between U.S. and Japan; Connections between Sino-Soviet and Sino-American relations; U.S. relations with South Korea, Burma, the Philippines, and Cambodia; Future outlook.

**Rogers, L., "How to get along with Japan," *World Press Review*, December 1990, p. 30.**

Presents an interview with Mitsuko Shimomura, editor in chief of the liberal weekly *Asahi Journal* in Tokyo. United States-Japanese relations; Dispute with the Soviet Union over four Kuril Islands; Concern over the environment in Japan.

### Economic relations

**Fingleton, E., "Eastern economics," *The Atlantic*, October 1990, p. 72.**

Examines the United States' inability to break into Japan's market by comparing it to mercantilism, suppressing consumption while blocking imports. Also blames Japan's high land prices and retail-space shortage. IBM given as example.

**Gest, T., Boroughs, D. L., et al., "How to beat the Japanese (a drama)," *U.S. News & World Report*, July 9, 1990, p. 14.**

Reports that United States and Japanese negotiators have capped a year of intense discussions with an ambitious pact aimed at quietly reducing economic tensions and that T. Boone Pickens staged a noisy walkout from a board meeting to protest protectionist business practices.

**Neff, R., Magnusson, P., et al., "Rethinking Japan: A new, harder line toward Tokyo," *Business Week*, Aug. 7, 1989, p. 44.**

Discusses how a fundamental rethinking of Japan is now under way at the highest levels of U.S. government, business, and academia. The standard rules of the free market simply don't work with Japan and revisionists feel that import restrictions and managed trade are games that the U.S. may also be forced to play. INSETS: People; Politics; Economy; Military; The Elite.

**Thurow, L. C., "American mirage: a post-industrial economy?" *Current History*, January 1989, p. 13.**

Argues that the growth of service employment in the U.S. economy will begin to decline and manufacturing jobs will increase. Post-industrial era; U.S. trade deficit; How service employment grew; Demand; Falling U.S. productivity; Comparison to West Germany and Japan; Workers and wages; Cost of capital; Capital per worker; Future outlook.

### Export-import trade

**"A cautionary tale," *Economist*, June 30, 1990, p. 34.**

Reports on the continuing problems with the U.S.-Japan trade talks. Accusations by U.S. of Japanese foot-dragging; Broad economic habits that create the imbalance; Japanese claim they owe it to the world to maintain a big current-account to spend for worthy causes; Shin Kanemaru; Bitterness of present and past negotiations.

**Barnes, F., "Laying off," *The New Republic*, May 21, 1990, p. 9.**

Examines a move away from confrontation and toward cooperation in United States trade policy with Japan. New attitudes reflected by President Bush and Japanese Prime Minister Toshiki Kaifu; Overview of new trade policies between the two nations; Focus on the United States' decision to refrain from naming Japan as an unfair trader.

**Dentzer, S. and Tharp, M., "Trade's most wanted list," *U.S. News & World Report*, May 22, 1989, p. 50.**

Reports that Japan, South Korea, Brazil, and India are likely to be cited as "trade-liberalization priorities." If named as such, U.S. Trade Representative Carla A. Hills must begin negotiating with each to dismantle tariffs, taxes, or other obstacles deemed to be either blocking U.S. imports or limiting expansion of services such as banking or accounting. Super 301.

**Drummond, J., "Hazardous to whose health?" *Forbes*, Dec. 11, 1989, p. 89.**

Reports on the United States tobacco industry's infiltration of Japan, Taiwan, and South Korea due to U.S. trade representative negotiations in the past three years. Growth in foreign markets offsetting waning sales in the United States; Hypocrisy of the U.S. government; Foreign governments and promotion of smoking.

**Holzinger, A. G., "Trading views with Japan," *Nation's Business*, May 1989, p. 34.**

Discusses the controversy provoked at the *Nation's Business* video conference, Dialogue on Japan-U.S. Trade, by U.S. perceptions that Japan engages in unfair trade practices.

**Javetski, B., Harbrecht, D. A., et al., "Can they douse the flames?" *Business Week*, March 12, 1990, p. 36.**

Reports on how the sudden Bush-Kaifu summit may not cool U.S.-Japan feuding, and is likely to make little headway on tough U.S.-Japan trade issues. Weaker yen; Little to offer; Japan-bashing. INSET: Where tensions are hottest.

**Kinsley, M., "Unilateral disarmament," *The New Republic*, March 4, 1991, p. 4.**

Calls for unilateral disarmament in the United States trade wars with such countries as Japan and Germany. Why protectionism is not a solution; How open borders are the best route to prosperity regardless of what policy other countries pursue.

**Kondracke, M., "Trade gales," *The New Republic*, April 2, 1990, p. 12.**

Studies the controversy over a recent meeting between President Bush and Japanese Prime Minister Toshiki Kaifu. Key disagreements; Fears of an oncoming crisis in United States-Japan trade relations; Japan's reluctance to take United States demands for reform seriously; American public's negative impressions of Japan; Projected implications of a trade crisis.

**Makin, J. H., "Let's keep our cool on U.S.-Japan trade," *Fortune*, July 3, 1989, p. 147.**

Opinion. Argues for the continuation of free trade between the United States and Japan, to avoid an application of Cold War rhetoric to the economic troubles between the two countries.

**Pear, R., "Far-off silver lining in dispute with Japan," *The New York Times*, May 27, 1989, p. 29.**

Analyzes the U.S. decision to name Japan as an unfair trading partner. Response of Japan and the European Community; Projected impact on U.S.-Japan economic relations.

**Powell, B. and Thomas, R., "The trade charade," *Newsweek*, March 5, 1990, p. 24.**

Examines the most recent meetings between Japanese and United States trade negotiators, round three of the Structural Impediments Initiative, originally aimed to address the trade imbalance, and rapidly deteriorating relations. No long-term United States goals; Historical unwillingness to take trade talks a seriously as arms negotiations; Outright protectionism.

**Powell, B., Thomas, R., et al., "Japan makes the hit list," *Newsweek*, June 5, 1989, p. 48.**

Reports that President Bush named Japan a "priority" violator under the so-called Super 301 law. The designation could lead to general trade retaliation after 18 months and angered many in Congress. India and Brazil were also named trade villains. Specific grievances; Fight over designation.

## International economic relations

**Bergsten, C. F., "The world economy after the Cold War," *Foreign Affairs*, summer 1990, p. 96.**

Looks at various global transformations currently under way and how the world of the 1990s will be changed. How power of United States, Soviet Union, and Japan will be altered; Potential of economic issues; Effects of unified Europe and unified Germany; Importance of United

States, Japan, and united Europe providing collective leadership.

**Tanzer, A., "What's wrong with this picture?"** *Forbes*, **Nov. 26, 1990, p. 154.**

Shows how, not by bureaucratic or military design but by spontaneous human action, Japan is remaking the face of Asia. The remaining question is, however, where Americans fit into the picture. How Asia's economies are transforming themselves so rapidly; Asian trade-bloc is developing; Intra-Asian trade is booming; Why American business is playing a diminished role; More.

**Tarnoff, P., "America's new special relationships,"** *Foreign Affairs*, **summer 1990, p. 67.**

Discusses how Japan and Germany have become the second and third most powerful economies in the world, countries whose international influence is exceeded only by that of the United States. Examines need for United States to engage both countries in all major discussions about the shape of the post-Cold War world; Why Japan and Germany have grown more rapidly since 1945 than their Western partners; Objectives of new triangular diplomacy.

## Public opinion

**"The yen menace,"** *The Nation*, **March 12, 1990, p. 331.**

Editorial. Discusses the United States' anti-Japanese feelings due to Japan's economic success. They have become successful using the United States' idea of the open world-trade system.

**Buckley, W. F. Jr., "What does Japan owe us?"** *National Review*, **Oct. 15, 1990, p. 94.**

Editorial. Criticizes Japan's offer of one billion dollars to help finance the Persian Gulf operation. American resentment at Japan's unwillingness to pay a fair share; How the Japanese will profit from the U.S. operation; How the U.S. should respond.

**Powell, B. and Martin, B., "What Japan thinks of us,"** *Newsweek*, **Apr. 2, 1990, p. 18.**

Presents an unflattering view which the Japanese have of the United States now — the U.S. seems unable to bear either its ills or the cures for them. An easy target; At work; Bad image; Losing face; Imbalance of trade; Includes statements by several prominent Japanese men.

**Smith, L., "Fear and loathing of Japan,"** *Fortune*, **Feb. 26, 1990, p. 50.**

Examines the growing intensity of anti-Japanese sentiment in the United States among politicians, white-collar workers, and journalists. Japan's grand design; Alleged racism; Expected actions by Congress; Benefits of Japanese expansion and investments; Adjustments to be made in the United States and Japan. INSETS: Japan and the U.S.: Misinformation age; How it looks to an American in Tokyo.

**Stokes, H. S., "Stock prices and Springsteen,"** *New Perspectives Quarterly*, **summer 1988, p. 20.**

A look from Tokyo on how the Japanese view America's declining power. Why Japanese invest in U.S.; Turning profits into investments; The myth of Japanese technological superiority; U.S. dependence on Japanese capital; Dangers of Japanese isolationism; Symbols as essence in Japan.

## Technological aspects

**"Tokyo talks fail to resolve patents row,"** *New Scientist*, **July 14, 1990, p. 30.**

Describes unsuccessful talks in Tokyo concerning U.S.-Japan patent disputes. Long delays in Japan allow exploitation of foreign inventions.

**Ferguson, C. H., "Computers and the coming of the U.S. keiretsu,"** *Harvard Business Review*, **July/August 1990, p. 55.**

Portrays the state of global competition: technology, manufacturing, and industrial structure all favor the Japanese in the race for supremacy in the information industry. The only sensible U.S. response is to shape an industry-led keiretsu — new alliances among U.S. companies. Cooperate or become vassals of Japanese competitors; Playing to Japanese strengths. INSETS: A brief history of Japan's keiretsu, by M. Anchordoguy.

**Leventer, M., "The 'Amerippon' alliance,"** *World Press Review*, **August 1989, p. 48.**

Examines relations between the United States and Japan. Cooperation and competition; U.S.-Japanese agreement on science and technology; Case study on the field of semiconductors in relation to U.S.-Japanese attitudes. INSET: Winning over the Americans, by K. Kawai.

**Powell, B. and Thomas, R., "Taking Japan off the hit list,"** *Newsweek*, **May 7, 1990, p. 50.**

Reports that Japan has announced that it would open its market wider in three areas (supercomputers, satellites, and wood products) and the Bush administration decided last week not to cite Japan as subject to special sanctions under the 1988 trade bill. Trade hawks in Congress; Relief among Japanese diplomats.

# Back Issues

*Great Research on Current Issues Starts Right Here... Recent topics covered by The CQ Researcher are listed below. Issues dated before May 10, 1991, were published under the name of Editorial Research Reports.*

**NOVEMBER 1989**
Balkanization of Eastern Europe
Dealing With the Underclass
America Turns to Recycling
New World Economy

**DECEMBER 1989**
North America Trade Pact
Influence Peddling
German Reunification
Learning Disabilities

**JANUARY 1990**
Higher Education Curriculum
Photonics
Age of 'Infotainment'
Abortion: Politicians' Nightmare

**FEBRUARY 1990**
Politics and Economic Growth
Free Agency in Sports
Repetitive Motion
War on Drugs

**MARCH 1990**
Asbestos: Are Risks Acceptable?
Public Health Campaigns
South Africa's Future
Homeless Need More Than Shelter

**APRIL 1990**
How Fair is the Tax Burden?
Workers' Compensation
U.S. Pacific Forces
Curbing Insurance Premiums

**MAY 1990**
Should Teaching Be a Profession?
Will Canada Fall Apart?
Is U.S. Patent System Outdated?
Federal Funding for the Arts

**JUNE 1990**
Downsizing America's Armed Forces
Progress In Weather Forecasting
S & L Bailout
Bio-Chemical Disarmament

**JULY 1990**
Do Americans Still Love Marriage?
Death Penalty Debate
Decline of Rural America
United Nations in the 1990s

**AUGUST 1990**
Democracy in the Philippines
Initiatives: True Democracy?
Hard Times at Newspapers
Teens Balance School & Jobs

**SEPTEMBER 1990**
Dangers of Alcohol
Western Alliance After the Cold War
Tobacco Industry
Right to Die

**OCTOBER 1990**
Organ Transplants
Energy Policy Options
Search for Arab Unity
Child Support

**NOVEMBER 1990**
Lotteries and Gambling
Post Cold-War Choices
Setting Limits on Medical Care
Multicultural Education

**DECEMBER 1990**
Cable TV Regulation
Americans' Search For Their Roots
Is Insurance System a Failure?
Why Schools Still Have Tracking

**JANUARY 1991**
Growing Influence of Boycotts
Should the U.S. Reinstate the Draft?
America's Archaeological Past
Peace Corps' Challenges in '90s

**FEBRUARY 1991**
Regional Impact of Recession
Puerto Rico's Status
Redistricting: Mapping Power
Nuclear Power

**MARCH 1991**
Acid Rain
Cost of the Gulf War
Reassessing Gun Laws
Future for Man in Space

**APRIL 1991**
Social Security
Canadian Crisis Over Quebec
California Drought
Electromagnetic Radiation

**MAY 1991**
School Choice
Racial Quotas
Animal Rights

Back issues are available for $4.00 (subscribers) or $7.00 (non-subscribers). Quantity discounts apply to orders over ten. To order, call Congressional Quarterly 1-800-432-2250.

# Future Topics

▶ *Divorce and Children*

▶ *Endangered Species*

▶ *Teenage Suicide*

# Children and Divorce

## What can be done to help children of divorce?

D
IVORCE CAN BE A WRENCHING EXPERIENCE
for children. New studies suggest the painful
effects of their parents' breakup can stay with
children for years. Many will not do well in school
or jobs, and some will fail in their own marriages later on.
The studies have intensified the debate over the "no-fault
divorce" laws that made it easier for couples to dissolve their
marriages. Some experts say the new findings on the effects
of divorce on children are exaggerated, and no one expects a
substantial movement away from liberalized divorce laws.
But some therapists are urging couples in distress to try
harder to resolve their problems rather than get a divorce.
And there is broad agreement that children of divorce need
greater support — financial, social and psychological — to
avoid becoming innocent victims of their parents' breakup.

C_Q **June 7, 1991 • Volume 1, No. 5 • 349-368**

*Formerly Editorial Research Reports*

COVER ART: BARBARA SASSA-DANIELS

June 7, 1991
Volume 1, No. 5

**EDITOR**
Sandra Stencel

**ASSOCIATE EDITOR**
Richard L. Worsnop

**STAFF WRITERS**
Charles S. Clark
Mary H. Cooper
Rodman D. Griffin
Patrick G. Marshall

**PRODUCTION EDITOR**
Laurie De Maris

**EDITORIAL ASSISTANT**
Thomas H. Moore

**GRAPHICS**
Jack Auldridge

**PUBLISHED BY**
Congressional Quarterly Inc.

**CHAIRMAN**
Andrew Barnes

**VICE CHAIRMAN**
Andrew P. Corty

**EDITOR AND PUBLISHER**
Neil Skene

**EXECUTIVE EDITOR**
Robert W. Merry

**PUBLICATIONS MARKETING/SALES**
Robert Smith

**EDITOR, EBSCO PUBLISHING**
Melissa Kummerer

The CQ Researcher (ISSN 1056-2036). Formerly Editorial Research Reports. Published weekly (48 times per year, excluding March 1, May 3, Aug. 2 and Nov. 1, 1991) by Congressional Quarterly Inc., 1414 22nd St., N.W., Washington, D.C. 20037. Rates are furnished upon request. Application to mail at second-class postage rates is pending at Washington, D.C. POSTMASTER: Send address changes to The CQ Researcher, 1414 22nd St., N.W., Washington, D.C. 20037.

# Children and Divorce

BY KENNETH JOST
AND MARILYN ROBINSON

## THE ISSUES

When a marriage breaks up and the family breaks down, many people can't help but ask, "What about the children?"

Liberalized attitudes toward divorce in the 1950s, '60s and '70s tended to minimize the harmful effects of marital dissolutions on children. Many experts even argued that the emotional damage of living with hostile or abusive parents was just as traumatic, if not more so, than a family breakup.

In the past decade, however, some social scientists have suggested that divorce may have greater and longer-lasting negative effects on children than previously thought. These findings, combined with a renewed emphasis on the importance of family life, have contributed to a questioning of the wide acceptance of divorce as a recommended course of action for families in distress.

The divorce rate in the United States remains high — in fact, higher than in other industrialized countries. (*See graph, p. 356.*) Government statistics indicate that nearly 1.2 million Americans were divorced in 1990, and about half of those divorces involved children under the age of 18. Experts project that 40 percent of children 17 years old or younger will experience divorce during the next decade.

Children's responses to divorce vary greatly, of course, and divorce can't be blamed for all the problems a child may experience after a family breakup. But concern about the well-being of children is at the heart of the renewed debate over divorce. These are among the key questions:

***Does divorce have long-term ad-***

***verse psychological effects on children?***

Judith S. Wallerstein, a California psychologist, touched off a sometimes polarized debate among social scientists, psychologists and family therapists with the publication of a book in 1989 described as the first-ever long-term study of children of divorce. In the book, *Second Chances: Men, Women and Children a Decade After Divorce*, Wallerstein and her co-author, journalist Sandra Blakeslee, reported that many of the children of 60 middle-class divorced families from the San Francisco area studied over a 12-year period experienced difficulties in education, career and interpersonal relationships.[1] Many of the children felt intense rejection, anger and loneliness at the time of the divorce. While some of them resolved these problems over time, other children who had seemed to be adjusting well developed severe emotional reactions to the divorce 10 or 15 years later.

Wallerstein found that 10 years after their parents had divorced, only 34 percent of the children in the study were doing well. Another 37 percent were depressed, could not concentrate in school, had trouble making friends and suffered a wide range of other behavioral problems. (The remaining children were doing well in some areas but faltering in others.) In a magazine article drawn from the book, Wallerstein described the 37 percent figure as "a powerful statistic" and declared: "It would be hard to find any other group of children — except perhaps the victims of a natural disaster — who suffered such a rate of sudden serious psychological problems."[2]

Wallerstein's findings drew a flurry of media attention, but some researchers immediately questioned her methodology, criticizing the sample of families studied as too small and not representative. Two years later, this disagreement persists. "It is highly likely that [Wallerstein's] study exaggerates the prevalence of long-term problems," sociologists Frank F. Furstenberg Jr. and Andrew J. Cherlin write in their just published book, *Divided Families*.[3]

Furstenberg, a professor at the University of Pennsylvania, and Cherlin, a professor at Johns Hopkins University, note that the 60 families Wallerstein studied had all been referred to a clinic for counseling and that many had "extensive psychiatric histories." In addition, the two sociologists argue that since Wallerstein had no control group of intact families for her study, she had no basis for depicting all of the problems that emerged after divorce as attributable to the family breakups. (*See At Issue, p. 361.*)

In an academic publication a year earlier, however, Furstenberg noted that several studies had found evidence of adverse long-term effects of divorce in two areas: educational attainment and family formation. The studies showed what Furstenberg called a "fairly consistent" pattern of more school problems, grade failure, lower attendance and school dropout among children of divorce than among children of intact families. Similarly, children of divorced families had a higher incidence of early sexual activity, premarital pregnancy, early marriage and later marital instability.[4]

In her book, Wallerstein identified two other phenomena among children of divorce. The first — which she dubbed the "overburdened child syndrome" — relates to children taking on the role of caretaker for one or both parents; 15 percent of the children in her study held their parents together psychologically after the divorce. This caretaker role, which sometimes lasts for years, can cripple the child's own emotional and social progress. "Instead of gathering strength from their childhood and adolescent experiences," Wallerstein said, "these young people are seriously weakened by the demands made on them within the divorced family."[5]

Wallerstein also found evidence of what other researchers had called "the sleeper effect" — a fear of betrayal that surfaced, especially among young women, well after their parents had divorced. Wallerstein said she documented the pattern in 66 percent of the young women in her study between the ages of 19 and 23. The fear usually surfaced when the young women became concerned with commitment, love and sex in an adult context and began to make connections between their fears and their parents' divorce.

Wallerstein's confirmation of the delayed effects of divorce on girls was considered an important research finding because it undercut the commonly held belief that boys react worse to divorce than girls.

Furstenberg, one of Wallerstein's critics, acknowledges the point. "The hazards of divorce may not be greater for boys than for girls — only different," he says. "Boys 'act out' in response to divorce, while girls exhibit less socially visible forms of maladjustment."[6]

To some extent, the dispute between Wallerstein and her critics is one of perspective: whether the glass is half-empty or half-full. Neil Kalter, director of the Center for the Child and Family at the University of Michigan in Ann Arbor, studied more than 1,000 youngsters over a 10-year period and found that 30 percent to 50 percent experienced "the painful and disruptive legacy" of their parents' divorce for years. But he added: "If 30 percent to 50 percent of children of divorce experience lasting, divorce-linked difficulties, then it follows that 50 percent to 70 percent do not."[7]

What is clear from all the studies is that divorce has an enormous impact on children, greater in many ways than the impact on the separating parents. "Almost all children of divorce regard their childhood and adolescence as having taken place in the shadow of divorce," Wallerstein says.[8] Furstenberg and Cherlin write of the "wrenching period of upset and adjustment" that children of divorce are likely to experience whether or not they suffer long-term effects.[9]

In that sense, Wallerstein's book has fundamentally changed the public policy debate by putting somewhere higher on the social agenda the issue of promoting the welfare of children in divorce.

### Should more marriages be saved for the sake of the children?

The American public has apparently undergone a sharp change of opinion on this issue. This was dramatically suggested by the results of surveys conducted more than two

decades apart of a random sample of young white mothers from the Detroit area. In 1962 — as liberalized attitudes toward divorce were beginning to gain ground — nearly half of the mothers surveyed agreed with this statement: "When there are children involved, parents should stay together even if they don't get along." When the same group of women was asked the same question in 1985, however, 82 percent disagreed.[10]

Despite her work in documenting the adverse effects of divorce on children, Judith Wallerstein also rejects this once well accepted prescription for couples with children. "When people ask whether they should stay married for the sake of the children, I have to say, 'Of course not,' " she wrote in her book. "All our evidence shows that children turn out less well adjusted when exposed to open conflict, where parents terrorize or strike one another, than do children from divorced families."[11]

Nonetheless, the effects of divorce on children are being cited today by many family therapists and social conservatives in arguing for changing the law to make it harder to get a divorce or urging couples considering a divorce to use counseling to try to stay together.

"We need some sort of braking mechanism on divorce," says David L. Levy, president of the National Council for Children's Rights. "We have 2 million marriages a year and a million divorces. Families are being wrecked. Maybe we need to go back to 'fault' divorce so that couples won't enter divorce quite so lightly."[12]

"Divorce is not all it is cracked up to be in terms of a solution: In many cases, it's created more problems than it has solved," says Michele Weiner-Davis, a family therapist in Woodstock, Ill., whose keynote address to the 17,000-member American Association for Marriage and Family Therapy last fall was entitled "Divorce-Buster."

When children are involved, Weiner-Davis adds, "there is no such thing as divorce. Unless one parent leaves the scene completely . . . you will have your ex-spouse in your life forever, on less friendly terms. You may terminate a relationship with a document, but you can't terminate a history. The history lives on."

For their part, Furstenberg and Cherlin insist they — like the public at large — are not oblivious to the detrimental effects of divorce on children. "Many of us recognize that children often are the casualties of this new marriage system . . . ," they write. "We feel uneasy about how this system is working out for children. At the same time, we don't quite know what to do about it." [13]

Like Wallerstein and other experts, however, Furstenberg and Cherlin reject the idea of staying together for the children's sake. So does Edward W. Beal, a Bethesda, Md., psychiatrist whose new book, *Adult Children of Divorce*, parallels Wallerstein's in many of its findings on the adverse effects of divorce on children.[14] The key to avoiding or minimizing those effects, Beal says, is for parents to make a clean break in their relationship. "The problem is that parents get legal divorces, but they don't get emotional divorces," he says. As a result, their children "have emotional problems."

### *What can be done to reduce the negative effects of divorce on children?*

Despite the differing perspectives on the magnitude of the problem, the studies on the effects of divorce on children tend toward common recommendations: greater sensitivity to the problems encountered by parents and children, greater emphasis on open and non-judgmental communication and greater willingness

# Grim Statistics

*Both the number of divorces in the United States and the number of children affected by divorce rose sharply in the 1960s and early 1970s. The number of children involved in divorce has been declining since the early 1980s. This drop can be attributed partly to a slight decline in the divorce rate and the concurrent decline in the number of children in married-couple families. However, both the number of divorces and the number of children involved in divorce still exceed one million per year.*

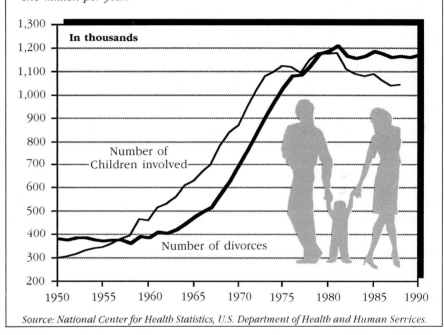

*Source: National Center for Health Statistics, U.S. Department of Health and Human Services.*

to seek support or counseling from outside experts or groups. In addition, some of the experts make broader public policy recommendations for helping families withstand the problems of divorce, especially the economic pressures on the growing number of single-parent families.

In her book, Wallerstein lays out a detailed list of psychological "tasks" for children themselves to help them get through a divorce. Among the most important:

■ **Understanding the divorce.** Perceiving the immediate changes and over time evaluating and drawing useful lessons from their parents' actions.

■ **Strategic withdrawal.** Removing the divorce from the center of their thoughts and getting back to their own interests and peer relationships.

■ **Dealing with loss.** Overcoming the "profound sense of rejection, humiliation, unlovability and powerlessness" that often accompanies the departure of one parent.

■ **Accepting the permanence of divorce.** Getting over the denial that persists in many children for years after a divorce.

■ **Taking a chance on love.** Venturing into relationships despite anxieties and fears of betrayal.

Parents, Wallerstein says, must help their children through this process. Children need to be told repeatedly that the divorce does not weaken the tie between parent and child and must not be burdened with one parent's anger against the other. And while parents should involve children in some of the important household decisions stemming from a divorce, parents also should help their children avoid the "overburdened child syndrome" by encouraging them to remain children.

Furstenberg and Cherlin similarly stress the need to protect children from the "emotional fallout" of a divorce, but note that the advice is "not easy to follow." And, despite the recommendations for both parents to remain part of their children's lives, they note that the most common pattern is for the non-custodial parent — typically, the father — to "abdicate virtually all responsibility" for child-rearing.[15]

As a result, the two sociologists emphasize steps they say are needed to help the resulting single-parent families. The most oft-cited problem — the lax enforcement of child support orders — has been the focus of intense attention at the state and federal levels over the past decade (*see p. 359*). A 1988 federal law requires states to implement child-support guidelines and also provides for a system of automatic withholding of child-support payments — initially only for parents whose children are receiving welfare but beginning in 1994 for all new child-support payments.

While commending these efforts, Furstenberg and Cherlin go further and endorse a plan devised by Columbia University sociologist Irwin Garfinkel to create an assured child-support benefit — to be paid by the federal government if not by the non-custodial parent. Legislation along those lines is being considered in Congress, but its cost may be too much for budget-strapped lawmakers to buy.

Furstenberg and Cherlin also call for employers to make the workplace more responsive to parents' needs — through flexible work schedules, leave for infant care and part-time work with fringe benefits. And they urge efforts to provide more affordable child care, citing one study that found single mothers spent 17 percent of their weekly earnings on child care compared

with the 9 percent spent by mothers living with partners.

But even the most progressive social and economic policies cannot prevent divorce from being a time of pain and stress for children. And, as psychiatrist Neil Kalter concludes,

the responsibility for helping children through those difficulties ultimately rests with their parents. "Who else knows their child so well?" Kalter asks. "Who does the child depend on more? And who cares so deeply?"[16] ∎

# BACKGROUND

## History of Divorce

Since ancient times, divorce has been perceived as a threat to social stability and order and has been condemned or prohibited by many religions, including Roman Catholicism. But some form of divorce has always prevailed despite restrictive laws and penalties and social ostracism for couples who dissolve their marriages.

This historic opposition to divorce did not derive, however, from a concern for the well-being of children. Historically, the welfare of children did not become a major issue in the debate over divorce until the 17th or 18th centuries, according to historian Roderick Phillips, whose book *Putting Asunder* traces the history of divorce in Western civilization.[17] The Roman Catholic Church's theologically based opposition to divorce viewed children in a relatively impersonal, abstract manner. Procreation was one of the purposes of marriage, but there was little emphasis on the social obligations of parenthood.

Protestant reformers disagreed with the Catholic interpretation of marriage as a holy sacrament. Viewing it more as a contract, they maintained that a marriage could be dissolved as a result of matrimonial "fault" or crime against the marriage, such as adultery. The rearing and education of children were

viewed as the principal purposes of marriage, but, once these functions were completed, it was thought there was no reason why a marriage should not be terminated.

The Protestant Reformation thus began the process of taking decisions about divorce away from the ecclesiastical realm and giving them to secular institutions. So the divorce policies brought to the shores of the New World by the mostly Protestant émigres from Europe were substantially secularized. Marriage in the American colonies was typically a civil affair performed by magistrates. Divorce, too, was a civil matter, with adultery at the top of a short list of grounds for dissolving a marriage.

After the American Revolution, the now independent states legalized divorce more widely. Divorces — rare and scandalous in Colonial times — became more common and somewhat less stigmatized. In a fluid and mobile pioneer society, desertion became the most common of offenses cited in divorce petitions. Other grounds were added over time, and divorce petitions became so numerous that divorce-granting authority had to be shifted from state legislatures to courts. By the end of the 19th century, every state but South Carolina had rejected the view of marriage as indissoluble and adopted divorce laws that appeared strict on paper but that were routinely circumvented without challenge.

The first tremors of anxiety about

*Continued on p. 356*

# Chronology

## 1800s
Early in the century, children still are considered property belonging to the father and usually remain with the father upon divorce. By the end of the century, however, many states have embraced the "tender-years" doctrine that says young children should stay with their mothers upon divorce.

### 1860
U.S. divorce rate reaches 0.2 per 1,000 population.

### 1881
New England Divorce Reform League is formed to lobby for more restrictive divorce laws.

### 1889
First national survey in the U.S. documents a 150 percent increase in divorce over a 20-year period.

## 1900-1910s
U.S. divorce rate reaches 0.9 per 1,000 population.

## 1920s-1930s
U.S. divorce rate continues to climb through the 1920s and, despite a dip during the Depression, through most of the '30s.

### 1932
"Quickie divorce" wars break out among states that need revenue.

### 1936
Gallup Poll registers 75 percent opposition to liberalized divorce laws.

## 1940s-1950s
Divorce rate begins to level off and, after a postwar spurt, it begins a 10-year decline.

## 1960s
Americans adopt more liberal attitudes toward divorce.

### April 27, 1966
New York Gov. Nelson A. Rockefeller signs a law widening the grounds for divorce in the state from adultery to include cruel and inhuman treatment, abandonment for two or more years, confinement in prison or an agreed upon separation of two years.

## 1970s
Courts begin to look favorably at joint custody arrangements.

### Jan. 1, 1970
The nation's first no-fault divorce law goes into effect in California. The law was signed by California's once-divorced governor, Ronald Reagan, on Sept. 5, 1969. Forty-five states adopt some form of no-fault divorce over the next five years.

### 1971
Number of children involved in divorces granted that year tops 1 million for the first time.

### Dec. 20, 1974
Congress clears legislation to establish a parent-locator service for finding fathers who are delinquent in their support payments and whose children receive Aid to Families with Dependent Children (AFDC).

### 1979
U.S. divorce rate hits peak of 5.3 per 1,000 population.

## 1980s
U.S. divorce rate levels off but remains at historically high levels.

### Aug. 8, 1984
Congress approves Child Support Enforcement Amendments aimed at beefing up states' collection of child-support payments. Amendments require automatic wage-withholding in some cases where a parent is delinquent in support payments.

### Sept. 30, 1988
Congress clears welfare reform bill with child-support provisions. Among other things, the bill expands the use of wage-withholding of child-support payments.

### Feb. 17, 1989
Judith S. Wallerstein publishes *Second Chances: Men, Women and Children a Decade After Divorce.* She claims many children of divorce have long-term emotional and psychological problems.

## 1990s
Debate over the effects of divorce on children continues.

### Oct. 27, 1990
Congress passes $22.5 billion child-care assistance package.

# U.S. Couples More Likely to Divorce

*The divorce rate in the United States has declined slightly in recent years, but American couples are still far more likely to divorce than are those in other industrialized countries.*

**Divorce rate per 1,000 existing marriages, 1986**

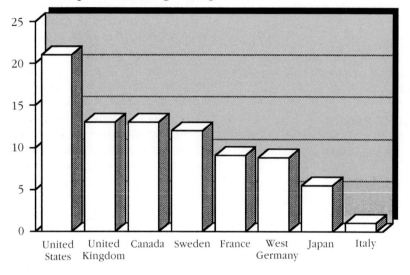

*Source: House Select Committee on Children, Youth and Families.*

*Continued from p. 354*

the rising divorce rate came in the 1850s from conservatives who were worried about the social consequences. The furor died down during the Civil War but flared up again with a postwar rise in divorce. During the latter part of the relatively conservative 19th century, divorce became a social issue along with sexuality, venereal disease, prostitution and temperance. Concern about the issue led the New England Divorce Reform League, an anti-divorce group, to urge Congress to do a study documenting the incidence of divorce. That report, released in 1889, confirmed that divorce had risen dramatically in the United States: from 9,937 in 1867 to 25,535 in 1886 — more than a 150 percent increase.[18] *

---

*By modern standards, however, the divorce rate in the late 19th century was low: 0.4 per 1,000 population in 1880 or 1.2 per 1,000 existing marriages compared with the current level of 4.7 marriages per 1,000 population or 20.7 per 1,000 married women 15 years of age and older.

The trend that so alarmed many Americans was occurring in other industrializing societies as well: Divorces in France tripled from 1885 to 1910 and increased fivefold in England and Wales between 1867 and 1910. Still, the U.S. divorce rate exceeded that of European countries, and America's high rate was cited as an ominous warning by social conservatives in many countries, including nearby Canada and far-distant New Zealand.

### Changing Attitudes

Around this time, another important development occurred: a fundamental change in the law governing custody of children of divorce. Until the early 19th century, children were considered to be the property of their fathers and remained with the father upon divorce. The shift in the 19th century from a mostly agrarian society to a more industrial society put more emphasis on the mother's role. At the same time, the early feminist movement brought women

more political and economic power.

Responding to these social changes, the courts in England and in the United States tended to promote maternal custody, especially for young children ages 6 to 12. This "tender years" doctrine evolved into a broader maternal preference almost universally recognized by family courts in the United States through the middle of the 20th century.

Child welfare issues also first came onto the national agenda around the turn of the 20th century, but with limited results until the 1960s. A White House conference on care for dependent children in 1909 helped win enactment of pension programs for widowed mothers by some 40 states. In 1912, legislation established the federal Children's Bureau to investigate and report on "all matters pertaining to the welfare of children." But the bureau was widely viewed as hidebound before it was submerged under the new Office of Child Development in 1970.

The progressive movement and organized labor joined to lobby for a federal law to prohibit child labor, but the U.S. Supreme Court struck down two statutes as unconstitutional before finally upholding such a provision in 1937. During World War II, Congress established the first program to provide federal assistance for child care, but it was motivated primarily by the need to get women into wartime factories rather than by broader concern about children's well-being.[19]

Meanwhile, the U.S. divorce rate had more than doubled in three decades — to 2.0 per 1,000 population in 1940. World War I had brought about a spike in the rate, but it continued to climb through the 1920s and, despite a dip at the start of the Depression, through most of the '30s. The end of World War II brought another sudden spike: 610,000 divorces were granted in

1946, for a rate of 4.3 per 1,000 population. The divorce rate then leveled off and actually declined slightly during the 1950s, a decade of relative social conservatism, but it began to increase again in the '60s.

The 1960s were a decade of change in many aspects of social life in the United States and other Western countries. Social policies became more liberal. Widespread use of birth control changed sexual attitudes and practices. More women entered the work force. And the traditional social and political dominance of men was challenged by a new vigorous feminist movement. These liberal attitudes touched off a re-evaluation of marriage and divorce, culminating in a fundamental transformation of U.S. divorce law: no-fault divorce.

## No-Fault Divorce

No-fault divorce allowed a couple to dissolve their marriage without assigning blame or responsibility to either party. First adopted in California in 1970, the concept spread quickly to other states. "Within five years, most states had adopted at least one no-fault ground," notes Franklin E. Zimring, director of the Earl Warren Legal Institute at the University of California in Berkeley.[20]

Proponents of no-fault divorce cited a number of reasons for shifting from adversarial proceedings in which one spouse accused the other of one or more of the statutorily recognized grounds for divorce. They argued that fault-finding ignored the reality that both parties to a marriage were likely to bear responsibility for its breakdown and that the adversarial process in any event intensified the recrimination and bitterness accompanying most divorces. They

also pointed out that strict divorce laws — such as New York's, which up to 1966 recognized only the ground of adultery — were routinely circumvented by couples who could afford to go to states such as Nevada with minimal residency requirements and broader grounds for divorce. Finally, these reformers noted, the fault-based laws did not correspond to actual practice, since the vast majority of divorces were uncontested.

**Opponents of no-fault divorce warned that it would lead to "divorce on demand," and critics cite the subsequent statistics as proof. The divorce rate, which had climbed slowly in the late 1960s, jumped by almost 40 percent from 1970 to 1975.**

Opponents of no-fault divorce warned at the time that it would lead to "divorce on demand," and critics cite the subsequent statistics as proof. The divorce rate, which had climbed slowly in the late 1960s, jumped by almost 40 percent from 1970 to 1975. It continued to climb, although at a slower rate, for the rest of the decade. (*See graph, p. 353.*) Since 1975, more than a million couples have been divorced in the United States each year. The number of children affected by divorce also increased in the 1970s. Beginning in 1972, more than 1 million children were involved in divorces granted each year — a rate of around 16-18 per 1,000 children under 18 years of age.

Both the number of divorces and

the number of children affected by divorce leveled off and then declined during the 1980s, but they remained at historically high levels. The high divorce rate fed the fears not only of social conservatives but also of many mental health professionals and the public at large. In a survey of members of the American Psychological Association in early 1991, for example, the demise of the nuclear family was listed most often as the greatest threat to America's mental health — cited far more often than the next most frequent responses of unemployment, drug abuse and alcohol abuse.[21]

### *Economic Impact on Women and Children*

A different, feminist critique of no-fault divorce emerged in the mid-1980s — chiefly with the 1985 publication of *The Divorce Revolution* by a Stanford University sociologist, Lenore J. Weitzman. After analyzing alimony awards, property settlements and child-support orders in California over a 10-year period, Weitzman concluded that women's economic interests were being ill-served under the no-fault system.

The plight of women was dramatized by one statistic: Divorced women and their children experienced a 73 percent decline in their standard of living after divorce, while men experienced a 42 percent increase. Alimony, when granted, was low and often short-lived, Weitzman contended. Child-support orders were inadequate and poorly enforced, she said. And equal division of marital property, she concluded, operated unfairly for many women, whose earning power was adversely affected by years spent on household and child-rearing duties.

Stephen D. Sugarman, director of the family law program at the Earl

# Financial Consequences of Divorce

The psychological effects of divorce on children may still be debated, but a new study by the U.S. Census Bureau shows that their parents' breakup will probably bring some painful financial consequences.

The family income of children whose parents separated dropped an average of 37 percent within four months and remained 30 percent below the pre-separation level 16 months later, according to the study, *Family Disruption and Economic Hardship: The Short-Run Picture for Children.*

The study also found that the percentage of children living in poverty increased from 19 percent to 36 percent at the four-month mark after separation. The percentage of families receiving food stamps jumped from 10 percent to 27 percent at the four-month mark and stayed at that level for one year.

The report, prepared by researchers Suzanne Bianchi and Edith McArthur, tracked a sample of 2,800 children whose parents had separated and covered a period from October 1983 through May 1986.

About 90 percent of children live with their mothers after their parents break up, so the financial pinch results directly from the household's loss of the father's income. The researchers said the income loss was offset by women going to work or finding additional work, turning to welfare programs such as Aid to Families with Dependent Children and food stamps or receiving child support.

The report showed that only 44 percent of children were receiving child support from the absent father after four months. Concern about lax enforcement of child support laws led Congress to pass laws in 1984 and 1988 to require states to set guidelines for judges to follow in awarding support and to institute automatic wage withholding of support payments. The withholding requirements are already in effect for some support payments and will apply to all new support orders beginning in 1994.

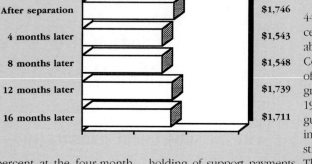

**Monthly Family Income After Marital Separation**

| | |
|---|---|
| Before separation | $2,435 |
| After separation | $1,746 |
| 4 months later | $1,543 |
| 8 months later | $1,548 |
| 12 months later | $1,739 |
| 16 months later | $1,711 |

Source: *Family Disruption and Economic Hardship*, U.S. Census Bureau, 1991.

Warren Legal Institute in Berkeley, Calif., has disputed Weitzman's contention that women have fared worse economically under California's no-fault law than under its earlier divorce law. Sugarman says Weitzman's data actually shows that both before and after no-fault divorce was introduced in California, most couples had little property to divide and that alimony was the exception, not the rule. Measured in constant dollars, he says, spousal support awards actually were higher in 1977 than in 1968, and the greater use of temporary awards was of minimal importance since as a practical matter alimony payments either ended with a woman's remarriage or stopped being enforced after 10 years or so.[22]

Despite his disagreement over the statistics, Sugarman agrees with Weitzman's ultimate point: that women and children suffer economically from divorce and divorce law needs to be changed to cushion that blow. Weitzman's prescription included child-support awards and property settlements designed to equalize the standard of living in the custodial and non-custodial households. Sugarman believes support and property settlements should be based to some extent on the post-divorce financial prospects for both spouses, but he also calls for some type of social insurance system to protect lower-earning spouses from the financial shock of divorce.

"[W]ith such a public financial base in place, the debate over new ways of allocating private financial interests between divorcing husbands and wives would be much less divisive," Sugarman writes. "Those championing women's interests would feel less of a need to reach so far, and those defending men's interests would feel less threatened." As for how the government should finance this social insurance benefit, Sugarman merely says: "I save [that] for another time."[23]

## Support and Custody

As no-fault divorce was being adopted, lawmakers and judges also were changing another component of family law: child custody. The shift from finding one spouse at fault, combined with the women's movement's emphasis on sex-neutral laws, led to a widespread view that fathers should be given greater consideration in deciding custody of children in divorce cases. By the mid-1970s, the stated maternal preference in custody cases had been replaced in most states with a new, supposedly sex-neutral standard: "the best interests of the child." Later case law, as well as state statutes, tried to define the best-interests approach by listing specific factors courts should consider in awarding custody, such as the continuity of a child's relationships and environment.

A second change in divorce law was the introduction of joint custody, which was supposed to give mothers and fathers equal time with the child and equal parenting functions after the divorce. The hope was that joint custody would reduce disputes over custody and help children by keeping both parents involved in their upbringing. California introduced joint custody in 1970. By 1989, 34 states had statutorily recognized joint custody — 12 states gave preference to the arrangement — and no state prohibited such an arrangement when both parents agreed.[24]

The promised benefits of joint custody, however, have not materialized. In California, for example, it resulted in a new battleground for couples when judges began to interpret the law in a way that favored joint custody even if one of the spouses objected. California women's rights groups pushed through an amendment in 1980 that explicitly states there is no preference for joint custody unless both parents request it.

Joint residential custody arrangements often proved to be expensive, emotionally wrenching, logistical nightmares for parents and children. Many parents are now settling for less complicated arrangements, with one parent being the "primary caretaker" of the child but both parents having joint legal custody and an equal say in the child's health, education, religious upbringing and so forth.

Although joint custody rouses strong passions among divorced couples and lawyers, it is still a relatively rare phenomenon — even in California. A 1989 study found that only 16-18 percent of all custody agreements in two Northern California counties included dual living arrangements. A much larger proportion of the same group of families (79 percent) had joint legal custody, however. Robert Mnookin, law professor at Stanford Law School and co-author of the study with Stanford psychologist Eleanor Maccoby, believes the incidence of joint custody is probably similar in other urban-suburban areas of California. The number of joint custody arrangements appears to be even lower in other states. Experts say only about 2 percent to 6 percent of all divorce filings call for joint residential custody.[25]

### Child Support Enforcement

Despite the shift to sex-neutral standards and the agitation of fathers' rights groups, judges continue to demonstrate a marked maternal preference in awarding custody. Children still end up with the mother in about 90 percent of all custody cases.

For that reason, enforcement of child support has been a key issue for women's groups as well as child welfare organizations and the social service community. Their combined lobbying on the issue resulted in enactment of two federal laws in the 1980s aimed at remedying the problems of inadequate child-support awards and lax enforcement.

The Child Support Enforcement Amendments of 1984 created incentives for the states to expand collection enforcement. It also required states to develop guidelines with numerical formulas for judges' optional use in setting support awards. And automatic wage withholding was put into effect for welfare families or cases being handled by state enforcement agencies when absent parents fell one month behind in their support payments.

The Family Support Act of 1988 strengthened the 1984 law. It required judges to use the state guidelines on support awards unless they explained in writing reasons for departing from the formulas. Beginning in late 1993, states will have to review support awards in welfare cases at least every three years and in non-welfare cases whenever requested by a parent or enforcement agency.

The 1988 law also expanded automatic wage-withholding. This provision applied immediately to all support orders being enforced by a state agency, not just those where the absent parent fell behind. Beginning in 1994, wage-withholding will apply to all newly issued child-support orders whether or not a state agency is helping enforce them.[26]

The gap in child support is most pronounced for children born out of wedlock. The number of never-married mothers soared more than 25 percent between 1986 and 1988 — from 2 million to 2.6 million — and only 19.7 percent of never-married mothers were awarded child support. For children of divorce, the child-support system appears to be working somewhat better, although awards still sometimes fall well short of children's needs. In 1987, the latest year for which Census Bureau figures are available, nearly 80 percent of the 5.8 million divorced or remarried women had been awarded child support, as were about 55 percent of the 1.4 million women separated from their husbands. About half of those women were receiving full payments, a quarter were receiving partial payments and another quarter were receiving nothing at all. The actual amounts received averaged $3,073 for divorced women and slightly less for separated women.[27]■

# CURRENT SITUATION

## Helping Children Cope

Children tuned in to a recent episode of "Sesame Street" saw Kermit the Frog interviewing a young bird who chirped cheerily, "Mom's tree is over there; back there is Daddy's tree. They live in different places, but they both love me." The program also included a segment on children's drawings that showed a family could be one or more children living with both parents, with one parent, with an aunt, an uncle or one or both grandparents.

The segments exemplify one major recommendation from experts on divorce being adopted in any number of guises: provide positive reinforcement for children to overcome the common feelings of loss and betrayal after parents break up. "Children of divorce see themselves as being different from children whose families have stayed together," writes psychiatrist Edward Beal. "They mourn their lost childhood and what they perceive as the richness and protection of a family that stays together." [28]

Schools provide a natural site for helping children through these problems. The National Education Association since 1987 has advocated more school-based programs to serve both the educational and psychological needs of "students from families that no longer fit the Norman Rockwell image." [29]

One example of such a program is "Banana Splits," a support group for children of divorce that has spread to more than 100 schools since its creation in 1978 by social worker Elizabeth McGonagle of Ballston Spa, N.Y. The idea is for students to get together with someone from the school — a psychologist, counselor or teacher — and with other children of divorce to talk in a supportive, confidential atmosphere about problems and experiences they may not have talked about with anyone else. "There's still a stigma attached," says school psychologist Susan Kosser, who runs the Banana Splits program at Vanderbilt Elementary School in Dix Hills, N.Y., a small Long Island community. "Lots of times they still haven't faced it themselves."

Parents must give permission for their children to participate in the once-a-week sessions and must meet periodically with Kosser. Children are encouraged to open up lines of communication with their parents, but anything said in the sessions is confidential unless the child agrees to let Kosser bring it up with his or her parents.

Kosser believes the program is successful. "It's nothing you can measure scientifically or empirically," she says. "But as a result of Banana Splits, we see less absenteeism, less homework undone and [fewer] trips to the school nurse."

Kids Turn, a San Francisco-area program created by several family law attorneys, tries to accomplish similar goals. The program brings children and parents together for a series of six 90-minute sessions to learn about divorce, including the legal process, and to share their experiences. "We talked about stuff about our parents, and we had puppet shows about it," one 5-year-old participant told a newspaper interviewer. "It made things much happier." [30]

## Help for Parents

More parents are turning to therapy before and after divorce in order to help their children. Psychiatrist Neil Kalter says the most common complaint that child and family therapists hear from divorcing or already divorced parents is that it is difficult to talk with children about important changes in the family.

Charlotte McConnell, a therapist with Family and Child Services of Washington, D.C., says she tells parents to talk to the children about the decision to divorce when the decision is final and to tell them what they can expect. McConnell says parents should emphasize that they still love the children, while explaining that the breakup is a grown-up matter. She also helps parents in a sort of pre-mediation session to think through possible living situations and other matters that will have an impact on the children, such as visitation.

Once parents have separated, McConnell says, a common difficulty is the child's desire for parents to reunite — a source of tension exacerbated when one or both parents decides to date again. She says she advises parents to avoid having "a revolving door" of people that children may become attached to and to delay trying to create "a sort of little happy unit" until they know the relationship is going to work out.

Parents need support for themselves as well. One group that tries to provide that support is Parents Without Partners, an organization founded in 1975 by two single parents in New York City that now has about 135,000 members in the United States and Canada. "Your morale is important, because it will set the tone for the entire family," the organization's promotional brochure says. Included in its 40 practical tips for single parenting are advice on dealing with stress and anger and a strong recommendation for beginning a new social life: "You need friends your own age, and your children need the same."

Between 40 percent and 45 percent of the group's members are single fathers, according to spokesman

*Continued on p. 362*

# At Issue:

## Does divorce always have long-term effects on children?

**JUDITH S. WALLERSTEIN AND SANDRA BLAKESLEE**

*Wallerstein is executive director of the Center for the Family in Transition, Corte Madera, Calif.; Blakeslee is a free-lance journalist*
FROM *SECOND CHANCES: MEN, WOMEN AND CHILDREN A DECADE AFTER DIVORCE* (1989).

*a*lmost all children of divorce regard their childhood and adolescence as having taken place in the shadow of divorce. . . .

For the children in our study, the postdivorce years brought the following:

Half saw their mother or father get a second divorce in the 10-year period after the first divorce.

Half grew up in families where parents stayed angry at each other.

One in four experienced a severe and enduring drop in their standard of living and went on to observe a major, lasting discrepancy between economic conditions in their mothers' and fathers' homes. . . .

Three in five felt rejected by at least one of their parents . . . sensing that they were a piece of psychological or economic baggage left over from a regretted journey.

Very few were helped financially with college educations, even though they continued to visit their fathers regularly. . . . But because their fathers were relatively well-off, they were ineligible for scholarships. . . .

Almost half of the children entered adulthood as worried, underachieving, self-deprecating, and sometimes angry young men and women. Some felt used in a battle that was never their own. Others felt deprived of the parenting and family protection that they always wanted and never got. Those who were troubled at young adulthood were more depleted by early experiences before and after their parents' divorces, had fewer resources, and often had very little help from their parents or anybody else. Some children literally brought themselves up, while others were responsible for the welfare of a troubled parent as well.

Finally, and perhaps most important for society, the cumulative effect of the failing marriage and divorce rose to a crescendo as each child entered young adulthood. It was here, as these young men and women faced the developmental task of establishing love and intimacy, that they most felt the lack of a template for a loving, enduring, and moral relationship between a man and a woman. It was here that anxiety carried over from divorced family relationships threatened to bar the young people's ability to create new, enduring families of their own.

**ANDREW J. CHERLIN AND FRANK F. FURSTENBERG JR.**

*Cherlin is professor of sociology, Johns Hopkins University; Furstenberg is professor of sociology, University of Pennsylvania.*
FROM *THE WASHINGTON POST*, MARCH 20, 1989.

*a*t current rates, 40 percent of American children will experience the breakup of their parents' marriage. Studies show that their responses will vary greatly. Unfortunately, only the most negative outcomes of divorce are receiving attention right now, particularly with the publication of . . . *Second Chances: Men, Women, and Children a Decade After Divorce,* by psychologist Judith S. Wallerstein and Sandra Blakeslee.

*Second Chances* is an impassioned, often insightful study of a serious problem, and many of its conclusions are wise and warranted. But it also needlessly exaggerates the problem. Regrettably, the authors ignore the limitations of their exploratory study and generalize to the nation as a whole. . . .

We do not doubt that many young adults retain painful memories of their parents' divorce. But it doesn't necessarily follow that these feelings will impair functioning as adults. Had their parents not divorced, they might have retained equally painful memories of a conflict-ridden marriage. . . . These alternative outcomes cannot be examined in a study like Wallerstein and Blakeslee's, which has no comparison group of children from intact, unhappy marriages. But in . . . other studies, those in intact families where the parents fought continually were doing no better than the children of divorce. . . .

Government can do more to reduce the economic inequity after divorce between men, on the one hand, and women and children on the other. . . . Beyond economic measures, however, we don't know enough about long-term consequences of divorce to provide a public agenda. Without doubt, many children and families need help and support in managing the crisis of divorce. Increases in funding for counseling and mediation services, information hot-lines and self-help groups are warranted.

But it would be a mistake to assume the need for near-universal therapeutic services for the vast population of maritally disrupted families on the basis of Wallerstein and Blakeslee's overstated conclusions about the long-term consequences of divorce. Their findings are inconsistent with other research and are undercut by the peculiar nature of their sample. When more representative studies are carried out, the problem is likely to look less severe than Wallerstein and Blakeslee suggest.

## Should It Be Harder to Get a Divorce?

*Recent polls indicate that both adults and teenagers think it's too easy to get a divorce in the United States.*

**ADULTS**

Should divorce in this country be easier or more difficult to obtain than it is now?

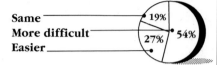

Same — 19%
More difficult — 27% 54%
Easier

*Source: National Opinion Research Center, General Social Survey, 1989.*

**TEENAGERS, AGE 13-17**

Do you think it is too easy or not easy enough for people in this country to get divorced?

Too easy — 76%
Too hard — 24%

**TEENAGERS, AGE 13-17**

Do you think that most people who get divorced have tried hard enough to save their marriages?

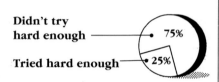

Didn't try hard enough — 75%
Tried hard enough — 25%

*Source: Survey by Gallup Youth Survey, 1989.*

Continued from p. 360

Tony Gallagher, a single father who has been a member since 1971. He says the organization helped him appreciate the importance of fathers staying involved with their children after divorce. "Sending a child-support check every month was a very nice thing to do," Gallagher says, "but it does not take the place of taking the child to the doctor when he or she gets sick in the middle of the night, or going to school for a parent/teachers meeting." ∎

# OUTLOOK

## Trends in Divorce

The U.S. divorce rate leveled off in the late 1980s, and some experts believe it will remain steady for a while. Sally Cunningham, a statistician with the U.S. National Center for Health Statistics, notes that young "baby boomers" — in their 20s and 30s — are divorcing less, possibly "profiting from watching those just ahead." Economic hard times may also deter some couples from seeking a divorce. "The middle class is finding that the money to support two households just isn't there," says David Mattenson, a Chicago matrimonial attorney.[31]

A somewhat lower percentage of children under 18 are being affected by divorce as well — down from 18.7 per 1,000 children in 1981 to 16.4 per 1,000 in 1988. Still, the sobering statistics indicate that half of all new marriages in the United States will end in divorce. Divorce is "here to stay," says psychiatrist Beal. "On an individual basis, the most you can say is that people should make an informed decision. On a societal basis, it's a disaster."

Despite dire assessments, however, no major change in divorce law appears to be in the works. Even Judith Wallerstein, whose book on the adverse effects of divorce on children touched off a nationwide debate, does not advocate making divorce more difficult to obtain. "Our findings do not support those who would turn back the clock," she writes.[32]

### Legislative Outlook

Children's welfare issues, on the other hand, are getting increased attention, especially at the federal level. In a report issued in July 1990, the House Select Committee on Children, Youth and Families gravely warned that compared with children in other developed countries, "children in the United States are frequently at greater risk for a host of social, economic, and health problems."[33] Sentiments like those have led a number of lawmakers to introduce "children's rights" legislation in recent years, and in 1990 Congress approved legislation to provide $22.5 billion in child-care assistance over a five-year period.[34]

One proposal to alleviate poverty in single-parent families being touted around Capitol Hill is called "Child Support Assurance." The plan basically calls for the federal government to take over from the states the collection of billions of dollars that non-custodial parents owe. An absent parent — most commonly, the father — would be required to pay a fixed percent of his income. If he could not pay the full amount, the government would step in and provide a minimum benefit to the mother. Rep. Thomas J. Downey, D-N.Y., who chairs the House Ways and Means Subcommittee on Human Resources, is drafting legislation along those lines for likely introduction sometime in 1991.

Congress will also receive recommendations in early 1992 from a special commission on child support established under the 1988 child-support amendments. Margaret Haynes, the head of the commission and director of the American Bar Association's child-support project in Washington, says the 15-member panel is likely to recommend a stronger federal enforcement program along with steps such as automation of child-support records and better training of judges, lawyers and caseworkers to improve collection efforts at the state level.

On an individual level, therapists and family counselors may be moving toward a more activist role in trying to repair strained marriages and steer couples away from divorce. Michele Weiner-Davis says a growing number of her therapist colleagues are recognizing that "divorce is not the answer we thought it would be." In her practice, she counsels couples to concentrate on what is working in their marriage and then to examine where they get stuck — the negative cycle that aggravates what they are doing wrong.

For couples who do decide to get divorced, the debate over the adverse effects on children has sensitized therapists, counselors, teachers and others on the need to help young people cope with their particular problems. More fathers are staying active in parenting after divorce, and efforts such as mediation are being taken to reduce disputes over child custody.

Still, the experts are repeating their strong warnings about the well-being of children in divorce. "A high proportion of parents are unable to manage the divorce in a way that protects the child's economic and emotional interests," sociologists Furstenberg and Cherlin

*Kenneth Jost, a lawyer, is a free-lance journalist in Washington, D.C. Marilyn Robinson also is a free-lance journalist in Washington.*

write.[35] Wallerstein says the rising divorce rate and other changes in family life have created "unprecedented dangers for society, especially for our children." And she concludes with only partial optimism that the actions taken to date by judges, lawmakers, teachers, therapists, counselors and society at large "still do not measure up to the magnitude of the problem." [36]

## Notes

[1] Judith S. Wallerstein and Sandra Blakeslee, *Second Chances: Men, Women and Children a Decade After Divorce — Who Wins, Who Loses — and Why* (1989), pp. 10-15.

[2] Judith S. Wallerstein, "Children After Divorce: Wounds that Don't Heal," *The New York Times Magazine*, Jan. 22, 1989, p. 20.

[3] Frank F. Furstenberg Jr. and Andrew J. Cherlin, *Divided Families: What Happens to Children When Parents Part* (1991), p. 68.

[4] Frank F. Furstenberg Jr., "Divorce and the American Family," *Annual Review of Sociology*, 1990, pp. 393-394.

[5] Wallerstein and Blakeslee, *op. cit.*, pp. 184-185.

[6] Furstenberg, *op. cit.*, pp. 392-393.

[7] Neil Kalter, *Growing Up With Divorce: Helping your Child Avoid Immediate and Later Emotional Problems* (1990), p. 2.

[8] Wallerstein and Blakeslee, *op. cit.*, p. 298.

[9] Furstenberg and Cherlin, *op. cit.*, p. 96.

[10] Arland Thornton, "Changing Attitudes toward Family Issues in the United States," *Journal of Marriage and the Family*, November 1989, cited in Furstenberg and Cherlin, *ibid.*, pp. 100-101.

[11] Wallerstein and Blakeslee, *op. cit.*, p. 305.

[12] Quoted in William Raspberry, "Everybody's 'Pro-Family'," *The Washington Post*, March 20, 1991, p. A19.

[13] Furstenberg and Cherlin, *op. cit.*, p. 2.

[14] Edward W. Beal and Gloria Hochman, *Adult Children of Divorce: Breaking the Cycle and Finding Fulfillment in Love, Marriage and Family* (1991).

[15] Furstenberg and Cherlin, *op. cit.*, pp. 27-28.

[16] Kalter, *op. cit.*, p. 395.

[17] Roderick Phillips, *Putting Asunder: A History of Divorce in Western Society* (1988).

[18] Phillips, *op. cit.*, p. 462.

[19] Gilbert Y. Steiner, *The Children's Cause*, Brookings Institution, 1976, pp. 4-8.

[20] "Foreword," to *Divorce Reform at the Crossroads* (1990), Stephen D. Sugarman and Herma Hill Kay, eds., p. vii.

[21] *USA Today*, March 19, 1991, p. 1A.

[22] Sugarman and Kay, *op. cit.*, pp. 131-135.

[23] Stephen D. Sugarman, "Dividing Financial Interests on Divorce," in Sugarman and Kay, *ibid.*, p. 164.

[24] See Sarah Glazer, "Joint Custody: Is It Good for the Children?", *Editorial Research Reports*, Feb. 3, 1989, pp. 58, 65-66.

[25] *Ibid.*, pp. 64-65.

[26] See Robert K. Landers, "Child Support: Payments, Progress and Problems," *Editorial Research Reports*, Oct. 26, 1990, pp. 622-623.

[27] *Ibid.*, p. 619.

[28] Beal, *op. cit.*, p. 27.

[29] *Educating Students From Divorced and Single-Parent Homes: A Literature Review and Resource Guide*, National Education Association, October 1988, p. 2.

[30] Quoted in the *Los Angeles Times*, Aug. 26, 1990, p. A1.

[31] Cunningham and Mattenson were quoted in *USA Today*, May 21, 1991, p. 1D.

[32] Wallerstein and Blakeslee, *op. cit.*, p. 305.

[33] U.S. House Select Committee on Children, Youth and Families, *Children's Well Being: An International Comparison*, July 1990, p. 1.

[34] *1990 Congressional Quarterly Almanac*, p. 547.

[35] Furstenberg and Cherlin, *op.cit.*, p. 399.

[36] Wallerstein and Blakeslee, *op.cit.*, pp. 305-306.

# Bibliography

## Selected Sources Used

### Books

**Beal, Edward W., and Hochman, Gloria, *Adult Children of Divorce: Breaking the Cycle and Finding Fulfillment in Love, Marriage, and Family*, Delacorte Press, 1991.**

Divorce has deep, lasting effects on children, according to psychiatrist Edward W. Beal, but they must be understood in terms of the family's pattern of dealing with problems before, during and after divorce. With his journalist collaborator Gloria Hochman, Beal stresses that children of divorce need not repeat the past and provides practical advice — drawn from research and more than 300 case studies — on breaking the cycle of divorce.

**Furstenberg, Frank F. Jr., and Cherlin, Andrew J., *Divided Families: What Happens to Children When Parents Part*, Harvard University Press, 1991.**

Sociologists Frank Furstenberg of the University of Pennsylvania and Andrew Cherlin of Johns Hopkins University are not alarmed about the U.S. divorce rate — likening the figures to trends in other developed countries — or about the effects of divorce on children. They are more concerned about the economic consequences of divorce and advocate a "child support assurance" plan as one way to help protect the economic as well as emotional well-being of children of divorce.

**Kalter, Neil, *Growing Up With Divorce: Helping Your Child Avoid Immediate and Later Emotional Problems*, Free Press, 1990.**

Neil Kalter, director of the Center for the Child and the Family at the University of Michigan, views parents as the key to helping children cope with the stresses of divorce. His detailed clinical accounts illuminate both the "environmental stresses" — arising from parental conflicts, the loss of the non-custodial parent and the like — and "internal stresses" in the form of the child's own beliefs, fantasies and inner conflicts.

**Phillips, Roderick, *Putting Asunder: A History of Divorce in Western Society*, Cambridge University Press, 1988.**

This authoritative work by historian Roderick Phillips of Canada's Brock University details the theological, legal and social treatment of divorce from the Middle Ages to modern times in Europe, North America and Australia. Phillips statistically documents the rise of divorce in modern society and links it to other historical trends, including secularization, industrialization and feminism.

**Sugarman, Stephen D., and Kay, Herma Hill (eds.), *Divorce Reform at the Crossroads*, Yale University Press, 1990.**

This collection of essays by family law experts opens with Professor Stephen D. Sugarman's excellent overview of current law on divorce, custody and support. The articles that follow offer a variety of provocative analyses of current issues and prescriptions for future reforms.

**Wallerstein, Judith S., and Blakeslee, Sandra, *Second Chances: Men, Women & Children a Decade After Divorce — Who Wins, Who Loses — And Why*, Ticknor & Fields, 1989.**

Judith Wallerstein's controversial findings on the long-term psychological effects of divorce on children, drawn from her experiences as a family therapist in Northern California, changed the shape of the debate over the issue. Despite the criticism that an unrepresentative sample skewed her statistics, Wallerstein's work has helped force greater attention to children's well-being by the legal system, government policy-makers and the social services community.

**Weitzman, Lenore J., *The Divorce Revolution: The Unexpected Social and Economic Consequences for Women and Children in America*, Free Press, 1985.**

Stanford University sociologist Lenore Weitzman challenges the no-fault divorce revolution from a feminist perspective, arguing that divorced women in California fared better economically under the old law than under no-fault.

### Reports and Studies

**National Center for Health Statistics, *Advance Report of 1988 Final Divorce Statistics*, May 1991.**

The latest statistics show that the U.S. divorce rate dropped in 1988 for the third consecutive year. Preliminary data indicate the rate leveled off in 1989 and 1990. The proportion of children affected by divorce has also dropped over the past decade, but the figure is twice what it was a generation ago.

**U.S. Census Bureau, *Child Support and Alimony: 1987*, June 1990.**

The Census Bureau's latest figures indicate a payoff from efforts to improve the enforcement of child-support awards. The aggregate amount of child support received (adjusted for inflation) increased 32 percent from 1985 to 1987, while average support payments — which had been declining for several years — increased 16 percent.

# The Next Step

## Additional Articles from Current Periodicals

### Books & reading

**Kaplan, L. & Ade-Ridder, L., "Book briefs," *Family Relations*, October 1990, p. 467.**
Reviews the book *Men and Divorce*, by Michael F. Myers.

**Redfield, C. L., "For young children: Books on divorce," *Single Parent*, July/August 1989, p. 7.**
Book reviews. Presents short reviews on several books on divorce for young children. *God, Where's My Daddy*; *Dinosaurs Divorce*; *Son For a Day*.

**Stuttaford, G., "Forecasts: Nonfiction," *Publishers Weekly*, Jan. 18, 1991, p. 49.**
Reviews the book *Adult Children of Divorce: Breaking the Cycle and Achieving Success in Love, Marriage and Family*, by Edward W. Beal and Gloria Hochman, introduction by Robert Coles.

**Tavris, C., "A remedy but not a cure," *The New York Times Book Review*, Feb. 26, 1989, p. 13.**
Reviews *Second Chances: Men, Women, and Children a Decade after Divorce*, a study by Judith S. Wallerstein and Sandra Blakeslee on the long-term effects of divorce on families. INSET: Unpredictable fathers (book excerpt).

### Case studies

**Marks, J., " 'We have a problem,' " *Parents*, February 1991, p. 60.**
Recounts how a counselor helped a child of divorce come to terms with parents battling for his affections. The article also describes how the counselor helped the parents overcome their guilt and tension.

**Parker, L., "Picking up the pieces," *Single Parent*, September/October 1990, p. 40.**
Presents a fictional story "Picking Up the Pieces," about a child's view of divorce, by Linda Parker with an illustration by Joan Waites.

### Custody issues

**Christensen, D. H., Dahl, C. M., et al., "Noncustodial mothers and child support: Examining the larger context," *Family Relations*, October 1990, p. 388.**
Examines the differences in treatment of non-custodial mothers and non-custodial fathers by courts at the time of divorce. 1,043 randomly selected court cases; Single variable of child support; Methods; Findings; Conclusion and discussion; Implications for policy.

**Derdeyn, A. P., "The post-divorce family, legal practice, and the child's needs for stability," *Children Today*, May/June 1989, p. 12.**
Discusses the situation of children in divorced families. Seeking to ensure stability for children; Child custody issues; Protecting the custodial parent-child unit; Legal issues.

**Ferreiro, B. W., "Presumption of joint custody: A family policy dilemma," *Family Relations*, October 1990, p. 420.**
Traces the debate over whether joint custody should be mandated by state law as the norm for divorcing couples. Debate between fathers' and mothers' rights groups and among mental health and legal professionals. Public policy implications; Policies for strengthening co-parenting after divorce; Types of joint custody statutes; Research evidence; Discussion and policy recommendations; Conclusions.

**Gibson, J. T., "Weekend dads," *Parents*, March 1989, p. 188.**
Gives advice on handling visits between a toddler and a father after parents divorce. Planning activities; Showing love and concern.

**Greif, G. L. & DeMaris, A., "Why fathers gain custody," *Single Parent*, September/October 1990, p. 12.**
Reports on why fathers gain custody of children following a divorce. Money factor; More emotionally competent; Housing and location; Children's wishes; How parents can decide custody situations.

**Nordheimer, J., "Summer, children and 'war of the exes,' " *The New York Times*, July 12, 1990, p. C1.**
Discusses summer visits of children with divorced fathers. Differing viewpoints of the fathers and mothers; Why the visits are sometimes painful.

**Powell, T. R., "Fathering is not always traditional," *Single Parent*, January/February 1990, p. 28.**
Reflects on the author's maturing perspectives concerning his children with the passage of time after divorce. Accepting a limited role of influence; Importance of forgiving spouse and self; Emotional release and love.

**Seltzer, J. A., "Legal custody arrangements and children's economic welfare," *American Journal of Sociology*, January 1991, p. 895.**
Investigates the effects of legal custody arrangements on the amount of child support fathers pay after divorce,

contrasting the experiences of families in which parents share authority over children through joint legal custody and those in which mothers have sole legal custody. Implications of joint custody for children's opportunities; Child support; Data; Results.

**Seltzer, J. A., "Relationships between fathers and children who live apart: The father's role after separation,"** *Journal of Marriage & the Family*, **February 1991, p. 79.**

Uses data from the 1987-88 National Survey of Families and Households to describe three components of nonresident fathers' involvement with children: social contact, economic involvement, and participation in childrearing decisions. The analysis shows that fathers' involvement with children varies depending on the circumstances of the children's birth and their current living arrangements. Results.

## Debates & issues

**"The case against divorce,"** *Utne Reader*, **November/ December 1990, p. 68.**

Contends that issues beyond family must be critically examined before divorce rates can come down.

**Brodkin, A. M., "Helping students cope with divorce,"** *Instructor*, **January 1991, p. 18.**

Interviews Dr. Judith S. Wallerstein on the impact of divorce on children. Dr. Wallerstein has conducted a decade-long study on the subject of divorce and its long-term effects on children of divorced parents. She explores some reactions and behaviors students may exhibit and suggests ways in which teachers can help them adjust to changes at home. INSET: Starting a support group.

**Cain, B. S., "Older children and divorce,"** *The New York Times Magazine*, **Feb. 18, 1990, p. 26.**

Examines the recurrent themes found after an analysis of college-age children whose parents underwent a midlife divorce. Initial reactions of shock; Dismantling of the family house; Moral reversals in parent's behavior; No guilt or blame; Concern for single parents; Altered attitudes toward love and marriage.

**Franklin, K. M., Janoff-Bulman, R., et al., "Long-term impact of parental divorce on optimism and trust: Changes in general assumptions or..,"** *Journal of Personality & Social Psychology*, **October 1990, p. 743.**

Conducts two studies to examine the long-term impact of parental divorce on beliefs about the self and others. Children of divorce reported less trust of a future spouse and were less optimistic about marriage. Exploratory analyses found that continuous conflict in family of origin

adversely affected all levels of trust.

**Furstenberg, F. F. Jr., "Divorce and the American family,"** *Annual Review of Sociology*, **1990, p. 379.**

Reviews the demographic, cultural, economic and social factors that have resulted in the transformation of the institution of marriage over the past century. Altering the life course of children in families; Problems interpreting the effects of divorce on children; Alterations in kinship systems; Public policy issues; Sources of marital instability.

**Kitson, G. C. & Morgan, L. A., "The multiple consequences of divorce: A decade review,"** *Journal of Marriage & the Family*, **November 1990, p. 913.**

Focuses primarily on adults and how they deal with the consequences of divorce. Controversy and new emphases in studies of divorce; Methodology and suggested directions for future research; More.

**Ligammare, M., "To everything there is a season,"** *Single Parent*, **March/April 1989, p. 16.**

Discusses the importance of not thrusting too much responsibility on children as confidants or emotional supporters after divorce or death of a spouse. Importance of childhood and adolescence.

**Segal, J. & Segal, Z., "Dealing with divorce,"** *Parents*, **September 1989, p. 201.**

Discusses the emotional effects of divorce on 5- and 6-year-old children. How available resources and relationships can help a child fare better; Advice on how parents can help a child cope.

**Smolowe, J., Dolan, B., et al., "Can't we talk this over?"** *Time*, **Jan. 7, 1991, p. 77.**

States that the fear of AIDS, a general maturing of the baby-boom generation and a growing awareness of the problems divorce poses for children have all conspired to make divorce a less attractive option. Therapists encouraging troubled couples to stay together; *The Case Against Divorce*, by Diane Medved; Traditionalists and quick-fix approaches.

**Springen, K., "Fight for a name of his own,"** *Newsweek*, **Nov. 5, 1990, p. 71.**

Explores the battle over what name a child should take in a divorce case. Divorce attorneys predict that disputes between biological parents will grow more common as women try to extend gender equality to their children's names. Court's decision to give a child one of the parent's names seen as a victory; Argument that the key issue should be neither men's rights or women's right but continuity for the child.

**Theroux, P., "When the bough breaks...," *Parents*, February 1989, p. 59.**

Discusses the effects of divorce on children, even when parents hurt children inadvertently and gives advice on minimizing hurt. Examples.

**Toufexis, A., "The lasting wounds of divorce," *Time*, Feb. 6, 1989, p. 61.**

Discusses a 15-year study on the effects of divorce on children, which says youngsters suffer the consequences many years after the breakup. Psychologist Judith Wallerstein's book, *Second Chances*; Disagreement from other psychologists.

**Trueman, D., "Protecting the children of divorce," *USA Today*, May 1989, p. 74.**

Examines the emotional impact of divorce on children. How parents can help their children in a divorce situation; Importance of effective co-parenting with suggestions on how to accomplish this.

**Wallerstein, J. S., "Children after divorce," *The New York Times Magazine*, Jan. 22, 1989, p. 18.**

A report on a 10-year study of the effects of divorce on children. Case studies; Relationship between the quality of life in post-divorce families and the psychological condition of children; Fear of betrayal in relationships; The "overburdened child" syndrome; The sleeper effect; Statistics; Other studies that support these findings.

## Parental relationships

**Bay, R. C. & S. L. Braver. "Perceived control of the divorce settlement process and inter-parental conflict," *Family Relations*, October 1990, p. 382.**

Determines if perceived control over the settlement process during divorce is related to the degree of conflict reported by divorcing parents, as predicted by the theory of "psychological reactance." Representative sample of divorcing couples with children; Method; Results; Discussion; Implications for practice; Summary.

**Masheter, C., "Postdivorce relationships between ex-spouses: The roles of attachment and interpersonal conflict," *Journal of Marriage & the Family*, February 1991, p. 103.**

Examines post-divorce relationships between ex-spouses, using survey data from 265 respondents (154 women and 111 men) from a random-selection sample of 550 couples who had been divorced for two to two-and-a-half years. Method and results. Fragment relationships.

**Meredith, G. R., "Caught in the middle: A dangerous game," *Single Parent*, November/December 1990, p. 38.**

Gives advice to divorced parents caught in the middle between children and ex-spouse. Determining seriousness of the problem; Getting accurate information; Urging children to talk with their other parent; Learning from the situation.

**Stark, E., "Friendship after divorce," *Single Parent*, May 1988, p. 12.**

Discusses the relationship of divorced couples. One of eight such couples still remain friends. Explains why it's OK to have a good relationship with an ex-spouse and how this can be beneficial to the children.

## Research

**Amato, P. R., "The 'child of divorce' as a person prototype: Bias in the recall of information about children...," *Journal of Marriage & the Family*, February 1991, p. 59.**

Uses the perspective of cognitive social psychology to explore the "child of divorce" prototype. In the first study, a free-recall task was used to generate descriptions of children from divorced families. The second and third studies tested the hypothesis that people recall information about children from divorced families in a biased manner. The third study found that a cognitive bias against children of divorce exists among those holding positive and negative attitudes.

**Kurdek, L. A., "The relations between reported well-being and divorce history, availability of a proximate adult...," *Journal of Marriage & the Family*, February 1991, p. 71.**

Examines the relations between reported well-being (global happiness, depression, and general health) and divorce history (0, 1, or 2 divorces), the availability of a proximate adult, and gender in a sample of 6,573 primary respondents from the National Survey of Families and Households. Methods and results.

**White, L. K., "Determinants of divorce: A review of research in the eighties," *Journal of Marriage & the Family*, November 1990, p. 904.**

Encompasses work published in the 1980s that concerns the causes of divorce. Substantive findings are reviewed under three broad headings: macrostructure, demographics and the life course, and family process. Trends in methods, samples, and theory are also reviewed. Recommendations for future research.

# Back Issues

*Great Research on Current Issues Starts Right Here... Recent topics covered by The CQ Researcher are listed below. Issues dated before May 10, 1991, were published under the name of Editorial Research Reports.*

**NOVEMBER 1989**
Balkanization of Eastern Europe
Dealing With the Underclass
America Turns to Recycling
New World Economy

**DECEMBER 1989**
North America Trade Pact
Influence Peddling
German Reunification
Learning Disabilities

**JANUARY 1990**
Higher Education Curriculum
Photonics
Age of 'Infotainment'
Abortion: Politicians' Nightmare

**FEBRUARY 1990**
Politics and Economic Growth
Free Agency in Sports
Repetitive Motion
War on Drugs

**MARCH 1990**
Asbestos: Are Risks Acceptable?
Public Health Campaigns
South Africa's Future
Homeless Need More Than Shelter

**APRIL 1990**
How Fair is the Tax Burden?
Workers' Compensation
U.S. Pacific Forces
Curbing Insurance Premiums

**MAY 1990**
Should Teaching Be a Profession?
Will Canada Fall Apart?
Is U.S. Patent System Outdated?
Federal Funding for the Arts

**JUNE 1990**
Downsizing America's Armed Forces
Progress In Weather Forecasting
S & L Bailout
Bio-Chemical Disarmament

**JULY 1990**
Do Americans Still Love Marriage?
Death Penalty Debate
Decline of Rural America
United Nations in the 1990s

**AUGUST 1990**
Democracy in the Philippines
Initiatives: True Democracy?
Hard Times at Newspapers
Teens Balance School & Jobs

**SEPTEMBER 1990**
Dangers of Alcohol
Western Alliance After the Cold War
Tobacco Industry
Right to Die

**OCTOBER 1990**
Organ Transplants
Energy Policy Options
Search for Arab Unity
Child Support

**NOVEMBER 1990**
Lotteries and Gambling
Post Cold-War Choices
Setting Limits on Medical Care
Multicultural Education

**DECEMBER 1990**
Cable TV Regulation
Americans' Search For Their Roots
Is Insurance System a Failure?
Why Schools Still Have Tracking

**JANUARY 1991**
Growing Influence of Boycotts
Should the U.S. Reinstate the Draft?
America's Archaeological Past
Peace Corps' Challenges in '90s

**FEBRUARY 1991**
Regional Impact of Recession
Puerto Rico's Status
Redistricting: Mapping Power
Nuclear Power

**MARCH 1991**
Acid Rain
Cost of the Gulf War
Reassessing Gun Laws
Future for Man in Space

**APRIL 1991**
Social Security
Canadian Crisis Over Quebec
California Drought
Electromagnetic Radiation

**MAY 1991**
School Choice
Racial Quotas
Animal Rights
U.S. and Japan

Back issues are available for $4.00 (subscribers) or $7.00 (non-subscribers). Quantity discounts apply to orders over ten. To order, call Congressional Quarterly 1-800-432-2250.

# Future Topics

▶ *Teenage Suicide*

▶ *Endangered Species*

▶ *Europe 1992 Update*

# Teenage Suicide

*What can be done to identify and help potential victims?*

A DEATH IN THE FAMILY IS ALWAYS DEVASTATING, even if extreme old age or terminal illness is the cause. But the shock of bereavement is infinitely greater when a teenage family member commits suicide. Relatives are left to cope as best they can with feelings of grief and guilt. Once unusual, teenage suicide has become increasingly common in recent decades. Suicide now ranks as the third leading cause of death among people ages 15 to 24. Programs designed to identify and help at-risk youths have proliferated nationwide. Though no one challenges the goal of dissuading young people from taking their lives, experts disagree on whether prevention programs should include all teenagers or only those thought to be at greatest risk.

C Q | **June 14, 1991 • Volume 1, No. 6 • 369-392**

*Formerly Editorial Research Reports*

June 14, 1991
Volume 1, No. 6

**EDITOR**
Sandra Stencel

**ASSOCIATE EDITOR**
Richard L. Worsnop

**STAFF WRITERS**
Charles S. Clark
Mary H. Cooper
Rodman D. Griffin

**PRODUCTION EDITOR**
Laurie De Maris

**EDITORIAL ASSISTANT**
Thomas H. Moore

**GRAPHICS**
Jack Auldridge

**PUBLISHED BY**
Congressional Quarterly Inc.

**CHAIRMAN**
Andrew Barnes

**VICE CHAIRMAN**
Andrew P. Corty

**EDITOR AND PUBLISHER**
Neil Skene

**EXECUTIVE EDITOR**
Robert W. Merry

**PUBLICATIONS MARKETING/SALES**
Robert Smith

**EDITOR, EBSCO PUBLISHING**
Melissa Kummerer

The CQ Researcher (ISSN 1056-2036). Formerly Editorial Research Reports. Published weekly (48 times per year, excluding March 1, May 3, Aug. 2 and Nov. 1, 1991) by Congressional Quarterly Inc., 1414 22nd St., N.W., Washington, D.C. 20037. Rates are furnished upon request. Application to mail at second-class postage rates is pending at Washington, D.C. POSTMASTER: Send address changes to The CQ Researcher, 1414 22nd St., N.W., Washington, D.C. 20037.

COVER ART: BARBARA SASSA-DANIELS

# Teenage Suicide

BY RICHARD L. WORSNOP

## THE ISSUES

This year more than 5,000 American teenagers and young adults will take their own lives and perhaps 50 times that number will make serious but unsuccessful attempts to do so. Suicide now ranks as the third leading cause of death among people ages 15 to 24, trailing only accidents and homicide. Among white non-Hispanic youths in that age bracket, suicide is the No. 2 cause of death, after accidents.

These figures are disturbing enough when viewed out of context. They become even more worrisome when one learns the teenage suicide rate has tripled since the 1950s.* Although there are indications the growth curve may be flattening, the number of youth suicides remains far too high to permit any complacency on the part of suicide-prevention experts.

Young people who commit suicide are not easily pigeonholed. Self-inflicted deaths occur within all social, ethnic and economic classes. As a recent report noted: "Adolescents who have all the 'right' friends and are academically and athletically successful kill themselves" as do "youths who come from divided families, have few friends and are failing in school-related activities." [1]

Nonetheless, certain generalities hold true for all age groups — including teenagers. Women, for instance, attempt suicide about three times as often as men. On the other hand, men complete suicide about three times as often as women. About 20 percent of the individuals who attempt suicide repeat the behavior, and each attempt tends to be more dangerous than the preceding one.

A recent nationwide survey by the Gallup Organization drew attention to the extent of suicidal behavior among American young people. [2] Six percent of the respondents, who ranged in age from 13 to 19, said they had tried to commit suicide and 15 percent said they had "come very close to trying." Gary Hoeltke, a senior vice president at the Gallup Organization and a former school psychologist, says he was not surprised at the study's results. In fact, he believes the reported 6 percent attempt rate understates the actual extent of the problem.

If nothing else, the Gallup findings underscored the need for community- or school-based suicide prevention programs aimed specifically at young people. Youth suicide prevention "really is in its infancy," says Karen Dunne-Maxim, co-coordinator of the Suicide Prevention Project at the University of Medicine and Dentistry of New Jersey. Alan Berman, a clinical psychologist at the Washington (D.C.) School of Psychiatry, estimates that only about 200 youth suicide-prevention programs are currently operating across the country, though the number of participating high schools probably is somewhat higher. (*See At Issue, p. 385.*)

Some experts derive cautious satisfaction from the fact that the youth suicide rate has leveled off in the past decade. Berman says there is no single factor to explain the trend, though he speculates it may have something to do with the general reduction in teenage drug use. "If you were to plot the pattern of drug use among adolescents over time and plot the rate of [adolescent] suicide, you would see some correspondence in the curves," he says. "The two variables seem to parallel."

But many experts still are hesitant to say the tide has turned. One reason is that the youth suicide rate shot up — from 12.9 to 13.2 per 100,000 persons ages 15-24 — in 1988, the most recent year for which complete data are available. This may be only a random fluctuation, or it could signal the start of another long-term trend.

Because their field is relatively new, suicide-prevention experts are cautiously feeling their way as they search for the most effective methods of identifying and counseling "at risk" youths. A vast body of historical and literary lore about suicide has accumulated since ancient times, and much of this material still speaks to the human condition as it exists today. But professionals specializing in suicide prevention — and youth suicide prevention in particular — must also sort out and evaluate a host of contributing fac-

---

*U.S. suicide rates, derived from figures compiled by the Department of Health and Human Services' National Center for Health Statistics, are expressed as the number of deaths per 100,000 population.

tors of distinctly modern origin. As a result, the professionals confront a number of questions to which there are only partial answers at present.

### What has caused the great increase in teenage suicide in recent decades?

The first question that arises when a teenager commits suicide is "why?" The fact that a person on the threshold of adulthood would choose to end his or her life is and always has been deeply troubling — not only to the deceased's immediate family but also to friends, classmates and members of the community at large. In nearly every case of youth suicide, there is no single cause but rather a "constellation" of causes that interacted in various ways over time.

Some psychologists relate America's postwar baby boom to the increase in youth suicide. Children born between 1950 and 1955 passed through their teens and early 20s during the late 1970s, the period when the youth suicide rate was rising most quickly.

Disappointment in love — the so-called "Romeo and Juliet" syndrome — is often cited as a factor, but many experts regard it as an unsatisfactory explanation for the upsurge in teen suicides in recent decades. "Teenage romances broke up 25 years ago," says Dr. George Weiner, chairman of the psychiatry department at George Washington University. "Is there something different [today] about the sense of despair, the sense of hopelessness . . . that youngsters feel suicide is a reasonable solution?" [3]

A 1986 government survey attempted to answer this question.[4] Experts in suicide research and prevention were asked to list the characteristics of youth at risk of killing themselves. Half of the respondents cited family conflicts, more than one-third mentioned physical or sexual abuse, and 17 percent named

alcohol or drug abuse. All three problems have become especially prominent in the postwar period.

Many see the breakdown in the nuclear family — manifested by high rates of divorce and remarriage, more children living in single-parent families, multiple changes of residence and school, and child abuse — as leading to emotional isolation, a key factor in youth suicide.[5]

Many young people who commit suicide are drug or alcohol abusers. Although their drug abuse may not have been the chief cause of death, the same inner anguish that led the youngsters to drugs or alcohol probably influenced their decisions to kill themselves. In this way, excessive drug or alcohol use may act as a suicide trigger.

Sexual orientation may also play a role in youth suicides. In a recent study, researchers at the University of Minnesota and the University of Wisconsin found that 41 of 137 young homosexual or bisexual males interviewed said they had attempted suicide.[6] Their findings paralleled those of a 1989 U.S. Department of Health and Human Services (HHS) study that found male and female homosexual teenagers were three times as likely as heterosexual teenagers to attempt suicide. According to the HHS study, homosexuals accounted for 30 percent of all completed teenage suicides.[7]

Other factors often cited by the experts have figured in youth suicide through the ages: depression, low self-esteem, difficulty in controlling impulses, inadequate coping skills, inability to communicate, lack of hope for the future, desire for instant gratification and unrealistic perceptions of death.

Such traits are often found among low achievers in school, but as the participants in the 1986 government survey pointed out, some high achievers also are at risk of suicide. That is because such youths tend to

impose unrealistically high standards on themselves or feel a need to impress family members and school peers by excelling academically or socially. Since their concept of self-worth is so heavily oriented toward achievement, teenage perfectionists often cannot come to grips with being even second-best.

In an undetermined number of cases, the root cause of suicidal behavior in teenagers may be biological or genetic. Recent research has uncovered evidence that suicidal teenagers have markedly different brain chemistry from that of other youngsters. This tentative finding seems to buttress earlier research indicating that depression is often accompanied by abnormalities within and between the brain's neurotransmitting systems (*see p. 380*).

If the origins of depression do turn out to be biological, genetic factors may be involved. Some studies have shown that children of depressed or manic-depressed parents may be 30 percent to 50 percent more likely to become depressed as the children of other parents. To many researchers, such a finding indicates genetics at work. However, it is also possible that the children's depression may be caused by the depressed parents' emotional limitations and the resulting home environment.

### What are the warning signs that a teenager is at risk of suicide, and how should one respond to them?

Although a teenager's suicide always comes as a great shock, the victim typically drops numerous clues before committing the fatal act. The trouble is that family members and friends often fail to detect these telltale signs or, if they do, disregard them. This is a tragic oversight, mental health professionals say, since experience shows that most young people are ambivalent about taking their lives. It is believed that few really want to die; they simply want to put an end to their emotional pain.

Suicidal people sometimes communicate a subtle or indirect message about their intent. Verbal clues might include statements like: "I might as well be dead," "you won't have to worry about me much longer," or "you'll be sorry when I'm gone." The widely held belief that "people who say they are going to kill themselves never do" is a myth, experts insist. A young person who talks about wanting to die is likely to attempt suicide.

Another suicide signal is preparation for death, which for a young person might entail giving away prized possessions like a CD player or mountain bike. Sudden changes in mood or behavior that last a long time are also suspect. Shy people who become outgoing and adventurous for no apparent reason or friendly people who become withdrawn and apathetic may be depressed and considering suicide.

Other clues indicating depression are uncommunicativeness, irritability, fatigue, changes in eating and sleeping habits, reckless or abusive behavior, a marked increase or decrease in sexual activity, loss of interest in school, friends and other activities, preoccupation with death and lessened fear of death. Increased use of drugs or alcohol, although not necessarily evidence of suicidal thoughts, may precede a suicide attempt or signal a deep depression that could become suicidal when the drugs no longer ease the emotional pain they were intended to relieve.

In some cases, the most ominous sign of suicidal intent is the sudden onset of apparent peace of mind after a long period of troubling behavior. Such a mood change may indicate the person has finally resolved to commit suicide and thus has achieved a kind of tranquility.

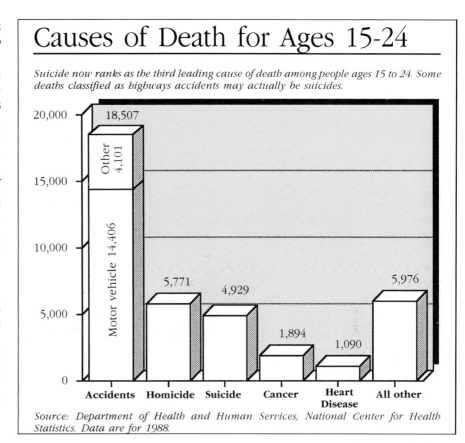

# Causes of Death for Ages 15-24

*Suicide now ranks as the third leading cause of death among people ages 15 to 24. Some deaths classified as highways accidents may actually be suicides.*

Accidents: 18,507 (Other 4,101; Motor vehicle 14,406)
Homicide: 5,771
Suicide: 4,929
Cancer: 1,894
Heart Disease: 1,090
All other: 5,976

*Source: Department of Health and Human Services, National Center for Health Statistics. Data are for 1988.*

Experts in mental health care say the most important response to suicidal young people is to take them seriously. All too often, parents or friends dismiss suicidal clues because the person giving them does not seem to be unhappy or the "type" to commit suicide. Parents and friends also may dismiss distress signals as adolescent melodrama, overreaction or attempts to get back at them.

Experts agree that people who have made suicidal comments or who display evidence of severe depression (either directly or by acting out) should be asked if they are contemplating suicide and if they are, what plans — if any — have been made. If the person has a definite plan, if the means are easily available, if the method is a lethal one, and the time is set, the risk of attempted suicide is very high. Consequently, it is vital not to miscalculate the danger by failing to probe for details.

Rather than implant the idea of suicide, as some people assume, such questions will relieve young people by letting them know they are being taken seriously. Open dialogue also gives disturbed youngsters an opportunity to talk about their suicidal feelings and impulses. But the person doing the questioning should observe certain guidelines.

For instance, experts advise against telling at-risk youngsters that suicide is wrong or sinful, that they should be grateful for what they have since so many others of their age are worse off, or that everything is basically all right. If the potential victim believed all that, he or she would not be suicidal in the first place. Such statements only add to troubled youngsters' feelings of hopelessness and worthlessness and reinforce their belief that no one understands them.

By the same token, people talking

# Literary References

*". . . And Richard Cory, one calm summer night,
Went home and put a bullet through his head."*

— *Edward Arlington Robinson, "Richard Cory"*

In literature as in life, suicide inspires feelings of sorrow, awe and pity. Dante's thoughts on the subject, as expressed in the *Inferno*, reflect Christian doctrine of the early 14th century. As Virgil conducts Dante through the various regions of hell, they find that suicides occupy the fiery seventh circle, along with murderers, blasphemers and perverts.

In his tragedies, Shakespeare employed suicide as a dramatic device again and again. The Bard of Avon's roster of self-inflicted deaths includes the title characters in *Romeo and Juliet* and *Antony and Cleopatra*; Cassius and Brutus in *Julius Caesar*; Goneril in *King Lear*, Ophelia in *Hamlet*; Othello; and Lady Macbeth. Unlike Dante, Shakespeare was non-judgmental. A. Alvarez observed that Othello's suicide "weighs not at all" for Shakespeare; "what matters is its tragic inevitability and the degree to which it heightens his heroic stature. Instead of damning him, [Othello's] suicide confirms his nobility." †

The literary treatment of suicide underwent another change with the publication in 1774 of Goethe's novel *The Sorrows of Young Werther*. The book was written after the author's unrequited love for Charlotte Buff and seems to have helped him regain his emotional equilibrium. But *Werther's* effect on the reading public was just the opposite. The romantic tale of the doomed young man in the blue tail coat and yellow waistcoat impelled dozens of young men throughout Europe to commit suicide in emulation.

Two of the finest novels of the 19th century, *Anna Karenina* and *Madame Bovary*, featured heroines who killed themselves. American authors of the 20th century also have explored the subject with sensitivity. They include novels by Edith Wharton (*The House of Mirth*), William Faulkner (*The Sound and the Fury*), John O'Hara (*Appointment in Samarra*), and short stories by Willa Cather ("Paul's Case") and J. D. Salinger ("A Perfect Day for Bananafish").

Perhaps the most famous suicide in modern literary annals is the young American poet Sylvia Plath. Shortly before her senior year in college, Plath made a serious suicide attempt (with sleeping pills) and was found barely in time to save her life. The attempt, and the events leading to it, found fictional expression in her posthumously published novel, *The Bell Jar*. Esther Greenwood, the narrator and central character, likens madness to the descent of a stifling bell jar over her head.

**Poet Sylvia Plath**

In this state, she says, "wherever I sat . . . I would be sitting under the same glass bell jar, stewing in my sour air." And she adds, "To the person in the bell jar, blank and stopped as a dead baby, the world itself is the bad dream."

In February 1963, Plath again attempted suicide (by gas from her kitchen range), and this time she was successful. The irony is that she probably wanted to be rescued; a note found near her body said, "Please call Dr. ---" and gave his phone number. But gas from her apartment had seeped into the bedroom of a neighbor living one floor below, knocking him out. Otherwise, the man might have been able to help save her.

† A. Alvarez, *The Savage God: A Study of Suicide* (1972), p. 152.

with youngsters contemplating suicide should not attempt to analyze their behavior or try to shock or challenge them out of the idea. The danger here is that the youngsters may decide to accept the challenge. Moreover, experts caution that arguing with teenagers about whether they should live or die also runs a high risk of backfiring.

Those dealing with a suicidal young person should reassure him or her that depressed feelings are temporary and that there is always a chance that problems can be resolved as long as life exists. It should also be mentioned that if death is the choice, it is a final one and cannot be reversed. If the young person displays symptoms of acute distress, he or she should not be left alone.

People who are uncertain about what the youngsters they are attempting to comfort intend to do should summon outside help. Doctors, members of the clergy or mental health professionals contacted through a community health center, suicide prevention center or a telephone crisis "hotline" can offer advice about what to do in various situations. Professional assistance is essential for people who already have attempted suicide.

***Why do some teenage suicides occur in closely related "clusters"?***

A relatively rare phenomenon, the youth suicide "cluster," has become a focus of research since the early 1980s. By one definition, a suicide cluster is "a group of suicides, suicide attempts, or both, that occur closer together than would normally be expected in a given community." [8] Such clusters account for only about 1-2 percent of all suicides among adolescents and young adults. But the inherent drama of suicide claiming the lives of a locality's young people as if by contagion ensures that a cluster will receive wide coverage in the local — and sometimes the national — news media.

Charlotte Ross, executive director of the Youth Suicide National Center in San Mateo, Calif., cites a number of theories as to why a suicide cluster develops.* "[A]t any given time [there are] a number of people who are particularly vulnerable," she says. The triggering mechanism could be the sudden death of a friend or acquaintance, or even "a story in a newspaper, a film, a TV show, that either deliberately or inadvertently suggests that suicide is a solution to a problem."

Ross herself feels the forces setting a suicide cluster in motion are more complex than that. "One of the things that's not been sufficiently explored is the grief reaction of young people," she says. "It has certainly been underestimated how much young people grieve for their friends, how much they identify [with them]." Guilt also may play a pivotal role. "Many times, young people feel they should have done something" to prevent a friend's sui-

cide, Ross says, "so they become depressed themselves."

While a suicide cluster is in progress, it can seem unstoppable as it seemingly feeds upon itself. But eventually it does end, prompting suicide-prevention experts to ask themselves, once again, "why?" Ross suggests the answer may be disarmingly simple: "You run out of highly vulnerable kids who are susceptible."

A 1989 study of two teenage suicide clusters that occurred in Texas earlier in the decade indicated how difficult it is to draw an all-purpose profile of at-risk young people. On the one hand, the 14 youngsters who committed suicide were more likely "to have had more than two different adults in the role of parents" than were the non-suicidal teenagers in a control group. This seemed to suggest a potential source of intra-family conflict. On the other hand, the "school performance, work performance [and] overall social relationships" of the suicides were similar to those of the control-group members. Some of the suicides were close friends, but others had had no direct contacts with the rest of their cluster. Further clouding the picture was a finding that the youths who committed suicide were less likely than control-group members to have watched television programs about suicide.[9]

### How effective are suicide-prevention programs designed for teenagers?

Though no one argues with the goal of dissuading teenagers from taking their lives, some professionals insist that prevention programs are so ill-conceived that they may encourage suicide rather than deter it. Others do not go that far, saying only that teenage suicide-prevention programs tend to be too broadly or too narrowly focused.

Teenagers themselves appear to take a more positive view of such

programs. Participants in the recent Gallup survey were asked what they thought their school should do to prevent teenage suicide. Three main suggestions emerged: (1) creating a special program for teenagers with problems, (2) holding a course for parents on how to be better parents, and (3) alerting students to such outside sources of help as hot lines and counseling groups.

Alan Berman of the Washington School of Psychiatry also reports that teenagers generally think well of suicide-prevention programs. "Most youngsters seem to find the programs of value to them," he says. "They enjoy being attended to and being given information and [coping] skills." He adds, however, that the youngsters most at risk of committing suicide "are the hardest to get involved."

At-risk teenagers also tend to be more critical of youth suicide-prevention programs than are teenagers in general. That was the conclusion of a study of three such programs conducted by Dr. David Shaffer of the Columbia University College of Physicians and Surgeons and five colleagues. Of the teenagers in the programs who had attempted suicide, 26.7 percent agreed with the statement "talking about suicide in the classroom makes some kids more likely to try to kill themselves." By contrast, only 11.5 percent of the entire group of teenagers in the programs agreed with the statement.[10]

Karen Dunne-Maxim of the University of Medicine and Dentistry of New Jersey makes the point that school-based prevention programs should eschew statistical data on youth suicide. "You don't want to give those statistics to kids in a classroom," she explains, "because you're saying, in effect, 'Everybody's doing it.' The numbers somehow make suicide seem normal."

Much of the fire directed at youth

---

*Margaret O. Hyde and Elizabeth Held Forsyth, authors of *Suicide: The Hidden Epidemic*, theorized that the second and subsequent suicides in a cluster represent "a tragic plea for positive attention, an attempt to enjoy in death the same high status as the first suicide." They also suggested that some youngsters who are pulled into a suicide cluster "may harbor the 'magical' or juvenile belief that they are all-powerful and can reverse death, can have death without dying." See Margaret O. Hyde and Elizabeth Held Forsyth, *Suicide: The Hidden Epidemic* (1986 edition), p. 32.

# Youth Suicide Rate, 1950-1988

*The youth suicide rate — expressed as the number of deaths per 100,000 population — has nearly tripled in the past 40 years. It rose from 4.5 in 1950 to 13.2 in 1988, the last year for which complete statistics are available. One fact has remained constant over the decades: White teenage boys and young men are far more likely to commit suicide than are other youths.*

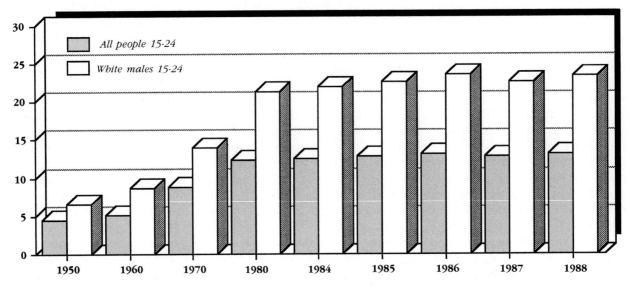

Key:
- All people 15-24
- White males 15-24

*Source: Department of Health and Human Services, National Center for Health Statistics.*

suicide-prevention efforts centers on classroom materials. Of particular concern are films that inadvertently sensationalize or glamorize the subject. After viewing such a film, some experts say, at-risk youngsters may be more inclined to consider suicide than before. Many youth suicide-prevention programs are faulted for being too short. Berman notes that the typical school-based program lasts only four to eight hours in all. "We know that to truly change attitudes and behavior requires much more time than a few hours," he says.

The question of whether school-based suicide prevention programs should be broadly or narrowly focused may never be answered to the satisfaction of all concerned. Everyone agrees the primary aim of prevention programs is to identify and help the teenagers most at risk of suicide. Thus many professionals contend that prevention programs, which usually have limited resources to begin with, should concentrate on the youngsters most in

need of assistance.

Berman, on the other hand, says exposing all students to suicide-prevention techniques can benefit the at-risk minority. If a student spots a classmate or peer who is troubled and urges him or her to seek help "that may be a significant intervention," Berman says, "because these at-risk youth often are not help-seeking kinds of kids."

Dr. Weiner of George Washington University takes a dim view of prevention programs that deal exclusively with suicide. "Except on a very individual basis, there isn't anything that really represents suicide prevention," he says. On the other hand, "it would be extremely constructive and positive if [suicide-prevention instruction] were included in the context of educating students about mental illness and how suicide may be related to mental illness."

***What can be done to ease the impact of teenage suicide on family members?***

In the aftermath of a teenage suicide, the needs of the dead youngster's immediate family tend to be overlooked. Many friends assume (sometimes correctly) that the family does not want to talk about what happened. As a result, the friends may make a point of avoiding the subject. Sometimes, they go so far as to suspend all social contact with the family. The trouble is that such behavior may reinforce whatever guilt feelings the family already harbors. Moreover, sidestepping the question of suicide prevents family members from working out their grief as they would do in the case of a death from natural causes.

Research has established that suicide, especially of a young person, gives rise to a complex blend of reactions among family members and close friends. These generally include: (1) strong feelings of loss, accompanied by sorrow and mourning; (2) anger at being made to feel responsible or at being rejected, in that whatever help had been offered was refused; (3) guilt, shame or embarrassment; (4) relief that the nagging, insistent demands of the deceased have ended; (5) feelings of desertion, a common reaction among children in particular; (6) self-questioning as to whether everything possible had been done to forestall suicide; (7) arousal of one's own suicidal impulses.

Numerous communities across the country have taken steps to provide grief counseling to family survivors of a teenage suicide. Whether it is provided through survivors' organizations, mental health centers, churches or crisis intervention programs, the counseling is aimed at easing the emotional turmoil that a suicide inevitably generates. Above all, the objective is to make sure that family members and friends do not take their own lives because of the anguish they feel.

On the basis of a study of parents who had lost children through suicide, psychiatrist Harvey L. P. Resnik and author Arthur Herzog recommended that a trained professional should visit the parents within 24 hours of the death. Several parents in the study said they would have appreciated and benefited from immediate counseling. Resnik and Herzog said the first visit should be supportive, with later ones devoted primarily to exploring guilt feelings and correcting distorted attitudes toward the deceased. After perhaps six months, the consultations could become less frequent. But Resnik and Herzog stressed that the counselor should take care to schedule a visit close to the anniversary of the death, as this is a time when painful memories are likely to resurface.[11] ∎

# BACKGROUND

## Attitudes Toward Suicide

Efforts to reduce high suicide rates have long been impeded by the stigma still attached to disorders of the mind. In a classic social and historical study of suicide, Henry Romilly Fedden traced the prevalent attitude toward suicide to primitive tribal superstitions concerning ghosts of the dead, particularly ghosts of persons who had been murdered. These superstitions often required that elaborate purification rites be performed.

"If such precautions were taken to calm the ghosts of the murdered . . . how disturbing to primitive minds must the suicide ghost have been," Fedden wrote. "Whereas the ghost of the murdered man bore malice only against his executioner, the ghost of the suicide was believed to harm society in general, and the latter was held to be indiscriminately and collectively responsible for his death." [12]

Indeed, the primitive suicide frequently was a "revenge" suicide in which the victim believed his ghost would haunt and plague his enemies. The only recourse for the latter was to mutilate or destroy the corpse, so the risen ghost would be incapable of inflicting harm.

Traditional feelings about suicide, it has been suggested, may represent an instinctive reaction to the contempt for society implicit in the act of killing oneself. People are troubled by such conduct, and their natural reaction is to condemn the suicide. There may also be an unconscious wish to protect the community against the contagion of self-destruction. In primitive times, moreover, purely economic considerations were involved: An adult male suicide deprived the tribe of a warrior, and a woman's suicide represented the death of a potential mother.

Classical philosophers were the first to tie suicide to a system of morality. The ancient Greeks viewed life as a penitential journey, a discipline imposed by the gods to which a man must submit himself. Suicide thus amounted to rebellion, an unruly escape from a destiny laid down by superior powers.[13]

But some Greek and Roman philosophers also advanced the notion that suicide was justifiable if life became truly unbearable — because of a painful disease, for example. It was also widely believed in the ancient world that suicide was preferable to falling into enemy hands. Hundreds of Jewish defenders of the mountaintop fortress of Masada killed themselves in 73 A.D. rather than be captured and enslaved by attacking Roman legions.

Some customs of a suicidal nature were sanctioned by tradition. Conjugal martyrdom — a form of institutional suicide known as suttee — was practiced for centuries among Hindu women. As late as 1802, an estimated 270 wives willingly met death within 30 miles of Calcutta by throwing themselves on their husbands' funeral pyres.

In the Orient, Buddhist monks regularly sacrificed their lives in an effort to attain nirvana, the extinction of passion and desire. In the sixth century, monks who decided to immolate themselves would eat waxy and fatty foods for several years in order to burn better. A passage in sacred Buddhist writings reads: "Abandoning one's existence is to be looked upon as the best self-sacrifice, for to give one's body is better than to give alms. . . ."

### Christian Era

It remained for the Christian church to attach the onus of sin to suicide, although biblical scholars have found no specific anti-suicide teachings in the Old or New Testaments. By contrast, the Muslim prohibition is explicit. The Koran states: "O believers, says the Prophet, commit not suicide.... Whoever shall do this maliciously and wrongfully, we will in the end cast him into the fire."

The Christian church is believed to have offered no strong opposition to suicide before the first quarter of the fifth century. At that time, Saint Augustine, in the first book of his *City of God*, argued that suicide was "a detestable and damnable wickedness." Augustine believed anyone who took his own life was no better than a murderer who had violated the Sixth Commandment. A large number of the early Christian saints had put themselves to death, but Augustine excused their actions by saying they had been under secret instructions from God. His argument formed the basis of Christian condemnation of suicide that later led to the classification of suicide as a felony in civil law.

Even after Augustine's injunction, the church continued to countenance three types of suicide: voluntary martyrdom; that which ascetics inflicted on themselves by intense privations, especially starvation; and the suicide of a virgin to preserve her chastity. By the end of the fifth century, however, suicide had become so tainted that not even the virgin, ascetic or martyr could take this way out with impunity. In 533 A.D., the Council of Orleans* denied funeral rites to suicides, though it allowed them to ordinary criminals. The Council of Braga in 566 penalized all suicides without distinction or exception of any sort.

---

*A church council is an assembly of ecclesiastics convened to consider matters of doctrine, discipline, law or morals.

And in 693 the Council of Toledo ordained that even the attempted suicide should be excommunicated.

Everywhere in Europe from the Middle Ages to the 18th century, suicide entailed seizure of goods or land, or both, depending on local custom. Under the feudal system, everyone was somebody else's "man," so any suicide, however humble,

> **The weakening of ancient taboos against suicide opened the door to research on ways of identifying and treating persons at risk of taking their lives. Much of this work has centered on mental depression.**

amounted to robbery of some superior. As time passed, however, more and more juries managed to avoid confiscating the property of suicides by handing down verdicts of lunacy. Furthermore, religious and civil penalties for suicide never were enforced vigorously against the nobility.*

### Modern Era

With the 19th century, suicide entered a new phase. The British Parliament in 1823 revoked an ancient requirement that the body of a suicide be buried at a crossroads with a stake driven through the heart to pin down the ghost. But Britain still re-

---

*One of Shakespeare's gravediggers in *Hamlet*, speaking of the recently drowned Ophelia, says, "If this had not been a gentlewoman, she should have been buried out o' Christian burial." *Hamlet*, Act V, scene 1.

quired that a victim of suicide be interred in the "suicides' corner" of the cemetery without religious rites between the hours of 9 p.m. and midnight.

Forfeitures and confiscations of suicides' property were abolished in 1870; the rationale was that they upset the quiet course of society, which depended upon inheritances.

In 1879, suicide ceased to be legally considered as homicide, and the maximum sentence for attempted suicide was reduced to two years. In addition, suicides finally were granted the right of burial at normal hours and the question of religious rites was left to the discretion of clergymen. Although laws and practices changed, public opinion continued to regard suicide as somehow dishonorable. And it was not until 1961 that criminal sanctions against attempted suicide were removed from the statute books in England.

With some exceptions, the religious and legal view of suicide was more tolerant in the United States. The Massachusetts Legislature decreed in 1660 that suicides should be buried in some common highway and a cartload of stones laid upon the grave "as a brand of infamy and as a warning to others to beware of the like damnable practices." The statute was not enforced for long, however, and it was repealed in 1823.

Modern thinking about suicide has been largely shaped by Emile Durkheim, a French sociologist, and Sigmund Freud, the father of psychoanalysis. Durkheim felt suicide was basically a sociological phenomenon. In *Le Suicide*, published in 1897, he listed three types of suicide: (1) *altruistic suicide*, where the customs and mores of a particular society facilitate and even de-

Continued on p. 380

# Chronology

## CHRISTIAN ERA

**Church thinking about suicide hardens.**

### 415
St. Augustine declares that suicide is "a detestable and damnable wickedness."

### 533
Council of Orleans denies funeral rites to suicides, though it allows them to ordinary criminals.

### 566
Council of Braga penalizes all suicides, without distinction or exception of any sort.

### 693
Council of Toledo ordains that a person who merely attempts suicide should be excommunicated from the church.

## 1600s-1800s

**Most people continue to regard suicide as somehow dishonorable.**

### 1660
Massachusetts Legislature decrees that suicides should be buried in some common highway with a cartload of stones laid upon the grave "as a brand of infamy and as a warning to others to beware of the like damnable practices." (The law was not enforced for long and was repealed in 1823.)

### 1774
Goethe's novel *The Sorrows of Young Werther* is published. Dozens of young people in Germany and other European countries commit suicide in emulation of the book's hero.

### 1823
British Parliament revokes an ancient requirement that the body of a suicide be buried at a crossroads with a stake driven through the heart to prevent the ghost from returning to haunt the community.

### 1851
Rejecting the conventional arguments against killing oneself, German philosopher Arthur Schopenhauer asserts: "There is nothing in the world to which every man has a more unassailable title than to his own life and person."

### Jan. 25, 1897
In his General Decrees Concerning the Prohibition and Censorship of Books, Pope Leo XIII declares: "Those books are prohibited which defend suicide as lawful."

### 1897
French sociologist Emile Durkheim's landmark study, *Le Suicide*, is published. Durkheim argues that suicide is essentially a sociological phenomenon.

## 1920
*Sigmund Freud, the father of psychoanalysis, sets forth his theory that suicide represents the precocious victory of the inner drive toward death in* **Beyond the Pleasure Principle**.

## 1960s-1970s

**Youth suicide rate climbs sharply.**

### 1977
Youth suicide rate reaches a historic peak. Among people ages 15-24, there are 22.9 suicides per 100,000 whites males; 15.5 per 100,000 black males; 5.5 per 100,000 white females; and 4.0 per 100,000 black females.

## 1980s-1990s

**Youth suicide rate begins to level off, but concern about the problem leads many communities to establish suicide prevention programs.**

### 1983
California becomes first state to enact a law providing public funds for youth suicide prevention programs.

### Aug. 7, 1986
A Los Angeles superior court judge dismisses a lawsuit against British heavy-metal singer Ozzy Osbourne. The suit charged that Osbourne had contributed to the suicide of a 19-year-old man who shot himself in 1984 after listening to an Osbourne record.

### March 11, 1987
Four teenagers from Bergenfield, N.J., a New York City suburb, commit suicide by locking themselves in a garage and sitting in a car with a running engine. A note written by all four leaves no doubt that the deaths were self-inflicted.

### Aug. 24, 1990
A state district judge in Reno, Nev., rules that Judas Priest, a British heavy-metal group, is not responsible for the deaths of two young men who had shot themselves after listening to the group's album *Stained Class*.

Continued from p. 378

mand the practice (suttee, hara-kiri); (2) *egotistic suicide*, in which the victim is not sufficiently identified with the institutions of society and is forced to assume more individual responsibility than he can handle; and (3) *anomic suicide*, in which an individual's adjustment to society is suddenly broken or changed, as by financial reverses or even sudden and unexpected prosperity.

To Freud, suicide represented the precocious victory of the inner drive toward death. He argued in *Beyond the Pleasure Principle*, published in 1920, that "Death is the aim of all life." Man's inner destructivity, he wrote, is like every other instinctual tendency, rooted in both the primary drive to live and its opposite, the tendency to return to the inorganic matrix.

## Suicide and Depression

The weakening of ancient taboos against suicide opened the door to research on ways of identifying and treating persons at risk of taking their lives. Much of this work has centered on mental depression.

Recent research supports the view that depression is often accompanied by abnormalities within and between the brain's neurotransmitting systems. These systems include billions of nerve cells, their projections and interconnections with other nerve cells, and neurotransmitters, which are composed of chemical compounds called amines. Neural impulses traveling in and out of the brain are accompanied by the release of these amines — manufactured and stored within nerve cells — which convey information from one nerve cell to another. The chemical messages of these neurotransmitters are passed along from cell to cell out across the synapse, a

small gap between nerve cells. The synapse is the critical spot, where the chemical action is completed or goes awry.

An imbalance of brain amines or an imbalance between the systems they are connected with may impair the transmission of messages across the synapse, thus affecting the entire central nervous system and possibly producing symptoms of depression. Three amines in particular — dopamine, norepinephrine and serotonin — have been identified with symptoms of depression. Norepinephrine is what is released by nerve cells when a person gets "high" from amphetamines; this compound is related to stimulation and mania, a kind of hyperactivity of the emotions. Serotonin has been implicated in sleep disturbances and the presence or absence of pain, as well as personality disturbances. Researchers have related serotonin deficiencies to people with aggressive or impulsive behavior. Specifically, serotonin levels have been found to be low in people who commit violent suicides or make violent suicide attempts.

Most research to date on the brain chemistry of persons who have killed themselves has involved adults. One notable exception was a study of teenagers conducted in the 1980s by two University of Pitts-

burgh psychiatrists. From 1980 to 1987, Drs. Neal D. Ryan and Joaquim Puig-Antich monitored the growth hormone secretion of 140 boys and girls ranging in age from 12 to 17. The 34 youngsters in the group who suffered from major depression and had attempted suicide or devised a suicide plan secreted less growth hormone than the 40 depressed but non-suicidal students and 66 healthy children, whose levels were about the same. The subjects' sex was not a factor.

Growth hormone, a chemical secreted by the pituitary gland at night, affects every cell in the body. Its primary role is to promote muscle development and bone growth. But because the gland resides in the brain, abnormal growth-hormone levels can also be a warning sign that mental processes are out of sync.

Though the findings of the University of Pittsburgh study were tentative, they could hold significant implications for teenage suicide prevention. That is because different aspects of brain chemistry often are related. "We hypothesize that lower growth-hormone levels may reflect changes in serotonin function," Dr. Ryan noted.[14] In the future, this connection could help identify teenagers at risk for suicide. ■

# CURRENT SITUATION

## Responding to Suicides

Pinpointing youngsters who fit the at-risk profile is only half the battle. The other, more difficult half consists of trying to persuade them that suicide is not the only option

when emotional anguish seems unbearable. Many of the difficulties arise from the fact that youth suicide prevention is still a relatively new field. As a result, prevention specialists tend to disagree about which treatment methods are the most effective.

Consider, for example, the suicide crisis hotlines operating in many communities across the country. These telephone services are open to callers of all ages, and typically operate around the clock. But they

# The Rock Music Connection

The already long list of factors contributing to teenage suicide has gained a startling new entry in recent years. Some families of young suicide victims say their children were driven to kill themselves by the lyrics of songs performed by certain rock groups. In a few cases, the families filed suit against the offending groups as well as the companies that produce their records.

One case that attracted extensive media coverage involved James Vance and Raymond Belknap of Sparks, Nev., who spent six hours one day in December 1985 listening to the *Stained Class* album of Judas Priest, a British heavy-metal group. The young men smoked marijuana and drank a lot of beer while they listened. Afterward, they went to a churchyard in nearby Reno and took turns shooting themselves in the head with a shotgun. Belknap died instantly; Vance, though horribly injured, survived.

Belknap's family and Vance subsequently sued Judas Priest and CBS Records for damages. They contended that the *Stained Class* album in effect hypnotized the youths through a subliminal message that caused them to form a suicide pact. For their part, the defendants cited their constitutional right to free speech.

Ruling on the case last Aug. 24, Judge Jerry Whitehead of Washoe District Court in Nevada said Judas Priest and CBS Records were not to blame for the actions of young Belknap and Vance.† At the same time, he said that hidden words did indeed exist on the album but that the group had not placed them there deliberately. He said the subliminal message "do it" recurred throughout the album but that it resulted from a chance combination of sounds.

The members of Judas Priest are not the only rock performers to be sued in connection with the suicide of a young fan. Ozzy Osbourne, a British heavy-metal singer whose on-stage antics have included biting the head off a bat, was the target of such litigation in 1986. He, too, was accused of encouraging young people to kill themselves, in his case with a song entitled "Suicide Solution." That case was dismissed Aug. 7, 1986, by a Los Angeles superior court judge who upheld Osbourne's First Amendment right to free speech.

Osbourne also was the defendant in a suit filed by a Georgia couple who claimed their 16-year-old son had committed suicide in 1986 after repeatedly listening to "Suicide Solution" on the singer's *Blizzard of Ozz* album. In a decision handed down in early May, Judge Duross Fitzpatrick of U.S. District Court in Macon, Ga., said the couple could not prove conclusively that Osbourne's music caused their son's death. The judge also held that the music is free expression protected by the First Amendment.

---

† James Vance died before the case was decided.

---

do not necessarily follow the same approach. Some hotlines advocate "active listening" with a guarantee of anonymity designed to help the caller work through a crisis and reach his own decision. No advice is offered on the ground that it could make a troubled person feel misunderstood. In contrast, certain other hotlines aggressively trace calls when they believe the caller is at immediate risk of suicide. Moreover, they do not hesitate to summon the police or other emergency-response units to intervene in such cases.

Mental health professionals also are of two minds as to whether anti-depressant drugs should be administered to teenagers. Some psychiatrists believe that since there is growing evidence that depression is biochemically based, it would be foolish not to use drugs to combat depression's harmful effects. But other doctors believe such drugs are dangerous because they can easily be given to youngsters for whom depression is not the primary problem, or because the wrong drug could be prescribed to a psychotically depressed child with disastrous effects.

Controversy also surrounds youth suicide-prevention programs and "postvention" programs that are set up to deal with a suicide's aftermath. Some of the most significant advances in the latter category have occurred after cluster suicides. A widely publicized example is the cluster that developed in 1987 in Bergenfield, N.J., a suburb of New York City. It began March 11, 1987, when the bodies of four teenagers — two sisters and two young men — were found seated in a car with its engine running in a garage at a garden apartment complex.* A lengthy suicide note, written on a brown paper bag and signed by all four, had been left on the front seat. Although the garage where the simultaneous suicides occurred was locked and put under periodic police surveillance, a 20-year-old man and a 17-year-old woman managed to attempt suicide there by the same means six days later.

The Bergenfield suicides galvanized the entire community. Dr. Thomas Kavanagh, a psychologist in charge of special education services for the Bergenfield public schools, later told a congressional subcommittee that a counseling team of

---

*Three of the four victims had dropped out of Bergenfield High School. Bergen County Prosecutor Larry J. McClure, speaking at a post-suicide news conference, characterized all four as "very troubled."

## Suicide Rates by Age Groups

*An old rule of thumb held that suicide rates generally increased for each decade of age, starting with the below-14 age bracket and ending with the over-85 age group. That pattern has changed somewhat in recent decades. The suicide rate for Americans ages 15 to 24 has tripled since the 1950s, bringing it within striking range of the rate for the next age bracket (25-34). The suicide rate then declines slightly until age 55, when another steep rise begins, culminating with persons between ages 75 and 84. This group contains a large proportion of people that have just lost spouses or are seriously ill or depressed.*

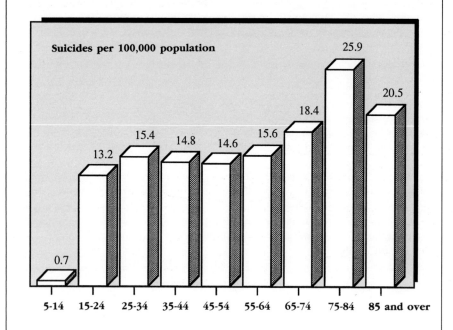

**Suicides per 100,000 population**

| | | | | | | | | |
|---|---|---|---|---|---|---|---|---|
| 0.7 | 13.2 | 15.4 | 14.8 | 14.6 | 15.6 | 18.4 | 25.9 | 20.5 |
| 5-14 | 15-24 | 25-34 | 35-44 | 45-54 | 55-64 | 65-74 | 75-84 | 85 and over |

*Source: Department of Health and Human Services, National Center for Health Statistics. Data are for 1988.*

four social workers, three psychologists, three nurses and four guidance advisers was formed within an hour after word of the quadruple suicide was received. "What was especially helpful," Kavanagh said, "were the ongoing meetings between the school and community response team which were held to formulate a response to this crisis. In the evening, clergy, community mental health [workers] and police worked actively in counseling the youth, identifying ones who were 'at risk' and reaching out to them and their families." [15]

A number of Bergenfield High School students interviewed by *The New York Times* on the day of the four suicides complained that the crash counseling program was overdue. They said the school had made no concerted effort to channel their grief after the sudden deaths several months earlier of four other area youths. Though the earlier deaths were officially classified as accidents linked to alcohol or other drugs, some observers suggested that suicidal intent may have been present as well.

### New Guidelines

In November 1987, the New Jersey Department of Health and the U.S. Centers for Disease Control (CDC) cosponsored a workshop on community responses to cluster suicides.

The workshop led, in turn, to the publication of a set of proposals for preventing or containing such clusters. Most of the recommendations are equally valid as community guidelines for dealing with isolated teenage suicides.

One of the main suggestions was that "all concerned sectors" of the community should take part in a youth suicide-prevention program. "No single agency ... has the resources or expertise to adequately respond to an evolving suicide cluster," the CDC stated. "Moreover, the emergence of one agency as the sole focus for responding to an apparent suicide cluster" runs the risk of making that agency and its representatives "scapegoats for a community's fear and anger." [16]

The CDC went on to suggest that representatives of the local news media be invited to take part in developing the suicide-prevention plan. If this is done, newspapers and broadcasters may be less likely to cover suicides in an inadvertently sensational manner. Participants in a 1989 workshop on the reporting of suicide noted that providing specific information on how a suicide occurred could well be harmful. "A detailed description of the suicide method could be used as a 'how-to' manual by persons contemplating suicide," the workshop concluded. "This does not mean that general information about the method used should not be reported, but information such as the type of hose used, where it was purchased, and how it was hooked up to the exhaust, should be avoided." [17] The workshop also cautioned that a suicide should never be described as "successful," a word that connotes approval. "Completed" is the term most professionals use.

The need to avoid sensationalism extends to community and school officials as well. Fulsome eulogies, the CDC observed, "might increase

# Statistics May Understate Extent of Problem

Experts generally agree that official statistics on suicide greatly understate the dimensions of the problem. For instance, many highway accidents are believed to stem in part from suicidal tendencies, for recklessness often affords an easy exit from life. Barbiturate users and some alcoholics fall into the same category.

Still other patently suicidal deaths are classified as "accidental" or "natural" because of strong local taboos regarding self-destruction. In some instances, physicians will cover up poison and barbiturate suicides out of regard for the families of the victims or to protect the families from loss of insurance benefits. The deception is made easy by the similarity between symptoms of poisoning and symptoms of various natural diseases.

Suicide investigating teams have reported encountering evasion, denial, concealment, and even direct suppression of evidence by friends and relatives. Suicide notes may be deliberately destroyed. Letters may be written to the coroner protesting in advance a possible ruling of suicide, and sometimes such protests are accompanied by petitions from a whole neighborhood. Because of all these factors, those who study suicide estimate the actual number of self-inflicted deaths in the United States each year is several times greater than the official total issued by the National Center for Health Statistics on the basis of death certificates.

In an effort to establish uniform standards for determining whether a suicide has occurred, the U.S. Centers for Disease Control assembled a task force whose recommendations were published by the *Journal of the American Medical Association* early in 1989. The task force said a finding of suicide required evidence that the death was *self-inflicted.* This could be determined through an autopsy, by toxicologic, investigatory and psychological evidence, and by statements of the decedent or witnesses.

The task force also stated that a finding of suicide required clear evidence of *intent.* This could include, among other things:

■ Explicit indications of a desire to kill oneself.
■ Unexpected or inappropriate preparations for death.
■ Expressions of hopelessness or of great emotional or physical pain.
■ Efforts to learn about or procure means of killing oneself.
■ Evidence that the decedent recognized the chosen instrument's lethality.
■ Precautions to avoid rescue.
■ A previous suicide threat or attempt.
■ Recent stressful events or significant losses in the decedent's life.
■ Serious depression or mental disorder.†

---

† "Operational Criteria for Determining Suicide," *Journal of the American Medical Association,* Jan. 20, 1989, p. 360.

---

the likelihood that someone . . . who is having suicidal thoughts will also commit suicide, so as to be similarly glorified or to receive similar positive attention." At the same time, the CDC advised against vilifying the deceased: "In addition to being needlessly cruel . . . such an approach may only serve to make those who do identify with the [suicide] feel isolated and friendless."[18]

The ideal response, the CDC suggested, should combine sympathy and restraint in near-equal measure. For instance, a high school student's death "should be announced privately to those students who are most likely to be affected by the tragedy — close friends, girl friends, boy friends, and the like." After teachers are briefed, the news can be broken to other students in small, supervised groups. And finally, funeral services "should not be allowed to unnecessarily disrupt the regular school schedule."[19]

## State and Federal Initiatives

In the United States, youth suicide prevention has long been the province of traditional care providers at the local level — churches, community mental health centers, survivors' self-help groups, and so on. But over the past decade, the federal government and state governments have begun to enter the field in a modest way.

Consider the proposed Youth Suicide Prevention Act, a bill introduced in Congress in 1986. The purpose of the measure was to enable the secretary of Education to make grants to local educational agencies and private nonprofit organizations. The funds were to be earmarked for programs to increase community awareness of youth suicide and to train school personnel and community leaders in methods of devising suicide-prevention strategies. Hearings on the bill in May 1987 gave Congress an opportunity to examine the quadruple suicide that had occurred in Bergenfield, N.J., two months earlier (*see p. 381*).

Eventually, the legislation was folded into a 1988 bill reauthorizing most federal elementary, secondary and adult education programs. Federal aid for youth suicide prevention became part of the Chapter 2 program of block grants to state and local education agencies established in 1981.

State governments have displayed more initiative on suicide prevention than Washington has. California led the way in 1983 with the first state-funded pilot programs, developed by the state Department of Education and county suicide prevention agencies under a law passed that year. At school, teenagers received instruction in sound decision-making, how suicide can be related to alcohol and drug abuse, suicide warning signs, community suicide services, and ways of improving interaction among students, teachers and school counselors. Related community projects included peer-group programs, 24-hour suicide-prevention hotlines, data collection on youth suicide attempts, and training sessions for parents and teachers.

The 1983 California law was a pilot effort covering only two counties. A law approved by the Legislature two years later was more ambitious, directing the California Department of Mental Health to set up a five-year, statewide suicide-prevention program. Its main features were substantially the same as those of the more limited 1983 program.

Another state with a highly regarded youth suicide-prevention program is New Jersey. Under a law enacted in 1985, a statewide program was set up by the New Jersey Department of Human Services and administered by community mental health service providers in cooperation with local boards of education. The aim was to develop classroom materials, training programs for teachers and counselors, and other community-based ventures. Mental health care providers were urged to submit proposals for suicide-prevention projects, including recommendations on how to evaluate their effectiveness.

The 1985 law also created a Governor's Advisory Council on Youth Suicide Prevention in the Department of Human Services. Two years later, the advisory council helped Bergenfield residents and students to cope with the town's multiple youth suicides. Its work there attracted the attention of the federal Centers for Disease Control, which asked the council to organize a workshop on cluster suicides. The meeting, held in Newark in November 1987, drew officials from across the country. In 1989, the council published a how-to manual, *Youth Suicide Prevention: Meeting the Challenge in New Jersey Schools*, summarizing what it had learned up till that time.

More than a dozen other states besides California and New Jersey have enacted youth suicide-prevention laws since 1983, according to the National Conference of State Legislatures. The states are Connecticut, Florida, Illinois, Maine, Maryland, New York, North Carolina, Oregon, Rhode Island, Texas, Utah, Virginia and Wisconsin. But the pace of activity seems to have slowed recently. The 1990 NCSL survey of new laws on children, youth and family issues found no new laws on youth suicide prevention, nor does the organization know of any such laws under consideration this year.* The American Association of Suicidology, a Denver-based group, also reports that it has not heard of any pending suicide-prevention bills at the state level.

Nearly all the state laws on the subject call for drafting policies or establishing programs to increase public awareness of the conditions that can lead to youth suicide. Illinois goes further, requiring that selected school personnel undergo training on how to recognize suicidal behavior and how to intervene should a suicide attempt occur. Another Illinois law provides grants for evaluating the effectiveness of youth suicide-prevention programs in the state. Oregon requires hospitals that treat youths under age 18 for a suicide attempt to refer the youths to inpatient or outpatient community treatment facilities. Oregon hospitals also are required by law to report statistical data about such cases to state authorities. ■

_____

*NCSL stresses that its legislative surveys are not necessarily comprehensive. On occasion, it fails to detect a recently enacted statute.

# OUTLOOK

## Will Rate Remain Steady?

Looking ahead, suicide prevention experts offer varying scenarios. One area of research that may hold particular promise has to do with pinpointing the biological factors that predispose some youths toward suicidal behavior. Future discoveries of this nature may make it easier to identify at-risk youth and begin treating them in a timely fashion.

Dr. David Shaffer of Columbia University's College of Physicians and Surgeons is cautiously upbeat about progress along this line. "We are getting much more sophisticated in deciding who is at risk" for suicide, he says, noting that impulsive suicidal behavior is associated with low levels of a particular kind of neurotransmitter. "At the moment, the only way we have of measuring those neurotransmitters is through a spinal tap, which obviously can't be done routinely," he says. "But it could be that down the line we'll find less intrusive ways of identifying the personalities that are at greatest risk for suicide."

*Continued on p. 386*

# At Issue:

## Are school-based suicide-prevention programs effective?

MARGARET HYDE AND ELIZABETH FORSYTH

*Hyde and Forsyth have collaborated on several books*
FROM *SUICIDE: THE HIDDEN EPIDEMIC* (1986).

**a** growing number of communities are accepting the idea of teaching suicide prevention in the schools as part of their health education programs. Individuals who are concerned about the possible increase in youth suicide or simply want to save even one life, can suggest such programs to their counselors, health education teachers, and principals. They can ask their parents to bring up the subject at Parent-Teacher Association or other organization meetings.

Schools where one (or more) students have committed suicide can galvanize the attention given to the tragedy and start a teaching program. After four young people took their lives within an 18-month period, the Cherry Creek school district in Denver . . . began a program of class discussions with students and held parent workshops and volunteer training seminars for teachers, counselors and nurses. . . .

Students, in their seventh- and eighth-grade suicide-prevention discussions, learn the danger of keeping threats as secrets and are encouraged to tell a counselor of threats they hear. They learn to openly discuss their feelings about depression and suicide. These students know not to panic if they feel depressed or overwhelmed and how to use community resources to help themselves and others. They learn alternatives to suicide. There are ways of dealing with a painful life. Having those insights, and better ways to cope with life's stresses, brings these students closer together.

A parent who attended a workshop learned the way to cope with her child's statements about suicide and how to help. She asked questions about her 12-year-old, a boy who had threatened suicide. It turned out that he even had a plan to hang himself in the garage. Immediate action led to hospitalization where medication and counseling lessened his depression in a period of three weeks. A life was saved.

Teachers learn to spot suicidal themes in writing assignments and artwork and to take action to help troubled young people. . . . Other school systems are working with similar programs. All such programs broaden the students' vision of life and increase the values we call ''human'' — hope, imagination, and care for others.

WILLIAM R. MATTOX JR.

*Policy analysis director of the Family Research Council in Washington, D.C.*
FROM *POLICY PERSPECTIVES*, MAY 1987.

**i** f good intentions were the only prerequisite for initiating a new government program, then many suicide-prevention efforts would be worthy of taxpayer funding. But good intentions alone do not insure good programs. And while there is reason to be concerned about the problem of teen suicide, there is even greater reason to be concerned that some efforts to attack the problem head-on may do more harm than good.

Dr. Steven Stack, an Auburn University sociologist, has conducted a series of research studies on suicide during the last decade. In his most recent study, he found that national news stories and televised dramas about suicide often trigger an increase in the suicide rate among many young people. This funding suggests that public discussion of suicide often exacerbates the problem.

Accordingly, efforts to reduce teen suicide through classroom discussion or increased public awareness may not only fail — they may backfire. As Mitch Anthony of the National Suicide Help Center put it, ''Programs that merely teach teens facts about suicide are more destructive than helpful.''

This does not mean that there is nothing that can be done to stem the tide of youth suicides. Instead, it means that efforts to reduce teen suicide should seek to address many of the root causes of suicide rather than attacking the problem through well-meaning public awareness campaigns and classroom discussions. . . .

Based on the research evidence, it appears that society's two bedrock institutions — the family and religion — hold the key. Just as the demise of these two institutions has greatly contributed to the current problem, it stands to reason that a reinvigoration of family life and religious activity in this country would, among other things, bring down the teen suicide rate.

This recommended antidote for addressing the teen suicide problem does not readily lend itself to significant government intervention. Instead, it requires a wider cultural transformation of the way our society views the family and religion.

*Continued from p. 384*

Shaffer also is mildly encouraged about the overall trend of youth suicide in the United States. He does not believe the increase in the youth suicide rate in 1988 represents the beginning of another upward cycle. Shaffer bases his optimism on the recent decline in illegal drug use among teenagers. "This should bring the suicide rate down with it," he says.

While the number of young people using marijuana, cocaine and other illegal drugs has dropped, alcohol use among teenagers remains a serious problem. A pair of studies recently issued by the Department of Health and Human Services estimated that 8 million teenagers consume alcohol weekly and 454,000 of them qualify as "binge drinkers." [20]

Alan Berman finds the statistics on teenage drinking distressing, but he doesn't think they have much relevance to the youth suicide problem. With completed teenage suicides, he says, "you're more likely to find significant and frequent use of [illegal] drugs" than a similar pattern of alcohol use.

Like Shaffer, Berman predicts the number of teen suicides will remain fairly constant in the years ahead, but he says there's no way to know for sure. The leveling of the youth suicide rate in the 1980s "may just be the eye of the storm," he says. "There's no way of knowing."

The prognosis for youth suicide-prevention programs nationwide seems guarded at the moment. Because of current economic conditions, George Weiner is somewhat pessimistic. "Schools are under enormous [budgetary] pressures now," he notes, "and they really are retrenching. When schools retrench, [suicide prevention] is an area that is usually the first to go."

That is not the only reason why many schools still lack such a program. According to the U.S. Depart-ment of Health and Human Services, some schools are under heavy parental pressure to focus exclusively on academic matters. Other schools shy away from establishing a suicide-prevention program out of fear of becoming exposed to liability suits. [21]

But even if all the nation's high schools had suicide-prevention programs, some teenagers would continue to kill themselves. That realization has made many mental health professionals view the issue philosophically. Speaking of suicide prevention in general, Berman says, "It's an ocean of problems and we're just throwing pebbles." ∎

## Notes

[1] Governor's Advisory Council on Youth Suicide Prevention and the New Jersey Adolescent Suicide Prevention Project, *Youth Suicide Prevention: Meeting the Challenge in New Jersey Schools,* 1989, p. 15.

[2] The Gallup Organization solicited written responses from a random sample of 1,152 youngsters ages 13 to 19. Results of the survey, which was conducted from November 1990 to January 1991, were released in early April. The poll was conducted for Empire Blue Cross and Blue Shield.

[3] Quoted in the *Los Angeles Times,* May 13, 1991.

[4] Office of Inspector General, U.S. Department of Health and Human Services, *Youth Suicide: National Program Inspection,* November 1986.

[5] See Gerald L. Klerman and Myrna M. Weissman, "Increasing Rates of Depression," *Journal of the American Medical Association,* April 21, 1989, p. 2234.

[6] Gary Ramafedi, James A. Farrow and Robert W. Deisher, "Risk Factors for Attempted Suicide in Gay or Bisexual Youths," *Pediatrics,* June 1991. The study was conducted among homosexual or bisexual males ages 14 to 21; about 79 percent of the subjects were white.

[7] U.S. Alcohol, Drug Abuse and Mental Health Administration, Department of Health and Human Services, *Report of the Secretary's Task Force on Youth Suicide,* January 1989.

[8] Association of State and Territorial Health Officials and the New Jersey Department of Health, *Recommendations From a Workshop on Suicide Contagion and the Reporting of Suicide,* March 1991, p. 1.

[9] Lucy E. Davidson, *et al.,* "An Epidemiologic Study of Risk Factors in Two Teenage Suicide Clusters," *Journal of the American Medical Association,* Nov. 17, 1989, pp. 2690, 2691.

[10] David Shaffer, *et al.,* "Adolescent Suicide Attempters: Response to Suicide-Prevention Programs," *Journal of the American Medical Association,* Dec. 26, 1990, pp. 3151-3155. Shaffer is director of the division of child and adolescent psychiatry at the College of Physicians and Surgeons.

[11] Arthur Herzog and Harvey L. P. Resnik, "A Clinical Study of Parental Response to Adolescent Death by Suicide With Recommendations for Approaching the Survivors," *Proceedings of the Fourth International Conference of Suicide Prevention,* 1967.

[12] Henry Romilly Fedden, *Suicide: A Social and Historical Study* (1938), p. 35.

[13] In the *Phaedo,* Plato quotes Socrates as saying: "But I do think . . . it is true that the gods are our guardians, and that we men are a part of their property. . . . If one of your possessions were to kill itself, though you had not signified that you had wished it to die, should you not be angry with it? Should you not punish it, if punishment were possible? . . . In the same way perhaps it is not unreasonable to hold that no man has a right to take his own life, but that he must wait until God sends some necessity upon him, as has now been sent upon me."

[14] Quoted in *American Health,* May 1989.

[15] Testimony before U.S. House Subcommittee on Elementary, Secondary and Vocational Education, Committee on Education and Labor, May 13, 1987.

[16] U.S. Centers for Disease Control, *CDC Recommendations for a Community Plan for the Prevention and Containment of Suicide Clusters* (supplement to the *Morbidity and Mortality Weekly Report*), Aug. 19, 1988, p. 3.

[17] Association of State and Territorial Health Officials and the New Jersey Department of Health, *op. cit.,* p. 4.

[18] Centers for Disease Control, *op. cit.,* p. 7.

[19] *Ibid.,* p. 7.

[20] Office of Inspector General, U.S. Department of Health and Human Services, *Youth and Alcohol: A National Survey — Drinking Habits, Access, Attitudes and Knowledge* and *Youth and Alcohol: A National Survey — Do They Know What They're Drinking?* Both studies were published in June 1991.

[21] See *Youth Suicide: National Program Inspection, op. cit.,* p. 11.

# Bibliography

## Selected Sources Used

### Books

**Alvarez, A., *The Savage God: A Study of Suicide,* Random House, 1971.**

Alvarez, an English poet and critic, begins his book with a brief account of the life of Sylvia Plath, the American poet who committed suicide in London in 1963 at the age of 30. He then launches into a historical and literary survey of suicide. He concludes by disclosing that he, too, had once tried to kill himself.

**Barrett, Terence, *Life After Suicide: The Survivor's Grief Experience,* Aftermath Research, 1989.**

The purpose of this work is to make people more aware of the emotional plight of suicide victims' loved ones. "Although the impact of a suicide is greatly determined by the closeness of the relationship which had been formed with the decedent," Barrett writes, "no one associated with this form of death can escape its effects, regardless of distance from the deceased. Suicide touches something deep in the core of our humanness, and we can, none of us, be neutral to its occurrence."

**Hawton, Keith, *Suicide and Attempted Suicide Among Children and Adolescents,* SAGE Publications, 1986.**

After examining the causes of teenage suicide and ways of trying to prevent it, Hawton stresses how much remains to be learned: "[I]n terms of prevention of both attempted suicide and completed suicide by children and adolescents, we are only at the stage of conjecturing about possible strategies rather than being able to offer firm guidelines based on research findings."

**Husain, Syed Arshad and Vandiver, Trish, *Suicide in Children and Adolescents,* SP Medical and Scientific Books, 1984**

Husain and Vandiver explain why suicide apparently remains quite rare among children but has become increasingly common among adolescents. One reason is that "Western culture, in general, tends to underestimate the strength of children's emotions and motivations; therefore, suicidal motives in children are usually unthinkable — and therefore uninvestigated."

### Articles

**Macy, Marianne, "Lives on the Line: How the City's Suicide Hot Lines Pull People Back From the Brink," *New York,* April 22, 1991.**

Macy describes the operations and guiding principles of New York City's two main suicide hotlines, Samaritans and Help Line. The chief difference between them concerns intervention. Samaritans does not try to trace a call when a person seems poised to commit suicide; Help Line does attempt to trace calls in such cases.

**Shaffer, David, et al., "Adolescent Suicide Attempters: Response to Suicide-Prevention Programs," *Journal of the American Medical Association,* Dec. 26, 1990.**

Shaffer and his colleagues set forth the results of a study of three suicide-prevention programs aimed at ninth- and 10th-grade students. "There is a clear need to evaluate such programs to determine their efficacy and safety," they write. "With respect to safety, an a priori objection to such programs is that they are unselective and that the large group of adolescents they engage are, for the most part, not at risk for suicide."

### Reports and Studies

**Governor's Advisory Council on Youth Suicide Prevention and the New Jersey Adolescent Suicide Prevention Project, *Youth Suicide Prevention: Meeting the Challenge in New Jersey Schools,* 1989.**

This report, describing New Jersey's experience with school-based suicide-prevention programs, could serve as a how-to manual for schools in other states that are planning to establish such programs.

**U.S. House Subcommittee on Elementary, Secondary and Vocational Education, Committee on Education and Labor, *Hearing on H.R. 457, the Youth Suicide Prevention Act,* (published proceedings of a hearing held May 13, 1987).**

This hearing, held just two months after four teenagers committed suicide in Bergenfield, N.J., includes extensive testimony on the tragedy. Of particular interest is the statement of Dr. Thomas Kavanagh, director of special education for Bergenfield's public schools.

**Office of Inspector General, U.S. Department of Health and Human Services, *Youth Suicide: National Program Inspection,* November 1986.**

The authors of this study concentrate on community-based mental health services, which they see as the backbone of youth suicide-prevention efforts. "Public education should not focus solely on youth suicide," the study says, "but should address related problems, such as the extent of self-destructive behavior among the nation's youth and removing the stigma associated with mental health treatment."

# The Next Step

## Additional Articles from Current Periodicals

### Addresses & essays

**Greenhagen, S., "That's no way to end a good life,"** *Newsweek*, **summer/fall 1990, p. 74.**
Presents a short essay concerning teenagers' thoughts about committing suicide. Problems; Support from family and peers; Adjusting personality according to the friends you are with; "If you let time pass, your problem will seem less serious."

**Hoagland, E., "The urge for an end: contemplating suicide,"** *Harper's*, **March 1988, p. 45.**
Essay. All aspects of suicidal thoughts in the later years; Child suicide; Love for the living as an answer to suicidal thoughts.

### Books & reading

**Breed, W., "Book reviews,"** *Social Forces*, **September 1990, p. 328.**
Reviews the book *Suicide From A Sociological Perspective*, by David Lester.

**Meister, J. S., "Book department: Sociology,"** *Annals of American Academy of Political & Social Sciences*, **March 1991, p. 203.**
Reviews the book *Self-Destruction in the Promised Land: A Psychocultural Biology of American Suicide*, by Howard I. Kushner.

**Weinstein, S. R., "Book reviews,"** *New England Journal of Medicine*, **March 15, 1990, p. 785.**
Reviews the book *Suicide Among Youth: Perspectives on Risk and Prevention*, edited by Cynthia R. Pfeffer. A book for scholars, professionals, and laypeople, working toward a deeper understanding of this escalating social issue.

**Zabel, R. H., "Media reviews,"** *Exceptional Children*, **September 1990, p. 78.**
Reviews the books *Depression in Suicide in Children and Adolescents: Prevention, Intervention, and Postvention*, by P. G. Patros and T. K. Shamoo, and *Suicide Intervention in the Schools*, by S. Poland.

### Case studies

**"The sorrows of Cobb County,"** *Time*, **Nov. 14, 1988, p. 29.**
Discusses the alarming suicide rate in Cobb County, Ga., where 51 suicides, including six teens, were recorded.

**Bergman, B. and J. Dunn, "Northern agony,"** *Maclean's*, **June 4, 1990, p. 14.**
Examines the social and psychological problems besetting Canada's northern native peoples. Deterioration of the traditional lifestyle; Recent conference in Whitehorse, Yukon Territory; Comments by spokespeople from Inuit, Dene, and other native groups; Suicide rate; Child sexual abuse; Family violence; Alcoholism; Venereal diseases, and AIDS; Need for economic independence.

**Couchman, G. C., "Trying to live with suicide,"** *Newsweek*, **Oct. 8, 1990, p. 12.**
Opinion. Offers a personal response from a wife whose husband killed himself six years ago as she describes her attempts to grapple with the pain, other people's casual use of the word "suicide," and her feelings of having neglected her spouse. Argues that the horror of the grief that comes with suicide is anything but healing.

**Hevesi, D., "Running away,"** *The New York Times Magazine*, **Oct. 2, 1988, p. 30.**
Tells the tragic story of April Savino, runaway at 15, drug addict, suicide at 19 in New York City. Mental illness; Homelessness; Drug addiction; Broken families.

**Wolfle, J., "Adolescent suicide — an open letter to . . . ,"** *Phi Delta Kappan*, **December 1988, p. 296.**
A mother of a teen suicide victim asks school and professional counselors to let parents know when their teenagers seem troubled or claim to be considering suicide.

### Debates & issues

**Blumenthal, S. J., "Youth suicide: The physician's role in suicide prevention,"** *Journal of the American Medical Association*, **Dec. 26, 1990, p. 3194.**
Editorial. Comments that the prediction and prevention of youth suicide is one of the most difficult clinical problems facing the physician. Risk factors; Interventions.

**Elkind, D., "The facts about teen suicide,"** *Parents*, **January 1990, p. 111.**
Discusses teenage suicide, which claims over 5,000 lives a year and has tripled since the 1950s. The many reasons that lead to suicide; Warning signs; What parents can do to help a suicidal teen overcome the crisis.

**Shaffer, D., Vieland, V., et al., "Adolescent suicide attempters,"** *Journal of the American Medical Associ-*

*ation*, Dec. 26, 1990, p. 3151.

Studies the impact of suicide education programs on high-risk teenagers, defined as those who admitted to having made a suicide attempt. Methods; Results; Comment.

## Drama

**Feinour, P., "A high school play helps suicidal teenagers," *Education Digest*, May 1989, p. 50.**

Describes a play, "Empty Chairs," which has won national acclaim for its message of the tragedy and futility of suicide. Videotaped version is being shown in schools. Provides address.

**Glantz, S., "Audiovisual review," *School Library Journal*, May 1990, p. 64.**

Reviews the videotape series "Second Wind," by Youth Vision. Deals with teen suicide, and the feelings of parents and teens involved.

**Pond, S., "Student body count," *Rolling Stone*, April 20, 1989, p. 38.**

Discusses making the film "Heathers," a black comedy about teenage suicide and murder. Comments by producer Denise Di Novi, screenwriter Dan Waters, and director Michael Lehmann.

## Drug use

**Crumley, F. E., "Substance abuse and adolescent suicidal behavior," *Journal of the American Medical Association*, June 13, 1990, p. 3051.**

Examines the evidence for an association between psychoactive substance abuse/dependency and adolescent suicide attempts/completions. Link between substance abuse and depression and/or conduct and personality disorders; Association between alcohol abuse and firearm suicide; Limitations and artifacts of studies; Conclusions.

**Goodwin, F. K., "Cocaine and suicide attempts," *Journal of the American Medical Association*, Nov. 21, 1990, p. 2495.**

States that scientists report for the first time that using cocaine dramatically increases the likelihood that a suicide attempt will be made. The National Institute on Mental Health and the National Institute on Drug Abuse find that cocaine use elicits a greater chance of suicide than clinical depression or alcohol abuse.

**Toufexis, A. and Purvis, A., "Warnings about a miracle drug," *Time*, July 30, 1990, p. 54.**

Discusses recent reports of suicide attempts in Prozac users which have raised doubts about the popular antidepressant. Leading antidepressant; Several confounding

factors; New product literature to alert physicians.

## Mass media coverage

**Gundlach, J. H. and Stack, S., "The impact of hyper media coverage on suicide: New York City, 1910-1920," *Social Science Quarterly*, September 1990, p. 619.**

Presents a time series analysis, finding that substantial media coverage of the suicides of ordinary people, during 1913-1914 in New York City, increased suicides. The relationship follows a non-linear, combined threshold-ceiling effect. It is estimated that the period of "hyper" coverage resulted in an additional 89 suicides in New York City.

**Weiss, R., "Teen suicide clusters: More than mimicry," *Science News*, Nov. 25, 1989, p. 342.**

Reports on a new study that reveals that teenage suicide victims who were already at risk of suicide are not more likely to take their own lives after exposure to other suicides. Flaws in past studies; Excesses in public exposure to suicide should be curtailed.

## Physiological aspects

**"Suicide brains: Naturally prone to pain?" *Science News*, Nov. 10, 1990, p. 301.**

States that a new study indicates that brain cells that mediate the perception of pleasure and pain in suicide victims differ markedly from the same cells in people who die of natural causes. New work looks at opioid receptors in victims' brains.

**Charles, D., "Opium deprivation could make you suicidal," *New Scientist*, Nov. 10, 1990, p. 23.**

Describes research by Anat Biegon showing that the brains from many suicide victims contain abnormal levels of opioid receptors. Potential use for monitoring depression in psychiatric patients; Finding the physical causes of depression.

## Prevention

**Blumenthal, S. J., "Youth suicide: The physician's role in suicide prevention," *Journal of the American Medical Association*, Dec. 26, 1990, p. 3194.**

Editorial. Comments that the prediction and prevention of youth suicide is one of the most difficult clinical problems facing the physician. Risk factors; Interventions.

**Edwards, T. K., "Providing reasons for wanting to live," *Phi Delta Kappan*, December 1988, p. 296.**

A research psychologist believes that giving teens time

with caring adults, such as teachers or administrators, can make the difference between a well-adjusted or a suicidal teen.

**Frymier, J., "Understanding and preventing teen suicide," *Phi Delta Kappan*, December 1988, p. 290.**

Interviews Barry Garfinkel, M.D., a psychiatrist who works with teens. Dr. Garfinkel gives several signs to watch for and courses of action for educators to take when a teen may be considering suicide. INSET: Publications on suicide available.

**Goldsmith, M. F., "Focus on adolescent health enrolls school helpers," *Journal of the American Medical Association*, May 16, 1990, p. 2609.**

Reports on the Centers for Disease Control's Division of Adolescent and School Health that will encourage America's schools to make children and adolescents healthier. Major health problems of students include car crashes, injuries, homicide, suicide; Division has set up systems to disseminate information; Additional initiative focus on college students and others.

**Parachin, V. M., "How to 'suicide-proof' your child," *Single Parent*, July/August 1989, p. 16.**

Presents advice from an ordained minister who works as a bereavement counselor and grief therapist on how to prevent a child's suicide.

**Rotheram-Borus, M. J. and Bradley, J., "Triage model for suicidal runaways," *American Journal of Orthopsychiatry*, January 1991, p. 122.**

Evaluates a triage model for suicidal youths at four community-based agencies over a 30-month period. The program screened youths for suicidal ideation, trained staff in assessment, instituted agency protocols for triage, and established a multilevel mental health service network. How and why the number of suicide attempts decreased after implementation of the program; Program description; Discussion.

## *Psychological aspects*

**Charles, G., and Matheson, J., "Suicide prevention and intervention with young people in foster care in Canada," *Child Welfare*, March/April 1991, p. 185.**

Discusses the risk of suicide among foster children. Suicide prevention and intervention with foster children; Helping foster parents understand the dynamics and assessment of suicidal behaviors; Development of supporting interventions, policies and procedures; Episodes of isolation, helplessness and ambivalence; Relationship between suicide rate and hostility and anger; Warning signs; More.

**Herskowitz, J., "Cries for help," *Learning*, January 1990, p. 34.**

Discusses the importance of recognizing childhood depression, a disorder that is sometimes overlooked or misinterpreted and can lead to suicide. Causes and symptoms of childhood depression. INSETS: Checklist for recognizing childhood depression; Helping students cope with depression, by C. Carlile.

**Schotte, D. E., Cools, J., et al., "Problem-solving deficits in suicidal patients: Trait vulnerability or state phenomenon?" *Journal of Consulting & Clinical Psychology*, October 1990, p. 562.**

Presents a short-term, longitudinal study that examines the stability of interpersonal problem-solving skills of hospitalized suicide ideators (N=36). Data shows interpersonal problem-solving deficits may be a concomitant, rather than a cause, of depression, hopelessness, and suicide intent. Method and results.

**Spirito, A., Hart, K., et al., "Social skills and depression in adolescent suicide attempters," *Adolescence*, Fall 1990, p. 543.**

Examines the relationship among depression, social skills, and suicidal behavior in a sample of 41 adolescents hospitalized in a general medical setting following a suicide attempt. These subjects were compared with 40 nonsuicidal psychiatrically hospitalized adolescents. Assesses the social skills using the Matson Evaluation of Social Skills with Youngsters (MESSY).

**White, W., "Teen suicide," *Teen Magazine*, January 1988, p. 70.**

Discusses the problem of teenage suicide. Possible emotional reasons for suicide; Warning signs; What to do if a friend is suicidal; Myths about suicide.

## *Research*

**Davidson, L. E., Rosenberg, M. L., et al., "An epidemiologic study of risk factors in two teenage suicide clusters," *Journal of the American Medical Association*, Nov. 17, 1989, p. 2687.**

Discusses an epidemiologic study of the risk factors involved in two clusters of teenage suicides that occurred in Texas between February 1983 and October 1984. Background; Methods; Results; Comment.

**Dixon, W. A., Heppner, P. P., et al., "Problem solving appraisal, stress, hopelessness, and suicide ideation in a college population," *Journal of Counseling Psychology*, January 1991, p. 51.**

Expands prior research linking problem solving skills to suicide by looking at the role of problem solving appraisal. Study involving 1,277 students enrolled in introductory psychology courses; Separate study involving 2,383 students; Problem solving appraisal and negative life stress as independent predictors of suicide ideation and hopelessness; Method; Results; Discussion; More.

**Domino, G., "Popular misconceptions about suicide: How popular are they?" *OMEGA*, September 1990, p. 167.**

Explores the prevalence of misconceptions about suicide in a sample of 643 United States residents who were administered the Suicide Opinion Questionnaire (SOQ). Twenty SOQ items; Looking for differences in gender, age, and ethnic background; Method; Results; Discussion.

**Howe, H. II, "Thinking about the Forgotten Half," *Teachers College Record*, winter 1990, p. 293.**

Presents the main findings and recommendations of a study of American youth done by an independent commission appointed by the William T. Grant Foundation. Two reports sharing the title "The Forgotten Half"; The shortchanging 50 percent of America's young; Inadequate service; Statistics on dropout rate, teenage births; Drug abuse, annual suicide rate of youth; Economic situation of children and youth in the US; More.

**Rogers, J. R., "Female suicides: The trend toward increased lethality in method of choice and its implications," *Journal of Counseling & Development*, September/October 1990, p. 37.**

Presents a brief review of analyses of statistics on suicide in the United States that have documented a trend toward increased lethality in the method of choice in female suicides. Implications for female suicidal risk assessment.

**Rotheram-Borus, M. J., Trautman, P. D., et al., "Cognitive style and pleasant activities among female adolescent suicide attempters," *Journal of Consulting & Clinical Psychology*, October 1990, p. 554.**

Compares cognitive style and pleasant activities of 77 suicide-attempting female minority adolescents with those of two groups of non-suicide-attempting female minority adolescents, 39 of whom were psychiatrically disturbed and 23 of whom were non-disturbed. Results suggest using different cognitive-behavioral interventions with depressed and non-depressed minority female adolescent suicide attempters. Method and results.

**White, G. L. Jr., Murdock, R. T., et al., "Development of a tool to assess suicide risk factors in urban adolescents," *Adolescence*, fall 1990, p. 655.**

Describes tools to examine the differences between adolescents who have attempted suicide and other teenagers. Eighty-two teenagers between the ages of 14 and 19 participated in the test for this instrument; Questions were sorted into three domains: family environment, social environment, and self-perceptions; Method; Results.

## Rock music

**"Ozzy: Read my lyrics," *Rolling Stone*, July 26, 1990, p. 88.**

Discusses three separate cases in which rock star Ozzy Osbourne's song "Suicide Solution" is alleged to have caused the suicides of teenagers. Deaths of John McCollum, 19, of Calif., Michael Waller, 16, of Ga., and Walter Kulkusky, 16, of N.J.

**Billard, M. and Paraskevas, M., "Heavy metal goes on trial," *Rolling Stone*, July 26, 1990, p. 83.**

Probes the 1985 suicide of Raymond Belknap, 18, and the attempted suicide of Belknap's friend Jay Vance, then 20. Both from Sparks, Nev.; Lawsuit filed four years ago by Aunetta Roberson, Belknap's mother and Vance, now dead; Allegations that the music and lyrics of Judas Priest, a British heavy-metal band, caused Ray Belknap to shoot himself. Judas Priest's 1978 album "Stained Class"; Details of the case; CBS Records; Young men's backgrounds.

**Burns, C. and Considine, J. D., "Metal mania," *Rolling Stone*, Nov. 15, 1990, p. 100.**

Traces the evolution of heavy metal music in Britain and the U.S. The music's appeal to the alienated adolescents of the 1980s caused distress among parents and authorities. Lawsuit involving Ozzy Osbourne's song "Suicide Solution" and the band Judas Priest; Bands including Def Leppard, Iron Maiden, Metallica, Van Halen, and others.

**Henry, W. A. III, and Pappa, E., "Did the music say 'do it'?" *Time*, July 30, 1990, p. 65.**

Reports on the trial in Reno, Nev., of four of the five members of the British heavy metal rock band Judas Priest, who are accused of "mind control" in the suicide deaths of two Sparks, Nev., teenagers. Secretly encoded subliminal images not protected by the First Amendment.

# Back Issues

*Great Research on Current Issues Starts Right Here... Recent topics covered by The CQ Researcher are listed below. Issues dated before May 10, 1991, were published under the name of Editorial Research Reports.*

**DECEMBER 1989**
North America Trade Pact
Influence Peddling
German Reunification
Learning Disabilities

**JANUARY 1990**
Higher Education Curriculum
Photonics
Age of 'Infotainment'
Abortion: Politicians' Nightmare

**FEBRUARY 1990**
Politics and Economic Growth
Free Agency in Sports
Repetitive Motion
War on Drugs

**MARCH 1990**
Asbestos: Are Risks Acceptable?
Public Health Campaigns
South Africa's Future
Homeless Need More Than Shelter

**APRIL 1990**
How Fair is the Tax Burden?
Workers' Compensation
U.S. Pacific Forces
Curbing Insurance Premiums

**MAY 1990**
Should Teaching Be a Profession?
Will Canada Fall Apart?
Is U.S. Patent System Outdated?
Federal Funding for the Arts

**JUNE 1990**
Downsizing America's Armed Forces
Progress In Weather Forecasting
S & L Bailout
Bio-Chemical Disarmament

**JULY 1990**
Do Americans Still Love Marriage?
Death Penalty Debate
Decline of Rural America
United Nations in the 1990s

**AUGUST 1990**
Democracy in the Philippines
Initiatives: True Democracy?
Hard Times at Newspapers
Teens Balance School & Jobs

**SEPTEMBER 1990**
Dangers of Alcohol
Western Alliance After the Cold War
Tobacco Industry
Right to Die

**OCTOBER 1990**
Organ Transplants
Energy Policy Options
Search for Arab Unity
Child Support

**NOVEMBER 1990**
Lotteries and Gambling
Post Cold-War Choices
Setting Limits on Medical Care
Multicultural Education

**DECEMBER 1990**
Cable TV Regulation
Americans' Search For Their Roots
Is Insurance System a Failure?
Why Schools Still Have Tracking

**JANUARY 1991**
Growing Influence of Boycotts
Should the U.S. Reinstate the Draft?
America's Archaeological Past
Peace Corps' Challenges in '90s

**FEBRUARY 1991**
Regional Impact of Recession
Puerto Rico's Status
Redistricting: Mapping Power
Nuclear Power

**MARCH 1991**
Acid Rain
Cost of the Gulf War
Reassessing Gun Laws
Future for Man in Space

**APRIL 1991**
Social Security
Canadian Crisis Over Quebec
California Drought
Electromagnetic Radiation

**MAY 1991**
School Choice
Racial Quotas
Animal Rights
U.S. and Japan

**JUNE 1991**
Divorce and Children

Back issues are available for $4.00 (subscribers) or $7.00 (non-subscribers). Quantity discounts apply to orders over ten. To order, call Congressional Quarterly 1-800-432-2250.

# Future Topics

▶ *Endangered Species*

▶ *Europe 1992 Update*

▶ *Parental Consent*

PUBLISHED BY CONGRESSIONAL QUARTERLY INC., IN CONJUNCTION WITH EBSCO PUBLISHING

# Endangered Species

*Can we protect biological diversity without undue economic sacrifice?*

T HE ENDANGERED SPECIES ACT OF 1973 GIVES
federal agencies and environmental groups a
powerful weapon in the fight to rescue animals and
plants from the brink of extinction. But biologists
and conservationists say the federal program focuses too
much on individual species. They would like the emphasis to
shift to preserving entire ecosystems that support a range of
plants and animals. Business interests, on the other hand,
would like Congress to give the government more flexibility
to balance ecological needs with economic concerns. This
conflict pits the goal of preserving grizzly bears, wolves,
owls, salmon and other threatened and endangered species
against the need to protect workers' jobs and the economic
well-being of their communities and states.

  **June 21, 1991 • Volume 1, No. 7 • 393-416**

*Formerly Editorial Research Reports*

COVER ART: BARBARA SASSA-DANIELS

# CQ Researcher

June 21, 1991
Volume 1, No. 7

**EDITOR**
Sandra Stencel

**ASSOCIATE EDITOR**
Richard L. Worsnop

**STAFF WRITERS**
Charles S. Clark
Mary H. Cooper
Rodman D. Griffin

**PRODUCTION EDITOR**
Laurie De Maris

**EDITORIAL ASSISTANT**
Thomas H. Moore

**GRAPHICS**
Jack Auldridge

**PUBLISHED BY**
Congressional Quarterly Inc.

**CHAIRMAN**
Andrew Barnes

**VICE CHAIRMAN**
Andrew P. Corty

**EDITOR AND PUBLISHER**
Neil Skene

**EXECUTIVE EDITOR**
Robert W. Merry

**PUBLICATIONS MARKETING/SALES**
Robert Smith

**EDITOR, EBSCO PUBLISHING**
Melissa Kummerer

The CQ Researcher (ISSN 1056-2036). Formerly Editorial Research Reports. Published weekly (48 times per year, excluding March 1, May 3, Aug. 2 and Nov. 1, 1991) by Congressional Quarterly Inc., 1414 22nd St., N.W., Washington, D.C. 20037. Rates are furnished upon request. Application to mail at second-class postage rates is pending at Washington, D.C. POSTMASTER: Send address changes to The CQ Researcher, 1414 22nd St., N.W., Washington, D.C. 20037.

# Endangered Species

BY TOM ARRANDALE

## THE ISSUES

It's been nearly 20 years since Congress passed the Endangered Species Act of 1973* and, by some measures, the legislation has been a great success. The bald eagle, peregrine falcon, brown pelican, American alligator and a number of other species have been brought back from the edge of extinction. The grizzly bear, gray wolf, black-footed ferret and the California condor may make it, too. But a host of birds, mammals, insects and plants still are in trouble and are not likely to survive.

The U.S. Fish and Wildlife Service currently lists more than 1,100 species as either endangered or threatened; more than 600 of them are found in the United States. (*See table, p. 398.*) Government biologists are studying another 3,700 species as candidates for protection under the law.

Species have been vanishing ever since life on Earth began. No government program can prevent all losses. But conservationists and biologists fear that human population growth and economic development are now speeding the rate of extinction to a catastrophic level, destroying the biological diversity that is essential to the balance of nature.

"Biodiversity is no frill," says Reed Noss, a biologist in Oregon who directed studies on ecological diversity for the U.S. Environmental Protection Agency (EPA). "It is life, and all that sustains life."

The Endangered Species Act is up for renewal next year and environmentalists would like to see it ex-

*The comprehensive 1973 law was preceded by simpler acts in 1966 and 1969.

panded to protect not just individual species but also whole ecosystems that support a range of plants and animals. Business interests, on the other hand, would like Congress to give the government more flexibility to balance ecological needs with economic concerns. What's at stake, they argue, are workers' jobs and the economic survival of hundreds of communities across the nation. "The Endangered Species Act now threatens to devastate economies based upon altering nature — logging, mining, and damming rivers," says Seattle economist John Baden.

The competing demands of wildlife protection and economic development are seen most vividly in the Pacific Northwest. On April 29, the Fish and Wildlife Service, which is responsible for protecting and restoring most endangered species, proposed declaring 11.6 million acres of forest in Washington, Oregon and Northern California as "critical habitats" essential to the survival of the threatened northern spotted owl. Only 2,100 pairs of

northern spotted owls remain in the region's ancient forests of Douglas fir and mixed conifer trees.

Timber industry officials claim that setting that much forest aside could cost as many as 131,000 jobs, mostly in small towns that depend on logging and milling. "In our zeal to protect this bird, we may cripple the timber industry" and "destroy the lifestyles of the loggers and millworkers who built the Pacific Northwest," says Sen. Slade Gorton, R-Wash.[1]

Environmentalists say it's not just the owl that is at stake. Biologists consider the spotted owl an "indicator species" whose dwindling numbers reflect the deterioration of the "old growth" forest ecosystems.

The spotted owl is not the only source of conflict in the Pacific Northwest. Conservation groups in the region are campaigning to have several species of salmon put on the endangered species list. That step could force the federal government to revamp its operations at eight major dams on the Columbia River. Critics say this could lead to sharp increases in electricity rates and hurt the region's industrial development. Protecting the salmon also would affect logging, cattle grazing and other regional businesses. (*See story, p. 406.*)

Struggles between environmentalists and economic interests are not limited to the Pacific Northwest. Similar controversies have arisen over reintroducing wolves to Yellowstone National Park, building a mountaintop observatory in Arizona that threatens the habitat of an endangered red squirrel, and protecting desert tortoises in areas where ranchers graze cattle and off-road motorcyclists race across the federally owned rangelands.

Many more conflicts are likely in

the future, says Jay Sheppard, a biologist with the Fish and Wildlife Service who helps oversee the 1,134 species already listed as endangered or threatened. "As we pour more concrete, cut more forests and build more dams, it restricts species to smaller and smaller areas," Sheppard says.[2]

The United States has set aside millions of acres in national parks, forests, wildlife refuges and wilderness areas, but those systems preserve only a fraction of the continent's original ecological richness. Already the nation has lost half its fertile wetlands — swamps, bogs, coastal salt marshes, river bottoms and other low-lying, moisture-laden lands. In the Southeast, 98 percent of the longleaf pine forests are gone. The Midwest has lost 98 percent of the original tallgrass prairie. Some ecosystem types like the Midwest oak savanna are virtually extinct.

"We are on the verge of massive biological impoverishment, nearly on a par with that forecast for developing nations in the tropics," says Montana biologist and writer Douglas H. Chadwick. "The truly frightening thing … is that we ended up here … despite the Endangered Species Act."[3]

While conservationists want to strengthen the Endangered Species Act to help restore the country's dwindling biodiversity, Pacific Northwest loggers, Wyoming ranchers and other economic interests are protesting that the existing law already demands too stiff a price to save what they see as reclusive owls, destructive wolves and little-known plants and animals that have no demonstrable value to humans. Neither side is satisfied with current wildlife management, but efforts to change the system could spark all-out political wars over balancing ecological goals with economic objectives.

*Is the Endangered Species Act working?*

The 1973 Endangered Species Act requires the federal government to list species of wild plants and animals that are in danger of extinction and it directs the Fish and Wildlife Service and the National Marine Fisheries Service to draft "recovery plans" for protecting survivors and increasing their numbers to the point where their future is assured.*

The law's most crucial provision, Section 7, forbids federal funding or other government participation in projects that jeopardize threatened species or intrude on habitats critical to their survival. Section 7 also allows citizens to sue to enforce the law's requirements. This has given environmental groups a powerful weapon for challenging dams, timber harvests, livestock grazing, mining and other economic development on federal lands that could harm a listed species. (*For more information on the 1973 law, see p. 399.*)

The Endangered Species Act clearly has given some species the chance they needed to recover. The bald eagle and peregrine falcon have come back from the brink of extinction. The whooping crane population on the Texas Gulf Coast is expanding. "For the most part, the law has worked, particularly when we've been able to protect habitat because of the listing of species," says Frank Bond, vice president of the Peregrine Fund, a private group of falconers that has bred endangered peregrines, alplomado falcons and other birds of prey for reintroduction to the wild.

Supporters of the law say it gives the nation the chance to make deliberate choices about saving threatened wildlife. When disease, habitat loss and population growth threat-

---

*The U.S. Fish and Wildlife Service protects most endangered plants and animals; the National Marine Fisheries Service takes care of endangered marine mammals.

ened the last free-flying California condors, the last colony of black-footed ferrets, and some of the last remaining red wolves and Mexican gray wolves, government biologists trapped the animals rather than let them die in the wild. In alliance with American zoos, federal and state wildlife officials are trying to preserve those species' genetic stocks through captive breeding so they eventually can be reintroduced to the wild. The Fish and Wildlife Service has successfully released captive red wolves in North Carolina and the agency now is considering restoring a population of red wolves to the Great Smoky Mountain National Park on the Tennessee-North Carolina border.

Some conservationists have criticized the government for concentrating its recovery efforts on a few "charismatic" species — like the eagle, grizzly bear and spotted owl — while allowing countless other endangered species to slide silently toward oblivion. For example, the U.S. Forest Service is spending $10 million a year to inventory, monitor and finance research on spotted owls — more than it commits to all other threatened and endangered species in the national forests.[4]

Critics also say it takes too long to get animals on the endangered species list. Biologist Douglas Chadwick says as many as 300 species that are candidates for the list "may already be extinct."[5] And countless more animals and plants may be slipping away without the government even knowing about their plight. Among the neglected species, biologists say, are songbirds, reptiles and amphibians. Last year, for example, biologists began noting a rapid decline across the world in amphibian species like frogs and toads.[6]

John F. Turner, an eagle biologist and former Wyoming state senator who is now director of the Fish and Wildlife Service, shares his col-

# Listed Threatened and Endangered Species

*Much progress has been made in identifying and protecting endangered and threatened species, but the number of listed species in 1991 (1,134) dwarfs the number for which there are recovery plans (358).*

| Category | Endangered U.S. | Endangered Foreign | Endangered Both | Threatened U.S. | Threatened Foreign | Threatened Both | Species Total† | Species Having Recovery Plans†† |
|---|---|---|---|---|---|---|---|---|
| Mammals | 36 | 249 | 19 | 5 | 22 | 3 | 334 | 31 |
| Birds | 57 | 153 | 16 | 7 | 0 | 5 | 238 | 67 |
| Reptiles | 8 | 58 | 8 | 14 | 14 | 4 | 106 | 25 |
| Amphibians | 6 | 8 | 0 | 4 | 0 | 1 | 19 | 6 |
| Fishes | 51 | 11 | 2 | 27 | 0 | 6 | 97 | 49 |
| Snails | 4 | 1 | 0 | 6 | 0 | 0 | 11 | 7 |
| Clams | 38 | 2 | 0 | 2 | 0 | 0 | 42 | 30 |
| Crustaceans | 8 | 0 | 0 | 2 | 0 | 0 | 10 | 5 |
| Insects | 10 | 1 | 1 | 9 | 0 | 0 | 21 | 12 |
| Arachnids | 3 | 0 | 0 | 0 | 0 | 0 | 3 | 0 |
| Plants | 184 | 1 | 6 | 51 | 2 | 9 | 253 | 126 |
| TOTAL | 405 | 484 | 52 | 127 | 38 | 28 | 1,134 | 358 |

† *Separate populations of species, listed both as "endangered" and "threatened," are tallied twice. Those ten are: chimpanzee, grizzly bear, leopard, gray wolf, bald eagle, piping plover, roseate tern, Nile crocodile, green sea turtle and olive ridley sea turtle.*

†† *More than one species may be covered by some recovery plans, and a few species have more than one plan covering different parts of their ranges. So far, 286 recovery plans have been approved.*

*Source: U.S. Fish and Wildlife Service. Figures are current as of June 4, 1991.*

leagues' concern about neglected species. He points to the plight of such birds as warblers, scarlet tanagers, wood thrushes, bobolinks, grosbeaks, orioles, and ruby-throated hummingbirds, which he says are being threatened because of heavy development around their wintering grounds in Latin America and summer habitats in the United States. "At this rate," Turner says, "the only Baltimore orioles kids will see in the next century will be baseball players."

Many conservationists would like to see the Endangered Species Act expanded to cover entire ecosystems. "I don't think the law is working the way it was intended," says Sara Vickerman, Pacific Northwest regional representative for Defenders of Wildlife, a national environmental organization. "They'll never have enough time, or enough people, or enough money to deal with species one at a time."

More is at stake than the survival of wolves or grizzly bears. In a report issued last September, the EPA's Science Advisory Board ranked the loss of biological diversity among the nation's most serious environmental problems. "Although natural ecosystems — and the linkages among them — are not completely understood," the report noted, "there is no doubt that over time the quality of human life declines as the quality of natural ecosystems declines." [7]

### Can we afford the human costs of protecting wildlife habitats?

Some critics have accused environmental groups of misusing the Endangered Species Act and other federal laws to accomplish broader objectives — such as stonewalling development — that lack as much public support as saving endangered wildlife. Economist John Baden, who directs the Seattle-based Foundation for Research on Economics and the Environment, says environmentalists are trying to capitalize on the appeal of the northern spotted owl to stop logging in old-growth forests. "No one cares about the spotted owl, nobody," Baden says.

Baden warns environmentalists that their tactics could backfire. Fear of job losses and economic disruption could create a backlash, he says, that eventually could endanger the Endangered Species Act itself. "Environmentalists don't understand that environmental sensitivity and concern for ecological integrity are hostages to prosperity," he adds.

There's no question that the human costs of protecting wildlife habitats can be high. Timber industry officials have estimated that blocking harvests on lands proposed as critical habitat for the spotted owl could cost more than 131,000 jobs that depend directly or indirectly on logging and sawmill operations. Others put job loss estimates at around 30,000.[8] Whatever the final figures prove to be, people in the small logging towns that dot the Northwest already are feeling uncertain about how they will earn their living.

The human costs of wildlife protection were described by Sen. Gorton, who told his Senate colleagues about the owner of a sawmill in his state who was forced to lay off 33 of his 40 employees in 1989 "partly as a result of U.S. Forest Service spotted owl management decisions." The sawmill lost a significant source of timber after 3,000 acres in the Olympic National Forest were designated a spotted owl habitat. "[P]reservation of the spotted owl is a worthy goal," Gorton said. But "if the choice is exclusively between setting aside a portion of our habitat for a small woodland creature ... or the hardworking families which form the backbone of my state's rural communities and timber industry, I will choose people."[9]

Under 1978 amendments to the Endangered Species Act, federal officials are required to take economic consequences into account when they designate critical habitat and draft "recovery plans" to ensure a species' survival (see p. 404). The Fish and Wildlife Service has not yet completed its study of the economic impact of its April 1991 proposal to set aside 11.6 million acres of old-growth forest as critical habitat for the spotted owl. After the analysis is completed, it's likely the proposed acreage will be reduced. In the end, the plan "might be much, much different than it is now," says Interior Secretary Manuel Lujan Jr.[10]

Meanwhile, political and legal jockeying continues over how much old-growth logging can proceed without driving the spotted owl to extinction. (See Chronology, p. 401.)

Most environmentalists express sympathy for the plight of workers who may lose their jobs because of the requirements of the Endangered Species Act. But while economic dislocation is regrettable, they add, the spotted owl controversy is calling public attention to the loss of an irreplaceable ecological system. Whatever the spotted owl's fate, they say, if logging in old-growth forests is allowed to continue at current levels, the West's timber resources will soon be exhausted and the mills and other lumber-related businesses will close down anyway.

Similar impassioned disputes are developing in New Mexico and Arizona, where the Fish and Wildlife Service is processing a petition to list the Mexican spotted owl, a separate subspecies, for protection. In the interim, the Forest Service has revised planned timber harvests on Southwestern national forests to maintain old-growth habitat for the owl and other dwindling species. The regional economic stakes are not as high as in Oregon and Washington, but logging companies contend that slowing down planned timber sales will force them to shut down sawmills that provide most of the jobs in Arizona and New Mexico communities.

"I'm sympathetic to the workers out there," says David Henderson, the National Audubon Society's New Mexico staff representative. "But for years, industry has gotten everything they wanted [from timber sales] without regard for sustainability" of harvest levels over the long term. "And here we are, hitting the wall."

### Should wetlands regulations be weakened?

Of all types of habitats, the country's low-lying wetlands probably provide the most productive wildlife environment. Coastal salt marshes, New England swamps and bogs, Midwestern prairie "potholes," South-

western playa lakes, Mississippi Valley bottomland hardwood forests, and Alaska's wet tundra rank among the nation's most vital ecosystems. Nearly one-third of the country's endangered or threatened species live in wetlands or depend on them for at least part of their habitat.[11]

For generations, Americans treated swamps, bogs, prairie "potholes" and other low-lying lands as wastelands. They routinely filled them in to create farmland, build shopping centers and eliminate breeding sites for disease-carrying mosquitoes. Fish and Wildlife Service studies have found that the country already has destroyed more than half of the 221 million acres of wetlands that the lower 48 states held during Colonial times.

Unfortunately, biologists now are finding that wetlands support an irreplaceable web of life for waterfowl, amphibians, insects and other species. They also help control floods and cleanse rivers and streams of impurities.

Two decades ago, Congress gave the U.S. Army Corps of Engineers power to regulate "dredge-and-fill" operations in U.S. waters under Section 404 of the federal Clean Water Act of 1972. The courts have interpreted that authority broadly to take in any lands that biologists define as wetlands.

The corps is not, however, alone in its oversight of wetlands. Congress gave the EPA authority over wetlands regulation, and the Fish and Wildlife Service consults with the corps to help determine whether projects on either private or public lands will damage important wetlands.

The overlapping authorities have often pitted these government agencies against each other. Corps district engineers, particularly in Southern states, have generally defined wetlands narrowly. The corps usually has granted permits to fill in wetlands to developers who drew up "mitiga-

# 1973 Endangered Species Act

The Endangered Species Act of 1973 directs the U.S. government to evaluate the biological status of wild plants and animals and list them for protection if their survival is in jeopardy. The law sets up two protected categories: "endangered species" that are already in danger of disappearing throughout all or a significant portion of their range, and "threatened species" that are likely to reach that point in the foreseeable future. In addition to entire species, the agencies can list subspecies or even geographically distinct populations that are disappearing, even when they are abundant in other areas.

The U.S. Fish and Wildlife Service, an Interior Department agency, is responsible for listing most animals and plants; the U.S. Commerce Department's National Marine Fisheries Service lists marine mammals. The law allows private individuals to petition those agencies to list a species they contend is in danger or to change the protected status of a species.

In amending the law in 1978, Congress expanded the listing process by directing the agencies to designate critical habitat essential for preserving the species they are listing. Other changes also enacted in 1978 require officials to draft recovery plans setting out the steps required to increase listed species' populations to healthy levels.

Once fish and wildlife are listed, the law prohibits killing, capturing, harassing, or otherwise "taking" individual members of those protected species. The "taking" prohibition applies to listed plants only on federal lands.

The law also forbids trading in endangered species, including importing or exporting protected species or products made from them. In 1982 amendments, Congress set up an elaborate process for granting permits for "incidental takings" of protected animals or plants by private persons who submit plans for accompanying steps to conserve the species affected.

The law also directs all federal agencies to make sure their actions will not contribute to a listed species' extinction. The provision, Section 7 of the law, requires other agencies to consult with the Fish and Wildlife Service or the National Marine Fisheries Service while considering actions that might threaten protected species or disturb critical habitat. Those agencies then can suggest alternative plans to avoid affecting protected wildlife. If no alternative exists, the project cannot proceed.

Responding to the Tellico Dam controversy of the 1970s — which pitted the fate of a small fish called the snail darter against a dam being constructed by the Tennessee Valley Authority (*see p. 404*) — Congress in 1978 amendments set up a federal Endangered Species Committee — widely dubbed the "God Committee" — to grant exemptions for Section 7 if a project's benefits outweigh the preservation of a species.

---

tion" plans to minimize impacts or offset damage by preserving other tracts or even creating artificial wetlands. The EPA and the Fish and Wildlife Service haven't agreed with corps policy, and have pushed for tougher action against wetlands destruction. The EPA has even stepped in from time to time to overturn corps decisions to approve permits.

In one continuing battle, the EPA in January vetoed a Section 404 permit that the corps had granted for building the controversial Two Forks Dam on the South Platte River to supply water to Denver and its suburbs. In another noteworthy case, a Massachusetts developer bought a wetland site and obtained a corps permit to build a shopping mall. But the EPA vetoed the project, ruling that the company could have moved the mall to another upland site that a competing firm controlled.

During the 1988 presidential campaign, George Bush pledged to allow "no net loss" of the country's remaining wetlands. After Bush's election, the corps shifted gears and accepted the EPA's proposal for "sequencing" wetlands mitigation steps. Before permits are granted, that policy requires federal officials to first determine whether a project could just as easily be built elsewhere.

In another move toward tougher regulation, the corps, the EPA, the Fish and Wildlife Service and the U.S. Soil Conservation Service in 1989 jointly drafted a technical Wetlands Delineation Manual that agency officials in the field use when they rule whether property qualifies as wetlands. The manual has significantly broadened the kinds of terrain the government considers wetlands where owners must obtain permits before they can develop property.

As the EPA and the corps have implemented tighter regulations, farmers, oil companies, construction contractors, real estate agents and individual homeowners have complained that federal officials have needlessly stalled plans for making use of privately owned lands by denying dredge-and-fill permits. Farmers have complained about federal officials declaring low spots in their fields that fill up after heavy rains to be regulated wetlands. Landowners have objected that the government has been expansively defining wetlands to include man-made drainage ditches, pine flats and forested bottomlands that are dry for most of the year.

The 1989 manual "leads to a lot of areas that are exceptionally dry being considered wetlands," contends Michael Luzier, director of the environmental regulatory department for the National Association of Home Builders.

The agencies drafted the manual as a technical document, but critics contend that officials have used its expansive definition to effectively extend the reach of wetlands regulations without going through the process of public notice and comment that federal administrative law requires. As a result, "a lot of people have found that they're in wetlands when they don't expect to be," says Susan Tomasky, the Washington, D.C., counsel to the National Wetlands Coalition, an industry lobbying group comprised of oil and gas companies, real estate developers, home builders, mining companies, utilities, port authorities and some city governments. The coalition estimates that 75 percent of wetlands in the lower 48 states lie on private property.

Coalition officials also cite "horror stories" about homeowners and owners of small businesses who run afoul of the law for failing to obtain permits before developing land they later discovered was covered by wetlands regulations. As federal prosecutors have stepped up enforcement, at least five landowners have received jail terms for refusing to comply with wetlands regulations, coalition officials say. In one instance, the corps denied an "after-the-fact" permit to a Louisiana farmer who had mortgaged his home and converted an unauthorized trash dump into commercial crawfish ponds that provide habitat for river otters. "I guess if a crawfish pond is found to be destruction of a wetland, you just begin to see how pervasive this can be, and to some people fairly nonsensical," says Robert Szabo, a coalition attorney.

Luzier says that the procedures set up under the law are also a problem. Getting a permit can take a year or 18 months, which Luzier says discourages landowners from developing their properties. Federal policies also force developers to finance costly studies of alternative sites, he adds, consuming money that could be spent to buy or create new wetlands for preservation.

Benjamin H. Grumbles, assistant Republican counsel to the House Public Works Subcommittee on Water Resources, argues that the Section 404 regulation "has become a federal land-use planning statute" that corps and EPA officials use to tell private landowners what they can and cannot do with wetlands they own.[12] Even if a permit is granted, Grumbles says, it often sets conditions that make the property less attractive to buyers. "There's a very real stigma attached to it. People know there are very serious restrictions on what you can do with those lands," he says.

Responding to the outcry, the White House in 1989 set up an interagency task force to review wetlands policies and come up with ways to meet the president's "no net loss" objective without imposing undue burdens on property owners. But conservation groups are already complaining that the administration has gone too far. In particular, they complain that the White House staff last year forced the EPA and the corps to weaken the new mitigation policy by exempting small tracts and entire regions that have high proportions of wetlands.

Oliver A. Houck, a law professor at Tulane University and an expert in wetlands law, says those changes essentially barred the agencies from applying the sequencing procedure for the type of small-scale projects "that have gobbled up coasts and inland waterways, quarter-acre by quarter-acre."

The congressional Office of Technology Assessment has estimated that 300,000 acres of wetlands are still being destroyed each year. "We've already written off half the wetlands in the United States," says Houck, a former National Wildlife Federation attorney. "We've got to be talking about bringing wetlands back, but instead they're putting more under."

EPA Administrator William K. Reilly puts himself right between the developers and the environmental groups when he says that the recent revisions in the department's wetlands policies will correct "overreaching" by wetland regulators without excluding "genuine wetlands" from protection. "I would caution those who want wetlands protection to avoid overreaching to include so much land that they bring the system crashing down," Reilly warned.[13]    ■

# BACKGROUND

## Government Regulation

Since the Pilgrims landed at Plymouth Rock, roughly 500 animals and plants have disappeared from North America. By the end of the 19th century, trappers had depleted beaver in Rocky Mountain streams, buffalo hunters had decimated the mighty bison herds on the Great Plains, and overhunting and Eastern woodland logging had eliminated the once-plentiful passenger pigeon. Deer, elk, and antelope herds had dwindled to perilous levels.

Even in Colonial times, Americans recognized that uncontrolled slaugh-

*Continued on p. 402*

# Chronology

## 1970s
*Federal environmental protection laws force government agencies to pay more attention to wildlife protection. Fate of the endangered snail darter captures public attention.*

### Dec. 28, 1973
President Nixon signs the Endangered Species Act of 1973, which greatly strengthens federal protection for plant and animal species threatened with extinction.

### Fall 1976
Congress passes the National Forest Management Act and the Federal Land Policy and Management Act, which require that national forests and federal rangelands be managed under "multiple-use" policies that provide room for wildlife as well as grazing, logging, and mining.

### June 15, 1978
U.S. Supreme Court rules the Endangered Species Act prohibits the Tennessee Valley Authority from destroying the habitat of a rare, three-inch long fish — the snail darter — by finishing the Tellico Dam on the Little Tennessee River (*Tennessee Valley Authority v. Hill*).

### Oct. 15, 1978
In response to the Supreme Court's decision, Congress amends the Endangered Species Act to set up a committee empowered to grant exemptions for specific projects.

### Jan. 23, 1979
In its first decision, the committee established by Congress in 1978 votes against granting an exemption for the Tellico Dam.

### Sept. 25, 1979
The snail darter saga finally ends when President Carter reluctantly signs a bill directing that the Tellico Dam be completed. Biologists subsequently find several new snail darter populations, and the Fish and Wildlife Service downgrades the snail darter from endangered to threatened status.

## 1980s
*Despite the Reagan administration's deregulation drive, Congress twice extends the Endangered Species Act without major changes. Plight of the northern spotted owl comes to the public's attention.*

### 1984
National Wildlife Federation and other conservation groups appeal U.S. Forest Service guidelines for managing national forests in the Pacific Northwest, saying they would reduce the number of northern spotted owl pairs the agency intends to protect. In response, the Forest Service agrees to draft a separate environmental impact statement for managing spotted owls.

### 1986
U.S. Forest Service releases a draft of its environmental impact statement for spotted owls. The document draws the fire of both conservation groups and the timber industry.

### 1987
GreenWorld, an environmental group, petitions the Fish and Wildlife Service to list the northern spotted owl as endangered. On Dec. 17, the agency says the listing is not warranted.

### Nov. 9, 1988
U.S. District Judge Thomas Zilly rules the Fish and Wildlife Service has violated the law by failing to list the spotted owl for protection.

## 1990s
*Biologists and conservationists express concern about the country's steady loss of biological diversity.*

### September 1990
Environmental Protection Agency's Science Advisory Board says the agency has neglected the threats to wildlife and human welfare posed by the loss of ecological diversity.

### June 26, 1990
Fish and Wildlife Service lists the northern spotted owl as a threatened species.

### March 26, 1991
Secretary of the Interior Manuel Lujan Jr., in a speech to the San Francisco Commonwealth Club, says the rigidity of the Endangered Species Act prevents the government from balancing species protection with economic concerns.

### April 29, 1991
Fish and Wildlife Service Director John Turner announces his agency's proposal to consider 11.6 million acres in California, Oregon and Washington as protected critical habitat for the spotted owl.

### May 23, 1991
U.S. District Judge William Dwyer issues an injunction barring the Forest Service from selling timber on 66,000 acres of old-growth forest in the Pacific Northwest until the government completes plans for protecting the spotted owl.

# Number of Species Placed on Endangered List Per Year

*The U.S. Fish and Wildlife Servie began listing animals and plants as endangered or threatened in 1967, a year after the first Endangered Species Act was passed. From fiscal 1967 to fiscal 1990, a total of 1,189 species were listed as endangered or threatened. If a threatened species becomes endangered, it counts as a second listing. Only 15 species have been removed from the list and six of those were extinct.*

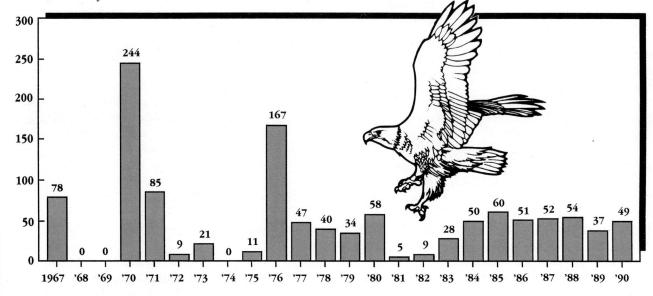

*Source: U.S. Fish and Wildlife Service.*

*Continued from p. 400*
ter was depleting valuable wild populations. Twelve of the 13 original British Colonies passed wildlife-management laws to control the slaughter of deer and other species. But indiscriminate hunting continued into the 1900s, when state governments created game departments to issue licenses, set hunting and fishing seasons and station wardens in the back country to enforce regulations.

It is, in fact, state wildlife agencies — not the federal government — that manage most species found within their boundaries. In addition to enforcing game laws, state wildlife agencies run fish hatcheries, conduct biological research and buy critical big-game habitat for wildlife refuges.

As the nation's largest landowner, the federal government also plays a major role in protecting wildlife habitats. Congress set Yellowstone National Park aside in 1872, and President Theodore Roosevelt in 1903 proclaimed the first national wildlife refuge, on Pelican Island off the Florida coast. Congress now has set aside 49 national parks where National Park Service rangers manage 47.2 million acres to restore or preserve natural ecological systems. In addition, the federal government has created 450 wildlife refuges containing 90 million acres and set aside 32 million acres of its national forests in wilderness areas that Congress has designated for preservation.

What's more, through treaties and legislation, Congress has asserted federal authority to protect wildlife that migrates across international or state boundaries. The Weeks-McClean Act of 1913 declared protecting migratory waterfowl a federal responsibility. The Migratory Bird Treaty Act of 1918 gave the Fish and Wildlife Service power to set limits that states observe when they set hunting seasons for ducks, geese and other migratory birds.

### Habitat-protection measures

With game numbers still plummeting, groups like the National Wildlife Federation formed to support habitat-protection measures. Gun and ammunition manufacturers also saw declining game-bird populations as threatening their business. With their support, Congress in 1934 required every waterfowl hunter to buy a "duck stamp," now priced at $12 annually, to generate funds for protecting wetlands as migratory waterfowl habitat. Three years later, hunters and arms manufacturers supported adoption of the Pittman-Rob-

*Continued on p. 404*

# Who's Who

The following organizations and government agencies are concerned with the endangered species issue.

## GOVERNMENT

**Interior Department:** The government's chief conservation agency. Administers the U.S. Fish and Wildlife Service, the National Park Service and the Bureau of Land Management. Contact: Main Interior Building, Washington, D.C. 20240, (202) 208-3171.

**U.S. Fish and Wildlife Service:** Responsible for carrying out laws designed to protect endangered plants and animals. The service maintains the endangered species list. Contact: Main Interior Building, Washington, D.C. 20240, (202) 208-5634.

**National Park Service:** Administers the nation's national parks, which provide habitats for many endangered species. Contact: Box 37127, Washington, D.C. 20013, (202) 208-4747.

**Bureau of Land Management:** Handles the government's public lands and federally owned mineral resources. The Land and Renewable Resources Office designs conservation and management plans for endangered species. Contact: Main Interior Building, Washington, D.C. 20240, (202) 208-4896.

**U.S. Department of Agriculture (USDA):** Administers the Forest Service, which manages the habitats of hundreds of endangered species. The Forest Service spent over $8 million in fiscal year 1990 on research and management of the northern spotted owl alone. USDA also has an office that coordinates its resource management programs. Contact: Assistant Secretary's Office for Natural Resources and Management, 14th St. and Independence Ave. SW, Washington, D.C. 20250, (202) 447-7173.

**Other** government agencies also reported spending money in fiscal year 1990 on endangered species: Animal and Plant Health Inspection Service (USDA), Bureau of Indian Affairs (Interior Dept.), Bureau of Reclamation (Interior Dept.), U.S. Army Corps of Engineers, U.S. Customs Service (Treasury Dept.), Department of Defense, Environmental Protection Agency, Federal Highway Administration (Transportation Dept.), National Oceanic and Atmospheric Administration (Commerce Dept.), Tennessee Valley Authority.

**In Congress,** committees with oversight over endangered species are the Senate Environment and Public Works Committee (and its Subcommittee on Environmental Protection), the House Merchant Marine and Fisheries Committee (and its Subcommittee on Fisheries and Wildlife Conservation and the Environment) and the House Government Operations Committee, which oversees the U.S. Fish and Wildlife Service.

## NONGOVERNMENT

**The Nature Conservancy:** The Conservancy seeks to protect endangered species and preserve natural diversity by buying up tracts of land and setting them up as wildlife sanctuaries. It owns 5.5 million acres of land in the U.S. alone, and much more internationally in conjunction with other groups. Contact: 1815 North Lynn St., Arlington, Va. 22209, (703) 841-8745.

**World Wildlife Fund-U.S.:** The Fund is associated with the Conservation Foundation and is the largest private U.S. group working worldwide to protect endangered species. The Fund helps protect parks and preserves, supports research, monitors international trading in wildlife and lobbies government and business. Contact: 1250 24th St. NW, Washington, D.C. 20037, (202) 293-4800.

**National Wildlife Federation:** Organized in 1936 and boasting 5.8 million members, the NWF attempts to raise public awareness of ecological problems through publications and education programs. The Federation is also active in litigating environmental disputes in many areas including endangered species. Contact: 1400 16th St. NW, Washington, D.C. 20036, (202) 797-6800.

**The Wilderness Society:** The Society dedicates itself to protecting America's prime wilderness and seeks to foster an American land ethic. Contact: 1400 I St. NW, Washington, D.C. 20005, (202) 842-3400.

**Greenpeace:** Founded in 1970, Greenpeace concentrates on saving endangered water animals such as whales, seals and dolphins — often by direct intervention. The group also works against nuclear and toxic pollution. Contact: 1436 U St. NW, Washington, D.C. 20009 (202) 462-1177.

**Sierra Club:** Founded in 1892, the Club attempts to preserve nature by focusing on legislation, litigation, public information, wilderness outings and conferences. Contact: 730 Polk St., San Francisco, Calif. 94109, (415) 776-2211.

**Natural Resources Defense Council:** The Council combines scientific and legal approaches to the problems of the environment; it conducts studies, brings legal actions and informs the public. Contact: 40 20th St., New York, N.Y. 10011, (212) 727-2700.

Continued from p. 402

ertson Act, imposing an 11 percent excise tax on rifles, shotguns, ammunition and archers' bows. That measure now generates $120 million a year in federal matching grants to help state game departments preserve habitat, conduct big-game research and teach hunter safety.

Anglers and fishing equipment manufacturers lobbied for a 1950 law, the Dingell-Johnson Act, that imposed a similar tax on fishing gear for restoring sport-fish habitat. And starting in the mid-1980s, the Wallop-Breaux Act tripled such funding to $110 million a year by imposing additional taxes on sport fishing boats and tackle.

Through various government reorganization laws in the 1950s, Congress created the Fish and Wildlife Service within the Interior Department to manage federal wildlife refuges and administer other wildlife programs. The Fish and Wildlife Coordination Act, passed in 1934 and strengthened in 1958, requires other federal agencies to consult with the service to determine whether their projects will influence wildlife populations or habitat. The service also regularly reviews environmental impact statements that other agencies prepare under the National Environmental Protection Act of 1969. A 1970 reorganization transferred authority over commercial fisheries, whales, seals, and other marine mammals to the National Marine Fisheries Service, a Commerce Department agency.

A more fundamental and far-reaching sort of federal involvement in protecting wildlife came with passage of the Endangered Species Act of 1973. This act significantly expanded the federal role by declaring that the national interest required saving threatened wildlife and mandating protections for species listed as endangered. (*For a complete de-* *scription of the law, see story, p. 399.)*

## Economic Tradeoffs

Since the enactment of the Endangered Species Act in 1973, the politics of wildlife preservation have revolved largely around debates over the economic costs.

In the mid-1970s, the nation's commitment to the Endangered Spe-

> **The 1973 Endangered Species Act requires the federal government to list species of plants and animals that are in danger of extinction. The act also requires the government to take steps to protect wildlife habitats that are critical to the survival of endangered species.**

cies Act was tested by a controversy over whether the federally run Tennessee Valley Authority should finish building Tellico Dam in Tennessee, thereby flooding a critical habitat for the snail darter, a tiny fish species listed for protection. The U.S. Supreme Court in 1978 held that the Endangered Species Act barred completing the project even though the government had already invested $100 million in construction.

Congress in 1978 set up an interagency panel — quickly dubbed the "God Committee" — to consider exempting projects from the law's provisions. After the panel ruled against exempting the Tellico project, however, Tennessee's congressional

delegation the next year attached a rider to federal appropriations legislation that cleared the way for finishing the dam.[14]

In extending the Endangered Species Act in 1978, Congress took steps to force federal agencies to resolve potential conflicts before the government invested substantial amounts in new projects. The new language aimed at keeping backers from "steamrolling" projects by making irreversible commitments that foreclosed alternative designs less damaging to critical habitat. At he same time, an amendment to the act required officials to take economic consequences into account when designating critical habitats and designing recovery plans.

### Political Pressures

After the Reagan administration took office in 1981, Interior Secretary James G. Watt and other conservatives attempted to weaken the Endangered Species Act, which they viewed as too burdensome on business. But the administration backed off in the face of congressional determination to keep the law intact; Congress extended the law twice during Ronald Reagan's two terms, in 1982 and again in 1988, without seriously considering major amendments.

But conservation groups sparred with the White House and the Interior Department throughout the 1980s over funding levels for endangered species protection. In its yearly budgets, the administration proposed spending cutbacks and sought to divert funds from listing new species to protecting ones already designated for protection. Congress consistently put money for endangered species back into the budget. After slowing dramatically in the early 1980s, the pace of listing species picked up toward the end of

Reagan's tenure. (*See graph, p. 402.*)

Conservationists say things have improved noticeably under President Bush. The Bush administration has accepted higher funding for endangered species, and government biologists say John Turner, who was named director of the Fish and Wildlife Service by Bush in 1989, is more supportive of the endangered species program than his predecessors. The backlog of candidate species continues to expand, but "the program has pretty much returned to its pre-Watt standards," says Michael Bean, an attorney with the Environmental Defense Fund.

## Lingering Tensions

But environmentalists and many in Congress have still found fault with federal agencies' actions. At the top of the list are complaints about the agencies' lackadaisical attitude toward protecting endangered species. Federal "recovery teams" have completed recovery plans for barely a third of the listed species, and the government's track record on implementing those recommendations has been spotty. For instance, Fish and Wildlife Service wolf recovery plans drafted a decade ago call for reintroducing northern Rocky Mountain gray wolves in Yellowstone National Park and captive-bred Mexican wolves to the Southwest. But reintroduction remains in the planning stages because of ranchers' opposition.

Congress last year had to order the Fish and Wildlife Service — along with the National Park Service, state game agencies, conservationists and livestock interests — to come up with a Yellowstone reintroduction plan. The joint effort stalled when representatives of the National Wildlife Federation and Defenders of Wildlife refused to accept the pan-

el's proposal to allow unlimited hunting of gray wolf packs that have moved into Montana and Idaho by themselves from Canada.

Similarly, in New Mexico, Wolf Action, an offshoot of the Earth First environmental activist group, filed a lawsuit in 1990 charging that the service and the U.S. Army violated the law by failing to implement the Mexican wolf recovery plan by releasing captive animals on the White Sands Missile Range. The service's Southwestern regional office has responded by gearing up wolf recovery planning.

But it's in the Northwest that the biggest battles have been fought. Since the early 1980s, environmental groups have been challenging federal timber harvest plans in the region that they contend are rapidly cutting down the country's last old-growth stands of trees. Conservationists won several court rulings against the Forest Service and the U.S. Bureau of Land Management, an Interior Department agency that manages some productive Oregon timberlands. Despite the rulings, however, Sen. Mark O. Hatfield, R-Ore., a powerful member of the Senate Appropriations Committee, succeeded in adding riders to annual appropriations bills that allowed timber sales to proceed and logging to continue.

But conservationists have been fighting old-growth harvests on another front by demanding protection for the spotted owl. In 1987, environmentalists brought the Endangered Species Act into play. A Massachusetts-based conservation group called Greenworld petitioned the Fish and Wildlife Service to list the owl for protection.

That set the stage for four lawsuits that at least temporarily halted most timber sales on Pacific Northwest national forests that are the nation's most productive remaining sources of lumber.

### Wetlands Disputes

The other major battleground of the late 1980s and early '90s has been wetlands. As evidence accumulated that wetland losses threatened waterfowl populations, including the ducks and geese that sportsmen like to hunt, steps were taken to protect wetlands habitat on a comprehensive basis. In conjunction with state and provincial wildlife agencies, the Interior Department and Canada's environmental agency in 1986 signed a North American Waterfowl Management Plan for protecting and restoring 5.5 million acres of wetlands and adjoining upland habitat as breeding and wintering grounds for hard-pressed waterfowl species.

At the same time, Congress set up a federally financed National Fish and Wildlife Foundation that matches with government funding donations from corporations and Ducks Unlimited, a sportsmen's group, to acquire critical waterfowl habitat in California's Central Valley, the Gulf Coast, the Great Lakes, and the prairie "pothole" wetlands of the upper Midwest and Canada. In addition to protecting habitats, the foundation finances research on sea turtles, mountain lions, black-footed ferrets, wolves, and other species.

But federal efforts to regulate development on privately owned wetlands remain mired in controversy. The most vocal criticism has come from outraged landowners who contend that the federal government has taken their private property rights without compensation when it denies permits for developing their lands as they see fit. Indeed, in two 1990 decisions — *Florida Rock Industries v. United States* and *Loveladies Harbor Inc. v. United States* — the U.S. Supreme Court ruled that the federal government had unconstitutionally taken private property without just compensation

*Continued on p. 406*

# Salmon Spawn New Controversy

As the debate over the northern spotted owl intensifies, the Pacific Northwest is facing a new controversy. The National Marine Fisheries Service is considering a request to add five species of salmon that spawn in the freshwater headwaters of the Columbia River system to the endangered species list. That step could force wrenching changes in dams operating along the rivers. The dams, which generate cheap electric power, are credited with spurring the growth of Seattle, Portland and other communities, as well as the region's important aircraft and aluminum industries.

The salmon hatch in fresh upstream waters, migrate downstream during springtime runoffs to live in the Pacific Ocean, then make a remarkable return journey to deposit their eggs in the headwaters of the Salmon and Snake rivers, 900 miles from the Columbia's mouth.

Between 1938 and 1975, the U.S. Bureau of Reclamation and U.S. Army Corps of Engineers built eight major dams and several smaller dams on the Columbia and its major tributaries. The structures, which generate power and store water for irrigation and municipal uses, have inundated roughly a third of the salmon's spawning habitat. They've also made the upstream journey more difficult, even though some dams include "fish ladders" and other devices to permit migrating salmon to pass through them. The dams also store up springtime snowmelts from Pacific Northwest mountains, slowing the annual surge of water that newly hatched salmon once rode downstream.

Before the rivers were dammed, fish could travel to the sea in about one week. With current slower flows, the journey takes about six weeks. And most of the fish that leave Idaho spawning grounds die without reaching the Pacific. According to one study, annual runs of salmon "had dwindled to 2.5 million [by 1980], less than a quarter (and by some estimates only 15 percent) of the run sizes 100 years earlier." [†]

Alarmed by the trend, conservation groups, wildlife organizations and the Shoshone-Bannock tribe in Idaho petitioned the government to list the Snake River sockeye, the lower Columbia River coho, and the spring, summer, and fall chinook salmon species as endangered.

If the National Marine Fisheries Service lists the species, a process that could take another year to complete, the government could curtail salmon fishing and order that dam operations be changed to enlarge springtime surges and accommodate salmon migrations. A consortium of public utilities that market power from Columbia system dams has predicted that such changes could raise electricity rates for the region by 33 percent.

"Everybody west of the Mississippi who turns on a light switch is in some ways responsible for what happened and may in some ways end up paying for it," says Rolland A. Schmitten, Western regional director for the National Marine Fisheries Service. "This doesn't mean we are going to start closing down dams or shutting down the whole West Coast fishery, but it will require sacrifice." [††]

Regional leaders now are trying to come up with a salmon rescue plan that will head off a bitter fight like the one over protecting the spotted owl in old-growth forests. In 1980, Congress authorized the four states that share the Columbia system — Washington, Oregon, Idaho and Montana — to set up the Northwest Power Planning Council to work with federal water management agencies to coordinate river management policies. Earlier this year, Idaho Gov. Cecil D. Andrus, who served as secretary of the Interior under President Jimmy Carter, proposed lowering the reservoirs behind four Snake River dams to strengthen downstream currents.

"The salmon is the ultimate symbol of the Pacific Northwest," Andrus told a reporter for *The New York Times*. "These stalwarts have fought all the obstacles we've put before them in order to return to the spawning grounds of their birth. We ought to be ashamed of ourselves if we can't save them."

Dams in the Columbia River Basin would be forced to change their operations if the government adds five species of salmon to the endangered list.

---

[†] Northwest Power Planning Council, *Columbia River Basin Fish and Wildlife Program,* 1987, p. 3.

[††] Quoted by Timothy Egan in *The New York Times*, April 1, 1991.

*Continued from p. 404*

when the Corps of Engineers denied permits to fill in wetlands.

But it's not just private owners who've run up against the wetlands conflict. In some disputes, state governments and even federal highway and energy projects have run afoul of wetland regulations. Four years ago, corps and EPA officials in New England ordered New Hampshire highway engineers to abandon a partly built bridge in the Bloody Brook Swamp in the southeast corner of the state because they had failed to obtain a Section 404 permit to build it.

If wetlands and the spotted owl are the highest-profile disputes of the past decade, there are still a host of other, less publicized cases. In recent years, other controversies have developed over transplanting sea otters along the California coast, preserving the Florida panther habitat, and designating the Louisiana black bear for protection.

Environmental groups are still trying to halt plans by the University of Arizona to build an observatory in endangered red squirrel habitat on Mount Graham near Safford, Ariz. When conservationists came up with data showing that desert tortoise populations were plummeting in southeastern California, the Fish and Wildlife Service in August 1988 listed the species as threatened. ■

date agencies that insist on promoting big-game hunting while depleting the rest of the nation's wildlife heritage. Animal-welfare activists have been harassing hunters in the field, and California voters last year canceled mountain lion hunts that the state Fish and Game Department had scheduled.

Biologists and environmentalists have long objected that state game departments have all but ignored threats to songbirds, snakes, frogs and other "non-game" wildlife that may be well on their way toward extinction. In Colorado alone, "there are about 250 species we don't know anything about," says Judy L. Sheppard, one of the state's three non-game specialists. "We don't know if they're on the brink or not."

# CURRENT SITUATION

## State Wildlife Agencies

W hile controversy continues over protecting particular endangered species, federal and state wildlife agencies are searching for ways to broaden their missions to take responsibility for preserving all the nation's biological wealth.

Two major trends can be discerned. State governments retain primary responsibility for protecting most wildlife, and their wildlife agencies are struggling to make a subtle but important shift from being "fish and game" departments that cater to sportsmen to agencies that focus on broader ecological concerns. Secondly, federal agencies have been gradually changing their focus from protecting single endangered species to preserving the habitats they share with other wildlife. Both shifts have generated signifi-

cant political conflicts.

The original orientation of state wildlife agencies toward recreational concerns should be no surprise, in light of the fact that state fish and game departments have — since early in the century — financed their operations primarily by selling hunting and fishing licenses. Nationally, fish and game departments rely on license sales to fund more than half their annual budgets. The agencies, in return, have spent most of their resources providing the deer, elk, grouse, bass, trout and other game species that their "hook and bullet" constituency covets.

William A. Molini, director of the Nevada Department of Wildlife, says while his agency doesn't "like to make species value judgments ... there's a demonstrated demand for more elk, and the hunters are willing to pay for it." So if biologists find that clearing sagebrush will improve elk habitat, Molini adds, "we're more apt to do it for elk and not worry too much about the sage sparrow."

Because of such attitudes, state game departments are now being characterized by critics as out-of-

### Changing Their Priorities

The complaints and protests seem to have had some effect. Some states have renamed "fish and game" agencies "wildlife" departments with missions to protect all species. All 50 state agencies now have launched formal non-game programs, even though some officials fear that diverting resources to those programs will anger the sportsmen who now pay the bills by buying licenses and paying excise taxes.

Missouri since 1976 has dedicated one-eighth of 1 percent of sales tax revenues to wildlife and land conservation programs, and Florida now charges newly arriving residents a fee to register their cars, a portion of which is used to offset the toll that rapid population growth is taking on the state's non-game wildlife. "We've been trying to become a holistic resource management agency, and that means taking care of all the critters," says Robert M. Brantly, executive director of the Florida Game and Freshwater Fish Department.

Most states fund non-game programs primarily through contributions generated by wildlife "check-

# "Gap Analysis"

For all their splendid scenery, America's national parks, wilderness areas and wildlife refuges protect only fragments of North America's original biological wealth. Recognizing that gaps remain, the U.S. Fish and Wildlife Service is launching a systematic search to find the country's last biological frontiers before it is too late to preserve their full complements of native plants and animals.

Working with state wildlife agencies and university scientists, federal biologists are now surveying the remaining strongholds of biodiversity in Idaho, California, Oregon and Utah. They are using a technique known as "gap analysis," pioneered by Fish and Wildlife Service biologist Michael Scott at the University of Idaho. The technique combines satellite maps and computer technology to identify species-rich regions. Biologists then compare those areas with land ownership patterns to determine where biological systems are in danger of damage by human intrusion.

President Bush's proposed fiscal 1992 budget for the Fish and Wildlife Service includes $1 million to be used to expand gap analysis work to 17 other states, primarily in the West but also including West Virginia, Vermont, Massachusetts, Arkansas, Tennessee and New Hampshire. Defenders of Wildlife, a nationwide conservation organization, is asking Congress to appropriate $4 million so the Wildlife Service can fund gap analysis work in 14 more states. Scott says with a funding level of $4 million a year, gap analysis could be completed for the entire nation within six years "for less than a penny an acre."

Once the analysis is completed, the question becomes how to protect the ecosystems that have been identified as being vulnerable to human intrusion. Interior Secretary Manuel Lujan Jr. has made it clear that he opposes solutions that involve the federal government buying land from private owners, and the wetlands controversy demonstrates the fierce resistance government programs encounter when they attempt to regulate how landowners use private property. But gap analysis at least could let the American people know what's at stake when they decide between economic growth and protection.

offs" on state income tax forms. Revenues have been falling in recent years, however, primarily because wildlife programs compete with checkoffs that legislatures have added for other causes.

To cultivate broader public support among people who don't go hunting and fishing, game departments now have started wildlife viewing programs and promoting backyard habitat conservation in urban areas. Through the International Association of Game and Fish Agencies, they also are asking Congress to help finance non-game protection, perhaps through some kind of tax on "non-consumptive use" of wildlife resources by photographers, birdwatchers and hikers.

Congress in 1980 passed a federal non-game law that authorized $5 million a year in federal support for state programs. But the act has never been funded, and proposals to finance non-game assistance through various mechanisms are still being debated. The Fish and Wildlife Service in 1984 released a report analyzing potential revenue sources that included annual congressional appropriations, new mining fees on federally owned lands, sale of special postage stamps,and taxes on birdseed, bird houses, binoculars, backpacking equipment, wild animal furs, cameras and film, camping trailers, snowmobiles, or off-road vehicles. But manufacturers have opposed taxing outdoor equipment they sell, and national environmental groups have yet to unite behind one revenue package.

Across the country, however, state wildlife agencies are now recognizing that they cannot maintain wildlife populations if habitat losses continue. And, more and more, state game managers see habitat being lost as suburban development spreads into wildlife habitat. Near big cities, game wardens respond to a growing number of complaints when deer browse through homeowners' gardens or bears seeking food or water wander down from mountains and foothills to residential streets now occupying their valley habitats. State game departments have responded by running their own refuges, many acquired with federal revenue-sharing funds financed by taxes on firearms and fishing tackle. But the numbers of refuges that have been created are clearly insufficient.

Bill Montoya, director of the New Mexico Game and Fish Department, says when he took that post in 1988, "I realized we had gone up against a brick wall in our ability to increase wildlife populations by just managing the animals. Without habitat, there's no sense in having wildlife. And we've got to be in on the ground floor to look at things that threaten it."

No longer willing to stand by while habitat is destroyed, game department officials now are speaking up when unplanned urban growth, accelerating timber harvests, and oil and gas drilling threaten both pri-

*Continued on p. 410*

# At Issue:

## Are the human costs of protecting the northern spotted owl too high?

**SEN. SLADE GORTON, R-WASH.**

FROM *THE CONGRESSIONAL RECORD*, MARCH 15, 1989.

### yes

*a* constituent of mine who owns [a sawmill] in Beaver, Wash., has been forced to lay off 33 of his 40 employees since the first of the year, partly as a result of U.S. Forest Service spotted owl management decisions. [This] is but one example of the crippling economic and social effects that spotted owl management is having on Washington state and elsewhere. . . .

The battle I have described takes places in our National Forests; the conflict is over the extent to which we use these forests to provide jobs for our citizens against protected habitat for the spotted owl. This conflict has ramifications in any part of this nation in which growth and commerce may affect local wildlife.

For much of my state's history — beginning long before Bill Boeing located his factory near a steady source of lumber for his first airplanes — forest formed the foundation of our state's economy. Years of prosperity were based on the felling and milling of trees. . . .

In our zeal to protect this bird, we may cripple the timber industry by unnecessarily setting aside tens or hundreds of thousands of acres of valuable timberland, above and beyond the millions of acres already set aside as parks and wilderness.

I am not speaking here of huge, faceless timber corporations — most of them own and harvest their own lands. It is thousands of individual Washingtonians . . . who will lose their jobs, and they are good jobs: cutting, hauling and milling timber. We will lose homes and communities. . . . We will endanger school systems, we will hurt people — loggers, truckers and their families. We will contribute to alcoholism, child abuse and suicide.

Mind you, preservation of the spotted owl is a worthy goal. I hope and I believe that it can be preserved without devastating our timber industry and its good people. But . . . if the choice is exclusively between setting aside a portion of our habitat for a small woodland creature after we have already set aside millions of acres of wilderness, or the hardworking families which form the backbone of my state's rural communities and timber industry, I will choose people.

**THE EDITORS OF THE SEATTLE POST-INTELLIGENCER**

FROM *AN EDITORIAL IN THE SEATTLE POST-INTELLIGENCER*, MAY 27, 1991.

### no

*u* S. District Judge William Dwyer has taken the only reasonable course in ruling that the Forest Service must prepare a plan to save the northern spotted owl before allowing more cutting in the owl's habitat.

In one sense, Dwyer's ruling was a difficult one, since many residents of this state's timber-dependent communities remain ill-prepared to engage in other occupations. The issue of assistance to residents of these communities is one that should command the attention of Congress.

This ruling will, for the time being at least, shut down logging operations on almost 80 percent of 17 forests in western Washington, western Oregon and Northern California.

The judge ruled that a "substantial risk" exists that the owl would be wiped out if logging continued on those parcels while the agency tried to fashion a habitat preservation plan. Obviously, if the planners discovered that the owl for its survival needed trees that had been felled in the interim, no amount of judicial restraint would bring back either the bird or the trees.

However, the picture is not quite as bleak as it seems. Some harvesting would continue on federal lands, since 4.8 billion board feet of timber has been sold that has not yet been felled. Dwyer put 66,000 acres off limits until the new rules are in place.

In another sense, the ruling was an easy one. The Forest Service blatantly has flouted the law and ignored the directive of Congress to prepare the plan. . . . Dwyer pinned the blame for what he called "deliberate, systematic" violations of the law not on Forest Service personnel but on "higher authorities" in the executive branch of government.

If the Forest Service now abides by the law and moves along as smartly as it should have from the outset to prepare a cutting and habitat conservation plan, the pain caused by uncertainty can be somewhat lessened.

Stability is needed in the Northwest timber harvest regime and the judge has made it crystal clear that it is the Forest Service's responsibility to stop stalling and provide that stability.

*Continued from p. 408*

vate and public lands essential to wildlife populations. "State game agencies in the West are starting to show some backbone," says Jim Norton, the Southwest representative for The Wilderness Society.

In the Southwest, the New Mexico and Arizona game departments have appealed planned U.S. Forest Service timber sales, arguing that logging would destroy deep-forest habitat for the Mexican spotted owl, pygmy nuthatch, black bear and other hard-pressed species. Environmentalists in the Pacific Northwest credit the Washington Department of Wildlife with helping build scientific groundwork on the spotted owl issue. The Wyoming Game and Fish Department last year negotiated an agreement that requires the U.S. Bureau of Land Management to give state biologists a chance to review potential wildlife impacts before federal land managers approve oil and gas drilling leases.

## Federal Focus

Local governments now play a growing role in preserving habitat through zoning regulations and land conservation programs that preserve greenbelts in urban areas. But the federal government is by far the country's largest landowner, and the way it manages its vast holdings determines the fate of many species.

Over the past several years, the federal Fish and Wildlife Service has been struggling with a shift in focus from single endangered species to new initiatives that focus more attention on keeping ecological systems intact. The service has been putting more resources into "pre-listing" efforts to protect declining species that might become endangered. In some cases, biologists are combining work on several candidate spe-

cies that share the same habitat.

Along with the Forest Service, the EPA, the Agency for International Development and other agencies, the service on May 14 launched an international Neotropical Migratory Bird Conservation Program that aims at protecting 200 or so warblers, vireos, tanagers, grosbeaks, and other forest-dwelling songbird species.

Between 1978 and 1987, 44 of 62 neotropical species found in Eastern states declined; in some states, populations fell off for 70 percent of neotropical species during the 1980s. The program aims at halting habitat losses in U.S. forests as well as Latin American countries where neotropical species spend the winter. "As a result of that strategy, we will wind up addressing some pretty critical biodiversity issues," says Robert J. Shallenberger, the Fish and Wildlife Service's deputy assistant

regional director for refuges and wildlife in Texas, Oklahoma, Arizona and New Mexico.

But some federal agencies are finding themselves increasingly at odds with the administration over protecting habitats, particularly wetlands.

For example, when EPA officials this spring rewrote the wetlands delineation manual to narrow the scope of regulations, Fish and Wildlife Service Director Turner refused to sign proposed revisions, now under White House review, that biologists say will exempt as much as 10 million acres of land from wetlands regulations. EPA officials at Washington headquarters say they are making merely technical changes, but EPA and Fish and Wildlife Service officials in the field say the administration is caving in to developers' pressure. ∎

# OUTLOOK

## Wetlands Debate

With the Clean Water Act and Endangered Species Act both up for renewal by 1992, Congress will be confronting the long-building conflicts over how the nation should manage its lands to protect wild species and their habitat. Wildlife experts are generally agreed there will have to be significant changes in policies, and they are likely to be controversial.

The wetlands issue has already been heating up as House and Senate committees prepare to consider revising the Clean Water Act authority for the Section 404 program. Rep. Jimmy Hayes, a Louisiana Democrat, and more than 100 House cosponsors are pushing legislation that the National Wetlands Coalition attor-

neys drafted to replace the existing wetlands program. "We need Congress to speak to the issue of what is a wetland," says Luzier of the home builders association.

But environmentalists and biologists view the legislation as an unworkable scheme designed to make effective regulation impossible. In essence, the measure — HR 1330 — would require the federal government to inventory all wetlands and classify them in three categories. The law would open the lowest-value wetlands for development and require the government to compensate the owners of high-value wetlands that would be set aside for preservation. It also would strip the Environmental Protection Agency of its oversight role and give the Corps of Engineers primary responsibility for wetlands regulation.

Environmental group lobbyists see little chance that Congress will approve the Hayes bill. But they worry that the number of congressmen supporting the legislation will force federal agencies to back off from aggressively enforcing existing regulations. Meanwhile, the White House interagency task force on wetlands is expected to have recommendations for meeting Bush's "no net loss" goal ready for Cabinet consideration sometime this summer, but conservationists are skeptical about the outcome.

## Legislative Outlook

The emotions stirred by the spotted owl issue will be a factor when Congress debates renewing the endangered species program. Interior Secretary Lujan has called the existing law "too tough" [15] and has urged Congress to provide more flexibility so the government can take economic impacts into account before it lists a species for protection, not just in designating critical habitat.

In the past, Congress has consistently refused to open the law to special-interest amendments, and conservation lobbyists are confident this Congress will not accept major changes. Down the road, however, more controversy could weaken congressional support for keeping the law intact. Frank Bond, the Peregrine Fund official, worries that environmentalists' tactics — such as using the spotted owl to force changes in forest management — eventually will backfire by convincing Congress to weaken the statute.

Even if the Endangered Species Act is preserved, conservationists now recognize that further steps are required. Proposals are numerous. Rep. James H. Scheuer, D-N.Y., chairman of the House Science, Space and Technology Subcommittee on Environment, has proposed a National Biodiversity Conservation and Research Act that calls for developing national plans for conserving ecological diversity. The bill also would direct federal land agencies to maintain the biological diversity on public lands "to the extent practicable."

Defenders of Wildlife and other groups have called for protecting corridors between existing natural areas so that populations can exchange genetic stock and move if climatic changes alter habitat conditions. Other groups have proposed that government wildlife agencies could protect key habitats by buying tracts of land, purchasing conservation easements, restricting resource development on public lands or developing cooperative efforts with private landowners.

All of these proposals will undoubtedly meet resistance because they can be expected to carry rather high price tags. Ultimately, their chances of success rest on whether the voting public is convinced of the need to pay the price. For the past century, hunters and fishermen have provided the backbone of political and financial support for wildlife management in this country. Wildlife experts say that constituency, with its relatively narrow wildlife interests, is no longer enough, if it ever was.

Turner, the Fish and Wildlife Service director, sees a need to educate an increasingly urbanized population about the threat that declining ecosystems pose to all kinds of life on the planet. "While we laboriously list species and undertake costly recovery programs for species that already need intensive care, we may be losing the bigger war for preservation of ecosystems and biodiversity," Turner told those attending a wildlife conference in Denver last year. "In the long run we need to look much harder for ways to save groups of species that are beginning to decline before they are so far gone." [16] ∎

## Notes

[1] *Congressional Record*, March 15, 1989.

[2] Quoted by The Associated Press, April 12, 1991.

[3] Douglas H. Chadwick, "The Biodiversity Challenge," *Defenders Magazine*, May/June 1990.

[4] There are more than 170 threatened and endangered species in the 191 million acres of the national forest system, but the Forest Service currently has programs in place to preserve habitat for a only dozen. See *Biological Diversity on Federal Lands*, The Keystone Center, Keystone, Colo., April 1991, p. 71.

[5] Chadwick, *op. cit.*

[6] See Kathryn Phillips, "Where Have All the Frogs and Toads Gone?" *BioScience*, June 1990.

[7] U.S. Environmental Protection Agency, Science Advisory Board, *Reducing Risks: Setting Priorities and Strategies for Environmental Protection*, September 1990, p. 9.

[8] See Mike Mills, "Spotted Owl Gains Ground in Timber Controversy," *Congressional Quarterly Weekly Report*, May 4, 1991, p. 1127.

[9] *Congressional Record, op. cit.*

[10] Quoted in Mills, *op. cit.*

[11] See The Conservation Foundation, *State of the Environment: A View Toward the Nineties*, 1987, p. 290.

[12] Benjamin H. Grumbles, "Wetlands, Waste Sites, and Oil Spills: To Federalize or Not to Federalize," *Environmental Law Reporter*, December 1990, p. 10513.

[13] Quoted in *The Boston Globe*, May 14, 1991.

[14] For background, see Steven Lewis Yaffee, *Prohibitive Policy: Implementing the Federal Endangered Species Act*, 1982, p. 165.

[15] Interview with the *Denver Post*, May 11, 1990.

[16] Turner spoke March 19, 1990, at the 1990 North American Wildlife and Natural Resources Conference.

*Tom Arrandale is a free-lance writer who lives in Albuquerque, N.M.*

# Bibliography

## Selected Sources Used

### Books

**Chandler, William J., ed., *Audubon Wildlife Report, 1989/1990*, Academic Press Inc., San Diego, Calif., 1989.**

The latest in a series of annual reports first printed in 1985, this edition contains a chapter on old-growth forests in the Pacific Northwest. Chapters by Michael Bean, an attorney for the Environmental Defense Fund, in each year's edition provide useful analysis of recent legal developments in enforcing the Endangered Species Act and other wildlife protection laws.

**Norse, Elliott A., *Ancient Forests of the Pacific Northwest*, The Wilderness Society and Island Press, Washington, D.C., 1990.**

Norse, a senior ecologist for the Wilderness Society, sums up the environmentalist case for preserving old-growth forests in the Pacific Northwest.

**Rohlf, Daniel J., *The Endangered Species Act, A Guide to Its Protections and Implementation*, Stanford Environmental Law Society, Stanford, Calif., 1989.**

Rohlf's legal handbook provides an exhaustive review of the political and legal issues posed by the Endangered Species Act. It discusses the administrative decisions and court rulings that have shaped how government officials go about listing species, drafting recovery plans and implementing the law's restrictions on federal activities that threaten endangered wildlife. Rohlf maintains the 1973 law is "still the most forceful declaration in favor of wildlife conservation made by any nation."

### Articles

**Chadwick, Douglas H., "The Biodiversity Challenge," *Defenders Magazine*, May/June 1990.**

Chadwick outlines the case for looking beyond managing single species to policies aimed at keeping entire ecosystems intact and maintaining protected corridors linking similar types of systems. "Our challenge now is to conserve the very nature of nature," Chadwick writes, "which is the power to connect, to sustain, to heal and to invent; to keep filling the world with an infinite variety of wonders. . . . That is what biodiversity and landscape linkages are all about."

**Cohn, Jeffrey P., "The Politics of Extinction," *Government Executive*, October 1990, p. 18.**

Cohn reviews ongoing controversies over protecting the spotted owl, desert tortoise and the gray wolf. "For government agencies, controversial species such as the northern spotted owl symbolize the problems and politics of managing endangered wildlife when no consensus exists between conservationists and economic interests," Cohn writes.

**Scott, J. Michael, et al., "Beyond Endangered Species: An Integrated Conservation Strategy for the Preservation of Biological Diversity," *Endangered Species Update*, July 1989, p. 43.**

The authors argue that governments will never be able to muster enough resources to save most endangered species by protecting them one at a time. They outline gap analysis procedures for mapping U.S. ecosystems and determining which systems lack adequate protection in existing national parks, refuges, wilderness areas and other conservation lands.

### Reports and Studies

**Defenders of Wildlife, *Preserving Communities and Corridors*, Washington, D.C., 1989.**

"Our intention here is to report on and applaud the efforts of federal and state wildlife agencies to save all wildlife species, while giving special attention to their efforts to protect diverse habitats," M. Rupert Cutler, then president of the national conservation organization, writes in an overview.

**U.S. Congress, Office of Technology Assessment, *Technologies to Maintain Biological Diversity*, 1987.**

OTA assesses the accelerating loss of biological diversity, in this country and abroad. The report calls for a national commitment to conserving diversity and outlines technologies for accomplishing that goal, including setting aside parks and preserves, maintaining species in botanic gardens and zoos, and freezing genetic materials in seed banks and sperm banks.

**U.S. Environmental Protection Agency, Science Advisory Board, *Reducing Risk: Setting Priorities and Strategies for Environmental Protection*, September 1990.**

The Science Advisory Board urges the EPA to focus its resources on environmental problems, including loss of biological diversity, that pose the most serious long-term risks. "Over the long term, ecological degradation either directly or indirectly degrades human health and the economy," the report concludes.

# The Next Step

## Additional Articles from Current Periodicals

### Birds

**Budiansky, S., "More environmental than thou," *U.S. News & World Report*, Mar. 26, 1990, p. 10.**

Examines the recent history of the bald eagle, rescued from the brink of extinction by the intervention of man (who caused the problem in the first place), tripling its numbers in the past 15 years. Of the more than 500 species placed on the endangered-species list in the United States, only a handful have ever recovered to the point they can be removed or downgraded; Doomed by human existence.

**Byrnes, P., "Spotted Owl 'threatened,' " *Wilderness*, fall 1990, p. 4.**

Reports that the Fish and Wildlife Service will list the Northern Spotted Owl as a threatened species and will develop a recovery plan for the owl. Listing implications; Possible exemptions; Alternative recovery plan.

**Emerson, K., "Seen any warblers lately?" *The New York Times Magazine*, Sept. 2, 1990, p. 26.**

Reports on the threat to North American songbirds from deforestation in South America and suburbia in the north. Dwindling species; Problems from pesticides; Vulnerability to predators; The parasitic brown-headed cowbird.

**Jackson, L., "Flying with falcons," *Canadian Geographic*, August/September 1990, p. 28.**

Describes a helicopter search for endangered birds in Labrador. Peregrine falcons and harlequin ducks; Mapping peregrine distribution; Indirect victims of the pesticide DDT.

**Turbak, G., "A reason to whoop," *International Wildlife*, January/February 1990, p. 12.**

Describes biologist Ernie Kuyt's efforts over the last 23 years to save the endangered whooping crane from extinction. It's one of the world's 15 crane species, stands five feet tall, with wings spanning seven feet, and evolved during the epoch of the saber-toothed cat and the mastodon.

### Case studies

**Brower, K., "Losing paradise," *Wilderness*, winter 1989, p. 20.**

Discusses the island ecosystems of Hawaii, the most isolated archipelago on the planet, with 96 percent of its native species found nowhere else on earth, and many of them facing extinction. Destruction by people; Natural enemies; Biosphere reserves and national parks; Ocean mining, helicopter overflights, and other threats.

**Cohn, J.P., "An island for conservation," *Bioscience*, May 1990, p. 342.**

Describes the ongoing work in conservation, research and education on St. Catherine's Island, a privately owned barrier island about 50 miles south of Savannah, Georgia. From hunter-gatherers to scientists; Native ecology; Bronx Zoo breeds rare and endangered species on the island; Relics of Indian society; Ecology education.

### Debates & issues

**Adler, J. & Reiss, S., "They've paved paradise . . ." *Newsweek*, Aug. 13, 1990, p. 62.**

Discusses the development of the Florida Keys and how it has caused the animal inhabitants to compete with humans. Six endangered species which are found nowhere else inhabit the islands; Curious range of environmental problems; Key deer; Key rabbit; Destruction of the United States only living coral reef; Water pollution.

**Bowermaster, J. & Mahurin, M., "All creatures great and dying," *Rolling Stone*, May 3, 1990, p. 78.**

Presents a partial list of threatened and endangered species. Discusses mankind's past and present destruction of animal and plant species and their habitats. Number of extinct and endangered species; Acceleration of the extinction rate; Need to save plants for medical research.

**Cowen, R., "Rodents and telescopes: A squirrelly issue," *Science News*, July 7, 1990, p. 7.**

Reports on a bitter debate among researchers over the merits of construction on a portion of Mt. Graham in Arizona. Plans to place seven large telescopes on the mountain; Endangered species of a red squirrel inhabits the mountain.

**Dayton, L., "On the saving of the species," *New Scientist*, Jan. 19, 1991, p. 25.**

Reports on the opinions of scientists gathered at the meeting of the World Conservation Union (IUCN) in Perth last month. Scientists were told they must rethink their research methods and deal with the political and economic aspects of the problem. Opinion of Jeffrey McNeely, the chief conservation officer of IUCN; Establishing a rate of extinction; Joining forces with universities, botanical gardens, and research stations. INSET: Documenting disappearing species.

**Diamond, J., "Playing dice with megadeath," *Discover*, April 1990, p. 54.**

Discusses the increasing problem of species extinction. Majority of species undiscovered; Human arrival in an area historically coincides with mass extinctions; Overhunting, relocation of predators, destruction of habitat, and disturbance of food chain; The great auk, the Nile perch and the African elephant.

## Economic aspects

**"Endangered species," *Life*, January 1991, p. 52.**

Comments on the conflict between environmentalists and loggers over ancient forests in the Pacific Northwest. How it reflects the larger debate between those trying to save jobs and those trying to save the wild.

**"Poached? Moi?" *Economist*, Oct. 13, 1990, p. 92.**

Examines the current state and future of ivory trade in the world. Impact of the two-year moratorium on ivory trade begun last year by the Convention on International Trade in Endangered Species (CITES); Work in identifying where ivory comes from by Dr. Nikolaas van der Merwe; Details of the process; Proposal that ivory should be traded by auction by the Southern African Centre for Ivory Marketing (SACIM); Outlook.

**Gup, T., "Owl vs man," *Time*, June 25, 1990, p. 56.**

Describes the controversy in the Pacific Northwest, between the logging industry and environmentalists, which will not end when the US Fish and Wildlife Service announces whether it will list the northern spotted owl as a threatened species. Fundamentally different philosophies about the place of man in nature; Export of logs to Japan; Ignorance, arrogance and greed; Contradictory statistics; Economics and politics controlling decisions of BLM, Fish and Wildlife.

**Neff, C., "A cutting issue," *Sports Illustrated*, July 2, 1990, p. 13.**

Reports that more environmentally sensitive approaches to logging may have to be used following the U.S. Fish and Wildlife Service's recent decision to declare the spotted owl a threatened species, and destroying its natural habitat illegal. An estimated 20-50,000 loggers could lose their jobs due to the decision.

**Udall, J.R., "A wild, swinging river," *Sierra*, May/June 1990, p. 22.**

Reports on the negative effects irregular flows from the Glen Canyon Dam are having on the Colorado River and Grand Canyon National Park. Erosion of beaches; Endangered species; Disturbance of raft trips; Environmental Impact Statement ordered; Irregular flows used to meet peak power demands.

## Endangered Species Act

**Carlston, J., Bean, M., et al., "A hard act to follow," *Backpacker*, October 1990, p. 86.**

Examines the Endangered Species Act, passed in December 1973. Includes comments by some environmentalists. Confusion; Endangered Species Committee, sometimes called the 'God Committee.'

**Gup, T., "Down with the God squad," *Time*, Nov. 5, 1990, p. 102.**

Opinion. Considers the current call by some Bush administration officials to amend the Endangered Species Act, a move that will greatly expand the powers of a committee of political appointees to exempt species from the protection of the act when man's economic interests so dictate. Northwestern loggers and the spotted owl; Arizona and the Mount Graham red squirrels; Species preservation depends on political resolve.

## Fish

**Gantenbein, D., "Salmon on the spot," *Sierra*, January/ February 1991, p. 31.**

Explains why several conservation groups and the Shoshone-Bannock tribe of Idaho filed petitions seeking Endangered Species Act protection for five wild salmon runs in the Pacific Northwest. Farmers, utilities, fishermen and recreationists may be affected; Problem is not new; Extinction jeopardizes hatchery runs; Recovery measures suggested.

**Hoke, F., "Intemperate fish loss," *Environment*, November 1990, p. 21.**

Reports that the huge numbers of endangered and extinct species of fish in the tropics have commanded great media attention but a new study suggests that the rate of biodiversity loss in temperate aquatic ecosystems is at least as dramatic. Survey details.

**Tudge, C., "Underwater, out of mind," *New Scientist*, Nov. 3, 1990, p. 40.**

Examines the controversies surrounding the conservation of freshwater fish, one of the most endangered and least understood animals. Saving species and habitat; Problems facing freshwater fish such as loss of habitat, over-fishing and non-native species introduction. INSET: Can amateurs conserve rare fish?

## Mammals

**"The ivory paradox," *Economist*, Mar. 2, 1991, p. 16.**

Contends that ending all trade in elephant tusks (ivory) would be more harmful to elephants as a species than setting up a toughly controlled trading system to market a limited quantity of sustainably harvested ivory. African elephant placed on Appendix I of the Convention on International Trade in Endangered Species (CITES); Findings of the Wildlife Trade Monitoring Unit; New markets developing for ivory; Idea of an Ivory Exchange; Details.

**Balog, J., "A personal vision of vanishing wildlife," *National Geographic*, April 1990, p. 84.**

Presents a photo essay with startling portraits of animals in captivity that may be among the last of their species. Includes the Florida panther; West Indian manatee; Hamadryas baboon; Grizzly bear; Asiatic black bear; Black rhinoceros; Others.

**McDonald, K.A., "U. of Arizona gets go-ahead to build its telescope on Mt. Graham as agencies rule out more study," *The Chronicle of Higher Education*, Sept. 5, 1990, p. A4.**

Discusses a decision by the U.S. Forest Service and the Agriculture and Justice Departments which ruled that the University of Arizona could begin construction of a controversial observatory on Mount Graham because a 1988 federal law specifically exempted the observatory from additional biological studies. Endangered Species Act; Transplanting criticized.

**Williams, T., "Waiting for wolves to howl in Yellowstone," *Audubon*, November 1990, p. 32.**

Examines the political reasons why wolves still have not been reintroduced to Yellowstone National Park (Wyoming, Montana, Idaho). National Park Service's duty to enforce the Endangered Species Act; Public support for reintroduction versus the attitudes of ranchers and politicians; Natural-fire policy controversy; Idaho Senator James McClure's bill; Political haggling over an environmental impact study; Hunters; Comments by Dick Mader, founder of the "Common Man Institute."

## Marine mammals

**Elmer-Dewitt, P., Dorfman, A., et al., "Are sharks becoming extinct?" *Time*, Mar. 4, 1991, p. 67.**

Details how commercial shark fishing has begun to threaten several species, including the thresher, mako and hammerhead. Marked decline which may become extinction; National Marine Fisheries Service (NMFS) management plan for the fishery; Jump in US catch; Fin-hunting and valuable meat; Vulnerability to fishing assault; Infant mortality rates; Vital role in ocean ecology; Immune systems.

## Reptiles

**Martin, J. & Wolfe, R., "The engaging habits of**

**chameleons suggest mirth more than menace," *Smithsonian*, June 1990, p. 44.**

Reports on chameleons, the color-changing lizards whose survival is threatened by loss of habitat in areas like Madagascar and Africa. Characteristics and habits of different species; Vulnerability and breeding in captivity; Toll of the pet trade; Research on chameleons; Ability to change color.

## Restoration

**Arrandale, T., "A new breed of zoo," *Sierra*, November/December 1990, p. 26.**

Examines the role of zoos in offering hope for the survival of endangered species with breeding programs to return healthy populations to natural habitats. Some conservationists call for saving expanses of human-free habitat instead of zoo programs; Zoos aid in public education; Simulated natural habitats.

**Cohn, J.P., "The new breeding ground," *National Parks*, January/February 1991, p. 20.**

Explains how zoo research and captive breeding programs are helping to save endangered species. The national parks provide sanctuary for the declining species zoos work with and a home for their reintroduction into the wild. Describes the black-footed ferret breeding program at the National Zoo (Washington, D.C.). Florida panthers; Red wolves.

**Griffith, B., Scott, J.M., et al., "Translocation as a species conservation tool: Status and strategy," *Science*, Aug. 4, 1989, p. 477.**

Examines several translocation efforts to establish, re-establish or augment a population of certain species. Factors associated with successful translocations; Evaluating alternative strategies; Enhancing the chances of success.

**Hinrichsen, D., Bomford, L., et al., "How Poland rescued Europe's largest mammal," *International Wildlife*, July/August 1990, p. 36.**

Recounts how Poland launched one of the world's first attempts to resurrect a species, the European Bison, already extinct in the wild by 1919. Today about 400 European bison live in the Polish and Soviet parts of Bialowieza Forest.

**Kleiman, D.G., "Reintroduction of captive mammals for conservation," *Bioscience*, March 1989, p. 152.**

Offers detailed guidelines for reintroducing endangered species into the wild. Conditions which will lead to successful reintroduction; Examples from recent reintroduction efforts; Habitat protection and restoration; Education and public relations.

# Back Issues

*Great Research on Current Issues Starts Right Here... Recent topics covered by The CQ Researcher are listed below. Issues dated before May 10, 1991, were published under the name of Editorial Research Reports.*

**DECEMBER 1989**
North America Trade Pact
Influence Peddling
German Reunification
Learning Disabilities

**JANUARY 1990**
Higher Education Curriculum
Photonics
Age of 'Infotainment'
Abortion: Politicians' Nightmare

**FEBRUARY 1990**
Politics and Economic Growth
Free Agency in Sports
Repetitive Motion
War on Drugs

**MARCH 1990**
Asbestos: Are Risks Acceptable?
Public Health Campaigns
South Africa's Future
Homeless Need More Than Shelter

**APRIL 1990**
How Fair is the Tax Burden?
Workers' Compensation
U.S. Pacific Forces
Curbing Insurance Premiums

**MAY 1990**
Should Teaching Be a Profession?
Will Canada Fall Apart?
Is U.S. Patent System Outdated?
Federal Funding for the Arts

**JUNE 1990**
Downsizing America's Armed Forces
Progress In Weather Forecasting
S & L Bailout
Bio-Chemical Disarmament

**JULY 1990**
Do Americans Still Love Marriage?
Death Penalty Debate
Decline of Rural America
United Nations in the 1990s

**AUGUST 1990**
Democracy in the Philippines
Initiatives: True Democracy?
Hard Times at Newspapers
Teens Balance School & Jobs

**SEPTEMBER 1990**
Dangers of Alcohol
Western Alliance After the Cold War
Tobacco Industry
Right to Die

**OCTOBER 1990**
Organ Transplants
Energy Policy Options
Search for Arab Unity
Child Support

**NOVEMBER 1990**
Lotteries and Gambling
Post Cold-War Choices
Setting Limits on Medical Care
Multicultural Education

**DECEMBER 1990**
Cable TV Regulation
Americans' Search For Their Roots
Is Insurance System a Failure?
Why Schools Still Have Tracking

**JANUARY 1991**
Growing Influence of Boycotts
Should the U.S. Reinstate the Draft?
America's Archaeological Past
Peace Corps' Challenges in '90s

**FEBRUARY 1991**
Regional Impact of Recession
Puerto Rico's Status
Redistricting: Mapping Power
Nuclear Power

**MARCH 1991**
Acid Rain
Cost of the Gulf War
Reassessing Gun Laws
Future for Man in Space

**APRIL 1991**
Social Security
Canadian Crisis Over Quebec
California Drought
Electromagnetic Radiation

**MAY 1991**
School Choice
Racial Quotas
Animal Rights
U.S. and Japan

**JUNE 1991**
Children and Divorce
Teenage Suicide

Back issues are available for $4.00 (subscribers) or $7.00 (non-subscribers). Quantity discounts apply to orders over ten. To order, call Congressional Quarterly 1-800-432-2250.

# Future Topics

► *Europe 1992 Update*

► *Parental Notification*

► *Soviet Nationalities*

# The CQ Researcher

PUBLISHED BY CONGRESSIONAL QUARTERLY INC., IN CONJUNCTION WITH EBSCO PUBLISHING

# Europe 1992

*The European Community faces new challenges to unification*

IN 1985 THE 12 MEMBERS OF THE EUROPEAN
Economic Community embarked on an ambitious path
to more fully integrate their economies by Dec. 31,
1992. The slogan "EC-92" quickly became a rallying cry
for member nations that were struggling with slow economic
growth and declining competitiveness. In the past six years,
the EC has made great progress in removing obstacles to
internal trade and it looks like the community will accomplish
most of its goals by the deadline. But new developments are
threatening the process of European integration. The nations
of Eastern and Central Europe have broken free from decades
of Soviet domination and they have joined other non-member
European countries in seeking closer ties with the European
Community. These developments also pose new challenges to
U.S. interests in Europe.

 **June 28, 1991 • Volume 1, No. 8 • 417-440**

*Formerly Editorial Research Reports*

COVER ART: BARBARA SASSA-DANIELS

# CQ Researcher

June 28, 1991
Volume 1, No. 8

**EDITOR**
Sandra Stencel

**ASSOCIATE EDITOR**
Richard L. Worsnop

**STAFF WRITERS**
Charles S. Clark
Mary H. Cooper
Rodman D. Griffin

**PRODUCTION EDITOR**
Laurie De Maris

**EDITORIAL ASSISTANT**
Thomas H. Moore

**GRAPHICS**
Jack Auldridge

**PUBLISHED BY**
Congressional Quarterly Inc.

**CHAIRMAN**
Andrew Barnes

**VICE CHAIRMAN**
Andrew P. Corty

**EDITOR AND PUBLISHER**
Neil Skene

**EXECUTIVE EDITOR**
Robert W. Merry

**PUBLICATIONS MARKETING/SALES**
Robert Smith

**EDITOR, EBSCO PUBLISHING**
Melissa Kummerer

The CQ Researcher (ISSN 1056-2036). Formerly Editorial Research Reports. Published weekly (48 times per year, excluding March 1, May 3, Aug. 2 and Nov. 1, 1991) by Congressional Quarterly Inc., 1414 22nd St., N.W., Washington, D.C. 20037. Rates are furnished upon request. Application to mail at second-class postage rates is pending at Washington, D.C. POSTMASTER: Send address changes to The CQ Researcher, 1414 22nd St., N.W., Washington, D.C. 20037.

# Europe 1992

BY MARY H. COOPER

## THE ISSUES

On Dec. 31, 1992, the 12 nations that make up the European Community (EC) will arrive at a milestone in the community's 35-year history.* That is the deadline the EC has set for removing all remaining barriers to free trade within the community. If this deadline is met, the EC will have moved one step closer toward the goal of European unity advanced by French economist and diplomat Jean Monnet and other European leaders after World War II.

The European Community began its program of market integration, popularly known as "EC-92," in 1985. At that time, the Far East, led by Japan, and North America, led by the United States, were consolidating their powers as regional trade blocs. The European Community, on the other hand, was bogged down by internal disputes and stagnant economic growth. Community leaders feared that unless Europe took immediate steps, it would fall even further behind the Far East and North America in the emerging world trade regime.

Since adopting its unification program, the community has accomplished many of its goals. Many barriers to cross-border trade have been eliminated or simplified. (*See table, p. 429.*) The prospect of heightened competition already has boosted economic activity in Western Europe. Companies doing business there, including U.S. multinationals and exporters, have taken steps to

improve their positions in the new market, producing an unprecedented number of mergers and acquisitions on the continent.

But recent events have created new challenges to the community's ability to shape Europe's future. Many of the challenges stem from the political and economic upheavals in Eastern Europe and the Soviet Union. With the fate of reform in the Soviet Union still uncertain, Eastern European nations are doing all they can to plant their feet firmly in the West. They are joining the ranks of other non-member European countries that would like to become part of the European Community.

For the architects of European unity at work at EC headquarters in Brussels, the calls for help from the East are sounding just when they expected to be putting the finishing touches on the EC-92 program. They believe the drive toward a barrier-free internal market must be completed before they can consider enlarging community membership.

The decisions the European Community makes about its future will almost certainly affect the United States. According to a recent report by the Congressional Budget Office, the efficiencies associated with the EC-92 program will "make the European Community a more formidable competitor in international trade." [1]

### Can the European Community accomplish what it has set out to do by the 1992 deadline?

A 1985 "white paper" drawn up by the Commission of the European Communities identified 300 barriers — later reduced to 282 — that stood in the way of full economic integration of the European Community. The commission set the deadline for achieving their removal and thus "completing the internal market" for Dec. 31, 1992. The commission then submitted its proposals to the European Community's Council of Ministers, which is responsible for enacting EC legislation. (*For a description of the duties of the commission and the Council of Ministers, see story, p. 421.*)

The Council of Ministers already has adopted two-thirds of the commission's proposals. Among the more significant directives the council has approved are: (1) elimination and simplification of customs and tax procedures on goods traded within the community; (2) deregulation of the transportation sector and (3) elimination of technical standards member states had adopted over the years to block imports and protect local industries.

But council adoption of the commission's proposals does not complete the legislative process. Each of the member governments also has to approve the directives and it is at this stage that the drive toward EC-92 has run into roadblocks.

---

* The 12 members of the European Community are Belgium, Britain, Denmark, France, Germany, Greece, Ireland, Italy, Luxembourg, the Netherlands, Portugal and Spain. See map, p. 424.

According to Don R. Wright at the U.S. Commerce Department's office of EC affairs, only 24 of the 184 directives the Council of Ministers had approved by the end of February had actually gone into effect in all 12 member countries. This delay, he emphasized, was not due to intentional obstruction but rather the lack of adequate administrative procedures to deal with the plethora of new rules coming out of Brussels.[2]

Most member states acted quickly to simplify customs formalities, a major impediment to the rapid transit of goods across borders. But they have fallen behind in removing certain technical barriers, especially the national product and certification standards that have forced manufacturers to make different products for different nations.

More administrative delays are likely in the future as the Council of Ministers begins work on some of the more controversial components of EC-92, particularly those that threaten the survival of domestic industries. For example, a heated dispute has arisen over a proposal to impose new standards for high-definition television (HDTV), an area in which European producers are far behind their competitors in the United States and Japan.[3] France, Germany and the Netherlands support the adoption of standards that would tend to keep out non-community HDTV technology and thus help their own struggling HDTV producers survive. But they are opposed by the governments of Britain, Denmark, Spain and other countries that have little or no domestic HDTV capability and are more interested in opening their consumer markets to non-EC products.

Gary Clyde Hufbauer, a professor of international financial diplomacy at Georgetown University's School of Foreign Service, singles out several other areas on which it will be especially hard to find agreement

among all 12 members. Tax rates are one example. Spain, which now has a 12 percent sales tax, opposes a recent proposal to set a 16 percent communitywide sales tax. Spain fears the four-point increase would fuel inflation at home.

Auto emissions and safety regulations also are sources of controversy. Some member states — primarily France and Italy — have fashioned their standards to protect domestic automakers. Changing the standards would make non-domestic autos much more competitive.

Those same national interests will make it hard for the community to agree on a common policy toward imports of products from outside the EC. There already are lively debates over Japanese automobiles and Third World textiles, both of which have been largely excluded from European markets in order to protect local producers.

Despite these difficulties, Hufbauer is optimistic that the European Community will meet most of its goals by the 1992 deadline. "The momentum seems to be in place to probably overcome these difficulties in the next year and a half," he says. Although he predicts the EC-92 program will probably spill over into 1993, Hufbauer expects the Council of Ministers will enter into a "nonstop negotiating session in the last quarter of 1992. It will get very electric, considering all those difficult decisions it will have to make."

### How is the peaceful revolution in Eastern Europe affecting the process of European integration?

Before 1989, the European Community was able to focus its unification efforts almost exclusively on the 12 existing member states. Since then, the world has witnessed the fall of communist governments throughout Eastern Europe and the desperate efforts of Soviet President Mikhail Gorbachev to integrate his

country's economy into the global market. As a result of these political changes, the European Community has broadened its concerns to include what Stephen L. Cooney Jr., director of international investment and finance for the National Association of Manufacturers, calls three circles of expanding relationships: the EC and its program of internal unification; the non-EC countries of Western Europe, including the six members of the European Free Trade Association (EFTA)*, another Western European trade group; and now Central and Eastern Europe.

"The old communist model is gone and discredited," Cooney says, "There is no longer a Europe of two models or multiple models, but a Europe with one driving engine, and that is the European Community. Everybody else is trying to figure out how best to hook up to it."

The European Community has long spoken of its unification efforts as a process of both "deepening and broadening" the community by improving market efficiency within its boundaries and adding new members. Today the focus is on "deepening" existing relations among the 12 current members by making the internal market more competitive. This is the goal of EC-92.

The "broadening" side of unification involves relations with the non-EC countries of Europe. This has been a secondary focus of community concern in recent years as some of these free-market, Western European nations have applied for association with the EC. The community has already doubled its membership since it was formed in 1957 and it has responded to the recent requests with a commitment to eventually add new members.

---

*EFTA includes Austria, Finland, Iceland, Norway, Sweden and Switzerland. EFTA also has an economic cooperation agreement with Yugoslavia.

# How the European Community Is Governed

The 12 countries that comprise the European Community (EC) are a highly diverse group. In terms of industrial development, they range from Germany, Europe's industrial powerhouse, to the largely agricultural economies of Portugal and Greece. EC citizens speak 11 different official languages and many more dialects, and they represent very different and often incompatible cultures. Uniting these conflicting interests is a bureaucracy based in Brussels, Luxembourg and France.

The **Commission of the European Communities**, based in Brussels, is the community's main administrative body. It ensures that all decisions and treaty provisions are implemented. The commission also has responsibility for proposing new policies. It was the commission, for example, that produced the 1985 white paper outlining the goals for market integration by Dec. 31, 1992.

There are 17 commissioners, who are appointed by EC member governments, subject to the approval of them all. Once appointed to their four-year terms, commissioners serve the community and act independently of their national governments. The commission is led by a president, appointed from among the commissioners to renewable two-year terms. The current president, Jacques Delors of France, has held office since January 1985.

The **Council of Ministers** meets twice a year in Brussels to enact the legislative proposals it receives from the commission. The 12 member nations usually send their foreign ministers to represent them on the council, but ministers of finance, agricultural affairs, transportation or other areas are sometimes sent instead when the council is discussing their areas of interest.

The council enacts legislation under a system of weighted voting that gives countries with larger populations more votes than smaller countries. Britain, Germany, France and Italy get 10 votes each. Spain gets eight votes, Belgium, Greece, the Netherlands and Portugal five each, Denmark and Ireland three each and Luxembourg two. A total of 54 votes out of the 76 constitutes a "qualified majority."

The **European Council**, made up of the 12 heads of government and the president of the European Commission, meets at least twice a year to discuss questions concerning the community and political cooperation among the member nations. It was created by the 1987 Single European Act.

The **European Parliament** is made up of 518 members who, since 1979, have been elected directly by universal suffrage. The members, who serve for five-year terms, are grouped by political affiliation rather than by nation. There are currently 11 groups, ranging across the political spectrum from the Group of the United European Left to the Technical Group of the European Right. The Socialist Group, with 180 members, and the Group of the European People's Party (Christian Democrats), with 121, are the largest.

The European Parliament has long served as a public forum in which the commission's proposals and the council's actions are subject to debate. The Parliament also can amend or reject the community's budget. The 1987 Single European Act granted the European Parliament greater legislative powers, including the power of assent to applications for membership in the community and association and cooperation agreements with non-member governments. The Parliament normally meets for one week each month in Strasbourg, France.

The **Court of Justice of the European Communities**, made up of 13 justices appointed and approved by the member governments, acts as the community's supreme court. Based in Luxembourg, the court interprets community laws. Its decisions are binding and they overrule judgments made by national courts.

The **Court of Auditors**, also based in Luxembourg, is responsible for auditing the community's general budget. The European Parliament uses the auditors' annual reports and other investigations in deciding whether to accept, amend or reject the community budgets.

---

The countries of the EFTA already are closely linked to the European Community through a reciprocal free-trade agreement. They also participate in organizations that are setting up common industrial standards for all of Europe. Since 1989, EFTA as a group has been negotiating with the EC to create a common "European Economic Area," which would have the effect of expanding the European Community without formally joining the two trade groups. The original goal was to complete these negotiations by the EC-92 deadline, but reluctance on the part of some of the EFTA countries to accept the sweeping deregulation that is part of the European Community's agenda may push this deadline later into the 1990s.

At the same time, individual members of EFTA are forging their own relations with the European Community. Austria has already applied for full membership. Sweden is expected to do so this summer, while the issue is the subject of discussions currently under way in Switzerland, Norway and Finland. Among non-EFTA members, Malta and Turkey have also applied to join the community. Of all the applicants, Austria appears to top the community's list for acceptance. But even Austria will have to wait until at least 1993. "The

EC has placed its priority on 1992," Andreas van Agt, head of the EC commission's delegation to the United States, explained at a recent forum in Washington.[4] "Countries that have already applied for full membership, such as Austria, can't be processed while the EC is engrossed in its deepening process."

If Austria, Sweden and other EFTA countries must wait at least two years to join the European Community, the delay will likely be much longer for the countries of Central and Eastern Europe. Until recently, most of the region was tied economically to the Soviet Union through the Council for Mutual Economic Assistance, or COMECON, the communist trade bloc that exchanged goods largely according to the dictates of Moscow. In this so-called command economic system, the nations of Eastern Europe — East Germany, Poland, Hungary, Czechoslovakia, Bulgaria and Romania — for 45 years conducted most of their trade within COMECON through a barter arrangement that shielded domestic industries and currencies from the rigors of the international marketplace dominated by the capitalist principles of free competition and trade.

Since 1989, however, the communist governments of Eastern Europe have fallen like dominoes, COMECON has virtually ceased to exist and the region's new, democratically elected governments have introduced painful economic reforms in an effort to open their economies to the world trading system. As the Soviet Union is embroiled in a tumultuous reform process of its own, Eastern Europe is looking to the West — and chiefly the European Community — as its lifeline to the future.

Over the longer term, the European Community supports the unification of all Europe, including the countries of Eastern Europe. "All of the former Soviet-dominated states in Central and Eastern Europe now regard the European Community as a safe haven, both politically and economically," Henning Christophersen, vice president of the EC commission, said at a recent seminar held by the Institute for International Economics.[5] "They wish to join the community because they are confident that we can protect their newly-won freedom and their newly-won democratic identity and because they view themselves a fully paid-up European nations, just like Belgium, Denmark or the United Kingdom. . . . In all these views, they are perfectly correct."

In an attempt to help these countries reform their economies to the point where they could gain admission to the community on an equal footing with the West, the community led an effort to set up the European Bank for Reconstruction and Development. Funded with $12 billion from 39 countries and two community organizations, the bank opened April 15 with a mandate to help Eastern Europe and the Soviet Union reform their economies.

To date, however, the only former East-bloc nation to join the European Community is East Germany. It did so by ceasing to exist Oct. 3, 1990, when Germany was reunified. As for the rest of the former East-bloc nations, the EC has adopted a wait-and-see attitude. "The community in its present structure isn't capable of absorbing a great number of new members," van Agt said. He added that the delay would not hurt the countries of Eastern Europe, "for they would not qualify for membership in the short term because of the state of their economies."

There is another reason for the European Community's reluctance to embrace the nations of Eastern Europe. With the future of reform in the Soviet Union still up in the air and the pain of economic and political change only now becoming apparent, the situation in Eastern Europe is unstable. Dismayed over the loss of services and jobs that is accompanying the shift from command to free markets, East Europeans are facing the prospect of even greater deprivation before the situation improves and many may try to move to the West. And last month the Soviet Union passed a law making it easier for Soviet citizens to emigrate.

All this makes Western Europe nervous. "There is a growing concern about immigration in Western Europe," van Agt said. "How can we face mass immigration from Eastern Europe, not to mention the Soviet Union?" Pointing to recent riots in Brussels by immigrants from North Africa, he added, "They are all heading for the land of milk and honey that many people think is Western Europe."

### How will EC-92 affect American business and America's trade balance?

When the European Commission made public its plan for removing all remaining barriers to trade within the community by the end of 1992, reactions in the United States were ambivalent. On the one hand, a more efficient economic environment in Europe would make it easier for highly competitive American firms to do business there. With fewer bureaucratic hassles to deal with, U.S. multinational corporations with subsidiaries in the EC welcomed the program as a way to improve their own access to European markets.

But U.S. exporters were less sanguine about their prospects in Europe. They feared that as the European Community tore down barriers to internal trade, it would throw up new ones to protect the unified market from outside competitors, creating a "Fortress Europe" that could only cut into the European sales of U.S. exporters.

# Trading Partners

*The European Community is the largest trading partner of the United States, taking 24 percent of total U.S. exports and providing 18 percent of U.S. imports. By way of comparison, Canada takes about 22 percent of U.S. exports and provides 19 percent of U.S. imports. Japan supplies 20 percent of U.S. imports, but takes only 12 percent of U.S. exports. The United States takes 19 percent of EC exports and provides 19 percent of EC imports.*

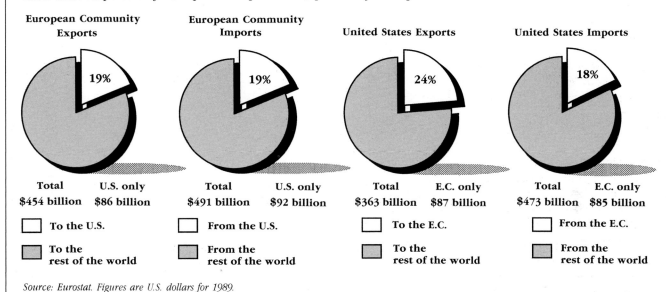

**European Community Exports**

19%

| Total | U.S. only |
|-------|-----------|
| $454 billion | $86 billion |

☐ To the U.S.
▨ To the rest of the world

**European Community Imports**

19%

| Total | U.S. only |
|-------|-----------|
| $491 billion | $92 billion |

☐ From the U.S.
▨ From the rest of the world

**United States Exports**

24%

| Total | E.C. only |
|-------|-----------|
| $363 billion | $87 billion |

☐ To the E.C.
▨ To the rest of the world

**United States Imports**

18%

| Total | E.C. only |
|-------|-----------|
| $473 billion | $85 billion |

☐ From the E.C.
▨ From the rest of the world

*Source: Eurostat. Figures are U.S. dollars for 1989.*

As EC-92 has progressed, however, those fears have greatly subsided. American exports have actually risen in recent years, reversing a downward trend in sales abroad that characterized most of the 1980s. According to the Office of the U.S. Trade Representative, the United States exported more than $98 billion worth of goods and services to the European Community in 1990, up 14 percent from the year before. It was the second straight year in which the United States enjoyed a trade surplus with the community.[6] Much of the rise in exports was due to the fall in value of the U.S. dollar. The cheaper dollar reduced the prices of U.S. goods sold overseas.

While fears of a Fortress Europe have subsided among many U.S. businesses, they have wasted little time in devising defensive strategies to deal with the changing economic environment they expect to face in 1993 and beyond. "Virtually every

company I've talked to has taken some kind of action," Cooney says, "and they've all come to different decisions."

According to surveys conducted by KPMG Peat Marwick, an international accounting firm, more than 80 percent of American companies are following events as they unfold in the community and are reviewing their positions in Europe.[7] Generally, this review is leading companies to try to increase their exports to European markets and to consider investing in firms already operating in the community or setting up production facilities there. Last year, for example, Ford Motor Co. acquired the British automaker Jaguar, Texas Instruments Inc. invested more than $1 billion to build semiconductor and calculator plants in Italy, and International Paper spent $300 million to buy out Aussedat Rey, a French paper producer.[8]

The EC Council of Ministers still

has to settle many issues of concern for U.S. businesses, such as the scope of banking deregulation and whether to allow free trade in financial services. Some manufacturers are also still in limbo. Mark Grayson, a spokesman for the Pharmaceutical Manufacturers Association, says his industry is worried about how EC-92 will affect the European market for drugs. "We don't know how they are going to regulate drugs, so for us none of the issues has been resolved," he says, even though American drug companies do not depend as much on exports as some other manufacturers because the biggest firms already have subsidiaries in Europe.

Like the big pharmaceutical companies, computer and business equipment manufacturers like International Business Machines Corp. already have production facilities in the EC. Their strategy has been to join forces with their European

# The 12 Members of the European Community at a Glance

| EC countries | Area (square miles) | Population (millions) | Projected Per capita GDP (US $) 1990 | Projected unemployment %, 1990 | Projected Trade Balance 1990 (US $ billions) |
|---|---|---|---|---|---|
| Germany | 137,755 | 78.3 | 24,003† | 6.4† | 65.4† |
| France | 211,207 | 56.4 | 17,019†† | 9.0 | - 14.8†† |
| United Kingdom | 94,249 | 57.4 | 11,755†† | 6.5†† | - 37.6†† |
| Italy | 116,303 | 57.7 | 14,990†† | 12.0†† | - 10.8†† |
| Netherlands | 13,103 | 15.0 | 14,887†† | 5.6†† | 2.6†† |
| Belgium | 11,781 | 9.9 | 17,375 | 8.8 | - 2.9 } |
| Luxembourg | 998 | 0.4 | 19,898‡ | 1.6†† | |
| Denmark | 16,629 | 5.1 | 22,368†† | 9.3†† | 3.1†† |
| Greece | 50,944 | 10.0 | 5,611 | 8.6 | - 9.5 |
| Ireland | 27,136 | 3.5 | 11,272 | 17.0 | 3.5 |
| Spain | 194,896 | 39.3 | 12,442 | 16.3 | - 37.0 |
| Portugal | 35,553 | 10.8 | 5,053 | 5.8 | - 5.2†† |

*GDP, gross domestic product, is the total value of goods and services produced by a country's domestic businesses.*
† *Excludes Eastern Germany.*
†† *1989 figures.*
‡ *1988 figures.*

Source: U.S. Department of Commerce.

counterparts to lobby the Council of Ministers for changes that will favor the industry as a whole. Mary Ann Karinch, a spokeswoman for the Computer and Business Equipment Manufacturers Association, says the reform process already has changed the way American computer firms do business in Europe. "We are becoming involved ... with our counterparts overseas to make our views on issues like standards, testing and insurance known and to make sure those directives reflect the views of industry," she says.

For American manufacturers as a whole, the outlook for EC-92 is distinctly positive. Companies generally see Europe 1992 "as something that is going to facilitate business rather than close it out," says Cooney of the National Association of Manufacturers. American manufacturers of capital goods — machine tools and other factory equipment — have fared especially well in the recent export boom. Cooney traces much of that performance to

rising investment in new factories in Europe spurred by EC-92.

Just as EC-92 presents both opportunities and pitfalls for U.S. business, so does the prospect of the community's expansion in coming years. "As [other countries] hook up to the EC, obviously that is going to expedite their development and expedite opportunities for U.S. companies," says Cooney. "The bad news is that practices that we object to in the EC will be shadowed to some degree in those countries. . . . To the degree that they want to get Common Market benefits, they have to play ball with the EC."

As individual companies have stepped up their lobbying efforts in Brussels, so, too, has the U.S. government. While the actual negotiations on EC-92 are conducted solely among representatives of the 12 member governments, the United States maintains a mission in Brussels with a staff of 45. "We make our voices heard in the commission ... if the negotiations affect external re-

lations," says David Michael Wilson, counselor for public affairs at the Brussels mission.

While he declined to comment on the thornier directives the community is still negotiating, Wilson says U.S. efforts have paid off in the past. For example, he says the second banking directive, approved two years ago, originally contained no provisions for reciprocal national treatment. That is, European governments were not required to grant the same privileges to U.S. bank subsidiaries in the community as their own bank subsidiaries received in the United States. "We managed to work with the community ... so that the legislation ended up being modified in a way that resulted in the community adopting the principle of reciprocal national treatment," Wilson says. "That worked out fine from our perspective."

While U.S. businesses and the U.S. mission to the European Community are focusing on EC-92, America's overall trade position with the European Community is being decided not in Brussels but in Geneva. There negotiators for the United States, members of the European Community and the other members of the General Agreement on Tariffs and Trade, or GATT, are trying to remove non-tariff barriers to global trade and bring trade in agriculture, services, intellectual property rights and investment under the rules of the multilateral trade agreement. Called the Uruguay Round of trade negotiations after the country where they began in 1986, these talks bogged down last December over the European Community's unwillingness to accept U.S.-supported cuts in the community's agricultural subsidies. Talks recently resumed in Geneva, but their outcome remains in doubt, largely because of the EC-U.S. dispute. ∎

# BACKGROUND

## EC's Postwar Origins

Long before the 1992 deadline was established, European statesmen had dreamed of political union on the continent. That vision was particularly strong in the mid-1940s after World War II.

To help rebuild the continent after the war, the United States stepped in with the Marshall Plan, a program of economic aid first proposed in 1947 by Secretary of State George C. Marshall. The same year, British Prime Minister Winston Churchill expressed a sense of dismay at Europe's apparent inability to determine its own political future. "Has Europe's mission come to an end?" Churchill asked. "Are the states of Europe to continue forever to squander the first fruits of their toil upon the erection of new barriers, military fortifications and tariff walls and passport networks against one another? Do we imagine that we can be carried forward indefinitely upon the shoulders — broad though they may be — of the United States of America?"

Churchill's exhortation expressed the desires of many European statesmen, including Jean Monnet of France and Konrad Adenauer of West Germany. They wished to rebuild Europe's economic and political structures in ways that would help unify the continent and overcome the divisive national interests that had precipitated both world wars.

Their goals were shared by the United States, which hoped that a united Europe would serve as a bulwark against Soviet expansion. On the economic front, the United States also looked with favor upon Western Europe's attempt to remove trade barriers. U.S. businesses were so dominant in world trade at the time that the potentially negative effects of European unification were outweighed by the promise of growing European demand for U.S. products that a more efficient market would bring.

The first concrete plan to reach this goal emerged on May 9, 1950, when French Foreign Minister Robert Schuman proposed the pooling of Europe's coal and steel industries. Schuman declared that "the gathering of the nations of Europe requires the elimination of the age-old opposition of France and Germany," and proposed the creation of a European authority to oversee these industries that were crucial to both the civilian and defense industries.

Schuman's plan led to the creation in 1951 of the European Coal and Steel Community (ECSC), which initially included Belgium, Italy, Luxembourg, the Netherlands, France and West Germany. Under the auspices of the ECSC High Authority, trade in coal and steel among the six signatory nations more than doubled within the next five years.[9]

The six members of the Coal and Steel Community tried soon thereafter to take a bigger step toward European unity by signing a common defense treaty and laying out plans for political union. But after the French Parliament rejected these attempts at military and political integration in 1954, the ECSC members decided instead to concentrate their efforts toward unification on the economic front.

Negotiations begun in June 1955 produced the Treaty of Rome that the six members signed in 1957. The treaty established two additional European communities: the European Economic Community (EEC) and the European Atomic Energy Community (Euratom). The EEC was designed to set up a regional free-trade area, or "common market," without barriers to the free movement of goods and services, capital and people among the six member countries. Euratom's goal was to pool their technological expertise to produce nuclear energy for peaceful purposes.

Although the three separate "communities" set up in the 1950s still exist, the EEC, commonly referred to as the European Community, or EC, is the one that has assumed the central role in the process of postwar European unification. Since the original six members signed the Treaty of Rome in 1957, the community's membership has doubled. Denmark, Ireland and the United Kingdom joined in 1973. Greece was accepted in 1981. Portugal and Spain joined in 1986, bringing the European Community to its current membership of 12 countries. With the unification of East and West Germany in October 1990, the five eastern states that had made up the German Democratic Republic enlarged

German participation in the community as well.

As the community's membership was broadened over the years, so too were the terms of cooperation among community members. The original six members took the first major step toward unifying their economies on Jan. 1, 1959, when they began eliminating customs duties imposed on each other's exports and set up a common tariff on imports from outside the community. This process was completed on July 1, 1968, when all customs duties on goods traded within the community were dropped. Three years later, they adopted the Common Agricultural Policy (CAP) to foster trade in agricultural products within the community and protect that market from foreign competition. The CAP policy consists of government subsidies aimed at supporting certain agricultural products to enable European farmers to sell them at competitive prices on world markets. It has emerged as one of the main bones of contention between the United States and the European Community.

A truly common market requires a common currency, and this has long been one of the European Community's central goals. But adopting a common currency requires member nations to cede authority over an essential power of sovereign nations, that of minting currency and setting monetary policy through a central bank. It was not until March 1979 that the community reached agreement on a less ambitious step toward monetary union and created the European Monetary System.

Instead of a currency to replace the British pound sterling, French franc and German mark, the community adopted a currency "basket" called the "European Currency Unit," or ECU. Each member nation's central bank uses the ECU to settle accounts with the other members' central banks. The central banks are also required to peg the value of their own currencies to the ECU so they fluctuate in value against the ECU only within an established range.

## Boom to Bust

Judging from trade statistics of the time, the Common Market was a huge success. Between 1958 and 1972, internal trade among the original six members grew from $6.8 billion to $60 billion.[10] But the member nations' rapid economic growth did not spring form the community's existence alone. While not all the countries of Western Europe progressed at the same rate, they all enjoyed to some degree the effects of the postwar boom. Fueled by U.S. assistance through the Marshall Plan and the release of pent-up demand for consumer goods and protected by the security structures of the North Atlantic Treaty Alliance (NATO), the economies of Western Europe grew rapidly during the 1950s and '60s.

America's gamble on improved business opportunities through a unified market in Europe also paid off. As demand for U.S. goods grew in the 1960s, large American manufacturers established multinational corporations as a less costly way to serve the European market than by shipping their products across the Atlantic. Automakers like Ford and General Motors Corp., followed by other U.S. manufacturers, began setting up factories in their major European markets, using mainly local labor to produce goods for sale in local markets.

Economic growth in Western Europe began to slow in the early 1970s. When the members of the Organization of Petroleum Exporting Countries (OPEC) pushed up energy prices in the the mid-'70s, inflation rose to double-digit levels. The resulting economic "stagflation" — characterized by high inflation, high interest rates and slow economic growth — heightened labor unrest across the continent. These domestic problems preoccupied the governments of community nations and slowed the momentum of European unification. At the same time, disagreements arose within the community over Britain's contributions to the EC budget and over the effects of agricultural subsidies.

The early 1980s marked the European Community's low point. The combination of inflation, high unemployment and high labor costs had undermined Western Europe's ability to compete on international markets with the United States and Japan, which was growing faster in economic clout than either of the other two regional giants. Meanwhile, the push toward European unity had stalled. In the place of tariffs on goods sold among community members, a plethora of non-tariff barriers had been thrown up to protect domestic markets. These included national technical standards for electrical and automotive components that served primarily to keep competitors' products off local markets. In the public eye, the postwar miracle had given way to "Euro-slcerosis," a kind of chronic progressive disease of the economy that seemed certain to leave Europe at a permanent disadvantage if nothing was done to correct it.

## Deadline Set for EC-92

Concerned by these developments, the community decided to make an effort to restore the momentum toward European unification that had emerged in the early postwar

Continued on p. 428

# Chronology

**1950s** *Fearful that uncontrolled competition among European countries could lead to a third world war, the leading nations of Western Europe strive to coordinate their economic policies.*

### April 18, 1951
France, West Germany, Belgium, Italy, Luxembourg and the Netherlands set up the European Coal and Steel Community pooling their coal and steel industries.

### March 25, 1957
The same six countries sign the Treaty of Rome establishing the European Economic Community and the European Atomic Energy Community.

**1960s** *The postwar economic miracle facilitates the process of European integration.*

### July 1, 1968
All customs duties on goods traded within the European Community are lifted and a common tariff on imports to the community goes into force.

**1970s** *"Eurosclerosis" sets in with sluggish economic growth in Western Europe.*

### Jan. 1, 1973
Denmark, Ireland and the United Kingdom join the European Community. Norway's electorate rejected their country's admission to the EC in a referendum three months earlier.

### March 13, 1979
European Monetary System (EMS), a system for regulating exchange rates within the European Community, enters into force. The same year, the first direct elections are held for the European Parliament.

**1980s** *Growing competition from East Asia and North America encourages the European Community to take unprecedented steps to unify its markets.*

### Jan. 1, 1981
Greece becomes a member of the European Community.

### June 29, 1985
The European Commission issues *Completing the Internal Market*, a blueprint for economic integration among the 12 community members to be completed by Dec. 31, 1992. The same year the community adopts the Single European Act enhancing the powers of the European Parliament and introducing a series of reforms aimed at achieving political and monetary union as well.

### Jan. 1, 1986
Portugal and Spain join the EC.

### July 1, 1987
The Single European Act, which amends the EC treaties to give the European Parliament greater power, goes into effect.

**1990s** *The European Community moves closer to its goal of market integration and begins the process of political and monetary union.*

### October 1990
Britain links the pound sterling to the EC's Exchange-Rate Mechahnism (ERM), eroding longstanding British opposition to monetary union with the community. German reunification on Oct. 3 brings the states of eastern Germany into the European Community.

### April 15, 1991
European Bank for Reconstruction and Development (EBRD), a multilateral financial institution set up to facilitate East Europe's transition to a market economy, opens in London.

### Dec. 31, 1992
Deadline for completion of the single market among the 12 member nations of the European Economic Community, known popularly as "EC-92."

### 1994
Target date for the creation of a European central bank which initially would take over monetary policy from the member governments and hold all foreign exchange reserves for the community. The bank would later issue all currency, first in national currency denominations, to be replaced later with European Currency Units or ECU.

Continued from p. 426

period. In 1985, a committee led by Lord Cockfield of Britain issued a white paper outlining the steps that were required to remove the remaining obstacles to economic integration and setting a deadline of Dec. 31, 1992, for their removal.[11]

The white paper identified three types of barriers to internal trade in the EC: physical, technical and fiscal. Although tariffs and restrictions on the number of goods imported into member countries had been largely eliminated in the 1960s, physical barriers remained, chiefly in the form of customs and immigration controls. Technical barriers posed even greater obstacles to intra-community trade. Each country had its own list of technical specifications for every kind of consumer product imaginable as well as safety standards, so that manufacturers often had to alter their products for export to other community nations. Philips N.V., the Dutch electronics firm, for example, had to produce seven different types of television sets incorporating different plugs, semiconductors and tuners to sell to its 12 EC partners.[12]

National licensing systems and public procurement practices constituted another kind of technical barrier to trade inside the community. Procurement of telecommunications equipment, military hardware and other goods and services purchased by governments has been almost exclusively directed to domestic firms. At the same time, licensing procedures have been skewed to benefit domestic interests and close out other community providers of such services as airline service and telecommunications and to prevent the immigration of professional workers from other member countries.

The third category of barriers the white paper addressed were the difficulties faced by exporters because of differences in the kinds and rates of taxes collected by member governments. Many EC members, for example, in the 1980s adopted the value-added tax, or VAT, an indirect tax on the consumption of goods and services that is applied at each point in the chain of production and distribution. Each country sets its

> **The most dramatic moment of Eastern Europe's peaceful revolution occurred on Nov. 9, 1989, when East Berliners tore down the Berlin Wall, which had stood for more than two decades as the main symbol of Europe's division.**

own tax rates for the VAT and for excise taxes, creating a paperwork nightmare for exporters within the community.

To garner support for the community's ambitious new agenda, the commission published another study in 1988, known as the Cecchini report, that predicted the removal of trade barriers set forward in the white paper would raise economic output in the member nations by around 5 percent, create almost 2 million new jobs and reduce inflation. The report also quantified the costs of existing barriers to community trade. For example, it set the cost of delays at national borders, where in some cases trucks are held up for days at a time, at $10 billion a year.[13]

Even before the report was published, supporters of a renewed effort to complete the Common Market set to work to jump-start the unification process. They met with surprising success in gaining the support of member nations, which agreed to revise the Treaty of Rome to permit far more economic and political unity than had been envisioned in the past. With the Single European Act, community members adopted a series of reforms "to transform relations as a whole among their States into a European Union...." The act, which took effect July 1, 1987, conferred greater legislative powers to the European Parliament (*see story, p. 421*). It also stipulates that only a qualified majority* is needed to enact directives aimed at creating a unified market, so that no single member state can hold up the process.

### New Life for the EC

As the campaign for EC-92 took off during the closing years of the 1980s, Eurosclerosis became a thing of the past. Under the strong leadership of Commission President Jacques Delors, the unification process has been enhanced by other measures. Responding to the fears of the community's poorer members, whose industries have enjoyed especially strong government support, the Council of Ministers in 1988 agreed to double the community's funding aimed at helping these weaker economies sustain the intense competition EC-92 is expected to unleash. As a result, the less industrially advanced countries, such as Portugal and Greece, will receive special funding from their wealthier partners to help them adjust to the changing competitive environment.

Another initiative that helped

Continued on p. 430

---

*Countries with larger populations, such as West Germany and Britain, have more votes than smaller ones such as Portugal and Luxembourg.

# 1992 At a Glance

The European Council has adopted about two-thirds of the 282 regulations it plans to put into place by Dec. 31, 1992, in order to remove all remaining barriers to trade among the European Community's 12 member states. The following chart lists some of the most significant elements of the EC-92 program, grouped by type and status. Except where noted, the new rules "harmonize," or make identical, divergent national rules and standards among the member states.

## ADOPTED OR MOSTLY ADOPTED

### Product standards, testing and certification

Simple pressure vessels
Toys
Construction products
Tractors
Machine safety
Cosmetics
Quick frozen foods
Flavorings
Food emulsifiers, preservatives
 and additives
Jams and fruit juices
Food inspection
Definition of spirits and
 aromatic wines
Coffee extracts
Materials and articles
 in contact with food
Noise levels for tower cranes,
 household appliances, hydraulic
 diggers and lawn mowers
Tire pressure gauges
Detergents
Radio interference
Automobiles, trucks,
 motorcycles and emissions
Fertilizers
Lifting and loading equipment
Measuring instruments
Gas appliances
Telecommunications
Earthmoving equipment
Medicinal products and
 medical specialties
Personal protection equipment

### Packing, labeling and processing requirements

Food and beverage ingredients
Irradiation
Nutritional labeling
Dangerous preparations packaging
 and labeling

### Government Procurement

Coordination of procedures for award
 of public works and supply contracts
Extension of EC law to
 telecommunications,
 utilities services

### Services

Mutual funds
Broadcasting
Tourism
Air transport
Electronic payment cards
Information services
Life and other insurance
Banking
Securities
Maritime transport
Road passenger transport

### Liberalization of capital movements

Long-term capital, stocks
Short-term capital

### Consumer protection regulations

Misleading definitions of products
Price indications

### Corporate conduct laws

Trademarks
Cross-border accounting operations

### Customs practices

Single Administrative Document for
 intra-EC trade
Customs presentation charges
 abolished
Customs formalities eliminated

### Free movement of EC professional and workers

Higher education diplomas recognized
Vocational training qualifications

Training for general medical practice
Training for engineers
Activities in field of pharmacy
Commercial agents' activities

## PROPOSED OR DUE TO BE PROPOSED

### Product standards, testing and certification

Global approach to testing and
 certification
Medical devices
Infant formula

### Packing, labeling and processing requirements

Extraction solvents

### Government Procurement

Extension of EC law to transport
 services

### Services

Railways

### Taxation

Value-added taxes
Excise taxes

### Corporate conduct laws

Protection of computer programs
Transaction taxes
Company law
Mergers and acquisitions
Copyrights
Cross-border mergers
Bankruptcy

### Free movement of EC professional and workers

Income taxation
Elimination of residence
 permit requirements

*Source: Don R. Wright, "The EC Single Market in 1991 — Status Report," Business America, Feb. 25, 1991.*

Continued from p. 428

push the community toward its 1992 deadline was the adoption of the principle of mutual recognition of standards, certification and testing. Under this principle, member governments can no longer disallow the importation of goods from other community nations if those goods meet the standards of the country where they were produced. The principle of mutual recognition changed the rules of the game for doing business in Europe.

As corporate leaders came to terms with the changing environment, they began to take steps to adapt. An unprecedented wave of cross-border mergers and acquisitions appeared in the late 1980s, as strong companies bought out their competitors in other countries, smaller firms sought partners to strengthen their competitive presence and makers of specialized products tried to enhance their edge in niche markets throughout the community.

Many of the white paper proposals were adopted quickly. Before the end of the 1980s, the community had "harmonized" standards for a wide range of goods, including toys, cosmetics, many food products, motor vehicles and their emissions, as well as noise levels for household appliances and construction cranes. (*See table, p. 429.*) It had also harmonized many health regulations, some VAT rates, rules on misleading consumer product information and rules governing the provision of certain services, including air transport, electronic payment cards and tourism. Customs formalities and paperwork at national borders were eliminated or simplified.

At the same time the 12 members of the European Community were agreeing to measures that promised to improve their economic conditions, a peaceful revolution was building in the Soviet Union that promised to relax the East-West ten-

sions that had dominated the continent since the end of World War II. The rise to power of Soviet leader Mikhail S. Gorbachev in 1985 was followed by a series of diplomatic initiatives from Moscow that resulted in new agreements to reduce nuclear and conventional forces in Europe. Gorbachev also signaled a new Soviet desire to make political and economic reforms necessary to integrate the country more fully into the global trade system.

What began as a Soviet diplomatic initiative quickly became a mass movement for political and economic reform throughout the Soviet

Union and its military and trade allies of Eastern Europe. Demands for democratization spilled into the streets throughout Eastern Europe, where communist administrations were overthrown and replaced by freely elected parliamentary governments. The most dramatic moment of Eastern Europe's peaceful revolution occurred on Nov. 9, 1989, when East Berliners tore down the Berlin Wall, which had stood for more than two decades as the main symbol of Europe's division. A new sense of optimism swept Western Europe. Eurosclerosis had been transformed in only a few years into Europhoria.■

# CURRENT SITUATION

## New Realities

The peaceful revolution in Eastern Europe that paved the way for German reunification was greeted enthusiastically throughout Europe as it unfolded in 1989. With the incorporation into western Germany of the five eastern *Länder*, or states, that had made up the German Democratic Republic, the European Community gained more territory, consumers and the most advanced industrial base in Eastern Europe. But as the costs of reunification began to mount, its luster began to fade. German Chancellor Helmut Kohl, lauded as a national hero when Germany was reunited last October, was greeted with rotten vegetables and protests when he visited industrial centers in the eastern region of his country in April.

Germany, which last year surpassed the United States as the world's leading exporter, is the un-

disputed locomotive of the European Community. But the costs of reunification are distracting the German government from its leadership role just when that leadership is most needed to push through the remaining elements of EC-92.

This year alone, the German government is expected to invest $58 billion in the eastern region to help dismantle the old state-run economy and privatize industry. In addition, Germany has committed $50 billion for investment in the Soviet Union and Eastern Europe, more than any other Western nation.

Germany is not the only country in the EC to experience a slowdown in economic activity. In its most recent outlook, published May 22, the European Commission predicted that economic growth throughout the community will reach a mere 1.25 percent this year, down 50 percent from 1990. Unemployment is expected to reach 8.8 percent this year and 9.25 percent in 1992.

The rise in oil prices and subsequent fall in business and consumer confidence that accompanied the war in the Persian Gulf explain part of Europe's economic slowdown. The recession in the United States and the dollar's low value also make it hard for European exporters to sell their products in the U.S. market. The jobless ranks are expanding in several EC countries, including Italy and the Netherlands, where EC-92 is already causing a shakeout in the manufacturing sector that has shut down inefficient businesses. In Britain, whose economy is actually contracting, unemployment may exceed 10 percent next year.[14]

### Talks on Political and Monetary Union

While the European Community works toward meeting its deadline for EC-92, it has launched two new initiatives that go far beyond the goal of completing the internal market. Last Dec. 15, Jacques Delors, president of the European Commission, launched two separate conferences, one to achieve political union within the community, the other to achieve economic and monetary union with the ultimate goal of establishing a single European central bank authorized to coin a single currency for the entire community. The commission set a tentative deadline for both political and monetary union for the mid-1990s.

The political and monetary conferences mark a milestone in the community's history, for they signal a new willingness on the part of its members to at least discuss giving up major elements of national sovereignty. Only a month before, the most vociferous opponent of such concessions to the notion of European unity, British Prime Minister Margaret Thatcher, resigned her office after her objections to the plans for monetary union were overridden by the other community members.

While still skeptical about the prospects for political and monetary unity, Thatcher's successor, John Major, has proved far more supportive of the commission's efforts to press forward toward these goals. He pro-

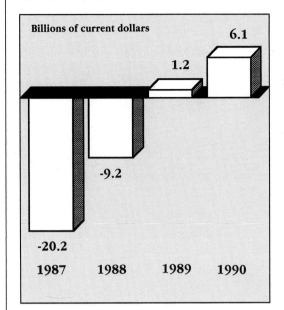

## U.S.-EC Trade Balance

Billions of current dollars

6.1
1.2
-9.2
-20.2

1987    1988    1989    1990

*The balance of U.S.-EC trade has gone through roughly three phases: The first one from the 1950s until the early 1980s was characterized by a chronic EC deficit. The second phase, from 1984 to 1988, was characterized by a U.S. deficit. Since 1989, as the dollar's value has weakened, the U.S. has enjoyed a growing trade surplus with the European Community. The weaker dollar has made American exports more attractive to European consumers.*

Sources: U.S. Department of Commerce; Office of the U.S. Trade Representative.

poses that before going to full monetary union the community temporarily adopt a "parallel currency" that member nations could use at will.

For now, the conferences on political and monetary union are taking a back seat to EC-92 and the more immediate challenges posed by economic reform in Eastern Europe. "I would say that the political and monetary conferences are useful forward momentum, but they're sort of a distraction from the really tough work," says Gary Clyde Hufbauer. In contrast to the hard negotiations that await community members before December 1992, he says, "they occupy a kind of high, lofty level of things that don't really concern the man in the street or the company in the street."

## Aid to Eastern Europe

More pressing, Hufbauer says, is the clamor among other European nations, including those of

Eastern Europe, to join the community. As close neighbors to the Soviet Union's former allies, the European Community has a special stake in the region's peaceful transition to a free-market economy and absorption into the rest of Europe. Hufbauer foresees tough bargaining with these countries over access to community markets of farm produce, such as pork products from Poland. "But my guess is that they will deal with such complications by simply postponing any meaningful talks," he says.

For now, the European Community is elaborating a plan for closer "association" of Eastern European countries to its market that would go beyond existing bilateral free-trade agreements between the community and the single nations of the region. The association agreements now being drawn up also call for industrial, technical and scientific cooperation, long-term financial assistance and negotiations on political issues. "Implementing these agreements will help bring their economies up to the level of competition of the West," says Andreas van Agt. For its part, the EC Council has agreed to eliminate tariffs on steel and textile imports from Eastern Europe by 1996.

In the long run, the European Community has a bigger financial stake in Eastern Europe than the United States does. But it is pressing the United States to be more forthcoming in assisting the region to make the difficult transformation to a free-market economic system, arguing that the region's peaceful integration into the rest of Europe is essential to global stability.

Van Agt points out that 78 percent of the ECU 23 billion ($37 billion as of June 10) pledged so far to assist Eastern Europe has come from the European Community. An additional ECU 25 billion ($40 billion) are needed, he says, between now and the end of 1992. "If the West were to provide $20 billion to Central and Eastern Europe and $30 billion to the Soviet Union each year, this would be less than 10 percent of their defense expenditures and less than half of 1 percent of our gross national product," he says.

The Bush administration makes a clearer distinction than does the EC between the reform efforts under way in the Soviet Union and those of its former allies in Central and Eastern Europe. The administration approved $369.7 million in direct foreign aid to Eastern Europe in 1991 and contributed $70 million to the European Bank for Reconstruction and Development.

Aid to the Soviet Union, however, is a far more controversial subject. Recently, however, the Bush administration has softened its opposition to providing trade concessions to the Soviets until they introduce more significant reforms to their economic system and pay off more of their mushrooming foreign debt. Earlier this month, Bush extended

trade benefits and approved $1.5 billion in credit guarantees to enable the Soviets to purchase U.S. grain. He also reversed his earlier opposition to Gorbachev's request to meet in July with the top industrial nations' leaders when they attend their annual economic summit.*

Differences over aid to Eastern Europe and the Soviet Union are only one area of concern for U.S. policymakers dealing with EC relations. Earlier this year, the Bush administration and members of Congress were highly critical of what they saw as the community's belated and inadequate response to U.S. requests for help in the Persian Gulf War.

---

*The leaders of Britain, Canada, France, Germany, Italy, Japan and the United States — the so-called G-7 — will meet July 15-17 in London.

Their criticism was aimed primarily at Germany, which has come under fire in Washington for failing to assume a degree of responsibility in global security matters commensurate with its overwhelming economic clout within the EC. German Chancellor Kohl also faces the reproach of official Washington for failing to lower German interest rates, a step his critics say would help bring Europe out of the current recession — and fuel demand for U.S. exports to the community. During a visit to Washington in May, Kohl deflected both U.S. complaints of German policy. He defended the German central bank's high interest rate policy as necessary to contain inflation, and he pointed to recent efforts to develop an independent defense policy under the auspices of the European Community. ∎

# OUTLOOK

## Japan's Challenge

Since 1989, the most apparent challenge to the European Community's ability to complete its internal market by the Dec. 31, 1992, deadline has been the rapid pace of change in Eastern Europe and the Soviet Union. As long as the peaceful revolution in the former East bloc continues, the community will face only an unanticipated financial drain as it extends economic assistance to its neighbors to the east. In the long run, the community stands to gain from closer association with the region, which it sees as part of its own area of eventual unification. "It is in our self-interest to provide avenues of development to Central and Eastern Europe," says Andreas van Agt. "The EC will continue its march to unification and open its doors to

all of Europe."

But while the community has been focusing its attention on EC-92 and the eventual enlargement of its area, Japan has been making impressive inroads into the community that are only now being fully recognized. European governments have long protected domestic industry from the onslaught of high-quality Japanese consumer products that overran the U.S. market in the 1970s and '80s. But EC-92 promises to break down some of the barriers that have kept the Japanese out of Europe for so long. Under the EC-92 directives, countries like Italy and France, which have imposed strict quotas on Japanese autos and VCRs, for example, will be forced to bring their quotas closer in line with countries like Britain that have maintained less stringent barriers to Japanese products.

But the Japanese are not simply awaiting the easing of export re-

*Continued on p. 434*

# At Issue:

## Does the European Community have a definite role to play in the new world order?

### yes

**JACQUES DELORS**

**President of the Commission of the European Communities**
FROM *FOREIGN POLICY*, FALL 1990.

*t*he European Community is not simply a fruit of the Cold War, and so must not die with the Cold War's end. It is the fruit of an ideal that was alive even in the last century, that was carried forward by a growing minority of politicians, that found institutional expression after the war, and that remains very much alive today. Were it not alive we would never have made such progress in the face of so many pessimistic predictions.

The countries of Europe can cooperate in several ways even though the level of ambition and the search for essential common interests are not viewed in the same way by every country. Similarly, several forms of cooperation are possible with and within the other regional groupings in the world. The growth of these groupings, which are motivated by the same type of issues that inspired and necessitated the EC, shows that the world is in a process of reorganization.

Only through sharing the burden can global problems be addressed and can the EC itself continue to gain influence. This will be done primarily through the reorganization of the world economy. And as long as the member states of the European Community do not agree on the direction of this reorganization, progress will be stalled. Whatever progress has been made in recent years, the world economic system is still unjust, and therefore inefficient. . . .

[T]he organization of the EC, in particular its federal structure, remains an idea full of possibilities.

A federal Community is not an idea of the past, but of the future. It is perfectly compatible with accepting the global responsibilities I mentioned above.

History has not rendered it obsolete. After all, the Community was not simply a product of the Cold War; and the federal approach has demonstrated its value, as seen in the efficiency of the Community's organization in comparison to organizations established purely on an intergovernmental basis. The Community's experience has shown that it can reconcile the union of people and the closer association of nations. Jean Monnet used to say that it was a question above all of uniting people. Today, with the perspective of realism, I would add, "and of bringing nations together."

### no

**JEANE J. KIRKPATRICK**

**Director of international programs, American Enterprise Institute for Public Policy Research**
FROM *THE WASHINGTON POST*, MAY 13, 1991.

*n*ot so long ago, it seemed to many that then-Prime Minister Margaret Thatcher of Britain was the principal obstacle to construction of a federal union of the European Community's 12 member states. In Brussels today, those must seem like the good old days.

This is a time of trouble for the EC. The gulf war was the first test of the community's capacity to forge a common foreign and military policy. It flunked. The very effort revealed that there is no common European diplomacy or military policy because there are no foreign policy views shared by all members. In addition, there are no shared military forces — nor will there be in the foreseeable future. . . .

In a divided Europe, the European Community united democracies of the West against the dictatorships of the East. It was NATO against the Warsaw Pact, translated into the political and economic spheres. Once the people of eastern Europe were free to choose their own governments, they chose democracy. Once they were free to choose their own associations, they chose the European Community.

Their desire for membership puts heavy moral and political pressure on EC members. Will they turn away the new democracies, whose economic and political development is so vital in the long term to the continent? Dare they?

The very thought of admitting eastern [European countries] brings opposition from those who, like Portugal, Spain and Greece, fear that poor eastern European countries would divert EC funds that might otherwise go to its own poorest members — Portugal, Spain and Greece. It arouses opposition as well form ardent "Euro federalists" who are convinced that "widening" membership before "deepening" it would weaken already weak ties within the community. . . .

Today, the most important questions about the European Community remain open — its powers, members, borders and relations with others are not decided. In fact, the EC was an important product of the old world order. Can it survive the end of the era in which it was born?

*Continued from p. 432*

straints that EC-92 is likely to bring. Japanese manufacturers of automobiles, computers and myriad other products are investing heavily in Europe to set up production facilities inside the community. As of April, they had spent $54 billion in new factories and acquisitions of European companies, such as Fujitsu's buyout of ICL, Britain's only computer manufacturer and NEC's attempt to acquire part of Groupe Bull, France's large computer conglomerate.[15]

While some European governments see less reason for alarm — Britain is home to many Japanese subsidiaries — France is sounding the clarion call for the community to shut out the Japanese before it is too late. On May 15, French President François Mitterrand chose as the new French prime minister Edith Cresson, a longstanding critic of Japanese policy and supporter of protectionist policies to keep Japanese financial interests out of Europe. She has accused the Japanese of trying to take over the continent and calls for defensive action by the European Community, including the creation of an industrial policy to protect domestic high-tech industry and other sectors that are vulnerable to Japanese competition. She has already created a new "super-ministry" in France to coordinate policy in telecommunications, finance, foreign trade and industry.

## Bottom Line for the U.S.

It is too soon to tell whether Cresson's militantly protectionist policy toward Japan will spill over into the European Community's relations with the United States and reignite fears in this country that EC-92 may ultimately produce a Fortress Europe. Barring a drastic change in

approach, European integration is not expected to have a major impact on the health of the U.S. economy. According to the Congressional Budget Office, "large overall effects on the economy of the United States are unlikely."[16]

For the present, American firms are busy dealing with the changes due to take effect Jan. 1, 1993, or soon thereafter. And the most prescient of these, says Steve Cooney of the National Association of Manufacturers, are adopting innovative strategies to deal with an increasingly complex global trading system that will be dominated by three major trade blocs: North America, where the existing U.S.-Canadian free-trade area may soon be expanded to include Mexico; the European Community, which may eventually include Eastern Europe; and the Far East, a less formally structured trade area dominated by Japan.

In this emerging trade system, Cooney says, the multinational corporation is no longer an adequate vehicle for companies to penetrate overseas markets. "The old approach by which you invest in a market in order to jump the tariff wall to produce and sell in that market alone is going the way of the dodo in most companies," he says. "You have to have an integrated presence in each of these three areas." That may mean setting up facilities to make some components in one trade area that will be shipped to another area for assembly with other components for final sale to all three areas. The need for U.S. companies to adjust to this new trade system will persist, whether the European Community meets its deadline for reform or not.■

## Notes

[1] Congressional Budget Office, *How the Economic Transformations in Europe Will Affect the United States*, December 1990, p. xi.

[2] Dixon R. Wright, "The EC Single Market in 1991 — Status Report," *Business America*, Feb. 25, 1991.

[3] For background information on high-definition television, see Patrick G. Marshall, "A High-Tech, High-Stakes HDTV Gamble," *Editorial Research Reports*, Feb. 17, 1989, pp. 89-104.

[4] Van Agt spoke at a seminar on the outlook for Central and Eastern Europe held May 21, 1991, at the Brookings Institution.

[5] Christophersen, a former deputy prime minister of Denmark, is responsible for economic and financial affairs in the European Commission. He addressed a seminar titled "Europe toward Year 2000" held April 29, 1991, in Washington.

[6] See Office of the U.S. Trade Representative, *1991 Trade Policy Agenda and 1990 Annual Report of the President of the United States on the Trade Agreements Program*, pp. 25-29.

[7] KPMG Peat Marwick, *The New Europe*, 1990, and *EC 1992: Strategic Implications for American Business*, 1989.

[8] See "America's New Rush to Europe," *Business Week*, March 26, 1990, pp. 48-49.

[9] *A Guide to the European Community*, EC Delegation to the United States, 1991, p. 3.

[10] *Ibid*, p. 10.

[11] E.C. Commission, *Completing the Internal Market: White Paper from the Commission to the European Council*, 1985.

[12] See Gary Clyde Hufbauer, ed., *Europe 1992: An American Perspective*, 1990, p. 6.

[13] Paolo Cecchini *et al.*, *The European Challenge 1992: The Benefits of a Single Market*, 1988.

[14] See Amy Kaslow, "Visiting Experts Describe European Scene," *The Christian Science Monitor*, May 30, 1991.

[15] See "The Battle for Europe," *Business Week*, June 3, 1991, pp. 44-52.

[16] Congressional Budget Office, *op. cit.*, p. 9.

# Bibliography

## Selected Sources Used

## Books

**Burstein, Daniel, *Euroquake*, Simon & Schuster, 1991.**

The author examines the repercussions of economic integration in Western Europe scheduled to take place at the end of next year with completion of the single market within the 12-nation European Economic Community (EEC). He emphasizes the leading role that Germany will play in the unified market but predicts that Germany's economic clout will not be matched by an equivalent strength in political cohesiveness, which is being undermined by the difficulty of incorporating eastern Germany.

**Freney, Michael A., and Hartley, Rebecca S., *United Germany and the United States*, National Planning Association, 1991.**

U.S.-German relations are changing following the reunification of East and West Germany last year. Burdened by the cost of integrating the formerly communist eastern states into the rest of the country's booming market economy, Germany is resisting pressure from the United States to bring down high interest rates and support U.S. foreign policy objectives as enthusiastically as the Bush administration would like. Likewise, Germany's role as the lead economy in the European Economic Community is being undermined by the high cost of the unification process.

**Hufbauer, Gary Clyde, ed., *Europe 1992: An American Perspective*, The Brookings Institution, 1990.**

Hufbauer traces the history of the European Community's program for unification. The book also contains detailed analyses of the program's potential impact on various sectors of American industry, including banking, automobiles, telecommunications and semiconductors, all of which are vulnerable to protectionist policies the EC Council is currently considering.

## Articles

**Richman, Louis S., "Managing for a Second Miracle," *Fortune*, April 22, 1991, pp. 221-226.**

Integrating what was once East Germany into the German economy is proving more difficult than expected. Although it boasted the most advanced industrial base in Eastern Europe, the region's factories are burdened with obsolete equipment and poor productivity. The German government has set about liquidating inefficient industrial conglomerates and retraining workers.

## Reports and Studies

**Central Intelligence Agency, *Eastern Europe: Coming Around the First Turn*, Report to the Technology and National Security Subcommittee of the Joint Economic Committee, U.S. Congress, May 16, 1991.**

The CIA reports that Eastern Europe faces an even more difficult series of reforms in 1991 than it did last year, including the elimination of price subsidies and centralized economic planning that were essential to the region's command economies while under Soviet control. The United States and Western European countries, led by the European Community, have already provided or pledged almost 45 billion in assistance to the region.

**Congressional Budget Office, *How the Economic Transformations in Europe Will Affect the United States*, December 1990.**

Although the European Community's program to unify its internal market by 1992 is expected to have a "modest" impact on U.S. international output and trade, broader changes now taking place on the continent may have a far bigger effect. Economic reform in Eastern Europe designed to bring the region into the world trading system and Germany's absorption of the former German Democratic Republic, together with EC-92, "could have significant effects on particular industries and sectors in the United States," CBO reports. U.S. firms with a presence in the EC stand the best chance of benefiting from the changes.

**Cooney, Stephen, *EC-92: New Issues and New Developments*, National Association of Manufacturers, April 1991.**

Cooney, director of international investment and finance at NAM, outlines the progress made by the European Community as it nears its goal of unifying the internal market by the end of 1992. He emphasizes the uncertainties on the final outcome of this process by the interest among other European countries in joining the EC and the community's recent drive to unify its political and monetary structures as well.

**Office of European Community Affairs, *A Guide to the European Community*, 1991.**

This recently published description of the community and its institutions encompasses the latest developments in the drive toward political and monetary union. The guide also examines the state of relations with the Soviet Union and Eastern Europe and focuses on statements of support from the Bush administration for unification.

# The Next Step

## Additional Articles from Current Periodicals

### Addresses & essays

**"Charging ahead,"** *Time*, Sept. 18, 1989, p. 40.

Summarizes the increasingly unified Europe that is becoming less reliant on the superpowers and more of a global power. Changes that are occurring; European Community unification in 1992; How the U.S. is perceived.

**Fink, D. E., "Meeting the 1992 challenge,"** *Aviation Week & Space Technology*, **June 12, 1989, p. 51.**

Editorial. Discusses the challenges Europe faces in meeting the 1992 deadline for eliminating economic, trade and social barriers that currently restrict commerce among the 12 European Community nations. Need for innovative strategies; Problems in China.

### Books & reading

**Kirkpatrick, C., "On Europe,"** *Current History*, **December 1990, p. 425.**

Reviews several new books about post-World War II Europe. Includes *After 1992: The United States of Europe*, by Ernest Wistrich; *Europe 1992: An American Perspective*, edited by Gary Clyde Hufbauer; *The Bloc that Failed: Soviet-East European Relations in Transition*, by Charles Gati; Others.

**Thomsen, S., "Book reviews: Economics, development, energy and environment,"** *International Affairs*, **January 1991, p. 158.**

Reviews the book *Europe 1992: an American perspective*, edited by Gary Clyde Hufbauer.

### Case studies

**Greenhouse, S., "1992 whets BSN's big appetite,"** *The New York Times*, **July 25, 1989, p. D1.**

Discusses the raft of deals involving France's largest food company, BSN group and its chairman Antoine Ribaud, 70, that is an attempt to position themselves for the European Community unified market in 1992. Company history; Market strategy.

**Greenhouse, S., "Deutsche Bank's bigger reach,"** *The New York Times*, **July 30, 1989, Section 3, p. 1.**

Discusses Alfred Herrhausen's plans as head of West Germany's Deutsche Bank, to turn the bank into a pan-European giant as the continent's trade and financial barriers tumble down in 1992 and into a global banking titan. Deutsche Bank's acquisitions; Risks in plans; Background of Herrhausen.

**Sanger, D. E., "Daimler-Benz and Mitsubishi negotiating cooperative plan,"** *The New York Times*, **March 7, 1990, p. A1.**

Discusses a plan of 'intensive cooperation' in automobile technology, aerospace, microelectronics, and a number of service industries, which is being negotiated by Mitsubishi in Japan and Daimler-Benz in West Germany. If completed, it will create a series of joint ventures that will give Daimler access to some of Japan's best technology and give Mitsubishi a desperately needed foothold in Europe before that market is integrated in 1992.

### Debates & issues

**"Old Italian customs,"** *Economist*, **March 23, 1991, p. 100.**

Comments on the debate between various European Community governments over what kind of export regulations should apply to works of art once Europe becomes a single market in 1992. Position of the Italians, who have the most severe restrictions on free movement of their works of art; Smuggling figures from Interpol; Looking for a common policy for the art trade; Position of Britain; Tzannis Tzannetakis, the Greek minister of culture; Details.

**"Sell by 1992,"** *Economist*, **March 2, 1991, p. 14.**

Contends that subsidizing state-owned firms is incompatible with the European Community's goal of establishing a genuinely free internal market after 1992. Difficulties in restricting the flow of subsidies; Letting companies raise new money by selling shares; Situation in France and Italy; Suggestions of France's Industry Minister Roger Fauroux; Sir Leon Brittan, the competition minister; Belief that some state firms deserve support; Outlook.

**Brimelow, P., "The dark side of 1992,"** *Forbes*, **Jan. 22, 1990, p. 85.**

Reports on the creation of a boundary-free European community in 1992 which could turn Europe into a protectionist, corporatist and anti-American entity. European court whose rulings are binding on member countries'; British resistance and reasons for it; Jacques Delors who heads the European Commission and his ambitions for a superstate; British Prime Minister Margaret Thatcher's fears. INSET: One currency or many?

**Haberman, C., "Europeans fear '92 economic unity may benefit Mafia,"** *The New York Times*, **July 23, 1989, Section 1 p. 1.**

Outlines how the deregulation of European markets in

1992 may make it easier for drug traffickers to move contraband and cash. Possible solutions; Mafia's current role in Italy.

**Riemer, B., Templeman, J., et al., "So long, 'Europhoria' — it was nice while it lasted," *Business Week*, Oct. 15, 1990, p. 46.**

Observes how pricier oil, inflation fears, and sluggish growth have torpedoed the wild optimism about Europe in 1992. Cutting back investment plans; Consumers are slowing spending and boosting savings; Slashing expenditures; Thinking of raising taxes; Plans put on hold; Exports slowing.

**Rosenbaum, A., "Fortress Europe for 1992," *The Nation*, Dec. 18, 1989, p. 748.**

Discusses the potential impact of the European Community's plans for economic unity by 1992, on European civil liberties. Prospects of a pan-European police organization, using computerized ID cards; Perceived barriers to refugees; Human rights violations of increased security measures.

**Templeman, J. and Smith, A. D., "German unity: A threat to Europe 1992?" *Business Week*, Jan. 22, 1990, p. 40.**

Discusses how the first half of 1990 is crucial to determining whether the European Community can make its move to a single market over the next three years. The biggest worry is that the linchpin of the Common Market, the French-German relationship, is in its worst condition in years. Other tensions that must be dealt with in preparation for 1992.

**Templeman, J., Peterson, T., et al., "The shape of Europe to come," *Business Week*, Nov. 27, 1989, p. 60.**

Reports how melding Eastern Europe with the West is a tantalizing idea, but the political and economic problems are staggering. How salvaging the wrecked economies of the East bloc is a challenge akin to postwar reconstruction; Why the European Community is worried that its plan for unity in 1992 could fall apart.

**Tully, S., "Europe hits the brakes on 1992," *Fortune*, Dec. 17, 1990, p. 133.**

Details how the European Community's drive toward an open market by the end of 1992 is suddenly starting to bump hard against the very barriers that the EC is trying to tear down. As the deadline nears, powerful cartels — especially in automaking, agriculture, and aviation — are fighting ferociously to hang on to their privileges, and the community is caving in to them. Gives examples.

**Valls-Russell, J., "Europe's bumpy road to '92," *New Leader*, Sept. 4, 1989, p. 8.**

Discusses key obstacles to be overcome in Europe's plans for economic and monetary union by 1992, as outlined in the Single European Act. Inconsistencies among the 12 member nations in defense and foreign policy; Disagreement on scheduling individual steps toward unity; Concerns about eroding local identity; Environmental issues.

**Wittenberg-Cox, A., "Europe's price for free trade," *Canadian Business*, June 1990, p. 27.**

Describes how Andre Kirchberger, a member of a social affairs Cabinet of the European Community, and his colleagues will propose legislation within two years to the two central bodies of the EC, the Council of Ministers and the European Parliament. While other commissioners are preparing the economic integration of Europe, Vasso Papandreou's Cabinet is readying the social side of 1992, setting the rules on everything from working hours to social security.

## Economic aspects

**"Single, but not level," *Economist*, Feb. 23, 1991, p. 83.**

Reports on why the earliest that the whole of the European Community's financial-services industry will be able to take advantage of its single market now looks like being mid-1994. The European Commission's timetable for EC member countries to implement its third life-insurance directive, whose draft was published on Feb. 20; The commission had hoped to have all the main services liberalized together by the end of 1992; Problems; Details; Outlook.

**Koretz, G., "1992 promises a rich harvest for Europe . . . ," *Business Week*, Jan. 22, 1990, p. 20.**

Discusses estimates by Italian economist Paolo Cecchini that the European Community can expect a rise in total income in the range of 2.5 percent to 6.5 percent over the next few years. Arguments by economist Richard E. Baldwin that Cecchini's estimates are too conservative.

**Lawday, D., "It's a bird, it's a plane, it's Euroman," *U.S. News & World Report*, Dec. 25, 1989, p. 45.**

Comments on the rise of ambitious American businessmen set on seizing the opportunities provided by Europe's goal of a unified market by 1992. Importance of understanding European culture and economy; Role of the Euroman as seen by entrepreneur Douglas Hamilton.

**Riemer, B., Melcher, R. A., et al., "Will the franc, the lira, and the pound become collector's items?" *Business Week*, Oct. 1, 1990, p. 53.**

Addresses how as adoption of its ambitious plan for free trade in 1992 draws closer, the European Community is moving forcefully to adopt a single currency and a central bank modeled on the U.S. Federal Reserve Board. If all goes according to plan, Europe in 10 years could be the home not only of the world's largest financial market but also of a Eurofed and a supercurrency rivaling the Federal Reserve and dollar in global influence.

**Riemer, B. & English, V., "Investors are grabbing their checkbooks — and heading for Europe,"** *Business Week,* **Dec. 25, 1989, p. 118.**

Reports how the opening of Eastern Europe and the approach of the European Community's 1992 deadline for dropping internal barriers are fueling visions of a megaboom in Europe. Reasons for investing in Europe; Analysts' outlook for various European markets and industries.

**Szamuely, G., "The politics of 1992,"** *Commentary,* **October 1989, p. 42.**

Discusses likely effects of European unity, which is foreseen in terms of trade by 1992. European Economic Community (EEC); Single European Act; Involvement with the Soviet bloc.

## Investments, Foreign

**"A spring in Europe's step,"** *Economist,* **Aug. 18, 1990, p. 41.**

Discusses the recent strengthening and growth of Western Europe's economies resulting from the investment boom in preparation for the single market of 1992, and German reunification. Describes the economic success or failure of various countries.

**Kosnett, J. and Goldwasser, J., "The time is now,"** *Changing Times,* **January 1990, p. 64.**

Discusses how Americans should start investing now in order to take advantage of Europe's economic marriage in 1992. How Americans will benefit from changes; Best investment strategies and opportunities.

**Work, C. P., "Jumping into the Euromarket: Is it cheaper by the dozen?"** *U.S. News & World Report,* **July 3, 1989, p. 44.**

Discusses efforts of U.S. and Japanese firms as they scramble for a place in Europe's unified market before 1992. Reason for economic unification; Examples of recent activity by U.S. and Japanese firms.

## Italy

**Rossant, J., "Can Italy catch up? "** *Business Week,* **June 11, 1990, p. 34.**

Describes how Italy's economy is slowing, its business leaders aren't thinking globally, and it may not be ready

for Europe 1992. With Europe on the brink of a new economic era, Italy's problems may catch up with it. Its labor is less productive, its services are more expensive, and its markets are less liberal than those of its rivals. Other changes that need to be made; Outlook.

## Germany

**Egan, J., "The awesome German giant,"** *U.S. News & World Report,* **April 1, 1991, p. 50.**

Presents an interview with David Burstein, analyst of global business and financial issues, concerning Germany and its future. Includes such subjects as German economic success, weaknesses of Germany's economy, German economic hegemony in Europe after 1992 and the limits of Germany's role in Europe.

## Great Britain

**Powell, B., Pedersen, D., et al., "The Japanese invade Europe,"** *Newsweek,* **Oct. 2, 1989, p. 28.**

Talks about British Prime Minister Margaret Thatcher's visit to Japan and her warning to Japanese businessmen that the integration of Europe at the end of 1992 gives them all an opportunity, but also invites risks and problems Thatcher wants to avoid. INSET: Target industries.

**Melcher, R. A., "More than ever, Thatcher is odd woman out,"** *Business Week,* **July 3, 1989, p. 40.**

Discusses British Prime Minister Margaret Thatcher's Conservative Party defeat in recent European Parliament elections. The loss is certain to intensify calls for Thatcher to ease her opposition to further economic and monetary integration with Europe as the European Community's 1992 free-trade deadline approaches.

## United States

**Cooney, S., "The impact of Europe 1992 on the United States,"** *Proceedings of the Academy of Political Science,* **January 1991, p. 100.**

Reviews the nature of the 1992 European Community (EC-92) program and its relative success to date. The primary U.S. interest in 1992 is economic; EC-92 as an expanding concept; The impact of EC-92 on U.S. international economic interests; Specific EC-92 concerns of U.S. interests.

**Forrestal, R. P., "Europe's economic integration in 1992,"** *Vital Speeches,* **Aug. 1, 1989, p. 633.**

Presents a speech given by Robert P. Forrestal, President of the Federal Reserve Bank of Atlanta, to the Alston & Bird 1992 Strategy Seminar, dealing with the implications for the U.S. in Europe's planned economic integration in 1992.

**Friedrich, O., Behar, R., et al., "Freed from greed?"** *Time*, **Jan. 1, 1990, p. 76.**

Recounts the financial estimates of debt, poverty, and ethical misdeeds of the 1980s which the United States will be paying for during the '90s. Booming international trade; U.S. trade deficit increasing; Spend now, pay later; Difficulties foreseen with the opening up of Eastern Europe, and the initiation of the European Community in 1992.

**Hale, D. D., "Global finance and the retreat to managed trade,"** *Harvard Business Review*, **January/February 1990, p. 150.**

Explores how the rise of Japanese financial power and the contradictions of United States economic policy are weakening the competitive position of the United States financial services industry. Potential for the emergence of a new managed trade system; Need to develop truly free markets; Suggested resolutions. INSETS: Banking on 1992: Europe embraces managed trade, by D. D. Hale; The Basle Accord and financial competition, by R. Bhala & E. B. Kapstein.

**Prokesch, S., "Europe taking a lead in growth,"** *The New York Times*, **Jan. 15, 1990, p. D1.**

Says that economists predict that Western Europe's economic growth will exceed that of the U.S. in the 1990s. The prediction is based on the benefits already flowing from the European Community's continuing effort to create a single market by 1992, and the changes in Eastern Europe.

**Shelburne, R. C. and Schoepfle, G. K., "The European Community 1992 program and U.S. workers,"** *Monthly Labor Review*, **November 1990, p. 22.**

Presents highlights of the conference "EC 1992: Implications for U.S. Workers" held in March 1990. Economic relationship between the European Community (EC) and the United States; Projected impact on investments; Social dimension of EC 1992; Common concerns expressed by participants; How the United States should respond to several unanswered questions.

## Technological aspects

**"Europe and Japan,"** *Nature*, **July 27, 1989, p. 247.**

Opinion. Discusses the fears of Europe over the prospect of ruinous technological competition with Japan after it becomes a true common market by the end of 1992. Study diagnosing competitive disadvantages; Challenges awaiting Europe.

**Chow, S. C., "Joint ventures with the EC,"** *High Technology Business*, **July/August 1989, p. 10.**

Presents an overview of legal obstacles faced by high-tech businesses in technology transfers to Europe in 1992. Legal guidelines to follow; Key restrictions.

**Madia, W. J., "Technology and the European market of 1992,"** *Vital Speeches*, **Feb. 1, 1990, p. 238.**

Presents speech by William J. Madia, senior vice president of Battelle Memorial Institute, given before the Planning Forum, dealing with the issue of the super economic and technological team that will result from the joined forces of the 12 European Community nations, and the three necessary characteristics, U.S. companies need to compete in the European technological market.

**Peterson, T. and Maremont, M., "Adding hustle to Europe's muscle,"** *Business Week*, **Special Innovation Issue 1989, p. 32.**

Discusses how Europe is funneling money into promising new technologies, hoping to get back into the high-tech race with Japan and the U.S. How the move toward a unified market by 1992 is forcing European labs and factories to get bigger and meaner in a hurry.

**Peterson, T. and Maremont, M., "Suddenly, high tech is a three-way race,"** *Business Week*, **June 15, 1990 (Bonus Issue), p. 118.**

Describes how, in key fields such as high-technology, Europe is catching up fast to Japan and the U.S. With Eastern Europe opening up and the unified market looming in 1992, Europe's prospects of shrugging off its recent lethargy have never been better; Pouring money into risky high-tech projects. INSETS: The search for the grail of particle physics, by T. Peterson; Hanging tough by teaming up, by J. B. Levine; High tech seems to be a dirty word, by J. B. Levine.

# Back Issues

*Great Research on Current Issues Starts Right Here . . . Recent topics covered by The CQ Researcher are listed below. Issues dated before May 10, 1991, were published under the name of Editorial Research Reports.*

**DECEMBER 1989**
North America Trade Pact
Influence Peddling
German Reunification
Learning Disabilities

**JANUARY 1990**
Higher Education Curriculum
Photonics
Age of 'Infotainment'
Abortion: Politicians' Nightmare

**FEBRUARY 1990**
Politics and Economic Growth
Free Agency in Sports
Repetitive Motion
War on Drugs

**MARCH 1990**
Asbestos: Are Risks Acceptable?
Public Health Campaigns
South Africa's Future
Homeless Need More Than Shelter

**APRIL 1990**
How Fair is the Tax Burden?
Workers' Compensation
U.S. Pacific Forces
Curbing Insurance Premiums

**MAY 1990**
Should Teaching Be a Profession?
Will Canada Fall Apart?
Is U.S. Patent System Outdated?
Federal Funding for the Arts

**JUNE 1990**
Downsizing America's Armed Forces
Progress In Weather Forecasting
S & L Bailout
Bio-Chemical Disarmament

**JULY 1990**
Do Americans Still Love Marriage?
Death Penalty Debate
Decline of Rural America
United Nations in the 1990s

**AUGUST 1990**
Democracy in the Philippines
Initiatives: True Democracy?
Hard Times at Newspapers
Teens Balance School & Jobs

**SEPTEMBER 1990**
Dangers of Alcohol
Western Alliance After the Cold War
Tobacco Industry
Right to Die

**OCTOBER 1990**
Organ Transplants
Energy Policy Options
Search for Arab Unity
Child Support

**NOVEMBER 1990**
Lotteries and Gambling
Post Cold-War Choices
Setting Limits on Medical Care
Multicultural Education

**DECEMBER 1990**
Cable TV Regulation
Americans' Search For Their Roots
Is Insurance System a Failure?
Why Schools Still Have Tracking

**JANUARY 1991**
Growing Influence of Boycotts
Should the U.S. Reinstate the Draft?
America's Archaeological Past
Peace Corps' Challenges in '90s

**FEBRUARY 1991**
Regional Impact of Recession
Puerto Rico's Status
Redistricting: Mapping Power
Nuclear Power

**MARCH 1991**
Acid Rain
Cost of the Gulf War
Reassessing Gun Laws
Future for Man in Space

**APRIL 1991**
Social Security
Canadian Crisis Over Quebec
California Drought
Electromagnetic Radiation

**MAY 1991**
School Choice
Racial Quotas
Animal Rights
U.S. and Japan

**JUNE 1991**
Children and Divorce
Teenage Suicide
Endangered Species

Back issues are available for $4.00 (subscribers) or $7.00 (non-subscribers). Quantity discounts apply to orders over ten. To order, call Congressional Quarterly 1-800-432-2250.

# Future Topics

▶ *Parental Notification*

▶ *Soviet Nationalities*

▶ *Mexico's Emergence*

# Researcher

PUBLISHED BY CONGRESSIONAL QUARTERLY INC., IN CONJUNCTION WITH EBSCO PUBLISHING

# Teenagers and Abortion

*State laws requiring parental involvement stir opposition*

LAWS REQUIRING TEENAGERS TO INVOLVE THEIR parents in abortion decisions have become the object of widening controversy. The debate over parental involvement laws is taking place against the backdrop of the volatile abortion issue. Polls indicating strong public support for such laws have supplied new ammunition to anti-abortion activists. Many politicians who generally support abortion rights also support parental consent and notification laws. But an organized campaign of abortion-rights activists and professional groups is seeking to head off or repeal the laws, calling them a violation of minors' rights and a threat to adolescent health. Many families have a stake in the outcome of this debate: Every year, more than a million American girls under age 20 become pregnant.

 **July 5, 1991 • Volume 1, No. 9 • 441-464**

*Formerly Editorial Research Reports*

COVER ART: BARBARA SASSA-DANIELS

# CQ Researcher

July 5, 1991
Volume 1, No. 9

**EDITOR**
Sandra Stencel

**ASSOCIATE EDITOR**
Richard L. Worsnop

**STAFF WRITERS**
Charles S. Clark
Mary H. Cooper
Rodman D. Griffin

**PRODUCTION EDITOR**
Laurie De Maris

**EDITORIAL ASSISTANT**
Thomas H. Moore

**GRAPHICS**
Jack Auldridge

**PUBLISHED BY**
Congressional Quarterly Inc.

**CHAIRMAN**
Andrew Barnes

**VICE CHAIRMAN**
Andrew P. Corty

**EDITOR AND PUBLISHER**
Neil Skene

**EXECUTIVE EDITOR**
Robert W. Merry

**PUBLICATIONS MARKETING/SALES**
Robert Smith

**EDITOR, EBSCO PUBLISHING**
Melissa Kummerer

The CQ Researcher (ISSN 1056-2036). Formerly Editorial Research Reports. Published weekly (48 times per year, excluding March 1, May 3, Aug. 2 and Nov. 1, 1991) by Congressional Quarterly Inc., 1414 22nd St., N.W., Washington, D.C. 20037. Rates are furnished upon request. Application to mail at second-class postage rates is pending at Washington, D.C. POSTMASTER: Send address changes to The CQ Researcher, 1414 22nd St., N.W., Washington, D.C. 20037.

# Teenagers and Abortion

BY CHARLES S. CLARK

## THE ISSUES

Battles over abortion are being waged in an ever-shifting theater of operations. As combat moves from the courts to state legislatures to Congress to the ballot box, one issue is drawing especially heavy firepower: laws that require teenagers to involve their parents in abortion decisions. Forty-one states have enacted laws that prevent minors — generally anyone under age 18 — from obtaining abortions unless they either notify their parents or get the consent of one or both parents.*

The issue of teenagers and abortion stems from a problem welcomed by no one: Every year in the United States more than a million girls under age 20 — about one in every 10 — become pregnant. About 82 percent of these pregnancies are unintended and about 42 percent of them are aborted.[1] (*See graph, p. 454.*) The Children's Defense Fund, a Washington advocacy group, estimates that at least 40,000 teenage girls drop out of school every year because of pregnancy.

Though a majority of the public continues to favor a legal right to abortion,** opinion polls indicate the public supports parental involvement in teen abortion decisions by majorities as high as 81 percent (*see p. 458*). "Parents have a right to be involved in life-and-death decisions such as abortion," says Rep. Christopher H. Smith, R-N.J., a longtime

abortion opponent and author of a federal parental notification bill.

Critics say that while parental involvement laws may be well-intentioned, they sometimes force young women to resort to illegal abortions or expose them to abuse from hostile family members. "Parental involvement is ideal, but sometimes it's impossible," says Jane Hodgson, a St. Paul obstetrician whose name is attached to a court case that unsuccessfully challenged a parental notification law in Minnesota (*see p. 450*). "... We have to face the reality that a teen may encounter violent abuse if she is forced to bring an estranged parent into the process."[2]

It is difficult to separate the debate over parental involvement from the broader and highly emotional issue of abortion. One reason is that the most vocal lobbyists for such laws are anti-abortion activists. Galvanized by a 1989 Supreme Court ruling that upheld state restrictions on abortions and two 1990 decisions affirming the constitutionality of parental involvement laws, the anti-

abortion movement has stepped up its lobbying efforts. According to the National Conference of State Legislatures, 226 abortion-related bills have been introduced this year, 34 of which deal with the issue of parental involvement.

A number of states enacted parental involvement statutes in the 1970s and '80s, but many of them are not being enforced because of court challenges. (*See table, p. 445.*) The laws vary widely in their restrictiveness. Some require physicians to telephone or write to parents before performing abortions on teenagers. In some states, doctors must wait 24 to 48 hours after alerting the parents before performing the procedure. Some states require written, even notarized, proof of the parents' consent. In some states both parents must give their consent. Some allow one parent to make the decision; others allow the role to be filled by grandparents, clergy or other adults. A growing number of states permit minors to have an abortion without parental involvement if they first appear before a judge, a procedure known as a judicial bypass.

Many politicians would like to avoid the question of parental involvement altogether. The abortion issue is complicated enough, they say, without piling on such delicate questions as the proper role for government in intimate communications between parent and child. Even politicians who generally favor abortion rights may find it difficult to oppose laws that require some parental involvement in such decisions.

"The idea that parents are ultimately responsible for their children is so ingrained that even a pro-choice politician could gain with the electorate" by backing parental involvement laws, says Gary Bauer, president of the Family Research

---

*Because of court challenges, only 19 states currently are enforcing the laws (*see table, p. 454*). Nebraska will become the 20th in September.

**Sixty percent of those responding to a May 1991 NBC News-*Wall Street Journal* poll said abortion should not be made illegal.

July 5, 1991   443

Council in Washington and formerly President Ronald Reagan's domestic affairs adviser.

On the other hand, opponents of such laws can point to a victory last fall indicating strong citizen sentiment that government should stay out of such issues. Last November, Oregon voters rejected a proposed parental notification law that had been garnering strong approval in opinion surveys (*see p. 454*).

Citizens, legal experts and state and federal legislators are likely to be grappling with abortion and parental involvement issues for the foreseeable future. Here are the central questions on which the outcome will hinge:

### Are parental involvement laws needed?

"Mom, Dad, I'm pregnant." The reluctance of teens to pronounce the dreaded words is serious enough without the moral vagaries of abortion. For many girls, the revelation is also a first admission of sexual activity. "They're going to kill me," "My Dad will throw me out" are common reactions among pregnant teens. "It's not the eventual reaction but the initial reaction they're worried about," says Cynthia Waszak, research director for the Center for Population Options in Washington.

Most unmarried teenage girls who become pregnant *do* tell their parents.* It's the remaining girls who need the protections offered by parental involvement laws, supporters of the laws say. Most teens are too immature to make such decisions on their own, they argue, and the laws encourage parent-child communication.

Backers of parental involvement laws say adolescents tend to underestimate their parents' supportive-

ness. The first reaction is usually anger, but when the turmoil subsides, anywhere from two-thirds to four-fifths of parents have been found to be supportive.[3] "Many times, [family members] are forced to communicate because of a crisis and are actually brought together by the very hardship they wished to hide," writes Samona J. Smit, a lobbyist for the Iowa Right to Life Committee.[4]

Opponents of such laws say research does not support the notion that teenagers are too immature to make such an important decision. According to a committee of the American Psychological Association, a teenager's fear of family conflict, lack of experience in dealing with medical professionals and lack of money were much more likely to affect her decision about abortion than was her psychological maturity.[5]

A 1989 study by the Johns Hopkins School of Hygiene and Public Health monitored 360 black teenage girls of similar socioeconomic backgrounds who sought pregnancy tests at Baltimore clinics. Two years later, the study found, those who had had abortions were far more likely to have graduated from high school than those who had given birth. They also were better off economically, were no more likely to have had psychological problems and were less likely to have experienced another pregnancy.[6]

Those who support parental involvement often justify such laws on medical grounds. They say adolescents who undergo abortions have a greater risk of complications in future pregnancies. According to another Johns Hopkins University study, girls under age 18 who have abortions are two and a half times more likely than women ages 20-29 to acquire the inflammation of the uterus known as endometritis.[7] But opponents of parental involvement say abortions actually are safer for adolescents than childbirth is.

Infact, they say, girls ages 15-19 are about 24 times more likely to die from childbirth than from first-trimester legal abortions.[8]

The most emotional argument in favor of protective abortion laws involves the rights of parents. "Parents always had [the right] to bring up their children and oversee their medical treatment," says Richard Doerflinger, an abortion policy director for the U.S. Catholic Conference. In recent decades, he says, minors have been given rights by government. "How did government get the right to kick the parents out in the first place?" he asks.

Many parents are amazed that a teenager who needs permission to get an aspirin from the school nurse or get her ears pierced could go to an abortion clinic and, in the words of one anti-abortion activist, "have her delicate reproductive organs tampered with without my consent."[9]

Opponents of the laws reply that most states have legislation protecting the confidentiality of a minor's decision to seek health care for sex-related medical problems, birth control, drug and alcohol abuse and for medical emergencies. The distinction, they say, is that if health care will suffer, confidentiality is honored. They add that school nurses who supply aspirin and jewelers who offer ear piercing are most likely concerned about liability.

### Are efforts to enact parental involvement laws really attempts to restrict abortion?

Many abortion-rights advocates say parental involvement laws are just another means of restricting access to abortion. In contrast with other proposed abortion restrictions, such as limits on public funding and mandatory waiting periods, parental involvement laws are considered easiest to pass because they draw support from those on both sides of the abortion question, particularly

---

*A 1980 survey, the most recent available, found that 55 percent of teenage girls who became pregnant voluntarily told their parents.

among parents.

"It's a right-to-life effort to chip away at abortion, a war of attrition," says Eleanor Smeal, president of the Fund for a Feminist Majority, a legislative interest group based in Arlington, Va. Janet O'Keeffe, a legislative analyst at the American Psychological Association, and Kathryn Kolbert, state coordinating counsel for the American Civil Liberties Union's Reproductive Freedom Project, express similar views. "It's all a secondary strategy to banning abortion," Kolbert says.

Anti-abortion groups deny that their interest in parental involvement laws stems from anything but the issue's merits. "Obviously the laws don't go far enough" to accomplish a total ban on abortion, says Mary Spaulding Balch, state legislative coordinator at the National Right to Life Committee. "We do think it will save lives, and it will make the situation better for vulnerable teens," she adds. "[But] they're not the laws we would use as a vehicle to reverse" *Roe v. Wade*, the 1973 Supreme Court decision that legalized abortion. Balch acknowledges that most of the lobbying for parental involvement laws is done by anti-abortion activists.

The anti-abortion movement is not unanimous on the value of parental involvement laws. Paul Brown, executive director of the American Life League, a Virginia group that opposes both abortion and contraception, says last year's Supreme Court decisions upholding parental involvement laws "were not such a big deal." The restrictions only "give the parents the right to okay the killing of their grandchild." [10]

Doerflinger of the U.S. Catholic Conference says his group's support for parental involvement laws is part of a broader agenda. "The idea that parents have certain basic rights to be involved with their children is a

# State Parental Involvement Laws

*Although a majority of states have such laws, only 19 currently are enforcing the laws because of court challenges. Nebraska will become the 20th in September.*

| State | Status of law | Year enacted | Requirement | Number of parents | Judicial bypass |
|---|---|---|---|---|---|
| Alabama | enforced | 1987 | consent | one | yes |
| Alaska | not enforced | 1970 | consent | one | no |
| Arizona | enjoined | 1989 | consent | one | yes |
| Arkansas | enforced | 1989 | notice | two | yes |
| California | enjoined | 1987 | consent | one | yes |
| Colorado | enjoined | 1967 | consent | one | no |
| Connecticut | enforced | 1990 | other† | NA | no |
| Delaware | not enforced | 1970 | consent | two | no |
| D.C. | none | NA | NA | NA | NA |
| Florida | enjoined | 1988 | consent | one | yes |
| Georgia | enjoined | 1988 | notice | one | yes |
| Hawaii | none | NA | NA | NA | NA |
| Idaho | not enforced | 1983 | notice | two | no |
| Illinois | enjoined | 1983 | notice | two | yes |
| Indiana | enforced | 1984 | consent | one | yes |
| Iowa | none | NA | NA | NA | NA |
| Kansas | none | NA | NA | NA | NA |
| Kentucky | enjoined | 1986 | consent | two | yes |
| Louisiana | enforced | 1981 | consent | one | yes |
| Maine | enforced | 1989 | other†† | one | yes |
| Maryland | enforced | 1991 | notice | one | no‡ |
| Massachusetts | enforced | 1980 | consent | two | yes |
| Michigan | enforced | 1990 | consent | one | yes |
| Minnesota | enforced | 1981 | notice | two | yes |
| Mississippi | enjoined | 1986 | consent | two | yes |
| Missouri | enforced | 1979 | consent | one | yes |
| Montana | not enforced | 1974 | notice | one | no |
| Nebraska | enforced | 1991 | notice | one | yes |
| Nevada | enjoined | 1985 | notice | one | yes |
| New Hampshire | none | NA | NA | NA | NA |
| New Jersey | none | NA | NA | NA | NA |
| New Mexico | not enforced | 1969 | consent | one | no |
| New York | none | NA | NA | NA | NA |
| North Carolina | not enforced | 1967 | consent | one | no |
| North Dakota | enforced | 1981 | consent | two | yes |
| Ohio | enforced | 1985 | notice | one | yes |
| Oklahoma | none | NA | NA | NA | NA |
| Oregon | not enforced | 1969 | consent | one | no |
| Pennsylvania | enjoined | 1988 | consent | one | yes |
| Rhode Island | enforced | 1982 | consent | one | yes |
| South Carolina | enforced | 1990 | consent | one (or grandparent) | yes |
| South Dakota | not enforced | 1973 | consent | one | no |
| Tennessee | enjoined | 1988 | consent | two | yes |
| Texas | none | NA | NA | NA | NA |
| Utah | enforced | 1974 | notice | two‡‡ | no |
| Vermont | none | NA | NA | NA | NA |
| Virginia | not enforced | 1970 | consent | one | no |
| Washington | enjoined | 1970 | consent | one | no |
| West Virginia | enforced | 1984 | notice | one | yes |
| Wisconsin | enforced | 1985 | other† | NA | no |
| Wyoming | enforced | 1989 | both | one | yes |

*Note: Where a state has more than one law on the books, only the most recent has been included.*

† *Provider must counsel and encourage minor to notify a parent or other adult family member. In Connecticut, the law applies only to minors under age 16.*
†† *Consent of one parent or other adult family member or counseling of minor.*
‡ *Physician decides if minor is mature, or if notification of parents would be harmful.*
‡‡ *Currently being applied to require notice to one parent.*

*Sources: Alan Guttmacher Institute; American Civil Liberties Union*

basic tenet of Catholic thought,'' he says.

The wide appeal of parental involvement laws in opinion polls is a sign that many people don't perceive the parental involvement question as the abortion debate in disguise. "Parental consent is a lot more about values and parenting than it is about abortion," says Celinda C. Lake, a Democratic pollster for Greenberg/Lake: The Analysis Group in Washington.

### Do parental involvement laws reduce teen abortion rates and birthrates?

A federal study released in August 1990 indicated the teen birthrate rose in 1988 for the first time in 18 years, particularly among girls ages 15-17. Jacqueline Darroch Forrest, vice president for research and planning of the Alan Guttmacher Institute, a nonprofit research group once affiliated with the Planned Parenthood Federation of America, expressed concern that stepped-up publicity about parental notification and consent laws may have dissuaded pregnant teens from seeking abortions. "Young kids who may be hearing this discussion may get the wrong understanding that either abortion is not allowed for them or they have to have the consent of their parents," she said.[11]

The actual impact of parental notification and consent laws on teen birthrates and abortion rates is difficult to determine. Detailed information is available from just three states.

The earliest study deals with a parental consent law in place in Massachusetts since April 1981. Published in 1986, it found that abortions to minors had declined by 43 percent since the law was enacted. However, the study was limited by the fact that Massachusetts is a small state bordered by five neighboring states; many pregnant girls could have

gone out of state to get abortions rather than tell their parents about their pregnancies.[12]

In Missouri, where a parental consent law took effect in 1986, a state study found that the number of teen pregnancies ending in abortion declined from 38.3 percent in 1985 to 33.5 percent in 1988. Teen birthrates rose slightly from 33.0 percent in 1985 to 35.6 percent in 1988, but on the whole continued a decline that began in 1980.

The Missouri Health Department attributed the trends both to improved contraception use and the parental consent law. The department added that the parental consent law had produced a 36 percent increase in the number of Missouri girls going across the border to Kansas to obtain abortions. The study also noted a slight increase in the percentage of abortions to minors occurring in the second trimester. This is a more dangerous procedure. It speculated that some teens may have delayed telling their parents about their pregnancies and that this led to later abortions. The number of teens obtaining second-trimester abortions in the state rose from 19.3 percent in 1985 to 22.8 percent in 1988.

The state with the most elaborate data is Minnesota. Its parental notification law was enacted in 1981, was struck down in 1986 and became the basis for the most important Supreme Court case on parental involvement in abortion (*see p. 450*). Tracking more than 16,000 pregnant teens, the Minnesota Health Department found that abortion rates declined slightly, with the percentage of pregnant minors having abortions falling from 54 percent in 1980 to 48 percent in 1986. However, the proportion of teens having abortions during the second trimester rose by 19 percent during this period.

The Minnesota data, heavily publicized because of the Supreme Court case, was also notable because Min-

nesota, unlike Massachusetts, is a large, mostly rural state where teenagers are not likely to find it easy to travel out of state for an abortion. That heightened the interest of James L. Rogers, a psychology professor at Wheaton [Ill.] College, who, in a project financed by the antiabortion group Americans United for Life, performed his own analysis of the effect of Minnesota's parental notification law. Noting the decline in the teen abortion rate and a drop in the teen birthrate, Rogers concluded that the parental consent law had "encouraged responsible sexual behavior among teenagers."[13]

Rogers' conclusions are not shared by Janet O'Keeffe of the American Psychological Association. She says teenagers' decisions to use contraceptives are very complex and depend on psychosocial attitudes, communication between partners and availability. The decline in teen birth and abortion rates at the time that Minnesota's notification law was in effect "is very likely a spurious relationship," she says. "Correlation doesn't equal causation. It's like noting that there is a higher incidence of births and storks in rural areas as compared with urban areas."

The Alan Guttmacher Institute issued a memorandum in March rebutting Rogers' conclusions. It asked why there was no sudden increase in abortion or pregnancy rates after the law was blocked by the courts. It noted that Minnesota has a higher-than-average rate of contraceptive use. And it argued that Rogers' hypothesis that the fear of having to notify parents will cause teens to be more sexually responsible assumes that "a large number of very young teenagers followed carefully the actions of the Supreme Court or the debates in the state legislature, read or listened to the news regularly, understood the information correctly, and acted with a prudence and foresight not normally found in older teenagers or even adults."

Rogers concedes it can be difficult to prove causation, but says as a scientist he is obligated to offer an explanation once he's established a relationship. "It's like rising temperatures and ice cream sales," he says, "a very strong correlation."

### Do parental involvement laws harm teenagers?

Opponents of parental involvement say the laws are not only ineffective and unfair but can actually harm adolescents. According to Marcia D. Greenberger and Katherine Connor, attorneys for the National Women's Law Center, the laws "can spark a family upheaval that would otherwise not occur and can be extremely dangerous for young women who live in homes where physical, psychological and sexual abuse is present." [14]

Associate Justice Harry A. Blackmun, in a dissenting opinion to a 1990 Supreme Court ruling upholding a parental involvement law, wrote: "For too many young pregnant women, parental involvement in this most intimate decision threatens harm, rather than promises comfort. The court's selective blindness to this stark social reality is bewildering and distressing." [15]

To some, laws that require parental notification may seem less onerous than laws requiring parental consent. But as a practical matter, says Rachael Pine, an attorney for the American Civil Liberties Union (ACLU), there is little distinction between them. "Teenagers are emotionally and economically dependent on their parents," she says. "Once you require them to tell their parents, you are in effect giving the parents the opportunity for a veto." [16]

Laws requiring teenagers to involve both parents in an abortion decision are considered particularly onerous, especially in cases where the parents are divorced. Such laws

# Number of Teen Abortions

*The number of abortions performed on women ages 19 and younger rose sharply following the 1973 Supreme Court decision legalizing abortion. The number of teen abortions declined in the 1980s. In 1987, the last year for which complete statistics are available, more than 406,000 women under the age of 20 had abortions.*

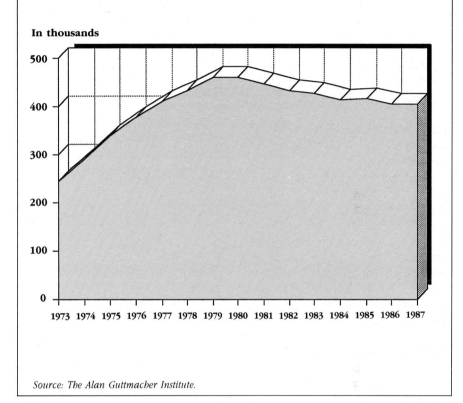

*Source: The Alan Guttmacher Institute.*

"disrupt carefully tailored joint custody agreements in which one parent has been awarded the legal authority to make decisions about a child's health care," attorneys Greenberger and Connor note.

The biggest danger of parental involvement laws, critics maintain, is that they can delay a girl's access to medical care. Adolescents, particularly younger teens, often don't recognize the signs of pregnancy. Legal and judicial barriers further delay their seeking help, critics say, and could push an abortion into the second trimester, when it is more dangerous and more expensive. Although only 10 percent of all abortions in the United States are performed in the second trimester,

23 percent of the abortions performed on adolescents under age 15 are in the second trimester. [17] Deaths caused by abortion are estimated to rise about 20 percent for each week of gestation from the 8th to the 15th week of pregnancy, and 50 percent after that, according to the American College of Obstetricians and Gynecologists.

Some opponents of parental involvement say such laws force adolescents to seek dangerous, illegal abortions. They often cite the case of Becky Bell, a 17-year-old Indianapolis girl whose 1988 death following a secret abortion has been blamed on Indiana's parental consent. (*See story, p. 453.*)

Opposition to parental involvement laws comes from a wide range of professional and civic groups, including the American Academy of Family Physicians, the American Academy of Pediatrics, the American Psychiatric Association, the Organization for Obstetric, Gynecological and Neonatal Nurses, the National Medical Association, the American Association of University Women, the American Jewish Congress and the League of Women Voters.

The National Association of Social Workers has issued a statement saying parental involvement laws interfere with their work "by restricting the options that are available to clients, substituting the judgment of others for that arrived at through careful assessment by worker and client." A statement issued by the YWCA argues that a pregnant adolescent "will sense when and if it is appropriate to consult her parents." Roselyn Payne Epps, president of Girls Incorporated, an advocacy group for girls, told congressional staff members earlier this year that "parental notification causes serious medical, economic and social consequences for several groups — the teenagers who are pregnant and who

do not feel able to deliver and care for a child; the children to whom they give birth; and the society at large, particularly in terms of the cost to taxpayers for services to these young women and their children."

Confronted with this roster of opponents, Mary Spaulding Balch of the National Right to Life Committee said: "We're surprised that these groups are against them because the laws are working. Teen pregnancy rates are down, while national rates are up." Backers of the laws say individual tragedies, even if traceable to parental involvement requirements, do not invalidate the laws. "It's like a seat belt law," Balch says. "A small percentage of people die because they're wearing seat belts, but the vast majority of people using them are prevented from sustaining injuries."

***Should judges be able to take the place of parents in helping a minor decide on having an abortion?***

The Supreme Court has ruled that parental involvement laws are constitutional as long as they include a "judicial bypass." This procedure permits underage girls who seek an

abortion to go before a judge instead of involving their parents. The judge first must decide whether the girl is mature enough to make the abortion decision on her own. If it is decided the girl is not mature enough, the judge must decide whether the abortion would be in her best interests.

Many health clinics provide legal counseling to help young women use the judicial bypass. In some states, courts appoint a lawyer to help the woman. Despite such help, some opponents of parental involvement laws say the procedure still is too complex and daunting for a minor to negotiate while in a crisis. They say many girls are traumatized by the thought of going before a judge and discussing their sex lives. The ACLU has estimated that a girl might have to discuss her pregnancy with as many as 23 strangers before obtaining a judicial bypass, not to mention the embarrassment of being seen awaiting an abortion hearing by court clerks, police officers, public defenders and others.

Some critics of the procedure also complain that judges apply their own values to the girl's situation. A judge in Indiana asked a pregnant Hispanic minor the race of her sexual partner, making the point that the baby would be more adoptable if it were white. In Ohio, a judge determined that one pregnant 17-year-old was not a "mature minor" and denied her an abortion even though she worked outside the home 35 hours a week and paid rent to her parents.

Anti-abortion groups also oppose the judicial-bypass requirement, saying it enables minors to skirt parental involvement laws. "The judge only works with the information that the girl tells him," says Ruth Pakaluk, president of Massachusetts Citizens for Life ". . . Parents have no way to get any other information to a judge." [18]

# Teenagers and Abortion

*In 1987, the last year for which complete statistics are available, about 26 percent of abortions performed in the United States were on women under age 20. This was down from about 33 percent in 1973.*

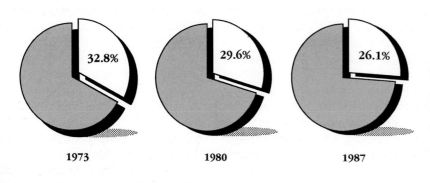

1973     1980     1987

*Source: The Alan Guttmacher Institute.*

Many judges themselves say they would rather avoid the moral responsibility such hearings entail. "I don't want to be the fall guy and have blood on my hands," Francis Bourrisseau, a judge in Mason County, Mich., told the Ludington *Daily News.*[19] ∎

# BACKGROUND

## Parental Rights

I n 1973, in the watershed *Roe v. Wade* decision legalizing abortion, the Supreme Court said a woman's right to decide whether to have an abortion "is not unqualified and must be considered against important state interests." The ruling left open many abortion-related issues. Challenges and proposed refinements began immediately in courts and legislatures throughout the country. Proposals for parental notification and consent laws were among the first challenges (though several states had put such laws on the books in the late 1960s). The debate revolved around concepts of minors' rights vs. parental rights.

Minors' rights is a modern-day concept. For most of American Colonial and republican history, youth were considered under the complete control of their parents, who were even entitled to the fruits of their children's labor. It wasn't until 1967 that the Supreme Court endowed minors with the right to claim protections as "persons" under the Bill of Rights and the 14th Amendment. The case, known as *In re Gault*, involved a 16-year-old Arizona boy who had made an obscene phone call and was deprived of his rights during his trial. In 1969, the Supreme Court further affirmed the rights of minors in *Tinker v. Des Moines Independent Community School District*, in which it recognized the free speech rights of high school students whose principal had barred them from wearing black armbands to protest the Vietnam War.

Parental rights are derived more by tradition. A heritage of family autonomy from government is imbedded in Anglo-American law. Beginning in the 1920s, the Supreme Court began to speak of parents as having a federal constitutional right to direct the upbringing of their children free from state intervention unless there was a constitutionally derived justification for such state intervention. In a 1972 case in which the Court determined that Amish parents could not be compelled to send their children to school beyond eighth grade (*Wisconsin v. Yoder*), the justices noted that the "primary role of the parents in the upbringing of their children is now established as an enduring American tradition."

### Age of Majority

Today, each state has a definition of "the age of majority," a point at which a teenager is seen as having the legal rights of an adult. For decades, the age of majority was 21, but after the 26th Amendment gave 18-year-olds the vote in 1971, most states lowered the age of majority to 18.*

Parents generally are given the right to make health-care decisions for their underage children by virtue of maturity and experience and because parents are financially liable for such treatment.[20] Depending on the state, laws or health department regulations may require parental consent for minors to undergo an appendectomy, cosmetic surgery, dental work, ear piercings or even a

_____

*The age of majority in Alabama, Nebraska and Wyoming is 19.

visit to a tanning salon. Exceptions, however, are often made for treatment of sexually transmitted diseases, drug or alcohol abuse, or use of birth control. The reasoning in such cases is that lack of confidentiality might deter the minor from seeking health care.

Attached to the concept of the age of majority is the notion of an "emancipated minor," a teenager whose characteristics give him or her legal rights beyond those afforded others the same age. Traditionally, an emancipated minor had to be living apart from parents with their permission and earning his or her own support through traditional employment. By implication, he or she was above the age of compulsory school attendance.

In the past two decades, the concept has broadened to permit the minor some role in determining his or her status. Though definitions vary by state, in principle, a judge can declare a minor emancipated if he or she is married, has been inducted into the armed forces, has established a home away from that of the parents or has achieved economic independence with or without parental consent.

Another term that figures in parental involvement debates is the "mature minor." Defined primarily by the courts, this status and accompanying freedom to make health-care decisions may be conferred by judges and doctors based on the minor's intelligence and documented knowledge of the risks and benefits of the treatment under discussion.

## Courts as Battlegrounds

A ll of these concepts were given a thorough working over in courts and legislatures after the 1973 legalization of abortion. Anti-abortion activists took to the courts and began circulating model bills in legislatures seeking to undo the effects of *Roe v. Wade* and to implement restrictions on abortion. This prompted an organized response by abortion rights advocates.

The first time the Supreme Court addressed the parental involvement issue was in 1976, in *Planned Parenthood of Central Missouri v. Danforth.* It was a victory for opponents of parental involvement laws. The Missouri branch of the national group of family planning clinics had challenged the constitutionality of a Missouri law requiring parental consent for unmarried minors seeking an abortion. Defenders of the law spoke of "safeguarding the authority of the family relationship." The court disagreed, saying the parental consent policy was "no more weighty than the right of privacy of the competent minor mature enough to have become pregnant." It said that "constitutional rights do not mature and come into being only when one attains the state-defined age of majority. Minors as well as adults are protected by the Constitution and possess constitutional rights."

In 1979, in *Bellotti v. Baird,* the Supreme Court overturned a parental consent statute in Massachusetts that had never gone into effect. However, the court acknowledged that under certain circumstances parental consent might be appropriate, citing "the peculiar vulnerability of children," "their inability to make critical decisions in an informed, mature manner," and "the importance of parental role in childrearing." It was in the *Belloti* case that the court determined that parental consent laws would be constitutional only if they offered the procedure known as a judicial bypass for emancipated or mature minors and minors whose best interests might be served by confidential abortions.

In 1981, the Supreme Court began to shift its views on teenagers and abortion. In *H. L. v. Matheson,* it upheld a Utah law making it a crime for doctors to perform an abortion on an unemancipated minor without informing her parents. It rejected a woman's contention that abortion was being singled out for special treatment in contrast to surgical procedures that did not require parental notice.

In 1983, the court in *City of Akron v. Akron Center for Reproductive Health* struck down regulations requiring physicians to obtain one parent's consent before performing an abortion on anyone under 15 because a judicial bypass was not offered. This was a victory for opponents of the laws. The same day, however, in *Planned Parenthood of Kansas City v. Ashcroft,* the court upheld the constitutionality of a parental consent law that included a judicial bypass.

It was in July 1989, 16 years after *Roe v. Wade,* that anti-abortion forces got their biggest boost from a Supreme Court decision. The court ruled in *Webster v. Reproductive Health Services* that states could put some restrictions on publicly funded abortions. In the 1990 state legislative session following the *Webster* ruling, 250 abortion-related bills were introduced in the United States, more than twice as many as in 1989.

The *Webster* decision also marked a shift in tactics by some anti-abortion groups. Confronted with polls that consistently showed the public as opposed to a ban on abortion, some anti-abortion activists scaled back their short-term agenda to the politically possible. "They are no longer saying, 'Let's make abortion illegal' because the general public will not stand for that," said Richard E. Ryan, a pollster in Houston who works with anti-abortion groups.[21]

### Hodgson Case a Turning Point

A year after the *Webster* ruling, the Supreme Court ruled for the first time on parental involvement laws "as applied." Because previous cases dealt with parental consent laws, the court had agreed to hear cases involving notification statutes in Ohio and Minnesota. In *Ohio v. Akron Center for Reproductive Health,* Planned Parenthood argued that Ohio had "no compelling interest in requiring a pregnant girl to talk with her parents since that conversation would pose a danger to her health." The court disagreed. On June 25, 1990, it upheld the constitutionality of Ohio's one-parent notification law, which included a 24-hour waiting period between notification and performance of the abortion and a judicial-bypass mechanism. However, the court left open the question of whether a judicial bypass was constitutionally required under a one-parent notification law.

On the same day, the court decided what many experts say is the most significant parental involvement case to date, *Hodgson v. Minnesota.* Minnesota's two-parent notification law had been challenged by obstetrician Jane Hodgson, who in 1970 had become the first doctor in the country convicted of performing an abortion in a hospital. Since that conviction was thrown out, she had performed or supervised thousands of abortions. Minnesota's law had been in effect from 1981 to 1986, when a challenge from Hodgson and the ACLU was successful in district court; the judge struck down the law.

During the subsequent appeal of that ruling, the ACLU presented voluminous testimony from Minnesota girls who had had abortions and from judges who expressed displeasure with the law and its judicial bypass. A three-judge panel of the 8th U.S. Circuit Court of Appeals agreed that the law did not further "the state's interest in protecting pregnant minors or assuring family

*Continued on p. 452*

# Chronology

## 1970s
*Major Supreme Court rulings prevent states from outlawing abortion in the first trimester of pregnancy. Several states pass parental consent and notification laws.*

### Jan. 22, 1973
Supreme Court rules the Constitution protects a woman's decision to abort a pregnancy (*Roe v. Wade*). In a separate decision, the court rules a state may not interfere with the exercise of that right by prohibiting or limiting access to the means of abortion (*Doe v. Bolton*).

### July 3, 1976
Supreme Court, in its first ruling on parental involvement in abortion, holds a one-parent consent requirement unconstitutional. It recognizes that a "mature" unmarried minor has the constitutional right to choose abortion in consultation with a physician (*Planned Parenthood of Central Missouri v. Danforth*).

### July 2, 1979
Supreme Court strikes down a Massachusetts parental consent statute because it lacks a provision giving minors access to a confidential, expeditious proceeding before a judge (*Bellotti v. Baird*).

————— • —————

## 1980s
*Supreme Court's position on abortion and parental involvement laws begins to shift.*

### June 30, 1980
Supreme Court rules government can refuse to fund abortions, rejecting a challenge to the Hyde amendment barring federal Medicaid funds for abortion (*Harris v. McCrae*).

### March 23, 1981
Supreme Court upholds a Utah law making it a crime for doctors to perform an abortion on a dependent minor without notifying her parents (*H. L. v. Matheson*).

### June 15, 1983
Supreme Court reaffirms *Roe v. Wade* and strikes down as unconstitutional five sections of an Akron ordinance restricting a woman's right to an abortion, including a parental notication requirement (*City of Akron v. Akron Center for Reproductive Health Inc.*). But in a separate decision, the court upholds the constitutionality of a parental consent law that includes a judicial-bypass provision (*Planned Parenthood of Kansas City v. Ashcroft*).

### Dec. 14, 1987
In a deadlocked decision, the Supreme Court effectively strikes down an Illinois statute requiring that parents be told 24 hours before a physician performs an abortion on a minor (*Hartigan v. Zbaraz*).

### July 3, 1989
In a key victory for abortion opponents, the Supreme Court upholds the constitutionality of Missouri's statute banning abortion in public facilities, opening the gates to new state restrictions on abortion (*Webster v. Reproductive Health Services*).

### Oct. 5, 1989
Florida Supreme Court declares the state's parental consent law unconstitutional.

————— • —————

## 1990s
*Bills to create or strengthen parental notification and consent laws are introduced in many states.*

### June 25, 1990
Supreme Court upholds Minnesota's two-parent notification requirement as long as it includes a judicial-bypass option and it affirms the constitutionality of Minnesota's 48-hour waiting period (*Hodgson v. Minnesota*). The same day, the court upholds an Ohio statute requiring one-parent notification 24 hours before an abortion (*Ohio v. Akron Center for Reproductive Health*).

### Oct. 12, 1990
Senate passes a federal parental notification amendment attached to an amendment favored by abortion rights advocates to permit federal funding of abortions in cases of rape or incest. The amendment is later dropped in conference with the House.

### Nov. 6, 1990
Oregon voters reject a measure that would have prohibited a minor from obtaining an abortion until 48 hours after one of her parents had been notified by her physician.

Continued from p. 450

integrity." The following year, however, the composition of the Circuit Court changed, gaining appointees from President Reagan. In August 1988, the full court met and reversed the district court's decision, sending the case to the Supreme Court.

### Complicated Ruling

The final ruling was a complicated defeat for Jane Hodgson and the ACLU. The Minnesota abortion law under review had parental notification requirements in two separate provisions. The Supreme Court struck down one of the provisions because it lacked a judicial bypass. Writing for that majority, Justice John Paul Stevens argued that "not only does two-parent notification fail to serve any state interest with respect to functioning families, it disserves the state interest in protecting and assisting the minor with respect to dysfunctional families."

A different majority, however, then upheld other provisions of the Minnesota law, including one that contained a parental notification requirement and a judicial bypass. The Court said two-parent notification with a judicial bypass is constitutional because, in the words of Justice Sandra Day O'Connor, the Minnesota government's "interference with the internal operation of the family . . . does not exist where the minor can avoid notifying one or both parents by use of the bypass procedure."

Anti-abortion activists cheered the ruling. "A victory for family unity," said Archbishop Daniel E. Pilarczyk, president of the U.S. Catholic Conference. The Women's Legal Defense Fund expressed dismay. "The Supreme Court action has put teen women at greater risk," its statement said. "It has struck a blow at the underpinning principle of *Roe v. Wade*."

## Political Hot Potato

In Congress, parental involvement issues have provoked debate but no laws. Still, measures to require parental involvement have been a powerful tool of anti-abortion members and they have kept abortion rights members on the defensive. "It's a tough vote," says Rep. Ron Wyden, D-Ore., because "it takes some time to explain" the issue to constituents.

Parental notification amendments have been offered on several occasions to appropriations bills that include federal money for abortion-related programs. Last fall, a notification bill was twice approved by the Senate on a voice vote. The debate revealed the passion surrounding the abortion issue and the complex and shifting positions it forces on politicians. Sen. William L. Armstrong, a Colorado Republican who has since retired, ambushed Sen. Tom Harkin, an Iowa Democrat who was embroiled in a close re-election campaign in which his pro-abortion rights position was under attack.

Harkin and other abortion rights advocates had attached their most popular abortion amendment, one permitting use of federal funds for abortions in cases of rape or incest, to the spending bill for the Labor, Health and Human Services and Education departments. In a sort of "poison pill strategy," Armstrong intertwined his parental notification bill with Harkin's amendment.

Armstrong's plan would have required doctors treating teenage girls seeking abortions to provide written parental notification and to wait 48 hours before operating in states where no parental notification or consent laws were in effect. "I am gravely concerned about the permissiveness of our country toward abortion," Armstrong said at the time. "This national calamity . . . is a trag-

edy for the effect on the parents of the unborn child, and the grandparents of the unborn child." Armstrong made no secret of the fact that though the amendment dealt solely with notification, a ban on abortion was what was "in my heart."

In opposing Armstrong while keeping an eye on Iowa voters (who just three weeks later would re-elect him), Harkin said the amendment was "cruel, heartless and uncaring." But he also made it clear he favored parental notification laws if they contained a judicial bypass. He said the Armstrong plan did not provide for any leeway for children from broken homes or dysfunctional families. Therefore, he said, the states ought to decide the parameters of parental notification and consent.

The result was a 48-48 vote against Harkin's move to table the Armstrong proposal, which was then approved on a voice vote along with the abortion rights advocates' rape or incest language. Both were later dropped in conference with the House.

### Battles in the States

Parental involvement laws emerge more frequently as a state issue. In governors' races where abortion has been important — the 1989 races that elected Democrats James J. Florio in New Jersey and L. Douglas Wilder in Virginia, for example — the eventual winners favored abortion rights, but each felt it wise to express a receptivity to some form of parental involvement laws. (Neither New Jersey nor Virginia has such a law in effect.)

In Michigan, by contrast, incumbent Gov. James J. Blanchard in December 1989 had vetoed a parental consent law. After petitions were gathered under a state constitutional provision that allows citizens to put an issue on the ballot, the bill was repassed by the Legislature in September 1990. Blanchard and his

Continued on p. 454

# The Case of Becky Bell Mobilizes Parents

Abortion battles are often waged with the weapons of personal testimony. In the debate over parental involvement laws, nothing gets more personal than the story of Bill and Karen Bell, an Indianapolis couple whose 17-year-old daughter became pregnant, secretly sought an abortion and suddenly died. The Bells blame their tragedy on Indiana's parental consent law and have launched a campaign to repeal such laws nationwide.

Becky Bell was a high school sophomore when she became pregnant in the spring of 1988. That July, she went to the local Planned Parenthood clinic, where counselors laid out her options and told her of Indiana's law requiring the written consent of one parent for an abortion. Becky, who'd already had one pregnancy scare and had been in a drug detoxification program, had been frightened, according to a close friend, by a warning from her father not to "mess up" again.

When she told her boyfriend of her condition, he abandoned her. Becky was confused, the friend recalled, and undecided over whether to carry to term and put the baby up for adoption, or to travel out of state for an abortion. Though Indiana's law included a judicial bypass, she was apparently told that Indiana judges were issuing few abortion waivers to minors.

In September, two weeks into her junior year, Becky came home from a party crying and complaining of symptoms her parents took to be the flu. The next day, she fainted at her job as a part-time grocery cashier. She was running a high fever and spent the next few days in bed. She resisted her parents' urging that she go to a doctor.

The next day, Becky began hemorrhaging and had to be helped to the bathroom. She and her mother thought it was her menstrual period. But she was wheezing. This time she didn't object when her parents rushed her to the doctor. She was diagnosed with severe pneumonia and hospitalized. That evening, while her parents were out at dinner, she became unconscious and was put in intensive care, her lungs filled with fluid. That was when an examining doctor discovered her pregnancy. She died that night.

The coroner's report gave the cause of death as "septic abortion with pneumonia." The autopsy revealed a genital infection, which the forensic pathologist ruled as having resulted from an illegal abortion. It is a statement that has divided medical experts and activists in the parental involvement debate. It would not have been easy for a 17-year-old to locate a "back-alley" abortionist in Indianapolis, though this is what Becky's parents believe happened. Some surmise that Becky herself may have inserted a foreign object into her uterus. Others think she spontaneously miscarried.

After a year and a half of retracing their daughter's steps, the Bells began their campaign against parental involvement laws in early 1990. They are accepting funding from the Fund for a Feminist Majority, working in cooperation with local affiliates of the National Abortion Rights Action League and the National Organization for Women. Their daughter's death has been the theme of television advertisements from Planned Parenthood. The fund featured Becky Bell in a video on parental involvement laws and has launched a national campaign to enlist high school and college students to fight the laws.

Anti-abortion groups have attacked the campaign. A newsletter published by the National Right to Life Committee says there is no solid evidence that Becky Bell died of an illegal or self-induced abortion. "Clearly, Becky's parents are still in a stage of profound denial over their daughter's death and are being used shamelessly by pro-abortion forces for their own anti-life goals," wrote John C. Willke, a physician who recently retired as president of National Right to Life.

"It's a weak reed on which to base an entire public policy campaign," says Richard Doerflinger, a director of abortion policy at the U.S. Catholic Conference. "It's a tragic situation, but it's one sensationalized case."

Activists working to repeal parental involvement laws say opposition from anti-abortion forces will not deter their campaign. "With the Bell case, people see it could happen to their own child," says Eleanor Smeal, president of the Fund for a Feminist Majority.

Parents who favor parental involvement laws have their own organization, though it is still struggling for a national presence. Eileen Roberts is a Fredericksburg, Va., mother of a teenage daughter whose secret abortion at age 14 was followed by years of expensive medical bills for her family. In 1987, Roberts founded a parental support group called Mothers Against Minors' Abortions (MAMA). She has collected more than 3,000 signatures on a petition backing a parental notification bill in the Virginia legislature and hopes to collect 100,000 by the start of the 1992 session.

Recruiting parents in other states, however, has not been fruitful, she says. Personal experiences with abortion are "difficult to talk about," she says. "Mothers are not willing to come forward."

Roberts' personal experience has led to her focus on the importance of providing medical histories before surgery to avoid what she sees as the often-tragic aftermath of teenagers' abortions. Opponents of parental involvement, she says, are "giving our daughters secret abortions and then dumping them on our driveways for us to take care of them for the rest of their lives."

# Percentage of Pregnancies Terminated by Abortion

*Young women ages 15-19 are far more likely to get abortions than are older women, as the bar chart below left indicates. In 1987, the last year for which complete statistics are available, 41.6 percent of teen pregnancies were terminated by abortion. As the line graph below right indicates, the percentage of pregnancies terminated by abortion has remained fairly constant for all groups, including teenagers.*

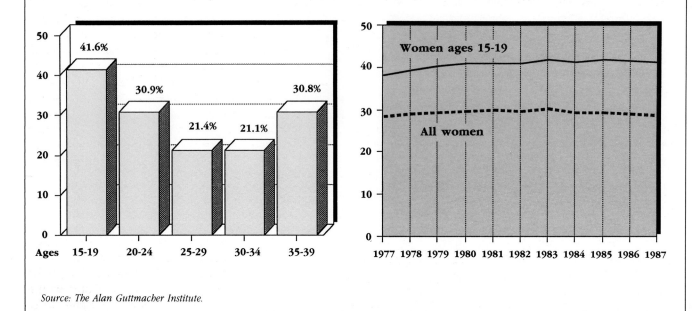

Source: The Alan Guttmacher Institute.

Continued from p. 452
staff, according to Carol King, executive director of the Michigan Abortion Rights Action League, were mindful of the popularity of parental consent. So they were shy about associating Blanchard's most recent act on abortion with that issue and softpedaled it in a campaign that focused on economic issues. Republican John Engler, a supporter of parental consent, won the governorship in November. The bill became law and took effect in April 1991.

Popular as they are, parental involvement requirements are not necessarily decisive in the political arena. This was clear in last fall's governor's race in Texas between businessman Clayton Williams and the eventual winner, state Treasurer Ann W. Richards. At the start of that campaign, the Texas Poll had showed that 70 percent of Texans favored parental consent for abor-

tions for women under 18. The Texas Republican Party had adopted a legislative plan that included a call for parental consent legislation. (Bill Price, president of Texans United for Life, said it was the best hope anti-abortion rights advocates had of getting through the Legislature in 1991. It was a compromise that alienated more conservative anti-abortion groups.)

Clayton Williams drew an ovation from the party convention in July 1990 by charging: "In the 'New Texas' envisioned by Ann Richards you won't have the right to know if your 13-year-old daughter is about to receive an abortion. Don't let Ann Richards tell you that your child's future is none of your business." (Newspapers reported that Williams' own daughters disagreed with him on parental consent.)

Opponent Richards took a consistently strong position against any re-

strictions on abortion rights, but she also foiled Williams' efforts to portray her as out of the mainstream. "We all support and encourage young people talking to their parents about any critical situation, including a pregnancy," Richards said continually during her campaign. "But parent-child communication cannot be forced through legislation."

Though the race was eventually decided on issues of crime, drugs and verbal gaffes by Williams, observers in both camps agreed that Richards deflected the parental consent issue effectively. "She did it with authenticity so that people felt she wasn't being permissive," said Wendy Sherman of EMILY'S List, a Washington group that raises funds for women Democratic candidates.

### Oregon Ballot Initiative

For opponents of parental involvement laws, the biggest news in recent years has been the defeat of a ballot initiative in Oregon last Fall, the only time a parental involvement law has been tested at the ballot box.

Most citizens of Oregon favor abortion rights. Republican Sen. Bob Packwood actively supports them, and in 1978 and 1986, Oregonians rejected efforts to ban state funding for poor women seeking abortions. In the summer of 1990, however, polls showed that more than 70 percent of Oregonians favored a parental notification law.

Anti-abortion activists from Oregon Right to Life succeeded in accumulating enough names on a petition to put a parental notification measure on the November ballot. Measure 10, as it was called, would have required doctors to notify one parent of a minor seeking an abortion 48 hours before operating. It offered no judicial bypass. Failure to notify could bring suspension of the doctor's medical license and would expose him to lawsuits. Insurance companies would not insure against such suits. Exceptions would be made in cases of rape or incest and abuse reported to state authorities, and the 48-hour waiting period could be waived if the girl's life or health was in danger.

To complicate the political situation, another anti-abortion group, the Oregon Citizens Alliance, succeeded in getting a separate measure on the ballot that would have banned abortion except in cases of rape, incest or danger to the mother's life. It was known as Measure 8. The polls indicated it had little chance of winning.

The fight was on. Packwood struck a staunchly neutral position, calling parental notification "a state issue." The conservative, Pennsylvania-based DeMoss Foundation sent in money for anti-abortion television commercials, and straw votes were held at high school campuses. Both sides took out radio and television ads and proponents on talk shows. Planned Parenthood officials and anti-abortion activists vied for time with editorial writers, and Bill and Karen Bell, parents of the Indiana teenager who died from an abortion, spoke at rallies and on college campuses. The ACLU sent staff to the polls on Election Day with posters telling voters to vote no on both Measures 8 and 10.

Measure 10 lost 52 percent to 48 percent.* Lynda Herrington, executive director of Oregon Right to Life, said her group had tried to distinguish between parental notification and the ban on abortion, but "the

_____

*Measure 8 lost 68 percent to 32 percent.

opposition succeeded in linking the two measures, using ads of a dark back alley that said, 'Don't send your daughter back to the alleys.' That's what tipped the scales."

Opponents of parental involvement laws were excited by the opportunity Oregon offered them to execute a detailed education campaign on the issue. Rachel Garland, legislative director to Rep. Les Aucoin, an Oregon Democrat, says the lesson of Measure 10 is that "when people really focus on what the consequences are, the issue looks quite different. It was the one time they had enough time to go around and make the case." ■

# CURRENT SITUATION

## Congress and the Court

Today's abortion debate continues to be fought on subsidiary issues — who pays for abortions, who has access to them and under what conditions. Hence parental involvement proposals continue to stir complex, compromise ingredients into a mixture many see as made from absolutes. The central issue of whether abortion should continue to be legal, however, is lurking not far below the surface.

The current Supreme Court — with its majority of Reagan-Bush appointees, its inclusion of David H. Souter in the seat long occupied by abortion rights advocate William J. Brennan Jr., and the nomination of Clarence Thomas to replace retiring Associate Justice Thurgood Marshall — is moving, many believe, toward a reconsideration of *Roe v. Wade.*

Challenges to bans on abortion in Alabama, Louisiana, Pennsylvania, Utah and Guam are working their way through the courts and might be heard by the Supreme Court within the next year. Abortion rights advocates, for their part, are seeking to write *Roe v. Wade* into law. The 1991 Freedom of Choice Act, sponsored by Rep. Don Edwards, D-Calif., and Sen. Alan Cranston, D-Calif., would simply declare that states may not restrict the right of a woman to choose to terminate a pregnancy. Both sides agree, however, that its passage would probably invalidate state parental involvement laws.

On the secondary issues, recent battles offer hope to both sides. Abortion rights advocates took heart in May when the House passed an amendment requiring military health facilities overseas to provide abortions to service members and their dependents. But the next day, the anti-abortion forces were rejoicing in the Supreme Court's decision, in *Rust v. Sullivan,* to uphold federal regulations that prohibit federally funded family planning counselors from discussing abortion with patients. Abortion rights backers were plainly worried. "*Rust* is a clear indicator of the Supreme Court's hostility to abortion and of its understanding of the doctor-patient relationship," said Kathryn Kolbert of the ACLU.

Even if the Supreme Court decides there is no constitutional right to an abortion, each state would still be left to enact its own abortion laws. So parental involvement issues are apt to continue as bones of contention. To elements of the anti-abortion movement who believe a complete ban on abortion is politically unrealistic, parental involvement laws remain a popular vehicle for reaching out to Americans who are ambivalent on abortion.

In Congress last month, anti-abortion members waging the annual fight over spending for the federal family planning program had planned to try to attach a parental notification amendment to a major appropriations bill in conjunction with the abortion-rights backers' amendment to overturn the Bush administration's restrictions on abortion counseling. Offered by Rep. Vin Weber, R-Minn., it would have required physicians at clinics receiving funds under the federal Public Health Service Act to notify one parent 48 hours before performing an abortion on a minor. It was ruled out of order, and anti-abortion members contented themselves with allowing the abortion counseling amendment to pass in the knowledge that President Bush planned to veto the spending bill.

## Action in the States

On the state level, the action is more furious. More than 220 bills dealing with abortion have been introduced this year in state legislatures. Thirty-four of the bills

deal with either enacting, strengthening or repealing parental involvement laws. More are possible this fall, though proposals on such a politically sticky issue are likely to taper off as the 1992 campaigns get under way.

Since the 1989 *Webster* ruling permitted state restrictions on abortion, parental involvement laws have

---

**The abortion debate continues to be fought on subsidiary issues — who pays for abortions, who has access to them and under what conditions. But the central issue of whether abortion should continue to be legal is lurking not far below the surface.**

---

been enacted in Maine, South Carolina, Connecticut, Michigan, Maryland and, most recently, Nebraska. Legislatures in Mississippi, Tennessee, Kentucky and Pennsylvania have acted to put laws that have been blocked by the courts into effect; their cases are moving through the courts.

Many other parental involvement proposals have been killed at the committee level before the full legislatures ever voted on them.

Opponents of such laws credit their successes to the fact that women have been gaining election to legislatures and to key committee posts in greater numbers. "It's not a Democratic-Republican issue," says Tamar Raphael of the Fund for a Feminist Majority. "The majority of women oppose the bills. It's Republican males who are the worst."

### Political Compromises

Sometimes, the laws that emerge are a compromise between abortion rights and anti-abortion considerations. When Maryland enacted its parental notification law in February, its lawmakers were still smarting from a tumultuous eight-day filibuster the previous year by abortion opponents. It had produced a compromise abortion bill so schizophrenic (it would have combined a *Roe v. Wade* guarantee of abortion rights with a package of abortion restrictions) that it quickly sunk in committee.

This time, a group of anti-abortion strategists decided that parental notification was the only step possible politically, and abortion rights forces, though divided, acceded to their leaders' judgment that acceptance of parental notification was the only way to pass legislation guaranteeing Maryland women access to legal abortions.

The result was a law that gives physicians leeway to decide whether the girl seeking an abortion is mature enough to proceed without her parents. Opponents of parental involvement laws applaud the Maryland compromise; some anti-abortion activists call it "the abortionist's consent" law and have been circulating a petition to repeal it.

As more states become experienced with parental involvement laws, the laws also get more sophisticated. The Nebraska bill signed into law on May 29, for example, contained a one-parent notification requirement for girls under 18 seeking an abortion, a 48-hour waiting period and a judicial bypass, as well as a provision, similar to one in Michigan, that requires the state education department to provide students with information on the law. ∎

# At Issue:

## Are parental involvement laws a positive force in helping teenagers deal with abortion?

### *yes*

HUGH L. CAREY

**Former governor of New York**
FROM *CATHOLIC NEW YORK*, JULY 27, 1989.

*n*ot too long ago, a mother in Connecticut was shocked to receive a call advising her that her 15-year-old daughter was in a White Plains hospital awaiting corrective surgery to repair a botched abortion after being transferred to the hospital from a Planned Parenthood facility in Greensburgh. The doctors at the hospital wanted the mother's consent to operate because the girl was a minor.

That mother was caught up in New York's bizarre law, which allows a 15-year-old from Connecticut to come to an abortion clinic in New York and have an abortion without her parent's consent, but requires that same parent's consent if surgery is needed to repair the damage done by the abortion. Indeed, New York requires parental consent if that same young girl wanted to have a cavity filled or needed her appendix removed or simply wanted to go on a field trip with her school class. But not if she seeks an abortion.

Do parents have a right to know if their teenage daughter is pregnant? Do parents have a right and obligation to be involved in every problem that affects their minor child? My answer is a resounding "yes."

There's a dividend that could flow from a parental consent law. When Massachusetts adopted a parental consent law — providing the court permission option — there was a 19 percent drop in teenage pregnancies. And the same thing happened in Minnesota. Do I believe some children behave differently just because what Mom would say if she found out? You bet I do. I believe it because that's what I was like growing up. And children are the same today.

Parenting a minor means knowing and helping — not being left in the dark only to be shocked, like that mother in Connecticut, to learn too late, that things have gone so terribly wrong for her child. But it's when things have gone wrong that parents must know, so they can help the child they love. When the issue is a surgical procedure on the person of a minor child, let it be said loud and clear that mother knows best. And it is best that mother knows — and father, too.

### *no*

AMERICAN CIVIL LIBERTIES UNION,
REPRODUCTIVE FREEDOM PROJECT

FROM A PAMPHLET TO BE PUBLISHED THIS YEAR.

*r*equiring a young woman to involve her parents or a judge before obtaining an abortion may sound harmless at first, for it would be better if every young woman could discuss an unwanted pregnancy with loving and caring parents. Sadly, too many parents react with hostility or violence to the news of their daughter's pregnancy.

More than half of the young women seeking abortion tell at least one parent about their decision. The younger the woman, the more likely her parents are to know about, and even suggest, the abortion. Nevertheless, mandatory notification laws will cause some young women who are unable to tell their parents about their pregnancies to seek medical care from unlicensed, illegal abortionists or to attempt self-abortion — risking death or permanent injury.

Instead of offering support to their pregnant daughters, some parents lash out violently. Particularly where there is a history of physical or sexual abuse in the family, this violence can jeopardize the life and health of a young woman or destroy her future. For a variety of compelling reasons, rape and incest survivors are often unable to discuss the abuse with anyone. Telling their abusers about a pregnancy is unthinkable. Because most teenagers have no means of providing for their own food and shelter, the fear of being kicked out of their homes is especially acute.

Daughters often refuse to discuss their pregnancies with parents who are substance abusers or who are physically ill or emotionally unstable, feeling the need to shelter their parents from further trauma. Even in families where there are close ties, young women may decide not to tell their parents about a pregnancy. Often, these young women want to live up to their parents' expectations and preserve good family relationships.

With more than one million young American women becoming pregnant each year — most of whose pregnancies are unplanned and unwanted — teenage pregnancy is a societal problem that is not likely to disappear soon. Nevertheless, we can substantially reduce unwanted pregnancies by making a full range of reproductive health care options more accessible to young women. Repeal or modification of all parental notification and consent laws is a crucial first step.

# OUTLOOK

## Powerful Polls

Parental involvement laws derive their political forcefulness from their consistent appeal in opinion polls. In focus groups conducted for the National Abortion Rights Action League, pollster Harrison Hickman found that parental consent is an issue that "strikes deep in the heart of all parents' fears and uncertainties about their role as guides, arbiters, protectors and shapers of their children."

Hickman adds, "Parents of teenagers almost always have a sense of losing touch with their child and many are deeply concerned about their child's safety. To questions about adolescent abortion, a parent most often will respond that they 'don't want my child to go through something like that without me.' Parental consent laws give these parents hope that they will still be able to exercise some control." [22]

A May 1990 Yankelovich Clancy Shulman poll for Cable News Network and *Time* magazine showed the public by 50 percent to 46 percent believes both parents, not simply one, should give permission for an abortion. The poll also indicated that the public views abortion differently from other medical procedures. It asked whether a teenager under 18 should be able to consent to various medical procedures without parental permission. Only 38 percent said teenagers should be able to have an abortion without parental consent. The percentages were much higher for other medical procedures: 63 percent said parental consent shouldn't be required have a tooth pulled; 59 percent, to donate blood; 53 percent, to obtain birth control; 45 percent, to take medication.

Of the commonly offered restric-tions on abortion, parental involvement laws are clearly the most attractive. A CBS News-*New York Times* poll in July 1989 asked respondents which of four restrictions they would endorse. Requiring parental consent drew 71 percent; requiring a test to make sure a fetus is not developed enough to live outside the womb, 60 percent; prohibiting employees of public hospitals from performing abortions, 35 percent; and passing laws that would make it difficult for private clinics to perform abortions, 41 percent.

To abortion rights groups battling parental involvement laws, such polls are merely a "first-take opinion" that can be changed, in the words of Eleanor Smeal of the Fund for a Feminist Majority. "After some education on the issue, many people say, 'Oh my god, give the girl what she needs,'" Smeal says.

## Politicians under Pressure

Statistics show that middle- and upper-income pregnant teens are 2.5 times as likely as low-income counterparts to obtain abortions. This hints that teen abortion will remain an issue among the politically active. Many observers on both sides of the issue see a repeal campaign as an uphill battle. Following a nationwide poll and set of focus groups conducted in 1989, EMILY'S List concluded that voters favor abortion rights but warned that "voters will not forgive candidates who appear to be working against responsible parents." The group noted that a Democrat who opposes parental consent loses ground against an anti-abortion Republican who supports parental consent laws. It advised Democratic candidates to "take concrete steps to affirm parental responsibility," such as backing parental consent laws with a judicial bypass.

Republican pollster Linda DiVall of American Viewpoint says the compromises and exceptions to the abortion debate represented by parental involvement laws are very important politically. "The American people are very centrist" on abortion, she says. "They're looking for reasonable behavior and judgment, so abortion becomes a character-defining issue."

But those running the campaign against the laws won't be discouraged. "Politicians lag behind public opinion," says Eleanor Smeal. "They play it safe. They want to be able to tell the right-to-lifers, 'I'm with you on this one,' and pick up support here and there. But on the abortion issue, it's increasingly hard. There's pressure to be either" in favor of abortion rights or anti-abortion.

Janet O'Keeffe of the American Psychological Association says politicians are scared of 30-second television sound bites from their opponents. "Those with children can't step out of their feelings as parents — that they'd like to know" about a daughter's abortion, she says. On the other hand, O'Keeffe adds, lawmakers have an obligation to look at the facts. The judiciary looks at legal, constitutional issues, but they don't have to consider the effects. "Lawmakers do."

## Issue Won't Go Away

The problems that prompt parental involvement laws are not easing. In 1988, 50 percent of unmarried 15-to-19-year-old women and 60 percent of unmarried 15-to-19-year-old men reported they had had sexual intercourse. From 1982 to 1988, the percentage of unmarried 15-year-old women who had had intercourse rose from 19 percent to 27 percent. [23] The Center for Population Options puts the annual cost to government for Medicaid, food stamps and welfare payments to families in which the mother first gave birth as a teen at $21.5 billion.

Conducting any kind of education campaign around such issues is tough, says Sally Patterson, vice president for public affairs at Planned Parenthood. "Abortion is not an accepted medical practice in this country, even though it's legal; women are reluctant to discuss it," she says. "We're not a society that encourages women to talk about sexuality." Barbara Radford, executive director of the National Abortion Federation, which opposes parental involvement laws, says opposing such laws is the "most difficult part of" her work because it requires "making people see that many young women are not able to communicate with their families on sexual issues, particularly pregnancy."

"So much education is needed to defeat parental consent laws outright, we have a long way to go," says pollster Celinda Lake. "Where we can be successful is passing broad-based laws," such as in Maine, Connecticut and Wisconsin, where health-care providers, clergy, social workers, even boyfriends' mothers are able to stand in for parents.

Such compromises, however, don't satisfy supporters of parental involvement laws. "In some ways this compromise makes everything worse," says Edie Palmer, a lobbyist for Maine Right to Life. "These women can drag out a great aunt's second cousin and get consent, or waltz into some clinic and find a doctor to give the OK. It's simple to skirt the idea of family involvement." [24]

Given the public's support for legal abortion, anti-abortion activists can't be certain that parental involvement will lead to fewer abortions. As Harvard University law Professor Lawrence H. Tribe points out, a minor who is too young to consent to an abortion or any other medical procedure is also too young to refuse them. "This suggests," Tribe concludes, "that parental consent requirements, whatever might be said for them as a matter of parental authority generally, cannot plausibly be defended as part of a 'pro-life' compromise since the premises on which such consent requirements rest equally support parentally compelled abortions." [25]

Fear of the anti-abortion movement's long-term agenda leads many opponents of parental involvement laws to believe that compromises are not advisable. "Compromises aren't compromises, they're an attempt to deny a basic fundamental right," says Eleanor Smeal.

Rachel Garland of Rep. AuCoin's staff says lawmakers may have to face the fact that parental involvement laws "won't get the right-to-lifers off their backs. "When the issue is killing babies and ninth-month abortions, parental notification doesn't get you very far," she says.

For the moment, supporters of parental involvement laws feel they're in the catbird's seat. "I don't see repeal happening in any state," says Balch of the National Right to Life Committee. "We have the support of the people. It doesn't matter what your position on abortion is. It is an issue that will not go away." ∎

## Notes

[1] S. K. Henshaw and J. Van Vort, "Research Note: Teenage Abortion, Birth and Pregnancy Statistics: An Update," *Family Planning Perspectives*, March/April, 1989.

[2] Quoted in *Scholastic Update*, April 20, 1990.

[3] Frank Bolton, *The Pregnant Adolescent*, Russell Sage Foundation, 1980, cited in a fact sheet published by the National Right to Life Committee.

[4] *Des Moines Register*, Dec. 27, 1989.

[5] Gary B. Melton and Nancy Felipe Russo, "Adolescent Abortion: Psychological Perspectives on Public Policy," *American Psychologist*, January 1987.

[6] Laurie Schwab Zabin, Marilyn B. Hirsch and Mark R. Emerson, "When Urban Adolescents Choose Abortion: Effects on Education, Psychological Status and Subsequent Pregnancy," *Family Planning Perspectives*, December 1989.

[7] Burkman *et al.*, "Morbidity Risk Among Adolescents Undergoing Elective Abortion, *Contraception*, Vol. 30, 1984, p. 99.

[8] *Adolescents and Abortion: Choice in Crisis*, Center for Population Options, July 1990, p. 7.

[9] Quoted in *Scholastic Update, op. cit.*

[10] Quoted in *Newsweek*, July 9, 1990, p. 23.

[11] Quoted in *The New York Times*, Aug. 17, 1990.

[12] V. G. Cartoff and L. V. Klerman, "Parental Consent for Abortion: Impact of the Massachusetts Law," *American Journal of Public Health*, Vol. 76, p. 397.

[13] James L. Rogers, Robert F. Boruch, George B. Stoms and Dorothy DeMoya, "Impact of the Minnesota Parental Notification Law on Abortion and Birth," *American Journal of Public Health*, March 1991.

[14] Writing in *Family Planning Perspectives*, January/February, 1991.

[15] *Ohio v. Akron Center for Reproductive Services*, July 1990.

[16] Quoted in *The New York Times*, July 16, 1989.

[17] Alan Guttmacher Institute, *Teenage Pregnancy: The Problem that Hasn't Gone Away*, 1981.

[18] Quoted in *The Wall Street Journal*, Nov. 29, 1989.

[19] Cited in *The New York Times*, May 3, 1991.

[20] See *Adolescent Health Care Decision Making: The Law and Public Policy*, a June 1990 report prepared by the Office of Technology Assessment for the Carnegie Council on Adolescent Development a program of Carnegue Corporation of New York.

[21] Quoted in *Newsweek, op. cit.*

[22] Summarized by the Center for Population Options in *Adolescents and Abortion*, 1990, p. 11.

[23] *1988 National Survey of Family Growth*, cited by the Alan Guttmacher Institute.

[24] Quoted in *The Wall Street Journal*, Nov. 29, 1989.

[25] Lawrence H. Tribe, *Abortion: The Clash of Absolutes* (1990), p. 199.

# Bibliography

## Selected Sources Used

### Books

**National Research Council,** *Risking the Future: Adolescent Sexuality, Pregnancy and Childbearing,* **National Academy Press, 1987.**
A committee of medical and psychiatric experts surveys current literature on teenagers' sexual behavior, pregnancy rates, use of abortion and experience in childbearing.

**Tribe, Lawrence H.,** *Abortion: The Clash of Absolutes,* **W. W. Norton & Co., 1990.**
Tribe, a Harvard University law professor, examines basic arguments in the abortion debate.

### Articles

**Greenberger, Marcia D., and Connor, Katherine, "Parental Notice and Consent for Abortion: Out of Step with Family Law Principles and Policies,"** *Family Planning Perspectives,* **January/February 1991.**
Attorneys at the National Women's Law Center argue that parental involvement laws violate the privacy of minors and disrupt the principles of traditional family law.

**Halpern, Sue, "The Fight Over Teenage Abortion,"** *New York Review of Books,* **March 29, 1990.**
A background discussion of parental notification abortion cases in Ohio and Minnesota written before they were decided by the Supreme Court in June 1990. It examines the pros and cons of the judicial bypass mechanism.

**Melton, Gary B., and Russo, Nancy Felipe, "Adolescent Abortion: Psychological Perspectives on Public Policy,"** *American Psychologist,* **January 1987.**
Two psychologists examine empirical research they say the Supreme Court has neglected in deciding adolescent abortion cases.

**O'Keeffe, Janet, and Jones, James M., "Easing Restrictions on Minors' Abortion Rights,"** *Issues in Science and Technology,* **fall 1990.**
Two analysts from the American Psychological Association survey psychological and legal literature to argue that forced parental involvement in pregnancy decisions is counterproductive and harmful.

**Rogers, James L, Boruch, Robert F., Stoms, George B., and DeMoya, Dorothy, "Impact of the Minnesota Parental Notification Law on Abortion and Birth,"** *American Journal of Public Health,* **March 1991.**
A team of psychologists and statisticians evaluates data from the Minnesota Center for Health Statistics on the effects of Minnesota's parental notification law. They suggest the law prompted adolescents to be more responsible in avoiding pregnancy.

**Worthington, Everett L. Jr. et al., "The Benefits of Legislation Requiring Parental Involvement Prior to Adolescent Abortion,"** *American Psychologist,* **December 1989.**
A team of psychologists surveys academic literature to argue that parental notification and consent laws can help adolescents gain support from their parents in dealing with abortion decisions.

### Reports and Studies

**American Civil Liberties Union Reproductive Freedom Project,** *Parental Notice Laws: Their Catastrophic Impact on Teenagers' Right to Abortion,* **ACLU, 1986.**
Legal activists working to preserve abortion rights compiled these arguments against parental involvement laws in the course of prolonged litigation in the *Hodgson v. Minnesota* case.

**Gittler, Josephine, Quigley-Rick, Mary, and Saks, Michael J.,** *Adolescent Health Care and Decision Making: The Law and Public Policy,* **Office of Technology Assessment, U.S. Congress, working paper prepared for the Carnegie Corporation of New York, June 1990.**
Three law professors examine the legal history and reasoning behind state laws and regulations affecting health care decisions affecting minors. They discuss parental roles in procedures used in treatments for sexually related health problems, drug and alcohol abuse and mental health problems.

**National Abortion Rights Action League,** *Who Decides?: A State-by-State Review of Abortion Rights,* **The NARAL Foundation, 1991.**
A major abortion rights activist group compiled this description of each state government's current attitudes on abortion, abortion laws in effect and pending legislation. It also gives each state's figures on the number of abortion providers.

# The Next Step

## Additional Articles from Current Periodicals

### Case studies

**"Kathy's day in court,"** *Ms.*, **April 1988, p. 46.**

Gives an account of "Kathy" a 17-year-old from Birmingham, Ala., and her request before a judge for permission to obtain an abortion. Examines the effectiveness of the parental consent abortion laws on the books in 20 states. Comments by pro-choice and right-to-life spokespeople. INSET: A state-by-state guide to parental consent and notification laws for minors' abortions.

**Greenhouse, L., "Abortion law fight turns to rights of teen-agers,"** *The New York Times*, **July 16, 1989, Section 1, p. 1.**

Analyzes two upcoming cases before the Supreme Court that could restrict the rights of teenagers to obtain an abortion without parental consent. Poll results indicating parental consent favored by a majority; Statistics on current parental involvement; High rate of teenage sexual activity; Impact of childbirth on teenagers.

**Greenhouse, L., "Abortion: A new round,"** *The New York Times*, **Nov. 24, 1989, p. A1.**

Recounts details of the two abortion cases to be heard by the Supreme Court this session, and covers the out-of-court settlement in Illinois earlier this week. Ohio and Minnesota cases rooted in parental notification of an impending abortion for minors; Where the public stands; Bush administration brief.

**Halpern, S. and Cates, G., "Teen-abortion laws turn trauma to tragedy,"** *Rolling Stone*, **Aug. 9, 1990, p. 43.**

Opinion. Recounts the case of Becky Bell, an Indiana high school student who died of an illegal abortion on Sep. 16, 1988. Her parents, Karen and Bill Bell, have become vocal activists who lobby against parental consent laws. Uses the Bell case as an example of family situations caused by such laws.

**Mackey, L., "Court fails to block abortion,"** *Christianity Today*, **Sept. 8, 1989, p. 65.**

Reports that Canadian Chantal Daigle, involved in a legal battle with her boyfriend who did not want her to abort their child, crossed the border into the U.S. and had an abortion. The abortion debate in Canada; Pro-life group Campaign Life.

**Marek, E., "The lives of teenage mothers,"** *Harper's*, **April 1989, p. 56.**

Presents an account of the author's visit to the Teen Parenting Program in the Bronx at the Kingsbridge Heights Community Center where she met with a group of teenage mothers. Problems the mother's face; Brief profiles of mothers, their education, feelings on abortion and birth control; More.

**Schmalz, J., "U.S. Supreme Court clears way for Florida teen to have abortion,"** *The New York Times*, **May 19, 1989, p. A12.**

Reports that the U.S. Supreme Court has opened the way for any Florida girl, regardless of age, to have an abortion without the approval of a parent or judge. Case of T. W. discussed; Probable changes in law discussed.

**Sharpe, R., " 'She died because of a law,' "** *Ms.*, **July/August 1990, p. 80.**

Tells the story of Indianapolis, Ind., housewife Karen Bell, 46, who travels the country lobbying against parental consent abortion laws. Bell's daughter Rebecca (Becky), 17, died of a septic abortion. Relationship with daughter; How Rebecca's death changed Bell's life.

**Zirkel, P. A., "In loco parentis,"** *Phi Delta Kappan*, **March 1990, p. 563.**

Reports on a court case that arose when an Alabama school helped one of its minority students obtain an abortion. The girl's parents, as well as the parents of the father, alleged they were 'coerced' into the abortion, and an appellate court ruled that the school acted improperly in loco parentis.

### Debates & issues

**Arkes, H., "How to roll back Roe,"** *National Review*, **Oct. 28, 1988, p. 30.**

Opinion. A report on abortion laws in the U.S. today. Examines what the Supreme Court decision in *Roe v. Wade* (1973) actually established. When human life begins; Right of a pregnant woman over the unborn child.

**Colen, B. D., "Mother, may I?"** *Health*, **October 1990, p. 42.**

Argues against recent state laws and Supreme Court rulings requiring parental notification of an adolescent girl's plans to have an abortion. Realities of American life; Adolescent's right to privacy; Criticism of right-to-life advocates.

**Greenhouse, L., "Oblique clash between 2 justices mirrors tensions about abortion,"** *The New York Times*, **Nov. 30, 1989, p. A1.**

Describes the clash between Supreme Court Justice

Sandra Day O'Connor and Justice Antonin Scalia on the issue of a Minnesota law requiring that parents be notified before a teenager may have an abortion. Pros and cons; *Webster v. Reproductive Health Services*; *Roe v. Wade*. INSET: Survey finds split on abortion persisting.

**Greenhouse, L., "States may require girl to notify parents before having abortion," *The New York Times*, June 26, 1990, p. A1.**

Discusses the Supreme Court ruling that states may require a teenage girl to notify both parents before obtaining an abortion, as long as the alternative of a judicial hearing is provided for those who do not want to inform their parents.

**Gruber, E. and Anderson, M. M., "Legislating parental involvement in adolescent abortion," *American Psychologist*, October 1990, p. 1174.**

Discusses the comment by Worthington, et al. in the December 1989 issue of the *American Psychologist* dealing with mandatory parental involvement in the decision-making process preceding adolescent abortion. No way to legislate "involvement"; Decision-making competence; More.

**Harrington-Lueker, D., "The Supreme Court, abortion, and schools," *Education Digest*, March 1990, p. 40.**

Discusses what costs and controversies are posed for schools by the U.S. Supreme Court's limitations on abortion rights. Welfare costs and teenage pregnancy.

**Lawton, K. A., "Scanning the prolife battlefields," *Christianity Today*, June 16, 1989, p. 52.**

Examines the current battles over the issue of abortion. U.S. Congress debates on the issue; The RU 486 abortion pill; Fetal-tissue research; Requiring parental consent for abortion; Sex-selection procedures; Operation Rescue.

**McAnarney, E. R. and Hendee, W. R., "Adolescent pregnancy and its consequences," *Journal of the American Medical Association*, July 7, 1989, p. 74.**

Discusses adolescent pregnancy and its consequences. Obstetric and neonatal outcome; Developmental status of the children of adolescents; Psychosocial outcome of young parents; Maternal educational and economic status; Repetition; Abortion; Adolescent fathers.

**Orenstein, P., "Does father know best?" *Vogue*, April 1989, p. 314.**

Examines the legal rights of fathers to prevent the abortion of their unborn children. Position of men's rights groups; Two cases pending in the Indiana Supreme Court; Involvement of the American Civil Liberties Union and the National Right to Life Committee.

**Pickett, J., "Who's raising my granddaughter?" *Christianity Today*, Jan. 14, 1991, p. 26.**

Considers the debate on abortion from the perspective of an adoptive parent. Experiences adopting and raising two children that might have been aborted; Helping her adopted daughter deal with a pregnancy out of wedlock; Daughter's decision to place her child for adoption; Why Christians should focus on adoption as a positive alternative to abortion.

**Salholz, E., King, P., et al., "Teenagers and abortion," *Newsweek*, Jan. 8, 1990, p. 32.**

Discusses the Supreme Court rulings expected on a set of cases involving parental notification and consent before teenagers can obtain an abortion. Privacy vs. the right to know; More than a million teenage pregnancies every year; Current restrictive laws in effect; Some pros and cons of parental consent. INSET: Young and pregnant.

**Salholz, E., King, P., et al., "The right-to-lifers' new tactics," *Newsweek*, July 9, 1990, p. 23.**

Discusses the right-to-life groups' feelings about the Supreme Court decision to require parental consent for teenage girls who have an abortion. Gives parents the right to kill their own grandchild; Change in tactics; *Webster v. Reproductive Health Services* case; National Right to Life Committee; National Abortion Rights Action League.

**Szegedy-Maszak, M., "Calm, cool and beleaguered," *The New York Times Magazine*, Aug. 6, 1989, p. 16.**

Profile of Faye Wattleton, president of the Planned Parenthood Federation of America, and her plans to mobilize for the next abortion rights campaign. Three abortion-related cases to be heard by the Supreme Court; History of Planned Parenthood; Funding for the organization; Personal history and career as a nurse; Plans to propose a constitutional amendment guaranteeing freedom of reproductive choice.

**Watzman, N., "When sex ed becomes chastity class," *Utne Reader*, July/August 1990, p. 92.**

Reports on the "abstinence-based" sex education curriculum called "Sex Respect" which is an alternative to programs that include information about abortion and contraception. Premise of "Sex Respect"; Backing of conservative groups; Criticism of program. INSET: Education needed as incidence of AIDS rises among teens, by B. B. Kelley.

## Law & legislation

**"Chipping away at Roe v. Wade," *Christianity Today*, Aug. 20, 1990, p. 37.**

Considers the prospects for a reversal of the 1973 *Roe v. Wade* Supreme Court decision legalizing abortion. Impact of the resignation of liberal Justice William J. Brennan; Recent cases on parental notice requirements; Role of Justice Sandra Day O'Connor.

**Carlson, M., Cramer, J., et al., "Abortion's hardest cases," *Time*, July 9, 1990, p. 22.**

Discusses a recent Supreme Court decision which upheld a Minnesota law requiring unwed teenagers to notify both parents before an abortion if the law allows minors to go to a judge instead. It also upheld an Ohio law requiring physicians to notify one parent of a pregnant minor of her intent to have an abortion, and provided for a judicial bypass. Wedge issues: dealing with rape, incest and parental involvement.

**Greenhouse, L., "States may require girl to notify parents before having abortion," *The New York Times*, June 26, 1990, p. A1.**

Discusses the Supreme Court ruling that states may require a teenage girl to notify both parents before obtaining an abortion, as long as the alternative of a judicial hearing is provided for those who do not want to inform their parents.

**Kaplan, D. A. and McDaniel, A., "The family vs. the state," *Newsweek*, July 9, 1990, p. 22.**

Reports on two Supreme Court rulings: The right to die and the abortion issue. Upheld state laws requiring a teenage girl to notify at least one parent before having an abortion; Missouri can prohibit the parents of Nancy Cruzan from removing feeding tubes because of no definitive evidence that she would have wanted treatment stopped. INSET: Living wills.

**Rovner, J., "Family planning is catalyst to a simmering feud," *Congressional Quarterly Weekly Report*, April 6, 1991, p. 86.**

Discusses a new legislative strategy for reauthorizing the federal family planning program that is the first tangible evidence of a shift in Republican leadership on one of the House's busiest subcommittees. Polarization of Energy and Commerce Subcommittee on Health and the Environment; Moderate Edward Madigan; Role of family planning; Parental notification for abortions; Family planning advocates; Abortion opponents. INSET: Gearing up for another round.

**Schreiber, L., "Teenage and pregnant," *Glamour*, March 1991, p. 236.**

Examines the U.S. Supreme Court's decision to uphold the Minnesota law that requires doctors to notify both of a minor's biological parents before performing an abortion. Parental notification hearings; Example cases; Dangers;

Minnesota teen birthrates. INSET: The politics of judicial bypass: A national update (judicial-bypass laws and abortion).

**Whitman, D., "When pregnant girls face mom and dad," *U.S. News & World Report*, Dec. 4, 1989, p. 25.**

Examines an upcoming U.S. Supreme Court case on the role of parents when a minor daughter is seeking an abortion. Minnesota state statute that requires parental consent; Obstetrician Jane Hodgson's challenge of the law; Pro-life and pro-choice arguments. INSET: Jane Hodgson's odyssey.

## Moral & religious aspects

**Doerr, E., "Bad news in bunches," *Humanist*, September/October 1990, p. 33.**

Opinion. Reports on recent court rulings harmful to religious liberty. Peyote case and the American Indians; Upholding of the 1984 Equal Access Law; Upholding of parental notification laws in abortion cases; Reviews of various books.

## Research

**Miller, B. C. and Moore, K. A., "Adolescent sexual behavior, pregnancy, and parenting: Research through the 1980s," *Journal of Marriage & the Family*, November 1990, p. 1025.**

Summarizes research from the 1980s on the topics of adolescent sexual activity, conception, abortion, marriage, adoption, and childbearing. Research about the antecedents of adolescent sexual and conceptive behavior is emphasized because they are the key risk factors in adolescent pregnancy. Discusses advances in data and methods, and highlights research gaps.

## Social aspects

**Chelala, C. A., "Teenage pregnancy in New York," *World Health*, April/May 1990, p. 21.**

Analyzes the factors that have contributed to the high rate of teenage pregnancy and abortion in U.S. lifestyles; Lack of parental involvement; Lack of adequate sex education and effective contraceptives; Poverty; How to deal with adolescent sexuality; Suggested programs.

# Back Issues

*Great Research on Current Issues Starts Right Here. . . Recent topics covered by The CQ Researcher are listed below. Issues dated before May 10, 1991, were published under the name of Editorial Research Reports.*

**DECEMBER 1989**
North America Trade Pact
Influence Peddling
German Reunification
Learning Disabilities

**JANUARY 1990**
Higher Education Curriculum
Photonics
Age of 'Infotainment'
Abortion: Politicians' Nightmare

**FEBRUARY 1990**
Politics and Economic Growth
Free Agency in Sports
Repetitive Motion
War on Drugs

**MARCH 1990**
Asbestos: Are Risks Acceptable?
Public Health Campaigns
South Africa's Future
Homeless Need More Than Shelter

**APRIL 1990**
How Fair is the Tax Burden?
Workers' Compensation
U.S. Pacific Forces
Curbing Insurance Premiums

**MAY 1990**
Should Teaching Be a Profession?
Will Canada Fall Apart?
Is U.S. Patent System Outdated?
Federal Funding for the Arts

**JUNE 1990**
Downsizing America's Armed Forces
Progress In Weather Forecasting
S & L Bailout
Bio-Chemical Disarmament

**JULY 1990**
Do Americans Still Love Marriage?
Death Penalty Debate
Decline of Rural America
United Nations in the 1990s

**AUGUST 1990**
Democracy in the Philippines
Initiatives: True Democracy?
Hard Times at Newspapers
Teens Balance School & Jobs

**SEPTEMBER 1990**
Dangers of Alcohol
Western Alliance After the Cold War
Tobacco Industry
Right to Die

**OCTOBER 1990**
Organ Transplants
Energy Policy Options
Search for Arab Unity
Child Support

**NOVEMBER 1990**
Lotteries and Gambling
Post Cold-War Choices
Setting Limits on Medical Care
Multicultural Education

**DECEMBER 1990**
Cable TV Regulation
Americans' Search For Their Roots
Is Insurance System a Failure?
Why Schools Still Have Tracking

**JANUARY 1991**
Growing Influence of Boycotts
Should the U.S. Reinstate the Draft?
America's Archaeological Past
Peace Corps' Challenges in '90s

**FEBRUARY 1991**
Regional Impact of Recession
Puerto Rico's Status
Redistricting: Mapping Power
Nuclear Power

**MARCH 1991**
Acid Rain
Cost of the Gulf War
Reassessing Gun Laws
Future for Man in Space

**APRIL 1991**
Social Security
Canadian Crisis Over Quebec
California Drought
Electromagnetic Radiation

**MAY 1991**
School Choice
Racial Quotas
Animal Rights
U.S. and Japan

**JUNE 1991**
Children and Divorce
Teenage Suicide
Endangered Species
Europe 1992

# Future Topics

▶ *Soviet Nationalities*

▶ *Mexico's Emergence*

▶ *Athletes and Drugs*

PUBLISHED BY CONGRESSIONAL QUARTERLY INC., IN CONJUNCTION WITH EBSCO PUBLISHING

# Soviet Republics Rebel

*The 15 Soviet republics are pressing for greater autonomy*

THE MANY REGIONS AND ETHNIC GROUPS OF the Soviet Union are calling for enhanced rights. Some of them, especially the Baltic republics of Latvia, Estonia and Lithuania, want all-out independence. Others seek increased autonomy that would wrest some control away from Moscow. Complicating this push for a realignment of power are ethnic clashes in several republics. Such militancy represents a bold challenge to the Soviet state. It threatens the central command in Moscow and may hasten the political demise of Mikhail S. Gorbachev. A proposed treaty defining the powers of the central government and the rights of the republics has further kindled the debate. Though the treaty improves the republics' stature, it makes secession difficult to achieve. How this conflict is resolved will help define the future shape of the Soviet Union.

 **July 12, 1991 • Volume 1, No. 10 • 465-488**

*Formerly Editorial Research Reports*

Cover Art: Barbara Sassa-Daniels

# CQ Researcher

July 12, 1991
Volume 1, No. 10

**EDITOR**
Sandra Stencel

**ASSOCIATE EDITOR**
Richard L. Worsnop

**STAFF WRITERS**
Charles S. Clark
Mary H. Cooper
Rodman D. Griffin

**PRODUCTION EDITOR**
Laurie De Maris

**EDITORIAL ASSISTANT**
Thomas H. Moore

**GRAPHICS**
Jack Auldridge

**PUBLISHED BY**
Congressional Quarterly Inc.

**CHAIRMAN**
Andrew Barnes

**VICE CHAIRMAN**
Andrew P. Corty

**EDITOR AND PUBLISHER**
Neil Skene

**EXECUTIVE EDITOR**
Robert W. Merry

**PUBLICATIONS MARKETING/SALES**
Robert Smith

**EDITOR, EBSCO PUBLISHING**
Melissa Kummerer

The CQ Researcher (ISSN 1056-2036). Formerly Editorial Research Reports. Published weekly (48 times per year, excluding March 1, May 3, Aug. 2 and Nov. 1, 1991) by Congressional Quarterly Inc., 1414 22nd St., N.W., Washington, D.C. 20037. Rates are furnished upon request. Application to mail at second-class postage rates is pending at Washington, D.C. POSTMASTER: Send address changes to The CQ Researcher, 1414 22nd St., N.W., Washington, D.C. 20037.

# Soviet Republics Rebel

BY VICTORIA POPE

## THE ISSUES

In varying degrees, the Soviet Union's 15 republics are pressing for greater power. The autonomous regions within the republics, many of which are inhabited by ethnic minorities, also want greater freedom. This push for a new balance of power reflects a search for regional and ethnic identity denied the republics for many decades.

But the quest for self-determination is as diverse as the 15 republics themselves. Some would be placated by less interference from Moscow in their political and cultural lives. Others are pressing for all-out independence, including the right to mint their own currency and operate their own borders. As Soviet Deputy Prime Minister Vladimir Shcherbakov noted recently, "Everybody has a different idea of sovereignty."

Shcherbakov made his comments following months of consultations to try and hammer out consensus on a new draft Union Treaty, which would replace the one that created the Union of Soviet Socialist Republics (U.S.S.R.) in 1922, five years after the Bolshevik Revolution brought the Communists to power. From the standpoint of the 15 republics, the most positive innovation of the draft treaty is its declaration that their laws will take precedence over the laws of the union. However, politicians in the republics are wary of specifics in the treaty that appear to contradict or undermine the promise of republican leadership in key areas, including the economy and foreign trade (*see p. 480*).

Talks between the center and the "periphery" — the term many Soviet commentators use when describing the non-Russian regions of the

U.S.S.R. — are further complicated by the uneasy relations between Russia, the country's most populous and largest republic, and the rest of the country. While the non-Russian republics are sullen about the favored status of Russia, the Russians, in turn, are testy about the nationalist backlash aimed at Russians living in other republics. As republican self-assertion has swelled, so has Russian nationalism. (*See story, p. 479.*)

Amid such tensions, Soviet President Mikhail S. Gorbachev faces difficult political choices. He appears to recognize the necessity of ceding power to the republics. Yet he would like to hold as much decision-making as possible in the hands of federal authorities and would like to protect the Communist Party of the Soviet Union (CPSU) from a sudden collapse. The CPSU has renounced its constitutional monopoly on power, but many in the party still want to set the policy agenda. The country also faces the real danger of economic collapse if the republics were to break away simultaneously.

Gorbachev's apparent strategy is to try and forestall such a free fall through concessions to the republics. Still, he is ever mindful of conservatives in the party who accuse him of too much leniency in dealing with the unrest. Gorbachev's opponents say anarchy is inevitable unless Moscow asserts its control immediately. They would like to see a tough policy, perhaps even a martial-law crackdown, against the states — principally the Baltic republics — seeking independence. These hard-liners also view the new union treaty as a threat to their existence because it would signal a new constitution and the dissolution of the current Soviet legislature. They say Gorbachev has brought shame on the country by encouraging republican autonomy, which they believe will lead to the destruction of the Soviet Union as a superpower.

Even Soviet reformers sympathetic to pro-independence sentiments are quick to admit that the trend toward self-determination threatens to create as many problems as it has solved. A desire to settle old scores pervades many of the upheavals besetting the country. In the Central Asian republics of Tajikistan, Kirgizia, and Uzbekistan, for example, the fighting between groups stems from historic, sometimes ancient, disputes over territory. These ethnic schisms were made worse when the Soviet authorities forced massive migrations from one Central Asian republic to another in the 1920s. The official rationale was that a new population mix was needed in the region for economic and political reasons. The outcome was large numbers of disaffected, displaced people who today are fighting to get back their historic lands.

Given the complexity of the Soviet nationalities issue, the West has had to walk a fine diplomatic line that neither satisfies the radical republicans nor the anti-independence forces. U.S. and Western European policy-makers applaud the move for self-determination in the republics as a hopeful sign for the emergence of democratic institutions and ideals, but they worry about republican aims destabilizing the Soviet Union.

Some further argue that trying to accommodate the yearning for nation-states along ethnic lines opens the Pandora's box of national rivalries that has plagued Europe many times in the past. Indeed, some political pundits have even sought to liken the beleaguered Gorbachev to Abraham Lincoln in his quest to keep the union together.[1] But many foreign policy analysts say the Soviet Union is doomed to fall apart because it is an artificial union without legitimacy. For both sides, the great imponderable is how great an erosion of Soviet territory will take place, and how fast.

### What's behind the republics' push for greater autonomy?

Since the Bolshevik Revolution, the Soviet Union has been held together by the oppressive force of totalitarianism. In the present period of openness, known as *glasnost*, ushered in by Mikhail Gorbachev, the Kremlin is allowing for more freedom. But without the mortar of coercion, the Soviet Union is beginning to break apart.

Not only has *glasnost* allowed local populations to criticize the central government, it has helped them to define who they are as people and what they would like to become. This reassertion of cultural and ethnic values has sparked a revitalization of local folk traditions that were long overshadowed by Russian or Soviet culture. Many Soviet national groups view their own culture as superior to that of Russia and they resent the decades when they were

forced to bow to Russia's interests. This attitude is particularly prevalent in the Baltic States, the Western Ukraine and Georgia.

A specific bone of contention is the domination of the Russian language.* Another affront to republican pride has been the treatment of local, non-Russian populations as second-class citizens by Russian settlers who were moved deliberately to areas where they were given plum jobs and above average living conditions.

Today's restiveness in the republics is the product of many years of seething resentment. The oftentimes brutal history of Soviet communism has left its scars. With the unfettering of historical inquiry under Gorbachev, factual evidence has bolstered what many had already learned in the privacy of their homes: The creation of the Soviet state was frequently violent. Almost without exception, the different republics can point to less-than-fair treatment by the central government.

The grievances against the Soviet system are particularly strong in the Ukraine. At the time of the civil war that followed the Bolshevik Revolution, Ukrainians resisted reincorporation into Russia. As a result, Stalin considered the region turncoat and unleashed on it the full fury of his terror. Another hard-hit area during the Stalin era was the North Caucasus. It had also fought for independence, and toward that goal had allied itself at times to the anti-Soviet Russian white army, a strategy Stalin could never forgive.[2]

In Kazakhstan, too, the Stalinist period is remembered with anger. In terms of their population, a larger proportion of Kazakhs perished or went abroad (many to China) as a result of Stalin's crimes than any other national group in the Soviet Union. Memories

---

*A point of antagonism in the non-Russian republics is the large number of Russians living there who never learn the local language.

of this period can be viewed as a factor in the riots that shook the Kazakh capital of Alma-Ata in 1986. Though the immediate cause of these disturbances was the replacement of a Kazakh party chief by a Russian, the festering resentment, decades old, also was responsible.

It is not just the past that makes the present state of affairs in the republics so agitated: The social and economic reforms ushered in under Gorbachev also have encouraged the assertion of national rights. Economic reform has produced hardships with few countervailing material benefits. Consequently, the level of disenchantment throughout the Soviet Union has risen sharply.

Many politicians on the republican level have begun speaking on behalf of their constituents when they question the fairness of Moscow reaping most of the profits from exports, such as cotton, that come from the republics. They are demanding a greater share of the proceeds from both agriculture and manufactured goods. Along with these rising economic expectations, Gorbachev's political reforms have created ideal conditions for the mobilization of ethnic identity by activists intent on redressing festering disagreements with Moscow or with rival ethnic groups.

Given the breadth and diversity of the Soviet Union, national tensions are perhaps inevitable. The country stretches from Moldavia next to Romania at the U.S.S.R.'s westernmost rim, to Kirghizia, bordering China, in the east. (*See map, p. 476.*) It has a population of a staggering 290 million people. It is a complex ethnic mosaic with more than a hundred national groupings. Fifteen of these constitute over 90 percent of the population, but they, too, are characterized by many religious, cultural and linguistic differences.

In Estonia, for example, the language is part of the Finno-Ugric group, which is related to Finnish and more distantly to Hungarian. Only the native tongues of Byelorussia and the Ukraine are Slavic languages like Russian. The U.S.S.R. is also comprised of many different religions, including the Ukrainian Uniate Church, which is the name for the Catholic Church of the Western Ukraine, as well as the Georgia Orthodox Church and Moslem sects in the Central Asian republics. However, the most dominant force in the religious landscape is the Russian Orthodox Church.

According to the 1989 census, Russians accounted for just over 50 percent of the population. The two other Slavic groups — Ukrainians and Belorussians — formed roughly 20 percent, the Moslem nationalities approximately 15 percent, the Baltic nations 3 percent, and the Christian peoples of the Caucasus — Armenians and Georgians — another 3 percent.[3]

An estimated 60 million Soviets live outside their home ethnic territory. "The complexity of the nationalities question in contemporary Soviet politics stems from the fact that the key actors are not merely dispersed ethnic groups, as in the United States, but nations and nationalities inhabiting or laying claims to historical territorial homelands," writes Gail Lapidus, a professor of political science at the University of California at Berkeley.[4]

Another point of tension stems from the way different parts of the U.S.S.R. are officially categorized. The 102 nations or ethnic groups listed in the 1989 census do not all enjoy equal status. An elaborate pecking order positions the 15 republics at the top of the power structure. These republics are comprised of the Russian Soviet Federative Socialist Republic (RSFSR) and the 14 Soviet Socialist Republics (SSRs).

They alone among the Soviet peoples have the right, on paper anyway, to secede from the Soviet Union as well as to engage in relations with foreign states.[5]

Following the 15 republics in the hierarchy are the 20 Autonomous Soviet Socialist Republics (ASSRs). In

**Given the breadth and diversity of the Soviet Union, national tensions are perhaps inevitable. Another point of tension stems from the way different parts of the U.S.S.R. are officially categorized.**

many instances, the ASSRs are included in the territory of the Union Republics. For example, Russia has 16 such regions. These units have their own constitutions, but clearly have less stature than the republics. This inequality is a source of friction and increases the chances of internecine fighting between groups. And the hostility only gets worse among groups of the bottom tier. These units are known as Autonomous Regions and the 10 National Districts.

Perhaps most embittered are the national groups that have no territorial units to call their own. The Crimean Tartars number over 130,000, but haven't had an Autonomous Region since theirs was abolished after World War II. The Soviet Union's large ethnic German population, officially estimated at over 2 million, also doesn't have its own territory. It was stripped of its status as an auton-

omous region during the Stalin years. Lowest of all in the Soviet hierarchy are such groups as the Poles, numbering over a million, and the Kurds, at around 150,000, which aren't even listed on the census as distinct nationalities.

In many instances, there are specific claims to sovereignty based on historical fact. A recent article in *Moscow News*, an independent weekly newspaper, counted at least 70 such disputes over territory or sovereignty based on longstanding claims.[6] Of these, the most straightforward and well-documented is the Baltic position that their inclusion in the Soviet Union is an artificial construct of the Molotov-Ribbentrop pact worked out by Adolph Hitler and Josef Stalin before the outbreak of World War II. (*See story, p. 472.*)

Most parts of the Soviet Union, however, are generally less radical than the Baltic States, and they aren't so adamantly against the present configuration of power. For example, some of the poorer Central Asian republics are less active in the independence movement. Byelorussia, which lacks the nationalism of Georgia or the Ukraine, has remained a bulwark of conservatism, though its opposition movement is growing. But even in republics supportive of Gorbachev, militancy is replacing complacency. By the end of last year, all 15 republics had adopted declarations of sovereignty, saying their laws take precedence over national laws.

### Will the push for more autonomy lead to civil war?

Unrest is already a way of life in many areas of the U.S.S.R. On any given week, there are reports of outbreaks of ethnic violence or other forms of protest in some part of the union. *Moscow News* recently reproduced a map of the Soviet Union showing 76 cities, towns, districts or regions where "Soviet people are in mortal conflict on ethnic grounds." [7] Out of 23 inter-republican borders, only three are not contested: Lithuania-Latvia, Byelorussia-Latvia, Russia-Byelorussia. (*See map, p. 476.*) With such mounting chaos, many Soviet and Western analysts warn of the inevitability of civil war — or of martial law — if the center cannot hold.

In a landmark essay in 1989, foreign policy expert Zbigniew Brzezinski warned that the "rising tide of nationalism" in the Soviet Union could be convulsive. "Whereas [Communist theorist Karl] Marx once described the tsarist Russian empire as a prison of nations, and Stalin turned it into a graveyard of nations, under Gorbachev the Soviet empire is rapidly becoming the volcano of nations," Brzezinski wrote.[8]

Brzezinski, a professor at the Paul Nitze School of Advanced International Studies at Johns Hopkins University and formerly national security adviser to President Jimmy Carter, speculated that liberation movements in the Soviet republics, coupled with new national passions in Eastern Europe, would "soon make the existing Soviet bloc the arena for the globe's most acute national conflicts."

Brzezinski's prediction of unrest in the Soviet Union becomes more accurate with each passing month. But how the Kremlin will ultimately respond to the unrest is less clear. A consistent policy has yet to emerge. Indeed, the potential for civil war cannot be gauged without a clear sense of how far the Kremlin would go to preserve the status quo.

Many of Gorbachev's public statements have been blunt. "To exercise self-determination through secession is to blow up the union, to pit peoples against one another and sow discord, bloodshed and death," he said in a 1989 speech. The current unrest in Yugoslavia appears to have toughened Gorbachev's resolve. Answering a question about the ethnic fighting in that country at a news conference in the Ukraine on July 5, Gorbachev said, "I vote for unity under any circumstance. The tense situation [in Yugoslavia] is a sorrow and a warning for all the nationalities of the Soviet Union." Gorbachev added: "I came to the conclusion that we cannot live apart. [Dissolution of the Soviet Union] would provoke great risk and unpredictable consequences." [9]

The crackdown in the Baltics at the beginning of this year indicates that the federal authorities will use force, if necessary, to keep the union together. In January, troops of the Soviet Interior Ministry stormed facilities in Latvia and Lithuania, killing 20 people. Despite that action, pro-autonomy forces, at least in the Baltics, are standing firm on their goal of independence. Many analysts believe another confrontation in the Baltics is only a matter of time.

Such tests of wills between the center and the periphery could easily lead to outbreaks of protracted fighting, such as is occurring in the breakaway Yugoslav republic of Slovenia. As in Yugoslavia, the use of federal troops to stop secession is fraught with dangers. Many factors could mitigate against a quick resolution of an armed conflict. Though Moscow's soldiers would have the advantage of better equipment, the republican troops would be fighting for what they viewed as a "just cause."

In the Yugoslav case, Slovenian troops were able to besiege a quickly demoralized federal army. While there is no way of knowing how the Soviet army would handle a similar mission, the ordinary soldier might be tempted to desert, or carry out his duties with something less than zeal, as happened in Yugoslavia. Such a reaction would set the stage for a long, bloody conflict that could easily spread, or spin out of control.

French scholar Hélène Carrère D'Encausse, who in a 1975 book on the Soviet nationalities problem correctly predicted the present-day turmoil, believes a non-violent solution is still possible. "What's left is compromise, which would allow different communities to live side by side, often in multi-ethnic states," she wrote recently in *The New Republic*. "It is clear that if they want to develop any equilibrium between communities, the [republics] have everything to gain by forming larger aggregates, in which particular conflicts would carry less weight." [10]

D'Encausse, a professor at the Institute of Political Science in Paris, believes nationalism is a necessary stopping place on the road to democracy. "It is natural," she writes "that . . . people in the throes of liberation finds traces of conflicts and resentments that have set [them] against other peoples. . . . A peaceful open nationalism comes only later, when certainty that the nation can flourish has been guaranteed by time."

"If we forget this," D'Encausse adds, "and imagine that these peoples, experiencing a rebirth of their own life, might . . . accede to democracy while bypassing the nation and its consolidation around powerful national feeling, we are once again reasoning like Lenin, thinking that in the name of a simple postulate we can dispense with certain stages of social development." [11]

### Should the West support the independence movements?

Handling the nationalities question is a delicate balancing act for the Western alliance. Discussing allied aid to the Soviet Union recently, U.S. Secretary of State James A. Baker III underscored the importance of helping the Soviets and the Eastern Europeans make a peaceful transition to democracy. He said a way needs to be found whereby groups will be able to express their long-suppressed ethnic and national identities. He further suggested that the Conference on Security and Cooperation in Europe* (CSCE) be used as the venue for the possible development of a peacekeeping force to help defuse ethnic and national tensions and settle border disputes.[12]

But some policy-makers view the situation as one in which the West is by and large on the sidelines. The hard reality, they say, is that there is little the West can do to bring about major reforms in the structure of decision-making in the Soviet Union.

For the Bush administration, the issue boils down to a central question: Will helping the republics destroy Gorbachev's political career? President Bush and his policy-makers have largely cast their lot with Gorbachev and the reform process they believe he is especially capable of carrying out. The United States and the rest of the Western alliance fear the rise of conservative, repressive forces should Gorbachev be forced out of power. The president has said on repeated occasions that he would like to see the Soviet leader succeed in transforming the Soviet Union.

Critics of the administration say too much good will toward Gorbachev amounts to the neglect of some highly legitimate claims for sovereignty, for example in the Baltic republics. These critics include quite a few Republicans, who have

urged President Bush to take a stronger position on the Baltics. "If our-Gorbachev-at-any-price policy" enables him to get away with repression at home, "then we might as well have the hard-liners back," Sen. Malcolm Wallop, R-Wyo., said last year. "At least under the hard-

**The United States considers the Baltic republics "captive nations" that were unfairly seized by the Soviet Union during World War II. Baltic leaders would like the U.S. and other Western powers to go one step further and formally recognize their independence.**

liners we were less prone to self-delusion." [13]

On March 21, 1990, following Lithuania's declaration of independence and the Soviet Union's subsequent economic blockade of the republic, Sen. Jesse Helms, R-N.C., proposed a resolution demanding recognition of the new government. After much backdoor jockeying, Bush administration officials convinced senators to reject it, 36-59. The next day, the Senate adopted a much milder resolution urging the president to "consider" Lithuania's appeal for recognition. The House followed suit on April 4, 1990, passing a resolution urging the president to "plan for and take those steps, at the earliest possible time," that would create normal diplomatic relations with Lithuania.[14]

The United States considers the Baltic republics "captive nations" that were unfairly seized by the So-

viet Union during World War II. Baltic leaders would like the United States and other Western powers to go one step further and formally recognize their independence.

In an April 1991 speech in Los Angeles, Lithuanian President Vytautas Landsbergis complained about Western faintheartedness on the question of Baltic independence. "Those who did not recognize the incorporation of Lithuania (into the Soviet Union) should be prepared to recognize its independence today," he said. "But we are always confronted by arguments from the West that such a move would not be liked by Mr. Gorbachev, that it might create difficulties for him at home." [15]

Despite Landsbergis' criticism of Western policy toward the Baltics, there is mounting evidence that Washington would like to develop better direct ties to the wayward republics. In May 1991, Deputy Assistant Secretary of State Curtis Kamman visited Latvia, Lithuania and Estonia to assess the political situation in the Baltics. A U.S. fact-finding team, led by Under Secretary for Agriculture Richard Crowder, was also in Lithuania in early 1991 to tour a modern grain storage facility built with American venture capital.[16]

Those visits followed calls from some members of Congress that Washington should demand that any financial or humanitarian aid it sends to Moscow must be distributed equitably to all the republics. In particular, liberal lawmakers have said that the United States needs proof that the Baltic nations are not discriminated against when aid is parceled out.

Some American legislators, including Sen. Bill Bradley, D-N.J., believe aid to the Soviet Union should be targeted through the republics to

---

*The Conference on Security and Cooperation in Europe includes the 15 members of the North Atlantic Treaty Organization (NATO), the Soviet Union and the neutral and non-aligned nations of Europe, including the former members of the Warsaw Pact. The conference produced the 1975 Helsinki Accords, which called for advance notification of troop maneuvers in Europe. Signatories also agreed to allow the free movement of people and information across national boundaries.

# The Molotov-Ribbentrop Pact

On the night of Aug. 23, 1939, while Soviet dictator Josef Stalin looked on, the foreign minister of the Soviet Union, Vyacheslav M. Molotov, and the foreign minister of the German Reich, Joachim von Ribbentrop, signed a German-Soviet non-aggression pact in Moscow. The published text of the treaty pledged both nations to refrain from aggressive action or attack against the other and to lend no support to a third party should either "become the object of belligerent action" by one.

The pact allowed Adolf Hitler's army to invade Poland on Sept. 1, 1939, without the risk of Soviet military support in defense of its Western neighbor. The invasion marked the start of World War II.

The Molotov-Ribbentrop pact also contained a secret protocol that set forth the details of a Soviet-Nazi plan to carve Eastern Europe into spheres of influence. The secret agreement, which gave most of Poland to the Germans, placed Finland,† Bessarabia and the Baltic States of Latvia, Lithuania and Estonia in the Soviet sphere of influence (*see map*). Soviet troops occupied Bessarabia and the Baltic countries in 1940 and subsequently absorbed them into the U.S.S.R. as republics.

The Soviet Union has only recently admitted to the existence of the secret agreement. In June 1989, the Soviet Congress of Peoples' Deputies created a commission authorized to investigate the Molotov-Ribbentrop pact. In July of that year, a high-ranking Communist, Valentin Falin, said on West German television that there was no doubt the pact included the secret agreement. He also acknowledged that a West German microfilm of the protocol appeared authentic. Soviet officials had earlier dismissed the microfilm as a forgery.

The Soviet admission gave pro-autonomy forces in the Baltic republics substantiation from the Kremlin itself that their countries were illegally annexed. This injected new vigor into the Baltic liberation movement. On the 1989

**Results of the Nazi-Soviet Pact August 23, 1939**

- Germany, 1936
- German gains in Poland
- Soviet gains in Poland, Latvia, Lithuania, Estonia and Bessarabia

anniversary of the signing of the Molotov-Ribbentrop pact, thousands of protesters wearing black ribbons marched in the Baltic capitals of Tallinn, Riga and Vilnius. As long as Estonia, Latvia and Lithuania remain part of the U.S.S.R., many in the Baltic republics will view the Molotov-Ribbentrop pact as an abiding symbol of their servitude to Moscow.

---

† The U.S.S.R. invaded Finland in November 1939 after Finnish leaders rejected Soviet proposals to alter the Finnish-Soviet border. The Finns were forced to capitulate in March 1940 and surrendered thousands of square miles of territory to the Soviets.

---

help build up their political influence. Critics of this idea say it is difficult to imagine how such a policy could work diplomatically under the present governmental configuration. Still, reform politicians in key Soviet cities such as Leningrad and Moscow have already succeeded in getting Western philanthropies to give directly to local projects, thus establishing a model for how U.S.

government aid might someday be handled. Upon returning from the Soviet Union recently, former U.S. President Richard M. Nixon urged Washington to "diversify, intensify and multiply" its contacts with the Soviet republics.

Yet legislators on both sides of the political divide remain skeptical of the Soviet Union's ability to use aid wisely. (Many discussions on help-

ing the Soviet Union and its republics are peppered with arguments that the money would be better used at home.) They say if the West wants to support reform in the Soviet Union, it should provide incremental aid such as credits and grain.

Whatever sympathies are felt in the West for the republican push for independence, many Western countries worry that the secession of individual republics from the union would spell economic disaster. Because of the high degree of economic interdependence between the republics, Western business leaders in particular advise the creation of a closely knit network of horizontal ties, especially bilateral and multilateral treaties that would require minimal input from the central government in Moscow. These structures would replace the vertical structures that have traditionally placed the Kremlin and the Communist Party on the top and the nationalities and their local governing councils on the bottom.[17]

But such structures are yet to be formed. And until that time when a true rehaul of the system is implemented, the West may well be responding to crisis, not orderly reform.■

---

# BACKGROUND

## Bolshevik Era

Russia was traditionally an empire, and the panoply of nations today known as the Soviet Union first came together under the imperialist policies of the czars. In 1900, Russia had a vast colonial empire. Its reach extended beyond even the present-day borders of the Soviet Union, and included Poland and Finland. The czarist government kept control over its disparate holdings through repressive measures. Czar Nicolas I promoted a policy of "official nationalism," which viewed cultural imperialism by the conquering power as an important feature of creating a nation-state. Russia imposed its language, culture and religion on the periphery with a vengeance. Non-Russian languages were banned in publishing and education.

The Bolshevik Revolution, which ended czarist rule in February 1917, was first seen as a golden opportunity for the national groups that made up the Russian empire. Vladimir Ilyich Lenin, the leader of the revolution, appeared open to greater freedom for the republics. In his early writings, the founder of the Soviet state took a favorable view of self-determination. He specifically applauded Norway's secession from Sweden in 1905 as an example of how the nationalities problem could be solved. He also looked up to Switzerland as a model of a polyglot country that had handled problems of multi-ethnicity with sensitivity. At the same time, he was eager to promote the cause of national emancipation to show up the transgressions of the czars. He described the republics as "stolen property," the booty of czarist conquests.[18]

But the Bolshevik Revolution and the nationalities policy forged by Lenin were in time to disappoint the many patriotic organizations hoping for a new dawn of national awakening to arrive. The policy took a fateful turn when a leading figure of the Bolsheviks, Josef Stalin, was appointed the People's Commissar for Nationality Affairs. He was to prove a harsh critic of republican assertiveness, which he viewed as a threat to his consolidation of power.

One early stumbling block was that the Bolsheviks' sympathy with the concept of self-determination clashed with their most fervent mission for "workers of the world to unite." The idea of internationalism — implying common values of the proletariat everywhere — would by its definition de-emphasize matters like cultural and religious differences. Marxism-Leninism considered nationalism as a "survival of the past," something destined to disappear under the progressive force of socialism. The Communist leaders fervently promoted the ideal of a "New Soviet Man," whose loyalties were meant to be supranationalist.[19]

Whatever Lenin's personal sympathies to the question of national identity, the Bolsheviks' early application of the nationalities policy would place them on a path that would emphasize the pre-eminence of Russia and strong rule by a central authority. Kremlin policy would ebb and flow between a regard for pragmatic politics that viewed autonomy as a necessary bone to the nationalities to discourage efforts to put down national aspirations, to an orthodox policy that gave the republics little maneuvering room. Time and again, the early Communist leaders promised sovereignty and the right to secession to all the nations of the U.S.S.R., but their quest to consolidate power made them wary of the dissolution of the empire. They reached out to the new Bolshevik groups in all of the republics and bypassed the local councils that had been hoping to receive enhanced power.

Tensions between the central authority and the republics never really went away. But the temperature rose especially quickly as the Bolsheviks attempted to consolidate power. In the Ukraine, the local council, the Ukrainian Rada, was one of the first to test Moscow: It blocked the free passage of the Red Guards through Ukrainian territory. The Bolsheviks treated this comeuppance as grounds for an escalation of hostility. They issued an ultimatum, and invaded the Ukraine. Similar force was used in many regions, including Latvia, Lithuania and Estonia.

Under various forms of duress, sometimes even under the threat of the bayonet, a union of Soviet states was cobbled together. Moscow's meddling in the republics, though not constant, was persistent. But at times there were efforts at a policy responsive to local desires. In the 1920s, education in the non-Russian republics was carried out in the native tongues of the regions.

But these periods of relative calm were followed by assertions of power from the center. Purges, disappearances and other retaliations against nationalist leaders quickly characterized Moscow's relations with the republics. Even provincial officials who got their start as Bolsheviks were often, when they showed some conviction about national rights, branded nationalists.

### Stalin's Crackdown

By the 1930s the Stalinist terror crushed what was left of reform. The intellectuals and artists of the non-Russian republics came under particularly fierce attack in this period. Some minority groups in the autonomous regions like the Crimean Tartars, Kalmyks, Chechen, Ingush, Volga Germans and Meskhehan Georgians — the so-called "punished people" — faced mass deportations and other reprisals.

During this period, the Kremlin created a special niche for Russia and the Russians. It openly espoused the idea of Russia as a first among equals. By adopting this stance, successive generations of Kremlin leaders were recalling Stalin's famous 1945 speech about the Russians following the surrender of Nazi Germany in 1944. In it, Stalin toasted the Russian people saying, "[They] are the most outstanding nation of all the nations comprising the Soviet Union."

After the death of Stalin in 1953 and the rise of Nikita S. Khruschev as Stalin's successor, republican hopes were pinned on the new communist leadership. Khrushshev's "secret speech" at the Twentieth Soviet Party Congress in February 1956 de-

cried the excesses of Stalinism and signaled a more thoughtful approach to the nationalities question. In the speech, Khrushchev acknowledged the shame of wide-scale deportations and criticized prior Soviet policy in other ways.

At first, the period of relaxation spawned a flowering of local cultures. There was less interference from Moscow on local administrative matters. But this relative absence of tension was short-lived. By late 1956, the Kremlin had changed course again. The government began promoting a new concept, "the fusion of nations," which called for an amalgamation of the Soviet Union's disparate groups in a Communist melting pot.

In dealing with the nationalities, a pattern of repression emerged. The Kremlin often clamped down on their republics when they felt insecure in other ways. This was particularly true when social unrest in another area threatened Soviet stability. In 1956, when Hungarians took to the streets and tried to overthrow the communist system, and Poland experienced its own anti-Communist riots, Khrushchev bore down hard on the nationalities.

> How much leeway Gorbachev wants to give the nationalities is difficult to assess. Since he took power in 1985, the Soviet leader has shown ambivalence toward the issue. Some analysts believe he was unprepared for the fervor of nationalist sentiment.

When shipyard strikes in Gdansk, Poland, in 1980 ushered in the Solidarity labor movement, the Soviet leadership once again tightened its grip on the republics.

## Gorbachev's Position

Conditions changed suddenly last year with the unraveling of communism in Eastern Europe. Anti-Communist forces, emboldened by Gorbachev's reform policies, and bolstered by enormous popular support, toppled the pro-Soviet Communist parties ruling the countries of the former Warsaw Pact. Gorbachev faced immediate blame for this receding of the Soviet Empire. His military and security forces spoke bitterly about the loss. They began to pressure Gorbachev not to allow the republics to stage a similar exit.

How much leeway Gorbachev wants to give the nationalities is difficult to assess. Since he took power in 1985, the Soviet leader has shown ambivalence toward the issue. Many political analysts believe he was unprepared for the fervor of nationalist sentiment. Paul A. Goble, a State Department official specializing in the nationalities question, points out that until the 1970s, the career track of aspiring Russian politicians required some service in the non-Russian areas. In the last 20 years, however, this pattern broke down, lessening the central government's grasp of ethnic issues.

Gorbachev's career illustrates Goble's point. The Soviet leader spent his formative political years in Stavropol, in the Caucasus, an area where 90 percent of the population is Russian. Then he moved to Moscow. Goble cites figures showing

Continued on p. 478

# Chronology

## 1920s
Bolsheviks consolidate their hold over the Soviet republics in the years following the 1917 Russian Revolution.

### 1922
Union of Soviet Socialist Republics (U.S.S.R.) is formed. Josef Stalin becomes General Secretary of the Central Committee of the Communist Party.

## 1930s-1940s
Under the iron rule of Stalin, the Kremlin implements harsh measures in the republics. Tens of millions of political opponents and peasant farmers are killed.

### Aug. 23, 1939
U.S.S.R. and Nazi Germany sign a non-aggression pact. A secret protocol divides Eastern Europe into Soviet and German spheres. Under this arrangement, the Soviets will annex the Baltic States of Latvia, Estonia and Lithuania in 1940.

### June 27, 1940
U.S.S.R. invades Romania. Bessarabia and Northern Bukovina are annexed by the Soviets.

## 1950s
After Stalin dies in 1953, Nikita S. Khrushchev loosens the state's grip on the nationalities, but unrest in Eastern Europe makes the Kremlin uneasy about republican aspirations for self-determination.

## 1960s-1970s
After Khrushchev's ouster from office in October 1964, the new collective leadership of Aleksei N. Kosygin and Leonid I. Brezhnev adopts a hard-line approach to the nationalities. Many republican groups react with public protest.

### April 14, 1978
Thousands of angry demonstrators take to the streets of Tbilisi, Georgia. The protest centers on the omission in the new draft constitutions of Georgian, Armenian and Azerbaijani as official languages of their respective republics.

## 1980s
Republican fervor grows. Under glasnost, marches and other public demonstrations of anti-Soviet sentiments proliferate.

### Aug. 23, 1987
Estonians, Latvians and Lithuanians demonstrate on 48th anniversary of the 1939 Molotov-Ribbentrop pact.

### Sept. 28, 1988
Riot police storm peaceful, pro-independence rallies in the Lithuanian capital of Vilnius.

### April 9, 1989
Soviet troops use what is widely believed to be toxic gas to quell a demonstration in Soviet Georgia. Twenty people die and some 4,000 are taken to hospital.

### September 1989
A pro-independence rally organized by the Azerbaijani Popular Front in Baku draws tens of thousands.

## 1990s
Soviet Union's constituent republics step up their efforts to win independence.

### March 11, 1990
Lithuania issues a declaration of independence. Soviet authorities respond with an economic blockade, which ends 72 days later when Lithuania announces a moratorium on the declaration of independence.

### June 12, 1990
The Russian parliament proclaims its republic a sovereign country.

### Dec. 17, 1990
Congress of People's Deputies begins debate on draft Union Treaty.

### Jan. 7, 1991
An attack in Lithuania by Soviet military units leaves 14 people dead and more than 160 wounded.

### March 17, 1991
In a nationwide referendum, the majority of Soviets vote in favor of keeping the union. But results indicate many also want heightened republican autonomy.

### April 1991
Gorbachev reaches agreement with nine of the 15 republican leaders to work out the terms of an economic treaty that would give the republics a greater voice in how they will reform their economies.

### June 12, 1991
Boris N. Yeltsin becomes freely elected president of Russia, making that republic the first in the U.S.S.R. to hold direct presidential elections.

# The 15 Soviet Republics At A Glance

The
Soviet Union

① Estonia
② Latvia
③ Lithuania
④ Byelorussia
⑤ Ukraine
⑥ Moldavia
⑦ Russia
⑧ Georgia
⑨ Armenia
⑩ Azerbaijan
⑪ Kazakhstan
⑫ Turkmenistan
⑬ Uzbekistan
⑭ Tadzhikistan
⑮ Kirghizia

★ Moscow

SWEDEN • FINLAND • White Sea • Baltic Sea • POLAND • CZECHOSLOVAKIA • HUNGARY • ROMANIA • YUGOSLAVIA • BULGARIA • ITALY • ALBANIA • GREECE • TURKEY • Black Sea • Mediterranean Sea • SYRIA • IRAQ • IRAN • Caspian Sea • AFGHANISTAN • PAKISTAN • KASHMIR • CHINA

## ① Estonia

**Population:** 1.6 million.
**Ethnic breakdown:** 65% Estonians, 30% Russians, 3% Ukrainians, 2% Byelorussians.
**History:** ruled by Germany, Sweden or Russia until 1918, when it became independent. Annexed by Soviets as part of 1940 deal with Nazi Germany.
**Recent events:** In March 1990, declared Soviets an occupying power and pledged to restore independence gradually. Rejected Gorbachev's offer of "special status" if it would drop secession movement.
**Importance to union:** Big exporter of dairy products to other republics. Oil shale provides electric power for Leningrad.

## ② Latvia

**Population:** 2.7 million.
**Ethnic breakdown:** 54% Latvians, 33% Russians, 5% Byelorussians, 3% Ukrainians, 3% Poles.
**History:** Occupied from 1200s to 1920, when it became an independent country. Annexed by Soviets in 1940.
**Recent events:** Independence declared in May 1990, but leaders said actual secession would come only after negotiation with central government.
**Importance to union:** Riga is an important port; Latvia manufactures machinery, scientific instruments and consumer goods.

## ③ Lithuania

**Population:** 3.7 million.

**Ethnic breakdown:** 80% Lithuanians, 9% Russians, 8% Poles, 2% Byelorussians.
**History:** An independent country before Russians ruled after 1795. Restricted democracy from 1920 to World War II. Claimed by Soviets in agreement with Nazi Germany in 1940.
**Recent events:** Leader of Baltic drive for independence; declared independence in March 1990. Soviets tried to stem revolt with economic embargo.
**Importance to union:** Provides 66% of the world's amber.

## ④ Byelorussia

**Population:** 10.2 million.
**Ethnic breakdown:** 79% Byelorussians, 12% Russians, 4% Poles, 2% Ukrainians.

**History:** Never independent, it was taken over by Russia in 1772 and was one of four union republics when U.S.S.R. was started in 1922.
**Recent events:** In July 1990, Parliament adopted a declaration of sovereignty, saying its laws supercede national ones.
**Importance to union:** Heavily industrial, producing 13% of nation's motors, 12% of TVs.

# ❺ Ukraine

**Population:** 51.7 million.
**Ethnic breakdown:** 74% Ukrainians, 21% Russians, 1% Jews.
**History:** Home to famous Cossack warriors in 1500s, it's been dominated by Russia since 1667 and was one of four original republics.
**Recent events:** Declared sovereignty of its laws in July 1990. Now calling for its own army and currency.
**Importance to union:** Agricultural heart of the nation, producing 56% of corn, 25% of wheat. Also mining center, making 47% of nation's iron ore, 25% of its coal.

# ❻ Moldavia

**Population:** 4.3 million.
**Ethnic breakdown:** 64% Moldavians, 14% Ukrainians, 13% Russians, 4% Gagauzi (Turkish Christians), 2% Jews.
**History:** Once known as Bessarabia, it was controlled by the Turks or Russians until becoming part of Romania after World War I. Soviets seized area in 1940.
**Recent events:** Declared sovereignty of its laws in June 1990. Moldavians want to reunite with Romania. Russians and Ukrainians in east want to stay in Soviet Union. Gagauz set up own republic in south.
**Importance to union:** Heavily agricultural, producing 33% of the nation's wine and grapes.

# ❼ Russia

**Population:** 147 million.
**Ethnic breakdown:** 83% Russians, 4% Tatars, 3% Ukrainians.
**History:** Ivan IV (the Terrible) founded Russian state in 1500s. Its greatest expansion came in the 1800s.
**Recent events:** Slow to respond to reforms, republic is now home to several parties in opposition to communists. Parliament declared sovereignty in June 1990, claiming the right to control its natural resources.
**Importance to union:** Produces 91% of nation's oil, 76% of natural gas, 57% of steel and 55% of coal.

# ❽ Georgia

**Population:** 5.4 million.
**Ethnic breakdown:** 69% Georgians, 9% Armenians, 7% Russians, 5% Azerbaijanis, 3% Ossetians, 2% Abkhazians.
**History:** A Caucasian empire in the late 1100s, until it was invaded by Mongols. Turks and Persians fought over it, so Georgia turned to Russia and was annexed in the 1800s. It beame a republic in 1936.
**Recent events:** Declared independence in April. Calling for talks with Soviets to restore independent state.
**Importance to union:** Produces 95% of nation's tea.

# ❾ Armenia

**Population:** 3.3 million.
**Ethnic breakdown:** 90% Armenians, 5% Azerbaijanis, 2% Russians, 2% Kurds.
**History:** Armenia was the first state to adopt Christianity, in about A.D. 300. It has had various rulers since it was first conquered in 1375. Became a republic in 1936.
**Recent events:** Declared independence in August 1990. Slow to revolt since it is caught between historical enemy Turkey and largely Moslem Azerbaijan. The republics have fought over Armenian enclave in Azerbaijan.
**Importance to union:** Fruit-growing, manufactures motors.

# ❿ Azerbaijan

**Population:** 7 million
**Ethnic breakdown:** 78% Azerbaijanis, 8% Armenians, 8% Russians
**History:** Ruled by Arabs, then Turks for 1,200 years. Russians gained control in 1700s. Made a republic in 1936.
**Recent events:** First republic to declare independence, in September 1989. Mostly Shiite Moslem population hopes to reunite with historical kin in Iran.
**Importance to union:** Large oil producer; grows cotton, grapes and silk.

# ⓫ Kazakhstan

**Population:** 16.6 million.
**Ethnic breakdown:** 41% Russians, 36% Kazakhs, 6% Ukrainians, 2% Tatars.
**History:** Moslem people of Mongol heritage, Kazakhs were nomadic people brought into Russian empire in 1800s. It became a republic in 1936.
**Recent events:** Declared its laws to be sovereign in October 1990.
**Importance to union:** Large oil and coal producer, and grows one-third of nation's wheat.

# ⓬ Turkmenistan

**Population:** 3.5 million.
**Ethnic breakdown:** 68% Turkmen, 13% Russians, 9% Uzbeks, 3% Kazakhs.
**History:** Populated largely by nomadic tribes, this mostly desert area was invaded by Russia in 1800s; made a republic in 1925.
**Recent events:** In August 1990, it declared its laws to be sovereign. Calmest republic.
**Importance to union:** Largest sulfur deposits in world.

# ⓭ Uzbekistan

**Population:** 19.9 million.
**Ethnic breakdown:** 69% Uzbeks, 11% Russians, 4% Tatars, 4% Kazakhs, 4% Tadzhiks.
**History:** Ruled by a succession of conquerors from Central Asia until Russians gained control in late 1800s. Became a republic in 1936.
**Recent events:** In June 1990, Parliament declared that its laws took precedence over central government. Dissent centers on pollution (overfarming, excess of pesticides), ethnic problems.
**Importance to union:** Grows 67% of nation's cotton.

# ⓮ Tadzhikistan

**Population:** 5.1 million.
**Ethnic breakdown:** 59% Tadzhiks, 23% Uzbeks, 10% Russians.
**History:** Once part of the Persian Empire, this land was won by Russia in a war with Central Asians after the revolution in 1917. Became a republic in 1929.
**Recent events:** In August 1990, Parliament declared that its laws took precedence over central government's.
**Importance to union:** Highest birthrate in nation. Produces 11% of nation's cotton.

# ⓯ Kirghizia

**Population:** 4.3 million.
**Ethnic breakdown:** 48% Kirghiz, 26% Russians, 12% Uzbeks, 3% Ukrainians, 2% Tatars.
**History:** Kirghiz are Moslem people who were conquered by the Russians in the late 1800s. It became a republic in 1936.
**Recent events:** Declared its independence in December 1990, the last republic to state intentions.
**Importance to union:** Mines coal and mercury ore, produces wool.

Source: *The St. Petersburg Times.* Information current as of spring 1991.

Continued from p. 474

that in the 1970s, one-third of the top party elite was non-Russian, one-third was Russian, but with significant experience in the non-Russian republics, and one-third were like Gorbachev. By the end of the 1980s, however, Gorbachev had presided over a recomposition of the leadership that left only 20 percent fitting the first two categories. Thus Gorbachev's myopia on the nationalities question was reflected in the officials surrounding him.[20]

This lack of exposure to the republics may have compounded the difficulties that Gorbachev faced in coping with the burgeoning liberation movements in the republics. New national elites, represented by such groups as Lithuania's Movement to Support Perestroika, known as Sajudis, pressed for more freedom for the republics.* At the same time, and perhaps more worrisome, were the spontaneous expressions of anger in the republics.

Soviet troops using what was thought to be highly toxic gases, broke up demonstrators in the Georgian city of Tbilisi in April 1989. Nineteen were killed in the pro-independence rallies. In the Ukraine in October 1990, tens of thousands poured into the streets of Kiev and Lvov to demonstrate against the domination of the Communist Party. And ethnic unrest shook the republic of Moldavia in late 1990, leaving four dead after Soviet troops moved in to quell the unrest. Coal miners' strikes in the Ukraine in the spring of 1991 must have brought vividly to mind the memory of Poland's feisty Solidarity movement, which began with spontaneous expressions of dissatisfaction with the Communist system and ended eventually as an organized movement that in time toppled the Communist Party in Poland.  ■

Gorbachev to address them on details of the new Union Treaty as a way of making peace with the republican representatives.

Chaos over the chain of command has sparked many tests of will between the supreme soviets of the various republics and the central ministries. For example, in Kazakstan, where an anti-nuclear lobby is growing, the Kazakhstan Supreme Soviet and the U.S.S.R. ministry of defense are at loggerheads over the scheduling of a nuclear-weapons test at the Semi-Palatinsk test site. Public sentiment is against it, and local leaders are responding to the public pressure. The U.S.S.R. finally suspended nuclear tests for four months in reaction to this protest.

## Face-Off in the Baltics

Gorbachev's most vexing problem is doubtless the Baltic republics. Restiveness in the region came as no surprise: Lithuania, Latvia and Estonia had led the march for republican freedom for several years.

In an early act of quiet defiance, four Estonian Communist economists in 1987 presented a plan to turn their republic into a free-trade zone. It was a draft blueprint for the concept of economic autonomy which all the Baltics, including Estonia, would refine and radicalize over the ensuing months. But the quest for self-determination was not only expressed in treatises. Demonstrations erupted throughout 1987, and culminated in autumn protests in the Estonian cities of Voru and Parnu and in the Latvian capital of Riga.

The many expressions of Baltic self-assertion reached a turning point when the Lithuanian parliament issued a declaration in March 1990 announcing the re-establish-

*Sajudis was formed on June 3, 1988, when a group of 500 academics met at the Academy of Sciences in Vilnius and hammered out a charter that called for more autonomy for Lithuania. That same summer, a second more radical group was formed. Called the Lithuanian Freedom League, it espoused an immediate withdrawal of Soviet "occupation forces" from Lithuania, and Lithuania's independent membership in the European Community.

# CURRENT SITUATION

## Challenges to Gorbachev

The last 12 months have presented many challenges to Mikhail Gorbachev. Even his legitimacy as Soviet president was called into question by the contrasting example of relatively free elections to the republic's supreme soviets, or councils.

In June Boris N. Yeltsin, a Gorbachev rival, was elected president of Russia in the republic's first-ever direct, popular election.* Gorbachev, by contrast, was not elected by popular vote.

Further fueling the difficulties of ruling the country has been the so-called "war of laws," in which feisty republics overturn every new law in the Supreme Soviet, or parliament, by insisting that local laws take precedence. In fact, on Nov. 14, 1990, the parliament temporarily collapsed because of the war of legislation. Dispirited legislators, weary of this legal logjam, simply canceled the legislative docket and asked

*The Russian parliament had elected Yelstin president of the republic on May 29, 1990. Yeltsin resigned from the Soviet Communist Party on July 12, 1990.

Continued on p. 480

# Mother Russia: A Search for Roots

Feodor Dostoevsky devotedly called it "Mother Russia," and under the Communist system the Russian republic has enjoyed a position of "first among equals." With the emergence of strong nationalist movements all over the Soviet Union, however, non-Russian Soviets are openly rejecting the preferential treatment of their "elder brother."

Nationalist slogans in the republics are often accompanied by anti-Russian tirades. The complaints include the way in which Russians were moved into their regions to act as a skilled labor force loyal to Moscow; the way that Russian politicians have dominated the ranks of the Kremlin elite; and even, the way in which they have been assigned to read Dostoevsky and other Russian writers to the exclusion of their own indigenous literary figures. Faced with this hostility, the Russians are on the defensive. They say their republican neighbors are "Russophobic" and jealous of their success.

On one level, Russia's dominant position is only natural. The Russian Soviet Federated Socialist Republic (RSFSR) is the largest and most important union republic. With 6.5 million square miles, it contains about 75 percent of the Soviet land mass and 51 percent of the population (147 million, according to 1988 Soviet statistics). Its power is also derived from its abundance of natural resources. It boasts huge deposits of coal, diamonds, one-fifth of the world's known gold deposits and many other minerals. Such bounty amid the Soviet Union's near-economic collapse has sparked political wrangling between the republic and the central government over who should control these commodities and their hard-currency revenues.

Russia's capital, Moscow, is also the capital of the U.S.S.R., giving the city twin roles that serve to blur the distinction between Russia the republic and Russia the heartland of Kremlin power. Yet it is just that distinction that Russian politicians are trying to underscore.

Many Russians chafe at the common Western misperception that the names "Soviet Union" and "Russia" are interchangeable. By the same token, there is a groundswell of support for moves to separate Russia's institutions and ministries from those of the central government. Last year, Russia's police force began reorganizing so that it could be independent from the Soviet state's security apparatus, for example, the KGB — the security police and intelligence agency of the U.S.S.R. Many other institutions are following suit.[†]

In this drive for greater independence, the Russians are led by a dynamic helmsman. Boris N. Yeltsin, the charismatic president of the Russian Republic, is an extroverted politician who has roused anger in the Kremlin and cheers from the crowd. He was dismissed as Moscow party boss in

November 1987. In May 1990, however, parliament elected him president of the Russian republic. Then, in a startling move just two months later, he announced his resignation from the Communist Party. In the spring of 1991, he was re-elected president of the republic by popular vote. He has made a career of criticizing President Mikhail S. Gorbachev as too slow on reform, and his popularity is in part a protest vote against the Soviet leader.

Yeltsin has assembled around him a team of imaginative young bureaucrats who are willing to go head-to-head with Kremlin *apparatchiki* (officials of the Communist Party) when it comes to defending the interests of Russia. A case in point was a July 1990 transaction between the national government and the De Beers diamond concern. The Kremlin agreed to sell $5 billion in diamonds exclusively through De Beers' Swiss subsidiary. When the Russian republican government found out, they protested that *their* natural resources could not be sold without their consent. Gorbachev shot back with an equally stiff statement saying, "foreign economic deals" . . . "shall be strictly fulfilled."[††] The Russians backed down, in so much as they haven't tried to block the transaction, but they still won't deem the sale valid.

Though many Russians are proud of this new assertiveness, some are worried about the rise of chauvinism, especially on the cultural front. Many popular Russian writers and artists treat the homeland as a sacred entity and write about its traditions in worshipful tones. More troublesome, loving Russia has at times amounted to hating others, as the anti-Semitic, xenophobic, and anti-Western diatribes of the ultra-nationalists have shown.

But some Russian intellectuals counsel patience before judging this strain too harshly. Russian writer Yuri Afanes'yev sees the rise of extremist groups like the chauvinist, anti-Semitic Pamyat as an outgrowth of the Soviet Union's "identity crisis," and its loss of "historical memory." From this vantage point, nationalism is a search for roots.[‡] But many political scientists view a shift of emphasis as crucial to a true turn to democracy in Russia. It would mean replacing the idea of nationalism, which can pit one group against another, with patriotism, which leaves ample room for peaceful coexistence.

---

† See Mark Galeotti, "Russia's Police Move Toward Independence," *Report on the U.S.S.R.*, a weekly publication of Radio Free Europe/Radio Liberty, Oct. 26, 1990, p.4.

†† See Paul Hofheinz, "The New Russian Revolution," *Fortune*, Nov. 19, 1990, p. 127.

‡ For a detailed discussion of this point, see Roman Szporluk, "Dilemmas of Russian Nationalism," *Problems of Communism*, July-August 1989. p. 16.

Continued from p. 478
ment of their independence. The Kremlin responded with an economic embargo of the region that lasted 72 days until the Lithuanians declared a moratorium on their call for independence. But tensions continued to mount.

In January 1991, Gorbachev ordered Soviet airborne troops into seven Soviet republics, including the Baltics. A pre-dawn attack in Lithuania by Soviet military units left 14 people dead and more than 160 wounded. The Soviet president later denied responsibility for the crackdown, claiming he had never been informed of the planned assault. Despite these denials, many commentators in and outside the Soviet Union speculate that Gorbachev must have known.

Despite the crackdown, the Baltic States have kept up their campaign for independence. They are displaying the flags of their "countries" on walls of schools and in doorways. In Lithuania, pictures of ancient kings and other patriotic figures hang in many households. For the Balts, as the people of the Baltic republics are known, an important incentive for keeping faith is that many of their older citizens can remember the existence of an independent state before 1940. (*See story, p. 472.*)

Without a doubt the Balts have staked a radical position. Leaders like Lithuanian President Landsbergis believe the economic and political deterioration of the Soviet Union offers them a chance to break free. Some Western analysts think that full independence is within the realm of possibility, although they say Baltic pressure could also trigger a military backlash. However, Landsbergis and other leaders counter that even as a martyr, the Baltic States would keep alive the idea of independence for future generations.

The immediate danger of new reprisals is still at hand. In March, 1991, Landsbergis warned that the Kremlin was preparing "for a new strike, perhaps more sophisticated than in January." In late June, communication outages between Moscow and the Lithuanian capital of Vilnius sparked fear of a new crisis. But at present, the assault on Lithuania and the other Baltic republics appears mainly to be harassment rather than confrontation.

The Bush administration and the West in general have backed Baltic aspirations, but the support has been at times tempered by political considerations. Secretary of State Baker told the Baltic foreign ministers at a Paris meeting of the CSCE in the fall of 1990 that Washington was not willing to risk a confrontation with Moscow over the Baltic States. Baker said he felt that such a conflict would be counterproductive for everyone involved.[21]

But at other times, U.S. policymakers have gone to pains to differentiate between justified and unjustified Kremlin intervention. At a Nov. 29, 1989, White House briefing, a little over a month before Soviet troops attacked facilities in Lithuania and Latvia, Baker was asked whether there were circumstances under which the United States would support Gorbachev if he cracked down against people in his own country.

The secretary of state answered: "It depends what you mean by crackdown. . . . Suppose you have Azerbaijanis and Armenians actively fighting each other. Would it be inappropriate for the central authority to try and restore peace, whether it was through martial law or otherwise? That's far different from using force — in my view it is far different than using force to suppress the peaceful dissent from policies that the central government might be pursuing."

## The Union Treaty

The proposed draft Union Treaty, outlining the terms for the "Union of Sovereign Republics," was passed by the Congress of People's Deputies at the end of 1990. It must now be ratified by the 15 constituent republics. Six have already rejected the draft outright: the three Baltic republics plus Armenia, Georgia and Moldavia.

In May, Gorbachev said ratification proceedings would go on without the six rebel republics. Though the Soviet president did not say the six would be excluded from the terms of the treaty, he pointed out that the breakaway republics would have to be treated differently in terms of tariffs, customs and other essential functions of the union.

Several republics now supporting the treaty say their support is contingent on revisions. On July 5, the parliament of the Russian republic, at Yeltsin's urging, voted to back the treaty in principle, but said final approval was dependent on changes to key provisions related to control of taxation and foreign trade. Yeltsin's appeal for the treaty's approval surprised many observers. "The Union Treaty is an act of huge political importance and just to reject it would mean political collapse and the destabilization of the country," Yeltsin said during debate on the issue.[22]

Though it's officially called "A Law on Resolving Questions Connected with the Exit of the Union Republic from the USSR," the draft treaty does little to clarify how and under what conditions a republic of the Soviet Union can secede. "To secede from the union," writes *New York Times* Moscow correspondent Bill Keller, the republics "would still be obliged to follow a daunting legal procedure that includes satisfying all financial claims of the center

Continued on p. 482

# At Issue:

## Is the disintegration of the Soviet Union inevitable?

### yes

GABRIEL SCHOENFELD

*Editor of Soviet Prospects and a senior fellow at the Center for Strategic and International Studies.*
FROM *THE NEW REPUBLIC*, JAN. 21, 1991.

*i*f the recent chaotic Congress of People's Deputies taught us anything, it is that the Union of Soviet Socialist Republics is no more. To paraphrase what Voltaire once said about the Holy Roman Empire, it is no longer a Union, no longer Soviet, and no longer Socialist. Only the republics remain, but some are nascent states and others are in danger of splintering themselves. Whatever happens now — crackdown, chaos, even Gorbachevite success — there is a sense that a Rubicon has been crossed. The U.S.S.R. is over. . . .

By lifting the pall of repression and fear, Gorbachev dried up the fuel that the old system ran on. His tinkering with the economy replaced torpor with scarcity and chaos.

. . . After maintaining for seven decades that the problem of multinationalism had been "solved," the Kremlin finally admitted that its interethnic fraternity of brotherly love was based upon terror and lies. But the very process of attempting to account honestly for what Moscow now describes in official publications as "Stalinist ethnocide" involved unraveling the various myths that bound together the U.S.S.R. . . .

The instruments of coercion that were once the pride of Soviet totalitarianism are themselves divided and faltering. The former Interior Minister, Vadim Bakatin, says that the militia — the Soviet local police — is infected with "primeval nationalism." . . .

As the possibility of a crackdown emerges, the question before the Kremlin is the same as in February 1917: Will the Cossacks obey an order to fire on the crowd? Even if the answer is yes, the second question is more pertinent: What then? There is no longer something called communism to justify spilling new rivers of blood. Russian nationalism in both its benign and malignant varieties is one potential substitute for ideology, but it has little appeal in the sizable non-Russian areas where competing nationalisms flourish. The best that imperial-minded Russians can hope for is a pan-Slavic confederation of nations, but given the embarrassment of socialism, it will approximate the Solzhenitsyn rather than the Soviet variety. Either way, the 12 non-Slavic republics would not be willing members of this particular club.

### no

PAUL A. GOBLE

*Special Assistant for Soviet Nationalities in the U.S. Department of State.*
FROM *PROBLEMS OF COMMUNISM*, JULY/AUGUST 1989.

*t*he disintegration of the U.S.S.R. remains just as unlikely now as it was in the past. Despite a willingness to tolerate more diversity in the Soviet republics than ever before, Moscow would clearly sacrifice almost all its other policy goals in order to maintain the integrity of the Soviet Union. . . .

The U.S.S.R. is not now and is not likely in the future to become a liberal society in Western terms, so discussions about a "return" to repression are misplaced. At the same time, a simple restoration of the past — be it Brezhnevism or Stalinism — probably is impossible, except at costs far beyond the ability of the authorities to pay. As a result, we are likely to be entering a period where there will be a series of ratchet-like adjustments of freedom and repression, as both Moscow and the other actors feel the situation out. No one event is likely to mark a turning point in either direction, and we will have to develop tolerance for a certain amount of messiness if we are to understand the situation. . . .

Further devolution of power to the republics is likely, although it may be combined with recentralization in some areas, such as key economic sectors. The existing federal system is likely to be simplified, with some autonomous soviet socialist republics raised to union-republic status, and sub-union republic groups put in a single category. At the same time, a variety of mechanisms to protect extraterritorial groups — for example, through the creation of regional national soviets or republic supreme soviets of nationalities, or through the expansion of central supervision of ethnic rights for individuals — is likely. . . .

The result . . . will not be some "solution" to the nationality problem. The days when it could be declared "solved" are over. The best Moscow and the two other players [Russians and non-Russians] can hope for is an institutionalization of the current messiness and a growing acceptance of limits by all three. To the extent that this happens, the rise of ethnic politics in the U.S.S.R. may point to a more thoroughgoing reconceptualization of Soviet political life. . . .

Continued from p. 480
and giving minority enclaves in the republic a chance to opt out."[23]

Still, the draft treaty gives the republics in principle more power than they have under the current constitution, but less than the increasingly bold republics want. The central authorities would continue to control military and foreign affairs, banking and monetary policy, borders and customs. The center would also have the final say in economic, environmental and industrial policy. Moscow also would fashion a uniform budget.[24]

Gorbachev proposed a popular referendum on the Union Treaty in all of the republics in part to build credibility. On March 17, 1991, a majority of the country's voters said they favored the continuation of the union. Though that vote appears to contradict the spirit of autonomy sweeping the republics, many political observers note that the specific

wording of the referendum question was a key factor in the way people voted. It asked: "Do you think it is necessary to preserve the Union of Soviet Socialist Republics as a renewed federation of equal sovereign republics in which the rights and freedoms of individuals of all nationalities will be fully guaranteed?" Many observers said this sentence could be interpreted in many ways, depending on which parts of it were taken as most important.[25]

Despite the referendum's outcome, President Gorbachev remains on the defensive. At his July 5 news conference in the Ukraine, Gorbachev heatedly defended the treaty, which he said would "create a safe atmosphere for every nationality." Referring to events in Yugoslavia, Gorbachev added, "And that is why I think . . . we have chosen the right way, of renewal, not disintegration. And I will not deviate from this way no matter how hard the pressure on me."[26] ∎

# OUTLOOK

## Possible Outcomes

The nationality question, as with other festering problems in the U.S.S.R, is becoming progressively less manageable. On one side, there is pressure from government conservatives who believe a firmer hand with the nationalists is necessary to stop a descent into anarchy. On the other end of the political spectrum, the republican leaders are growing less and less interested in cooperation with the center. The only inducement Gorbachev really has to offer them is the potential advantages of a common all-union market.

Some analysts believe the Soviet Union in its present configuration cannot last. (*See At Issue, p. 481.*)

Now that all 15 republics have adopted resolutions on "sovereignty," a push for outright secession looms on the political horizon. The Baltic nation of Lithuania has already declared its independence, and negotiations between its leaders and Moscow are ongoing. Whether the Kremlin will let the Baltics go is an open question. But many Soviet experts believe it is not outside the realm of possibility.

Far more nettlesome would be a defection by the Ukraine. At a time of a rapidly shrinking Soviet gross national product (GNP), the Ukraine's economic strengths are important assets for the Kremlin. (*See At A Glance, p. 476*). Such a basic challenge to Kremlin authority as a defection by the Ukraine might spark a declaration of martial law. "The existence of a serious separatist movement in the Ukraine would

be intolerable for [Gorbachev], as it would be to any Russian leader because for 1,000 years Kiev has been the mother of the Russian church and the cradle of Russian culture," writes Martha Brill Olcott, a Soviet scholar at Colgate University.[27]

Some scholars believe it would be easiest for the Soviet Union to split into several entities characterized by common heritages. One such grouping might be a Slavic confederation linking Russia, the Ukraine and Byelorussia, and perhaps Moldavia. These republics share a Byzantine Christian heritage, as well as linguistic and cultural similarities. The Lithuanians, Latvians and Estonians represent another distinctive group. Further south, the people of Central Asia share Sunni Muslim traditions but are perhaps too ruled by tribal traditions to join together in a broad regional fashion. Still more difficult to characterize is the Caucasus, a region of varied populations and marked by ethnic strife. The Armenians, for example, are the proud heirs of the oldest established church in Christendom, the Armenian Catholic Church. Their neighbors and rivals, the Azerbaijanis, are Shiite Muslim, and closely linked to Iran in culture.

Most experts on the Soviet Union agree on the possible scenarios that could play out in the coming months and years in the Soviet Union. First, it is possible that a federal union scheme will prevail minus the rebellious six republics that seek full independence. Or expectations in the republics may be scaled back to endorse a confederation where horizontal relationships — that is, republic-to-republic agreements — would serve to diminish domination by the center.

Brzezinski believes a confederation or commonwealth scheme would benefit all. "It is the only option that can combine some degree of continued unity with democracy," he writes. "For the Russians, it would mean that democracy and prosperity would no longer be impossible goals, as the Russians would no longer have to bear the consequences of being the oppressor of others. For the non-Russians, it would provide genuine political and economic power within their homelands." [28]

But if a peaceful solution is not reached, a violent resolution may play itself out. An authoritarian dictatorship might wipe out all vestiges of *glasnost*, and the wayward republics would be forced back into the fold. But even without such an apocalyptic vision, the future may prove grim. For if nothing is done, with both sides becoming increasingly adverse to compromise, the disintegration of the world's last empire, would gain fresh momentum.

Western policy-makers are afraid the momentum for a breakup may already be there. Casting a wary eye at strife-torn Yugoslavia, they worry that the Soviet republics may find themselves in armed confrontation with the federal authorities. Such apprehensions may spur the Western powers to give the Soviet Union an infusion of funds to help stabilize the situation.[29] But given the thicket of ethnic and political problems facing the Soviet nationalities, money alone may not be enough. ∎

*Victoria Pope is a free-lance writer based in Moscow.*

# Notes

[1] See Ronald Steel, "Pax Sovietica," *The New Republic*, Jan. 21, 1991, pp. 17-20.

[2] See Bohdan Nahaylo and Victor Swoboda, *Soviet Disunion* (1990), pp. 60-80. Also see Robert Conquest, *Harvest of Sorrow: Soviet Collectivization and the Terror-Famine* (1986) and Roy A. Medvedev, *Let History Judge: The Origins and Consequences of Stalinism* (1971).

[3] Paul A. Goble, "Gorbachev's National Problem," in Jed Synder, ed., *Soviet Politics Under Gorbachev* (1990), reprinted in *Soviet Nationalities Issues*, a compilation of essays and other materials prepared for the American press corps by the Center for War, Peace and the News Media for a Moscow meeting in May 1990.

[4] Gail W. Lapidus, "Gorbachev's Nationalities Problem," *Foreign Affairs*, fall 1989, p. 95.

[5] These rights are granted them under the 1977 Soviet Constitution. See Nahaylo and Swoboda, *op. cit.*, p. 360.

[6] *Moscow News*, No. 11, March 1991. *Moscow News* is an English-language publication.

[7] *Ibid.*

[8] Zbigniew Brzezinski, "Post-Communism Nationalism," *Foreign Affairs*, winter 1989/90, pp. 1-25.

[9] Quoted in *The Washington Post*, July 6, 1991.

[10] Hélène Carrère D'Encausse, "Springtime of Nations," *The New Republic*, Jan. 21, 1991, p. 21.

[11] *Ibid.*, p. 22.

[12] Quoted in *The New York Times*, June 19, 1991.

[13] Quoted in "Lithuanian Events Highlight U.S. Stake in Gorbachev," *Congressional Quarterly Weekly Report*, April 7, 1990, p. 1085.

[14] *Ibid.*

[15] Quoted in *The Washington Times*, May 13, 1991.

[16] *Ibid.*

[17] Deutsche Bank, Economics Department, *Focus Eastern Europe*, June 1991.

[18] See Nahaylo and Swoboda, *op. cit.*, p.14.

[19] Nadia Duik and Adrian Karatnycky, *The Hidden Nations* (1990), p. 30.

[20] Goble, *op. cit.*, pp. 3 and 19.

[21] *Report on the U.S.S.R.*, a weekly publication of the federally funded Radio Free Europe/Radio Liberty Research Institute on Current Soviet Affairs, Jan. 4, 1991, p. 50.

[22] Reuter story printed in *The Washington Post*, July 6, 1991.

[23] *The New York Times*, Dec. 18, 1990.

[24] *Ibid.*

[25] See *Christian Science Monitor*, March 19, 1991.

[26] Quoted in *The Washington Post*, July 6, 1991.

[27] Martha Brill Olcott writing in *The New York Times*, March 24, 1990.

[28] Brzezinski *op. cit.*, p. 21.

[29] See Craig R. Whitney, "Spur to Summit Action," *The New York Times*, July 5, 1991.

# Bibliography

## Selected Sources Used

### Books

**Diller, Daniel C., ed., *The Soviet Union*, 3rd edition, Congressional Quarterly, 1990.**

A comprehensive look at the Soviet Union's history, geography and politics with special educational features such as a chronology, biographies and excerpts from important statements, treaties and other documents. The book covers a wide range of topics, from women in Soviet society to the problem of alcohol abuse.

**Diuk, Nadia and Karatnycky, Adrian, *The Hidden Nations: The People Challenge the Soviet Union*, William Morrow and Company, 1990.**

The authors look at the resurgence of nationalism in the Soviet Union through firsthand reporting in the republics. Written from a position of advocacy, the book explains why the republics feel thwarted by Kremlin policy. Interviews with pro-autonomy leaders provide a fascinating glimpse into the independence movements in the U.S.S.R.

**D'Encausse, Hélène Carrère, *The Great Challenge: Nationalities Versus the Bolsheviks, 1917-1930*, Holmes & Meier, 1990.**

An examination of a critical period in the history of the Soviet Union's nationalities problem by a leading French scholar on the Soviet Union. D'Encausse's pioneering 1975 book on the restive republics, *Decline of an Empire: The Soviet Socialist Republics in Revolt*, was published in English in 1979.

**Nahaylo, Bohdan and Swoboda, Victor, *Soviet Disunion: A History of the Nationalities Problem in the U.S.S.R.*, The Free Press, 1990.**

Nahaylo, a senior research analyst for Radio Liberty in Munich, and Swoboda, an Honorary Research Fellow at the School of Slavonic and Eastern European Studies at the University of London, are well-seasoned experts. Their book, *Soviet Disunion*, is a detailed, chronological examination of the Soviet nationalities. The authors' intimate knowledge of the subject matter is manifest in their careful analysis of events from the time of Lenin to the end of the 1980s.

### Articles

**Brzezinski, Zbigniew, "Post-Communist Nationalism," *Foreign Affairs*, winter 1989/90.**

Brzezinski, national security adviser to President Jimmy Carter and author of *The Great Failure: The Birth and Death of Communism in the Twentieth Century*, analyzes

the rise of nationalism in the Soviet Union and Eastern Europe today. In this highly articulate, well-paced essay, he urges the West not to sit on the sidelines. "A great historic drama is in the process of unfolding — and it can have benign or malevolent international consequences," he writes.

**Burg, Stephen "The Soviet Union's Nationalities Question," *Current History*, October 1989.**

Burg, an associate professor of political science at Brandeis University, traces the career of Soviet President Mikhail S. Gorbachev and his reaction to nationalist dissent. Burg provides an especially engrossing discussion of the situation in the Ukraine.

**Goble, Paul, A., "Ethnic Politics in the U.S.S.R," *Problems of Communism*, July-August 1989.**

Goble is special assistant for Soviet Nationalities in the U.S. Department of State and a leading expert on the nationalities question. This article takes an exhaustive look at ethnic politics, and thoroughly examines the likelihood of such apocalyptic scenarios as the complete disintegration of the U.S.S.R.

**Lapidus, Gail W., Gorbachev's "Nationalities Problem," *Foreign Affairs*, fall 1989.**

Lapidus, a professor of political science at Berkeley, provides a valuable historical perspective on the nationalities problem. From a policy perspective, she believes the West has a limited role to play. "The United States would be well-advised . . . to refrain from aligning itself in support of one or another national group," she writes.

**Schoenfeld, Gabriel, "The End," *The New Republic*, Jan. 21, 1991.**

Schoenfeld, a senior fellow at the Center for Strategic and International Studies, views the U.S.S.R. as effectively finished. As he puts it in his witty opening paragraph: "To paraphrase what Voltaire once said about the Holy Roman Empire, [the Soviet Union] is no longer a Union, no longer Soviet, and no longer Socialist."

### Reports and Studies

**Deutsche Bank, *The Soviet Union at the Crossroads: Facts and Figures on the Soviet Republics*, June 1991.**

A valuable report on the republics by the economics department of Deutsche Bank in Frankfurt, Germany. Particularly worthwhile are the sections offering an economic prognosis for each republic and the section giving facts and figures on the republics.

# The Next Step

## Additional Articles from Current Periodicals

### Addresses & essays

**Brzezinski, Z., "The Soviet Union: Three scenarios," U.S. News & World Report, April 23, 1990, p. 48.**

Opinion. Zbigniew Brzezinski muses that because of intense nationalism in the Soviet Union, Mikhail Gorbachev's task of reforming his country is made much more difficult. Inevitable collision between the Russian center and the non-Russian periphery. Remain an empire, or fragment, or have a Romanian type of revolution.

**D'Encausse, H. C., "Springtime of nations," The New Republic, Jan. 21, 1991, p. 20.**

Calls for dismemberment of the Soviet Union. Why its nation-states should be allowed to break away; Challenges such a disintegration would cause; Proposed compromise that would blend independence with mutual assistance; Dangers of suppressing nationalism.

**Mandelbaum, M., "Shaky empires, then and now," Time, Oct. 29, 1990, p. 93.**

Suggests that the Kremlin and the West would both do well to study what happened to the Ottoman Turks at the beginning of the century. Argues that while the survival of the Soviet Union in its present form is threatened by unrest among its non-Russian minorities, the Ottoman Empire ultimately could not withstand the nationalist aspirations of its non-Turkish peoples; Economic backwardness, resentment of central authority.

### Azerbaijan

**Watson, R., Coleman, F., et al., "Gorbachev's civil war," Newsweek, Jan. 29, 1990, p. 38.**

Discusses the recent outbreak of fighting in the Soviet Republic of Azerbaijan and how it signals another painful setback for Mikhail S. Gorbachev and his stalled reforms, and threatens his leadership. Ethnic strife; Reactions at home and abroad; Programs; Press coverage. INSET: About Azerbaijan.

**Wilson-Smith, A., "A seething rage," Maclean's, Feb. 5, 1990, p. 32.**

Reports on continued fighting between Armenians and Azeris in the Soviet republic of Azerbaijan and the conflict's political implications for President Mikhail S. Gorbachev. Armenian and Azeri reaction to Gorbachev's decision to send troops and to declare martial law; Azeri and Armenian fighters; Soviet and foreign reaction; How Gorbachev has consolidated his power.

### Baltic region

**Gray, M., "Danger zones," Maclean's, Feb. 11, 1991, p. 16.**

Discusses Baltic nationalists' resistance to the Soviet crackdown on their fight for independence. Rebel barricades around the parliament buildings in Estonia, Latvia, and Lithuania; Withdrawal of some Soviet troops; Domestic criticism of President Mikhail Gorbachev's policies; Recent violence in Riga, Latvia, and Vilnius, Lithuania; Pro-independence referendums in Estonia and Lithuania; Soviet black-beret unit base near Riga.

**Rubinfien, E., "Holding the empire together," National Review, Feb. 11, 1991, p. 21.**

Considers the implications of the Soviet Union's hardline policy against independence movements in the Baltic republics. How recent crackdowns reflect the true position of Soviet President Mikhail Gorbachev; What the West's response should be.

**Tutwiler, M., Baker, J. A. III, et al., "Situation in the Baltics," Dispatch, Jan. 28, 1991, p. 58.**

Presents statements by State Department spokeswoman Margaret Tutwiler, Secretary of State James A. Baker III, and White House spokesman Marlin Fitzwater, Jan. 22, 1991, concerning the Soviet Union's use of force in the Baltic States. Hopes for a peaceful resolution to this situation; Discussions on the strategic arms treaty; Support of various international agencies to drive home the point that the legitimate aspirations of the citizens of Latvia, Lithuania and Estonia must not be denied.

**Vesilind, P. J. and Price, L. C., "The Baltic nations," National Geographic, November 1990, p. 2.**

Reports that Estonia, Latvia, and Lithuania, after 50 years of Soviet domination, are struggling to regain their lost sovereignty. How their newly elected leaders face the twin challenges of repairing ravaged lands and economies and restoring trust in the government. INSET: Bold moves for pawns of the empire.

### Debates & issues

**Luers, W. H., "Reading a road map of human misery," U.S. News & World Report, Nov. 19, 1990, p. 49.**

Lists the forces behind the mounting migration and emigration in the collapsing political and economic system of the Soviet Union. Nationalism and ethnic conflict; Military demobilization; Environmental damage; Economics; Fear and disorientation.

**Parker, J., "United in disunion," *Economist*, Oct. 20, 1990, Soviet Union survey, p. 4.**

Analyzes the forces that are driving the process of disintegration in the Soviet Union, nationalism and the devolution of authority from the center to local authorities. National diversity in Soviet Union; Comparison with America; President Mikhail Gorbachev's desire to rule by consent; The danger of the country becoming ungovernable; The proposed "new Union Treaty," which would turn the country into the U.S.S.S. (Union of Sovereign Soviet States); Details; Outlook.

**Stanglin, D., Knight, R., et al., "Into the Soviet centrifuge," *U.S. News & World Report*, April 23, 1990, p. 46.**

Describes the restive Soviet republics and considers the possibility of civil insurrection. Nationalities issue; Generation gap in the military; Radical economic reform.

## Georgia

**Wilson-Smith, A., "A separatist drive," *Maclean's*, Apr. 23, 1990, p. 24.**

Reports on the growing independence movement in the Soviet republic of Georgia. Commemoration of the April 9, 1989, shooting of demonstrators by Soviet troops; Soviet Union's takeover of Georgia in 1921; Soviet government's response to the independence movement; Anti-Russian sentiment in Georgia.

## International aspects

**"Bust-up in the Balkans," *Economist*, Oct. 13, 1990, p. 17.**

Opinion. Contends that the current troubles erupting in Yugoslavia are presenting Europe with many of the issues that might also come from the Soviet Union in the near future. Yugoslavia's history as a collection of nationalities; Little chance that it could lead to a superpower conflict; Danger of conflict spilling over into other countries; First test of the new "European security order"; Possible roles for the United Nations, European Community, and others; Outlook.

**Bierman, J., "Jaded liberty," *Maclean's*, Nov. 26, 1990, p. 32.**

Examines the disillusionment that is sweeping Eastern Europe a year after the collapse of communism. Rise of nationalism and racial prejudice; Attempts to create a market economy; Soviet economy; Industrial pollution; Poland; Romania; Anti-Semitism; Crime.

**Hawkins, W. R., "New enemies for old?" *National Review*, Sept. 17, 1990, p. 28.**

Stresses the importance of America's maintaining a strong army despite the recent breakup of the Communist world. Addressing the resurgence of militant Islam; Rising nationalism around the world; Dangers still posed by the Soviet Union; Why the United States must help maintain world order; Proposed new military strategy. INSET: The enemy within? (conflicts within the Soviet army), by B. Crozier.

**Sikorski, R., "The Red Army remains," *National Review*, Feb. 25, 1991, p. 22.**

Considers the potential impact of Soviet crackdowns in Lithuania and Latvia on the future of Poland. Current Soviet inflexibility about the terms and timing of withdrawing its troops from Poland and Germany; Polish fears that the army will stay; Future forecast.

**Talbott, S., "Best of times, worst of times," *Time*, Jan. 7, 1991, p. 39.**

Discusses the political climate in Eastern Europe that threatens the glorious cause of freedom from communistic rule. Hating, fearing and fighting each other; Soviet disunion; The 1990 resurgence of nationalism in its most divisive, destructive forms has also brought an increase in the willingness of many nations to pool energies, resources, political will, and even sovereignty on behalf of shared objectives and mutual interests.

## Lithuania

**" 'Lithuania is again independent,' " *America*, March 31, 1990, p. 307.**

Editorial. Comments on Lithuania's declaration of independence from the Soviet Union. History of Lithuanians; United States' refusal to recognize the original Soviet takeover; Reaction from Moscow; Negotiations planned.

**Ignatiev, N. and Laskas, J. M., "The singing revolution," *Life*, April 1991, p. 78.**

Traces Lithuania's struggle for freedom, after the onset of World War II. Three successive occupations, by the Soviet Union, Germany, and then the Soviet Union again. Frustrations under Soviet rule; Break for independence, by peaceful means; Violent crackdown by the Soviet army; Current status.

**Stanglin, D., Trimble, J., et al., "Making his move," *U.S. News & World Report*, Jan. 21, 1991, p. 30.**

Details the Soviet crackdown in Lithuania the previous week when President Mikhail Gorbachev sent armored vehicles into Vilnius, showing that holding the country together by any means is more important than nurturing either reforms or Moscow's new partnership with the West. Muting criticism; February arms control meetings; Spreading crackdown: Latvia, Kiev, Georgia; Sharp turn to the right.

## Moldavia

**"You from him, I from you,"** *Economist*, Nov. 3, 1990, p. 59.

Looks at how recent moves of the Soviet republics of Georgia and Moldavia toward independence have demonstrated that nationalism is a sword that can cut both ways. Results of recent Georgian elections; Violence in Moldavia between the Moldavians and the minority Gagauz; Problems with minority clashes; Impact of democratization; Details; Outlook.

**Crowther, W., "The politics of ethno-national mobilization: Nationalism and reform in Soviet Moldavia,"** *Russian Review*, April 1991, p. 182.

Explores what the relationship between political reform and nationalist mobilization is under the impact of *glasnost* and *perestroika* in the Soviet Union, and why the numbers of those supporting nationalist movements have grown so explosively. Analysis of the dynamics of change in Soviet Moldavia; Restructuring and popular mobilization in Moldavia; State and popular mobilization; Conclusion.

## Political aspects

**Brady, R., "A wrenching tug-of-war with Moscow,"** *Business Week*, Jan. 14, 1991, p. 32.

Examines conflicts over sovereignty that are flaring across the Soviet Union. Breakaways expected in 1991; New presidential powers; Gorbachev's ability to set agenda waning; Momentum for change is growing stronger; Greatest pressure from Russian republic; Separate tax policies; Russian parliament slashing its contribution to the national budget; Crucial test; Better distribution of food; Last-ditch effort to keep control.

**Cullen, R., "Laying that burden down,"** *Atlantic*, March 1990, p. 32.

Describes how the Soviet Union may react to demands for secession by the Soviet republics. Pressures on Soviet leader Mikhail Gorbachev; Revolution in the republics; Russian nationalists; Demands for a show of authority.

**Trimble, J., "Feuds now, fights later?"** *U.S. News & World Report*, Jan. 14, 1991, p. 38.

Considers the escalating war of Moscow with the republics, the key being whether the power will flow from Moscow to the republics or vice versa. Boris Yelstin charges "a war with the center" has begun; Tensions rise as central controls weaken; Increasing Mikhail Gorbachev's political risk along with his power; Increasing pressure in the Baltics. INSET: Capitulating to capitalism, by J. Marks.

## Russia

**Bogert, C., "Wanting out of Russia,"** *Newsweek*, Nov. 12, 1990, p. 40.

Reports that Soviet Tatars join the hordes demanding more independence from Boris Yeltsin's Russian republic. Once the republic asserted its own sovereignty, the rush to redraw the border turned the republic into a map maker's nightmare. Background on the ancient battle between Russians and Tatars; Tatars expecting more money and power; Question of how much authority they will actually gain from Moscow. INSET: Breaking away (map showing regions thinking of declaring autonomy).

## Ukraine

**"A giant starts to stir,"** *Economist*, Oct. 6, 1990, p. 55.

Reports on the nationalistic stirrings in the Soviet republic of the Ukraine, most markedly demonstrated by a series of strikes and demonstrations held October 1st. Growing support and membership in Rukh, the nationalist movement; Role of the Uniate church; Rumors of troop movements and increased KGB activity in the region; Rukh Chairman Ivan Dracz; Move toward free elections; Outlook. INSET: Monument to terror (discovery of communal graves adding to political upheaval in the Ukraine).

**Gray, M., "The Ukrainian factor,"** *Maclean's*, Dec. 3, 1990, p. 26.

Discusses the Ukraine's growing nationalist movement and its implications for the rest of the Soviet Union. Implementation of the Ukraine's own rationing system; Food shortages; Bilateral trade pact between the Ukrainian and Russian republics; Ukraine's role as the Soviet Union's breadbasket. INSET: Unearthing mass murder (remains of political prisoners found in Zolochev, the Ukraine).

**Karatnycky, A., "Rukh awakening,"** *The New Republic*, Dec. 17, 1990, p. 16.

Probes the re-emergence of the Ukraine, long considered Europe's hidden nation. Long-suppressed desire of the Ukrainians to reclaim independence; Overview of the Rukh movement, the political force behind the Ukrainian revival; Prospects for secession.

**Sikorski, R., "Why Ukraine must be independent,"** *National Review*, Nov. 5, 1990, p. 74.

Examines the Ukrainian national movement, known as Rukh. Historical misfortunes suffered by the Ukraine; Why the Soviet Union needs the Ukraine to remain a superpower; Arguments in favor of making the Ukraine an independent state.

# Back Issues

*Great Research on Current Issues Starts Right Here... Recent topics covered by The CQ Researcher are listed below. Issues dated before May 10, 1991, were published under the name of Editorial Research Reports.*

**JANUARY 1990**
Higher Education Curriculum
Photonics
Age of 'Infotainment'
Abortion: Politicians' Nightmare

**FEBRUARY 1990**
Politics and Economic Growth
Free Agency in Sports
Repetitive Motion
War on Drugs

**MARCH 1990**
Asbestos: Are Risks Acceptable?
Public Health Campaigns
South Africa's Future
Homeless Need More Than Shelter

**APRIL 1990**
How Fair is the Tax Burden?
Workers' Compensation
U.S. Pacific Forces
Curbing Insurance Premiums

**MAY 1990**
Should Teaching Be a Profession?
Will Canada Fall Apart?
Is U.S. Patent System Outdated?
Federal Funding for the Arts

Back issues are available for $4.00 (subscribers) or $7.00 (non-subscribers). Quantity discounts apply to orders over ten. To order, call Congressional Quarterly 1-800-432-2250.

**JUNE 1990**
Downsizing America's Armed Forces
Progress In Weather Forecasting
S & L Bailout
Bio-Chemical Disarmament

**JULY 1990**
Do Americans Still Love Marriage?
Death Penalty Debate
Decline of Rural America
United Nations in the 1990s

**AUGUST 1990**
Democracy in the Philippines
Initiatives: True Democracy?
Hard Times at Newspapers
Teens Balance School & Jobs

**SEPTEMBER 1990**
Dangers of Alcohol
Western Alliance After the Cold War
Tobacco Industry
Right to Die

**OCTOBER 1990**
Organ Transplants
Energy Policy Options
Search for Arab Unity
Child Support

**NOVEMBER 1990**
Lotteries and Gambling
Post Cold-War Choices
Setting Limits on Medical Care
Multicultural Education

**DECEMBER 1990**
Cable TV Regulation
Americans' Search For Their Roots
Is Insurance System a Failure?
Why Schools Still Have Tracking

**JANUARY 1991**
Growing Influence of Boycotts
Should the U.S. Reinstate the Draft?
America's Archaeological Past
Peace Corps' Challenges in '90s

**FEBRUARY 1991**
Regional Impact of Recession
Puerto Rico's Status
Redistricting: Mapping Power
Nuclear Power

**MARCH 1991**
Acid Rain
Cost of the Gulf War
Reassessing Gun Laws
Future for Man in Space

**APRIL 1991**
Social Security
Canadian Crisis Over Quebec
California Drought
Electromagnetic Radiation

**MAY 1991**
School Choice
Racial Quotas
Animal Rights
U.S. and Japan

**JUNE 1991**
Children and Divorce
Teenage Suicide
Endangered Species
Europe 1992

**JULY 1991**
Teenagers and Abortion

# Future Topics

▶ *Mexico's Emergence*

▶ *Athletes and Drugs*

▶ *Sexual Harassment*

PUBLISHED BY CONGRESSIONAL QUARTERLY INC., IN CONJUNCTION WITH EBSCO PUBLISHING

# Mexico's Emergence

*Will economic reform work? Can democracy wait?*

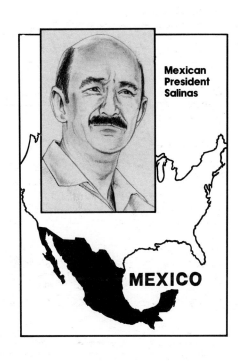

Mexican President Salinas

MEXICO

F IVE YEARS AGO, MEXICO WAS A CLASSIC
example of everything wrong in the developing
world: The country's centrally planned economy
had collapsed, political leadership was wanting and
government inefficiency and corruption were rampant. Many
Mexicans believed their country would never recover. Now,
suddenly, Mexico has emerged as one of the world's most
promising economies. Carlos Salinas de Gortari, Mexico's 43-
year-old president, has embarked on a bold course toward
modernization. By opening up the economy and proposing a
free-trade agreement with the United States, he hopes to lure
foreign investment and liberate his impoverished country
from decades of underdevelopment. In the process, he is
altering the nature of U.S.-Mexican relations. He is also
creating pressures for political change.

C_Q    **July 19, 1991 • Volume 1, No. 11 • 489-512**

*Formerly Editorial Research Reports*

COVER ART: BARBARA SASSA-DANIELS

July 19, 1991
Volume 1, No. 11

**EDITOR**
Sandra Stencel

**ASSOCIATE EDITOR**
Richard L. Worsnop

**STAFF WRITERS**
Charles S. Clark
Mary H. Cooper
Rodman D. Griffin

**PRODUCTION EDITOR**
Laurie De Maris

**EDITORIAL ASSISTANT**
Thomas H. Moore

**GRAPHICS**
Jack Auldridge

**PUBLISHED BY**
Congressional Quarterly Inc.

**CHAIRMAN**
Andrew Barnes

**VICE CHAIRMAN**
Andrew P. Corty

**EDITOR AND PUBLISHER**
Neil Skene

**EXECUTIVE EDITOR**
Robert W. Merry

**PUBLICATIONS MARKETING/SALES**
Robert Smith

**EDITOR, EBSCO PUBLISHING**
Melissa Kummerer

The CQ Researcher (ISSN 1056-2036). Formerly Editorial Research Reports. Published weekly (48 times per year, excluding March 1, May 3, Aug. 2 and Nov. 1, 1991) by Congressional Quarterly Inc., 1414 22nd St., N.W., Washington, D.C. 20037. Rates are furnished upon request. Application to mail at second-class postage rates is pending at Washington, D.C. POSTMASTER: Send address changes to The CQ Researcher, 1414 22nd St., N.W., Washington, D.C. 20037.

# Mexico's Emergence

BY RODMAN D. GRIFFIN

## THE ISSUES

For more than a century, Mexico and the United States have gazed uneasily across their common border, never quite prepared to accept that they are neighbors. Mexico has always made a point of asserting its independence from the country that seized half its territory in the Mexican-American War of 1846-1848. For its part, the United States has tended to ignore the impoverished land to the south, partly out of arrogance but mostly because for six decades it has been able to count on Mexico's basic stability. As former Arizona Gov. Bruce Babbitt once noted, "The great paradox of Mexico is that in our minds it might easily be 10,000 miles away."

In fact, it is only a footstep away. Although both nations boast proud traditions of revolution and independence, they are — whether they like it or not — entwined in a knot of interdependence. Not only do they share a 2,000-mile border, which stretches from San Diego on the Pacific to Brownsville, Texas, on the Gulf of Mexico, they straddle one of the few frontiers that separate an economically advanced country from a developing one. Mexico is its northern neighbor's third largest trading partner and a critical source of imported oil.

World events are fast pushing these distant neighbors closer together, both culturally and economically. Mexican President Carlos Salinas de Gortari, challenging a long tradition of state control and anti-Americanism, is transforming Mexico — and U.S.-Mexican relations — more profoundly than any of his predecessors in this century. Despite taking office with a reputation as a

Mexican President Salinas

MEXICO

cautious technocrat, Salinas has wielded the enormous power of the Mexican presidency to impose a remarkable overhaul of the economy.

Not yet halfway through his six-year term, Salinas has moved decisively to arrest corrupt union bosses, drug traffickers and repressive government officials. He has deregulated large sectors of the economy, lowered trade and investment barriers and sold off state corporations, including such politically sensitive ones as telephones, mines, steel mills and airlines.

Equally impressive, Salinas has curbed bureaucratic growth, restructured the tax system and slashed the fiscal deficit to its lowest level in a quarter century. In doing so, he has won the applause of the World Bank, President George Bush and leaders of other industrialized nations, who now hold Mexico up as a textbook example of modernization for the rest of the developing world to follow.

Salinas' boldest step — and biggest gamble — is his proposal for a free-trade agreement (FTA) with the

United States. Salinas is betting that a free-trading Mexico, bordering the world's largest and richest market, will divert the river of money and technology that now is flowing into low-cost havens in Asia and, for a while at least, Eastern Europe. With the trade pact negotiations, which have been expanded to include Canada, Salinas is preparing to write a new page of North American history that would push two uneasy and often distrustful neighbors into a permanent embrace.

Despite these extraordinary accomplishments, however, Mexico's domestic situation remains precarious. Economic hardship is as severe as ever; the political process is changing but is still far from democratic; corruption is endemic; and drug traffic has corrupted many official institutions, including the police. Moreover, the standard of living of the average Mexican is 40 percent lower than it was in 1982 and there is some question as to how long Mexicans will be willing to endure.

It seems the more Salinas does, the more he needs to do. The opening of the economy has unleashed pent-up demands for a more open political system. The 43-year-old president faces a difficult choice: either further accelerate the pace of reform, which is already intense by Mexican standards, or risk losing the gains he has promised the Mexican people. A lot is on the line, especially for the ruling Institutional Revolutionary Party (PRI). After more than 60 years of unbroken rule, the party's hold over Mexico has weakened in recent years and Salinas barely squeaked into office in 1988 amid widespread allegations of election fraud. If Salinas and his economic program stumble, the party would likely face further erosion.

***Given Mexico's long history of opposing foreign investment, what is the likelihood that the economic opening will be sustained?***

"In the old days," Jesus Silva-Herzog, a minister of finance in the previous government, said recently, "we . . . were taught that Uncle Sam and foreign investment were the problem. Now we are being told that they are the solutions." [1] Indeed, within the past three years, Mexico has gone from being one of the world's most protected, closed markets to one of the most open.

In July 1990, *Forbes* magazine told American businessmen to "forget Eastern Europe. The next great economic miracle will take place right on our borders." Mexico, it declared, had become "a revolution you can invest in."

Some investors wonder how stable that investment will be. Throughout this century, Latin American economies have shifted between being open and closed to foreign investment. Peru opened up sectors of its economy in 1981, only to close them five years later; Brazil liberalized its foreign investment laws in 1985, then passed a new constitution in 1988 that was more restrictive.

Mexico, for the most part, has consistently tried to limit outside investment, particularly in strategic sectors, such as natural resources, railroads and telecommunications, which are closely tied to Mexican sovereignty. This worries many potential investors and U.S. officials because there is always the chance the present economic opening will be reversed. In addition, there is a danger in stopping the reforms halfway, as happened in both Argentina and Brazil. Each curbed raging inflation three or four years ago, only to collapse into hyperinflation even more ruinous than before. That, critics say, is still a possibility for Mexico.

On the other hand, the Mexican government has taken a series of important steps to ensure that the opening is not reversed. Under Salinas' predecessor, Miguel de la Madrid Hurtado, Mexico joined the General Agreement on Tariffs and Trade (GATT) in 1986, committing the country to free trade — and a more open economy. That same year Mexico also accepted a $500 million loan from the World Bank to liberalize its trade regime. Since then, Salinas has signed a number of bilateral trade agreements with the United States and other countries that have become part of the internal law of Mexico. Collectively, these actions have helped attract foreign capital. According to the Banco de Mexico, direct foreign investment increased from $2.6 billion in 1988 to more than $4.6 billion in 1990.

"The risk of the opening being reversed is greatly minimized because there is consensus in Mexico in favor of what Salinas has done," says Susan Kaufman Purcell, vice president for hemispheric affairs at the Americas Society. "After a decade of despair, they see light at the end of the tunnel." Sidney Weintraub, author of *A Marriage of Convenience: Relations between Mexico and the United States*, agrees. "The shift in approach is not a one-shot affair . . . but a continuing reordering of the economy," he writes. "Whatever the durability of the present phase of modernization, there is no looking back." [2] Recent polls indicate that over 70 percent of Mexicans now favor a trade agreement with the U.S. — which would lock in the changes even tighter. [3]

Economic performance could prove to be the real litmus test for the durability of Mexico's trade opening, says Nora Lustig, a visiting fellow at the Brookings Institution in Washington. "So long as the economic performance is good, the opposition will not be able to use the economic opening as a way to criticize the ruling government," she adds.

At present, most economic indicators are quite favorable. During the last three years, the economy has grown at more than 3 percent a year and inflation has averaged roughly 20 percent, compared with 160 percent in 1987. Rudiger Dornbusch, an international economist at the Massachusetts Institute of Technology (MIT), predicts that growth rates will soar to 6 percent annually through the decade.

But, unfortunately, Salinas' economic reforms have not yet translated into an immediate economic boon — particularly not for the average Mexican, who still struggles just to survive. Twenty percent of working-age Mexicans are unemployed and 50 percent live in poverty, according to the World Bank. The risk, of course, is that if expectations of a payoff are not met soon, Mexicans will blame the government and its policy of economic integration.

Perhaps more important, certain powerful elements within Mexican society — protected industrialists, organized labor and the bureaucracy — stand to lose as a result of the trade opening. During the past few decades, they have come to rely on a system of controlled imports, reinforced by an overvalued exchange rate, and thus never had to compete in the marketplace. Unless they can be convinced to become more efficient, they may balk as the impact of the economic opening strikes home.

***What impact will a free-trade agreement have on Mexico — and on U.S.-Mexican relations?***

Most analysts agree that a free-trade agreement is much more crucial to Mexico's longer-term development and stability than it is to the United States. But the consequences of what happens in Mexico will inevitably be felt north of the border. Numerous studies conclude that a free-trade accord will result in more jobs in both countries. "More jobs will mean higher wages in Mexico, and this in turn will mean fewer migrants to the United States and Canada," Salinas told a group of U.S. newspaper editors in April. "We want to export goods, not people." [4]

Free trade is the linchpin of President Salinas' strategy to snap Mexico out of economic stagnation. Many economists say a free-trade pact and related U.S. aid, debt relief and investment could make or break hopes for a stronger economy.

Mexican objectives are quite specific. First, a trade agreement with the United States would yield more open and secure access to a market that accounts for nearly three-quarters of total Mexican trade. The agreement would eliminate non-tariff barriers to exports, reduce the high maximum tariffs on items such as orange juice, asparagus and certain textiles, and create a mechanism for the bilateral resolution of trade disputes. One of the "most important" goals of the negotiations, says Herminio Blanco Mendoza, Mexico's chief negotiator, is to minimize the possibility the United States will impose trade barriers in the future. [5]

Second, a trade pact would help lock in domestic reforms instituted over the past six years. Investors from Europe and Japan — as well as the United States — would be encouraged by the added security of knowing the current favorable climate toward trade and investment is unlikely to be overturned.

And third, a free-trade accord would set up a psychology of permanence that goes beyond the here-to-day, gone-tomorrow mentality of *maquiladoras*, Mexico's assembly plants clustered along the border (*see p. 498*). According to a U.S. International Trade Commission report, lower tariffs on U.S. components sold in Mexico would provide an incentive to locate new facilities in Mexico's interior, near population centers where consumers are concentrated

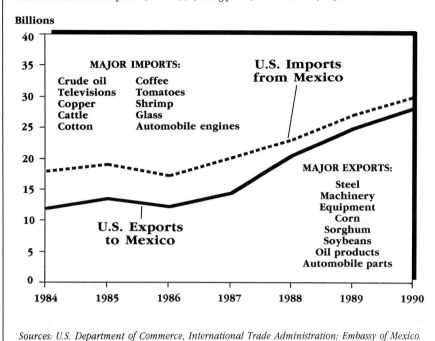

# U.S.-Mexico Trade

*The U.S. still imports more from Mexico than it sells to Mexico, but the gap is closing. U.S. exports to Mexico almost doubled from 1987 to 1990, rising from $14.6 billion to $28.3 billion.*

**Billions**

**MAJOR IMPORTS:**

| Crude oil | Coffee |
| Televisions | Tomatoes |
| Copper | Shrimp |
| Cattle | Glass |
| Cotton | Automobile engines |

**U.S. Imports from Mexico**

**U.S. Exports to Mexico**

**MAJOR EXPORTS:**
Steel
Machinery
Equipment
Corn
Sorghum
Soybeans
Oil products
Automobile parts

*Sources: U.S. Department of Commerce, International Trade Administration; Embassy of Mexico.*

and where there is better access to low-wage labor.

Already the talk of free trade has boosted confidence in Mexico's future. Mexico's stock market, the *Bolsa*, doubled in value in 1990 and as of June was up another 78 percent this year, a performance better than any other market in the world. [6] The renewed confidence should also help encourage the return of capital that left the country in the 1980s, as well as inspire new lending from international financial institutions, both of which are needed to bankroll Mexican economic development.

However, not everyone in Mexico endorses the free-trade pact, or the concept of economic integration. Cuauhtémoc Cárdenas, the leader of the leftist opposition in Mexico, said negotiations "would signify annexation to the United States." [7] Others have questioned whether the pace of negotiations is too fast. "We have already given too much unilaterally in

the trade field. ... We must avoid being more Catholic than the pope," warns former Finance Minister Silva-Herzog. [8]

Should the agreement fail, experts say, one certain casualty would be the current policy of cooperation with the United States, since the failure would strengthen the cluster of political groups traditionally suspicious of U.S. motives. Furthermore, although too much has changed for Mexico to revert entirely to the pre-reform era, those opposed to economic reform and to the trade agreement would more than likely join forces in an effort to return the economy to relative isolation and bureaucratic control.

## Has Mexico made real progress toward political reform?

As a presidential candidate in 1988, Salinas vowed not only to open up the economy, but also to reform the country's political system. He pledged to end corruption, and to have free elections, ultimately leading to multiparty government. "We are going to respect the citizens' vote and carry out clean and transparent elections," he said. "I prefer the risk of reform to the risk of inactivity."

Despite widespread claims of fraud in his own election, which some people feel was actually won by Cuauhtémoc Cárdenas, many experts feel Salinas has taken steps to "modernize" Mexico's Tammany Hall-style* political system:

■ In mid-1989, Salinas' political party, the PRI, recognized an opposition gubernatorial victory for the first time since the party was founded in 1929. Ernesto Ruffo Appel, the nominee of the center-right National Action Party (PAN), defeated candidates of the PRI and the nationalist Democratic Revolutionary Party (PRD) in Baja California Norte.

■ Salinas also made good on his anti-corruption campaign and removed a number of the most notorious party bosses. He even deployed the army to oust the powerful chief of Mexico's oil workers' union, Joaquín Her- nández Galicia. The union, with a reputation for corruption and nepotism, had in the past been treated with care by the government in exchange for stability among oil workers.

■ In July 1989, the PRI forged a congressional coalition with several opposition parties to obtain passage of a new election law, the Federal Code of Electoral Institutions and Procedures. The new code mandates the creation of a multiparty federal electoral commission and a "new and reliable" electoral list. It was widely touted by the PRI as evidence that the party is committed to reform.

"There is no question that Mexico is much more pluralistic today than it

was 10 years ago," says M. Delal Baer, director of the Mexico Project at the Center for Strategic and International Studies. "But it is still not perfect. You have to remember that Mexico has no history of electoral democracy at all." In fact, each of the reforms mentioned above can be matched by striking examples of how Mexico's politics haven't changed.

First, by most accounts, the vast majority of state and local races held since 1988 have been marked by blatant fraud, and in some cases violent crackdowns, including the use of army tanks to quell protests.

Second, despite progress in rooting out corruption, the fact remains that the PRI's octopuslike system of patronage remains largely intact. Critics contend that the cleansing efforts serve other political purposes. For example, they say, Galicia was sacked not so much because he was corrupt, but because he supported Cárdenas in the 1988 presidential election.

And third, the new electoral law also stipulates that the party with the most support in congressional elections will enjoy an absolute majority of the seats, provided that the party's nominees receive at least 35 percent of the popular vote. In other words, the PRI has virtually guaranteed itself control of the federal government.

Salinas' delicate balancing act of permitting some reforms, while resisting others, has not appeased Cárdenas and his leftist coalition. Nor

has it pleased his critics on the right, who complain that the pace of reform is too slow — and that Salinas' real intent is to preserve the PRI's iron grip on Mexican politics. Says Adolfo Aguilar Zinser, a professor of political science at Mexico City's National Autonomous University and one of Salinas' most vocal critics: "He is as dictatorial as his predecessors. He's just changed the messages." [9]

Many observers contend there are limits on how far Salinas and pro-reform technocrats can go in curbing the authoritarian practices of old-line politicians, including labor and peasant leaders who constitute the party's so-called dinosaur wing.

"Salinas clearly wants to open the system, but he is not about to gamble on broad political changes," says John Bailey, a professor of government at Georgetown University. The reason: a serious political challenge may jeopardize the economic opening, something Salinas has explicitly stated is a precondition for democracy.

Ultimately, how much change Salinas might be willing to propose may depend on the progress of the free-trade negotiations, his perception of how many concessions will be necessary to keep the U.S. Congress happy, and whether the economic changes in Mexico are producing sufficient results to give the PRI a reasonable chance of prevailing in open elections. ■

# BACKGROUND

## Political Evolution

In order to understand Mexico, it is imperative to know something of its history. Octavio Paz, Mexico's Nobel laureate poet, argues that the United States was founded in a land

without a past, whereas precisely the opposite was true for Mexico, which is a land of superimposed pasts. Mexico, he once said, must find its own way to modernity, making the "past . . . not an obstacle but a starting point." [10]

To this day, one Mexican in four is a full-blooded Indian. More important, the Indian presence still haunts

Continued on p. 496

---

*Tammany Hall was a powerful Democratic political organization in New York that is often associated with political corruption.

# Chronology

## 1500s-1800s *The defeat of the Aztecs and the birth of Mexico as a nation.*

### 1521
Spanish conquistador Hernán Cortés kills Aztec Emperor Cuauhtémoc and overtakes the Aztec capital of Tlatelolco.

### 1820
Mexico achieves independence from Spain.

### 1848
Treaty of Guadalupe-Hidalgo cedes half of Mexico's territory to the United States.

## 1900-1930s *Mexico passes from dictatorship to revolution to a one-party state.*

### 1910
The working classes rebel against the dictatorship of Porfirio Díaz. After seven years of chaos, the revolution is consolidated and a new constitution is written in 1917.

### 1929
The Institutional Revolutionary Party (PRI) is founded.

### 1938
President Lázaro Cárdenas nationalizes the oil industry and puts control of foreign firms in hands of a government-owned concern called Petróleos Mexicanos, or Pemex.

## 1940s-1960s *The economy grows at an average rate of 6 percent a year, with minimal inflation.*

### 1968
Troops fire on a peaceful demonstration in the capital, killing more than 300 people.

## 1970s *Mexico becomes dependent on oil exports and borrows heavily from international financial institutions.*

### 1973
A huge oil field is discovered near the southeastern town of Villahermosa, giving Mexico the sixth-largest petroleum reserves in the world.

## 1980s *Referred to as the "lost decade." The economy stagnates, relations with the United States deteriorate and the government falls into crisis.*

### August 1982
The Mexican government announces it is no longer able to service its $80 billion debt.

### September 1982
In his last state of the union address of his presidency, José López Portillo announces the nationalization of Mexico's banks.

### May 1986
U.S. Customs Commissioner William von Raab accuses Mexican officials of complicity in the drug trade.

### July 1986
As part of President de la Madrid's more open economic policy, Mexico joins the General Agreement on Tariffs and Trade (GATT).

### July 1988
Carlos Salinas de Gortari wins Mexican presidential election with 50.4 percent of the vote.

### July 1989
The PRI forges a congressional coalition with several opposition parties to "reform" the electoral system.

### August 1989
For the first time since its founding 60 years earlier, the PRI recognizes an opposition gubernatorial victory.

## 1990s *Salinas accelerates the economic opening and opposition groups focus on the need for electoral reform.*

### May 13, 1990
The Mexican Congress approves a constitutional amendment that returns to private hands two-thirds of the equity in 18 banks nationalized in 1982.

### Sept. 21, 1990
Salinas formally notifies George Bush that he wants to begin talks on a U.S.-Mexico free-trade agreement.

### May 1991
The House and Senate approve so-called fast-track legislation to extend for two years the president's authority to negotiate trade accords.

### June 12, 1991
Trade negotiations between the United States, Mexico and Canada officially begin in Toronto.

# Mexico At A Glance

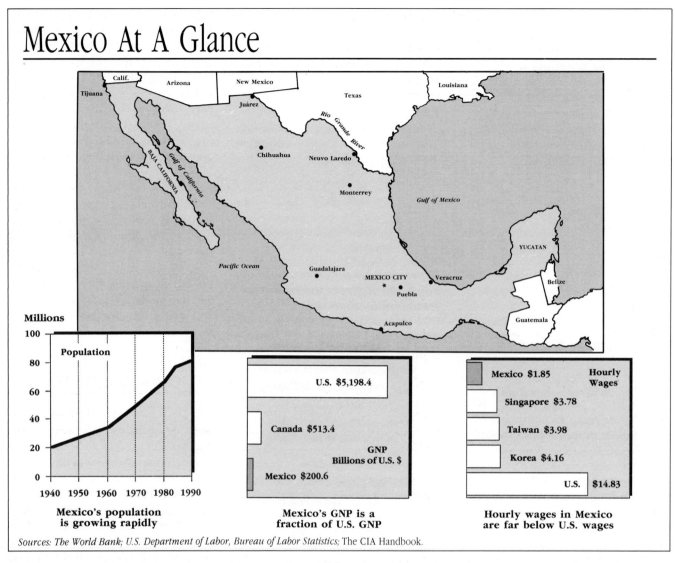

**Millions**

Mexico's population
is growing rapidly

Mexico's GNP is a
fraction of U.S. GNP

Hourly wages in Mexico
are far below U.S. wages

*Sources: The World Bank; U.S. Department of Labor, Bureau of Labor Statistics; The CIA Handbook.*

---

*Continued from p. 494*

the soil, mingling with the ghosts of the Aztecs and the Spanish conquistadores to produce a mestizo country never too distant from its past. Mexicans like to point out that they had a thriving capital and a bustling university when the land to the north was still a barren plain. Even now, the fall of that Aztec city and its last emperor, Cuauhtémoc, 470 years ago at the hands of Hernán Cortés and his band of 700 men, is remembered as the paradigm of the country's central myth: the confrontation between native culture and foreign imperialists.

The Mexican Revolution (1910

17) was a popular reaction to the dictatorship of Porfirio Díaz, under which private, often foreign, capital had been allowed free rein. The revolution, it is contended, rid Mexico of a feudal order and established a regime dedicated to social justice for all Mexicans. When Mexico finally struggled free after a century of invasions and insurrections, it named streets after its revolutionary heroes — Pancho Villa, Emiliano Zapata and the rest — and made self-determination its highest national goal.

The irony of the revolution is that Mexico's form of government since 1920 has been much closer to the

*porfiato*, as Díaz's dictatorship is commonly known, than most Mexicans would ever admit. Mexico still relies on one man to hold the destiny of the nation in his hand. But the system has been depersonalized. Instead of having a series of dictators, Mexico invests one office — the presidency — with immense power.*

The PRI, which was founded under a different name in 1929, eventually consolidated power and built a

---

*Although there are elections in Mexico, it is a foregone conclusion that the victor will be the candidate of the ruling PRI, who is handpicked by the outgoing president.

centralized state in which high tariff walls permitted impressive growth and authoritarian rule ensured stability. More a revolutionary organization than a political party, the PRI draws support from unions representing the sprawling bureaucracy, the peasantry and labor, based on an elaborate system of patronage.

For almost 50 years, from 1930 to the late 1970s, Mexico's domestic economy grew at an average annual rate of 6 percent. This sustained growth altered Mexico from an economic backwater to a potential middle-level power. It also helps explain the durability of the PRI.

## Oil: Blessing and Curse

Deposits of crude oil large enough to export were first discovered in Mexico near the southeastern town of Tampico in 1901. But oil has been both a blessing and a curse to Mexico. It provided resources for the nation's development, but it also was the lightning rod for foreign interference and the basis for some of the most egregious indignities inflicted on Mexico by the United States. The best-known public example was the Bucareli agreements of 1923, under which Mexico was forced to make concessions to U.S. oil interests in return for U.S. recognition of the government of President Alvaro Obregón.

In 1938, however, after American and British companies, including Standard Oil, Texaco and Gulf, had moved in for a killing, Mexico struck back by nationalizing the foreign firms and placing them under the control of a government-owned concern called Petróleos Mexicanos, or Pemex. This bold stroke by Lázaro Cárdenas, who was then president, is the paragon to which all national leaders since have aspired.

Just before the 1973 Arab embargo left Western nations searching for new sources of petroleum, Mexico struck oil again, this time near the southeastern town of Villahermosa. By the end of the decade, the country was pumping oil out of the sixth-largest reserves in the world and was launched upon a giddy carnival of high living. During those profligate years, hundreds of thousands of phony jobs were created in the oil industry to provide pocket money for government officials. As revenue increased, so did graft. One mid-level Pemex official was charged with embezzling $97 million. Oil helped to corrupt the system, and corruption helped to oil it.

Soon enough, many chieftains of Pemex and its union, one of the largest in Latin America, had established themselves as the sheiks of Mexico — and as exemplars of extortion, patronage and bribery. By the early 1970s, mismanagement and inefficiency had become so crippling that the country was forced to import 62,000 barrels of oil a day. Pemex's woes were symptomatic of a much greater malaise: corruption pervaded every sector of the PRI bureaucracy.[11]

### Economic Collapse

Buying much more than it could pay for, borrowing promiscuously and frantically printing more and more pesos, the government of President José López Portillo tried to sustain its extravagant spree even after a glut of oil began to develop in 1981. Eventually, the economy crashed. By August 1982, Mexico could no longer pay interest on its $80 billion in foreign debt, and international banks and governments had to come to the rescue with a $6 billion emergency loan package. By the end of that year, when López Portillo handed over power to his chosen successor, Miguel de la Madrid, inflation had hit 100 percent, the peso had been devalued by 40 percent and growth had slipped into reverse.

Over the next few years Mexico had to accept austerity measures prescribed by the International Monetary Fund (IMF) and foreign creditors, particularly U.S. banks, to obtain foreign loans. The measures included new taxes, a steep reduction in imports and a nearly 10 percent cut in the federal budget.

The severity of Mexico's economic collapse in the 1980s is the key to understanding the current economic opening — as well as the incremental political changes inside Mexico. "If there wasn't a profound restructuring tied to the debt crisis throughout Latin America, the statist* model of development would not have become obsolete," explains Purcell of the Americas Society.

## 'Distant Neighbors'

Despite their proximity, the United States and Mexico have never understood each other. The vast majority of U.S. citizens are ignorant of Mexican culture, history and geography. Foreign policy experts say even when U.S. policies have helped Mexico, the benefits have occurred inadvertently rather than as a function of thought-out policy.

For their part, Mexicans have always distrusted their northern neighbor and resented U.S. meddling. They claim there is more than a little truth to Porfirio Díaz's famous lament, "Poor Mexico, so far from God, and so close to the United States." Mexican desire for independence from the United States shows up in many ways. For example, Mexico refused to accept bilateral U.S. aid under the Alliance for Progress, but accepted U.S. assis-

---

*Statism is a political system under which economic planning is in the hands of a highly centralized government.

tance given indirectly through multilateral institutions such as the World Bank and the Inter-American Development Bank.*

While Mexico has never been able to escape its dependence on its northern neighbor, U.S. policy has vacillated between indifference and overbearing paternalism. The asymmetry has forced an uneasy friendship that, until recently, seemed always on the brink of rupture. "When Mexico becomes the focus of U.S. media and political attention, the relationship's delicate balance is impaired by emotional outbursts and mutual recriminations," writes Adolfo Aguilar Zinser.[12]

U.S.-Mexican relations reached a low ebb in the mid-1980s, when disagreements over foreign policy, mainly Mexico's support for Nicaragua, overwhelmed the relationship. By 1985, de la Madrid had moderated his support for the leftist Sandinista government, but the U.S. position "hardened," according to a senior U.S. official in Mexico City at the time. He said, "We feel that Mexico is continuing to pressure us to negotiate directly with the Sandinistas. But the issue has polarized. If you're not our friend, you're our enemy." [13]

Meanwhile, the number of Mexicans arrested along the border increased from 750,000 in 1982 to a high point of more than 1.6 million in 1986. (*See story, p. 499.*) At the same time, a steadily rising tide of drugs was flowing northward. According to the U.S. Drug Enforcement Agency, Mexico accounted for roughly one-third of all the heroin and marijuana pouring into the United States in the mid-1980s and served as a transshipment point for 30 percent of the cocaine flown from

---

*On March 13, 1961, President John F. Kennedy spelled out a 10-point program of Inter-American cooperation, known as the Alliance for Progress. Under this program, the U.S. allocated $500 million in aid for Latin American nations to help them toward self-sustaining growth.

Colombia and farther south.

Both the rash of drug smuggling and flood of "illegals" drove Washington to express, with unprecedented frankness, its anxiety and even its anger toward Mexico. The bitterness was reflected in May 1986 hearings on Mexico's economic crisis before a Senate Foreign Relations subcommittee chaired by Sen. Jesse Helms, R-N.C. Testifying before the committee, William von Raab, the U.S. commissioner of customs, accused Mexican officials of complicity in the drug trade, touching off a dark phase in U.S.-Mexican relations.

### Maquiladoras: Bright Spot

One bright spot in the U.S.-Mexico relationship has been the *maquiladora* program. Set up in 1965, the program's idea is simple. Duty-free imports of components are allowed into Mexico, where they are assembled into finished products and exported. If exported to the United States, which the vast majority are, these products are assessed for duty only on the value added in Mexico.

Trade unions in the United States have long argued that the program encourages American firms to export jobs across the Rio Grande. Critics in Mexico contend the program has resulted in excessive pollution in Mexico (*see story, p. 503*) and has not stimulated real employment growth. Moreover, they say that most *maquila* work is simple assembly, which does not bring high-technology skills to Mexico.

These criticisms notwithstanding, the *maquiladora* industry has experienced phenomenal growth (over 20 percent a year). There are presently about 2,200 *maquiladoras*, mostly near the U.S. border, that employ some 560,000 Mexicans. The industry contributed more than $2 billion to Mexico's economy last year and has become the country's second-largest source of foreign exchange earnings, after oil.[14]

*Maquiladoras* offer benefits to the United States, too. A 1988 study by the U.S. International Trade Administration indicated that the vast majority of the 900 firms surveyed felt that assembly plants in Mexico had improved their international competitiveness. A separate study on *maquiladoras* conducted by Wharton Econometrics and the Center for Econometric Research on Mexico, based in Philadelphia, said that eliminating the program would cost the United States $2.6 billion in gross national product and 76,000 jobs.

## 'Salinastroika'

As long as the PRI could guarantee annual growth rates of 6 percent, as it did for many decades, Mexicans were willing to accept its paternal rule. But the economic collapse in the 1980s threw the entire system out of whack. By the 1988 presidential election, it was readily apparent that there were serious cracks in the PRI's armor.

Though Mexico has long had opposition parties, both on the left and the right, it wasn't until recently that they became a more potent force in Mexican politics. The conservative National Action Party (PAN), founded in 1939, has long served as the leading opposition party. While the PAN's strength has traditionally come from the northern border states, where it won numerous local elections, the party was able to expand its appeal in the '80s to include large segments of the urban middle classes, who were frustrated by the loss of their hard-won financial gains in the '70s.

By the 1988 election, when the PRI won barely one-quarter of the vote in Mexico City, it was clear that the PRI's hegemonic status had ended; it had lost its traditional claim to be the "party of majorities."

# Immigration: A Fixture in U.S.-Mexican Relations

Nearly five years ago, the U.S. Congress passed a landmark immigration law in an effort to stem the flow of illegal aliens crossing the U.S.-Mexico border. The 1986 law, the Immigration Reform and Control Act (IRCA), sought to weaken the economic magnet that draws illegal aliens to the United States by prohibiting the employment of people who cannot document their immigration or citizenship status. In a departure from previous policy, which had focused on border enforcement, IRCA was backed up with stiff fines on employers who hire illegal aliens.

Despite early success, a growing number of scholars and policy-makers have recently concluded that the law's deterrent effect was only temporary. "Employer sanctions may have seemed a real barrier at first, but now they are just one more hurdle to overcome," says Wayne A. Cornelius, director of the Center for U.S.-Mexican Studies at the University of California at San Diego.

Before the law was enacted, apprehensions of people crossing the border reached more than 1.6 million a year, provoking the Reagan administration to declare the border

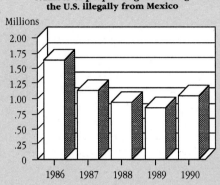

**Number of people caught entering the U.S. illegally from Mexico**

Millions
2.00
1.75
1.50
1.25
1.00
.75
.50
.25
0

1986   1987   1988   1989   1990

*Source: U.S. Border Patrol.*

"out of control." After three years of steady declines, there was an increase in 1990 (*see graph*).

"The problem," writes Jorge G. Castañeda, one of Mexico's leading political analysts, "is that both the supply and demand sides of the immigration equation continue to favor greater flows, and the strictures provided by the 1986 law are severely flawed." †

Castañeda says there are "push" and "pull" factors operating beyond the control of either the United States or Mexico: the shift in the United States from a manufacturing to a service economy, which created a demand for low-skilled workers; the aging of the U.S. population; and the growth of the Mexican population. Furthermore, the case can be made that so long as wages are 10 times higher in the United States than in Mexico, mass immigration will continue, regardless of U.S. immigration policy or Mexican economic policies.

---

† See Jorge G. Castañeda and Rafael Alarcon, "Workers are a commodity, too," *The Los Angeles Times*, April 22, 1991.

---

However, the threat to the PRI didn't come from the center-right PAN, but from the left.

Earlier in 1987, a group of prominent PRI members announced the formation of the "Democratic Current," which would seek to reform the structure of the party from within. Following the selection of Salinas as the PRI's official candidate to the presidency and the refusal by central party authorities to recognize the legitimacy of the dissidents, several of them left the PRI and founded the National Democratic Front (FDN).

In alliance with several previously marginal parties and the bulk of the Mexican left, the FDN supported the presidential candidacy of Cuauhtémoc Cárdenas, an ex-member of the PRI elite and son of Lázaro Cárdenas, Mexico's most revered president. Cárdenas ran an extremely popular campaign which advocated greater social justice, writing off Mexico's debt and closing the economy to foreign investment. Salinas was elected by a bare majority (50.4 percent) in an election fraught with charges of vote fraud.

Under Salinas, who holds a Ph.D. in business from Harvard, Mexico has achieved a remarkable degree of success in turning around the economy. To institute his program of economic liberalization and austerity, commonly referred to as "Salinastroika," * he has brought in a dynamic team of young free-market economists, many of whom were educated in the United States. Many

---

*The phrase refers to Soviet President Mikhail S. Gorbachev's economic reform program, *perestroika*.

---

of these reforms were actually begun by de la Madrid, Salinas' predecessor and mentor, but the new president quickened the pace.

### Progress on the debt

One of Salinas' first priorities was to bring the country's $100 billion debt under control. In February 1990, Mexico was the first to negotiate debt relief under the Brady Plan, a massive debt-relief program initiated by U.S. Treasury Secretary Nicholas F. Brady. External debt was reduced 20 percent, about $20 billion, which will result in savings of about $4 billion in debt service each year from 1990 to 1994.

When Mexico was negotiating its historic debt-reduction agreement with its 470 commercial bank creditors in 1989, Salinas and his economic team predicted that a burst of growth was imminent, fueled both by a surge of foreign investment and the return of Mexican capital that had gone abroad. The National Development Plan sent to the Mexican Congress predicted that the $26.5 billion that foreigners have invested in Mexico would double by 1994, the end of Salinas' term.

What Salinas could not anticipate, however, was that communism would collapse in Eastern Europe and present Mexico with a whole new set of rivals. Overnight, state-owned companies were on the block around the world, offering the foreign investor attractive new possibilities. In addition, Europeans were preoccupied with opportunities presented within the European Community in 1992[15] — and Japanese and other East Asian investors were reluctant to move into Mexico too fast, for fear of angering Washington.

As a result, Salinas began contemplating closer economic ties with the United States. His government also intensified its assault on the domestic sector. The government raised revenues 13.4 percent by enforcing the tax laws for the first time in Mexican history, and cut expenditures.[16] Three-quarters of the state's corporations were privatized, and deregulation permitted businesses to respond to the market rather than to bureaucrats. All told, the government has cut the number of state-run companies from 1,155 to fewer than 280.

In addition, trade and investment barriers have been substantially lowered. Today, 1.7 percent of goods imported into the country require licenses, down from 100 percent in 1982, and the maximum tariff has been sliced to 20 percent from 100 percent (the average is 10 percent, compared with 4 percent for the United States).[17] Some two-thirds of the economy is now open to foreign ownership.

Since 1989, when he set out to liberalize foreign investment regula-

tions, $5.2 billion in new capital has flowed into Mexico, along with consumer goods once unavailable. Salinas has also rectified a dangerous reliance on oil, which produced 78 percent of Mexico's export income in 1982. Today it accounts for less than 35 percent.

This year, the economy is growing at an annualized rate of 3.9 percent, the third straight year of growth after nearly a decade of stagnation. "Mexico has discovered there is life after debt," Miguel Leaman, a Mexican trade official, quipped recently.[18]

Yet though expectations have improved, investment has not yet increased sufficiently to bring Mexico prosperity. Employment in manufacturing has grown, but not as fast as

the labor force. The country's imports have nearly doubled, thanks to economic liberalization, but exports have grown slowly. As a consequence, Mexico's trade deficit mushroomed to $3 billion in 1990. Foreign debt payments eat up almost a fourth of its export earnings and, as world interest rates rise, each percentage-point increase swells its annual debt payments by nearly $1 billion.

"If the Mexican economy is to be jump-started through foreign investment," says James P. Womack, research director of the international motor vehicle program at MIT, "the major source of funds will be American firms, and the major market for the products produced will be the United States and Canada." ∎

# CURRENT SITUATION

## Free-Trade Debate

Over the past five years, Mexico has been erecting a new trade policy while chiseling away at its trade barriers. Since joining GATT in 1986, Mexico has signed a series of bilateral trade agreements with the United States: the 1987 Framework Understanding, the 1987-88 sectoral accords on steel and textiles, and the 1990 Memorandum of Understanding on Textiles, to name a few. But proponents of a North American free-trade agreement say more economic integration is needed, especially in agriculture, automobiles and textiles.

In 1987, President de la Madrid told *The Economist*, the British magazine, that a free-trade zone between Mexico and the U.S. was "not a possibility," because Mexicans could not

tolerate the thought of delivering their economy and society to what they believed would be American hegemony. By February 1990, the government's position, as well as the tide of public opinion, had shifted dramatically. The Salinas administration — facing a new inflationary threat, high unemployment and an expanding trade deficit, and fearing for its political survival — broached the idea of a U.S.-Mexico free-trade agreement with President Bush.

Despite some trepidation among U.S. trade officials that the economic and political disparities between the two countries are too great, Bush notified Congress on Sept. 25 that the administration planned to enter into trade talks with Mexico.

After several months of acrimonious debate, which pitted organized labor, environmental groups and textile organizations against the administration, Hispanic organizations and numerous business groups, Congress voted in May to authorize "fast track" negotiations between the United States and Mexico. "Fast

*Continued on p. 502*

# Would a Free-Trade Agreement Be Good for the U.S.?

The prospect of a free-trade zone spanning all of North America, an issue that was on the back burner just last year, has suddenly emerged as one of the hottest and most contentious political issues of the year. "Nobody expected this thing to move very quickly, and all of a sudden here it is, coming like a bullet train," says Robert M. Stern, an economist at the University of Michigan.[†]

Since Mexico began economic reform in 1986, opening its economy to foreign investment and goods, U.S. exports have risen from $12 billion to $28 billion and its trade deficit with Mexico has dropped from $4.9 billion to $1.8 billion. Citing these improvements, advocates of closer economic integration argue that a more prosperous Mexico is good for North Americans.

More specifically, they claim a U.S.-Mexico-Canada free-trade agreement (FTA) promises a huge, thriving North American market that surpasses anything the European Community or Japan can hope for. But foes warn that such an accord would trigger an exodus of U.S. factories to south of the Rio Grande, inspire a flood of Mexican imports and significantly increase pollution along the border (*see story, p. 503*).

The Bush administration has made a trade accord with Mexico a cornerstone of its foreign policy. "By eliminating trade and investment barriers, we will stimulate the dynamism of our economies, enhance the competitiveness of our businesses and farmers, and set a standard for trade liberalization for the hemisphere and the world," exuded Carla A. Hills, the U.S. trade representative, while lobbying lawmakers this spring.

A February 1991 report by the U.S. International Trade Commission (USITC) concludes that an FTA "will benefit the U.S. economy overall by expanding trade opportunities, lowering prices, increasing competition, and improving the ability of U.S. firms to exploit economies of scale." By the year 2000, Mexico is expected to have 100 million consumers who want more goods and services. Already, the Commerce Department estimates that 538,000 U.S. jobs are related to exports to Mexico, with half those jobs a direct result of Mexican trade liberalization.[††]

Many Democrats from border states have joined Republicans in supporting a free-trade pact because it would mean more jobs for their districts. But Democrats from the industrial North, along with organized labor, argue that such a pact would mean a loss of jobs. Mexican labor costs are about 10 percent of those in the United States. And though it varies widely from industry to industry, the cost of labor makes up roughly two-thirds of U.S. manufacturing costs overall.

"No matter how productive, U.S. workers cannot compete with labor costs of less than $1 an hour," says Mark A. Anderson, an international economist with the AFL-CIO. "A free-trade agreement will only encourage greater capital outflows from the United States." According to labor leaders and environmentalists, lax enforcement of environmental and tax laws in Mexico, as well as the absence of the kinds of worker protection laws and other benefits Americans enjoy, also will encourage the migration of U.S. jobs to Mexico.

Even fervent promoters of free trade concede there will be losers. To exploit lower Mexican wages, American manufacturers of autos, glass, apparel, electronics, toys, and other labor-intensive goods would probably shift more low-paying jobs to Mexico. In the industrial Midwest, where manufacturing accounts for 30 percent of employment, compared with 16 percent nationwide, the fallout could be staggering.

But even without a trade agreement, the incentives for U.S. companies to move south are significant and have been increasing since Mexico began lowering its tariffs three or four years ago. "The choice is not so much to keep jobs here or lose them to Mexico," says Rudiger Dornbusch, an economist at the Massachusetts Institute of Technology. "Competition from low-wage countries has been going on for more than a decade. The right question to ask about free trade with Mexico is whether we should prefer that, when jobs do go abroad, that they go south rather than to Asia."

Indeed, many trade experts say if it weren't for Mexico many low-skilled jobs would have migrated to the Far East years ago. Moreover, they are quick to point out that money will be allocated for retraining and there will be a long transition period — at least 10 years — for import-sensitive industries.

Eliminating trade barriers would also probably harm farmers who grow crops currently protected by tariffs and quotas, such as avocados, oranges and sugar. At the same time, certain U.S. industries and geographic areas, notably the Southwest, stand to benefit from a U.S.-Mexico trade accord. For example, U.S. farmers who grow grain and soybeans probably would see a surge in exports to Mexico.

Looking at the U.S. economy as a whole, many economists say a U.S.-Mexico free-trade pact won't be terribly significant. The U.S. economy is 25 times the size of the Mexican economy, and many trade barriers already have been dismantled. In this sense, U.S. objectives in pursuing an FTA may be more political than economic. By supporting Salinas at this critical time, the United States may achieve one of its chief foreign policy goals: Mexico's political stability. Moreover, a free-trade pact would promote economic growth in Mexico, and thus reduce the pressures for emigration by Mexico's fast-growing labor force.

---

[†] Quoted in *Business Week*, Nov. 12, 1990.

[††] See *North American Free Trade Agreement*, U.S. Department of Commerce, May 1991, p. 25.

*Continued from p. 500*

track" gives the administration authority to negotiate a trade agreement on the understanding that the final document will be voted up or down by Congress and not be subject to amendment.

"Without the fast track, we would be dead in the water," Under Secretary of State Robert B. Zoellick told a Senate Foreign Relations subcommittee in April. "It would kill [the free-trade agreement], it would kill the [GATT] and it would kill jobs." No country would negotiate a trade agreement, he said, if it were subject to multiple amendments in Congress.[19]

Dividing more along regional than party lines, both the House and the Senate rejected resolutions that would have denied Bush's request for a two-year renewal of fast-track procedures. On May 1, roughly three weeks prior to the vote, the president presented Congress with an "action plan," an 80-page document explaining U.S. motives for a free-trade pact, and including pledges to spend money on worker retraining, if need be; to reject any weakening of U.S. environmental laws; and to negotiate safeguards designed to lessen the impact on U.S. industries that feel threatened by a trade agreement. Bush's action plan effectively undercut the opposition coalition.

Canada formally joined the talks this spring, broadening the debate to a North American Free Trade Agreement. (A U.S.-Canadian Free Trade Agreement took effect in 1989.[20]) The vision is to craft the biggest open market in the world, from the Yukon to the Yucatan, with a combined gross national product of $6 trillion and some 360 million consumers.

Under the envisioned agreement, the U.S.-Mexico border ultimately would disappear for purposes of trade and industry. Tariffs would be lowered and eventually eliminated; restrictions against U.S. investment would be reduced; and the Mexican

market would be "freed up" for U.S. agricultural products. Some problem areas, such as petroleum, transportation and migration, will probably have to be handled by exemption from the FTA or through special provisions. But other difficult issues will have to be ironed out. For example: How will Japanese and other foreign *maquilas* operate within the confines of a trilateral agreement? What rules will be established to protect intellectual property?[21]

Though opponents are still threatening to reopen the issue in the Senate later this year, most experts believe the fast-track vote put Congress firmly in the background on trade negotiations — at least until the proposed agreements are sent to Congress. The negotiations, even on the fast track, will take at least a year to complete, according to U.S. trade officials.

If a pact isn't signed, it could be disastrous for Salinas, who has invested an enormous amount of political capital in its success. The economic opening has already had great impact at all levels of society. For the average Mexican, the transition to a freer economy has been accompanied by a collapse of purchasing power; for Mexico's elite, it has meant a dramatic change in the power structure. For decades the political system has served the interests of a relatively small cluster of political and industrial groups. As economic reform has progressed, it has forced development of new alliances and constituencies to sustain the governing coalition in power.

The cement that holds the new coalition together is the expectation of economic recovery — and the distribution of the benefits among the coalition partners, including large sectors of the middle classes and parts of the working class. "The timing is critical for Mexico because expectations are so high," says Greg Rocha, a political scientist at the University of Texas at El Paso. "If it

takes too long, the coalition supporting Salinas may unravel."

## Qualified Democracy

Peruvian novelist Mario Vargas Llosa caused a furor during a forum in Mexico City in August 1990 when he described Mexico as "the perfect dictatorship . . . camouflaged so that it appears not to be a dictatorship." His harsh words contained an element of truth. Yet the Mexico of today might be more accurately described as a "qualified democracy." The country's political system is dominated by one party, but there is a significant — and increasing — degree of pluralism.

To be sure, Mexico does have repressive features, such as summary arrests and muzzling of dissent. A detailed report issued in June 1990 by Americas Watch, a human rights organization, concluded that an array of human rights violations have become institutionalized in Mexican society, including killings and torture by police, and violations of civil liberties by the judicial system.

Nevertheless, Mexico does have a functioning judicial system and an active legislature. While the press usually echoes the government line, opposition news media do exist, and are becoming much more prevalent.

In the case of electoral reform, "Salinas is neither a brutal autocrat nor a revolutionary democrat," says Baer at the Center for Strategic and International Studies. "Rather, he is a gradualist." He has undertaken measured reforms to open the political process while at the same time ensuring that the PRI maintains control over the government.

Thus, while Salinas and other PRI leaders emphatically promise clean and fair elections, the PRI machinery regularly steals them. For exam-

*Continued on p. 504*

# Mexico's Polluted Environment

Every society that has gone through an industrial revolution has paid a price in terms of pollution and environmental degradation: 18th-century Britain had its soot-spewing textile mills just as 20th-century China has its fetid coal-fired factories. Developing nations take the position that only after they have attained the standard of living that rich countries enjoy will they adopt more restrictive environmental policies.

Mexico is no exception. For more than a decade, Mexico City, with a metropolitan area population approaching 20 million, has had a well-deserved reputation as one of the world's most polluted cities. But recent studies indicate that Mexico City's foul air is just the tip of the country's environmental woes.

Mexico's pollution problems — ranging from groundwater contamination to unmonitored disposal of hazardous waste to smog wafting as far north as the Grand Canyon — are so grave that they have emerged as a major issue and potential obstacle to the North American free-trade agreement currently being negotiated. (*See story, p. 501.*)

If the trade pact is signed, environmental groups on both sides of the border have warned, the problems could get much worse. Environmentalists argue that the border infrastructure already cannot handle the number of cars, people and industry. Moreover, they fear that unfettered Mexican access to U.S. markets will lead to a rapid expansion of pollution-prone industries, such as steel and chemical manufacturing. They also complain that free trade is likely to spur greater mining and timbering of an already scarred landscape.

President Bush has taken environmentalists' concerns seriously enough that he promised in a May 1 report to members of Congress that he would not accept an accord that involved lower environmental standards than in current U.S. law, and that he would pursue parallel talks to address Mexico's environmental problems.

The brunt of the debate has focused on Mexico's 2,200 *maquiladoras*, or assembly plants, situated along the border. Nearly 80 percent of the companies surveyed for an April 1991 General Accounting Office study cited air pollution laws as a major factor in their relocation decisions.[†]

Despite the fact that Mexico's environmental laws have been modeled after those in the United States and are quite stringent, the U.S. spends 50 times more per capita on enforcement. Until recently, the Secretariat of Urban Development and Ecology (SEDUE), Mexico's equivalent of the Environmental Protection Agency (EPA), had just five employees to regulate 300 *maquiladoras* as well as other environmental problems in Ciudad Juarez, a city of 1.5 million.

The exodus of manufacturing plants to Mexico's border region already has had significant consequences for communities on both sides of the frontier:

■ At least 12 million gallons of raw sewage from Mexico flows into the Tijuana River every day, polluting San Diego's beaches. The Mexican government is so hard pressed to deal with the problem that the U.S. government, the state of California, and the city of San Diego have agreed to pay most of the $192 million cost of a treatment plant on the border.[††]

■ More than 1,000 American-owned plants in Mexico generate hazardous waste but only 19 percent could show they had complied with Mexican law and disposed of wastes properly, according to a report issued by SEDUE last November.

■ Industrial wastes and untreated sewage flowing into Nogales, Ariz., from Mexico have been blamed for hepatitis rates 20 times the national average.

■ The EPA says the New River, which traverses the U.S.-Mexico border and provides irrigation for California crops in the Imperial Valley, contains more than 100 toxic pollutants, including PCBs, vinyl chloride, and nitro-benzene.[‡]

Amid growing concern about the environment, President Salinas stepped up his anti-pollution policy. To beef up environmental enforcement, the government has increased SEDUE's budget by 600 percent over the last two years and says it will add 100 new inspectors. In March, Salinas launched a program to replace outmoded buses and taxis and permanently shut down Mexico City's largest oil refinery.

At the direction of Presidents Bush and Salinas, the EPA is working with Mexico to develop an integrated environmental border plan. The U.S. Congress is now considering legislation to set up a permanent U.S.-Mexican environmental health commission, in which the EPA and SEDUE would work jointly to evaluate the *maquiladoras* and explore ways of preventing environmental abuse along the border.

In April, Fernando Menéndez, chief air-pollution monitor for Mexico City, announced that any company seeking to relocate to Mexico would have to comply with emission standards at least as strict as where it came from. Since then, 226 factories in the Mexico City area — including international companies such as General Motors, DuPont and Coca-Cola — have been hit by partial or total closure orders for failing to comply with Mexico's environmental laws.

Critics remain skeptical. "For decades nothing happened on environmental issues. Now this. There's no question the free-trade negotiations are pushing the changes," says Armando Baez, director of Atmospheric Sciences at the National Autonomous University of Mexico.[‡‡]

† *U.S.-Mexico Trade: Some Wood Furniture Firms Relocated from Los Angeles Area to Mexico*, General Accounting Office, April 1991.

†† See Joseph LaDout, "Deadly Migrants," *Technology Review*, July 1991.

‡ See Stanford J. Lewis, *et al.*, *Border Trouble: Rivers in Peril*, National Toxic Campaign Fund, May 1991.

‡‡ Quoted in *The Christian Science Monitor*, June 4, 1991.

Continued from p. 502

ple, in elections in the state of Mexico last November, the PRI claimed victory in 116 out of 120 municipalities by such unbelievable margins that virtually all independent observers, including the Organization of American States, cried foul.

One interpretation of what is presently occurring is that popular discontent has forced the PRI to reform, albeit reluctantly. Experts say Salinas would probably prefer to postpone free elections until the economic reforms restart the economy, raise wages and bring people back to the PRI. But both domestic and international pressures for immediate change are too strong. So the PRI has made the ultimate pragmatic decision: The PRI now fields better candidates than in the past — and accepts fairer elections in areas where the press and the opposition can readily monitor vote tallies, mostly in the north. "The PRI leadership has a history of moving just enough to adjust to the circumstances, but not so much that they reform the system," says Rocha.

One potential obstacle to a more democratic system is the apparent inability of the two opposition parties to collaborate in forcing the PRI to deliver on its promises of political reform. Whereas the extreme conditions in which most Mexicans live have provided fertile ground for the populist demagoguery of Cárdenas, chronic rifts within the PRD have left the party in disarray. And rather than negotiate political reforms with the PRI, which the PAN has done, Cárdenas has preferred to label the PRI "unreformable." By doing that, he is holding himself out as an alternative in 1994 should the PRI's economic reforms fail. But he has also forced the PRI into a defensive posture.

Meanwhile, voter apathy is so high that turnout in state elections has slumped to as little as 22 percent.[22] To its credit, however, over the past few years the PRI has permitted an increasing number of opposition victories in local contests. This is significant because the PRI no longer controls a two-thirds majority in the Congress, and thus must form alliances with opposition parties in order to pass constitutional amendments.

Whether these changes signify substantive reform depends on one's point of view. One thing that is certain is that they have loosened the PRI's absolute grip on power. Polls indicate that Salinas is extremely popular both inside and outside of Mexico, but that popularity has not translated into popularity for the PRI, which remains largely discredited.

The PRI will face another crucial test this August, when midterm elections for the entire Chamber of Deputies (lower house), one-half of the Senate, and seven governors are decided. The stakes are high for Salinas because now more than ever his party needs legitimacy. If the U.S. Congress deems the elections unfair, there will be pressure to make political reform a condition for signing a free-trade agreement, which most experts believe would scuttle the negotiations.

### Reform From Within?

Thus far, PRI reformers seem to have focused their attention more on the party than on the electoral system. "The PRI must be in the vanguard of democracy in Mexico," explained Sen. Luis Donaldo Colosio. "The PRI [must] engage in its own internal reform." [23] Even opposition leaders concede that the PRI, and the PRI alone, holds the key to democratization in Mexico.

Oddly enough, in order to democratize itself, many observers feel the party must first impose more centralized control over its regional representatives, some of whom may not share the president's goals. Since taking office, Salinas has used his immense presidential power to root out corruption and inefficiency both in the unions and in the PRI bureaucracy. Not only has he jailed tax evaders and corrupt union bosses, he systematically attacked the PRI's entrenched system of patronage. For example, on May 31, 1991, the president closed down the union-run port of Veracruz, which had become notorious for graft and inefficiency. The port, which employed more than 1,500 day laborers, will be modernized and turned over to private companies.

"Salinas is taking selective steps to root out bottlenecks — pockets of corruption and inefficiency that jeopardize his economic project," says John Bailey at Georgetown.

The stakes in moving Mexico from a statist system to one based on an open market and individual accountability are quite high. Some experts say too high. "Change will mean committing political suicide for those in power," says one Mexican analyst who requested anonymity. "There is an intrinsic contradiction in political reform in Mexico. In order for change to happen, leaders will have to be willing to lose personally. The new leadership is more in agreement on the vision for what will make a modern Mexico, but the political procedures are still unchanged."

In any event, there are bound to be winners and losers — and Salinas has been cautious not to alienate his power base. Organized labor fears that structural reforms will mean the continued loss of jobs and buying power; inefficient manufacturers fear competition in a less protected marketplace; bureaucrats fear that trimming the state's economic role will diminish their influence; and many PRI stalwarts fear that expanding the private sector at the expense of the state will shrink the patronage and bribe money essential to lubricating the party's creaky machinery.

The reduction or elimination of

Continued on p. 506

# At Issue:

## Is Mexico moving toward democracy?

### LUIS RUBIO

**Political scientist and general director of CIDAC, an independent research center in Mexico City**
FROM *THE LOS ANGELES TIMES*, Aug. 6, 1990.

*t*ime seems to be running out for the old political ways of Mexico. President Carlos Salinas de Gortari recently appointed a commission of impeccable individuals to monitor human rights violations in an effort to clamp down, once and for all, on all abuses, whether by private groups or public agencies. Then, Congress passed a new electoral law that eliminates all the devious instruments through which the ruling Institutional Revolutionary Party (PRI) used to rig elections. . . .

Given the size of Mexico, human rights violations have been relatively few, but nonetheless serious, in recent years. Police and government officials, particularly at the state and local levels, have killed dissidents and threatened whomever they deemed stood in [their] way.

Typical of the style of the Salinas administration, the government response has been neither shy nor complacent. Rather than simply solving the one or two cases that have attracted particularly strident public opinion, the president went all the way to create a commission that has no legal hindrances to carrying out any investigation. . . . The quality of the commission members guarantees, if nothing else, that they are not going to shy away from anything. . . .

In the realm of elections, there had been so many instances of rigging in the past 50 years that elections no longer fulfilled the democratic role of conferring legitimacy on the political system. Here, too, Salinas went for consensus rather than a quick fix. . . .

The PRI began to negotiate even with the most radical opposition. By the end of the congressional term, the PRI had conceded the most fundamental strongholds of electoral control. As a result, voters have to present a registration card with picture; preliminary election results will be announced the same day; the entity responsible for certifying the results will not be skewed in favor of the PRI by the presence and votes of government people; and all parties will share equally in the nomination and selection of electoral supervisors. . . .

These two actions show a clear line of departure from the good old days of easy PRI rule. Most important, however, they demonstrate a clear understanding by the administration that it is impossible to be successful in the new era of economic competition and involvement with the rest of the world if Mexico's political house is not kept in perfect order.

### ANDREW REDING

**Director of the Mexico project of the World Policy Institute, a public policy organization**
FROM *THE NEW YORK TIMES*, NOV. 17, 1990.

*w*hen Salinas took office in 1988, he was widely expected to revolutionize politics. With "Salinastroika" in full gear, it was thought, Mexican *glasnost* could not be far behind. Yet even as democratic transformations sweep the globe, Salinas has done little or nothing to move Mexico toward democracy. If anything, he has tightened the ruling Institutional Revolutionary Party's (PRI) control over political life. The prime bulwark of Mexican authoritarianism remains the PRI's control of the electoral machinery. It dominates all electoral commissions, and the interior minister presides over the Federal Electoral Council, a condition found among other Latin nations only in Cuba.

As documented by official precinct tally sheets in the hands of the opposition, the government used the power [in November 1990] to steal elections from both the center-right National Action Party (PAN) and the center-left Revolutionary Democratic Party (PRD). . . .

Protests against electoral fraud are repressed. Police and para-military groups killed more than 60 PRD sympathizers [last] year. In April [1990], Salinas sent tanks into Michoacan to retake town halls occupied by protesters.

Salinas' electoral reform bill, rubber-stamped by the PRI-dominated Congress, increases the share of PRI-controlled seats on the Federal Electoral Council . . . and effectively insures the PRI an absolute majority of seats in Congress regardless of its percentage of the vote. To preclude opposition alliances like those that have triumphed in Chile and Nicaragua, the law bars joint candidacies. It forbids opposition parties to publicize vote totals that differ from the electoral council's, and criminalizes peaceful protests against the official determinations of the electoral authorities.

The Salinas administration's hostility to democratic process extends to control of the news media. The government denies the major opposition parties access to state television channels, even though it is legally mandated. . . . The state controls most of the print media through subsidies, bribes and paid (though unidentified) insertions of government-supplied "news." . . .

In view of Mexico's slide toward political unrest, the Bush administration and Congress should insist on international observation of future elections in order to encourage them to come into conformity with international standards.

Continued from p. 504
Mexico's many subsidies, import permits, regulations and licenses will, over time, substantially reduce opportunities for the collection of bribes by bureaucrats and party stalwarts. At the same time, the fact that Mexicans are being given a louder voice in economic decision-making may engender greater citizen participation in public affairs over the years. ■

# OUTLOOK

## Ongoing Problems

Even if a free-trade agreement is reached, it will not be a panacea. Mexico faces a gamut of structural problems that will test Salinas' political resolve and his reputation as an innovator and reformer. Despite Salinas' immense popularity inside Mexico, political and social pressures have continued to mount. One of the most unpopular aspects of Salinas' reforms is his inflation-fighting wage controls, imposed with the acquiescence of the PRI-controlled labor federations. Coupled with price increases, wage limits have obliterated workers' purchasing power and weakened the authority of the PRI's labor bosses.

At the same time, there are fewer jobs. The U.N. Economic Commission on Latin America estimates that prolonged recession has left nearly 20 percent of the work force unemployed, and a staggering 40 percent underemployed, most of them in the informal economy of street vendors, which may account for one-third to one-half of Mexico's gross domestic product (GDP). The chasm between the haves and the have-nots remains one of the widest in the world. Mexico has the world's 13th largest economy, yet over half of its population now lives in poverty, without adequate housing or access to health care and other social services.

Salinas is caught in a Catch-22. He cannot increase wages for fear of setting off another wave of runaway inflation, which crippled the economy in the mid-1980s. For the same reason, he cannot increase state spending to create new jobs. His only recourse is continued austerity until the anticipated surge of foreign and domestic investment. This explains why Salinas is so aggressively pursuing a free-trade agreement now.

Another daunting challenge for Salinas lies in Mexico's agricultural system. More than half the country's arable land is held as *ejidos*, a pre-Columbian form of land tenure in which a peasant community collectively owns a piece of land and the natural resources and houses on it. As Mexico's population has grown, the parcels worked by individual peasants have shrunk in many cases to an acre or less, thus making economies of scale impossible. Combined with a tradition of low prices for agricultural producers and large subsidies for consumers, the result is that Mexico had to import more than 10 million tons of grain last year.

The flow of immigrants to "El Norte," which abated briefly after the 1986 Immigration Act was passed, has picked up again. (*See story, p. 499.*) While a porous border with the United States is welcomed by Mexicans, since it serves as a social and economic pressure release, there is also a flip side. Mexico loses many of its most talented and motivated citizens.

Forty percent of Mexicans are under the age of 15, with 1 million entering the job market every year. At best, experts say, employment will grow at half a percentage point yearly, but the working-age population will continue to increase by more than 3 percent a year.

### U.S.-Mexican Relations

Even if all illegal immigration to the United States were stopped tomorrow, demography would continue to make contacts between Mexico and the United States deeper than that between almost any other pair of countries. David Hays-Bautista, a demographer at the University of California at Los Angeles, calculates that by 2030, 40 percent of the population of California will be of Spanish-speaking origin, compared with about 20 percent in 1980. This group will be mainly — perhaps more than 80 percent — of Mexican origin. Clearly the days of ignoring Mexico's influence on the United States are in the past.

Virtually everyone agrees that U.S.-Mexican relations are the best they've been in years, perhaps decades. Part of the reason is that the focus has shifted from irritants, such as foreign policy, drugs and immigration, to trade, which holds vast opportunities for both countries. "FTA negotiations have taken over the bilateral agenda," explains David Ronfeldt, a researcher at the RAND Corp. "Even though immigration and drug numbers are up, the relationship has improved." Mexico is the centerpiece of President Bush's Enterprise for the Americas Initiative to encourage free trade, provide debt relief and stimulate investment throughout the Western Hemisphere.[24]

Despite the improved atmosphere, there is always the danger of rupture. According to Weintraub and others, the United States still looks down at Mexico, and threatens to punish the country if it does not cooperate in whatever field happens to be the current fancy, whether it is the momentary politics of drugs, the treatment of particular foreign investors or the refusal to adopt a pro-U.S. foreign policy.[25]

Moreover, at a time when Mexico is looking outward, many politicians in the United States are threatening trade protectionism. "Ironically, the biggest potential stumbling block to Mexico's modernization may be the U.S. Congress," says Purcell at the Americas Society. "Too many of our leaders do not recognize the importance of FTA for the U.S. People only respond to economic arguments without talking about political arguments, such as the stability of Mexico."

Few analysts, however, seriously believe Mexico's stability is in jeopardy. Despite U.S. preoccupation with the issue, Mexico has proved to be as stable as the pyramids of Teotihuacán. Of course, that could all change if the economy again slips into stagnation, and the government backslides on political reform.

### Can Democracy Wait?

In many ways, Salinas is a lot like Soviet President Mikhail S. Gorbachev: constantly testing the system even while he embraces it. But unlike Gorbachev, Salinas opened the economy first, and he has been hesitant in opening the political system. Many analysts agree that this strategy might work better than Gorbachev's, whose economic reforms are now stuck because he cannot muster the necessary political support from his demoralized party and divided country. Salinas is no doubt mindful of the experience of Chile and South Korea, where economic reforms implemented under strict political control have survived transitions to democracy.

Until Salinas' economic program is secure, and yields tangible results for the average Mexican, free elections are unlikely. For now at least, the economic changes are pushing the political changes. "Mexico has a long way to go in terms of modernizing itself socially and politically,"

says Lustig at Brookings. In the long run, however, most analysts feel the pressures for political reform — and electoral democracy — will prevail.

In Mexico, the basis of political legitimacy is shifting from an omnipotent patronage state, where loyalty is rewarded above merit, to an electoral democracy, where programs and ideas make the difference. There is a certain historical irony at work. Mexico was the first nation to undergo a modern 20th-century social revolution with the attendant development of a single party, welfare state. Now, in the late 20th century, Mexico has rediscovered 19th-century liberal ideas such as limited government, a strong civil society and electoral democracy.

Whether through cable TV, Mexicana flights from New York to Cancún or midnight border crossings at San Ysidro and El Paso, constant contact with the United States is erasing cultural, geographical and political borders. And if a free-trade agreement is reached, it will only accelerate the process. For, along with investment dollars will come democratic norms. Once opened, most experts believe the Pandora's box of democracy may be impossible to close. "If you go into a supermarket and have a choice of 40 different cereals, it is only natural to expect to have a choice between more than one [political] party," says Bailey. ■

## Notes

[1] Quoted by Robert Pastor in "Salinas Takes a Gamble," *The New Republic*, Sept. 10 & 17, 1990.
[2] Sidney Weintraub, *A Marriage of Convenience: Relations between Mexico and the United States* (1990), p. 209.

[3] One survey revealed that nearly 60 percent of Mexicans would actually support forming a single country with the U.S. and Canada if it meant better living standards. See Douglas W. Payne, "Mexico: The Politics of Free Trade," *Freedom Review*, July-August 1991, p. 29.
[4] Comments made in an address before the American Society of Newspaper Editors at Harvard University, April 10, 1991.
[5] Quoted in *The Christian Science Monitor*, June 11, 1991.
[6] *Business Week*, June 24, 1991.
[7] Quoted in the Mexican newspaper *Excelsior*, July 7, 1990.
[8] Interview in *New Perspectives Quarterly*, winter 1991, p. 29.
[9] Quoted in *Time*, Nov. 19, 1990.
[10] Cited in Weintraub, *op. cit.*, p. 56.
[11] *Ibid.*, p. 58.
[12] Adolfo Aguilar Zinser, "Mexico: The Presidential Problem," *Foreign Policy*, winter 1987/88, p. 57.
[13] Cited in Robert A. Pastor and Jorge G. Castañeda, *Limits to Friendship: The United States and Mexico* (1990), p. 162.
[14] Khosrow Fatemi, *et al.*, *The Maquiladora Industry: Economic Solution or Problem?* (1990), p. 3.
[15] For details, see "Europe 1992," *The CQ Researcher*, June 28, 1991, pp. 417-440.
[16] See "Mexico: A New Economic Profile," *Mexican Ministry of Finance*, April 1991.
[17] Cited in " Viva Free Trade with Mexico!" *Fortune*, June 17, 1991.
[18] Quoted in *The Wall Street Journal*, April 22, 1991.
[19] Quoted in *The Washington Post*, April 12, 1991.
[20] For background, see "North America Trade Pact: A Good Idea?" *Editorial Research Reports*, Dec. 8, 1989, pp. 681-696.
[21] For background on intellectual property rights, see "Artists' Rights and Copyrights," *Editorial Research Reports*, May 13, 1988, pp. 245-256.
[22] See *The New York Times*, April 4, 1991.
[23] Quoted in Miguel Angel Centeno, "Mexico in the 1990s: Government and Opposition Speak Out," an issue brief prepared by the Center for U.S.-Mexican Studies at the University of California at San Diego, 1991, p. 21.
[24] Under the Enterprise for the Americas Initiative, the United States recently signed a debt-reduction agreement with Chile and framework trade agreements with Nicaragua and Panama. See *The Washington Post*, June 28, 1991.
[25] Weintraub, *op. cit.*, p. 209.

# Bibliography

## Selected Sources Used

### Books

**Pastor, Robert A., and Castañeda, Jorge G.,** *Limits to Friendship: The United States and Mexico,* **Vintage Books, 1990.**

The two political analysts offer their views on the most salient issues that affect the U.S.-Mexico relationship: foreign policy, economic integration, drugs, the border, etc. Each section contains two parts, one from the U.S. perspective, written by Pastor, and the other from the Mexican perspective, written by Castañeda. The book is informative despite its awkward structure and uneven content.

**Riding, Alan,** *Distant Neighbors: A Portrait of the Mexicans,* **Alfred A. Knopf Inc., 1984.**

This well-written, incisive book is a must read for anyone interested in Mexico. Though it predates the Salinas presidency, it contains invaluable history and insights into Mexican society and culture. Many of Riding's interpretations are useful in understanding Mexico's bumpy road toward modernization.

**Weintraub, Sidney,** *A Marriage of Convenience: Relations between Mexico and the United States,* **Oxford University Press, 1990.**

This is a very thorough, cogent, albeit somewhat dry, account of U.S.-Mexican relations. Weintraub makes some balanced recommendations on how to improve the relationship.

**Weintraub, Sidney, with Rubio F., Luis and Jones, Alan D., eds.,** *U.S.-Mexican Industrial Integration: The Road to Free Trade,* **Westview Press, 1991.**

For those interested in a detailed analysis of how U.S.-Mexico free trade will affect various economic sectors, this volume is a useful source. The chapters on the environment by Roberto A. Sánchez and C. Richard Bath are particularly instructive.

### Articles

**Baker, Stephen, "Mexico: A New Economic Era,"** *Business Week,* **Nov. 12, 1990.**

This cover story on Mexico is a good starting point for understanding the business impact of Mexico's economic opening.

**Cárdenas, Cuauhtémoc, "Misunderstanding Mexico,"** *Foreign Policy,* **spring 1990**

Cárdenas, the leader of the leftist opposition in Mexico,

presents the greatest electoral threat to the ruling Institutional Revolutionary Party (PRI) in 1994. This article is extremely critical of Salinas' embrace of the United States and serves as a useful guide to the Mexican left's political platform.

**Grayson, George W., "Mexico Moves Toward Modernization,"** *Current History,* **March 1991.**

The author is a leading Mexico scholar and offers a comprehensive and unbiased account of the steps Mexico has taken toward economic and political modernization.

**Payne, Douglas W., "Mexico: The Politics of Free Trade,"** *Freedom Review,* **July-August 1991.**

In this article, Payne applauds Salinas' economic reforms but takes a harsh view of Mexico's "dictatorial" political system and human rights situation. Payne concludes that the viability of U.S.-Mexican economic relations will hinge on Salinas' commitment to opening the political system.

### Reports and Studies

**Angel Centeno, Miguel,** *Mexico in the 1990s: Government and Opposition Speak Out,* **Center for U.S.-Mexican Studies, University of California at San Diego, 1991.**

In 1990, the Center for U.S.-Mexican Studies conducted a series of seminars on the status of political change inside Mexico. This report offers a synopsis of the positions of the three major political parties, as defined by some of their more prominent leaders.

**Lustig, Nora,** *Bordering on Partnership: The U.S.-Mexico Free Trade Agreement,* **Brookings Discussion Paper, Feb. 25, 1991.**

Lustig, an economics professor and visiting scholar at the Brookings Instution, takes a broad look at the free-trade agreement focusing on the costs and benefits in both the United States and Mexico.

***North American Free Trade Agreement: Generating Jobs for Americans,* U.S. Department of Commerce, May 1991.**

The U.S. Commerce Department makes its case for how free trade will benefit the U.S. economy. This study includes useful data on *maquiladoras* and U.S.-Mexican trade.

# The Next Step

## Additional Articles from Current Periodicals

### Borders (Geography)

**"Whose dirt?"** *Economist*, **Aug. 18, 1990, p. 20.**
Describes the threats to the water supply that runs along the 1,000-mile border between Texas and Mexico. Spread of infectious diseases; "Maquiladoras," the Mexican assembly plants; Population growth; A rural development bill now in Congress that could help the problem.

**Barich, B., "La frontera,"** *New Yorker*, **Dec. 17, 1990, p. 72.**
Describes the most heavily traveled border in the world, the border between Mexico and the United States, and the towns along it, where the people pass through. Town of San Ysidro and the border patrol; What illegal aliens do to elude the border patrol; Smugglers or "coyotes"; La Libertad; Fears of the Central Americans; Both sides of Otay Mesa; Aliens from Oaxaca; What the aliens do for work; Migrant camps; Workers with and without documents.

**Scott, W. C., Bernstein, S. L., et al., "A permanent U.S.-Mexico border environmental health commission,"** *Journal of the American Medical Association*, **June 27, 1990, p. 3319.**
Presents the American Medical Association's Council on Scientific Affairs report on the need for a permanent U.S.-Mexico border environmental health commission. Environmental health concerns; Historical perspective on prior control measures; Political support; Alternatives; Other.

### Education

**Tangeman, M., "Educators see chance for better academic relations between Mexico and U.S. as economic ties improve,"** *The Chronicle of Higher Education*, **Feb. 6, 1991, p. A35.**
Reports that in the face of the widely anticipated signing of a U.S.-Mexico free-trade agreement, educators in Mexico see an opportunity to improve academic relations between the two countries as they work toward major expansion of their economic and cultural ties. Mexico in a clear commercial disadvantage with Canada and the U.S.; Cultural imperialism; U.S. grants; Soviet aid.

### Debts, Public

**Karmin, M. W., "Half a loaf for Third World debtors,"** *U.S. News & World Report*, **Aug. 7, 1989, p. 48.**
Discusses debt deal with Mexico which Treasury Secre-

tary Nicholas F. Brady hailed as "a model" for aiding other debtor nations. Why the plan may not be so good; Other Latin American countries.

### Economic aspects

**"The new model debtor,"** *Economist*, **Oct. 6, 1990, p. 85.**
Explores the remarkable economic reform of Mexico in the past five years. President Carlos Salinas de Gortari's modernization of the economy through deregulation, privatization, and tax reform. Outlines the new economic strategy, which focuses on reforms in public spending, devaluation of the peso, prices and wages, imports, and foreign debt; The free-trade agreement and its impact; The National Solidarity Programme; Details; Outlook.

**Smolowe, J., Dabrowski, A., et al., "In a hurry or running scared?"** *Time*, **Nov. 19, 1990, p. 58.**
Comments on the modernization of Mexico's economy that President Carlos Salinas de Gortari has achieved so far, but states that he is not nearly as far along in reforming the country's antiquated political system. Polarization between the haves and the have-nots; Asking for sacrifices the people do not understand; Arbitrary detentions, disappearances and political assassinations.

### Foreign relations

**"Congress must call the tune on Mexican talks,"** *Business Week*, **April 15, 1991, p. 102.**
Editorial. Talks about how the economic and social disparities between the United States and Mexico are creating the potential for lost jobs and departing industry, as well as side-effects such as worsening environmental problems. To ease such worries, the administration is expected to promise that it will expand programs such as retraining for laid-off American workers and insist that Mexico improve its performance in areas from workers' rights to environmental protection.

### Free-trade agreement

**Allard, C., "Mexico for sale: Gringos welcome,"** *Canadian Business*, **November 1990, p. 72.**
Reports on Canadian Trade Minister John Crosbie's announcement that Canada would join the Mexican-U.S. free-trade talks. Mexico has embarked on the capitalist road to rapid prosperity; Issue of how Canadian companies can exploit opportunities in a Mexico that now has money to spend; Continental prosperity.

**Barone, M. and Baer, D., "Free trade con salsa," *U.S. News & World Report*, Nov. 26, 1990, p. 36.**

Comments on the upcoming visit of George Bush to Monterey (Mexico) and the push for free trade with Mexico which is coming from Bush, Secretary of State Baker and Secretary of Commerce Mosbacher. Support strong in states along the border, and opposition from the United Auto Workers is fierce.

**Cloud, D. S., "Congress wary of Bush plan to open doors to Mexico," *Congressional Quarterly Weekly Report*, Feb. 23, 1991, p. 451.**

Addresses President Bush's push for a free-trade agreement with Mexico to speed the flow of goods and services from the "Yukon to Yucatan." Thinking locally not globally; Deep misgivings about the possible loss of U.S. jobs; Arguments of proponents; Coalition groups to stifle talks; Stalemate of General Agreement on Tariffs and Trade fueling the drive; The procedural angle; Regional interests; Border problems; More.

**Daly, J., "A triple threat? " *Maclean's*, Oct. 8, 1990, p. 48.**

Examines the reasons why Canada is entering into three-way free-trade talks with the United States and Mexico. Advocates and opponents of free trade; Canadian and U.S. corporations taking advantage of Mexico's "maquiladora" program; Canadians' disapproval of the Canada-U.S. free-trade agreement and fear of job loss.

**Dornbusch, R., "It's time to open up trade with Mexico," *Challenge*, November/December 1990, p. 52.**

Argues that the liberalization of trade between the U.S. and Mexico would be mutually beneficial. Advantages of Mexico as a market; Effect on U.S. labor; Europe's free-trade agreement; Direct foreign investment; More.

**Johns, R. and Graham, R., "Drawing closer to Mexico," *World Press Review*, August 1990, p. 58.**

Discusses the potential bilateral agreement on free trade between the United States and Mexico. Mutual benefits; Criticisms; Good relationship between Presidents Bush and Carlos Salinas de Gortari; Maquiladora border industry. INSET: Mexican and Canadian views.

**Kinsley, M., "Holy guacamole!" *New Republic*, April 1, 1991, p. 6.**

Praises the Bush administration's proposal for a free-trade zone with Mexico. Advantages of the agreement for both countries; Refutes several arguments against free trade with Mexico, as put forth by the AFL-CIO and other protectionist groups.

**Levinson, M. and Thomas, R., "Guess who's mad about trade," *Newsweek*, April 22, 1991, p. 50.**

Examines how President Bush's Mexico plan has angered people and created an opposition group. As Congress wrestles with the president's plan to eliminate trade barriers between the U.S. and Mexico, labor, environmental and religious groups have joined to put the outcome in doubt. The unlikely coalition has formed to keep Bush from ramming through the Mexico deal. Environmental concerns; Labor fears; Church groups' worries.

**Rutledge, J., "Driving away more jobs," *U.S. News & World Report*, April 8, 1991, p. 56.**

Focuses on the free-trade agreement between the United States and Mexico. The agreement would make it initially more attractive to move labor-intensive businesses from California to Mexico. The sources of lasting prosperity; The rising costs of conducting business in California.

**Wickens, B., Conger, L., et al., "A giant marketplace," *Maclean's*, June 25, 1990, p. 20.**

Reports on the recent agreement between the United States and Mexico to begin negotiations for a free-trade pact between the two nations. Discusses Canadian reaction to the trade initiative and debate over Canada's possible participation in a North American common market.

**Wood, N. and Fulton, E. K., "Reopening the trade wounds," *Maclean's*, March 18, 1991, p. 42.**

Examines the pros and cons of a possible free-trade agreement between Canada, the United States and Mexico. Trade talks; International Trade Minister John Crosbie; Critics and proponents on the proposed trade pact; Auto-parts industry; Fear of lost jobs, etc.; Possible advantages for Canada.

## Immigration & emigration

**Vernez, G. and Ronfeldt, D., "The current situation in Mexican immigration," *Science*, March 8, 1991, p. 1189.**

Reviews various aspects of Mexican immigration and their meaning for policy considerations. How and why Mexican immigration has grown; Characterizing Mexican immigrants; Three areas of particular national concern; Conclusions and implications.

## Industry

**Banning, K. and Wintermantel, D., "Motorola turns vision to profits," *Personnel Journal*, February 1991, p. 50.**

Examines how Motorola's Guadalajara, Mexico, discrete semiconductor plant adopted a U.S. program which strengthened its competitive position. Role of Dick Wintermantel, director of sector organizational and human resources effectiveness at Motorola's semiconductor product sector's headquarters in Phoenix, Ariz.; Details.

**Dalglish, B., "Open borders," *Maclean's*, Dec. 3, 1990, p. 48.**

Discusses Mexico's modern industrial revolution and the possibility of U.S.-Mexico-Canada free-trade agreement. Mexican President Carlos Salinas de Gortari's economic policies; Young, educated Mexican professionals; Mexico's "maquiladora" program; Canadian and American union leaders' fears about lost jobs; INSETS: Gaining a new lease on life (profile of Mexican worker Gustavo Gonzalez), by B. D.; Shadows over the future (profile of Canadian worker Ronald Trudell), by J. Daly.

**Middlebrook, K. J., "The politics of industrial restructuring," *Comparative Politics*, April 1991, p. 275.**

Analyzes industrial restructuring in the Mexican automobile industry beginning with an overview of key developments in the industry from the 1960s through the early '80s. Political and economic consequences of industry reorganization; Export promotion and industry reorganization in the 1980s; Post-Fordist labor relations and the search for flexible production; Mexican case in comparative perspective.

**Sklair, L., "Transnationals across the border: Mobilizing U.S. support for the Mexican Maquila industry," *Journal of American Studies*, August 1990, p. 167.**

Examines one fraction of transnational capital, that involved the Mexican maquila industry, mainly concentrated along the U.S.-Mexican border, and analyzes how it has striven to safeguard and advance its economic interests. By focusing on this regional manifestation of the global capitalist system, some light may be thrown on the increasingly difficult task that confronts U.S. corporations in their attempt to retain their hegemony in the system.

**Tolan, S. and Kammer, J., "Life in the low-wage boomtowns of Mexico," *Utne Reader*, November/December 1990, p. 42.**

Illustrates the conditions of workers employed by companies such as ITT, IBM and Kodak, lured south by the fall of the Mexican peso. Rep. Jim Kolbe, R-Ariz., supports the maquiladora program of assembly in Mexico at low cost for manufacturers; Wages have plummeted in the last eight years.

## Moral & religious aspects

**Grayson, G. W., "Meet me in church," *Commonweal*, Aug. 10, 1990, p. 439.**

Studies the relationship between church and state in

Mexico's national politics. Historical conflict between the two; How that is changing under the leadership of Carlos Salinas de Gortari of the Institutional Revolutionary Party (PRI); Response of Cuauhtemoc Cardenas, leader of a nationalist-leftist coalition Democratic Revolutionary Party (PRD); How Cardenas should change his stand.

**Schwartz, S. A., "Paz in our time," *American Spectator*, December 1990, p. 32.**

Profiles Octavio Paz, 1990 Nobel laureate in literature, Mexican poet and critic. Radical leftist youth; Fervent anti-communist and loving defender of the U.S. and its world role after 1945; Vision of pluralistic order and its religious underpinnings in post-Columbian Mexico; Commitment to the reintroduction of Catholic culture in the open marketplace of ideas.

## Social life & customs

**Foley, M. W., "Organizing, ideology, and moral suasion: Political discourse and action in a Mexican town," *Comparative Studies in Society & History*, July 1990, p. 455.**

Analyzes an organizing effort in a Mexican community to show how the terms with which villagers and organizers represent their situation might succeed in transforming generalized discontent into a concrete program of action — and how efforts to do so might fail. Assesses recent work on peasant resistance and protest and argues the need for a fresh approach; The exigencies of organizing in the town and focuses attention on moral appeals in the efforts to generate solidarity; More.

**Goethals, H., "Mexico's stroke of genius," *Americas*, July/August 1990, p. 3.**

Reports that Mexico has taken a giant step toward upgrading its cultural and scientific profile in the United States by converting the "House of Mexico" into a center for the dissemination and promotion of the country's rich heritage in art, the sciences and technology. History of the house; House was formally inaugurated as the Mexican Cultural Institute on June 11, 1990; Variety of purposes.

**Plagens, P., Belejack, B., et al., "Mexico on five galleries a day," *Newsweek*, Oct. 29, 1990, p. 70.**

Criticizes the Metropolitan Museum's idea of attempting to squeeze Mexico's art history of nearly 90,000,000 people and three distinct civilizations into part of a floor of their museum called "Mexico: Splendors of Thirty Centuries." Possibility of a free-trade pact between Mexico and the U.S. that set the project in motion; Details how the exhibition tells a fascinating story; Pre-Columbian art and post-conquest art; Frida Kahlo's work; More.

# Back Issues

*Great Research on Current Issues Starts Right Here... Recent topics covered by The CQ Researcher are listed below. Issues dated before May 10, 1991, were published under the name of Editorial Research Reports.*

**JANUARY 1990**
Higher Education Curriculum
Photonics
Age of 'Infotainment'
Abortion: Politicians' Nightmare

**FEBRUARY 1990**
Politics and Economic Growth
Free Agency in Sports
Repetitive Motion
War on Drugs

**MARCH 1990**
Asbestos: Are Risks Acceptable?
Public Health Campaigns
South Africa's Future
Homeless Need More Than Shelter

**APRIL 1990**
How Fair is the Tax Burden?
Workers' Compensation
U.S. Pacific Forces
Curbing Insurance Premiums

**MAY 1990**
Should Teaching Be a Profession?
Will Canada Fall Apart?
Is U.S. Patent System Outdated?
Federal Funding for the Arts

**JUNE 1990**
Downsizing America's Armed Forces
Progress In Weather Forecasting
S & L Bailout
Bio-Chemical Disarmament

**JULY 1990**
Do Americans Still Love Marriage?
Death Penalty Debate
Decline of Rural America
United Nations in the 1990s

**AUGUST 1990**
Democracy in the Philippines
Initiatives: True Democracy?
Hard Times at Newspapers
Teens Balance School & Jobs

**SEPTEMBER 1990**
Dangers of Alcohol
Western Alliance After the Cold War
Tobacco Industry
Right to Die

**OCTOBER 1990**
Organ Transplants
Energy Policy Options
Search for Arab Unity
Child Support

**NOVEMBER 1990**
Lotteries and Gambling
Post Cold-War Choices
Setting Limits on Medical Care
Multicultural Education

**DECEMBER 1990**
Cable TV Regulation
Americans' Search For Their Roots
Is Insurance System a Failure?
Why Schools Still Have Tracking

**JANUARY 1991**
Growing Influence of Boycotts
Should the U.S. Reinstate the Draft?
America's Archaeological Past
Peace Corps' Challenges in '90s

**FEBRUARY 1991**
Regional Impact of Recession
Puerto Rico's Status
Redistricting: Mapping Power
Nuclear Power

**MARCH 1991**
Acid Rain
Cost of the Gulf War
Reassessing Gun Laws
Future for Man in Space

**APRIL 1991**
Social Security
Canadian Crisis Over Quebec
California Drought
Electromagnetic Radiation

**MAY 1991**
School Choice
Racial Quotas
Animal Rights
U.S. and Japan

**JUNE 1991**
Children and Divorce
Teenage Suicide
Endangered Species
Europe 1992

**JULY 1991**
Teenagers and Abortion
Soviet Republics Rebel

Back issues are available for $4.00 (subscribers) or $7.00 (non-subscribers). Quantity discounts apply to orders over ten. To order, call Congressional Quarterly 1-800-432-2250.

# Future Topics

▶ *Athletes and Drugs*

▶ *Sexual Harassment*

▶ *Fetal Tissue Research*

# THE CQ Researcher

PUBLISHED BY CONGRESSIONAL QUARTERLY INC., IN CONJUNCTION WITH EBSCO PUBLISHING

# Athletes and Drugs

*Problem persists despite new testing requirements*

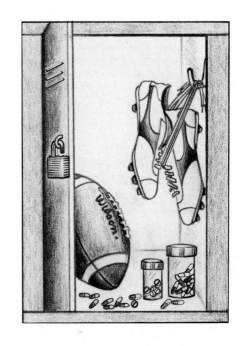

EVERY YEAR, IT SEEMS, DOZENS OF well-known athletes get in trouble because of drugs. Sometimes drug use costs athletes their careers. Sometimes it costs them their lives. For every professional athlete caught using drugs — whether "recreational" drugs such as cocaine or performance-enhancing drugs such as steroids — there are hundreds of college and high school athletes who are risking the same fate. Concerned about the effects of drug use on athletes' health and on the integrity of sports competition, sports officials have instituted testing programs and severe penalties in an effort to bring the problem under control. But some experts feel drug use will remain rampant in sports as long as top athletes are lionized by fans and richly rewarded by team owners and corporate sponsors.

C_Q **July 26, 1991 • Volume 1, No. 12 • 513-536**

*Formerly Editorial Research Reports*

July 26, 1991
Volume 1, No. 12

**EDITOR**
Sandra Stencel

**ASSOCIATE EDITOR**
Richard L. Worsnop

**STAFF WRITERS**
Charles S. Clark
Mary H. Cooper
Rodman D. Griffin

**PRODUCTION EDITOR**
Laurie De Maris

**EDITORIAL ASSISTANT**
Thomas H. Moore

**GRAPHICS**
Jack Auldridge

**PUBLISHED BY**
Congressional Quarterly Inc.

**CHAIRMAN**
Andrew Barnes

**VICE CHAIRMAN**
Andrew P. Corty

**EDITOR AND PUBLISHER**
Neil Skene

**EXECUTIVE EDITOR**
Robert W. Merry

**PUBLICATIONS MARKETING/SALES**
Robert Smith

**EDITOR, EBSCO PUBLISHING**
Melissa Kummerer

The CQ Researcher (ISSN 1056-2036). Formerly Editorial Research Reports. Published weekly (48 times per year, excluding March 1, May 3, Aug. 2 and Nov. 1, 1991) by Congressional Quarterly Inc., 1414 22nd St., N.W., Washington, D.C. 20037. Rates are furnished upon request. Application to mail at second-class postage rates is pending at Washington, D.C. POSTMASTER: Send address changes to The CQ Researcher, 1414 22nd St., N.W., Washington, D.C. 20037.

COVER ART: BARBARA SASSA-DANIELS

# Athletes and Drugs

By Richard L. Worsnop

## The Issues

Five years after University of Maryland basketball star Len Bias died from an overdose of cocaine, drug abuse by athletes still plagues U.S. colleges and professional sports teams. Indeed, studies show that consumption of performance-enhancing drugs is on the rise in high schools as well. The pattern has held despite stepped-up efforts to detect and punish use of banned substances and warnings from medical experts about the health effects of profligate drug use.

According to Dr. Charles E. Yesalis, a professor of health and human development at Pennsylvania State University, "drug use among athletes has gone up dramatically" in recent years. Athletes also are becoming more venturesome about mixing different types of drugs — amphetamines and steroids, say. One reason is that new drugs keep coming on the market, and some turn out to be of help in giving athletes a competitive edge — even if that is not the drugs' primary purpose.

The substance-abuse problem in sports is by no means confined to the United States. Some of the more flagrant examples of sports-related drug abuse over the years have occurred in bicycle racing, whose primary fan base is in Europe, and at the Olympic Games, where athletes from around the world compete. One of the "highlights" of the 1988 Summer Olympics at Seoul was the disqualification of Canadian sprinter Ben Johnson after he won the 100-meter dash in world-record time. Johnson was forced to surrender his gold medal after tests determined he had taken a prohibited anabolic ste-

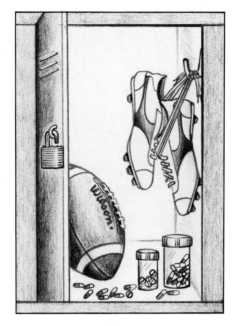

roid prior to the race.

Drug scandals doubtless will surface again at the 1992 Olympics in Barcelona, Spain. International Olympic Committee drug sleuths will set their sights on events where power or endurance are crucial — sprints, distance races, shot put, javelin, discus, hammer, weightlifting, swimming and cycling. And, in all likelihood, most of their efforts will go for naught because world-class athletes are skilled at adjusting their doses to escape detection. In some instances, athletes get help in hiding their drug use from coaches or other professionals. According to Thomas H. Murray, a member of the U.S. Olympic Committee's substance abuse committee, "there is growing evidence that use of banned performance aids is tolerated, and perhaps even encouraged, by some coaches, trainers and physicians." [1]

Nevertheless, sports officials feel they have no choice but to try to combat drug use in sports with every legitimate weapon at their command. They are motivated in part by concern for the athletes' well-being. Most performance-enhancing agents have side-effects that can pose an immediate or long-range threat to health.

But the officials are driven by self-interest, too. If the public comes to perceive track and field, professional football or some other major sport to be hopelessly drug-ridden, attendance and television viewership are likely to plummet. And that could lead to financial ruin for athletes and sports promoters alike.

The monetary stakes are higher today than ever before. Many star baseball, basketball and football players earn more than $1 million annually, and a select few command huge additional sums from product endorsements. Pro team owners, meanwhile, are constantly scrambling for more income from broadcasting and other sources to meet their burgeoning payrolls and still turn a profit. A series of drug scandals might well cause media outlets and corporate sponsors to re-evaluate their financial commitment to sports.

Similar trends are under way at the Olympics. Relaxation of International Olympic Committee rules on amateurism has opened the games to athletes whose chief livelihood is sport. This, in turn, has brought increasing emphasis on winning and breaking records. Since there often is little innate difference among top athletes in any sport, even a fractional improvement in performance may be decisive in championship events. It follows that gaining that slight competitive edge can lead to substantial increases in performance and endorsement fees. Many athletes have concluded that the quickest way to reach these goals is through performance-enhancing drugs.

Recognizing this, sports officials have adopted a number of strategies for combating drug abuse by athletes. Major U.S. professional sports leagues, the National Collegiate Athletic Association and international sports federations have compiled ever-lengthening lists of banned substances and instituted testing procedures. Furthermore, the federal government and more than 40 states have enacted laws to control anabolic steroids, one of the chief performance-enhancing drugs. The aim of all this activity is to forestall the situation envisioned in 1984 by Peter Lawson, who was then secretary of the United Kingdom Central Council for Physical Recreation. "Unless something is done soon," Lawson warned, "international sport will be a competition between circus freaks manipulated by international chemists." [2]

Though the hazardous consequences of drug abuse are beyond dispute, questions persist about the effectiveness and propriety of drug testing. Some experts say the constant flow of new and improved drugs into the marketplace will always leave the drug-taker a step or two ahead of the drug-tester. Others argue that random testing constitutes an unacceptable violation of privacy. (*See At Issue, p. 529.*) But even as debate rages on these issues, more basic questions about drug abuse in sports also continue to provoke comment.

### Why do athletes take drugs?

Like other people, athletes take drugs for a variety of reasons. **Recreational use** covers all those occasions when drugs are taken to "get high" or "have fun." This is what Len Bias was doing when he died from a cocaine overdose on June 19, 1986. Bias and some friends were celebrating his selection by the Boston Celtics as the first player chosen in that year's National Basketball Association draft. Another case of recreational drug use by an athlete ended trag-

ically only eight days later. Don Rogers, a defensive back for the Cleveland Browns, died on the eve of his wedding from what was determined to be "cocaine poisoning."

Drug use for the purpose of **pain relief** also is widespread among athletes, virtually all of whom suffer injuries of some sort during their careers. The ability to "play hurt," much prized by coaches and fans, is often reinforced by painkillers and tranquilizers.

In most cases, athletes take drugs for **performance enhancement**. This can mean a number of different things, depending upon the sport. Weightlifters, bodybuilders and football linemen want to put on more muscle; sprinters want to make a more explosive start out of the blocks; cyclists and long-distance runners and swimmers seek greater endurance; archers and shooters strive for a steadier aim; and so on. In each of these sports, and others as well, drugs are at hand to achieve the desired end.

Some performance-enhancing drugs are effective only if taken shortly before the start of a race or a game. They usually are easy to detect through post-competition testing of urine. Other performance-enhancers serve mainly as training aids. By helping muscles to recuperate more quickly from exhaustion or injury, these substances enable users to train more frequently and for longer periods at high intensity.

Nearly all the drugs used in organized sport have potentially serious side-effects, and some athletes decline to use them for that reason. But other athletes take drugs with little or no hesitation. To a large extent, their attitude has been shaped by society. "Drugs are used to soothe pain, relieve anxiety, help us to sleep, keep us awake, lose or gain weight," noted the British authors of a book on drug abuse in sports. "For many problems, people rely on drugs rather than

seeking alternative coping strategies. It is not surprising that athletes should adopt similar attitudes." [3]

Athletes may also turn to drugs to relieve stress generated by the conflicting demands of sports competition and ordinary life. "There is tremendous psychological pressure on athletes," says John C. Weistart, a Duke University law professor and co-author of *The Law of Sports.* "They are surrounded by people boosting their egos and telling them they're invulnerable to the ordinary pressures that we all face. An athlete has to deal with the disjunction between the outside world, which says he's exceptional, and what he feels inside, which is he's just as human as the rest of us." [4]

Still, the nature of sports competition provides the main impetus for athletes to turn to drugs. As former National Football League Commissioner Pete Rozelle observed, "Professional athletes are an ideal target for drug use. They fall within the susceptible age group, 20 to 35. They receive inordinate salaries. They have free time due to the short length of the professional sports seasons. . . ." [5]

Paul Tagliabue, the current NFL commissioner, makes the further point that athletes face continual peer pressure to take drugs. "If you use steroids, you get a competitive advantage," he said. "And if you use them, you force the other guy to use them. That's why it threatens the integrity of . . . athletic competition." [6]

### What kinds of drugs do athletes take and what are their effects?

For performance enhancement, **anabolic-androgenic steroids** are today's sports drugs of choice. Steroids are a family of synthetic compounds formulated to mimic the male sex hormone testosterone. The term **anabolic** refers to the ability of steroids to build up muscle tissue, thus increasing body size and strength. This is done by utilizing

# How Drugs Affect Sports Performance

*The table below describes various drugs athletes take to improve their sports performance. It also describes the health risks associated with each drug.*

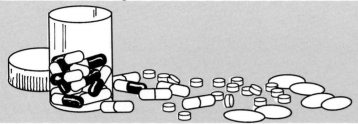

| Drug | Sports in which drug is used | Performance-enhancing effects | Negative effects |
|---|---|---|---|
| Steroids | Bodybuilding, football, track and field "power" events, weightlifting. | Increases muscle mass and strength, helps muscles recover more rapidly from fatigue or injury. | Men: Acne, hair loss, testicular atrophy, " 'roid rage"; women: irreversible masculinization, including deepening of voice. Both sexes: Increased risk of heart and liver disease, sterility. |
| Amphetamines | All sports except those in which steady nerves and concentration are required. | Heightens alertness and postpones onset of fatigue. | Feelings of anxiety and restlessness, accompanied by rapid heartbeat and breathing; risk of addiction. |
| Beta-blockers | Archery, shooting, ski jumping, figure skating. | Slows the heartbeat and steadies body movements. | Can cause asthma symptoms, impair mental alertness, lead to impotence. |
| Human growth hormone | Sports where steroids are widely used; viewed as a steroid substitute. | Promotes muscle growth and strength. Not detectable by present testing methods. | Thickens skin, internal organs, bones and facial features. Extreme cases of overuse can lead to diabetes, heart disease, impotence and shortened life span. |
| Diuretics | Bodybuilding, boxing, weightlifting, wrestling — all sports in which competitors are grouped in weight classes. | Reduces weight quickly by hastening the excretion of urine; masks the presence of certain other prohibited drugs. | Can result in dehydration, leg and stomach cramps, excessive loss of sodium and potassium; kidney damage. |
| Erythropoietin | Long-distance running, cycling and cross-country skiing events. | Bolsters endurance by increasing the blood's supply of oxygen-carrying red cells. Not detectable by current testing methods. | Thickening of the blood to a point where clots may form, triggering a stroke or heart attack. |

*Source: U.S. Olympic Committee.*

the nitrogen that builds proteins more effectively. The **androgenic** effects of steroids are those that relate to the development of male sex characteristics.

There are few appropriate medical applications for steroids. Perhaps the most generally accepted use is for deficient endocrine function of the testes. More controversial uses include stimulation of red blood cell production in aplastic anemia victims; growth acceleration in growth-retarded children; and treatment of breast cancer, osteoporosis and a hereditary form of fluid retention.[7]

By far the most common use of steroids is by athletes and others who want to improve body strength and image. Although precise information is hard to come by, it is believed that athletes generally take the drugs in dosages 10 to 100 times greater than would be prescribed for therapeutic purposes. Furthermore, athletes often take more than one type of steroid at a time — a practice known as "stacking."

Steroids usually are taken in cycles lasting six to eight weeks, interspersed with rest periods ranging from weeks to months. To minimize adverse side-effects, athletes typically start steroid training at a low dosage and gradually build toward a peak intake. The dosage then is lowered in stages, completing a "pyramiding" pattern.

Steroids may be taken orally or by injection. For years, injectables were the preferred form because the drug remained potent longer than orals did. But longevity became a disadvantage once steroid-detection methods were perfected. Many steroid-using athletes have since switched to the shorter-acting but less detectable pills.

Increasing muscle mass and strength requires a good deal more effort than merely taking steroids on a regular basis. To produce the wanted bulk, the drugs must be combined with a high-calorie, high-protein diet and a strenuous training regimen that usually involves weightlifting. Because steroids help muscles recover rapidly from fatigue, users are able to train harder than they could if they were not taking the drugs.

But the sleek, powerful body that steroids help to mold is not achieved without cost. Even when administered in low therapeutic doses, steroids may cause unwanted side-effects. For male users, these include sterility, hair loss, acne, reduction of sex drive, development of female-type breast tissue, atrophy of the testicles and enlargement of the prostate gland. Liver cancer has been reported in persons who have used steroids, as have heart disease, stroke and vascular disorders.

Female steroid users also run serious risks. They may experience such undesirable side-effects as excessive growth of body and facial hair, deepening of the voice to a masculine timbre and enlargement of the clitoris. Research indicates that these changes often are irreversible.

Disturbing as the physical consequences of steroid use can be, many experts say the drugs' psychological side-effects are their worst feature. "The mind is affected tremendously," said Richard L. Sandlin, a one-time heavy steroid user, in testimony before a congressional subcommittee last year. "While taking steroids you can experience increased hostility, increased irritability, increased aggressiveness — you

go attack the weights at the gym; then go home and attack family and friends." [8] The behavior described by Sandlin is so common among heavy steroid users that it has acquired a catchy name: " 'roid rage."

For some athletes and coaches, steroid-inspired combativeness is a desirable trait. This is especially so in football, with its stress on bone-crunching tackling and blocking. The trouble is that the euphoria that accompanies heavy steroid use often turns to deep depression once an individual ceases taking the drug. When this happens, the athlete is powerfully tempted to resume steroid use, if only to ease his emotional distress. In this way, steroids become psychologically addictive.

To a large extent, steroids have supplanted **amphetamines** as the performance-enhancing drug most favored by athletes. First chemically synthesized in 1887, amphetamines belong to a class of drugs that has many of the same properties as adrenalin, a stimulant that occurs naturally in the body. Amphetamines act mainly on the central nervous system and the sympathetic nervous system, which regulates many of the body's unconscious functions.

Known also as "pep pills" or "speed," amphetamines cause increases in breathing and heart rate when taken in relatively low doses. Blood pressure rises, too, and appetite decreases. The drugs also dull pain and heighten feelings of assertiveness.

The golden age for amphetamine use in American sports was the 1960s and '70s. Football players in particular took them for what one authority on sports drug use called "a jolt of get-up-and-kill." [9] Tolerance to amphetamines sets in rapidly, however, so athletes soon find themselves taking steadily higher doses to experience the highs produced by the drug's ability to release

and sustain adrenalin and adrenalin-related chemicals in the body. As the upward spiral of dosage proceeds, users may suffer severe weight loss and personality distortion.

These side-effects persuaded many amphetamine users to swear off the drug. The ex-users were also influenced by the advent of testing methods that made it easy to detect amphetamines after a game or a race. Steroids, which induce mood swings much like those from amphetamines, strike many athletes as being less harmful to their health.

The amphetamine threat still exists, though. Charles Yesalis of Penn State reports that the drug is used even now in the National Football League. In Yesalis' opinion, amphetamines are one of the two most dangerous substances currently taken by athletes, along with erythropoietin (see below).

**Cocaine**, the drug that killed Len Bias and Don Rogers, is more of a recreational than a performance-enhancing agent. An odorless powder extracted from the leaves of the coca plant, which is native to the Andean region of South America, cocaine is classified as a stimulant. Like its chemical cousins, amphetamines, cocaine increases body temperature, heart rate and blood pressure and curbs the appetite.

Cocaine is not addictive in a strictly physical sense. That is, the body does not develop a physical dependence on it nor is there physical withdrawal when a cocaine user stops taking it. But cocaine is psychologically addictive. Heavy users often come to treat it as an emotional crutch, exhibiting what is called "behavior dependence." This has been demonstrated in laboratory tests where monkeys starved themselves to death so as to keep getting cocaine.

According to Thomas Murray, cocaine "never has been a big factor" in sports competition, although its

# Athletes and Alcohol

Sports drug programs focus mainly on controlled substances — drugs whose distribution and use are prohibited or closely regulated by law. But many authorities argue that the chief drug problem in sports, as in society at large, is alcohol. Because alcohol is legal, athletes and others are free to consume as much beer, wine and distilled spirits as they wish. The trouble is that a minority of users cannot control themselves and become "problem drinkers" or alcoholics.

Some athletes say they take a drink or two before competing to relieve tension. Numerous studies have shown, however, that a drink or two is enough to impair reflexes, balance and hand-eye coordination. Moreover, a few drinks can dull the senses of sight, hearing and touch. This can put the athlete at a serious disadvantage in fast-paced sports like hockey, auto racing, basketball and tennis.

Many sports heroes of the modern era were known for their fondness for drink. They included baseball greats Babe Ruth, Grover Cleveland Alexander and Hack Wilson, all members of the Hall of Fame at Cooperstown, N.Y. In more recent times, pitchers Ryne Duren of the New York Yankees and Sam McDowell of the Cleveland Indians grappled with drinking problems.

Like other people, athletes who drink to excess gamble not only with their health but with their very lives. Consider, for example, what happened to hockey star Pelle Lindbergh. A highly regarded goaltender for the Philadelphia Flyers, Lindbergh was fatally injured in November 1985 when his sports car slammed into a concrete wall in southern New Jersey; he died two days later without regaining consciousness.

The Flyers' team physician announced after the accident that Lindbergh's blood alcohol content had been measured at .24 percent, far in excess of the .10 percent legal threshold for determining drunkenness. Medical experts calculated that a person of Lindbergh's weight (166 pounds) would have to consume 15 drinks in four hours to achieve the alcohol level found in Lindbergh's blood.

On Aug. 1, 1988, diver Bruce Kimball, a silver medalist at the 1984 Olympics, lost control of a car, killing two people and injuring six. Kimball's blood-alcohol content was tested at .20, twice Florida's legal limit. He was charged Aug. 16 with driving under the influence, manslaughter and other crimes. Five days later, he failed to qualify for the 1988 U.S. Olympic team.

According to police, drinking also contributed to a fatal traffic accident in Boston last March involving Charles Smith, a guard for the Boston Celtics. Police said a van driven by Smith struck and killed two Boston University students and then sped away. After being apprehended, Smith was charged with motor-vehicle homicide, leaving the scene of an accident and drunken driving.†

For many substance-abusing athletes, alcohol and "hard" drugs go hand and hand. Earlier this year, boxing champion Sugar Ray Leonard admitted to excessive use of alcohol and cocaine. The widely publicized drug problems of pro football stars Dexter Manley, Lawrence Taylor and Charles White also involved the alcohol-cocaine combination.

---

† Smith's Breathalyzer reading was .06 percent, under the .10 legal level for drunken driving in Massachusetts. Below .05, a person is not considered drunk. But under state law, when a Breathalyzer reading falls between .06 and .09, police can presume alcohol has been consumed and may charge a person with drunken driving.

---

stimulative properties could have some value in enhancing short-term performance. The traces of cocaine found in athletes, Murray says, have been mostly "the residue of recreational use." Like amphetamines, cocaine is easy to detect in post-competition testing. Consequently, says Murray, "The athletes we find it in usually are addicted or extremely careless."

For a time, some athletes were drawn to cocaine because of its glamorous aura. That image stemmed largely from cocaine's high cost, which gave it a cachet that street drugs like marijuana could never possess. But cocaine's reputation has taken a pounding in recent years, in part because of what happened to Bias, Rogers and some other prominent athletes who used it. Moreover, introduction of the relatively cheap, smokable form of cocaine called crack dimmed the drug's luster by putting it within reach of the non-affluent.

To produce short-term improvement in athletic performance, a drug need not be a stimulant like cocaine or amphetamines. Consider **beta-blockers**, a class of anti-anxiety drugs prized by athletes whose events require high levels of motor control under conditions of emotional stress. These events include archery, pistol shooting, ski jumping, diving and combination sports like the modern pentathlon (which includes shooting) and the biathlon (shooting and cross-country skiing).

Beta-blockers are prescribed for certain heart conditions because they lower blood pressure, decrease the heartbeat rate and block stimulatory responses. They do this by preventing some of the body's adrenalin from binding to sites on the heart known as beta-receptors. As a result, beta-blockers are useful for steadying the aim of shooters and archers and for calming the nerves of divers and ski-jumpers.

For athletes in most other types of events, beta-blockers would be counterproductive. Experience shows they reduce aerobic power and endurance, though muscle strength apparently is unaffected. Because they interfere with the action of adrenalin, beta-blockers can nudge the hormone system slightly out of sync. Also, the drugs retard production of a liver enzyme needed for eliminating wastes.

A drug of more recent origin, **human growth hormone** (HGH), is a genetically engineered equivalent of the substance produced naturally by the pituitary gland. Since artificial HGH is relatively new, not much is known about its effects on athletes over long periods. It is known, however, that athletes have tried HGH in the belief it will help augment strength and lean muscle mass in much the same way steroids do. In addition, anecdotal reports suggest athletes take the hormone: (1) to prevent the breakdown of muscle tissue after steroids are discontinued; and (2) to strengthen tendons and ligaments so as to guard against ruptures or tears caused by added muscle. A further attraction is that no test has yet been devised for detecting synthetic HGH in the body.

Once again, though, HGH use entails considerable risk to the athlete's health. The primary hazard is acromegaly, a disorder that occurs spontaneously when excess growth hormone is secreted by a pituitary tumor. Acromegaly symptoms also can be induced by taking large doses of synthetic HGH. Adult sufferers experience runaway bone growth in the feet, hands, nose and jaw. Soft facial tissues expand, too, creating a characteristic "Frankenstein" look. Diabetes, heart disease

and impotence often follow; premature death is the prognosis in nearly all acromegaly cases.

Perhaps the most dangerous drug now being used by athletes is **erythropoietin** (EPO), another product of biotechnology. EPO is a synthetic preparation of the identically named natural human hormone, which stimulates the production of red

> Beta-blockers are prescribed for certain heart conditions because they lower blood pressure, decrease the heartbeat rate and block stimulatory responses. As a result, they are useful for steadying the aim of archers and calming the nerves of divers.

blood cells from bone marrow. It thus lends itself readily to the treatment of certain blood disorders, notably the anemia associated with chronic kidney failure.

Athletes in endurance events were quick to recognize EPO as a potentially powerful performance aid. By adding more red cells to the bloodstream, EPO increases the blood's oxygen-carrying capacity. The added capacity, in turn, translates into greater reserves of aerobic power for marathoners, cross-country skiers and long-distance bicycle racers. EPO already has supplanted **blood-doping**, whereby endurance athletes received pre-competition transfusions of their own stored blood. Blood-doping is prohibited by the International Olympic Committee and other major sports bodies. EPO, like HGH, is undetectable by cur-

rent testing techniques.

Specialists in sports medicine are unanimous in condemning the EPO craze. "EPO will be a more dangerous drug than anything we've seen," says Dr. Robert Voy, medical director of the Las Vegas (Nev.) Institute of Physical Therapy and Sports Medicine. "It has the potential to kill athletes." [10]

The alarm voiced by Voy and his peers stems from the fact that higher concentrations of red cells thicken the blood. And the thicker the blood, the greater the chance of developing clots that could lead to a stroke or heart attack. Murray suggests one likely scenario: "In the course of an endurance event, like the marathon or a long road race in bicycling, it's imaginable that somebody [on EPO] would sweat away a lot of fluid," making the blood still more viscous. That is why, Murray says, EPO is "probably the most lethal sports drug right now."

### Where do athletes obtain their drugs?

For obvious reasons, none of the performance-enhancing substances favored by athletes are obtainable over-the-counter at the corner drugstore. Nonetheless, supplies of the more popular drugs usually stay in rough balance with demand. Steroids provide a current case in point. Over the past three years, a number of federal and state laws have been enacted for the purpose of curbing steroid use and distribution. (*See story, p. 528.*) Yet anecdotal reports from around the country indicate steroids are as easy to obtain as before — perhaps even more so. As in the case of cocaine, a major frustration for drug enforcement authorities is that many of the steroids consumed in the United States come from abroad.

Richard Sendlin testified last year

that U.S. athletes obtain steroids from four main sources: doctors, friends, mail-order firms and the black market. Most of the drugs, he said, come from underground laboratories in the United States and foreign countries, chiefly Mexico.* Furthermore, steroids that originate in such labs often contain "unknown or unexpected ingredients." Physicians, in Sendlin's opinion, account for only a small percentage of illicit steroid traffic.

Sendlin's testimony parallels the findings of others who have traced the paths by which steroids reach athletes. For instance, a study of steroid users who competed in the 1987 national championships of the U.S. Powerlifting Federation found that 73 percent identified the black market as their drug source.[11] In the study, "black market" was defined as other athletes and gym owners or managers.

Through investigations conducted since 1985, the Justice Department and the U.S. Food and Drug Administration have observed significant changes in the clandestine distribution of steroids. At the beginning, people without prior criminal records diverted legally produced steroids of domestic origin to black-market channels. Next came smuggling into the United States of steroids manufactured abroad; domestic production of counterfeit steroids in underground labs; and, finally, the involvement of criminals. According to Justice Department officials, the black market in steroids operates in all parts of the country.

Less is known about the ways athletes obtain other major performance-enhancing drugs. Limited amounts of synthetic human growth hormone are available from illicit

---

sources for $500 to $1,500 per unit — a price range that reflects the great gap between supply and demand. Genentech Inc., a biotechnology company that manufactures HGH under the trade name Protropin, believes there are three main reasons why so little of the drug finds its way into the black market: (1) The technical knowledge required to make HGH is not widely diffused, even within the pharmaceutical industry; (2) building a facility to produce the drug illegally would be prohibitively expensive; and (3) the company's strict distribution controls have been highly effective so far.[12]

### How effective is drug testing of athletes?

Because athletes intent on using performance-enhancing drugs usually have little trouble obtaining them, drug testing by necessity becomes the last line of defense against rampant sports doping. But testing is no panacea and likely never will be. Even with the advanced equipment now in use at the Olympics and other major sports competitions, some drugs cannot be detected at all and others elude the testers if taken in low to moderate dosages.

Complicating matters is the availability of drugs that mask the presence of performance-enhancing substances. Many of these masking agents are diuretics, which reduce the concentration of drugs in the urine by inducing a more rapid excretion of urine. Diuretics also are used as emergency slimming aids in sports with several weight classes, such as boxing and weightlifting. Because of this, the International Olympic Committee has placed diuretics on its list of banned drugs.

Many authorities on sports medicine say the drug-taker will always be a step or two ahead of the drug-tester, if only because new drugs

---

and new masking agents keep appearing on the market. Testers thus are reduced to playing a never-ending game of catch-up. "It's not a fair fight," says Yesalis. "It's not even a close fight." In his view, drug testing at the Olympic level "is pretty much a farce." Citing another sport to illustrate his point, Yesalis says some pro football players are sending urine specimens to private labs for analysis. In that way they learn what constitutes an undetectable, but still effective dose for their particular body chemistry.

When athletes are caught with banned substances in their urine, they often say the laboratory made an error or sabotage occurred. Ben Johnson made such a complaint after being confronted with evidence of steroid use at the 1988 Olympics. So, too, did swimmer Angel Myers, who was dropped from the 1988 U.S. Olympic team because of a positive test for nandrolone, a steroid. Myers said the birth-control pills she was taking at the time metabolized in her body in such a way that they resembled nandrolone.

Ethical considerations prevent drug-testing officials from routinely responding to such charges. But their defenders insist that testers do as well as they can with the equipment at their disposal, and that they do not see themselves as being on a witch hunt for drug miscreants. On the contrary, Murray says the guiding principle of the U.S. Olympic Committee's testing program is that "we never want a false positive" test result, even if this means some athletes on performance-enhancing drugs receive a clean bill of health.[13]

Drug-testing technology, which also is used for tracing hazardous industrial pollutants, has grown highly complex. Ben Johnson got his comeuppance from an analytical instrument consisting of a gas chromatograph linked to a mass spec-

---

*Confiscated steroids also have come from Belgium, Brazil, Britain, Canada, France, Germany, Italy and Switzerland. The Justice Department reports that most confiscations of steroids take place in California.

trometer. In tandem, the machines can detect substances in concentrations as low as one part per billion, which *Forbes* magazine likened to "finding a teaspoon of sugar dissolved in a 50-meter Olympic-size swimming pool." [14]

In the first stage of Olympic drug testing, a sample of urine is injected into a heated tube that vaporizes the liquid into its chemical components. Each substance takes a characteristic amount of time to reach the bottom of the tube, affording an opportunity for preliminary analysis. In the second stage, mass spectrometry, the compounds emerging from the tube are bombarded by electrons. The resulting molecular debris is then subjected to final analysis and identification. If a banned drug is found, a second test is conducted in the presence of the athlete, his or her coach and officials of the national team.

One reason why drug testing of

athletes has turned up relatively few offenders is that it usually takes place at a predetermined time — shortly after a race or a game. Thus, athletes can escape detection by suspending drug use for a few days or weeks before the event. To close this gaping loophole, some sports officials advocate random drug testing, also called out-of-competition testing. This approach largely eliminates the athlete's assured margin of safety and presumably forces him or her to reconsider the pluses and minuses of drug use. However, some civil libertarians oppose random testing on the ground that it violates the athlete's Fourth Amendment protection against "unreasonable searches and seizures." *(See At Issue, p. 529.)* Until this dispute is settled, an effective international drug-testing system for sports that includes the United States may be impossible to implement. ∎

muscular development that steroids help to promote.

### Use in College and by Pros

Circumstantial evidence indicates steroids also are widely used in professional and college football. Lyle Alzado, a former defensive end for the Los Angeles Raiders, said in a nationally televised interview June 29 that his inoperable brain cancer had been caused by "a certain steroid" he took during a comeback attempt in 1990. The drug, he charged, weakened his immune system. In an article published in the July 8 issue of *Sports Illustrated,* Alzado went further. "I lied," he said. " . . . I lied to a lot of people for a lot of years when I said I didn't use steroids. I started taking anabolic steroids in 1969, and I never stopped. . . . I couldn't [stop], and then I made things worse by taking human growth hormone, too." [15]

Just in the past six years, drug abuse twice has cast a shadow on the NFL championship game. On Jan. 28, 1986, the day after his team lost Super Bowl XX to the Chicago Bears, coach Raymond Berry of the New England Patriots revealed that five Patriots players had serious drug problems and that five to seven more were suspected of having problems. At a meeting the same day, the entire squad voted to become the first NFL team to adopt a voluntary testing program. The drug jinx struck again three years later, when running back Stanley Wilson of the Cincinnati Bengals was kicked off the team on the eve of Super Bowl XXIII for taking cocaine in his hotel room.[16]

Cocaine has tainted or ruined the careers of numerous other star athletes in pro sports. Bob Hayes, the winner of two Olympic gold medals in 1964 and for 10 seasons a leading wide receiver for the Dallas Cowboys, was arrested and convicted in

# BACKGROUND

## An Old Problem

Athletes have taken natural or synthetic performance aids since the earliest days of organized sports competition. In ancient Greece and Rome, athletes believed that if they consumed certain body organs of animals they would automatically acquire a desired trait — courage, say, in the case of a lion's heart. Greek athletes of the third century B.C. ate mushrooms before competing and gladiators took stimulants to enable them to keep fighting despite fatigue and injury. Similarly, ancient Romans tried to increase the speed and endurance of their horses in chariot races by feeding them a mixture of water and honey.

More complex substances came

into general use in the 19th century, when athletes experimented with alcohol, caffeine, opium, nitroglycerine, cactus-based stimulants, sugar cubes dipped in ether and even brandy laced with strychnine.* German scientists isolated the male hormone testosterone in 1935, but synthetic testosterone compounds apparently were not used in strength sports on a regular basis until the mid- to late 1950s.

From that time to the present, use of performance-enhancing drugs has grown steadily. Throughout the period, weightlifters and bodybuilders — and, lately, professional wrestlers — have been the athletes most closely linked to steroids. That stands to reason, since those sports put a premium on the strength and

---

*Strychnine, a powerful poison, acts as a stimulant in small doses.

*Continued on p. 525*

# Chronology

**1970s** *Drug abuse by athletes reaches alarming levels, prompting sports organizations to take countermeasures to preserve to the integrity of competition.*

## 1971
The National Football League formally bans the use of amphetamines.

## 1976
The Summer Olympic Games in Montreal are the first at which athletes are tested for use of anabolic steroids. The hazards of steroid use had been known for years, but no effective way of detecting them in an athlete's body existed.

———————•———————

**1980s** *The battle against sports drug abuse escalates.*

## Jan. 28, 1986
The day after his team lost Super Bowl XX to the Chicago Bears, coach Raymond Berry of the New England Patriots discloses that five Patriots players have a serious drug problem and five to seven more are suspected of having a problem. At a meeting held the same day, the entire squad votes overwhelmingly to become the first National Football League team to accept voluntary drug testing.

## April 1, 1987
New York Mets pitcher Dwight Gooden is placed on the disabled list after testing positive for cocaine use. He later undergoes treatment and makes a successful return to the team.

## April 1987
Birgit Dressel, one of West Germany's finest Olympic-class athletes, dies unexpectedly at age 26. Investigators discover that she had been swallowing, injecting and inhaling some 100 different drugs as part of her training regimen.

## Sept. 27, 1988
Canadian sprinter Ben Johnson is stripped of the Olympic gold medal he won two days earlier in the 100-meter dash because post-race testing of his urine indicated he had taken Stanozolol, a prohibited anabolic steroid.

## Nov. 18, 1988
President Ronald Reagan signs into law the Anti-Drug Abuse Act of 1988, which makes it a crime to distribute steroids for uses other than those prescribed by a physician.

## Jan. 21, 1989
Stanley Wilson, a running back for the American Football League champion Cincinnati Bengals, is kicked off the team on the eve of Super Bowl XXIII for allegedly taking cocaine in his hotel room.

## 1989
The U.S. Olympic Committee and the National Olympic Committee of the Soviet Union sign an agreement aimed at reducing the use of performance-enhancing drugs by Olympic and other world-class athletes in the two nations.

———————•———————

**1990s** *The federal government and dozens of states declare war on steroids.*

## 1990
The National Football League initiates a policy of subjecting all players to year-round, unscheduled testing for steroid use.

## Nov. 29, 1990
President Bush signs into law the omnibus Crime Control Act of 1990, which adds more than two dozen steroid compounds to Schedule III of the Controlled Substances Act.

## March 30, 1991
Former Olympic gold medalist and professional boxing champion Sugar Ray Leonard acknowledges that he used cocaine and drank heavily from 1983 to 1986, following surgery for a detached retina.

## June 3, 1991
Jamie Astaphan, a physician who prescribed steroids for Ben Johnson and other Canadian athletes, is suspended from practicing medicine for 18 months and fined $5,000.

## June 27, 1991
Dr. George Zahorian III is convicted by a U.S. District Court jury in Harrisburg, Pa., of violating a 1988 federal law that prohibits giving steroids for performance enhancement or other non-medical reasons. Zahorian is the first doctor to be found guilty under the law. He was charged with selling steroids to four professional wrestlers and a weightlifter.

## June 29, 1991
In a television interview, former Los Angeles Raiders defensive end Lyle Alzado says his inoperable brain cancer was caused by "a certain steroid" he took during a comeback attempt in 1990. The drug, he charges, weakened his immune system. In a subsequent magazine article, Alzado discloses he also has taken human growth hormone.

# Hall of Shame

*The list below is just a small sample of the professional and college athletes who've been caught using drugs — "recreational" drugs such as cocaine or performance-enhancing drugs such as steroids — in recent years.*

**Len Bias**
**(with Celtics Head Coach K.C. Jones)**

**Len Bias** — Although he played on generally mediocre University of Maryland teams, Bias was a basketball All-America selection. The Boston Celtics made him the No. 1 pick in the 1986 National Basketball Association draft. While celebrating his good fortune with friends, Bias ingested cocaine, suffered a seizure and died.

**Dexter Manley** — The Washington Redskins defensive end was suspended for 30 days in 1988 after failing a test for cocaine use. Cocaine again was found in his system in 1989, triggering a "lifetime" suspension from the National Football League. But NFL Commissioner Paul Tagliabue reinstated Manley in 1990, and the player signed with the Phoenix Cardinals.

**Ben Johnson** — The duel that track fans were waiting for at the 1988 Seoul Olympics — Canadian Ben Johnson vs. American Carl Lewis in the 100-meter dash — was no anticlimax: Johnson won in world-record time. But subsequent analysis of Johnson's urine showed he had taken performance-enhancing steroids before the race. He was forced to surrender his medal to Lewis, and his record was stricken from the books.

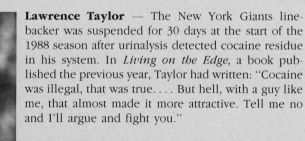

**Ben Johnson**

**Brian Bosworth**

**Brian Bosworth** — Bosworth, known to college football fans nationwide simply as "the Boz," cultivated a brash image by wearing earrings, thumbing his nose at authority and tinting strips of his hair various unnatural hues. Before the 1987 Orange Bowl game, a drug test revealed Bosworth had been using steroids, with the result that he was barred

from playing. University of Oklahoma football coach Barry Switzer later kicked Bosworth off the team.

**Diego Maradona** — Maradona, an Argentinian, was acclaimed in recent years as world soccer's brightest star, much as Pelé from neighboring Brazil was two decades earlier. But the cheering stopped in March, when Maradona tested positive for cocaine and was suspended

**Diego Maradona**

for 15 months by the Italian Soccer Federation and FIFA, the sport's international governing body. Returning to Argentina, Maradona was arrested in April on drug charges resulting from a police raid.

**Lawrence Taylor** — The New York Giants linebacker was suspended for 30 days at the start of the 1988 season after urinalysis detected cocaine residue in his system. In *Living on the Edge*, a book published the previous year, Taylor had written: "Cocaine was illegal, that was true. . . . But hell, with a guy like me, that almost made it more attractive. Tell me no and I'll argue and fight you."

**Charles White** — The Los Angeles Rams running back was arrested by police in Brea, Calif., in 1987 and charged with being under the influence of a controlled substance (cocaine). To stay with the Rams, White agreed to undergo drug counseling and urinalysis daily (later changed to three times a week) for the rest of his career. In 1988, test results indicated he had drunk a large amount of alcohol. White was suspended for 30 days.

**Lyle Alzado** — A fierce pro football defensive end, most memorably for the Los Angeles Raiders, Alzado made an unsuccessful comeback attempt last season. In recent weeks he disclosed that he had taken steroids since 1969 and used both steroids and human growth hormone to aid his comeback. He blames the drugs for causing his inoperable brain cancer.

**Lyle Alzado**

**UPI/Bettman and Reuters/Bettman Newsphotos**

Continued from p. 522
1978 on charges of selling cocaine. New York Mets fans were shocked when the team's top pitcher, Dwight Gooden, was placed on the disabled list in April 1987 after testing positive for cocaine use. The Gooden story had a happy ending, however. After undergoing treatment, he rejoined the Mets and successfully resumed his career.

More recently, Sugar Ray Leonard disclosed that he used cocaine from 1983 to 1986. Speaking at a March 30, 1991, news conference, the former Olympic gold medalist and professional boxing champion said he also drank heavily during the period, which followed surgery for a detached retina. Earlier in March, world soccer superstar Diego Maradona tested positive for cocaine and was suspended for 15 months by the Italian Soccer Federation and FIFA, the sport's international governing body. After returning to his native Argentina, Maradona was arrested in late April on drug-possession charges resulting from a police raid.

Inescapably, perhaps, drug abuse by athletes has filtered down to college sports programs, which act as finishing schools for the pros. For instance, University of Oklahoma linebacker Brian "the Boz" Bosworth was banned from the 1987 Orange Bowl game after flunking a test for steroid use mandated by the National Collegiate Athletic Association. The following season saw the publication of a *Sports Illustrated* article on steroid use that elicited much comment nationwide. It was a harrowing first-person account by Tommy Chaikin, a University of South Carolina linebacker, who recounted how steroids drove him to violence and nearly to suicide.[17]

The drug problem affects college coaches as well as athletes. After Georgetown University basketball coach John Thompson learned in 1989 that two members of his team

were socializing with Rayful Edmond III, a major Washington drug lord, he arranged a meeting with Edmond and persuaded him to break off contact with the players. Kevin Mackey, former basketball coach at Cleveland State University, was not so fortunate. He was fired last July when Cleveland police found traces of cocaine in a sample of his urine taken after a drunken-driving arrest. Mackey later acknowledged that he had abused alcohol and cocaine for the previous three years.

### Adolescent Steroid Use

Although drug abuse by pro and college athletes provides ample cause for concern, sports medicine specialists are even more disturbed by evidence that high school students are turning to performance-enhancing drugs. According to one widely cited study of steroid use among high school senior boys, 6.64 percent of the respondents — about 1 of every 15 — reported current or prior use of steroids.[18] Applying that usage rate to the total U.S. population of secondary-school boys, the study's authors concluded that between 250,000 and 500,000 youngsters were taking or had taken steroids.

The largest group of users in the study (47.1 percent) said their main reason for taking steroids was to improve athletic performance. Another 26.7 percent said their chief objective was to improve personal appearance. Approximately 44 percent of the users said they had taken more than one steroid at a time. Moreover, 38.1 percent had used both the oral and injectable forms. As for sources, 60.5 percent of the users named the black market, defined as "other athletes, coaches, gyms, etc." About 20 percent said they obtained their steroids from a health-care professional, defined as a physician, pharmacist or veterinarian.

Adolescent steroid users are sub-

ject to the same side-effects that adult users face, as well as a few peculiar to their age group. Almost all college and professional athletes have reached their full adult height, so they do not have to worry about steroids' tendency to stunt growth by hastening bone maturation. But the drugs may keep some adolescent users from ever attaining the stature heredity intended. Medical experts speculate also that steroids may interfere with the youngsters' still developing reproductive systems. And because the liver of an adolescent is somewhat smaller than an adult's, the teenage steroid user may be at correspondingly greater risk of liver dysfunction.

## Attitudes Toward Drugs

Despite all the medical hazards, which by now are widely known in sports circles, athletes persist in taking steroids and experimenting with other drugs that may be even more harmful. One reason is that aspiring athletes hope to share in the acclaim and riches showered on established sports stars. In this connection, some say Ben Johnson's disgrace at the 1988 Olympics may have done more to encourage than to discourage steroid use. Johnson evidently managed to pass previous drug tests while on steroids and stood to make an estimated $18 million in endorsement fees if he had been able to pass the fateful test at Seoul. Thus, other sprinters could have concluded that the rewards of becoming "the world's fastest human" outweigh the risks of trying to do it with the aid of banned drugs.

Another reason why many athletes are nonchalant about drugs is that they are young and in top physical condition. This can lead to feelings of invulnerability. In his congressional testimony, Richard Sandlin said athletes who take steroids are convinced that "anything that could make you look so good and feel so strong could never be bad for you." When side-effects do appear, steroid users tend to discount them. Samuel Wilson Fussell, a former body-builder and steroid user, recalled the reaction of "Vinnie," a fellow bodybuilder who developed acne from steroids: "You know, Sam, I think muscles are worth a few zits, don't you?" [19]

The main reason why drug-taking athletes disregard the warnings of sports scientists is that many of the experts talk down to athletes and, worse still, have sometimes been glaringly wrong. "Most scientists are not held in high esteem by athletes," says Yesalis, because the scientists have "clearly misspoken on several matters where it turned out the athletes knew what they were talking about." That being the case, "sports scientists' credibility with athletes is not great."

A prime example of what Yesalis was referring to is the medical profession's flip-flop on steroids. In 1977, the American College of Sports Medicine issued a position statement on "The Use and Abuse of Anabolic-Androgenic Steroids in Sports." It said in part:

"(1) The administration of anabolic-androgenic steroids to healthy humans below age 50 in medically approved therapeutic doses often does not of itself bring about any significant improvements in strength, aerobic endurance, lean body mass or body weight.

"(2) There is no conclusive scientific evidence that extremely large doses of anabolic-androgenic steroids either aid or hinder athletic performance." [20]

As far as steroid-using athletes were concerned, those two sentences were preposterous. Their experience left no doubt in their minds that steroids, when combined

with a strict dietary and exercise regimen, did indeed build muscle mass, strength and overall performance. The circumstantial evidence supporting their view was so overwhelming that the College of Sports Medicine issued a revised position paper on steroids in 1984. The first two paragraphs read:

"(1) Anabolic-androgenic steroids in the presence of an adequate diet can contribute to increases in body weight, often in the lean mass department.

"(2) The gains in muscular strength achieved through high-intensity exercise and proper diet can be increased by the use of anabolic-androgenic steroids in some individuals." [21]

The revised position statement conforms much more closely to what athletes have long known to be true. Nonetheless, the credibility gap remains in place; athletes still tend to take medical experts' warnings of steroid-caused health calamities with a grain of salt. As British Broadcasting Corporation sports commentator Ron Pickering put it, "It's no use trying to scare them by saying their balls will drop off." [22] ∎

# CURRENT SITUATION

## Drug Policies

D rug use by athletes has prodded sports governing bodies in the United States and abroad to take corrective action. Although provisions vary somewhat from sport to sport, most programs involve publishing a list of prohibited drugs, establishing testing procedures for substances that can be detected and laying down penalties for athletes found in violation of the code. The main drug-control rules of selected U.S. sports organizations follow:

**National Basketball Association (NBA).** Instituted in September 1983 by agreement of the NBA and the NBA Players Association, pro basketball's drug policy is widely viewed as the most progressive in all sports. Any NBA player who is convicted of, or pleads guilty to, crimes involving the use or distribution of cocaine or heroin is immediately and permanently banished from the league. On the other hand, any

player who comes forward voluntarily to seek treatment for a drug problem will receive counseling and medical help at the league facility set up for that purpose. Under the terms of the management-union agreement, the player's club pays for the treatment, the player continues to collect his salary, and no penalty of any kind is imposed so long as the player complies with the terms of his treatment.

The league, however, reserves the right to administer drug tests to players if it feels there is reasonable cause to do so, and any individual failing a test is banned from the NBA for two years. He may apply for reinstatement at the end of that period, subject to the approval of both the NBA commissioner and the players' union. Factors to be taken into account in deciding such cases include the circumstances of the player's dismissal, his conduct and abstinence from drug use during the suspension period, and whether he satisfactorily completed drug treatment in accordance with NBA procedures. In 1988, the league expanded its policy to include random drug testing of rookies.

**Major League Baseball.** Baseball's drug-testing program is grounded on this premise, set forth in a 1988 news release from the Office of the Commissioner: "There is no place for illegal drugs in the game. The use of illegal drugs by players, umpires, owners, front office personnel, trainers or anyone else in the game will not be condoned or tolerated."

In practice, the program is far less sweeping than that language implies. Because the Major League Baseball Players Association opposes mandatory drug testing as an invasion of privacy, only players who have testing clauses written into their contracts or who volunteer to be tested run the risk of disciplinary action for drug use.

One exception occurred in February 1986, three months after drug trials in Pittsburgh implicated 21 major-league players in cocaine use or distribution. The trials gave Baseball Commissioner Peter V. Ueberroth a pretext for disciplining the athletes, which he proceeded to do. He suspended the seven chief offenders for one year and told them they would be reinstated only if they donated 10 percent of their 1986 base pay to a drug-abuse prevention program, agreed to random drug testing and performed 200 hours each of drug-related community service. Ueberroth also took drug testing out of the hands of individual ball clubs and put it under the control of the commissioner's office.

**National Football League (NFL).** Since it includes steroids, the NFL's drug policy is the most comprehensive of any U.S. professional team sport. Current NFL procedures for detecting steroid use, put into effect last season, call for increased testing on a year-round basis. For first offenders, a positive result brings a four-game suspension; second offenders face suspension for the rest of the season, including the playoffs, or four games — whichever is greater.*

A separate set of rules governs what the NFL terms "drugs of abuse," including marijuana, cocaine, opiates (chiefly heroin) and phencyclidine (PCP). All players are tested for these substances in the preseason. Those whose test results are positive, or who have a prior record of drug use or treatment, automatically become subject to reasonable-cause testing during the season and afterward.

A player who tests positive for the first time will be notified by the NFL drug adviser to undergo medical evaluation and treatment; a second

---

*Dr. Forrest Tennant, the NFL's former drug adviser, was quoted on July 3 by *The New York Times* as saying the league's approach to steroid-use testing was not tough enough. "Random testing only tests a handful of people, and it doesn't get to the guys who are known to have used them," he said. He recommended that a player who tests positive for steroids be tested monthly thereafter.

**Drug use by athletes has prodded sports governing bodies in the United States to take corrective action. Most programs involve publishing a list of prohibited drugs, establishing testing procedures and laying down penalties for athletes found in violation of the code.**

positive result brings removal from the active roster for 30 days or four games, whichever is greater, plus additional drug treatment; a third positive result means immediate suspension from league play, subject to possible review after one year. Under NFL policy, moreover, failure or refusal to take a preseason or reasonable-cause test is seen as tantamount to a positive test result and exposes the player to the appropriate degree of disciplinary action.

**National Hockey League (NHL).** If nothing else, pro hockey's drug policy is short and to the point. In a statement issued in 1989, NHL President John A. Ziegler Jr. said: "Our official policy is well-defined. If a player uses or gets caught with illegal drugs, he will be suspended." Ziegler went on to say that "Our policy is also explicit on the question of rehabilitation programs. We have none. That is a conscious policy decision because we believe it only offers an excuse. We want our players to know from the start that if you want to play in the NHL, say no to drugs."

**National Collegiate Athletic Association (NCAA).** The NCAA, whose membership consists of more than 1,000 four-year colleges and universities, operates a drug program that combines education and testing. Since 1973, the NCAA Drug Education Committee has supplied material to grade school, high school and college athletes. The NCAA Committee on Competitive Safeguards and Medical Aspects of Sports is in charge of testing. More than 70 substances, including stimulants, steroids, beta-blockers, diuretics and street drugs, are on the organization's prohibited list.

At its 1990 national convention, the NCAA adopted a hard-line policy on steroids. The policy calls for Divi-

# Federal and State Steroid Regulations

The Crime Control Act of 1990, signed into law by President Bush last Nov. 29, placed more than two dozen steroid compounds on Schedule III of the Controlled Substances Act of 1970. Persons convicted of unlawful use or distribution of the substances face up to five years in prison.

The Controlled Substances Act (CSA) is an amalgam of earlier laws aimed at regulating substances with powerful psychoactive effects. All drugs covered by the CSA are capable of inducing physical or psychological dependence. Schedule I of the CSA is reserved for those drugs with both a high potential for abuse and no currently accepted medical applications. Schedules II through V include drugs with legitimate medical uses and decreasing levels of addictiveness. Drugs other than steroids on Schedule III include amphetamines and barbiturates.

Even before the 1990 federal law took effect, numerous states had taken action to regulate steroids. At the start of 1991, 19 states had placed steroids under the jurisdiction of their own controlled substances laws: Alabama, Arizona, California, Connecticut, Florida, Idaho, Kansas, Kentucky, Louisiana, Minnesota, Nebraska, Nevada, New York, North Carolina, Oregon, Pennsylvania, Tennessee, Texas and Utah.

Twelve states had outlawed steroid distribution and use except for valid medical reasons: Arkansas, Colorado, Georgia, Hawaii, Illinois, Iowa, New Hampshire, New Jersey, North Dakota, Oklahoma, South Carolina and South Dakota. Six states specifically outlawed the distribution of steroids for the purpose of bodybuilding or sports performance enhancement: Delaware, Indiana, Massachusetts, Ohio, Rhode Island and Washington. Michigan outlaws steroid use except in livestock and other non-human species. Virginia outlaws all manufacture and distribution of steroids.

Several states have enacted steroid-related legislation this year. For instance, Arizona moved steroids from Schedule IV to Schedule III of the state controlled substances law; Georgia placed steroids on Schedule III of its controlled substances law; and Maryland put 27 steroids on Schedule III of its law. In all states that have not yet added steroids to Schedule III, the Crime Control Act of 1990 takes precedence over state law.

---

sion I football players to undergo year-round, mandatory testing for steroids on a random basis. A player testing positive for the first time faces suspension for a year; a second positive test for steroids, steroid masking agents or other performance-enhancing drugs calls forth the "death penalty" — a lifetime ban from NCAA competition.

The NCAA drug-testing program is being challenged in court by Stanford University. In August 1988, Judge Conrad Rushing of Santa Clara (Calif.) Superior Court issued a permanent injunction allowing all Stanford athletes to compete in intercollegiate sports events without submitting to the NCAA's mandatory drug tests. Rushing said the NCAA program "invades student-athletes' privacy." Frank D. Uryasz, the NCAA's director of sports science, reports that the Stanford case is now before the California Supreme Court. He does not expect oral arguments to take place until late this fall

at the earliest. As Uryasz sees it, "There really is overwhelming support for drug testing in college athletics. Stanford clearly is in the minority on this issue."

**United States Olympic Committee (USOC).** The USOC's drug-control program (effective from 1989 through 1992) is modeled on that of the International Olympic Committee. For the most part, USOC drug tests occur only at the Olympic Festival and during trials for the World University Games, Pan American Games and Olympic Games.*

USOC penalties for use of a banned substance are severe. For steroids, amphetamines, diuretics, beta-blockers and certain other drugs, the recommended sanction for first use is

suspension from competition for two years; a second offense brings a lifetime ban. For lesser drugs, such as codeine and caffeine*, the maximum penalty for the first positive test result is a three-month suspension; for the second offense, a two-year suspension; and for the third offense, a lifetime ban. Furthermore, any physician, coach, trainer, or other attendant who is found to have aided or abetted an athlete's drug infraction faces suspension for at least the same length of time as the athlete does. Failure to comply with USOC testing procedures also invites punishment. In most cases, refusal to be tested after signing a testing consent form

Continued on p. 530

---

*Pursuant to plans announced in November 1989, the USOC hopes to begin out-of-competition drug testing by October for 10 sports — bobsledding, boxing, cycling, rowing, speedskating, swimming, track and field, volleyball, weightlifting and wrestling.

---

*Caffeine was added to the list of banned substances because it is a stimulant. To test positive for caffeine, a person would have to consume the equivalent of 6-8 cups of coffee in one sitting and be tested within 2-3 hours. Caffeine is also found in many other products, including soft drinks, chocolate and some over-the-counter medications.

# At Issue:

## Is random testing the right way to combat drug abuse by athletes?

**BILL FRALIC**

*Offensive guard for the Atlanta Falcons*
FROM TESTIMONY BEFORE THE SENATE
JUDICIARY COMMITTEE, MAY 8, 1989

*i* believe steroid use is rampant . . . [in the National Football League], and that includes my own team. . . . In our league, random testing is the only way to stop the steroid madness. . . . There are players who justify steroid use. They have a doctor monitor them and believe they are "protected" because they're being responsible in their use of steroids. There is no responsible use of steroids in football. . . .

I want the game rid of steroids, and I don't care how it's done. I'm willing to test every day. I once polled our players about random testing and 80 percent were in favor of random testing. The other 20 percent were more concerned with how the testing would be done. I find this significant because public perception is just the opposite. Fans believe players are fighting random testing. I'm certain players favor random testing so they can get off steroids. But unless they can be certain that the guy across from them is off steroids, then there is no hope.

Some people brag that they have bulked up without steroids, and they'll even give you a grocery list of foods they eat to support their claim. I submit that this is a farce. This player may in fact be consuming 10,000 to 12,000 calories a day, but I would bet everything I had that this consumption is supplementary to his use of steroids and growth hormones.

Growth hormones are a frightening development. The synthetic development of growth hormones has dropped prices to very affordable levels. It's another avenue players will take to beat the system.

What it means is that the NFL will become something of a freak show. Eventually, there will be disgrace in the game, much like we have seen disgrace in the Olympics.

And what happens if the game ever became clean of steroids? You might see 300-pound players become 270-pound players. You might see 240-pounders shrink to 220 or 215. And so forth.

But the game won't change. If anything, the game will be better because there will be less injuries.

Again, I personally don't care how we rid the game and society of steroids. I just want it done. We need help.

**ALAN L. SACK**

*Honors Program chairman at the
University of New Haven*
FROM *THE NEW YORK TIMES*, NOV. 25, 1988.

*n* othing better illustrates the low regard that the National Collegiate Athletic Association has often had for the rights of student-athletes than its random drug-testing policy. There are a number of alternatives for addressing the problem of substance abuse. Unfortunately, the NCAA chooses an approach that protects the public-relations image of its member institutions but shows little or no concern for the dignity and privacy of the vast majority of hard-working young athletes who are drug-free. . . .

Why should an athlete who has exhibited no behavior that would give rise to suspicion of illegal activity have to submit to . . . humiliation, inconvenience and violation of privacy? Why should athletes who only an hour before may have participated in the greatest athletic event of their careers have to agree to be herded like cattle into a urine-collection station and be treated like common criminals?

One way to justify the extreme diminution of Fourth Amendment rights implicit in a search without probable cause is to argue that random drug testing of college athletes is crucial to public safety. Few people oppose the kinds of general searches that are carried out at airports while passengers are preparing to board planes. . . . The case for testing college athletes without probable cause seems far less compelling. . . .

It is not my intention here to cover the many complex constitutional issues surrounding random drug testing. My argument is simple. The vast, vast majority of college athletes are good, decent, dedicated and drug-free. If the NCAA had respected those athletes as students and as sensitive human beings, random drug testing would have been instituted only as a last resort, and even then, only after encouraging athletes to consider the constitutional issues involved.

Efforts to fight substance abuse in college sports must be concerned with more than keeping athletes drug-free in the short term. The goal should be to help athletes understand the role that drugs play in our society and to prepare them to fight drug abuse throughout their lives. The NCAA should take the hundreds of thousands of dollars that are going into random drug testing and undertake a massive program in drug education.

Continued from p. 528
automatically triggers a two-year sanction.

## Legislative Action

The federal government and most state governments have moved decisively in recent years against two key performance-enhancing drugs — steroids and human growth hormone. Congress led the way with the Anti-Drug Abuse Act, which was signed into law by President Ronald Reagan on Nov. 28, 1988. The law penalized distribution of steroids for uses other than those prescribed by a physician. Violators face prison terms of up to three years in cases involving adult steroid users, and up to six years in cases involving persons under age 18.

The Crime Control Act of 1990, signed into law by President Bush last Nov. 29, placed more than two dozen steroid compounds on Schedule III of the Controlled Substances Act of 1970.* Persons convicted of unlawful use or distribution of the substances face up to five years in prison. The measure also outlawed the distribution of human growth hormone for any use in people other than the treatment of a disease or other recognized medical condition. Violators of the HGH provision were made liable to prison terms of up to

---

*The Controlled Substances Act (CSA) is an amalgam of earlier laws aimed at regulating substances with powerful psychoactive effects. All drugs covered by the CSA are capable of inducing physical or psychological dependence. They include heroin, marijuana and cocaine, which previously were controlled under the Harrison Act and Marijuana Tax Act, and a number of other substances listed in the Drug Abuse Control Amendments of 1965. Schedule I of the CSA is reserved for those drugs with both a high potential for abuse and no currently accepted medical applications. Schedules II through V include drugs with legitimate medical uses and decreasing levels of addictiveness. Drugs other than steroids on Schedule III include amphetamines and barbiturates.

five years. In HGH offenses involving individuals under age 18, the maximum prison term rises to 10 years.

Steroid-control efforts at the state level parallel what Congress has done. More than 40 states have enacted laws or adopted regulations since 1986, with most of the activity occurring in the past three years. About 20 states have placed steroids on their controlled substance lists, which follow the federal model. Louisiana and New York are the only states to list steroids under Schedule II, a more stringent classification than Schedule III. Eight states — Arizona, Connecticut, Florida, Idaho, Kansas, Minnesota, Tennessee and Texas — placed steroids on Schedule IV or lower. Accordingly, they will have to amend their statutes to conform with federal law, which sets minimum enforcement standards binding on the states. Arizona took such action in April.

It may be too early to say whether the new toughness on steroids will actually curb use of the drugs, but two recent developments may turn out to be significant. Jamie Astaphan, a physician who prescribed steroids for Ben Johnson and

other Canadian athletes, was suspended June 3 from practicing medicine for 18 months and fined $5,000. The penalty was imposed in Toronto by a panel of four doctors from Ontario's College of Physicians and Surgeons.

Then, on June 27, George Zahorian III, an osteopath and urologic surgeon, was convicted by a U.S. District Court jury in Harrisburg, Pa., of violating the 1988 federal law that prohibits giving steroids for performance enhancement or other non-medical reasons. Zahorian was the first doctor to be found guilty under the law. He was charged with selling steroids to four professional wrestlers (including Hulk Hogan) and a weightlifter.[23]

Murray, for one, feels sure that going after the doctors, trainers, coaches and others who supply drugs to athletes — or who condone or willfully ignore drug use — will lead to "real changes." If such individuals know they can be banned from sport for at least as long as athletes are, he says, "those people will begin to get nervous about it and will begin to pay more attention to whether the athletes training under them are using drugs or not." ∎

# OUTLOOK

## No Easy Answers

In future years, chances of bringing drug use by athletes under firm control may hinge on international cooperation on testing procedures. The United States and the Soviet Union took a step in this direction by signing an agreement in 1989 designed to rid sports in the two nations of performance-enhancing drugs by Olympic and other world-class athletes. The program

features out-of-competition testing on short notice for athletes selected by each nation, plus additional testing at selected competitions involving U.S. and Soviet competitors. Moreover, scientists from each country are to live in the other country on a long-term basis to permit joint analysis of drug-test data.

Murray believes this pact will be productive. He also thinks the collapse of communism in Eastern Europe will have similarly beneficial effects. One of the consequences of communism's demise, he notes, has been "the exposure of state-supported efforts to evade drug testing.

It was a big embarrassment in East Germany and the Soviet Union."

In Murray's opinion, "the opening up of Eastern Europe provides possibilities for getting serious about drug control that we didn't have before," in that it may now be easier to persuade American athletes competing against Eastern Europeans to stay off drugs. In past years many U.S. athletes were convinced, with good reason, that their Eastern European counterparts enjoyed a built-in competitive advantage because of performance-enhancing drugs supplied by the state. Murray also feels that "athletes themselves, for the most part, would like to compete against other athletes who they knew were free of drugs."

Yesalis, on the other hand, doubts whether any international agreement on drug testing can be effective. "First of all, I question the sincerity of it," he says, citing track and field as an example. "Track and field is a big business because people watch it not to see somebody run but to see records broken. And without drugs, you're not going to have records broken." Also, he points out, some anabolic steroids still can't be detected in low to moderate doses.

Yesalis makes the further point that an athlete — a football player, say — who uses steroids in high school but then ceases using them before entering college still may enjoy an unfair competitive advantage throughout his sports career. Someone who stops taking steroids after prolonged use typically retains 25 to 75 percent of his added muscle mass, provided he continues to adhere faithfully to his dietary and exercise regimen.

Realizing this, Yesalis says, high school athletes are encouraged "to bulk up [on steroids] before they get their [college athletic] scholarships." The college coach then can say he doesn't have any steroid users on his team — a claim that is, of course, not strictly true. "If you recruit a kid who has used steroids," says Yesalis, "you have just as much of [an ethical] problem as if he had used them yesterday."

Murray, an ethicist by training, says significant reduction of sports drug use will require a change of heart above all else. "Athletes are going to have to decide that they are just not going to tolerate cheating by their competitors — and that they are not going to cheat, either," he says. Outsiders can try to buttress those decisions by devising drug-testing methods that make it less likely cheaters will escape punishment. Murray acknowledges that "We'll never be able to do that perfectly, because people will discover new drugs and new ways of disguising drug use." All the same, he considers it a battle well worth fighting and feels "we've made some progress." ∎

## Notes

[1] Thomas H. Murray, "The Ethics of Drugs in Sport," *Drugs and Performance in Sports*, Richard H. Strauss, ed., 1987, p. 13.

[2] Quoted by Tom Donohoe and Neil Johnson in *Foul Play: Drug Abuse in Sports* (1986), p. 125.

[3] *Ibid.*, pp. 126-127.

[4] Quoted in *Time*, Aug. 25, 1986.

[5] *Ibid.*

[6] Quoted in *Sports Illustrated*, July 9, 1990.

[7] George L. White, *et al.*, "Preventing Steroid Use in Youth: The Health Educator's Role," *Health Education*, August-September 1987, p. 33.

[8] Testimony before Subcommittee on Crime of the House Judiciary Committee, March 22, 1990. Sandlin is a former assistant coach for strength and fitness at the University of Alabama.

[9] Bob Goldman, *Death in the Locker Room: Steroids, Cocaine & Sports* (1984), p. 76.

[10] Quoted in *Business Week*, Dec. 11, 1989.

[11] Charles E. Yesalis, *et al.*, "Self Reported Use of Anabolic-Androgenic Steroids by Elite Power Lifters," *The Physician and Sportsmedicine*, December 1988, pp. 91-94.

[12] U.S. General Accounting Office, *Drug Misuse: Anabolic Steroids and Human Growth Hormone*, August 1989, p. 35.

[13] Quoted in *Journal of the American Medical Association*, June 23, 1989.

[14] Kathleen K. Wiegner, "Gotcha!" *Forbes*, Nov. 28, 1988, p. 240.

[15] Lyle Alzado (as told to Shelley Smith), "I'm Sick and I'm Scared," *Sports Illustrated*, July 8, 1991, p. 21. Dr. Robert Huizenga, Alzado's personal physician and formerly a Raiders team doctor, said in an accompanying interview that he knew the player was on steroids. He also said there was "no question" steroids could have caused Alzado's cancer. "We know anabolic steroids have cancer-forming ability," Huizenga said. "We know that growth hormones have cancer-growing ability."

[16] Wilson was banned from the league for life in November 1989. He was sentenced this June 20 in Long Beach, Calif., to a four-year suspended term for burglary. As a condition of his sentence, Wilson was ordered to remain in a drug rehabilitation program.

[17] Tommy Chaikin (with Rick Telander), "The Nightmare of Steroids," *Sports Illustrated*, Oct. 24, 1988, pp. 84-102.

[18] William E. Buckley, *et al.*, "Estimated Prevalence of Anabolic Steroid Use Among Male High School Seniors," *Journal of the American Medical Association*, Dec. 16, 1988, pp. 3441-3445. The study was based on questionnaires completed by 3,403 male seniors at 46 private and public high schools across the nation.

[19] Samuel Wilson Fussell, *Muscle: Confessions of an Unlikely Bodybuilder* (1991), p. 121.

[20] For the full text of the 1977 position statement, see *Medicine and Science in Sports*, winter 1977, p. xi.

[21] For the full text of the 1984 position paper, see Richard H. Strauss, ed., *Drugs & Performance in Sports* (1987), p. 199.

[22] Quoted by Donohoe and Johnson, *op. cit.*, p. 52.

[23] The weightlifter and wrestlers were not charged in the case because the offenses occurred before enactment of the 1990 federal law putting steroids on Schedule III of the Controlled Substances Act.

# Bibliography

## Selected Sources Used

### Books

**Donohoe, Tom, and Johnson, Neil, *Foul Play*, Basil Blackwell, 1986.**

Donohoe and Johnson are British researchers with a special interest in the problems of drug use. They conclude that "The use of drugs in sport cannot be examined in isolation from the general problems which have afflicted sport. International sport has become increasingly *professional* and *political*."

**Francis, Charlie (with Jeff Coplon), *Speed Trap: Inside the Biggest Scandal In Olympic History*, St. Martin's Press, 1990.**

The book's interest derives chiefly from the identity of its author. Francis was the coach of Ben Johnson, the Canadian sprinter who was forced to return his 1988 Olympic gold medal after tests showed he had taken steroids shortly before competing.

**Fussell, Samuel Wilson, *Muscle: Confessions of an Unlikely Bodybuilder*, Poseidon Press, 1991.**

Fussell, a spindly Oxford University graduate, decides to take up bodybuilding at age 26 because he is afraid he will be assaulted on the streets of New York City (where he works) if he does not. In due course, thanks to weightlifting, diet and steroids, he develops the kind of competition-class body that no street tough would dare mess with. But then, at age 30, Fussell goes cold turkey and watches without regret as his hard-won muscles gradually melt away.

**Meer, Jeff, *Drugs & Sports*, Chelsea House Publishers, 1987.**

Like other writers on drug abuse by athletes, Meer focuses on the headline-making substances — cocaine, steroids, beta-blockers and so on. But he reminds his readers that alcohol and nicotine also have shortened the careers of competitors in numerous sports.

### Articles

**Alzado, Lyle, (as told to Shelley Smith), "I'm Sick and I'm Scared," *Sports Illustrated*, July 8, 1991.**

Alzado, a former All-Pro defensive end for the National Football League's Denver Broncos, Cleveland Browns and Los Angeles Raiders, discloses that he was lying when he repeatedly denied using anabolic steroids during his playing days. He now acknowledges he was a heavy steroid user, and also took human growth hormone during a comeback attempt last season. He blames the two drugs

for causing his inoperable brain cancer. "I was a giant," he says. "Now I'm weak. And I'm scared."

**Buckley, William E., "Estimated Prevalence of Anabolic Steroid Use Among Male High School Seniors," *Journal of the American Medical Association*, Dec. 16, 1988.**

This widely cited study documents what many observers suspected — that anabolic steroids are used by a small but significant percentage of high school students. The evidence suggests that efforts to combat steroid use by teenagers should begin as early as junior high school and should not be confined to athletes.

**Chaikin, Tommy (with Rick Telander), "The Nightmare of Steroids," *Sports Illustrated*, Oct. 24, 1988.**

Chaikin describes his experiences with steroid use as a member of the University of South Carolina football team. Of particular interest is his account of the psychological changes wrought by the drug, bringing him at one point to the verge of suicide.

### Reports and Studies

**U.S. General Accounting Office, *Drug Misuse: Anabolic Steroids and Human Growth Hormone*, August 1989.**

A concise but thorough survey of what is currently known about the extent of steroid and HGH use as well as the health consequences of taking the drugs. A short bibliography is attached.

**U.S. Olympic Committee, *Drug Free*, 1989.**

This booklet is a handy guide to the substances that are banned — as well as those that are permitted — by the U.S. Olympic Committee (USOC). Also included are details of the U.S.-Soviet agreement on drug testing of athletes and the USOC's drug-control policies and procedures for the 1989-92 period.

**U.S. House Subcommittee on Crime, Committee on the Judiciary, *Anabolic Steroid Restriction Act of 1989* (published proceedings of hearing held March 23, 1989).**

Witnesses discuss whether federal control of steroid use and distribution is needed. The following year, Congress did in fact approve legislation to that end. At this hearing, the most interesting witnesses are Dr. Charles E. Yesalis, a drug expert from Pennsylvania State University, and Olympic gold medalist Carl Lewis, who has thought-provoking things to say about drug use at the highest levels of track and field.

# The Next Step

## Additional Articles from Current Periodicals

### Anabolic steroids

**"Athletics notes: Steroid use at colleges is said to exceed previous estimates," *The Chronicle of Higher Education*, Dec. 19, 1990, p. A28.**

Comments on a study by the NCAA which found the use of anabolic steroids by college athletes may be significantly higher than previously estimated. Estimating opponent's use of muscle-building drugs.

**"Teenagers blase about steroid use," *FDA Consumer*, December 1990, p. 2.**

Reports that American teenagers are turning a deaf ear to the dangers of anabolic steroids and are using the drugs in increasing numbers to build athletic prowess and improve their appearances, a 1990 Department of Health and Human Service report concludes.

**Cowart, V.S., "Ethical, as well as physiological, questions continue to arise over athletes' steroid abuse," *Journal of the American Medical Assn.*, June 16, 1989, p. 3362.**

Discusses the ethics involved in the use of anabolic steroids by athletes. Role of coaches and physicians; Ethics in research.

**Hallagan, J.B., Hallagan, L.F., et al., "Anabolic-androgenic steroid use by athletes," *New England Journal of Medicine*, Oct. 12, 1989, p. 1042.**

Discusses anabolic-androgenic steroid use, regulation of its use, including the federal Anti-Drug Abuse Act of 1988, and its implications for physicians. Includes state regulation of anabolic-androgenic steroids and the need for education and testing programs.

**Pfotenhauer, P., "Steroids: The power drugs," *USA Today*, March 1989, p. 88.**

Reports on the increase of anabolic steroid use by today's athletes, despite well-known health risks. Pressure on US athletes to remain competitive with their European counterparts. INSET: The size enhancers: A steroid glossary.

### Actions & defenses

**Janofsky, M., "Rule that will strip Johnson of his world records is approved," *The New York Times*, Sept. 6, 1989, p. D21.**

Discusses a ruling passed by the International Amateur Athletic Federation that nullifies any mark held by someone who admits to having used performance-enhancing drugs and which strips Ben Johnson, the Canadian sprinter, of his world records in the 100-meter dash and the indoor 60-meter event.

**Underwood, N. and Anderson, A., "Starting over," *Maclean's*, Sept. 18, 1989, p. 66.**

Discusses the International Amateur Athletic Federation's decision to revoke all records set by athletes who have admitted to using steroids and other drugs, retroactive to Jan. 1, 1984, from Jan. 1, 1990. Canadian sprinter Ben Johnson's loss of two world records; Testimony of Johnson and Canadian runner Angella Issajenko before the Dubin inquiry; New IAAF random drug-testing policy.

### Case studies

**"A crash course in drug testing," *Time*, Feb. 5, 1990, p. 25.**

Reports on Homewood-Flossmoor High School outside Chicago, which began random testing of all who take part in athletics for ten common drugs, including marijuana, cocaine, and alcohol. Details of the Flossmoor plan; Question as to whether it is a violation of the students' rights.

**"A day of reckoning," *Maclean's*, June 26, 1989, p. 32.**

Reports on disgraced sprinter Ben Johnson's testimony before the Dubin inquiry into drug use by Canadian athletes. Johnson admitted that he used banned anabolic steroids. Loss of his Olympic gold medal for the 100-m dash at the 1988 Summer Olympic Games in Seoul, South Korea; Johnson's doubtful status as an athlete.

**Burfoot, A. and Wischnia, B., "Not his cup of tea," *Runner's World*, March 1990, p. 12.**

Profiles Jeff Scuffins, a US distance runner, who was recently suspended for illegal drug use, yet who maintains he only drank some herbal tea. Athletics Congress; Substance abuse rulings.

**Dawidoff, N., "Bad example," *Sports Illustrated*, Oct. 29, 1990, p. 13.**

Presents the case of Brian Lee Tribble, who was recently convicted on drug charges. Involvement in the drug overdose of basketball player Len Bias; Influence of drug dealers as role models.

**Lupica, M., "David Thompson, back to earth," *Esquire*, March 1990, p. 73.**

Profiles ex-basketball player David Thompson and his

problems with drugs. When he first started using cocaine; His bankruptcy; How he got help.

**Noden, M., "A dirty coach comes clean," *Sports Illustrated*, Mar. 13, 1989, p. 22.**

Describes Coach Charlie Francis' recent testimony before Canada's Commission of Inquiry when he admitted that sprinter Ben Johnson had used steroids since 1981.

**Reilly, R., "A visit to hell," *Sports Illustrated*, Aug. 29, 1988, p. 52.**

Profiles Charles White, the National Football League's leading rusher, and his battle with drug abuse. Heisman trophy winner in 1979.

**Scarpino, V., Arrigo, A., et al., "Evaluation of prevalence of 'doping' among Italian athletes," *Lancet*, Oct. 27, 1990, p. 1048.**

Reports on the results of a survey requested by the Italian National Olympic Committee and the National Research Council to investigate the knowledge about and attitudes of Italian athletes to illegal drugs and other forms of 'doping' in sports. Subjects and methods; Results; Discussion.

**Steptoe, S., "He's pitching a different game," *Sports Illustrated*, Sept. 10, 1990, following p. 143.**

Discusses how Sam McDowell, 47, an ex-major league pitcher who spent 15 years in professional baseball, overcame alcohol and drug addiction and is now a professional counselor.

**Sullivan, R., "Gambling, payoffs and drugs," *Sports Illustrated*, Oct. 30, 1989, p. 40.**

Discusses the NCAA investigation of major violations involving the University of Florida's athletic department. Recent drug investigations and indictment; Recent resignation of football coach Galen Hall; NCAA suspension of quarterbacks Kyle Morris, Shane Matthews, G.A. Mangus, and receiver Brady Ackerman; Florida's basketball program.

**Wickens, B., "A deepening scandal," *Maclean's*, June 5, 1989, p. 48.**

Reports on testimony by Dr. George Mario (Jamie) Astaphan before Dubin inquiry into the use of drugs in sports. Astaphan is disgraced Canadian sprinter Ben Johnson's personal physician; Johnson's positive steroid test during the 1988 Summer Olympics in Seoul, South Korea; Tape recording of a conversation between Astaphan and Johnson.

**Wulf, S., "Positive and negative," *Sports Illustrated*, Apr. 8, 1991, p. 15.**

Reports that soccer star Diego Maradona and boxer

Sugar Ray Leonard have both used cocaine. Maradona tested positive for the drug and went into seclusion; Leonard admitted to using cocaine between 1983 and 1986.

## Debates & issues

**"NFL drug problem faces allegations of racism," *Jet*, Feb. 12, 1990, p. 46.**

Presents comments on the alleged racial bias of the NFL drug tests and treatment program, after a television program claimed three white quarterbacks tested positive for cocaine use but weren't counseled or sanctioned; 26 of the 30 players who have been publicly sanctioned are black.

**Gambaccini, P., "Drugs," *Runner's World*, October 1990, p. 85.**

Deplores the focus on drugs and drug testing in the media concerning running. Accusations; The Athletics Congress (TAC); Steroids and stimulants; Coach Chuck DeBus; Policy and protest; More.

**Jereski, L., "It gives athletes a boost — maybe too much," *Business Week*, Dec. 11, 1989, p. 123.**

Discusses how many athletes are using erythropoietin (EPO) a drug created for kidney patients that boosts the body's production of oxygen-carrying red blood cells to improve their performance. Because EPO is made naturally by the body, tests don't show if someone has taken it, causing concern among coaches, doctors, and athletic association officials that EPO may eventually supersede anabolic steroids as the top performance-enhancing drug among athletes. Deadly side effects.

**Winner, L., "The era of the enhanced athlete," *Technology Review*, February/March 1989, p. 22.**

Opinion. Comments on the legitimate role of performance-enhancing technology in sports. Drug scandal surrounding Canadian sprinter Ben Johnson; Social pressure and winning; Proposal for 'Natural Olympics' and 'Enhanced Olympics.'

## Football

**Breo, D.L., "The other Super Bowl question — can the NFL police its drug policy?" *Journal of the American Medical Association*, Jan. 23, 1991 & Jan. 30, 1991, p. 506.**

Explains the controversy about the alleged shortcomings in the National Football League's (NFL) drug program. The NFL's drug adviser is Dr. Forest S. Tennant who believes that his testing program is successful.

**Cowart, V.S., "Professional football player suspen-**

sions re-emphasize problems of steroid abuse," *Journal of the American Medical Association*, Oct. 6, 1989, p. 1743.

Discusses the 30-day suspensions of 13 players in the National Football League who had positive tests for anabolic steroids. Testing process.

**Demak, R. and Kirshenbaum, J., "The NFL fails its drug test,"** *Sports Illustrated*, **July 10, 1989, p. 38.**

Presents a special report on the National Football League's (NFL) drug program based on transcripts of hearings in NFL drug cases and on interviews with players, agents, team doctors, and other officials. Results of findings; League commissioner Pete Rozelle; Drug adviser Dr. Forest Tennant Jr.; Opposition by the NFL Players Association. INSET: A doctor and his critics.

**Johnson, W., "Hit for a loss,"** *Sports Illustrated*, **Sept. 19, 1988, p. 50.**

A report on the growing number of National Football League players suspected of drug abuse. Lists 17 players who have been suspended this season; Drug testing procedures; Steroid problems downplayed; Role of public relations; Inequitable penalties.

**Lederman, D., "University of Notre Dame says 5 of its football players tested positive for use of anabolic steroids,"** *The Chronicle of Higher Education*, **Sept. 5, 1990, p. A37.**

Reports that a 'Sports Illustrated' article, quoting a former football player, has accused Notre Dame football coach Lou Holtz with caring more for winning than about the well-being of his players, and the university has admitted that five players had tested positive for the use of muscle-building drugs (anabolic steroids) since 1987. Coach 'had to have known'; No further checking planned.

## Testing

**"NCAA tightens drug rules for collegiate gridders,"** *Jet*, **Feb. 12, 1990, p. 48.**

Reports on the random, year-round drug testing and stiffer penalties voted in by the National Collegiate Athletic Association (NCAA) for college football players.

**Cowart, V.S., "Athlete drug testing receiving more attention than ever before in history of competition,"** *Journal of the American Medical Association*, **June 30, 1989, p. 3510.**

Discusses drug testing of athletes. Reliability of results; Questions about testing; Pro and con viewpoints; International agreement on testing; Need for universal protocol.

**Lederman, D., "Appeals court upholds decision barring the NCAA from administering drug-testing plan**

at Stanford," *The Chronicle of Higher Education*, Oct. 3, 1990, p. A43.

Comments on the California appeals court decision upholding a 1988 barring of the National Collegiate Athletic Association from forcing Stanford University's athletes to participate in the association's mandatory drug-testing program. Violation of the right to privacy; No adequate consideration of other deterrents to drug use; NCAA reviewing the court's decision.

**Neff, C. and Noden, M., "Test case? "** *Sports Illustrated*, **Apr. 16, 1990, p. 14.**

Discusses how the Athletic Congress's year-round, out-of-competition drug-testing program, admirable in its intent, is turning out to be flawed. Specifics of the program; Problems in implementation; Victim of program, Henry Marsh.

**Rhoden, W.C., "N.C.A.A. stiffens drug penalties and expands testing in football,"** *The New York Times*, **Jan. 11, 1990, p. A1.**

States that the National Collegiate Athletic Association voted to require random, year-round testing of players in major football programs for performance-enhancing drugs, and to impose stiffer penalties for violators. The progress of the year-round testing will be monitored, and if the program proves successful, it will be expanded to other sports.

## Track & field

**Henderson, J., "Users and losers,"** *Runner's World*, **March 1989, p. 14.**

Opinion. Expresses view that recent publicity of drug use at 1988 Summer Olympics has cost the sport of running its good name. Drug problem in the sport is real, but limited in scope; Drugs tempt elite runners; Distance running drug free; Proposed suggestions on ways to use drug testing and penalize offenders.

**Neff, C., "Drugs and track,"** *Sports Illustrated*, **Oct. 2, 1989, p. 25.**

Reports on allegations made by former US 400-meter standout Darrell Robinson linking Olympic gold medalists Carl Lewis and Florence Griffith Joyner and other American athletes to a variety of performance-enhancing substances.

**Noden, M., "Positively negative,"** *Sports Illustrated*, **Nov. 19, 1990, p. 22.**

Reports that two United States track stars, Randy Barnes and Butch Reynolds, recently tested positive for steroids. Suspension by the International Amateur Athletic Federation; Appeal.

# Back Issues

*Great Research on Current Issues Starts Right Here... Recent topics covered by The CQ Researcher are listed below. Issues dated before May 10, 1991, were published under the name of Editorial Research Reports.*

**JANUARY 1990**
Higher Education Curriculum
Photonics
Age of 'Infotainment'
Abortion: Politicians' Nightmare

**FEBRUARY 1990**
Politics and Economic Growth
Free Agency in Sports
Repetitive Motion
War on Drugs

**MARCH 1990**
Asbestos: Are Risks Acceptable?
Public Health Campaigns
South Africa's Future
Homeless Need More Than Shelter

**APRIL 1990**
How Fair is the Tax Burden?
Workers' Compensation
U.S. Pacific Forces
Curbing Insurance Premiums

**MAY 1990**
Should Teaching Be a Profession?
Will Canada Fall Apart?
Is U.S. Patent System Outdated?
Federal Funding for the Arts

**JUNE 1990**
Downsizing America's Armed Forces
Progress In Weather Forecasting
S & L Bailout
Bio-Chemical Disarmament

**JULY 1990**
Do Americans Still Love Marriage?
Death Penalty Debate
Decline of Rural America
United Nations in the 1990s

**AUGUST 1990**
Democracy in the Philippines
Initiatives: True Democracy?
Hard Times at Newspapers
Teens Balance School & Jobs

**SEPTEMBER 1990**
Dangers of Alcohol
Western Alliance After the Cold War
Tobacco Industry
Right to Die

**OCTOBER 1990**
Organ Transplants
Energy Policy Options
Search for Arab Unity
Child Support

**NOVEMBER 1990**
Lotteries and Gambling
Post Cold-War Choices
Setting Limits on Medical Care
Multicultural Education

**DECEMBER 1990**
Cable TV Regulation
Americans' Search For Their Roots
Is Insurance System a Failure?
Why Schools Still Have Tracking

**JANUARY 1991**
Growing Influence of Boycotts
Should the U.S. Reinstate the Draft?
America's Archaeological Past
Peace Corps' Challenges in '90s

**FEBRUARY 1991**
Regional Impact of Recession
Puerto Rico's Status
Redistricting: Mapping Power
Nuclear Power

**MARCH 1991**
Acid Rain
Cost of the Gulf War
Reassessing Gun Laws
Future for Man in Space

**APRIL 1991**
Social Security
Canadian Crisis Over Quebec
California Drought
Electromagnetic Radiation

**MAY 1991**
School Choice
Racial Quotas
Animal Rights
U.S. and Japan

**JUNE 1991**
Children and Divorce
Teenage Suicide
Endangered Species
Europe 1992

**JULY 1991**
Teenagers and Abortion
Soviet Republics Rebel
Mexico's Emergence

Back issues are available for $4.00 (subscribers) or $7.00 (non-subscribers). Quantity discounts apply to orders over ten. To order, call Congressional Quarterly 1-800-432-2250.

# Future Topics

▶ *Sexual Harassment*

▶ *Fetal Tissue Research*

▶ *Oil Imports*

# THE CQ Researcher

PUBLISHED BY CONGRESSIONAL QUARTERLY INC., IN CONJUNCTION WITH EBSCO PUBLISHING

# Sexual Harassment

*Men and women in workplace power struggles*

IN THE DECADES SINCE WOMEN SWEPT INTO THE American work force, sexual harassment has continued to make disturbing, if sometimes titillating, headlines. But the classic scenario of bosses blackmailing subordinates for sex has steadily broadened. Legally defined sexual harassment now includes lascivious comments, off-color jokes and "leering," murky areas that raise debates over freedom of speech. With employers being held responsible for sexual harassment on the job, many companies have adopted guidelines and grievance procedures. Still, courts are crowded with sexual harassment cases. In fact, the debate in Congress over the 1991 civil rights bill has turned partly on the issue of whether victims ought to collect damages when they successfully sue.

 **August 9, 1991 • Volume 1, No. 13 • 537-560**

*Formerly Editorial Research Reports*

August 9, 1991
Volume 1, No. 13

**EDITOR**
Sandra Stencel

**MANAGING EDITOR**
Thomas J. Colin

**ASSOCIATE EDITOR**
Richard L. Worsnop

**STAFF WRITERS**
Charles S. Clark
Mary H. Cooper
Rodman D. Griffin

**PRODUCTION EDITOR**
Laurie De Maris

**EDITORIAL ASSISTANT**
Thomas H. Moore

**GRAPHICS**
Jack Auldridge

**PUBLISHED BY**
Congressional Quarterly Inc.

**CHAIRMAN**
Andrew Barnes

**VICE CHAIRMAN**
Andrew P. Corty

**EDITOR AND PUBLISHER**
Neil Skene

**EXECUTIVE EDITOR**
Robert W. Merry

**PUBLICATIONS MARKETING/SALES**
Robert Smith

**EDITOR, EBSCO PUBLISHING**
Melissa Kummerer

The CQ Researcher (ISSN 1056-2036). Formerly Editorial Research Reports. Published weekly (48 times per year, excluding March 1, May 3, Aug. 2 and Nov. 1, 1991) by Congressional Quarterly Inc., 1414 22nd St., N.W., Washington, D.C. 20037. Rates are furnished upon request. Application to mail at second-class postage rates is pending at Washington, D.C. POSTMASTER: Send address changes to The CQ Researcher, 1414 22nd St., N.W., Washington, D.C. 20037.

COVER ART: BARBARA SASSA-DANIELS

# Sexual Harassment

BY CHARLES S. CLARK

## THE ISSUES

History did not record the name of the first boss who told an underling, "Have sex with me or you're fired." But it is safe to assume the employee did not file a formal complaint with her employer, even though the threat probably caused her great emotional anguish. For decades, many victims felt the only way to cope with sexual harassment at work was to quit their job or suffer in silence.

Not any more. Women, who now make up nearly half of the nation's work force, are demanding that employers take steps to prevent harassment and punish offenders. Victims of sexual harassment are also showing an increased willingness to take their cases to court.

But while there is a new sensitivity to sexual harassment in the workplace, the problem has not gone away. "Sexual harassment exists . . . at all levels of the corporate hierarchy," says Peter Eide, manager of labor relations at the U.S. Chamber of Commerce. "It's not just high-level executives trying to grope their secretaries."

From the executive suite to the construction site, from the campus to the industrial park, sexual harassment manifests itself in all sectors of society. Two years ago midshipmen at the U.S. Naval Academy in Annapolis, Md., chained a woman classmate to a urinal as a prank, prompting disciplinary action and a Navy investigation. Last September, several members of the New England Patriots football team made obscene comments and gestures to a female sportswriter from the *Boston Herald* who was interviewing another player in the team's locker

room. The reporter, Lisa Olson, has filed a lawsuit against the team. This spring, neurosurgeon Frances Conley announced she was resigning from her 25-year teaching post at Stanford University's medical center because of what she called "pervasive sexism." Among other things, Conley claimed her male colleagues would rub her leg under the operating table, call her "honey" and speak openly of the shape of her breasts.

As more victims of harassment have gone public, the damage the practice causes has become clearer. "It can destroy lives," says Diane Halpern, a California State University psychologist with a specialty in gender differences. People switch majors, drop out of college, quit their jobs.

Many people assume sexual harassment is an expression of sexuality. But most experts see it as a reflection of unequal power in the workplace. Most victims are "women in lowly positions," says Susan Rubenstein, an attorney in San Fran-

cisco who specializes in sexual harassment cases. "A secretary will get harassed before a lawyer, a paralegal will get harassed before an associate and a mechanic will get harassed before an engineer."

"It's not a battle of the sexes, it's about change — women and men learning new ways to act," says Susan L. Webb, a Seattle-based consultant on sexual harassment. "When you have a group dominated by one sex or race, when a minority comes in, it's likely that the majority will bother or harass the minority."

The surge of women into the labor force — and their increased presence in the ranks of managers and supervisors — has been going on for a quarter of a century. Yet some attitudes have been slow to change. "Old gentlemen from a different generation need to be taught and enlightened that women are equal, they . . . are not playthings or second-class citizens," says Eide of the Chamber of Commerce. Linda Chavez, staff director for the U.S. Civil Rights Commission during the Reagan administration, says many men still are confused about what is and is not acceptable behavior around female co-workers. "There's no Emily Post you can go to for rules of behavior in the workplace," she says.

The number of sexual harassment complaints filed with the Equal Opportunity Employment Commission (EEOC) — the federal agency charged with investigating workplace discrimination around the country — has risen slightly in recent years (*see graph, p. 541*). But women's groups say society still has a long way to go in spreading awareness among would-be harassers and among victims, who often are hesitant to report abuses and brave the long, expensive and emotionally stressful legal process. (*See story, p. 549.*)

August 9, 1991    **539**

In judging sexual harassment cases, courts can consider the victim's sexual history, whether she dressed in a sexually provocative manner, whether she used sexually oriented language, was willing to engage in sexual banter in the workplace, her past conduct with the harasser and her overall personality. "We're at the point now with sexual harassment that we were 10 or 15 years ago with rape," says Patricia Oreland, executive vice president of the National Organization for Women. "There's still an inclination to blame the victim." [1]

Although most people acknowledge that incidents of sexual harassment do happen, some accuse the women's movement of exaggerating the problem. "The entire issue is a perfect example of a minor special interest group's ability to blow up an 'issue' to a level of importance which in no way relates to the reality of the world in which we live and work," said a 38-year-old male plant manager for a manufacturer of industrial goods. [2]

Others say employers and university officials have overreacted to alleged incidents of sexual harassment, creating an environment that demands what detractors of feminism deride as "political correctness." Nicholas Davidson, author of several books critical of feminism, writes woefully of a University of Toronto math professor who in 1989 was accused of sexual harassment for having stared at a part-time female student at the university swimming pool. He was reprimanded and required to undergo counseling. [3]

The issue of sexual harassment has also raised complicated legal and constitutional questions. When a Florida judge last January ruled in favor of a female shipyard welder who had brought a sexual harassment suit because pinups of nude women had been posted at her work site, attorneys for the American Civil Liberties Union (ACLU) expressed concern that such decisions might violate the right of free speech and expression (see p. 550).

Others think the courts have gone too far in awarding damages to victims of sexual harassment. Suing under state laws, plaintiffs have won as much as $3.1 million in punitive and compensatory damages (see story, p. 542). As sexual harassment cases have developed over the years, courts have established that companies can be financially liable for the behavior of their employees, even if they were unaware of it and even if they have a policy against sexual harassment. The Supreme Court has also affirmed that companies can be liable if they tolerate a "hostile atmosphere" in which sexual harassment can flourish.

Many companies find it difficult to investigate harassment complaints. "Most often, you have a woman who says something has happened [and] a man who says it didn't," says a vice president for human resources for an auto plant that was involved in a sexual harassment case. "[A]s an employer you have the obligation to protect them both." [4]

The result is that most companies have erred on the side of caution; more than three-quarters of the *Fortune* 500 companies surveyed in 1988 by *Working Woman* magazine had instituted sexual harassment policies. "It's a lawsuit waiting to happen if they do nothing," says Diane J. Generous, senior associate director of employee relations at the National Association of Manufacturers in Washington.

Men and women are learning — sometimes the hard way — what is the proper relationship between sex and work. "The contours of appropriate behavior between the sexes ... are not a fixed, universally known, or widely shared set of rules," writes Lloyd R. Cohen, a professor at Chicago-Kent School of Law. [5] As society seeks such rules, these are some of the issues that are likely to be discussed:

### What constitutes sexual harassment?

It is relatively easy to theorize about the motivation for sexual harassment — power struggles, stereotyping, resentment of non-traditional workers — but defining it can be like trying to capture smoke in a jar. The difficulty stems in part from what sociologist and sexual harassment specialist Barbara A. Gutek describes as the "high incidence of sex at work that represents caring, intimacy, flattery and plain physical attraction." [6]

The fact that the workplace is often a milieu for meeting people of the opposite sex means some people may confuse harassing behavior with courtship. What is seen as flirtation or innocent joking by one person may be viewed as harassment by another.

The most frequently cited definition of sexual harassment was put forward by the EEOC in 1980 during the Carter administration. It read: "Unwelcome sexual advances, requests for sexual favors, and other verbal or physical conduct of a sexual nature constitute sexual harassment when 1) submission to such conduct is made either explicitly or implicitly a term or condition of an individual's employment, 2) submission to or rejection of such conduct by an individual is used as the basis for employment decisions affecting such individual, or 3) such conduct has the purpose or effect of unreasonably interfering with an individual's work performance or creating an intimidating, hostile, or offensive working environment." [7]

This definition and general EEOC guidelines on sexual harassment were affirmed by the Supreme Court in its 1986 ruling in *Meritor Savings Bank v. Vinson*, in which the court held that sexual harassment in the workplace is sex discrimination barred by Title VII of the 1964 Civil Rights Act (*see p. 548*). The court also ruled that such harassment is illegal not only when it results in the loss of a job or a promotion, but also when it creates an offensive or hostile working environment.

Since 1986, the EEOC has elaborated on its sexual harassment guidelines. The agency has noted that both men and women can be victims or perpetrators of harassment. Harassers need not be the victim's supervisor, but can be a co-worker, or, in some cases, even an outsider, such as a customer or a consultant. EEOC guidelines also say there can be illegal sexual harassment between people of the same sex. Further, the victim does not have to be the person at whom the unwelcome sexual conduct is directed. For example, the sexual harassment of one female employee may create an atmosphere that is intimidating to another employee.

Potentially liable employers are also on notice that a finding of sexual harassment does not require that the victim suffer a concrete economic injury, the reasoning being that the victim need not wait for evidence of damage to complain.[8] Finally, a victim seeking redress is not required to have complained to the harasser or to a supervisor, though in determining an organization's liability courts usually take into account whether the company had been informed and whether a suitable grievance procedure existed.[9]

It took years of court decisions before the distinction was formalized between sexual harassment that involves a direct demand for sex in return for advancement or job security and "hostile environment" harassment, which can include lewd remarks and displays of obscene pictures or cartoons. It is the "hostile environment" notion, enunciated by the Supreme Court in the *Meritor*

# Complaints Filed With the EEOC

*The number of sexual harassment complaints filed with the federal Equal Employment Opportunity Commission has increased in recent years. A 1986 Supreme Court decision expanding the definition of sexual harassment to include incidents that create a hostile work environment may account for some of the increase.*

**Sexual harassment complaints filed with the EEOC**

| 1981 | 1982 | 1983 | 1984 | 1985 | 1986 | 1987 | 1988 | 1989 | 1990 |
|------|------|------|------|------|------|------|------|------|------|
| 3,661 | 4,233 | 4,385 | 4,380 | 4,953 | 4,431 | 5,336 | 5,215 | 5,204 | 5,557 |

*Source: Equal Employment Opportunity Commission.*

case, that sometimes creates tough calls involving culture and speech. For example, is it sexual harassment if a male boss calls a woman "babe" or "honey" or if a co-worker exposes his undershorts that are covered with hearts?

Many borderline cases involve behavior less easily dismissed as harmless. Judges have ruled that a hostile environment existed when a supervisor peered over a bathroom stall when a female employee was using the toilet, when a supervisor rubbed up against an employee and talked constantly about sex and when a supervisor kept track of a female employee's menstrual cycle on his office calendar. But in most cases, such behavior was considered harassment only if it was part of an overall pattern that was seen as destructive.

The courts have also ruled that employers can be held liable if they impose improper demands on employees. In 1981, the EEOC successfully sued the owners of a New York City office building because they had required a female lobby attendant, over her protestations, to wear a "short, revealing and sexually provocative" uniform (*EEOC v. Sage Realty*). The woman filed charges after her employer ignored her complaint that she was subjected to propositions and lewd comments from people in the lobby.[10]

Though legally both sexes can be victims of harassment, the overwhelming majority of cases involve men harassing women. Still, female-to-male harassment does occur. In 1982, a federal judge awarded $25,000 to a 33-year-old Wisconsin

# Top Awards to Victims

Though many court awards for sexual harassment are kept secret as a term of settlement, some sums that have been made public are substantial. Following are the top damages imposed on individual harassers and/or their companies in the past five years under state laws. The information was compiled by Jury Verdict Research Inc., a Solon (Ohio) firm that tracks data on personal injury litigation.

*Moore v. Cardinal Services Inc.*
Settled December 1986
Richland, Ohio
A female suffered emotional distress after her former supervisor allegedly forced her to perform oral sex by threatening her with the loss of her job.
Award: **$3,100,000** ($2,800,000 compensatory and $300,000 punitive)

*Bihun v. AT&T Information Systems*
Settled May 1990
Los Angeles
A 37-year-old female personnel manager went on worker's compensation following emotional distress allegedly caused by unwelcome sexual advances from her supervisor. When she returned, her job had been eliminated, and she was transferred to a lateral position with the same pay.
Award: **$2,000,000** ($1,500,000 compensatory and $500,000 punitive)

*Gaffke v. U-Haul of Oregon*
Settled February 1988
Multnomah, Ore.
A female executive suffered emotional distress and lost wages after a shipping and vehicle rental company and its subsidiary discriminated against her in the form of lesser wages, sexual advances from managers and subsequent wrongful termination.
Award: **$1,448,969** ($198,969 compensatory and $1,250,000 punitive)

*O'Connell v. Local Union 25*
Settled October 1989
Wayne, Ill. ·
A 30-year-old female apprentice asbestos worker claimed she suffered sexual harassment, sex discrimination and wrongful discharge. The defendant said she was dismissed for excessive absenteeism.
Award: **$1,100,000** compensatory

*Preston v. Douglas; Soncrant; City of Detroit*
Settled April 1987
Wayne County, Mich.
A 32-year-old female police officer claimed she was sexually solicited by her commander and that her rejection of him resulted in hostility from co-workers, which caused her to be hospitalized for emotional distress.
Award: **$900,000** compensatory

state social security office employee who had charged that he had been demoted after refusing sexual demands from his female supervisor.[11]

### How pervasive is sexual harassment?

Gauging the actual incidence of sexual harassment is difficult, both because definitions of the term are mercurial and, according to some critics, because the problem's seriousness may be exaggerated by ideologues or management consultants who specialize in sexual harassment cases.

Several surveys covering disparate sectors of society have varied widely in their findings. The first broad-scale effort to measure sexual harassment was conducted by *Redbook*

magazine, which surveyed 9,000 women in 1976. Eighty-eight percent of the respondents said they had been victims of harassment and 52 percent said they had been fired or induced to quit a job because of it.[12]

In 1980, a survey was conducted among 20,000 federal workers by the U.S. Merit Systems Protection Board (MSPB), the grievance arbitration board for government employees. Forty-two percent of the females and 15 percent of the males responding said they had been sexually harassed. (An updated, smaller survey conducted by the board in 1987 produced nearly identical results.) According to the MSPB, victims of harassment tended to be young, not married, college-educated, members

of a minority racial or ethnic group (if male), in a trainee position (or office/clerical positions, if male), in a non-traditional position (female law enforcement officers or male secretaries), to have an immediate supervisor of the opposite sex or to have an immediate work group composed predominantly of the opposite sex.[13]

The most recent large-scale survey of sexual harassment was released in September 1990 by the Department of Defense. Of 20,000 U.S. military respondents around the world, 64 percent of the females reported having been sexually harassed, some directly, others in subtler ways such as being subjected to catcalls, dirty looks and teasing. (Only 17 percent of the males reported being harassed.) Of those women reporting direct harassment, 38 percent said they had been touched or "cornered," 15 percent said they had been pressured for sexual favors (compared with only 2 percent of males) and 5 percent said they had been victims of rape or attempted rape.[14]

In the corporate world, recent surveys indicate that 15 percent of women have been sexually harassed within the past year, according to Freada Klein, an organizational development expert who specializes in sexual harassment.[15]

Surveys on college campuses show the number of respondents reporting to have been sexually harassed ranging from 40-70 percent. Bernice R. Sandler, a college specialist at the Center for Women Policy Studies in Washington, says only 2 percent of campus harassment cases involve a professor demanding sex in return for a good grade. Most sexual harassment on campus involves male and female students, she says. On several campuses recently, college men have been taken to task for a practice known as "scoping" — loudly rating the physical attributes of women as they walk by. Sometimes the men will surround a woman and demand that she bare her breasts.

The steadiest barometer of the ebbs and flows of sexual harassment is the number of such complaints filed with EEOC offices. The number of complaints (of which those found to have merit is a fraction) has risen slightly in recent years, reaching 5,557 in 1990 (*see graph, p. 541*). The 1986 Supreme Court decision expanding the definition of sexual harassment to include incidents that create a hostile work environment may account for some of the increase.

The relatively small number of complaints to the EEOC was cited by *Forbes* in a 1989 article that said management consultants specializing in sexual harassment were blowing the problem out of proportion. If the ex-

perts are to be believed, the article stated, at least 35 percent and possibly as many as 90 percent of American women get harassed. If this was true, the article said, the total number of harassment victims could be as high as 49 million. But based on the number of EEOC complaints, the article said, the number of victims would be only 0.0091 percent of the female work force.[16]

Women's groups and others who favor an activist approach to combating sexual harassment say the incidence is significantly underreported. "Women used to think there was nothing they could do about it," says Isabelle Katz Pinzler, director of the women's rights project at the ACLU. Many women decline to file charges for fear of confronting superiors, being labeled a troublemaker or subjecting their personal lives to scrutiny.

The American population at large does not appear to believe that sexual harassment is rampant. Only 26 percent of the women responding to a national survey conducted in September 1986 said they had experienced sexual harassment at work. Only 17 percent of the women and 16 percent of the men thought sexual harassment was "a big problem"; 67 percent of both men and women said it was "somewhat of a problem."[17]

### Do men and women view sexual harassment differently?

Though modern workplace policies seek to minimize distinctions between men and women, sexual harassment is an issue that brings out the contrasts between the sexes. Indeed, today's courts, after decades of striving to treat men and women equally under the law, have begun articulating a doctrine in the sexual harassment area that acknowledges female sensitivities not necessarily shared by men (*see p. 550*). This aspect of the sexual harassment debate divides feminists and revives age-old debates over whether gen-

der traits are inbred or learned.

Perhaps the nub of the sexual harassment issue is the fact that certain types of sexual behavior are interpreted differently by men and women. In a survey of more than 1,200 working men and women in Los Angeles County in 1980-81, sociologist Gutek recorded the reactions of men and women to a sexual proposition from a co-worker: 67 percent of the men but only 17 percent of the women said they would be flattered by a proposition; 63 percent of the women but only 15 percent of the men said they would be insulted by it.[18] Another survey described a man in an office eyeing a women's body up and down; 24 percent of the women respondents characterized such behavior as harassment, but only 8 percent of the men did.[19]

Surprisingly, however, men and women were roughly in agreement about what qualifies as sexual harassment in a nationwide poll taken for *Time* in 1986. Majorities of both sexes agreed that sexual harassment occurs if a male boss or supervisor makes remarks to a female worker that contain sexual references or double meanings; frequently puts his arm around the woman's shoulders or back; insists on telling her sexual jokes; pressures her to go to dinner with him; or asks her to have sex with him. Pollster Hal Quinley speculates that the responses of men and women were similar because men are more suspicious of such behavior when they see it in other men.

Some differences between the genders are observable in everyday life — the fact that men are raised to be the sexual aggressor, that men more than women overtly ogle the opposite sex in public and the fact that men more than women like to look at naked pictures of the opposite sex. "It is difficult to imagine a suit by a longshoreman complaining of mental stress due to the display of nude male centerfolds by female co-workers," writes Ellen Frankel Paul, a political scientist at Bowling Green State University in Ohio.[20]

Why these differences exist is a question for biologists, philosophers and theologians. What is clear to those who study sexual harassment is that the effects of these sex differences are thrown into sharp relief in the workplace. The work world continues to be dominated by men, and many women still are looking over their shoulders worrying whether they have established their professional worth. "Studies show that men view sexual harassment as less serious, that it's merely pleasantries and teasing, whereas women see it as more threatening, because men are in power," Sandler notes.

Gutek agrees. "In Western society, men are 'naturally' viewed as serious workers, and a sexual overture or proposition from a woman does not alter that view of them," she writes. ". . . A man can relish an overture from an attractive young woman . . . without having to wonder if she will fire him when the affair is over." [21]

What's more, it has long been noted that women, more often than men, are reluctant to challenge authority figures, while men, often in positions of power, are reluctant to relinquish their authority. Research published this year confirms that differences in degrees of assertiveness persist. A laboratory experiment by Linda L. Carli, a psychology professor at Wellesley College, consisted of having men and women watch the same videotapes showing a colleague deliver a persuasive talk. Male and female viewers relied on different non-verbal cues for determining status of the male and female presenters. Carli concluded that women are more influential with men when their facial expressions

are warm, their posture is relaxed and their speech is tentative. In other words, women are less threatening to men when they are perceived as less competent, a value that gets absorbed by both men and women.[22] As women begin to break out of the non-assertive mold, Carli

> As women begin to break out of the non-assertive mold at work, some men may attempt to trivialize the contributions of women by treating them as sex objects.

says, some men may be tempted to "trivialize the contributions of women by treating them as sex objects."

Men who pursue women sexually at work often accuse women of dressing seductively and "asking for it." * "If a woman dresses to kill . . . hoping to arouse the interest of those men she likes, non-targeted men receive many of the same visual cues," writes Frederic Hayward, executive director of Men's Rights Inc. in Sacramento, Calif. "More and more men are, in fact, complaining that provocative dress constitutes sexual harassment against them." [23]

Women, by contrast, may view dressing as a challenge or even a burden

---

*About half of the people responding to the September 1986 survey conducted for *Time* — 49 percent of the women and 53 percent of the men — agreed with the following statement: "Women who complain about sexual harassment have often asked for trouble by the way they dress or behave."

needed to maximize their marketability. Feminist journalist Naomi Wolf writes in her new book, *The Beauty Myth: How Images of Beauty Are Used Against Women*, of how women are expected to complement their job skills with a "professional beauty qualification" that entails great psychic and financial costs.

Still, the idea persists that women more than men are more likely to use sex to get ahead professionally. Seventy-eight percent of the women and 86 percent of the men responding to a 1981 *Harvard Business Review* survey agreed with the statement, "Women can and often do use their sexual attractiveness to their own advantage." [24]

### How are organizations dealing with sexual harassment?

"Sexuality is emotional, not rational," Gutek writes. "It may be an important aspect of life, but can be viewed as a frivolous concern at work compared to weighty matters of commerce, government and education." [25]

Since those words were written in 1985, American companies have been examining sexual harassment with an eye on the bottom line. Ignoring sexual harassments can cost the average company up to $6.7 million a year in absenteeism, employee turnover, low morale and low productivity.[26] A psychology professor who gives seminars on sexual harassment told a reporter for *Fortune* that her biggest problem was getting male managers to take the subject seriously. "I'm glad we're getting a course on this so I can finally figure out how to do it," they would joke, until she reminded them of the latest settlement figures.[27]

Many of the hundreds of companies that have adopted sexual harassment policies do more than post the policy on a bulletin board. Aware that courts may hold them responsible for their managers' effectiveness in maintaining a work environment free of harassment, firms such as International Business Machines Corp. and E. I. du Pont de Nemours & Co. regularly put on training seminars and hire consultants with a specialty in the subject to show videos and act out hypothetical scenes. Disciplinary actions may save much in litigation costs; the *Working Woman* survey of *Fortune* 500 companies found that 20 percent of sexual harassers were fired.

The federal government, in general, has blazed a trail ahead of private business in clamping down on sexual harassment. Federal agencies have had policies against sexual harassment in place since 1980.* States are starting to take action, too. California has had a law in effect since 1985 that makes it an unlawful employment practice to fail to take reasonable steps to prevent sexual harassment. Minnesota enacted a law in 1989 requiring all educational institutions in the state to develop policies on sexual harassment and sexual violence. This spring, Maine passed a law requiring all employers to post a sexual harassment policy and to provide training seminars in the topic for new employees.

In government as in the private sector, establishing a policy does not guarantee that supervisors and victims of sexual harassment will make use of grievance procedures. The 1980 survey by the Merit Systems Protection Board found that only 2 percent of those who claimed to have been harassed took action. By 1987, seven years after federal policies against harassment were introduced, only 5 percent of those surveyed had reported complaints.

On college campuses, numerous codes against sexual harassment are

now in effect. Policies at Harvard University and the University of Iowa prohibit "amorous relationships between faculty members and anyone under their supervision." A similar ban at Antioch College and Kalamazoo College forces professors to steer clear of all students. At the College of William and Mary, freshman students beginning this fall will be required to attend a workshop on sexual assault and harassment.

Antioch has one of the most far-reaching policies. Urged on by a campus feminist group called Womyn of Antioch (the spelling is intended to be non-sexist), the college calls for the removal of all sexual offenders from the campus within 24 hours of an allegation. Offenses include rape and assault but also leering or pressure for dates, and the determination of guilt is made by a single person, an appointed "advocate." The ACLU has called Antioch's policy "incredibly harsh" and says it denies due process.[28]

Organizations that want to do something about sexual harassment often turn to outside groups for help. The Association for the Sexually Harassed in Philadelphia puts on seminars, conducts support groups, advises businesses on sexual

harassment policies and conducts statistical research. President Cheryl Gomez-Preston founded the group in 1988 after she successfully sued the Detroit police department for sexual harassment, winning $675,000. The organization called 9to5, the National Association of Working Women, in May 1989 created a hotline for victims of abuse in the workplace. It gets as many as 420 calls a day dealing with sexual harassment, pregnancy discrimination and layoffs.

Costly, multi-level efforts to organize against sexual harassment have prompted critics to argue that women, instead of demanding a workplace perfectly cushioned against all bumps along life's road, should learn to handle sexual harassment on their own. "A girl in high school should learn to deal with unwanted overtures before she gets to the work world," says anti-feminist Phyllis Schlafly, head of the conservative Eagle Forum. "People don't need a federal policeman standing at every watercooler."

"I'd rather see the man and woman resolve it between themselves," acknowledges consultant Susan Webb. "Everybody loses when it's reported to a supervisor. Half the group is mad at him, half at her." ∎

# BACKGROUND

## Women at Work

I ncidents that today would be called sexual harassment show up in American history as far back as Colonial times, when court records mentioned cases of servants being seduced by employers. In 1734, a group of female servants published a notice in the New York *Weekly Journal* saying, "We think it reasonable

we should not be beat by our mistresses' husbands, they being too strong and perhaps may do tender women mischief."[29] In 19th-century mill towns, single girls living in boardinghouses and working in low-paying jobs as seamstresses were often pressured for sex by factory supervisors who viewed them as having looser morals than "proper ladies" who lived with their families.

The desire to protect working women from illicit sex was one motivator in the "Purity Crusade" of the turn-of-the-century Progressive Era and in the unionization and workplace protection struggles of the early 20th century. A court case that resonates in modern times was recorded in Chicago in 1908, when two women took a saloon keeper to court on behalf of a young immigrant woman who had been fired from the saloon when he learned she was pregnant with his illegitimate child. The women lost.[30]

It wasn't until the early 1960s that women began entering the work force in numbers large enough to create a societal consciousness that would formalize sexual harassment as a problem in need of a remedy. In 1959, there were 22 million women in the American work force, or 33 percent, according to the Labor Department. By 1991, working women numbered 57 million, or 45.5 percent of the work force. Whereas in the past women often worked in entry-level jobs and then quit when they got married, most women now work out of economic necessity. In today's inflationary economy where two-income families are the norm, 11 million families are headed by women, compared with 1.5 million in 1950. Fifty-eight percent of women in today's labor force are either single, divorced, widowed, separated or have husbands earning less than $15,000.[31]

The seeds of future sexual harassment adjudication were planted during debate over the monumental 1964 Civil Rights bill. Though most of the debate revolved around the goal of protecting blacks in the segregated South, the bill's impact was broadened significantly when Title VII, dealing with discrimination in employment, was expanded to include sex discrimination. The 1964 bill also created the Equal Opportunity Employment Commission to investigate discrimination complaints against individuals, though initially it was given no enforcement powers.

In society at large during the 1960s, the availability of the birth control pill meant women could postpone childbearing and launch a career. The sexual revolution brought heretofore behind-the-scenes sexual behavior into the open, and the rise of the women's movement heightened demand for equality of the sexes.

## '70s Activism

The 1970s ushered in an era of dramatic efforts to curb workplace discrimination of all forms, as government and private employers launched affirmative action programs. In 1972, Congress passed the Equal Employment Opportunity Act. It gave the EEOC a presidentially appointed independent general counsel with authority to bring cease-and-desist orders and bring suit in federal court against employers judged guilty of workplace discrimination. The same year, Congress passed the Education Act Amendments, which prohibited sex discrimination at schools and universities receiving federal funds.

Within a few years, sexual harassment complaints had begun working their way through the courts. The first case was brought in Arizona when two female employees of a manufacturer of eye-care products resigned because of repeated verbal and physical advances of their supervisor.[32] The district court declined to hold the company liable because the supervisor's conduct served no employer policy and didn't benefit the employer. It called the supervisor's conduct "a personal proclivity, peculiarity or mannerism."

Sexual harassment victims during these years began suing under a variety of laws, principally Title VII of the 1964 Civil Rights Act. In 1977,

the U.S. Court of Appeals for the District of Columbia held in *Barnes v. Castle* that sexual harassment constitutes sex discrimination under Title VII if it "adversely affects job condition." Plaintiffs also sued under state anti-discrimination laws, state fair employment practice laws and other state tort or contract laws citing infliction of emotional distress, assault and battery or breach of employment contract.

It was in 1977 that the first charge of sexual harassment of students was brought under Title IX of the 1972 Education Amendments. In *Yale v. Alexander*, an undergraduate at Yale University said her professor offered her an "A" in his course if she would accept his sexual proposition. She refused and received a "C." Her suit demanding that the grade be removed from her transcript was joined by four other students and a faculty member. In 1980, the suit was dismissed because the plaintiff had graduated and because Yale in the meantime had established a sexual harassment grievance procedure.

With momentum from court action, it was only a matter of time before the first major studies of sexual harassment appeared. Lin Farley's *Sexual Shakedown: The Sexual Harassment of Women on the Job* (1978) defined the concept and compiled anecdotes, while Catherine A. MacKinnon's *Sexual Harassment of Working Women: A Case of Sex Discrimination* (1979) argued for legal remedies. Famed anthropologist Margaret Mead weighed in with a widely noted article calling for a taboo on sexual relations in the workplace.[33]

Also at this time, sensational news accounts of sexual harassment prompted a congressional investigation into harassment in the federal government. In 1978, federal contractors were required by regulation to ensure a working environment free

*Continued on p. 548*

# Chronology

**1960s** *Women begin surging into the work force. The women's movement gathers steam.*

### July 2, 1964
President Lyndon B. Johnson signs the Civil Rights Act prohibiting employment discrimination and creating the Equal Employment Opportunity Commission (EEOC) to investigate complaints.

———•———

**1970s** *Sexual harassment cases begin flooding the courts. Women's groups and academics formalize the concept of sexual harassment.*

### March 24, 1972
President Richard M. Nixon signs the Equal Employment Opportunity Act, giving the EEOC enforcement powers and expanding coverage of Title VII of the Civil Rights Act.

### June 23, 1972
Nixon signs the 1972 Education Amendments. Title IX forbids any education program receiving federal funds from discriminating on the basis of sex.

### 1975
First reported court case on sexual harassment arises when two female employees in Arizona resign because of verbal and physical advances from their supervisor (*Corne v. Bausch & Lomb*).

### November 1976
*Redbook* magazine publishes the results of the first major survey on sexual harassment in the workplace.

### 1977
A Yale University undergraduate and four other students file the first sexual harassment charges under Title IX of the 1972 Education Amendments. D.C. Circuit Court of Appeals rules that sexual harassment constitutes sex discrimination under Title VII of the Civil Rights Act if it "adversely affects a job condition" (*Barnes v. Costle*).

### June 30, 1978
President Jimmy Carter issues an executive order consolidating the government's fair employment enforcement under the EEOC.

### Oct. 13, 1978
Carter signs the Civil Service Reform Act prohibiting personnel practice from discriminating on the basis of "race, color, religion, sex or national origin." The law creates the Merit Systems Protection Board as the government's board of appeal for grievance procedures.

### Dec. 12, 1979
Office of Personnel Management issues policy statement defining sexual harassment and noting that the practice is unacceptable.

———•———

**1980s** *Supreme Court issues its first major ruling on sexual harassment.*

### Nov. 10, 1980
EEOC publishes guidelines defining sexual harassment.

### June 19, 1986
Supreme Court, in its first sexual harassment case, rules that sexual harassment in the workplace is sex discrimination in violation of Title VII of the Civil Rights Act. Such harassment is illegal not only when it results in the loss of a job or promotion, but also when it creates an offensive or hostile working environment (*Meritor Savings Bank v. Vinson*).

### December 1988
*Working Woman* magazine publishes a major survey on sexual harassment in *Fortune* 500 companies.

———•———

**1990s** *Stepped-up government action against sexual harassment. Feminists win in the courts.*

### September 1990
Pentagon releases largest military survey on sexual harassment.

### March 19, 1990
EEOC issues updated guidelines on preventing sexual harassment.

### Jan. 18, 1991
Sixth U.S. Circuit Court of Appeals in Florida rules that nude pinups in the workplace constitute illegal sexual harassment (*Robinson v. Jacksonville Shipyards*).

### Jan. 23, 1991
Ninth U.S. Circuit Court of Appeals recognizes doctrine of the "reasonable woman" in considering what qualifies as sexual harassment (*Ellison v. Brady*).

Continued from p. 546

from harassment. In 1979, the House Post Office and Civil Service Committee held hearings on sexual harassment, and the Office of Personnel Management issued a government-wide directive warning of the problem. Meanwhile, the EEOC's powers were again boosted when it was handed what had previously been the Labor Department's responsibilities for enforcing the 1963 Equal Pay Act and the 1967 Age Discrimination in Employment Act.

In the closing weeks of the Carter administration in November 1980, the EEOC, then chaired by Eleanor Holmes Norton,* issued its influential guidelines on sexual harassment (*see p. 540*). They were adopted by most federal agencies and many private organizations.

### Reagan-era Reverses

When the Reagan administration came to power, the EEOC's activism against workplace discrimination was curbed. Sen. Orrin G. Hatch, R-Utah, in April 1981 held Labor Committee hearings to study the EEOC's new sexual harassment guidelines to determine whether they were too inclusive and might create more antagonism against women, place too great a burden on employers and, in Hatch's words, "have the potential for infringing upon freedom of expression of others." [34]

Among those testifying at Hatch's hearing was anti-feminist Phyllis Schlafly. "Sexual harassment on the job is not a problem for the virtuous woman, except in the rarest of cases," Schlafly said. "When a woman walks across the room, she speaks with a universal body language that most men intuitively understand. Men hardly ever ask sexual favors of women from whom the certain answer is no."

---

*Norton currently is the non-voting delegate from the District of Columbia in the House of Representatives.

In 1982, President Ronald Reagan named Clarence Thomas to head the EEOC. (Thomas, now an appeals court judge, is President Bush's nominee to the Supreme Court.) During his eight-year tenure, Thomas sharply cut the agency's reliance on goals and timetables in affirmative action cases. Many Carter-era staff members who had been activists against sex and race discrimination left the agency. Because of budget cuts, EEOC spending on training, investigation and travel were trimmed, and agency public service announcements to combat discrimination were ended. Staff began to shrink (it would drop from 3,777 in 1980 to 2,853 in 1990[35]). The number of charges of race, sex, religious and age discrimination that were investigated and litigated also shrunk, while the number that were found to have "no cause" increased. The EEOC's backlog of unresolved cases doubled during the 1980s.

In 1986, Ralph G. Neas, director of the Leadership Council on Civil Rights, called Thomas a "disappointment," saying he had failed to vigorously prosecute job biases against minorities and the aged.[36] Thomas defended his record by saying the agency had restructured to process its caseload faster and more efficiently while investigating complaints more thoroughly.

## Meritor Ruling

The most important development of the 1980s in the sexual harassment area was the Supreme Court's 1986 ruling confirming a body of case law that had considered sexual harassment a violation of federal sex discrimination law. The facts in *Meritor Savings Bank v. Vinson* were as follows: Mechelle Vinson was hired as a teller-trainee at a bank

that was later merged with others to form Meritor. Within four years, she became an assistant branch manager. Soon after her first promotion, her supervisor, Sidney L. Taylor, invited her to dinner and then to a motel. At first, she refused, then she agreed, fearing for her job. They had sex 40-50 times over the next few years. He embarrassed her in front of co-workers and, according to her testimony, forcibly raped her. She then went on a two-month leave of absence during which she was fired.[37]

After she filed suit for sexual harassment, the supervisor denied the charges and accused her of retaliating for a different office dispute. His witnesses testified that Vinson had dressed provocatively, and spoken of her sexual fantasies. The district court concluded that Vinson had not proved her case because the involvement had been voluntary. Because the bank had a policy against discrimination and she had not used the bank's grievance procedure, the district court ruled the bank could not be held liable. But an appeals court reversed the lower court because it had not considered the hostile environment brand of sexual harassment. It held that the employer is liable for a hostile environment whether or not it knew about the sexually harassing behavior.

As the Supreme Court took on the case, women's groups and government and business groups watched with interest, waiting to see whether the court would confirm the EEOC's 1980 guidelines on sexual harassment and find employers liable for harassment conducted by employees. The EEOC worked with the Justice Department in submitting an amicus brief, seeking a middle course between extremes. As EEOC Commissioner Rosalie Gaull Silberman recalled, on one side was the narrow view that sexual harassment cannot constitute unlawful sex discrimina-

*Continued on p. 550*

# Two Trips Through the Courts

Most sexual harassment incidents are never reported and those that are often get resolved by managers on the scene. Victims who seek legal redress face a hard road — the average civil lawsuit for sexual harassment takes two to three years. To many, this reality is evidence that few women "cry wolf" and spend years of time, money and anguish pursuing charges that were fabricated. "It takes a superhuman effort to go to court," says Alison Wetherfield, legal director of the NOW Legal Defense and Education Fund in New York City. "It would have to be one enormous vengeance suit to get that far." Here are two case studies of women who saw themselves as sexual harassment victims and went to court.

**Catherine A. Broderick** was a 28-year-old attorney who went to work in the Arlington, Va., office of the Securities and Exchange Commission (SEC), the federal agency that enforces government regulations on corporate financial transactions. It soon became apparent that some of the chief attorneys in the 40-person office were having affairs with their secretaries and junior attorneys and were giving them cash awards and promotions. Drinking parties and long afternoon jogs were common during the work week for those lower-level females who cooperated. The agency was run "like a brothel," with managers competing to acquire mistresses, Broderick recalled.†

She began complaining about sexual harassment by the managers. She was soon enduring poor performance reviews and threats that she would be fired and was called a "festering morale problem." In 1984, having failed to win any promotions, Broderick was transferred to SEC headquarters. When she took her complaint to court, she financed her counsel by selling some of her possessions while the defendants relied on government attorneys. In her suit, Broderick cited sexual overtures between supervisors and underlings in the office and the fact that an attorney working under her who was thought to be having an affair with the boss won promotions that were denied Broderick. It was a notable example of the "hostile" work environment that had been included in the Supreme Court's 1986 definition of sexual harassment (*see p. 548*).

In May 1988, nine years after the case began, a district court judge ruled in Broderick's favor. The SEC was required to pay her $128,000 in back pay and give her a promotion. The three SEC attorneys found to have committed sexual harassment were later cleared by a special counsel investigation, and so no SEC action was taken against them. In the aftermath, Broderick, who had begun therapy, expressed pessimism that her career would ever recover.

**Kathleen Neville** was a 27-year-old television advertising saleswoman working for what was then Taft Broadcasting in Buffalo. In 1981, her supervisor kissed her against her wishes and repeatedly demanded sexual favors, which she rejected. Soon, the supervisor began finding fault with her work, citing an unexcused absence from the office. When she finally reported the situation to the station manager, he confronted her supervisor, who denied all.

Despite excellent performance reviews, Neville was abruptly given two weeks to find another job. Pointing to the company's written sexual harassment policy, she countered that she would challenge the decision. Neville was then placed on leave while a female accountant investigated the charges as an "impartial" arbiter.

In November 1981, her termination for "poor performance" was made official. Working with her lawyer, Neville then filed a complaint with the Equal Opportunity Employment Commission (EEOC). In the meantime, she received anonymous death threats by phone late at night, and her new employer was approached with commentary on her work history by an employee of the station that had fired her.

Receiving a right-to-sue letter from the EEOC, she filed in federal court in Buffalo in mid-1982, claiming sex discrimination in violation of Title VII of the 1964 Civil Rights Act. After six postponements, the trial began in December 1984. The defense attorneys brought in a surprise witness, the manager of a gas grill company who said he had received poor service from Neville when purchasing advertising on the TV station where she worked. Neville said the testimony was made up. Nevertheless, her own lawyer said it was damaging.

Next came a wait of more than two years for the judge's ruling. Neville had moved to Washington, and was told to fly back to Buffalo as her lawyer picked up the verdict. "A favorable decision would not return me to my role as a valued employee of Channel 2," she later wrote of her thoughts while waiting. "It would not give me back the lost years. It would not take away the gossip, and the whispers, and the stigma of being 'the sexual harassment lady.' " ††
Her lawyer told her that after waiting seven years and spending $500,000, she'd lost. The judge had made some technical criticisms of her defense and noted that in Title VII cases, the burden of proof is on the plaintiff.

With a more specialized team of lawyers on board, the oral arguments for her appeal were presented in May 1987, in New York City. The district court's ruling that Taft had legitimate business reasons for terminating her was affirmed. Two months later, she was asked to appear in court in Buffalo again to answer Taft's suit seeking payment for the company's legal costs. Though she was already $138,000 in debt, Neville was required to pay partial fees. She later wrote a book about her case.

---

† Quoted in *The Washington Post*, June 6, 1988.

†† Kathleen Neville, *Corporate Attractions* (1990).

Continued from p. 548

tion under Title VII. On the other was "the overly broad view that would have made employers strictly liable for all sexual conduct in the workplace. If employers, public and private, were made liable for everything, in practice they might feel liable for nothing, and do nothing."[38] Too much policing might also limit women's career advancement and infringe on their social life, Silberman wrote. There was concern that Title VII's provisions not be trivialized by being used to police flirtation, sexual innuendo or vulgar language.

In handing down the ruling, the court confirmed that the sex discrimination provisions of Title VII do apply to sexual harassment. Associate Justice William H. Rehnquist wrote that the language of Title VII is not limited to "economic" or "tangible" discrimination, and that an employer is responsible for maintaining "an environment free from discriminatory intimidation, ridicule and insult." The majority agreed with EEOC guidelines that employers were not automatically liable, but cautioned that the mere existence of a policy against sexual harassment and an internal grievance procedure did not insulate an employer from liability, though such facts are relevant. ∎

Numerous observers commented on the freedom of speech question raised by the *Robinson* case. There are no easy answers to banning tasteful nudes, said Dianna Johnston, an assistant legal counsel at the EEOC. "It's all on a case-by-case basis, and to make a determination, you'd have to know more. One consideration is how much, how often, the offensive behavior is. And is the picture sitting on a guy's desk facing him, or is it on a wall where no one can miss it?"[40]

### The 'Reasonable Woman'

A far-reaching sexual harassment ruling in California in January altered a legal doctrine that goes back to the early 19th century. Students of American law have long been taught to analyze behavior that is being legally challenged through the eyes of the "reasonable man." After the rise of feminism in the 1960s and '70s, most legal writers replaced the "reasonable man" concept with the gender-neutral "reasonable person." But in *Ellison v. Brady*, the 9th U.S. Circuit Court of Appeals formalized the doctrine of the "reasonable woman."

The case involved Kerry Ellison and Sterling Gray, both employees of the Internal Revenue Service office in San Mateo, Calif. They were not working together and were not well acquainted when they chanced to have lunch together. He asked her out for a drink. She refused. She then began receiving unwelcome love letters. He frightened her and she thought he was crazy. "I know that you are worth knowing with or without sex," Gray wrote. "I have enjoyed you so much over the past few months. Watching you. Experiencing you from so far away."

After Ellison complained to her supervisor, Gray was transferred to another office, but after he filed a union grievance, he was scheduled

# CURRENT SITUATION

## Free Speech Issues

Proponents of strong action to combat sexual harassment have been buoyed in recent months by developments in the courts, government and Congress.

In January, feminists hailed a first-of-its-kind court ruling from Florida upholding a female ship welder's complaint about having to look at pinups of nude women while on the job. In *Robinson v. Jacksonville Shipyards*, Lois Robinson, one of six women on a shipyard staff of 846, testified that she had complained repeatedly to her supervisors about sexual teasing and the presence of pictures, many from calendars published by equipment supply companies, displaying such images as a nude woman's body stamped with "USDA Choice" and a dartboard made from a drawing of a woman's breast. In response, her supervisors

said the workers had a constitutional right to post the pictures. Robinson filed suit in 1986.

The trial was notable because it was the first time expert witnesses were permitted in a sexual harassment case. The experts introduced the sociologist's notion of "sex role spillover," a term referring to the intrusion into the workplace of gender-based roles of female as sex object and male as sexual aggressor.

In a verdict that has caused employers to re-examine their policies, Judge Howell W. Melton rejected what he called the shipyard management's "ostrich defense."[39] He barred the shipyard from permitting calendars and posters with nude or partially clad women, held two employees personally liable and ordered the shipyard to pay Robinson's legal fees. "Pornography in the workplace may be far more threatening to women workers than it is to the world at large," Melton wrote. "Pornography on an employer's wall or desk communicates a message about the way he views women, a view strikingly at odds with the way women wish to be viewed in the workplace."

Continued on p. 552

# Harassment in the Halls of Congress

egal remedies for sexual harassment are available to all members of the American work force — except in the Washington enclave known as Capitol Hill. Congress has always exempted its own employees from laws it passes to protect U.S. workers against discrimination, health and safety risks and unfair labor practices. Hence there is no small irony in the emergence in recent years of reports of sexual harassment by members of Congress themselves.

Three incidents surfaced in 1988 alone. Rep. Floyd H. Flake, D-N.Y., was accused by a former aide at the Queens (N.Y.) church where he is pastor of harassing her into leaving her job after she ended a sexual affair with him. Rep. Gus Savage, D-Ill., was accused of making persistent, unwelcome sexual demands on a Peace Corps volunteer during a trip to Africa (the House ethics committee later expressed disapproval of his conduct but imposed no punishment). And in the episode with the most lasting impact, then-Rep. Jim Bates, D-Calif., was accused by two female aides of fondling them and commenting on their anatomy in the presence of others.

The Bates case was a turning point because the chief accuser, Dorena Bertussi, became the first to file a sexual harassment charge with the House ethics committee. Bertussi said she decided to come forward because she was angry and felt that if someone didn't do it, other women would be hurt. She later learned that female colleagues in Bates' office had had similar experiences. "We used to write the poor guy memos since we didn't want to be with him," Bertussi recalls.

After she had gone to work for another House member, Bertussi agreed to speak anonymously for a story in the Capitol Hill newspaper *Roll Call.* Then everything mushroomed. When Bates didn't take any responsibility for his acts, she filed the complaint. Bates denied the story and executed what Bertussi calls a damage control strategy. The ethics panel rejected Bertussi's initial complaint because it wasn't notarized. A second one was filed, but it wasn't acknowledged for almost a year. Bertussi never testified to members, only to staff, she says, and she learned of results only through the press. Meanwhile, Bates' staff warned her that Bates was planning to release damaging information about her past. That led her to believe he'd hired a private detective to probe her, a charge Bates denies.

In October 1990, two years after Bertussi filed her complaint, the ethics committee sent Bates a "letter of reproval," one of its lightest penalties. In accepting the committee's resolution, Bates said: "Times are changing. Members of Congress will be carefully scrutinized on personal and professional behavior."

Bertussi was not satisfied. She made plans to sue Bates civilly but abandoned them when the four-termer lost his re-election bid. Bates, who says the case was not a major factor in his losing race, appeared this May on Cable News Net-

work's "Larry King Live." He said he didn't think Bertussi's charges were accurate, but admitted that some of his actions had crossed bounds and that he had learned a lot about sexual harassment and paid a price with his family.

Bertussi, who now works for a trade association, spoke about sexual harassment at a February 1990 meeting of the Capitol Hill branch of the National Women's Political Caucus. Numerous women approached her, many in tears, to tell of their own sexual harassment experiences. Many said they were surprised to see how many women "buy into the system," how female supervisors would tell them, "What's wrong with you, honey, can't you take a joke?"

The caucus appointed a task force to study sexual harassment on the Hill, where more than 20,000 people are employed. This spring, it launched a petition drive urging members to pledge to remove sexual harassment from their offices. In announcing the pledge drive, the caucus was joined by Rep. Mary Rose Oakar, D-Ohio, who criticized the "plantation mentality" of Congress, and Del. Eleanor Holmes Norton, D-D.C., head of the Equal Employment Opportunity Commission during the Carter administration, who noted that sexual harassment flourishes in "male bastions" such as Congress.

As of early August, 200 of 535 members had signed the pledge. Despite the caucus' efforts at bipartisanship, however, political forces entered the picture. House Speaker Thomas S. Foley, D-Wash., citing a Speaker's general policy of detachment, declined to sign the pledge, though he commended the caucus' work and urged members to take sexual harassment seriously. He was immediately attacked by Rep. William E. Dannemyer, R-Calif., for his "lukewarm" support of the effort to eliminate sexual harassment, prompting the caucus and other women's groups to defend Foley by calling Dannemeyer a political opportunist.

Though the Dannemayer flap passed, a more substantive area of contention remained. Foley's statement praised the women's caucus for highlighting existing procedures for handling sexual harassment complaints under House rules and through the Office of Fair Employment Practices, an entity set up temporarily in 1988 and made permanent this year. To Bertussi and others in the National Women's Political Caucus, the existing House and Senate procedures represent "a sham and a false hope." Victims of sexual harassment on Capitol Hill are still denied outside legal recourse, they point out, and accused members are judged by other members who are reluctant, for political reasons, to be severe. "Records are sealed, and nothing gets out to change anyone's behavior," Bertussi said. As a plaintiff, "you're forbidden to talk about it or carry it any further."

Rep. Andy Jacobs Jr., D-Ind., over the years has repeatedly introduced a bill that would extend to the legislative branch the workplace protections of the 1964 Civil Rights Act and other laws. It has never emerged from subcommittee.

Continued from p. 550

to return. He sent her another letter. Ellison then filed a suit against the IRS citing sexual harassment. Her case was dismissed in a summary judgment by the district court, but on appeal the 9th U.S. Circuit Court ruled that the district court should hear the full case.

"Because women are disproportionately victims of rape and sexual assault," wrote Judge Robert R. Beezer, "women have a stronger incentive to be concerned with sexual behavior. Women who are victims of mild forms of sexual harassment may understandably worry whether a harasser's conduct is merely a prelude to a violent sexual assault. Men, who are rarely victims of sexual assault, may view sexual conduct in a vacuum without a full appreciation of the underlying threat of violence that a woman may perceive." [41]

Like the shipyard pornography ruling, the *Ellison* case caused ambivalence among legal observers. Pinzler at the ACLU, while applauding the judge's intent, worries that it sets up a double standard. "The reasonable woman standard suggests that reasonable women and reasonable men can't see things the same way," she says. ". . . A reasonable woman might be seen as more prudish, which is not true."

# Government Actions

In Washington this spring, the EEOC, citing a rise in sexual harassment complaints, implemented new procedures to accelerate complaint processing (from one to two years to as little as a month) and sent packets of sample legal pleadings to women's groups and lawyers. "Sexual harassment is the crime of discrimination which keeps on hurting," said current EEOC Chairman Evan J. Kemp Jr. "No time should be

wasted in protecting its victims and bringing an employer who harasses to court." [42]

Kemp, however, has complained that 1980s budget cuts have continued to crimp the amounts his agency can spend on litigation. And some outside critics call the new EEOC activism a public relations stunt launched at a time when the Bush administration has been opposing provisions in the current civil rights bill that would permit punitive and compensatory damages in sex discrimination cases (*see below*). "Evan Kemp is more accessible, more high-profile than [Clarence] Thomas," says Claudia Withers of the Women's Legal Defense Fund, but "the EEOC has yet to exert the leadership function that is its right."

## '91 Civil Rights Bill

This summer's debate in Congress over the civil rights bill was dominated by the issue of racial quotas in hiring. [43] But sexual harassment issues arose in the debate over punitive and compensatory damages.

Title VII of the 1964 Civil Rights Act contains no damage remedies for victims of race, sex, age, religious and disability discrimination who suffer medical, psychological or financial harm; it awards only "make-whole relief," such as back pay and attorney's fees. (Victims of race discrimination can sue for damages under Section 1981, a Civil War-era statute.)

In the weeks leading up to the floor debate on this year's bill, three substitute versions of the damages provisions of the bill were prepared. The version offered by House Minority Leader Robert H. Michel, R-Ill., and backed by President Bush and many in the business community, included up to $150,000 in damages for harassment but none for other gender discrimination. It would generally avoid jury trials. A version offered by Reps. Edolphus Towns, D-N.Y.,

and Patricia Schroeder, D-Colo., and backed by the National Women's Law Center would have offered unlimited damages for discrimination. A third version, offered by House Judiciary Committee Chairman Jack Brooks, D-Texas, and Rep. Hamilton Fish, R-N.Y., would have limited punitive damages to $150,000, or the amount of compensatory damages, whichever is greater.

Arguing for unlimited damages, Rep. Patsy T. Mink, D-Hawaii, said: "Times have changed since Title VII was first enacted. Millions and millions of women have gone into the workplace. ... They are harassed, they are not given job opportunities, they are not given promotions, they are not considered equal at the job site. ... All we are saying is, if a worker can go today to court and recover unlimited damages which they have personally suffered and punitive damages against their employer for having perpetrated those injustices if they come in under race discrimination, why should they not be able to do this under sex discrimination?"

Opponents derided the damages proposals, which would require jury trials, as a way to "pad the pockets of trial lawyers," as Rep. Steve Gunderson, R-Wis., put it. "A jury will go for a deep pocket and bring a skewed view to the issue," said Diane Generous of the National Association of Manufacturers, which led a coalition against the Democrats' bill. "A lot of individuals don't have a lot of sympathy for corporations and whether or not in fact there has been wrongdoing, they say the company can afford to pay."

It was the Brooks-Fish version, with limited damages, that was voted into the bill that finally passed the House, 273-158, on June 5. "Unfortunately, we have to face reality," Brooks said before the vote. "A provision that provides unlimited damages for women in a bill would

Continued on p. 554

# At Issue:

## Is sexual harassment primarily a "woman's problem"?

SANDRA THOMPSON

*Assistant managing editor/newsfeatures,*
*St. Petersburg Times*
FROM *ST. PETERSBURG TIMES,* APRIL 4, 1991.

### yes

**e**very woman I know has been sexually harassed in the workplace. We talk about it among ourselves — in private — but not to anyone in a position to challenge such behavior, even if that person is us. . . .

The obvious reason we don't talk is that we don't want to lose our jobs. We don't want to confront our bosses or more powerful colleagues about inappropriate behavior, because we fear getting fired or being blocked from advancement. That's one reason, and it's 100 percent valid.

But there is another less obvious, more insidious, reason we don't talk. We don't talk because we are used to making excuses for men's behavior. We're taught to do it from the time we are little girls. "Your father had a hard day at the office, the factory, the hospital, the courtroom" we were told to explain away the kind of behavior by our fathers that we'd never accept from our mothers. . . .

We wanted to believe the excuses, not because we depended on our father (or our grandfather or uncle) for financial support — children aren't that calculating — but because we loved our father and wanted to respect him. We were told to respect him, and to admire him, because he was our father. Therefore, anything he did that was not deserving of our respect didn't count. We later transferred our ability to deny reality into the workplace, to our bosses and to public officials and other men in positions of power.

A woman professor I know told me that when she was a graduate student her master's thesis adviser leaned across his desk and grabbed and squeezed one of her breasts. At the time, she didn't acknowledge to him that it had happened, and she didn't report it to any authority. . . .

What astonished me was not so much what had happened, but that the woman spoke so highly of her adviser — of his brilliance in his subject area and the intellectual thrill of working for him. . . . Her admiration for the man, who was still on the university staff, was untarnished by an action that on the street would qualify as sexual assault.

Women of my generation learned not to allow a man's "private" actions (even when done in a public place by a man in a position of power over a woman) to tarnish our admiration and respect. Men make lewd comments? Inappropriate advances? Disparaging remarks about women? Hey, we all *know* that happens! Some men — not all, not even most — are jerks. We expect it. We would certainly not be so humorless as to object to it.

FREDERIC HAYWARD

*Executive director of Men's Rights Inc.,*
*Sacramento, Calif.*
FROM *THE (SACRAMENTO) BUSINESS JOURNAL,*
OCT. 8, 1990.

### no

**i**f you stare at a man and he doesn't like it, you risk a punch in the jaw. If you stare at a woman and she doesn't like it, you risk a megabuck financial settlement and/or a ruined career.

The problem is not, of course, that we make too much of sexual harassment; rather, the problem is that our perspective is biased by narrow, sexist, political interests.

A less-biased look at sexual harassment reveals, among other things, a host of women and men who are victimized by female abuse of sexual power. . . . Feminist protestations of women's powerlessness (hence innocence) notwithstanding, most of us personally know of women who have used and abused their sexual power. . . .

We do not even have a name for it, let alone a law against it. Any analysis of sexual office politics that ignores this component might be "politically correct," but is woefully inadequate. . . .

In essence, sexual harassment means requiring a person to carry out a traditional sex role as a subcondition for employment. Since a main component of the traditional female role is to provide sexual gratification, women usually find themselves caught in the well-publicized trap of providing sex as part of a job.

A main component of the traditional male role, on the other hand, is to bear physical risk and undertake heavy labor. The twin brother of sexual harassment, then, entails the primary assumption of dangerous and beast-of-burden tasks as a condition for a man's employment. . . .

The bottom line is that men suffer a disproportionate share of work-related accidents. The male-centered form of sexual "harassment" kills. . . .

Even when the concern is limited to only female victims of only-female defined sexual harassment, moreover, the male perspective needs to be included before effective solutions can be developed. Blaming one gender exclusively (men) is as politically popular as it is specious. . . .

If a woman dresses to kill, for example, hoping to arouse the interest of those men she likes, non-targeted men receive many of the same visual cues. More and more men are, in fact, complaining that provocative dress constitutes sexual harassment against them. Furthermore, sexual harassment is not necessarily a physical attack; it can even be an unwanted glance. Yet, the only purpose of showing cleavage is to have people admire it; can we really place all the blame on the man for looking?

*Continued from p. 552*

mean that bill could not garner enough votes to carry the day."

The compromise, however, is still bothersome to some. Peter Eide of the U.S. Chamber of Commerce said the cap on punitive damages isn't really a cap if it can be raised to the level of uncapped compensatory damages. Women's groups say puni-

tive damages are needed to force corporations to right their ways. "$150,000 is cost of doing business for a large corporation," says Alison Wetherfield, legal director of the NOW Legal Defense and Education Fund in New York City. "It's less than they spend on their lawyers." The Senate will take up its version of the bill this fall. ∎

sensitized to women's concerns about sexual harassment, a judge's gender is not always a good predictor of thinking. Judge Edith H. Jones of the 5th Circuit, long mentioned as a possible Supreme Court candidate, made headlines trying a sexual harassment case involving International Paper Co. When the plaintiff's attorney argued that a male co-worker had grabbed her client's breasts, pinched her buttocks and scrawled obscenities about her continually, Jones interrupted her to say, "Well, your client wasn't raped." [48]

# OUTLOOK

## Problem Persists

The drumbeat of news stories on sexual harassment has not let up. This spring, in Tallahassee, Fla., the state capital was riveted by testimony from a former legislative committee analyst about pressure from legislators for sexual favors and the payment of $47,000 in hush money. In San Diego, a member of the city's planning and community development department was forced to resign in May after it was revealed he had an affair with a female assistant and made a secret payment to her after she had filed a sexual harassment complaint. At Emory University in Atlanta, a top law professor resigned in April "to start the healing process" following an uproar over his having been cleared of complaints that he kissed students without their consent and called them at home to invite them on dates.

Many people continue to treat sexual harassment as a joke. In Mort Walker's ageless comic strip "Beetle Bailey," General Halftrack persists with his chronic leering at his secretary, Miss Buxley.

What stands out today, however, is a heightened public awareness of sexual harassment and a new willingness among victims to go public. In the legal area, Wetherfield reports,

many attorneys are bringing both Title VII and state tort claims together as a way of winning compensation for pain and suffering of sexual harassment victims. Clients may win more money using state laws, she says, but the cases lose the political statement they make at the federal level. Allan Seigel, a Washington D.C., labor attorney, says federal courts are mildly antagonistic toward sexual harassment suits, while state courts are even more so. [44]

In either venue, the going is rough. A study by management professors released in 1989 surveyed the outcome of every sexual harassment case filed with the Illinois Human Rights Department for two years. It found that only 31 percent had outcomes favorable to the plaintiff. [45]

Judges' attitudes still vary widely when they're interpreting the sexual behavior of men and women and deciding such procedural issues as the relevance of a female plaintiff's sex life to a sexual harassment charge. A 6th Circuit judge in 1986 ruled against a woman's sexual harassment complaint by saying she wasn't the kind of person who would find such conduct unwelcome. [46] By contrast, a 4th Circuit judge in 1987 ruled it was improper for a lower court to admit evidence of the plaintiff's past sexual conduct when there was no evidence that the harasser knew or had reason to know of it. [47]

Though many activists argue that male judges need to become more

### Will Education Work?

In 1988, former EEOC Chairman Norton told *Working Woman*, "Sex harassment has developed as one of the great lessons in how education can have an effect on an offensive practice." And many activists on the issue are putting their faith in education campaigns. "Whether or not there are differences between men and women, we come to work to work," says Withers of the Women's Legal Defense Fund. "Anyone can be educated that there will be consequences for inappropriate behavior."

To critics, elaborate policies, education campaigns and corporate sensitivity training sessions dealing with sexual harassment can be abusive and patronizing. "It's totalitarian mind control as in China or the Soviet Union in the Stalinist era," says Linda Chavez. "There will be a backlash reaction." Many commentators wrote mockingly this spring about a sexual harassment policy now in effect at Amherst Regional High School in Massachusetts that prohibits students from staring at each other in the hallways or exchanging intimate gossip. "Slow Times at Amherst High," read a headline in *Harper's* magazine. [49]

"Women cannot expect to have it both ways: equality where convenient, but special dispensation when the going gets rough," writes political scientist Ellen Frankel Paul. "At some point the price for such protection is the loss of both liberty and privacy rights." [50]

A sign that efforts against harassment are paying off might be seen in the fact that 35,000 women participated in the Persian Gulf War this year and, according to the Pentagon, there were no major reports of sexual harassment. But evidence of scant progress can be found in a situation in California, where the state government recently reported that its decade-old effort to recruit women into state construction apprenticeship programs had fallen way short of its goals. Women construction workers "are sent for coffee, they're put off by themselves, they're sexually harassed, men urinate next to them," said Helen R. Neuborne, executive director of the NOW Legal Defense Fund, which compiled statistics on the program. "There is so very little incentive for them to stay." [51]

Corporate consultant Webb says companies should be given credit for clamping down on sexual harassment. "Maybe in the beginning, they were dealing with it out of fear, but I see today's company wanting to be more aware," she says. Peter Eide agrees. "The deterrent is already built into this economy," he says. "Everyone agrees that at the turn of the century, there will be a shortage of competent, qualified and trainable employees. No one in their right mind will engage in any conduct that will make people not want to work for their company."

As women take on more traditionally male roles, power relations in society are likely to change, and the phenomenon of sexual harassment may dwindle, or take on new forms. As a 36-year-old government administrator told the *Harvard Business Review*: "The more power people have, the more able they are to let go of their inhibitions and act on their desires. As a woman manager, I must admit to temptation! It is when the overtures are unwanted, persistent, and power-based that they are unhealthy organizationally." [52] ■

# Notes

[1] Quoted in *The Miami Herald*, April 30, 1991.

[2] Quoted by Eliza G. C. Collins and Timothy B. Blodgett in "Sexual Harassment ... Some See It ... Some Won't," *Harvard Business Review*, March-April 1981, p. 76.

[3] Cited in "Feminism and Sexual Harassment," *Society*, May-June 1991, p. 39.

[4] Quoted by Ronni Sandroff in "Sexual Harassment in the Fortune 500," *Working Woman*, December 1988, p. 74.

[5] Lloyd R. Cohen, "Sexual Harassment and the Law," *Society*, May-June 1991, p. 8.

[6] Barbara A. Gutek, *Sex and the Workplace: The Impact of Sexual Behavior and Harassment on Women, Men and Organizations* (1985), p. 60.

[7] Section 1604.11, *Code of Federal Regulations*, Vol. 29, Ch. XIV, July 1990 edition.

[8] D.C. Circuit Court, *Bundy v. Jackson*, 1981.

[9] EEOC memo of March 19, 1990, "Policy Guidance on Current Issues of Sexual Harassment."

[10] See Margaret S. Garvey, "The High Cost of Sexual Harassment Suits," *Personnel Journal*, January 1986, p. 75.

[11] See *The Washington Post*, Aug. 29, 1982.

[12] Claire Safran, "What Men Do to Women on the Job: A Shocking Look at Sexual Harassment," *Redbook*, November 1976.

[13] *Sexual Harassment in the Federal Workplace: Is It A Problem?* A report of the U.S. Merit Systems Protection Board, Office of Merit Systems Review and Studies, March 1981, p. 6.

[14] Defense Manpower Data Center, *Sexual Harassment in the Military: 1988,* September 1990.

[15] Quoted in *Working Woman, op cit.*

[16] Gretchen Morgenson, "Watch That Leer, Stifle That Joke," *Forbes*, May 15, 1989, p. 69.

[17] Unpublished poll taken for *Time* by the polling firm of Yankelovich Clancy Shulman.

[18] Gutek, *op. cit.*, p. 96.

[19] *Harvard Business Review, op. cit.*, p. 76.

[20] Ellen Frankel Paul, "Bared Buttocks and Federal Cases," *Society*, May-June 1991, p. 7.

[21] Gutek, *op. cit.*, p. 35.

[22] Paper presented to the Eastern Psychological Association, April 1991.

[23] Frederic Hayward, "A Case Against Society's Sexual Harassment of Men," *The (Sacramento) Business Journal*, Oct. 8, 1990.

[24] *Harvard Business Review, op. cit.*

[25] Gutek, *op. cit.*, p. 5.

[26] Figure cited in *Working Woman, op. cit.*

[27] *Fortune*, Sept. 14, 1987, p. 147.

[28] For details, see the *Dayton Daily News*, Nov. 14-17, 1990.

[29] Mary Bularzik, "An Historical Analysis of Sexual Harassment in the U.S." *Aegis*, January-February 1979.

[30] *Ibid.*

[31] Cited in a fact sheet by 9to5, National Association of Working Women.

[32] Garvey, *op. cit.*, p. 75.

[33] Margaret Mead, "A Proposal: We Need Taboos on Sex at Work," *Redbook*, April 1978, p. 31.

[34] Quoted in *The Washington Post*, April 22, 1981.

[35] Cited in "Unequal Justice: Why Women Need Stronger Civil Rights Protections," a brief by 9to5, National Association of Working Women.

[36] Quoted in *The New York Times*, Feb. 8, 1987.

[37] John D. Rapoport, and Brian L. P. Zevnik, *The Employee Strikes Back* (1989), p. 73.

[38] *Sexual Harassment: How to Develop and Implement Effective Remedies*, National Association of Manufacturers, p. 9.

[39] Quoted in *The New York Times*, Jan. 23, 1991.

[40] Quoted in *The New York Times*, Feb. 8, 1991.

[41] Quoted by Howard A. Simon in "*Ellison v. Brady*: A 'Reasonable Woman' Standard for Sexual Harassment," *Employee Relations Law Journal*, summer 1991, p. 71.

[42] Quoted in *The Washington Times*, March 18, 1991.

[43] For background, see "Racial Quotas," *The CQ Researcher*, May 17, 1991, pp. 277-300.

[44] Quoted by Kathleen Neville in *Corporate Attractions* (1990), p. 222.

[45] *Psychology Today*, May 1989, p. 16.

[46] *Rabidue v. Osceola Refining Co.*

[47] *Swentek v. U.S.Air.*

[48] Quoted in *The Washington Post*, June 29, 1991.

[49] *Harper's*, April 1991, p. 32.

[50] Paul, *op cit.*, p. 7.

[51] Quoted in *The New York Times*, Feb. 15, 1991.

[52] *Harvard Business Review, op. cit.*, p. 76.

# Bibliography

## Selected Sources Used

### Books

Dzeich, Billie Wright, and Weiner, Linda, *The Lecherous Professor: Sexual Harassment on Campus*, Beacon Press, 1984.

Two university officials offer a sociological, cultural and historical analysis of sexual relations and sexual harassment between faculty and students. The book includes numerous anecdotes and personal recollections from surveys.

Gutek, Barbara A., *Sex and the Workplace: The Impact of Sexual Behavior and Harassment on Women, Men and Organizations*, Jossey-Bass Publishers, 1985.

A sociologist analyzes results of a representative survey of Los Angeles County men and women on their experiences with sexual harassment, offering theories to explain harassment's origins and functions.

McWhirter, Darien A., *Your Rights at Work*, John Wiley & Sons Inc., 1989.

McWhirter, an employment attorney, surveys case law affecting victims of sexual harassment and other workplace discrimination.

Neville, Kathleen, *Corporate Attractions: An Inside Account of Sexual Harassment with the New Sexual Rules for Men and Women on the Job*, Acropolis Books Ltd., 1990.

The book recounts the personal experience of a television advertising saleswoman who spent years taking her supervisor to court for sexual harassment. It includes how-to procedures for filing complaints with the Equal Opportunity Employment Commission.

Rapoport, John D. and Zevnik, Brian L. P., *The Employee Strikes Back!*, Collier Books, 1989.

An overview of case law and remedy procedures for victims of sexual harassment, age discrimination, drug testing, polygraph abuse, unfair performance appraisals and wrongful firing.

### Articles

Collins, Eliza G. C., and Blodgett, Timothy B., "Sexual Harassment ... Some See It ... Some Won't," *Harvard Business Review*, March-April 1981.

This article reports statistical results and quotes extensively from a survey of American business executives on their experiences with and attitudes toward sexual harassment.

Garvey, Margaret S., "The High Cost of Sexual Harassment Suits," *Personnel Journal*, January 1986.

Garvey provides anecdotes and a history of sexual harassment cases that moved through the courts. The article includes a checklist for employers to use in avoiding liability.

Sandroff, Ronni, "Sexual Harassment in the Fortune 500," *Working Woman*, December 1988.

A detailed report on a survey of corporate policies and experiences with sexual harassment. It includes a lengthy case study and analysis by consultants in the field of sexual harassment.

Simon, Howard A., "Ellison v. Brady: A 'Reasonable Woman' Standard for Sexual Harassment," *Employee Relations Law Journal*, summer 1991.

Simon explains the precedents set and the legal implications of the sexual harassment ruling by the 9th U.S. Circuit Court of Appeals this January replacing the traditional "reasonable man" standard with a "reasonable woman" standard.

*Society*, Vol. 28, No. 4, May-June 1991.

This issue of the social science journal includes five articles on sexual harassment, discussing its impact on the law, the church and feminism.

### Reports and Studies

National Association of Manufacturers: *Sexual Harassment: How to Develop and Implement Effective Policies*, 1987.

This legal and historical analysis of sexual harassment in the corporate world offers overviews of how several major corporations implemented their sexual harassment policies.

National Women's Law Center, *Title VII's Failed Promise: The Impact of the Lack of a Damages Remedy*, March 1991.

Timed to have an impact on Congress' debate over the 1991 civil rights bill, this treatise uses case law and anecdotes to argue that a federal damages award is needed to redress victims of sex discrimination.

Women's Legal Defense Fund, *Sex Discrimination in the Workplace*, 1988 edition.

This legal handbook outlines procedures, answers questions and reproduces addresses and forms needed by victims seeking remedies for sex discrimination.

# The Next Step

## Additional Articles from Current Periodicals

### Actions & defenses

**Bacon, D. C., "See you in court," *Nation's Business*, July 1989, p. 16.**

Examines the rising number of lawsuits filed by employees against their employers. Impact of a litigious atmosphere on workplace relations; Causes of the increase in lawsuits; Emphasis on "wrongful discharge" cases, discrimination, sexual harassment and privacy charges. INSETS: Your firm may need a "legal checkup," by K. V. Rea; State your case on workers' suits; Laws protecting employees' rights; Useful books on employment law, by J. R. Beales.

**Koen Jr., C. M., "Sexual harassment claims stem from a hostile work environment," *Personnel Journal*, August 1990, p. 88.**

Discusses recent court decisions that have made it clear that employers can be held liable for sexual harassment. Research; Title VII; EEOC; Case descriptions; Guidelines.

**Tifft, S., E. Rudulph, et al., "A setback for pinups at work," *Time*, Feb. 4, 1991, p. 61.**

Reports that the federal district court in Jacksonville, Fla., ruled that pictures of naked women and scantily clad women displayed at the Jacksonville Shipyards qualify as harassment under Title VII of the 1964 Civil Rights Act. Landmark case brought by welder Lois Robinson; Judge Howard Melton ruled "females in a 'sexually hostile' workplace are a captive audience for pornography and are usually reluctant to challenge superiors over the issue."

### Armed forces

**"Naval assaults," *Time*, Nov. 5, 1990, p. 37.**

Notes that the Navy's Inspector General has released a report which finds that the Orlando Naval Training Center, which includes the only boot camp for women, is the site of at least six rapes and no prosecutions. Servicewide review due to allegations of sexual harassment at the U.S. Naval Academy in Annapolis, Md., and of rape aboard two Navy ships.

**Moskos, C., "Army women," *Atlantic*, August 1990, p. 70.**

Examines the life, the sentiments, and the aspirations of women in the U.S. Army. Women in combat and changes in the role of women in the military; Background; Daily life; Sexual harassment; Proposal for a trial program of women in combat.

### Case studies

**"Eliminating sexism at Annapolis," *U.S. News & World Report*, Oct. 22, 1990, p. 16.**

Comments on a recent Pentagon study that found that "there is a breakdown in civility and discipline which contributes to an environment conducive to sexual harassment and discrimination" at the U.S. Naval Academy in Annapolis, Md. Congressional oversight; Eliminating bigotry, prejudice and sexism.

**"Limousine libertine? " *Time*, July 31, 1989, p. 21.**

Outlines sexual harassment allegations against Chicago, Ill., Democratic Rep. Gus Savage who reportedly made advances on a 28-year-old Peace Corps volunteer in Kinshasa, Zaire.

**"Report faults Naval Academy on treatment of women," *Congressional Quarterly Weekly Report*, Oct. 13, 1990, p. 3442.**

Highlights a civilian review committee's report that the U.S. Naval Academy still lags behind the rest of the Navy in according equal treatment to women. Investigations triggered by an incident last December; Sexual harassment punishable by expulsion.

**"Sex charges against TV's Mr. Conservative," *Newsweek*, Aug. 15, 1988, p. 22.**

Reports that John McLaughlin, 60, of "The McLaughlin Group," is the target of a $4 million sexual-harassment charge by former office manager Linda Dean, 35.

**Amiel, B., "Here's looking at you, kid," *Maclean's*, Apr. 10, 1989, p. 9.**

Opinion. Discusses the sexual harassment case filed by part-time student Beverley Torfason against University of Toronto Professor Richard Hummel. Criticizes the case as a debasement of the serious problem of sexual harassment. University of Toronto's Sexual Harassment Review Board; Outcome.

**Blum, D. E., "Medical professor, U. of Iowa face aftermath of bitter sexual-harassment case," *The Chronicle of Higher Education*, March 13, 1991, p. A15.**

Considers the sexual-harassment lawsuit filed by Jean Y. Jew (involving charges dating back to 1973) which was settled in her favor by a federal court last August. Case serving as a lightning rod for faculty concerns about the way the university handles professors' grievances; Raising awareness of the issues of sexual harassment; Mishandling of the case by the university not extraordinary; Clear guidelines issued; Divisions and cynicism.

**Kenny, J. D., "Bennington's lost innocence," *Rolling Stone,* Oct. 4, 1990, p. 125.**

Novelist Bret Easton Ellis, a Bennington College graduate, examines the new conservatism at Bennington following the dismissal of tenured drama professor, Leroy Logan, 54, after a male student filed sexual-harassment charges against him. Bennington's reputation as a free-spirited liberal-arts college; Logan's denial of the charges; Comments by Bennington President Dr. Elizabeth Coleman; Students' comments; The alleged incident at Booth House.

**Kittay, J., "Professors, students, and sex," *Harper's,* October 1990, p. 26.**

Interviews Leon Botstein, president of Bard College and Simon's Rock of Bard College, by *J'accuse,* a magazine about academic life. He talks about accusations of sexual harassment against four professors at the school.

**Lake, A., "One woman's battle against an obnoxious boss," *Woman's Day,* Sept. 5, 1989, p. 92.**

Reports on a lawsuit filed on behalf of Linda Schultz, a saleswoman for Sigma Circuits in Santa Clara, Calif., against her boss and employer because of a sexually offensive workplace. Discusses her lawsuit, her filing and winning the suit. INSETS: If you're sexually harassed . . . ; What is sexual harassment?

**McIntosh, C., " 'Please leave me alone,' " *Working Woman,* December 1988, p. 74.**

Describes a case history of a $2.5 million sexual harassment lawsuit and lists recommendations by experts on what the company could have done to avoid the suit. Chronology of events; Confidential reporting of complaints; Educating workers as well as supervisors; Developing sexual harassment policies and procedures. C. Breslin and M. Morris. INSETS: Resources for managers: Videos; Resources for managers: Publications; Resources for managers: Training programs.

**Olson, K., "Harassment by mail," *Woman's Day,* May 22, 1990, p. 50.**

Recounts the story of writer Kiki Olson, who was the target of sexual harassment through the mail. How the man obtained personal numbers and addresses; How he was caught. INSET: Is obscene mail legal?

## Colleges & universities

**Decker, R. H., "Can schools eliminate sexual harassment?" *Education Digest,* January 1989, p. 59.**

Offers guidelines for school board members and employees concerning sexual harassment. Equal Employ-

ment Opportunity Commission guidelines; Recommendations for victims of sexual harassment.

**Magner, D. K., "Update on minority groups: New anti-harassment policy goes into effect at Stanford University," *The Chronicle of Higher Education,* Aug. 1, 1990, p. A26.**

Discusses a new policy approved by Stanford University's Student Conduct Legislative Council that seeks to protect students from harassment or intimidation on the basis of their race, sex, handicap, religion, sexual orientation, or national or ethnic origin.

**Starr, M., "The writing on the wall," *Newsweek,* Nov. 26, 1990, p. 64.**

Reports that women at Brown University began a list of male names on a bathroom door, claiming the male students to be rapists. Formation of the group Brown Against Sexual Assault and Harassment; Difficulty women have had with the justice system at Brown; Comments by men who were on the list.

**Warshaw, R., "Greek system under fire," *Utne Reader,* May/June 1990, p. 69.**

Covers the problems posed by Greek-letter organizations, especially fraternities, on university campuses across the United States. Contrasting the bias-free goals of the 1990s with the exclusionary policies of the Greek-letter system; Reports on fraternity culture involving, hazing, sexism, and drug abuse; Bans on Greek-letter systems. INSET: Harassing women becomes a sick college sport, by J. O. Hughes & B. Sandler.

## Debates & issues

**"But you only meant it as a compliment," *U.S. News & World Report,* Aug. 1, 1988, p. 58.**

Consideration of what does or does not constitute sexual harassment in the workplace from the man's point of view. Questions to ask oneself to help define boundaries; Questions of physical contact; Dating; Comments on clothing or appearance; Swearing and dirty jokes.

**Bozzi, V., "Harassment charges: Who wins?" *Psychology Today,* May 1989, p. 16.**

Discusses how anyone contemplating the decision to file a sexual-harassment charge is probably wasting time unless they are sure they have a cut-and-dried case. According to a recent study, all but the strongest cases fail.

**Haiman, F. S., "Sexist speech and the first amendment," *Communication Education,* January 1991, p. 1.**

Focuses on an analysis of sexist expression by men against women. This includes, at one extreme, direct intimidation or harassment and, at the other extreme, utterances that, though derogatory, are statements of an ideology or point of view. Problems of analysis arise when considering a school context, whether a classroom, a dormitory, or open spaces on campus.

**Kannapell, A., "Outrage over omnipresent violence: Where to aim it?" *Utne Reader*, November/December 1989, p. 46.**

Describes the author's personal anger at sexist treatment by men including verbal and physical violence molestation and rape. Reaction to the Central Park rape; Response to sexual harassment on the street; Facing the truth of omnipresent violence. INSET: Sexism comes in all colors, by J. Morgan.

**Leo, J., "What qualifies as sexual harassment?" *U.S. News & World Report*, Aug. 13, 1990, p. 17.**

Opinion. Responds to Michelle Locke's Associated Press story on the new sexual harassment code at Amherst-Pelham Regional High School in Mass. Author's own look into this strange social obsession; Role of feminist ideology; Criticism of the rules.

**Sanders, A. L. and Cramer, J., "A quotas-vs.-voters dilemma," *Time*, Oct. 29, 1990, p. 42.**

Considers the Civil Rights Act of 1990 that seeks to overturn some recent Supreme Court decisions and would ban racial harassment on the job and expand existing laws to permit victims of race, religious or sex bias to win judgments against their employers and collect damages. Political impasse; Reimposing on business the burden of showing that their racially or sexually imbalanced work forces result from "business necessity," not bias.

## *Workplace*

**"Hands off at the office," *U.S. News & World Report*, Aug. 1, 1988, p. 56.**

Advice on how to complain about sexual harassment in the workplace. Ways to nip it in the bud; Background to the problem; Tough legal standards; Statistics on complaints filed with Equal Employment Opportunity Commission. A. Saltzman. INSET: How women react: Ways to handle harassment and percentages used by women.

**"Pull down the pinups, raze the glass ceiling," *Business Week*, March 18, 1991, p. 140.**

Editorial. Talks about how the problem of sexual harassment in the workplace is gaining new attention thanks to some recent court rulings. Discusses the rulings; Benefits; Necessary steps now being taken.

**Galen, M., Schiller, Z., et al., "Ending sexual harassment: Business is getting the message," *Business***

**Week, March 18, 1991, p. 98.**

Highlights rulings from court decisions that are rewriting the rules governing conduct between the sexes in the workplace. During the 1980s, the rules governing sexual harassment grew tougher, and now courts are stretching the definition of harassment even more. Employers' efforts; Concern reflects the growing ranks of females in non-traditional jobs. INSET: Sex still sells — but so does sensitivity.

**Goodyear, M. L. and Black, W. K., "Combating sexual harassment: A public service perspective," *American Libraries*, February 1991, p. 134.**

Addresses the problem of sexual harassment in libraries and details how Iowa State University library deals with the problem. Writing a harassment policy to raise consciousness in the library; Provide a statement of intolerance for harassment; Develop an operating definition; Encourage staff; Clarify actions; Offer development sessions for public service staff. INSET: Iowa State University policy on harassment.

**McDonald, K. A., "Many female astronomers say they face sex harassment and bias," *The Chronicle of Higher Education*, Feb. 13, 1991, p. A11.**

Describes some of the results of two studies done by the American Astronomical Society concerning sexual harassment and discrimination of females by their male colleagues. Reports that 40 percent of the women in the first survey and 71 percent in the second survey, reported experiencing or witnessing some form of discrimination or harassment against women in the profession. Dual-career couples; Overt discrimination becoming more subtle; France and Italy.

**Morgenson, G., "Watch that leer, stifle that joke," *Forbes*, May 15, 1989, p. 69.**

Reports on sexual harassment in the U.S. workplace. Equal Employment Opportunity Commission guidelines and Title VII of the Civil Rights Act of 1964; Consultants who make money giving advice; Decline in federal cases alleging harassment; Examples; History. INSET: Advice to women: Act like a freight train (discusses two women in the finance industry).

**Padavic, I. and Reskin, B. F., "Men's behavior and women's interest in blue-collar jobs," *Social Problems*, November 1990, p. 613.**

Examines whether men's reactions to women who worked temporarily in plant jobs discouraged women from returning permanently to those jobs. Hostility, sexual harassment; paternalism and functional differentiation experienced; Reasons why some women lack interest in male blue-collar jobs; Male responses to women entering sex-atypical jobs; More.

# Back Issues

*Great Research on Current Issues Starts Right Here. . . Recent topics covered by The CQ Researcher are listed below. Issues dated before May 10, 1991, were published under the name of Editorial Research Reports.*

**JANUARY 1990**
Higher Education Curriculum
Photonics
Age of 'Infotainment'
Abortion: Politicians' Nightmare

**FEBRUARY 1990**
Politics and Economic Growth
Free Agency in Sports
Repetitive Motion
War on Drugs

**MARCH 1990**
Asbestos: Are Risks Acceptable?
Public Health Campaigns
South Africa's Future
Homeless Need More Than Shelter

**APRIL 1990**
How Fair is the Tax Burden?
Workers' Compensation
U.S. Pacific Forces
Curbing Insurance Premiums

**MAY 1990**
Should Teaching Be a Profession?
Will Canada Fall Apart?
Is U.S. Patent System Outdated?
Federal Funding for the Arts

**JUNE 1990**
Downsizing America's Armed Forces
Progress In Weather Forecasting
S & L Bailout
Bio-Chemical Disarmament

**JULY 1990**
Do Americans Still Love Marriage?
Death Penalty Debate
Decline of Rural America
United Nations in the 1990s

**AUGUST 1990**
Democracy in the Philippines
Initiatives: True Democracy?
Hard Times at Newspapers
Teens Balance School & Jobs

**SEPTEMBER 1990**
Dangers of Alcohol
Western Alliance After the Cold War
Tobacco Industry
Right to Die

**OCTOBER 1990**
Organ Transplants
Energy Policy Options
Search for Arab Unity
Child Support

**NOVEMBER 1990**
Lotteries and Gambling
Post Cold-War Choices
Setting Limits on Medical Care
Multicultural Education

**DECEMBER 1990**
Cable TV Regulation
Americans' Search For Their Roots
Is Insurance System a Failure?
Why Schools Still Have Tracking

**JANUARY 1991**
Growing Influence of Boycotts
Should the U.S. Reinstate the Draft?
America's Archaeological Past
Peace Corps' Challenges in '90s

**FEBRUARY 1991**
Regional Impact of Recession
Puerto Rico's Status
Redistricting: Mapping Power
Nuclear Power

**MARCH 1991**
Acid Rain
Cost of the Gulf War
Reassessing Gun Laws
Future for Man in Space

**APRIL 1991**
Social Security
Canadian Crisis Over Quebec
California Drought
Electromagnetic Radiation

**MAY 1991**
School Choice
Racial Quotas
Animal Rights
U.S. and Japan

**JUNE 1991**
Children and Divorce
Teenage Suicide
Endangered Species
Europe 1992

**JULY 1991**
Teenagers and Abortion
Soviet Republics Rebel
Mexico's Emergence
Athletes and Drugs

Back issues are available for $4.00 (subscribers) or $7.00 (non-subscribers). Quantity discounts apply to orders over ten. To order, call Congressional Quarterly 1-800-432-2250.

# Future Topics

▶ *Fetal Tissue Research*

▶ *Oil Imports*

▶ *Palestinians*

# THE
# CQ Researcher

PUBLISHED BY CONGRESSIONAL QUARTERLY INC., IN CONJUNCTION WITH EBSCO PUBLISHING

# Fetal Tissue Research

*Should we permit research on fetal tissue transplants?*

F ETAL TISSUE RESEARCH HOLDS THE PROMISE of medical miracles — transplants to treat a host of diseases including parkinsonism and diabetes. But anti-abortion groups say the use of fetal tissue from induced abortions will encourage more women to have abortions and lead to a multimillion-dollar fetal harvesting industry. Two advisory bodies at the National Institutes of Health say adequate controls could be established to prevent abuses, but abortion opponents have persuaded the Reagan and Bush administrations to block federal funding for the research. Some privately funded research and clinical studies are continuing, but scientists and others want Congress to lift the funding moratorium to allow expanded research. President Bush is expected to use a veto if necessary to preserve the funding ban.

C Q | **August 16, 1991 • Volume 1, No. 14 • 561-584**

*Formerly Editorial Research Reports*

COVER ART: BARBARA SASSA-DANIELS

CQ Researcher

August 16, 1991
Volume 1, No. 14

**EDITOR**
Sandra Stencel

**MANAGING EDITOR**
Thomas J. Colin

**ASSOCIATE EDITOR**
Richard L. Worsnop

**STAFF WRITERS**
Charles S. Clark
Mary H. Cooper
Rodman D. Griffin

**PRODUCTION EDITOR**
Laurie De Maris

**EDITORIAL ASSISTANT**
Thomas H. Moore

**GRAPHICS**
Jack Auldridge

**PUBLISHED BY**
Congressional Quarterly Inc.

**CHAIRMAN**
Andrew Barnes

**VICE CHAIRMAN**
Andrew P. Corty

**EDITOR AND PUBLISHER**
Neil Skene

**EXECUTIVE EDITOR**
Robert W. Merry

**PUBLICATIONS MARKETING/SALES**
Robert Smith

**EDITOR, EBSCO PUBLISHING**
Melissa Kummerer

The CQ Researcher (ISSN 1056-2036). Formerly Editorial Research Reports. Published weekly (48 times per year, not printed the first Friday of any month with five Fridays) by Congressional Quarterly Inc., 1414 22nd St., N.W., Washington, D.C. 20037. Rates are furnished upon request. Application to mail at second-class postage rates is pending at Washington, D.C. POSTMASTER: Send address changes to The CQ Researcher, 1414 22nd St., N.W., Washington, D.C. 20037.

# Fetal Tissue Research

BY KENNETH JOST

## THE ISSUES

The doctors who perform the operation describe it as straightforward, almost simple. The patient, suffering from a degenerative nerve disorder called Parkinson's disease, is prepped for the surgery with a local anesthetic that numbs the skull. Surgeons drill a hole about the size of a quarter in the skull and, guided by a computer-generated image of the brain, use a long needle to insert tiny bits of tissue they hope will graft onto the patient's brain. The tissue contains cells that will enable the brain to begin producing a chemical that Parkinson's patients lack and that nerve cells need to control muscle movement. If the transplant succeeds, the uncontrollable shaking characteristic of Parkinson's disease may be reduced and the patient may be able to resume something like a normal life.

The procedure still is highly experimental, but researchers say they are encouraged by the results of 16 transplant operations performed since 1987 in Sweden and the United States. But the politics of the research are anything but simple — because the tissue used in the transplants comes from aborted fetuses.

To anti-abortion groups, such research raises the specter of a multimillion-dollar fetal harvesting industry and an increase in the number of abortions performed in the United States. They say women considering abortion will be influenced by the argument that "something good" may come from their decision to end a pregnancy. "It is unworthy of us, as a nation, to kill our unborn children and then use them for spare parts," says John C. Willke, former president of the country's largest anti-

abortion group, the National Right to Life Committee.

Members of the medical and scientific communities say the issue is not abortion but research — research that offers hope of treating Parkinson's and many other currently irreversible diseases, including diabetes, Alzheimer's and a number of genetic disorders. They insist few women, if any, would be moved to have an abortion by a charitable impulse to donate fetal tissue. And they contend that a ban on the sale of fetuses can prevent any commercialization or profiteering — just as has been done with organ transplants from adult donors.

Those arguments satisfied two advisory groups that studied the issue for the National Institutes of Health (NIH), the federal agency that provides roughly one-third of the nation's health research funding. In 1988, a special commission appointed to study the issue voted 18-3 to pronounce fetal tissue transplant research "acceptable public policy" — a position then unanimously en-

dorsed by the standing advisory committee to the director of the NIH.

That advice, however, was rejected in November 1989 by Louis W. Sullivan, the Bush administration's secretary of Health and Human Services (HHS), NIH's parent department. Sullivan decided instead to extend, indefinitely, the moratorium on NIH funding of fetal tissue research first ordered by the Reagan administration in March 1988. The moratorium barred NIH funding of clinical transplantation studies using tissue from induced abortions.

The NIH moratorium did not affect privately funded research in the United States. And fetal tissue transplantation research continues in more than a dozen other countries around the world.

Bush administration officials and anti-abortion groups depict the NIH funding moratorium as a limited one. The current director of the NIH, Dr. Bernadine Healy, says the agency allotted $8 million to other fetal research for fiscal 1990. Healy, who headed a research clinic in Cleveland, was a member of the special NIH commission and joined in its recommendation to approve funding fetal tissue transplant research. As NIH director, however, she has fallen in place behind the moratorium, promising senators in her confirmation hearing to support and enforce it.

Efforts are under way in Congress to reverse the moratorium. A provision to lift it was included in an NIH reauthorization bill approved by the House in 1990, but it was dropped in order to avoid a possible presidential veto. House opponents of the ban — led by Rep. Henry A. Waxman, D-Calif., chairman of the House Commerce Subcommittee on Health and the Environment — renewed the fight in 1991. A similar provision was again included in an NIH reauthorization bill approved by the House on July 25.

Opponents of the moratorium are also laying plans for a legal challenge if the Waxman bill stalls. Several organizations are preparing a suit contending that HHS imposed the moratorium without complying with the requirements of the federal law governing administrative rule-making. Anti-abortion groups predict the moratorium will pass legal muster.

Here are some of the major questions raised in the debate over fetal tissue research:

### Is the use of fetal tissue from induced abortions morally or ethically wrong?

Anti-abortion groups and the medical research community approach the question from fundamentally opposing viewpoints. To those who view the fetus as an unborn human being from the moment of conception, any use of its tissue after it has been deliberately killed — anti-abortionists call it nothing less than murder — amounts to complicity with an absolute moral wrong. Issues of consent, safeguards and the like simply do not matter.

"Our position is premised on the view that a fetus is a living human being, and taking that life without sufficient justification is morally objectionable," says James Bopp Jr., general counsel of the National Right to Life Committee and a dissenting member of the NIH advisory panel. Trying to separate the abortion from the subsequent research, Bopp wrote in his dissent, is no more morally valid than Nazi researchers' rationalizations for using Holocaust victims for scientific experiments.

Some researchers, on the other hand, view the aborted fetus as indistinguishable from any other ca-

daver whose cells, tissues and organs can be used in medical research or treatment with proper consent — from the donor's family in the case of an adult, the mother in the case of a fetus. Dr. John F. Enders, who shared in the Nobel Prize for his work in developing the polio vaccine based on research with fetal cells, stated the view strongly in a 1974 letter arguing against a bill in the Massachusetts legislature to ban fetal research. "From the ethical standpoint . . . ," Enders wrote, "the use . . . derived from the aborted fetus, whether the tissue becomes available through natural or artificial means . . . differs in no moral or social aspect from the use of tissue from persons who die postnatally." [1]

Most people who have studied the issue fall between these two polarized positions. Anti-abortion groups generally do not object to the use of fetal tissue from spontaneous abortions or stillbirths.

Medical organizations, disease groups and most ethicists who have studied the issue believe the use of fetal tissue is clearly justified, but they now generally endorse procedural requirements on abortion providers and researchers before fetal tissue can be retrieved or used in experimentation or treatment. "I see the use of tissue from dead aborted fetuses as a rather clear-cut ethical question provided that safeguards are built into public policies to prevent potential abuses," says LeRoy Walters, director of the Kennedy Institute of Bioethics at Georgetown University.

### Does fetal tissue research offer substantial promise for developing new ways to treat diseases?

Fetal tissue transplant research dates to the 1920s, when Italian researchers sought to transplant insulin-producing pancreatic cells in a diabetic patient. That experiment failed, as did subsequent experi-

ments in the United States using cells derived from fetuses and still-born infants.

By the 1960s, however, transplants using fetal liver or thymus tissue had become an established treatment for one rare genetic disorder. More recently, researchers have reported encouraging results from experimental fetal pancreatic transplants for diabetics and fetal brain cell transplants for Parkinson's patients. The experiments have fed optimistic news accounts, but scientists have generally tried to adopt a cautionary attitude. "It's very important because of the political and social controversy that we be very cautious about reporting results," says Dr. Eugene Redmond Jr., a Yale neurosurgeon who has performed nine fetal neural cell transplants.

Fetal tissue is appealing for transplants because it grows rapidly and is less likely to be rejected by the body's immune system — the major medical difficulty in transplant operations. But the transplants attempted so far are all experimental, and researchers have encountered many problems. In diabetics, for example, transplantation of fetal pancreatic cells has not eliminated the need for insulin and has led to rejection problems that researchers do not completely understand. The reported results of fetal tissue transplants on Parkinson's patients in Sweden and the United States are mixed, and the claimed success by a Mexican surgeon has been met with skepticism (see p. 570).

Opponents of fetal tissue research do not directly challenge the scientists, but point to the speculative nature of the research as further reason for hesitation. "The procedures, as applied to humans, are essentially untried and untested; therapeutic benefit is, as yet, undetermined," said Rabbi J. David Bleich of Yeshiva University's Benjamin Cardozo School of Law, another dissenting member of the NIH panel.

Scientists and groups representing people with serious diseases, however, say the many questions still unanswered about the potential benefits and risks of fetal tissue transplants underscore the need for more research — and for federal funding to give the research both tangible and symbolic support. "'We don't know that [fetal pancreatic transplants] will work," says Kenneth Farber, executive director of the Juvenile Diabetes Foundation, "but the way we can find out is to do the research."

### Would the wide use of fetal tissue transplants encourage more women to have abortions?

Supporters and opponents of fetal tissue transplant research disagree as heatedly on this question as on any other point in the debate. Opponents maintain that women would inevitably be influenced to have more abortions by altruistic appeals to make "something good" come from their decision. Supporters of the research say that that argument "trivializes" the real reasons why women have abortions.

Douglas Johnson, legislative director for the National Right to Life Committee, says studies show women are "ambivalent" before deciding to have an abortion and "come under pressure" from others, such as boyfriends or parents. "The argument that some good may come from this procedure … is an argument that would be employed and in some cases would prevail," he says. "It would provide a rationalization and a rationale that would lead to the death of many unborn children."

A somewhat similar conclusion was voiced from a feminist, pro-abortion-rights perspective by Dr. Janice Raymond, a professor of women's studies and medical ethics at the

University of Massachusetts in Amherst. Testifying before the House Commerce Health Subcommittee in April, Raymond said the practice of donating fetal tissue would reinforce "the expectation on women … that they ought to meet the needs of others." The result, she said, would be to make an already difficult decision harder and to alter the abortion procedure in ways that might be harmful

**Fetal tissue transplants are appealing to medical researchers because fetal tissue grows rapidly and is less likely to be rejected by the body's immune system.**

to women in order to preserve the fetus more nearly intact.

Several bioethicists who testified before the Health Subcommittee disagreed with the argument that women's abortion decisions might be influenced by the possibility of donating fetal tissue. Among them was Dr. Arthur Caplan, director of the University of Minnesota's Center for Biomedical Ethics. "People get abortions for reasons that have nothing to do with helping science," Caplan said. "It's a distortion, a malicious one, of the motives that bring women to abortion."

One scientific question bears on the issue: How many fetuses will be needed if fetal tissue transplantation becomes widespread? Raymond calculates that of the 1.5 million elective abortions performed annually in the

United States, only 90,000 early fetuses would be available for transplantation under current practices. She contrasted that figure with the 60,000 new cases of Parkinson's and 15,000 new insulin-dependent diabetics diagnosed each year and the tens or hundreds of thousands of people with other diseases potentially curable with fetal tissue transplants. "Where are all these fetuses going to come from?" she asked.

Researchers say fetal transplants are so far from becoming established treatment that any such statistical calculations are meaningless. But they also say experiments may show how to reduce the number of fetuses needed in transplants. Researchers also say that growing cells in cultures may reduce the demand for fetuses. Anti-abortion groups join in endorsing that line of inquiry, which they say might mean demand for fetal material could be met by tissue from spontaneous abortions, ectopic pregnancies and stillbirths.

### Can adequate controls be established on procedures for obtaining and using fetal tissue for transplants to prevent or minimize ethical problems?

The NIH advisory panel recommended a series of guidelines to keep abortion decisions and procedures separate from procurement and use of fetal tissue. The guidelines, paralleling recommendations by such groups as the American Medical Association, would prohibit payment for fetal tissue other than "reasonable expenses" incurred in retrieval, storage, preparation and transportation. They would also require that maternal consent be obtained for use of the tissue but only after the woman has made the decision to undergo the abortion. And they would prevent the woman from designating the recipient of the tissue.

Research supporters liken the ban on buying fetuses to the federal National Organ Transplant Act, which prohibits the sale of organs for transplant. "There's no billion-dollar industry in organ transplants," says Dr. Kenneth J. Ryan, chairman of Harvard Medical School's department of obstetrics and gynecology and a key member of the NIH advisory panel. "That's something the government has been able to regulate."

But anti-abortion activists say the analogy is wrong. "It's not optional whether someone is going to die because of an auto accident or something," James Bopp argues. "It is optional whether someone is going to have an abortion. It's simply a different context. ... When you look at the fact that the current amount of fetal tissue would be woefully inadequate, there would be lives to be saved and money to be made."

The guideline to keep abortion procedures independent of any use of the fetal tissue stems from the belief that second-trimester fetuses might yield more valuable tissue than earlier fetuses and that the standard techniques for the operation would fragment the fetus too much for it to yield useful tissue.

However, a report by the University of Minnesota's Center for Biomedical Ethics suggests that the most common technique for first-trimester abortions in the United States — vacuum aspiration — does yield usable tissue, as does the most common second-trimester procedure — dilatation and evacuation (D & E). ∎

# BACKGROUND

## Early History

Medical research involving use of tissue from aborted fetuses has been going on at least since the 1920s. There have been some successes and some failures, but until the heating up of the abortion issue in the 1970s, there was scant public debate about the ethics and morality of the research.

The most important medical advances attributable to fetal tissue research have been in the development of vaccines. Studies of fetal tissue in the 1930s by Albert B. Sabin and Peter K. Olitsky ushered in a new era of immunological approaches to combating viral diseases. Research using human embryonic tissue over the next decade by John F. Enders, Thomas Weller and Frederick C. Robbins laid the groundwork for the development of the anti-polio vaccine in the 1950s. Enders, Weller and Robbins were awarded the 1954 Nobel Prize in medicine for their work.[2]

Fetal tissue transplant research has been less successful. The first reported attempt to transplant fetal tissue to cure disease was aimed at diabetes, which is caused by the failure of the pancreas to produce insulin needed by the body to break down sugars. Insulin was discovered in 1921, and in 1928 Italian researchers transplanted tissue taken from three human fetuses to an insulin-dependent diabetic. They found no effects, however. U.S. doctors reported in 1939 on two similar, unsuccessful fetal transplants. And in 1959, two U.S. doctors reported they had transplanted tissue from six stillborn infants to their diabetic mothers but had found only a transitory reduction in insulin requirement in just one case.[3]

Liver and thymus transplants became the next focus of fetal tissue research. Because the liver and thymus play a central role in the development of immune and blood systems, it was thought transplanted tissue could help treat patients with a number of blood or immunological diseases.

In 1959, an American researcher reported attempts to use fetal liver cells in patients with leukemia — cancer of the blood — but with no lasting benefit. Two years later, another U.S. doctor reported no success in using a fetal liver transplant to try to treat aplastic anemia, a disease caused by the failure of bone marrow to produce blood cells.

In 1968, however, fetal liver transplants were found to help restore immune functions in patients with a rare congenital condition called DiGeorge's syndrome, which is caused by abnormal development of a portion of the upper digestive tube. Further research showed that fetal thymus transplants could be used for DiGeorge's patients, and today that procedure is the treatment of choice for severe forms of the disease.[4]

### New Sensitivities

The limited fetal tissue research through the 1960s proceeded largely out of the public eye, with more attention focused, for example, on bone marrow transplants as treatment for blood and immune disorders. In 1968 and 1969, however, two important vaccines emerged from fetal research: one against rubella, or so-called German measles, and another against Rh hemolytic disease, the condition that results when mother and fetus have incompatible blood types. The effectiveness of those two vaccines is evident today, but both then and now their origins in laboratory work on human fetuses were largely unrecognized. Indeed, fetal research was so obscure that it was completely overlooked by congressional inquiries into emerging bioethical issues in

*Continued on p. 568*

# Chronology

**1950s** *Vaccine for polio developed using tissue from human fetal kidneys; researchers awarded 1954 Nobel Prize in medicine.*

———•———

**1960s** *Fetal research yields vaccine against German measles, improved treatment of Rh blood disease and advances in prenatal diagnosis of genetic defects.*

———•———

**1970s** *Controversy over fetal tissue research first becomes a public issue.*

**Jan. 22, 1973**
U.S. Supreme Court recognizes constitutional right to abortion in *Roe v. Wade.*

**July 1975**
Department of Health, Education and Welfare issues regulations effectively barring research on live fetuses but allowing research involving dead fetuses or their tissues if permitted by state law.

———•———

**1980s** *Doctors and scientists in several countries accelerate research on fetal tissue transplants. Anti-abortion groups in U.S. vigorously oppose use of fetuses from induced abortions in fetal cell transplants.*

**March 22, 1988**
Robert E. Windom, assistant secretary of Health and Human Services (HHS), imposes moratorium on funding by the National Institutes of Health (NIH) of fetal tissue transplant research involving aborted fetuses.

**September 1988**
NIH advisory panel completes hearings, votes to declare use of aborted fetuses in fetal tissue transplants "acceptable public policy."

**November 1988**
Dr. Curt Freed at the University of Colorado performs first U.S. fetal neural cell transplant on patient with Parkinson's disease; patient gradually improves, but by summer 1991 is still unable to return to work.

**Jan. 19, 1989**
NIH director forwards recommendation of advisory panels to HHS secretary, urging restoration of funding for fetal tissue transplant research.

**1989**
Dr. Hans Sollinger at the University of Wisconsin and Dr. Kevin Lafferty at the University of Colorado continue animal studies on fetal pancreatic cell transplants to treat diabetes after halting clinical studies because of unsolved rejection problems with human patients.

**June 1989**
In first detailed report of fetal neural cell transplants, Swedish researchers report limited success in two patients with Parkinson's disease. Better results described to news media in spring 1990 from transplant performed on Parkinson's patient in 1989.

**June 1989**
American Medical Association endorses use of tissue from aborted fetuses as "promising area of clinical investigation that should continue to receive federal funding."

**Nov. 2, 1989**
HHS Secretary Louis W. Sullivan extends moratorium on federal funding of fetal tissue transplants "indefinitely."

———•———

**1990s** *Research continues, controversy grows.*

**May 23, 1990**
Dr. Robert Nathan Slotnick of University of California-Davis performs first fetus-to-fetus transplant in U.S. in effort to cure prenatally diagnosed genetic disorder. Child born Oct. 30, 1990; outcome of procedure still uncertain.

**May 1991**
House Commerce Subcommittee on Health and the Environment approves NIH reauthorization bill with provision to lift NIH funding moratorium. Opponents of moratorium leak plans to file suit to overturn funding curb on administrative law grounds.

**June 4, 1991**
House Energy and Commerce Committee votes 26-17 in favor of lifting NIH funding moratorium.

**July 25, 1991**
House approves NIH reauthorization bill that would lift ban on funding research using tissue from aborted fetuses. Bill awaits Senate action; opponents anticipate a presidential veto.

# Fetal Tissue Transplants: Status Report

*Fetal tissue transplants have been studied as a possible treatment for several diseases, but with one exception the procedures are still experimental.*

| Clinical illness | Incidence or prevalence in the U.S. | Status of fetal tissue as therapy |
|---|---|---|
| DiGeorge's syndrome | Very rare | Accepted |
| Severe combined immune deficiency (SCID) | Rare. In one of more common forms, between 1 per 10,000 and 2 per 1,000,000 live births | Experimental, perhaps alternative |
| Acute leukemia | 24,000 new cases per year | Experimental |
| Aplastic anemia | 1,200-2,400 new cases per year | Experimental |
| Inherited storage disorders | Variable, generally quite rare. Exceptions in certain ethnic groups | Unknown |
| Radiation accidents | Episodic, unpredictable. Small numbers to date | Unknown |
| Parkinson's disease | 500,000 existing cases | Early experimental |
| Insulin dependent diabetes mellitus | 325,000-645,000 | Experimental |

*Sources: Center for Biomedical Ethics, University of Minnesota; National Diabetes Information Clearinghouse*

*Continued from p. 566*
the late 1960s and early '70s.[5]

In Britain, however, regulating fetal research became a public issue after reports in 1970 that abortion clinics had been selling fetuses for use in research. In May 1972, a royal commission endorsed the use of fetuses obtained in abortions if the sale of fetuses or fetal tissue was prohibited. The commission said any payments to abortion clinics should be limited to meeting administrative costs and "in no other circumstances should there be monetary exchange." The group also urged that for purposes of permitting research, the definition of viability — when a fetus is considered capable of independent life — be moved up to 20 weeks rather than 28 weeks. No research should be conducted on viable fetuses inconsistent with promoting its life, the commission said.

Bioethical issues became more urgent in the United States with the disclosure in 1972 of a shocking public health research scandal: a U.S. Public Health Service study initiated in the 1930s on the effects of syphilis on 400 black men from Tuskegee, Ala., none of whom was ever told he had the disease or offered treatment. Legislation to establish a panel of experts at the Department of Health, Education and Welfare (HEW, now the Department of Health and Human Services — HHS) to study the legal and ethical issues was introduced in Congress.

The bill did not pass, but HEW did establish an ad hoc advisory group to report to Congress. Again, however, fetal research was not on the agenda. That changed in 1973 — thanks to the U.S. Supreme Court.

## Abortion Rights Fallout

Abortion reform had been a liberal cause for decades in the United States. In the 1960s, reformers succeeded in getting several state legislatures to ease laws that restricted or in some cases virtually prohibited abortion. Reformers were also pursuing legal challenges to restrictive abortion laws and in 1971 got two cases — from Georgia and Texas — to the Supreme Court. The justices were divided after oral argument and requested an unusual second round of arguments from the opposing lawyers. When the decision was finally announced on Jan. 22, 1973, it was a bombshell that instantly transformed abortion into a political issue.

The 7-2 decision in *Roe v. Wade* recognizing a woman's constitutional right to abortion gave abortion reformers more than most of them had ever expected. States were essentially barred from regulating first-trimester abortions and severely limited in regulating second-trimester abortions. Virtually all state abortion laws had to be rewritten, and the burden of drafting and lobbying for legislation was now on opponents of abortion rather than abortion rights groups.

Anti-abortion groups protesting the Supreme Court's decision needed ways to dramatize the issue and, as Diana S. Hart of the Alan Guttmacher Institute wrote, fetal research was "perhaps an inevitable target. It fit in with the anti-abortionists' position that the fetus was a person from the moment of conception . . . ; and the issue promised to provide plenty of the kind of dramatic examples that congressmen seek when arguing for a measure." [6]

Rep. Angelo D. Roncallo, R-N.Y., introduced legislation to ban fetal research on April 13, 1973. The day before, about 200 persons had gathered at the NIH to protest the use of live aborted human fetuses in research.* The protest, organized by students from a Roman Catholic school for girls, won a pledge from a high NIH official that the agency would not fund any research on living human fetuses.

Roncallo got a floor vote on his proposal the next month, as an amendment to an omnibus bill aimed at expanding biomedical and behavioral research training. Like the high school protest, Roncallo aimed his rhetoric at research on live fetuses, casting his bill as a plea on the part of a fetus: "Do not cut tissue samples while I still have a heartbeat."

The bill's sponsors urged House members to defer any action on fetal research until Senate hearings on a broad range of bioethics issues

---

*One particularly controversial experiment, called "The Artificial Placenta," used living fetuses to simulate the role of the placenta in supplying oxygen to the immature fetus. Researchers constructed an elaborate circulation system and then maintained the fetuses long enough to test the circuitry. The research was widely criticized on ethical grounds, although it also won an award from the American College of Obstetricians and Gynecologists. See Maggie Scarf, "The Fetus as Guinea Pig," *The New York Times Magazine*, Oct. 19, 1975.

could be completed. But Roncallo had touched a nerve: His amendment carried 354-9. The next month, he attached a similar ban on fetal research funding to the appropriations bill for the National Science Foundation (NSF). The rider, which had no effect since the NSF had not funded any fetal research, was included in the final bill passed by the Senate a week later.

The Senate spent more time, however, debating the fetal research issue as part of companion bills developed by Sen. Edward M. Kennedy, D-Mass., to expand funding for health research and training and to create a commission to study bioethics issues. In September, Kennedy beat back an effort to attach a fetal research funding ban to the bill with a compromise, adopted 53-35, that imposed a moratorium on fetal research "before or after induced abortion" until the commission had developed policies in the area.

Other differences delayed the legislation, but it was finally enacted in July 1974. The measure banned HEW-supported research involving "the living human fetus, before or after abortion," unless aimed at assuring the survival of the fetus. The ban was intended as a temporary measure pending the new advisory commission's development of policies covering the area.[7]

### 1975 Federal Regulations

The commission — formally called the National Commission for the Protection of Human Subjects of Biomedical and Behavioral Research — submitted its recommendations just within the May 1, 1975, deadline. As part of its study, it received a report from a private research institute that documented wider-than-recognized fetal research over several decades. The report credited the research with having saved thousands of lives through such developments as amniocentesis — the technique for di-

agnosing fetal defects early in pregnancy; the vaccine against rubella; and better treatment of Rh disease and newborn respiratory distress syndrome.

Influenced by that report, but also under pressure from anti-abortion groups focusing on research involving live fetuses, the commission recommended lifting the moratorium in favor of guidelines that ostensibly would permit some such research to continue. But the recommendations, adopted as regulations in July 1975, were so restrictive that they virtually barred any research involving live fetuses or their tissue.

Research had to be directed at the health needs of the fetus or the mother, could pose no added risk to the fetus and could not involve terminating the heartbeat or respiration of the non-viable fetus. Artificially maintaining the vital functions of living, non-viable fetuses was also prohibited. The regulations required a separation between the persons performing the abortion and the persons removing tissue from live fetuses. And the regulations prohibited any inducements, monetary or otherwise, and any change in abortion procedures that would hurt either the fetus or the pregnant woman.

The regulations referred only briefly, however, to use of tissue from dead fetuses. The one clear requirement in the regulations was that research involving dead fetuses had to conform to any applicable state or local laws. Otherwise, it was a matter of uncertainty and dispute whether the other procedural provisions — such as the ban on payment or the mandatory separation between the abortion and the personnel using the tissue — applied to research involving dead fetuses.[8]

Abortion opponents had already been lobbying for state legislation and by the time of the commission's report had pushed through laws in

15 states restricting research involving the fetus in utero or research involving the aborted fetus. One state — Massachusetts — did specifically permit research on dead fetuses as part of a compromise law negotiated between abortion opponents favoring an across-the-board ban and scientists urging leeway for some continued research.[9]

Political activity on the issue died down until a resurgence of anti-abortion agitation in the early 1980s. Research was continuing in other countries and, to some extent, in the United States with private funding. But scientists complained that the regulations had essentially taken the NIH out of the business of funding any significant fetal research.

## Research Continues

Anti-abortion forces renewed the fight in Congress against fetal research in 1982 and three years later succeeded in codifying part of the regulations that HEW (now HHS) had issued in 1975. But laboratory scientists and clinical researchers in the United States and other countries were pushing forward with work that would change the focus of the debate to fetal tissue transplants.

Diabetes continued to present the most alluring possibility of a disease that could be treated by transplanting fetal tissue. Diabetes is relatively widespread: About 1.5 million people in the United States have Type I diabetes, the most serious form of the disease, which is caused by a lack of insulin. Transplantation of the pancreas, the organ that produces insulin, theoretically offered a direct method of treating the disease, but transplanting the entire pancreas was a technically difficult

procedure. There were substantial problems with rejection, and the drugs used to deal with the problems had their own serious side-effects. A less invasive procedure was to transplant only the insulin-producing cells from an adult pancreas — so-called islets. Early experiments were unsuccessful, however. In any event, the limited availability

*Fetal tissue transplants have been studied as a possible treatment for several diseases, most notably diabetes and Parkinson's disease.*

of donor organs from adult cadavers made it unlikely that either procedure would offer widespread help to diabetics in the near future.[10]

So researchers in several countries resumed the experiments with transplanting fetal islets into adult diabetics. In the United States, researchers at the University of Colorado Health Sciences Center performed 16 such transplants between 1984 and 1989. The results were encouraging, according to Dr. Kevin J. Lafferty, an immunologist who directed the privately funded research with Dr. Everett Spees, a surgeon at St. Luke's Medical Center in Denver.

The experiments showed that the transplanted fetal pancreatic tissue would engraft, differentiate into insulin-producing islets and survive. The ultimate question, though, was whether the transplanted cells

would produce enough insulin to maintain the patient. "The answer to that is yes and no," Lafferty explains. Patients needed less insulin than before the transplant, "but no one came off insulin."

Dr. Hans Sollinger was conducting similar research at the University of Wisconsin Medical School under a grant from the NIH. He performed four transplants before stopping the research, in part, he says, because of the controversy over NIH funding of fetal tissue transplants but primarily because of scientific problems. "We realized we hadn't overcome the problems as far as rejection was concerned," he says.

In a survey of the research in the field, the University of Minnesota's Center for Biomedical Ethics counted some 600 fetal tissue transplant procedures worldwide through 1989, including 38 in the United States. It called the results of the research "disappointing," noting in particular rejection problems like those Lafferty and Sollinger described. "Evidence indicates . . . that fetal pancreatic tissue may be as immunogenic [producing an immune response] or more so than adult cadaveric islet cells and adult pancreatic organs," the report concluded.[11]

### Parkinson's Research

Parkinson's disease provided a similarly tempting area of research for fetal tissue transplants. As with diabetes, it could be traced to the lack of a specific chemical — dopamine, produced by the brain and needed by nerve cells to control muscle movements. The disease is widespread: About 500,000 cases are counted in the United States today.[12] And, like diabetes, Parkinson's is currently incurable.

One established treatment for Parkinson's is Levodopa, or L-dopa, a medicine that can replace dopamine. The benefit is only temporary, however, and many patients suffer even worse symptoms after taking the medicine for awhile. So, as with diabetes, researchers focused on tissue transplants as a way to stimulate the brain to produce the needed dopamine on its own.

In 1985 a team of Swedish doctors reported the results of one experimental technique: transplanting tissue from the patient's own adrenal gland — a small gland located above each kidney — into the brain. The results of these adrenal autografts were inauspicious: a temporary halt in the patients' deterioration but no long-term clinical improvement. The Swedish team published a second report in 1987 on two more adrenal autografts with similar results. A Mexican team, however, reported more positive results in 1987, and their claimed success with 12 patients led to wider experimentation. By 1988, more than 100 adrenal autografts had been performed worldwide, but researchers had been unable to match the Mexican team's reported results and began to doubt the study.

Doubts about adrenal autografting contributed to interest in transplanting fetal brain tissue into Parkinson's patients. The same Mexican team performed two such operations in 1987. By 1988, similar operations had been reported by the Swedish team and by British researchers. And in November 1988, Dr. Curt Freed of the University of Colorado in Denver performed the first such operation in the United States.

More than two years later, the patient in that operation, Don Nelson, a former factory manager 52 years old at the time of the operation, shows signs of improvement. "His hands work much better. He's doing some woodworking," Freed explains. "We've reduced his drug dose. . . . We have not cured his par-

kinsonism, but we did secure some modification of it."

Freed, using private funds and requiring patients to pay the actual costs of the operations themselves, has since performed two more fetal tissue transplants. One patient has shown no improvement, but Freed says the other — operated on in January 1991 — is showing signs of "an excellent outcome."

Meanwhile, at Yale University, Eugene Redmond was designing a more ambitious study, aiming at up to 20 fetal tissue transplants to test the procedure. Redmond has now performed nine operations and has prepared an article for publication later this year describing the results. In part because of the seeming exaggerations about some of the other clinical studies, Redmond has declined to be specific about the results. But he suggests they were encouraging. "It's reasonable to assume that if our efforts were not encouraging, we would not continue," he says.

### NIH's Role

Freed's and Redmond's work was the type often funded by the NIH. Indeed, the NIH had been continuing to support fetal research since adoption of the 1975 guidelines, which prohibited research on living fetuses but left the study of dead fetuses up to state and local laws. And an NIH-funded tissue and organ registry played an important role in assisting the early tissue transplant research.

The National Disease Research Interchange (NDRI) had been established in 1980 with NIH funding as a clearinghouse for human cell, tissue and organ retrieval for use by U.S. researchers. The Philadelphia-based organization helped establish the national network for adult pancreases, for example, to support the research on islet transplantation in diabetes. In 1984, in response to sci-

entists' urgings, NDRI turned to setting up a similar network for fetal cadaver tissue. Over the next three years, the NDRI provided 2,000 to 3,000 fetal samples to 23 researchers. In June 1987, however, the NDRI discontinued collection of fetal samples "because of concerns expressed by NDRI's NIH advisers," according to the group's president, Lee Ducat.[13]

Around the same time, NIH researchers were preparing to perform what would have been the first U.S. fetal neural transplant on a Parkinson's patient. According to reports, the researchers were told two days before the operation was to take place that it had been postponed while the Reagan administration reviewed the proposal.[14] That review broadened into a full examination of the issues of fetal tissue transplants and an officially declared moratorium on NIH funding of research in the field.

## NIH Funding Moratorium

The Reagan administration's controversial decision to bar NIH funding of fetal tissue transplant research came in an undramatic form: a three-page internal memorandum from Robert E. Windom, assistant secretary for health, to Dr. James E. Wyngaarden, the NIH director. "I have given careful thought to your request to perform an experiment calling for the implantation of human neural tissue from induced abortions into Parkinson's patients to ameliorate the symptoms of this disorder," Windom wrote.

The proposal, he continued, "raises a number of questions — primarily ethical and legal — that have not been satisfactorily addressed. . . ." For that reason, Windom said, he wanted Wyngaarden to convene "one or more special outside advisory committees" to "comprehensively" examine the use of fetal tissue from induced abortions in transplantation and "to advise us on whether this kind of research should be performed, and, if so, under what circumstances." The memorandum, dated March 22, 1988, listed 10 questions for the advisory groups to consider, including:

■ Is an induced abortion of moral relevance to the decision to use human fetal tissue for research?

■ Does the use of fetal tissue in research encourage women to have an abortion?

■ Would abortion clinics change procedures for performing abortions — for example, deliberately delay an abortion — if fetal tissue transplants became common?

Other questions focused on current practices regarding payment for fetal tissue, the impact of state and local laws on fetal research and the possible development of fetal cell cultures as an alternative to fresh fetal tissue. Pending the report and Wyngaarden's reconsideration of the issue, Windom said he was withholding his approval of any experiments involving transplantation of fetal tissue if obtained from induced abortions — though not, he emphasized, if obtained from spontaneous abortions or stillbirths.

News of Windom's decision was first published by *The Washington Post* on April 15, and scientists reacted sharply. "NIH sets the pace, and this will cripple fetal research in the United States," said Dr. Bernard Liebel, a professor of medicine at the University of Toronto and an expert on fetal research and juvenile diabetes.[15]

Anti-abortion groups praised the administration's decision. Willke of the National Right to Life Committee urged members of his organization to write President Reagan and urge him to make the funding ban permanent.

Meanwhile, Wyngaarden had appointed a 21-member panel to study the issues Windom had listed. The head of the panel was a retired federal appeals court judge from Philadelphia, Arlin Adams. In addition, two members of the panel were picked to chair committees focusing respectively on the scientific and legal/ethical issues: Kenneth Ryan of Harvard Medical School and LeRoy Walters of the Kennedy Institute of Bioethics. Other panel members included eight physicians or medical researchers, three law professors, three theologians, two leaders of minority organizations, a psychologist, James Bopp, general counsel of the National Right to Life Committee, and Notre Dame University theologian James T. Burtchaell.

The panel held two days of public hearings Sept. 14 and 15, taking testimony or statements from more than 50 individuals or organizations representing all areas of research and a wide range of views. But just a week before the scheduled hearings, news leaked that the White House had already drafted a broadly worded, permanent ban on federal support for any research involving electively aborted fetuses and had told HHS Secretary Otis R. Bowen that it wanted to issue the directive "as soon as possible."[16]

The White House backpedaled the next day. Spokesman Marlin Fitzwater described the draft order as "a very first cut." And policy adviser Gary Bauer, who had supervised the preparation of the proposal, said it would be all right for HHS to await the report from the advisory committee before responding.[17] For his part, HHS Secretary Bowen told a congressional committee Sept. 15 that he had "no position absolutely as yet."

"The big danger that needs to be prevented is the possibility of any sale of fetal tissue by those who would become pregnant with intent

to sell," Bowen said. Then, after listing a number of benefits from fetal tissue research, Bowen concluded by referring to its possible use in treating Parkinson's disease: "I know if I had Parkinson's, I'd be grateful for [fetal] cells. . . ."

The benefits of further study were also emphasized by the medical researchers who dominated the witness list in the two days of hearings by the advisory committee. Among the witnesses were Lafferty from Colorado, Sollinger from Wisconsin and Redmond from Yale. Along with other medical experts and representatives of groups like the Juvenile Diabetes Foundation and the United Parkinson Foundation, they urged the advisory panel to recommend resumed NIH funding of the fetal tissue transplant experiments.

Some of those witnesses, as well as a handful of others who avoided a direct response on the funding issue, called for a variety of safeguards on gathering fetal tissue and deciding on its use. But strong opposition to federal funding of the research came only from anti-abortion groups, including the National Right to Life Committee, the American Life League and the National Conference of Catholic Bishops' Committee for Pro-Life Activities.

### Panel's Recommendations

Three months later, the advisory panel completed its report, presented not as a unified narrative but as a series of answers to the 10 questions Windom had propounded. The panel's conclusion came in its answer to the first question: "It is of moral relevance that human fetal tissue for research has been obtained from induced abortions," the panel said. "However, in light of the fact that abortion is legal and that the research in question is intended to achieve significant medical goals, the panel concludes that the use of such tissue is acceptable public policy."

The panel said four guidelines were appropriate in light of "the moral convictions deeply held in our society":

■ The decision to terminate a pregnancy and the procedures for abortion should be independent from retrieval and use of fetal tissue.

■ Payments should be prohibited, except payment for expenses associated with retrieval, storage, preparation and transportation of tissue.

■ Potential recipients should be properly informed of the source of the tissue.

■ Procedures should be adopted that "accord human fetal tissue the same respect accorded other cadaveric human tissues entitled to respect."

The panel said it doubted that use of fetal tissue for research would lead to an increase in the number of abortions but endorsed two guidelines to safeguard against that possibility: requiring that any discussion of donating fetal tissue come only after the decision on terminating the pregnancy and prohibiting the woman from designating the transplant-recipient of the fetal tissue.

The panel answered Windom's other questions by recommending other procedural guidelines and pronouncing the previous scientific research with animals sufficient to justify human clinical studies. But it ended with no explicit recommendation on resuming NIH funding of the research.

In a separate statement, Adams, the chairman of the panel, noted his long opposition to abortion but endorsed federal funding of fetal tissue research as a means to regulate what would otherwise be "completely unsupervised" private research. Safeguards developed by NIH, Adams said, "would protect pregnant women and fetuses in a far more circumspect and intelligent manner

than if the NIH did not participate in any way."

In a harshly worded dissent, Bopp and Burtchaell accused the panel's majority of "a raw and ruthless determination 'to achieve significant medical goals' no matter what the moral consequences." They argued that fetal tissue transplant research was unacceptable because of the woman's inability to give proper consent for use of the fetus, the likely incentive to future abortions and "complicity with abortions al-

> **The NIH advisory panel noted it was "of moral relevance" that fetal tissue for research was obtained from abortions, but the panel concluded that the use of such tissue was "acceptable public policy."**

ready performed" — which they likened to Nazi researchers' experiments on Holocaust victims.*

The NIH director's standing advisory committee quickly — and unanimously — endorsed the advisory panel's findings Dec. 14, adding an explicit recommendation to lift the moratorium on NIH funding. A

---

*Rabbi Bleich of Yeshiva University issued a separate dissent, predicting the research would "have the effect of increasing instances of feticide. . . ." A fourth panel member, Daniel Robinson, chairman of the department of psychology at Georgetown University, filed a letter to state his "personal" opposition to abortion or to any federal funding for research involving fetuses from induced abortions. As a panel member, however, he said he had tried to address the "public policy" questions apart from the question of the morality of abortion.

month later, with President-elect Bush about to take office, NIH Director Wyngaarden formally transmitted the report and recommendation to HHS.

The presidential transition delayed action on the recommendation, but anti-abortion groups were cheered by the appointment of a strong opponent of abortion, James O. Mason, to be assistant secretary of health. While the issue was pending, however, two medical groups weighed in with recommendations for continuing fetal tissue transplant research under ethical safeguards. In April, the Stanford University Medical Center Committee on Ethics published its conclusion that human fetal tissue "can be used ethically for medical research and treatment."[18] And in June the American Medical Association (AMA) declared fetal tissue transplants "a promising area of clinical investigation that should continue to receive federal funding."[19]

### Administration's Response

Mason finally announced his position Nov. 1, 1989. He told reporters he was recommending an indefinite extension of the moratorium, saying that funding of fetal tissue transplant research would amount to government encouragement of elective abortion and that successful research would create a demand for fetuses that would likely lead to more abortions.

The next day, HHS Secretary Sullivan, who had already indicated he would defer to Mason on the issue, concurred, saying "the limited moratorium" would be continued "indefinitely." In a three-page letter to Acting NIH Director William H. Raub, Sullivan said he, too, was convinced fetal tissue transplants might increase the number of abortions. "Providing the additional rationalization of directly advancing the cause of human therapeutics cannot help but tilt some already vulnerable women toward a decision to have an abortion," he wrote.

Anti-abortion groups praised the decision, but the medical and research communities were outraged. "It's like the Middle Ages," said Dr. Birt Harvey, president of the American Academy of Pediatrics.[20]

Among the public critics were current and former high-ranking NIH officials. "Banning federal funds will shut this field down," said Florence Haseltine, director of the Center for Population Research at the NIH's National Institute of Child Health and Development.[21] "I know of no precedents of repression of federal science like this one," said Dr. John Fletcher, director of the Center for Biomedical Ethics and Religious Studies at the University of Virginia and former chief ethics officer for NIH's clinical center.[22]

### Congress Reacts

With the administration's decision finally made, attention shifted to Congress. The House Commerce Subcommittee on Health and the Environment, chaired by Rep. Waxman, called on Mason to defend the policy in a hearing April 3, 1990, that also included testimony from opposing members of the NIH advisory panel and representatives of medical and disease groups.

Waxman, a strong supporter of abortion rights and federal health research funding, derided the funding ban, calling it a "know-nothing policy" adopted with "no evidence, no backing in the NIH director's advisory committee, and against the recommendations of its own expert panel." But, under relentless questioning by Waxman, Mason clung to the policy and the administration's rationale. "I don't believe that a practice which, to succeed, must have a continuous supply of aborted

fetuses is one that this nation wants or needs," Mason said. He reiterated that fetal tissue transplants could tilt some women to have an abortion and argued that the recommended "wall" between the abortion procedure and use of the donated tissue "cannot be built."

Four months later, Waxman introduced legislation to overturn the funding moratorium. He succeeded in attaching the repealer to a three-year NIH authorization bill that won approval in the Health Subcommittee on Sept. 18 and in the full En-

ergy and Commerce Committee on Sept. 26.

The companion Senate bill contained no similar provision, however, and the Bush administration staunchly opposed the provision. Facing a likely veto, Waxman and others decided to drop the fetal tissue research funding provision and a host of other controversial sections. The stripped-down measure cleared Congress in October, leaving the fetal tissue research issue to be debated again when the 102nd Congress convened in 1991.[23] ■

# CURRENT SITUATION

## Science Issues

The NIH moratorium frustrated researchers and scientists — none more than the NIH team whose proposal had prompted the review in the first place. "Science is driven by enthusiasm, and this has really suppressed enthusiasm," Dr. Edward H. Oldfield, chief of neurosurgery at the NIH, told the Los Angeles Times.[24]

Both Freed at Colorado and Redmond at Yale say the need to rely on private funds has affected their studies on Parkinson's patients. Freed got seed money from a local philanthropist whose brother suffered from Parkinson's but he has since required patients themselves to pay the cost of the operation — about $24,000, a hefty sum although far less than most transplant operations. "It is influencing the nature of the study," Freed says. "It's biasing the study toward an older and richer group."

The two U.S. researchers focusing on diabetes — Lafferty at Colorado and Sollinger at Wisconsin — both

halted their work because of scientific problems. But Sollinger, whose NIH funding would not have been affected by the moratorium, says the controversy was also a factor in his decision. "I thought [halting the research] would be a prudent thing to do until the issues were resolved," he says.

Work was proceeding in other countries, though, and the latest reported results from the Swedish team on their work with Parkinson's patients were encouraging. The patient they operated on in 1989 showed marked improvement by the spring of 1990. Previously unable to walk and rarely able to control his muscles, the patient was described in news accounts as having recovered enough to carry out extensive renovations on his home. "After only a year it is far too early to say he is cured," said Ollie Lindvall, professor of neurology at University Hospital in Lund in southern Sweden. "But we are on the threshold of something very important." [25]

Sweden is one of six countries where parliamentary or medical society committees have adopted statements approving fetal tissue research. (The others are Australia, Britain, Canada, France and the

Continued on p. 576

# Tough Choices

Guy and Terri Walden, devout Christians strongly opposed to abortion, have confronted in the starkest possible terms the question of using tissue from an aborted fetus in experimental medicine. When tests early in Terri's pregnancy last year showed the fetus had the same rare genetic disorder that had already taken the lives of two of their children, the couple had to decide whether to allow the use of tissue from an aborted fetus for an in utero transplant to treat or possibly prevent the disease.

"A lot of the objections [to fetal research], when it's a matter of life or death for your child, don't hold much water," says Guy Walden, pastor of a small Baptist church in Houston.

The Waldens decided to try the transplant. A little more than a year after the operation — the first reported fetus-to-fetus transplant in the United States — the Waldens and their doctors are encouraged, but do not know yet whether the operation was a success.

"I wish I could tell you unambiguously this baby is engrafted and the engrafted cells are generating the [desired] enzyme," says Dr. Robert Nathan Slotnick at the University of California-Davis School of Medicine, who performed the transplant on May 23, 1990. "We have very promising signs, but I can't tell you that."

The Waldens date their "pilgrimage" from 1980, when their first child, Jason, was diagnosed with a fatal genetic disorder called Hurler's syndrome, which is caused by the absence of an enzyme needed to break down one of the body's sugars. Without the enzyme, the sugar accumulates in the body's cells and causes progressive infections, mental retardation and other problems. About 40 to 80 cases are reported in the United States every year. The disease is said to be invariably fatal by the age of 10.

The Waldens were missionaries in Costa Rica when they learned of Jason's illness. After Terri became pregnant again, they returned to the United States for tests to see whether this child would also have Hurler's syndrome. The diagnosis was positive, and doctors counseled the Waldens to have an abortion. "We told them that due to our religious convictions, abortion was not an option for us," Walden said at an April 15 hearing before the House Commerce Subcommittee on Health and the Environment.

After Angie was born, Guy and Terri considered not having any more children. But they read in the Bible, "Children are an heritage of the Lord," and decided that they would. When Terri became pregnant in 1986, the couple decided to forgo genetic screening. Hannah was born in September; she does not have Hurler's. Nor does their fourth child, John, born in November 1988. Jason died in January 1989 — eight years, nine months old. Angie died in September 1990, two months short of her eighth birthday.

Meanwhile, Terri had become pregnant again. One of the doctors that Guy and Terri had consulted put them in touch with Slotnick as someone who might be able to treat the disease in the womb. "We are getting very good" at diagnosing genetic diseases before birth, Slotnick says. "Our interest now has been: Is there much we can do beyond diagnosis and offering termination of pregnancy?"

Postnatal bone marrow transplants are one way to treat some genetic diseases, including Hurler's, but there are problems, including finding a match and undergoing radiation or chemotherapy to kill the existing bone marrow.

So Slotnick explored the idea of an in utero bone marrow transplant — to be performed in the first trimester of pregnancy, before the fetus was likely to reject non-matching donor tissue. He performed the procedure successfully on monkeys and then scouted for parents who would agree to participate in a clinical experiment.

Nearly 20 couples were interviewed; all except the Waldens decided to have an abortion instead. Guy and Terri had to wrestle with a different issue: whether the experiment could be squared with their anti-abortion views. They consulted other pastors and fellow Christians, lawyers and other people they trusted. And they also looked to the Scripture — and reread the story of God's creation of Eve from Adam's rib. "God formed one human being from the tissue of another," Guy Walden said. "Not only does God approve of this, but he himself performed the first one."

Slotnick then had to find a donor. Luckily, a patient came to him with an ectopic or so-called tubal pregnancy — implantation of the fetus in the fallopian tube rather than the uterus. Abortions are necessary to protect the mother in such cases and, for that reason, anti-abortion groups do not oppose use of resulting fetal tissue in transplant research. As Guy Walden acknowledged in an interview, however, "Had the only tissue been from an electively aborted fetus, . . . we would have used it."

Slotnick says the half-hour surgery itself was "rather unremarkable." The rest of Terri's pregnancy was also unremarkable, although Nathan was born in October three weeks premature with an underdeveloped respiratory system that Slotnick believes to be unrelated to the genetic disease or the transplant operation.

Both Slotnick and the Waldens favor lifting the federal funding moratorium to enable research to be stepped up. "I feel that if the technology could be brought about that we could heal diseases in the womb, a lot of parents would not get abortions," Guy Walden explains.

"We're getting better at handling fetal tissue and storing it," Slotnick adds. "It's certainly possible that cell cultures could be grown so that you wouldn't need aborted fetuses. . . . But if you can't do the research, you can't answer the question."

Continued from p. 574
Netherlands.) The Council of Europe Parliamentary Assembly — with representatives from 14 European countries — adopted a similar recommendation in 1986. And, according to Walters, the 41st World Medical Assembly, with representatives from 140 countries, also endorsed fetal tissue transplant research in September 1989. The current U.S. funding moratorium, he says, "is out of step with the international consensus on this topic."

A congressional hearing on April 15 called to focus attention on the funding moratorium provided the setting for the dramatic announcement of the latest area of experimentation. The parents of a child diagnosed before birth with a rare and fatal genetic disorder told the House Commerce Subcommittee on Health of their decision to permit a surgical team to perform the first U.S. fetus-to-fetus transplant. The story drew added political significance from the fact that the couple agreed to the experiment only after reconciling it with their strongly held views opposing abortion. (See story, p. 575.)

## Political Issues

The Health Subcommittee's hearing also gave the new NIH director, Bernadine Healy, an opportunity to reaffirm her promise to abide by the fetal tissue transplant moratorium — which she had opposed as a member of the NIH advisory panel.

Healy had first promised to support the moratorium during her confirmation hearing before the Senate Labor and Human Resources Committee on March 14. "I firmly believe that much of the success of science in this country is that it has largely been non-political and non-partisan," Healy told the senators. "But there are circumstances that

arise where the moral or ethical concerns of the society may appear to collide with the pursuit of science." Departing from her prepared text at that point, Healy added: "Sometimes this results in a timeout, as with the fetal tissue moratorium imposed by Secretary Sullivan, which I am prepared to support."

To Waxman's Health Subcommittee, Healy repeated that she had "a moral responsibility to abide by the ban," but she sought to minimize its effects by pointing out that the NIH was continuing to fund a "substantial portfolio" of fetal tissue research within the limits of the moratorium.[26]

Healy also indicated that her thinking had shifted somewhat on the question of whether fetal tissue transplants might cause some women to have an abortion — a possibility she had at first rejected. "I must say that I was shocked and distressed in the course of the dialogue that followed those panels to hear that in fact there are some women who would willingly get pregnant in order to terminate a pregnancy for the purposes of helping a kin who has one of these dread diseases," Healy said during questioning by Rep. Ron Wyden, D-Ore. "As a woman, I believe that is exploitation of women. I found that offensive, unimaginable at the time."[27]

Waxman had included a provision to lift the moratorium in a new NIH reauthorization bill (HR 1532), coupling it with a broader provision to block the HHS secretary from rejecting the ethical recommendations of expert panels. In a letter the day before the scheduled markup of the bill, Secretary Sullivan warned that the president would veto the bill because of those and other provisions limiting administration discretion over NIH funding and policies.

Republicans on the subcommittee took up Sullivan's warning, depicting the bill as "micromanagement"

of NIH by congressional Democrats. But Waxman's bill passed largely intact. An amendment by Rep. William E. Dannemeyer, R-Calif., to strike the provision lifting the fetal research moratorium failed 7-13, with just one Democrat — Gerry Sikorski of Minnesota — breaking party lines to vote for it.[28]

The full Energy and Commerce Committee approved the bill a month later, on June 4. Dannemeyer's amendment to preserve the moratorium failed again on a largely party-line vote of 17-26.[29]

Afterward, opposing camps put differing spins on the committee breakdown. Douglas Johnson of the National Right to Life Committee said he was encouraged by the near party-line vote. "It would indicate that [Waxman] would not be anywhere near veto-override strength on this issue," Johnson said. But Sally Rosenberg, general counsel for the Juvenile Diabetes Foundation, one of the groups lobbying for Waxman's bill, noted with satisfaction that three anti-abortion lawmakers — Democrats Terry L. Bruce of Illinois, Ralph M. Hall of Texas and Thomas J. Manton of New York — voted to overturn the fetal research funding curb.

When the NIH bill reached the House floor July 25, fetal research opponents made a tactical decision not to try to remove the provision repealing the moratorium. Rep. Christopher H. Smith, R-N.J., co-chairman of the Congressional Pro-Life Caucus, explained that anti-abortion forces chose to spare lawmakers a bruising fight because they expected the bill to be vetoed.

Waxman countered that anti-abortion lawmakers feared they would not get the one-third vote on the fetal research issue that would be needed to sustain a veto. "We had many pro-life members tell us they just didn't see this as an abortion issue and they

Continued on p. 578

# At Issue:

## Should the federal government lift its moratorium on funding research using tissue from aborted fetuses?

### REP. HENRY A. WAXMAN

*Waxman, D-Calif., is chairman of the House Energy and Commerce Subcommittee on Health and the Environment.*
FROM *FETAL TISSUE TRANSPLANTATION RESEARCH HEARING,* HOUSE HEALTH SUBCOMMITTEE, April 2, 1990.

**yes**

Spinal cord injury, Parkinson's disease and diabetes cripple and kill millions of Americans. For years, people with these conditions have hoped for medical breakthroughs, and for years nothing was found.

Breakthroughs are now being found. But the Bush administration has ordered the National Institutes of Health to ignore them — not because of concern about their scientific merit but because of misplaced allegiance to the most extreme elements of the anti-abortion movement. Because these research projects involve the transplantation of fetal tissue rather than organs or tissue from adults, the Bush administration has decided to abandon all such research and give up hope.

This is wrong, scientifically and ethically.

Let's be clear at the outset: This is not research on living fetuses, on potentially living fetuses, or on newborn babies. This is research on tissue on fetuses that are dead, with no viability, and not even "potential life."

. . . The rationalization of this "know-nothing" policy is that, despite all scientific advice and evidence to the contrary, the administration fears that American women might have more abortions so that they can contribute tissue to science. The administration has concluded this with no evidence, no backing in the NIH Director's Advisory Committee and against the recommendation of its own expert panel. The policy is comparable to one of banning lifesaving organ transplants to limit traffic accidents, and it is equally ludicrous. . . .

There are legal questions regarding the administration's ability to issue such far-reaching prohibitions with no authority, no publication and no procedures. There are policy questions on censorship, chilling of research and scientific freedom. But, most important, there are questions of science and morality regarding the decision to abandon research and hope for millions of Americans.

We should not hold greater reverence for dead tissue than for living people. And we should not resign our public health responsibilities in favor of political rhetoric. This ban should be rescinded, and research should go on.

### JAMES O. MASON

*Mason is assistant secretary for health, U.S. Department of Health and Human Services.*
FROM *FETAL TISSUE TRANSPLANTATION RESEARCH HEARING,* HOUSE HEALTH SUBCOMMITTEE, April 2, 1990.

**no**

Human fetal tissue has been used in biomedical research for many years. More recently, researchers have explored transplantation of fetal tissue in patients with Parkinson's disease, diabetes and Alzheimer's. It is this transplantation of human fetal tissue from induced abortions, as distinguished from other fetal tissue research, which is the subject of the moratorium. . . .

We are persuaded that one must accept the likelihood that permitting the human fetal tissue research at issue will increase the incidence of abortion. We are particularly convinced by those who point out that most women arrive at the abortion decision after much soul searching and uncertainty. Providing the additional rationalization of directly advancing the cause of human therapeutics cannot help but tilt some already vulnerable women toward a decision to have an abortion.

The proponents of fetal tissue transplantation research acknowledge that a strict wall would have to be erected between the abortion decision and the decision to donate fetal tissue to research. While such a distinction may be easy to theorize, we doubt that such a neat separation can be accomplished.

For example, because there is often a need to utilize post-mortem tissue promptly, it may be necessary to consult pregnant women before the abortion is actually performed. This will potentially influence the decision-making process despite the safeguards recommended by the NIH advisory panel. In addition, should the research efforts in question prove successful, a greater need for aborted fetuses could result. . . .

The Department, through the NIH, has a longstanding commitment to sponsoring innovative research approaches to diabetes, Parkinson's and other diseases. Many different avenues are being explored to prevent, treat and cure these disabling conditions. . . .

Extending the moratorium was not an easy decision. The Secretary [Louis W. Sullivan] and I are staunch supporters of biomedical research. In the case of fetal tissue transplantation research, however, these research objectives conflict with administration policy that seeks to ensure the protection of all human life.

Continued from p. 576

were with us," he said. "That's why there wasn't a vote."

Waxman sought to pick up support for the bill by agreeing to an amendment to extend to private-sector research the bill's provisions barring sale of fetal tissue and preventing pregnant women from designating the recipient of fetal tissue. But the 274-144 vote for the bill on final passage was short of the two-thirds margin that would be needed to override a veto. Afterward, Dannemeyer confidently predicted, "The policy of this administration will be sustained." [30]

## Legal Issues

While the NIH bill was moving in the House, word had leaked that a number of groups opposed to the moratorium, led by the Chicago-based United Parkinson Foundation, were preparing to go to court to overturn the funding curb on administrative law grounds. Judy Rosner, the organization's executive director, said the suit would contend that HHS did not follow the requirements of the Administrative Procedure Act in imposing the indefinite moratorium and erred in going against the advice of the commission it created to consider the issue. Rosner said timing of the suit would depend on what happened in Congress. "We're waiting to see what happens to Mr. Waxman's bill," she said.

The legal issues had been considered — and viewed as problematic — within HHS prior to Secretary Sullivan's decision. In a memorandum dated Oct. 4, 1989, Richard J. Riseberg of the HHS general counsel's office advised that if the March 1988 moratorium were made permanent, "consideration would have to be given" to the Administrative Procedure Act's formal rulemaking procedures "in order to maximize our legal position in case the moratorium is challenged under that Act."

The 1946 act, the basic law governing federal regulatory proceedings, generally requires agencies to give the public notice and an opportunity to comment on proposed new rules before adopting them. It also gives courts power to overturn new regulations if, for example, they go beyond the agency's statutory authority or are not supported by the evidence the agency gathers.

Riseberg's four-page options paper noted that formal procedures would be more time-consuming and possibly lead to more publicity than the alternative of "simply mak[ing] the temporary policy permanent." But he said that such an extension "likely fits within the definition" of a rule under administrative law requiring either publication in the *Federal Register* or formal rule-making procedures. "To the extent any of these are not taken," Riseberg warned, "it opens a window of potential legal vulnerability in the event of litigation." [31]

In extending the funding curbs a month later, Sullivan said he was extending the moratorium "indefinitely." But when Assistant Secretary Mason appeared before the Health Subcommittee in April 1990, he acknowledged to Waxman that the action amounted to a permanent ban. "Mr. Chairman, seeing the short-term now and the long-term effects, I don't see a change in that moratorium," Mason said.                                                                ∎

# OUTLOOK

## Will Moratorium End?

The prospects for fetal tissue transplant research are clouded by political controversy and scientific difficulty. But the consensus within the medical research community is that the studies conducted so far provide encouraging signs that in the future some patients with serious diseases may be treatable with transplants using cells derived from fetal tissue. With research continuing in other countries and, with private funds, in the United States, continuing, slow progress is likely in dealing with the medical and scientific difficulties of such procedures even if the federal ban on funding such experiments remains in effect.

In Congress, the odds of overturning the HHS moratorium are no better than even despite the House's approval of a bill to lift the funding curb. The decision by the administration's supporters not to contest the issue on the House floor appeared to recognize a weak political position, but they did muster 144 votes against the bill on final passage — just two votes short of the number that would be needed to sustain a presidential veto even if all members voted.

The companion Senate bill (S 1523) introduced July 22 does not contain a provision to lift the fetal research moratorium. The principal staffer working on the issue for the Senate Labor and Human Resources Committee was said to believe that a measure lifting the moratorium could probably not be passed on the Senate floor. Sen. Kennedy, the committee's chairman, had previously criticized political restrictions on NIH funding. But the committee's ranking Republican, Orrin G. Hatch of Utah, was a strong anti-abortion lawmaker and had played a key role in the 1985 measure codifying the previous HHS rules restricting research on live fetuses.

Even if Congress did pass a bill to

lift the funding curb, anti-abortion groups say they expect President Bush would veto it. HHS Secretary Sullivan cited the fetal research issue as one of many sections of the Health Subcommittee bill that would lead "the president's senior advisers" to recommend a veto. Bush had used his veto to kill several abortion-related provisions objected to by anti-abortion groups, and through July Congress had never overridden a Bush veto.

That calculation left opponents with the probable need to go to court if they wanted to overturn the moratorium while Bush remained in office. The groups planning the suit declined to discuss it in detail, but on the surface their legal theory had a plausible basis. Predicting any legal issue is hazardous, however, and the administration might be able to impose a similar funding restriction through more formal procedures if the moratorium were overturned.

### *Research Continues*

Clinical studies were continuing despite the lack of NIH funding. Perhaps the most eagerly awaited experimental results were from Yale's Redmond on the half dozen fetal neural transplants performed on Parkinson's patients. The other principal researchers with Parkinson's patients — Freed at Colorado and the Swedish team — had also described encouraging results from some, though not all, of their transplant procedures.

The results of fetal cell transplants with diabetics were more mixed. Two U.S. scientists — Sollinger at Wisconsin and Lafferty at Colorado — had both suspended clinical studies because of difficulties in overcoming rejection problems with transplant patients. But both researchers are continuing animal studies in hope of surmounting the problems.

The fetus-to-fetus transplant performed in May 1990 indicated the continuing interest in exploring fetal cell transplants to treat genetic disorders. But in this area too, wide use of fetal cell transplants is still far down the road. And for other diseases, the potential is even more speculative.

AIDS groups, for example, publicized an NIH official's statement in fall 1989 that fetal liver cell transplants might offer hope for treating the disease: "[F]etal liver cells ... very well may be able to completely suppress the virus and allow reconstitution," Dr. Anthony Fauci, director of the National Institute of Allergy and Infectious Diseases, told the group ACT-UP (AIDS Coalition to Unleash Power). Afterward, however, Fauci stressed to a reporter that the therapy was not proven and described the publicity as "a lot of to-do about absolutely nothing." [32]

The progress in fetal cell transplant procedures has been slow. But fetal research in this and other fields has been accelerating in recent years, and the scientific work is not going to be stopped by the lack of federal funding in the United States. As breakthroughs are achieved, the pleas from researchers, disease groups and individuals suffering from some of mankind's most debilitating diseases will grow stronger — testing the ability of anti-abortion forces to keep the funding ban in effect. ∎

## Notes

[1] Writing in *The New England Journal of Medicine,* May 23, 1974, p. 1199.
[2] Diana S. Hart, "Fetal Research and Anti-abortion Politics: Holding Science Hostage," *Family Planning Perspectives,* March/April 1975, p. 73.
[3] Center for Biomedical Ethics, University of Minnesota, *The Use of Human Fetal Tissue: Scientific, Ethical, and Policy Concerns,* 1990, pp. 65-66.
[4] *Ibid.,* pp. 21, 28-29.
[5] Hart, *op. cit.,* pp. 73-74, 75.
[6] Hart, *op. cit.,* p. 76. The Alan Guttmacher Institute is a nonprofit research group once affiliated with the Planned Parenthood Federation of America.
[7] *Ibid.,* pp. 76-78.
[8] Rachel Benson Gold and Dorthy Lehrman, "Fetal Research Under Fire: The Influence of Abortion Politics," *Family Planning Perspectives,* January/February 1989, p. 8; Center for Biomedical Ethics, *op. cit.,* pp. 170-172.
[9] Hart, *op. cit.,* pp. 78-79.
[10] Center for Biomedical Ethics, *op. cit.,* pp. 59-60.
[11] Center for Biomedical Ethics, *op. cit.,* pp. 66-67.
[12] *Ibid.,* p. 101.
[13] Statement of Lee Ducat, *Report of the Human Fetal Tissue Transplantation Research Panel, Vol. II,* December 1988, p. D107.
[14] *Los Angeles Times,* Oct. 17, 1990, p. A18.
[15] Quoted in *The Washington Post,* April 15, 1988, p. A20.
[16] *The Washington Post,* Sept. 9, 1988, p.A1; *The New York Times,* Sept. 9, 1988, p. A10.
[17] *The New York Times,* Sept. 10, 1988, p. 6.
[18] *The New England Journal of Medicine,* April 20, 1989, p. 1093.
[19] *Chicago Tribune,* June 25, 1989, p. 16. Also see *Journal of the American Medical Association,* Jan. 26, 1990, p. 565.
[20] Quoted in *The New York Times,* Nov. 2, 1989, p. A1.
[21] Quoted in *The Washington Post,* Nov. 2, 1989, p. A3.
[22] Quoted in *The New York Times,* Nov. 2, 1989, p. B19.
[23] *Congressional Quarterly Weekly Report,* Aug. 25, 1990, p. 2719; *1990 Congressional Quarterly Almanac,* p. 600.
[24] *Los Angeles Times,* Oct. 17, 1990, p. A18.
[25] Quoted in *The Washington Post,* March 27, 1990, p. A1.
[26] See *The Washington Times,* April 26, 1991, p. A3.
[27] Partial transcript of hearing provided by National Right to Life Committee.
[28] *Congressional Quarterly Weekly Report,* May 11, 1991, p. 1204.
[29] *Congressional Quarterly Weekly Report,* June 8, 1991, p. 1505.
[30] *Congressional Quarterly Weekly Report,* July 27, 1991, p. 2078.
[31] House Energy and Commerce Subcommittee on Health and the Environment, Fetal Tissue Transplantation Research Hearing, April 12, 1990, 213-218.
[32] *New York Newsday,* Nov. 3, 1989, p. A8. A longer excerpt of Fauci's comments to the group appears, along with the *Newsday* article, in Health Subcommittee, *Ibid.,* pp. 169-171.

# Bibliography

## Selected Sources Used

## Articles

**National Right to Life Committee, "Scavenging Aborted Babies: The Myth and the Reality of Fetal Tissue Transplants," *NRL News*, Jan. 22, 1989.**

This special report by the National Right to Life Committee newspaper contains articles critiquing the arguments for fetal tissue transplants and describing from a critical perspective the status of the medical research, including possible alternatives to fetal tissue transplants.

**Donovan, Patricia, "Funding Restrictions on Fetal Research: The Implications for Science and Health," *Family Planning Perspectives*, September/October 1990.**

This article from the magazine of the pro-abortion rights Alan Guttmacher Institute examines from a critical perspective the effects of the moratorium on federal funding for fetal tissue transplant research.

**Gold, Rachel Benson, and Lehrman, Dorothy, "Fetal Research Under Fire: The Influence of Abortion Politics," *Family Planning Perspectives*, January/February 1989.**

This article traces the history of fetal research and political developments in the United States from the 1973 abortion rights ruling *Roe v. Wade* through the report of the National Institutes of Health special advisory committee on fetal tissue transplants.

**Kolata, Gina, "Miracle or Menace?" *Redbook*, September 1990.**

Kolata, who has covered the fetal research issue as a science reporter for *The New York Times*, provides a good overview of the issue. The magazine also asked readers to respond to a series of questions on the issue and published the results of that survey in December 1990.

## Reports and Studies

**American Medical Association, Council on Scientific Affairs and Council on Ethical and Judicial Affairs, "Medical Applications of Fetal Tissue Transplantation," *Journal of the American Medical Association*, Jan. 26, 1990.**

This report by two AMA councils finds use of fetal tissue for transplant purposes ethically permissible if seven conditions are met. As background to these guidelines, the councils' report provides useful though technical detail on the status of transplant research as of mid-1989.

**National Institutes of Health, Consultants to the Advisory Committee to the Director, *Report of the Human Fetal Transplantation Research Panel*, December 1988.**

The NIH advisory panel's 73-page report (Vol. I) consists of its responses to the 10 questions posed by Robert Windom, assistant secretary of Health and Human Services, in creating the panel in March 1988, along with separate concurring and dissenting statements by various members. The second volume of the report contains statements from 35 witnesses representing all areas of research and all points of view.

**National Institutes of Health, Advisory Committee to the Director, *Human Fetal Tissue Transplantation Research*, December 1988.**

This is the report of the standing advisory committee to the director of NIH, recommending adoption of the recommendations of the special advisory committee that funding of fetal tissue transplant research be deemed "acceptable public policy." Included are statements from members of the special advisory committee urging adoption or rejection of the report that provide additional insights into their deliberations and disagreements.

**U.S. House Subcommittee on Health and the Environment, Committee on Energy and Commerce, *Fetal Tissue Transplantation Research*, published proceedings of hearing in Washington, D.C., April 2, 1990.**

The House Health Subcommittee's hearing on legislation to lift the moratorium on federal funding for fetal tissue transplant research included testimony from 10 witnesses and statements from 13 organizations. Among the witnesses were the assistant secretary of Health and Human Services who recommended the moratorium and majority and dissenting members of the National Institutes of Health advisory committee on the issue. (The subcommittee held a second hearing on the issue on April 15, 1991; those proceedings have not been printed yet.)

**Center for Biomedical Ethics, University of Minnesota, *The Use of Human Fetal Tissue: Scientific, Ethical and Policy Concerns*, 1990.**

This 271-page report provides a comprehensive account of the history and status of fetal tissue research and a thorough and objective analysis of the ethical issues the research poses. The report also contains a lengthy, well-organized bibliography and a concise chronology.

# The Next Step

## Additional Articles from Current Periodicals

### Actions & defenses

**Gershon, D., "Will ban provoke challenge?"** *Nature,* **Sept. 6, 1990, p. 4.**

Reports that the Parkinson's Disease Foundation will soon decide whether to sue the U.S. administration over its ban on the use of federal funds to support fetal tissue transplantation research. Background of the ban; legal issues.

### Addresses & essays

**"Fetal flaw,"** *New Republic,* **Jan. 1, 1990, p. 7.**

Editorial. Criticizes the Department of Health and Human Services' extension of the Reagan administration's ban on federal funds for fetal tissue research. Refutes Republican right-to-lifers' claim that using the tissue will encourage abortions; agrees that moral issues must be addressed but urges stringent oversight rather than an outright ban.

### Case studies

**Hansen, J. T. and Sladek, J. R. Jr., "Fetal research,"** *Science,* **Nov. 10, 1989, p. 775.**

Reviews some of the significant contributions of fetal research and fetal tissue research over the past 20 years. Prenatal diagnosis; surgical intervention; vaccine development; future of fetal and fetal tissue research.

**Langone, J., "One womb to another,"** *Time,* **April 3, 1989, p. 71.**

Describes a historic fetal-cell transplant performed on a pregnant French woman in Lyon by Drs. Jean-Louis Touraine and Daniel Raudrant. How it was done.

**Marx, J., "Fetal nerve grafts show promise in Parkinson's,"** *Science,* **Feb. 2, 1990, p. 529.**

Reports on research by Swedish scientists in which fetal nerve tissue transplanted into the brain of a patient with severe Parkinson's disease produced a significant improvement in the patient's condition. Effects of dopamine-secreting neuron transplantation; grafting procedures; Mexican research report.

**Weiss, R., "Fetal-cell recipient showing improvements,"** *Science News,* **Feb. 3, 1990, p. 70.**

Reveals that a tiny sample of human fetal cells transplanted into the brain of a man with Parkinson's disease appears to have survived and grown there for at least eight months, significantly reducing his symptoms.

### Debates & issues

**"Fetal tissue wrangle,"** *Nature,* **Nov. 9, 1989, p. 104.**

Opinion. Opposes the U.S. secretary of Health and Human Services' decision to ban exploratory use with federal funds of fetal tissue transplants. The National Institutes of Health's reputation for intellectual independence will be seriously undermined. Comparison with British tissue regulations.

**"U.S. squeamishness,"** *Nature,* **Jan. 17, 1991, p. 181.**

Opinion. Criticizes the U.S. government for timidity over the use of fetal tissue in research. United States has ethical responsibilities in advising all researchers not just those supported by private funds.

**Annas, G. J. and Elias, S., "The politics of transplantation of human fetal tissue,"** *The New England Journal of Medicine,* **April 20, 1989, p. 1079.**

Discusses the use of fetal tissue in experimental transplantation and research. Report by the Human Tissue Fetal Transplant Research Panel created by the National Institutes of Health. Refers also to report of the Stanford University Medical Center Committee on Ethics in this issue of the Journal. Federal regulations; ethical issues.

**Beardsley, T., "Aborted research,"** *Scientific American,* **February 1990, p. 16.**

Discusses the controversy over fetal tissue research, as a result of the actions of abortion opponents and politicians, as well as in the face of stringent regulations by the National Institutes of Health. The controversy is hampering work on various diseases, fetal abnormalities research, and infertility.

**Budiansky, S., McAuliffe, K., et al., "The new rules of reproduction,"** *U.S. News & World Report,* **April 18, 1988, p. 66.**

Analysis of the field of reproduction in the modern world. Surrogate motherhood, frozen human embryos and fetal-tissue transplants were never envisioned by laws written in simpler times. As the technology of reproduction continues its rapid advancement, experts warn of "anarchy" — unless the law and ethics can catch up. The Vatican's stance; future reproductive possibilities.

**Kolata, G., "More U.S. curbs urged in the use of fetal tissue,"** *The New York Times,* **Nov. 19, 1989, Section 1, p. 1.**

Discusses a growing controversy over federal financing for fetal tissue research. Opponents' ethical concerns;

proponents' emphasis on the value of fetal tissue in medical research; how tissue is currently obtained and sold.

**Palca, J., "Fetal debate continues," *Nature,* June 8, 1989, p. 411.**

Reports on the U.S. controversy over abortion and government consideration of a moratorium on the use of human fetal tissue for transplantation. Problems for researchers; federally supported fetal research.

**Post, S.G., "Fetal tissue transplant: The right to question progress," *America,* Jan. 5, 1991 and Jan. 12, 1991, p. 14.**

Presents the opposition toward the use of fetal tissue transplants for research and disease therapy. Reasons include possible abortion encouragement, a link between the abortion centers and biomedical science and political turmoil. Benefits of fetal tissue transplants; issue of elective abortion.

**Thorne, E.D., "Regulating commerce in fetal tissue," *Society,* November/December 1988, p. 61.**

Doctors are fairly confident that within the next few years they will be able to transplant brain tissue from aborted human fetuses to alleviate, perhaps cure, several crippling diseases of the brain and central nervous system. A debate on the proper uses of fetal tissue is taking shape, and several states have already proposed regulatory initiatives.

**Weiss, R., "Bypassing the ban," *Science News,* Dec. 9, 1989, p. 378.**

Discusses the use of non-fetal cell substitutes due to the extended, indefinite ban on federally funded fetal tissue transplants. Therapeutic potential for Parkinson's disease; success with stimulating neuronal repair in animals.

**White, R., "The aborted fetus: a commercial prize," *America,* Jan. 23, 1988, p. 53.**

Discussion of the serious questions now being raised about the ownership and appropriate use of tissues removed from the human body during surgery or autopsy. And now the question of use of tissue of aborted fetuses is being raised; possibility of commercialization of aborted fetuses.

## Government policy

**"Federal fetal transplant ban continues," *Science News,* Nov. 11, 1989, p. 310.**

Reports that the Bush administration has extended a 20-month ban on federal funding for research involving fetal tissue transplantation. Criticism from scientists.

**Hilts, P.J., "Citing abortion, U.S. extends ban on**

**grants for fetal tissue work," *The New York Times,* Nov. 2, 1989, p. A1.**

Reports that Dr. James O. Mason, assistant secretary for health in the Department of Health and Human Services, extended a 20-month-old ban on federal financing of research using transplanted fetal tissue, overriding recommendations by medical panels that such work go ahead because of its promise for treating diabetes and other diseases. Criticism from medical professionals; conflict discussed.

**Marwick, C., "Ban to be lifted on research use of fetal tissue?" *Journal of the American Medical Association,* Jan. 20, 1989, p. 342.**

Reports on the National Institute of Health's advisory committee unanimously recommending lifting the moratorium on the use of human fetal tissues in clinical research studies.

**Myers, C., "NIH nominee voices support for moratorium on fetal-tissue research," *The Chronicle of Higher Education,* March 20, 1991, p. A28.**

Details some comments from Bernadine P. Healy at her confirmation hearings before the Senate Labor and Human Resources Committee. Nominee for director of the National Institutes of Health would support a controversial moratorium on federal support of fetal-tissue-transplantation research; Direct role in determining how much universities could charge for overhead; criticism of the administration; women's health a priority.

**Palca, J., "Fetal tissue transplants remain off limits," *Science,* Nov. 10, 1989, p. 752.**

Discusses the decision by Health and Human Services Secretary Louis W. Sullivan to indefinitely extend a moratorium on federal funding for research in which fetal tissue from recent abortions is transplanted into human patients. Ethical questions; uses of fetal tissue; special panel report.

**Rovner, J., "NIH nominee averts battle over fetal research ban," *Congressional Quarterly Weekly Report,* March 16, 1991, p. 686.**

Reports that a much-anticipated showdown over abortion and research using fetal tissue has been averted at least for the moment as President Bush's nominee to head the National Institutes of Health (NIH), who twice voted to overturn a ban on funding of research that uses aborted fetal tissue, promises to support the ban. Bernadine P. Healy; breezed through the rest of her questioning; on her way to becoming the first woman to head the NIH; anti-abortion groups wary.

**Weiss, R., "Panel recommends resuming fetal studies," *Science News,* Sept. 24, 1988, p. 197.**

Covers the National Institutes of Health advisory panel's decision to encourage use of cells and tissues from aborted fetuses in biomedical research. Fetal cell transplants; anti-abortion groups; uses for fetal cells.

Wheeler, D. L., "2 groups form a panel to set ethical guidelines on use of fetal tissue," *The Chronicle of Higher Education,* Jan. 16, 1991, p. A4.

Describes the National Advisory Board on Ethics in Reproduction (formed by the American College of Obstetricians and Gynecologists and the American Fertility Society) whose aim is to set standards for the regulation of experiments with fetal tissue and embryos. Federal government "moral and scientific vacuum"; diverse representatives; non-binding opinions.

## International policies

"Using fetal tissue," *Nature,* Aug. 3, 1989, p. 327.

Opinion. Discusses more restrictive rules for the use of fetal tissue in Britain. Basis of proposals; difficulty for government.

Coles, P., "French fetal cell transplant operations," *Nature,* Dec. 20, 1990 and Dec. 27, 1990, p. 667.

Reports that a French national ethics committee for life sciences and health has overturned its ban on the use of fetal brain tissue grafts for medical treatments. Doctors plan to carry out pilot operations to treat Parkinson patients.

Dickson, D., "Fetal tissue transplants win U.K. approval," *Science,* Aug. 4, 1989, p. 464.

Reports on a British government committee's approval of research involving fetal tissue from induced abortion. Response to ethical concerns; unlikelihood of the United States following Britain's lead. INSETS: Germany to ban embryo use, by D. Kirk; funding fight over facilities (conflict over use of National Science Foundation funds for university research facilities) by M. Crawford.

## Law & legislation

"The research freedom act," *Hastings Center Report,* January/February 1991, p. 2.

Discusses plans by Rep. Henry A. Waxman, D-Calif., to reintroduce the federal Research Freedom Act which was defeated last term. Moratorium on funding of fetal tissue transplantation; ethical safeguards of the Research Freedom Act of 1990; more.

Gershon, D., "Move to overturn ban," *Nature,* Aug. 16, 1990, p. 598.

Reports on legislation introduced by Rep. Henry A. Waxman, D-Calif., to overturn the moratorium on the use of federal funds to support fetal tissue research. Wax-

man's bill would also establish a mechanism for the review and approval of experiments in biomedical and behavioral research.

## Moral & religious aspects

"Fetal tissue panel organized," *Family Planning Perspectives,* January/February 1991, p. 4.

Reports on the announcement on Jan. 7 that there would be an assembly of a 15-member board to establish ethical standards for research involving human embryos and fetal tissue. American College of Obstetricians and Gynecologists; American Fertility Society; panel to consist of scientists, ethicists, lawyers, and religious leaders; federally funded fetal research.

Gershon, D., "New panel for ethical issues," *Nature,* Jan. 17, 1991, p. 184.

Reports that two U.S. medical organizations will establish a national advisory board to set ethical guidelines in reproductive and fetal tissue research. The founding societies are the American College of Obstetricians and Gynecologists and the American Fertility Society; the new board will be known as the National Advisory Board on Ethics in Reproduction.

Simons, A., "Brave new harvest," *Christianity Today,* Nov. 19, 1990, p. 24.

Explores the controversial issue of fetal-cell research. Determining the relationship between abortion and fetal-cell implants; potential benefits for victims of diabetes, Parkinson's disease and Alzheimer's disease; ethical concerns posed; opposing viewpoints, those that view the fetus as a cadaver and those that see it as a victim; role of the church.

## Office of Technology Assessment

Hamilton, D. P., "OTA quietly backs fetal tissue work," *Science,* Oct. 12, 1990, p. 201.

Focuses on the Office of Technology Assessment's (OTA) report on "neural grafting" using fetal central nervous system (CNS) tissue. OTA's recommendations for fetal tissue research; congressional options.

Wheeler, D. L., "Oversight of tissue transplants may be inadequate, report says," *The Chronicle of Higher Education,* Oct. 17, 1990, p. A10.

Examines a report from the Office of Technology Assessment which found that the federal government may not be adequately overseeing experimental transplants of tissue into the human brain. Treatment for Parkinson's disease; Sale of fetal tissue; Justification for new procedures on human subjects.

# Back Issues

*Great Research on Current Issues Starts Right Here. . . Recent topics covered by The CQ Researcher are listed below. Issues dated before May 10, 1991, were published under the name of Editorial Research Reports.*

**FEBRUARY 1990**
Politics and Economic Growth
Free Agency in Sports
Repetitive Motion
War on Drugs

**MARCH 1990**
Asbestos: Are Risks Acceptable?
Public Health Campaigns
South Africa's Future
Homeless Need More Than Shelter

**APRIL 1990**
How Fair is the Tax Burden?
Workers' Compensation
U.S. Pacific Forces
Curbing Insurance Premiums

**MAY 1990**
Should Teaching Be a Profession?
Will Canada Fall Apart?
Is U.S. Patent System Outdated?
Federal Funding for the Arts

**JUNE 1990**
Downsizing America's Armed Forces
Progress In Weather Forecasting
S & L Bailout
Bio-Chemical Disarmament

**JULY 1990**
Do Americans Still Love Marriage?
Death Penalty Debate
Decline of Rural America
United Nations in the 1990s

**AUGUST 1990**
Democracy in the Philippines
Initiatives: True Democracy?
Hard Times at Newspapers
Teens Balance School & Jobs

**SEPTEMBER 1990**
Dangers of Alcohol
Western Alliance After the Cold War
Tobacco Industry
Right to Die

**OCTOBER 1990**
Organ Transplants
Energy Policy Options
Search for Arab Unity
Child Support

**NOVEMBER 1990**
Lotteries and Gambling
Post Cold-War Choices
Setting Limits on Medical Care
Multicultural Education

**DECEMBER 1990**
Cable TV Regulation
Americans' Search For Their Roots
Is Insurance System a Failure?
Why Schools Still Have Tracking

**JANUARY 1991**
Growing Influence of Boycotts
Should the U.S. Reinstate the Draft?
America's Archaeological Past
Peace Corps' Challenges in '90s

**FEBRUARY 1991**
Regional Impact of Recession
Puerto Rico's Status
Redistricting: Mapping Power
Nuclear Power

**MARCH 1991**
Acid Rain
Cost of the Gulf War
Reassessing Gun Laws
Future for Man in Space

**APRIL 1991**
Social Security
Canadian Crisis Over Quebec
California Drought
Electromagnetic Radiation

**MAY 1991**
School Choice
Racial Quotas
Animal Rights
U.S. and Japan

**JUNE 1991**
Children and Divorce
Teenage Suicide
Endangered Species
Europe 1992

**JULY 1991**
Teenagers and Abortion
Soviet Republics Rebel
Mexico's Emergence
Athletes and Drugs

**AUGUST 1991**
Sexual Harassment

Back issues are available for $4.00 (subscribers) or $7.00 (non-subscribers). Quantity discounts apply to orders over ten. To order, call Congressional Quarterly 1-800-432-2250.

# Future Topics

▶ *Oil Imports*

▶ *Palestinians*

▶ *Police Brutality*

# THE
# CQ *Researcher*

PUBLISHED BY CONGRESSIONAL QUARTERLY INC., IN CONJUNCTION WITH EBSCO PUBLISHING

# Oil Imports

*U.S. energy dependence remains high after the gulf war*

WHEN SADDAM HUSSEIN SENT HIS troops across the border into oil-rich Kuwait on Aug. 2, 1990, the stage was set for yet another global oil shock. To most everyone's surprise, the gulf war's impact on oil supplies was less traumatic, in the long run, than expected. But the situation nonetheless forced the United States to confront its continued dependence on oil imports. During the last major energy crisis, in 1978-79, oil shortages resulted in higher prices and prompted Americans to save energy. Oil imports shrank. But the subsequent fall in oil prices prompted consumers to return to bigger, less-efficient cars, and oil imports climbed back up. Then Saddam plundered his neighbor, putting the torch to more than 500 Kuwaiti oil wells and sparking the U.S. to re-examine its energy policies.

CQ  **August 23, 1991 • Volume 1, No. 15 • 585-608**

*Formerly Editorial Research Reports*

COVER ART: BARBARA SASSA-DANIELS

August 23, 1991
Volume 1, No. 15

**EDITOR**
Sandra Stencel

**MANAGING EDITOR**
Thomas J. Colin

**ASSOCIATE EDITOR**
Richard L. Worsnop

**STAFF WRITERS**
Charles S. Clark
Mary H. Cooper
Rodman D. Griffin

**PRODUCTION EDITOR**
Laurie De Maris

**EDITORIAL ASSISTANT**
Thomas H. Moore

**GRAPHICS**
Jack Auldridge

**PUBLISHED BY**
Congressional Quarterly Inc.

**CHAIRMAN**
Andrew Barnes

**VICE CHAIRMAN**
Andrew P. Corty

**EDITOR AND PUBLISHER**
Neil Skene

**EXECUTIVE EDITOR**
Robert W. Merry

**PUBLICATIONS MARKETING/SALES**
Robert Smith

**EDITOR, EBSCO PUBLISHING**
Melissa Kummerer

The CQ Researcher (ISSN 1056-2036). Formerly Editorial Research Reports. Published weekly (48 times per year, not printed the first Friday of any month with five Fridays) by Congressional Quarterly Inc., 1414 22nd St., N.W., Washington, D.C. 20037. Rates are furnished upon request. Application to mail at second-class postage rates is pending at Washington, D.C. POSTMASTER: Send address changes to The CQ Researcher, 1414 22nd St., N.W., Washington, D.C. 20037.

# Oil Imports

BY MARY H. COOPER

## THE ISSUES

American oil consumers — that is, practically everyone — have ridden a roller coaster over the past 12 months. With the energy crises of the 1970s just a memory, they had enjoyed five straight years of plentiful, cheap gasoline. They received a rude jolt on Aug. 2, 1990, when Iraq invaded Kuwait, its neighbor to the south and fellow member of the Organization of Petroleum Exporting Countries (OPEC).* After taking over the country, Iraqi forces cut off Kuwait's oil production, some 1.6 million barrels a day. The United Nations, under pressure from the Bush administration, imposed a trade embargo against Iraq in retaliation for its aggression, removing 2.8 million barrels a day of Iraqi oil from the world market.[1]

The shut-off of oil in Iraq and Kuwait — compounded by fears that production throughout the Mideast could be affected — caused a panic in world oil markets. The price of crude jumped from $13 a barrel in June to $40 early in the confrontation. By October it had leveled off at $33. Gasoline prices followed suit, rising from a pre-invasion national average of $1.08 cents a gallon for self-service, regular unleaded to $1.39 by late November.

On Aug. 8 President Bush launched Operation Desert Shield, deploying U.S. military forces to prevent Iraq from pushing beyond Kuwait into Saudi Arabia, a stalwart U.S. ally and oil supplier. In January the

---

*OPEC is made up of the Arab nations of Abu Dhabi, Algeria, Iraq, Kuwait, Libya, Qatar, Saudi Arabia and the United Arab Emirates, as well as Ecuador, Gabon, Indonesia, Iran, Nigeria and Venezuela.

president went on the offensive, launching Operation Desert Storm with widespread international support. The president assured the public that the action was not to protect American oil supplies but rather to counter aggression and safeguard both Saudi Arabia and the precarious tranquility — dubbed by Bush the New World Order — that had nudged aside the Cold War.

Whatever the motive behind Desert Storm, the crisis in oil supplies was resolved even before the 100 days of fighting stopped. A grateful Saudi Arabia increased its own production to compensate for the loss of Iraqi and Kuwaiti oil, alleviating the panic that had sent oil prices soaring in August. Additional downward pressure on prices came from a recession beginning last fall in the United States and some other major oil-consuming nations, reducing overall demand. By March 1991 world oil prices had fallen to about $17 a barrel, only $4 more than before the gulf crisis began. Since then, prices have stabilized at

around $21-$22 a barrel.

As in the past, U.S. interest in reducing the country's dependence on foreign suppliers escalated along with the price of oil during the latest crisis. In the fall of 1990, Congress passed a 5-cent-a-gallon increase in the tax on gasoline paid by consumers at the pump and imposed a steep tax on the purchase of luxury automobiles, which tend to consume more fuel than less expensive models.

In February, the Bush administration published its long-awaited National Energy Strategy, and several legislative proposals aimed at least in part at reducing oil imports were introduced. "Never before," said Secretary of Energy James D. Watkins, "has there been a strategy compiled to reach the objectives of energy security, environmental quality, affordable energy through an integrated approach combining free-market incentives, reduced regulation, increased federal investment in R & D."

The fall in oil prices, not surprisingly, has been accompanied by signs that consumer support for aggressive legislative action to cut oil imports has weakened. As the debate over energy policy continues in Congress, analysts are stepping back to re-evaluate, yet again, how best to address the issue of energy dependence.

### Just how vulnerable is the United States to a sudden cutoff of foreign oil?

The oil markets reacted dramatically to Iraq's invasion of Kuwait largely because the United States, the world's biggest oil consumer, relies so heavily on imported oil. While imports accounted for only a quarter of U.S. oil consumption as recently as 1985, the figure had jumped to 42 percent in 1989. During the same four-year period, Americans' thirst for oil grew by more than 1.5 million barrels to 17.3 million barrels a day, more than a quarter of all the oil consumed worldwide.[2]

At first glance, new statistics suggest that American consumers may have learned a lesson from the gulf war and cut back on their purchases of petroleum imports. Last year, the Energy Department reports, U.S. demand for oil fell by 2.4 percent to 16.9 million barrels a day. The agency projects demand will fall an additional 200,000-400,000 barrels a day this year.[3]

But upon closer examination, the slight gain in energy independence over the past year does not seem to indicate a shift away from oil products out of concern arising from the war. Higher gasoline prices and lower income due to the recession have merely forced motorists temporarily to cut back on vacation driving and other unnecessary travel. At the same time, Americans today are buying heavier cars with higher horsepower than they did three years ago, so that fuel efficiency has actually declined since 1988.

The Energy Department predicts demand will grow by as much as 520,000 barrels a day next year if the recession ends as anticipated, more than making up for the decline of the past year. "The war has had essentially no impact, either on production or on consumption trends," says Christopher Flavin, vice president for research at the Worldwatch Institute in Washington. "We seem to be pretty much back on the path that we've been on since 1986, which is a path of rapidly rising oil imports. Domestic production is declining rapidly, while consumption is growing slowly."

Apart from the Mideast's political instability and the consequent uncertainty of its oil availability, the short-term prospects for adequate and relatively inexpensive oil supplies are good. True, Iraq cannot re-

sume exporting oil until the U.N. sanctions are lifted, and Kuwait's sabotaged oil fields have only recently begun to produce small amounts of oil for export. But the oil shortfall stemming from the hostilities will not affect consuming nations.

"We weren't buying a lot of oil from Kuwait anyway," says John H. Lichtblau, president of the Petroleum Industry Research Foundation in New York City. "When you're talking about the United States, the question is not Kuwait, because at the moment there's enough oil around in the world. That's why oil prices are where they are."

Lichtblau says the loss of production from Iraq and Kuwait has had a greater impact on OPEC, which currently is operating near capacity and may reach capacity in the fourth quarter of this year if Iraq is still out of the market at that time.* Boosted by increased production from Saudi Arabia, OPEC increased its output in June to 22.9 million barrels a day.

When the political realities of the Persian Gulf region are taken into account, however, American vulnerability to a sudden cutoff is more worrisome. Optimists point out that there is always the Strategic Petroleum Reserve, established in 1975 to meet U.S. oil demand in case of a major disruption in supplies. The reserve contains about 580 million barrels of crude oil, enough to last 34 days. Optimists also note that even when significant oil supplies are abruptly interrupted, as in the gulf war crisis, other suppliers can quickly cover the loss.

But it all depends on the political issues at stake. During the latest cri-

sis, replacing the West's lost Iraqi and Kuwaiti oil happened to serve the interests of Saudi Arabia, OPEC's and the region's leading producer. But the gulf war was unusual in the history of Middle Eastern conflicts and oil crises, which typically have arrayed Arab producers against the United States and other oil consumers. "How [OPEC producers] choose to use their power is basically unknown," says James J. MacKenzie, an energy expert at the World Resources Institute, an environmental research group in Washington. "All we know is, wars there are totally unpredictable. And I expect the next one will be unexpected, too. . . . And we will then say it's time we develop an energy policy."

### Can the United States satisfy its oil needs without relying on imports?

Official statistics paint a bleak picture of what lies ahead if no significant steps are taken to reduce oil imports. More than a third of world oil production comes from OPEC, which controls three-quarters of the proven reserves of crude oil in the world. Two-thirds of the oil in the world is in the Persian Gulf region, site of all the major disruptions in oil supplies to date. Of course, previous crises in the Middle East spurred consuming nations to seek alternative sources of petroleum. To a great extent they were successful. In 1990, for example, the major industrial nations obtained 31 percent of their oil imports from non-OPEC sources. The United States did even better, obtaining 45 percent of its daily 8.4 million imported barrels from non-OPEC sources, mainly Canada and Mexico.[4]

But this diversification in foreign oil purchases cannot last. Non-OPEC production is expected to decline, not increase, in the future. Oil production in the United States peaked in 1970 at 11.3 million barrels a day and fell to 8.9 million barrels a day

---

*The U.N. Security Council voted Aug. 15 to allow Iraq to sell up to $1.6 billion worth of oil to buy food and medicine for the country's desperate citizens. But it remained uncertain whether the Iraqi government would accept the proposal because it imposes restrictions on the use of the oil revenues.

# U.S. and Oil: Production, Consumption and Imports

*U.S. production has declined since output peaked in 1970. While completion of the trans-Alaskan pipeline reversed the steep decline of the 1970s, falling prices in 1986 led many domestic operations to close. U.S. oil imports tend to mirror consumption patterns. As oil use rose in the '70s, imports also increased, largely because domestic production had peaked. In the early 1980s, recession and the abandonment of fuel efficiency standards contributed to drops in consumption and imports. Falling prices in 1986 pushed oil use and imports back up, but they fell following the onset of recession in 1990.*

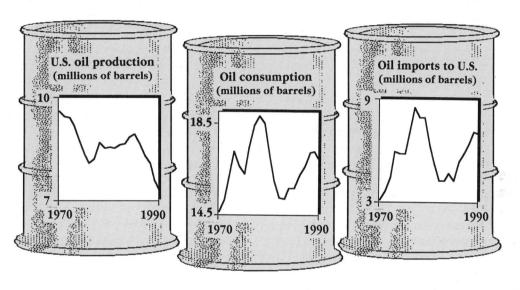

*Source: Energy Information Administration.*

in 1990, the lowest level since 1964.[5] Proven oil reserves here have fallen almost steadily from 34.3 billion barrels in 1975 to 25.9 billion last year. Although geologists estimate that significant reserves may remain to be discovered in Alaska, these estimates have yet to be proven.

The North Sea offshore oil rigs controlled by Britain and Norway — erected in response to earlier crises in the Middle East — produce more than 3 million barrels a day. But the North Sea's proven reserves have shrunk from their peak of 25 billion barrels in 1978 to 16 billion last year. The other major non-OPEC oil-producing region, the Soviet Union, was turning out 12 million barrels a day in 1988, but economic turmoil has forced the country to reduce its output to under 11 million barrels. There, too, proven reserves peaked in the mid-1970s, at 83 billion barrels, and now stand at 58 billion. By

contrast, proven reserves in OPEC nations have grown from 398 billion barrels in 1970 to 767 billion. Fully 85 percent of OPEC's reserves lie in the Persian Gulf region.[6]

To James MacKenzie, these data point to but one conclusion: "Within five or six years — certainly within this decade — the OPEC countries, especially those in the Persian Gulf, are going to have total control over prices and in a sense the economic and political destinies of the Western nations and Eastern Europe."

Other analysts take a more optimistic view of U.S. dependence on oil imports. "Dependence by itself is not exactly something that you have to spend sleepless nights over," says Lichtblau of the Petroleum Industry Research Foundation. "Japan is 99 percent dependent on foreign oil, mostly from the Middle East, and yet their economy is not exactly in sham-

bles. And all of Western Europe, with the exception of the United Kingdom, is much more dependent on foreign oil than we are." He points out not only that the war caused no shortage of petroleum products in the United States but also that the price fluctuations might have been less severe if the president had released oil from the Strategic Petroleum Reserve earlier in the crisis.

As for those who want the United States to end its vulnerability to foreign turmoil by becoming energy self-reliant, Lichtblau says, "They don't know what they're talking about." Energy independence, he maintains, is a particularly unrealistic goal over the next 15 years because of the continuing U.S. need for gasoline, heating oil and jet and diesel fuel. Since the country produces only about 8 million barrels of the 17 million barrels of oil it uses each day, Lichtblau says, "There's no way you could cut back to the domestic level or anywhere close to it. It would be an incredible hardship for the public, it would require enormous increases in price and it would require mandated shifting to other fuels.''

### What are the alternatives to imported oil?

It is just such alternative fuels that many people say could and should be more aggressively developed to reduce, if not eliminate, the country's dependence on oil imports. To get an idea how big a task replacing foreign oil would be, look at petroleum's place in the overall energy picture. Fossil fuels — oil, coal and natural gas — provide 89 percent of the country's energy supply. Of the three, oil is the main source of energy, accounting for 41 percent of the total energy supply. Coal supplies 23 percent of the nation's energy and natural gas supplies 24 percent.[7]

Coal and natural gas are attractive alternatives to oil in at least one respect. Though, like oil, they are finite energy sources and will run out some day, both are in abundant supply over the medium term. The problem with replacing imported oil with domestic fossil fuels is that they are not as well-suited to the main user of oil, the automobile. The transportation sector, including cars, trucks, ships and aircraft, accounts for 64 percent of U.S. petroleum use. Cars alone consume more than half that total. Many other oil consumers — industries, electric utilities and residential and commercial users — switched to alternative fuels, including natural gas, coal and nuclear energy, in past energy crises when oil prices rose.

If the country is to reduce its dependence on foreign oil, then, it must focus on oil consumption by automobiles. One way to do so is to cut back on driving. Many communities have done this through car-pool incentives and expansion of mass transit. But such incentives have drawbacks. Except for older urban centers, mass transit has limited appeal. Life in the suburbs and newer communities, built on the premise of easy access to cheap gasoline, would be unthinkable without some form of personal transit.

> The main problem with replacing imported oil with domestic fossil fuels is that they are not as well suited to the main user of oil, the automobile. The transportation sector accounts for 64 percent of U.S. petroleum use.

Another approach to reducing auto consumption of oil — improving fuel efficiency — has also been tried. The same law that set up the Strategic Petroleum Reserve in 1975 defined standards that required the auto industry to double new cars' fuel efficiency from the average 13 miles per gallon of the time to 27.5 miles per gallon by 1985. This change alone reduced oil consumption in the United States by a third.[8] A bill now before Congress would improve these Corporate Average Fuel Economy (CAFE) standards (see p. 598). But as long as gasoline is used to fuel cars, the United States likely will continue to depend on foreign oil. For while auto efficiency improvements reduce oil consumption, the rising number of cars on the road more than makes up for the savings in fuel.

In recent years, scientists have made progress in developing alternative fuels for cars. Two forms of alcohol, methanol and ethanol, are being added to gasoline in smog-polluted cities in an effort to comply with the Clean Air Act Amendments of 1990, thus reducing the amount of gasoline consumed. Another promising fossil fuel is compressed natural gas. Pilot programs featuring fleets of natural-gas-powered delivery vehicles are being introduced in New York and other smoggy cities. It may be some time, however, before this fuel can used as a gasoline substitute for private cars because a distribution system for natural gas must be set up.

Consequently, many bets are on electricity rather than alcohol. Several automakers have already developed electric-powered prototypes that could be available to the public by the mid-1990s. Because they can only travel for about a hundred miles before recharging — a process that lasts several hours — electric cars are envisioned as second cars, suitable primarily for commuting.

Because only 5 percent of the oil consumed in the United States is used by electric-generating plants, which rely primarily on coal, natural gas and nuclear energy, environmentalists see vast potential oil savings. "We could run tens of millions of cars on just the surplus generation capacity we have in our electric-generating plants such as they are without having to build any more new plants," says Charlie Garlow, an officer in the Sierra Club's Washington, D.C., chapter who actively supports the organization's push for electric cars. Alternatively, solar panels could be installed on the cars themselves, providing a steady source of electrical energy.

The most promising new energy source for electric cars is the fuel cell, a batterylike device that can convert a gaseous fuel, such as hydrogen or natural gas, into electricity in a process that emits little more than water vapor. The fuel cell would be more attractive to consumers than the conventional battery for an electric car because its range would be about three times as great. "In the long run, the fuel cell makes the most sense, because it would be a virtually no-emission car, with a range of 300 miles, and you could use any energy source to produce the gas," says Flavin of Worldwatch. This technology, however, is not expected to provide a feasible alternative to the gasoline-driven engine until well into the 21st century.

### How do oil imports affect efforts to protect the environment?

With evidence mounting that auto emissions are the major source of air pollution as well as an important contributor to global warming, the benefits of alternative energy sources must be weighed against their environmental impact. Burning fossil fuels of any kind releases large amounts of carbon dioxide, carbon monoxide, chlorofluorocarbons and other gases that in large quantities pollute the environment and contribute to the "greenhouse effect," an alteration of the atmosphere that many scientists say is causing a potentially catastrophic rise in global temperatures. The United States uses more than 35 percent of the world's transport energy, which in turn accounts for almost a third of total energy use in the world.[9]

So-called "clean gasoline," containing alcohol-based additives such as ethanol or methanol, are now being distributed by several oil companies in an effort to curtail auto emissions. In June, the Environmental Protection Agency (EPA) proposed new regulations requiring the intro-

duction of oxygenated gasoline in 41 cities with high carbon monoxide levels by November 1992. Under the Clean Air Act Amendments of 1990, reformulated gasoline must be available in nine cities with very high ozone levels by January 1995.* But clean gasolines can only help reduce certain kinds of pollution. The National Academy of Sciences estimates that reformulated gasoline would cut carbon dioxide emissions by 1.7 percent at most.[10] Thus, environmentalists stress, the search for alternatives to gasoline for transport in the United States is especially urgent.

Switching entirely from gasoline to ethanol or methanol would sharply reduce the need for oil imports. But these are the least effective alternatives to gasoline from the environmental viewpoint, producing a high percentage of the gases that cause the greenhouse effect as they are currently produced. According to the Environmental Defense Fund, methanol, derived from coal, would produce up to 80 percent more greenhouse gases than gasoline. Ethanol, produced mainly from corn but distilled using fossil fuel, produces 25 percent more greenhouse gases. In both cases, pollution caused by gasoline used to transport the gases must be factored into the equation.[11]

Better than all these alternatives, in Flavin's view, is compressed natural gas, which is less polluting and, at the equivalent of $9 a barrel of oil, far less expensive than gasoline. Natural gas is also in abundant supply in the United States, and production is not expected to begin declining un-

---

*The EPA is expected to identify the 41 cities at the end of August. Nine cities that the EPA already has identified as having unacceptably high levels of ozone are Baltimore, Chicago, Hartford, Houston, Los Angeles, Milwaukee, New York, Philadelphia and San Diego. Under a binding agreement reached Aug. 15 by the oil industry and environmental groups, refiners will be required to provide reformulated gasoline that emits 15 percent fewer ozone-producing substances in these nine cities.

til after the year 2000. By 2010 the United States is expected to be relying on imports to meet its demand for natural gas. But most of it would probably come from Canada, one of the nation's most reliable foreign energy suppliers.[12] "We've got a lot of gas, it's extraordinarily cheap and from an air-pollution standpoint it's better than all the alternatives except electric cars," Flavin says.

Electric cars emit no polluting gases, which makes them especially attractive for smog-ridden cities such as Los Angeles and Denver. The only emissions associated with their use would occur at the power plants that provide the electricity for their batteries, and these are generally located far from the urban centers where air pollution is heaviest. Electric cars charged with electricity from coal-fired plants would be more polluting than cars charged from natural gas-fired or nuclear power plants. But even if the current mix of coal- and gas-fired plants is used, there would be a reduction in pollution for every electric car that replaces a gasoline-driven car. "These vehicles, which can ultimately be run from renewable resources or even nuclear power if that industry can ever get its act together, would lead to enormous reductions in urban air pollution, oil imports and climate warming," says MacKenzie.

Whatever alternative fuels are developed for environmental reasons, their use can only help curtail U.S. dependence on foreign oil. "If we say we have to reduce our consumption of oil products because it affects the environment, then of course it also means we'll import less because at the margin every barrel of oil that is consumed is imported," Lichtblau explains. "So if we reduce our consumption by 100,000 barrels a day, that means exactly 100,000 barrels a day less imports because we would always produce the maximum level possible domestically." ∎

# BACKGROUND

## U.S. Oil Dominance

It is an irony of today's energy predicament that the United States, which now depends on imported oil, was the first major exploiter of crude oil. After it was discovered that kerosene, a byproduct of "rock oil," or crude, provided excellent artificial illumination, early oilmen set out to find a way to extract the substance. The first successful oil well, dug in Titusville, Pa., in 1859, launched a highly profitable business that soon came under the almost exclusive control of John D. Rockefeller and his Standard Oil Co. The search for new sources pushed the oil boom west, where enormous reserves were found in California, Oklahoma and Texas. As news of kerosene's superior lighting quality spread, the American oil industry quickly found overseas markets for its product. Within a decade of the Titusville find, kerosene was the fourth-largest U.S. export, and more than half the industry's output went overseas, mainly to Europe.[13]

With Thomas Edison's invention of the electric light bulb around the turn of the century, the oil industry's future looked bleak. Up to that time, oil producers had concentrated on refining crude oil into kerosene for illumination. They were saved by another invention of the late 1800s, the automobile. Gasoline, up to then a largely useless byproduct of the kerosene refining process, was soon found to be the ideal fuel for cars. When Henry Ford streamlined auto production with the assembly line, demand for the horseless carriage mushroomed, and with it the demand for gasoline.

As world demand for oil and gasoline mounted, other sources of petroleum were discovered, notably in Russia. By 1917 the United States still accounted for nearly 70 percent of global oil output, and a quarter of its production was sold abroad.[14] World War I cut off Russian oil supplies just as the belligerent powers of Europe needed vast quantities to fuel their new oil-driven ships. As a result, the European allies turned to the United States to power their war efforts. In response, President Woodrow Wilson appointed the nation's first energy official to allocate the precious resource between the European allies and U.S. consumers, who were increasingly turning to oil to fuel factories and home furnaces as well as the rapidly growing numbers of cars.

As industrial development and the sales of autos took off in the 1920s, demand for oil continued to climb. Only now the American producers were faced with foreign competitors, who sold at lower prices. It was then that American fear of overreliance on foreign sources of oil developed in earnest. In 1920, as domestic supplies dwindled, oil prices rose by half to $3 a barrel. Public attitudes toward oil companies, which had been highly negative before the breakup of Standard Oil in 1911, shifted amid growing support for corporate efforts to find new oil wells abroad. By this time, however, U.S. producers, who still accounted for two-thirds of the world's oil output, had to compete with British concerns in the Middle East and the Dutch in the East Indies (modern Indonesia). The vast reserves of the Middle East, which came into play with the discovery of oil in Bahrain in 1923, gradually eroded American dominance in oil exports.

When the Depression hit, demand for oil fell, creating a glutted market that further drove down prices. In an effort to break the vicious cycle of overproduction, lower prices and further overproduction to make up for the losses caused by falling prices, the government in 1933 imposed quotas on all the oil-producing states. To prevent foreign suppliers from taking advantage of this new restriction on domestic oil producers, Congress passed a tariff on oil products. As a result, oil imports fell.

Despite the growth of oil imports during the early years of the century, the United States continued throughout the 1930s to export more gas and oil than it imported. This stemmed in large part from the discovery of vast oil fields in East Texas. But as producers flocked to the region, output quickly exceeded demand, and prices fell as a result. By 1931, East Texas was producing about half the country's oil. Crude oil prices had plummeted to 13 cents a barrel, 67 cents less than it cost to produce. If nothing was done to bring production into line with demand, oil producers would essentially drown in their own oil, unable to cover the cost of operating their wells.

Declaring East Texas in a state of insurrection, Texas Gov. Ross Sterling sent in the National Guard to shut down the oil fields. He also ordered the Texas Railroad Commission to bring order to the oil market. The commission used a system of prorationing that was to serve as a model for OPEC two decades later. By establishing production ceilings that were targeted to meet existing demand, the commission could effectively control the price of East Texas crude. Less than a year after its creation, the Texas Railroad Commission had restored order — and profitability — to the oil industry.[15]

## Postwar Import Quotas

The expansion of industrial development following World War II boosted demand for oil, especially

Continued on p. 594

# Chronology

## 1859-1960s The U.S. "discovers" oil and becomes the world's leading oil producer and consumer.

### Aug. 28, 1859
The first successful oil well is drilled in Titusville, Pa.

### February 1865
John D. Rockefeller launches his successful bid to control the oil and kerosene industry, resulting in the creation of Standard Oil.

### 1896
Henry Ford begins the mass production of automobiles, launching a revolution in transportation and ensuring the world's reliance on oil.

### 1948
The U.S. becomes a net importer of oil but continues to provide about half the world's oil into the 1950s.

### March 10, 1959
President Dwight D. Eisenhower imposes quotas on imported oil to protect domestic producers from lower-priced imports.

———— • ————

## 1970s Oil crises push up the prices of gasoline and other oil products.

### 1970
U.S. oil production peaks at 11.3 million barrels a day and begins its inexorable decline as the pool of proven reserves dwindles.

### October 1973
The Organization of Petroleum Exporting Countries (OPEC) demands a 70 percent increase in the price of oil to $5.11 a barrel. The subsequent oil embargo against the U.S. and other countries that support Israel in the Yom Kippur War launched against Israel by Arab states pushes the price above $17 a barrel. Earlier that year, President Richard M. Nixon abolished oil import quotas.

### 1975
President Gerald R. Ford sets up the Strategic Petroleum Reserve to protect the U.S. from interruptions in international oil supplies. Congress also establishes fuel-efficiency standards for cars.

### 1977
President Jimmy Carter launches his ambitious National Energy Plan, calling it the "moral equivalent of war." The trans-Alaskan pipeline is completed, allowing crude oil from the North Slope to reach the Lower 48.

### December 1978
Revolution in Iran cuts off that country's output of 5 million barrels a day from world markets.

### June 1979
OPEC, now in control of 90 percent of world oil output, raises the price of crude from $14.50 to up to $23.50 a barrel. Consumers in the U.S., which imports 46 percent of its oil, line up at gasoline stations.

———— • ————

## 1980s As world oil prices fall, so does support for a national energy policy. Oil imports climb with U.S. demand for foreign oil.

### 1981
President Ronald Reagan, reacting to a surplus of oil on world markets, begins to dismantle much of Carter's energy plan.

### 1986
Oil prices plummet to their lowest level since the first oil crisis in 1973.

———— • ————

## 1990s The gulf war prompts renewed calls for greater energy independence.

### Aug. 2, 1990
Iraq occupies Kuwait, cutting off 1.6 million barrels of oil a day from the world market. A U.N.-sponsored embargo also removes Iraqi oil from world markets. Panic buying pushes oil prices up from $13 a barrel to $40.

### February 1991
Sen. J. Bennett Johnston, D-La., introduces a sweeping energy bill based on President Bush's National Energy Strategy. It calls for opening the Arctic National Wildlife Refuge to oil drilling, a tax on oil imports and tax incentives for energy producers. An alternative bill, introduced by Sen. Richard H. Bryan, D-Nev., would raise the CAFE standards for fuel efficiency from 27.5 to 40 miles per gallon by the year 2000.

### March 1991
Oil prices return to near pre-invasion levels. Gasoline prices follow.

# Chief Sources of U.S. Oil Imports

*Following the oil shocks of the 1970s, when crude oil prices skyrocketed, the U.S. began turning to non-Arab members of the Organization of Petroleum Exporting Countries (OPEC) and other markets. The exception was Saudi Arabia, which continues to be the leading U.S. source of foreign oil.*

| Country | | Imported crude oil and petroleum products (thousand barrels/day, 1991) |
|---|---|---|
| Saudi Arabia | Arab OPEC | 1,822 |
| Canada | Non-OPEC | 984 |
| Venezuela | Other OPEC | 944 |
| Mexico | Non-OPEC | 693 |
| Nigeria | Other OPEC | 653 |
| Angola | Non-OPEC | 235 |
| Colombia | Non-OPEC | 165 |

*Source: Energy Information Administration.*

Continued from p. 592

in Western Europe and North America. Patterns of development, urban growth and suburban expansion — all based on access to the automobile and cheap fuel — became ever more entrenched in the American way of life and cemented the country's dependence on oil. In 1948 the United States became a "net importer" of oil, importing more oil (mostly from Venezuela) than it exported. But the change was hardly noticed, as the United States continued to provide about half the world's oil into the 1950s.

Just as the demand for oil grew after the war, so too did the number of international oil companies. With more players in the world market, competition for sales mounted, pushing down oil prices. Throughout the two decades following World War II, the supply of oil tended to exceed demand, further dampening prices and adding new impetus to the expansion of industries, utilities, home construction and especially automobile sales — all based on the premise of cheap and plentiful oil.

The fall in world oil prices after the war dealt a blow to U.S. oil companies, mostly Texas-based independents whose high extraction costs prevented them from selling as cheaply as foreign producers, especially those from the Middle East. There, vast quantities of high-quality crude were being tapped from easily accessible reserves at very low prices. Although President Dwight D. Eisenhower initially rejected import quotas as disruptive to the emerging system of global free trade, he bowed to pressure from the American independents and in 1959 imposed quotas on oil imports. Eisenhower's reluctant decision marked a turning point in U.S. energy policy. The quotas, which initially limited oil imports to 9 percent of U.S. consumption, were relaxed somewhat during the Kennedy and Johnson administrations, but they remained in force for 14 years.

The imposition of import quotas by the United States, still the world's biggest oil market by far, did protect domestic producers from cheap foreign oil and allowed them to stay in business. But in the long run they also hurt the U.S. economy. For one thing, while quotas drove up the price of oil on the U.S. market, they drove them down elsewhere. With the world's largest oil market closed to all but a fraction of world oil supplies, producers competed with one another to sell to other markets. In this sense, U.S. oil quotas helped fuel the economic booms in Japan and Western Europe, which became America's chief economic competitors.

## Birth of OPEC

Oil quotas also had political ramifications that were to run counter to U.S. interests two decades after they went into effect. When Eisenhower exempted Canada and Mexico from the quotas, a strong protest came from the government of Venezuela, which was then the second-largest oil producer after the United States and sold 40 percent of its oil exports to the U.S. market.

The Eisenhower administration's refusal to accommodate Venezuela's demands prompted its minister of mines and hydrocarbons, Juan Pablo Pérez Alfonzo, to establish an energy policy that was to form the rationale for OPEC. His country's oil resources, Pérez Alfonzo said, should be in the hands of its government, not foreign oil companies, which kept about half the revenue from the crude they produced there. Only the government, he reasoned, would serve the public interest by restricting output to prolong the life of the country's reserves and funneling the profits of oil sales into industrial development and modernization that would leave Venezuela with a broader economic base when the oil eventually did run out.[16]

In April 1959 Pérez Alfonzo signed a "gentlemen's agreement" with several Middle Eastern nations that called for the nationalization of oil interests then controlled by the major American oil companies, known as the "seven sisters," as well as by other countries, notably Britain and the Netherlands. The agreement also called for the creation of an international commission — OPEC — to set prices among the members.

But OPEC was not to bring its power to bear on the world oil market for more than a decade. In 1956, when Egyptian President Gamal Abdel Nasser closed the Suez Canal to oil shipments from the Persian Gulf, the United States and European nations organized a successful oil allocation scheme that mitigated the effects of the cutoff. What had begun as a downward trend in oil prices during the 1950s became a major slide by the end of the '60s as the glut of oil supplies on an unregulated world market depressed prices. The discovery of large oil reserves in Libya in the early 1960s further accelerated the trend toward lower crude prices.

The next oil crisis grew out of Arab-Israeli tensions, which had been building ever since the creation of the Jewish state in the aftermath of World War II. During the 1967 Six-Day War, Arab oil producers called for an oil embargo against supporters of Israel, chiefly the United States and Britain. By this time, Western Europe had grown dependent upon the region for 75 percent of its oil. But once again, the oil consumers were saved by their ability to organize alternative means of obtaining their fuel, this time using supertankers to transport Persian Gulf oil to markets in Europe. Within a month of its inception, the Arab oil embargo had failed. The Arabs then raised production to compete among themselves for market share, creating a period of oversupply, which pushed down world prices.[17]

While the industrial nations were able to weather the supply disruptions of the 1960s, conditions in the United States, still the world's biggest oil consumer, changed in ways that would tip the balance of power between oil producers and consumers. In 1970, American oil production

peaked at 11.3 million barrels a day and began a decline that continues today. Although new reserves were later found on Alaska's North Slope, these would never boost U.S. production to such heights again. The boom that had been fueled by the oil fields in the Lower 48 was over.

Because the growth in oil consumption did not slow with dwindling domestic reserves, the United States could no longer insulate itself from the world oil market. The Texas Railroad Commission stopped enforcing its production allocations, and the import quotas that had held cheap foreign oil to just 9 percent of the domestic market were eased to allow more oil in to meet demand. The share of U.S. oil consumption met by imports grew rapidly, from 19 percent in 1967 at the close of the Six-Day War to 36 percent by 1973.[18]

### '73 Arab Oil Embargo

Pressed to find new policy solutions to tight oil market conditions, President Richard M. Nixon in 1973 abolished the oil import system that Eisenhower had adopted 14 years before. At the same time that the industrial Western nations were consuming more and more oil, the Middle Eastern oil-producing nations were capturing a growing portion of the world market. Conditions finally were ripe for them to wield the "oil weapon," and they did so with a vengeance. Arab producers made their move after Egypt and Syria launched a surprise attack against Israel on Oct. 5, as the country was observing the Yom Kippur holiday.

The Yom Kippur War coincided with a crucial meeting between the major international oil companies and the members of OPEC, who de-

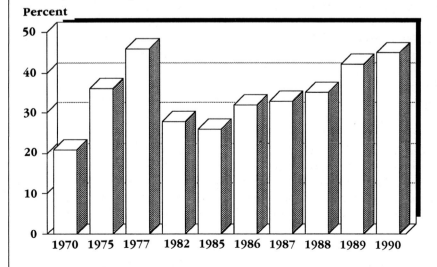

## Growing U.S. Dependence on Foreign Oil

*U.S. dependence on foreign oil has increased ever since 1970, when domestic production reached its peak. The 1973 oil crisis led to a dramatic rise in imported oil in 1975 and '77. A sharp drop in the use of foreign oil in 1982 was caused by the recession. In the mid-1980s, several factors led to increased dependence on imports: low prices, falling U.S. production and OPEC's inability to control production.*

**Percent**

*Source: Energy Information Administration.*

manded a much higher percentage of the price of a barrel of crude than the companies were willing to grant. In mid-October, OPEC unleashed its power with an unprecedented unilateral increase in the price of oil to $5.11 a barrel — a 70 percent hike.[19] At the same time, the Arab producers agreed to an embargo against the United States and other countries that supported Israel. The inability of other suppliers to make up the resulting shortfall precipitated the first major oil crisis.

The panic buying of limited oil supplies following the embargo's announcement pushed up oil prices much further than OPEC had demanded. Within a month, they had skyrocketed to above $17 a barrel, more than triple OPEC's stipulated price. Despite government efforts designed to distribute tight oil supplies efficiently, American motorists were for the first time forced to line up at gas stations.

On November 17 Nixon responded to the first energy crisis by calling on the American people to conserve energy by car-pooling to work and turning down thermostats in winter and up in summer. "Let us set as our national goal," Nixon declared in setting out Project Independence, "in the spirit of Apollo, with the determination of the Manhattan Project, that by the end of this decade we will have developed the potential to meet our own energy needs without depending on any foreign energy source."

By the time the embargo ended, in March 1974, oil prices had quadrupled. For the next five years, the world oil market resumed its normal course — only at prices three times what they had been before. As the consuming nations began to discover and exploit new oil reserves, notably in Alaska, Mexico and the

North Sea, world prices remained steady and even fell slightly for the remainder of the 1970s. In 1978 the trans-Alaskan pipeline was completed, allowing crude from the North Slope reserves to reach consumers in the Lower 48.

### '78 Energy Crisis

But early the next year, another crisis in the Middle East roiled the oil markets and the entire world econ-

> President Nixon responded to the 1973 Arab oil embargo by urging Americans to develop "the potential to meet our own energy needs." President Carter called the development of an effective energy policy "the moral equivalent of war."

omy. This time the trouble arose in Iran, where the U.S.-backed shah was ousted from power by a popular revolution inspired by the fundamentalist Islamic teachings of the Ayatollah Ruhollah Khomeini. The revolutionaries cut off the country's exports, removing 5 million barrels a day from the world market, and later renewed production at far lower levels.

The loss of Iranian oil supplies drove up oil prices, and OPEC followed suit in June 1979 with another price hike from $14.50 a barrel to a range of between $18 and $23.50 a barrel. By this time, OPEC controlled more than 90 percent of the world's output of oil, so it was in even a better position to set prices than before. The United States was importing 46 percent of its oil, more

than half of which came from Arab members of OPEC.

As part of his policy response to the second OPEC price hike, President Jimmy Carter reimposed oil import quotas. In agreement with the other major industrial nations, the Carter administration pledged to hold oil imports to no more than 8.5 million barrels a day through 1985. Carter had entered the White House in 1977 saying the need for an effective energy policy was "the moral equivalent of war." He called for an intensified federal role in regulating the energy market and increased funding for this purpose. By the end of his term, annual federal spending for energy programs stood at $3.5 billion, more than four times the spending level of 1974.[20]

As a result of Carter's National Energy Plan, the Department of Energy was created to centralize energy planning efforts. Programs were set up to foster consumer conservation of electricity through tax incentives for improved home and office building insulation, set energy efficiency standards for major appliances and require factories and electric utilities to switch back to coal from oil. Carter also initiated the gradual dismantling of oil and natural gas prices put in place as part of the Nixon administration's anti-inflation campaign. The Carter years saw a vast increase in federal spending for research into alternative fuels such as solar energy.

## Reagan's Energy Policy

Despite the reappearance of gas lines during the oil crisis of 1978, the American public was less concerned about the country's energy dependence than their president, whose popularity also suffered from his inability to free the American hostages held in Iran. In his place, American voters in 1980 chose Ronald Reagan, whose views on the federal government's role in the energy market were the antithesis of Carter's. Holding true to his campaign promise to deregulate industry and leave American business affairs to "the magic of the marketplace," Reagan immediately set about dismantling much of his predecessor's energy program upon entering the White House in 1981.

Reagan failed to convince Congress to abolish the Department of Energy. But he did succeed in cutting federal spending for energy programs and redirected what remained of the federal effort in energy affairs toward exploiting potential oil reserves in the outer continental shelf and in federal lands previously protected from development. One of Reagan's targets was the EPA, where budget cuts impeded its ability to enforce remaining regulations aimed at curbing air and water pollution, much of which derives from the burning of oil and other hydrocarbons.

### Oil Glut

The Reagan administration's dismantling of energy programs was facilitated by a new oversupply of oil on world markets. This oil glut resulted in large part from the higher prices OPEC had exacted from consuming nations in 1978. Hit with bigger oil bills, the industrial world, including the United States, plunged into the most severe recession since the Great Depression of the 1930s. With economic activity in decline, demand for oil plummeted.

At the same time, consumer nations were looking to non-OPEC sources for their oil, such as the North Sea and Alaska. They also continued to switch to alternative fuels, especially natural gas, nuclear power and even back to coal. OPEC was

losing its grip over the world oil market, and its members began to cheat on their quota system, introduced to keep prices from eroding. As a result, the glut grew larger. In November 1985 OPEC announced it would no longer try to defend the price it received for oil, then almost $32 a barrel, and would instead loosen its production quotas to regain its former share of the world market. Prices fell to $10 a barrel.

The result: yet another oil shock. Good news in the short term for consumers, who paid less for gasoline and home heating oil, the price drop spelled trouble for domestic producers and for the country's ability to reduce its dependence on oil imports. Oil exploration and production from marginal wells — those that yield appreciable amounts of oil only after using expensive extraction methods — became too costly and fell off. As prices dropped, so too did the improvement in energy efficiency that had begun following the first big oil crisis in 1973. To satisfy its demand for oil — now on the upswing again because of low prices — the United States turned increasingly to foreign sources, including the Persian Gulf, to meet its energy needs.

### Persian Gulf War

When Iraqi forces under President Saddam Hussein invaded Kuwait in August 1990, another oil crisis seemed inevitable. Now dependent on the Persian Gulf for 13 percent of its oil, the United States was more vulnerable to a cutoff from the region than it had been during the first major crisis in 1973. Indeed, oil prices rose from $14 a barrel on the eve of the invasion to $40 by November. Gasoline prices rose as well.

But the nature of this conflict helped the consuming nations avoid a full-scale crisis. Unlike previous conflicts in the region, when the Arab OPEC producers were united in their stand against Israel and its Western allies, the gulf war found OPEC's leader, Saudi Arabia, arrayed in full support of the oil consumers in their effort to oust Iraqi forces from Kuwait. Although the invasion and a United Nations embargo against Iraqi oil and other exports cut off oil supplies from both Kuwait and Iraq, Saudi Arabia and other oil producers were able to fill the shortfall. Even before U.S. forces entered the conflict in January or the outcome of the war became clear, oil prices had begun to fall. ∎

# CURRENT SITUATION

## Bush's Energy Strategy

Congress reacted to the crisis atmosphere that forced up oil prices after Iraq's invasion of Kuwait with several measures aimed at reducing the country's dependence on oil imports. Lawmakers increased the federal gasoline tax by 5 cents a gallon, doubled the excise tax on luxury gas-guzzling automobiles and passed a production credit for "enhanced oil recovery" as an incentive for oil companies to extract hard-to-obtain crude from domestic wells. Congress took two other key actions in 1990. It increased the Strategic Petroleum Reserve's capacity to 1 billion barrels as a buffer against sudden cutoffs of foreign oil and it enacted the Clean Air Act Amendments. These require the use of additives in gasoline sold in smog-ridden cities and mandate fuel switching to alternative sources in the longer term.

This year Congress is also consid

# U.S. Energy Sources

*The U.S. uses more oil, by far, than any other energy source. Forty-one percent of the nation's energy comes from oil — 40 percent of it imported in 1991. But oil is the only U.S. energy source dependent on foreign markets. The United States is virtually self-sufficient for all its other energy needs — natural gas, coal, nuclear and hydroelectric. (Some natural gas and hydropower are purchased from Canada.)*

*The Bush administration's proposed National Energy Strategy would curtail oil consumption by increasing federal gas mileage standards and by giving tax breaks for conservation efforts. To encourage the development of alternative fuels, the policy also would support the construction of new natural gas pipelines and ease restrictions on licensing nuclear power plants. Meanwhile, California's strict energy regulations mandate that by the year 2003 10 percent of all new cars sold in the state must have zero emissions. Given current technology, that means electric cars; 12 states and the District of Columbia are considering similar legislation.*

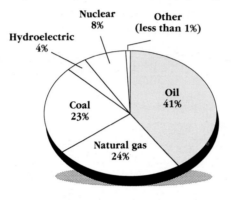

Source: Energy Information Administration.

ering a broad new energy initiative launched in February by the Bush administration. The National Energy Strategy, the product of a year and a half of extensive field hearings, includes several measures aimed specifically at reducing the country's reliance on foreign energy sources.

The strategy's main elements are the centerpiece of an energy bill introduced by Sen. J. Bennett Johnston, D-La., in February. The National Energy Security Act (S 1220) would try to boost domestic oil output by opening the Arctic National Wildlife Refuge (ANWR) to oil and gas drilling, give tax breaks to energy producers and impose a tax on oil imports. At the same time, the bill would attempt to curtail oil consumption by increasing the federal CAFE standards for gas mileage, establish energy-efficiency standards for appliances and buildings and give tax breaks for conservation efforts. In an effort to encourage the development of alternative fuels, the

bill would phase in requirements for their use in vehicles, boost construction of natural gas pipelines and make it easier for nuclear power plants to obtain operating licenses.

The Johnston energy bill, like the Bush energy strategy on which it is based, has come under attack from environmentalists for emphasizing steps that would favor the energy sector — oil companies and the nuclear industry — over more aggressive measures to reduce consumption and encourage the switch to renewable energy sources. The critics' main complaint focuses on the opening of ANWR to drilling for oil and gas, which they say will jeopardize the wilderness area for an as yet undetermined quantity of crude. Supporters of the measure point to geological data indicating that between 1 billion and 9 billion barrels of oil may lie beneath the refuge.[21] "The geologists are very optimistic about a huge field, and if they are right it would be the biggest find

since the first Alaskan [discovery] in 1968 at Prudhoe Bay," says oil analyst John Lichtblau.

As for the bill's provision for enhanced oil recovery, Christopher Flavin of Worldwatch says history provides no indication that these incentives would yield significant amounts of new oil, especially at today's moderate prices. "It really defies logic, because we came through a period of very high oil prices in the early 1980s, and there was very little enhanced oil recovery going on even at those high prices," he says. "The administration's assumption that enhanced oil recovery would yield several million barrels a day strikes me as preposterous."

Even where the Johnston bill does promote alternative fuels, critics say, it promotes the wrong ones for reasons having more to do with politics than sound energy policy. James MacKenzie of the World Resources Institute, for example, says the bill's promotion of ethanol as a viable alternative fuel is "just craziness." Farmers would receive federal support for growing corn to produce ethanol under the proposal, but ethanol as currently produced would actually give off more greenhouse gases than the gasoline it would replace. "Ethanol is the pits," MacKenzie says, noting the fuel's volatility and propensity to emit ozone. "It's just a political solution to a physical problem. Ethanol is a farm-support program that has nothing to do with energy."

## Gas Mileage Standards

Another bill now before Congress would tighten the CAFE standards. Unlike the Johnston bill, which bows to the Bush administration's opposition to fuel-efficiency standards, the Motor Vehicle Fuel Ef-

*Continued on p. 600*

# California Leads the Way to Alternative Fuels

While Congress will not get down to serious consideration of proposals to reduce oil imports and harmful auto emissions until this fall, California has already enacted the most far-reaching air-quality standards in the country. Beginning in 1993, the state will start phasing in cuts in allowable auto emissions that will force automakers and energy producers alike to either clean up the products they sell in California or lose their share of this lucrative market. At the same time, the rules will reduce the state's reliance on oil as an energy source.

California's new energy regulations result in part from changes mandated by the federal Clean Air Act Amendments of 1990. That law requires automakers to produce 150,000 low-emissions vehicles by 1996 for sale in California, home of the most polluted city in the country, Los Angeles. It also requires that cleaner-burning, reformulated gasoline (which contains a different mix of aromatics and olefins to emit slightly less carbon dioxide than conventional gasoline blends) be made available for these vehicles.

**GM's electric car, the Impact**
*Photo courtesy General Motors Corporation*

But California's sweeping standards also stem from the state's longstanding support of the California Energy Commission, which was created in 1974 in the wake of the first national energy crisis. The results have been impressive. In the late 1970s California's utilities used oil to generate more than half the state's electric power, compared with just 6 percent today. The commission succeeded by using both alternative non-renewable energy sources such as natural gas and renewable sources such as solar and wind power. By emphasizing improved energy efficiency, the commission reports, California has reduced its per capita energy consumption by 15 percent since 1978.[†]

California's energy commission is now concentrating on transportation, which accounts for almost half the energy consumed in the state. Californians used 13 billion gallons of gasoline in 1989, making the state the third-largest gasoline consumer in the *world*, after the United States as a whole and the Soviet Union. At the same time, air pollution caused by auto emissions has worsened.

In September 1990 the state adopted new emissions standards for cars and small trucks sold in the state, to be phased in over the next 13 years. These standards are stricter than those imposed nationwide by the Clean Air Act Amendments. In 1998, 2 percent of all new vehicles sold in California must have zero emissions. Given today's technology, that means electric cars. But by the year 2003, all new vehicles sold in the state must have low or ultra-low emissions, while 10 percent must have zero emissions.

In the short term, the California Energy Commission has put forward a plan to reduce vehicle use, make fuel use more efficient and speed the shift to alternative fuels. In its most recent report, the commission recommends that California tighten the Corporate Average Fuel Economy (CAFE) standards for cars sold in the state, even if Congress fails to better fuel efficiency nationwide (*see p. 598*).

The new energy report calls for the state to issue by next year a plan for adapting all state government vehicles to alternative fuels. By 1993 all local governments are to presenttheir plans for switching to alternative-fuel fleets that meet or exceed California's air quality standards.

Although California is far ahead of the country, 12 states and the District of Columbia have indicated they will also enact legislation requiring cleaner fuels and, eventually, electric cars. These include every state along the Eastern seaboard from Virginia to Maine, plus Colorado, Illinois and Texas.[††]

While oil companies and automakers are busy lobbying Congress to ward off some of the costlier provisions of the energy policy proposals under consideration by lawmakers, they are also busy vying for market share in areas like California, where strict standards are scheduled to go into force in the 1990s. Arco, for example, announced in early July that it has developed a gasoline that would reduce pollutants by a third and could be used in today's cars. General Motors (GM) has developed an electric car called the Impact that will be ready for sale in 1993 — five years before they will be required in California — as part of its plan to introduce zero-emissions vehicles.

GM will find a formidable competitor in Nissan, which plans to set up battery-recharging stations in California. The Japanese automaker is developing a quick-charging battery that would eliminate one of the major drawbacks of electric cars, the long recharging time that leaves these vehicles out of operation for several hours every 100 miles or so.[‡]

---

[†] See California Energy Commission, *California's Energy Plan*, 1991 Biennial Report, July 1991.

[††] See Matthew L. Wald, "When the E.P.A. Isn't Mean Enough About Cleaner Air," *The New York Times*, July 21, 1991.

[‡] See "Nissan Jolts Detroit," *Business Week*, June 3, 1991.

Continued from p. 598
ficiency Act (S 279), proposed by Sen. Richard H. Bryan, D-Nev., would require auto manufacturers to achieve an increase in the average automobile gasoline mileage of their entire fleet of cars from 27.5 to 40 miles per gallon by the year 2000.

Environmental organizations and their supporters in Congress launched a grass-roots letter-writing campaign in June opposing the Johnston bill and supporting Bryan's CAFE standards proposal. They say that improving fuel efficiency is the single most effective way to protect the environment while reducing oil imports.

Bryan says the Reagan administration's rollback of fuel standards from 27.5 to 26.5 miles per gallon for the 1989 model year means the country will consume 900 million gallons of gasoline more than it would have if the standards had remained unchanged. According to the Sierra Club, one of the efficiency bill's leading supporters, the improved CAFE standards alone would save 2.5 million barrels of oil every day by the year 2005, more oil than the entire list of proposals contained in Johnston's bill.

Not all environmentalists agree with this assessment. MacKenzie, for example, says the emphasis on CAFE standards is a mistake because it does no more than simply slow down the growth of gasoline consumption. "Instead of facing the fact that gasoline here is cheaper than bottled water, we are attempting to basically force consumers to buy more efficient vehicles without in any way affecting how they drive those vehicles," he says. Rather than trying to "regulate our way into this more efficient future," MacKenzie advocates raising the price of gasoline with higher taxes at the pump. "The problem is that our fuel is too cheap, it doesn't reflect the security costs or the pollution costs or the climate costs of consuming it," he says.

In other industrial nations, where gasoline prices do reflect these costs, MacKenzie says, consumers voluntarily demand more efficient cars, drive them less and use mass transit to a greater extent than do Americans. In Italy, for example, consumers pay more than $4 a gallon for gasoline, most of which is the government fuel tax. As a result, the vast majority of Italians drive small, fuel-efficient cars. The same kind of energy policy, based mainly on excise taxes on gasoline at the pump, is in effect in most other industrial nations, including Japan and Germany.

MacKenzie says a similar approach based on oil pricing is the best solution for America's dual energy problems — the growing dependence on imports and the relentless degradation of the environment caused by burning fossil fuels. He proposes a gradual rise in the federal tax on gasoline sales at the pump by 10 cents a year over the next decade at least. In order to make the gasoline tax revenue-neutral and soften the blow to lower-income groups, he says, Social Security taxes could be reduced by an amount that varies according to personal income. ∎

# OUTLOOK

## Continued Dependence

There is little evidence of support in Congress for the pricing approach to energy policy that MacKenzie espouses. Even the 5-cent increase introduced last winter found grudging support, and that was at the height of concern over future availability of oil supplies from the Persian Gulf. "There are plenty of people in Congress who understand this, but they are still in a great minority and together they don't have enough courage to do what makes sense," MacKenzie says.

For its part, the Bush administration is strongly opposed to any energy policy that relies on new taxes. In early August, House Democratic leaders withdrew from floor consideration a highway reauthorization bill that would have included an additional 5-cent gasoline tax. Bush had threatened to veto the bill because of the tax increase.

Because oil prices have stabilized and supplies are adequate for the foreseeable future, the energy debate this year seems likely to focus

primarily on Bryan's proposed improvements in fuel-efficiency standards and Johnston's big national energy bill, which is expected to come before the Senate this fall.

By that time, the recession may be considerably weaker. Already, auto sales are beginning to climb, and gasoline demand will likely follow suit. That means oil imports will soon resume their upward path. Oil analyst Lichtblau, who along with the Bush administration supports the Johnston bill, says even if significant amounts of oil are discovered in the Arctic National Wildlife Refuge, oil imports will climb over the next decade. "I think it is quite likely that there will be an increase in our dependence on foreign oil from the current 40-42 percent range to the mid-50 percent range by the year 2000," he says. "No matter what happens in Alaska, we will continue to depend on foreign oil as far ahead as you can look."

The Energy Department not only agrees with Lichtblau's assessment but also predicts that by 2010 the United States will depend on imports for up to 74 percent of its oil.[22] Both falling U.S. oil output and rising consumer demand for gasoline

Continued on p. 603

# At Issue:

## Should drilling for new domestic oil be allowed in Alaska's Arctic National Wildlife Refuge?

### CITIZENS FOR THE ENVIRONMENT

*A research and educational organization that promotes environmental stewardship consistent with economic growth.*
**FROM POLICY STATEMENT ISSUED APRIL 17, 1991.**

*yes*

east of Prudhoe Bay, along the northeastern coast of Alaska, lies America's most promising onshore prospect for substantially increasing domestic oil production. Geological surveys indicate the area may contain major oil fields, even some chance for a huge, Saudi Arabian-size field. Yet, development of these potential fields is controversial because the area falls within the boundaries of the Arctic National Wildlife Refuge (ANWR). The resulting, sometimes acrimonious debate has tended to obscure the basic policy issues involved. . . .

ANWR (pronounced "an-wahr") . . . encompasses over 19 million acres, an area about the size of the state of South Carolina, bordered by the Beaufort Sea and Arctic Ocean on the north and Canada on the east. The Brooks Mountain Range divides the more mountainous interior of ANWR from its coastal plain region north of the mountains. The debate focuses on the so-called "1002 area" (named after Section 1002 of the Alaska National Interest Lands Conservation Act of 1980 . . .), where potential oil resources are located. The 1002 area covers about 1.5 million acres on the coastal plain.

Twenty years of oil company operations on Alaska's North Slope show that development in the 1002 area should not lead to significant damage to either wildlife populations or the land. The range of the Central Arctic caribou herd includes the North Slope area and the western part of ANWR. The herd has increased in population from about 3,000 animals in 1972 to more than 18,000 animals. This simple statistic captures the essence of what several detailed studies report: The caribou seem to have adapted well to roads, pipeline, and other facilities required by development. Oil operations on the North Slope have caused localized displacement of wildlife, but no significant long-term harm.

Responsible oil exploration and development in the 1002 area makes sense because the potential benefits to the country are great while the potential risks to the environment are minimal. Obtaining balance in our environmental policies requires that we carefully weigh the best estimates of both the potential risks and benefits of all activity. Unnecessary damage to the environment and unnecessary denial of economic growth are wastes we should seek to avoid.

### SIERRA CLUB

*An environmental-protection advocacy group that considers the region "our last Arctic wilderness."*
**FROM POLICY STATEMENT ISSUED JANUARY 1991.**

*no*

the Arctic National Wildlife Refuge is one of the few remnants of true wilderness left in America. The U.S. Fish and Wildlife Service calls the Arctic Refuge "the only conservation system unit in North America that protects, in an undisturbed condition, the complete spectrum of arctic and subarctic ecosystems."

The wildlife here is unique and abundant. Polar bears den on the arctic plains, musk-ox roam along glacial rivers and wolves prowl the foothills. Grizzly bears haunt the open tundra, Dall sheep scale the mountaintops and moose range in the Taiga forest, south of the mountains.

Most notable of all is a herd of 180,000 caribou known as the Porcupine herd. The caribou of the Porcupine herd migrate hundreds of miles annually between their wintering grounds and the coastal plain of the Arctic Refuge, where they give birth to their young every spring.

The oil industry believes that oil also lies underneath the Arctic Refuge's coastal plain and is urging Congress to allow them to drill there. However, by all accounts, there is less than a one-in-five chance that any economically recoverable oil exists in the Arctic. Despite these odds the oil industry and its supporters tout the Arctic Refuge as "another Prudhoe Bay." In actuality, according to Interior Department figures, there is only a 1-in-100 chance of another find that size in the Arctic Refuge.

Oil companies are now trying to use the crisis in the Middle East to push Congress into opening up the Arctic Refuge to development. If oil were found in the Arctic, it would take another 10 years of exploration and development before that oil could be recovered and used.

We wouldn't flood the Grand Canyon to build a hydroelectric dam. We wouldn't plug Yellowstone's Old Faithful to tap its geothermal energy. Why should we irreparably harm this unique wilderness for a short-term supply of oil that wouldn't be available for another 10 years? There are other options and resources that can permanently reduce this country's dependence on oil.

Rather than follow the oil industry's "drain America first" philosophy, the Sierra Club supports the safer and more long-lasting alternative of energy efficiency. Greater fuel efficiency and the increased use of renewable, nonpolluting energy alternatives, such as solar power, will save this country much more oil than could ever be taken from the Arctic.

# How Oil Companies Have Weathered Desert Storm

In August 1990, when gasoline prices took off following Iraq's invasion of Kuwait, angry consumers and their representatives in Congress accused the oil companies of price-gouging — taking advantage of the crisis to make unfair profits. Actually, the Persian Gulf War had an uneven impact on the oil industry. While some sectors of the industry did indeed reap windfall profits during the early stages of the crisis, others actually suffered losses.

From August through January, oil producers — companies that extract crude oil from the ground — reaped high profits because crude prices soared and remained high during that period. After January, prices returned to prewar levels and have remained there ever since. "So the benefits of the war in terms of shortages driving up prices lasted five months, and then they went away," says John H. Lichtblau, president of the Petroleum Industry Research Foundation.

Oil producers typically enjoy high profits during such crises. "It's perfectly consistent with the behavior of oil purchasers in ... 1973 and 1979, when we had a massive increase in inventories, which had the effect of pushing up prices," explains Bernard Picchi, an oil analyst at the New York investment firm of Salomon Brothers. Worried about the future availability of crude, buyers tried to build their inventories at once.

For the buyers themselves, chiefly oil refiners — companies that transform crude oil into gasoline, heating oil, jet fuel and other products — the gulf crisis was less beneficial. "As crude oil prices went up, gasoline prices increased by much less, so that the profit margin was squeezed from August through November before picking up again somewhat," Lichtblau says. The same profit squeeze was felt by refiners selling the other oil products, whose prices also rose less than that of crude oil.

The fall in crude oil prices in early 1991 allowed refiners and retailers of oil products to recapture some of their losses from the last half of 1990. "In mid-January the crude oil price collapsed, and retail prices did come down, not immediately, but within three to four weeks," Lichtblau explains.

Today, consumers complain that despite the fall in oil prices, gasoline remains more expensive than it was before the gulf war. The American Automobile Association reports that a gallon of self-serve, regular unleaded costs an average $1.15. That is just over 6 cents more than this time last year. But 5 cents of that increase is claimed by the new federal gasoline tax, which went into effect last December. Also, while oil prices have fallen, they have not returned to their prior level but stabilized at $3 to $4 dollars a barrel above

last year's price. So refiners and gasoline retailers are not gouging consumers, Lichtblau says. "The increase in the crude oil price plus the increase in taxes actually make the margin on the sale of gasoline lower than a year ago."

Picchi goes even further to defend the behavior of U.S. oil companies, saying they "exercised enormous restraint" during the gulf war. If price-gouging occurred anywhere during the crisis, he says, it was in the oil markets of Singapore and Northern Europe, where jet-grade kerosene reached $42 a barrel in February, a time when crude oil prices had already fallen back to about $20 a barrel.

"Never in my 13 years covering the oil industry have I seen that wide a spread between the price of a product and the price of crude oil," Picchi says. But partly because the Bush administration pressed domestic oil firms to hold down retail prices, he says, this spread was never felt in the U.S. "The issue of price-gouging is something that these flower children of the 1960s are making up. There's no statistical evidence to show that whatsoever."

Those data do show that the gulf war has not given a lasting boost to the U.S. oil industry. After enjoying windfall earnings in the first quarter of this year, several large integrated companies — those that are involved in the oil trade from the ground to the gas pump — reported a fall in earnings during the second quarter. Part of the reason for the decline stems from the rising cost of exploring for new oil and natural gas reserves. Another factor is the low price of natural gas, now at about $1.05 per thousand cubic feet — the equivalent of oil selling for about $7 a barrel.

Whatever happens to efforts to reduce American dependence on oil imports, Picchi adds, the United States will provide less and less of the integrated oil companies' earnings in coming years. "The reality is that production and refining are increasingly moving away from the United States." Even the sale of oil products in the world's biggest oil-consuming nation is not expected to enrich these companies as it has in the past.

But while U.S. oil consumption falls, other countries will take up the slack. Portugal, Spain and the Soviet Union, not to mention all of Africa and Southeast Asia, Picchi says, "should all enjoy fairly good growth rates in oil consumption." So while some domestic refiners and many independent oil producers may go under as U.S. reserves run dry, the big integrated companies should weather the market changes. "The lesson in the last few years is that integration is a formula for stability for major oil companies."

> While some sectors of the industry did indeed reap windfall profits during the early stages of the crisis, others actually suffered losses.

*Continued from p. 600*

and other oil products will cause this growing energy dependence, the department predicts.

If two decades of recurrent crises characterized by tight supplies, volatile prices and even the involvement of American soldiers in a major war in the Middle East have failed to curb Americans' appetite for foreign oil, will anything? James MacKenzie says it will take the threat of environmental cataclysm to make consumers change their driving habits, the chief contributor to the country's energy dependence. "The only thing that I think will kick off a grass-roots effort will be recognition that the climate change is occurring so fast that we've got to do something," he says. "When that happens, then maybe there is some hope we can deal with it. But time is running out." ■

## Notes

[1] Central Intelligence Agency, Directorate of Intelligence, *International Energy Statistical Review*, April 30, 1991, p. 1. Figures are for 1989.

[2] Arthur Andersen & Co. and Cambridge Energy Research Associates, Inc., *World Oil Trends* (1991), pp. 6, 32.

[3] Energy Information Administration, U.S. Department of Energy, *Short-Term Energy Outlook, Second Quarter 1991*.

[4] CIA, *op. cit.*, p. 4.

[5] Energy Information Administration, *Annual Energy Review 1990*, May 1991, p. 117.

[6] Oil reserve data from Arthur Andersen and Cambridge Energy Research Associates *op. cit.*, pp. 38, 40; production figures from CIA, *op. cit.*, p. 1.

[7] See Energy Information Administration, *op. cit.*, p. 7.

[8] See Daniel Yergin, *The Prize: The Epic Quest for Oil, Money, and Power* (1991) p. 718.

[9] See Michael P. Walsh, "Motor Vehicles and Global Warming," in Jeremy Leggett, ed., *Global Warming: The Greenpeace Report* (1990), p. 261.

[10] National Academy of Sciences, National Academy of Engineering and Institute of Medicine, *Policy Implications of Greenhouse Warming: Report of the Mitigation Panel* (1991), pp. 5-12.

[11] From testimony presented by Diane C. Fisher, staff scientist of the Environmental Defense Fund, at hearings before the House Energy and Commerce Subcommittee on Energy and Power, June 19, 1991.

[12] Energy Information Administration, *1991 Annual Energy Outlook, with Projections to 2010*, March 1991, pp. 22-23.

[13] Yergin, *op. cit.*, p. 56.

[14] *Ibid*, p. 178.

[15] *Ibid*, pp. 250-251.

[16] *Ibid*, p. 000.

[17] *Ibid*, pp. 557-558.

[18] *Ibid*, p. 567.

[19] *Ibid*, p. 606.

[20] See Walter A. Rosenbaum, *Energy, Politics, and Public Policy* (1987), p. 8.

[21] M. Lynne Corn, Claudia Copeland and Pamela Baldwin, *Arctic Resources: Over a Barrel?* CRS Issue Brief, Congressional Research Service, May 10, 1991, update, p. 4.

[22] Energy Information Administration, *1991 Annual Energy Outlook*, p. 20.

# Bibliography

## Selected Sources Used

### Books

**Leggett, Jeremy, *Global Warming: The Greenpeace Report*, Oxford University Press, 1990.**

Although the report details the environmental problems thought to contribute to global warming, a chapter on the role of motor vehicles thoroughly analyzes the various gases that gasoline-driven vehicle engines emit. These gases are among the major causes of urban air pollution, atmospheric ozone depletion and the greenhouse effect that produces global warming.

**Yergin, Daniel, *The Prize: The Epic Quest for Oil, Money, and Power*, Simon & Schuster, 1991.**

After the 1978-79 oil crisis, Yergin co-authored *Energy Future* (Random House, 1979), a well-regarded analysis of the potential for developing alternative energy sources. In the present volume, he presents an exhaustive but fascinating history of the oil trade from its beginnings in western Pennsylvania to its role in the gulf war, focusing on the personalities involved in oil's development and the politics that have encouraged its use.

### Articles

**Easterbrook, Gregg, "Waste of Energy," *The New Republic*, March 18, 1991, pp. 26-31.**

The Bush administration's long-awaited National Energy Strategy, the author writes, lacks the most-needed reforms of all: conservation incentives and energy-pricing mechanisms that make the price of oil reflect the social costs of its use. "There is no sentence in the 214-page document that would displease any monied interest group — the sure sign of a failed policy."

**Verleger, Philip K., "The Oil Vortex: A Way Out?" *International Economic Insights*, September/October 1990, pp. 3-7.**

The author, an analyst for the Institute for International Economics and a former energy policy official in the Carter administration, is optimistic about the long-term availability of oil. But he advocates an oil import fee as part of a stronger system for responding to sudden crises.

### Reports and Studies

**Arthur Andersen & Co. and Cambridge Energy Research Associates, *World Oil Trends*, 1991 edition.**

These two research and consulting firms present a comprehensive analysis of the world oil market, including producer and consumer data, reserve estimates, pricing trends and information on refining capacity and transportation. By presenting data for every year since the early 1970s, the volume presents a comprehensive view of trends in each aspect of the oil business.

**California Energy Commission, *California's Energy Plan*, 1991 Biennial Report, July 1991.**

At the vanguard of U.S. energy policy, California has reduced its per capita energy consumption by 15 percent since 1978 while the rest of the country is increasing its energy consumption. The state's approach includes a variety of initiatives to promote conservation and the use of "cleaner" fuels in an effort to reduce oil dependency as well as improve environmental conditions.

**Congressional Budget Office, *Carbon Charges as a Response to Global Warming: The Effects of Taxing Fossil Fuels*, August 1990.**

The budget office, which provides nonpartisan analyses of economic issues to Congress, examines the economic effects of various taxes on the use of fossil fuels, including oil, coal and natural gas. One of these options, aimed at reducing the global emission of carbon dioxide, would tax fossil fuels according to their carbon content. Such a tax would have to be phased in gradually to mitigate its damage to the economy.

**MacKenzie, James J., "Toward a Sustainable Energy Future: The Critical role of Rational Energy Pricing," *WRI Issues and Ideas*, May 1991.**

The author, an associate with the World Resources Institute's program in climate, energy and pollution, contends that "low gasoline prices in the United States fail to reflect the full social costs of driving and contribute to urban sprawl and almost total reliance on motor vehicles to meet daily needs." Only by raising gasoline prices, he writes, will the country reduce its consumption of oil.

**National Academy of Sciences, National Academy of Engineering and Institute of Medicine, *Policy Implications of Greenhouse Warming: Report of the Mitigation Panel*, National Academy Press, 1991 (prepublication manuscript).**

This new report by three leading scientific research organizations compares different options for curtailing the release of greenhouse gases as part of its framework for international negotiations on global warming. The chapter on transportation energy management concludes that radical improvements in vehicle efficiency will come slowly because of the slow turnover of vehicles in use.

# The Next Step

## Additional Articles from Current Periodicals

### Addresses & essays

**"Wasting opportunities,"** *Economist,* Dec. 22, 1990, p. 14.

Comments on the United States' need for an intelligent strategy for energy. How President Bush should react to the Department of Energy's National Energy Strategy; dangers of a tariff on oil imports; too much use of energy by United States; need for greater energy efficiency; fuel taxes must rise; details.

**Kuttner, R., "How we can break the cycle of oil crunches,"** *Business Week,* Sept. 17, 1990, p. 18.

Comments on a sound strategy that would reduce dependence on imported oil, develop domestic alternatives, and ensure stable prices through a long-term contract with oil-exporting nations. Using a minimalist energy policy; steps toward self-sufficiency; captive commodity; no surprises.

**Lawson, R. L., "Energy for America and world economic cooperation,"** *Vital Speeches,* April 15, 1990, p. 410.

Presents a speech by Richard L. Lawson, president of the National Coal Association, delivered as the Inaugural Address in the Distinguished Lecturer Series of the University of Kentucky Mining Engineering Foundation, which proposes an energy plan similar to the 1947 Marshall Plan; using coal resources and clean coal technology to eliminate imported oil dependency.

**Mack, T., "A microchip in hand beats oil in the ground,"** *Forbes,* Oct. 30, 1989, p. 150.

Interview with John Lichtblau, president of the Petroleum Industry Research Foundation Inc. and longtime observer of the world energy industry. U.S. economy; importing oil; oil dependence; Middle East; OPEC.

### Debates & issues

**Barrett, W. P., "Domestic blockade?"** *Forbes,* Sept. 3, 1990, p. 36.

Reports how the United States is nearing the limits of its ability to move and process imported oil, and the Iraq-Kuwait crisis will only delay the crunch. How our transportation, storage and refinery facilities are running at or near capacity; storage capacity; tanker situation getting tight; if U.S. economy would slow, demand for oil would slow.

**Gaffney, J., "The moral equivalent of war in the Middle East,"** *America,* Sept. 8, 1990 and Sept. 15, 1990, p. 125.

Opinion. Suggests that President Bush call for a conservation of energy derived from imported oil as a moral equivalent to full-scale war in the Middle East.

**Hayes, T. C., "Putting the oil reserve to the test,"** *The New York Times,* Sept. 28, 1990, p. D1.

Discusses the government's intention to sell oil from the nation's Strategic Petroleum Reserve. Experts agree that the extra oil should prevent any shortages even if there is a prolonged loss of imports from Iraq and Kuwait, but they warn that distribution difficulties in the first few weeks of the program could lead to spot shortages early on and that hoarding by speculators could be a problem.

**O'Reilly, B. and Pare, T. P., "The coming gush of oil imports,"** *Fortune,* May 7, 1990, p. 127.

Discusses rising United States oil imports, expected to account for over half the oil used in the United States this year, and almost half of the U.S. trade deficit. Forecasters say, however, that the United States will take rising oil imports in stride, and that the deficit may correct itself by the end of the decade. Dropping U.S. production; energy policy and economics; conservation; gas tax; fuel-efficient cars; OPEC prices; effect of U.S.-Soviet relations.

**Rudolph, B., "Step on the gas, pay the price,"** *Time,* April 3, 1989, p. 40.

Discusses how, as the use of oil increases in the United States, less domestic oil is being discovered, causing a need to purchase more imported oil. Fears of overdependence on foreign sources like in the 1970s; what the U.S. government is doing.

**Sheets, K. R. and Pasternak, D., "America's great pipeline war,"** *U.S. News & World Report,* July 30, 1990, p. 38.

Describes the controversy over a natural-gas project which pits self-interest against national energy needs. Iroquois natural-gas pipeline, 370 miles from Canada to Connecticut; federal approval expected this week; influence of the wealthy on the route; curbing oil imports.

**Wald, M. L., "Lower oil prices thwart U.S. energy goal,"** *The New York Times,* March 4, 1991, p. D1.

Analyzes the growing American reliance on imported oil. Need to conserve, despite the lower prices.

**Wald, M. L., "U.S. imports record 49.9 percent of oil,"** *The New York Times,* July 19, 1990, p. D1.

Discusses the decline of the U.S. oil industry. The half-year statistics confirm a trend that has been evident in fits and starts for months. Chart shows petroleum products in the U.S., both domestic and imported.

## Economic aspects

**"Curbed drills," *Economist*, July 14, 1990, p. 74.**

Reports that soaring oil imports and slumping prices are combining to make life a misery for U.S. oilmen. Their pleas for help are falling on deaf ears. Predictions of U.S.'s reliance on foreign oil coming true; study by Arthur Andersen on 236 publicly owned companies; fall in U.S oil production; difficulty of staging a quick recovery; handicap of import taxes and the tax on petrol; role of the Congress.

**"Scorecards on the oil giants," *Fortune*, Sept. 10, 1990, p. 45.**

Presents 10 scorecards comparing the top oil companies doing business in the United States, the world's largest market for oil and the biggest importer as well. How some will have to change their sources of crude from month to month; how, as petroleum prices rise, the big profits will go to companies that produce high percentages of the crude their refineries need.

**"Weaning the U.S. from its oil addiction," *Business Week*, Aug. 20, 1990, p. 106.**

Editorial. Covers how the explosion in oil prices that has followed the embargoes on Iraqi and Kuwaiti oil confronts Washington with a thorny policy issue. The justification for raising gasoline taxes to conserve energy and minimize the growing U.S. dependence on oil imports is stronger than ever.

**Cooper, J. C. and Madigan, K., "The cold wind of the economy is putting prices on ice," *Business Week*, Dec. 3, 1990, p. 27.**

Reports that the chill that is sweeping through the U.S. economy is, in fact, cooling down inflation. States how the sluggish economy had already produced some moderation in the pace of goods prices. Non-energy prices remain tame; housing is skewing service inflation; higher prices inflate inventories; a setback in foreign trade; pricier oil means skimpier imports.

**Dentzer, S., Cook, W. J., et al., "The economic perils ahead," *U.S. News & World Report*, Aug. 20, 1990, p. 29.**

Examines the economic effects of Saddam Hussein's invasion of Kuwait and assesses future problems. Serious weaknesses in the United States economic policy; dependence on imported oil; possible effects on the fiscal 1991 budget; price changes in oil; possible measures. INSETS: Good deals at the gas pump?, by K. Sheets; sluggish growth or a worsening downturn?

**Elving, R. D., "Budget talks reawaken oil-import fee debate," *Congressional Quarterly Weekly Report*, July 7, 1990, p. 2124.**

Discusses the issue of a possible oil-import fee and asserts that the likelihood of one being passed is very small. Tariff on imported oil; President Bush, a Texan and former oilman; arguments for tax have been around for years; every new budget deal gives oil tariff new life; favorable report; changing politics; more.

**Finney, B., "The dragon within," *Mother Earth News*, May/June 1990, p. 14.**

Discusses how politicians and engineers would like to use geothermal technology to reduce Hawaii's dependence on imported oil. Controversy brewing because Wao Kele O Puna rain forest, the last major lowland tropical rain forest in the United States, lies over much of the proposed drilling zone.

**Koretz, G., "Oil imports are setting an ambush for the economy," *Business Week*, March 13, 1989, p. 26.**

Discusses how the chances are growing that a rising oil import bill will seriously retard improvement in the trade balance in 1989 and beyond.

**Labaton, S., "Trade deficit increases modestly," *The New York Times*, July 18, 1990, p. D1.**

Reports that the nation's trade deficit rose modestly in May, to $7.73 billion, fueled by the economy's heavy reliance on oil imports and foreign automobiles. However, it also showed a healthy growth in imports, particularly in manufactured goods.

**Sheets, K. R., "America's oil-chill factor," *U.S. News & World Report*, March 27, 1989, p. 54.**

Report that steeper petroleum prices and rising imports threaten to increase the trade gap between Americans and foreigners. Analysis of trade deficit; curbing energy consumption.

**Sheets, K. R., "Calm waters, troubled oil," *U.S. News & World Report*, July 9, 1990, p. 35.**

Discusses the announcement by President Bush to place most of the United States coastline off-limits to oil and natural-gas exploration for the rest of this century, ensuring the import, by tanker, of more foreign oil. Economic implications of a drain on our balance of payments in trade; energy consumption increasing; development of other energy resources lagging.

## Environmental aspects

**"A one-legged energy policy," *Business Week*, Feb. 25, 1991, p. 116.**

Editorial. Comments on how the Bush administration is striving to produce its way out of excessive dependence on imported oil, at the probable cost of increased offshore drilling and opening up the Arctic National Wildlife Refuge. Environmental safeguards needed; whether augmenting supplies or restraining demand will be a faster, cheaper and easier way of cutting dependence.

**Lemonick, M. D. and Borg, J., "Hot tempers in Hawaii," *Time*, Aug. 13, 1990, p. 68.**

Reports that plans in Hawaii to replace much of the island's imported foreign oil with a supply of clean, natural and endlessly renewable power by tapping geothermal power in molten rock has concerned conservation groups. Unsafe and unnecessary project and will harm the precious Wao Kele O Puna rain forest. Further arguments for and against the project; individual and groups involved.

**Mack, T., "Connecticut Yankees in Saddam's court," *Forbes*, Nov. 12, 1990, p. 154.**

Studies how, in theory, the Northeastern states should cut their dependence on imported oil by burning more Canadian natural gas, but in practice the vested interests are digging in their heels. Benefits of using gas over oil; natural gas pipeline project; how many of the same people who want a greener environment and less dependence on Middle Eastern crude oil don't want a pipeline soiling their back yard; examples.

## *International aspects*

**"Where the oil flows," *Fortune*, Sept. 10, 1990, p. 48.**

Lists the world's major crude oil importers and exporters — and who gets what from whom.

**Cook, W. J., "The oil market at peace," *U.S. News & World Report*, March 11, 1991, p. 53.**

Considers the effects of the short Persian Gulf War on long-range oil prices. The Saudis are now likely to control the pricing, and their belief that moderate pricing ($20/barrel) is in their long-term interest will discourage development of other high-cost oil reserves, alternative energy sources and fuel conservation. Cheap oil a mixed blessing; fuel economy standards and a price-floor for imported oil.

**Feron, J., "Energy Commission gives final approval to gas pipeline," *The New York Times*, Nov. 15, 1990, p. B1.**

Reports that the Federal Energy Regulatory Commission gave final approval to the construction of a pipeline that will carry natural gas from western Canada to six Northeastern states, eventually replacing 100,000 barrels of imported oil a day. The Iroquois Gas Transmission System, a partnership of U.S. and Canadian energy companies, hopes to begin work in the spring.

**Kuntz, P., "Unstable Mideast oil supply rocks the world market," *Congressional Quarterly Weekly Report*, Jan. 5, 1991, p. 21.**

Presents questions about the nature of the United States' interests in oil. The administration has never denied oil's central importance to the gulf conflict, but they tend to avoid the issue. Rhetoric containing synonyms for oil; why is oil so important?; why is the oil in the Middle East so important?; why does the U.S. care who controls oil?; is the American response an attempt to protect cheap oil?

**Uri, N. D., "Factors affecting adherence to the 55 MPH speed limit," *Transportation Quarterly*, October 1990, p. 533.**

Discusses a variety of programs that emerged in the United States after the Arab oil embargo in 1973-74 aimed at reducing dependence on imported crude oil. The 55 mph national limit; factors affecting highway speed; estimation results; more.

## *Persian Gulf War, 1991*

**"Don't save this face," *Economist*, Jan. 12, 1991, p. 11.**

Argues that there are reasons important enough to justify going to war against Iraq in the gulf. Dangers of Saddam Hussein being left unchallenged in Kuwait; Resolution 678 of the United Nations Security Council; failed meeting between Secretaries of State James A. Baker III and Tariq Aziz; fundamental importance of oil; danger of face-saving measures for Saddam Hussein; details.

**Maynes, C. W., "Dateline Washington: A necessary war? " *Foreign Policy*, Spring 1991, p. 159.**

Considers the four factors identified as those behind the American decision to go to war in the Persian Gulf: oil, order, security and Israel. Questions if the gamble was prudent; curbing or deterring Saddam Hussein's ability to threaten his neighbors; curbs on arms shipments to the Middle East; doctrine of collective security; regional or global; Iraqi dependence on imports; security of Israel; pronounced religious divide; France's four-stage program; controversial proposals.

**Meldrum, A., "The ripple effect," *Africa Report*, January/February 1991, p. 34.**

Considers how soaring oil prices from the Persian Gulf crisis have dealt a blow to southern Africa's precarious economies, as limited resources earmarked for other areas have had to be diverted to pay inflated fuel costs. Most southern African countries must import all petroleum; Angola's rich supply of oil makes it stand to benefit; worst off is Mozambique, then Zambia and Zimbabwe; Zambia continues restructuring program; great deal of aid needed.

# Back Issues

*Great Research on Current Issues Starts Right Here. . . Recent topics covered by The CQ Researcher are listed below. Issues dated before May 10, 1991, were published under the name of Editorial Research Reports.*

**FEBRUARY 1990**
Politics and Economic Growth
Free Agency in Sports
Repetitive Motion
War on Drugs

**MARCH 1990**
Asbestos: Are Risks Acceptable?
Public Health Campaigns
South Africa's Future
Homeless Need More Than Shelter

**APRIL 1990**
How Fair is the Tax Burden?
Workers' Compensation
U.S. Pacific Forces
Curbing Insurance Premiums

**MAY 1990**
Should Teaching Be a Profession?
Will Canada Fall Apart?
Is U.S. Patent System Outdated?
Federal Funding for the Arts

**JUNE 1990**
Downsizing America's Armed Forces
Progress In Weather Forecasting
S & L Bailout
Bio-Chemical Disarmament

Back issues are available for $4.00 (subscribers) or $7.00 (non-subscribers). Quantity discounts apply to orders over ten. To order, call Congressional Quarterly 1-800-432-2250.

**JULY 1990**
Do Americans Still Love Marriage?
Death Penalty Debate
Decline of Rural America
United Nations in the 1990s

**AUGUST 1990**
Democracy in the Philippines
Initiatives: True Democracy?
Hard Times at Newspapers
Teens Balance School & Jobs

**SEPTEMBER 1990**
Dangers of Alcohol
Western Alliance After the Cold War
Tobacco Industry
Right to Die

**OCTOBER 1990**
Organ Transplants
Energy Policy Options
Search for Arab Unity
Child Support

**NOVEMBER 1990**
Lotteries and Gambling
Post Cold-War Choices
Setting Limits on Medical Care
Multicultural Education

**DECEMBER 1990**
Cable TV Regulation
Americans' Search For Their Roots
Is Insurance System a Failure?
Why Schools Still Have Tracking

**JANUARY 1991**
Growing Influence of Boycotts
Should the U.S. Reinstate the Draft?
America's Archaeological Past
Peace Corps' Challenges in '90s

**FEBRUARY 1991**
Regional Impact of Recession
Puerto Rico's Status
Redistricting: Mapping Power
Nuclear Power

**MARCH 1991**
Acid Rain
Cost of the Gulf War
Reassessing Gun Laws
Future for Man in Space

**APRIL 1991**
Social Security
Canadian Crisis Over Quebec
California Drought
Electromagnetic Radiation

**MAY 1991**
School Choice
Racial Quotas
Animal Rights
U.S. and Japan

**JUNE 1991**
Children and Divorce
Teenage Suicide
Endangered Species
Europe 1992

**JULY 1991**
Teenagers and Abortion
Soviet Republics Rebel
Mexico's Emergence
Athletes and Drugs

**AUGUST 1991**
Sexual Harassment
Fetal Tissue Research

# Future Topics

▶ *Palestinians*

▶ *Police Brutality*

▶ *Advertising Under Fire*

PUBLISHED BY CONGRESSIONAL QUARTERLY INC., IN CONJUNCTION WITH EBSCO PUBLISHING

# The Palestinians

*Will they ever get an independent homeland of their own?*

T he U.S.-led rout of Iraq in the gulf war has reshaped the geopolitical map of the Middle East. Among other things, the crisis has focused attention on one of the region's most intractable problems: what to do about the Palestinians. Having rallied behind Iraq in the war, the Palestinians are now politically isolated and economically ravaged. The nearly four-year-old uprising, or *intifada*, in the occupied territories has begun to sputter, leaving the Palestinians' dream of an independent state as distant as ever. Recognizing the urgency of the situation, President Bush has proposed a regional peace conference, tentatively scheduled for October. The Palestinians' current weakness could work in their favor. As one expert says, it allows them "to pursue the attainable rather than the ideal."

 **August 30, 1991 • Volume 1, No. 16 • 609-632**

*Formerly Editorial Research Reports*

COVER ART: BARBARA SASSA-DANIELS

*CQ Researcher*

August 30, 1991
Volume 1, No. 16

**EDITOR**
Sandra Stencel

**MANAGING EDITOR**
Thomas J. Colin

**ASSOCIATE EDITOR**
Richard L. Worsnop

**STAFF WRITERS**
Charles S. Clark
Mary H. Cooper
Rodman D. Griffin

**PRODUCTION EDITOR**
Laurie De Maris

**EDITORIAL ASSISTANT**
Thomas H. Moore

**GRAPHICS**
Jack Auldridge

**PUBLISHED BY**
Congressional Quarterly Inc.

**CHAIRMAN**
Andrew Barnes

**VICE CHAIRMAN**
Andrew P. Corty

**EDITOR AND PUBLISHER**
Neil Skene

**EXECUTIVE EDITOR**
Robert W. Merry

**PUBLICATIONS MARKETING/SALES**
Robert Smith

**EDITOR, EBSCO PUBLISHING**
Melissa Kummerer

The CQ Researcher (ISSN 1056-2036). Formerly Editorial Research Reports. Published weekly (48 times per year, not printed the first Friday of any month with five Fridays) by Congressional Quarterly Inc., 1414 22nd St., N.W., Washington, D.C. 20037. Rates are furnished upon request. Application to mail at second-class postage rates is pending at Washington, D.C. POSTMASTER: Send address changes to The CQ Researcher, 1414 22nd St., N.W., Washington, D.C. 20037.

# The Palestinians

**BY RODMAN D. GRIFFIN**

## THE ISSUES

For more than 40 years, Palestinians have been a disenfranchised, displaced people, yearning for a homeland. So when Iraqi President Saddam Hussein attempted to link his Aug. 2, 1990, invasion of Kuwait to the Palestinian cause, he found a receptive audience. Saddam promised to withdraw Iraqi troops if Israel relinquished Arab lands it took in the 1967 Arab-Israeli War. But instead of liberating the occupied territories, the gulf war has left the Palestinians even more in crisis — economically destitute, bereft of financial backers and torn apart by internal strife.

"Politically and economically, the plight of Palestinians across the board has no equivalent since 1948, when [Israel declared the establishment of a Jewish state and the Palestinians] were dispossessed," says Hisham Sharabi, a professor at Georgetown University and editor of the *Journal of Palestine Studies.* "This is a human tragedy on a grand scale." (*For background on the establishment of Israel, see p. 616.*)

The decision to back Iraq in the gulf war has cost the Palestinians much of the sympathy and support they had earned during the *intifada,* the nearly four-year-old popular uprising in the occupied territories. "It certainly did the Palestinian cause no good for the Palestinians themselves to appear to be using the violation of another people's sovereignty to redeem their own," writes George Abed, director of the Palestine Welfare Association, a Geneva-based development-assistance foundation.[1]

The consequences for the Palestinians living in the occupied territories — the West Bank and the

Gaza Strip (*see map, p. 613*) — have been severe. The Palestinian economy, already crippled by the *intifada,* was virtually destroyed by Israel's wartime emergency measures, which included a 40-day, dawn-to-dusk curfew, a ban against travel outside the territories and severe work restrictions. Arab economists estimate that fewer than 200,000 of the 1.7 million Palestinians in the occupied territories now have jobs. That brings unemployment among adults to roughly 60 percent. While about 110,000 Palestinians worked in Israel last year, only 35,000 now have army permits to enter Israeli territory for jobs. But even many of those cannot get regular work, their jobs having been filled by Soviet Jewish immigrants, who numbered some 200,000 last year.[2]

The economic devastation caused by the war, the intractable political deadlock with Israel and the recent influx of Soviet Jews have created unparalleled frustration and desperation among Palestinian Arabs. In the

last three years, the suicide rate in the Gaza Strip has quadrupled. Even more disturbing, the *intifada* seems to be turning inward: Palestinians suspected of collaborating with Israel are being killed by other Palestinians. Some 400 have been murdered since the *intifada* began, and the pace has been accelerating. In Gaza, 59 Palestinians have been killed by other Arabs so far this year, compared with 15 killed by Israeli soldiers.[3]

The gulf war has also created a new diaspora.* Hundreds of thousands of Palestinians — as well as Jordanians and Yemenis (who also supported Iraq) — have been expelled from Saudi Arabia, Kuwait and other gulf states. The Palestinian community in Kuwait, considered the most prosperous in the diaspora, has been fractured. Since Saddam's invasion last August, more than half of its 400,000 residents have fled and many of those who have remained have been abused. "The Palestinians are weak, and they have nobody to protect them," says Rashid Khalidi, a professor of Middle East Studies at the University of Chicago. "It [has been] like anti-Semitism, like pogroms in Europe."

The Palestinians, of course, are no strangers to economic hardship — or controversy. For decades the Palestinian issue has occupied center stage in the Middle East drama. Since 1948, the Arab states have justified their continuing hostility toward Israel on the grounds of defending the rights of the Palestinians to return to the land whence they came. But now, in the aftermath of the war, some experts say support for that cause has waned — and, along with it, Arab financial aid for the Palestinians.

---

*Diaspora means the scattering of people with a common origin, background, set of beliefs, etc.

With nowhere else to turn, moderate Palestinians are pinning their hopes on the United States — and the newly invigorated Middle East peace process. Hoping to translate momentum from the allied victory into a broader peace between Arabs and Israelis, President Bush has proposed a regional peace conference, tentatively scheduled for October, sponsored by Washington and Moscow. Bush is pursuing a "two-track strategy," parallel talks between Israel and the Palestinians on the one hand and between Israel and the Arab states on the other.

Many analysts, including those in the Bush administration, believe the gulf war has created a historic opportunity. For the first time in 43 years, Syria appears willing to talk peace with Israel. For different reasons, some Palestinians also are more willing to negotiate than they have been in the past. Disarray among Palestinian leaders, including those in the Palestine Liberation Organization (PLO), the mass exodus from the gulf states, the exhaustion of the *intifada* — all have combined to open the way for flexibility. Says Palestinian journalist Daoud Kuttab, "We're almost dying for any solution, and therefore we're willing to make almost any concession." [4]

Some Palestinians even appear willing to negotiate without a direct presence by the PLO and its leader, Yasir Arafat. This would remove an impediment that has confounded Middle East peace negotiations for the past decade. But even if the Palestinians decide to attend the conference, the road to peace will be rocky.

It's not yet clear, for example, whether the conference will be delayed because of the recent three-day coup attempt in the Soviet Union. Some Palestinians expressed support for the eight-man committee that tried to oust Soviet President Mikhail S. Gorbachev, which could further

weaken the Palestinians' negotiating position at a peace conference.

Progress toward resolving the Palestinian problem also depends on whether Israel is willing to compromise on the notion of "land for peace," embedded in United Nations Resolutions 242 and 338, which call for withdrawal of Israeli forces from occupied Arab areas, an end to the state of belligerency between the Arab nations and Israel, and acknowledgment of and respect for the sovereignty, territorial integrity and political independence of every nation in the area. [5] Israel has agreed to attend the conference, but thus far has shown no inclination toward compromise on substantive issues. In fact, in the three months following Kuwait's liberation, Israel earmarked more occupied land in the West Bank for Jewish settlement than it did in the preceding year. [6]

Historically both sides have found war easier to wage than peace. And breaking that cycle will require unprecedented diplomatic efforts — far more than the usual diplomatic talks. As the various parties jockey for position at the peace table, here are some issues that must be addressed.

### Who is the legitimate representative of the Palestinian people?

Whether living under Israeli occupation, confined in squalid refugee camps in Lebanon or Jordan or working as aliens in other Arab countries, most Palestinians still identify their struggle for self-determination with the Palestine Liberation Organization. Denied a homeland, the Palestinians have considered the PLO as their only national emblem for more than 20 years. In poll after poll, even informal surveys conducted after the gulf war, the vast majority of Palestinians have consistently affirmed that the PLO represents their political aspirations.

"Those much sought-after alternatives to the PLO do not exist," writes

Rami Khouri, a well-known Palestinian author living in Jordan. "The PLO commands the trust and allegiance of the overwhelming majority of Palestinians.... It is more than a collection of politicians or ideas; it is a symbol of our very being as a national community." [7]

Nevertheless, since the PLO emerged as a guerrilla force in the 1960s, Israel has steadfastly refused to recognize it, much less negotiate with it, out of concern that its members were determined to destroy the Jewish state. "The PLO is a terrorist organization," says Elie Kedourie, a scholar at the pro-Israeli Washington Institute for Near East Policy. "Furthermore, its leadership is self-appointed. It does not represent a democratic organization in any real sense."

Palestinians respond that the PLO is more democratic than most Arab governments. They claim their nationalist movement does find political expression in the sometimes stormy sessions of the Palestine National Council, the PLO's 450-member parliament-in-exile, where votes are taken and the losing minority abides by the majority decision.

Despite Israel's concerns, many Middle East experts believe the PLO's legitimacy should no longer be questioned. In 1974, Arab heads of state recognized the PLO as "the sole legitimate representative of the Palestinian people." One month later, the organization received international recognition when Yasir Arafat spoke before the U.N. General Assembly, which granted the PLO observer status.* In 1976, the PLO became the twenty-first full member of the Arab League, and by 1977 more than 100 nations had granted

---

*U.N. observer status entitles the PLO to maintain a mission at the U.N. and participate in all U.N. functions except voting. The vote on the PLO's observer status was 105-4 with 20 abstentions. Only Israel, the United States, Bolivia and the Dominican Republic voted against the PLO.

# Israel and the Occupied Territories

**West Bank:** This area, along with the Gaza Strip, was part of the larger Arab state envisioned in the 1947 United Nations plan to partition Palestine (see map, p. 617). It was annexed by Jordan after Israel drove back attacking Arab forces in the first Middle East war in 1948, and has been administered by Israel since the 1967 war. Many Israelis consider control of the West Bank, which now has about 100,000 Jewish settlers, a strategic asset to be bargained away only for the firmest guarantees against a new military threat. Some Israelis also see it as part of the biblical Land of Israel and are reluctant to give back any of it.

**Gaza Strip:** This 140-square-mile area along the Mediterranean coast came under Egyptian military control after the 1948 war and has been administered by Israel since 1967. It contains some of the most embittered and squalid Palestinian refugee camps.

**Jerusalem:** Israel is adamant that its reunification of Jerusalem after the 1967 war and designation of the reunited city as its capital are not subject to negotiation. This clashes with Arab assertions that East Jerusalem should be treated as part of the West Bank. Israelis bitterly remember that they were prevented from visiting Jewish holy places in the Old City while Jordan controlled the eastern half of Jerusalem from 1948 to 1967. The United States has never recognized Israel's annexation of East Jerusalem.

**Golan Heights:** This strategic high ground was wrested from Syria in the 1967 Six-Day War. Israel, in effect, annexed it in 1981, and 11,000 Jews have settled there. Syria has made recovery of the Golan Heights a major goal. Israelis fear that Syria might again shell northern Israel from the heights, as it often did before 1967.

**Sinai Peninsula:** In 1967, Israel also took control of the Sinai Peninsula from Egypt. The expansive Sinai is mostly desert but contained Egyptian air bases and was considered an important strategic buffer. As part of the Egyptian-Israeli peace treaty of March 26, 1979, Israel returned the Sinai Peninsula to Egypt in exchange for peace.

**Israeli "Security Zone":** Since 1985, Israeli forces, with the aid of Lebanese militia forces, have patrolled a narrow border strip of Lebanese territory to prevent cross-border guerrilla raids.

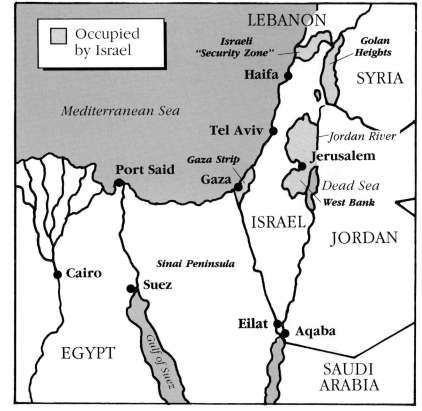

the PLO some form of diplomatic recognition.

By far the PLO's most significant step toward legitimacy was made in December 1988 when Arafat recognized Israel's right to exist, provided an independent Palestinian state was created alongside it. In an address before a special U.N. General Assembly session in Geneva, Arafat renounced terrorism and accepted Resolutions 242 and 338 — a profound policy shift that cleared the way for then U.S. Secretary of State George P. Shultz to enter into official dialogue with the PLO.*

---

*The U.S.-PLO dialogue was curtailed six months later when Arafat refused to condemn outright a terrorist raid at a Tel Aviv beach thought to have been conducted by an Iraqi-backed PLO faction (see p. 622).

But Israel questions the genuineness of the PLO commitment to a negotiated agreement. Most Israelis, both on the left and the right, are convinced the changes reflect a shift in tactics rather than policy. They say deeds, not words, represent the PLO's true intentions. Indeed, many Palestinian leaders have been intimidated, or even assassinated, by one or another radical faction of the PLO in the past. For example, recent evidence suggests that intelligence chief Salah Khalaf (Abu Iyad), the PLO's No. 2 in command, was assassinated last January for his moderate stance on Arab-Israeli negotiations and his role in disrupting terrorist operations.[8]

If the PLO isn't the legitimate representative of the Palestinians, who is? Israelis say that has been the problem all along. They say there have been no legitimate "interlocutors" to represent the Palestinians in negotiations. Israel's critics respond that it has served their interests to deny Palestinians national identity. Even today, there are Israelis, such as Housing Minister Ariel Sharon, a former defense minister, who believe that Palestinians do not represent a national entity and ought to be incorporated into other Arab states, primarily Jordan, which is more than 50 percent Palestinian. These views, however, represent the fringe, even in Israel.

The current Israeli government, led by Yitzhak Shamir, favors elections in the occupied territories that would lead to some sort of limited autonomy, short of a Palestinian state. The PLO's weakened image as a result of its stance in the gulf war has made this scenario more plausible. Although few Palestinians are willing to repudiate the PLO publicly, many believe the organization's leadership is increasingly ineffective, corrupt and out of touch. To some degree, the PLO's missteps have allowed West Bank Palestinians freedom to pursue their own interests, and possibly to negotiate their own settlement with the Israelis (*see below*).

But as Graham Fuller, a senior analyst at the RAND Corporation, a think tank in Santa Monica, Calif., points out, "West Bankers are not the sum total of the Palestinian peo-

ple." Fuller says elections in the West Bank and Gaza would effectively ignore the roughly 3.5 million Palestinians who live outside the territories (*see table, p. 621*), and over the long run would create more problems than they solved.

### How has the intifada altered the political equation in the occupied territories?

What the Arab armies had failed to do with planes and missiles, the Palestinians under Israeli military rule

> **What Arab armies had failed to do with planes and missiles, the Palestinians accomplished with stones, metal pipes and knives: They attracted attention and sympathy for their plight in the occupied territories.**

in the occupied territories accomplished with stones, metal pipes and knives: They attracted attention and sympathy for the plight of Palestinians.

The *intifada* erupted in December 1987. Some analysts say the uprising was inevitable, a spontaneous outburst caused by prolonged, intense poverty and social injustice. Others say it was orchestrated by PLO "insiders" operating out of Israel's prisons.[9] Whatever its origins, the *intifada* has had a profound impact on world opinion, on Palestinians and on Israeli society.

"The *intifada* brought the Palestinian issue front and center for the world to see," says Helena

Cobban, a scholar-in-residence at the Middle East Peace Foundation, a Washington-based organization that supports peace and security in the region. "Until 1987, Israeli leaders had convinced the world — and the Israeli public — that their occupation in the territories was the most benign in history." That image dissolved as scenes of Palestinian teenagers being beaten by the Israeli Defense Forces flashed across television screens around the world.

Israel's violent crackdown against bands of stone-throwing youths aroused criticism from all quarters. "Before 1987, the occupation was morally comfortable for Israel, and considered viable over the long term," says Cobban. "The *intifada* shattered those perceptions."

As the uprising stretched on from month to month, serious fissures in the body politic began to emerge. For example, hundreds of senior Israeli reserve officers who had done duty in the territories formed the Council for Peace and Security, which urged an exchange of territory for peace. In March 1989, the Israeli newspaper *Ha'aretz* became the first Israeli publication to call on Shamir to drop his opposition to talks with the PLO.

While most Israelis didn't feel immediately endangered, the *intifada* served notice that the threat to the Jewish state did not come exclusively from surrounding countries. The war could come to the "home front" even if it wasn't raging on the borders.[10]

The stones of the *intifada* also sent ripples through the Arab world, most notably Jordan, which had been seen by Israel and the United States as the most appropriate state with which a Palestinian entity could be linked. The uprising's relentless force persuaded King Hussein to remove Jordan from consideration as a surrogate ruler of the territories. In July 1988, the king announced that "Jordan is not Palestine" and that his kingdom would relinquish its historic links to the West Bank. He said he could no longer speak for the Palestinians and that the world would have to accept a separate Palestinian state.*

The political vacuum created by King Hussein's withdrawal was quickly filled by the PLO, which was embraced by the *intifada's* leadership. Most experts believe the PLO had little or nothing to do with the outbreak of the uprising. On the contrary, it is the *intifada* that had a major impact on the PLO leadership, forcing it to abandon its long-trumpeted "military solution" against Israel and adopt a more pragmatic policy, including Arafat's acceptance of Resolutions 242 and 338.

The *intifada* represents the first large-scale independent political action by the West Bank to assert control over its own destiny. Indeed, for the first time, the West Bank has begun to think of itself as a distinct Palestinian political entity, rather than simply as part of the broader Palestinian people. That, according to scholars at the Washington Institute for Near East Policy, has created a real opportunity. Executive Director Martin Indyk says the *intifada* precipitated a shift in the balance of power in the Palestinian national movement from the PLO, based in Tunis, Algeria, to a local leadership in the territories.[11]

Indyk also believes the *intifada* ultimately will force the combatants to negotiate. "The combination of Palestinian desperation and Israeli discomfort has produced for the first time an agreement on the objective: a transitional negotiation that would end the military occupation and provide self-government for the Palestinians in the territories," he writes.[12]

Other Middle East experts are not so optimistic. The fact that the *intifada* began to sputter even before Iraq invaded Kuwait has led some to conclude that Israel has little incentive to compromise with the Palestinians. "Israel has crushed the *intifada*, and in my opinion has no intention of giving the Palestinians anything tangible," says Noam Chomsky, a political scientist at the Massachusetts Institute of Technology (MIT). "So long as Israel has U.S. support, it can maintain the occupation indefinitely."

### What will the Palestinians bargain for eventually?

The demand for a Palestinian state is almost surely non-negotiable in the eyes of most Palestinians. "They have not come this far and waited so long for something less," says Fuller at the RAND Corporation. "Any other arrangement, like some kind of local autonomy in confederation with Israel or Jordan, is strictly interim — a way station before a more permanent settlement."

On the other hand, some Western observers argue that the "Palestinian tragedy" lies in their decades-long failure to accept the various deals that have been put to them. As Abba Eban, a former Israeli foreign minister, once quipped: "The Palestinians never miss an opportunity to miss an opportunity." In 1937, when Britain's Peel Commission suggested dividing Palestine between Arabs and Jews, they said "no." They said "no" on at least three subsequent occasions: in 1947, when the United Nations proposed the idea; in 1967, after the Six-Day War, when they told Israel, "no conciliation, no negotiation and no recognition"; and in 1977, when Egyptian President Anwar el-Sadat tried to coax the PLO into his peace diplomacy with President Jimmy Carter at Camp David.*

It is tempting, surveying this history, to accuse the Palestinians of having inflicted most of their miseries upon themselves. By insisting on the whole loaf, they have ended up with no loaf. Palestinians, of course, see it differently. Dividing Palestine between its Arab and Jewish inhabitants may sound fair now, but it did not seem that way in the 1930s and '40s when most of Palestine's people were Arabs and most of the Jews were new arrivals from Europe. Ever since Israel's creation in 1948, Arabs have dreamed of recovering the land that they believe was unjustly taken from them. Instead of partition, they favored abolishing Israel and establishing a democratic, binational Palestinian state, as expressed in the PLO's National Charter.

For many Palestinians, that dream died in 1988, when the PLO accepted Resolutions 242 and 338. By declaring statehood and recognizing Israel, the PLO signaled its hope that a diplomatic settlement to the Israeli-Palestinian conflict might be found. Early in 1989, intelligence chief Salah Khalaf, in a dramatic videotaped address to an Israeli-Arab symposium in Jerusalem, said: "In the past we believed that this land was ours alone, and we did not believe the idea of coexistence between states ... [Today] we have come to believe in the necessity of coexistence."[13]

Not all Palestinians, however, are prepared to accept coexistence. Radical PLO factions, such as the Popular Front for the Liberation of Pales-

---

*Since Secretary of State James A. Baker III began his peace diplomacy in March, King Hussein has signaled a new willingness to accept a confederation of his country and the West Bank in order to achieve a breakthrough toward a Middle East peace settlement. Ultimately, however, the king still advocates a separate Palestinian state.

---

*On March 26, 1979, Egyptian President Sadat, Israeli President Menachem Begin and U.S. President Jimmy Carter signed the Camp David Agreements in Washington. In return for peace and the establishment of diplomatic relations, Israel agreed to withdraw from the Sinai Peninsula (*see p. 620*).

tine,* still advocate "total armed struggle." Moreover, the Palestinians in the West Bank and Gaza, generally speaking, have always had a slightly different political agenda than those Palestinians living in the refugee camps of Jordan, Syria and Lebanon. Because most of the refugees were from those parts of Israel that fell within the pre-1967 boundaries — from places like Haifa, Jaffa or the Galilee — the only way they would ever feel truly at home again was if Israel disappeared entirely and they were allowed to return to their original villages.

---

*Founded by George Habash in 1967, the Popular Front for the Liberation of Palestine is the main rival of al-Fatah, the comparatively moderate PLO group that Arafat heads. The Popular Front is pro-Marxist and headquartered in Syria.

Many of the 1.7 million Palestinians in the West Bank and Gaza, however, could feel at home again in the fullest sense if Israel's occupation of the West Bank and Gaza ended. "Their immediate problem was Israel's occupation, not its existence," explains Cobban. "Therefore, they are much more receptive to a two-state solution."

How this dichotomy within the Palestinian community will be handled is one of the most serious challenges that the Palestinian leadership faces today. Obviously, a settlement that satisfies only the narrower interests of the Palestinians in the occupied territories, without dealing with Palestinians in the diaspora, would expose the PLO to internal stress and factionalism. ■

# BACKGROUND

## Roots of the Conflict

The collision between Jews and Palestinian can be traced to the late 19th century. It was then that Jews from around the world began flocking back to their ancient biblical homeland in Palestine, drawn by a modern Jewish nationalist movement known as Zionism. The Zionists called for the ingathering of the Jews in Palestine and the creation there of a modern Jewish nation-state. The movement met resistance, faint at first, from the indigenous Arab population of Palestine (see story, p. 621), whose own national awakening had begun amidst the gradual collapse of the Ottoman Empire.

Following World War I, Palestine fell under British control. In 1917, in what has come to be known as the Balfour Declaration, British Foreign Minister Arthur James Balfour announced Britain's support for the "establishment in Palestine of a national home for the Jewish people." Out of the broad region known as Palestine, Britain carved two political entities in 1921. One territory consisted of the region east of the Jordan River; it was named the "Emirate of Transjordan," and later simply "Jordan."* There, the British enthroned Abdullah ibn Hussein, a Bedouin tribal chieftain educated in Istanbul, whose family came from what is now Saudi Arabia. Half of Jordan's original 300,000 population were nomadic Bedouins and the other half "East Bankers," or Palestinian Arabs from the East Bank of the Jordan.

In the western half of Palestine, between the Mediterranean Sea and the Jordan River, Palestinian Arabs and Zionist Jews wrestled for control under the British umbrella. As the

---

*Under a treaty signed with Britain in 1946, this area became the independent Hashemite Kingdom of Transjordan.

Jewish-Palestinian conflict sharpened in the wake of a massive influx of European Jewish survivors of World War II, Britain announced its intention to withdraw from the western half of Palestine.

London turned over responsibility for determining the fate of this disputed territory to the United Nations, and on Nov. 29, 1947, the U.N. General Assembly voted 33 to 13 with 10 abstentions to partition western Palestine into two states — one for the Jews, which would consist of the Negev Desert, the coastal plain between Tel Aviv and Haifa and parts of the northern Galilee, and the other for the Palestinian Arabs, comprising primarily the West Bank of the Jordan, the Gaza District, and the Arab sectors of the Galilee. (See map, p. 617.) Jerusalem, cherished by both Muslims and Jews as a holy city, was to become an international enclave under U.N. trusteeship.

The Zionists, then led by David Ben-Gurion, accepted this partition plan even though they had long dreamed of controlling all of western Palestine and Jerusalem. "We could hold out for all the land of Israel," he said, "but if we did that we might lose everything." [14]

But the Palestinian Arabs and the surrounding Arab states rejected the partition proposal on the ground that it would legitimize the Jewish state. They felt that Palestine was all theirs, that the Jews were interlopers and that they had the strength to drive them out.

On May 15, 1948, the day after the Jews declared establishment of Israel, the armies of Jordan, Egypt, Syria, Lebanon, Saudi Arabia and Iraq invaded Palestine with the declared intention of wiping the Jewish state off the map. Many Palestinians fled to neighboring Arab countries to wait out the war, hoping to return as victors.

Toward the end of the war, with the Jewish troops in control, Ben-

Gurion sought to expand and secure Israel's highly vulnerable borders by taking more territory and expelling Palestinians from their villages — especially those near border areas. By the time a U.N.-mediated armistice ended the conflict in 1949, some 600,000 to 760,000 Palestinians had fled or been expelled from the region.[15]

Meanwhile, the other areas designated for the Palestinians by the United Nations were taken by Jordan and Egypt; Jordan annexed the West Bank, while Egypt assumed control of Gaza. Neither Arab state allowed the Palestinians to form their own independent government in these areas.

Jordan's annexation of the West Bank dramatically altered its own ethnic makeup. The 450,000 Bedouins and East Bank Palestinians who had made up Jordan's population before 1948 were joined by some 300,000 Palestinian refugees. In 1951, King Abdullah was assassinated by a disgruntled Palestinian in Jerusalem. He was soon succeeded by his grandson Hussein, who is the present king of Jordan.

Following the 1948 fighting, Israel signed separate armistice agreements with Egypt, Lebanon, Jordan and Syria. These agreements notwithstanding, the Arab states frequently allowed various Palestinian resistance groups to use their territory to launch raids against Israel, particularly from the Egyptian-occupied Gaza Strip.

Eventually, in 1964, the Arab League, inspired by Egyptian President Gamal Abdel Nasser, an ardent advocate of Arab unity,[16] organized the Palestinian resistance groups under one umbrella, which later became known as the Palestine Liberation Organization. In those days, ironically, the PLO was essentially a tool of the existing Arab regimes — intended to control the Palestinians as much as to support them.

## Proposed Partition of Palestine, 1947

*On Nov. 29, 1947, the U.N. General Assembly voted to partition Palestine into two states — one for the Jews and one for Palestinian Arabs. The proposed Palestinian state — indicated by the darker shaded areas on the map below — covered an area larger than the West Bank and Gaza Strip today.*

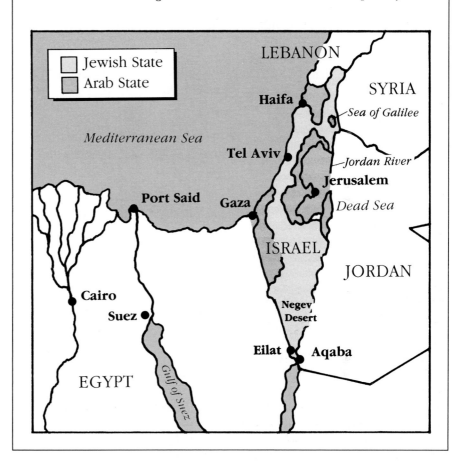

### The Six-Day War

In June 1967, Israel launched a pre-emptive strike against Egypt, Syria and Jordan. The attack came after Nasser declared his intention to annihilate the Jewish state and forged military alliances with Syria and Jordan for that purpose, building up troops along his border with Israel and blockading shipping at the Israeli port of Eilat. The war that followed Israel's surprise attack, known as the Six-Day War, ended with the Israeli army occupying Egypt's Sinai Peninsula, Syria's Golan Heights and Jordan's West Bank.

While the Six-Day War was a triumph for Israel's small but well-equipped army, it also contained foreboding elements. The Arabs' defeat "awakened widespread national consciousness, especially among the Palestinians," writes Don Peretz, director of the Middle East Program at the State University of New York at Binghamton. "The anti-Israel virus spread from the Arab East across all North Africa, and ardent Arab nationalist through the Middle East and North Africa joined in support of the Palestinian guerrilla movements."[17]

The 1967 defeat also resulted in a

radicalization of the Palestinian movement. After the war, says William Quandt, a senior fellow at the Brookings Institution, a think tank in Washington, "the Palestinians took a somewhat different tack. They said, 'We can't wait for the Arab regimes, because the Arab regimes are all . . . self-interested. Even though the Arab masses may be with us, the regimes have to be forced to join us, and therefore we have to ignite something, a revolution.'" Palestinians continued to seek money and support from Arab governments, but they no longer looked to those governments for leadership.

## Rise of the PLO

For the Palestinians, dislocation, dispossession and exile had rendered their society politically weak and physically divided. In the longer term, however, occupation at home and harassment abroad strengthened their socio-political identity, assuring the psychological and political foundations upon which continuing demands for self-determination would be based.

In 1969, a little-known Palestinian guerrilla by the name of Yasir Arafat, who headed the al-Fatah ("Conquer") guerrilla group, was elected chairman of the PLO's executive committee. Then, as now, the PLO was composed of many different political camps. Although Arafat carried the title chairman of the executive committee, he would never wield complete and uncontested control over all the PLO factions.

The PLO guerrilla groups were granted significant economic aid by the Arab states in order to press the battle with Israel. The Arab states also backed PLO efforts to take control of Palestinian refugee camps in the weaker Arab countries, particularly Lebanon and Jordan, and to use those camps as bases of operation against Israeli targets at home and abroad. In both Jordan and southern Lebanon, the Palestinian guerrillas assumed quasi-sovereign authority over certain regions bordering on Israel. Their raids on Israel brought about fierce Israeli retaliation, which created tensions between the Palestinians and the Lebanese and between the Palestinians and Jordanians.

Matters came to a head in Jordan in September 1970, when radical Palestinian guerrillas brought to Jordan three hijacked airliners and prevented the Jordanian army from getting near the planes or rescuing the passengers. Recognizing that he was on the verge of losing control over his whole kingdom, King Hussein decided to wipe out Arafat and his men once and for all by launching a full-scale offensive against the PLO-dominated Palestinian refugee camps and neighborhoods in the Jordanian capital, Amman. The PLO responded by calling for Hussein's overthrow. In what became known as "Black September," Bedouin troops killed thousands of Palestinians while crushing the PLO's attempt to topple Hussein.

But Arafat was not to be counted out. He and the PLO immediately fell back on their other "state-within-a-state," which they had established in the Palestinian refugee districts of Beirut and southern Lebanon. More than 150,000 Palestinians had fled to Lebanon after the 1948 war, and by 1975 their numbers — increased by a high birth rate and by refugees from Jordan — had risen to nearly half a million.

After the 1973 Yom Kippur War,*

---

*Unlike the Six-Day War, the Yom Kippur War had nothing to do with the struggle for a Palestinian homeland. On Oct. 6, 1973, Egyptian and Syrian troops launched a surprise attack on Israeli-occupied territory in the Sinai Peninsula and the Golan Heights in an attempt to regain territories lost in 1967. The Arab nations inflicted heavy damage on Israeli defenses, but were ultimately defeated.

when it became obvious to Palestinians that they could no longer count on Arab states to regain their land by force, Palestinian guerrilla groups stepped up their own actions against Israel. Israel, in turn, launched raids against Palestinian camps in Lebanon.

As a result of political deadlocks inside Lebanon, the Lebanese government was paralyzed — a situation that served Arafat's interests. As the fighting escalated, divisions between Muslim and Christian communities in Lebanon deepened. "For a decade, from the mid-1960s, the expanding Palestinian presence served increasingly to polarize Lebanese opinion," writes Patrick Seale. "Muslims, sharing Arab nationalist sentiments, were committed to their cause, but Christians on the whole were not, and the more importunate the Palestinians became, the wider grew the Muslim-Christian cleavage." [18] It was at this point that the Lebanese civil war became fully intertwined with the Israeli-Palestinian conflict.

In 1982, Israel invaded Lebanon in an attempt to destroy the PLO leadership and infrastructure. As a result, the PLO was forced to leave Beirut, depriving Arafat of his last base in the Arab world from which to make direct attacks on Israel. It appeared that the PLO's significance to the Arab-Israeli conflict had greatly diminished. This was an illusion, however, because the strength of the PLO, although founded on the concept of armed struggle against Israel, had never rested with its military capability. The broad range of international diplomatic support the PLO had garnered over the years as the institutional symbol of Palestinian nationalism had become the principal basis of its legitimacy.

Meanwhile, throughout the 1970s and early '80s, Egypt, Jordan and Syria unsuccessfully attempted to negotiate for the return of the terri-

Continued on p. 620

# Chronology

**Late 1800s** European Jews begin to migrate to Palestine in large numbers.

———•———

**1900-1930s** As plans crystallize for a Jewish homeland, the conflict between Jews and Palestinians grows more intense.

**Nov. 2, 1917**
British Foreign Secretary Arthur J. Balfour issues the Balfour Declaration, endorsing the idea of establishing a "national home" for the Jewish people in Palestine.

**1920**
Under a League of Nations mandate, Britain carves up Palestine into two entities, Transjordan (now Jordan) and Palestine.

**1936-39**
The Arabs of Palestine revolt in an attempt to halt the establishment of a Jewish homeland. Britain crushes the rebellion and expels Palestinian leaders.

———•———

**1940s-1950s** Hopes for a diplomatic resolution to the Palestinian problem recede.

**Nov. 29, 1947**
United Nations votes to partition Palestine into two states, one for the Jews and one for the Palestinian Arabs, with Jerusalem to become an international enclave. The Jews accept partition, but the Palestinians reject it.

**May 14, 1948**
The British withdraw from Palestine and Israel declares independence. The following day, five Arab states invade Israel.

**January 1949**
War ends with an indefinite cease-fire. Jordan occupies the West Bank and Egypt occupies the Gaza Strip. Some 600,000 to 760,000 Palestinians become refugees.

———•———

**1960s-1970s** The Palestinian nationalist movement gains momentum.

**June 5, 1967**
Israel launches a pre-emptive strike against Egypt, Syria and Jordan as they are preparing for war against the Jewish state. The Six-Day War ends with Israel occupying the Sinai Peninsula, the Golan Heights, the Gaza Strip and the West Bank.

**November 1967**
United Nations passes Resolution 242 as a formula for bringing peace to the Middle East.

**February 1969**
Yasir Arafat is elected chairman of the executive committee of the Palestine Liberation Organization (PLO).

**1970**
King Hussein's army defeats Arafat's PLO guerrillas in a civil war for control of Jordan.

**October 1974**
An Arab summit conference in Rabat, Morocco, affirms that the PLO is the "sole legitimate representative" of the Palestinian people.

**1980s** With economic and social conditions deteriorating in the occupied territories and the likelihood of a military victory diminishing, the PLO adopts a more moderate position.

**June 6, 1982**
Israel invades Lebanon and forces the PLO to evacuate its headquarters in Beirut.

**Dec. 9, 1987**
The Palestinian uprising, or *intifada*, erupts in the West Bank and Gaza Strip.

**Dec. 14, 1988**
Arafat renounces terrorism and recognizes Israel's right to exist. U.S. Secretary of State George P. Shultz authorizes the opening of a dialogue with the PLO.

———•———

**1990s** Palestinians grow increasingly desperate as Jewish settlements in the territories continue and prospects for an independent Palestinian state fade.

**June 20, 1990**
President Bush suspends U.S.-PLO dialogue after a radical PLO faction launches a terrorist attack on Israel.

**Aug. 2, 1990**
Iraq invades Kuwait; Palestinians back Iraq in the war with U.N. coalition forces.

**July 31, 1991**
President Bush and Soviet President Mikhail S. Gorbachev formally propose a regional Middle East peace conference to include talks between Israel and the Palestinians.

*Continued from p. 618*

tories occupied by Israel. Israel made it clear, however, that it had no intention of returning to the so-called Green Line, the borders set in the 1949 armistice. Israel cited security concerns and the unwillingness of neighboring Arab states to recognize the legitimacy of Israel.

## Under Occupation

Israel's treatment of the lands captured in 1967 is highly controversial. History records numerous other instances when territories gained during war have been incorporated against their will within the victorious country's boundaries — as in the Soviet occupation of the Baltic republics of Estonia, Latvia and Lithuania during World War II. But in such cases, the populations of the conquered territories generally are made citizens of the conquering state and are granted some degree of equality with the rest of the citizenry of the country. In other instances, for example the U.S. occupation of Japan after World War II, the occupation is short-term, and the actions of the occupying power are constrained by international law. Neither description fits the Israeli occupation of the West Bank (including East Jerusalem), the Gaza Strip and the Golan Heights.

There have been changes in official Israeli policies toward the occupied territories. The Sinai was returned to Egypt as part of the 1978 Camp David agreements, negotiated by President Jimmy Carter, Egyptian President Anwar el-Sadat and Israeli President Menachem Began. Israel extended its legal jurisdiction to East Jerusalem in 1967 and officially annexed it in 1980; the Golan Heights region was annexed in 1981. The basic approach, however,

has been to rule the Palestinian population through harsh military laws, while giving all rights and benefits of citizenship to those Jewish Israelis who chose to establish settlements.[19]

In spite of Palestinian absence at the negotiations, the Camp David Accords had recognized the "legitimate rights of the Palestinian people" and affirmed that the Palestinians would be allowed to establish a self-governing authority in the West Bank and Gaza for a transitional period, after which the final status of these territories would be negotiated. Since he could not annex the West Bank, but had no intention of giving it back or even allowing the Palestinians the real autonomy promised them under Camp David, Israeli Prime Minister Begin simply left the final status of the West Bank formally open, meanwhile building a whole new reality on the ground: more roads connecting the territories to Israel, more land expropriations from Palestinians and more Jewish settlements.[20] By 1987, there were 67,000 Jewish settlers in the West Bank and roughly 50 percent of the land and most of the area's water sources were under Israeli control.

### Beginning of the Intifada

As the Palestinian population ballooned during the 1970s and '80s, conditions inside Palestinian villages, towns and refugee camps were deteriorating. Stifling pressures of life in this cramped environment were exacerbated by Israeli policies that restricted local economic development. The Palestinians' frustrations needed only a catalyst to create the long-anticipated explosion. That spark occurred on Dec. 9, 1987, in a refugee camp in Gaza, when four Arab workers returning from their jobs in Israel were killed in a collision with an Israeli truck. Thousands of mourners marched on an Israeli army camp, convinced that the acci-

dent was deliberate.* The Israeli army fired on the demonstrators, killing four of them.

What began as sporadic protests by random groups of restless youth not only spread but developed into an organized resistance movement with an underground leadership, a definite political objective and a well-planned and integrated strategy. From rock throwing, insults and the illegal display of national colors and patriotic slogans, tactics were devised to extend participation to the entire Palestinian community. These included an economic boycott of many Israeli products, nonpayment of taxes to Israel and weeklong strikes closing down public facilities.

As the first long-term, deep-rooted expression of political protest against Israeli occupation, the *intifada* began a process of psychological and political transformation among Palestinians who had always looked to external actors for salvation from Israeli control. "The Palestinians came to understand through the uprising what made the Israeli occupation work — it was themselves and their own cooperation with the whole Israeli system," says Sari Nusseibeh, a Palestinian professor at Bir Zeit University on the West Bank. "The most important achievement of the *intifada* was to show Palestinians where their chains were and how they could remove them." [21]

The uprising has hastened remarkable changes in the socio-political structure of Palestinian society under occupation. Virtually all age groups and social classes were mobilized in its support. But the uprising also signaled the coming of age of a new

*Continued on p. 622*

---

*Three days earlier an Israeli merchant had been stabbed to death in Gaza, and Gazans believed the truck driver was a relative of the merchant intent on avenging his death.

# Who Are the Palestinians?

Israeli Prime Minister Golda Meir once declared: There is "no such thing as Palestinians." Her blunt comment in 1969 caused a furor in the Arab world, but it reflected what many Israelis then felt. Even today, there are Israelis, such as former Defense Minister Ariel Sharon, who believe the Palestinians do not represent a distinct national entity and ought to be incorporated into other Arab states, primarily Jordan, which is more than 50 percent Palestinian.

Though it is true that the creation of a Jewish state galvanized Palestinian consciousness, most historians call Meir's statement a gross inaccuracy. "That argument is pure polemics," says Laurie Brand, a political scientist at the University of Southern California. "The overriding point today is that more than 5 million Palestinians around the world trace their roots to the area west of the Jordan River that now constitutes Israel and the occupied West Bank."

Both Arabs and Jews lived in that region thousands of years ago. But the area has been predominantly Arab and Islamic since the end of the 7th century and — despite the steady arrival of Jewish colonists beginning in the late 19th century — had an Arab majority until 1948.[†]

The word "Palestine" is of Roman origin, referring to the biblical land of the Philistines. The term fell into disuse for centuries, but the British revived it as an official designation for the area that the League of Nations mandated to their supervision in 1920, following the World War I breakup of the Turkish-Ottoman Empire.

Because the league's mandate applied to both Transjordan (now Jordan), east of the Jordan River, and Palestine, west of the river, the argument was made that the term "Palestinian" applied to persons east as well as west of the Jordan River. Thus, it was argued, the designation applied not just to the Arab inhabitants — as is the common practice today — but also to Jews and Christians living in the former mandated area.[††]

Palestine as a legal entity ceased to exist in May 1948 when Britain, unable to control Arab-Jewish hostility and the influx of Jewish immigrants, relinquished its mandate, and Israel declared its independence. The United Nations had voted in 1947 to partition Palestine into Arab and Jewish sectors.

During 1948-49, Israel enlarged its territory in a war of independence with neighboring Arab nations. By war's end, some 600,000 to 760,000 Palestinians had fled or been expelled from Israel. But Israel did not take control of all of Palestine. One region, the West Bank, came under the control of Jordan, which later annexed the territory, and another, the Gaza Strip, came under Egyptian control. These territories later were occupied by Israel during the 1967 Six-Day War.

Although the Palestinians are physically dispersed — mostly in Israel, the occupied territories, Jordan, Kuwait and other Arab states — and more than 2.3 million live in refugee camps, they are unified by a common dream of a national homeland. "Unlike other Arabs," writes James Akins, the former U.S. ambassador to Saudi Arabia, "Palestinians have retained a pure nationalism. They have been deprived of their homes, and their nationalism represents their only hope of regaining their homeland." [‡]

Palestinian refugees have been eligible for Jordanian citizenship since 1952, and they are prominent in Jordanian government and business. But even in that country, says Ele Saaf, director of the United Nations Relief and Works Agency in Jordan, the Palestinians have never been "psychologically integrated." [‡‡]

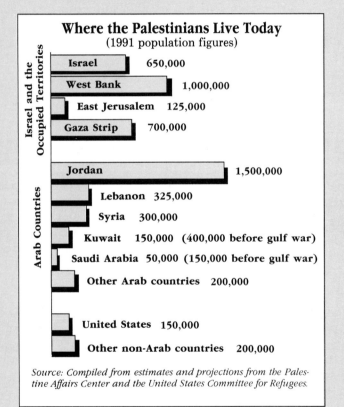

**Where the Palestinians Live Today**
(1991 population figures)

Israel and the Occupied Territories

- Israel 650,000
- West Bank 1,000,000
- East Jerusalem 125,000
- Gaza Strip 700,000

Arab Countries

- Jordan 1,500,000
- Lebanon 325,000
- Syria 300,000
- Kuwait 150,000 (400,000 before gulf war)
- Saudi Arabia 50,000 (150,000 before gulf war)
- Other Arab countries 200,000

- United States 150,000
- Other non-Arab countries 200,000

Source: Compiled from estimates and projections from the Palestine Affairs Center and the United States Committee for Refugees.

---

† See Edward Said and Christopher Hitchens, eds., *Blaming the Victims* (1988), p. 236.

†† See Congressional Quarterly, *The Middle East*, 7th ed., 1990, p. 9.

‡ James E. Akins, "The New Arabia," *Foreign Affairs*, summer 1991, p. 39.

‡‡ Quoted in Robert I. Friedman, "The Palestinian Refugees," *The New York Review of Books*, October 1990, p. 40.

*Continued from p. 620*
generation of activists. They represent a potent social force, one with little respect for Israeli administrative authority and one less responsive to Israeli coercive measures.[22]

While the *intifada* raised Palestinian national consciousness, it has carried a heavy price. Since its inception, some 950 Palestinians, mostly teenagers, have been killed by Israeli forces, more than 110,000 have been injured and 15,000 are held in administrative detention.[23] The *intifada* has also taken a toll on the precarious economies of the West Bank and Gaza. Since 1987, unemployment has soared to 75 percent in some areas, and the gross national product in Gaza has declined by at least 30 percent.[24]

By mid-1990, many Palestinians had begun to feel that their struggle was losing its force — and its balance. The *intifada's* singular strength had been its ability to sustain an unarmed, civil rebellion against what Palestinians considered a cruel and unjust occupation, and to do so with extreme restraint. But after nearly three years of mounting self-sacrifice, the *intifada* was careening out of control. The uprising had stopped delivering headlines in the world press, and increasingly there were reports of infighting over the merits of reverting to a strategy of "armed struggle." ∎

# CURRENT SITUATION

## The Gulf War

It was at this critical juncture in the Palestinian national movement that the gulf crisis occurred. The PLO's recognition of Israel and acceptance of a two-state solution, announced by the Palestine National Council in November 1988 and further elaborated by PLO Chairman Arafat at a special U.N. General Assembly session in Geneva the following month, had produced no tangible political gains. Moreover, Palestinians felt deep resentment at the failure of Egypt and the gulf states to use their influence with Washington to find a just resolution to the Palestine question.[25]

In 1989, as the Palestinian leadership grew more disenchanted, it began to draw closer to Iraq. The choice was reinforced by necessity, given the deadly hostility of Syria on the one hand and the disengagement of Jordan from the Palestine issue in 1988 on the other. Iraq gradually became a hospitable base for logistical and political support for the PLO, as well as a source of financial aid to the *intifada*. A strategic alliance of convenience, if not of objectives, had been forged.

It was a clear sign of the direction events in the region were taking when an Iraqi-based PLO faction carried out an unsuccessful attack against civilians at a Tel Aviv beachfront during the summer of 1990. The PLO, unwilling or unable to alienate Iraq, did not condemn the raid. This silence persuaded the Bush administration to break off the dialogue it had been pursuing with the PLO. Experts say this convinced the Palestinians that the United States was not genuinely interested in a balanced solution to their problem.

It was within this context of utter frustration, economic deterioration and political impasse that Palestinians rallied behind Iraq's occupation of Kuwait. While many Palestinians opposed the actual invasion, they were even more opposed to the U.S.

occupying force in the region. "Westerners underestimate the Arab fear of outside domination," explains Sara Roy of the Center for Middle East Studies at Harvard University. Saddam Hussein, she says, offered an alternative; finally an Arab leader had stood up to Israel and U.S. hegemony. Furthermore, it was viewed as hypocritical that the United States would so boldly enforce U.N resolutions in Kuwait while ignoring those relating to Palestine.

Whether one sympathizes with Palestinians for their stance in the war or not, one thing is certain: They are paying dearly for it. During the war, the Israeli army resumed its highly criticized policy of deporting Palestinians considered security risks, imposed Draconian security measures and enforced an unprecedented 40-day curfew and travel ban that effectively sealed off the territories. "Conditions in the West Bank and Gaza are as bad or worse than I have ever seen them, probably worse even than the aftermath of the 1967 war," says Peter Gubser, who heads American Near East Refugee Aid, a private relief group.

The consequences have been greatest for Palestinians in the gulf states. The once-prosperous Palestinian community in Kuwait has lost an estimated $10 billion.[26] "Kuwait was the bedrock, a place of unquestioned stability for Palestinians," says Helena Cobban. "For 40 years, it was always the place where a substantial number of Palestinian professionals or technical people could find jobs." That haven of stability has disappeared. Some 250,000 Palestinians have either been expelled or fled for fear of reprisals. Although a very small percentage of Palestinians in Kuwait collaborated with the Iraqi invaders, the common Kuwaiti line now is to condemn all Palestinians: "We took them in; we gave them good jobs; and now they stab us in the back. Never again will

# What Can Be Gained at a Peace Conference?

Undoubtably, everybody in the Middle East has at least some interest in a genuine settlement of the Palestinian problem. If the various factions actually end up at the peace table, here are some of the things the key players hope to get out of the process:

**THE PLO.** The Palestine Liberation Organization hasn't been invited to directly participate in negotiations. But its position is important because most Palestinians will consider the Palestinian negotiating team that will participate to be legitimate only if it is blessed by the PLO. The Palestinians ultimately hope to gain an independent state but might be willing to settle for less — so long as the door is left open for statehood at some point down the road. Having lost international credibility since the gulf crisis, the PLO is under great pressure to approve a Palestinian delegation, even if it means compromise.

**ISRAEL.** Prime Minister Yitzhak Shamir's hard-line government has been leery of international peace conferences for years, and insists it will not trade land for peace. Nevertheless, Israel can't afford to be seen as a spoiler. No longer the sole U.S. ally in the region, Israel has asked the United States for $10 billion in loan guarantees to build housing for the influx of Soviet immigrants. By appearing to support U.S. peace diplomacy, Israel greatly improves its chances for getting the U.S. aid. Israel is clearly more interested in one-on-one peace talks with its Arab neighbors than in talks with the Palestinians, which could eventually lead to territorial concessions.

**SYRIA.** The gulf war has convinced Syria that the United States is now the pre-eminent foreign power in the Middle East. President Hafez al-Assad knows where the money is and wants to curry U.S. favor. Assad also wants to shed Syria's image as a terrorist state. He may pay lip service to the Palestinians, but reportedly detests PLO leader Yasir Arafat and might be satisfied with the return of the Golan Heights in exchange for peace with Israel.

**JORDAN.** King Hussein needs to recover from the gulf war debacle, when he lost political standing throughout the West for supporting Iraq. Jordan also needs cash to repair the damage the war dealt to its economy by curtailing trade with Iraq and shutting down the flow of money sent home by Jordanian workers in Iraq and Kuwait. Participating in a U.S.-led peace process could rehabilitate Jordan politically and also would help reopen the spigots of U.S. aid. Obviously, by agreeing to take part in a joint delegation with Palestinians, Jordan would re-emerge as a pivotal player in determining the future of the West Bank and Gaza. Few experts, however, believe King Hussein wants to incorporate a Palestinian state into Jordan.

**SAUDI ARABIA.** Publicly, the Saudis espouse strong support for the Palestinian cause. But since the end of the gulf war they have been ridding their kingdom of thousands of Palestinians and replacing them with Egyptian workers. Above all, the Saudis want stability for the region and might prefer that the fate of the Palestinians be controlled by the Israelis rather than by Yasir Arafat or Jordan's King Hussein.

**UNITED STATES.** By organizing a peace conference, the United States would enhance its own reputation as the superpower most able to control events on the world stage. Israel is still a close strategic ally, and it is unclear how hard President Bush is willing to push Prime Minister Shamir on the issue of land for peace.

---

we do anything for them." [27]

The expulsion of Palestinians from the gulf states has also added to the region's already seething refugee problem. Since the end of the war, Jordan has taken in more than 200,000 refugees, a burden its anemic economy can hardly bear. Jordan lost about $600 million in aid from Saudi Arabia and the gulf states for having backed Iraq in the war. Saudi Arabia and Kuwait used to pour more than $120 million a year into the Palestine National Fund, which financed the PLO. That fund-

ing has stopped, as have the remittances from Palestinian workers in the gulf states.

Economically devastated, the Palestinians are also isolated politically. "The Arab leaders have always used the Palestinian issue for their own purposes," says Chomsky of the Massachusetts Institute of Technology. "They've made gestures to appease their own populations, who support Palestinian nationalism, but they've never had any use for Palestinians as a people. Now, after the gulf war, they aren't even making gestures."

## Baker Peace Plan

When the gulf war ended in March, Washington had high hopes that the allied victory would provide the momentum for Arabs and Israelis to seek a more lasting peace. In May, the United States proposed holding a regional peace conference under American and Soviet auspices that would address both the future of the occupied territories and the larger question of Israel's relations with the Arab states.

Since May, Secretary of State James A. Baker III has made seven trips to the region, shuttling between the various capitals to line up the conference's principal participants: Syria, Israel, Jordan, Kuwait, Saudi Arabia, Egypt and Lebanon. Apprehensive as the Arabs and Israelis may be, they haven't turned down Baker's offer. The first encounter is expected to be a one-day multilateral conference, followed by direct talks between Israel and Syria and Israel and a joint Jordanian-Palestinian delegation.

Only the Palestinians have yet to agree to attend. The sticky question of who will represent them at the conference has yet to be resolved. Though the Palestinians haven't requested direct PLO participation, Israel still adamantly refuses to sit down with Palestinians from the diaspora or East Jerusalem for fear of signaling that the area, won in the 1967 war and now annexed to Jewish West Jerusalem, is open to negotiation.

Angry at being frozen out, PLO Chairman Arafat has threatened that no Palestinians will attend the conference unless Washington asks him to choose the Palestinian delegates. "In effect, what Arafat is saying is, 'I'm important; pay attention to me,'" says Brookings' William Quandt. But most analysts predict that the Palestinians, weakened and isolated after the gulf war and under fierce pressure from the United States and the Arab states, will eventually bow to the inevitable. "It's hard for the Palestinians to accept how much their position has eroded," says Quandt. "But they want in the game, and in the end they will have to swallow it."

But even if such procedural gaps are bridged, numerous impediments remain. A peace conference is not the same thing as peace. U.S., Arab and Israeli officials have expressed concern that progress in bringing the parties to the table has done nothing to change the fundamental attitudes of Israel and its neighbors or narrow the gap between their views on territory, security and coexistence.

Instead, some officials say, both Israel and the Arab states have accepted the U.S. plan solely to improve their relations with the Bush administration, or out of fear of the consequences of defying Washington. Israel, Egypt and Saudi Arabia are all heavily reliant on U.S. aid, and Syria has a keen interest in improving U.S. ties. Once the conference begins, officials fear the attention and tactics of the parties may remain focused on Washington rather than on each other, making progress on substantive issues, such as the question of Palestine, nearly impossible.

## Land for Peace?

Washington's foundations for a comprehensive peace settlement, Bush has recently reiterated, are Security Council Resolutions 242 and 338, which call on Israel to trade land it has occupied since 1967 for security guarantees from the Arab states. In the U.S. view, the West Bank, Gaza, the Golan Heights and East Jerusalem are all negotiable. But Prime Minister Shamir has repeatedly vowed to oppose any territorial concessions, offering only what he calls "peace for peace." In April, Shamir told the French newspaper Le Monde: "I will never abandon the territories. I wouldn't want to enter national memory as someone who sold off part of Israel cheaply." [28]

Meanwhile, every day approximately 50 new Jewish settlers move to the occupied territories, bringing the total Jewish population to more than 100,000.[29] According to recent data, Israel now owns title to 68 percent of the land in the West Bank.[30] And if current settlement activity continues, Palestinians will within three years become a minority in East Jerusalem, which was Arab until the 1967 war.

In testimony before the Foreign Operations Subcommittee of the House Appropriations Committee on May 22, Secretary of State Baker said: "I don't think that there is any bigger obstacle to peace than the settlement activity that continues not only unabated but at an enhanced pace." Although the United States has repeatedly condemned the expansion of Jewish settlements in the territories, even hinting that U.S. aid to Israel could be affected if the practice continues, the real heat is on the Palestinians. Increasingly, say local residents and foreign diplomats involved in the peace process, Arabs are realizing that if they don't strike a deal with Israel now, there may be a lot less to deal for later.

"The settlement activity is tantamount to the liquidation of the Palestinian people, acre by acre," said Ibrahim Mattar, a Palestinian economist who monitors Israeli settlements. "The giant condos are more than an obstacle to peace; they are facts we cannot change."[31] Palestinians are also terrified by the mass immigration of Soviet Jews to Israel and by Shamir's comment last year about needing a "big Israel" to settle them. As many as 1 million Soviet Jews are expected to settle in Israel and the occupied territories during the next five years. Palestinians had always counted on demographics to work in their favor, noting the high Palestinian birth rates in Israel and the territories. The massive influx of Soviet Jews could take away what some PLO strategists called their "secret weapon."

Many Israelis feel a deep religious attachment toward the West Bank,

*Continued on p. 626*

# At Issue:

## Is "land for peace" still a valid concept?

ABDEL RAOUF EL REEDY

*Egypt's ambassador to the United States*
FROM *THE WASHINGTON POST,* JUNE 18, 1991

**O**n numerous occasions, President Bush has pledged that once the gulf crisis was over, the United States would be fully engaged in a process aimed at solving the Palestinian problem and the Arab-Israeli conflict. Bush was true to his word; as soon as the crisis was over Secretary of State James A. Baker III travelled to the region several times seeking to convene a peace conference among the parties to the conflict.

A basis for settlement already exists with all the parties accepting Security Council Resolutions 242 and 338. Resolution 242 emphasizes " . . . the inadmissibility of the acquisition of territory by war and the need to work for a just and lasting peace in which every state in the area can live in security." In application of these principles, Israel is to withdraw its forces from the territories it occupied in 1967, and the Arab states are to end the state of war and accept Israel as a state in the region. This formula has come to be known as "exchanging territory for peace" and was faithfully followed by Egypt and Israel in their negotiations leading to the Egyptian-Israeli peace treaty. . . .

This formula is as valid today, in relation to the other fronts, as it was in 1979. To say otherwise would be in contradiction to the principle of the inadmissibility of the acquisition of territory by war, which is a cardinal principle of the United Nations Charter. . . .

As someone who attended the deliberations leading to the adoption of Resolution 242 . . . I can assert that there was never any doubt that the resolution meant Israel's withdrawal on all fronts, including the West Bank, Gaza and the Golan Heights. . . . President Bush, in his address before a joint session of Congress on March 6, stated that "a comprehensive peace must be grounded in United Nations Security Council Resolutions 242 and 338 and the principle of territory for peace."

Resolution 242 recognized the security needs of all states. It referred to the necessity of guaranteeing the territorial inviolability and political independence of every state in the area through measures including the establishment of demilitarized zones. The Egyptian-Israeli peace treaty provides a model for such measures. Entering its 13th year, the treaty is a testimony that security is derived more from peace rather than from territorial acquisition.

At this crucial juncture it is essential that both sides avoid reinforcing each others' fears by words or deeds. The formula of land for peace remains the essence of the solution to the conflict. After so many wars and so much suffering in the region, time is not only ripe for peace in the Middle East, it is also running out.

*Israel's ambassador to the United States*
FROM *THE WASHINGTON POST,* JUNE 9, 1991.

**r**esolution 242 is often referred to as a supposedly clear and unequivocal affirmation of the principle of "territory for peace." This certainly is not the case. While "242" does stipulate the inadmissibility of the acquisition of territory by force, there must be a clear distinction between territories acquired through aggression and those that are held as a consequence of legitimate self-defense against aggression, as Israel was subjected to in 1967 and could be again in the future. . . .

Furthermore, though Israel's main concern in the "territories" was and is security, it should not be forgotten that from a strictly legal standpoint — as well as in the light of history — Israel's claim to the West Bank is at least as good as anyone else's.

But "land for peace" is more than simply a misreading of "242." It is also a non starter as a negotiating position. . . . It forgets that ultimately the nature of any final settlement will not hinge on a debate over the legalistic complexities of a resolution, but on Israel's ability to ensure peace by establishing secure borders and on the willingness of the Arabs to accept the existence of a sovereign Jewish state in their midst.

And if the Gulf war has taught us anything, it is the important role that geography plays in the defense of a country. Those who argue that the Scud attacks on Israel prove that intercontinental missiles make territory an obsolete deterrent, I would remind that this war, like all its predecessors, was started and finished on the ground. . . .

The value of the West Bank from a strategic perspective has, therefore, only been reaffirmed by this war.

But did Israel not set a precedent by withdrawing from all of Sinai? No, it did not. Israel may have been justified in the context of "242" to consider the pre-1967 international frontier with Egypt, with the hundreds of miles of desert stretching beyond it, to be reasonably secure — while the pre-Six Day War Green Line between Israel and the West Bank, only minutes away from most of Israel's population centers, is anything but.

Where real peace is a possibility, Israel has long declared a willingness to compromise. But compromise is a two-way street. There may indeed now be a "window of opportunity" before us, but if our Arab neighbors and those who support their views insist that "242" means only "land for peace," they will have prejudged the outcome of the proposed peace talks and prevented genuine progress toward a lasting settlement.

**August 30, 1991  625**

Continued from p. 624
known in Israel as the biblical area of Judea and Samaria. To a majority of Israelis, however, maintaining the territories is basically a matter of security. And in the aftermath of the gulf war, there is no longer any certainty that land buys security. If the Israeli state can give up most of the West Bank for genuine peace, and if the security threat of a West Bank in Palestinian hands can be reasonably

resolved, then experts say many would settle for resolving the national crisis by handing the territories over to the Palestinians as the lesser evil. In a poll published in June by the Institute of Applied Social Research at Hebrew University, one-third of Israelis favored a demilitarized Palestinian state, 69 percent favored some territorial concessions and 78 percent favored letting go of the Gaza Strip. ■

he says. "No Arab can accept what he considers unjust treatment of another Arab. There will be no peace in the region until the Palestinian issue is resolved, and every Arab leader knows that."

In an ironic twist, the Palestinians' current weakness may ultimately work in their favor. On their own, they've never made enough concessions to satisfy Israel or, for that matter, the United States. Now that they are politically emasculated and economically desperate, says William Quandt, they may for the first time actually get to the negotiating table. Paradoxically, he points out, their weakened position permits them to "pursue the attainable rather than the ideal."

Israel, which emerged from the gulf war strategically strengthened and morally vindicated, is in less of a mood for compromise. "The Shamir government has no intention of giving up one inch of territory. There will be deadlock within the first 30 seconds of sitting down at the table," says Zachary Lockman, a professor of Middle East Studies at Harvard. "Israel has been able to have its cake and eat it, too — absorb new immigrants, keep the territories and still get U.S. aid."

Lockman argues that the outlook for resolving the Palestinian problem will remain bleak until the United States uses aid as a carrot, or stick, to coerce the Israeli government to compromise. At present, that is not too likely. Publicly, the Bush administration insists it will not link aid with progress toward peace. More important, by agreeing to attend a conference, Israel boosted prospects for U.S. congressional approval of a much-needed $10 billion program of loan guarantees to help it absorb the expected influx of Soviet immigrants.[32] Congress is expected to consider the package in September, before the peace conference is scheduled to convene.

# OUTLOOK

## Window of Opportunity

In essence, the Palestinian problem is straightforward: two peoples, Jews and Palestinian Arabs, vying for the same turf, which since the 1967 Six-Day War has been controlled by Israel. For half a century, it has been essential to the psychology and mental security of each side to absolutely deny the existence — and the rights — of the other. At some point this vicious circle has to be broken.

In the Middle East, however, optimists are a scarce commodity. History seems more on the side of conflict than peace. Despite the emergence of the United States as the pre-eminent foreign power in the region, there are roadblocks at every turn. Radical Islamic factions could easily launch a campaign of violence, either against Israel or against Palestinians willing to cooperate with the United States, in an effort to sabotage the process. And though some Palestinian leaders have sounded positive, the conference still could fall apart over the problem of choosing Palestinian negotiators acceptable to both Israel and the PLO.

Clearly, the easing of Cold War tensions and the U.S. triumph in the

gulf war have jumbled the Middle East chessboard. The region's principal players — Syria, Israel, Saudi Arabia, Jordan and Egypt — have at least some interest in a genuine settlement to the disputes that have left their region roiling for decades.

But there are also compelling reasons not to settle, not least being the sheer complexity of the issues and the risks of failure. Explosive questions need to be answered: Should Palestinians in the diaspora be allowed their "right of return"? Should Jerusalem, revered by Jews and Arabs alike, be shared between the two states? Can Syrian President Hafez al-Assad be trusted? Who will control the Golan Heights, the West Bank and Gaza? What security arrangements will be in place? If and when peace talks begin, the real issues of contention will be these, not the composition of the negotiating teams.

Despite frequent speculation that the Palestinian cause will be abandoned by the Arab states, most experts doubt that will happen. "The Palestinian issue remains the linchpin of the entire region," says Sara Roy. "It is still the only issue Arab governments can use to legitimize themselves to their constituencies." Graham Fuller agrees. "We must look beyond the fact that many Arabs dislike Palestinians and are bitter over Arafat's stance in the gulf war,"

Lockman contends that the most likely scenario is that Prime Minister Shamir will attend a ceremonial conference, and even enter into a few months of bilateral negotiations, but never yield on the territories question — knowing full well that with elections coming up in 1992, the United States is unlikely to pressure Israel too hard. By then there would be another 20,000 or so Jewish settlers in the territories, and there also would have been elections in Israel, meaning Shamir might not personally have to preside over any territorial concessions.*

### Is the status quo tenable?

If the Palestinian issue is not resolved now or in the near future, most observers believe it will become even more volatile. The stakes for both Israelis and Palestinians are tremendous. Secretary of State Baker has warned Palestinians that this may be their "last chance" to obtain autonomy, a necessary step before achieving their dream of an independent state. According to Palestinians, it may also be the last chance before Israeli settlement activity and repression create new and even uglier political dynamics.

"In the fervor to initiate a process, attention has focused on procedural issues that have nothing to do with the fundamental problems of the territories," says Roy. "People in Gaza and the West Bank live miserable lives. The status quo is not tenable."

If peace talks fail to take place because either Israel or the Palestinians refuse to budge, experts say diplomacy will be discredited in the Arab world, further radicalizing young Palestinians inside and outside the occupied territories. The refugee camps will then continue to be the seeds of intense Palestinian resentment, frustration and terror.

---

*Israeli elections must take place no later than the fall of 1992.

The reality in the West Bank and Gaza is that time is on no one's side. Georgetown's Hisham Sharabi says this may be the last time that a relatively moderate PLO will still be able and willing to make a deal that involves territorial compromise. And it may be the last chance before Palestinians become so desperate and so radicalized that groups advocating "no negotiation, no compromise" come to reflect the majority view in the territories. Says Sharabi: "If this initiative fails, there is no doubt that fundamentalism will gain. More and more Palestinians are already turning to Islam as the only solution."

No matter how unappealing Arafat may be to Americans or Israelis, and no matter when or why Palestinian nationalism arose, that nationalism is staring the world in the face now. The histories of South Africa, Northern Ireland, Lebanon, the Soviet Union and many other nations show that suppressed nationalism can be a powerful revolutionary force that is dangerous to ignore. ∎

## Notes

[1] George Abed, "Palestinians and the Gulf War," *Journal of Palestine Studies,* spring 1991, p. 30.
[2] *The New York Times,* May 25, 1991.
[3] See *The Economist,* June 29, 1991, p. 36, and *The New York Times,* Aug. 8, 1991.
[4] Quoted in *The Wall Street Journal,* May 10, 1991.
[5] The U.N. Security Council unanimously approved Resolution 242 on Nov. 22, 1967. Resolution 338, approved on Oct. 22, 1973, basically reaffirms Resolution 242 and calls for negotiations among the parties in the region.
[6] Cited in *The Wall Street Journal,* Aug. 1, 1991.
[7] "The Palestinians After the Gulf War: The Critical Questions," collection of articles published by The Center for Policy Analysis on Palestine, Washington, D.C., March 27, 1991, p. 16.
[8] See *The Washington Post,* July 23, 1991.
[9] See "Israel's Prison Academies," *The Atlantic,* October 1989, p. 22.
[10] See Ze'ev Schiff and Ehud Ya'ari, *Intifada: The Palestinian Uprising — Israel's Third Front* (1989).
[11] See Martin Indyk, "Peace Without the PLO," *Foreign Policy,* summer 1991, p. 30.
[12] Martin Indyk, "Half-Bakered: The Administration's Fanciful Peace Plan," *The New Republic,* May 27, 1991, p. 8.
[13] Quoted in Michael C. Hudson, *The Palestinians: New Directions (1990),* p. 160.
[14] Quoted in Thomas Friedman, *From Beirut to Jerusalem* (1989), p. 253.
[15] For a detailed account see Benny Morris, *The Birth of the Palestinian Refugee Problem, 1947-49* (1987).
[16] For background on Nasser and the history of Pan-Arabism, see "The Elusive Search for Arab Unity," *Editorial Research Reports,* Oct. 19, 1990, pp. 602-616.
[17] Don Peretz, *The Middle East Today* (1988), p. 146.
[18] Patrick Seale, *Assad: The Struggle for the Middle East* (1988), p. 271.
[19] See Deborah J. Gerner, *One Land, Two Peoples* (1991), p. 89.
[20] Friedman, *op. cit.,* p. 266.
[21] *Ibid.,* p. 386.
[22] See Hudson, *op. cit.,* p. 7.
[23] These figures were as of May 31, 1991. Provided by the Palestine Human Rights Information Center, Jerusalem/Chicago.
[24] Sara Roy, "The Political Economy of Despair: Changing Political and Economic Realities in the Gaza Strip," *Journal of Palestine Studies,* spring 1991, p. 61.
[25] See Rashid Khalidi, "The Palestinians and the Gulf Crisis," *Current History,* January 1991, p. 19.
[26] *The Washington Post,* March 2, 1991.
[27] James E. Akins, "The New Arabia," *Foreign Affairs,* summer 1991, p. 37.
[28] Quoted in *The Nation,* July 1, 1991, p. 11.
[29] See "Israeli Settlement in the Occupied Territories," Report prepared for the Committee on Appropriations, U.S. House of Representatives, March 19, 1991. This figure doesn't include East Jerusalem, which has a Jewish population of approximately 120,000. Washington has not recognized Israel's annexation of East Jerusalem.
[30] *The Wall Street Journal,* May 10, 1991.
[31] Quoted in Judith Miller, "Nowhere to Go: The Palestinians After the War," *The New York Times Magazine,* July 21, 1991, p. 32.
[32] See *Congressional Quarterly Weekly Report,* July 27. 1991, p. 2094.

# Bibliography

## Selected Sources Used

### Books

**Brynen, Rex, ed., *Echoes of the Intifada: Regional Repercussions of the Palestinian-Israeli Conflict*, Westview Press, 1991.**

This collection of essays by Palestinian experts concentrates specifically on the origins and ramifications of the *intifada*, or uprising. Essays on the *intifada's* impact on the United States and Israel are particularly interesting.

**Congressional Quarterly, *The Middle East*, Seventh Edition, 1990.**

An excellent compendium of facts about the Middle East, this book contains a detailed chapter on the evolution of the Arab-Israeli conflict and the various Middle East peace proposals. It also contains useful background on the various factions within the Palestine Liberation Organization.

**Friedman, Thomas, *From Beirut to Jerusalem*, Farrar Straus Giroux, 1989.**

Thomas Friedman offers readers a vivid picture of his life as a foreign correspondent for *The New York Times*, first in Beirut and, later, in Jerusalem. This is journalism at its best — observant, objective and sensitive.

**Hudson, Michael C., ed., *The Palestinians: New Directions*, Center for Contemporary Arab Studies, Georgetown University, 1990.**

The essays in this collection cover a wide range of topics relating to Palestinians and their quest for an independent state. Focusing on both history and the future, several of the essays offer provocative analysis of the thinking within the Palestinian nationalist movement.

**Schiff, Ze'ev, and Ya'ari, Ehud, *Intifada: The Palestinian Uprising — Israel's Third Front*, Simon & Schuster, 1989.**

A very readable account of the uprising by two Israeli journalists, generally sympathetic to the Palestinians but still from an Israeli point of view. The book is extremely informative but may overstate the *intifada's* impact on Israeli society.

### Articles

**Abed, George T., "The Palestinians and the Gulf Crisis," *Journal of Palestine Studies*, spring 1991.**

An excellent article on the losses the Palestinian community has endured in the aftermath of the gulf war. The author is critical of the PLO leadership yet compellingly explains their predicament prior to the crisis.

**Akins, James E., "The New Arabia," *Foreign Affairs*, summer 1991.**

The former U.S. ambassador to Saudi Arabia offers an interesting analysis of the geopolitical map in the Middle East following the defeat of Saddam Hussein. Akins examines the future of inter-Arab relations as well as the fate of Palestinians following the war.

**Friedman, Robert I., "The Palestinian Refugees," *The New York Review of Books*, March 29, 1990.**

Robert Friedman presents an in-depth, well-researched account of how the Palestinian refugee problem evolved from 1947 to 1990. Published prior to Saddam Hussein's invasion of Kuwait, this article is nonetheless a timely chronicle of conditions inside the refugee camps.

**Miller, Judith, "Nowhere to Go: The Palestinians After the War," *The New York Times Magazine*, July 21, 1991.**

Judith Miller's article focuses on the plight of Palestinians in Kuwait and their sense of despair and hopelessness.

### Reports and Studies

**Fitzgerald, Garret, *The Israeli-Palestinian Issue*, Trilateral Commission, May 1990.**

This report is particularly useful in describing how the various parties in Israel, the Arab states and the Palestinian community perceive the Palestinian issue.

**Fuller, Graham, *The West Bank of Israel: Point of No Return?* RAND Corporation, August 1989.**

Though a bit dated, this report contains a superb analysis of the forces at play in the Israeli-occupied territories. Fuller contends that the *intifada* has made a Palestinian state on the West Bank inevitable.

**United Nations, *The Origins and Evolution of the Palestine Problem, 1917-1988*, 1990.**

This U.N. study is tedious and poorly written but still serves as an invaluable resource for background on the Palestinian issue.

**U.S. Department of State, *Israeli Settlement in the Occupied Territories*, March 19, 1991.**

This study of Israeli settlement activity in the occupied territories was written at the request of the House Committee on Appropriations. The report contains useful background data and up-to-date information on the status of Soviet immigrants living in the occupied territories.

# The Next Step

## Additional Articles from Current Periodicals

### Debates & issues

**"A lost voice,"** *The New York Times Magazine,* **April 28, 1991, p. 34.**

Palestinian novelist Anton Shammas contends that language lay at the heart of the Persian Gulf War and may hold the key to peace in the Middle East. Arab-Israeli-Palestinian disputes and the role of language; use of the word "linkage"; more.

**"UN Security Council resolution on Israel,"** *Dispatch,* **Dec. 24, 1990, p. 358.**

Presents the text of U.N. Security Council Resolution 681 (Dec. 20, 1990) expressing grave concern over the rejection by Israel of Security Council Resolutions 672 and 673 and deploring the decision by the government of Israel to resume deportations of Palestinian civilians in the occupied territories.

**Dickey, C., "Keeping up appearances of movement,"** *Newsweek,* **April 22, 1991, p. 26.**

Assesses the current relationship between the Arabs and Israel, contending that even though Israel's most threatening enemy, Iraq, is now in ruins, the central problems between Israel and the Arabs remain. Questions if Israel has a right to exist and the Palestinians a right to a state. Confusing debates; efforts made by U.S. Secretary of State James A. Baker III; U.N. Security Council Resolution 242; more.

**Goode, E. E., "Israel's willful conscience,"** *U.S. News & World Report,* **April 15, 1991, p. 62.**

Profiles Amos Oz, Israel's most celebrated and controversial novelist, an outspoken dove, the "conscience" of his country, the man who "is determined above all to tell the truth regardless of whom it offends." Supporter of a Palestinian homeland and a negotiated peace; founder of the organization Peace Now; blunt, arrogant, naive, dreamer, death threats in the mailbox; his newest novel "To Know a Woman."

### Israel

**"Security Council asks for urgent efforts to monitor Palestinian civilian situation,"** *UN Chronicle,* **March 1991, p. 55.**

Summarizes the U.N. Security Council's unanimous vote to make new, urgent efforts to monitor the situation of Palestinian civilians under Israeli occupation, and to ensure respect by Israel for Geneva Convention obligations.

**"That man again,"** *The Economist,* **April 13, 1991, p. 40.**

Reports on the visit of U.S. Secretary of State James A. Baker III to Israel. Israeli reaction; Israel's Likud-led coalition government; Prime Minister Yitzhak Shamir; Foreign Minister David Levy; outlook for a successful Arab-Israeli peace conference; question of who would speak for the Palestinians; position of PLO leader Yasir Arafat; details.

**Doherty, C. J., "U.S.-Israeli relations cool after heat of war,"** *Congressional Quarterly Weekly Report,* **May 4, 1991, p. 1145.**

Declares that although at the height of the Persian Gulf War the Bush administration drew close to the Israeli government of Prime Minister Yitzhak Shamir, like the war itself, the era of warm relations passed quickly. Battling a common enemy; at odds again with Shamir government; compromise on conditions for peace talks between Israel and its neighbors; barring contacts between U.S. officials and the Palestine Liberation Organization; expanding role of Rep. Mel Levine, D-Calif.

**Elon, A., "Letter from Jerusalem,"** *The New Yorker,* **Dec. 24, 1990, p. 80.**

Describes the current political and social conditions in Jerusalem. Palestinian uprising on the West Bank and the Gaza Strip; relationships between Jews and Arabs; riots and other forms of violence; United States policy toward Israel; more.

**Elon, A., "Report from Jerusalem,"** *The New Yorker,* **April 1, 1991, p. 80.**

Presents a report on the current political situation in Jerusalem after the end of the Persian Gulf War. Sense of civilian vulnerability in the area; President Bush's promised new world order; damage to Tel Aviv area houses; lack of Israeli preparation for the war; continuation of immigration from Soviet Union; Palestinian support of Saddam Hussein; Arab-Israeli conflict.

### Land disputes

**"Next stop Palestine,"** *The Economist,* **March 9, 1991, p. 17.**

Examines how the end of the gulf war will impact the long-standing argument between Israel and the Palestinians. Why the Israelis don't want to give the West Bank back to the Palestinians; benefits from the defeat of Iraq; loss sustained by Palestine Liberation Organization leader Yasir Arafat; change in Palestinian leadership; value of

American friendship; stance of the present Israeli government; outlook.

**"Shamir talks about talks," *U.S. News & World Report,* April 8, 1991, p. 15.**

Notes Israeli Prime Minister Yitzhak Shamir's stance in relation to controversies between Israelis and Palestinians. His refusal to hold direct talks with Arabs; no sympathy for the idea of swapping land for peace; comments on the anticipated U.S.-Soviet offer to host Middle East peace talks.

**Church, G. J., Fernandez, M., et al., "Does land still buy security?" *Time,* April 1, 1991, p. 39.**

Considers the raging debate over whether Israel could safely return even a demilitarized Golan Heights to Syria. The heretics: (1) Bassam Abu Sharif, adviser to PLO Chairman Yasir Arafat, hinting a Palestinian state did not have to include every last bit of the West Bank; (2) Ehud Olmert, Health Minister of Israel, proclaiming Israel ready for negotiations with Syria; (3) Dan Shomron, chief of staff, remarking "one can speak about risk vs. territory."

**Doherty, C. J., "Disputes over settlements strain the peace process," *Congressional Quarterly Weekly Report,* March 30, 1991, p. 802.**

Discusses the issues that strained relations between the United States and Israel before the Persian Gulf War and that have begun to cause renewed friction now that the conflict has ended. Prime Minister Yitzhak Shamir continuing to expand housing settlements in Israel's occupied territories; determined to halt violence by Palestinians against Israelis; Israeli request for new loan guarantees later this year; expanding settlements; more settlers planned.

**Zuckerman, M. B., "New thinking, old realities," *U.S. News & World Report,* March 25, 1991, p. 76.**

Editorial. Argues that in the wake of the Persian Gulf War the United States should not blindly buy into the notion of land for peace. Saddam Hussein has united the Jews of Israel, left and right, in the belief that a Palestinian homeland would be suicide, and that the Palestinians will never accept the coexistence of Israel. Fundamental hostility of Syria toward Israel; importance of the West Bank to Israel's defense; new respect for the old realities.

## Middle East relations

**Lane, C. and Warner, M. G., "Your wish is my demand," *Newsweek,* May 20, 1991, p. 34.**

States that Washington still hopes for a breakthrough in the Middle East, but reveals that the area is reverting to its old, intransigent form. Secretary of State James A. Baker III's fourth diplomatic tour last week; the behavior of the

Saudis; Egyptian President Hosni Mubarak; Arab and Israeli relations; security and the peace process; Prince Bandar bin Sultan; Kuwait.

**Reed, S. and Javetski, B., "The gulf: What America should do now," *Business Week,* April 15, 1991, p. 32.**

Reports on the battle still raging in the Middle East and tells how President Bush is doing almost nothing to help. Losing some of the respect he earned during the war; his inaction could doom thousands of Iraqis and Palestinians to refugee camps or death; killing hopes for progress on Arab-Israeli peace and for reforming the region's medieval political system; what should be done.

**Robbins, C. A., Makovsky, D., et al., "In search of tiny openings," *U.S. News & World Report,* May 6, 1991, p. 44.**

Details the most recent Middle East trip of Secretary of State James A. Baker III that failed to break the deadlock on two key questions: who would represent the Palestinians at any talks and what role would the United Nations play in any peace conference. Sorting out the various players; keeping the agenda intentionally vague; Palestinians appear willing to accept a gradualist approach. INSET: photo essay of Baker's trip.

## Moral & religious aspects

**Budiansky, S., "Bowed heads and golden rules," *U.S. News & World Report,* March 25, 1991, p. 10.**

Comments that Western expectations for a Middle East peace remain peculiarly Christian ones, based at heart on the premise that if only the Israelis and the Palestinians would sit down and talk they would learn to love their neighbors as themselves. Fundamental differences between the Semitic and the Western world views; the essence of Jewish morality: to perfect this world, one must hate evil, not forgive it; "What is hateful to you, do not do to your fellow man."

**Landes, D. S., "Islam dunk," *The New Republic,* April 8, 1991, p. 15.**

Analyzes the religious overtones of the gulf war, which pitted the Western infidels against Muslims even though one was a tyrant. History of Muslim conquest; Western influence; importance of Saddam Hussein's move into Kuwait; impact of war on Middle Eastern politics; role of Israeli-Palestinian conflict; other religious obstacles.

## Palestine Liberation Organization

**"Arafat's dangerous ploy," *Time,* Oct. 15, 1990, p. 55.**

Discusses the problems arising because of the refusal of the Palestine Liberation Organization's leader Yasir Arafat to condemn Iraq's conquest of Kuwait. Infuriated Arab backers; Kuwait and Saudi Arabia cut off funds; thousands of Palestinians lose their jobs on the gulf; political squeeze; covering all bets; internal radicals who would like to depose him.

**"Life after Arafat," *The Economist*, Feb. 2, 1991, p. 20.**

Assesses the likelihood of Yasir Arafat remaining as the leader of the Palestine Liberation Organization (PLO). Recent criticism of Arafat's judgment; impact of PLO support for Iraqi President Saddam Hussein; impact to Palestinians; need for the PLO to economize; potential new leaders; killings of several senior PLO men; details; outlook.

## Persian Gulf War, 1991

**"Revenge is blind," *The Economist*, March 30, 1991, p. 39.**

Describes mistreatment of Palestinians in Kuwait. Accused of collaboration with Iraqis; many cases of unjust accusation.

**"The other occupation," *The Economist*, March 9, 1991, p. 40.**

Looks at what the end of the gulf war means for the 1.7 million Palestinians living in the West Bank and Gaza Strip, which are occupied by Israel. Visit by U.S. Secretary of State James A. Baker III; position of the government of Prime Minister Yitzhak Shamir; signs of cautious independence among the Palestinians living under occupation; signs that the *intifada* is reviving; details.

**Bollag, B., "Gulf crisis may leave deep scars on higher education in the Middle East," *The Chronicle of Higher Education*, April 3, 1991, p. A1.**

Details some of the massive destruction the Persian Gulf crisis has caused in Iraq and Kuwait and suggests the biggest losers may be Palestinians, as hundreds of Palestinian teachers find themselves unable to reclaim jobs they were forced to give up because of the conflict. Financial aid for the six Palestinian universities in the West Bank and Gaza Strip in doubt; problems in Egypt and Saudi Arabia; persecution of Palestinians in Kuwait; positive developments.

**Dowell, W., "Life under a cloud," *Time*, April 29, 1991, p. 42.**

Describes Kuwait today, a sky of charcoal cloud dripping white ash and underneath scores of flashy cars and motorcycles, running water, electricity and telephones, fresh vegetables in the supermarket. Meeting the country's basic requirements; much Iraqi damage was superficial; persecution by Kuwaitis enraged by Palestinian support of Saddam Hussein; continuing retribution and government

incompetence; resignation of the Cabinet; Parliamentary elections, fall 1992.

**Kirk, D., "Saddam boosters," *The Nation*, April 1, 1991, p. 400.**

Reports how the Palestinians and Bedouins in Jordan see Saddam Hussein as a hero and feel that they have won a victory. Their attitude toward "enemy" nations; why they feel they have won; the danger to Jordan from these two groups.

**Peretz, M., "Worst enemy," *The New Republic*, March 25, 1991, p. 13.**

Argues that the Palestinians have severely damaged world support for their cause due to their decision to side with Saddam Hussein in the gulf war. How their joyous response to Iraqi Scud attacks on Israel has reinforced that country's fears of living in close proximity to a hostile state; recommended Western policy toward Palestinians and Jordan, which also exhibited support for Hussein.

**Warner, M. G., Pedersen, D., et al., "With friends like these," *Newsweek*, May 6, 1991, p. 42.**

Looks at the problems facing Kuwait since the withdrawal of Iraqi troops. Rebuilding infrastructure to make progress in political reform; Emir Jabir al-Ahmad al-Sabah grudgingly entertaining idea of "a new Kuwait"; Kuwait's nascent opposition pushing for reopening of Parliament; American displeasure; recent Amnesty International report; misery of 600 people, mostly Palestinians; inability of al-Sabah family to keep its own house in order.

## Protests, demonstrations, etc.

**"A most exploitable massacre," *The Economist*, Oct. 13, 1990, p. 41.**

Details the Oct. 8, 1990, killing of 19 Palestinians by Israeli police in Jerusalem. President Bush's response and his dismissal of the idea that the event had undermined his strategy in the gulf; Iraqi President Saddam Hussein's use of the massacre by linking his fate to that of Palestine's; comments of Prime Minister Yitzhak Shamir; accusations against the Palestine Liberation Organization and the *intifada*.

**Stanger, T., "New mandate: Shoot to kill," *Newsweek*, Apr. 8, 1991, p. 38.**

Details the violence in Israel between Palestinians and Jews and the hard line Israeli police are taking on Arab violence. Anger over renewed attacks against soldiers and civilians; the *intifada* since 1987; Israel struggling for three years to contain Arab attacks on Jews; surge in gun-license applications for self-defense.

# Back Issues

*Great Research on Current Issues Starts Right Here... Recent topics covered by The CQ Researcher are listed below. Issues dated before May 10, 1991, were published under the name of Editorial Research Reports.*

**FEBRUARY 1990**
Politics and Economic Growth
Free Agency in Sports
Repetitive Motion
War on Drugs

**MARCH 1990**
Asbestos: Are Risks Acceptable?
Public Health Campaigns
South Africa's Future
Homeless Need More Than Shelter

**APRIL 1990**
How Fair is the Tax Burden?
Workers' Compensation
U.S. Pacific Forces
Curbing Insurance Premiums

**MAY 1990**
Should Teaching Be a Profession?
Will Canada Fall Apart?
Is U.S. Patent System Outdated?
Federal Funding for the Arts

**JUNE 1990**
Downsizing America's Armed Forces
Progress In Weather Forecasting
S & L Bailout
Bio-Chemical Disarmament

**JULY 1990**
Do Americans Still Love Marriage?
Death Penalty Debate
Decline of Rural America
United Nations in the 1990s

**AUGUST 1990**
Democracy in the Philippines
Initiatives: True Democracy?
Hard Times at Newspapers
Teens Balance School & Jobs

**SEPTEMBER 1990**
Dangers of Alcohol
Western Alliance After the Cold War
Tobacco Industry
Right to Die

**OCTOBER 1990**
Organ Transplants
Energy Policy Options
Search for Arab Unity
Child Support

**NOVEMBER 1990**
Lotteries and Gambling
Post Cold-War Choices
Setting Limits on Medical Care
Multicultural Education

**DECEMBER 1990**
Cable TV Regulation
Americans' Search For Their Roots
Is Insurance System a Failure?
Why Schools Still Have Tracking

**JANUARY 1991**
Growing Influence of Boycotts
Should the U.S. Reinstate the Draft?
America's Archaeological Past
Peace Corps' Challenges in '90s

**FEBRUARY 1991**
Regional Impact of Recession
Puerto Rico's Status
Redistricting: Mapping Power
Nuclear Power

**MARCH 1991**
Acid Rain
Cost of the Gulf War
Reassessing Gun Laws
Future for Man in Space

**APRIL 1991**
Social Security
Canadian Crisis Over Quebec
California Drought
Electromagnetic Radiation

**MAY 1991**
School Choice
Racial Quotas
Animal Rights
U.S. and Japan

**JUNE 1991**
Children and Divorce
Teenage Suicide
Endangered Species
Europe 1992

**JULY 1991**
Teenagers and Abortion
Soviet Republics Rebel
Mexico's Emergence
Athletes and Drugs

**AUGUST 1991**
Sexual Harassment
Fetal Tissue Research
Oil Imports

Back issues are available for $4.00 (subscribers) or $7.00 (non-subscribers). Quantity discounts apply to orders over ten. To order, call Congressional Quarterly 1-800-432-2250.

# Future Topics

► *Police Brutality*

► *Advertising Under Attack*

► *Rain Forests*

# THE CQ Researcher

PUBLISHED BY CONGRESSIONAL QUARTERLY INC., IN CONJUNCTION WITH EBSCO PUBLISHING

# Police Brutality

*Los Angeles incident raises questions across the nation*

AS FRONT-LINE TROOPS IN THE WAR ON CRIME, police officers must stand tough in an environment that doesn't forgive mistakes. But do the police go overboard? Recent headlines have forced police and citizens alike to confront an unpleasant reality: The use of excessive force by police, if not on the rise, is far from rare. The beating last March of Rodney G. King, a black man from Los Angeles, seemed to corroborate charges of routine police abuse of civilians, especially minorities. The King incident has prompted calls for improved police training and administration in Los Angeles and other cities. Some experts say a whole new approach is needed. One technique gaining favor, known as "community policing," holds that greater interaction between police and community residents will lead to more evenhanded law enforcement.

## I N S I D E THIS ISSUE

CQ   **September 6, 1991 • Volume 1, No. 17 • 633-656**

*Formerly Editorial Research Reports*

COVER PHOTO: © DARROW MONTGOMERY

September 6, 1991
Volume 1, No. 17

**EDITOR**
Sandra Stencel

**MANAGING EDITOR**
Thomas J. Colin

**ASSOCIATE EDITOR**
Richard L. Worsnop

**STAFF WRITERS**
Charles S. Clark
Mary H. Cooper
Rodman D. Griffin

**PRODUCTION EDITOR**
Laurie De Maris

**EDITORIAL ASSISTANT**
Thomas H. Moore

**GRAPHICS**
Jack Auldridge

**PUBLISHED BY**
Congressional Quarterly Inc.

**CHAIRMAN**
Andrew Barnes

**VICE CHAIRMAN**
Andrew P. Corty

**EDITOR AND PUBLISHER**
Neil Skene

**EXECUTIVE EDITOR**
Robert W. Merry

**PUBLICATIONS MARKETING/SALES**
Robert Smith

**EDITOR, EBSCO PUBLISHING**
Melissa Kummerer

The CQ Researcher (ISSN 1056-2036). Formerly Editorial Research Reports. Published weekly (48 times per year, not printed the first Friday of any month with five Fridays) by Congressional Quarterly Inc., 1414 22nd St., N.W., Washington, D.C. 20037. Rates are furnished upon request. Application to mail at second-class postage rates is pending at Washington, D.C. POSTMASTER: Send address changes to The CQ Researcher, 1414 22nd St., N.W., Washington, D.C. 20037.

# Police Brutality

BY RICHARD L. WORSNOP

## THE ISSUES

Six months ago 25-year-old Rodney G. King was just another anonymous Californian. Then, on the night of March 3, King was stopped by police after a high-speed auto chase. As 11 Los Angeles police officers stood by and watched, four baton-wielding policemen savagely beat and kicked King. All the police officers were white; King is black. The incident might have attracted no more than passing local attention but for one thing: A resident of a nearby apartment building was standing on his balcony trying out his new video camera. Plumbing-store manager George Holliday recorded the appalling scene and sold the tape to a local television station. On March 5, when the Cable News Network (CNN) aired the two-minute tape, Rodney King was no longer a nobody.

Reaction across the country was swift and nearly unanimous. News commentators, public officials and ordinary citizens condemned the beating and demanded that the Los Angeles Police Department (LAPD) take steps to prevent any similar incidents. Then-U.S. Attorney General Dick Thornburgh announced that the Justice Department would review every police brutality complaint to the federal government over the past six years.[1] And there were calls, particularly in Southern California, for the resignation of Daryl F. Gates, police chief of Los Angeles since 1978.

On April 1, Los Angeles Mayor Tom Bradley established an independent commission to conduct "a full and fair examination" of the police force. (The panel, headed by former Deputy Secretary of State

Warren Christopher, became known as the Christopher Commission.) In its subsequent report, the commission called the King beating "a landmark in the recent history of law enforcement, comparable to the Scottsboro case in 1931 and the Serpico case in 1967."[2]

Many outside experts agreed. James Fyfe, a 16-year veteran of the New York City Police Department who is now a professor of justice, law and society at American University in Washington, regards the King case as a "watershed" in police-community relations comparable to the urban disorders of the 1960s. Before the 1960s, Fyfe says, people assumed "the police knew best." But a decade-long period of urban turmoil showed that assumption "was not necessarily so," and "police practice was changed as a result." Fyfe believes the King beating will bring further changes. In the past, he says, police officers "always got the benefit of the doubt" when accused of

misconduct. "Today, the citizen's and the police officer's words are being given equal weight. That is going to require police departments to re-examine the way they operate."

American police are no strangers to innovation born of scandal. Since the turn of the century, U.S. law enforcement agencies have been repeatedly shaken up and forced to reorganize by reformers. In most instances, the changes stemmed from popular outrage over police misconduct, chiefly corruption or brutal treatment of suspects. Sometimes the police are faulted for inaction, as in the current serial-murder case of Jeffrey L. Dahmer. Three Milwaukee police officers have been suspended for failing to rescue one of Dahmer's victims, a 14-year-old Laotian boy. *(See story, p. 637.)*

Most police-reform movements are locally based. Over the past 30 years, however, the federal government has sought to improve police performance on a nationwide basis. In the 1960s, the U.S. Supreme Court issued a set of rulings enumerating suspects' rights that police must respect during the arrest and interrogation stage. *(See story, p. 643.)* More recently, the court has tried to delineate the boundary between acceptable and "excessive" use of force by police officers. *(See story, p. 647.)* Congress, meanwhile, provided aid to local police departments for 14 years starting in 1968 through the now-defunct Law Enforcement Assistance Administration. Guided by a similar impulse, the crime bill approved by the Senate July 11 would establish a federally funded Police Corps as a source of college-educated recruits for police departments across the country *(see p. 647).*

Such initiatives have had generally positive effects. Police are now more sophisticated about combating crime, and have more resources for doing so than ever before. By most accounts, they also are more aware of the rights of criminal suspects.

Nonetheless, the problem of police misconduct persists, as the Rodney King beating so vividly showed. Even before the Christopher Commission issued its report, the King incident had prompted law enforcement experts to ponder anew the root causes of police misbehavior and to re-examine old assumptions about the most effective ways of preventing it.

### Why does police brutality occur?

Law enforcement officials are of several minds about the reasons behind the overuse of force that is labeled "police brutality." According to Robert Scully, president of the Detroit-based National Association of Police Organizations, "there obviously has to be some kind of stress factor" at work in brutality cases because stress is an "inherent part" of policing.

Los Angeles Police Chief Gates agrees. "We operate in a far more complicated and difficult arena than almost any other profession," he said recently. "Nobody else has to make the kinds of decisions that police officers do. Nobody else has to get his blood pressure and his pulse rate up so high, and then drop it down and make an immediate decision based on a variety of factors."

For this reason, Gates gives his officers considerable latitude in performing their duties. "If I think they were doing their very best to deal with a tough situation, and they used some force, and perhaps they got the last whack in . . . ," he said, it can be "tough to distinguish whether the last whack was necessary. I give them the benefit of the doubt. I think they deserve it." [3]

Hubert Williams, president of the Washington-based Police Founda-

tion, a research group that studies ways to improve police performance, says brutality also may occur if police leaders don't make clear to officers on the beat that excessive force will not be condoned.

Police officers learn the fundamentals of departmental policy — what they are supposed to do and not supposed to do — during training. "The problem," says Williams, a former police chief in Newark, N.J., "is that sometimes training formally says one thing and the actual operation of the department says another. When that happens, reality often speaks louder than words."

According to Fyfe, some such clash between theory and practice may have contributed to the Rodney King beating. "There's no doubt that police officers in other places have beaten people," he says. "But to do it in public, and in front of so many other officers, betrays an absolute confidence that citizens' versions of what happened would not be believed and that other officers would not be informants. I don't think you can do that without working in an organizational culture that has let officers know that that kind of behavior will be tolerated."

The reluctance of police officers to inform on their colleagues not only allows misconduct to go undetected but also may encourage its spread. The Christopher Commission reported that "Virtually all of the FTOs [field training officers] interviewed stated that they would report serious police misconduct." Yet the fact that few FTOs had ever filed a complaint against a fellow officer, the panel said, clearly indicated that a "code of silence" was observed throughout the force.[4]

The commission blamed some of the LAPD's problems on a "significant number" of officers cited in a disproportionate number of citizen brutality complaints. "The department not only failed to deal with the

problem group of officers but it often rewarded them with positive evaluations and promotions," the commission said.

Such attitudes are by no means confined to the LAPD. Most U.S. police departments provide incentives for their officers, including promotions, merit pay raises and "officer of the month" recognition. Nearly always, the incentives reward aggressive acts leading to numerous arrests, the capture of a dangerous felon or some other extraordinary feat. The cited act frequently entails force, which police officials tend to justify after the fact as appropriate in the circumstances.

In any event, police officers often can evade disciplinary action for the use of unnecessary force by filing "cover charges" against the suspect. "If they shoot somebody," says Ira Glaser, executive director of the American Civil Liberties Union, "they usually charge him with attempted murder; if they beat him, they charge him with resisting arrest and assaulting a police officer." [5] In the absence of eyewitness testimony or physical evidence to the contrary, the police officer's word usually prevails.

Since 1980, a recent *Los Angeles Times* study found, the Los Angeles County district attorney's office has declined to prosecute at least 278 police officers and sheriff's deputies accused of assaulting civilians. At least 41 other officers were prosecuted on excessive-force charges, and about half of them were convicted. According to the *Times,* "the district attorney's office commonly accords accused officers a benefit of the doubt when debating whether to file police brutality charges." [6]

A survey by *The Washington Post* uncovered a similar local pattern.[7] Of the 61 police-brutality cases heard in 1990 by the District of Columbia's Civilian Complaint Review Board, excessive force was found in 18. Because the board has a backlog

# The Jeffrey Dahmer Case: When Police Fail to Act

Police misconduct usually stems from an act contrary to law or departmental policy. Occasionally, misconduct stems from an officer's failure to act. That's one of the more troubling aspects of the case of Jeffrey L. Dahmer, the Milwaukee man charged with murdering at least 15 young males.

Among Dahmer's victims was Konerak Sinthasomphone, a 14-year-old Laotian boy. On May 27, three Milwaukee police officers were dispatched to Dahmer's neighborhood in response to telephone calls from concerned neighbors about a naked young male who was in the middle of the street, bleeding and unable to stand. It was Sinthasomphone.

When the officers arrived on the scene, Dahmer persuaded them that the boy was a young adult who was his live-in lover. The officers returned Sinthasomphone to Dahmer's apartment and left after spending a short time inside. Dahmer told police after his arrest that he killed Sinthasomphone almost immediately upon the officers' departure.

The officers' behavior aroused a storm of protest, especially from Milwaukee's minority and homosexual communities. Since the two women who alerted the police were black, Sinthasomphone was Asian and Dahmer was white, the officers were accused of displaying racial prejudice. By accepting Dahmer's version of the situation, it was said, the police implicitly showed that they disbelieved the complainants. The officers were also criticized for dismissing the incident as "a boyfriend-boyfriend thing."

James Fyfe, a former New York City policeman who is a professor of justice, law and society at American University in Washington, says the incident reflects an apparent failure of police policy. "The Milwaukee Police Department operates on a must-arrest policy in domestic cases," he says. "The paper directive in Milwaukee is that when police encounter violence that involves a domestic situation, they must arrest. They must treat it like other types of violence. Clearly, those cops did not go along with it, so that raises a whole lot of questions about just what the policy means."

Responding to the wave of criticism, Milwaukee Police Chief Philip Arreola suspended the three officers, with pay, and filed administrative charges against them for failing "to conduct a proper investigation." Meanwhile, Wisconsin Attorney General James Doyle announced that the officers would not be prosecuted. Doyle said state investigators had concluded that the officers had used poor judgment in handling the situation. But, he added, "failing to make the correct judgment is not a violation of the criminal law."

---

of more than 800 cases — four new complaints are filed for each old one resolved — most complaints are not investigated until two years or more after the incident occurred. When police-misconduct cases go to civil court in the Washington area, judges and juries tend to side with the police.

Although they seldom are prosecuted for brutality, Los Angeles police officers consider excessive force a problem meriting attention. In an internal survey conducted in May and June, more than two-thirds of the approximately 650 LAPD officers who responded attributed excessive force in the department to "overaggressiveness or lack of self-control." Almost 30 percent viewed it as a "serious problem" for the department. About half of the respondents cited job-related stress, off-duty personal problems, lack of self-confidence and fear of personal injury as factors that can trigger the use of excessive force. About one-fourth identified racial prejudice as a contributing factor.

Whatever the cause, the problem of police brutality is a costly one for Los Angeles. In 1972 the city paid $553,340 in judgments and settlements for the actions of the police department. In 1990, by comparison, the city paid out more than $8 million.

### How can police brutality be reduced?

Excessive force can be reduced, James Fyfe believes, only "by holding officers more closely accountable for what they do." He says police administrators are coming to realize that if they "don't do things to control police behavior and increase accountability, people outside the department will."

It is during the training period that police recruits learn the fundamentals of departmental policy and relevant sections of local, state and federal law. The attitudes and habits formed at this time are likely to shape the officers' conduct throughout their law enforcement careers.

One way to improve police training, experts say, is to make sure that the ethics and policy lessons taught in police academies guide behavior when recruits go on duty. "Police must learn in field training the truth of their academy lessons," ethicist Edwin J. Delattre wrote in *Character and Cops*. "Without coherence between academy preparation and field training, and cooperation between teachers and [field training officers], even very good academy programs will soon be forgotten by officers in the field." [8]

Police training has evolved over the years in response to changing social and legal conditions. Today's recruits are "trained to be cautious, not macho," says Patrick V. Murphy, former head of the Washington and New York City police departments. "Most progressive chiefs won't discipline a cop if someone gets away . . . but they will be tough if an officer is too aggressive." [9]

As the ethnic makeup of urban neighborhoods changes, police training officers are putting more stress on cultural awareness programs. Ignorance of differences between racial, ethnic, religious and other identifiable groups may lead a police officer to misjudge the danger — or absence of danger — in a particular situation. Conversely, knowledge of intergroup differences could help the officer deal with volatile incidents like domestic squabbles. An added benefit is that any improvement in relations between police and the minority community is almost sure to result in fewer hostile acts directed at officers.

Another proposal for guarding against police misbehavior calls for changing or expanding the types of conduct that are rewarded by raises and promotions. Instead of bestowing laurels primarily for deeds of derring-do, said the authors of a 1988 study of urban law enforcement, police departments should give serious thought to honoring "exemplary service to the community."

"An institutional reward system should be established for officers who avoid or reduce violent situations, and who avoid the use of force, especially deadly force where it is justifiable," wrote Geoffrey P. Alpert and Roger G. Dunham in *Policing Multi-Ethnic Neighborhoods*. "Once command officers, from the [police] chief to the sergeants, support and reward violence reduction,

it is possible to enlist the support of private business and service groups to provide symbolic and monetary rewards for such behavior." [10]

More rigorous recruitment and personnel-review procedures could help combat police misconduct by identifying individuals who are likely to draw complaints of physical or verbal abuse. Studies have shown that a relative handful of officers on urban forces are named in a disproportionate number of such complaints. For instance, the Christopher Commission found that of the approximately 1,800 LAPD officers against whom an allegation of excessive force or improper tactics was made from 1986 through 1990, more than 1,400 were named in only one or two complaints. "But 183 officers had four or more allegations, 44 had six or more, and one officer (whose initial background investigation indicated he had a problem controlling his temper) was the subject of 19 personnel complaints, including at least three shootings and 11 complaints of excessive force in his first two-and-a-half years on the force." [11]

A similar pattern exists in other cities. In Washington, D.C., for example, 44 officers each were the subject of three or more complaints alleging excessive force, verbal abuse or harassment, according to the city's Civilian Complaint Review Board. The 44 represent less than 1 percent of the 4,800 officers on the force, but the complaints against them account for almost 25 percent of those pending before the review board.

To combat the "problem officer" situation, the Christopher Commission recommended that the LAPD's initial psychological evaluation process for applicants focus "less on test and oral interview results and more on an analysis of past behavior." The panel also recommended that veteran officers be retested every three years "to uncover both psy-

chological and physical problems."

Fyfe endorses these proposals. "A cop's job is much more dangerous psychologically than it is physically," he says. "But once a person becomes a police officer, they just throw him out into this psychologically demanding environment and never look at him again."

Routine psychological testing may be a difficult reform to institute, however. "In most places," Fyfe notes, "an acknowledgment by a police officer of a psychological or emotional problem means the end of his career." For that reason, police departments have hesitated to set up psychological screening programs.

### What effect does police misconduct have on public opinion?

Almost invariably, the public responds negatively to allegations of police brutality. In a *Los Angeles Times* poll published three weeks after the Rodney King beating, 31 percent of the respondents said they thought Police Chief Gates should resign immediately because of the incident. Another 31 percent said Gates should step down if an investigation found LAPD officers guilty of misconduct.

Significantly, the poll indicated anti-Gates sentiment had risen since a similar survey taken only days after the beating. In that survey, 13 percent of those polled said Gates should quit immediately, and 27 percent said he should if the charges against his officers were upheld.

However, the respondents' ire was not directed solely or even primarily at Gates. Asked whether LAPD misconduct was "due more to the policies of those who run the department or more to the beliefs and personalities of the average police officer," 58 percent cited officers' beliefs and personalities and 29 percent named departmental leadership.

Though the *Times* poll results undoubtedly reflected area public

# A Black and White Issue?

*Polls indicate that blacks are more likely than whites to think that people in their neighborhoods are roughed up unnecessarily by police. Blacks also are more likely than whites to believe that charges of police brutality are justified.*

Question: Some people say the police rough up people unnecessarily when they are arresting them or afterwards. Do you think this happens to people in your neighborhood?

Question: When you hear charges of police brutality, how likely do you think it is that the charges are justified?

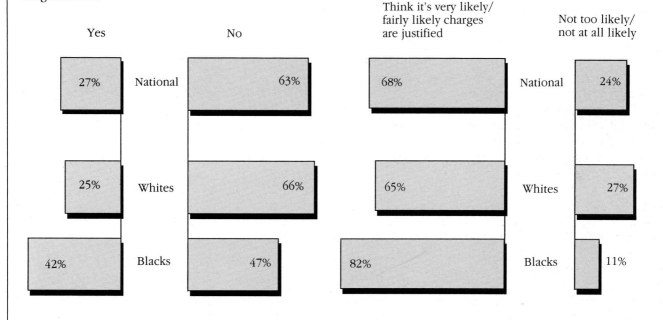

Yes    No

Think it's very likely/
fairly likely charges
are justified

Not too likely/
not at all likely

National    27%    63%    68%    National    24%

Whites    25%    66%    65%    Whites    27%

Blacks    42%    47%    82%    Blacks    11%

*Source: Survey by CBS News/New York Times, April 1-3, 1991, reprinted in The American Enterprise, July/August 1991.*

opinion, they tended to obscure the generally favorable view most people in Los Angeles (and elsewhere in the United States) hold about police officers. This more positive attitude was reflected in another *Los Angeles Times* poll released July 16, nearly a week after the Christopher Commission report was issued. Asked to rate the LAPD's performance in holding down crime "in your neighborhood," 65 percent of those surveyed said "very favorable" or "somewhat favorable." Moreover, the police received a "favorable" rating from majorities in each of the three population groups identified in the survey — Anglos, blacks and Latinos.

The recent *Los Angeles Times* poll corresponds to the findings of national opinion surveys conducted over the years. These indicate that police are generally perceived as honest and ethical. For instance, 37 percent of the respondents to a 1977 Gallup poll rated police honesty and ethical standards as "very high" or "high," while 12 percent said they were "low" or "very low." Responding to the same question in a 1990 Gallup poll, 49 percent answered "very high" or "high," and 9 percent said "low" or "very low." [12]

According to law enforcement experts, the public's antipathy to police brutality but its positive view of overall police behavior are not as contradictory as they may seem. Speaking from the perspective of a former police officer, Fyfe says: "I don't think the poll results are inconsistent, because a good part of the public wants the police to be brutal sometimes."

Fyfe cites the case of two police officers assigned to adjoining foot beats in Harlem in the mid-1960s. The two were frequently the subject of citizen complaints about minor physical abuse. Finally, the precinct captain shifted the officers to different beats pending an investigation. Within days, a group of citizens petitioned the captain to bring the pair back. "But these are the guys that people say are slapping people around," the captain said. "That's right," said one of the petition-bearers. "But they know *who* to slap around."

The moral of the story, as Fyfe sees it, is that "It's terrible for the police to be brutal, but if you have to be brutal to make the streets safe for me, it's not so bad." ∎

# BACKGROUND

## Law and Order

Organized law enforcement in the United States dates back barely 150 years. The first American police force was established in New York City in 1844 by an act of the state legislature. (Before then, large American cities had loosely organized systems for maintaining order, such as night watchmen. Texas established a state police force, the Texas Rangers, in 1835.) New York's original 800 policemen, identifiable only by their star-shaped copper badges (hence the nickname "cop"), were divided into a day shift and a night shift. Not long afterward, other large cities set up similar police forces — Chicago (1851); Cincinnati and New Orleans (1852); Philadelphia and Boston (1854); Newark and Baltimore (1857).

From that time to the present, policing has been largely a local responsibility. As the country's population grew, the trend in police organization was to establish new forces rather than to centralize or consolidate existing ones. Today there are more than 12,000 city, county and state police agencies.

The development of law enforcement in the American West may have laid the groundwork for the often uneasy police-community relations of today. "In many a frontier town in the West, the man with the fastest gun was made sheriff, to tame the other rowdies," historian Ralph Lee Smith wrote in *The Tarnished Badge*. "Many western lawmen were themselves lawbreakers, criminals, killers and fugitives. The old system of using criminals as 'thief-takers' enjoyed a new lease on life in the American West." [13]

Even in their infancy, big-city police forces often encountered citizen hostility and violence. The Civil War draft riots in New York City, for instance, had distinct anti-police overtones. With insufficient police or troops to cope with the situation, the city for several days in July 1863 was virtually given over to mobs. They wrecked the draft offices, invaded the arsenal, sacked the mayor's residence and looted and burned many stores. Blacks were beaten and killed. Before order could be restored, several police stations were burned to the ground.

### Police Corruption

Corruption, either by citizen bribes or through criminal interference, surfaced early on as a recurrent problem. In most Western towns in the 19th century, it was relatively easy to "buy" the sheriff. "This situation led straight to a close tie between crime and the police as Western settlements grew into modern cities," Smith observed. [14]

The extent of police corruption at the turn of the century was laid bare by the celebrated muckraking author Lincoln Steffens in *The Shame of the Cities,* a collection of articles written for *McClure's* magazine. One piece, focusing entirely on police scandals in Minneapolis, created a nationwide sensation.

The story began early in 1901, when physician Alfred Elisha Ames became mayor of Minneapolis. Ames "laid plans," Steffens wrote, "to turn the city over to outlaws." To this end, Ames dismissed 107 of the best officers on the 225-man police force, and those kept on the payroll were charged a fee for the privilege. Gambling, prostitution, pickpocketing and cardsharping were all organized under the detective bureau. Criminals from across the country came to Minneapolis to negotiate for "concessions" of one kind or another. A grand jury investigation in 1902 led to Ames' downfall. The scandals uncovered by the jury, shocking as they were, had their counterparts in other large cities of the time.

Matters did not improve much over the next quarter-century. Consider this account by social historian Robert M. Fogelson of typical big-city police of the 1920s: "Now and then, when pressure from reformers built up, they raided a joint or arrested a crook; but most of the time they kept out of sight and away from trouble. If they ran into a jam, they asked the ward leaders for help.... As the patrolmen well knew or soon found out, they were no match for an influential gambler, liquor dealer or other disreputable businessman, let alone a well organized, highly mobile, fully armed gang of criminals closely allied with the ward leader." [15]

## Police-Reform Movement

Even in the 1920s, however, police-reform sentiment was gathering force throughout the nation. A prime objective was to sever the ties between politicians and police that were seen as the wellspring of all the troubles plaguing urban law enforcement. The city charter adopted by Los Angeles in 1925 was hailed as a milestone in police reform. The charter (which is still in force) placed the police department under the control of a five-member Board of Police Commissioners appointed by the mayor. In addition to its function as "head" of the department, the Police Commission was given the power to name, discipline and remove the police chief.*

*Continued on p. 642*

*The commission's authority has since been undermined. In 1937, the Los Angeles police chief acquired civil service protection, which had the practical effect of giving the incumbent chief lifetime tenure. The chief cannot be suspended or removed except for "good and sufficient" cause based on an act or omission that occurred during the previous year. Furthermore, the commission must prove such cause exists in a hearing before the Board of Civil Service Commissioners.

# Chronology

## 1800s

*Cities across the country set up police departments, some of which soon become involved in corruption and clashes with the public.*

### 1844
The first modern American police force is established in New York City. Officers are identifiable only by their star-shaped copper badges, giving rise to the nickname "cop."

### 1894
A special committee of the New York state Senate investigates complaints of corruption in the New York City Police Department and is told that officers regularly obtain appointments and win promotions through political influence and cash payments.

———— • ————

## 1960s
*The Supreme Court hands down a series of decisions expanding the rights of criminal suspects and limiting police authority. Police handling of civil rights protests in the South and urban unrest in the North provokes criticism.*

### 1961-1966
Seven major Supreme Court decisions define the rights of criminal suspects in police custody. The best-known is *Miranda v. Arizona* (1966), which held that a suspect must be informed of his right to remain silent and of his right to have counsel present during interrogation and must be warned that anything he says may be held against him.

### May 3, 1963
Police in Birmingham, Ala., use high-pressure fire hoses and police dogs to repulse groups of black civil rights marchers, mostly high school and college students.

### June 20, 1968
President Lyndon B. Johnson signs into law the Crime Control and Safe Streets Act, which creates the Law Enforcement Assistance Administration. The agency allocated federal grants to state and local governments to help them upgrade their police forces.

### August 1968
Chicago law enforcement officers take part in what is later called a "police riot" to quell demonstrations during the Democratic National Convention. A panel that investigated the incident reports that some officers responded to provocation with "unrestrained and indiscriminate police violence . . . often inflicted upon persons who had broken no law, disobeyed no order, made no threat."

———— • ————

## 1980s
*As various federal courts grapple with the question of what constitutes excessive use of force by law enforcement officers, police departments begin to experiment with "community policing" programs.*

### 1983
Los Angeles Police Chief Daryl F. Gates and the Los Angeles Unified School District introduce DARE (Drug Abuse Resistance Education), a program taught in schools by police officers. Numerous communities across the country soon institute similar programs.

### 1985
U.S. Supreme Court strikes down a Tennessee statute that authorized the use of deadly force to apprehend a non-dangerous fleeing suspect *(Tennessee v. Garner)*. The court makes it clear that deadly force is to be used only when apprehending offenders who are known to be violent.

———— • ————

## 1990s
*The beating of a black motorist by white police in Los Angeles stirs nationwide concern about police brutality.*

### March 3, 1991
Rodney G. King, 25, is severely beaten by Los Angeles police officers after being stopped for a speeding violation. A videotape of the incident is shown repeatedly on television over the next few days.

### March 14, 1991
Four Los Angeles policemen are indicted by a grand jury in connection with the Rodney King beating.

### July 9, 1991
The Independent Commission on the Los Angeles Police Department (known as the Christopher Commission) condemns the repeated use of excessive force by a significant minority of police officers.

### July 11, 1991
U.S. Senate approves a comprehensive crime bill including a provision to set up a Police Corps that would provide law enforcement agencies with a steady supply of college-educated patrol officers.

### July 22, 1991
Los Angeles Police Chief Daryl F. Gates says he plans to retire in 1992.

*Continued from p. 640*

The police-reform movement was gaining strength elsewhere as well. One goal was to make officers measure up to professional standards. Until about 1930, amateurism and incompetence held sway. Most officers lacked even a high school education, received little training, earned low pay and remained on the force well beyond normal retirement age.

The most widely copied formula for police professionalism was the model used by Orlando Wilson when he was police chief of Wichita, Kan., from 1928 to 1939. Wilson advocated a clear-cut chain of command, specialization of tasks, delegation of authority and responsibility and close supervision of officers on patrol duty. He also stressed the importance of higher education and personal integrity for police officers. Law enforcement agencies nationwide remade themselves in the Wilsonian image in the 1930s, '40s and '50s, a period when crime rates were relatively low.

The nation's favorite police officer of the 1950s probably was the unflappable and thoroughly professional Sgt. Joe Friday of the LAPD, lead character of the weekly television series *Dragnet*. Friday's oft-repeated line, "All we want are the facts, Ma'am," became a national catch phrase.

At about that time, Fyfe says, people "came to believe, and so did the police, that the increased professionalism of the police was responsible for keeping crime rates low." Events were to show, however, that "the level of professionalism of the police didn't matter very much" in controlling crime or curbing the incidence of police misconduct.

### Misconduct Problems Persist

In 1961, a grand jury in Kansas City, Mo., reported that "Sometime in 1953 a 'deal' was made between the 'syndicate' and certain members

... of the police department which led to the 'syndicate' being permitted to operate a number of gambling and after-hours liquor establishments, control prostitution, and fence stolen merchandise." For its part, the syndicate "supposedly promised to commit no major robberies or burglaries within the city limits."

Chicago's police force became ensnarled in a major corruption scandal in 1960, when eight officers were arrested on charges of burglary; thousands of dollars' worth of loot was recovered from the homes of seven of them. In the ensuing uproar, Mayor Richard J. Daley announced the resignation of the police chief and the appointment of a five-man committee to designate a successor. The committee's choice: Orlando Wilson, then dean of the University of California School of Criminology.

During Wilson's seven years as Chicago police superintendent, the force acquired the reputation of being one of the most modern and efficient in the country. Both the organization and the operating methods of the department were thoroughly reformed. He established an Internal Investigation Division to root out corruption; doubled the number of civilians in clerical jobs, freeing up a thousand regular officers for patrol duty; and promoted racial integration of the department. Most significant of all, Wilson moved the superintendent's office in April 1960 from City Hall to police headquarters, symbolizing the divorce of police administration in Chicago from politics.

For the remainder of the 1960s, allegations of police misconduct in the United States focused mainly on brutality rather than corruption. Many of the charges stemmed from police mistreatment of civil rights demonstrators in the South, urban rioters and anti-war protesters. The

Chicago Police Department, fresh from its restructuring by Wilson, was not immune to attack. In 1968, several members of the Chicago force were indicted in connection with a "police riot" to quell demonstrations during the Democratic National Convention.[16]

## Rulings on Suspects' Rights

In 1968, President Lyndon B. Johnson signed into law the Crime Control and Safe Streets Act, which embodied a number of recommendations made the previous year by the President's Crime Commission. Title I of the act created the Law Enforcement Assistance Administration (LEAA) to help state and local governments upgrade their police forces. More controversial was Title II, which tried to soften the effects of several Supreme Court decisions in the 1960s on the rights of criminal suspects during police interrogation. *(See story, p. 643.)*

The LEAA survived for 14 years, dispensing almost $8 billion for everything from improved police equipment to shelters for homeless youths and special task forces to prosecute "career criminals." By the late 1970s, the agency had come under fire for generating too much red tape in its grant program and for wasting money on gadgetry of little actual use in reducing or preventing crime. The LEAA closed down in 1982.

The Supreme Court's rulings on suspects' rights remain in force, though subsequent decisions have modified them to some extent. When the earlier rulings were first handed down, some police officials expressed fear that they would make their job more difficult. Much of the criticism was directed at *Miranda v. Arizona* (1966), which held, in part, that a suspect must be told of his

# Key Supreme Court Decisions on Suspects' Rights

***Mallory v. U.S.*** (1957). A suspect must be taken before a magistrate as soon as possible after his arrest. Any "unnecessary delay" will invalidate a confession obtained from the accused person prior to his appearance before a magistrate. (The court nullified the death sentence imposed on Andrew Mallory, a young man who "confessed" to rape to Washington, D.C., police during a delay of more than 18 hours between his arrest and his arraignment.)

***Monroe v. Pape*** (1961). Any person whose constitutional rights have been violated by a police officer may bring the officer into federal court and sue him personally for damages. (James Monroe, a black handyman, claimed his apartment had been broken into by 13 Chicago police officers who had no arrest or search warrants and that he and his wife had been forced to stand naked while the apartment was ransacked. The court held that Monroe could sue the police officers as individuals but not the city.)

***Mapp v. Ohio*** (1961). Evidence may not be used in any court, state or federal, if collected in a search and seizure that is "unreasonable" under the Supreme Court's interpretation of the Fourth Amendment. (The court's decision reversed the conviction of Dollree Mapp, whose house had been entered without a search warrant by police looking for gambling materials. Instead, they found some obscene books, which were admitted as evidence in a trial that resulted in Mapp's conviction under an Ohio law that made it a crime to possess obscene literature.)

***Gideon v. Wainwright*** (1963). Any indigent person brought to court, state or federal, on a felony charge is entitled to have counsel appointed for him by the court. (The decision was elicited by a handwritten petition from Clarence Earl Gideon, a Florida State Prison inmate who had been convicted of breaking and entering a poolroom with intent to commit petty larceny. His appeals for a lawyer and for *habeas corpus* had been refused prior to his Supreme Court petition.)

***Massiah v. U.S.*** (1964). Incriminating statements obtained by federal agents from a person after he has been indicted but in the absence of his attorney cannot be used against him in federal courts. (The decision reversed the narcotics conviction of Winston Massiah, a seaman who had made incriminating statements to a co-defendant in a car in which a federal agent had hidden a listening device.)

***Malloy v. Hogan*** (1964). The bar to self-incrimination, set forth in the Fifth Amendment, applies to state as well as to federal courts. (William Malloy had refused, on the grounds that he might incriminate himself, to answer the questions of a Connecticut state investigator. His subsequent contempt conviction had been upheld by the Connecticut Supreme Court of Errors, whose decision was reversed by the U.S. Supreme Court.)

***Escobedo v. Illinois*** (1964). Any confession is inadmissible as evidence if the police have questioned the suspect without letting him see a lawyer and without warning him that he has a right to remain silent. (The decision was based on an appeal by Danny Escobedo, who had been arrested on suspicion of murder in Illinois. Police reportedly had not allowed his lawyer to see him until after he had confessed, and he reportedly had not been advised of his constitutional right to remain silent.)

***Miranda v. Arizona*** (1966). (1) A suspect must be informed of his right to remain silent and to have counsel present during interrogation and must be warned that anything he says may be held against him; (2) defense counsel must be provided if the suspect wants, but cannot afford, counsel; (3) the prosecution must prove that a suspect knowingly waived his rights if he confessed without counsel present; (4) prolonged interrogation must be construed as lack of such waiver; (5) if a suspect indicates "in any manner" that he wants to remain silent, even after starting to talk, questioning must end. (The decision reversed the conviction of Ernesto A. Miranda, who had confessed to rape under police interrogation in Phoenix. Retried for the same crime in 1967, Miranda was convicted on the basis of evidence unrelated to his confession.)

right to remain silent and to have counsel present during interrogation. Testifying before a subcommittee of the Senate Judiciary Committee a month after the decision was issued, special agent Alvin A. Dewey of the Kansas Bureau of Investigation said police officers who adhere to the *Miranda* guidelines "are really talking the defendant out of telling us anything."

In the intervening years, most police have learned to live with *Miranda* and the other decisions commonly lumped with it. Fyfe, in fact, takes the position that the rulings on suspects' rights have had a "beneficial effect" on police operations. He says they compelled U.S. police departments "to improve training regarding searches and interrogation — and that is a good thing."

## Excessive Force Rulings

During the 1970s and '80s, the Supreme Court and certain lower federal courts turned their attention to the question of what constitutes "excessive force" by police officers. (See story, p. 647.) In 1973, the 2nd U.S. Circuit Court of Appeals held in *Johnson v. Glick* that a determination of excessive force must depend on whether the amount of force used "shocks the conscience." [17]

Recognizing that it had laid down a rather vague standard and that excessive-force cases often were not clear-cut, the court went on to list four factors for courts to take into account: "(1) the need for the application of force, (2) the relationship between the need and the amount of force that was used, (3) the extent of injury inflicted and (4) whether the force was applied in a good-faith effort to maintain or restore discipline or maliciously and sadistically for the very purpose of causing harm." This formula has gained wide acceptance among federal appeals courts nationwide.

In *Tennessee v. Garner* (1985), the Supreme Court struck down a Tennessee statute that authorized the use of deadly force to apprehend a non-dangerous fleeing suspect. The case concerned the shooting and killing by a Memphis police officer of an unarmed 15-year-old fleeing from a house burglary. He had stolen two $5 bills and a purse. The use of deadly force in such circumstances, the court held, represented an "unreasonable seizure" under the Fourth Amendment.

Fyfe, who served as the Garner family's expert witness in *Tennessee v. Garner,* argued then and still believes the decision worked in police officers' favor. It did so, he says, by making it clear that deadly force was to be used only when apprehending offenders who were known to be violent. No longer would police have to decide whether to shoot at a fleeing suspect when lives were not at risk. Speaking of *Garner* and other rulings affecting police conduct, Fyfe says: "There's no evidence that

any decision of the U.S. Supreme Court has [adversely] affected public safety or the effectiveness of the police in any way whatsoever."

## Rodney King Case

The "excessive force" issue looms large, of course, in the Rodney King beating. In its report on that incident and the overall operation of the Los Angeles Police Department, the Christopher Commission found that "a significant number of officers in the LAPD . . . repetitively use excessive force against the public and persistently ignore the written guidelines of the department regarding force." [18] Those guidelines state, in part: "While the use of reasonable physical force may be necessary in situations which cannot be otherwise controlled, force may not be resorted to unless other reasonable alternatives have been exhausted or would clearly be ineffective under the particular circumstances. Officers are permitted to use whatever force . . . is reasonable and necessary to protect others or themselves from bodily harm."

The commission's reconstruction of the King beating was based largely on the videotape taken by George Holliday from his balcony. According to police, King was ordered out of his car after the high-speed chase and told to lie flat on the ground. Failing to do this to the police officers' satisfaction, he was struck twice by a Taser electric stun gun. When that didn't subdue him, he was beaten repeatedly with police batons. "Finally, after 56 baton blows and six kicks, five or six officers swarmed in and placed King in both handcuffs and cordcuffs restraining his arms and legs. King was dragged on his stomach to the side of the road to await arrival of a rescue ambulance." [19]

Significant though it was, the King beating served mainly as a starting point for the Christopher Commission's wide-ranging investigation into the LAPD. Among other things, the panel called attention to some of the messages transmitted over the department's Mobile Digital Terminal (MDT) system. This high-speed communications network links patrol cars not only to headquarters but also to each other through a computer terminal in each vehicle. Messages sent over the MDT system are stored on computers and thus can be reviewed long afterward, which is what Christopher Commission staffers did. In preparing the panel's report, they scanned all MDT messages between LAPD patrol cars for approximately 180 days during the period from November 1989 to February 1991.

Numerous messages bespoke a callous attitude toward suspects: "Capture him, beat him and treat him like dirt"; "What, did U beat another guy." The commission was troubled that police officers would readily put such thoughts on record, knowing as they did that the messages could be monitored far into the future. "The apparent confidence of these officers that nothing would be done about their inflammatory statements suggests a tolerance within the LAPD of attitudes condoning violence against the public." [20]

Other LAPD messages published in the commission's report betrayed contempt for racial and ethnic minorities, women and homosexuals. These messages attracted particular attention in the news media, given the circumstances of the King case: The suspect was black, while all the arresting officers were white. The messages lent substance to complaints by area minority groups of unfair treatment at the hands of the police.

To counteract the attitudes expressed in the second set of MDT

*Continued on p. 646*

# Two Cases: Did Police Use Excessive Force?

**Don Jackson** was riding in a car driven by a friend two years ago when they were stopped by police in Long Beach, Calif., allegedly for straddling traffic lanes. Jackson, 30, a police officer and a self-styled crusader against police brutality, had arranged beforehand to have a television camera crew following him in another car.

The tape the TV crew made, subsequently broadcast on NBC's "Today" program, showed Jackson, who is black, becoming involved in a heated exchange with officer Mark Dickey, who is white. It also showed the plate-glass window of a motorcycle shop breaking around Jackson as Dickey searched him. Some viewers thought the tape clearly showed Dickey shoving Jackson's head through the window.

Three days after the incident, the Long Beach City Council asked the Los Angeles County district attorney's office to investigate. Jackson, for his part, remained on stress-related disability leave from the police department in nearby Hawthorne, where he held the rank of sergeant. He was suing the department for harassment, alleging racism.

Initially, Jackson's "sting" operation appeared to be an unqualified victory for him. Dickey was charged with assault on the basis of the NBC tape. In addition, he and his partner, Officer Mark Ramsey, were charged with falsifying their police report on the incident. And the Long Beach city prosecutor dropped the resisting-arrest charges against Jackson.

But the final disposition of the case was less clear-cut. In November 1990 Long Beach city officials decided that Dickey, 29, and Ramsey, 28, were eligible to receive half of their pay for life because of stress-related disability.

Commenting on the Dickey-Ramsey settlement, the *Los Angeles Times* said in an editorial: "Half salaries for the two young officers will cost taxpayers more than $36,000 every year for decades. The very thought is outrageous. What sort of mixed message is Long Beach or any city sending in a case like this? How can such disability retirements not be seen by many as almost a reward for alleged police misconduct?" †

Dickey and Ramsey received more good news last May, when the criminal charges against them were dropped after a Long Beach Municipal Court jury split 11-1 in favor of acquittal. "The public has not gotten the message," Jackson said afterward. He characterized the mistrial as "an endorsement for police abuse, for racism," and said he probably would return to Long Beach to stage more stings.

The 11 jurors who voted for acquittal were influenced by a slow-motion version of the NBC tape of the Jackson-Dickey encounter. They concluded that Dickey did not deliberately push Jackson into the shop window and that Jackson broke the glass with his elbows, not his head.

**Arthur McDuffie**, a black insurance agent from Miami, died after a high-speed police chase 12 years ago. To this day, no one knows exactly what happened. After visiting a female friend, McDuffie headed home on his motorcycle

about 1 a.m. on Dec. 17, 1979. A police field report said the chase began when McDuffie ran a red light and sped away with the officers in hot pursuit. After about eight minutes, the report said, McDuffie lost control of the motorcycle and

**Arthur McDuffie**

was thrown to the ground. He suffered severe head injuries and died on Dec. 21 without regaining consciousness.

Ten days after the incident, the four white officers involved in the chase were suspended following an investigation. Arthur McDuffie's death, declared Bobby Jones, acting director of the Dade County Public Safety Department, "may have been caused by police instead of an accident."

The following day, manslaughter charges were filed against the four officers. Investigators charged that the four beat McDuffie with batons and flashlights and that they smashed his motorcycle with their clubs to make his injuries appear to be the result of a traffic accident. The victim's skull was "cracked like an egg" by "long, heavy, blunt objects," said Ronald Wright, the chief deputy medical examiner. "This was a melee." (Police records showed that the four officers had each been named in numerous misconduct complaints.)

Because of the intense media coverage in the Miami area, the trial of the four officers was shifted to Tampa, more than 200 miles away. Wright testified that the blows suffered by McDuffie were equivalent to falling from a four-story building and that McDuffie's brain damage was the worst he had seen in 3,600 autopsies.

On May 17, 1980, after only two hours and 45 minutes of deliberation, an all-white jury found the four defendants not guilty. Within hours, violent protests broke out in black Miami neighborhoods, especially Liberty City. For the next three days, the city was wracked by violence, arson and looting that left 18 persons dead and more than 300 injured. The rioting also led to some 1,000 arrests and caused property damage estimated at $100 million.

Some good did come of the McDuffie tragedy. Responding to the recommendations of state and local task forces, police departments in the Miami area took steps to improve their procedures, attitudes and community relations. Changes also were made in the recruitment, selection and training of police officers, including the promotion of minority officers to command-level positions.

---

† *Los Angeles Times,* Nov. 29, 1990.

*Continued from p. 644*

messages, the commission recommended changes in the training of new officers. At present, the training curriculum includes an eight-hour cultural-awareness class in which minority-group representatives instruct recruits about cultural differences. Eight hours is "insufficient," the commission said, since no more than 1½ hours is spent on any one ethnic group.

Of the structural changes proposed by the commission, the most controversial was a recommendation that the police chief serve a five-year term, renewable for only one additional term. The panel also urged that the power to appoint the police chief be shifted to the mayor from

the Police Commission and that the chief's civil service protection be eliminated.

Declaring that the current system of handling complaints against the police "does not work," the commission prescribed a major overhaul. It ruled out proposals for a civilian complaint review board on the ground that such an approach might encourage police officers to adopt an "us against them" attitude. Instead, it recommended a "civilian oversight process" under the aegis of the existing Police Commission. To this end, the panel said the Police Commission should establish an Office of the Inspector General to track complaints and any resulting disciplinary action. ■

would also have to take a look at the arsenals of weapons police have at their disposal," she adds, "and [learn] how and when they are used and what the policies are for their use."

High-level opposition to some parts of the Christopher Commission reform package already has surfaced. A City Council committee headed by Councilman Richard Alatorre recently rejected the proposal to have the mayor name future police chiefs. The committee also turned down a recommendation that Police Commission decisions be exempted from City Council review. On June 4, Los Angeles voters approved a city charter amendment giving the council authority to override the actions of municipal commissions — including the Police Commission.

In contrast to the council's foot-dragging, the King incident has brought high-profile action on other fronts. After many weeks of resisting demands that he step down, Police Chief Gates announced July 22 that he will retire next April, provided a successor has been selected by then. "Maybe [my retirement] will stop all the nonsense that's been going on," Gates said in a videotaped message to his 8,300 troops.

Preparations for prosecuting the four police officers directly involved in the King beating are under way, too. All have been charged with assault with a deadly weapon likely to cause great bodily injury and one count of unnecessary assault or beating by a police officer. Three of the officers were also charged with inflicting great bodily injury; two were charged with filing a false police report; and one was charged with being an accessory after the fact, for allegedly trying to cover up his own involvement and that of other officers.

The defendants scored a preliminary victory in July, when a state appellate court ordered the trial to take place outside of Los Angeles County. "There is a substantial probability

# CURRENT SITUATION

## Fallout From King Incident

Today, two months after the Christopher Commission's study, its recommendations are in limbo. The Los Angeles City Council is debating putting some of the proposals before the voters in a 1992 referendum. But a number of observers are pessimistic over the prospects for meaningful reform.

One skeptic is Karol Heppe, executive director of the Police Misconduct Lawyers Referral Service, a Los Angeles-based organization that advises victims of police abuse about their rights. The Christopher Commission report was "more than we expected," Heppe says, but she still regards it as "a watering down" of citizen demands and fears it is "going to be watered down still further." She also thinks it likely that

"many of the reforms are never going to take place."

Heppe is especially disappointed that the commission did not urge the creation of an independent civilian review board. She advocates a review board that would have authority to make recommendations for disciplinary action against police officers and have independent investigators of its own to look into complaints. "Most civilian review boards have to rely on the police to investigate themselves," she says, "and we think that's part of the problem."

Heppe also sees the need for "an independent prosecutor who will take the responsibility to prosecute police officers." The district attorney has a "built-in conflict of interest," she says, because he has to rely on police officers to testify in court on the government's behalf.

Finally, Heppe calls for the "demilitarization" of the LAPD — shifting "the paramilitary-style training that recruits go through now" to a "more community-oriented" approach emphasizing verbal skill as a tool for defusing disputes. "You

# Controlling the Use of Force

Controlling the use of force — especially deadly force — has always been one of the most difficult tasks facing any police department. And the problem is not limited to the discharge of firearms. As the International Association of Chiefs of Police and the U.S. Bureau of Justice Assistance point out, "uses of force may range from verbal persuasion or coercion ... to the use of ... more aggressive measures involving baton, stun gun, Taser, tear gas or other nonlethal equipment." †

Regardless of the type of force employed, the rule of thumb is that no more of it should be applied than is needed to deal with the situation at hand. This is the approach generally favored in departmental policy statements and in court decisions and state laws on the subject. Obviously, no single formula can cover every situation that a police officer might encounter in the line of duty. In some instances, a few soothing words will suffice to cool off a domestic dispute. But at a time when big-city drug dealers are armed with automatic weapons and do not hesitate to commit "drive-by" shootings, police officers are clamoring for bulletproof vests and advanced weaponry of their own.

A typical police department policy on the use of force holds that officers *shall not* (1) fire warning shots; (2) draw or point their weapons at unarmed persons suspected of misdemeanors; (3) fire at or from moving vehicles; (4) fire at an escaping or fleeing felon if the person is known to the officer as a juvenile (unless the individual poses a deadly threat to others); or (5) fire at an escaping or fleeing felon if the felony committed is a non-forcible property crime (unless the individual poses a deadly threat to others).

These guidelines generally are applicable everywhere in the United States, though differences in state law should always be taken into account.

As a general rule in most states, police officers may legally apply lethal force *as a last resort* in these situations: (1) self-defense against threatened death; (2) self-defense against great bodily harm; (3) prevention of the unlawful killing of another; (4) prevention of unlawful great bodily harm to another; (5) prevention of the commission of a felony; (6) apprehension of a fleeing felon; (7) overcoming of fierce resistance to arrest; (8) prevention of a felon's escape; (9) recapture of an escaped or fleeing felon; or (10) suppression of a riot.

Violation of departmental regulations or state law on the use of deadly force exposes an officer to a variety of sanctions ranging in severity from departmental discipline to civil or criminal action in a local, state or federal court. Indeed, depending upon circumstances, the officer may be found culpable by more than one tribunal. The most common action taken against police officers who have used deadly force is a civil suit initiated by the survivor or his family, or by innocent parties inadvertently injured during the incident.

† Joint policy statement issued January 1989, published in International Association of Chiefs of Police, *Project Response: IACP Responds to the Police Brutality Issue,* May 1991.

---

Los Angeles County is so saturated with knowledge of the incident, so influenced by the political controversy surrounding the matter and so permeated with preconceived opinions that potential jurors cannot try the case solely upon the evidence presented in the courtroom," the California 2nd District Court of Appeal said in its decision.*

---

*The move to a different jurisdiction will be the first in almost 20 years for a Los Angeles County criminal trial. Ordinarily, defense requests for a change of venue are rejected on the ground that the county has such a large number of potential jurors — some 6½ million — that pretrial questioning surely can produce 12 unbiased ones. Thus, such notorious criminal defendants as Charles Manson, the "Night Stalker" (Richard Ramirez), the "Hillside Strangler" (Angelo Buono Jr.) and the alleged McMartin Preschool child molesters all were tried in Los Angeles County despite heavy pretrial media coverage.

The King case, meanwhile, has prompted some LAPD housecleaning. To curb abuse of its patrol-car communications system, the department set out to identify and discipline the officers who sent the offensive personal messages cited by the Christopher Commission. Message traffic over the computer network reportedly has declined by about 25 percent since the crackdown began.

The LAPD also made personnel changes in its Foothill Division, where the King beating occurred. The number of black patrol officers assigned to the division increased from 10 to 16, and the number of Hispanic patrol officers rose from 39 to 46. At the same time, the number of white patrol officers fell from 121 to 98. "What we're after," said Deputy Police Chief Mark A. Kroeker, "is a sensitizing to the demographics of the service population." [21]

## Police Corps Proposal

The objectives cited by Kroeker appear compatible with those of the omnibus crime bill now pending in Congress. The Senate version of the bill, approved July 11, aims to reduce violent crime by raising the number of police with advanced education and training assigned to community patrol and providing educational aid to students intending to become police officers. The Senate-passed bill also would establish a $30 million grant program under the Justice Department for tuition aid to law enforcement personnel and correctional officers seeking college degrees.*

The most controversial police-related provision of the bill calls for setting up a Police Corps, a concept modeled on both the Reserve Officers' Training Corps (ROTC) and the Peace Corps. Successful applicants would receive college scholarships worth up to $7,500 a year, with an overall limit of $30,000. In return, students would have to serve four years in a state or local police department. Failure to serve the full term would obligate the student to repay the scholarship in full.

The Police Corps idea originated with Adam Walinsky, a New York lawyer and former aide to the late Sen. Robert F. Kennedy, D-N.Y. James Fyfe, for one, fervently supports the proposal, arguing that "education serves to make people more well-rounded," and "we need well-rounded individuals to be police officers." [22]

The chief benefit of a Police Corps, Fyfe believes, would come from making law enforcement officers more representative of the citizenry they serve. At present, the police "really don't reflect the composition of our society, especially in terms of social class. My students [at American University] are privileged kids, and virtually none of them considers a police career a viable option. That's terrible. One thing we need to do is gentrify the police a little bit."

Fyfe waves aside the criticism that Police Corps members will go on to more lucrative pursuits as soon as their four-year terms are over. In his opinion, that really makes no difference. He says the important thing is that Police Corps members, much like the Army draftees of old, will undergo an experience that will remain with them through life. What Police Corps enlistees learn first-hand about crime and justice, he feels, could well translate into more meaningful support for the police in future years. "The war on drugs would be a whole lot more sophisticated," Fyfe says by way of example, "if a few of the people who debate what to do about it had spent a little time as undercover drug cops in Chicago."

Still, many police officials oppose the Police Corps concept, in part because they consider it a rebuke to today's police officers. Robert Scully of the National Association of Police Organizations testified against proposed Police Corps legislation two years ago, and his views have not changed. Police departments nationwide are hobbled by hiring freezes and layoffs, he notes, so money earmarked for the Police Corps "could be much better used for maintaining and training police officers who are already on the force and have chosen law enforcement as a career."

Scully also faults Police Corps proponents for encouraging "kids right out of high school" to make a career decision. "These are kids 18, 19 years old," he says. "Most of them can't even decide where they want to go to college. And you're asking them to make a career decision to become a police officer!" Instead of "looking for people who want to make law enforcement a part-time job to pay for an education," Scully says, "we should be looking for people who are dedicated to crime-fighting [and] who want to be here for the long run." ∎

# OUTLOOK

## Community Policing

Whether or not it becomes a reality, the Police Corps idea dovetails with what many experts see as the wave of the future in American law enforcement. Usually called "community policing," it seeks to involve members of the community in carrying out the police mission.

One part of the community-policing agenda calls for increasing the number of officers walking a beat — the preferred mode of crime-prevention in many urban areas until about half a century ago. One reason for the shift from foot patrols to cruisers was that many beat officers were taking payoffs on duty. Another reason was budgetary — fewer officers could cover more territory in a motor vehicle. Today, with the 911 system for emergency calls in operation almost everywhere, big-city police spend much of their time rushing from one crime scene to another.

Nowhere has the vehicle-based, reactive approach to policing been embraced more enthusiastically than in Los Angeles. Among other innovations, the LAPD pioneered the use of paramilitary Special Weapons and Tactics (SWAT) teams, helicopters and motorized battering rams. The department's wide array of vehicles and support equipment enables it to respond to reported crimes rapidly and in impressive force. At the same time, though, police officers have come to be viewed by many Los Angeles residents as alien figures who show up in the neighborhood only when trouble does.

Ironically, one of the nation's

Continued on p. 650

---

*The House Judiciary Subcommittee on Crime and Criminal Justice approved a draft crime bill on July 31. The full Judiciary Committee is expected to take up the measure after the House reconvenes in September.

*"Community policing" also is referred to by other names, including "positive policing."

# At Issue:

## Would a Police Corps lead to improved law enforcement?

**REP. ROBERT K. DORNAN**

*Republican U.S. Representative from California*
FROM A HEARING OF THE HOUSE JUDICIARY
COMMITTEE, NOV. 2, 1989

*t*he Police Corps is an idea whose time has come. . . . [It] will establish opportunities for meaningful community service with a police department in exchange for a college education. But as worthy as that goal may be, in my mind the Police Corps is necessary for one overriding reason: We need more "cops on the beat" on American streets, especially in our major cities, which as we all know have been torn apart by the drug trade and the crime drugs breed.

If we are going to make a commitment to put more cops on the beat, then we should seek to attract the most qualified candidates to fill those positions. And as the Police Corps' candidate-selection process is designed to be very competitive, we can be reasonably certain to attract excellent people. . . .

[T]his in no way implies that our current crop of police officers is anything but a well-trained, highly motivated and caring group of professionals. It is merely recognizing that our law-enforcement officials need to keep pace with the growing sophistication of criminals. For instance, the FBI used to accept high school graduates as trainees. Now they accept only college graduates, and if those graduates are not lawyers or accountants, they must have three years of administrative work experience before they can become agents. We need that same commitment to improving the educational excellence of our local and state police. . . .

[T]here is a national crisis in recruiting police personnel. In one department after another, massive retirements are expected . . . and many departments are already scrambling to replace retirees. When it is up and running, the Police Corps will help plug this manpower gap by putting 25,000 college-educated police on the streets each year.

After four years, this means we will increase the number of police on America's streets by about 20 percent. And because graduates would be placed almost exclusively on foot patrol and not added to police bureaucracies, the corps should increase cops on the front lines by about 40 percent. Most of these extra cops will be in our highest crime areas. And they are desperately needed, especially when you consider how the demands on the job have changed.

**ROBERT SCULLY**

*President, National Association of
Police Organizations*
FROM *THE NEW YORK TIMES,* JUNE 25, 1990.

*t*he Police Corps bill . . . is a misconceived proposal that would do nothing to advance law enforcement or educational policy. Under the plan, high school students would receive $40,000 in college loans, which would be forgiven by the federal government if they served as police officers for four years after college graduation. . . .

A major assumption underlying the Police Corps proposal is that there is a national problem in recruiting qualified police officers. While we agree that in certain areas in which police wages are low it is difficult to find qualified officers, in others there are far more qualified applicants than there are positions. For example, Detroit's Mayor Coleman Young . . . ordered the layoff of 500 highly qualified police officers for budgetary reasons. And in New York City, Mayor David N. Dinkins imposed a moratorium on hiring new police officers. Police Corps graduates could not be hired under these circumstances. And even where there is a shortage of officers, improved police compensation would quickly succeed in solving the problem.

Another assumption of the proposal is that college graduates entering police service for four years after graduation would contribute to the quality of police protection and service. But it is usually only after at least four years that police officers are considered to have enough seasoning not to be prone to errors of inexperience. The departure of Police Corps members after four years would forfeit their best potential years of service. True career officers could not be expected to give the kind of support to short-term "cadets" that they normally provide to new recruits.

The idea that the corps would be a cheaper way of providing police protection because Police Corps recruits would be gone after four years is also wrongheaded. Under the proposal pending in Congress, recruits would receive the same benefits as other officers. That they would not be around to collect a pension would not mean that pension contributions would not be made in their behalf. We need better trained and educated police officers, but on-the-job experience and training are more important in police work than a college degree.

Continued from p. 648
most successful community-policing programs was introduced by the LAPD. Police Chief Gates and the Los Angeles Unified School District began the Drug Abuse Resistance Education (DARE) program in 1983. DARE, which is taught in schools by police officers, has been adopted by communities across the country.

The Christopher Commission paid tribute to the DARE program and urged the LAPD to approach policing in the same spirit. "LAPD officers are encouraged to command and to confront, not to communicate," the panel stated. "Community policing concepts, if successfully implemented, offer the prospect of effective crime prevention and substantially improved community relations." The department, it added, "must gain an adequate understanding of what is important to particular communities."

Beyond Los Angeles, clashes between police officers and neighborhood residents have been traced to mutual misunderstandings that a community-policing program might have cleared up. Miami was torn repeatedly by racial disorders in the 1980s. In the process, animosity between the city's Cuban-American and black communities came to light. To uncover the causes of the ill-feeling, researchers Geoffrey P. Alpert and Roger G. Dunham examined how Miami's different ethnic communities view the police.

They found that residents of Cuban-American neighborhoods generally agree that "the responsibility for crime control rests mainly with the police."[23] These attitudes are held even by the *Marielitos,* the lower-class Cuban immigrants who came to Miami in the 1980 boatlift.

Residents of Miami's black neighborhoods, on the other hand, are "much more negative and suspi-cious toward the police than the Cubans." Alpert and Dunham surmised that the blacks they interviewed do not regard police as "agents of social control" but rather as "representatives of the majority class."[24]

Ethnically tinged views about the police also surfaced after an outburst of violence this spring in a Washington, D.C., neighborhood heavily populated by blacks and Hispanics. The trouble erupted after a black female police officer attempted to arrest and handcuff a Hispanic man who had disregarded her order to stop drinking in public. Hispanic residents later complained that Washington's police force, which is about two-thirds black, is insensitive to their culture. Drinking out of doors is an acceptable practice in much of Latin America, these residents said, and assigning a female police officer to handcuff a Hispanic man could be taken as an insult.

Community policing is designed to detect and defuse misunderstandings like these. Under the model proposed by Alpert and Dunham, officers would be assigned to a neighborhood for an extended period, supervised by command staff and advised by neighborhood groups. The aim is to reduce isolation between police and the residents they serve. Other elements of the program include frequent contacts between police and neighborhood groups as well as improved police training, feedback mechanisms and a reward system pegged to crime prevention.

### Implementation Problems

According to the Police Foundation's Hubert Williams, community policing is the "most promising" new concept in law enforcement to emerge thus far "because it's consistent with our democratic system of government — where the people have the ultimate say." But shifting from a military-type structure to a neighborhood-based system could be jarring for veteran officers. Williams points out that the typical U.S. police department is "an authoritarian system where orders come down from the command hierarchy to the officer on the beat." The officer "is controlled largely by a dispatch system that tells him where to go and how to handle the complaint. He's also told that he's got to get back on the air as soon as possible. He doesn't have time to get to the underlying causes of the incidents he investigates."

Under the community-policing concept, by contrast, officers are expected "to interact with community representatives or to try to arrange multi-party involvement" in resolving disputes. In short, Williams says, "community-oriented policing requires the officer of the future to have greater discretion and to work with the citizens he is sworn to protect in a collaborative way."

Though the transition to community policing may prove rocky, Fyfe feels the outcome will make the effort worthwhile. "If the cop is part of

> The main obstacle to the spread of community policing is likely to be cost. Given today's economic climate, few communities may be prepared to make the necessary outlays for retraining and additional officers.

the community and becomes a fixture there, it's good for him because he begins to see the neighborhood as more than just a bunch of people who call him when there's trouble. And it's good for the residents because the cop becomes a trusted institution."

Some officers feel community policing has been oversold as a crime-prevention measure. Consider this harsh appraisal by Sgt. John Karshner of the Houston Police Department, which pioneered the concept: "Neighborhood policing is a fallacy. It sounds real good, but it can't work, and it has significantly contributed to bad morale here. It's a silly, pseudo-scientific philosophy rife with inconsistencies and half-truths." [25]

The main obstacle to the spread of community policing is likely to be cost. Because of its stress on police interaction with neighborhood groups, an effective community-policing program probably would require the hiring of additional officers as well as the retraining of those already on the force. Given today's economic climate, few communities may be prepared to make the necessary outlays. As always, such decisions ultimately are made by individual citizens. Police officials, knowing full well where the buck stops, are fond of pointing out that the public can have the police protection it is willing to pay for. ■

# Notes

[1] Thornburgh resigned effective Aug. 15 to run for the Pennsylvania Senate seat of the late Sen. John Heinz, who died April 4 when his helicopter collided with a light plane. The Justice Department review of police brutality complaints is still in progress. There is no deadline for completion.

[2] Independent Commission on the Los Angeles Police Department, *Report of the Independent Commission on the Los Angeles Police Department,* July 9, 1991, p. i. The Scottsboro case concerned nine black youths convicted of raping two young white women in Alabama. The belief that the case against them was unproved and that the verdicts were the result of anti-black prejudice in Alabama brought the case national attention. The U.S. Supreme Court reversed the convictions twice on procedural grounds. At the second trial, one of the girls recanted her previous testimony. In 1937, charges against five of the men were dropped and the state agreed to consider parole for the others. Three were freed in the 1940s. When the fourth escaped to Michigan in 1948, the state refused to return him. In the Serpico case in New York City, Detective Frank Serpico was a leading witness in the corruption probe by the Knapp Commission, which reported in 1972 that high police officials did nothing after learning that some officers were suspected murderers, extortionists and heroin dealers.

[3] Diane K. Shah (interviewer), "Playboy Interview: Daryl Gates," *Playboy,* August 1991, p. 60.

[4] Independent Commission, *op. cit.,* p. 132.

[5] Quoted in *USA Today,* March 12, 1991.

[6] *Los Angeles Times,* July 7, 1991.

[7] *The Washington Post,* Aug. 18, 1991.

[8] Edwin J. Delattre, *Character and Cops: Ethics in Policing* (1989), p. 189.

[9] Quoted in *The New York Times,* Sept. 2, 1990.

[10] Geoffrey P. Alpert and Roger G. Dunham, *Policing Multi-Ethnic Neighborhoods: The Miami Study and Findings for Law Enforcement in the United States* (1988), p. 140.

[11] Independent Commission, *op. cit.,* p. 36.

[12] Responses were similar in Gallup surveys conducted in 1981, 1983, 1985 and 1988.

[13] Ralph Lee Smith, *The Tarnished Badge* (1965), p. 9.

[14] *Ibid.,* p. 10.

[15] Robert M. Fogelson, *Big City Police* (1977), p. 51.

[16] The "police riot" charge was contained in a Dec. 1, 1968, report by a special panel of the National Commission on the Causes and Prevention of Violence. The report asserted that some Chicago officers had responded to provocation by demonstrators with "unrestrained and indiscriminate police violence . . . often inflicted upon persons who had broken no law, disobeyed no order, made no threat."

[17] The "shocks-the-conscience" standard was first propounded by the U.S. Supreme Court in the 1952 case *Rochin v. California.*

[18] Independent Commission, *op. cit.,* p. iii.

[19] *Ibid.,* p. 7.

[20] *Ibid.,* p. 54.

[21] Quoted in the *Los Angeles Times,* July 22, 1991.

[22] Testimony before the House Judiciary Subcommittee on Crime, Nov. 2, 1989.

[23] Alpert and Dunham, *op. cit.,* p. 121.

[24] *Ibid.,* p. 125.

[25] Quoted by John F. Persinos, "The Return of Officer Friendly," *Governing,* August 1989, p. 59.

# Bibliography

## Selected Sources Used

### Books

**Alpert, Geoffrey P., and Dunham, Roger G.,** *Policing Multi-Ethnic Neighborhoods: The Miami Study and Findings for Law Enforcement in the United States,* **Greenwood Press, 1988.**

Seeking the underlying causes of the police-citizen violence that plagued Miami in the 1980s, Alpert and Dunham found that members of the local black and Cuban-American communities hold sharply opposing ideas about law enforcement. The authors also propose a community-policing program that they feel would help defuse Miami's explosive tensions.

**Delattre, Edwin J.,** *Character and Cops: Ethics in Policing,* **American Enterprise Institute for Public Policy Research, 1989.**

Although Delattre includes a broad historical overview of law enforcement in the United States and takes a close look at such perennial problems as corruption and the use of deadly force, the main focus of his book is on moral issues and personal character. "That we cannot entirely accomplish our purposes — that the mission of the police cannot be fully realized — is no reason for despair or cynicism," he concludes.

**Fogelson, Robert M.,** *Big-City Police,* **Harvard University Press, 1977.**

This is a detailed historical study of professional policing in the United States, with particular emphasis on the reform movement that began in the late 19th century and never has really ended.

**Geller, William A., ed.,** *Police Leadership in America: Crisis and Opportunity,* **Praeger, 1985.**

This collection of essays, organized under eight general headings, concentrates on the role of the police chief in modern law enforcement. In some sections, the lead essay is followed by a response — and occasionally even by a rejoinder to the response.

**Trautman, Neal E.,** *Law Enforcement Training,* **Charles C. Thomas, 1986.**

Intended mainly for law enforcement professionals, this manual stresses the importance of training as a legal shield against citizen allegations of police misconduct. "Training in itself cannot eliminate or drastically reduce the number of civil suits brought against law-enforcement agencies," Trautman writes. "It can, however, greatly reduce the potential for awarding large financial damages."

### Articles

**Shah, Diane K. (interviewer), "Playboy Interview: Daryl Gates,"** *Playboy,* **August 1991.**

This interview, conducted before the King beating, was updated by three conversations that took place after the incident. On the printed page, Gates comes across not only as blunt and occasionally tactless but also as proud and supportive of his officers.

**Freyermuth, R. Wilson, "Rethinking Excessive Force,"** *Duke Law Journal,* **September 1987.**

Freyermuth explores the Supreme Court's evolving position on what constitutes excessive force by concentrating on two decisions — *Tennessee v. Garner* (1985) and *Whitley v. Albers* (1986). He also discusses a number of relevant U.S. appeals court decisions on the issue.

### Reports and Studies

**Independent Commission on the Los Angeles Police Department,** *Report of the Independent Commission on the Los Angeles Police Department,* **July 9, 1991.**

This report would not have been issued without the Rodney King beating as a trigger. In turn, as the commission notes here, the King beating might well have gone unnoticed except for the videotape taken by George Holliday, a civilian onlooker: "[W]ithout the Holliday videotape the complaint might have been adjudged to be 'not sustained,' because the officers' version [of the beating] conflicted with the account by King and his two passengers, who typically would have been viewed as not 'independent.'"

**International Association of Chiefs of Police,** *Project Response: IACP Responds to the Police Brutality Issue,* **May 1991.**

This collection of position papers and model policies was issued in response to the King beating and the interest it aroused in what constitutes reasonable force by a police officer making an arrest.

**U.S. House Subcommittee on Crime, Committee on the Judiciary,** *The Police Corps Act* **(published proceedings of hearing held Nov. 2, 1989).**

Supporters and opponents of an ROTC-like Police Corps spar in this hearing on the merits of legislation to create such an institution. The 1989 measure got nowhere, but a slightly modified version has been folded into this year's omnibus crime bill.

# The Next Step

## Additional Articles from Current Periodicals

### Actions & defenses

**Fried, J. H., "5 officers charged with murder in slaying of a suspect in Queens," *The New York Times*, March 21, 1991, p. A1.**

Says that five New York City police officers were arraigned on murder charges in the death of Federico Pereira, 21, a car-theft suspect who was punched, kicked, and strangled as he was being arrested. This is the latest in a string of accusations of brutality to be made against New York City officers in recent years.

**Sullivan, R., "Jury awards $2 million to man beaten by police," *The New York Times*, April 19, 1991, p. B1.**

Reports that a Manhattan jury awarded $2 million to Leroy Williams, a 36-year-old truck driver, whom it found had been beaten by Port Authority officers in 1984. The verdict was meant to both penalize the Port Authority of New York and New Jersey and to send a message to police departments that such brutality will no longer be tolerated.

### Case studies

**"Beating crime," *Economist*, March 23, 1991, p. 28.**

Discusses how the videotaped beating of Rodney King by four officers of the Los Angeles police continues to grow as a national issue. Announcements from then-U.S. Attorney General Dick Thornburgh; Los Angeles Police Chief Daryl Gates; Los Angeles Mayor Tom Bradley.

**"More hardball ahead," *Time*, April 8, 1991, p. 33.**

Addresses the Los Angeles policemen accused in the videotaped beating of Rodney King and the repercussions of their act. Pleaded not guilty; reports of taunting King in the hospital; demand for resignation of Police Chief Daryl Gates; prevention of further brutality.

**Baker, J. N., Wright, L., et al., "Los Angeles aftershocks," *Newsweek*, April 1, 1991, p. 18.**

Reports that the impact of the recent video showing Rodney King being brutally beaten by Los Angeles police is being felt in courts and precinct houses across the country. How a transcript of dialogue among officers has made the drama even more chilling; the Justice Department's sweeping national investigation of police brutality; listing of disclosures piling up at the LAPD; image problem.

**Brady, D. and Gregor, A., "The LAPD video," *Maclean's*, April 1, 1991, p. 42.**

Discusses reaction to an amateur videotape showing several Los Angeles police officers brutally beating a black man, Rodney King, who had been stopped for speeding. The Los Angeles Police Department (LAPD) also released police-radio tape recordings of the incident. Plumbing supplier George Holliday captured the beating on videotape; debate over police brutality in the United States and Canada; calls for the resignation of Los Angeles Police Chief Daryl Gates.

**Contreras, J., "Cracking heads in South Africa," *Newsweek*, Sept. 17, 1990, p. 43.**

Reports on the continued fighting in South Africa, especially last week when soldiers in Sebokeng township opened fire with live rounds on a crowd of angry hostel dwellers during a factional clash. Government's final recognition that it has a problem with police brutality; skepticism over what President F. W. de Klerk preaches in public and says in private; African National Congress leader Nelson Mandela's response to the incident.

**Gonzalez, D., R. Blumenthal, et al., "In officers' murder case, a tangle of contradictions," *The New York Times*, March 24, 1991, p. 1.**

Details controversy surrounding a struggle New York City police had with Federico Pereira that led to his death. The police involved have been indicted on murder charges. Effects of police brutality in a Los Angeles case; lack of video footage in the Queens case; deepening controversy.

**McKinley, J. C. Jr., "Debate over police review board heats up while complaints fall," *The New York Times*, March 27, 1991, p. A1.**

Says that New Yorkers are filing far fewer complaints alleging police brutality and misconduct, but this trend has intensified rather than dissolved the debate about brutality and the board that investigates it. Statistics on complaints.

**Morganthau, T. and Katel, P., "Looking for a place in the sun," *Newsweek*, Dec. 17, 1990, p. 32.**

Describes polyethnicity in South Florida that has Miami's many ethnic groups fighting for power. Puerto Ricans in the Wynwood community feeling outnumbered and ignored; descriptions of fighting; rage over police brutality and Hispanic hostility; incident in which suspected crack dealer Leonardo "Cano" Mercado was beaten and kicked to death by six police officers; the trial and acquittal of the police; how the tragedy has triggered more violence.

**Mydans, S., R. Stevenson, et al., "Videotape of beating by officers puts full glare on brutality issue," The New York Times, March 18, 1991, p. A1.**

Presents a special report on police brutality in Los Angeles on March 3, in which Rodney King, a black man, was beaten and kicked for nearly two minutes. Details of the incident; videotape; police chief's views questioned; steady increase in lawsuits over the years.

**Prud'Homme, A., Booth, C., et al., "Police brutality!" Time, March 25, 1991, p. 16.**

Describes the nationwide reaction to the television screening of a videotape record of Los Angeles policemen taking turns kicking an unarmed black man and smashing him in the head, neck, kidneys and legs with their truncheons. While a helicopter bathed the scene in a floodlight, 11 other policemen watched, and Rodney King, 25, suffered 11 fractures in his skull, a broken ankle, and some brain damage. Nationwide debate over excessive police violence.

**Sullivan, R., "Prosecuting police: New unit, new cases," The New York Times, April 4, 1991, p. B1.**

Tells about the Official Corruption Unit, a special unit that has been created in New York City to investigate and prosecute police misconduct cases, including accusations of brutality and corruption. Increase of cases since the videotaped incident in Los Angeles; more distance between investigators and police.

**Suro, R., "3 ex-policemen are convicted in Texas killing," The New York Times, May 4, 1990, p. A1.**

Reports that three former police officers, all of them white, were found guilty of murdering Loyal Garner Jr., 34, a black truck driver, who was severely beaten in an East Texas jail more than two years ago in a case that provoked sharp racial tensions in the region.

**Taliaferro, J. and Murr, A., "After police brutality: L.A.'s identity crisis," Newsweek, May 20, 1991, p. 32.**

Examines how the brutal police beating of Rodney King in Los Angeles has exposed the city's troubles. What is wrong with L.A. involves its structure under a reform-era system that divides power among the mayor, City Council and department heads protected by civil service; Roland Coleman of the Southern California Civil Rights Coalition; laws that barred Mayor Tom Bradley from firing Police Chief Daryl Gates; Rep. Maxine Waters.

**Turque, B., Buckley, L., et al., "Brutality on the beat," Newsweek, March 25, 1991, p. 32.**

Details anger against the Los Angeles Police Department for the vicious March 3 beating of 25-year-old Rodney King. Principal charge against four L.A. officers in the grand jury indictment; demands for the resignation of Police Chief Daryl Gates; how the videotape of the King beating confirms the violence and abuse that L.A. blacks and Hispanics have long alleged; other issues the King assault has sparked; Newsweek poll of police force.

## Debates & issues

**"A rising storm in L.A.," U.S. News & World Report, March 25, 1991, p. 12.**

Reveals that two minutes of a home videotape may become the catalyst for a nationwide crackdown on police brutality. The sight of Los Angeles police pummeling a defenseless black man sickened even hard-line Police Chief Daryl Gates; four of the officers indicted in the controversy.

**"From flag-waving to dark frenzy," Maclean's, April 1, 1991, p. 56.**

Opinion. Presents columnist Allan Fotheringham's comments on his belief that the recent beating of a black man by a group of white Los Angeles police officers and the American patriotism-gone-wild reaction to victory in the Persian Gulf War are connected.

**"Law breakers and law makers," National Review, April 15, 1991, p. 11.**

Considers two recent instances of faulty justice. Beating of a suspect by Los Angeles police officers; British appeals court decision that the Birmingham Six — opposed Irish Republican Army terrorists who have been imprisoned for more than a decade — are in fact not guilty; analysis of justice systems in the two countries.

**Bishop, K., "Police attacks: Hard crimes to uncover, let alone stop," The New York Times, March 24, 1991, Section 4, p. 1.**

Examines the national outrage the videotape of white Los Angeles police officers beating a black man has provoked. Demands for a citizen review board or complaint office to monitor police practices in Los Angeles; nationwide survey showing variations in the ways complaints of police misconduct are classified and kept; how Los Angeles and New York cases hint at the limitations of remedies.

**Blumenthal, R., "Police feel haunted by specter of brutality," The New York Times, March 30, 1991, p. 21.**

Presents a periodic visit to one New York City police precinct, and tells of ambivalent feelings of New York City police officers about accusations of brutality. In cases where wrongdoing is clear-cut they are fierce in their condemnation, but the police officers say they are nevertheless constantly second-guessed by outsiders with the luxury of hindsight.

**Bruning, F., "The enemy is us, not the L.A. police force,"** *Maclean's,* **April 15, 1991, p. 11.**

Opinion. Discusses reaction to the videotape showing Los Angeles police officers beating Rodney King. Concludes that the United States remains a society defined by race, class and income in which police brutality is inflicted upon those deemed undesirable. Los Angeles Police Chief Daryl Gates; police brutality in other cities.

**Buckley Jr., W. F., "L.A. law,"** *National Review,* **April 29, 1991, p. 62.**

Editorial. Examines the case for the defense of the Los Angeles police officers charged with beating suspect Rodney King. Overview of the incident; why the defense case is faulty.

**Gest, T., "The battle over criminal law,"** *U.S. News & World Report,* **April 8, 1991, p. 14.**

Asserts that, despite the police brutality in Los Angeles that is causing Americans to seriously question the way in which U.S. police work, the U.S. Supreme Court decided last week that "coerced confessions" can be admitted at criminal trials if there is other overwhelming proof of a defendant's guilt. How some predict officers will view the decision as a green light to abuse suspects; decision shows how the court's conservative majority views crime issues.

**Gest, T., Whitman, D., et al., "Why brutality persists,"** *U.S. News & World Report,* **April 1, 1991, p. 24.**

Notes that although Congress has convened hearings into police brutality and the president has denounced the videotaped bludgeoning of Rodney King, police brutality has declined in recent years in New York City, Chicago, New Orleans, and even Los Angeles. Curbing police abuse; relatively small number of repeat offenders responsible for most police abuse; costs of police brutality; chronic urban tensions. INSET: a mixed picture on police conduct.

**Lacayo, R., Booth, C., et al., "Law and disorder,"** *Time,* **April 1, 1991, p. 18.**

States that to watch the videotape of Los Angeles policemen kicking and clubbing Rodney King was to suddenly explore a dark corner of American life. Undermining the image of cool professional police, an occasion for dismay, soul searching and defensiveness. Evidence growing that the officers involved expected their behavior to be winked at; other brutality cases; weeding out problem officers. INSETS: Untitled (communications tape from L.A.); writing on the wall.

**Monroe, S., "Complaints about a crackdown,"** *Time,* **July 16, 1990, p. 20.**

Reports that minorities charge that the Los Angeles Police Department's war on gangs has become a war on their communities. Lawsuits claiming violations of civil rights; brutality suits against the sheriff's department; controversial bar-arm chokehold.

**Morrow, L., "Rough justice,"** *Time,* **April 1, 1991, p. 16.**

Asks the question of the Los Angeles police beating of a motorist, "how does a group of otherwise normal people turn into a mob capable of this kind of savagery?" Social and personal dimensions; dangerous, brutalizing work American police do; fighting an unwinnable war with atrocities committed on both sides; exerting social control by exemplary doses of terror, on the conceit that violence is the only language the victim understands.

**Roberts, S., "Brutal question: Police violence, public trust,"** *The New York Times,* **March 21, 1991, p. B1.**

Comments on police brutality in New York City. Statistics; rejection of proposal to revamp the review board; "mussing" suspects.

**Yocum, S., "Why it happened: An L.A. cop's view,"** *Newsweek,* **March 25, 1991, p. 34.**

Presents the view of an officer with the Los Angeles Police Department concerning the brutal beating of 25-year-old Rodney King. How the officers who beat King are no better than the worst criminal she's put in jail; why the whole LAPD shouldn't be blamed; why it happened; how any officer would be angered by a vehicle endangering the lives of others; the darkest side of police work; support the LAPD deserves.

## Training

**Blumenthal, R., "Police plan new version of foot duty,"** *The New York Times,* **Feb. 14, 1991, p. B1.**

Discusses the plan of New York City police for restructuring the department into a modernized version of the beat system abandoned decades ago. Details of the plan.

**Lacayo, R., Shannon, E., et al., "Back to the beat,"** *Time,* **April 1, 1991, p. 22.**

Details some actions cities across the United States are taking to put visible police back into the communities to protect, serve, and befriend local residents. Rigorous training in the basics of policing; Boston, Houston and San Francisco: Community Patrol Officer Programs — the beat cop is back; community policing as a deterrent; discouraging crimes before they happen; new yardsticks needed to measure individual performance; the macho image.

# Back Issues

*Great Research on Current Issues Starts Right Here. . . Recent topics covered by The CQ Researcher are listed below. Issues dated before May 10, 1991, were published under the name of Editorial Research Reports.*

**FEBRUARY 1990**
Politics and Economic Growth
Free Agency in Sports
Repetitive Motion
War on Drugs

**MARCH 1990**
Asbestos: Are Risks Acceptable?
Public Health Campaigns
South Africa's Future
Homeless Need More Than Shelter

**APRIL 1990**
How Fair is the Tax Burden?
Workers' Compensation
U.S. Pacific Forces
Curbing Insurance Premiums

**MAY 1990**
Should Teaching Be a Profession?
Will Canada Fall Apart?
Is U.S. Patent System Outdated?
Federal Funding for the Arts

**JUNE 1990**
Downsizing America's Armed Forces
Progress In Weather Forecasting
S & L Bailout
Bio-Chemical Disarmament

**JULY 1990**
Do Americans Still Love Marriage?
Death Penalty Debate
Decline of Rural America
United Nations in the 1990s

**AUGUST 1990**
Democracy in the Philippines
Initiatives: True Democracy?
Hard Times at Newspapers
Teens Balance School & Jobs

**SEPTEMBER 1990**
Dangers of Alcohol
Western Alliance After the Cold War
Tobacco Industry
Right to Die

**OCTOBER 1990**
Organ Transplants
Energy Policy Options
Search for Arab Unity
Child Support

**NOVEMBER 1990**
Lotteries and Gambling
Post Cold-War Choices
Setting Limits on Medical Care
Multicultural Education

**DECEMBER 1990**
Cable TV Regulation
Americans' Search For Their Roots
Is Insurance System a Failure?
Why Schools Still Have Tracking

**JANUARY 1991**
Growing Influence of Boycotts
Should the U.S. Reinstate the Draft?
America's Archaeological Past
Peace Corps' Challenges in '90s

**FEBRUARY 1991**
Regional Impact of Recession
Puerto Rico's Status
Redistricting: Mapping Power
Nuclear Power

**MARCH 1991**
Acid Rain
Cost of the Gulf War
Reassessing Gun Laws
Future for Man in Space

**APRIL 1991**
Social Security
Canadian Crisis Over Quebec
California Drought
Electromagnetic Radiation

**MAY 1991**
School Choice
Racial Quotas
Animal Rights
U.S. and Japan

**JUNE 1991**
Children and Divorce
Teenage Suicide
Endangered Species
Europe 1992

**JULY 1991**
Teenagers and Abortion
Soviet Republics Rebel
Mexico's Emergence
Athletes and Drugs

**AUGUST 1991**
Sexual Harassment
Fetal Tissue Research
Oil Imports
The Palestinians

Back issues are available for $4.00 (subscribers) or $7.00 (non-subscribers). Quantity discounts apply to orders over ten. To order, call Congressional Quarterly 1-800-432-2250.

# Future Topics

▶ *Advertising Under Attack*

▶ *Threatened Forests*

▶ *Foster Care*

# The CQ Researcher

PUBLISHED BY CONGRESSIONAL QUARTERLY INC., IN CONJUNCTION WITH EBSCO PUBLISHING

# Advertising Under Attack

*Critics organize around race, sex, health and the environment*

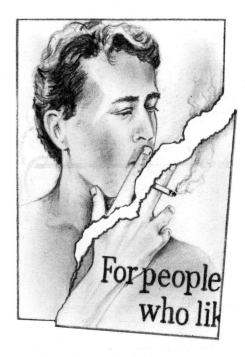

For people who lik[...]

ADVERTISING HAS LONG BEEN A LIGHTNING rod for social criticism. But today's advertisers push their wares in a landscape teeming with well-organized critics. Their concerns range from sexual and racial stereotyping to the promotion of health-threatening products, from hollow claims of environmental sensitivity to the explosion of advertising clutter. To bring about change, activist critics commit civil disobedience, lobby for restrictions on advertising and organize boycotts and letter-writing campaigns against offending corporations and the media. Beleaguered firms and advertising professionals are fighting back, claiming their First Amendment right of free speech is being trampled. But as ads are altered, or pulled from the market, it's clear the critics are having an impact.

September 13, 1991 • Volume 1, No. 18 • 657-680

*Formerly Editorial Research Reports*

COVER ART: BARBARA SASSA-DANIELS

# CQ Researcher

September 13, 1991
Volume 1, No. 18

**EDITOR**
Sandra Stencel

**MANAGING EDITOR**
Thomas J. Colin

**ASSOCIATE EDITOR**
Richard L. Worsnop

**STAFF WRITERS**
Charles S. Clark
Mary H. Cooper
Rodman D. Griffin

**PRODUCTION EDITOR**
Laurie De Maris

**EDITORIAL ASSISTANT**
Thomas H. Moore

**GRAPHICS**
Jack Auldridge

**PUBLISHED BY**
Congressional Quarterly Inc.

**CHAIRMAN**
Andrew Barnes

**VICE CHAIRMAN**
Andrew P. Corty

**EDITOR AND PUBLISHER**
Neil Skene

**EXECUTIVE EDITOR**
Robert W. Merry

**PUBLICATIONS MARKETING/SALES**
Robert Smith

**EDITOR, EBSCO PUBLISHING**
Melissa Kummerer

The CQ Researcher (ISSN 1056-2036). Formerly Editorial Research Reports. Published weekly (48 times per year, not printed the first Friday of any month with five Fridays) by Congressional Quarterly Inc., 1414 22nd St., N.W., Washington, D.C. 20037. Rates are furnished upon request. Application to mail at second-class postage rates is pending at Washington, D.C. POSTMASTER: Send address changes to The CQ Researcher, 1414 22nd St., N.W., Washington, D.C. 20037.

# Advertising Under Attack

BY CHARLES S. CLARK

## THE ISSUES

Brown & Williamson Tobacco Corp. is courting trouble with its current billboard advertisements for Kool cigarettes. The eye-catching ads feature a lithe blonde slipping off a pink sweatshirt to reveal a skimpy bathing suit. Cigarette makers are accustomed to protests, but this campaign is a likely target for a full-scale attack — from health officials concerned about the glamorization of cigarettes among youth, inner-city community leaders who link smoking to high cancer rates among blacks, environmentalists opposed to billboard blight and feminists and conservative religious leaders who are upset about sexual exploitation.

In the past few years, anti-advertising activists have taken to the streets — literally. In Washington, for example, a feminist group called Women Fighting Back has slapped a sticker on the Kool ad reading, "Keep your ads off my body." In several cities, activists — including the Rev. Calvin O. Butts in Harlem and Michael Pfleger, a Chicago priest — have painted over ads promoting tobacco and alcohol products in inner-city neighborhoods. Such ads promote the lethal message "that success and glory and power come from alcohol and smoking," says Alberta Tinsley-Williams, a Wayne County [Mich.] commissioner who has led ad protests in Detroit.

The advertising industry calls such actions vigilante censorship, but it has not been able to ignore the protests. "I have never seen such a volume and intensity of troubles with advertising," says John O'Toole, president of the American Association of Advertising Agencies (AAAA).[1]

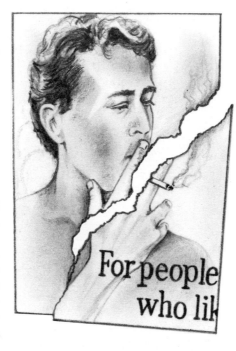

For people who li[k]

Twice in 1990, R. J. Reynolds Tobacco Co. came under attack for appealing to population groups seen as vulnerable to the seduction of cigarette ads. Uptown cigarettes, whose stylish ads seemed to target blacks, never made it to the marketplace after a roar of protests from a coalition of community groups. Just weeks later, RJR's Dakota brand, reportedly aimed at non-college-educated "virile young women,"[2] was withdrawn from a planned marketing test in Philadelphia following protests from groups such as Dakotans against Dakota Cigarettes and the Women vs. Smoking Network.

And this July, in the wake of a nationwide protest led by religious leaders and 21 health groups, the federal Bureau of Alcohol, Tobacco and Firearms forced the G. Heileman Co. to stop selling a high-alcohol malt liquor called PowerMaster, which Heileman was promoting to blacks.

Today's advertising protesters run the gamut from liberal to conservative, nationwide to community-based, professionally staffed to volunteer-driven. But these well-organized and vocal critics have some things in common: They have learned to work the news media effectively and to target their protests, much as advertisers now target well-defined segments of the population. As management theorist Peter F. Drucker wrote in 1989: "The single-cause group derives its power from . . . its single purpose rather than its numbers. Its task is almost never to get something done. It is to stop, to prevent, to immobilize. This is the new 'mass movement' that increasingly dominates the political process."[3]

Today's advertising critics operate in an environment characterized by what some are calling the "fragmenting of America" — a period when economic, social and technological trends are prompting Americans to emphasize their differences rather than nurture their similarities. The recent debate over multicultural education underscored the phenomenon,[4] but it has become part of the general public policy climate.

Advertising has been drawn into the fray for essentially the same reason. "Because [advertising] stands at the intersection of industry, communications and group interactions, [it] can come under attack from anyone who is upset about any feature of these three domains," William Leiss, Stephen Kline and Sut Ghally write in *Social Communication in Advertising*.

Advertising, in the words of English author Norman Douglas, reflects "a nation's ideals." Thus it should come as no surprise that Madison Avenue becomes embroiled in social conflict when the ideals advertisers emblazon on billboards and television screens don't reflect the lives of average people. "We tend to see advertising as a metaphor for a greater society," says New York University law Professor Burt Neuborne, the First Amendment counsel for the Association of National Advertisers (ANA), "and if it's doing its job, it is the ideal. But if you have doubts about the quality of life, you'll criticize ads. When you argue about targeting, what you're complaining about is that society hasn't found a way to integrate 'out' groups into the mainstream."

Advertising experts have long recognized that individual elements of ads often become more important than the placement of the product. Ads depict who uses the product, how a family looks, what is beautiful and the roles played by men and women. "That's why blacks and women" get upset over certain ads, says Duke University Professor William M. O'Barr. "The proper role model for blacks doesn't have a lot to do with a product, but it does have to do with who's dominant and who's subordinate."

Historically, advertising has been "a whipping boy for what critics see as society's ills," says ANA President DeWitt F. Helm Jr. "There's a tendency to legislate behavior, and when there's a failure to achieve these objectives, [the critics] try to regulate or censor ads."

The critics' outspokenness has forced many corporations to become savvy about social issues in ways they might never have imagined. The Oregon-based Nike Co. ran smack into social controversy with its $60-million-a-year advertising campaign for expensive sneakers featuring basketball superstar Michael Jordan and other celebrities. In the spring of 1990, Nike came under fire on two fronts. Sportswriters began blaming its ads for a spate of killings involving young inner-city blacks fighting over the high-

*This ad for Kool cigarettes could invite criticism from inner-city community leaders who link smoking to high cancer rates among blacks; feminists and religious leaders upset about sexual exploitation; and environmentalists concerned about billboard blight.*

priced shoes. Then Jesse Jackson's Chicago-based Operation Push announced a boycott of Nike, demanding that the company hire more black executives and channel more capital into minority businesses and publications. In response Nike launched an extensive media campaign highlighting its affirmative action programs and its $5 million "stay in school" advertising campaign. As Nike public relations Director Liz Dolan recalls, "We never expected athletic shoes to become a political issue, but they did."

Today's critics are building on the bedrock of public skepticism toward advertising. (The Gallup poll has continually ranked advertising near the bottom among professions evaluated by the public for honesty and ethical standards.) Also, many observers blame the declining quality of American political debate on simplistic, and frequently negative, campaign advertisements. *(See story, p. 668.)* At the same time, critics are capitalizing on resentment over the fact that "ads are appearing in more and more places than ever before,"

says Kim B. Rotzoll, a professor of advertising at the University of Illinois at Urbana/Champaign. *(See story, p. 661.)*

Given the controversy surrounding so many ads, it's not surprising that 1990 saw more legislative proposals than ever before to ban ads, restrict the content of ads, tax ads or end tax deductibility for ads. And for the first time, the advertising industry began systematically tracking court cases involving advertising issues *(see p. 666)*.

As long as Madison Avenue continues to turn out ads that push society's "hot buttons," critics of all sorts will continue to press their demands for more honesty and sensitivity to health, social and environmental issues. Here are some of the key issues in the debate:

### What changes in advertising have provoked the new critics?

There was a time when advertisers could reach the masses in America simply by taking out a two-page spread in *Life* magazine or placing a 60-second spot on "The Ed Sullivan Show." That was before the 1960s and the advent of the civil rights movement, organized feminism and environmentalism. Back in those days, when the arrival of television inaugurated the modern advertising era, American consumers were seen as a relatively homogeneous group. "The American consumer is not a moron, she is your wife," advertising guru David Ogilvy counseled Madison Avenue.

By the early 1970s, the America of Ed Sullivan — and David Ogilvy — had changed. The acquisitive middle class that had expanded so steadily after World War II had entered a period of economic stagnation. The once-typical consumer was suddenly an elusive creature. The subsequent segmentation of the market meant the demise of mass-

*Continued on p. 662*

# Is American Society Smothered in Advertising?

*It's 7 A.M. as America's kid awakens on Ninja Turtle sheets. He rises, dons Superman underwear, a Dick Tracy T-shirt, and sits down to Nintendo breakfast cereal with his Simpsons bookbag beside him. His sister downs her pink Breakfast with Barbie cereal, ready to pick up her Garfield notebook and catch the school bus. . . . It's 9 A.M., and our American kid is in school, settling down to watch a 12-minute news program produced just for kids — with two minutes of ads. . . . School is out for the day, and our American kid rushes home, grabs a magazine, turns on the TV, and plops down on the couch for heavy-duty advertising pressure. . . . It's early Friday evening, and our American kid, his sister and friends head out to the movie theater. They see a Coke commercial before the movie starts. Will the kids have a three-hour respite from the commercial barrage of the day as they watch a double-feature? Not with Domino's Pizza, Pepsi and Burger King as part of the action in "Teenage Mutant Ninja Turtles." Nor with Lucky Strike and Camel cigarettes prominently featured in "Who Framed Roger Rabbit?" . . . It's 10 P.M., and our American kid is curled up in bed, solving a maze in a children's magazine. Is he finally safe from commercial messages? No. The maze itself is an ad for Hershey's chocolate.*

Consumers Union created this scenario for a pamphlet called "Selling America's Kids." The group has joined a growing chorus of critics who say there simply are too many ads. "It's time we said, 'Enough!' " shouts a brochure from the Center for the Study of Commercialism, formed last year as an offshoot of the Washington-based Center for Science in the Public Interest.

The Federal Express Orange Bowl. The Virginia Slims tennis matches. The Anheuser-Busch Rolling Stones concert. They're all screaming at us to "buy, buy, buy," the center says. This "crass commercialism creates an insatiable appetite for more and fosters feelings of envy, anxiety and insecurity."

Such critics are furthering the time-honored view that advertising preys on human vulnerability to create a society of passive consumers enslaved by corporate dictates They have data to prove their point. Since 1965, the number of network TV commercials has tripled and is increasing 20 percent a year.† Signs of a dramatic increase in commercial saturation can be traced to the 1980s. In 1984, during the Reagan administration, the Federal Communications Commission dropped the limits on the number of minutes per hour TV networks could devote to commercials. (Radio ad time had been deregulated the year before.)

According to the Center for the Study of Commercialism, the amount spent on media advertising in the United States has doubled since 1982, jumping from $66 billion to $130 billion in 1990. The arrival of cable TV networks devoted to home shopping and the placement of advertisements on videocassettes and in movie theaters has become visible to all but the most isolated consumer. "It was clear even years ago that ours is the world's most commercial-saturated society," notes Michael Schudson, a professor of communications and sociology at the University of California-San Diego and author of a book on advertising.

If critics of advertising overkill have a field marshal, it is Michael F. Jacobson, the Massachusetts Institute of Technology-trained microbiologist who helped found the Center for Science in the Public Interest in 1971. "Advertisers take advantage of innate desires for the good life," Jacobson says, "and there was nothing pushing on the other side for a moderate, more civic-oriented life."

The center sponsors conferences, publishes books and advocates hikes in luxury taxes and an end to the tax deductibility of advertising expenses. It also develops public service messages to encourage Americans to consume less, turn off their TVs and "relearn" the values of community and cooperating with others.

The advertising industry views Jacobson as an extremist. "Not many consumers share Michael Jacobson's knee-jerk view," says John O'Toole, president of the American Association of Advertising Agencies. According to O'Toole, consumers accept corporate sponsorship of events such as the Sunkist Fiesta bowl because they get to see them for free on television.

O'Toole also points to the economic benefits of advertising. "The more ads, the more sales; and the more sales, the more tax revenues in state coffers," he says. But even he believes there can be too many ads. "Yes, I'd like to see fewer ads," he says, "because then each would have more impact."

Kim B. Rotzoll, a professor of advertising at the University of Illinois at Urbana-Champaign, says advertisers should ask themselves whether their heightened visibility is really welcome. "People get blasé, the ads become like wallpaper," he says. Rotzoll argues, however, that Jacobson's group oversimplifies things. "Where's the evidence that we're even close to a consumer revolt over advertising saturation?" he asks.

Jacobson acknowledges that evidence of a consumer revolt is "pretty spotty." But he sees signs of hopeful moderation. "The recession," he concludes, "has let some air out of the greed balloon."

---

† Peter F. Eder, "Advertising and Mass Marketing: The Threat and the Promise" *The Futurist*, May-June 1990, p. 38.

Continued from p. 660

circulation magazines such as *Life*, *Look* and *The Saturday Evening Post*. What was the point of spending money to reach so many readers, argued advertisers, if they weren't all the "right" buyers, if they were all different?

In response, Madison Avenue adopted elaborate systems that divided the buying population into distinct, targetable groups. The best-known system was dubbed VALS, because it zeroed in on consumers' "values and lifestyles." Created in 1978-79 by the Stanford Research Institute in Palo Alto, Calif., VALS identified nine lifestyle groups ranging from "survivors" just eking out a living to "the integrated," those wealthy few who have it all.[5]

Whereas in the 1950s Detroit might design a new tail fin in hope of attracting waves of new buyers, today's auto marketers must create a whole line of products, each catering to a demographic niche, or category, and each with a unique advertising strategy for reaching, say, young singles who want luxury and high style, or parents who want cars that are simple and practical.

Reaching the already fragmented American marketplace became more difficult during the 1980s, when the proliferation of cable television channels ate into the mass-audience reach of the three major TV networks. As a result, advertisers who wanted to reach that newly fragmented audience had to buy time selectively, a technique known as "narrowcasting." In the words of New York adman Steve Seiter, they turned to "a combined-arms approach" — some television, some print, some direct mail — to "catch the consumer in a cross-fire of communications."

Adapting to the new multicultural American bazaar caused a sea change in the ad industry. The transformation, as O'Toole of the AAAA

After a nationwide protest led by religious leaders and 21 health groups, the federal Bureau of Alcohol, Tobacco and Firearms forced the G. Heileman Co. to stop selling PowerMaster, a high-alcohol malt liquor being targeted to blacks.

noted, created "a bewildering new world of advertising."

Advertising trade journals today commonly tout new opportunities in the $278 billion market of black consumers or the $141 billion Hispanic market. Each niche requires advertising with tailored images, personalities and music. Black households, for example, watch 27 percent more television than white households, according to the Arbitron rating service,[6] indicating a TV-oriented strategy for black-oriented products. "We're changing from the melting-pot theory to a kind of salad bowl," says Gary Berman, president of Market Segment Research.[7]

It is targeting, more than any other factor, that draws critics' ire. Because smoking and alcohol abuse are more prevalent among minorities and low-income groups, liquor and cigarette ads represent what New York University's Neuborne calls "banners of an unfair world."

On the surface, health concerns are the central issue for such organizations as the Coalition on Smok-

ing OR Health (made up of the American Heart Association, the American Cancer Society and the American Lung Association) and the Center for Science in the Public Interest, a 20-year-old group of consumer-activist scientists. But underlying their clashes with advertisers are the larger issues of power, social class and economic inequality.

The critics waging front-line campaigns against alcohol and tobacco ads are flanked by comrades in arms fighting on behalf of myriad other social issues, adding to the advertising industry's siege mentality. Madison Avenue braces as Women Against Pornography issues its "plastic pig" awards to "deserving" advertisements. Action for Children's Television attacks Saturday morning cartoon shows featuring heroes that double as retail products for kids, like G. I. Joe "action" figures. And Scenic America, a Washington-based environmental group, calls for new legislation to further restrict billboards, which it calls "the most intrusive and offensive form of advertising."

One of the most vocal ad critics on the scene today is the Rev. Donald Wildmon, head of the conservative American Family Association in Tupelo, Miss. His group threatens boycotts of national advertisers whose ads — or the programs or publications they appear in — promote sex, violence or abuse of alcohol. It recently demanded that Calvin Klein's Obsession perfume stop using sexually graphic magazine ads featuring intertwined nude bodies. Wildmon boasts that he can "call 20 to 25 of the largest advertisers in the country and be on a first-name basis with their top ad guys."

In this climate, some advertisers so fear controversy that even individual consumers can bring about sweeping change. In 1989, Pan American World Airways reportedly canceled a "lighthearted" radio campaign after a phone call from a woman complaining about sexism in the ad. It featured a businessman who looks forward to traveling with his secretary but is disappointed when his wife is booked to accompany him. "I call [such complaints] advertising terrorism," says Jack Trout, a marketing executive in Greenwich, Conn. "A lot of folks have realized they can get their point of view across by jumping on the phones and threatening a boycott. The more it happens, the more it gets in the press, the more it's going to feed highly organized attempts to intimidate advertisers." [8]

Of course, there's also a positive way to look at the situation. "The new twist now is that advertisers are sensitive," says adman Seiter, "but for their own selfish reasons." They don't "want to put ads out there that are going to backfire."

### Do advertisers have a social responsibility?

The late Howard Gossage, a veteran copywriter who became an advertising industry critic, once said that trying to explain responsibility to advertisers was "like trying to convince an eight-year-old that [sex] is more fun than [eating] a chocolate ice cream cone." [9]

As Gossage was suggesting, advertisers view social responsibility differently than their critics. They see it in utilitarian terms: They believe free-market forces, if left unencumbered by government regulation, will produce the greatest good for the greatest number. That's why, for example, they oppose limits on the number of commercials in children's television programming. "If a program has 'too many' commercials, children will stop watching it," says the AAAA. [10]

Similarly, Anheuser-Busch spokesman Stephen J. Burrows is unfazed by feminists' criticisms of beer ads featuring women in bikinis. "We

don't think we depict any individual in a less-than-responsible fashion in ads," he told *Business Week*. [11]

When critics seek to restrict advertising to protect what they see as a vulnerable group, defenders of advertising often respond with charges of elitism. "To suggest that blacks or Hispanics or other minority groups are not capable of receiving information — in this case, advertising — and making an informed decision based on that decision smacks of a plantation-type of mentality," says Helm of the ANA. [12]

But some advertising professionals acknowledge a need for self-restraint. Recent controversies over the targeting of minorities for products that are considered harmful, John O'Toole concedes, have added "a new dimension of consideration that complicates marketing. The question of whether they should target these groups raises questions of sensitivity, if not legality."

Rather than burden advertising with the nation's social problems, ad executives often prefer to emphasize its primary responsibility: producing ads that are accurate and fair. Doing that, says Helm, largely eliminates the "bad apples," the deceptive ads. "It's usually the . . . mail-order ads for things like bust-enhancers that people are concerned about, not national advertisers," he explains.

Some critics argue, however, that even if advertisers have good intentions, the unintended effects are important as well. Feminists bristle at advertisements that dehumanize women and overemphasize physical perfection. "I know very few young women with healthy attitudes toward their bodies," says Jean Kilbourne, a media critic and producer of documentaries on sex in advertising. "To sell products, you have to make women obsessed about a small amount of weight. Now, the advertisers didn't set out to cause eating disorders. But the damage is done, and

it will take a while to undo."

Sociologist Gail Dines, who heads a Cambridge, Mass., group called Challenging Media Images of Women, contends that many depictions of women in ads border on the pornographic, encouraging sexual degradation or even rape. Dines also decries the way advertisements prey on low-income women. The message that this "product will empower you to catch a man speaks to poor women on a real level, teaches them they can buy into the middle class," she says.

Advertising professionals, not surprisingly, are unwilling to take responsibility for general social and economic ills, arguing that advertisements reflect rather than create cultural norms. "It would be ludicrous to portray unattractive people, be they male or female, in advertisements," says Helm. "All of us have a desire to be attractive and presentable. It's a matter of taste."

O'Toole agrees — to a point. "The fact that society has decided slenderness is standard for feminine beauty is not the fault of advertising," he says. On the other hand, the use of sex, "if it has nothing to do with the benefit being communicated, is bad advertising as well as tasteless."

### How have advertisers responded to criticism?

Corporations do respond to critics — but usually only when they perceive it to be in their own interests. Two years ago Pepsico threw out its $25 million TV ads for its soft drink featuring pop singer Madonna when religious groups threatened a boycott. They were offended by religious references in one of the irreverent singer's typically risqué music videos.

And remember the Maidenform woman? The famous lingerie ads ("You'll never know where she'll turn up") ran from 1971 to 1982, featuring an attractive woman parading confidently down the avenue or working in her office — in just her bra and panties. Though the ad had become a classic, feminists felt it trivialized women in the workplace. The campaign was finally discontinued when a Maidenform "doctor," sitting at a patient's bedside in her red lace unmentionables, drew complaints from the National Organization for Women and the American Medical Women's Association.

Other advertisers have sought to placate feminists by creating ads showing "liberated" women. This summer, brewery giant Anheuser-Busch responded to charges of sexism in its bikini-adorned Bud Dry ads with an ad showing two women at the beach rating the men who walk by, which prompts a male surfer to complain, "Why can't they just love us for our minds?"

Facing the volatile debate over tobacco and alcohol ads, the Outdoor Advertising Association of America (OAAA) also took the compromise route. In June 1990 the group adopted voluntary guidelines recommending that ads promoting products illegal for sale to minors not be located on billboards within 500 feet of churches, schools and hospitals. Two months later the OAAA announced it would begin identifying such billboards by tagging them with the international children's symbol. But Scenic America blasted the guidelines as ineffective and a "smokescreen" designed to divert attention from the problem. While outdoor advertisers claim a decline in the percentage of billboards devoted to alcohol and tobacco products, critics counter with studies showing a continuing high proportion of such billboards in minority neighborhoods.

Compromises not withstanding, most advertisers under heavy attack have manned the barricades to defend their right to commercial free speech. "The tobacco industry has

Targeted at non-college educated "virile young women," R.J. Reynolds Tobacco Co.'s Dakota brand sparked the ire of women's groups and health activists.

stonewalled," says Michael Pertschuk, a former chairman of the Federal Trade Commission who now co-directs the Advocacy Institute, a grass-roots lobbying group. "They've gotten more sophisticated — saying they're not interested in selling to kids — but since they won't admit that smoking is harmful, they can't argue for moderation."

The Tobacco Institute, the cigarette industry's Washington outpost, has produced public relations campaigns discouraging youths from smoking. To fend off future restrictions on cigarette advertising, the institute joined forces with the American Civil Liberties Union, which says bans on cigarette ads violate constitutional protections of free speech. The improbable alliance gives tobacco advertising "a powerful cloak of respectability," Pertschuk says.

Tobacco's rapport with the First Amendment reached a new level of intimacy in 1989, when Philip Morris, the big cigarette maker, agreed to sponsor the National Archives' celebration of the bicentennial of

the Bill of Rights. The company's print and television ads and $60 million national tour featuring the original Virginia Bill of Rights (on which the first 10 amendments to the Constitution were modeled) drew outrage from members of Congress and critics of smoking. "This joint venture smears the Bill of Rights with the blood of all Americans killed as a result of smoking Marlboro and other Philip Morris cigarettes," fumed Dr. Sidney Wolfe of the Public Citizen Health Research Group. Other health activists followed the tour and protested at each stop.

The alcohol industry, unlike tobacco sellers, acknowledges that its product poses a health problem but takes pains to point out that more people enjoy alcohol in moderation than abuse it. The industry wages "very subtle, sophisticated corporate damage control," Pertschuk observes. Liquor and beer makers maintain a code of ethics (not always adhered to) that among other things discourages ads that trivialize inebriation or link alcohol to sexual arousal. Both groups have produced major advertising campaigns to curb drunken driving and promote moderation in drinking. Many alcoholic beverage companies support the Los Angeles-based Century Council, which fights alcohol abuse. And the liquor industry voluntarily refrains from advertising on television.

As fans of Smokey the Bear have known for years, the advertising industry itself spends considerable money on public-interest advertising, enhancing its image in the process. In 1990, the industry-supported Advertising Council spent a record $1.34 billion for ads promoting the Partnership for a Drug-Free America, AIDS prevention and other causes.[13]

Individually, companies in the industries most under attack by advertising critics rank among the top backers of nonprofit groups in minority communities. Alcohol and tobacco companies support Black History Month activities, the Congressional Black Caucus Foundation, the National Council of La Raza and the U.S. Hispanic Chamber of Commerce, to name a few.

To Michael Jacobson, executive director of the Center for Science in the Public Interest, such largess represents an attempt to take advantage of groups struggling to survive. "It has two benefits," Jacobson says, "standard PR and marketing, plus it silences effective critics. The National Urban League might get in-

volved in beer controversies, except that they get beer money." Jacobson also contends that ads promoting the Partnership for a Drug-Free America emphasize the need to combat illegal drugs and thus distract people from the dangers of alcohol and tobacco.

Walker Merryman, vice president of the Tobacco Institute, says there is no evidence that corporate giving is an effort to co-opt minorities. "Anyone reckless enough to make a charge like that should be obligated to prove it," he says. ■

on: emotional security, reassurance of worth, ego gratification, creative outlets, love objects, sense of power, sense of roots and immortality.

The advertising community responded with skepticism toward Packard, much as it scoffed at the criticism of Madison Avenue values then widespread in films and literature. In the late 1950s the influential Young & Rubicam ad agency took out an advertisement in *The Wall Street Journal* that complained: "There is no chestnut more overworked than the critical whining: 'Advertising sells people things they don't need.' We, as one agency, plead guilty. Advertising does sell people things they don't need. Things like television sets, automobiles, catsup, mattresses, cosmetics, ranges, refrigerators and so on.... People don't really need these things. People don't really need art, music, literature, newspapers, historians, wheels, calendars, philosophy, or, for that matter, critics of advertising. All people really need is a cave, a piece of meat, and possibly, a fire."

# BACKGROUND

## Everyone's a Critic

Advertising has generated criticism from the day it began grabbing consumers' attention with one-sided messages from someone wishing to sell something, which is to say, since advertising began. Educated observers were immediately contemptuous of advertising, which was born in 16th-century English coffee houses in the form of handbills touting such products as a dentifrice that gave users a lifetime without toothaches.[14]

Advertising's excesses continued to disgust many members of society. After the Civil War, Gen. Robert E. Lee declined an offer to endorse life insurance and other products, rejecting such opportunities as undignified. By the 1950s, the dawn of the modern advertising era, historian Arnold Toynbee would comment: "[T]he destiny of our Western Civilization turns on the issue of our struggle with all that Madison Avenue represents, more than it turns on the issue of our struggle with Communism." [15]

In the civic arena, legions of critics of advertising emerged during

the hyperbolic heyday of patent medicines, around the turn of the century. Still more critics spoke out during the 1920s, when the American mass market was forming and the technique of targeted marketing was already in use by cigarette manufacturers eying newly enfranchised women.

The Depression years of the 1930s, which led many Americans to question the country's economic system, saw anti-capitalist critiques of advertising by mainstream thinkers as well as Marxists, including a bestselling critique of American advertising published in 1933, *100,000,000 Guinea Pigs*. And the founding of the Consumers Union of the United States, also in the 1930s, launched the consumer movement.

The 1957 publication of sociologist Vance Packard's famous exposé of advertising, *The Hidden Persuaders*, became an overnight sensation. It added a "Big Brother" threat to the ad critic's arsenal by describing advertising's use of "motivational research" techniques to "channel our unthinking habits, our purchasing decisions, and our thought processes by the use of insights gleaned from psychiatry and the social sciences." Packard identified eight hidden human needs that admen play

A few years later, an advertising superstar published what many took as a response to Packard's claim to have exposed the ad industry's inner workings. In his popular 1963 book, *Confessions of An Advertising Man*, David Ogilvy discussed how "the Avenue" worked, hoping to add respectability to advertising's tarnished image.

In the modern era, most critics of advertising have concentrated less on conspiracies and more on individual instances of advertising's social effects, ethics and deceptiveness. One of the most infamous deceptions was brought to light by a small, modestly financed group — the same kind of organization making headlines today. In the late 1960s, Campbell Soup ads featured bowls of vegetable soup brimming with vegetables. In fact, clear marbles had been put in the bottom of the bowl to make the vegetables appear more abundant than they really were. Confronted by a barrage of negative publicity orchestrated by Students Opposed to Unfair Practices (SOUP), a group led by John Banzhaf, a professor at George Washington University Law School, Campbell entered into a consent agreement with the Federal Trade Commission (FTC) and halted the ads.

### Most Regulated Industry?

Advertising practitioners often respond to criticisms and proposals for restrictions by calling themselves "the most regulated industry." They point out that the time, place and manner of advertisements are commonly policed by law and regulation. Primary responsibility for curbing deceptive advertising practices resides with the FTC. In addition, the Securities and Exchange Commission regulates advertising of stocks and bonds, the Transportation Department regulates airline advertising, the Federal Communications Commission (FCC) oversees children's TV ads, the Food and Drug Administration regulates prescription drug ads and the Treasury Department's Bureau of Alcohol, Tobacco and Firearms regulates most aspects of tobacco and alcohol advertising. There are also a number of state and local regulations, and under the 1946 Lanham Trademark Act, anyone injured by an advertiser's false or misleading claim may bring action in a federal court.

On top of all the governmental controls, advertisers also impose their own self-regulation. Print ads are typically reviewed by legal departments of agencies and advertisers, and often by technical and scientific staffs. Broadcast networks review storyboards of TV ads before they are produced. At the Council of Better Business Bureaus, complaints from consumers or competing advertisers are reviewed by the Na-

tional Advertising Division and National Advertising Review Board, which negotiate with the offending advertiser and, if there's still an impasse, forward the case to the FTC. Since 1971, more than 2,800 cases have been handled by the council, which also has a special unit for children's advertising.

The editors, owners and publishers of broadcast and print media that carry ads constitute a further set of controls on advertising. They have the power (if not the financial incentive) to reject ads they deem inappropriate. Such judgments, however, are often highly subjective. This summer, for example, the Italian sportswear company Benetton riled a chorus of critics with a $3.5 million ad campaign featuring such graphic images as a nun and a priest kissing and a newborn baby with an intact umbilical cord. Many publications rejected the ads, but some saw no problem and published them.[16]

## Free Speech Argument

The concept of "free commercial speech" forms the bedrock upon which advertisers operate. (See At Issue, p. 673.) Historically, Anglo-Saxon law has regarded advertising as "*mere* commercial speech," subject to restrictions against fraud but not deserving of the sacred status of free speech in the political realm. The U.S. Supreme Court affirmed this principle in 1942 in *Valentine v. Chrestensen*, a case involving the right to distribute commercial handbills, and again in 1951 in *Breard v. Alexandria*, in which a magazine salesman claimed his right to free speech had been infringed by ordinances prohibiting door-to-door salesmen. The court held in *Breard* that commercial speech was outside the realm of First Amendment protection. The court's landmark libel

ruling in 1964 in *The New York Times v. Sullivan,** distinguished between "commercial" and "editorial" advertisements, arguing that editorial ads, at least, warranted First Amendment protection.

In 1975, the court moved closer to protecting commercial speech in *Bigelow v. Virginia*. The case involved advertisements informing Virginia residents that they could go to New York to obtain an abortion (abortions were illegal in Virginia at the time). The court ruled that the information in the ad was clearly factual material of public interest and more than simple commercial speech.

Five years later the Supreme Court ruled on what became the touchstone case involving commercial free speech. The 1980 case revolved around New York state's attempt to block a utility company from promoting the use of electric power during a time when the state was promoting energy conservation. In *Central Hudson Gas and Electric v. Public Service Commission of New York*, the Supreme Court established a four-part test for determining the constitutionality of government restrictions on commercial speech. The test required a determination that the commercial speech at issue was protected by the First Amendment (in other words, whether it concerned lawful activity and was not misleading) and a determination of whether the government's measure was reasonable.

In 1985, the advertising industry was cheered again when the Supreme Court ruled that ads could

*Continued on p. 669*

---

*The court ruled that the First Amendment guarantee of freedom of the press protects the press from libel suits for defamatory reports on public officials unless the officials prove that the reports were made with actual malice. Actual malice was defined as "with knowledge that it [the defamatory statement] was false or with reckless disregard of whether it was false or not."

# Chronology

**1920s** *Cigarette ads aimed at women draw criticism. Advertisers begin to design ads around people rather than products.*

---

**1930s** *The Depression forces advertisers to scale back and emphasize frugality. Consumer movement is launched. Social critiques of advertising appear.*

---

**1950s** *Postwar prosperity creates booming ad market. Television sets arrive in average American households.*

**1957**
Vance Packard publishes *The Hidden Persuaders*, which becomes a best-seller.

---

**1960s** *Rise of feminism and civil rights movement. Ralph Nader invigorates the consumer movement.*

**1963**
David Ogilvy publishes *Confessions of an Advertising Man* and Betty Friedan publishes *The Feminine Mystique*, which includes a chapter called "The Sexual Sell."

**Jan. 11, 1964**
U.S. Surgeon General issues a report on the dangers of smoking.

**July 27, 1965**
President Lyndon B. Johnson signs federal Cigarette Labeling and Advertising Act requiring warning labels on cigarette packages.

**Oct. 22, 1965**
Johnson signs Highway Beautification Act calling for reduction of billboard blight.

**1969**
Federal Communications Commission (FCC) bans ads for products that are based on characters featured in a television program from being shown during that TV program.

---

**1970s** *Rise of organized consumer groups and environmentalists.*

**April 1, 1970**
President Richard M. Nixon signs Public Health Cigarette Smoking Act banning tobacco ads on TV and radio.

---

**1980s** *Reagan administration relaxes broadcasting regulations and the policing of unfair advertising. The fitness movement and other trends increase public opposition to smoking and drinking.*

**June 20, 1980**
Supreme Court lays down four criteria for restricting commercial free speech (*Central Hudson Gas and Electric v. Public Service Commission of New York*).

**June 27, 1984**
FCC removes limits on the number of ads that can appear per hour on television, reasoning that "commercial levels will be effectively regulated by marketplace forces."

**Oct. 12, 1984**
President Reagan signs bill requiring health warning labels to appear on cigarette ads.

**June 13, 1988**
A U.S. district judge in Newark, N.J., awards $400,000 in damages to widower Thomas Cippolone, who claimed his wife died from smoking caused by cigarette ads.

**Nov. 5, 1988**
President Reagan pocket-vetoes the Children's Television Act, which would have required federal regulators to consider, at the time a broadcaster applied for renewal of a license, whether the station had served "the educational and informational needs of children in its overall programming."

**March 5, 1989**
Whittle Communications begins test-marketing Channel One, its controversial school television service that includes commercial advertising.

---

**1990s** *Advertising critics organize and target their attacks.*

**Oct. 1, 1990**
Congress again passes the Children's Television Act, which President Bush allows to become law without his signature.

# Political Ads and the Willie Horton Factor

Americans raised on the jingles of soap advertisements have long been accustomed to equally upbeat pitches touting candidates for public office. But more and more, cheery slogans like "I like Ike" and the gauzy Norman Rockwellesque scenes favored by President Ronald Reagan are giving way to a virulent brand of campaign promotion: the attack ad.

The controversial negative ads reached new visibility during the 1988 presidential campaign, when supporters of Republican candidate George Bush ran the much-criticized "Willie Horton" commercial. Shown on national cable TV for 28 days, the ad painted Democratic candidate Michael S. Dukakis as soft on crime because during his administration as governor of Massachusetts, convicted murderer Horton, who is black, had stabbed and raped a woman while on furlough from a Massachusetts prison.

"[Such] commercials make the American public captive in two respects," writes Curtis Gans, director of the Committee for the Study of the American Electorate. "Since they occur in the midst of regular programming, they cannot be readily shut off. And since their primary appeal is not to reason but rather to emotions, they are virtually unanswerable." †

If there were any doubts about the emotional impact of the Horton ad, a recent study dispels them. G. David Hughes, a University of North Carolina media analyst, electronically monitored the reactions of 23 subjects to several commercial and political advertisements. The Horton ad produced strong responses when words from the ad — "kidnapping," "stabbing" and "rape" — flashed across the screen.

The Bush campaign officially disavowed the Horton ad, but the conservative activists who produced it decided to keep the spot on the air. Some of the same individuals recently produced a negative ad supporting Bush's Supreme Court nominee, Clarence Thomas. The 60-second spot calls into question the moral character of three of Thomas' critics: Sens. Edward M. Kennedy, D-Mass.; Joseph R. Biden Jr., D-Del.; and Alan Cranston, D-Calif. White House Chief of Staff John H. Sununu asked the producers to drop the ad, but they refused.

Among the many critics of such ads is TV commentator Bill Moyers, a former White House press aide under President Lyndon B. Johnson. According to Moyers, negative political advertising "is wrecking the polity of America, destroying our ability as a cooperative society to face reality and solve our problems."

Efforts to clean up political advertising, ironically, have drawn support from many of the much-maligned professionals on Madison Avenue. Advertising giant David Ogilvy once called political spots the "only really dishonest kind of advertising that's left." They're "virtually unregulated," complains DeWitt F. Helm Jr., president of the Association of National Advertisers. "The public at large gets its image of all advertising from political ads."

John O'Toole, president of the American Association of Advertising Agencies, favors free airtime for candidates as an alternative to the current system of privately funded ads.

Many lawmakers are concerned about the anonymous nature of negative ads — which rarely identify the candidate benefiting from the attack. An added worry is that the ads have turned off voters (turnout in 1988 was the lowest in 40 years). Now Congress is considering legislation that would provide candidates with free airtime to respond to attacks, issue publicly funded vouchers for campaign ads at least one minute long and require candidates to appear personally in all their campaign advertising. Such provisions became part of a major overhaul of congressional campaign financing rules that the Senate passed this May. A House task force is considering a similar plan.

But some observers, among them University of Virginia political scientist Larry J. Sabato and communications expert Kathleen Hall Jamieson of the University of Pennsylvania, say restricting negative ads would violate constitutional rights to free speech. And at least one observer thinks such ads have a legitimate role to play. Says political commentator Charles Cook: "Negative ads deliver more information than do the soft fuzzy images of candidates walking along the beach." ††

Even if Congress' plan becomes law, negative advertising is not likely to disappear from American politics. "Clever media people will find a way to structure ads so that the candidate's fingerprints won't be on the negative part," says political consultant Vic Kamber.

Professor Jamieson sees another problem with pulling the plug on attack ads: Many negative ads, she says, are based on solid evidence, while others are deceptive but not easily preventable. The Horton ad, for example, is accurate, she points out. "I'm personally appalled by the ad, but it would pass every test against deceptive ads. What people find offensive is use of the black face of Willie Horton, which Bush then used to stand for all crime."

---

† *The Washington Post*, Feb. 12, 1989.

†† *Campaign*, September 1990, p. 1.

‡ *Campaign*, June 1991, p. 25.

Continued from p. 666

not be restricted to text merely to soften the impact of powerful images. The case, *Zauderer v. Office of Disciplinary Counsel of the Supreme Court of Ohio*, involved a lawyer whose newspaper ads seeking new clients included a photo of the Dalkon Shield intrauterine device, then the subject of multiple lawsuits. The state of Ohio had sought to restrict the use of the photo, claiming it was misleading. But the court ruled that "the use of illustrations or pictures in advertisements serves important communicative functions; it attracts the attention of the audience to the advertiser's message."

The next year, however, the court gave a boost to proponents of restrictions on advertising. That case, *Posadas de Puerto Rico Associates v. Tourism Council of Puerto Rico*, involved a gambling casino's challenge to a Puerto Rican law forbidding it from advertising. The court held that if government has the power to restrict such conduct as gambling or consumption of alcoholic beverages or smoking, it also has the power to regulate advertising intended to encourage that conduct.

## Advertisers and Children

The issue of freedom of commercial speech for advertisers enjoy weighs heavily on critics of advertising. Action for Children's Television (ACT), for example, is careful to avoid calls for censorship in its fight to improve children's programming. But along with groups like Consumers Union and the Center for Science in the Public Interest, ACT argues that children need special protection from authoritative-sounding communications that they may not recognize as coming from someone with something to sell. "Unlike

adults, children do not zap the ads when they use a remote control device," says ACT founder Peggy Charren. "The ads feature more children and better animation than the programs they interrupt. Children like commercials, and corporations know how to take advantage of this sad fact of TV life." [17*]

In addition to working to reduce the number of children's commercials, ACT's staff of four in Cambridge, Mass., lobbies the FTC to stop deceptive advertising, produces educational materials about the uses of television, petitions the FCC to require more public service broadcasting and presses for more minorities and women on TV. Charren finds it ironic that in the past 20 years, the "consumer movement has gotten more sophisticated while advertisements have gotten worse and more powerful."

ACT's biggest victory was passage in 1990 of the Children's Television Act, sponsored by Rep. Edward J. Markey, D-Mass. Reflecting concerns in Congress that American children are falling behind children in other countries in educational achievement, the law requires children's television fare to be a consideration in a TV station's license renewal. It also limits commercials to 10½ minutes per hour on weekends and not more than 12 minutes on weekdays, and establishes a national endowment for children's educational television.

"The legislation addresses congressional concerns about overcommercialization ... but avoids unnecessary and unconstitutional programming standards," said Edward O. Fritts, president of the National Association of Broadcasters.[18] An earlier version of the law was vetoed by Pres-

ident Ronald Reagan, who worried about regulatory interference and violations of broadcasters' rights to free speech. President Bush cited similar concerns, but he agreed to let the new version become law without his signature.[19]

ACT lost its fight to have the bill include restrictions on so-called program-length commercials, the half-hour cartoon shows whose heroes are also popular toys — such as He-Man, G. I. Joe and Ghostbusters. "Because full enjoyment of these shows will require buying the interactive toys, these programs will hit a new extreme as 30-minute commercials and put children who cannot afford the products at a disadvantage," Charren told *TV Guide*.[20]. Toy companies defend the shows as superior to reruns and note that psychologists review the plots for entertainment quality.

ACT has also been at the forefront of efforts to beat back the headway made by Channel One, the controversial school television service launched by Nashville-based Whittle Communications in 1989. Whittle supplies school classrooms with free video equipment on the condition that students watch a daily 12-minute world news summary that includes two minutes of paid commercials.

ACT and other critics object to "privatizing" American education and forcing a "captive audience" of young people to see commercials, particularly when the audience is often low-income kids watching ads for expensive running shoes and stereo equipment. "We're afraid that commercialism will corrupt the whole educational process," said Bill Honig, superintendent of public instruction in California, which threatened to dock funds from school districts if they subscribed.[21]

As an alternative to Channel One, ACT promotes Cable News Network's "CNN Newsroom," a daily, 15-minute commercial-free news-

---

*A recent survey by *Advertising Age* magazine indicates that 62 percent of Americans want children's ads taken off the air entirely. And the American Academy of Pediatrics is calling for a ban on children's food ads, saying the many candy and sugar-coated cereal messages contribute to a national obesity problem.

cast. It boasts more than 21,000 subscribers, who use TVs supplied by the schools or local cable companies. But Whittle is winning converts and now claims more than 8,200 schools in 47 states and the District of Columbia. "Denying students access to technology to help them learn more is a greater ethical risk than controlled exposure to ads," says Stan Jasinskas, a middle school principal in Kansas City, Kan.[22] ∎

# CURRENT SITUATION

## Legislative Attacks

Government efforts to tax, restrict or ban certain types of advertising — particularly for alcohol and tobacco products — have long been opposed by most advertising professionals. They cite what they call the "slippery slope" argument. If bans on advertising for legal products are approved, they argue, products in murkier areas of health concern — such as high-cholesterol food — will be swept up in restrictions. If alcohol and tobacco products are harmful, then ban *them*, goes the argument advanced by such industry groups as the American Advertising Federation, the Freedom to Advertise Coalition and the Ad Tax Coalition.

Legislation to restrict tobacco ads was introduced last year by Sen. Edward M. Kennedy, D-Mass. Among other things, the proposed legislation called for the removal of federal control over tobacco advertising, thus allowing individual states to enact their own ad restrictions. It also called for disclosure of additives in tobacco products and more-prominent health warning labels on cigarettes. The bill also would establish a center for tobacco studies within the Public Health Service to inform the public on the hazards of tobacco.

This year's version of the bill, which cleared the Senate Labor and Human Resources Committee on June 19, is similar, but its restrictions would apply only to outdoor advertising and ads on buses and subway trains. It is backed by the Coalition for Consumer Health and Safety, a group of 38 organizations led by the Consumer Federation of America.

On the House side, a sweeping anti-tobacco bill stalled last year after clearing the Energy and Commerce Subcommittee on Health and the Environment. Introduced by Chairman Henry A. Waxman, D-Calif., and Mike Synar, D-Okla., the bill would have banned most cigarette sales by vending machines, ended public distribution of free tobacco product samples and outlawed the sale of candy and gum in packages designed to resemble tobacco products. Tobacco lobbyists, however, succeeded in getting provisions removed that would have banned tobacco industry sponsorship of sporting events and eliminated all photographs and graphics from tobacco advertising. Synar and Waxman have yet to introduce their bill in the current Congress.

Alcohol ads are also getting congressional attention. An unlikely pair, Sen. Strom Thurmond, R-S.C., and Rep. Joseph P. Kennedy II, D-Mass., have introduced bills in the current Congress to require health warning labels on alcoholic beverage ads. Advertisers argue that such warnings dampen companies' willingness to advertise, and that in the case of broadcast ads, the health warnings would eat up large portions of an ad's expensive airtime. This, they argued, would amount to an advertising tax. Noting that an FTC survey of scientific literature in 1985 found little evidence that advertising increases consumption or abuse of alcohol, the industry argued instead for separate ads devoted to the dangers of alcohol abuse. Reducing alcohol abuse "will not be achieved by warning labels that hitchhike on brand advertising messages," AAAA Vice President Harold A. Shoup has argued.

Last year, a previous version of the labeling-requirement initiative was the subject of extensive House hearings in the Energy and Commerce Subcommittee on Transportation, Tourism and Hazardous Materials. The liquor, beer and wine industries teamed up with advertising associations and broadcasters to defeat the bill, citing the free commercial speech argument. The National Association of Broadcasters (NAB) also testified that requiring labels on ads would cause advertisers to withdraw them, costing broadcasters $762 million in annual revenues.[23].

This was not the first time the advertising and broadcast industries banded together to fight alcohol ad restrictions. In December 1988, then-U.S. Surgeon General C. Everett Koop convened a panel of experts on drunken driving that recommended severe restrictions on wine and beer advertising. However, following opposition by the NAB, the AAAA, the OAAA and the Television Bureau of Advertising, the recommendations died on the vine.

Congressional opponents of alcohol and cigarette advertising also hope to effect change through taxation. Sen. Bill Bradley, D-N.J., and Rep. Ted Weiss, D-N.Y., have introduced bills to eliminate the tax deduction for tobacco advertising expenses. A House task force working on campaign finance reform is considering a national tax on all commercial advertising to finance federal election campaigns. Bills to tax ads or end tax deductibility have been introduced in several states that are facing budget crises. In Pennsylvania, the legislature is considering a tax on business advertising and public relations expenditures.

### 'Billboard Blight'

America's billboard industry, now embroiled in the fight over alcohol and tobacco ads in the inner city, has for decades been battling activists on a more fundamental issue: government efforts to rid the country of billboards everywhere. The "billboard blight" issue came up this year during Congress' debate over reauthorization of the five-year Surface Transportation Act.

In the years immediately following the 1965 Highway Beautification Act, thousands of billboards across the country were dismantled. Their owners were sometimes compensated directly by state or local governments. But financially strapped local governments often preferred to "amortize" the costs, compensating owners by letting them keep the billboards up past the deadline. In 1978, following strong lobbying by outdoor advertisers, the highway act was amended to eliminate the amortization option.

In June Sen. John H. Chafee, R-R.I., offered an amendment to restore the option, but again the OAAA prevailed, arguing that amortization violated the Fifth Amendment's prohibition against taking private property without compensation. Action on a companion bill is expected this fall in the House.

To Robert Bonnie, a policy associate with Scenic America, billboards are "visual pollution" and "an important quality-of-life issue." He points to the four states and the hundreds of cities that have banned billboards entirely. "Many people think it's a conservation and garden

The environmental group Friends of the Earth recently released a 112-page critique of E.I. du Pont de Nemours & Co.'s "green" marketing claims and environmental record. Du Pont's recent TV ads, featuring engaging animals in the wild is "a distortion of environmental fact," the groups said. "In reality, Du Pont is the single largest corporate polluter in the United States. Using seal pups and dolphins to gloss over that fact is disingenuous and misleading."

club issue," he adds, "but it has become a huge issue in minority and low-income neighborhoods." *

Ruth Segal, acting president of the OAAA, not surprisingly, rejects the "visual pollution" characterization. She points out that billboard users are often small businesses — campground operators, car dealers and local hotels — that can't afford ads on television. "It's the only cost-effective way to catch families traveling because they don't read local newspapers or watch local TV," she says.

## Policing 'Green' Ads

Rising public interest in the environment has spawned a hot new trend on Madison Avenue — "green advertisements," which promote the

*States and cities that have banned billboards include Vermont; Hawaii; Alaska; Maine; Houston; Charlottesville, Va.; Santa Monica, Calif.; Santa Fe, N.M.; and Durham, N.C.

environmental virtues of companies and products. As green ads have proliferated, environmental activists have begun monitoring them to make sure they're accurate in their use of "green" terminology (is the product really "recyclable" and "ozone friendly"?) and their portrayal of corporate behavior.

Environmental activist Denis Hayes, organizer of the first Earth Day in 1970, leads a new California-based organization called Green Seal, which plans to use the Underwriters Laboratories Inc. to evaluate products and then issue a seal of approval to worthy products. Friends of the Earth is also embarked on an evaluation campaign. The group recently released a 112-page critique of E. I. du Pont de Nemours & Co.'s environmental marketing claims and environmental record. "Du Pont's feel-good advertising is a distortion of environmental fact," charged the group's senior analyst, Jack Doyle. "In reality, Du Pont is the single largest corporate polluter in the United States. Using seal pups and dolphins [in its television advertising] to gloss over that fact is disingenuous and misleading."

Concerned over increasing instances of false advertising, California, Florida, Minnesota, New York and other states have passed laws defining green terms. At the same time, groups of state attorneys general have taken legal action against false ads. Last year, one group forced Mobil Chemical Co. to stop labeling its Hefty trash bags as "degradable" in landfills because the claim was untrue.

To advertisers seeking to market uniform products in all regions, the activism of the attorneys general creates an unworkable patchwork of laws, some harsher than others. "We have to have national standards," says Helm at the Association of Na-

tional Advertisers. "We've got 50 umpires calling balls and strikes with no defined strike zone."

Last November the National Association of Attorneys General released a "Green Report" outlining the need for a uniform set of definitions of green terms that could be used nationwide. In a follow-up report this May, the association offered specific definitions for green terms and recommendations for handling legal claims. They also endorsed legislation proposed by Sen. Frank R. Lautenberg, D-N.J., and Rep. Gerry Sikorski, D-Minn., that would require the Environmental Protection Agency to define green terms. The FTC, meanwhile, is also exploring the issue. In June, a parade of some 50 corporations appearing at an FTC hearings agreed almost unanimously on the need for national standards for green ads. ∎

Recent Camel ads have been condemned by health activists. "People are turned off by . . . the cartoons that appeal to kids," says Michael Pertschuk of the Advocacy Institute. Women's groups have charged that some of the ads in the campaign also are sexually degrading.

# OUTLOOK

## Critics' Success Stories

This June, the Rev. Pfleger was acquitted of property-destruction charges stemming from his arrest for painting over billboard ads for Smirnoff vodka and Newport cigarettes near his Chicago church. In New York City, Calvin Butts watched with satisfaction as the billboard companies whose signs he had defaced grew weary of issuing refunds to advertisers and began replacing liquor and cigarette billboards with public service advertisements. He was never prosecuted.

Advertising critics with an eye on help from Washington are optimistic about the future, in part because of President Bush's appointment of Janet Steiger to head the FTC. Nearly all agree that Steiger has departed

from the Reagan-era laissez-faire mind-set and is more aggressively going after deceptive advertisements. The FTC recently negotiated a consent agreement with a maker of so-called "infomercials" — long TV ads in a news or talk-show format that resemble an actual television show. The agency said the infomercials violated the Federal Trade Commission Act, which says advertisers can't fool the audience with ads that don't look like ads. The agreement calls for the ad maker to redress consumers with a $1.5 million fine.

The FTC also recently pressured telephone services companies to discontinue "900" phone numbers featuring the "voices" of such characters as Woody Woodpecker and the Easter Bunny, which encourage children to run up their parents' long-distance bills. Art Amolsch, editor of the *FTC:WATCH* newsletter, says Steiger's FTC is reinstituting a policy

from the late 1970s that holds advertising agencies as well as sponsors responsible for deceptive ads. Congress, meanwhile, is considering letting the FTC resume a discarded policy of banning certain classes of ads on an industrywide basis.

Still other encouraging signs for critics of alcohol and tobacco ads have come from Surgeon General Antonia Novello and Health and Human Services Secretary Louis W. Sullivan. In April Sullivan came out strongly against tobacco-sponsored sports events. Michael Pertschuk of the Advocacy Institute says the credibility of tobacco advertisers has never been lower. "People are turned off by the Camel campaign of jazz musicians, the cartoons that appeal to kids," he says.

Many advertisers are worried that the Supreme Court is increasingly inclined toward the federal government's support of legal restrictions on commercial speech. In the coming term, the court will hear an appeal in the case of Rose Cippolone, a New Jersey woman who died in

*Continued on p. 675*

# At Issue:

## Should advertisers enjoy constitutional rights to free speech?

**BURT NEUBORNE**

*Professor of law, New York University*
FROM *FREE MARKETS, FREE CHOICE*, ESSAY ON COMMER-
CIAL SPEECH WRITTEN FOR THE ASSOCIATION OF NA-
TIONAL ADVERTISERS, APRIL 1987.

**STEVEN H. SHIFFRIN**

*Professor of law, Cornell University*
FROM AN INTERVIEW IN *MEDIA AND VALUES*,
SPRING/SUMMER 1991.

Speech enjoys a uniquely favored status in democratic culture. While the bulk of significant human
behavior, like eating or sleeping or working or
traveling or sex, is subject to substantial — though not
unlimited — regulation by the political majority, speech is
singled out and insulated from the general regulatory
power by a series of highly protected taboos — both legal
and social.

When religion, politics, science or art is the topic of
speech, the lessons of our cultural past and our political
present powerfully reinforce the anti-censorship ground
rules. Speech about commercial choice doesn't always
receive the same protection. Commercial speech has constantly been subjected to a series of censorship attempts,
often by persons who would bridle at an attempt to censor
"first-class" speech about religion, science, politics or art.
Although calls for the censorship of commercial speech
are generally well-intentioned, at bottom they are classic
attempts by well-meaning . . . elites to substitute their
conception of harm for that of individual hearers.

The free flow of speech about commercial choice deserves special protection because it is integral to our
culture's commitment to individual autonomy. Free societies make a linked political and economic decision to
govern the polity and the economy by deferring to the sum
of individual preferences. We trust individuals to evolve
those preferences in a rational manner and have pledged
to respect them through a combination of political democracy and consumer sovereignty.

Banning commercial speech from mass media will inevitably be self-defeating. Instead of utilizing society's capacity to transmit information in the most effective manner, selective media bans cause ignorance. The net result
must always be a less-informed hearer who is forced to
make decisions on a second-best basis.

The linked experiments in political democracy and
consumer sovereignty that characterize free societies are
premised on a leap of faith in the capacity of the individual
to assimilate information and to make rational, informed
choices. In place of faith in the individual, censors propose a vote of "no confidence" in the capacity of individual hearers to decide for themselves whether or not
speech is worth listening to. . . . Sooner or later, censorship corrodes the foundations of a free society by gnawing
away at the faith in the individual on which all free
institutions are ultimately based.

Alcohol and cigarette producers have tried to wrap
themselves in the First Amendment. One would
think from their pronouncements that it protects
all their activities. Commercial speech is commercial advertising, or, in the words of the U.S. Supreme Court,
"speech that proposes a commercial transaction." However, the Supreme Court stated in 1986 that what's called
the commercial speech doctrine does not protect their
advertising.

For most of the history of the republic, commercial
speech received no legal protection whatsoever. Today, it
occupies a subordinate position in the hierarchy of First
Amendment values. Specifically, a law that promotes a
substantial state interest, and by means that are no more
extensive than necessary to serve that interest, is not
contrary to First Amendment protections. The "interest,"
of course, in this case would be the public health. . . .

As U.S. Supreme Court Justice Tom Clark once said,
"There is no war between the Constitution and common
sense. "Cigarettes and alcoholic beverages present a major
health problem. Nothing in the commercial speech doctrine prevents Congress or the states from taking reasonable steps to address the genuine public health problems
associated with alcohol and cigarettes, and the Supreme
Court has so recognized.

Cigarette companies have used reverence for the First
Amendment to get broadcasters to air what functions as
image advertising. By sponsoring advertising that says
"We're for the First Amendment," a cigarette company
such as Philip Morris can get its name on television in a
favorable context, one which assists its lobbying on Capitol Hill. . . . [T]he advertising conducted by tobacco companies does have an effect. Most Americans think, given
this blitz of advertising, that the First Amendment must
protect cigarette advertisers.

An outright ban on alcohol and tobacco advertising
would clearly be constitutional under a doctrine propounded in a 1986 Supreme Court decision about a law
regulating gambling, *Posados de Puerto Rico Associates v.
Tourism Council of Puerto Rico*. In it the court stated: "It
would be a strange constitutional doctrine which would
concede to the legislature the authority to totally ban a
product or activity but deny to the legislature the authority
to forbid the stimulation of demand for the product or
activity or advertising on behalf of those who would profit
from such increased demand."

# An Education in Advertising

Samuel Johnson, the 18th-century English writer, may have set a standard for lay critics of advertising when he noted in *The Idler* (1759): "Advertisements are now so numerous that they are very negligently perused, and it [has] therefore become necessary to gain attention by magnificence of promise and by eloquence sometimes sublime and sometimes ridiculous."

But today's scholarly study of advertising is a new and improved pursuit. "There's been a huge surge of interest in advertising and consumer culture from historians, sociologists and anthropologists," says Roland Marchand, a professor of history at the University of California-Davis.†

It wasn't until the late 1970s and early '80s, two decades after Vance Packard published his groundbreaking book *The Hidden Persuaders*, that academics such as Marchand (*Advertising the American Dream*), Hunter College's Stuart Ewen (*Captains of Consciousness*) and Rutgers University's T. J. Jackson Lears (*Some Versions of Fantasy: Toward a Cultural History of American Advertising*) dug up and interpreted the ads that shaped the modern mass market.

It is in such works that critics of advertising's effects on society see a solution: educate consumers in what they call "media literacy" to allow them to "decode" the subtle effects of ads.

In Los Angeles, the Center for Media and Values works to create "values-based media literacy curricula and resources" for high schools, colleges, religious institutions and community centers. Founded in 1989 by Sister Elizabeth Thoman, the center warns that Americans lag behind their European, Canadian and Australian counterparts in establishing media studies programs in public schools. Through its quarterly magazine, *Media and Values,* and other publications, the center raises awareness of ads that are deceptive or sexist or that promote use of alcohol and tobacco.

A similar group, the Media Foundation in Vancouver, British Columbia, Canada, publishes *Adbusters* magazine, which critiques ads that are sexist, anti-health or anti-environment. The foundation supports the airing of "alternative" public interest advertising and organizes letter-writing campaigns against offending companies.

Not to be outdone on the education front, the U.S. advertising industry has its Advertising Educational Foundation, which since 1983 has sponsored visiting lecturers on campuses and encouraged academics to study ad agencies. The foundation's initiatives are part of an industry effort to alleviate what DeWitt F. Helm Jr., president of the Association of National Advertisers, calls an "information gap" in the public mind that leaves people "jaundiced" about advertising and its role in the U.S. economy.

In the past few years, several archives of print and broadcast advertisements have been established, notably at the American Advertising Museum in Portland, Ore.; the Smithsonian Institution in Washington, D.C.; Duke University, in Durham, N.C.; and the University of British Columbia. The Smithsonian describes its Center for Advertising History as "a unique window on America's past ... a record of our desires and aspirations, our values and fears." Curators examine and document the creative process that produced famous ad campaigns such as Nike's use of sports celebrities, Alka Seltzer's "Speedy" and Federal Express' fast talker.

**Alka Seltzer's "Speedy"**

"There are no obvious, clear-cut answers to the important questions" about advertising's effects, notes the Smithsonian's chief archivist, John A. Fleckner. "People 50 to 100 years from now will have a good deal more insight into what advertising meant in the late 20th century, when they can see where the next century is going." ††

William O'Barr is trying to find some answers in his Duke University classroom. O'Barr, a professor of cultural anthropology and sociology and curator of the 2-million-piece J. Walter Thompson archive of advertising history, teaches a course on the effects of advertising on society. He finds the attitude of his students instructive."They all say they hate ads, never watch them and are not affected by them, but they're very attracted [to the class]. They're trying to understand something they already know intuitively."

---

† Quoted in *The New York Times* Oct. 9, 1988.

†† Quoted in *Express Magazine*, September 1989.

Continued from p. 672
1984 from cancer. Her husband sued the manufacturer of her favorite cigarettes, blaming their advertisements for her death. A lower court awarded him $400,000. In the appeal, *Thomas Cippolone v. Liggett Group Inc.*, the Supreme Court will decide whether the health warnings on the cigarette pack required under the federal Cigarette Labeling and Advertising Act prevent such tort claims for damages. During the trial, an advertising historian testified that from 1940-60, half of all cigarette ads had used healthiness as a theme.

"The climate for us is never easy," says the Tobacco Institute's Merryman. "New restrictions or a ban could come tomorrow." Tobacco companies received good news this July, however, when a judge in Canada ruled that the country's three-year-old ban on tobacco advertising was unconstitutional. Canada's ban is frequently cited as a model by American proponents of a ban on tobacco ads.

Because advertising is a major component of the U.S. economy (it has been called the "lifeblood of capitalism"), efforts to restrict ads or wean society from its dependence on advertising face tough going. Magazines such as *Reader's Digest* make huge financial sacrifices when they refuse to accept alcohol and tobacco ads. Also, corporations with mammoth advertising budgets have tremendous clout in the marketplace. Two years ago that fact was driven home to Saatchi & Saatchi, one of the world's largest ad agencies, when it wrote an ad for Northwest Airlines announcing its new no-smoking policy. In apparent retaliation, RJR Nabisco canceled contracts worth $84 million with the London-based agency, contracts not for tobacco ads but for Nabisco food products.[24]

Corporations complain that while their ads sometimes highlight social problems, they aren't to blame. Liz Dolan, public relations director for embattled Nike, says black children in the inner city are killing themselves not over running shoes but "over 10 cents." "If you want to address the problem of hopelessness in the inner city," she adds, "you have to start with education, basic nutrition and an intact family structure."

Indeed, the advertisers' embrace of the First Amendment strikes a chord with many Americans. As a result, says media critic Jean Kilbourne, there is much "confusion today about what censorship is. People feel that if they speak out against something, or leaflet a porno theater, it's censorship."

Nevertheless, six out 10 Americans say advertising insults them.[25] "We're reaching the point," says Professor Rotzoll at the University of Illinois, "where decisions should be made as to what the proper limits of commercial content are. There are all sorts of values in our rich society, and the commercial ones are getting drummed in more and more at the expense of more-enduring values."

While they still defend what they see as their central place in American society, advertisers have learned to acknowledge their critics. "Americans have had a love affair with advertising," DeWitt Helm told the Association of National Advertisers annual meeting last October. "They laugh at our jokes. They sing our jingles. And they buy the products and services we tell them about. Advertising is an old friend. But as with any long-term friendship, disagreements arise, disillusionments occur. It's now up to us to woo the public and restore its confidence in the integrity of our messages." ∎

## Notes

[1] Quoted in *Business Week*, April 30, 1990, p. 70.
[2] The marketing plan for Dakota, leaked to the Washington-based Advocacy Institute, described the target user.
[3] Peter F. Drucker, *The New Realities* (1989), p. 99.
[4] For background, see "Controversy Over Multicultural Education," *Editorial Research Reports*, Nov. 30, 1990, pp. 681-696.
[5] Eric Clark, *The Want Makers* (1989), p. 169.
[6] *Television/Radio Age*, March 3, 1986, p. 104.
[7] Quoted in *Newsweek*, Aug. 14, 1989, p. 34.
[8] Quoted in *The Washington Post*, April 4, 1989.
[9] Quoted in Kim B. Rotzoll, *Advertising and Ethics: Observations on the Dimensions of a Cluttered Battleground* (1989), p. 2.
[10] *Ibid.*, p. 27.
[11] *Business Week*, March 19, 1991, p. 100.
[12] Quoted in *The New York Times*, April 4, 1990.
[13] Figures cited in *The New York Times*, Aug. 12, 1991.
[14] Joseph Seldin, *The Golden Fleece: Advertising in American Life* (1963), p. 14.
[15] Philip Gold, *Advertising, Politics and American Culture* (1987), p. 31.
[16] See *The Washington Post*, Aug. 10, 1991.
[17] Quoted in *Christian Science World Monitor*, December 1990, p. 28.
[18] Quoted in *The New York Times*, Oct. 19, 1990.
[19] See *The Washington Post*, Aug. 2. 1991.
[20] Quoted in *TV Guide*, June 13, 1987, p. 8.
[21] Quoted in *U.S. News & World Report*, Nov. 6, 1989, p. 34.
[22] *Ibid.*
[23] From *Broadcasting Advertiser Reports*, cited by NAB President Edward O. Fritts.
[24] Richard W. Pollay, "Cigarettes Under Fire: Blowing Away the PR Smoke Screen," *Media and Values*, spring-summer 1991, p. 13.
[25] Results of a survey last year by the DDB Needham ad agency.

# Bibliography

## Selected Sources Used

## Books

**Barthel, Diane, *Putting on Appearance: Gender and Advertising*, Temple University Press, 1988.**

A study of the role of beauty in advertising and how Madison Avenue draws from and influences men and women's notions of gender ideals. The book contains ad industry anecdotes, particularly from women's magazines.

**Clark, Eric, *The Want Makers: The World of Advertising, How They Make You Buy*, Viking, 1989.**

A British journalist lays out in great detail the central issues confronting the advertising industry and its critics. He says the proliferation of electronics means that the real explosion in advertising is still to come.

**Gold, Philip, *Advertising, Politics and American Culture: From Salesmanship to Therapy*, Paragon House Publishers, 1987.**

An examination of the interaction of advertising with social and political conflict through several decades of American history, with an emphasis on psychology.

**Liess, William; Kline, Stephen; and Ghally, Sut, *Social Communication in Advertising: Persons, Products & Images of Well-Being*, Methuen, 1986.**

A scholarly survey of literature on advertising's effects on culture and social and economic issues. It recounts the common attacks on advertising as well as the counter-arguments.

**Meyer, William, *The Image Makers: Power and Persuasion on Madison Avenue*, Times Books, 1984.**

A veteran journalist and advertising man surveys contemporary advertising techniques and issues, providing insider details of how advertising agencies create campaigns.

**Schudson, Michael, *Advertising, The Uneasy Persuasion: Its Dubious Impact on American Society*, Basic Books, Publishers, 1984.**

A sociologist and communications professor at the University of California-San Diego surveys advertising issues. He concludes that ads reinforce rather than create consumer needs.

**Seldin, Joseph, *The Golden Fleece: Advertising in American Life*, The Macmillan Co., 1963.**

A veteran advertising man surveys the history of advertising and highlights marketplace trends up to the early 1960s.

## Reports

**Hacker, George A.; Collins, Ronald; and Jacobson, Michael, *Marketing Booze to Blacks*, Center for Science in the Public Interest, 1987.**

Citing government health statistics and analyzing corporate advertising strategies, this report lays out the case of health activists who oppose alcohol advertising that targets blacks.

**Maxwell, Bruce, and Jacobson, Michael, *Marketing Disease to Hispanics: The Selling of Alcohol, Tobacco and Junk Foods*, Center for Science in the Public Interest, 1989.**

Case studies and critical analysis of how corporations are targeting the newly emerging Hispanic market.

**Rotzoll, Kim B., *Advertising and Ethics — Observations on the Dimensions of a Cluttered Battleground*, Department of Advertising, College of Communications, University of Illinois at Urbana-Champaign, 1989.**

This report attempts to explain the motivations of both advertisers and the critics of advertising. It explores why advertising always has been, and probably always will be, controversial.

# The Next Step

## Additional Articles from Current Periodicals

### Alcohol

**"Broadcasters face growing pressure on alcohol ads,"** *Broadcasting*, April 22, 1991, p. 68.

Discusses how legislation that would require health warnings in alcohol advertising is gaining support within Congress, according to members of the House Energy and Commerce Committee see it; the growing pressure surrounding the issue of alcohol advertising; Bill Richardson (D-N.M.) said restrictions on alcohol advertising are an infringement of the First Amendment; more.

### Children

**Colford, S.W., "Top kid TV offender: Premiums,"** *Advertising Age*, Apr. 29, 1991, p. 52.

Presents the results to a recent study which showed that fast-food marketers and 900-number services most often violate the voluntary guidelines of the National Advertising Division's Children's Advertising Review Unit. Also includes a list of advertisements in violation of NAD guidelines.

**Kunkel, D. and D. Roberts, "Young minds and marketplace values: Issues in children's television advertising,"** *Journal of Social Issues*, spring 1991, p. 57.

Reviews research on young children's responses to television commercials in the context of the history of attempts to regulate television advertising directed to children. Examines the use of research in the policymaking process; uses a developmental perspective in addressing the research evidence; assesses the role of research while providing an historical overview of the key regulatory decisions affecting children's television advertising.

### Debates & issues

**Beschloss, S., "Making the rules in prime time,"** *Channels*, May 7, 1990, p. 23.

Examines the ongoing battle between program producers and censors about what is acceptable content on television. Pressure on programmers to bolster flagging ratings by pushing the medium's boundaries; concern of advertisers; transferring standards responsibilities from censors to programmers. INSET: A partial who's who in network standards.

**Colford, S.W., "Protests of CNN hit advertisers,"** *Advertising Age*, Feb. 18, 1991, p. 1.

Discusses why several national advertisers, including Nabisco Brands, have received many angry letters urging them to pull their advertising from the Cable News Network, because of correspondent Peter Arnett's reports from Baghdad. Some of the calls and letters expressed concern that Arnett was serving as a mouthpiece for Iraqi propaganda. Interview with Saddam Hussein; ratings; letters not from organized boycott groups; advertising influencing editorial?

**Horton, C., "Hyundai pulls planned ad in L.A. beating aftermath,"** *Advertising Age*, April 22, 1991, p. 2.

Features the decision of Hyundai Motor America to withdraw one commercial from their newest advertising campaign, at the last second. The decision followed a Los Angeles newspaper report linking the commercial to a recent incident in which white Los Angeles police officers brutally beat Rodney G. King, a black driver said to have been pulled over for speeding. The ads' connection to the incident; description of the ad; more.

**Schiller, Z. and M. Landler, "P&G can get mad, sure, but does it have to get even? "** *Business Week*, June 4, 1990, p. 65.

Describes the strident attack on one of the nation's most powerful advertisers, Proctor & Gamble, by a liberal political group called Neighbor to Neighbor. Out of 30 television stations asked to air an ad boycotting Folgers coffee, all but two refused. P&G, in return, pulled all their other ads from the stations which aired the ad.

### Elections

**"Myths unmasked,"** *Broadcasting*, March 25, 1991, p. 114.

Editorial. Focuses on a current study by the 'Los Angeles Times,' revealing that just over one-third of the money spent in Senate races and only about one-fourth of the money spent in House races was spent on advertising in all media (television, radio, newspapers and billboards). Opposes the campaigns that are financed by special interest groups that supply candidates with more and more money.

**"Pol ads: Right fight, wrong reason,"** *Advertising Age*, May 13, 1991, p. 20.

Editorial. Addresses the accusation of Alex Kroll, incoming chairman of the American Association of Advertising Agencies, that political advertisers are ruining the reputation of advertising. Author's opinion that the media and advertising should present the truth about politicians; unfair to put down only political advertisers when some others also give advertising a bad name; work for better political ads as a step toward better government.

**Kamber, V., "Political discourse descends into trivia," *Advertising Age*, Feb. 25, 1991, p. 20.**

Opinion. Debates whether or not negative campaign advertising is the prime cause of declining voter turnout and increased alienation from the political process. States that the true cause of the problem is not negative advertising, but the absence of any substantive discussion of issues in campaigns. Includes several recommendations which would elevate the quality of political discourse.

## Environment

**Beers, D. and C. Capellaro, "Greenwash! " *Mother Jones*, March/April 1991, p. 38.**

Criticizes the recent trend in advertising known as greenwashing, which attempts to co-opt environmentalism. Gives examples of its use by such companies as Arco, Chevron, Mobil, Texaco, Waste Management Inc., Louisiana Pacific, IBM, The Nuclear Regulatory Commission, GE, and the Chemical Manufacturer's Association.

**Colford, S.W., "Greening of NAD? " *Advertising Age*, Feb. 11, 1991, p. 3.**

Examines how the ad industry's scramble to develop environmental marketing guidelines took a new twist last week when the Association of National Advertisers asked the industry's self-regulatory arm to consider issuing green guidelines. The ANA's request to the National Advertising Division of the Council of Better Business Bureaus comes as the Federal Trade Commission this week is expected to receive a similar request from a group of major marketers and trade associations.

**Landler, M., Z. Schiller, et al., "Suddenly, green marketers are seeing red flags," *Business Week*, Feb. 25, 1991, p. 74.**

Shows how after a decade of complacency, the Federal Trade Commission is clamping down on advertisers that make false or deceptive claims. Explains why the FTC has done a 180-degree turnaround on false advertising. Examples of prosecution are given; heightened vigilance comes after a five-year stretch in which advertisers made increasingly farfetched health claims; hefty damages; drafting guidelines. INSET: Ads under attack.

**Lawrence, J., P. Sloan, et al., "Toiletries to strip excess packaging," *Advertising Age*, May 13, 1991, p. 3.**

Highlights how Procter & Gamble Co. and other marketers, both in the U.S. and around the world, are removing excess packaging from brands to reduce solid waste in the latest "green marketing" trend. Source reduction efforts are taking hold because of increasing concerns about solid waste. In the next few months, consumers will start to see more unboxed or cartonless products on store shelves — particularly in the health and beauty care category.

**Levin, G., "Think twice about ad claims," *Advertising Age*, Feb. 4, 1991, p. 13.**

Advises advertisers to use green claims with great caution for their products. One should be certain a product offers a significant environmental, health or human service advantage before launching a green campaign. Lists the questions the Environmental Protection Agency uses to gauge a product's safety; legitimate green products with identifiable benefits.

**Mark, K., "Canada plans ads for green logo," *Advertising Age*, April 8, 1991, p. 18.**

Discusses the Canadian government's plan to promote its Environmental Choice Program's EcoLogo with a multimillion-dollar ad campaign starting in June. The goal of the voluntary program; what is required of companies seeking approval for the green EcoLogo; how the TV, radio and print campaign will help consumers better understand the meaning behind the EcoLogo; environmentally safe labels help to sell a product.

## Health aspects

**Lawrence, J. and S. Hume, "Texas notches a win over Kellogg," *Advertising Age*, April 8, 1991, p. 6.**

Reports that U.S. District Judge A. Joe Fish denied Kellogg's motion for a preliminary injunction that would have prevented the Texas Department of Health from detaining Heartwise cereal, a product that contains the "drug" psyllium. Judge Fish ruled Kellogg misrepresented Heartwise and promoted it as a cholesterol-reducing product based on its psyllium content; promotes state law enforcement against food marketers.

**Liesse, J. and J. Dagnoli, "Kraft, Campbell on health kick," *Advertising Age*, Feb. 11, 1991, p. 1.**

Summarizes how Kraft General Foods and Campbell Soup Co. are targeting ConAgra's popular Healthy Choice brand in what looks like a game of catch-up in the food industry. As ConAgra tests Healthy Choice line extensions in a variety of product categories, No. 1 food marketer Kraft General Foods is ready to test a broad line of "foods for healthier eating" called Kraft Alternatives. Features; outlook; competition.

## Moral & religious aspects

**Alster, N., "Crude doesn't sell," *Forbes*, Jan. 21, 1991, p. 60.**

Reports that sex and smut, which were going to win

back audiences for TV networks, hasn't worked. "Hull High" and "Doctor, Doctor," resounding flops; cable having enormous success with old-fashioned family programs; sex and profanity the reason for woes; American parents change channels when watching with children; letters to advertisers; successful and clean shows rate over smutty material; ignoring shift in audience tastes; pursuit of younger viewers out of hand; more.

Ramirez, A., "Burger King ads help end boycott by religious group," *The New York Times,* Nov. 7, 1990, p. D1.

Discusses the skirmish between Burger King Corporation and the Christian Leadership for Responsible Television. Earlier this year, the group had accused the company of sponsoring television shows that were "against family values" and began a boycott of the chain in September. Burger King's large newspaper advertisement saying it supported "traditional American values on television" helped end the boycott.

## Racism

"Billboard battle won," *Christian Century,* April 11, 1990, p. 361.

Covers Metropolitan Outdoor Advertising Company's decision to stop displaying billboards which advertise alcohol and cigarettes near schools and churches in Harlem. Campaign against minority-targeted advertisements.

Morganthau, T., "Sullivan: Bush's aide makes waves," *Newsweek,* March 5, 1990, p. 19.

Discusses the attack of secretary of Health and Human Services Dr. Louis W. Sullivan on R.J. Reynolds for test-marketing a new brand of cigarettes aimed specially at African-Americans, and his recent protest of the Virginia Slims women's tennis tour, sponsored by Philip Morris. Once powerful tobacco lobby in obvious disarray; industry's marketing practices. INSET: Cigarettes in search of a target.

## Sponsorship of athletics

"Corralling tobacco's sports ties," *Advertising Age,* April 22, 1991, p. 22.

Editorial. Comments on the latest pressure campaign being launched by U.S. Health and Human Services Secretary Louis Sullivan, which opposes the idea of tobacco companies sponsoring sporting events. Tells how Sullivan, a powerful anti-cigarette force, is calling for fans and athletes to boycott such activities. Pressure expected to mount against governments, stadium owners, teams, and athletes; what the campaign calls for; a question of where the campaigns will end.

Cohen, S., "Smoke screen," *Women's Sports & Fitness,* May/June 1991, p. 54.

Examines the growing controversy over the link between cigarettes and tennis. Pressure to withdraw from sponsorship of cigarette firms; Virginia Slims' sponsorship; Philip Morris' contribution to women's tennis. INSET: Under fire (cigarette sponsorship), by S.C.

## Tobacco

Amos, A., B. Jacobson, et al., "Cigarette advertising policy and coverage of smoking and health in British women's magazines," *Lancet,* Jan. 12, 1991, p. 93.

Compares the results of a 1989 survey of cigarette advertising and coverage of health aspects of smoking in British magazines with a large female readership with the results of a 1985 survey which led to new voluntary restrictions in 1986 on cigarette advertising in magazines. Restrictions appear to have had a small effect on cigarette advertising and have failed to achieve their aim.

Colford, S.W., "Tobacco group ends paid placements," *Advertising Age,* Dec. 17, 1990, p. 31.

Examines the Tobacco Institute's announcement of a series of voluntary youth-oriented restrictions on cigarette sampling, movie placements, and other marketing practices. Federal legislation introduced in recent congressional sessions; seen as "smoke screens" by anti-tobacco lawmakers; ads to run in major magazines; focus of the drive to help parents help their children resist peer pressure to start smoking; changes in marketing; supervision of vending machines; more.

Colford, S.W. and Dagnoli, J., "Surgeon general raps ad shops," *Advertising Age,* Oct. 8, 1990, p. 77.

Profiles how Surgeon General Antonia Novello, in her first policy address against tobacco advertising, targeted for special criticism the ad agencies that handle tobacco accounts. Softer stand than predecessor, C. Everett Koop; attack on agencies is called unfair; more.

Mintz, M., "Marketing tobacco to children," *Nation,* May 6, 1991, p. 577.

Reports on the alarmingly successful advertising and promotion of tobacco to children by the tobacco companies. Lawsuit in Canada that challenged the constitutionality of its Tobacco Products Control Act of 1988; why adolescents are targeted; industry techniques for targeting children.

# Back Issues

*Great Research on Current Issues Starts Right Here. . . Recent topics covered by The CQ Researcher are listed below. Issues dated before May 10, 1991, were published under the name of Editorial Research Reports.*

**MARCH 1990**
Asbestos: Are Risks Acceptable?
Public Health Campaigns
South Africa's Future
Homeless Need More Than Shelter

**APRIL 1990**
How Fair is the Tax Burden?
Workers' Compensation
U.S. Pacific Forces
Curbing Insurance Premiums

**MAY 1990**
Should Teaching Be a Profession?
Will Canada Fall Apart?
Is U.S. Patent System Outdated?
Federal Funding for the Arts

**JUNE 1990**
Downsizing America's Armed Forces
Progress In Weather Forecasting
S & L Bailout
Bio-Chemical Disarmament

**JULY 1990**
Do Americans Still Love Marriage?
Death Penalty Debate
Decline of Rural America
United Nations in the 1990s

**AUGUST 1990**
Democracy in the Philippines
Initiatives: True Democracy?
Hard Times at Newspapers
Teens Balance School & Jobs

**SEPTEMBER 1990**
Dangers of Alcohol
Western Alliance After the Cold War
Tobacco Industry
Right to Die

**OCTOBER 1990**
Organ Transplants
Energy Policy Options
Search for Arab Unity
Child Support

**NOVEMBER 1990**
Lotteries and Gambling
Post Cold-War Choices
Setting Limits on Medical Care
Multicultural Education

**DECEMBER 1990**
Cable TV Regulation
Americans' Search For Their Roots
Is Insurance System a Failure?
Why Schools Still Have Tracking

**JANUARY 1991**
Growing Influence of Boycotts
Should the U.S. Reinstate the Draft?
America's Archaeological Past
Peace Corps' Challenges in '90s

**FEBRUARY 1991**
Regional Impact of Recession
Puerto Rico's Status
Redistricting: Mapping Power
Nuclear Power

**MARCH 1991**
Acid Rain
Cost of the Gulf War
Reassessing Gun Laws
Future for Man in Space

**APRIL 1991**
Social Security
Canadian Crisis Over Quebec
California Drought
Electromagnetic Radiation

**MAY 1991**
School Choice
Racial Quotas
Animal Rights
U.S. and Japan

**JUNE 1991**
Children and Divorce
Teenage Suicide
Endangered Species
Europe 1992

**JULY 1991**
Teenagers and Abortion
Soviet Republics Rebel
Mexico's Emergence
Athletes and Drugs

**AUGUST 1991**
Sexual Harassment
Fetal Tissue Research
Oil Imports
The Palestinians

**SEPTEMBER 1991**
Police Brutality

Back issues are available for $4.00 (subscribers) or $7.00 (non-subscribers). Quantity discounts apply to orders over ten. To order, call Congressional Quarterly 1-800-432-2250.

# Future Topics

▶ *Threatened Forests*

▶ *Foster Care*

▶ *Pay-Per-View TV*

# THE CQ Researcher

PUBLISHED BY CONGRESSIONAL QUARTERLY INC., IN CONJUNCTION WITH EBSCO PUBLISHING

# Saving the Forests

*Conservation efforts are mounting, but so are the losses*

FOR THE PAST DECADE, ENVIRONMENTALISTS have been warning that the world's forests are being eradicated. Seemingly insatiable demands for timber, fuel-wood and other products are only part of the problem. Forests also face growing pressure, especially in developing countries, from cattle ranchers and farmers. Now scientists' warnings about "global warming" are giving new urgency to deforestation concerns. Evidence is mounting that tree loss intensifies the so-called greenhouse effect because burning and decaying trees release heat-trapping carbon dioxide. The causes of deforestation are clear, but they are complex and interrelated, and efforts to stem the tide have been largely ineffective. A worldwide environmental summit on global warming scheduled for next year is likely to focus new attention on forest destruction.

September 20, 1991 • Volume 1, No. 19 • 681-704

*Formerly Editorial Research Reports*

COVER ART: BARBARA SASSA-DANIELS

*CQ Researcher*

September 20, 1991
Volume 1, No. 19

**EDITOR**
Sandra Stencel

**MANAGING EDITOR**
Thomas J. Colin

**ASSOCIATE EDITOR**
Richard L. Worsnop

**STAFF WRITERS**
Charles S. Clark
Mary H. Cooper
Rodman D. Griffin

**PRODUCTION EDITOR**
Laurie De Maris

**EDITORIAL ASSISTANT**
Thomas H. Moore

**GRAPHICS**
Jack Auldridge

**PUBLISHED BY**
Congressional Quarterly Inc.

**CHAIRMAN**
Andrew Barnes

**VICE CHAIRMAN**
Andrew P. Corty

**EDITOR AND PUBLISHER**
Neil Skene

**EXECUTIVE EDITOR**
Robert W. Merry

**PUBLICATIONS MARKETING/SALES**
Robert Smith

**EDITOR, EBSCO PUBLISHING**
Melissa Kummerer

The CQ Researcher (ISSN 1056-2036). Formerly Editorial Research Reports. Published weekly (48 times per year, not printed the first Friday of any month with five Fridays) by Congressional Quarterly Inc., 1414 22nd St., N.W., Washington, D.C. 20037. Rates are furnished upon request. Application to mail at second-class postage rates is pending at Washington, D.C. POSTMASTER: Send address changes to The CQ Researcher, 1414 22nd St., N.W., Washington, D.C. 20037.

# Saving the Forests

By Mary H. Cooper

## The Issues

Dramatic satellite photographs of Brazilian rain forests spewing flames and black smoke shocked the globe into a sudden and grim awareness in 1987: The Earth's forests are being destroyed at a startling pace. That year, cattle ranchers and farmers eager to exploit the land under the thick forest canopy put the torch to millions of acres of the Amazon Basin's pristine woodland.

But deforestation — and its awesome consequences — is hardly limited to Brazil. Events the world over can be traced to deforestation: last spring's disastrous floods in Bangladesh; the uprooting of forest dwellers from their ancestral lands in northern Borneo; the relentless southward spread of the Sahara Desert in Africa, encouraging famine; and, in the Northwestern United States, the destruction of an evergreen that is the only known source of a newly discovered cancer-treatment agent.

Forest destruction causes many less visible, but potentially more devastating, environmental problems. It dooms thousands of plant and animal species to extinction, often before they have been discovered. It often triggers a reduction in local rainfall. Perhaps most damaging of all, deforestation may hasten the process of global warming, a potentially catastrophic trend that may soon distort weather patterns in many parts of the world.

Forestry experts agree that the 1980s have seen a rapid acceleration in the pace of deforestation throughout the 7 percent of the Earth's land surface that is still forest-covered. In 1987 alone, some 17 million hectares (a hectare is the metric equivalent of 2.47 acres) of so-called

closed, or dense, tropical forest were destroyed, up from 7.5 million hectares in 1981.[1]

Although these figures are only estimates, they indicate a trend that is not open to question. If destruction of the world's forests continues at today's pace, Costa Rica, El Salvador, Haiti, Paraguay, Côte d'Ivoire (Ivory Coast) and Nigeria will have no more forests at all within the next 30 years.[2] According to the environmental group Greenpeace, 14.2 million hectares of the world's forestland disappear every year, or 1.8 percent of the total.[3]

Gauging just how fast Earth's forests are shrinking nonetheless stymies the experts because reliable information is hard to obtain. In some countries facing deforestation, officials either can't or won't measure the pace of destruction. Even satellite imaging techniques don't work well because smoke from fires set to clear away trees screens vast areas from view. Published statistics aren't too much help either. Most publica-

tions still cite figures published by the United Nations' Food and Agriculture Organization (FAO) in 1970 and 1980. But more recent data suggest that these earlier figures greatly understate the extent of the problem. FAO is scheduled to release new findings next year. Meanwhile, other organizations agree that the pace of deforestation quickened during the 1980s.

One thing is clear: Governments have tolerated the destruction of their forests for decades, unable or unwilling to stop the cutting because it often has served useful purposes.

Until recently, forest clearing in newly emerging nations was seen primarily as a positive step, necessary for industrial and agricultural development and for building roads, dams and other vital infrastructure. Now, however, as populations in many developing countries skyrocket, forests offer a convenient "safety valve," a place where the poor can eke out a living far from overcrowded cities and a government that can't afford to help them.

The obstacles to halting deforestation have seemed insurmountable. "It's almost in danger of becoming one of those topics like the weather, that everyone talks about but no one does anything about," says Gareth Porter, project director of the Environmental and Energy Study Institute.* He and other environmentalists hope next summer's scheduled Earth Summit in Rio de Janeiro, Brazil, will focus the world's attention on deforestation and find ways to combat the related social and eco-

*The institute is an independent research organization that was created by Congress in 1984 to help produce policies for environmentally sustainable development. Porter spoke at a meeting of congressional staff members held by the institute July 26.

nomic problems. (*See p. 696.*) Here are some of the questions they'll be trying to answer:

### Where does most deforestation occur?

Deforestation hits hardest in tropical forests, those vast tracts bordering the equator. (*See map, p. 692*). One variety, the rain forest of the Amazon and Congo basins, receives large amounts of rainfall and remains warm year-round. Tropical forests also include the dry savanna type found in India and Africa, as well as the mostly evergreen variety of the Andes and Himalaya mountain ranges.

Tropical forests cover 780 million hectares (35-43 percent of the world's forests) in more than 70 countries. But more than 97 percent of the tropical forests lie within the boundaries of 34 countries in three global regions: Latin America, Southeast Asia and Africa. And it is forests in these 34 countries that draw the greatest concern about deforestation. Most are moist lowland rain forests, which are disappearing the fastest — fully 20.4 million hectares annually, according to the World Resources Institute (WRI).[4]

Latin America suffers the world's highest rate of deforestation. The WRI estimates that this region loses about 1.3 percent of its forests each year, compared with 0.9 percent in Asia, 0.6 percent in Africa and 0.1 percent in the United States.[5]

In 1987, *Time* magazine dedicated a cover story to the burning of vast forest tracts in Brazil's Amazon Basin.[6] The country's forest loss that year alone was an unprecedented 9 million hectares. Although its rate of deforestation has since subsided, due in part to development-policy changes, Brazil still destroys more forestland than any country in the world. Most of the devastation has been in four states of northwestern Amazonia — Rondônia, Acre, Mato

Grosso and Para — at the hands of loggers, cattle ranchers and poor farmers who have fled overcrowded cities and barren fields in other parts of the country. Because Brazil contains fully a third of the world's remaining tropical forests — and more than the rest of Latin America combined — it gets most of the world's attention.

The pattern of deforestation seen in Brazil is common to much of the tropics. Typically, the forest's margins are destroyed by mechanized operations, such as commercial logging and road-building. Once the big trees are removed, landless "colonists" burn away the remaining brush and smaller trees to settle and cultivate the land.

Although Brazil, because of the vastness of its forests, leads the world in total acres deforested, other countries of Latin America are losing their forests at faster rates. Costa Rica, one of Central America's most affluent countries, razes 6.9 percent of its forests each year, the highest deforestation rate of any country on Earth. Its dry tropical forest, rich in tropical hardwoods, is disappearing even faster than the moist forests of Amazonia and parts of Southeast Asia and Africa. (*See table, p. 693.*)

In South Asia, the devastation has reached the point where no primary rain forest survives outside parks and reserves in Bangladesh, India and Sri Lanka. In Southeast Asia in particular, logging is the leading culprit. Indonesia, for example, contains the largest forested area in the world after Brazil, officially covering 140 million hectares of the country's total area of 190 million hectares. But vast stretches of this officially sanctioned area have been depleted by commercial logging operations.[7] Indonesia is not alone. In Malaysia, stands of prized Philippine mahogany trees are disappearing so fast that some timber-importing countries have bowed to pressure from environmental

groups and now boycott Malaysia's timber products — which constitute half the hardwood used in the world.

Coastal tropical forests are also being destroyed at an alarming rate. Mangroves, which thrive in tidal areas, today are even rarer than tropical timber. Mangrove swamps have made way for rice paddies and shrimp farms in Burma, Thailand and other Southeast Asian countries where mangrove swamps once rimmed the coastline, providing a line of defense against flooding.

Central Africa is the third major region that is undergoing rapid deforestation. There the focus of concern is sprawling Zaire, which like Brazil has vast tropical forest and a rapidly growing and impoverished rural population. While commercial logging takes a toll in Zaire, the rural poor cause the worst damage as they seek land for grazing and cultivation. Tropical forests, which covered about 1 million square kilometers in Zaire a decade ago, have been reduced to an estimated 70 million hectares.[8]

In West Africa, the never-ending search for fuel causes the deforestation problem. As the region's population increases, the number of trees cut for wood and charcoal exceeds the number of seedlings that survive to replenish the forests. The resulting deforestation is concentrated around urban areas, where wood gatherers have stripped the countryside bare of trees for many miles.[9] Deforestation from excessive removal of wood for fuel mainly occurs in dry forests, which also include the highland forests of the Hindu Kush, Andes and Himalayas. Even alpine forests have not been spared: Large stands of trees in the Himalayan highlands of Nepal are rapidly disappearing.

Forests in temperate climates, mostly in the more heavily industrialized Northern Hemisphere, have already been largely destroyed in the process of industrialization.

# The Deforestation Fighters

Several surprisingly dissimilar groups now fight to block deforestation; each one has its own special agenda. The following organizations have led the campaign to curb deforestation:

**United Nations Food and Agriculture Organization (FAO)**: The FAO's Committee on Forest Development in the Tropics has emerged as a leading force in the fight against deforestation. It is most commonly known by the acronym of a June 1985 agreement it supported, the Tropical Forestry Action Plan, or TFAP. The plan calls for reversing forest destruction throughout the world and improving the lives of forest dwellers by increasing food production while encouraging sustainable use of the forests. Critics fault the TFAP, however, for spending a third of its funds to support logging and fuel-wood plantations. These enterprises often involve the destruction of original forests even as they promote the planting of new trees. Less than 10 percent of TFAP resources are targeted for conservation.

**International Tropical Timber Organization (ITTO)**: Japan and Western industrial nations began negotiations for an International Tropical Timber Agreement in 1978. Largely reflecting the interests of the Japanese timber industry, which depends heavily on imports, the organization sought to preserve enough stands of tropical forest to assure an adequate and affordable supply of timber. When deforestation emerged as a pressing environmental issue in the 1980s, environmental organizations successfully lobbied ITTO to include forest conservation as well as "sustainable utilization," or managed harvesting, as two of the agreement's aims. Funded mostly by Japan, ITTO had a project budget of less than $5 million in 1990.

**International Monetary Fund, the World Bank and Other Multilateral Institutions**: Forestry and forest conservation projects account for a very small portion of development aid provided by such multilateral institutions as the International Monetary Fund, the World Bank and the regional development banks. Even though the World Bank instituted lending reforms in 1987 aimed in part at preserving the environment, the new policies have yet to have much impact on deforestation. Similarly, the regional development banks — the African, Asian, and Inter-American banks — have not acted on their stated commitment to lend money for conservation projects.

**Agency for International Development and Other Government Aid Programs**: Projects to curb deforestation also represent a small portion of aid provided by donor countries directly to Third World countries. The biggest single source of such grants and low-cost loans is the U.S. Agency for International Development (AID), which includes tree-planting projects in its budget. Japan, Scandinavian countries and Britain also earmark funds for forest management in developing countries, though critics charge these funds are often spent on reforestation projects aimed at enhancing timber supplies rather than preventing the clearing of natural forests.

**Environmental and Development Organizations**: Private groups that promote environmental protection, forest conservation and economic development in the Third World are largely responsible for pushing governments and international agencies to change their policies in ways that protect forests. For example, the World Resources Institute, an environmental-policy research organization based in Washington, D.C., worked with the United Nations Development Program and the World Bank to draw up the TFAP. The Worldwatch Institute, the World Wildlife Fund and the Conservation Foundation are among the other big groups that support scientific research and conservation projects to save tropical forests. In addition, many local environmental organizations around the world help carry out forest conservation projects that are funded by the World Bank and donor governments.

---

† For more information on these organizations, see Brian Johnson, *Responding to Tropical Deforestation: An Eruption of Crises — An Array of Solutions* (1991).

However, some temperate forests, such as the old-growth forests of the Pacific Northwest, are still being depleted by logging, though at a slower rate than many tropical forests. In addition, acid rain and air pollution are thinning the already diminished forests of Central Europe, as well as some areas of the United States and Canada.

Deforestation may now threaten the huge stands of evergreen and deciduous trees that make up the hemisphere's boreal, or northern, forests. Also known as the taiga, they account for a quarter of the world's remaining forests and stretch across vast, largely uninhabited regions of Alaska, Canada, Scandinavia and the Soviet Union south of the Arctic Circle. The Soviet taiga alone, with more than 1.6 billion acres, is three times bigger than Brazil's rain forest. Although these woodlands have largely escaped damage to date, they are coming under increasing pressure from industrialization, such as the construction of dams and factories in Siberia and the search for oil and other natural resources.[10]

## How does deforestation happen?

Although natural disasters, such as floods, volcanoes and forest fires set by lightning, destroy large areas of forests each year, they do not cause deforestation. Left to themselves, decimated woodlands replace themselves. Human activity causes true deforestation — the permanent loss of forested lands.

Commercial loggers were long thought to be the principal culprits in deforestation. Environmentalists point to the irreversible damage being wrought today in Indonesia and Malaysia, where government-sanctioned logging is removing great quantities of valuable tropical hardwoods for export to Japan and other timber importers in the industrial world.

While it is true that modern logging operations entail the use of large machines that destroy many trees besides the ones being extracted, the timber industry actually removes relatively few trees from the forests. Exports of tropical timber account for no more than 4 percent of all trees removed from the forests.[11] According to the U.N.'s Food and Agriculture Organization, more than 80 percent of the trees taken out of the world's forests are used for firewood, not lumber. Especially in Africa and India, rapidly growing populations of poor people often travel great distances to gather wood for cooking and heating.

It is not the loggers or fuel-wood gatherers, however, who deliver the death blow to the forests, but the ranchers and colonists, eager to exploit the forestland itself for grazing or agriculture. Typically, deforestation follows a similar pattern the world over. First, commercial loggers open tracts of forest by building logging roads, removing desirable trees and destroying undesirable ones with their heavy machinery. The forests, usually publicly owned, are then settled by impoverished colonists, who burn the partially cleared land much as forest dwellers have done for millennia. Then the newcomers plant crops.

But the slash-and-burn technique that has worked so well in the past quickly backfires for the colonists. Traditionally, forestland that was cleared in this way was used for only a season or two and then left fallow to recover, a process that took many years. Soil poor in the nutrients needed by grass and crops made the delay necessary. Colonists tend to exploit their cleared holdings for as long as possible, however, and after a few years they, too, must abandon the land. By then it is often so depleted that it can no longer support the vegetation that makes up the tropical forest. The colonists then leave their ruined lands to move further into the forest, often on the heels of commercial loggers.

Cattle ranchers often follow in the colonists' footsteps. Unlike the farmers, who typically are refugees from depleted land in other parts of the country or from unemployment in the cities, ranchers are often cattle barons, wealthy landowners who raise large herds of cattle, mostly for export. Because they can raise cattle at lower cost than their counterparts in the industrial world, these tropical ranchers are a favored source of beef for the hamburger sold in fast-food restaurants, mainly in the United States and Canada. But the depleted soil of former forestland cannot even support grasses for more than two or three years. So the ranchers and their cattle also move on, following in the footsteps of the loggers and colonists, leaving behind a wasteland and completing the process of deforestation.

## What are the underlying causes of deforestation?

Loggers, fuel-wood gatherers, colonists and ranchers may be the main agents of deforestation worldwide, but they aren't the cause. Fundamental reasons draw them to the forests in the first place. For the most part, these root causes of deforestation revolve around the whole problem of underdevelopment in the Third World. The first and most obvious cause in many countries undergoing rapid deforestation is poverty. Colonists and fuel-wood gatherers are most active in the least developed countries, where economic output, or gross national product (GNP), is less than $500 per capita. Such countries include Myanmar (Burma), India, Indonesia, Vietnam and virtually all the nations of East and West Africa. Among the world's wealthiest countries, with a per capita GNP of $6,000 or more, only the United States figures among the top 10 countries experiencing the greatest loss of forested land.[12]

Closely related to poverty is rapid population growth. In many regions of the world, especially Africa, large families are virtually the only source of social services for the elderly. Under these conditions, says Twig Johnson, chief of the Office of Forestry, Environment and Natural Resources at the U.S. Agency for International Development (AID), "the only assistance people have for sure is children, so they will have as many as they can."

But as the population increases, governments are harder pressed than ever to meet citizens' needs. As the population rises, the poorest people are pushed out of the cities and fertile agricultural areas to marginal lands. In countries where large forests still survive, desperate refugees head for these last untapped sources of sustenance. Clearing the forests for agricultural and other uses, however, is nothing more than a stopgap solution to poverty because the cleared land becomes barren within a few years. Johnson calls the combination of poverty and population growth a "negatively reinforcing system that is extremely powerful."[13]

# 'Debt-for-Nature' Swaps: An Ingenious Approach

In the late 1970s, hopeful Third World nations borrowed vast sums for development. But prosperity was elusive, and now many can't even make interest payments on the more than $1 trillion they owe to banks and governments of industrial nations, let alone pay off the principal. Much of the outstanding debt is unlikely ever to be repaid.

Although the so-called "debt crisis" has delayed economic development throughout the Third World, it also has inspired an ingenious response to the problem of deforestation, the "debt-for-nature swap." Introduced in 1987, the financial sleight-of-hand technique works like this: A private organization in the industrial world, usually an environmental group, buys a developing country's debt at discounted rates. (Banks that hold "bad" loans, as many Third World loans are classified, are eager to wipe them off their books). The environmental group then gives the loan agreement back to the indebted country in exchange for its commitment to complete a reforestation project or protect a given forested area from destruction.

One such swap was concluded between the government of Ecuador and two environmental groups, the U.S.-based World Wildlife Fund (WWF) and Fundación Natura of Ecuador.† WWF bought $1 million of Ecuador's debt on the open market for $353,500. In exchange, the central bank of Ecuador issued bonds in Fundación Natura's name for $1 million in local currency. Fundación Natura uses the interest income from the bonds to pay for forest protection projects in Ecuador and, when the bonds mature, will receive the principal for its endowment.

The debt-for-nature swap is a win-win transaction — the developing country owes less money to foreign lenders and receives "free" development aid, the bank gets back at least a portion of its original loan and the environmental organizations further their goal of curbing deforestation and promoting sustainable development. So far, however, debt-for-nature swaps have made little headway, mainly because the funds available to environmental groups through donations are a drop in the bucket compared with outstanding Third World debt.

All this may change, however, following the June announcement by BankAmerica Corp. that it would donate up to $6 million of its outstanding loans to Latin American countries to save the rain forests. The main beneficiaries of this year's donations, totaling $2 million, will be Mexico and Ecuador. BankAmerica, the holding company of Bank of America, is the first commercial financial institution to initiate a debt-for-nature swap. If other banks follow its example, swaps could provide a needed boost to the campaign against deforestation while offering some relief to indebted nations.

---

† See Nick Lenssen, "Debt-for-Nature Swaps," *World-Watch*, December 1988.

The potency of that system is seen in the rapid increase of the world's population, which has grown from 2 billion people to more than 5 billion over the past 50 years. Of the 2.6 billion people who live in the tropics, where most of the remaining forests stand, 750 million live in absolute poverty.[14] Most of the countries with high rates of deforestation are undergoing rapid population increases, notably in East and West Africa. But except for the United States and Thailand,[15] in no country among those experiencing the most extensive deforestation is the population at stable levels.

Some governments of countries already beleaguered by poverty and rapidly growing populations actually hasten the process of deforestation by encouraging the migration of landless poor to the forests. "Many of the root causes of deforestation lie outside the forests," says Howard Heiner, assistant director of the American Society of Foresters, who has worked extensively with international agencies and national forestry officials in Central America. He identifies tax breaks given to cattle ranchers and cultivators for clearing forest lands as a leading government incentive for deforestation in that region as elsewhere. The reason, he explains, is that governments often view the forests as untapped reserves where the unemployed poor can eke out a living and pose less of a threat to stability than they would in the cities.

"The forests are a social relief valve that drain off the landless poor from the cities," Heiner says. Brazil, for example, launched an extensive development plan for Amazonia to open up "land without people for people without land." New roads facilitated the migration of colonists to the northwestern states that became the symbol of deforestation in 1987.

More fundamentally, governments often perpetuate a social system that concentrates land ownership in the hands of a minuscule portion of the population. In Indonesia, where the government forced more than 2 million poor Javanese to resettle in the rain forests of southern Borneo, 1 percent of the population owns a third of the land.[16] Social injustice thus compounds the pressures of poverty and overpopulation that are building to erode the remaining forests in many countries. In many cases, indigenous forest dwellers are the main victims.

A symbol of their plight was Chico Mendes, a leader of the Brazilian rubber tappers, who was murdered in 1988 for his role in opposing the wholesale destruction by cattle ranchers and land speculators of the forests on which he and his supporters depended for a living. (*See p. 694.*) Since 1900, according to Cultural Survival, a human rights advocacy group in Cambridge, Mass., one Indian tribe in Brazil has been "destroyed" *every* year.

Until recent years governments found support for policies that threaten forests from the World Bank and other international development agencies that financed the construction of hydroelectric dams, roads and other large projects aimed at speeding industrialization in the Third World. Many of these projects were undertaken in forested areas and caused widespread destruction of the forest habitat.

The governments of industrialized countries and commercial banks have also, indirectly, fostered deforestation by extending excessive loans to many developing nations during the 1970s. Set back by the oil crises and global recession of the 1970s and early '80s, many countries have been unable to meet their repayment schedules, precipitating the Third World debt crisis. This indebtedness has impeded development in many nations with tropical forests, notably Brazil, and thus aggravated the conditions of poverty that favor deforestation. It has also blunted the sensitivity of many governments to environmentalists' warnings about the dangers posed by deforestation.

In the industrialized world, it is development pressure, not poverty, that lies at the root of deforestation. In the Eastern United States, southeastern Canada and Central Europe, acid rain is the big problem. Caused by the burning of coal and other fossil fuels, acid rain increases soil acidity and damages the leaves of trees for miles within heavily industrialized areas. (*See p. 690.*)

### How does deforestation affect the global environment?

Widespread destruction of forested land profoundly affects the surround-

© Plowden/Greenpeace 1989

*A towering old-growth tree in an African rain forest dwarfs a chainsaw-wielding logger. Logging is often the first step in the deforestation cycle, followed by farming.*

ing area. When loggers use clear-cut logging techniques, leaving few trees standing, the exposed topsoil easily washes away in heavy rains. Erosion occurs especially quickly on steep slopes and is aggravated when colonists move in to uproot any remaining vegetation. The soil ends up in streams and rivers, and eventually clogs downstream dams. Rising water levels eventually cause floods that are often far from the site of forest destruction. The flooding that devastated Bangladesh in 1988, for example, has been attributed to deforestation in the Nepalese Himalayas, hundreds of miles away.

Destruction of forests also has an immediate impact on local climate: There is less rain. Trees give off water vapor as a product of photosynthesis, and in rain forests they are a vital link in the hydrologic cycle. In the first phase, convection moves water through the roots of trees, then it enters the atmosphere by transpiring through the leaves. In the second phase of the cycle, the atmospheric water vapor collects in clouds and finally falls back to earth as rain. Deforestation reduces the amount of water released into the air, disrupting the cycle. The arid conditions that result prevent the regeneration of the plant species that once made up the forest, even after the cattle ranchers and cultivators move on.

Scientists do not know how many species of plants and animals live in the world's forests. But it is known that many species live only in limited areas and that the destruction of even small ecosystems can lead to the extinction of many species. Considering the extent of deforestation today, it is possible that thousands of plant and animal species, many of them not yet identified, are being lost each year.

The dangers of species reduction was made clear recently in the case of the Pacific yew tree, which lives only in the Pacific Northwest. Medical researchers recently discovered that a substance found only in the Pacific yew's bark may be one of the most effective agents ever found for treating certain types of cancer. But in the process of harvesting the region's towering Douglas firs with heavy machinery, loggers commonly destroy the little yew.

Environmentalists point to the rapid disappearance of this valuable plant as a symptom of the drain on the world's "gene bank" caused by deforestation. They point out that tropical forests contain a far greater number of species of plants and animals — offering as yet unknown advantages to mankind — than temperate forests, such as those of the Pacific Northwest. Thus their destruction poses an especially grave threat to the world's biodiversity. According to one recent estimate, the clearing of tropical rain forests eradicates at least 4,000 species each year.[17]

But the greatest potential damage caused by deforestation is its impact on the global environment. Mounting evidence that a buildup of certain gases in the atmosphere is causing global temperatures to rise is focusing growing concern on deforestation. These gases trap the sun's heat inside the Earth's atmosphere, causing temperatures to rise much as a glass roof keeps a greenhouse warm by trapping heat inside. The gas that contributes most to this greenhouse effect is carbon dioxide ($CO_2$). A natural product of respiration in animals, carbon dioxide is also released by burning fossil fuels such as coal and gasoline. Abnormal amounts of $CO_2$ are building in the atmosphere today as a result of industrialization. Deforestation also contributes to $CO_2$ buildup because forests, together with oceans, are essential "sinks," or absorbers, of this gas.

During photosynthesis, plants absorb carbon dioxide. As the plants decay or burn, the carbon stored inside plants is released back into the atmosphere as $CO_2$. Because deforestation destroys great numbers of large trees containing vast stores of carbon, it is an important contributor to $CO_2$ buildup. Although estimates vary, deforestation is thought to be responsible for 10-30 percent of the buildup. ■

# BACKGROUND

## Early Use of Forests

Deforestation has gone hand in hand with human development. Early hunter-gatherers were dependent on woodlands. But according to biologist Paul B. Sears, the next steps in human evolution marked the beginning of our ambivalent attitudes toward forests.* "By a curious paradox," he writes, "it was only by loosening those ties [to the forest] that [humans] began the slow and painful upward climb toward civilization."

---

*Some early civilizations developed far from heavily forested land. Because the Nile River delta lacked woodlands, the ancient Egyptians used their military might to obtain wood from other parts of the Middle East, notably Syria.

Agriculture required treeless space, and armed with fire and primitive axes, early humans began to clear the forests. "Thus the forest early assumed an equivocal role in human culture," Sears continues. "It was prized for the materials it yielded and for some of the functions it performed, but it was also regarded as a rival for the space needed for crops and flocks. This two-mindedness about the forest has continued to confuse humanity down to the present day, with sorry results."[18]

Forests, even in temperate zones, require heavier rainfall than either grasslands or scrubland to thrive. For this reason a protracted dry spell lasting a millennium throughout Europe after the last glaciers receded about 11,000 years ago killed off some of the dense forests that had covered the continent. This deforestation by natural causes allowed early farmers of the Neolithic Age to migrate. Many of them moved northwest from Asia Minor through central Europe toward the Baltic Sea.

The pace of deforestation accelerated, however, following the development of metalworking in bronze, and later iron. Fuel wood was required not only for heating and cooking but also for the metalworkers' forges. At the same time, the metal tools they fashioned made forest clearing easier. Specialized tools enabled these early Europeans to replace their mud and stone huts with more durable wooden structures. Thus demand for timber further hastened the forests' destruction.

But according to Sears, "it was the invention of steel, an alloy of iron and carbon, which was most devastating to the forests of Europe. Armament and empire went hand in hand, and the age of Charlemagne is no more notable for its military exploits than for its wholesale destruction of forests for the manufacture of steel."[19] Since charcoal was the principal source of carbon, large quantities of wood were needed to produce enough charcoal.

While the feudal era brought with it a sharp increase in deforestation in Europe, it also saw the first awareness of the need to conserve forest resources, which were valued as hunting preserves for the nobility. "Both on the Continent and in England," Sears writes, "the chief areas where forests were protected against the insatiable demand for charcoal and timber were those ... reserved for the sport and recreation of the ruling class."

Modernization and wars continued to take their toll on Europe's forests. While significant stands were to survive over the centuries in northern Europe, the southern part of the continent never recovered. The forests of the Mediterranean region are among the most heavily damaged in the world, according to a recent World

Bank study, which found that only 5 percent of the land is covered by trees. The rest, the study found, has been largely denuded of forest cover by natural and man-made fires, as well as poor forestry management and overgrazing.[20]

## Development's Impact

While industrial progress continued to take its toll on the forests of the Northern Hemisphere, the vast woodlands of the South were spared until modern times. Deforestation in Third World countries began increasing when the developed countries of Europe and North America began seeking hardwood timber, rubber and other commodities offered by the vast rain forests of the tropics. The demand for rubber, for example, exploded following Charles Goodyear's invention of the vulcanization process in 1839. Because rubber was found only in Amazonia at that time, Brazil enjoyed an economic boom based chiefly on exports of latex. But by the early 1900s trees that had been taken by British smugglers to East Asia also began to produce latex, and at lower cost. As a result, Brazil lost its grip on the crucial rubber market, and the country suffered a severe economic setback.

Although rubber was one of the key products that lured entrepreneurs to Brazil, its cultivation had a relatively minor impact on the rain forests. But later development, in Brazil and throughout the Third World during the 1960s and '70s, was to prove disastrous. Many of the development schemes were as concerned with moving poor people out of the crowded cities and into the sparsely populated forests as they were with modernizing the countries' economies.

This sudden concern with reloca-

tion was spurred by the unprecedented growth in the world's population since the mid-1800s, largely the result of advances in technology and medicine. By the year 2000, the World Bank estimates there will be 6.2 billion people on Earth. That's an annual increase of about 100 million people, the vast majority of whom reside in the developing world. These are the very regions that are least able to sustain population increases without suffering environmental damage, notably deforestation. According to one source, for every tree planted in the tropical regions, 10 are destroyed.[21]

### Brazil's Operation Amazonia

In the mid-1960s, the Brazilian government launched Operation Amazonia, an ambitious plan to develop the sparsely populated rain forests that covered much of the country. The project called for the construction of roads linking the urban centers on the Atlantic coast to the interior; encouraging landless farmers to move inland; and tax incentives to attract new industries and ranches to the region. With the completion of the 1,900-kilometer Belém-Brasília highway in 1964, the country's new capital was linked to the shores of the Amazon River, deep in the interior. Large numbers of migrants used the road to colonize the northwestern states of Amazonia, and by 1970 wide swaths of devastated wasteland on either side of the highway signaled the beginning of Brazil's progressive deforestation.[22]

Despite the rapid degradation of Amazonia, colonists continued to migrate to the region. Not surprisingly, social unrest soon developed over land rights and overcrowding of villages. The Brazilian government responded in 1981 with a massive new project to accelerate development in the region. Called the Northwest Brazil Integrated Development Program,

or Polonoroeste, the $1.5 billion project received a third of its funding from the World Bank. Among its aims was the replacement of forest clearing for unsustainable agriculture with tree planting.

Polonoroeste failed, however, and became instead a synonym for misguided development principles. The shift from agriculture to tree farming never occurred, while most of the infertile farmland was converted into pasture, a move that only further reduced its eventual regenerative ability. Far from preventing further deforestation, the project accelerated the destruction of wooded land. By 1988, cleared land accounted for almost a quarter of Rondônia's total area, up from only 3 percent following the first wave of migration in 1980.[23]

Such massive relocation efforts, also known as transmigration projects, have not been confined to Latin America. Since the early 1980s Indonesia has relocated large numbers of landless Javanese to several sparsely inhabited islands. By 1985, some 2.5 million people had been moved to Indonesian Borneo and other heavily forested islands. The same year, Indonesia reached an annual deforestation rate estimated at 700,000 hectares, by far the highest rate in Southeast Asia. Although extensive commercial logging operations accounted for part of the loss, most destruction of Indonesia's forests is attributed to agriculture.[24]

## Pollution's Role

In North America, early settlers found dense woodlands along most of the Atlantic coast. Pushing the frontier westward meant clearing forests virtually to the Mississippi River. The Great Plains and the Southwest were largely grassland,

*Continued on p. 692*

# Chronology

## 1960s
*Rapid population growth and economic development in the Third World encourage deforestation.*

### 1964
The Brazilian government completes construction of the Belém-Brasília highway linking the urban coastal cities with the heavily forested interior. The road is a key component of Operation Amazonia, a development project involving the relocation of poor farmers and urban unemployed to the rain forests.

### Mid-1960s
The first signs of damage from acid rain appear among high-elevation fir and spruce forests in the Eastern United States.

## 1970s
*World Bank and regional development banks provide loans to developing countries for massive projects that result in widespread deforestation.*

### 1977
Green Belt, an environmental movement in Kenya, begins employing women — who traditionally gather wood for fuel throughout sub-Saharan Africa — to plant trees in deforested areas.

### 1978
Timber importers and exporters from Japan, the U.S. and Western Europe begin negotiations to create the International Tropical Timber Organization to assure the continued availability of valuable hardwoods. An agreement creating the Yokahama-based ITTO is finally signed in December 1988.

### Late 1970s
Air pollution and acid rain caused by the burning of fossil fuels for industry and transportation begin to kill vast areas of West Germany's Black Forest, one of the last remaining large forests in Western Europe. The damage soon spreads to other European forests.

## 1980s
*The pace of forest destruction suddenly accelerates, and world attention focuses on deforestation as a major factor in environmental degradation.*

### 1980
The "Global 2000" report, commissioned by President Jimmy Carter, identifies deforestation as the biggest environmental threat for the next two decades.

### 1982
Brazil, with World Bank funding, launches the vast Polonoroeste project, a road-construction and resettlement campaign in the Amazon basin that will cause widespread deforestation.

### 1985
As a result of Indonesia's relocation project, 2.5 million Javanese inhabit the undeveloped outer islands. Some 700,000 hectares of forested land are cleared, the highest deforestation rate in Southeast Asia. In Brazil, Chico Mendes, leader of the rubber-tappers, calls for the creation of "extractive reserves," areas of the forest to be closed to modern development and set aside for the sole use of the local gatherers of latex, nuts, fruit and other forest products.

### May 1987
Responding to growing criticism of the World Bank's support of development projects that degrade the environment, Bank President Barber B. Conable Jr. announces reforms in the institution's lending practices that would commit it to financing more environmentally beneficial projects.

### 1987
A record 20.4 million hectares of forests are destroyed worldwide. Much of the damage occurs in Brazil, where loggers, ranchers and farmers clear an unprecedented 9 million hectares of forest in the Amazon region. The Earth's population reaches 5 billion, twice the 1950 figure. Inhabitants of northern Borneo begin to blockade logging roads into their forest homelands.

### December 1988
Chico Mendes is assassinated following his extensively publicized campaign to curtail forest clearing in the Amazon.

## 1990s
*Threat of global warming heightens awareness of deforestation.*

### June 1-12, 1992
The United Nations Conference on Environment and Development is expected to be the biggest meeting ever held on threats to Earth's environment, with the main emphasis on global warming. Because of its contribution to this phenomenon, deforestation likely will be an important focus of debate.

# The World's Dwindling Forests

*Around the globe, the rate of forest loss varies widely. Countries shown on the map are experiencing the most serious losses. Tiny Costa Rica destroys its forests faster than any country on earth. While its total loss is a comparatively* *low 124,000 hectares per year, the annual rate of loss is 6.9 percent of Costa Rica's forests. (A hectare is equal to 2.47 acres.) Giant Brazil, on the other hand, loses a staggering 9,050,000 hectares annually, but because Brazil's total* *fores perc perc 295,*

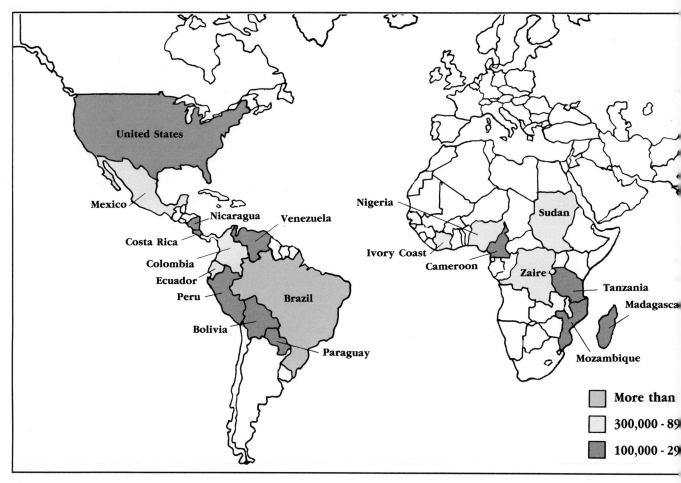

Source: World Resources 1990-91: A Guide to the Global Environment, *The World Resources Institute in collaboration with the United National Environment Programme and the United Nations Development Programme, 1990.*

*Continued from p. 690*
but forests covered most of the Pacific Northwest.

Throughout most of the United States, forests have been cleared for agriculture and, chiefly in the Southeast and Northwest, for timber. But in recent years another agent has been silently destroying the country's woodlands — air pollution and acid rain produced by the combustion of fossil fuels.

The extent of the damage began to be apparent in the mid-1960s, among high-elevation fir and spruce forests in the Eastern United States. Since then, air pollution has been identified as a major killer of trees throughout the country. The worst damage has been found in California and at upper altitudes of the Appalachian Mountains, from North Carolina to New England. Low-elevation evergreens, including white pine and commercial stands of yellow pine, as well as sugar maples in the Northeast and in Canada, are also victims of air pollution emanating from industrial centers in the Midwest and along the Eastern seaboard.[25]

Similar destruction has been noted with greater alarm in Germany and other countries of Central and Western Europe, whose forests have already been exhausted by earlier civilizations and, more recently, by the devastation of two world wars. Deforestation from air pollution and acid rain has taken an even greater toll in Europe than it has in North America because it has affected virtually all species of trees.

First evident in the late 1970s, as large stands of silver fir began dying in West Germany's Black Forest, for-

# A Country-By-Country View

*vast, the rate of loss is a more modest 1.8*
*S. suffers an even lower rate of loss, 0.1*
*00 hectares out of the U.S. forest total of*
*ctares are lost each year.*

Myanmar (Burma)

Vietnam

Philippines

nd
alaysia

Indonesia

ectares lost

tares lost

tares lost

| Country | Extent of forest, 1980s Total acres, hectares (in thousands) | Deforestation, 1980s Acres lost per year, hectares (in thousands) | Percentage of total lost |
|---|---|---|---|
| **AFRICA** | | | |
| Cameroon | 23,300 | 190 | .8% |
| Ivory Coast | 9,834 | 518 | 5.2 |
| Madagascar | 13,200 | 156 | 1.2 |
| Mozambique | 15,435 | 120 | .8 |
| Nigeria | 14,750 | 400 | 2.7 |
| Sudan | 47,650 | 504 | 1.1 |
| Tanzania | 42,040 | 130 | .3 |
| Zaire | 177,590 | 370 | .2 |
| **NORTH AND CENTRAL AMERICA** | | | |
| Costa Rica | 1,798 | 124 | 6.9 |
| Mexico | 48,350 | 615 | 1.3 |
| Nicaragua | 4,496 | 121 | 2.7 |
| United States | 295,989 | 159 | .1 |
| **SOUTH AMERICA** | | | |
| Bolivia | 66,760 | 117 | .2 |
| Brazil | 514,480 | 9,050 | 1.8 |
| Colombia | 51,700 | 890 | 1.7 |
| Ecuador | 14,730 | 340 | 2.3 |
| Paraguay | 19,710 | 212 | 1.1 |
| Peru | 70,640 | 270 | .4 |
| Venezuela | 33,870 | 245 | .7 |
| **ASIA** | | | |
| India | 64,200 | 1,500 | 2.3 |
| Indonesia | 116,895 | 920 | .8 |
| Malaysia | 20,996 | 255 | 1.2 |
| Myanmar (Burma) | 31,941 | 677 | 2.1 |
| Philippines | 9,510 | 143 | 1.5 |
| Thailand | 15,675 | 397 | 2.5 |
| Vietnam | 10,110 | 173 | 1.7 |

est depletion quickly spread to include Norway spruce and pine. By 1982, Europe's hardwoods, mainly beech and oak, were also affected. By the end of the decade, all the major tree species in West Germany showed signs of damage. The situation is less dire in other parts of Western Europe, including France and Britain. But in Eastern Europe, where environmental protection has not been a high priority, the damage to remaining forests may be far more serious. It will be years before the full extent of the damage is known.

## Curbing Deforestation

Plato blamed the drying up of ancient springs on deforestation of the Grecian hills. But sophisticated knowledge of deforestation's role in erosion and water flow is relatively recent. It was just a few decades ago, for example, that scientists proved there was a connection between clearing rain forests and local weather conditions.

Similarly, only now do they understand why most deforested land is less fertile for cultivation after a few growing seasons than grassland that has been converted to agriculture. The soil in forests is shallower than the soil in grasslands, and it is more acidic. It yields heavy crops for a few years — until the rich, thin topsoil is destroyed by oxidation and erosion. Then costly fertilization is needed if farming is to continue. This is especially true of moist tropical forestland, where the thin humus layer is quickly destroyed by exposure, and nutrient minerals are quickly washed out by heavy rains.

Armed with their new understanding of deforestation's awesome impact and rapid spread, environmentalists stepped up their rescue efforts in the early 1970s. But their warnings fell on deaf ears among the governments and international agencies best equipped to act. Countries that relied heavily on earnings from timber exports, such as Indonesia and Malaysia, ignored calls for conservation. For their part, importers of tropical timber, chiefly the United States, Western Europe and Japan, also showed scarce interest in conservation measures that might diminish the available supply, and thus raise the cost, of harvestable timber.

Consuming nations only began to listen to the warnings in 1980, when the "Global 2000" report commissioned by President Jimmy Carter identified widespread destruction of rain forests as the most serious immediate threat to the environment. At the time, deforestation's role in global warming was not yet widely recognized. The main worry was that rapid clearing of tropical forests would deplete the supply of valued hardwood. Nonetheless, this concern led timber importers and exporters to begin negotiations in 1978 for the International Tropical Timber Agreement. The final agreement called for "sustainable utilization and conservation of tropical forests and their resources, and maintaining the ecological balance in the regions concerned."[26]

### Role of International Agencies

It was not until the late 1980s that the forces best equipped to curb deforestation — governments and international development agencies — began to make significant policy changes aimed at forest protection. The World Bank (officially, the International Bank for Reconstruction and Development), the Asian Development Bank, the African Development Bank and the Inter-American Development Bank all had poured billions of dollars into large projects following World War II. In so doing they had often contributed to deforestation. The World Bank, for example, had assisted Brazil's infamous Polonoroeste project as well as other schemes in Asia and Africa involving the transmigration of hundreds of thousands of people to rain forests, resulting in deforestation and other environmental damage.

Under the bank's new president, Barber Conable, the World Bank began assessing the environmental impact of potential projects as well as their potential economic benefit. "If the World Bank has been part of the problem in the past," Conable announced in May 1987, "it can and will be a strong force in finding solutions in the future."[27] Among the reforms he introduced were new positions for environmentalists within the bank bureaucracy and a commitment to fund more projects that benefit the environment. Projects that contributed to deforestation, including Polonoroeste and a cattle ranching program in Botswana, were suspended. ∎

# CURRENT SITUATION

## Third World Response

Some developing nations facing severe deforestation are beginning to heed the calls for new conservation policies coming both from local environmental groups and the original forest dwellers whose lands have been invaded by loggers, colonists and cattle ranchers.

Before he was murdered in 1988, Chico Mendes organized his fellow rubber tappers in the northwest Brazilian state of Acre into a potent resistance movement whose appeals to the government attracted international attention. The nation's estimated 80,000 tappers, mostly indigenous forest inhabitants who collect latex from wild rubber trees, depend on the forest's survival for their livelihood. "They had been in conflict for decades with cattle ranchers who were burning down the forests and driving them out," says Stephan Schwartzman, a senior scientist with the Environmental Defense Fund (EDF). "They saw this as a way of getting land rights that would then allow them to improve their standard of living on an environmentally sustainable basis."

In 1985 Mendes called on the Brazilian government to set aside large areas of the rain forest to be used as "extractive reserves" as an alternative strategy for developing Amazonia. These reserves would be used solely for the harvesting of forest products, such as latex and Brazil nuts by the local inhabitants. Such sustainable development would avoid deforestation while protecting both the environment and the forest inhabitants' livelihood.

After receiving numerous threats from cattle ranchers, Mendes was murdered, one of an estimated 1,000 Indians, farmers, rubber tappers and union officials who have been killed in the Amazon since 1980.[28] But his campaign for extractive reserves seems to have begun paying off. Schwartzman says there are now 10 reserves covering 3 million hectares in Brazil. "There is no place you can point to and say this is an extractive reserve the way Chico Mendes thought of it," he says. "There are further legal and administrative steps that have to be taken that are quite important that the government has been slow to take. But at least

# Flavor of the Month: Rainforest Crunch

It's not just clever marketing that makes Rainforest Crunch different — not the unusual name and not the colorful tin decorated with exotic animals and plants. Rainforest Crunch *is* different: This crunchy candy is made with Brazil nuts and cashews that were collected by the indigenous people of the Brazilian rain forest region of Amazonia.

Rainforest Crunch is one of a growing number of consumer items that aim to halt deforestation by making the rain forests valuable as a source of profit. If forest products can be sold on world markets, it is reasoned, deforestation may be slowed and with it the hardship it brings to indigenous forest-dwellers. In the case of Rainforest Crunch, the Brazil nuts are gathered from trees native to the forest, while cashews come from trees that are frequently planted in reforestation projects.

The candy is made by Community Products Inc., a company run by ice cream maker Ben Cohen, the co-founder of Ben & Jerry's Homemade. The company buys the Brazil nuts and cashews from Cultural Survival, a nonprofit group in Cambridge, Mass., that was founded in 1972 by social scientists at Harvard University to aid tribal peoples and ethnic minorities. The group procures rain forest products from Brazilian rubber tappers and other rain-forest dwellers around the world and donates part of the profits to rain forest conservation projects.

Next on Ben & Jerry's menu: rain forest sherbets made with tropical fruits provided by Cultural Survival. The group also provides the oils, fruits, fragrances and pigments for a new line of products made by the Body Shop, an English cosmetics maker.

Some retailers buy rain forest products directly from the producers themselves. Smith & Hawken, which sells garden equipment through catalogs, now sells garments with buttons made from the nut of the tagua tree, a palm that grows in the rain forests of northern Ecuador. Smith & Hawken buys tagua nuts from a cooperative run by local forest inhabitants.

Forest-dwellers often have no legal claim to their territory, no voice in national legislatures and no alternative sources of income after the bulldozers, machetes and fires destroy their homelands. Nowhere is their plight worse than in the rain forests of South America, central Africa and Southeast Asia. According to Cultural Survival, these regions are home to some 200 million people belonging to about 2,000 known tribes.

---

the first steps have been taken."

One step the Brazilian government has taken is to suspend the tax incentives that had long been offered to cattle ranchers who cleared forests for grazing. The incentives had been designed to boost the production of beef for export, which was a lucrative source of foreign exchange. Brazilian President Fernando Collor de Mello — following a state visit to Washington in June, where he came under criticism for his country's lax environmental policies — signed a decree prohibiting fiscal incentives for any project that causes deforestation.

Although Schwartzman emphasizes that the tax incentives for clearing forests have been only suspended and not eliminated, he calls the decree "heartening, at least. It still has to be enforced, which is liable to be a good trick, but finally there is legal recognition that deforestation is an issue."

Resistance to destructive development among native forest dwellers is growing in other countries as well. In India, widespread illegal logging has come under attack from a nationwide movement that originated in the 1970s when a group of women — dubbed "the tree huggers" — formed human chains around trees to prevent loggers from harvesting the already depleted forests of the Himalayan foothills. In Malaysia, members of the Penan and Kayan tribes have repeatedly tried to blockade cutting in their homeland in northern Borneo. Many have been arrested for violating a Malaysian law that prohibits interfering with logging operations. In Kenya, an environmental movement called the Green Belt has employed women to plant trees across the country since 1977. Because women traditionally have been the main gatherers of fuel-wood in Africa, the movement may satisfy two goals by offering alternative employment for women while reforesting damaged lands.

These and other grass-roots movements to protect natural resources in the Third World have had little impact on the rate of deforestation. While they enjoy the support of local and international environmental organizations, they haven't forced much change in their governments' forestry or social policies. Heavily indebted governments that are hard-pressed for export earnings are unwilling to curb logging operations or stop using the forests as a social relief valve. As a result, global deforestation continues to accelerate.

## U.S. Stand

During his campaign for the presidency in 1988, then-Vice President George Bush placed heavy emphasis on the need to protect the environment. Upon entering the White House, Bush repeated this message and appointed William K. Reilly, a respected environmentalist and critic of the Reagan administration's environmental policies, to head the Environmental Protection Agency.

But since then, the Bush administration has assumed a more ambivalent stance on environmental issues, including deforestation. The president has identified deforestation as an area of special concern, and in 1990 — during the Houston economic summit of the seven leading industrial nations* — he announced he would support the negotiation of a world forestry agreement.

But the administration's first official proposal for such an agreement, issued in June, appeared to severely limit its scope. The U.S. Proposal on Forest Principles made no specific mention of the old-growth forests where most deforestation occurs. Instead, the proposal merely suggests that signatory governments have a "general obligation" to establish national strategies to improve the management of their forests.

The administration's weak response, critics say, reflects pressure from the domestic timber industry, which opposes recent moves to restrict logging in the old-growth forests of the Pacific Northwest. The reduction of allowable timber harvests, aimed at saving the endangered northern spotted owl from extinction, also threatens the livelihood of many logging communities in Washington and Oregon.[29] Several bills now before Congress would provide financial assistance to these communities while limiting the amount of timber that can be removed from spotted owl habitat.

Many environmentalists say the

*The seven leading industrial nations, known as the G-7, are the United States, Japan, Germany, Britain, Italy, France and Canada.

United States must do more to protect its own forests if it expects to obtain a world agreement. "Some of the worst forest destruction in the world is taking place in this country," says Nels Johnson, manager for biological diversity at the World Resources Institute's Center for International Development and Environment. "If the United States is to provide leadership, we'd best start at home. Malaysia, Indonesia and Brazil are watching what the Pacific Northwest does."[30]

The United States also came under fire from other industrial nations on a related issue, global warming. Trees absorb carbon dioxide, and their destruction is believed to contribute to the accumulation of excessive amounts of this gas in the atmosphere. The job of curbing deforestation would fall primarily to the developing countries. But industrial nations would have to reduce the amount of gasoline and other fossil fuels they consume. Burning fossil fuels accounts for most of the carbon dioxide emitted into the atmosphere.

Eager for an agreement to reduce carbon emissions, most industrial nations have either adopted or promised to adopt ceilings on the amount of carbon dioxide they emit by the year 2000. Even Britain, which had resisted making such a commitment, agreed to do so this summer. But the Bush administration has refused to go along with such a commitment, citing the need for further research into the phenomenon of global warming. According to White House Chief of Staff John H. Sununu, the mathematical models that predict global warming are unrealistic and have led to assessments that are "either incomplete or inconclusive."[31] Because the United States alone accounts for almost a quarter of the world's carbon dioxide emissions, its participation is seen as essential to the success of a world climate agreement. ∎

# OUTLOOK

## Earth Summit 1992

Deforestation promises to rank among the most pressing items on the agenda of the U.N. Conference on Environment and Development, scheduled to take place June 1-12, 1992, in Rio de Janeiro. Also known as the Earth Summit, the meeting promises to be the biggest international meeting on this issue ever held. Some 7,000 delegates, including heads of state, from more than 150 nations are expected to participate.

The conference will focus on global warming and the steps all nations would have to take to curb the rise in temperatures. It is not yet clear whether deforestation will be addressed in the context of climate change or in a separate convention on forests. But because tropical deforestation contributes as much as a third of the buildup of carbon dioxide, developing nations will undoubtedly be asked to protect their forests and stop offering incentives for landless colonists, loggers and ranchers to clear the trees for development. Eleven developing countries recently linked to 82 percent of the carbon dioxide buildup due to deforestation will likely come under the greatest pressure for change: Brazil, Indonesia, Colombia, Côte d'Ivoire, Thailand, Laos, Nigeria, Vietnam, Philippines, Myanmar (formerly Burma) and India.[32]

But the developing world is likely to make demands of its own on the

Continued on p. 698

# At Issue:

## Does current policy allow for the sustainable harvest of the Pacific yew as a source of an effective cancer-fighting drug?

**JAMES OVERBAY**

*Deputy chief, National Forest System, Forest Service, U.S. Department of Agriculture.*
FROM HEARINGS ON THE PACIFIC YEW AND THE DEVEL-OPMENT OF TAXOL, HELD JULY 29, 1991, BEFORE THE HOUSE SMALL BUSINESS SUBCOMMITTEE ON REGULA-TION, BUSINESS OPPORTUNITY AND ENERGY.

*yes*

*t*axol, a chemical extracted from the bark of the Pacific yew, has proven to be an extremely effective anti-cancer drug. Although Pacific yew occurs on all major ownerships in the Northwest, the majority of the trees large enough to provide significant quantities of bark are located in the national forests along the west side of the Cascade Mountains in Oregon and Washington. Other locations are in the Blue Mountains of Eastern Oregon and Washington, on the west side of the Rocky Mountains in Idaho and Montana, and in Northern California. . . .

For the most part, Pacific yew has been harvested from timber sales of other major timber species such as Douglas fir and hemlock. Contractors obtain permits and harvest the yew either before or after the main logging operation. Harvesting yew bark is expected to increase dramatically from last year's 90,000 pounds to meet the estimated need of 750,000 pounds in 1991.

The Forest Service's Pacific Northwest region is initiating a multi-regional effort to develop and coordinate a program to manage the collection of Pacific yew bark on National Forest System lands, in coordination with other land management agencies and landowners. The 750,000 pounds of dried yew bark that will be collected during the 1991 field season will produce about 25 to 36 kilograms of pure taxol, or enough to treat 12,500 to 18,000 patients. Bark must be removed from at least 38,000 yew trees to meet this objective. It is estimated that this amount of bark will be required annually for the next few years, then a reduced amount [will be needed] as alternative sources of taxol become available.

To put this in perspective, we estimate there are about 23 million Pacific yew trees growing on suitable National Forest System lands in the Oregon Coast Range and the Cascades of Oregon and Washington. If only 10 percent were actually available for harvest, and 38,000 trees were harvested each year it would take about 60 years to deplete the supply, not counting regeneration.

**JESSICA MATHEWS**

*Vice president, World Resources Institute.*
FROM *THE OREGONIAN,* June 19, 1991.

*no*

*t*he *Wall Street Journal* calls it "the ultimate confrontation between medicine and the environment." *The New York Times* warns that "recovery for sick people may mean death for the spotted owl." The controversy could make earlier battles over endangered species and habitats look tame.

This time the subject is a drug called taxol. The head of the National Cancer Institute says it's the most import new cancer drug in 15 years. It has been shown to fight ovarian, breast and lung cancer and is only beginning to be tested.

The difficulty is that taxol comes from the bark of the Pacific yew, a rare tree found in endangered, ancient forests. It is a complex molecule that so far has stymied chemists' best efforts to synthesize it in the lab. A breakthrough might be around the corner or years away.

The yew is a slow-growing, shade-loving tree, which makes it a poor candidate for plantations devoted to producing the drug. That leaves the natural forests as the only source of taxol for the indefinite future.

But the yew grows sparsely, and six 100-year-old trees are needed to treat one patient. Harvesting enough for the vast potential market, at an affordable cost, could mean clear-cutting all the remaining ancient forests in the Northwest.

Until now, loggers have treated the Pacific yew as a trash tree, ripping it out and burning it along with other underbrush. Though taxol's potency was established in 1989, the Forest Service has been slow to respond, trapped by a mind-set that prizes lumber above all other forest products and services. Almost 2 billion board feet of ancient-forest timber is under contract to be cut this year and next, yet it took intense pressure from environmental groups to produce a government moratorium on burning yews just two months ago. Only now is the Forest Service proposing an inventory to discover how much yew is in the forests, and where. . . .

The formula for balancing immediate human needs with environmental values and long-term human well-being is . . . to save, study and use — not use up now, rue later.

Continued from p. 696

industrial nations. One will likely be that the United States set an example by stopping deforestation at home. For one thing, says Schwartzman of the Environmental Defense Fund, the United States and the rest of the industrial world can better afford to pay the price of environmental protection. "The social costs to us of forgoing cutting down old-growth forests are much less than they are in other places."

The Third World is also likely to demand financial assistance from the industrial nations in carrying out programs to curb deforestation. Many governments are loath to interfere with export earnings, such as logging. Heavily indebted countries like Brazil, which owes $120 billion to outside creditors, are particularly reluctant. Meanwhile, a group of 41 developing countries has already called on the industrial nations to help them pay for programs promoting sustainable development. At a June meeting in Beijing to prepare for the summit, the group blamed most of the world's pollution on the industrialized nations and said they should shoulder much of the burden of cleaning it up.

### Bleak Outlook for Forests

If the Earth Summit fails to garner support for an effective campaign to stop deforestation, many observers rate the prospects for much of the world's forests as poor indeed. Of course, current damage estimates are sketchy at best, and predictions of future deforestation are even hazier. Nonetheless, some experts paint a bleak picture of the coming 21st-century world if trees continue to fall at anything close to today's rate. Greenpeace, for one, paints a cataclysmic picture. By the year 2000, the group estimates, forests will be gone from many parts of the globe, including Thailand, Vietnam, East and West Africa, Madagascar, Ecua-

dor, Peru and Bolivia.

The forest survival prospects are only slightly better for many other regions, Greenpeace estimates. By 2020, Malaysia and most of Indonesia will be deforested, and virtually no primary forest will remain in the Philippines and Myanmar, the group says . In the vast forests of the Congo Basin (made up of the Congo, Gabon and Zaire) the future is slightly better, but only because the regions involved are so mammoth. In Brazil, similarly, Amazonia's forests will stand longer simply because of their incredible scope; but the country's peripheral states may be devastated.

Stopping the onslaught won't be easy, given the colonization pressure of millions of people, and the equally intense needs of financially devastated developing nations to produce revenue through cattle raising and other means. But the price of doing little or nothing, many scientists warn, could be global warming and other climatic changes. "We need action, not more research," says Nels Johnson of the World Resources Institute. ∎

## Notes

1 Norman Myers, "Tropical Forests," a chapter in Jeremy Leggett, ed., Global Warming: The Greenpeace Report (1990), pp. 384-386.
2 See World Resources Institute, United Nations Environment Programme and United Nations Development Programme, World Resources 1990-91 (1990), p. 7.
3 Myers, op. cit., pp. 384-386.
4 World Resources Institute, op. cit., p. 102.
5 Ibid., p. 42.
6 Time, Oct. 19, 1987.
7 Myers, op. cit., p. 383.
8 Ibid., pp. 382-383.
9 See Dennis Anderson, The Economics of Afforestation: A Case Study in Africa, The World Bank, 1987, p. 8.
10 See Mark Cheater, "Save That Taiga," World-Watch, July-August 1991, p. 10.
11 See Brian Johnson, Responding to Tropical Deforestation: An Eruption of Crises — An Array of Solutions, World Wildlife Fund and The Conservation Foundation, 1991, p. 10.
12 For poverty figures, see The World Bank, The World Bank Atlas 1990 (1990), pp. 10-11.
13 Johnson spoke at the July 26 meeting of congressional staffers held by the Environmental and Energy Study Institute.
14 See Brian Johnson, op. cit., p. 14.
15 Ibid, pp. 22-23. In these two countries the fertility rate — measured according to the number of children a woman will bear during her lifetime — stands at fewer than three children.
16 Ibid., p. 14.
17 See Paul R. Ehrlich and Edward O. Wilson, "Biodiversity Studies: Science and Policy," Science, Aug. 16, 1991, pp. 758-761.
18 Paul B. Sears, writing in Stephen Haden-Guest, John K. Wright and Eileen M. Teclaff, eds., A World Geography of Forest Resources (1956), pp. 3-4.
19 Ibid, p. 5.
20 The World Bank and The European Investment Bank, The Environmental Program for the Mediterranean: Preserving a Shared Heritage and Managing a Common Resource (1990), p. 30.
21 See Ivan Head, "South-North Dangers," Foreign Affairs, summer 1989, p. 78.
22 See Dennis J. Mahar, Government Policies and Deforestation in Brazil's Amazon Region, 1989.
23 Ibid, p. 34.
24 See Robert Repetto, The Forest for the Trees? Government Policies and the Misuse of Forest Resources, World Resources Institute, May 1988.
25 See James J. MacKenzie and Mohamed T. El-Ashry, Ill Winds: Airborne Pollution's Toll on Trees and Crops, World Resources Institute, September 1988, and "Acid Rain: New Approach to Old Problem," Editorial Research Reports, March 8, 1991, pp. 129-144.
26 See Johnson, op. cit., pp. 21-22.
27 Quoted by Pat Aufderheide and Bruce Rich, "Environmental Reform and the Multilateral Banks," World Policy Journal, spring 1988, p. 301.
28 Amnesty International's estimate, cited in World Resources Institute, op. cit., p. 110.
29 For background, see "Endangered Species," The CQ Researcher, June 21, 1991, pp. 393-416.
30 Johnson spoke at the July 26 meeting of congressional staffers held by the Environmental and Energy Study Institute July 26.
31 Quoted in The New York Times, Sept. 10, 1991, p. C9.
32 World Resources Institute, op. cit., p. 109.

# Bibliography

## Selected Sources Used

### Books

**Leggett, Jeremy, ed., *Global Warming: The Greenpeace Report*, Oxford University Press, 1990.**

The chapter on tropical forests recommends large-scale reforestation in the tropics as a cost-effective and technically feasible way to reduce atmospheric carbon dioxide. Reforestation would only be effective, the author stresses, if deforestation is curbed at the same time.

### Articles

**Aufderheide, Pat, and Rich, Bruce, "Environmental Reform and the Multilateral Banks," *World Policy Journal*, spring 1988, pp. 301-321.**

The World Bank and the smaller regional development banks for several decades encouraged the construction of huge development projects in the Third World that resulted in massive deforestation and did little to address the root causes of poverty in those countries. Since the late 1980s, however, the banks have begun targeting their funds toward environmentally sound projects.

**Ehrlich, Paul R., and Wilson, Edward O., "Biodiversity Studies: Science and Policy," *Science*, Aug. 16, 1991, pp. 758-761.**

The authors estimate that at least 4,000 species become extinct each year as a result of tropical deforestation. Why should we care? "Because *Homo sapiens* is the dominant species on Earth, we and many others think that people have an absolute moral responsibility to protect what are our only known living companions in the universe."

**Postel, Sandra, "A Green Fix to the Global Warm-up," *World-Watch*, September-October 1988, pp. 29-36.**

Reforestation, the large-scale planting of trees to replace those lost to logging operations and clearing for agriculture and grazing, can reduce the amount of carbon dioxide in the atmosphere and thus slow global warming, Postel argues. This is because trees remove carbon dioxide from the atmosphere during photosynthesis.

**Ryan, John C., "Goods from the Woods," *World-Watch*, July-August 1991, pp. 19-26.**

This article describes the emergence of extractive reserves as viable alternatives to logging and other activities that cause deforestation. In the reserves, local inhabitants collect nuts, resins and other products of tropical forests without destroying the trees themselves. First proposed by a Brazilian rubber tappers' union, extractive reserves are gaining recognition as one way to exploit forest reserves while preserving the forest habitat.

### Reports and Studies

**Environmental and Energy Study Institute, *Partnership for Sustainable Development: A New U.S. Agenda for International Development and Environmental Security*, May 1991.**

The institute, an independent organization created by Congress to present policy options on environmental issues, recommends 12 changes in U.S. development policies for the Third World. One is the establishment of a global partnership to save tropical forests, which would combine developing countries' plans for halting deforestation with U.S. financial and technical support and forgiveness of outstanding debt.

**Gregersen, Hans, Draper, Sydney, and Elz, Dieter, eds. *People and Trees: The Role of Social Forestry in Sustainable Development*, Economic Development Institute of the World Bank, 1989.**

Social forestry, defined as the exploitation of tree products to generate income for communities, can help combat deforestation in virtually every region of the world. An example is the planting of trees between cultivated fields to prevent erosion, provide windbreaks and assure an adequate supply of fuel-wood.

**National Academy of Sciences, National Academy of Engineering and Institute of Medicine, *Policy Implications of Greenhouse Warming: Report of the Mitigation Panel*, National Academy Press, 1991.**

The study recommends steps governments and consumers can take to reduce the emission of greenhouse gases, such as carbon dioxide, that are thought to cause global warming. In a chapter on deforestation, the study concludes that the United States should encourage the sustainable development of tropical forests through appropriate economic aid to the Third World.

**World Resources Institute, *World Resources 1990-91*, Oxford University Press, 1990.**

This annual guide, prepared in collaboration with the United Nations Environment Programme and the United Nations Development Programme, focuses this year on environmental problems in Latin America. Deforestation in the region is most evident in Brazil, where recent policy changes have as yet had little impact on that country's destruction of rain forests.

# The Next Step

## Additional Articles from Current Periodicals

### Books & reading

**Graber, D., "A jungle of competing interests," *Sierra*, March/April 1991, p. 76.**

Reviews three books about the South American rain forest. "The Fate of the Forest," by Susanna Hecht and Alexander Cockburn; "The Burning Season: The Murder of Chico Mendes and the Fight for the Amazon Rain Forest," by Andrew Revkin; "The World is Burning: Murder in the Rainforest," by Alex Shoumatoff.

**Mathews, T., Kepp, M., et al., "A life under fire in Brazil," *Newsweek*, Sept. 3, 1990, p. 62.**

Discusses the recent release of books on the death of Chico Mendes and the destruction of Brazil's rain forest. "The World is Burning," by Alex Shoumatoff; "The Burning Season," by Andrew Revkin; "The Decade of Destruction," by Adrian Cowell.

**Maxwell, K., "The tragedy of the Amazon," *The New York Review of Books*, March 7, 1991, p. 24.**

Reviews several books on rain forest deforestation including: "The Last Rain Forest: A World Conservation Atlas," edited by Mark Collins, foreword by David Attenborough; "Neotropical Rainforest Mammals: A Field Guide," by Louise H. Emmons, illustrated by François Feer; "The Fate of the Forest: Developers, Destroyers and Defenders of the Amazon," by Susanna Hecht and Alexander Cockburn; others.

### Debates & issues

**"The dwindling forest beyond Long San," *Economist*, Aug. 18, 1990, p. 23.**

Reports on the increasing depletion of the tropical rain forests in Malaysia, particularly in Sarawak on the island of Borneo. Malaysian Prime Minister Mahathir Mohamad's views on Western nations' motives and timber exports; reactions of the forests' natives; outlook.

**Burman, A., "Saving Brazil's savannas," *New Scientist*, March 2, 1991, p. 30.**

Asserts that human activities are threatening Brazil's savannahs as well as its rain forests. The biological potential of the area; a fascinating ecosystem; description; the Serra do Espinhaco; the primary stress factors; a unique source of life.

**Goethals, H., "Preserving a Paraguayan paradise," *Americas*, November/December 1990, p. 3.**

Reports on the threats posed to several rare animals by deforestation in Paraguay. Protection efforts; rain forests of Eastern Paraguay; Mbaracayu reserve.

**Green, G. M. and Sussman, R. W., "Deforestation history of the eastern rain forests of Madagascar from satellite images," *Science*, April 13, 1990, p. 212.**

Presents statistics on the rate of deforestation in the eastern rain forests of Madagascar, one of the most rich areas on Earth biologically, over a 35-year period, using satellite images and maps of vegetation based on earlier aerial photographs. 50 percent reduction; average yearly deforestation; areas with most rapid cutting.

**Joyce, S., "Snorting Peru's rain forest," *International Wildlife*, May/June 1990, p. 20.**

Covers the destruction of Peru's jungles and the Andean rain forest in order to grow coca, worth billions of dollars when processed into cocaine. Describes the Huallaga Valley, now known as the "Valley of Death," because of the cocaine grown there. Damage caused by coca production; Indian uses of coca; Peruvian and United States police efforts.

**Monastersky, R., "The fall of the forest," *Science News*, July 21, 1990, p. 40.**

Examines new reports that warn that the world's tropical forests are disappearing much faster than scientists and policy-makers thought. Chopping and burning annually consume about 1 percent of the remaining rain forests and dry forests in the tropics.

**Nicolai, D., "The destruction of America's rain forest," *Utne Reader*, July/August 1990, p. 23.**

Reports on how American timber companies are successfully lobbying Congress and the U.S. Forest Service (USFS), to let them cut the last ancient rain forest in the United States, located in the Pacific Northwest. Debate over logging plans in the Pacific Northwest; reasons for lost jobs in the timber industry; split among environmentalists.

**Radulovich, R., "A view on tropical deforestation," *Nature*, July 19, 1990, p. 214.**

Presents a commentary that raises questions about tropical deforestation in developing countries. Global effect; severity of problem in the tropics.

**Raymond, C., "Researchers see loss of cultural diversity in destruction of world's rain forests," *The Chronicle of Higher Education*, Dec. 12, 1990, p. A5.**

Comments on the annual meeting of the American

Anthropological Association where scholars noted that environmental scientists should be paying as much attention to cultural diversity as to biological diversity in their efforts to save the world's tropical forests. One acre lost every second; wastage; environmental degradation and the loss of cultural diversity; overexploitation, conservation and preservation.

**Shabecoff, P. "Loss of tropical forests is found much worse than was thought,"** *The New York Times,* **June 8, 1990, p. A1.**

States that tropical forests, which play a vital role in regulating global climate, are disappearing much more rapidly than previously estimated — 40 to 50 million acres vanishing each year recently.

## *Economic aspects*

**Katzman, M. T. and Cale, W. G. Jr., "Tropical forest preservation using economic incentives,"** *Bioscience,* **December 1990, p. 827.**

Demonstrates how economic analysis can provide useful insights into policies to protect specific rain forest habitats. The problem in economic terms; suggested systems and their limitations; conservation easement proposal; an example of easement.

**Mardon, M., "Maneuvers in the teak wars,"** *Sierra,* **May/June 1991, p. 30.**

Focuses on the decimation of Myanmar's forests that supply Thailand's logging companies with teak and raise money for the Myanmar government's fight against pro-democracy insurgents. Response from U.S. conservation groups like the Sierra Club; The Rainforest Alliance, a conservation group based in New York; San Francisco-based Rainforest Action Network; Sen. Daniel Patrick Moynihan's (D-N.Y.) trade bill to restrict import of Myanmar timber.

**Mardon, M., "Steamed up over rainforests,"** *Sierra,* **May/June 1990, p. 80.**

Reports on a proposed large-scale geothermal project in the Wao Kele O Puna rain forest on the Big Island of Hawaii. Ecological danger of development; need for environmental impact studies; energy efficiency as a low-cost alternative.

**Morell, V., "Bringing home a piece of the jungle,"** *International Wildlife,* **September/October 1990, p. 12.**

Discusses ways in which people can use rain forest products, like palm frond shoots and Brazil nuts, to help preserve the rain forests and bring money to the poor towns and governments.

**Pearce, F., "Brazil, where the ice cream comes from,"** *New Scientist,* **July 7, 1990, p. 45.**

Reviews a conference on "The Rainforest Harvest" in London. Environmentalists excited about Rainforest dairy ice-cream that uses two fruits of the Amazon; economic lifeline for the forests, an alternative to destruction by chainsaws and firebrands; making money out of the rain forests without upsetting the ecology; conservation meeting capitalism; servicing Western consumers; work of Jason Clay; products from the rain forest.

**Smith, E. T., "Will these buttons help save the rain forests?"** *Business Week,* **Sept. 24, 1990, p. 137.**

Reports that with the forests threatened and imports of elephant ivory banned in the U.S. an environmental group and two clothing makers are reviving the tagua-nut industry to save the trees and the animals while improving rural economics. The tagua nut, an ivorylike nut found in the rain forests of Ecuador and Colombia can be processed into products. Benefits; cost.

## *Environmental aspects*

**"Monkeying around with oil wells,"** *Environment,* **April 1991, p. 22.**

Considers how officials at Conoco, a subsidiary of Du Pont, want to build an oil pipeline and 100-mile road into Ecuador's pristine Yasuni National Park, and claim that the project will not endanger the rain forest and its inhabitants.

**Babbitt, B., "Amazon grace,"** *New Republic,* **June 25, 1990, p. 18.**

Explores the devastation caused by the construction of BR 364, a major road project in Brazil. Environmental costs; impact on local Indian tribes; why the Inter-American Development Bank and the World Bank are helping to fund the project; efforts of Project Acre, a program designed to control the forest destruction that will accompany the road building; questions the value of BR 364. INSET: Rain forest chic (about cultural survival, a project run by Jason Clay), by O. Feldman.

**Bloyd-Peshkin, S., "Grazing our way to disaster,"** *Utne Reader,* **January/February 1991, p. 15.**

Warns that the cattle business is destroying U.S. public lands along with the Amazon rain forest. The small amount of beef that is actually produced from these areas; governments' encouragement of development for cattle; costs to taxpayers in terms of dollars and environmental damage.

**Charles, D., Dickson, D., et al., "Local 'prospectors' seek the fruits of the rainforest,"** *New Scientist,* **Feb. 23, 1991, p. 22.**

Reveals that speakers told the American Association for the Advancement of Science (AAAS) that biologists are planning to do "chemical prospecting" in the tropics in the next decade. New drugs, food, and industrial products from the rain forest; plans of academics for a combination of classification and harvesting; possible funding by pharmaceutical companies; issues of the indigenous peoples; more.

**Linden, E., "Good intentions, woeful results," *Time*, April 1, 1991, p. 48.**

States that a new threat to the world's fast-diminishing rain forests has united the normally fractious environmental community, now arrayed against the Tropical Forestry Action Plan, sponsored in 1985 by the United Nations, World Bank and other groups. A plan devised according to the needs of the aid agencies rather than the needs of the countries; benefits to adoption of programs stressing forestry over conservation; based on a flawed premise; scattershot approach.

## Native peoples

**Dorfman, A. and Maier, J. Jr. "Assault in the Amazon," *Time*, Nov. 5, 1990, p. 100.**

Reports that Brazil is making an effort to drive gold miners from the rain forest home of the Stone Age Yanomami tribe who are succumbing to malaria, tuberculosis and venereal disease, as well as malnutrition brought by the miners. Government assault on airstrips; preservation of Indian land in protected parks in Brazil and Venezuela.

**Dufour, D. L., "Use of tropical rainforests by native Amazonians," *Bioscience*, October 1990, p. 652.**

Explores the diverse use of rain forests by Amerindians. History of native Amazonians; use of forests for agriculture; use of forests for hunting, fishing, collecting; contrasts with non-indigenous farmers; changing views of native Amazonian resource use.

**Reiss, S., "The last days of Eden," *Newsweek*, Dec. 3, 1990, p. 48.**

Describes how the Yanomami Indians' land, 60,000 square miles of rain forest straddling the Venezuelan-Brazilian border, sits in the path of the onrushing juggernaut of development. As the world's largest remaining group of unacculturated tribal people, the Yanomami represent a last chance for the modern world to atone for the savage obliteration of so many of the original Americans, North and South. The Yanomami's physical survival; land rights.

**Underwood, N., Ashford, M., et al., "Beauty endangered," *Maclean's*, May 21, 1990, p. 60.**

Discusses the Amazon native people's demands that

environmentalists who are trying to save the Amazon rain forest support the Indians' right to control their lands. Recent meeting between ecologists and natives in Iquitos, Peru; foreign-debt-for-nature exchanges; Brazilian government policies; Yanomami of Brazil's Roraima state; Lima, Peru-based Indigenous People's Organizations of the Amazon Basin.

## Organizations

**Carpenter, B., "Faces in the forest," *U.S. News & World Report*, June 4, 1990, p. 63.**

Reviews the work of the United States Agency for International Development in Guatemala's forested Peten province, where scientists are striving to preserve as much of the tropical rain forest as possible, yet attend to the economic needs of the Peteneros. Short profiles of four interested parties. INSET: The planet's vanishing species.

**Sattaur, O., "Last chance for the rainforest plan?" *New Scientist*, March 2, 1991, p. 20.**

Ponders whether the Tropical Forestry Action Plan (TFAP), currently on the verge of failure, can be reformed. Planned meeting of forestry experts and environmentalists in Geneva to attempt to salvage the plan; creating a new strategy for development work in Third World countries; history of the TFAP; increases in deforestation; the role of the World Resources Institute (WRI); lack of impact of TFAP on deforestation; more.

**Sayer, J., "Plans alone will not save the rainforests," *New Scientist*, March 2, 1991, p. 10.**

Comments on the Tropical Forestry Action Plan (TFAP) which was agreed to in 1985 and on the meeting scheduled for Geneva which will discuss the future of this plan. Failures and success in the TFAP; the policy issues underlying forest mismanagement; reviews of TFAP by Friends of the Earth; moving the debate into the tropical countries themselves.

**Sun, M., "How do you measure the Lovejoy Effect? " *Science*, March 9, 1990, p. 1174.**

Profiles biologist and Amazonian rain forest crusader Tom Lovejoy, initiator of the 20-year Minimum Critical Size of Ecosystems (MCSE) Project in the Amazon. Lovejoy is equally at home in the Amazon and as a motivator of powerful public figures for his cause. Scientific and social background; early career; test for conserving biological diversity; debt-for-nature swap; work at Smithsonian.

## Preservation

**"Rainforests saved by satellite," *New Scientist*, April 13, 1991, p. 15.**

Describes the role of satellite photographs in Brazil's crackdown on illegal burning in the Amazon rain forest. What pictures taken by the American satellite NOAA 9 show about the location of the fires; role of Brazil's environmental agency Ibama; statistics of reductions of the burning in the last year; "Operation Amazonia"; the chestnut industry as a beneficiary of the decrease in burnings.

**Calderazzo, J., "Meditation in a Thai forest," *Audubon,* January 1991, p. 84.**

Examines the current state of conservation efforts in Thailand. Loss of forests to unwise logging practices; development in Phi Phi Islands National Park; Buddhist monk Ajarn Pongsak's Tu Bou Forest Monastery; environmentalist Nancy Nas; "A Buddhist Perception of Nature" education program; logging on the Malay peninsula; Khao Yai National Park; air pollution in Bangkok.

**Gibbons, B. and Blair, J.P., "The plant hunters," *National Geographic,* August 1990, p. 124.**

Reports that the Missouri Botanical Garden, a leading center for tropical botanical research, has expanded its mission to educating the world about the effects of rain forest destruction. Reports on the progress being made. INSET: The garden's global mission.

**Roberts, L., "Ranking the rain forests," *Science,* March 29, 1991, p. 1559.**

Describes the Rapid Assessment Program (RAP) an ecological SWAT team put together by four of the world's foremost tropical biologists to do quick and dirty surveys of disappearing tropical forests. Support from systematists and conservationists; setting conservation priorities; origins of RAP; first mission to Bolivia; results of first mission; second mission in Ecuador; criticisms of RAP.

**Stanford, B., "My air, your rainforest: An experiment in global responsibility," *Educational Leadership,* November 1990, p. 97.**

Reports on an effort by the Arkansas International Center of the University of Arkansas at Little Rock and members of Programa Latinoamerica Nino-a-Nino (PLANAN) to develop a program to foster a sense of global responsibility for the environment in students. The ATLAS project; exploring the environment through art, literature and sociology; PLANAN seminar in Guatemala; differences in perspective; ongoing projects with the teachers of Guatemala.

**Worcman, N. B., Ramid, J., et al., "Brazil's thriving environmental movement," *Technology Review,* October 1990, p. 42.**

Assesses Brazil's environmental movement which despite some victories must still overcome fundamental problems which threaten long-term progress. Emergence of the movement; environmental Secretary Jose Lutzenberger; destruction of the rain forest; factors contributing to Brazil's environmental problems; changes under democratic rule; Our Nature Program; efforts to save the Amazon rain forest.

## Research

**Bell, A., "On the roof of the rainforest," *New Scientist,* Feb. 2, 1991, p. 48.**

Explores the story of the "raft of the treetops," a craft that can land on top of trees to aid in the exploration of the South American rain forest. The origin of the idea; expedition to French Guiana sponsored by UNESCO in 1986; success of the mission; vulnerability of the airship during inflation and deflation; rewards of night flights; trees too shy to touch.

**Colinvaux, P. A. and Bush, M. B., "The rain-forest ecosystem as a resource for hunting and gathering," *American Anthropologist,* March 1991, p. 153.**

Refutes the arguments of Bailey et al. in a recent issue of "American Anthropologist" that rain forests can never have supported human populations reliant solely on hunting and gathering. Belief that many tropical rain forests are highly productive of the resources needed for hunting, gathering, and fishing. Movements of peoples at end of last glaciation; food resources of rain forests; more.

**Hurrell, A., "The politics of Amazonian deforestation," *Journal of Latin American Studies,* February 1991, p. 197.**

Seeks to review some recent work on the politics of deforestation and to suggest directions for further research. Suggests a number of themes that need to be explored in assessing Amazon policy during the Sarney period (1985-90). More.

**Merewood, A., "The tropical pharmacy," *Health,* December 1990/January 1991, p. 46.**

Explores the healing possibilities of many tropical rain forest plants, which are being destroyed. Role of rain forests; extracts of plants in powerful drugs; anti-cancer properties; studies at National Cancer Institute (NCI); role of native healers in finding effective medicines; lack of natural plant testing by drug companies; examples.

**Wise, J., "Hotline from Brazil helps to model the climate," *New Scientist,* April 6, 1991, p. 24.**

Reveals that a set of British-designed automatic weather stations will soon be helping study issues involving the deforestation in Brazil. Study of atmospheric changes above the Amazonian forest canopy; more.

# Back Issues

*Great Research on Current Issues Starts Right Here... Recent topics covered by The CQ Researcher are listed below. Issues dated before May 10, 1991, were published under the name of Editorial Research Reports.*

**MARCH 1990**
Asbestos: Are Risks Acceptable?
Public Health Campaigns
South Africa's Future
Homeless Need More Than Shelter

**APRIL 1990**
How Fair is the Tax Burden?
Workers' Compensation
U.S. Pacific Forces
Curbing Insurance Premiums

**MAY 1990**
Should Teaching Be a Profession?
Will Canada Fall Apart?
Is U.S. Patent System Outdated?
Federal Funding for the Arts

**JUNE 1990**
Downsizing America's Armed Forces
Progress In Weather Forecasting
S & L Bailout
Bio-Chemical Disarmament

**JULY 1990**
Do Americans Still Love Marriage?
Death Penalty Debate
Decline of Rural America
United Nations in the 1990s

**AUGUST 1990**
Democracy in the Philippines
Initiatives: True Democracy?
Hard Times at Newspapers
Teens Balance School & Jobs

**SEPTEMBER 1990**
Dangers of Alcohol
Western Alliance After the Cold War
Tobacco Industry
Right to Die

**OCTOBER 1990**
Organ Transplants
Energy Policy Options
Search for Arab Unity
Child Support

**NOVEMBER 1990**
Lotteries and Gambling
Post Cold-War Choices
Setting Limits on Medical Care
Multicultural Education

**DECEMBER 1990**
Cable TV Regulation
Americans' Search For Their Roots
Is Insurance System a Failure?
Why Schools Still Have Tracking

**JANUARY 1991**
Growing Influence of Boycotts
Should the U.S. Reinstate the Draft?
America's Archaeological Past
Peace Corps' Challenges in '90s

**FEBRUARY 1991**
Regional Impact of Recession
Puerto Rico's Status
Redistricting: Mapping Power
Nuclear Power

**MARCH 1991**
Acid Rain
Cost of the Gulf War
Reassessing Gun Laws
Future for Man in Space

**APRIL 1991**
Social Security
Canadian Crisis Over Quebec
California Drought
Electromagnetic Radiation

**MAY 1991**
School Choice
Racial Quotas
Animal Rights
U.S. and Japan

**JUNE 1991**
Children and Divorce
Teenage Suicide
Endangered Species
Europe 1992

**JULY 1991**
Teenagers and Abortion
Soviet Republics Rebel
Mexico's Emergence
Athletes and Drugs

**AUGUST 1991**
Sexual Harassment
Fetal Tissue Research
Oil Imports
The Palestinians

**SEPTEMBER 1991**
Police Brutality
Advertising Under Attack

Back issues are available for $4.00 (subscribers) or $7.00 (non-subscribers). Quantity discounts apply to orders over ten. To order, call Congressional Quarterly 1-800-432-2250.

# Future Topics

▶ *Foster Care*

▶ *Pay-Per-View TV*

▶ *Youth Gangs*

# Foster Care Crisis

*Experts stress need for more programs aimed at keeping families together*

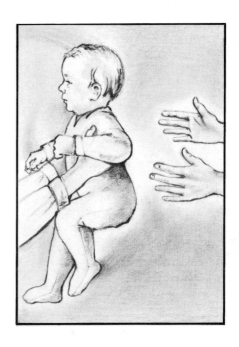

THE NUMBER OF CHILDREN IN THE NATION'S foster care system has risen sharply in recent years. Child welfare agencies face a crisis brought on by deteriorating social conditions and budgetary constraints. Rising teen pregnancies and maternal drug abuse mean increasing numbers of infants abandoned at birth. Reported cases of child abuse or neglect also are on the rise. With state and local agencies unable to adequately supervise foster homes or arrange adoptions, many children will spend much of their lives in foster care, often with lasting emotional scars. Child welfare groups favor a large increase in federal funding and a greater focus on services aimed at keeping families together. Legislation pending in the House and Senate calls for such changes, but finding the money will be difficult.

September 27, 1991 • Volume 1, No. 20 • 705-729

*Formerly Editorial Research Reports*

COVER ART: BARBARA SASSA-DANIELS

September 27, 1991
Volume 1, No. 20

**EDITOR**
Sandra Stencel

**MANAGING EDITOR**
Thomas J. Colin

**ASSOCIATE EDITOR**
Richard L. Worsnop

**STAFF WRITERS**
Charles S. Clark
Mary H. Cooper
Rodman D. Griffin

**PRODUCTION EDITOR**
Laurie De Maris

**EDITORIAL ASSISTANT**
Thomas H. Moore

**GRAPHICS**
Jack Auldridge

**PUBLISHED BY**
Congressional Quarterly Inc.

**CHAIRMAN**
Andrew Barnes

**VICE CHAIRMAN**
Andrew P. Corty

**EDITOR AND PUBLISHER**
Neil Skene

**EXECUTIVE EDITOR**
Robert W. Merry

**PUBLICATIONS MARKETING/SALES**
Robert Smith

**EDITOR, EBSCO PUBLISHING**
Melissa Kummerer

The CQ Researcher (ISSN 1056-2036). Formerly Editorial Research Reports. Published weekly (48 times per year, not printed the first Friday of any month with five Fridays) by Congressional Quarterly Inc., 1414 22nd St., N.W., Washington, D.C. 20037. Rates are furnished upon request. Application to mail at second-class postage rates is pending at Washington, D.C. POSTMASTER: Send address changes to The CQ Researcher, 1414 22nd St., N.W., Washington, D.C. 20037.

# Foster Care Crisis

BY KENNETH JOST

## THE ISSUES

The public service ads used to recruit foster parents evoke heart-warming images: A loving couple takes in a troubled child, provides a comfortable home and emotional support and, after a while, sends the now-healthy child back to his family or on to a permanent adoptive family.

But the picture of foster care that emerges from congressional committees, study commissions and child advocacy groups is starkly different: Unwanted children shuttled from one foster home to another, separated from their siblings, often abused or neglected, and deeply scarred by the pain of separation and rootlessness.

Many child welfare experts call the bleaker picture the more realistic one. In fact, they say the nation's foster care system is in crisis, overloaded despite a 1980 federal law aimed at putting children into more-permanent family situations. They argue that limited funding at the federal and state levels prevents social service agencies from helping troubled families stay together or giving children the support they need while in foster care. "Foster care, intended to protect children who are abused and neglected by their parents, is too often an equally cruel form of abuse and neglect," the National Commission on Children charged in its report on the needs of the nation's children, issued in June.[1] "This is intolerable, and it must not continue," said Sen. John D. Rockefeller IV, D-W.Va., the commission chairman.

There are more than 400,000 children in foster care today, up from 270,000 in the early 1980s. (*See*

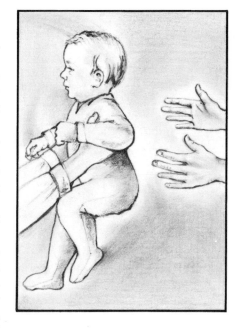

*graph, p. 709.*) But according to the National Commission on Family Foster Care,* the number of qualified foster parents has decreased by 25 percent — falling from 134,000 in 1984 to 100,000 today.[2]

"The child welfare system is in crisis," Wade Horn, commissioner of the federal Administration on Children, Youth and Families (ACYF), told a House subcommittee in March. ". . . [T]he number of children in care is increasing at an alarming rate, with children entering foster care at younger ages and with more complicated problems."

State and local officials confirm the sense of crisis. "The increasing number of children entering or re-entering foster care threatens our ability to make a permanent, positive difference in lives of troubled children and families," warns the American Public Welfare Association,

---

*The commission is a joint project of the Child Welfare League of America and the National Foster Parent Association.

which represents state and local welfare offices.

There is also wide agreement on the causes of the crisis:

■ A sharp increase in the number of reported cases of child abuse or neglect, prompted in part by a 1974 federal law mandating that teachers, doctors and others notify authorities of any suspected abuse or neglect cases;

■ Alcohol and drug abuse, especially "crack" cocaine addiction among women, which experts blame for the large number of infants born drug-exposed and the rising number of infants abandoned at birth;

■ AIDS and the number of children born exposed to the AIDS virus, many of them abandoned at birth;

■ An increase since 1985 in the number of children born to teenage girls, reversing a three-decade decline;

■ An increase over the past decade in the number of children born to unmarried women;

■ An increase in the number of homeless children and children living in poverty.[3]

There is even a measure of agreement on how to deal with the crisis: Put greater emphasis on family services aimed at giving troubled families the social skills — and, to a lesser extent, the tangible assistance — they need to make it on their own, psychologically and financially.

That solution requires money, though, and funding for social services was cut at the beginning of the Reagan years and has remained stagnant since then. Foster care, on the other hand, benefits from a federal funding provision that guarantees states partial reimbursement for expenditures on children in group and foster homes or other institutions.

The result, critics say, is a skewed incentive for state and local agencies to place children in foster care —

September 27, 1991 707

# Federal Funding at a Glance

Three major federal programs provide funds for state and local child welfare agencies to operate foster care systems and provide other social services to children and families:

**Foster Care.** Authorized under Title IV-E of the Social Security Act, this program provides at least 50 percent matching funds to states for maintenance payments for children eligible for Aid to Families with Dependent Children (AFDC). As an "open-ended entitlement," the program does not require annual appropriations from Congress but provides reimbursement for whatever level of qualified expenditures are submitted by the states. It was funded at $1.8 billion in fiscal 1991.

**Child Welfare Services.** Authorized under Title IV-B of the Social Security Act, this program provides 75 percent matching funds to states for direct child welfare services including preventive services (such as counseling or improving parenting skills); placement of children in foster care or adoption; and services to reunify families with children in foster care. The fiscal 1991 appropriation was $273.9 million.

**Social Services Block Grant.** Under Title XX of the Social Security Act, each state receives a block grant to spend on any social services it chooses. There are no comprehensive data on how much of the money is spent for child welfare services. The fiscal 1991 appropriation was $2.7 billion.

ultimately at greater expense to the government — rather than to try to keep the children with their families. These critics, including several key lawmakers in the House and Senate, want to counteract that effect by passing legislation to increase federal funding for social services. But the Bush administration is dubious about the bills, questioning the projected cost of between $3 billion and $6 billion over five years.

Meanwhile, experts warn that the already overloaded foster care system continues to grow, often hurting the very children it is supposed to help. Here are some of the major issues in the debate:

### Are too many children placed and kept in foster care unnecessarily?

Throughout the 20th century, child welfare policy has been torn between the sometimes conflicting goals of preserving families and protecting children — which sometimes meant removing children from their homes. In 1980 Congress sought to put the federal government firmly on the side of keeping families together. The Adoption Assistance and Child Welfare Act passed that year required welfare agencies to make "reasonable ef-

forts" to keep families intact before placing a child in foster care.

Eleven years later, however, the number of children in foster care has increased, not decreased. Not only are more children entering foster care for the first time, and apparently staying for longer periods, but statistics indicate that more children are re-entering foster care after unsuccessful attempts to return to their families.

"We remove too many children from their families, place them too far away, spend too much money doing so, and unnecessarily hurt children and parents in the process," says Peter Forsythe, vice president of the Edna McConnell Clark Foundation, a New York-based group that supports intensive family preservation services.[4]

In addition to its goal of keeping families intact, the 1980 child welfare act promoted adoption for children who could not be reunited with their families. But this goal, too, has not been met. Only 8 percent of children in foster care are eventually adopted, according to Brenda G. McGowan, a professor at Columbia University's School of Social Work.[5]

Despite such problems, even the

critics acknowledge that foster care must continue to play a part in child welfare policies. And foster care is generally recognized as a great improvement over the housing of children in orphanages and other large institutions that were common in the first half of the 20th century.

"Despite its problems, [foster care is] not the pits," says David Fanshel, a professor at Columbia's School of Social Work. "Many people are rescued by the system. It picks up the pieces where many other social systems have failed, and it can't be blamed for the problems of those systems."

### Does federal funding for foster care encourage unnecessary placements?

State and local governments traditionally played the major role in operating and paying for child protection and welfare services. In 1961, however, the federal government assumed a major role in the process. An amendment to the Social Security Act gave states substantial federal matching funds for foster care expenditures on children from families eligible for Aid to Families with Dependent Children (AFDC).

McGowan says the law had "unintended" results. "Although the program provided significant relief to states for the costs of children in placement, it offered no incentive to states to develop alternatives to foster care," she wrote in a report for the National Center for Children in Poverty. "Consequently, it had the effect of encouraging too frequent and too extended foster care placements for children at risk." [6]

Then, in 1980, following two decades of research and commentary about the foster care system — most of it critical — Congress passed the Child Welfare Act, a law explicitly aimed at promoting adoption and reducing the number of children in foster care. The new law restructured the AFDC-Foster Care program under a new Title IV-E of the Social Security Act, and put a cap on federal matching payments for foster care if funding for child welfare services under Title IV-B reached specified levels.[7]

Funding for social services, however, has never reached the levels set in the law, so the cap on federal reimbursements has not gone into effect. As a result, say McGowan and other critics, state and local agencies have no financial incentive to reduce foster care placements. "Right now," says Sen. Rockefeller, "it's cheaper for states to place children in foster care than to provide the support and services that can keep many families safely together."

### Do intensive family preservation services reduce the need for foster care placements — and save states money?

The Children's Defense Fund (CDF) and CWL are among the major groups that have called for state and local agencies to reduce the number of children placed in foster care through expanded use of "family preservation services" aimed at keeping families intact. These programs deliver intensive, short-term help

from a caseworker with as few as two or three cases at a time. The caseworker makes in-home visits and is available to the family around the clock for periods of 30-45 days.

This approach is sometimes called a "Homebuilders model," after a program that has been operating in Tacoma, Wash., since 1974. The Clark Foundation, which helps to start such programs, counts more than 40 states where either Homebuilders is the primary family preservation program or at least one Homebuilders-type program is in place.

Advocates of this approach contend that despite the heavy staffing costs, it saves money by preventing

unnecessary foster care placements. "The minute that a child is headed toward placement, you can place a dollar figure on the child," the foundation's O'Malley explains. Typically, family preservation services cost $3,000 to $7,000 per family — compared with a range of $10,000 to as high as $17,500 per child per year for foster care. "Even given some margin of error," O'Malley says, "you can be sure that you're going to be saving money on a per-child basis."

Foundation Vice President Forsythe claims that Homebuilders-type programs have achieved "almost unbelievably high rates of success" in preventing placements in the 17

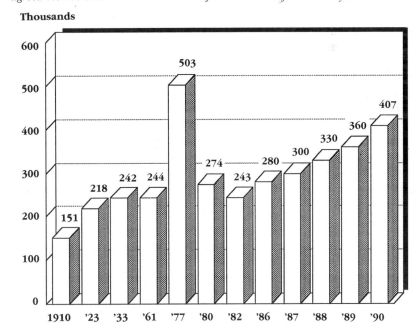

# U.S. Foster Care Population, 1910 - 1990

*The number of children in foster care in the United States rose slowly from 1910 through the 1950s. The number grew more rapidly in the '60s and '70s, reaching a peak of 503,000 in 1977. Efforts to preserve or reunify families, reinforced by the 1980 Adoption Assistance and Child Welfare Act, brought the number of children in foster care down. By the mid-1980s, however, such problems as homelessness and drug and alcohol abuse caused the numbers to rise again. By the end of the decade, policy-makers and experts agreed the increase had created a crisis for the nation's foster care system.*

**Thousands**

|  |  |
|------|-------|
| 1910 | 151 |
| '23 | 218 |
| '33 | 242 |
| '61 | 244 |
| '77 | 503 |
| '80 | 274 |
| '82 | 243 |
| '86 | 280 |
| '87 | 300 |
| '88 | 330 |
| '89 | 360 |
| '90 | 407 |

*Sources: Leroy Pelton, For Reasons of Poverty: A Critical Analysis of the Public Child Welfare System in the United States, 1989 [1910-1982]; Toshio Tatara, "Child Substitute Care Flow Data for FY 1990 and Child Substitute Care Population Trends Since 1986 (Revised Estimates)," VCIS [Voluntary Cooperative Information System] Research Notes, May 3, 1991 [1986-1990].*

years they have been operating. According to the foundation, 90 percent of the children at risk in all such programs remained with their families immediately after intervention; 85 percent were still with families a year later. At the same time, the programs are said to have kept children safe — the driving goal behind all child protection and welfare services. According to O'Malley, no child has been killed or seriously injured by a family member during a Homebuilders intervention.

Not everyone is convinced about the effectiveness of family preservation services, however, including the Bush administration. In a February speech to an American Enterprise Institute symposium on child welfare reform, Horn questioned "the current excitement" over such services. Evaluations had not shown "substantially lower rates" of placement four to six months after services were terminated, he said. "What is needed is not a grand rush to 'fully fund' family preservation services," he concluded, but additional experimentation and more careful evaluation of the results.

The claims of success for family preservation services may indeed be overblown. The supposed cost savings, for example, depend on the assumption that the programs accurately identify children who would be placed in foster care but for the intervention. Department of Health and Human Services program analyst Karl Ensign noted a California study that found a 25 percent placement rate after three years among families served by family preservation programs. This was higher than the 20 percent placement rate found among families randomly assigned to non-specialized services.

The skeptics may challenge the cost-saving claims, but they do not disagree with the goal of keeping troubled families together and providing them with better social ser-

vices. Both sides in the debate also recognize the underlying crisis confronting child welfare agencies: the growing number of children in foster care and the dearth of places to put them. And any solution other than keeping children in their families entails more money — which

neither federal nor state governments can easily provide. That makes the goal of family preservation not so much a choice as a necessity. The challenge for lawmakers and child welfare experts is to identify the social service approaches that can accomplish the goal. ■

# BACKGROUND

## Early History

Foster care has been an important component of child welfare policy in the United States since the mid-19th century. Before then, needy and homeless children had been housed in private or public orphanages or in public almshouses along with the adult poor and the mentally retarded.

Public concern about conditions in these large institutions led to the idea of recruiting farmers, typically in the Midwest, to shelter and care for children in need. "Home-finding" agencies were formed to help ship children to what was depicted as a wholesome life in a bucolic setting. In reality, many of the children found themselves virtually indentured to farmers who cared little for them except as cheap help.[8]

Late in the 19th century, the child welfare movement assumed a more aggressive stance with the founding of child-rescue agencies. The first — the Society for the Prevention of Cruelty to Children — was established in New York City in 1874. By 1900, there were some 250 such agencies around the country.

The growing national concern about child welfare led President Theodore Roosevelt to convene a White House conference on children in 1909. It laid the groundwork for the first federal child welfare agency,

the U.S. Children's Bureau, which was established in 1912. The conference also went on record as supporting the principle of maintaining children in their own families whenever possible and not depriving them of home life "except for urgent and compelling reasons."[9]

The federal role in child welfare policy, however, was largely symbolic for the next two decades. Resistance from state welfare agencies concerned about federal intrusion and from states opposed to proposed anti-child labor laws kept the Children's Bureau weak and poorly funded.

Still, the 1909 White House conference did manage to give a helpful push to one concrete policy innovation affecting children and families. So-called mother's pension laws, enacted in 40 states by 1920, provided public funds to help "fit" and "proper" mothers maintain dependent children in "suitable" homes.

According to Professor Leroy Pelton of Salem State College in Massachusetts, the laws were aimed at preventing the breakup of families for reasons of poverty alone. But Pelton says the continued strength of the child protection societies undermined the "pension" laws. Operating through newly established juvenile courts, the societies continued to press for child removal, contributing to a rise in the overall U.S. foster care population from 151,000 in 1910 to 243,000 in 1933.[10]

Institutional foster care was declining, however, while foster family

*Continued on p. 712*

# Chronology

## 1800s
*Concern over conditions in large orphanages leads to the use of "free foster homes" — typically on Midwestern farms — to care for abandoned children.*

### 1874
The child rescue movement is founded and spreads throughout the country, concentrating on removing children from problem families and prosecuting unfit parents.

———— • ————

## 1909-1930s
*Foster care population slowly rises, but the proportion of the foster care population in institutions drops.*

### 1909
White House Conference on Children says children should be kept with natural families "except for urgent and compelling reasons."

### 1935
Federal Social Security Act of 1935 provides funding for Aid to Dependent Children, allowing more mothers to keep their children at home.

———— • ————

## 1950s
*Number of children in foster care remains fairly steady, but concerns grow.*

### 1959
*Children in Need of Parents*, a critical study of family foster care, depicts children as adrift in the system and urges greater emphasis on family support services.

## 1960s-1970s
*Growing concerns about child abuse bring new pressures to remove children from families when abuse or neglect is suspected.*

### 1961
An amendment to the Social Security Act provides federal reimbursement for state foster care expenditures for children eligible for Aid to Families with Dependent Children (AFDC).

### 1967
Congress establishes the Title IV-B program under Social Security Act to fund state child welfare services.

### 1974
The Child Abuse Prevention and Treatment Act lays down strict requirements for doctors, teachers and others to report suspected child abuse or neglect; such reports quadruple over the next 15 years.

### 1975
Title XX of the Social Security Act is enacted to provide funds for states' social services, including child welfare programs.

### 1977
Foster care population hits all-time peak of 503,000 children.

———— • ————

## 1980s
*Foster care population declines slightly early in decade, then begins to climb again.*

### 1980
Congress passes Adoption Assistance and Child Welfare Act, requiring states to make "reasonable efforts" to reunite foster children with their families or place them in adoption. Title IV-E program is established under the Social Security Act to partially reimburse states for their foster care maintenance payments and administrative and training costs.

### 1983
Foster care population begins to rise again. Experts blame flood of abuse and neglect complaints, increase in teen pregnancies, rising drug and alcohol abuse by parents and inadequate housing.

———— • ————

## 1990s
*Child welfare experts say the overloaded foster care system is in crisis.*

### June 26, 1990
House subcommittee passes $4.5 billion bill to increase funding for child welfare social services, but the measure goes no further.

### Jan. 14, 1991
New child welfare legislation introduced in Senate seeking to increase funding for social services; House bill introduced June 6 following hearings in spring.

### June 24, 1991
National Commission on Children recommends federal funding for family support and preservation services be nearly quadrupled over five years and urges other reforms to reduce the foster care population.

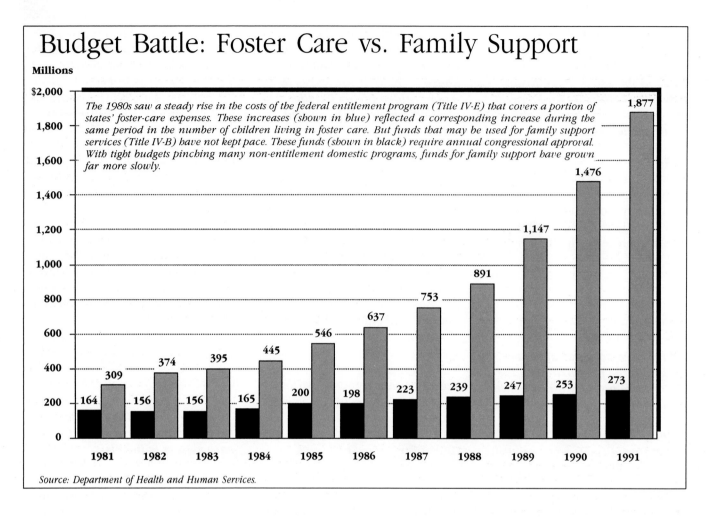

# Budget Battle: Foster Care vs. Family Support

**Millions**

*The 1980s saw a steady rise in the costs of the federal entitlement program (Title IV-E) that covers a portion of states' foster-care expenses. These increases (shown in blue) reflected a corresponding increase during the same period in the number of children living in foster care. But funds that may be used for family support services (Title IV-B) have not kept pace. These funds (shown in black) require annual congressional approval. With tight budgets pinching many non-entitlement domestic programs, funds for family support have grown far more slowly.*

| Year | Black | Gray |
|------|-------|------|
| 1981 | 164 | 309 |
| 1982 | 156 | 374 |
| 1983 | 156 | 395 |
| 1984 | 165 | 445 |
| 1985 | 200 | 546 |
| 1986 | 198 | 637 |
| 1987 | 223 | 753 |
| 1988 | 239 | 891 |
| 1989 | 247 | 1,147 |
| 1990 | 253 | 1,476 |
| 1991 | 273 | 1,877 |

*Source: Department of Health and Human Services.*

Continued from p. 710
care was on the upswing. In 1910, nearly three-fourths of the foster care population of 151,000 were in institutions. By 1933, institutional care accounted for just under half the total of children in foster care. Beginning that year, the population in institutions began an absolute decline — falling from 140,000 children to 110,000 in 1950 and roughly 80,000 in 1960. At that point, institutional care accounted for less than one-third of the total foster care population of 268,000.[11]

One important factor in the reduction in institutional care was the decline of orphanhood and orphanages. The number of "full orphans" — children who had lost both parents by death — dropped from 750,000 in 1920 to 60,000 in 1954.[12]

Income-maintenance programs enabled more women to keep dependent children at home. As Pelton notes, however, it was the federal government, not the states, that contributed most. State widows' pension laws served relatively few families — roughly 94,000 in 1931. But the federal Social Security Act of 1935 provided wider funding for Aid to Dependent Children (ADC, later changed to Aid to Families with Dependent Children, AFDC). By 1940, 372,000 families were receiving ADC benefits; by 1950, the figure had increased to 651,000.[13]

The Social Security Act of 1935 also provided an important spur to the expansion and professionalization of state child welfare services. McGowan notes, for example, that there was little coordinated plan-

ning before passage of the act, but by 1938 all but one state had submitted the coordinated service delivery plans needed to establish eligibility for receipt of federal funds. Over the next two decades, trained staff replaced volunteers, and states took on more responsibility for financing, regulating and delivering services.

Nonetheless, McGowan concludes, child welfare in the early 1960s was still oriented to the care of children outside their homes, seldom integrated with voluntary family services and providing "no public family services as such." Some private agencies, she says, offered high-quality services to children, but public agencies and many of the voluntary agencies as well "provided minimum care and protection to large numbers of poor, often minority, children."[14]

## Conflicting Pressures

Initially viewed as an improvement over institutional care, foster family care began receiving more critical scrutiny in 1959 with the publication of a book-length study by Henry S. Maas and Richard E. Engler Jr. of the University of California-Berkeley School of Social Welfare. They found that as many as half of the children in the nine communities they examined lived "a major part of their childhood" in institutions or foster families — with negative effects on their future development. "Children who move through a series of families or are reared without close and continuing ties to a responsible adult have more than the usual problems in discovering who they are," they wrote. "These are the children who learn to develop shallow roots in relationships with others, who try to please but cannot trust, or who strike out before they can be let down." [15]

In a set of policy recommendations accompanying the study, which was funded by the Child Welfare League, Executive Director Joseph H. Reid noted that marital breakdown had emerged as the most important factor in foster care placements. "By the time the family and child are known to the social agency, in a large percentage of cases family disintegration is already so great that remedial efforts are almost hopeless," Reid wrote. He argued that agencies should extend "imaginative outreaching services" to families in their homes at "the first sign of family breakdown." [16]

But Reid also argued for a more clear-cut severance of parental rights in cases where it was clear that parents were not going to take responsibility for a child. He advocated greater use of group homes for long-term foster care — homes for four to six children with full-time agency employees serving as foster parents. As for foster parents themselves,

Reid argued that they needed greater support, including regular baby-sitting services financed by the agency to give them "sufficient freedom to maintain their own emotional health." [17]

## Crusade Against Child Abuse

When the Maas-Engler study appeared, the nation's substitute-care rate for children — the proportion of children in institutions or family foster care — had fallen to 3.7 per 1,000, the lowest figure since 1910. Their study, and Reid's recommendations, prescribed reducing the placement rate even further. Over the next two decades, however, an aggressive campaign against child abuse offset those arguments and contributed instead to a steady rise in the number of children removed from families and placed in foster care.

The crusade against child abuse began with the "discovery" by Henry Kempe, a physician at the University of Colorado School of Medicine in Denver, of what he called the "battered child syndrome." In a paper presented to the American Academy of Pediatrics in 1961, Kempe used the term to refer to cases of serious physical abuse of children by parents or foster parents and called it "a frequent cause of permanent injury or death." He urged physicians to take steps to ensure a complete investigation of unexplained injuries "so that a decision can be made as to the necessity of placing the child away from the parents until matters are fully clarified." [18]

In 1963, the U.S. Children's Bureau developed the first model reporting statute in an effort to create more uniformity among the states in the reporting of suspected cases of child abuse and neglect. Ten years later, every state had passed a mandatory reporting law. The federal government followed in 1974 with the Child Abuse Prevention and Treatment Act, which expanded the

types of suspected maltreatment that had to be reported as well as the groups of professionals covered by the reporting requirement. [19]

Leroy Pelton argues that abuse and neglect were defined and construed more broadly than necessary. Media attention and reporting laws combined to bring thousands of suspect families to the attention of protective agencies. These agencies had few if any social services to offer families, Pelton says. But they did have resources, including federal funds under a 1961 amendment to the Social Security Act, for foster care. "Having only a hammer," Pelton concludes, "they perceived every problem to need hammering." [20]

More sympathetic assessments of the agencies serve nonetheless to validate Pelton's essential point. The Child Welfare League, for example, reported in a 1968 survey that many placement agencies would have preferred to maintain more children in their homes but found "a lack of community resources to strengthen and support family functioning." [21] Social service caseworkers were pictured as underpaid, undertrained and overworked. A 1978 report by the Children's Defense Fund found child welfare workers facing "impossibly large caseloads" and having "no time to get to know children ..., no time to visit families, and no training to deal with complex family problems." [22]

Whatever the causes, the foster care population rose steadily through the 1960s and most of the '70s. By 1977, 503,000 children were in foster care, and the placement rate stood at a record 7.6 per 1,000 children. The recurrent criticisms about the quality of care intensified. They merged with the growing children's rights and legal aid movements to produce tangible pressure in the form of class action suits aimed at improving conditions for children in foster care. And by the end of the decade Congress stepped in to try to solve the problem.

## Congressional Action

Congress contributed, seemingly unintentionally, to the rise in foster care with what Brenda McGowan calls "a little-noticed, little-debated amendment" to the Social Security Act in 1961. The legislation, enacted first as a temporary measure and made permanent the following year, gave states substantial federal matching funds — 50 percent or more — against their expenditures on foster care for children from AFDC-eligible families. McGowan reflects the prevailing view among child advocacy groups today in saying that the law's failure to provide incentives for alternatives to foster care had the effect of encouraging too frequent and too extended foster placements.[23]

Leroy Pelton, on the other hand, places greater weight on the infusion of federal funds for child welfare services under 1962 and 1967 Social Security amendments. The Public Welfare Amendments of 1962 provided open-ended, 75 percent federal matching funds for state spending on "social services," a term that Pelton says was left ill-defined. The 1967 amendments further expanded the scope of spending. States tapped into the federal spigot for $194 million in 1963, $354 million in 1969 and then $1.7 billion in 1972 before Congress finally set a ceiling of $2.5 billion per year on the program. (The ceiling was reached in 1977.) Pelton says it is not known exactly how the states spent the money, but he cites other studies as indicating that "a large proportion" was spent on foster care.[24]

Congress created an additional federal funding stream for child welfare programs as part of the Child Abuse Prevention and Treatment Act in 1974. The act authorized a relatively small grant program — totaling about $25 million in FY '91 —

for state anti-child-abuse projects. Also in 1974, Congress set up a new program of federal aid to state social services. Reflecting the Nixon administration's "New Federalism," the law carried over the 75 percent federal matching provision — and the $2.5 billion ceiling — for state social service expenditures aimed at preventing abuse and neglect, preserving families and preventing or reducing inappropriate institutional care.

Title XX — and its Reagan administration reconfiguration, the Social Services Block Grant — has been a major source of child welfare funds for many states. But McGowan notes that the relatively stagnant funding level — $2.7 billion in FY '89 — has meant that interest groups have been competing for what became more limited social service funds.[25]

By the late 1970s, Congress was being lobbied by a broad coalition of public officials and child welfare professionals to bring the foster care system under control. Critics pointed not just to the rising overall population but also, in particular, to the apparent increase in the length of time children stayed in foster care. In 1977, a study sponsored by the old Department of Health, Education and Welfare (HEW), found that 58 percent of all children in foster care had been there for more than two years and that the median length of stay in substitute care was two and a half years.[26]

The critics focused as well on the federal funding mechanisms. Expenditures under the AFDC-Foster Care maintenance reimbursements program had risen sharply from $40 million in 1971 to $205 million in 1979 while funds for social services had lagged. The child welfare services program under Title IV-B had been authorized at $266 million in 1972, but actual program funding was well below that amount — just $56.5 million in 1979. States spent much of

that money for foster care maintenance for children not covered by AFDC. That left little federal money to help pay for social services that, the critics contended, could actually reduce foster care costs by keeping families intact.[27]

Legislative efforts over a five-year period culminated in 1980 with the enactment of the Adoption Assistance and Child Welfare Act, now frequently referred to by its public law number: PL 96-272. The act sought to get children out of foster care and either back to their families or into adoption by requiring individualized case planning and reviews and by simultaneously authorizing more money for social services and setting a conditional ceiling on foster care maintenance reimbursements.

### Unfulfilled Promises

Eleven years after its enactment, PL 96-272 is credited with a number of positive effects. As Beverly McGowan notes, it helped create opportunities for subsidized adoption of special-needs children. States acted to take advantage of the federal reimbursements; by 1989, federal adoption assistance expenditures totaled $112 million. McGowan says the law has also ensured more careful review of the actions of child welfare agencies, focused greater attention on the need for placing children in a permanent setting after foster care, and created an impetus for development of preventive and after-care services.[28]

Many promises of the 1980 law, however, have gone unfulfilled. After dropping for several years, the foster care population — and the placement rate — has been rising since the mid-1980s. The ceiling on foster care reimbursements has never taken effect because Title IV-B appropriations have never reached the authorization levels. Title XX funding, meanwhile, actually de-

# Bring Back Orphanages?

A small but growing number of child welfare experts want to turn back the clock to solve the foster care crisis: They want to bring back the orphanage. But in their modern version, there are no bleak, overcrowded dormitories where stern matrons dispense harsh discipline and little, if any, loving care. Instead, smaller group homes create a semblance of family life for children who are unlikely to rejoin their natural families or be adopted into new ones.

Those who advocate modern-day orphanages say there simply is no alternative to long-term group care for many abandoned or neglected children. "In a well-meant effort to recognize the rights of parents and the potential benefits of a family setting, we have consigned infants and youths to a foster care system that, by its design, cannot provide the continuity and care so many children desperately need," said Joyce Ladner, a professor of social work at Howard University in Washington, D.C.†

When orphanages were being established in the mid- and late 19th century, they were an improvement over the alternative: the poorhouse, where abandoned children were thrown in with alcoholics and the mentally retarded. But with the maturing of the child welfare movement in the 20th century, warehousing yielded to the more enlightened policies of family foster care. Orphanages became virtually extinct, their buildings converted into residential treatment facilities for children needing special social services.

David Liederman, executive director of the Child Welfare League of America, says group care for children with special needs is still one essential part of a child welfare system's mix of services. But the new orphanages generally offer no specialized care, merely a long-term residential setting.

In Kansas, for example, The Villages, a nonprofit social service agency, contracts with the state to operate a handful of facilities staffed by full-time professional "parents" where 10 or so children live for anywhere from two to eight years.†† The Los Angeles County Infant and Therapeutic Shelter, also operated by a private agency under contract with the county, houses 45 infants and toddlers in nursery units with a substitute mother for each child.‡

MaryLee Allen, child welfare director for the Children's Defense Fund (CDF), sees risks in establishing such facilities. "They generally start with a burst of enthusiasm, but then the care starts to deteriorate," she says.

"It's a trap," Allen adds. "If you start even a small congregate care facility, once those beds are there, those beds are going to be filled." Gary Stangler, director of Missouri's Department of Social Services, voices the same concern: "Once that orphanage is built, I guarantee I'll fill it, and it will never go away." ‡‡

For her part, Allen is unconvinced that there really is an orphanage revival. CDF is currently conducting a survey to try to document the number of long-term group-care facilities in operation. Whether or not they constitute a trend, the proponents of such facilities make no apologies for the care they provide, especially in the inner cities where the problems of dysfunctional families, parental substance abuse, poverty and homelessness are most acute.

"When I got started, I was very apologetic about putting children in a group setting," Sheila Anderson, director of the Los Angeles infant shelter, told *The Washington Post*. "Now I'm very proud of what we do. It's an alternative for some children. We don't have to go back to the horrors of some institutions of the 1940s."

---

† Op-ed article in *The Washington Post*, Oct. 29, 1989.

†† See Penelope Lemov, "The Return of the Orphanage," *Governing*, May 1991, pp. 31-32.

‡ See Marcia Slacum Greene, "Rebirth of Orphanages Is Reviving Old Fears," *The Washington Post*, Jan. 9, 1990, p. A6.

‡‡ Quoted in Lemov, *op. cit.*, p. 35.

---

clined — from $3 billion in fiscal 1981 to $2.7 billion in fiscal 1989.

Federal review of state programs has been criticized as lax. A 1989 report by the General Accounting Office (GAO), for example, prompted a frustrated Congress that year to impose a moratorium on penalties against the states for non-compliance. Meanwhile, new studies, congressional hearings and a flurry of court cases were documenting that many children in foster homes receive inadequate care or worse, and little attention or help from the agencies charged with protecting them.

What happened? Democratic lawmakers have placed much of the blame on the Reagan administration for cutting social services funding and being slow to implement — and loath to enforce — the provisions of the 1980 law. "Frankly, we don't know whether or not the law works, because the Department of Health and Human Services (HHS — formerly HEW) throughout the 1980s failed to enforce compliance," Rep. George Miller, D-Calif., chairman of the House Select Committee on Children, Youth and Families, testified in a hearing before the Ways and Means Subcommittee on Human Resources in April 1990.

Miller criticized HHS for initially allowing states to "self-certify" compliance with the law. When auditing procedures were set up, he said, they were "lax and ineffective." State officials told his committee in 1988 that HHS failed to explain reasons for denying state claims or to give technical assistance to correct problems. And data on the number of children in foster care remained hard to get, Miller said. In 1988, HHS's most recent data was for 1985.[29]

Child advocacy groups make the same criticisms, charging both the Reagan and Bush administrations with failing to provide leadership as the foster care crisis developed. "They have not taken the required steps to ensure compliance with the protections that are in place," says MaryLee Allen, child welfare director for the Children's Defense Fund. ACYF Commissioner Horn acknowledged some of the criticisms in his appearances before the Human Resources Subcommittee in April 1990 and again last March, but he insisted HHS was moving to solve some of the problems. He said his agency was conducting tests in several states to improve review of state child welfare programs by developing ways to evaluate the quality of services rather than mere technical compliance with the statute. Efforts were also under way, he said, to improve so-called Section 427 reviews. These reviews set out procedural protections for children in foster care, such as formal case planning, permanency planning and periodic case review. And, in his most recent appearance, Horn promised that the long-delayed rule on a uniform data-collection system would be implemented by Oct. 1.[30]

## Increase in Placements

Regulatory delays and difficulties did not, however, create the foster care crisis. The triggering cause was the doubling of child abuse and neglect cases reported to child welfare agencies since passage of the 1980 child welfare act — from 1.2 million cases in 1981 to 2.5 million cases in 1989. Experts and advocacy groups disagree on whether those statistics reflect an increase in abuse and neglect or merely better reporting.

Some observers — including conservative Douglas Besharov, who headed the National Center on Child Abuse and Neglect in the Reagan administration, and liberal academic Leroy Pelton — argue that child abuse and neglect are being "overreported" and that a high proportion of reports go unsubstantiated.

But according to Mark Testa of the University of Chicago, substantiated abuse and neglect cases rose during most of the 1980s. Addressing a February conference on foster care issues sponsored by the American Enterprise Institute, he noted that national figures show a 68 percent increase in substantiated cases from 1982 to 1987 — roughly equal to the increase in total cases reported.[31]

Whether or not abuse and neglect cases are being overreported, the statistics add up to huge increases in the numbers of children being processed by the agencies supplying the foster care network. Public opinion, caseworker attitudes and bureaucratic imperatives all operated to emphasize child safety as the major criterion in dealing with those cases. Even without any other considerations, the predictable result was an increase in placements.

Two of the decade's biggest social crises — drugs and homelessness — have added to the pressure to put more children in foster care. In a study of black children in foster care in five major cities, the National Black Child Development Institute found parental drug abuse and inadequate housing the most frequent factors contributing to foster care placements. Drug abuse was cited as a factor in 37 percent of the foster care placements overall — and 52 percent of New York City's cases. Poor housing was given as a factor in 30 percent of the cases, including 11 percent of the children in foster care listed as homeless.[32]

The increased caseloads fell on child welfare agencies that were ill equipped to provide the social services that families needed. Agencies were understaffed, in part because of state budget problems and in part because of recruitment difficulties caused by low salaries. An American Public Welfare Association (APWA) commission reported in 1990 that the average salary for entry-level child welfare workers was $17,000 to $25,000 and that salaries had kept pace with inflation since 1987 in just 17 of 44 states surveyed. And job stress and burnout caused in part by higher-than-recommended caseloads contributed to high turnover, especially among front-line caseworkers.[33]

The agencies were also finding it harder to recruit foster parents. One factor was low pay. The Senate Finance Committee reported in 1990 that the nationwide average reimbursement rate was $268 per month for a child under 6, $292 for 9-year-olds, and $338 for 16-year-olds.[34] In addition, greater numbers of working women means fewer mothers are at home to care for foster children. And an average 60 percent of foster parents quit within a year. "My wife and I did foster care for 17 years," says Gordon Evans, information director of the National Foster Parent Association, "and I don't believe we could handle today's children." [35]

The many pressures on child welfare agencies produced horror stories chronicled by court cases throughout the decade. In New York City, caseworkers found themselves forced to herd hundreds of children into offices during the day and move them to temporary beds every night. A federal judge ruled in 1987 that the city had violated the children's constitutional rights.[36] A suit filed in Washington, D.C., in 1989 showed that the

Continued on p. 718

# Kinship Care: Does Grandmother Know Best?

When Clarence Thomas' mother realized she could not give him the care he needed, she sent him to live with his grandparents. Today, the traditional practice of extended family care, especially common among black Americans, is playing a key role in the government-supported foster care system. But the increased use of "kinship," or "grandmother," care has child welfare experts puzzling over a host of policy issues:

■ Are children better off if they are removed completely from their natural families and routed into non-family foster care as a transition toward adoption? Or does kinship care preserve an important link with the natural family while ensuring proper care in a nurturing home environment?

■ Do understaffed child welfare agencies adequately supervise the care being given to children who are placed with relatives? Or do they assume that a child's extended family is going to take good care of the child and focus their limited resources on other problems?

■ Does the use of kinship care increase the overall capacity of the foster care system? Or does it merely incorporate informal arrangements into the formal system — at government expense?

Caught unprepared by the sudden increase in kinship care, the experts have been unable to give hard answers to these questions. But one thing is certain: In the past five years, placement with relatives has been the fastest growing component of the foster care system.

In New York City, the number of children placed in foster care with relatives shot up from 1,000 in 1986 to more than 20,000 in 1990. During the same period, Illinois recorded a 121 percent increase in kinship care — from 3,707 children placed with relatives in 1986 to 8,205 in 1990.

The trend is most pronounced in urban ghettos, where it carries on the tradition of "taking care of our own" stressed by black self-help advocates from Booker T. Washington to Clarence Thomas. The Supreme Court nominee spoke movingly of his grandfather's influence on his life during recent Senate confirmation hearings.

Some experts worry, however, that extended family care is now being encouraged, unintentionally, by government income-support systems that allot more money for children in foster care than in their own families. In New York, for example, the monthly payment for an additional child under Aid to Families with Dependent Children (AFDC) is $109 while the foster care payment for the same child is $371.

As Mark Testa, an associate professor at the University of Chicago notes, the disparity has generated rumors that signs have been posted in New York apartment houses saying, "Grandparents, you can receive money by taking care of your grandchildren." † But Testa concludes that financial incen-

tives cannot be the only explanation. Foster care payments were available to relatives in Illinois as early as 1973, he says, but the increase in kinship care began only after 1986.

The uncertainty over the causes of the trend is matched by uncertainty about its effects on children. Some officials and experts are convinced of the benefits of kinship care. Barbara Sabol, commissioner of New York City's Human Resources Administration, says kinship foster care offers "important advantages" over regular foster care and calls it "the preferred response when placement is necessary." ††

But advocates of family preservation say kinship care can discourage family unification by making it easier for parents to maintain contact with their children without regaining full custody. Some experts believe kinship care tends to discourage planning for adoption, since a family member is unlikely to take part in a legal action severing the parental rights of a relative.

Testa cited statistics indicating that kinship care does tend to leave children in limbo for longer periods. A study in Illinois showed that children cared for by relatives left their care at one-fifth the rate of children in regular foster care. One proposed solution to the problem: create a new status like legal guardianship that would offer financial support for the child's care while eliminating the government's role in supervising the arrangement.

For now, the length of time that children may live in kinship care underscores the concerns about the quality of care they receive. "There's a feeling that it's being done without good study of the homes," says David Fanshel, professor of social work at Columbia University. "It's very convenient for public departments because it spares them the very real difficulty of finding suitable foster parents."

As Fanshel notes, however, there has been relatively little research done on this issue. That gap may explain the tentative conclusions that study groups offer about kinship care. The report in May by the National Commission on Children, for example, said kinship care is "often a desirable arrangement," but added that states need to provide support and services for the children in kinship care and continue efforts to reunite the children with their natural families.‡

---

† Task Force on Permanency Planning for Foster Children Inc., *Kinship Foster Care: The Double Edged Dilemma*, October 1990, quoted by Mark Testa in "Conditions of Parents and Children at Risk of Substitute Care," American Enterprise Institute Conference on Child Welfare Reform Experiments, Feb. 20-21, 1991.

†† Testimony before House Ways and Means Subcommittee on Human Resources, April 30, 1991, p. 3.

‡ National Commission on Children, *Beyond Rhetoric: A New American Agenda for Children and Families*, May 1991, p. 299.

Continued from p. 716

had an average monthly backlog of 1,200 uncompleted child neglect investigations and, typically, a four-day delay before acting in emergency cases when its own law required action within 24 hours. Another federal judge ruled in April 1991 that the District, too, was violating children's constitutional rights; he particularly upbraided D.C. officials for failing to file for the recovery of an estimated $21 million per year in available federal reimbursements.[37]

In the wake of the scandals came recommendations for "new" solutions that in fact harkened to old patterns of substitute care. Some experts called for greater use of group, or congregate care, foster homes that in effect were updated, smaller-scale versions of the traditional orphanage, each accommodating 10-20 children cared for by paid staff. (*See story, p. 715.*)

Child advocacy groups, however, have spoken out sharply against the idea. "I'm passionately opposed to the expansion of congregate care, particularly for very young children," Carol Williams, a senior research analyst at the Center for Study of Social Policy, told a National Commission of Children hearing in April. "We are seeing children in institutions that are [technically] not called orphanages, and the children are not doing well."

Child welfare experts have also been debating another placement option for troubled children: "kinship care." Putting children in the care of other relatives, such as grandparents, has been growing in a handful of cities, particularly New York, where officials now describe it as the preferred option. (*See story, p. 717.*) Some administrators and experts see the trend as mirroring the pattern in black families of caring for their own and offering a more family-like setting than placement with a non-related foster parent.

But experts such as Gordon Berlin, senior vice president of the Manpower Research Demonstration Program, a nonprofit organization that designs employment-focused programs for disadvantaged groups, have raised a host of questions about kinship care. Testifying before the Human Resources Subcommittee in March, Berlin said kinship care appeared to last longer than foster care with a non-relative and was less likely to result in adoption. At the same time, he said, the foster care payments to the relative created a financial disincentive to returning the child to the family.

These debates about kinship care took place in the late 1980s against the backdrop of the sharp rise in the foster care population and the even sharper increase in federal spending for foster care maintenance. According to government and private data, the number of children in foster care rose from 280,000 in 1986 to at least 360,000 at the end of 1989 and perhaps 407,000 at the end of 1990. Federal spending on foster care maintenance under Title IV-E nearly tripled during the five-year period — from $637 million in 1986 to $1.877 billion for fiscal 1991. Meanwhile, spending on social services under Title IV-B rose more slowly, from $198 million in 1986 to $273 million in 1991. The Children's Defense Fund said that measured in constant dollars, federal social services spending had increased just 6 percent since 1981.

By the end of the decade, Congress was being urged to address the foster care crisis. In response, the House Ways and Means Subcommittee on Human Resources fashioned legislation, sponsored by Acting Chairman Thomas J. Downey, D-N.Y., to boost spending for social services. The bill would have made Title IV-B a "capped entitlement" — not requiring annual appropriations — that would be set initially at $500 million and rise to $1 billion by fiscal 1994. Funds for the Title XX Social Services Block Grant were also to be increased — from $2.8 billion to $3.1 billion by fiscal 1993. States would also be given new mandates to emphasize family reunification (including follow-up care) as well as drug and alcohol abuse treatment programs.[38]

The subcommittee approved the measure by voice vote June 27, 1990, with only one Republican — Tennessee's Don Sundquist — opposing it. But the Bush administration strongly opposed the bill. "Such large program expansions under current budget conditions would be imprudent," HHS Secretary Louis W. Sullivan wrote the subcommittee. With Congress embroiled in a yearlong struggle over the budget deficit, the bill died with no further action. ■

# CURRENT SITUATION

## In the Trenches

For many children today, the child welfare system can offer only a choice between unacceptable alternatives: a troubled, possibly dangerous life with families who cannot or will not be helped to overcome problems of drugs, violence or poverty; or placement in a foster care system that cannot help the children of dysfunctional families to heal and grow.

Caseworkers confront conditions that one child welfare administrator — returning to day-to-day operations with a county welfare department after a five-year hiatus — described as

# D.C. Lawsuit Underscores National Problem

LaShawn A. was 2 ½ years old when her homeless and emotionally troubled mother relinquished her to the Washington, D.C., Department of Human Services (DHS). The agency placed the little girl in a foster home. Three years later, evidence indicated LaShawn had been beaten and possibly sexually abused, but the agency did not remove her from the home.

Kevin E. was placed with DHS in 1978, when he was 3 weeks old. By 1989, 11 years later, he had been shuttled to 11 different foster care placements. The agency's legally required case plan for Kevin listed adoption as the goal, but as of 1989 he had never been referred to the agency's adoption unit.

LaShawn and Kevin were two of seven plaintiffs in a class action suit filed in 1989 by the American Civil Liberties Union (ACLU) against the District of Columbia. The suit charged that the city's inadequate treatment of foster care children violated the children's civil rights and demanded improvements in the system.

The suit was one of many brought in recent years by the ACLU's Children's Rights Project and other legal aid organizations that have led to changes in foster care systems around the country, including those in Alabama; Connecticut; Georgia; Kansas City, Mo.; and New York City.

In the Washington suit, U.S. District Judge Thomas F. Hogan ruled in favor of the plaintiffs following a three-week trial in February that produced damning testimony about indifference and ineptitude in the DHS. In a blistering, 102-page opinion, Hogan called the city's foster care system "a travesty" that had violated children's rights under the Constitution and federal and D.C. law. He ordered the ACLU and city to work out a settlement plan to improve the system.

The 84-page agreement approved by Hogan in August calls for doubling the number of child social workers over three years. Among its other major provisions:

■ Caseloads of foster care social workers will not exceed 20 cases. Previously, caseloads had been as high as 120 cases.

■ No more than three unrelated children will be placed in a single foster home. The previous limit had been four, but it was routinely exceeded.

Under the agreement, the nonprofit Center for the Study of Social Policy will draft a detailed implementation plan by the end of the year. The center will monitor compliance with the plan, but D.C. officials will retain day-to-day administrative control over the foster care system. A similar ACLU suit against the state of Connecticut ended earlier in the year with an outside group actually running the state's system.

"Washington's system was one of the worst in the country, if not the worst," said Marcia Robinson Lowry, director of the Children's Rights Project. "The new proposal will help to make it one of the best."

The District's foster care problems had festered during Mayor Marion S. Barry Jr.'s final years in office. Pleading financial problems, his administration had left vacant up to 40 percent of the city's child welfare social worker positions. Evidence uncovered by ACLU lawyers showed routine failure to comply with deadlines for handling cases.

When Mayor Sharon Pratt Dixon took office in January 1991, she asked the Bush administration for help in turning the system around. Following Judge Hogan's ruling in April, a Bush administration official on loan to the District government, D. Ray Sirry, the associate commissioner of the U.S. Children's Bureau, helped mediate the settlement during three months of difficult negotiations. He said D.C. officials under Dixon had already begun moving to increase staffing but that it would take a year for major changes to be visible.

As if to underscore the urgency of the ACLU suit, a 3-year-old child housed in an overcrowded D.C. foster home died in a fire the weekend before Hogan's hearing to approve the settlement. Marcus Brooks was one of eight children living in a home that had lost its foster care license in 1989 because of overcrowding.†

---

† See *The Washington Post*, Aug. 27, 1991, p. B1

---

"culture shock." Beverly Jones, assistant director for child welfare services in Maryland's Anne Arundel County, told an American Enterprise Institute (AEI) forum in February that she found "significant and striking" differences when she returned "to the trenches" in 1989.

"Poly drug use" — alcohol along with other drugs — was common, Jones said, as was the use and acceptance of violence. Caseworkers would not go into the community alone — or unarmed. Families were poorer "not only in terms of material goods but also in spirit." And extended family members were increasingly unwilling — or unable — to care for children who needed help.

Jones' department was in a better position to deal with these problems than many other child welfare agencies, especially in large cities. Her caseworkers had a low average caseload of 25-33 cases. In Los Angeles, the average caseload in 1988 was about 75 cases. In Washington, D.C., caseloads reached 125 cases per caseworker. (The Child Welfare League recommends a caseload of 28 cases, a figure that is currently under review.)

The neglect and abuse cases handled by welfare caseworkers must move through a juvenile court system that also is overwhelmed by the caseload. During field hearings in Los Angeles last year, the National Commission on Children visited juvenile courts where judges routinely processed 35-40 cases per day — about 10 minutes per case. In some jurisdictions, the numbers are higher — as many as 100 cases in a day.

Judge Paul Boland, presiding judge of the Los Angeles County Juvenile Court, told the commission that 90 percent of the court's cases involve parental substance abuse. And about 4,000 drug babies — babies with drugs in their systems because of the mother's drug use during pregnancy — were expected to enter the Los Angeles system in 1990. These babies, Boland said, would need more services, be more difficult to return home or place for adoption and be likely to stay in the system much longer than other abused or neglected children. But drug treatment services were not available to all the mothers and children who needed them, Boland said.

Homelessness adds to the foster care overload as well. One-third of the estimated 2.2 million homeless people in the United States are families with children. And homelessness was found to be a factor in 11 percent of the 1,000 foster care cases studied in five cities for 1986.[39] In 1988, a New Jersey official told the House Ways and Means Subcommittee on Public Assistance that homelessness was a factor in 40 percent of foster care placements in the state and the sole precipitating cause in 18 percent of the cases.[40]

Once again, government services are inadequate to cope with the problem. But efforts to provide housing and thus avoid placing a child in foster care collide with budget realities. In New York, Democratic Gov. Mario M. Cuomo vetoed a bill in 1990 that would have funded subsidized housing for families at imminent risk of foster care

placement, saying it would cost too much. New York City does have a program, however, to help pay for housing in cases where its lack is preventing the return of the child from foster care.

Despite the problems, some experts maintain that children in foster care generally are doing well. "There are over 150,000 foster families taking in children unrelated to them, and for the most part doing quite well with them," says Columbia University's David Fanshel.

Former Reagan administration official Douglas Besharov agrees — in part. "The vast majority of children in the system receive good physical care, often substantially better than their parents can provide," he wrote in a 1990 article. The problem, he said, lies with the emotional impact foster care has on children, especially older children who have been through multiple placements. For them, he said, foster care is often an "unsettling" experience that "den[ies] them the consistent support and nurturing they desperately need."[41]

## In Congress

The House Select Committee on Children opened the current push for federal legislation to stem the foster care crisis with a strongly worded report in January 1990 decrying the system's "extraordinary failings" — weak federal oversight, inadequate resources and services that are "uncoordinated, inefficient and ultimately ineffective." In line with recommendations of child advocacy groups, the committee's Democratic majority concluded that federal funding mechanisms created disincentives to keeping families together and urged that more money be given to intensive family preservation services to prevent removal of children from their natural families.[42]

Legislation reflecting those goals was introduced in the Ways and Means Human Resources Subcommittee by the panel's acting chairman, Thomas Downey, following two days of hearings in April. But the bill's price tag — $4.5 billion in additional spending over five years — was too much in a year when controlling the budget deficit was the major preoccupation for Congress and the administration. While the subcommittee approved the bill by voice vote in June, no further action was scheduled; and no comparable legislation was introduced in the Senate in 1990.

Parallel bills were introduced in the House and Senate in 1991. Both measures called for making the Title IV-B social services funding program a "capped entitlement" — one not requiring annual appropriations. Both bills would raise funding gradually over the next four years: to $1 billion in fiscal 1995 in the House bill and to $725 million in the Senate bill. Both bills seek to ensure that states do not use the new funds to supplant their own spending but fund new or expanded programs, especially in drug treatment and family preservation. The House measure would move toward that goal by setting aside specified percentages of Title IV-B funding for family services — 30 percent in fiscal 1992 rising to 50 percent in fiscal 1995. The Senate bill stipulates that the increased Title IV-B funding would be designated for five areas, including family preservation services. It also sets up a separate new entitlement program for substance abuse treatment programs for pregnant women and caretaker parents to be funded initially at $75 million in fiscal 1992 and increasing to $125 million by fiscal 1996.

The House measure, in addition, would expand eligibility for federal foster care reimbursement by eliminating the current limitation of Title

*Continued on p. 722*

# At Issue:

## Do family preservation services reduce the number of children placed in foster care?

### Peter Forsythe

*Vice President, Edna McConnell Clark Foundation*
FROM *A PAPER PRESENTED AT AN AMERICAN ENTERPRISE INSTITUTE FORUM ON "CHILD WELFARE REFORM EXPERIMENTS,"* FEB. 20, 1991.

*f*amily preservation services have three goals: (1) safety of the child, family, worker and community; (2) keeping the family together and avoiding placement; (3) improving the skills of family members so they will be better able to handle this and other similar problems in the future.

The safety success has been virtually 100 percent. . . . I am not aware of a single child who has ever been seriously hurt . . . during the period while family preservation services were being provided. . . .

The placement prevention figures are just as impressive as the safety record. Homebuilders [a model family preservation program developed in Washington state in the late 1970s] has a composite 17-year record of preventing placement over 90 percent of the time, measured at the end of the intervention. A year after completion, some families have resorted to placement, but the avoidance rate is still about 85 percent. Because numbers vary by geography, culture . . . and referral agency, the composite numbers are just that — but their consistency and almost unbelievably high rates of success give great hope for a substantial impact on placement numbers if such services were in fact available to many more families. . . .

Measurement [of better family functioning] is much more difficult, but all evidence points to impressive gains. One of the most thorough analyses of this issue is the federally funded *Families In Crisis*. . . . That study . . . found statistically significant and measurable gains in many areas, from less use of physical punishment to the condition of the family home. . . .

Another factor not to be overlooked in times of troubled budgets is the cost-effectiveness of Family Preservation Services. Family foster care averages more than $10,000 per child per year, and the average stay is more than a year. . . . Family preservation, on the other hand, costs from $3,000 to $5,000 per family. . . . Therefore, even in times of fiscal constraint, there is no excuse not to expand the availability of services. Michigan, Missouri and others have continued their expansion of Family Preservation Services this year in spite of budget cutbacks overall. In tough times, it is indefensible to ignore cheaper alternatives, especially when they meet society's need for safety and avoid the disadvantages of family dismemberment.

### John R. Schuerman

*Faculty Associate, Chapin Hall Center for Children, University of Chicago*
FROM *A PAPER PRESENTED AT AN AMERICAN ENTERPRISE INSTITUTE FORUM ON "CHILD WELFARE REFORM EXPERIMENTS,"* FEB. 20, 1991.

*e*arly evaluations of family preservation programs were positive, suggesting that services were quite effective in preventing the placement of children. However, these studies have been criticized as scientifically flawed and their results must be viewed with suspicion. Recent studies in California and New Jersey, employing more rigorous research methods, tell a different story. In both of these studies, random assignment of subjects to family preservation or to regular services were employed. These studies found little difference in the proportion of children placed in these two groups. . . .

It is evident that many, if not most, of the families in the control groups in these experiments did not have children "at imminent risk of placement." Since the cases were randomly assigned, those receiving family preservation services were also not at imminent risk of placement. This observation has important implications for both evaluation and service planning. If few cases in the control group are placed, it is much more difficult for an evaluation to detect placement prevention effects. . . . More importantly, it is evident that the services are not being delivered to those for whom they were intended, those most likely to experience placement. . . .

We do not suggest that these services are necessarily being wasted. The families receiving them often have great needs, and the programs may well benefit them. . . . Many workers believe that when placement occurs, involvement in programs of this kind results in "better" placements, that is, placements of shorter duration or of greater stability. . . .

Our message is that there are limits to the technology of family preservation services. We believe that it is unlikely that these services will have a substantial direct effect on overall placement rates or on the numbers of children in substitute care. . . .

Even though placement prevention is unlikely to be a major result, the proliferation of these programs has resulted in a badly needed increase in the resources available to these families. But family preservation services should take their place in a larger agenda of reform of the child welfare system, an agenda that should include improvements in a now neglected substitute care system and attention to improving the communities in which our children live.

**September 27, 1991   721**

*Continued from p. 720*

IV-E to AFDC-eligible children. To balance the cost of this proposal — called "delinking" foster care and AFDC — the House bill would somewhat lower the Title IV-E reimbursement rates.

Both bills also contain a host of detailed provisions aimed at improving federal oversight and state implementation of the provisions of the 1980 law. And both bills call for an administration study of one of the most important, and most litigated, mandates of the 1980 law: the requirement that states make "reasonable efforts" to keep a child in the family before placing him or her in foster care.

Despite the early introduction of the Senate bill, the Senate Finance Committee had not held or scheduled hearings on the bill by the August congressional recess.

In the House, however, Downey's bill was approved by the Human Resources Subcommittee Sept. 24 following three sets of hearings by the panel in the spring. As approved by the subcommittee, the bill's total cost was put at $6.8 billion over five years. Downey said the question of how to pay for the new program would have to be addressed by the full Ways and Means Committee.

The administration restated its opposition to the measure in a letter delivered on the eve of the markup. HHS Secretary Sullivan, citing what he termed the bill's "excessive costs and highly prescriptive provisions," said he would recommend the president veto the bill as currently written.

### *In the Courts*

Meanwhile, court actions continued to provide the most immediate prospect of bringing about administrative or funding changes in state foster care systems. Connecticut officials agreed in December 1990 to a plan developed by a court-appointed mediation panel that sets limits on caseworker caseloads; specifies timetables for handling cases; prescribes new steps to recruit and retain foster and adoptive homes; and mandates establishment of a statewide training academy for current and future child welfare employees. Marcia Robinson Lowry, director of the American Civil Liberties Union (ACLU) Children's Rights Project, which brought the court action, estimated the cost to Connecticut at $10 million per year.

Project lawyers also won a similar suit against the District of Columbia's child welfare agency this year. D.C. officials agreed in June to a plan that, among other things, will more than double the number of child welfare caseworkers in order to reduce caseloads from 120 per worker to around 20. The agreement came after the federal judge in the case issued a stinging ruling in April finding that D.C. officials had violated children's constitutional and statutory rights by, among other things, failing to move children out of foster care and failing to act within mandated time limits in emergency cases.

In August, Illinois officials agreed to a similar settlement to end a three-year-old suit brought by ACLU lawyers. Under the plan, the state's Department of Children and Family Services promised to reduce the caseloads of foster care workers from the present level of 50-75 cases down to 25 and to limit child protective service investigators to 12 new cases per month. The plan also called for appointment of an outside monitor to oversee implementation of the accord through at least 1999. A federal judge tentatively approved the settlement Aug. 29 and scheduled a hearing on the plan for Nov. 8. ■

# OUTLOOK

## No Easy Answers

The social and economic conditions that have fed more children into foster care over the past five years — in particular, drug use, inadequate housing and the growing number of dysfunctional families in minority communities — show no sign of relenting.

Based on growth rates since 1986, the U.S. foster care population could exceed 500,000 in 1995. Whatever the rate of growth, there is wide agreement that the child welfare system needs more money today and much more in the future. "The first need is more bucks," says former Reagan official Besharov. "The states and state child welfare programs are in as close to a state of depression as one could imagine — I mean that fiscally and morally."

"We have been starved for resources," says David Liederman of the Child Welfare League. "I think we need billions, not millions, and that is the nub of it." [43]

Even the Bush administration has recognized the need for more spending. In the face of bipartisan criticism, it has stopped pushing its proposal to cut reimbursement for state administrative expenses. But it offers no substantial initiatives of its own and remains opposed to the spending increases proposed in the Democratic-sponsored House and Senate bills. In any event, new spending measures face the hurdle of pay-as-you-go budget rules that will require the tax-writing committees to find revenue sources or offsetting budget cuts if federal funds for child welfare services are to be increased.

With or without more federal money, state and local governments will bear the brunt of the foster care crisis. Family preservation services hold out the promise of stemming the crisis — and controlling the costs — by keeping at-risk children in families. The Children's Defense Fund reports that 10 states are moving to adopt such services on a statewide basis. But new studies cast doubt on the cost-saving claims. Without those savings, the high-intensity casework thought necessary to get a troubled family back on track may be viewed as desirable but not affordable.

Meanwhile, the optimistic premises of the 1980 child welfare act — keeping families together whenever possible and moving toward adoption when children are removed from their homes — are yielding to a pessimism brought on, in particular, by maternal drug use. The plight of drug-exposed infants abandoned at birth is one factor in growing calls to make it easier to terminate parental rights, permitting a child to be taken permanently from its parents. Yet child welfare experts recognize that these "special needs" children will be hard to place in adoption and in the meantime will require expensive care.

The foster care crisis has produced a consensus on the need for action. This seeming agreement has yet to produce tangible legislative results at the federal level, however, leaving state and local governments overwhelmed by the needs of today's generation of vulnerable children.

"Examples from real life defy the notion that there is a quick fix," Beverly Jones, assistant director of child welfare services in Anne Arundel County, Md., told an AEI forum in February. "What I do know is that far too many children are unprotected and that their quality of life is unacceptable." ∎

*Kenneth Jost is a free-lance writer in Washington.*

## Notes

[1] Congress established the commission, known as the Rockefeller Commission, in 1987 to examine such areas as health, education and tax policy as they relate to the needs of the nation's children.

[2] From an "executive summary" of the commission's report, released in February 1991.

[3] Nearly one in five children, or 19.6 percent, in the United States live in families with incomes below the federal poverty rate ($12,700 for a family of four); this number is below the peak level of 22.2 percent in 1983 but higher than any time between 1966 and 1980. See Children's Defense Fund, *The State of America's Children*, 1991, pp. 22-23.

[4] Testimony before the Senate Labor and Human Resources Subcommittee on Children, Families, Drugs and Alcoholism, Feb. 20, 1991.

[5] Brenda McGowan, "Child Welfare Reform," in *A Children's Brief: Child Welfare Reform Resource Guide*, National Center for Children in Poverty, July 1991.

[6] *Ibid.*, p. 15.

[7] *Ibid.* See also *1980 Congressional Quarterly Almanac*, pp. 417-18.

[8] McGowan, *op. cit.*, p. 13.

[9] See Robert H. Bremner, *Children and Youth in America: A Documentary History*, Vol. II, p. 365.

[10] Leroy Pelton, *For Reason of Poverty: A Critical Analysis of the Public Child Welfare System in the United States* (1989), pp. 6-7, 10-13.

[11] *Ibid.*, p. 21; Bremner, *op. cit.*, Vol. III, p. 634.

[12] *Ibid.*, pp. 637-638.

[13] Pelton, *op. cit.*, p. 15.

[14] McGowan, *op. cit.*, p. 14.

[15] Henry S. Maas and Richard E. Engler Jr., *Children in Need of Parents* (1959), p. 356.

[16] *Ibid.*, p. 382.

[17] *Ibid.*, pp. 383-390.

[18] Kempe's paper, as published in the *Journal of the American Medical Association* in 1963, appears in Bremner, *op. cit.*, Vol. III, pp. 868-873.

[19] Pelton, *op. cit.*, p. 22; National Association of Public Child Welfare Administrators, *Guidelines for a Model System of Protective Services for Abused and Neglected Children and Their Families*, pp. 16-17.

[20] Pelton, *op. cit.*, pp. 23-30.

[21] Quoted in Bremner, *op. cit.*, Vol. III, p. 676.

[22] Quoted in Edna McConnell Clark Foundation, *Keeping Families Together: The Case for Family Preservation*, 1985, p. 3.

[23] McGowan, *op. cit.*, p. 15.

[24] Pelton, *op. cit.*, p. 24.

[25] McGowan, *op. cit.*, p. 16.

[26] Cited in Senate Finance Committee, *Foster Care, Adoption Assistance, and Child Welfare Services*, September 1990, p. 5.

[27] *Ibid.*, p. 4.

[28] McGowan, *op. cit.*, p. 17.

[29] House Ways and Means Subcommittee on Human Resources, *Federally Funded Child Welfare, Foster Care, and Adoption Assistance Programs*, April 4-5, 1990, p. 36.

[30] Horn's 1990 testimony appears in Human Resources Subcommittee, *op. cit.*, pp. 6-33; the 1991 hearings have not yet been printed.

[31] Mark F. Testa, "Conditions of Parents and Children at Risk of Substitute Care," American Enterprise Institute Conference on Child Welfare Reform Experiments, Feb. 20-21, 1991.

[32] National Black Child Development Institute, *Who Will Care When Parents Can't? A Study of Black Children in Foster Care*, 1989, p. 36.

[33] National Commission on Child Welfare and Family Preservation, *Factbook on Public Child Welfare Services and Staff*, 1990, pp. 71-73.

[34] Senate Finance Committee, *op. cit.*, p. 24.

[35] Quoted in Penelope Lemov, "The Return of the Orphanage," *Governing*, May 1991, p. 33.

[36] *The New York Times*, Sept. 26, 1987, p. 1.

[37] *The Washington Post*, April 19, 1991, p. A1.

[38] *Congressional Quarterly Weekly Report*, June 30, 1990, p. 2073.

[39] National Black Child Development Institute, *op. cit.*, p. 36.

[40] Cited in House Select Committee on Children, *No Place to Call Home: Discarded Children in America*, January 1990, p. 29.

[41] Douglas J. Besharov, "Crack Children in Foster Care," *The American Enterprise*, January/February 1990, p. 15.

[42] House Select Committee on Children, *op. cit.*, pp. 2-3, 9-12.

[43] Quoted in *Congressional Quarterly Weekly Report*, March 30, 1991, p. 797.

# Bibliography

## Selected Sources Used

### Books

**Bremner, Robert H. *et al.* (eds.), *Children and Youth in America: A Documentary History*, Harvard University Press, 1971 (Vol. II), 1974 (Vol. III).**

This monumental compilation of original source materials chronicles foster care from the "home-finding agencies" and child-rescue movements of the 19th century through the decline of the orphanage, institutionalization of child welfare agencies and development of family foster homes in the 20th century.

**Pelton, Leroy H., *For Reasons of Poverty: A Critical Analysis of the Public Child Welfare System in the United States*, Praeger, 1989.**

Professor Pelton combines a thorough and insightful history of foster care in the United States with a strongly argued thesis that the merger of child protection and child welfare functions has operated to remove too many children from families, especially poor families, while failing to provide those families needed social services.

### Articles

**Besharov, Douglas J., "Crack Children in Foster Care," *The American Enterprise*, January/February 1990.**

The skyrocketing number of female drug users has presented America's social-service providers with fresh and puzzling challenges. The foster-care system must be restructured, says the author, who was the first director of the National Center on Child Abuse and Neglect.

**Cohen, Deborah L., "Foster-Care Reforms Often Ignore Problems Children Face in School," *Education Week*, June 5, 1991.**

The educational needs of children in foster care have been ignored as legislators and social workers try to solve the foster-care crisis, say many experts.

**Lemov, Penelope, "The Return of the Orphanage," *Governing*, May 1991.**

The failures of other social service systems have led to the re-emergence of the "orphanage" — or its modern equivalent — as a solution to the foster care crisis.

**Rovner, Julie, "Children in Crisis Overwhelm Foster-Care Programs," *Congressional Quarterly Weekly Report*, March 30, 1991.**

This article gives an overview of the foster care crisis with detailed reporting on legislative activity on the issue.

### Reports and Studies

**Children's Defense Fund, *The State of America's Children 1991*, 1991.**

In its annual report, this major advocacy group surveys the crisis confronting foster care systems in the United States, highlights reforms in several states and makes its own recommendations for federal, state and local governments, the private sector and community organizations.

**Committee on Finance, United States Senate, *Foster Care, Adoption Assistance, and Child Welfare Services*, September 1990.**

This staff-written document details the somewhat complex federal programs for funding and regulating state and local foster care systems, including state-by-state and year-by-year data on federal spending under those programs.

**Edna McConnell Clark Foundation, *Keeping Families Together: The Case for Family Preservation*, 1985.**

In this pamphlet, the foundation explains the goals and operation of family preservation services and also includes a brief history of child welfare services and an overview of current federal laws.

**National Commission on Child Welfare and Family Preservation, *Factbook on Public Child Welfare Services and Staff*, American Public Welfare Association, 1990.**

This important survey documents, state by state, the services, policies and personnel practices of child welfare agencies.

**National Commission on Children, *Beyond Rhetoric: A New American Agenda for Children and Families*, May 1991.**

Declaring that too many children in foster care are "faceless and forgotten," this congressionally established commission recommended comprehensive reforms to aid children in troubled families and improve care for children in substitute care.

**Select Committee on Children, Youth and Families, United States House of Representatives, *No Place to Call Home: Discarded Children in America*, January 1990.**

This forceful critique of the implementation of the 1980 child welfare reform act also contains a wealth of statistical data, a comprehensive listing of court cases over care of children in substitute care and an extensive listing of sources.

# The Next Step

## Additional Articles from Current Periodicals

### Case studies

**Aguilar, L., "Helping their way off welfare,"** *Newsweek,* **May 7, 1990, p. 70.**

Describes the new Michigan program L.I.F.E. (for Living in Family Environments) which pays 14 welfare recipients $21,500 a year to become foster mothers to severely disabled children. Role model; funded by a $200,000 grant from the state Department of Mental Health.

**Blakeslee, S., "Child-rearing is stormy when drugs cloud birth,"** *The New York Times,* **May 19, 1990, p. 1.**

Reports on couples who become adoptive and foster parents of drug-exposed babies. Difficulty in rearing them; returning the children; unresponsiveness of the children; frustration; lack of advice and support services.

**Bondy, D., D. Davis, et al., "Mental health services for children in foster care,"** *Children Today,* **September/October 1990, p. 28.**

Examines the treatment approach developed by the Queens Child Guidance Center in Jamaica, N.Y., to promote children's adjustment to foster care. Working with children and foster parents; working with birth parents; the role of the play room.

**Chamberlain, P. and Weinrott, M., "Specialized foster care: Treating seriously emotionally disturbed children,"** *Children Today,* **January/February 1990, p. 24.**

Demonstrates how Specialized Foster Care (SFC) programs have effectively helped seriously emotionally disturbed children. Use of homelike foster family setting and proven methods of behavior change; natural family often cares for the child; highlights "Transitions" and "Monitor," two SFC programs based at the Oregon Social Learning Center (OSLC) in Eugene, Oreg.

**Conniff, R., "Families that open their homes to the sick,"** *Time,* **Dec. 5, 1988, p. 12.**

A report on a group of 18 foster mothers in Connecticut who care for children with AIDS or AIDS-related illnesses, never telling their neighbors or extended families. How they cope.

**Kantrowitz, B., McCormick, J., et al., "Children lost in the quagmire,"** *Newsweek,* **May 13, 1991, p. 64.**

Presents details of an Illinois foster-care case that highlights controversy over reuniting foster children with birthparents they barely know. Foster parents Joseph and Marjorie Procopio adopted a baby from a drug addict mother who was a prostitute. They were later ordered by a judge to return the child to the biological mother. Redefining the "best interest of the child"; statistics from the Child Welfare League of America; more.

**Nelson, I. and Andersson, M., "Fostering new hope,"** *New Choices,* **January 1990, p. 52.**

Interviews Phyllis and Joe Hazard, an older Worcester, Mass. couple who have cared for more than 30 foster children over 13 years. The Hazards discuss how they became foster parents, the advantages and the disadvantages. INSET: Foster care: Some risks, many rewards.

**Rimer, S. "Woman overcomes bureaucratic odds to regain her children,"** *The New York Times,* **Jan. 25, 1991, p. B3.**

Tells how Michelle Rogers, 31, got her four children out of foster care by overcoming her addiction to drugs, navigating through an overburdened social-services bureaucracy, and finding an apartment in Brooklyn, where landlord after landlord told her they preferred not to rent to mothers on public assistance.

**Whitmore, J., "Mobilizing training resources for rural foster parents, adoptive parents, and applicants in . . . ,"** *Child Welfare,* **March/April 1991, p. 211.**

Describes a program for legally mandated training of foster and adoptive applicants in a vast rural territory. Development and funding of the program; the Eastern Region Children Services of the Oregon Department of Human Resources; size and description of the area; program outline; training library; contracted training; more.

### Child welfare

**Benedict, M. I. and White, R.B., "Factors associated with foster care length of stay,"** *Child Welfare,* **January/February 1991, p. 45.**

Examines what is presently known about accurate estimates of children's length of stay in foster care and presents new data in a cohort of Maryland children. Methods; child and parental characteristics; agency service factors; multivariate analysis; more.

**Carbino, R., "Advocacy for foster families in the United States facing child abuse allegations,"** *Child Welfare,* **March/April 1991, p. 131.**

Discusses the role of the agency in assisting foster care families faced with maltreatment allegations and calls for a revision of policy and procedures governing agency response. Pioneering efforts of a few states revealed in a 1989 national survey; need for development, evaluation and dissemination of more constructive response models; lack of attention to this issue in the professional literature; more.

**Katz, L. and Robinson, C., "Foster care drift: A risk-assessment matrix," Child Welfare, May/June 1991, p. 347.**

Presents a matrix which is intended to improve permanency planning practice by early identification of foster children who are least likely to return to their families. For use with children eight and under who are already in foster care; lack of matrix application to most child-protective service cases; case plan; more.

## Debates & issues

**"Foster homes may not be safe," USA Today, December 1990, p. 4.**

Presents highlights of research on foster homes conducted by Nolan Rindfleisch, a social work professor at Ohio State University. Examples of mistreatment in child welfare institutions; call for stricter standards for state-governed facilities.

**"Paradise lost," New York, Oct. 23, 1989, p. 100.**

Report by New York City council President Andrew Stein on the foster-care system. Removing of children from loving homes; the Dade case; accountability in NYC foster-care system.

**Barden, J.C., "When foster care ends, home is often the street," The New York Times, Jan. 6, 1991, p. 1.**

Considers how a large and disproportionate number of the nation's homeless are young people who have come out of foster care programs without the money, skills or family support to make it on their own. Foster care systems around the country are being overwhelmed; four studies confirming that people formerly in foster care are vastly over-represented among the homeless.

**Beck, M., "Willing families, waiting kids," Newsweek, Sept. 12, 1988, p. 64.**

Discusses the nation's system of foster and adoptive placements and policies discouraging inter-racial placements despite willing parents and long lists of children waiting for adoption. Controversy; court cases; changes over the years in placement.

**Besharov, D.J., "Crack children in foster care," Children Today, July/August 1990, p. 21.**

Examines the role of foster care in serving the needs of "crack babies." Balance between children's and parents' rights; abuse and neglect; impact on foster care; goals of

foster care; need for high-quality, long-term care; adoption and permanent guardianship.

**Charles, G. and Matheson, J., "Suicide prevention and intervention with young people in foster care in Canada," Child Welfare, March/April 1991, p. 185.**

Discusses the risk of suicide among foster children. Suicide prevention and intervention with foster children; helping foster parents understand the dynamics and assessment of suicidal behaviors; development of supporting interventions, policies and procedures; episodes of isolation, helplessness and ambivalence; relationship between suicide rate and hostility and anger; warning signs; more.

**Daley, S., "Few are getting rent subsidies to avoid foster care," The New York Times, Dec. 7, 1989, p. B1.**

Reports that a year after a rent subsidy became available to help families get their children out of foster care, the program is barely off the ground. The subsidy, which was designed to help parents whose children remained in foster care only because they had no place to house them, has been given to just 33 families. The program had been expected to help as many as 1,000 children return to their families within a few months. Complicated forms; details.

**Daley, S., "Foster placement by skin shade is charged," The New York Times, Jan. 18, 1990, p. B1.**

Reports that the American Civil Liberties Union claims that in an effort to place hundreds of abused and neglected children into foster care each week, New York City has resorted to distributing them to private foster-care agencies on the basis of gradations of skin color and hair texture.

**Farber, M.A., "A growing foster-care program is fraught with ills," The New York Times, Nov. 22, 1990, p. B1.**

Describes New York City's kinship approach to caring for children, whereby Grandmothers, aunts, and other relatives are paid to take in and care for abused or neglected children in their families. But whatever its merit in principle, the program appears to have had practical problems from the beginning.

**Harris, M., "Where have all the babies gone?" Money, December 1988, p. 164.**

Thousands of children find themselves bouncing between foster families while waiting for permanent homes. They're trapped in a failed adoption system, beyond the reach of couples who plead to give them homes. INSETS: No two states agree on adoption; adoption was born on a train.

**Hill, B.K., Hayden, M.F., et al., "State-by-state data on**

children with handicaps in foster care," *Child Welfare*, September/October 1990, p. 447.

Reports on a national survey which updates until December 31, 1985 the available information on children with handicaps in foster care. New kinds of handicaps, number of children with handicaps and kinds of foster care needed; effects of AIDS and crack addiction; types of placement including residential treatment centers and family foster homes; mandated state reporting systems; method; results; discussion.

**Mica, M.D. and Vosler, N.R., "Foster-adoptive programs in public social service agencies: Toward flexible family resources," *Child Welfare*, September/November 1990, p. 433.**

Details findings of a survey of state public social service agencies regarding the issue of foster-adoptive placement. Legal and social work issues in this type of placement; the "flexible family" resources program implemented by the Foster Care and Adoption Units of the St. Louis County Office of the Division of Family Services; historical developments; more.

**Navarro, M., "AIDS children's foster care: Love and hope conquer fear," *The New York Times*, Dec. 7, 1990, p. A1.**

Tells about the growing number of foster parents who are raising young children with AIDS. Why they volunteer; emotional challenge of a sickly child; their hopes.

**Stehno, S.M., "The elusive continuum of child welfare services: Implications for minority children and youths," *Child Welfare*, November/December 1990, p. 551.**

Discusses the increase in minority youths in the foster care population and the implications for child welfare agencies. Worsening well being of the nation's minority populations; statistics from the Children's Defense Fund; shortage of qualified foster parents; more.

**Taylor-Brown, S., "The impact of AIDS on foster care: A family centered approach to services in the United States," *Child Welfare*, March/April 1991, p. 193.**

Looks at the challenges presented to the foster care system by Acquired Immune Deficiency Syndrome (AIDS). Current changes in understanding of HIV infection in children; implications for foster care; reviewing training needed by foster care personnel and foster parents to enable them to provide competent services; placement for infected children; placement of uninfected children when mothers die of AIDS; more.

**Yost, D.M., Hockstadt, N.J., et al., "Medical foster care: Achieving permanency . . . ," *Children Today*,**

September/October 1988, p. 22.

Describes the Chicago, Ill.-based Medical Foster Parent Program, designed to find foster homes for seriously ill children who are hospitalized, but are alert and responsive and can benefit greatly from a family environment. Examples; challenges.

## *Government policy*

**Barden, J.C., "Foster care system reeling, despite law meant to help," *The New York Times*, Sept. 21, 1990, p. A1.**

Says that, ten years after the signing of a federal law meant to reduce the need for foster care by helping troubled families stay together, the system has grown into a multibillion-dollar maze of confusion and misdirection, overwhelmed by the profusion of sick, battered and emotionally scarred children who are becoming the responsibility of the public.

**Sack, K., "New York City now backs family-aid bill," *The New York Times*, July 21, 1990, p. 23.**

Reports that New York City officials helped keep a state foster-care prevention bill alive by dropping their opposition to it and encouraging Gov. Mario M. Cuomo to sign it. Bill would grant subsidies to parents who risk losing their children to foster care because of lack of housing; opposition.

## *Orphanages*

**Creighton, L.L., "The new orphanages," *U.S. News & World Report*, Oct. 8, 1990, p. 37.**

Discusses the rise in "parentless families" in the United States and the crisis in foster care that have led to a return of orphanages. Hale House in New York City; St. Ann's Infant and Maternity Home in Hyattsville, Md; collapsing child protection system; staggering reports of child abuse; loving the abandoned; William Bennett. INSETS: Patricia; Michael; James; Diane; challenging the myths.

# Back Issues

*Great Research on Current Issues Starts Right Here... Recent topics covered by The CQ Researcher are listed below. Issues dated before May 10, 1991, were published under the name of Editorial Research Reports.*

**MARCH 1990**
Asbestos: Are Risks Acceptable?
Public Health Campaigns
South Africa's Future
Homeless Need More Than Shelter

**APRIL 1990**
How Fair is the Tax Burden?
Workers' Compensation
U.S. Pacific Forces
Curbing Insurance Premiums

**MAY 1990**
Should Teaching Be a Profession?
Will Canada Fall Apart?
Is U.S. Patent System Outdated?
Federal Funding for the Arts

**JUNE 1990**
Downsizing America's Armed Forces
Progress In Weather Forecasting
S & L Bailout
Bio-Chemical Disarmament

**JULY 1990**
Do Americans Still Love Marriage?
Death Penalty Debate
Decline of Rural America
United Nations in the 1990s

**AUGUST 1990**
Democracy in the Philippines
Initiatives: True Democracy?
Hard Times at Newspapers
Teens Balance School & Jobs

**SEPTEMBER 1990**
Dangers of Alcohol
Western Alliance After the Cold War
Tobacco Industry
Right to Die

**OCTOBER 1990**
Organ Transplants
Energy Policy Options
Search for Arab Unity
Child Support

**NOVEMBER 1990**
Lotteries and Gambling
Post Cold-War Choices
Setting Limits on Medical Care
Multicultural Education

**DECEMBER 1990**
Cable TV Regulation
Americans' Search For Their Roots
Is Insurance System a Failure?
Why Schools Still Have Tracking

**JANUARY 1991**
Growing Influence of Boycotts
Should the U.S. Reinstate the Draft?
America's Archaeological Past
Peace Corps' Challenges in '90s

**FEBRUARY 1991**
Regional Impact of Recession
Puerto Rico's Status
Redistricting: Mapping Power
Nuclear Power

**MARCH 1991**
Acid Rain
Cost of the Gulf War
Reassessing Gun Laws
Future for Man in Space

**APRIL 1991**
Social Security
Canadian Crisis Over Quebec
California Drought
Electromagnetic Radiation

**MAY 1991**
School Choice
Racial Quotas
Animal Rights
U.S. and Japan

**JUNE 1991**
Children and Divorce
Teenage Suicide
Endangered Species
Europe 1992

**JULY 1991**
Teenagers and Abortion
Soviet Republics Rebel
Mexico's Emergence
Athletes and Drugs

**AUGUST 1991**
Sexual Harassment
Fetal Tissue Research
Oil Imports
The Palestinians

**SEPTEMBER 1991**
Police Brutality
Advertising Under Attack
Saving the Forests

Back issues are available for $4.00 (subscribers) or $7.00 (non-subscribers). Quantity discounts apply to orders over ten. To order, call Congressional Quarterly 1-800-432-2250.

# Future Topics

▶ *Pay-Per-View TV*

▶ *Youth Gangs*

▶ *Gene Therapy*

# THE CQ Researcher

PUBLISHED BY CONGRESSIONAL QUARTERLY INC., IN CONJUNCTION WITH EBSCO PUBLISHING

# Pay-Per-View TV

*It won't replace "free" TV any time soon*

AMERICANS HAVE ALWAYS GROWN UP THINKING they should be able to watch television for free. Cable TV shook that cherished assumption, and now pay-per-view (PPV) telecasts threaten to topple it once and for all. Championship prizefights, star-studded pro wrestling shows and current hit movies are all standard fare on pay-per-view, generating hundreds of millions of dollars annually. Next year's Summer Olympics in Barcelona, Spain, will be the first ever shown on PPV as well as on broadcast television. Still, limited channel capacity threatens to retard pay-per-view expansion in the years just ahead. And professional team sports are under heavy pressure to keep their championship events — especially the Super Bowl and the World Series — available to all TV viewers at no charge.

## INSIDE THIS ISSUE

CQ   October 4, 1991 • Volume 1, No. 21 • 729-752

*Formerly Editorial Research Reports*

COVER ART: BARBARA SASSA-DANIELS

### CQ Researcher

October 4, 1991
Volume 1, No. 21

**EDITOR**
Sandra Stencel

**MANAGING EDITOR**
Thomas J. Colin

**ASSOCIATE EDITOR**
Richard L. Worsnop

**STAFF WRITERS**
Charles S. Clark
Mary H. Cooper
Rodman D. Griffin

**PRODUCTION EDITOR**
Laurie De Maris

**EDITORIAL ASSISTANT**
Thomas H. Moore

**GRAPHICS**
Jack Auldridge

**PUBLISHED BY**
Congressional Quarterly Inc.

**CHAIRMAN**
Andrew Barnes

**VICE CHAIRMAN**
Andrew P. Corty

**EDITOR AND PUBLISHER**
Neil Skene

**EXECUTIVE EDITOR**
Robert W. Merry

**PUBLICATIONS MARKETING/SALES**
Robert Smith

**EDITOR, EBSCO PUBLISHING**
Melissa Kummerer

The CQ Researcher (ISSN 1056-2036). Formerly Editorial Research Reports. Published weekly (48 times per year, not printed the first Friday of any month with five Fridays) by Congressional Quarterly Inc., 1414 22nd St., N.W., Washington, D.C. 20037. Rates are furnished upon request. Application to mail at second-class postage rates is pending at Washington, D.C. POSTMASTER: Send address changes to The CQ Researcher, 1414 22nd St., N.W., Washington, D.C. 20037.

# Pay-Per-View TV

BY RICHARD L. WORSNOP

## THE ISSUES

When it comes to heavyweight title fights, last April's Evander Holyfield-George Foreman bout deserves an asterisk — but not for the pugilism. The 15-round bout grossed $48.9 million from home viewers, making it the most lucrative pay-per-view (PPV) attraction ever held.

Chances are that Holyfield-Foreman will not remain No. 1 on the PPV Hit Parade for long. Former heavyweight champion Mike Tyson is scheduled to fight current champ Holyfield on Nov. 8, a match that some say could attract the largest PPV audience ever. *(See list, p. 733.)* There is also speculation that Tyson's recent indictment on rape charges in Indianapolis will help to swell the home audience.*

Such box-office successes suggest only one conclusion to many industry observers: After many false starts, pay-per-view television seems poised at last to become a major force in home entertainment. Some 18.8 million American homes are now equipped to receive PPV, and the number is expected to grow to 35.9 million by 1996. Overall PPV revenue is expected to reach $435 million in 1991, and $1.1 billion by 1996.[1]

Will pay-per-view grow to the point where it challenges broadcast and conventional cable TV? Few telecommunications experts would dare make such a prediction at this time. For despite its robust growth in recent years, PPV currently ac-

counts for only about 3 percent of overall cable revenue. And the immediate future doesn't look much different, says John M. Mansell, an analyst for Paul Kagan Associates, a leading cable TV investment research firm based in Carmel, Calif. He predicts that PPV "is still going to be a relatively small percentage of the total a decade from now."

Meanwhile, the growth goes on. NBC and Cablevision Systems Corp., the country's ninth-largest operator of local cable systems, are planning to show much of the 1992 Summer Olympics in PPV packages costing as much as $170 each. If all goes reasonably well, the first pay-per-view Olympics could establish a marketing strategy — and new price scale — for the entire PPV industry.

At present, the industry is hobbled by insufficient channel capacity on cable television systems. About one-fifth of all cable systems offer fewer than 30 channels — not enough, in most cases, to allow for regular PPV service.

However, technological innovations on the horizon promise to open a broad window of opportunity for pay-per-view. The most significant innovation is video signal compression, which will permit as many as eight television signals to fit into the space now occupied by a single channel. This will mean, eventually, many more channels per system. In major urban areas, cable systems may have 150-plus channels, including a dozen or more set aside for PPV.*

According to a recent Federal Communications Commission working paper, additional channel capacity will enable local cable systems to schedule staggered starting times for pay-per-view showings of popular movies. "In other words," the paper said, "a pay-per-view programmer could transmit a box-office hit several times each night, with starting times every 15 minutes or half hour of prime time. Since viewers would never have to wait very long for their chosen movie to begin, this service can be characterized as 'near video-on-demand.' "[2]

Pay-per-view's prospects are not unclouded, however. A major ongoing problem is the movie studios' insistence on releasing new features to home video stores 45 to 60 days before their premiere on PPV. Sports programming, PPV's current mainstay, is another source of concern. Over the past several years, pay-per-view has established itself as the medium of choice for prizefighting and professional wrestling. On the other hand, playoff and championship games of the three main professional team sports — baseball, basketball and football — remain out of reach

---

*In the Sept. 23 issue of *Sports Illustrated,* Rick Reilly estimated the gross from the upcoming fight at up to $100 million, which would be far more than any previous fight.

---

*Time-Warner Inc., the nation's second-largest operator of cable TV systems, plans to begin 150-channel service in part of the New York City borough of Queens in late December. The service will be provided by existing technology.

for a number of reasons. But some analysts predict that mutual economic need will force an accommodation between the Big Three and PPV. The reasoning is that PPV presentation of key pro games will give both parties lucrative new sources of revenue.

On balance, pay-per-view's strengths seem to outweigh its shortcomings. Richard A. Gershon, an assistant professor of telecommunications management at Western Michigan University, sees PPV playing a "very significant" role in two areas. One is "special events" like championship prizefights, where pay-per-view already reigns supreme. The other is motion pictures, where PPV is only a minor factor at present. But in Gershon's opinion, pay-per-view showings of recent films will take off once cable systems become "interactive," permitting instantaneous two-way communication between cable households and system operators. With the arrival of interactivity, says Gershon, "pay-per-view will have some tremendous opportunities."

Interactive television on a broad scale still appears several years away. In the meantime, projections for pay-per-view growth range from guarded to bullish. At a February cable industry seminar called "PPV Events: How Healthy is the Golden Goose?" participants concluded that competitive pressures and sluggish economic conditions will slow the spread of PPV until at least 1995. Only three months later, though, participants in the Cable Television Administrative and Marketing Society's second annual conference on pay-per-view were decidedly more upbeat. Their confidence was fueled by reports that PPV events grossed more than $130 million in 1990.*

All the same, PPV still suffers from a fundamental problem. Many consumers have only a vague notion of how pay-per-view works. "It doesn't matter what the schedule is if people don't know what pay-per-view is," says Lloyd Werner, the president of Request Television, a PPV network.[3] Werner feels the industry should launch a marketing campaign aimed at answering people's questions about pay-per-view and learning what kinds of programming they want to see on it.

### How is pay-per-view television delivered to the home?

Most pay-per-view programming is transmitted via cable to the consumer's television set by the local cable system. The programs are scheduled to begin (but not necessarily to end) at fixed times, just as with "free" TV programming. The major difference is that the consumer must first decide whether he wants to pay to watch the event being marketed. If the program in question is a movie, he must also decide when he wants to see it. PPV movies typically are shown several times a day.*

The next step is to contact the cable company. For most cable subscribers, this involves calling in the order by telephone. When the attraction is a popular one, such as the Holyfield-Foreman fight, the customer who fails to place his call well in advance runs the risk of being put on hold or encountering repeated busy signals. To eliminate the bottleneck, some cable systems have adopted the American Telephone & Telegraph Co.'s Automatic Number Identification (ANI) system. This enables the customer to dial an 800 number that takes orders by computer.

ANI is by no means the last word in PPV order-placing technology. "Impulse" ordering allows the customer to make a spur-of-the-moment purchase by pushing buttons on a remote-control device. Programs purchased this way can be delivered within seconds.

Market research shows that PPV purchases per customer increase whenever ordering is made easier.[4] Consequently, PPV executives and motion-picture studios have been urging cable systems to shift more rapidly to ANI and impulse ordering technology. Many cable operators are reluctant to do this, saying the technology's cost cannot be offset by additional PPV revenue and higher buy rates. (The buy rate is the percentage of PPV households that purchase a particular pay-per-view program.)

Regardless of how a pay-per-view program is ordered, it reaches the customer's television set through the same cable that carries regularly scheduled cable fare. To make PPV feasible, the customer's TV set must be "addressable" — that is, the cable operator must be able to turn the PPV channel on and off from a remote location. According to Don Mathison, senior vice president for marketing and programming at Media General Cable Inc. of Chantilly, Va., addressability "means that we can 'talk' to the customer's converter box. The box has that capability, whereas limited-service customers have a converter box that we cannot talk to remotely."

Paul Kagan Associates estimates there are 17.7 million addressable households nationwide at present, representing 34 percent of all basic cable TV subscribers. By the end of 1992, the organization projects these numbers to rise to 23.2 million and 41 percent. The 1992 pay-per-view Olympics package being marketed by NBC and Cablevision Systems is expected to spark some of the growth.

---

*PPV events include boxing, wrestling, concerts and other kinds of live entertainment. Movies form a separate programming category.

*Some cable systems with several PPV channels have adopted a multiplex format for exhibiting movies. The approach allows each channel to show only one feature on a continual basis, as do the individual units of a multiplex movie-theater complex.

# What People Watch: The Top PPV Events

*When it comes to pay-TV revenue, sports events are king. Of the 10 leading revenue-earning events of any kind that have been shown on pay-per-view TV, all were sports events—either boxing or wrestling. Concerts bring in considerably less.*

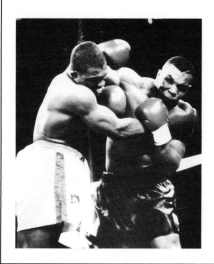

| TOP 10 REVENUE-EARNING SPORTING EVENTS | | | | TOP 10 REVENUE-EARNING CONCERT EVENTS | | | |
|---|---|---|---|---|---|---|---|
| Event | Date | Price | Total revenue (millions) | Event | Date | Price | Total revenue (millions) |
| Holyfield-Foreman | 4/91 | $35.95 | $48.9 | New Kids on the Block | 3/90 | 19.95 | 5.5 |
| Douglas-Holyfield | 10/90 | 36.50 | 38.6 | Moscow Music Festival | 8/89 | 19.95 | 4.3 |
| Tyson-Ruddock | 3/91 | 34.95 | 33.4 | Rolling Stones | 12/89 | 22.50 | 4.0 |
| Leonard-Duran | 12/89 | 35.00 | 24.3 | New Kids on the Block 2 | 12/90 | 19.95 | 3.1 |
| Wrestlemania VII | 3/91 | 29.95 | 22.9 | The Who: "Tommy" Live | 8/89 | 19.95 | 3.0 |
| Spinks-Tyson | 6/88 | 34.95 | 21.0 | Grateful Dead | 12/87 | 19.95 | 1.5 |
| Wrestlemania VI | 4/90 | 29.95 | 20.2 | Live Turtles | 10/90 | 14.95 | 1.0 |
| Leonard-Hearns | 6/89 | 35.00 | 19.3 | Phil Collins | 10/90 | 22.50 | 0.9 |
| Wrestlemania IV | 3/88 | 19.95 | 18.1 | Grateful Dead | 6/89 | 19.95 | 0.8 |
| Summer Slam '90 | 8/90 | 27.50 | 17.7 | Rap Mania | 4/90 | 9.95 | 0.7 |

*Source: The Pay TV Newsletter, April 30, 1991. Photo by Will Hart/Showtime.*

Also hoping to capitalize on the PPV Olympics are suppliers of addressable converters. Jerrold Communications is pushing the Olympian 2000, a no-frills model. At $70, it costs slightly more than half the price of a standard unit. Not to be outdone, Zenith is offering its Pay Master for as little as $35 apiece in volume discount orders. The sales pitch to cable companies stresses that addressability will enable them to make money not just from the Olympics but from subsequent PPV events as well.

Nevertheless, many smaller cable systems remain unpersuaded that addressability is for them. These systems often lack the channel capacity or subscriber base to make pay-per-view a reliable source of income year after year. They also balk at spending as much as $30,000 for the processing and signal-encoding equipment that an addressable system needs at the point of program distribution. To overcome such objections, Zenith has lowered the equipment's price to $2,500 in certain cases.

Though cable systems serve the vast majority of pay-per-view customers, they may never reach a small but significant part of the market — an estimated 15 million homes in sparsely settled rural areas. Many of these out-of-the-way households rely on outdoor dish antennas to relay signals from communications satellites to their TV screens. Now TVN Entertainment Corp., which began full-time operation in May, supplies the dish antenna market with 10 channels of PPV programming beamed from space.

To place an order, the customer tunes his set to the desired TVN channel and then dials an ANI number. Once the caller's identity is verified and the order approved, TVN activates a descrambler mounted on the caller's dish antenna and the program appears on his screen. Elapsed time is only a few seconds. The TVN descrambler, based on technology developed about two years ago, is said to be highly resistant to signal piracy.

Because TVN has been in business for only a few months, it is too soon to say how well it is doing. Some prospective customers undoubtedly will find the $19.95 installation charge and the $3.99 per-movie viewing fee excessive. On the other hand, the convenience of PPV ordering may be a big selling point in areas where home video stores are few and far between.

Turning their attention to still another group of deprived viewers, some television executives are exploring the possibility of bringing pay-per-view to households that once had cable but now have neither cable nor a dish antenna. If the occupants of such a home wanted to see a pay-per-view event, all they would have to do is connect the "dead" cable wire to their cable-ready set and place their order with the cable company.

### What sort of programming is best suited for pay-per-view?

Virtually all pay-per-view programming currently can be classified as either recently released motion pictures or "events." Since pay-per-view movies are usually shown numerous times and at different hours, it can be difficult to assess a film's popularity nationwide on any given day or week. This year movies are projected to gross $127 million on pay-per-view, up from $103 million in 1990.

PPV events are one-time-only performances or events presented live. Because the programming is shown everywhere simultaneously, audience and revenue figures provide a detailed profile of popular taste at a particular day and hour. In the history of PPV to date, three types of events have been the biggest draws by far: championship boxing, professional wrestling and — a distant third — concerts by popular music groups.

Events are expected to gross $295 million this year, more than double the 1990 total of $137 million. Seven of the Top Ten (including the first five) events were championship prizefights; the remaining three featured pro wrestling. The highest-rated concert event, No. 27 on the list, was a March 1990 performance by the rock band New Kids on the Block. (See table, p. 733.)

For sports historians, boxing's popularity among PPV customers comes as no surprise. During the formative years of broadcast television, boxing was the premier sport on the home screen. In 1948, NBC telecast fights on Mondays and Fridays, the DuMont network broadcast them on Tuesdays and Wednesdays, and CBS did so on Wednesdays. But overexposure ultimately dimmed the sport's allure. The last weekly boxing show went off the air in 1964.

Boxing has been a pay-per-view hit because most of the fights have been title contests featuring well-known boxers like Tyson, Holyfield and Sugar Ray Leonard.

Pro wrestling, while still a strong second to boxing on pay-per-view, may be experiencing the effects of overexposure. "The buy rates are falling with every show," says Dave Meltzer, the editor and publisher of

*Wrestling Observer Newsletter.* "It's a combination of there being so many wrestling shows on pay-per-view and so many more events [of other kinds] as well. Soon, with the Olympics and all, wrestling is going to drop down the list — not far down, but down."

The top three wrestling events on pay-per-view have been three of the four most recent productions of Wrestlemania, an annual showcase of talent sponsored by the World Wrestling Federation (WWF). Wrestlemania, Meltzer says, is the pro wrestling fan's Super Bowl; indeed, each edition of the event is identified by a Roman numeral, as are National Football League (NFL) championship games.

Wrestlemania VII, staged last March, grossed $22.9 million; Wrestlemania VI grossed $20.2 million in 1990; and Wrestlemania IV grossed $18.1 million in 1988. These figures, while they show a steady upward revenue progression, actually are somewhat misleading. For one thing, viewers paid $19.95 to see Wrestlemania IV but $29.95 to see Wrestlemania VI and VII. Also, the number of PPV households rose by 6 million between 1988 and 1991.

Consequently, Meltzer feels the key measure of audience acceptance is the buy rate — the percentage of PPV households that actually order an event. From this standpoint, the WWF has reason to worry about pro wrestling's pay-per-view prospects. Wrestlemania posted its best buy rate in 1987, when 10.2 percent of potential viewers signed on. Over the next four years, the rate steadily fell, to 9.0, 5.6, 5.0 and 4.6 percent. Wrestling isn't the only attraction with PPV box-office blues.

Many TV industry analysts attribute the failure of pop-music concerts to hit it big on PPV to poor promotion. The principal failing, they say, is promoters' overriding emphasis on filling seats when a group is on tour. By

taking this blinkered approach, promoters often give little advance attention to the concert that will be shown on pay-per-view. Furthermore, the PPV concert usually is scheduled at a tour's conclusion, when fan enthusiasm is likely to have waned. This seems to have been what happened when the Rolling Stones appeared on pay-per-view at the end of their "Steel Wheels" tour of North America in December 1989. The concert, priced at $22.50, grossed about $4 million but had a buy rate of only 1.3 percent.

Scott Kurnit, president of Showtime Event Television, the PPV division of the Showtime cable network, feels that concert promoters have much to learn about the production requirements of pay-per-view. "For music, it can't *just* be music," he says. "It has to be an event, something that is compelling television. Music by itself is not as compelling as a boxing match." [5]

Some pay-per-view events have been assailed by television critics for their questionable taste. A prime example is "Thunder and Mud," a 1989 production featuring heavy-metal bands and mud-wrestling by women clad in string bikinis. Commentary was provided by hostess Jessica Hahn, best known for her role in the downfall of television evangelist Jim Bakker. Potential viewers were unimpressed. Only 23,000 people — one-fifth of 1 percent of all PPV households — paid to see "Thunder and Mud," which *Washington Post* TV critic Tom Shales blasted as "tawdry and amateurish." He went on: "Pay-per-view is in its early stages as a business and already it sinks to this." [6]

Now pay-per-view is targeting a more upscale market segment: opera lovers. On Sept. 23, a four-hour gala marking the 25th anniversary of the Metropolitan Opera House at Lincoln Center was offered for $34.95. The first of what may be an ongoing series of pay-per-view opera presentations, the gala was seen on some 35,000 cable homes around the country and brought in $1.2 million. Cablevision Systems, one of the show's sponsors, has signed a long-term agreement with the Met to broadcast two or three opera events a year on PPV, provided revenues are high enough to make the undertaking worthwhile.

As the number of pay-per-view households increases, promoters will be tempted to explore other uncharted areas. Jeffrey Reiss, whose Reiss Media Enterprises is a co-owner of the Request Television pay-per-view network, suggests a major auction by Sotheby's or the opening of a Broadway show as PPV possibilities. "If Prince Charles and Diana were getting married now, it would be on pay-per-view," he says.[7] Industry analyst John Mansell has his doubts. "It would be kind of difficult," he says, "to show what is arguably a public news event on a pay-per-view basis."

Even if Princess Di makes it to PPV, many PPV executives feel sports programming will continue to be the mainstay of their industry. Seth G. Abraham, president of Time Warner Sports, the sports marketing arm of Time Warner Inc., says the broadcast networks "have lost their grip on logic and their wallets" with the amounts being spent for the rights to broadcast sports events. "The future will be with PPV, which will alter the sports landscape," he predicts.[8]

***Will premier sports events like the World Series and the Super Bowl ever shift from "free" television to pay-per-view?***

When it comes to inalienable rights, few are more sacred than being able to plop down in your easy chair on a Sunday afternoon to watch a *free* football game. Nobody's likely to put a price tag on the Super Bowl,

## Who Subscribes to PPV

*The number of PPV subscribers is expected to grow from 15.4 million in 1990 to 50 million in 1999, according to industry projections. During that period, the percentage of cable households that subscribe to PPV will rise from 27.9 percent to 74.2 percent while the percentage of households with TV that subscribe to PPV will jump from 16.7 to 48.8 percent.*

|  | 1990 est. | 1995 proj. | 1999 proj. |
|---|---|---|---|
| PPV subscribers (millions) | 15.4 | 33.0 | 50.1 |
| PPV subscribers/Basic cable subscribers (%) | 27.9 | 54.1 | 74.2 |
| PPV subscribers/TV households (%) | 16.7 | 33.6 | 48.8 |

*Source: Paul Kagan Associates,* The Kagan Cable TV Financial Databook, *June 1990.*

at least not anytime soon. But things are changing.

Since 1984, the San Diego Padres have offered as many as 50 home baseball games per season through a local cable sports channel. Single games cost $7.95, and multi-game packages are available. Sales per game average 15,000 to 20,000 households. Pro basketball's Dallas Mavericks, Houston Rockets, Portland Trail Blazers, San Antonio Spurs and six teams in college football's powerful Southeastern Conference (including Alabama, Auburn and Georgia) also are involved in pay-per-view.

Last season, the National Hockey League's Minnesota North Stars showed all home playoff games on PPV (away games were on free TV). The buy rate, or percentage of PPV customers who paid for the game, started out at 2.5 percent in the first round and peaked at 15 percent at the final round, the Stanley Cup, according to Pat Forciea, the team's vice president for communications. This season, the North Stars will offer 13 home games on pay-per-view at $9.95 each. The North Stars are the only NHL team on PPV, although the Chicago Black Hawks are considering it, Forciea says.

But that's only the beginning of what could be a PPV sports deluge. Some media analysts predict that several of broadcast television's premier

sports attractions, including the Kentucky Derby, the Indianapolis 500 and Wimbledon, eventually will migrate to pay-per-view. Moreover, professional sports leagues see PPV as a new revenue source that can help bridge the difference between what the broadcast networks pay them and the sums they need to keep pace with escalating player salaries.

In another possible scenario, regular-season athletic events would be available on PPV on an "out-of-market" basis, or away from a team's home turf. For example, Boston Celtics fans in Omaha would be able to buy a package of Celtics games delivered by pay-per-view. But out-of-market broadcasts may prove unworkable if they cannibalize the TV audience in areas where the games can be purchased.

With TV audiences potentially at stake, pro sports leagues are understandably closemouthed about their PPV plans. "We're not really ruling out much," says Ed Desser, head of the National Basketball Association's television ventures division, "with one caveat: We are committed to national over-the-air TV. We are committed to national basic cable, and we are committed to local TV in various forms. We're not going to take the [NBA playoff] finals and put them on pay-per-view." [9]

Desser's comments obviously were intended to reassure sports

## Average Revenues from PPV Events

*Although average boxing revenues fell from 1989 to 1990, revenues for wrestling and concerts posted strong gains. Overall, average per-event revenues jumped 13 percent over 1989, with boxing still in the lead.*

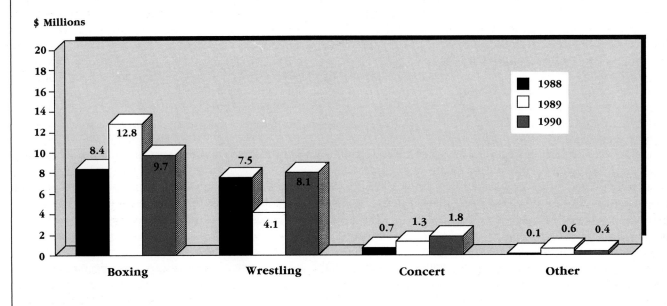

$ Millions

| | 1988 | 1989 | 1990 |
|---|---|---|---|
| Boxing | 8.4 | 12.8 | 9.7 |
| Wrestling | 7.5 | 4.1 | 8.1 |
| Concert | 0.7 | 1.3 | 1.8 |
| Other | 0.1 | 0.6 | 0.4 |

*Source: The Pay TV Newsletter.*

fans and public officials worried that pro playoff and championship games are all destined to end up on pay-per-view someday. Concern centers on what John Mansell calls the "crown jewels" of American sport: the World Series and the Super Bowl. The concern is well founded, according to some television insiders. "The Super Bowl will eventually be on pay-per-view," says Winston H. Cox, chairman of the Showtime cable network. "They don't want to hear that in Washington, but if the economics make sense and the technology is there, you can't stand in the way of it." [10]

Others are not so sure. What will happen in the future, says Western Michigan University's Richard Gershon, will be influenced by American broadcasting history. "There is no law that says the World Series and the Super Bowl will forever be made available on a free, advertiser-supported basis," he says. "It's just that

that has been the tradition of broadcasting in this country for well over 60 years. It is accepted as the norm."

Mansell says the World Series and Super Bowl may appear on pay-per-view someday, but not on an exclusive basis. He foresees a television option not unlike the one viewers will have next year with the Olympics — a pay-per-view edition shown simultaneously with the free, over-the-air broadcast. "That could be done if an upscale version of the game was carried on pay-per-view," says Mansell. "The pay-per-view version might allow viewers to select camera angles. It could be on high-definition TV with fancier graphics, and perhaps stereo sound."

Sports officials have long insisted they have no plans to move their championship games to pay-per-view. Former NFL Commissioner Pete Rozelle set the pattern in 1961 while testifying on behalf of legislation authorizing single-network tele-

vision contracts with professional sports leagues. Asked by the House Antitrust Subcommittee's counsel whether he understood "that this bill covers only the free telecasting of professional sports contests, and does not cover pay TV," Rozelle said: "Absolutely."

The NFL has adhered to Rozelle's position in subsequent congressional testimony. Responding to a question posed by Sen. Arlen Specter, R-Pa., at a 1982 Senate Judiciary Committee hearing on pro sports antitrust immunity, then-NFL counsel Paul Tagliabue declared that "the words 'sponsored telecasting' in [the 1961 act] were intended to exclude pay and cable. This is clear from the legislative history and from the committee reports. So, that statute does not authorize us to pool and sell to pay and cable."

The catch is that the NFL has since signed broadcast-rights contracts with two cable channels, ESPN

(Entertainment and Sports Network) and TNT (Turner Network Television). And the National Basketball Association has a four-year, $275 million contract, signed in 1989, to show selected regular-season and playoff games on TNT.

To some members of Congress, such arrangements have unsettling implications. Sen. Howard M. Metzenbaum, D-Ohio, spoke for many when he asked Rozelle at a 1987 hearing "whether this is the proverbial story of the camel's nose under the tent, and whether this is the first move to cable television, pay television, and then a second step and a third step to the point where football cannot be seen across the breadth of this nation unless you are willing to pay for it." [11]

Apprehension about the NFL's long-range intentions regarding pay-per-view surfaced again after Tagliabue, who became NFL commissioner in 1989, addressed the Federal Communications Bar Association in Washington last November. He indicated that the NFL was exploring the feasibility of out-of-market PPV sales. There are "growing pressures to make games available on a select and targeted basis," he said, citing "the mobility of American society where we have Cleveland [Browns] fans in San Diego."

Tagliabue's remarks before the lawyers' group and in a later interview on ESPN triggered an exchange of letters with Rep. Edward J. Markey, D-Mass., chairman of the House Energy and Commerce Committee's Telecommunications and Finance Subcommittee, who expressed concern about the league's pay-per-view strategy. Calling Markey's fears misplaced, Tagliabue said PPV would be a market test that would not alter existing broadcast contracts and that any PPV games would be in addition to the present broadcast and cable schedule. In another conciliatory gesture, the commissioner said on Aug. 27 there would be no pay-per-view telecasts of NFL games before 1994, at the earliest.

In any confrontation with professional sports leagues over pay-per-view, Congress has a powerful though never-used weapon at its disposal. As league executives are well aware, Congress has the power to enact legislation stripping a professional sport of its protection from federal antitrust laws, which allow the leagues to act as an entity for purposes of negotiating broadcasting contracts. Thanks to a controversial 1922 Supreme Court decision,[12] major-league baseball enjoys blanket antitrust immunity. Pro basketball, football and hockey enjoy immunity only when negotiating leaguewide contracts involving the sale of national TV and radio rights. Removal of the antitrust shield, team owners say, would be economically ruinous.

Congress could also enact a law requiring Major League Baseball and the NFL to keep their championships on free television even if the games were also offered on pay-per-view. A bill that would do just that was introduced May 8 by Sen. John McCain, R-Ariz. "[A]ccess to the World Series and the Super Bowl should not be determined by an income test," McCain declared. "These traditions have always been available to all Americans, regardless of their income level. This access should remain unchanged." McCain's bill was referred to the Senate Committee on Commerce, Science and Transportation, which has taken no action on it.

Even in the absence of federal legislation, some media experts say the broadcast networks have a powerful incentive to keep the "crown jewels" on free TV. If a pay-per-view promoter made a serious bid for the NFL championship game, wrote the authors of a historical survey of pay TV, "it is hard to imagine ABC, NBC and CBS not falling over each other to score the public relations coup of being the Network That Saved the Super Bowl." [13] On the other hand, declining viewership and advertising revenue have weakened the broadcast networks' ability to outbid competitors for major attractions.

In Gershon's view, offering championship sports events exclusively on pay-per-view could undermine interest in sports programming generally. He reasons that many fans will come to feel "disenfranchised," with the result that they will eventually stop going to the stadium to see regular-season games and will even stop watching games on television.

Most viewers of televised sports, says Gershon, "want to be able to tune in for a couple of innings. If the game interests them they'll continue to watch, and if it doesn't, they'll turn it off. If the game is part of a sports package they pay for on cable, that's fine." Fans have a "casual commitment" to sports, Gershon adds. "They don't want to have to exercise pay-per-view decision-making each time they turn on the set." ∎

# BACKGROUND

## Early Experiments

Although pay-per-view television is only now hitting its stride, TV viewers have had the chance to pay for the programs they watch since the earliest days of commercial broadcast television. In 1949, Zenith Radio Corp. petitioned the Federal Communications Commission (FCC) for authority to field test its Phonevision pay TV service, delivered through telephone lines to subscribers' home screens. Phonevision offered three films daily in the Chicago area, each costing $1 per showing — a substantial price at the time. To order a film, a subscriber called Phonevision, where an operator unscrambled the video signal being carried over the subscriber's telephone line.[14]

In a decision reflecting its long-time ambivalence about pay television, the FCC approved Zenith's application but gave the company only 90 days to conduct the Phonevision experiment. When the results were tallied, the average rate of movie watching by the 300-family Phonevision test group was three times greater than the national average attendance at movie theaters during the trial period. That prompted Zenith to call the future of pay TV bright, but the FCC disagreed and refused to extend the company's permit.

Two other experimental pay-TV systems appeared in 1950-51. To purchase a program from Skiatron Electronics & Television Corp.'s Subscribervision, broadcast over WOR-TV in New York City, a viewer inserted a plastic punch card, paid for in advance, into a device attached to the TV set, activating a decoder that released a viewable picture to the television tube. A rival pay-TV system, International Telemeter Corp.'s Telemeter, broadcast over KTLA-TV in Los Angeles, represented pay-per-view in perhaps its purest form. Customers requested programs simply by dropping coins into a meter on the TV set.

It was not until February 1955 that the FCC announced that it was trying to determine whether, in fact, it had legal standing to regulate what was then called subscription TV (STV). In May 1957 the commission said the Communications Act of 1934 gave it such authority.

Five months later, the FCC set forth the ground rules for conducting tests of STV systems. Authoriza-

tions for tests were to be granted for three years and were not automatically renewable, the commission said. Moreover, STV trials were limited to markets that already had a substantial amount of free television programming. The restriction was designed to protect existing broadcast channels.

Though the FCC's criteria for STV seemed cautiously framed, they unleashed a storm of criticism from broadcasters and theater owners. *(See story, p. 740.)* Both groups feared pay television would make unacceptably large inroads into their markets. The FCC reacted to the furor by announcing in February 1958 that it would not process any STV applications until Congress had considered the issue.*

Once it became clear Congress would take no legislative action, the FCC returned to the STV issue. In March 1959 the FCC limited field trials to one market per subscription system.[15] In December 1968 the FCC reiterated that policy and imposed tough restrictions on the kinds of programs STV systems could carry. The commission's aim, it acknowledged, was "to protect the existing TV structure."

The FCC, in fact, succeeded in killing off nearly all interest in STV. But another development also contributed to subscription television's demise. By the early 1970s, pay cable (including pay-per-view and premium channels) had established itself as broadcast television's chief competitor for quality programming. The focus of FCC regulatory policy

---

*During hearings in January 1958 before the House Interstate and Foreign Commerce Committee, Rep. Emanuel Celler, D-N.Y., said conversion "to the service of toll television will only increase viewers' costs and broadcasters' profits, without producing any long-term improvement in programs." In a similar vein, FCC Chairman John C. Doerfer testified pay TV should be halted if field tests showed it would replace free TV.

shifted accordingly.

Initially, the commission was prepared to grant pay cable more leeway than it ever gave STV. In 1969, it concluded the public interest would be served if cable programming content was free from outside restrictions. Broadcasters pleaded with the FCC to reconsider, arguing that pay cable was just as liable to "siphon" desirable programs from them as STV was. After a long delay, the commission announced it was re-evaluating its position on pay cable.

### The FCC's Tough Rules

The product of this review was the FCC's final set of pay-cable rules, issued March 20, 1975. The rules made it extremely difficult to show recent or vintage movies and many popular sports events. The rules also banned series-type programs with interconnected plots and set casts of characters and limited movies and sports events to a maximum of 90 percent of the total hours telecast.

As the broadcasters had done five years earlier, Home Box Office Inc. and several motion picture distributors petitioned the FCC for reconsideration. Their request was denied. The FCC's decision then was appealed to the U.S. Court of Appeals for the District of Columbia circuit, which issued its ruling in the case of *Home Box Office v. Federal Communications Commission* on March 25, 1977. The court found for the plaintiffs, delivering a stinging rebuke to the FCC and a sharp setback to the broadcast television industry.

"[T]he Supreme Court recognized in *U.S. v. Midwest Video* that the [FCC] can act only for ends for which it could also regulate broadcast television," the appeals court noted in its decision. "It is clear that the thrust of the commission's [pay-cable] rules is to prevent any competition by pay cable entrepreneurs for film or sports material that has been

*Continued on p. 741*

# Chronology

## 1940s-1950s

*As the U.S. TV industry grows after the war, the first pay video ventures are launched.*

### July 3, 1947

Zenith Radio Corp. announces it is working on a system for scrambling broadcast TV signals. Two years later, it files a petition with the Federal Communications Commission (FCC) requesting authority to field test the system, called Phonevision.

### Oct. 17, 1957

The FCC announces conditions under which trial applications for subscription television (STV) systems will be considered. It limits requests to cities with at least four commercial television stations.

## 1960s

*A California experiment with pay TV is shot down at the ballot box, nearly killing the concept.*

### March 1960

Zenith announces plans for a pay-TV test in Hartford, Conn. The experiment helps shape subsequent federal policy on STV and pay cable.

### July 17, 1964

Subscription Television Inc. begins pay-per-view telecasts of baseball, movies and other entertainment fare in Los Angeles and San Francisco.

### Nov. 3, 1964

By a 2-to-1 margin, California voters approve a ballot proposal to outlaw pay TV.

### May 19, 1965

Judge Irving H. Perluss of California Superior Court rules the six-month-old ban on pay TV unconstitutional.

### Dec. 12, 1968

The FCC limits subscription TV to a single channel in communities with at least five commercial TV stations. The overall aim of the restrictions, the commission acknowledges, is "to protect the existing TV structure."

## 1970s

*The regulatory straitjacket stunting the growth of pay television begins to loosen.*

### March 20, 1975

The FCC prevents cable systems from offering feature films and sporting events on a subscription basis to prevent cable systems from "siphoning" programs that might otherwise be available for broadcast use.

### March 25, 1977

The U.S. Court of Appeals for the District of Columbia Circuit, in *Home Box Office v. FCC,* holds that the commission lacks jurisdiction under the Communications Act to issue regulations restricting the programming offered by pay-TV cablecasters in order to prevent the "siphoning" of popular fare from conventional broadcast television to pay TV.

## 1980s

*For the first time, pay-per-view TV demonstrates its ability to generate substantial revenue for sports and entertainment performers and promoters.*

### Nov. 25, 1980

Approximately 170,000 pay-per-view households (out of a nationwide total of 400,000) pay $15 each to watch the Sugar Ray Leonard-Roberto Duran fight. It is the first multimillion-dollar attraction in PPV history, with revenue of more than $2.5 million.

### March 1985

Wrestlemania I attracts an audience of 30,000 households. The "gate" of $300,000 establishes pro wrestling as a viable PPV event.

## 1990s

*Revenue from PPV continues to rise, feeding speculation that the industry's long-awaited boom is near.*

### April 19, 1991

The Evander Holyfield-George Foreman fight generates $48.9 million in pay-per-view TV revenue, a PPV record.

### June 1991

An FCC working paper on television's future predicts a diminished role for broadcast stations and a more prominent one for cable TV, including pay-per-view.

### Aug. 27, 1991

National Football League Commissioner Paul Tagliabue says the NFL will have no pay-per-view television, in any form, until at least 1994. Earlier in the year, Tagliabue had hinted at the possibility of NFL games on PPV as early as 1992.

# They Didn't Want Their STV

There were big promises in 1964 when Subscription Television Inc. (STV) came to the Los Angeles and San Francisco Bay areas. The main attraction of the new cable TV system was commercial-free telecasts of Los Angeles Dodgers and San Francisco Giants baseball games, priced at $1.50 each. Headed by Sylvester L. "Pat" Weaver, a former president and chairman of NBC, STV pledged to provide each team with 20,000 paying home viewers in its first year of operation. By the fifth year, the company said, the Dodgers would have 700,000 subscribers and the Giants 500,000.

It soon became clear that STV would fall well short of its goals. When service began that July in Los Angeles,† only about 2,500 homes had signed up. The firm's failure to obtain the broadcast rights to recent Hollywood films proved critical. The lackluster opening night lineup on STV's three channels reflected STV's undistinguished fare: One channel showed a Dodgers-Chicago Cubs game; another carried a surfing program and a film about ancient Egypt; and the third broadcast a drama about racial troubles in South Africa and a satiric revue from Upstairs at the Downstairs, a New York cabaret.

Despite STV's inauspicious start, movie studios and theater owners felt threatened by pay television. They helped to organize and fund the Citizens Committee for Free TV, which gathered enough signatures to put an initiative on the November 1964 ballot prohibiting pay TV from challenging free TV in California. Supporters of the proposal argued that a successful pay-TV system, with its vast subscription revenues, would buy up the most popular shows and performers seen for free on advertiser-supported television. For its part, STV said it would continue to stress programming rarely seen on broadcast television — chiefly opera, serious drama and sports events blacked out in the local broadcast market.

Both sides expected a close race. Instead, the initiative swept to victory by a margin of more than 2 to 1. Voters apparently were swayed by warnings that they would soon have to pay to watch sports, movies and even regular series like "Perry Mason" and "The Donna Reed Show" unless STV was stopped in its tracks.

The triumph was short-lived, however. On May 19, 1965, Judge Irving H. Perluss of California Superior Court ruled that the state's ban on pay television was unconstitutional. Characterizing the TV networks' concern about program siphoning as "speculative and illusory," Perluss said "it would appear that the charges here made could have been made by the radio industry when television was made available for the home and by the producers of silent pictures on that memorable day when Al Jolson appeared on the motion picture screen and sang in 'The Jazz Singer.'" Perluss added that "Invention and progress may not and should not be so restricted, at least when they are cloaked with the immunity of the fundamental freedom."

The judge's ruling, however, came too late for STV. Soon after voters passed the initiative, the company went out of business in California.

In an ironic twist, the National Association of Theater Owners (NATO), one of the leaders of the 1964 campaign against pay TV in California, has since undergone a change of heart. Executive Director Mary Ann Grasso says experience shows pay television has little effect on the motion picture box office. "We have found that people still like to go to the movies [in theaters], and we're obviously glad about that," she says. Consequently, NATO has taken no formal policy position on pay-per-view. (The group is more concerned about the possible impact of high-definition television, Grasso says, but has adopted no policy on that either.††)

Coincidentally, several National Football League teams in 1964 experimented with pay telecasts of selected home games, which were blacked out on local broadcast television. The Baltimore Colts, Chicago Bears, Detroit Lions and New York Giants showed the games in movie theaters via closed-circuit television. Only one-fourth of the 25,600 available theater seats in New York City were filled for the Giants-Washington Redskins game. On the other hand, the Lions-Green Bay Packers game sold three-fourths of the seats in Detroit. Still, overall results were deemed disappointing, and the experiment was not repeated.

> **Voters apparently were swayed by warnings that they would soon have to pay to watch sports, movies and even regular TV series when STV was stopped in its tracks.**

---

† STV began operating in the San Francisco area a month later.

†† For background on high-definition television (HDTV), see "A High-Tech, High Stakes HDTV Gamble," *Editorial Research Reports*, Feb. 17, 1989, pp. 89-104.

*Continued from p. 738*

shown on conventional television or is likely to be shown there."

The court also challenged the validity of broadcasters' claims that pay-cable operators would try to monopolize all the best programming. "The commission," it declared, "has not demonstrated whether the alleged 'siphoning' phenomenon is a real or merely a fanciful threat."

Standing the broadcasters' argument on its head, the court observed that "cablecasters are unlikely to withhold feature films and sports material from markets they do not serve since broadcast of this material would undoubtedly have a substantial value."

The *Home Box Office* decision, which the Supreme Court declined to review, was virtually an Emancipation Proclamation for cable TV. Previously, it had been treated as a supplement to broadcast television, whose interests received priority consideration from federal regulators. Now cable would be treated as an equal competitor in the media marketplace. Since 1977, with only occasional prodding from the courts, the FCC has removed all major restrictions on cable TV operations.

The industry received another major boost with the passage of the Cable Telecommunications Policy Act in 1984. In one stroke, the law eliminated many of the restrictions imposed on cable operators by local governments. While it recognized the power of cities to grant and renew cable TV franchises, the law made cable companies less vulnerable to the whims of local officials by outlining uniform operating and licensing requirements. The new law also limited the control cities had over cable programming, barred regulation of rates after two years and capped the franchise fees they can charge at 5 percent of local revenues.[16]

### Satellites Play Crucial Role

If deregulation helped spark the explosive growth of cable television since the late 1970s, the advent of satellite transmission of programs to local cable systems literally put cable into orbit.[17] Pioneered by HBO in 1975, satellites made it possible to deliver economically a vast array of national programming services, including movies, sports, news and material designed for specialized audiences.

Having lost the battle to limit cable TV's expansion, broadcasters moved to grab part of the cable action. For instance, ABC now owns the Entertainment and Sports Network (ESPN), which carries major-league baseball and NFL football games, and in 1989 NBC introduced CNBC (Consumer News and Business Channel).

NBC also submitted the winning $401 million bid in 1988 for U.S. broadcast rights to the 1992 Olympics in Barcelona, Spain. The network subsequently transferred the cable rights to Cablevision Systems of Woodbury, N.Y., the parent company of SportsChannel America. NBC and Cablevision are now trying to market a pay-per-view Olympics package, an ambitious undertaking that could lead to similar joint ventures in the future.  ■

# CURRENT SITUATION

## Selling the Olympics

Less than a year before the Summer Olympics are due to begin, the NBC-Cablevision pay-per-view experiment remains in a state of flux. The original plan called for a 16-day, three-channel package of Olympics coverage for as much as $170. NBC officials touted the package as costing less than $10 a day and as "a fraction of the cost of attending a single major sporting event."

Ronald Hawkins, New York bureau chief for *Cable TV Business* magazine, scoffed at that rationale. "What we're talking about is watching a television program — not attending an event — that costs nearly $10 a day," he wrote. "For people who don't live on expense-account lunches, $10 per day is a significant amount of money — even for something as prestigious as the Olympics.

And remember, NBC will be showing the big events and highlights on 'free' television anyway."[18]

Still, many cable TV executives are enthusiastic. Don Mathison of Media General Cable says his Fairfax County, Va., company is "very excited" about the PPV Olympics: "We think there are a lot of people who would like to follow specific sports from beginning to end and not look at an edited version of what took place."

Mathison's cable system, with 94 channels in operation, already has set aside three of them for its Olympic "triplecast." Few systems have that much channel capacity and thus may have difficulty making room for two weeks of pay-per-view programming.

In fact, trouble caused by the extra programming already has emerged, forcing NBC and Cablevision to readjust their marketing strategy. Initially, they planned to show the pay-per-view Olympics on national cable networks, notably C-SPAN, the Discovery Channel and the Family Channel. This would have been a simple way of gaining access to local cable systems nationwide. But when Discovery balked at the idea of suspending

# A 'Ticket' Price for Every Pocketbook

When it comes to the price of a "ticket" on pay TV, there's something for every pocketbook. Movies anchor the low end of the scale. According to Paul Kagan Associates of Carmel, Calif., one of the cable TV industry's leading investment research firms, the average price of a pay-per-view movie this year is $4.30, up from $4.25 in 1988. By the year 2000, Kagan Associates expects the price to rise only to $4.75.

Prices leap skyward for pay-per-view "event" programming. Recent championship prizefights have been in the $35 range. Professional wrestling earns a somewhat lower tariff. The two most recent editions of Wrestlemania, the annual showcase that has been called pro wrestling's Super Bowl, each cost $29.95. The typical charge for concerts by top-rated popular performers generally hovers around $20. The highest-priced concert to date, at $22.50, was a December 1989 appearance by the Rolling Stones.

Because PPV is an emerging industry, program suppliers and cable system operators still are experimenting with different pricing formulas. Prices may never be the same after the upcoming 1992 Summer Olympics "package" being offered by NBC and Cablevision Systems Corp., the country's ninth-largest multiple-system cable TV operator. The two

companies plan to show 1,080 hours (540 live and 540 taped replay) of Olympic events from Barcelona on three cable channels over a 15-day period beginning next July 26.

The Olympics "triplecast" will be the most expensive programming package ever carried on pay-per-view. The "bronze" package, at $95, includes either the first seven days of the Olympics or seven weekend days. The "silver" package, at $125, includes all 1,080 hours of coverage plus a 50 percent discount on certain merchandise in the NBC Olympics catalog. The "gold" package, at $170, includes everything in the silver package as well as a commemorative book, a set of Olympics pins and a videotape of Olympics highlights to be delivered after the Games.

Heavy promotion of the triplecast is planned to coincide with Christmas, the Super Bowl and other major events — including Mother's Day and Father's Day. The overall objective is to get commitments from subscribers as early as possible and avoid a last-minute deluge of orders by impulse buyers.

Ellen Cooper, NBC vice president for public relations, says the hope is to sign up between 2.5 million and 3.5 million households; the break-even point is estimated at 2.75 million homes.

service for two weeks, NBC and Cablevision announced they would let participating local systems find space on channels of their choosing.

The two PPV Olympics partners will be able to lend a helping hand in some cases. NBC plans to combine its own CNBC and American Movie Classics (AMC) on a single channel for the duration of the Olympics, leaving the second channel open for PPV use. Similarly, Cablevision could make its SportsChannel America available. The trouble is that these cable services are not carried on many smaller cable systems — the very ones that will be hardest pressed to accommodate the pay-per-view triplecast.

By itself, solving the channel-clearance problem would not ensure a financially successful PPV Olympics. For one thing, some observers question the NBC-Cablevision as-

sumption that a substantial market exists for Olympic events that are generally considered minor sports in this country. "Lots of people will think the [free] network Olympic programming is enough," says Rex Lardner, senior vice president and general manager of the Goodwill Games, a division of TBS Sports. "From the Goodwill Games [a sort of mini-Olympics], we have learned that Americans are interested in amateur sports, but their favorites are [still] football, basketball and baseball." [19] Gymnastics and track and field will attract pay-per-view customers, he predicts, but sports like judo and weightlifting will not draw.

If the PPV Olympics buy rate fails to meet NBC-Cablevision's 10 percent target figure, it will not be for lack of promotional effort. Potential subscribers will be offered a 112-page book on the history of the

Olympics, plus a guide to the PPV programming; a set of Olympics collector pins; and a variety of items marketed in cross-promotions with businesses interested in reaching the same consumers that NBC and Cablevision are aiming at. Prospective customers also will be reminded that part of their subscription fee is earmarked for support of the U.S. Olympic program and thus may be tax-deductible.

Many television industry analysts believe the value of the PPV Olympics cannot be measured in terms of revenue alone. Sid Amira, vice president of the Madison Square Garden cable network, says NBC and Cablevision do not need to achieve a 10 percent buy rate for the event to be judged a success. "If they get a 2 or 1 percent buy rate, if they really satisfy those viewers and disseminate knowledge that the Olympics do exist on pay-per-view, that will be successful."[20]

John Mansell of Paul Kagan Associates takes a similar position. Most people expect the PPV Olympics to lose money, he says, so failure to meet revenue goals would "not be viewed as any kind of a setback or black mark for pay-per-view." In his opinion, what NBC and Cablevision are doing should be regarded as "very much of an experiment." Richard Gershon of Western Michigan University agrees, characterizing the pay-per-view venture as "part of the learning curve."

## New Movie Option

Another experiment that may influence the course of PPV is video-on-demand (VOD), which would enable home viewers to order any one of hundreds or even thousands of movies at any time of day or night. Denver-based Tele-Communications Inc. (TCI), the nation's largest operator of cable TV systems, announced in May it would gauge consumer interest in VOD through two tests conducted in cooperation with AT&T Network Systems and U.S. West, a regional telephone company.[21]

One group of 225 homes in the Denver area will be offered an enhanced PPV service with frequent starting times, 15 different movies a day and at least six different titles available at any hour. A second group of 225 homes will be offered a more advanced system that closely approximates true VOD. Viewers in the second group will be able to choose from among some 1,000 films for delivery to their sets at any time. They will also have limited use of the pause button on their remote-control units — one 10-minute break per film.

John C. Malone, TCI's chief executive officer, likens VOD to patroniz-ing a video store without having to leave home. In fact, some television industry analysts predict that a nationwide network of VOD systems could spell serious trouble for home video chains like Blockbuster. But home video executives profess to be unconcerned, asserting that video-on-demand really threatens movie-oriented "premium" cable channels like Home Box Office, Cinemax and Showtime. ∎

# OUTLOOK

## FCC Studies TV's Future

Video-on-demand is just one of several emerging technologies that are reshaping the contours of American television. And according to a working paper issued in June by the FCC's Office of Plans and Policy, the future may be different indeed. "Over the past 15 years the range of broadcast, cable and other video options available to the American viewer has increased dramatically," it said. "Broadcast television, however, has suffered an irreversible long-term decline in audience and revenue share, which will continue throughout the current decade."

The paper went on to predict that "television broadcasting will be a

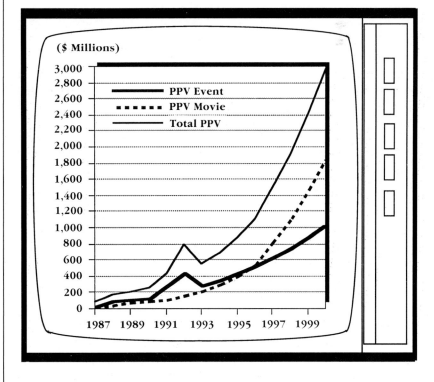

# Looking Into PPV's Future

*Pay-TV revenues should skyrocket in the next few years, according to projections. From $435 million this year, total revenues should hit $789 million next year, $1.1 billion in 1996 and nearly $3 billion by the year 2000.*

($ Millions)

PPV Event
PPV Movie
Total PPV

*Source: The Pay TV Newsletter.*

smaller and far less profitable business in the year 2000 than it is now. Although broadcasting will remain an important component of the video mix, small-market stations, weak independents in larger markets and UHF independents in general will find it particularly difficult to compete, and some are likely to go dark." [22]

Because television is rapidly evolving, the working paper urged the FCC to re-examine its regulatory premises. "Many of the FCC's broadcasting rules were adopted when there were far fewer channels per market, and the three networks dominated the supply of programming," it said. "Much of the FCC's broadcast regulation was motivated by a desire to limit economic market power and concentration of control over program content on the part of broadcast stations and networks. These concerns appear misplaced, or at best of greatly diminished importance, in a world where broadcast stations and networks face dozens of cable channels and program networks." [23]

FCC Chairman Alfred C. Sikes agrees. "We've got to have reality-based regulation, and the reality is fragmentation, intense competition," he said shortly after the working paper was issued. "The transmission medium that had been dominant is now secondary. Broadcasting has been eclipsed by cable." [24]

Acting unanimously on July 11, the five FCC commissioners voted to launch a study of current rules on TV station ownership. The commission will solicit comments on whether it should scrap rules that bar an individual from owning more than one station of the same type in the same market and that prohibit television stations from owning cable systems. The latter change would require congressional assent.

The FCC inquiry also will examine technological advances that will greatly enlarge the number of chan-

nels cable systems can offer, such as digital-signal compression (a technique for sending several signals at once). "The video marketplace is going through changes as significant as any in its history, and it is incumbent upon the commission to monitor these changes and adjust its policies accordingly," Commissioner James H. Quello said.

Signal compression should be of particular help in facilitating the spread of pay-per-view, as the experience of Media General Cable's 94-channel system suggests. Because it has so many channels, the Fairfax system is able to devote seven of them to PPV. An eighth "barker" (promotional) channel carries information about what is being shown on pay-per-view. Don Mathison of Media General says market research indicates viewers depend at least as much on the barker channel for PPV schedules as they do on the printed monthly program guide.

## Technology Must Keep Up

According to the FCC working paper, pay-per-view faces a bright future if related technological developments proceed on schedule. One such development concerns addressable converters.

"In 1990, only 38 percent of basic subscribers had addressable converters; in 1999, 84.4 percent are projected to be so equipped," the paper said. "Also, since programmers and cable operators find it advantageous to be able to cater to the impulse buyer, the ability to process a large number of orders almost instantaneously is important. Various methods . . . have been developed to handle the last-minute bulges in orders. As these become more widely applied, the pay-per-view ordering process will become easier, which should spur demand." [25]

Pay-per-view is also expected to benefit from the advent of interactive television, which allows home viewers, using a key pad or home computer, to bank and shop from home. In fact, they can even choose camera angles in telecasts of sporting events. "Interactive video plus video compression could allow the viewer to 'direct' his or her own telecast of a football game or other sporting event," the working paper noted. "Interactive television could also be used for polling viewers on various subjects, ranging from local or national political issues to how to end a television program to voting for contestants in a talent contest." [26]

As Mathison sees it, interactivity will be the ultimate achievement in television technology. "I don't think anyone would question that," he says. "The future [of television] is clearly interactive. People want greater control of their time, of the quality of their time, of what they are viewing. If you can give them that electronically, you've really hit a home run."

Broadcast television, on the other hand, may find itself in danger of striking out. According to the FCC working paper, "Broadcast television stations will experience declining revenues and increasing program costs" over the next 10 years. "Network compensation will fall with network advertising revenues, and national sport advertising will erode partially to cable. The potential for greatly increased competition from cable in local advertising is clear as well." [27]

The bad news may not end there. As programming choices multiply, the television market is likely to fragment along ability-to-pay lines. At the top of the heap will be the affluent households that can afford the latest in big-ticket technology — big-screen, high-definition receivers

*Continued on p. 746*

# At Issue:

## Does pay-per-view television have a promising future?

**TOM ROGERS**

*President, NBC Cable*
FROM *LUNCHEON ADDRESS BEFORE NATIONAL ACADEMY
OF TELEVISION ARTS AND SCIENCES*, SEPT. 25, 1991.

**M**ost of us here are in some sector of electronic communications, a business that involves itself in offering choices to the public. . . . There was a brand-new choice on Monday night [Sept. 23]. A first. Pay-per-view opera. On cable. Placido Domingo, Luciano Pavarotti and a cast of 30 of the world's most distinguished singers in a four-hour cablecast celebrating the 25th anniversary of the opening of the Metropolitan Opera at Lincoln Center. . . .

We don't expect a major buy rate with this kind of offering. We didn't get one on Monday — yet we did establish a new choice for a small but very select audience.

Digital [signal] compression is on the horizon, and compression is going to make it possible to shoehorn four to eight channels into the space that one channel now occupies. Our 35-channel cable systems could grow to 280 channels. Our present major-capacity systems could expand to 600 or 1,200 channels. And that increased capacity, beyond being able to accommodate more cable networks and niche programming of all kinds, is going to let PPV take off and grow to full potential.

A system with a few hundred channels will be able to put aside 30 to 40 channels for PPV and to initiate video-on-demand — literally the ability to order exactly what you want from a cable system's library of hundreds of titles and types of programs, and to watch what you've selected whenever you say go. . . .

PPV is not a new territory. It's been around for years. But as I noted before about PPV opera, and as you well know if you've been following the trials and tribulations we've had getting the PPV Olympics up to speed, NBC and Cablevision are bringing a lot of original thought and organizational skill to the job of getting PPV firmly established in this country as something more than an occasional Mike Tyson fight.

The Olympics on PPV . . . is now only 10½ months away from happening. So far we have 80 of the top 100 MSOs [multiple-system cable TV operators] signed to carry the triplecast. We expect at the end to have 2,000 individual systems signed. . . . Long term, NBC wants to be able to reach viewers across a multiplicity of channels — on free network TV, on basic cable, on pay cable, and in the PPV environment of special events or video-on-demand.

**KEITH DAWSON**

*New York correspondent for* **Cable TV Business**
FROM *CABLE TV BUSINESS*, FEB. 1, 1990.

**I** venture to make two predictions. First, in 10 years, pay-per-view as we know it today will not exist. Second, it will be even more difficult for some pay services to attract new viewers and keep the old ones as the VCR/movie rental boom continues. . . .

[T]here has to be some compelling reason to continue buying a pay service. Consumers constantly reassess their commitments to cable each time the monthly bill is delivered. Perhaps more new, original programming by the pay services will lure them in, but with basic channels committing so much money to original programming, competition for that programming is fierce.

And by extension, the same logic holds with pay-per-view. Is there really any reason for a consumer to pay $5 for a PPV movie when the same movie around the corner costs half that? The PPV services claim that convenience is worth the extra cost. But is there any reason to expect that if a consumer's disposable income dried up that he wouldn't be willing to trade that small convenience for the selection and savings of the video store?

Because with both pay and PPV, the reality of the situation is that the only choice a viewer has at any given moment is the movie that is showing right then and there. Some services may claim that they show hundreds of movies each month. A careful consumer would say that is irrelevant, because he cannot watch hundreds of movies a month even if he wanted to. And if the movies he wants to watch and the movies the pay or PPV channel is showing right now are not the same, he will feel like he is wasting his money.

A similar consumer reaction is reflected by PPV big-ticket events — the concerts and spectacles. When a consumer gets a cable bill inflated by $25 or $30 for a concert, then finds the concert showing on Fox or MTV not too many weeks later, is there any reaction but anger? Is there much chance that customer is going to feel friendly toward the medium enough to part with his money again in the near future?

It is of course premature to sound the death knell for this kind of cable viewing. But disconcerting signs are there. . . . Considering how important the revenue from these services is to both operators and programmers, executives should keep that fact in mind.

Continued from p. 744

with quadraphonic sound and a full array of interactive features. This will be the main target audience for pay-per-view programmers.

The middle tier of TV consumers will comprise viewers whose sets are not so fancy and who subscribe only to basic cable plus a few premium channels, like Showtime and HBO. For such families, a PPV program will be a special treat — one budgeted for rather than ordered on impulse.

The low-income homes at the bottom level of TV viewership will rely mainly on broadcast stations. Unable or unwilling to subscribe to cable, they will be of less interest to advertisers than other households. As the FCC working paper gently put it, "Broadcast television will have its place in this new world but as one player among many." [28]  ∎

## Notes

[1] All figures are year-end projections (as of June 30, 1991) by Paul Kagan Associates Inc., a cable TV investment research firm based in Carmel, Calif.

[2] Office of Plans and Policy, Federal Communications Commission, *Broadcast Television in a Multichannel Marketplace*, June 1991, pp. 49-50.

[3] Quoted in *Broadcasting*, April 30, 1990. Werner's remarks were made at the Cable Television Administration and Marketing Society's first annual conference on pay-per-view, held in Orlando, Fla., in April 1990.

[4] A 1989 study by Paramount Pictures' video division found impulse devices produced a 13 percent buy rate for top movies, almost double the rate of ANI and almost three times that of phone calls to customer-service representatives.

[5] Quoted in *The Washington Post*, Dec. 17, 1989.

[6] Writing in *The Washington Post*, Nov. 14, 1989.

[7] Quoted in the *Los Angeles Times*, Aug. 13, 1989.

[8] Quoted in *Communications Daily*, March 1, 1991.

[9] Quoted in *Cablevision*, May 6, 1991.

[10] Quoted in *The Wall Street Journal*, Jan. 24, 1991.

[11] Testimony before Subcommittee on Antitrust, Monopolies and Business Rights of the Senate Judiciary Committee, Oct. 6, 1987.

[12] The case was *Federal Baseball Club of Baltimore Inc. v. National League of Professional Baseball Clubs*. For details, see "Free Agency: Pro Sports' Big Challenge," *Editorial Research Reports*, Feb. 9, 1990, pp. 88-89.

[13] Peter J. Fadde and James C. Hsiung, "Pay TV: A Historical Review of the Siphoning Issue," *Communications and the Law*, April 1987, p. 24. At the time the article was written, Hsiung was an assistant professor in Purdue University's department of communication; Fadde was an M.A. student in Purdue's department of education.

[14] Much of the material in this section is derived from Richard A. Gershon, "Pay Cable Television: A Regulatory History," *Communications and the Law*, June 1990.

[15] The FCC's Fourth Report and Order spelling out the limited field trials was released shortly before a pay TV channel in Hartford, Conn., went out of business after six and a half years. Customers could view up to 30 hours of subscription programming a week for between $1 and $3 a program. The channel's failure to break even helped defuse fears that pay television threatened the continued existence of advertiser-supported broadcast TV.

[16] Many consumers complained that deregulation of the cable TV industry led to rapidly rising prices and reduced service. This led to efforts in Congress to re-regulate the industry. See "Does Cable TV Need More Regulation?" *Editorial Research Reports*, Dec. 7, 1990, pp. 697-712.

[17] HBO's first satellite feed was the Muhammad Ali-Joe Frazier heavyweight championship fight from the Philippines ("The Thrilla in Manila").

[18] Ronald Hawkins, "PPV Olympics: Trouble Ahead?" *Cable TV Business*, March 1, 1990, p. 17.

[19] Quoted in *Cable TV Business*, Sept. 1, 1990.

[20] *Ibid.*

[21] AT&T Network Systems is providing software, remote-control units and switching boxes; U.S. West is providing fiber-optic transmission cable.

[22] Office of Plans and Policy, *op. cit.*, p. vii.

[23] *Ibid.*, p. 3.

[24] Quoted in *Broadcasting*, July 8, 1991.

[25] Office of Plans and Policy, *op. cit.*, pp. 83-84.

[26] *Ibid.*, pp. 59-60.

[27] *Ibid.*, pp. 159-160.

[28] *Ibid.*, p. 161.

# Bibliography

## Selected Sources Used

### Articles

**Fadde, Peter J., and Hsiung, James C., "Pay TV: A Historical Review of the Siphoning Issue,"** *Communications and the Law,* **April 1987.**

Fadde and Hsiung analyze TV broadcasters' argument that pay-television systems would be able to outbid over-the-air stations and networks for premium programs. According to the broadcasters, "Such 'siphoning' of programs from 'free' television would deny access to those viewers who could not receive or could not afford the subscription service."

**Gershon, Richard A., "Pay Cable Television: A Regulatory History,"** *Communications and the Law,* **June 1990.**

This detailed survey of pay television since World War II focuses on Federal Communications Commission rules that protected over-the-air broadcasters from such competitors as subscription television, pay cable and pay-per-view.

**Hawkins, Ronald, "Cable's Sports Dilemma,"** *Cable TV Business,* **Feb. 15, 1990.**

Cable TV values sports programming for the same reason broadcast TV does: It is a proven draw with viewers and advertisers. At the same time, cable operators and pro sports league executives don't want to provoke Congress into passing legislation limiting "sports siphoning" from broadcasters or stripping pro sports of antitrust protection. Hawkins, New York bureau chief for *Cable TV Business,* looks into these touchy questions.

**Holm-Hansen, Vibeke, "Cable's Sleeping Giant: Waking Up Pay-Per-View,"** *Cable TV Business,* **July 15, 1990.**

The author, Denver bureau chief of *Cable TV Business,* examines what consumers like — and dislike — about pay-per-view. The overall conclusion is that PPV executives must improve their marketing techniques if they hope to meet their growth objectives.

**Johnson, William Oscar, "Sports in the Year 2001,"** *Sports Illustrated,* **July 22, 1991.**

Johnson speculates on what watching sports on television will be like 10 years from now, when pay-per-view, digital signal compression, interactivity and high-definition TV may be in place. Fans will be intrigued by the wonders coming their way, but perhaps they will also be sobered by what it is likely to cost.

**Lichtenstein, Bill, "The Censor Within,"** *Channels,* **Nov. 5, 1990.**

Lichtenstein, a New York-based writer and TV producer, wonders whether local agitation against adult programming will discourage PPV programmers from offering such fare.

**Ross, Stephen F., "An Antitrust Analysis of Sports League Contracts With Cable Networks,"** *Emory Law Journal,* **Spring 1990.**

Ross, an associate law professor at the University of Illinois, sets out to determine whether the National Football League's decision to show some games on cable television constitutes an antitrust violation. He concludes that the argument is not without merit.

**Tedesco, Richard; Moozakis, Chuck; and Applebaum, Simon, "Ready, Set, Grow!"** *Cablevision,* **May 6, 1991.**

In this special report, Tedesco writes that the PPV Olympics will spur the migration of other sporting events to pay-per-view; Moozakis examines how suppliers of addressable converters hope to increase sales in conjunction with the Olympics; and Applebaum speculates on the type of programming that might be shown on cable systems with 40 or more pay-per-view channels.

### Reports and Studies

**Federal Communications Commission, Office of Plans and Policy,** *Broadcast Television in a Multichannel Marketplace,* **June 1991.**

This working paper, the authors stress, does "not necessarily reflect the views of other members of the Office of Plans and Policy, other commission staff, or the commission itself." It concludes that broadcast television will continue to lose ground to cable, though at a slower rate than previously, and that cable's days of runaway growth are coming to an end.

**Subcommittee on Antitrust, Monopolies and Business Rights, Senate Judiciary Committee,** *Antitrust Implications of the Recent NFL Television Contract* **(published proceedings of hearing held Oct. 6, 1987).**

The National Football League's then-commissioner, Pete Rozelle, and its then-counsel, Paul Tagliabue (the present commissioner), are grilled by senators concerned about the NFL's decision to show games on cable TV. The main thrust of the senators' questions is whether this development portends an eventual move of the Super Bowl to pay-per-view.

# The Next Step

## Additional Articles from Current Periodicals

### Debates & issues

**"1992 PPV Olympics: The long road to Barcelona,"** *Broadcasting*, March 25, 1991, p. 50.

Discusses the controversy behind NBC's plans for the 1992 pay-per-view Olympics, and how these plans are now accepted by the cable industry, especially the top multiple system operators (MSOs). The price of the event has decreased since last spring; states that there is still a long way to go to settle revenue splits and channel capacity; more.

**"A technical knock-out for the networks?"** *Economist,* March 23, 1991, p. 31.

Looks at how the growing popularity of pay-per-view television (PPV) is posing a threat to America's big three networks and cable television. Recent pay-per-view fight between Mike Tyson and Donovan "Razor" Ruddock; two leading pay-per-view channels, Request and Viewers Choice; details.

**"Adult programing, B movies fill gaps in PPV menu,"** *Broadcasting*, Aug. 27, 1990, p. 51.

Asserts that although pay per view is not a mature business, niche services are beginning to fill the programming holes that mainstream PPV leaves behind. Benefits of adult programming; escalation of interest in adult services; B-movie service; more.

**"Cable executives focus on future of cable programing,"** *Broadcasting*, Oct. 1, 1990, p. 73.

Covers the recent National Academy of Cable Programming's annual fall luncheon and its panel discussion on "Life After 35 Channels: The Future of Cable Programming." Panel members; topics; pay-per-view outlook.

**"Hollywood tries to fit PPV into its game plan,"** *Broadcasting*, April 29, 1991, p. 37.

Reports that with an explosion in pay-per-view (PPV) channels expected during this decade, movie studios are eyeing ways to make sure they are helping to light the fuse. Future of PPV networks; cable operator control; a desire for studios to control their own PPV channels. INSETS: Is PPV networks' merger in cards? (Viewer's Choice and Request Television); Queens helpers (Time Warner's plans for its 150-channel television).

**"Last hurrah for the four-year cycle?"** *Broadcasting*, Feb. 25, 1991, p. 43.

States that broadcasters are looking forward to 1992, because it will be the last time the Fifth Estate will get a three-event boost from a presidential election year and both the Summer and Winter Olympics. Fragmentation must be considered among cable and pay-per-view; media stocks have shown good gains; possible negative impact broadcasters will feel from the increased scrutiny from politicians and agencies; free-time-for-politician proposals; projection of gains.

**"Lloyd Werner: Sold on Group W,"** *Broadcasting*, July 8, 1991, p. 71.

Profiles Lloyd Werner, senior vice president, sales and marketing, Group W Satellite Communications, and president, Request Television. Werner likes instant gratification; his educational and professional background; how some of the mistakes Group W made has helped Werner; opinion on pay-per-view; plans at Group W.

**"PPV and DBS: Partners in uncertain future,"** *Broadcasting*, Feb. 18, 1991, p. 49.

States that competitive pressures and the hard realities of a worsening economy will slow development of direct broadcast satellite (DBS) and Pay-Per-View (PPV), according to cable and DBS executives at last Tuesday's Future Of DBS & Pay-Per-View seminar in Beverly Hills. Comsat Video Enterprise's president and CEO, Robert Wussler wary of DBS industry; more.

**"Wireless cable: The 'will-carry' medium,"** *Broadcasting*, July 15, 1991, p. 17.

Reports that Wireless Cable Association (WCA) President Robert Schmidt stated that his industry "will carry" all broadcast signals, and talked of other potential synergies with broadcasting, including increased pay-per-view opportunities. Lists the problems the industry still faces; the other major obstacles that have been repaired by the new Federal Communications Commission (FCC) rules.

**Davis, E., "TV's fascinating, frightening future,"** *Utne Reader,* July/August 1990, p. 86.

Presents an essay on the future of television watching as technology becomes more interactive. Range and depth of programming; blending of television with computers and game interfaces; how data is delivered to homes.

**Katz, R., "PPV keeps pace,"** *Channels*, Dec. 3, 1990, p. 50.

Questions whether or not the pay-per-view industry will be ready for the 1992 Olympics. NBC will offer parts of the games via PPV and wants 25 million addressable homes to make the Olympics work; promotional efforts are raising awareness of pay-per-view.

**Lichtenstein, B., "The censor within," *Channels*, Nov. 5, 1990, p. 16.**

Questions whether fear of offending the community and self-censorship will defeat diversity in television. Independent Entertainment Group's attempt to produce a pay-per-view concert featuring "2 Live Crew"; looks at several stations and networks affected by censorship controversy.

## Economic aspects

**"Boxing's a hit in June PPV flurry," *Broadcasting*, July 8, 1991, p. 48.**

Details the busy pay-per-view (PPV) month of June that included five boxing matches and specials. Tyson-Ruddock II still managed to generate a $43 million take, the second largest of the year behind the nearly $50 million for the Holyfield-Foreman match in April. Buy rates approaching Tyson-Ruddock I; the number of buyers.

**"Cable finances: Getting past the credit crunch," *Broadcasting*, April 1, 1991, p. 45.**

Discusses the opening session of the National Cable Television Association (NCTA) convention, moderated by ABC political and media analyst Jeff Greenfield. The bleak aspects of the finances of the cable business; the credit crunch that is affecting cable; the success of the pay-per-view (PPV) Olympics that could have an effect on what happens to PPV; ways to improve and expand cable multiple system operators' (MSOs') existing core businesses.

**"Cable rates rising faster than perceived value," *Broadcasting*, Jan. 14, 1991, p. 108.**

Studies the increase in cable rates over the past few years, which has exceeded many cable subscribers' perceived value for their service, according to a new "attitudes and usage study" commissioned by the Cable Television Administration & Marketing Society (CTAM). Price value is the main reason for dissatisfaction; pay-per-view (PPV) needs improvement; CTAM's plans to improve the price value relationship. INSET: Fourth-quarter cable network ratings: 1990 vs. 1989.

**"Pro leagues readying to enter PPV waters," *Broadcasting*, May 13, 1991, p. 54.**

Reports that professional sports leagues may enter the pay-per-view (PPV) world in the 1990s by offering out-of-market games to displaced sports fans. The National Hockey League (NHL) is looking to experiment with PPV packages to dish owners next fall, and the National Bas-

ketball Association (NBA) and the National Football League (NFL) may follow suit in the next several years; rising salaries and prices new owners are paying for teams are fueling interest in PPV; Major League Baseball (MLB) will stay local.

**"Sports: Ticket for tough times," *Broadcasting*, March 4, 1991, p. 53.**

Reports that regional sports networks and pay-per-view can be counted on to "balance the sports checkbook," as rights fees skyrocket and broadcast networks continue to lose money and viewers on their sports packages. Comments from Seth Abraham, president and chief executive officer of Time Warner Sports.

**"Warner Bros. on the stump for PPV movies," *Broadcasting*, Feb. 18, 1991, p. 50.**

States that Warner Bros. is determined to improve pay-per-view movie buy rates. It has spent the past 10 weeks on the road visiting nine of the top 15 multiple system operators (MSOs) and presenting the results of a study of 11 of the top pay-per-view (PPV) cable systems in the country. Warner wants to share its knowledge to boost their business; response from MSOs is positive; more. INSET: Operators given price ranges for PPV Olympics.

**Baker, J., "Up, up and away," *TV Guide*, Feb. 2, 1990, p. 7.**

Discusses the high cost of televising National Football League games, and the probability that this year's contract will be even higher, probably $25 million or more per season for each league team, and the possibility of making football a pay-per-view (PPV) sport. INSET: 23 years of winners and losers (Superbowl matchups), by M. Dougherty.

**Katz, R., "Look who's discounting," *Channels*, Sept. 24, 1990, p. 42.**

Calculates the profitability of discounting pay-per-view (PPV) movies. Success of Columbia Pictures' "Look Who's Talking" discount campaign; pros and cons of several discounting options. INSET: A theater nearer you.

## General

**"Expanding niche: College football PPV," *Broadcasting*, Aug. 20, 1990, p. 47.**

Reveals that Host Communications plans to expand its pay-per-view (PPV) package for coverage of college football games in 1990. Host programming schedule last year; LSU's Tigervision PPV network; more.

**"Government roadblock," *Broadcasting*, May 6, 1991, p. 8.**

Reports that talks over the past couple of months to

bring Hollywood studios and cable operators together, possibly via merger of pay-per-view (PPV) networks Viewer's Choice and Request Television, were a culmination of conversations that began six to eight months ago; how to get together without raising antitrust problems.

**"More PPV gospel from Bleier,"** *Broadcasting*, **Sept. 10, 1990, p. 76.**

Summarizes the findings of Ed Bleier, president of Warner Pay TV, Animation, and Network Features, who says movies and events are the big earners for pay per view (PPV) cable.

**"PPV networks, standalones: Noting differences,"** *Broadcasting*, **Dec. 3, 1990, p. 43.**

Cites the differences between pay-per-view (PPV) networks and cable systems that use standalone PPV channels. The corporate structures of Request and Viewer's Choice. INSET: HBO helping hand.

**"TCI to test PPV, video on demand in Denver,"** *Broadcasting*, **May 6, 1991, p. 23.**

Reports that Tele-Communications Inc. announced plans to test video-on-demand and multichannel pay-per-view PPV) in United Artists' suburban Denver system later this year, assisted by both AT&T and US West. AT&T Network Systems will provide the hardware and software to deliver the Viewer Controlled Cable Television (VCTV) services; US West will provide the optical-fiber transmission from the VCTV test center to UA's head end facilities.

**"Wussler says PPV will strengthen DBS,"** *Broadcasting*, **Dec. 3, 1990, p. 43.**

Presents comments from Robert Wussler, president and chief executive officer of Comsat Video Enterprises, at the CTAM 1990 PPV (pay-per-view) conference in Anaheim, Calif. The future of PPV.

**Katz, R., "Pay cable's chameleon,"** *Channels*, **Oct. 22, 1990, p. 8.**

Reports that the Movie Channel has gone pay-per-view (PPV) as an innovative marketing tactic to draw subs into the service with the sampler and then convince them to sign on full time. Several dozen systems have begun using the sampler; operators love the concept and are happy with the results.

**McManus, J. & S. Donaton, "Time Warner creates new unit for sports punch,"** *Advertising Age,* **Aug. 6, 1990, p. 4.**

Explains how Time Warner hopes to score a knockout punch for a new business venture, with the help of former heavyweight boxing champion Mike Tyson. With an eye toward becoming a major force in the lucrative pay-per-

view (PPV) TV business worldwide, Time Warner last week formed Time Warner Sports to expand existing sports operations and to buy sports properties. Gives details.

**Rudolph, I., "Vanilla icing for video upstart,"** *TV Guide*, **Dec. 7, 1990, p. 50.**

Looks at the astonishing success of rap singer Vanilla Ice, which industry insiders attribute to The Video Jukebox Network, a new pay-per-view cable service.

## Technological aspects

**"Compression, boxing light operators' PPV fire,"** *Broadcasting*, **May 20, 1991, p. 50.**

Reports that the Cable Television Administrative and Marketing Society's second pay-per-view (PPV) conference in Orlando, Fla., finds cable bullish on PPV's future. One reason is three boxing bouts over the past two months that grossed well over $100 million in revenue; the advances in digital compression that can make 100-channel cable systems a reality in the near future could open a whole new world for PPV opponents. INSET: PPV notes (Global Sports Promotions news).

**"Digital compression makes PPV future brighter,"** *Broadcasting*, **May 6, 1991, p. 39.**

Discusses the new way of looking at the world that cable operators are anticipating if digital compression produces hundreds of channels in the 1990s. Operators see expanded scheduling of hit movies, different movie genres and other programing to fill the vast increase in pay-per-view (PPV) channels.

**"Moving up the timetable on DBS,"** *Broadcasting*, **Aug. 20, 1990, p. 27.**

Reports that SkyPix is planning an 80-channel pay-per-view system in less than a year and is stressing the value of compression technology as a key to medium power service to small dishes. Long lead in developing video compression chips; origins of SkyPix; more.

**"New carriage options for PPV Olympics,"** *Broadcasting*, **April 8, 1991, p. 53.**

Reports on the channel capacity issue, which continues to be the most perplexing one for the pay-per-view (PPV) Olympics. The PPV Olympics began polling the top 100 multiple system operators (MSOs) last week to get their reaction to the several proposed ideas to get channel capacity, the most controversial being the plan in which four top 10 basic networks give up their channel space and combine on one composite channel leaving three channels for the Olympics triplecast; more.

**"TW's plan for Queens: 150 channels, 40 of PPV,"**

***Broadcasting*, March 11, 1991, p. 21.**

Announces Time Warner's plans to build a 150-channel cable system in New York's borough of Queens, using a combination of coaxial cable and fiber optics. It is being constructed primarily to deliver 40 channels of pay-per-view (PPV). Describes the company's current Queens system — with 270,000 subscribers; the technology Time Warner uses; the cost of the system; plans to expand the enhanced channel capability further into New York City; more.

**Angus, R., "Cable TV's high-tech gamble," *Video*, July 1991, p. 22.**

Reports on new technology that cable companies will soon be offering, such as high-definition televison (HDTV) and interactive television. Fiber-optic networks; onscreen program guides; pay-per-view (PPV) prices.

## Television programs

**"Cable systems to be offered a choice of Olympics packages," *Broadcasting*, Sept. 3, 1990, p. 41.**

Asserts that the 1992 pay-per-view (PPV) Olympics will be offered to systems in a variety of license fee packages designed to give operators more pricing flexibility. Various options described; more.

**"PPV Olympics talks start with Family, Discovery," *Broadcasting*, June 10, 1991, p. 74.**

Discusses the efforts of NBC and Cablevision's pay-per-view (PPV) Olympics to secure carriage for the three-channel event for non-addressable cable homes. Their efforts has led Olympics executives to formally sit down with both the Family Channel and The Discovery Channel; Olympics executives are offering to buy their respective ad inventories at market rates, paying for every subscriber affected by the Olympics; more.

**"PPV Olympics targets basics in quest for channel space," *Broadcasting*, April 29, 1991, p. 22.**

States that NBC and Cablevision's pay-per-view (PPV) Olympics will try to convince four of the largest cable networks to give up their channel space to carry the event for two weeks in 1992.

**Rosenthal, H. M., "Pay-per-view services may shun rap concert by 2 Live Crew," *TV Guide*, Sept. 28, 1990, p. 42.**

Reports that major pay-per-view (PPV) cable services are deciding whether to offer the controversial rap group "2 Live Crew's" Nov. 8 live concert.

**Rudolph, I., "Tina struts into new PPV era," *TV Guide*, Jan. 4, 1991, p. 44.**

Looks at the current state of pay-per-view (PPV) televi-sion events and contends that if Tina Turner's Jan. 4 PPV concert is successful, it will be the beginning of wide-scale PPV success.

**Wulf, S., "Coming into view," *Sports Illustrated*, April 29, 1991, p. 15.**

Discusses the television coverage of the George Foreman-Evander Holyfield fight. TVKO, a pay-per-view (PPV) boxing network that attracted nearly 2 million viewers; President Seth Abraham; adding legitimacy to PPV; poor quality of the telecast was covered up by the exciting match.

**Wulf, S., "Hitting the fan," *Sports Illustrated*, March 4, 1991, p. 11.**

Reports that the National Football League will soon introduce pay-per-view (PPV) telecasts of its games. PPV as the wave of the future; impact on television viewers; possibility of other sports moving toward PPV.

# Back Issues

*Great Research on Current Issues Starts Right Here. . . Recent topics covered by The CQ Researcher are listed below. Issues dated before May 10, 1991, were published under the name of Editorial Research Reports.*

**MARCH 1990**
Asbestos: Are Risks Acceptable?
Public Health Campaigns
South Africa's Future
Homeless Need More Than Shelter

**APRIL 1990**
How Fair is the Tax Burden?
Workers' Compensation
U.S. Pacific Forces
Curbing Insurance Premiums

**MAY 1990**
Should Teaching Be a Profession?
Will Canada Fall Apart?
Is U.S. Patent System Outdated?
Federal Funding for the Arts

**JUNE 1990**
Downsizing America's Armed Forces
Progress In Weather Forecasting
S & L Bailout
Bio-Chemical Disarmament

**JULY 1990**
Do Americans Still Love Marriage?
Death Penalty Debate
Decline of Rural America
United Nations in the 1990s

**AUGUST 1990**
Democracy in the Philippines
Initiatives: True Democracy?
Hard Times at Newspapers
Teens Balance School & Jobs

**SEPTEMBER 1990**
Dangers of Alcohol
Western Alliance After the Cold War
Tobacco Industry
Right to Die

**OCTOBER 1990**
Organ Transplants
Energy Policy Options
Search for Arab Unity
Child Support

**NOVEMBER 1990**
Lotteries and Gambling
Post Cold-War Choices
Setting Limits on Medical Care
Multicultural Education

**DECEMBER 1990**
Cable TV Regulation
Americans' Search For Their Roots
Is Insurance System a Failure?
Why Schools Still Have Tracking

**JANUARY 1991**
Growing Influence of Boycotts
Should the U.S. Reinstate the Draft?
America's Archaeological Past
Peace Corps' Challenges in '90s

**FEBRUARY 1991**
Regional Impact of Recession
Puerto Rico's Status
Redistricting: Mapping Power
Nuclear Power

**MARCH 1991**
Acid Rain
Cost of the Gulf War
Reassessing Gun Laws
Future for Man in Space

**APRIL 1991**
Social Security
Canadian Crisis Over Quebec
California Drought
Electromagnetic Radiation

**MAY 1991**
School Choice
Racial Quotas
Animal Rights
U.S. and Japan

**JUNE 1991**
Children and Divorce
Teenage Suicide
Endangered Species
Europe 1992

**JULY 1991**
Teenagers and Abortion
Soviet Republics Rebel
Mexico's Emergence
Athletes and Drugs

**AUGUST 1991**
Sexual Harassment
Fetal Tissue Research
Oil Imports
The Palestinians

**SEPTEMBER 1991**
Police Brutality
Advertising Under Attack
Saving the Forests
Foster Care Crisis

Back issues are available for $4.00 (subscribers) or $7.00 (non-subscribers). Quantity discounts apply to orders over ten. To order, call Congressional Quarterly 1-800-432-2250.

# Future Topics

▶ *Youth Gangs*

▶ *Gene Therapy*

▶ *World Hunger*

# THE CQ Researcher

PUBLISHED BY CONGRESSIONAL QUARTERLY INC., IN CONJUNCTION WITH EBSCO PUBLISHING

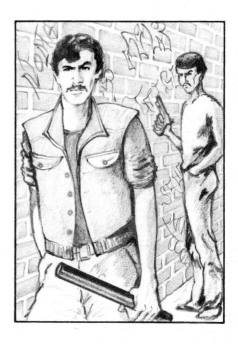

# Youth Gangs

*Worsening violence prompts crackdowns and community mobilization*

D RIVE-BY SHOOTINGS AND ASSAULTS BY GANGS now routinely make headlines in dozens of American cities. But today's gangs differ from the classic switchblade-toting packs of the 1950s. Many are tightly organized, mobile criminal units that carry semiautomatic weapons and run sophisticated drug-trafficking operations. Police, government officials, community leaders and academics can't agree on a solution to the gang problem. Does it lie in tougher police tactics, more effective social work or a combined approach that involves the whole community? As drug arrests and murders by teenagers continue to mount, some police officials refuse to acknowledge the existence of gangs while others call for a coordinated national effort to combat them.

October 11, 1991 • Volume 1, No. 22 • 753-776

*Formerly Editorial Research Reports*

October 11, 1991
Volume 1, No. 22

**EDITOR**
Sandra Stencel

**MANAGING EDITOR**
Thomas J. Colin

**ASSOCIATE EDITOR**
Richard L. Worsnop

**STAFF WRITERS**
Charles S. Clark
Mary H. Cooper
Rodman D. Griffin

**PRODUCTION EDITOR**
Laurie De Maris

**EDITORIAL ASSISTANT**
Thomas H. Moore

**GRAPHICS**
Jack Auldridge

**PUBLISHED BY**
Congressional Quarterly Inc.

**CHAIRMAN**
Andrew Barnes

**VICE CHAIRMAN**
Andrew P. Corty

**EDITOR AND PUBLISHER**
Neil Skene

**EXECUTIVE EDITOR**
Robert W. Merry

**PUBLICATIONS MARKETING/SALES**
Robert Smith

**EDITOR, EBSCO PUBLISHING**
Melissa Kummerer

The CQ Researcher (ISSN 1056-2036). Formerly Editorial Research Reports. Published weekly (48 times per year, not printed the first Friday of any month with five Fridays) by Congressional Quarterly Inc., 1414 22nd St., N.W., Washington, D.C. 20037. Rates are furnished upon request. Application to mail at second-class postage rates is pending at Washington, D.C. POSTMASTER: Send address changes to The CQ Researcher, 1414 22nd St., N.W., Washington, D.C. 20037.

# Youth Gangs

BY CHARLES S. CLARK

## THE ISSUES

Los Angeles police called it "the hammer," a series of squad-car sweeps through the city's dangerous south-central neighborhoods, home to such notorious gangs as the rival Crips and Bloods. In February 1988, a 1,000-member police task force on one such sweep arrested 121 suspected gang members on charges ranging from traffic and curfew violations to narcotics and handgun possession. During the same evening, two young men were shot in gang-related incidents in the area. In the weeks that followed, most of the charges stemming from the sweep were dropped. But no arrests were made in connection with the two shootings. And so the gang-related homicide rate in Los Angeles County continued its unchecked climb, reaching a record 690 murders in 1990.

Already this year, Los Angeles has racked up 520 gang-related murders, solidifying its place as the unofficial "gang capital of the United States." Gang membership in L.A. is thought to have doubled in the past five years, leading to a chilling estimate: Some 950 gangs involving 100,000 youths plague the city. The rampant growth of gangs frustrates police officials. "[We] miscalculated the situation," says Los Angeles County Undersheriff Robert Edmonds. "Our expertise is ill-suited to preventing the emergence of new gangs or the increased membership of existing gangs." [1]

The 1990s have witnessed a dramatic surge in public awareness of youth gangs. Only 10 cities had serious gang problems a decade ago, but youth gangs now operate in 125 U.S. cities, according to University of

Southern California sociologist and gang expert Malcolm W. Klein. The cities with the worst gang problems lie in the Midwest and West. Chicago alone has about 125 gangs with an estimated 12,000-15,000 members, while New York, the classic setting for gang violence for much of U.S. history, reports only 37 gangs with about 1,000 members. *(See map, p. 757.)* Gangs are now challenging community peace in cities unaccustomed to organized crime; Omaha, Neb., in one four-day period last year, experienced nine drive-by shootings by gang members.

The most visible reason for gang expansion is the spread of the drug trade, particularly the easy availability of crack cocaine (called "rock" on the street). Because cocaine can be easily "cooked" by street-smart chemists and then sold in inexpensive, easy-to-conceal doses, crack offers attractive financial opportunities for gang members in poverty-stricken, jobless neighborhoods. Because crack is addictive, its peddlers

can look forward to steady profits from repeat sales in neighborhoods whose turf they have staked out. Indeed, the vast amount of money to be made from the drug trade, in turn, has increased the trade in illegal firearms: Gangs once typified by switchblades and baseball bats now often outgun the police, commonly carrying AK-47 and Uzi assault weapons.

Modern youth gangs are not only better armed than their street-corner ancestors but also noticeably more violent and cruel. "When I was a kid and someone in the neighborhood was killed, they would talk about it for months," says Chicago police Lt. Frank Trigg. "Now when someone is killed, it's nothing. They seem to have lost the value of life." [2]

The everyday quality of gang murders — often provoked by seemingly trivial insults — intimidates average citizens in gang-dominated communities and schools. Not long ago, a 310-pound high school football player in Compton, Calif., stood passively as he was beaten by members of a local street gang; he was afraid to fight back because the gang has a reputation for killing its enemies. [3]

Though soured drug deals and neighborhood turf battles cause much of the publicized gang violence, police report that most gang-related homicides are random and spontaneous, often perpetrated by one gang member against a particular foe — or any member of the rival gang who happens along. Tragically, many victims of gang shootings are innocent bystanders. In 1989, only half of the victims of gang-related violence in Los Angeles had any connection to gangs. L.A. police reported 1,112 drive-by shootings in the county that year, accounting for 1,675 casualties.

Because gang members are usually young (ages typically range from

**October 11, 1991    755**

13-24) police can't easily monitor and control their activities. It's more difficult, for example, to plant an agent inside a gang than to infiltrate adult criminal groups. As Jerome H. Skolnick, a law professor at the University of California at Berkeley, points out, "You get to be known [in the neighborhood] when you're 14 years old." The juvenile status of most gang offenders also means they often receive relatively light sentences to correctional facilities.

The extent of the gang problem in any given city can be difficult to gauge. One thing that makes gang rosters hard to compile, experts point out, is the many levels of membership, ranging from hard-core leaders ("original gangsters," as gang founders are called) to part-timers, departed members, would-be members ("wanna-bes") and younger, aspiring members ("gonna-bes"). *(See glossary of gang terms, p. 758.)*

Regional and ethnic differences add to the risk of confusion. A 1989 Justice Department survey estimated that about 50 percent of the nation's gang members are black, 35 percent are Hispanic and the rest white or Asian.[4] University of Chicago sociologist Irving A. Spergel says minority youth who commit crimes are more likely to be assumed to be members of a gang, even though such white groups as the "skinheads" and neo-Nazis often commit the same crimes.[5]

Asian gangs present police with tremendous language and cultural barriers. Increasingly, highly mobile Chinese, Vietnamese, Laotian and Cambodian gangs (such as the Flying Dragons and the Ghost Shadows) are invading the homes of other Asians, raping and threatening to shoot women and children if valuables aren't surrendered. The Asian victims are mistrustful of the justice system and often fear that reporting the crimes will lead to retaliation.

In Los Angeles, the Hispanic barrio gangs and the black Bloods and Crips have developed complex subcultures, dress codes and rituals. *(See story, p. 767.)* In New York City, by contrast, the gangs are likened more to "pickup basketball teams." Unlike the gangs of the 1960s and the current Los Angeles gangs, a New York state task force recently wrote, "today's gangs are ... loosely organized and change constantly.... Violence or criminal activity can indeed happen anywhere at any time, and require only a requisite number of aggressive, disenfranchised youth and a target of opportunity." [6]

In Washington, D.C., which has one of the country's highest homicide rates and a serious problem with drug rings, police for years maintained that there were no traditional youth gangs with special names or turf. This September, however, Police Chief Isaac Fulwood Jr. announced that Washington's drug trade was now, in fact, being fueled by youth gangs using names tied to individual neighborhoods.[7]

The mercurial nature of gang membership makes it difficult to determine whether a particular assault, homicide, rape or auto theft was committed by an individual who happens to be in a gang, or by an individual acting *because* of his gang membership. Los Angeles uses a "broad and inclusive" definition of a gang incident and attributes 20-30 percent of homicides to gangs, according to Armand Morales, a psychiatry professor at the University of California at Los Angeles and an expert on gang behavior. Chicago, by contrast, uses a narrow definition, and gangs are said to account for only 10 percent of the city's homicides.

Police departments vary widely in their general approach to handling gangs. Special gang units of as many as 400 officers may be assembled in Chicago, for instance, while New York and Philadelphia designate fewer than 10 officers as gang specialists. As some critics point out, special gang units often help in attracting funding for law enforcement, but they also may exaggerate the problem and cause fear in the community.

In Tulsa, Okla., for example, police purposefully avoid "getting on the gang bandwagon," in the words of police Maj. Carolyn Kusler. "If there's a criminal, we'll go after the crime. If he did it with other people, we'll go after conspiracy," she says. But when police departments try random gang crackdowns, "any young black male wearing red is automatically suspect and is thrown up against a wall. We discourage that."

On the other hand, police can face criticism for denying a gang problem exists in the face of mounting evidence. Often it takes a galvanizing event to provoke action. In Columbus, Ohio, police organized a special gang unit in the mid-1980s after gang members assaulted the mayor's son at a high school football game and attacked the governor's daughter at a fast-food restaurant. In Boston, police began a crackdown in November 1990 after 19-year-old Hector Morales, a member of a Jamaican gang called the X-Men, was killed by police after he wounded two officers. And in Los Angeles, the extra funding and police manpower came in 1988 after a Japanese-American woman walking in the posh Westwood neighborhood was killed in black gang cross-fire.

In the 1950s and '60s, the primary approach to the gang problem was intervention: trying to prevent youngsters from joining gangs or using social services to work with gang members themselves. In the 1970s and '80s the emphasis changed to police suppression. According to University of Chicago sociologist Spergel, "there is no clear evidence that either approach was successful." [8] As the latest efforts to tackle the gang problem take shape, here

# Cities Under Attack

*In a survey conducted for the Justice Department in 1988-89, 21 major U.S. cities were linked to "chronic" gang problems (shown by a dot) and 24 cities were identified as having "emerging" gang problems (shown by a square). Since the survey, says lead researcher Irving A. Spergel of the University of Chicago, the number of cities coping with gang problems probably has doubled.*

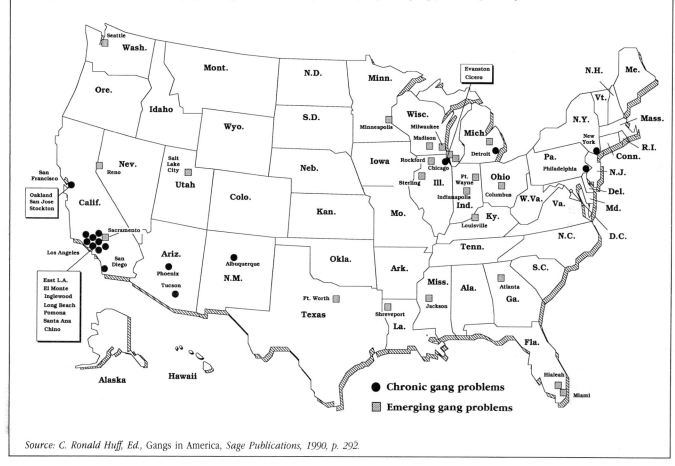

● Chronic gang problems
▨ Emerging gang problems

*Source: C. Ronald Huff, Ed.,* Gangs in America, *Sage Publications, 1990, p. 292.*

are the issues on which the outcome will hinge:

### Why do young people join gangs?

"Gangs don't have membership drives," says Léon Bing, author of *Do or Die*, a new book of interviews with Los Angeles gang members. "Kids drift toward gangs. Organizations like the Crips and the Bloods are the only option. There is no Little League in Watts. There are no programs. Those streets are stultifying. And there's no way for kids to get out their natural aggression." [9]

Classic social theory holds that gangs appeal to kids in low-income, inner-city neighborhoods beset by poverty, racial strife, broken families and meager job opportunities. That such conditions are widespread today is amply documented by the news media, by such scholars as University of Chicago sociologist William Julius Wilson, author of *The Truly Disadvantaged: The Inner City, the Underclass and Public Policy* (1987), and by gang specialists.

Recent field studies in Brooklyn and Milwaukee point to the rise of gangs in areas where the rapid loss of manufacturing jobs during the 1980s produced a segmented labor force, with whites dominating bet-ter-paying positions and minorities trapped in low-wage jobs, welfare and the illegal, underground economy.[10] With today's higher unemployment, says Washington State University criminologist James F. Short, fewer young men "grow out of" gangs than was the case 20 and 30 years ago.

"Many people here have no jobs, no responsibility, nothing to do but stand on the corner and get into trouble," laments the Rev. Jerry Kroeger, pastor of St. Basil/Visitation Catholic Church in Chicago. "When they do not have education, they try to show their power in other

# A Glossary of Gang Slang

**Act hard:** to act tough

**Basehead:** cocaine addict

**To 'dis someone:** to show disrespect toward someone

**To be down:** to do right for your gang, to protect your turf

**Gangbanging:** hanging out with gang members

**Getting a body:** killing

**Gonna-be:** youngster likely to join a gang

**Good from the shoulders:** good at fighting

**Greasy mitt:** car thief

**To head up:** to fight someone one on one

**Hemmed up:** to be hassled or arrested by the police

**'Hood:** neighborhood, turf

**Homeboys:** fellow gang members

**To jack someone:** to rob someone

**Jacket:** a record or reputation within the gang or in police files

**Jumped in:** initiated into a gang

**Kickin' it:** relaxing with your gang members

**Nation:** a league of gangs spread throughout a city

**Mad-dogging:** staring someone down

**Make a move:** commit a crime

**Old head:** experienced gang member

**Original Gangster (OG):** founding member of a gang

**Rep:** reputation

**Set:** the gang

**Sagging:** wearing pants very low on hips

**Shanking:** knifing

**Shot callers:** gang leaders

**To smoke someone:** to shoot someone

**Snaps:** money

**Sock-eye:** a strong fighter

**Strawberry:** a girl who gives sex for drugs

**Take him out of the box:** to kill a rival

**Wanna-be:** youngster who hopes to join a gang someday

ways." [11] Gang members themselves make the same point. "When you join a gang you feel like somebody," said a Los Angeles gang member. "Especially in South-Central, people feel like if you're not a movie star or a professional sports player, you not nothing. . . . So a gang, it like gives you something." [12]

Because gangs also show up in middle-class areas, however, poverty alone doesn't account for their attraction. Growth in gangs historically has coincided with surges in immigration. "When any ethnic group was at the bottom, they formed gangs — the Jews, the Irish, the Italians," notes Larry Rawles, deputy director of the Crisis Intervention Network, a Philadelphia social service program. [13]

"Youths in recently immigrated families want friends and find them quickly in gangs that share similar cultures," write psychologist Gerhard Kohn and retired Long Beach, Calif., police officer Carroll Shelly. "With the housing shortage in Southern California, families crammed into small dwellings have made the streets a more desirable place to be and a living room for many of the youths from these families." [14]

On a personal level, it is also clear that gangs provide companionship, training, activities, protection and a sense of belonging. "So much of what gangs build on is based on adolescent development, the tension between dependence and independence, rebellion, the need to be connected, the need for approval from peers," says David Dawley, who as a community organizer in the 1960s worked with Chicago's Vice Lords gang and now chairs the National Center for Gang Policy in Bethesda, Md. "At age 13 or 14, parents lose control to the peer structure, and the peer culture in the inner city is in the street."

Research has shown that many gang members come from fatherless

households. The gang "was a second family in a sense," a gang member told a reporter. "My mother was working a lot. I was always with [the gang], basically spending more time with them than at home." [15]

The elaborate culture and secret folklore that accompany the criminal acts of many gangs can be seen as typical of the adolescent need for rebellion and the tendency to magnify the notoriety of neighborhood heroes. "Movements of collective defiance," write sociologist Jack Katz and anthropologist Daniel Marks, "initially draw young people by their cultural power: dress and hair styles, distinctive walks and favorite music, a semiotics of graffiti and hand signals and a shared store of historical events that may be recounted endlessly." [16]

In the adolescent peer group in many communities, gang members are envied because, proverbially, they get the girls. Asked by a Michigan State University criminologist whether she would date a boy who was not in a gang, a Detroit teenager replied: "If a guy ain't got no crew, he probably ain't got no cash. Guys with no paper don't interest us." [17]

There is also a more general peer pressure. "A kid who doesn't want to [join] still has to be friendly with the gang," said a Boston youth worker. "He's got to respect those kids, show concern, not turn up his nose at them." [18] Sometimes the peer pressure leaves the realm of pressure and enters the realm of threat. In Chicago last year, a 14-year-old boy got a phone call from a gang leader asking him if he wanted to get involved in drug dealing. As politely as he could, the boy refused. "Well, then," the gang leader asked, "who's going to fight for you?" [19]

For many young people, hanging out with the gang is simply a fun way to formalize a sense of peer brotherhood. Asked what being a "homeboy" meant to him personally, a San

Francisco gang member told researcher Dan Waldorf that the key is "being down," or sticking up for fellow gang members. "It means I am down for him and he down for me and my partners and my buddies. Just like any social group, that is the way we are."

A less sympathetic view of why kids join gangs is offered in a pamphlet published by the Chicago Police Department. "Simply put," it says, "the hard-core gang member is a loser. Lacking recognition in the family, school athletics or employment, the member seeks the acceptance, support and protection of other losers and cowards."

### Are youth gangs making the nation's drug problem worse?

Few would deny that American youths commit an alarming share of the nation's crime. (See chart, p. 760.) Where experts are deeply divided, however, is on the degree to which youth gangs contribute to those crimes — particularly those associated with illegal drugs. "Kids who are into violence do the same whether they're in gangs or not," says Rutgers University criminologist Jeffrey Fagan. "Wearing [gang] colors may make them more newsworthy."

Certainly the public's current impression of a national gang crisis is, in part, the product of extensive news media coverage given to such dramatic events as drive-by shootings and the government's War on Drugs. But some experts argue that the media exaggerate the criminal role of gangs.

Martín Sánchez Jankowski, a sociologist at the University of California at Berkeley and author of a new book recounting his years researching and living with gangs, says reporters overemphasize the violent nature of gangs. He quotes an Irish gang member in New York City: "When we do an interview with a reporter, we act out as crazy as we can and as mean as we can because that way we get to send a message to everybody who might want to come into our neighborhood and try something that if we catch them they ain't going to be given any mercy." [20] Others have noted that gang members often seek out reporters, and that many keep scrapbooks of clippings about their exploits.

Experts seeking to replace anecdotal impressions with hard data on gang crime have produced inconclusive results. A 1989 study by the RAND Corporation's Peter Reuter, who has written widely about drug trafficking, said the question of how much the drug problem is the result of gangs could not yet be answered. On the one hand, Reuter wrote, gangs appear to be more interested in flamboyance and establishing a highly visible identity than they are in maintaining the discretion needed to operate successfully in the drug trade. On the other hand, the neighborhood roots of the gangs and their reputation for coercive violence make effective tools for a drug ring to use to intimidate potential informants.

The view that gang organizations facilitate drug trafficking — and thus send crime to other cities around the country — is advanced most prominently by Berkeley's Skolnick. He bases many of his conclusions on interviews conducted with gang members in California prisons in the late 1980s. Skolnick distinguishes between the "cultural gang" and the "entrepreneurial gang," between gangs formed to protect neighborhoods and provide adolescent male cohesiveness and gangs more strictly designed as criminal drug-trafficking organizations.

Chicano gangs, for example, "have a history that predates involvement with contemporary drug trafficking," he notes. "For these gangs, drug selling is usually an incidental feature of gang life. Traditional gang values of machismo and being a 'warrior for the barrio' still appear to dominate."

The entrepreneurial gangs, by contrast, have established elaborate hierarchical organizations made up of members who often eschew drugs themselves on the ground that being "high" hinders effectiveness in doing business. Bound together by business considerations, Skolnick says, these "professionalized" gangs, many of whom are black, often tap into networks of kin in other cities, establishing new markets and using local gangs for protection from police. In Los Angeles, such gangs often funnel the proceeds of drug sales into legitimate businesses such as car washes, beauty parlors and automotive stores. These gangs, the argument goes, are a chief cause of recent increases in drug crime.

USC sociologist Klein disputes Skolnick's view. Klein's researchers have combed arrest records in Los Angeles County and the city to gauge the proportion of drug offenders who belong to youth gangs. Their research showed that "while the cocaine business was increasing dramatically and gang members were becoming more involved, they were not becoming a larger proportion of all who were involved; rather, there is evidence of increasing non-gang presence even in gang-involved cases." [21]

Skolnick says that by relying only on arrest records, Klein fails to factor in the presumably high numbers of drug dealers who have not been arrested precisely because their gang membership helps them avoid police. Klein counters that one could also assume just the opposite: that the arrest records overcount the proportion of gang drug dealers because gang members who commit crimes are more visible to police and hence are more likely to be arrested.

Many police chiefs have adopted Skolnick's view of drug-inspired mi-

# Murder on the Rise

*National statistics on youth crime are not broken down between gang-related and non-gang-related crimes. But among youths under 18, one of the crimes most often associated with gangs — murder — has been rising for several years, after a steep decline in the early 1980s. As the nation's gang problem worsens, criminologists estimate that 70 percent of youth crimes are committed by only 7 percent† of the nation's youths.*

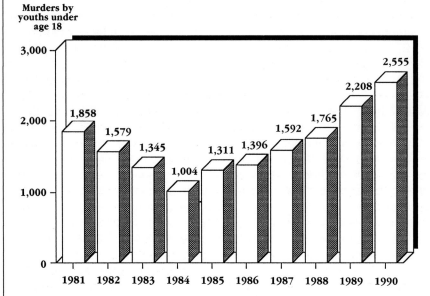

**Murders by youths under age 18**

1981: 1,858
1982: 1,579
1983: 1,345
1984: 1,004
1985: 1,311
1986: 1,396
1987: 1,592
1988: 1,765
1989: 2,208
1990: 2,555

† *National School Safety Center,* Gangs In Schools: Breaking Up Is Hard To Do, *1990.*
*Source: FBI Uniform Crime Reports*

gration of gangs. They note that the cocaine that comes into the United States (mostly from Colombia) is now so plentiful in Los Angeles that gangs can transport it to other cities and sell it at five or six times the L.A. price. Gangs with links to L.A.'s Bloods and Crips have been reported in 48 states.

Many observers, however, say the migration issue has been exaggerated. People in other cities use Los Angeles gangs as a "scapegoat" for the problem of home-grown gangs, says Steve Valdivia, executive director of Community Youth Gang Services in Los Angeles.

"Cultural symbols and associations run through our culture very fast through music and television," says gang expert Dawley. "There are Crips in Portland that can't find Los Angeles on a street map and Vice Lords in Columbus or Cleveland who have never been to Chicago and who would never let a Chicago Vice Lord come in and tell them what to do." Certainly, few if any L.A. Crips and Bloods have been spotted in such longtime gang cities as San Francisco or New York, quite likely because they are put off by the tough local gangs that are already in the drug game.

Arguing against the notion that gang violence is traceable to drugs are statements by many gang members that violence is a bad idea because it brings publicity and hence police. In September 1990, Los Angeles County Sheriff Sherman Block told a gathering of educators that the misconception that drugs are the chief motivator for gang violence has hobbled police efforts to combat the problem. "The cause for the majority of the violence is pure and simple: fascination and excitement,

coupled with deep-seated hatred of one gang for another," Block said.[22]

Whether or not gangs exacerbate the drug problem, students of gang problems say that the arrival of drugs definitely has altered the gang scene. A gang member told Skolnick's researchers: "The big change that came, came in 1984. That's when the drugs started hittin' the street, [and] everybody got into it. Back in the old days it was like everybody was together, like a big, old family. Now ever since the drugs hit the street, everybody wants to go their own way, forget about the neighborhood. ... People get a lot of money, [and] sometimes the homeboys get jealous and stuff ... and sometimes my own homeboys take from the homeboys."

### What remedies to the gang problem work best?

This summer, when the city of Chicago appointed veteran police official Robert Dart to buck up the police department's Community Concentrated Gang Enforcement Unit, he declared: "It is my philosophy that we attack gangs on two levels. We cut the leadership head off and remove them from the community while we beleaguer and attack the body and legs of the creature."[23]

Chicago's get-tough policy, while acknowledged as necessary, competes with a widening array of additional approaches to the gang problem. Among them: preventing kids from joining gangs, redirecting existing gangs into positive activities and trying to alter the socioeconomic conditions in which gangs breed. All of these alternatives require help not just from police but from schools, businesses, social service agencies and community and political leaders.

The most common method used by cities with gang problems remains suppression through law enforcement. It was cited by 44 percent of officials responding to a 45-city Justice Department survey conducted in 1988-89. *(See map, p. 757.)* The least-tried approaches, the survey showed, were those that rely on community mobilization and providing new social opportunities for gangs. Interestingly, the least-tried approaches were rated as the most effective.[24]

The law enforcement approach concentrates on eliminating a gang's leadership. The pamphlet published by the Chicago police describes the rationale for this approach: "The leadership is directly related to the character and number of members of the gang. The core members, whose entire ego is involved in the gang's identification, are generally the most violent members. ... The marginal or fringe members drift in and out of the gang according to their needs. These members lack direction and, unlike the hard-core members and leaders, can be positively influenced to a constructive role in society."

In the endless debate over what works best, police work or social work, the new consensus is that both approaches are needed. "We have to prevent more kids from getting into gangs while addressing the hard-core leaders," says Carol Behrer, associate commissioner of the federal Family and Youth Services Bureau in Washington, which administers a grant program in gang prevention. "As we like to say, to empty the bathtub, you both turn off the tap and pull the plug."

In the law enforcement area, officials battling gangs have won new powers in recent years. In September 1988, then-California Gov. George Deukmejian signed a legislative package that gave police such tools as the ability to seize arrestees' drug-related assets and suspend their driving privileges. The package also added a new law to the California penal code: the Street Terrorism Enforcement and Protection Act

(known as the STEP Act). It allows local district attorneys who determine that a particular gang is involved in criminal activity to distribute a letter to gang members warning them that such a determination has been made. If these individuals are later convicted of a crime, the STEP Act provides what are called "enhancers" — additional penalties for gang membership — that can tack on up to five extra years in prison.* California officials report that the STEP Act has improved their opportunities for keeping gang criminals off the streets. (In one instance, a gang member who received his letter from a district attorney crumpled it up and tossed it away, resulting in an arrest for the less-than-macho crime of littering.)

In Tulsa, Maj. Kusler reports that the police made progress by educating district attorneys about enforcement problems with gangs. Several years ago, Tulsa police noticed that they had arrested a lot of gang members for drive-by shootings but that the shootings continued. It turned out, she said, that the district attorney's office was dismissing many of the cases because the victims were declining to press charges, preferring instead to get even with their enemies by themselves. By bringing once-reluctant witnesses into the DA's office, Kusler said, they were able to prosecute enough offenders to disrupt the economy of the local drug business. "It took 8-9 months to put a lid on it," she says, "but finally the gangs came into our office to say, 'We quit.'"

Other promising new approaches, according to sociologist Spergel, involve "vertical case management," which both prosecutors and probation officers can use. Typically, a repeat offender during his crime ca-

---

*Laws directly banning gang membership have not withstood court challenges on civil liberties grounds.

reer deals with an ever-shifting staff of prosecutors or probation officers. Under the vertical method, the same official is assigned to the same repeat offender to provide a continuity that may enhance prospects for breaking the offender's crime pattern.

In the social services arena, programs to get gang members into jobs or back into school are reported to be most effective when they employ gang peers as counselors and therapy for family members. A psychologist's recent study in Long Beach, Calif., (home to 9,000 gang members) reported a 92 percent rehabilitation rate using such counseling.

One of the great success stories has been Philadelphia's House of Umoja (Unity), an African-American community shelter and counseling center that was given credit for much of the gang decline in the City of Brotherly Love in the 1970s. Founded in 1969, Umoja provided job placement and sporting events for gang members and arranged a major summit meeting in 1974 to stop violence among rival gangs. (It has since been folded into the city government gang program.)

In Los Angeles, the city-funded Community Youth Gang Services, founded in 1981, organizes graffiti cleanup teams, provides job placement and sponsors sporting events between gangs (the "midnight basketball" program schedules games at times that drug deals ordinarily occur). In late 1986, the agency negotiated what was called the December Season of Peace meeting, in which 125 members of 52 L.A. street gangs, mostly Hispanic, gathered at a church to forge a truce for the Christmas holidays.

In many cities with gang problems, community groups — including clergy, political activists, parents of gang members and ex-gang members — have patrolled the streets with walkie-talkies to monitor gang activity. They must strike a balance between the need to earn the trust of gangs and the need when trouble looms to relay information to police. The use of former gang members in social work and on neighborhood patrols has raised questions about whether ex-offenders can be trusted. But Lt. Bob Ruchhoft, a gang specialist with the Los Angeles police, says their contribution to peace-keeping is invaluable. "You cannot hire people born and raised in the middle class to go into these neighborhoods," he says.[25]

Officials have had some success in focusing on schools, where they have recommended aggressive steps to discourage gang recruiting. One of the most important tactics is to remove gang graffiti as soon as it appears, according to a handbook published by the National School Safety Center, a group sponsored by the Justice and Education departments that works with Peppardine University in Malibu, Calif.

But overly tough measures will not remove gangs from schools, according to Alan McEvoy, a sociologist at Wittenberg University in Springfield, Ohio. He recommends establishing the school as a neutral zone for rival gangs while recognizing the unique ethnic or social-class characteristics of each gang. He discourages the practice of suspending students who are gang members, arguing that they will simply hang around and encourage peers to drop out.

McEvoy also says schools should consider giving gangs a measure of legitimacy if gang members agree to take on school-approved tasks or roles. Offering gangs certain resources and privileges — a faculty adviser, access to facilities, even a limited share of school funds — "is a way for the school to channel group behavior in positive directions and to define goals for the group," he writes.[26]

Channeling gangs in a positive direction is the approach used by the Boys & Girls Clubs of America. Its nationwide network of 1,100 recreation and youth centers operates a "targeted outreach" program, which recruits "at-risk" youngsters as well as established gang members to provide a constructive peer community that offers the same prestige, excitement and camaraderie as gangs. It has been cited by Congress as one of the most effective anti-gang efforts.

The issue of conferring legitimacy on gang culture has long been the subject of debate. The notion is favored by California sociologist Jankowski, who points out that the gangs he lived with offer escort services, help people move or give poor families money. "They offer the neighborhood protection. They're like a volunteer militia," he says.

Similarly, David Dawley, who spent two years with Chicago's Vice Lords, says he "would rather use the positive characteristics of gangs to redirect behavior than try to eliminate them. Certainly the idea of colors raises fear when we associate them with certain gangs, but it sells tickets when we're talking about the Fighting Irish of Notre Dame." The challenge, he adds, is to "have some programs that compete with the street. You have to start with where people are, not where we want them to be."

The legitimizing approach, however, meets understandable resistance from observers who've long associated gang names and colors with violent crime. Police often resent probation officers or counselors who become too closely identified with gang members. Sociologist Klein says he once favored legitimizing gangs but changed when data began to show that a certain proportion of delinquency is caused by gang cohesiveness. "The recognition of names and territories increases identity and cohesiveness and helps recruiting so that the gang gets larger," he says. ■

# BACKGROUND

## Gangs Through History

The youth gang phenomenon dates back at least to St. Augustine (A.D. 354-430), who wrote in his *Confessions* of the pleasures of stealing pears in the company of his adolescent accomplices: "My pleasure was not in those pears, it was in the offense itself, which the company of fellow sinners occasioned." [27]

Records of life in 17th-century London mention youth gangs with such names as the Mims, the Bugles and the Dead Boys who terrorized the citizenry by breaking windows, destroying taverns and fighting, each group wearing different-colored ribbons.

Those early English gangs gave rise to the modern era's "Teddys." They have counterparts in Japan (the Mambos), Germany, (Halbstarke), Italy (Vitelloni), South Africa (Tsotsio) and France (Blousons Noirs).

In the United States, the first recorded youth gang was the Forty Thieves, founded in about 1825 in New York's Lower Manhattan. Others appeared in Philadelphia in the 1840s, growing out of volunteer fire departments. Taking such names as the Bouncers, the Rats and the Skinners, they defaced walls with graffiti and carried pistols and knives.

Also in this period, the waves of Irish immigrating to New York soon begat such gangs as the Bowery Boys and the Dead Rabbits, who waged three-day rumbles that forced help-

*Continued on p. 764*

# Chronology

**1920s** *Chicago becomes the nation's gang capital during Prohibition; Mexican immigrants form first Hispanic gangs in barrios of Los Angeles; Eastern and Southern European immigrants continue flocking to ethnic enclaves in New York City that gave rise to many gangs.*

### 1927
Criminologist Frederick M. Thrasher publishes first major study of gangs.

---

**1950s** *Southern blacks migrate to Northern inner cities; classic era of teen street gangs counseled by social workers; wave of Puerto Rican immigrants arrives in New York City.*

---

**1960s** *Gangs take on traits from civil rights, Black Muslim and radical youth movements; government channels some gangs into anti-poverty work.*

### 1961
President John F. Kennedy signs the Juvenile Delinquency and Youth Offenses Control Act creating a federal committee to address youth crime.

### 1965
Blacks riot in the Watts section of Los Angeles causing 34 deaths and $40 million in damage; riots also occur in other cities beset by gangs, including Detroit, Chicago, New York and Newark.

### 1967
President's Task Force on Juvenile Delinquency calls for community efforts to curb youth crime; Senate probes fraud in federal grant program for Chicago's Blackstone Rangers gang.

---

**1970s** *Police officials and academics shift their strategies on gangs from social work to suppression and control.*

### Aug. 21, 1974
Congress passes Juvenile Justice and Delinquency Prevention Act creating a federal Office of Juvenile Justice and Delinquency Prevention.

### 1975
Justice Department's first attempt to survey gang problem nationally.

---

**1980s** *Los Angeles takes its place as gang capital of the nation; crack cocaine arrives in inner cities; Reagan administration declares war on drugs.*

### 1982
FBI officially designates outlaw motorcycle gangs as a national investigative priority within its organized crime program.

### 1985
California creates a State Task Force on Youth Gang Violence; Los Angeles Police Chief Daryl F. Gates vows to eliminate gangs in five years.

### 1988
President Reagan signs Anti-Drug Abuse Act; California convenes a State Task Force on Gangs and Drugs; Los Angeles cracks down with sweeps through gang neighborhoods.

### May 15, 1989
Bush administration announces ban on imports of semiautomatic assault weapons used by many street gangs.

---

**1990s** *Gang membership continues to rise; federal, state and local governments organize with police, social workers and academics to coordinate comprehensive approach to the gang problem.*

Continued from p. 762

less police to call in the Army. Their nonchalance toward violence was remarkable: A member of the Plug Uglies is said to have seized a stranger on the street and cracked his spine in three places just to win a $2 bet.[28] Female gang members also were known in the mid-19th century. Hellcat Annie and Battle Annie earned reputations as tough street fighters.[29]

New York gangs in this period were not above selling their services to labor unions and company operators maneuvering in the rough and tumble world of politics. "By 1855," a city historian wrote, "it was estimated that the Metropolis contained at least 30,000 men who owed allegiance to gang leaders and through them to the leaders of Tammany Hall and the Know Nothing, or Native American Party."[30] During the Civil War, Irish gang members were blamed for the anti-conscription riots in which many blacks were lynched.

The arrival of German and Italian immigrants in the late 19th century produced equally violence-prone gangs, some of whom would commit crimes for hire; a slash on the cheek with a knife cost $10, throwing a bomb, $50, and murder, $100. Social reformer and photographer Jacob Riis, a concerned observer of these early New York gangs, wrote: "It might be inferred that the New York tough is a very fierce individual.... It is only when he hunts with the pack that he is dangerous."[31]

By the turn of the century, Jewish gangs and Chinese gangs had been added to the ethnic stew in New York's Chinatown and in such rough neighborhoods as Hell's Kitchen on the West Side. In the 1920s, with Prohibition the law of the land, youth gangs in many cities became involved with adult bootleggers. In Southern California, waves of Mexican immigrants arrived to form the first barrio gangs.

But the worst gang problems at this time were found in Chicago. Criminologist Frederick M. Thrasher in 1927 published the first major book on the problem, *The Gang: A Study of 1,313 Gangs in Chicago*. He described Polish, Irish, Anglo-American, Jewish, Slavic, Bohemian, German, Swedish, Lithuanian, black, Chinese and Mexican gangs. "The gang is a conflict group," Thrasher wrote. "It develops through strife and warfare." He pointed to some success in turning cohesive gangs into Boy Scout troops.

The ethnic character of American gangs continued to manifest itself. In the 1930s, the rising numbers of blacks migrating from the South to New York, as well as new immigrants from the British West Indies, set up the first rivalries among black gangs. In the early 1940s, U.S. servicemen stationed in Southern California clashed violently with gangs of Hispanic youths in the so-called Zoot Suit Riots, after a clothing style popular among Hispanics.

It was after World War II, when Americans began to move from farms to cities, that the classic gang era began. The first "teenage" subculture emerged in the postwar period, and gangs severed their earlier ties to adult organized crime. In Los Angeles, two black gangs called the Businessmen and the Home Street Gang appeared. It was during the 1950s that CBS News correspondent Edward R. Murrow drew nationwide attention to the conditions that produce gangs with his documentary "Who Killed Michael Farmer?" about the death of a handicapped young man at the hands of a Bronx street gang.

Society's response to gangs was typified by the detached-worker program of the New York City Youth Board. It sought to reduce gang tensions by building long-term relationships with gang members and by sponsoring dances or athletic con-

tests. "Participation in a street gang or club," a 1950 Youth Board document read, "like participation in any natural group, is part of the growing-up process.... Within the structure of the group the individual can develop such characteristics as loyalty, leadership and community responsibility.... Some gangs ... have developed patterns of anti-social behavior.... Street members can be reached and will respond to sympathy, acceptance, affection and understanding when approached by adults who possess those characteristics and reach out to them on their own level."[32]

## Efforts at Respectability

In the 1960s, the Hell's Angels motorcycle gang gained national exposure and greatly influenced the younger, more ethnic gangs in cities. "By 1965," wrote counter-culture journalist Hunter S. Thompson, later of *Rolling Stone* fame, "[gangs] were firmly established as All-American boogeymen." At the same time, the decade's civil rights movement, urban riots and radical politics spilled over into the world of gangs, particularly among blacks, many of whom would become attracted to revolutionary groups such as the Black Panthers. With President Lyndon B. Johnson's War on Poverty, millions of federal grant dollars were pouring into inner cities, and some criminal youth gangs decided to join the Establishment.

In New York City in 1967, leaders of the Puerto Rican gang Spartican Army decided they wanted a role in bettering the social and economic conditions of their Lower East Side neighborhoods. Borrowing from Johnson's Great Society rhetoric, they took the name the Real Great Society and applied for a grant from

Continued on p. 766

# Gangs on Film: A Legacy of Violence

Gangs create their subculture from many sources — members' ethnic heritage, peers, popular music, television — but clearly one of the most powerful influences is the movies. It wasn't long after "The Godfather" hit the theaters in 1972 that a Detroit gang began calling itself the Corleones, after that movie's Mafia family.

Impressionable gang members across the country pick up mannerisms and names from Los Angeles movie gangs, says Steve Valdivia, executive director of Community Youth Gang Services in Los Angeles. And sometimes they pick up more than that. From "Blackboard Jungle" in 1955 to this year's "New Jack City" and "Boyz 'n the 'Hood," big-screen violence often has translated into real violence outside the theaters.

Rapper Ice Cube portrays a gang member in "Boyz 'n the 'Hood," a film about black youths in Los Angeles. (Photo © 1991 Columbia Pictures)

Humphrey Bogart starred in the first major American street-gang film, "Dead End," about a hardened criminal who returns to his decrepit New York neighborhood and is resented for setting a bad example for local youth. The 1937 film launched the careers of Leo Gorcey and other actors dubbed the Dead End Kids (also called the Bowery Boys). The following year, Spencer Tracy and Mickey Rooney starred in "Boys Town," in which a trouble-maker living at a boys' rehabilitation community returns to New York and gets entangled with his brother's gang.

In 1954, the prototypical image of the American motorcycle gang was established with the "The Wild One," starring Marlon Brando as the leather-jacketed leader of the Black Rebels. When a girl in the film asked Brando's character what the Rebels were rebelling against, his famous reply was: "What have you got?" That theme continued the following year with another Hollywood milestone, "Rebel Without a Cause," starring James Dean.

The year 1955 also brought the most controversial gang film of all, "Blackboard Jungle." It starred Glenn Ford as a high school teacher confronted by Vic Morrow and Sidney Poitier as inner-city toughs who are tamed only when their allegiance to their gang leader is broken. The film was widely criticized for what many saw as sensationalized violence (some movie theaters issued disclaimers assuring patrons that no such violence could be found locally). Frightened civic leaders couldn't have predicted that the near-riots that did result from "Blackboard Jungle" were actually inspired by the film's use of Bill Haley and the Comets' song "Rock Around the Clock," the first rock soundtrack ever.

Gang dramas became a B-movie staple for the rest of the '50s and early '60s (typical were such titles as "High School Hellcats" and "Devil's Angels"), before culminating in 1961 with the most enduring gang film of all, "West Side Story," based on the stage play. Starring Natalie Wood and Richard Beymer, the Romeo and Juliet story set in New York City portrayed the era when street workers tried to cure gangs of their "social disease." Lyrics sung by the white gang (the Jets) and their Puerto Rican rivals (the Sharks) are still quoted by today's gang members, though some actual gang members scoff at the fictional toughs who sang "Deep down inside us there is good!"

The 1970s crop of gang films mostly recalled the earlier days. The 1974 release "The Lords of Flatbush" (starring Sylvester Stallone and Henry Winkler) was a nostalgic musical set in the 1950s, while "The Wanderers" in 1979 portrayed New York City's ethnic gangs at the time of the assassination of President John F. Kennedy (1963). Also in 1979, actual violence was reported following showings of "The Warriors," the story of a charismatic hood who's killed while trying to organize all New York gangs into an army against police. The same year, the Los Angeles gang scene was portrayed in "Boulevard Nights," the tale of a young Chicano who tries to break away from street life but is lured back by his brother.

In the 1980s, the new visibility of gangs and violence fueled by the drug trade spawned a rash of gang movies. In 1981, "Fort Apache, The Bronx," starring Paul Newman, explored the ethnic tension and poverty that breed gangs. Notable in 1988 was "Colors," starring Sean Penn and Robert DuVall, which told the story of two cops in grim black neighborhoods of Los Angeles. The L.A. police and others warned that it glorified violence and would cause trouble. "It's almost like a how-to movie," said Curtis Sliwa, founder of the Guardian Angels. A gang member in Stockton, Calif., was shot and killed while standing in line to see the film.

In 1991, two major gang films appeared, and both led to violence and canceled screenings. "New Jack City," written and directed by blacks, attracted large numbers of blacks with its story of a cruel drug lord and his showdown with a New York City cop. It caused riots in several cities and one death. In July came "Boyz 'n the 'Hood," regarded as a poignant portrayal of the misery permeating gang neighborhoods. Despite a pacifist message, its opening caused riots, two deaths and a reported 30 injuries.

The recent wave of gang films shows no signs of cresting. A major film on Hispanic L.A. gangs, "American Me," is due out in January, and director Oliver Stone is also developing a film about Los Angeles' Crips.

Continued from p. 764
the federal Office of Economic Opportunity (OEO). They were turned down, but their well-publicized efforts (profiled in *Life* magazine) did attract private foundation money. They opened a Real Great Society nightclub, a child-care service and a leather goods store, all of which blossomed briefly but failed within a year.[33] They then organized summer classes for inner-city youths and finally won an OEO grant.

By this time, gangs in other cities had begun the quest for War on Poverty dollars. The Real Great Society joined with the Vice Lords (Chicago), the Mission Rebels (San Francisco) and the Sons of Watts (Los Angeles) and other gangs to set up Youth Organizations United, an anti-poverty organization with headquarters in Washington.

In Chicago, meanwhile, another experiment in gang respectability was under way. In 1967, the Blackstone Rangers, led by a fervent black nationalist named Jeff Fort, began toying with the notion of doing anti-poverty work with a radical white clergyman named John Fry. Fry was affiliated with a community organizing group named for Chicago's Woodlawn neighborhood. Because this group opposed Chicago's powerful mayor, Richard J. Daley, its anti-poverty programs had never received federal grant money, over which Daley had de facto control. But the prospective turnaround of the Blackstone Rangers changed the picture. In June 1967, the OEO awarded the Woodlawn Organization and the Blackstone Rangers $927,000 to operate anti-poverty programs for one year.

Daley was furious at fellow Democrats in the Johnson administration, but he did not have to fume for long. The Woodlawn program quickly became known to the public as a monumental failure.[34] Only 76 of 800 participants in its jobs program got

jobs. Bookkeeping was lax. Gang members were heard to encourage each other to quit school and be paid from the federal grant, and many of them clearly reveled in the national publicity being given their gang. At the same time, the Blackstone Rangers, continually harassed by Chicago police, continued their violent feud with the rival Disciples. By the fall of 1967, Jeff Fort had been arrested on murder charges.

In Washington, Sen. John L. McClellan, D-Ark., chairman of the Government Operations Committee, held widely publicized hearings about the Woodlawn grant. Many blamed the OEO for poor judgment. While under indictment, Fort appeared as a witness but refused to speak. (The murder charges against him were later dismissed.) In May 1968, OEO shut down the Woodlawn project, just weeks after the Blackstone Rangers were given credit for keeping Chicago relatively calm during the urban riots that followed the assassination of the Rev. Dr. Martin Luther King Jr. The idealistic notion of giving government money to reformed gang members had suffered a crippling blow.

### Roots of Today's Violence

The impact of Chicago's gang experiment during the days of the War on Poverty would be felt for decades.

Chicago gang members continued to receive foundation money for nearly 20 years. Jeff Fort was sentenced to prison in the early 1970s for fraud committed with the OEO grant. In prison, he converted to Islam and changed the Rangers' name to El Rukns (Arabic for "the Foundation").

When he and other El Rukns emerged from prison in the late 1970s, they were "meaner and tougher than ever," in the words of David Dawley, and they threw themselves into the violence of the drug trade. Dozens were sent to prison in the early 1980s. In 1987, Fort was charged with conspiring to commit terrorist bombings around the United States on behalf of Libyan leader Muammar el-Qaddafi. Today, Fort is in prison for drug trafficking, where, with his right to use a telephone, he continues to run the El Rukns.

In August 1991, the Chicago homicide rate hit a record annual high of 609, as gangs from the feuding People and Folk "nations" continued their violence apace. In response, Mayor Richard M. Daley recalled the gang grant scandal from the era when his famous father ran City Hall. The younger Daley lashed out at the liberal "social workers" of the 1960s and '70s who had "coddled" teenage gang members who today, as adults in their 40s, are the kingpins of Chicago's drug trade. ■

# CURRENT SITUATION

## Spending to Fight Gangs

"Violent street gangs have been identified as a priority for funding and program development," declares U.S. Assistant Attor-

ney General Jimmy Gurulé. Before his appointment in 1990 to head the five Justice Department bureaus with jurisdiction over youth gangs, Gurulé spent four years as an assistant U.S. attorney in Los Angeles, where he saw firsthand the city's efforts to thwart gang violence.

Gurulé says the Bush administration has realized that the War on Drugs alone, with its emphasis on tougher law enforcement, will not

Continued on p. 768

# A Dossier on Gang Subcultures

In trying to understand and control youth gangs, investigators and scholars have assembled what amounts to anthropological studies of gang characteristics. Police files record everything from the fact that the Crips in Los Angeles wear blue while rival Bloods wear red to intricate details of the Satanic rituals and grave desecrations committed by white gangs known as "stoners" or "heavy metalers." These and other rituals make it clear that youth gangs are far more than mere social clubs or business organizations — they are highly developed subcultures.

A key determinant of a gang's culture is the neighborhood, known by blacks and Hispanic gang members as "the 'hood." Hispanic gangs, especially, identify strongly with their "barrios," swatches of land often sandwiched between freeways and railroad tracks in which the same gang might have lived and fought for several generations.

The nature of the 'hood can make a difference in how police approach gang crime. Hispanic gangs that sell drugs are more likely to consummate deals with friends and acquaintances inside selected shops, restaurants or apartments, according to San Francisco gang researcher Dan Waldorf. Doing business this way requires police to have insider knowledge — to know a gang's secret hand signals, for example. Black gangs, by contrast, usually make sales out in the open, often to strangers, in front of housing projects or small stores.

A gang's name also reveals much. Names are often designed to inspire fear (as in New York City's Savage Nomads), to boast about a gang's modus operandi (Miami's Mazda Boys steal Mazda cars) or to celebrate the gang's street or housing project (as in the Main Street Crips or the 11-Deuce Hoovers, in the neighborhood of 112th and Hoover Streets in Los Angeles).† In many cities, police seek to avoid publicizing the names of gangs because, as Boston police spokesman Scott Gillis said, "It gives them undue notoriety."

The dress codes and colors provide further evidence that gangs are determined to thrive in their own cultures — gang members persist in wearing their distinctive colors even though it helps police keep track of them. Today's gang members frequently wear baggy khaki pants riding low on the hips, patterns shaved into their heads, a single glove or earring and shoelaces laced to one side or the other. They also sport bandanas and colored rags hanging from their back pockets. Many have cigarette burns on their hands to signify courage, while others display knife cuts. Tattoos are popular with black gangs. Some members wear rapper-style sunglasses and "cake cutter" combs with sharp metal tines.

Quite often they wear expensive sneakers (the BK on British Knights sneakers means "Blood Killer" to the Crips). Hats and jackets with the names of rival professional football teams have been known to provoke fights between gangs. Asian gangs are known to color and spray their hair in bizarre styles, a disguise that can be altered quickly by the wind as their speeding car leaves the scene of a crime.

Graffiti, as Los Angeles Police Chief Daryl F. Gates has said, "is the essence of gang membership, the essence of gang fear." For many gangs, the act of marking graffiti is a declaration of control of a neighborhood. Defacing a rival gang's graffiti can provoke deadly retaliation. Common images in graffiti include pitchforks, guns, dollar signs, profanity and sometimes the name of a targeted shooting victim. Hispanic graffiti is characterized by stylized, three-dimensional or block lettering with serifs. Black graffiti, L.A. police say, has fewer flourishes.

Gang culture can be highly ceremonial. Many gangs have daunting initiation rites that require an aspiring member to steal a car, fight the gang's leaders or participate in a drive-by shooting. Gang marriage ceremonies have also been recorded; one in New York City involved the sharing of blood from knife cuts and the pouring of a can of beer over the the couple's heads. At gang funerals, a booklet with photos and a rhyming tribute to the deceased is often distributed.††

Though the vast majority of gang members are male, many gangs have female associates, and there are some all-female gangs. (Los Angeles is said to have 20-30 female gangs.) Female gang members often hide and protect male members, or carry concealed weapons or narcotics for them, police say, because they are less likely to be searched. They also cater gang parties. Gang girls are often the objects of fights between jealous rival gangs. They are sometimes used as sexual lures, and are often expected to provide sex to multiple gang members.

Female gang members are often teen mothers with drug problems who, faced with the alternative of prostitution, use gangs to support themselves. Though they are increasingly as prone to fighting as male gang members, females continue to play a secondary role in most gangs. As a 19-year-old male Hispanic gang member from Santa Ana said: "We're the ones who take care of the 'hood; we protect them. They ain't got nothing to say." ‡

---

† The origin of the name Crips is uncertain. One theory traces it to the comic book "Tales from the Crypt." Another says it is short for kryptonite, the comic book mineral that can kill Superman, and a third says it is short for cripple, as the gang's original members in 1969 were said to have been handicapped.

†† See Anne Campbell, *The Girls in the Gang* (1984), p. 23.

‡ Quoted in James Diego Vigil, *Barrio Gangs* (1988), p. 102.

Continued from p. 766
solve the gang problem. He is eagerly pursuing three initiatives: 1) a national field study to hold hearings and hear testimony from police and community leaders in cities affected by gang crime; 2) a "weed and seed" program, in which neighborhoods with the worst gang problems will have their law enforcement intensified to "weed out" gang leaders followed by a "seed" program of economic development, prevention and education; and 3) a three-year, $8 million Justice Department partnership with New York University, the Ford Foundation and the Pew Charitable Trusts to produce a national long-term strategy for prevention of youth gang crime.

Gurulé and the administration, however, are at odds with Sen. Joseph R. Biden Jr., D-Del., chairman of the Judiciary Committee. When the Senate this July passed its version of a major crime bill, Biden made sure it included authorization for $100 million to provide formula grants to states and local governments for a major education, prevention and treatment effort involving youth gangs and youth drug sales. (A similar plan passed the Senate in 1990 but died.) In introducing his bill in June, Biden attacked the Justice Department's "lack of leadership," noting that the president's budget had called for slashing the Office of Juvenile Justice and Delinquency Prevention from $72 million to $7.5 million.

Gurulé says the administration opposes Biden's anti-gang grant program. "It's an oversimplification that more money is the answer," he says. The fate of the plan lies with the House, which is considering its own crime bill this fall. A version that passed the Judiciary Committee Sept. 26 did not include Biden's plan. It did, however, include several gang-related measures, such as a new federal penalty for drive-by shootings and funds for "midnight basketball" programs.

It also included a provision to stiffen the sentences for offenders convicted of state or federal crimes if the offender committed the crime on behalf of or in association with a criminal street gang. The plan, originally introduced by Rep. Esteban E. Torres, D-Calif., who counts many gangs in his Los Angeles district, carefully avoids violating constitutional rights to freedom of association.

The House crime bill also includes a proposal by Rep. Charles B. Rangel, D-N.Y., to provide federal grants to promote "community policing." Already in use in New York City and elsewhere, the approach moves away from the use of highly specialized police officers working on gang and drug problems in isolation and instead regularly sends officers out into the same neighborhoods to maintain relations with local citizens.[35]

## Coordinating Approaches

The U.S. Health and Human Services Department (HHS), meanwhile, is awaiting a House-Senate conference to learn whether the Youth Gang Drug Prevention grant program run by its Administration on Children, Youth and Families will see its funding cut to half of last year's amount. The authorization bill calls for $15 million to renew grants to some 83 state and local organizations that do research, organize neighborhood coalitions and provide counseling to families troubled by gangs. A House Appropriations subcommittee, however, has sought to divert some $7 million to programs for child development and runaway youths.

This year's authorization of the program includes what are called "consortium grants," which divide up funds from the same grant among diverse public and private community groups and state or local agencies. The effect, a House aide says, is to bring law enforcement people into contact with community groups, creating essential new links between people working to combat gangs.

This notion of multi-agency efforts against gangs is exactly what is missing from the current federal effort, according to sociologist Spergel. The social agencies reach out only to young people, yet don't provide jobs and schools, he notes. At the same time, the police say they need community collaboration, but they're interested in information on gangs, not providing gang members with jobs. "We've got to loosen the roles of these people," Spergel says. He calls for a collaboration between the Education, Labor, and Housing and Urban Development departments in addition to Justice and HHS. The Office of Juvenile Justice is supposed to coordinate interagency efforts, Spergel says, but it is weak.

Spergel's views are shared by many in the National Governors' Association, which organized, with the Justice Department, the state of Nevada and the National Criminal Justice Association, a national conference this October in Reno to compare notes on the country's myriad strategies for approaching the gang problem. Similarly, the National Association of Counties, which has repeatedly called for boosts in funding for programs under the Juvenile Justice and Delinquency Prevention Act, this year passed a resolution calling on Congress and the administration to create a national "front-end" policy that invests in long-term *preventive* programs for troubled youth, one that would include shelter, education and employment.

Assistant Attorney General Gurulé agrees with the criticism that there

Continued on p. 770

# At Issue:

## Is tougher law enforcement the best solution to the youth gang problem?

### DARYL F. GATES

*Chief of Police, City of Los Angeles*
FROM *THE POLICE CHIEF*, NOVEMBER 1990.

*j*ust as there is no single solution to the ills of society, there appears to be no single solution to the gang problem. Many "tried and true" law enforcement tactics have met with limited and rather temporary success. However, there is no question that strict enforcement of all applicable laws to curtail gang activity, as well as a commitment to a complete prosecution policy, are absolutely essential. . . .

Many experts agree that a key factor in the elimination of gang violence is prevention. But it is also true that prevention programs need time to work. Their impact can be measured only through a long-term reduction in the number of gang members. Consequently, law enforcement strategies directed toward stopping the violence remain the primary tool in our battle against street gangs. When the influence of narcotics trafficking and the lure of vast amounts of money are added to current levels of street gang activity, the violence is magnified. This type of behavior is most difficult to deter and adds unrelenting responsibilities to the few hundred officers currently assigned the primary duty of combating the gang problem.

Perhaps the greatest obstacle is the inability of an overburdened criminal justice system to effectively prosecute and incarcerate convicted gang members for the length of time necessary to have an impact on the problem. The courts and jails are so inundated with cases and arrestees that the system has become a revolving door for criminals. Jail overcrowding is so acute that only the most recalcitrant and violent offender spends appreciable time in custody. Most of the arrested gang members are returned to the streets to prey on the community and rival gang members. Probation lacks sufficient penalties to deter criminal activity, since a violation simply puts the criminal back through a system that is still unable to hold him.

Law enforcement and social agencies cannot assume total responsibility for addressing gang violence. The solution must be rooted in the gang-infested neighborhoods. Gangs do not survive in areas where the citizens unite and work with law enforcement against gang activity.

The battle against gangs cannot be won overnight, nor can it be won by a half-hearted effort. However, concerted commitment from law enforcement, other governmental agencies and the community can begin to solve the gang problem and reduce the level of fear.

### REP. CHARLES B. RANGEL, D-N.Y.

FROM THE *CHICAGO TRIBUNE*, APRIL 4, 1991

*d*espite the pervasiveness of drug-related gang activities throughout the United States, the problem is treatable. By employing well-balanced, community-based, anti-gang programs, some cities have succeeded in abating and preventing the spread of drug-dealing gangs.

Columbus, Ohio, for example, addressed its nascent gang problem with a two-tiered approach that is gaining national recognition. The city of Columbus began by recognizing the need for a law-enforcement unit specializing in gangs. The police needed to institutionalize a method for sharing information with many disparate community and government organizations. Next, the city introduced a parallel prevention program based on community outreach to youth. By emphasizing close contact between police, schools, the juvenile courts and youth outreach programs, the city involved law enforcement with the prevention process.

The youth gang/drug problem needs this kind of coordinated, inter-agency approach to thwarting gang activities while preventing youths from becoming involved in gangs and drugs. Government programs are most effective when they recognize the root causes of drug use and gang participation; young people need to feel they have opportunities. Gang members have the potential and desire to leave the streets if they are shown the pathway out.

The federal government can support community efforts to stop gangs and drugs. I have recently introduced the Community Police Partnership and Drug Abuse and Crime Prevention Act of 1991 to help police become involved in helping young people avoid criminal activities. By developing mentor relationships between law enforcement and youths, improving police accessibility to neighborhood information and expanding access to needed social services, community/police partnerships can help reduce crime, including youth involvement in gangs and drugs.

Youth gangs' involvement with drugs is yet another manifestation of our country's dire need to focus more attention on young people before they get sucked into addiction and crime. The first step to curing any ailment is to recognize the problem. The cities and towns that have confronted their gang/drug phenomenon succeeded in diminishing drug-related gang activity. We must recognize this development on a national level by providing federal assistance while maintaining decision-making power at the community level.

Continued from p. 768
hasn't been enough coordination on solving the youth gang problem. "The millions to fund the War on Drugs has not had an impact," he says. "It's a learning process."

An example of this inability to coordinate can be found in the status of the proposal, favored by Spergel and other gang specialists, for a national computer data base on gangs. Sen. Dennis DeConcini, D-Ariz., has introduced the Outlaw Street and Motorcycle Gang Control Act of 1991, which would make the federal

Bureau of Alcohol, Firearms and Tobacco the keeper of a national gang analysis center. (BATF agents arrest many youth gang members on federal firearms possession charges.) The legislation would facilitate shared access to the 140-odd crime data bases maintained around the country, relieving the overburdened Los Angeles police from having to provide gang data to police in other cities. The DeConinci bill is stalled, sources say, because the FBI, which has elaborate data bases of its own, sees it as a "turf" problem. ∎

"finding jobs for the good people," not the "bums. They ought to go to prison." [37]

Skolnick sees more reason for hope. "These kids are dangerous to themselves and to others, but they're still kids," he says. "We can shape them." Innovative approaches to leading young people away from gangs have borne fruit in many cities. Since 1982 the San Francisco-based Breakthrough Foundation has run a Youth at Risk program to combat gangs, drug abuse, the school dropout problem and teen suicide. Now working in 28 cities, its volunteer counselors have taken more than 1,800 children with police records on out-of-town retreats and then followed their cases for a year. They report great success in job placement and in lowering repeat offenses.

# OUTLOOK

## Reasons for Optimism

In the Boston suburb of Randolph, a disco club has been holding dances since last year at which a strict dress code is enforced. Worked out in cooperation with youth gang specialists among local police, the policy bans jeans, sneakers, T-shirts, sweatshirts, sweatpants and hats and stipulates that all boys wear shirts with collars. The Massachusetts branch of the American Civil Liberties Union (ACLU) said the rules were constitutional as long as they were clearly intended to maintain security at the dance. "But if it becomes a ruse for keeping out blacks or any other groups that are protected under civil rights laws," said the ACLU's local executive director, John Roberts, "that would be something else." [36]

The civil liberties issues that arise with the gang problem represent only a fraction of the obstacles society faces in the search for large-scale solutions. "Gangs are a byproduct of things going on with respect to the inner city, the urban underclass and isolation," says USC's Malcolm

Klein. "It's an impossible thing to tackle. We can't change the whole American economic system."

"It really is a macro problem," agrees Berkeley's Jerome Skolnick. It's one thing to give gang members cultural counseling to change their values, he says, "but it's hard to say you ought to go work when there's not much work."

Efforts by legislatures and city councils to create jobs programs for gang members often meet resistance because of tight budgets and the judgment that, with black and Hispanic unemployment already disproportionately high, former gang members are among the least attractive to employers. "Gang members are not interested in challenges," says Stephan Fleisher, executive director of the San Fernando Valley Child Guidance Clinic. "They reject school, they reject jobs because [jobs] are beneath them. They have a very superior conception of themselves, and that's what allows them to kill people, because they see themselves as above ordinary persons."

Los Angeles Police Chief Daryl F. Gates is more blunt: "There are plenty of jobs out there" for those who are willing to work, he has said. Efforts should be concentrated on

The Community Day Center in Bellflower, Calif., puts gang members in charge of providing exercise and entertainment to handicapped children. As the gang members' self-esteem improves, many of the high school dropouts have returned to graduate.[38] Since 1980 in Silver Lake, Calif., current and former gang members have participated in an annual ethnic street fair in conjunction with local gay activists. The event provides neutral ground on which members can meet people outside the narrow gang universe. "Some of our kids didn't know anybody besides their own neighbors," recalled a former gang member who now directs a community center there. "They didn't know how to socialize." [39]

Prominent among the people fighting back against gangs are mothers. As Patricia Patrick, director of an L.A. group called Mothers Against Gangs in the Community, said: "We came forth as citizens, concerned citizens and parents to address the issues of gang violence because we feel that the police, anybody that's in office, cannot conquer this problem alone, because it starts in the home."[40]

Celebrity role models also play a part. National Football League Hall of Famer and actor Jim Brown works with gang members in Los Angeles in a program he created called Amer-I-Can. It borrows the wisdom of self-reliance from such varied sources as black revolutionary Malcolm X and Alcoholics Anonymous. "Some nights you will come up here and you will see the baddest cats in the city . . . the brothers society says you cannot do anything with," Brown says. "Yet we know these young men with their negative power, if turned positive, can change our communities."[41]

Assistant Attorney General Gurulé says he's hopeful that gang violence can be reduced if there is close coordination between police and advocates of long-term prevention. Steve Valdivia of Los Angeles' Community Youth Gang Services says that "the neighborhoods are healable and the people salvageable" if politics are removed. If enough resources were directed in, he says, they could solve the problem in five to ten years.

The University of Chicago's Spergel also finds grounds for optimism in the long term. Look back in history, he says, and think of the gangs of Irish immigrants that fought police and militia in 19th-century New York, or the Jewish and ethnic gangs. The Asians, blacks and Hispanics, he points out, are still adjusting to the urban migration. "It's part of the American system," he says.

The solution to the gang problem may well remain elusive, if for no other reason than the fact that the gang phenomenon is a vicious cycle. In a California corrections facility last year, 13-year-old Henry, a Grape Street Crip from south-central Los Angeles, was doing time for shooting rival gang members from the nearby Florencia neighborhood. In-

side the institution, he met one of the enemy, 15-year-old Saoul, whom he had once shot at a park. "Say, ain't you from Grape Street? Didn't you shoot at me?" Saoul asked him.

After a silence, Henry recalled, they both started laughing. "He's a nice guy — you know, normal," Henry said. "We don't fight each other anymore, but I'll fight his friends."[42] ∎

# Notes

[1] Quoted in the *Los Angeles Times*, Jan. 16, 1991.

[2] Quoted in the *Chicago Tribune,* April 8, 1991.

[3] *The Wall Street Journal*, April 23, 1991.

[4] Information on the survey is reported in Irving A. Spergel and G. David Curry, "Strategies and Perceived Agency Effectiveness in Dealing with the Youth Gang Problem," *Gangs in America* (1990), C. Ronald Huff, ed., pp. 288-309.

[5] For background on the "skinheads" and neo-Nazi groups, see "Growing Danger of Hate Groups," *Editorial Research Reports*, May 12, 1989, pp. 261-276.

[6] *Reaffirming Prevention: Report of the Task Force on Juvenile Gangs*, New York State Division for Youth, March 1, 1990.

[7] See *The Washington Post*, Sept. 29, 1991.

[8] Irving A. Spergel and Ronald L. Chance, "National Youth Gang Suppression and Intervention Program," *National Institute of Justice Reports*, June 1991, p. 22.

[9] Quoted in the *Los Angeles Times*, Aug. 27, 1991.

[10] John M. Hagedorn with Perry Macon, *People and Folks: Gangs, Crime and the Underclass in a Rustbelt City* (1988).

[11] Quoted in the *Chicago Tribune*, April 8, 1991.

[12] Quoted in Jerome H. Skolnick, *Gang Organization and Migration*, State of California Department of Justice, p. 17.

[13] Quoted in *Gangs in Schools*, National School Safety Center, 1990, p. 11.

[14] "Juveniles and Gangs," paper presented at the 1991 annual convention of the American Psychological Association.

[15] Quoted in the *Los Angeles Times*, June 26, 1988.

[16] Column in *Los Angeles Times*, Jan. 25, 1989.

[17] *Harpers*, July 1990, p. 32, from the book by Carl S. Taylor, *Dangerous Society*, 1990.

[18] Quoted in *The Boston Globe*, July 14, 1991.

[19] Quoted in *The New York Times,* Jan. 4, 1990.

[20] Martín Sánchez Jankowski, *Islands in the Street* (1991), p. 306.

[21] Malcolm W. Klein, Cheryl L. Maxson and Lea C. Cunningham, "Crack, Street Gangs, and Violence." The paper is scheduled to be published in the Nov. 4, 1991, issue of *Criminology*.

[22] Quoted in *Los Angeles Times*, Sept. 20, 1990.

[23] Quoted in the *Chicago Tribune*, June 23, 1991.

[24] Spergel and Chance, *op. cit.*, p. 21.

[25] Quoted in *The New York Times Magazine*, May 22, 1988. p. 30.

[26] Alan McEvoy, "Combating Gang Activities in Schools," *Education Digest*, October 1990, p. 31.

[27] Quoted in Armando Morales and Bradford W. Sheafor, *Social Work: A Profession of Many Faces* (1989), p. 415.

[28] Haskins, *op. cit.*, p. 31.

[29] Anne Campbell, *The Girls in the Gang* (1984), p. 9.

[30] Quoted in Irving A. Spergel, "Youth Gangs: Continuity and Change," in *Crime and Justice: A Review of Research*, Michael Tonry and Norval Morris, eds., Vol. 12, 1990, p. 172.

[31] Quoted in James Haskins, *Street Gangs: Yesterday and Today* (1974), p. 48.

[32] Quoted in Haskins, *op. cit.*, p. 99.

[33] *Ibid.*, p. 112.

[34] See Nicholas Lemann, *The Promised Land* (1991), p. 245.

[35] For background on the community policing concept, see "Police Brutality," *The CQ Researcher*, Sept. 6, 1991, pp. 633-656.

[36] Quoted in *The Boston Globe,* April 8, 1990.

[37] Quoted in the *Los Angeles Times*, Aug. 18, 1988.

[38] *Newsweek*, May 7, 1990, p. 70.

[39] Quoted in the *Los Angeles Times*, June 1, 1988.

[40] California Council on Criminal Justice, State Task Force on Gangs and Drugs, Final Report, January 1989, p. 89.

[41] Quoted in the *Los Angeles Times*, Sept. 24, 1991.

[42] Quoted in *Time*, June 18, 1990, p. 50.

# Bibliography

## Selected Sources Used

### Books

**Campbell, Anne, *The Girls in the Gang*, Basil Blackwell Inc., 1984.**

A Rutgers University social psychology professor who lived with four female gang members in New York City analyzes gang phenomena from a feminist perspective.

**Haskins, James, *Street Gangs: Yesterday and Today*, Hastings House Publishers, 1974.**

An illustrated, popular-style history of street gangs throughout American history that shows similarities between gangs past and present.

**Huff, C. Ronald, ed., *Gangs in America*, Sage Publications, 1990.**

The most up-to-date anthology of writings on youth gangs by anthropologists, sociologists and criminologists who discuss the state of scholarship and policy issues.

**Jankowski, Martin Sanchez, *Islands in the Street: Gangs and American Urban Society*, University of California Press, 1991.**

An insider's account and analysis of the gang phenomena by a sociologist who lived and fought alongside street gangs in Los Angeles, New York and Boston. He examines why some gangs thrive while others die out.

**Vigil, James Diego, *Barrio Gangs: Street Life and Identify in Southern California*, University of Texas Press, 1988.**

A University of Southern California anthropologist examines the roots and culture of Hispanic gangs.

### Articles

**Spergel, Irving A., "Youth Gangs: Continuity and Change," *Crime and Justice: A Review of Research*, University of Chicago Press, 1990.**

A comprehensive tour of current issues involving gangs by the sociologist who is principal investigator for the Justice Department's National Youth Gang Suppression and Intervention Program.

**Morales, Armando, "Urban Gang Violence: A Psychosocial Crisis," *Social Work: A Profession of Many Faces*, Allyn and Bacon, 1989.**

A historical overview of the gang phenomena and gang behavior with an emphasis on their treatment by the mental health profession.

### Reports and Studies

***Gangs in Schools: Breaking Up is Hard to Do*, National School Safety Center, Pepperdine University Press, 1990.**

A handbook of analysis with quotations from school administrators and law enforcement officials about how gangs threaten schools and what is being done about it.

***National Institute of Justice Reports* 7, No. 224, June 1991.**

Two gang-related articles appeared in this issue of the Justice Department monthly, one reporting on a 45-city survey of anti-gang efforts and another detailing the Bush administration's efforts at solving the gang problem.

***Reaffirming Prevention: Report of the Task Force on Juvenile Gangs*, New York State Division for Youth, March 1, 1990.**

A survey of gang membership and characteristics around the state of New York that includes recommendations on improving existing programs and launching new ones.

***State Task Force on Gangs and Drugs*, Final Report to the California Council on Criminal Justice, January 1989.**

This analysis of the gang problem in the state with the largest gang problem offers strategic recommendations for action. Margins contain substantive quotations from dozens of observers of gangs.

# The Next Step

## Additional Articles from Current Periodicals

### Case studies

**"Straight outta south-central,"** *Newsweek,* July 1, 1991, p. 63.

Comments on the work of Tracey Morrow, more widely known as Ice-T, the "thinking person's glorifier of gang violence." Title song to "O.G. Original Gangster," Ice-T's fourth album; comparison to N.W.A.

**"When you're a Crip (or a Blood),"** *Harper's Magazine,* March 1989, p. 51.

Recounts the conversation between Los Angeles gang members who talk about the world in which the drive-by killing is an admirable act. Description of the participants. INSET: A gangbanger's glossary.

**Barron, J., "Tourist-slaying suspects are tied to a gang of ritualistic muggers,"** *The New York Times,* Sept. 5, 1990, p. A1.

Reports that the eight black and Hispanic youths arrested in the fatal stabbing of a 22-year-old tourist from Utah in a midtown subway station belonged to a gang with a singular initiation ritual — would-be members had to mug someone to get in. The gang, FTS, is a racial and ethnic mix which, at its peak a couple of years ago, numbered 250.

**Barron, J., "Youth slain in gang fight outside a junior high school,"** *The New York Times,* Dec. 21, 1990, p. B1.

Reports that Michael Moore, 15, was killed and another teen-ager was wounded outside a Bronx junior high school when two teen-age gangs got into a fight 'about girls.' Details.

**Collier, A. "To deal and die in L.A.,"** *Ebony,* August 1989, p. 106.

Discusses drug dealing by gangs in the Los Angeles, Calif. area. Comments by Lt. Hourie Taylor of the Special Investigation Division of the Compton, Calif. Police Department; reasons why teenagers join gangs and sell drugs; comments by former gang members; reasons why they lift gangs.

**Hays, C.L., "Chinatown's old gangs give way to violence and fear,"** *The New York Times,* July 31, 1990, p. B1.

Discusses the recent surge in violence in New York City's Chinatown, which was once considered an oasis from many kinds of crime. Vietnamese gangs are blamed; Born to Kill gang.

**Kaihla, P., "'Violence is nice. Honestly,'"** *Maclean's,* May 22, 1989, p. 40.

Discusses youth gangs in Toronto, Ont. "Swarmings" (mass attacks on victims); Toronto discotheque called Club Focus; gangs called The Untouchables, The Markham Massive, The Goofs; Black or Jamaican "posses"; white gangs; gang violence at the Eaton Centre shopping area; comments by gang members.

**Lorch, D., "Mourners returned fire, police say,"** *The New York Times,* July 30, 1990, p. B1.

Discusses a shootout in a New Jersey cemetery. Mourners at a gang member's funeral apparently shot back at two or three men, believed to be from rival groups, who opened fire at graveside in what law-enforcement officials say is an escalating Chinatown feud.

**Morganthau, T., Beachy, L., et al., "New York's nightmare,"** *Newsweek,* Sept. 17, 1990, p. 35.

Reports on Brian Watkins, a 22-year-old tennis instructor from Utah who, after attending the U.S. Open tennis championships in Queens, was killed by a gang when he tried to protect his mother. Steady erosion of basic law and order in New York; murder suspects; Mayor Dinkins' response.

**Mydans, S., "As cultures meet, gang war paralyzes a city in California,"** *The New York Times,* May 6, 1991, p. A1.

Discusses the gang war going on in Long Beach, Calif., between Hispanic and Cambodian residents, two immigrant cultures with almost nothing in common except their attempts to build a new life in the same neighborhood. Since tensions escalated into war 18 months ago, more than 55 drive-by shootings have claimed victims. Fears of violence have nearly paralyzed the Cambodian population.

**Mydans, S., "Trophies from the gang wars: Wheelchairs,"** *The New York Times,* Dec. 6, 1990, p. A1.

Says that paralyzed young men in wheelchairs are one of the new signs of the gang warfare in Los Angeles. Tells how they are supported by their gang members who visit them in the hospital and offer them a surrogate family that will support them when they return to the streets.

**Shorris, E., "The priest who loves gangsters,"** *Nation,* Dec. 18, 1989, p. 737.

Describes the efforts of a young Jesuit priest, Gregory J. Boyle, to work with gang members in Los Angeles. Use of his church, the Dolores Mission, to provide an alternate lifestyle for the gangsters; gang members' experiences of police brutality and harassment; conflicts faced by Boyle in his work.

**Stanley, A. and Nachtwey, J., "All ganged up," *Time*, June 18, 1990, p. 50.**

Describes South Central Los Angeles where more than 500 gangs with some 80,000 known members infest Los Angeles county. Bitter rivals; 462 gang-related murders in 1988; drive-by shootings; hate isn't personal, it's an attitude; late teens and early twenties, but as young as ten or eleven; the enemies keep changing.

**Terry, D. "As many fall, project's survivors struggle on," *The New York Times*, Feb. 6, 1991, p. A1.**

Presents the last of three articles on life in the Martin Luther King Jr. Towers in Harlem. Tells about some of the people who have lived there for a long time and have survived the hard times, the gang fights, the closed factories, and the bitter disappointments that have fallen on them.

**Terry, D., "Youth gang gives a name to students' fear of crime," *The New York Times*, March 1, 1989, p. B1.**

Describes a youth gang in New York City called the Decepticons. Members mug high school students on their way home from school, stealing anything from their shoes to their earrings. Many students fear violence.

**Yalowitz, G., Robinson, L., et al., "Hong Kong shoot-outs," *U.S. News & World Report*, Oct. 1, 1990, p. 49.**

Discusses the recent resurgence of the Triad gangs, often recruiting children as young as 12, thought to be responsible for a wave of violent crime marked by armed jewelry heists, homicides, and Mafia-style gang wars in Hong Kong, where police fear the lawlessness will increase. Demoralized police force.

## Debates & issues

**"Selling fear to L.A.'s poor," *Newsweek*, Oct. 22, 1990, p. 33.**

Reports that Los Angeles' American National Insurance Co. and Golden State Mutual Life have been using fear tactics to sell policies to families with children at risk from gang- or drug-related violence. Agents from American National's Inglewood office are reportedly cashing in on the bloodshed by presenting clippings in troubled neighborhoods to persuade frightened families to buy $5,000 or $10,000 policies.

**Baker, S. and Gore, T., "Some reasons for 'wilding,' " *Newsweek*, May 29, 1989, p. 6.**

Discusses the teenage random crime called "wilding."

Gives examples of teen-gang-related attacks and suggests they stem from strained family relations, drugs, rock lyrics, videos, "slasher" films, and lack of adult responsibility.

**Bremner, B., "Murder on main street," *Business Week*, Jan. 14, 1991, p. 42.**

Reports that in 1990, once-safe smaller cities nationwide saw dramatic increases in drive-by shootings, gang rampages, and other violent behavior that was long the province of major urban centers. Example in Fresno, Calif.; fighting back with neighborhood watches and youth programs; why that kind of violence is spilling over into smaller communities; special drug courts to speed prosecutions; community-based policing; in for more mayhem.

**Byron, C., "Where have you gone Roger Maris?" *New York*, June 10, 1991, p. 20.**

Offers a nostalgic look at New York City as it was in the Summer of 1961, when gangs could be romantic, a la "West Side Story" and there was no crack, homelessness, or AIDS to eviscerate communities. Looks at the city's 1961 budget and compares spending then with spending now.

**Came, B., Gillies, L., et al., "Gang terror," *Maclean's*, May 22, 1989, p. 36.**

Examines the terror and violence caused by youth gangs in Canada's major cities. Forming along racial and ethnic lines, gangs include Asian, Latin American, black, and middle-class white youths. Skinheads; gang warfare; alienation of immigrant youths; comments by police and other experts; breakdown of traditional family and social values; comments by gang members. INSET: Death among the innocent, by A. Gregor (gang-related deaths in Los Angeles, Calif.).

**Hedges, S.J., "When drug gangs move to nice places," *U.S. News & World Report*, June 5, 1989, p. 42.**

Discusses the appearance of violent youth gangs in nice areas. Anti-gang campaign; growing crack trade; gang activity.

**Johnson, D., "Teen-agers who won't join when drug dealers recruit," *The New York Times*, Jan. 4, 1990, p. A1.**

Says that teen-agers everywhere contend with peer pressure to use drugs just to fit in. But in the inner city, where poverty and frustration can make a drug high seem all the more appealing, there is also the pressure of street gangs, whose threats can be more ominous than any anti-drug message. Examples.

**Monroe, S., "Complaints about a crackdown," *Time*, July 16, 1990, p. 20.**

Reports that minorities charge that the Los Angeles police department's war on gangs has become a war on their communities. Lawsuits claiming violations of civil rights; brutality suits against the sheriff's department; controversial bar-arm chokehold.

**Whitaker, C., "The new generation of the '90s," *Ebony*, August 1990, p. 29.**

Introduces a special 'Ebony' issue on the new generation of young black people who will come of age in the 1990s. Attitude towards the civil rights struggles of the past; social and economic perils such as drug addiction, gang warfare, etc.; new activism; rap music; generation at the crossroads; technological advances.

**Witkin, G., Hedges, S.J., et al., "Kids who kill," *U.S. News & World Report*, April 8, 1991, p. 26.**

Discusses the prevalence of youths killing with and being killed by guns. States that every 100 hours, more youths die on the streets than were killed in the Persian Gulf. Focuses on several youths who have been killed within the last year by youths with guns; the reasons why youths feel the need to carry a gun; the gang connection; easy access to the purchase of guns; the schools crack down; violence prevention; more.

## *International aspects*

**Kaihla, P., "'Imprisoned' prostitutes," *Maclean's*, March 25, 1991, p. 24.**

Discusses the networks of brothels, often disguised as massage parlors, which are run by Asian gangs in such Canadian cities as Toronto, Vancouver, and Calgary. Importation of young women from Hong Kong, Malaysia, Thailand, etc.; brutal conditions; Chinese gangs, such as the Dai Huen Jai, or Big Circle Boys.

**Wilson-Smith, A., "Gang warfare, Soviet-style," *Maclean's*, May 22, 1989, p. 44.**

Discusses teenage gangs in the Soviet Union. The "Lyuberi," a gang from the Lyubertsy suburb of Moscow; gangs in the city of Kazan; gangs in other cities; consumer-oriented youths; black market activities; reaction of Soviet officials.

## *Mass media coverage*

**"Let's take back our streets," *Ebony*, April 1991, p. 106.**

Proposes various solutions to the nation's crime and drug problems. Reprinted from the book "Let's Take Back Our Streets," by Reuben Greenberg, the first black police chief in Charleston, S.C. Drug gangs; how to deal with drunk drivers; penalties for crime; how individual citizens can help.

**"'New Jack City' film shows new approach to drugs and gangs," *Jet*, March 11, 1991, p. 54.**

Examines 'New Jack City' a movie that reportedly takes a fresh look at inner city drugs and gang problems. Description of term 'New Jack'; appearance of black stars in movie; comments by director and star Mario Van Peebles; comments from star Wesley Snipes; film debut.

**Collier, A., "'Boyz 'n The 'Hood' shows how danger, pain and love make men out of boys," *Jet*, July 15, 1991, p. 56.**

Describes the debut film on gang violence from filmmaker John Singleton, "Boyz 'n The 'Hood." Story of three boys' lives as young teens; positive aspects of black males; comments by actor Cuba Gooding Jr.; screen debut of rapper Ice Cube; messages of film.

**Mahurin, M., "Do or die," *Rolling Stone*, July 11, 1991, p. 72.**

Presents an excerpt from the book "Do or Die," by Leon Bing, which is the first-ever inside account of day-to-day life among the rival Los Angeles gangs, the Bloods and Crips.

## *Prevention*

**McEvoy, A., "Combating gang activities in schools," *Education Digest*, October 1990, p. 31.**

Summarizes some of the measures schools and communities have taken to address gang problems, and how some measures inadvertently made matters worse.

**Monaghan, P. "Summer programs at Portland campus aims to help poor teen-agers steer clear of gangs' violence," *The Chronicle of Higher Education*, Aug. 15, 1990, p. A23.**

Describes a summer program at the Cascade campus of Portland Community College which pays students to attend, and has 16 students identified by school counselors, police gang units or other agencies as at risk of becoming involved with gangs. Improving writing and math skills; facing the hazards of growing up poor; keeping track of the students through high school.

**Reinhold, R., "In the middle of L.A.'s gang war," *The New York Times Magazine*, May 22, 1988, p. 30.**

A street-smart diplomatic corps, that includes former gang members, aims to defuse tensions and steer kids away from joining gangs. They work for Community Youth Gang Services, an agency funded by the city and county of Los Angeles, Calif.

# Back Issues

*Great Research on Current Issues Starts Right Here... Recent topics covered by The CQ Researcher are listed below. Issues dated before May 10, 1991, were published under the name of Editorial Research Reports.*

**APRIL 1990**
How Fair is the Tax Burden?
Workers' Compensation
U.S. Pacific Forces
Curbing Insurance Premiums

**MAY 1990**
Should Teaching Be a Profession?
Will Canada Fall Apart?
Is U.S. Patent System Outdated?
Federal Funding for the Arts

**JUNE 1990**
Downsizing America's Armed Forces
Progress In Weather Forecasting
S & L Bailout
Bio-Chemical Disarmament

**JULY 1990**
Do Americans Still Love Marriage?
Death Penalty Debate
Decline of Rural America
United Nations in the 1990s

**AUGUST 1990**
Democracy in the Philippines
Initiatives: True Democracy?
Hard Times at Newspapers
Teens Balance School & Jobs

**SEPTEMBER 1990**
Dangers of Alcohol
Western Alliance After the Cold War
Tobacco Industry
Right to Die

**OCTOBER 1990**
Organ Transplants
Energy Policy Options
Search for Arab Unity
Child Support

**NOVEMBER 1990**
Lotteries and Gambling
Post Cold-War Choices
Setting Limits on Medical Care
Multicultural Education

**DECEMBER 1990**
Cable TV Regulation
Americans' Search For Their Roots
Is Insurance System a Failure?
Why Schools Still Have Tracking

**JANUARY 1991**
Growing Influence of Boycotts
Should the U.S. Reinstate the Draft?
America's Archaeological Past
Peace Corps' Challenges in '90s

**FEBRUARY 1991**
Regional Impact of Recession
Puerto Rico's Status
Redistricting: Mapping Power
Nuclear Power

**MARCH 1991**
Acid Rain
Cost of the Gulf War
Reassessing Gun Laws
Future for Man in Space

**APRIL 1991**
Social Security
Canadian Crisis Over Quebec
California Drought
Electromagnetic Radiation

**MAY 1991**
School Choice
Racial Quotas
Animal Rights
U.S. and Japan

**JUNE 1991**
Children and Divorce
Teenage Suicide
Endangered Species
Europe 1992

**JULY 1991**
Teenagers and Abortion
Soviet Republics Rebel
Mexico's Emergence
Athletes and Drugs

**AUGUST 1991**
Sexual Harassment
Fetal Tissue Research
Oil Imports
The Palestinians

**SEPTEMBER 1991**
Police Brutality
Advertising Under Attack
Saving the Forests
Foster Care Crisis

**OCTOBER 1991**
Pay-Per-View TV

Back issues are available for $4.00 (subscribers) or $7.00 (non-subscribers). Quantity discounts apply to orders over ten. To order, call Congressional Quarterly 1-800-432-2250.

# Future Topics

▶ *Gene Therapy*

▶ *World Hunger*

▶ *Fast-Food Business*

# THE CQ Researcher

PUBLISHED BY CONGRESSIONAL QUARTERLY INC., IN CONJUNCTION WITH EBSCO PUBLISHING

# Gene Therapy

## Scientific advances raise searing ethical and legal questions

I
F A DISEASE IS CAUSED BY FAULTY GENES, THEN why not just replace the bad ones with normal genes? That's the seductive idea behind gene therapy, a conceptually simple way of treating everything from hereditary disorders such as cystic fibrosis to more common ailments like heart disease. Now, after years of clinical tests in animals, scientists actually are inserting genes into people. But experts say formidable technological hurdles still remain and that it may be years before there are practical medical applications. In the meantime, the Human Genome Project is unleashing a flood of information about our genetic makeup that raises wrenching ethical and legal questions. Ethicists say that choosing where to draw the line between alleviating suffering and controlling human destiny will be one of society's most daunting challenges in the 1990s.

$C_Q$  **October 18, 1991 • Volume 1, No. 23 • 777-800**

*Formerly Editorial Research Reports*

COVER PHOTO: NATIONAL INSTITUTES OF HEALTH

# CQ Researcher

October 18, 1991
Volume 1, No. 23

**EDITOR**
Sandra Stencel

**MANAGING EDITOR**
Thomas J. Colin

**ASSOCIATE EDITOR**
Richard L. Worsnop

**STAFF WRITERS**
Charles S. Clark
Mary H. Cooper
Rodman D. Griffin

**PRODUCTION EDITOR**
Laurie De Maris

**EDITORIAL ASSISTANT**
Thomas H. Moore

**GRAPHICS**
Jack Auldridge

**PUBLISHED BY**
Congressional Quarterly Inc.

**CHAIRMAN**
Andrew Barnes

**VICE CHAIRMAN**
Andrew P. Corty

**EDITOR AND PUBLISHER**
Neil Skene

**EXECUTIVE EDITOR**
Robert W. Merry

**PUBLICATIONS MARKETING/SALES**
Robert Smith

**EDITOR, EBSCO PUBLISHING**
Melissa Kummerer

The CQ Researcher (ISSN 1056-2036). Formerly Editorial Research Reports. Published weekly (48 times per year, not printed the first Friday of any month with five Fridays) by Congressional Quarterly Inc., 1414 22nd St., N.W., Washington, D.C. 20037. Rates are furnished upon request. Application to mail at second-class postage rates is pending at Washington, D.C. POSTMASTER: Send address changes to The CQ Researcher, 1414 22nd St., N.W., Washington, D.C. 20037.

# Gene Therapy

BY RODMAN D. GRIFFIN

## THE ISSUES

On Sept. 14, 1990, a 4-year-old girl in the Clinical Center at the National Institutes of Health (NIH) in Bethesda, Md., made medical history. With a simple blood transfusion, she became the first human patient to receive gene therapy. Normal by any obvious standard, the brave little girl with brown hair and big dark eyes lives under a genetic curse. She suffers from adenosine deaminase (ADA) deficiency, a rare, incurable and deadly genetic disease that results from the lack of a gene that regulates production of an enzyme needed to keep the immune system functioning properly. It is the same disorder that in 1984 claimed the life of David, a 12-year-old boy who had become famous as the "Bubble Boy" because he spent most of his life in a plastic chamber to protect him from infection.

This little girl, whose name is withheld at the request of her parents, may be more fortunate. After a year of gene therapy, her immune system is beginning to produce the white blood cells necessary to ward off infection. She is now attending kindergarten and taking ice-skating lessons. For the first time in her life her parents feel she can interact with other children without the risk of infection.

The medical procedure itself was hardly awe-inspiring. In a 30-minute blood infusion, the child received about 1 billion blood cells that had been outfitted with copies of the gene she lacked. That was it. But if the technique works, and doctors are "extraordinarily encouraged," the results could be little short of miraculous. She may eventually begin to lead a normal life, without need for

the costly and only partly effective drug now used to extend the lives of young victims of the disease.

The landmark experiment, led by Dr. W. French Anderson, a pioneering advocate of gene therapy, and Drs. R. Michael Blaese and Kenneth Culver, raised the curtain on what some experts believe will be a new era in medicine, when many previously incurable genetic diseases will be contained or even conquered. "This is not Buck Rogers stuff for 50 years from now," says Anderson, "but a technology that is successfully under way right now."

"The genetics revolution will change medicine more in the next 20 years than it has changed in the past 2,000," predicts Dr. Leroy Hood, a molecular biologist at the California Institute of Technology. Although ADA deficiency afflicts fewer than 60 people worldwide, recent studies indicate that many more common disorders, such as heart disease, high blood pressure, diabetes, some cancers and even alcoholism are genetically linked — and

may eventually be targets for gene therapy.

The era of genetic medicine is upon us. Indeed, last January Dr. Steven Rosenberg, chief of surgery at the National Cancer Institute at NIH, began using gene therapy to treat patients with advanced skin cancer. And this month, three more clinical trials for human gene therapy were approved by the NIH Recombinant DNA Advisory Committee (RAC), the principal review body that must approve all federally funded experiments with altered DNA. Two of these trials involve genetically engineered vaccine for cancer patients, and the other involves genetic treatment for patients with a severe form of high cholesterol that can lead to heart attacks in children.

The long-term impact of these efforts on society could be enormous. Approximately 5 percent of the infants born in the U.S. are afflicted with often debilitating and sometimes fatal genetic diseases. In most cases, no effective treatment exists for these disorders, which are caused by one or more faulty or missing genes among the estimated 50,000 to 100,000 genes in human DNA. Even more frightening, one out of every four people will contract cancer, which last year claimed more than half a million Americans.

The object of gene therapy, simply put, is to provide the body with healthy genes that can fulfill the role of defective ones. "Gene therapy is actually a sophisticated drug-delivery system," Anderson explains. "Anything given now by injection, you can engineer the patient's own cells to pump out. The advantage is that eventually it will be a one-time treatment." The idea is to insert particular genes into genetically normal cells so that they can produce a therapeutic protein.

October 18, 1991   779

It all sounds rather straightforward, but medical researchers will have to overcome some formidable technological barriers before gene therapy becomes commonplace. Delivering replacement genes to particular cells, inserting them into the correct place in the DNA of those cells and then coaxing the genes to function properly are goals that still often elude scientists.

And there are risks. If a gene is accidentally spliced into a vital segment of the cell's DNA it could disrupt the functioning of another critical gene. Or it might activate a nearby oncogene, a gene that can initiate the growth of a tumor. Transplanted without other genes that regulate the function of that gene, the new gene might order the production of too much or too little of a protein, with unforeseen consequences.

The ability to tinker with genes will reach deep into the fabric of society, affecting law, ethics and personal choice. Until now, the technology has been so limited that it hasn't created serious alarm. Testing couples and fetuses with a family history of hereditary disease is becoming standard practice. But what if the gene map becomes much more detailed, leaving almost nothing to chance? And what if gene therapy becomes widely accessible, not only for an array of diseases but also to prevent allergies, to induce growth or to enhance intelligence?

Over the next decade, the Human Genome Project, a multibillion-dollar, international effort to understand the language of human genetics, will unleash a torrent of information about human nature — everything from predisposition to disease to hair color to shoe size. *(See story, p. 787.)*

Questions are just starting to arise about who will be privy to genetic information, whether individuals will know who has access to their genetic makeup and how such data

will be used. The dilemmas could be acute, given that for many diseases a bad gene doesn't guarantee that the affliction will develop but is merely an indicator that it might. Make too much of that, ethicists warn, and "defective" genes could be used to justify unwarranted discrimination. Insurers might deny coverage, for instance, and employers might withhold jobs.

As more and more scientists queue up to perform clinical trials for human gene therapy, here are some of the questions being asked:

## Is it ethical to tamper with human nature?

To unlock the secrets hidden in the chromosomes of human cells is to open up a host of thorny legal, ethical and religious issues. Chief among them is the question of whether man has the right to play God with his genes. "Genetic manipulation seems artificial in ways that aren't representative of the natural order," says Arthur Caplan, director of the Center for Biomedical Ethics at the University of Minnesota. "The public has this perception that somehow it's wrong to manipulate the natural order, that we ought not to muck around there."

Such concerns haven't stopped man from tampering with the genes of crops and farm animals to suit human needs. In agriculture, biotechnology firms and universities are working on everything from tougher tomatoes to leaner pigs to plants that can make their own pesticides. Critics say tinkering with human genes can't be far behind.

"Recent discoveries about the biological reasons for homosexuality, intelligence and mental illness are setting the plate for more genetic intervention," says Dr. Paul Billings, director of genetics at Pacific Presbyterian Hospital in San Francisco. "It is still far from clear just how far society wants to go with gene therapy."

Crossing the threshold into direct genetic manipulation, society may be headed down a slippery slope in which the outcomes cannot be easily controlled, warns Jeremy Rifkin, president of the Foundation for Economic Trends and a longtime opponent of genetic engineering. Rifkin raises the specter of "engineering" workers to render them less susceptible to chemical carcinogens in lieu of cleaning up the workplace.

Most ethicists, however, believe such Orwellian nightmares are far-fetched. Even if they were desired, the technology is decades if not centuries away. "Some people pander to fears about eugenics or Frankenstein monsters or researchers playing God," says LeRoy Walters, director of the Center for Bioethics at Georgetown University. "Their extrapolations go far beyond what has been proposed — or what would even be considered — by review committees."

In the 19th century, new discoveries about heredity and evolution gave rise to the eugenics movement — a misguided pseudoscience whose followers thought that undesirable traits should be systematically purged from the human gene pool. Under the aegis of eugenics, at least 29 states in the early part of this century passed mandatory sterilization laws affecting people thought to be genetically predestined to be alcoholic, feebleminded or possessing criminal tendencies. As a result, tens of thousands of people in the U.S. were sterilized against their will.[1]

Fearful of where gene therapy could lead, many ethicists — and scientists — want to limit gene therapy to the treatment of the somatic (body) cells of individuals currently suffering from genetic disease. If gene transplants are performed on tissue, or somatic, cells, the altered genes will die with the patient; they cannot be passed on to any children the patient might subsequently have.

"Somatic gene therapy is not qualitatively different from other medical treatments, such as bone marrow transplants, and should not be treated as if it is," says George Annas, who directs the law, medicine and ethics program at Boston University School of Medicine.

Someday, however, it may be possible to change genes in "germ" cells, which give rise to sperm or eggs. If that feat is accomplished in humans — it already has been successfully done in animals — the new genes would be transmitted down through the generations. Already some investigators say that if and when the scientific obstacles can be overcome, germ-line therapy could be the best approach for certain diseases — perhaps those that affect multiple organs — and they balk at the notion of shutting the door on it.

Though germ-cell gene therapy might seem like the ultimate in preventive medicine, critics focus on its darker side. If biologists can change the course of heredity, they can try to play God and influence human destiny. It would permanently change the gene pool of the species — no doubt with some totally unpredictable results. "Are we wise enough to ignore millions of years of evolution, which has brought us to the point of having recessive traits?" asks Rifkin.*

Genes that are detrimental under certain conditions, he argues, may turn out to have hidden benefits. Sickle-cell anemia, for instance, is a debilitating blood disease suffered by people of African descent who have two copies of an abnormal gene. A person who has only one copy of the gene, however, will not be stricken with anemia and will in fact have an unusual resistance to

*In 1983 Rifkin and several dozen theologians mounted an unsuccessful effort to persuade Congress to ban all experiments on human germ cells.

# Gene Therapy for a 4-Year-Old

*The first patient to receive gene therapy was a little girl whose body didn't produce the enzyme ADA, vital to her immune system, because of an inherited defective gene. At the National Institutes of Health in Bethesda, Md., doctors put normal ADA genes into some of her white blood cells, then injected the modified cells back in her body. After a year of gene therapy, doctors say her immune system is beginning to produce the white cells needed to ward off infection.*

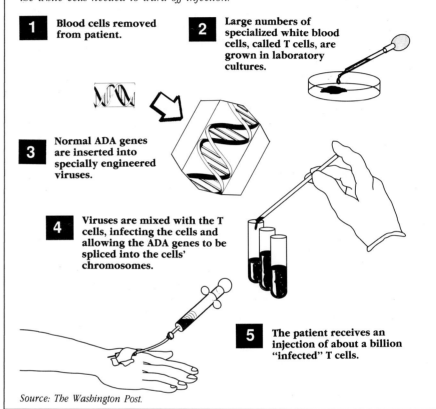

**1** Blood cells removed from patient.

**2** Large numbers of specialized white blood cells, called T cells, are grown in laboratory cultures.

**3** Normal ADA genes are inserted into specially engineered viruses.

**4** Viruses are mixed with the T cells, infecting the cells and allowing the ADA genes to be spliced into the cells' chromosomes.

**5** The patient receives an injection of about a billion "infected" T cells.

*Source: The Washington Post.*

malaria. That is why the gene remains common in African populations. Similar benefits may account for the existence of other recessive genes as well, which to the unknowing eye seem only detrimental.

No geneticist is currently known to be planning to transfer genes to human germ cells. But medical scientists have an obligation to protect humanity against disease and dysfunction. "What if doctors could use germ-line therapy to cure Lesch-Nyhan syndrome,* a disease where

*Lesch-Nyhan syndrome is considered one of the most devastating disorders. Symptoms include mental retardation and self-mutilation.

children suffer horribly?" says Caplan. "Wouldn't they have a moral obligation to use it?"

## Is there sufficient public debate over the merits — and risks — of human gene therapy?

The path leading up to the first human gene therapy experiment was long and tedious. Drs. Anderson and Blaese first submitted a trial-run proposal for treating ADA deficiency in April 1987. It was reviewed a dozen times by seven local and national regulatory committees and altered again and again to meet their requirements. In all, it took three years and three months before the proposal

## Common Genetic Diseases

*Humans suffer from some 4,000 genetic diseases ranging from ADA deficiency, which afflicts fewer than 60 people worldwide, to common disorders such as heart and kidney disease. Heredity may play a role, along with environment and other factors, in many other diseases, including hypertension and Alzheimer's.*

| Disease | Incidence | Nature of Illness |
| --- | --- | --- |
| Adult polycystic kidney disease | 500,000 | Kidney damage and failure |
| Down syndrome | 250,000 | Range of mental retardation |
| Sickle-cell anemia | 100,000 | Impaired circulation, anemia, pain |
| Cystic fibrosis | 30,000 | Chronic respiratory infections and digestive problems |
| Duchenne muscular dystrophy | 25,000 | Muscular degeneration, weakness |
| Huntington's disease | 25,000 | Progressive mental and neurological degeneration |
| Hemophilia | 20,000 | Uncontrolled bleeding |
| Phenylketonuria (PKU) | under 10,000 | Mental deficiency |
| Retinoblastoma | under 10,000 | Cancer of the eye |
| †Hypertension | 58 million | High blood pressure that results in increased risk of stroke |
| †Dyslexia | 15 million | Disturbance of the ability to read |
| †Atherosclerosis | 6.7 million | Vascular disease caused by the deposition of fatty substances of the inner layer of the arteries |
| †Cancer | 5 million | An uncontrolled growth of cells |
| †Alzheimer's disease | 2-4 million | Progressive mental degeneration |
| †Schizophrenia | 1.5 million | Psychotic disorder demonstrated by disintegration of personality |
| †Diabetes (Type 1) | 1 million | A pancreatic gland disorder characterized by inadequate secretion or utilization of insulin |
| †Multiple sclerosis | 250,000 | Loss of myelin sheath in central nervous system |

*† Heredity may account for only a fraction of these cases.*
*Source: International Biotechnology Associaton.*

was approved last September.

In contrast, five months earlier, with nothing more than permission from their own hospital's ethics committee, Dr. Peter Law and his colleagues at the University of Tennessee inserted normal muscle cells — with their full complement of genes — into a boy with muscular dystrophy. The theory was that the transplanted cells would make a protein the boy's own muscle cells could not.

Why is it that anyone wanting to replace a single gene in a patient's cells must negotiate a maze of federal reviews while someone wanting

to put in all the genes at once can simply do it?

The key to the paradox is the word "gene." The muscular dystrophy therapy, with its more benign name, "cell therapy," slipped by unnoticed because it did not conjure up Frankenstein images of messing with genes. "I call it genophobia," quips Caplan.

Actually, in the muscular dystrophy case, cell therapy was not anyone's first choice. "It is like giving a whole library when all you want is one book," said Dr. Leon Charash, chairman of the National Medical Advisory Board of the Muscular Dys-

trophy Association.[2] Doctors say it would make more sense simply to transplant the gene that produces the needed protein, but it has only recently been isolated, and animal experiments are still under way.

Because gene therapy is a new and potentially risky treatment, the NIH has put gene therapy proposals through a rigorous review process that includes at least five separate regulatory bodies.

"The emotional impact of having somebody manipulate the fundamental blueprint of a human being is very frightening," Anderson acknowledges. "We need to have the public understand it and to have adequate safeguards."

"Gene therapy is the most extensively debated therapy in history," says Robert Cook-Deegan of the Institute of Medicine in Washington. "I don't know of any biomedical science that has had the detailed scrutiny that human gene therapy has had." At each stage of a research plan, he says, geneticists are called before committees of ethicists, lawyers, physicians and other scientists and forced to defend their work.

"The [RAC review] is a political process as much as a thoughtful social review," counters geneticist Paul Billings. Billings argues that the RAC is stacked to support internal programs at NIH, the principal federal funding source for biomedical research in the United States. "We are talking about broad-ranging public policy decisions, like abortion. These decisions shouldn't be made by people at NIH. We need input from a broader range of opinions, such as the disabled," he says.

Although Cook-Deegan believes the review process in place for human gene therapy is a "model" for other innovative technologies, he agrees that more debate is crucial. "We need people around with resources at hand to think through the policy consequences of these issues," he says. Part of the problem is that for many issues that relate to gene therapy, like genetic screening, privacy of genetic information and discrimination, it is not at all clear where to turn. The Congressional Biomedical Ethics Board, which was created by Congress in 1985, fell apart over the abortion issue three years later without having accomplished anything.* Similarly, the proposed Ethics Advisory Board within the Department of Health and Human Services has become mired in the contentious debate over fetal research and in vitro fertilization and is now moribund.

Although 83 percent of the public say they support gene therapy to cure usually fatal genetic disease, according to a 1987 survey by the Office of Technology Assessment, few people really understand it. "This is one area of science that could potentially cause more harm than good," says Boston University's George Annas. "We need to broaden the public debate now before we have those techniques. Once they are available, it's over. You won't be able to prevent their usage. Gene therapy could become the cosmetic surgery of the next century."

### Does the enthusiasm over gene therapy raise false hopes for cures to diseases?

You can barely open the newspaper without reading about some genetic breakthrough that explains one human fault or another. With impressive regularity, science is finding ways to identify seemingly healthy individuals who are likely to develop a deadly hereditary disease or to pass it on to their offspring.

But unfortunately, science's ability to spot these diseases is outstripping

---

*The board, composed of six senators and six representatives, split equally on abortion and right-to-life issues and spent nearly three years haggling over who should be on the committee.

by many years its ability to do very much to prevent or treat them. "In fact, with virtually every genetic disorder, we are going to have an uncomfortable window that may extend over decades, when we can diagnose but not treat," says the University of Michigan's Francis Collins, who co-discovered the cystic fibrosis gene in 1989. This lag is creating complex medical, legal and moral dilemmas involving family relationships, confidentiality of medical data and proper counseling.

And as the ever increasing array of genetic tests becomes available, the gap between the number of people diagnosed to have disease and the number for which there are available cures is bound to grow. "If you can't do anything about it, how much is knowledge worth?" asks Daniel Wickler, director of the Program in Medical Ethics at the University of Wisconsin School of Medicine. "The sheer amount of genetic data is mindboggling."

Most researchers say any promises of medical miracles must be taken with a large dose of caution. "The idea that gene therapy will be available to a sizable number of people any time in the near future is pie in the sky," says Teri Liegler, a geneticist at the University of California at San Francisco. "At best, it's decades away." The reason, she says, is that most of the 4,000 or so genetic disorders involve more than one gene and are not very well understood. Moreover, practical gene therapy will require treated cells to survive more than a few months, which scientists haven't yet shown.

"We have this enormous preoccupation with genes," adds New York psychologist Joan Rothschild. "The lay public thinks that everything is genetic — and it isn't. Other environmental factors are critical; we're spending all this money on research, and we don't have decent prenatal care in this country. It's scandalous,

14-year-old teenagers are giving birth to children with brain damage."

According to the Council for Responsible Genetics, in Cambridge, Mass., the exaggerated emphasis on genetic diagnosis draws attention away from the social measures that are needed to ameliorate most diseases, including equitable access to health care. The council declares: "Once socially stigmatized behaviors, such as alcoholism or other forms of addiction or mental illness, become included under the umbrella of 'genetic diseases,' economic and social resources are likely to be diverted into finding biomedical 'cures' while social measures will be shortchanged." [3]

For those in the disability community, misleading promises of a "cure" can be disturbing. Marcia Saxton, a disability-rights activist who has spina bifida, says preoccupation with finding "cures" for a myriad of disorders, some of which are not debilitating, itself perpetuates bias against the disabled. "In the end, quality of life has little to do with severity of disability and everything to do with how that person is treated in the community," she says.

"I am sure research will result in therapeutic benefits for some people," adds Deborah Kaplan of the World Institute on Disability in Oakland, Calif., "but gene therapy has attracted hype like a magnet. Unfortunately, it fosters a public attitude that views disability as pathology — that we as a society can't afford for people with disabilities to be born. Having a disability is not necessarily the worst thing in the world." [4]

If society focuses on cure, as opposed to care, disability-rights advocates say the disabled will suffer more in the future. "The issue of 'cure' is not clear-cut. There are trade-offs," Kaplan says. "Not everyone offered a cure will take it. We are concerned about pressure to undergo treatment as it becomes available." ∎

# BACKGROUND

## Cracking the Code

To understand gene therapy, it is important to know a little about the underlying biology. The concept of heredity first arose in the mind of Gregor Mendel, an Austrian monk. In 1865, after observing the flower colors and other characteristics of many generations of pea plants, Mendel formulated the laws of heredity and suggested the existence of packets of genetic information, which became known as genes. Soon afterward, chromosomes were observed in the nuclei of dividing human cells, and scientists later discovered a chromosomal difference between the sexes. One chromosome, which they named Y, was found in human males' cells, together with another, called X. Females' cells, on the other hand, had two copies of X.

But it was not until 1911 that a gene, only a theoretical entity at the time, was correctly assigned to a particular chromosome. After examining the pedigrees of several large families with many color-blind members (males are primarily affected), Columbia University scientist E. B. Wilson applied Mendelian logic and proved that the trait was carried on the X chromosome. In the same manner over the next few decades, several genes responsible for such gender-linked diseases as hemophilia were assigned to the X chromosome and a few others attributed to the Y.

In 1953, the door to genetic understanding was blown open when Jim Watson and Francis Crick discovered the double helix of DNA twisting like a fateful serpent through human cells. For centuries, scientists have known that traits are inherited, among them many diseases. What the discovery of DNA made clear was why. Genes are chunks of DNA that serve as blueprints for the production of proteins and chemicals essential for life.

The human genetic landscape — our genome — consists of all the DNA information carried on the 22 pairs of chromosomes in our cells plus the X and Y chromosomes involved in determining sex. Each chromosome is studded with genes, found in the nucleus of every one of the body's 100 trillion cells.* And each gene is responsible for the manufacture of a particular protein that contributes to either the structure or the functioning of the body. But the body is so finely tuned that fatal disorders can arise from a mix-up in just one base pair among the 3 billion base pairs in the body.

For example, researchers believe that cystic fibrosis, the most common fatal genetic disease in the United States today, is often caused by one defective base pair in a gene located somewhere along chromosome 7. Most of the more than 4,000 genetic disorders, however, are more complex and often are associated with more than one gene.

Biologists first conceived of manipulating genes as a form of therapy 30 years ago, when they began to trace the crippling symptoms of sickle-cell anemia, which affects one in every 500 American blacks, to its genetic roots. They discovered that this blood disease stems from a tiny mutation in one of the genes for human hemoglobin.

"Knowing this," says Richard Mulligan, a noted biologist at the Whitehead Institute for Biomedical Research at the Massachusetts Institute of Technology (MIT), "people immediately imagined a way of curing sickle-cell patients. Get a normal copy of a human hemoglobin gene in hand, then stick this gene into the blood-forming cells of the bone marrow." These cells, called stem cells, produce all the cells in the blood. In the sickle-cell victim, stem cells with the transplanted normal gene would make red blood cells packed with normal hemoglobin protein — and the anemia would be overcome.[5]

Curing the disease by replacing the mutant gene responsible for it seemed an intricate but straightforward solution. But 30 years ago no one had yet figured out how to isolate and clone a mammalian gene in the lab. That achievement had to wait until 1975, when a group of researchers at Harvard University finally managed to clone a beta-globin gene from the blood of a rabbit. Two years later the human beta-globin gene was identified and cloned. But even once the healthy genes could be obtained, no one knew how to get them to work in the impaired cells. The solution to that puzzle still largely eludes scientists.

### Regulatory Web

Though French Anderson started the first gene therapy lab at NIH in 1968, public acceptance — even among fellow scientists — didn't come until later. "Twenty years ago, you couldn't utter the phrase 'gene therapy' without being told you were talking nonsense," says Dr. Theodore Friedmann, a molecular geneticist at the University of California at San Diego. "Now it's taken for granted that it's coming."

Ethicists and scientists trace the roots of the debate over the issue to a trailblazing conference in Pacific Grove, Calif., in 1975, when molecular biologists tried to forestall public opposition by voluntarily regulating their newfound ability to cut and splice genes and insert them into bacteria.[6] The scientists helped set up a federal review process to ensure that they would not inadvertently cre-

---

*Red blood cells have no nuclei, and thus do not have genes.

Continued on p. 786

# Chronology

## 1860s-1940s
**Scientists begin to understand the principles of heredity, triggering medical advances — but also the birth of the eugenics movement.**

### 1865
While studying the patterns and relationships of pea plants, Austrian monk Gregor Mendel formulates the laws of heredity. These units of inheritance later became known as genes.

### 1910
Mendel's work is rediscovered, launching modern genetic research with fruit flies and ultimately leading to the sex-linked nature of chromosomes.

### 1927
In *Buck v. Bell*, the U.S. Supreme Court upholds the constitutionality of the Virginia sterilization statute, reflecting public acceptance of eugenics, the science of improving the genetic qualities of humans.

## 1950s-1960s
**Researchers unravel the genetic code and begin to correlate genetic traits to certain illnesses.**

### Feb. 28, 1953
James Watson and Francis Crick unveil the structure of deoxyribonucleic acid, or DNA, the material from which genes are made.

### 1968
First gene therapy lab set up at NIH under Dr. W. French Anderson.

## 1970s
**As molecular biologists develop the tools for splicing genes, public-policy groups begin to debate the social and ethical implications of gene therapy.**

### 1974
The Recombinant DNA Advisory Committee (RAC) is established within the National Institutes of Health to develop guidelines for the safe conduct of gene research.

### 1975
Researchers at Harvard University clone a beta-globin gene from the blood of a rabbit; two years later the human beta-globin gene is identified and cloned.

## 1980s
**Paced by genetic breakthroughs, the regulatory review process for human gene therapy experiments is established.**

### 1980
Religious leaders send a letter to then-President Jimmy Carter expressing concern about the potential consequences of genetic engineering; Dr. Martin Cline's unapproved attempts to perform gene therapy on two patients in Israel and Italy arouse public uproar.

### November 1982
The President's Commission on Bioethics releases landmark report on gene therapy, called *Splicing Life*. The report articulates the principal public policy positions on gene therapy that stand to this day.

### Jan. 22, 1985
The RAC publishes the first national guidelines for human gene therapy. This document, "Points to Consider," sets the criteria for the ethical and scientific safeguards that must be met before new medical experiments are tried.

### May 22, 1989
The first human gene transfer experiment takes place at NIH. Doctors remove cells from a person with cancer, genetically alter those cells and then put them back into the patient. The so-called "marking" study paves the way for human gene therapy.

## 1990s
**The human gene therapy frontier opens, initiating what many experts are convinced will be a new era in medicine.**

### Sept. 14, 1990
The first human gene therapy experiment begins with treatment of a 4-year-old girl with adenosine deaminase (ADA) deficiency, a rare condition that makes her unable to manufacture an enzyme that helps regulate the immune system.

### October 1990
NIH announces official launch of the Human Genome Project, a $3 billion, 15-year endeavor to map and sequence human genes.

### Jan. 29, 1991
Dr. Steven Rosenberg at NIH treats the first cancer patients using gene therapy.

### October 1991
The RAC approves three gene therapy protocols, two for treating cancer and one for treating severe high cholesterol.

Continued from p. 784

ate a monster strain of bacteria.

"The concern was that once you can start doing genetic engineering in bacteria you then develop the potential capability of manipulating genes and redesigning human beings," says Anderson.

By June 1980, a letter to then-President Jimmy Carter from leaders of the Jewish, Catholic and Protestant religious communities had sparked renewed interest in the ethics of human gene therapy. The letter expressed concern about the potentially dangerous consequences of genetic engineering and the lack of adequate government review.[7]

The letter proved to be prophetic. Within four months, the *Los Angeles Times* broke a long story that confirmed one of the religious leaders' worst fears — a maverick scientist striking out on his or her own. Dr. Martin Cline, at the time a leading hematologist at the University of California at Los Angeles, applied for permission to insert new genes into patients with beta-thalassemia, a blood disorder that causes severe anemia. When UCLA denied permission, saying the animal data were insufficient to justify trying it on human beings, Cline went abroad to treat patients in Italy and Israel. The treatment had no effect on the patients one way or the other, but the lack of peer approval created a public uproar. When his actions came to light, Cline was sternly disciplined by NIH.[8]

The ensuing scandal chastened scientists and triggered a complex federal review process for gene therapy. In late 1980, the President's Commission on Bioethics began a two-year study that culminated in the publication of *Splicing Life: The Social and Ethical Issues of Genetic Engineering with Human Beings.* The landmark report concluded that somatic cell gene therapy was morally no different from other forms of

medical therapy. It also inspired then-Rep. Al Gore (D-Tenn.), chairman of the Subcommittee on Investigations and Oversight of the House Committee on Science and Technology, to take the congressional lead on gene therapy in 1982 and convene a hearing. In 1984, the committee asked the Office of Technology Assessment to study gene therapy,[9] and Gore sponsored legislation setting up the Biomedical Ethics Board, which would in part be responsible for evaluating the ethical implications of genetic breakthroughs.

From the *Splicing Life* report of the president's commission and the congressional hearing of 1982 one can draw a straight line to the review process for gene therapy proposals currently in place in the United States. For a gene therapy protocol — or proposal for research — to pass muster, it must be approved by at least five separate bodies: the local institutional biosafety committee (which concerns itself with the impact of using recombinant DNA technology), the local institutional review board (which reviews research on humans), the Human Gene Therapy Subcommittee of the RAC, the RAC itself and the Food and Drug Administration (FDA).[10] Finally, the director of the NIH must sign off on all experiments. These procedures were put into place to assure the public that there would be no repeat of the Cline debacle.

### Fields Converge

As the political and regulatory framework for approving gene therapy was being devised, scientists were grappling with a more fundamental problem: how to make gene therapy work in lab cultures and in animal studies. Several labs were also competing to be the first to conduct an actual human gene therapy experiment.

Before patients could be treated, appropriate genes had to be isolated

and understood. It was then necessary to identify and collect appropriate target cells and to develop safe and efficient vectors, or "delivery trucks," with which to introduce foreign genes. Finally, there must be unequivocal evidence from animal experiments that the inserted gene functions adequately, that the recipient cells have a reasonably long life span, and that the foreign genes have no dangerous side effects. These requirements still pose daunting challenges to scientists.[11]

In the early 1980s, Richard Mulligan at MIT had a novel idea. Why not use retroviruses to shuttle healthy genes to ailing cells? All retroviruses — the most notorious of which is the AIDS virus — can penetrate the cell nucleus and insert retroviral DNA into the cell's own chromosomes. They are smaller than most other viruses and, unlike most other viruses, usually do not kill the cells they infect.

After years of lab manipulations — in which the virus' inner workings were stripped away bit by bit — the retroviruses now used in gene therapy have been reduced to shells for carrying foreign genes and getting them into the cell's nucleus.

The retroviral vector has the desired gene spliced directly into its nucleus. Then begins the process known as transduction — in which the cells designated to receive the gene are mixed with the gene-boosted vector in a culture dish.

In 1988, Mulligan's success at engineering viruses that can transplant human hemoglobin genes into developing blood cells in a mouse, producing cells with perfectly functioning hemoglobin, brought gene therapy a giant step closer to reality. "To the guy on the street, who thinks of viruses just as agents of disease," says Mulligan, "using them to perform gene therapy may sound like science fiction. But 10 years

Continued on p. 788

# Human Genome Project: Mapping Our Future

Ten or 15 years from now — barring unforeseen technical setbacks — scientists will have mapped every bump on our complex genetic landscape. Genetic breakthroughs like the isolation of the cystic fibrosis gene will soon be overshadowed by the avalanche of genetic information flowing out of research labs.

The engine that will drive these advances in gene analysis is the biologists' moonshot, the Human Genome Project.† The ambitious goal of this international effort is to read out the sequence of the 3 billion bases of DNA that, strung end to end, carry the information of all the body's genes. Given a clear, easily read atlas of our genetic endowment, researchers will be able to accelerate the rate at which they discover important genes.

In the 38 years since James Watson and Francis Crick first discerned the complex structure of DNA, scientists have deciphered only 1,700 of the 50,000 to 100,000 genes that contain our genetic information. The broad range reflects how little is actually known about the genome.

Genome? The word causes the eyes of most Americans, whose taxes will largely support the project's estimated $3 billion cost, to glaze over. Explains biochemist Robert Sinsheimer of the University of California at Santa Barbara: "The human genome is the complete set of instructions for making a human being." Those instructions are tucked into the nucleus of each of the human body's 100 trillion cells and written in the language of deoxyribonucleic acid, the fabled DNA molecule.

When the project was officially launched in 1989, James Wyngaarden, former director of the National Institutes of Health (NIH), predicted that it would make "major contributions to understanding growth, development and human health, and open new avenues for gene therapy." One of the early benefits will be the identification of more and more of the defective genes responsible for the thousands of known inherited diseases, and development of tests to detect them. Like those already used to find Huntington's and sickle-cell markers, for example, these tests will allow doctors to predict with near certainty that some patients will fall victim to specific genetic diseases and that others are vulnerable and could be stricken.

The search for genes involves two arduous endeavors: mapping and sequencing. In mapping, researchers use what they've learned from studying inheritance in families to determine which of the 23 pairs of chromosomes might hold the gene they're trying to find. But to truly understand the gene, researchers must pinpoint its location among the 4,000 others on a chromosome and unravel the exact sequence of its four constituent base molecules — called A, C, T and G — that control everything from eye color to who gets cancer.

But finding a gene is no simple task. It often lies somewhere between two known so-called markers that are separated by millions of bases. When asked how difficult it was to locate the cystic fibrosis gene, for example, University of Michigan geneticist Francis Collins described it as the equivalent of knowing a light bulb is out and having to check every house in the United States to find it.

"The Human Genome Project is probably the most politically delicate, and arguably the most important government science program since the Manhattan Project," writes Robert Wright in *The New Republic*.†† It is often mentioned in the same breath with "big science" projects such as the superconducting supercollider and the space station. In financial terms it's smaller than these two ($3 billion vs. $6 billion and $20 billion, respectively), but in economic and social significance it could be much bigger.

University of Utah geneticist Mark Skolnick says that genome mapping will change the way medicine is practiced. "Right now," he says, "we wait for someone to get sick so we can cut them and drug them. It's pretty old stuff."

Eventually, says Mark Guyer of the NIH's Human Genome Office, people might have access to a computer readout of their own genome, with an interpretation of their genetic strengths and weaknesses. At the very least, this would enable them to adopt an appropriate lifestyle, choosing the proper diet, environment and — if necessary — drugs to minimize the effects of genetic disorders.

The very thought of reading the entire genetic message, and perhaps altering it, alarms those who fear the knowledge could create ethical problems. Does genetic testing constitute an invasion of privacy, for example, and could it lead to more abortions and to discrimination against the "genetically unfit"? Should someone destined to be stricken with a deadly genetic disease be told about his fate?

These questions inspired the Human Genome Committee to pledge to spend 3 percent of the genome budget studying ethical and social implications. But that hasn't quieted critics. "The project is a costly, unsuitable use of precious research funds," says Martin Rechsteiner, co-chair of the University of Utah department of biochemistry.‡

Indeed, mapping the genome will not automatically translate into understanding how proteins interact. Nor will it lead to immediate cures. For instance, scientists have known the general location of the sickle-cell gene since 1949, but a cure to the disease still eludes them.

"It's critical that people appreciate the limits of what can be done, so that their fears don't intrude on the benefits that could come out of genetic research," cautions Nancy Wexler, a psychologist and hereditary-disease specialist who sits on the Genome Project's advisory board.

---

† For a detailed description, see *National Research Council, Mapping and Sequencing the Human Genome*, 1988.

†† See Robert Wright, "Achilles' Helix," *The New Republic*, July 9, 1990, pp. 21-31.

‡ *The New Scientist*, Sept. 15, 1990, p. 20.

*Continued from p. 786*

from now he's going to see it as just another fancy medical procedure doctors use to treat sick people." [12]

That same year, French Anderson and Michael Blaese, at NIH's National Cancer Institute (NCI), approached Dr. Steven Rosenberg, also at NCI, with an idea they thought would bring them another step closer to human gene therapy — but also help Rosenberg in his cancer research. They wanted to piggyback gene-transfer technology onto Rosenberg's successful anti-cancer techniques. As Anderson puts it, their goal was "to start with a target cell we knew we could hit" — the cells that Rosenberg was working with.[13]

Rosenberg was well-known for his innovation with "adoptive immunotherapy," a cancer treatment that involves culturing huge quantities of a patient's own natural cancer-fighting cells — tumor-infiltrating lymphocytes, or TIL cells. Anderson and Blaese's plan was to add a genetically engineered virus to the TIL cells before giving them back to patients. The project would begin by simply tacking on a gene that would tag the TIL cells, to help trace their progress through the body. This would be followed by insertion of a therapeutic anti-cancer gene.

In May 1989, the three NIH scientists treated the first of 10 cancer patients with gene-engineered TIL cells — and then used the gene to track the cells' progress in the body. It wasn't actual gene therapy — because the implanted gene wasn't designed to help arrest the cancer — but it was very close. The success of the marking study convinced the RAC that gene therapy just might work.

### Genetic Politics

The approval for treatment of ADA deficiency has moved gene therapy

"from abstract science to research and patient care," said Gerard McGarrity, chairman of the RAC, in September 1990. "The field of medicine has been looking for this kind of therapy for a thousand years. This is a historic moment."

A debate that began nearly two decades earlier had reached its resolution, but it did not come easily. By most accounts, the first human gene therapy experiment wouldn't yet have happened if it were not for the vision — and dogged persistence —

**The debate was dominated by a clash between two cultures — physicians anxious to treat dying patients and laboratory scientists insistent on perfecting their techniques.**

of one man: French Anderson. Alexander Capron, co-director of the Pacific Center for Health Policy and Ethics at the University of Southern California, claims that Anderson almost single-handedly moved gene therapy through the regulatory labyrinth to the point of acceptability. "For a serious scientist to have mastered the bureaucratic review process is truly extraordinary," he says.

During the months preceding approval, as the protocol was sent back and forth between researchers and the committee, RAC members grappled with questions of ethics, safety, politics, money and even professional competition. Throughout, the debate was dominated by a clash between two cultures — physicians anxious to treat dying patients and laboratory scientists insistent on perfecting their techniques.

The questions of what diseases are appropriate for treatment, who

should be treated and what techniques should be used are critical for any other innovative medical procedure. But with gene therapy, due to the potential risks, they took on a special political significance. "The overriding factor," according to Walters, "was that the risk/benefit assessment work in favor of the patient." Other diseases being considered for the first human gene therapy experiment included cancer and severe high cholesterol.

ADA deficiency seemed an ideal candidate because it is caused by a single faulty gene that was cloned a decade ago and is well understood by scientists. At the same time, however, the proposed experiment raised the ethical dilemma of whether it is appropriate to try experimental treatments on children, something the medical community frowns upon.*

Anderson's chief critic, MIT's Mulligan, contended that Anderson's ADA deficiency experiment is premature, calling it "technically and scientifically a bad idea." Mulligan, a laboratory scientist, argued that more preliminary research is necessary before experiments are undertaken on humans.** Ultimately, the proponents of the ADA gene therapy trial prevailed. "Within the past two years, as results from animal experiments have turned out positive, the pendulum has swung in favor of the clinicians," says LeRoy Walters. ∎

---

*In addition, while the protocol was in the review pipeline a new drug called PEG-ADA was developed that helped affected children fight off infection so long as they received weekly injections. The approval of the new drug by the FDA almost derailed the ADA gene therapy trial as reviewers wrestled with conflicting opinion about just how good the drug was and whether it constituted an alternative therapy.

**Mulligan was the only member of the Human Gene Therapy Subcommittee to vote against the ADA deficiency experiment. For a more detailed account of the debate, see "Breaking the Code," *The San Francisco Examiner,* May 19, 1991.

# CURRENT SITUATION

## The New Frontier

On Sept. 14, 1990, the frontier of human gene therapy was officially opened. The trio of NIH doctors, led by Anderson, began treatment of the 4-year-old with ADA deficiency — the first time genes were transferred into a human being for a therapeutic, rather than purely informational, purpose. At the experiment's one-year review at NIH last month, Dr. Blaise stopped short of declaring the girl "cured" but said the NIH team was "extraordinarily encouraged" by her progress. Indeed, "cure" isn't even the goal of gene therapy for this child. At best, the doctors hope to put her on a schedule of gene-boosted infusions every few months.

Since the experiment began, she has continued to receive standard care for ADA deficiency: weekly injections of the drug PEG-ADA, which generally keeps the immune system functioning at about half its normal level. Her immune function is now producing its own ADA, and the doctors have decided to temporarily stop the gene therapy to observe how long the genes are surviving. Ultimately, if all continues to go well, the girl will be able to rely on gene therapy alone and eliminate the weekly shots of PEG-ADA, which cost $250,000 a year. In January, a 9-year-old girl became the second gene therapy patient to be treated for ADA deficiency.

The promising results have led the National Heart, Lung and Blood Institute — one of 13 institutes at the National Institutes of Health — to ascribe gene therapy as its "highest priority." This year the institute officially dropped heart-surgery functions in order to dedicate $3-$5 million to a bone marrow-transplantation unit that would pursue gene-therapy technology.

In January, NIH's Rosenberg used gene therapy for the first time to treat cancer. Two patients with malignant melanoma, a severe form of skin cancer, received immune-system cells that had been bolstered with the gene for a potent anti-cancer substance called tumor necrosis factor. Within the next two years, a total of 50 melanoma patients are scheduled to receive gene therapy. According to the American Cancer Society, there is no conventional cure for melanoma, which afflicts 28,000 Americans annually and kills more than 6,000.

"Should this therapy work," Rosenberg says, "it could provide a powerful new treatment for other malignancies, including breast and colon cancers."

So-called "disease" genes have been tied to Alzheimer's disease, coronary heart disease, emphysema, multiple sclerosis and diabetes. "If we could find a cure for a disease with a genetic component such as diabetes," says Abbey Meyers, executive director of the National Organization for Rare Disorders, "that would probably be the most important medical advance of the century, if not of all time." [14]

In the case of cancer, and other complex diseases, gene therapy has a slightly different mission than it has with diseases that are strictly genetic. Curing the disease may not be the goal, at least not initially. By locating genes that suppress tumors, doctors hope to be able to predict how successfully many cancer patients will fight their disease. Knowing that, they might modify chemotherapy treatments, prescribing the most aggressive doses for patients without tumor-suppressor genes. In effect, gene therapy would work in tandem with other more conventional therapies.*

Scientists suspect that the genes involved in most complex illnesses, like manic depression, schizophrenia and many cancers, confer only a susceptibility to illness. The disease may not occur unless some harmful environmental factor triggers it. So people predisposed toward lung cancer may not get the disease unless they smoke, for example.

As the Human Genome Project pinpoints these culprits, it will also open up important avenues for diagnosis and treatment *(See p. 787)*. The pace of scientific discovery is dizzying. All across the United States — as well as in Canada and in Europe — scientists are preparing for gene therapy experiments, some using retroviruses, others creating synthetic carriers or experimenting with chemical, electrical and even mechanical techniques to insert genes into cells. Substantial progress toward gene therapy applications have been made in the following areas:

■ Cystic fibrosis — In 1989, teams at the University of Michigan and the Hospital for Sick Children in Toronto discovered the gene responsible for the most common fatal genetic illness of young Americans. Cystic fibrosis afflicts 30,000 victims; their average life span is 26 years. The basic gene defect leads to many problems, including secretions that form a thick mucus, clogging the lungs and causing chronic infection.

One new treatment, involving a genetically engineered protein called DNase, was tested on 12 patients last year. DNase facilitates the thinning of mucus. Using an aerosol spray, researchers led by NIH's Dr. Ronald Crystal inserted the protein directly into the patients' airways.

*Continued on p. 791*

---

*Cancer surgery, radiation therapy and chemotherapy can cure only half of those with cancer.

# Genetic Screening Provokes Anxious Debate

Well before gene therapy cures any disease, genetic information will be used by society, both for good and for bad. The opportunities and dilemmas created by the new genetic knowledge begin even before birth. It is already possible, through a variety of prenatal tests, to determine whether a child will be a boy or a girl, retarded or handicapped, or the victim of some fatal genetic disorder. So far, genetic screening can detect the presence of genes that cause about 200 diseases.

According to a recent study by Johns Hopkins geneticist Neil A. Holtzman, almost 2.8 million women will be tested to see if they carry the gene for one of four major inherited disorders: cystic fibrosis, sickle-cell anemia, hemophilia and muscular dystrophy.† If the fetus carries a gene that could lead to disease, the parents will face the difficult decision of whether to abort the pregnancy.††

Complicating such decisions is the fact that genetic prognostication will probably never be an exact science. For instance, the cystic fibrosis test is complex, and currently identifies only about 85 percent of those who harbor the gene for the illness. Yet even as hospitals and doctors move toward widespread screening, propelled in part by profit motives (the test costs $125-$250) and a fear of lawsuits, the test itself is being both damned and praised. "I'm not sure we are confident we can communicate risk [of actually passing on a disease] accurately to people," says Holtzman.

And the cystic fibrosis test marks only the beginning. Parents-to-be in the latter part of the 1990s will confront an ever-expanding menu of prenatal genetic tests that will affect a variety of reproductive decisions. Terminating a pregnancy may come relatively easily to some whose offspring carry genes dooming them to crippling diseases that appear early in life, such as Tay-Sachs and cystic fibrosis. But what about other disorders that are not so debilitating or life-threatening? The mutant gene leading to Huntington's disease usually permits normal life until one's 40s or 50s, typically after the trait has been passed on to the next generation.

Woody Guthrie, the legendary American folk singer and composer, died of Huntington's in 1967 at the age of 55. Would the world really have been better off if he were never born? And what about fetuses predisposed to manic depression, which some believe boosts creativity?

One fear is that prenatal diagnoses could push parents into abortions they don't want. "As soon as these tests become available, they take on the character of an obligation," warns Harvard biologist Ruth Hubbard. "If a woman doesn't use them, we may blame her for burdening society with a disabled child." ‡ Already one case has been reported where a health maintenance organization (HMO) threatened to refuse medical coverage to a couple unless they terminated a pregnancy where the fetus carried the gene for cystic fibrosis. Under pressure of lawsuit, the HMO backed off.

Dr. Paul Billings, chief of genetic medicine at Pacific Presbyterian Medical Center in San Francisco, believes such stories may be warning signs of a coming wave of genetic discrimination. "Once genetic information is gleaned about someone," Billings says, "there will be no way to keep it private."

Life- and medical-insurance companies base coverage decisions on genetic information and might one day require that potential customers have their genes screened, presumably so that people likely to develop fatal or disabling diseases could be charged higher premiums, or possibly turned away. Insurers already have used a similar policy to avoid covering individuals at high risk for AIDS, a practice now banned in several states. Ethicist John Fletcher at the University of Virginia predicts that "the confusion caused by widespread testing for genetic flaws will lead inevitably to national health insurance."

Bitter controversies also are brewing over genetic testing in the workplace.‡‡ At the moment, there is nothing to keep employers from using tests to screen out prospective hires with genes for heart disease, for instance — even though there's no guarantee that these people will ever fall ill. At the extreme, Nachama Wilker, executive director of the Council for Responsible Genetics, worries about creating "cadres of the genetically unemployable."

Once someone's genes have been screened, the results could find their way into computer banks. Without legal restrictions, these personal revelations might eventually be shared among companies and government agencies. Just like a credit rating or an arrest record, a DNA analysis could become part of a person's permanent electronic dossier.

Concerns over these issues led Rep. John Conyers Jr., D-Mich., to introduce the Human Genome Privacy Act in April. The legislation is designed to protect an individual's right to privacy and prevent genetic discrimination. A public hearing before a subcommittee of the House Government Operations Committee is scheduled for this week.

"But it is not just a matter of regulating or not regulating genetic screening," notes Arthur Caplan, director of the Center for Biomedical Ethics at the University of Minnesota. "The issue is much more complex than what Congress must or can do. That underestimates the impact of the genetic revolution on society. Genetic testing will enable scientists to tease apart cause and effect. It will challenge the way we think about what constitutes disease — and, ultimately, make us reconsider what it is to be human."

---

† Neil A. Holtzman, *Proceed with Caution*, 1990, p. 152.

†† In some cases, such as with phenylketonuria (PKU), screening allows for early utilization of dietary therapy that prevents the onset of mental retardation normally associated with the disease.

‡ Quoted in *Business Week*, May 28, 1990, p. 82.

‡‡ See Office of Technology Assessment, *Genetic Monitoring and Screening in the Workplace*, October 1990.

Continued from p. 789

All of the patients were able to breathe easier, and now a much larger DNase study is under way.

Besides this promising drug treatment, progress also has been made toward finding a cure. Last fall, two teams of investigators used gene transfer to correct the cystic fibrosis defect in cells in lab cultures. And this spring, researchers developed genetically engineered cold viruses that they believe may serve as Trojan horses, carrying healthy genes into genetically defective lung cells.[15]

■ High cholesterol — A medical team led by Dr. James Wilson, a University of Michigan geneticist, received approval from the RAC this month to treat human patients with familial hypercholesterolemia, a metabolic disorder that results in hardening of the arteries and increased risk of heart attacks.

Wilson is trying to transfer good genes into defective liver cells that, when functioning properly, help clear cholesterol from the blood. Eschewing a retrovirus vector, he and two University of Connecticut scientists have developed a synthetic protein-DNA complex to deliver the healthy genes. If successful, this treatment could be widely applicable to people with less severe, but still threatening, cholesterol levels.

■ AIDS — More than 100,000 Americans have lost their lives to this disease, and another million or so may be infected — plus countless more millions worldwide. Researchers now know that the human immunodeficiency virus (HIV) enters the body's white blood cells primarily through a receptor called CD4.

One promising approach to curing AIDS, currently being pursued by French Anderson and Robert C. Gallo of the National Cancer Institute, involves a white blood cell genetically engineered with a decoy CD4 receptor. If enough mock CD4 can be kept circulating in the blood-stream, these decoys may snare the AIDS virus and keep it from penetrating the white blood cells.

■ Cardiovascular disease — Bypass surgery is a common treatment for blocked blood vessels. Under this procedure, a new vessel, known as a vascular graft, is inserted to replace a clogged one. But in one-third of the 300,000 bypass surgery operations performed each year, blood clots eventually develop. Scientists at NIH are trying to coat the implant with cells containing the gene for TPA, a natural clot dissolver, to avoid this complication of surgery. "Here we are not talking about gene transfer to cure a disease, but as a way to prevent a complication of another therapy," says Anderson.

## Economic Issues

For most single-gene disorders, modern medicine and surgery have very little to offer. Thus, gene therapy offers a tantalizing — if expensive — prospect for cure. So long as gene therapy is a high-tech procedure practiced in a few sophisticated labs around the country, however, it will not be clinically available to a wide segment of the population. Nor will it be commercially viable.

Most scientists agree that finding a cure for ADA deficiency is a medical steppingstone to finding cures for other more common disorders. But even with ADA deficiency, alternative drug treatment is only partially effective and exorbitantly expensive. Although an effective gene therapy could have a very high one-time cost, it may still be more cost-effective than years of repeated hospitalizations experienced by children with debilitating diseases such as severe combined immune deficiency and leukemia. Bone marrow transplants, which are fairly common treatments for these diseases, cost between $100,000 and $200,000.

"We actually may end up saving money," says Caplan at the University of Minnesota. "Rather than dealing with symptoms, we will be able to alter or even cure some diseases." The economic benefits of gene therapy would be most striking for patients who would otherwise require long-term institutional care. For example, dialysis treatment for patients with polycystic kidney disease costs roughly $35,000 per year. Overall, some $5 billion is spent each year in the United States on renal failure (including diabetes), according to Caplan.

If advances in gene therapy produce the results researchers hope for, it is not only the medical profession and the U.S. taxpayer who stand to benefit. The pharmaceuticals industry will be changed dramatically. The prospect of huge profits from the new genetic drugs has fostered the rapid growth of an industry that had estimated earnings of more than $1 billion in the U.S. last year.

Although venture capitalists thus far have been leery of the commercial risks of gene therapy, experts say pharmaceutical companies are waiting in the wings, poised to snap up companies that make therapeutic breakthroughs. Says Philip Leder, chairman of the genetics department at Harvard Medical School: "We are suddenly presented with a whole new set of tools for curing disease." To many scientists, the prospect of harnessing the human body to produce its own therapeutic drugs represents the most exciting prospect of all.

The new class of drugs relies on the technology of recombinant DNA, pioneered in the mid-1970s, which allows scientists to identify, reproduce and re-engineer the genes that create proteins, which in turn control human bodily functions. Researchers say that unlike the chemicals used in traditional drugs, the engineered proteins are the same as those that already exist in the body.

During the past 15 years, scientists have spliced and cloned genes to create copies of the proteins in the human body. Already, about a dozen of the new, genetically engineered drugs are on the market, and industry experts say that the flow could grow to include hundreds of new substances. "After the year 2000, one of every two or three ethical drugs will turn genes on or off," says Wally Steinberg, chairman of Health Care Investment Corp., an Edison, N.J., venture capital firm. "The end game of molecular biology will be genetic therapy." [16]

The genetically derived pharmaceutical products on the market today include human insulin, hepatitis B vaccine, human-growth hormone and an antibody that helps prevent rejection of kidney transplants. Other genetically derived substances are now under development as cures or vaccines for several types of cancer, for Alzheimer's disease and for AIDS. For example, Viagene, a company in San Diego, Calif., may soon test a therapy for HIV infection in which a gene taken from a virus is inserted into the DNA of infected people. In cells of the immune system, it will produce viral antigens to provoke the body to mount a cellular immune response that, theoretically, could wipe out the virus.

At present, half a dozen biotechnology firms are actively involved in gene therapy, but Bruce Merchant, vice president for regulatory affairs at Viagene, suspects that number will double or triple within the next few years. And, increasingly, government scientists and private corporations are forging alliances to bring medical advances from the lab bench to the doctor's office.

Back in 1986, Congress, concerned that many potentially useful discoveries were languishing in government labs, passed the Technology Transfer Act to facilitate the marketing of government inventions. Without a profit motive, the legislation's backers reasoned, what company would be willing to invest the millions usually required to bring a new invention to the marketplace? Indeed, the costs of developing the new genetic drugs are huge: Officials at Silicon Valley-based Genentech Inc., say that the firm spent at least $100 million in the development of tissue plasminogen activator, a protein that dissolves blood clots in heart-attack victims.

The U.S. Congress' solution to the funding problem was the so-called CRADA (an acronym for Cooperative Research and Development Agreement), which allows companies to hold licensing rights to patents held by government agencies. French Anderson was the first scientist at NIH to have such an agreement with a private company, Genetic Therapy Inc., a biotechnology firm based in Gaithersburg, Md.; now more than 150 others do as well. [17]

Under this sort of arrangement, the private firm helps fund the research and in return gains exclusive rights to the gene therapy technology developed. Using technology licensed from NIH, Genetic Therapy has developed three of the four gene therapy vectors approved by the federal government for use in humans. Its goal is to develop an injectable viral vector, a sort of "smart bomb" for gene delivery that heads straight to the spot on the chromosome where the new gene belongs.

"When you have to remove cells and treat them in the lab and return them to the patient," Anderson says, "you can only do gene therapy at a handful of high-tech medical centers. The ideal is to engineer everything in advance so that all you have to do is grab a syringe off the shelf and inject the genes into whoever needs them." ∎

# OUTLOOK

## Technical Obstacles

After years of peering into cells and figuring out how they work, scientists are now able to arrange and rearrange the basic building blocks of life. "We are going to be able to predict who is likely to develop certain cancers and screen those individuals so that we detect them early and do appropriate procedures to make sure that this cancer never occurs or is unlikely to occur," predicts geneticist Michael Hayden of the University of British Columbia. If perfected, doctors say gene therapy could be preventive medicine in its purest form.

"This is intellectually the most exciting time in science since Darwin," says John Fletcher at the University of Virginia. Virtually all experts agree that we are in the midst of a genetic revolution. There is considerably less consensus, however, on when gene therapy's tremendous potential will be realized. Even French Anderson, gene therapy's biggest booster, counsels patience for parents of children with genetic diseases other than ADA deficiency — such as sickle-cell anemia and cystic fibrosis. "Gene therapy for other conditions is not going to happen tomorrow," he says. "We must be careful not to oversell gene therapy to a hopeful public."

The notion of a genomic Xanadu, where the scientists possess a vast library of vectors that can efficiently insert genes either throughout the

Continued on p. 794

# At Issue:

## Should scientists conduct experiments on the germ-line of humans?

**DANIEL F. KOSHLAND JR.**

*Professor of Biochemistry, University of California at Berkeley, and editor of* Science *magazine*
FROM AN ARTICLE IN *MBL SCIENCE*, WINTER 1988-89.

*i*n gene therapy, there is an obvious clash between cultures. Some groups oppose any genetic engineering, arguing that it is an ill-concealed approach to biological warfare, and an equally bad attempt to permanently change the gene-line of Homo sapiens for the worse.

Some scientists, put on the defensive by this attack, are giving a curious answer. They are saying genetic engineering to produce somatic mutations in the individual human is fine, but genetic engineering in the germ-line is bad. There is a logic in that position: Changing an individual can only do damage to that individual whereas changing the germ-line can influence future generations. That is a conservative position, and, possibly, a politically motivated compromise that will allow genetic engineering to go forward. But I wonder whether it is a wise compromise.

We are already keeping alive a number of people who, in previous generations, would have died in infancy or early childhood. Kept alive, these individuals produce genetically defective offspring. I am a good example. I can't see very well, and I certainly would have been eaten by a saber-toothed tiger if I didn't wear glasses and live in a safe environment. Civilization affects the germ-line just as much as genetic engineering. Keeping diabetics alive with insulin, which increases the propagation of an inherited disease, seems justified only if one is willing to do genetic engineering to remove diabetes from the germ-line and thus to save the anguish and cost to millions of diabetics.

I am not advocating that one introduce genes into the germ-line quickly, without a great deal of thought. But I am trying to illustrate that hastily contrived political compromises may have unintended and adverse long-range implications. . . . If a child destined to have a permanently low IQ could be cured by replacing a gene, would anyone really argue against that?

Let us proceed a little toward the science of the future with a genetic engineering problem. If I asked an audience largely favorable to science whether one should be allowed to substitute a good gene for a bad gene that causes diabetes in the germ-line, I would guess that the overwhelming answer would be yes. Such a surgical replacement of a defective gene by a good one, which is not present in our methodology today but probably is coming, would allow diabetics to become parents with the knowledge that their children would not inherit this disease. The inverse of that decision — denying to help diabetics — is actually affecting the germ-line in a worse way.

**STUART NEWMAN**

*Professor of cell biology and anatomy, New York Medical College*
FROM A POSITION PAPER PREPARED FOR THE COUNCIL FOR RESPONSIBLE GENETICS, SEPT. 26, 1991.

*i*t is difficult to argue against manipulation of somatic (body) cells to treat life-threatening disorders. However, germ-line modification is another story. It has not yet been overtly attempted in humans, and there is no current social consensus that supports it. Arguments against germ-line modification include the following:

First, it is not needed in order to save the lives or alleviate suffering of existing people. Its target population is "people" who have not even been conceived yet.

Second, the cultural impact of treating humans as biologically perfectible material artifacts would be very negative. Those people who fall short of some technically achievable ideal would be seen as "damaged goods."

And third, there is a real possibility of mistakes that introduce additional susceptibility to cancer and other diseases into the human gene pool. A good case can be made that at least some of the changes that may be induced by inserting large segments of DNA into the germ-line are different in kind from those that occur spontaneously, and could have major, unpredictable consequences for both the individual and the future of the species. . . .

No published reports have yet appeared on germ-line modification in humans, but there appear to be no technical obstacles. In mice and other vertebrate animals, germ-line gene modification has actually proved technically easier than somatic modification because the cells of early embryos are better at incorporating foreign DNA. . . . Procedures [that could be used] for germ-line therapy are well-established for humans and are widely used in in vitro fertilization clinics.

Some people say it is desirable to "cleanse" the gene pool of "deleterious" genes. Although the techniques are new, this is similar to the policy of "scientific" eugenics that was fashionable before World War II. . . . In addition, genes could be introduced into the germ-line to enhance certain characteristics desired by parents. Indeed, some have suggested future "needs" to design individuals "better at computers, better as musicians, better physically."

It should be noted that in almost all cases, parents carrying "deleterious" versions of a gene could arrange to have unaffected offspring without germ-line modification. If an appropriate prenatal diagnostic is available, selective abortion is the most straightforward means. Or, embryo selection following in vitro fertilization could be used.

Continued from p. 792

body or into specific tissues, may be pure fantasy. Although scientists agree that current experiments are a step in the right direction, it will take a leap in biotechnological abilities before gene therapy can be customized to treat many human diseases. Anderson predicts that an injectable vector for humans will not be ready for clinical trial for at least seven or eight years — and most scientists say that's optimistic.

Gene transfer is not the same as pushing the search-and-replace key on your computer. It is still very much a hit-or-miss proposition. Take cystic fibrosis. The scientific community was euphoric when the gene was discovered in 1989. Since then, there have been major breakthroughs toward treatment. At the same time, however, it has been discovered that the original mutation causes only about 75 percent of the cases; about 100 other mutations have been found that also cause cystic fibrosis, and no single one is responsible for more than a few percent of the remaining cases.

Much has yet to be learned about how genes interact, particularly those for more complex disorders, such as cancer and heart disease. And, the long-term effects of incorporating new genetic material into cells of humans are still largely unknown. "The Holy Grail is to infect the stem cell, which gives rise to the whole blood system; then we can say the patient has been cured long-term," says Dusty Miller, a geneticist at Seattle's Fred Hutchinson Cancer Research Center. Thus far, scientists haven't yet located stem cells in humans. And once they do, there is no assurance that any of the techniques currently being used will be of any use.

In the near term, the more likely impact will be found in the area of diagnostics. Studies show that when prenatal diagnosis has been done in conjunction with adequate public education, there has been a remarkable reduction in the births of the severely disabled. This has been achieved through selective abortion. And in many cases, knowledge of a predisposition to disease will enable the individual to make changes in lifestyle and diet to reduce risks of the onset of disease. In some instances, such as ADA deficiency, science will produce therapies that will end extended suffering.

Nevertheless, experts say it is important to keep the field in perspective. Breakthroughs must be put in the context of advances in other alternative therapies, such as bone marrow transplants and drugs that might alleviate suffering in a less invasive — and less risky — way.

## Ethical Concerns

In Edward Albee's 1962 play, "Who's Afraid of Virginia Wolfe?" George (a historian) describes the agenda of modern biology to alter chromosomes: "All imbalances will be corrected, sifted out ... propensity for various diseases will be gone, longevity assured. We will have a race of men ... test-tube-bred ... incubator-born ... superb and sublime." That is the nightmare scenario that many people fear.

Already, prenatal diagnosis raises perplexing ethical dilemmas. Such decisions will become even more difficult when genetic testing detects the presence in a fetus of diseases that are not life-threatening, but produce a child that is less than perfect. "As the years pass, this gray area of decision-making will widen inexorably," notes Robert Weinberg, a molecular biologist at MIT's Whitehead Institute. "Sooner or later, an enterprising graduate student will uncover a close association between a [gene] marker and some benign aspect of human variability like eye color. And then genetic decision-making will hinge on far more than avoiding dread disease." [18]

Is society prepared to handle the flood of genetic information that the Human Genome Project will provide? Dr. Billings says it isn't. "There is a gulf between what is technically possible and what is practical in this society," he says. "The technology is developing so quickly that we fail to realize that the application side — how much people know about genetics, about the accuracy of genetic testing, about the regulatory framework that is required — is lagging far behind." At present, a private company could hire a private physician to carry out gene therapy in a private hospital with no public review or oversight whatsoever.[19]

If gene therapy develops as a standard medical technology, other nettlesome issues will emerge regarding who is to pay for it, how to assure equitable access to it, who is qualified to perform it, how to regulate its proper use, and which diseases merit its applications.

Moreover, if somatic cell gene therapy is found to be useful in treating severe childhood disease, there will be strong incentive to develop techniques for gene therapy in fetuses. Scientists have extensive evidence that the metabolic abnormalities associated with some genetic diseases cause serious damage before birth.[20] But in order to correct those malfunctions, scientists need more information about gene expression during normal human development. Many believe that the only way to obtain such information will be through fetal research, which is currently banned in this country.*

---

*The United States has had a legislative ban on federally supported fetal research since November 1985. In addition, 25 states have statutes that limit or prohibit such research. See "Fetal Tissue Research," *The CQ Researcher*, August 16, 1991.

"We are mapping the human genome with one hand and cutting off opportunities to use that knowledge with the other," comments ethicist John Fletcher.

### Germ-line Therapy

During the next decade, experts say the real battle in human gene therapy will be waged over the issue of manipulating the germ-line of humans. Fortunately, some of the most ardent supporters of genetic research are the first to admit the potential for abuse and see the need for ground rules. "With regard to human therapeutics, no reasonable, rational or ethical scientist is currently contemplating germ-line therapy," says Viagene's Bruce Merchant. "It will open a Pandora's box of public debate that will go on for decades. The abortion issue will pale by comparison."

Nevertheless, successful germ-line experiments are already being conducted in animals — and critics say it is only a matter of time before it will be done with humans. "Many scientists recognize the broader social repugnance of germ-line therapy, but if the technology is available, I'm not so sure they will be able to resist it," cautions Nachama Wilker, executive director of the Council for Responsible Genetics.

Ethicist LeRoy Walters envisions two possible rationales for using germ-line therapy to treat genetic diseases. The first would arise if some genetic diseases were found to be resistant to somatic cell gene therapy, such as those involving the central nervous system. In those cases, it might be necessary to insert genes into the cells of a very early embryo. The second rationale involves the issue of efficiency. If somatic cell gene therapy became a successful cure for some of the more prevalent genetic diseases, such as cystic fibrosis, the treated patients would constitute a new group of de-

fective gene "carriers." It might be more efficient, socially as well as clinically, to correct the flaw in the embryo, according to Walters.[21]

This summer, the RAC's Human Gene Therapy Subcommittee appointed a panel to determine how to broach the volatile issue. But so long as there are federal restrictions on fetal tissue research the debate may be moot, says Fletcher. "Until we restore areas of scientific and clinical inquiry in the federal sector," he adds, "I see no plausible hypothesis for trying germ-line therapy for a long time to come."

"At some point, we must ask ourselves what is worth trying to fix — to engineer out of the human genome," says ethicist Arthur Caplan. "The real issue is not germ-line therapy versus somatic therapy. It is: What is the risk/benefit ratio for the individual? What degree of uncertainty is there with the therapy?" Over the next decade, one of society's greatest challenges will be deciding where to draw the line.

For those with children who suffer from a cruel disease or who themselves are predisposed toward cancer or some ravaging mental disorder, that decision may be less complicated. Human gene therapy offers the most tangible — albeit distant — prospect for an improved life. ∎

## Notes

[1] In 1927, the U.S. Supreme Court assessed the constitutionality of the Virginia sterilization statute. In *Buck v. Bell*, the court upheld the statute, which allowed the involuntary sterilization of patients of state institutions who suffered from hereditary insanity or mental deficiency. See Lori B. Andrews, *Medical Genetics: A Legal Frontier*, 1987, p. 13.

[2] Quoted in *The New York Times*, Sept. 16, 1990.

[3] See Council for Responsible Genetics, *Position Paper on Genetic Discrimination*, 1990.

[4] For background on an interesting case where this debate is currently being played out, see "Should Bree Walker conceive a child?" in the *Los Angeles Times*, Aug. 17, 1991.

[5] Quoted in "The Ultimate Medicine," *Discover*, March 1990, p. 62.

[6] See Institute of Medicine, *Bio-Medical Politics*, 1991, pp. 258-298.

[7] See LeRoy Walters, "The Ethics of Human Gene Therapy," *Human Gene Therapy*, summer 1991, p. 116.

[8] See the *Los Angeles Times*, Oct. 8, 1980.

[9] See Office of Technology Assessment, *Human Gene Therapy: Background Paper*, 1984.

[10] See Walters, *op. cit.,* p. 116. The Recombinant DNA Advisory Committee (RAC) of NIH is the most critical regulatory hoop. By early 1983 the RAC had already functioned for almost eight years as the national standard-setting and review body for laboratory research for the early efforts to use DNA technology in manufacturing pharmaceuticals. The RAC, however, oversees only research proposals that involve federal funding.

[11] For a more detailed description of the scientific challenges of gene therapy, see "Gene Therapy in Perspective," *Nature*, January 1991, p. 275.

[12] Quoted in *Discover, op. cit.,* p. 62.

[13] Quoted in Robin Marantz Henig, "Dr. Anderson's Gene Machine," *The New York Times Magazine*, March 31, 1991, p. 34.

[14] Quoted in *Time*, Sept. 24, 1990, p. 76.

[15] See *Science*, Sept. 28, 1990, p. 1503, and *Science News*, April 20, 1991, p. 246.

[16] Quoted in *The New York Times*, Aug. 5, 1990.

[17] Henig, *op. cit.,* p. 35; see also *The Washington Post*, Aug. 26, 1991.

[18] Robert A. Weinberg, *Technology Review*, April 1991, p. 48.

[19] Concern about this issues was expressed in an editorial by Dr. French Anderson in *Human Gene Therapy*, autumn 1991, p. 194.

[20] Eve Nichols, *Human Gene Therapy*, 1988, p. 168.

[21] For a discussion of germ-line gene therapy, see LeRoy Walters, "Ethical Issues in Human Gene Therapy," *Journal of Clinical Ethics* (to be published December 1991).

# Bibliography

## Selected Sources Used

### Books

**Andrews, Lori B., *Medical Genetics: A Legal Frontier*, American Bar Association, 1987.**

Andrews, a lawyer and expert on biomedicine, offers a detailed and well-documented account of the legal issues associated with genetic research.

**Holtzman, Neil A., *Proceed with Caution: Predicting Genetic Risks in the Recombinant DNA Era*, Johns Hopkins University Press, 1989.**

This thoughtful book takes a wide-ranging look at the role of genetics in human disease. It explains how recombinant DNA technology has revolutionized the ability to identify the genes that predispose to or cause illness. The author also makes specific recommendations toward reducing the risk of genetic technology misuse.

**Nichols, Eve, *Human Gene Therapy*, Harvard University Press, 1988.**

This is an excellent primer on gene therapy. Nichols explores the potential for gene therapy and provides useful background on various technologies involved.

### Articles

**Anderson, W. French, "Genetics and Human Malleability," *Hastings Center Report*, January/February 1990.**

Dr. Anderson has written extensively on the subject, but this article in particular provides insight into where he believes the field of gene therapy is going, and where he feels the ethical boundaries should be drawn.

**Fletcher, John C., "Evolution of Ethical Debate about Human Gene Therapy," *Human Gene Therapy*, spring 1990.**

Fletcher presents a succinct summary of the events leading up to the first human gene therapy trial. He has been an important voice in the debate since its inception.

**Henig, Robin Marantz, "Dr. Anderson's Gene Machine," *The New York Times Magazine*, March 31, 1991.**

Henig offers a colorful — and fascinating — profile of Dr. W. French Anderson, concentrating on the long journey to public acceptance for the gene therapy field.

**Roberts, Leslie, "Ethical Questions Haunt New Genetic Technologies," *Science*, March 3, 1989.**

This is an excellent account of the acrimonious battle between gene therapy supporters at NIH and opponent Jeremy Rifkin. The author ultimately concludes that there is a need for a forum to debate the ethical issues that surround the new genetic technologies.

**Walters, LeRoy, "Human Gene Therapy: Ethics and Public Policy," *Human Gene Therapy*, summer 1991.**

The author explores on the ethical debate over gene therapy but also encourages that society look forward — and discuss the potential for germ-line gene therapy.

**Weinberg, Robert A., "The Dark Side of the Genome Project," *Technology Review*, April 1991.**

Weinberg, a noted molecular biologist, takes a very critical view of the Human Genome Project; he warns that the capabilities of genetic technology are advancing faster than society's ability to react.

**Wilfond, Benjamin S., and Fost, Norman, "The Cystic Fibrosis Gene: Medical and Social Implications for Heterozygote Detection," *The Journal of the American Medical Association*, May 23, 1990.**

In this detailed and heavily footnoted article, the authors address the principal issues concerning genetic screening, including the vast potential for stigmatization and discrimination.

**Wright, Robert, "Achilles' Helix," *The New Republic*, July 9, 1990.**

This article focuses on the politics as well as the personalities behind the Human Genome Project.

### Reports and Studies

**Council for Responsible Genetics, "Position Paper on Genetic Discrimination," 1990.**

This position paper focuses on the vast potential for abuse of genetic information and urges a cautionary approach.

**Industrial Biotechnology Association, "Gene Therapy and Genetic Screening: Issues to Consider," 1991.**

This brief report touches on all the main scientific, social and ethical issues raised by human gene therapy.

**Office of Technology Assessment, "Genetic Monitoring and Screening in the Workplace," October 1990.**

The OTA is one of the best sources for information on genetics research. Its exhaustive report on genetic screening outlines the major policy issues that society will confront *before* gene therapy becomes commonplace.

# The Next Step

## Additional Articles from Current Periodicals

### Cancer therapy

**Ames, K. and Crandal, R., "On the trail of an elusive killer," *Newsweek,* Nov. 26, 1990, p. 68.**

Announces that a powerful weapon in the war against cancer — gene therapy — received the Food and Drug Administration's go-ahead. By year-end, scientists at the National Institutes of Health (NIH) intend to work with the first of 50 terminal patients with advanced melanoma, a virulent skin cancer that does not respond to any other form of treatment. Head of the research team, Steven A. Rosenberg; tests on rhesus monkeys; details.

**Corelli, R., "Advancing on cancer," *Maclean's,* Aug. 13, 1990, p. 48.**

Discusses the National Institutes of Health's authorization for gene-therapy experiments on children with ADA (adenosine deaminase) deficiency and patients with melanoma, a fatal form of skin cancer. Implications for gene therapy; research teams. INSET: The drug war against AIDS (Abbott Laboratories AIDS-fighting compound called A-74704).

**Culliton, B. J., "Gene therapy: Into the home stretch," *Science,* Aug. 31, 1990, p. 974.**

Describes gene therapy that researchers hope will treat cancerous tumors and immune deficiency, which has been approved after a long and difficult review process. Marker genes for bone marrow transplants; TNF gene experiment and ADA protocol; discussions with NIH's Institutional Biosafety Committee (IBC).

**Jereski, L. and Freundlich, N., "Stopping cancer in the starting blocks," *Business Week,* April 2, 1990, p. 82.**

Reviews some genetic research which shows unusual promise in a frustrating search for cancer cures. Money spent on research; identifying cancer-causing genes; a disease that kills 500,000 people annually; no miracles; striking results; gap between research and cancer therapies. INSETS: New tools for fighting cancer; the case of the missing gene: How doctors trace cancer's family ties.

**Karp, J. E. and Broder, S., "Oncology," *Journal of the American Medical Association,* June 19, 1991, p. 3141.**

Summarizes the use of principles of molecular biology for the treatment and care of patients with cancer. Evolution of gene therapy; insights into the forces that drive normal and abnormal cell division; practical applications including the drug taxol; chemoprevention.

**Weiss, R., "Cancer war escalates to genetic weapons," *Science News,* Feb. 2, 1991, p. 69.**

Reports on the first use of genetically engineered white blood cells in two cancer patients with advanced melanoma. The experimental approach's objectives; how the therapy works; Food and Drug Administration (FDA) concerns about toxicity of tumornecrosis factor (TNF); plans for continued experimental therapy.

### Case studies

**Angier, N., "For first time, gene therapy is tested on cancer patients," *The New York Times,* Jan. 30, 1991, p. A1.**

Reports that a 29-year-old woman and a 42-year-old man were the first two cancer patients to receive gene therapy in an attempt to defeat otherwise incurable tumors. Details of the procedure; researchers cautious.

**Ezzell, C., "Scientists seek to fight cancer with cancer," *Science News,* May 25, 1991, p. 326.**

Describes a proposed experiment in which cancer-fighting genes will be inserted into tumor cells taken from advanced melanomas, then put into cancer patients. Reasons for experiment; previous work with genetically modified tumor-infiltrating lymphocytes (TIL); results of TIL experiments; direct insertion of tumor necrosis factor (TNF); approval needed for experiment.

**Jaroff, L., Dorfman, A., et al., "Giant step for gene therapy," *Time,* Sept. 24, 1990, p. 74.**

Summarizes the use of gene therapy at the Clinical Center of the National Institutes of Health on a 4-year-old girl suffering from ADA deficiency, a rare, incurable and deadly genetic disease (similar to the one that claimed the life of David, the "bubble boy"). Landmark experiment; providing the body with healthy replacement genes that can fulfill the intended role of defective ones; Drs. W. French Anderson, R. Michael Blaese and Kenneth Culver.

**Marwick, C., "Two more cell infusions on schedule for gene replacement therapy patient," *Journal of the American Medical Association,* May 8, 1991, p. 2311.**

Reports that a 4-year-old girl with adenosine deaminase deficiency is being treated with gene replacement therapy at the National Institutes of Health in Bethesda, Md. Researchers plan to perform two more cell infusions on the patient. Minimal nature of adverse effects from the treatment.

## Cystic fibrosis therapy

**"Cystic fibrosis: towards the ultimate therapy, slowly,"** *Lancet*, Nov. 17, 1990, p. 1224.

Editorial. Offers physicians information on recent developments in cystic fibrosis research. Cautions that gene therapy is a long way off.

**Angier, N., "Team cures cell in cystic fibrosis by gene insertion,"** *The New York Times*, Sept. 21, 1990, p. A1.

Reports that scientists have cured cystic fibrosis cells in the laboratory by inserting a healthy version of the gene that causes the disease. The latest experiments were performed under test-tube conditions, and researchers warn that clinical therapies based on the new results are several years in the future. Also, there could be side effects that are yet to be discovered.

**Beardsley, T., "Clearing the airways,"** *Scientific American*, December 1990, p. 28.

Discusses the possible role gene therapy might play in correcting the genetic defect found in cystic fibrosis (CF) patients. Cystic fibrosis transmembrane regulator (CFTR); results of recent research; regulation of CFTR gene; drawbacks of gene therapy; research into introduction of CFTR gene into CF patients' lung cells.

**Brady, D., "Signals of hope,"** *Maclean's*, Oct. 1, 1990, p. 52.

Discusses recent gene therapy breakthroughs that could produce a cure for cystic fibrosis. Research conducted independently by teams at the universities of Michigan and Iowa; comments by Toronto-based CF researcher Lap-Chee Tsui and Dr. James Wilson of the University of Michigan.

**Brownlee, S., "People to watch: James Wilson,"** *U.S. News & World Report*, Dec. 31, 1990, p. 80.

Profiles James Wilson, 35, who, with colleagues at the University of Michigan, successfully inserted a gene into cells taken from people with cystic fibrosis, restoring the sick cells to health. Gene-therapy trial at the National Institutes of Health; breaking down cholesterol in rats; tinkering with the human genetic legacy; gene therapy's potential.

## Debates & issues

**Angier, N., "Gene implant therapy is backed for children with rare disease,"** *The New York Times*, March 8, 1990, p. A1.

Reports that the Institutional Biosafety Committee at the National Institutes of Health held the nation's first public hearing on a human gene therapy project and then approved it as safe without opposition. Under the proposal, children with a severe genetic disease would be treated by inserting new genes into their blood cells. If initial experiment proves successful, scientists say it will open a new chapter in treating hereditary diseases.

**Weatherall, D. J., "Gene therapy in perspective,"** *Nature*, Jan. 24, 1991, p. 275.

Presents a commentary on the reasons for the delays in human gene therapy even after the successes of molecular medicine and the recent announcement of a human gene transfer protocol. Ethical aspects; difficulties; progress.

**Wheeler, D. L., "Debate begins over who should pay for experimental gene therapy,"** *The Chronicle of Higher Education*, Feb. 13, 1991, p. A7.

Questions whether patients or their insurance companies should pay for some of the costs of experimental treatments in human gene therapy. University of Pittsburgh researchers; experiments at the National Institutes of Health financed by the federal government; "A major unresolved issue for all experimental treatments"; holding gene therapy hostage to a flaw in the American health-care system; third parties; consent forms.

## Research

**"More problems than products,"** *Nature*, Jan. 3, 1991, p. 5.

Reviews recent disappointments in the field of biotechnology. Genetically engineered L-tryptophan; takeovers and mergers; Bovine sumatotropin banned; gene therapy trial; regulations causing some progress and also restrictions in Europe. INSET: Engineering trouble? (L-tryptophan).

**Angier, N., "Drug cuts deaths tied to infection,"** *The New York Times*, Feb. 14, 1991, p. A1.

Discusses a new genetically engineered drug that significantly cuts the death rate from septic shock, a quick and overwhelming infection of the bloodstream that kills tens of thousands of people each year and is an especially great threat for hospital patients and wounded soldiers. The novel treatment is a human protein, called a monoclonal antibody, that has been manipulated in the laboratory to home in with a sharpshooter's precision on the bacterial toxin.

**Armstrong, L., " 'Antisense': A drug revolution in the making,"** *Business Week*, March 5, 1990, p. 88.

Reports how companies like ISIS Pharmaceuticals and others are trying to design antisense compounds to seek and destroy genes that carry viruses — including AIDS. Gene targeting is the inevitable next step in human therapeutics; research being done; how antisense drugs work; the cutting edge.

**Beardsley, T., "Profile: Gene doctor," *Scientific American*, August 1990, p. 33.**

Profiles gene therapist W. French Anderson, chief of the molecular hematology branch of the National Heart, Lung and Blood Institute, who expects to begin gene therapy on a young, severe combined immunodeficiency (SCID) patient this fall. Career at Harvard; research on DNA; work at NIH; work on regulatory approval for gene therapy; risks of therapy.

**Carey, J., Hamilton, J. O., et al., "The genetic age," *Business Week*, May 28, 1990, p. 68.**

Describes how science is making huge strides in linking genes to disease. New tests, drugs, and treatments promise to revolutionize medicine. INSETS: Fatal attraction: When deadly genes get together, by J. Carey; Closing in on disease-causing genes; Gene therapy: Cells that carry messengers of health, by J. Carey; Rooting out a cause of mental retardation, by J. Carey; The technology behind the breakthroughs, by J. O. Hamilton and N. Freundlich.

**Hughes, M. R. and Caskey, C. T., "Medical genetics," *Journal of the American Medical Association*, June 19, 1991, p. 3132.**

Highlights several selected genetic developments of 1990. Molecular genetics of cancer predisposition; human Genome Initiative; clinical trends on gene replacement therapy initiated.

**Verma, I. M., "Gene therapy," *Scientific American*, November 1990, p. 68.**

Details research into somatic cell therapy for genetic defects. Problems controlling the fate of DNA introduced into cells; gene augmentation; methods of non-targeted delivery of genes; Retrovirus gene delivery system; treatment of beta thalassemia research; precise regulation of expression; genetic alteration of skin cells; liver cell gene therapy. INSET: Further reading.

**Wheeler, D. L., "Gene-therapy trials in human subjects backed by NIH panel," *The Chronicle of Higher Education*, Aug. 8, 1990, p. A1.**

Reports that the Recombinant DNA Advisory Committee (NIH) has recommended granting permission for two human gene-therapy experiments that would add the alteration of genes in human cells to the repertoire of treatments that can be used to fight disease. Need approval from Food and Drug Administration.

## Transplantation

**Chen, I., "Rabbit trail may lead to human gene therapy," *Science News*, Nov. 10, 1990, p. 294.**

States that scientists have temporarily abated an inherited, cholesterol-elevating disease in rabbits using transplants of genetically modified liver cells. Disease known as familial hypercholesterolemia is now treated only moderately successfully by liver transplantation.

**Ezzell, C., "Gene therapy meets liver transplants," *Science News*, April 13, 1991, p. 228.**

Reports on approval by the National Institutes of Health's (NIH) Human Gene Therapy Subcommittee of a new cell-transplant technique that would seed the failing livers of very sick children with healthy, genetically marked liver cells. Alternative to whole-liver transplants; treatment plans; opposing votes; approval of other gene-marker experiments.

## Viruses

**Ezzell, C., "Genetic therapy: Just a nasal spray away?" *Science News*, April 20, 1991, p. 246.**

Looks at the possible use of genetically engineered cold viruses to help treat inherited lung diseases such as cystic fibrosis by carrying normal genes into the lungs by a nasal spray. Details of research; possible applications.

**Hoffman, M., "New vector delivers genes to lung cells," *Science*, April 19, 1991, p. 374.**

Describes research which shows that viruses have the potential to cure disease as well as to cause it. Delivery of "therapeutic" gene by coldlike virus in rats; potential pitfalls of more common gene-delivery systems; using adenoviruses; treatment of hereditary emphysema; questions about virus' safety and effectiveness.

**Montgomery, G., "The ultimate medicine," *Discover*, March 1990, p. 60.**

Discusses research that is using viruses, nature's genetic parasites, to carry beneficial genes into sick cells, or gene therapy, and its applications for treatment of genetic disorders. Studies of hemoglobin; problems facing researchers; Retroviral trucks; switches and enhancers; first human gene transplant; drawbacks of gene therapy.

**Tiollais, P. and Buendia, M., "Hepatitis B virus," *Scientific American*, April 1991, p. 116.**

Contends that new vaccines produced by genetic engineering hold the promise of eradicating liver diseases and a common form of cancer caused by the hepatitis B virus. Explanation of HBV infection; expression of the various HBV genes; how HBV induces cancers; Molecular hybridization technique; more.

# Back Issues

*Great Research on Current Issues Starts Right Here... Recent topics covered by The CQ Researcher are listed below. Issues dated before May 10, 1991, were published under the name of Editorial Research Reports.*

**APRIL 1990**
How Fair is the Tax Burden?
Workers' Compensation
U.S. Pacific Forces
Curbing Insurance Premiums

**MAY 1990**
Should Teaching Be a Profession?
Will Canada Fall Apart?
Is U.S. Patent System Outdated?
Federal Funding for the Arts

**JUNE 1990**
Downsizing America's Armed Forces
Progress In Weather Forecasting
S & L Bailout
Bio-Chemical Disarmament

**JULY 1990**
Do Americans Still Love Marriage?
Death Penalty Debate
Decline of Rural America
United Nations in the 1990s

**AUGUST 1990**
Democracy in the Philippines
Initiatives: True Democracy?
Hard Times at Newspapers
Teens Balance School & Jobs

**SEPTEMBER 1990**
Dangers of Alcohol
Western Alliance After the Cold War
Tobacco Industry
Right to Die

**OCTOBER 1990**
Organ Transplants
Energy Policy Options
Search for Arab Unity
Child Support

**NOVEMBER 1990**
Lotteries and Gambling
Post Cold-War Choices
Setting Limits on Medical Care
Multicultural Education

**DECEMBER 1990**
Cable TV Regulation
Americans' Search For Their Roots
Is Insurance System a Failure?
Why Schools Still Have Tracking

**JANUARY 1991**
Growing Influence of Boycotts
Should the U.S. Reinstate the Draft?
America's Archaeological Past
Peace Corps' Challenges in '90s

**FEBRUARY 1991**
Regional Impact of Recession
Puerto Rico's Status
Redistricting: Mapping Power
Nuclear Power

**MARCH 1991**
Acid Rain
Cost of the Gulf War
Reassessing Gun Laws
Future for Man in Space

**APRIL 1991**
Social Security
Canadian Crisis Over Quebec
California Drought
Electromagnetic Radiation

**MAY 1991**
School Choice
Racial Quotas
Animal Rights
U.S. and Japan

**JUNE 1991**
Children and Divorce
Teenage Suicide
Endangered Species
Europe 1992

**JULY 1991**
Teenagers and Abortion
Soviet Republics Rebel
Mexico's Emergence
Athletes and Drugs

**AUGUST 1991**
Sexual Harassment
Fetal Tissue Research
Oil Imports
The Palestinians

**SEPTEMBER 1991**
Police Brutality
Advertising Under Attack
Saving the Forests
Foster Care Crisis

**OCTOBER 1991**
Pay-Per-View TV
Youth Gangs

Back issues are available for $4.00 (subscribers) or $7.00 (non-subscribers). Quantity discounts apply to orders over ten. To order, call Congressional Quarterly 1-800-432-2250.

# Future Topics

▶ *World Hunger*

▶ *Fast-Food Business*

▶ *Eastern Europe's Environmental Problems*

# THE CQ Researcher

PUBLISHED BY CONGRESSIONAL QUARTERLY INC., IN CONJUNCTION WITH EBSCO PUBLISHING

# World Hunger

*New questions arise about ways to fight food shortages*

THE SOVIET UNION, CRIPPLED BY CROP failures and a virtual breakdown of its economic system, is appealing for massive shipments of food and medicine to help the Soviet people get through the winter without serious shortages. With world attention riveted on the Soviets, hunger in other parts of the world has almost been forgotten. Yet the United Nations reports that 30 million Africans face starvation unless massive shipments of food aid reach them soon. U.S. policy-makers are at odds over the proper role of aid in overcoming famine and promoting self-sufficiency in countries with chronic food shortages. Meanwhile, eager to encourage the Soviets' move toward democracy and free markets, the United States and other countries with surplus food have promised to help.

## THIS ISSUE

C Q   **October 25, 1991 • Volume 1, No. 24 • 801-824**

*Formerly Editorial Research Reports*

COVER ART: BARBARA SASSA-DANIELS

# CQ Researcher

October 25, 1991
Volume 1, No. 24

**EDITOR**
Sandra Stencel

**MANAGING EDITOR**
Thomas J. Colin

**ASSOCIATE EDITOR**
Richard L. Worsnop

**STAFF WRITERS**
Charles S. Clark
Mary H. Cooper
Rodman D. Griffin

**PRODUCTION EDITOR**
Laurie De Maris

**EDITORIAL ASSISTANT**
Thomas H. Moore

**GRAPHICS**
Jack Auldridge

**PUBLISHED BY**
Congressional Quarterly Inc.

**CHAIRMAN**
Andrew Barnes

**VICE CHAIRMAN**
Andrew P. Corty

**EDITOR AND PUBLISHER**
Neil Skene

**EXECUTIVE EDITOR**
Robert W. Merry

**PUBLICATIONS MARKETING/SALES**
Robert Smith

**EDITOR, EBSCO PUBLISHING**
Melissa Kummerer

The CQ Researcher (ISSN 1056-2036). Formerly Editorial Research Reports. Published weekly (48 times per year, not printed the first Friday of any month with five Fridays) by Congressional Quarterly Inc., 1414 22nd St., N.W., Washington, D.C. 20037. Rates are furnished upon request. Application to mail at second-class postage rates is pending at Washington, D.C. POSTMASTER: Send address changes to The CQ Researcher, 1414 22nd St., N.W., Washington, D.C. 20037.

# World Hunger

BY MARY H. COOPER

## THE ISSUES

At a time when food shortages are threatening millions of people in developing nations with starvation, the Soviet Union faces its own crisis. The beleaguered nation has launched an appeal for help from the United States, Western Europe and Japan to avert massive shortages of food and medicine this winter. Unless they soon receive nearly $15 billion worth of supplies, the Soviets warn, popular discontent over deteriorating living conditions may evolve into a revolt that could scuttle recent political and economic reforms.

The world's "donor" countries — the United States and others with food surpluses that traditionally provide the bulk of emergency food aid — are responding quickly to the Soviets' pleas. Once reluctant to assist this former adversary until it had proved its commitment to democratic reform, the United States was jolted into action after the failed coup by Communist hardliners against the government of Mikhail S. Gorbachev.

During their three days in power, the coup's instigators made clear their intention to reverse the democratic and economic reforms Gorbachev had introduced since taking power in 1985. Once reinstated as the head of an interim government in a much looser confederation of Soviet republics, Gorbachev took several radical steps that convinced the Bush administration of his government's commitment to reform. The transitional State Council recognized the independence of the Baltic republics of Latvia, Lithuania and Estonia, promised to remove Soviet troops from Cuba and began work on an economic plan that would

lead the country into the free-market global economy.

Eager to encourage the reform process and fearful that food shortages might undermine its legitimacy in the eyes of the Soviet people, American officials promised on Sept. 18 that the United States would help with direct food deliveries and suggested that the Soviet Union might also receive easier financing terms on U.S.-backed loans for food purchases. The Bush administration also sent a mission of agricultural experts to the Soviet Union to determine the country's immediate needs.

While Soviet citizens facing winter shortages of food have captured the attention of the media and politicians, other peoples have far more serious problems. Far from the limelight, 30 million Africans face the real and immediate menace of starvation, according to the United Nations. Only five years ago, victims of famine in the Horn of Africa (Somalia, Ethiopia and Djibouti) received huge shipments of food aid from the United States and Western European

nations. Since then, however, their plight has actually worsened, while deteriorating economic conditions throughout sub-Saharan Africa have extended the threat of famine to additional millions in other areas of Africa as well.

Famine is the final, most critical stage of the suffering caused by the lack of nutritious, affordable food. But the list of suffering people goes well beyond famine victims. The U.N. Food and Agriculture Organization (FAO) estimates that as many as 550 million people around the world suffer from chronic hunger. That means that about one in 10 of the world's population does not get enough food to eat. Those figures do not even include the additional hundreds of millions of people — mainly children — who suffer blindness, goiter, anemia and other diseases due to poor diet.

The persistence of hunger at a time when technological advances have improved agricultural productivity has sparked a debate among U.S. policy-makers and agricultural experts about the causes of hunger and the Earth's ability to support its growing population. Some observers say that food crops are a finite resource whose availability is threatened by global warming and other forms of environmental degradation. Others maintain that rising crop yields and declining population growth rates argue against such dire predictions. They say that apart from natural disasters such as drought and floods, remaining pockets of hunger are due primarily to local political and social circumstances — for example, government interference in the free market, as in the Soviet Union, or civil war, as in the Horn of Africa. Here are some of the major questions being raised in the debate:

**October 25, 1991    803**

**How severe is the food shortage in the Soviet Union?**

The Soviet Union, with its advanced industrial base and vast agricultural resources, faces food problems that are short-term in nature. The transition from a state-controlled economy to a free market will be wrenching and may yet fail. But the country's long-term ability to feed its 290 million citizens is not in question.

What many observers do question is the amount of political fallout that could accompany short-term food shortages. The concern is not so much that people will die of hunger during the harsh northern winter but rather that they will withdraw their support for the economic-reform process and prompt a return to totalitarian rule.

Although there was little variety in the food sold in state stores before the Soviet Union embarked on its road to economic reform, the centrally controlled agricultural system did offer a fairly reliable supply of affordable food. *(See story, p. 818.)* The government subsidized food and other basic commodities to keep prices low for consumers. Meat and other items that were in short supply at subsidized prices could be obtained at higher prices from cooperative markets that sold products from farmers' private plots.

Today, the old economic system survives, but it has been crippled by a breakdown in the food distribution network, caused mainly by hoarding at both ends of the supply chain. "A lot of the problem in distribution is that the currency is valueless," says Carol G. Brookins, president of World Perspectives, Inc., an agricultural consulting firm in Washington. If state subsidies for consumer items are removed, she explains, prices for these items can be expected to rise, and rise fast — producing runaway inflation and devaluation of the ruble, the Soviet Union's currency. "In

any country where there is runaway inflation, commodity producers hold on to their products, because once they sell it they get something for it that becomes valueless," Brookins adds.

As one measure of the extent of hoarding, a government official in the Ukraine, the Soviet Union's bread basket, reported in mid-September that his region's granaries held only 6.5 million of the 17 million tons of grain it will need this winter.[1]

As they learn that farmers are hoarding their produce, consumers at the other end of the distribution chain follow suit, buying up canned food and other durable goods at current prices in anticipation of later shortages and higher prices. "Hoarding is a normal instinct of people when their currency is valueless and when they don't know what is going to happen," says Brookins, who visited the Soviet Union in August. As the ruble loses its value and the distribution system breaks down, managers of collective farms and factories are taking matters into their own hands, bartering manufactured goods for food.

This is not to say that the food situation in the Soviet Union is not precarious and, in certain areas, critical. Bartering may work in the countryside, but it does little to alleviate the situation in the cities. As food supplies disappear from the shelves of state stores, some essentials, such as flour, butter, oats and cereal, are being rationed in St. Petersburg (formerly Leningrad), Russia's second-largest city.[2]

The Soviet Union has long been the world's biggest grain importer, accounting for a fifth of global grain sales. This year, the grain crop amounted to only 190 million tons, down 20 percent from last year's record level of 235 million tons, so the country's need for imports will be even greater. Overall food pro-

duction, by Soviet accounts, is down by more than 10 percent since last year, and the remaining 12 republics are said to need grain and sugar.*

Over the past few weeks estimates of the amount of food the country will need have mushroomed. Gorbachev originally asked for $7.4 billion in food aid, already a massive amount. Then, on September 19, his government doubled the request, saying $14.7 billion worth of food in direct aid and credits to buy grain on the world market would be required to make it through the winter.

The credits are needed because the Soviet Union is not producing enough oil, its main source of hard currency, to pay for its food needs. Long the world's biggest oil producer, the Soviet Union used dollars earned from oil exports to pay for the grain it bought from the United States and other grain producers. But the Soviets' oil reserves have been dwindling for several years, reducing output.

In addition, the turmoil that has accompanied the breakdown of the centrally planned economy has disrupted the supply of oil-drilling machinery, replacement parts and transportation equipment, further reducing oil output.

**How severe are food shortages in the rest of the world?**

Media attention to the dramatic, recent events in the Soviet Union obscures a stark reality: More than 17 million people around the world will die this year from starvation. Most other nations affected by hunger fall into the more common pat-

---

*Under the reorganization of the Soviet Union announced Sept. 6, the transitional State Council headed by Gorbachev includes representatives of all 15 republics that made up the Soviet Union before the coup except Lithuania, Latvia and Estonia, whose independence the council recognized the same day. The remaining 12 republics must decide whether to be part of the new "Union of Sovereign States."

# Hunger Spans the Globe

*More than 550 million people in 31 countries need what the United Nations Food and Agriculture Organization calls "exceptional assistance" in food supplies. Shortages are triggered by a number of factors, including crop failures, natural disasters and distribution disruptions caused by civil strife and influxes of refugees.*

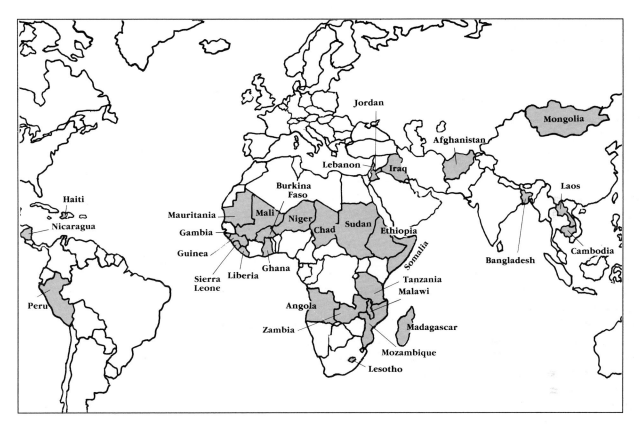

*Source: United Nations Food and Agriculture Organization.*

tern of poverty, underdevelopment and poor growing conditions that have destroyed their ability to feed their populations. And while world attention is focused on the needs of the Soviet Union, some of these countries face far more serious problems. Famine threatens 30 million people in Africa alone, especially in the Sudan and Ethiopia. "People there are dying ... and they are mostly small children under the age of five," says Rob Buchanan, program director for the Horn of Africa at Oxfam America, a relief organization that distributes food aid worldwide.

Civil war in Sudan and, until the

fall of the government in May, in Ethiopia as well, is the main cause of famine conditions in the region because of the massive logistical problems it has created. The needs of some 9 million refugees and displaced people in each of these countries, Buchanan says, have put a tremendous strain on their food distribution systems.

Although the situation in the Horn of Africa is almost as bad as it was in the mid-1980s, few people in the industrial world are aware that food shortages even exist there today. "The media tend to treat famine in Africa as an old story," Buchanan says. "There is nothing really new

about it, so it's not very newsworthy." Buchanan blames the media's simplistic approach to famine and its causes for this information gap.

When the story of famine in Ethiopia was picked up back in the mid-1980s, he says, "it was presented in a sensationalistic way so people felt there was a chance to solve the problem once and for all if [everyone] contributed money and if governments gave food relief."

At the time, people were poorly informed about the basic causes of the famine — mainly civil war and debt — problems Buchanan says "are very difficult to explain in two or three sentences in a newspaper."

## Big Food Donors

*The United States is the biggest giver of food aid by far, followed by the European Community, Canada, Japan and Australia. Most of the world's grain aid goes to developing nations in Africa, Asia and Latin America.*

| DONORS | 1989-1990 (000 tons of grain) |
|---|---|
| Australia | 305 |
| Austria | 18 |
| Canada | 930 |
| European Community Total † | 3,293 |
| EC as a group | 2,547 |
| Individual EC nations | 747 |
| Belgium-Luxembourg | 18 |
| Denmark | 1 |
| France | 170 |
| Germany | 259 |
| Greece | 3 |
| Italy | 90 |
| Netherlands | 98 |
| Spain | 25 |
| United Kingdom | 83 |
| Finland | 27 |
| Japan | 430 |
| Norway | 31 |
| Saudi Arabia | 8 |
| Sweden | 82 |
| Switzerland | 35 |
| United States | 6,147 |
| U.N. World Food Program purchases | 19 |
| Others | 65 |
| **TOTAL SHIPMENTS** | 11,390 |
| Wheat | 7,875 |
| Rice | 691 |
| Coarse grains | 2,823 |
| **RECIPIENTS** | |
| Developing countries † | 9,806 |
| Africa | 4,595 |
| Asia | 3,213 |
| Latin America | 1,781 |
| Other regions | 219 |

† *Total inexact due to rounding.*

*Source: Food and Agriculture Organization of the United Nations.*

Because the public was left with the idea that the massive food aid of the mid-1980s had solved the problem, he adds, "it's very difficult now to mobilize international support that really needs to be mobilized."

About a third of Africa's 500 million population is undernourished, according to FAO. But more than half the 550 million undernourished people in the world live in Asia. Other regions affected by hunger are Latin America, the Caribbean and the Near East. Most hungry people live in rural areas of developing countries and tend to belong to families of landless farm workers and animal herders.

The vast majority — 11 million — of the 17 million people who die each year of starvation or, more commonly, of hunger-related diseases, are children under the age of five. These deaths could be prevented by adequate supplies of food. That's because most of the diseases that cause death among the hungry — diarrhea, measles and respiratory infections — are not life-threatening in the absence of malnutrition.

In Africa, the damage to crops and food distribution systems caused by civil war ranges far beyond Sudan and Ethiopia, affecting Liberia, Angola, Mozambique and other nations. In Asia, Afghanistan and Cambodia are suffering from food shortages caused primarily by the disruption of planting, transportation and distribution of crops because of ongoing civil conflict. The Persian Gulf War has pushed much of the population of Iraq to the brink of famine while refugees from that conflict are straining Jordan's ability to feed them.

Although human actions are most often the leading cause of hunger today, adverse weather conditions continue to play an important role. Drought has reduced food supplies in much of Africa as well as in Southeast Asia this year, while summer floods have destroyed crops in China, and last spring's devastating cyclone in Bangladesh wiped out vast areas under cultivation.

### What motivates the major food "donor" countries?

Countries that grow surplus food crops typically set aside more than 10 million tons of grain each year for aid. FAO estimates that this year's supply of emergency grain will reach 11.2 million tons.[3] With heavily indebted developing countries unable to buy the food they need on the commercial market, it is expected that even greater amounts of food aid will be required in the future.

Although food aid most directly benefits the recipient nation's hungry population, it also helps the donor nations maintain their agricultural stabilization policies. The United States, the 12-nation European Community (EC) and most other food exporters subsidize agricultural production within their own territory. By assuring farmers of receiving a certain price for the commodities they grow, governments guard against potentially devastating price swings that result from unexpected changes in weather patterns or global supplies.

Unusually good weather in wheat-producing nations, for example, often results in a global bumper crop of wheat. When world supplies exceed demand for the grain, wheat prices fall. If prices fall far enough, farmers who have already invested in fertilizer, harvesting equipment and other agricultural "inputs" may not receive enough money for their wheat crops to cover their investment. In some years, prices fall so low that many farmers are driven out of business.

In an effort to stabilize agricultural-commodity prices, and thus protect the farmers, the United States controls production of so-called target-price commodities, including wheat, feed grains, cotton and rice. Each year the secretary of Agriculture determines whether production of these commodities should be limited.

This year, for example, it was decided that only 5 percent of the land used to cultivate wheat should be taken out of production for the recently planted 1992 wheat crop. Since wheat acreage was reduced by 15 percent last year, the 1992 wheat crop should be about 10 percent bigger than this year's. The decision was made to leave more land in cultivation mostly because of low stocks in the United States and "to assure ourselves of sufficient stocks to meet not only commercial sales but any food aid and donations that we would be involved in," said Randy Weber, assistant deputy administration of the Agricultural Stabilization and Conservation Service, which administers the U.S. farm program.

The EC also has an agricultural subsidy program, known as the Common Agricultural Policy (CAP). Like the U.S. farm program, CAP is designed to prevent wide fluctuations in world agricultural commodity prices. By paying relatively high prices for EC farm products, CAP is also intended to protect European farmers, whose land holdings typically are much smaller than those of American and Canadian farmers and who are thus less able to exploit the economies of scale available to their North American competitors on the world market. Partly because of the generous subsidies offered by CAP, however, EC farmers regularly produce surplus amounts of certain commodities, notably meat, butter and grain, which become available for food aid and assistance.

This year, the European Community has taken the lead in responding to Soviet appeals for food aid and has already promised $300 million in free food. The EC has also announced plans to buy surplus food from Eastern Europe and ship it to the Soviet Union, a transaction that shows how the system of agricultural subsidies in producer nations can help all parties.

The surplus food in question was produced in Poland, Hungary and Czechoslovakia, which wanted to sell it to EC countries as part of the effort to break free of their 45-year economic dependence on the Soviet Union. Citing the community's policy of protecting domestic farmers from low-price imports, however, France blocked an EC initiative to buy the food, even though the EC had enthusiastically supported Eastern Europe's economic reform programs. The compromise is not fully acceptable to Poland and the other East European producers, who would prefer to establish normal trade relations with the EC. But by purchasing the food and then giving it to the Soviet Union, the EC can honor its food aid commitment and continue to protect its farmers while offering the East Europeans a market for their products.

Outright food aid, provided free in emergency situations, is less common than food assistance programs, in which grain and other food supplies are sold on favorable terms to needy countries. "There is a tendency to assume that anything that involves a government program is by definition aid, and that is much too broad an assumption," says Robert Kohlmeyer, vice president of World Perspectives.

In addition to emergency aid, donor nations with food surpluses also offer government-guaranteed loans to countries with food shortages so that they can buy surplus grain and other food on a commercial basis. Kohlmeyer adds that the only assistance programs the Bush administration has so far made available to the Soviet Union are the credit guarantees. "Those are clearly commercial in nature," he says.

President Bush authorized U.S. loan guarantees for the Soviet Union totaling $1.5 billion on June 11. So far, the Soviet Union has received $600 million in such loans, all from European banks. An additional $500 million in loan guarantees became available October 1, and a final installment of $400 million is due in February. In the event that the Soviet Union defaults, the U.S. government assumes responsibility for 98 percent of the loan principal as well as 4.5 percentage points of the interest charged. But so far U.S. banks have balked at lending to the Soviet Union, even with the guarantees. The country's foreign debt has been rising quickly over the past few years because dwindling oil exports have failed to generate enough foreign exchange to buy grain and other food.

### What blocks food aid from getting where it is needed?

Two practices by food-exporting nations suggest that there is plenty of food available in the world — stockpiling surplus production and paying farmers not to cultivate available land when world food surpluses begin driving down commodity prices. The FAO estimates, in fact, that 10 percent more food is typically produced than is needed to feed all the world's inhabitants.

The problem, simply, is a chronic inability to distribute the food where it is needed. International trade conditions prevent many developing nations from acquiring adequate supplies from exporters. This obstacle can be traced in large part to the Third World debt crisis, which began in the late 1970s when developing countries that had borrowed large amounts of money were unable to keep up with payments on their debts. As a result of recent oil price increases, many of these countries were spending more on oil and other imports than they could earn

# Food Aid Agencies and Organizations

Before the 1960s, food aid was largely a matter of individual governments' initiative. The United States and other food exporters would donate their surplus harvests directly to countries beset with temporary food emergencies. In 1961, however, the United Nations and its affiliated agency, the Food and Agriculture Organization, set up the World Food Program to collect surplus food and cash from U.N. member nations to provide relief in food emergencies. In 1974, following widespread crop failures in the early 1970s, the U.N. General Assembly created the 36-member World Food Council to coordinate food assistance and help governments in longer-term efforts to eliminate hunger and malnutrition.

Once donor nations send food aid to needy countries, either directly or through the U.N. agencies, their role in the relief effort typically ends. Once the food arrives at the port of destination, other agencies assume responsibility for its distribution. When the emergency is the result of a natural disaster such as a cyclone or drought, it is generally the government of the recipient nation that receives and distributes food aid to famine victims, often in centralized camps located in remote rural areas.

But when famine is the result of civil strife, as is often the case today, local government agencies are often unwilling or unable to participate in the relief effort. In these cases the job of distributing food aid falls to non-governmental organizations, such as the Red Cross, which provide trucks

and also can offer medical assistance to famine victims. Specialized private relief agencies have also emerged in recent decades to facilitate food distribution efforts worldwide.

Some of the best-known agencies originated during World War II. This list includes Oxfam (originally the Oxford Committee for Famine Relief), Catholic Relief Services and CARE (Cooperative for American Relief Everywhere Inc.). Today, these agencies and numerous others are focusing their work on sub-Saharan Africa.

Additional information on current food relief efforts may be obtained from:

U.S. National Committee for World Food Day, 1001 22nd St., N.W., Washington, D.C. 20437, (202) 653-2404.

CARE, 660 First Ave., New York, N.Y. 10016, (212) 686-3110.

Oxfam America, 115 Broadway, Boston, Mass. 02116, (617) 482-1211.

Catholic Relief Services, P.O. Box 2045, Church Street Station, New York, N.Y. 10008, (212) 838-4700.

Africare, 1601 Connecticut Ave., N.W., Washington, D.C. 20009, (202) 462-3614.

American Friends Service Committee, 1501 Cherry St., Philadelphia, Pa. 19102, (215) 241-7000.

Lutheran World Relief, 360 Park Ave. South, New York, N.Y. 10010, (212) 532-6350.

---

on exports. The crisis has continued over the past decade, contributing to the decline of living conditions in much of the Third World. Unable to buy food on conventional terms, many developing countries appeal for assistance in buying food and, in emergencies, for direct food aid.

To add to their woes, developing countries also face barriers to selling what few goods and commodities they are able to produce. These take the form of tariffs, taxes that many nations still impose on imports in order to protect agricultural and industrial interests at home. Because of such tariffs, developing countries are often unable to sell their goods abroad and thus cannot earn the foreign exchange necessary to buy food.

But eliminating tariffs to improve

the efficient movement of food and goods in the world trading system is not an easy matter. Peter Day, an agricultural scientist at Rutgers University, explains the dilemma for the EC, which maintains one of the world's highest tariff barriers to outside agricultural commodities. "The EC faces the problem of keeping their farmers busy and productively employed," he says. "The fact that they can't produce on a large scale comparable to their North American cousins means that they have to be protected by these economic barriers and that if the economic barriers were torn down, then 90 percent of those farmers would probably go out of business and you would have all kinds of economic chaos. So it's a very real problem, and it isn't one that you can easily solve by saying

how ridiculous it is."

Once food supplies, either emergency aid or commercially purchased, arrive in port, more obstacles to efficient distribution frequently spring up. Underdeveloped countries, where hunger and famine most often strike, are unable to quickly move food from dockside to countryside. Railways, roads and trucks are few and in disrepair, while the hungry are usually far from the ports of entry. What has happened in the Sahel region of northern Africa is typical. "They would get large amounts of food to ports and to airfields, but distributing it out to where it was needed was extremely difficult because of the lack of infrastructure," Day says.

Ironically, a similar problem stymies the Soviet Union, whose role as a global superpower provides it with a vast industrial base and its own fuel supplies. But as the country's resources were diverted to the military sector during the Cold War, the consumer side of the economy, including food production and distribution, suffered. Once one of the world's leading grain producers, the Soviet Union was forced to begin importing grain in 1972 and has depended on imports ever since. The country's distribution system, never particularly efficient, has deteriorated even further during the past few years of economic upheaval and was a major cause of last winter's food shortages. As much as half the vegetable crops are said to have rotted in the fields, and a third of the harvested grain perished in leaky silos or was lost in transport to mills.

As a result of such problems, food donors worry that shipments they make to the Soviet Union this year may never reach consumers. To allay these concerns, Soviet officials have invited the International Red Cross to distribute donated food once it arrives in the country. The Soviet republics also agreed to overlook their differences with the central government in Moscow and coordinate the receipt and distribution of food aid throughout the coming winter.

### Should the United States provide food aid, considering its own domestic needs?

The United States has long taken the lead in providing emergency food aid to countries in distress. While few Americans oppose granting emergency food assistance to avert famine, the Soviet request has prompted a lively debate over the proper use of food aid. Along with emergency supplies, the Soviets are requesting longer-term assistance aimed at helping them dismantle their state-controlled system and build a market-based economy, a process that will undoubtedly entail

hardship for Soviet citizens.

Aside from humanitarian considerations, supporters of food aid stress that stocking store shelves will discourage hoarding and the consequent shortages of essential items and thus contribute to the success of economic reform. "The absence of food from store shelves is the most destabilizing force any society can ever confront," says Dwayne O. Andreas, chairman of Archer Daniels Midland, a U.S. food-products conglomerate that sells grain to the Soviets. "Confronted with food shortages, people quickly progress from anger, to hunger, to violence. The risk, of course, is that the seedling of Soviet democracy might be lost." [4]

But longer-term donations and credit for food purchases to help countries develop the capacity to feed their populations are controversial. Continuing to provide food aid after emergency needs are met, critics say, removes the incentive for recipient governments to invest in agricultural development. Even some Soviet officials concede this point. "We need to organize a sound economic life mostly on our own," Moscow Mayor Gavril Popov said recently. Emphasizing that the Soviet Union has enough food to feed its citizens, Popov noted the downside of food aid and assistance. "The best way for foreigners to help is to come in and invest for profit. Western aid in the past only postponed the necessary reforms." [5]

Many Americans agree with Popov's reasoning and oppose giving the Soviet Union more than emergency supplies for this winter, even though such aid would be aimed at helping the country become a productive member of the international trading system. According to a recent poll, 75 percent of the public opposes giving additional foreign aid in the form of cash grants to the Soviet Union, and only 40 percent favor giving the country low-

interest loans to help it adjust to a market system. [6]

Soviet appeals for food aid have been greeted with ambivalence in the United States. Many critics point to the unmet needs of poor people at home, many of whom suffer chronic malnutrition. Last year more than 33.5 million people in the United States lived below the official poverty line (which is $12,675 for a family of four), up 5.5 percent from the year before, according to a recent report to Congress. [7] The poor include a quarter of all children under six. Each month, according to the Physicians Task Force on Hunger in America, a half-million children suffer malnutrition.

While he voiced support for helping to avert famine in the Soviet Union, if necessary, Rep. David Bonior, D-Mich., the House majority whip, urged the administration to hold off on longer-term aid as long as domestic poverty is so great. "For 45 years ... the United States has rightfully extended a hand to much of the world. Now, until we have addressed our more pressing domestic problems, aid to other nations simply has to take second place. It took Dorothy a trip to Oz to discover that there is no place like home. We don't have to go any place to learn the same lesson or to see that it is time we began taking care of our own." [8]

But some agricultural analysts stress that there need be no contest between domestic and international programs for the needy. The "aid" being provided to the Soviets, for example, consists mostly of credit guarantees for commercial loans, not outright grants; thus it would not add to the federal budget deficit. "We're not giving the money away if it's a credit and the Soviets are to pay it back," says Carol Brookins of World Perspectives. "And there is no reason to believe that they won't pay it back." ■

# BACKGROUND

## The Green Revolution

Until the mid-20th century the world's growing population was able to satisfy its expanding food needs by clearing new land for cultivation. But around 1950 the supply of unexploited, easily utilized, arable land ran out. Ever since then, most increases in food supplies have come from gains in crop productivity.

The global effort to increase crop yields that began in the 1960s, known as the "Green Revolution," involved the development of new varieties of grains that were resistant to drought and insect infestation and produced high yields at harvest. At the same time, tractors, combines and other mechanized equipment have saved labor costs and time, chemical fertilizers and pesticides have become more widespread and irrigation has brought previously infertile desert lands under cultivation.

In the mid-1960s the main focus of concern over future food availability was Asia, where populations were growing faster than in other parts of the developing world. At the same time, the output of rice, the main source of food for most Asians, was stable. Scientists feared that widespread famine would ensue unless ways were found to greatly increase rice production. To do that they launched a massive research project, which became the basis of the Green Revolution.

In 1966, the International Rice Research Institute, based in the Philippines, crossed a dwarf Chinese variety with an Indonesian variety to produce IR8, the first high-yielding rice for tropical regions. A later hybrid, IR36, produces as many as three harvests a year, and is now the most widely cultivated crop in the world. Current research is expected to yield yet another rice variety that may increase rice output by 20-30 percent by the year 2000. The new plant would be more resistant to insects and diseases and could be seeded directly rather than propagated from seedlings, relieving rice farmers of one of their most tedious tasks — planting individual rice plants by hand.[9]

### Famines of the 1970s

The Green Revolution and other efforts to improve crop yields greatly increased food production for two decades. Between 1950 and 1971, global grain production almost doubled, growing from 631 million tons to 1.2 billion tons. Despite a rapid population increase during the same period, the improvements brought about a 30 percent increase in grain yields on a per-person basis. With higher grain output, livestock herds grew and diets improved in many developing countries.[10]

But between 1971 and 1980, grain production barely kept pace with the increase in world population. At the same time, food prices rose rapidly, in large part because of the quadrupling of oil prices during that decade. Higher oil prices pushed up the cost of producing grain and other food crops. As a result, the dietary improvements witnessed during the preceding two decades stalled.

Oil price increases do not fully explain the sudden rise in food prices in 1972. Regional crop failures that year drastically cut the world food supply. Even the Soviet Union, long a leading grain exporter and the main source of food for many of its economic and political allies, reversed its role in the world grain market and began importing large shipments of grain from the United States and other exporters.

The massive Soviet grain purchases of 1972 placed a further drain on the world's grain supply, resulting in a doubling of the price of wheat. Without affordable food supplies, India and parts of Africa that had been spared widespread hunger during the preceding quarter century of crop improvements suffered famine.[11] Famine struck in Bangladesh twice during the 1970s, once in 1971-72 and again in 1974-75, resulting in the loss of more than 750,000 lives. Even more people died in neighboring India.

During the same period, famines occurred in several countries south of the Sahara Desert. The first of a series of droughts in this region — the Sahel — began claiming lives in the mid-1970s. The worst hit countries were Chad, Mali, Mauritania, Niger, Senegal and Upper Volta. Farther east, in the Horn of Africa, droughts in Ethiopia and Somalia began taking their deadly toll in 1975. More than a million people died in 1984-85 alone, the peak year of the region's chronic famine.

## Food Aid Initiatives

The sudden disruption of world grain supplies in 1972, together with regional crop failures that year and in 1974, brought to a close the 20-year period of adequate global food supplies and stable food prices made possible by the Green Revolution. The crisis spread as dwindling food reserves forced the food-exporting nations to reduce shipments of food aid at a time when they were most needed.

Under the threat of widespread famine, the U.N. General Assembly convened a World Food Conference in Rome in November 1974. As a result of the meeting, the General Assembly in December established the World Food Council to coordinate actions by member nations and international agencies to deal with food emergencies as well as improve

*Continued on p. 812*

# Chronology

## 1960s
**With little unexploited land left for additional cultivation, scientists attempt to increase crop yields with new varieties of grain, launching the Green Revolution in agriculture.**

### 1961
The United Nations creates the World Food Program to collect food and cash from U.N. members to provide food relief in emergencies.

———— • ————

## 1970s
**The Soviet Union, once a leading exporter of grain, emerges as a leading grain importer while Third World nations face mounting difficulties in meeting food needs.**

### 1972
Poor harvests lead the Soviet Union to import a huge amount of grain, 22.8 million tons. The United States grants the Soviets $500 million in credits to buy U.S. grain.

### 1973
World Bank President Robert S. McNamara announces a shift in bank lending toward agricultural and rural development with the aim of reducing malnutrition and "absolute poverty" in much of the Third World.

### Oct. 20, 1975
The United States and the Soviet Union sign a long-term grain agreement calling on the Soviets to purchase at least 6 million tons of U.S. grain (wheat and corn) annually for the next six years. The annual sales over that period actually average 11 million tons. The agreement is subsequently extended.

## 1980s
**Famine strikes in sub-Saharan Africa.**

### 1981
Upon McNamara's departure from the World Bank, the bank's lending for agriculture and rural development begins a decade-long decline.

### Aug. 25, 1983
The United States and the Soviet Union sign a second grain sales agreement calling for minimum annual sales of 9 million tons for five years.

### 1984-85
Hundreds of thousands of people die of starvation in Ethiopia, Sudan, Chad and Mozambique as a result of a five-year drought in much of sub-Saharan Africa. Prompted in part by televised fund-raising efforts such as the Live Aid rock concert July 13, 1985, international donors send about 7.5 million tons of food to the region in 1985.

### April 1985
Mikhail S. Gorbachev assumes leadership of the Kremlin.

### Sept. 30, 1985
The United States exports a record 18.6 million tons of grain to the Soviet Union.

### August 1986
The collapse in world commodity prices hits bottom; wheat, which sold for $218 a ton in the early 1980s, costs $125 a ton.

### Sept. 30, 1989
The Soviet Union buys a record 21.7 million tons of American grain.

## 1990s
**Food needs in Eastern Europe and the Soviet Union divert world attention from continuing famine in sub-Saharan Africa.**

### June 1, 1990
The third long-term grain agreement, due to go into effect Jan. 1, 1991, is signed by the U.S. and Soviet governments.

### Jan. 8, 1991
The Bush administration extends $1 billion in credits to the Soviet Union for purchasing U.S. agricultural commodities. The credits are used to buy feed grains, wheat and wheat flour, protein meals, poultry meat, soybeans and almonds as well as pay for some transportation costs.

### June 11, 1991
President Bush grants the Soviet Union an additional $1.5 billion in credit guarantees through Sept. 30, 1992.

### Mid-1991
An estimated 30 million people face starvation in sub-Saharan Africa, and food aid requirements of some 5.7 million tons approach the levels recorded during the 1984-85 famine.

### Aug. 19-21, 1991
Communist Party hardliners stage an unsuccessful coup attempt against the reformist government of Mikhail Gorbachev.

### Sept. 6, 1991
The Soviet legislature disbands, ending 74 years of centralized rule in the Soviet Union and passing political power to the 12 republics.

Continued from p. 810

food production and trade. The following year the FAO set up the Global Information and Early Warning System on Food and Agriculture to warn of impending food shortages and allow donor nations to provide food aid before famine set in.

The World Food Council has since worked with the FAO and the World Food Program, both older U.N. agencies, to predict and recommend remedies for food shortages before they result in famine. The World Food Program, established in 1961, uses agricultural commodities and cash from U.N. member nations to provide relief in food emergencies. FAO, created in 1945, is the U.N.'s main agency aimed at increasing food production and improving the standard of living in the areas where famine most often strikes.

For its part, the United States, which had emerged in the postwar period as the world's leading grain exporter, has long taken the lead in providing emergency food aid — as well as longer-term assistance to hungry nations trying to become self-sufficient in food production. The first major initiative came in 1948 with the Marshall Plan, which transferred $12.5 billion in investment capital and technology to help the nations of Western Europe rebuild their economies after World War II. Although the effort focused U.S. resources on reconstructing war-torn industrial facilities, it also helped affected countries to restore their agricultural production and served as an important precedent for later U.S. food aid initiatives.

During the 1960s, the Agency for International Development (AID) assumed responsibility for helping developing nations, shifting the focus from Europe to Asia, Africa and Latin America. Under the 1973 Foreign Assistance Act, U.S. development aid shifted away from industrial development toward rural development and improved food production. AID projects concentrated on agricultural research to boost crop yields, population control and improvements in nutrition and health care. AID played an important role in spreading technologies developed during the Green Revolution to many Third World countries that were dependent on food imports.

### Changing Policies

During the 1980s, the U.S. government and international agencies such as the World Bank and the International Monetary Fund shifted their focus from providing direct assistance to the poor in recipient nations to requiring changes in the economic policies in those nations. Nonetheless, AID continued to spend about half its resources on agricultural development and nutrition projects. A third of this assistance goes to countries in Asia and the Middle East, a quarter to Latin America and the Caribbean and one-fifth to Africa.[12]

In addition to AID assistance programs that aim at improving food self-sufficiency in the Third World, the United States distributes food aid directly to countries experiencing short-term food shortages under the Food for Peace program (created under Public Law 480), which was modified by the 1966 Food for Peace Act. The program was designed both to dispose of surplus agricultural commodities and to develop future markets for these commodities overseas.

Most of the food provided under Food for Peace is actually sold to recipient countries under Title I of the law, which extends low-interest loans for buying U.S. food on a commercial basis. The other main component of Food for Peace, Title II, provides donations for emergency disaster relief and for less urgent nutrition and economic development programs. Private, voluntary organizations, such as Oxfam (originally the Oxford Committee for Famine Relief) and CARE (Cooperative for American Relief Everywhere Inc.), as well as recipient governments and international agencies actually deliver the donations under Title II.

Since the 1960s, according to the Congressional Budget Office, food aid has declined significantly, both as a form of economic assistance and in relation to U.S. agricultural exports. Food aid accounted for a third of U.S. economic assistance in 1970, but only one-fifth by 1980. As a share of total agricultural exports, food aid declined from about a third in the early 1960s to just one-twentieth by the mid-1980s, the CBO reports.[13] Congress acted last year to partially reverse the trend away from food grants, however. Under the 1990 Food, Agriculture, Conservation and Trade Act, the minimum amount of grants will increase slightly from 1.9 million tons in 1991 to 2 million tons in 1995.

### Food Aid Drops

The United States is not the only food donor to have reduced the volume of commodities it donates to developing countries. While food aid accounted for more than a third of all food imports of developing nations in the early 1960s, less than 10 percent of food imports are now provided as grants today.

The shift away from grants came as the negative effects of food aid started to become apparent. While food aid is unquestionably required to help starving populations survive sudden shortages, free shipments of food can, perversely, damage the ability of recipient nations to feed themselves. If food aid continues to arrive on local markets after the emergency has passed, food prices fall, discouraging local farmers from planting crops. This causes indigenous food stocks to dwindle, making the country more dependent on

# Link Between Population and Food Production

*As population growth rates have declined in Asia and Latin America, per capita food production in each area has increased. Asia benefited enormously from the Green Revolution, which focused on improving rice production. In Africa, conversely, the continent's rising population growth rate contributed to its increasing inability to produce enough food.*

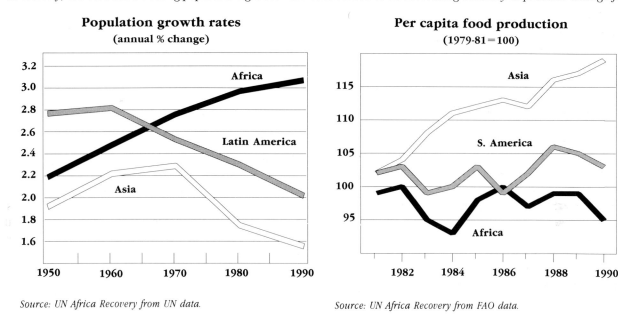

**Population growth rates**
(annual % change)

**Per capita food production**
(1979-81 = 100)

*Source: UN Africa Recovery from UN data.*

*Source: UN Africa Recovery from FAO data.*

food aid than before.

The danger that mismanaged food aid programs can undermine developing nations' ability to feed themselves is not lost on food recipients themselves. Even India, one of the world's leading recipients of food aid in the postwar period, has for several years tried to free itself from dependence on outside food sources. Under the government of Prime Minister Rajiv Gandhi, India instituted economic policies designed to increase the country's self-sufficiency in food production. Following the May 21 assassination of Gandhi, who had lost power and was seeking a return to office, the new prime minister, P.V. Narasimha Rao, reiterated these policies. "My objective is to make India truly self-reliant," he declared in a recent address. Self-reliance for India, he said, "means the ability to pay [for] our imports

through exports. My motto is, trade not aid. Aid is a crutch. Trade builds pride. And India has been trading for thousands of years." [14]

## Continuing Shortages

These and other efforts among food-importing nations to develop their own food production systems have been greatly aided by the agricultural advancements ushered in with the Green Revolution. Since 1965, world grain production has grown by more than 70 percent, and it has more than doubled in developing countries where crop improvements can mean the difference between famine and survival. Not surprisingly, Asia, the revolution's first testing ground, has seen the greatest improvements in crop yields.

Because grains provide about half the calories of the human diet, the huge increases in grain crop yields have improved global nutrition. Other food products have shown significant, if less impressive, gains. Harvests of root crops and tubers, such as potatoes, have increased since 1965, especially in Asia. Meat, milk and fish production has more than doubled in developing countries over the period. Other food crops, including fruits and vegetables, have almost doubled since 1965 throughout the Third World. [15]

However, it is also apparent that the Green Revolution's most dramatic impact has passed. At the same time that oil price increases and new Soviet demands on world grain supplies were disrupting global markets in the mid-1970s, the improvements in crop yields produced by the Green Revolution were already ta-

# Desperate Times in Africa

*While some 30 million people in 17 African nations face food shortages, the situation is especially critical in the 10 nations listed below. The gravest problems plague Sudan, Ethiopia, Angola, Mozambique, Liberia and Somalia — all afflicted by civil strife. Drought has also hurt harvests in several countries. According to the relief organization Oxfam America, only 2.2 million tons of the 4 million tons of food needed have been pledged.*

| Country | Total population (millions) | Affected population (millions) | (% of total) | Food needed (000 tons) | Food pledged (000 tons) | (% of need) |
|---|---|---|---|---|---|---|
| Sudan | 26 | 8 | (31) | 1,194 | 557 | (47) |
| Ethiopia | 49 | 7 | (14) | 1,353 | 806 | (60) |
| Somalia | 8.4 | 4 | (48) | 130 | 29 | (22) |
| Angola | 9 | 2 | (22) | 109 | 54 | (50) |
| Mozambique | 15 | 2 | (13) | 281 | 130 | (46) |
| Liberia | 2 | 1.4 | (68) | 224 | 90 | (41) |
| Niger | 7 | 1.8 | (26) | 107 | 87 | (81) |
| Malawi | 8 | 1 | (12) | 174 | 160 | (92) |
| Burkina Faso | 9 | 1.5 | (17) | 100 | 80 | (80) |
| Mauritania | 2 | 0.9 | (45) | 95 | 70 | (74) |

*Source: Oxfam America.*

pering off. Although global production of grains continued to increase in the 1980s, the pace of that increase slowed after 1983. The record 1989 crop of 1.88 billion metric tons was only 4 percent higher than the 1984 crop of 1.8 billion tons. Global production of meat, milk, fish, vegetables and fruits increased slowly, while world root crops have actually declined since 1984.[16]

While the specter of famine lifted from most parts of Asia in the 1980s, it did not disappear but rather settled on Africa. There, alone, the percentage of undernourished people actually increased over the decade. Sub-Saharan Africa's inability to feed itself stems in large part from rapid population growth. While the population growth rate is falling in every other region of the world, in Africa it is increasing by 3 percent each year. *(See graph, p. 813.)* The continent's population, 481 million in 1981, will exceed 800 million by the turn of the century, according to U.N. projec-

tions.

The World Bank estimates that food production must increase by 4 percent a year from now until 2020 if the region's inhabitants are to escape hunger. To promote this growth in output, the bank in 1988 launched an African Agricultural Services Initiative charged with disseminating new and existing technology, appropriate to local conditions, to African farmers. The bank is attempting to correct its past mistakes by training local staff to work with farmers rather than relying on foreigners from the industrial world, who often are unfamiliar with African food preferences and work habits.

## Africa's Plight

After more than a decade of periodic famine in the Horn of Africa and other parts of the continent, the United Nations held a special session on Africa's economic crisis in June 1986. The meeting adopted the Program of Action for African Eco-

nomic Recovery and Development, which called on African recipients of food aid to make policy changes that would encourage self-sufficiency. One change called for the removal of food price subsidies that make food affordable for city dwellers but reduce farmers' incomes and thus discourage domestic food production. Donor nations agreed to help by removing barriers to their exports, thus enabling them to earn foreign exchange.

Five years after the program began, however, the plight of hungry sub-Saharan nations has deteriorated even further. The U.N. secretary-general reported in August that most African countries today are more dependent on food imports and food aid than they were in 1986.[17]

The underlying causes of Africa's inability to attain food self-sufficiency are complex. "The main reason why people are hungry in Africa today is civil war and conflict," says Oxfam's Rob Buchanan. "Moving beyond that, there are issues of resource distribution, of trade and debt, which are having long-term depressing effects on the African economy."

Buchanan says Sudan's experience is typical in much of sub-Saharan Africa, where monoculture — the large-scale cultivation of a single crop for export — is degrading land that could otherwise be used to produce food for domestic consumption.

Since the 1960s, Sudan has reserved much of its best agricultural land for large commercial plantations to grow cotton, the country's chief export. Cotton depletes the soil, and excessive use of pesticides and other chemicals has further degraded the soil for other crops.

Because the world price for cotton

has plummeted in recent years, Sudan's export earnings have sunk. At the same time, prices for food and other items the country must import have risen, further straining its trade balance. In order to buy needed food, the Sudanese government has gone heavily into debt to foreign lenders and currently owes more money to the International Monetary Fund than any other government in the world.

The IMF, in turn, is requiring Sudan to develop export industries as a way to boost the country's foreign earnings. But the IMF policies, in Buchanan's view, "would simply push them farther down that road of growing less food for domestic consumption, which would tend to make people even more hungry." ∎

notably Canada and Australia, which have long criticized subsidized food export programs as unfair trading practices. Another solution would be to distribute the food through Food for Peace, which governs the disposal of U.S. agricultural surpluses to needy countries. The United States could also quickly provide food aid to the Soviet Union by declaring it eligible for disaster relief.

But the administration continues to evade requests for a specific commitment of aid for the Soviets. During the president's first official exchange with a high Soviet official since the coup, Foreign Minister Boris Pankin asked the United States in late September to make a firm commitment to provide immediate humanitarian aid as well as "massive" long-term economic assistance. Bush reportedly made no such commitment but rather restated his previous position that a plan to provide emergency aid is still in the planning stages and that further assistance will depend upon the pace of economic reform in the individual Soviet republics and at the national level.[18]

# CURRENT SITUATION

## Soviets Seek Help

As the Soviet request for food aid mushroomed, from $2 billion in early September to $7.4 billion in mid-September to $14.7 billion by Sept. 19, the European Community was joined by the United States and Japan in promising to help. The Bush administration, however, continues to emphasize its offer of loan guarantees and has not yet specified how much free food assistance the United States will offer its former Cold War adversary if the banks continue to balk at lending the Soviets money under the loan guarantee program.

In early September, with no breakthrough in the loan programs in sight, Soviet Prime Minister Ivan S. Silayev told food exporters that his country needed 5.5 million tons of

grain, 800,000 tons of meat, 900,000 tons of sugar and 15 other food items. In response, the European Community announced a plan to buy surplus food from Poland, Hungary and Czechoslovakia, former Soviet allies in Eastern Europe, and ship it to the Soviet Union (see p. 807).

President Bush offered one enticement to reluctant banks shortly after the coup failed, making immediately available $315 million of the $500 million in agricultural loan guarantees for the Soviets that had been planned for Oct. 1. There are, however, several ways the Bush administration could speed up the transfer of U.S. food aid to the Soviets. One solution, favored by American banks, would be to guarantee the entire Soviet loan program, instead of guaranteeing just 98 percent of the loan amount.

The Agriculture Department has balked at this proposal, however, saying it would set a precedent for other hard-pressed countries to ask for loans on easier terms. The change also would irritate other grain exporters,

Meanwhile, members of Congress are proposing other ways to help the Soviet Union rebuild its agricultural sector. Sen. Richard G. Lugar, R-Ind., has introduced a bill — the 1991 Support for Emerging Democracies Act — that would send American farmers and transportation experts on lengthy visits to Soviet republics undertaking market reforms in order to teach their skills to local farmers and officials. Rep. Jim Leach, R-Iowa, has proposed trading U.S. surplus grain for Soviet oil, a barter arrangement he says would ease U.S. energy dependence at the same time it eases the Soviets' entry into the world trading system. Leach also has urged the administration to establish formal agricultural aid links with all 12 current Soviet republics as well as the three Baltic states of Latvia, Lithuania and Estonia.

Some lawmakers are evoking the memory of the Marshall Plan as a model for U.S. assistance to the Soviet Union today. Sen. Bill Bradley, D-N.J., has proposed launching a similar program, in collaboration with the European Community and Japan. Bradley would condition the program's funds and technical assistance on the republics' willingness to adopt free-market economies, cut defense spending and engage in free trade.

However, many Democrats, as well as the Bush administration, oppose U.S. participation in a major aid program for the Soviet Union as a misguided use of federal funds, at least until the pace of economic reform picks up in the Soviet Union. Perhaps the most controversial proposal for helping the Soviet Union has come from Rep. Les Aspin, D-Wis., who urged that $1 billion be taken from the 1992 defense budget and spent on humanitarian aid. (See At Issue, p. 817.)

## African Woes

While lawmakers and the media focus U.S. attention on the Soviets, the chronic hunger that plagues millions of Africans south of the Sahara continues unabated and largely unnoticed. Despite the warning by U.N. Secretary-General Javier Perez de Cuellar that Africa faces "an unrelenting crisis of tragic proportions," the five-year U.N. Program of Action for African Economic Recovery and Development was deemed a failure by a recent meeting called to assess the program's effects.[19] Since the program began in 1986, participants concluded, food shortages have mounted and financial assistance from the industrial nations has actually diminished.

Participants in the U.N. program

agreed on a new set of goals for 1996, including a reduction in Africa's $270 billion debt. The revised plan also calls on donor nations to increase their development assistance from $21 billion in 1989 to $30 billion by 1992, and by an additional 4 percent annually until the year 2000.

But relief workers and supporters of food aid to Africa worry about the prospects of the 30 million Africans facing starvation, including 16 million in the three countries in the war-torn Horn of Africa — Ethiopia, Somalia and Djibouti. Bread for the World, a Washington lobbying group, is backing legislation that would re-

quire the United States to provide emergency food aid to all needy citizens of the region. The Horn of Africa Recovery and Food Security Act was included in the foreign aid authorization bill and awaits House action.

The measure calls for an increase in U.S. food aid pledges for the Horn of Africa as well as the shipment of mine-detecting equipment, trucks and fuel to facilitate inland transport of food. It also calls for negotiations among the United States and other arms exporters aimed at ending arms shipments to warring factions in the region. ∎

# OUTLOOK

## Debating Soviet Aid

Beyond providing emergency food aid, the proper role for donor nations in fostering self-sufficiency among food importing nations remains much debated. Proponents of enhanced long-term technical and financial assistance say that promoting self-sufficiency among developing nations is in the best interests of the United States because it encourages global stability. Critics of such assistance are skeptical about spending money on programs that may have little benefit to recipient nations. Long-term assistance to help the Soviet Union reform its vast agricultural system, many say, would be a poor investment before the central government and the 12 remaining republics undertake their own difficult reforms.

It is not yet clear, even to the Soviet republics themselves, what path agricultural reform will take. "You may [find] that the republics just don't want free competition, and that they want to control all or

certain aspects of the agriculture," says agricultural consultant Carol Brookins. "The republics have viewed economic reforms as ways to gain economic independence from the center, but they have not — especially where food is involved — really thought about wanting to just open up food distribution to privatization and open competition."

Whatever path the Soviets follow, Brookins cautions, it will take a long time. "Although the Soviet Union is a resource-rich part of the world and has a middle-income economy with a highly educated people, it's probably going to take five to 10 years of massive economic reform and restructuring," she says.

"But that doesn't mean that they are going to need assistance," Brookins adds, "apart from possibly some emergency food shipments, if there are problems in specific areas."

## Green Revolution's Future

As for the developing nations that continue to suffer from hunger, the prospects for gaining food self-

Continued on p. 819

# At Issue:

## Should the U.S. spend some of the "peace dividend" resulting from the end of the Cold War to help the Soviet Union?

### REP. LES ASPIN, D-WIS.

**Chairman of the House Armed Services Committee**
FROM A MEMORANDUM TO COMMITTEE MEMBERS, AUG. 28, 1991.

recent events in the Soviet Union will prove to be among the most important of the 20th century. The government of the Soviet Union is undergoing great changes. While we cannot see how it will all work out, we can definitely see one source of trouble ahead — there will be enormous dislocation.

I am suggesting the following course of action to my colleagues in the conference on the Fiscal 1992 Defense Authorization Bill. We should provide some money — I am suggesting $1 billion — from the defense budget for fiscal year 1992 for a Humanitarian Aid and Stabilization Fund. This new fund would be available to the Bush Administration to use as it sees fit for aid to the Soviet people — for humanitarian purposes and to promote stability. . . .

Preventing more instability and chaos in the Soviet Union is in our security interest. Events during the abortive coup have underscored forcefully the nuclear risks stemming from chaos in the Soviet Union. We have much to fear from further outbreaks of instability. . . .

Earlier this year we airlifted emergency relief to over a million Iraqi refugees who fled to the mountainous areas along the Turkish-Iraq border. $1 billion in U.S. humanitarian assistance by itself will not solve the food and medicine crisis facing the Soviet people. But it would make a big dent in it and show the way for our fellow allies. It was U.S. leadership that made possible the multinational coalition that reversed Saddam Hussein's aggression against Kuwait and helped care for the Kurdish people in northern Iraq. It can also help the Soviet people survive the coming winter.

I also want to make clear what my proposal is not. The Humanitarian Aid and Stabilization Fund is not for long-term economic aid. It is true that the failed coup and the events that have followed it mean we are more likely to see economic reforms and more likely to see them sooner. But I agree with those who say we need to see the reforms before we send the economic aid. . . .

Giving short-term humanitarian assistance to the Soviet Union is not an exercise in American altruism. Rather, it is an attempt to prevent further instability in the Soviet Union. Since helping the Soviet people survive the coming winter will contribute to a less threatening environment, this program should be funded out of the defense budget, not domestic spending or other foreign aid accounts. It is defense by other means.

### SEN. BOB DOLE, R-KAN.

**Senate Minority Leader**
FROM A STATEMENT ISSUED AUG. 29, 1991.

over the past couple of weeks, all eyes have been focused on the Soviet Union.

Sooner than any of us thought, we move from the transition era of Mikhail Gorbachev to the revolutionary era of Boris Yeltsin and his democratic allies. . . .

[I]t is going to be a challenging time for U.S. policy, too. I said we needed to stay cool. Not everyone is heeding my advice.

Already people are out there advocating a billion dollars in new aid — in taxpayers dollars — for the Soviet Union. . . .

[W]e should . . . avoid the temptation to start grabbing money out of the defense budget to fund some new multibillion foreign aid program.

I'd like to offer this revolutionary idea. If we want to provide foreign aid to the Soviet Union, how about taking it out of the foreign aid budget? That's a pot of nearly $15 billion. If our priorities for spending that money are changing, as the world changes — and I believe those priorities are changing — let's make some slight readjustments in our individual foreign aid programs. That's the way to fund new foreign aid — not through new taxes, or cutting our still vital defense.

Let's not forget: A couple of weeks ago, we had no idea who had his finger on the button of the Soviet missile and nuclear arsenal. And it is not inconceivable that, tomorrow, or next week, or next month — we're going to be wondering about this question again. Even failing some new coup attempt or widespread instability, can anyone guarantee that some disgruntled local commander in one of the rebellious republics is not going to grab a couple of nuclear armed missiles; can anyone guarantee that some stubborn hard-line submarine commander is not going to create his own "Red October" — and start engaging in a little game of deadly bluff or blackmail?

This is not the time to rush to disarm. Maybe, if things work out right in the Soviet Union — and in the Middle East, and a couple of other places, for that matter — maybe then we can start examining whether we can slash our defense spending. But let's at least wait until the dust settles in Moscow before we start pulling the plug on our own nation's security.

# Death of the Soviet Agricultural System

The Soviet Union's request for food aid from the West is a telling indictment of the agricultural system as it evolved under Communist Party leadership. Simply put, mismanagement transformed one of the world's largest grain exporters into its biggest grain importer.

Before the 1917 Bolshevik revolution, Russia was a predominantly agrarian society. A relatively small number of landowners controlled its vast agricultural resources while millions of peasants living in conditions of semi-slavery worked the land. The revolution stripped the landowners of their holdings, which became state property.

In the late 1920s, Soviet leader Josef V. Stalin collectivized agricultural production throughout Russia and the other Soviet republics, placing planting and distribution under central authorities. Stalin wanted to improve food production to support his goal of quickly turning the country into an industrial power. By placing cultivation under the central government and setting low market prices for food, he could be sure the growing work force in the cities would have enough to eat.[†]

The basic production unit thus became the collective farm, a cooperative organization of farmers who were told each year how much of what commodities they were expected to produce for the state, and at what price. In return for free machinery, fertilizers and seeds, as well as a guaranteed buyer, farmers were expected to meet production quotas and hand over the harvest to the state.

For about 30 years, central planning and collectivization worked well. The Soviet Union increased its industrial output in isolation from the erratic swings of the business cycle that during the 1930s hurled the capitalist world into the Great Depression. Not even the devastation caused by World War II, in which more Soviet citizens died than all other war casualties combined, stopped the growth.

During the 1950s, the Soviet Union enjoyed record grain harvests, and Nikita Khrushchev, Stalin's successor, further boosted production by developing previously uncultivated lands in the Asian republics of the Soviet Union.

But even as agricultural production increased, a food crisis was already in the making. In the mid-1960s, the Soviet Union reversed its traditional pattern and became a net grain importer, buying more grain than it sold on world markets. Poor growing conditions were a factor. Outside the breadbasket regions of the northern Caucasus, the southern Ukraine and the Crimea, much of the Soviet Union is unsuited for cultivation, and harvests are especially vulnerable to drought and other adverse growing conditions. (Bad weather, for example, damaged Soviet harvests for seven years in a row beginning in 1979.)

The country's expanding animal husbandry program also contributed to the grain crisis. While the greater availability of meat, poultry and dairy products improved the diets of many Soviet citizens, the country's production of fodder grains could not keep up with the growing demand for animal feed.

Peasant resentment of Stalin's collectivization program is another frequently cited reason for the decline in Soviet harvests in recent years. Millions of peasants starved in Stalin's campaign to centralize agriculture, and the continued resistance to the change influenced the way collectivized agriculture emerged. For example, few silos and other storage facilities were built in the countryside because of Stalin's fear that the peasants would steal the food before it could reach the cities. Even after Stalin's death, there was little improvement in the situation. As a result, much of the food rotted in the fields or in transit between the farms and the processing plants.

In 1982, the government began trying to recapture the country's self-sufficiency in grain. The Food Program introduced that year called for increased production, mostly in feed grains such as corn. It also targeted the distribution system for streamlining. New storage facilities were to be built in the countryside, while the collective farms were slated for more equipment. In 1985 all agricultural sectors were coordinated under a single central agency.

Like previous overhauls of the agricultural system, the reforms of the 1980s failed to restore the Soviet Union's ability to feed itself. They failed in large measure because they ignored one basic element of the Soviet system: food subsidies. Ever since Stalin decided to favor the urban proletariat over the peasantry, the Soviet government has subsidized food products at the point of sale. While it may have bought support for the system among city dwellers by making food cheap, food subsidies eventually undermined the efficient allocation of resources in the countryside and ultimately doomed the entire system. By the 1980s, for example, price distortions were so great that rather than growing grain to feed their animals, farmers found it more profitable to sell their grain to the state and then feed their cattle loaves of bread they bought at subsidized prices at state stores.

The price distortions also have encouraged farmers to work harder on their private plots than they did on the collective farms. Although these private plots account for only 3 percent of the country's land under cultivation, they are the source of about 60 percent of its potatoes, 40 percent of its fruit and eggs and 30 percent of its milk, meat and vegetables.[††] Meanwhile, shelves lie empty in state stores that sell the products of collective and state farms at subsidized prices.

---

[†] See Marshall I. Goldman, *Gorbachev's Challenge* (1987), p. 10.

[††] Goldman, *op. cit.*, p. 33.

Continued from p. 816
sufficiency are more problematic. A recent study by the Center for Global Food Issues at the Hudson Institute, a conservative research group based in Indianapolis, challenges traditional theories that link the ability of developing countries to feed themselves with efforts to control population growth. It also identifies political policies and civil strife as the main causes of food shortages. The report advances the optimistic prediction that the world is not in danger of running out of food despite its growing population. For one thing, the study reports, growth trends are leveling off. For another, the advances of the Green Revolution have not ended and can be expected to continue raising crop yields through new strains of cereals and other commodities.[20]

While other food experts agree with the institute on the causes of hunger, they say technology alone can't end the problem. "The high levels of productivity brought by the Green Revolution have an environmental cost," cautions Peter Day of Rutgers University. Widespread use of chemical fertilizers and pesticides has caused water pollution. But even the creation of new strains of drought- and insect-resistant cereals, the heart of the Green Revolution's agenda, carries a great risk in Day's view. "The Green Revolution poses problems, especially genetic vulnerability, which stems from the uniformity that results when massive agricultural projects are superimposed on the environment," Day says.

Because farmers generally want to cultivate the newest, highest-yielding varieties, only a few strains of a given cereal account for the bulk of global production. "If you have hundreds of square miles planted to one genotype," Day says, "it's an invitation to all kinds of disasters, from pests and diseases to climatological problems, that a mixture of different types of

plants may not be so subject to."

If technology alone cannot provide the tools for hungry nations to feed themselves, the United States and other donor nations will continue to face the issue of world hunger and the debate over how best to help those countries avert famine. ∎

# Notes

[1] Amb. Guennadi I. Oudovenko, the Ukraine's permanent representative to the United Nations, testified before the Senate Finance Committee Sept. 12 at hearings on U.S.-Soviet trade.

[2] See Felicity Barringer, "Wide Bartering Keeps Leningrad Going," *The New York Times*, Sept. 4, 1991.

[3] Food and Agriculture Organization of the United Nations, Global Information and Early Warning System on Food and Agriculture, *Food Outlook*, June 1991.

[4] Andreas testified Sept. 12 before the Senate Finance Committee.

[5] Quoted by William Drozdiak, "Winter Famine Seen Unlikely in U.S.S.R.," *The Washington Post*, Oct. 3, 1991.

[6] *Washington Post*-ABC News poll conducted Aug. 23-27. See Richard Morin, "Most in Poll Reject Giving Soviets Cash," *The Washington Post*, Aug. 29, 1991.

[7] Rebecca M. Blank, *Growth Is Not Enough: Why the Recovery of the 1980s Did So Little to Reduce Poverty*, Joint Economic Committee, Sept. 26, 1991.

[8] Writing in *The Washington Post*, Sept. 19, 1991.

[9] The World Bank, *World Development Report 1991: The Challenges of Development*, 1991, p. 74.

[10] See Lester R. Brown, *Building a Sustainable Society* (1981), p. 90.

[11] Brown, *op. cit.*, p. 91.

[12] See Congressional Budget Office, *Agricultural Progress in the Third World and its Effects on U.S. Farm Exports*, May 1989, pp. 64-65.

[13] *Ibid*, p. 70.

[14] From a July 9 address to the nation, published in *India News*, July 1-15, 1991, p. 1.

[15] See World Resources Institute, *World Resources 1990-91* (1991), p. 84.

[16] *Ibid*, p. 84.

[17] From *Economic Crisis in Africa*, Report of the U.N. Secretary-General, Aug. 28, 1991.

[18] See Ann Devroy and John M. Goshko, "Soviet Seeks U.S. Aid, Shows New Cooperation," *The Washington Post*, Sept. 25, 1991.

[19] A committee representing all 160 members of the U.N. General Assembly met Sept. 5-15 to assess the U.N. Africa Recovery Program.

[20] See Dennis T. Avery, *Global Food Progress 1991* (1991).

# Bibliography

## Selected Sources Used

## Books

**Avery, Dennis T., *Global Food Progress 1991: A Report from Hudson Institute's Center for Global Food Issues*, Hudson Institute, 1991.**

The author challenges the theory of Thomas Malthus, a 19th-century English scientist who predicted that Earth's resources would run out if the world's population continued to grow. Avery cites advances in food science, exemplified by the increase in crop outputs brought about by the Green Revolution of the past three decades, as evidence that Malthusian doctrine is flawed.

**Brown, Lester R., *Building a Sustainable Society*, W. W. Norton & Company, 1981.**

Brown, director of the Worldwatch Institute in Washington, D.C., argued in this classic work that population growth was causing environmental pressures that undermined Earth's ability to feed itself. Widespread famine could be averted, he wrote, only if people learned to exploit the planet's resources on a sustainable basis.

**Fowler, Cary, and Mooney, Pat, *Shattering: Food, Politics, and the Loss of Genetic Diversity*, University of Arizona Press, 1990.**

Beginning in the 1960s, scientists began improving the crop yields, durability and resistance to drought of the world's main food grains. But according to Fowler and Mooney, the Green Revolution poses a threat as well. As more farmers plant only the latest varieties of grain, the older varieties are disappearing, leading to a loss of genetic diversity among food grains and making crops vulnerable to disease.

**Giorgis, Dawit Wolde, *Red Tears: War, Famine and Revolution in Ethiopia*, Africa World Books, 1989.**

Giorgis, a former Ethiopian government official who was responsible for coordinating relief efforts during the famines of the mid-1980s, describes the obstacles that prevented donated food from reaching many of his starving countrymen — impassable roads, inadequate transportation equipment, lack of storage facilities and deliberate sabotage — all resulting from the protracted civil war of the time.

**Goldman, Marshall I., *Gorbachev's Challenge: Economic Reform in the Age of High Technology*, W. W. Norton & Company, 1987.**

Goldman, a Harvard University economist who specializes in the Soviet Union, analyzes Soviet agricultural policy in this overview of *perestroika*.

## Articles

**Ehrlich, Paul R., and Wilson, Edward O., "Biodiversity Studies: Science and Policy," *Science*, Aug. 16, 1991.**

Earth's exploding population is causing a largely undetected but massive extinction of plant and animal species, the authors note. "Every new shopping center built in the California chaparral, every hectare of tropical forest cut and burned, every swamp converted into a rice paddy or shrimp farm means less biodiversity," they write. Stopping this loss will require a wide range of policy measures amounting to "nothing less than the kind of commitments so recently invested in the Cold War."

## Reports and Studies

**Congressional Budget Office, Congress of the United States, *The Outlook for Farm Commodity Program Spending, Fiscal Years 1991-1996*, June 1991.**

This report examines changes introduced by the 1990 farm bill (the Food, Agriculture, Conservation, and Trade Act of 1990) in U.S. agricultural subsidies.

**International Bank for Reconstruction and Development (World Bank), *World Development Report 1991: The Challenge of Development*, Oxford University Press, 1991.**

The World Bank's annual report on global development issues focuses this year on policies to enhance development. In the agricultural sector as elsewhere, the Bank reports, government policies have often posed more obstacles than enhancements to progress. Many Third World governments, for example, have favored industry over agriculture by subsidizing food prices in cities while paying farmers too little for their crops to make farming a profitable enterprise.

**U.N. Secretary-General's Report, *Economic Crisis in Africa: Final Review and Appraisal of the Implementation of The United Nations Programme of Action for African Economic Recovery and Development 1986-1990 (UNPAAERD)*, Aug. 28, 1991.**

This report summarizes progress made over the past five years since the United Nations General Assembly met in special session to consider ways to help Africa resolve the severe economic crisis that had brought poverty and famine to much of sub-Saharan Africa. Despite many reforms undertaken by African nations to improve economic management, the economic and social conditions have actually worsened.

# The Next Step

## Additional Articles from Current Periodicals

### Africa

**Cater, N., "The forgotten famine," *Africa Report*, May/June 1991, p. 60.**

Considers the "donor fatigue" that many Western nations are suffering despite a two-year drought that puts 20 million in the Sahel at risk of famine.

**Cherfas, J., "FAO proposes a 'new' plan for feeding Africa," *Science*, Nov. 9, 1990, p. 748.**

Looks at the proposal of 'aid-in-kind' fertilization of African soil by the U.N. Food and Agriculture Organization (FAO) to stop nutrient erosion and boost food supplies. Criticisms of proposal; plan to stop continent-wide agricultural collapse; erosion statistics; previous soil conservation schemes; new approach to fertilization; techniques instruction.

**Davidow, J., "The Horn of Africa," *Dispatch*, May 20, 1991, p. 363.**

Presents a statement by Jeffrey Davidow, Acting Assistant Secretary for African Affairs, before the Senate Foreign Relations Committee, May 1991, concerning food shortages and wars plaguing the countries of the Horn of Africa. Sudan, Ethiopia, Somalia.

**Krauss, C., "Ethiopians have new rulers, but famine's specter lingers," *The New York Times*, June 14, 1991, p. A1.**

Discusses the situation in Ethiopia, where up to 15 percent of the population may need emergency food assistance if substantial rains do not begin in the next four weeks or if the new provisional government is unable to establish order. Shipments of food and water interrupted by looting and ambushes; Kebri Beyah refugee camp.

### Books & reading

**Radu, M., "Brief reviews: Africa," *ORBIS*, spring 1991, p. 316.**

Reviews the book "Reluctant Aid or Aiding the Reluctant: U.S. Food Aid Policy and Ethiopian Famine Relief," by Steven L. Varnis.

### Debates & issues

**"Tragic relief," *New Republic*, June 3, 1991, p. 9.**

Evaluates the effectiveness of the United Nations Disaster Relief Office (UNDRO) in light of the Kurdish refugee crisis and cyclone devastation in Bangladesh. Organization's inability to effectively coordinate efforts; recommendation that the U.N. establish a permanent undersecretary general in charge of disaster relief; How the new program would function.

**Bierman, J., Brady, D., et al., "The victims," *Maclean's*, May 20, 1991, p. 36.**

Discusses the wars, natural disasters and famine that threaten several Third World nations. Also examines "compassion fatigue" among Western governments and relief organizations. Cyclone in Bangladesh; famine and civil wars in the Sudan and Ethiopia; Iranian obstructionism in Kurdistan; Kurdish refugees; Western perception that Third World governments don't do enough to help themselves or prepare for predictable disasters; environmental degradation.

**Cloud, D.S., "Who should get U.S. food aid? Congress wants to decide," *Congressional Quarterly Weekly Report*, Sept. 1, 1990, p. 2767.**

Considers the perils of food aid, the reason why Congress is overhauling the nation's principal program for distributing the bounty of its farmland to famine-stricken, less productive regions of the world. Omnibus farm bills; 1954 law, Food for Peace; convenient disposal chute for surplus crops; food sold on easy credit; Congress wants to curtail the president's broad authority; political tool; who actually runs the program; side effects of generosity.

**Crossette, B. "Relief officials say bad planning proves calamitous in Bangladesh," *The New York Times*, May 5, 1991, p. 1.**

Reports on criticisms of the Bangladesh government's slow response in assessing needs and moving supplies to survivors of the cyclone that struck on Monday. Death toll; concern that those who survived the storm's huge waves and floodwaters would succumb to disease and exposure; no Bangladesh official given authority to coordinate and command relief efforts.

**Grey, S., "Food aid that fails to feed the hungry," *New Scientist*, April 6, 1991, p. 12.**

Reveals that John Seaman of the British charity Save the Children Fund believes that 100,000 refugees may have died needlessly because of mistakes.

### Economic aspects

**Lawton, K.A., "A world of hurts stretches relief groups and givers to their limits," *Christianity Today*, June 24, 1991, p. 48.**

Studies the impact of numerous global catastrophes on international relief-and-development groups. Reduced giving among secular organizations; fear of public burnout; determining where and how to spend limited resources; frustration with dependence on the media to enlist public support; internal fatigue experienced by many relief groups; how two Christian organizations are faring. INSET: A case for family planning? (Bangladesh).

## Iraq

**"U.S. humanitarian assistance to Iraqi refugees,"** *Dispatch*, **April 8, 1991, p. 233.**

Presents a statement by President Bush released April 1991, concerning Air Force distribution of food, blankets, clothing, tents and other relief-related items for Iraqi refugees in northern Iraq. Assistance of military forces; economic and food assistance to the government of Turkey.

**Burleigh, N., "Watching children starve to death,"** *Time*, **June 10, 1991, p. 56.**

Describes conditions inside the pediatric ward at Baghdad's Qadissiya Hospital, which has scant medicine and no food, fighting a battle against epidemic disease and starvation, whose principle victims are children. Hospitals damaged by allied bombing, and civilian uprisings; dysentery the No. 1 killer in Iraq; demoralization among medical workers; reliance on relief aid.

**Gordon, M.R., "G.I.'s in Iraq, hands tied, try to aid the refugees,"** *The New York Times*, **April 2, 1991, p. A1.**

Discusses the Iraqi refugee situation. Nobody wants them — not the Kuwaitis, the Saudis, or the U.S. Army. The Army is providing them with food, water and emergency medical care, but says it cannot offer the political asylum and shelter from civil strife that many seek.

**Rosenthal, A., "A risky undertaking,"** *The New York Times*, **April 18, 1991, p. A1.**

Analyzes the Kurdish relief plan. President Bush presented the plan as a straightforward and limited humanitarian operation, but it has raised the possibility of snaring him in just the kind of political and military tangle that he has been trying to avoid.

## Political aspects

**"Relief workers flee Sudan,"** *U.S. News & World Report*, **Feb. 4, 1991, p. 16.**

Reports that the decision of the military government of Sudan to ally itself with Saddam Hussein has caused most foreign relief workers and agencies to flee the country. As many as one in three of Sudan's 26 million people will

need food assistance, and relief agencies have pledged only 80,000 of the 1.2 million tons of food needed.

**Borrus, A., Dwyer, P., et al., "Bush and Soviet aid: The clamor for an about-face,"** *Business Week*, **Dec. 17, 1990, p. 41.**

Highlights how President Bush, who has flip-flopped on taxes and reversed himself on negotiating with Iraq, is reluctantly getting ready for another political somersault. The issue is economic help, especially food shipments, for a cold and hungry Soviet Union. The President will waive the Jackson-Vanik Amendment — a move that would make Moscow eligible for favorable trade treatment and cheap credit for the purchase of agricultural commodities.

**Doherty, C.J., "Bush lifts Soviet credit ban to ease food shortage,"** *Congressional Quarterly Weekly Report*, **Dec. 15, 1990, p. 4144.**

Considers President Bush's suspension of a 15-year-old ban on extending commercial credits to the Soviets, enabling them to buy up to $1 billion worth of U.S. agricultural goods. Members of Congress were generally supportive. Also supplying technical experts and financial aid for medical equipment; 1974 Jackson-Vanik amendment; a show of support after Strategic Arms Reduction Treaty (START); more evidence of the passing of the Cold War; more.

**Riding, A., "Baltic assaults lead Europeans to hold off aid,"** *The New York Times*, **Jan. 23, 1991, p. A1.**

States that the European Parliament blocked a $1 billion European Community food-aid package for the Soviet Union to protest the crackdown by Moscow against pro-independence groups in the Baltic republics.

## Relief organizations

**Sloane, J., "The hunger-fighters,"** *Farm Journal*, **Jan. 15, 1990, p. 32.**

Describes projects and networks such as the Farmer-to-Farmer Program of Volunteers in Overseas Cooperative Assistance (VOCA), in which U.S. farmers help fight hunger in Third World countries by introducing more productive farming techniques.

**Wirt, G., "The fuel-efficient Sudanese cookstove,"** *Whole Earth Review*, **summer 1991, p. 108.**

Addresses how CARE, the international relief and development organization, is helping skilled craftsmen to produce stoves that use little fuel, are cheap to operate, and help slow the loss of Sudan's dwindling forests. Mohammed Hassan, a tinsmith; the making of a stove; Sudan's drought.

## Soviet Union

**"Help for Russia,"** *Economist*, Dec. 1, 1990, p. 14.

Looks at the mobilization of emergency aid for the Soviet Union, which is facing a winter of possible famine. Reasons why Germany is leading the aid parade; meetings between President Mikhail Gorbachev and Germany's Helmut Kohl; problem in Soviet Union is in distribution, not lack of food; need to control the aid; fears of a Soviet collapse; dangers of giving aid as a way of helping to prop up Gorbachev; details.

**"The wrong word,"** *Economist*, Dec. 1, 1990, p. 47.

Investigates the potential for famine in the Soviet Union this winter. Comments from Valentina Gudilina to the Soviet parliament; emergency food aid being sent in response to requests from President Mikhail Gorbachev; record grain harvest this year; estimates of waste from agricultural economist Vladimir Tikhonov; warning signs of famine; potential for food aid to simply worsen the situation; details; outlook.

**Bilski, A., Gray, M., et al., "Bracing for a flood,"** *Maclean's*, Jan. 14, 1991, p. 22.

Discusses recent rumors that large numbers of Soviet refugees are set to inundate Eastern Europe. Food shortages in the Soviet Union; foreign aid; concern in Poland, Czechoslovakia and Hungary; Soviet President Mikhail Gorbachev's efforts to deal with the food crisis. INSET: A perilous winter exodus (exodus of ethnic Greeks from Albania), by J. Bierman.

**Friedman, T.L., "Moscow asks U.S. for food supplies; Baker hints at aid,"** *The New York Times*, Dec. 11, 1990, p. A1.

States that, for the first time, the Soviet Union publicly asked the U.S. for food supplies to help it overcome shortages in major cities. The Bush administration indicated it would provide some kind of aid, although it has said that aid is really not needed because there are no production shortages, only a breakdown in the distribution system.

**Gray, M., "A hunger for change,"** *Maclean's*, Dec. 17, 1990, (following) p. 27.

Explains how President Mikhail Gorbachev is using his new increased emergency powers to seek solutions to the Soviet Union's food shortages and distribution problems. Fear of famine; aid from the West; restive republics; land privatization issue.

**Haberman, C., "Europe supports $2.4 billion plan to assist Kremlin,"** *The New York Times*, Dec. 15, 1990, p. 1.

Discusses the European Community's agreement to give the Soviet Union $2.4 billion in emergency food and medical aid and technical assistance. Possibility of emergency aid to beleaguered Eastern Europe; summit meeting of 12 national leaders in Rome.

**Rosenbaum, D.E., "U.S. plans to send people, not cash, to assist Soviets,"** *The New York Times*, July 9, 1990, p. A1.

Says that President Bush is prepared to send teams of experts to the Soviet Union to help it rebuild rail and communications networks, grain storage sites, food distribution systems and other essential services, but he opposes a move for large financial aid to the Soviets, as proposed by West Germany and France.

**Trimble, J., "Hungry for handouts,"** *U.S. News & World Report*, Dec. 10, 1990, p. 38.

Outlines some foreign aid currently being offered to Moscow from sheep from Australia to credit from Canada and the European Community to buy food. Ominous signs of internal collapse; Western aid turning up on Moscow's black market; Soviet distribution system; reliance on Soviet military to move aid.

## United Nations

**"Economic and Social Council holds second session in Geneva,"** *UN Chronicle*, December 1990, p. 59.

Reports that the United Nations Economic and Social Council adopted 171 resolutions and decisions on subjects ranging from transnational corporations to the consequences of the Chernobyl accident. Other key issues included food aid for Palestinians, drug abuse control, capital punishment and economic and humanitarian assistance.

**"Who helps?"** *Economist*, June 8, 1991, p. 45.

Examines the difficulties facing the World Food Program (WFP), a United Nations agency that is the world's biggest deliverer of emergency food aid. Controversy surrounding non-emergency food aid; work in Iraq and Turkey; Ethiopia; food pledged; impact of civil wars and unhelpful governments in Africa; details.

**Khan, S.A., " 'Operation Salam': To build a future,"** *UN Chronicle*, June 1990, p. 22.

Discusses the United Nations office set up in Afghanistan to co-ordinate humanitarian and economic assistance, known as "Operation Salam." Main activities in 1990; U.N. response to emergency food needs; food shortages; continued hostilities and U.N. efforts.

# Back Issues

*Great Research on Current Issues Starts Right Here... Recent topics covered by The CQ Researcher are listed below. Issues dated before May 10, 1991, were published under the name of Editorial Research Reports.*

**APRIL 1990**
How Fair is the Tax Burden?
Workers' Compensation
U.S. Pacific Forces
Curbing Insurance Premiums

**MAY 1990**
Should Teaching Be a Profession?
Will Canada Fall Apart?
Is U.S. Patent System Outdated?
Federal Funding for the Arts

**JUNE 1990**
Downsizing America's Armed Forces
Progress In Weather Forecasting
S & L Bailout
Bio-Chemical Disarmament

**JULY 1990**
Do Americans Still Love Marriage?
Death Penalty Debate
Decline of Rural America
United Nations in the 1990s

**AUGUST 1990**
Democracy in the Philippines
Initiatives: True Democracy?
Hard Times at Newspapers
Teens Balance School & Jobs

**SEPTEMBER 1990**
Dangers of Alcohol
Western Alliance After the Cold War
Tobacco Industry
Right to Die

**OCTOBER 1990**
Organ Transplants
Energy Policy Options
Search for Arab Unity
Child Support

**NOVEMBER 1990**
Lotteries and Gambling
Post Cold-War Choices
Setting Limits on Medical Care
Multicultural Education

**DECEMBER 1990**
Cable TV Regulation
Americans' Search For Their Roots
Is Insurance System a Failure?
Why Schools Still Have Tracking

**JANUARY 1991**
Growing Influence of Boycotts
Should the U.S. Reinstate the Draft?
America's Archaeological Past
Peace Corps' Challenges in '90s

**FEBRUARY 1991**
Regional Impact of Recession
Puerto Rico's Status
Redistricting: Mapping Power
Nuclear Power

**MARCH 1991**
Acid Rain
Cost of the Gulf War
Reassessing Gun Laws
Future for Man in Space

**APRIL 1991**
Social Security
Canadian Crisis Over Quebec
California Drought
Electromagnetic Radiation

**MAY 1991**
School Choice
Racial Quotas
Animal Rights
U.S. and Japan

**JUNE 1991**
Children and Divorce
Teenage Suicide
Endangered Species
Europe 1992

**JULY 1991**
Teenagers and Abortion
Soviet Republics Rebel
Mexico's Emergence
Athletes and Drugs

**AUGUST 1991**
Sexual Harassment
Fetal Tissue Research
Oil Imports
The Palestinians

**SEPTEMBER 1991**
Police Brutality
Advertising Under Attack
Saving the Forests
Foster Care Crisis

**OCTOBER 1991**
Pay-Per-View TV
Youth Gangs
Gene Therapy

Back issues are available for $4.00 (subscribers) or $7.00 (non-subscribers). Quantity discounts apply to orders over ten. To order, call Congressional Quarterly 1-800-432-2250.

# Future Topics

▶ *Fast-Food Business*

▶ *Eastern Europe's Environmental Problems*

▶ *Business and Education*

# THE CQ Researcher

PUBLISHED BY CONGRESSIONAL QUARTERLY INC., IN CONJUNCTION WITH EBSCO PUBLISHING

# Fast-Food Shake-Up

*Beleaguered chains improve nutrition, environmental impact and job quality*

FASTER THAN YOU CAN SAY "CHEESEBURGER, fries and a Coke," the fast-food industry built itself into a fixture on the American scene. But almost from the start, the industry's phenomenal rise was accompanied by hefty servings of criticism. Nutritionists attacked the greasy, high-calorie menus, environmentalists blasted the high consumption of disposable packaging and career counselors scorned the monotonous, low-paying jobs. Now the industry is taking major steps to satisfy critics. It is offering more nutritionally balanced menus, reducing packaging waste and improving benefits to retain workers longer. The motivation goes beyond good citizenship — fast food is a fiercely competitive business driven by powerful consumer demands.

 **November 8, 1991 • Volume 1, No. 25 • 825-848**

*Formerly Editorial Research Reports*

COVER ART: BARBARA SASSA-DANIELS

November 8, 1991
Volume 1, No. 25

**EDITOR**
Sandra Stencel

**MANAGING EDITOR**
Thomas J. Colin

**ASSOCIATE EDITOR**
Richard L. Worsnop

**STAFF WRITERS**
Charles S. Clark
Mary H. Cooper
Rodman D. Griffin

**PRODUCTION EDITOR**
Laurie De Maris

**EDITORIAL ASSISTANT**
Thomas H. Moore

**GRAPHICS**
Jack Auldridge

**PUBLISHED BY**
Congressional Quarterly Inc.

**CHAIRMAN**
Andrew Barnes

**VICE CHAIRMAN**
Andrew P. Corty

**EDITOR AND PUBLISHER**
Neil Skene

**EXECUTIVE EDITOR**
Robert W. Merry

**PUBLICATIONS MARKETING/SALES**
Robert Smith

**EDITOR, EBSCO PUBLISHING**
Melissa Kummerer

The CQ Researcher (ISSN 1056-2036). Formerly Editorial Research Reports. Published weekly (48 times per year, not printed the first Friday of any month with five Fridays) by Congressional Quarterly Inc., 1414 22nd St., N.W., Washington, D.C. 20037. Rates are furnished upon request. Application to mail at second-class postage rates is pending at Washington, D.C. POSTMASTER: Send address changes to The CQ Researcher, 1414 22nd St., N.W., Washington, D.C. 20037.

# Fast-Food Shake-Up

BY CHARLES S. CLARK

## THE ISSUES

In unappetizing language and large, jarring type, ads warning about "The Poisoning of America!" appeared in newspapers across the country in the spring of 1990. Their author, Phil Sokolof, a 68-year-old Omaha, Neb., millionaire who had survived a heart attack, was sending a message to McDonald's from his National Heart Savers Association: Stop cooking french fries with high-cholesterol beef fat and reduce the fat content of your hamburgers. "High cholesterol kills!" the ads shouted. "500,000 heart attack deaths every year."

McDonald's threatened legal action and claimed Sokolof's figures on fat content were wrong. A national poll conducted by *Advertising Age*, however, showed high consumer awareness of the ads and 38 percent of respondents saying the series had prompted them to avoid fast-food restaurants.[1]

In July 1990, just three weeks after Sokolof took out a second round of ads, McDonald's and two other fast-food chains, Burger King and Wendy's, all switched from beef tallow to vegetable oil. (Another chain, Hardee's, had switched earlier.) And more changes were in store. Last April, McDonald's came out with the "McLean Deluxe," its 91 percent fat-free hamburger, the leanest in the business.

McDonald's executives sought to minimize the credit given to Sokolof and other health critics, insisting that both changes had been in the research stage for years. Undeterred, Sokolof took out another set of ads to celebrate his new respect for McDonald's. "Now we're on the same team," he effused to reporters. The

"whole food industry is moving in the right direction."

The move toward sounder nutrition is only one of many changes coming thick and fast in the fast-food industry. An institution long derided (even by its patrons) for its greasy-spoon menus, wasteful packaging and low-skill, monotonous jobs is now scrambling to catch a wave of aging baby-boomers with a new range of convenient, tasty but healthful products. Offerings being tested range from "fast" fettuccine Alfredo to fresh vegetables, already dubbed "McSticks" at McDonald's. Last February, an American icon known as Kentucky Fried Chicken changed its name to KFC to avoid the unhealthy sounding "fried" and, as KFC public affairs director Richard Detwiler explains, to reflect long-term plans to offer chicken cooked in other ways.

The changes are more than culinary. After years of negative publicity and protest letters from schoolchildren, McDonald's last November set a new environmental pace for the in-

dustry by joining with the nonprofit Environmental Defense Fund in an initiative to eliminate 80 percent of the waste generated by its 8,500 domestic restaurants and 600 suppliers.

Leo J. Shapiro, a Chicago consultant who has studied U.S. eating habits for 40 years, says consumers now demand that fast-food companies be good citizens. His surveys show that 85 percent of Americans think that consumers should get more than product for their money, that their support should go to companies that don't harm the environment or hurt people.

"Consumerism has come back, like in the late '60s and early '70s," says Michael Evans, a spokesman for Burger King, noting that his Miami-based company's toll-free number for customer feedback gets 4,000 calls a day.

The impact of these consumer trends is hardly small potatoes. An estimated 46 million Americans patronize the nation's 160,000 fast-food restaurants every day, each spending an average of $250 a year.[2] Only 4 percent of Americans say they never visit them, a National Restaurant Association (NRA) survey revealed.

The share of the family food budget spent on eating out has shot up from 25 percent in the late 1960s to 40 percent now, egged on by the proliferation of two-income families grabbing meals on the go. The insatiable demand for speed and convenience revved up in the late 1980s with the expansion of "drive-thru" facilities. A remarkable 62 percent of fast food was ordered "to go" in 1990, compared with 23 percent in 1982.[3] The same period witnessed a spectacular rise in pizza home-delivery services, many of them catering to baby-boomers "cocooning" in front of their VCRs. (Pizza Hut, which didn't even offer delivery five years ago, now depends on it for 40 percent of its business.)

Food in the age of the microwave oven has created new expectations for speed. To increasingly harried Americans, time considerations are paramount. (A Harris Poll shows that the average American work week grew from 41 hours in 1973 to 47 hours in 1989, with available leisure time declining 37 percent.)

Fast food's hassle-free quickness is winning consumers away from intricately prepared meals in which fine food is savored. In a 1988 *Consumer Reports* survey, three of five respondents said they went to fast-food restaurants "to get in and out quickly" rather than for quality; 40 percent admitted they were getting only fair or poor quality food.[4] "We used to eat when the food was ready," market researcher Shapiro says. "Now we eat when we're ready." [5]

With speed the name of its game, the fast-food industry is running to keep up. Carl's Jr., a West Coast fried-chicken and burger chain, has installed huge stopwatches at its drive-through windows, guaranteeing that if food is not served within a minute, customers get a $1 coupon. Atlanta-based Arby's, the roast beef specialist, allows customers to order by pushing computer buttons, thus eliminating the inefficiency of talking. At some Wendy's outlets, clerks offer to take your order while you're standing in line to save "think time" at the counter. Other outlets have removed seats to make room for customers who eat standing up.

Gimmicky as some of these changes may seem, they reflect the competitive nature of the $74 billion fast-food industry, which can never rest on the warm glow of yesterday's meal. The once-almighty hamburger, for example, is now on fast food's back burner: Americans eating outside the home consume 46 percent more pizza, 52 percent more Mexi-

can food and 13 percent more chicken than they did in 1984, but 6 percent less beef, according to NPD Crest, a Chicago consulting firm.[6] Not only are fast-food companies in a cook-off against one another, together they are competing for what they call "share of stomach" against the rival formats that also offer convenience — quick-service delis, all-you-can-eat buffets and supermarket salad bars.

After a healthy growth rate that reached 21 percent annually in the early 1970s, the industry in the past two years has tapered off to about 6 percent annually. (This spring, McDonald's, the world's largest restaurant chain, reported a first-quarter drop of 2 percent in operating revenues, its worst performance in years.) The fast-food industry is still burned by an employee turnover averaging 140 percent a year, and some analysts argue that it has now saturated the U.S. market, forcing more concentration on expansion overseas. *(See story, p. 839.)*

The shrinking profits, worsened by the current recession, have kicked off a price war. Taco Bell fired the first shot in 1988, offering such out-of-the-past come-ons as 39-cent bean burritos. For the last quarter of 1990, the Irvine, Calif., chain saw its sales improve at five times the industry rate.

McDonald's and Hardee's have answered Taco Bell with 59-cent hamburgers, and Wendy's now serves a baked potato for 99 cents. The price war played right to the strengths of Louisville-based Rally's, a back-to-the-basics chain with a low-overhead, drive-through approach; it sells a quarter-pound cheeseburger, large Coke and fries for 85 cents less than McDonald's. Some competitors, however, warn that discounts harm long-term profitability, arguing that quality is a better selling point in the never-ending battle for the allegiance of the American palate.

One thing is certain: With so many business, consumer and lifestyle issues piled on the table, the fast-food industry will be cooking up new surprises in the years ahead as it fights to preserve its place on the American scene. Its future will hinge largely on the following issues:

### Can the fast-food industry satisfy complaints from nutritionists?

That Americans are acquiring a taste for nutrition is clear to both dietary purists and libertarians. National Restaurant Association polls in 1989 found that nearly 70 percent of Americans worry about nutrition, up from 62 percent in 1986. Nutrition issues have also been gaining visibility since many fast-food companies began posting nutritional information in stores. *(See p. 840.)* McDonald's devoted a special section of its 1990 annual report to the nutrition discussion.

Nutritionists have long complained that fast food contains too much fat, sodium, sugar and calories. Medical experts have warned eaters to go easy with these dietary bugaboos because, as a fast-food eating guide published by the Washington-based Center for Science in the Public Interest noted, they promote obesity, high blood pressure, stroke, heart disease and probably cancer of the colon, breast and prostate.

Federal officials have added to critics' ammunition. Agriculture Department spokeswoman Karen Bunch said in 1990: "The trend toward eating more fast food reduces the variety in our diets and may increase the risk of nutritional deficiency. A typical fast-food meal contains half the recommended daily allowances (RDA) of calories and protein, but only a third of the RDA of vitamin C, thiamine and niacin, and lesser amounts of iron, calcium and vitamin A." [7]

Fast food's nutritional risks are difficult to gauge, however, because, as KFC's Detwiler points out, "You can't look at diet in terms of one meal. It's a continuum." And, as fast-food marketers know better than anyone, nutrition is only one issue on customers' minds. "Clearly, consumers are more nutrition-conscious," Detwiler says, "also convenience-conscious, plus taste-conscious. To succeed, [a food company] has to balance these very powerful consumer interests. It's not enough to make a product healthier. If it doesn't taste good, no one will buy it."

Nor do fast-food firms consider nutrition their sole responsibility. As a Wendy's spokesman said, eating out is viewed "more as entertainment," while nutrition is reserved for the home.[8] Finally, despite lofty nutritional rhetoric, many consumers indulge in breaded chicken skins and fatty beef if that's where the taste is. Says Charles Bernstein, editor of *Nation's Restaurant News*, "Customers often talk healthy and light foods, but eat heavy." [9]

Nevertheless, while the "tastes great/less harmful" debate goes on, fast-food chains clearly have made a strategic decision to cater to nutrition-minded patrons. "Our strategy is not necessarily to move towards healthier items," said John Merritt, senior vice president of public affairs for Hardee's, soon after Hardee's introduced the "Lean 1" hamburger, which claimed 30 percent less fat than its quarter-pound burger. "Our strategy is to move towards more choice. We found ourselves in a situation where one in three people was on some kind of diet, which meant that every time a party of three came in there was one who wanted a different choice."

Many fast-food critics share Phil Sokolof's enthusiasm and are highly pleased with the recent avalanche of "lite" fast food — the diet burgers, salad bars, frozen yogurt and apple

# Fast-Food Giants

*When fast-food chains are ranked according to total sales (both foreign and domestic), McDonald's towers over the competition, with nearly $19 billion in revenues. No. 2 Burger King posted just over $6 billion in revenues. The rankings remain the same for sales only in the United States.*

| Company headquarters | Major product | 1990 sales ($ millions) | Number of outlets | Ownership |
|---|---|---|---|---|
| **McDonald's** Oak Brook, Ill. | hamburgers | $18,759 | 11,803 | Public |
| **Burger King** Miami, Fla. | hamburgers | 6,100 | 6,200 | Grand Metro-politan PLC |
| **KFC** Louisville, Ky. | chicken | 5,773 | 8,187 | PepsiCo |
| **Pizza Hut** Wichita, Kan. | pizza | 4,900 | 8,040 | PepsiCo |
| **Hardee's** Rocky Mount, N.C. | hamburgers | 3,158† | 3,622† | Imasco Ltd. |
| **Wendy's International** Dublin, Ohio | hamburgers | 3,070 | 3,727 | Public |
| **Domino's Pizza** Ann Arbor, Mich. | pizza | 2,650 | 5,376 | Privately held |
| **Taco Bell** Irvine, Calif. | Mexican food | 2,400 | 3,273 | PepsiCo |
| **Dairy Queen** Bloomington, Minn. | sweets | 2,316† | 5,207 | Public |
| **Arby's** Atlanta, Ga. | sandwiches | 1,430 | 2,420 | DWG Enterprises |
| **Little Caesars Pizza** Detroit, Mich. | pizza | 1,400 | 3,173 | Privately held |
| **Subway** Milford, Conn. | sandwiches | 1,100 | 5,380 | Doctors Associates Inc. |

*Source:* Restaurants and Institutions *magazine.*     † *Estimate*

bran muffins. "I've been amazed," says Michael Jacobson, executive director of the Center for Science in the Public Interest. "Five years ago, the fast-food industry didn't even know what the word 'nutrition' meant. Now it's a top consideration whenever they're introducing a new product or revising an old one."

Jacobson gives special credit to McDonald's for McLean Deluxe, for its 99.5 percent fat-free milkshakes, and for dropping the high-fat "McDLT" hamburger. As part of its "food for a new attitude" campaign, McDonald's now displays nutritional information on posters, distributes an educational package for school-

children called "Eating Right, Feeling Fit" and answers consumer questions through its Nutrition Information Center.

McDonald's decision to stop frying in beef fat has been widely emulated. By February 1991, an NRA survey would show that 89 percent of chain operators had switched to vegetable oil, up 27 percentage points from the previous year. McDonald's is the arbiter of taste, Jacobson says. It can change its milkshake and keep it that way even if people say they don't like the taste. McDonald's can say, "That's what a shake is," Jacobson says.

The industry makes sure its

changes don't go unnoticed. At a 1990 conference of the American Dietetic Association (ADA), Wendy's surveyed 341 dietitians and found that 92 percent said the fast-food industry had taken major steps in recent years toward improving nutrition. A heartening 90 percent said fast food can fit into a well-balanced diet, and 33 percent of the conference-goers even admitted to once-a-week fast-food habits.

Still, Jacobson notes that the move toward nutrition has not been flawless. "Wendy's has a fabulous salad bar, but its double cheeseburger is horrendous," he says. "Most products are still pretty junky. KFC fried sandwiches are awful, and a Big Mac is nothing for nutritionists to write home about."

The new edition of Jacobson's guide to fast food picks the worst fast-food offenders: Carl's Jr.'s Double Western Bacon Cheeseburger (1,030 calories, 14 teaspoons of fat); Jack in the Box's Ultimate Cheeseburger (942 calories, 16 teaspoons of fat); and Burger King's Double Whopper with Cheese (935 calories, 14 teaspoons of fat).[10]

But KFC's Detwiler dismisses Jacobson for being unrealistic about the kinds of products consumers are willing to buy.

"What Michael Jacobson wants to eat for lunch isn't exactly what the rest of the world wants to eat for lunch," he says.

Most experts handle the fast-food conflict with a call for moderation. "Consumers must recognize that even though these [new and improved] foods are better for you, they *do* have shortcomings," says Neva Cochran, an ADA spokeswoman. "They are still lower in some important nutrients and higher in calories, fat and sodium than a well-balanced, home-cooked meal. If a person's total diet is balanced, then *any* fast food is okay once in a while. Just not three times a day."[11]

## Is the fast-food industry making a substantive effort to protect the environment?

Waste material generated by fast-food companies, the industry is quick to point out, represents less than 1 percent of the country's total landfill volume.[12]

Nevertheless, fast food draws the wrath of environmentalists because its packaging waste is so visible to average consumers. And, because so much waste is taken off-premises by customers, the industry has been under pressure both to recycle its own packaging waste and reduce the waste it generates in the course of bringing food to customers.

McDonald's, as the industry leader and the critics' most visible target *(see story, p. 831)*, scored big points with the environmental community Nov. 1, 1990, when it announced radical changes in its packaging. "McDonald's has seen the future, and it's green!" proclaimed Fred Krupp, executive director of the Environmental Defense Fund (EDF), which helped develop the new packaging policy. "McDonald's Surrenders!" trumpeted the newsletter for the Citizens Clearinghouse for Hazardous Waste, a grass-roots group based in Falls Church, Va., that for three years coordinated much of the nationwide "McToxics" protests against McDonald's. Members picketed stores, fought for local ordinances against Styrofoam and organized "send-it-back" campaigns to return used packaging to McDonald's headquarters to protest the symbol of "the throwaway society."

The previous April, McDonald's had marked Earth Day 1990 by announcing that it was setting up its "McRecycle" program, committing $100 million to helping create suppliers for its newly adopted recycled napkins, shipping materials, drink trays and carry-out bags, which, because they do not come in direct contact with food, can be made of recycled materials and still meet health standards.

Though McDonald's would become the largest user of recycled paper in its field, McRecycle still depended on cooperation from established companies and recycling entrepreneurs to provide collection, processing and composting services, which vary regionally. Hence McDonald's was still under attack for continuing to generate large amounts of packaging used to serve food. As consumer advocate Ralph Nader charged, "By concentrating on waste *management* rather than offering to end the production of waste, McDonald's ignores the human health dangers posed by hazardous chemical emissions produced as McDonald's unneeded plastic and Styrofoam packing is manufactured."[13]

The company's breakthrough 40-point agreement with the EDF called for the redesign and reuse of such items as condiment containers and lids for drinking cups; the substitution of unbleached paper for paper coated with toxic inks and waterproofers; and composting programs for such organic waste as coffee grinds and egg shells.

The centerpiece, however, was McDonald's decision — agreed to at the eleventh hour — to abandon its well-known clamshell-shaped hamburger container made from polystyrene plastic. The clamshell, in use since the 1970s, outperformed paper in retaining heat and cold, protecting food from contamination and repelling grease stains. Critics argued, however, that producing polystyrene wasted energy and increased air pollution, that clamshells whose useful life can be measured in seconds might endure for centuries buried in landfills, and that as a plastic, the clamshell was difficult and costly to recycle.

For most of the six months that McDonald's worked with EDF, the

*Continued on p. 832*

# Fast Food's Most Visible Target

In the fast-food world, McDonald's relishes its role as the storybook business success, the speedy-food pioneer, the essential presence on Main Street USA. With glory, however, have come the inevitable brickbats — from food critics, neighborhood activists and frustrated minority investors.

Perhaps the chief reason McDonald's seems to embody everything negative about fast food is the chain's sheer visibility. "They have establishments on every street corner," a National Restaurant Association official once said. "They're easy-to-identify targets, like the oil companies, for anyone who wants to throw criticism." (When *USA Today* was created by the Gannett Co., the new formula featuring super-short, easy-to-read articles prompted detractors to nickname it "McPaper.")

McDonald's faced its first major public relations challenge in 1968, a time when racial tensions were high following the assassination of the Rev. Dr. Martin Luther King Jr. In Cleveland, black activists began a boycott of McDonald's to protest the fact that whites owned six McDonald's stores in the city's black neighborhoods. Picket signs went up, riot police gathered and the city polarized along racial lines.

Newly elected Mayor Carl Stokes, a black, set up negotiations between the company and the protesters at City Hall. But Stokes had permitted the activists to bring guns to the tense meeting, and it stalemated. Only when a prominent local black physician labeled the boycott "a shakedown" did the deadlock ease. McDonald's had thwarted the activists' demands for a role in choosing franchisees, but it did replace the six white owners with blacks.[†]

The spotlight of unwanted publicity glared on McDonald's again in 1972, when the corporation's patriarch, Ray Kroc, donated $25,000 to President Richard M. Nixon's re-election campaign. Before Congress that year was a bill to hike the minimum wage, a move actively opposed by many of McDonald's independent franchisees, who had joined other small businesses in lobbying for a subminimum training wage to be offered to part-time student workers. Organized labor and other critics of the special training wage derided it publicly as "the McDonald's bill."

Against the backdrop of the debate over wages, Nixon's Wage and Price Control Board granted McDonald's an exception on prices and permitted a 5-cent price increase for the chain's Quarter Pounders. Syndicated columnist Jack Anderson got wind of the price hike and linked it to Kroc's donation to Nixon. The affair tainted McDonald's with the campaign-finance scandals of the Watergate era.

In 1974 McDonald's took yet another public relations drubbing. Plans had been laid for a Manhattan store at 65th Street and Lexington Avenue. The tony neighborhood boasted a historic armory, a fashionable apartment building, the venerable Cosmopolitan Club for women and Chase Manhattan Bank's headquarters. Suddenly, an angry New York elite of writers, architects, lawyers and stockbrokers organized the Friends of Sixty-Fifth Street and collected 15,000 signatures. As picketing began, McDonald's proceeded with plans, feeling safe in the knowledge that it owned the property and had met all zoning requirements.

Then editorials in *The New York Times* denounced the project as an eyesore. *Times* food critic Mimi Sheraton warned of the litter and unsavory characters that would be drawn to the neighborhood. She called McDonald's food "irredeemably horrible," the hamburgers "rubbery," the lettuce like "wet confetti" and the shakes like "aerated Kaopectate." Around the same time, the weekly business newspaper *Barron's* published a scathing critique of McDonald's accounting practices. After the company's stock dived, McDonald's surrendered. The building instead became home to a women's clothing store.

For McDonald's officials who had embraced the heartwarming tale of the small-town hamburger chefs who changed America, such hostility was tough to swallow. "All things that made McDonald's successful — its predictability, uniformity and controls — were perceived by some people as lacking individuality, stamped out and mass-produced," a beleaguered McDonald's publicist remarked in the mid-1970s. "We were tagged as part of a plastic society some social observers were condemning. For the first time, we were on the defensive." [††]

In recent years, community resistance to fast-food "tackiness" has continued. Last year, little New Market, Md., a historic village of 450 people, dozens of antique shops and rows of 18th- and 19th-century homes — successfully fought off a McDonald's plan to open a new store by threatening to go to court. "It's just not consistent with what we're doing here," said Mayor Franklin Shaw. "I have yet to see an 18th-century McDonald's." [‡] The opening of a McDonald's in Rome, Italy, prompted the founding of the Slow Food Society in the late 1980s. With nearly 30,000 members in 26 countries (including a branch in New York City), it circulates light-hearted exhortations warning that "fast-food is one of the most powerful and destructive components of our speeded-up modern lives."

Today, McDonald's is careful to scout out locations and communicate with locals to try to avoid clashes. And the company's public affairs officers, as they fend off attacks on McDonald's environmental policies and other issues, try to apply a positive spin. "As my Dad used to tell me," says McDonald's spokeswoman Terri Capatosto, "pioneers take all the arrows."

---

† John F. Love, *McDonald's: Behind the Arches*, 1986, p. 363.
†† Ibid, p. 359.
‡ Quoted in *The New York Times*, Oct. 21, 1990.

Continued from p. 830

company was leaning toward retaining the clamshells and launching a national program to recycle them. It cited scientific studies and had set up a regional recycling experiment. But the EDF's arguments — and, most important, public perception of the foam container as wasteful — changed McDonald's mind. "We were literally within hours of deciding to go with a national plastic recycling program," said McDonald's President Edward Rensi. "We had it well-developed and ready to go. But the public tipped us over the edge, into paper." [14]

Clamshell supporters, as represented by the Polystyrene Packaging Council, argue that McDonald's made the wrong move. They point to polystyrene recycling initiatives already in effect as well as to studies. One, by Franklin Associates Ltd. of Canada, shows that it takes 30 percent less energy to produce polystyrene containers, and that they burn more cleanly. Another study, from an independent German research firm, says the use of paper packaging could end up costing consumers twice as much.[15]

In any case, the agreement by the industry's pace-setter "far exceeded our expectations and original goals," the EDF-McDonald's task force commented. It predicts that the switch to paper will reduce packaging volume by 70 to 90 percent and that McDonald's will meet its 1991 goal of creating suppliers for its $100 million commitment to purchasing recycled products. According to task force member Richard A. Denison, an EDF scientist, "McDonald's continues going great guns on the implementation" and maintains frequent contact with the EDF. He even suggests that the company should promote its deeds more in advertising.

Michael Williams, a spokesman for the Clearinghouse on Hazardous Waste, says that nearly all the fast-food companies were either already active environmentally or are now following McDonald's lead. He criticized Hardee's, however, for declining to switch from polystyrene to paper packaging. Hardee's argues that polystyrene is 100 percent recyclable, has been approved by the Food and Drug Administration as safe and contains no chlorofluorocarbons (CFCs), a material commonly used in foam packaging that is believed to harm the Earth's protective ozone layer. Hardee's 1990 environmental efforts, such as switching from a paper carton to wax wrap for its biscuits and decreasing packing in cleaning supplies, reduced its annual waste stream by 3 million pounds, the company says.

On the day McDonald's announced it would stop using clamshells, California-based Jack in the Box said it would drop polystyrene, too. It has now eliminated carry-out bags and modified packaging to eliminate more than a million pounds of waste per year. International Dairy Queen, meanwhile, in 1989 had launched a waste-reduction program expected to lower waste by 1.7 million pounds each year. Taco Bell has announced that it has set up a task force on "source reduction," to consider such "primary packaging" changes as reducing the number of condiment packages given to consumers as well as "secondary packaging" changes such as shipping soft drink syrup in tanker trucks instead of polyethylene bags inside cardboard boxes. This July, Burger King began switching from paperboard to paper in its 6,500 restaurants to save 300,000 pounds of paper a year.

Putting to rest an environmental issue raised loudly in the 1970s, most fast-food companies proudly declare that none of their beef comes from cattle in Latin America that graze on land that has been denuded of rain forests.

## Is the fast-food industry providing desirable jobs?

When economists grow concerned about U.S. competitiveness in world trade, they often raise the specter of "a nation of hamburger flippers." In many circles, the fast-food industry does not enjoy a reputation for offering high-skilled jobs, generous wages or lofty career potential to its 3.5 million employees (more than the electronics and steel industries combined). Staffed to a large degree by teenagers working their first jobs, the industry battles an unusually high employee turnover rate.

Workers in eating and drinking establishments in general are at the bottom of the Bureau of Labor Statistics' list of low-paying industries, earning an average of $5.17 per hour. Because labor represents a significant 20 percent of fast-food retailing costs, owners are determined to keep wages low. (Compliance with the 1990 federally mandated hike in the minimum wage caused 59 percent of restaurants to raise menu prices, 49 percent to reduce employee hours and 27 percent to cut employee benefits, according to the NRA.)

Not one of the fast-food chains is unionized, laments Keith Mestrich, director of special services for the Food and Allied Services Trades Department of the AFL-CIO, "and there are no workers with a greater need." Not only are the benefits and job security poor, he says, but teen-agers often lack the courage to refuse an unreasonable demand: "Their status is left completely up to the employer."

Fast-food work is also scorned for its monotony, its "fool-proof" cash registers with buttons showing pictures instead of numerals and its production drills that leave little to chance or individual discretion. In declining to include McDonald's in their 1985 book, *The 100 Best Companies to Work for in America*, business journalists Robert Levering, Milton Moscowitz and Michael Katz wrote of the company's "dehumanizing assembly-line operation that leaves the employee with little or no time to think." [16]

Industry representatives, not surprisingly, offer a brighter view. Fast-food jobs are an "Ellis Island" for workers wishing to participate in our growing services economy," effuses a Taco Bell pamphlet. First jobs in the fast-food industry are said to teach young people responsibility, teamwork and interpersonal skills. Such views are backed by some scholars, writers and conservative policy advocates. McDonald's has replaced the U.S. Army as the nation's largest job-training program, writes business reporter John F. Love in his history of the chain, and one of every 15 U.S. workers first entered the work force under the Golden Arches.[17] McDonald's is also the largest employer of black Americans and has been featured in *Black Enterprise* magazine as one of the 50 best places for blacks to work.

Fast-food skills are transferable in today's shifting economy, says conservative economist Marvin Kosters of the American Enterprise Institute for Public Policy Research, with the low pay a form of indirect payment for the broad skills learned.[18] Finally, one of the common recruiting arguments advanced by fast-food companies is that many of their top executives got their start as members of store crews. Pizza Hut, for example, says more than 40 percent of its managers began as drivers, waiters, waitresses or cooks.

In a well-known study in the early 1980s, analysts Ivan Charner and Bryna Shore Fraser of the National Institute for Work and Learning in Washington surveyed 7,741 people

working at 279 fast-food restaurants in seven chains. In results pleasing to the industry, 67 percent said they enjoyed the work, 50 percent said they were proud to work in the industry and only 14 percent said they were embarrassed. About 25 percent said the job helped them get along better with families, while 61 percent of teachers and 64 percent of guidance counselors surveyed said they approve of fast-food jobs.[19] The industry can also point to a July 1987 Gallup Poll commissioned by the restaurant industry in which the most frequently cited reasons fast-

> McDonald's has replaced the U. S. Army as the nation's largest job-training program. McDonald's is also the largest employer of black Americans.

food workers liked their jobs were 1) to gain job experience; 2) to learn responsibility; and 3) to have a good time.

As Herbert R. Northrup of the Wharton School of Business writes: "It is perhaps ironic that many of the most insistent advocates of job-training programs in this country are the same academics, journalists and government administrators who condemn the fast-food job as, at best, a meaningless dead-end and thus fail to see that the object of their contempt has in effect become one of the most massive, cost-efficient and racially equitable job-training pro-

grams in our nation's history." [20]

In recent years, the debate over teens working in fast food has shifted dramatically as the industry has experienced a labor shortage. The number of 16-to-24-year-olds dropped from 38.7 million in 1980 to 33.7 million in 1990, the Census Bureau reported, and is projected to drop to 32.9 million by the year 2000. In 1988 the NRA estimated that fast-food outlets were short 200,000 laborers, leading many chains to actively recruit. In scarce labor markets such as Boston and Atlanta, entry-level jobs were suddenly offered at $6 to $7 an hour. More important, many firms began recruiting not just teens but recent immigrants, college students, housewives with children at school, adult moonlighters and the elderly. Today, more than 9 percent of all fast-food employees are 55 or older, according to a federal survey.[21]

The labor shortage and the more varied work force explain why several fast-food companies have begun improving employee benefits. In July 1989, for example, Pepsico, owner of Taco Bell, Pizza Hut and KFC, began awarding stock options to all full-time employees. A year later Wendy's followed suit, having extended medical, dental and retirement benefits to its rank-and-file employees the previous year. Many local franchises now offer to pay college tuition for their employees.

At a Burger King store in Detroit, for example, turnover in recent years had hit 179 percent, forcing the replacement of each worker nearly twice a year. Noting that many quit to attend school, owner Herbert Schervish offered to pay for tuition and books at either of two local community colleges. In a two-year period, turnover among program participants dropped below 40 percent.[22]

A sign of the fast-food industry's desperation for employees is its frequent reliance on the youngest who apply for its jobs. In 1990, when Labor Department agents conducted sweeps of work sites around the country, 80 percent of the 40,000 child labor law violations they uncovered were in the fast-food industry. (The department hit Burger King with a lawsuit alleging violations; its dismissal by a federal judge is under appeal.)

Last March, Sen. Howard M. Metzenbaum, D-Ohio, held a hearing on his legislation to increase penalties for violating child labor laws. James M. Coleman, general counsel of the National Council of Chain Restaurants, representing 37 of the largest restaurant and hotel companies, testified that the violations represented only a fraction of the 3.5 million 16- and 17-year-olds lawfully working and the millions under 16 who are permitted to work under certain circumstances. He said the violations were unintentional and argued that some regulations are open to different interpretations. For example, he said, 14- and 15-year-olds are prohibited from cooking and baking in working kitchens but are permitted to do so at lunch counters.

Another area where many see a need for progress in fast food is in minority ownership of franchises. Though racial and ethnic minorities accounted for 25.4 percent of the U.S. population in the 1990 census, only 8.5 percent of restaurant franchises are owned by minorities.[23] Burger King is currently being sued for racial discrimination and restraint of trade practices by some minority licensees, and critics argue that fast-food companies are willing to set up white operators in inner cities but are reluctant to put minority operators in white communities. To remedy the situation, KFC, for

example, is offering a $60 million guaranteed-loan program to help minorities open stores. Jesse Jackson's Operation PUSH in Chicago is working with Burger King to create an industry model for minority-run restaurants more in line with consumer demographics. "It's not really necessary to have black operators to cater

to black customers," said W. Maurice Bridges, a spokesman for Hardee's. "But it is important to have black operators, in our view, because it brings in a loyal minority-customer base if it is generally well-recognized that Hardee's is sensitive to black concerns and is working to develop black entrepreneurs." [24]  ■

# BACKGROUND

## Fast Food's Ancestors

Food that Americans can eat on the go — without getting dressed up and without taxing one's brain with complicated menu choices — traces its roots to the early 19th century, when the railroads were first offering average citizens the chance to travel across the country. Quick lunches were served at rail stops to hungry passengers who had only minutes to gobble before they had to return to their trains.

A British naval officer, Capt. Frederick Maryat, described the scene in a letter in 1839: "The cars stop, all the doors are thrown open, and out rush all the passengers like boys out of school, and crowd round the tables to solace themselves with pies, patties, cakes, hard-boiled eggs, hams, custards and a variety of railroad luxuries too numerous to mention. The bell rings for departure, in they all hurry with their hands and mouths full, and off they go again until the next stopping place." [25]

Americans in this period were already demonstrating impatience when it came to eating. "Back in 1830," says food historian Harvey Levenstein of McMaster University (Hamilton, Ontario), "the idea was, 'Why not get it over with?' You don't like the taste, and you can get on with the things you enjoy more."

Only in the late 19th century did the family meal emerge as an American ritual, he says.[26]

By the 1920s, Levenstein writes, the increased proportion of single women in white-collar occupations in the middle and lower-middle class fueled a boom in cafeterias, lunch counters and sandwich shops.[27] Non-franchised establishments labeled "quick lunch rooms" were common in cities. The number of unskilled workers ready to take jobs in informal restaurants began a rise that would dramatically outpace any rise in the number of trained gourmet chefs.

### Industry Takes Shape

The first documented drive-in eating establishment appeared in Dallas in 1921, when visionary entrepreneur Royce Hailey started a "Pig Stand" at which automobiles, newly common, could pull up for barbecued sandwiches.[28]

The first outlet for fast food as we know it today was opened in Wichita, Kan., in 1921 by E. W. "Billy" Ingram. He served small 5-cent hamburgers at his White Castle and encouraged customers to buy them by the bag. Within a few years he had a chain stretching to 11 states. Customers were mostly male — often truck drivers, for example — and not families.

Ingram spawned a slew of imitators in the late 1920s. A&W Root Beer didn't serve food initially, but when it opened a Washington, D.C.,

*Continued on p. 836*

# Chronology

**1920s** *Single women enter the work force; automobile ownership widens.*

**1921**
First fast-food chain, White Castle, founded in Wichita, Kan.

**1925**
Franchising pioneer Howard Johnson opens his first eatery in Quincy, Mass.

———— • ————

**1940s** *Return of GIs from war prompts new enterprises; rise of "teenage culture."*

**June 22, 1940**
First Dairy Queen soft ice cream store opens in Joliet, Ill.

**1948**
Richard and Maurice McDonald open the first hamburger drive-in in San Bernardino, Calif.

———— • ————

**1950s** *Development of suburbs, interstate highways.*

**1954**
Burger King launched in Miami; Shakey's first pizza parlor founded in Sacramento, Calif.

**1955**
Ray Kroc opens his first McDonald's in Des Plaines, Ill.

**1958**
Pizza Hut founded by Frank L. Carney in Wichita, Kan.

**1960s** *Fast-food chains expand rapidly; Americans step up travel.*

**1960**
Hardee's founded in Rocky Mount, N.C., by Wilbur Hardee.

**1961**
McDonald's sets up Hamburger University in Oak Brook, Ill.

**1962**
McDonald's introduces filet of fish sandwich.

**1963**
Ronald McDonald mascot introduced in Washington D.C., by TV personality Willard Scott.

**1967**
McDonald's opens in Canada, begins national advertising in U.S.

**1968**
McDonald's introduces Big Mac and hot apple pie.

**1969**
White House Conference on Food, Nutrition and Health draws attention to widespread malnutrition.

———— • ————

**1970s** *New chains fold during fast-food shakeout; environmentalists become vocal; fast food served in schools.*

**1971**
First McDonald's in Japan and Australia.

**1972**
McDonald's introduces Quarter Pounder and develops the Egg McMuffin.

**1973**
Food and Drug Administration creates first regulations for nutrition labeling.

**1977**
McDonald's introduces Egg McMuffin nationally, launching breakfast fast-food market.

**1979**
Sen. George McGovern, D-S.D., praises fast food at hearing. FDA rejects mandatory nutrition labeling in restaurants.

———— • ————

**1980s** *Nutrition consciousness rises; movement launched to require food labeling.*

**1982**
McDonald's introduces Chicken McNuggets.

**1985**
FDA and Agriculture Department reject restaurant nutrition labeling. Wendy's introduces salad bar.

**1987**
McDonald's introduces salads. Domino's begins 30-minute delivery policy.

———— • ————

**1990s** *Fast-food chains answer critics on nutrition, environment.*

**Nov. 1, 1990**
McDonald's retires the polystyrene "clamshell," switches to paper.

**Nov. 8, 1990**
President Bush signs Nutrition Labeling and Education Act.

Continued from p. 834
branch in 1927, a young franchisee named J. Willard Marriott converted his outlet to something called Hot Shoppes, serving barbecue sandwiches. Thus was born the Marriott hotel and restaurant chain.

The most successful early attempt at franchising can be traced to Quincy, Mass., where in 1924 one Howard Johnson began expanding his menu from ice cream to full meals. He soon persuaded a Cape Cod restaurateur to use the Howard Johnson name and supply network. By 1934 he had 25 Howard Johnsons; by 1940 there were 100 along the East Coast.

In California, meanwhile, in the late 1930s, restaurateur Bob Wian began a chain of restaurants that offered a large hamburger with "the works" — two patties on a triple-decker bun. By the 1940s, his "Big Boy" chain and others were joined by Joliet, Ill.-based Dairy Queen, whose soft ice cream machines and limited menu gave GIs returning from World War II an easy franchise opportunity. In 1948, Dairy Queen splintered and created rival Tastee Freeze. The food fight was on.

## The Age of McDonald's

As their modern culinary history unfolded, Americans seemed increasingly destined to abandon the pioneer spirit of experimenting with unfamiliar new restaurants. Instead, millions and millions opted for the security of known-quantity fare. No restaurant chain played a bigger role in this transformation than McDonald's, whose Horatio Alger success story is an oft-told classic in fast-food lore.

The tale begins in the late 1940s with the New Hampshire-born McDonald brothers, Richard and Maurice, who ran a small barbecue par-

lor in San Bernardino, Calif. It was a time when quick restaurants strived to create the atmosphere of home cooking. The McDonald brothers served their food on plates, with silverware and glasses, but it was delivered by teenage carhops.

The brothers were modestly successful, but there was a problem. "The fry cooks were always trying to date the carhops," Richard, now 82, recalled in a recent interview.[29] If a carhop snubbed a fry cook, he would fill her orders last, and customers complained. Not only that, silverware was constantly being stolen. And customers also complained that the pork, ham, beef and chicken being served was greasy or stringy. So the brothers set out to find a food item that would be the same every day of the year, and never too tough.

What the McDonalds did was design the first "limited-menu restaurant." At night, after closing their barbecue place, they would take the crew home and, using chalk outlines on their tennis court, walk them through a theoretical hamburger-production drill inside a tiny, 600-square-foot space designed to eliminate all unnecessary movement. Their plan: retire the carhops, reduce the menu options from 25 to 9, standardize the condiments on hamburgers for speed's sake and minimize the need for dishwashing by using paper cups and plastic flatware. There would be no juke boxes, no cigarette machines and no pay telephones to encourage loitering. It worked.

Opening in 1948, McDonald's was able to offer hamburgers for an amazingly low 15 cents with only 20 seconds' waiting time. The brothers' well-lit, ultra-clean work space (the stainless-steel fixtures fairly radiated hygiene) and their insistence on well-groomed crews allowed them to go after the family clientele, offering an eatery young kids couldn't mess up.

After some initial resistance from customers who missed the carhops, the brothers were soon selling burgers by the thousands under the trademarked Golden Arches. Publicity in trade publications brought franchise offers, and by the early 1950s they had begun doing business with an Illinois milkshake-machine salesman named Ray Kroc. It was Kroc who, licensing the McDonald's name and concept, capitalized on the opportunities for nationwide franchising brought about by the country's new demographic trends — mobility via the new highway system and the spread of suburbia.

Kroc didn't insist on expensive corner locations for his U-shaped drive-ins, and he went for solid middle-class communities with informal lifestyles and disposable income. "When we looked for a site, we counted church steeples, not autos," he said.[30]

Kroc opened his first McDonald's in Des Plaines, Ill., in 1955, and launched 228 more during the next five years. In the process he began a trend that, while working wonders at feeding an America on the go, would spell the end for countless mom-and-pop restaurants while creating fast-food highway strips through small towns that many would regard as eyesores.

McDonald's successful strategy was maddeningly simple. "What we have attempted to do is eliminate the things people don't eat," Kroc would later say. "You can't eat a 20 percent tip, or a perfumed finger bowl. It isn't the cost of food that's gone up, it's the service. We're in the meat and potato business, and meat and potatoes are not a fad."

The rise of McDonald's as a corporation under Kroc also revolutionized the world of food suppliers. When a beef or cheese producer wouldn't conform to McDonald's specs, Kroc went to small, non-mainstream operators. Today, they may lack name recognition (Keystone Foods supplies the hamburgers, Jack Simplot the potatoes, Schreiber the cheese), but they are giants in their fields.

In 1960 Kroc bought out the McDonald brothers for what at the time was an astonishing $2.7 million, nearly all of it borrowed. (For decades, company histories — including Kroc's autobiography — would credit Kroc with founding the McDonald's chain. Finally, this October, in the wake of newspaper stories recounting the brothers' role, McDonald's annual founder's day advertisements acknowledged Richard and Maurice McDonald.)

By this time, McDonald's had competition from chains offering everything from donuts to fish sticks to tacos. In 1954 Shakey's launched the first pizza chain, and Burger King began crowding McDonald's by offering larger, broiled hamburgers. In 1955 Harlan Sanders, a former service station and restaurant owner who had earned the governor's title of Kentucky Colonel for creating a secret recipe for fried chicken (and enriching the state's cuisine), at age 65 cashed his first Social Security check and took to the road to offer his recipe and cooking demonstration to restaurateurs. By 1960, Kentucky Fried Chicken had 200 franchises.

The revolution spawned by Ray Kroc and the McDonald brothers had forever changed the culture of America, not least by homogenizing eating habits.

"In the 1920s critics complained that restaurant-goers in the farthest reaches of the country faced similar meals," writes food historian Levenstein. "Now, the meals are not just similar, they are identical, for the success of the new systems is based on the customer's certainty that wherever he or she goes, the product will indeed be exactly the same."[31]

# Convenience Is Where You Find It

*Appearances to the contrary, fast-food chains don't have a monopoly on prepared foods the public buys to consume at home. But in recent years the chains have acquired an increasingly large slice of the market, growing from a 41 percent share in 1989 to 51 percent this year. By comparison, table-service restaurants had 23 percent of the market, with supermarkets a distant third at 14 percent.*

**Major Sources of Prepared Food**

|      | Fast-food restaurants | Table-service restaurants | Supermarkets |
|------|-----------------------|---------------------------|--------------|
| 1991 | 51%                   | 23%                       | 14%          |
| 1990 | 46                    | 27                        | 14           |
| 1989 | 41                    | 33                        | 12           |

*Source:* Restaurant Business, *July 1, 1991.*

# Boom Years

In the economic go-go years of the 1960s, the movement of large numbers of women from the kitchen into the work force heightened America's appetite for quick-service food. The hamburger was establishing itself as king. (U.S. ground-beef consumption increased by 50 percent from 1965-75, according to the Institute of Policy Planning at Pennsylvania State University.)

The Arby's roast beef sandwich chain was launched in 1964, to be answered in 1968 when Marriott and Roy Rogers teamed up to launch a chain. (The chain named after The Singing Cowboy was gobbled up by Hardee's in 1990). The fast-food chains were also becoming large corporations with their own cultures. In 1961 McDonald's founded Hamburger University in Oak Brook,

Ill., where employees could study "hamburgerology," learn the management skills needed for running a franchise and generally absorb "a family feeling and a sense of belonging." Burger King would follow suit in 1964 by opening "Whopper College."

During these heady times — McDonald's grew from 300 outlets in 1961 to 1,000 in 1969 and Kentucky Fried Chicken from 1,000 in 1965 to 4,000 in 1971 — both chains went public, offering stock to hungry investors. McDonald's also became a major presence in advertising. Its Ronald McDonald character — created in the Washington, D.C., area by current NBC weatherman Willard Scott, then a local TV personality — was criticized for preying on children ("Hey kids, get Mom and Dad to take you to McDonald's!") but was highly successful. It prompted Jack in the Box to create Jack the

Clown and set the stage for children's product premiums and tie-ins that continue in fast food today. McDonald's is now one of the country's top 10 advertisers, spending more than $1.1 billion in 1990, and its several generations of jingles are nearly as familiar as the national anthem.

Beginning in the 1960s, many fast-food outlets received facelifts. Gone were the chintzy plastic and neon signs. Drive-through stands were replaced with more permanent-looking buildings with indoor seating, complete with potted plants and wood paneling. The chains became familiar enough to their customers that they could tailor their decor locally. Today, wrought-iron stairways and balconies bedeck a Wendy's in historic New Orleans, for example, and a KFC in Miami features an art deco theme.

By the early 1970s, all the major U.S. food companies had invested in the fast-food business, and many were expanding overseas. As competition grew, new names appeared, monikers like seafood specialists Long John Silver's and Arthur Treacher's. In the subsequent industry shakeout, many chains died quick deaths, among them Burger Chef and Gino's. By the mid-1970s, fast food was enough of a fixture on the American landscape that school menu planners were using it to lure back students who had stopped eating the cafeteria lunch. Fast food received another nudge toward respectability in 1979, when Sen. George McGovern, D-S.D., during a hearing on nutrition needs, proclaimed before TV news cameras that fast food was healthy.

## Nutritional Labeling

It was in the early 1980s that the nation witnessed the first stirrings of the nutrition activism that has en-gulfed the fast-food industry today. The country had embarked on a physical-fitness kick, and the first legislation had been introduced to improve ingredient labeling on food packaging.

Dietary habits were clearly changing. Surveys showed, for example, that from 1983 to 1986, the number of Americans concerned about fats and calories almost doubled, and the number of people avoiding cholesterol rose by more than 150 percent.[32] Concerns were also rising about an area where nutrition is often poorest — the inner city — which had become an important setting for chains no longer wedded to the suburbs.

For many inner-city residents, fast-food outlets are oases of comfort — well-lit, heated, clean — and their food is often the best nourishment available on a budget. Operation PUSH calculated that the inner city represented about 25 percent of McDonald's business, and that inner-city minorities spend 20 percent more than the average customers on fast food. Black males, a Burger King manager says, are two-and-a-half times more likely than whites to order the high-fat "double whopper" with cheese, for example.

Critics grew concerned. "The too-powerful presence of the fast-food industry in this community is the major challenge to good health," said Pedro Expada, president of the Soundview Health Center in the South Bronx. "Our people don't go to fancy restaurants. They're fighting off the temptation of the fast-food industry."[33]

Nutrition activists sought to protect Americans of all income levels by calling on chains to disclose their ingredients on the packaging. Such requirements have long been resisted by the restaurant industry as expensive and cumbersome. (See At Issue, p. 841.)

In the mid-1980s, there was little evidence that fast-food customers wanted nutritional disclosures. In fact, McDonald's Chairman Michael Quinlin candidly told a group of Wall Street money managers that he "couldn't care less" about the proposals.[34] In 1985, the Center for Science in the Public Interest approached the Food and Drug Administration (FDA) with a new labeling proposal. The plan was rejected, as a similar one had been in 1979. While the FDA did have the legal authority to require the labels, went the explanation, they presented tricky enforcement problems, and, anyway, such a decision was best left to state regulators.

Soon afterward, however, New York State Attorney General Robert Abrams began investigating McDonald's advertising claims implying that Chicken McNuggets were made from pure chicken. In negotiating withdrawal of the ads, Abrams helped orchestrate a one-year experiment on nutritional disclosure in New York. At the same time, attorneys general in California, Texas and eight other states threatened five limited-menu restaurant chains with requirements that they provide nutrition ingredients. In a settlement still in effect today, McDonald's, Burger King, Jack in the Box, Kentucky Fried Chicken and Wendy's agreed to offer separately printed nutrition information in pamphlets or on posters in stores around the country.

The New York experiment with McDonald's, the Center for Science in the Public Interest (CSPI) maintained, not only gave New Yorkers a new basis on which to choose their fast food but also resulted in menu changes. McDonald's, it says, cut back on its beef-fat frying and stopped using Yellow Dye No. 5, which can touch off allergies. "The companies had been keeping their ingredients a secret," Jacobson says, "and once we found out the ingredi-

*Continued on p. 840*

# To Russia, With Cheese

Political scientists researching the collapse of Communism in the Soviet Union will have many landmarks to point to. But the fatal blow may have come during the August coup attempt when someone on Russian President Boris N. Yeltsin's staff picked up a phone in the besieged Russian Parliament building and ordered a few hundred pizzas from the neighborhood Pizza Hut.

If nothing else, the delivery demonstrated how successfully American fast-food chains have invaded the rest of the world.

Our fast-food giants — McDonald's, Kentucky Fried Chicken and Pizza Hut — have discovered that thinking globally pays off. The Moscow McDonald's is the chain's busiest; it has served almost 50,000 Muscovites a day since it opened in January 1990.

More than half of Kentucky Fried Chicken's profits come from abroad, and its foreign sales are growing at more than 20 percent a year. Pizza Hut is the top pizza chain in 53 countries. The Beijing Pizza Hut is one of the chain's busiest — even though the Chinese have relatively low levels of disposable income, and many Chinese think of cheese as unfit-to-eat spoiled milk.

Why is U.S. fast food doing so well overseas? "There is a much lower level of competition" abroad, says Robert Emerson, author of *The New Economics of Fast Food.* "The U.S. is pretty saturated, but that's not true in most parts of Europe." There are not only relatively few chain restaurants, he says, "there are not really a lot of mom-and-pop operations at the low end, either. To try to have a meal for $2 to $3 in France or Germany is pretty tough, unless you are willing to patronize a fast-food restaurant."

This wide-open market may make fast food one of America's few truly successful exports. "There is a small number of things that we do very well in a global competitive sense," says Emerson. "Certain kinds of retail, aircraft building, producing innovative medicines and growing grain very efficiently. That's it."

Sears, K-mart and other American retailers that have tried to expand abroad haven't been as successful as fast-food operations, Emerson says. "Real estate costs are much higher, and, in certain markets, the issue of uniformity of supply is a tricky one. McDonald's has dealt with that successfully, but it took them a while."

Indeed, when McDonald's expanded into Europe in the 1970s, it found that the infrastructure needed to produce a Big Mac and fries simply did not exist. The company ended up having to build bun factories, potato-storage facilities and syrup plants.† The slow pace of McDonald's progress frustrated investors used to quick profits, but according to Emerson the strategy paid off. "Having built slowly, their position is now unassailable," he says.

To be successful abroad, American fast-food purveyors have to walk a fine line: They cannot be too American, lest the locals take offense at a Yankee giant moving in, but they have to be American enough to separate themselves from the pack. "People abroad are sensitive about Americans owning their local businesses," said Brent Cameron, president of McDonald's International. "Americans didn't understand that sensitivity until the Arabs came over and started buying *our* businesses." ††

McDonald's kept Canadian fears of being overrun by America in mind when it began its expansion there in the early 1970s; it set up restaurants with Canadian partners, using Canadian labor, Canadian suppliers and Canadian foodstuffs. It kept its money in Canadian banks, and the president of McDonald's Canada even became a Canadian citizen.

By contrast, in the low-income Philippines, McDonald's worried less about anti-Americanism than about pricing itself out of the market. Since pasta is a lot cheaper than beef, McSpaghetti was whipped up for the market. The dish was such a success that McDonald's abandoned its original expansion plan calling for 10 Filipino outlets. Its new goal is 200 stores.

American fast-food companies can even be successful in selling non-traditional food abroad. Taco Bell has 52 stores in nine foreign countries — Canada, Britain, Japan, Guatemala, the Philippines, South Korea, Guam and Aruba; the Qatar outlet is set to open next month.

"Our food is very different from traditional Mexican fare," a company spokesman points out. "In fact, we have created something called 'Taco Bell food.'" It's so different that the company thinks the new cuisine may have appeal south of the border: Taco Bell has its eye on Mexico as a possible future market.

*— Thomas H. Moore*

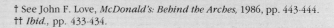

† See John F. Love, *McDonald's: Behind the Arches,* 1986, pp. 443-444.
†† *Ibid.,* pp. 433-434.

Continued from p. 838
ents, we knew why."

Compliance by the fast-food chains on the national level, however, has been inconsistent. In the spring of 1990, the CSPI surveyed 65 of the restaurants party to the agreement with the attorneys general and concluded that only Jack in the Box had lived up to it. Pamphlets were available at just 44 percent of McDonald's, 43 percent of Burger Kings and 23 percent of KFCs.

The movement toward greater nutrition consciousness, meanwhile, continued to gather steam. In 1988, a version of nutrition-labeling legislation passed Congress but was vetoed by President Ronald Reagan, who cited potential harm to the reputations of commodities industries.

Two federal studies, the 1988 *Surgeon General's Report on Nutrition and Health* and the 1989 National Research Council's *Diet and Health: Implications for Reducing Chronic Disease Risk*, added fuel to arguments that cardiovascular disease, cancer, stroke, diabetes and obesity are linked to excessive intake of calories, fat, cholesterol and sodium. More people began demanding that food labeling requirements be updated to reflect such beliefs and to prevent inaccurate health claims. Grocery manufacturers weighed in with concerns that labeling requirements would be too expensive for small companies to implement.

### 1990 Legislation

The Nutrition Labeling and Education Act was finally signed into law in November 1990, after highly visible lobbying by Phil Sokolof of the National Heart Savers Association, whose newspaper ads backed the bill. (Rep. Henry A. Waxman, D-Calif., chairman of the Energy and Commerce Subcommittee on Health and the Environment, called the bill a tribute to Sokolof's tenacity.) "This

legislation will have an empowering effect on consumers," said Dr. Virgil Brown, president of the American Heart Association.

The law required most processed foods to display specific nutrition information, including the amount of fat, saturated fat, cholesterol, sodium, sugars and dietary fiber. The Health and Human Services secretary is required to define such terms as "light" and "low-fat." The law will preempt most state nutrition-labeling laws, relieving manufacturers from having to tailor labels to markets in different states.

Those observers concerned with fast food, however, noted that the law applies to processed foods only. Out of reluctance to load up the bill and risk sinking it, explains Scott Ballin, vice president of the American Heart Association, the decision was made not to try to broaden the bill to cover meat and poultry, or restaurants of any type. That, many nutrition activists hoped, would come later.   ∎

# CURRENT SITUATION

## Package-Labeling Debate

Topping the agenda of many fast-food critics is winning passage of a requirement that chains list nutrition ingredients on the packaging for all food items. According to the Heart Association, expansion of the law's coverage to restaurants is needed because 40 percent of American meals are consumed away from home. Fast-food restaurants, AHA's Ballin adds, are already highly standardized, making the addition of labels relatively easy. In June, the FDA announced it was considering a new rule requiring restaurant disclosure; the Agriculture Department, which can require disclosure by purveyors of fresh meat and poultry, is set to release proposed regulations this month.

Rather than wait idly for federal action, however, nutrition activists are moving on the state and local levels. In what Michael Jacobson calls "the breakthrough we've been waiting for," New York City Consumer Affairs Commissioner Mark

Green this August proposed legislation to require every fast-food restaurant in the city to disclose ingredient and nutrition information on posters, tray liners and brochures. He was joined by Burger King Chief Executive Officer Barry J. Gibbons, who has promised that Burger King will abide by the plan without waiting for its enactment.

"Consumers should be able to make educated choices easily," Green said. "It's difficult in many fast-food restaurants because they aren't always given the user-friendly information they need. How many people know, for example, that a full packet of salad dressing is about equal in fat content to a hamburger and french fries, and don't know that low-calorie dressing is available?"

Whether the New York bill will pass, and whether it will be extended to require such labels on individual food items in all restaurants, will largely depend on the opposition from the restaurant industry. In comments filed with the FDA in July, NRA Executive Vice President William P. Fisher warned that "singling out any one segment of the food-service industry is illogical, inequitable and would ultimately result in a federally imposed market disadvantage." He was

Continued on p. 842

# At Issue:

## Should the government require the fast-food industry to put ingredient labels on the packages of individual food items?

**Michael F. Jacobson and Sarah Fritschner**

*Executive Director, Center for Science
in the Public Interest
Food Writer, Louisville Courier-Journal*
FROM *THE COMPLETELY REVISED AND UPDATED
FAST-FOOD GUIDE*, 1991

traditional restaurants have never been required to reveal what's in their food, principally because ingredients could change daily and there is really no place for a label, as such, to appear. Fast-food restaurants are a whole different ball game, however, one that federal regulators knew little about when they came up with their labeling rules in 1938. Fast-food restaurants can be compared to mini food factories, but instead of turning out cans of chicken and tomato soup, they are producing boxes of cheeseburgers and pouches of fries. Instead of selling via supermarkets, they sell directly to consumers. Most of these foods come in wrappers or containers that could accommodate ingredient labeling.

. . . Numerous health and other problems associated with the ingredients in fast food make it important for consumers to know what they are getting when they order chicken nuggets and a shake. Many people concerned about heart disease would want to know that the nuggets may be fried in saturated beef fat. People sensitive to Yellow No. 5 dye need to know when to avoid milk shakes, and those with dietary and religious concerns would like to know how to avoid beef, pork or dairy products. . . .

By reading labels, consumers who are allergic to specific ingredients can find out instantly if they should avoid a certain product. Most consumers don't know the trauma of food allergy. But chronic diseases have reached epidemic proportions — heart disease, hypertension, diabetes and cancer touch all of our lives and often are related to the food we eat. As a result many people choose to avoid foods that promote those diseases. Labels disclosing the ingredients of foods, including the fats in which they are fried, would benefit millions of people. . . .

Labeling would be even more useful if it included information about calories and specific nutrients, such as protein, fat and vitamins. . . . Many people would be surprised to learn that the stuffed baked potato they ordered contained 500 calories, the shake 600 and the burger 700. Wouldn't it be nice (and, sometimes, depressing) to have a big, bold calorielisting on menu boards and on every package as a reminder? . . . Until all fast-food chains reveal all the ingredients and nutrients in their foods, consumers will not always be able to make intelligent purchasing decisions. . . .

**John R. Farquharson**

*President, National Restaurant Association*
FROM *NATION'S RESTAURANT NEWS*, AUG. 12, 1991

undaunted by their own previous rulings, the Food and Drug Administration has recently asked for comment on the feasibility of ingredient labeling in fast-food restaurants. . . . We at the National Restaurant Association feel that the issue of ingredient labeling has been put to rest more times than Zachary Taylor. We realize that our customers deserve to know what is in the food they are eating, but a mandate is not the answer. . . .

The FDA, the Agriculture Department and the Federal Trade Commission have previously acknowledged that such a requirement would not be feasible and, if imposed, would bring huge added costs to restaurants and the consumer. The FDA rejected such proposals in 1979 and 1986, saying that the agency had "significant reservations as to whether it would be practical or equitable to enforce such a requirement against one segment of the food-service industry. . . ." In addition, Congress exempted restaurants from the labeling requirements of the Nutrition Labeling and Education Act of 1990.

Such a mandate would create an operational nightmare for restaurants. And for many restaurant owners, the cost of logistics of such labeling would be overwhelming. . . . In a collective finding, the FDA, USDA and FTC have determined labeling to be unworkable, saying that "not only is there a multitude of ingredients in each food on a menu, but many restaurants also vary menus frequently or change recipes according to the availability of raw commodities."

We object to the FDA's current proposal because there is no workable definition of a fast-food restaurant. The agency has no guidelines for such an establishment — not annual sales, not numbers of units, not price range. Apparently the agency is attempting to focus on restaurants that serve standardized menu items. But standardization in the food-service industry does not mean identical ingredients. Food products, even among franchised and corporate-owned restaurants, are often obtained locally and can contain different ingredients. . . .

In addition, approval of mandatory labeling in fast-food outlets would likely be only the government's first step toward even greater labeling regulation in the future. As has been shown in previous matters, Uncle Sam will not be satisfied until his grip is firmly around all segments of our industry.

Continued from p. 840

joined by the National Council of Chain Restaurants, which added that its companies would be forced to stock thousands of different sizes and types of boxes or labels for each type of beverage.

The fast-food industry also argues that offering nutrition information is already common on a voluntary basis. A recent NRA survey reported that 78 percent of chain operators currently provide nutrition information: 81 percent through their corporate headquarters, 76 percent on separate printed material, 67 percent on site, 24 percent via toll-free telephone requests, 24 percent on wall posters, 19 percent on tray liners, 10 percent on the package, 10 percent on interactive computers, and 5 percent on the back of menus. What's more, says a McDonald's spokeswoman, to read the label in a fast-food restaurant you would have to buy the item first, so what good does it do?

Jacobson counters that labels received after purchase can be useful to consumers in deciding their next purchase. Nutrition activists also argue that the industry's voluntary compliance is spotty and lacks the uniformity that inexpert consumers need to make comparisons. What's most important, Jacobson says, is that labeling requirements will give fast-food chains a new incentive to improve nutritional quality to compete with other chains. Consumers everywhere, especially in the inner city, will then benefit, he says, whether or not they care about nutrition.

## Pizza in Schools

A sign of the fast-food industry's status can be found in a battle currently being waged in Washington: Pizza Hut versus the U.S. Department of Agriculture. Since 1966, the government has sought to protect schoolchildren from the temptations of junk food by requiring outside food vendors serving schools to meet the same criteria on food content that is required of in-school food operators. Commercial vendors say they should have no restrictions, all the while tempting school-lunch officials with food that is popular among students and often delivered at good prices. Pizza Hut is currently seeking to respond to customer demand — and boost profits — by including more pepperoni in the pizzas it delivers to public schools, many of them part of the $14 billion federal program that serves 28 million children daily.

Currently, Pizza Hut puts only largely meatless toppings on school pizzas. That's because USDA rules would require an expensive third inspection for meat that, though already inspected once at the slaughterhouse and again at the processing plant, is then prepared with other food products for resale to schools. An alliance of consumer groups and the rival frozen-pizza industry has backed USDA, citing a need for safety precautions. Hence Pizza Hut would be forced to keep its pepperoni below 2 percent of the pizza, even though hot dogs, sandwiches and burritos are exempt from the rule.

"If they accept the fact that we can sell a pizza with 20 pieces of pepperoni on it, why can't we put 25 or 30 or 60 pieces on it?" asked Larry Whitt, a Pizza Hut vice president.[35] An exemption to the inspections for the fresh-pizza industry, introduced by Rep. Charles W. Stenholm, D-Texas, and modified by Dan Glickman, D-Kan., Pizza Hut's home-state representative, was added to a bill designed to make technical corrections in last year's farm bill. It has passed the House and is pending in the Senate Committee on Agriculture, Nutrition and Forestry. ∎

# OUTLOOK

## Menu of Options

In today's society, "Hunger is a chore to be finished rather than an event to be savored and enjoyed," laments Robert B. Cialdini, a social psychologist at Arizona State University. "It is a regrettable but necessary feature of modern life that we don't take time to smell the roses. We gulp things down that are worth savoring." [37]

Still, fast-food operations will have to scramble to retain "share of stomach" from grocery stores, convenience stores and vending machines. Most fast-food customers are 18 to 24 years old, notes industry researcher Robert L. Emerson. They consume 4.8 fast-food meals every week, compared with 3.7 per week for all consumers. The size of this age group doubled from 1960 to 1980 but will drop 20 percent by the year 2000. The growing population group will be people over 65, and they eat out only 1.8 times per week.[38]

Today's industry faces high real-estate prices and highway strips teeming with fast-fooderies (there is now one restaurant for every 2,700 Americans, compared with one for every 7,000 in the late 1970s).[39] Chains have been branching out into sports arenas, airports, hospitals, colleges, turnpike stops, mall food courts, kiosks, airline in-flight meal services and even zoos. KFC, Pizza Hut and Dairy Queen are even sending 42-foot mobile coaches equipped with cooking facilities to fairgrounds and rock concerts.

For some chains, a huge underexploited market is the dinner clientele. McDonald's, for instance, only makes 30 percent of its sales during the dinner hour, far below Kentucky Fried Chicken (65 percent) or Pizza Hut (73 percent). Fast food for dinner may require a different mindset; it's slower, says Michael Evans of Burger King, which is considering serving its BK Broiler at dinnertime with a bun and salad in a basket.

From the all-important consumer's point of view, the gut issue for the industry will still be food and its quality. Nutrition activists are excited about prospects for even wider, healthier choices. Michael Jacobson hopes to see bean burgers, hot vegetables, fruit salads and more pasta. Pizza Hut is already planning a 90 percent fat-free pizza. Indeed, activists expect the fast-food industry to play a key role in the improvement of national nutrition.

"American taste buds will have to change," declares the Heart Association's Ballin. "Fatty foods taste great. So the industry has to come up with ways to remove the fat and cholesterol but still cater to consumer taste buds." In doing so, the industry's claims may sometimes outpace its actual nutritional changes. In October, for example, KFC, Dunkin Donuts and Nestle's backed down from low-fat claims for products that are still, in the view of New York Attorney General Abrams, high in fat. KFC agreed to change the name of a new chicken product from "Lite 'N Crispy" to "Skinfree Crispy."

Faced with new conditions, the industry in general has shown an astonishing ability to adapt what began as a purposefully narrow idea. To counter the charge of menu homogenization, Burger King pushes its "olive burgers" in Detroit and its "breakfast burritos" in San Antonio. And the industry is just as ready to

help the American family. Pizza Hut spokesman Roger Rydell speculates that if, tomorrow, Americans decide that food preparation makes for a rich family experience, Pizza Hut would create a pizza-making kit for the home.

Fast food's core achievement — efficiently served, inexpensive food — will likely endure. But will its menus continue to offer a never-ending feast of consumer choices? Too much choice invites the risks of delay and inefficiency that fast food was originally intended to avoid. The industry "is undergoing a midlife crisis," writes Joseph Durocher, a professor of hotel administration at the University of New Hampshire. Some outlets take a shocking 12 minutes to serve a hamburger, he says. "Its attempts to be all things to all people have caused erosion. There's been a shakedown in the fast-food business because, when it began it made some promises to the American public. It was supposed to be fast, inexpensive, prepared quickly and offer a limited menu that could stand relatively long holding periods. The fast-food organizations have broken their promises.[39] ∎

## Notes

[1] *Advertising Age*, July 2, 1990, p. 1.

[2] Cited in Michael F. Jacobson and Sarah Fritschner, *The Completely Revised and Updated Fast-Food Guide*, 1991, p. 10.

[3] *Business Week*, Oct. 21, 1991, p. 116.

[4] *Consumer Reports*, June 1988, p. 355.

[5] Quoted in *Forbes*, Oct. 1, 1990, p. 186.

[6] *Fortune*, March 11, 1991, p. 62.

[7] Alan J. Miller, *Socially Responsible Investing*, 1991, p. 88.

[8] *Consumer Reports*, June 1988, p. 355.

[9] Quoted in *USA Today*, Aug. 19, 1991.

[10] Jacobson and Fritschner, *op. cit.*

[11] Quoted in *American Health*, June 1991, p. 60.

[12] Study by William Rathje, University of Arizona anthropologist, cited in a pamphlet on the environment by Hardee's.

[13] Quoted in *Everyone's Backyard*, Citizens Clearinghouse for Hazardous Wastes, December 1990, p. 2.

[14] Quoted in *Restaurant Business*, July 1, 1991, p. 114.

[15] Studies cited by Harvard Business School professors Jeffrey F. Rayport and George C. Lodge in "Fed a Line, Ronald Goes Green," *Los Angeles Times*, Nov. 26, 1990.

[16] For more background, see "Teens Work to Balance School and Job," *Editorial Research Reports*, Aug. 31, 1990, pp. 494-508.

[17] John F. Love, *McDonald's: Behind the Arches* (1986), p. 5.

[18] Quoted in Ben Wildavsky, "McJobs: Inside America's Largest Youth Training Program," *Policy Review*, summer 1989, p. 30.

[19] Ivan Charner and Bryna Shore Fraser, *Fast Food Jobs*, National Institute for Work and Learning, 1984.

[20] Quoted in Wildavsky, *op. cit.*, p. 30.

[21] See *The New York Times*, Nov. 19, 1990.

[22] *Nation's Business*, August 1989, p. 25.

[23] *Nation's Restaurant News*, Sept. 2, 1991, p. 1.

[24] *Ibid.*, p. 42.

[25] Quoted by Daniel J. Boorstin in *The Americans: The National Experience* (1965), p. 110.

[26] Quoted in *The New York Times*, Dec. 6, 1989.

[27] Harvey Levenstein, *Revolution at the Table: The Transformation of the American Diet* (1988), p. 208.

[28] Joseph Monninger, "Fast Food," *American Heritage*, April 1988, p. 69.

[29] Quoted in *The Wall Street Journal*, Aug. 15, 1991.

[30] Quoted in *McDonald's 25th Anniversary History*, 1980.

[31] Levenstein, *op. cit.*, p. 208.

[32] *Ibid.*, p. 209.

[33] Quoted in *The Wall Street Journal*, Dec. 19, 1990.

[34] Quoted in Jacobson and Fritschner, *op. cit.*, p. 102.

[35] Quoted in *The Washington Post*, Oct. 11, 1991.

[36] Quoted in *The New York Times*, Dec. 6, 1989.

[37] Robert L. Emerson, *The New Economics of Fast Food* (1990), p. xix.

[38] *Business Week*, Jan. 9, 1989, p. 86.

[39] *USA Today* magazine, April 1990, p. 3.

# Bibliography

## Selected Sources Used

### Books

**Charner, Ivan and Fraser, Byrna Shore Fraser,** *Fast Food Jobs,* **National Institute for Work and Learning, 1984.**

Results of a national survey of teenage fast-food workers, describing their demographics, attitudes toward work and effects of the work experience on their lives.

**Emerson, Robert L.,** *The New Economics of Fast Food,* **Van Nostrand Reinhold, 1990.**

The president of the Stonehill Capital Management research firm has compiled a business-oriented analysis and comprehensive set of tables on the history and current state of the fast-food industry.

**Institute of Medicine,** *Nutrition Labeling: Issues and Directions for the 1990s,* **National Academy Press, 1990.**

Report of a committee of experts from the National Academy of Sciences detailing all policy issues surrounding food labeling. Published just after passage of the 1990 Food Labeling and Education Act.

**Jacobson, Michael and Fritschner, Sarah,** *The Completely Revised and Updated Fast-Food Guide,* **Workman Publishing, 1991.**

The executive director of the Center for Science in the Public Interest and a food writer (and professional nutritionist) at the Louisville *Courier-Journal* outline the policy issues surrounding fast food and rate each chain's products on nutritional quality.

**Love, John F.,** *McDonald's: Behind the Arches,* **Bantam Books, 1986.**

A former reporter provides a detailed, behind-the-scenes history of the rise of America's premiere fast-food chain, offering a wealth of data about McDonald's.

**Miller, Alan J.,** *Socially Responsible Investing: How to Invest with Your Conscience,* **New York Institute of Finance, 1991.**

This is a guidebook for investors who wish to support companies that have good records on such issues as environmentalism, sexism, workers' rights, shareholders' rights and foreign policy. Several fast-food companies' policies are evaluated.

### Articles

**Graham, Ellen, "McDonald's Pickle: He Began Fast Food but Gets No Credit,"** *The Wall Street Journal,* **Aug. 15, 1991.**

How McDonald's under Ray Kroc has downplayed the role of the original McDonald brothers in the corporation's development. Kroc bought the brothers out in 1960.

**Hume, Scott, "McDonald's: The Green Revolution,"** *Advertising Age,* **Jan. 20, 1991.**

The behind-the-scenes story of the fast-food leader's bid to be the industry leader in environmentally sensitive marketing. The article provides background on the decision to abandon polystyrene packaging.

**Lerch, S. and McArthur, P., "Brave new fast food,"** *American Health,* **June 1991, p. 58.**

Looks at the "lighter menu" the fast-food industry is marketing in an effort to accommodate America's growing health consciousness. Examples of successful "health food" in fast-food restaurants (Burger King's BK Broiler, Kentucky Fried Chicken's Lite 'N Crispy Chicken, Wendy's Grilled Chicken Sandwich); question of significant health improvements.

**Monninger, Joseph, "Fast Food,"** *American Heritage,* **April 1988.**

A novelist marvels on the history of fast food and its place in American society.

**Schlesinger, Leonard A., and Heskett, James L., "The Service-Driven Service Economy,"** *Harvard Business Review,* **Sept.-Oct. 1991.**

Two business professors examine the role of fast-food jobs in an economy increasingly devoted to services, criticizing McDonald's management for inflexibility and praising Taco Bell for service-sector innovations.

**Wildavsky, Ben, "McJobs: Inside America's Largest Youth Training Program,"** *Policy Review,* **Summer 1989.**

An editor of a conservative journal seeks to rebut popular notions that fast-food jobs are dead-end jobs, highlighting the benefits of working at McDonald's.

# The Next Step

## Additional Articles from Current Periodicals

### Competition

**Crain, R., "Food, folks and . . . Sparky's? "** *Advertising Age*, **Sept. 24, 1990, p. 34.**

Discusses how, for the first time in recent history, McDonald's is putting another name on a new restaurant idea it's trying. The company is testing a 1950s diner under the Golden Arch Cafe label in Hartsville, Tenn. The idea is to see if McDonald's Corp. can put a different kind of unit in smaller towns and still make acceptable profits and gain customer approval. Other companies looking for new ways to grow.

**Hume, S., "McD's latest: Cold McSubs,"** *Advertising Age*, **Dec. 17, 1990, p. 3.**

Considers how McDonald's Corp. is taking on the fast-growing submarine sandwich chains in one market while increasing its challenge to Pizza Hut in two others. McDonald's, working to revamp its menu and lower prices to boost domestic sales, has started testing a line of cold sandwiches under the McSubs name in a dozen stores in Madison, Wis. Ongoing battle between Pizza Hut and McDonald's; competition; other product-line extensions; target consumers.

**Hume, S. and Geiger, B., "McDonald's takes nip at supermarkets,"** *Advertising Age*, **March 11, 1991, p. 1.**

Shows how McDonald's Corp. is now trying to compete with convenience and grocery stores, both of which are increasing their sales of prepared foods and which now account for more than 20 percent of the takeout market. In one restaurant, the fast-food leader is testing McExtras, a refrigerated case containing basic grocery items like milk, eggs, bread and butter. How rival chains are competing; challenges; other plans.

**Hume, S. and Serafin, R., "Burger King attacks Big Mac with brands,"** *Advertising Age*, **July 16, 1990, p. 3.**

Describes how Burger King Corp. is upping the ante in its battle to gain ground on fast-food market leader McDonald's Corp. The No. 2 hamburger chain is looking to add brand name products to its mix of offerings. Testing Domino's pizza in four of the restaurants; frozen yogurt; other possibilities.

**Johnson, B. and Hume, S., "Dueling chicken,"** *Advertising Age*, **April 15, 1991, p. 4.**

Discusses the increased competition with Kentucky Fried Chicken Corp., the top fast-food chicken chain, by Taco Bell. Taco Bell has recently released several new chicken items at a reduced rate. Details several of Taco Bell's television ads, which will run in spot markets nationally in a multimillion-dollar campaign. McDonald's testing of new chicken products; reaction from KFC.

**McKay, S., Allen, G., et al., "Eating on the run,"** *Maclean's*, **Oct. 22, 1990, p. 52.**

Discusses the proliferation of fast-food alternatives to burgers and fries. Competition that has cost the burger chains some large profits; response of Wendy's Restaurants of Canada Inc., and the Burger King and McDonald's chains.

**Ramirez, A., "In the orchid room . . . Big Macs,"** *The New York Times*, **Oct. 30, 1990, p. D1.**

Describes the new McDonald's restaurants in New York City that cater to adults. Facing flattening sales growth and a falling stock price, the chain is experimenting with radical changes in location, decor, food and service. It is also test-marketing pizza, pasta, seafood and other dishes that might attract the entire family to the slow dinnertime hours.

### Debates & issues

**"The health nut who took a bite at Big Mac,"** *Newsweek*, **April 16, 1990, p. 64.**

Discusses the $500,000 worth of newspaper ads that millionaire health advocate Phil Sokolof took out last week. The ads claimed that fast-food companies are killing us with cholesterol and fat. Shows an example of the ad; response from the companies involved.

**Castro, J., Dolan, B., et al., "One big mac, hold the box!"** *Time*, **June 25, 1990, p. 44.**

Profiles Kids Against Pollution, started three years ago by a fifth-grade civics class at the Tenakill School in Closter, N.J., which urged a ban on polystyrene at the school. 800 chapters in United States and Europe; campaign against McDonald's, the Send-it-back campaign.

### Economic aspects

**"High costs slow down fast food,"** *USA Today*, **April 1990, p. 3.**

Comments on a slowdown in the fast-food industry; high labor costs; efforts to adjust to changing consumer demands; future prospects.

**Berg, E. N., "An American icon wrestles with a troubled future,"** *The New York Times*, **May 12, 1991,**

**Section 3, p. 1.**

Reports that for two years, the McDonald's restaurants in the U.S. have been struggling to prevent a decline in their business from snowballing. Reasons for the fall; comparison to Taco Bell's sales in the last quarter; McDonald's Corp.'s success abroad.

**Duffy, B., Knight, R., et al., "Fast food skids into the slow lane," *U.S. News & World Report*, Feb. 12, 1990, p. 16.**

Reports that despite opening a new restaurant in Moscow, McDonald's and other fast-food chains are wallowing in the worst slump in a decade, and the Marriott Corp. sold its Roy Rogers chain to concentrate on hotels.

**Hume, S., Johnson, B., et al., " 'Value' trend nibbles at fast-food profits," *Advertising Age*, May 6, 1991, p. 20.**

Deals with how McDonald's, Burger King, and other fast-food restaurants who've entered into the discounting game cannot sustain these price cuts for much longer. Looks at whether the incremental volume can offset the food giveaways; whether or not the outlets can remain profitable for much longer; outlook; changes.

**Therrien, L., "McDonald's isn't looking quite so juicy anymore," *Business Week*, Aug. 6, 1990, p. 30.**

Discusses how the latest financial results reveal that McDonald's, the once invincible fast-food champ, is losing some of its punch. How sales are growing, but they've lost their sizzle; growing nutritional concerns affecting McDonald's; testing pasta dishes, fish and chips and pizza in several stores.

## Environmental aspects

**"One big McBow to environmentalism," *Newsweek*, Nov. 12, 1990, p. 59.**

Notes that McDonald's announced it will trash its familiar "clamshell" boxes made of polystyrene. President of McDonald's U.S.A. Ed Rensi's comments; pressure from customers and environmentalists to make the change; Environmental Defense Fund's role in the decision.

**Gifford, B., "The greening of the golden arches," *Rolling Stone*, Aug. 22, 1991, p. 34.**

Examines the recent rise in McDonald's consciousness concerning environmental issues stemming from a task force's 138-page report on ways in which the fast-food restaurant chain can reduce its almost 2 million-pound-per-day flow of waste. Environmental Defense Fund (EDF); immediate benefits for McDonald's; EDF's General Counsel Shelby Yastrow; McDonald's previous links with environmental groups; work of the task force; consumer reaction; effect on other firms; details.

**Hocking, M. B., "Paper versus polystyrene: A complex choice," *Science*, Feb. 1, 1991, p. 504.**

Presents an analysis of paper vs. polystyrene foam as the material of construction for hot drink containers in fast food or other single-use applications. Takes into account the environmental impact, manufacturing stages, recycling and disposal of each product.

**Hoke, F., "Corporate America buys in," *Environment*, June 1990, p. 21.**

Reports that some U.S. corporations, recognizing that recycling cannot succeed without markets for recycled products and that recycling programs are good for public relations, are changing the way they do business. Programs by McDonald's USA and Rubbermaid Commercial Products Inc.

**Holusha, J., "Coming clean on products: Ecological claims faulted," *The New York Times*, March 12, 1991, p. D1.**

Discusses the changes that many companies, under pressure to make their goods look clean and green, are making in their packaging — more on the basis of marketing studies than environmental findings. Cites McDonald's Corp., Procter & Gamble Co. and other companies as examples.

**Wirka, J. and Collaton, L., "Seamy 'solutions,' " *Environmental Action*, March/April 1991, p. 28.**

Questions the recycling solutions proposed by several industries and companies. Includes plastics industry, drink-box makers, polystyrene industry, McDonald's and Procter & Gamble.

## Health aspects

**"Fast food: How lean is lean?" *Consumer Reports*, July 1991, p. 453.**

Examines the new lean foods from major fast-food chains to see if they are as healthful and tasty as they claim. "McLean Deluxe"; "BK Broiler"; "Lite 'N Crispy Chicken."

**Burros, M., "The slimming of fat fast food," *The New York Times*, July 25, 1990, p. C1.**

Comments on the changes in fast food — use of vegetable oil for frying, and more nutritious alternatives to double cheeseburgers and fried chicken — which were brought about by the greater public awareness of the hazards of a diet high in fat and cholesterol, and because of the pressure applied by consumer groups and health professionals.

**Ramirez, A., "When fast food goes on a diet," *The***

***New York Times,*** **March 19, 1991, p. D1.**

Says that, with its lower-fat hamburger, McDonald's is entering a "healthy fast-food" market that other chains have entered with mixed results. Kentucky Fried Chicken's Lite 'N Crispy chicken has had strong sales, but Pizza Hut's "light" pizza stumbled and was taken off the menu. People don't buy as healthy as they talk.

**Roberts, M., "Health food?"** ***U.S. News & World Report,*** **May 20, 1991, p. 73.**

Considers fast food and the new, lower-fat versions of best-sellers that turn out to win hearts but aren't saving any. McDonald's new McLean Deluxe, Hardee's Real Lean Deluxe, Kentucky Fried Chicken's Lite 'N Crispy; partially reformed fat depots.

## *International business ventures*

**"McGoulash to go,"** ***Economist,*** **April 6, 1991, p. 70.**

Looks at why franchising has become the most popular way of investing in Hungary, focusing on the success of McDonald's restaurants in that country.

**"Sunrise on Gorky Street,"** ***Canadian Business,*** **May 1991, p. 65.**

Looks at the problems and satisfactions involved in being a manager of a McDonald's restaurant in Moscow.

**Blackman, A., "Moscow's Big Mac attack,"** ***Time,*** **Feb. 5, 1990, p. 51.**

Reports on the opening of a McDonald's fast-food store in the Soviet Union. Located on Pushkin Square, just a few blocks from the Kremlin; problems encountered; prices; the process of opening.

## *Social aspects*

**"The decline and fall of the hamburger,"** ***Consumer Reports,*** **May 1990, p. 303.**

Reviews specialty foods for the microwave that aim at the market of fast food created by McDonald's and Burger King. The makers; description of the food; cost; nutrition.

**Harris, J., "I don't want good, I want fast,"** ***Forbes,*** **Oct. 1, 1990, p. 186.**

Reports that research shows that Americans care less about what they eat than how they eat it. The fast-food industry is paying very close attention and adapting to fit those particular needs. Drive-through windows; customers want things quick, cheap and easy, and they don't really care how it tastes; three most important factors in a customer's decision.

**Kleiman, D., "Fast food? It just isn't fast enough anymore,"** ***The New York Times,*** **Dec. 6, 1989, p. A1.**

Gives a look at the changing relationship of Americans with food, and how fast-food companies and food manufacturers are being forced to offer consumers faster and faster options.

**Manzl, H., "Feeding on fast food and false values,"** ***Education Digest,*** **January 1990, p. 40.**

Discusses the unrealistic attitudes and expectations students have as a result of such sources of popular culture as the electronic media, advertising and fast food. Effect on the educational system; immediate gratification.

## Statement of Ownership, Management, Circulation

*Act of Aug. 12, 1970: Section 3685, Title 39, United States Code*

Title of publication: The CQ Researcher. Date of filing: October 31, 1991. Frequency of issue: Weekly (Except for 3/1, 5/3, 8/2, 11/1/91). No. of issues published annually: 48. Annual subscription price: $285.00. Location of known office of publication: 1414 22nd Street N.W., Washington, D.C. 20037-1097. Location of the headquarters or general business offices of the publisher: 1414 22nd Street N.W., Washington, D.C. 20037-1097. Names and addresses of publisher, editor and managing editor: Publisher, Neil Skene, 1414 22nd Street N.W., Washington, D.C. 20037-1097; Editor, Sandra Stencel, 1414 22nd Street, N.W., Washington, D.C.: 20037-1097; Managing Editor, Thomas J. Colin, 1414 22nd Street N.W., Washington, D.C. 20037-1097. Owner: Times Publishing Company, P.O. Box 1121, St. Petersburg, Florida 33731. Known bondholders, mortgagees, and other security holders owning or holding 1 percent or more of total amount of bonds, mortgages or other securities: Citicorp/Citibank (Mortgage Holder), 2000 L Street, N.W., Washington, D.C. 20036.

| Extent and Nature of Circulation | Average Number of Copies Each Issue During Preceding 12 Months | Actual Number of Copies of Single Issue Published Nearest to Filing Date |
|---|---|---|
| A. Total number of copies printed (Net Press Run) | 6,654 | 6,460 |
| B. Paid Circulation | | |
|     1. Sales through dealers and carriers, street vendors and counter sales | — | — |
|     2. Mail subscriptions | 5,079 | 4,783 |
| C. Total paid and/or requested circulation | 5,079 | 4,783 |
| D. Free distribution by mail carrier or other means. Samples, complimentary, and other free copies | 72 | 72 |
| E. Total distribution (Sum of C and D) | 5,151 | 4,855 |
| F. Copies not distributed | | |
|     1. Office use, left over, unaccounted, spoiled after printing | 1,503 | 1,605 |
|     2. Returns from news agents | — | — |
| G. TOTAL (sum of E & F — should equal net press run shown in A) | 6,654 | 6,460 |

# Back Issues

*Great Research on Current Issues Starts Right Here... Recent topics covered by The CQ Researcher are listed below. Issues dated before May 10, 1991, were published under the name of Editorial Research Reports.*

**APRIL 1990**
How Fair is the Tax Burden?
Workers' Compensation
U.S. Pacific Forces
Curbing Insurance Premiums

**MAY 1990**
Should Teaching Be a Profession?
Will Canada Fall Apart?
Is U.S. Patent System Outdated?
Federal Funding for the Arts

**JUNE 1990**
Downsizing America's Armed Forces
Progress In Weather Forecasting
S & L Bailout
Bio-Chemical Disarmament

**JULY 1990**
Do Americans Still Love Marriage?
Death Penalty Debate
Decline of Rural America
United Nations in the 1990s

**AUGUST 1990**
Democracy in the Philippines
Initiatives: True Democracy?
Hard Times at Newspapers
Teens Balance School & Jobs

**SEPTEMBER 1990**
Dangers of Alcohol
Western Alliance After the Cold War
Tobacco Industry
Right to Die

**OCTOBER 1990**
Organ Transplants
Energy Policy Options
Search for Arab Unity
Child Support

**NOVEMBER 1990**
Lotteries and Gambling
Post Cold-War Choices
Setting Limits on Medical Care
Multicultural Education

**DECEMBER 1990**
Cable TV Regulation
Americans' Search For Their Roots
Is Insurance System a Failure?
Why Schools Still Have Tracking

**JANUARY 1991**
Growing Influence of Boycotts
Should the U.S. Reinstate the Draft?
America's Archaeological Past
Peace Corps' Challenges in '90s

**FEBRUARY 1991**
Regional Impact of Recession
Puerto Rico's Status
Redistricting: Mapping Power
Nuclear Power

**MARCH 1991**
Acid Rain
Cost of the Gulf War
Reassessing Gun Laws
Future for Man in Space

**APRIL 1991**
Social Security
Canadian Crisis Over Quebec
California Drought
Electromagnetic Radiation

**MAY 1991**
School Choice
Racial Quotas
Animal Rights
U.S. and Japan

**JUNE 1991**
Children and Divorce
Teenage Suicide
Endangered Species
Europe 1992

**JULY 1991**
Teenagers and Abortion
Soviet Republics Rebel
Mexico's Emergence
Athletes and Drugs

**AUGUST 1991**
Sexual Harassment
Fetal Tissue Research
Oil Imports
The Palestinians

**SEPTEMBER 1991**
Police Brutality
Advertising Under Attack
Saving the Forests
Foster Care Crisis

**OCTOBER 1991**
Pay-Per-View TV
Youth Gangs
Gene Therapy
World Hunger

Back issues are available for $4.00 (subscribers) or $7.00 (non-subscribers). Quantity discounts apply to orders over ten. To order, call Congressional Quarterly 1-800-432-2250.

# Future Topics

▶ *Eastern Europe's Environmental Problems*

▶ *Business and Education*

▶ *Cuba's Dilemma*

# The Greening of Eastern Europe

*Devastated countries try to reverse Communism's environmental toll*

E
ASTERN EUROPE ENDURED THE POLITICAL
and economic oppression of Communism for some
40 years — until the revolutions of 1989. But human
freedom wasn't the only victim of the Communist
regimes. The environment, too, suffered greatly under
centrally planned economies that put a priority on
production quotas and developing heavy industries while
providing no incentives for conservation or pollution
controls. Now two huge tasks confront Eastern Europeans as
they try to bring order to their countries: They must energize
crippled economies and find the resources to clean up four
decades of profligate pollution. Western nations are
providing help, but far less than is needed. Some experts
worry that without more aid, some countries in the region
may not hold together under the economic stresses.

 **November 15, 1991 • Volume 1, No. 26 • 849-872**

*Formerly Editorial Research Reports*

COVER ART: BARBARA SASSA-DANIELS

# CQ Researcher

November 15, 1991
Volume 1, No. 26

**EDITOR**
Sandra Stencel

**MANAGING EDITOR**
Thomas J. Colin

**ASSOCIATE EDITOR**
Richard L. Worsnop

**STAFF WRITERS**
Charles S. Clark
Mary H. Cooper
Rodman D. Griffin

**PRODUCTION EDITOR**
Laurie De Maris

**EDITORIAL ASSISTANT**
Thomas H. Moore

**GRAPHICS**
Jack Auldridge

**PUBLISHED BY**
Congressional Quarterly Inc.

**CHAIRMAN**
Andrew Barnes

**VICE CHAIRMAN**
Andrew P. Corty

**EDITOR AND PUBLISHER**
Neil Skene

**EXECUTIVE EDITOR**
Robert W. Merry

**PUBLICATIONS MARKETING/SALES**
Robert Smith

**EDITOR, EBSCO PUBLISHING**
Melissa Kummerer

The CQ Researcher (ISSN 1056-2036). Formerly Editorial Research Reports. Published weekly (48 times per year, not printed the first Friday of any month with five Fridays) by Congressional Quarterly Inc., 1414 22nd St., N.W., Washington, D.C. 20037. Rates are furnished upon request. Application to mail at second-class postage rates is pending at Washington, D.C. POSTMASTER: Send address changes to The CQ Researcher, 1414 22nd St., N.W., Washington, D.C. 20037.

# The Greening of Eastern Europe

BY PATRICK G. MARSHALL

## THE ISSUES

The revolutions in Eastern Europe that swept away the Iron Curtain of Soviet political oppression also exposed shocking economic and social conditions. It's now clear that the 40-plus years of Communist rule took a devastating environmental toll as well.

In Poland 65 percent of the rivers are so polluted that industries can't even use the water because it corrodes machinery. In Czechoslovakia a third of the rivers are so far gone they are devoid of life. And in Hungary, more than 700 communities import water because pesticides contaminate their wells.

Forests and wildlife are succumbing, too. Acid rain has claimed broad swaths of the region's forests. In Bulgaria, 40 percent of the bird species are endangered, according to the National Academy of Sciences, along with a quarter of all mammal, reptile and amphibian species.

The human toll is also tragically high. In some industrial areas life expectancy has dropped a full eight years. The air in many Eastern European cities is so bad that children are routinely sent to rural camps simply to breathe relatively clean air. (Poles who are severely affected by pollution sometimes recuperate in specially outfitted salt mines deep below the surface.) And a recent survey of 13,000 Polish schoolchildren found that a quarter of them had pollution-related diseases.

While the full magnitude of the damage was hidden by the governments of Eastern Europe, citizens did protest in the late 1980s. The region's environmental groups often became a vehicle for political dissent. *(See story, p. 860.)* In Ruse,

Bulgaria, for example, a 1987 citizens' protest against pollution from a chemical plant across the Danube River in Romania led to the formation of Ecoglasnost, the nationwide environmental group that contributed to the overthrow of Bulgaria's Communist regime. Similarly, protests in Hungary over plans to dam the Danube sparked broader opposition to the government that eventually led to its fall.

Now, with the Communist governments out of power, many of the environmental groups have begun to fragment as once-angry protesters find other causes. Unfortunately, the fragmentation is taking place just as the immensity — and cost — of the environmental cleanup is becoming clear. And with most Eastern European economies nearly comatose, resources are scarce. But many observers believe that ecological and economic reconstruction must be handled simultaneously, however daunting the challenge.

The stakes are high, and not only for Eastern Europeans. Much of their pollution drifts into the West. What's more, an unstable Eastern Europe represents a threat to Western Europe. At the very least, continued instability would likely send more refugees fleeing westward.

Given strong U.S. security interests in a stable Europe, the environmental situation in Eastern Europe is of considerable concern to Washington. As the debate heats up over what the United States can and should do to help, here are some of the questions being raised:

### Can Eastern Europe afford to clean up its environments?

In a word, no. The cost of raising Eastern Europe to the environmental standards of the European Community (EC) clearly surpasses current resources.

Estimates for cleaning up Poland made by international agencies generally begin at $100 billion. Polish economist Zbigniew Bochniarz puts the tab at up to $300 billion. A draft report by the World Bank and several European and U.S. government agencies estimates the cost of environmental aid for Czechoslovakia at $50-$100 billion.[1] And the price tag for cleaning up to the former East Germany could reach $300 billion, according to a detailed study by the Berlin-based Institute for Ecological Economics.[2]

According to many in the environmental community, these estimates are merely shots in the dark — but more likely low than high. And there's not enough information to make even ballpark estimates for many of the region's countries, including Romania, Yugoslavia and Albania.

Unfortunately, the environmental bill is coming due just as Eastern European countries are undertaking major economic restructuring *and*

# An Environmental Box Score

*According to six key indicators, Czechoslovakia and Poland have the most serious environmental problems in Eastern Europe. The two countries are heavily industrialized and heavily dependent on high-sulfur brown coal. Hungary, Bulgaria and Romania face lesser but still-serious problems.*

|  | Czechoslovakia | Poland | Hungary | Bulgaria | Romania |
|---|---|---|---|---|---|
| Atmospheric pollution | +++ | +++ | + | + | ++ |
| Water pollution | ++ | ++++ | ++ | ++ | ++ |
| Soil degradation | + | +++ | + | + | + |
| Waste disposal problems | ++ | ++ |  | + | ++ |
| Habitat and species destruction | ++ | +++ |  | ++ | ++ |
| Forestry damage | +++ | +++ |  | + | + |

Key: + significant   ++ serious   +++ major   ++++ catastrophic

*Source:* Environmental Issues in Eastern Europe: Setting an Agenda, *The Royal Institute of International Affairs and World Conservation Union, 1990.*

---

trying to deal with already massive foreign debts.

To make matters worse, the 1990 gross domestic product of every country in Eastern Europe declined between 3 percent (Czechoslovakia) and 12 percent (Poland), and even worse figures are expected this year. As for a recovery, the World Bank predicts it won't take place until 1996 or later.[3]

While the huge sums required for cleaning up the region may be beyond the reach of Eastern European countries, they are also not likely to come from the international community. "The West Germans probably can afford to [help] East Germany, but nobody can afford to pay that amount of money for the rest of Eastern Europe," says Barbara Jancar Webster, a specialist on Eastern Europe at the State University of New York at Brockport. "Certainly the United States isn't going to, and there's no other big source of money."

To date, a few hundred million dollars in environmental aid for Eastern Europe has come from international banks, Western Europe and the United States, but that's only "a

drop in the bucket" compared with what's going to be needed, says Carl Mitchell, a consultant to the U.S. Agency for International Development (AID), which oversees most U.S. environmental aid.

Faced with such a stark scenario, Eastern Europeans will have to make some hard choices, according to the experts. "The first thing for the countries to do is to sort out their priorities," says Samuel Hale Jr., an AID adviser in Czechoslovakia and Hungary. "Most of them haven't even done that yet."

But once enough information is gathered to set priorities, the shortfall of funds is so great that, according to Hungarian environmentalist Janos Vargha, "most of the problems will not go away within an imaginable range of time."

### Are Eastern Europeans willing to make the necessary sacrifices?

Environmental issues were a major rallying point for the political opposition in many Eastern European countries, and according to opinion polls they continue to be important, especially in Poland, Czechoslovakia

and Hungary. For example, a Czech poll taken in early 1990 found that improving environmental conditions was the country's No. 1 priority to 83 percent of the respondents.[4]

Nonetheless, support for environmental reform under the new governments appears to be waning. "The people who were the scientists in the environmental movements have been recruited into the governments," explains Webster. "The other people, for whom the environment was a symbol of protest, have gone back to worrying about their daily tasks."

Poland, Czechoslovakia and Hungary each have new environmental ministries, she notes, but government interest in what they are accomplishing is "more symbolic than anything else."

"My fear is that in order to get the economy going, they'll grasp at anything just to get their factories working and people paid," Webster adds. Indeed, with a host of competing needs crying out for limited funds, officials of the new governments are showing an increasing tendency to push aside environmental issues.

It's a classic problem, says Clyde Hertzman, an environmental-health researcher at the University of British Columbia at Vancouver. While the money spent on the environment may do more for the economy than the money spent on subsidizing an inefficient manufacturing plant, the immediate benefits are harder to see. "When a thousand people get laid off, that's concentrated," Hertzman says. "If tourism in an area goes up 5 percent a year over 10 years because people hear that the air has gotten better, that the monuments are cleaner, it may have a bigger impact, but it doesn't land with a bang."

Fearful that such attitudes will erode support for environmental reforms, environmental groups and some academic analysts believe that both economic and environmental aid should be increased.

According to Polish economist Bochniarz, the economic and environmental strains are already showing. "We've already had unrest related to the building of a nuclear power station in Poland, and to the building of a waste plant," he says. "Those are just examples, in some cases violent examples. It's a tough issue in terms of losing jobs. It's very delicate."

If Poland and the rest of Eastern Europe are to clean up and maintain some semblance of stability, Bochniarz argues, governments will need courage, and the people will need patience. And, he adds, "We need more aid, especially technological assistance."

### Can Eastern Europe's economies recover without cleaning up?

Officials may well be tempted to focus on reviving their economies, but environmentalists warn that full economic recovery may not be possible *without* stopping pollution.

"You can't have a successful economy without instituting pollution-control devices; it's not sustainable," says Margaret Bowman, an attorney with the Environmental Law Institute (ELI) in Washington. Bowman, who has been helping the Czech government write new environmental legislation, adds that while the Ministry of the Environment understands the point, it escapes the Finance Ministry. "Their view is, 'We'll wait until we're a rich country, and then we'll worry about environmental issues,' " Bowman says. "But the issues are so fundamental that you can't wait. There's only so much you can do to damage your environment before it gets very expensive."

According to Bowman and others, pollution must be tackled now for two reasons: It's a major drag on a country's economy, and it scares away much-needed foreign investors.

Pollution imposes many economic costs, but mainly it damages public health and natural and cultural resources. According to a recent study of Poland, for example, "virtually all of the nationwide health data ... showed evidence of poorer health status in areas of ecological concern or disaster." [5]

Environmentally induced illnesses — from minor skin irritations to lung and heart disease and a variety of cancers — require significant health-care costs. Not only do they need medical treatment, but the chronic and sometimes deadly illnesses caused by pollutants often require costly, long-term care. Environmental illness imposes another, more hidden cost on society: When workers are out sick — and Eastern Europe has very high absenteeism rates — productivity declines.

Pollution also damages a wide range of resources. Industrial and agricultural toxins leaching into the sea, for example, have reduced populations of sturgeon and other commercial fish in the Caspian Sea by more than two-thirds over the past 20 years. Sulfur dioxide emissions have destroyed huge forest tracts, crippling lumber industries in some areas. Air pollution also has damaged architecture and statuary, necessitating costly repairs and causing a drop in tourism revenues. And contaminated soil has reduced crop yields.

Though putting a dollar figure on the damage is as much art as science, the U.S. Environmental Protection Agency estimates that pollution has eroded Eastern Europe's gross national product by as much as 15 percent.[6] Polish officials estimate their losses at that rate.[7] Czechoslovakia puts its decline at between 5 and 7 percent.

The need for foreign investment — the second major reason why experts say Eastern Europe requires prompt anti-pollution action — is also difficult to quantify. Western in-

vestors have shown a clear reluctance to do business in Eastern Europe for fear of liability suits. They want responsibility for previous pollution clearly spelled out before they invest in existing companies. Even when Western firms are establishing new plants, they want reliable environmental standards.

"Businesses would rather know what the standards are at the start," says Bowman, "and incorporate them into their capital investment than have standards that are going to increase over the years, but not in any predictable way. But the governments are hesitant to provide that."

AID adviser Samuel Hale Jr. believes the new governments of Eastern Europe are realizing that they can't postpone pollution cleanups. "Most of the governments are starting to recognize that environmental damage imposes real costs — health-care costs, having to buy bottled water, and so on," he says. "Hopefully that appreciation will grow in the next year or so."

### Should the West put environmental conditions on aid?

Many environmentalists worry that hard-pressed Eastern European governments will, in the end, divert available funds from pollution action to short-term economic "fixes," such as subsidizing inefficient — and often polluting — industries in an ultimately vain effort to save jobs.

Accordingly, some analysts have suggested that donor governments should put strict environmental conditions on general aid packages for those countries. The World Bank, for example, requires an environmental impact statement on all its project loans. But such conditions are not currently attached to U.S. aid, or to aid from most other major donors.

"They're going to have to borrow money, and that borrowed money can have an environmental clause in it," says Barbara Jancar Webster. "It's the greatest leverage we have. Anybody that lends money should put in requirements so that whatever is built new is built properly. That's a beginning."

Such conditions might indeed be useful, says Steve Wassersug, program manager of the Regional Environmental Center (REC) in Budapest, Hungary, which is funded by the United States and other countries to provide aid for environmental programs in Eastern Europe. "It would make [loan recipients] focus on the environment as a condition of their aid."

Even if Eastern European governments don't need to be pushed into investing in the environment, antipollution requirements could still be attached to general aid and trade packages. Such conditions would give Eastern European governments an excuse for pursuing unpopular environmental reforms.

Some analysts warn, however, that heavy-handed requirements could backfire, worsening relations with Eastern Europe. "The question is, do you use a carrot or a stick?" asks Richard Liroff, director of the World

Wildlife Fund's Central and Eastern Europe program. "All we have to do is provide as many carrots as we possibly can." That, he says, will trigger "smart choices about how to use very limited resources for environmental cleanup."

Some Eastern European environmentalists feel, however, that while blatant Western pressure might be offensive, Western governments can help Eastern European countries resist pressure from Western business. "We are afraid some Western companies that use technologies not welcomed by the public in the [West] will regard Eastern Europe as a last chance," says Janos Vargha, founder of the Danube Circle environmental group and president of East European Environmental Research, a private think tank in Budapest. Vargha points to French, American and German firms that want to build nuclear power plants in Eastern Europe and sell half the electricity to the West. Those companies, with the help of their governments, are pressuring Hungary right now, says Vargha, and "the Hungarian government is not so strong." ∎

detailing its pollution problems and recommending steps for cleaning up. "We were told almost immediately to destroy all the copies," he told a magazine reporter. "It would have cost too much and slowed down production. Everything was produce, produce, produce — and to hell with the rest." [9]

This focus on production at all costs, in virtually every industry from steelmaking to mining, shipbuilding to agriculture, produced two clear results: an extraordinary amount of pollution and industries that quickly became technologically obsolete.

According to a recent Worldwatch Institute report, Eastern European countries use 50 to 100 percent more energy than the United States to produce goods, and up to 300 percent more than Japan.[10] And in the process, they create much more pollution. "Ranked by both emissions per dollar of GNP and emissions per capita, East European countries are the most heavily polluting," the report says. "A single lignite-burning power plant in the former East German town of Boxberg emits 460,000 tons of sulfur dioxide annually, more than total emissions in Denmark and Norway combined." Similarly, a single chemical plant in East Germany was found to be discharging as much mercury into nearby rivers each day as a comparable plant in West Germany discharged in a year.

To make pollution matters worse, prioritizing production meant not burdening industries with expensive requirements for pollution controls, such as regulations on dumping hazardous wastes.

The geology of Eastern Europe has contributed to the pollution problem. The lignite, or brown coal, found throughout the region contains a high degree of sulfur and consequently is significantly more polluting than the hard coal that fueled

# BACKGROUND

## Communism's Legacy

The root cause of Eastern Europe's environmental woes is no secret: four decades of centralized economic planning controlled by the Communists.

After World War II, most of the governments of Eastern Europe — and especially the more populated countries of Poland, Czechoslovakia and Hungary — hung their hopes for economic success on the development of heavy industry. In accordance with the Communist system,

government — not the marketplace — set prices for raw materials and energy. To ensure success, many nations contributed heavy subsidies — a trend that continues. Throughout the 1980s, for example, Poland paid for 83 percent of the cost of natural gas sold to industry, as well as 49 percent of the coal costs and 27 percent of the electricity costs.[8]

Such subsidies, of course, gave engineers little incentive to make manufacturing more energy-efficient. And, in the short run, at least, the inefficiency had no economic price. The former director of environmental protection for a major film factory in East Germany recalls that his staff prepared a report in the early 1980s

Continued on p. 857

# Chronology

**1980s** *Growing environmental awareness leads to the formation of environmental groups throughout Eastern Europe.*

## 1980

Polish legislature, dominated by the Communist Party, passes the Law on the Protection and Shaping of the Environment, which designates 27 areas of the country as environmental danger zones and establishes fines for polluters. Polish Ecological Club, an offshoot of the Solidarity trade union, is founded.

## 1984

Opposition to the construction by Hungary and Czechoslovakia of a huge hydroelectric project on the Danube River leads to the founding of the influential Danube Circle environmental group in Hungary.

## 1987

Citizens of Ruse, Bulgaria, protest pollution coming from a Romanian chemical plant across the Danube River, which leads to the formation of Ecoglasnost, the country's first nationwide environmental group.

## Summer 1989

Two environmental parties are founded in Czechoslovakia: the Green Party and the Alternative Green Party.

## September 1989

Poland's first Solidarity government assumes control and quickly convenes a meeting of environmental groups to discuss environmental problems. The government also initiates an ambitious privatization program for industry and business.

## November 1989

The Communist government of Czechoslovakia hands power over to Civic Forum, the strongest opposition group. Elections in June 1990 confirm Civic Forum as the country's leading party, and the government embarks on a program of economic liberalization. In the United States, Congress passes and President Bush signs into law the Support for East European Democracy Act of 1989, which includes $60 million for environmental problems in Poland and Hungary.

————— • —————

**1990s** *In the wake of political changes throughout the region, more aggressive environmental efforts are undertaken in several countries, as well as steps toward free markets and privatization.*

## March 1990

Elections in Hungary result in the first non-Communist government since World War II. With the Communist bloc's freest markets, Hungary plans still further liberalization.

## May 1990

The European Community announces more than $80 million in environmental and privatization aid for Poland and Hungary.

## June 1990

The reformed Communist Party in Bulgaria, renamed the Bulgarian Socialist Party, wins a majority in the first elections held since the fall of the Communist government.

## September 1990

The Regional Environmental Center is established in Budapest, Hungary. Funded by the United States and other Western countries, the center encourages the development of non-governmental environmental organizations.

## October 1990

East Germany becomes part of the Federal Republic of Germany, which assumes responsibility for cleaning up pollution in Eastern Germany.

## November 1990

Polish government releases its sweeping National Environmental Policy, which calls for greater energy efficiency in industry, strict limits on air pollutants and a long-term cleanup program.

## January 1991

Czechoslovakia adopts the Charter of Fundamental Rights and Freedoms assuring citizens of the right to live in a "favorable environment" and obtain information about the environment.

## February 1991

Bulgaria frees prices of most goods, relaxes import and export restrictions.

## May 1991

Czechoslovakia's Parliament passes the country's first law governing the disposal of hazardous wastes, followed two months later by a rigorous air-quality law.

# Eastern Europe's Battered Environment

The Communist regimes of Eastern Europe treated data on environmental problems as state secrets, but the fall of the Iron Curtain opened the door on information. Though some of the damage — especially that resulting from the dumping of hazardous wastes — may never be documented, a picture is nonetheless emerging of widespread ecological devastation.

## Bulgaria

Bulgaria is among the cleanest countries of Eastern Europe, not because of enlightened environmental policies but because it is less industrialized and also less dependent on high-sulfur brown coal.

Still, the absence of environmental regulation that is endemic to the region has caused significant pollution "hot spots." According to Richard Liroff of the World Wildlife Fund, "Bulgarians living near industrial complexes have markedly higher instances of numerous diseases and, in some cases, body-tissue levels of heavy metals two to four times standards set by the World Health Organization."[1]

Aside from the hot spots, environmental damage is worst in the Rhodopes Mountains, where lumbering, mining and 20 hydropower dams have taken a heavy toll. Tourism on the Black Sea is suffering because of pollution from Bulgarian sources as well as from countries upstream on the Danube River.

## Czechoslovakia

Czechoslovakia and Poland are the two most polluted countries in Eastern Europe. Shortly after becoming president of Czechoslovakia, Vaclav Havel reportedly said the Czech landscape looked like "the end of World War III."[2] According to several sources, more than 70 percent of the country's forests are damaged, and one-third of the trees are dead. Thirty percent of the rivers cannot sustain fish, and half the drinking water is sub-standard.[3]

The major pollutants are industrial effluents, especially sulfur dioxide and nitrogen oxides, and trace metals. Major cities in both the Czech and Slovak republics are suffering. Because of industrial emissions and the widespread use of coal for heating, the capital city of Prague and Bratislava, Slovakia's largest city, each lose about two hours of daylight in winter.

## Hungary

Hungary is in decidedly better shape than Czechoslovakia or Poland, largely because it has become less reliant on brown coal. Nevertheless, in areas where coal is still heavily used,

problems persist. The conversion from coal to natural gas and other energy sources has been slowest among heavy industries, including steel, cement, aluminum processing, chemical production and mining.

Hungary's biggest environmental problem is water quality. Untreated sewage from Czechoslovakian as well as Hungarian sources heavily contaminates the Danube. Only one-third of Hungary's industrial wastewater is treated at all, and one-third of the municipal sewage dumped into the river is completely untreated. In addition, an estimated 60 to 75 percent of all groundwater is polluted by sewage, agricultural chemicals, animal wastes and industrial discharges.[4] As a result, hundreds of towns use bottled water.

## Poland

In October 1990, Poland's Ministry of the Environment, Natural Resources and Forestry called Poland a "country confronted with ecological disaster." The biggest contributor to the widespread air pollution is sulfur dioxide from brown coal. Poland relies on coal for nearly 80 percent of its energy. By itself, Poland accounts for 10 percent of Europe's total emissions of sulfur dioxide. Air pollution affects roughly half the country, especially the industrial region of Silesia, in the southwest. Forest damage is widespread.

Poland's water supply is in bad shape, too. Between 1967 and 1987, river waters classified as not needing any treatment fell from 31 percent to 5 percent. At the same time, water unfit for any use rose from 29 percent to 42 percent.[5] The primary contaminants are industrial wastes and sewage. About 40 percent of industrial wastes are untreated before being dumped into rivers.

The government has designated 27 areas as ecologically "hazardous." They comprise 11 percent of the land and about a third of the population. Five other areas are designated ecological "disaster" areas: Gdansk, Legnica-Glogow, Upper Silesia, Krakow and Rybnik.

## Romania, Yugoslavia and Albania

Relatively little information is available on environmental conditions here. It is known that Romania is much less dependent on coal than most of Eastern Europe and generally has fewer air pollution problems, except in industrial areas. Ecologists are concerned about the Danube Delta, where the river pours into the Black Sea. Environmentalists worry that the delta has been damaged by large agricultural irrigation projects. Romanians also face the hidden threat of hundreds, if not thousands, of illegal, unrecorded toxic waste dumps.

Continued from p. 854
the industrial revolutions in Western Europe and much of the United States. And coal accounts for fully 80 percent of the energy resources in Poland, 72 percent in Eastern Germany and 41 percent in Czechoslovakia. "The result is air pollution and acid rain that blackens buildings, kills trees and shortens lives," notes the Worldwatch report.[11]

Ironically, Eastern Europe's single-minded concentration on production led to new and renovated plants that quickly became outmoded. Western steel makers, for example, responded to high market prices for energy by refining technologies in an attempt to reduce their energy costs. In the process they learned to make steel not only cheaper but better. Their progress made Eastern European industry even less competitive, which in turn worsened the economy of each country and made governments still more reluctant to divert money to environmental purposes, even in the face of public outcry.

## Extent of the Damage

The consequences are not hard to find. Respiratory illnesses, for example, are significantly more common in most Eastern European cities than in the West. And other environmentally related diseases are also appearing with high frequency, including skin conditions, lung cancer, heart disease and low birth weight.

The impact of air pollution on the region's natural resources is even deadlier. In 1987 it was estimated that 10 percent of Poland's forests were under serious stress from air pollution,[12] a figure many environmentalists consider too low. A 1988 United Nations survey found that 70 percent of Czechoslovakia's forests had been damaged, and more than 5 percent were classified as dead or dying.[13] A more recent report estimates that fully one-third are dead or dying.[14]

The statistics for water pollution are equally disturbing. According to one report, 9,000 lakes and a third of the rivers in Eastern Germany are biologically dead.[15] Seventy percent of Czechoslovakia's rivers are described as badly polluted, with the result that about 50 percent of the nation's drinking water does not meet minimum standards — standards a Czech government report says are already "outdated." [16]

In fact, treatment of wastewater is woefully lacking throughout Eastern Europe. Half of Poland's cities and 35 percent of its industries don't even treat their wastewater at all before discharging it into rivers, according to Worldwatch. In Czechoslovakia, only 40 percent of the wastewater is adequately treated. Groundwater, too, is being severely affected, primarily by contamination from pesticides and fertilizers that leach into underground aquifers.

What's more, like air pollution, water pollution tends to ignore borders. Toxins in many rivers float downstream to Western Europe, and to the oceans. Large sections of coastline on the Baltic and Black seas have been significantly affected by sewage, agricultural runoff and industrial effluents. According to Worldwatch, more than half the floor of the central Baltic Sea is now "devoid of life."

But even that doesn't define the problem. Eastern Europe is dotted with hundreds of pollution "hot spots" — pockets of intense pollution from local factories, aluminum plants, mine tailings — plus probably thousands of sites contaminated by illegal dumping of hazardous wastes.

"In very few cases have these dumps even been discovered," says Janos Vargha.

### Government Response

Just as there is a remarkable similarity to the environmental problems facing the industrial countries of Eastern Europe, a common pattern tends to define the government response to those woes. Often, the initial reaction to pollution was denial. Environmental and public health data were collected sporadically. Moreover, they were classified as state secrets, creating a crucial lack of information that still plagues attempts to deal with the problems in Eastern Europe.

While the secrecy continued, governments were forced to take some measures to control pollution. Between 1965 and 1980, for example, Czechoslovakia adopted standards for pollutants in the air, water and ground. Some of those regulations — especially those for air quality — were more stringent than in most Western industrial countries.

Poland took an equally tough stance. A sweeping 1980 law designated 27 areas in the country as environmental danger zones and established provisions regulating future development. The law also set fines for polluters and charges for the use of natural resources. In the mid-1980s, Poland adopted a national program aimed at dramatically cutting coal-burning emissions.

Unfortunately, the regulatory systems set up by the Communist governments in Eastern Europe proved ineffective in enforcing the new standards. Polluting industries, unable to meet the stringent standards set out in Czechoslovakia, were still required to meet production quotas and regularly "obtained 'exceptional permissions' and thus avoided compliance," according to a report published by the current Czechoslovak government.[17]

In Poland, the fines actually imposed on polluting companies by the government averaged well under 1 percent of the production costs of

## Air Pollution at a Glance

*Levels of sulfur dioxide pollution in Eastern Europe are among the highest in the world due to coal dependence, few pollution controls and energy inefficiency. In 1988 the former East Germany was the region's leading polluter. After reunification, West Germany agreed to help clean up the contamination.*

| Country | Emissions (thousand tons) | Emissions per capita (kilograms) | Emissions per dollar GNP (grams) |
|---|---|---|---|
| East Germany | 5,258 | 317 | 31 |
| Czechoslovakia | 2,800 | 179 | 24 |
| Bulgaria | 1,030 | 114 | 21 |
| Poland | 4,180 | 110 | 20 |
| Romania | 1,800 | 78 | 19 |
| Hungary | 1,218 | 115 | 17 |
| Soviet Union | 10,124 | 35 | 5 |
| United Kingdom | 3,664 | 64 | 5 |
| United States | 20,700 | 84 | 4 |
| Sweden | 214 | 25 | 1 |
| France | 1,226 | 22 | 1 |
| West Germany | 1,300 | 21 | 1 |

*Source: Worldwatch Institute. Figures are for 1988.*

those companies, a level that is unlikely to deter a polluter. Poland also found the goals laid out in the 1987 air pollution abatement program too expensive, and three years later the government eased the regulations, permitting sulfur dioxide emissions at 40 percent of the tougher level and nitrogen oxide at one-fourth the original level.[18]

Indeed, as economic conditions in Eastern Europe worsened during the 1980s, even the little that had been spent on the environment shrank. In Hungary, for example, funds for environmental protection were cut by 15 percent in 1981 and 21 percent in 1982. In the best of times, Hungary has devoted only 1 percent of its GNP to environmental protection, compared with an average level of 1.7 percent for Western industrial countries.[19]

In Poland, the figures are even lower. In the late 1970s, Poland's investment in environmental protection was 0.37 percent of the GNP,

and it increased only to 0.73 percent by the mid-1980s.[20] Czechoslovakia's public investment in environmental protection averaged about 1.4 percent between 1971 and 1975, but by 1980 the figure was down to less than 1 percent, where it remained throughout most of the 1980s.[21]

## Activists Unite

Despite government attempts to hide the environmental damage taking place, some incidents could not be kept secret. In 1987, for example, angry citizens in Ruse, Bulgaria, banded together to protest pollution from a chemical plant across the Danube River in Romania. Faced with pressure from the group, Bulgarian Prime Minister Todor Zhivkov promised to raise the issue with Romania. His failure to do so provoked further outrage and contributed to the founding of the na-

tionwide environmental organization Ecoglasnost.

Similarly, local opposition to the construction of a hydroelectric power station on the Danube in Hungary led to the founding of the Danube Circle environmental group. Dozens of smaller, local groups formed throughout Eastern Europe to protest other pollution problems. *(See story, p. 860.)*

Environmental groups actually were nothing new to the industrialized countries of Eastern Europe. Poland's first environmental group — the League for the Protection of Nature — was founded in 1912. And even during the years of Communist rule, Poland, East Germany, Czechoslovakia and Hungary all permitted government-sanctioned environmental groups, whose main role was advocating nature preserves, conservation and nature education for children.

But in the 1980s, as economic stresses weakened the regimes, environmental groups became the focus of broader political dissent. "There are several reasons that may explain this big green wave," says Janos Vargha. "For one thing, the public was closed off from a large amount of relevant information about the environmental problems, and the weakening of the system made it possible to publish more. Second, the environmental activity was regarded as less dangerous for the state than direct political action of dissident movements, which means that a number of people who wanted to do something for democracy did it within the environmental movement."

Indeed, in Czechoslovakia, Bulgaria and Hungary — and in the Baltic republics of the Soviet Union — environmental movements played key roles in the political opposition that unseated the Communists.

And in Poland, while the biggest national environmental organization, the Polish Ecological Club, was not in the vanguard of dissent, it was important. Founded in 1980 during the blossoming of the Solidarity trade union movement, the club managed to survive after the suppression of Solidarity itself in 1981. By the late 1980s the group had 17 branches and more than 3,000 members. When Solidarity returned to prominence in 1989, the club played a major role in establishing the Solidarity Commission on Environmental Protection and Natural Resources.

In light of the "opposition" role played by environmental groups, says Vargha, "there were many hopes that [they] would play an important role in the new political systems" that have emerged in the last two years.

That's not the way things turned out, however. Wherever a Communist regime fell, environmental groups have lost members and fragmented into smaller groups. Vargha blames the fragmenting on the sudden loss of a common opponent. "Under the totalitarian system there was a certain pressure to keep to-

gether very different people working in the green movement," he says. "[Now] there is no totalitarian system and there is freedom of press and association; there's no more need for such strong cooperation."

There are two major consequences of this fragmentation, says Vargha. "One is a negative effect: There's been a decrease in the importance or the visibility of environmental issues. The second is a positive effect: The environmental movement started an evolutionary process of developing different institutions, like pressure groups, networking groups."

The irony is that just when making political headway against environmental damage seemed possible, there was neither the economic capability nor the organizational potential to do so. "In the Communist system," Vargha notes, "the people lost the skill, education and knowledge of how they can organize themselves. Their autonomous behavior disappeared." Simply changing the laws is not the answer, Vargha adds. "People have to learn how to use the laws." ∎

In addition to the EC aid, the countries of Europe are also helping on an individual basis. The most generous so far has been Germany which, in addition to assuming responsibility for cleaning up Eastern Germany, has promised $120 million to Poland. Poland will also receive $60 million from Sweden, $70 million from Denmark and $35 million from Finland for environmental projects.

The United States has allocated $60 million in environmental aid for the region, most of it earmarked for a handful of demonstration projects in Poland and for the Regional Environmental Center in Budapest. As AID consultant Carl Mitchell notes, the $60 million "isn't enough money to clean up more than a few sites."

The international banks are providing somewhat larger amounts, but as loans instead of grants. The World Bank already has loaned $358 million to Poland for environmental projects over the last year, and is expected to extend environmental help to other countries in the region next year. The European Bank for Reconstruction and Development is also expected to begin making loans there in 1992.

# CURRENT SITUATION

## International Aid

Today, the countries of Eastern Europe are in a quandary: They must undertake radical economic reconstruction *and* massive environmental cleanup efforts with inadequate resources. Clearly, massive doses of international aid will be required to achieve anything significant. It is equally clear, however, that the funds from Western coun-

tries and international banks are falling far short of what is needed.

The total amount of aid from the international community — in the form of grants and loans — that has gone to Eastern Europe for environmental purposes over the past year adds up to no more than about $1 billion. That includes roughly $100 million from the EC, a figure EC program analyst Sylvie Motard says "was too little, and which was spread too widely." According to Motard, environmental aid from the EC is expected to more than double this year, to about $250 million. Yet cleanup costs are estimated on the order of $100 billion each just for Poland and Czechoslovakia.

### A Strategy for Progress

If there is a bright spot in the picture, it is that the countries and the aid donors appear to be in general agreement as to the broad outlines of a strategy for economic and environmental reconstruction. The strategy has three major legs:

∎ **Legislating standards, enforcement and incentives**: For the most part, the problem is not one of setting sufficiently stringent pollution standards. "In some cases the standards are already higher than EC standards," notes Polish economist Bochniarz. "They're just not respected."

What is desperately needed in the region, experts say, are realistic en-

*Continued on p. 861*

# Environmental Activism

Eastern Europe's most active environmental groups are in Bulgaria, Czechoslovakia and Poland. Romanian activists are just beginning to organize.

## BULGARIA

**Ecoglasnost** is one of the few nationwide environmental groups in Eastern Europe. Founded in April 1989, it has 70 chapters around Bulgaria and about 15,000 members. The group was formed to protest the environmental policies of the Communist regime and ultimately helped in its overthrow. According to Richard Liroff of the World Widlife Fund, the organization has only two half-time paid employees, but "the expertise and activity of its volunteer activists is extraordinary." †

Several other new groups are noteworthy:
■ **The Independent Society of Ecoglasnost Varna.** An offshoot of Ecoglasnost in the resort of Varna on the Black Sea; about 550 members.
■ **The Bulgarian Society for Conservation of the Rhodope Mountains.** A group of 10 local groups; 1,500 members.
■ **The Wilderness Fund.** A group of about 15 scientists dedicated to saving endangered species.
■ **The Bulgarian Federation for Environmental Protection.** Formerly a state organization; sponsors youth projects.

## CZECHOSLOVAKIA

The closest thing Czechoslovakia has to a truly national environmental group is **Green Circle**, an umbrella organization for the three biggest organizations and about 30 smaller groups. Some cities and villages also have local Green Circles, which operate with considerable autonomy.

The biggest environmental organizations in Czechoslovakia are the **Czech Union of Nature Protectors**, the **Brontosaurus Movement**, the **Slovak Union of Protectors** and the **Tree of Life**. The first two groups operate exclusively in the Czech Republic, the latter two in Slovakia.

Dozens of smaller local groups have sprung up in recent years, including the **Prague Mothers**, the **Prague Energy Efficiency Center** and **Green Telephone**, a group of students at Prague's Charles University who answer environmental questions from the public.

Just before the 1989 revolution, two environmental political parties were formed: the **Green Party** and the **Alternative Green Party**, which split off from the Green Party amid concerns over police infiltration. Many in Czechoslovakia expect the two parties will reunite after next June's elections.

## HUNGARY

Hungary's best-known environmental group is the influential **Danube Circle**. Founded in the mid-1980s by environmentalist Janos Vargha, it gathered broad public support when it opposed a huge hydroelectric system Hungary was planning to build with Czechoslovakia. Hungary backed out of the project in 1989.

The **Nature Conservation Group** of Eotvos University in Budapest, founded in 1983 by a group of young biologists, campaigned to protect Szarsomlyo Mountain from limestone mining. Since the revolution, the group has tried to establish a network with other Eastern European groups.

Many who joined Hungary's environmental groups in the 1980s did so to oppose the government. Since its ouster, environmental groups have lost members and have fragmented.

## POLAND

Poland's oldest environmental group is the **League for the Protection of Nature**, which was founded in 1912 and is funded by the government.

The appearance of real political opposition and the founding of Solidarity in 1980 prompted the birth of non-governmental environmental groups. The first was the **Polish Ecological Club** (PEC), a Krakow-based Solidarity spinoff that is Poland's most popular group. Though the club suffered during the crackdown against Solidarity in 1981, it did not disband, and by the late 1980s it had 17 branches and 3,000 members.

In addition to the PEC, there are more than 30 smaller environmental groups in Poland, including:
■ **The Franciscan Movement for Ecology.** A Gdansk-based independent group founded in 1986; it has ties to the Roman Catholic Church. The group focuses on pollution of the Baltic Sea and Poland's coastline.
■ **The National Foundation for Environmental Protection.** Founded in 1989 and based in Warsaw; it has 26 branches and provides anti-pollution training to local governments and private groups.

On the political front, the **Solidarity Commission on Environmental Protection and Natural Resources** convened many of the larger, independent environmental groups for talks with the government in 1989. Poland also has two official green parties: the **Polish Green Party**, founded in 1988, and the **Independent Green Movement Party**.

## ROMANIA

The environmental movement is still in its infancy in Romania, with a large number of newly formed and poorly organized local groups. The most notable is the **Ecological Movement of Romania**, which is both an environmental group and a political party.

† Richard Liroff, "Environmental NGOs [Non-Governmental Organizations] in Bulgaria," draft manuscript, Aug. 5, 1991.

*Continued from p. 859*

forcement mechanisms. Agencies with real power must be created to enforce the standards, and fines for violating them must be raised to realistic levels and then enforced.

Finally, a host of other legislative measures could help. A recent EPA report makes a number of suggestions: "Fiscal policy, including broad-based taxes, can be introduced to improve the efficient use of resources. A surtax on hydrocarbon fuels and differential taxing for leaded fuels, a tax on the production of hazardous materials and a surtax on power utilities could be developed to generate short-term revenues for environmental investments and affect long-term consumption patterns." [22]

■ **Institution Building**: "Environmental issues are not well-represented by political structures," says Janos Vargha. "Which means that initiatives will come from the grassroots movements. Pressure from these groups will improve the environmental activity of the state."

At the same time, understaffed and undertrained government agencies are not doing an adequate job of collecting information and enforcing environmental regulations that already exist. That, says Carl Mitchell, is why most U.S. funding has been directed to training programs for governmental and non-governmental organizations, primarily through the REC. "The thought has been that most of the funding would go to strengthening the ability of the public sector to respond, strengthening the ability of the private sectors to provide services and training, to improve the understanding of how to deal with the problem."

■ **Establishing Free Markets**: Both donor countries and Eastern Europeans are pinning their greatest hopes on the establishment of free markets bearing not only political but also environmental fruits. The expecta-

tion is that two key measures in particular will be most effective: market pricing of energy and labor and privatization of businesses.

Market pricing would provide incentives for the development of more energy-efficient processes, and for shutting down businesses that can't grow more efficient. "As the government reduces subsidies for energy and other production materials, unprofitable state enterprises will fail and pollution will diminish," writes Liroff of the World Wildlife Fund. "This outcome already is evident in the former German Democratic Republic, where large portions of the outmoded chemical industry have been shut down, and discharges are estimated to have tumbled by 50 to 60 percent." [23]

Also, Western analysts are hopeful that Eastern Europeans' need for Western capital may help convince their governments to clean up and to establish legal liabilities for pollution. "There is a great deal of reluctance [from Western investors]," says Liroff. "I think it's not a matter of whether cleanups take place, but a question of who bears responsibility. The Western investors want a pretty good record of what the baseline conditions are, where they're starting from, and how much if at all they'll be expected to pick up the bill for damage in the past. Maybe they can live with certain existing damaged conditions. But they want to make sure whether or not it's going to cost them."

AID consultant Samuel Hale agrees and thinks the liability fears will have the most impact specifically on the privatization efforts. "If Eastern European governments don't assess the environmental liabilities of the companies they're trying to privatize, then they're not going to get privatized," he says. "Until they have some sort of environmental legislative baseline in place, companies are going to be

hesitant about making long-term capital investments."

## Legislative Action

The Eastern European countries differ significantly in the amount of progress they've made toward each of these goals.

Though it might seem that the legislative front would be the easiest arena in which to make some headway, most countries have accomplished little. "People are concerned about environmental issues, but there are other things that take precedence in a society that's trying to make so many changes at once," explains an EPA analyst who asked not to be identified.

Poland has passed some general environmental legislation, and a more sweeping omnibus environmental law is currently in its fifth draft. But more specific laws and regulations were put on hold until after the recent October elections. "It has created a lot of uncertainty, and I really don't know what's going to happen with that act," the EPA analyst said shortly before the elections. "Nobody knows what's going to happen after the elections, how they're going to change the government and legislative proposals. It's a big mystery."

Hungary has yet to get even as far as draft legislation of a national environmental law. According to Margaret Bowman of the ELI, "There has been an internal dispute between the Ministry of the Environment and the Parliament about who would have the authority to draft an environmental law." Bowman says they finally resolved that dispute by farming out the drafting of a law to a professor at the Hungarian Academy of Sciences, "but the process has been slow."

And, as in Poland, Hungarian politicians are awaiting the outcome of elections expected to take place before the end of the year. Until then, no serious legislative action is likely.

### Czech Legislative Progress

The one place where significant legislative action has occurred is Czechoslovakia. In May, the Parliament passed the first waste law in the nation's history. The act regulates the production, transport and disposal of hazardous wastes, requires permits for waste handlers and regulates the import and export of wastes.* In July, the Czechoslovak Parliament followed up the waste act with an air quality law setting more rigorous emissions standards to be phased in over the next five years and providing for taxes to support monitoring and enforcement.

Will these laws be any more effective than earlier ones that were ignored? Margaret Bowman believes they will. "The problem with the old laws was twofold," she says. "First, the legal system in Czechoslovakia prior to last year wasn't really a legal system. It's like a lot of Communist countries. They have the auspices of having an actual system, of having a constitution that gives rights to people, but it's all just on paper, not an actuality. In addition, the previous laws had no grounding in reality when it came to reasonable limits for hazardous waste, or emissions from the factory. When you have standards that there's no way to achieve, then they lack legitimacy."

What will really determine the fate of Czechoslovakia's new environmental legislation, however, is whether it is also adopted by the Czech and Slovak republics that comprise Czechoslovakia. Czechoslovakia is actually ruled by three

---

*According to Eastern European environmentalists, much of the illegal dumping in Poland and Czechoslovakia was of wastes exported by West Germany for disposal.

governments — the federal government, the Czech government and the Slovak government — and the governments of the republics have a good deal more autonomy vis-à-vis the federal government than do, for example, the states of the United States. To be effective, the federal legislation must be backed up by the passage of implementing legislation in the republics.

Unfortunately, political tensions are further complicating matters. According to Bowman, the environmental ministries in the republics are very serious about the legislation. "The difficulty is that the finance ministries and the economic ministries don't want to be serious about environmental issues," she says. "There is an internal struggle, and because of it you're not going to see as strong standards and laws being passed as the environmentalists in Czechoslovakia would like." And the republics are very jealous of federal powers. After the waste act was passed by the federal Parliament, for example, it came under immediate attack from Slovak politicians, who felt the law went further than the Parliament had a right to go.

Despite the new legislation under consideration throughout the region, many Western analysts are concerned that Eastern European countries don't have the legal infrastructure to make them work effectively. While the Czechoslovakian Charter of Fundamental Rights and Freedoms, adopted in January 1991, specifically allows citizens to enforce their right to live in a "favorable environment" and to receive information about the environment in the courts, the legal system is another matter.

"They don't have any system for citizen suits and civil enforcement," says Bowman. Even in Poland and Hungary, where there is a Roman law tradition that gives citizens the right to come into the courts for en-

forcement of laws, in actual practice the courts haven't been used that way on environmental issues. "In all of Europe the concept of citizen involvement in environmental decision-making isn't a strong concept the way it is in the United States," Bowman notes.

# Environmental Agencies

While major environmental legislation is still in the gestation stage in most Eastern European countries, reform of the environmental agencies has progressed a bit more rapidly. But there is a still a long way to go.

According to Rich Liroff, the most serious steps have been taken in Poland and Czechoslovakia, where the environmental ministries are being strengthened. One characteristic of all the countries is that responsibility for environmental management is shared at lower bureaucratic levels. Liroff sees that as a positive development because "there's such a strong distrust of the center. There's a potential for having more legitimized, credible work done at the subnational level." Still, he adds, "there is a lack of both knowledge and financial resources at the local level."

As for the rest of the region, Liroff says Bulgaria, Hungary and Romania are moving more slowly on institutional reforms. "Hungary still has a relatively ineffective environment ministry that, until September of last year, was combined with a public-works-style water development agency," he says. "Unfortunately, the environment ministry has now merged with the ministry of construction. As one Hungarian environmentalist has said, 'This could be a new fox in the henhouse.'"

In general, experts seem to agree that, while environmental institutions are being strengthened somewhat, they are losing the political battles with other ministries. In the face of economic stagnation, people are demanding jobs rather than action on the environment. As one recent report noted of Czechoslovakia, "Citizens' general desires to have Western goods [have] pushed environmental concerns to a lower priority within the government." [24]

Though Western aid is funding workshops for government-agency staffs throughout the region in an attempt to raise the standards of those institutions, Western governments and environmental groups alike are putting more hopes on building up environmental groups. "The problem is that there is not enough pressure from the [people]," Janos Vargha told a reporter. "I don't wait for a leading role from the state administration — this is not its nature — but more and more environmental associations, institutes and groups will be established and cooperate with one another." [25]

The environmental groups, however, like the environmental ministries, face a severe lack of resources. "Volunteers upon whom they rely have become more difficult to find because people must work multiple jobs to feed their families," says Liroff. "And soaring paper prices restrict the publication of documents and newspapers. Even before these economic difficulties, most environmental groups operated without the resources that Western environmental movements take for granted — a steady flow of information; access to computers, copy and facsimile machines and telephones; and funding from foundations." [26]

As a sign of the hard times, Ecoglasnost, the national environmental group in Bulgaria, has been unable to publish its weekly newspaper and has asked Western environ-

mentalists to send a copying machine so they can resume publishing.

In Czechoslovakia, too, "basic Western consumer and office supplies are often not yet available," reports the Washington-based Center for International Environmental Law. "For example, copy machines are virtually non-existent in entire

**The environmental groups face a severe lack of resources. Volunteers are getting harder to find, and paper, computers, telephones and copy and facsimile machines are in short supply.**

regions of the [country]. Available equipment and supplies are prohibitively expensive." [27]

The primary Western effort to encourage environmental groups in Eastern Europe is through funding of the REC in Budapest. With its $14 million in contributions, the center is providing grants to environmental groups and conducting extensive workshops on organizing.

Some analysts, however, doubt the effectiveness of such efforts to build environmental groups in the region. "The notion behind the Regional Environmental Center is that by providing small seed money for little projects of environmental groups, the center will renew the environmental movement, which virtually collapsed after the transition," says Webster. "This renewal, then, will produce the public pressure on the

governments. They're also hoping that this will tie in the international environment groups. There's a great deal of belief — and I think it's almost too much faith — in this sort of global environmental movement. That it, by being so global and raucous, will prevent governments from taking other sorts of actions."

Does Janos Vargha see much likelihood that public pressure for environmental reform will increase in the near future? "I'm very pessimistic," he says.

## Free Markets

Many experts believe the development of free markets and privatization may be the best hope for environmental reform. But while environmentalists agree that such economic factors as market pricing of energy and the closing of heavily polluting industries could significantly reduce pollution in a relatively short time, the process of economic liberalization is one that may take decades.

Czechoslovakia, Hungary and Poland — the three countries in the region that have taken the lead in economic reform — have already started down the road to privatization and free markets. All have made their currencies convertible (but only for businesses, not for consumers), lowered trade barriers and freed most prices. And all three have begun limited privatization efforts. Poland and Czechoslovakia plan to privatize businesses over the next few years. Hungary has had a small stock market for several years, Poland has had one for a few months, and Czechoslovakia is expected to start one soon.

But the governments of these three countries are beginning to hedge on initial plans for a rapid privatization and further freeing of markets. Their hesitancy is understandable. After all, privatizing businesses and freeing markets is generally an expensive undertaking, and most citizens will suffer a lower standard of living before the reforms improve things. And, unfortunately, the recession that has nagged Western Europe and the United States in recent months has been much more severe in Eastern Europe. The combined domestic product of Czechoslovakia, Bulgaria, Hungary, Poland and Yugoslavia declined a dramatic 8 percent in 1990 and will likely take a similar beating this year. Industrial production has dropped even more, falling 17 percent in 1990 and a projected 11 percent this year.[28]

"While still paying lip service to rapid privatization, many officials have quietly begun to advocate a more gradualist approach," notes *The Economist*, a London-based magazine. "Most have been horrified by the collapse of industry in the former East Germany, once considered the most industrially advanced country in Eastern Europe. Others naturally worry about how much more upheaval an already moody and dispirited populace can tolerate. Though quickly rejecting the communists, voters have not yet given any East European government a clear mandate. All are, in some sense, divided."[29]

Indeed, that division was clearly visible during the October elections in Poland. More than 60 percent of Polish voters decided not to cast ballots. Those that did split their votes among so many parties that none arguably has a mandate for leadership. And if there was a trend in the voting, it was that the parties that did best advocated backtracking on economic reforms. "In the best case, one may expect a defense of present achievements," former Deputy Minister of Finance Marek Dabrowski told reporters. "In the worst case, one may

expect an attempt at turning back from the path of reforms."[30]

### Steps Toward Privatization

Even if the governments were committed to rapid economic change, however, many economists are skeptical that liberalization could take place without severe dislocations. The magnitude of the task is incredible, and the brave steps that have been taken so far seem small by comparison.

In Hungary, which has long had the most open economy of the Eastern bloc, even after years of gradual privatization the private sector accounts for only about one-third of the nation's annual domestic product. Though the agency supervising privatization has approved the sale of 360 state businesses, only two of those companies have been sold. According to *The Economist*, 90 are still owned completely by the government, and the rest have private stockholders but are still controlled by the government.

Poland's recent privatization efforts have resulted in a private sector that accounts for a sizable 40 percent of the country's economic production. But here, too, the numbers mask some underlying problems. Between 75 and 90 percent of industrial output — the most polluting kind — is state-owned, and those firms are so uncompetitive that their sale to Western investors is unlikely.

Czechoslovakia has much farther to go than either Hungary or Poland. The private sector accounts for only about 2 percent of the economy and, as in Poland, virtually all of the industrial concerns are state-owned and unlikely to attract buyers.

In all, Hungary has about 2,300 state-owned companies, Poland 7,500, Czechoslovakia 4,800, Bulgaria 5,000 and Romania 40,000. Bulgaria and Romania have yet to undertake any privatization, while Poland, Czechoslovakia and Hun-

gary plan to privatize a total of about 7,000 businesses by 1994. "At their current pace," says *The Economist*, "they will be lucky to reach that goal in 30 years, never mind three. In practice, selling state-owned firms has proved time-consuming, frustrating and expensive."

Given that scenario, it's also going to be quite a long time before privatization of industry will significantly affect environmental problems in the region.

Even if market reforms could take place more quickly, some experts remain unconvinced that they would be a cure-all for Eastern Europe's environmental ills. "Market incentives on their own certainly aren't going to work," argues Bowman of the ELI. "They've never worked in the United States, so I don't know why everyone thinks that Eastern Europe is going to be any different. Even in the United States, market incentives work because you have a series of regulations and standards supporting them."

### Need for Financial Aid

Regulations and standards can only be effective, however, if businesses can afford to meet them. Otherwise, they are ignored. That is the fundamental quandary facing Eastern Europe. It cannot in the short-term afford the measures — both legislative and economic — that will be most effective over the long-term in cleaning up the environment.

It's clear that current levels of aid are not enough to deal with the situation. "My impression is that the funds that have been contributed by all the banks together are probably going to be a drop in the bucket compared to what they need," says AID consultant Carl Mitchell. "They're going to have to generate a lot of this capital on their own, through their own economies. And in the long run through borrowing."

*Continued on p. 866*

# At Issue:

## Are debt-for-nature swaps a bad idea?

**LAURA CALDWELL**

*Research Associate, Council on Hemispheric Affairs*
FROM *THE CHRISTIAN SCIENCE MONITOR,* SEPT. 11, 1990.

Persuading debtor nations to preserve specified regions of their deteriorating environment, in exchange for a slight reduction in their often massive foreign debt, has become a popular concept embraced by environmentalists, creditor banks and the governments of a number of debtor and creditor nations. . . .

Debt-for-nature swaps, the code name for the deals, may superficially appear to be the solution to . . . environmental and economic woes. But they often fail to fully handle the complex nature of the problems they attempt to address.

The idea for these swaps arose in 1984 when it was hypothetically proposed by Thomas Lovejoy, then vice president of the World Wildlife Fund. Suggesting that "debtor nations willing to protect natural resources could be made eligible for discounts or credits against their debts," Mr. Lovejoy triggered the interest of international conservation organizations. . . .

Numerous problems plague these agreements. Programs mandated by international environmentalists often do not fit the needs of local organizations or the individual country's political and economic agendas. A simple government proclamation to protect a specified area of land, or the allocation of funding for environmental programs, frequently will not withstand internal and external pressures for attention to other areas, such as creating hydroelectric power, development of roads and additional social programs. Local nationalists may charge that their country's sovereignty is being demeaned when a government adopts conservation programs developed by foreign organizations. . . .

Economically, the benefits for the debtor nations are slim. Only a small percentage of the nation's foreign debt is actually relieved, the maximum to date being 10 percent, since swaps affecting more than that amount of a country's foreign debt could induce runaway inflation. Additionally, most swaps require that the debt bought off by a conservation organization, or relieved by a foreign government, be converted into national currency bonds and sold to the public, a process that only adds to domestic debt. . . .

Debt-for-nature swaps have not yet proven themselves. Simply demanding the preservation of land cannot inculcate in the local population the value of conservation or the importance of irrigation and crop rotation.

**STEVE RUBIN**

*Director of Conservation Finance, Conservation Foundation*
FROM *AN INTERVIEW,* NOV. 1, 1991.

I don't think anybody these days is claiming that debt-for-nature swaps are, by themselves, the only approach to conservation. They are simply one tool, an important tool, that can be used to address some of the issues. Principally, it's a financial mechanism. It leverages local currency, and provides more local currency than would otherwise be received if you exchanged dollars through the normal exchange system.

What happens is that when you buy debt at a discount, and the debt is exchanged into local currency through the central bank, you ultimately wind up with something that is equivalent to a better rate of exchange. All you're doing with these programs is creating local currency that finances conservation programs.

It's very important to realize that complaints of outsiders forcing policies on countries simply don't apply anymore. In our case, in Madagascar [and] in Mexico, we had to run a very severe gauntlet of approval by the government. We have to have a financial proposal that's approved by the central bank of the country involved. We also do an environmental proposal that's approved by the environmental authorities. . . .

The way this thing works is not that you exchange debt for a policy change. That happened in the very first swap that our organization did in Bolivia. But in all of the others, it has been debt for local currency. So that the idea that you got an unenforceable policy change for the money simply is irrelevant. And so far there hasn't been a single default or suspension of payments on the conservation bonds that have been created. . . .

As for charges that these swaps are a violation of sovereignty, some local nationalists in any country can charge anything. The question is the truthfulness of the charge. I think international organizations help local organizations to carry out their conservation objectives, and this is done with the explicit approval of their governments. So I don't think it's a legitimate argument. . . .

Do these swaps benefit the recipient countries? First of all, I'd say 10 percent of a country's foreign debt being relieved through debt-for-nature swaps is an unbelievably major contribution. Secondly, these swaps have become catalysts for loans from other governments in addition to actually reducing commercial debt. We're beginning to see a real contribution from this one technique. It's really quite impressive.

Continued from p. 864

There is, however, another kind of assistance that some in Eastern Europe consider more important than loans and grants — trade. Indeed, according to some observers in Eastern Europe, the Western industrialized countries are adding insult to the injury of inadequate aid by preaching the value of free markets while maintaining trade barriers with the struggling economies of the region.

There is no small irony in the fact that environmental groups and some government agencies in the West have stressed that Eastern Europe's economic recovery and environmental rehabilitation will both require de-emphasizing heavy industry in favor of areas in which these countries can be more competitive internationally. "The biggest single benign environmental impact would be to restructure their economies ... into things like agriculture and light industry like textiles," says AID consultant Hale. But those are sectors that face the highest protectionist barriers in Western Europe and the U.S. "So they're stuck," says Hale.

"We need to have serious assistance instead of lip service," argues Zbigniew Bochniarz. "The EC wants to give us some aid, but they don't want to liberalize the access of our agriculture and textiles to the EC market."

erate trade between the EC and these countries, but they don't go much further than that."

As if the economic and environmental problems weren't enough, the prognosis for Eastern Europe's rebirth seems even bleaker when possible ethnic and nationalistic tensions are factored in. A number of experts worry that if the economies do not stabilize relatively soon, the many stresses that divide Eastern European countries — both internally and among themselves — may erupt as they have in Yugoslavia. Already Romania has experienced violent protests in response to hardships from economic reforms.

∎

# OUTLOOK

## European Community

There is no escaping the fact that Eastern Europe is facing hard times for years to come. The recently gained political and economic freedoms hold out the promise of better times ahead, but in the meantime — possibly one or two decades — the dislocations resulting from the transition will call for great sacrifice and patience.

The demands placed on Eastern Europeans by the change to freer markets will almost certainly lower their commitment to environmental reform, at least until their economies stabilize. Already, signs of wavering on measures that would help the environment are evident in government ministries.

Meanwhile, environmentalists both in the West and the East have held out the hope that the lure of membership in the European Community will encourage Eastern Europeans to hold the line on environmental re-

forms. But other observers doubt the EC will throw open its doors soon. "The EC itself is in a very difficult period right now," says Barbara Jancar Webster. "What's more, the EC doesn't need anything that Eastern Europe has. And Eastern Europe doesn't represent a consumer market. So there's no benefit to the EC to admitting these countries."

But that's just as well, adds Webster, because the countries of Eastern Europe are far from ready to join the EC. "To bring Eastern Europe into the Community means that they would have to standardize all kinds of things, like wages and social security and pensions and medical, which is impossible at the present time," she says. "In fact, it would completely wipe them out."

Instead of membership, the EC is negotiating "association agreements" with some of the Eastern European countries. According to EC analyst Sylvie Motard, the Eastern Europeans "perceive association agreements as a sort of first step toward membership." But, Motard adds, "this is not at all the idea of the EC institutions. The association agreements try to lib-

## Signs of Hope

Still, bleak as the outlook seems, some Western environmentalists glimpse silver linings in the dark clouds. First, since Eastern Europe has virtually no pollution-control hardware in place, it may do things right the first time.

"It may mean we won't commit some of the same mistakes in the East that we made in the West because of haste," says Steve Wassersug of the Regional Environmental Center. "We went through a fragmented and expensive process of building the laws — the Clean Air Act, the clean water act, the 'superfund' law — because we didn't understand the relationship between each one."

Environmentalists also hope that Easterners avoid another mistake that Westerners made and are now struggling with: cutting support for public transportation. "Eastern Europe still relies primarily on public transportation systems, but there is a risk that this pattern will change as consumers opt for car travel, and budget-conscious finance ministries cut subsidies for buses, subways, trolleys and trains," writes Hilary French of the Worldwatch Institute. "Two decades of choking on automotive pollution and trying to deal with traffic congestion in the United States have led transportation planners to regret abandoning comprehensive public transportation systems."[31]

Yet another silver lining stems, ironically, from the same Cold War mentality that encouraged the region's polluting habits. "The lifting of the Iron Curtain has also revealed a more positive legacy — the 'no-man's lands' of international borders," notes the World Wildlife Fund's Liroff. Now that the soldiers, mines and fences are largely gone, many of these ecologically rich regions are vulnerable to development pressures.

"There's a window of opportunity here, the opportunity of a lifetime to [protect] large swaths of very valuable habitat," says Liroff. The fund cites 24 natural areas that deserve protection, including the Bavarian Forest and the Mur floodplain in western Hungary and northern Yugoslavia.

While no lands have yet been saved by purchases, Poland seems to have caught the environmental spirit, entering into two pace-setting agreements. Under one, the World Wildlife Fund will give Poland $50,000 for projects on the Vistula River if Poland establishes a protected park in the Biebrza wetlands in northeastern Poland. In the other deal, a so-called "debt-for-nature swap," Germany will wipe out $60 million of Polish debt if Poland undertakes environmental projects. *(See At Issue, p. 865.)*

Despite all the silver linings, most experts agree the road to recovery won't be easy, or fast. Ventures Clyde Hertzman, the Canadian health researcher, "If the region can stay out of war, given about a 20-year time horizon I'm reasonably optimistic." ∎

## Notes

[1] *Czech and Slovak Federal Republic: Joint Environmental Study*, draft report by the governments of Czechoslovakia, the Czech and Slovak republics, the European Community, the United States government and the World Bank, March 1991.

[2] *Umwelt Report DDR: Bilanz der Zerstorung.*

[3] See "Survey of Business in Eastern Europe," *The Economist*, Sept. 21, 1991, p. 4.

[4] Steven Dickman, "Pollution as Czech Public Enemy Number One," *Nature*, March 8, 1990.

[5] Clyde Hertzman, *Poland: Health and Environment in the Context of Socioeconomic Decline*, Health Policy Research Unit, University of British Columbia, January 1990, p. 19.

[6] U.S. Environmental Protection Agency, *Environmental Conditions in Poland and Hungary*, summer 1991, p. 9.

[7] A more recent estimate by the World Bank puts the figure at about 5 percent, a figure the Environmental Protection Agency report notes is "still two or three times that of OECD [Organization for Economic Co-operation and Development] countries generally and thus severely impedes Poland's prospects for development." *Ibid.*, p. 32.

[8] U.S. Environmental Protection Agency, *op. cit.*, p. 40.

[9] Andrew Phillips, "A Terrible Price: Neglect in East Germany Is Poisoning the Heart of a Continent," *MacLean's*, Sept. 17, 1990, p. 82.

[10] Hilary French, *Green Revolutions: Environmental Reconstruction in Eastern Europe and the Soviet Union*, Worldwatch Institute, Paper 99, November 1990, p. 13.

[11] *Ibid.*, p. 21.

[12] U.S. Environmental Protection Agency, *op. cit.*, p. 33.

[13] *Czech and Slovak Federal Republic: Joint Environmental Study*, op. cit., p. 8.

[14] David B. Hunter and Margaret B. Bowman, *An Overview of the Environmental Community in the Czech and Slovak Federal Republic*, Center for International Environmental Law, August 1991, Part III, p. 1.

[15] French, *op. cit.*, p. 17.

[16] Czechoslovak Department of the Environment, *The Environment in Czechoslovakia*, p. 33.

[17] *Czech and Slovak Federal Republic: Joint Environmental Study*, op. cit., p. 16.

[18] U.S. Environmental Protection Agency, *op. cit.*, p. 39.

[19] *Ibid.*, p. 46.

[20] *Idem.*

[21] *Czech and Slovak Federal Republic: Joint Environmental Study*, op. cit., p. 16.

[22] U.S. Environmental Protection Agency, *op. cit.*, p. 141.

[23] Richard Liroff, "From Iron Curtain to Green Tapestry?" *Brandeis Review*, summer 1991, p. 29.

[24] Hunter and Bowman, *op. cit.*, Part IV, p. 1.

[25] S. Marc Miller, "A Green Wind Hits the East," *Technology Review*, October 1990, p. 57.

[26] Richard Liroff, "Environmental Legacy Mixed in Eastern Europe," draft article, Aug. 8, 1991, p. 11.

[27] Hunter and Bowman, *op. cit.*, Part IV, p. 1.

[28] *The Economist*, *op. cit.*, p. 5.

[29] *Ibid.*, p. 9.

[30] *The New York Times*, Oct. 29, 1991.

[31] Hilary French, "Eastern Europe's Clean Break With the Past," *Worldwatch*, March-April 1991, p. 24.

## Notes to story, p. 856:

[1] Richard Liroff, "Eastern Europe: Restoring a Damaged Environment," *EPA Journal*, July-August 1990, p. 50.

[2] Gergen, David R. "Cleaning up the Fouled Workers' Paradise," *U.S. News & World Report*, April 30, 1990, p. 27.

[3] Czechoslovak Department of the Environment, *The Environment in Czechoslovakia*, undated, p. 47.

[4] U.S. Environmental Protection Agency, *Environmental Conditions in Poland and Hungary*, summer 1991, p. 84.

[5] *Ibid.*, p. 29.

*Patrick G. Marshall is a free-lance writer in the Washington, D.C., area.*

# Bibliography

## Selected Sources Used

## Articles

**"Don't Give Up Now: A Survey of Business in Eastern Europe,"** *The Economist*, **Sept. 21, 1991.**

An excellent analysis of the economic plight facing the countries of Eastern Europe. The article also offers a useful discussion of the difficulties facing these countries in their attempts to privatize their economies.

**Miller, Marc S., "A Green Wind Hits the East,"** *Technology Review*, **October 1990.**

This article is a roundup of three interviews by the author with figures central to Eastern European environmental issues: Imre Szabo, an official of the Hungarian government responsible for the country's energy system; Bedrich Moldan, minister of environment for the Czech Republic; and Janos Vargha, founder of the Danube Circle environmental group in Hungary. Though seriously dated by events, the interviews offer a firsthand view on the seriousness of the environmental problems facing Eastern Europe.

## Reports and Studies

**French, Hilary F.,** *Green Revolutions: Environmental Reconstruction in Eastern Europe and the Soviet Union*, **Worldwatch Paper 99, November 1990.**

This report presents a brief (62-page) summary of the environmental problems in Eastern Europe and their origins. It's very well footnoted, which makes it a valuable resource for those looking for background sources. The only real weakness of the report is that it's already a year old, and much has happened since it was published.

**European Community,** *The European Community and its Eastern Neighbors*, **Office for Official Publications, August 1990.**

This slim (34 pages) volume offers a useful summary of relations between the countries of Western and Eastern Europe. It also includes numerous trade statistics, and the results of post-Communist elections in Eastern Europe.

**Hertzman, Clyde,** *Environment and Health in Czechoslovakia*, **Health Policy Research Unit, University of British Columbia, December 1990.**

Amply illustrated with maps and bolstered with statistical data, this report represents the most up-to-date and authoritative compendium available on the health effects of pollution in Czechoslovakia. Hertzman has also produced reports on two other countries in the region: *Hungary Report* (October 1990), and *Poland: Health and Environment in the Context of Socioeconomic Decline* (January 1990).

**Hunter, David B., and Bowman, Margaret B.,** *An Overview of the Environmental Community in the Czech and Slovak Federal Republic*, **Center for International Environmental Law, August 1991.**

Hunter and Bowman provide a very detailed look at the environmental groups in Czechoslovakia. The report also provides valuable background on the environmental issues in the country, and of legislative attempts to deal with them.

**Russell, Jeremy,** *Environmental Issues in Eastern Europe: Setting an Agenda*, **Royal Institute of International Affairs, London, 1990.**

A useful summary of the types of major environmental damage documented in each Eastern European country.

**U.S. Environmental Protection Agency,** *Environmental Conditions in Poland and Hungary*, **summer 1991.**

This is a report to Congress mandated under the Support for East European Democracy (SEED) Act of 1989, which provided funding for environmental programs in the region. It represents the most up-to-date compendium of environmental conditions in the two countries, and includes many maps, graphs and detailed statistical data.

**U.S. State Department,** *U.S. Assistance to Central and Eastern Europe*, **October 1991.**

This draft report provides details on all U.S. assistance to Eastern Europe, including that devoted to environmental problems.

**World Bank,** *The World Bank and the Environment: A Progress Report*, **1991.**

This report is the World Bank's response to critics that it has not taken sufficient precautions to ensure that projects it funds do not adversely affect the environment. It outlines the bank's policy guidelines, and includes a region-by-region breakdown detailing loans and casting them in their best environmental light.

**World Wildlife Fund,** *Ecological Bricks: For our Common House of Europe*, **October 1990.**

Sponsored by the World Wildlife Fund, this report describes 24 regions of Eastern Europe that the group argues should receive protection as nature preserves. The report also describes the environmental hazards that threaten these areas.

# The Next Step

## Additional Articles from Current Periodicals

### Cleanup

**Dickman, S., "Western help comes slowly,"** *Nature*, **Dec. 6, 1990, p. 472.**

States that an expert task force on the environment in Eastern Europe is urging governments and potential Western benefactors to focus on the dangerous areas that threaten public health. Plans for a monumental clean-up of polluted air, water and land.

**Schwartz, J., C. Koehl, et al., "Cleaning up by cleaning up,"** *Newsweek*, **June 11, 1990, p. 40.**

Reports on the efforts being put forth in Eastern Europe by U.S. companies to clean up the pollution of the past decades. Toxic waste dumps; devastation in Eastern Europe worse than once feared; estimated cost at $200 billion; suffering of children and environment; International Waste Management System; Browning-Ferris; Martech USA; Clean-/Flo Laboratories; Waste Management, Inc. INSET: The money in the mess.

**Walmsley, A., "Cleaning up on dirt,"** *Maclean's*, **June 18, 1990, p. 40.**

Discusses the Canadian companies that are taking the lead in the environmental and pollution-control markets. United States and Eastern European markets; inroads made by Union Carbide Canada Ltd. and TransAlta Utilities Corp. in the acid-rain-control market; former polluters that now export environmental know-how; Solarchem Environmental Systems' groundwater purification method; more.

### Czechoslovakia

**Bingham, S., "Czechoslovakian landscapes,"** *Audubon*, **January 1991, p. 92.**

Discusses Czechoslovakia's environmental crisis and the nation's efforts to stop pollution and protect its natural resources. Observes that the health of the landscape mirrors a nation's morality more than ideology or wealth. President Vaclav Havel's ecological awareness; the people's love of nature; air pollution, deforestation, disease, etc.; Civic Forum; Green Party; comments by Minister for Environment Bedrich Modlan and other activists and experts.

**Rich, V., "Bad neighbors taken to task over Polish pollution,"** *New Scientist*, **Oct. 13, 1990, p. 10.**

Reports on the problem of Czechoslovakia's pollution affecting neighboring Poland; need for Western help; cleanup process to take up to 10 years; Stefan Kozlowski,

vice president of Parliament's Commission on Environmental Protection states that two most effective proposals have fallen by the wayside.

**Simons, M., "Central Europe's grimy coal belt: progress, yes, but at what cost? "** *The New York Times*, **April 1, 1990, p. 1.**

Reports on the coal industry of Eastern Europe and its effects on the environment and the people. For three decades, nothing has been allowed to stand in the way of Czechoslovakia's hunger for coal. And in the mountains of Bohemia alone, 28 villages have been destroyed and 80,000 people evicted from their homes in the name if five-year energy plans. Effects in East Germany; mining; economic effects.

**Waters, R., "A new dawn in Bohemia? "** *Sierra*, **May/June 1990, p. 34.**

Describes the disastrous ecological situation in Czechoslovakia. Repressive control of environmental information under former Communist Party; high rates of cancer, cardiac disease, and respiratory ailments; effects of brown coal mining, power stations, and petrochemical plants; environmental priority under President Vaclav Havel.

### Debates & issues

**"European firms 'lack environmental strategy,' "** *New Scientist*, **July 20, 1991, p. 17.**

Highlights the results of a survey conducted by BDA Deloitte & Touche, an international environment auditing and consultancy agency, which found that 50 percent of Europe's big industrial groups have no environmental strategy. British firms and their health-and-safety policy; beliefs of British industrialists that public demand for environment-friendly goods has reached a peak; environment consciousness in Hungary; more.

**"The West must help a poisoned East,"** *Business Week*, **March 19, 1990, p. 146.**

Editorial. Discusses how, as Western governments try to help foster the revival of Eastern Europe, they are learning a dark lesson: the frightening damage that environmental degradation can do to the physical well-being of a nation's people and to its economic health. The lesson for the West.

**Boehmer-Christiansen, S.A., "Curbing auto emissions in Europe,"** *Environment*, **July/August 1990, p. 16.**

Reports how economic considerations and political indifference have long hindered the use of auto emission controls and regulations in Europe. How the demand for stricter regulations and better enforcement is growing with shifting political winds, the opening of Eastern Europe and the single market coming in 1992.

**Gergen, D.R. and Andrews, A.E., "Cleaning up the fouled workers' paradise," U.S. News & World Report, April 30, 1990, p. 27.**

Discusses the environmental damage and devastation that Communism loosed on Eastern Europe, and outlines several ways to begin correcting the damage. European regional EPA to assess problems and map out priorities; attach environmental conditions to loans and foreign investment.

**Jensen, H. and Wilson-Smith, A., "The cost of neglect," Maclean's, May 7, 1990, p. 54.**

Discusses the nightmarish environmental problems facing the nations of Eastern Europe and the Soviet Union. Communist regimes' neglect of the environment; examples from Poland, East Germany, Czechoslovakia, the Soviet Union; lack of funds for the cleanup; need for Western aid; infant deformities; cancer and other diseases.

**Kratochvil, A., "The polluted lands," The New York Times Magazine, April 29, 1990, p. 30.**

Presents a photo essay of polluted Eastern Europe. Denial of hazards under Communist regimes; worst pollution in Poland; new governments creating environmental departments; some call for an ecological Marshall Plan.

**Painton, F., J. Borrell, et al., "Where the sky stays dark," Time, May 28, 1990, p. 40.**

Presents a country by country rundown on environmental pollution in Eastern Europe, after more than 40 years of official silence, which includes whole valleys enveloped in clouds from belching smokestacks, obsolete and unsafe nuclear reactors decaying, lakes and streams fishless and dying forests. Cleanup efforts will clash with the desire to boost consumption of food and manufactured products.

**Simons, M., "Rising Iron Curtain exposes haunting veil of polluted air," The New York Times, April 8, 1990, p. 1.**

Reports on the widespread and dangerous poisonous gases that float freely in industrialized area of Eastern Europe, the reason that this problem has been kept hidden, and the affects on the population. Opinions of health specialists; study on mothers in the area and their fetuses; treatment underground; effects on water and food.

**Thompson, J., "East Europe's dark dawn," National Geographic, June 1991, p. 36.**

Examines how Eastern European nations that have been freed from decades of Communist rule and unrestricted industrialization confront a harrowing legacy: air, water, and land deadened by pollution. Problems caused by burning of coal; health problems because of pollution; controversy over nuclear power. INSETS: Pollution's long shadow; where night falls all day long.

## Germany

**Meyer, M., "The hollow society," Newsweek, Feb. 26, 1990, p. 26.**

Reports how, after 40 years of Communism, East Germany is imploding. Factories are falling apart, pollution is the worst in Europe, and thousands are fleeing the country each day. Description of the situation; what needs to be done. INSET: "Kultur" bridges a political canyon, by S. Sullivan.

## Hungary

**Bohlen, C., "As Soviets leave Hungary, dispute arises over the bill," The New York Times, July 4, 1990, p. 1.**

Says that Soviet troops who are pulling out of Hungary are leaving behind a legacy that to Hungarians somehow befits the 45-year occupation — rows of grubby, rundown barracks, shoddy apartment buildings, fields of unexploded artillery shells, and waste dumped directly into the ground. The Soviet Army is asking the Hungarians to foot the bill for what is termed 'Soviet investment' in Hungary.

**Smith, D., "Launching Hungarian ReLeaf," American Forests, August 1991, p. 33.**

Insists that even as Hungary rises from the rubble of the Iron Curtain, it is proving anew that trees are a unifying influence everywhere in the world. Hungarian environmental leaders Judit Vasarhelyi and Gyorgy Gado; strategies for targeting the Hungarian people; overwhelming response to the project by people from all walks of life in Hungary. INSET: Ultess Fat Utodaidnak: Trees for people.

## International aspects

**"The dirty dozen," Rolling Stone, May 3, 1990, p. 64.**

Opinion. Lists and discusses the 12 most environmentally damaged places on earth. Tells where to write with comments, etc. Drift netting in the Pacific Ocean; Lenin Steelworks in Nowa Huta, Poland; Penan rain forest in Malaysia; Fresh Kills Landfill on Staten Island, N.Y.; Chernobyl, U.S.S.R.; more.

**Aldhous, P., "Environmental aid 'a priority,'" *Nature*, June 21, 1990, p. 655.**

Reports that the European Community's (EC) environment ministers have agreed that environmental protection should be given priority in the EC aid package for Eastern Europe.

**Benderly, J., "Bush's brainchild in Budapest," *Environmental Action*, May/June 1991, p. 12.**

Focuses on the Regional Environmental Center for Central and Eastern Europe that opened in September 1990 in Budapest, Hungary as part of President George Bush's economic aid package. Backed by the U.S. Environmental Protection Agency; main projects are international conferences and environmental vehicles; activists concerned by elitist approach; controversy surrounding Executive Director Peter Hardi.

**Gray, C.B., "A 'no regrets' environmental policy," *Foreign Policy*, summer 1991, p. 47.**

Suggests that unilateral action may address some problems in the short term, but is fundamentally incapable of providing a long-term solution to global environmental problems. Difficulties in reaching an effective international agreement on global climate change; the greenhouse effect; true environmentalism and skeptics; Bush administration policy; East European environmental problems; environmental expenditures; the market approach to pollution.

**Morgenson, G., "'Profits are for rape and pillage,'" *Forbes*, March 5, 1990, p. 94.**

Discusses the reasons the government is doing such a poor job legislating the cleanup of the environment, and at such a high cost, and gives examples. Alternative fuel program; Eastern European free market approaches to environmental issues; pollution by entire population; adding cleanup costs to offending products; pollution taxes; Emission-Reduction Credits for industrial pollution.

**Vavrousek, J., "Europe must unite on environment issues." *New Scientist*, July 6, 1991, p. 12.**

Opinion. Calls for the establishment of a coordinated pan-European effort to create a better environment. Improving existing European environmental institutions; need to develop an environmental program for Europe; the decline of Comecon; inadequate support of environmental activities by the UN system; cleaning of the Rhine catchment area; more.

## Poland

**"U.S. mission studies hazwaste in Poland," *Civil Engineering*, September 1990, p. 21.**

Outlines reasons why the Polish government is considering five projects that would apply U.S. engineering and technology to Poland's hazardous and solid-waste management problems. The U.S. Trade and Development Program (TDP) will pay for the studies. Poland's extensive environmental problems; reaction of local governments.

**Fischhoff, B., "Report form Poland," *Environment*, March 1991, p. 12.**

Examines how Poland's new government has the will but very little money to clean up the country's environment, which the communist regime left severely contaminated for the sake of industrial production. Because the old regime suppressed data on pollution, Polish doctors and scientists can only guess at what terrible health hazards abound.

**Fuhrman, P., "Breathing the Polish air," *Forbes*, June 24, 1991, p. 40.**

Reports that since the collapse of socialism, emissions of dust and most other pollutants in Poland have dropped greatly. The biggest factor in the improvement in Poland is the phasing out of industrial subsidies and centrally controlled energy prices. This helps the environment by first forcing conservation and then, as the market decrees, the closure of old, inefficient and polluting plants.

**Maremont, M., J. Kapstein, et al., "Eastern Europe's big cleanup," *Business Week*, March 19, 1990, p. 114.**

Reports how a few weeks ago, Bronislaw Kaminski, Poland's environmental minister, issued a list of Poland's 80 worst polluters, fueling outrage — and support for a cleanup plan he hopes to offer by July. A grim tale; no more nukes; outlook.

**Sweeney, P., "Krakow at the crossroads," *Sierra*, March/April 1991, p. 56.**

Reports on the pollution and environmental issues facing Krakow, Poland. Unregulated heavy industry and low-quality coal burning have caused heavy air pollution; the Polish Ecological Club and the environmental magazine *Aura* were founded in Krakow; government issues; help from the United States.

## Romania

**Laurent, C., "Ceausescu's poisonous bequest to the nation," *New Scientist*, Feb. 9, 1991, p. 22.**

Comments on the first detailed report on the Romanian environment since the overthrow of the Ceausescu dictatorship a year ago. Air pollution and dead rivers; report by Dan Manoleli and others at the University of Bucharest; sulfur and nitrogen oxides and other chemicals in the air; antiquated industries as cause of pollution.

# Back Issues

*Great Research on Current Issues Starts Right Here. . . Recent topics covered by The CQ Researcher are listed below. Issues dated before May 10, 1991, were published under the name of Editorial Research Reports.*

**MAY 1990**
Should Teaching Be a Profession?
Will Canada Fall Apart?
Is U.S. Patent System Outdated?
Federal Funding for the Arts

**JUNE 1990**
Downsizing America's Armed Forces
Progress In Weather Forecasting
S & L Bailout
Bio-Chemical Disarmament

**JULY 1990**
Do Americans Still Love Marriage?
Death Penalty Debate
Decline of Rural America
United Nations in the 1990s

**AUGUST 1990**
Democracy in the Philippines
Initiatives: True Democracy?
Hard Times at Newspapers
Teens Balance School & Jobs

**SEPTEMBER 1990**
Dangers of Alcohol
Western Alliance After the Cold War
Tobacco Industry
Right to Die

**OCTOBER 1990**
Organ Transplants
Energy Policy Options
Search for Arab Unity
Child Support

**NOVEMBER 1990**
Lotteries and Gambling
Post Cold-War Choices
Setting Limits on Medical Care
Multicultural Education

**DECEMBER 1990**
Cable TV Regulation
Americans' Search For Their Roots
Is Insurance System a Failure?
Why Schools Still Have Tracking

**JANUARY 1991**
Growing Influence of Boycotts
Should the U.S. Reinstate the Draft?
America's Archaeological Past
Peace Corps' Challenges in '90s

**FEBRUARY 1991**
Regional Impact of Recession
Puerto Rico's Status
Redistricting: Mapping Power
Nuclear Power

**MARCH 1991**
Acid Rain
Cost of the Gulf War
Reassessing Gun Laws
Future for Man in Space

**APRIL 1991**
Social Security
Canadian Crisis Over Quebec
California Drought
Electromagnetic Radiation

**MAY 1991**
School Choice
Racial Quotas
Animal Rights
U.S. and Japan

**JUNE 1991**
Children and Divorce
Teenage Suicide
Endangered Species
Europe 1992

**JULY 1991**
Teenagers and Abortion
Soviet Republics Rebel
Mexico's Emergence
Athletes and Drugs

**AUGUST 1991**
Sexual Harassment
Fetal Tissue Research
Oil Imports
The Palestinians

**SEPTEMBER 1991**
Police Brutality
Advertising Under Attack
Saving the Forests
Foster Care Crisis

**OCTOBER 1991**
Pay-Per-View TV
Youth Gangs
Gene Therapy
World Hunger

**NOVEMBER 1991**
Fast-Food Shake-Up

Back issues are available for $4.00 (subscribers) or $7.00 (non-subscribers). Quantity discounts apply to orders over ten. To order, call Congressional Quarterly 1-800-432-2250.

# Future Topics

▶ *Business' Role in Education*

▶ *Cuba's Dilemma*

▶ *Retiree Medical Benefits*

# Business' Role In Education

*President's plan for greater business involvement generates controversy*

USINESS HAS BEEN A LEADING FORCE IN THE decade-old educational reform movement. Worried that high school graduates lack the skills needed to enable the United States to compete in the 21st century, business leaders have pressed hard for changes aimed at upgrading the nation's schools. Educators have welcomed some partnerships between schools and business, but often resisted structural changes pushed by business interests. Now, President Bush has given business the lead role in creating a private corporation to select designs for more than 500 "break-the-mold" schools slated to be in operation by 1995. Educational groups have reacted warily, raising questions about whether the 10-year commitment to educational reform promised by major business organizations will produce collaboration or confrontation.

November 22, 1991 • Volume 1, No. 27 • 873-896

*Formerly Editorial Research Reports*

COVER ART: BARBARA SASSA-DANIELS

*The CQ Researcher*

November 22, 1991
Volume 1, No. 27

**EDITOR**
Sandra Stencel

**MANAGING EDITOR**
Thomas J. Colin

**ASSOCIATE EDITOR**
Richard L. Worsnop

**STAFF WRITERS**
Charles S. Clark
Mary H. Cooper
Rodman D. Griffin

**PRODUCTION EDITOR**
Laurie De Maris

**EDITORIAL ASSISTANT**
Thomas H. Moore

**GRAPHICS**
Jack Auldridge

**PUBLISHED BY**
Congressional Quarterly Inc.

**CHAIRMAN**
Andrew Barnes

**VICE CHAIRMAN**
Andrew P. Corty

**EDITOR AND PUBLISHER**
Neil Skene

**EXECUTIVE EDITOR**
Robert W. Merry

**PUBLICATIONS MARKETING/SALES**
Robert Smith

**EDITOR, EBSCO PUBLISHING**
Melissa Kummerer

The CQ Researcher (ISSN 1056-2036). Formerly Editorial Research Reports. Published weekly (48 times per year, not printed the first Friday of any month with five Fridays) by Congressional Quarterly Inc., 1414 22nd St., N.W., Washington, D.C. 20037. Rates are furnished upon request. Application to mail at second-class postage rates is pending at Washington, D.C. POSTMASTER: Send address changes to The CQ Researcher, 1414 22nd St., N.W., Washington, D.C. 20037.

# Business' Role in Education

BY KENNETH JOST

## THE ISSUES

Think of a school as a factory. The principal is the foreman; the teachers are the workers. After a 12-year manufacturing process, the factory turns out graduates who go on to fill places in the larger economy: some in blue-collar jobs, others in white-collar positions. The education factory certifies — by means of a diploma — that the graduates it produces will meet the needs of the factories, shops and service industries that employ them to keep their businesses strong and growing.

Business has viewed public education in these terms for most of the 20th century. As the United States emerged as a world economic power at the turn of the century, business recognized that it depended on the schools to produce a labor pool to fill its need for assembly-line workers, plant foremen, craftsmen, technicians and professionals. If the business of America was business, the schools were an essential part of the enterprise — just as important as the investment capital, natural resources and banking system that were transforming the United States into an economic colossus.

The business sector's newfound interest in public education produced mandatory attendance laws and vocational education — an attempt to match the job training achieved under the apprenticeship system used by Germany, America's chief economic competitor at the time. It also marked the beginning of a half-century period in which businessmen and other middle-class professionals dominated local school boards and shaped the public schools to meet the needs of the growing U.S. economy.

Beginning in the late 1970s, however, American business began to think that something was wrong with what it was getting from the public schools. The United States was no longer paramount in the global marketplace, no longer preeminent in science and technology and, despite the continued strength of its higher education system, no longer first in educational achievements of its public school graduates. Test scores were down, dropout rates high and many graduates seemingly unprepared to step into an increasingly sophisticated and competitive workplace. Business leaders who had withdrawn from involvement in educational issues since the 1960s came to believe that their economic future — and the nation's — depended on fundamental changes in the nation's schools.

In the 1980s, business played a lead role in shaping the debate over educational policy in the states and at the national level. The factory model was obsolete, business people said. The modern school needed less cen-

tralized management, greater teacher autonomy and more active involvement by students in the learning process. At the same time, business leaders demanded strengthened accountability through performance-based pay incentives for teachers and greater stress on "educational outcomes" as measured by scores on standardized tests.

As the decade progressed, elements of this business-backed agenda were included in education reform packages adopted in several states. Business groups often provided the political clout needed to override opposition from the education bureaucracy and overcome anti-tax sentiment among the public at large.

At the same time, business groups and individual businesses began to play a more active role in education policy at the local level. Partnerships between business and education expanded in number and scope. Traditional business projects, such as helping schools pay for band uniforms, were supplemented by business-funded experimentation with new curricula and teaching methods and broader "compacts" promising money and jobs in return for structural changes and improved performance by the schools.

Then in 1988, George Bush made education reform a key plank of his presidential campaign, promising to serve as "the education president" if elected. Once in the White House, Bush sought to fulfill that pledge by convening a high-visibility summit with the nation's governors on education issues in September 1989 and embracing a set of six national education goals in his State of the Union address in January 1990. But Bush's concrete legislative proposals were less ambitious than his rhetoric and, in any event, died at the hands of senators from his own party as Con-

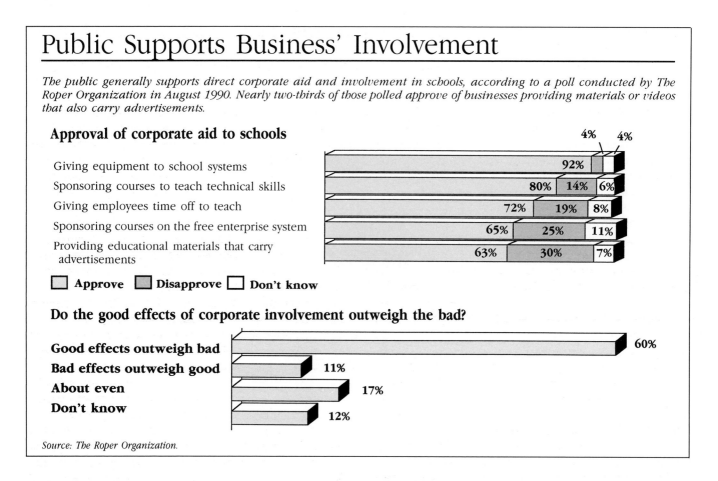

## Public Supports Business' Involvement

*The public generally supports direct corporate aid and involvement in schools, according to a poll conducted by The Roper Organization in August 1990. Nearly two-thirds of those polled approve of businesses providing materials or videos that also carry advertisements.*

**Approval of corporate aid to schools**

| | Approve | Disapprove | Don't know |
|---|---|---|---|
| Giving equipment to school systems | 92% | 4% | 4% |
| Sponsoring courses to teach technical skills | 80% | 14% | 6% |
| Giving employees time off to teach | 72% | 19% | 8% |
| Sponsoring courses on the free enterprise system | 65% | 25% | 11% |
| Providing educational materials that carry advertisements | 63% | 30% | 7% |

☐ Approve   ☐ Disapprove   ☐ Don't know

**Do the good effects of corporate involvement outweigh the bad?**

| | |
|---|---|
| **Good effects outweigh bad** | 60% |
| **Bad effects outweigh good** | 11% |
| **About even** | 17% |
| **Don't know** | 12% |

*Source: The Roper Organization.*

---

gress adjourned in October 1990.

Bush turned to business leaders as he sought to regain momentum on the issue this spring. Bypassing Congress, he moved to create a private corporation, the New American Schools Development Corporation, to spearhead research and development of 535 new "break-the-mold" schools — one in each of the nation's congressional districts, and an additional two for each state. Business was to raise $150 million to $200 million for the enterprise, and business leaders were to staff and oversee its operations.

The "special place" that Bush said he was giving to the corporate community raised many questions. Some business leaders wondered whether the administration was foisting public-policy questions onto the private sector. On the academic front, Michael Timpane, president of Colum-

bia University's Teachers College and co-author of a positive assessment of business initiatives in education reform, asked how the private corporation could be expected to take account of the public interest.

A more critical academic observer of business, Robert B. Reich of Harvard University's John F. Kennedy School of Government, questioned the business community's sincerity in promoting educational reform while sometimes failing to support tax and bond measures needed for adequate school funding.

These questions, combined with reservations about the Bush plan voiced by education organizations and leading Democratic lawmakers, indicated the uncertainty about how far education reform would go — or in what direction. As specific proposals are developed, the questioning can be expected to increase, and

resistance can be anticipated from many quarters. Here are some of the issues that will underlie the coming debate:

***What distinctive contribution can business make to the current debate over education policy?***

The business community's growing involvement in educational reform stems directly from self-interest: concern about the size and quality of the work force. Major employers have been reporting increasing difficulty in finding qualified applicants even for clerical jobs. But the business groups working on the issue say they are interested in more than improved vocational education.

"The driving force that has gotten most businesses involved is concern about the work force," says R. Scott Fosler, vice president and director of government studies for the Washington-based Committee for Economic Development (CED). "But it's not limited to that. They are also concerned about producing capable citizens."

David T. Kearns, the former Xerox Corp. chairman now serving as deputy secretary of Education, says that narrowly defined vocational education is "the last thing" that high-tech companies need. In his book *Winning the Brain Race*, Kearns said a broad liberal education "teaches people to think, to solve problems, to take risks" — the entrepreneurial and innovative attributes that U.S. companies need to succeed in the global marketplace.[1]

Some educators question whether the business community as a whole shares this broad view. Gary Marx, associate executive director of communications for the American Association of School Administrators, says business people have to be reminded of the schools' role in preparing students for citizenship and for their self-fulfillment. "They are not simply creatures of or captives of a job or business," Marx says.

Other education experts raise fears that business involvement in education issues may lead to creeping commercialism in the classroom and ideological influence on the curriculum. Alex Molnar, a professor in the department of education at the University of Wisconsin-Milwaukee, warns that schools are being caught in "corporate marketing wars" ranging from Whittle Communications' controversial advertiser-supported Channel One news program for classrooms to such seemingly innocuous projects as grocery store receipts to pay for computers. And Molnar warns that businesses are pressuring legislatures and school boards to adopt business-oriented economic curricula and encouraging schools to use materials representing corporate viewpoints on public issues.[2]

But John Chubb, a politically conservative education policy expert at the Brookings Institution in Washington, sees little danger that businesses will influence either the ideological or moral content of public schooling. "Business demands are by and large pretty basic," says Chubb. "They want to see students read and write and calculate. If they have a bias in curriculum, it's toward math and science."

Business organizations, in fact, generally disclaim any ideological motivation in their push to restructure the nation's schools. They depict political advocacy as the business community's most important contribution to the cause: elevating the issue, forging coalitions with other groups and maintaining sustained pressure on legislatures and school boards for systemic reform.

Chubb agrees that business' political clout will be a key factor in determining how far educational reform goes. "If the status quo is to change, it's going to require more than irate parents," he says. "It requires irate pressure. And business is capable of doing that."

## Would the policies being advocated by many business leaders and organizations be good for U.S. schools?

Education is a big business. Spending on public elementary and secondary education totaled $195 billion in fiscal 1990. Business leaders looking at the problems currently facing the nation's school systems can see problems that have parallels in their own companies and industries: low morale among an aging work force, crumbling infrastructure, ineffective quality control, inadequate investment in new technology and wasteful layers of middle-level management.

Many business leaders believe the solutions to these dilemmas can be found in the same wisdom U.S. com-

panies are now being taught: Decentralize the factory. Bring front-line workers into the problem-solving and decision-making processes. Create pay incentives for superior performance. Make the investments needed to modernize plant. Bring the latest technology into the production process. And recognize that the marketplace will mete out harsh discipline to any company that fails to learn these lessons.

In educational policy, these lessons are embodied in a cluster of reforms that business-minded critics and political conservatives have been pushing over the past decade or longer. School-based management calls for reducing the role of central administrators and giving principals and teachers greater responsibility — and accountability — for what goes on in their schools. Pay-for-performance embraces several plans — merit pay, career ladders, master teachers — intended to give pay incentives for superior teaching. National testing is designed to foster quality control and make school boards and individual schools more accountable for student achievement levels. And school choice is aimed at introducing the discipline of the marketplace into public education by giving parents the right to take their children out of inferior schools.[3]

The educational establishment has generally opposed or resisted these changes, and the political debate has sometimes been heated. Efforts to reshape teacher pay brought forth strong opposition from teachers' unions such as the National Education Association (NEA) and the American Federation of Teachers (AFT) in the first half of the 1980s. School choice, which President Bush and Education Secretary Lamar Alexander have strongly endorsed, is being opposed by an array of educational groups and political liberals.

Each of the issues is more complex

# Assessing Graduates' Skills

*Some experts have questioned the prevailing view that today's graduates are leaving high school with weak academic skills. But a recent survey indicates that the business community still is deeply concerned about their level of preparation for the job market.*

**How Employers Rated Recent High School Graduates**

| | Positive % | Negative % |
|---|---|---|
| Being able to work cooperatively with fellow employees | 57 | 41 |
| Having both the desire to learn more and the capacity to keep learning more on the job | 46 | 50 |
| Good attitude in dealing with those under them | 42 | 45 |
| Learning how to dress and behave well | 39 | 58 |
| Having a good attitude toward supervisors | 39 | 58 |
| Ability to read and understand written and verbal instructions | 33 | 64 |
| Having the capacity to concentrate on work done over an extended period of time | 30 | 66 |
| Learning how to read well | 30 | 67 |
| Motivated to give all they have to the job they are doing | 25 | 71 |
| Being capable of doing arithmetic functions | 25 | 72 |
| Learning mathematics well | 22 | 74 |
| Having a real sense of dedication to work | 20 | 78 |
| Having real discipline in their work habits | 19 | 78 |
| Learning how to write well | 12 | 84 |
| Learning how to solve complex problems | 10 | 86 |

*Source: "An Assessment of American Education: The View of Employers, Higher Educators, The Public, Recent Students and Their Parents," Louis Harris & Associates, Inc., September 1991. The survey was sponsored by the Committee for Economic Development.*

than the politicized debate sometimes suggests. School-based management, for example, has perhaps the widest appeal of the items on business' agenda. Speaking for the school administrators' group, Marx agrees that schools need to be "streamlined." But he adds that school systems still must be responsible for setting and enforcing goals. "That means in some cases monitoring and providing substantial encouragement to perform," he concludes.

Merit-pay plans for teachers, adopted in some states as an alternative to lock-step pay systems tied solely to longevity, have now largely been abandoned, according to a report by The Business Roundtable and the National Alliance of Business.[4] The plans proved to be both unpopular with teachers and difficult to administer. Two other less sweeping pay reforms are now viewed as more promising, the report says. Career ladders create new job structures over the course of a teacher's career, with higher pay for greater duties. And master-teacher plans designate exemplary teachers to take on additional responsibilities in such areas as curriculum development and peer assistance, again at higher pay.

National testing — included in President Bush's plan on a voluntary basis — is aimed at spurring educational performance by giving parents, students and educators a universal measure of student achievement. Low scores, it is argued, will bring forth demands for improvement that school systems or individual schools will find harder to ignore or deflect.

As The Business Roundtable report notes, however, existing tests are not seen as good indicators of reasoning and analytic skills. "New measures of student performance are necessary," the report concludes.[5] From a different perspective, national testing raises fears of usurping the traditional local control over curriculum — fears that unite many educators with political allies ranging from the progressive left to the libertarian right.

As for school choice, business organizations have somewhat distanced themselves from the politically charged debate between conservatives who view it as vital to educational reform and educators and political liberals who regard it as a threat to public education. The Business Roundtable does not list choice in its nine-point education agenda, but describes it in a separate policy statement as "one part of a broader reform movement."[6] Similarly, the Committee for Economic Development says choice plans should be limited to public schools and implemented only as part of an overall plan where "accountability measures are clearly laid out" and "the special needs of the disadvantaged are taken into account."[7]

## Is more money needed to solve the education system's problems?

Despite their disagreements about specifics, educators have adopted a posture of generally welcoming greater business involvement in the education reform movement. But they also say that structural changes alone will not solve the schools' problems without more money: money to repair and renovate aging buildings, buy computers and other modern equipment, increase teacher pay, maintain or improve teacher-student ratios and so forth. The test of the business community's sincerity, education groups argue, is its willingness to push hard for taxes and bond measures the schools need to pay for needed improvements.

Historically, business interests have not met that test, according to Michael Timpane of Columbia University's Teachers College and Laurie Miller McNeill, a research associate at the college. They note that business groups were among the strongest supporters of state tax-limitation measures in the late 1970s and early '80s that are contributing to fiscal constraints on state and local governments today. In the mid-1980s, however, businesses sometimes joined in supporting gubernatorial and legislative reform initiatives that included tax increases to help pay for them, particularly in Southern states. By the end of the decade, though, business support for revenue measures was becoming rarer, Timpane and McNeill conclude.[8]

National business organizations today take an ambivalent position on the need for funding increases. In its discussion of school financing, for example, The Business Roundtable stresses the need for more money for early childhood education and points to the wide disparity in per pupil expenditures between wealthy school districts and poorer areas. But it makes no direct call for businesses to support broad-based revenue measures or school financing equalization efforts. And it concludes by skeptically noting that studies "have not been able to show a direct correlation between dollar input and school output."[9]

For his part, President Bush has strongly questioned the need for more money. "Let's stop trying to measure progress in terms of money spent," Bush said in announcing his education plan at the White House April 18. Saying that per pupil spending on education increased 33 percent — in constant dollars — over the past decade, Bush concluded, "I don't think there's a person anywhere who would say . . . that we've seen a 33 percent improvement in our schools' performance."

Education groups and liberal players in the education debate deride the skepticism toward additional spending. "One of the shibboleths is that you can't solve problems by throwing money at the schools," Wisconsin's Alex Molnar says. "Well, if they [business leaders] really believe that, I'd like to see them send their kids to schools in the districts that spend less money on education than the schools where they're sending their kids now."

Molnar particularly emphasizes the question of equalizing school funding — an issue on which neither the administration nor business groups have played a significant role. That issue gained new attention this fall with the publication of a book by social critic Jonathan Kozol, *Savage Inequalities*, which graphically depicts inadequate school conditions in six inner-city districts and documents the disparity in spending compared with wealthier districts in adjoining suburban areas.[10] "If the president wanted to do something about education," Molnar says, "he'd go on television and say, 'This is intolerable. . . . Let's equalize educational funding.'"

The business community has recently supported tax measures in some states — Kentucky and Oklahoma, for example — that will help increase state funding for schools in part to remedy financing inequities. But business interests played no part in the litigation that has helped bring the issue to the fore in many states, and they have not put it at the top of their agenda today. To critical observers, that suggests that business is taking on more manageable problems — such as improving curriculum and teaching methods and promoting more effective management and accountability — while giving less attention to more difficult problems arising from the social and economic conditions affecting children and youth, especially in the inner city.

Business groups' support for more money for early childhood education programs such as the Head Start program partly belies that argument. But the broader point is well taken that the critical test for educational reform is how much improvement it brings to the schools in less advantaged areas where student achievement levels are now the lowest. American business needs for those students to do better in school if they are to do better in the workplace and in the larger society. Timpane and McNeill note disappointedly that to date business involvement in education has produced "no widespread impact" on educational outcomes. "The results of such efforts," they conclude, "may not be visible for generations."[11]                    ∎

# BACKGROUND

## Early History

Business played an important part in a fundamental transformation of public education in the United States at the turn of the century. The conditions that drew business leaders into educational policy then parallel the concerns facing business and society today.

An influx of immigrants was making the U.S. population more heterogeneous, producing concerns about how to integrate the new

Americans into the workplace and civic life. The child welfare movement helped raise concerns about family life and the role of the schools in children's moral development. And U.S. manufacturers, jealous of America's growing economic strength, felt apprehensive about Germany's rise as a world power and saw in its system of trade schools a model for the United States if it was to compete effectively in the global marketplace.[12]

As compulsory attendance laws increased the number of children in public schools, the business community saw a direct stake for itself in the work training that students received. "The nation that wins success in competition with other nations must train its youths in the arts of production and distribution," the National Association of Manufacturers wrote in a 1905 tract arguing for increased "industrial education" in the schools. The German technical and trade schools, the report noted, "are at once the admiration and fear of all countries." [13]

The debate over vocational education involved pedagogical and economic issues. While many educators had supported "manual education" as one part of a student's development, they opposed using the classroom to teach specific job skills. Organized labor shared that concern and also bristled at the overt anti-unionism that business brought to its support for vocational education programs.

But the American Federation of Labor was eventually brought into a coalition supporting vocational education, and Germany's growing economic and military might heightened the sense of urgency over the issue. In 1917, Congress embraced the arguments by passing legislation, the Smith-Hughes Act, that provided $1.7 billion in federal aid to states to train and pay salaries for vocational teachers in the high schools.[14]

### The Factory Model

Around the same time, business was bequeathing a broader legacy to public education: the top-down organizational theory that American corporations had adopted at the end of the 19th century. The principal, teacher and student took their places in what has more recently been labeled the "factory-floor" model of public schools.[15]

Despite some progressive experiments in allowing students to set their own pace, most schools operated like assembly lines, with the school day rigidly divided into hour-long classes and students progressing in lock step grade by grade.

After World War I, the so-called administrative progressives — composed of businessmen and professional elites — added one more businesslike feature: professional administration. School administration became a separate function from teaching, and professional superintendents and managers were hired to enhance quality control and accountability. At the top of the organizational chart were elected school boards, independent of other government bodies and typically dominated by the business and professional classes.

This system of public education was generally thought to have served business and the larger society well. Combined with the surge in post-secondary education brought on by the GI Bill of Rights after World War II, the nation's public schools could reasonably claim to have created a well-educated mass citizenry that supported the world's most stable democracy and a well-trained work force that ran the world's strongest economy.

### Sputnik Scare

Public confidence in the schools was shaken in 1957, however, with the Soviet Union's launch of its first sputnik satellite. Suddenly, the United States confronted the notion that it was behind its major international adversary in educating its young people in science and mathematics.

The government's response was the National Defense Education Act of 1958, providing federal grants to improve education in science, math and foreign languages. Most of the money was directed toward college education, however. Broader aid to elementary and secondary education was pushed over the next decade, but fell victim to opposition from states' rights-minded lawmakers and anti-tax business organizations.

Indeed, the business community generally retreated from public education during the 1960s and most of the '70s. Public/Private Ventures, a social policy research organization that has evaluated recent business-education partnerships, links the retreat to the rise of collective bargaining by teachers and the growth of aggressive parent and community groups, especially in urban areas. These trends complicated educational policy-making in the major cities at the same time that businesses and their employees were moving to the suburbs. "The distance between the business community and urban schools grew, and a period of disaffection was under way," the group concluded.[16]

## Business Gets Involved

By the end of the 1970s, the business community was beginning to recognize that it could not walk away from the problems of the public schools. The realization led to an increase in the number and scope of business-education partnerships. And it brought major businesses and business organizations in as major players in a surge of efforts by gover-

Continued on p. 882

# Chronology

## 1880s-1910s

*U.S. public education is transformed as compulsory attendance laws increase school enrollment and progressive-education movement reshapes curriculum. Business interests push for vocational education to give students training for the workplace.*

### 1917

Smith-Hughes Act provides federal aid for state vocational education systems.

———— • ————

## 1920s-1950s

*School systems come under the control of elected school boards, typically dominated by middle-class professionals and businessmen, and operated by professional administrators.*

### 1944

G.I. Bill of Rights promises education benefits to veterans returning from World War II. Enrollment in nation's colleges and universities doubles during the seven years in which benefits are available.

### 1957

The Soviet Union's launch of sputnik satellite shakes U.S. confidence in science education in high schools and colleges.

### 1958

Congress passes National Defense Education Act providing federal aid for teaching science, mathematics and foreign languages.

## 1960s-1970s

*Business community retreats from urban public education as employers move to suburbs and power shifts to teachers' unions and parents' groups.*

### 1965

Congress establishes Head Start preschool program.

———— • ————

## 1980s

*Worried that a "work force skills gap" is hampering U.S. competitiveness, business becomes a major player in efforts to improve the nation's schools.*

### 1982

Boston school system and business community agree on "compact" establishing hiring goals for high school graduates in exchange for commitment to increase graduation rate and student achievement. When school system falls short of goals, a new pact is negotiated in 1989 requiring further changes.

### 1983

*A Nation at Risk*, published by the National Commission on Excellence in Education, warns of "rising tide of mediocrity" in education.

### 1988

George Bush campaigns on pledge to be "education president" if elected. He repeats the promise in speech to educators two days before inauguration in January 1989.

### June 1989

The Business Roundtable is challenged by Bush to draw up specific plan for educational reform. The Roundtable's nine-point plan is presented to Bush in September.

### Sept. 27-28, 1989

President Bush holds "education summit" with nation's governors.

———— • ————

## 1990s

*Business groups commit to 10-year campaign to improve nation's schools and are given major responsibility in Bush education initiative.*

### Feb. 28, 1990

National Governors' Association adopts six national education goals for the year 2000 as listed by Bush in his State of the Union address.

### February 1991

Report by Committee for Economic Development counts more than 73,000 school-business partnerships, but calls many superficial and finds no evidence of overall improved student achievement.

### April 18, 1991

President Bush announces education initiative, including plan for business group to create New American Schools Development Corp. to develop designs for "break-the-mold" schools.

### Sept. 30, 1991

Educational-testing scores released by U.S. Department of Education show student achievement levels rose slowly during 1980s, returning to levels of 1970. "That's not nearly good enough for the 1990s," Education Secretary Lamar Alexander says.

### Oct. 15, 1991

New American Schools Development Corp. prepares 64-page "request for proposals" and sets deadline of Feb. 14, 1992, for grant applications.

Continued from p. 880

nors and state legislatures to upgrade school systems in their states.

Demographic changes were the critical factor in the business community's actions, as the report by Public/Private Ventures describes. Businesses had benefited for more than a decade from the growing number of women and young people entering the labor pool. With that growth tapering off, businesses saw that their entry-level labor force was diminishing and, most significantly, changing — becoming more racially and ethnically mixed. Companies run by white, middle-class managers realized that they were "ill prepared to effectively recruit and train the minority and poor population" in this new labor pool.[17]

In addition, business saw an urgent need for better education because of the economic shocks of the 1970s — the oil price embargo, stagflation and the declining strength of the U.S. economy vis-à-vis such major trading partners as West Germany and Japan. America's inability to maintain a competitive edge in manufacturing and commerce was blamed on a shortage of skilled workers, which was in turn was blamed on the poor quality of American schools. Business leaders who had been content to send their children to private or suburban public schools now came to believe that the U.S. position in the world economy required "renewed attention to the entire educational system."[18]

### 'A Nation At Risk'

A commission appointed by President Ronald Reagan's first secretary of Education, Terrell H. Bell, made this point the opening cry of its call for upgrading the nation's schools in its 1983 report, *A Nation at Risk*. "Our once unchallenged pre-eminence in commerce, industry, science and technological innovation is being overtaken by competitors

throughout the world," the 18-member National Commission on Excellence in Education warned. "What was unimaginable a generation ago has begun to occur — others are matching and surpassing our educational attainments."[19]

The report urged schools to stiffen curriculum requirements in the "new basics" — English, mathematics, science and social studies. It urged school districts and state legislatures to consider lengthening the school day to seven hours and the school year to 200 or 220 days instead of 180. It called for higher standards, and higher salaries, for teachers. And it concluded by recommending "that citizens provide the fiscal support and stability" needed to bring about the reforms.

President Reagan embraced the report's conclusion that the quality of education had been declining for two decades. But the Republican chief executive said the responsibility for solving the problem rested with parents and state and local officials rather than the federal government.[20] Democrats criticized Reagan's failure to offer any large-scale federal program to deal with the problems.[21]

Many states had begun their own work on educational reform, however, before the commission's report. As Denis P. Doyle and Terry W. Hartle reported in their 1985 summary of state educational reform, the states also were motivated by economic concerns: the need for a well-trained work force to maintain economic competitiveness.[22] Reform efforts were especially strong in the Southeast, where traditionally lagging schools posed an obstacle to intensifying efforts to attract new business and industry from other states and from abroad. Among the governors pushing strong educational reform initiatives were two who continued as players into the 1990s: Republican Lamar Alexander

of Tennessee, named secretary of Education in 1990; and Democrat Bill Clinton of Arkansas, his party's principal spokesman during the 1989 "education summit" between President Bush and the National Governors' Association.

Business groups typically joined rather than initiated such reform efforts. But in the South and elsewhere, they provided critical support — even to the point of backing tax increases to pay for the changes. In some states — most notably, California — business groups even provided the impetus for educational improvement. The California Business Roundtable helped push through an ambitious agenda of higher standards, teacher and school improvements and funding increases in the early 1980s. But as Columbia's Michael Timpane and Laurie Miller McNeill note, the California business community failed to sustain a leadership role on the issue. And as economic conditions worsened nationally toward the end of the decade, businesses became less willing to support tax measures to pay for better schools.[23]

### Partnership Programs

The business community was also crafting its own initiatives in educational improvements. At the local level, major businesses and business leaders had long been education boosters. In the 1980s, such boosterism became more widespread and more organized. Business-education partnerships occurred in 17 percent of the nation's schools in 1984 and 40 percent today.[24] Local chambers of commerce sometimes played the organizing role: The Dallas chamber, for example, organized a program that matched virtually every school in the district with a business partner.[25]

The most common business-education partnership was the so-called adopt-a-school program, where a

# Chicago Experiment Produces Mixed Results

A wealthy Chicago businessman who dropped out of high school at the age of 14 believes that corporate-minded management is what today's troubled schools need to succeed. But the elementary school he helped found in an inner-city Chicago neighborhood in 1988 — despite its corporate funding and management — has yet to show that it can improve students' education without an increase in costs.

Joseph Kellman, a blunt-talking, 71-year-old businessman and philanthropist, was the driving force behind the Corporate/Community School in the poor, predominantly black North Lawndale neighborhood on Chicago's West Side. As he worked to raise funds for the school from the Chicago business community, he preached a message appealing to fellow executives. "Public schools don't need education reform," Kellman said. "They need management reform." †

The school — tuition free, with students chosen randomly from neighborhood applicants — put into operation several ideas that major business groups have included in their agenda for educational reform: It is governed by a board of directors composed of business executives, educators and community representatives. Teachers are given one-year renewable contracts and merit pay rather than permanent tenure and seniority-based salaries. Classrooms emphasize teamwork and student discussion rather than teacher lectures. Students progress through the curriculum at their own rate and receive written evaluations rather than grades.

The school runs year-round, with a three-week vacation. And the building is open from 7 a.m. to 7 p.m., allowing operation of a full-day preschool and giving older kids an alternative to the distractions of the street.

In its first year, results appeared promising. Students showed gains in achievement-test scores, discipline improved and staff and parent morale was high. Operating costs averaged $5,100 per pupil, compared with the city-wide average of $4,100.†† But the gap was blamed on start-up costs, and the average fell to $4,644 in the 1991-92 school year. One reason for the drop was that the school reached its target enrollment of 300.

As the school moved into its fourth year of operation, however, it faced the problem of finding long-term financial support. A spokesman says pledges from corporate sponsors are "well short" of the school's needs for 1992-93 and that a full-time fundraiser will be hired to oversee a five-year, $25 million drive aimed primarily at foundations. "The main core of corporate support is still there," says spokesman Steve Weiner, "but corporate giving programs are rarely geared toward long-term commitments."

William Ayers, an assistant professor of education at the University of Illinois in Chicago and a former deputy mayor for education, has credited Kellman for having "a good idea." But, he adds, critics of waste and bureaucracy in the public schools need to recognize that better management alone will not solve all the problems of the schools. "They haven't captured the complexity of why urban schools fail," he says.‡

---

† Quoted in *The New York Times,* Dec. 6, 1989, p. B14.
†† See *The Wall Street Journal,* Feb. 9, 1990, p. R24.
‡ Quoted in *Education Week,* Dec. 5, 1990, p. 11.

---

company paired itself with an individual school and provided assistance ranging from tutoring or classroom assistance to materials and money. As Timpane and McNeill conclude, such "helping-hand" relationships provide help in achieving "peripheral goals" but do not aim at systemic reform. Still, the assistance is not insignificant. "A single computer donation in the hands of a creative school staff," they write, "can make a significant difference in the day-to-day business of teaching and learning." 26

Some business initiatives went further with programs — variously labeled "compacts" or "collabora-tives" — aimed at systemwide changes. Most early programs were cooperative efforts between business groups and schools. Businesses provided money, expertise and political support for projects aimed at goals that school officials fully embraced. But in some cities, business organizations took a more challenging approach, offering the schools money and support only in return for meeting specific goals or adopting structural changes that educators had previously resisted.

The Boston Compact was the most prominent example. The 1982 agreement committed Boston businesses to giving high school graduates jobs and college aid if the school system lowered dropout rates and raised student achievement scores. After six years, businesses exceeded the hiring goals, but the school system fell short on its promises. The reading ability of graduates showed only marginal improvements, while the dropout rate actually rose.

Business leaders responded in 1989 by demanding a renegotiation of the compact to include school decentralization and creation of "school improvement councils" including parents, educators and business and community representatives.

The experience showed, as Timpane and McNeill conclude, "that the expectation of change and the reality of change are two different things." [27]

At its inception, however, the Boston Compact was viewed as a model for local business communities to follow. Using federal and foundation funds, the National Alliance of Business began a program in 1986 to set up similar compacts in seven — later expanded to 12 — cities. That experience also demonstrated the gap between hope and reality. In its 1991 final report on the project, the alliance acknowledged that progress "has occurred more slowly than anticipated originally." Only one of the 12 cities — Louisville — got a glowing report. In many of the other cities, goals were not met and support from businesses or schools was weak.[28]

Most significantly perhaps, the report concluded that the promise of jobs was not enough to keep potential dropouts in school. "Those students already turned off by schools that did not address their needs, either their different learning styles or social or health problems, still dropped out as before," the report said. To reach these "at-risk" students, the report recommended a "whole-student" focus that would include mentoring, specialized counselors and other social services provided through the schools for students and their families alike.

## Presidential Politics

The sobering conclusions about the difficulty of achieving measurable progress — even with unified action by the business and education communities — were forming at the same time that the mid-decade surge of educational reform efforts in the states seemed to be ebbing. But the 1988 presidential campaign provided a new forum for elevating the issue. And one of the many voices heard from in the renewed debate was an influential business leader, David T. Kearns, chairman and chief executive officer of Xerox.

Kearns used a speech to the Detroit Economic Club in October 1987 to get presidential candidates' attention. The first wave of educational reform, he said, had produced only incremental changes while leaving "an outmoded educational structure . . . still firmly in place." Public schools were not providing business the quality work force it needed, but business had been "disappointingly unspecific" in pushing for change. To fill the need, Kearns offered a six-point agenda that he said amounted to a "complete restructuring" of the schools.

Kearns' speech, expanded the next year into the book *Winning the Brain Race*, co-authored by political scientist Denis Doyle, opened with a free-market plea for school choice: Students should be free to pick any public school in their district, with funding following the student to the chosen school. Schools would be run by teachers and principals, operated as magnet schools free to design their own curriculum and kept open all year. Students would advance at their own pace rather than according to a traditional grade structure. Standards for teachers would be raised, and pay would be based in part on performance. Academic standards would be stiffened, and a core curriculum required: English, math, science, history, foreign language and computer science. Moral and democratic values would be taught. And federal support for research and demonstration projects would be modestly increased.[29]

Education proved to be a popular topic among candidates of both parties in 1988, but there was more rhetoric than specifics. Democrats faulted Bush for the Reagan administration's record of cutting federal funding for education, which fell from $32.3 billion in 1981 to $27.8 billion in 1988 measured in constant 1989 dollars. Bush pledged to become the "education president" but was vague on what that promise would entail. He repeated the pledge two days before his 1989 inauguration, however, in a meeting with educators. And as the year progressed, he laid plans for a fall "education summit" with the nation's governors.

A less prominent but perhaps equally significant meeting occurred in June 1989 when Bush was the featured speaker before a session of The Business Roundtable, an organization comprising chief executives of 210 of the nation's biggest companies, devoted solely to education. Bush challenged the business executives to come forward with a specific plan for educational reform. The group took up the task and presented its platform to Bush three months later — just two days before the Sept. 27-28 summit with the governors.

Despite their general phrasing, the Roundtable's nine "essential components of a successful education system" clearly denoted a direction for schools to follow: greater responsibility for school-based staff rather than central administration, better preparation and in-service training for teachers, higher academic standards, better methods of testing student achievement and a system of rewarding schools that succeed and penalizing those that fail. Significantly, the business group also called for expanding preschool programs to reach all disadvantaged students and for increasing health and social services beginning with prenatal care for mothers and affordable child care for working parents. To heighten the sense of commitment to reform, the Roundtable pledged a 10-year effort to work toward its goals.

# Half Full or Half Empty?

*American elementary and secondary pupils have made some gains in four key areas — science, math, reading and writing — according to a recent Department of Education report. But the report also shows that overall academic progress has been essentially flat over the past 20 years. "Today's students seem to know about as much math and about as much science and read about as well as their parents did at that age 20 years ago," Education Secretary Lamar Alexander said of the report. "That's not nearly good enough."*

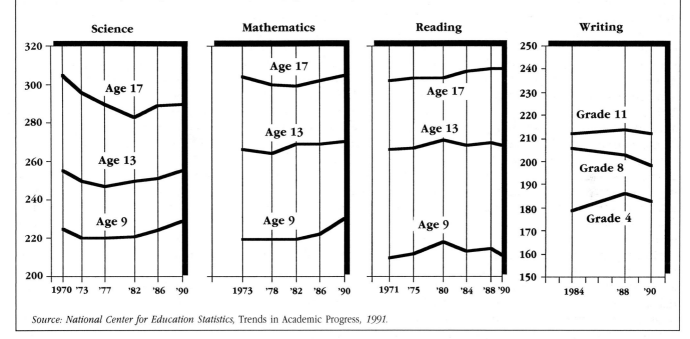

Source: *National Center for Education Statistics,* Trends in Academic Progress, *1991.*

### School Choice

The report, formally adopted by the Roundtable in June 1990 and embraced by such other major business groups as the U.S. Chamber of Commerce and National Alliance of Business, skirted the most sensitive political issue: school choice. Instead, the Roundtable drafted a separate statement describing choice as "one part of a broader reform effort" but only "a means not an end." The priority to be given to the issue proved to be a point of contention between the business groups and the administration.

In a meeting with business leaders in October 1989, Bush's chief domestic policy adviser, Roger Porter, touted choice as the most important element in school reform efforts and maintained that additional funding was not needed to improve the

schools. Several executives present disagreed. "I get upset when I see our nation's leaders acting as if choice will solve all the problems," said Owen Butler, chairman of the Committee for Economic Development. Butler also called for "much stronger leadership" on school funding.[30]

Bush himself had avoided any commitment to more federal spending for education at the summit with the governors. The meeting did yield a plan to formulate early in 1990 national educational goals that the president and the governors would jointly endorse. The six goals, announced by Bush in his State of the Union address in January and formally adopted by the governors in February, called for ensuring that all children enter school ready to learn; raising the high school graduation

rate to 90 percent; requiring "demonstrated competency" by fourth-, eighth- and twelfth-grade students in specified core curriculum subjects; making U.S. students first in the world in science and mathematics; achieving universal adult literacy; and making every school free of drugs and violence. The target date for reaching the goals was the year 2000.[31]

The president's immediate proposals to Congress had been less ambitious: a $441 million package introduced in 1989 to encourage anti-drug efforts, magnet schools, teacher certification, science and math achievement and so forth. Democratic lawmakers said the plan was too modest and was to be paid for only by stripping funds from other, more worthwhile programs. The maneuvering over Bush's proposals and Democratic alternatives lasted more than a year, with only one piece enacted: increased math and science scholarships. The bulk of the president's proposals died on the Senate floor in October 1990 when Republican senators, worried about the cost, blocked consideration of the bill containing the surviving pieces of his initiative.[32]

## New Corporate Strategies

For its part, business seemed to be faltering a bit as well in its efforts to promote educational reform. Timpane and McNeill said the number of chief executive officers actively working on education issues had fallen from the peak period in the mid-1980s. They attributed the decline to concerns about the sagging domestic economy and impatience and frustration with the slow pace of change.[33] As 1990 ended, the leading national business groups were trying to shore up the campaign efforts. The Business Roundtable, for example, published a "participation guide" for business on education issues, with a personal message from IBM Chairman John F. Akers asking business leaders to get involved in the reform drive.

Many businesses were, in fact, already involved in specific projects in their communities. The General Electric Foundation committed $20 million to its College Bound program aimed at doubling the number of university entrants from poor or inner city schools. Honeywell worked with government and community leaders in Minneapolis to establish a program — called Success by Six — to improve the school readiness of young children, especially in the city's poorest neighborhoods. In California, Pacific Telesis funded an experiment to create "leadership councils" — composed

of parents, teachers and principals — to design curriculum and management improvement strategies at selected elementary and middle schools.[34]

While these and many similar business-backed projects looked for discrete improvements within the existing public education system, some in the business community sought more radical changes. In Chicago, local businessman Joseph Kellman spearheaded a $3 million fundraising drive to set up a brand-new school aimed at showing that application of corporate management principles could improve student achievement at the same cost as public schools. Now in its third year, the Corporate/Community School is showing some improvement in test scores and hoping to bring average

costs down to public school levels as it reaches its target enrollment of 300. *(See story, p. 883.)*

The same search for radical change led the RJR Nabisco Foundation in November 1989 to launch a five-year, $30 million grant program for innovative school projects aimed at creating "fundamentally new learning environments." RJR Nabisco Chairman Louis V. Gerstner Jr. said the Next Century Schools program was intended as a catalyst for concrete changes. "No more prizes for predicting rain," he said, "prizes only for building arks."[35] A year and a half later, Gerstner would be among the business executives tapped by President Bush to put that same attitude to work in a bigger project to design a new generation of schools for America. ■

# CURRENT SITUATION

## The Bush Initiative

Business leaders were at President Bush's side as he announced his new education initiative April 18. The White House had consulted closely with key business organizations in developing its proposals. And the business community was being given the responsibility for carrying out the one new feature of the president's plan: a privately funded corporation to develop designs for what Bush called "break-the-mold" schools to be in operation within five years.

An 11-member "business core group" was named to spearhead the establishment of the New American School Development Corp., including the chairmen of several major

business organizations: The Business Roundtable, the U.S. Chamber of Commerce, the National Federation of Independent Business and the American Business Conference. RJR Nabisco chairman Gerstner was also named to the core group, and a senior vice president from the company, Roger D. Semerad, was chosen to head the working group charged with the day-to-day details of getting the corporation up and going.

The official response from major business groups was enthusiastic. But the newspaper *Education Week* found some questions being quietly raised among people in the business and philanthropic communities, such as whether the federal government was shirking its own responsibilities for educational design, whether the new corporation would simply embrace pet projects of key business leaders and whether the corporation would push controversial school-choice plans.[36]

Most broadly, some questioned whether a big research effort was

# Chris Whittle's Latest: For-Profit Schools

Media entrepreneur Chris Whittle thinks there's big money to be made in education. He plans to spend $60 million over the next three years to lay the groundwork for a multibillion-dollar chain of for-profit schools.

Whittle's idea appeals to the business people working on President Bush's initiative to develop designs for a new generation of American schools, but the reaction from public educators ranges from polite skepticism to outright opposition.

"To organize schools on the basis of a profit motive is truly anathema to me," says Sharon Robinson, director of the National Education Association's National Center for Innovation. "The opportunity to become educated should be so highly cherished that we should try to give it away every which way we can."

Whittle, chairman of Knoxville, Tenn.-based Whittle Communications, first stirred controversy among educators when he introduced a commercially sponsored newscast, Channel One, into public classrooms.

**Chris Whittle**

In announcing his new project May 16, Whittle again ruffled educators' feathers by saying he would do a better job than existing schools by using innovative technology and classroom methods. "These won't look like schools you know," he told reporters.†

Whittle's plan calls for a three-year, $60 million research-and-design project involving about 100 educators and others. His firm would then try to raise $2.5 billion to $3 billion to open 200 private schools in major urban areas by the fall of 1996. The plan envisions serving about 150,000 students, 1 to 6 years of age initially, with an eventual goal of 2 million students at 1,000 campuses when all grades have been added by the year 2010.

Whittle said the tuition charged would be just below the per-pupil cost of public education in each community, typically around $5,600. Cost-saving techniques would be one focus of the initial research. Whittle suggested shaving costs by having students work in cafeterias or clerical jobs and using older students to help teach younger ones.

Whittle's initiative was welcomed by Roger D. Semerad, head of the working group for the New America Schools Development Corporation created at President Bush's behest to design a new generation of American schools. "Between the Whittle effort and America 2000," Semerad told the newspaper *Education Week*, "I am more encouraged that some group is going to come up with very practical yet ambitious plans for designing these new learning environments." ††

Whittle said his project was designed both to make money and to demonstrate a better way of operating schools without unnecessary educational bureaucracy. And he indicated that he was motivated in part by the negative reaction educators had to his Channel One newscast. (Now in nearly 9,000 schools nationwide, using TV monitors donated by Whittle, the 12-minute newscasts include two minutes of commercials.) "We got angry at some of the bureaucracy in education," he said.‡

California Superintendent of Instruction Bill Honig, one of the opponents of using Channel One in classrooms, is also among the critics of Whittle's new project. "While theoretically you could run a for-profit operation that offers quality," he said, "my experiences with Chris Whittle lead me to be suspicious of the whole thing. He tends to let the commercial side take precedence over the educational side." ‡‡

---

† Quoted in *The Wall Street Journal*, May 17, 1991, p. A10.

†† *Education Week*, May 22, 1991, p. 14.

‡ *Ibid.*

‡‡ Quoted in *The Wall Street Journal*, May 15, 1991, p. B1.

---

needed at all. "Parents, students and educators know what works to a large extent," said Sandra Kessler Hamburg, education-studies director for the Committee on Economic Development. "Now they need to be shown how they can make it work in their own schools."

Reaction from education groups reflected ambivalence because of both policy and practical considerations. Leaders of the two biggest teachers' groups — Albert Shanker of the American Federation of Teachers and Keith Geiger of the National Education Association —

both gave Bush credit for getting personally behind what Geiger called "a bold and far-reaching initiative." [37] But Bush's proposals on school choice and national testing and his failure to propose new federal funding drew critical responses.

As for the new schools corporation, Gary Marx of the American Association of School Administrators said many teachers and administrators raised concerns that the project would divert business funding from other ongoing business-education partnerships.

Roger Semerad acknowledges that risk. "That's entirely possible," he said in September, when fundraising for the corporation had reached about $40 million. But Semerad said RJR Nabisco made a $1 million contribution without reducing its funding of its own Next Century Schools project and that other businesses should follow that example. "We found another pocket," he said.

Meanwhile, the corporation had held three meetings, attended by more than 1,500 people, to get input on drafting the formal request for proposals from grant applicants. The 64-page report completed in mid-October admonished bidders to "go far beyond the expectations of prior education reform efforts" and propose "break-the-mold" designs, not research projects or mere modifications of existing educational models. The deadline for bids was set at Feb. 14, 1992.

Sharon Robinson, director of the NEA's National Center for Innovation, said the process made her "more confident" that the corporation would "have a chance to look at serious and substantive proposals." But she added, "The jury is still out. ... If all we see come out of this is funding of symbolic experimentation of choice and technology, and nothing speaks to core issues like what is taught and how, then it will be [nothing but] a grand gesture."

## 'Crisis' Questioned

While the president's business-backed initiative was moving forward, however, a new debate

gradually emerged over some of its basic premises: the asserted decline in U.S. educational achievement, the blame placed on schools for gaps in work force skills and the sincerity of the business community's commitment to educational reform.

An article last spring in the *Harvard Business Review*, written by Managing Editor Nan Stone, questioned the conventional wisdom that today's students were leaving high schools with lower academic skills. In fact, Stone stated, student achievement levels had changed very little since the 1970s. Math, reading and writing scores were stable, she said, while science and civics scores fell in the 1970s but regained lost ground in the '80s.[38]

New statistics released by the U.S. Department of Education in the fall somewhat confirmed Stone's view. The department's "Trends in Academic Progress" showed achievement scores in reading, math and science generally rising during the 1980s and more than offsetting the declines in the 70s except for high school seniors' scores in science, which remained below the 1970 level. *(See graphs, p. 885.)*

Administration officials viewed the data less favorably than Stone, however. "The achievement trend lines are essentially flat over the past 20 years," said Diane Ravitch, assistant secretary of Education for educational research and improvement. "What was good enough 20 years ago is not good enough anymore."[39]

Stone also argued that the claimed work force skills gap was exaggerated. She cited surveys by the federal Commission on the Skills of the American Workforce that found only 15 percent of employers reporting trouble finding workers with appropriate skills. And although 80 percent of employers said they were worried about work force skills, the problems they cited most frequently were not academic but social: work

habits and demeanor.

Stronger business criticism of students' academic skills did emerge, however, in a new survey by Louis Harris & Associates sponsored by the Committee for Economic Development and released in September. Out of 402 employers surveyed, only 33 percent reported that recent high school graduates have "the ability to read and understand written and verbal instructions" and just 25 percent said they are "capable of doing arithmetic functions." *(See table, p. 878.)*

"This means that most employers have serious doubts about the functional literacy of the vast majority of the labor pool from which they must find new employees," the survey concluded.

### *Financing Controversy*

Another debate between business and educators was stirred by Robert Reich of Harvard's John F. Kennedy School of Government over corporations' financial support for schools. In his book *The Work of Nations*[40] and opinion pieces in several publications, Reich argued that business was doing less than met the eye to support America's schools. Despite the lobbying for educational reform, he said, corporate giving to education had risen a scant 3 percent in 1988 and 5 percent in 1990, and only a tiny fraction — $156 million out of $2.6 billion — went to public grade schools.

At the same time, Reich said, major businesses were undermining local school financing by routinely demanding property tax abatements as a condition for remaining in or coming into an area. "Instead of supporting the public schools," Reich wrote in *The Washington Post*, "U.S. corporations are busily siphoning state and local tax dollars that might otherwise prop them up."[41]

Christopher Cross, a former assistant secretary of Education now

*Continued on p. 890*

# At Issue:

## *Does business really care about education?*

### WILLIAM H. KOLBERG

*President and CEO, The National Alliance of Business*
WRITTEN FOR *THE CQ RESEARCHER*

*t*he business community has an enormous stake in the quality of the U.S. education system. . . . The question is: Given the importance of an educated work force, is the U.S. business community doing its fair share in upgrading the K-12 system?

The answer depends on what one believes to be the solution to the problem we have. Some people believe that the solution lies in spending more money on education and that the business community should be a stronger advocate for larger budgets and higher taxes. Others simply want business people to be more forceful advocates for change, leaving the solution to the education experts.

The business community believes the answer is somewhere between these extremes. Business people must demand better educated high school graduates, and then they must help those educators who are trying to improve the education process. If this reformation requires more money in a state, a district or a school, business must be there to help. Whether this financial assistance is in the form of direct grants or endorsement for higher taxes depends on the need.

The fact of the matter is that business has a good record of endorsing higher school budgets and taxes where that need has been demonstrated. . . .

In most states, business supplies about 50 percent of the tax dollars used for education. Beyond that, business last year donated about $264 million directly to the nation's K-12 system and another $200 million to organizations working to improve K-12 education. Additionally, business has been asked by President Bush to provide $150 million to $200 million to fund the New American Schools Development Corporation.

But money isn't the only answer for the problems that plague education. Accordingly, businesses throughout the United States have formed coalitions with educators and others to upgrade schools. Companies have poured staff support, money and clout into these projects. The Business Roundtable and the National Alliance of Business have launched a 10-year effort to work with state and local governments to achieve educational excellence.

If a "silver bullet" existed to fix America's educational system, business would buy it. Just as the education community is experimenting with solutions, business is trying to discover the most efficient combination of action programs it should take to spur our nation to quality education.

### ROBERT B. REICH

*Lecturer in political economy and management, Harvard's John F. Kennedy School of Government*
FROM *THE WASHINGTON POST*, April 21, 1991

*g*eorge Bush's new plan for reforming American education places much responsibility — and hope — on the private sector. . . . But is corporate America really all that concerned about the state of education?

Yes, American business talks a good game. It seems like every conference I attend on the subject of American competitiveness begins or ends with a speech by a prominent chief executive of a major American corporation about his business's stake in improving the quality of the American work force. . . .

I'm reasonably sure that the CEOs who deliver these speeches are sincere. Some are actively committed to the task. And . . . many of these programs are undoubtedly accomplishing some worthy objectives. . . . But the suggestion that the private sector is taking — or will take — substantial responsibility for investing in America's work force is seriously misleading. . . .

[T]he rate of corporate giving to American education declined markedly in the 1980s, even as the economy boomed. In the 1970s and through the start of the 1980s, corporate giving to education jumped an average of 15 percent a year. But in 1990, corporate giving was only 5 percent more than in 1989; and in 1989, only 3 percent over 1988.

Most of this money never finds its way to public primary and secondary schools anyway. Of the $2.6 billion that corporations contributed to education in 1989, only $156 million went to support public grade schools. The rest went to private schools or to colleges and universities. . . .

Ironically, instead of supporting the public schools, U.S. corporations are busily siphoning off state and local tax dollars that might otherwise prop them up. Corporations do this by demanding tax breaks and subsidies as a condition for remaining in or coming to the area. . . .

The inescapable conclusion is that American business isn't really worried about the future of the American work force? Why? One reason is that U.S. corporations are finding the workers they need outside the country, often at a fraction of the price. . . .

So don't be fooled by all the rhetoric surrounding corporations and the public schools. As corporate America finds ever more of its skilled workers overseas, it has become less — not more — concerned about whether it has a skilled work force at home. That means several thousand fewer points of light for George Bush to count on.

*Continued from p. 888*
heading The Business Roundtable's educational reform efforts, countered that the government authorities offering the tax concessions were also to blame. "It's one arm of the public sector undermining the other," he said. "Reich overlooks that significant part of the equation."

Cross also insisted that major businesses have shown their willingness to support tax increases to pay for educational reforms. Ashland Oil Co. was a major contributor to lobbying efforts to pass a one-cent sales tax hike to pay for a school financing reform plan in its home state of Kentucky, he said, while Oklahoma's business community helped pay for the successful campaign to defeat a September referendum that would have repealed a sales tax hike enacted as part of an educational reform package the year before.

### New Learning Methods

Despite the arguments over test scores and school funding, educators and business did seem to agree on one element of the educational reform agenda: the need for new learning methods in the schools.

The "factory-floor" model and rigid division of the school day would no longer suffice, argued education experts from across the political spectrum. Students need to be more actively engaged in the learning process. They need to develop problem-solving skills that present curricula largely ignore. And they need to be evaluated on the basis of performance rather than grades and machine-scorable standardized tests.

The NEA's Sharon Robinson warns, however, that translating this broad agreement into concrete changes in the classroom will not be easy. "It would be ridiculous for me to say that we are graduating a generation of problem-solvers when they [the schools] don't have the capacity to

teach problem-solving skills," Robinson says. "They don't have the resources to do that: I mean money, materials, and sometimes I mean skills, and sometimes I mean authority to make it happen."

The architects of the new schools corporation answered that their effort was focused precisely on solving

# OUTLOOK

## Politics and Economics

Business and education have been thrown into the common enterprise of improving the nation's schools at a time when both are under external pressures and critical scrutiny. And, despite the history of ties between the two institutions, they have not been so close in recent years. As David Kearns and Denis Doyle wrote in *Winning the Brain Race*, "no two groups in America know less about each other than business leaders and educators." [42]

Business leaders such as Kearns angered many educators over the past decade with harsh attacks on the public schools and insistent calls for higher standards and improved performance. Since taking office as deputy secretary of Education in March, however, Kearns has softened his rhetoric a bit. And business and education groups alike seem to be making a similar effort to move from wariness and distrust to positive collaboration. "Business does not seem to be saying [anymore] that we know how to fix it, you educators just need to do what we say," the NEA's Robinson says.

Despite an improved business-education relationship, broader economic and political conditions pose major obstacles to new educational reform initiatives at the national,

those problems. "Nobody's doing what [the New American Schools Development Corp.] proposes to do," says Roger Semerad, "which is leapfrog over our current problems . . . use our best minds to determine what is the best method of learning for the future, not just fix the current system." ∎

state and local levels. The federal budget deficit limits Washington's ability to support new programs, and bold policy moves are in any event unlikely because of partisan rivalry and disagreements between the Republican administration and the Democratic-controlled Congress.

As for the states, fiscal problems stemming from declining revenues and increasing demand for health and social services are putting many educational reform initiatives in jeopardy. "There still is an intense interest in education improvement," says Gene Wilhoit, executive director of the National Association of State Boards of Education. "It is just butting up against a terrible economy." [43]

The sluggish economy affects business support for educational reform, too: Witness the slowing rise in corporate contributions to education over the past two years. Equally important, a depressed job market reduces the incentives for students in school to do their best. "Today, we have people who graduate from our schools moving into jobs that are now part-time that used to be full-time or that have low pay and no benefits," says Gary Marx of the school administrators' group. "That tends to be discouraging to people who graduate from school."

With business and education both under the spotlight, partnerships at the local level can be expected to continue to rise. So far, however, these partnerships have been relatively superficial and, as Teachers

College President Timpane observes, have not resulted in measurable improvements in student achievement. And even if the new ideas coming from individual business projects or the New American Schools Development Corp. prove to be more far-reaching, they, too, are unlikely to produce the kind of short-term statistical progress that business executives are accustomed to seeing in the corporate world.

In that sense, the key question is whether the business community will stay the course on educational reform. The political and financial clout that business brings to education policy-making can make a difference in winning public support for goals that educators share or overcoming educators' resistance to policies they oppose. But the 10-year campaign promised by The Business Roundtable will require extraordinary efforts to maintain interest and support, especially if concrete progress is hard to document. Anything less, however, may leave the nation's schools little changed — and little improved — as America enters a new century. ■

# Notes

[1] David Kearns and Denis P. Doyle, *Winning the Brain Race: A Bold Plan to Make Our Schools Competitive* (1989), p. 2.

[2] Alex Molnar, "No Business," *The Wall Street Journal*, Feb. 9, 1990, p. R32.

[3] For a full discussion of the school choice issue, see *The CQ Researcher*, May 10, 1991.

[4] *The Business Roundtable Participation Guide: A Primer for Business on Education*, 1991, pp. 16-17.

[5] *Ibid.*, p. 37.

[6] *Ibid.*, pp. 97, 103-04.

[7] Committee for Economic Development, *The Unfinished Agenda: A New Vision for Child Development and Education*, 1991, pp. 47-50. Four members of the CED's Re-

search and Policy Committee filed separate statements objecting to limiting choice to public schools. See pp. 92-94.

[8] Michael Timpane and Laurie Miller McNeill, *Business Impact on Education and Child Development Reform*, Committee for Economic Development, 1991, pp. 23-24.

[9] The Business Roundtable, *op. cit.*, pp. 43-49.

[10] Jonathan Kozol, *Savage Inequalities: Children in America's Schools* (1991). In an appendix, Kozol cites statistics showing, for example, that per-pupil spending in suburban Manhasset, N.Y., in 1991 came to $15,084 compared with $7,299 for New York City and that the gap between spending in the two districts has increased over the past five years. See p. 237.

[11] Timpane and McNeill, *op. cit.*, p. 32.

[12] Marvin Lazerson and W. Norton Grubb, *American Education and Vocationalism: A Documentary History, 1870-1970* (1974), pp. 1, 18-19.

[13] *Ibid.*, pp. 91-92.

[14] Harry G. Good, *A History of American Education*, 2d ed., (1962), pp. 304-306. Historian Lawrence A. Cremin provides illuminating, chapter-length discussions of the vocational education debates in two of his works: *The Transformation of the School: Progressivism in American Education, 1876-1957* (1961), and *American Education: The Metropolitan Experience, 1876-1980* (1988).

[15] Edward B. Fiske, "Retooling America's schools by shifting from the 'factory floor' model to the power-sharing one," *The New York Times*, Jan. 4, 1989, p. B10.

[16] Public/Private Ventures, *Allies in Education: Schools and Businesses Working Together for At-Risk Youth*, fall 1987, pp. 7-8.

[17] *Ibid.*, p. 11.

[18] *Ibid.*

[19] National Commission on Excellence in Education, *A Nation at Risk: The Imperative for Educational Reform*, April 1983, p. 5.

[20] See *The New York Times*, May 1, 1983, p. A1; May 18, 1983, p. A1.

[21] See *The New York Times*, May 10, 1983, p. A1.

[22] Denis P. Doyle and Terry W. Hartle, *Excellence in Education: The States Take Charge*, American Enterprise Institute, 1985, pp. 13-14. At the time the report was published, Doyle was director of education policy studies at AEI and Hartle was a resident fellow at AEI. Doyle is now at the

Hudson Institute in Washington, D.C., and Hartle is senior consultant to the Senate Labor and Human Resources Committee.

[23] Timpane and McNeill, *op. cit.*, pp. 21-22.

[24] *Ibid.*, p. 9.

[25] Public/Private Ventures, *op. cit.*, p. 13.

[26] Timpane and McNeill, *op. cit.*, p. 10.

[27] *Ibid.*, p. 17. See also National Alliance of Business, *The Compact Project: School-Business Partnerships for Improving Education*, 1989, pp. 2-3.

[28] National Alliance of Business, *The Compact Project: Final Report*, 1991, p. 5. The other areas in the program are Albuquerque, N.M.; Cincinnati; Detroit; Indianapolis; Memphis, Tenn.; Miami-Dade County, Fla.; Pittsburgh; Providence, R.I.; Rochester, N.Y.; San Diego; and Seattle.

[29] Kearns and Doyle, *op. cit.*, pp. 139-143 (text of speech).

[30] Quoted in *Education Week*, Nov. 8, 1989, p. 1.

[31] The text of the National Governors' Association statement on the goals can be found in *Education Week*, March 7, 1990, pp. 16-17.

[32] *1990 Congressional Quarterly Almanac*, p. 610.

[33] Timpane and McNeill, *op. cit.*, pp. 6-7, 33.

[34] See Ronald E. Berenbeim, *Corporate Strategies for Improving Public Education*, The Conference Board, 1991.

[35] *Ibid.*, pp. 41-42.

[36] *Education Week*, May 8, 1991, p. 1.

[37] *Congressional Quarterly Weekly Report*, April 20, 1991, p. 986.

[38] Nan Stone, "Does Business Have Any Business in Education?" *Harvard Business Review*, March/April 1991, p. 47.

[39] Quoted in *The New York Times*, Oct. 1, 1991, p. A1.

[40] Robert B. Reich, *The Work of Nations: Preparing Ourselves for 21st-Century Capitalism* (1991).

[41] Robert B. Reich, "Big Business Cuts Class," *The Washington Post*, April 21, 1991, p. B1.

[42] Kearns and Doyle, *op. cit.*, p. 13.

[43] Quoted in *Education Week*, June 19, 1991, p. 26.

*Kenneth Jost is a free-lance writer in Washington.*

# Bibliography

## Selected Sources Used

### Books

Cremin, Lawrence A., *American Education: The Metropolitan Experience, 1876-1980*, Harper & Row, 1988.

This third volume in the comprehensive history of American education by Lawrence Cremin, a professor and former president of Teachers College, Columbia University, includes a chapter on schools as "places of work." Cremin's earlier work, *The Transformation of the American School: Progressivism in American Education, 1876-1957* (Alfred A. Knopf, 1961), contains a chapter on early efforts to integrate schooling and the world of business.

Kearns, David T., and Doyle, Denis P., *Winning the Brain Race: A Bold Plan to Make Our Schools Competitive*, Institute for Contemporary Studies Press, 1988.

Kearns, then chairman of Xerox Corp. and now deputy secretary of Education, and Doyle, a senior fellow at the Hudson Institute, collaborated in producing this strongly argued tract calling for a "total restructuring of our schools."

### Articles

Stanfield, Rochelle, "School Business," *National Journal*, July 27, 1991.

The article describes and assesses business' role in the current drive to improve the nation's schools.

Weisman, Jonathan, "Businesses Sign On to Bush Plan, But Many Also Raising Concerns," *Education Week*, May 8, 1991, p. 1.

This is one of several thorough and insightful articles by reporters for this influential newspaper chronicling the current educational reform initiatives and business' role in them.

### Reports and Studies

Business Roundtable, *The Business Roundtable Participation Guide: A Primer for Business on Education* (2d ed.), April 1991.

This primer, prepared for The Business Roundtable by the National Alliance for Business, systematically summarizes the major areas in the current debate over education policy: curriculum, management, accountability, financing, infrastructure, technology, early childhood development and auxiliary social services. Each chapter specifies the role business can play in the area, while an appendix

details the Roundtable's nine-point education reform agenda. The book also contains a seven-page bibliography.

Committee for Economic Development, *Investing in Our Children: Business and the Public Schools*, 1985.

This influential report by the nonpartisan, business-backed research organization describes the importance of educational reform for the future of U.S. business and details recommendations for business involvement in a strategy to improve U.S. schools "from the bottom up." Two subsequent CED reports elaborate on and update these themes: *Children in Need: Investment Strategies for the Educationally Disadvantaged* (1987) and *The Unfinished Agenda: A New Vision for Child Development and Education* (1991).

National Alliance for Business, *The Compact Project: School-Business Partnerships for Improving Education*, 1989; *The Compact Project: Final Report*, 1991.

The National Alliance of Business stimulated development of education reform demonstration projects in 12 U.S. cities based on business-education partnerships similar to that adopted in the Boston Compact in 1982. The group's detailed 1989 report and briefer final report this year describe the 12 projects with a measure of optimism tempered by the conclusion that progress had been slower than anticipated.

Public/Private Ventures, *Allies in Education: Schools and Businesses Working Together for At-Risk Youth*, fall 1987.

This Philadelphia-based research organization conducted a three-year assessment of nine business-education partnerships and found only limited benefits for the school systems or the students participating in the programs. An updated assessment of the programs is to be published in spring 1992.

Timpane, Michael, and McNeill, Laurie Miller, *Business Impact on Education and Child Development Reform*, Committee for Economic Development, 1991.

Timpane, president of Columbia University Teachers College, and McNeill, a research associate at the college, conclude that business involvement fundamentally changed the politics of education policy-making during the 1980s. They say business initiatives have been beneficial but limited and warn that a sustained commitment will be needed to produce measurable results. The report also contains a well-organized, 15-page bibliography.

# The Next Step

## Additional Articles from Current Periodicals from EBSCO Publishing's Database

### Addresses & essays

**Brown, S., "Business and education," *Vital Speeches*, June 15, 1991, p. 538.**

Presents a speech by Steve Brown, "Business and Education," delivered at the National Business Education Association Annual Convention in Nashville, Tenn., on March 28, 1991, dealing with the issue of re-establishing our educational system's credibility.

**Munro, J. R., "Troubled urban schools and American business," *Vital Speeches*, June 1, 1991, p. 495.**

Presents a speech by Time Warner Inc. Chairman J. Richard Munro entitled "Troubled Urban Schools and American Business," delivered at the Business Forum on Education, Allegheny Conference on Economic Development, in Pittsburgh, Pa., on March 5, 1991, dealing with issue of the cost of academic excellence.

**Rist, M. C., "Business 'takes action' in school reform," *Education Digest*, November 1990, p. 47.**

Presents an article condensed from *The American School Board Journal*, by Marilee C. Rist concerning the business aspects of school reform. School-business partnerships; The Boston Compact; Chicago and Mississippi compacts; The Corporate/Community School; central issue of business involvement in school.

**Schroeder, K., "Early, early education," *Education Digest*, April 1991, p. 73.**

Discusses a report from the Committee for Economic Development, a national business organization, on preparation of young children for school. The report, entitled "The Unfinished Agenda: A New Vision for Child Development and Education," makes several recommendations.

### Books & reading

**"Resources," *Educational Leadership*, April 1991, p. 91.**

Reviews the book *Guidelines for School-Business Partnerships in Science and Mathematics*, by Louis H. Blair, Paul J. Brounstein, Harry P. Hatry, and Elaine Morley.

Case studies

**Branch, E., "Can business save our schools?" *Black Enterprise*, March 1991, p. 38.**

Explores the business community's efforts to upgrade education in the public schools. Why corporate America is concerned about the quality of education; 12 diverse programs established, such as IBM's Project A+, Procter & Gamble's Aspire, and Eastman Kodak Co.'s Kodak 21st Century Learning Challenge; implications for the black community. INSETS: What the CEOs have to say; contacts to help you get involved.

**Braxton, L., "Plan for kids soars," *Black Enterprise*, June 1991, p. 44.**

Describes Opportunity Skyway, a business and educational partnership that encourages minority and disadvantaged students to stay in school and focus on career alternatives. How it was founded by the Landover, Md.-based Prince George's Private Industry Council Inc. (PIC); benefits of the program.

**Recio, I., "Beyond day care: The company school," *Business Week*, May 20, 1991, p. 142.**

Talks about how a handful of companies are joining forces with school districts to set up classes inside the front gates. Looks at how Miami community leaders, frustrated over tight budgets and overcrowded classrooms, came up with the idea. Benefits for parents who work in the companies and for the school administrators; how the plan works; what employers get out of the deal; encouraging more companies to adopt the practice.

**Solomon, C. M. and Archambault, C., "New partners in business," *Personnel Journal*, April 1991, p. 56.**

Looks at the ways in which corporate America is taking a leading role in education through the formation of business-education partnerships. Diminishing quality of students entering the work force; different levels of business involvement; role of human resources (HR); profiles of the programs of six companies, including Fannie Mae (Federal National Mortgage Association), Burger King Corp., and Cray Research Inc.; details.

### Corporate aid to education

**"Bush challenges business to back new schools," *Congressional Quarterly Weekly Report*, July 13, 1991, p. 1906.**

States that President George Bush took his quest to be the education president to the nation's boardrooms by announcing July 8 that the business community has so far raised $30 million to pay for special "break the mold" schools. New American Schools Development Corp; fundraising campaign at a Rose Garden ceremony.

**Atkins, A., "Big business and education," *Better Homes & Gardens,* March 1991, p. 32.**

Reports on the recent surge in aid for education from corporate America. Why the corporations are supporting education; business/education partnerships; company's motives; suggestions for playing a role in school/business partnerships. INSET: Getting the best business deal for your school.

## *Debates & issues*

**Celis III, W., "Despite touted gifts, business tax breaks cost schools money," *The New York Times,* May 22, 1991, p. A1.**

Discusses company donations to schools, saying that many companies that give gifts extract as many sizable tax breaks as they can from their communities, cutting off money needed to finance public education. Now, educators are fighting back, trying to make businesses pay their full share of taxes.

**Cetron, M. J. and Gayle, M. E., "Educational renaissance: 43 trends for U.S. schools," *Futurist,* September/October 1990, p. 33.**

Lists 43 trends for United States schools. More business-and-school partnerships; increased parental participation; lifelong learning emphasis; more. INSETS: The connection to jobs and work; the family connection.

**Davies, G. K., "The president's 'bold educational reform' is a scam," *The Chronicle of Higher Education,* May 15, 1991, p. A44.**

Opinion. Argues that the "bold educational reform" plan proposed by President Bush is flawed in ways that make it unnecessary even to begin detailed analysis of its 44 distinct elements. A national dilemma is being treated as a public relations issue rather than as a problem that business could help solve. Public schools run by those with an enormous stake in the status quo; suggested positive program; no simple formula.

**DeLoughry, T. J., "President proposes education reforms," *The Chronicle of Higher Education,* April 24, 1991, p. A1.**

Details President George Bush's blueprint for a "populist crusade" to reform U.S. schools. Heavy reliance on the involvement of education leaders, business leaders and scholars; mixed reviews from college officials; the right to choose schools; no additional money for student aid.

**Hoerr, J., "Business shares the blame for workers'**

**low skills," *Business Week,* June 25, 1990, p. 71.**

Describes how businesses and schools are equally sharing the blame for workers' low skills these days. Schools are continuing to turn out poorly educated young people, and employers continue to reject the idea of spending large amounts of money to train workers and upgrade skills. Problems of training people; studies done. INSET: The low priority companies give skills.

**Johnson, J. L., "Essay," *Scientific American,* October 1990, p. 135.**

Opinion. Recommends steps to be taken to improve science education in schools and to avoid the problem of technical illiteracy in U.S. students. Business-sponsored programs in schools; employee training; development of innovative educational programs; examples.

**Lewis, A. C. and Pett, J., "*America* 2000: What kind of nation?" *Phi Delta Kappan,* June 1991, p. 734.**

Evaluates President Bush's new education policy "America 2000: An Education Strategy." Four goals of the proposal; projected impact on school administrators, teachers, researchers, the business community, parents and children; failure to address the needs of the most vulnerable children in society.

**Lewis, A. C., "Business as a real partner," *Phi Delta Kappan,* February 1991, p. 420.**

States that the business community's work in the reform of schools is well intentioned, but that it will not bring about the fundamental changes that the business community says are needed. Transition from school to work; beginnings of an apprenticeship movement.

**Pipho, C., "Business leaders focus on reform," *Phi Delta Kappan,* February 1991, p. 422.**

Contends that the transformation of state education systems through a wide array of reform efforts may have reached a crucial fork in the road. Survey of state reforms; recommendations for reform.

**Shapiro, B., "The wrong choice," *Nation,* May 20, 1991, p. 652.**

Editorial. Denounces President Bush's call for big business to manage the nation's schools. What Bush proposed for school reform; the lack of spending by the United States on education compared with 15 industrialized countries; the disparity between suburban and city schools.

**Stanfield II, J. H., "American businesspeople and the ambivalent transformation of racially segregated public schools," *Phi Delta Kappan,* September 1990, p. 63.**

Analyzes the business community's historical and contemporary interests in schooling and the integral roles businesses play in creating or transforming the racial stratification of public schools.

**Stone, N., "Does business have any business in education?"** *Harvard Business Review,* **March/April 1991, p. 46.**

Asks the fundamental question, "Does business have any business in education?" Focuses on two often unexamined assumptions in the current debate over the quality of the public schools; why business must intervene; basic academic skills lacking in today and tomorrow's workers; problems with business' current efforts at education reform; recommended strategy. INSET: Untitled (list of related publications).

**Szabo, J. C., "Do public schools miss the mark?"** *Nation's Business,* **October 90, p. 37.**

Highlights results of a survey on public attitudes toward education conducted by the Roper Organization for the Center for Workforce Preparation and Quality Education, established by the U.S. Chamber of Commerce. How Americans link businesses and schools; major concerns; response toward suggested reforms. INSET: Helping business in education reform.

**Waddell, G., "Preparing workers for century 21,"** *Education Digest,* **December 1990, p. 62.**

Discusses the trends now affecting work force training needs and how community colleges need to make additional efforts to meet growing business needs. Gives examples of successful, innovative programs colleges are using to train workers for the 21st century.

## *Economic aspects*

**"Skills lacking for tomorrow's jobs,"** *USA Today,* **December 1990, p. 12.**

Observes that many of present and future members of the American work force are lacking the necessary skills for tomorrow's jobs. Current trends that will affect the U.S. education system in the near future; importance of business contributions to educational reform.

**Jacob, J. E., "Developing productive people,"** *Vital Speeches,* **Aug. 1, 1991, p. 623.**

Presents a speech by John E. Jacob, "Developing Productive People," delivered to the American Assembly of Collegiate Schools of Business in St. Louis, Mo., on April 22, 1991, dealing with the issue of education and social issues critical to business.

## *International aspects*

**Baggott, J., "The customer is always right,"** *New Sci-*

*entist,* **Aug. 3, 1991, Vol. 131 Issue 1780, p. 46.**

Presents the author's perceptions of what would happen if the British system for science education were run according to business principles. The British Association for the Advancement of Science and the establishment of a National Commission on Education; grant from the Paul Hamlyn Foundation; review of the A-level system; more.

**Hamilton, S. F., "Apprenticeship in Germany: How can we use it here?"** *Education Digest,* **February 1991, p. 22.**

Describes the system of apprenticeship in West Germany, and examines how it might be implemented in the United States. Schooling and worksite experience; tracking effects of apprenticeship; some U.S. programs that resemble West German apprenticeship; opportunities offered by apprenticeships; guidelines for setting up an apprenticeship-type program; cooperation with business.

**Massey, A. T., "In break with past, many Soviet institutions of higher education plan to impose tuition,"** *The Chronicle of Higher Education,* **July 17, 1991, p. A29.**

Details a Soviet Council of Ministers authorization aimed at granting more independence to academic institutions that will allow tuition charges as part of contractual arrangements with business enterprises who agree to subsidize future employees. Many universities to charge students tuition who have no outside sources of financial support; expected change in the demographics of the schools.

# Back Issues

*Great Research on Current Issues Starts Right Here... Recent topics covered by The CQ Researcher are listed below. Issues dated before May 10, 1991, were published under the name of Editorial Research Reports.*

**MAY 1990**
Should Teaching Be a Profession?
Will Canada Fall Apart?
Is U.S. Patent System Outdated?
Federal Funding for the Arts

**JUNE 1990**
Downsizing America's Armed Forces
Progress In Weather Forecasting
S & L Bailout
Bio-Chemical Disarmament

**JULY 1990**
Do Americans Still Love Marriage?
Death Penalty Debate
Decline of Rural America
United Nations in the 1990s

**AUGUST 1990**
Democracy in the Philippines
Initiatives: True Democracy?
Hard Times at Newspapers
Teens Balance School & Jobs

**SEPTEMBER 1990**
Dangers of Alcohol
Western Alliance After the Cold War
Tobacco Industry
Right to Die

**OCTOBER 1990**
Organ Transplants
Energy Policy Options
Search for Arab Unity
Child Support

**NOVEMBER 1990**
Lotteries and Gambling
Post Cold-War Choices
Setting Limits on Medical Care
Multicultural Education

**DECEMBER 1990**
Cable TV Regulation
Americans' Search For Their Roots
Is Insurance System a Failure?
Why Schools Still Have Tracking

**JANUARY 1991**
Growing Influence of Boycotts
Should the U.S. Reinstate the Draft?
America's Archaeological Past
Peace Corps' Challenges in '90s

**FEBRUARY 1991**
Regional Impact of Recession
Puerto Rico's Status
Redistricting: Mapping Power
Nuclear Power

**MARCH 1991**
Acid Rain
Cost of the Gulf War
Reassessing Gun Laws
Future for Man in Space

**APRIL 1991**
Social Security
Canadian Crisis Over Quebec
California Drought
Electromagnetic Radiation

**MAY 1991**
School Choice
Racial Quotas
Animal Rights
U.S. and Japan

**JUNE 1991**
Children and Divorce
Teenage Suicide
Endangered Species
Europe 1992

**JULY 1991**
Teenagers and Abortion
Soviet Republics Rebel
Mexico's Emergence
Athletes and Drugs

**AUGUST 1991**
Sexual Harassment
Fetal Tissue Research
Oil Imports
The Palestinians

**SEPTEMBER 1991**
Police Brutality
Advertising Under Attack
Saving the Forests
Foster Care Crisis

**OCTOBER 1991**
Pay-Per-View TV
Youth Gangs
Gene Therapy
World Hunger

**NOVEMBER 1991**
Fast-Food Shake-Up
The Greening of Eastern Europe

Back issues are available for $4.00 (subscribers) or $7.00 (non-subscribers). Quantity discounts apply to orders over ten. To order, call Congressional Quarterly 1-800-432-2250.

# Future Topics

▶ *Cuba in Crisis*

▶ *Retiree Medical Benefits*

▶ *Asian Americans*

# THE CQ Researcher

PUBLISHED BY CONGRESSIONAL QUARTERLY INC., IN CONJUNCTION WITH EBSCO PUBLISHING

# Cuba In Crisis

*Will Fidel Castro share the fate of other Communist leaders?*

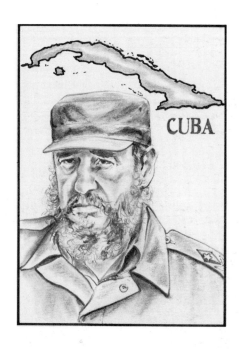

CUBA

A DECADE AGO CUBAN PRESIDENT FIDEL CASTRO was a leader of almost mythical proportion. Today, with the worldwide collapse of Communism and the loss of the Soviet Union as Havana's chief patron, Cuba is at a crossroads. With few reliable trading partners and even fewer political allies, Castro faces the most serious challenge of his 33-year rule. Thus far, his answer has been an odd mix of anti-capitalist rhetoric, subtle efforts to lure foreign investors and not-so-subtle political repression. Whether the aging guerrilla leader will be able to salvage his country — and its revolution — will depend on many factors, including U.S. policy. For its part, Washington is trying to isolate Castro and accelerate his demise, raising the prospect of a popular rebellion or overthrow attempt.

CQ **November 29, 1991 • Volume 1, No. 28 • 897-920**

*Formerly Editorial Research Reports*

COVER ART: BARBARA SASSA-DANIELS

# CQ Researcher

November 29, 1991
Volume 1, No. 28

**EDITOR**
Sandra Stencel

**MANAGING EDITOR**
Thomas J. Colin

**ASSOCIATE EDITOR**
Richard L. Worsnop

**STAFF WRITERS**
Charles S. Clark
Mary H. Cooper
Rodman D. Griffin

**PRODUCTION EDITOR**
Laurie De Maris

**EDITORIAL ASSISTANT**
Thomas H. Moore

**GRAPHICS**
Jack Auldridge

**PUBLISHED BY**
Congressional Quarterly Inc.

**CHAIRMAN**
Andrew Barnes

**VICE CHAIRMAN**
Andrew P. Corty

**EDITOR AND PUBLISHER**
Neil Skene

**EXECUTIVE EDITOR**
Robert W. Merry

**PUBLICATIONS MARKETING/SALES**
Robert Smith

**EDITOR, EBSCO PUBLISHING**
Melissa Kummerer

The CQ Researcher (ISSN 1056-2036). Formerly Editorial Research Reports. Published weekly (48 times per year, not printed the first Friday of any month with five Fridays) by Congressional Quarterly Inc., 1414 22nd St., N.W., Washington, D.C. 20037. Rates are furnished upon request. Application to mail at second-class postage rates is pending at Washington, D.C. POSTMASTER: Send address changes to The CQ Researcher, 1414 22nd St., N.W., Washington, D.C. 20037.

# Cuba In Crisis

By Rodman D. Griffin

## THE ISSUES

In Cuba, the Western Hemisphere's last bastion of Marxism-Leninism, billboards promote Communism, not consumerism. The first thing a visitor sees after the airplane lands at Havana's José Martí Airport is a giant broadside proclaiming *Socialismo o muerte* — Socialism or death. The bleak choice underscores Cuba's current crisis. As the countries of Eastern Europe and Latin America have succumbed one by one to the winds of democracy and the free market, Cuban President Fidel Castro has stood defiant and uncompromising.

"We are going to defend ourselves alone, surrounded by an ocean of capitalism," Castro declared in a five-hour speech at Cuba's Fourth Communist Party Congress in October.* "Our greatest historical responsibility is the fight for our ideas, which is the fight of all the exploited, subjugated, hungry people of the world. They are not simply ideas. They are our destiny, our independence, our revolution."

Such platitudes may have satisfied the 1,800 party stalwarts who attended the five-day conference, but they will do little to cure Cuba's multiple ills. The country's highly centralized and grossly inefficient economy is crumbling. The extent of the malaise became all too apparent to average Cubans last January when a single Soviet ship carrying grain and flour showed up behind schedule, forcing the Cuban government to cut bread rations and raise the price of eggs by 50 percent. "We can't eat pride," lamented one Cuban at the time.[1]

CUBA

At stake is not only the shape of Castro's revolution but also its survival in a world turned upside down. Cuba, an island of 10.7 million people that for three decades has defied American power and pressure and stood as a beacon for Latin leftists and Third World revolutionaries, has become a crippled icon, staggering grimly toward economic despair and social chaos. "Not only is there no light at the end of the tunnel," commented one Western diplomat, "but the light inside the tunnel has now been switched off."

Determined to end the hemorrhaging of his own country's economy, and hopeful of gaining U.S. aid, Soviet President Mikhail S. Gorbachev has decided to pull the plug on Cuba. This September he announced the planned withdrawal of 11,000 Soviet military personnel from the island and signaled the end of Cuba's $1.5 billion trade subsidy, already down from $4 billion in 1988.[2]

Since the early 1960s Cuba has depended on barter with the former Soviet bloc for roughly 85 percent of

its trade, including nearly all of its oil. Soviet oil deliveries fell 20 percent last year and may slip even further this year.*

Without the Soviet lifeline, experts say the Cuban economy, which was already sputtering, may be doomed. "People were willing to live at a subsistence level so long as there was a safety net — the Soviet Union," says Susan Kaufman Purcell, vice president for Latin American affairs at the New York-based Americas Society. "Now the future is totally uncertain. I don't see how this can go on for another year."

Over a year ago, Castro began preparing for a possible Soviet pullout, instituting an emergency program called the "special period in peacetime," which blends wrenching economic austerity with redoubled efforts at political control and mobilization. The special period calls for an all-out effort to cut fuel consumption and to solve food shortages by increasing domestic agricultural output. Cuban officials have begun moving thousands of city dwellers to the countryside to boost food production. Factories have been closed to save fuel. Ships in the harbor are being loaded and unloaded by hand instead of cranes. Oxen are replacing tractors. And some 750,000 bicycles have been imported from China to replace buses and taxis.

In one of the country's many paradoxes, the special period also includes a massive effort to boost foreign-currency earnings by attracting tourism and specialized foreign investment — activities that blatantly contradict Castro's strident rhetoric.

Politically and economically isolated, the regime is calling for extraordi-

---

*The Cuban Communist Party Congress meets every five to 10 years to discuss party strategy and set policy for the next several years.

*As of October, Cuba had received less than half of the 10 million tons of Soviet oil it was scheduled to receive in 1991.

nary sacrifice from citizens already weary of long lines, scarcity and general dilapidation. In recent months, as the list of rationed goods has swollen, new limits have been placed on everyday items like tobacco, soap, gasoline and cooking fuels. The lack of spare parts for 5,000 Hungarian buses has idled much of Cuba's public transport fleet, and the shortage of Czech tires for cane-cutting machines has slowed the sugar harvest.

Castro's political stock also seems to be nearing depletion. The ouster of Panama's Gen. Manuel Antonio Noriega in 1989 and the 1990 electoral defeat of the Sandinistas in Nicaragua have deprived Castro of his last remaining strategic allies. The election in Nicaragua, coupled with the defeat of Gen. Augusto Pinochet and his anointed successors in Chile, has left Castro groping to explain why in Cuba alone it is unnecessary to vote.

So far, Cubans seem disinclined to duplicate Eastern Europe's overthrow of socialism. No angry demonstrations fill the plazas, no anti-Castro graffiti appears on the walls, no evident spark is about to ignite an uprising. But if the economy deteriorates much further, and most Western experts predict that it will, Castro could be in trouble.

Already this year more than 1,900 Cubans, mostly young people, have fled to Florida aboard rubber tires, wooden rafts and makeshift boats — four times the total of all of last year.[3] The U.S. Coast Guard estimates that half that many may have perished in the treacherous Straits of Florida. In a country that suppresses free expression, the frenzied rush to exit is perhaps the most tangible measurement of the simmering discontent.

Castro's conundrum is that while nothing less than a radical overhaul of the nation's economy can reverse its free fall, renunciation of state-run economics could trigger a political

chain reaction with unpredictable consequences. Castro fears the creation of a broad political opposition and a serious challenge to Cuba's one-party rule. As experts watch events unfold in Cuba, here are some of the questions they are asking:

### Will Cuba be the next Communist domino to fall?

Given the loss of its chief patron, the Soviet Union, U.S. officials believe the fall of Cuba's current government is inevitable. "The system is a dinosaur in today's world," says Bernard Aronson, U.S. assistant secretary of State for the Western Hemisphere. "When and how it will change you can't predict, but it *will* change."

Many in the Cuban-American exile community are convinced that change will happen sooner rather than later. "In a few months, days, at any moment, there will be a revolt in Cuba," says José Carreño, a political prisoner in Cuba for 16 years and now news producer at WQBA, a commercial radio station in Miami.

"The failed Soviet coup attempt ... has intensified the march toward freedom and democracy in Cuba," adds José Cárdenas, research director of the powerful Cuban American National Foundation, which has already begun drafting suggestions for revisions to the Cuban Constitution. The Kiwanis Club of Little Havana in Miami has even gone so far as to plan a *Cuba libre* celebration at the Orange Bowl.

Such exuberance, of course, could be misplaced. Miami's Cuban-American community has been predicting "Christmas in Havana" for years. More to the point, parallels with Eastern Europe are misleading. Whereas socialism was imposed by Soviet force in Poland, Hungary and Czechoslovakia, Castro's rule came as a nationalist reaction to the brutal dictatorship of Fulgencio Batista.

Many Cubans can recall their

own sacrifices in the fight against Batista, and those who can't are constantly reminded of what others suffered in the revolution and its aftermath. Fidel Castro is inseparable from the Cuban revolution. In fact, Cubans call themselves *'fidelista'* much more often than *'comunista'* or *'socialista.'*

And although the Cuban leadership has lost much popular support, few Cubans openly criticize Castro personally, and most experts contend the regime still probably has more backing than most of its Communist counterparts in Eastern Europe before the reforms. "Castro is still very entrenched in Cuba," says Cristina Garcia, a Cuban-American author in Los Angeles. "People may be dissatisfied, but there is still a deep personal loyalty for Fidel. He is Cuba's Teflon president."

Furthermore, neither Cuba's Catholic Church nor trade unions have the strength of these institutions in Poland. And economic reform in Cuba never led to the degree of domestic liberalization and contacts with the West as in Hungary and Poland. Moreover, Gorbachev's declaration that he would not intervene militarily in Eastern Europe to halt reform was seen as a green light to move; Soviet troops have never been a factor in Cuba.

"The government is certainly going through a major crisis," says Ramón Cernuda, a U.S. representative for a coalition of four anti-Castro organizations in Cuba. "There is a growing dissident movement and discontent among the young people. But that doesn't mean the government will fall tomorrow. There is a strong nationalist sentiment in Cuba — and there is still the military."

The significance of Castro's traditional role as David to the U.S. Goliath cannot be ignored. The U.S.-backed Bay of Pigs invasion in 1961, the CIA's assassination schemes against Castro in the early 1960s and the ongoing economic embargo* have all helped Castro to justify his continued demands for revolutionary sacrifice and vigilance. An exceedingly nationalistic people, Cubans reportedly were horrified by the U.S. invasion of Panama in December 1989 and fear that Cuba could be next.

Experts say the majority of Cubans, while hopeful for changes, seem prepared — or resigned — to trust Castro to make them. This is not surprising since many of them can argue, as Eastern Europeans cannot, that they are better off now than before the revolution. For all its shortcomings, Castro's regime has provided Cubans with free housing, health care and education and a small, but guaranteed, income. Using these measuring sticks, Cubans fare better than many of their Latin American neighbors. The island is among the 20 nations in the world with the lowest infant mortality, and among Third World nations it has the highest literacy rate, the highest doctor-patient ratio and the longest life expectancy.

For the moment, the consensus among most experts is that the Castro regime is not on the brink of collapse. "The situation is fraught with dangers [for Cuba]," says Andrew Zimbalist, an economist and Cuba expert at Smith College. "But the analogy that Cuba is a house of cards about to come tumbling down isn't apt. It's a house of iron. But that doesn't mean the people inside the house are happy."

### What political alternatives are there to Castro?

If conditions are bleak in Cuba, the alternatives appear even bleaker

*The embargo was imposed in 1962. For details, see p. 905.

as Cubans scan the horizon. "If we had capitalism, it would be the capitalism of Haiti, El Salvador and Honduras, not of the United States and France," says Dr. Jaime Bernaza, a kidney specialist and 25-year member of the Cuban Communist Party. "We do not have what a consumer society has, but we have the necessities." [4]

"Even those who were enthusias-

> **Experts say the majority of Cubans, while hopeful for changes, seem prepared — or resigned — to trust Castro to make them. This is not surprising since many of them can argue, as Eastern Europeans cannot, that they are better off now than before the revolution.**

tic about *perestroika* are now beginning to wonder as they look at Eastern Europe, which has 40 percent unemployment," says Alicia Torres, executive director of the Cuban American Committee Research and Education Fund, a Washington lobby group that favors closer U.S.-Cuban relations. "That is not an alternative many Cubans want."

An obvious impediment to change in Cuba has been the lack of an organized political opposition. "Castro has so dominated the political landscape for 30 years that even those who disagree with him don't see an alternative," says Wayne Smith, former head of the U.S. Interests Section in Havana and now director of

the Cuban Studies Program at Johns Hopkins University.

"There is no Boris Yeltsin in Cuba and no organization that could mobilize the opposition," adds William LeoGrande, a political scientist at American University in Washington. "Cuba thus far has no mass-opposition movement comparable to Solidarity or the Catholic Church in Poland, or the intellectuals in Czechoslovakia. It has been able to prevent a credible focal point of opposition from coalescing."

One of the effects of Cuba's Communist Party monopoly and absolutist political culture has been to give critics of the government and independent thinkers two options: silence or exile. Some 10 percent of the population — most of whom would have been part of an internal opposition — now live in exile. *(See story, p. 908.)* Moreover, the relaxation of emigration restrictions over the past four years has enabled Castro to rid his country of potential opponents. Recently he lowered the minimum age for exit visas from 60 to 20, inspiring the largest migration since 1980.*

The role the exile community will play in fostering or abetting change in Cuba is itself a contentious issue. Ever since the Bay of Pigs invasion, when some 1,200 U.S.-backed exiles invaded the island in an unsuccessful attempt to oust Castro, Cuba has used the prospect of invasion to stir nationalist fervor. "Although some in the conservative exile community dream of returning to power in Havana, that is an illusion," says Torres. "The future leaders will come from

*In late July, the U.S. State Department suspended applications for visitor visas after issuing 40,000. Roughly one-third of the Cubans who come to the United States on visitor visas never return to Cuba.

inside the country."

The problem, of course, is that Cuban society has become atomized, crippled by a limited tradition of representative government and years of systematic political policing. On every block, a Committee for the Defense of the Revolution reportedly takes notes on all suspicious behavior and the comings and goings of all visitors. "If I had to use one word to describe the Cuban people," a senior Roman Catholic official noted recently, "it would be fear. We have no leaders."[5]

After a brief liberalization that allowed dissident groups more freedom to organize and operate in 1987 and 1988, the government has stifled internal dissent and all but silenced the island's incipient human rights movement. Today open opposition is limited to about 15 small human rights and political groups that are often harassed by the regime. As Communist governments abroad have fallen, and conditions inside Cuba have worsened, Castro has clamped down even harder. "The political repression and human rights situation has deteriorated since the changes in the Soviet Union," says Ramón Cernuda. Before 1988, Cuba had more political prisoners per capita than Augusto Pinochet's repressive regime in Chile.

At the same time, it is not entirely clear that Cubans want a U.S.-style democracy. "The key thing is putting bread on the table," says Wayne Smith. "No one in Cuba is talking about democratic elections. They want a more open political system, but a multi-party system is not one of the top five items on anyone's agenda."

Realistically, the most palpable alternative to Castro in the short term is the military, one of the largest, most experienced and well-disciplined in Latin America. But just as Castro lacks prominent opposition outside the government, no one inside the regime appears conspicu-

ously ready or willing to fill his shoes. Within the last two years, Castro has installed trusted top army commanders, all of whom fought at his side in the revolution, in the most critical government positions. And unlike in Romania, military experts say there seems to be no split in Cuba between the armed forces and the security police. "The military has been remarkably loyal to Castro," says Jorge Domínguez of Harvard University, a leading Cuba expert. "I don't see a coup coalition in the making."

### What are the chances for normalizing relations between Cuba and the United States?

Since the late 1970s, the principal U.S. conditions for improving bilateral relations were that Cuba: 1) begin to remove its troops from Africa; 2) not support efforts to overthrow other governments in this hemisphere; 3) reduce its ties with the Soviet Union; and 4) show greater respect for human rights — especially by releasing political prisoners.[6]

Over the last couple of years the global picture has changed dramatically. The end of the Cold War, the collapse of communism in Eastern Europe and growing accommodation between the United States and the Soviet Union have all had a big impact on Cuba. The Cuban-Soviet relationship, long seen as a security threat to the United States, is itself in a state of steady disintegration. In addition, Cuba is out of Africa and apparently not supporting revolutionary forces in the hemisphere, including the guerrilla insurgency in El Salvador.* Finally, though Cuba's human rights record is spotty, the State Department's own report for 1988 acknowledged that the situation had improved.

---

*The Cuban government officially supports negotiations between the Salvadoran rebels and the U.S.-backed government.

In a 1988 poll, 51 percent of Americans favored normalizing relations between Cuba and the United States, compared with 31 percent against.[7] Nevertheless, experts say the prospects for normalization are minimal. In fact, in March 1990 President Bush ratcheted up the requirements for any re-engagement between the two countries. Now, Bush said, Cuba must first have a market economy; second, hold fully democratic, internationally supervised elections; and third, reduce its armed forces.

The shrinking of the Soviet-Cuban relationship does pose some delicate questions for U.S. policy-makers. Already some Latin American leaders are urging Washington to relax its economic embargo of Cuba in response to the recent changes — and some in the United States have argued for the same thing to prevent another mass exodus of Cubans from pouring into Florida, recalling the 129,000 refugees who arrived via the 1980 Mariel boatlift and caused severe problems in South Florida.

"One aspect of the embargo that is remarkably dumb deals with communications," says Domínguez. "Not only should the U.S. stop preventing [companies like] AT&T from modernizing communication links to Cuba, we should be donating fax machines to Cuba. It is ridiculous to support Castro's blockade of information. We should allow U.S. citizens to visit Cuba, to tell them there is a better way."

Critics of the current U.S. policy argue that the administration is guilty of moving the goal posts to suit an ineffective — and outdated — anti-Castro agenda. "The United States would lose nothing by trying engagement," says Smith. "It should deal at least as pragmatically with Cuba as it does with China and South Africa, which suffer some of the same defects as does Cuba."

*Continued on p. 904*

# The Castro Mystique: Crusader and Pragmatist

He is a man Americans love to hate, an enduring symbol of totalitarianism whose full beard and olive-green fatigues seem to shout Karl Marx and revolution for export. In a 1988 survey of U.S. public opinion, 85 percent of those responding had an "unfavorable" impression of Fidel Castro — putting him neck and neck with Libya's Muammar el-Qaddafi for dead last.†

The fact that Castro is reviled by so many Americans probably enhances rather than diminishes his stature. More important, a majority of Cubans still revere him, despite his country's repressive regime and woeful economy.

No reigning leader in the Third World — perhaps the entire world — has compiled such impressive accomplishments. Castro reached power with heroic status and without foreign help, gained enormous worldwide influence with his revolutionary fervor and declarations of autonomy and at one time had troops in Angola, Yemen, Ethiopia and Vietnam. The Soviet Union and the United States treated him as a power to be reckoned with.

"Without Fidel Castro's advice and support, there would have been no Nicaraguan Sandinistas, no invasion of Grenada, no guerrilla movements from El Salvador to Uruguay to Chile, no destruction of democracy in [Argentina and Chile], no Marxist Angola, Mozambique, or Ethiopia," writes syndicated columnist Georgie Anne Geyer in a recent — and highly critical — biography. "In short, he devised virtually every twentieth-century technique with which the weak now fought the strong. From 1959 on, wherever the United States had a watershed foreign-policy crisis, Castro's formative hand could be found." ††

Born on Aug. 13, 1926, the son of wealthy sugar plantation owners who had emigrated to Cuba from Spain, Castro became a lawyer and was involved in politics from a young age. From the beginning he has seemed impervious to fear — and either destined for glory or the grave. In 1953, in his trial following the failed attack he led on Moncada Barracks, an outpost of the Batista dictatorship, Castro declared defiantly, "Condemn me, it does not matter! History will absolve me!"

Granted clemency after serving two years of his 15-year sentence, Castro went into exile in Mexico where he continued planning for Batista's overthrow, which he eventually engineered in 1959. Initially, at least, Castro was far from being a Marxist; instead he belonged to Cuba's vague populist political tradition. José Martí and Eduardo Chibás — the forerunners of this tradition — had called for the elimination of political corruption, an end to Cuba's dependence on sugar and the development of a nationalist identity.

Castro is a man of action, of tactics, of strategies. He declared himself a socialist the day before the Bay of Pigs invasion, which he knew was coming, and has cloaked the revolution in socialism ever since. "Fidel is not a doctrinaire ideologue," says Mike Mazarr, a Cuba expert at the Center for Strategic and International Studies in Washington. "He adapts to circumstances as they develop. He's always been a Castroist, first and foremost."

"Castro is an extremely talented leader ... who is driven by profound hatred of the United States," adds Susan Kaufman Purcell at the New York-based Americas Society. "He has an uncanny knack for tapping into vulnerabilities and insecurities of the Cuban people."

Given his ambition and ego, analysts say, it is difficult to imagine that he would ever have been content to play exclusively on a small domestic stage. Commenting on Castro's "Messiah complex," Herbert Matthews, one of Castro's most sympathetic chroniclers, wrote: "Fidel has all along felt himself to be a crusader, if not a savior. He is out to achieve a second liberation of Latin America."‡

That clearly failed, as has economic socialism, but Castro has still managed to hold on. Fueling his staying power is his fanatical resolve, which has carried him through the initial six-year struggle against Batista and the subsequent three decades of U.S. economic warfare and CIA assassination plots. But Castro turned 65 this summer, and he has taken to expressing his will more and more apocalyptically. It's been a long, dark journey from his pre-revolutionary cry, "History will absolve me," to "Socialism or death."

Beyond the mystique of Castro as hero, two fears sustain his power: fear of repression and fear of change. Today, Castro is more entrenched and isolated than at the start of his rule. Just as he molded the revolution, he could as easily choreograph its collapse.

The question now is whether he can adapt to the modern world and accept a lesser global role. When China's Mao Tse-tung found his "revolutionary immortality" fading away, he launched the horrendous Cultural Revolution, destroying an entire generation of intellectuals. Will Castro do the same? Probably not. His biographers say he has always been more the pragmatist and less the ideologue. That explains how he can stridently denounce capitalism, yet attempt to lure foreign investment to Cuba.

Of course, Castro's actions are never to be counted on — and he is never to be counted out. "Castro's career has been marked by numerous sharp turns in both domestic and foreign policy," notes Douglas Payne of Freedom House, a conservative think tank. "The possibility cannot be excluded that he might suddenly declare himself a champion of *perestroika* and swear, in typically egotistical fashion, his *perestroika* is the best."

---

† Poll cited in *U.S. News & World Report,* Jan. 9, 1989, p. 37.
†† Georgie Anne Geyer, *Guerrilla Prince: The Untold Story of Fidel Castro* (1991), p. 4.
‡ Herbert Matthews, *The Cuban Story* (1961), p. 191.

## Cuba At A Glance

**Population:** 10.7 million

**Total Area:** 44,220 square miles

**Capital:** Havana

**Armed Forces:** 180,500 in mid-1990, of whom 79,500 were conscripts. In 1991, in an effort to save money, compulsory military service was cut from three years to two.

**Infant Mortality Rate:** 10.7 per 1,000 live births. Cuba is the only Latin American country to have been included by UNICEF in the category of countries with the lowest infant mortality rates in the world, on par with the industrialized nations.

**Life Expectancy:** 76, the highest in Latin America

**Illiteracy Rate:** 1.9 percent

**Principal Export:** Sugar accounts for about 75 percent of Cuba's exports. Cuba produces 7 percent of world sugar output and is the world's largest exporter.

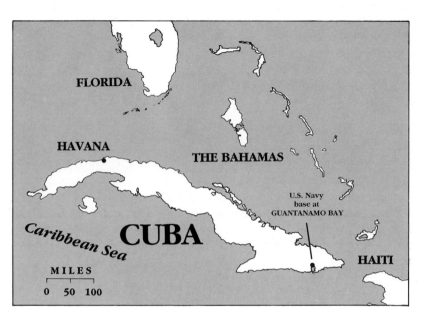

*Sources: The Economist Intelligence Unit,* Cuba: Country Profile 1991-92; *Population Reference Bureau.*

*Continued from p. 902*

Smith concedes, however, that such a policy shift is unlikely. "First, the administration sees no constituency advocating more open, relaxed relations with Cuba," he says. "There would be no collective heartache if Castro withers. In fact, a policy turnaround might alienate the right-wing exile community. And second, the administration has an emotional quest to see Castro's head delivered on a platter."

The crisis in Cuba has enlivened the debate between those who say it is time to tighten the screws to quicken Castro's fall and those who want to open dialogue to ease peaceful transformation rather than to push for violent transformation. *(See At Issue, p. 913.)*

For his part, President Bush is dismissing calls for a gentler Cuba policy but so far has also resisted calls to tighten the embargo. "Let me tell you something," he said in a speech in October. "I'm not going to change [our policy] one single bit." [8] The United States, having intensified its longstanding goal of keeping Castro isolated and under pressure, seems to have given up hope for a peaceful transition to democracy. "We can't manage the change," explains one State Department official. "We just have to wait for it." ∎

# BACKGROUND

## Cuban Revolution

The Cuban Revolution is often viewed as having begun on Jan. 2, 1959, when Fidel Castro and his guerrillas marched triumphantly into Havana after forcing dictator Fulgencio Batista to flee to the Dominican Republic. In fact, the origins of the revolution go back to Cuba's fight against 400 years of Spanish colonial occupation and some 60 years of U.S. domination.

Similarly, the revolution cannot be reduced to a single and superficial factor — such as Castro's charisma, Communist ideology or U.S. hostility. Rather, it is the combination of all of these things, conspiring with the collective will of the Cuban people, that enabled the revolution to occur — and to endure three decades of U.S. pressure and growing isolation.

Inspired by Simón Bolívar's 19th-century struggle for national liberation throughout the hemisphere, and, late in the century, by José Martí's vision for an independent Cuba, Cubans fought two wars of independence with Spain, in 1868 and 1895. But though the Cubans won the long and bloody conflict, they lost their struggle for nationhood when, in 1902, the United States transformed the island from a colony to a protectorate.

### U.S. Protectorate

Back in 1823, when the Monroe Doctrine was proclaimed to limit European influence in the Western Hemisphere, John Quincy Adams declared that Cuba had "an importance in the sum of our national interests, with which that of no other foreign territory can be compared." He described it as a "ripening apple" that "cannot choose but to fall to the ground."[9] By the end of the century, the United States was not about to let Spain's receding empire interfere with its evolving sphere of influence. Following its victory in the Spanish-American War of 1898, the U.S. plucked Cuba from Spain's domain.

Ever since, Cuba and the United States have shared a large part of their respective histories. The United States occupied the island from 1898 to 1902 and from 1906 to 1909. It maintained a formal "protectorate" there from 1902 to 1934, landing troops seven times during those years. As one legacy, the United States continues to operate a military base at Guantanamo under a treaty that has no termination date. In addition, the U.S. government and U.S. private firms played a significant role in Cuba's domestic affairs throughout the first half of the century. Between 1909 and 1929, U.S. capital investments in Cuba increased sevenfold.[10]

U.S. investments and tutelage, however, did virtually nothing to change Cuba's stratified class structure. As a result, Cubans fared little better under Washington's watchful eye than they had under Spain. Declining economic conditions in the 1920s, corruption and repression by the local government and recurring U.S. intervention spawned a new generation of reformers and revolutionaries. Their rejection of foreign domination and demands for worker reforms led to the Revolution of 1933, which fostered some economic and social progress and an increased state role in economic affairs. At the same time, however, it gave the Cubans a taste of nationalism.

### Batista Overthrown

Unfortunately, the reforms did not hold. Faced with the prospect of losing an election, Fulgencio Batista, an army officer and former president, abrogated the constitution and staged a military coup on March 10, 1952. After a quixotic six-year struggle, Fidel Castro, a young, charismatic lawyer, led a guerrilla force called the Movement of July 26* that ultimately overturned Batista's brutal and corrupt dictatorship in 1959.

The young revolutionaries, driven more by Cuban nationalism than Marxism-Leninism, proclaimed armed insurrection the only viable path toward full national and social liberation. But their triumph in 1959 did not end the revolutionary process. While the victory closed the country to foreign domination and led to improved living standards, it also ushered in an era of totalitarianism and political repression — and exacerbated relations with the United States.

## U.S. Pressure

Initially, Castro reasserted his independence of the United States but maintained diplomatic relations. By early 1960, however, it was clear the honeymoon wouldn't last. A high-level Soviet mission had visited the island in February, and U.S. public opinion had begun to shift against the new Cuban government, inspired by "show" trials of former Batista soldiers* and press reports that Cuba might become socialist. That summer, the United States ordered American oil companies in Cuba not to refine any crude oil from the Soviet Union. Castro retaliated by nationalizing the refineries, and soon thereafter the United States canceled the quota on Cuban sugar, cutting off the U.S. market.

On Jan. 3, 1961, President Dwight D. Eisenhower formally broke off relations with Cuba, 10 months after he had authorized preparations for an invasion of the island by some 1,200 Cuban exiles who were trained and supplied by the CIA. In the ill-fated Bay of Pigs invasion, which began on April 17, 1961 — three months after John F. Kennedy took office as president — invading forces were routed within 72 hours.

Most experts agree that U.S. support for the invasion — and then the failure to act decisively to ensure its success — gave the Soviets a green light in Cuba. "The Bay of Pigs fiasco was the single most important event that encouraged and accelerated Soviet involvement in Cuba," says Jaime Suchlicki, executive director of the North-South Center at the University of Miami. The bungled invasion damaged U.S. credibility in the hemisphere and legitimized Castro's revolution. In addition, the subsequent repression of dissenters inside Cuba stunted the growth of a significant organized opposition.

Following the debacle, the United States turned to other methods of dealing with Cuba, even sanctioning CIA attempts to assassinate Castro. On the diplomatic front, the govern-

---

*The Movement of July 26 is named after a band of less than 200 rebels who on July 26, 1953, attacked Moncada Barracks, a military base in eastern Cuba. The attack failed but inspired popular support for the revolution and recognition for Castro.

---

*More than 600 Batista soldiers were executed.

ment sought to isolate the Cuban regime and strangle it economically. Washington pressured its allies throughout the world to reduce their commerce with Cuba and instituted a full embargo in 1962.[11]

In the Organization of American States (OAS), the United States forced the suspension of Cuban membership by a slim majority in January 1962. Furthermore, all OAS countries that had not already done so severed diplomatic relations with Cuba — except Canada and Mexico, which refused to bow to U.S. pressure.

## Soviet Friendship

Meanwhile, the Soviet Union moved quickly to solidify its strategic relationship with Castro. New trade and cultural agreements were signed, and increased economic and technical aid was sent to Cuba. By mid-1962, at the height of the Cold War, the Soviets embarked on a dangerous gamble by surreptitiously introducing nuclear missiles and bombers onto the island.

On Oct. 22, President Kennedy confronted the Soviet challenge, instituting a blockade of the island and demanding the withdrawal of all offensive weapons. With the world watching the tense standoff, Soviet Premier Nikita S. Khrushchev blinked and ordered the missiles removed, but only after gaining Kennedy's assurance that the United States would not invade Cuba.

"It is ironic that the crisis — hailed at the time as a U.S. victory — was nothing more than an ephemeral victory," writes Suchlicki. "In return for the removal of offensive weapons from the island, the United States was satisfied to accept a Communist regime only a few miles from its shores."[12]

From Havana's perspective, the Soviet alliance provided security from the threat of U.S. intervention. But Castro also effectively used the Cold War to catapult his personal agenda onto the international stage.

As Jorge Domínguez has noted, massive Soviet support over the next three decades has enabled this small country to have a big foreign policy. Indeed, Cuba has had international power and prestige that far exceeded the scope of its economic or military might.

### Exporting Revolution

During most of the 1960s, Castro's stated goal was to turn the Andes into Latin America's own Sierra Maestra, the mountains from which Castro launched his revolution in 1959. In the Second Declaration of Havana in 1962, Castro virtually declared war on the other governments of the hemisphere and vowed to lend support to guerrillas anywhere and everywhere.

Cubans were in the Congo in the early 1960s, in the Middle East during the 1973 Yom Kippur War and in revolutionary insurgencies throughout Latin America, the most famous being Che Guevara's failed 1967 campaign in Bolivia. Some 250,000 Cubans saw combat in Angola between 1975 and 1989, and tens of thousands more in Ethiopia. In all, Cuban soldiers fought in 17 African nations.[13]

As Cuban forces fanned the globe, Castro's international prestige soared in the Third World. In 1961 Cuba was the only Latin American country among the 25 founding members of the Nonaligned Movement (which Castro later chaired).

Needless to say, Cuba's export of revolution served Soviet interests and bridled U.S. policy-makers, who were concerned about the spread of communism in the hemisphere — most recently in Grenada, Nicaragua and El Salvador. Castro became America's *bête noire,* and for most of the past 30 years prevention of "another Cuba" has been *the* principal goal behind U.S. policy in the hemisphere.

The arrival of Jimmy Carter in the White House in 1977 heralded an attempt to normalize relations between the two countries. But though official "interest sections" were established in Washington and Havana in 1977,* relations improved only marginally. One major setback came in 1980 when Castro temporarily lifted restrictions on emigration and opened the port of Mariel, allowing some 129,000 disgruntled Cubans to flee the island. This includeed 2,700 "undesirables" — common criminals and the mentally disturbed. The Mariel boatlift, as it is called, caused economic and social havoc in South Florida.

During the last two years of the Reagan administration, there again was some movement toward negotiating U.S. differences with Cuba. An immigration agreement was restored in 1987;** talks were begun on an array of broadcasting problems; and, most important, agreement was reached in 1988 on withdrawing Cuban troops from Angola and creating an independent Namibia. At the time, many experts believed the incoming Bush administration would expand the negotiating agenda. Instead, it quickly ruled out the diplomatic track and said there would be no thaw in relations.

## Castro's Pragmatism

Over the years, changing circumstances, pressure from the Soviets and the failure of his own tactics

*Continued on p. 908*

---

*Interest sections enable the two countries to have direct communications but carry a lesser diplomatic status than embassies. This spring, following changes in Eastern Europe, the Cuban Interest Section in Washington was moved from the Czechoslovak Embassy to the Swiss Embassy.

**The earlier 1984 immigration agreement, which allowed for the repatriation of Mariel "undesirables" and 20,000 entry visas for Cubans wishing to emigrate to the United States, was suspended by Cuba when the Voice of America's anti-Castro Radio Martí went on the air in 1985.

# Chronology

## 1890s–1930s
*Cuba achieves independence from Spain but becomes a U.S. protectorate.*

### Feb. 15, 1898
The U.S. battleship *Maine* explodes in Havana harbor, ultimately triggering the Spanish-American War and U.S. occupation of Cuba.

### May 28, 1901
Platt Amendment is added to the Cuban Constitution, giving the United States the right to intervene in Cuba at will.

### Aug. 12, 1933
The dictatorship of Gerardo Machado is overthrown by the "Revolution of 1933," which ushers in an era of modest reforms.

---

## 1950s
*Cuba passes from dictatorship to revolution.*

### March 10, 1952
Fulgencio Batista abrogates the Cuban Constitution and stages a military coup, prompting a new generation of Cubans to take up arms.

### July 26, 1953
Band of revolutionaries led by Fidel Castro undertakes failed attack at the Moncada Barracks.

### Jan. 2, 1959
Fidel Castro's reconstituted forces march triumphantly into Havana after forcing Batista to flee into exile.

## 1960s–1970s
*U.S.-Cuban relations freeze in Cold War rhetoric as Castro embraces Marxism-Leninism and attempts to spread revolution throughout the globe.*

### Jan. 3, 1961
President Eisenhower breaks diplomatic relations with Cuba.

### April 17, 1961
A CIA-sponsored invasion force of 1,200 Cuban exiles lands at the Bay of Pigs and is defeated in 72 hours.

### 1962
The U.S. imposes full economic and political blockade of Cuba.

### October 1962
President Kennedy confronts the Soviets over nuclear missiles in Cuba. Khrushchev blinks first, but only after Kennedy gives assurances that the U.S. will not invade Cuba.

### Nov. 5, 1975
Castro sends 18,000 troops to Angola to back the government in its war against rebels backed by South Africa and the United States.

### Sept. 1, 1977
The U.S. and Cuba open "interest sections" in each other's capitals in what appears to be a step toward normal relations. That sours after Cuba dispatches 18,000 troops to Ethiopia.

---

## 1980s
*As glasnost and perestroika sweep the Communist world, Fidel Castro begins to moderate foreign policy but reaffirms commitment to state-controlled economy.*

### April 21, 1980
Castro opens the port of Mariel, leading to the exodus of some 129,000 Cubans to Florida, including many criminals.

### May 19, 1985
Radio Martí begins broadcasting anti-Castro programs to Cuba; Castro retaliates by suspending 1984 immigration agreement.

### 1986
Castro launches "rectification campaign" to eliminate all traces of liberal economics.

---

## 1990s
*Increasingly isolated, both politically and economically, Cuba suffers severe economic crisis, prompting some to predict Castro's downfall.*

### March 27, 1990
TV Martí goes on the air in Cuba; 23 minutes later, Cuba begins jamming the electronic signal.

### October 1990
Castro declares a "special period in peacetime," a draconian austerity program designed to increase Cuban self-sufficiency.

### July 1991
The last 17,000 Cuban soldiers depart from Angola, ending Cuba's 16-year presence.

### Sept. 11, 1991
Soviet President Gorbachev announces that his country plans to withdraw 11,000 troops from Cuba and end its trade subsidy.

### Oct. 10, 1991
Fourth Communist Party Congress convenes; minor political and economic reforms are announced.

# Florida's Cuban-American Community ...

For three decades, Cuban exiles have clustered in front of coffee stands on Calle Ocho (Eighth Street) in Miami's Little Havana section and talked about returning to their homeland. "Next Christmas in Havana" is the common refrain, emblazoned on bumper stickers throughout Miami.

Now, buoyed by socialism's worldwide decline, South Florida's 700,000 Cuban exiles are no longer just talking about Fidel Castro's fall but euphorically planning for the day that he does. There is even an official 18-member Free-Cuba Commission, appointed by Gov. Bob Martínez, charged with assessing the impact of Castro's fall on Florida.

A post-Castro constitution has been sketched out (reportedly with the help of Nobel laureate economist Milton Friedman), business plans drafted, corporate investments lined up and the words to popular songs rewritten in excitement over the prospect of a free Cuba. A local joke is that so many Cuban Americans are planning vacation homes in Cuba that its coastline will have to be doubled to accommodate them.

"The conventional wisdom in the Miami exile community is that the guy cannot last a year," Miami Mayor Xavier Suárez, himself a Cuban exile, told *Newsweek* some 21 months ago. Obviously, the pundits were wrong: The "Maximum Leader" (formally, Castro is Cuba's president and first secretary of the Community Party) is still firmly entrenched in power.

Nonetheless, the exile community is not deterred. Waiting for Castro's demise has become part of the culture, just like *media noches* (Cuban sandwiches) and *los quince* (Miami's debutante balls). "The exile community has a very partial view of their homeland that may not be in touch with reality," explains Lisandro Pérez, a Cuba specialist at Miami's Florida International University.

For the Cuban Americans who fled the island after Castro took power in 1959, virulent anti-communism is a way of life. Miami is probably the only U.S. city where foreign policy is a paramount issue in local politics. The political voice behind the Cuban-American community,

which has become a potent economic and social force, is the Cuban American National Foundation (CANF), a conservative, anti-Castro lobby group that claims some 50,000 members.

With close links to the Bush administration, the CANF wields undeniable power. Among other accomplishments, the foundation successfully got Radio Martí and TV Martí on the air in 1985 and 1990, respectively, and in 1985 was instrumental in lifting a congressional ban on U.S. aid to Jonas Savimbi's anti-Communist guerrillas, who were fighting Cuban troops in Angola.

This spring the organization scored another big win when Czechoslovakia agreed to stop serving as Cuba's diplomatic representative in Washington after CANF's founder and president, Jorge Mas Canosa, promised to buy the Czechs a building for their consulate in Miami and to promote trade and investment.

Needless to say, the CANF also has been in the vanguard of those preparing for a post-Castro Cuba. "We are the West Germany of Cuba," says Mas Canosa, referring to his fellow exiles prospering in the United States. The CANF claims to have buyers willing to pay $15 billion for 60 percent of Cuba's land and assets. Although foundation leaders deny it, in private they reportedly advocate armed U.S. intervention — the solution favored by 56 percent of Miami's Cuban exiles in a recent poll.†

Mas Canosa's talk of rescue from the outside worries other influential Cuban-American leaders. "For better or worse, the future of Cuba is going to be decided by the people living on the island," says Arturo Villar, publisher of *Vista*, a Miami-based Hispanic-American magazine. "By promoting the sense that an overthrow of Fidel Castro means the triumphant return to Havana by the Miami exiles, the [CANF] is only increasing the chances that events in Cuba will eventually turn violent." ††

In fact, the presumption that the CANF speaks for a majority of Cuban-Americans, something which has been taken for granted for years, is itself questionable. A 1988 poll of Cuban-Americans found that only 36 percent believe that rightist groups, such as the CANF, reflect their

---

induced Castro to moderate his stance. For the aging guerrilla leader, the countries of Latin America no longer loomed as potential converts to Cuba's revolutionary gospel but rather as sources of economic salvation for the Cuban regime itself. By 1984, relations were restored with most of the countries of the region.

At that time, it had become clear that Castro's adventurist ideology was bankrupt. Following the collapse of the Cuban-supported revolutionary government in Grenada in October 1983, Cuban activities in the hemisphere were cut back drastically. And even in El Salvador, Cuba has indicated its preference for a ne-

gotiated solution.[14]

Castro's pragmatic changes in foreign policy were not matched on the home front. In 1986 when Mikhail Gorbachev embraced *perestroika* and *glasnost,* Castro instead decreed a "rectification campaign" — a return to communist orthodoxy, reining in private initiative and rooting out the

# ... Exiles or Immigrants?

thinking.‡

Moreover, some observers say moderate voices in the Cuban community have been silenced by anti-Castro elements who have sometimes punctuated the political debate with a bomb blast.‡‡ The subsequent lack of dialogue, ironically, has legitimized the extreme right as the voice of all Cuban Americans.

"If *perestroika* and *glasnost* come to Cuba, I hope for the sake of Cubans that they come to Miami first," says Delores Prida, a well-known Cuban-American playwright who resides in New York. She says any dissent from the hard-line, anti-Castro position is not tolerated in Miami. For instance, she says, exhibitions of post-revolutionary Cuban art at Miami's Cuban Museum of Art and Culture have been canceled because of death threats, and artists who have performed in Cuba are shunned publicly and refused grants.

The times, however, are changing. Now more than ever, there seems to be a clearly visible split within the community between those who want to tighten the screws on Castro and others who favor open dialogue and negotiation. The split has caused bitter feuds over such issues as the handling of Radio Martí, which critics say Mas Canosa controls as if it were part of his personal fiefdom, and the direction of U.S. policy.

To be sure, the CANF still has a strong and voluble following. But today, a second generation of Cuban Americans, born in the United States or just babies when they left the homeland, are coming into their own. And although they carry with them some of the angst of their exile parents, they have lost much of the anger.

"The younger generation doesn't have the same stake in the old fight," says Cristina Garcia, a Cuban-American author and former Miami bureau chief for *Time*. "We talk about Cuba, but it's not the same. The interest is more and more casual and familial than political."

The so-called "yucas" — young, upwardly mobile Cuban Americans — are cautiously embracing the freedom of the American political system and, increasingly, voicing a more moderate line toward Cuba.

"The old generation represented by the CANF still has an *exile* agenda," says Alicia Torres, executive director of the Cuban American Committee, a Washington lobby group that favors closer relations with Cuba, "whereas the younger generation has an *immigrant* agenda."

These younger, 30-something Cuban Americans are bilingual, bicultural and, for the most part, economically secure. The majority wouldn't go back to Cuba even if Fidel Castro and communism disappeared overnight.

The same can't be said for many older exiles, and some recent arrivals who haven't found the prosperity they expected. A 1990 poll taken for a Spanish-language television station in Miami, WLTV, suggested that as many as one of every five South Florida Cubans would return to the island if Castro left power.

As Cuban Americans grapple with their split identity, one thing can be agreed upon. More than the Straits of Florida separate a generation of Cubans reared on communism from those steeped in American life. "The Cuba we left has disappeared," comments businessman Carlos Pérez, a leader in exile. "Everybody knows it's going to be a mess. It's a different people, a different system."

Indeed, after nearly 33 years of communism, Cuba may no longer be the Cuba they remember. For many Cuban-Americans, particularly those in the CANF camp who left the island three decades ago, the Havana of yesterday is more likely to be found in the Miami of today.

---

† Cited in *The New York Times*, Sept. 6, 1991.

†† Quoted in *Forbes*, Jan. 21, 1991, p. 55.

‡ Poll conducted by the Gallup Organization for Potomac Associates. See William Watts, *The United States and Cuba: Changing Perceptions, New Policies?*, The Johns Hopkins University School of Advanced International Studies, 1989.

‡‡ In 1989, 18 bomb blasts directed at "traitors," some of whom merely advocated dialogue with Cuba, led the FBI to declare Miami the terrorism capital of the United States.

---

profit motive. Many experts interpret Castro's recalcitrance as a last-ditch effort to salvage his revolution. "If the Soviet Union were our neighbor," a high-level Cuban official attempted to explain last year, "we could well experiment with *glasnost, perestroika* and who knows what else. But, unfortunately, only 90 miles away lies the United States. And there is the problem." [15]

### Domestic Crackdown

The rectification campaign summarily shut down private farmers' markets, first opened in 1980 to stimulate production and ease chronic food shortages. It restrained private entrepreneurship and outlawed cottage artisans making everything from shoes and keys to safety-glass windshields. Production bonuses, overtime pay and other profit incentives were also cut back. In their place, Castro urged a return to socialist ideals and self-sacrifice, what one young electrician in Havana wearily called "working harder for less."[16]

Besides revolutionary morality, Cuban officials argue that they have strong economic reasons for the domestic crackdown. Corruption was rampant under the more liberal system. Factory managers kept production quotas ridiculously low so they could overproduce and reap hefty bonuses. Middlemen dominated the free markets, buying produce from farmers, then jacking up retail prices to more than five times the wholesale rate.

Though some of these allegations may have been true, economists say the reassertion of rigid bureaucracy plunged the economy into a tailspin. Between 1986 and 1989 the economy declined at an annual rate of almost 1 percent, labor productivity fell by 2.5 percent and the budget deficit increased 4.5 times.[17]

Politically, the rectification campaign entailed a fierce repression of the small human rights movement that had been given a breathing spell between 1987-89. The Cuban government has worked hard to limit news about Soviet reforms. Soviet magazines sympathetic to Gorbachev's reforms, like *New Times* and the *Moscow News,* were removed from newsstands. The term *perestroika* itself didn't appear in the Cuban press until November 1987, long after it had become a household word in the United States.

One of the more important indicators of Castro's desperation was the 1989 public trial and execution of Gen. Arnaldo Ochoa Sánchez, a much decorated hero of the Angola war, and other senior officers on drug and self-confessed treason charges. It is widely believed that the apparently trumped-up charges, and subsequent purges throughout the regime, were designed to reaffirm the absolute political domination of Fidel Castro and his brother Raúl, his heir apparent.[18]   ■

# CURRENT SITUATION

## Collapse of Communism

Having successfully resisted the *Yanquis* and eight of their presidents for three decades, Fidel Castro is now finding that it is the collapse of communism in the Soviet Union and Eastern Europe that represents the greatest danger to the Cuban revolutionary society. "Thirty years after he aligned Cuba with the Soviet Union, [Castro] must worry not only whether he hitched Cuba's fate to a falling star but also whether his own historical mission will vanish into the black hole of world communism," writes Edward Gonzalez, a political scientist at the University of California at Los Angeles.[19]

International trends have left Castro politically isolated. Democracy has swept through Latin America, from Chile to Nicaragua.* The civil war in El Salvador is inching toward a negotiated settlement. The African theater no longer presents inviting targets for Cuban internationalism, and Cuban troops have withdrawn from Angola.

Once referred to as the Soviet military's "unsinkable aircraft carrier," Cuba has lost its geopolitical importance in the post-Cold War era. In addition, the December 1989 U.S. invasion of Panama deprived the Cubans of the "supermarket" through which they were able to import high

_____

*The only two governments in the hemisphere that were not democratically elected are in Cuba and Haiti. Haiti's elected president, Jean-Bertrand Aristides, was ousted in a coup this September.

technology and partially breach the U.S. economic embargo.

Experts say it is the economic isolation that ultimately may spur Castro to change — or fall. The radical transformations of the Soviet Union and Eastern Europe, which accounted for 85 percent of Cuba's trade, have had a crushing effect on the Cuban economy. Eastern European countries now deal with Cuba on a cash basis, and the changed terms of trade with the Soviet Union are expected to cut $1 billion from Cuba's foreign-exchange earnings this year alone.[20]

In order to keep his country afloat, Castro has had to institute the "special period in peacetime," an austerity program intended to guide Cuba toward self-sufficiency. But that alone won't be enough. Cuba must start competing against all the other poor countries trying to earn hard currency. "It's a nasty situation," says Gillian Gunn, a Cuba expert at the Washington-based Carnegie Endowment for International Peace. "Not even a market-economy person would have a solution to this."

Moscow has repeatedly promised not to abandon its Cuban allies, who provide an important listening post on the United States as well as much of the Soviet Union's sugar, citrus fruit and nickel. But despite such assurances, the two countries' trade relations are being adversely affected by Soviet decentralization.

While Cuban trade officials used to deal with 65 Soviet agencies to coordinate supplies of everything from air conditioners to sheet metal to canned beef, today they must contract with about 1,500 Soviet trading companies, in addition to 35 government agencies. For the first five months of the year, almost all Soviet supplies to the island were halted as the two countries negotiated specific dollar values for products that in the past had been exchanged on a barter basis.[21]

## The Soviets' Hard Line

After the failed Soviet coup in August and the ascent of reform forces led by Russian President Boris N. Yeltsin — who has said repeatedly that Moscow cannot afford to maintain charitable trade relations with Cuba — the Soviet Union has taken an even harder line.

"Cuba has survived repeated crises since Castro took power in 1959, but this is the worst ever," says American University's William LeoGrande. "The loss of the Soviet subsidy is a very bad blow to Cuba. It's the equivalent of lopping off 5 percent of gross national product at a time when the economy is in recession and trying to absorb the dislocation from the loss of trade from Eastern Europe."

Meanwhile, Castro is scrambling to find new trading partners, looking primarily to China, Latin America and Europe. Cuba sold $100 million in medical vaccines to Brazil in 1990, and there is talk of increased trade with Venezuela and Mexico.

"These are only minor ventures," comments Antonio Jorge, an economist at Florida International University in Miami. What's more, they would not give Cuba what it really needs: spare parts, heavy chemicals and pesticides from Eastern Europe. And besides, experts doubt Havana will get trade subsidies. Already, Cuba owes $1 billion to Argentina and $300 million to both Brazil and Mexico.

Cuba's economic woes, of course, are caused by more than the loss of trading partners. "Castro's zigzag course in economic policy has stalled the economy," Jorge adds. "From an economic standpoint, his policies have been completely irrational." Years of dependence on Soviet subsidies have compounded Cuba's inherent Communist tendency to shelter inefficiency. What productive capability Cuba does have was geared, at Soviet insistence, largely

# Tourism on the Rise

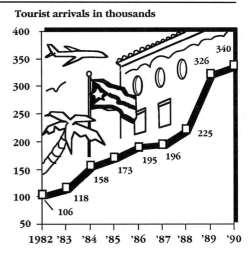

**Tourist arrivals in thousands**

By 1995, Cuba hopes to attract a million tourists a year. Of the 340,000 visitors to Cuba in 1990, 26 percent came from Canada. Others came from Germany, Spain, Mexico, Italy, Brazil and Argentina.

The rapid growth in tourism has caused difficulties for the Cuban government. Concerned that the tourism industry was creating an elite group with access to foreign currency, the government in mid-1989 took steps to restrict ordinary Cubans' access to foreign exchanges.

*Source: The Economist Intelligence Unit, Cuba: Country Profile 1991-92.*

to sugar — hardly a scarce commodity. And the U.S. trade embargo excludes Cuba from its best market.

## Mixed Messages

Through five years of reforms in the Soviet Union, a wary Castro has refused to emulate Mikhail Gorbachev's political and economic changes. In July, when the Soviet leader was spurning Marxism-Leninism, Castro declared in his state-of-the-nation address that "a revolution like ours changes neither its names nor its ideas."

Castro's fiery oratory, along with the defiant "Socialism or death" slogan that is plastered on billboards all around the country, gives the impression that Cuba isn't budging. "The reality, of course, is that Cuba is changing," says William LeoGrande. "Castro has no choice."

At home the Cuban leader has given the tourism industry rare freedom to form joint ventures with foreign firms to build and renovate hotels. A joint Cuban-Spanish hotel, the Sol Palermas, opened in May

1990 at Varadero Beach; Cubanacán, the state tourism company, is discussing plans with other Western European, Jamaican and Brazilian firms.

"This is a momentous change for a country founded on the expropriation of foreign property," says Harvard's Domínguez. By 1995, Cuba expects to attract about 1 million tourists a year from Europe, Latin America and Canada and gross up to $800 million, compared with 340,000 tourists last year who generated $250 million.[22]

Aware of tourism's limitations, the Cuban government is aggressively pursuing joint ventures in other sectors, including medical technology, light industry and construction. As a result, Britain and Mexico have dispatched trade delegations, Colombia has offered to refine Cuban oil and Venezuelan businessmen are pressing their president to pry open Cuban markets.[23] A French firm has entered into an agreement with the Cuban government to explore for oil off Cuba's shores.

So while the regime insists on a one-party Communist system and central planning, it is welcoming foreign investment, encouraging maximum profits, liberalizing travel restrictions and building luxury hotels. Mixed messages? Certainly. But in 1991, Cuba is a country of contradictions, a schizophrenic island that seems to operate on many levels.

The Pan American Games, hosted by Cuba this summer, provided perhaps the most glaring set of paradoxes. The country managed to build 21 new sports facilities — including a 35,000-seat stadium and a 55-building Pan Am village — and renovated 46 more buildings, all at a time when it still has trouble getting fruit and vegetables to markets.

In theory, Cuba's balmy beaches could once again make the island a mecca for fun-seekers. But visitors from rich, democratic countries are also agents of change. Attempts to seal off hard-currency hot spots from Cubans have caused local resentment at what are cynically called "green zones" where "tourism apartheid" rules.

There are other contradictions, too. Castro recently announced that the Communist Party's staff would be cut in half. That saves money but also converts thousands who once had a stake in the system into disgruntled job-seekers. Under the so-called "special period" of austerity, new investments in health care have been put on hold, and scarce medical supplies are being rationed. But that reduces the one aspect of Cuban socialism that everyone likes. And using ox-carts saves gas but bogs down an already sluggish distribution system. More and more Cubans are saying that, given the uncertainty of Cuba's relationship with the Soviet Union, the island must adapt to new global realities.

### Fourth Party Congress

At last month's Fourth Communist Party Congress, an important five-day conference where 1,800 party delegates met in Santiago de Cuba to discuss party strategy, the Castro regime again sent mixed signals to the Cuban public. Prior to the congress, there was some hope that Castro would use the opportunity to announce a new direction for Cuba.

That was not to be. As many analysts expected, the congress was a balancing act in which Cuban leaders permitted more public participation in decision-making while at the same time keeping the process from escalating out of control. During the closed meeting, Castro severely criticized the United States and endorsed the draconian special period, but at the same time he accepted a measure of domestic capitalism by agreeing to allow handymen, plumbers, carpenters and other tradespeople to work for their own profit. Other changes endorsed by the congress include:

■ Approval in principle of direct election of lawmakers in the National Assembly.

■ Adoption of a series of internal changes, including lifting of a ban on party membership for religious believers (called the "atheist clause").

■ Election of a 225-member party Central Committee and Politburo, which for the first time includes younger political leaders.

Permitting a glimmer of entrepreneurship in effect gives official sanction to an already vibrant black market. "This isn't the first time Castro has tinkered with elements of a market economy," says LeoGrande. "He is fundamentally a political pragmatist."

Most observers believe Castro's tinkering won't begin to brake the nose-diving economy. "The regime still has control of who is elected at a local level," says Susan Kaufman Purcell at the Americas Society. "The changes are cosmetic. Those who expected real grappling with economic problems must be disappointed."

"But," says Harvard's Jorge Domínguez, "there were some important, substantive changes. This was not a trivial event." For example, he says, removal of the atheist clause enables non-Communist Party members to hold important administrative posts. Before, professional advancement in all fields, including medicine and education, was reserved for the 600,000 party members. "Castro made disparaging remarks about multiparty systems, but he didn't shut the door on a more open political system," Domínguez adds.

## Cuba Isolated

The Bush administration has isolated Cuba and has encouraged its Latin American allies — as well as the Soviet Union — to follow suit. For example, when U.S. officials caught wind of a proposed partnership between Brazil's VASP airline and Cuba's state airline earlier this year, they threatened to block VASP's projected purchase of American aircraft, and the negotiations were ended. And just last month the administration flatly rejected an offer by Mexico, Venezuela and Colombia to broker an end to the 30-year U.S. standoff with Castro.

Rather than normalize relations, current U.S. policy is to pressure Cuba through isolation — "to force Castro to fall under his own weight," as one administration official puts it. To stir the political pot inside Cuba, the United States has begun beaming TV Martí to Cuba, a $16-million-a-year project to inform Cubans about life in the free world through programs like "Three's Company" and MTV. The predawn broadcasts have been jammed easily by Cuba's military. Jamming has also affected Radio Martí, which since 1985 has played an important role informing Cubans of global events.

Clearly the most contentious policy issue has been the U.S. embargo,

*Continued on p. 914*

# At Issue:

## Should the United States normalize relations with Cuba?

TOM SCHIERHOLZ

*Former staff writer for* **The Christian Science Monitor**
**FROM** *THE WALL STREET JOURNAL*, **AUG. 8, 1991.**

*i*f the Bush administration were interested in creative American diplomacy, it would engage Fidel Castro in dialogue, negotiation and compromise. Instead, Bush seems content to leave American policy toward Cuba on auto-pilot, going nowhere.

Inaction on America's Cuba policy is not merely careless, it is dangerous. It makes the president and the American people appear duplicitous and insincere as they fashion the "new world order." While Castro's Cuba remains subject to Washington's trade embargo, China — the new headquarters of world communism — enjoys most favored nation trading status. Iraq — which has yet to surrender its chemical, biological and nuclear arms — receives food and medical aid despite a worldwide prohibition on trade with Saddam Hussein. Cuba cannot.

The double standard is confusing to the Cuban leadership and counterproductive to long-term U.S. interests. The Bush administration asks Cuba to develop a market economy, to hold internationally supervised relations and to reduce its armed forces. But it makes no such demands of China. ... Cast in terms of individual lives, the Bush position is even more regrettable, given the suffering the embargo inflicts on innocents. ...

Opponents of a new Cuba policy give several reasons when they argue that the U.S. should not normalize relations. They say Cubans will not negotiate in good faith. They charge that Castro continues to support subversive groups. And they charge negotiations would offer a cure to a dictator on his political deathbed.

The facts suggest the opposite is true. Cubans have proven they can make and keep commitments, when it is in their interest to do so. ...

The biggest loss in the current policy is America's. Without normal relations, the U.S. loses its best opportunity to shape a post-Castro Cuba. With full diplomatic business and cultural ties, the U.S. would have access to the Cuban people — and the influence that goes along with it. Our [current] policy gives Castro the luxury of painting the U.S. as the global bully.

Castro has succeeded in mending fences with the other nations of the hemisphere — the only countries he ever really threatened. The U.S. should take a cue from its Latin American neighbors and make peace with Havana.

JOSÉ S. SORZANO

*Former deputy ambassador to the U.N. and a former*
*president of the Cuban American National Foundation*
**FROM TESTIMONY BEFORE THE HOUSE SUBCOMMITTEE ON**
**WESTERN HEMISPHERE AFFAIRS, JULY 31, 1991.**

*t*here are those who wish to take advantage of Castro's weakened position. They advocate a radical shift in the American policy of containment and isolation of Cuba which has been in force for over a quarter of a century. Their view is that the United States should repeal its economic embargo, lift the travel restrictions and start a dialogue with Castro. It is also argued that, if nothing else, these measures will unleash within Cuba the same or similar forces which now threaten Gorbachev's rule. ...

Setting aside the question of why Castro — an astute and experienced political operator — would permit the entry of such an obvious Trojan horse, there is the issue of whether there are quicker and surer ways of profiting from Castro's current problems.

Why change a policy with solid bipartisan support ... which clearly has been instrumental in creating the dead-end situation that Castro now faces?

Regardless of the desirable transformations the proposed policy changes may eventually have on Castro's Cuba, in the short run they have the perverse effect of legitimizing Castro's dictatorial rule, providing him with a desperately needed breathing spell and, tragically, prolonging his grip on power.

That is not an appealing scenario to those who believe that more than 30 years of economic deprivation and political repression are enough. There are, therefore, no persuasive policy reasons for altering course now. The United States should continue to insist that Cuba respect human rights, and that Castro call for internationally supervised elections. ...

To ask for anything less is to weaken the U.S. policy of support for the region's democratic processes. By maintaining the economic embargo the probability is that Cuba's collapsing economy, increased internal discontent and the changes in Eastern Europe and the Soviet Union will finally topple Castro's regime or force him to accept an electoral outcome.

All indications are that American patience and perseverance will hasten the day when the Cuban people will be able to determine their preferred form of government and freely select their legitimate leaders through electoral mechanisms. If anything, rather than relaxing U.S. pressures on Cuba as is being argued, American policy should be tightened a few final turns to hasten Castro's demise.

which Cuba has declared "illegal, unjust and a violation of the U.N. Charter." Taking the matter before the U.N. General Assembly this month, Havana hopes to derail legislation pending in Congress that would close one of the last embargo loopholes — one that amounted to $700 million in trade for Cuba last year.*

### Embargo's Future

An amendment sponsored by Sen. Connie Mack, R-Fla., would close that loophole and expand the embargo against Cuba to the level now imposed against North Korea, Vietnam and Cambodia. The Bush administration, while eager to keep the economic pressure on Cuba, is opposed to the legislation because of pressure from allies. Nevertheless, the Mack bill passed the Senate and the House this autumn as part of the Export Administration Act. The bill is now before a House-Senate conference committee, but final action is not expected to occur this year.

"If the foreign policy objective is to return Cuba to democracy, like in Chile and Nicaragua, the U.S. should tighten the embargo," says Jaime Suchlicki at the University of Miami. Suchlicki argues that reducing pressure on Castro would, in effect, reward him for his authoritarian rule. Purcell at the Americas Society agrees. "There will be no change until there is unrest," she says. "It could be bloody, but lifting the embargo without political change will only reinforce that man."

At the same time, a growing number of Cuba experts believe the embargo has ceased to make sense. Says Smith College's Andrew Zimbalist: "If

our policy were more benign, it would remove Castro's pretext for not changing." Inside Cuba, Oswaldo Payá, leader of the Christian Liberation Movement, says that because of the way Fidel stands up to the gringos, "the blockade strengthens Castro."[24]

Other critics of the embargo make humanitarian arguments. "Increased U.S. pressures may impede rather than encourage the kind of reforms we need," writes Elizardo Sánchez,

one of Cuba's most outspoken dissidents, who has spent nine of the last 10 years in Cuban prisons. "Tightening the embargo, far from producing rapid changes in the regime, could bring about even greater privations for the already suffering Cuban people."[25] Sánchez argues that excluding foods and medicines from the embargo would have a greater impact on fostering change and gaining the trust of the Cuban people. ∎

# OUTLOOK

## The "Zero Option"

While the spasms in the Soviet Union have shocked Cubans, Castro for the past 18 months has been warning them to expect the worst. In rhetoric that has verged on the apocalyptic, the "Maximum Leader" has been preparing Cubans recently for what he calls the "zero option"— the possible elimination of all oil and food shipments from the Soviet Union. Cuban officials insist the island is ready to live without electricity rather than return to capitalism or cave in to Washington's "imperial" designs.

But ordering bureaucrats to work on farms and in factories to prepare for life without energy is not a solution. "Ad hoc adjustments to a deteriorating economic situation, combined with the selective use of repression, are little more than stopgap measures," says Purcell. "As the crisis deepens, Castro will eventually face a choice between using Cuba's already weakened institutions to mobilize and control an increasingly desperate population, or loosening political and economic controls in order to raise productivity."

Both choices represent challenges to Castro's rule. As much as he may

fear — and loathe — the demon of capitalism, most analysts believe he has no choice but to embrace it. "I don't see how Cuba can increase productivity without introducing private initiatives," says Wayne Smith of Johns Hopkins University. In the near term, a lot will depend on Castro's efforts to attract foreign investment.

Economist Antonio Jorge predicts that by early next year Castro will indeed be forced to adopt the zero option. "If at that point, Cuba is forced to cut back an additional 25 to 30 percent of oil and industrial raw materials, the Cuban economy will break," he says. "I'm not talking about idle industrial capacity which countries experience during recession, but a radical change. Cuba may simply end up as another Haiti."

Unlike the early phase of the revolution, when sacrifice was accepted willingly in anticipation of some payoff down the road, the zero option offers little, if any, benefit. "Sacrifice was okay so long as ice cream was available and they had three pairs of shoes," says Laurence Birns, executive director of the left-leaning Council for Hemispheric Affairs. "As life becomes more stringent, Cubans will ask, 'Sacrifice for what?' Are they willing to go to the wall for a now-obsolete political credo?"

The answers to these questions are basically unknowable, especially

---

*When imposed in 1962, the embargo applied to U.S. citizens, companies and their foreign subsidiaries. But under pressure from allies, Washington in the mid-1970s eased some restrictions. The relaxed guidelines applied the ban only on those foreign subsidiaries of U.S. companies headed by U.S. citizens and allowed trade with Cuba so long as U.S. currency or manufactured goods were not involved.

given the lack of free expression on the island. Too little is known outside that closed society about the post-revolutionary generation, people in their late 20s or younger, to be able to predict what they will do. The members of this generation, who make up more than half of Cuba's population, have regarded free education and medical care as their birthright. On the other hand, many, if not a majority, can be expected to be impatient with the incessant shortages and to hanker for the consumer goods and political freedoms they know exist 90 miles away.

### Castro's Last Stand

The issue is further complicated by U.S. policy, which will undoubtedly play an instrumental role in determining Castro's next move. "Castro sees the U.S. as a historic enemy of Cuba," says LeoGrande. "A large part of the revolution is breaking the hegemony of the United States. ... [T]he foremost concern is the U.S. re-establishing dominance over Cuba."

The likelihood of Castro bowing to U.S. demands for multiparty elections and a free-market economy, especially in the face of U.S. hostility, is practically nil. Castro's intentions were made clear at a Latin American summit this summer when he declared: "We are preparing ourselves economically, preparing ourselves politically, preparing ourselves morally and preparing ourselves militarily. ... What are we going to do? Anything is possible except that Cuba should raise the white flag."

Everyone, even proponents of current U.S. policy, agrees that Castro will not quietly back down. "He's not the kind of revolutionary leader who retires to the Riviera," says Wayne Smith. Nor does the Bush administration seem the least bit interested in taking any steps to improve relations with Cuba, for fear of prolonging Castro's rule.

For the United States, the hardline policy carries real risks. At 65, Castro will not be around forever, and the embargo, which is opposed by dissident groups inside Cuba and causes serious hardship for the Cuban people, could alienate the next generation of Cubans. Or, in the event of insurrection, some even see a threat to the Florida coast.

Obviously, the dangers from such unrest are much greater for Cuba. "If you squeeze Castro, producing an explosion, half a million Cubans could die," warns Enrique Baloyra, a political scientist at the University of Miami. "Ultimately, it could prolong Castro's political career."

In the interim, conditions are likely to worsen before they get better. Even if the Cuban government successfully realigns its trade relations and lures new foreign investment, it will take years before the efforts bear fruit for average Cubans.

"I don't believe Castro's fall is imminent or even inevitable," says Smith, "but if he digs in his heels, if he doesn't move far enough in two or three years, popular frustration will reach a point of desperation that any spark will touch off a rebellion." ∎

## Notes

[1] Quoted in *U.S. News & World Report,* Jan. 7, 1991, p. 60.
[2] See *The New York Times,* Sept. 12, 1991.
[3] *The New York Times,* Oct. 10, 1991.
[4] Quoted in the *Los Angeles Times,* April 7, 1991.
[5] Quoted in *The New Republic,* Jan. 7, 1991, p. 28.
[6] See Wayne S. Smith, "A Pragmatic Cuba Policy," *Foreign Service Journal,* April 1991, p. 22.

[7] The poll was conducted by The Gallup Organization for Potomac Associates. The findings were first presented at a June 1988 conference at The Johns Hopkins University School of Advanced International Studies. See William Watts, *The United States and Cuba: Changing Perceptions, New Policies?,* The Johns Hopkins University School of Advanced International Studies, 1989.
[8] Quoted in *The Wall Street Journal,* Oct. 9, 1991.
[9] Cited in *The Nation,* Oct. 24, 1988, p. 385.
[10] See Philip Brenner, et al., *The Cuba Reader* (1989), p. 2.
[11] For background on the U.S.-Cuban relationship, with chapters written from both the U.S. and Cuban perspectives, see Jorge I. Domínguez and Rafael Hernandez, *U.S.-Cuban Relations in the 1990s* (1989).
[12] Jaime Suchlicki, "Cuba and the United States," in Georges Fauriol and Eva Loser, eds., *Cuba: The International Dimension* (1990), p. 47.
[13] See Pamela S. Falk, "Cuba in Africa," *Foreign Affairs,* summer 1987, p. 1077.
[14] See Wayne S. Smith, "Washington and Havana: Time for Dialogue," *World Policy Journal,* summer 1990, p. 557.
[15] Quoted in *The Progressive,* June 1990, p. 18.
[16] Quoted in *U.S. News & World Report,* Jan. 9, 1989, p. 37.
[17] See Carmelo Mesa-Lago, "Countdown in Cuba," *Cuba in the Nineties* (1991), p. 72.
[18] Details of the trial, which caused an uproar in Cuba, remain shrouded in mystery. See Julia Preston, "The Trial that Shook Cuba," *The New York Review of Books,* Dec. 7, 1989.
[19] Edward Gonzalez, "The Beginning of the End for Castro?" in *Cuba in the Nineties, op. cit.,* p. 10.
[20] The Economist Intelligence Unit, *Cuba: Country Profile,* 1991, p. 11.
[21] See *The Washington Post,* Aug. 27, 1991.
[22] For a more detailed account of Cuba's efforts to expand its tourism industry, see *The Wall Street Journal,* Sept. 11, 1991.
[23] See *The Miami Herald,* Oct. 25, 1991.
[24] Quoted in *Fortune,* Aug. 26, 1991, p. 97.
[25] From an op-ed article in *The Miami Herald,* Oct. 3. 1991.

# Bibliography

## Selected Sources Used

## Books

**Brenner, Philip, et. al. eds., *The Cuba Reader: The Making of a Revolutionary Society*, Grove Press, 1989.**

This is a compendium of articles and book excerpts representing a wide array of viewpoints and covering all aspects of Cuba, its history and foreign relations. The volume is generally sympathetic to Castro and the Cuban Revolution. The book includes writings by José Martí, Che Guevara and Fidel Castro.

**Domínguez, Jorge I., and Hernández, Rafael, eds., *U.S.-Cuban Relations in the 1990s,* Westview Press, 1989.**

This collection of scholarly essays focuses on the relations between the United States and Cuba in the coming decade. Half of the essays are authored by Cubans.

**Fauriol, Georges, and Loser, Eva, eds., *Cuba: The International Dimension,* Transaction Publishers, 1990.**

Another collection of scholarly essays. The authors in this volume generally take a more critical view of Castro. The book is particularly useful as background on Cuba's foreign policy during the 1980s.

**Geyer, Georgie Anne, *Guerrilla Prince: The Untold Story of Fidel Castro,* Little, Brown and Co., 1991.**

Geyer's anti-Castro bias is obvious throughout this recent biography. She relies heavily on interviews from the Cuban exile community. The book does provide interesting insights and personal details on Castro's life.

**Suchlicki, Jaime, *Cuba: From Columbus to Castro,* Brassey's Inc., 1990.**

A standard history of Cuba since Spanish-colonial times, this work is particularly good on pre-revolutionary Cuba. Though Suchlicki is a harsh critic of Castro, the book presents a balanced overview.

## Articles

**Gunn, Gillian, "Will Castro Fall?" *Foreign Policy,* summer 1990.**

Gunn's analysis of Castro's dilemma is informative and thoughtful.

**Preston, Julia, "The Trial that Shook Cuba," *The New York Review of Books,* Dec. 7, 1989.**

The trial and execution of Gen. Arnaldo Ochoa Sánchez is one of the most fascinating episodes in recent Cuban history. Preston's account helps explain some of the mystery behind the trial and Castro's apparent effort to consolidate power and root out opposition.

**Purcell, Susan Kaufman, "Cuba's Cloudy Future," *Foreign Affairs,* summer 1990.**

Purcell anticipates Castro's steady economic and political isolation and advocates continued U.S. pressure. She urges the United States to avoid "a premature reconciliation that snatches defeat from the jaws of victory by allowing Castro to substitute U.S. trade for declining Soviet aid and thereby prolong his undemocratic personalistic rule."

**Smith, Wayne S., "Washington and Havana: Time for Dialogue," *World Policy Journal,* summer 1990.**

Smith, a former chief of the U.S. Interests Section in Havana, argues that U.S. policy toward Cuba is misguided. Instead of bellicose rhetoric, he says Washington should engage in dialogue with Havana on an issue-by-issue basis.

## Reports and Studies

**Economist Intelligence Unit, *Cuba: Country Profile 1991-92,* 1991.**

This annual survey of political and economic background contains some of the more current economic data on Cuba.

**Freedom House, *Cuba in the Nineties,* 1991.**

This report, basically a compilation of articles that have been published elsewhere, provides various opinions on the durability of Castro's rule. For the most part, the authors conclude that his fall is inevitable, if not imminent.

**Gonzalez, Edward, Ronfeldt, David, *Castro, Cuba, and the World,* RAND Corporation, June 1986.**

Gonzalez and Ronfeldt profile Castro's mindset and world view. This study attempts to explain the Cuban leader's ambitions and patterns of behavior as a political actor with the goal of interpreting Cuba's policy decisions.

**Watts, William, *The United States and Cuba: Changing Perceptions, New Policies?* 1989.**

Watts analyzes public opinion data compiled for Potomac Associates by The Gallup Organization in 1988. The data offers insight into public attitudes about what the U.S. policy toward Cuba ought to be. Some of the more interesting survey results are those from the Cuban-American community.

# The Next Step

## Additional Articles from Current Periodicals from EBSCO Publishing's Database

### Books & reading

**Zimbalist, A., "Reviews,"** *Economic Development & Cultural Change,* **January 1991, p. 462.**

Reviews the books "To Make a World Safe for Revolution: Cuba's Foreign Policy," by Jorge I. Dominguez and "Measuring Cuban Economic Performance," by Jorge F. Perez-Lopez.

### Debates & issues

**"Making the best of Cuba's bad job,"** *Economist,* **Jan. 26, 1991, p. 37.**

Focuses on the problems facing Cuba's Caribbean version of socialism as Fidel Castro's revolution enters its 33rd year. Economy in trouble, as a Third World Communist nation; changing foreign trade; Castro's "peacetime special period," which involves drastic measures to cut the use of energy and materials; biotechnology; trade with former Communist nations; lesson's drawn from communism's demise; details.

**Reiss, S., "The only dream left is to get out,"** *Newsweek,* **Aug. 12, 1991, p. 38.**

Reports on how Cuban President Fidel Castro spent an estimated $150 million on the Pan American Games in Havana, while cutting the food supply to his people. Many Cubans desire to leave Castro's antique Marxist economics; the problem of thousands of illegal immigrants flowing into Florida from Cuba; tourism apartheid.

**Robinson, L., "Castro's new revolution,"** *U.S. News & World Report,* **June 24, 1991, p. 38.**

Examines the new revolution of Cuba's leader, Fidel Castro. Volunteers have always been a trademark of Castro's do-it-yourself revolution; Cubans now have to give so much under such difficult circumstances; Cuba can no longer depend on its socialist allies for food; more than 100,000 Cubans have volunteered to plant and harvest their country's crops; every sector of Cuba's economy is suffering; predictions of how things in Cuba will suffer. INSET: The Miami to Moscow shuttle.

### Economic conditions

**"Tighten belts, gather herbs,"** *Economist,* **Sept. 8, 1990, p. 54.**

Discusses a plan implemented by President Fidel Castro, which he calls "a special period in a time of peace," which has rationed petrol and diesel supplies and restricted power use in Cuba. Details of plan; weakening ties between Cuba and the Soviet Union and other Eastern-bloc countries; impact of the plan.

**Bruce, M.R., "Cuba's open boats,"** *American Spectator,* **September 1991, p. 12.**

Presents a report from the rescue effort concerning Cubans who are paddling out to sea in hopes of reaching southern Florida as Cuba's society collapses. Thousands make it but many more die, and estimates of people who survive range from 1-in-3 to 1-in-10; Balseros, the Cuban "raft-people"; the belief that Cuban President Fidel Castro's days are numbered.

**Main, J., Harris, C., et al., "Cuba: Pushing for change,"** *Fortune,* **Aug. 26, 1991, p. 90.**

Details the problems Cubans are still facing in their everyday life — from standing in long food lines to employment changes — and looks at how Cuba is finally beginning to deal with these issues. Where to place the blame for Cuba's problems; collapse of the public transit system; shifting toward a freer market; alternatives to Fidel Castro; the U.S. trade embargo on Cuba; more.

**Padgett, T., Katel, P., et al., "Glasnost hits Castro's Cuba,"** *Newsweek,* **Sept. 10, 1990, p. 40.**

Reports on the growing discontent in Cuba sparked by a reduction in Soviet aid. Fidel Castro recently called on Cubans to voice their opinions; reports from recent defectors to the United States; committees for the Defense of the Revolution have grown less intrusive.

**Reyes, G., "Cuba in crisis,"** *World Press Review,* **January 1991, p. 59.**

Reports on the austerity plan Fidel Castro has put into effect in Cuba. Some visible effects of the program; why it was instituted; Cuba's tightening of economic ties with China and Canada.

**Robinson, L., "Fidel Castro's last battle,"** *U.S. News & World Report,* **Dec. 31, 1990, p. 60.**

Comments on the longtime holdout of Cuba's Fidel Castro who may be unable to resist change for much longer. Daily fight for survival: rationed food, gas allowances, reductions in power consumption, furloughs of office workers to grow food; Soviet support based on barter but expected to change to hard currency slowly; managing internal dissatisfaction; joining the world trading community.

White, P. T., "Cuba at a crossroads," *National Geographic*, August 1991, p. 90.

Examines how Cuba, nearly 30 years after the missile crisis sent the world to the last tick before nuclear war, remains stubborn, socialist, and alone. How this last bastion of Marxism-Leninism skirts economic collapse as Caribbean rhythms of life continue to pulse on this island of tropical beauty. INSET: Cuba.

## Economic relations — Soviet Union

"The Miami trail," *Economist*, Oct. 20, 1990, p. 48.

Comments on the impact to Fidel Castro's government of the Soviet Union's decision to cease giving Cuba subsidies to keep the government afloat. Announcement by the Cuban Communist Party that it will shed almost half its bureaucrats; Dropping supplies from the Soviet Union; rationing instated; announcement from Czechoslovakia's foreign minister and Deputy Prime Minister Jiri Dienstbier that the old ties with Cuba were to be cut; more; details.

Farber, S., "No more Soviet aid for Cuba?" *Nation*, Oct. 29, 1990, p. 482.

Examines what options are open to Cuba if it is to maintain its present degree of independence now that the Soviet Union has decided that subsidizing Cuba is a luxury it can no longer afford. Cuts in energy and food; choices it has to make; description of a minimum program of national survival.

Fins, A. N., Brady, R., et al., "Gorbachev will soon make Castro more of an island," *Business Week*, July 16, 1990, p. 47.

Describes how, battered by economic troubles at home, Mikhail S. Gorbachev intends to turn off the spigot of Soviet aid and trade subsidies, worth upwards of $3 billion annually, that have kept Cuba's Marxist economy afloat for 30 years. The phaseout, starting next year, will severely squeeze the island's rickety economy, which is already hurt by disruptions in trade with Eastern Europe. Cuba's outlook; adjustments to be made.

Katel, P., "One man is an island," *Newsweek*, Sept. 9, 1991, p. 39.

Considers if Cuban leader Fidel Castro can maintain relations with the Soviet Union. Declaration in response to communism's collapse in the Soviet Union that Cuba will "continue its independent, Cuban, socialist line." Soviet oil deliveries; Soviet-supplied grain; the Moscow-Havana connection; three of Asia's last Communist states that are reeling from the Soviet collapse: Afghanistan, Vietnam and North Korea.

Pearson, J., DeGeorge, G., et al., "Now Fidel really has to tough it out alone," *Business Week*, Sept. 16, 1991,

p. 51.

Comments on the possible effects of the drastically shrinking ties between Cuba and the Soviet Union. Cuba's proposed market-oriented reforms; Moscow's sharp cuts in military and economic aid to Cuba; the Cuban American National Foundation.

Tifft, S., Booth, C., et al., "So long, amigos," *Time*, Sept. 23, 1991, p. 36.

Details the announcement by Soviet President Mikhail S. Gorbachev that thousands of Soviet servicemen stationed in Cuba would be coming home, and his vow to cut economic ties. Coupled with a U.S.-Soviet agreement to halt arms shipments to Afghanistan, the Cuban pullout signaled Moscow's desire to disengage from costly commitments abroad and concentrate on priorities at home. Havana's reaction; Soviet imports from Cuba; Castro's armed forces.

## Foreign relations — United States

"Havana night," *Economist*, Aug. 31, 1991, p. 20.

Discusses American-Cuban relations. U.S. President George Bush's comments on the economic isolation of Fidel Castro's Cuba; Cuban "balseros" (rafters) washing up on the shores of Florida; Cuba's economy; the Mariel episode in 1980; hostage crisis at the Talladega federal jail in Alabama involving Cuban prisoners; details.

Banks, A., "Inside Gitmo," *The New York Times Magazine*, March 31, 1991, p. 26.

Discusses the military base in Guantanamo Bay, Cuba, asserting that it is the U.S. military outpost that time continues to forget. Traditional institutions of American community life; future of the base and U.S.-Cuban relations.

Kozak, M. G., "Cuba: An anachronism in today's world," *Dispatch*, Oct. 22, 1990, p. 211.

Michael G. Kozak, deputy assistant secretary of State for inter-American affairs, comments on U.S. policy toward Cuba before the Cuban-American National Foundation, October 1990. Cuba's time warp and U.S. policy; Cuban support for subversion abroad; human rights abuses and political repression in Cuba; Cuban military ties with the Soviet Union. INSET: Country profile: Cuba.

## Immigration & emigration

"Raft people," *Economist*, April 6, 1991, p. 42.

Reports that Cuba's Fidel Castro has announced that he was considering allowing all Cubans ages 18 or over to travel wherever they want. Concern of American officials; recent incidents of Cubans escaping to Florida; problems facing Cuba and the Communist Party government; case of Maj. Orestes Lorenzo Perez, a Cuban Air Force pilot who defected to the United States; details.

**Reiss, S. and Katel, P., "The plane people of Miami,"** *Newsweek,* **May 20, 1991, p. 41.**

Reports on the influx of Cubans into Miami and the unpopularity of Cuba's leader Fidel Castro. People arriving in Miami by both plane and boat; charter flights that are legal under the 28-year-old U.S. embargo against Castro because tourism was never banned; one charter company that processes visa applications; anti-Castroism; exile leader Jorge Mas Canosa, president of the Cuban-American National Foundation, and other leaders who are opening up.

## International relations

**"Cuba checks out,"** *Economist,* **April 27, 1991, p. 49.**

Looks at how the upcoming removal of Cuban troops from both the Congo Republic and Angola marks the end of Fidel Castro's military adventures in Africa. History of Cuban involvement in Africa; details.

**"The self-laceration of Cuba,"** *Economist,* **July 28, 1990, p. 31.**

Reports that it looks like Cuba has been cast aside by its latest protector, the Soviet Union and it is now more important than ever to cultivate their relationship with the few countries in the West that have languidly reached out a helping hand. Cuba's quarrel with Spain; relationship with the Soviet Union after the expiration of the latest five-year plan in 1991; trade with Eastern Europe; Castro's plans for the country that demand sacrifice.

**Brady, R., Borrus, A., et al., "Will Moscow someday decide: 'Yanqui si, Fidel no'?"** *Business Week,* **June 17, 1991, p. 52.**

Explains how Soviet support for Cuba looms once more as a serious political hurdle to the new Moscow-Washington warmup that the Soviets desperately want. States that there is just so far the U.S. will go without some fundamental progress with regard to Soviet policy in Cuba. Part of the economic squeeze is due to shrinking Soviet-Cuban trade; wave of Cuban refugees into the U.S.

## Politics & government

**Gunn, G., "Cuba in crisis,"** *Current History,* **March 1991, p. 101.**

Assesses the view that the Cuban Revolution will collapse in the near future. Aid from Soviet Union cut sharply; serious foreign debt problems; ruling Communists too dogmatic; will survive only if economy stays relatively healthy and Cuban people continue to support Castro.

**Landau, S., "Fidel will be around awhile,"** *Nation,* **June 25, 1990, p. 884.**

Examines the political strengths of Cuba even though political fortunetellers inside Washington declare that Fidel

Castro and the Cuban Revolution are "about to hit the wastebasket of history." Myths about Cuba; Castro's strategy for Cuba; political shake-up in Cuba.

## Religion

**Maust, J., "Freedoms only for show?"** *Christianity Today,* **June 24, 1991, p. 64.**

Investigates recent developments toward religious freedom in Cuba. New approval for the entry of large quantities of Scripture into the country; beliefs of some that President Fidel Castro is only making surface changes due to Cuba's hosting of the upcoming Pan American Games; status of Christianity in Cuba.

**Woehr, C., "Churches gain favor with Castro, see spiritual awakening,"** *Christianity Today,* **Jan. 14, 1991, p. 46.**

Studies a series of unprecedented developments in Cuban church/state relations. Spiritual awakening in the church in 1988; government response; challenges facing the growing number of believers; common fears.

## Social conditions

**Lowenthal, A. and Gardels, N., "Cuba's predicament: A fate worse than imperialism?"** *New Perspectives Quarterly,* **winter 1991, p. 10.**

Interviews Cuba's Vice President Carlos Rafael Rodriguez who gives his opinions on the proposed free-trade agreement between the United States and Mexico and why the Cuban lifestyle is more equitable than that of the United States A poor country but one of equality; education of Cuban youth; Jeb Bush; relationship with the Soviet Union.

**Rhoden, W. C., "17 hours across rural Cuba: The revolution lives,"** *The New York Times,* **Aug. 18, 1991, p. 1.**

Reports that although Cuba's roads are potholed and the luxuries are few, there are doctors and less poverty. Cuba's largest cities, Havana and Santiago de Cuba over the last two decades; sense that support for Castro and his revolution 32 years ago remains strong in the Cuban countryside; the Cuban campesino; details offered by Cubans concerning their plight.

# Back Issues

*Great Research on Current Issues Starts Right Here... Recent topics covered by The CQ Researcher are listed below. Issues dated before May 10, 1991, were published under the name of Editorial Research Reports.*

**MAY 1990**
Should Teaching Be a Profession?
Will Canada Fall Apart?
Is U.S. Patent System Outdated?
Federal Funding for the Arts

**JUNE 1990**
Downsizing America's Armed Forces
Progress In Weather Forecasting
Sir &s tL Bailout
Bio-Chemical Disarmament

**JULY 1990**
Do Americans Still Love Marriage?
Death Penalty Debate
Decline of Rural America
United Nations in the 1990s

**AUGUST 1990**
Democracy in the Philippines
Initiatives: True Democracy?
Hard Times at Newspapers
Teens Balance School & Jobs

**SEPTEMBER 1990**
Dangers of Alcohol
Western Alliance After the Cold War
Tobacco Industry
Right to Die

**OCTOBER 1990**
Organ Transplants
Energy Policy Options
Search for Arab Unity
Child Support

**NOVEMBER 1990**
Lotteries and Gambling
Post Cold-War Choices
Setting Limits on Medical Care
Multicultural Education

**DECEMBER 1990**
Cable TV Regulation
Americans' Search For Their Roots
Is Insurance System a Failure?
Why Schools Still Have Tracking

**JANUARY 1991**
Growing Influence of Boycotts
Should the U.S. Reinstate the Draft?
America's Archaeological Past
Peace Corps' Challenges in '90s

**FEBRUARY 1991**
Regional Impact of Recession
Puerto Rico's Status
Redistricting: Mapping Power
Nuclear Power

**MARCH 1991**
Acid Rain
Cost of the Gulf War
Reassessing Gun Laws
Future for Man in Space

**APRIL 1991**
Social Security
Canadian Crisis Over Quebec
California Drought
Electromagnetic Radiation

**MAY 1991**
School Choice
Racial Quotas
Animal Rights
U.S. and Japan

**JUNE 1991**
Children and Divorce
Teenage Suicide
Endangered Species
Europe 1992

**JULY 1991**
Teenagers and Abortion
Soviet Republics Rebel
Mexico's Emergence
Athletes and Drugs

**AUGUST 1991**
Sexual Harassment
Fetal Tissue Research
Oil Imports
The Palestinians

**SEPTEMBER 1991**
Police Brutality
Advertising Under Attack
Saving the Forests
Foster Care Crisis

**OCTOBER 1991**
Pay-Per-View TV
Youth Gangs
Gene Therapy
World Hunger

**NOVEMBER 1991**
Fast-Food Shake-Up
The Greening of Eastern Europe
Business' Role in Education

Back issues are available for $4.00 (subscribers) or $7.00 (non-subscribers). Quantity discounts apply to orders over ten. To order, call Congressional Quarterly 1-800-432-2250.

# Future Topics

▶ *Retiree Medical Benefits*

▶ *Asian Americans*

▶ *Obscenity Issues*

# Retiree Health Benefits

*Companies are cutting benefits, adding fuel to calls for reform*

A CHANGE IN CORPORATE ACCOUNTING RULES MAY
have a profound effect on health insurance for
retired workers. Under the new rule, due to take
effect at the end of next year, companies will have
to show the projected costs of providing health insurance
benefits to their retirees as a liability on their annual financial
statements. In many cases, the change will result in a
significant loss in reported earnings. To minimize the potential
losses, a number of firms have begun asking retirees to
shoulder a greater part of the costs of their coverage. Some
companies have dropped coverage for retirees altogether. The
drop in retiree health benefits adds one more dilemma to the
broader crisis of health care in America. An estimated 37
million people lack any insurance at all to cover health-care
costs, which now are rising by about 20 percent each year.

 **December 6, 1991 • Volume 1, No. 29 • 921-944**

*Formerly Editorial Research Reports*

COVER ART: BARBARA SASSA-DANIELS

December 6, 1991
Volume 1, No. 29

**EDITOR**
Sandra Stencel

**MANAGING EDITOR**
Thomas J. Colin

**ASSOCIATE EDITOR**
Richard L. Worsnop

**STAFF WRITERS**
Charles S. Clark
Mary H. Cooper
Rodman D. Griffin

**PRODUCTION EDITOR**
Laurie De Maris

**EDITORIAL ASSISTANT**
Thomas H. Moore

**GRAPHICS**
Jack Auldridge

**PUBLISHED BY**
Congressional Quarterly Inc.

**CHAIRMAN**
Andrew Barnes

**VICE CHAIRMAN**
Andrew P. Corty

**EDITOR AND PUBLISHER**
Neil Skene

**EXECUTIVE EDITOR**
Robert W. Merry

**PUBLICATIONS MARKETING/SALES**
Robert Smith

**EDITOR, EBSCO PUBLISHING**
Melissa Kummerer

The CQ Researcher (ISSN 1056-2036). Formerly
Editorial Research Reports. Published weekly (48
times per year, not printed the first Friday of any
month with five Fridays) by Congressional Quarterly Inc., 1414 22nd St., N.W., Washington, D.C.
20037. Rates are furnished upon request. Application to mail at second-class postage rates is pending at Washington, D.C. POSTMASTER: Send
address changes to The CQ Researcher, 1414 22nd
St., N.W., Washington, D.C. 20037.

# Retiree Health Benefits

By Mary H. Cooper

## THE ISSUES

Tales of corporate insensitivity are not uncommon on Capitol Hill, but at recent congressional hearings on health-care costs, the case of a 64-year-old retiree in DeLand, Fla., struck many observers as especially outrageous.[1] The hapless man, identified only as Mr. Knox, had received a letter from his former employer on Oct. 1, informing him that his health benefits had been canceled — 10 days earlier. He had no alternative but to seek coverage for himself and his wife on his own. At the least, Knox was faced with the prospect of paying much more for coverage, perhaps more than he could afford on a retiree's income.

But the reality proved even more devastating. Because Knox's wife suffers from Parkinson's disease, local insurers told him that no one would cover her at any price. And because Mrs. Knox is not yet 65, she is not yet eligible to receive health insurance coverage under Medicare, the federal health insurance program for those 65 and older and the disabled.

Knox is one of 5 million retirees who rely on health insurance benefits provided by their former employers. Like him, thousands of retirees will lose health-care coverage before they become eligible for Medicare benefits.

Many of these early retirees, who left the work force before reaching age 65, were lured into retirement during the 1980s by companies eager to downsize their operations by reducing payroll costs. Part of the lure was the assurance of continued medical coverage in retirement, a traditional benefit companies have long offered as a natural extension of the benefits they offer active employees.

All that is changing now, as com-

panies — faced with seemingly endless double-digit health-care inflation — look for ways to cut their liabilities for health coverage.

For most of the past decade, these efforts focused on ways to cut insurance costs for active workers. In most cases, employers terminated traditional insurance policies, which paid for physician care and hospital stays with seemingly little thought to the cost, and bought coverage for their employees with health maintenance organizations (HMOs), preferred provider organizations (PPOs) and other so-called managed-care insurance plans. These cut costs by requiring policyholders to use member physicians and hospitals, who charge set fees and stress preventive medicine in an attempt to reduce policyholders' need for these services in the first place.

The search for ways to cut health-care costs for current employees has more recently led employers to look at retiree health benefits as well. As a result, more and more workers are receiving a disturbing message from

their employers: Don't expect to enjoy the same level of health benefits once you retire.

It's a message that outrages Uwe Reinhardt, a health economist at Princeton University's Woodrow Wilson School of Public and International Affairs. "I can guarantee you that no other country would allow this," Reinhardt says. "But the American set-up allows shysters routinely to victimize decent, small people, the people who are not plugged in. This [health insurance] thing is exactly the same flim-flam that the savings and loan executives pulled off. It's shameful, but what can you do? I've said these same words in front of Congress. The fact is American workers are really treated harshly. Here, every time a CEO messes up, they fire a thousand secretaries."

The trend toward less health coverage and higher premiums for the insurance that workers and retirees do receive is being accelerated by a new accounting rule, which will require corporate balance sheets to reflect a company's liability for post-retirement benefits. Under the new rule, issued by the Financial Accounting Standards Board (FASB), expenses for current retiree benefits must be disclosed as well as the projected costs of such coverage for current employees once they retire.

Here are some of the questions being raised about the new accounting rule and other retiree health-care issues:

### How common are health insurance benefits for retirees today?

Employer-sponsored health insurance is the most common form of health insurance used by working Americans and their dependents today. More than half of all companies provide health coverage to active

December 6, 1991    923

# Retiree Health Coverage at a Glance

*In 1988, 42.8 percent of Americans age 40 and over had retiree health benefits through their own or their spouse's current or former employer. This included both private and public employees.*

| Coverage | Total | Men | Women |
|---|---|---|---|
| Total | 89,964,438 | 41,273,463 | 48,690,975 |
| No retiree health coverage | 57.2% | 53.1% | 60.6% |
| Workers | | | |
| Covered by employer's plan | 16.3 | 23.4 | 10.4 |
| Covered by spouse's employer plan | 11.7 | 5.0 | 17.3 |
| Retirees | | | |
| Covered by employer's plan | 11.5 | 17.3 | 6.6 |
| Covered by spouse's employer plan | 3.3 | 1.2 | 5.0 |

*Source: Employee Benefit Research Institute, EBRI Issue Brief, March 1991*

workers, and nearly two-thirds of workers in the private sector are covered by employer health plans.

Of the nation's 96 million private-sector workers, about 30 million are enrolled in plans that provide for continued coverage in retirement. According to the General Accounting Office, about 5 million private-sector retirees currently are covered by employer-sponsored health insurance.[2] Virtually all Americans age 65 and older are covered by Medicare, the federal insurance plan that today covers 34 million Americans. Most also have additional insurance to pay for health-care needs not covered by Medicare, either through employer-sponsored retiree health plans or through supplemental insurance they buy on their own.

As health costs have risen, however, fewer employers have been offering retiree health benefits. According to a recent survey by A. Foster Higgins & Co., a New York consulting firm, the percentage of firms offering retiree health benefits dropped between 1987 and 1989, from 64 to 60 percent for retirees under age 65, and

from 57 to 52 percent for Medicare-eligible retirees. The survey found that most of these companies were cutting benefits for future retirees, not for current retirees like Mr. Knox.[3]

A retiree's vulnerability to the squeeze on health benefits hinges on a number of factors — all of them beyond the individual's control. Age is a key factor. "Young" retirees are far more vulnerable than those who have reached age 65, when they can tap into Medicare. A retiree who leaves the work force at 55, for example, must depend on employer-provided insurance for 10 years. If the employer cancels that coverage, the retiree must look elsewhere for insurance, often to no avail because individual coverage is often prohibitively expensive and because older people commonly have chronic illnesses that insurers refuse to cover. About 2 million retirees currently covered by employer-sponsored plans fall into this under-65 age group.

In addition to age, a retiree's health coverage depends greatly on his employment situation prior to retirement. A survey conducted by the

Employee Benefit Research Institute (EBRI) in 1988 found that 43 percent of people age 40 and over had retiree health coverage through their own or their spouse's employer.[4] But the quality of coverage differs significantly according to such variables as whether the workplace is covered by a union contract, the industrial sector to which it belongs and the size and age of the company involved.

As a group, employees covered by union contracts are far more likely than non-union workers to get health benefits as a binding condition of employment. Contracts negotiated by the United Auto Workers, for example, generally provide health insurance coverage for retired workers and their families. Retirees who are not yet eligible for Medicare receive the same coverage as active workers. Once they reach 65, these retirees continue to receive the same health coverage with so-called wrap-around benefits, which make up the difference between what Medicare covers and what active workers receive.

However, current workers who belong to labor unions cannot expect the same level of health coverage when they retire. That's because employers have begun in recent years to try to shift the cost of insurance to the employees themselves.

"We cannot overstate the difficulties that retiree health benefits present at the bargaining table," Meredith Miller, assistant director of the AFL-CIO's department of employee benefits, said at recent congressional hearings on retiree health coverage. "Warmed up by a rash of cost-shifting in the 1980s, employers are characterizing ... their promise to provide retiree health benefits as 'unfortunate mistakes' in foresight." [5]

### Do some industries offer better benefits than others?

Certain industries are more likely than others to offer retiree health coverage. Utilities, insurance companies and energy and petroleum firms are the leading providers.[6] Retiree benefits in general, including health insurance, are less common in the rapidly growing services sector, even in union shops.

In the health-care and building-maintenance industries, "low wages and minimal benefits are the norm," says Peggy Connerton, director of public policy for the 975,000-member Service Employees International Union. "This is the new service economy, where three-quarters of all the jobs are. When these workers retire, they fall off a cliff. Pension coverage in the service-producing sector is lower than in the goods-producing sector. If you have a pension, but your wages were low, then maintaining health coverage is usually impossible. Some of our members have spent their lives working in the health-care industry but can't afford coverage after they retire." [7]

Coverage also depends upon the makeup of a company's work force. The more retirees there are compared with the number of active workers, the less likely the employer

is to offer retiree health insurance to new hires. Thus, older companies, often with a large number of retirees, are less likely than newer ones to offer this benefit.

This distinction is even more pronounced in the aging industries of the Rust Belt, whose profitability declined during the 1980s in the face of strong foreign competition. In an effort to boost profits, many of these companies downsized, encouraging active workers to retire early. As a result, the ratio of retirees to active workers at companies such as Bethlehem Steel and Chrysler is about 2 to 1. At AT&T, which expanded during the years of growth in service industries, the ratio is five active

workers for each retiree. Retiree health coverage is far less burdensome for such companies.

Company size is another important variable in retiree health insurance. Generally, the bigger the firm, the more likely it is to offer coverage to retirees. The EBRI study found that 62 percent of the retirees receiving health benefits from a past employer had worked in firms with more than 1,000 employees, and three-quarters had worked for companies employing 100 or more. According to The Wyatt Company, a Boston-based employee-benefits consulting firm, 70 percent of the country's largest industrial companies provide retiree health benefits.[8]

Government workers with health

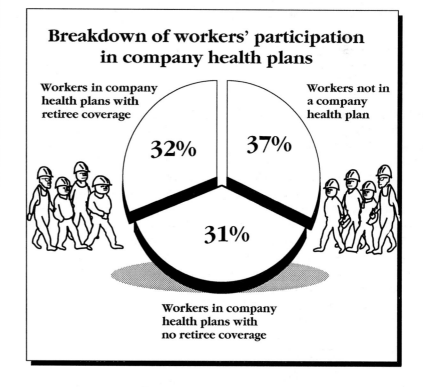

# Most Workers Don't Have Coverage

*In private industry, about 32 percent of the nation's 96 million active workers, or 30 million workers, belong to company health plans with retiree coverage. The remaining 68 percent either are not in company health plans or are in plans without retiree coverage.*

### Breakdown of workers' participation in company health plans

**Workers in company health plans with retiree coverage**

**32%**

**Workers not in a company health plan**

**37%**

**31%**

**Workers in company health plans with no retiree coverage**

*Source: General Accounting Office*

# Who Gets Retiree Health Benefits

*When it comes to health-care benefits, workers who retire from large organizations fare best: Nearly 20 percent of retirees from organizations with more than 1,000 employees have employer-provided health-care coverage, far more than any other group. Nearly 17 percent of retirees from the private sector have employer-provided health coverage, compared with 10.7 percent of retired government workers.†*

| Organization size and industry | Covered by own employer plan |
| --- | --- |
| **Organization size** | |
| Fewer than 20 employees | 1 % |
| 20-99 | 1.5 |
| 100-249 | 1.5 |
| 250-499 | 1.2 |
| 500-999 | 1.5 |
| 1,000 or more | 19.4 |
| Don't know/no response | 6.7 |
| **Type of industry** | |
| Private | 16.7 |
| Government | |
| federal | 4.9 |
| state and local | 5.8 |
| Self-employed | 0.4 |
| Don't know/no response | 5.4 |

† *These figures apply to individuals age 40 and over.*

*Source: Employee Benefit Research Institute*

benefits fare slightly better in retirement than their counterparts in the private sector. In 1987, 48 percent of participants in state and local government health plans enjoyed retiree health benefits.[9] However, because health benefits are not given to all active public employees, overall retiree coverage among government employees is actually very low. EBRI found only 16 percent of all federal retirees and 19 percent of all retirees from state and local government received health-care benefits.[10]

While a significant portion of U.S. firms provide retiree health coverage, they are under no more legal obligation to do so than they are to offer health insurance to active workers.

Unlike pension benefits, which are subject to stringent funding requirements, the vast majority of health benefit plans for retirees are funded on a pay-as-you-go basis. That is, the companies offering these benefits pay for them out of current earnings.

Likewise, there are few legal restrictions on companies that wish to terminate retiree health benefits. However, one powerful constraint is a labor contract that contains no escape clause allowing the employer to change benefits at a later date. "If your union leader did the deal for you, you may have protection," says Princeton's Uwe Reinhardt. "Some of them were smart and put ironclad legal protections in their contracts so

the corporations cannot break their promises. Others were trusting, and those promises were broken."

If retirees from healthy firms have little recourse when their former employers cancel promised benefits, those who worked for firms that have since gone under are in an even worse bind. Despite changes made to the bankruptcy code in 1988 aimed at protecting retirees, the General Accounting Office reports that almost half the bankrupt companies it surveyed terminated retiree health benefits, leaving 91,000 retirees without coverage permanently or for periods ranging from one to 16 months.

### What caused the crisis in retiree medical benefits?

Rapid increases in health-care costs in recent years — the same phenomenon that is causing employers to reduce health benefits for active workers — also put the squeeze on retiree health benefits. Since 1960, health costs have risen steadily, from $27.1 billion to $666.2 billion last year.

Health costs also have climbed as a percentage of the gross national product (GNP), the nation's total economic output, from 5.3 percent to a record 12.2 percent over the same period. The pace of inflation in health costs quickened in the 1980s and has been in the double digits since 1988. At this rate, The Wyatt Company predicts, the entire GNP will be spent on health care by about 2070 if nothing is done to break the inflationary spiral.[11]

According to the Department of Health and Human Services, half the rise in health costs in the 1980s was due to general inflation. The other half was attributed equally to medical-care inflation and to increases in the use of medical services — more tests and more visits to the doctor. More than a third of health expenditures last year went to hospitals, a fifth went to doctors and the remainder was paid for nursing home care and other health services, the Department of Health and Human Services reports. Paperwork and other administrative functions have been reported to account for 10 percent of all health costs in the United States, a claim the government disputes.[12]

Retirees' health-care costs are rapidly rising at many companies for two fundamental reasons. First, the general population is aging. That is, there is a growing number of older people in the population as a whole. This phenomenon will become even more evident early in the next century, when members of the postwar baby boom begin to reach retirement age. Demographers liken this trend to a pig passing through a python: Before and after the bulge created by the baby boomers, the age groups are less populous.

In 1960, 9 percent of the population was 65 or older. By 1990, the percentage had risen to 12 percent. By 2030, almost one American in four will be elderly. Further, as the ranks of retirees swell over the next two decades, the cost of providing health care for them will rise astronomically. That is because older people require more medical care than the rest of the population. Even today, the elderly account for 12 percent of the population but a third of all medical costs.[13]

In addition to demographic trends, the growing number of retired people is a result of corporate decisions in the 1980s, when many companies tried to cut payroll costs by actively encouraging employees to retire early. (Since the early 1970s, the number of people who retire at age 62 has doubled.[14]) But for companies that provide health care for retirees, this move is proving to be a double-edged sword. While they can thus remove these workers from the active payroll, employers are finding that the cost of providing health coverage for early retirees is much higher than it is for older retirees who

are eligible for Medicare.

According to Lawrence H. Thompson of the General Accounting Office (GAO), companies pay on average $3,323 to cover each young retiree, compared with just $992 for retirees 65 or over. That is because company benefits for older retirees generally are limited to services that are not covered by Medicare.[15]

### How does the new accounting rule affect retiree health benefits?

Since the 1970s, health-care inflation and growth in the retiree population have prompted employers to reconsider their promises of medical coverage for retirees. Benefit cuts have become increasingly widespread since the mid-1980s, when health-care costs accelerated. In the past two years, however, companies have pointed to a new accounting rule to justify decisions to cut back on retiree health benefits.

The new rule, issued in December 1990, will require most companies to recognize health liabilities for current and future retirees on their financial statements after Dec. 15, 1992. (Some small, privately held companies will have until Dec. 15, 1994, to comply with the regulation.) Employers may either set the money aside to pay for these benefits or treat them as unfunded liabilities against their earnings.

The new rule (known as FAS 106) was issued by the Financial Accounting Standards Board (FASB), a private, nonprofit organization based in Norwalk, Conn., that sets the standards for accounting procedures throughout the private sector. Because FASB is not a government agency, its rules technically do not have the force of law. But its indirect authority is such that any entity that issues annual financial statements, including both businesses and not-for-profit organizations, is virtually required to observe FASB regulations.

Two organizations enforce FASB rules. The Securities and Exchange Commission, an independent agency set up in 1934 to protect the public against fraud in the stock market, requires all publicly held companies to follow FASB standards in drawing up their financial reports. And the American Institute of Certified Public Accountants requires its members to see that FASB standards are followed when they audit both publicly and privately held entities.

"Neither of these involve force of law in the sense of our having direct authority over the way financial statements are drawn up," says FASB Chairman Dennis Beresford. "Rather, we issue the pronouncements and others enforce them."

Unlike pension plans, which companies are required by law to prefund to assure that the money will be there for employees once they retire, retiree health plans do not have pre-funding requirements. As a result, the vast majority of companies have funded and accounted for retiree health costs on a pay-as-you-go basis, listing only the current year's retiree health costs on annual balance sheets. Thus, the cost of providing promised health insurance benefits for future retirees never has been reflected on corporate balance sheets.

Beresford offers two reasons why corporations failed to account for retiree health costs on their financial statements. One is the relatively low cost of these benefits, at least until recent years. "They just weren't that big of a deal 10 years or more ago," he says. But there are less benign reasons for the oversight as well, in Beresford's view. "The companies in many cases frankly saw that there was a benefit in giving away something that was going to cost them 10 cents 10 years from now, as opposed to 10 cents now. They were more inclined to do the former, especially if they didn't have to account for it."

The lax accounting practices also have held open an escape hatch allowing employers to run away from their promises to workers as health costs escalated. "Many people took the position that these were not real liabilities," Beresford says, "but rather plans that were predicated on the company's having the ability to make the payments and that the company could discontinue at any time." These companies, he adds, have viewed retiree health benefits "almost as a gratuity that if we feel like it we'll keep paying."

Although FAS 106 does not require companies to make new investments in retiree health benefits, it has caused a furor among many corporations that provide these benefits. The new regulation will force employers to acknowledge to shareholders their liabilities for retiree health benefits and thus to report significantly reduced earnings.

According to one study, the total accrued liability for U.S. companies offering retiree health benefits amounts to $332.1 billion, based on 1988 medical expenses. If FAS 106 had been implemented in 1988, according to the study, it would have reduced total reported earnings by 15 percent.[16] However, the Employee Benefit Research Institute estimates these liabilities totaled substantially less — about $241 billion in 1988. Because of health-care cost inflation, the institute says that sum will be substantially higher when the rule takes effect in December 1992.

But many analysts dispute the notion that FAS 106 will hurt corporate performance in the stock market. "My hunch is that 90 percent of that has already been fully taken into account in the stock price, that when the change comes the world will yawn," predicts Princeton health economist Uwe Reinhardt. "Any good analyst will already have taken this into account.... It's the first thing

they'll look at."

No one disputes the enormity of the accrued costs of retiree health benefits. For some large companies it runs into billions of dollars. General Electric Co., for example, announced Sept. 16 that it would take a one-time, pretax charge against earnings for the first quarter of 1991 of $2.7 billion — the company's estimate of the cost of retiree health benefits for

current and future employees — to comply with FAS 106.

Some other corporate behemoths reported similarly huge liabilities for their retiree health commitments to present and future workers. These amounted to $2.3 billion at International Business Machines Corp., $2 billion to $3 billion at USX and $1 billion each at Lockheed and the Aluminum Co. of America (Alcoa). ∎

# BACKGROUND

## Early Aid for Retirees

Until 1935, few American workers could look forward to income security upon retirement. That's why barely a third of men over age 60 were retired at that time. They well knew the enormous financial burdens faced by older people who left the work force before age and poor health forced them to quit.

As part of its effort to protect citizens from the devastation caused by the Great Depression, the administration of Franklin D. Roosevelt moved to help retirees. The Social Security Act, passed in 1935, established the federal retirement income system, funded by employer and employee payroll taxes. Since disbursements began in 1940, Social Security benefits have provided the principal source of income for retirees age 62 and over.

In 1940, an increase in federal corporate income tax rates and tax breaks for corporate pension contributions prompted companies to set up pension plans for their employees to supplement Social Security benefits. Labor unions began winning pension benefits in contract negotiations in the late 1940s, and employer-sponsored pension plans became increasingly common, especially among large companies, during

the 1950s and '60s.

But these private pension plans were vulnerable to dips in the economy and corporate mismanagement. Companies were under no requirement to pre-fund their pension plans. As a result, retirees from firms that ran into financial trouble or went bankrupt could suddenly find their pensions gone, along with their ability to pay for health care.

### Unions Win Benefits

For many years, advances in health care for retirees went hand in hand with expanded pension rights. Beginning in the 1940s, labor unions won employer-sponsored health insurance coverage as important new benefits in contracts with industry. Frequently, insurers sold employers group coverage, which costs less than individual policies, and employees typically paid half the premium costs. Under later contracts, many employers picked up the entire cost of coverage, both for workers and their dependents.

During the late 1950s and '60s, companies began offering retirees the same health coverage they gave to active workers. The economy was expanding rapidly, boosting corporate earnings, and there were relatively few retirees on company payrolls. Health care was still affordable, so corporate liabilities for retiree health coverage were not significant.

Continued on p. 930

# Chronology

**1930s** *President Franklin D. Roosevelt sets up a federal pension system to help assure retirees of adequate income in their old age.*

### 1935
Congress passes the Social Security Act, providing income for retirees through payroll taxes paid by employers and employees.

— • —

**1950s-1960s** *During two decades of rapid economic growth, unions win employer-sponsored pension and health benefits to bolster benefits available to retirees.*

### July 30, 1965
President Lyndon B. Johnson signs into law the Medicare bill providing federal health insurance to people 65 and older and the disabled. The same year Medicaid is enacted to cover health care for the poor.

— • —

**1970s** *Retirees gain important protection for their employer-sponsored pension benefits.*

### 1974
Congress passes the Employee Retirement Income Security Act (ERISA), which tightens funding and disclosure requirements for private pension plans and creates the Pension Benefit Guaranty Corporation to insure pension funds.

**1980s** *Hurt by growing foreign competition and the worst recession since the 1930s, U.S. companies attempt to cut payroll costs by encouraging workers to retire early and reducing benefits.*

### 1984
The United Auto Workers brings suit against Yard-Man Inc., a subsidiary of Montgomery Ward, to prevent it from terminating its retiree health plan. The court's landmark ruling holds that even when contracts don't describe plan benefits, promises of retiree benefits made in oral statements, memos and pamphlets can be legally binding.

### 1985
Retirees gain limited health protection with passage of the Consolidated Omnibus Budget Reconciliation Act (COBRA), which requires employers to offer retirees and other terminated employees the opportunity to continue participating in their company's health plan for 18 months at their own expense.

### July 17, 1986
LTV Corp. files for reorganization under Chapter 11 of the bankruptcy code and terminates all health insurance coverage for its 78,000 retirees.

### 1988
Congress passes the Retiree Benefits Bankruptcy Protection Act, which restricts the ability of employers to change or terminate retiree health plans during bankruptcy proceedings and retroactively reverses the LTV action. Congress also passes (and later repeals) the Medicare Catastrophic Coverage Act capping the amount of out-of-pocket expenses the elderly would have to pay for health care not covered by Medicare. Also in 1988, the 2nd U.S. Court of Appeals rules in *Moore v. Metropoli-*

*tan Life Insurance Company* that employers can alter retiree health benefits if they have explicitly reserved the right to do so in plan documents.

— • —

**1990s** *Health-care costs rapidly increase, prompting employers to make deeper cuts in retiree benefits.*

### December 1990
The Financial Accounting Standards Board (FASB) announces a new accounting standard, FAS 106, that will force employers to reflect on financial statements the costs of providing health-care benefits to current and future retirees.

### 1991
Rep. Dan Rostenkowski, D-Ill., introduces the Health Insurance Coverage and Cost Containment Act, which, among other things, would lower Medicare eligibility from age 65 to 60.

### Nov. 12, 1991
Chrysler, Lockheed, Xerox and other large corporations join a coalition of unions, lawmakers and two former presidents — Gerald R. Ford and Jimmy Carter — in endorsing the "pay-or-play" health insurance concept. Under such plans, employers would have to either provide health insurance for their workers and retirees or pay a tax to help government provide health coverage.

### Dec. 15, 1992
The new FAS 106 accounting rule goes into effect for most employers.

### Dec. 15, 1994
FAS 106 takes effect for small, privately held firms.

# The High Cost of Health Care

*Health-care costs shot up for all Americans between 1977 and 1987, but the elderly were hardest hit. For those 65 and older, per capita spending jumped from $1,785 in 1977 to $5,235 in 1987, a 193.3 percent increase. The increase for those under 65 was substantially less: 138.9 percent.*

| Year | Total (billions) | | Per capita | |
| | Age 65 and over | Under age 65 | Age 65 and over | Under age 65 |
| --- | --- | --- | --- | --- |
| 1977 | $ 43.4 | $105.7 | $1,785 | $ 537 |
| 1984 | 119.9 | 221.9 | 4,202 | 1,024 |
| 1988 | 158.2 | 284.3 | 5,235 | 1,283 |
| Total growth | | | | |
| 1977-1987 | 264.5% | 169.0% | 193.3% | 138.9% |

*Source: Employee Benefit Research Institute,* EBRI Issue Brief, *March 1991*

*Continued from p. 928*

As unions won retiree health benefits as part of negotiated contracts with private industry, non-union employees also began to look forward to continued health coverage when they retired. At General Motors, for example, non-union, salaried employees have long received the same health benefits as hourly workers who belong to the United Auto Workers and are covered by contracts negotiated by the UAW.

## Medicare Passes in 1965

As part of his Great Society program, President Lyndon B. Johnson in 1965 pushed two new health insurance programs for the disabled, the indigent and the elderly. Medicaid, administered by the states and funded mostly by the federal government, pays the cost of medical care for the nation's poor. Medicare was devised as an insurance plan for those over 65, including retirees. Upon signing Medicare into law on July 30, Johnson proclaimed, "The specter of catastrophic hospital bills can be lifted from the lives of our older citizens."

Medicare became the largest source of health insurance for retirees and now covers some 34 million people. It is funded through a combination of payroll taxes, general federal revenues and premiums charged to Medicare participants.

Medicare does not pay for all retirees' health-care needs, however. Only 80 percent of physicians' "reasonable" fees are reimbursed, and patients must pay the difference out of pocket or through additional health coverage provided by their former employers or by private Medigap insurance.*

When Medicare became available, many employers who provided health insurance to their retirees con-

---

*As part of the 1990 Omnibus Reconciliation Act, Congress tightened regulations covering Medigap insurance to help the elderly avoid paying for coverage already provided by Medicare. The move came a year after Congress repealed another measure aimed at helping to reduce health-care costs for the elderly, the 1988 Medicare Catastrophic Coverage Act. The law, which had capped the amount Medicare beneficiaries could be required to pay for health care not covered by the federal program, was opposed by middle- and upper-income senior citizens who would have been charged an income surtax to finance catastrophic coverage.

tinued to do so, offering wrap-around coverage for services not provided by Medicare, such as routine preventive care, most outpatient prescription drugs, dental care and the cost of eyeglasses, hearing aids and other health-care supplies commonly required by the elderly. As deductibles were introduced by Medicare, wrap-around benefits often paid for these as well.

The cost to employers of providing retiree health benefits remained low until the 1980s. For a new company with a relatively young work force, the cost was negligible. In addition, employers were simply required to report retiree benefit costs on a pay-as-you-go basis, listing in their balance sheets the current year's payouts for retiree health coverage. And even these figures only appeared in a footnote to the financial statement.

### ERISA Passed in 1974

Since 1974, Congress has accorded greater protection to retirees' pension benefits than to their health benefits. That year it passed the Employee Retirement Income Security Act, better known as ERISA, which established pension plan disclosure and reporting requirements, trust responsibility and enforcement rights.

ERISA also established the Pension Benefit Guaranty Corporation (PBGC) to insure pension funds and set standards for participation, vesting and funding. In particular, ERISA requires employers to "vest" — render non-forfeitable — pension benefits for employees after five years.

Under the original law, a worker had to be employed by one company for 10 years before being vested with pension benefits. A subsequent amendment halved the vesting period.

ERISA also requires employers to pre-fund their pension plans, regularly setting aside money for employees' future retirement, to assure that the benefits are there when employees become eligible to receive them. Federal protection of pension funds and tax incentives for employers to provide pensions have greatly increased retirees' access to benefits.

The number of pension plans in the United States has grown from fewer than 700 in the 1930s to almost a million today. The vast majority of employees of companies with 100 workers or more are covered by pension plans.[17]

But ERISA is silent on the issue of retiree health benefits. There is no enforceable vesting period and no funding requirement for health plans under the law. This leaves retirees vulnerable to corporate decisions to eliminate their coverage. As K. Peter Schmidt, an expert in employee benefits at the Washington law firm of Arnold & Porter, points out, "If the employer goes out of business or benefits are otherwise curtailed there, retired workers don't have the option of retiring from somewhere else."[18]

## Benefits Cut in the '80s

The recession of 1981-82 and the rapid incursion of Japanese and other manufacturers into the American market for consumer goods caused a setback to U.S. industry from which it has yet to recover. Manufacturers of some of the coun-

> During the 1980s, many employers terminated or reduced retiree health benefits, often on the occasion of plant closings or bankruptcy proceedings. Such actions prompted Congress to pass the 1988 Retiree Benefits Bankruptcy Protection Act.

try's core goods, including steel and automobiles, were forced to go out of business or cut costs by closing factories or otherwise reducing their payrolls.

In either case, workers and sometimes retirees paid a heavy price for the decade-long restructuring of American industry. Even as companies were encouraging older workers to retire before the normal retirement age of 65, they were beginning to reduce fringe benefits, requiring active employees to pay a higher share of health-care costs and reducing health benefits for retirees.

"Though we have fought off cuts in retiree health benefits wherever

we could, we have seen 10 years of significant erosion," says one union official who asked not to be identified. "Whereas a few years ago I would have said coverage was virtually universal among our members, I'm a lot softer on that now. A lot of plants have closed, and the opportunity to lose your coverage has been greatly expanded in this country."

During the 1980s, many employers unilaterally terminated or reduced retiree health benefits, often on the occasion of plant closings or bankruptcy proceedings. Congress stepped in to help in 1985, when it passed the Consolidated Omnibus Budget Reconciliation Act (COBRA). This law requires employers to offer terminated employees, as well as retirees, the option of continuing to participate in the company's health plans for a limited period, generally 18 months, at their own expense.

### The LTV Case

One of the most notorious cases of unilateral termination of retiree health benefits involved LTV Corp., which on July 17, 1986, filed for reorganization under Chapter 11 of the bankruptcy code. At the same time, the company terminated all health insurance coverage for its 78,000 retirees and their dependents. The company claimed that continuing to pay premiums on retiree insurance would unfairly prevent them from meeting their obligations to other creditors and that, in any case, maintaining retiree coverage was not necessary to the company's continued operation during the bankruptcy proceedings.

LTV's action led Congress in 1988 to pass the Retiree Benefits Bankruptcy Protection Act. This law prohibits companies from unilaterally terminating health coverage for retir-

Continued on p. 933

# How the Courts Treat Retirees' Claims for Benefits

All isn't always lost when employers renege on their health-care promises to current and future retirees. Although the legal status of claims against companies that alter or eliminate health benefits is still unfolding, recent rulings suggest that some claims are likely to stand up in court, particularly those of current retirees.

For the most part, courts have followed the general principles of contract law, ruling that employers have the right to make changes in retiree health benefits if that right is clearly stated in documents describing the benefits plan.

This legal concept was reflected in a precedent-setting 1983 ruling in a class-action lawsuit brought against Bethlehem Steel Corp. The suit was filed after the company reduced medical benefits for 18,000 retirees and required them to make contributions to the plan. A federal District Court decided against the company because it had issued written and oral statements to employees promising that the benefit plan would cover retirees free of charge for the rest of their lives.

But what happens when employers don't distribute official plan descriptions to their employees? In a landmark case, *United Auto Workers v. Yard-Man, Inc.* (1984), the 6th U.S. Circuit Court of Appeals ruled that such "extrinsic," or informal, evidence as oral statements, memos and pamphlets could be considered the legal equivalent of documents defining plan benefits in the absence of language spelling out those benefits in labor contracts.

In 1988, however, the 2nd U.S. Circuit Court of Appeals, in *Moore v. Metropolitan Life Insurance Company*, rejected the legal validity of similar evidence because the plan documents included a clause in which the employer reserved the right to alter benefits. Thus, plaintiffs appear to have a stronger case when employers have failed to include an escape clause in their retiree health plans.†

Plaintiffs' lawyers invariably cite the 1984 Yard-Man ruling when they make the case that retirees have a right to promised coverage for as long as they live. In that case, the court ruled that if retiree health benefits are paid for out of funds that otherwise would have been part of their earnings, there is an inference that the payments constitute "status benefits" that will continue throughout retirement.

But courts both have accepted or rejected this concept in subsequent cases. In *Anderson v. Alpha Portland In-*

> **The legal status of claims against companies that alter or eliminate health benefits is still unfolding, but recent rulings suggest that some claims are likely to stand up in court.**

*dustries, Inc.* (1988), for example, the 8th Circuit Court cited the intent of Congress in rejecting the status-benefit inference. If Congress had intended for retiree health benefits to be status benefits, as are pension benefits, the court found, it would not have explicitly excluded health benefits from the funding requirements spelled out in the 1974 Employee Retirement Income Security Act (ERISA).

Also in 1988, Congress moved to protect benefits facing elimination during bankruptcy proceedings. Two years after the LTV Corp. tried to terminate its retiree health plan when it filed for bankruptcy under Chapter 11, Congress passed the Retiree Benefit Bankruptcy Protection Act, putting a stop to all such unilateral cancellations.

Under the new law, any employer undergoing bankruptcy proceedings must maintain all retiree health benefits unless they prevent the company from reorganizing and unless a court approves the shift. In addition, all benefit changes are subject to the approval of the retirees or their representatives, such as a union.

Employees who retire before age 65 are especially vulnerable to changes in retiree health benefits because they are not yet eligible for insurance coverage under Medicare. Their concerns were addressed in *Armistead v. Vernitron Corp.* (1989). Vernitron, a New York-based medical equipment manufacturer, announced in 1987 that it was transferring its Nashville operation to a plant with lower labor costs. Believing they would receive the lifetime health benefits promised in a benefits description booklet, 33 employees took early retirement. But the day the plant closed the company announced those benefits had been terminated.

Some of the new retirees immediately tried to get their jobs back but were denied reinstatement. The 6th U.S. Circuit Court of Appeals decided in the employees' favor, citing both the contract provisions of the 1947 Labor Management Relations (Taft-Hartley) Act and ERISA's provisions on terminating benefits plans. The court said that the employees had been induced to retire early with the understanding that they would enjoy those benefits.††

---

† See Employee Benefit Research Institute, *EBRI Issue Brief,* March 1991.
†† See "Unilateral Termination of Benefits Violates ERISA, Taft-Hartley, Court Says," *BNA Pension Reporter,* Oct. 14, 1991.

Continued from p. 931
ees upon filing for bankruptcy, as LTV did. Under the new law, employers must continue to pay benefits until the affected retirees — or a court — agree to changes in the benefit plan that are equitable and that permit the company's restructuring under Chapter 11. LTV, for example, eventually was required to continue paying premiums on its retirees' health insurance.

Although LTV's action was notable for the number of people it affected, the company was not alone in terminating or drastically cutting retiree health benefits. Many companies have done the same, often citing foreign competition as their primary motive. The auto industry, for example, cited Japan's competitive edge in health costs in its efforts to cut benefits. Health-care costs in Japan, which has a national health insurance system, are about a third of those in the United States.

U.S. automakers also pointed to the low health costs of Japanese auto plants set up in the United States during the 1980s as a means of overcoming trade barriers to this market. Because they have been in operation for only a few years, these facilities lack significant retiree populations and thus have much lower retiree health benefit costs than the Big Three automakers.

With employers focusing on cutting retiree benefits in attempts to reduce costs, strikes by U.S. workers have increasingly been called specifically to protect those benefits. The Service Employees International Union found that almost two-thirds of the 43 big strikes in 1989 were called over disputes involving health-care benefits, including those for retirees. These include a nine-month walkout by the United Mine Workers against the Pittston Coal Co. in Kentucky, Virginia and West Virginia.

The same year 60,000 members of the Communications Workers of America staged a 17-week strike against Nynex Corp., the regional telephone company serving New York and New England, until the company withdrew its proposal to cut health-care benefits. The extent of employers' legal obligations to keep their promises of health benefits to current and future retirees has also been the subject of numerous court cases. *(See story, p. 932.)*

## Pension Troubles

The erosion of retiree health benefits comes at a time when pensions — the mainstay of many retirees' financial well-being — are facing financial troubles as well. An estimated 50 major pension plans were underfunded by $21.5 billion in 1990, according to the federal Pension Benefit Guaranty Corporation. While it is true that these are only a small fraction of the 95,000 pension plans insured by the PBGC, it is also true that the agency currently guarantees a maximum payment of $27,000 a year on each pension it insures. And only a third of American employees belong to plans that are insured by PBGC.

The insurance also is limited to so-called defined-benefit pension plans, those that pay out a specific, predetermined sum to retirees. It does nothing to protect the assets of defined-contribution plans, which are increasingly popular among employers because they are less risky.

Such uninsured retiree pension plans include 401(k) plans, named after a clause in the tax code, under which employees and employers contribute a defined amount of pre-tax income to a long-term fund. While they look like a good deal to active workers because participation reduces current taxable income, 401(k)s may be less attractive than defined-benefit pensions because they offer no guarantee of a set income upon which a worker can rely upon retirement.[19]

Because of widespread bankruptcies during the 1980s among large employers in the steel, airline and other industries, the premiums charged to companies for PBGC coverage have risen from $1 per employee when the agency was formed to as much as $72 per employee today. Even so, continuing bankruptcies among large companies are threatening the agency's ability to guarantee these funds. The PBGC now has an accumulated deficit of almost $2 billion, and its accounting system is in such disarray that federal authorities are unable to audit the books.[20]

At the same time, many workers today lack pension coverage at all. Pension benefits first appeared in contracts negotiated for workers in the manufacturing sector.

Today, as those industries have declined and new jobs have expanded most rapidly in the service sector, fewer workers can look forward to retirement income beyond Social Security and whatever savings they have managed to put away while still employed.

Even retirees who collect pension benefits are having trouble meeting expenses, especially health-care fees. According to the Employee Benefit Research Institute, health-care costs are rising much faster than retirees' incomes. Health-care inflation has long outpaced increases in Social Security benefits, pension distributions and income from investments.

From 1977 to 1988, EBRI reports, total expenditures for health care by those age 65 and over rose by 265 percent — to $158.2 billion from $43.4 billion. During the same period, the portion of total personal income used to pay out-of-pocket health costs rose from 9 percent to 13 percent.[21]                    ∎

*Continued on p. 935*

# Chrysler Puts the Brakes on Retiree Benefits

Like other big U.S. manufacturers that have been in business for many years, Chrysler Corp. has a large retiree population. The payroll currently includes 68,000 retirees and 90,000 active workers — all covered by Chrysler's retiree health plan. With its growing numbers of retirees and rising health costs, the company has seen the plan's costs skyrocket. Chrysler estimates, in fact, that retiree health benefits add about $700 to the sticker price of every car it sells.

In an effort to reduce these costs, the automaker began scaling back retiree health benefits several years ago. In 1988 the company introduced a $200 deductible in its health-care plan for active workers and retirees and a requirement that future retirees share the costs of health coverage. In 1990 a "flexible-benefits" plan was introduced that includes deductible amounts ranging from $200 to $1,500. Workers and retirees who opt for coverage with higher deductibles — which costs the company less than coverage with low deductibles — receive added benefits, such as dental coverage.

Many companies have adopted similar changes in their health plans for active and retired workers. But this year Chrysler introduced a complex new plan that goes beyond typical cost-cutting measures, targeting non-union workers and retirees for draconian health benefit reductions. The cuts only affect the 18,000 retirees and 20,000 active workers who are not covered by a labor contract negotiated with the United Auto Workers. Chrysler's union members will continue to enjoy the more generous retiree health benefits offered under the old plan.

To launch the change, Chrysler switched from a defined-benefit plan to a defined-contribution plan. The difference is crucial: Defined-benefit plans assure retirees of a certain coverage, no matter what the cost to the employer. A defined-contribution plan, on the other hand, only assures retirees how much the employer will pay toward that coverage. Costs that exceed the employer's contribution must be met by the retiree, either out of pocket or by additional insurance coverage the retiree buys on his own.

To help workers and retirees pay for the coverage no longer provided by the plan, Chrysler now offers an array of special-funding accounts they can use to set aside in-

> **This year Chrysler introduced a complex new plan that goes beyond typical cost-cutting measures, targeting non-union workers and retirees for draconian health benefit reductions.**

come for that purpose. As a result, Chrysler workers and retirees must make what Hewitt Associates, Chrysler's benefits consultant, candidly calls "a complex array of decisions" from among the plan's "numerous movable parts" in choosing how they wish to finance their health coverage in retirement.[†] If, for example, employees choose to set aside part of their salaries in tax-deferred savings accounts for retirement health expenses such as 401(k) plans or voluntary employee beneficiary associations (VEBAs), the company will make matching contributions as an incentive for them to do so.

Chrysler is also planning to peg retiree health benefits to age and length of service. Under the old plan, retirees who qualified for pensions received medical coverage with no out-of-pocket payments. Under the new plan, an employee who retires at age 60 with 30 years of service with the company will receive the maximum insurance while someone the same age with only 10 years with Chrysler will get only half that coverage. This change, to go into effect in 1993, penalizes workers who retire early and who have not worked for the company for 10 years or more.

In yet another major cost-cutting change targeting current retirees, the company automatically enrolled all the workers who retired after Feb. 1, 1988, in the new defined-contribution plan; about 3,000 people were affected. The 15,000 who retired before that date, however, must choose between continuing in the old benefit plan or joining the new one. Chrysler offers several sweeteners to entice these older retirees to come on board and levies substantial penalties against those who do not.

For example, old retirees who join the new plan can choose from among a wider array of health-care providers, buy long-term-care policies (for nursing-home care) and receive a cash bonus. Those who don't enroll will continue to receive the old benefits with no deductibles and no copayments. However, the company says it reserves the right to change those benefits in the future. As a result, retirees who stay in the old plan conceivably run the risk of losing all coverage down the road.

---

[†]Hewitt Associates, "Chrysler Restructures Retiree Medical — for Retirees and Actives," *On Employee Benefits,* Spotlight Edition, 1991.

# CURRENT SITUATION

## Corporate Options

The Financial Accounting Standards Board rule requiring employers to list the current and future costs of retiree health benefits on their financial statements will take effect Dec. 15, 1992. Although the deadline is just a year away, relatively few companies have decided how to adjust to FAS 106, and fewer still have acted on the upcoming change in accounting standards. "The vast majority of companies that do provide retiree health benefits have yet to do anything," says EBRI President Dallas Salisbury.[22]

Employers have the choice of continuing their current retiree health plans but making changes in the way they fund them, cutting benefits or doing both. Employers can pre-fund their retiree health benefit plans in several ways. Some analysts propose granting employers tax incentives to do so, much as they receive tax breaks for their contributions to pension funds. Supporters of this approach say that employers might be more likely to provide health coverage for their retirees if it resulted in lower corporate taxation.

But others dispute this claim. David Hirschland, assistant director of the UAW's Social Security Department, points out that older manufacturing companies, which already are under competitive pressure to cut health benefits for their sizable retiree populations, cannot afford to pre-fund retiree benefits, even under favorable tax conditions.

Companies that choose to cut retiree health benefits are generally focusing on future rather than current retirees. "New hires and workers with relatively short seniority are the most likely to lack benefits so far," Salisbury says. Most of these workers will continue to receive some kind of retiree benefits. According to Hewitt Associates, a consulting firm in Lincolnshire, Ill., only about 1 percent of companies have chosen to eliminate all health coverage for retirees. The most common change in benefit plans, made by two-thirds of the 922 large employers Hewitt surveyed in 1989 and 1991, is an increase in retiree contributions.

IBM, for example, recently announced it would cap benefits for anyone who retires after Dec. 31, 1991. Employees who retire before the end of the year will receive the more extensive benefits provided under the current plan. This type of scheduled cutback has an additional effect of encouraging early retirement among eligible workers, especially if they are in ill health. "If you're 61 years old and not in great health at IBM, you'll be leaving this year," says Eugene Flegm, assistant controller at General Motors.

A slightly different approach has been taken by AT&T, which kept its retiree health plan in effect for the company's more than 100,000 current retirees. For employees who retired after March 1, 1990, however, the company pays retiree premiums only up to a fixed amount, based on the retiree's age and dependent status. The retirees themselves are responsible for any additional costs.

Other companies are switching from a defined-benefit to a defined-contribution approach to retiree health coverage. By agreeing to pay a fixed amount toward retiree insurance — rather than paying for health benefits regardless of their cost at the time they are received — employers can defend themselves from health cost inflation.

Many companies that are adopting this approach are also redesigning their benefits plans to condition coverage based on seniority. Quaker Oats, for example, introduced a defined-contribution plan under which the employer pays most costs of coverage while retirees pay the remainder based on their years of service. The longer the retiree was employed by Quaker, the less he must pay for coverage. Rewarding longer-service employees with better retiree benefits is a change that 10 percent of the firms in the Hewitt survey have already made.

Flegm says GM as well as the other two big U.S. automakers are also considering cutbacks in health benefits for retirees. But they will be unable to act as quickly as IBM, whose employees are not represented by a union. Negotiating with the United Auto Workers is not "a simple task," he says. "It's almost like negotiating with the elderly over reducing Social Security benefits."

GM's non-union, salaried workers may not be so fortunate. "Over the years, it's been true that whatever the hourly workers negotiated in terms of pensions and benefits, the salaried workers got," Flegm says. He suggests, however, that salaried workers' benefits may begin to suffer as a result of cost-control efforts. "We do not have a salaried workers' union, but they've gotten benefits without negotiating. That's been the past practice. Whether that stays in place or not is a different question."

### Impact on Active Workers

Union representatives confirm the growing pressure from employers to reduce health benefits for retirees. "With the current trend of health-care cost acceleration as well as the upcoming accounting regulation, there has been a dramatic increase in negotiations on retiree health care," says Claudia Bradbury, a policy associate for employee benefits at the AFL-CIO. "Health-care cost escalation and benefit reductions are the No. 1 issue on the bargaining table right now, and an integral part of this issue is retiree health."

What all this means to retirees and active workers today depends on several factors. Because court challenges to changes in promised retiree health benefits have tended to be more successful when made on behalf of retirees than active workers, most employers are maintaining their benefit plans for current retirees and focusing cutbacks on active workers.

Union members are less likely to face retiree health benefit cuts than non-union workers. "It is less likely that the benefit itself will be cut" for union workers, Bradbury says. However, union members can be expected to pay a greater share of the costs of retiree health benefits than they have in the past, as employers attempt to shift these costs during contract negotiations.

### Medicare Changes Asked

Critics of the current system of health care for retirees, based on company-by-company decisions regarding coverage and costs, are looking to Congress for help. Rep. Dan Rostenkowski, D-Ill., chairman of the House Ways and Means Committee, for example, has introduced the Health Insurance Coverage and Cost Containment Act of 1991 (HR 3205), which, among other things, would lower Medicare eligibility from 65 to 60. This would at least reduce the vulnerability of retirees who lose their employer-sponsored health benefits before they can receive federal coverage. Congress has not yet acted on the measure.

The measure has been endorsed by the AFL-CIO as an intermediate step toward broader health-care reform. According to the Employee Benefit Research Institute, the legislation, if it had been in effect in 1989, would have increased total Medicare enrollment by as many as 5 million people, including two-thirds of the 1.2 million individuals age 60-64

who were then uninsured.

Covering younger retirees in Medicare would benefit employers as well as reduce this group's vulnerability to catastrophic health-care costs. The General Accounting Office estimates that companies that provide retiree health coverage would have saved $4 billion of their total

pay-as-you-go costs of $11.4 billion for this coverage in 1991 if HR 3205 had gone into effect Jan. 1. These employers' accrued retiree health liabilities — that is, their liabilities for current and future retirees — which GAO estimated at $335 billion this year, would have dropped by 30 percent under the measure.[23] ∎

# OUTLOOK

## Calls for Reforms

Support is growing for broader reform of the nation's health-care system that would protect not only retirees but the entire population. The most sweeping reform proposals, modeled after health-care systems in Canada and other industrial nations, would set up a national health insurance plan covering all U.S. citizens.

Under a sweeping bill introduced by Rep. Marty Russo, D-Ill., the Universal Health Care Act of 1991 (HR 1300), a single federal insurance plan, supported by payroll, corporate and personal income taxes, would replace the current mix of private and public insurers to cover all health-care costs. Because all citizens would depend on a single public insurer for care regardless of age, ability to pay or employment status, certain segments of the population, such as retirees, would no longer receive less coverage than others.

The recent victory of Harris Wofford, D-Pa., in his Senate race against Dick Thornburgh, a former governor of Pennsylvania and U.S. attorney general, has underscored the growing concern in the United States over the cost and availability of health care. Wofford is thought to owe his victory in large measure to his strong support for national health insurance.

But Americans have mixed feelings over the notion. A recent survey conducted by the Gallup Organization and the EBRI found that a majority of Americans rate the health-care system in this country as fair or poor. Sixty percent said the federal government should provide health coverage for everyone, up from 54 percent two years ago. But only 48 percent said they would support a national health program if it meant paying higher taxes.

### The 'Pay-or-Play' Plan

This ambivalence is prompting many supporters of national health insurance to proceed toward their ultimate goal by incremental steps. One such measure is the "pay-or-play" concept advanced by many congressional Democrats. Under this proposal, employers would have to either provide health insurance for their workers and retirees or pay a tax to help government provide health coverage.

The AFL-CIO and many individual unions endorse national health insurance but also favor pay-or-play and lowering the Medicare eligibility age as interim measures. Speaking for corporate interests, the National Association of Manufacturers (NAM) in October came out against both national health and pay-or-play proposals and for continuing the current mix of public and private health insurance. "The U.S. voluntary health-care system is the envy of other

Continued on p. 938

# At Issue:

## Should the U.S. adopt Canada's national health insurance program?

REP. MARTY RUSSO, D-ILL.

*Vice chairman of the House Ways and Means Subcommittee on Health and sponsor of the Universal Health Care Act of 1991 (HR 1300).*
FROM *THE WASHINGTON POST*, SEPT. 10, 1991.

*e*veryone agrees that this country needs to reform its health-care system. Everyone also agrees that this reform should guarantee high-quality health care to all Americans without increasing current health-care spending. Only a single-payer health-care system can expand health care to every American while saving billions of dollars without causing rationing and without requiring cost sharing. . . .

Critics cite waiting lines in Canada, which they say are caused by the Canadian single-payer system. In fact, Canada has few waiting lines; the Canadians never have to wait for emergency care. . . .

Those who focus on rationing in Canada tend to ignore the rationing Americans face daily from their insurance companies. Unable to control runaway medical inflation, insurance companies protect their profit margins through rationing. Their tactics include denying care, even when prescribed by a physician, increasing cost sharing and refusing to cover preexisting conditions. The high co-payments and deductibles force hard-working families to wait months before they can afford to go to the doctor. . . .

Americans dependent on private health insurance are only an illness or a job away from losing coverage. In 1990, more than 37 million Americans had no health insurance, and millions more were underinsured. Canadians, on the other hand, never worry about whether their medical bills will be covered or about losing their coverage when they get sick.

The truth is, Canada's health-care system is more efficient than ours. Canada spends 40 percent less per person on health care than the United States, yet Canadians visit their physicians more often then people do in the United States. Furthermore, nearly all expectant mothers in Canada receive prenatal care. In the United States, only 76 percent of women who had live births in 1988 received prenatal care starting in the first trimester. . . .

We can't afford to do anything less than single-payer. According to the General Accounting Office, the only way we will ever slow health-care inflation in the U.S. is through comprehensive reform. And, as the Congressional Budget Office has testified before the Ways and Means Committee, single-payer is the only system that can provide high-quality care to all Americans for less than we currently spend on health. No other health-care proposal — neither mandated benefits nor pay-or-play — can make this claim.

REP. BILL GRADISON, R-OHIO

*Ranking Republican member of the House Ways and Means Subcommittee on Health.*
FROM *THE WASHINGTON POST*, SEPT. 28, 1991.

*i* agree with Marty Russo that the U.S. health-care system needs major reform. Far too many people lack health insurance, costs continue to skyrocket and essential-care providers are experiencing deteriorating financial conditions.

I disagree, however, with Russo's sincere but Utopian notion that the solution to our problems is a single-payer system such as that used in Canada.

First of all, the track record of our government in dealing with social-welfare programs should give us considerable pause at such a prospect. The government has failed to carry out the promises already made to provide health care to the poor and other social populations.

Fewer than 50 percent of the poor are covered by Medicaid, where limitations on eligibility, the scope of benefits and the level of reimbursement undermine its value to those it was intended to serve. And Medicare . . . has become such a stingy payer that if a hospital were to serve only Medicare patients, it would soon have to close its doors.

We would be far better off with a system of multiple payers. Such a system provides for some self-correcting mechanisms that are impossible under a single-payer system, which is, after all, essentially a price-control system in disguise.

The solution to U.S. health-care problems will be one that fits our culture, our circumstances and our needs. The Canadian plan, even for Canada, is not without its shortcomings or its critics. . . . Health rationing in Canada, for example, is not just an unfortunate byproduct in the Canadian system — it is a chronic problem. . . .

Advocates of the Canadian system generally understate the cost of adopting the Canadian approach. The extent of the administrative savings that might be achieved is questionable but will certainly fall well short of what is needed to fill in the extensive gaps that exist in our system. Thus, we would still need to raise substantial new sums.

Does anyone really believe the United States will abolish all private health insurance (as would be required under a single-payer system)? Does anyone really believe that our states would approve a system that sends their health budgets soaring?

Simple solutions won't work. What is needed is to examine the factors that drive costs — state health insurance mandates, tort laws that boost medical-malpractice insurance premiums and a third-party payer system that promotes unnecessary and inappropriate services.

# Future Shock: How Benefits Will Change

*A new accounting rule that takes effect at the end of 1992 is likely to prompt major changes in retiree health benefits. At least 60 percent of the firms responding to a recent survey say they will increase the contributions active employees will have to make when they retire. And at least 45 percent of the firms plan to hike current retirees' contributions.*

| | **Employee Group Affected** | | | |
| | | **Active employees** | | |
| | Current retirees | Eligible to retire | Not yet eligible to retire | Future hires |
|---|---|---|---|---|
| Will make a plan design change in the next two years | 63% | 77% | 80% | 74% |
| Will increase retiree contribution for dependent coverage | 48 | 61 | 63 | 62 |
| Will increase retiree contribution for single coverage | 45 | 60 | 61 | 60 |
| Will increase deductible or coinsurance | 30 | 42 | 44 | 43 |
| Addition of utilization management (also called "managed care") | 19 | 24 | 23 | 23 |
| Will change types of benefits offered (e.g., dental, outpatient psychiatric) | 19 | 26 | 29 | 29 |
| Choice of coverage options | 17 | 25 | 26 | 26 |
| Addition of PPO (Preferred Provider Organization) | 15 | 18 | 18 | 18 |
| Will change coordination with Medicare | 13 | 16 | 17 | 17 |
| Will tie retiree contribution amount to length of service | 11 | 26 | 32 | 32 |
| Addition of HMO (Health Maintenance Organization) | 8 | 9 | 10 | 9 |
| Will provide additional non-medical benefits to offset medical benefit cutbacks | 3 | 4 | 4 | 4 |

*Source: Hewitt Associates*

Continued from p. 936

nations, producing the latest in technological advances, yet it falls short in certain critical areas," the association declared in a statement issued Oct. 19. "While NAM continues to oppose mandating health-care costs, all employers and employees should share in the financing of such benefits."

But some major corporations are beginning to break ranks with the traditional approach supported by NAM. Some firms that do provide health benefits for workers and retirees see pay-or-play proposals as a way to save money. They claim that businesses that do not insure their workers and retirees push up their own insurance costs because doctors and hospitals make insured individuals — and their employers — pay for services rendered to the uninsured.

Numerous large corporations, including Chrysler, Bethlehem Steel, Lockheed, Westinghouse and Xerox, joined a broad coalition of unions, lawmakers and two former presidents — Gerald R. Ford and Jimmy Carter — in endorsing the pay-or-play concept in a statement issued Nov. 12.

"I believe we all recognize the fact that our nation's fragmented health-care system is simply not working," said Walter F. Williams, Bethlehem's chairman and chief executive officer, at a news conference.

The coalition would require all employers to either provide private health coverage to their employees or pay a new 7 percent payroll tax to help the government provide insurance. Employees of firms that fail to provide insurance would also pay a 1.75 percent payroll tax. The funds generated by the new taxes would be used by the states to purchase private insurance policies for these workers.

While Congress failed to tackle any of these proposals this year, health-care reform is emerging as a key issue in next year's presidential campaign. The Bush administration, which has come under growing criticism for failing to present a comprehensive health-care reform measure of its own, opposes the pay-or-play option as too expensive for small businesses.

On the other hand, many supporters of national health insurance are lending their support to such pay-or-play proposals as a more realistic legislative goal for the near term. If support for these broad reforms gains ground, measures aimed specifically toward protecting retiree health benefits may be pushed aside. ∎

## Notes

[1] This case was described by Rep. Pete Stark, D-Calif., at hearings on retiree health costs held Nov. 5, 1991, before the House Ways and Means Subcommittee on Health.

[2] General Accounting Office, *Employee Benefits: Extent of Companies' Retiree Health Coverage,* March 1990.

[3] A. Foster Higgins & Co., *Health Care Benefits Survey 1989, Report 4: Retiree Health Care* (1990).

[4] The Washington-based Employee Benefit Research Institute, a nonprofit, nonpartisan, public-policy research organization, included both public and private employers in its survey.

[5] Miller testified at the Nov. 5 hearings on retiree health costs.

[6] Foster Higgins, *op. cit.*

[7] Connerton testified at the Nov. 5 hearings.

[8] The Wyatt Company, *Managing A Changing Work Force: It's Time to Take a Look At Your Retiree Health Benefits* (undated).

[9] U.S. Department of Labor, *Employee Benefits in State and Local Governments, 1987* (1988).

[10] Data presented in testimony by Dallas L.

Salisbury, president of the Employee Benefit Research Institute, at the Nov. 5 hearings.

[11] The Wyatt Company, *Employer-Sponsored Health Benefits Programs: A Chronic Affliction or a Growing Malignancy?* This undated report is one in a series entitled "Management USA: Leading a Changing Work Force," published by Wyatt, a benefits consulting firm.

[12] See "Medical Costs Rising Twice as Fast as the Economy's Average," *The Nation's Health,* published by the American Public Health Association, November 1991.

[13] U.S. government figures quoted by Dallas L. Salisbury, president of the Employee Benefit Research Institute at the Nov. 5 hearings.

[14] See American Federation of Labor and Congress of Industrial Organizations (AFL-CIO), *Danger Ahead: Negotiating for Retiree Health Care Benefits* (undated).

[15] Thompson, assistant comptroller general for GAO's human resources division, testified at the Nov. 5 hearings.

[16] The results of the study, conducted by the Washington-based American Enterprise Institute for Public Policy Research, were presented at the Nov. 5 congressional hearings by Howard C. Weizman, president of the Association of Private Pension and Welfare Plans.

[17] See The Wyatt Company, *Retirement Policy Schizophrenia: Does America Want Its Elderly to Work or Retire?* (undated), one of a series of reports entitled "Management USA: Leading a Changing Work Force.

[18] Schmidt testified at the Nov. 5 hearings.

[19] See Jeremy Main, "Is Anything Safe Anymore?" *Fortune: 1992 Investor's Guide,* pp. 49-56.

[20] See Albert B. Crenshaw, "Pension Agency's Books In Disarray, Study Finds," *The Washington Post,* Nov. 8, 1991.

[21] Employee Benefit Research Institute, "Retiree Health Benefits: Issues of Structure, Financing, and Coverage," *EBRI Issue Brief,* March 1991.

[22] Salisbury testified at the Nov. 5 hearings on retiree health benefits.

[23] From testimony presented Nov. 5 by Assistant Comptroller General Lawrence H. Thompson before the House Ways and Means Health Subcommittee.

# Bibliography

## Selected Sources Used

## Articles

**Connelly, Mary, et. al., "Big 3 Must Book Huge Losses: Retirees' Health-Care Costs to Slash Equity by Billions,"** *Automotive News,* **Nov. 4, 1991.**

The Big Three U.S. automakers, General Motors Corp., Ford Motor Co. and Chrysler Corp., will have to record a total $20 billion loss on their balance sheets for 1993 as a result of the new accounting rule on retiree health benefits. The rule will require employers who provide health coverage for retired workers to begin listing the current and projected cost of that coverage as a liability on their annual financial statements in 1993. Although all U.S. firms operate under the same accounting rules, the change will have its greatest effect on automakers and other large and older industries, which have large retiree populations.

**Laugharn, Gary L., "Caught in the FASB Crossfire,"** *HRMagazine,* **July 1990.**

The author, an actuary and consultant on retiree benefits with Hewitt Associates, describes the impact of the new accounting rule issued by the Financial Accounting Standards Board (FASB) that requires employers to account for the cost of current and future retiree health benefits. Current retiree health plans typically have a single age-and-service requirement for eligibility: Age 55 and 10 years of service with the employer. But future retirees can look forward to stricter eligibility requirements. Employees will have to retire later and stay with the same employer for a longer time to get the broadest medical benefits when they retire.

**"Ouch! The Squeeze on Your Health Benefits,"** *Business Week,* **Nov. 20, 1990.**

Health benefits for active workers and retirees are becoming increasingly costly to employers and beneficiaries alike. As employers try to contain health costs, workers and retirees find their out-of-pocket costs rising while their access to care and choice of providers are shrinking.

**Sullivan, Louis W., "Health Care Reform,"** *Health Insurance Underwriter,* **June 1991.**

Sullivan, the current secretary of Health and Human Services, has been directed by President Bush to come up with a health-care-reform initiative, which is still in preparation. In a series of speeches this year, Sullivan has discussed the need to cut health costs, called on individuals to help reduce those costs by adopting "lifestyle changes" and claimed that a "significant percentage" of the 34 million uninsured people in this country really do have access to affordable health care. In this article, he praises the current system of public and private insurance as "fundamentally sound."

**Taulbee, Pamela, "What's Ahead for Retiree Health,"** *Business & Health,* **December 1990.**

FAS 106, the FASB's new accounting rule, will become a major issue in contract negotiations in the 1990s. This collection of interviews with a number of union and management representatives as well as outside analysts reveals agreement on one point: Even in union shops, employees will be asked to shoulder a greater part of the cost of these benefits.

**Watzman, Nancy, "Socialized Medicine Now, Without the Wait,"** *The Washington Monthly,* **October 1991.**

With a few adjustments, Canada's health-care system would work very well in the United States, according to Watzman, who works for Public Citizen, a consumer-advocacy group. In addition to covering all citizens, regardless of job status or wealth, Canada's national health insurance system spends only a penny for every dollar used for health services. Such low administrative costs would help cut health costs in the United States, where up to 24 cents is used for paperwork for every dollar spent on treatment.

## Reports and Studies

**Employee Benefit Research Institute, "Retiree Health Benefits: Issues of Structure, Financing, and Coverage,"** *EBRI Issue Brief,* **March 1991.**

EBRI, a Washington-based research group, analyzes the impact of the new accounting rule affecting retiree health benefits. The report describes the extent of coverage today and the options employers have for pre-funding their retiree plans. It concludes that Congress is unlikely to grant special tax concessions to employers as a means of encouraging them to pre-fund retiree health benefits because it would cost the Treasury $37 billion a year to do so.

**U.S. General Accounting Office,** *Employee Benefits: Extent of Companies' Retiree Health Coverage,* **March 1990.**

This report to Congress found that more than half the companies in the United States provide health coverage to active workers, but only 4 percent offer health benefits to retirees. Because most of the companies that do offer retiree health plans are large corporations, the number of people who receive health benefits in retirement are more than these figures would suggest. About 40 percent of private-sector workers are covered by retiree health plans.

# The Next Step

## Additional Articles from Current Periodicals from EBSCO Publishing's Database

## Advice

**Kirkpatrick, D. and Langan, P.A., "Retirement: Save until it's painful," *Fortune*, Feb. 25, 1991, p. 121.**

Reflects on how retiring with a moderate income takes a lot of money and preparation these days. Only savvy investing and will power can put you there. What to think about when preparing your retirement package. Medical expenses on the increase; unexpected costs; why you need to start saving now.

**Luciano. L., "Covering your longer life," *Money*, fall 1989, p. 91.**

Gives advice on planning retirement health costs. Company coverage; individual coverage; HMOs; Medigap insurance; long-term-care coverage; continuing-care communities. INSETS: Insurance to the rescue; what you need to know about Medicare, by F.C. Marshman.

**Wilcox, M.D. and Kainen, B., "Medical coverage for early retirees," *Changing Times*, February 1991, p. 82.**

Considers various medical-insurance options for people who retire before age 65, when Medicare coverage takes effect.

## Bankruptcy

**Lyons, J., "Triage on trial," *Forbes*, May 13, 1991, p. 104.**

Asserts that the 1988 Section 1114 of the bankruptcy code, designed to protect retirees of bankrupt companies, is not working very well. Bankruptcy judges are dealing with a sticky issue: whether to use assets to pay the health benefits of retirees who have worked faithfully for the failed company; how the law is affecting Eastern Air Lines; the situation confronting Federated Department Stores Inc. and Allied Stores Corp. in their Chapter 11 reorganization.

**Salpukas, A., "Retirees' plight in bankruptcies," *The New York Times*, July 2, 1991, p. D1.**

Discusses the issue of how long bankrupt companies should be financially responsible for providing medical benefits to retirees. Many retirees cannot afford the cost of private insurance plans, and many plans will not accept retirees with serious illnesses. Gives the example of Eastern Airlines.

## Case studies

**Barker, R. and Griesing, D., "Are investors liable for LBOs gone bust?" *Business Week*, Aug. 5, 1991, p. 74.**

Debates whether or not public investors, and even their brokers, can be held liable for money they made on a leveraged buyout (LBO) if it later goes sour, and includes the story of 7,000 Kaiser Steel Corp. retirees who were left with slashed pensions and no medical coverage when Kaiser was bought in 1984. Retirees hoping to recapture some of the $160 million in case that the LBO paid to stockholders; opposition; fraudulent-conveyance cases.

**Dentzer, S., "A healthy settlement for mine workers," *U.S. News & World Report*, Jan. 15, 1990, p. 45.**

Studies the continuing debate over how to share the burden of skyrocketing health-care costs for employees and retirees, in the wake of a tentative settlement between the United Mine Workers and the Pittston Coal Company. Highlights of the settlement; history of the industry's benefits program.

**Garland, S.B., "The retiring kind are getting militant about benefits," *Business Week*, May 28, 1990, p. 29.**

Reports on the militancy of several thousand GM retirees who are giving pause to other companies that want to unload some of the cost of current and future retirees' health care. Describes the new standards that would force companies to post dramatically increased long-term liabilities by disclosing projected retiree health-care costs on their financial statements. Side effects. INSET: Cutting retiree benefits: How companies can avoid trouble.

**Hayes, T.C., "LTV puts top assets on block," *The New York Times*, May 21, 1991, p. D1.**

Discusses the LTV Corp.'s decision to sell its once-renowned aircraft and military electronics operations. Anxiety of the company's 16,100 employees; income and health benefits pledges for retirees.

**Santora, J.E., "American opts for flex," *Personnel Journal*, November 1990, p. 32.**

Discusses a flexible-benefit program and a retirement health care pre-funding program implemented by American Airlines on Jan. 1, 1990. Details of program, which allows employees to decide exactly where their company-paid benefits will be spent and whether they want to purchase additional benefits at their own expense. INSET: Pre-funding ensures retirement medical benefits.

## Debates & issues

**"When retirees demand their medical rights,"** *Business Week,* **May 28, 1990, p. 114.**

Editorial. Tells how, as more and more companies try to cut medical coverage for retirees or make them pay some of their health-care costs, retirees are hauling former employers into court. Judges are thwarting management's efforts to curb soaring costs, ruling in many cases that companies made binding promises of lifetime medical coverage.

**Berkman, S., Mark, E., et al., "New health insurance plan for retirees,"** *Good Housekeeping,* **April 1991, p. 237.**

Investigates long-term-care insurance and points that should be examined about this type of policy. Benefit limit; daily benefit; waiting period.

**de Lissovoy, G., Kasper, J., et al., "Changes in retiree health benefits: Results of a national survey,"** *Inquiry,* **fall 1990, p. 289.**

Provides some background on retiree health benefits and reasons for their emergence as a central issue in health plan benefit design. Describes the survey and its findings. Concludes with a discussion of policy implications.

**Dentzer, S., "How we will live,"** *U.S. News & World Report,* **Dec. 25, 1989, p. 62.**

Studies growing fears of a retirement crisis among baby boomers. Four key factors considered; savings; Social Security; pensions; health care.

**Freeman, L. and Steenhuysen, J., "ESOP's fables,"** *Advertising Age,* **Feb. 25, 1991, p. 26.**

Shows how several companies are turning to employee stock-ownership plans to fund retiree medical benefits. Also includes other motives for turning to ESOPs; why employees should be wary when presented with such options; downside risks; how ESOPs work. INSETS: How plans work; what makes ESOPs safer.

**Loomis, C.J., "The killer cost stalking business,"** *Fortune,* **Feb. 27, 1989, p. 58.**

Discusses the retiree health benefits' crisis companies are facing; analyzes the effect the Financial Accounting Standards Board (FASB), which considers these benefits as compensation, will have on companies.

**McNatt, R., "The coming squeeze in retirement benefits,"** *New Choices,* **July/August 1991, p. 98.**

Discusses a change in a Financial Accounting Standards Board (FASB) rule that could affect medical expenses after retirement. Debits for 20 years of future health benefit expenses; shrinking benefit liabilities; growth of health-care

costs; possible effects on current retirees.

**Schurenberg, E., "On your mark, get set, go!"** *Money,* **fall 1989, p. 8.**

Presents guidelines for retirement plans in the 21st century, and lists the five most prominent features. Less Social Security; role of company pensions; cutbacks in retiree health benefits; longer life spans; less time to save in 50s.

**Thompson, R., "Benefits update,"** *Nation's Business,* **July 1990, p. 22.**

Summarizes some of the current trends and developments in the field of employee benefits, including self-funded, multiple-employer health plans, shrinking retiree health-care plans, and Medicare cost shifting.

**Todd, J.S, "The American health-care system,"** *Vital Speeches,* **Feb. 15, 1990, p. 276.**

Presents a speech by James S. Todd, M.D., senior deputy executive vice president, American Medical Association, delivered to the National Education Association 1989 Retirement and Benefits Forum in San Antonio, Texas, about the need to strengthen the American health-care system, the problems and concerns it faces, and how the United States system compares with the Canadian one.

**Warner, D., "Benefits update,"** *Nation's Business,* **April 1991, p. 32.**

Presents several brief articles on benefits issues for small employers. Health benefit cost increases; new accounting rule on retiree health insurance; cutting costs of workers' compensation; importance of being able to screen workers' histories; parental leave bill in Kansas; more.

## Law & legislation

**Ferrara, P.J., "The catastrophic health care fiasco,"** *Consumers' Research Magazine,* **February 1990, p. 28.**

Opinion. Criticizes the catastrophic health insurance initiative passed in August 1988. Reaction of senior citizens; benefits provided; American Association of Retired Persons.

**Freudenheim, M., "New rule on benefits approved,"** *The New York Times,* **Oct. 18, 1990, p. D1.**

Says that the Financial Accounting Standards Board voted to require employers to subtract from each year's earnings reports a portion of the costs of the health benefits that they have promised to future retirees. Reason for the change.

**Garland, S.B., "Bitter choice: Broken promises or broken budgets,"** *Business Week,* **Dec. 10, 1990, p. 34.**

Declares that in early December, the Financial Accounting Standards Board is expected to approve a controversial rule requiring companies to account for long-term retiree health costs on their balance sheets, starting in December 1992. How those unfunded liabilities — totaling as much as $400 billion — could wipe out many companies' net worth; how changes could spell trouble for current workers. INSET: Retirees start to feel the pinch.

**Hanks, C.A., "Before the well runs dry: Cutting the cost of retiree health benefits," *USA Today,* May 1989, p. 86.**
Discusses the growing costs of retiree health benefits facing today's employers. Why retiree medical costs are rising; recommendations to employers.

**Kaiser Jr., C., "Start planning for new rules on benefits," *Business Month,* May 1989, p. 87.**
Discusses how companies should start planning for the Financial Accounting Standards Board's proposal requiring companies to reflect in their balance sheets the cost of employees' post-retirement medical and insurance benefits.

**Nathans, L.J., "Soothing the sting of an accounting rule," *Business Week,* Sept. 18, 1989, p. 106.**
Discusses a new accounting rule that requires companies to write off the future cost of retirees' medical benefits far in advance, rather than simply paying them as they come in. How Standard & Poor's Corp., Moody's Investors Services Inc. and others are handling the rule.

**Norman, J.R., "Retiree benefits: this footnote doesn't have to become a nightmare," *Business Week,* Feb. 27, 1989, p. 39.**
Opinion. Discusses a proposed ruling by the Financial Accounting Standards Board regarding retiree health benefits that could virtually wipe out profits for the top 1,000 public companies.

**Novack, J., "Now you see it..," *Forbes,* Aug. 21, 1989, p. 57.**
Reports on a largely unused 26-year-old tax break that would have enabled companies to fund post-retirement health-care costs in advance, and how Congress is moving to wipe out the tax break.

# Back Issues

*Great Research on Current Issues Starts Right Here... Recent topics covered by The CQ Researcher are listed below. Issues dated before May 10, 1991, were published under the name of Editorial Research Reports.*

**MAY 1990**
Should Teaching Be a Profession?
Will Canada Fall Apart?
Is U.S. Patent System Outdated?
Federal Funding for the Arts

**JUNE 1990**
Downsizing America's Armed Forces
Progress In Weather Forecasting
Sir &s tL Bailout
Bio-Chemical Disarmament

**JULY 1990**
Do Americans Still Love Marriage?
Death Penalty Debate
Decline of Rural America
United Nations in the 1990s

**AUGUST 1990**
Democracy in the Philippines
Initiatives: True Democracy?
Hard Times at Newspapers
Teens Balance School & Jobs

**SEPTEMBER 1990**
Dangers of Alcohol
Western Alliance After the Cold War
Tobacco Industry
Right to Die

**OCTOBER 1990**
Organ Transplants
Energy Policy Options
Search for Arab Unity
Child Support

**NOVEMBER 1990**
Lotteries and Gambling
Post Cold-War Choices
Setting Limits on Medical Care
Multicultural Education

**DECEMBER 1990**
Cable TV Regulation
Americans' Search For Their Roots
Is Insurance System a Failure?
Why Schools Still Have Tracking

**JANUARY 1991**
Growing Influence of Boycotts
Should the U.S. Reinstate the Draft?
America's Archaeological Past
Peace Corps' Challenges in '90s

**FEBRUARY 1991**
Regional Impact of Recession
Puerto Rico's Status
Redistricting: Mapping Power
Nuclear Power

**MARCH 1991**
Acid Rain
Cost of the Gulf War
Reassessing Gun Laws
Future for Man in Space

**APRIL 1991**
Social Security
Canadian Crisis Over Quebec
California Drought
Electromagnetic Radiation

**MAY 1991**
School Choice
Racial Quotas
Animal Rights
U.S. and Japan

**JUNE 1991**
Children and Divorce
Teenage Suicide
Endangered Species
Europe 1992

**JULY 1991**
Teenagers and Abortion
Soviet Republics Rebel
Mexico's Emergence
Athletes and Drugs

**AUGUST 1991**
Sexual Harassment
Fetal Tissue Research
Oil Imports
The Palestinians

**SEPTEMBER 1991**
Police Brutality
Advertising Under Attack
Saving the Forests
Foster Care Crisis

**OCTOBER 1991**
Pay-Per-View TV
Youth Gangs
Gene Therapy
World Hunger

**NOVEMBER 1991**
Fast-Food Shake-Up
The Greening of Eastern Europe
Business' Role in Education
Cuba In Crisis

Back issues are available for $4.00 (subscribers) or $7.00 (non-subscribers). Quantity discounts apply to orders over ten. To order, call Congressional Quarterly 1-800-432-2250.

# Future Topics

▶ *Asian Americans*

▶ *Obscenity Issues*

▶ *The Disabilities Act*

# CQ Researcher

PUBLISHED BY CONGRESSIONAL QUARTERLY INC., IN CONJUNCTION WITH EBSCO PUBLISHING

# Asian Americans

*America's fastest-growing minority seeks more political clout*

SINCE 1980 THE NUMBER OF ASIAN AMERICANS IN the United States has more than doubled, making them the nation's fastest-growing minority group, by far. They are, in addition, the nation's best-educated and most prosperous minority. But the widely circulated stereotype of a "model minority" is misleading. The Asian-American community actually is a mosaic of nationality groups with differing cultural and linguistic backgrounds. Many newly arrived Asian immigrants are poor and barely literate. Lacking job skills, some young men from this disadvantaged group join gangs that prey upon Asian-American families and businesses. Since they have limited political influence, Asian Americans feel their needs are overlooked. Now, though, they are becoming more aggressive in using their economic clout to achieve their aims.

 December 13, 1991 • Volume 1, No. 30 • 945-968

*Formerly Editorial Research Reports*

COVER ART: BARBARA SASSA-DANIELS

# CQ Researcher

December 13, 1991
Volume 1, No. 30

**EDITOR**
Sandra Stencel

**MANAGING EDITOR**
Thomas J. Colin

**ASSOCIATE EDITOR**
Richard L. Worsnop

**STAFF WRITERS**
Charles S. Clark
Mary H. Cooper
Rodman D. Griffin

**PRODUCTION EDITOR**
Laurie De Maris

**EDITORIAL ASSISTANT**
Thomas H. Moore

**GRAPHICS**
Jack Auldridge

**PUBLISHED BY**
Congressional Quarterly Inc.

**CHAIRMAN**
Andrew Barnes

**VICE CHAIRMAN**
Andrew P. Corty

**EDITOR AND PUBLISHER**
Neil Skene

**EXECUTIVE EDITOR**
Robert W. Merry

**PUBLICATIONS MARKETING/SALES**
Robert Smith

**EDITOR, EBSCO PUBLISHING**
Melissa Kummerer

The CQ Researcher (ISSN 1056-2036). Formerly Editorial Research Reports. Published weekly (48 times per year, not printed the first Friday of any month with five Fridays) by Congressional Quarterly Inc., 1414 22nd St., N.W., Washington, D.C. 20037. Rates are furnished upon request. Second-class postage paid at Washington, D.C. POSTMASTER: Send address changes to The CQ Researcher, 1414 22nd St., N.W., Washington, D.C. 20037.

# Asian Americans

BY RICHARD L. WORSNOP

## THE ISSUES

Connie Chung is a familiar presence on television. Amy Tan's first two novels of Chinese-American life were best-sellers. And David Henry Hwang has written several internationally acclaimed plays, including the 1988 Broadway hit "M. Butterfly."

All this shows — doesn't it? — that Asian Americans have become a respected and influential presence in American society. Well, yes — but make that a decidedly qualified yes. As Asian Americans have learned over many years, the attitudes that their fellow Americans harbor about them are subject to abrupt and unsettling change. For instance, the economic success of Asian immigrants often inspires admiration, but that sometimes curdles into envy.

The great surge of immigration from across the Pacific in recent decades has thrown the country's mixed feelings about Asian Americans into sharp relief. In the 1980s alone, the Asian-American population more than doubled, outpacing all other racial or ethnic groups. Assuming U.S. immigration policy undergoes no major change, the Asian-American growth rate is expected to remain robust through the 1990s and beyond.

By most measures, the newcomers' impact has been positive. Asian-American children do well in school, and their older brothers and sisters get into and excel at the nation's elite colleges and universities. Asian-American families are uncommonly stable and tend to have incomes well above the U.S. median.

Willingness to work hard, defer gratification and adapt their skills to new situations have enabled thou-

sands of Asian-American entrepreneurs to realize the American dream. Korean Americans own and operate hundreds of small grocery stores in Los Angeles, New York, Washington and other big cities; Indian Americans run many of the small motels in California and other states; Indians and Pakistanis own newsstands, stationery and card shops in New York City and its suburbs; Cambodians dominate the doughnut-shop business in Southern California; and Vietnamese immigrants have become a major force in the Texas shrimp-fishing industry. These economic achievements have earned Asian Americans a seemingly enviable reputation as America's "model minority."

That shorthand description assumes that Asian Americans are a single cultural entity. Nothing could be further from the truth. The Asian-American community actually is a mosaic of ethnic, national and racial groups: highly educated, prosperous third-generation Japanese Americans; impoverished, illiterate Hmong tribespeople from Laos; second-generation Chinese-American college students attending top universities; recently emigrated Filipino physicians struggling to learn English; Chinese-speaking emigrants from Hong Kong and Taiwan working long hours for low pay in restaurants and garment factories in big-city Chinatowns; New Delhi-born psychiatrists opening their own practices. There are Vietnamese-American street toughs and Chinese-born Nobel Prize winners. There are Christians, Buddhists, Hindus, Shintoists, Taoists, Confucians and Muslims.

Above all, first-generation Asian Americans are divided by language. "Each [Asian-American] community has not only its own language but also its own alphabet," notes Jerry C. Yu, president of the Korean-American Coalition, a civil rights organization based in Los Angeles. The lack of a common tongue makes it difficult for the various Asian-American groups to take concerted action on issues of common interest.

The growing diversity of Asian America was the subject of a recent symposium in Los Angeles sponsored by the Asia Society. "It's all changed now," said one participant, associate law Professor Bill Ong Hing of Stanford University. "The reality is that the community is hugely different. No one can claim to speak for Asian America anymore." Arthur Hu, a columnist for *Asian Week,* a San Francisco newspaper, agreed: "You've got fragmentation across generations, across regions, across nationalities, East Coast vs. West Coast."[1]

Though Asian Americans still account for less than 3 percent of the country's total population, their increasing visibility seems to have triggered a resurgence of hate crimes directed expressly at them. Anti-Asian violence dates back to the mid-19th century, when Chinese laborers first came to the United States in large

# The Diversity of Asian Americans

*The number of Asian Americans in the U.S. has more than doubled since 1980. The economic success enjoyed by many Asian Americans has left the impression that all Asian Americans are prospering. In fact, this so-called "model minority" is a culturally diverse group divided by language and other customs, with many members of its ethnic subgroups struggling to survive.*

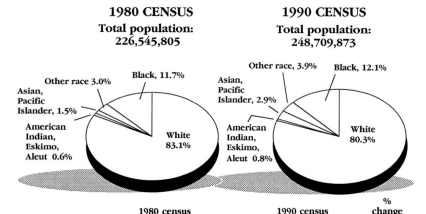

**1980 CENSUS**
Total population:
226,545,805

**1990 CENSUS**
Total population:
248,709,873

|  | 1980 census |  | 1990 census |  | % change |
|---|---|---|---|---|---|
| White | 188,371,622 | 83.1% | 199,686,070 | 80.3% | 6.0% |
| Black | 26,498,025 | 11.7 | 29,986,060 | 12.1 | 13.2 |
| Hispanic origin | 14,608,673 | 6.4 | 22,354,059 | 9.0 | 53.0 |
| American Indian, Eskimo, Aleut | 1,420,400 | 0.6 | 1,989,234 | 0.8 | 37.9 |
| Asian, Pacific Islander | 3,500,439 | 1.5 | 7,273,662 | 2.9 | 107.8 |
| Chinese | 806,040 | 0.4 | 1,645,472 | 0.7 | 104.1 |
| Filipino | 774,652 | 0.3 | 1,406,770 | 0.6 | 81.6 |
| Japanese | 700,974 | 0.3 | 847,552 | 0.3 | 20.9 |
| Asian Indian | 361,531 | 0.2 | 815,447 | 0.3 | 125.6 |
| Korean | 354,593 | 0.2 | 798,849 | 0.3 | 125.3 |
| Vietnamese | 261,729 | 0.1 | 614,547 | 0.2 | 134.8 |
| Cambodian | 16,044 | † | 147,411 | 0.1 | 818.8 |
| Hmong | 5,204 | † | 90,082 | † | 1,631.0 |
| Laotian | 47,683 | † | 149,014 | 0.1 | 212.5 |
| Thai | 45,279 | † | 91,275 | † | 101.6 |
| Hawaiian | 166,814 | 0.1 | 211,104 | 0.1 | 26.5 |
| Samoan | 41,948 | † | 62,954 | † | 50.1 |
| Guamanian | 32,158 | † | 49,345 | † | 53.4 |
| Other | 69,625 | † | 343,910 | 0.1 | 394.0 |

*† Less than one-tenth of 1 percent*
*Sources: U.S. Census Bureau;* The Washington Post

erupted between Korean shopkeepers in run-down neighborhoods and their poor, mostly black, clientele. Blacks complain that the Koreans treat them with disrespect and siphon money out of the community. The shopkeepers retort that black customers often are rude and not averse to shoplifting.

If nothing else, such clashes reveal a chasm of misunderstanding between the two sides. Community organizations in some cities have launched outreach programs in an attempt to bridge the gap, and these efforts may eventually bear fruit. But the long history of anti-Asian sentiment in the United States suggests that a more broadly based educational effort may be needed. For while Asians have lived in the United States in significant numbers for a century and a half, many Americans know less about them than about any other prominent minority group. Here are some of the major questions being asked about today's Asian Americans.

## Where are Asian immigrants coming from, and where are they settling?

Even for experts on Asian-American demographics, the profile that emerged from 1990 census data was startling. Exceeding projections made only a year or two earlier, the Asian-American population* rose from 3.5 million in 1980 to 7.3 million in 1990 — a growth rate of 108.6 percent. The Asian-American rate of increase was twice that of Hispanics, six times that of blacks and 20 times that of non-Hispanic whites. The net gain of 3.8 million Asian Americans represented 17 percent of overall U.S. population growth (22.2 million) during the decade.

The Asian-American community

*The term Asian American is identical to the U.S. Census Bureau category of "Asian or Pacific Islander." The 1990 census reported 28 different Asian groups and 21 different Pacific Islander groups.*

numbers. The chief motivation then, historians agree, was white America's fear of being overwhelmed by the "Yellow Peril."

Racist feelings of that kind still exist, fueled in part by fading memories of World War II and the Korean and

Vietnam wars. However, discrimination against Asian immigrants also stems from concern among some Americans — blacks and Hispanics as well as whites — that Asians are taking over businesses and jobs. In several cities, violent disputes have grew not only in size but also in diversity of national origin. The 1.6 million people of Chinese descent counted in 1990 topped the list, followed by Filipinos (1.4 million), Japanese (848,000), Asian Indians (815,000) and Koreans (799,000). The largest population gains in percentage terms were recorded by Hmong tribespeople from the mountains of Laos, who increased from 5,200 in 1980 to 90,000 in 1990, and Cambodians, who increased from 16,000 in 1980 to 147,000 in 1990. All told, nine different Asian-American population groups numbered more than 100,000 persons in 1990.

If current growth patterns continue, Asian America's diversity will become even more pronounced by the end of the century. Chinese and Filipinos doubtless will remain the two most populous groups, but Japanese probably will be overtaken by Asian Indians, Koreans and possibly Vietnamese.

As their numbers swelled in the 1980s, Asian Americans put down roots in all sections of the country. The 1990 census counted 2.8 million Asian Americans in California, the largest state total by far. New York was in second place, with 694,000, followed closely by Hawaii, with 685,000. Together, those three states accounted for 58 percent of all Asian Americans. Hawaii is, and always has been, the only state with an Asian-American majority.

Except in California, where they constitute 9.6 percent of all residents, Asian Americans account for less than 5 percent of the population of every state in the lower 48. Nonetheless, they are gaining on other minority groups in some areas. Asian Americans outnumber blacks in 10 states — California, Hawaii, Idaho, Maine, Montana, New Hampshire, Oregon, Utah, Vermont and Washington. And they outnumber Hispanics in four states — Alaska, Hawaii, Maryland and Minnesota.

Asian Americans could become a significant force in several additional states if 1980s growth rates can be sustained. Between 1980 and 1990, Asian Americans increased by 246 percent in Rhode Island, 219 percent in New Hampshire and 210 percent in Georgia. The growth rate in 27 other states ranged between 100 percent and 194 percent. The lowest growth rate for any mainland state, 43 percent, was in Wyoming, which also has the smallest Asian-American community (2,806).

For the most part, Asian America's presence is felt most keenly at the local level. That is because newly arrived immigrants tend to cluster in communities where others from their native land settled before them. Cosmopolitan cities like New York and San Francisco have long had their Chinatowns. Now other Asian immigrant groups are forming similar cities-within-a-city. They include Koreatown in Los Angeles, Little Saigon in the Virginia suburbs of Washington, D.C., and the desperately poor Hmong community in Fresno, Calif.

One of the most remarkable enclaves is Flushing, a sprawling residential and commercial neighborhood in the New York City borough of Queens. Formerly home to immigrants from various European countries, Flushing was sliding downhill in the 1970s as crime soared and shops closed for lack of patronage. Meanwhile, housing prices stagnated.

It was at this point that Asian Americans in the New York area discerned Flushing's underlying strengths as a place to live and do business. Besides having an ample stock of residential and commercial property, the huge Long Island neighborhood is situated near LaGuardia Airport, Shea Stadium and the affluent commuter suburbs on the north shore of Nassau County. In addition, Flushing is easily reached by subway, commuter railroad and highway.

Having noted all this, immigrants from Asia began to buy homes and open small businesses in Flushing. Today, most of the storefront signs on Main Street, the chief shopping artery, display signs in Chinese, Korean and other Asian languages. The area has become a popular shopping destination, especially on weekends, for Asian Americans from all over the New York metropolitan area. It is estimated that almost 100,000 Chinese and Koreans have moved into Flushing since the late 1970s.

Some New Yorkers credit Asian Americans with rescuing Flushing from further decay. Others contend neighborhood improvement has been a mixed blessing. The Asian influx drove up the prices of homes and commercial property, forcing many established residents and merchants to move elsewhere. There are strains within Flushing's Asian community as well. Those who arrived in the area early on profited handsomely by buying and reselling real estate. The catch is that escalating home values have made Flushing unaffordable for many Asian-American families of modest means — at least for the time being.

In some respects, Flushing is a microcosm of recent Asian-American experience in the United States. That Asian immigrants were able to revive a down-at-the-heel neighborhood in so short a time speaks volumes about their industriousness and willingness to take calculated risks.

At the same time, the turnaround stirred resentment among some white and black residents who felt that the Asians' success must have been achieved by unfair means — through government aid not available to other U.S. population groups, perhaps. Similar suspicions color many people's attitudes about Asian-Americans' performance in the classroom and on the job. These attitudes, Asian Americans say, have inspired a subtle form of discrimination against them.

## How extensive is anti-Asian discrimination in education?

The academic success of Asian-American young people should come as no surprise, considering that education ranks near the top of all the values cherished by Asian-American families. Statistics show that Asian Americans score higher than any other ethnic group in high school mathematics tests and trail only whites in verbal testing. Asian Americans also have the nation's highest high school graduation rates, and a large percentage of them go on to college.*

Parental pressure to study hard is not the only explanation for Asian-American academic success. U.S. immigration policies act as a magnet, attracting some of the best and brightest Asians. In a process that some have called "selective immigration," the United States each year takes in thousands of young scientists, engineers, managers and other professionals from many countries, including South Korea, Taiwan, India and the Philippines.** The children of these well-educated new immigrants tend to do well in school. In addition, outstanding Asian students are gaining admission to U.S. universities by the thousands; many of them stay after graduation.

The stress on education also has been strong among the approximately 1 million Vietnamese, Cambodians and Laotians who have entered the United States since the Communist takeovers of those countries in 1975. Many of these "boat people" were poor, uneducated and spoke little or no English on arrival in America. But studies have shown that their chil-

dren are succeeding in school. Federal programs to help refugee children learn English and adapt to the U.S. educational system are part of the reason for the success of many Indochinese students.

Despite their academic achievements, Asian Americans say they experience discrimination on U.S. campuses ranging from racial harassment to unstated admissions quotas. Asian-American leaders believe that some of the nation's best universities have deliberately held down the number of Asian students they accept.

According to Kathryn Imahara, a lawyer for the Los Angeles-based Asian Pacific Legal Center, such admissions quotas are "a prevalent problem across the United States." * She adds that news accounts of alleged quotas have done nothing to alleviate the situation.

One difficulty in proving discrimination is that "the admissions process is so subjective," says Imahara. "Most of the people doing the application reviewing are Anglo-Saxon and have a tendency to [think], 'Oh, well, we haven't admitted enough whites.' That isn't always the case, but it happens a lot." Some colleges have added Asian Americans and other minorities to their admissions staffs, but Imahara feels more needs to be done to make the process fairer.

For their part, college officials insist the allegations of admissions quotas are unfounded. Ira Michael Heyman, former chancellor of the University of California at Berkeley, took the position that "there should always be a 'mix' of students" and that "factors other than scores and grades should be considered." This approach, followed at Berkeley and other University of California campuses, "is not unlike the admissions patterns at the best-known private

universities, which have always selected for diversity — including geographical representation, athletic ability and other special talents, and increasingly for economic and ethnic diversity," Heyman said.[2]

Rejecting this rationale, Asian Americans say "diversity" is a code word for a discriminatory policy that violates federal law. Under Title VI of the Civil Rights Act of 1964, recipients of federal funds may not discriminate on the basis of race, color or national origin. In 1988, the U.S. Education Department's civil rights office launched investigations to ascertain whether Harvard University and the University of California at Los Angeles (UCLA) had established illegal quotas limiting the number of Asian-American students they admit.

The inquiries produced differing conclusions. Michael Williams, the assistant secretary of Education for civil rights, said on Oct. 1, 1990, that the department's probe had found discrimination at UCLA. He noted "an inconsistency in how Asian and white applicants [to the graduate mathematics department] who received the same evaluation ratings were treated." Williams added that there was "insufficient evidence to show a nondiscriminatory basis for this pattern."

Because of these findings, Williams said, UCLA must (1) offer admission to five Asian-American students who had been discriminatorily denied admission; (2) establish a uniform admissions procedure; and (3) improve record-keeping "to allow us to determine whether or not [UCLA] is observing the civil rights laws."

Harvard, in contrast, received a clean bill of health. The Education Department's civil rights office reported Oct. 7, 1990, that Asian-American undergraduate applicants to Harvard College were admitted "at a significantly lower rate than white applicants," but it concluded that the disparity reflected "the preference given to children of alumni and re-

---

*According to a 1985 study conducted for the American Educational Research Association, 51 percent of all 1980 Asian-American high school seniors enrolled in four-year colleges by February 1982, as compared with 37 percent of white seniors, 33 percent of black seniors and 20 percent of Hispanics.

**The 1990 Immigration Act established five categories for job-based visas, including "aliens with exceptional ability or members of the professions."

---

*The center provides legal assistance to Asian Americans and monitors bias against Asian Americans in higher education.

cruited athletes," not discriminatory policies. Noting that Asian Americans constituted 19.7 percent of the 1990-91 Harvard freshman class, up from 5.5 percent for the class of 1983, the office said the trend "doesn't support a hypothesis that ceilings are placed on the number of Asian Americans admitted."

### How extensive is anti-Asian discrimination in employment?

Asian Americans complain that they face discrimination in the workplace as well as on campus. "In both government and private employment," the California attorney general's Asian and Pacific Islander Advisory Committee declared in a 1988 report, Asian Americans "remain clustered in the lower and mid-level ranges, poorly represented at the higher-level management and leadership level, and often experiencing what has been referred to as a 'glass ceiling,' a barrier that prevents them" from rising above a certain job plateau.[3]

The report went on to observe that, "the stereotype of Asian/Pacific Islander Americans as subservient, unassertive and lacking communication skills can create institutional bias that makes it more difficult for Asians to pass the subjective portions of the screening process." Asian Americans often do poorly on the oral portion of such tests "either because of limited English language skills or accent bias on the part of the interviewer, or both."[4]

Accent discrimination, a problem faced by many newly arrived immigrants, is one of the civil rights issues that Kathryn Imahara of the Asian Pacific Legal Center deals with frequently. A related employment barrier that she battles is English-only rules in the workplace.

Asian Americans with special skills confront one of the most frustrating types of job bias. When they arrive in the United States, they usually expect to resume their careers. Instead, they

## Asian Immigration By Decade

*The first Chinese immigrants were lured by the Gold Rush, and then by work on the transcontinental railroads. But anti-Asian sentiment and laws kept immigration low in the early and mid-20th century. The number of Asians allowed to enter the U.S. increased dramatically in the 1970s and '80s. Recent immigrants included thousands of Vietnamese "boat people."*

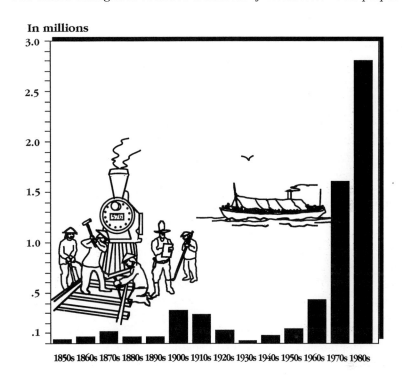

**In millions**

1850s 1860s 1870s 1880s 1890s 1900s 1910s 1920s 1930s 1940s 1950s 1960s 1970s 1980s

*Source: U.S. Immigration and Naturalization Service*

find their educational credentials discounted, their professional qualifications called into question and their work experience dismissed as irrelevant. Furthermore, many of those who do meet the educational requirements on licensing examinations fail to earn a passing grade because of limited proficiency in English and lack of familiarity with U.S. testing procedures.

"The unemployment and underemployment of these foreign-born and educated Asian/Pacific Islander professionals deprives their communities not only of health care and other professional services but also of much-needed bilingual/bicultural

skills in the provision of these services," the advisory committee's report noted.[5]

An unintended consequence of the 1986 Immigration Reform and Control Act was the erection of new barriers to hiring recent immigrants from Asia and Latin America. The primary purpose of the law was to penalize employers who knowingly hired undocumented aliens. In this way, the measure's sponsors hoped to eradicate the "shadow society" of illegal immigrants living in poverty and constant fear of deportation.

According to a 1990 study by the

*Continued on p. 953*

# Asian Americans: A Coast-to-Coast Phenomenon

*In the past decade, most states have experienced unprecedented growth in the number of Asian immigrants. The states with the highest overall percentages of Asian Americans are Hawaii, California, Washington and New York.*

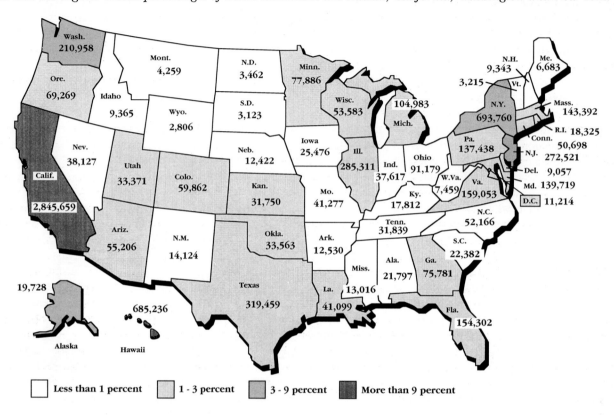

| Less than 1 percent | 1 - 3 percent | 3 - 9 percent | More than 9 percent |

| State | % Asian | % change 1980 - 1990 | State | % Asian | % change 1980 - 1990 | State | % Asian | % change 1980 - 1990 |
|---|---|---|---|---|---|---|---|---|
| Alabama | 0.5 | 123.9 | Kentucky | 0.5 | 78.7 | Ohio | 0.8 | 90.7 |
| Alaska | 3.6 | 144.9 | Louisiana | 1.0 | 72.8 | Oklahoma | 1.1 | 94.3 |
| Arizona | 1.5 | 150.6 | Maine | 0.5 | 126.8 | Oregon | 2.4 | 99.2 |
| Arkansas | 0.5 | 85.9 | Maryland | 2.9 | 117.4 | Pennsylvania | 1.2 | 113.5 |
| California | 9.6 | 127.0 | Massachusetts | 2.4 | 189.7 | Rhode Island | 1.8 | 245.6 |
| Colorado | 1.8 | 100.1 | Michigan | 1.1 | 84.9 | South Carolina | 0.6 | 89.1 |
| Connecticut | 1.5 | 167.3 | Minnesota | 1.8 | 193.5 | South Dakota | 0.4 | 79.7 |
| Delaware | 1.4 | 120.3 | Mississippi | 0.5 | 75.6 | Tennessee | 0.7 | 128.0 |
| District of | | | Missouri | 0.8 | 78.7 | Texas | 1.9 | 165.5 |
| Columbia | 1.8 | 69.0 | Montana | 0.5 | 70.2 | Utah | 1.9 | 121.4 |
| Florida | 1.2 | 171.9 | Nebraska | 0.8 | 77.4 | Vermont | 0.6 | 137.3 |
| Georgia | 1.2 | 209.9 | Nevada | 3.2 | 169.2 | Virginia | 2.6 | 140.2 |
| Hawaii | 61.8 | 17.5 | New Hampshire | 0.8 | 219.0 | Washington | 4.3 | 105.7 |
| Idaho | 0.9 | 57.4 | New Jersey | 3.5 | 162.4 | West Virginia | 0.4 | 43.6 |
| Illinois | 2.5 | 78.7 | New Mexico | 0.9 | 106.9 | Wisconsin | 1.1 | 195.0 |
| Indiana | 0.7 | 83.0 | New York | 3.9 | 123.4 | Wyoming | 0.6 | 42.5 |
| Iowa | 0.9 | 120.1 | North Carolina | 0.8 | 146.3 | | | |
| Kansas | 1.3 | 110.6 | North Dakota | 0.5 | 74.9 | U.S. TOTAL | 2.9 | 107.8 |

*Source: U.S. Census Bureau*

*Continued from p. 951*

Rand Corp. and the Urban Institute, the employer-sanction provisions of the 1986 law have done little to deter illegal immigration.[6] On the other hand, says Jerry Yu of the Korean-American Coalition, the sanctions have made many employers wary of hiring "anyone who doesn't look 'American' — that is, white." Yu says he knows "for a fact" that "a lot of Asians" have been denied jobs because of employer uneasiness about the law's application. A 1990 U.S. General Accounting Office report came to the same conclusion.[7] The 1986 law, it said, has caused "widespread discrimination" against legal job applicants who appear "foreign."

### Why do so many Asian Americans establish small businesses?

Job discrimination against immigrants helps explain why thousands of newly arrived Asian Americans go into business for themselves. For many, the choice between working for a "glass-ceiling" company and starting from scratch as one's own boss is no choice at all. Though the risks of failure are high, ambitious Asian newcomers often see the opportunity to strike it rich through entrepreneurship as the most attractive option they have.

Start-up money may be scarce, so the vast majority of newly formed Asian-American businesses are "mom and pop" operations. The authors of a 1986 study of minority-owned businesses in California found Asian-controlled enterprises there are primarily sole proprietorships that use family members and other non-paid employees.[8] Even so, profits generally are small. Many of the businesses are eating or drinking establishments, food stores or health clinics.

Whether the Asian-American enterprise is large or small, different groups tend to gravitate toward different specialties, the California study concluded. The Chinese, for instance, are often found in retail, wholesale and financial enterprises, but rarely in construction or transportation. The Japanese prefer construction and transportation to retail and service establishments. Retail-oriented Korean Americans have become a major force in food marketing.

A Census Bureau report issued this summer cast additional light on the explosive growth of Asian-American business formation during the past decade. The report, derived from the bureau's 1987 Survey of Minority-Owned Business Enterprises, showed that Asian-American businesses increased nationwide from 187,691 to 335,331 between 1982 and 1987. The 79 percent growth rate exceeded that of any other U.S. population group.

Combined receipts of the firms owned by Asian Americans rose by nearly 162 percent during the period, as against a nationwide average increase of 14 percent. In 1987, Asian-American entrepreneurs made the greatest share of their money, $3.8 billion, from food stores. Census data also indicate that approximately 6 percent of Asian Americans own businesses of some kind, compared with about 6.5 percent of whites, 2 percent of Hispanics, 1.5 percent of blacks and 1 percent of Native Americans.

Surprisingly, many Asian-American entrepreneurs "don't have much training in business," says Jerry Yu. But if language and cultural barriers prevent them from getting a satisfactory job working for someone else, "they go into business with a friend or their family." Furthermore, many Asian immigrants who do find jobs with a corporation eventually quit and open a business of their own "because they feel their opportunities [for advancement] are limited."

Asian-American professionals who abandon salaried jobs to start a business seldom have second thoughts, Yu says. "Once they're out there on their own, and if they're successful, why would they want to go back?

There is almost no incentive for them to return to a professional job."

Yu notes, however, that fewer professionals from South Korea are coming to the United States than in the past, largely because the Korean economy is flourishing. When highly trained Koreans do emigrate to the United States, they often conclude they would be better off going home. The returnees include an uncle of Yu's. "So the immigrants we see more and more of now are those that have less to lose by leaving Korea," he says.

The hectic pace of business formation by Asian Americans has fueled speculation that they have access to clandestine sources of start-up money. Asian Americans scoff at the notion. Actually, they say, many would-be Asian entrepreneurs have difficulty borrowing money because they are viewed as poor credit risks.

To get around this obstacle, Asian immigrants turn to their own communities for financial help. Korean Americans have learned to pool their money in a *keh*, or cooperative, typically comprised of about 20 members. Members contribute a fixed sum (usually $100 to $1,000) every month to the pot, which is awarded in full to a different member each month. Once the monthly payout cycle is completed, the *keh* disbands.

It's little wonder money-pooling arrangements appeal to immigrants with scant knowledge of English or the U.S. banking system: *Kehs* provide a source of interest-free venture capital as well as a forum for exchanging business tips. Also, there is little chance that a member would dare to stop contributing to the pot after getting his share. Reneging on a financial pledge to others violates Asian concepts of personal and family honor.

Like other immigrant groups, Asian Americans have formed credit unions to provide loans and other financial services to community members who are wary of dealing with established banks. One such institution, the Korean Federal Credit Union of Washington, D.C., recently was forced to close. The National Credit Union Administration, which insures federally chartered credit unions, attributed Korean Federal's failure to faulty management, inadequate record-keeping and an unusually high percentage of business loans, which are riskier than other types. Because it was federally insured, nearly all the credit union's depositors will be reimbursed.

Owners of large Asian-American businesses also rely on community-based networking. Consider the Asian-American Manufacturers Association (AAMA) of Menlo Park, Calif. Formed in 1980 out of concern that Asian Americans were not getting a fair share of federal aid to ethnic groups, AAMA now boasts a membership of about 500 manufacturers of high-technology products like computers, microprocessors and semiconductors. The association's concerns have since broadened to include discrimination in employment and higher education, hate crimes aimed at Asian immigrants and support of Asian-American political candidates. Most AAMA members are of Chinese origin, though some came from India, Japan, Pakistan, the Philippines and South Korea.

### Are Asian Americans truly a "model minority"?

The AAMA is one of the success stories that lends substance to the notion that Asian Americans are America's "model minority." Data showing the median family income of Asian Americans to be higher than that of any other U.S. population group would seem to clinch the argument.

Far from being flattered by the "model" tag, Asian Americans resent it. They insist it is just another ethnic stereotype. Like other stereotypes, they say, it distorts reality and discourages people from viewing members of

the targeted group as individuals with differing needs, wants and abilities.

Roger Daniels and Harry H. L. Kitano, who have written extensively on Asian Americans, make the further point that notions of what constitutes a "successful minority" are subject to change. "At one time," they note, "a good Indian was a dead Indian; a common goal regarding Asian Americans was that of total exclusion from American society; and blacks were supposed to be almost totally segregated. Or on a more subtle level, Asian Americans and blacks who behaved according to dominant-group role prescriptions, such as those who 'knew' their place, might be considered as more successful than their more non-conforming counterparts. Even today, success may be equated with those who have opted to become more like members of the dominant group or those who have adjusted to minority status through conflict-free behavior."[9]

While not disputing the accuracy of the family-income figures, Asian-American advocacy groups contend the numbers are misleading. For one thing, they say, a majority of Asian Americans live in California, New York and Hawaii — states with incomes and living costs well above the national average. Moreover, they point out that an Asian-American family often has several breadwinners, not just one or two.

A more serious failing of the family-income figures is that they suggest all Asian-American families are affluent. In truth, income levels vary widely within the Asian-American community. People of Chinese and Japanese origin whose forebears came to this country more than a generation ago generally are much better off than recent Asian immigrants. At the bottom of the income heap are Indochinese refugees, many of whom remain mired in poverty long after they arrive in the United States. The most destitute of all are

members of the Hmong tribe from the mountains of Laos. An estimated 90 percent of the Hmong community in Fresno, Calif., is on welfare. But since Asian Americans are generally perceived as being successful, they often find it difficult to obtain needed social services and may be denied access to affirmative-action programs.

Asian community leaders say the academic feats of Asian-American young people also need to be examined more closely. That is because the classroom performance of Asian-American students at elite campuses has led some observers to assume that all Asian youths are innately brainy.

Here again, Asian-American leaders say, the accomplishments of some obscure the difficulties faced by many. Chang-lin Tien, now the chancellor of the University of California at Berkeley, addressed the issue in 1988. "Certainly Asian Americans have done very well," he said. "But the stereotype of the model minority disadvantages some groups very deeply. The [newly arrived] immigrant groups, especially, have many problems. They have incredible family pressure to do well; they have language problems; they suffer from major cultural differences; they have to work to help out financially. But the feeling is that, because Asians in general are doing so well, they don't need extra help."[10]

Indeed, Asian-American students' reputation for excelling at mathematics and science — fields in which English-language proficiency is not essential — can be a burden. Some Asian youths decide to major in math or science out of concern that they will not succeed in another specialty. By the same token, some high school counselors routinely steer Asian Americans toward those fields because they feel Asians are too introverted and submissive to become top-rank performing artists, lawyers or business executives. In sum, the various facets of the "model minority" image all too often function as a trap. ■

# Chronology

## 19th Century

*Soon after the first Chinese immigrants arrive in the United States, racially grounded bias surfaces and restrictive laws are enacted.*

### 1848-49
Large numbers of Chinese come to the United States to strike it rich in the California Gold Rush.

### 1854
In *The People v. George W. Hall,* the California Supreme Court states that "Chinese, and all other people not white, are included in the prohibition from being witnesses against whites."

### 1868
Under the Burlingame Treaty, Chinese laborers are encouraged to enter the United States to help build the transcontinental railroads but are denied citizenship.

### Oct. 16, 1876
The Workingman's Party of California, advocating an end to Chinese immigration, asserts: "To an American death is preferable to life on a par with the Chinaman. Treason is better than to labor beside a Chinese slave."

### 1882
The Chinese Exclusion Act bans immigration of all Chinese laborers and miners for 10 years. The law is extended for 10 years in 1892, for two years in 1902 and indefinitely in 1904.

### 1884
The Democratic National Platform declares, "American civilization demands that against the immigration or importation of Mongolians to these shores our gates be closed."

## 1920s

*With one notable exception, the prohibition against immigration from Asia remains firmly in place during the decade following World War I.*

### 1924
Congress passes the National Origins Act, prohibiting nearly all immigration by Asians.

### 1924-29
More than 24,000 Filipinos emigrate to California in response to a shortage of low-wage labor.

———— ● ————

## 1940s

*Americans of Japanese descent are persecuted during World War II. But there is new respect for China, a U.S. ally in the war.*

### Feb. 19, 1942
President Franklin D. Roosevelt signs an executive order giving the U.S. Army authority to intern "any and all persons" living near "military areas." Some 110,000 men, women and children of Japanese descent are moved to 10 large relocation camps.

### 1943
Congress repeals the Chinese Exclusion Act and also permits Chinese residents to become naturalized U.S. citizens.

———— ● ————

## Postwar Era

*Legal barriers to Asian immigration are dismantled after World War II. But a residue of anti-Asian prejudice remains.*

### 1952
The Immigration and Nationality (McCarran-Walter) Act makes foreign-born persons of all Asian groups eligible for U.S. citizenship.

### 1957
Tsung Dao Lee of Columbia and Chen Ning Yang of Princeton's Institute for Advanced Study are awarded the Nobel Prize in physics. Both were born in China and became naturalized U.S. citizens.

### Aug. 21, 1959
President Dwight D. Eisenhower proclaims Hawaii the 50th state. The territory's Asian-American majority impeded its long effort to join the Union.

### 1965
The Immigration Act opens the way to large-scale immigration from Asian countries for the first time.

### June 19, 1982
Vincent Chin, a Chinese American, is fatally beaten in Detroit by two white autoworkers. Asian Americans are outraged when the two are sentenced to only three years' probation.

### Aug. 10, 1988
President Ronald Reagan signs into law a bill providing $1.25 billion in reparations to Japanese Americans interned during World War II.

### Feb. 15, 1990
Professor Chang-Lin Tien, a mechanical engineer born in China, is named chancellor of the University of California at Berkeley. He is the first Asian American chosen to head a University of California campus.

### Nov. 29, 1990
President Bush signs into law a bill allowing immigration to climb from about 500,000 persons annually to about 700,000 for the first three years of the act.

# BACKGROUND

## 19th-Century Bias

Long before Asian immigrants became a "model minority," most Americans looked on them with disdain. "The Chinese were objects of racist thought even before they arrived in America," wrote one observer.[11] New England merchants and shippers who did business with the Chinese in the late 18th century considered their trading partners to be crafty, scheming, dishonest and cowardly.

Early American diplomats, intellectuals and government officials generally shared and spread this attitude. U.S. Protestant missionaries tended "to impugn the morality of the whole Chinese nation," historian Stanford M. Lyman wrote. "To missionaries bent on conversion, the ordinary Chinese were debased heathens awaiting divine rescue from their unholy condition of 'lechery, dishonesty, xenophobia, cruelty, despotism, filth and intellectual inferiority.'"

Chinese immigration to the United States began in 1848, when two men and one woman landed in San Francisco, beginning a flow that lasted three decades.[12] The journey was arduous and costly, and there were family and social pressures against going abroad. But the lure of the California Gold Rush induced thousands of Chinese to pull up stakes and head across the Pacific. When "the merchant ships pulled into Canton with exaggerated tales of the gold discovery in California, mountains crumbled, oceans dried up, distances shrank and dangers were shrugged off for men of ambition quick to take advantage of a situation that promised fortunes in nothing less than gold," historian Betty Lee Sung wrote.[13] By 1851, there were 25,000 Chinese in California, more than 90 percent of them men.

When the Chinese found that the "strike-it-rich" stories had been overblown, many turned to the backbreaking work of building transcontinental railroads and farming. Encouraged by the railroad barons who valued their cheap labor and industrious work habits, the Chinese continued to book passage to America. By 1870 their population in the United States stood at 63,000, and 99 percent of them lived in California.

### Railroad Jobs Disappear

As the Chinese immigrant population increased in the 1870s, railroad jobs began to disappear, and the welcome mat was rolled up. Chinese who sought work in mines, domestic service and factories encountered fierce discrimination. The 1876 manifesto of the Workingman's Party of California, a political group advocating an end to Chinese immigration, declared: "To an American death is preferable to life on a par with the Chinaman. Treason is better than to labor beside a Chinese slave." Labor leaders and newspapers added their voices to the hostile chorus, accusing the Chinese of driving wages to a substandard level and of taking jobs away from whites.

The anti-Chinese movement of the last quarter of the 19th century fostered a number of atrocities: In 1871 in Los Angeles some 20 Chinese were hanged or burned to death; in 1885 in Rock Springs, Wyo., at least 28 Chinese coal miners were shot to death; and in 1887 at Hell's Canyon, on the Idaho-Oregon border, 31 gold miners were robbed and killed.[14]

"In general," Lyman wrote, "Chinese immigrants were held to be servile as laborers, unfair in their competition with white workingmen, vicious in their ethics, immoral in their conduct, contagious and disease-ridden and subject to a private government outside the control of American law. In addition, the fact that they send much of their earnings to China

and that they were regarded as an unassimilable people, aroused concern, indignation and contempt."[15]

## Anti-Chinese Laws

Early on, anti-Chinese sentiment was codified in federal and state law. From 1854 to 1874, a California statute barred Chinese from testifying in court against whites. The 1868 Burlingame Treaty with China blocked Chinese from becoming American citizens. Congress passed the Chinese Exclusion Act of 1882, which banned immigration of all Chinese laborers and miners for a decade.[16] It also formally mandated that "no state court or court of the United States shall admit Chinese to citizenship." The Chinese Exclusion Act was extended for an additional 10 years in 1892, for two more years in 1902, and indefinitely in 1904.

According to the Census Bureau, the annual number of Chinese immigrants coming into the United States fell from a high of 39,579 in 1882 to just 10 in 1887. This virtually total exclusion had "devastating long-run effects on Chinese-Americans," economist Thomas Sowell noted. "Because the early Chinese immigration was almost exclusively male, all hope of a normal social or family life was destroyed for the great majority of the Chinese population" of the U.S.[17]

Amendments to the Chinese Exclusion Act permitted a few thousand Chinese to immigrate annually from 1896 to 1924 — a period when millions of Southern and Eastern Europeans came to the United States. Then the Immigration Acts of 1917 and 1924 shut down Chinese immigration altogether. The 1917 act set up a "barred zone" in Asia, including most of China, from which immigration was forbidden. The 1924 law excluded all foreigners not eligible to be U.S. citizens.

These harsh restrictions left countless Chinese men virtually marooned in this country, living alone in big-city Chinatowns, working in low-paying, menial jobs in laundries and restaurants. "Never in the history of the United States had the nationals of another friendly, sovereign state been so humiliated, so disgraced," Betty Sung wrote. "The Chinese were the only people specifically named in legislation to be excluded from the United States."[18]

## Arrival of Japanese

The history of Japanese immigration to the United States closely parallels the Chinese experience. The first Japanese to settle here were young men who came to work on sugar plantations in the Hawaiian Islands in 1868. Traffic quickened in the 1880s after the Japanese government made emigration legal. By the early 1900s, about 100,000 Japanese — called Issei, a combination of the Japanese words for "one" and "generation" — had come, mostly from the Japanese countryside.*

"Most seem to have come from somewhere above the lowest socioeconomic strata of the population," University of Cincinnati historian Roger Daniels wrote, "and most exhibited that combination of energy and ambition which has made the Japanese Americans the most upwardly mobile nonwhite minority in the United States."[19]

Like the Chinese, Japanese immigrants were welcomed initially. In Hawaii (which became a U.S. territory in 1898), California and other

---

*Second-generation Japanese-Americans are called Nisei, and third-generation Japanese are called Sansei.

Western states, the Japanese worked as common laborers and domestic servants. Those who saved enough from their low-paying jobs started laundries, restaurants, gardening services, retail stores and other small businesses. By all accounts the Issei were hard-working, productive members of society who lived quiet, family-oriented lives.

> **Anti-Japanese feelings escalated in 1905 following the Russo-Japanese War, in which Japan quickly and easily defeated imperial Russia.**

Nevertheless, a vicious anti-Japanese movement emerged in California around the turn of the century. Politicians and newspapers railed against the Japanese, predicting they would take over the state. Anti-Japanese feelings escalated in 1905 following the Russo-Japanese War, in which Japan quickly and easily defeated imperial Russia. Japan's triumph, Daniels said, "effectively challenged for the first time white military supremacy in Asia and raised the specter of the yellow peril."[20] In 1908 President Theodore Roosevelt, under pressure from Californians, concluded an agreement with Japan in which Japan would no longer issue passports to laborers for travel to the United States.

The agreement did not bar the immigration of Japanese women and children. As the number of Japanese Americans increased, so did anti-Japanese agitation in California. The Legislature enacted a law in 1913

that barred aliens ineligible for citizenship from owning property. In 1920 the state's voters, by a margin of 3 to 1, approved a stronger Alien Land Act prohibiting non-citizens from leasing and sharecropping as well as purchasing land. Moreover, anti-Japanese Californians continued to press for exclusionary immigration legislation. The 1924 Immigration Act, which put a halt to virtually all immigration from Asia, was enacted in large part to meet these demands.

By the time of the Japanese attack on the American fleet at Pearl Harbor in Hawaii on Dec. 7, 1941, some 127,000 Japanese lived in the United States. With the ensuing declaration of war against Japan and Japanese military advances in the western Pacific, anti-Japanese feelings ran rampant throughout the country, especially on the West Coast, where residents feared a Japanese invasion.

### FDR Orders Internment

On Feb. 19, 1942, President Franklin D. Roosevelt signed an executive order giving the U.S. Army authority to evacuate, relocate and intern "any and all persons" living near "military areas." The Japanese were not mentioned in the order, which nonetheless became the legal instrument for putting some 110,000 Japanese men, women and children into 10 large relocation camps in isolated areas of Arizona, Arkansas, California, Colorado, Idaho, Utah and Wyoming. More than 150,000 Hawaiians of Japanese ancestry were not interned, and many servicemen from this group served with distinction in the armed forces during the war. One of them was Sen. Daniel K. Inouye, D-Hawaii, who lost his right arm while fighting in Europe with the Japanese-American 442nd Regiment.

It was clear, too, that implementation of Roosevelt's directive was based solely on racial considerations. No other American ethnic groups whose countries of origin were at war with the United States — namely, Germany and Italy — were subjected to similar treatment. As a result, many of the Japanese-American internees were forced to sell their homes and businesses at a fraction of market value.

Ironically, World War II also brought a softening of anti-Chinese sentiment in this country. Because it was a U.S. ally in the conflict with Japan, China and its leader, Chiang Kai-shek, received sympathetic coverage from the American news media. In 1943, Congress repealed the Chinese Exclusion Act and allowed up to 105 Chinese a year to immigrate to the United States. More important, the 1943 law permitted Chinese residents to become naturalized U.S. citizens.

The following decade saw American public opinion toward the two main Asian powers change direction once again. When China entered the Korean War late in 1950 on the side of North Korea, anti-Chinese feeling soared. Japan, then still under postwar U.S. occupation, was increasingly seen as America's best friend in Asia and an emerging bulwark of democracy in the region.

## Quota Laws Eased

But the most important development in U.S.-Asian relations during the Korean War years was passage of the Immigration and Nationality (McCarran-Walter) Act of 1952. The law made it possible for any person, regardless of race, to become a naturalized citizen. Thus, immigrants from Japan, Korea and other Asian countries became eligible for U.S. citizenship for the first time. McCarran-Walter also did away with the blanket exclusion of immigrants

from Asia, although discrimination against this group continued because of the national origins system.*

Immigration policy was further liberalized in 1965, when Congress abolished the 1924 quota system and set an annual quota of 170,000 immigrants from the Eastern Hemisphere. No more than 20,000 persons were to be admitted from any one country. In addition, the 1965 act based immigration on a "first come, first admitted" basis, without regard to place of origin. It also made special provision for the admission of refugees. Immigration from Asia zoomed. According to the U.S. Immigration and Naturalization Service, Asian immigrants numbered 445,300 between 1961 and 1970. The total rose to 1.6 million between 1971 and 1980 and to 2.8 million between 1981 and 1990.

After the defeat of South Vietnam in 1975, resettlement of Indochinese refugees became the overriding concern of U.S. immigration officials. During 1975 alone, some 130,000 Vietnamese, Laotians and Cambodians came to the United States. They were admitted under the attorney general's parole authority, whose original intent was to facilitate the entry of persons not necessarily eligible for immigration. In 1977 and 1978, Congress approved bills directing the attorney general to grant permanent-resident status to Indochinese parolees.

### Refugee Act of 1980

Going beyond this ad hoc approach, Congress passed the Refugee Act of 1980. The law broadened the definition of refugees to include persons who are persecuted or fear persecution "on account of race, religion, nationality, membership in a

---

*The 1924 Immigration Act established the national origins system, which fixed quotas in direct proportion to the "number of inhabitants in the continental United States in 1920 whose origin by birth or ancestry is attributable to such geographic area." This resulted in the allocation of three-fifths of the total number of quota immigrants to Great Britain and Germany.

particular social group, or political opinion" if they remain in their country or have no choice but to return there. Another provision allowed Indochinese parolees to change their status to permanent resident after one year in the United States. From 1961 to 1970, only 19,895 Asians were admitted to this country as permanent residents under various refugee acts. The number soared to 210,683 between 1971 and 1980 and to 796,722 between 1981 and 1990.

In 1986, Congress made it unlawful for any person knowingly to hire, recruit or refer for a fee any alien not authorized to work in the United States. Consequently, many employers are now reported to be wary of offering a job to anyone who doesn't "look American." On the other hand, Asian Americans benefited from a provision increasing the legal immigration ceilings for colonies from 600 to 5,000; the aim was to help prospective immigrants from British-administered Hong Kong, which is due to revert to Chinese control in 1997.

The most recent legislative revision of immigration policy, signed into law by President Bush on Nov. 29, 1990, allowed immigration to rise from about 500,000 people to about 700,000 for each of the first three years. Thereafter, an annual ceiling of 675,000 is to apply. The law also allowed Hong Kong to be treated as a separate foreign state, not as a colony, for purposes of visa allocations. However, the number of visas available to Hong Kong natives was not to exceed 10,000 a year between fiscal years 1991 and 1993. In addition, the law provided up to 12,000 visas a year between fiscal 1991 and 1993 for Hong Kong nationals who are high-level employees of large U.S. corporations in the territory.

### Reparations to Internees

Besides making it easier for Asians to become permanent residents of

*Continued on p. 960*

# Asian Americans Break into the Arts

It's hard to say who delivered the most inscrutable performance in "The Son-Daughter," a 1932 film set in San Francisco's Chinatown. Was it Helen Hayes, the title character? Or was it one of her co-stars, who included Warner Oland, Ramon Navarro and Lewis Stone? All four were white actors pretending to be Chinese.

That was par for the Hollywood course at the time, and for many years afterward. Consider Oland, the first "Charlie Chan" of the sound-film era. The actor, Swedish by birth, portrayed a Chinese-American detective who was fond of spouting fortune-cookie wisdom ("Insignificant molehill sometimes more important than conspicuous mountain") for the enlightenment of his "Number One Son," Keye Luke, who actually *was* Chinese.

When Oland died in 1937, Sidney Toler (another Caucasian) took over the role and was almost as effective in it as his predecessor. Roland Winters, yet another non-Asian, succeeded Toler and guided the series to its unmourned demise in 1949.

The "Chan" pictures were not deliberately offensive, though some modern viewers may think otherwise. Similarly, the 1936 film version of Pearl S. Buck's novel about Chinese peasants, *The Good Earth,* was made with the best of intentions. Again, though, the leads were played by white actors — Luise Rainer and Paul Muni. The same pattern held eight years later with the Chinese-peasant movie "Dragon Seed," starring a laughably unconvincing Katharine Hepburn.

The post-World War II years brought no immediate change in Hollywood's casting habits. In 1946, the English actor Rex Harrison played the male lead in "Anna and the King of Siam," a movie that inspired the 1951 Rodgers and Hammerstein Broadway musical, "The King and I." While Harrison made a convincing Asian character, the same could not be said of Lee J. Cobb as the king's Siamese adviser, or of Linda Darnell as a royal concubine. Even as late as 1956, Marlon Brando played an Asian in the film version of John Patrick's hit play, "The Teahouse of the August Moon."

Not surprisingly, many Asian Americans were offended at how white Americans portrayed them. The editors of an anthology of Asian-American writing charged in 1974 that "American culture, protecting the sanctity of its whiteness, still patronizes us as foreigners. America does not recognize Asian America as a presence, though Asian Americans have been here seven generations. For seven generations we have been aware of that refusal, and in-

ternalized it, with disastrous results." [†]

But Asian-American writers were soon to seize the initiative by portraying themselves and their culture on their own terms. The breakthrough work was Maxine Hong Kingston's *The Woman Warrior* (1976), a collection of short stories that mixed memories of the author's childhood in San Francisco with mystical tales of female warriors and monkey kings. More recently, Amy Tan made the best-seller list with her first two novels of Chinese-American life, *The Joy Luck Club* and *The Kitchen God's Wife.* "M. Butterfly," by Chinese-American playwright David Henry Hwang, was a Broadway hit in 1988 and has been successfully produced overseas.

A common theme of recent Asian-American writing is the clash of attitudes between long-established and newly arrived immigrants or between different generations of the same family. One example is "Yankee Dawg You Die," a 1989 play by Philip Kan Gotanda, a third-generation Japanese American. One of the play's two characters is a young Japanese-American actor who, in Gotanda's words, "will take only roles he thinks are correct, are dignified. There are certain roles he will never play — the Ching Chong Chinaman houseboy, the stereotypical evil Japanese World War II general, the Fu Manchu villain from outer space." The other character, an older Japanese-American actor, is not so choosy because he represents the old guard. "They would take any role they could get," says Gotanda, "because they were actors and they were going to survive." [††]

Despite the increasing visibility of Asian Americans in the arts, they still experience the kind of slights that were commonplace in the Hollywood film studios of old. In August 1990, for example, theater producer Cameron Mackintosh announced he was canceling the planned Broadway production of the hit British musical "Miss Saigon." He made the threat in response to a demand by the American Actor's Equity union that he replace the white actor Jonathan Pryce with an Asian in the principal role of a half-French, half-Vietnamese pimp. The dispute eventually was settled in Mackintosh's favor, and the play opened with Pryce in the role he had originated in London. Mackintosh did agree, however, not to use yellow makeup in an effort to make Caucasian actors appear Asian.

> A common theme of recent Asian-American writing is the clash of attitudes between different generations of the same family.

---

[†] Frank Chin, Jeffery Paul Chan, Lawson Fusao Inada and Shawn Hsu Wong, eds., *Aiiieeeee! An Anthology of Asian American Writers* (1974), pp. viii-ix.
[††] Quoted in *The New York Times,* June 7, 1989.

Continued from p. 958
the United States, the federal government has made belated amends to Japanese-Americans interned during World War II. On Feb. 19, 1976, the 34th anniversary of Roosevelt's executive order on internments, President Gerald R. Ford revoked the wartime document and apologized for the relocation. Calling attention to the bicentennial celebrations scheduled later that year, Ford said "an honest reckoning" must take account of "our national mistakes as well as our national achievements."

Still, it was not until 1988 that Congress enacted legislation providing $1.25 billion in reparations to the Japanese-American internees. Under the law, each of the estimated 60,000 surviving internees was to receive $20,000. "On behalf of the nation, the Congress apologizes," the bill declared. Two of the measure's chief supporters, Reps. Robert T. Matsui and Norman Y. Mineta, both California Democrats, are Japanese Americans who as children were interned with their families.  ∎

# CURRENT SITUATION

## "Hate Crimes"

Despite their achievements, and to some extent because of them, Asian Americans remain vulnerable to violent "hate crimes." Reliable figures on such offenses are hard to come by, since reporting criteria vary from jurisdiction to jurisdiction, and many Asian-American victims hesitate to approach the police because they fear retaliation or feel ashamed.* But anecdotal evidence from across the country strongly suggests that attacks on Asian Americans are on the rise.

Within the Asian-American community, one hate crime stands out above all others: the 1982 slaying in Detroit of Vincent Chin, 27, a U.S.-born draftsman of Chinese ancestry. On June 19, 1982, Chin and three friends visited a topless bar to celebrate his impending marriage. Two white men got into an argument with

---

*Under legislation signed into law by President Bush in April 1990, the Justice Department was directed to gather and publish hate-crime statistics for each of the following five years.

Chin, using racial slurs. A scuffle ensued, and the participants were ejected from the bar. Later that night, the two whites spotted Chin at a fast-food restaurant. When he left, one of the assailants held him while the other struck him repeatedly with a baseball bat. Chin died four days later.

### Attackers Get Probation

Chin's attackers, who were laid-off autoworkers, apparently believed he was Japanese and blamed him for the U.S. auto industry's troubles. Originally charged with second-degree murder, the two were subsequently allowed to plead guilty to a lesser offense, manslaughter. Wayne County Circuit Judge Charles Kaufman placed them on three years' probation and fined each of them $3,780.

The Asian-American community reacted with fury to what it viewed as a miscarriage of justice. A "Justice for Vincent Chin" committee was formed, petitions were circulated and pressure was brought to bear on the Justice Department to enter the case. The protests eventually yielded a federal indictment charging Ronald Ebens, the bat-wielding assailant, with depriving Chin of his civil rights. Ebens was tried, found guilty and sentenced to 25 years in prison, but judicial errors caused the conviction to be reversed on appeal.

At the 1987 retrial, Ebens' attorney persuaded the jury that the assault on Chin was not racially motivated. The autoworker went free. A subsequent civil suit was settled by a court-approved agreement under which Ebens agreed to pay, in installments, $1.5 million to Chin's estate.

Though the Chin tragedy occurred nearly a decade ago, it has left an enduring mark on the Asian-American community. Now, as then, it is perceived as evidence that Asian Americans are still not regarded as U.S. citizens worthy of equal protection under the law. Chin's death also underscored the need to identify and eliminate the causes of hate crimes directed at Asian Americans and to take vigorous countermeasures whenever such crimes occur.

Stanley Mark, a staff member of the Asian-American Legal Defense and Education Fund, a nonprofit civil rights organization based in New York, feels hate crimes are caused by "bias, just bias; it's not rational." He adds, "There is a stereotype that Asians are foreigners even though they've been here many generations. There is a sense that they are competing for jobs, that there are too many of them even though the number is under 4 percent of the whole population of the United States. Many people feel they are the cause of job layoffs and other economic ills. These stereotypes feed into a biased context, and some people act on it violently."

## Black-Asian Tensions

The violence is by no means one-sided. Soon Ja Du, a Korean-born grocer in Los Angeles, was convicted of voluntary manslaughter Oct. 11 in the shooting death of a 15-year-old black girl the merchant had accused of stealing a $1.79 bottle of orange juice. The incident occurred in Du's

Continued on p. 962

# At Issue:

## Is it accurate to call Asian Americans a model minority?

ANTHONY RAMIREZ

*Associate Editor,* Fortune *magazine*
FROM *FORTUNE,* NOV. 24, 1986.

*w*hy is it that Asian Americans tower above the rest of the population in both dollars and sense? Their speeded-up realization of the American dream is due in great measure to hard work, dedication to education, a willingness to adapt to a predominantly white culture — and, not least, to brains.

The evidence is persuasive that Asian Americans are smarter than the rest of us — the 98 percent of the population not from the Far East. Asian-American children and grownups consistently outscore whites, the population as a whole, and other racial minorities on a wide variety of tests that are used to assess intelligence, scholastic ability and cognitive development. Says Philip E. Vernon, a psychologist at the University of Calgary: "Their intelligence can't be denied."

In 1980, for example, the U.S. Department of Education found that Asian-American high school students got A's more often and failed less than whites or any other racial group in eight subjects, ranging from English to art. Asian Americans particularly stood out in subjects requiring non-verbal skills. Similarly, on the Scholastic Aptitude Test, which is used to measure college potential, Asian Americans have the highest average math score.... Asian Americans perform just as impressively in tests of cognitive development, designed to measure thinking ability rather than how much a child has learned....

Psychologist Vernon is one of a flock of social scientists who are intrigued with the riddle of how Asian Americans got so smart. Most of these scientists agree that the answer lies in some mixture of heredity and upbringing, but they tie themselves in knots arguing about the relative importance of the two....

Among the social scientists who think Asian-American braininess is largely hereditary is Arthur Jensen, a University of California psychologist who has published controversial studies on the variation in intelligence by race. For evidence Jensen points to the wide variety of tests in which Asian Americans as a group excel. Although no single test proves the dominance of heredity, Jensen contends that taken together the tests span such a broad range of skills and abilities that no large group could ever be taught to ace all of them.

RONALD TAKAKI

*Professor of Ethnic Studies, University of California at Berkeley*
FROM *STRANGERS FROM A DIFFERENT SHORE,* 1989.

*a*sian-American "success" has emerged as the new stereotype for this ethnic minority. While this image has led many teachers and employers to view Asians as intelligent and hardworking and has opened some opportunities, it has also been harmful. Asian Americans find their diversity as individuals denied: Many feel forced to conform to the "model minority" mold and want more freedom to be their individual selves, to be "extravagant."

Asian university students are concentrated in the sciences and technical fields, but many of them wish they had greater opportunities to major in the social sciences and humanities.... Asian Americans find themselves all lumped together and their diversity as groups overlooked. Groups that are not doing well, such as the unemployed Hmong, the downtown Chinese, the elderly Japanese, the old Filipino farm laborers, and others, have been rendered invisible.

To be out of sight is also to be without social services. Thinking that Asian Americans have succeeded, government officials have sometimes denied funding for social service programs designed to help Asian Americans learn English and find employment. Failing to realize that there are poor Asian families, college administrators have sometimes excluded Asian-American students from Educational Opportunity Programs (EOP), which are intended for all students from low-income families.

Asian Americans also find themselves pitted against and resented by other racial minorities and even whites. If Asian Americans can make it on their own, pundits are asking, why can't poor blacks and whites on welfare? Even middle-class whites, who are experiencing economic difficulties because of plant closures in a deindustrializing America and the expansion of low-wage service employment, have been asked to emulate the Asian-American "model minority" and to work harder....

Significantly, Asian-American "success" has been accompanied by the rise of a new wave of anti-Asian sentiment. On college campuses, racial slurs have surfaced in conversations on the quad: "Look out for the Asian Invasion." "M.I.T. means Made in Taiwan." "U.C.L.A. stands for University of Caucasians Living among Asians."

Continued from p. 960

store in the south-central section of the city, where animosity between Korean shopkeepers and their black customers runs deep. Similar tensions have been noted in other cities with sizable numbers of Asian Americans and African Americans.

Du's shooting of Latasha Harlins was recorded on videotape, which was shown at the trial. On the tape, Du is seen firing a .38 caliber handgun she has retrieved from under the counter. According to the *Los Angeles Times'* description of the videotape: "At that point, the teenager turns toward the camera, which is mounted over the entrance to the store, and appears to be walking away from Du. Then, the gun in Du's hand is seen firing. The girl falls, a single mortal wound to the back of her head." Although Du's attorneys argued that she acted in self-defense and that the gun fired accidentally, the jury came to a different conclusion. It found Du guilty of voluntary manslaughter. In doing so, it rejected a more serious charge of second-degree murder as well as a lesser chage of involuntary manslaughter.

Du was sentenced to five years' probation, creating outrage in the black community. Los Angeles County District Attorney Ira Reiner said on Nov. 26 that he would appeal the sentence.

In the opinion of Jerry Yu of the Korean-American Coalition, the main cause of friction between Korean shopkeepers and the black community in Los Angeles is "economic disempowerment." He notes that "south-central L.A. is a huge area, and yet it has no major employers. It doesn't even have a bank. People have no hope. And that was true even before Korean-Americans started moving into the area and opening businesses. In 1965, when the Watts riots occurred, there weren't any Korean merchants there."

Because Koreans have established businesses in the area, Yu says, "We do have an interest in trying to improve the situation. The Korean community is trying to reach out, to work with the black community." At the same time, though, he says there is "no way that one or two communities are going to solve a problem this big. It will require a concerted effort at the local, state, regional and federal levels."

Meanwhile, many Asian Americans are increasingly concerned about intra-community crime. Street gangs, many composed of young Vietnamese men, have been preying upon other Asian immigrants in a number of major cities. One favored tactic is the home invasion, in which gang members burst into a house in an Asian neighborhood, tie up family members and threaten or beat them until money and other valuables are surrendered. Before leaving, the thieves threaten the family with reprisals if the crime is reported to police.

Oftentimes, the warning is heeded. California Rep. Matsui has observed that many Asian Americans "came from totalitarian regimes where going to the police is simply not standard practice. Tragically, many of these immigrants also believe that the violence they face here is simply part of life in America."[21]

# OUTLOOK

## Disinterest in Voting?

Some Asian Americans believe concern about crime could help mold the community into a potent political force. Bill Wong, a columnist for *The Oakland Tribune* and *Asian Week,* says crime is "a potential unifying issue" because it "has affected all Asian-American groups."

Crime is not the only issue of communitywide interest; others include discrimination in employment and higher education. Immigration policy holds somewhat less appeal. Because only a few thousand people a year immigrate from Japan, Wong doesn't think Japanese Americans care much about immigration questions. "On the other hand," he says, "Koreans, Filipinos and Chinese do care." Similarly, U.S.-born Chinese Americans and Japanese Americans, already fluent in English, are less concerned than recent immigrants about English-only rules, bilingual ballots and the like.

Many recent immigrants have yet to become citizens and registered voters. In addition, some of those who are eligible to vote neglect to do so out of lack of interest or unfamiliarity with the American political system. This disinterest in voting is the main reason why Asian Americans have yet to show much muscle in the political sphere.

Asian Americans have long been politically prominent in Hawaii, where they are the majority ethnic group. California is a different story. Although the state has an Asian-American population of 2.8 million, not one person of Asian descent currently holds a seat in the 120-member Legislature. California's highest-ranking Asian-American public official is Secretary of State March Fong Eu. Wong sees no Asian-American breakthrough in the Legislature in the immediate future. He notes, however, that "more Asian Americans are running for local offices. So at some point we will have a growing pool of Asian-American local officials, and some of them will have statewide ambitions — not only in California but in other states."

### San Francisco Mayoral Race

As a rule, Asian-American candidates should not assume that members of their ethnic group will automatically vote for them. Wong cites the experience of San Francisco Supervisor Tom Hsieh, a Chinese American who finished fifth in the recent mayoral election. "Some ethnic Chinese weren't willing to support Hsieh because his politics were thought to be moderate-conservative, and some Chinese Americans in San Francisco are liberal-progressives," Wong says.

Looking to the future, Wong believes it will be "a humongous political challenge" to forge a pan-Asian voting bloc. He feels there will be "some individual instances where Asians may coalesce around a candidate at a local level and be able to provide that candidate a very good plurality of support." But he doubts that the Asian-American community, diverse as it is, "will ever vote for one of its own as overwhelmingly as the African-American community voted for Jesse Jackson."

Dr. Kyo R. Jhin, a former chairman of the Asian-American Voters Coalition, a voter-education group based in the Washington, D.C., area, is more sanguine about the Asian-American community's ability to put aside ethnic differences when pursuing common goals. Noting that Asian Americans are concentrated in such pivotal states as California, New York and Texas, he says Asian voters could hold the balance of power in some close elections.

Jhin adds that the voters' coalition itself has demonstrated Asian Americans from different backgrounds can work together for political ends. When the group was formed nine years ago, he recalls, trust among its component nationality groups was in short supply. "But we quickly learned we wouldn't get anywhere by fighting our battles individually."

### *Key Test in Delaware*

One key test of Asian-American political prowess will come next year when S.B. Woo, a Chinese-American physics professor, runs for Dela-

ware's at-large U.S. House seat. Delaware voters elected Woo as lieutenant governor in 1984 by fewer than 500 votes; in 1988 he won the Democratic primary for a U.S. Senate seat by 71 votes but lost the general election to Republican incumbent William V. Roth Jr. Delaware's Asian-American community is minuscule, comprising only 9,057 persons, or 1.8 percent of the state's population.

Woo's 1992 campaign should show once and for all whether he has a future in national politics. It may also show whether Asian Americans in other parts of the country are willing to help a candidate whose only link to them is a shared ethnic identity. Woo recently completed a fundraising trip to California, where he appealed for support from Chinese-American and other Asian organizations. Bill Wong, for one, feels it is "conceivable" that an Asian-American candidate can win the support of different Asian groups nationwide "if the office is high-profile enough and if these groups feel there is some reason to come together."

At the same time, Wong cautions against assuming that increasing political visibility means bias against Asian Americans is fading. He cites President Bush's appointment of Elaine L. Chao* to be the new director of the Peace Corps as "the kind of event that deflects attention from everyday discrimination" against Asian Americans who are not in the public spotlight.

Similarly, the S.B. Woo candidacy may be less significant than it seems. In Wong's view, "Where there are very few people of a certain ethnic background, it is not remarkable to see them become 'assimilated' and 'accepted.'" Inter-group conflicts arise, he says, when the minority community grows larger and becomes more competitive in the local economy.

---

*Chao, who formerly served as deputy secretary of Transportation, is the highest-ranking Asian American in the Bush administration.

In sum, Wong foresees continuing "overt and subtle discrimination" against Asian Americans for the foreseeable future. Still, he feels that "people of Asian backgrounds will keep on rising and becoming successful."

## Notes

[1] Hing and Hu were quoted in the *Los Angeles Times,* Oct. 27, 1991.

[2] Article written for the *Los Angeles Times,* Feb. 7, 1989.

[3] [California] Attorney General's Asian and Pacific Islander Advisory Committee, *Final Report,* December 1988, p. 6.

[4] *Ibid.,* p. 76.

[5] *Ibid.,* p. 96.

[6] The Rand Corp. and the Urban Institute, *The Effect of Employer Sanctions on the Flow of Undocumented Immigrants to the United States,* April 1990.

[7] U.S. General Accounting Office, *Immigration Reform: Employer Sanctions and the Question of Discrimination,* March 29, 1990.

[8] Bruce E. Cain and D. Roderick Kiewiet, *Minorities in California* (1986).

[9] Harry H. L. Kitano and Roger Daniels, *Asian Americans: Emerging Minorities* (1988), p. 160. Kitano is a professor of social welfare and sociology at the University of California at Los Angeles; Daniels is a professor of history at the University of Cincinnati.

[10] Quoted in *The New York Times,* July 10, 1988.

[11] Stanford M. Lyman, *Chinese Americans* (1974), p. 56.

[12] Kil Young Zo, *Chinese Emigration Into the United States, 1850-1880* (1978), p. 82.

[13] Betty Lee Sung, *Mountain of Gold: The Story of the Chinese in America* (1967), pp. 21-22.

[14] Kitano and Daniels, *op. cit.,* p. 22.

[15] Lyman, *op. cit.,* p. 62.

[16] In 1882, approximately 105,000 persons of Chinese descent lived in the United States, of whom 100,000 were male.

[17] Thomas Sowell, *Ethnic America* (1981), p. 138.

[18] Sung, *op. cit.,* p. 57.

[19] Roger Daniels, *Concentration Camps U.S.A.: Japanese-Americans and World War II* (1972), p. 7.

[20] *Ibid.,* p. 10.

[21] Testimony before Subcommittee on Civil and Constitutional Rights of the House Judiciary Committee, Nov. 10, 1987.

# Bibliography

## Selected Sources Used

## Books

**Daniels, Roger, *Asian America: Chinese and Japanese in the United States Since 1850,* University of Washington Press, 1988.**

Daniels, a University of Cincinnati history professor, reviews the progress of the nation's two oldest Asian immigrant groups: Chinese Americans and Japanese Americans. "There has been ... no significant assimilation of Asian ethnicity into a pan-Asian bloc," Daniels writes. "Although Europe-centered scholars of ethnicity may treat 'Orientals' as a cohesive group, what Asian-American cohesion does exist has been largely imposed from without by discrimination."

**Hsia, Jayjia, *Asian Americans in Higher Education and at Work,* Lawrence Erlbaum Associates, Publishers, 1988.**

Hsia debunks the notion that Asian Americans are born to succeed in the U.S. job market. "Well-qualified, United States-educated Asian immigrants still face bleak employment opportunities compared to immigrants from the Western Hemisphere and the native-born majority," he writes. "Asian immigrants or refugees educated abroad must settle for jobs far below their training and experience. Immigrants or refugees with limited education and few marketable skills are only a little better off than 19th-century coolies."

**Kitano, Harry H. L., and Daniels, Roger, *Asian Americans: Emerging Minorities,* Prentice Hall, 1988.**

The authors examine the adjustment problems of all the leading Asian-American immigrant groups. They write that their purpose is "to place in one volume the material on Asian Americans that is currently scattered in widely disparate sources" and "to provide a cohesive, interdisciplinary account, tying in historical and social psychological perspectives."

**Takaki, Ronald, *Strangers From a Different Shore: A History of Asian Americans,* Little, Brown and Co., 1989.**

Takaki, an ethnic-studies professor descended from a Japanese-American family that labored on Hawaiian plantations, traces the evolution of America's principal Asian immigrant groups: Chinese, Japanese, Filipinos, Asian Indians, Koreans and Vietnamese. "In America," he writes, "Asian immigrants encountered long hours of labor and racial discrimination, but they did not permit exterior demands to determine wholly the direction and quality of their lives. Energies, pent up in the old countries, were unleashed, and they found themselves pursuing urges and doing things they had thought beyond their capabilities."

## Articles

**Gurwitt, Rob, "Have Asian Americans Arrived Politically? Not Quite," *Governing,* November 1990.**

"Immigrants outweigh the native-born in every Asian ethnic group except Japanese Americans," Gurwitt writes. "That single fact goes a long way toward explaining why the growing mass of Asian Americans are only now starting to turn their attention to American politics in a concerted way."

## Reports and Studies

**[California] Attorney General's Asian and Pacific Islander Advisory Commission, *Final Report,* December 1988.**

Examines anti-Asian sentiment and hate crimes as well as related criminal justice and civil rights issues. The chief focus is on developments in California.

**Subcommittee on Civil and Constitutional Rights, House Judiciary Committee, *Anti-Asian Violence,* Nov. 10, 1987.**

Representatives of Asian-American organizations and public officials express their views on the nature and causes of hate crimes directed at Asian Americans. A common observation is that Asian Americans' apparent success in school and on the job has "provoked the envy and resentment of less high-achieving Americans."

**U.S. Commission on Civil Rights, *The Economic Status of Americans of Asian Descent,* October 1988.**

Examines the impact of legal protection of Asian Americans against economic discrimination, particularly since the passage of the Civil Rights Act of 1984.

**U.S. Commission on Civil Rights, *Recent Activities Against Citizens and Residents of Asian Descent,* 1987.**

The commission presents a broad historical overview of Asian immigration to the United States since the mid-1850s and the violence it provoked almost from the start. It then examines today's Asian-American community and proposes reasons for the anti-Asian violence, harassment and intimidation of recent years.

# The Next Step

## Additional Articles from Current Periodicals from EBSCO Publishing's Database

### Affirmative action programs

Dwyer, P. and Cuneo, A. Z., "The 'other minorities' demand their due," *Business Week,* July 8, 1991, p. 62.

Looks at the claims of 'other minority' groups who are feeling left out in regards to affirmative action. Women, Hispanics and Asian Americans; statistics; problems faced by each group; growth of the populations; competition for a limited number of jobs; more.

Jaschik, S., "New federal challenge programs for minorities seen in Education Dept. memo on Oregon plan," *The Chronicle of Higher Education,* Jan. 16, 1991, p. A1.

Considers a memo from the Education Department that criticizes an Oregon program providing tuition waivers to minority students as being illegal in part because the "actual goal ... is to increase enrollment of blacks, Hispanics and Native Americans." Complaint concerning exclusion of Asian and Asian-American representation; Office of Civil Rights and the NAACP Legal Defense Fund; investigation to kill the program.

### Books & reading

Daniels, R., "Book reviews," *Journal of Higher Education,* July/August 1990, p. 481.

Reviews the book "Asian Americans in Higher Education and at Work," by Jayjia Hsia.

Rose, P. I., "Some Americans from Asia," *Reviews in American History,* September 1990, p. 430.

Reviews the book "Asian Americans: Chinese and Japanese in the United States since 1850," by Roger Daniels.

Taylor, P. A. M., "Reviews and short notices: The Americas," *History,* October 1990, p. 450.

Reviews the book "Asian Americans: Chinese and Japanese in the United States since 1850," by Roger Daniels.

### Debates & issues

Allis, S., "Kicking the nerd syndrome," *Time,* March 25, 1991, p. 64.

Profiles several Asian-American students who are rejecting the science stereotype and the ethic behind it. Tohoru Masamune, 31: MIT degree in chemical engineering — actor. David Shim, 21: government major, Harvard Law. Hei

Wai Chan, 28: Ph.D. electrical engineering, MIT: social worker. Cara Wong, 20: Harvard-Radcliffe biochemistry major — reading history and government. Over-achievers settling into the mainstream; strong parental pressure.

Bagasao, P. Y., "Opening minds — and doors," *Change,* November/December 1989, p. 4.

Editorial. Discusses the need for open minds and open doors concerning Asian and Pacific Americans and their "whiz kid" stereotypes, admissions controversies, and Asian American studies programs.

Coughlin, E. K., "Burgeoning Asian population in America proves a challenge and a boon to scholars" *The Chronicle of Higher Education,* April 10, 1991, p. A5.

Details the dramatic reshaping of Asian-American studies in the wake of the 1965 change in US immigration law which saw Asians begin emigrating to America in significant numbers. Rapid growth of the field in recent years; rise in ethnic studies; correcting pervasive stereotypes about Asians; evolution of Asian-American studies over the past 20 years; diversity of the new Asian immigrants; flowering of literary and artistic creation.

Hsia, J. and Hirano-Nakanishi, M., "The demographics of diversity," *Change,* November/December 1989, p. 20.

Examines the diverse demographics of Asian Americans in the US in such areas as immigration, birth and refugee admissions since 1970. The new classification of specific Asian American groups beginning in 1980; variations between the groups; characteristics shared by most groups that impact higher education; high value placed on education.

Jaschik, S. and Schonberger, B., "U.S. finds Harvard did not exclude Asian Americans," *The Chronicle of Higher Education,* Oct. 17, 1990, p. A1.

Reports that the Education Department has concluded that Harvard University does not discriminate against Asian-American applicants, a finding that was attacked by Asian-American leaders. Preference to children of alumni longstanding and legitimate; similar investigation at the University of California at Los Angeles; alumni-admissions preferences a fact of life.

Jen, G., "Challenging the Asian illusion," *The New York Times,* Aug. 11, 1991, Section 2 p. 1.

Criticizes the way Asian Americans are represented in American films. Asserts that the stage and screen still deal in stereotypes. Keeping the East mysterious; how Asian and Asian-American images are symptomatic of a more profound invisibility.

**Pang, C.J., "Theater departments can help combat the dearth of Asian Americans in the entertainment industry," *The Chronicle of Higher Education*, April 17, 1991, p. B1.**

Opinion. Argues that the widely publicized controversy over producer Cameron Mackintosh's casting of English actor Jonathan Pryce in the leading role of the play "Miss Saigon" raises fundamental concerns about the small number of Asian-American actors in mainstream American theater. Percentage of Asians belonging to Actors' Equity; Asian-American performance shaped by non-Asians; university departments promoting sensitivity to Asian aesthetic traditions.

**Saigo, R.H., "The barriers of racism," *Change*, November/December 1989, p. 8.**

Opinion. Discusses ways in which racist attitudes toward Asian Americans in official U.S. policy and the media, have also pervaded higher education. Entrance denial; employment in higher education; author's experiences with racism.

**Suh, M., "The many sins of 'Miss Saigon,'" *Ms.*, November/December 1990, p. 63.**

Criticizes the racial and sexist stereotypes in the British musical "Miss Saigon." Stereotyped Asian women's roles; casting of British actor Jonathan Pryce, a Caucasian, as a Eurasian; Actors' Equity's compromise with producer Cameron Mackintosh; comments by Japanese-American actress Kim Miyori.

**Suzuki, B.H., "Asian Americans as the 'model minority,'" *Change*, November/December 1989, p. 12.**

Examines the reputation Asian Americans have received as a "model minority." The evolution of the image; its acceptance by the American public; social reality of the image; effect on Asian Americans in higher education. Results of studies on image's accuracy; conclusions. INSET: Model minority? Getting behind the veil, by R. Lou.

**Takagi, D.Y., "From discrimination to affirmative action: Facts in the Asian American admissions controversy," *Social Problems*, November 1990, p. 578.**

Looks at the history of claimsmaking activity in regard to Asian American organizations, university officials, state and federal institutions, and neoconservatives. Discrimination against Asian Americans, 1983-1986; pressure to justify admissions practices at America's elite universities; more.

**Ueda, R., "False modesty," *New Republic*, July 3, 1989, p. 16.**

Examines growing Asian American dissatisfaction with their successful assimilation into American culture. Economic and educational rewards weighed against loss of identity; claims that full equality and non-discrimination have yet to be reached.

## Economic aspects

**Cuneo, A.Z., "Companies disoriented about Asians," *Advertising Age*, July 9, 1990, Special Report, p. S-2.**

Describes the rapidly growing, well-educated and financially well-endowed Asian-American population that has a combined purchasing power of $30 billion. How some marketing experts believe Asian Americans will be one of the most influential consumer groups in the next 10 years; prime concerns; what brands they look for.

**Kerr, P., "Cosmetic makers read the census," *The New York Times*, Aug. 29, 1991, p. D1.**

Comments on the way cosmetics companies are designing cosmetics for black, Hispanic and Asian women because of the rising number of Americans of non-European descent, and because minority women are becoming increasingly desirable customers. Competition; population growth from 1980 to 1990.

**Shao, M., Power, C., et al., "Suddenly, Asian-Americans are a marketer's dream," *Business Week*, June 17, 1991, p. 54.**

Discusses how well-educated, affluent Asian Americans now represent a dream population for US marketers. Tells how companies are now targeting this group through elaborate combinations of advertising, promotions, and community events. Marketing consultants reporting increasing interest; Asian Americans growing at the fastest rate of any group; expected growth; helping maintain ties to home; formulas for success.

## Education

**Bagasao, P.Y., "Student voices breaking the silence," *Change*, November/December 1989, p. 28.**

Interviews several Asian American students on their college experiences, major studies, opinions on the Asian "whiz kid" myth and racial incidents. Offers suggestions for improving the educational and counseling needs of these students. INSETS: Don't fix anything that isn't broken; overcoming the fear of writing; Do the right thing!; from Honolulu to New York City; learning English, learning in English; the education of a leader.

**Buderi, R., "Berkeley's changing student population," *Science*, Aug. 18, 1989, p. 694.**

Discusses the current controversy at the University of California at Berkeley over admissions procedures for Asian

Americans, and charges of overt racism against the students, both by students, and by the university's tendency to steer Asian Americans toward science and engineering. INSET: Concern in Washington (Congressional review of Asian-American college admissions procedures), by C. Holden.

**Goleman, D., "Probing school success of Asian-Americans," *The New York Times*, Sept. 11, 1990, p. C1.**

Explains the reasons behind the dazzling academic performances of Asian-American students.

**Hune, S., "Opening the American mind and body," *Change*, November/December 1989, p. 56.**

Discusses the renewed interest in, and resistance to, Asian American studies in U.S. higher education. How it began; effects of the studies; its form today in higher education; emphasis on education theories; future. INSETS: Asian/Pacific Islander Student Groups, by A. Espiritu; Asian American Studies Programs, by A. Espiritu.

**Liu, I., "A distinction between early and late educational achievements," *American Psychologist*, August 1991, p. 876.**

Comments on Sue's and Okazaki's attempt to explain the high academic achievements of Asian Americans. Report by Arbeiter (1984); problem of directly comparing socioeconomic standings across cultures; ancestors of Asian-American college-bound seniors from a select group; relative functionalism as a partial explanation.

**Lynn, R., "Educational achievements of Asian Americans," *American Psychologist*, Aug 1991, p. 875.**

Contends that the evidence cited in support of Sue's and Okazaki's conclusion concerning the issue of high educational achievement of Asian Americans is so selective that it is seriously misleading. Hypothesis of high genotypic IQ in Asians; world literature on the question; Sue's and Okazaki's preference given to the study by Stevenson et al.

**Sue, S. and Okazaki, S., "Asian-American educational achievements," *American Psychologist*, August 1990, p. 913.**

Comments on various hypotheses regarding the educational achievement of Asian Americans. Hereditary differences; cultural values; restrictions of upward mobility in other fields; achievement levels; lack of evidence for genetic explanation; more.

**Sue, S. and Okazaki, S., "Explanations for Asian-American achievements: A reply," *American Psychologist*, August 1991, p. 878.**

Presents a reply to comments on these authors' earlier work concerning Asian Americans, as a group, exhibiting high levels of academic achievements. Nature and nurture revisited.

## Political activity

**McGurn, W., "The silent minority," *National Review*, June 24, 1991, p. 19.**

Documents Republican efforts to recruit Asian Americans to their political party. Common factors that create a natural affinity between many Asian Americans and Republican principles; how Asian Americans can enhance the Republican Party; why Asian Americans have had little political interest to date.

**Rothenberg, S., "The invisible success story," *National Review*, Sept. 15, 1989, p. 43.**

Discusses the increased political importance of Americans of Asian descent. Political voting trends; economic successes; great diversity among different nationalities; enormous, untapped financial and enthusiastic potential for political parties to consider and court.

## Social aspects

**Abe, J. S. and Zane, N. W. S., "Psychological maladjustment among Asian and White American college students," *Journal of Counseling Psychology*, October 1990, p. 437.**

Discusses differences in psychological maladjustment among foreign-born Asian-, U.S.-born Asian- and white American college students after controlling for variables that have been confounded with ethnicity. Psychological maladjustment in terms of interpersonal and intrapersonal distress; confounding variables found in other studies; co-variation due to generation level; method; results; more.

**Lee, F. R., "'Model minority' label taxes Asian youths," *The New York Times*, March 20, 1990, p. B1.**

Shows how Asian-American students have been burdened by the myth that they are the "model minority." They face harassment in school and pressure at home. Dropout rate.

**Zane, N. W. S., Sue, S., et al., "Asian-American assertion: A social learning analysis of cultural differences," *Journal of Counseling Psychology*, January 1991, p. 63.**

Assesses differences in self-reported assertion by Asian and Caucasian Americans across nine different situations. Cultural differences in assertiveness; relationship of assertiveness behavior to expectancy outcomes and self-efficacy beliefs; greater anxiety and guilt reported by Asians; more.

# Back Issues

*Great Research on Current Issues Starts Right Here... Recent topics covered by The CQ Researcher are listed below. Issues dated before May 10, 1991, were published under the name of Editorial Research Reports.*

**JUNE 1990**
Downsizing America's Armed Forces
Progress In Weather Forecasting
Sir &s tL Bailout
Bio-Chemical Disarmament

**JULY 1990**
Do Americans Still Love Marriage?
Death Penalty Debate
Decline of Rural America
United Nations in the 1990s

**AUGUST 1990**
Democracy in the Philippines
Initiatives: True Democracy?
Hard Times at Newspapers
Teens Balance School & Jobs

**SEPTEMBER 1990**
Dangers of Alcohol
Western Alliance After the Cold War
Tobacco Industry
Right to Die

**OCTOBER 1990**
Organ Transplants
Energy Policy Options
Search for Arab Unity
Child Support

**NOVEMBER 1990**
Lotteries and Gambling
Post Cold-War Choices
Setting Limits on Medical Care
Multicultural Education

**DECEMBER 1990**
Cable TV Regulation
Americans' Search For Their Roots
Is Insurance System a Failure?
Why Schools Still Have Tracking

**JANUARY 1991**
Growing Influence of Boycotts
Should the U.S. Reinstate the Draft?
America's Archaeological Past
Peace Corps' Challenges in '90s

**FEBRUARY 1991**
Regional Impact of Recession
Puerto Rico's Status
Redistricting: Mapping Power
Nuclear Power

**MARCH 1991**
Acid Rain
Cost of the Gulf War
Reassessing Gun Laws
Future for Man in Space

**APRIL 1991**
Social Security
Canadian Crisis Over Quebec
California Drought
Electromagnetic Radiation

**MAY 1991**
School Choice
Racial Quotas
Animal Rights
U.S. and Japan

**JUNE 1991**
Children and Divorce
Teenage Suicide
Endangered Species
Europe 1992

**JULY 1991**
Teenagers and Abortion
Soviet Republics Rebel
Mexico's Emergence
Athletes and Drugs

**AUGUST 1991**
Sexual Harassment
Fetal Tissue Research
Oil Imports
The Palestinians

**SEPTEMBER 1991**
Police Brutality
Advertising Under Attack
Saving the Forests
Foster Care Crisis

**OCTOBER 1991**
Pay-Per-View TV
Youth Gangs
Gene Therapy
World Hunger

**NOVEMBER 1991**
Fast-Food Shake-Up
The Greening of Eastern Europe
Business' Role in Education
Cuba In Crisis

**DECEMBER 1991**
Retiree Health Benefits

Back issues are available for $4.00 (subscribers) or $7.00 (non-subscribers). Quantity discounts apply to orders over ten. To order, call Congressional Quarterly 1-800-432-2250.

# Future Topics

▶ *Obscenity Issues*

▶ *The Disabilities Act*

▶ *Term Limitations*

# ERRATA

Corrections for "The Obscenity Debate," Dec. 20, 1991, *CQR:*

1. Reference to Learned Hand, p. 977:

Learned Hand was never a member of the Supreme Court. He was known, however, as the court's "10th justice," and during more than 40 distinguished years as a federal judge he delivered some 2,000 opinions and gained a reputation as a defender of free speech.

2. Reference to Sheena Easton, p. 982:

Sheena Easton is a pop singer, not a country singer.

# The Obscenity Debate

*Crackdowns on pornography and lewdness draw cries of censorship*

F
IVE YEARS AFTER A CALL TO ARMS FROM A
federal commission on pornography, the war over
obscenity is at full tilt. Justice Department
prosecutors are putting heat on pornography
purveyors nationwide, and an alliance of religious activists
and political conservatives is blasting the work of avant-garde
artists, raunchy rap singers and on-the-edge filmmakers. A
counterattack has been launched by the sex-film industry as
well as a diverse coalition of artists, publishers and librarians
who see censorship as a threat to First Amendment rights to
free speech. As similar fights in the past have shown,
obscenity is a gray legal area that is highly politicized. A
national consensus on the issue remains elusive.

 December 20, 1991 • Volume 1, No. 31 • 969-992

*Formerly Editorial Research Reports*

COVER ART: BARBARA SASSA-DANIELS

December 20, 1991
Volume 1, No. 31

**EDITOR**
Sandra Stencel

**MANAGING EDITOR**
Thomas J. Colin

**ASSOCIATE EDITOR**
Richard L. Worsnop

**STAFF WRITERS**
Charles S. Clark
Mary H. Cooper
Rodman D. Griffin

**PRODUCTION EDITOR**
Laurie De Maris

**EDITORIAL ASSISTANT**
Thomas H. Moore

**GRAPHICS**
Jack Auldridge

**PUBLISHED BY**
Congressional Quarterly Inc.

**CHAIRMAN**
Andrew Barnes

**VICE CHAIRMAN**
Andrew P. Corty

**EDITOR AND PUBLISHER**
Neil Skene

**EXECUTIVE EDITOR**
Robert W. Merry

**PUBLICATIONS MARKETING/SALES**
Robert Smith

**EDITOR, EBSCO PUBLISHING**
Melissa Kummerer

The CQ Researcher (ISSN 1056-2036). Formerly Editorial Research Reports. Published weekly (48 times per year, not printed the first Friday of any month with five Fridays) by Congressional Quarterly Inc., 1414 22nd St., N.W., Washington, D.C. 20037. Rates are furnished upon request. Second-class postage paid at Washington, D.C. POSTMASTER: Send address changes to The CQ Researcher, 1414 22nd St., N.W., Washington, D.C. 20037.

# The Obscenity Debate

BY CHARLES S. CLARK

## THE ISSUES

The Justice Department has added a twist to Supreme Court Justice Potter Stewart's famous "definition" of pornography: "I know it when I see it." The department's obscenity unit is currently prosecuting interstate distributors of sex films with the aid of beefed-up resources and a new certitude. "All we have to do is hear the titles and we know," says department spokesman Doug Tillett.

Justice's crackdown is the most concrete legacy of the 1986 federal commission on pornography, which sought to document pornography's "corrosive harms," among them causing aggression toward women.[1] Joining in the fight is the Federal Communications Commission (FCC), which is seeking a round-the-clock ban on broadcasting that it deems indecent. In the past two years, the FCC has been issuing stiff fines to drive-time radio deejays prone to routines laced with crudity.

Manning the same anti-pornography barricades are cadres of private citizens. This October, during National Pornography Awareness Week, billboards proclaiming "Real Men Don't Use Porn" went up in 23 states, accompanied by photographs of celebrity endorsers. The billboard backers included such groups as New York City-based Morality in Media and the National Coalition Against Pornography, in Cincinnati, Ohio.

In numerous cities, religious groups such as the Rev. Donald Wildmon's American Family Association, based in Tupelo, Miss., have orchestrated letter-writing campaigns and boycotts of bookstores that sell such magazines as *Playboy* and *Pent-*

*house* and video stores that rent films rated X or NC-17.

Perhaps the most visible activist has been conservative Sen. Jesse Helms, R-N.C., a passionate critic of explicit art funded by the National Endowment for the Arts. For the third year in a row, Helms has stood on the floor of the Senate and, holding works of art depicting human genitals, decried the country's descent to "Sodom and Gomorrah."[2]

The smut-busters' resurgence has created what to some is a worrisome social climate. These are times in which a Florida record vendor can be fined for selling a raunchy but million-selling album by the rap group "2 Live Crew." These are times in which the respected director of a Cincinnati arts center can be brought to trial for exhibiting the homoerotic photographs of the late Robert Mapplethorpe — to some 80,000 willing visitors.*

"The past five years have brought

---

*Museum Director Dennis Barrie was acquitted of pandering obscenity in October 1990.

some of the heaviest attacks on freedom of expression that this country has seen in a generation," says Christopher M. Finan, executive director of the Media Coalition, a New York-based group of publishers, booksellers and periodical distributors formed in 1973 to lobby for First Amendment rights. "We're in a period of reaction," of what's been called "sex panic," says Marjorie Heins, director of the Arts Censorship Project at the American Civil Liberties Union (ACLU).

The anti-censorship forces have formed their own advocacy groups and filed lawsuits on behalf of artists who were denied government grants because their work was deemed obscene. In 1990, People for the American Way, a liberal advocacy group based in Washington, commissioned radio spots against book banning read by celebrities Kathleen Turner, Garrison Keillor and Colleen Dewhurst. Playboy Enterprises joined with *The Nation* magazine to sponsor a colloquium in the fall of 1990 entitled "The First Amendment in Crisis."

This fall, during the American Library Association's annual Banned Books Week, many libraries displayed books that have been banned in some regions (including works by Mark Twain, John Steinbeck and Judy Blume). And the Adult Video Association, headquartered in Beverly Hills, Calif., this month staged a censorship protest outside a Los Angeles federal building.

To observers on both sides, the current obscenity debate is a Reagan-Bush era rehash of the larger issues that exploded during the divisive 1960s and early '70s — the sexual revolution, legal abortion and gay rights. Gary Bauer, a former adviser to President Ronald Reagan and now president of the Washington-based Family Research Council, calls it "an

# Oft-Confused Terms

**O**bscenity, derived from the Greek for "filth," is the legal term for written or photographic materials that have been determined by the judicial system not to warrant protection by the First Amendment. The term is reserved mostly for sexual materials, though some people favor including materials depicting violence.

**Pornography,** derived from the Greek for "writing about prostitutes," is a broader term used for all material that is intended to be sexually arousing. To most people, the word is pejorative, though many works labeled por-nographic have artistic merit. Modern-day pornography is generally divided into two types: "hard-core," typified by explicit depictions of sex acts, and "soft-core," character-ized by nudity and simulated sex.

**Indecency,** derived from Latin for the opposite of something that is "fitting," refers to language or images that are morally unfit to be seen or heard. Broadcasters, particularly, are forbidden by law from transmitting sexu-ally indecent material, except under conditions set out by the Federal Communications Commission.

ongoing cultural civil war revolving around morality," one that pits Americans "with a fairly traditional religious faith, who feel that the culture is out of control, against secular people who believe in a pluralistic society."

Obscenity is a mercurial concept whose nature has evolved through different periods of history. The Supreme Court's definition of the term, in the 1973 case *Miller v. California,* gives individual communities the task of determining what is obscene. Hence, what would quickly land someone in jail in Salt Lake City might be routine fare on New York's 42nd Street.

But a community's standards on obscenity are notoriously difficult to determine, even after someone goes to the trouble of going to court. In May 1989, for example, a U.S. district judge in Los Angeles dismissed racketeering charges against an adult video distributor because, he said, the sprawling Los Angeles area is too diverse to give him "positive evidence of what the entire community believes in."[3]

Critics of obscenity crackdowns worry that the cures being offered are worse than the disease. An example they cite is a bill sponsored by Sen. Mitch McConnell, R-Ky., that would allow victims of sexual assaults (or their survivors if they are killed) to seek monetary damages

from producers, distributors, exhibitors and sellers of child pornography or obscene adult pornography if a jury is convinced that the attacker was influenced by the pornography. *(See p. 984.)*

Critics also target the Justice Department, whose newly renamed Child Exploitation and Obscenity Section is spearheading the crackdown on pornography using the controversial tactic of multiple prosecutions of the same defendant in different states. The obscenity unit also is employing techniques that critics say produce overly severe penalties and lead to entrapment.

Some have criticized the department's crackdown as an overexuberant use of taxpayer dollars intended to win political points. In December 1990, after three Los Angeles video companies were indicted in Dallas for allegedly distributing hard-core pornography, their attorney blasted the Bush administration. "For what we believe is the most cynical of political reasons," the attorney said, the administration "is attempting to impose a national censorial stranglehold on the citizens of America to vindicate the beliefs of a small radical group of constituents."[4]

As the war over obscenity continues, the direction the pendulum swings next will be decided largely on the following issues:

## Does the political climate favor the crackdown on obscenity?

There is little doubt that campaigns against pornography and sexually explicit art have a political foundation under their moral and social pillars. Conservative columnist Patrick J. Buchanan, a recently announced presidential candidate, argued last year that "conservatives need to exploit this mood of national rage against filthy and blasphemous art, against general coarseness and crudity, to rally a movement to recapture America's culture."[5]

The mood Buchanan speaks of "has something to do with election of a conservative administration in 1980," says Finan of the Media Coalition, "but it's also the reaction among some groups to the liberalization of the 1960s."

To Finan and others in the arts, publishing and film communities, "the censors," with their large mailing lists and well-publicized protest tactics, are clearly winning — and controlling — today's battle. "They set the terms of debate in the form of 'pornography and obscenity,' which is highly charged language," says Rick Karpel, director of government relations for the Video Software Dealers Association. "No one will defend pornography and obscenity. It's difficult to turn the debate around."

The ability of the political right to set the obscenity agenda is also reinforced by the large numbers of conservative judges appointed by the Reagan and Bush administrations. On June 22, for example, the Supreme Court, in a 5-4 vote, ruled that Indiana may ban nude dancing in nightclubs. Chief Justice William H. Rehnquist wrote that "public indecency statutes such as the one before us reflect moral disapproval of people appearing nude among strangers in public places."*

The public, however, appears split on obscenity issues. When a September Gallup Poll asked respondents whether the standards in their communities regarding the sale of sexually explicit material should be stricter, 43 percent said yes while 47 percent said keep them as they are. That's a slight increase in tolerance from 1977, when 45 percent wanted stricter standards, and only 35 percent said don't change them.

"Americans are ambivalent," says Bauer, whose Family Research Council publishes educational materials denouncing pornography. "But the average American is not exposed to material we're concerned about. Most imagine the *Playboy* centerfold they snuck a look at 25 years ago and say, 'Well, I don't like it, but it's not dangerous, and a free society should err on the side of letting things through.' But these people change when they see the child porn, the sadomasochism and the hard-core porn that exploits women and children."

Anti-obscenity activists can take heart in the public's recent buying patterns. In 1990, adult videos represented just 7 percent of the video rental market, down from 13 percent in 1984, according to the Video Software Dealers Association. Industry surveys show that the dollar volume generated by adult films declined steadily from 11.4 percent in 1987 to 7 percent in 1990.

Still, the apparent cooling of interest in celluloid sex may be only a short-term dip. A whopping 400 million adult tapes were rented from mainstream video outlets in 1990, according to the Adult Video Association, compared with only 54 million in 1980, when videocassette recorders were less common.* And *Playboy's* pay-per-view soft-core porn television service is now available to 5 million American households, compared with 3.2 million in June 1990.

Government crackdowns and citizen protests may win converts to the view that sexually oriented materials are harmful, but there is some evidence that Americans' attitudes about obscenity and crackdowns are heavily influenced by what their neighbors think. Communications expert Daniel Linz calls the phenomenon "prosecution-induced intolerance." According to Linz, a professor at the University of California at Santa Barbara, the greater the media attention given law enforcement activities against pornography, the more the average observer may assume that the citizens of a community are intolerant.

To evaluate a jury's application of community standards, Linz recently surveyed a group of adults in Mecklenburg County, N.C., where state prosecutors in 1989 had charged Cinema Blue, a now-defunct adult theater and bookstore, with selling obscene materials. The survey subjects were divided into two groups. One group of 129 was shown the films that had led to the indictment,

and a control group was shown a non-explicit film. After surveying both groups' attitudes about whether explicit films should be permitted in the community, Linz found that fewer members of the group that had actually seen the films, as compared with the control group, felt that they appealed to a "morbid, shameful or unhealthy interest in sex."[6]

## Is pornography harmful?

This question has long divided experts, prompted reams of studies and inspired endless debate over whether freedom of speech considerations should be overridden by a need to protect the public.

The bulk of the 1,960-page *Final Report* of the 1986 commission on pornography led by Attorney General Edwin Meese III asserts that pornography harms both the individual and society. "A person who learned about human sexuality in the 'adults only' outlets of America," University of Virginia law and psychiatry Professor Park Elliot Dietz told the commission, "would be a person who had never conceived of a man and woman marrying or even falling in love before having intercourse, who had never conceived of tender foreplay, and who had never conceived of procreation as a purpose of sexual union. Instead, such a person would be one who had learned that sex at home meant sex with one's children, stepchildren, parents, siblings ... pets, and with neighbors, milkmen, plumbers, salesmen, burglars and peepers."[7]

Pornography's religious critics emphasize the warping of the user's view of sex. "Pornographic material is one weapon in the arsenal of Satan designed to undermine moral purity in the human will by encouraging lust," says a pamphlet from the Christian Life Commission of the 15-million-member Southern Baptist Convention. Marital life is spoiled as pornography causes users to becomed-

---

*Conservative judges, however, are not always predictable in their rulings on obscenity issues. The newest Supreme Court member, Clarence Thomas, ruling as an appeals court judge last August, voted with the majority in overruling the FCC's effort to ban indecent radio broadcasts 24 hours a day.

*Blockbuster Video, a Florida-based chain that serves 13 percent of the U.S. market, does not rent or sell movies rated NC-17. The Rev. Wildmon claims credit for the policy, but a Blockbuster spokesman says it predates Wildmon's campaign.

ddissatisfied with their real-life sex partners, the pamphlet says.

In addition, argues Victor Cline, a University of Utah psychologist who has treated sex offenders, pornography becomes addictive, requiring the user to seek rougher and more sexually shocking material to achieve the same effect. Eventually, the user is prompted to act out what he has seen, often forcing wives to submit to degrading or dangerous sex acts.[8]

To this indictment, the Meese commission — backed by many feminists — added the charge that pornography perpetuates the "rape myth," the notion that every woman secretly desires to be sexually taken by force. It is a common element in the scanty plots of pornographic movies. Feminists also argue that pornography degrades women by portraying them as sexually insatiable objects of male pleasure in a world of sexual inequality, a view summed up in the title of Andrea Dworkin's 1981 book, *Pornography: Men Possessing Women.*

Thirdly, feminists argue that pornographic movies are dangerous and exploitative to the often unwilling participants. Former porn actress Linda Marchiano (better known as Linda Lovelace) described in her 1980 book, *Ordeal,* how she was held against her will for two and a half years while she performed on camera for the legendary pornographic movie "Deep Throat."[9]

On the social level, critics of pornography point out that the $10 billion porn industry is heavily controlled by organized crime. They also cite a link between pornography and violent crime, noting that serial killers such as John Wayne Gacy and Ted Bundy were consumers of pornography. A frequently cited 1988 FBI study found that 81 percent of violent sexual offenders regularly used violent pornography. In 1985, researcher Sara Lee Johann examined 2,380 cases of abuse, battering and sexual assault in Minnesota and

found that 68 percent of the abusers beat or sexually abused the victim after viewing pornographic materials (58 percent of the abusers actually showed pornographic pictures or articles to their victims).[10]

When the Meese commission cited such studies, detractors pounced on it for assuming a single causal link between pornography and rape. They also ascribed alarming implications to the implied proposals for widespread banning of porn. "Pedophiles, child molesters, who have been arrested are often found to have in their homes not simply commercial child pornography, but scrapbooks containing department store underwear advertisements," scoffed Barry Lynn of the ACLU.[11] Skeptics can also point to studies that conclude just the opposite of the anti-porn activists' assertions. A 1989 study by Cynthia Gentry of Wake Forest University examined areas with high rape rates and found "no evidence of a relationship between [sales of] popular sex magazines and violence against women."[12]

Perhaps the best-known national studies of pornography and rape rates showed some correlation. But a strong association does not mean that one causes the other, cautioned the authors, Yale University's Larry Baron and the University of New Hampshire's Murray Straus.[13] They and other researchers have pointed out that the high porn-consumption rates in high-rape states are accompanied by other "hypermasculine" aspects in those states, such as a large number of subscriptions to *Field and Stream* magazine.[14]

Most expert judgments on the effects of pornography result from a series of laboratory film-viewing experiments. Typically, the scientists subjected male college students to selected films with varying degrees of soft- and hard-core sex and violence and then measured their heartbeats and aggressive feelings toward an annoy-

ing woman (a laboratory confederate acting the part). Other experiments measured the subjects' degree of sympathy toward a rape victim portrayed on film, or their willingness to intervene to stop a rape.

The results, compared with reactions of men in control groups, are contradictory. The soft-core erotica in many of the experiments reduced feelings of aggression. But after seeing several types of films, many of the subjects reported increased feelings of aggression, particularly those predisposed to aggression. Several experiments showed that, under laboratory conditions, ability to empathize with a rape victim was diminished.

This body of data, according to communications professor Edward Donnerstein of the University of California at Santa Barbara, was oversimplified by the Meese commission, whose leap to pornography as a cause of rape he called "bizarre."[15] Furthermore, Donnerstein argues, the sex in the laboratory films seemed to have less impact on the subjects than the violence. "It should be obvious to anyone with a television set that the mass media contain an abundance of violent non-sexually explicit (and thus non-obscene) images and messages," he writes. "These ideas about rape and violence may be so pervasive in our culture that it is myopic to call them the exclusive domain of violent pornography, much less the domain of the broader category of legally obscene materials."[16]

The charge that pornography harms individual users is also rejected by a sizable body of scholarship. "No research I've seen supports the idea that non-violent pornography is addictive and destructive," says Lloyd G. Sinclair, a sex therapist in Madison, Wis. Sinclair previews sex films for adult movie distributors to block ones that use underage models or actors who show signs of coercion. "The idea that porn is so powerful anyone with average ideas can become addicted to it is frankly ludicrous."

In fact, a serious school of thought argues for pornography's positive effects. Stag films "permit mental adultery while preserving monogamy," wrote Joseph Slade in an oft-quoted 1970 essay about New York's porn district.[17] Others have cited the "cathartic effect" of pornography on users who release their fantasies through masturbation instead of going out and committing sex crimes.[18]

Finally, experts have observed positive effects on the conjugal lives of couples who watch adult movies that feature mainstream sexual activity. According to Sinclair, both men women are generally aroused by such films and often increase their lovemaking for a day or so after viewing. Verbal communication about sex is enhanced, he adds, and the viewers experience an increased acceptance of the idea that it's OK to look at such material.

### Is the Bush administration using reasonable tactics in its pornography crackdown?

This September, Dick Thornburgh, who had just quit as U.S. attorney general to run for a Senate seat, sent a fundraising letter to Pennsylvania voters touting his crackdown on pornography as a reason to support him. Among the Justice Department's accomplishments, Thornburgh said, were persuading Congress to pass the 1988 Child Protection and Obscenity Enforcement Act; increasing child pornography prosecutions by almost 60 percent in a single year; shutting down the nation's only satellite broadcaster of pornography; collecting more than $6 million in fines and seized properties; and nearly eliminating mail-order pornography distribution.

The Justice Department currently has 13 pornography prosecutors, almost double the number under Attor-

ney General Meese. Its child and adult pornography activities have ballooned in the past five years: There were 1,422 child-porn investigations from 1987-91, almost double the 1980-84 number, according to the U.S. Postal Inspection Service, which has responsibility for policing ob-

scenity sent through the mail. Adult pornography investigations jumped from 81 during 1981-85 to 222 in the past five years.

Bill Kelly, now retired after running the FBI's anti-obscenity efforts for 18 years, says "the situation has completely turned around." Kelly

## Mixed Attitudes About Sexual Freedom

*Americans' attitudes about sexually explicit material have become slightly more tolerant since 1986, according to a recent Gallup Poll. However, an overwhelming 76 percent want to ban dial-a-porn telephone numbers, and at least 45 percent would ban performances by female and male strippers.*

*For each of the following, do you feel it should be totally banned, sold to adults as long as there is no public display or sold to adults with no restrictions?*

|  | Total ban | No public display | No restrictions | No opinion |
|---|---|---|---|---|
| Magazines that show nudity |  |  |  |  |
| 1991 | 29% | 49% | 20% | 2% |
| 1986 | 29 | 51 | 18 | 2 |
| Magazines that show adults having sexual relations |  |  |  |  |
| 1991 | 45 | 41 | 13 | 1 |
| 1986 | 49 | 40 | 9 | 2 |
| Theater showings of X-rated movies |  |  |  |  |
| 1991 | 42 | 39 | 17 | 2 |
| 1986 | 43 | 38 | 16 | 3 |
| Sale or rental of X-rated video cassettes for home viewing |  |  |  |  |
| 1991 | 33 | 47 | 18 | 2 |
| 1986 | 36 | 43 | 19 | 2 |

*Do you think each of the following activities and services should be legal or not legal for sale to adults?*

|  | Legal | Illegal | No opinion |
|---|---|---|---|
| 900 telephone numbers offering sexually explicit talk | 23% | 76% | 1% |
| Performances by female strippers or nude dancers in bars or clubs | 51 | 46 | 3 |
| Performances by male strippers or nude dancers in bars or clubs | 52 | 45 | 3 |

*Source: The Gallup Poll, Oct. 6, 1991*

## Parents Concerned about Popular Entertainment

*A recent Gallup Poll found that more than half of the parents surveyed were "somewhat" or "very" concerned about the possible negative impact of sexual images. Heavy metal rock music was of greatest concern, with 67 percent of parents registering concern.*

***How concerned are you that the sexual content of the following forms of entertainment might have a negative effect on our nation's children?***

|  | Very concerned | Somewhat concerned | Not concerned | Not at all concerned | No opinion |
|---|---|---|---|---|---|
| Heavy metal rock music | 45% | 22% | 16% | 12% | 5% |
| Music videos | 33 | 31 | 19 | 12 | 5 |
| Rap music | 32 | 28 | 21 | 13 | 6 |
| Popular TV programming | 28 | 33 | 22 | 15 | 2 |
| Rock music in general | 26 | 30 | 24 | 18 | 2 |
| Hollywood movies | 26 | 35 | 24 | 12 | 3 |
| Stand-up comedy | 24 | 32 | 24 | 18 | 2 |

*Source: The Gallup Poll, Oct. 6, 1991*

says the Justice Department has been working with local officials and citizens' groups in successful operations like the one in Oklahoma City, "where they've gotten rid of all massage parlors, strip joints and adult bookstores."

Two initiatives in particular have won the department kudos: Project Looking Glass, a crackdown on child-porn users in 1987-88 that tallied 202 searches and 147 convictions; and Project PostPorn, a crackdown on interstate mail-order pornography during the same period that resulted in the prosecution of 11 companies, 50 convictions and fines as high as $2 million. Officials deny that the crackdown was initiated by politicians in Washington. "It's a response to citizen complaints," says Raymond Smith, a program manager

for the Postal Inspection Service who works with Justice on obscenity.

Among the probe's targets was Phil Harvey, the owner of Adam and Eve, a major mail-order adult film distributorship based in Carrboro, N.C. Harvey does $30 million a year in sales to 2 million customers who order videos with such titles as "Toy-Loving Lesbians." In 1986, he watched as 32 state and federal agents raided his warehouse, led by a former aide to Sen. Helms. Harvey was prosecuted under a new North Carolina obscenity law. A jury in Alamance County screened his films and acquitted him in less than an hour.

Last year, however, the Justice Department began prosecuting Harvey in conservative Utah, where he last shipped a film in 1986. "The indictment is politically motivated," Harvey

says, noting that the government knows his screening process tries to prevent circulation of films depicting children, violence or bestiality.

Several months before he was indicted, Harvey himself sued the department, charging it with misuse of prosecutorial powers. His attorneys have a deposition from several disgruntled FBI agents, among them Robert Marinaro, who ran the FBI's anti-obscenity operations. Marinaro says the bureau engaged in a "running battle" with Justice's obscenity unit and that he refused to participate in investigations of companies whose material met Supreme Court standards. "They became zealots about this area of pornography," Marinaro says, "and their religious beliefs overstepped good judgment in terms of how they should go about looking at this material."

The Justice Department's use of multi-state prosecutions against pornographers has brought disapproval from legal scholars, who deride it as "forum shopping," an effort to go after national porn purveyors in conservative states, where juries are more apt to convict. To Maxwell Lillienstein, counsel to the American Booksellers Association, it's "a kind of entrapment." He warned that prosecutors may extend "this kind of censorship by intimidation to mainstream wholesalers and booksellers who sell art books, sex education books."[19] Others say it is a waste of taxpayers' money to go after run-of-the-mill adult films instead of the hard-core variety that feature sadomasochism, coprophilia and bestiality.

Rebutting the forum-shopping charge, department spokesman Tillett points out that anti-porn prosecutions have taken place in Alexandria, Va., Las Vegas and Minneapolis, "hardly hotbeds of conservatism. The beauty of the whole thing is the local community standards. We believe in a fairly bright line as to what is obscene." People like Phil Harvey "would have you believe it's all garden variety hetero sex," Tillett adds, "but there's bestiality, homosexuality, child porn and violence."

The Justice Department doesn't make distinctions, charges Marjorie Heins of the ACLU. "It cuts deals, attempts multiple prosecutions · and drives people into settlements" using tactics that have been condemned as unconstitutional by two federal judges. In one case, the ACLU says, the Justice Department demanded as part of a settlement that a company stop distributing constitutionally protected material such as *Playboy* and *The Joy of Sex.* "They want a bright line," Heins says, that would deem as obscene "12-13 titles now available in your Walden Books store, including *Any Woman Can!, How to Satisfy a Woman Every Time,* the high-art drawings of Aubrey Beardsley and the Kama Sutra."

Since the debate began over federal funding of sexually explicit art, the Justice Department has raided the homes and studios of artists, the ACLU says, prompting the group to file a Freedom of Information Act request for documents from Justice's obscenity unit.

Justice's pursuit of users of child pornography has not escaped criticism, despite the fact that materials showing pedophilia and produced with models below the age of consent are scorned by many in the adult pornography industry. Keith Jacobson, a farmer in Newman Grove, Neb., has taken the department to the Supreme Court, charging its agents with entrapment. Jacobson was convicted of possessing child porn after ordering bogus catalogs fabricated by U.S. postal inspectors. He was sentenced to probation and 250 hours of community service. University of Arizona law Professor Paul Marcus, an expert on entrapment, called it "one of the most outrageous examples of government behavior that I have seen."[20] The Justice De-

partment and Postal Inspection Service say such stings are justified when the victim is predisposed to commit the crime.

The Justice Department's critics are not all from the left. Libertarian commentator Doug Bandow has faulted the department's use of the 1970 Racketeer Influenced and Corrupt Organizations law (RICO) to go after pornographers, arguing that its severe property-forfeiture provisions should be reserved for organized crime.

In 1987, the department convicted a Virginia couple for selling six sex magazines and four videos valued at about $100 and ended up seizing their three bookstores containing a

non-pornographic inventory worth more than $1 million. The big advantage of using RICO against pornographers, counters Robert Showers, former head of Justice's obscenity section, is that it allows you to "take out the unit as a whole."[21]

Government enforcers are also permitted to seize property from obscenity-law violators under the 1988 Child Protection and Obscenity Enforcement Act. But in Dallas last month, a federal judge refused to confiscate millions of dollars' worth of non-obscene videotapes from a convicted California distributor, noting that only two videos in the company's inventory of 5,700 titles were obscene.  ∎

# BACKGROUND

## Early Obscenity Bans

Long before the age of erotic home videos, there was sexually explicit art and literature. The Kama Sutra sex manual in ancient India, the promiscuous romps of John Cleland's *Fanny Hill* in 18th-century England, the sexual-torture writings of the Marquis de Sade in 18th-century France, all, at some point, were banned. In colonial America in 1711, the government of Massachusetts prohibited publication of "wicked, profane, impure, filthy and obscene material."

The earliest recorded obscenity case in the United States was *Commonwealth v. Sharpless* in 1815, in which the Pennsylvania Supreme Court ruled that a merchant could not exhibit a picture of a nude couple for a profit. In 1821, two Boston booksellers were convicted of selling *Fanny Hill,* and by 1843, the first federal obscenity law had been passed, regulating the trade in risqué French postcards.

The first legal definition of obsceni-

ty was set forth by the British, in an 1868 case, *Regina v. Hicklin.* Chief Justice Lord Cockburn declared material obscene if it tended to "deprave and corrupt" the minds of readers open to immoral influences. That definition was imported by American jurists and was used well into the 20th century. It was challenged in 1913 by U.S. Supreme Court Justice Learned Hand, who complained that the *Hicklin* definition took allegedly obscene quotations out of context and didn't factor in children as the most easily influenced of people, thus reducing all adults to the level of children in order to police a salacious few.[22]

The archetype of American anti-obscenity legislation was the 1873 Comstock Act, named for its chief lobbyist, Anthony Comstock, the 28-year-old founder of the New York Society for the Suppression of Vice. It became a model for state laws well into this century, and "Comstockery" entered the lexicon as a name for crusaders against obscenity.

### *Artistic Challenges*
In the 1920s and '30s, the question of defining obscenity and pornogra-

phy was debated widely among publishers, the mass media and intellectuals. The controversial British author D. H. Lawrence, who saw some of his works banned, among them *Lady Chatterley's Lover,* wrote that "what is pornography to one man is the laughter of genius to another." Such groups as the Society for the Suppression of Vice staged book burnings.

In 1933, an effort to ban James Joyce's *Ulysses* was struck down by Judge John Woolsey in the Southern District of New York. He set forth a new test, saying that a work was obscene if it was written with pornographic intent and if it tended to "stir the lustful thoughts" of the reader.[23]

Also during this period, the film industry, in 1931, issued its first "Code to Govern the Making of Major Motion Pictures." It laid down a strict but hard-to-enforce rule that "obscenity in word, gesture, reference, song, joke or by suggestion is forbidden." In 1936, the Catholic Church's Legion of Decency began issuing its own "moral" ratings of popular films, a practice continued today by the U.S. Catholic Conference.

The mainstream film industry, of course, had no control over the underground production of stag films or "blue" movies, often distributed in the 8mm format for home projectors. To a large extent, it was the post-World War II prosperity that created the market for these low-budget sex films as well as the mass market for magazines and rock music.

In 1957, the Supreme Court ruled for the first time on an obscenity case. In *Roth v. the United States,* it upheld the obscenity conviction of New York bookseller Samuel Roth. In writing the majority opinion, Associate Justice William J. Brennan authored a new test, making obscenity depend on "whether to the average person, applying contemporary community standards, the dominant theme of the material taken as a whole appeals to the prurient interests."

In the next few years, a series of court battles ensued over publishers' rights to market Lawrence's *Lady Chatterley's Lover,* Henry Miller's novel *Tropic of Cancer,* and once again, *Fanny Hill,* sold under its original title, *Memoirs of a Woman of Pleasure.* The trend was clearly toward liberalization. It was in ruling on a 1964 case, *Jacobellis v. Ohio,* in which a French film, "The Lovers," was deemed not obscene, that Justice Stewart issued his famous "I know it when I see it" comment about pornography.

## Liberalism's Heyday

The political upheavals, the sexual revolution and the rise of the counterculture in the 1960s wrought many changes in mainstream arts — the musical "Hair" brought nudity to Broadway, and Hollywood films broke new ground for frankness. *(See story, p. 980.)* Graphic sex films from Europe, among them "I Am Curious (Yellow)," were now advertised in daily newspapers. With the new artistic freedoms came a new, multi-billion-dollar pornography industry, whose XXX-rated movie houses, peep shows and live-sex stage acts flashed their neon lights openly in Times Square and other neighborhoods. The country remained as divided as ever over obscenity, as did the Supreme Court: In one day in 1967, it issued 14 separate opinions in three obscenity cases.

The trends were alarming enough that in 1968, during the latter part of the Johnson administration, a federal commission was convened. The President's Commission on Obscenity and Pornography was given a $2 million budget and two years to work. It sponsored original physiological and psychological research and surveyed the effects of pornography laws in other countries. It found no proof that

pornography was harmful or linked to violence, and it recommended the repeal of "federal, state and local legislation prohibiting the sale, exhibition, or distribution of sexual materials to consenting adults." *

By the time the Democratic-appointed commission delivered its report, however, it was 1970, and a conservative administration had come to Washington. "I totally reject this report," Richard M. Nixon declared. "So long as I am president, there will be no relaxation of the national effort to control and eliminate smut from our national life."[24]

The reaction among conservatives to the commission's "morally bankrupt conclusions" was intense and enduring enough that several would form anti-pornography organizations to call for a new crackdown on obscenity as part of the Reagan Revolution. Recalls Christopher Finan of the Media Coalition, the commission "was the high-water mark of liberalization."

### Defining Obscenity

As the 1970s got rolling, pornography began to change. Underground stag films and cheap foreign imports were giving way to big-budget, widely publicized American-made porn featuring full-length plots and close-up photography of genitals during orgasm. As feminists would note, many of the newer films used substantially more violence against women in their sex scenes. By this time, the marquees on Main Street theaters across the country beckoned average moviegoers to such titles as "Deep Throat," "The Devil In Miss Jones" and "Inside Marilyn Chambers." These and similar films were subject-

*Continued on p. 981*

---

*There were some dissenters on the commission, notably land developer Charles H. Keating Jr., the founder of Citizens for Decency Through Law, who later was instrumental in convening the Meese pornography commission and who gained national notoriety for his role in the recent savings and loan scandal.

# Chronology

## 19th Century
**British and American courts begin defining obscenity.**

### 1815
In the earliest U.S. obscenity case, the Pennsylvania Supreme Court rules that a merchant can't exhibit pictures of a nude couple for profit.

### 1868
British court defines "obscenity." Definition is then borrowed by American jurists.

### 1873
Congress passes the first U.S. anti-obscenity act, named for anti-porn crusader Anthony Comstock.

## 1920s-1930s
**Anti-obscenity crusaders burn books; bans are challenged in courts; motion picture industry launches code of morals.**

### 1933
New York court rules James Joyce novel *Ulysses* is not obscene.

## 1950s-1960s
**Postwar economy fuels rise of sex books, magazines, stag films.**

### 1957
Supreme Court rules for the first time on an obscenity case, upholding the conviction of New York bookseller Samuel Roth.

### March 21, 1966
Supreme Court declares *Fanny Hill* is not obscene.

### April 22, 1968
In *Ginsberg v. New York*, the Supreme Court upholds a law prohibiting the sale of "girlie" magazines to anyone under the age of 17.

## 1970s
**Porn films become more mainstream, more violent.**

### Sept. 30, 1970
First federal pornography commission issues its report.

### June 6, 1973
Supreme Court's landmark decision in *Miller v. California* provides current working definition of obscenity.

### July 3, 1978
Supreme Court in *FCC v. Pacifica Foundation* upholds Federal Communications Commission's authority to prohibit indecent broadcasting.

## 1980s
**Reagan era invigorates anti-obscenity activists.**

### July 2, 1982
In *New York v. Ferber*, the Supreme Court rules that authorities can prohibit sexually explicit materials involving children without showing that material is obscene.

### May 21, 1984
President Reagan signs the Child Protection Act toughening penalties and broadening Postal Service investigative powers.

### July 9, 1986
Meese commission on pornography releases its *Final Report*.

### Feb. 25, 1986
In *City of Renton v. Playtime Theatres Inc.*, the Supreme Court upholds an ordinance banning adult theaters in Washington state within 1,000 feet of a residential zone, church, park or school.

### May 4, 1987
In *Pope v. Illinois*, Supreme Court determines that community standards should not be applied to obscenity cases in determining whether a work has scientific, artistic or literary value.

### Nov. 18, 1988
Reagan signs omnibus drug bill containing Child Protection and Obscenity Enforcement Act.

### Oct. 1, 1988
Reagan signs appropriations bill containing 24-hour ban on indecent broadcasting, which is then challenged in courts.

### June 23, 1989
Supreme Court in *Sable Communications of California v. FCC* protects indecent but not obscene telephone conversations.

## 1990s
**Bush administration continues crackdown on child and adult pornography.**

### Nov. 29, 1990
President Bush signs Crime Control Act containing Child Protection Restoration and Penalties Enhancement Act.

### Oct. 5, 1990
Cincinnati jury acquits gallery director who exhibited Mapplethorpe photographs.

# Fine-Tuning the Movie Rating System

One of the Solomonic compromises in the censorship debate has been the film rating system administered by the Motion Picture Association of America (MPAA). Since 1968, it has helped the public decide which movies are suitable for minors without dictating content. The system has been dogged by controversy, however, requiring several moves to fine-tune it.

The need for standardized ratings first became clear with the newly daring films of the turbulent 1960s. At the time, the industry's 1920s-vintage system of self-regulation was still in effect, and MPAA President Jack Valenti found himself negotiating with Hollywood executives over the final editing of Mike Nichols' "Who's Afraid of Virginia Woolf?" which contained the word "screw" and the phrase "hump the hostess," and Michaelangelo Antonioni's "Blow-Up," the first mainstream film featuring nudity.

Valenti's uneasiness at making judgments on art and censorship set in motion a search for a better system.† Congress was also moving to require a rating system.

In 1968 the MPAA, with the approval of film distributors and theater owners, unveiled a system that broke films into four categories, to be used voluntarily by film marketers. The ratings would be derived by majority vote of an anonymous panel representing a national cross-section of parents. (Today's panel ranges in age from 33 to 70 and consists of two homemakers, a cabinet-maker, a children's book illustrator, a postal worker, a college teacher, a social-service administrator, a news reporter and a hairdresser.) Producers or distributors who object to a rating may re-edit the film or appeal to the Rating Appeals Board. As of June 1991, 102 of 235 appeals had been granted.

More than 10,000 films have been rated over the past 23 years, with more than half receiving an R and only about 4 percent earning an X or the new NC-17 rating.

The biggest problem has been with the X rating. Though some mainstream films were rated X ("Midnight Cowboy" won the Academy Award for best picture in 1969), most Xs went to films with little content other than graphic sex. Moreover, the MPAA had not secured trademark protection for its system, which meant that marketers of unrated sex films could use the X rating as a selling point (XXX!! the marquees blared). To the public and to

| | |
|---|---|
| General audiences<br><br>**G**   G GENERAL AUDIENCES | **Nothing that would offend parents for viewing by children.** |
| Parental guidance suggested<br><br>**PG**<br><br>PG PARENTAL GUIDANCE SUGGESTED<br>SOME MATERIAL MAY NOT BE SUITABLE FOR CHILDREN | Parents urged to give **"parental guidance." May contain some material parents might not like for their young children.** |
| Parents strongly cautioned<br><br>**PG-13**<br><br>PG-13 PARENTS STRONGLY CAUTIONED<br>Some Material May Be Inappropriate for Children Under 13 | **Parents are urged to be cautious. Some material may be inappropriate for pre-teenagers.** |
| Restricted<br><br>**R**<br><br>R RESTRICTED<br>UNDER 17 REQUIRES ACCOMPANYING<br>PARENT OR ADULT GUARDIAN | **Contains some adult material. Parents are urged to learn more about the film before taking their young children with them.** |
| No children under 17 admitted<br><br>**NC-17**<br><br>NC-17 NO CHILDREN<br>UNDER 17<br>ADMITTED | **Patently adult. Children are not permitted.** |

serious filmmakers, the X was inextricably linked to pornography, a box-office kiss of death.

Then in 1990, a first-of-its-kind lawsuit was brought against the MPAA by the distributors of the Spanish film "Tie Me Up! Tie Me Down!" Though well-received by critics, it had been rated X because of a graphic scene involving a toy skindiver and a nude actress in a bathtub. The distributors' suit called the rating "arbitrary" and "capricious." †† A New York Supreme Court judge upheld the rating but admonished the MPAA, saying its system was out of date and unscientific.

That July, 30 Hollywood directors sent Valenti a letter denouncing the rating system, at the same time that religious and parents' groups were saying the system had become vague and permissive. Two months later, the MPAA changed the X rating to NC-17 and this time secured a trademark on the new system.

The change restored meaning to the top category and removed filmmakers' fears that being slapped with an X would harm marketability. "I think it would be hard to attract the raincoat crowd with a rating called NC-17," Valenti said.‡ At the same time, the MPAA added more-detailed explanations of its lower ratings.

While 74 percent of the public approve of the new system, according to a July 1991 poll,‡‡ many anti-pornography activists dislike the change to NC-17. "Lots of theaters wouldn't carry X-rated films because they carried a stigma," says Gary Bauer, president of the Family Research Council. Now, he says, more will carry NC-17 films. Such worries have prompted religious and conservative groups to threaten boycotts of theaters, video stores and even newspapers that advertise NC-17 films.

"The religious right wants to ruin the NC-17 rating" by failing to distinguish between pornography and non-pornographic films, says Rick Karpel, government relations director of the Video Software Dealers Association. "It's not the MPAA's fault. The NC-17 has meaning. The X had lost all meaning."

---

† Jack Valenti, *The Voluntary Movie Rating System* (1991).
†† *The New York Times,* July 20, 1990.
‡ *The New York Times,* Sept. 27, 1990.
‡‡ The poll was conducted for the MPAA by the Opinion Research Corp.

Continued from p. 978
ed to state and local challenges that filled court dockets for years.

It was in 1973, in *Miller v. California,* that the Supreme Court established the basis for obscenity law today. In upholding the conviction of a vendor who had mass-mailed brochures advertising sex books, the court created a three-pronged obscenity test for determining whether a work is beyond First Amendment protection: (1) "whether the average person, applying contemporary community standards, would find that the work, taken as a whole, appeals to prurient interest; (2) whether the work depicts or describes, in a patently offensive way, sexual conduct specifically defined by applicable state law; and (3) whether the work, taken as a whole, lacks serious literary, artistic, political or scientific value."

Writing for the majority, Chief Justice Warren E. Burger said the court had intended to deem only hard-core materials obscene, suggesting as a guideline that such materials included "patently offensive representations or descriptions or ultimate sexual acts, normal or perverted, actual or simulated" and "patently offensive representations or descriptions of masturbation, excretory functions and lewd exhibitions of the genitals." The court rejected the earlier test that to be obscene a work had to be "utterly without redeeming social value."

Four justices dissented in the *Miller* ruling, among them William O. Douglas, who wrote:

"The First Amendment was not fashioned as a vehicle for dispensing tranquilizers to the people. Its prime function was to keep debate open to 'offensive' as well as to 'staid' people. ... The materials before us may be garbage. But so is much of what is said in political campaigns, in the daily press, on TV or over the radio."

The *Miller* decision's chief importance came from the court's refusal to enunciate a national obscenity standard, leaving decisions on obscenity prosecutions and convictions up to district attorneys and juries in different communities. The ruling led to the closings of "adult" bookstores in many cities and the formation of the Media Coalition by worried members of the book and magazine industries.

## The Meese Commission

The arrival of the Reagan administration in 1981 cheered anti-pornography activists. In signing the 1984 Child Protection Act, which gave the Postal Inspection Service new investigative powers against child porn, President Reagan announced the formation of a new national commission to study pornography. Attorney General Meese convened it in May 1985. With 11 members, a one-year schedule and a budget of $500,000, the commission held six field hearings and heard 208 witnesses, most favoring tighter controls on pornography. The panel listened to wives who'd been sexually abused by pornography-addicted husbands and heard former *Playboy* bunnies describe the impersonal emptiness of group sex in Hugh Hefner's mansion.

Meese unveiled the commission's *Final Report* — to some chuckling from reporters — in July 1986 at the Justice Department, where he stood in front of a bare-breasted statue of the spirit of justice. The report contained lists of crude-sounding titles of pornographic films and reprinted graphic scripts. Its principal findings were that the hard-core material found in many adult bookstores and video outlets was much worse than the material reviewed by the 1970 commission and that contemporary pornography contained significant amounts of violence, incest, sodomy and bestiality. It recommended legislation and citizen action against por-

nography and led to the formation in January 1987 of the Justice Department's National Obscenity Enforcement Unit.

The Meese commission made at least one major tactical error. In February 1986, Executive Director Alan Sears had sent a warning letter to numerous U.S. corporations — including CBS, RCA, Warner Communications and Southland Corp. — all owners of retail outlets that sold soft-core men's magazines such as *Playboy* and *Penthouse.* The letter informed them that they had been identified as pornography distributors and gave them 30 days to prove otherwise — or they would be named as such in the commission's *Final Report.*

Immediately, more than 8,000 convenience stores stopped carrying the magazines. *Playboy* and *Penthouse* sued the Justice Department, calling the letter an unconstitutional restraint on trade. Justice lost the suit and was forced to send another letter nullifying the first letter, and Meese and other anti-pornography activists would later acknowledge that the air-brushed nude photos in soft-core men's magazines were not legally obscene. The stigma the commission's letter attached to *Playboy* and others has remained, however. Southland, owner of the 7-Eleven chain, still has a policy against selling such magazines.

### *Unlikely Alliance*
Politically, the Meese panel was remarkable for having cemented an unlikely alliance between conservative, religious anti-pornography activists and a diverse group of radical feminists. Its report drew heavily on the writings and testimony of writer Andrea Dworkin and law Professor Catherine A. MacKinnon, who were fresh from almost-successful efforts at passing anti-pornography ordinances in Minneapolis, Indianapolis and Cambridge, Mass. (MacKinnon's draft ordinance defined pornography as
Continued on p. 983

# The Flap Over Music Warning Labels

When rock star Prince sang about the girl in the lobby masturbating and country singer Sheena Easton sang of her "sugar walls," they created a legacy they could hardly have intended. It was these and other sexually blunt pop lyrics that shocked Tipper Gore and other parents in the Washington, D.C., area into forming the Parents' Music Resource Center (PMRC) in 1985, to raise public awareness of questionable record lyrics.

"Like many parents of my generation, I grew up listening to rock music and loving it," Gore wrote, "but something has happened since the days of 'Twist and Shout' and 'I Love Lucy.'"[†] Gore's efforts to organize parents against the music industry's "callousness toward children" drew cries of censorship and ridicule from many. Rock musician Frank Zappa blasted her "ill-conceived housewife hobby projects," and she was satirized as a prude in *Penthouse* and *Hustler*.[††]

But Gore had backing from parent-teacher associations around the country. After well-targeted public pressure and a widely publicized congressional hearing — Gore's husband, Sen. Al Gore, D-Tenn., was on the panel) — the PMRC, in its first year, got the recording industry to accept a system of voluntary parental-warning labels.

Record companies were given the option of using a self-designed label or including printed lyrics. But between January 1986 and August 1989, when 7,500 albums were released, only 49 had labels or lyrics. PMRC deemed 121 albums (about 2 percent) to be offensive.

Then, after a key endorsement from record retailers, the Recording Industry Association of America (RIAA) launched a strengthened system in May 1990, using a standardized label. In the first year, 93 major releases in the rap, heavy metal, comedy, pop and blues genres bore the "Parental Advisory: Explicit Lyrics" warning.[‡]

Record companies determined which albums would be labeled; some used individual "judges" while others convened committees from the recording industry. As predicted, a few artists, among them comedians George Carlin and Andrew Dice Clay, turned the new system into a marketing tool, producing album covers parodying the label.

The PMRC says it's pleased with results. "We're trying to talk to a younger crowd," says Executive Director Suzie Talaat. "Today's students and new parents don't see music as much of an issue, and they've been influenced by the negative press about us." Some of that negative press persists. Rock critic Dave Marsh charges PMRC with a "consistent Christian evangelical bias" and calls the group "the crucial link between the relatively respectable censors and the really frightening guys mumbling in the corner on the far right."[‡‡]

Consistent with its stated policy of supporting the First Amendment, the PMRC has opposed recent efforts to make warning labels mandatory. Fueled by the furor over the four-letter lyrics on "2 Live Crew's" "Nasty as They Wanna Be" rap album, lawmakers in 22 states in 1990 considered legislation to require warnings. In addition, some of the bills would have imposed a surtax on explicit recordings or allowed parents to bring civil actions against retailers who sell obscene recordings to minors.

The RIAA fought back, sending representatives — including popular singers EmmyLou Harris and Rosanne Cash — to state capitals to testify. The RIAA argued that the existing voluntary system makes legislation unnecessary; that parents, not record store owners or legislators, should decide what children hear; that store owners would face fines and imprisonment if their interpretation of obscenity differs from a jury's; and that such legislation would curtail the First Amendment rights of artists and audiences.

The RIAA also produced a national poll released in April 1990 showing that 52 percent of Americans support voluntary labeling, and 76 percent oppose the government getting involved in decisions about children's music. In 1990, only Louisiana passed a bill requiring warning labels, but it was vetoed by Gov. Buddy Roemer. The legislation was reconsidered in 1991 but failed in the Louisiana Senate by a single vote.

Meanwhile, evidence is mounting that concern over risqué lyrics may have been unnecessary. Several studies of teen music habits suggest that, unlike adults, kids listen more to the beat than the lyrics and tend to take off-color lyrics in stride.

A 1991 study by Peter Christenson of Lewis and Clark College led him to rebut what he calls the "forbidden fruit theory," the common notion that warning labels merely whet kids' appetites for controversial recordings. In his experiment involving a group of 145 middle-class children ages 11-15, half the subjects were exposed to a set of heavy metal and contemporary dance albums with warning labels and the other half to the same albums without the labels.

He concluded that the warning label to most of the teens was a turnoff. "If you would compare it to film ratings, a label would compare to an X rating, not an R," Christenson said. "Teenagers want something a bit racy. . . . But they are famous for rejecting extremes."

† Tipper Gore, *Raising PG Kids in an X-Rated Society* (1987), p. 11.
†† *Ibid.,* p. 26.
‡ *Billboard,* April 13, 1991.
‡‡ Dave Marsh, *50 Ways to Fight Censorship* (1991), p. 67.

Continued from p. 981
"the graphic sexually explicit subordination of women whether in pictures or words" and declared it a form of sex discrimination that women could fight in the courts.) Dworkin told the Meese commission that "the major motif of pornography as a form of entertainment is that women are raped and violated and humiliated until we discover that we like it and at that point we ask for more. . . . When your rape is entertainment . . . you have reached the nadir of social worthlessness."[25]

Other feminists, however, argued that such thinking leads to crackdowns against legitimate sexually oriented literature (such as the feminist health book *Our Bodies, Ourselves* and birth control literature) and hence violates the First Amendment. Feminism pioneer Betty Friedan called the Meese commission "a dangerous diversion of energy." A year after the panel adjourned, a group called the Feminist Anti-Censorship Taskforce (FACT) challenged Dworkin's approach by publishing a book of feminist erotica called *Caught Looking.*

Larry Baron, an expert on pornography and violence, wrote in 1987 that "a particularly insidious aspect of the [Meese commission's *Final Report*] is [its] use of feminist rhetoric to attain its right-wing objective. Replacing the outmoded cant of sin and depravity with the trendier rhetoric of harm, the commission exploited feminist outrage about sexual violence in order to bolster oppressive obscenity laws."[26]

## Indecent Broadcasts

As stewards of the public airwaves, broadcasters have special legal responsibilities on obscenity issues, particularly because radio and television programs are readily accessible to minors. It was in 1973 that comedian George Carlin's now famous "Filthy Words" monologue aired on Pacifica Radio's WBAI-FM in New York City. Containing seven commonplace dirty words, it was broadcast at 2 p.m. following warnings to listeners about explicit language. After a father complained that he and his son had heard the sketch on the way home from school, it took two years for the FCC to take action.

The FCC found the material "indecent within the meaning of the law" and reprimanded Pacifica. The radio network appealed to the U.S. Court of Appeals for the District of Columbia Circuit, and with backing by the National Association of Broadcasters, the Motion Picture Association of America (MPAA) and the three television networks, it won.

In 1978, however, the Supreme Court ruled against Pacifica, affirming the FCC's right to police indecent broadcasts. In the interim, the FCC began using the case and its list of seven dirty words to set forth its definition of indecency, which covered "language that describes, in terms patently offensive as measured by contemporary community standards for the broadcast medium, sexual or excretory activities or organs, at times of the day when there is a reasonable risk that children may be in the audience."

From 1975-87, broadcasters pretty much adhered to the guidelines, and no violations were prosecuted. (Meanwhile, the FCC had established a "safe harbor," from 10 p.m. to 6 a.m., when programs containing indecent material were permitted.)

Then in April 1987, during the Reagan administration, the FCC took action against three broadcasters, replacing the safe harbor with the more general concept of "when there is a reasonable risk that children may be in the audience." The three stations got off with a warning. After protests from broadcasters, the FCC in No-

vember 1987 reinstituted the safe harbor, this time from midnight to 6 a.m. Anti-obscenity activists such as Morality in Media began lobbying for a 24-hour ban on broadcast indecency.

Congress approved such a ban in the fall of 1988, and the FCC prepared to implement it in January 1989. But then a coalition of broadcasters and civil rights groups led by Action for Children's Television (ACT) of Cambridge, Mass., filed suit, calling the 24-hour ban unconstitutional. Peggy Charen, founder of ACT, said she prefers to have children exposed to "rotten television" rather than accept censorship. In July 1990, the FCC voted 5-0 for the 24-hour ban. In August 1991, however, a three-judge Circuit Court panel in Washington, D.C., ruled that indecent broadcasting is protected under the First Amendment and instructed the FCC to re-create a safe harbor. The commission is appealing to the Supreme Court.

## High-Tech Sex

Sex itself may be changeless, but society never stops inventing new ways to deliver the erotic message. Porn movies can now be beamed across the country by satellite.* The advent of personal-computer networks has introduced a world of electronic personal ads, interactive sex games and underground bulletin boards for seekers of child porn. *Penthouse* subscribers can order free computer software that allows them to "talk" electronically to the "Pet of the Month." And the proliferation of the home video camera has spawned a craze of amateur sex videos, which are now traded on the adult video

---

*This year, the New York City-based Home Dish Only Satellite Network was forced into bankruptcy when the Justice Department and an Alabama prosecutor went after its "Exxxtasy Channel."

market among consumers who seem eager to watch some less-intimidating sex performers in action.

But no technology has created more trouble for policy-makers than "dial-a-porn." Prompted by the impending deregulation of the telephone industry in 1982, dozens of telephone entrepreneurs entered government lotteries to win the right to market telephone sex services that include both live encounters (known as "junk sex") with audio-prostitutes and recorded conversations that offer users the sounds of sex in all its variety in the privacy of their own receivers. The obvious problem with such services, which began as prefix 976 numbers but now also use 900, is that minors have easy access to them. (Indeed, studies have shown that many if not most users are ages 10-16.)

Congress on no less than four occasions has attempted to curtail dial-a-porn, only to be challenged in court. In June 1989, the Supreme Court ruled in *Sable Communications of California v. FCC* that a ban on dial-a-porn obscenity was constitutional, but a ban on indecency was not. In other words, if the government wanted to protect minors from hearing explicit telephone conversations, it would have to draft a narrow law that wouldn't violate the free speech rights of adult listeners and services.

Later that year, Sen. Helms successfully pushed through an amendment that combined a ban on dial-a-porn obscenity and indecency. It has since been upheld by the 9th U.S. Circuit Court of Appeals, though another challenge is pending in a New York. An appeal to the Supreme Court is also possible. The FCC, meanwhile, has begun enforcing its telephone indecency rules. Many companies that market telephone information services, consequently, have cut back their dial-a-porn services.

To the telephone industry, the dial-a-porn question comes down to how customers are billed. Regional phone companies, until they won some recent court rulings, were required under the First Amendment to cooperate with dial-a-porn companies by including their billings on monthly statements to customers. Under the new FCC regulations prompted by the *Sable* ruling and the Helms amendment, phone companies will no longer bill for dial-a-porn unless

they receive a specific application requesting the service from an individual household. Requiring an advance application hampers the service's attractiveness, according to Washington attorney Melanie Haratunian, who represents information-industry clients, because it "ruins the spontaneous nature of such calls if you require a cooling-off period." ∎

# CURRENT SITUATION

## McConnell Bill

When Sen. Mitch McConnell introduced his Pornography Victims' Compensation Act this year, he drew backing from a familiar assortment of interest groups, among them the Family Research Council, Feminists Fighting Pornography and some 100 local chapters of the National Organization for Women. The bill, which would have allowed rape victims or their survivors to collect damages from producers, distributors, exhibitors and retailers of sexually explicit materials, was criticized as unconstitutional by an alliance of authors, publishers and distributors of books, magazines, recordings and videotapes. The opponents said "its imprecise and unworkable standards would deter citizens from reporting, writing and creating freely" and hence "would damage legitimate efforts to inform, educate and entertain the American public." [27]

In July, to the dismay of some of his backers, McConnell reintroduced the bill and narrowed it to apply only to material already deemed obscene by the Supreme Court. Under his new bill, the statute of limitations would run out two years after commission of the offense or a year after conviction.

For a conviction, the defendant would have to have reasonably foreseen that the material would create an unreasonable risk of such a crime, and the material would have to be a substantial cause of the crime.

The opponents are still not satisfied. A spokesman for the American Library Association told the Senate Judiciary Committee last July that the bill would put librarians in the position of being "indemnifiers of the victims of criminals who choose to copy conduct described or depicted in books, movies or television." ACLU President Nadine Strossen, debating McConnell this September on the CNN talk show "Crossfire," said that "causes of crime are complex and manifold, and the danger of this bill is displacing responsibility from a person who commits a violent act onto a third party who creates a work of art." In such civil lawsuits, says Finan of the Media Coalition, "the story of a terrible crime becomes the centerpiece of trial of whether material is obscene" so that works that are not criminally obscene often would become so.

McConnell says he can't guarantee that some legitimate filmmakers wouldn't be sued, but adds: "Critics don't give juries enough credit. If given proper instructions, they will give the proper result." When the law is applied in different regions, he also notes, it might become necessary to "separate out some of the parties," so

*Continued on p. 986*

# At Issue:

## Should Congress require purveyors of sexually explicit materials to compensate rape victims?

### SEN. MITCH MCCONNELL, R-KY.

*Sponsor of Pornography Victims' Compensation Act*
**FROM *SCRIPPS HOWARD NEWS SERVICE*, AUG. 8, 1991**

*a*merican women are in greater peril now from attack than they have ever been in the history of our
nation," a Senate Judiciary Committee report said
on May 21, 1991. The rape rate in the United States is four
times that in Germany, eight times France's, 15 times England's and 20 times Japan's. Last year's increase in rape
was three times that of the year before. In my home state
of Kentucky, reported rapes increased 43 percent.

The sex crimes do not occur in a cultural vacuum.
There is increasing evidence, and belief among Americans,
that violence in the media promotes violence against wom-
en and children. Hard-core pornography is the most dangerous aspect of this assault on women and children. In
response to this growing threat, I introduced the Pornography Victims' Compensation Act. This bill would give victims of sex crimes, or their survivors, the right to sue the
purveyors of hard-core pornography if a link could be
shown between the crime and specific pornographic material. This bill is designed to hit pornographers where it
hurts them most — their wallets. This bill does not ban
such material from being produced, it simply holds the
purveyors liable for the harm their businesses cause.

All women are victims in this culture of violence. Millions of American women are afraid to walk from their offices to their cars. They are afraid to go outside after dark.
They are afraid within their own homes.

Another dimension of the problem is the extent to
which it affects children. Each year, 1 million children from
six months to 16 years old are sexually molested and then
filmed or photographed. There is a large audience for this
filth, many of whom are themselves child molesters. Child
molesters are prolific, each averaging 117 child victims.

The pornography industry trades in the abuse, exploitation and degradation of women and children. Pornography
is not an expression of free speech, it is a lucrative business. The financial interest in fighting this bill is considerable. Pornography is a multibillion-dollar industry. A
witness from the Video Software Dealers Association testified before the Senate Judiciary Committee that 30 percent
to 50 percent of VSDA members sold hard-core pornography.

Pornography is fueling violence in this country, and it is
time the industry was held accountable for the harm it
causes. This bill is one thing we can do to protect women
and children from sexual predators, and give them some
recourse against those who profit from their victimization.

### DON ROSENBERG

*Executive vice president, Video Software Dealers Association*
**FROM *SCRIPPS HOWARD NEWS SERVICE*, AUGUST 1991**

*i*magine for a minute that you own a video store. Now
suppose that someone who rents a movie from your
business sexually assaults a person two years from
now and claims that watching the movie in 1991 caused
him to commit the offense. If Congress approves the Pornography Victims' Compensation Act, the victim of that assault could sue you and recover damages.

In essence, the bill would shift the blame for sexual assault from the criminal who committed the act to an innocent third party. The victim of a sex crime, or the victim's
family, could sue the creators and distributors of expressive
material (i.e., movies, books, recorded music) if they allege
that the material caused the assailant to commit the offense. In fact, the victim can sue even if the alleged criminal has not been convicted in a criminal trial!

What kind of material would be covered? Unfortunately,
nobody knows for sure. The bill refers to "obscene" material,
but "obscenity" statutes are inherently elusive and subjective.
Is "Debbie Does Dallas" obscene? How about "Last Tango in
Paris" or "Pretty Woman"? Whether a particular movie is legally "obscene" turns on a jury's determination of whether
the picture violates an ill-defined "community standard."

What would be the controlling "community" standard
under the McConnell bill? If your video store is in Chicago,
and a customer who rents a tape there later commits a sex
crime in a rural area of North Carolina, which community's
standard applies? The bill is silent on the issue. It certainly
would not be fair if a Chicago video store were forced to
deny customers a movie that is legal there because it is
considered "obscene" in North Carolina.

Video store owners would face the constant threat of
lawsuits by victims understandably seeking revenge and an
outlet for their emotional turmoil. Victims could allege that
almost any explicit movie is "obscene," in order to bring a
suit. Most video rental stores cannot afford the litigation, let
alone the risk that a jury may bend over backward to find
a film obscene out of sympathy for a rape victim.

So if you own a video store when the McConnell bill
takes effect, how do you protect yourself? Besides closing
up shop, there is only one thing you can do: Refrain from
carrying any films containing depictions of sex.

It is a longstanding principle of American jurisprudence
that individuals are held responsible for their own actions.
The McConnell bill violates that principle. It would be bad
policy for Congress to shift the focus of attention away
from the criminal's responsibility to the "bad influences."

that a jury might find a producer liable, but not a seller, who might have been less likely to foresee a work's harmful effects.

Another objection to McConnell's bill is the charge that it would encourage new litigation at a time when courts are already overburdened. McConnell says he opposes excessive litigation, but thinks this might be one area it would be beneficial. "I'll be candid," he says. "The purpose of the bill is to create a fear of litigation that will make certain illegitimate businesses discontinue." Sen. Joseph R. Biden Jr., D-Del., chairman of the Judiciary Committee, has expressed some practical concerns with the bill because of differing regional definitions of obscenity. He has agreed to take it up in January.

### Porn Record-Keeping

Some of the groups fighting the McConnell bill are active in another pornography controversy, this one over the Justice Department's quest to require record-keeping by producers and distributors of sexually explicit materials. The 1988 Child Protection and Obscenity Enforcement Act required the recording of names and ages of all models and performers who appear in explicit books, magazines, periodicals, films or videotapes created after 1978. It also gave law enforcement authorities new power to require convicted distributors of obscene material to forfeit personal property.

A coalition led by the booksellers' association filed suit, charging that the law was unconstitutional and warning that such record-keeping would unduly burden retailers and librarians and would affect mainstream works, including medical texts.

In May 1989, a district court in Washington, D.C., struck down the record-keeping provisions but left intact the property-forfeiture provisions. Then-Attorney General Thornburgh appealed, but in late 1990,

Congress passed an amended version of the record-keeping provisions, which were to take effect in February 1991. The Justice Department issued draft regulations to implement the law, but these were harshly criticized. In the meantime, a coalition that includes the booksellers, the American Library Association and Penthouse International has challenged the revised law. The lawsuit is on hold pending Justice's release of new regulations.

## Local Crackdowns

Because of the community-standards doctrine of obscenity law, states and localities in recent years have been taking advantage of their freedom to go further than federal law in restricting explicit materials, both to adults and to minors. According to FBI veteran Kelly, the recent crackdowns have earned six states top ranking as the strictest anti-obscenity enforcers: Utah, North Carolina, Indiana, Florida (except for Dade County), Virginia and Texas.

Encouraged by a 1990 Supreme Court decision (Osbury v. Ohio), 30 states have now made simple possession of child pornography a crime, according to the Phoenix-based Children's Legal Foundation. States are also considering legislation to limit displays of material "harmful to minors" and bills to give the MPAA film ratings force of law.

Perhaps the most publicized effort is in Michigan, which is considering a sweeping bill that would give police new powers to go after explicit material on records, computers, tapes and compact discs, and would raise fines against video stores that rent obscene movies from $5,000 to $100,000. It would also switch the state's test for community standards from state to local jurisdictions, allowing prosecutors to concentrate on the jurisdictions most likely to award convictions while complicating the distribution networks of chain stores.

In turn, the opponents of the crackdowns have become well-organized. In Oregon this June, the Senate rejected a minors'-access obscenity bill after video dealers and booksellers formed an Oregon Free Speech coalition. And in Fort Worth, the MPAA and the Video Software Dealers Association are actively opposing a proposed ordinance giving Fort Worth its own mandatory movie-rating system similar to one used in Dallas since 1966. It would create a 26-member board to screen films and add ratings such as S (sexual conduct), L (obscene language), V (violence), D (drug abuse), N (nudity) and P (perverse behavior).

It is favored by the National Coalition on Television Violence. Opponents say the system is too broad to pass First Amendment muster, that it interferes with parents' rights, creates confusion with the existing rating system and would restrict the number of movies in Fort Worth. ∎

# OUTLOOK

## Smut vs. Art

This November, when the county council in Prince George's County, Md., approved a ban on nude dancing in nightclubs, dissenting members worried that it might inhibit artistic endeavors such as nude modeling in art classes. Fundraisers for the New York City Opera last fall became concerned that new obscenity guidelines from the National Endowment for the Arts would force them to alter their production of Arnold Schoenberg's "Moses und Aaron," which calls for three naked virgins on stage. In Sacramento this fall, employees at a federal building grew divided over the wisdom of a new policy that put a sheet of black plastic over a painting of a partially nude woman after employees had complained.

Across the country, efforts to grapple with the offensiveness some see in explicit materials invariably trample on somebody's vision of free expression. And the regional variations of what constitutes obscenity show few signs of evaporating.

Feminists, too, continue to be divided by obscenity issues. At this July's National Organization for Women convention in New York, a proposal to launch a national campaign against sexually explicit material was defeated after lobbying by a contingent of prostitutes, porn stars and publishers. Elsewhere, various ad hoc feminist groups have been marching into shopping-mall bookstores and tearing up unpurchased copies of *Penthouse* or distributing buttons ridiculing the ACLU's defense of the First Amendment rights of pornographers.

### Alternatives to Bans

As an alternative to banning free expression, many in the anti-censorship camp call for more sex education. And some foresee a potential for mainstream Americans to become more vocal against overly broad restrictions. "We haven't yet reached the point where we're not embarrassed to say, 'I like sexually explicit material,' or even to defend it the way people defend the right to abortion," says sex-film distributor Phil Harvey.

Anti-pornography activists see much work still to be done. Betty Wein, a spokeswoman for Morality in Media, would target cable television. In New York City, the basic cable service includes a public access channel that late at night transmits nude talk shows and dial-a-porn ads that feature closeups of genitals in sexual motion.

Civil-liberties groups plan to continue countering the crackdown with what the ACLU's Heins says is "a plea for tolerance, not so much for sex." "The American people show a desire for increasingly frank portrayal of every subject, whether its sex or drugs," says the Media Coalition's Finan. "We don't defend any type of material. But if you start to censor "2 Live Crew" because it's crude, what is the standard?"

Freedom of expression, however, is not everyone's paramount consideration. "If we examine the First Amendment," says psychologist Victor Cline, "we will note that there are many kinds of democratically enacted prohibitions of speech and expression — libel, slander, perjury, conspiracy, false advertising, excitement to violence or other criminal activity, or speech that might create 'a clear and present danger,' such as yelling fire in a crowded theater." [28]

Others, however, worry that obscenity crackdowns are a sign of panicky thinking. "Society is uptight about sex, and pornography is a handy whipping boy," says sex therapist Lloyd Sinclair. "We sometimes overreact in an effort to find someone or something to blame for problems related to sexuality."

The Family Research Council's Bauer acknowledges that his fellow anti-obscenity activists have to be "discerning about what one lumps in with porn. But we're pretty far away from worrying about society erring on the side of too many restrictions. The pendulum is not moving that way. Popular culture is still in the other camp." That's why, he predicts, obscenity issues "will bedevil politicians for a long time." ■

## Notes

[1] Attorney General's Commission on Pornography, *Final Report,* July 1986, p. 324.

[2] For more information on recent attempts to restrict government funding of the arts, see "Tying Down Federal Funds for the Arts," *Editorial Research Reports,* May 25, 1990, pp. 302-315.

[3] Quoted in the *Los Angeles Times,* May 4, 1989.

[4] Quoted in the *Los Angeles Times,* Dec. 4, 1990.

[5] Quoted in the *Los Angeles Times,* Aug. 2, 1990.

[6] Daniel Linz, et al., "Estimating Community Standards: The Use of Social Science Evidence in an Obscenity Prosecution," *Public Opinion Quarterly,* spring 1991, p. 80.

[7] Quoted in document from the National Coalition Against Pornography.

[8] Cline's theory was summarized in a pamphlet published by Morality in Media.

[9] Linda Lovelace and Michael McGrady, *Ordeal* (1980).

[10] Study cited in a pamphlet published by Morality in Media.

[11] Quoted in Philip Nobile and Eric Nadler, *United States of America v. Sex: How the Meese Commission Lied About Pornography* (1986), p. 36.

[12] Cynthia Gentry, "Pornography and Rape: An Empirical Analysis," *Deviant Behavior,* 1991, Vol. 12., quoted in Marcia Pally, *Sense & Censorship: The Vanity of the Bonfires* (1991) p. 27.

[13] Cited in Edward Donnerstein, Daniel Linz and Steven Penrod, *The Question of Pornography: Research Findings and Policy Implications* (1987) p. 67.

[14] Joseph Scott and Loretta Schwalm, "An Examination of Adult Theater Rates and Rape Rates by State," *Controversial Issues in Crime and Justice* (1988), quoted in Marcia Pally, *op. cit.,* p. 26.

[15] Quoted in *The New York Times,* May 27, 1986.

[16] Donnerstein, et al., *op. cit.,* p. 178.

[17] Quoted in Susan Gubar and Joan Hoff, *For Adult Users Only: The Dilemma of Violent Pornography* (1989), p. 151.

[18] Gene Abel, professor of psychiatry at Emory University, in testimony before the Meese commission in Houston, cited in Nobile and Nadler, *op. cit.,* p. 252.

[19] Quoted in *The Washington Post,* March 26, 1990.

[20] Quoted in *The Washington Post,* Nov. 6, 1991.

[21] Doug Bandow, "RICO v. Porn: Penalties More Shocking Than the Crime," *The Wall Street Journal,* Dec. 20, 1988.

[22] Carol Gorman, *Pornography* (1988), p. 19.

[23] *Ibid.,* p. 19.

[24] Quoted in Nobile and Nadler, *op. cit.,* p. 24.

[25] Quoted in literature from the National Coalition Against Pornography.

[26] Quoted by Marcia Pally, *op. cit.,* p. 10.

[27] Quoted in *Free Expression,* newsletter for the American Booksellers Foundation for Free Expression, spring 1991.

[28] Quoted in literature from the National Coalition Against Pornography.

# Bibliography

## Selected Sources Used

### Books

**Donnerstein, Edward; Linz, Daniel; and Penrod, Steven, *The Question of Pornography: Research Findings and Policy Implications,* The Free Press, 1987.**

Three experts in communications and psychology have compiled an authoritative summary of the laboratory research and policy questions surrounding the question of whether pornography causes violence.

**Gore, Tipper, *Raising PG Kids in an X-Rated Society,* Abingdon Press, 1987.**

The co-founder of the Parents' Music Resource Center tells why and how she embarked on her campaign to clean up explicit rock lyrics. The book also is a resource for readers who want to become active on the issue.

**Gorman, Carol, *Pornography,* Franklin Watts, 1988.**

A generalist prepared this solid primer on the moral and policy issues that have surrounded obscenity over the past few decades.

**Gubar, Susan and Hoff, Joan, eds., *For Adult Users Only: The Dilemma of Violent Pornography,* Indiana University Press, 1989.**

In this anthology of academic writings, feminists and scholars explore the literary, political, psychological, legal and policy issues surrounding pornography in recent history.

**Marsh, Dave, *50 Ways to Fight Censorship,* Thunder's Mouth Press, 1990.**

A well-known rock music journalist and critic has assembled a resource book for people who want to take action against efforts to restrict access and moderate the content of popular music, books, television and films.

**Nobile, Philip and Nadler, Eric, *United States of America vs. Sex: How the Meese Commission Lied about Pornography,* Minotaur Press, 1986.**

Two editors of *Forum,* a sex journal published by Penthouse International, critique what they view as conservative biases in the work of the Reagan administration's pornography commission.

### Reports and Studies

**Justice Department, Attorney General's Commission on Pornography, *Final Report,* U.S. Government Printing Office, July 1986 (2 vols.).**

The full text of the report by the Meese commission contains profiles and testimony from the 11 commissioners and more than 200 witnesses as well as the panel's policy recommendations and a detailed survey of contemporary pornographic material.

### For More Information

**American Civil Liberties Union, 132 West 43rd St., New York, N.Y., 10036, 212-944-9800.**

Civil-liberties advocacy group that opposes efforts to curb pornography, citing the First Amendment.

**Children's Legal Foundation, 2845 E. Camelback Rd., Suite 740, Phoenix, Ariz., 85016, 602-381-1322.**

Assists with prosecutions and circulates information advocating restrictions on pornography, particularly child porn.

**Family Research Council, 700 13th St. N.W., Suite 500, Washington, D.C. 20005, 202-393-2100.**

Conducts research and issues policy advice to government officials, scholars and the public on family issues. Seeks restrictions on pornography.

**Media Coalition, 900 Third Ave., Suite 1600, New York, N.Y. 10022, 212-891-2070.**

Alliance of publishers, booksellers and periodical distributors seeking to protect rights to free expression. Opposes many efforts to curb pornography.

**Morality in Media, 475 Riverside Drive, Suite 475, New York. N.Y. 10115, 212-870-3222.**

Acts as a clearinghouse for information on the campaign against pornography.

**National Coalition Against Pornography, 800 Compton Road, Suite 9224, Cincinnati, Ohio, 45231, 513-521-6227.**

An alliance of religious groups that disseminates information kits to help citizens lobby for crackdowns on pornographers.

**Parents' Music Resource Center, 1500 Arlington Blvd., Arlington, Va. 22209, 703-527-9466.**

Monitors new recordings and alerts public to lyrics viewed as possibly obscene.

**People for the American Way, 2000 M St. N.W., Suite 400, Washington, D.C. 20036, 202-467-4999.**

Civil liberties advocacy group that opposes most current efforts to restrict sexually explicit materials.

# The Next Step

## Additional Articles from Current Periodicals from EBSCO Publishing's Database

## Actions & defenses

**Cohn, B. "The trials of Adam & Eve," *Newsweek,* Jan. 7, 1991, p. 48.**

Describes how Phil Harvey's business, PHE, Inc., also known as Adam & Eve, which is one of the nation's biggest mail-order pornography companies, has become a top target in the most aggressive federal attack on pornography in decades. Project PostPorn; actions of the National Obscenity Enforcement Unit in 1986; obscenity, a tricky area of the law; Adam & Eve's suit against the government.

**Linz, D., Donnerstein, E., et al., "Estimating community standards: The use of social science evidence in an obscenity prosecution," *Public Opinion Quarterly,* spring 1991, p. 80.**

Examines elements of the legal test for obscenity of sexually explicit material indicated in a criminal case. A cross-section of residents of Mecklenburg County (Charlotte, N.C.) were randomly assigned to view either one of the sexually explicit films and the sexually explicit magazine charged in the criminal case, or a control film. Methods; results.

## Addresses & essays

**Garvey, J., "Don't be offended," *Commonweal,* Sept. 28, 1990, p. 534.**

Discusses society's tendency to approve of an individual's right to be offended at slurs against women, racial minorities and homosexuals. Condemns society's tendency to criticize individuals who are offended at anti-religious language and behavior; why religious people should be offended by the ridicule of faith and religious symbols.

**Gergen, D., "Who should pay for porn?" *U.S. News & World Report,* July 30, 1990, p. 80.**

Editorial. Argues that some artists believe they can have it both ways — to engage in the wanton destruction of a nation's values, and then expect the nation to pay their bills. Congress should leave in place the current rules against funding obscene works and refrain from imposing new restrictions.

**Hyde, L., "The freedom to talk dirt," *Kenyon Review,* fall 1990, p. xii.**

Editorial. Talks about how the current debate over obscenity, government funding, and the arts has set the author to thinking about dirt, what it is and why we have such trouble with it. Keeping "dirt" out of sight; needing the very

things we once called "dirty"; candidates for dirt status.

**Jones, T.K., "Put up yer dukes," *Christianity Today,* Dec. 17, 1990, p. 14.**

Editorial. Fears that indecency is becoming "decent" in American society. Examples of broadening definitions of decency over the past year; new interpretations of the constitutional guarantee of free speech; resulting erosion of public standards; how Christians should respond.

**Lipman, S., "Can we save culture?" *National Review,* Aug. 26, 1991, p. 36.**

Observes that while conservatives are content to live their private lives, the Left is taking control of American culture. Differing responses of liberals and conservatives to the recent controversy over the National Endowment for the Arts (NEA) grants for sacrilegious and obscene art; how members of the Left enforce their cultural agenda; why conservatives have not influenced culture; resulting impact on society.

**O'Sullivan, J., "First amendment wrongs," *National Review,* July 9, 1990, p. 6.**

Editorial. Presents "National Review" editor John O'Sullivan's views on the constitutional amendment to prevent flag burning, "2 Live Crew" and obscenity, and the declaration that begging has been declared not to be a constitutional amendment.

**Saltzman, J., "Four-letter words," *USA Today,* September 1990, p. 87.**

Editorial. Supports the right of musicians and artists to describe or show sexual conduct in graphic terms. Examples of harassment of such artists as "2 Live Crew" and Robert Mapplethorpe; argument that the First Amendment protects their freedom of speech; offensive artists of the past that have gained respectability.

## Case studies

**Coughlin, E.K., "Zimmer, a poet and press director, takes on the arts endowment," *The Chronicle of Higher Education,* Oct. 10, 1990, p. A3.**

Profiles Paul Zimmer, director of the University of Iowa Press, who turned down a $12,000 grant from the National Endowment for the Arts rather than promise not to use the money for work that was obscene. Public notice and "nasty, angry reactions"; cherishing the First Amendment; poet first, publisher second; steady sources of support.

**Legman, G., "'Unprintable' folklore? The Vance Randolf Collection," *Journal of American Folklore*, July-September 1991, p. 259.**

Discusses the forthcoming publication of previously "unprintable" songs and other lore from Vance Randolph's collection. "Ozark Folksongs and Folklore"; obscenity; "Roll Me In Your Arms," and "Blow The Candle Out"; anti-sexual censorship; eroticism of work songs; Martha Wolfenstein's "Children's Humor"; John and Alan Lomax; prudery and its effect on publishing in the English-speaking world; more.

**Lewis, N. A., "Obscenity law used in Alabama breaks New York company," *The New York Times*, May 2, 1990, p. A1.**

Tells about the Home Dish Satellite Corporation, which was a flourishing New York City company beaming hardcore sex films to 30,000 subscribers around the country and soft-core ones to 1.2 million customers. But about 50 homes in Montgomery County, Ala., received the transmissions, and because the district attorney there has vowed to stamp out pornography, the company is facing criminal charges.

**Soocher, S., "2 Live Crew: Taking the rap," *Rolling Stone*, Aug. 9, 1990, p. 19.**

Examines the ruling by Broward County, Fla., Federal Judge Jose A. Gonzalez Jr. that "2 Live Crew's" rap album "As Nasty As They Wanna Be" is obscene. Details of the case and the decision; 1973 U.S. Supreme Court decision; nationwide anti-obscenity fervor. INSET: "Banned in the U.S.A." ("2 Live Crew" leader Luther Campbell's new single), by J. Ressner.

**Udesky, L., "When innocence is called obscene," *Progressive*, September 1990, p. 13.**

Reports on the April seizure of photographer Jack Sturges' photos and camera equipment by San Francisco police and FBI agents on child pornography grounds. Nude studies of children and their parents done with parental consent; effect on Sturges; response to right-wing efforts to undermine First Amendment.

## Censorship

**"A-Z of censorship," *New Statesman & Society*, April 5, 1991, Banned p. 5.**

Lists alphabetically over 30 examples of censorship. Included are: blasphemy, environment, gagging writ, jargon, libel, obscenity, pornography, self-censorship, underground and more.

**Conant, J., "Unholy alliances," *Harper's Bazaar*, February 1991, p. 144.**

Explores the recent wave of censorship attempts at works considered obscene by some. How censorship often leads to free publicity and increased sales; examples of such works, including Madonna's video "Justify My Love"; Bret Easton Ellis' novel *American Psycho*; and Painter Andres Serrano's "Piss Christ."

**Dority, B., "The war on rock and rap music," *Humanist*, September/October 1990, p. 35.**

Opinion. Argues against censorship of rock and rap music containing obscene or indecent lyrics. Parents Music Resource Center; first music obscenity trials; Music in Action and Rock & Roll Confidential; reaction to growing social and political involvement of rock musicians.

**McEntee, P., "Is pornography a matter of free expression?" *America*, Aug. 3, 1991, p. 66.**

Looks at censorship, the First Amendment, pornography and obscenity. Federal Communications Commission's (FCC) definition of indecency; FCC 24-hour ban on indecency challenged in federal court of appeals by American Civil Liberties Union, television networks, others; US Supreme Court obscene definition; increased law enforcement against pornography; damages pornography inflicts on society; misuse of the word, "censorship"; Morality In Media's White Ribbon Against Pornography.

**Neville, R., "Enough already!" *Utne Reader*, September/October 1990, p. 107.**

Offers insight into the ongoing debate over censorship and the implementation of current obscenity laws, which are somewhat vague and ambiguous in their treatment of First Amendment rights. INSETS: Why *Blue Velvet* is obscene, and *Debbie Does Dallas* is not, by D. Morris; Don't knock the rock: Music warning labels amount to censorship, by D. Marsh; the censors' sensibility, by C. Carr.

## Debates & issues

**"FCC gets copy of WGBH-TV Mapplethorpe broadcast," *Broadcasting*, Aug. 20, 1990, p. 59.**

Reports that media activist Donald Wildmon, of the Tupelo, Miss.-based American Family Association, filed a complaint which charges WGBH-TV with obscenity and indecency in regard to its airing a program that showed several pictures taken by the controversial artist Robert Mapplethorpe. Unique nature of the complaint explored; FCC precedents and their relation to this case.

**Clift, E. and Smith, V.E., "The right wing's cultural warrior," *Newsweek*, July 2, 1990, p. 51.**

Reports on Sen. Jesse Helms and his fight against obscenity, which has helped him raise $5.6 million in election funds. History of supporting hot-button issues to win votes; power over colleagues by threatening to portray them as pro-obscenity; power has its limits; Jesse Helms Citizenship Center.

**Drayer, M. "Monday memo,"** *Broadcasting,* **Jan. 21, 1991, p. 18.**

Presents a First Amendment/obscenity commentary from Michael Drayer of Mintz, Levin, Cohn, Ferris, Glovsky & Popeo, in Washington, D.C. Discusses how some obscenity cases, such as rap group, "2 Live Crew's" album "As Nasty As They Wanna Be," receive more attention than other cases, primarily the case involving Home Dish Satellite Networks Inc.'s (HDSN) potent mixture of sex and politics. How technology has outpaced the law; solutions to the problem.

**Grundberg, A., "Art under attack: Who dares say that it's no good?"** *The New York Times,* **Nov. 25, 1990, Section 2 p. 1.**

Argues that art labeled obscene has given attention to artists and blinded critics from arguing about esthetics, causing them to focus on defending the notion that artists can do and say whatever they please. Considers specific individuals, noting that the artists whose work is at the center of controversy are by no means representative of the best talents in their fields.

**Klein, M., "Censorship and the fear of sexuality,"** *Humanist,* **July/August 1990, p. 15.**

Discusses the psychological factors that typically underlie the desire to suppress sexually explicit materials. How pornography triggers people's fear of losing control of sexuality; cultural context of "bad" sexuality; fear of sexual abnormality.

**Mathews, T., Glick, D., et al., "Fine art or foul?"** *Newsweek,* **July 2, 1990, p. 46.**

Discusses the current uproar over the place of the arts in society and what role the government should assume in supporting them. Battle of art and obscenity; rap group "2 Live Crew"; artist Robert Mapplethorpe; battle over freedom of expression; Andres Serrano's "Piss Christ"; reference to Big Brother; "Artbusters"; Sen. Jesse Helms. INSETS: A quick look at the history of smut, by D.A. Kaplan; to see or not to see.

**Plagen, P., Lewis, S.D., et al., "Mixed signals on obscenity,"** *Newsweek,* **Oct. 15, 1990, p. 74.**

Reports that the Cincinnati's Contemporary Arts Center and its director, Dennis Barrie, were acquitted of obscenity charges for displaying graphic photographs by the late Robert Mapplethorpe while Charles Freeman, a Fort Lauderdale record-store owner, was convicted for selling a copy of "2 Live Crew's" "As Nasty As They Wanna Be" album to an undercover policeman.

**Saunders, D., "Copyright, obscenity and literary history,"** *ELH,* **summer 1990, p. 431.**

Explores the appearance of works by Shelley and Byron alongside mass-produced pornography that will clarify a detail of English literary historiography, drawing attention to the specific intersection of copyright and obscenity law in the English civil-law doctrine. Outlines various juridical thresholds bearing on English writing and writers: the first criminalization of obscene publication, the first Copyright Act, the Obscene Publications Acts of 1857 and 1959; more.

**Shulins, N., "Rated X,"** *Family Circle,* **Nov. 27, 1990, p. 63.**

Focuses on the battle being waged against obscenity today and what you can do to stop it. Experts' warnings about today's X-rated climate; anti-obscenity movement; how accessible it is to the young; what recourse the public has against obscenity.

## Federal aid to art

**"It's art,"** *Economist,* **Oct. 13, 1990, p. 98.**

Discusses the outcome of the trial involving Dennis Barrie, director of the Contemporary Art Center in Cincinnati, Ohio, stemming from an exhibit of the works of the late Robert Mapplethorpe. Found not guilty; controversy involving the National Endowment for the Arts (NEA); the question of obscenity; details.

**Berke, R.L., "House approves compromise bill to continue the Arts endowment,"** *The New York Times,* **Oct. 12, 1990, p. A1.**

Says that, after hours of emotional debate over what is art and what is pornography, the House of Representatives approved a bill to extend the life of the National Endowment for the Arts for three years and leave judgments about obscenity to the courts.

## Law & legislation

**Rosen, J., " 'Miller' time,"** *New Republic,* **Oct. 1, 1990, p. 17.**

Examines the Supreme Court's obscenity test, created in 1973 in the case *Miller v. California.* Purpose of the test as a means of distinguishing art from obscenity; original objections to the *Miller* test expressed by the arts community; efforts to now use the test to support current works deemed to be obscene; flaws in the test; suggested reform.

**Vance, C.S., "Misunderstanding obscenity,"** *Art in America,* **May 1990, p. 49.**

Examines the legal definition of obscenity in view of recent attacks on the National Endowment for the Arts (NEA). Senator Jesse Helms' influence; photographers Robert Mapplethorpe and Andres Serrano; confusing wording of the compromise bill following the Helms Amendment; 1973 *Miller vs. California* case; examples of self-censorship.

# Back Issues

*Great Research on Current Issues Starts Right Here... Recent topics covered by The CQ Researcher are listed below. Issues dated before May 10, 1991, were published under the name of Editorial Research Reports.*

**JUNE 1990**
Downsizing America's Armed Forces
Progress In Weather Forecasting
S & L Bailout
Bio-Chemical Disarmament

**JULY 1990**
Do Americans Still Love Marriage?
Death Penalty Debate
Decline of Rural America
United Nations in the 1990s

**AUGUST 1990**
Democracy in the Philippines
Initiatives: True Democracy?
Hard Times at Newspapers
Teens Balance School & Jobs

**SEPTEMBER 1990**
Dangers of Alcohol
Western Alliance After the Cold War
Tobacco Industry
Right to Die

**OCTOBER 1990**
Organ Transplants
Energy Policy Options
Search for Arab Unity
Child Support

Back issues are available for $4.00 (subscribers) or $7.00 (non-subscribers). Quantity discounts apply to orders over ten. To order, call Congressional Quarterly 1-800-432-2250.

**NOVEMBER 1990**
Lotteries and Gambling
Post Cold-War Choices
Setting Limits on Medical Care
Multicultural Education

**DECEMBER 1990**
Cable TV Regulation
Americans' Search For Their Roots
Is Insurance System a Failure?
Why Schools Still Have Tracking

**JANUARY 1991**
Growing Influence of Boycotts
Should the U.S. Reinstate the Draft?
America's Archaeological Past
Peace Corps' Challenges in '90s

**FEBRUARY 1991**
Regional Impact of Recession
Puerto Rico's Status
Redistricting: Mapping Power
Nuclear Power

**MARCH 1991**
Acid Rain
Cost of the Gulf War
Reassessing Gun Laws
Future for Man in Space

**APRIL 1991**
Social Security
Canadian Crisis Over Quebec
California Drought
Electromagnetic Radiation

**MAY 1991**
School Choice
Racial Quotas
Animal Rights
U.S. and Japan

**JUNE 1991**
Children and Divorce
Teenage Suicide
Endangered Species
Europe 1992

**JULY 1991**
Teenagers and Abortion
Soviet Republics Rebel
Mexico's Emergence
Athletes and Drugs

**AUGUST 1991**
Sexual Harassment
Fetal Tissue Research
Oil Imports
The Palestinians

**SEPTEMBER 1991**
Police Brutality
Advertising Under Attack
Saving the Forests
Foster Care Crisis

**OCTOBER 1991**
Pay-Per-View TV
Youth Gangs
Gene Therapy
World Hunger

**NOVEMBER 1991**
Fast-Food Shake-Up
The Greening of Eastern Europe
Business' Role in Education
Cuba In Crisis

**DECEMBER 1991**
Retiree Health Benefits
Asian Americans

# Future Topics

▶ *The Disabilities Act*

▶ *Term Limitations*

▶ *Oil Spills*

# The Disabilities Act

*Protecting the rights of the disabled will have far-reaching effects*

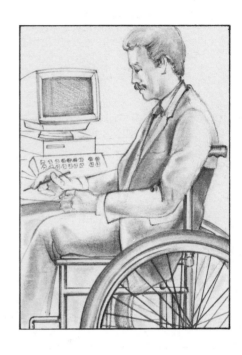

T
HE AMERICANS WITH DISABILITIES ACT IS THE
most sweeping piece of civil rights legislation since
the 1964 Civil Rights Act. It has the potential to
change the face of America, not only by requiring
that private businesses be accessible to the disabled but also
by changing attitudes and perceptions of disability. The
bipartisan bill zipped through Congress in 1990 with the
president's full support. Implementation, however, may not be
so swift — or so popular. As the Jan. 26 deadline for
compliance with the ADA's public accommodation provisions
approaches, companies are scrambling to make changes
necessary to comply with the statute's "vague" guidelines.
Meanwhile, lawmakers are pondering the costs of this
landmark legislation, and the courts are bracing for an
onslaught of lawsuits.

C_Q December 27, 1991 • Volume 1, No. 32 • 993-1016

*Formerly Editorial Research Reports*

Cover Art: Barbara Sassa-Daniels

**CQ Researcher**

December 27, 1991
Volume 1, No. 32

**EDITOR**
Sandra Stencel

**MANAGING EDITOR**
Thomas J. Colin

**ASSOCIATE EDITOR**
Richard L. Worsnop

**STAFF WRITERS**
Charles S. Clark
Mary H. Cooper
Rodman D. Griffin

**PRODUCTION EDITOR**
Laurie De Maris

**EDITORIAL ASSISTANT**
Thomas H. Moore

**GRAPHICS**
Jack Auldridge

**PUBLISHED BY**
Congressional Quarterly Inc.

**CHAIRMAN**
Andrew Barnes

**VICE CHAIRMAN**
Andrew P. Corty

**EDITOR AND PUBLISHER**
Neil Skene

**EXECUTIVE EDITOR**
Robert W. Merry

**PUBLICATIONS MARKETING/SALES**
Robert Smith

**EDITOR, EBSCO PUBLISHING**
Melissa Kummerer

The CQ Researcher (ISSN 1056-2036). Formerly Editorial Research Reports. Published weekly (48 times per year, not printed the first Friday of any month with five Fridays) by Congressional Quarterly Inc., 1414 22nd St., N.W., Washington, D.C. 20037. Rates are furnished upon request. Second-class postage paid at Washington, D.C. POSTMASTER: Send address changes to The CQ Researcher, 1414 22nd St., N.W., Washington, D.C. 20037.

# The Disabilities Act

By Rodman D. Griffin

## The Issues

On May 23, 1988, 19-year-old Lisa Carl, who has cerebral palsy, wheeled herself to her neighborhood movie theater in Tacoma, Wash. She waited patiently in her wheelchair until she reached the front of the line, then handed up her money. The theater owner refused to admit her. "I asked her, 'Why?' She said, 'You just can't.' I left. I felt embarrassed," Carl told a Senate committee. "I was not crying outside, but I was crying inside. I just wanted to be able to watch the movie like everyone else."[1]

Similar humiliations, experienced thousands of times a day by the nation's 43 million disabled, fueled a political movement that brought the United States to a historic moment. On July 26, 1990, President Bush signed the sweeping Americans with Disabilities Act (ADA), which extends to the disabled the same protections against discrimination that were given to blacks and women in the 1960s and '70s. It is, Bush has said, "one of the most important pieces of legislation to ever reach Capitol Hill."

When the first stage of the ADA goes into effect on Jan. 26 *(see timetable, p. 1000)*, the sort of blatant discrimination experienced by Lisa Carl will not only be rude, it will be against the law. The legislation represents a profound rethinking of how this country views disabled people, broadly defined as anyone with a physical or mental impairment that "substantially limits" everyday living. For the first time, America is saying that the biggest problem faced by the disabled may not be their own blindness, deafness or mental condition — but discrimination.

"You can't legislate attitudes," says

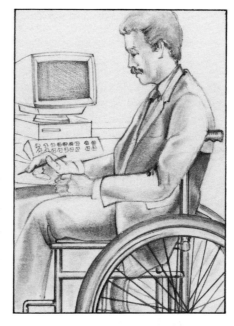

Pat Wright, director of governmental affairs at the Disability Rights Education and Defense Fund, based in Berkeley, Calif. "But you can level the playing field, and that's what the ADA is all about. It signifies the end of second-class citizenship for people with disabilities in this country."

For two decades, disabled people have been partially protected against discrimination by other civil rights laws — and a patchwork of local and state laws that vary across the country. But never before has the private sector had to comply with a comprehensive anti-discrimination mandate concerning disability. The legislation, to be phased in over several years, requires employers with 15 or more employees and virtually all providers of services available to the general public to take affirmative steps to make sure that jobs and facilities are available to those with disabilities.

Much of the public debate over the law has been dry and legalistic, centering on questions of appropriate remedies and definitions of such terms as "readily achievable" and

"undue hardship." But in contrast to many bills considered on Capitol Hill, the ADA has the potential to alter dramatically the way millions of Americans go about their everyday lives. Some 4 million businesses and 5 million buildings will be affected one way or another by this far-reaching statute.

The scope of the ADA extends far beyond the construction of wheelchair ramps and special parking spaces. It covers every facet of life. Restaurants, hotels, stores and theaters can no longer turn away a person with cerebral palsy, epilepsy, AIDS* or any other disability. Employers will be prohibited from rejecting qualified workers just because they are disabled, and they will be required to fashion generally inexpensive modifications to the workplace to make it accessible to the disabled, such as putting a desk on blocks to raise it for a wheelchair user.

Department stores will have to rearrange merchandise, car rental agencies will have to equip some autos with hand controls, telephone companies must provide operators to pass on messages from speech-impaired persons who use special phones with keyboards and more buses will be equipped with electronic lifts for wheelchairs. The changes ultimately will affect enterprises of all types and sizes, from basement hair parlors to large companies such as Safeway, Eastman Kodak and Citibank.

Though hailed by Republicans and Democrats alike, the legislation sends shivers through members of the business community. To them, the law is

---

*Although support for the ADA originated within the traditional disability community, the bill received the backing of groups seeking to bar discrimination against people with AIDS or HIV. Inclusion of people with AIDS was a controversial issue during congressional debate over the ADA.

a nightmare of details and definitions that will dictate what this latest public-policy pledge of equal opportunity means in practice. "We're all floundering in a sea of confusion," says Wendy Lechner, legislative representative for the National Federation of Independent Business (NFIB), which represents half a million small to mid-size businesses. "The lack of knowledge about how to comply is tremendous."

The business community is not alone in its confusion. According to a recent survey conducted for the National Organization on Disability, only 18 percent of the public know that the ADA was passed.[2] Serious questions about how much the law will cost, how it will be implemented and how it will be enforced remain unanswered. Critics have called it "feel-good legislation" that few could oppose politically, but that the country cannot afford economically.

As various government agencies step up the campaign to inform the public about the regulations and businesses scramble to come into compliance, here are some of the questions that business owners — and policy-makers — are asking:

### What are "reasonable accommodations" and what constitutes "undue hardship"?

Since passage of the ADA 18 months ago, the federal enforcement agencies involved have drafted detailed guidelines for compliance. The Equal Employment Opportunity Commission (EEOC) has prepared rules on employment (Title I) and the Department of Justice has dealt with public accommodation (Title III). But in both cases, the guidelines raise questions about the full extent of business' obligations under the law.

For example, the employment title requires employers to make "reasonable accommodations" for job applicants with disabilities who request them, unless such changes impose "undue hardship" on the organization.

Where exactly is the dividing line? An accommodation is deemed unreasonable under the ADA only if it places undue physical or financial hardship on the employer. Three factors must be considered: (1) The overall size of the business in proportion to the number of employees; (2) the number and type of facilities and size of the budget; and (3) the nature and cost of the accommodation.

Thus, under the ADA, it might be considered undue hardship for a small day-care center to equip a hearing-impaired operator with amplification equipment. A large private school, however, might be required to do so. Or, in a separate instance, the private school might be required to hire someone who knows sign language to help a deaf applicant for a teaching job.

Similarly, the public accommodation rules require that firms remove barriers to the disabled wherever their removal is "readily achievable" — defined as not causing "significant loss of profit" or reduced efficiency. "The law was designed to be a flexible standard," explains Pat Wright. "A mom-and-pop store should not carry the same burden as IBM. That would be unfair."

While disability rights advocates say the ADA's regulations allow for unforeseen situations, many in the business community see them as vague and confusing. The regulations, critics argue, contain no solid benchmark for determining what is reasonable or undue. Says David Copus, a Washington, D.C., employment attorney: "Instead of guidance, the EEOC has given us the case-by-case method." He suggests that many companies cited for discrimination can expect to make a costly defense in court of their actions.

"We'd have preferred specifics over complete uncertainty," adds the NFIB's Lechner. "The onus to make changes is on business, based on

knowledge that doesn't exist." Business groups worry that while Congress may have one idea of what is a reasonable accommodation or an undue burden, a regulator may have another and a judge still another. "We would have preferred knowing an amount or range of things that should be accomplished — a percentage of gross profits or a checklist of things to do," Lechner says. "As it is, it's anyone's ball game. The first one to court will draw up the rules. It's a very expensive way to determine what accommodation is."

During the congressional debate, there was concern that any specific dollar figure to be spent on complying with the law would become the standard, whether or not it actually resulted in access for the disabled. In other words, compliance efforts would focus on the costs rather than on the accommodations.

"I believe we've adopted the right approach," says John Wodatch, director of the ADA office at the Department of Justice. "It's important to give flexibility to the various enterprises. This is a comprehensive piece of legislation. More specifics that would apply across all enterprises could create unfair burdens. For example, a 500-room Hyatt hotel shouldn't have the same requirements as a 10-room bed and breakfast, even though they are both similar businesses."

### How much will it cost to implement the law?

"The ADA is the nicest bill to come along in a long time," editorialized *Reason* magazine in 1989. "Only the scum of the earth would oppose protecting [the disabled] from discrimination. It wouldn't be nice."[3]

Critics of the ADA invariably describe it as well-intentioned. What they fear, especially the business community, is the cost of compliance. Depending on how the law is interpreted by regulators and courts, it could spell staggering costs and liabilities that few businesses can afford, especially during recessionary times. Unlike other civil rights legislation, the ADA not only bans overt discrimination and exclusion but also requires accommodation, and thus imposes costs.

"These costs will be unrelated to the productivity of disabled workers," notes Carolyn Weaver, an economist with the American Enterprise Institute, a public-policy research organization in Washington.[4] As such, she argues, the legislation will secure higher wages and expanded employment opportunities for some disabled people while imposing a net economic drain on society.

Exactly what the ADA will cost is unclear. Before President Bush signed the law, the White House estimated that the employment and public accommodation provisions would require between $1 billion and $2 billion. Most economists, however, call those figures extremely low. "That amount would barely cover the cost of one industry to achieve compliance," says Roy Cordato, a senior economist at the Washington-based Institute for Research on the Economics of Taxation. Some healthcare providers have put compliance costs for their industry alone at $80 billion over the next decade.

"There are many hidden costs that won't be attributable to this law," says Cordato. "The ADA would have never passed Congress if it had put its true cost in the budget. Instead, the costs appear to have been heaped on the backs of business. But in reality the costs will be passed on to consumers — people will pay more for goods, and economic growth will be impeded. What this amounts to is a mandated benefits program for the disabled."

Counters John Wodatch at the Justice Department: "It is impossible to know the costs before you factor in the benefits. Any numbers being ban-

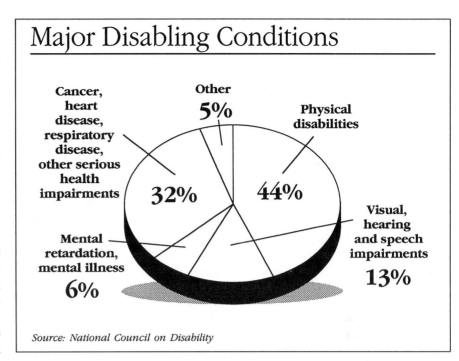

# Major Disabling Conditions

Cancer, heart disease, respiratory disease, other serious health impairments — 32%

Other — 5%

Physical disabilities — 44%

Visual, hearing and speech impairments — 13%

Mental retardation, mental illness — 6%

*Source: National Council on Disability*

died about are abstract, and thus suspect." As more disabled people enter into the mainstream of society, he adds, there will be economic as well as psychic benefits. Those who do not work now collect federal disability and welfare checks, costing nearly $60 billion a year. If more disabled people enter the work force, Wodatch says, that drain on society will surely lessen.

For individual businesses, of course, the potential costs of the ADA are very real, if not exactly quantifiable. The intercity bus industry, for example, which may face specific mandates under the new law, predicts disaster. "There can be no doubt about what is ahead for us," Fred Currey, chairman of Greyhound Lines, told a House subcommittee in 1989. If the bill requires that all new motor coaches be equipped with wheelchair lifts, he said, Greyhound, which recently came out of bankruptcy, would pull out of the smaller 5,000 of the 10,000 communities it serves and terminate some 10,000 workers. Curry estimated that the ADA would cost Grey-

hound $78 million a year in added expense and lost revenue.

"We already serve the very young, the very old, the very poor and the very rural," says Susan Perry, vice president of the American Bus Association. "We can't add cost and pass it on. Profitability is already marginal." Concerns about the potential burden of the ADA on the private bus industry led Congress to grant it an exemption, pending the results of a three-year study being conducted by the federal Office of Technology Assessment.*

But the bus lobby was not the only industry to cry poverty. Christopher Hoey, assistant general counsel for the F. W. Woolworth Co., which operates 5,700 retail stores, told another House subcommittee that if the law means all aisles and shelves must be accessible to a person in a wheelchair, the loss of display room would be "drastic, and in some cases ruinous." Retailers, he said, could lose one-third to three-fifths of productive

---

*Results from the OTA study are due in July 1993.

space, "the functional equivalent — in lost sales and employment — of closing a substantial fraction of the nations's stores, or even outlawing some types of stores."[5]

Backers of the law insist that compliance will not be as onerous as opponents claim. "It makes me chortle when I hear people say it will put them out of business," says Wright of the Disability Rights Education and Defense Fund. "That has never been the bill's intent. It will open the doors of society, not close the doors of business."

Supporters of the law say workplace accommodations — such as altering schedules, providing interpreters for the deaf or readers for the blind and installing special equipment — need not be expensive or difficult. They cite as evidence the compliance expenses related to the 1973 Rehabilitation Act, which the ADA was modeled after.* "Not one federally assisted program has gone bankrupt as a result of serving the disabled," says Wright. "We have a 15-year demonstration project. Businesses aren't going to go bankrupt."

According to numerous federal studies, access features, when designed into new construction, on average add less than 1 percent to the total cost.[6] For instance, a spokesman for Marriott Corp. says the added expense of providing such features as 40 wheelchair-accessible rooms and Braille panels in the elevators at a multimillion-dollar hotel it opened in San Francisco in 1989 was "insignificant." And when Marriott hired James Burtnett, who uses a wheelchair, as a telephone operator in its Bethesda, Md., headquarters, the company needed only to widen a phone cubicle, at a cost of less than $50.

While it costs more to revamp an existing building, the new law does not require "retrofitting" if it means an "undue hardship" for the business. Moreover, companies that have begun to meet access rules say accommodation is worth it because the customer base and labor pool are enlarged. "Hiring and accommodating people with disabilities as well as designing facilities accessible to all simply makes good business sense," says Richard E. Marriott, vice chairman of Marriott.

Paul Hearne, president of the Washington-based Dole Foundation for the Employment of People with Disabilities,* agrees. "The ADA will provide opportunities for employers, employees and public officials to work together to create a more productive and decent American workplace," he says. It will give the business community access to a "reliable work force" of disabled individuals who will "enter the marketplace both as employees and as consumers."

## Will the ADA lead to an explosion of lawsuits?

Many employers worry that the ADA will spur a rash of lawsuits. "Through its lack of fundamental guidelines and parameters for businesses, the law promotes lawsuits as a way of handling disputes between employers and the disabled," says Nancy Fulco, an attorney at the U.S. Chamber of Commerce. "Basically, the bill is an invitation to litigation, and it will take the courts 20 years to sort out the mess."

Those who choose not to make a good-faith effort to comply with the law may indeed be slapped with a lawsuit. In such cases, companies could be ordered to construct facilities, remove alleged barriers, hire personnel or take other steps to comply. They also may have to pay plaintiffs' attorneys' fees. For example, when a Berkeley, Calif., restaurant owned by the nationwide chain Specialty Restaurant Corp. remodeled its building but failed to comply with California's disability access law, a wheelchair-bound woman sued. In a 1988 jury verdict, she was awarded $36,000 in compensatory damages and half a million dollars in punitive damages. The jury also ruled that the restaurant had to pay the plaintiff's $191,000 in legal fees.

Under the ADA, cases concerning public accommodation compliance will not go before juries, and individuals cannot collect punitive damages. All the winning plaintiff can expect is that the non-complying business will be forced to comply — so long as the changes are "readily achievable." Nevertheless, the ADA will spur greater awareness of state laws governing disability access, which often carry harsher penalties for non-compliance.

It is in the employment area where the greatest increase in lawsuits is most likely to occur. The ADA offers a legal remedy for a much larger pool of people than the 1973 Rehabilitation Act, which has engendered fewer than 400 suits over nearly two decades.[7] That law has had "very limited applicability to the private sector and didn't provide nearly as much access to the courts as the new law," says Edward Potter, president of the National Foundation for the Study of Employment Policy, a pro-business research group in Washington. In contrast, the new law not only expands liability to virtually all private employers but also permits individuals seeking redress to sue on their own.*

Business groups fear the stakes in such litigation will be considerable.

Continued on p. 1000

---

*The 1973 law protects disabled people from discrimination by institutions that receive federal funding (see p. 1002).

---

*The Dole Foundation was established by Sen. Bob Dole, R-Kan., in 1983 to provide financial assistance to nonprofit organizations committed to helping disabled persons find jobs.

---

*Under the earlier law, disabled individuals who worked for federal contractors could seek redress from the Labor Department, which in turn could sue the company on the person's behalf.

# Who Are the Disabled?

"It is very difficult to define a disabled person," notes Evan J. Kemp Jr., chairman of the Equal Employment Opportunity Commission. "There are 43 federal definitions and literally thousands of state, county and local ones." In the early 1980s Kemp, who himself is disabled, cynically defined the category as including everyone but the mythical American — a 5-foot 10-inch, 160-pound, 28-year-old white male with no physical or mental impairments.[†]

Congress' definition is significantly narrower than that but encompasses many more people than are normally considered disabled. Under the Americans with Disabilities Act (ADA), an individual is classified as disabled if he or she has a physical or mental impairment that "substantially limits one or more of the major life activities," has a record of such an impairment or is regarded as having such an impairment.

"The definition is broad," concedes Sandra Swift Parrino, chairperson of the National Council on Disability, "but we didn't want to leave out populations. We wanted to include rather than to exclude."

According to Congress' count, the ADA covers some 43 million people, or one in every six Americans. Other organizations, however, cite different numbers. For example, a survey published by the National Center for Health Statistics in 1984 estimated that there were more than 160 million people in the non-institutionalized population who suffer from chronic impairments. Yet in the 1980 census only 22.5 million people identified themselves as disabled.

Critics of the ADA object to the broad classification. They differentiate between people who are disabled through no fault of their own and others, such as substance abusers and those with AIDS, who, these critics say, brought maladies on themselves and are not deserving of anti-discrimination protections.

"If Americans knew that reformed alcoholics are considered disabled with the same status as other disabled, I think they'd be appalled," says Walt Williams, an economics professor at George Mason University in Fairfax, Va. "The definition is not the man-on-the-street definition of a disabled person. It opens the door to all kinds of problems — including lawsuits."

Although a definition of disability that would yield a precise count (either you're in or you're out) would appease the desire for precision and quantification, experts say it would negate an important component of this public policy: the understanding that disability itself is not always precise and perfectly quantifiable. Disabilities are not necessarily immutable characteristics, like sex and race. A particular disability may limit functioning in one situation, such as riding a bus, while having no impact in another, such as using a word processor.

Moreover, disabled people are by no means a homogeneous group; they differ markedly in extent of impairment and range of potential abilities. This point is often missed by non-disabled persons, who tend to lump most types of disability into a single "handicapped" category.

"Two people with the same disability may respond differently," says Pat Morrissey, a disability consultant in Washington. "One may be disabled from birth — and have a lifetime of appropriate support and coping strategies — and not require special accommodations. Another with the same impairment may need extensive help.... Whereas employers want something finite, disability by nature is relative and personal."

Among disabled persons of working age, estimates show that fewer than 10 percent of those with physical limitations use a wheelchair. Equally small proportions of people with visual and hearing impairments are actually blind or deaf, while only one out of 10 people with mental retardation is severely retarded. And among individuals with learning disabilities, many have conditions that may impede reading, writing or computation, but that otherwise do not interfere with their intellectual and reasoning capabilities.

Contrast this set of disabilities with the variety of work opportunities likely to arise over the coming decade, and the possibilities for job-matching become plain. According to the U.S. Bureau of Labor Statistics, more than 90 percent of the new job openings through the year 2000 will be in information-intensive and service-intensive occupations. In these positions, brain power, not physical dexterity, will be the prime requirement.

Whatever the exact figure for the number of disabled, the overriding point is that the disability community is large — and growing. At least 60 million Americans between the ages of 18 and 64 will experience a mental disorder during their lifetimes, according to government economists.[††] And the explosive growth in the number of people with AIDS and HIV infection has already added hundreds of thousands more disabled to the population.

More important, the intent of the broad definition of disability is not to provide entitlements but to protect against discrimination. "People with disabilities really don't want any special treatment," says Kemp. "We want to blend in, to be treated like everybody else. We're a special-interest group that wants to lose its status as a special-interest group."

---

[†] Evan J. Kemp, Jr., "Disability in Our Society," in Carolyn Weaver, ed., *Disability & Work* (1991), p. 56.
[††] Cited in *The New York Times*, Sept. 23, 1991.

# Timetable for ADA Implementation

| | Brief description | Law's effective date(s) | Enforcement jurisdiction |
|---|---|---|---|
| **TITLE I Employment** | Provides that no covered entity shall discriminate against a qualified individual with a disability because of the disability in regard to job-application procedures, hiring, advancement, employee compensation, job training and other privileges of employment. | Takes effect July 26, 1992, for employers with 25 or more employees, and on July 26, 1994, for employers with 15 or more employees. Employers with fewer than 15 workers are exempt. | Equal Employment Opportunity Commission |
| **TITLE II Public Services** | Provides that no qualified individual with a disability shall be excluded from participation in or be denied the benefits of the services, programs or activities of public entities, including transportation facilities. | As of Aug. 26, 1990, all new public buses and light and rapid rail vehicles ordered are to be accessible; one car per train must be accessible by July 26, 1995; key commuter stations must be retrofitted by July 26, 1993; all existing Amtrak stations must be retrofitted by July 26, 2010. | Department of Transportation; Department of Justice |
| **TITLE III Public Accommodation** | Provides that people with disabilities should have access to existing private businesses that serve the public, so long as required accommodations are "readily achievable." The list includes hotels, restaurants, theaters, laundromats, museums, zoos, private schools and offices of health-care providers. | Takes effect Jan. 26, 1992, for businesses with more than 25 employees; on July 26, 1992, for businesses with 25 or fewer employees and annual revenue of $1 million or less; and on Jan. 26, 1993, for companies with 10 or fewer employees and annual revenue not exceeding $500,000. | Department of Justice |
| **TITLE IV Telecommunications** | Amends Title II of the Communications Act of 1934 by adding a section providing that the Federal Communications Commission shall ensure that interstate and intrastate telecommunications relay services are available, to the extent possible, to hearing-impaired and speech-impaired individuals. | By July 26, 1993, covered firms should have telecommunications services available 24 hours a day. | Federal Communications Commission |

*Continued from p. 998*

The disability law provides victims in employment cases with remedies established in the Civil Rights Act of 1991 — jury trials and up to $300,000 in punitive and compensatory damages. Factoring that in, Potter estimates the disability bill could generate more than $3.5 billion annually in damages and court costs.

"There were 115,000 discrimination cases filed at the federal and state level last year," Potter says. "If disability groups file charges at the same rate as other minority groups, and I see no reason to suspect less, they have the potential of more than doubling the caseload at the EEOC." EEOC Chairman Evan Kemp Jr. says he expects 12,000 to 15,000 new lawsuits a year once the ADA's employment provisions go into effect on July 26, 1992.

But despite predictions that lawyers lured by the scent of a generous award will rush to defend victims of disability bias, experts say discrimination cases are likely to remain unattractive. Results of racial harassment cases filed during the 1980s, when the courts allowed punitive damages, suggest that neither attorneys nor their clients will reap a financial bonanza. Two-thirds of the awards were $50,000 or less, and many large verdicts were later overturned, according to the National Women's Law Center in Washington.[8]

"I don't think there will be a flood of litigation," says John Wodatch at the Justice Department. "Rather, I see a great deal of interest in complying.

There seems to be a willingness to say, 'OK, what are the things that I need to do?' It's important to remember that this is a new concept for most organizations and enterprises. The confusion is over what they have to do."

"We don't want frivolous cases that would establish bad precedents. We don't want this to become a gravy train," adds Alexander Robinson, an attorney for the American Civil Liberties Union (ACLU), which is likely to bring many of the cases to court. "What is 'reasonable accommodation' inevitably will be figured out in the courts. But that is typical for this kind of legislation."

Most analysts — even those who opposed the ADA — agree that the vast majority of disabled people want access, not lawsuits. "But it takes just one lawsuit to devastate a business," notes Wendy Lechner at the NFIB. "This is not a carrot-and-stick piece of legislation; it's all stick and no carrot."

Disability rights advocates would prefer that businesses comply voluntarily. But with the ADA in hand, they are prepared to do battle in court if necessary. "This organization has trained 5,000 disabled people, educating them of their rights under ADA," says Pat Wright at the Disability Rights Education and Defense Fund. "We're creating an army of barrier-busters that will go business-by-business through their local communities." Wright says businesses have two options: They can pay for "reasonable accommodation" to make their buildings accessible or pay lawyers a lot more later, and still have to make the accommodations eventually. ∎

# BACKGROUND

## Isolated Minority

Americans with disabilities are the largest, poorest, least employed and least educated minority in America. Their history is largely one of isolation and segregation. Literally through institutionalization, and subtly through negative attitudes and treatment, persons with disabilities have been kept from the social mainstream and denied the benefits and opportunities available to non-disabled persons.

"They are a group of people who have been defined by what they are not, rather than by what they are," writes disability expert Jane West. "They have been described in terms of 'diseases, deformities and abnormalities,' identified by labels and diagnoses. They have been considered lifelong children who need to be taken care of and shielded from life's vi-

cissitudes."[9]

Indeed, the word "handicapped" itself implies dependency. The term originated in 19th-century England, when people with disabilities were forced to exist by begging "with cap in hand."

In early 19th-century America, taking care of the handicapped was left to their immediate families and a small band of social reformers, such as Thomas Hopkins Gallaudet, who opened a school for the deaf in Hartford, Conn., in 1817, and John Dix Fischer, who started the New England Asylum for the Blind in Boston in 1829.

For the most part, these individual acts of advocacy were not matched by government action. Indeed, after the crusading Dorothea Dix persuaded Congress to allocate funds for public mental hospitals, she was thwarted by President Franklin Pierce, who vetoed the measure in 1854. Caring for the physically and mentally disabled, the president declared, was not a federal responsibility.

### Impetus for Change

The ravages of World War I changed that. The many thousands disabled by war injuries provided the first strong impetus for federal aid to the handicapped. In response, the federal government expanded newly formed programs for vocational training. The Smith-Fess Veterans' Rehabilitation Act of 1920 established the first broad-based federal program to provide vocational training and job-placement to handicapped persons.[10]

The expansion of vocational rehabilitation continued through the Depression, when the Federal Board for Vocational Education initiated programs to help disabled persons who were also poor. In 1935, the programs received their biggest boost with the Social Security Act, which specified income-support benefits for disabled workers and authorized vocational rehabilitation programs on a permanent basis. Throughout the 1930s, '40s and '50s, training and counseling remained the central thrust of government policy toward the disabled.

From the early 1960s, however, the civil rights movement began to shape the aims of the disability rights groups. The direction of public policies to assist persons with mental or physical disabilities began to take a new slant, one that focused more on rights and protections than on services and income supports.

The disabled were not included as covered categories in the landmark Civil Rights Act of 1964, but the law's influence on them was nonetheless profound. The disabled saw their cause increasingly as an issue of equal opportunity, not rehabilitation. There was a recognition, particularly in the area of education for handicapped children, that society needed to do more than provide programs, many of which were perceived as "entitlements" similar in nature to welfare. Advocates saw the need for an attitudinal change, whereby persons with disabilities would be viewed as individuals with a wide set of abilities as well as one or more physical or mental impairments.

Some barriers erected by society were tangible in nature, including a variety of architectural designs and features that impeded the access of physically impaired persons to employment, social services and even voting. Architects and building contractors constructed buildings with an implicit model of the able-bodied adult in mind. Given their absence from most social settings and the lack of political and economic power, disabled persons were disregarded by those who designed buildings and public facilities.

## Early Laws

Congress' first response to this changing climate was the Architectural Barriers Act in 1968. It required federally funded or leased buildings to be accessible to the disabled. Next, the Urban Mass Transportation Act of 1970 required all public transportation services to be accessible to the disabled in order to qualify for federal funding.

As the idea of "mainstreaming" gained currency, so did initiatives to educate disabled children in the school system. The Education For All Handicapped Children Act of 1975 guaranteed disabled children a pubic education geared to their particular needs and abilities. It gave parents the right to dispute school programs with local administrators.

Though the Ford administration opposed the measure, many Republicans now hail its achievements. "This education law has been one of our modern success stories in the disability area," Attorney General Dick Thornburgh told the Senate Labor and Human Resources Committee June 22, 1989. Thornburgh noted that more than 150,000 disabled young

men and women complete their education each year under the act.

The linchpin event for advocates of the disabled, however, had come two years earlier with passage of the Rehabilitation Act of 1973. This act extended the authorization for federal aid programs for the handicapped, established the Office of the Handicapped within the Department of Health, Education and Welfare and moved from strict emphasis on vocational rehabilitation to broader programs to promote independent living.

### Importance of '73 Law

Little noticed at the time were the bill's final sections, which established protections for the disabled against discrimination in federal programs. Sections 501 and 503 prohibited employment discrimination on the basis of disability and required that recipients of federal contracts institute affirmative-action programs to hire and promote "qualified handicapped individuals." Section 504 provided a broader guarantee: "No otherwise qualified handicapped individual ... shall, solely by reason of his handicap, be excluded from the participation in, be denied the benefits of, or be subjected to discrimination under any program or activity receiving federal financial assistance."

Section 504 proved to be the most important public-policy edict affecting the rights of persons with disabilities to date. With it came the reserved parking places, curb cuts and wheelchair ramps that have become part of the landscape of federally funded construction. Over the last 18 years numerous court decisions have examined questions raised by Section 504, such as how to determine when a person with a disability is "otherwise qualified," when a "reasonable accommodation" crosses the line and becomes an "undue burden" and when a person with a disability presents a threat to the health and/or safety of others.

Implementation of the law was slow in coming, though. "It was 1977 before there were finally regulations," recalls Lex Friedan, executive director of the Institute for Rehabilitation and Research Foundation in Houston. Even today, many federal buildings fail to meet the guidelines due to lack of adequate enforcement provisions. "While Section 504 has unlocked the door for handicapped persons to enter the mainstream of society," writes B. P. Tucker, "it has failed in its goal of opening that door wide. Enforcement of Section 504 has been at best lethargic and at worst ineffectual." [11]

Part of the reason for that was the shift in the political environment in Washington. With the election of Ronald Reagan and the Republicans taking control of the Senate in the early 1980s, there was an effort at the Department of Justice as well as other federal agencies to roll back civil rights protections for disabled persons, including Section 504. [12] "There was little or no enforcement of disability legislation under the Reagan administration," comments disability rights activist Pat Wright.

## Fight for the ADA

Disability rights activists had hoped to amend the 1964 Civil Rights Act to include the disabled. As passed, the landmark law prohibited discrimination in employment, public services and public accommodations on the basis of race, sex, religion and national origin. As late as 1985, an amendment to the act remained a favored option among strategists for the movement. But by the late 1980s, that option was deemed impractical and potentially misguided. In particular, leaders of the traditional civil rights community were against reopening discussion of the 1964 law;

Continued on p. 1004

# Chronology

**1800s** *Responsibility for taking care of the handicapped is left to immediate families and a small band of social reformers.*

## 1817
Thomas Hopkins Gallaudet opens school for the deaf in Hartford, Conn.

---

## 1920s-1950s
*Returning war veterans prompt the federal government to play a role in vocational training and counseling of the disabled.*

### 1920
The Smith-Fess Act establishes the first broad-based federal program to assist handicapped persons.

### 1935
The Social Security Act allocates federal funds to assist indigent dependent children, elderly adults and blind citizens.

---

**1960s** *The "war on poverty" shifts public-policy direction to focus more on rights and protections than on services and income supports.*

### 1964
Disability community is influenced by passage of the Civil Rights Act, which prohibits discrimination on the basis of race, color, religion or national origin.

### August 1968
President Johnson signs the Architectural Barriers Act into law, beginning the process of eliminating physical barriers encountered by disabled citizens in federal buildings.

---

**1970s** *The decade is marked by the passage of significant federal legislation to increase disabled access to public institutions.*

### 1970
Urban Mass Transportation Act goes into effect requiring all public transportation services to be accessible to the disabled in order to qualify for federal funding.

### Sept. 26, 1973
President Nixon signs the Rehabilitation Act into law. Sections 501 and 503 require federal contractors to take affirmative action to employ persons with disabilities. Section 504 prohibits discrimination against otherwise qualified persons from participation in any program receiving federal funds.

### 1975
The Education For All Handicapped Children Act is passed mandating free, appropriate public education for all children with disabilities.

---

**1980s** *As the Reagan administration rolls back federal regulations, disability rights groups unite and push for more sweeping anti-discrimination statutes.*

### February 1986
The National Council on the Handicapped proposes anti-discrimination legislation in its report to Congress and the president, *Toward Independence.*

### 1988
The Fair Housing Act Amendments add persons with disabilities as a group protected from discrimination in housing.

### April 1988
Sen. Lowell Weicker, R-Conn., and Rep. Tony Coelho, D-Calif., introduce first versions of the Americans with Disabilities Act (ADA).

---

**1990s** *The disability community — and the private sector — prepare for a new era after passage of the ADA.*

### July 26, 1990
After the final version of the bill passes the House and Senate by lopsided margins, President Bush signs the ADA into law.

### July 26, 1991
The Department of Justice and the Equal Employment Opportunity Commission publish guidelines for compliance with the ADA in the *Federal Register.*

### Nov. 21, 1991
President Bush signs the Civil Rights Act of 1991 into law, enabling disabled workers to bring cases of intentional bias under the ADA to recover compensatory and punitive damages.

Continued from p. 1002

they feared that protections for already covered groups might be watered down in the process.

Activists thus turned their attention to fashioning new anti-bias legislation. A leading force behind these efforts was the National Council on Disability, originally called the National Council on the Handicapped.* "When the president and Congress asked us to take a look at disability rights back in 1985, our No. 1 recommendation was that there be an ADA, but no one did anything about it," says Sandra Swift Parrino, chairman of the 15-member council. In 1986, the council published *Toward Independence,* a report assessing federal disability laws and suggesting legislative action. "In 1987," Parrino says, "we went to Sen. Lowell Weicker (R-Conn.) who finally drafted the first official version of the bill."

In the push for ADA passage, other traditional civil rights groups and AIDS-policy advocates teamed up with disability rights organizations. The coalition argued that the absence of special equipment and other accommodations stymied efforts of the disabled to get jobs or otherwise join the mainstream.

Despite the concerns of business groups, their opposition to a bill was surprisingly muted. For one thing, no one wanted to look like a bigot fighting a civil rights bill, particularly one that was rushing through Congress. More important, experts say, businesses in the last few years have seen disabled people as a new source of labor and customers. "If they can get to the stores, business is going to increase," concedes Nancy Fulco of the U.S. Chamber of Commerce, who nonetheless lobbied to limit the bill's impact on business.

The mixed feelings of the business groups underscored how disability rights is a civil rights movement different from any other. Unlike the African American and women's movements, disability rights groups have never filled the streets with hundreds of thousands of marchers. Instead, the disability movement boasts "a hidden army," says former Rep. Tony Coelho, who has epilepsy. Since a sixth of the nation's population has some form of disability, Coelho argues, "disability impacts practically every family."

## Bipartisan Support

Nowhere was that clearer than in Congress and the White House, where key supporters of the rights bill felt a particular need to win the bill's passage because they personally knew about disabilities. After Lowell Weicker lost his Senate seat in 1988, sponsorship of the Senate bill fell to Tom Harkin, D-Iowa, who has a hearing-impaired brother and a paralyzed nephew. When Coelho resigned in May 1989 because of ethics-related issues, he designated Steny H. Hoyer, D-Md., to take over the bill in the House. Hoyer's wife is epileptic. Two other key senators in the bill's progress were Labor Committee Chairman Edward M. Kennedy, D-Mass., whose sister Rosemary is mentally retarded and whose eldest son Teddy lost a leg to cancer, and Minority Leader Bob Dole, R-Kan., whose right arm was partially disabled by a World War II injury.

The most important ADA promoter was President Bush, who had a daughter die of leukemia and has two sons with disabilities.* Bush's strong statements in support of the bill during the 1988 campaign won him important support in the usually Democratic disability community.

Nevertheless, despite widespread bipartisan support, the bill was in trouble until mid-1989 because of business fears about the cost. In a compromise bill, certain businesses were granted temporary exemptions, the time frame for compliance was extended and the "undue hardship" clause was also added at the request of small-business lobbies. In July, after having survived one Senate committee, four committees in the House and two conference committees, the final version of the bill zipped through the House on a 377-to-28 vote and the Senate by a 76-8 margin, and was signed into law by President Bush on July 26, 1990.

## New Consciousness

The success of the disability movement is extraordinary because it sprang up with little noise and little notice. One essential ingredient has been the growth of a new class consciousness among the disabled: 74 percent of them feel they share a "common identity" with other disabled people, according to a 1986 poll.[13]

"All disabled people share one common experience — discrimination," says Pat Wright. Often it is crude bigotry. In January 1989, an airline employee in New York who resented having to help a 66-year-old double amputee board a plane instead put him on a baggage dolly. A New Jersey private-zoo owner refused to admit children with Down's syndrome to the monkey house because, he claimed, they upset his chimpanzee.[14]

It is that kind of outrage and countless more subtle discriminations that mobilized the movement that now wants to change the image of the disabled. Many now reject the traditional attitudes of society that suggested their lives were tragic and

*Many disability rights groups have tried to minimize use of the word "handicapped" because it perpetuates a negative attitude toward the disabled. The National Council on Disability was established as an advisory body to government in 1978 but became an independent federal agency under the 1986 Amendments to the Rehabilitation Act.

*Bush's son Neil had dyslexia — impaired ability to read — as a childd, while another son, Marvin, had a colostomy after he had part of his colon removed in 1986.

# Compliance Consultants: Watch Out for Scams

The U.S. economy may be mired in a recession, but there is at least one area where business is booming: the ADA industry. Spanking new consulting firms, legal departments and architectural concerns are popping up everywhere, peddling their expertise in disability access. Most prudent businesses have either attended or are planning to attend at least one of a multitude of seminars being held in metropolitan centers throughout the country to assist companies in complying with the Americans with Disabilities Act.

"An incredible industry has been created as a result of ADA," says Pat Wright, director of governmental affairs at the Disability Rights Education and Defense Fund. "There are now consultants [everywhere] charging exorbitant rates to provide guidance. My fear is that a lot have little or no experience with disabilities and are advocating more than needs to be spent to achieve compliance. I call it the 'vulture syndrome.'"

The potential peril of this burgeoning growth industry is one thing ADA proponents and critics can agree upon. "It's a great scam," says Wendy Lechner at the National Foundation for Independent Business. "Some lawyers are selling fear and doom to business owners, charging $300 to tell them they need to spend $5,000 to stay out of jail. These scare tactics are the last thing we need."

Examples of slippery marketing ethics include a large number of consulting companies that are claiming special status as ADA experts. For example, one St. Louis company has emblazoned on its brochures, "Certified ADA Consultant." The question is, certified by whom? "I don't know who is certifying these outfits, certainly not the Department of Justice," says John Wodatch, director of Justice's ADA office.

There is also a plethora of new products being introduced that may or may not actually benefit the disabled. One Chicago company is advertising a "state-of-the-art playground material" that disability experts say is obviously an unsuitable surface for a wheelchair user. Another company that manufactures TDD machines,† which enable people with hearing impairments to use telephones, insists in its marketing materials that all businesses need to have one to meet ADA standards, which isn't the case.

Though many reputable organizations and firms have extensive experience dealing with issues confronting people with disabilities, such as Mainstream, Inc., in Washington, D.C., and Barrier Free Environments in Raleigh, N.C., the field of disability access is relatively new. "I don't think most architects understand what the ADA is all about," says Pittsburgh architect Jim Lynch. "The obvious solution may be the most expensive and least appropriate. Sometimes architects exaggerate out of ignorance. I've heard knowledgeable architects say, 'If in doubt, put in an elevator.' That's a wrong-headed approach. Architects need to know the technology — and also the intent of the legislation."

One architect for a major oil corporation based in Fairfax, Va., admitted to a building tenant that while attending a two-day ADA seminar he was advised to pad renovation bills by as much as 30 percent to account for the costs of complying with the ADA. "I was flabbergasted," says Sharon Mistler, executive director of End Dependence Center, the tenant that was undertaking the renovation. "I've worked in disability for 20 years, so I know what is required under this law. But what about those businesses that don't?"

Flim-flam operations, of course, are nothing new. "This is reminiscent of the asbestos nightmare, when consultants came out of the woodwork — and people bought into it," comments Jim Dinegar, vice president for government affairs at the Building Owners and Managers Association, which has published a guidebook for ADA compliance.

Following enactment of the Rehabilitation Act of 1973, a number of consultants went door-to-door to "help" companies. Some large companies that made renovations based on bad advice, such as Texas Instruments in Houston, had to remodel a second time to come into compliance.

The shady operations cast a shadow over consulting groups that are providing a legitimate — and much-needed — service to businesses. Closing the information gap regarding the ADA is a daunting task. "Scam operators increase the risk of a backlash," says Lex Friedan at the Institute for Rehabilitation and Research Foundation in Houston. "Wise businesses will seek assistance from government-sponsored sources, rather than independent groups without references. It's a buyer-beware environment."

---

†A TDD (Telecommunications Device for the Deaf) machine includes a portable keyboard that can be plugged into phones.

---

pitiful. They loathe charitable appeals such as the annual Jerry Lewis Telethon that raised $45 million for the Muscular Dystrophy Association over the Labor Day weekend. Such extravaganzas seek funds by emphasizing the most desperate cases. That kind of approach, activists say, suggests that disabled people are to be cared for and cannot be contributing members of society. "We don't want to be dependent any more," says Lex Friedan, who is a quadriplegic wheelchair user, the result of an automobile accident. "We want to be part of society in every way."

But despite the consciousness-raising and renewed vigor of the disability rights movement, many perceptions and biases still hold. While 90 percent of the respondents in the 1991 survey conducted for the National Organization on Disability said they admired people with disabilities for the barriers they have overcome, the study found that the respondents generally felt guilt, pity and awkwardness around the disabled. Only 19 percent said they could feel comfortable around a mentally ill person.

This data reinforces the need for legislation protecting the disabled from discrimination, activists say. "When legal rights aren't there, people are less willing to sit down and be educated," Tony Coelho told fellow lawmakers in May 1990. "Without the law on our side, they don't have to, and many would just as soon not." [15] ■

# CURRENT SITUATION

## Law's Implementation

The ADA is a landmark more for its comprehensiveness than its conceptual novelty. What the ADA does, in essence, is (1) codify many regulatory concepts and guidelines from Section 504 of the Rehabilitation Act of 1973 and other predecessor laws and (2) extend the Section 504 prohibition against discrimination in the private sector.

As the law enters into the implementation phase, it is clear that many people either don't know about it or are confused by it. "I'd be surprised if even half of the building owners out there even know about the ADA," says Jim Dinegar, vice president for government affairs at the Building Owners and Managers Association International (BOMA). BOMA has already sold 20,000 copies of its *ADA Compliance Guidebook* and says it receives some 200 inquiries a day from its members requesting information.

Some of the confusion stems from the sheer comprehensiveness — and complexity — of the law, which is being administered by four separate federal agencies. *(See timetable, p.*

*1000.)* When the Department of Justice published its compliance guidelines in the *Federal Register* on July 26, 1991, they took up more than 300 pages and were written in legalese incomprehensible to many who are obliged to comply. "To be honest, it's not the Justice Department's fault," says Dinegar. "They were given an unrealistic timetable from Congress. After they published their proposed rules, they received 12,000 pages of comments from 12 separate hearings held around the country, and had just a couple of months to produce the guidelines."

"I have not encountered a single architect working for business that really knows disability access," says attorney Sid Wolinsky, who has litigated two dozen disability lawsuits in California. "One of the most startling things is the ignorance of architects. They've been drawing up plans as if people in wheelchairs didn't exist." Jim Lynch, an architect in the Pittsburgh area, agrees. "I know of no architecture school that teaches disability access as a part of its main curriculum," he says.

In a massive campaign to inform the public of the ADA's requirements, Congress appropriated more than $13 million for specific technical-assistance projects for fiscal year 1991. The Department of Education has awarded $4.5 million to support 16 projects, including the creation of one center in each of the 10 federal regions to help implement the law at the local level.

"With Section 504, technical assistance was basically helping people with disabilities understand their rights," says Lex Friedan. "Now it's a much more balanced approach, working with entities that need to make changes. A lot will depend ... on the willingness of the business community to work with the disabled community to devise effective and inexpensive ways to comply with the law."

Of course, no one presumed implementation of this sweeping statute would be easy — or painless. "Some businesses have been so battered with prophesies of fear that they are poised to take the blow rather than make changes," says Barbara Bode, vice president of the Council of Better Business Bureaus, which represents about 250,000 U.S. businesses and has received a technical-assistance grant from the Justice Department. "There's a lot of misinformation out there. Businesses should be advised to beware of scams." *(See story, p. 1005.)*

An informal survey of businesses that will be affected by the ADA seems to confirm that there's a huge information gap on the subject. Reactions to questions about the law range from "never heard of it," to "I'm grandfathered," to "they can go ahead and sue me," to "I'll just shut down." Experts say ignorance of the law's impact — as well as recalcitrance on the part of some businesses — will only exacerbate the issue, inspire lawsuits and, more than likely, inflate the cost of compliance. "Any business owner who doesn't start planning now and waits a year or two will get caught unaware of the law's rules and could pay heavily," warns Fulco at the Chamber of Commerce.

"It's too early to tell exactly how the law will be implemented," says Pat Morrissey, a former Senate staffer

# Where to Turn for More Information

The following organizations offer free information and guidance on how to comply with the Americans with Disabilities Act:

**The Job Accommodation Network,** West Virginia University, 809 Allen Hall, P.O. Box 6123, Morgantown, WV 26506; (800) 526-7234. Funded by the President's Committee on Employment of People with Disabilities, JAN offers free advice and information to business owners about how to accommodate disabled workers.

**The National Institute on Disability and Rehabilitation Research,** U.S. Department of Education, 400 Maryland Ave. S.W., Washington, D.C. 20202; (202) 401-1579. The institute has funded 10 regional centers to help inform business owners about their options and provide cost information.

**Equal Employment Opportunity Commission,** 1801 L Street N.W., Washington, D.C. 20507; (202) 663-4177. Check the regional office in your area or call (800) USA-EEOC for a copy of the EEOC's technical assistance manual.

**U.S. Department of Justice, Office of the ADA, Civil Rights Division,** Washington, D.C. 20530; (202) 514-0301. The Justice Department has published guidelines for implementing public accommodations provisions (Title III) of the ADA.

**The Architectural and Transportation Barriers Compliance Board,** 1111 18th Street N.W., Washington, D.C. 20036; (800) USA-ABLE. The board offers copies of the access standards it developed for the law.

**The President's Committee on Employment of People with Disabilities,** 1111 20th Street N.W., Washington, D.C. 20036; (202) 376-6200. The committee has a variety of publications and information available to employers seeking to provide employment opportunities for persons with disabilities.

**The Disability Rights Education and Defense Fund,** 2212 Sixth Street, Berkeley, CA 94710; (800) 466-4232. DREDF provides technical assistance and training related to the ADA and other disability laws.

**The National Leadership Coalition on AIDS,** 1730 M Street N.W., Suite 905, Washington, D.C. 20036; (202) 429-0930. This organization has a free, 12-page set of guidelines called "Small Business and AIDS: How AIDS Can Affect Your Business." It includes information on everything from basic principles for managing people with AIDS to the legal issues involved.

**The Mental Health Law Project,** 1101 15th St. N.W., Suite 1212, Washington, D.C. 20005; (202) 467-5730. This organization has information regarding the impact of the ADA on people with mental disabilities.

---

who worked on the legislation and is now a disability consultant in Washington. "The key thing is that businesses have to look at the requirements of the ADA differently from other civil rights legislation. Unlike race, gender or religion, disability poses the need for accommodation — an affirmative obligation on the part of employers. They must have a process in place to deal with the inequalities — and each case will be different."

## Public Accommodation

The public-accommodation portion of the ADA (Title III) will provide the law's first litmus test. The provision, which takes effect on Jan. 26, 1992, for businesses with more than 25 employees, guarantees disabled people the chance to partake "fully and equally," like anybody else, in a business' services and goods. Public places of all sorts, from restaurants to auto dealerships, are required to install ramps, widen doorways or make other "readily achievable" modifications to provide easier access for physically disabled people. The rules require that people in wheelchairs be admitted to general-seating areas of theaters and arenas, not segregated in special sections. Clothing stores must permit handicapped shoppers to take companions into dressing rooms if assistance is necessary.

The list of sites covered under Title III is exhaustive. Hospitals, homeless shelters, private schools, homes used for offices or day-care centers and rooms in churches and private clubs that are leased to groups for public functions are all covered. For existing buildings, a barrier must be removed only if it can be accomplished without much difficulty or expense. If a barrier is considered too costly to remove, other steps should be taken to provide comparable service to the disabled. Stricter standards, requiring a "high degree of convenient access," will be imposed for facilities being renovated and buildings that open after Jan. 26, 1993.

A host of questions face building owners, retailers and restaurant operators: Do all 95,000 door handles have to be refitted with levers at Rockefeller Center in New York City? Do menus need to be provided in Braille or is it enough to have a waiter tell a customer what is available? Can clerks retrieve merchandise for the disabled or must they be able to reach any item in the store? Is it permissible to seat those in wheelchairs wherever they can be accommodated or do they have to have access to the entire restaurant?

ADA advocates say the answers to many of these questions require little more than simple common sense. "What we are trying to do is to figure out the most cost-effective way of complying with the act," says Bode. "Cheap and easy is what we are interested in. What the feds are looking for are patterns of good-faith compliance, not patterns of discrimination. In most cases, accommodations are very modest."

For example, a store would not have to write all of its price tags in Braille for visually impaired customers; instead, a sales clerk simply would have to be on hand to read prices to such customers. Similarly, rather than lowering drinking fountains at a cost of hundreds of dollars each, building owners may need only to purchase paper cup dispensers to make the water fountains accessible to those in wheelchairs.

Since most big companies already provide accommodations for the handicapped, small businesses fear they will bear the biggest expenses, even though the bill does not require alterations to existing buildings that would be an "undue burden." "Unfortunately," says the NFIB's Wendy Lechner, "under the ADA the first remedy is court — and small businesses are the least able to make accommodations and the least able to incur legal liability if they don't."

"Small businesses could be hard hit," admits Justice's John Wodatch. "That's why there's a tax credit. It's a way to recoup on a yearly basis the expenses of complying with the ADA. There was recognition that the tax credit was a way to encourage entities to comply — and to spread the burden of compliance on all taxpayers." Under the law, small firms

that spend between $250 and $10,250 on access may claim a tax credit equal to as much as 50 percent of the cost.* "We think small firms will fare quite well under the ADA," adds Bode. "In fact, small businesses we've consulted with are finding that their attempts to comply can be a useful marketing tool."

## Employment Provisions

Beyond access to services, the new law will help provide the disabled with access to jobs. According to the U.S. attorney general's office, 58 percent of all disabled working-age men and 80 percent of all disabled working-age women were not employed at the beginning of 1990. This represents a higher non-employment ratio than for any other major demographic group between the ages of 18 and 65.

But while the public is divided over the issue of affirmative action for minorities, the recent poll conducted for the National Organization on Disability found that Americans recognize that "by their very condition disabled people face many more challenges than the rest of the population, and therefore steps ought to be taken to give them additional assistance … namely affirmative action." According to the survey, 78 percent of the public see the disabled more as having underused potential to contribute by working and producing as compared with 11 percent who see them more as a burden on taxpayers. And 82 percent think greater employment of the disabled would be "a boost to the nation."

The equal-employment protections (Title I) of the disabilities law will be phased in starting next July 26 and will cover all aspects of the work re-

*The credit is available only to firms with gross receipts under $1 million or with fewer than 30 full-time employees.

lationship, including hiring, firing, training, benefits and promotion. Under the law, a disabled candidate is considered qualified to be hired or promoted if he or she can carry out the "essential functions" of the job. An employer may have to offer training, or such aids as readers or interpreters, if these steps would enhance employment opportunities and not cause undue hardship to the company. And employers will no longer be permitted to use pre-employment medical examinations to screen out disabled candidates before making a job offer.

Business groups fear they will be forced to hire less qualified personnel, pay for costly accommodations and face higher insurance premiums. "Many of these fears are unfounded," responds Bode. "No employer will be required to hire unqualified job candidates. In fact, the burden of proof will be on the potential employee to show that he or she can perform the essential functions of the job."

Backers of the law say some elements in the business community are looking at the ADA backward — that it offers opportunities, not risks. "A lot of this country's largest corporations — IBM, Hewlett Packard, McDonald's, Wells Fargo — have experience to show that this law is not onerous," says Marilyn Golden, a policy analyst at the Disability Rights Education and Defense Fund. "They have developed model programs to integrate disabled people into their work force. It's not as if Congress woke up and decided to hinder business. They weighed the costs and concluded that it is genuinely worth it to integrate 43 million Americans into society."

"The biggest barrier to getting [disabled] people hired is the attitude of managers, not the cost," says Kathleen Alexander, Marriott's vice president for personnel services. A 1987

Continued on p. 1010

# At Issue:

## Will the American with Disabilities Act impose excessive economic costs on society?

CAROLYN L. WEAVER

*Resident scholar at the American Enterprise Institute in Washington, D.C.*
FROM *THE AMERICAN ENTERPRISE*, MAY-JUNE 1990

*i*t is easy to support the Americans with Disabilities Act [ADA] in principle and thus forgo the rigorous analysis of individual provisions that we demand on other issues. Some advocates are insisting on just this approach. But in a day of limited fiscal resources, intense international competition and demands for many new or expanded social programs — including programs to help the disabled live independently, or make transitions from education to work — it is irresponsible not to ask the difficult questions about the likely impact of this legislation.

We should know who will benefit from the legislation and who will not. We should know the cost of the legislation and who will be obligated to bear those costs. We should know whether segments of the disabled population will be adversely affected. We should know the effect on employers and on competitiveness. If the legislation has adverse economic or redistributive effects, the disabled will be affected by them, too.

The ADA is unlike traditional civil rights measures in that it imposes on employers an obligation to incur costs in hiring members of the protected class, in this case people with disabilities. These costs will be unrelated to the productivity of disabled workers and, as a result, will distort business decisions. While the wages and employment of many disabled people will surely rise, the economy as a whole as well as certain segments of the disabled population will suffer. Unskilled workers and people with severe impairments who are seeking entry-level positions are likely to be affected adversely. The ADA amounts to a mandated benefits program for the disabled that is an efficient and costly way to achieve unimpeachable objectives....

The ADA ... creates three serious problems: first, it makes some or all disabled workers more costly to hire. Second, it makes firms incur costs that are unrelated to expected benefits. And third, it imposes poorly defined obligations on employers....

The accommodation costs and who should be obligated to bear them are key issues. If resources are to be put to their best use, firms must be in a position to weigh expected benefits and expected costs and to make their decisions accordingly. In competitive markets, firms cannot incur the expense of an accommodation — or pension plan or on-the-job training program — unless they expect to recoup enough extra output or sales to make the investment worthwhile.

JAMES S. BRADY

*Former White House press secretary and current vice chairman of the National Organization on Disability*
FROM *THE NEW YORK TIMES*, OCT. 29, 1989.

*a*stonishingly, for years it has been legal under federal law for a restaurant to refuse to serve a mentally retarded person, for a theater to deny admission to someone with cerebral palsy, for a dry cleaner to refuse service to someone who is deaf or blind. People with disabilities — the largest minority in the U.S. — were left out of the historic Civil Rights Act of 1964. A quarter century later, discrimination against disabled people is still pervasive....

As a Republican and a fiscal conservative, I am proud that [the ADA] was developed by 15 Republicans appointed to the National Council on Disability by President Reagan. Many years ago, a Republican president, Dwight D. Eisenhower, urged that people with disabilities become taxpayers and consumers instead of being dependent upon costly federal benefits. The ADA grows out of that conservative philosophy.

Today 66 percent of working-age adults with disabilities are unemployed and dependent on federal subsidies. The ADA [will] save taxpayers billions of dollars by outlawing discrimination, putting disabled people on the job rolls and thereby reducing government disability payments.

Experience has shown that no civil right has ever been secured without legislation. The ADA will insure that facilities and employers — public and private — maintain minimum standards of accessibility.

By breaking down barriers in stores and offices, it [will] enable more disabled people to purchase goods and services — and thereby strengthen our national economy. By breaking down barriers in public transportation, the act [will] allow more people with disabilities to be employed and participate in community activities. The act [will] free hundreds of thousands of citizens who are virtually prisoners in their homes because of inaccessible transportation and public accommodations....

Since I took a bullet in the head eight years ago during the assassination attempt on Ronald Reagan, I have come to know the daily problems, frustrations and needs of those who live with disability. I have had to learn to talk again, to read again and to walk again. I have succeeded, and I know that everyone can learn to overcome the final obstacle to our equal inclusion in American life: prejudice toward people with disabilities.

Continued from p. 1008
analysis of more than 10,000 disabled employees by the Job Accommodation Network* showed 31 percent of them required no added cost for special training or facilities, 50 percent were under $50 and 69 percent cost less than $500. Only 1 percent cost over $5,000. What's more, the great majority of the 19 million working-age people with disabilities say they want to work. When Louis Harris surveyed Americans with disabilities in 1986, for example, two-thirds of those who were jobless said they would like to be employed.

Leading disability advocates, like Gallaudet University President Dr. I. King Jordan, insist that a large part of the problem is the widespread perception that people with disabilities can't do the job, or even if they can, that dealing with employees with disabilities is too much of an inconve-

---

*The Job Accommodation Network is a branch of the President's Committee on Employment of People with Disabilities. It offers free consulting to employers on the issue of accommodating disabled workers.

nience. "The most important barriers to the employment of disabled people are attitudinal barriers," Jordan, who is hearing impaired, told the May 1991 conference of the President's Committee on Employment of People with Disabilities. "Often we're judged unable to do something before we're given an opportunity to try."

Virtually every study of the issue has given people with disabilities high marks for their work attitudes, attendance and productivity. Most notable are the results obtained by Du Pont, based in Wilmington, Del., which has been an industry leader in recruiting disabled people. For three decades Du Pont has been systematically measuring the job performances of disabled employees. Tabulations from the firm's 1990 study provide clear evidence that its recruitment efforts have paid off. Managers rated 97 percent of disabled workers average or above average in terms of job safety, 86 percent average or above in attendance and fully 90 percent average or above in overall job performance.[16] ∎

Legal experts say the impact of the law will vary geographically. For instance, it is likely to have more impact in the South and Midwest than in places like California and New York, where extensive disability legislation is already in effect. Similarly, the public accommodation section of the law may cause greater concern in older cities, where buildings are generally less accessible, than in more recently settled areas.

"It's still not clear how the employment provisions will shake out," says economist Roy Cordato. "But if there are set-asides for the disabled, they could cause resentment among non-disabled. There is an incentive to find legal ways to circumvent the hiring of the disabled."

Few analysts actually believe that will happen. Over the long term, most experts believe more jobs will be made available to disabled people. At the same time, the law does contain risks — even for the disabled. "Some companies may have committed resources to doing what they believe is required under the ADA," says Friedan. "When a person comes through the door with more involved needs as a result of severe disability, the employer may pull out his checkbook and say, 'Look how much I've paid. I've already made my contribution. Anything else would create an undue hardship.'" In this sense, the broad definition of disability and unspecific regulations could conceivably hurt the more severely disabled, who are in the greatest need of help.

Eventually, however, advocates are confident that attitudes will change and aesthetically pleasing, barrier-free architecture will pervade the cityscape. Architects will be well-versed in ADA parlance, and disabled people will truly be able to expect equal opportunities. "Like with other civil rights statutes, there will be an initial period with a lot of litigation caused by defendants who ignore the law,"

# OUTLOOK

## Transition Period

Just four years ago, Edward Berkowitz began his book, *Disabled Policy,* with the statement, "America has no disability policy." He went on to describe the many contradictory, uncoordinated and disparate programs and policies intended to serve persons with disabilities, some promoting dependence and segregation and others supporting independence and integration.

Covering a variety of mental and physical impairments, the disabled community is large and diverse. Its interests were often fragmented by a

multitude of state and federal programs serving each subgroup — one program here for the blind, another there for the deaf. As a result, the movement had little occasion in the past to unite. The new law has changed that, galvanizing this diverse community into a more potent force.

"When the 1973 law was passed there wasn't a grass-roots phenomenon tied to it. Now there is," says disability consultant Pat Morrissey. "The expectations are a lot different. Many organizations, including those in the public sector, are in for a rude awakening." Despite government efforts to increase public awareness of the law, the majority of people — and businesses — thus far have failed to comprehend its sweeping nature.

predicts attorney Sid Wolinsky. "There will be a few high profile cases helping business to realize what has to be done. And then, eventually, access for the disabled will become part of the cost of doing business."

These changes, of course, will take time. "Many business will not be able to make changes overnight," says Friedan. "They will presumably develop transition plans." Friedan believes most of the structural changes will take place during the next three to five years. During that time, he says, there will be continuing refinements and interpretations of the ADA and existing statutes with regard to ambiguous areas, such as insurance and technology.

### Problem Areas

The law's impact on the insurance industry, in particular, could pose problems in the future. As it is, any question about medical or physical performance will have to be job-related. What worries businesses is that because they'll know less about the workers they hire, it will increase the potential of a wrongful-hiring lawsuit if they hire someone with mental problems or someone who is potentially unstable because of mental stress. The law could also cause health-care costs to balloon.

"Nothing will keep insurance companies from charging higher and higher premiums," complains NFIB's Wendy Lechner. Businesses may be forced to carry employees with a greater likelihood for high health costs on insurance policies. That, in turn, could affect collective bargaining issues and possibly result in a reduction of health-benefit policies for all employees.

"The real sleeper of this law will be its impact on employee evaluations," says Morrissey. "In jobs where the essential functions are clearly delineated, it will be easier to tell if they can be performed with or without accommodations. However, most office-

job evaluations are more subjective. How will employers measure performance in office jobs in order to protect themselves from discrimination charges?" This question has inspired many businesses to review job descriptions to make sure they can pass muster in an ADA compliance case.

"I don't think employers will notice any dramatic increases in the number of people with disabilities applying for jobs until the early 21st century," notes EEOC Chairman Kemp, who uses a wheelchair. "For many people with disabilities, marketing themselves will be a completely different way of thinking. Even if they want to work, many are used to being dependent on welfare, Social Security or disability benefits. They'll have to wean themselves off dependency before they can develop the self-confidence to go looking for work."[17]

It will also take time before discrimination cases go to court and legal precedents are established. There is no ADA police force going out to inspect buildings and enforce the law. Its success will be determined as much by collaboration between the disabled and business communities as it will by confrontation in the courts. "A lot depends on how technical assistance works out," says Lex Friedan. "Informal arbitration will save problems in court and in the administrative complaint departments. Informal mediation may be the key to preventing a breakdown in the judicial system."

Generally speaking, the debate over the ADA has been framed by the extremes: pessimists who feel the law will cripple businesses and optimists who feel it will liberate the disabled. In fact, it will probably do neither. Just as the 1964 Civil Rights Act did not make a colorblind society, neither will the ADA fully integrate the disabled into the mainstream. But it will change the landscape — and already has begun to change public attitudes.

Justin Dart, chairman of the President's Committee on Employment of People with Disabilities, summed it up this way: "The ADA is only the beginning. It is not a solution. Rather, it is an essential foundation on which solutions will be constructed."[18]  ∎

## Notes

[1] Testimony before the Senate Labor and Human Resources Committee, May 10, 1989.

[2] Louis Harris and Associates, "Public Attitudes Toward People with Disabilities," May-June 1991.

[3] "Disabled Politics," *Reason,* December 1989, p. 4.

[4] Carolyn Weaver, "The Politics of Good Intentions," *The American Enterprise,* May/June 1990, p. 84. For a more detailed analysis, see Weaver, *Disability & Work* (1991).

[5] Quoted in *Insight,* Oct. 30, 1989, p. 38.

[6] Jane West, ed., *The Americans with Disabilities Act: From Policy to Practice* (1991), p. 201.

[7] See *The Wall Street Journal,* May 23, 1990.

[8] Data cited in *U.S. News & World Report,* Nov. 18, 1991, p. 95.

[9] West, *op. cit.,* p. xviii.

[10] For details of early federal disability programs, see Stephen Percy, *Disability, Civil Rights, and Public Policy* (1989), p. 44.

[11] B. P. Tucker, "Section 504 of the Rehabilitation Act after Ten Years of Enforcement: The Past and the Future," *University of Illinois Law Review* (1989), p. 915. Tucker and other experts say universities, the National Park Service and organizations funded by the National Endowment for the Arts are notable for their compliance efforts.

[12] *Ibid.,* p. 104.

[13] Louis Harris and Associates, Inc., "The ICD Survey of Disabled Americans: Bringing Disabled Americans into the Mainstream," 1986. This poll was the first nationwide survey of people with disabilities.

[14] West, *op. cit.,* p. 186.

[15] Quoted in *Congressional Quarterly Weekly Report,* May 12, 1990, p. 1479.

[16] See "Equal to the Task II," *1990 Du Pont Survey of Employment of People with Disabilities.*

[17] From an interview printed in "Willing and Able," *Business Week,* special advertising section, Oct. 28, 1991, p. 19.

[18] Quoted in West, *op. cit.,* p. 334.

# Bibliography

## Selected Sources Used

### Books

**Percy, Stephen L., *Disability, Civil Rights, and Public Policy: The Politics of Implementation,* The University of Alabama Press, 1989.**

This book is particularly useful as background on the disability rights movement and the evolution of federal legislation affecting people with disabilities. The author also focuses on the philosophies that guide implementation.

**Weaver, Carolyn L., ed., *Disability & Work: Incentives, Rights, and Opportunities,* The AEI Press, 1991.**

This brief collection of essays on disability policy focuses primarily on labor and employment issues. Though many of the authors take an anti-regulation bent, they are followed by commentaries from other experts with opposing views. Overall, the book is a useful guide to the ADA employment provisions.

**West, Jane, ed., *The Americans with Disabilities Act: From Policy to Practice,* Milbank Memorial Fund, 1991.**

Jane West has put together an excellent primer on the ADA, including sections not only on the social policy context of this legislation but also detailed chapters on each of the act's provisions.

### Articles

**Freudenheim, Milt, "New Law to Bring Wider Job Rights for Mentally Ill," *The New York Times,* Sept. 23, 1991.**

Most state disability laws do not protect the mentally ill. Thus, the impact of the ADA on the mentally ill in terms of access to the workplace could be tremendous. This article does an excellent job of highlighting the critical issues, only minimally discussed elsewhere.

**Rovner, Julie, "Sweeping Law for Rights of Disabled," *1990 CQ Almanac,* pp. 447-461.**

Rovner has done much of the most detailed reporting on the passage of the ADA. This article gives extensive background on the legislative action leading up to its signing into law. Actual provisions of the bill are also included.

**Shapiro, Joseph P., "Liberation day for the disabled," *U.S. News & World Report,* Sept. 18, 1989, p. 20.**

This article came out almost one year before the ADA was signed into law but nonetheless covers most of the pertinent territory. It is particularly poignant in describing the mobilization of disability rights groups.

**Susser, Peter A., "The ADA: Dramatically expanded Federal Rights for Disabled Americans," *Employee Relations Law Journal,* autumn 1990, pp. 157-176.**

Susser offers a legalistic treatment of the ADA's employment provisions. Though a bit dry, the author provides interesting insights on the law's impact.

**Warner, David, "Rules on Medical Tests for New Hires," *Nation's Business,* August 1991, p. 29.**

*Nation's Business* is generally a good source for reportage on the issue of how the ADA will affect the business community. This article, in particular, may provide guidance on the subject of what business owners will be permitted to ask prospective employees.

**"Willing and Able: Americans with Disabilities in the New Work Force," *Business Week,* Special Advertising Section, Oct. 28, 1991.**

Despite its obvious promotional intent, this 37-page special advertising section provides much useful data on people with disabilities as well as useful references on model programs currently in place at some major U.S. corporations.

### Reports and Studies

**Jones, Nancy Lee, *The Americans with Disabilities Act (ADA): An Overview of Selected Major Legal Issues,* CRS Report for Congress, July 25, 1989.**

As the title implies, this report is a backgrounder on the legal issues that surround the ADA. The study discusses relevant court cases that have influenced the writing of the legislation.

**Louis Harris and Associates Inc., *Public Attitudes Toward People with Disabilities,* May-June 1991.**

This study, conducted for the National Organization on Disability, reveals data on the public's attitudes toward people with disabilities. Some of the conclusions are quite predictable, whereas others are surprising — such as the general ignorance of the ADA's passage.

**O'Quinn, Robert P., *The Americans with Disabilities Act: Time for Amendments,* Cato Institute Policy Analysis, Aug. 9, 1991.**

Robert O'Quinn takes a critical look at the ADA and concludes that it is too costly in its present form and in need of modification. His analysis also contains background on other legislation affecting the disabled.

# The Next Step

## Additional Articles from Current Periodicals
## from EBSCO Publishing's Database

### Addresses & essays

**"Americans with Disabilities Act,"** *Congressional Digest,* **December 1989, p. 289.**

Discusses the Americans with Disabilities Act then under committee consideration in the House of Representatives. Overview of advocate and opposition positions.

**"Monday memo,"** *Broadcasting,* **Feb. 25, 1991, p. 14.**

Presents a commentary on the Americans with Disabilities Act from Keltner Locke, King & Ballow, of Nashville. States that the FCC recognizes that individuals should be judged on their abilities, not on their disabilities; description of the Americans with Disabilities Act; how broadcasters will fare with this act.

**"Should the Senate approve the 'Americans with Disabilities Act of 1989'?"** *Congressional Digest,* **December 1989, p. 294.**

Presents arguments in favor of the passage of the Americans with Disabilities Act from Senator Edward M. Kennedy, American Telephone and Telegraph, Barrier Free Environments, Inc., Professors Edward D. Berkowitz and David H. Dean, and the Task Force on the Rights and Empowerment of Americans with Disabilities.

**Jensen, S., "Remove barriers from your church,"** *Christianity Today,* **Oct. 8, 1990, p. 12.**

Urges Christians to embrace the principles of the Americans with Disabilities Act (ADA). Common objections of the church toward the ADA provisions; how to overcome objections to ministry for the handicapped.

### Books & reading

**"Annotated listing of new books,"** *Journal of Economic Literature,* **June 1991, p. 707.**

Reviews the book "Americans with Disabilities Act of 1990: Law and explanation," published by the Commerce Clearing House.

### Case studies

**Ireland, K., "Du Pont anticipates ADA,"** *Personnel Journal,* **February 1991, p. 84.**

Reports that even before the Americans with Disabilities Act (ADA) was passed, Du Pont had a commitment to employing disabled workers. The Job Accommodation Network; details.

**Pati, G. C. and Stubblefield, G., "The disabled are able to work,"** *Personnel Journal,* **December 1990, p. 30.**

Discusses how a partnership between aerospace employers and the International Association of Machinists and Aerospace Workers (IAM) has succeeded in placing more than 5,000 disabled individuals in paying jobs. The Americans with Disabilities Act signed by President George Bush on July 26th; Projects with Industry (PWIs); details. INSETS: Injured mechanic becomes model for IAM's program; suggested contract language; good job fit helps the disabled find work.

**Vanderle, P., "Why business is hiring the mentally abled,"** *Canadian Business,* **May 1991, p. 19.**

Looks at Canadian business' hiring and training of workers with physical disabilities. Aside from morality and the law, Canada is faced with an aging population and shrinking labor pool; hiring the physically disabled makes sense.

### Colleges & universities

**Jarrow, J., "Disability issues on campus and the road to ADA,"** *Educational Record,* **winter 1991, p. 26.**

Discusses the impact of the Americans with Disabilities Act and Section 504 on colleges and universities. Putting a price tag on civil rights; the early days of Section 504; architectural and attitudinal barriers; the Supreme Court and the "Grove City" decision; the late 1980s; the Gallaudet controversy; more. INSET: How will the ADA affect us?

**Rothstein, L. F., "Campuses and the disabled,"** *The Chronicle of Higher Education,* **Sept. 4, 1991, p. B3.**

Opinion. Argues that it is increasingly important that administrators and faculty members understand what laws require of them concerning students, professors and staff members who are handicapped. The Americans with Disabilities Act, Section 504; job duties; architectural barriers; failure to make mandated changes could result in significant financial liability, costly litigation and loss of public image.

### Debates & issues

**"A business forced into bankruptcy can't provide opportunities to anyone,"** *Nation's Business,* **January 1990, p. 79.**

Editorial. Criticizes the provisions of the Americans with Disabilities Act then pending in Congress. Supports expanded business opportunities for the disabled; rejects the need for government intervention.

"Disabilities Act debated," *Christianity Today,* Sept. 22, 1989, p. 44.

Reports on the endorsement of the Americans with Disabilities Act of 1989 by Christian artist and author Joni Eareckson Tada. Criticism of the bill; what the church should do.

Cary, P., Lord, L., et al., "A bill of rights for the disabled," *U.S. News & World Report,* June 4, 1990, p. 14.

Reports on the recent passage of the Americans with Disabilities Act, to be signed this summer by President Bush, which is expected to cost upwards of $1 billion and trigger legal questions concerning its murky language.

Cryderman, L., "Worship in a wheelchair," *Christianity Today,* March 5, 1990, p. 11.

Editorial. Urges churches to support the Americans with Disabilities Act of 1989. Importance of treating handicapped worshippers as equal to others; churches' failure to accommodate the disabled without government requirements; refutes concerns that the act will increase state regulation of churches.

Johnson, M., "Disabled Americans push for access," *Progressive,* August 1991, p. 21.

Outlines the struggle by disability-rights groups to achieve wheelchair access to buildings and considers how local building officials thwart the law. The Americans with Disabilities Act, a federal law; organized business and the housing industry's claim that costs will be too high; an architectural study refuting this.

Lawton, K. A., "Churches 'live with' Disabilities Act," *Christianity Today,* Oct. 8, 1990, p. 71.

Observes the mixed responses of the Christian community over the recently approved Americans with Disabilities Act (ADA). Impact of the bill on Christian organizations; how the ADA can provide a good model for churches' ministries to the disabled.

Mandel, S., "Disabling America," *National Review,* Sept. 29, 1989, p. 23.

Discusses the negative implications of the Americans with Disabilities Act (ADA). Ambiguity of the bill; burdens it will impose; potential for numerous costly lawsuits.

McKee, B., "Achieving access for the disabled," *Nation's Business,* June 1991, p. 31.

Studies key details of the new Americans with Disabilities Act covering disabled customers and workers. Effective dates of the law's provisions; controversial edicts; defining "disabled"; employment protection; rules covering public access; required fixtures; tax deductions for companies; compliance advice for small businesses.

Williams, W. E., "The Santa Claus syndrome," *Success,* February 1991, p. 8.

Argues that the Americans with Disabilities Act, protecting the handicapped, is bound to backfire, hurting everyone. What the act says; the most insidious feature of the ADA; how it will affect the business world.

## Health aspects

"Disabilities," *Business Week,* Aug. 12, 1991, p. 33.

States that employers are worried about a key omission in the new regulations for the Americans with Disabilities Act, fearing that the law leaves them open to suits if they try to reduce health coverage for specific illnesses, such as AIDS. Holding off rules pending further study.

Orentlicher, D., "Genetic screening by employers," *Journal of the American Medical Association,* Feb. 16, 1990, p. 1005.

Opinion. Discusses concern over the possible misuse of genetic information by employers, and the expected passage of the Americans with Disabilities Act, which addresses the issue of employer-initiated testing. Discrimination prohibition; use of medical tests; loophole; other problems; employer burden; capacity testing.

Portner, J., "Fighting back," *Progressive,* August 1990, p. 30.

Describes recent efforts of AIDS activists. Impact of the Americans with Disabilities Act (ADA); civil rights protection to people with AIDS; ACT UP coalition; pressure on drug-testing regulations; emergency funds for hard-hit cities and states.

## Law & legislation

"Americans with Disabilities Act," *Congressional Quarterly Weekly Report,* July 28, 1990, p. 2437.

Details the major provisions of the American with Disabilities Act (ADA), cleared by the Senate July 13, which would provide sweeping protections against discrimination to 43 million disabled individuals. The bill (S 939 — H Rept 101-596) prohibits discrimination on the basis of disability in employment, public services and public accommodations. New buses and trains to be accessible to the disabled; telecommunications companies to operate relay systems.

"Summary of S. 933," *Congressional Digest,* December 1989, p. 292.

Summarizes the Americans with Disabilities Act of 1989 as prepared by the Senate Subcommittee on the Handicapped.

Beard, J. L., "U.S. moves toward barrier-free society," *Civil Engineering,* November 1990, p. 130.

Discusses the "Civil Rights Act for the Disabled," designed to eradicate discrimination against people with disabilities in areas of public access and employment and other laws that affect buildings and their accessibility.

**Beziat, C., "Educating America's last minority: Adult education's role in the Americans with Disabilities Act," *Adult Learning,* October 1990, p. 21.**

Highlights the Americans with Disabilities Act, which was signed into law by the president on July 26, 1990 and ensures that people with physical, mental and emotional disabilities will be protected against discrimination and will be ensured equal employment opportunities, the right to use public transportation, and the right to ready access to malls, stores, theaters and public buildings. The cause of discrimination; the role of education; 10 point action plan; details.

**Hunsicker, J.F. Jr., "Ready or not: The ADA," *Personnel Journal,* August 1990, p. 80.**

Describes the Americans with Disabilities Act (ADA) and its future impact for employers. Discrimination definitions; Title VII actions; Civil Rights Act of 1990. INSETS: Where to find help; ADA: Definition of disability; HR execs are ready for the ADA.

**Jaschik, S., "Washington update: Congress passes law barring discrimination against disabled," *The Chronicle of Higher Education,* July 25, 1990, p. A19.**

Reports that Congress has enacted legislation banning discrimination against the disabled in hiring, public accommodations, and transportation. Colleges could not refuse to hire people because of their disabilities; wheelchair, vision and hearing accessible; renovations; transportation.

**Johnson, M., "Enabling act," *Nation,* Oct. 23, 1989, p. 446.**

Editorial. Describes the Americans with Disabilities Act that passed the Senate and is assured to pass in the House. Disability rights groups wanted Title VII of the Civil Rights Act amended; Secretary of Transportation Samuel Skinner's opposition to ADA.

**Murphy, B.S., Barlow, W.E., et al., "ADA signed into law," *Personnel Journal,* September 1990, p. 18.**

Looks at the Americans with Disabilities Act (ADA) that was signed into law by President George Bush on July 26, 1990. The law prohibits discrimination against the disabled in private employment, public services and transportation, public accommodations and telecommunications. Definition of disability; details of the law; impact on employers.

**Murphy, B.S., Barlow, W.E., et al., "EEOC regulations on access to agency records," *Personnel Journal,* September 1991, p. 30.**

Comments on two final rules published by the Equal Employment Opportunity Commission (EEOC) on June 28, 1991. Non-disclosure rules applicable to information collected under the Americans with Disabilities Act; revision of regulations that implement the Privacy Act of 1974.

**Parmet, W.E., "Discrimination and disability: The challenges of the ADA," *Law, Medicine & Health Care,* winter 1990, p. 331.**

Presents an overview of the Americans with Disabilities Act of 1990 (ADA), which was signed by President George Bush last July 26. Regulation in employment, transportation, communications, health care, and public accommodations; background of the bill; definition of disability; exclusions; disability and the equal opportunity model; infectious diseases; more.

**Rovner, J., "Congress clears sweeping bill to guard rights of disabled," *Congressional Quarterly Weekly Report,* July 14, 1990, p. 2227.**

Examines landmark legislation cleared by Congress to extend broad civil rights protections to an estimated 43 million Americans with disabilities. Overcoming the two obstacles that blocked final action for more than a month; President George Bush in support; Americans with Disabilities Act (ADA); provisions; House and Senate approval; Sen. Tom Harkin, chief sponsor; covering Senate employees; food handlers with AIDS.

## Small business

**McKee, B.A., "A troubling bill for business," *Nation's Business,* May 1990, p. 58.**

Examines small businesses' concerns over the vague provisions of the Americans with Disabilities Act. Key clauses in the bill; costs of compliance.

**McKee, B.A., "Planning for the disabled," *Nation's Business,* November 1990, p. 24.**

Urges small-business owners to start plans to follow the basic measures of the recently enacted Americans with Disabilities Act. Importance of proper education on how to comply with the law; suggested resources for information; impact of the bill on employment and public accommodations; enforcement regulations and penalties. INSET: Resources for small firms.

# Back Issues

*Great Research on Current Issues Starts Right Here... Recent topics covered by The CQ Researcher are listed below. Issues dated before May 10, 1991, were published under the name of Editorial Research Reports.*

**JUNE 1990**
Downsizing America's Armed Forces
Progress In Weather Forecasting
S & L Bailout
Bio-Chemical Disarmament

**JULY 1990**
Do Americans Still Love Marriage?
Death Penalty Debate
Decline of Rural America
United Nations in the 1990s

**AUGUST 1990**
Democracy in the Philippines
Initiatives: True Democracy?
Hard Times at Newspapers
Teens Balance School & Jobs

**SEPTEMBER 1990**
Dangers of Alcohol
Western Alliance After the Cold War
Tobacco Industry
Right to Die

**OCTOBER 1990**
Organ Transplants
Energy Policy Options
Search for Arab Unity
Child Support

**NOVEMBER 1990**
Lotteries and Gambling
Post Cold-War Choices
Setting Limits on Medical Care
Multicultural Education

**DECEMBER 1990**
Cable TV Regulation
Americans' Search For Their Roots
Is Insurance System a Failure?
Why Schools Still Have Tracking

**JANUARY 1991**
Growing Influence of Boycotts
Should the U.S. Reinstate the Draft?
America's Archaeological Past
Peace Corps' Challenges in '90s

**FEBRUARY 1991**
Regional Impact of Recession
Puerto Rico's Status
Redistricting: Mapping Power
Nuclear Power

**MARCH 1991**
Acid Rain
Cost of the Gulf War
Reassessing Gun Laws
Future for Man in Space

**APRIL 1991**
Social Security
Canadian Crisis Over Quebec
California Drought
Electromagnetic Radiation

**MAY 1991**
School Choice
Racial Quotas
Animal Rights
U.S. and Japan

**JUNE 1991**
Children and Divorce
Teenage Suicide
Endangered Species
Europe 1992

**JULY 1991**
Teenagers and Abortion
Soviet Republics Rebel
Mexico's Emergence
Athletes and Drugs

**AUGUST 1991**
Sexual Harassment
Fetal Tissue Research
Oil Imports
The Palestinians

**SEPTEMBER 1991**
Police Brutality
Advertising Under Attack
Saving the Forests
Foster Care Crisis

**OCTOBER 1991**
Pay-Per-View TV
Youth Gangs
Gene Therapy
World Hunger

**NOVEMBER 1991**
Fast-Food Shake-Up
The Greening of Eastern Europe
Business' Role in Education
Cuba In Crisis

**DECEMBER 1991**
Retiree Health Benefits
Asian Americans
The Obscenity Debate

Back issues are available for $4.00 (subscribers) or $7.00 (non-subscribers). Quantity discounts apply to orders over ten. To order, call Congressional Quarterly 1-800-432-2250.

# Future Topics

▶ *Term Limitations*

▶ *Oil Spills*

▶ *Should Hunting Be Banned?*

# The CQ Researcher
## Subject Index
## January 1991 - December 1991

NOTE: Weekly CQ Researcher issues, indexed under **boldface** subject headings, are referenced by report title and date. Pertinent page numbers within each report are included in the citation. Cross references are used to direct the researcher from general to more specific subject headings, as well as from terms or phrases not used to terms or phrases that are used.